Our Twentieth Century's Greatest Poems

John Campbell, Editor & Publisher

Edited by Eddie-Lou Cole

Art Director Julie Joy

Library of Congress catalog card number: 82-050849
ISBN 0-910147-00-0
1982 Printing
Printed in the United States of America

Foreword

The Story Of the World Of Poetry

It's a wonderful thing to be part of the World of Poetry. I can remember when the first issue of our newsletter came whirring off the press, way back in August of 1975. We were so proud—and so excited! Our *entire* staff consisted of two poets: Yours Truly, Eddie-Lou Cole, Poetry Editor, and of course, John Campbell, Editor & Publisher. John had asked me to come aboard a few months earlier, to give him a hand with "a new poetry publication I have in mind."

Little did I know the publication he had in mind would grow, in a few short years, from one of "little magazine" status, to literally one of international prominence and prestige. In my years upon years of editing poetry journals and contributing to them, of writing poetry books, and publishing them, I have never seen anything like it. It is a success story of truly poetic proportions—and includes, among other things, the publishing of *Our Twentieth Century's Greatest Poems*, this magnificent anthology of over 7,000 beautiful poems!

With the publication of the Inaugural issue of the World of Poetry, on August 1, 1975, Editor and Publisher John Campbell launches a publishing empire, with Eddie-Lou Cole as Poetry Editor.

INAUGURAL ISSUE

World Of Poetry

A MONTHLY NEWSLETTER FOR POETS

VOL. 1, NO. 1 — 1 AUGUST 75

A NEW PUBLICATION FOR POETS

Here we are, O World, just about the newest and most best poetry publication around. We've been so busy here just getting our first issue out.

You should see our desk. Stacks of poems on it, and all kinds of letters and telegrams wishing us well. And phone calls offering help and good words. (Guess we'll keep the little guy on our masthead, as a reminder.) All we can say is, thanks—thanks for making us the happiest editors we know!

A few months ago we sponsored our first annual Poetry Competition. Hold on to your quills, because we've gotten entries from every state and province in the United States and Canada plus foreign countri... Sri Lanka...

The world has not grown so large nor man so old that there is no longer a place for old-fashioned values

JUST PLAIN FOLKS

by ROBERT MENDONCA

...thing like religio-patrio-matrio-socio-dociotic verse. I, for one (and I'm sure for all), prefer 'folksy.' At first glance it may not seem to have any redeeming social value. Yet it does provide a way for many to deal with grief, and joy, rejection and happiness:

We are just plain folks, your mother and me,
Just plain folks like our own folks used to be,
As our presence seems to
grieve you,
We will go away and leave you,
For we're sadly out of place here,
*'Cause we're Just Plain Folks.**

This song lyric might be laughed at today (I think lamentably so) whereas fifty years ago it would have produced characteristic crocodile tears. This is not the only example of this genre of verse whether musical or otherwise. We could have easily quoted such well-remembered tunes as, *Over the Hill To the Poor House, Home Sweet Home*, or *Silver Threads Among the Gold*—to name a few. People still like many of these songs—nay, they are favorites.

Have we changed so much as a people that we can no longer feel that pathetic plea, "we're just plain folks?" All propaganda to the contrary, I'm sure that most Americans still get a little sentimental when they think of their flag or their mothers; and although I'd prefer cheese cake to apple pie—but I think I've made my point. There is a place, a darn good place for folksy verse. Even our TV habits betray our love of the down-home, down-heart kind of stuff that has made *The Waltons* a top show. Or how about Stephen Foster's work, and gothic novels—they should have perished long ago, had they not touched us. What makes the difference is 'heart.'

What does this all mean, O poet? Well, first off, there is a market for your folksy verse—a considerable market. A good portion of the world population is still living on farms and in small cities. Places like Centerville, Dugganville, Porter's Corners, and Podunk still do exist, really [*continued on page 4*]

THE MONEY ISSUE

World Of Poetry — SEPTEMBER 1975

A MONTHLY NEWSLETTER FOR POETS

VOL. 1, NO. 2

AS YOU LIKE IT!

Earning money as a poet may take more ingenuity than merely writing poems

POETRY FOR PROFIT

by JOSEPH MELLON

Happy Thanksgiving!

VOL. 1, NO. 4

GOOD NEWS!

One of America's distinguished poets creates a successful sonnet form

THE AMERICAN SONNET

by IRMA G. RHODES

...d Of Poetry

...THLY NEWSLETTER FOR POETS — OCTOBER 1975

Our editor writes a few few rejection slips—to editors!

A TOUGH PILL TO SWALLOW

by JOHN T. CAMPBELL

By design World of Poetry is an exciting potpourri of poems, helpful articles on how to write (and sell) poetry, questions and answers, workshops, interviews with prominent poets, news items, market listings and contests—anything and everything we imagine a poet's heart could desire. Celebrities like Bobby Vinton, Red Skelton, Liberace, Tennessee Ernie Ford make their way into our pages, movie and television stars who are also quite good poets. It turns out they are attracted, many of them, by the glitter of the contests we sponsor, up to a dozen big ones a year, each boasting a grand prize of $1,000, with up to a hundred prizes totaling $10,000 or more. (Most of our contests are won, surprisingly enough, not by "name" or "celebrity" poets, but by housewives or students who've never entered a poetry contest before. One lady won with a poem she'd kept in a drawer for thirty years!)

***As host of the* Upstart Crow *television series, John Campbell talked poetry with guest stars Vincent Price, Steve Allen, Red Buttons, Richard Thomas and Leonard Nimoy. One of the results of the series was the production of John's Shakespeare album* "Perchance to Dream."**

One day, while I was in the middle of judging one of our contests, John came in the office with an idea. "Eddie-Lou," he said, "Why don't you write a book on how to write poetry, for the benefit of new poets who could use a few ideas." I took the suggestion under submission, and six months later emerged with a text, entitled *Now Technique For Today's Poets.* Like John predicted, it was another World of Poetry success.

Vincent Price

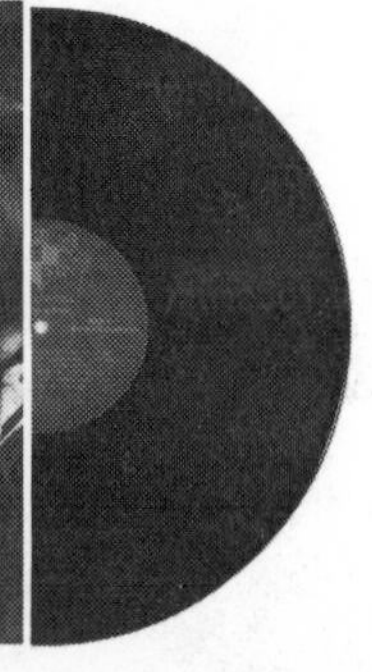
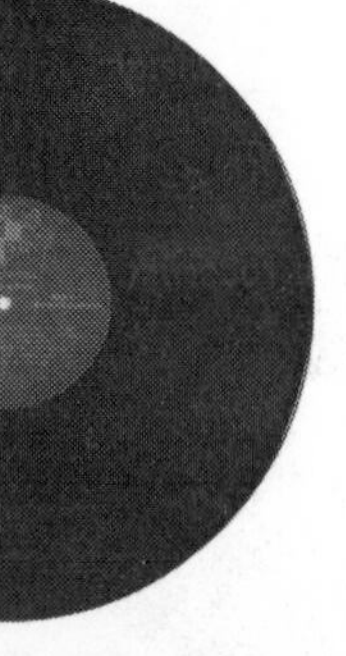

"Perchance to Dream"

Steve Allen

Leonard Nimoy

Red Buttons

Richard Thomas

Meantime, with the newsletter going great guns, and my book selling well, it was time for World of Poetry to venture again. John whose background includes acting (and Shakespeare), got a few of his friends together, and did a most phenomenal thing: he came up with a TV series on poetry, called the Upstart Crow (named after the criticism leveled at Shakespeare early in his career by one Mr. Green). As host of the weekly series, you could see John welcome such guest stars as Leonard Nimoy, Vincent Price, Richard Thomas, Red Buttons and Steve Allen. The first thing Mr. Allen said on the show was, "Congratulations that such a show exists!" As if this weren't enough to make everybody here at World of Poetry proud, out of the series, quite unexpectedly, came another success: John's hit Shakespeare album, "Perchance to Dream." J. C. Trewin, the doyen of London drama critics, honored John by writing the program notes to the album.

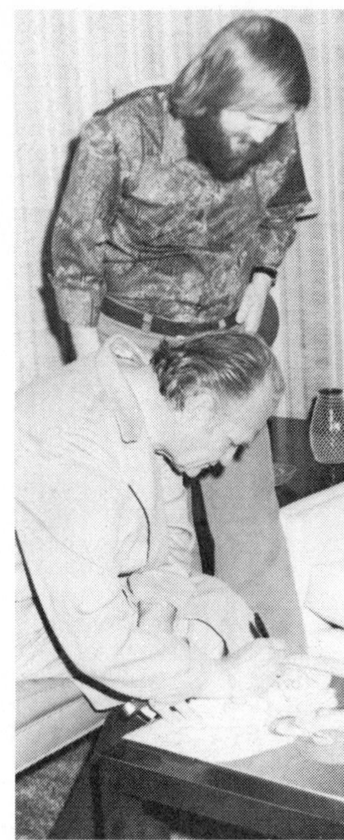
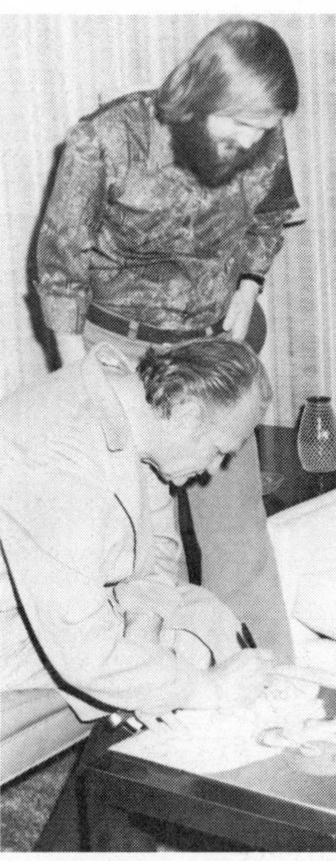

Red Skelton

Bobby Vinton Julie Joy

Liberace

Tennessee Ernie Ford

Bertha

Among the numerous celebrities to appear with our Editor and Publisher in the pages of the World of Poetry are Bobby Vinton (that's our Art Director Julie Joy, next to him), Red Skelton, Liberace, Tennessee Ernie Ford (all fine poets), and of course, Bertha, The Elephant.

Our Twentieth Century's Greatest Poems, which combines the talents of thousands of poets around the world, is our current success and our current joy. Like I said, it's a wonderful thing to be part of the World of Poetry.

—*Eddie-Lou Cole, Editor*
WORLD OF POETRY
Sacramento, Ca.
June, 1982

Our Twentieth Century's Greatest Poems

Joseph P. Kowacic
KEWEENAW
The warm
forest afternoon
was interrupted only
by the sound
of running water.
A fawn paused
to dip its fragile nose
into the rippling coolness.
A rabbit, unafraid,
lunched
upon his natural salad,
while a bear
lolled among the berry bushes.
A strong copper hand
reached
for a soft copper hand,
and four dark eyes
met.
The summer warmth
buzzed
with love. . . . .
This was long,
long ago. . .
when the forest
was savage.

Lorraine Lentz Rutter
PERILOUS TIMES
Storms are raging throughout the land,
With violence and crime on every hand.
Eruption is within the churches and within the family ties.
Unemployment is on the rise.
Let us not despair as God will keep us in his care.
He has wrought a wonderful creation.
Let us uphold in prayer the perils of the nation.
We can then obtain strength to conquer the attacks of the enemy.
Forever we can lean on the everlasting arms,
It is the best known remedy.

Edwin J. Harendza
MOTHER DEAR MOTHER
Oh, Mother, Dear Mother
Please forgive your son,
For I am truly sorry
For all the wrong I've done.
I've hurt you so often
In my childhood years,
Even when I grew up
I made you shed tears.
Oh, Mother, Dear Mother
How often I made you sad,
How often I disobeyed you
When I should have made you glad.
I know it's a little late now
After you're grey and old,
But this will make you feel better
If these things to you are told.
Oh, Mother, Dear Mother
It's never too late to start,
And so by this little verse
May I ease your heart.
May it grant me your forgiveness
And in a small way make you glad,
For Mother, Dear Mother
You're the best mother a son ever had.

John Campbell
TO ELLA IN OLIVEHURST
I am never at a loss for words and yet tonight there are no words.
Your mother tells me you are ill and too asleep to talk,
and I am heartsick at the thought.
I have loved you ever—and our sometime revels, on this earth and off, are so much a part of me that even now I live them and am fulfilled, like a flower long-rooted finally in the sun.
I had lifted high my head and the watery scenes were a blurr with happiness.
I could jump with frogs and take off on the backs of ever-winging birds.
But my attentions, all too happy, were a temporary thing, as who could desire so much of you and keep you long?
The pain before and after our affair lives with me, save for the sprinkling quiet in this toil of time, at whose soulful and forlorn end a mirror makes me up and in whose face an aging image comes.
I am taken with the flicker in a dancing candle; there is a message in my mind maddens me, and I stand in horror at my soul's quest; how easily it bores through monuments that mark us, and like a puff of smoke gives up in air.
The flicker in some remove, universes off, hath a pulse—and keeps its music ever, though the ear's asleep that once could hear it.
I am not now as I have been, and will not be as I am;
but that you are constant in my thought, believe it.
In that, dear and ever dearest one, I am as I am. . .
and love you still.

Steven McClain
ANGIE
Angie, will anyone ever understand
you're as simple as a ballerina
dancing in the sand
Angie, you're such a little girl
but a lady with so many high class ways
never quite sure if you want to leave or stay
so afraid of being alone
that you gave your love so freely
Angie, mostly giving and barely taking
Angie, you're a dream afraid of waking
so lost in your music
that you made your life a song
but is believing in dreams so very wrong
Angie
Angie will anyone ever understand
you're as simple as a ballerina
dancing in the sand
just a little girl
but a lady with so many high class ways
so lost in your music
That you made you life a song
but is believing in dreams so very wrong
Angie
Oh Angie, will anyone ever understand

John Campbell
TO REGGIE
I am not worded wisely or too well
As does appear in anything I say.
He died o' drowning, he that is my friend,
And fair as friendship is, as fast he was
In my soul a celebration, to this
That any day defines a tedious act,
So much is in the mouth with meaning mixed
Would think, in hearing of it, it were much;
But think you not it is, but in the tale,
As thus: as were the flea made furious
Suffers but a finger's flick, and then falls;
Nothing is now that little was before.
Bethink you now what I am in the tongue:
Too weak am I to weep, and too swollen
With sorrow e'en to sigh. My secret's out,
And blinks like a blasphemy in my brain.
Now sinks all sands life's structures stand upon;
Where late lived arsenals of ants, tiny
Upon a time; nor, tunnel-traveled, tired;
He among, now dear in the drink of death.
Follows from the first, and foot on foot in
The design of my dark destiny cries:
"Helpless am I, hot in the hell-hole, help!"

Winn Starr
SAINT WITH GUITAR
"Mendicant, itinerant evangelist"
He put in the "vocational objective" blank.
When the counselor figured it out,
He won a trip to the principal's office
For frivolity.
How can anyone chew out a fifteen-year old
Who is lucid, articulate, and adamant;
Who looks at him with wise eyes,
And understands and forgives him?
He didn't go to college
Or seminary —
Just dropped out of sight —
But he returned singing fluently of Love,
To braceros in their tongue,
And to beantniks, in theirs;
Accompanying his message
With strums seldom heard by the gringo.
Wearing old jeans,
Truck-tire sandals
And an air of sanctity,
Which he doesn't bother to fight,
He gives you a creepy feeling,
As he looks at you with wise eyes
And understands and forgives you.

JC
CONTEMPLATION
I fall in the dark halls
of my existence;
crowded from the top
with engines of destiny.
One provoked is enough.
That others die is no
comfort.
I see them carry you
as high as is my heart,
through the cemetery—
the naked branches
nodding
in their clinging to winter.
And the soiled shawls
denote the blackeness
of time to come;
and where the silence is
there you will find me,
like the wisp of fog
from the lips of one
who had said too much
too late
and wandered off
without applause.

J. A. Fowler
RIDING A FREIGHT
Have you ever rode a freight,
My friend?
Some say you're a bum
If you do.
And, maybe it's true.
But, between me and you,
There's nothin' like ridin'
A freight!
So, come on, jump inside.
It's only a ride.
And it might
Change your point
Of view,
Not about me, about
You.
You might find it takes
Spunk
To grab hold of a hunk
Of a freight moving out
On the fly.
You might be called bum
And nothin' but scum
By those that are better
Than you.
And there usually are
Quite a few.
But it don't matter
Too much in the passing
Of time,
For few lend thought
To the rhyme.
They're stuck in their shoals
And their personal hells.
And they can't see themselves
For the grime.
They're stuck in that thing
They call time.
But, between me and you
That's relative, too.
And we'll all get there
In the end.
So, ridin' a freight
Can be just as great
As ridin' a plane or a
Car.
They're all 'gonna' go
Just so far.

Y. Y. Wiley
TWIR LA LA TWIR LEE

An insect in a tree made a clicking sound
as it munched upon a leaf that it had found
and there seemed to be no other sound around.
Then a bird came and lit upon the branch
and pertly ate the insect when she had the chance.
So the little bird sat up in the tree
and she cocked her head as she sang to me,
"Twir la la, twir la la, twir lee."
Now you may not think that this is profound
but there seemed to be no other sound around.

Stephen Gianotti
BANQUET

Midnight motions to the dawn
As daybreak climbs aloft,
Horizon paints the resting place
Of sun, a firey soft.
A silver sliver moonlight slides
Then slips to yesterday,
Bleeding darkness from the dawn and
Giving us today.
Spiral sun-rays skyward soar
Crowning endless east,
Millions hungry wake but who
Will realize the feast?

Shari Forbes
ATTEMPTED ROBBERY

Sometimes I want to get into you
and I reach out,
touching you,
but you shoot across the room
without moving at all.
I look at my hand that is touching you,
the hand
that's a wooden growth
on my arm.
You are minute in the distance,
an image
in the wrong end of binoculars.
I hear your voice from across a sea,
the sound of it reaching me
long after your lips have stopped.
I laugh when I think of them up there,
whose room is directly above us.
I laugh so hard the tears come
until there is an aching
in my ribs.
I look at my hand touching you.
It moves across the room again,
and
the laughing
stops.

Connie Flint
YOU AND I

No one will ever know. . .
The dreams we've shared. . .
The hopes we've had. . .
The tears we've cried. . .
The times we've cared.
No one will ever know. . .
How we honestly tried. . .
How often we feared. . .
How we wanted to please. . .
How difficult it was.
No one will ever know. . .
When we laughed in joy. . .
When we shouted in anger. . .
When we held each other. . .
When we shook all over.
No one will ever know. . .
Except Our Father, who knows all. . .
Except our hearts, our soul, our being. . .
Except the people we've touched, wherever we were. . .
Except in all that we are today. . .WE KNOW.

Reinaldo Matos
A MOTHER CRYING

Do not make your moth... cry,
My little singing bird.
Instead, give her
All your love and affection.
You were still
Less than a tiny egg,
And she loved you.
It is not an ordinary branch
The mimosa tree of your nest.
Try always to be kind
And helpful
To her:
Don't let your mother cry.
If you can not love your mother,
You can not love anyone else.

Rosalie J. Bourne
FATALITY

Sorrow burned in the depth of her eyes,
Despair marked her very walk.
Hopeless her heart in rhythm moved,
Death hovered—her shadow to stalk.
She felt his grim presence by day and by night,
She prayed he would tire of this quest;
Search for another now ready to go,
Anxious to find peace, complete rest.
But he stayed by her side just out of her sight,
And whispered and called her by name.
Then tired of the struggle she faced with each breath,
She answered, thus ending the game.

Susie M. Werner
THE CRICKET

I heard a cricket chirping in the hall.
My husband said there wasn't one at all;
He said to dig the wax out of each ear—
And all imagined noises I'd not hear.
He said the noise was just the cuckoo clock,
And what I heard was just its slow tick-tock;
I could not understand his unbelief
And begged him listen, which he did—quite brief.
He still insisted, "There's no cricket there."
I knew there was and told him "You're not fair;
If you would listen closely, you would hear
Its loud chirping whene'er the coast is clear."
I moved the things; and in my husband's shoe
There was not only one cricket, but two;
I swatted both and showed them to him, dead—
But he still thinks the noise was in my head.
But why should we continue fuss and sass,
For as Abe Lincoln said, "This too, will pass";
And as the days go by, we will forget
Just what it was that made us fume and fret.

Nita M. Sodeman
TRUE LIVING

True living
Is giving
And giving, receiving.
Receiving just opens the door
For caring,
And sharing,
And oftentimes bearing
The burdens and needs of the poor.
Not poor in the sense
Of hunger for food,
Nor thirsty for water or wine.
But poor in the need
For people to care,
And thirsty for God's love divine.
Start living
By giving
What you've been receiving,
Walk through the wide open door
By caring,
And sharing,
And oftentimes bearing
The deep heart needs of the poor.

Peter C. Chapel
LOS ANGELES QUEEN OF ANGELS

When a tortoise carried the world on its back
and the world was known by all men to be flat
On the fringe of this world in the setting sun
In an island realm lived the Amazons.
This rugged island called California
This fabled gold-filled cornucopia
was plainly marked on map and chart
and fired adventure in a brave man's heart
Many tried and they failed to explore this fabled isle
and the lure of gold prevailed in Cibola for a while
Dauntless men braved the oceans, sunken galleons and starvation
Scurvy, was reward for most; upon land the hostile host.
Cortes found his El Dorado; others just the Colorado
From Mexico then came Portola, followed by Father Serra
and California then became a part of the Spanish Plan
To the glory and the honor of the sovereign land of Spain.
Dotting northward from the Baja rose the missions and the pueblos
And about the fairest one founded in 1781 was LOS ANGELES, LOS ANGELES,
NUESTRA SENORA LA REINA DE LOS ANGELES
Los Angeles, you're heaven blessed
From days of yore men sought your shore
Cibola's gold and Amazons have faded to where they began
You reign supreme; for you, the queen, ring out the chimes
LOS ANGELES, LOS ANGELES, SENORA LA REINA DE LOS ANGELES

Santa Monica, Santa Ana, Santa Barbara, Santa Clara
Santa Paula, Santa Rosa, Santa Margarita
San Gabriel, San Miguel, San Diego, San Antonio
San Fernando, San Francisco, Santa Maria—SENORA LA REINA DE LOS ANGELES
LOS ANGELES, LOS ANGELES, queen of the angels.
Los Angeles, to your esteem, you've made your children kings and queens
The world will remember
Mary Pickford, Greta Gargo, Charlie Chaplain, Clark Gable
Sonia Henie, Gilbert Roland, and Barrymores
Judy Garland, Shirley Temple, Ethyl Waters, Rita Hayworth
Sidney Portier, Bing Crosby, and Ann Miller
LOS ANGELES, LOS ANGELES, queen of angels
Los Angeles you are the hub of industry, commerce and arts
From coast to coast, across the seas, your products flow, and never cease
To find demand in all the lands of the world
LOS ANGELES, LOS ANGELES, queen of angels.
Los Angeles, though as you grew, your problems have multiplied too
But in the past you have been strong
and set things right where they belong.
The present, now, is not a joke
You have the heart, you have the brawn to bear the yoke
and you'll grow on and on
LOS ANGELES, LOS ANGELES, NEUSTRA SENORA LA REINA DE LOS ANGELES

Nancy Roulias
JESUS CHRIST
He was our saviour from his
birth;
Jesus who trod upon this earth,
He came to save us from our
sins,
And let our lives again begin.
Jesus was perfect in every way;
He walked and talked with God
every day.
He healed the sick—He made
the blind see,
He died on Calvary, for you and
me.
He fed the hungry, and carried
the weak,
He traveled near and far; sinners
he would seek.
Little children wanted to be
near him,
They felt his love, and He also
loved them.
For His second coming, we
patiently wait,
We will rush to meet Him—
open wide the gate.

Michael Bloom
TIME
Time is that, which even the
Shortest minute could be the
Longest moment spent—Time
may
Be the distance between two
Points, which may never be able
To attach—Or the immediate
Connection of something close
to
Your heart
Time could be measured in
one's
Mind by the way an individual
feels
About another, or the length to
which
All thoughts are closed, relating
to
A thing in reality

Time may never be a clock, a
watch
Or even a calendar, for time is
too
Dear to observe how it passes
Time is physical, by the use of
Our senses; Time is mental by
the
Existence of the mind; And time
Is reality, by the use of
Mechanical devices
Now in the present and as it
Extends into the future, time
Is insignificant when you are
With someone you love

Margaret M. Landry
ELDERLY PEOPLE
My heart feels out for the
Elderly People
People who have gone through
life as young once,
As they got older, they were
known as the
Elderly People,
They have accomplished a lot
for the world and
for their own children,
Seeing the Elderly People one
should know, that
someday all the young ones
would be called Elderly too,
As they get older in life and as
the years rolls along
Some Elderly People needs care
when they are unable
to care for themselves,
Some are lonely and all alone
with no one caring
or thinking of them,
It is sadness too my eyes to
see people get old but
we all happen to be one
later in life.

Scott Erickson
WILL YOU BE MY VALENTINE, AGAIN
In a past summertime
Back when we were in our
prime,
We would often wander about
And we would laugh, sing and
shout,
But now it seems when we kiss,
There is something we both
miss.
Tell me after I count to ten,
Will you be my valentine
again?
You know I would be blue,
If I had to go on without you.
I know you need some time,
So count the pennies in a
dime.
For each there is a reason why,
If you left me I would cry.
So think of us and how its been,
Will you be my valentine
again?
You remember that old oak tree,
We just lied there, you and
me.
We would talk for endless
hours,
Of senseless things and pretty
flowers.
When I asked you to be my
mate,
You didn't even hesitate.
Oh remember, remember back
when,
And say you will be my
valentine again.
I still love you, don't you see,
I want it to remain, you and
me.
Remember when you were nine,
I asked you to be my
valentine.
You giggled, and told me to
guess,
But before I could, you said
yes.
You were my valentine then,
Will you be my valentine,
again?

Linda L. Brown
SOLITARY
Solitary confinement,
fleeing from imaginary, invisible
germs,
I lay and look
for something different
to look at.
White everywhere,
spared by a two by four glass.
Green-gowned
faceless faces stare through
as if I have some rule
to break.
Air flows horizontally by me
quietly, as if to rob me
of noise as well,
I bitch for coffee
I can't drink
and space
in a room of space
to think.

Christine A. Doyle
LIFE
With all the beauty, elegance,
Mystique and gentleness,
It too has thorns surrounding
Yet they enhance its
preciousness.

Alberta A. Cox
APPRECIATION
I sat beneath a cloudless sky
In silent meditation.
I thought of all the blessings
Of my earthly habitation.
How God provided me with
sight
His glories to behold.
At first I thought of all the
trees
Too numerable to toll.
And then, I thought about the
flowers,
A million hues, dimensions.
Of the stature of the mountains
And the depth of seas and
oceans.
Of the greenness of the valleys
With the trickling little brooks.
Just sight alone endowed me
A million joys to span.
But I'm really just beginning
To tell what God has given
man!
For as I sat and pondered
Of the other gifts around us.
There is smell to reap and
enjoyment
From just numerous resources.
There is the ecstasy of flavor
From the pungent to the tasty.
Oh how fortunate the gift of
hearing
Of unending melody and song.
And above all the others
Is the one I cherish most!
It's the one that we call
feeling
For it merits endless scopes.
As the fingers of our hands
Feel the rough, the smooth, the
silky.
So the feelings of our spirit
unite in understanding.
And in closeness with our
Father,
It is forever binding.
As the gifts above He gave me
Are indeed each one a treasure.
To be used in exaltation
And in glory without measure.
I can climb the highest
mountain.
I can reach the deepest sea.
For if I belong to Jesus,
Then He also belongs to me.

Lloyd C. Bartholomew
THE SHADOW
My clip-board casts a shadow on
the wall.
Because it's not yet daylight and
my day's
Begun. Again today, to my
amaze,
My sleep is shorter than the
night. The call
That wakened me was not the
clock's alarm.
Too early I with finger stifled
it—
That jangle interrupting
Morpheus' bit
That rests the body for its
daylight charm.
But not the mind. The tensor
table lamp
Makes big and black a phantom
shade on wall
And ceiling. Like a giant bug
might crawl
And threaten occupation I hear
tramp
Ephemeral feet might make, see
shoulders square,
And rounded eyes unblinking in
their stare.

Glenda Lewman
WHISPERS
I am but a whisper
unto your soul.
A breeze gently flows
to your ear
and you hear it.
A cool, soft, white hand
caresses your face
and you feel it.
I am just
a whisper.
When your ears listen
and your heart
sheds its grief,
I will share
with you
secrets
of awesome beauty
and truth.

Alice B. Kendall
CHILDREN OF THE WILDERNESS
On the trail, the city street,
the freeway
hiking, running, driving
each one seeking his own end
pushing, struggling, striving
hoping for Utopia
around the bend. . . . .
all creatures lost and blind
to rainbows arching
overhead
and treasures left behind. . .
wildlings, leaderless
on singular stampede
through self-made
wilderness.

Craig Nagoshi
ISLAND
Broken winged,
I lie upon the barren rock
Beneath the silent azure sky,
Surrounded by the whispering
waves
Whose tongues I cannot fathom.
Broken winged,
Forsaken on this barren rock,
I watch by father circling above,
His feathers glistening in the
sunlight,
But his head is bent as he
wheels away
Into the far horizon.
Broken winged,
Shackled to this barren rock
By shattered pinions and melted
wax,
I gaze into the remorseless sun,
Whose perfect five I tried to
win,
That now descends beyond my

reach.
Broken winged,
I lie upon the barren rock
Beneath the silent evening sky,
Surrounded by the universe,
And wanting only shelter.

Alison S. Sloat
IF ONLY YOU COULD WAIT FOR ME

Today, yesterday, tomorrow—all the same
with thoughts of you, and wandering
when we'll meet again.
The tears so foolishly well up in me,
and I can't stop remembering
your look, your smile, the child in your eyes.
The two strongest feelings I've ever known—the warmth
of your touch, and the pain of letting go—are yours.
You hold a fragile piece of me.
Once. . .we were the perfect pair, but now I am here
and you are there.
If only you could wait for me.
I don't know why,
I do not know
why things have had to happen so
that I am lost without you.
I am lost, without you.

Arva R. Orman
FLIGHT OF THE SWAN

Beautiful swan—
Life beginning,
Years to conquer,
Always truth.
Elegant swan—
Eagerness pressing,
Future bright,
Promises to keep.
Magnificent swan—
Emotions burning,
Sadness dawns,
Truth defied.
Wondrous swan—
Beauty fading,
Love grown cold,
Gone forever.

Kathe' Fabry
THE GOOD LIFE

It's a good life.
Solitary at times,
But good.
Makes you a believer in Yourself,
Makes a survivor of you.
Beats you to submission,
Kicks your ass,
Then picks you up,
Dusts you off,
Ready to begin again.
It's a good life.
Solitude isn't unbearable,
Only lonely, at times.

Karl Bell
URGENCY

Let me hold your hand,
Before the universe
Collapses back upon itself.
Let me hear you laugh,
Before the forces of gravity
in that waiting black hole
Sucks us in forever.
Let me see your eyes aglow,
Before the orbit of the earth
goes awry
And the sun scorches us all.
Let me feel you closer,
Before some piece of cosmic
garbage loose in space for ages
Connects with Mother Earth.
Let me know your love,
Before the imponderable forces
out there join together
And whisk us away
Into a dimension which perhaps
does not know love.

Beth A. Crago
FOR MY RAINBOW

It's a gray and
rainy day
and I'm feeling a lot
like the day.
But I think of you
and the sun
shines through
making
a rainbow.
You are my
rainbow,
cheering me
after a
long rainy spell.
Bright and beautiful,
a promise of
better things to come.
And even as
others chase after
an elusive pot of gold,
I sit and wait
for the time we can
be together again.
For the time will come when
your treasure will be mine.

Billie Louise Parkison
To Honor Martha Rosie Gilbert (On Her Retirement)

Martha Rosie Dear it's been so
nice having you here
How willingly, and unselfishly
You share.
You have been so good,
And would help
Anybody, anytime, anywhere, if
You thought you should.
You have been so friendly
And kind indeed,
Always anxious, and so willing
To lend a helping hand
To those in need.

We have all enjoyed your
Friendship
Down through the years,
Now that you are leaving
There will
No doubt be tears.
In the southeast corner of our
Setting room, in your
Chair.
Each morning, when we all
Return for work, you are always
Setting there.
Now all we will see, will be
Your empty chair.
We will miss your smile, we
Will Miss your laughter, we
Will miss you
Being so kind.
When you get through, we will
All be thinking of you
Wherever you go, whatever you
Do please don't forget all us
Cannery Girls.
Your leaving makes us all kinda
Sad but on your retirement,
We know will make you glad,
Your long needed rest you will
Find but remember you will
Always be on our mind.
You, we will never forget,
In the mean time
We must stay on our Cannery
Job awhile yet.
August 21, 1977 you will
Adjourn and when to work we
Return
Your empty chair we all will
See, never again will you be
There,
To speak to me.
We just wanted you to know,
That we all love you so,
And we wanted to tell you
Before you go.
We will assure you that your
Retiring will not be the end
Because all of us Cannery Union
Members will still be your
Friend.
Well I am going to stop right
Here I won't say any more
I wouldn't want this reading to
Become a bore.
God Bless You

Annette R. LaCroix
I WANT TO FLY

I want to fly like Jonathan
Livingston Seagull
free as a breeze
unfettered—at ease
joyous—circling
balancing—dipping
soaring—sweeping
gliding on a cloud—feathered
and clear
crystalline droplets forming
The flight is rapturous unlike
the reality that plunges
one downward into the
labyrinthine depths and never
to surface in a completed
essence
I just want to fly

Joan Stephen
THE PAPER SANTA

I remember this paper Santa;
Made by a childish hand—
His beard was a blob of cotton
Put on with a flourish grand;
His smile was slightly tilted
One arm was fastened to move;
The other one seemed
immobile—
Two eyes looked out from a
groove.
His boots had faded the first
year
The top of his hat was gone
But, he was still a kindly being
When viewed in the early dawn.
I love this paper Santa
I've cared for him like a friend;
'Cause there never will be
another—
When he's gone it will be the
end.

Mary Dupont
THE WONDER OF IT ALL

I am seeking the days before us
As treasures yet to unfold. . .
Not knowing the shift of the
wind,
Or the golden ploy of each day's
setting sun.
I'm looking forward to the
unspent, new days before us—
As to promises of Spring's
Blossoming moments of
unquenchable bliss—
Not caring what's amiss.
What's tomorrow's triumphs
Without yesterday's
mistakes?
Laughter without love?
Tomorrow promises COTTON
CANDY,
SO, Where are you?
The summer will be too lonely
to endure.
The winter, in its cold, lameing
trek,
Will surely freeze this
numbing heart to peak.
Let not these new days of this
New year
Find us devoid of hope;
existing on empty hearted
memories
Of yesterdays.
We could approach each, new,
sunkist dawn, arm in arm,
And blend into its
wonderment. . .
OH! The wonder of it all—
The wonder of it all,
With you beside
me, LOVE.

Barbara Van Steenburgh
SUDDEN AUTUMN

Last night
a golden galleon came
to moor
in my grey yard.
A ship of birch, fullsail,

became
a Blackbeard's lure.
Tomorrow?
Long John Silver wind
will plunder it
for sure.

Nancy O'Neal
DELUGE

Rain patters at my window,
The sky turns a misty gray.
Thunder roars all around me,
On this gloomy, dreary day.
A certain serenity comes to me,
As lightning streaks the sky.
I feel warm and contented,
Watching raindrops fly.

Celia Hooper
KALEIDOSCOPE

(Dedicated to: "The Town Wanderer"

I look at you, and what do I see?
And why do I feel compelled
to view you so specially?
I see no similarity between the
looks of you and me:

(You have your world, and I
have my two).
And even your strange
personality finds no friend in
me.
So, why do I feel we somehow
belong together—to help each
other?
And what is the reason I relate
to you and feel a little less
alone and lonely when I look
at you?
Is it just that—in you—I see a
little bit of me. . .?

Lynn Slover

MY STYLE

I carry a continual love
for you.
I didn't know it showed.
But friends say it suits my
style.
Apparently I wear it well
If others can see it
Tell me. . .
Can you feel it?

Edna Bockmier

DECEMBER

With racing feet I danced
Through January's snow and
ice
Ran rampant through to March.
Her winds were gone within a
trice
And there was April's budding
larch
I stooped to gather April's
flowers
But flung them all aside
May beckoned with a jeweled
crown
If I'd with her abide.
I ran pell-mell through flowers
strewn
I clasped her adolescent crown
Then tossed away to reach for
June
For she was radiant in her glory
A bower, a ripening moon
And riches in her dowry
Alas I fled through July's heat
To find an August rich of
harvest
Upon the trees ripe peaches
hung
(My children's arms, my
children's eager eyes!)
Like giant beads the sun had
strung.
On now I raced with tiring feet
To reach maturity of thought
and duty
Desire I could not satiate
For only fall in all her harvest
beauty
Can give the melon and the
grape.
I held them, one and all
Quick, eager and delighted.
They slid so fast between my
fingertips,
Sweet wines of life invited
To my parched and eager
hungry lips.
October fled, I know not where
I glimpsed her golden leaves
I dimly understood the price
While picking up the sheaves
I feel the first cold chill of ice.
I lean my head into the wind
Feet firmly planting steps
November storms are racing
past
Her days, her hours eternal
debts
Until I faintly see the night at
last
December—Oh, December!

Helmut Callis

LONELY

There is so much
That must remain unsaid
That poisons us—
Because there is no friend
To lance the wounds
And heal them lovingly.

John E. Sanks

I NEED YOU

For years we've been together
now
in you I do confide,
Please discontinue your
wanderlust
cause I need you by my side.
It helps so much to have
someone
to share the things of life,
You know I really need you
through happiness and strife.
You've changed so much—its
hard to say
just what our future will be,
But if you'll only stop and think
you'll always stay with me.
I loved you when I married you
my love I just can't hide,
So lets please start all over again
cause I need you by my side.

Winifred A. Coburn

SNOW DAY

A fluffy white comforter covers
the ground.
The whispering breeze is an
awesome sound.
The sky ashen blue and full of
big puffy clouds.
The trees heavy with snow,
limbs are bowed.
Children making angels in the
soft white snow.
Children with sleds giving
others a tow.
Their face is a picture with their
twinkling eye,
And a nose that quivers as the
snowflakes go by.
Some say this day is not meant
for man nor beast.
The children gobble it up like a
Holiday feast.
Snowman, snowfort and hurling
missiles in the air,
The children think this is the
Best day to share.

Violet Warren Campos

PERSPECTIVES

"If you'll climb up to my garret,
Said the String-bean to the
Carrot,
I'll show you wonders you have
never seen:
You'll see Corn with silken
tresses
Fat Peas in tight green dresses
And Mister Scare-crow with his
grouchy mien.
You are such a stupid feller
To stay down there in your
cellar
Where it's dark and damp and
really not quite clean."
The Carrot tossed his greenery
And said, "Phooey on your
scenery
I'm satisfied with life down here
below.
In the Earth it is my pleasure
To conceal my golden treasure
I'd hate to imitate your brazen
show,
Up in your leafy tangle
Where so foolishly you dangle,
You're a tempting sight to every
hungry Crow."
Then the Scare-crow in vexation
Shouted, "Stop this conversation,
You are both as vain and foolish
as can be.
You insult my fine tradition
By your shameless exhibition
When you force me to descend
to Referee,
And if my pride you'll pardon
I'm protector of the Garden—
Your very lives, my friends,
depends on me."
The Sun smiled down in wonder
At this scene of bluff and
blunder,
It had happened many times in
days of yore.
Well he knew, ere summer
ended,
Bean and Carrot would be
blended
In a pot of soup beyond the
Kitchen Door—
And the Scare-crow'd be divested
Of his duties, as he rested
In the Tool-shed, 'til the Spring
returned once more.

Henry T. Jones, Jr.

GOD IS

God is the wind that touches
our face,
The rain, the cloud and the
storm,
God is the air we softly breathe,
The fire that keeps us warm.
God is the sun that gives us life,
The moon, the stars, and the
sky.
God is the bird that takes to
wings,
The sparrow and the hoot owl's
cry.
God is the ground on which we
tread,
The forest and the trees so tall.
God is the corn, the wheat, the
grain
That we gather to the barn in
the fall.
God is the child that lives next
door,
Who plays in the park and the
street.
God is the people we see each
day,
The high, the lowly and the
meek.
God is the earth and all it
contains,
The heavens, the universe and
beyond.
God is yourself, the body, the
mind.
And greatest of all He's your
soul.

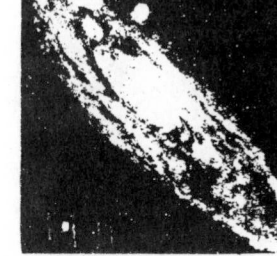

Kathleen M. LeCompte

GOODBYE TO GRANT

So long it seemed I walked the
earth
For sixteen years I felt cold and
alone
Wondering if there'd be one to
love
Someone to call my own
No Father had I, He'd long gone
away
His own blessing or maybe his
curse
My brothers, all older, had no
time
Yes, my family—for better or
worse
My sister, so footloose, but
never free
Just wandered the countryside
So close, yet so far apart were
we
Her own hurt she tried always
to hide
My father, my mother, even my
brother
Were lost mid the world's
flotsom it seemed
Gone were their visions, lost all
their hopes
Shattered was all they had
dreamed
Briefly I'd find fleeting
friendship
And laugh, if for a moment I
could
Oh, it's hard to be so alone
I hurt, though I tried hard to
be good
Ah, forget, yes, just forget for
awhile
Running madly against the wind
Being ill seemed at times to
bring loving care
Then followed guilt and a
feeling I'd sinned
Some said I was young with my
whole life ahead
But, Dear God, I felt really old
I'd longed for a little love and
a smile
Oh, God, I hurt, and the world
grows cold
Then a voice, "Come, Son, I
am your Father. . .
And My love is forever, you
see. . .
Come, see all the joys that await
you
Come, Grant, live in Heaven
with Me!

Midga

INTELLIGENCE IN EVOLUTION

Within the sphere of
intelligence
Resides two hemispheres of
knowing,
Recording its wisdom from
experience;
Pulsating electricity is
glowing!
Two hemispheres of
individualism,
Joined as two hemispheres in
unity,
Have evolved from blank

purism. . . .
Still in their infancy of maturity!
As the sands of an hour glass mount. . .
Through the passing of times,
So too, does the knowledge of recount
Grow as the mountain climbs.
Each has its purpose within age:
The right; construction and ideation,
The left; calculation and language,
Together, they know of the others creation!
Before the birth of the words spoken
Thought and communication traveled
In pictures, pure and unbroken. .
Perception and truth lived unchiseled!
Words have come to rule the thrown
Of thought and imagination
Cramping creativity that would of grown. . .
Like a seed sprouting from fertilization.
Little minds are taught to read and write
The language and history of our existence,
Learning to see and only recite. .
Denied the power of their adolescence!
Ridiculed and punished for day dreaming. . .
Denied the growth of their imaginations;
In the end. . .proves quite unredeeming,
For as they grow,
Dies the ability of their creation!
Genius immerges from a result of balance
Of maturation of both hemispheres;
Inbalance creates a vast disturbance
Within Nature and Her many gears!
Teach our children to view life imaged
Before they think in linguistics. . .
Intuition and perception must be encouraged,
If intelligence is not
To become eccentric!!!!!!

Donald D. Happel

YOU

Sometimes:
When a gentle breeze caresses my face,
Or the sun casts a golden haze on a silent stream,
The tears come to me
and I think of you. . . . .
Sometimes:
As I gaze into your eyes and look into your heart,
I see myself, but perhaps I am being vain.
Thinking, hoping that if I search your thoughts
I'll find myself. . . . .
Always:
I long to reach out and touch you softly.
To somehow show the feelings mere words don't convey.
A way to let you know what you mean and . . . . .
That I love you. . . . .
Always:
No matter what others may say or think,
If I feel like touching your shoulder
Or reach out and grasping your hand,
Then I will . . . . .
Never:
Not in this life or the better one to come
Will my love for you change, except to strengthen.
And if you should fall or lose your way,
You need but call and I'll be there. . .

Catherine Sedlak Ghiazza

KEEP THE "I" OUT OF IT

Who am I?
Am I a mystical dream or am I me?
Who is me?
"Me" is me!
A unique individual formed by the
Hands of God.
He loves me.
He cares for me.

He has promised me His strength and love.
With this promise in my heart, who could want more?
I am happy I am me!

Chani Susan Fischer

CONQUEROR

I have lived
A life of sorrow and loneliness,
Severed by hardships and maligning companions,
Until I quavered to continue
Life's inglorious battle.
But I will not surrender.
I am the Conqueror.
I have seen lust erupt
As mightily as a flaming volcano
Showering lava in burning destruction
As if to savor fear and submission
More heartily.
I have seen pain
As obliterating as a universe-quake:
The gentle moon and shimmering stars
Nestle in their comfortable surroundings
Emptied by a sudden shriek.
The bleak silence of nothingness prevails
Except for my screaming voice
And fragile body.
I have seen anger
Like a raging tornado
Sweep up the innocent and thoughtless,
Ruthlessly spilling their bodies
And years-earned possessions
On the shaken sand.
I have seen loneliness
Like a haunted night
Filled with wispy ghosts
Who speak in tremorous voices
And leave only
Memories and regrets.
But I will not surrender.
I am the Conqueror.
I am stubborn and courageous.
Some call me stupid.
I am honest and proud.
Some deem naive.
But I will never give in
To Life's commands:
"Forget!
Blind yourself in the
Dregs of drinks and mind-escaping drugs."
Until it screeches its final order:
"Kill yourself!"
I will make it
Far from the cry of
Eerie wails and unsettling disappointments
For the serenity of
An unquestioned existence
Of love, hope, and joy.
Yes—
The steps are difficult and long
Like a winding road
Along a series of mountains
Disappearing beyond the horizon
That a weary soul must climb.
But I will follow the road to its end
Where I will find:
Wind-flowing grasses
And rainbow-bright flowers;
Feel the sparkling-dancing water;
And touch others about me
In delighted communion.
And I will rejoice
Because I have made it.
I will never surrender.
I will always succeed.
I am the Conqueror.

Jeanine Ralstin

EMOTIONS

Personality is an embossed shield.
Something you can see and also feel.
Invisible, not to second sight.
To them, it's a little like flying a kite.

Steven Wayne Moore

TRUTH

I was a stranger, all alone.
Could not cope, was evil prone.
By nature I was a child of wrath.
Had no hope, my heart was stone,
And then the hands of time began to turn.
Truth of life and death was my concern.
So JESUS CHRIST revealed himself to me.
Abundant life I saw in him you see.
And then the light burst into my night
And all his glory shone.
God's love made known within his only Son.
And to my surprise, God opened my eyes
To watch him die and then arise.
On glorious power, I saw in that hour
As he ascended to Heavenly skies.
And then the hands of time began to turn.
Truth of life and death was my concern.
So JESUS CHRIST revealed himself to me.
"I'll come again to free, just wait and see.
As Lord of both the living and dead
I'll come again to your world.
Oh death where's thy sting, Oh grave thy victory?"
This truth I applied and could not hide.
In him I died, was crucified.
A new man was born, the old put aside.
The (white horse) of God's word I ride.
And as the hands of time begin to turn.
Truth of life and death is my concern.
So JESUS CHRIST reveals himself to me.
No greater friend there is that lives than he.
And even though he put on his show 2000 years ago,
He's the same yesterday, today, and tomorrow (I know).
His love I'll show. . . .until I go.

Tracy Pyles

TODAY ONLY

When times are hard and you feel blue
Think of others worrying too.
Just because your trials are many
Don't think the rest of us haven't any.
Life is made of joy and tears
Gladness and sorrows mixed up with fears
And tho to us it seems one sided
Trouble is pretty well divided.
If we could look into every heart
We find that each one has his part

And those who travel fortunes road
Sometimes carry the biggest load.
So my advice to those of you who needs some help to carry you through:
Don't carry the Past on your shoulder,
Don't double the load as you live and learn.
For Yesterday is dead and only memories
No way it can ever return.
When you carry a memory of

things that have been
You will be expecting
tomorrow to bring trouble
again.
All that has past and all that
has been
Can never return to be lived
again.
Living in the Future, which has
never been born
Invites uncertain fears,
borrowed distress and scorn.
Our Future lies ahead, or things
that will be
Are still in God's hands and
not up to me.
So all I should do is live for
Today
And trust God to show me
the truth and the way.

Eleanor Bash
HAIKU ONE—DOORS
When one door closes,
Another door will open.

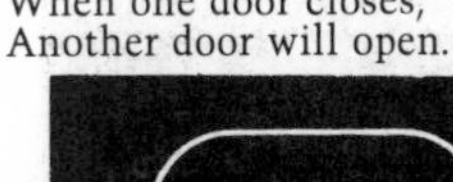

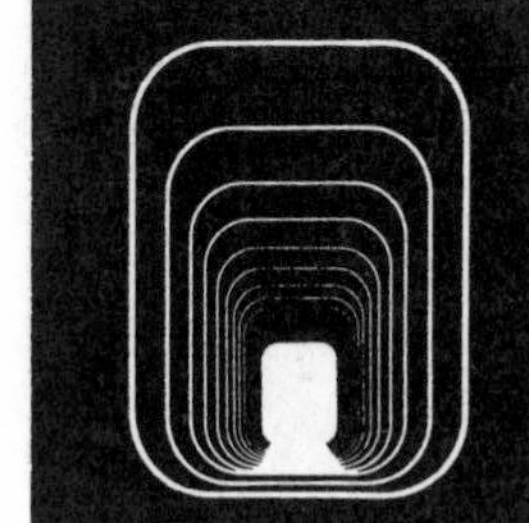

The inbetween hurts.

Elsie Halsey Lacy
POINTS FOR SALE OF POEMS
Know your chosen subject
and unfold its facts
ascertaining fascinations
with casts and attracts.
Picture with thoughts
imparted with imaginations
developed with supplies
from unfaltering ministrations
performed by the wise.
Though friends assign you
awards,
Remember sleek polish of poetic
themes
weave all rich rewards.
Too, it recompenses with
heightened
rise of the current sales
of your created poem.

Mable Hamblen
THE VICTROLA
We had a victrola of long, long
ago,
We'd crank it up, not too tight.
To listen to our favorite
records. . .
By lamplight. . .about every
night.
What happy memories came
along
When I listened to Kate or Bing.
I always played their records
And understood what they did
sing.
There was Enrico Caruso, of
opera fame
And cowboy ballads to hear. . .
"Red River Valley" or "Home on
the Range,"
And lots of songs of good cheer.
Then there were sad ones of
"Casey Jones"
And "The Baggage Coach
Ahead."
I'd listen to them all evening,
Until it was late and time for
bed.
Many of the old songs, that I
like to recall,
I whistled or hummed right
along.
And at times, I just couldn't
help it. . .
I'd burst right out loud, in
song.
I still have some very old
records,
But some, I really do miss.
When I recall the victrola of
yester-year. . .
And the music. . .I reminisce.
"May I Sleep in Your Barn
Tonight, Mister?"
As well as, "You Are My
Sunshine" and "Sweetheart."
It didn't take much time at all
For you to start and sing your
part.
We used to harmonize on all of
the songs. . .
Get up and waltz a while.
Or play, "Oh, Suzanna" and
square dance. . .
And sit down, puffing, and
smile.
Oh, it was fun playing all of
those records
On the victrola, so long ago.
You could sit so quiet in the
lamplight
And daydream a lot, I know.
Now, they have cassettes and
tapes
It's so different in every way.
That victrola had a special
sound. . .
I hear it, in memory, every day.

Barbara Lashbrook
WIZARD'S LULLABY
The legend is forgotten
In the dusty cornerstones.
The tombs of ancient rebels
Lie where grass is overgrown.
The twilight — so transparent;
'Neath the cradle of the sky,
The echo from the mountains
Whispers down a lullaby.
The fearless heart protected
By the magic of the wand.
The saga of adventure;
The unknown of what's beyond.
The father of the ages
Taught the children not to cry;
He soothed them with the
music
Of a wizard's lullaby.
The essence of a wizard;
Never fully understood.
Magician of concerto
Finds the gift in childhood.
Completed in the chapter
So the myth might never die;
A reckless preservation
Of the wizard's lullaby.

Paul J. Russell
THE SHELL
Sitting, wondering about life,
Madness slithers in with its
insideous smile,
Like the Cheshire Cat it
vanishes only to reappear.
I sit hoping that someone will
perceive the scream inside.
If only the shell would crack
and I could feel delight in
The nakedness of being one,
faceless in a crowd wondering
What will happen next.
Will I always be or will I cease?
How absurd existence when life
decays as awareness begins.

Virginia Green
TRY IT, YOU'LL LIKE IT
"Smile and the world smiles
with you,
Cry and you cry alone" so the
saying goes
'tis all too true for down
through the years
it has been shown.
Remember that a smile goes a
long, long way
So be sure to smile at some
one you meet
And wish them a happy day.
You will see in their eyes, an
expression of surprise
For that may be just what
they need
If their expression should
change and they smile back
You would have done
someone a good deed.
A babys smile shows
contentment
A parents smile shows love
A grandparents smile shows that
life has been well spent
While counting their
treasures given from above.
Now be sure to start your day
with a smile
And remember this quote that
some unknown poet has wrote
"It is easy enough to be pleasant
When life flows along like a
song
But the man worth while is one
who will smile
When everything goes dead
wrong."

Jenna V. Ownbey
MY FLAG IS FLYING. . .
My flag flings its living stars
Into the sunlit sky;

Its heart sings like a bird on
wing
To catch the wind rush by. . . .

John Joseph Burchek
ONE DAY
A sleepy dawn approaches us
waking from a splenderous
sleep
A new awakening, a new day, a
fresh start to explore
something new
Our eyes finally open to a gleam
of splendor looking at the
sunshine that fills our hearts
and knowing the treasures a
new day brings
All is behind us now except
memories of the past
One day is our day after our
life have begun, not as a new
born child but as we choose
one day be won
Our goals are set with new
strength, fastly our energies
proceed
To accomplish what may in our
one day that have just begun
One day whom might ask
should be the greatest day of
our lives
Our guess should not be maybe
tomorrow for now this day
have one
Our awakening from a splendid
bliss, renewed strength to go
on just for today, for
tomorrow may never come
Take your toll for all its
worth and one day can be
your continuous growth as we
take one day at a time
Tomorrow can be maybe a plan
but never one day in our life
Today is special from dawn to
dusk but when we retire our
next day may never come
So keep today as your special
goal and let tomorrow be only
a dream
For God in his holiness will
choose if that dream unfold to
a new day that may never
come

Eleanor Hughes
THE REFUGEE
The dawn will bring no joy to
them
these children of the Nile
The awful pain that hunger
brings
A mystery to the child
The mother's prayer, that used
to be
the answer to all things
Now goes all but unanswered
as death, the new day brings
Her children's swollen middles
and the tiny stick line limbs
cannot be helped by promises
or the singing of the hymns
It happened oh so slowly
and no one seemed to know
even as they watched it
The way the land would go
What once was green and fertile
aboundant in it's yield
Is now a barren wasteland
just waiting for the kill
The clouds that once were full
of rain
still hang there overhead
But empty now and hostile
They seem to mock the dead
The one's who could have
helped them
were to busy with their wars
and making people homeless
A drain on other shores
Now many more are dying
Not soldiers tall and strong
But helpless little children
who never made this wrong
In clusters there, they cling
to life
A sea of misery
A human tide of suffering
We call them Refugee

Austin Thomas
ZEST OF LIFE
The zest of life you are sure
to find,
If you have a feeling of love for
mankind,
People will respond to a smile
and a grin,

Treat them like brothers and
sisters,
And they will treat you like kin,
For love of life is a state of
mind,
Which you can have very
easily—or be left behind,
So why not live life to the
fullest,
Without a frown or a smirk,
To be complaining all the time
about things you can't change
is a silly quirk,
For if you approach a person
with a cheerful attitude,
He is infected—and that's the
end of my platitude.

Darlene Parkin
FEELING STRONG

Tonight the world
looked so microscopic,
As if I could
pat the hillside
with the palm of my hand,
Plug the smoke stacks
of the factory with my
little finger.
I felt above it all,
As if with one step
I could wipe out an
entire city.
Loving you has
helped me realize
my own power.

Carlton Ray Loftin
DIFFERENT

Differently we live our lives
With the passing of the days
Each of us struggling
In our differen't ways
Each with differen't goals
Embedded in our minds
Using differen't methods
To achieve them at the time
Touching different lives
Of their's that we see
Becoming part of them
And part of them we'll be
Traveling differen't paths
Reaching different ends
Then stopping to look back
To where it all began
Suddenly you realize
As your past you recall
All that you thought was
different
Wasn't that different after all

Karen Kay Bricker
OF TOMORROW AND TODAY

I ponder and think
Of tomorrow and today
Of yellows and greens
Daffodils and daisies
Of men and love
Jealousy and hate
Of wealth and poverty
Hopes and dreams
Shattered and broken
Scattered and torn
Of tomorrow and today
I ponder and think

Carolyn Nau Masters
THE WALL AT BERLIN

I stand beside a wall
A mass of brick and stone
That rises upward and divides
A city into two parts.
One side the East; one side the
West,
Two ideologies grappling for
A once-whole people who fear
the wall,
Who feel its throbbing in their
lives.
The swath is deep across this
land—
A massive, sanguine wound
festering with long life,
Quivering with swollen
exposure
To fierce tyrants and foreign
sway.
Before the wall there was a land
Of lofty aims and bold ideals,
Recently united and longing for
Fulfillment as a whole.
Beside me stands a crippled
man.
I look at him, then at the wall.
A wound has brought
unwholeness
To man and country both alike.

Joseph Ezzo
A WORD

is there a word
which says for me
what I have to say
there is
a universe of words
and yet none
I think
ride the wings of my thought
to my mouth
or pen
where heart
loins
and brain engender
I simply feel
a moment's glance
and gone
Wisdom I think
or nothing

Paul J. Lin
SUN DIAL

Each second, each moment
You jeer at the busy clock
Racing hopelessly with time.
You understand
The principle of steadfast
perserverance
And stand, erect, let time

Chase around the shadow of
your face,
Ever striving
To complete your solid life
Ever changing, moment after
moment
In your eternal existence.

Zona Albright Chedsey
MY MUSEUM

I paint the prairie sunset
That ushers in the night,
My canvas, magic memory,
My brush, the gift of sight.
The golden hues give softly
As the shaded pinks glide by,
Blending to a bursting brilliance
In the framed expanse of sky.
Though I am far from great
museums
With their Renoirs and Monets,
I have unsurpassed collections
Of the sunsets of June days.

Lisa Pietrocarlo
THE WHITE ROSE

I took a white rose
from out of the snow.
Where it came from
I didn't know.
I smelled its petals
and touched its leaves
As I saw a bird
fly out of the trees.
Could it be I wandered
that springs almost here.
No, it can't be
Oh, now it's clear.
This is a reminder
of times gone by
Laughter, sorrow
tears, a short cry.
This is a warning
not to forget
Happiness, sorrows
a kind person I'd met.
I saw a new light
in the life that I had.
Memories are'nt for forgetting
Some happy, some sad.
Reminders for sharing, loving,
growing
giving others something you
possess
Things you've experienced
and none of the rest.
With your heart
your thoughts can be shown.
And others will realize
how inside you've grown.
I turned with the rose,
still clenched in my hand
Then dropped it and placed it
for an unknown friend.
Let another gain
the wisdom I'd found
That happiness can't be
captured or bound.
I smelled the rose
just once again
And dreamt on to the future
but saved what had been.

Scott Beebe
UNTITLED

The seagull gently rose in the
air,
Calling to its mate,
As it majestically flew away.
The gentle breeze stirred the
sand,
Forever changing the way before
him,
He gazed at the seagull,
And the sand,
And a warmth flooded his soul.
He turned his gaze to the water,
But quickly turned away,
And the warmth returned.
The shifting sand gave way
under his footsteps,
Leaving his imprint as he moved
on.
He looked back to see his
footprints,
But the water had already
washed them away.
He wished for their existence.
Timidly he approached the
water.
It washed cold upon his feet.
He retreated one, then two
steps,
Until a huge boulder blocked
his way.
Standing there he looked at the
horizen,
So far away.
There, he suddenly knew, was
his destiny.
The water got colder with each
step.
He swam forward with little
conviction,
Trying to keep his destiny in
sight.
Periodically he would stop,
And look behind him.
But there was no trace of his
path.
He continued on.
Slowly darkness descended upon
him.
His destiny could no longer be
seen.
He could no longer even see
the beach,
From where he had come.
All was black.
He stopped swimming then,
Waiting for light to return.
He grew tired,
And the struggle to stay afloat,
Became increasingly difficult.
Slowly he began to sink.
"Help!" he cried, "Help me!"
Then, from the darkness, a light
appeared.
Slowly it grew in volume,
Until the light formed a hand.
A perfect hand.
The hand stretched itself out
to him.
Then a voice,
Coming from the blackness,
Surrounded him.
"Take my hand, and I shall save
you."
A great fear swept over him,
For he could not understand
what this was.
"Take my hand, and I shall save
you," repeated the voice.
"Come closer!" he cried.
"I cannot free myself enough
to reach!"
Then the darkness was split
with laughter.
From everywhere, all around
him,
Mocking him.
The water closed over him.

Florence E. Brytcuk
THE WIND

The wind is blowing a mad Pace,
It doesn't seem to get any place.
It blows your hair and slaps
your face,
Then never seems to leave a
trace,
Of it's departure to other lands.
To redden noses and freeze the
hands.

Kimberly B. Hanks
UNTITLED

Mommy why do you hit me if
you love me?
Is it like this with everyone
else?
If it is right then why does it
hurt so bad?
Mommy do you love me?
Do you just get mad or am I a
bad little girl?
Does this happen to every little
girl?
If it does then why doesn't
anyone else have scars and
bruises like me?
Mommy, please don't get mad!
Please don't hit me again!
Mommy it hurts!

Mommy!
I love you.

Tara G. Mullin
FRESHMAN

I want to go home
cries the freshman
I have no friends
the school is so big
the courses too hard
there's nothing to do
the cries of one
beginning again
a new life to
adjust to
to conquer
There's nothing there
to cushion you
when you fall
The dependence on Dad
has become
the independence on you
It's quite a big step
for those who have
no other siblings
to suddenly find themselves
with roomies
for those who have
never left home
to suddenly find themselves
with a new family
There are those who leave
walking away from
the constant pressures
But there are those
like you
who keep busy
be it politically
or playing ping-pong
that manage to stay
above
the drowning line

Mrs. James J. Bunner
THE GENTLE RAIN

The rain is falling, falling ever
so gently.
The Robin hops along, puts his
ear to the ground,
Where fishing worms abound.
Very quickly he pecks around,
Until his dinner he has found.

Then he flies up on a post,
Fluttering and spreading his
wings.
The rain falls gently on him
As he takes a refreshing shower,
And ever so beautifully he
sings.
No wonder he's so happy,
A nicer day I've never seen.
It is much cooler now, the air
is fresh and clean.
"Thank you God for such gifts"
You have given my spirits a lift,
As I watch the Robin in the
gentle rain.

Zane C. Chambers, Sr.
THE VALLEY OF TRANQUILITY

In my mind I shall paint a
picture
Of the most beautiful place that
ever can be,
Where there's joy, happiness,
and human understanding;
I shall call it the Valley of
Tranquility.
There is no government except
as people will;
For pardons there is no charge
or fee;
People ask forgiveness, and
forgiveness is given,
There in the Valley of
Tranquility.
No one places restrictions upon
me when I move;
I am free, free to roam, yes,
free to flee;
No one says I must go, no one
says I must stay;
It happens in the Valley of
Tranquility.
I fear not the taunts of bigotted
men,
For all are equal; there is no bias
causing misery;
There are no races, there are no
poor,
And no one will ridicule in the
Valley of Tranquility.
If I wish to build the smallest
of houses,
No one will laugh because it is
wee;
Each one builds the house he
wishes;
That's the way it is in the
Valley of Tranquility.
I shall build my house and build
my life;
I shall build in the best way I
see,
And there I shall choose to live
my life,
Nestled in the Valley of
Tranquility.
But there are others who may
not know
That this place is not just for
me;
It is within your heart if you
wish,
The place I call the Valley of
Tranquility.

Franco Buono
BEAUTIFUL BIRTH

The beauty of a newborn Child
Is astonishing grace of holiness.
The fascination of his magnetic
eyes
Is ocean of tenuous fluid.
The candor of his smile
Is recess of the Logos profound.
That's the miracle that parents
enjoy
Like Annette and David
Botindari.
The Lord comes to abide softly
In the loved Dave Baby deepest
within.
Like waves of moonlight so
precious is his grace.
Parents cradle him in arms
That make his welcome throne.
Their happiness is within a tiny
face,
Whose life is their charm
To fill the coming years in
blending memories,
That glorify in song the
mountains and the seas.
Time shall pass away so
magically,
As mountains whisper to the
rivers,
So shall one day sparkling little
beams
Of thoughts fill his manhood
grown.
Such pride in all that parents
have sown
May be their own
From that April day when he
was born.
That special day saw God's glory
in the dawn!

Elizabeth Nolan Wilson
THE CONNOR

O Symbol of a leisured time, of
elegance and grace,
O Rendezvous for celebrants,
where Titans set the pace,
What memories of glories past
illuminate your halls,
Of dancers, formally attired,
those wondrous Programme
Balls!
The magic rhythmic melodies
the music masters made,
The mellow, glowing ambiance!
The big bands! How they
played!
If ghosts could talk!
And then you stood
abandoned and alone.
Reduced by so-called progress to
nine cold floors of stone,
Your marble stairs, rotunda,
forgotten by your town
Like someone's poor relation in
tattered evening gown,
Besieged by taxes, changing
times, neglect and wind and
rain,
You stood erect, aloof and tall,
and tried to hide the pain.
No detonator, not for you, as
loomed the fated knell—
You bowed, disdainful, proud
throughout, and broken-
hearted,
Fell.

Jennifer L. Quass
MAINLINED

Glancing at the fine figure you
cut
Out of the darkness.
A hazy marijuana man
With chilling cocaine kisses
That numb my mouth and
tongue, I
Can't get enough of you.
In your arms opiated embrace,
I am a free-floater,
Watching as my fantasies play
back
In your hallucinogenic eyes.
Stripping to the flesh, you and I
Trace each other.
An amphetamine rush
Catches me and I'm set free.
My body a tourniquet, I am
Ready to receive
Your spilling morphine dream
life.
And I lay back,
Feeling no pain, yes
I am an addict.

Michelle L. Sullivan
ASPEN GROVE

The trembling aspens
Raise their white limbs
Above a carpet of dry grass.
Their coin-shaped leaves,
Touched with gold,
Send rustling music
Through the autumn air.
Could the aspens be shaking
With a feeling of cold and fear,
Or perhaps their tremble
Is a tremble of radiant joy?

Franco Buono
DEATH RITUAL

To live is of life the daily
anxiety
By looking at far, far past.
But stubbornly to it turning,
With unnecessary regret
Some wait the death.
Oh distressing thought!
To believe that almost
This should be supreme
freedom,
No!. . .It is not!
How much grateful to the sky
A generous gesture should be!
Rise up if the fate
Exhausted you on the ground!
It might happen that one day a
tear
Shall still appear around my
eyes
Wetting the age of my life.
In this case you, too, shall feel
A high warmth of youth.
If such is the effect of a tear,
That's what I call life to be
lived, yes,
Not to be consummated into
wretched idleness,
Not to be exhausted on the
ground,
Not to be felt in torment,
But to be extended to everyone
Of Orient and Occident!
That's what I call life to be kept
In serene spirit confidently
In the gladness and in the
sorrow!
Please confide! This is life!

Jon K. Shuppert
MY LADY

I am searching for a life in
heaven.
Because in heaven I know there
is you.
I am searching for a galaxy of
love.
I know that galaxy lies within
you.
You are like a beautiful flower
in full bloom and I want to be
your sun.
For me to be without your love
would be like living in a
world without the sun.
My lady, oh my lady you are the
blood within me!
Giving me life and always in my
heart.
You and I shall never ever part.
Because without your love life
would leave forever from my
heart.
My life was in a different world

before I met you.
In a world without the
happiness which you have
given me.
In a world without the love
which you have shown me.
In a world where I could only
imagine of a life with a angel
on earth.
Eternity life with you would be
a heavenly dream come true.
I truly wish to hold you forever
and ever.
I realize my life on earth will
not last forever.
But I have got the will and I
shall find the way to hold my
lady after I die, hold her
forever and ever!

Sher Clark
FIRE AND HONEY
Fire
and
honey. . .
he is
fire
and
honey. . .
when he
makes love
to me
he is
fire
and
honey. . .
and it is
warm
and
sweet
and
good. . .

Thomas Thorson
EASTER
A lily, o'ergrown,
Hidden by deceptive weeds,
Withers,
Forgotten by the sun.

Jane Aline Breaux
STOP AWHILE
Where is everyone going?
Rushing here and there,
They don't even know,
No one takes time to stop and
care.
Take some time for yourself,
It will do you good
To slow down,
Think for awhile,
And look around.
Go in a quiet room,
Turn the lights out
Pull yourself together,
And think things out.
You'll be surprised to find,
Some of the things in your
mind,
That's been sitting back,
Waiting to come out.
Don't hold anything inside,
While you take this little time
Concentrate, and see what you
find.
There could be another person
inside
Begging for your help,
Let him out!
Let him out!
Can't you hear him asking,
This little person inside?
Take some time out and
Listen to him for awhile.
Stop all the music and
Go inside yourself,
There's someone inside,
That needs your help.
Give him a chance,
He's waiting for you
Don't be afraid to face the truth,
You have nothing to lose.
Then turn the lights on,
And begin your life again
It could be different,
All the way to the end,
All the way to the end.

Karin Lindgren
UNTITLED
I stand very high from you,
whirlpool galaxy,
pinwheel of ocean agate and
foam.
White-fisted tentacles spin out
and fold in with centripetal fury;
Is your aura centered
in your emerald eye?
Alien cloud of water stars
skims the earth with its
tendril touch and snatches me
with its taloned promise.
Rabid maelstrom bends
the breakers of my laughter.

Lester Nicholas Recktenwald, Ph.D., F.I.A.L.
VICTORY
Defeat! defeat! defeat!
You have had it! Forget it! For—
Are you not alive and on your
feet?
If not, then arise on your feet
And strike with your hammer
On the anvil,
And beat, beat, beat
To the crackling of the heat
And greet, greet, greet
Your victory.

Michael J. Stanko
COMMUNICATION WITH CONSCIENCE
As I sat alone one Sunday
morning
Suddenly I sensed a hint of
warning,
And as my conscience began to
speak
Sad tears started to roll down
my cheek.
A little scolding here and there
Slowly, surely, my soul was laid
bare,
So here was that ugly part of me
None of us ever really care to
see.
True words, like a blackboard,
we can try to erase
But we all need the courage to
meet them face to face,
Oh yes, of course, I will try to
be good
Said by many of we mortals,
that's understood.
Blame it all on circumstances
beyond your control
But you can control your
conduct
to save your soul,
My conscience got these words
off his chest
Temporarily peaceful, my mind
was at rest.
Then much nicer thoughts came
to the fore
Recalling good deeds, nearly by
the score,
Then tears of joy down my
cheeks did roll
My conscience was salved, but
not the soul.
Thank you conscience, for the
short visit
It's been worthwhile, please
don't say "is it",
I know that you will be with me
to the end
Now and always need you, just
like a good friend.

Nina Di Lorenzo
THE COMMUNION OF LOVE
The communion of love
Is like the sea touching
The sands on a sunny day,
And this, my friend, is a form of
love
When all else is washed away.
The communion of love
Is like a covenant
Where unrehearsed promises are
made,
This too, my friend, is the kind
of love
That time will neither mar nor
shade.
The communion of love
Is like a tree
Both sturdy and unbending,
And through the years
My love shall be
A love that's never ending.

B. Frank
SONNET ON FREE VERSE
Free verse is fine for those
who want to let
Their words flow out like seeds
broadcast to earth
And land where'er they fall,
and never get
Down to the thinning out that
gives such worth
To gardens, having each plant in
its row
And every row the same length,
more or less,
With space between each plant
and row to grow
And lift the leaves which sun
and rain caress.
To scatter seeds is one way
to begin
To have some fruit, but
Nature's fruit is small,
Til Man steps in to train and
prune and thin;
And then he gets the fullest
fruit of all.
To sketch or practice with,
free verse is fine;
But sonnets are the masters'
high design.

John M. Cohen
Middle Age Awareness
I've grown too fond
of these walls I have built.
Cling to life
with no more than some hopeful
thoughts
and but a handful of
memories.
I walk blindly
and restricted
in no more than familiar
surroundings
with so few
accomplishments,
it's become hard
to imagine life has a future.
In this state, I can no longer
bear.
Have I surrendered.
surrendered,
damn,
oh help sweep me from
deep in this corner
where darkness hugs
serenity,
and the future,
a life style that takes a path
in which glory,
will play no part. . .

Ethel Hunt Street
CARE LESS
You seldom stop to say hello,
I see you passing by;
If you don't care to see me now
Don't bother when I die.
For then I cannot hear your
voice,
Nor see your look of sorrow;
Nor smell the flowers you
would bring
If I should live tomorrow.

M. J. Roedel
WHO AM I?
I am a mansion of many
windows,
some of which are cracked,
most of which are grimy,
each of which looks out on its
own universe.
Who am I?
I am a mansion
of many windows.

R. Michael Ingenito
REPERTOIRE
A carnival of shadows
filled to overflowing.
A tapestry of souls
ebbing with the tide.
A child acanter on horseback.
A ferris wheel afire
in the sky.
A life surviving on solitude.
A rowboat old and rotting.
A raven complaining
to the sunset.
A franscican alone
at service.
A young girl blushing,
nervous.

Cathleen Gail Cuppett
INSOMNIACS
Oh, pity those who cannot
sleep,
When all is dark, and darkness
deep.
When thoughtful thoughts ne'er
slow nor cease,
When tormenting worries
greatly increase,
When still is the night, and
loud is the mind,
The silent blackness is not kind.
Thy fellow creatures have no
rest,

But lie abed in anguished
distress.
The flesh fights soul; the soul
fights flesh,
And nightfall can neither one
refresh.
Oh agony, oh wretched grief,
Only in death is their relief.

Frances Dix
SOLITUDE
I sat one day upon a hill
searching for I knew not what
when suddenly my thoughts
took wings
and flew away like darting birds
to lands across the sea
Where dwelled I knew not who
to treasures yet to me unknown
to places where I longed to be
Then suddenly my thoughts
came rushing back again
like butterflies on velvet wings
as I sat upon the hill
and wished for things that
could not be.

Alessandra A. Poles
CIRCLE OF SPRING
Spring breathes in romance
Voices magnificant
Plants and trees flaunt charm
Like crystals reflect colors.
Summer blossoms out
All its cherished love
Paintings from its palette
Each season sheer delight.

Fall projects on earth
Lavish bronze from greens
Lazily hanging autumn
In shades of amber and reds.
Winter like galaxies
Glitters silvery white
Draws in snow for sleep
Fixed nature's way to blend.
Musical spheres are heard
Bells in cadence chime
Rains bring fresh new air
Thought of rebirth awakes.

Peggy Parker
ON A LAZY, LAZY SUMMER DAY
On a lazy, lazy summer day
I sat beneath the trees
And watched the placid river
Flow past with gentle ease.
My thoughts were mostly day
dreams,
Spinning cobwebs here and
there.
The bees' hum was monotonous;
Birds' songs filled the air.
My fishing pole lay idle
Beside me on the ground.
The fishing line curved loosely,
The float moved slowly 'round.
A Dragonfly lit on the line
And sent a lovely shiver
In ever widening circles
To arouse a sleeping river.
Now tell me truthfully, if you
can,
Is there a better place to be
Than on a shady river bank
'Neath the branches of a tree?

Majie Beard
JUST WONDERING
Think not for what tomorrow
may bring
It may be summer or winter
or spring
But the one who sends it
can see afar
The one who has moulded you
into what you are.
Sometimes you worry about
things unknown;
Fret not! for your efforts from
you are not gone
You can do many things you've
never tried
So don't just wonder, and ride
with the tide.
A glimpse of the future and
you wouldn't even go
But Great is the Archer that
bends the Bow
And swift as an arrow you
must be sent
For life goes forward, it's not
backward bent.
The length of the rainbow, the
width of the sky
Are some of the reasons that
we shouldn't shy——
And expect not the greatest, at
least be content
For the Blessings that come
The Master has sent.

Lauris Ann Hawkins
YOU ARE ALONE
I feel your tiny fingers wrapped
tightly around mine, secure,
knowing
I am with you. . .and I am.
Be with you as close as you
want
for as long as I am able to be
but I know I will have to
leave.
How do I explain that in the
end
no matter how many stand
beside you
nor how close they be. . .
you are alone.
Even I cannot accept this. All
life ends
and never will you have a true
friend
for eventually they will go
from you.

Judy Moffet
THE ROSE
The bud
Of beauty
Unfolds, glows.
Though one
Has faded,
Another grows.
Its scent
Penetrates
Deepest pain.
Passion
With promise,
Spring again.

Katherine Schultz
THE EQUALIZER
There once was a rich man
named Scotty,
Who was very self-centered and
haughty.
He's above me he thinks,
But his logic has kinks,
'Cause even a rich man goes
potty.

Tara Key
IT'S IN MY EYES
If you're waiting for words
To tell you how I feel
Just look into my eyes;
They are for real.
If I sometimes seem cold
Or like I don't care
Just look into my eyes;
Warmly waiting there.
If you ever want to tell me
Anything at all
Just look into my eyes;
I'll receive the call.
If you ever need
Someone to be there
Just look into my eyes;
They will always care.

Winnie Zerne
REGRET
With the first leaf that falls
Until in the spring, the leaves
turn green,
I wonder: How did Adam and
Eve Feel?"
Having never seen anything die;
They were expelled from
Paradise—
Together they experienced the
death of nature;
Eve must have wondered during
the long winter;
"When will the leaves return?—
We cannot bathe in the river
now—
It is covered with ice."
When the leaves returned, the
flowers bloomed,
The birds began to sing again—
They were glad and rejoiced,
But every fall they went through
the agony of regret—
And they laid aside fuel and
food for the winter ahead.

Robbin Leigh Hunt
MOMMY'S LITTLE GUN
Time to shoot, you have no say
First live action, then replay
We will be noticed by everyone
Got to find Mommy's Little
Gun.
I'm playing a deadly game
Close to you, a better aim
Where's the target, It's gonna
be fun
Got to find Mommy's Little
Gun.
Takes nerve to pull the trigger
Cut down a famous figure
Where's the bullets, I need
more than one
Got to find Mommy's Little
Gun.
I found it on Mom's
nightstand
Something special in my
hand— BLAM!
She'll be proud of a
murderous son
Got to use Mommy's Little
Gun.
With weapon I'm on patrol
To New York for rock and roll
Musical fame has he, I have
none
Glad to use Mommy's Little
Gun.
I love your movies, I'm sick
I'll nail the head Politic
I'm happy to be in Washington
Glad to use Mommy's Little
Gun.
In Rome I caused quite a scene
Then I bought blanks for the
Queen
My ammunition gave them a
stun
Glad to use Mommy's Little
Gun.
I found it on Mom's
nightstand
Something special in my
hand—BLAM!
Are you proud of your
murderous son?
Had to use Mommy's Little
Gun.

Dean Gehring
THIS IS WHAT I DREAD
I dread the day when I will be
gone.
As I'm sure men have since first
they saw dawn.
Yet, bad as it is, it is not my
worst fear.
The worst fear I have is that
no one will hear.
Hear the things that I have
to tell,
Forget them all as if they
never befell.
Then my life will have gone
for naught,
And all my battles will never
have been fought,
And all that I am, will have
been forgot.

Mary Langdell Marshall
I Dance On God's Carpet
The earth is God' footstool they
say,
And 'tis true that I like it this
way,
For I dance on God's carpet
when I am alone.
And I feel so much nearer His
throne.
I dance on His carpet so green
And the glorious sky is between.
But I'm sure way up there He is
sharing my prayer
Which is danced on His carpet
so green.
The earth is the Lord's I am sure
And each gift that He gives us
is pure
So I'll dance on His carpet the
song that I feel
And I'm sure He will know it is
real.
I dance on His carpet so bright
And the glorious stars in the
night
Whether shining or dim send
my message to Him,
As I dance on His carpet so
bright.

Drucilla Bain
THE STORM
I like to watch a storm begin
And watch the brilliant sun go in
And see the black clouds piling high
Like smoky screens across the sky.
I like to watch the birds seek shelter
And people scurry helter-skelter
To dodge the drops of falling rain
That soon beat on my window pane.
I like the sturdy gusts of wind
That make the trees and saplings bend
And see the flashing darts of light
That make the interim seem night.
I like to hear the steady pour
And know that I am safe-secure
Within my room.
And then when all the storm is past
And the rumbling thunder's gone at last,
I'm glad to know that soon again
I can watch another storm begin.

Connie M. Gibbens
LETTERS TO HEAVEN
Send these letters high aloft,
Into the ethers vast and far;
Give them passage on the breeze;
Send them hurtling on a star.
Or if a fleecy cloud drifts by—
He'd watch them often with me here—
Float them thereon to his new home
Beyond my sight yet very near.
He'd watch the jets streak thru' the sky,
White vapor trails against the blue,
Until they'd disappear from sight
His eyes would follow as if he knew
That soon he too would wing his way
Along that same bright blue sky trail;
So if one passes overhead
Take my letters and heart to him Air Mail.

Oran Bollinger
The Rise And Fall Of Man
It took a million million years, we're told
For God to create man.
With ooze and slime and muddy stuff
God's thoughts a million years did span.
A million more to spark some life
That neither thought nor ran.
What joy in heaven there must have been
When, BANG! Eternity began!
Another million years passed by
As single cells learned to unite;
And millions more to move those cells
From darkness into light.
With light to stimulate their growth,
Those simple cells became complex.
They took on form and swam about
With no awareness of a need for sex.
No simple task that was, you see,
to mold that mud into a shape—
Up through fish and frogs and flying things
The hand of God brought forth the ape.
The ape was not the image God had in mind
To oversee the wondrous earth,
So, onward through the passing years
The ape ascended to give man birth.
From trees to caves and prairie lands
The ancient form evolved to stand.
Discovering fire and stones and spears and guns,
Homo Sapiens at last controlled the land.
Science works from present to the past
by un-evolving modern shapes.
Consider this, with tongue in cheek,
Man, the orn'ry cuss, sprang direct from apes!
In reading this brief historic tale
You may rightly reject its hypothesis.
You've read of days from one to six
That told of instant man in Genesis.
It may not have taken those million million years
For God to finish out His Plan—
But it only takes a woman's passing glance
To make a monkey out of man!

Michael R. Burch
AT TWENTY—TWO
There are mountains purple and packed with time,
home to goats and misfit trees.
in lofty grandeur above vexed seas
they lift their haughty heads.
When the sun explodes above pale peaks
while clear fountains splash in crystal ruin
against the ancient nature runes
of tales to this day untold,
I taste with my eyes the dawn's fierce gold
and breathe the fragrant mountain air,
drinking deeply, wondering where
the magic days of youth have gone.

John R. Schofield
GREEN-EYED MICE
The green-eyed mice played leap-frog
Upon the elephant's trunk;
When they crawled inside, the elephant cried:
"This isn't any bunk!
This isn't any bunk-I-bunk,
This isn't any bunk!
I've told you once, you green-eyed mice,
And I'll be switched if I tell you twice,
This isn't any bunk!"
The green-eyed mice then went to sleep
Within the elephant's trunk;
And when they snored, the elephant roared:
"This isn't any bunk!
This isn't any bunk-i-bunk,
This isn't any bunk!
I've told you once, you green-eyed mice,
And I'll be switched if I tell you twice,
This isn't any bunk!"
The green-eyed mice then wakened up
Within the elephant's trunk;
And as they woke, the elephant spoke:
"This isn't any bunk!
This isn't any bunk-I-bunk,
This isn't any bunk!
I've told you once, you green-eyed mice,
And I'll be switched if I tell you twice,
This isn't any bunk!"
The green-eyed mice went out to play
Out of the elephant's trunk;
As they went away, they heard him say:
"This isn't any bunk!
This isn't any bunk-I-bunk,
This isn't any bunk!
I've told you once, you green-eyed mice,
And I'll be switched if I tell you twice,
This isn't any bunk!"

Candy McGee
THOUGHTS AT THE END OF DAY
The quiet at the end of day,
Lots of work and seldom play,
I'm on the run.
A pleasing sight, a pleasing sound,
The beauties of the world abound,
I share with none.
The pleasure of a fine ballet,
Mixed with a glass of good claret,
These things are fun. . .
A cozy fire, a glass of wine
A cigarette; these things are mine
Till they are done.
Rachmaninoff, Beethoven, too
Are my joys, but they please so few.
Am I just one?
Someone to share these small delights,
The hectic days and quiet nights
I have not won. . .
When lonely feelings come to me,
I search my soul and finally see
That it will come.

Helen C. Smith, Ph. D.
THE SOUNDING PRESENT
Here in the sod where Indian pinks once sprang
to vivid bloom, foundations of concrete
have sunk their mighty roots; the whir and clang
of industry supplants bird song once sweet
above the wild hay fields; and farmsteads, set
long years ago in poplar groves, now stand
only in dreams the old cannot forget. . .
New dreams have stamped their image on the land.
Yet in this metamorphosis one still
may vaguely trace the early patterning
of humble days, made beautiful by will
to see fresh hope in toil of each year's spring;
so shall the fortitude of dreamers last—
the sounding present holds the silent past.

Morell Kresser
HOW TO PAINT A POEM
Tell us how to paint a poem
From Earth's pregnant palette.
Sketch skids, scars and stars
With Zymurgy.
Splash emotions on canvas.
Mix wild moods from
Cadmium to Umber
With a handful of brushes.
Tell us how to quiver Our Peers.
Shiver Old Masters with
Alizerin pain.
Click typewriter keys in
rhythms of rain.
Research November's far-flung
sky———
Study Scorpio's Writing,
strung-out high!
How to paint a poem?
Give us a clue.
Scorpio's Answer!
Shatter the Cosmos
With Humor and Pathos
Into Prisms of Topaz.

Leoma Seibel Mola
SLEEP COWBOY SLEEP
It's time to lead your horse in,
You've ridden hard all day.
Time to hang your cowboy hat
On a peg, out of the way.
Time to take your boots off,
To rest your tired feet.
Time to lay back in your sack
To close your eyes and sleep.
God stands by your side
To take His cowboy home,
To let you ride upon His range
With your saddle and your roan.
Where the skies are always blue,
Where the grass stays fresh and green,

Where God is your Campfire Buddy
Who listens to your dreams.

John Sileno
LIKE LOVE, LIKE ROSES

True love
is full and fair.
Like a prize rose,
its existence is rare.
Tender care
will make it grow,
and with abundant love
its petals will glow.
Like love, like roses
the nectar is sweet,
The draught is given
as the lover's lips meet.
But also like roses
true love can perish,
if lovers neglect
what they used to cherish.
From experience we learn
to tend like the bee,
for it's love that nurtures
the fruit of the tree.
But every so often
tempers flare,
and the flower wilts
to the bee's despair.
And then one day
the vine is creased,
The flower blooms,
but the love has ceased.
The bee has left
and the lovers cry,
but it was carelessness
that caused the rose to die.

Patrice Gaudet
UNTITLED

Let me tell you a story
Of the way the world should be
I'm sure you'll find it fascinating
Not a one should disagree.
For all of life's confusions
Are just bottled in a jar
And everybody's problems
Are solved by falling stars.
This world is just too wonderful
For words alone to tell
So come with me and walk this land
For it casts a magic spell.
Only good things happen here
There's no sorrow and no pain
Once you've walked upon this land
You'll never be the same.
There are no wars upon this land
No tears are ever shed
The only catch to getting in
Is that you must be dead.

Benjamin Poff Draper
BENJAMINO

In the carefully planned ivory tower
High above the mundane sphere
Pen and paper and words abound
But poems seldom do appear.
My land is full of chattering folk
The clouds are low among the taxes
And full's the air with flying chips
From all my grinding axes.

James McNab Wilson
ENCOUNTER

The sky sank in the wild moor
Close by the shore where the sea sat
A maiden walked the silent sand
And knew not where her mind belonged.
A gull fell from the lowered sky
Crashed to the sand at her very feet
She backward sprang hand to her mouth
And tears began to flow her cheeks.
With trembled breath and beating heart
She to the broken bird did send
A hand so fine so free of toil
To touch its blood and broken wing.
Sky and sea and earth stood still
For a moment the maiden held her post
The bird caressing to her breast
She ran the way back to her host.

Winstead Doodle Weaver
Sonnet To Sweetheart Shelley Cindy

Thy cheek is soft, yet pale, as if some woe
Were tearing at thy sweet and tender heart;
But voices whisper that thou must not part
From paleness in thy beauty— were it so
'Twould taint the rose of whiteness— that I know.
Yet sorrow seems to live within thy soul.
And sadness of thy self is taking toll:
Cans't not thou order meloncholy go?
Like flaming orbs of fire thy deep brown eyes
Are burning darkness into me, and mine
Own are blinded as mists of love arise
And cloud my vision with the blackest line.
I look upon thy cheek, and my soul cries
For thee love. I live in distress divine.

Thomas V. Maloney
SHE CARED

There in her silence,
Lay her Bible with a note,
Her first and last request,
This is what she wrote:
"My beautiful Bible,
I leave in your care,
Holds the key to happiness,
That God let us share.
You'll find in my Bible,
Our wedding flowers,
All pressed,
Dear, that's all I leave,
You were my treasure chest."

Lin Salter Davis
WILL IT BE YOU

AAHHHHHH California sun. . .
.........warm breeze...present day memoirs. . . . .
how I need you today. . . .
.......for I am alone.......again...
Earlier, there were friends to chat with. . . .
...laugh with....wave to. . . .
But all in all........
...I'm all alone.
You blow over me and literally take my breath away.
Yes you did!
The one I breathed last......
...you took it!
Will it be this way....
....when all the life in me is gone?
Or will it be a Washington wind
..an Oregon gust.....
...or.....you again?
.....if it is you....
...blow lightly upon my face....
....like a kiss....good-bye. . .

Paulette Talboy Cary
CHILD OF THE HOLOCAUST
(Anne Frank)

What evil star were you born under
That such a fate should have been yours,
When this mad world was torn asunder
By demons risen from the sewers;
The tragedy of your existence is a
reflection of our time,
The evil things that did befall you
Were without reason, without rhyme;
Oh little Anne, child of disaster
What anger rises in my breast
To think that in these times so modern
You should have suffered such a test;
It's too late now for retribution,
It's too late too for hopeless tears,
But when I read your little Diary
My mind recalls those sad sad years;
The days of Holocaust are over, and they
must never be again,
This is my prayer, Oh God in Heaven,
May it come true, "AMEN AMEN"

William H. Schubert
CURRICULUM WITHIN: FROM WINDOWS TO PARADIGMS

Conceived codes on chromosomes
Multi-predispositions
Our windows on the world
(peep holes,
picture windows,
port holes,
French doors)...
Our receptors for experience
Experience—
That overlapping
ever-sliding-by
of interactions
interpenetrations
Some remains— fits
Part of the accumulating
apperceptive mass
Much bypasses
Analagous to the non-visual portion
Of the light spectrum—
unreceivable.
This array of pleasure—pain,
The continual flow of window panes
that multiplies focus on clarities
and distortions of life,
Is the curriculum!
The curriculum of life—
A bit planned
Some overt to our attention
Some due to intention
Some hidden
Much random fortune,
With unknown portions
Of grace.
All curricula are but subsets of
The life curriculum—
Curricula of:
School,
Home,
Occupation,
Church,
Social Clubs,
Media,
Love,
Marriage,
Social Interaction,
Self Education
All decision and action
Is regulated by
Paradigms within—
Neurological pillars
Formed by dominant
Experimental patterns
That guide subsequent experience.
If scholars search for the theory that
Guides the realm of action
That they study—they must
Find the paradigms within!

Donna Marie Hagan
POVERTY

There goes those awful people
they are packing their bags;
Gathering all their belongings
wearing clothes that are rags.
All those poor little children
who are hardly ever being fed;
Their parents can't afford food
they have to pay bills instead.
With so many mouths to feed
the mother's nerves are a wreck;
And over there sits the father
with his last unemployment check.
It's easy to sit and be silent
and play the part of a fool;
How very sad and cruel for them
the kids are too poor for school.
How can we just sit and watch
and pretend that we don't care;
These are the ones in real need
and the ones to be on welfare.

Fernando M. Serrano
WHEN YOU MISS THE ONE YOU LOVE

When you miss the one you love,
Suddenly you see the realism in life,
You see the dullness in her absence,
You see why you must spend the rest
of your life with her.
When you miss the one you love,
Suddenly you feel the utmost loneliness,
You feel the quickness of emptiness,
You feel the importance of being needed.
When you miss the one you love,
Suddenly you understand the meaning of
togetherness,
You understand your every

heartbeat,
You understand the obscure impulses of
your soul.
When you miss the one you love,
You see her and only her.
When you miss the one you love,
You feel the intense vibrations of her
love.
When you miss the one you love,
You understand why you must be with her.
But when you miss the one you love,
You suddenly realize, you're in love!

Marie Antionette Johnson
WORDS MEAN A LOT
From the day I was born and my mother saw I was a girl,
She said I'll fix her up with curls,
and I'll Make Her A Woman.
As I began to walk,
She said I'll teach her to walk like a lady
and this will Make Her A Woman.
As time went on and I began screaming,
She sat me down and said, ladies aren't loud,
so this helped to Make Me A Woman.
When I was old enough to know right from wrong,
She gave me chores to do, this was to accept responsibilities,
She said this will Make Her A Woman.
From my first year in school to my very last, She was always
on my back, saying do good in your grades, study hard, don't
give up, you've got to be strong. She would say, listen to
me, it won't hurt you.
It's just advice to help Make You A Woman.
Now that I'm finish with school and sort of on my own,
I can now sit back and think about the things she did
to help Make Me A Woman.

Edward W. Collins
A GOOD SUPERVISOR
A good supervisor has his employees at heart
He is well trained indeed to take a leader's part
In work methods and safety he his workers does train
A full knowledge of their job duties from him they gain.
He orders supplies and equipment on time
With human and technical skills he is well primed
He is a good communicator and motivator, too
His morale stays high in whatever he do.
A good supervisor keeps grievance down
He solves problems with judgement that's sound
Knowing that if on assumption he quickly acts
He may be put to shame and miss the real facts.
By him all rules are enforced indeed
To his work orders his workers gives strict heed
Because the buck he does not attempt to past
He is no more one of the boys but a leader at last.
No favoritism in him will anyone see
But a good example to his employees he will be
He keeps his work group from becoming a mob
And puts the right man on the right job.
A good supervisor is fair, firm and friendly
Maintaining good discipline in each employee
He stays in line with his superiors above
Knowing to give orders he must take orders in love.
His workers he tries hard to understand
He behaves maturely whether a woman or man
Whether legal, expert, reverent, rewarding or punitive power he use
His authority in leadership he does not abuse.
A good supervisor plans a job with thoughtful skill
Keeping in full line with his superiors rules and will
He directs, organize and keeps good control
Wise counsel he gives and fulfills his supervisor's role.

Margaret Christensen
TRAPEZE WALKER
Father, Grand father,
Great grand father,
An old man with a shovel
in his hands
and arthritis in his knees.
He hums a snatch of a tune
"Down in the Valley" while he
tends the evening water
on his salad garden.
With the skill of a cat
he walks a line
without a net
on a ground level six inch high
cement retaining wall,
stretched like a tight rope.
He sings "valley so low"
Using his shovel
as a balancing pole.

M. Elisabeth Steiner
NEW HAMPSHIRE
From across the boundless sea
They came, those dauntless settlers,
To this vast new wonderland,
Where white granite mountains
Reached high into drifting clouds,
And lush green meadows touched
Forests of birches, spruces,
Hemlocks and red maples.
The splendor of the foliage,
With its crimson, orange and gold,
Mirrored clear reflections
In the cool waters below.
Stretching through the country-side
Was that sparkling sapphire gem,
Lake Winnipesaukee,
With its myriad islands
Resting in its waterways.
Hidden in the mists above,
Sat Old weathered Stone Face,
Faithfully guarding his Notch.
What mattered nature's beauty,
Or feats of those native sons,
If missing was that freedom
So dear to everyone.
"Live free or die," rang out the cry
Of soldiers who gave their all,
That those who came thereafter
Might bask in God's new world.

Eileen B. Perry
MOTHER NATURE
I sought with nature to commune
At day's end, to dispell my gloom,
Needing courage to mend the rift
Of a broken relationship.
I watched the sun set in the west,
And birds fly homeward to their nests;
Listened to the bluejays' last cheeps
Before they settled down to sleep.
I saw twilight quickly recede,
Casting night's shadow over me.
My bitter feelings of distaste
Slowly began to dissipate.
I watched the evening star appear,
Millions of miles away, yet near
Enough that its eternal light
Dispelled the gloom of my dark night.

Arthur Charles Finmann
TO THE DEATH OF CHEAPNESS IN SEEING
In many ways the Mind can see,
In literature's sweetest phrase
Or in the calm of ordinary days;
In both can be felicity.
But man is such that he can choose
What deeply he prefers to know
And scorn with greatest inner woe
What he in fact prefers to lose.
So foolish are we in our mind
To make selective God's great gift
That, making in ourselves a rift,
We leave ourselves quite far behind.
The poet says — look at what's real!
This is the only, great appeal.

Donald E. Phillips
WOOD SIDE
Standing in the wood side
Between some pine and oak,
Thinking to myself
That life is just a joke.
Behold the oak leaves falling
From branches up on high
Revealing in their shedding
Great grandeurs of the sky.
Pine boughs though remain there,
Revealing not a trace
Of whats above their branches;
Dim shadows our disgrace.
The beauty of the pine tree
Out shines that of the oak,
And bows to false impressions
Of warmth within its cloak.

Marilyn J. Carrier
SO WILD MY LOVE
Her love is like no others.
She has the touch to melt your heart.
Eyes that can see into your soul.
Lips so soft and warm with glittering moisture.
Her heart, is to be given to one.
But when hurt, the fury begins.
So wild my love.

Eleanor Otto
FAITH AFTER VIETNAM
I take the river-lake route,
homecoming-reunion—in autumn.
Wet leaves swathe omniscient trees,
pine and oak. They know what I have seen.
Venerable buildings, unchanged on the outside,
quarried granite, flecked with slivers of quartz,
diamond eyes, glinting, scanning my being;
my life—shaped inside these stone enclosures.
I—once so frail—
still ignored, unknown, obscure;
now stronger than the rock;
think and purpose to banish carnage forever. . . . . .
Harder then the diamond flecks sealed in the rock,
once before, I tore myself out;
flew from the bouldered walls—
a comet slashing through black holes.
On this return—sobbing, dissolved in tears,
I throw myself against the rock.
It weeps and bleeds with me.
I stroke briny tears from the weathered furrows
and soothe the rough, aching crevices.
The stone is relieved;
I, uplifted, free again!
An armored galleon slides by on the lake.
My mind's compass spins;
then points beyond the brimming water,
where no death ship may carry me.
Henceforward, I shall sail by levitation,
bless and raise the martyred dead:
ascending, walk lightly over the sentient water,
as it leads unerringly to wide, illumined shores—
where choruses chant hymns of peace.

Daisy H. Alward
JUST A BOY
I see you yet,
lying inertly
between white sheets.
Brown and slender hands
rest limp beside
the bright orange ball.
No sounds are uttered.
Death overwhelms us all.
Spiritless boy,
do not be afraid.
I am your nurse.
I don't look, nor speak,
nor touch, nor smell
like anyone you've ever
encountered before.

Lifeless eyes forever.
The mouth that spoke,
the ears that listened,
seek not my voice,
nor smile to my words.
Eternity.
Drums of freedom roll.
Sweet lyrics of love
Await your youthful soul.

Jan Bratcher
OUR LEGAL LIVES

We legally take our lives apart.
I get the house, the kids, and
the car,
You get the child support
payments and
weekend privileges.
I get to find a new job.
You get to find an apartment.
I get to raise the kids alone.
You get the empty hours alone.
No one wins.
We only survive.

Louis Bascetta
MONTEZUMA

More than castle that sits on a
cliff,
of the Indian Pueblo the abode
as the proud, unreacheable eagle
all the valleys disdains and their
code.
O Montezuma!
I salute you from where I stand
in awe to observe and revere
the old Fate of the Indian tribe
which arrived to struggle in
your land.
O Montezuma!
They reclaimed the buttes and
the mesas
where the aroma of juniper and
yucca
with the agave adorns the
terrain
multicolored in amaranth stain.
O Montezuma!
Oak Creek Canyon, the pearl of
the region,
was sustaining their herds and
their children
with the prickly pear and the
maize
and the pods in a time of
friction.
O Montezuma!
Then, one morning, they rushed
in a flight
for a reason that man cannot
know,
and the desolate valleys still
show
the remains of their glory and
defeat.
O Montezuma!
Oh, reveal their wondrous
demise
that so drove their existence in
shadow,
they are burning my heart like a
fire
of youth that can love and
admire.
O Montezuma!

Glennie C. Larke
SEA GULL

Wing your elusive beauty,
Sail boat of the changing
sky,
Where the wind gods Blow.
None has ever sought
To imprison your demand
To glide, and fly,
Or to stay
Your perfection of motion,
Attained by the freedom of
your wing,
O Sea gull,
Sentinel of the sea!

Frances B. Thorn
THANKSGIVING PRAYER

We give our thanks today,
Dear God to Thee,
For Life, our greatest gift,
To hear and feel and see.
To hear the laughter,
Of a little child at play,
And the meadowlarks call,
At the break of day.
To feel the touch,
Of a loving hand,
And know that someone
Can understand.
To see the mountain's beauty,
Topped with a blanket of snow,
Sparkling in the sunshine,
From the valley here below.
For the gifts of plenty,
For food and the clothes we
wear,
For our home and loved ones,
Those who really care.
For living here in Utah,
Where we worship as we may,
We owe our gratitude,
On this special day.
For living in a land,
Where we can still be free,
With a right to do as we wish,
To be what we want to be.
We have so many blessings,
That we can only say,
Our thanks Dear God for
everything,
On this Thanksgiving Day.

Robert S. Hockberger
A SUMMER SMILE

Walking 'long the lakeshore
on a cold, grey, wintry day
Staring at the frozen waves
barren sky
empty benches
and wondering why
you went away
It happened here last summer
(seems like a hundred years
ago)
We built a castle out of sand
where now there's only ice
and snow
And I remember
one small tear that formed
though your smile refused
to fade
when one cruel wave crept in
to crush the castle that we
made
I think it was the tear
that made me fall in love that
day
Just as it was the smile
that made me hope that you
would stay
But love is like the seasons
ever changing
ever new
And now all I have are
memories
of a summer smile
a tear
. . . and you

Ron LeFevre
MY PEACE OF MIND

Water ebbs amid shimmering
stones;
Light-struck and clear, it slowly
hones
inlets edged by beach.
Granules of sand warm in the
sun,
To cool again when the day is
done,
but, till then, their warmth
soothes.
Green reeds contrast with the
sand,
As does blue sky with a faint,
white band
of windswept, hook-shaped
clouds.

Jewel Sullivan
MANKIND

Have you ever stopped and
given thought to the conditions
of Mankind today? Why they're
the most studied, yet misunder-
stood of all the species.
Take the wealthy businessman
the pauper on the street—
Can you see thru the individual
you might chance to meet?
Some make it good in life with
never a sway
From the rearing they got from
their 'yesterday'.
While others can't wait to boast
and brag
Of their good fortune, while
their character sags.
Seemingly running wild and
strong
Not thanking God from whom
their fortune comes.
Tooting their horns with a
thrusting sound
Not knowing or caring of their
"coming down."
Which is sure to happen as you
will see
Even to the best—both you and
me.
So whatever you may prosper in
this life
Give God the praise, cause He
made it so
That you may do well and have
good
As through this life you go.
Lift up His name and don't be
ashamed
Of giving Him thanks or
praising His name.
Be His humble servant, through
you let Him shine
Cause there's always *someone*
who's waiting in line;
To take up right where you left
off—
The price will be small,
regardless of the cost!

Diane B. Vaughan
IMAGES

images of broken fantasies
(in my head)
scattered and strewn
across my serenity
like distant stars
that once caressed my being
in their gentleness
(they make me forget)
find me longing for them
reality found me defenseless
smashed my dreams
with their cold bullets
of damnation and frustration
creating an existense
of non-existing
and fixed my mind into a
pattern
suited for society
locking away the fairy tale
schemes
that had heighted
my sense of
awareness

Pauline C. Bernot
A Living Entity In Time

All mysteries of time
Surface through God's work of
redemption.
A continuous rebirth of
creations,
Many un-noticed to the naked
eye of man.
Every living thing is a survivor
of another.
We are but minuscule
organisms,
A living entity in time.
Yet we are the center of all
things
As they revolve around us.
Everything that radiates,
radiates from us
Interwoven with all our senses.
The earth is an alive organism
and
We are its senses and conscious,
All else that moves and lives
Is its subconscious.
Yet we, the conscious organism
Alive only for a fleeting
moment in time,
Are just minuscule specks in
the universe.

Lynne C. Spence
A TOAST
FEBRUARY 5, 1981

Here's to drinking alone
And men who don't care,
Being fat and having short hair.
Here's to fallen dreams
And broken hearts,
Playing roles and living parts.
Here's to having no money
And needing to work
And going to bed with just any
old jerk.
Here's to Saturday nights
With an empty bookshelf,
Killing a fifth, and then
killing myself.

Otis Jackson
SURVIVAL OF THE QUAIL

Eleven sat but seven sprung,
From the dead the living run.
Among the green the young
sped,
Up and away the mother fled.
Hark to the setter, the hunter
called,
By now, you know, tis early fall.
With fear and fright, little
creatures be,
They dare not stay, yet scared
to flee.
As they wait in fear, small and
meek,
The hunter upon them, silently
creep.
Alas, together in a mighty rush,
They spring, headlong beyond
the brush.
Yet, together, they all took
flight,
That few be caught, in the
gunner's sight.
The hallowed would live to tell
the tale,
Of escape and survival of the
quail.

Frances Elizabeth Troxler
Captive Hearts In Song

A poem
you have written in my heart,
I keep for you—eternally, with
the rhythm of
a song written to the notes

that only love creates,
with gentleness that fawns know,
tenderness that only snow feels as it lands
on a leaf to rest—
and I,
with all the joy that they feel from this,
have captivated your song,
your joy, and gentleness, with tenderness
within me—
to only be played by you,
in the midst of our touch,
which sings the lyrics with the sweetness
and love of a mother's dear lullaby—
and never to sleep will they fall
separately or alone,
but entwined together
while our hearts love, beating,
to your song.

Nancy E. Girmus

MY GRANDFATHER AND I

A very smart man, my Grandfather was,
The kindest and most understanding person I ever knew.
My Grandfather and I were very close,
We shared many precious moments together.
I could always share problems with Grandfather,
That I sometimes couldn't share with anyone else.
My Grandfather fought in World War I,
He was injured in the war and later received an
honorable discharge.
In later years my Grandfather was in pain because of
the war,
But he never showed the pain he bore.
My Grandfather worked hard all year round,
He never let things get run down.
He fixed lots of toys for his Grandchildren,
When there wasn't work to be done.
He cared about other people first,
But he never seemed to get run down.
My Grandfather was well known,
Because of both small and large things he did for others.
Grandfather and I were so close that in 1975 when I
left for Excelsior Springs, Missouri, I told my Mother
something was going to happen to Grandfather and on
November 16, 1975, my Grandfather passed through Heaven's gates.
There is no doubt that my Grandfather received a Great
Reward in Heaven for all the things, both small and large,
He did while he walked on earth.
There are no other words to say, except, "My Grandfather Cared."

J. J. Jesberger

FOUND AND LOST

Unshackled now, by the whims
and fantasies of youth,
I have given way to the existence of a single urge.
As if held by some unsated
need,
My mind and my anatomy are surrounded.
Imprisoned amid honeyed
sensations
Ripened by the nearness and feel of you.
How is it, that I bring myself
to bear the anxiety?
Knowing that at any time,
You might slip from beneath
me and go.
Am I that sure that I will have you yet again,
Another time?
Do I love you so, that I grasp what joy I can,
Knowing I will make it last?
I can, you know.
I can make the sweetness last
for however long my need,
To fill any or every minute I am without you,
Even forever.
I do need to know that you love me,
At least for now.
And if it comes, that time of letting go,
Will the love we are today,
remain a chapter in your diary?
And will you turn back to that page
From time to time,
And love me still?

Robin Krams

ON MY WIFE'S DEATH

As one constantly finds himself faced with the unknown,
today I am faced with myself.
An anthology of opposing forces inhabit my insides
with nothing to hold them together but a hollow-feeling shell.
Confused by the actions of my outside inhabitants,
my mind is bound to question my internal thoughts.
And I, as an educated man,
feel compelled to question them also.
Today is a day like no other,
yet so similar to many previous ones.
It is a day that leaves me with a mass of thoughts
and simultaneously leaves me without a wife.
Often at times I wonder whom death is trying to hurt more.
the victim, or the family and friends of the victim.
Does the dying person actually realize that he is no more?
As he lies upon his deathbed, does he not just
lie back and take a comforting nap, never to realize that he will not again awake?
She is put at ease now.
She is put at her rest.
I shall try to remember her for the way she was
before the last few horrid moments. I shall try. It will not be easy.
These words do not sound as though they are
the words of a man who has just
lost his wife, yet they are.
Today I lost my wife.
I almost lost my mind.
I thought about it. I thought about her.
For a long time I spent the afternoon walking around in a daze.
I can not truthfully say that I was filled
with hostile emotions. In all candor, I felt empty.
That was what bothered me the most.
I had loved a woman
dated her
bore children with her and
lost her
to the fate of life.
I knew that I was suppose to feel something,
but I didn't.
Was the feeling that I should feel be the
hardship or insecurity of losing a loved one?
Or should I feel hatred for those who did not take her place?
Should I take my frustrations out on the Lord?
Why had he turned on us in our time of need?
Confusion.
That was what I felt the most.
In her last moments of terror, she turned to me with a yearn for rescue in her eyes.
But beyond that was a glimmer
as if to say, "Honey, look out for the kids while I'm gone.
I'll look after you.
And one more thing, darling.
Please know that I love you, and that I understand. . .
everything."
The mass began to decipher itself; A feeling of sorrow erupted. A feeling constituted with all others.
The only unanswered question was. . .
Sorrow for whom?
Her or me?

Nancy E. Grover

WATERS

The waters of the world— a lake, a sea, an ocean
Bring tranquility to those who walk along their shores
Or stand to gaze out 'oer the waves.
Its sacred body hides the mystery of the deep.
The blue, the green, the foam— tis nature's secret potion.
The roar as in concert
swells in crescendo—
then subsides in calm, quiet peace.
Bring your cares, your pain and vexation to the water
Wash them away as the waves slap the shore
As the gentle breeze blows cross'd your face
Let the water cleanse your soul.
Smell the air, feel the breeze, drink in the beauty of the brine.
Watch the setting sun cast shadows across the horizon
as it splashes reds and oranges in the sky that meets the endless sea.
The moon, too, adds its light and smiles down on
God's peaceful waters of the world.

Millie Craig

THE BRIDE

Just this time, I want to be alone,
Alone to think, to dream and to plan,
About the goodtimes, that tomorrow might bring.
The wondering, the waiting, the anxiety, will soon become real,
As real as the flesh, that I am able to touch on my body.
The memories of my high school years,
The junior and senior prom,
How lovely, how romantic.
That special guy, with all of his special way's.
When I think of all the things we did together, the places we went, the things we said.
Then there was the home coming queen, how I rushed to get ready, Oh! so excited.
Then it was over, another dream had passed and gone.
Will I be beautiful? am I sure?
Will I be frightened? Is this what I want for the rest of my life?
For tomorrow I will be a bride.

Carol Ann Cowan

Whispering Silhouettes

Breathlessly, we watched the moving sights
Of the city's silhouettes of lights;
They glistened like a whispered sigh
As they flickered softly in the evening sky.

Carol Ann Cowan

SOUNDS OF SILENCE

Early in the cool crisp light of dawn
A little chipmunk sat upon a rock
Nibbling noisily at an acorn;
He listened quietly to the sounds of silence
And then scurried away.

F. del Monte

FOR THE SPECIAL POETRY CONTEST

You're tempting me to send a verse?
I may have read of others worse
than these I write;
encouraged thus, I'll make a try. . . .
e'en though it might not satisfy
the ones you invite.
Not emulating Shakespeare,

I cannot gratify your ear;
and precious wit
to bring a subject of import
to all you folks who Muses
court. . . .
I have not it!
What can I tell you then you'd
care
to hear, if in my lines I dare
to but reveal
a simple bent for playful mirth,
a love for all I see on Earth
and hold it real?
Among the poems you collect,
it would be much in disrespect
to mine include. . . .
for truly, lines I write, not worth
are they to publicly unearth,
and show me nude.
Adornments none, and simple
word,
my very presence is absurd
in your Contest;
without guitar or harpsichord,
my voice can win me no
Award,—
nor Second-Best.
And kindly, though to qualify
you've eased the Rules,—I'll
just go by
and say Adieu!
For don't belong in company
of those who are, in Poetry,
selected few.

Amy McCarthy

FEED ALL PURPOSE

My spider plant was dying,
and you told me you cared too
much for me.
I watered it, perhaps too much,
and all this time I wanted to
make it with a stranger.
I tried to save it by repotting it,
and you told me you had to but
could not let me go.
I fed it the best kind of plant
food and the whole time I
pretended you were somebody
else.
My spider plant died.

John Von Ogden

Short And Meaningful

Will your waves of affection
ever curl for me again.
Will your eyes roll back in your
head, oh how long has it been.
The things we used to say to
each other do we say to
someone else.
Whenever I think so my mind
goes crazy and my hearts melts.
Sometimes the games of life can
be to difficult to play.
And if we gamble with it in the
end we all pay.
I'm doing well, I'm doing fine,
I try to keep you on my mind.

Lena London Charney

THE TRUTH

You want to see things
As they really are?
But can you?
How?
You look in the wall mirror,
Your own reflection you see.
I stare in the same mirror,
The counterpart, I view, is me.
You think about the country,
Recall mosquito bites and
ants in food.
I remember the country,
Relive the wondrous beauty
and peaceful mood.
You glance at the moon,
Of man's space conquest, you
dream.
I gaze at the moon,
Marvel in God's sublime
scheme.
You contemplate mankind,
Ponder injustice, prejudice,
and hate.
I meditate on mankind,
Perceive concern, love, and
hope in his fate.
You want to see things
As they really are?
But can you?
How?

DiAnne Denlinger Burchfield

SIMPLE PLEASURES

I remember when the whole
world
Was made just for me,
A big awesome playground
Full of simple pleasures.
Like swinging from Grandma's
willow tree,
Or baking mud pies in her
old stove,
And jumping out of Uncle Fred's
hay-loft,
Teasing that big black bull
he used to have,
That's when 4th of July meant
Pies and cakes at family
reunions,
When people still celebrated
their independence.
And the only problem I had
was that
My tiny tears doll got broken
and she wouldn't cry real tears
anymore.
Then I remember when the
world
Was made just for my love and
me.
A big awesome world to walk
In love and anticipations.
And life was full of simple
pleasures,
Like having a talk under
Grandma's willow tree,
Or baking him a cake in her
old stove,
And necking in Uncle Fred's
hay-loft,
Ignoring that big black
bull he used to have.
That's when 4th of July meant
Taking a slow walk by the
creek,
Ducking out of family
reunions
Declaring our own
independence.
And the only problem I had
Was convincing Dad that
I wouldn't turn into a pumpkin
after midnight.
And now I've but to remember
when
The world was made just for me.
Time in the guise of progress
came
To claim life's simple pleasures.
A new library sits where
Grandma's willow tree stood
And God only knows what
happened
To that old stove,
The hay-loft came down—
Uncle Fred died,
And so did that big black bull
he used to have
There's no more family reunions
On the 4th of July
And they don't make tiny tear
dolls anymore.
They buried that old stream
Under a super-highway,
And that old love is buried
there too,
And all the old things are
turning brand new
Simple pleasures come early
And leave too soon.

Dorothy Yoder

UNTITLED

We're all creatures.
Each must learn to become
his own person. True
to his own beliefs. Strong,
brave, and bold in God's
wisdom.

Edward Wielgus

IN LOVING MEMORY

Except for the doctor that we
both knew so well,
There was no one else there
to bid you farewell.
If I could have lifted your
head, kissed your brow—
And whispered. . .
"It's your hubby, darling
Josephine", and breathed a
prayer.
But you went away, without me
to speak a comforting word.
None, but Jesus, knows the
heartache it has brought.
Some may think the wound will
heal
But in my heart is a vacancy
which never can be filled.
Darling, you were always so
good and so kind
So thoughtful of me—and loved
us all.
But Jesus knew you would make
a jewel forever to shine.
And when I think of you my
darling,
And wonder why you went
away—
Although my heart is breaking,
I miss you more and more
each day.
When I go to the crypt where
you now lay,
It seems that I can hear you say
"Weep not for me, I suffer no
more
I will meet you in heaven some
sweet day"

Joel E. Ferrara

TODAYS MAN

He hurries through the gray of
every day
Too preoccupied to stop and
enjoy.
Time has left him gaunt and
wanting.
The more he runs to escape
the void
The louder are his own
footsteps.
Not to enjoy but to survive is
his quest.
No legacy has he left his heirs
Just hurried tracks on the
waters of time.
No sunlight pierces his almost
sightless world
This 20th. century product of
all lost ages.
He is more to be pitied
But would rather be loved.
The pity is lost on deaf ears
He does not know how to
accept love
He knows only to keep the
grueling pace
With his head held high
catching the mist of time
On his weathered face.
Never to smile, never to
enjoy, never to love. .

Wayne Bisek

EUTHANASIA?

Lay thoughtlessly, Lay silently,
Lay uncaringly exposed.
Body parched and shrunken.
Mind empty and unused.
Heart and soul long ago
abandoned. Life merely an
electronic existence.
Age rules rampant here. Slow
destruction its method.
Warp the spirit gradually.
Devour the body incessantly.
Loneliness and pain are constant
visitors Death stalks the
hallways.
Lay hopelessly. Lay helplessly.
Lay pitifully forgotten.
Death will visit here shortly—
Hopefully—Mercifully.

Connie Ratliff

DOES YOUR HEART HAVE A PADLOCK?

Does the door to your heart
have a padlock?
Have you hidden away the key?
O, what needless burdens
Doubt, guilt, and fear can be!
Christ stands knocking at the
door
Offering His Love and Blessings
free
But you must remove the
padlock
For, only *you* have the key!
He's waiting to take your
problems
He'll take away every care,
Where there was only pain in
your heart
He'll heal, placing His Peace
there!
So, why must there be a
padlock?
Take it off, let Him enter today,
Live *for* Him and *in* Him
He's The Truth, The Light, The
Way!

Sylvia Wright Lasher

THE AMERICAN MAN

In nights of velvet sleep
I remember him
My love for him
In a constant soft tiptoe

Across my heart and soul
I loved him as deeply
As the long blue night
And as wildly flaming
As each new days
Bursting light
Whenever I caught
A glimpse of him
My bones to butter turned
My blood raced
Like wildfire across
A parched forest burning
He was really something
Everything and all in one
Honor, love, gentleness and
strength
With sparkling eyes of morning
sun
And big strong hands
Creased with wear
That took time to show
Tiny sparrows that he cared.
He was womankind's dream
The strength of the forest
The gentleness of the sea
His love so strong
All fear became a fleeting thing
Who was he
You ask of me
He was a real man
And they have ceased to be
Yet the remembrance lingers on
Where have all the real men
gone
I cannot find them
Can you
It just seems so wrong
The perfumed dandys
Are here instead
With permanented hair
All over their heads
Its ends a kink
And around their necks
14 Karat chains of gold link
Empty vessels filled
Only with greed
Searching for only
Their self-centered needs
Weak and soft with souls
diseased
These fake men are all I see
And the man has ceased to be
He is gone from this land
Oh God
How did we lose this great and
gentle man
I loved him more
Than each mornings dawn
Oh God
Where have all the real men
gone!

Allene Marie Chabala

SAID THE VERY OLD MAN

Tell me about life, the old man
said,
let's see if it differs from the
one I have led.
Don't give me man's concept of
bad or good,
or a final summation of life
understood;
Or show me my errors and what
should have been done,
had I followed the shadows,
not reached for my sun.
And when you are finished,
please tell me what changes
the seasons—the movement of
plains and of ranges;
How long would it take for the
ocean to dry?
Could you bottle a rainbow if
you really would try?
And while heavenly bodies
pulsate a rhythm,
give me the meaning of all
that's within them.
But no matter my friend, I've
lived a life;
known all emotions—felt
usual strife.
I've run all the gamut of love
and of play;
I've reasoned with logic, and
what masters say.
Each age that I've come to I've
vented my rage,
challenged what was, and
doubted the sage!
But now I just wonder, and
smile in my heart;
what difference the goal or
specialized part?
You see, my good friend, there
is always a 'why'
for in every known truth
there's an innocent lie;
For how can 'truth' be fully well
known,
when secrets in crevices are
not always shown?
Yet, while I sit here in thoughts
retrospective;
reflecting on views of life in
perspective. . .
What difference the purpose—
no matter the stage,
your part has a meaning until
life's final page.

Billy J. Wallace

SONNET TO MARIAN

(Whose every word of encouragement is the strength I lack)

Much time I've spent
endeav'ring to employ
A language deft, inspired, and in
design
Abating agony, abetting joy—
Lines yet to be in sonnet's
measured line.
The message that would grant
my soul reprieve
And be for you eternally a sigh
Escapes this untrained layman
you believe,
Account your ardent servant
and ally.
Yet come repose and solace in
the thought
That numbers not unlike my
kind have sought
Such art. (It comes but seldom
to inspire
The lines whose beauty
compliments the lyre.)
And then I feel myself at least
a part
Of myriads whose verse does
sound the heart.
(heart)

Chuck Boerner

A MOMENT

The day having spent
A gentle breeze, not wasted
I gripped and ceased
The moment
A fleeting memory
of a day gone by
The sight of the woman
as she cries
For the moment
Something so special
Far beyond any words to create
The meaning of what we shared
and Together showed we truly
cared
for a moment
A one time love
In the graveyard of the past
Convincing ones self that
Things do last
For a moment

Gina Marie Pollichino

TWO HEARTS

When your heart pours
out its soul to me
And I listen very
very, very carefully;
I realize something
so very real and deep
Your heart has found a home
in mine, and is mine to keep.

Cheryl L. Grgich

IT'S NOT TIME

It's not time. . . .
for sad goodbyes
and tears.
It's not time. . . .
for unhappy smiles
and kisses goodbye.
It's not time. . . .
for memories to end
and fun times to be forgotten.
It's not time. . . .
for our love to end
and death.
So, why me? Why must I die?
It's not time.

Lynn Ann Sayre

LIFE THREADS

i step
from my
poem quiet room
into your
sports dominated
t.v. filled world
of people
newspapers
and current
events,
pretending
a sociality
i do not
own.

Jane Elizabeth Sayre

LETTER HOME

To all those near
Listen as I scream
in my sleep
As I see my backward sky
That flows winged toward
the earth,
I yell the petals to my hand
Where they lay
As I stroke them with
womanhood,
Velvet in my hand
I cry wonderful
As the words scale down
the mouth
That blows wishes
out
the door.
Because free is where I dance
With kisses on my toes
Meeting flesh and grass and
growth
That twirls
from dew to mouth
Coloring lips in pink pursuance
Of words I've never said,
Coloring cheeks in sun
That smoothes my lover's touch.
Yes, I scream in my sleep
For lovers never meet
And children never smile
As they walk
rooted to their destiny.
I yell wonderful to friends
Who hold my tears
As I watch the colors run,
my blurred insanity,
In figures clutching hearts and
heads
That throb with motherhood,
womanhood,
Scratching the surface
To find the colored core.
Yes, I chase the colors
For someone doesn't see
The color's meant for me.
I write you now,
to tell you this
Because few should know
The cry I hold in choking
throat,
The laughter in my arms,
That entangles vines and flesh.
Few should feel
the age in my pocket
Fingering my hair
In direction of where I've been,
look at loving.
Listen and you will hear
My kiss on windowpanes
That love your night.
your light
in color.

Leopoldo M. Hernandez

UNTITLED

She was a little girl
not much
a humble little thing
without shoes.
She used to wander around
and play
and laugh.
She never had the time to cry
enough.
Then she crossed.
The street was wide
perhaps too wide for her
perhaps as wide and deep
as death.
And that was all.
A muffled noise
a certain deaf and strange noise
which often precedes silence.
Then, nothing
A twisted body like a twisted
flower
without shoes.
A car beyond
stopped and cold,
its blind hatred of heaviness and
iron
already satisfied.
The sun had set
and she was dead
like the people who gathered at
once
like the flowers that withered at
once

like the afternoon that sank
into the night
like the earth that lost another
sun.
Somebody took his shirt and
covered her.
But she was warm.
The oncoming night was chilly.
But she was warm.
Warmed by the light of origin
warmed by the embrace of God.
Later
There was a cry piercing the air
a single and long cry.
There was a red star which
blinked
from a heaven of grief.
There was a somber car
which took the corpse away.
And nothing else
except
oblivion.
Yet
she would be there forever
like a blossom coming out of
the asphalt.
The little girl who was
not much
a humble little thing
without shoes.

Frances Crumley Hicks

THE LIVING FOOD WAY

I heard God's voice
To me He did say
"To obey My Will, you must
EAT—THE LIVING FOOD
WAY
I created the FOOD
Long before I created YOU,
To keep YOU healthy
Your EARTHLY journey
through.
YOU must NOT change MY
FOOD
To do so, you will soon see
YOU have brought upon
yourself
Sickness, disease and misery.
The FOOD I create for YOU
Contains a part of ME
Which will let YOU know My
Will
And draw Me closer to Thee.
I have given YOU every herb
And tree, bearing seed;
To EAT of these will
Supply ALL YOUR body
needs."

William J. Wood

ONE LIFE TIME IS NOT ENOUGH

For a life time I have loved
you.
But a life time is not enough.
You are the flower that
multiplied my lovely garden.
You are the sunshine that
nourished it with life.
You filled our home with
echos of love, and the pitter
patter of little feet.
And my garden flourished.
And though we grow old and
feeble—the sparkle is still in
your eyes, and your heart is
still a young and tender flower.
Love such as yours could
never grow old, and you are the
beauty of the garden.
When we are layed to rest—I
will need you by my side for
eternity.
For one life time is not
enough.

Charlotte Parker

BLUE SILENCE

The ocean has never moved
With such beauty and grace
The playful seal adds
A charming mole on its face.
The sand speaks only
As the wave retreats to sea
And then only gently. . .
Moving pebbles and debrie.
A gull guards the ocean front
Gliding to and fro. . .
And I gaze toward a surfer
Waiting. . .keeping low.
He seems so far away
And yet, he's very near.
So far because I think
Of my over-riding fear—
The ocean's such a beauty
And yet a threat to me,
I have such admiration
For all men of the sea.

Robert H. Burgoyne, M.D.

A BITTER INTERLUDE

It tastes bitter
As he knew it would.
The taste of unconditional love
Is sweet,
And denied not even
To the dead;
But was illegal,
So they said.
Dissatisfied with less,
He is alone.
How long will last, this
Bitter Interlude?

Paul Julian DuBois

REMEMBERED FRIENDS

Oh friends of yester years
We well remember you
Who shared our joys, our hopes,
our fears
And were to us so nobly true.
Your laughter rings through
the halls of time
That passed away far too soon.
Your music gave us thoughts
sublime
With the universe in tune.
From our homes we so
blithely came
To learn of life together,
And sometimes even dreamed of
fame
Through every kind of weather.
You gave us friendship's
priceless treasure
An ever guiding star within our
firmament:
Exceeding other gifts beyond our
power to measure
You helped us with life to be
content.

Jean Heaton Davidson

GOLDFISH

This pile of rocks
was once a goldfish pond.
This ring of green bricks
was the edge where
I hung for hours, watching
slick, red fish dart and
drift in and out
of my reflection, through
spirit walls of my eyes,
my nose, my mouth.
At times I forgot which was
reflection and which was fish.
The day I leaned too far,
fell in,
Father bellowed and banged
through the house with a
shovel,
yelled he knew this would
happen,
it was Mother's fault.
She cried and patted my wet
hair
with a green towel,
I was sure I was dead.

Phyllis A. Menna

A WEDDING PARODY

Two people meet
A friendship kindled
And love blooms
A ring for her finger
A 'date' is set
Announcements mailed
Plans organized
Nerves f a z e
r z l d;
the day arrives
Nuptial vows exchanged
Their union of love
Signed, sealed and witnessed
A scene of smiles, tears,
embraces;
The couple is swept away
In a modern chariot of white
For a trip into the future
As rice and rose petals
linger. . . . .
in the present.

Maro Rosenfeld

MANHATTAN

Manhattan. Fill me with your
love, your charm, your joy
Hide from me torment, grief and
sorrow
Take from me my heart, my
Soul, my person
Protect them from the Steepes
of Passion
Let your rising towers and
blinding lights
smoulder out the Sun, the Moon
and stars
They hold no beauty
comparable to your own
All the world has landed on
your shore
All life starts and ends like
a hurried subway ride
Share with me your peace with
time and space
Give to me peace of mind and
reason
Nurture me on the beauty of
your seasons
Speak to me. No, speak with me
Blot out the past of loneliness
and boredom
Hold out to me the fruits which
only you grow
Hate me not for asking all these
favors
I ask to share your crown only
because
I have given up everything to
wear it

Alice Denison Hackett

ON ANCESTRAL TRAIL

We whistle in the turbulent
winds
for haunting ghosts to
reappear
as solid personalities
with names blown out of
yesteryear.
Old truths still hang by fragile
threads—
threads time-weakened, faded;
long
enough to hold a tattered
piece
of a whole once bright and
strong.
As you, they built, begot and
buried;
wept beneath old willow trees
through which small stars
forever shine.
Where further seek a trace of
these?
Like you, they labored, loved
and laughed—
a mockingbird sings by a gate
that sags mid brambles—"late
too late"—
where lichen hides whose
name?—what date?

Gary W. Longrie

IN SILENCES CRYING

You came to me again,
In silences crying.
Warm light played
between the mirrors
and our eyes, and
lost itself in shadow.
The din of other voices
muted your strange hello.
We, like figured lamps
fought the gloom,
mute, porcelain children.

Isabelina Rodriguez

To My Future Husband

My love for you is very deep
much deeper than I've felt for
anyone.
Thus I promise you I'm yours to
keep,
forever more and then some.
I never stop thinking of you and
I,
and anxiously wait for the day,
that our loving knot we do tie
and each night next to you I lay.
My dreams have all come true.
You my love are everything I
need.
By being with and loving you,
my greatest dream has been
achieved.
You've filled a part of my life
that has been empty as a shell.
Thus I'd love to be your wife
so I may fill your life as well.
I love you more each second;
Each day I need you more.
You are my love, my only one.
You're the man that I adore.

Jim Stuart

AFTER QUARTER AFTER

Well, where is it this time?
They were supposed to be here
On the hour and now it's after
quarter
After and it's getting cold.
They said they'd tell me if
They got held up, unless they
lied again,
The little bastards. Well, I'll
give them another hour,
But they don't deserve it, and
if they don't
Bring it today, well, they'd
better tomorrow. Damned cold.

Clifford E. Sutton

A TRIBUTE TO ELVIS

Born in Mississippi
On a share-croppers farm;
He was lovingly cradled
On his Mothers arm.
A typical farm boy,
He helped his Dad do chores;

And practiced on a guitar
With his time indoors.
He loved to play and sing,
And was a religious boy;
Attended church with his
parents
Where he sang with great joy.
Moved to Memphis, Tennessee
When twelve years of age;
Went to high school there
And dreamed of the stage.
Became a truck driver
After high school days;
And cut his first record
In his own style and ways.
Cut a hit record
When only twentyone;
Sold a million copies—
And his career had begun.
For year after year
Great records he made;
And his fans lined up to see him
Where-ever he played.
He went to Hollywood
And became a movie star;
And his films were the best
Of ANY singers, by far.
Spent two years in the army,
But his fame did not sever;
For he came out of the army
More popular than ever.
He was gentle and religious,
Not effected by his fame;
And we honor his memory,—
Elvis Presley was his name!

K. M. Ozbirn

WINNIFRED

This was Winnifred's pen
and came from N.Y. as the
writing on its belly says
and I wonder what Liverpoole
Industries, Inc. is—
I think absurdly of Beatles,
but I know that's not it. . .
Before I got this pen it must
have been well used
as it is a little scratched and
tarnished—
the "Liverpoole" is fading after
all—either that, or
her dog slobbered on it and the
cat played mousey with it, or
maybe it is worn from
Winnifred's fingers
the logic of that is the only
thing that comes to mind. . .
But I wonder if anything could
be grander
than the essay I wrote with this
pen—
what a flash of black and gold it
was
sledding over the snowscape of
paper,
or the English notes I took with
it,
or the laughs I gave with it
across the miles at
my sister-in-love-with-the-boy-
next-door,
and next door, and next door—
Romeo and Juliet come to mind
even though I know that's not
it. . .
From the pen now worn into my
hands
were these lines predestined
Winnifred's?
I cry in sympathy for me and
tritely think of tea
and in anger use them to
admonish her to a posterity
because now I'll never be at
peace with her bad impression
of me
what a thing to live with,
forever
or the next fifty years at least—
but ten from now, will I or
anyone else have cared
of a young girl's problems with
pride and prejudice
they will be over and done with,
but is that it. . .
God, I am unspeakably angry
with her,
envious too for finding out
Oddly, I profoundly wish to
lie—
to anyone, myself, rather than
negotiate
the cruel aspects of all divorces
killing—
Last judgements come to mind,
but I don't believe in them. . .
And I wonder if I'm for all, after
all,
an unwanted stranger paying
sentimental tribute
that is, I suppose, the foremost
reason why
I did not join the others
and in my way wrote of a little
known woman
whose pen has fallen into my
hands—
is it enough to merely wonder
of how
instruments
are
rehandable. . .

Judy A. Rogers

DEATH'S BUTTERFLY

Too soon, too soon. . .It's time to
die
and listen to the earth slip by.
So silently that each earth's cry,
fluttering like the butterfly,
is ever echoed with a sigh.
No wings had I to rise and fly

to scan the earth
or reach the sky,
My failures too with me ly
Mere earthling grounded til I
die.

Betty J. Asbury

THE FLICKERING CANDLE LIGHTS

The flickering candle lights,
that are seen each night,
the sight of your lovely face,
are a welcome in this dark
place.
Stars are shining each night,
making it a lovely sight.
Your face is more gleaming
than anything in the sky.
We see the nearest star
from such a place so far.
Your eyes reflect the beauty
I see from within your soul.
Our hearts are kept beating,
even though the time is fleeting.
Every now and again
we see the love within.
Although the time for us is
passing,
as long as there is time,
the stars will shine.
Forget never my love,
for as long as candles will
flicker,
as long as the stars shine from
above,
we'll always be together.

Rachel A. Cox Williams

JON

JON is a naughty boy, he never
listens.
He is always dreaming of the far
away places.
Flying over the mountains,
skiing over the ridge.
Building skyscrapers, and the
worlds largest bridge.
Running across meadows
laughing with glee,
Picking wild flowers and giving
them to me.
No prettier picture could you
paint.
Its beauty and wonder make me
feel faint.
The wonders of childhood, its
joys and its tears.
Memories to last thru out all
my years.

Marge Naber O.P.

TREASURE

I feel numb, it is hard to think.
I know I was where I am now.
I had a treasure; It is no longer
there.
Your presence was growth for
me.
How will I grow in the absence
of you?
I can fall apart or know where
I've come.
Go backwards from where I've
come or
Go on to where I hope to be.
Loss is pain that causes me to
go on
And become more.
I have come too far and will
proceed to be all I can
Thanks to my lost treasure.
May I find a new treasure to
help me grow.
Lose it again I could
But never lose its affect on my
being.
Treasures are forever.

James S. LaSovage

FOR YE KNOW NOT. . .

The highway blurred with waves
of August sun
Outside the city where I'd
almost done
With biking for the day. A car
snaked round
The curves, invisible behind a
mound
To the small red squirrel
destined for the shade
Across the road. The hiss of
tires made
Too late a warning. Deadly
taking aim
A fang of bumper struck. A
morris came:
Three circles spun so quick they
seemed to melt
One to the other, like a coiled
belt,
Crescendoed by a backward
somersault
And climaxed in a concrete
thudding halt.
So comical it seemed, to see by
chance
This unrhapsodic, acrobatic
dance,
I blurted out a laugh—then
silent fell,
To recognize so plainly that
small hell,
And circled back again, again to
see
The evanescence of mortality:
Frenetic image never to be lost;
Dark pearl purchased at
exacting cost.

Lorna May Hanson

MR SPUD

A Spud is a Spud
no matter what
they use to call it
a lowly ground nut
But this old Spud
has been around
He's no dud
the Spanish found.
They took it to
Spain in 1538.
It went to Europe,
Germany and France.
They thought him so great,
They gave him a chance.
Before he left that port.
He came to court,
As a flower fair,
In Marie Antoinettes
beautiful hair.
In 1847 the Spud
hit a blite,
That almost put him
He caused an imigration.
A million and a half Irish
Faced Starvation
They brought the Spud
Back home.
Back to America,
No more to roam.
They boiled him and baked him,
Chipped him and dipped him,
Smashed him and mashed him.
He became a jet age Dandy,
He's very handy.
A might good Tater,
A real first Rater.
"MR. SPUD"

Artie Miller

CUT ME SOME SLACK

Please,
do not bind me
to an image:
they're too confining.
Today,
I want to be
all that I can honestly be,
at least
as much as I
can understand for now.
Give me a little space
to grow;
even if it's
in the far corner
of your mind.
Save the labels
for people who like
plaques, and signs, and titles.
The only authorization
I require
is the sincerity found in
you sharing you
and
me sharing me.

Linda L. Lasher

ODE TO CHILDHOOD

Perhaps the lasting gifts
One receives in a lifetime,
Are the treasures of

Happy childhood memories,
To be tucked away
Like outgrown toys;
Later, to be valued,
As symbols of. . . . . .
Love.

Betty Ruth Philips

SILENTLY

Voice that speaks to me from in the silence
Voice that speaks to me but makes no noise. . .
My listening heart slows gently to a rhythm;
A rhythm born of stillness, calm and poise.
My mantra, word of steadfast concentration
Usurps the idle plight of weary mind
And fills it with an all pervading quietness
That reflects the merge of self with the divine.
Is this the voice that draws us at transition,
That leads us safely to our promised land,
That bids us walk on waters yet uncharted,
The voice of Buddha, Tao, The Great I Am?
If this be so there is no room for sadness;
There's only celebration and new life. . .
The plane we go to be on will bring gladness
Life unto life. . .call softly once or twice.

John David Hogan

HOW MANY MORE

Music is said to soothe the savage beast
Such as a lion or tiger or a bear.
But there is one beast it doesn't soothe
In fact he doesn't seem to care.
The beast I speak of is homosapien
He walks on two legs not four.
But the music does not soothe his soul.
He marches on to war.
Does the music have no effect on him?
Or does he just not listen?
For the blood still pours in pools on the ground.
And the sun makes it glisten.
Or maybe man is the smartest beast in all the lands.
But then again a grown man cries
As a friend dies in his hands.
Hopefully one day we will learn
And put a stop to all this war.
But I think of all the people already dead
And I wonder how many more.

Elizabeth G. Pennington

GROWING OLD

I'm going *down* my Hill of Time
My days are growing fewer.
I must work fast ere they are gone,
And be a better doer.
No use to sit around and hope
That times will soon be better,
I must forget to groan and mope,
And be a real go-getter!
No matter if I don't feel well,
I *will not* yield to pain.
I'll drink a swig and take a pill
And feel OK again!
Three things God has given me:
Will-power that is strong,
Stern determination, and
Patience calm and long.
There's so much I would like to do
Before the final curtain
I must waste no precious time
Or I won't get done, that's certain!
Before I go, I hope to find
Some special thing to do
To help this ailing, tired old world
Present a brighter view.
No time to feel discouraged,
As fleeting moments fly,
Too soon the Clock of Life will stop,
And I'll be in the "Bye and Bye"!

Dr. Panos D. Bardis

The Second Golden Age

("The flower that once has blown for ever dies."
Omar Khayyam, Rubaiyat, 63.

A haunted British isle,
A lovely, sweet, enchanting northern nymph,
A golden cave.
But now, the Titan sleeps.
He sleeps and dreams a thousand dreams,
Prophetic dreams,
Portentious dreams,
Exotic reveries,
And eerie visions sparkling with the gems
Of wisdom and foresight.
While countless spirits, specters, phantoms, shades, and wraiths
Are dancing in the gloomy cave.
Too late!
Too late, too late, too late!
The sickle glows and glitters in his frozen hand—
The sickle forged by evil-eyed,
Dog-headed, flipper-handed creatures of the sea
That summon swirling snow
And clouds and hail and rain—
The adamantine scythe,
The silver crescent reaping corn
And the twin-berried, rootless mistletoe.
Too late, too late!
The northern nymph,
The haunting dreams,
The crescent moon
Will bring no feasts for kings and slaves.
Doomed Titan! Fallen, mantle-shrouded Lord!
Your scintillating star rose only for one age;
For history, to each of us, gives but one page!

Robert Hayward

The Two Of Us Forever

You know, it's funny,
Here I sit telling everyone
I don't want a lasting relationship
Yet,
All I do is think about you.
I can't get you off my mind.
It seems that with each passing day
I want to be with you, to hold you,
I want to feel your lips pressing into mine
and feel the touch of your caress.
I guess I am obsessed with the thought of you.
I feel as though I want to be a part of your life;
the permanent part.
But—
I'm afraid. Afraid to involve myself because of the mishaps of love
that I have already encountered,
And for fear of not meeting your style and standards.
Why can't life be easier?
Let us fall in love without worrying about
social standards,
religion,
and the almighty dollar.
Instead, let us worry about
each other,
happiness,
and love.
Let us put all thoughts aside
except the thoughts of the two of us living and loving life
as well as each other.
My promise to you
is love—for whatever it's worth.
And I hope it's worth a lifetime of us together,
totally,
just the two of us,
forever.

Charlotte Kay Mills

THE LITTLE BROWN SPARROW

The little Brown Sparrow that came for lunch
He flutters his wings then sits on a branch.
I love to watch him bring his friends
They all sit, have lunch, then they sing.
Off in a flash they all fly, not a single bird in sight!
But before you know it, they are back on a branch
Down to the bird feeder they fly, just for a bite;

They all gather in the feeder, then fly out of sight.
God has put such a tiny bird upon this earth
So many people do not take time to see.
I enjoy them coming each day just for me to feed.
The beauty that God has made,
I enjoy from day to day.
I'm glad I'm able to take a minute
To enjoy the things God has made.
I'm thankful for so many things each day.
Especially, the little Brown Sparrow that came today!

Lisa Marie Caswell

GRIEVANCE

Like furious racing rapids
My tears break through the sharp jagged rocks
Of uncontrollable emotions.
Anguish fills within my shattered heart
Crying for relief.
Yet no solace does my soul discover.
I pray faithfully that someone
Shall yield to my weeping,
But all are sources to my desperate call.
All faith now begins to descend
Into the deep black hole of fear,
Enveloping my body, soul, and mind.
I am numb.
No longer can I see the silken blue skies
Or feel the cool sand between my toes.
The sun does not shine
Nor the radiant moon glow.
The world is black.
I am gone.

Betty Van Lente Curti

THEY'RE MURDERING THE TREES

They're murdering the trees
on Oak Street today. . .
making room for
another expressway!. . .
so more cars can go faster
to get where they're going;
no need for stoplights,
not even of slowing!
Man's blueprint for "progress"
no more's just a dream:
the branches are crashing!
The saws! how they scream!
Yes, they're murdering the trees
on Oak Street today. . .
Progress. .Great Progress. . .
is having its way. . .
and, while all the trees
on Oak Street are dying. . .
I've pulled all the drapes,
and I'm crying!

Glenna Runkle McKee

SOLITUDE

Far up in the green mountains
stands a little cabin grey,
And it's there my heart is yearning
While time slips by day by day.
In this harried, hurried world where
I must deal with stress and strife,
always turning—ever yearning
for that quiet and peaceful life.
Standing here in this dim valley,
Full of noise and full of greed,
How I long for just one moment
for the solitude I need.
Yet I move not to that mountain,
my log cabin I never see,
It would seem that high ambition
has its hold also on me.
But I gain the strength I'm lacking
when to the hills I gaze,
for I know the time is coming when
I'll be there,
In the twilight of my days.

Laurie Carlson

DARK REALITY

Life may be a transient dream
But through it passes a sullen stream
And as one faces death eye to eye
A cold darkness draws ever nigh.
The cloud of grief grows ever thicker
The flame of hope begins to

flicker;
Life is so dark and bleak
As faith becomes so very
weak.
Trusted friends seem to
disappear,
While only sorrow is left near.
The family structure begins to
fold
As hearts recast dark and
cold.
A clear conscience is worth its
weight in gold,
But the fingers of guilt are
icy cold
As around my throat they
tightly clasp;
For breath of life they make
me gasp.
The dark, velvet canopy of
loneliness
Adds to my heart more
emptiness.
I no longer seem to find enough
love
Not even that given from him
above.
As sadness fills my empty heart
I ask only why he had to part,
I loved him oh so very much
I miss his kind words and
loving touch.
Now as my mind begins to stray
I think of how he brightened
my day,
As his smile, humor, and
contagious wit
Never ever seemed to quit.
His hands were hard, cracked,
and dry
But his touch was as soft as
the pastel sky.
From his arms poured bountiful
love,
Only matched by that from
above.
Finally, dark reality I again see
No longer on this earth is he.
But oh, what a beautiful
creature
Was my father, my friend, my
teacher.

Jane M. Johnston
WALDEN 1981
Extinguished, a writer's
world lay in empty
ruin—
The pond, still glistening,
weeps for the years of gentle
repose.
The path, barely recognized,
yearns for the solitary steps of
one man.
Invaded, a dreamer's
haven
wallows in
helplessness.

Chuck Chase
FORTY DAYS AND FORTY NIGHTS
Forty days and forty nights the
heat beat upon my head.
"That's only the beginning," the
weather showman said.
Forty days the mercury scorched
one hundred plus and more.
For forty sleepless nights the
heat continued to soar.
The mercury danced merrily up
past one hundred ten.
It may cool to one hundred four
just to climb back up again.
The water from my garden hose
is boiling my grass.
Trees are dripping leaves as
super-heated breezes pass.
Forty days and forty nights the
heat wave gains in clout.
If it scalds on forty more will we
last it out?
Cement blocks and all the
stones are melted in a pile.
Have to build a fire just to cool
things off awhile.
Raindrops are heading for a fall?
Dream on brother.
Hope when this heat wave ends
we don't have another.
This heat wave may burn on
another forty nights and days.
Finally ended in hell for not
mending my ways.

Barbara McFarquhar
MOURN NOT FOR ME
Mourn not for me
For I was three
And the world was very large.
Soon I was seven
Wearing shoes so hard
Blisters covered the heel.
But then I was thirteen
And knew the joys
Of a first sweet innocent kiss.
Mourn not for me
Though the years have passed,
For I have known joys and
sorrows.
I have sung in the morning
And danced in the night.
I have seen despair
And have had great hope.
My courage has been great
But it has failed also.
I have laughed and cried
I have rejoiced and mourned.
I have been born and seen many
births.
I have seen many deaths
And soon I will come full circle.
For when you read this
I too have died.
But weep not for me
Weep only for thee.
I have gone from your future
But I will always be in your
past;
For I have met you, and I have
changed you.
I made you laugh, I made you
cry.
You loved me, you hated me.
But just by being, I changed you.
And that change will last
forever.
Mourn not for me
Mourn only for thee.

Diane M. Civittolo
BUS STATION
the lonely man
in the corner
sees them come
he sees them go
sitting on his bench
no one bothers him
or bothers with him
except to inquire of
departures—
he knows them all
he sometimes smiles
a sign of senility they whisper
he's crazy
a sign of wisdom he knows
where they're going
and the time of arrival as well

Gilbert Creutzberg
NIGGER
Of course, that word is never
used
by liberal white folks
who read the New York Times.
It's a forbidden word.
But then, I wish I too could use
it
the way my black friends do—
without a trace of ugliness,
as an endearment, or in jest,
pure soul,
a word with warmth and gentle
sound
with feelings of a common bond.
I envy them.
I cannot say it
without sounding phoney,
and so
I *think* it sometimes
like a whisper in my mind.
Then, rather much to my
surprise
some of my friends say jokingly
to me,
"Hey, nigger!"
I take it as a compliment:
I have become an Oreo cookie
in reverse.

Deanna Frock
TOMORROW'S PROMISE
Yesterday—
I was like a child
So in love—so vital
I was engulfed in sunshine
Nothing seemed wrong
Although some things went that
way.
Today—
I'm grown up again
I'm tired and bored
I'm surrounded by gloom
Nothing seems right
Though everything is going
okay.
Tomorrow—
I'm not sure of whom I'll be
But the thought holds promise
Of pleasant things
Life will be good
Although I might not behave
that way.

Heidi Schwoch
UNTITLED
I was like an open wound,
so honest, so trusting.
But you changed all that,
didn't you?
I asked nothing but to feel.
Yet you gave me the gift of salt;
cauterized my one desire.
Yes, conspiracy's an evil word,
but it's an evil thing to conspire
with the world
to tear out the soul of one
so honest, so trusting.
I know it's naive to believe
in purity in a world
where old men are more than
willing
to send young men to their
deaths
by the hundreds.
And as if that wasn't enough,
forcing them to sing about it.
Giving those that survive to
grow old the same desire;
to send young men to their
deaths
by the thousands.
Yes, it was naive of me.
And worse still, I believed in
you,
and let myself be an open
wound to you.
Before you left I imagined
lonliness
to be a vast emptiness.
How was I to know hate could
be such a filling thing?
Time consuming.
I am no longer open, honest,
trusting,
But I do have the scar to prove
there was once such a fool.

Edward A. Gloeggler
YIELDING SEED
A lot is asked of a lowly seed
aspiring to be a seed:
Will you give up all that you
are
for what you may some day
be,
And fear no more the dark of
earth
to be buried with the dead,
And with your aim up in the
sky
dig down in the ground
instead?

Jolee H. Gregory
REFLECTIONS
The papers were finalized today.
Standing in a crowded room
suddenly I forget
what to say.
I'm lonely. . .again.
I wish. . .(if wishes were horses).
If. . .(the unforgiving minute). . .
He's gone.
I'm lonesome.
Again.

Anita Louise Virgil Avila
A PEACEFUL PLACE
If ever you seek a place for
piece of mind,
Let it be known to all mankind;
That the ocean at night is a
perfect place
to put your thoughts in order:
Walk along the beach barefeet,
feel the
sand creeping between your
toes,
Hear the waves in the breeze of
coldness;
See the shadows of the clouds
passing
through,
Watch the gleaming stars
outshine the moon;
As you're surrounded by this
quietness and
beauty:
Look out into the water at the
reflection
of the face that is yours,
Spend some time healing those
sores of
unhappy thoughts;
Bring in the joy within yourself:
Let peace into your mind, and
you will
find love in your heart,
And a satisfying soul,
Work up to your goals of
findings,
But best of all the ocean has
done your
unwiding:

Antonio Giraudier
LITTLE MOON
Little
Moon,
surging
inside
of
me,
when
you
said
so
many
essential
words.
Little
Moon,
of
a
romantic, yearning
quality.
Little Moon, growing. . .
Take care now,
be cautious,
before becoming
a Full Moon!

Susan Kuehl
RAINDROP
Funny little raindrop
coincidence how we meet
came close to my eyelid but fell
upon my cheek.
Should I let you wait there
Or should I dry you off?
Only made of water yet still
oh so soft.
Funny what a raindrop does to
your heart
makes it sad or happy, tastes
sour or tart.
So my little raindrop upon my
cheek you lay
contented I will always be if you
want to stay;
or until my hand with tissues
swishes you away.

Jinx Gollam
LEE'S SONG
you took the ring from your
finger
& placed it on my hand. . .
why you ever loved me
I shall never understand;
you came like a zephyr
on a hot & muggy night,
with open arms, reaching out,
you took me close, you held me
tight.
& gently, then softly,
you took my battered heart
& worked it with your hands
until the pain could no more
smart.
now you're gone, forever so,
God's will's been done, this I
know.
you took with you a part of me,
you gave to me a part of you.
I won't forget—because the rose,
where true love's sown, forever
grows.

Katrina Guffey
DESTRUCTION
A tear
slides slowly
from under a
closed lid.
It glides down
a saddened
face
slowly
leaving a path
of moisture.
Moving
unknowingly
to the destruction
of a silent
dry hand
wiping the moisture
away.

Letha Stone Harris
PEACE ON EARTH OR GOD'S WORTHY GOAL
Christmas is a time for peace—
Yet there's war on many
fields,
And war clouds threaten
everywhere.
Has this world's doom been
sealed?
Yes, according to our blessed
Lord,
Destruction will come in the
end;
Now—there'll only be peace on
earth
As it rules in the hearts of
men.
So remember the angel's
message
To shepherds so long ago:
"Peace on earth, good will
toward men";
God's will and His worthy
goal.
For during the last great
conflict.
(O, Praise His wonderful
name!)
The Prince of Peace, our Lord,
so dear,
Shall come again to reign.
While we're waiting for His
coming,
Let's do everything we can,
To let His peace rule in OUR
hearts,
And urge this upon every
man.

Patrick M. Sheridan
THE AWAKENING
Morning
The alarm rings
My hand reaches automatically
I am not yet awake
I'm in a half-sleep
with a pleasant dream
My heart is full of happiness
Today I have a date
With the love of my life.
I'm awake now
Where was I ten minutes ago
London, Paris, the moon
I can't remember
And I don't care
It doesn't matter now
We will soon be together
And my life
And my love
And my happiness
Will increase a thousandfold.

Dale Michael Brisson
MIRRORED TRAILS
I got another wrinkle today
and three more gray hairs
while you sat
whistling,
polishing your dancing shoes.

Bobbie S. Rahn
THOUGHTS OF DEANA
I snuggle down into the cozy
cocoon of our bed.
I touch the warm indention
made by your small body.
You are gone—I am so alone!
Suddenly inside as ache begins.
Swirling up from deep within it
consumes me.
Oh, agony! When will I hold you
again?
I must touch you, kiss you—
to survive.
I am only aching emptiness
without you.
I wait in a cold and lonely
void. . . . .

Kenneth Lafleur
THE HANDS OF NATURE
Trees have hands,
which are most matured in
May.
Like the hands of man,
but they need not pray.
They reach the heart of God
in another way.
By beautifying this Earth
from day to day.
God created trees for beauty,
oxygen, and shelter,
Which man will soon destroy
in his Helter Skelter.

Marjorie Graumenz
LIFE ON MARS
I know there is life on Mars
The seven lovely movie stars
They laugh and dance the whole
night through.
Oh, how I wish I were an
astronaut too.
The youngest sister she is a real
flirt.
She's always wearing her mini
skirt.
That girl I will have for me
When I'm an astronaut, you'll
see.

She skips from one place to
the other.
Guess she's looking for a fellow.
Hope she know's that I'm the
one,
way down here under the sun.
Wow, tonight she came a
streaking down
and landed beside me in my
home town.
She sure has filled my heart
with joy.
I've longed to touch her since I
was a boy.

Dale A. Hankey
THE ONLY ONE I KNOW
the circle on the ceiling
talks with the candle below
it will dance for as long
as the candle holds the glow
but now the candle's moving
or are my eyes the show
are the effects setting in
from the life i know
the lights are going out
they struggle to stay alive
but the powers are too strong
coming from the other side
so i pull myself together
to make one last stand
i want to go out happy
i want to die holding hands
rather than seeing the only face
that i've known thru time
the only one that i knew that
cared
the face of mine

Barbara R. Slater
HOPE
Oh moon, floating in the
endless skies,
Watching mankind and
hoping, hoping, hoping
What thoughts conceals your
unlined brow?
What sensations rise within
your golden globe?
What needs arouse your cool
serenity?
You lie suspended in the
couch of infinity.
Can we hope to rise one day to
your
Wisdom, peace and grace?
I believe that this may be, for
without hope,
I beat myself to death upon
The looking glass of life.

Doris A. Seymour
FOREIGN OR DOMESTIC
If I were an enemy of the U.S.A.
and seeking to destroy it
I would have created todays
dilemma
and sat back to enjoy it
I would have
upset the economy
increased taxes
encouraging strife
in all walks of life
I would have
clouded the vision of youth
with drugs
assuring them that they are
misunderstood
urging them to doubt basic
truths
proving to age that youth is
no good
I would have
started an arms race
to undermine stability
placing troups in far flung
fields
forcing debates on what
should be
I would have
backed both management and
labor
cheering victories on either
side
so long as they kept wrangling
and their common goals aside
I would have
allowed inflation
to take over

letting profits grow
in the hands of power
I would have
made transportation difficult
or next to impossible
by shortages and price hikes
to bring the country to a
standstill
Finally
I would have
placed good men in power
and promptly tied their hands
and while they struggled to
ease the world
I would ridicule and critize
them
Whether the dilemma is our
own or of foreign design
the results can be the same
some of the fault is mine

Lola M. Armstrong

GOOD NIGHT, MY LOVE

Good night, my love—
The lateness of the hour bids
me depart.
Conventions laws demand we
two should part.
Good night.
Farewell, my love—
E'en though my body rests long
leagues away,
Your love o'er all my being still
holds away.
Farewell.
I go, my love—
But only thoughts of claiming
you ere long,
To be forever mine, make me
this strong.
Good night.

Irene Sugranes Goulding

NEW HORIZONS

Behold my world of dreams!
What pleasant sights!
And all my life—it seems
Intoxicated with delights!
Long may it last!
Bright may it be!
A great forecast
Of things to see.
A great forecast
Of joys to come,
Forgotten past
And sorrows gone.

Stephen T. Hambey

WE DID NOT SAY GOODBYE

Alone I stand, alone I sigh
Elusive love doth make me cry.
A lover's dream, a midnight
madness
O' curse the ocean for my
sadness.
Be damned ye fate, so cruel,
unjust
That we should meet and leave I
must.
A blind man sings a poet's song
Of sirens and of seasons gone.
I did not say please wait for me
As Ulysseses to Penelope.
We did not say good-bye.

Louise P. Brown

LOST AND FOUND

Entangled by strands
of earthly desires
Pulsing with conscience
cooling the fires.
Material object
rag, bone, hank of hair
The body is mine—
but am I really there?
Child to my parents
friend to a friend
Bride, wife, then mother
where does it end?
Sweep clean the tangle
cut, tear and break free
When death makes a clearing
will it really find ME?

Nancy Brier O'Neal

AFFAIRS AND OTHER DEAD-END STREETS

We talk all around each other,
Like cars in a New Jersey Traffic
Circle,
Darting from the inner lane
To the outer lane,
Wanting to meet head-on
somehow
But never hitting the point. . .
We run like trapped mice in a
mad maze
Of obstacles and road blocks,
Blindly fumbling through
episodes
On one-way streets with no
exits
Before foolishly running out of
gas
During an energy shortage.

Patricia D. Drischel

THE WAY IT IS

I woke up this morning
Black as I could be—
And why not?
I was born to a black man
And his wife—
So I'll wake up that way
For the rest of my life.
The man who lives six blocks
From me wakes up white—
And why not?
We are as God made us
And the handiwork of
God is beautiful
Wouldn't life be dull
If all the trees were maple
And all the flowers
Were roses?

Kathryne Rees

ANTICIPATION

She was a strength to me,
And I to her.
Warm, close, clinging to one
another,
She needed me, and I her.
She loved to feel the warmth
Of a sunny day touch her hair
and ease her pain.
We had such good times
together,
She and I.
My thoughts are with her now
Even when I am not.
Impatiently waiting for the
restoration
That we might be one again,
A part of me is missing. . .
While I wait and wait
For the miracle that never
comes.

Deborah Ruth McManama

ATTRIBUTE

A stroke of passion created you,
Back in the days when passion
never ventured beyond
chamber walls.
How terribly gothic.
A Victorian lady, blessed with
all the attributes of your time
Excepting. . .the stilted diction.
'Grass roots' never harmed your
style.
One hundred strokes, made that
unloosened, comb-scarred hair
gleam—
A gleam matched only by Papa's
admiring double-vision.
He never could get enough of
you.
A stroke of color-rosy pastels,
Added radiance to that much
coveted skin,
Yet never masked the beauty
that it dusted.
A stroke of genius guided you.
You never were short on
wisdom.
And now. . .
Victoria is gone-and her era-your
era.
Gone too, your beauty, wisdom,
passion.
Papa's eyes still glisten at the
sight of you,
But tears shroud those hoped for
stars.
At least he can wallow-you can't
even remember what's
sorrowful.
Stilted diction. . .we envelope
you with it,
Though our conversations are
elementary.
Grand-daughter assisted blushes,
now melt in those facial
crevices—
And more aptly paint the
withered canvas.
A portrait faded by a palsy-
bearing stroke.

Nona Stillings

CAPRICE

I loved the rain before it came
for it would feed parched earth
like patting precious oils on
aging skin,
nourish plants,
cleanse the weary air,
bathe a flower face.
I loved the rain, and then it
came
pounding
on the world's floor.
Breaking, entering, running
to leave mud pies in houses,
cocoa pools in underpasses.
Slick the streets.
Steal a hill.
I saw it partner the wind
to strip trees,
play love me love me not
with petals, then
abandon them prettily.
Like excuses
for wanton acts.

Cheryl L. Becker

HAPPILY SPENT

If your love is as strong as mine
It will stand the test of time.
If we are there when we need
each other,
There will never be the other
lover.
As the sun rises and as it sets
It brings memories of when we
met.
Now everything is shared by
two,
Eternal love and gratitude.
As the years slowly pass me by
I can say I honestly tried.
To keep my man totally
content,
And these years were happily
spent.

William Edward Woodward

CHANCE

Chance,
Feeling out echoes
With a nickel and a dime
While substance
Skirts and flows
Beyond diurnal time;
Chance,
Hiding in the shadows,
Lurking in each moment,
Pure nonsense
To proud egos,
Yet a sporting page event;
A pair of dotted bones,
Sevens
And elevens,
Tips and meager loans,
Tidbits from the heavens;
The game parade of odds,
An ace,
A deuce,
A trey;
Cheap trinkets and trite nods
Dealt out, come what may—
Chance.

Roger Sorensen

FOR JOAN REYNOLDS

I wrote you a poem
But most women
Don't know
What a poem is
So, you won't see it
Unless
You do

Franklin G. Miller

THE ARCHITECT

Within the attic of his mind,
A man can build one fetid cell;
His own dark shadowed, narrow
hell—
Or yet erect so wide a place,
A silver dome where stars can
race;
Within the attic: his to find—
Within the attic of his mind.

Helen C. Kelley

TO PAULINE AND CLARK

No roses could be red enough
Nor chocolates be sweet enough
Nor other gifties good enough
To thank you for your gracious
hospitality,
But may you find a happiness
An everlasting happiness
In knowing that the happiness
You shared with me will fondly
grow in memory.
When I recall Reunion time
Our high school June Reunion
time
Our fiftieth Reunion time
I'll think of you and of your
hospitality.

Mildred Wickliff
MY TWISTLE TREE
All of my young life,
Through storm and strife,
I lived in an enchanted
make believe world.
In my garden of love,
God looked from above,
As my rambler rose around
the trellis was curled.
In the fluttering leaves,
Of the Twistle trees,
There sat a beautiful bird
so enchantingly rare.
I would gaze at this bird,
It seemed so absurd,
That it couldn't fly
through the air.
And there by the tower,
A most beautiful flower,
A rose of exotic fragrance
so sweet.
A soft little breeze,
Blew through the trees,
And scattered the petals
down at my feet.
In a far away place,
Where Queen Anne's lace,
Was a gossamer flower
white as snow.
In a land so divine,
I lived on cloud nine,
And where the cold winds
didn't blow.
The sun's golden beams,
The sparkling of the streams,
The azure blue of the skies
was aglow.
For in the days of old,
I believed a pot of gold,
Would be sitting at the end
of the rainbow.
I loved to play here,
Where fairies were near,
They were such lovely
playmates for me.
As I passed away time,
In my world so sublime,
Sitting and dreaming under
'My Twistle Tree.'

Viola Ruth Dawson
CATCHING COURAGE
The siren wailed the warning
loud and clear
The approaching tornado was
ever so near.
I called my dog and to my
shelter ran
To be as warm and safe as a
person can.
My heart was a drum, as loudly
it beat
Fear was as rampant as the
storm in the street
Came the silence of death in a
deadly quiet
That proceeds a tornado's
terrible bite.
My dog's hair bristled. She was
all upset.
"Be quiet," I said, "It's
all right, My Pet."
But upon her feet she whined
wierd and low
That funnel was near; and she
seemed to know.
Outside through the midst of
the raging gale
Through the noise of the wind's
fierce tail
Came the sweetest song that I've
ever heard
In the heart of that storm
sang a mocking bird.
Cheerfully, sweetly came the
tune through the squall
That bird made this person feel
humble and small
Such bravery and courage I've
never known
God sat with that bird on its
electric-wire throne.
"Be still," I said, to my throbbing
heart.
"Have faith; be brave"—"Fear
depart."
"Be still my body—cease to
quake.
Didn't the Master *you* also
make?"
The storm subsided, as storms
always do
And I'm here safe as can be
telling you
When something as frail as a
rain-soaked bird
Knows God so well—It my faith
has stirred.

John T. Hudelson
MT. ST. HELENS
The wooded valleys
and wooded hills
were freshened by the
morning dew.
The spring pools
reflected the mountain
peaks
As the sun came into
view.
Silver lined clouds
went drifting by
as birds took off
in flight.
The beginning of a
beautiful day,
after a dark and
lonely night.
The dew ladened blanket
that covered the earth
sparkled like diamond
studded sand.
In a panic filled
moment
this panoramic scene,
was changed into
desolate land.
For all hell broke loose
from the bowels of the
earth
As the mountain exploded
for all it was worth.
The wooded valleys, and wooded
hills, the spring pools and
the rocks and rills
Were shaken with a boisterous
shock
that filled the air
with ash and rock.
Life was destroyed for miles
around,
as floods of lava consumed
the ground.
All nature suffered within it's
wake,
from the aftermath of the
mighty quake.
Death and destruction
lie silent and bound;
buried uncoffin'd in an
ash covered mound.

Sherri L. Cole
CONFUSION
Mad or sad
Happy or excited
Which one is it?
I can't decide
or am I suppose to?
I don't know
Yes, I do
What should I do?
I want to grow up
But not old
I want to stay young
But not childish
I can't be scared
at least I shouldn't be
or is it all right?
Someone should be able
to tell me all the answers
or must I find them on my
own?
I have to get myself together
I don't want to be told how to
live
I have to be a strong individual
I don't need anyone else!
or do I?

Phyllis E. Schaber
GOD'S GIFTS
God does not compel us
To choose to follow Him;
Nor does He mean to go astray
To live a life of sin.
He gave us power of choice
To worship as we please;
To use our gifted talents
In christian love and peace.
We're tested by our faith
In what we do each day,
Searching for the stepping
stones
For each to find his way.
To live and grow in love and
knowledge;
In purpose and in plan,
There are many similarities
That God has given man.
For He who died upon the cross
Is our sustaining power;
Our lives are in His holy hands,
He knows the day and hour.

Kathy Phillips
FOR PHIL
What have I to lose in life?
each failure draws a poem,
a picture, thought, or paradise,
a fantasy my own.
Each memory evokes from me
a chorale painted blue,
a water color symphony,
a misty, passioned tune.
What have I to lose in love—
its habit is severe,
a junkie hooked on fairy tales,
a poet fed on tears.
What have I to lose in time—
each moment seems a year,
a rhythmic, four part harmony
set in an endless sphere.
So what have I to lose in life?
each day a dance unfolds
in high arched slippers poised
and straight
on concrete hard and cold.

Barbara A. O'Hara
WHAT AM I TO YOU
What am I to you?
The first sign of spring
The first robin to sing
Flowers that rains bring
What am I to you?
Free as birds in flight
Stars in the night
Dawn's first light
What am I to you?
Happiness holidays bring
A puppet on a string
A beautiful tiny thing
What am I to you?
Fireworks bright
Words that I write
A wonderful sight
What am I to you?

Madeline Ligammare
MY ENEMY, MYSELF
The mob's one face belonged to
me—
The voices? All my own.
There stood I, condemned to
die—
The stoned, the stoner, the
stone.

Louise I. Miller
TO AUNT GRACE
A gentle, happy spirit—
Her goal—
To make all others happy.
If she could bring a smile,
Better yet, a laugh—
Her day was then complete.
To give a single flower,
This was her favorite way
To say "I care."
She early learned to love,
So always loved.
She never learned to complain,
So never complained.

Stephen J. Panfil
LIMITLESS SKY
(Dedicated to the brave American Astronauts by trips to the Moon.)
O limitless sky, you are
a wonder to behold!
As man does explore, new
planets do unfold.
Your sea is infinite, in
God's firmament so clear,
His marvel and His mystery
seem ever so near.
O the beauty of the great
and wonderful sky
Seems to give the answer:
how we live and why.
The great eternal vastness
of human space
Is a reflection of His
beautiful face.
O sky, your depth of beauty
and of tone
Puts us in mind that we are
in God's zone.
As we travel, limitlessly,
eternally to and fro,
A little more of You, our God,
we see and know.
You are a part of His
eternal bliss
Which we, unborn, would
surely miss.
As we die, the shutter
closes in our face—
A wonder opens to us, as
it does in LIMITLESS SPACE.

Valerie A. Cole
DEATH OF A TREE
Standing still in the dark of night,
See the lightning flicker bright,
Frightened from the thunder boom,
Listening to its dreaded tune.
One quick second brought the crack,
Felt as a human, with broken back,
A pungent oder brought from the wood,
Wrenching with pain like nothing else could.
The rain felt good, it tasted cool,
Like drowning in a bottomless pool,
Bark burnt black, as it had bled,
The tree laid there desolate and dead.

Michael Galayda
JUST TO
I don't know what to say
about love,
about you.
But if I'm still alive,
it's just to
be near you.
What more can I say
about love,
about you?

Virginia E. Cruikshank
Miracle Upon Miracle
So seldom, dear God, are we aware
That miracles are at hand.
We do not detect the tiny buds
That secretly form in summer,
Until in spring, suddenly
Blossoms wave in the breeze.
We do not hear the sweet small voice
Of the purple finch
Offer its fervant praise to Thee.
The milkweed pod seems barren
Until its silken treasure bursts
Unexpectedly into our hands.
Seldom do we savor the wild strawberry
In its ripened meadow juice;
Nor do we sense golden honeysuckle
Making fragrant the breeze,
Tempting a multitude of bees.
The skies shine blue above,
But we look down.
Why then, God, do you think
We go our way unnoticing,
While continually, eternally,
You unfold miracle upon miracle?

Evelyn L. Bolin
TAINTED WORLD
O' dreary world so dark and cold,
what does for me the future hold?
Your mouth is full of sin and vile.
An honest man you will defile.
Yet, God through love so rich and deep
did give of you for man to keep.
Now, all nature in it's beauty
is marred by man's shirk of duty.
Once your fragrance so pure and sweet
has changed to naught but wicked feet
where men do roam and sin do pace.
In sight of God, tis' all disgrace.
O' weary soul, unselfish pride,
the Lord Himself is on your side.
Faint not from scorn and endless mock.
You're standing on a solid Rock.
Tread on your course. O' weary soul.
Your faith in God has made you whole.
Lift your eyes, with radiance give.
Praise the Lord for the life you live.
To you world! Life is just a span.
A course to lead for every man.
A testing ground that all must take.
A choice that each must choose to make.
Yes, for that Trumpet Sound I yearn.
The Time for our dear Lord's return.
I'll reap a place of perfect rest
and see you, nature, at your best.

Freda Holmes
SPRING AND IT'S BEAUTY
Against the blue blue sky the beautiful
Green of the trees. flare the sun against
The mountain side on the calm water beneath
The mountain side. oh what beauty spring
Brings as I stand on this great land. listen
So peaceful to the wondrous art of God's beautiful
Creation I could almost hear him call my name.

Mrs. June Niles
HEARTBEATS
The heartbeats of her soul kept time
Within the meters of a rhyme
Her eyes glanced deep emotions rare
Ones that robbed her senses bare
When to exchange them she would dare.
Brasen being she so much couquette
He drowned within the limpid pools
No escape from there-of all so far been met
And then forever more
The heartbeats of his soul kept time
Within the meters of her rhyme.

Ruth Innes
FOLLY
The racecourse road was smooth and straight.
Unheeding we hurried on down
The too-easy way. Had it been
Rough, full of obstacles, hurdles,
Holes, forbidding not beckoning,
And we had surmounted all, then
Perhaps we could excuse the race
We ran, the path we took. We could
have called it destiny or fate.
Now, having done it, we are done.

Jeff Edgerly
I LOVE YOU
Our love is something special.
Our feelings both are true.
So when and if I'm angry. . .
remember "I love you."
I know it isn't easy.
But still I'm very proud.
I know we as a couple,
will outlast all the crowd.
So when that you are doubted,
or someone says to you. . .
"Oh, how can you stay by him?"
Remember "I love you."

Margie M. Reese
NATURE AT ITS BEST
It's beautiful to perceive
The air gliding through the trees
In Autumn, when the leaves dry up
And crumble to the ground
Often forming a brown circle in fashionable design
As though they follow a plan
Passed down from a supreme hand
Flowers continue to bloom in a flourishing cycle
Never ending but enduring
Century after century
Throughout the universe, the seasons extend beyond eons
The earth revitalizes itself
And increases its seeds
So there will always be trees
Nature has beauty that man cannot create
It is really non-changing
Remaining perpetually stable
Man would have had paradise
Had it not been for sin
To allow a serpent to deceive him
Was a foolish and naive act
For which we have to suffer endlessly
Although redemption came through another man
Torment repeats itself making the world basically the same
If nature were left alone untouched by man
Perhaps paradise would return again

Colette Logue
THE LEGEND OF THE PALE MOON
Why is the moon so pale, my love?
Why is the moon so wan?
Is it the cold of the night, my dove?
Or missed it a sight of the sun?
Nay not so, dear heart of my heart,
List! I will tell you the tale
of One who bore a cruel part
that left the great moon so pale.
Long, long ago, the Savior lived
down on this world of ours;
the golden fleece of clouds were rived
as the angels sang of His powers.
He came to His own but His own would not.
They wanted the spoils of earth:
wealth, power, and pelf, the things that rot—
they rejected the things of worth.
For the wealth He brought was a wealth of Love
and power within His breast
The joys of heaven were stored above
for His Own who stood through Life's test.
Ah! Men were wicked; men were cold!
Warm love was thrown from the heart—
A shout was raised; a shout full bold!
"To the hills! Crucify Him, they barked!"
The moon saw the nails; the moon saw the spears
and the ruby-red flow of His Blood!
She hid her face from the evil sneers
that mocked at the Precious Flood.
The moon saw the Maid with the large, sad eyes
standing beneath His Cross!
The moon saw her tears and was petrified
at the pain of her great, great Loss!
So the moon grew pale for she understood
(and pale she remains to this day!)
That our God was stretched on the Holy Rood
To show us the Light and the Way!
Rood/Cross/Crucifix

Vera F. Miller
THE EYE OF GOD
As far as my heavens may stretch and my eyes can see, I know the face of God will always be.
As long as the wind is a friend of time and time the controller of life and death.
I know there is no reason for me to worry and fret.
Like the moon and stars that always shine, so will the eye of God be my guide in troubled time.

B. Eileen Kuchenreuther
LIKE NEVER BEFORE
Casually we met, simply by chance
you. . .your special charm
friendly attraction, very first glance

Quickly your love entered my soul
aware. . .like never before
willingly we accepted the couples role
Holding your hand, a pleasure held dear
our love. . .openly shared
friends for life, then, so simply clear
Wanting you, always fearful of tomorrow
desire. . .like never before
losing your love, created the ultimate sorrow
Gone from my life, still fantasies of more
physical passion. . .endless desire
momentarily I love you, then and now. . .
like never before

Phyllis Newton

THE SUN COMES UP THE SUN GOES DOWN

The sun comes up, the sun goes down
The cold and dark creeps into town
Many hastening homeward bound
Leaving no tracks upon the ground;
The sun comes up, the sun goes down.
Evening's darkness puts most to sleep
Save for willows alone to weep
Prowling mice from hiding places
Sitting owls in trees like vases;
Evening's darkness puts most to sleep.
Morning's brightness brings most alive
Some get ready for "eight to five"
Flowers lighten and wear a smile
Birds a-wing again for a while;
Morning's brightness brings most alive.

Marilyn Hare

FINALLY A BEGINNING (BECAUSE OF CHRIS)

The door opened fully for me that eve.
I crept out slowly and was welcomed.
No great fanfare awaited, only an extended hand.
With the touch received came a new friendship,
More gentle, yet stronger than any before.
Patience greeted words longed to be spoken.
No demands spurted forth,
Only accepting silence waited for me.
Slowly, the Past was uncovered and understood.
Ghosts, released, were swept away by the present living.
With the passing of Time came new moments
To be enjoyed and cherished as memories.
Sharing washed away the fear of "before."
Renewed strength filled the deep void within,
And the security of fearless expression grew.
I fear myself no longer.
The lock does not turn any more.
Freedom from being sad, lonely, frightened
Is once more a part of my being.
I am now able to say,
"I need to talk."
I have found my Friend.

Leisa Elliott-Johnson

UNTITLED

This ring I wear
once meant so much happiness to me.
As things changed,
the meaning became hazy through the tears in my eyes.
Remembering the times lately it was my source of hope,
doggedly trying to right the many wrongs
TRYING to regain your trust and love.
success evaded my choking grasp, But still I wasn't discouraged.
Not tonight,
in the cold blackness the ring glitters, taunting me
with failure dowsing the last spark of hope
smoking like the anger in my swollen eyes.
Times like this, I forget the love we've shared
Hearing only the echo of bitter accusations
My soul slowly dies. .
until all that is left is. . . . .
tears
falling on the ring you gave me in love. . . . .

W. C. NeSmith

SHELF BALM

If your fingers do the walking and your lawyers do the talking,
if your painters do the ceiling and your doctors do the healing;
If your waiters do the seating and your friends do the eating,
if your time is short abiding and your children do the 'ciding;
If your limits have contracted and your spirit has reacted,
if your role is swiftly fraying, you can still do the paying.

Margaret M. Verhulst

WAKE UP, WALT WHITMAN

My greeting is to you, Walt Whitman,
To your poem greeting me,
A reader drawn to you
Across distance, across time:
Your poem a delicate Brooklyn Bridge
A crowded Brooklyn Ferry,
A teeming Passage to India
On the airways of our minds:
My poems a bridge back to you,
A greeting through the barricade,
A shout:
And only folly warns me
The shout will not be heard.
My poems are a bridge between
Your Brooklyn Bridge
And my mad soul boat,
A brass bed sitting up in space
Up on the second floor of an apartment
Where I roost and write
Before dawn on a morning in the springtime
At the end of the century you began;
And here's an offer I've waked up to make you;
Wake up, Walt Whitman, wake up too,
For a few minutes this early morning, wake up:
Let's throw out a new span together
To another century beyond.

Dorthy M. Ross

PRAYER

Lord, let me be with children;
To know the touch of small, grimy paw
Against the unnecessary perfection of newly coiffed hair,
To see the milk-rimmed, gap-toothed smile
Of one who sees beauty in a frog.
Let me walk with children;
And feel the grass they understand
So well, beneath those bandaid-crowned knees,
And hear the lisping song of kool-aid sweet lips,
The unrehearsed purity of a raggedy doll's lullaby.
Lord, let me be with children;
To taste the gourmet kiss of peanut buttered
Lips against my own,
To sense the sheer delight in dimpled cheeks
Holding tight to a secret.
Let me kiss the tiny curl that hugs a baby's nape,
And be worthy of the infinite faith bestowed
When a small hand creeps into mine.

William L. Bennett

DAY OF RECKONING

Riding on the wind, roaring in the ears,
cacophonic, cataclysmic,
comes the sound of
Doomsday—
Rotating this sand-speck orb
until the sky becomes
the pit of Hell,
and the bottom the top!
Day of triumph, day of acclamation, day of
existential justice
when, at last, the man on the
bottom is on the top:
The scum in the pit is the Scarab,
the slime in the catch-basin
the Shechinah,
the scab in the blowhole
the shining symbol
on the zenith of
conformity's defeat!

Violet M. Wiita

A FRIEND

A friend is one who's always there,
When you are sad and blue.
He knows just when you need him,
So he stays close, close to you.
He leaves his work undone sometimes
To help you willingly.
Your troubles are his troubles too,
How thankful you should be.
He helps you through dark valleys, dear,
Lifts burdens hard to bear.
Rewards he never wants to have.
God keep you is his prayer.
Appreciate your good, true friend,
Like him help others too.
Our world a better place will be,
If that's what we all do.

James C. Goree, Jr.

HELLO

Presumptions, Assumptions, miss-construed—
Consume, diffuse and distribute the soul
and allow one
nothing.
Sadness reeks, seethes and emerges the catalyst
which brings the
sweetness of birth
after life.
The second arrival is peaceful
because, all is granted
where nothing is wished
and the absence
of feeling renders
all things
proper.

David Pilla

SOMEPLACE ELSE

Damn the setting sun
Which unlike
These empty hands
Will somewhere
Touch her golden hair.

Wilda M. Hively

LIFE'S LOVE SONG

We walked earths path together
Our life was like a song
The Master played the music
While we just hummed along,
Well—half way through the first verse
We missed a note or two
But got our hearts in tune again
As all true lovers do,
The song is almost over
Our story has been told
We held hands as we sang it
And watched our lives unfold,
Oh, what a magic love song
Our life has proved to be
Because He led the concert
And we tried to stay on key.

Philip King

SOCIAL MURDER

Sickle-cell sadness in an ivory world

breeds ebony contempt.
Beware the pseudo-servant
rebels
for hatred is hereditary,
and black is the dominant
colour
with power over guilty squire
kin.
Some are afraid of the dark
but we will never know their
fear,
they're experts.

Ondrea Tye

CLOUDS

Like clouds weaving their
canopy,
my thoughts of you.
Floating serenely,
they move in my mind's eye.
Threads of mist gathering,
afraid of what could be.
Is it a storm?
Tell me never.
You will know.

Joan Tyer

FREEDOM

freedom!
oh freedom
where is thy glow
tarnished, stained
impossible to know
you seduced me, tempted me,
lured me away
I didn't know freedom
felt this way
empty. . .
alone. . .
quiet
I don't like it
freedom—you're a
goddess
with feet of clay
give me back those
bonds—now—today

freedom!
oh freedom
where is thy glow?

Susan Kelly Jambard

UNTITLED

Her arm lays listless over the
chair
A letter crumbled in her hand
Lace and flowers lay on her
dress with care
Motionless, pain etched in her
face
Her cheeks still show a slight
glow
Perhaps from dance in graceful
flow
But again there is that letter
The background seems a blur
Yet every day I greet her, that
face so forlorn
And I never stop to ask and I
never will at all
For she is captured above my
bed, a picture on the wall!

Jeanne M. Halama

AUTUMN MEANS TO ME

Leaf-scent and merry-walking
autumn means to me.
The ancient gold of fallen
needles
beneath each pine-rank tree.
Distance-haze and moon-ring
skies
autumn means to me.
Bird-flock-flutter, fine as
feather,
rise and fall along the
hedgerows,
circle fields, bone-buff and
rattling
restlessly.
Wind-brisk and leafsmoke-
scented
autumn means to me.
Early evening ringed with
barking,
whispering hills and valleys
darkening
echoing tônes of gold and
golden,
autumn means to me.

Gary F. Gillespie

CONSIDER. . . .

Perhaps I'm not the greatest
thing
that God has ever made.
And I know there's many things
I've tried
that didn't make the grade.
I know that I am not so smart;
many things that I don't
know.
And many times I tried so hard,
but didn't place or show.
But just remember one thing,
dear;
a fact so very true.
If I were a perfect human being,
would I have a need for you?

Betty Williams

MARKUM

(As Told by the Cat)

It happened one cold bright
Christmas Eve,
As Santa was on his way,
He came across a little black cat
Who had no place to stay.
The cat was sad, his folks had
left—
The only folks he had.
And Santa, being the saint he
was,
Knew how to make him glad.
"That little black cat, if
you must know,
That very cat was *Me!*"
Santa stooped and stroked my
back
As gently as could be.
He softly spoke and said to me,
'How would you like to go
With me in my good aeroplane,
A-sailing over the snow?'
"Oh, yes, I'd like it very much!"
I quickly then replied.
He very gently picked me up,
And placed me safe inside.
At last, at last, I had a friend!
I was no longer sad.
It was the nicest way to feel
That I had ever had.
Santa Claus was happy, too.
He said he needed me.
He needed a gift for a lady dear,
Who's sweet as she can be.
'Would you be willing,' then
he asked,
'To go and live with her?
She'd like that very much,' he
said.
Again he stroked my fur.
"I surely would!" I then replied;
And that is how I came
To live with my sweet Ethel
then.
She chose "Markum" for my
name.
Though she calls me by her own
pet name:
'Marlie', she said, 'come here!'
And I so proudly went to her.
I now *belonged*! Did you *hear*!
Ethel was pleased with Santa's
gift.
And the *Gift* was happy, too.
It was love then at the very
first.
We both were glad. And so
would you.
One of the first things Ethel
said,
Was: 'How long your tail is!
Well!
And your legs, and your body!'
But she *liked* them. I could tell.
Then she said, 'So loud a *squeal!*'
But she didn't mind. I gave a
soft mew.
Sometimes my voice is soft
when I sing
And pat her face, with, "I love
you."
I think Ethel likes me as I am.
She doesn't mind my lengthy
size.

But the things she likes the
most
Are my beautiful bright green
eyes.
I'm sorry to say I'm not very
brave.
I'm so afraid of dogs.
At the thought of going outside
alone
My mind just simply bogs.
Once when my Ethel was very
sick
I got quite close to her
And put my arms around her
neck,
And warmed her with my fur.
Ethel's friends all love her, too,
Joy kept me for a month or so.
Evelyn has kept me, too.
I love them both, you know.
I'll be so happy when Ethel is
well
And we'll both of us go back
home.
She'll take me on my little leash
And around about we'll roam.

Karen M. Garcia

BE A FRIEND

Laugh with me when I'm cheery
Comfort me when I'm weary.
Help me learn right from wrong.
Walk beside me, make me
strong.
Hold my hand when I'm scared
Show me that you really care.
Let me in from the rain
Love me and I'll do the same.
Take me in and we will share
Together we will be a pair.
Stay with me until the end
In other words be a friend.

Mary A. Suttles

LONELINESS

Loneliness is naked branches
against a gray winter sky.
Loneliness is the ocean at
midnight, the breakers
crashing on a deserted beach.
Loneliness is the far-away
whistle of a night train,
echoing through the darkness.
Loneliness is the stillness of
a house, the
quiet ticking of a clock, a silent
phone.
Loneliness is an empty bed, the
forgotten touch
of someone dear.
Loneliness is headlights of a car
going by,
all the while knowing it won't
turn in.
Loneliness is wind whispering
through trees.
Loneliness is firelight flickering
on an empty chair,
an empty place at the table.
loneliness is a dog in the
distance,
howling at the full moon.

William John (B.J.) Sperle Jr.

DID I

Did I help a stranger on his way,
Did I say something nice
today
Did I smile to wipe away a tear,
Did I listen when was right to
hear
Did I sing when song was
needed most, and not a guest,
but gracious host
Did I lift someone when they
were down, Did I force a
smile, when I wished to frown
Did I say tomorrow, when I
should today, Did I hold a
hand not send away
Did I give a promise I can keep,
Did I laugh when tempted so
to weep
Did I these things attempt to do,
I say Did I—I ask, Did You?

Myra (York) (Barnum) Connell

REGRETS

If I could bring him back—
I'd sew the missing buttons,
keep my ice-cold toes away,
bake pies as often as requested,
yes, and waffles, too;
I'd unquarrel all the rows we
had,
unsnarl the tangled webs,
unbuild the walls we raised
together,
stone by stubborn stone.
If I could bring him back—
I'd do a better job of *loving!*

Cecilia Marchand
A VERY LUCKY MAN
He sits by himself in his well-ordered office,
On a quiet, lonely Saturday night,
Surrounded by the trappings of his social successes,
While he thinks over his weary life's flight.
He wonders from where the disenchantment has come,
And yet realizes it has been there for years,
From way back in the past to a young untried age,
When the future held very few fears.
He knows he has let others manipulate him,
And he's let them place him this way and that,
Until he has come near the end of his strength,
And his life feels so dull and so flat.
Yes, he sits quietly there in his well-ordered office,
While his life whirls in wild disarray,
And his house of cards crashes to pieces around him,
As he stares at it all in dismay.
He snatches at joy and tries to mend happiness,
And fumbles for peace, on the floor,
Until the pieces spin faster and faster and faster!
And they're just as out of place as before.
So he lets them lie there, where they've rolled and they've tumbled,
Scattered round his feet every which way,
And as he steps wearily over them, and he snaps off the light,
He says, "What a very lucky man, I am, today."

Terry Perkins Shirley
POEMS
There are poems about trees,
And poems about boys.
More poems about girls,
Then poems about toys.
There are poems about days
And poems about night.
A poem already written about everything in sight.
Some poems are tragic
Filled with lost love and war,
Many tell great stories
Of people near and far.
But within my heart,
And I know 'tis true—
There awaits a poem meant just for you.

Elton Daniel Spoon
GOD MADE MAN
God made man
Gentle and kind
Along came Satan
Changed man's mind.
God made man
Humble and small
But Satan said to man
That's not enough at all.
There is more to this world
That God made than you—
More than the Garden
And the sky's pretty blue.
When man heard this
He just couldn't wait
To cross-over through
That Garden gate.
When man left the
Garden of Eden that day
He'd wished and prayed
That he had stayed.
For in the Garden
Man saw through
God's eyes only.
Once crossed-over
To the other side,
Man saw through
The Devil's disguise.
That's why there are
Two sides to life this day.
Peace, Love, Happiness—
That's God's way.
War, Death, Hate—
Is the Devil's play.
Which will you choose
On your judgment day—
Remember it's not very
Far away.

Judith A. Robinson
DARK CLOUDS
Into ones life dark clouds appear.
and stay around for what seems like a year.
Though it isn't fair that some of us
have more despair, it makes one feel that God doesn't care,
but be aware, he is always there.
The clouds are not there to stay,
cause he's trying to move them away, to give you strength for sunny days.
For dark clouds return, maybe more
than you like, and it seems as though you've run out of fight.
But remember when they float by again
the sun is always at the other end.

Ada McCoy
Oh, Beautiful America
Oh, beautiful America; land that God has blessed
And shed His grace so wondrously
Oh North, East, South and West.
Your High Court led by Satan,
Has condemned you in His sight;
By saying evil's good making murder right.
Abortion is murder, a license to kill;
Slaughter of the innocent repeated o'er again.
These precious buds are blooming around God's mighty throne,
Carried there by angels to their eternal home.
The learned men, who say they are not human;
Will hear their cries throughout eternity.
They'll see them robed in white with crowns of victory
on their heads.
Oh, beautiful America, these precious jewels aren't dead.

Frederick E. Shaw
DESTINY
Yesterday is gone.
Should I listen for an echo
or lend ear to this day
that should I see tomorrow
it may blend with life's design?
I stand in the twilight of tomorrow
when I am to meet that which comes.
That which is to be.
The inevitable arrival of an infinity of joyous todays.

Margie Kane
I AM THE HOUSE
I am the house of your warmth
to be fulfilled soon;
I am the woman
of your womb.
Come fill me again
It is only then that I can feel the
risings of the tide and the
full blown moon
reach up to the sky and bring
the blessing of you
back to earth

back to me.
Come, appease me.
Make me strong.
To sing in the quiet of our love's
song;
and still awake
to yet another night.

Mrs. Julie Linzmaier
AUTUMN LEAVES
A Harvest moon was big and bright
The air was still, my heart was light
The clouds were fleecy and white
I thought to myself, what a beautiful sight
Jack Frost was busy with paint and brush
He took his time, no need to rush
Those pretty leaves I must not crush
As I walk in the twilight hush
Soon the cold north winds will blow
And the leaves will be covered with snow
Another long year will pass I know
Autumn leaves again with colors will glow

Georgene B. McKenzie
SEASON'S LOVE—AN ODE TO HAPPINESS
As I see your tender smile,
winter I recall awhile.
Planning dreams we hoped would grow,
throughout our lives as sunshine's glow.
Then came spring our plans to flourish,
soft embraces start to nourish.
A glance perhaps to summer's flowers,
and our many happy hours.
Together we can dream of love,
as fall presents it's morning dove.
The happiness we share this way,
fills the season's longest day.

Mary L. Hawkins
JESUS CHOSE TO LOVE ME
I'm so glad you chose to love me Jesus
Take my hand and let me walk with you.
Let me feed upon your whole word daily,
Let me learn your will you'd have me do.
If you hadn't chose to love me Jesus,
If you hadn't suffered, died and rose again,
There would be no answer to my problems,
There would be no forgiveness for my sins.
Since you chose to love me Jesus,
Your blood has covered all my sin,
I want to be a servant to you daily,
Your light of love to shine my heart within.
I'm so glad you chose to love me Jesus,
Your mercy and your love you've given me.
Here's my life, take it, remake and mold it,
In the person of yourself, reflect in me.

D'arlyn Lamphier Murphree
WYOMING WOMEN
Women in pickup trucks
Packing briefcases
Women in waiting lines
Packing babies on hips
Women docking sheep
Packing firearms for predators
Sharpshooting women
Shooting skeet/pheasants/and peeping toms
Women reaching out of their loneliness
To become somebody
Women haying/harvesting/
Harmonizing with the wind and the land
And sometimes
With their men.

Bebe Carroll
SUDDENLY A GAP
Falling on time
Soft and sure
Someone is with me.
Some bodies frail and distant
Some thoughts clear and close
One life to a card
Many smiles to a picture.
Three who are faithful
One who is loving
One who is cautious
One who is me,
Six moving as one.

The doors fly open
At the touch of a hand.
The running is swift
The doors open soon.
One in the center
Laying the ground,
Some on the edges
Searching the ground.
Faith and love fly in,
I fall aside,
And caution shuts the doors,
Six moving as one is no more.
Their cries are fierce and
painful,
I fear for the faithful and loving,
Fighting in the center and on
the edges.
Caution is with me on the
outside.

Dorothy E. Wright

BACKYARD BEAUTY

The dandelions open up their
yellow blooms
In the morning early as the sun
rises high;
So, I take the digger and go snip
a few
And flip them over to wither
and die.
This leaves the flowers without
the weeds,
The tall stalks stand with petals
unfurled;
So quiet and peaceful, the colors
blend
The most beautiful flowers in
the world.
The most relaxing of all the
places I've been
There's no other like my own
back yard;
With just the birds, my flowers
and me
It looks lived in without
working hard.

Raymond L. Posival

IVY COVERED WALL

Inside the Ivy Covered Wall,
Live hundreds of men; short and
tall,
Of every color: black, brown,
and white,
To whom the gate is locked
tight.
Because of some mistake he had
made,
A crime was committed; the
price had to be paid.
For many years, freedom will he
have not,
In his life there will always
be a blot.
When to him, the sentence first
was read,
His life had ended; he was dead.
Entrance he then made through
the penitentiary gate,
Wondered he what then would
be his fate.
Inside, the process, immediately
began,
For his belongings, a receipt
was in his hand.
Close to his scalp, his hair
they would shear,
His body shower and clad in
new gear.
In his uniform of white; a cap
on his head,
To the interviewer by a guard
he was lead.
Waiting in line, on a bench
he sat,
Until his turn, when the
interviewer he met.
A job there would he perform,
In the laundry, factory, or on the
farm.
Sheep, hogs, and cattle there
to feed,
Or plow the fields and plant the
seed.
His body so strong and seldom
sick,
Tanned when cotten he did
pick.
Outdoor labor, difficult though
it be,
Preferred he to a job in the
factory.
Labor must he, though he be
old,
Until time came for his parole.
With just a few years left in
his life's span,
Where could be found a job for
that old man?
Qualifications of reform,
experience and skill,
That old man will again head
for the hill,
The Federal Government, great
as it may be,
Refused him employment,
because a record has he.
To society a price he did pay,
Now he was free, but had no
place to stay.
No one seemed to care for him
at all,

Return would he to the Ivy
Covered Wall.

Leslie Criss, Sr.

I FIND YOU

I Find You,
Irresistibly attractive,
So interesting and kind;
I Find You,
Ever so Refreshing as a
Summer Day drenched in
Sunshine.
When I'm in your presence,
I'm helplessly captivated,
By the Intensity of You
That penetrates my soul
and mind.
Even in your absence I
Find You
Impossible to Forget.
Yet Distant from my grasp
I Find You
Forgiving of my Intrusion
Into your Existence
I Find You To Be
Life's sweet
Revelation
The Challenge of
My Expectation.

Robert T. Jones

THE RED, WHITE AND BLUE

Do not tread on me!
For I am strong!
And I am free!
I am strong
And I am free
For thy sign
Is liberty!
Flying high
Red, white and blue
My people fought
For freedom true!
Now I fly
On flagpole high
Popular! Proud!
For I can never die!

W. Henry Davis

NEANDERTHAL MY BROTHER

In all the legends I feel
anonymous.
I strive alone
To know the torso's riddle
Thru the craft of learned men
Who probe the thickets of
ancestral bone
And old fur in ambiguous earth
and fen.
Those legends gleaned elusive
as grabbling
After sunbeams in a darksome
cave;
Enigmas of abyssic glens and
fields
Of wind-blown desert wastes,
the relics
Of the phantom grave,
Yes, thru long forensic quest
Resolving old equations long
unguessed.
Am I colatteral to they who
ingested carnivores
And lard-fat mastodons;
Who left their mark on sooty
walls,
By foreign shores,
And homed in boundless
wilderness,
My brothers of the times named
Neanderthals.
Tell me the wonders of that
impelling spark
Which drives the Engine of the
Universe. .but hark,
Tonight the rhythm of the
stars wheel loftily and fair,
In symphonic beauty Bach and
Beethoven ride the air.

Michele C. Tillapaugh

SOMEBODY SAVED THE ROSE

A rose begins to grow—the bud
opens slowly
cautiously—guided by the
warmth of the sun and
gentle drops of rain. Each
petal begins to unfold—its
color is brilliant, its texture
is soft and delicate.
Gradually a chill comes in the
air—no rain comes,
no warmth, no sun, no gentle
loving touch to help the rose
to grow—the rose has been
neglected.
Will the rose just fade and die?
A tender, caring hand moves in
and clips the dainty
rose. Guided by a new loving
kindness the rose finds
protection from cruel
elements and neglect—the
rose finds a strong, yet loving
touch that gently urges the
rose to once again bloom.
The nearly lost and foresaken
rose once again brings
forth the beauty it once knew
how to give and receive, but
thought was long forgotten.
Somebody Saved the Rose!

Brian L. Newton

LOST IN INDIFFERENCE

Little boy lost in a world of
indifference,
Never knowing which way he
will go,
Trying to live his life to the
fullest,
Never letting his feelings show.
Little boy lost, but not in
indifference,
Lost in a world of hatred and
lies,
Trying to progress, but always
being held down,
Striving to attract their
attention,
No one seems to notice his
cries.
Little girl confused about her
purpose in life,
Never letting little boy
lost find his way,
Trying to decide what's best
for him,
Ignoring every word he might
say.
Little boys and girls who are
misinformed,
Dislikes little boy who is out
of the norm,
Trying to hurt him with
repeated tries,
Accusing him of things which
he denies,
Always attacked, but never
knowing why.

Leslie Dee Guessford

SWEET CHRISTMAS

Christmas time sure is dandy
With cakes and cookies, pies
and candy.
People baking. . .both North and
South
Goodies for me to stuff in my
mouth.
There's chocolate candy, free to
take
Tree-shaped cookies and wreath-
shaped cake.
But this steady "Here, I made
this—try it!"
Has absolutely blown my diet.
Plus all this luscious Christmas
cheer
Is going straight to my hips and
rear!
Which makes it obvious for all
to tell

I'm not putting enough "NO"
in my Noel!

Joan E. McCormick
FATHERHOOD
("Fathers, provoke not your children to anger, lest they be discouraged! Colossians 3:21.)
What constitutes fatherhood—
The physical seed of a selfish man,
Or the nurturing care and helping hand
Of one who provides the daily food?
Who is the true father of the child—
Bearer of seed, but the root of anguish,
Or the father figure, firm yet strong,
Who protects and shields the child from wrong?
On whom can the offspring depend—
Who cares enough to attend one's needs?
Who will vanquish doubts on which fear feeds—
Loving father, another kin or friend?
Who should enjoy the rights of fatherhood—
One who practices parenting as he should,
Or one who left his child to another's care,
Only to return the benefits to share?
Each man must answer and decide—
'What did I provide for my child?'
Was it sustenance and encouragement,
Or anger, hurt, and thus discouragement?

Nelda G. Wilson
YOU'LL ALWAYS FIND ME HOME
She was my dear Mother who lived all alone
With all her trinkets and little frills
A long way from the city life
Far up into the hills
She'd hold my hand as I sat down
In the comfort of her home
She'd say "Why don't you come more often?
You'll always find me home"
Her little house was always clean
And sparkled in the light
For she was up at sunrise
And worked far into the night
She'd say, My dearest daughter
Wherever you may roam
"Why don't you come more often?"
You'll always find me home."
I took those precious words she said
I locked them in my memory
I can still see her rocking
And singing merrily
I just had to go back and get her
And take her to my home
But she wasn't there to greet me
I didn't find her home
She had grown old and weary
She could no longer see
Her once strong heart had grown weak
She lost her memory
The grave finally claimed her
But it didn't have her long
For I'm sure God up in heaven
Sent an angel to take her home.

Samuel—H—Slattery
ITS GETTING LATE
As the years roll bye
It seems my longing for love will never die
In the eternal youth of my old age
I will not heed the words of the sage
And so I would prefer to be
An old fool in love
Than a wise man who knows no love
Yes it is getting late
But not late to find the glow
Of love in my heart
That fills the years with love
The memories of youth
And love like the embers of a fire
Seem to glow and brighten
As I gaze at you
Yes it is getting late
But I hope before it is too late
I shall remember the eternity of love
I found in You

Miss Catherine R. Cripe
LOOK AND YOU WILL SEE
you see me as
you want. . .
i see myself as
i wish. . .
GOD sees us as
we are. . .

Matthew Alan Noll
AFTER ME
Here I'll die,
Beneath the sky,
Where no one else can see.
Here I'll lie,
But don't you cry,
Because there will be somebody after me.

Sylvia England Grizzard
HOW DO I FEEL? LONESOME
How can mere words say how I really feel right now
The hours that pass slowly like days, as if they were my last—
The lonely ticking of the clock, as I watch the sun take a bow
The memories that flood my mind of things that make up my past—
What do I feel right now—
"LONESOME"
The stillness surrounds me as I sit here gazing out
I watch my child playing, so carelessly, running wild and free
And it hits me,—that *he* is what life is all about,
Then why am I feeling so useless, so unfullfilled, so unlovely—
How do I feel right now—
"LONESOME"
Shadows are creeping upon me from things I've said and done
Darkness falls all around me as I face them all alone—
I feel that I should cast them away and run—and run—and run—
But somewhere I know there's a place where the sun has shone
And yet, how do I feel right now—"LONESOME"
I think about the times I've loved, the saddness each time brought
And yet, I know there must have been some happiness—I just don't remember—
As I think back now, I realize that happiness was all I sought
But now, those things seem to fade away just like a dying ember
And now—Right Now—how do I feel?—"LONESOME"!

Miriam Sisson
THE GOLDEN AGE CLUB
See how they sit—so still
Hands folded, gnarled
Listening politely, but deafly
As youths mill about
To explain in vain
The problems of age

Their deaf ears lip reading, in pain,
The words from the stage
Hearing only the sweet music
Of their own youth
Drowning out the uncouth noise
Of lost hopes and forgotten dreams.

Susan M. Plut
SURVIVAL
Reflection on a lake—
It quivers, frightened;
It ripples, jumping;
It fades, running, seeking asylum.
The waters are now free of movement,
The reflection becoming but a mirage
Of what will never be again.
A single shot—ringing—reverberates
Through trembling timber.
The stalking has been played out.
Defenseless, the dear has fallen
victim to a scheme of cold-blooded
Self-indulgence.
The lake quivers once again,
Sensing that which man calls sport;
Innocent beauty becomes fair game for any
Sporting man.
Now, hastily, the hunter freshens up
At the waters of transgression,
Washing away the stains of his deed.
The lake transports this red offering
Over rocks,
Around weeds
Until it surrenders at the edge of a bend
Where land and water twist and turn
To ascertain which will dictate dominance.
And there lies the remains of ugliness
Of the truth
That nature must endure—
Endure and somehow survive.

Stella Caltha (Cathy) Collins
TOUCH A CHILD'S HAND
Touch a child's hand, a new world begins. . .
Full of laughter and small faces,
ice cream houses, books with live pages.
Storms of rain without any thunder,
Kings, Queens, Lords of Wonder.
Paper dolls that dance on their toes,
a winterland of everlasting snow.
A world that exists in continual peace,
where calm is every ocean, tame is every beast.
Clouds to ride on, to wish upon a star,
moonbeams to walk on, busy streets full of cars.
Where fairies, dragons, goblins, witches,
go along with pirates and kittens that hide in
Mom's kitchen.
A place where the endless play of summer,
is relived and renewed in each nights slumber.
Touch a child's hand. . . .
there's a world of sweet bliss, all is healthy
and happy in this world that exists.
An adventure awaits around each corner,
a place where your friends are, your never a loner.
You'll find this world in only one place,
those bright wondering eyes, a warm smiling face.
Yes, touch a child's hand, a new world begins.

George A. Murawski
LOVE
If the sun refused to shine
I would not mind,
If mountains should crumble to the sea
Then let it be,
For you hold the power to make me see
That life is loving you.
Man fails, man succeeds

But we decide which will lead,
Decisions are flirted with
To make souls unsure,
But you came along
And made me sure.
Life is a series of trials and
tribulations
Which lead us about aimlessly,
However, from me you get all
my adoration
For guiding me with your
magnetic charm,
Let the earth spin wildly then
While we pass time in each
other's arms.

Patricia A. Wilburn

TALKING TO ME AND GOD

The world can really get to me,
God.
Sometimes I feel like I have no
where to turn to.
I become worried and I don't
think,
Then I realize its time to have a
talk with you.
Maybe the talk is more to
myself, but you hear it.
I have to hurry here and there.
People demand more than I can
give.
Some people have no feelings, it
seems, they just don't care.
To sit and let my mind wander,
can get me by.
To watch the wind, the trees,
the animals outside.
To think of loved ones not so
near.
Remembering the times I've
laughed and cried.
Not really thinking, but then
my mind isn't blank.
No one can say the right words
when I need myself more.
We all need time alone
sometimes.
Simply turn the world off a
minute or two, just close the
door.
Take a deep breath, then let it
out slowly.
This help from you helps me
everyday.
This talk helps me in every way.
My blessings are many, for this I
am grateful,
Thank you God.

Kathleen A. Brothers

40TH STREET

When real thirsty, mom made
lemonade,
And hot butterscotch cookies
homemade,
But the fun was yet to start,
When from the shed, came the
go-cart,
Then watching kids gather from
blocks around,
Envious to ride, just from its
sound,
Or sometimes playing games,
like King of the Hill,
Getting bruises and bumps, I
remember still,
From fighting up the mounted
dirts top,
To be a King, that no one could
stop,
And to the couch, lonely at dad
I would stare,
Saying please, with your legs,
make a square,
Quickly crawling inside, feeling
warm, so content,
Remembering sometimes there,
half the day I spent,
Yes, the go-cart, the house,
the things we all done,
Recalling many memories of
growing up fun,
Now half of us gone, there, our
hearts will still meet,
At the house with no ending, on
40TH Street.

Margaret Tod Ritter

STORM CHANT

I am the trees of a forest blown
one way only.
I am the trees of a forest lonely,
lonely.
I am lashed by the darker winds,
I sway
To the earth, I am stricken, I
reel one way.
I am a forest of turbulent
trees.
I am bent double, the seven seas
Moan in the monsoon of my
tossing.
I am the trees of a forest
crossing
My rain stripped branches in
disarray,
I am black with rain, I am
hurled one way,
I am rooted and torn, I am
wrenched askew.
All of love's hurricane centered
on you.

Elizabeth Seifert Jones

THE SEEDLING

Into depths of darkness I plunge
to find a place of warmth,
I am the total epitomy of a new
revelation,
I cling to life, and gain a soul.
I begin, like the etching of a
portrait
Painted by an unknown hand.
I move silently, ever turning,
like a fish in a sea of
blackness.
I grow, the softness of love
touches me,
protects me,
and the drone of voices lulls me.
I grow, ever stronger, and Frail
Fingers reach
Out to touch, to love, and it
envelopes me. . .
New awakeness pushes me, and
the labor of
My host takes hold, and the
light is blinding. . .
All warmth grows cold and the
small being that is me, cries
out!
Suddenly, warm hands clasp me
and love flows thru me,
I reach out to grab the Universe,
and look upon this beautiful
one,
Who gave me breath, and
brought me life
My life. . . .my Mother.

Roberta Frisby

A FRIEND

Have you ever met a real friend,
one that is true?
One you know will always be
there, will always stand by
you.
One that is happy for you, when
things go your way,
One that doesn't cut you down,
no matter what you say.
A friend is someone who doesn't
talk behind your back,
Someone who doesn't laugh at
you because of what you lack,
One who understands you,
knows your smiles and your
frowns,
Be happy when you're up, be
sad when you're down.
It's really great to have a friend
to brighten up your day,
Someone you can talk to, who
will listen to what you say,
To have a friend. . .Be a friend. .
it really is a must.
It's nice to know there's
someone you can really trust.

V. S. "Vic" Hester

THE LAST HOUR

What would you do if you had
only one hour
On this earth before you die?
Would you spend this one hour
in idle regret
Or invest it in a home in the
sky?
I like to think I've invested
my time
As I've traveled the pathways of
life
In my heavenly home that my
Savior has made
Above this world of strife.
I like to think I've invested my
time
By doing the best that I can
To live close to God's golden
rule
And serving my fellowman.
So if I had only one hour left
Some I'd invest in praise to the
Lord,
Some I'd invest in thankfulness
And the reading of God's Holy
Word.
If I had only one hour left
I'd like to meditate for awhile
And talk to the Lord about
forgiving my sins
So I could leave this life with a
smile.
If I knew for sure that my time
had come
And I must prepare to take my
last breath
I would thank the Lord for His
blessings
And smiling I would go to meet
death.

Virginia Decot Dillingham

TRILOGY OF THE SKY

1932—Prom Night.
We sent a sigh up to the night,
A sweetly, pensive pair;
I said, "I want that tiny moon
to fasten in my hair;
How I should like two twinkling
stars
to place within my eyes;
I would that I could capture
Some magic from the skies!"
He held my face in tender
hands,
With wisdom spoke this truth,
"My love, you have earth's rarest
gifts
For you have dreams and youth."
1961—In our garden
We strolled into the garden
to gaze in outer space,
To search the sky for "Echo",
Its twinkling path to trace.
I felt his arms around me,
Our lips, in sweet alliance
Soon found that Mother
Nature
Was more interesting then
silence!
1980—On Daytona Beach.
(Dec. 7, 1980)
We sat upon the beach,
Our generations three,
We watched the Cape's new
satellite
Blaze to eternity.
The red tide's mist,
December's evening chill,
Did nothing to diminish
Our pride, our love, our
thrill!

Polly S. Owen

MY MOTHER

(Mae Stewart Perry)

Her hair is grey
Her eyes are hazel
Her lips are red as a rose
Her name is very short, 'tis Mae
But sweet as the sound
of the wind that blows
through the pines;
With a sobbing sigh and a
mystic murmer as it goes.
She is good
She is true,

And a wonderful smile has she;
That's not to be seen anywhere
not even in the depth of the
sea.
A light so tenderly deep
As the light in her eyes
When she looks at me;
And as a light that shines
to guide across the waves
the weary toil worn sailor
So shines her life
To brighten and to save.

Peggy Harris

UNTITLED

I watched
your tear
roll downward.
I saw your
pouting
frown.
Someone
broke your
heart.
Someone
stole
your crown.
Now I wipe
your
tear away.
And I
see you
smile.
Knowing
you'll

feel better.

But it's
only for
a while.

And now
you take
my hand.

Said walk
with me
a way.

We walked
along
the ocean.

And walked
into the
bay.

And two
lovers die.

In love
forever
more.

We found
them holding
hands.

washed
upon the
shore.

Charles W. Raymond, 2nd

TREASURE

The treasure chest, in days of
yore,
Was strapped secure with iron
bands;
Within slept bullion, guilders,
ore—
Handfuls of gems from distant
lands.

Its princely hoarders never
guessed
How time would change the
treasure chest!

The treasure chest of modern
day,
In yellow coat and trim of
chrome,
Goes wheeling down the right-
of-way
And, where it pauses, youngsters
come.

Carefully, traffic slows to rest
When stops this school bus
treasure chest.

Manuel D. Hornedo, MD

Show Us The Way—Mr. President*—Show Us The Way

Show us the way to regain the
health of our economy!
Ask Congress to establish a Soft
and a Hard Dollar—
A Soft Dollar for domestic use
for all our trade at home,
Backed up by all our tangible
assets—our homes, factories,
farms,
And all out Natural Resources—
forests, minerals, water
supplies,
And a high Protective Tariff on
all the things that we can
produce!
In this way we the people will
pitch in and conquer
inflation—
In the Good Old All-
American Way!
A Hard Dollar backed up by all
our Silver and Gold Bullion
Reserves—
To pay for needed luxuries from
abroad, including energy
products—
To conserve our own!
Show us the way to reduce our
Unemployment everywhere!
Ask Congress to establish a
National Apprenticeship
Program,
To place all our Unemployed
Teen-agers as apprentices,
In every office, factory and
farm— throughout the nation,
In short courses or long
courses—leading to valid
Graduation Certificates!
With full income tax credits to
the employers and
benefactors,
Thus in peace or war, you would
have a trained secondary labor
force
To back up and replace the
regulars—and the nation
would profit!
Show us the way—Mr.
President—Show us the way—
With you at the helm, we will
all work hard toward a strong
America!
We will all join hands behind
you and back you up all the
way,
To regain our Healthy Honor
and respect for our Flag
abroad!
Keep Showing Us The Way—
Mr. President—Keep Showing
Us The Way
In Conclusion—may the Good
Lord guide you for the Good
Health of Us All!
**Dedicated to Presdient-Elect Ronald Reagan, November, 1980*

Ann Webb

A PLACE TO RUN

A place to run.
Somewhere to go.
A gentle smile,
A peace to know.
The stillness of night,
The soft moonlight,
The listlessness
Of the plight.
A sea of stars
That light the sky.
The sleepy sounds
That keep sailing by.
Nothing so pure
As the night,
Except your love
That shines so bright.
Peace is mine
When death has bid
My life to take,
And my soul to rid.
Allow my spirit to ascend at
night,
To be with God,
To see the beauty of his work
So bright.
Let my eyes see the stars,
And the moon and the earth,
And all that he's given
Since before my birth.
We will be as one,
My father and I,
And forever can I feel
As the night of the sky.
(In memory of my Father
Luther Henry, Jr.
Passed Away—December 17,
1981)

B. W. Pfennig

THE LAST PARTING BREATH

Lying on the brink of death,
Panting to expel my final breath,
I return, reflect to those days
long ago,
Summer sunshine and winter
snow.
I relive those moments of joy
and defeat,
Times of inspiration, times
indiscreet.
My memories roll back like the
clouds of a storm,
Blackening, rumbling, sharp as a
thorn.
I remember the times both
joyous and glum,
Laugh at the things I've done
and were dumb,
Call back the love of my family
and friend,
Realizing now that this is the
end.
I wish I could change the things
that I've done,
Patch up mistakes and pray on
the run.
Just looking back, I can't see
why I've sat,
Putting off this and putting off
that.
Little can I say of what I have
made,
Nor what I have finished or
lifted a spade.
Few moments of my life were
really put to use,
More were left undone, just
taking abuse.
My life was like a shadow,
blackening itself,
Instead of a dream full of life
and of wealth.
Opportunities greater than
words to better myself have
passed by,
All that is left of me is now
going to die.
Happiness is a word I no longer
know,
Death is the word and soon I
must go.
I regret to expire leaving
nothing behind,
Not a shred of hope, not a piece
of my mind.
Again looking back at the past
and my life,
I have finally learned to take
things in strife.
Defeat has been my middle
name,
But what is left of it won't be
the same.
I'll look forward to life in
what lies ahead,
And no longer will I worry
about it after I'm dead.
I can see that what's to be done
won't be easy,
But what I have learned will
always stay with me.
I learned I could live if I
put my mind to it,
I can be important if I can
renew it.
Alas though, it's gone, my
life is now ended,
But what lies ahead will be
properly spended.
I know now that today is too
late,
But maybe next time I'll get
through the gate.
I'll start my life early and
end it all packed,
No one said it would be easy
but I've learned what I've
lacked.

Toucan Ry

THE BRIEFEST OF NAPS

I close my eyes to the sounds
Of gulls playing in the breeze,
The funneling tide and soaring
metal.
All goes on around me, me, here
in my sleep.
The peaceful joy of life
surrounds me.
Geese chasing one another
along their way,
Shadows dancing on the rippling
tide,
Wind sustaining their flight.
Furling flag snaps in the air.
All goes on around me, me, here
in my sleep.

Annie Lee Ray

THE SOLID ROCK

In sorrow some their vigil kept
On a dark day on Calvery's
Mount;
And a sad, broken Peter wept,
While there spilled out
Salvation's Fount.
Words of love spoken in soft
tone,
Heard by a tearful, faithful
flock;
From the cross, as the rejected
stone
Wondrously became the Solid
Rock.

Alice Johnson

A MODERN CHRISTMAS AND THE SECOND ADVENT

The snow falls
Softly on dirty streets
And trees and grass
Of the forest—
Stars sparkle
The moon gleams

The lights go out
Over country and town.
A few Christmas lights
Gleam on trees
In the silence
The wind blows the snow
In jagged patterns
A headlight gleams
Through the blackness—
Another winter
Night has come
Some say,
"Why Christmas?"
In Ward B
The legless, armless
Soldiers pray to die
T.V.'s blare
Church bells clang—
A choir prepares to sing.
Now you see Christ
Walking on the sea
You hear him call
Peter, James, and John
You see the fire loaves
And two fishes
That fed the five thousand
You hear him say
To the sea,
"Peace be still!"
You taste the water
Changed to wine
You see Lazarus
Who was dead
And you know
Miracles are true
You know
Jesus came one day
And died
An awful death
Between two thieves.
You hear the crowd
Yell, "Crucify him!"
And you touch
The hem of his garment
And are healed.
A huge ship
Is finally found
A trifle smaller
Than the Sagafjord—
Completely inclosed in ice
And half covered with
Glacial moraine
With many animal cages
Neatly arranged inside.
And all the world
Wanders and watches
On T.V.
The Russians are defeated—
The earth burns up.
The heaven rolls back
And down to earth
A new city wafts
Each side the length
Of the Alcan—
And the Spoke, the Head.
The King of Kings
Bedecked, berobed
And carrying crowns
Comes in his chariot
A fleecy cloud
With a reward
For each conquering hero!

Lucille Gilpin

SECRET LOVE

Suddenly my secret's out,
I admit without a doubt,
What keeps me going on and on,
When I feel so put upon.
Is it drugs, vodka or gin,
That some are sippin' and
poppin' in?
Is it a new love come to call?
A thrill to outshine and
surmount them all?
You've guessed, a whole new
life,
To bolster me up 'against' storm
and strife.
A friend always there, willing to
wait;
Companion, confidant, and
soulmate,
Who works in mysterious ways
Stirring new thoughts everyday.
Turn your life problems over to
Him.
A whole surge of strength enters
in.
If you're alone with no place
to turn,
Your body, soul and mind still
churn,
You can find solace and inner
peace
From pressures and hatred get
release.
Walking with Him the truth
you'll learn
You'll have the freedom for
which you yearn.
My Maker, my Helper lets me
live
With assurance the rest of the
world can't give.
His love is just as available
to you
Diligently seek Him, He is
your friend, too.

Wilma I. Brewer

HANDS

The tender hands of a mother,
As she smooths a child's fevered
brow,
Convey a love so deep and true,
Of selflessness before which we
bow.
Then there's the hand of a small
child,
Reaching out to his Dad with
trust,
Never doubting his ability
To solve all his problems; Dad
must.
The hands of sweethearts joined
together
With love that's beautiful and
true,
Believing in each others' plans,
In faith, that nothing could go
askew.
The doctor's hands, with such
precision,
As he works on those who are
broken,
Guided by a still higher hand,
Of whom no greater power is
spoken.
Nurse's hands that work
tirelessly,
To comfort those who are in
endless pain,
Sometimes to see a small
miracle
And to know that it was not in
vain.
Helping hands, stretched out to
others,
To respond to a person in need,
Always there to share a burden,
From which many would
quickly flee.
All the hands of the whole
world,
No matter the skin color they
are,
Are extensions of each other,
And through Christ, they are
near, not afar.
The greatest hands are the
Master's Hands,
As He shelters us in His loving
arms,
Protecting us 'til He takes us
home,
To His Kingdom, free from all
harm.

Betty Jean Lovelace

ROBE OF BABY BLUE

A pale green gown
And robe of baby blue,
I wear them in the moonlight
For the eyes of only you.
The pale green gown
Is very old you see.
The baby blue robe
Is new to you and me.

I wanted to wear
A robe like summer sun,
But you liked the baby blue
Your color is the one.
I wear it in the evening
And in the morning dew,
The pale green gown
And the robe of baby blue

Don R. Evans

THANKSGIVING CELEBRATIONS

Thanksgiving Day comes but
once a year,
Celebrated with thanks and
not fear.
Helping others to realize a
grateful need,
Emanating from true love and
not greed.
Always when the harvest is all
complete,
Living the good life, with
people to meet.
Never thinking of self, only of
another,
Either father or mother, sister
or brother.
Kindness to all regardless of the
station,
Beginning to love all who are
relation.
Starting with wife and children,
and then more,
Radiating spheres of influence
as never before.
Giving a life of service, a family
tradition,
Adding precept upon precept
without condition.
Including help to others
throughout the year,
To celebrate thanksgiving
without a tear.
Varying degrees of thanks we
give to all,
Involving the family and
having a big ball.
Increasing love by giving thanks
to our Lord,
Over and over, it is one thing
we can afford.
Naturally thanking God for a
land so good,
Never being ashamed of true
brotherhood.
Grateful at Thanksgiving to
make such a fuss,
Sincere and humble
opportunity for all of us.

Bonnie Bee Beard

MOVING THROUGH LIFE

At the threshold of life
I stand
Life is happening
All around me
I am a participant
The observer as well
I am the action.
Life constantly moves me
Along to new challenges
Doors open, doors close
I move through them
Always recognizing
A higher good awaiting
Behind each new door.
Crossroads ahead—
Which road do I choose?
Intuitively I know
My choice is
The very best way
I can go.
Obstacles appear
Along the way
Then melt into nothingness
As faithfully I march
With assurance
Knowing my most desired goal
Awaits at road's end
Yet, not the end
Only the beginning
Of a road still better
Than I've known before.
On and on life moves me
Through constant challenges
That only enhance
My spirit and my understanding
Of the universe
In which I live and move
And have my being.

Stanley A. Cassaday

PAINFUL THOUGHTS

I sit here in my home
with all the comforts
a man should own.
With pleasures and fantasies
at my finger tips.
From my eyes heavy tears drip.
My thoughts wonder not of
ecstasy
But of Vietnam where my
body
might still be.
A flash before me brings my
wife,
children, and a happy pain of
love within me.

And yet my heart misses a beat. . . . . .
When Roark, Meeham, Doc and the Infantry
Yells why not you
instead of me!
And I said Please let it be
For DEATH is quicker than destiny.
We fought together and side by side.
Our blood splattered on one another
as our weapons shouted
protection for the world
that didn't believe.
And yet you died while my heart still beats.
I never told you this you know.
But Guys. . .GOD I LOVED YOU SO!
Why couldn't I have told you then
Instead of searching for this END.
We met as strangers in that lost land.
But we greeted one another
with open hands.
We agreed one year from this date
we would meet here again to join the states.
I'm leaving now with my body whole
and just the memeories of
YOUR SOULS.

Gregor J. Verbinski
I CAN'T HEAR
I'm not a man or treated as such
My Heart is soon shattered with the wind's softest touch.
My eyes are the fire that smolders in rain
Thoughts of this life are deep in my brain.
I am the ill-fated puppet in tears
You're singing my song, but I can't hear.
Put down, kicked around, I live in a hole
What looks like the outside, is deep in my soul.
Those words of mimic mean nothing to you
I don't think know just what you can do.
Back talk, street talk, it's all just the same
I can't hear you talking, but I feel the pain.
I don't have to hear to know what is right
When your life is black, mine will be white.
I can't tell the sound of a seagull that calls
But, don't be deceived for I see it all.
Exquisite women with their heads held high
While deep inside they begin to cry.
And, the poor, poor boy who thinks he's a man
Has wasted his life just to do what he can.
Their words have no meaning to you or to me
The change in the latter is what I can see.
Music is nothing, the song's in my head
Through these few words you'll perceive what I've said.

Auguste Paul De Casas
A SONNET FOR PHYLLIS
The scent of morning fragrance in her hair,
The moist misty dew of dark brown eyes,
The soft velvet touch of flesh so fair,
Her exquisite embrace of rounded thighs;
Her hot zephyrs of breath against my face,
And throaty sounds of contented sighs;
The heavenly touch of satiny lace;

Her passionate feeling in muffled cries
In the rise and fall of regulated pace;
Her gentle quiet movement of a fawn,
Her poise, her beauty, her everlasting grace;
Shall I compare her to a rosy dawn?
So long as she is nestled in mine arm,
I have no need of sun to keep me warm.

June Pace
A STORY BOOK PLACE
Story, Wyoming is where they're at,
Roxy, Bob and Dusty the Cat.
Their little brown house is oh, so cute
with a stream running thru the yard, to boot!
The wooden bridge you have to cross
to get up to their door,
the pretty flowers, the bright green moss,
how, could you ask for more?
The trees are tall, the air is clear
the stream so swift it runs all year
the Robins are so fat and sassy
they'd steal the heart of any lassie.
The Antelope and White Tailed Deer
are creatures that are seen all year
they're full of pride, so soft and sleek
as they meander toward the creek.
Mother Natures' wild flower bed
with yellow, blue and scarlet red
sure makes you pause along the way
to thank Her for Her fine display.
A big bee buzzing all around
is such a peaceful, restful sound
the ring of a horseshoe sliding in place
causes a smile to split your face.
But the buzz of a saw, the crack of an axe
reminding you to face the facts
that (like the Ant) you'd better prepare
for that long Winter you know will be there.
When Winter comes and snow is deep
and Mother Nature's sound asleep
the wind does howl, the snow does blow
you bundle up from head to toe.
Long Winter evenings by the fire,
you rock and dream to your hearts' desire,
with Burpees' Catalogue in hand
you visualize that spot of land
as being a virtual Garden of Eden,
as soon as you can get to the seedin!
Evenings are great for playing cards or shooting the breeze
while the Winter wind howls thru the trees
the pot bellied stove is the Center attraction
while Jack Frost goes into action.
Morning comes, the air is clear
the world's a crystal chandelier
if Mother Nature was Jack Frosts' wife
I'll bet this world would know no strife.
I hope that as the years roll by
they'll never want to roam
there is no place in all the world
like Story, to call home.

Janet Hayes
ANGELS
She called you angel in the night,
her darlin' one.
She held you close and touched you
with her love.
But as you grew she turned and walked
away, closing the doors, she'd no time to play.
You told her many loving lies,
to quiet her cries.
But she called you angel one dark night.
Needing more, no time today,
She sent you far to find your way.
Wishing you had time to play
you plant the flowers on her grave.
You called me angel one winter day,
touched my fingers to your lips,
happy with an angel kiss.
Now your just a dream I had, so long to let you go.
I didn't know.
I lived my life while you did time,
learning to trust and love again.
(like way back then)
I grew up and so did you, alone.
But you called me angel one winter day.
Years had passed, you packed my dreams and then you turned away.
No more time to play, and all the flowers in the garden seemed to die.
Maybe it was just the times.
I called him angel one morning in spring.
And now we share his dreams.
There's been some pain but love has won,
I knew it would, he is our son,
and everyday we let him know we'll be here to help him, let him grow.
We take the time to say you're special as we play among the flowers in the garden.
And when the flowers die we'll make angels in the snow to pass the time.

Helen V. Pollack
A SENSE OF PLACE
A sense of place
What contentment at my age
To know that I belong
And even tho I may do wrong
It's my mistake to make
I've known many fruitful years
And as my end of time on earth appears
I have no fear
For in my mind I hold another sense of place.
This place that I now hold dear to me
was built with love and honesty
And pride to lift myself a notch or two
Above the life that I was used to
My goal has always been to reach as high as I could go
And know that I had done my very best
Then let it rest.
Upon my family I look with pride
And have earned a place by their side
But God forbid there come a day
Lest they forget I need my place
To do the little things I've always done
My way
Or just to sit and dream my dreams of yesterday.

Sandra Anne O'Neill
THE HEART SET FREE
A thought,
a special moment,
a joy,
a sadness,
a feeling,
an emotion.
When written down
everything close to the heart

can be re-lived, cherished.
Oh what beautiful things can happen
when the pen is put to the paper
and the heart is set free.

Grace Trapp
QUIESCENCE
Like a voluminous gray blanket
Fog rolled from the sea,
Sliding over
The throbbing mass
Of energy.
Sturdy pier-legs veiled to blurs,
Ships but ghosts of expired years.
All was still.
Gulls waiting on warm sand
Postponed their flight to sea.
Waves hushed.
Every Thing
Held softly
Under grey velvet.
My Self was still.

Mary Jane Fields
A HERITAGE OF FAITH
A few lapel pins for Sunday School attendance
A box of yellowing envelopes and paper,
A diary dated 1912
An old trunk to hold these things.....
A faded torn blue workshirt
A well worn Bible.....
Not much of value in the eye of the world,
The bankers, accountants and courts.
(The big people, who count!)
But what of the other things....
The true legacy?
If the wind is in the right direction
I can hear him whistling as he walks across the fields behind our house—
Or hear his voice clearly from the choir loft of his little church,
Singing "How Great Thou Art".. and meaning it!!
The walnut trees he planted as three inch sprigs
Now blow in the breeze nodding their approval
Of his faith.
The birds that still return to the boxes he built and the bushes he planted for their feathered forefathers
Sing their songs of thanksgiving
For his faith.
The leaves on the tall oaks he planted as twigs
Turn crimson each Fall in celebration
Of his faith.
The house he built wears a new coat of paint
And rings with the giggles of his own great-grandchild
As she learns to toddle on the floor he laid so many years ago,
In faith.
No old trunks or roomfuls of trunks
Could contain the faith he had during his eighty plus years—
Faith in his present,
Faith in the future,
Faith in his family,
Faith in his God......
He had enough for all
Because his faith lives on...
(Not in a rusting trunk or a pretentious bank vault)
In the lives of all he touched
In the soil he tilled
And in the seeds planted.
In the earth and in the hearts of all he touched;
There lies his legacy to mankind and to his heirs,
A fortune in memories.
(Dedicated to My Dad)

Lori A. Hobart
THE GOOD-BYE TIME
As the little boy
Sniffed his flower and
Watched the sunset
It reminded him
The flower's fragrance was
Like his mother's perfume
The sunset was like her
Going away
Now the tears are rolling down his face,
The flower is wilting, the sun is setting.
No longer can he see his mother's grave today.
No more can he see his mother.
As he leaves the grave site
Memories of his mother pass through his head.
He throws away the flower.
Now the sun, flower and his mother are gone.

Ann Gilchrist
BY GRACE OF GOD
An earlier bard wrote in despair,
"I'm nobody. Who are you?"
My friend, I am a child of God,
Undeservedly, but true.
His love gives meaning to my life—
To trust, to serve, to give.
My oneness with His universe
Sustains my will to live.
O struggling soul from caverns dark,
Lift up your eyes to see!
For all of time for humankind
God's grace flows full and free.
His own respond in joyful love
To better serve humanity.

Kathy Nash
A HURDLE CONQUERED
"Congratulations!" is what you hear,
As friends and family gather near.
They bear huge smiles, and gifts to please;
Their cameras aimed, they ask for "cheese."
This is the night you've waited for;
You've earned your key to the great door.
You're on your way to your success,
The rungs on your ladder becoming less.
Don't stop now, your goal is in sight;
Achievement can't be made with fight.
A few more steps, and you'll be there,
The place you've yearned for with great care.
Through all the schooling you have had,
You've met new people; good and bad.
The bad ones you just turned away,
The good ones you call "friends" have stayed.
Together, you have all matured
Through your experience endured.
You've learned new things in school (and out)
That someday will apply, no doubt.
Feelings seemed to always be
The cause of love, hurt, joy, envy;
But now you handle these real nice
(For some, you've had to pay the price).
And now the time has finally come
To say goodbye to everyone.
Each of your friends that you have known
Have plans in life; you're on your own.
You're times together have been fun;
They're all remembered, not just one.
Although your old friends are detached,
What you have had will not be matched.
Here come the tears, they won't stay back,
They each run it's own reckless track.
Now everyone gives hugs and tears
And promises of coming years.
Though things can never be the same,
You say it will; it's one big game.
The sun sets low, it ends the day.
The graduate is on his way.

Russell A. Novotny
LISTEN TO THE SNOW
Listen as the snow falls frozen without sound
Listen as the snow falls glistening on the ground.
Listen as the snow knits quilts of feather white
Listen as the snow knits mirrors in the night.
Listen as the snow mounts lightly in your hand
Listen as the snow mounts heavy on the land.

Dorothy R. Kujawski
SHAPE OF TOMORROW
Tomorrow's form by fear obscured,
Distrust, deception—all is blurred.
The awful bomb its shadows cast.
We cringe at what could be—aghast!
Tomorrow seen through children's eyes—
Hope builds a structure to the skies.
Incredible, what life might be
With peace to bless humanity.
Tomorrow's shape is in the mold,
In work we do, in dreams we hold.
In hearths we tend, in breaks we mend,
And over all, in prayers we send.
So take your pliant lump of clay,
And mold the best you can each day;
And pray the cast made in your span
Will fit in God's all seeing plan.
How great in God's eternal scheme
That man can always work and dream,
But final form and lasting trim
Are always, only, done by Him.

Carl P. Henry
DEATH BE THE PARDON
Someday I have a date to keep,
Beyond the touch of time;
Where breath of death,
Is overcome,
And prison left behind.
I don't know when
The gate of fate.
Will open wide for me;
Or what will come,
To take me from,
This place and set me free.
But I confess, it is my guess,
Sometime,
Long past, gone by;
A crime was done,
And I'm the one,
Who for that crime, did die.
I'm here on earth,
Confined by birth,
I cannot be set free;
'til the courts of time,
Rescind my crime,
And death doth pardon me.

Ken Parker
OZONE
Look up there! Look up there!
What has happened to the ozone layer?
It was there but they didn't care.
What have they done to our ozone layer?
They let it happen to you and me.
They were lookin' at money and didn't see
What the bible said would surely be;
And now we've had it don't you see!
Look up there! Look up there!
Has anybody seen our ozone layer?
It was there but they didn't care.
Oh my goodness we don't have a prayer!
There's just more people than I can stand;

All of them sprayin' as fast as
they can.
Who would have thought that
the end of man
Would have come about with a
little bitty can!

Mitzi Patterson
TO DEBBIE
(On Graduation from High School)
Like moving in a dream so clear,
You've done your thing through
every year,
Until today you do appear
To claim your prize—a
diploma!
The crystal ball is now unveiled,
No hint of all the work entailed,
No harp, no band, but you are
hailed

The Princess of Graduation!
In days ahead you will delight
In academic-campus sights
And magic scenes of college
nights,
Of pompous dress and flashing
lights.
You are there—Princess of
the ball!
And just ahead success will
loom,
Pink roses there for you will
bloom,
Reach out and pluck one for
your room
With quiet hand of
elegance,
Princess Debbie!

Virginia West
MOODS OF THE WINDS
Our lives interwoven like
moods of the winds
My happiness I owe to West
winds, calm wind.
For flowers and trees in her
warm breath shall grow,
And my heart shall be glad
where ever I go.
Contented and cheerful I live
with South wind, soft wind,
Tho' raindrops may splatter, no
sorrow they bring,
And the skylark shall soar on
his once broken wing.
Oh, it's easy to live in
moods of the wind
When the howling North wind
arrives in the night,
Purifying all earth and objects
with white.
What could keep spirits higher
than a hike in the snow,
Or to ski from the hilltop to
the valley below.
When South West winds are
angry like tempest rebel,
And paradise is lost in a torrent
of hell.
After the darkness we search for
the light,
For strength of his wrath rode
winds in the night.
Eastern winds can be pleasant,
all four winds combined,
From changeable sunny, to a gay
sort of time.
Cattle have fled, blizzards blown
by the East,
Heralding cold death for the
slow moving beast.
Our lives interwoven like
moods in the winds
A mood for each season, each
moment or whim.
The stone on the mountain, the
wave on the sea,
Are shaped by the wind for
eternity.

A. Jill Blow
Black Man/Black Lady On Mt. Olympus
She springs webs of love
misinterpreted
with a cracked sweaty pulse
for her children eat oatmeal
with powdered milk each
mornin' before
the smog rises from the closet
pollutin' their hog-washed skins
she prays more than most as she
scrubs
filth
from her wretchedness of a
home
fed on welfare checks and
unkept
unofficial promises
her windows crash with folks
cussin' about
whatever climate condition in
their souls
on alcoholic fantasies
some view her as no head or
heart
totally ignoring her personage,
her soul
as she walks her mind clean for
life
the world has eaten of her so
she's moved from reality
to a crack in the wall
and feels sufficient
but a strong black hand has
come about
dissipated by shattered hopes
sees her inner grief as his own
and quickly starts to mend the
crack
she drags her brittle body
straight for his head
down to his heart
and lays there still
as he loves
her
back
to
life
loves
her
back
to
life
as his own.

Patricia J. McElhinny
MY ANGEL BABY, DEAR
I never got to hold you close
Or touch your tiny hand
For you have gone to live with
God
In His most wondrous land.
I never saw your smiling face
Or kissed away a tear
Or heard your voice with
laughter ring
My angel baby, dear.
I never helped you pat-a-cake
Or sang you lullabies
Or rocked you fast to sleep at
night
Or comforted your cries.
But you've a place within my
heart
And always you'll be near
Until, one day, we meet at
last
My angel baby, dear.

Janet Pelletier
STILLNESS
Stillness,
A spector in my room.
Waiting,
For what. . .For whom?
Darkness,
A partner in the night.
Hovering,
Till the time is right.
Stillness,
Broken by a song.
The first rays of light,
Another dawn.

Kay Magenheimer
But One Reason For Writing Poems For The Dead
There is much more due
To one who dies
Than Death's *in transitu*
Closing of the eyes.
As silence falls
And words remain unsaid,
What trumpet calls the world
To the unspoken dead
Save a poet's heralded lines!
There, road the preface
To the book of their seasons.
There, sing the Preface
That signs the sacred canons
Of the graved and radiant dead,
Whose living caresses
Stamped on generations to come
The golden signet of talent,
Or bravely spun
The thread of discontent
That give rise to a rebel-son
Or an equal-minded daughter.
Ah, yes!
There is much more due
To one who dies
Than Death's *in transitu*
Closing of the eyes.

Nancy Anne Farrell
OF LOVE AND LIFE
You seek to find that perfect
union
how to know when it is there,
You find yourself in some
confusion
there seem to be many with
whom to share.
One takes you here, and there,
and everywhere
and you enjoy his company,
But for some reason, not too
clear you feel not true harmony.
Though you are with him every
day
and you like him, Oh, so
much,
You know deep down in every
way
that 'like' is not true loves
touch.
For true love is the vibrations
that with perfect undulations,
Make you feel so right at home
when you are with your love,
your own.
And when you are not with that
loved one
you both can feel the great
pain,
That can only be removed
when with that loved one you
remain.
Though you may hurt each
other dearly
and the anguish seems so hard
to bear,
You can overcome it merely
by staying together through
all fear.
For without each other
you are only drops of rain—as
in a storm,
But together
you are a river flowing with
life—creating form.
And when you are near each
other
there need no words be said
For all around you, you'll
discover!
you can feel that love is
spread.
But it is not just spread around
it pervades within you too,
Cause you know that with your
loved one
you are he and he is you.
For in love, we made
communion
of our mind, body, and soul,
And that, my love, is perfect
union
we are both each others goal.

Elizabeth Mowry
REFLECTIONS
Toddling little high-topped
shoes
Made of softest leather
Find their way across a room.
Then the tiny wearer turns to
smile
To proud faces that look on.
Delicately-fashioned evening
shoes,
Styled for young and slender
feet
Dance on with ease and
lightness.
And a young girl shares a
wordless secret
With her lover.
Faded, bulky slippers
Hug old and tired feet
That shuffle toward the warmth
of a fire.
An old woman has momentary
visions
Of baby shoes and dancing
slippers.

Linda Groce Bodiford

A CHRISTMAS EVE WISH

If there's one wish that I could
have, it would be this way.
I'd like to thank Dear Santa and
see him on his sleigh.
I know there is a Santa Claus,
cause every year you see,
there's o-o-oh so many toys and
a gre-a-t big Christmas tree!
So tonight I think I'll sit up and
wait for that jolly ole man.
I'll just put my pillow on the
stairs and stay awake if I can.
Maybe he'll come down the
chimney, or maybe through
the door.
I hope I can stay awake, cause
you see I'm only four.
So I'm sitting here waiting and
trying to get a peek,
but every time I blink my eyes,
I fall fast asleep.
Well I'm trying awful hard and
I'm getting a little mad
cause everytime that I wake up,
I just see my Dad.
He said, "Santa has gone son,
and you didn't see him at all."
All I could see was this
Christmas tree, and Boy, was
it tall.
He had left every thing that I
asked for, but there's one
thing
that puzzles me: How did he
bring all of these toys and
that
gre-a-t big Christmas tree?

Jon Firestone

AMERICA: A PROPHECY

A rustle of darkness & wires.
Our last will and testament lies
humming
and pulsing in its silo—
a deed which crouches in
expectancy,
urging to leap from the jaws of
the beast.
The law makers who drew up
this fatal charter hang beneath
silver
metal wings, explosive skin, jet
fuel
in their veins, they ride
vibrating
with high wind and
technological lust
to this malignant delivery.
The reading of the will consists
of
electrical whirrs & computer
insect clicks,
fire sings its song to god and the
sky chants with three tongues
of lightning;
the lawyers whistle down
disengaging their clawing light
from
shining bellies toward this
final rendering.
There is to be no contest to this
carnival
of splintered glass &
hyphenated hysterical light.
We have made this mutant
language because
we can no longer communicate
through our limestone hearts. . .
*(this poem was written three
weeks before the Damascus
missle silo explosion)*

Echo H. Van Riter

SEPTEMBER

The harvest fields are golden,
As they wait the gleaner's blade.
While smells of fern and clover
Drift up from the glade.
Altho our summer has lingered
late,
September now peers at the
garden gate,
Urging ahead a sharper breeze
To stir the flowers and lazy
trees.
Tomorrow he may try his hand
To paint new colors in the land.
Change green leaves to red and
gold
With bronze edges strong and
bold.
But there is mischief in his eye,
As a wedge of wild geese cross
the sky,
And he hears a new dressed leaf
declare,
"We too could fly if we'd only
dare."
Daring or not, September knew
They'd all drift down
When the cold winds blew.
Perhaps they would swirl around
for a day,
Then settle down by the tree to
stay;
And mother tree would moan in
the night
Over those leaves once fair and
bright.

Fred Jones

SEAMAN'S DREAM

There Is
An island in the sea
Somewhere waiting just for me
Somehow i knew that i had to
be true
Over the horizon ahead in the
blue
The Stars
And wind and seas all agreed
There must be someone real for
me
They were right without a doubt
Actually it was my only way
out
The Sea
Has a way of awakening a man
It's not so crowded as the land
Besides it offers a much better
view
Of everything—of reality and
you
In The Pacific
Under the Southern Cross
I discovered why i had always
been at a loss
A memory of her came back to
mind
Destiny told me that she was
my kind
I Must
Tell her before it's too late
And hope that she too believes
in fate
In Truth and Understanding and
True Love
And longs to be free like the
sea gulls above
Around The World
After many a port of call
I'm sure there's no one else
like her at all
I believe that i've found my
island in the sea
It's no secret——her name is
Rosemarie

Ronnie Page

DREAMS

As a child I hid from life in an
ocean of dreams,
believing Father-Time would
bear my precious schemes.
With innocence and faith I felt
in my young heart
that my dreams and reality
could not be far apart.
I toiled to sow good seeds in
life's fertile ground,
for to sow was to reap and
happiness to abound.
Yet in the autumn of life it
sadly comes to me
that my beautiful childhood
dreams I shall never see.
For as the body must turn to
dust, so it must be said,
man proposes—God disposes, as
my book of life is read.

Lori Therese Verner

BELIEVE IN MY LOVE

Believe in my love forever;
Like a bird, it has taken wing
And it soars on high,
But will never die,
And with a beautiful voice it
sings
Of memories and dreams,
Of stars and moonbeams.
Sure is the love for you have I.
Doubt never the love I give you;
The promises I tenderly make
Are gentle, but strong,
And my heart to you
belongs.
Even when my Maker shall take
My breath and my soul,
My love will never grow
cold
But will bloom, an eternity long.

Allene Marie Chabala

GOD'S COLORS

The trees and foliage give
colorful hues;
The sky is a spectrum in shades
of blues
I watch as a rainbow circles the
earth,
And I wonder. . .which shade
feels special worth?
Do greens or reds or blue carry
weight?
Should scarlet or purple indicate
fate?
Can I look at a sunset or sunrise
and see
A color that lessons it's beauty
so free?
And while yellow and red and
white intermesh,
Giving colorful races a tone of
flesh,
I close my eyes and wonder
what shade,
The Master made Angels—
which color he made!
I think of him saying, "They're
like you and me,
All differently colored as
meant to be."
All growth is in harmony with
natures light
From the dawning of day to the
darkest of night.
A symphony of sound without
start or end;
A tapesty of color with beautiful
blend
A circle of people holding hands
with each other,
Earth's feeling is one as we
touch one another.

Lila Tadlock

APRIL 19TH

In April's tender lilac frame
While waiting hopefully one day
God's gift to me became a name
And in my arms a baby lay.
This tiny breath designed from
clod
So fragile, so angelic, good!
Made life a rapture straight from
God
As if I in His presence stood.
Brief summer's sun lay soft and
warm
He loved and lived in afterglow
When death began its subtle
harm
Like winter's tide in ebb and
flow.
Through two score years my
hope, my dream.
My child in health and
happiness,
When heartbreak hid the
sunlight beam
For doctors tried with no
success.
I must wait for my Lord's
coming,
And hope for my Master's sweet
praise.
Only this to fill the longing
Only this for my aging days.

Carol Memmen

SOMEHOW, SOMETIME, SOME DAY

Somehow, sometime, some day,
the Lord will show you the
way—
The way to think, to act, to be,
following in faith where you
can not see.
When your will becomes His
will,
that is when a whole new you
will be born again.
If you will be still and learn to
pray,
somehow, sometime some
day—
When you say "Jesus I need
you,"
you will find Him at your
side;
When you say "Jesus, please lead
me,"
He will be there as your
guide;
When you say "Jesus forgive
me—
I'm sorry for what I have
done,"

All of your sins will be washed away—
Forgiven by Gods own son.
The time will come and you don't know when—
You will stand at the Judgement Throne.
You can have Jesus beside you then;
or stand trembling fearfully—alone.
Somehow, sometime, some day, it will be too late
to say "Jesus I need you"—
too late to let Him show the way—
Too late to say "Jesus forgive me."
and somehow, that some time could be today!

Jerrold Rubin

MY LOVE WENT ON A SAILING SHIP

My love went on a sailing ship
Over the silver sea.
He told me if I'd wait for him
He would return to me.
But those were only promises,
And men love to be free.
The sun has set three hundred times
Over the silver sea
Since my loved one steeled his heart
Against a lover's plea,
And still I sit and ponder
Where my heart-of-hearts might be.
I wonder if my lover's drowned,
Drowned in the silver sea,
And never in the passing years
Will he come back to me.
And never till the end of time
Will he come back to me.
(hesitation)
Then I must find another love,
As fine a one as he,
As gentle and as handsome
And as brave as brave can be.
And this one I will ne'er let sail
Over the silver sea.

Helene B. Walker

CHRISTMAS'S PAST

In the cold, cold moonlight, on a winters night
I see a cottage nestled in the glistening snow
Thru the memories I travel and its there I go
My Grandparents cheerful faces
and My Mother at the table set our places
The air is filled with heavenly smells
and how our hunger swells.
Dickie and I, our stockings hung
listen to the sings that all have sung
then after everything is said and done by all
we're up the steps to wait the morning call
nestled in a warm clean bed
we try to sleep as prayer is said.
My Dad, a slender man in a santa suit
My little brother gives a toy horn a loud loud toot
the morning filled with smells of home cooked sausage, Ham
and eggs too
Hot cakes on the griddle and all
eyes sparkling through
the hustle, bustle, fun, and mystery of things to come
it was a share of which we all had some.
Aunts, Cousins Uncles all came stomping in
Gifts, Goodies and cheerful grins
Gay packages and lots of happy chatter
total disaster, contented people no matter
outside the swirling snow and winter winds the only sound
within the cottage, Love, Peace, and contentment abound.

Jean J. Thacher

ODE TO A GIRL CHILD

Why the Lord chose me
I shall never know
To send me a flower
Which I've watched grow
From a very small bud
To a delicate bloom
Whose cheerful glow
Radiates the room
Your heart one day
Will do a twirl
When your eyes gaze upon
Your first born girl

Robert E. Griffis

FACE OF THE CLOCK

Little hand, big hand
they never seem to stop.
Time goes by so fast,
on the face of the clock.
Seconds turn into minutes,
minutes into hours.

Shadows of the day,
are like the fading flowers.
The weeks—the months,
make up the growing years.
Oh! how fast,
the decades do appear.
One look in the mirror,
you see what life has wrought.
Youth has escaped you,
on the face of the clock.

Marianne Duncan

KEEPSAKE

Our love
is a precious wildflower pressed
between the pages of our memories.
Occasionally
our thoughts touch
the dry and faded petals
and the withered leaves.
We remember
the warmth and joy
it brought
in blossom and bloom and
We smile.

Wilda Caplinger

PEACE

What is this peace
that will never depart?
It's a new lease
to a once troubled heart.
It's knowing the Lord,
and for him you now live.
It's reading his word,
being ready to give
whatever he asks,
whatever the task.
It's knowing in your heart
he's saved you from sin.
It's doing your part
a new soul to win.
It's being a Christian
and living for him.
It's asking for help,
and knowing he'll send
whatever you need
to finish the deed.
It's trying to please him
in every way.
It's knowing you'll see him
in Heaven some day.

Louise N. Justus

BEDROOM OF MY MIND

So softly you go walking
to the bedroom of my mind
In dreams we go back there
to another place and time
I see your face I love so dear
I take your hand in mine
as we walk away together
to the bedroom of my mind
Morning brings me sorrow
as the sun begins to shine
When darkness comes you'll call me
to the bedroom of my mind
Now your love is just memory
they say will fade in time
But there will never be another
I'm still yours and you're still mine
I guess I'll wait forever
though I know I'll never find
the kind of love that lived there
in the bedroom of my mind
For you've gone away forever
you never will be mine
And sadness fills the emptyness
in the bedroom of my mind.

Mildred Keil

THE BUD

God sent a tiny little bud
To make our lives more sweet,
He gave it arms and feet and hands
And a smile that was so neat.
We fed him love, he gave us joy
This tiny thing, our baby boy.
We watched him grow to a pint-sized tot
And many the times we laughed a lot.
He danced and played and made us glad
He was the smallest one we had
Then all too soon a change took place
No more a smile upon his face
Our hearts grew sad as days went by
For God had called our bud on high.

Frances Kay Ramey

HUMAN FACTOR

Silver sun sliding through the pine
A few hours before dawn
The world became yours and mine
Now, the day seeks to greet us
The egg has cracked
Yolk is shining through
Silver-not gold
A special issue
Silver sun sliding through the day
Music, laughter, chatter fill the air
People gathering round to play
Now, the world seeks to meet us
The egg has reached the bowl
Strongly whipped up
Add diced ham, spices, and cheese
Don't use a measuring cup
Silver sun sliding through to nightfall
See us—combinations—new casualties—old survivors
Listening to receive the right call
Mixed together—strength and safety in numbers
God helps us—it is Sunday
Tell me—have we made a mess
Or mixed a beginning
Life's omelette
cook egg mixture at medium consistent heat. . . . .

R. A. Younkin

CATERPILLARS

Caterpillars hung everywhere
by their silver threads
eating the woods all bare.
The lady and I went for a walk.
I would ask, "Was he good?"
as the hurt would burst into our talk.
I picked up a larvae, threw it on the lake
and wondered if it would drown,
how long it would take.
All along I thought, "How cruel,"
then I divorced myself from the scene,
wondering what we all would do.
I hoped that, perhaps, the breeze might float
the larvae to the other side.
I took her hand, faced her to say,
"I think I'll go tomorrow,
but I just can't leave you today."

Mary N. Saxon

THE BLOSSOMING

I am a painter.
I go out on the vast Wyoming plains,
and in one day record the

macro-scope
of rolling hills.
Beside the lake and river I sit down,
and duplicate with brush and board their mood.
I am a writer.
In mountain crofts the words leap from my pen!
In wild delight they skip and dance across
the rocky floor.
The lightening and the thunder, wind and rain,
and dark of night are fuel for my torch.
I am a gypsy.
The morning sun will never find my bed.
I never stay in any same locale
from day to day.
The calling trains invite me, "Come along!"
The friendly skies are mine. I ride the wind.
But I'm a prisoner.
In dreams I hurdle these four dingy walls,
attacking life, but only in my mind.
Yet my self-spoken sentence nears its end.
Tomorrow from tomorrow, I'll be free.
The hand that locked the door can open it.
That hand was mine. And I still hold the key.

Wilma Martin
PHOTOGRAPHS
I found an old photograph
with me, a tiny tot,
on the lap of Great-grandma,
a woman solid and serene as a
mountain rock.
On one side my mother so dear,
on the other Grandma,
who used to dry my childish tear.
As I sit and stare
the scene, like the years,
melts into air,
and suddenly—how can it be?—
the one in the center, Great-grandma,
is me!

Lori L. Cleveland
FRIENDSHIP
Friendship is not something
That can be taken or possessed,
Bought or sold,
It is just there.
It is not dominant but sharing.
It is not revengeful but forgiving.
It is not perfect but accepting.
Friendship is a gift from God,
A privileged way of saying. . . . .
You are special.

Clifford Roy Haight
NIGHT & DAY
NIGHT
Scabbard the day, with folds of night,
Stud the sheath, with diamond star,
Light the oceans tender waves,
Reflecting light both near and far.
Break the oceans' pressing swells,
Till folds of white fall into view.
And with each light, each star, each night,
I'll think of you!
DAY
Unsheath the day, pray let night go,
Suns' unleashed rays crush earth from far.
Behold the sight of cloud on high
Look past, perhaps, an earthly scar.
Let the heat waves shimmer on,
Heed not, for all is fair in view.
And on each way, each thought, each day
Will be of you!

Bhatkin Devi
WRITING
Writing is a conquest to me,
Why you may ask?
For it is an outlet for me
to let my emotions and energies
come out by pen.
Writing is the true essence of
one's expression to others.
Even in music there must be writing.
Even if you don't read or see
a line of sheet music.
Writing brings out your inner most
thoughts and actions.
Writing is like a drama, a song,
a novel, a play or anything else.
You must sit down and write it or
as they say compose it just so
If not, you do not love it
and you are short changing yourself
or even more, the world.
Oh, now I admit the world
don't give a damn now while you
are sitting there at a desk or kitchen
table writing whatever it is that you are writing.
However, one truly interested in it does
not let that discourage him or her.

Just wait until it reaches the bookstore
and bookracks and stands of say a Woolworth store.
Then and only then will you know if your work or works
are appreciated.
I'll betcha a hundred even a thousand, some eyebrows
will be raised. Either in complete delight of your
work or complete disgust and regret of it.
There may be a few (quite) in between neither delight
or disgust. Though I'll betcha a hundred even a
thousand, some eyebrows will be raised.
Now isn't that the plain old truth about writing?
even when composing.

Jeffrey S. Ruscio
THE BOYS ARE COMING HOME
Homeward bound creeps the train
with all it contains
young, innocent creatures
fear, shock and a stump
is all that remains
THE BOYS ARE COMING HOME
Faces so sad
for each dead comrade
ten, twenty heaping piles
blood that scars the field red
withdrawn, their visage is not glad
THE BOYS ARE COMING HOME
The letter was read that night
informing them their boy had lost the fight
killing three, their boy was a man
the tears, the sorrow, the guilty grief
now the train is out of sight
SOME BOYS ARE COMING HOME

Holly Trobaugh
MISCHIEF
The storm has rearranged the beach
As a child makes a salt-and-flour map.
Miniature mountain ranges end in cliffs
With broken shells hidden beneath.
The sand's white glare has mellowed
Under the brush of the rain;
The blue of the sea lies beyond the muddy path
Where the dye has run.
Neat haystacks of kelp
Shine orange in the sun;
Freshly washed rocks lie smooth in the froth
Like cobblestone roads of old English towns.
What mischief, what fun the storm spread on the beach!
If only the flies would remove
Their weight from the gull
Surely he would fly again
To laugh at the changes below.

Robyn G. Coultas
AUTUMN
Leaves turned red, gold, and brown,
Come softly tumbling to the ground.
Fragrances arising from burning leaves,
The liveliness of the chilling breeze.
With this season comes Halloween,
When little ghouls can be seen.
Also comes a great tradition,
The gathering of the kin,
When to God our thanks we pray,
We celebrate Thanksgiving Day.
The season soon becomes the past,
Time begins to grow so fast,
For those who await next year,
And the season they hold most dear,
Autumn.

Debbie Ziegler
DURING THE NIGHT
When the streets are empty
And the citys asleep,
All the houses are dark
And dreams are mysteriously deep.
I walk in the quiet,
I walk in the dark,
I hear nothing at all,
As I pass through the park.
I pass his house,
I pass it right by
Secret midnight visits,
Under a moonlit sky.
With one last look,
I begin my final stretch
I must get home,
Or hell I will catch.
Its time for a new day,
The perils of a citys sadness
The morning rush hour,
Its all city madness.
I think I will stick,
To the calmness in the night
The silence and darkness,
The stars and moonlight.

Irene C. Hesch
UNTITLED
Think of a small blade of grass
Think of me
Think of me
Picture it growing straight and fast
Think of me
Think of me
My face is upward to the sun
Shining on everyone. . .
The wind weaves softly through my hair
I laugh without a care. . .
If there can only be
Many more like me
We can be
We can be

Stephen Whyte
Unknown Destination
No port
for the ship on the sea
No nest
for the bird in a cloud
No hole
for the fox on the sand
No home
for the man in a cave
Forever wandering
running to, running from
Chased by fear
Drawn by dream
A sail
for the ship in a storm
A song
for the bird in the rain
A breeze
for the fox in the heat
A prayer
for the man in a rock
Never ceasing
climbing up, sliding down
Pushed by hate
Lured by love
The brine

for the bark as it sails
The wind
for the dove as it flys
The dunes
for the fox as it runs
The trees
for the man as he walks
Frequently swerving
turning right, twisting left
Marred by death
Lit by life
All who live must seek
The life of gladness
Waiting just for them,
And leave the sadness
Somewhere far behind.
Go, or never find!

Curtiss Paul DeYoung

Middle Class Morality

You buy T.V.'s, stereos and nice new cars
You go to movies and pay to see your favorite stars
You live in big houses on the right side of town
That Middle Class Morality will bring you down
Calvin Klein's, cowboy hats, the preppie look, it's the latest style
Breath mints, perfume and a shower with Dial
Make up, cover up that face and your frown
Your Middle Class Morality is bringing you down
You watched Civil Rights, Vietman and Watergate
You saw Boat People, Atlanta's children and a nation full of hate
What do you do except turn the channel on your console T.V.
You're another victim of Middle Class Morality
I was hungry, I was thirsty, I was a stranger
I was naked, I was sick, I was a prisoner
If you help the least of one of these, you will help Me
If not, you will die the death of Middle Class Morality

Addison T. Casey

GOD'S

I want to plant a garden.
I want to watch it grow.
I'll walk through my garden.
I'll watch God supply its water.
I'll watch him supply the sunshine.
I'll watch the plants sprout.
I'll watch the leaves grow.
I'll harvest the abundance of fruit;
I'll thank God and eat.
Oh just to sift dirt through my fingers
the rain the sunshine the land
It is all in God's hands.
All this he has created, and me.
Oh! how he gives so freely.
God is loving, he is willing, he is giving;
Truly our God is living.

Mary Frances Hardaway

DEATH/LIFE

Tiny seedling
Emerges from bare earth,
Wind laughing through its leaves.
Resplendent, in a blazing bier,
Red leafed maple,
Yellow sycamore.
Crackling leaves,
Severed twigs,
All on the ground.
Lifeless sticks
Pushed into naked earth
Silhouetted against the gray sky.
Death. Soon all
Is relinquished to finite memory,
Covered with white.
Life.
To live again, and die at last.
Perennial, not immortal.
Tiny seedling
Emerges from bare earth,
Wind laughing through its leaves.
Born, from a mother's womb
Red faced infant.
Laughing child.
Living promise,
Bright potential,
Rainbow possibilities.
Young adult,
Promise crumbles,
Hope is gone.
Mask is donned on plastic face,
Till eyes behold a Cross
Stark against the sky.
Death is life.
Soon all is new in Jesus,
Covered with His blood.
Life.
To live again, and live at last.
Eternal life.
Re-born, in Christ,
Transformed spirit,
Brand new home with God.

Ruth Hilda Paro

THE PRAYING NUN

Beyond a secluded garden wall
I saw a vision rare,
The face of a praying nun
As she knelt at evening prayer.
The garden shrine was her chapel,
A rose-hued sky formed the dome,
Sublime was this outdoor temple,
But she spoke to her God alone.
Clasped hands were of whitest marble,
Her face was of sculptured stone,
Her gleaming eyes were the candles,
And a halo about her shone.
Serenely she knelt in penance,
What sins had she to atone—
Her breath was the purest incense,
Rising on high to God's throne.
Tranquil, in deep meditation,
Close to her Master she stayed
Rapturous, silent Communion,
Long did the gentle nun pray.
Floating away like a Zephyr,
In the fast-dying rays of the sun,
Happy in sweet silence rapture,
Saintly, I know was this nun.
Sweet peace of the convent garden,
Brief glimpse of a Paradise,
Remote the world and all burdens,
Content was the Bride of Christ.

Patty Ryan Friedrich

HIDING

I'm a little mushroom,
Hiding in the woods.
No one can see me,
I'm hiding really good.
If I was in the city,
They'd pick me right away.
Cut me up in pieces,
And cook me the same day.
Sure glad no one can see me,
I'm hiding in the thicket's.
But if anyone comes up here,
I'd be the first they'd pick at!

/vjl

ME

Accept Me——
For what I am,
Imperfect I may be,
But, at least I am me,
Reject Me——
For what I am not,
Especially, if I am not
What you want,
But, please don't
Change Me——
Into someone that "you"
Want me to be,
I am an original individual
And, "I" like being me.

Nellie Hoyt

A DAY AT THE BEACH

How beautiful the sea; calm, serene. Far out, the fog hangs in a smooth barrier, muffling the fog horns low moan. The beach seems endless with promised treasures, precious shell, agates and the remnants of sailing ships who dared venture beyond safe harbor.
Driftwood lies scattered on the dunes far from native forests, carried by unknown streams to this final destination. Driftwood shells, agates; these I find half buried in drifting sands accompanied by Kleenex, the indispensible tissue. Peanut shells, half hidden, are companion to the brilliant gleam of ruby, emerald and sapphire glass; fragments waiting for unwary feet.
Gentle breezes stir torn pages of cast off newspapers thrown by careless hands. Perhaps hoping the news they bear could help some lone castaway thirsty for yesterdays stale news. Tread gently through empty beer cans resting in ashes of long dead campfires.
Ahead lies waters washing softly along shores, carving patterns in far reaching ocean beaches; gently shifting tiny shells along foaming waters. Shells? My shells become remnants of the ever present cigarette; filters, floating in water that retreats and advances. Filters that endlessly ride the ocean waves. They come from far away sewers. Washed in by countless rivers, fouling the shorelines; companions to cast off beer cans, broken glass and the news of yesterdays. Will the time arrive when we dare not walk unshod on wind strewn shores? Whose promise of adventure lures us, whose every wave mocks us with cast offs of a throw away civilization.
Will a few years of those who do not care ruin the beaches for those who do? Will broken glass, cans, be the norm for those who follow?

Rita Senn

REFLECTIONS

Silent fisher on the dock,

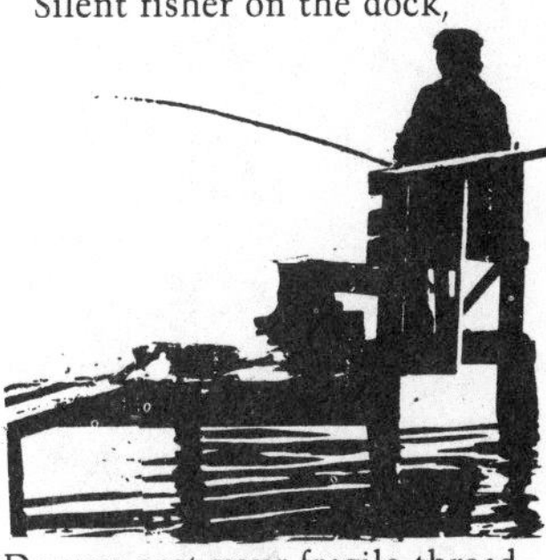

Do you cast your fragile thread
To catch the moon?

Michele Burns

SIMPLE VISION

Eyes closed,
the lids form an image
simply
pure
The quietest form of a white rose
dancing
in a water palace—
a
rustle of the faintest
petals
a ballet performed with
mystifying
beauty.
Eyes closed, the white rose
is the white wine
sipped
in private celebration.
Eyes open,
the white rose
is a swan
showing me all that is
part of
my dreamed reality.

Matthew A. Painter

ZIN-ZIN-BAR

She ventured out into the night,
Prowling for a mystery.
Every moment a life's adventure,
Until she killed my tenderness.
A hardened face, a saddened smile
Was all I had to give.
After all she had brought me,
I only wished that she live.

Stephen L. Bishop

A MOMENT

A moment my friend, for I've a story to share,
about that man you see lying there.
He's still, and silent with the machine breathing on,
left with memories of a youth

long gone.
He wasn't a general, a president, or lord.
He didn't move mountains with a single word.
He couldn't write songs or carry a tune.
He never did fly, or walk on the moon.
His wishes were simple, as were his dreams,
just a shirt on his back, and a pair of blue jeans.
What was so special about this old man?
What did he do that no others can?
He taught me what love can do for tears,
about the loneliness that leads to fears.
He showed me that people all in their own way,
dream of something better to come the next day.
He laughed, he cried, he bled, and healed
but all those memories within him are sealed.
He was patient and kind but yet human too,
and thats all I think he would ask of you.
So please touch him, and hold him, and show you care,
and look beyond the wrinkles and gray hair.
Look within the eyes, losing their sight,
and see his spirit still shining bright.

Arthur J. Nash

THE MELODY OF LOVE

The sounds of strings gently describe spring. The first buds slowly open to receive the rays of sun while still wet with morning dew. The laughing of the stream blends with the sounds of awakening. The flute sings the joy of life, like feathered friends which fly on high. The awakening is finding sun. There is dawn. Just for you my beloved, a melody of love.

The world is awake, alive. The woodwinds call and the reeds do play. The brass announces the sun is high. The drums sound the beat of day. Gone are the blossoms. The first fruit is on display.

The orchestra gives life to the Master's symphony. The sounds of summer paint a portrait of the productive years. The warm sun makes it clear; we stand at the noon of life, my dear. Just for you my love all of life does play, a melody of love.

The shifting leaves of gold and brown blend well with scent and sound. The crisp evening breeze like a marching band sets a brisk pace for harvest band. Now it is the trumpet and cornet with baton twirling majorette which calls the tune across the land.

The larder is full. The harvest home is richly blessed. The organ calls the faithful to prayer. The knurled laborers' hands gently entwine. The strong voices of hardy folk the psalms of joy do sing.

The brisk breeze and harvest song show that evening of life is here. Sip the cup of life my dear. Just for you, my love; just for you, a melody of love.

Softly the organ plays. Our hands entwine as memories we share. The falling snow like a lullaby played by a thousand violins which softly cry. The evening shadows turn to dark of night. Fear not. Does not the moon light on the snow a symphony inspire? The winter comes as night of life. Without fear we take our rest my dear. Night is but the soft refrain of eternal life. Love goes on. Just for you, my love; just for you, a melody of love.

Helen Simatos

ODE TO SHELBY

I never knew what terror was contained within your eyes;
beseeching me from under the sheath of black glass
Your death was mine
as I did not seek its confrontation
I have no consolation from pain and the dying fall.
I know there'd be no other
with that, and nothing more
I have nothing to remember
excepting the voices from the next room
that tell me
how I never knew of the pain
that passed from your soul into my heart.

Richard H. Hibbert

DAYDREAM REALITY

I contemplate the freedom
Of that dreamy, soaring bird;
Then ride upon the rhythm
Of all music I have heard.
I speculate on what might be
If I were just like they,
Until I have so fancifully
Consumed another day.
Yet freedom is not floating
On another creature's wings!
Joy comes not from listening
While other voices sing.
The fullest life consists of more
Than days piled up on days
Spent basking on a sheltered shore
In sunshine's borrowed rays.
I must float beside that lofty bird
To know how freedom feels;
Give music to the silent word
My buried soul conceals;
Discover what it's like to dive
Head first into the sea;
To find that life is still alive
Within the depths of me.

Coral Robinson

QUIET

Anticipating,
quiet voices
quiet moments
quiet light.
Dancing in the
quiet corners
quiet moods in
quiet night.
Illuminated
quietly for
quiet talks with
quiet eyes.
Quietly, to drift
away in
quiet love,
through
quiet skies.

Afton Potts

BABY

What does a baby look at
When it opens its big blue eyes
And smiles its sweetest smile
Straight up into the sky?
Could there be a fairy dancing?
Or an angel bending near?
To see it made the journey safe
From heaven down to here?
You say there are no fairies?
That angels never call?
Then to whom is a baby talking,
When it coos to a barren wall?
What causes that sudden dimpling,
Eyes to sparkle like the dew?
Who's closer to heaven than babies?
Perhaps to fairies, too?

Donald D. Warner

AND WHEN I DIE

And when I die
let those
who mock
my days
know that
the august
of my life
was made
beautiful
by the eventual
spring
that brought
with it
a new
refreshing destiny
And though joy
cometh
in the morning
and sadness
evaporates with
the dew
let those who mark
my grave
know that
only by loving
is love kept alive

Virginia Bahruth Holt

WITH THY GRACE

Lord, Thou knowst better than I, that each day I am growing older, and some day I, too, shall be old.

Until that day comes, help me to be compassionate to the elderly.

Guide me that I will not be sharp at their talkativeness, but be a gleaner of their rich stores of knowledge.

Allow me to be a sponge to soak up the wealth of their years of learning and wisdom.

Make me thoughtful and kind.

Let patience be my guide in dealing with the elderly.

For I, top, with thy grace, shall pass that way myself, in the not too distant future.

Marion Town Cairns

THROUGH A ROSE BUSH, DARKLY

Dark thicket of brambles,
Overgrown—centuries overgrown.
Paths hidden with weeds of ignorance;
Pools stagnant with slime of despair.
Behold the rose—seen darkly.
We must reach it—the lonely rose—
The hope of God held in its petals.
Kneel and weed—pull with patience
And exactness— the wildness grown.
Seen darkly—through haze of mesh of words—
Behold! The lonely rose—
stem straight, upright
And fused with love.

Fern Hamaker Wisotzkey

CARTING AWAY THE REMAINS

She has outlived her life
A relic
to be disposed of
like a broken plate
Her fate—a room,
all services provided,
in a home where she
and other relics wait
As she slips away,
groomed each day
by a stranger's hands,
other hands are busy
Pick, pick, grab, grab,
and she is not dead,
a clock, a dresser and a bed
are carted off
Hands that once were
warm, familiar,
pick, pick, grab, grab,
carting away the remains.

Gladys Willoughby Goins

WALKING ALONE

I walk alone in the stillness, of the evening afterglow,
To face the lonely night, of memories and heartbreak with woe.
I know that during the stillness, within the lonely home,

My heavy burdens will reappear,
as I live them all alone.
The hours tick by so slowly, as
I sit by the empty chair,
There is consolation in
knowing, that an unseen
presence seems so near.
I hold on to dreams that
tenderly, make life calm and
real,
Realization soon replace, and
the house is so dark and still.
As days pass on into years,
No time to measure human
tears,
So much of life has passed
beyond,
The happy part of life is gone,
As I walk this world alone.
There is a watchful eye that
guards,
As he sits upon his throne,
The lonely footsteps of the folk,
That walk this world alone.

Mrs. Luella Willems

SUN DRIED RAISINS

Grape drying time is special
It crowns the Thompson vine,
Sun's harvest in late summer
Is a favorite of mine.
The grapes take raisin image
When spread on paper trays,
From green, light gold, and
yellow
To brown in sun bright days.
The smell of drying raisins
Is carried through the air
From vineyards in the country—
Sweet fragrance everywhere.
The tasty little raisins
World wide consumers know
Are fit for all occasions
Good nourishment bestow.
Enriches fresh baked cookies
Gives flavor to a cake
Is used in garden salad
And added to a steak.
Quick energy for children
Who ask a snack to munch
And better than some candy
To take along for lunch.
How can a seedless Thompson
Turn color as it dries
Then lose its smooth round
shaping
Small wrinkled peanut size?
The raisin clusters drying
Hold mysteries devout
How does the sweetness enter?
What draws the moisture out?
The farmer sees the cycle
Of barren vines and canes
Its new green growth awakens
From cold mid winter chains.
The farmer in all seasons
Prepares his best known plan
With faith in God Creator
As partners—God and man.
Hard work before the harvest
A farmer understands
He takes the raisins gently
In his two calloused hands.
Depending on the weather
The water, sun, and rains
In sulphuring and spraying
The farmers hope remains.
Deep summer speaks
contentment
Suns harvest time is best
Abundance of the season
Sends peace and joy and rest.
These are the days of blessing
Sun's harvest holds design
Give praise to God, our maker
He prospers planted vine.

Deborah Smith

GUILTY

Your liquid of love became my
life:
You bled for my existence;
You sweated for my health;
You cried for my sanity.
And I did live.
And now I am ready
To take control. . .
To pour my own liquid.
The only way is to be cruel.
I must turn my back
On your liquid of pain. . .
I must forget
That is is *your* water flowing
through my veins.
You shed even more water for
my callousness
As I leave you.
What can I say?
I hear the accusations of cruelty;
The guilty feelings drown me.
Funny. . .
The first water I pour
Is tears for you.

Nancy Steele

MEMORIES

Running through a field of grass
Barefoot in the sun
Thinking thoughts of love and
you
Melting into one
Laughing in a summers wind
Crying sometimes too
Trust grows deep as through the
night
Love blooms sweet and new
Loving days and sleepless nights
Caring with a kiss
Wanting nothing giving all
Till sunshine turns to mist
Crying then forever
Into pillows warm with tears
And trying through the endless
nights
To quiet aching fears
Then praying for the pain to end
And dying deep inside
You think about him every day
You wonder why he lied
You weep for him each morning
You cry alone each night
Until one day the tears are gone
Until the day seems bright
And then you can't help
wondering
Just why it was you cried
And though you can't recall the
pain
A part of you has died
The little girl in you is gone
You have a womans heart
And though you'll always think
of him
You know you had to part
You think about the good times
then
Remembering a name
And saving faded photographs
That somehow never change
And so through years of pain
and joy
In moments tucked away
You'll fall in love with him
again
And live in yesterday
Until the time comes as it must
To put past love aside
Forgetting times you laughed
and sang
Forgetting times you cried
Remembering your duties now
You watch your children play
Forgetting all the years gone by
Remembering today

Lisa Beth Houle

A CAT POEM

I once saw a cat all fluffy and
gray, it was the month of May
He was very mute, also very
cute,
Looking outside that window
pane, wishing it would rain.
He watches a mouse run around
the house,
He watches a bug as it flies,
with his beautiful green eyes.
Everytime I pat his fur, he
begins to softly purr.
He stands upon that window
sill, very alert and very still.
He doesn't move, he doesn't
budge, unless you give him a
little nudge.
He sits there dreaming all day
long, sometimes he reminds
me of a little song.
He lives nearby, so I won't cry,
'cause I can see him again.

Kathryn Zimmerman

THE MARRIAGE

Someone spoke an unkind word,
Satan, standing nearby, heard,
Seized upon it gleefully,
Mixed it with some jealousy,
Blended in the cares of life,
Gave it to a tired wife,
And she watered it with tears,
Nurtured it with gnawing fears,
Spilled some on the children,
too,
Watched with horror as it grew
Into bitter fruits of strife,
Poisoning the family life.
Each with sobbing, broken heart,
Watched the marriage fall apart,
And with bitterness they
wonder
At what man has put asunder,
Blaming each and every one. . .
Even God. . .for what's been
done.
Yet if they had only heard
What God tells us in His Word;
How He has a perfect plan
For the wife and for the man,
For the children that He gave
them,
Oh, what heartaches it would
save them!
If they earnestly would pray,
Listening to what He'd say,
Look to Him in one accord,
Bring their marriage to the Lord,
In His Perfect Love to rest. . .
How that marriage would be
blessed!

Timothy Paul Riddle

WEBS OF LOVE

Winter brought the time
in the cold of December
When the windows reflect the
ice standing frozen and still;
but wait. . . .,I do remember.
(two winds in the valley
collided)
Said she, "In what tangled
circumstances do you
believe?"
(one hot; one cold)
Said I, "In webs of love I chose
to conceive."
On what tower do you stand?
I stand alone
then who are your masters?
I bow before only one throne.
In castle spires she dwelt
near the inner sea
She sailed a bitter salty ocean
from home
to wait in hope of me.
(the turn of the year)
Said she, "In what time do you
see us living
contemporaneously?"
(another turn of season)
Said I, "Soon, when Autumn
brings about my change of
scenery."
Will you come to see my
change?
I promise I will try
What promise of soul will you
hold to me?
the devotion of my love to
comply.
What wind of foreboding
brought the change?
in the deep wells of reason
that turned her face from me
What a torturous act of
unforgiven treason.
(a red mist of pain)
Said she, "Painfully I see a
change of course, where does
yours lead?"
(another warning)
Said I, "I follow no distinct
path, you were my need."
Did we not try hard?
perhaps too much so
what must we do, where to go,
to retrieve?
It is unknown;
tangled are the webs of love
that we conceive.

Ann Pedigo

MY BOY

My little boy with eyes so blue
brings me happiness the whole
day through
I work for him but it is only fun
for at the end of the day when
work is done
I look at him and smile with joy
how glad I am to have this boy
that romps and plays from morn
til night
and awakes each morning happy
and bright,
Not everyone has had the good
fortune as I
to hear a babys laugh and a
babys cry
it was such a thrill when he
began to talk and walk,
at christmas time he would
hang up his sock.
I was so proud when he started

to school,
he was kind to others he was no fool.
when I prayed at night to my God above
I would thank him so much for this child of love.
Then one very sad day he went away
but memories of him forever with me stay
like little boy blue, his books and toys
bring thoughts of him and other boys
that too were called to their heavenly place,
though I still long to see his dear face
and I can still see him through my tears
He has been with Jesus for many years.
I hope to meet him one day there
Where we will greet each other with a prayer.

Larry Tatge
WINTER COMES EARLY
You left me in November,
I really don't know why.
You never said you loved me,
But I always thought you did.
I guess I have to learn the hard way.
Now I go skating alone.
I only make one cup of hot chocolate.
We used to sit on the couch by the fire,
All bundled up with quilts.
I guess she's gone forever.
New Years was just another night.
I spent it all alone.
That winter came early,
And it lasted so long.
I guess it was meant to be.
Winter comes early.
No one out there seems to care.
Winters are cold.
They're all so very cold.
And Winter comes early.

Wendy McVicker Wagner
TIES
As droplets fall into the sea
and gently ripple toward me
in one unending tide,
so,
the ties of family
grow
from constant care
and dependability,
not from the blood
that is channeled through our veins.
Out there, somewhere, there is a man,
my father,
so they say.
But, I have never heard him call my name,
or seen his face.
He never tucked me into bed
or shared the pain of growing.
He never searched for me,
though I was always in this place,
and sometimes wished he would.
But no!
They tell me tales of him.
There never was a man like this,
this man who has no face, to me.
My father lies here in the ground!
who called me by my name,
who loved me
by the gentle care
he gave
to supervise my growing,
who, with his quiet dignity
commanded my respect
by respecting me.
Day by day
he grew to be my father.
Ties,
no blood can disentangle,
no death can sever.
That other man is dead to me,
though I am not sure he has died.

Bertha Czosnek Gromada
EVENING
The evening breeze is stirring
Perfume from the blooming grass;
From the distance draws the cooing
Of the night birds that pass;
The velvet coat of twilight
Puts on a deeper shade;
A diamond star pins back the folds
That on earth's crest are laid.

Carlos Leroy Hunsinger
I CAME WITH EMPTY HANDS
I came with empty hands your love to seek,
A stranger wandering from a world apart.
I came alone, unknown, and brought no price
Except a yearning and devoted heart.
I little knew such price could bring such love,
Or that a man could know such ecstasy.
I found a joy to ease the doleful heart,
And still the spirit longing to be free.
Where I have nobly wrought, your love inspired;
Where I have failed, 'twas I who missed the way.
Oh, lead me yet to reach the heights of gold,
And know the rapture of the splendrous day.

L. Cherny
AN ENDING
I walked down silver halls
Through golden walls
On the stairway to the Ending—
Turning, folding, and bending,
It wound its way through Dreams;
I followed it around laughter and screams,
Sold my soul along the way,
Stole its whole that I might stay,
And went on until the sky fell
And my castle slid into the fires of hell.
My ashes flew down silver halls
And golden walls of "To Remember. . ."
Frozen in a still December;
As the stairway crumbled,
My spirit stumbled
But turned its blind eyes away—
For it had arrived at the End, to stay.

Marva Louise Vedeler
ABIDING FAITH
Castles can tumble,
Houses can crumble,
But faith can abide,
When God's by thy side.
Horses can stumble,
People can grumble,
But faith can abide,
When God's by thy side.
A tree can fall,
A baby can bawl,
But faith can abide,
When God's by thy side.
A mother can call,
An infant can crawl,
But faith can abide,
When God's by thy side.
A freight train can haul,
A cradle can lull,
But faith can abide,
When God's by thy side.
A lion eats meat,
A gambler can cheat,
But faith can abide,
When God's by thy side.
A fighter can beat,
Satan can defeat,
But faith can abide,
When God's by thy side.
A boiler can heat,
Relatives can meet,
But faith can abide,
When God's by thy side.
Mansions can be built,
A tower can tilt,
But faith can abide,
When God's by thy side.
A woman can quilt,
A man can have guilt,
But faith can abide,
When God's by thy side.
A boyfriend can jilt,
A flower can wilt,
But faith can abide,
When God's by thy side,
A beggar can weep,
A sportsman can leap,
But faith can abide,
When God's by thy side.
A well can be deep,
A harvest can reap,
But faith can abide,
When God's by thy side.
Your faith you can keep,
Though trials do heap,
Your faith can abide,
When God's by thy side.

Jennifer Lue Olmstead
THE ROCKING CHAIR
It rocks
rocks
rocks,
in the empty air,
a forlorn little rocking chair.
To be free and see could be done;
so with might the fight should be won.
The small dove of love never came;
the chair was bare—always the same.
For hate and fate well played their role;
no hope to cope with this lonely soul.
It cries and tries but never hears;
the creaks it squeaks are really tears.
It rocks,
rocks,
rocks,
in the empty air.
A forlorn little rocking chair. . .

Myrtle Humber Polachek
SENIOR CITIZENS, AHOY!
To you I write (speak) this bit of verse
In the hope our understanding
Goes out in search of others' needs
And leads to great expanding
Of Christian love and worth and doing

In answer to the Spirit's wooing.
Your sabbath pattern does indeed
Bespeak a sacred trust
Tied up in deep commitments
We should regard as MUST'S,
Knowing the never-fail Recorder
Gives credit to the just.
May the marks you've made on the sands of time
Remind those prone to stumble:
Their real worth's found on firmer ground,
Made so by spirits humble,
And given to action by a heart-felt urge
Now free from groan or grumble.

J. Dominic Pricken
WINTER ROSE
Tedious trials at midnight hours,
Whispering breezes bring pleas from a heart.
Candle dimly flickers,
Window framed sky
Stands jury to it all.
A barrage of words and images
all brought from knowing lies,
storms arising with repetitious visions,
of deceiving elements
In the existence of blind trust.
To see love of harbor lights
Disappear behind preconceived masks,

And receive the decending
blows
With a scourging sense of fright.
Disolved dreams succumb
With reality's delight.
All neatly spoken with
Quick bold reply,
Maybe another day, maybe
another life.

Fred E. Royal

A RAINY DAY

Soft rain drops falling with,
Softness of body wet through
and through.
Brown hair straight and wet
with,
Young face straining in the rain.
Young breasts straining and,
Pushing out against the wetness.
Clinging jeans soaked through
and,
Youngness of thighs straining.
My God—where are you going,
So tense and strained.
With underwear so wet and
cold,
Against tenderness of youth.

Arthur P. Anderson

THE END OF THE ROAD

I'm a traveler on life's twisted
highway,
A rover alone in the cold.
You might say that I am the
blacksheep
Chased from the warmth of the
fold.
The passions of life were too
tempting,
Too weak was the will of the
mind.
I played like a toy with all
heartstrings;
New friends were easy to find.
Maybe this rogue's getting
mellow
Or the cold heart is faltering a
bit.
The pretty white snow is falling
All over the rock where I sit.
Life has been one big dinner—
I now have emptied my plate,

Please, Sir, help this poor
traveler—
Never mind— I think it's too
late!

Keli King

A DUET'S EPITAPH

At the end of every rainbow lies
a pot of gold,
For everything there is a valid
reason.
But that pot of gold isn't
always a material one,
And that reason isn't always
understood.
That pot of gold can be a friend,
It's rainbow a lost soul.
Or it can be the bloom of love
eminating from the bud of
caring,
A pot of gold worth more than
any other.
And for everything being, there
is a reason,
Trying to understand it is just
part of the game of life.
If it's understood, you move on
to the next space of advanced
self-understanding.
If it's not, then you forfeit
your move and try again as
your
next chance.
If you accept why, you're a
winner in the game.
If you refuse to, you're a loser
by bankruptcy.
Yet, the twosome do walk
hand-in-hand, the two do meet
in harmony,
A rainbow leads to a pot of gold,
the reason for what is.
And though some may say you
can't ever touch a rainbow,
moreover
grasp a pot of gold,
On the contrary. Just look
around you, the people are the
rainbows,
their reasons the pots of
gold.
You can touch a rainbow, you
already have.
And you already have inherited
that pot of gold because
you've
already answered the why's
and the why not's.
Yet one consistency doesn't
change.
The creator of rainbows, pots of
gold and valid reasons is still
the same, has always meant
the same.
The inventor of the game of life
and all life's plans is still the
giver of life.
Our Lord, God the Father
Almighty.

Laurence W. Martin

WENDY MARIE

Jesus loved her more than I
It's hard to comprehend
Her stay with us was not for
long
It totaled totaled three short
years plus ten
Tho I must go on by myself
With memories that she gave
He promised in his book of life
She is not in her grave
Born to this world with sin
from other times
He filled her heart with tender
love
From which he used to remold
mine
The world goes on each earthly
day
Tho we may often wonder why
For man was born into this
world
Predestined that he die
But Jesus sent his son to us
To pave a narrow road
That if we follow him each day
He'd surely save our soul
I know shes not the only child
The Lord has taken home
But my heart grieves each
passing day
For one I did not own
He loaned her to us for a time
So we would understand
That all things on this passing
earth
Were made for his own plan
The time will come when we'll
all know
What reasoning he had planned
To take this child that I
called mine
And place her in his hand

Barry

DREAMSONG

Soft shadows drift quixotic
through my mind—
Fanciful figures sway, bodies
entwined,
Dancing to music only I can
sense—
Imaginary rhythms played in
past tense. . .
Abstract inventions to mitigate
my pain—
Deceptive illusions smile with
disdain,
Illuminating dream's merry
rainbow,
Permitting delusive hopes to
grow. . .
Fantasies effervesce like
champagne bubbles,
Apparitions to disguise my
troubles—
Ideals that give my tattered
heart some peace,
An interlude to soothe my
soul's release. . .
Tomorrow my visions will melt
away—
They are but mirages that
came to play,
Content to stay for a short,
sweet spell—
Hallucinations will soon fade
into hell. . .

Madeline Rasmusson

ABIDE WITH ME

Simple and sweet was the song,
He sang in a wee little
trembling voice,
But the words were clear and
His smile made ever heart
rejoice.
"Abide With Me" he sang so
low,
And his voice did waver a bit,
As if his soul were full of love
And meant ever word of it.
He was only a child and he
Hardly knew the meaning of the
Prayer,
But our eyes were wet as we
Watched him in the Christmas
program there.
A light was shinning on his
brow,
As the last notes died away,
And every one who heard him
sing,
Bowed down his head to pray.
From the lips of this little boy,
Came the words of a mighty
plea,
Our souls were touched as he
sang,
These words, "O Lord Abide
with Me."
Now over twenty years have
passed,
Out in the world my son has
left me,
I still hear his voice in the
church,
Program, singing "O Lord Abide
With Me."

Donna Colwell Rosser

BY YOUR SMILE

It made my day,
That smile of yours,
As I walked through
Our little home's front door.
No tired, troubled lift
To the corners of your mouth,
But a broad, bright gift
That almost seemed to shout,
"Hooray, you're home!"
——A beautiful smile
To me, who'd been away
For awhile.
My heart was warmed
By your hug and your kiss,
But by your smile,
I knew I'd been missed.

Gwen Trimbell Pease

HOT FLASHES

Age of reckoning arrived already
progressing onward all unsteady
changing systems produce
symptoms
biological calendar moves
toward date
gain of unplanned weight a
woman's fate
hot flashes that steam the
glasses
half century passed actively
remarkable events positively
time of readjustment obviously
evident
all too visible complicated
simple phase
sweaty droplets dripping from
red face
frustrating confusion—memory
exclusion
graying hairs on tired head
with cause
proud Grandma passed
menopause
natural process complete, life
cycle does repeat
future pleasant times to
spend
golden years begin another trend
human development does define,
wise Creator design.

Diane Alison Blyth

THE MOMENTS OF TWO SISTERS

My sister: My bud my
friend. . . . .
I know it took years to tell
her— that I love her—and that I
will always be there for her
whenever she needs me.
Especially now when the time
has finally come to move away
from the close grasp of each
others hand, a hand you've
taken for granted for so many
years. . . . .
When that moment of departure
comes, when one must leave—to
seek new adventures and to lead
a new type of life—it isn't easy
for the one to pack up all the
belongings once shared and say
goodbye—for there are so many
more things that can't be packed
up and taken away. . . . .
You can't pack away those

memories; the sharing of material things, the idiosyncrasy's of one another, and the unspoken words..... You can't pack away the laughter, the giving, the tears, the love, and the moments only two sisters can understand..... The times when glances only needed to be exchanged to understand what one was saying to the other.....And then those memories of childhood secrets that only the two can trade and share.....
You can't pack away the growing times.....When projects were tackled together, and when we became involved in the same activities and learned to get a long, even though there were times of disagreement....The morning talks in the bathroom to catch up on the weeks gossip, and the ever present support and encouragement each always gave, those can not ever be packed away.....
There are many more things we could do and share, if we stayed together—but it is the time when one must go, the other is left to linger, in lonliness for awhile—but quickly continues on in a new way, with out the other.....
The two must separate, though painful for a moment or two—but what occurs next is a closeness—one which is new and different and one which only the distance between the two can bring, only the space of those miles can make the heart grow fonder—a love deeper and stronger than before.....

Harry Maizel
AFTER THE DELUGE
The waters still trembling
with sun-pleasure,
lave the peripatetic worm
undulating its way to Eden.
Skin, revoltingly ruddled,
was enough reason
for Paradise eviction——
Now he stretches spinelessly
to rest unnoticed
under green-pine flotsam,
but grackles gather
and myopically
gird for the kill.

Marian Parker
FELICITY
Thorton Plum allowed his
Sure-footed unicorn to
Race across embroidered clouds to
A land of fantasy and enchantment.
It was a place where dreams were
Realities and
Days knew no end.
Arthur Fudge, his brother-in-law,
Was a doubter and rarely
Allowed his mare out of her stall.
Well-shoed, the old nag grazed idly
On oats and hay for most of the day.
At night she had nightmares and
Leaned against her boards.
Plum and Fudge met each Tuesday for
Cribbage and croissants.
They discussed the time of day and
The climate to come.
When done, they would run home to curry and
Brush their respective beasties.
Each was glad that he was not the other.

Kimberly Ann Hunt-Strange
UNTITLED
A prayer. . .
To love and believe in a man
that i can not see, i can not feel or
touch but i can speak to at all times. . .i do.
To trust and seek refuge from the storm,
within him, to be in awe of his power but
comfortable to still ask of him "why me, lord". . .i have.
To know he is constant and consistent and will
forever be there, i need only to call out and i do.
Then surely my soul i give unto him.
Amen.

Dinah Renea Taylor
SILENTLY CRYING
A beautiful person, bringing joy and laughter to everyone you meet.
Your face, as beautiful as the rising sun yet you are not happy, Silently Crying.

A wonderful person, with a glow that outshines them all.
Your eyes, a lust of unexplainable beauty,
but you are not smiling,
Silently Crying.
A unique and intelligent person, with the potential to be the best there is.
Your style that is all your own, but where is the laughter,
Silently Crying.

Patrick J. Gallant
BEYOND DEATH'S DOOR, MY WIDOW WALTZES
Beyond death's door my widow waltzes.
Beyond the dark, in light and breath.
She casts white shadows on the walls,
attired in her wedding dress.
She speaks of past as though,
to hear the present brings the ending near.
In time of past she lives with me,
for my memory's as real as those
of withered blossoms pressed in books,
passe' though real I fear.
Oh, my maiden fair,
she sees me young in tie and tails
though I am lying here, a withered soul
and hence not standing there.
But for moments there my soul takes stance,
to make a bow, accept the dance.
Waltz to and fro and back again,
relive the past, relieve the pain.
And when the pain is dead and gone,
she sees me not through saddened eyes.
My youth she does no longer see;
now gray, forlorn, and old I be.
The dance it dwindles, still we stand.
Minds no longer filled with dreams.
Cares from past, on present lean,
the shadows have gone dark it seems.
We hand in hand walk through the door
of creaking hinge and darkened wood.
I felt the need to taste the past
and having done, take you to rest,
hold clasped your bosom to my chest.
Though death removed your soul from life,
it gave me back, my widowed wife.

Nancy Meese Stallsmith
FOREVER, MY LOVE—NO MATTER WHAT
Forever, my love—no matter what—
I want to be with you
Through rain and shine or ups and downs
Or joys and sorrows, too.
Forgive my human weakness
For getting upset and blue
'Bout some of the things you say to me
And some of the things you do.
Whenever I am acting like this,
The devil is having his say
And I'm listening to him instead of God
'Cause I've forgotten to pray.
I'm usually tired or feeling ill
And too weak to put up a fight
Forgetting to pray for God's guidance and help
To help me put things right.
Fortunately, most of the time,
During both day and night
I listen to the word of God
Then do and say what's right.
I know that things like houses and cars,
Trips, money and more clothes
Are not nearly half as important
As love that deepens and grows—
A love that patiently understands
Each other's hang-ups and woes
As well as every kind of mood
That often comes and goes—
A love that laughs with lots of joy
When sharing happiness—
A strong love that endures all things
Both failures and success.
Yes, my dear, I give to you
Myself from top to toe
The way the good Lord made me—
Not quite so perfect though.
I also give undying love
That never will depart
Forever, my love—no matter what—
From deep inside my heart.

Christine M. Kaminiski
UNTITLED
So sadly missed
the springtime of my life
youth has died
and how i mourn
its passing
young emotions
now gone
oh bring it all back
but it has all slipped-away from me
lost forever
now fading in the past
how fast
how fast
how fast
the years have
passed
i didn't know
my dreams were just for
dreaming
i didn't know my plans
were meant just for
planning
seeds to sow
but never reap
youth was mine
but not to keep
Time
You Thief

Sheila Sprague
ON SCIENCE
The flower is magestic
and soft and light to touch.
But to take each petal seperately
the flower isn't much.

Karen A. Smith
LIFE
Lord, I get so tired of my
seemingly worthless life,
with all its tribulations,
its quite hard to know whats right.
Just give me the strength to
make it as only you can do for
my body, is growing weak and
only you, can pull me through.

I've tried so hard to understand
to make each day worthwhile,
and show a little compassion to,
every man, woman and child.
For life is a matter of moments
just a glance or two away,
Don't let your life drift by
with nothing kind to say.

Ruth A. Arnaud

THE REDEMPTION

Upon the hill
stood the man,
His soul bared to the naked
light
and wind, as though He cared
nothing
of the indignity.
Beneath
the grass
the earth groaned it's
indifference
of His existence.
Shrouded in the cool mist
of Time,
the Soul of humility
transcended
the realities and truisms
and groped
for Eternity.

David K. Trites

SPRING GARDEN

A moment of time
Not yet made ready,
But bursting—a collection
Of nymphs, buds, suggestions,
Promises, promises of tomorrow;
In itself complete, though not.
With fulfillment a day, a month,
A season hence—perhaps?
Should God and gardener
Tend it well.

Dennis Paul McClellan

TIMELESS LOVE

Our Lord and God the King of
Kings
showed us all what true love
means;
He shed his blood upon a cross
to save all men whose hearts
were lost.
A man he was who knew no sin
died a propitiation for all of
men;
So man could live without this
death
the price of sin which Adam
did bequeath.

Taught us a life in which to live
to whom our souls we should
give;
Exposed the powers for which
we fight
and how to rid them from our
sight.
He sacrificed his life so we may
live
so unto him our love we give;
His love for us does so abound
till finally at last in our heart
it's found.
So spread the news of our good
Lord
his way of salvation no word
ignored;
Whose name our Father it so
pleases
of whom I speak is the
LORD JESUS.

Lynn E. Renner

WATERFALL

beautiful,
delightful,
glorious
deliver these
chains from
about my soul.
set free my spirit,
cast me in thyself
and make known
to mine eyes the
secrets you withhold.
let me ride upon
your silver-tipped wings
and let me dance
within your windy shoes.
be me the maker of
showers
and rainbows. be me
creator of thundering song.
a devine master of heavenly
valleys peaceful and green.
a zealous disciple to stately
walls
of precipitous grandeur.
majestically
powerful and
gracefully
sublime.
preserver
of sanctity,
filler of dreams
devoted to purity—eternally
free. . .
WATERFALL

William A. Pearl

THE TABERNACLE ON THE HILL

This morning God was here in
hundreds of voices
in the Tabernacle on the
Hill. . .
The place resounds with God's
love, I seem
to hear them still.
We heard the Blessings of God's
word, and
sang the songs of praise.
In this sacred spot, we love so
dear
We cherish every phrase. . .
We live again in memory, those
meetings
of yesteryear—
And feel the presence of God's
love in the
friendships we hold dear. . .
We say a silent prayer, and trust
that God,
will keep us in his love. .
And bring us back again next
year,
We pray to God above.
So homeward bound, we thank
God for
the blessings that gave us a
thrill,
And for the love of God we
found
in that TABERNACLE ON
THE HILL.

Diana Lyn Shew

THE FOUR SEASONS OF LOVE

We met, you and I.
Our love blossomed,
like a new bud on a tree.
Precious, fragile,
as a newborn kitten.
Quietly, softly,
as the floating clouds in the sky.
Was the springtime of our love.
We loved, you and I.
On the burning sands of love,
we thirsted for each other.
Passionately, aggressivily,
as a mother protects her young.
Heatedly,
as the blazing sun beats the
desert sands.
Was the summer of our love.
We became distant, you and I.
Our love flickered,
like the burning candle in a
breeze.
Cooling, changing,
as a flowing mountain stream.
Cold, blustering,
as the great northern wind.
Was the autumn of our love.
Our love was no more, dying.
Silently, swiftly,
as a thief steals away in the
night.
Smothered,
as the melting candle is
extinguished.
Dead,
like the blackened trees after a
forest fire.
Was the winter of our love.

Geneve Baley

Remember the Lilies of the Fields

(that they toil not)

When you know there are
Those that love you,
In God
You can think not in fear
Of tomorrow,
But see the
Lilies
Wearing a crown of
Glory,
In the
Fields. . . . .

Norma Claflin Trask

What Are Grandparents?

They are wonderful human
beings
Who always seem to have the
time
To do things for you and with
you,
That your parents never have
time to do.
Grandpa takes you fishing;
shopping;
To the circus.
He teaches you to whittle; to tie
flys,
How to milk the cows and feed
the hens.
How to run the tractor and till
the land.
Grandmas always seem to have
a cold
Glass of milk and a jar full of
home—
Made cookies her kitchen
smells of homemade
Bread, apple pies, and apple
tarts.
On Saturday you can be sure
that there
Will be homebaked beans and
either brown
Bread or hot biscuits—
Grandma makes dolls clothes
for the girls;
And teaches them how to sew
and do patchwork.
She shows the boys how to
make good kite tails,
Grandmas always have time to
teach a child
How to cook, but the best
things about
Grandparents are— The love
they have
For their grandchildren and the
stories
They spin about "when I was a
child."

Wendy Ann T. Stanz

OCTOBER REFLECTIONS

The tree is bare, naked.
Gusty Autumn has greedily
taken away the life of Summer,
forgetting the many faces of
flowers,
the greenness of the hillside,
and the laughter of lively
children.
It has, instead, given us Fall,
cold and crispy mornings
that bite at your ears
and nip at your nose.
Frosted, steamy windowpanes
stare out into a star-strewn
night,
awaiting the fast coming Winter
which will bring soft and silent
snowfalls. . .
The enduring, cold months that
lie ahead
inevitably happen—most
unexpectedly,
and leave us, exhausted,
with the beauty of a new and
blossoming Spring.

Denyille

THOUGHTS

An empty piece of paper
gives me
the impression
of a man without anything to
say.
Add a pen
and then
it is a man
who can't stop his thoughts
from having
their own way.
Soon he
has so much to say
that it takes
an eraser
to stop him.

Deborah Whittaker

WITHOUT YOU HERE

The clouds were crying for you
today,
Because they knew you went
away.
I want you back, it's true and
clear,
To me, you're someone that I
hold dear.
I wonder, can you see me from
where you are?
Right now, I'm looking for you
in the North Star.

I can't seem to find you
anywhere.
If I make a wish, can I come
there?
It's so lonely and I'm frightened
without you here.
Can't you come to wipe away
my tears?
I live my life in roles I play,
I live my life day by day.
It's a puppet world that we all
know,
We never take the time to grow.
I can't live my life without you
here,
I want you back, it's true and
clear.

Patricia Hoad

TO A DAUGHTER AT SUMMER'S END, 1981

You woke me
Early, as you'd
Said you would.
I sat reluctantly
For you
To make up my face
As you'd planned
For the last time
This year.
Later I found
You'd slipped
A Salt Water Taffy
Into my office lunch
And written "Pat"
On the brown bag.
When I got home
That evening
You were gone,
Of course—
That was also
Planned—
Back to live
With your Dad
And his new family
In San Francisco.
Moving onward, you and I
Know not when next
We'll meet, nor how.
But love it was that
Swung you first
Into the orbit of
My life—
Aching moments
Tense with love
Just before your
Life was launched
Are with me
Still.
Years later now
A different love
Still warming
And sustaining life
Brings you and me
Together
Time and again.

Kathryn Diehl Storrs

QUESTIONS

December half moons
reveal bared trees
once enhanced with
multi-colored hand painted
leaves.
Where is the hidden artist
who so bravely displayed
this array of colors?
Where is he hiding
with his paint brush
this cold, lonely winter eve?
Has he hibernated for the
duration?
How dare he tease us with such
splendor.
Awakening to the 1st frost bit
morn,
I catch my breath. . .and stand
amazed.
The once bared trees are now
filled
with glittering diamonds.
How dare I question
the maker and his ways.
He chose to share with us
another season:
and I chose to question why.

C. Robert Meyer

TO CHILDHOOD

I love to dream of Childhood
There weren't no worries then
Them's the days that's all gone
by
Them's the days that's been.
I 'member well my mother
How much she used to give.
And how my Pa would speculate
On how 'twas best to live.
I sure do miss their bein' round
To tell me how to be
To fill my house with love and
life
The way theirs was for me.

Winnie B.

EVERLASTING LOVE

A darling little angel in a land
so far away,
There's no pain and there's no
sorrow,
Only love to guide the way.
God called her home, she's not
alone,
Someone waited for her there
A dear one who had faith in
God
And seldom felt despair.
So she waits there, she and
Grampa,
With their arms opened wide,
To greet all their loved ones
When they cross the great
divide.
So have faith in God above
For life never really ends,
He calls us home to a land of
love
And it's there that life begins.

Margaret M. Huff

GIFTS OF GOLD

Imagine to walk along with
Jesus
And not know who He was,
And you'd sworn before you'd
know Him
Just by what He'd say or what
He does.
Imagine to look at his face or
speak with Him
And hear His heavenly voice,
Yet not know who was talking
And know not to rejoice.
Imagine telling Him your
troubles,
waiting to hear His advice
And realize deep down inside
that
you were seated in paradise.
As His eyes looked into yours—
a long, long story was told
Of suffering, of death
and of Gifts of Gold.

Margena Adams

TO JOHN

You'll be missed by everyone I
know.
Your music will remain to bring
back memories.
You beat the fans, the drugs and
booze.
You beat the break and
separation.
You beat it all.
But you couldn't beat the gun.
What we'll do without you, I
don't know.
You tried to bring peace to
everything and everyone.
But not everyone listened to
you.
You knew what you were doing.
I have the deepest sympathy for
Sean, Yoko, and Julian.
You gave five years of your life
to Sean.
He'll appreciate it when he's
older.
I'm glad you did.
If I'd known coming back would
endanger you,
I'd never have wanted it.
Your family needed you more, I
realize.
Thank you, John, for what you
did for us.
For bringing us Peace of mind.
We'll miss you very much.

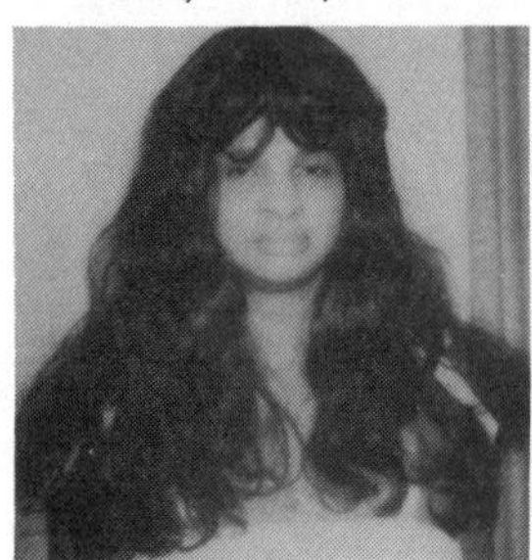

Bettye D. Little

A HOLY PRAYER

I have a prayer to give,
a holy prayer to God.
I have a love for Jesus,
"A Precious Love to hold."
I have a prayer to give,
a holy thought to God.
Love and Obedient,
I humbly give to you.
In all of thy holiness,
established in truth,
"You gave us Love"!
I give this to you dear Lord.
"A Holy Prayer."

B.M.S.

GOD HAS BLESSED ME

I met a man over the holidays
I hadn't seen since high school
days.
We dated—he gave me some
presents
He left—I tried sorting my
senses.
Dear God you have blessed me
Up until now I did not see.
I see, God, through this single
man
I shouldn't live my life alone.
I wish I had returned to this
man,
Much sooner, the love I had
been shown.
Dear God, you have blessed me
Up until now I did not see.
He seemed to want to know
me—
I took a ten-day vacation to see.
Up to the land of the last
frontier
That's where, on love's
adventure, he took me.
Dear God you have blessed me
Up until now I did not see.
I'd like to think our friendship
is strong
With no mysteries, black magic
or wand
Since the only chance for a
future marriage
Is when riding in God's
heavenly carriage.
Dear God you have blessed me.

Rebecca Kay Reed

SURVIVAL

After the shadows of night
have disappeared
The feeling of fear
will go with it.
That is when
we shall receive
the warming rays
of the bright star
in the sky.
It is then when the Evil things,
of night
will find their refuge
in cold, dark places,
until day has passed.
I shall know then
that it is safe,
and only then,
can I venture
from my hole
in this rock wall.
As time passed,
there are other creatures
waking and scampering around.
Hurrying to catch the dew
before it is lifted
into the clouds.
The star's rays are
warm on the ground under us
as we look for food.
I don't
have to look hard
as my meals
are the plants around me.
I am a
small, four-footed ball of fur.
When I was younger,
I had a tail,
but it is now gone,
it was bitten off
by a much larger
beast than I.
But wait!
My nose is picking up the odor
of something.
If I'm not mistaken
this creature would like
to have me for breakfast.
I must find
some place to hide,
out of nowhere
It jumps. . . .
I feel its teeth sink in
I'm gone. . . . .

Junie Gambs

TRANSITION TO TERROR

Early October sun,
shining with fiercest fires,
September heat will dissipate
Slight winds shake dim church
spires.
Violet-shaded bones
Covering moldy maws,
Emitting lusty groans
Unspeakable horrors cause.
Piercing, unseeing gaze

Of shapeless monstrous blots,
Seaching an endless haze
Transfixes tiniest tots
As late October moon,
horror in shadow creeps
Over the field of blood-black weeds
Where skeletal silence sleeps
Waiting to wake at day
With macabre ennui gone
The birds in joy sing songs
November's born at dawn.

Georgiana R. Fredrick

HUBBY ISN'T ALWAYS A HOBBY

There are hubbies and hobbies
Many married women will agree
And I confess, with tongue in cheek,
My hubby is one hobby for me.
Yet considering present-day pressures
When being liberated is the path to pursue
Away from the drudgery of housework
There is something more noble to do.
Thus, a fit of rebellion takes over
And a hubby seems less important
When a hobby becomes a more fun thing
A hubby can't confiscate, too.
"Just what is your hobby?"
"Haven't you guessed?"
It's writing, copiously filling pages with words
Only my eyes have scanned
And it satisfies the urge to do something
With whatever I can command.
Very often the routine to please hubby
Has been broken and been made more mundane
While thinking I'm being creative
By doing my very own thing.

Pixie Hammond

TIME IS STRANGE

Ten days
Till I'm with you.
A small forever, Dear.
Time is strange.
When we're together
It melts!

Charles Mark Morrison

YOURS IS. . .

Yours Is. . .
Yours is the First and Last
And all of the in between.
Yours is the Future and the Past.
And everything that's unseen.
And I can see what you really mean.
. . .Yours Is. . .
Yours Is. . .
Yours is the First and Last
And all of the in between.
Yours is the Future and Past
And everything that's unseen.
And I can see what you really mean.
. . .Yours Is. . .

Lisa Burke

MY LOVE

My love for you is with my heart and soul.
With my heart that which in me lies,
And with my soul that which never dies.
My love reaches out to eternity,
And lives free in serenity.
My love holds the very essence of life,
And treasures it without question.
My love is everlasting,
Like the seasons forever passing.
My love has magical moments,
Like the image of a rainbow across the sea.
My love has the majesty of the mountains,
And the wisdom they possess.
My love has the strength of my heart,
And the immortality of my soul.
My love will grow with that strength,
And with that immortality it will forever be.

Resa-Marie Georgian

SO LITTLE TIME

So little time to stop and look
There's hardly time to stop and cook.
So little time to stop and talk
There's barely time to stop and walk.
So little time to sit and think
There's barely time to even blink.
So little time to finish work
There's barely time for coffee to perk.
So as you can see
There really needs to be
More hours in a day
And not so much play.

Lizabeth Merritt

MOON BEAMS

It isn't the house we live in;
Though it's lined with silver and gold,
Nor is it a haunted image
Of the truth of a story told.
You may live in a big house
With a whole white loaf to eat,
Or you may live in a tall house
And may your rest be sweet;
But I will dine on the crust of the moon
And break the moon for my bread,
For my hunger is not of the world
As my table is strangely spread.
The moon has many stories
Of love fanciful and free,
And we see here
Life reflected
In truth's ₁irrored laughing sea.
So when its' silver reflection
Shines in your room at night,
I'll be there with all it's splendor
In the brilliancy of it's light
So don't close your curtain;
Let the moon shine in it's retreat,
For I'll smile at your head on the pillow
And know your dreams are sweet!

Julia Lee

LOVE

Love is the sunlight of the soul
That keeps us healthy, happy—whole;
Love is of God and thus ALL GOOD.
So let us thank God (as we should)
For love's abiding tender care
Found in all persons everywhere.

Tamara L. Serrano

THE FIRSTBORN CHILD

The sunlight reflection on her black silky hair
Her eyes always sparkling, seem to wander everywhere
Her frown, oh so sad, raising high her lips and cheeks
Her smile, just a twitch, shows the joy which she seeks
Her skin so tender and soft to touch
She glistens with beauty and I love her so much
Her hands so tiny, her long fingers hold tight
Grasping for security, to rid her of fright.
All day in her skin she struggles aware of a new world
At night she sleeps soundly, in her bed she lays curled
Her character building, unique in her ways
So quickly she grows, so quickly pass the days
She changes each day in so many ways
I watch her at sleep, for so peaceful she lays
In time she will grow, into a beautiful young miss
Too large to hold and to cuddle and kiss
She'll be her own person and guide her own life
And one day some man, she'll make a beautiful wife.

Hale Hamblen

THE UNKNOWN FACTOR—GOD

(The unknown factor (The Shadow of God) truly lays across the total universe and all the superficial knowledge of man.)

Into the great void of space that ₁ns eternity
Beyond where the light beams from the greatests suns reach
Beyond even where gravity fails to call
Things channeled into reverse rotation
Where things are totally consusin to man and in gestation
New worlds and universes, yet to be born
Where man cannot really imagine of or think of
With out his reason being shorn
New dimensions in both time and space
In the greatest of all space maelstroms
God only could think of or forment
A hellish truth in un-human humor
With which the soul of man to torment
For when man in his childish imaginings, thinks space
That he has reached the point in time and space
To try to kill off God in this earthly place
A great awakening has taken hold
For God must frown on man for his impunity to be so bold
Truly then the vastness, the wonder, of an unlimited Universe and space
Must come flowing through
For man has not really yet scratched the surface of anything for sooth
To destroy God in the hearts of man-thus in essence killing him
Or even be able to glimpse the master plan
Is beyond man's ken and leads to man's eternal fall
So really stand in awe, stop and think, of the totality
of a God, who is master of it all!!

Martine M. Gibbons

REFLECTIONS

I wonder sometimes if I pass through your mind
as often as you seem to visit mine.
Does the voice of Janis Joplin ever stir
the coals of your memory's fire?
It's strange, but no matter the years
that grow between us,
or those loves which burn to die,
I never do forget you.
I hear your name, and suddenly you are near.
You flood my present with our past.
I recall your cottage (to others it was a shack)
and I remember loving and laughter and whispering

in the dark, and I hurt. Is it ever such with you?
Now that I am older, as I fix meals or brush my hair,
I wonder "what did we ever argue about?"
I only meant to leave you for a little while.
When I returned, you'd left.
I thought throwing away your

pictures
would aid me to forget. . .
But you remain etched in my mind's eye
forever lingering—forever within my heart.
I remember crazy things, like dressing up in
rhinestones and satins to eat hamburgers in the park,
or watching butterflies. . .
or making love.
Have you found someone to replace me?
I remember how much you loved poetry,
maybe this page will catch your eye,
perhaps you'll know this is for you.
Perhaps the future will be ours.

Carlton C. Crank
VOICE OF THE MACABRE SILENT
Born in darkening darkness,
Naked ambivalence the passing moon.
Breezes of night ——
It clings to the warmth of a blade of grass,
Gently swaying.
As dawn in stealth awakens the world,
It will suffer, slowly die ——
Screams of agony never uttered, left unheard
As in the first rays of morning's light
The dance of death begins. . .
Vast all the oceans
Dancing upon a single blade of grass;
Prismatic in its light transforming movements,
Death throes glorious and exaltant ——
It vanishes, leaving no trace behind.
Forgotton treasure dead, lost and far away,
Its existence brief, plainly trivial. . .
The morning light prescind, still and silent
By the rustling of a memory,
A drop of dew.

Marianne Criswell
THE OLOGISTS ARE AT IT AGAIN
The ologists are at it again
This time it's the Eeks
Warning us the falling sky
Is high in strontium ninety.
Woe—woe—woeing us
About pollution, contamination, population;
Warning of shortages
Of everything but sin.
Sometimes I think an ologist
Is just Henny Penny with a Ph.D.
Whose word is always warning
Whose message is always doom.
Some when
Some now
Won't some ologist
Sound or sight salvation?

Mrs. V. W. Goodyear
OUR EASTER PRAYER
Heavenly Father,
Let us live precious life, as though newly born
As we welcome the Blessed Easter Morn.
In seeking Thy guidance in daily task
Let us be sincere in what we ask.
May new hope be instilled in the hearts of men
For Jesus, our Saviour, is risen again.
We would ask that Thy Love each one enfold
Today, as was in the times of old.
Be our shining example, that our thoughts be right
And our deeds acceptable in Thy sight.
With beauty and splendor Thyself we adorn
As we await the Eternal Easter Morn.
In Jesus' Name we pray.
Amen.

Camille Montant—McLauchlan
WITH YOU
Happiness is a cool summer rain
And walking on a grassy plain
And when the sun warms the air,
Entwining wild flowers in my hair.
Then riding a bike
While flying a kite
Love is doing these things with you.
Happiness is knowing that if I start to cry;
You'll always be nearby
To wipe away the bitter tears
And telltale mascara smears.
Then taking me in your arms
To keep me from all harm
Love is all these things about you.
Happiness is while growing old
We still treat each other like pure gold.
We'll both remember days when sad
But also the days when we were glad.
More hawk than dove
But it's you I love,
Love is being only with you.

Robert Klein Engler
CRICKETS
By a forest of clover,
on a continent of grass,
the bees are gathering their bread.
It is dry August and the days grow short.
On this planet of mites, where footfalls
come as earth quakes, the crickets sing.
You hear them in the bush
and hidden in the blades,
mysterious music in the wind.
Their song is buzz and saw and click,
and probably a love song,
music for metal colored flies
and silver-green beetles,
but especially a song for crickets.
One of these minstrels made its way
under my door while I was gone
to the mountains, found the basement
and trapped itself by the delicious warmth
of the water heater. The night I returned
I heard it chirp in the cinder bricks,
like one who sings alone in a deserted
city of the Gods, singing, waiting
for an answer, singing again.
I don't know what crickets do
when they come together,
these odd, black springs,
but unlike men who die
and leave off flesh
for a frame of white bones,
cricket insides turn to dust
and the black bodies of their profiles
stay memorial like an egg,
or shell, or broken violin.
I know, because just as I found
my father's violin in the basement
a few months after he died,
so, some days later,
I found the cricket dead and dry,
stretched out up side down
by the laundry sinks.
No one answered the song.
No one dare follow it past the door,
down the steps into the darkness
of wonderous ruins.
I was the one who had to pick it up,
wondering if it hurt to be a cricket,
polished like a machine, with hinges
and legs like locomotive shafts.
I had to walk the darkness
up the long stairs, past the door,
to toss the dust of songs
back to a forest of clover,
a continent of grass.

Dorothy Sammons
THE GARDEN SPIDER
The garden spider made a web,
Its silky threads sparkle with dew.
The spider is waiting for a tasty fly,
Or perhaps an insect or two.
The monster is big and ugly,
His web is between two trees.
Insects fly into the waiting trap,
They are pushed there by the breeze.
Mosquitos and flies become victims,
They are caught in the silky thread.
The spider is ready for breakfast,
Helpless insects have the monster to dread.

R. O. Wallace
AN ALLURING ZENITH
In souls eternal dwelling space
There is design in perfect harmony and pace
Innumerable stars live in shining praise
Reflecting light in timeless truth being but their way
Searching for the sake of searching
Man in all his glory ever reaching
Only seeking laughter of children playing in the rain
Whispers from soft breezes voicing endless change
Shadows of mind come to play in circles round the sun
Will O' the Wisp, becoming, fleeting near unseen
As clouds bank in imaginary voyage
Each scene unfolds, a living portion of the play upon
a stage of infinite dreams.

Pete Browne
SUMMA CUM LAUDE
Eight bears boogies in the forest wild
While eight inspectors through the forest filed.
The whole world stepped to a loud bassoon
That a monkey played from the face of the moon.
A chorus of gibbons in a glue nut tree
Sang verses high and loud and free
Sang verses wild and wide and free
Sang verses of nearer my God to thee.

Bernice Anderson
HEARKEN!
Learn to say "No, thank you!"
When the still small voice doth speak,
Keep moving ever onward—
'Tis your truth and way you seek.
Only you can hear the whisper
Of your inward self and soul,
Let others go their way, my dear,
Keep moving toward your goal.

Waste not your tears on pity
Nor your thoughts on vain regret.
Just lay them down and leave them.
Can you hear the music yet?
How wonderful the music,
How beautiful the way,
When we list to do the bidding
Of our heart and soul today!

Mindy Sue Pretzlspoon
LOVES' HARBOR
Here we two stand
Amidst a crumbling world,
Holding hands as partners
With our lives ahead.
There's no glimpse of light sometimes
other than my heart,
which glows ever bright throughout
this endless night of savage men and wars;
the light within my eyes is kindled by the Lord.

It knows no bounds-remains
everlasting—
to you, my love, and to our
world around us
which continues to dissolve.
It's our hope for resurrection,
beyond the hopelessness,
for God would not forsake the
children in His nest.
So, here we stand, you and I
amidst the crumbling Rome,
holding hands and holding hope
for something quite unknown.
I pray we maintain strength and
health
of body and of mind
to withstand the challenges of
our beliefs
caught flying in the wind,
to hang on tight to our loving
each other
and our friends.
You see, it's all got it's ending—
whatever it may be
and it's the gift of loving
that can set us free.
The gift of light within our
hearts
that guides us through the
harbor,
to see our lives through safely
to it's final hour.

Vincenzo Lxx Giallonardo
THE HANDWRITING ON THE WALL

O Supreme Sublime Glorious
Joyous Goddess of Creation O
Eartha and Skies O Embrace Me
and Enchant Me O Cherish Me
and Entrance Me with Thy
Beauty And Mutual Love O
from a Sunny Forest Vale by
Stream to the Vast Arched Stars
Where I Composed Spring 1975
Our "The Green Sperm and the
Golden Egg O Butterflies O My
Visions Body and Soul and Mind
and Spirit O Out Of the Womb
of the Ages O the Mongrel
Hordes Are Now Gathering and
Gallopping and Thundering
Through Eternities O Cultures
O Civilizations O Apocalypses
O Destinies O Forest Lanes
Stream Vortex Bridge O Swirling
Galaxies O Deep" etc O from
My August 13, 1913 Birth
About llam Along The Great
Valley Stream by the Barn Near
Valley Forge in Pennsylvania to
My July 4, 1976 Stand in Front
of Independence Hall in
Philadelphia, Pa. Where I Spoke
to About Four Billion Men and
Women and Children O'er
Planet Eartha etc "I Propose
an Amendment to the
Constitutions of the Nations of
Planet Eartha In That If a
Nation is Guilty of an
Impeachable Offense like
Permitting the Tyranny of
Desecrating Pollutions of Air
and Water and Food and Society
etc with the Tyrannies of
Maiming Deathly Violences
Wars etc and Thieving
Enslaving Outrageous Inflations

etc O a NEW SOLID 100%
HOLIDAY ELECTION is to
Take Place So That an
ORGANIZATION IN POWER
May Not Continue to Abuse Its
Position in This Ever Faster
WORLD of PRECISION VISION
DECISION. O in Truth and Love
etc O I AM M3-9 O the
Millbourne Millennium Master
Who is Now Maneuvering with
the Messiah at Midday and with
Mystique Mistress Mary with a
Mailing Address At 309 North
Simpson Street in Philadelphia,
Pennsylvania 19139 U.S.A."

Donna M. DeBoer
MY JOURNAL

Oh, friend of paper and pen
We have shared so much
answered so little
dreamed too soon.
We have crossed bridges
and burned them before we
dared
to concur them.
Friend of my dreams
a link to past, present, and
future.
You give me spaces to fill the
pieces of me, that don't fit
anywhere else.
It's nice having you around.

Catherine Joyce Haydu
INVESTIGATION ON THE PHENOMENON OF LIGHT

I see it—it is bright and warm.
Behold its brilliance
One who dares ruin this realm
of light
Will suffer the consequences of
anonymity
The equity of dominance
Is a mystery to all.

John J. Powers
NARROW ESCAPE

there is a way of feeling
which he knows, i do not,
a way of spending so much
time with a random supply
of people, places and beyond
the curved glass world—
yet he remains invisible
and even immune to love,
that love which surfaces
on top of old milk and layer-
cake
or curls its way in the gray
reach of his arms in the middle
of a splendid silent night;
unflappable and still young
he avoids as a rule
the look of age and sympathy
and simmering fear
served to him for my discreet
pleasure—there is a way of
feeling which he knows,
i do not; a way of the rare
widening of the mouth, the
watering, even the wincing—
i suppose i pale before him,
yet i remain awake, stirred,
curious and impassioned;
at night we trade thoughts
and play shuffle-board in
the light of the street,
we fall for the fantasy of being.

Bern A. Jackson
LOU WILLIE

Do you remember Lou Willie,
old Hank,
Goat Willie of the shadows,
wind-blown?
She tended a herd high in the
desolate crags
and lived in a cabin alone.
She gardened with only an old
rusty hoe
in such common raggedy clothes;
her wages were poor in food for
the shelf
but her yard held an old
fashioned rose.
She loved to be out in the wide
outdoors
where the view of the scenery
was rich;
she was a true friend of the
wilderness wild
through so often some called
her a witch.
The grazers are gone from the
crags,old Hank,
and the garden, thorn-woven and
dry;
a treasure is lost on the rimrock
bank
and the vultures all pass it by.
I think of Lou Willie of the
shadows, old Hank,
and the austere life she chose;
she favored us boys with
honeyed corn bread
and her heart was as warm as
the rose.

W. M. Tilley
SHORELINE

The smell of brine at water's
edge
Winds whipping up whitecaps
in the bay
Gray fog pushing in thru the
Golden Gate
Seagulls mewing, wheeling in
blue skies
A chill piercing coats and
rattling bones
The tantalizing aroma of coffee
from a thermos
As fishermen line up on an old
wooden pier
Shore birds foraging at the
water's edge
Life is filled with scenes such
as these.

David H. Berry
MEAT MONGER'S MUNCHOUT

Nothing for my dinner is quite
so sweet
as a thick red, juicy slab of
meat.
With every bite, juice dribbles
down my chompin chin.
Great grease globules sparkle
my grin.
A carnivorous creature am I
you'll see
the vegetarian life is not for me.
I'm found in McDonalds, Stead
Houses, and Burger Shacks.
Nothing beats my bacon
sandwich for a snack.
Years of meat contoured my
body
added a chin, padded by belly;
I'm a wee bit shoddy.
These nonsensical doctors
preach and say
"Curb the cholesterol or I'll
soon see my last day."
I care not cows are fed female
hormones
so my breasts grow a bit, voice
a bit higher—
I'm still normal.
The vegetarian life is not for me
meat eating's a big business in
this society.
Colonel Sanders, McDonalds
would run amock
if this silly vegetarian fad
came and stuck.
I need my meat.
It's not deceit—without it, I'm
too weak.
A vegetarian diet? Bite your
tongue! Of that I'll never
speak!

Vera M. Sponsler
SUNRISE GARDENER

Night left discreetly, crept into
the hills
Leaving her raindrop crystals,
swathing the daffodils.
Replenishing a lipstick stain
Provocatively on an early rose
Trailing a streak of misty light
Star-strewn from her sodden
clothes.
Night left, and gossiping birds
Heralded her flight
Greeting the young, unmarried
sun
Rolling the eastern light
Magnificent is nature's plan
Glutted with restless ease, I
bring
My mom made tools, and start
to dig
Filling my fingernails. . . .
with SPRING

Roxanne E. Meszaros
MY LOVE

My life has been so lonely,
Since you have gone away,
Everything is missing,
Your love and the words you
say.
I need you more and more each
day,
My time is spent alone,
I cannot smile without you,
And my loneliness is shown.
I know that some day you'll
come back,
And come and talk to me,
I'll tell you and I'll show you
too,
How unhappy I have been.
Your love is missed so greatly,
I find life hard to bear,

But when you do come back,
My love will be there.

Helene D. Brochu

THE ETERNAL CHILD

Walk softly child, for you do not know
For when winter comes, so does the snow.
Tread softly dear child upon the earth
For it is the place of eternal birth.
Though doomed you are because you are man
The quiet sands of time will always stand.
Find beauty in all that remains behind
Though fear and pain you shall always find.
Throughout the seasons of your lifetime
Choose the pathway which bares the least crime
Where you shall not waste the precious jewels
Of knowledge and wisdom and all that is well.
Search in the labyrinths within your mind
Release the shackles that society binds.
Walk softly child, for you do not know
For when winter comes, so does the snow.

Fran Weinberger

THE CITY

The City is my sanity as it surrounds, protects and comforts me.
It is my shelter against the unknown.
It is the sum of man's knowledge stacked high in skyscrapers
Jutting into the vastness above like fingers punctuating an instruction
Or a warning to the powers that be.
Each building an apostle of man-made miracles
Penetrating the boundary between reality and dreams,
Here and there, today and tomorrow.
Each building a guardian against infinity.
Sensuous in it's strength the city softens and spreads the sunlight,
Embracing me with it's shadows, shielding me from the rain,
Defining my world;
Changing the face of Nature's place and Me!

H. Leo Tewell

A TRUE FRIEND

If your life has been blessed
With But one true friend
Then, ah, what a blessing indeed
A friend who can share
All the times that are good
One to help you in times of need.
That someone who knows
And cares and responds
When it seems your back's to the wall
And they put out their hand
Their heart and their soul
And somehow you know
You won't fall.
Sure, there will be times
When you may not agree
When you won't see things
Quite the same
But you give and you take
And you show due respect
For you know it is part of the game.
What a beautiful world
If all could be blessed
With such a true friend in their life
Yes, I'll have a true friend
All the way to the end
And thank God, that true friend
Is my wife.

Inez (Green) Pinkney

MR CAN'T MR. CAN

"Mr. Can't" is a *great-big man!*

He'll upset your plans, if he can.
You want to do something, *"you can't,"* he'll say.

"You don't know how, and thats *not* the way."
"You *can't* be anybody, you *poor helpless thing."*

And more discouragements, Mr. Can't will bring.
So you *Cry*, be *miserable*, and think you'll *die*.
When along Comes *A Friend, "Little Miss Try,"*
With bundles of "Help you's," and things that are good.
She helps you get started as everyone should.
She shoves "Mrs. Can't" out, and slams the door,
Hoping your through with him, *Forever—more.*
She hustles about, worried you know,
Because its up to you, which way you go.
Slam the door on "Mr. Can't" and hurt his pride.
And ask *"Mr. Can"* to stay by your side.
Along with the help of *Little Miss Try*
You'll be a *great success by and by!*

Louise B. W. Woeppel

RESIGNED? OR RETIRED?

Tom never misses a cue,
In conversation or cards.
Onetime a top executive,
His mind still solves problems—
But no expert ever listens.
Ben haunts the laboratories,
Where he earned wide recognition,
Eager to use accumulated knowledge
To lessen humanity's woes—
But no foundation supports him.
Carl won a loyal following
As a pulpit orator who swayed many.
Now his influence is waning,
As ailments curtail activities—
And younger men choose to ignore him.
Retired?
No! Tired:
Of fresh-faced ridicule;
Of midlars' patronizing smiles;
Of stubborn, short-sighted cronies,
And over-possessive women!
Beth was called a master teacher,
Skilled in the needs of young children.
Her compassion and insight still alive,
But her techniques win few new diciples—
For teachers, unlike children, have changed.
Sue ran executive offices with zest,
Sure in experience and expertise.
But years and health have passed her by,
As do most of her early trainees—
Still uncomfortable with her strong standards.
Jane lived music for decades,
Thrilling audiences with lilting song.
But new stars hold the spotlight,
Forgetting whose traditions they inherit—
Eager to tune out memorable examples.
Retired?
No! Tired:
Of preoccupied grandchildren;
Of compulsive, concerned children;
Of restless, irritable spouses,
And complacent, fortunate friends!
EPILOGUE
Our weary world whirls on.
Generations come and go.
Those riding the crest of the wave
Forget predecessors below.
But no one works alone,
In any human endeavor.
And the wisdom and knowledge of all
Should enlighten us forever!

Susan E. Martin

IN THE NAME OF SPORT

God blessed our Indian fathers
With this virgin land;
The plains that teemed with bison,
Food in every hand;
Skies so wide with migrant flocks,
Rivers vast with life.
Then man hunted with innate skill,
A bow, a skinning knife.
In this, our world of modern times,
A hunter can delight;
His automatic guns and scopes
Make for an easy fight.
Hunters outnumber the hunted:
A sad, social report,
That man cruelly slaughters nature
All in the name of sport!

Stacy Mullaly

ILLUSIONS

The river flows by. . .
I think of you.
It tumbles over the rocks. . .
I hear your laugh.
A sweet musical sound caressing my ears.
I look deeper. . .
and see a shadow of you.
Deeper still. . .
I see your eyes
Warm and sensitive—beautiful green eyes.
Holding me close,
Keeping me safe.
It's hard to leave that lonely river.
It's musical depths,
make me feel complete.
At peace with myself.
I won't forget that river:
I will return again to it's warmth.
It makes me feel safe.
It makes me feel protected. . .
as I haven't felt for such a long time.
It flows gently through my memory.

J. Alfred Phelps

SOFT AS A BABY'S ASS

P.J., did you know that your lips are so soft and sweet
That just one of your kisses simply curled my feet?
Whether I kissed you slow or kissed you fast
It was just like kissing a baby's ass?
What do you know, P.J., of a baby's ass?
That round posterior so full of sass
A soft protuberence so all brand new
That's what I thought of when I kissed you.
It's been three hours since your lips met mine
I've been in a quandary all that time
Trying like hell to really understand
Why all that electricity from a little woman.
We said we'd be friends 'cause there's someone else
There's something the matter 'cause my heart really melts
When I think of you there and your upturned face

Your cherry-red lips make my heart really race!
P.J., are your lips really so soft and sweet
That one of your kisses simply curled my feet?
What is it that makes me want to kiss you so slow and fast?
By God, I believe that your lips *are* as soft as a baby's ass!

Jean M. Thieda
UNTITLED
Night's creeping in on silent feet
Drawing curtains over the sky,
Day, doggedly resists retreat
Holds its breath, departs with a sigh.
The many twinkling stars above
Spaced as lights on a christmas tree,
Best time of all to dream of love
As coming darkness sets souls free.

Susan Patricia Bell
AUTUMN STORMS
In the wind the leaves are spinning around desperately trying to land on the ground.
The sky is getting darker and the clouds are moving in ever closer.
The thunder crashes with terrible din
as the lightening brightens the world within.
And now at last the rain pours down
touching the leaves that lit on the ground.

Dena Gorrell
MEMORY'S JEWELS
Grieve not for the days that are past,
They are not really lost to you;
Change is a part of life,
And every dawning new.
But memories are a part of you,
And you can go back again.
The mind transcends both time and space—
To feel as you felt then.
So touch and feel and remember
Each moment fresh and new;
And on into the future
It will belong to you.
Now add it as a jewel
To an ever growing chain.
Lock the clasp and put it away,
Till you take it out again.

Denise Shaw
TAKING A CHANCE WITH YOU
Two souls brought together,
By a dominate force,
Willing to take a few chances,
A gamble that worked.
considering the odds,
And the fact that we won,
Love's the reward,
For each one of us.

Joan Betla Zygutis
BOYSCOUT'S MOTHER
On the 28th of August nineteen hundred and eighty-one
I welcomed home my boyscout son.
The form before me was something to behold,
I don't know if the description can be told!
One mass of dirt, dust, mud, and scum
That's what my boy had become!
Only the whites of his eyes could be seen
That was the only part of him that was clean!
He dropped his pack down with a thud
So weighted down with all that crud.
A thick, choking, cloud filled the air
I threw up my hands in utter despair!
How will I ever get him clean?
This filthy boy of just fourteen.
Soap him, scrub him, scour him well—
A bottle of Lysol to get rid of that smell!
Now to face that pile of clothes
I'll need a clothespin for my nose.
How can anything get so covered with grime?
So unidentifiable in one week's time.
My eyes could only see the complete disarray
Of socks, shirts, pants, that before me lay.
My task had just begun
Cleaning up after my Scout son!
Oh, Scoutmaster, have you no pity?
You must get together and form a committee
To get a merit badge in laundering made
To save us women in our crusade.
Camp Helendade needs washing machines
To teach the scouts to wash their jeans.
Give each boy a box of Tide
Instill in him a sense of pride
Let him go home as clean as he came
So all the Mothers won't have to exclaim—
"My God, is that my son under that dirty mess?"
They'll be able to see and won't have to guess!

Peter J. Bianchi
THE SYSTEM
Have you gotten word
of todays misconceptions?
We teenagers; all citizens
must alter directions.
The problem they say
is of the gravest importance.
For young people today
have too much reluctance.
Wanting only to gain
knowledge and wisdom,
Trying always to accomplish
the ruin of their system.
How could we reject
the ideas of our leaders?
We must remember and follow
the laws in our Readers.
And what of our future
of knowledge and wisdom?
Forget you have brilliance
for they have *The System!*

Bruce Casper
LAWS
Subject matter, if you will
The rules, the law in principal
Land or Man, or Biblical
All follow the master plan
Laws for protection
The rules of destruction
Convoluted, confusing standards
Shining stars, boots, belts, and lanyards
Laws of man, —Constitutions
Always faithful, never failing
Summer to Winter, morning sun shining
The laws of land are natural
Proven with the ages seasoning
With all the worlds pain and strife
A promise of eternal life
Loves faithful commitments—
Biblical Commandments

Ms. Merle Mason
CONTROL
When did I lose control?
I am no longer in charge.
When did I let this happen?
I follow, I flow, I bend.
I? I—no longer exist!

Sindjia Naing Topoian
GREEN TEA AND BUTTER COOKIES
Please be seated and accept my invitation for tea
Ease completed, selection repeated to be,
For here are cookies made of butter
Cut like the sea by the cookie cutter.

The guest accepted my urgent look
Less rejected this current cook;
Your presence delighted the very room
A menace in spite of merry gloom
Drawn to the table of moon-shaped delights
Pawn of this fable with moon-raped blights;
The sun skittered through the lacey dreams
That hung themselves, a face of schemes;
Steam swirled a signal from the cup
How enjoyable this little sup!
Answering in unison some as mine
Oh! This afternoon devine!
I enticed my guest to make a choice
Then spiced the rest to rejoice,
Selecting a cookie that you did choose
A butter delight which revealed no clues
A delicious morsel that melted its way
Down a convoluted path of sway
A suspicious eye held the course
A malicious sigh melted the force;
Playing the perfect host was I
Delaying a leisure boast to cry
That glee was mine and mine to give
The sea tea fine but not to live,
Laced with poison you could not detect
My charming smile was not suspect—
The tea was a colour of the sea
And green would kill this lover to be;
The room so sunny with opposite view
Oh gloom so funny! A positive hue—
Now a nauseous look convulsed a cry
How a cautious cook repulsed to die
Doubled in pain this wretched being
Troubled the mein and stretched seeing
Beyond the realm of this sweet death
Ceased the helm to beat the breath
Wretching in pain, fell to the floor
Stretching in vain, hell to deplore
An eye-look plea granted no grace
A sigh took tea planted no trace
For rigid of body and stare of eye
So frigid and solid this dare to die,
Pleading eyes caused contempt
Bleeding dies mauled attempt
As I laughed and howled
So daft and growled
As I crawled around to lick the corpse
And mauled abound to pick a force;
Eyes were staring, I ate them first
Like slippery marbles, palate cursed!
For the eyes were green as the tea
I suffered joy, mean as the sea—
The melted butter in cookies floated
I had won, how I gloated!
For eating the flesh also gave
A bleating mesh for the grave,
Osmosis caused the death of two
Prognosis paused a breath so blue
Dead were both and I howled with glee
For the lethal cookie cutter was me!

Gale Morrison
THE WIND
O—the wind does come
and the wind does go,
Spirits on the run
in the afterglow.
Wildly on a spree
moving fast, then slow,
Bringing you to me
better each to know.
So, the wind can be good
and the wind can be bad,
Never quite understood
maybe leaving one sad.
Leaving us as it should,
with hearts more glad,
Enjoying more, if we could
the things which we had.
Let it blow away all ill
thought act and deeds,
out o'er the windowsill,
better to join the weeds.
Ever anon, cheeks tan and brown,
having left its mark,
ere the wind went down
leaving its echo at dark.
Thence "Mama"m says a boy
while evincing a frown,
inwardly puffing with joy,
where goes, when the wind goes down?
Can one answer, now a man?
as another at ones knee,
try to answer, if you can,

"Wind going down?" Let's see.
So questions come ere winds do blow,
youths questions, so sincerely entitled to know, as up they grow
hoping the adults answer clearly.

Betty Nelson Hines

NIGHTCHILD

Come, sit with me tonight, Beloved
I plead that you tarry with me for a while
I am awake and cannot sleep, O gentle Dove
Someone calleth for Nightchild
Oh, if only you would accompany me tonight
On a drifting cloud traveling through the deep
Then would I not be alone or afright
Nor should the Nightchild have to weep
Beloved, my love, there is one that you love more than me
I see that her beauty is more virtuous than mine
She is no enemy for her name is Sleep
But of her I am jealous for thou art mine
Awake my love, come here to my side
Come share the moon and the stars for a while
Or let us ascend the clouds for a ride
Before dawn must it be, for I am Nightchild
Your precious footsteps I hear upon the floor
I regret that slumber coveteth my seducing smile
For it tis dawn, my Beloved and awake I cannot stay
Day is here, and you, Nightchild must sleep for a while
To my darling husband, Sidney

Susan M. Silver

LOVEMAKING

When you love me, my body
Spins in inner space.
Bound on a wheel of pleasure,
I feel a universal center in me.

Larry Roik

THE HUMBLING OF ARROGANCE

I have never lived in greatness,
Nor stood with much pride,
In my simple human acts I begin,
But never achieve.
I have not stood atop mountains
Or even grasped a shallow valley;
It is not any man's fault,
It is every man's fault
That I cannot love this world,
And I am subject to joy in only the Ideal;
Come now, sleep with me and learn
What a horrible pain that is.

Joy Elizabeth Thomas

NIGHT'S HUSH

The day is done
and all the busy folk
lay aside its heavy cloak
in twilight's happy hour.
Soft smiles, sweet grace, and
warming tones glow in dusk's sleeve,
slope down to garments laced
in midnight's sheerness.
Along the Milky Way
starbeams herald ethereal voices
sing lullabyes. Winds bade
interweave shadowy clouds of dreams
with gentle murmurs of spun moonmist
and sprinkles it over night's hush.

Robert Coleman Martin

THE MIME

Silent soul. . .white faced, gesturing to the crowd
Giving love. . .taking same. It's a game!
Look at him move. . .mimicing us all
Ever so careful not to fall
First he's a robot, then he's a clown
Picking up spirits, creating a frown
He knows a great deal the way that he walks
A lot of words said. . .yet he never talks
What mysteries lie behind the white face
always enclosed in a mystical space?
He draws us in with a sly little grin
We're captured unknowingly in a kind of charade
He's made us a part of his silent parade

Loretta M. Stiles

A SNOWY WHITE WORLD

Look out a frost covered window
Find a white world that's peaceful.
Trees covered by white sparklers,
That will melt away someday.
This world is icy cold, full of fun,
The sky is blue, full of glory.
Run out and build a frosty,
Feel the morning sun.
There, tracks of a deer,
That licked upon a salt block.
Winter goes on, the deer is tamed.
Trees covered with sparklers still.
Slowly, sunshine shall melt them away.

Jeannette Viola Unger Ewasyn

LAS VEGAS, NEVADA

Sitting at the gambling tables,
Really if one's soul comes back,
Several times as different characters.
That I don't believe.
But basically I always,
Felt a strong empathy,
Towards a man named Moses.
His was a hard, difficult journey,
But, oh glory, how close to God,
That man eventually became.
Most only get a glimpse of such mysteries,
When their soul departs this mortal body.
That is if they have kept the faith.
About the others it must be,
Worse than the most horrible, terrifying nightmare.
All I know is that some die calm and serene,
But a few scream worse than any insane person.
My active imagination can touch the heavens,
But such unnatural things it refuses to try to understand.

Bernice Morris Staples

THE KEY

Ah humanity! You overwhelm me in your colossal stupidity.
You wallow in the trough of life until death comes to end the strife.
Five senses then were given you and, even some have six,
And still you function without a chart, each life a hit or miss.
Why! Are the cries in life so helpless to heal one single sore,
And why the vast and empty space between you and the stars.
Yet, all the while you hold the key to open any door.
The key is LOVE, your answer YOU, for now and ever-more.

Elaney Roussopoulos

REFLECTIONS

The sun smiles sweetly
against my lips and the
orange's juices squeeze
against my finger tips;
the napkins play delightfully
with glee
upon my knee, as
I sit here
thinking
Where i should really be.
today is the sometime
i've been waiting for
although yesterday was and
tomorrow is no more
for time has come to
act upon the thought,
and brush aside all doubt
and old dependencies which
weaken me. for i have need
to be, to be unafraid and free
to be.

William H. Stockdale

HERE IS MY POEM

From Hiroshima to My Lai
In the burning of an eternal flame
Born of love's grace
For the hope of a
Gentle new morning sun

Roberta Norrell Rhodes

FREESPIRIT

Go with the wind Freespirit
Go with the restless sea,
Go where fate must lead you;
Your heart will ere be free.
Take your happy laughter, let others share your smile
And we will long remember
what we shared
With you awhile

Sidney Ganzler

RECKONING

And the knowledge thirst of Humankind
was not stayed
from stalking the grounding fire of creation
to its lair
exceedingly deep within the weave of matter,
but tore aside the seal from the furnace,
and in awe
looked upon That Light,
brighter than a thousand suns,
The Primordial Flower
which blossoms at the core of stars.
The reckoning of the New Age
was begun.

Debra Baldwin

HAIKU IMAGES

The artist reflects
Moods of the portraits he paints
Melancholy, joy
For one to be rich
Need he not of wealth possess
But love in his heart

Young girls, like flowers
Hide the woman in youth
Blossoming in spring

Franklin Sommers

MY LIFE

I wish I could express myself to others,
But my words fail myself:
My words fail my heart, mind, and soul,
And all that they hold I cannot express:
I die of frustration and loneliness,
But I live for love:
Written with eternal love and honor for God,
My Mother, and Nora Butler, for grace.

Bertie Ellen Floyd

SPRING IS COMING

Oh how the sun is shining through that big picture window in my room.
As I look out to greet such a beautiful day,
I see so many things to tell me spring is on its way.
The beauty of spring is coming soon,
already the daffodils are in bloom.
Outside a pretty sound I can hear,
the singing of the birds are so clear.
The bare looking trees with tiny buds beginning to spread,
will soon be loaded down with

blooms and green leaves
instead.
How soon the spring colors will
appear,
upon the flowers that God
made so dear.
The grass is turning green upon
the ground.
Spring is showing its coming
beauty all around.
As the brisk coolness of the
morning ends,
then the warmness of the
afternoon begins.
In a distance I can hear the
church bells ringing,
and seeing all these sights I
just feel Like singing.
From my window I feel that
spring is almost here.
So bowing my head I thank
the Lord for beauty so near.

Therese Cichon

MYREMECOPHILE

My belly,
still wet with the water
of our sweat,
and the juice from
your penis,
feels so good and
sticky,
like I'm covered with sweet,
sweet honey.
The ants crawl out from the
walls.
They are attracted by the
thick stickiness; and
come to nest,
like so many times before,
in and around
my navel.

Kay Ann Knowles—1951—1974

SKY

Walk slowly into the solitude,
that your soul provides
And the sky is deep
don't hide.
Walk slowly into that sky
Do you feel the door? Open it.
You have the magic key,
go through the door.
Play hide and seek, invite
yourself
to come and see
Who can find and who can keep.
But walk slowly in the sky,
quickness brings you down
To stand again high, hold your
breath
and laugh.
Walk slowly in the sky
See funny faces you once
knew,
Which one is you?
The sky is deep
you can't hide
The sky is you.

Janet Pembor

CHRISTMAS IN OTTAWA

Christmas in Ottawa!
Wish I was there
With the Brain and the Face,
The legs and the Hair;
A gallery housing
A fabulous group
Where Campbells do more
Than just brew a soup.
Christmas in Ottawa!
You're ten feet tall
Just breathing the air
And walking the mall
Where merchants, however
So classy and British
Are still only peddlars
With just the right finish.
Christmas in Ottawa!
French goods arrayed
Along with the English
So handsome displayed
In elegant shops
That are no vulgar home
To plastic and neon
And cheap, shiny chrome.
Christmas in Ottawa!
Where could you find
Three-hundred artists
At work at one time
Painting a fence
Not to wall themselves in,
But to buttress a
Hospital's charity binge.
Christmas in Ottawa!
Be of good cheer
Where china is cheap
And ladies are dear
And cigarettes aren't
Such a hazzard to health
As they are to your
Pocketbook's wavering wealth.
Christmas in Ottawa!
What is your fight,
Peace, Conversation
Or some kind of right?
You won't find it listed
Under a Cause,
It's a Regligion
Of unending pause.
Christmas in Ottawa!
Bless them, amen.
The YW's placed
Across from the M,
And they tell me in tones
So dulcet serene
Next year they're building
A subway between.
Christmas in Ottawa!
Hail and amen,
It's even worth crossing
The border again.
Christmas in Ottawa!
Don't be surprised
If next time I come
With a French Disguise.

A. L. Swanson

YE OLDE TYME NEW ENGLAND BARD

There was a bard of ye olden
tymes,
Whose task it was to spread
the news,
As he rode along he'd make up
rhymes,
Swap them for drinks at
rendezvous.
With horn and mailsack primly
displayed,
He at best sped at 1/2 horse
speed,
None could better this speed
nor exceed,
On the full rounds of the
tavern trade.
Ye olde skop on his horseback
shop,
Grinned as he galloped his
route,
At a clippety-clop, but always
he'd stop,
At horse-troughs for a few
swigs to boot.
As an olde tymer said, "without
a doubt,
Ye skop's tyme is about to run
out,
For one day a joker with a
prying mind,
A long string to a kite did
bind,
Some folks thought him a loony
lout,
When he got a sudden jarring
shock,
As down the wet, string the
current did sock,
Electrical energy was then
found out.
(Bard—an old time news vendor)
(Barde—old eastern packsaddle)
(Skop—a bard apprentice)

Esther Vanek (McGechie)

A SEED OF LOVE

From the moment of our first
meeting
in my soul was conceived a
seed,
Which drank the flowing
strength of your love;
on essence of kindess did feed.
Its roots grew deep as they
sapped upon
your fervent affectionate care,
And the soft, sweet, magical
music
of words whispered lovingly
fair.

Sprinkled daily with ardent
attention;
upheld by the warmth of your
smile;
Infused with the glow of
impassion;
it discovered a life
worthwhile.
Solely dependent upon your love
for the satiable desire you
nourish;
Only because of you will this
plant
continue to live and to
flourish.

Alexius M. Gallegos

WINGS

I want to feel my wings of
freedom
to soar into the sky
I need to kiss the lips of
freedom
before I start to die.
I feel the heavy weight of guilt
the heavy chains of here.
Surrounded by the high barb
fence
With only the sky to give me
cheer.
The stone brick walls that make
my cage
like a coil around my soul
The strict stern words of those I
hear
ring loudly, clear and cold.
I want to fly into the sky,
to feel my wings of freedom.
To fly along side next to you
and rule our tiny kingdom

Elizabeth C. Reed

HAIKU #1

Spring's nimbus; reigning.
New buds, the trees are birthing.
Winter's crown dethroned!

Alice H. Clark

KITCHEN QUALMS

Away from the kitchen with a
feeling of glee,
Concoctions prepared, let's
just wait and see;
Too small for two people, as
clear to the eye,
I pass in and out with never a
sigh.

David M. Singer

SAGITARIUS

Gracefully flowing, merging in
the winds,
Fleet of foot, noble of air;
Searching, probing, for his final
prey,
Will always search it is not
there.
Honest pure and open of soul,
Friendly, trusting; maybe too
much;
Looking for his fellow man,
Tracking the rabbit in his
hutch.
A paradox, an amusing one,
The archer would not harm his
prey;
But in his search, he follows
the rules,
And goes about a routine day.
Poor Sagitarius, fresh dew drops
on a flower,
Breathing life in a stale, dank
world;
The world closes in, and you
feel trapped,
Have no fear, you will last.
Gracefully flowing, merging in
the winds.

Enid Cohen

THE FRIGHTENED CHILD

A small boy walks alone—head
bowed,
Not seeing the wondrous world
around.
No trees, nor flowers, nor sky
above,
Clutching his books close to his
chest,
A single tear on his child's face,
Going to school—a fearful place,
By himself.

Melani Marie Mendoza

SEARCH

I am searching
for the meaning
of love within
myself. Sometimes,
I get frustrated
when I think
I am not flowing
with my feelings

or if my feelings
do not arise
the way I want
it to. There seem
to be reasons
I find so discouraging:
it is my weaknesses.
I know not the
right things to say
to tell you of
my feelings,
because deep inside
I really do not
know how to love.
So I thought about
what real love is
and I find that it
does not only
develop internally
but to have the
strength in knowing
how to relate
with you.
I realize that I
am not really strong
enough to withhold my
dreams of love.
I fight desperately
with my emotions and
become chaned to
only find meanings
I never been able
to live out.
I began to understand
parts of myself
in a way I thought
could never reveal
other possibilities.
My weaknesses are needs
to be fulfilled by love
or else there is no
giving or taking.
I find myself
relieved when I realize
that our love
does not necessarily
have to be perfect,
because our own
understanding of each
other only applies
to us. I find
that to only
expect from you
will destroy your
real character.
I will be overlooking
a greater beauty
that cannot be understood
unless I fully accept you.
I only need the patience,
because in us I see
our love that needs
strength, and in such a
relationship love will
definitely grow.
We need only to
be ourselves and
to understand the value
of our experiences.
This will lessen
the pain of
such a search:
I love you.

Paul Spencer
IN VINO VERITAS
Deep bitter is the sediment
That's left from making wine,
And bitter are the broken
dreams
Left hanging on the vine.
For Life is like a pendulum,
It swings, and none knows
where;
The Hand that moves it to and
fro,
Me thinks It does not care.
Then gather 'round you while
you may
The fruit, and not the pith,
For life is short, and death is
long,
And hell is not a myth.
Within each man, in life's
vineyard,
Is found both heaven and hell.
Look then for help within
yourself
For there's where God does
dwell.

Ranza Devereaux
NATHAN'S RETURN
Nathan, an elderly two-year old,
My devilish angel,
Watches the wind whistle
Through the evening shadows
of the tall trees
tossing balls of clouds
over the rolling hills.
Silently he yells
To the sun-lit moon.
Oh yes! He remembers this
friend—
their many games of hide and
seek
Played in yesteryear. Stranger
to none, living, this face,
but oblivious to the
unobservant,

He's full of nature's secrets,
giving the boy a knowing wink.
He'll never divulge his many
acts
of creative destruction.
The child has been here before;
Another time, another place—
Back from the living dead,
Back to another mom who
loves and adores this
big little parcel
of heavenly hell.

Donna L. Prestwood
LIGHTS
The tapeplayer is blasting
Smoke is circling above your
head
And the lights are flashing
As you lay upon your bed
You're in a world all your own
In your own special place
Where no man can enter
And only lights fill the empty
space
You see beautiful black lights
Some have yellow jackets, some
are only red
You look at your pretty lights
And wonder if you're dead
Will somebody help me?
No one knows if they can
Is this the way it should be?
Or is this the end for man?

Frank Babcock
ETERNITY
There is no light—no lack of
light—
no definition—
There is the fullness of the
Oneness
There is God—

Thomas W. Fuller
BEATITUDE
My writing shakes the empty
bottle of burgundy
The Grand Marnier, Courvoisier
aquiver
I thank you for the love I was
allowed to give
Bless your fortune, child, that
you could not return it
Bless your brother for the
impositions he allowed
On a lifelong friend and his
Scottish purse
Past and future are the inroads
that I make
On the ordered pursuit of his
life
Bless your mother for her heart
and love
And a constant river of support
For you and I—on different
roads
Bless your father with is
unflappable good will
And his willingness and passion
for his labors and his daughter
Bless their love for you, which
first checked mine
Bless you most as a jewel in
time

Irene Stalcup
THANKS
Pilgrims landed on the
Plymouth rock
Faced cold winter, hardships, but
through it all
Took stock and did recall
Blessings outweighed them all.
Thanks for twinkling stars and
moon at night
The sunrises, and then brings
daylight
Breezes blow, rains fall,
And crops, trees and grass
grows.
For families and kin
Neighbors and friends
With whom you can lend and
borrow
Share your tears, joy and sorrow.
In our rush and hurry
Have we forgot, to pause
And give thanks for
Our bountious lot.
Pilgrims had a feast and
celebration
To express gratitude and
appreciation
Let us not take our blessings
for granted
Gratitude makes our life
enchanted.

Gladys Holt
REALITY IS UNSEEN
Across the vast resources of the
mind,
Reality is unseen.
Hopes and dreams play in the
brain
Far and in between.
Bright dreams of the future; as
past, as gone;
Hopes of another world.
Nightmarish dreams of riches to
come;
All silvery, all ivory-pearled.
Voices of unseen persons whose
dreams have
Subsided or perished.
Paintings of loved ones some
fool before
Has so devotedly cherished.
Screams of agonized hopefuls in
vain who
Have dreamed before.
Keep dreaming; for the future
holds, for truth,
Unseen in reality; a door.
The future, holding truths for
persons to be;
Those unknown those not
seen.
The human mind molds dreams
and hopes and yet
Reality remains unseen.

Kenneth Graham
ONE DAY
Dreams from a lighter side
of darkness,
With little chance of
surviving,
Were captured at the home
where they were hiding.
The bugs were disturbed.
Sat and stared at stucco ceilings,
Plotting clever and wonderful
schemes.
But in my heart, I had a fear
The jester's laugh, one day I will
hear
Sulked through the familiar
community,
Without a trace of immunity.
Encountered my venerable
nemesis,
Supposedly purchasing
cigarettes,
But actually, enjoying my
frantic madness.
Returned to the cage in which
I'm kept
Twisted a key; the box fell open.
The paper arrived, marking an
exit.
Four moon since "Brown Rice"
had been labeled "The
Deceased,"
The righteous tributed still had
not ceased,
Coming mostly from dear
Brother Jack at the diocese.
Jack took the time to curse
"evil" karma
And claim His Word to be

undoubtedly dogma.
Is there a difference?
Sat alone in the corner pertinent to the universe
With vague intention of committing a crime.
As midnight oil kept burning,
I flicked a silver-plated button
And praised the echolalia of our fabulous convention,
Its message obliterated by time
The bugs were content once more.

Stanley A. Fellman

FOR A GROUP OF NAM MARINES BUT ESPECIALLY FOR MAC

With eyes as wide as World War,
Units of Honey jars move out to patrol poison;
They came back with tooth aches in their bones,
And badly sunburned inside their minds.

Instead of salutes, the veterans exchange tremples.
"If it was all for nothing, can we forget it ever was?"
Not if you prize your consciousness—
I only received an indirect reply:
"Poetry is real sounds entering a sleeper's dream."

Jacqueline E. Whitaker

GOD'S JUDGMENT

Can you see God in the midst of the universe?
Silence dissipated throughout the earth.
People crying and saying, "Lord save me!"
God answers, now it's too late to be free.
As God sits on the throne
People began to wonder and no place to roam.
I told you folks that I was coming back soon!
It's too late, so don't cry that tune.
Do you remember St. Matthew 25:13 and Revelation 22:12?
Watch therefore, for ye know neither the day
Nor the hour wherein the Son of man cometh.
And behold I come quickly and my reward is with me.
As God opens the gigantic Book of Life
Narrating our good works, faithfulness or vices
Did you put on the whole armour of Christ?
If not, your work of iniquity will surely fall.
Since you didn't answer God's call.
Let's examine ourselves and be sincere.
Don't be caught in Wrongdoings when He shall appear.
Have you heard the familiar remark?
I'm young and I have plenty of time.
Please surrender; it doesn't cost a dime.
Young folks, middle age and old, repent and yield.
Time isn't promised. God is our rescue and shield.
Accept Christ before Judgment Day
It's not too late, Christ is the way.

M. Junay Johanson

GENETIC RECOMBINATION

Looking down this trail,
a flash of light I saw in the dawn,
and to the rear I felt it,
universal law, time is gone.
And they united, time stood fast,
dropping feelings from the past.
Here they stood, a reaching hand apart,
the energy at start.
Combined a force, a touch of star,
from afar.
Combined of will, a touch of light,
to light the night.
A touch of hope, to see it blend,
at first as friends.
Then entity of both in form
had been reborn.
As now the wizard said, "I have a fill,
that is completely real."
As the light in the darkness
felt inner presence of your essence.
Outstretched arms he threw,
life that grew.
Glowing in the dark,
they shared one heart.
Only for a moment, on a beat,
everything complete.
Then the sparkles became what is known as a glow,
light flow.
The wizard outstretched his arms, his eyes became grey,
a changing day.
Sun comes, dashing light, from the distant hill,
then it spills.
As they, the wizard and the light,
came into each other in the night,
with great delight.

Esther Mazza

OUR HOME

OUR HOME—'Tis not just a house where people dwell
Nor, a fancy show-case for all to see;
From the windows come a delicious smell
Which seems to say stop for tea.
Each holiday fills it with song and laughter,
As family and friends come through the door
Happy memories last long, long after
'Tis not just for parties but much, much more.
On a cold winter's night, the fireplace glows;
At days end, oh! How good to get home
And sit by the fire to warm our toes,
With no worry or care if snow should come.
OUR HOME—is where the LORD lives too—
Where, we laugh, sing, plan and pray together
Where, we talk out all and be so true
Where, the sun always shines whatever the weather.

Larry E. Myers

MY SON

He's the one who makes me happy, when I'm feeling low,
He takes my hand, and wants to play, he's always on the go.
At times he makes me angry, for things that he may do,
But when it comes to punish him, I take the punish to.
He looks at me, those big blue eyes, as though they seem to say,
Why do you have to punish me, I just want to play.
Then he starts to pucker up, a tear upon his cheek,
That's when I hurt deep down inside, for words I couldn't speak.
I reach out to hold him close, and kiss away his tears,
Then the words, "I love you son," I whisper in his ear.
I love my son, so very much, and everybody knows,
His big blue eyes, his sandy hair, his little button nose.
And if he'd never have to hurt, or never have to cry,
I'd gladly give all I own, I'd even give my life.
He cuddles in my arms at night, I kiss his little hand,
And then he dozes off to sleep, "He's Daddy's little man,"
(My Pal, My Buddy, My Son.)

Estrella Besinga-Sybinsky

Of selves, of shadows, of trysts, of anomies: a tribute to the 3rd world

human frailty, human frailty
we make the song, and sing
and yet,
we do not pause to cheer
the diversity within the song
where would the
melody be,
without the differing
notes?
harmony is
you and i, them and us,
blending together
not as
beasts to
beasts.
"do unto others
as you would
want others do
unto you", a cardinal rule—
so simple, so profound,
alas, so easily forgotten.
but yet, a spark of hope
"we shall protect ourselves
and send untested pesticides
abroad"—and rome shall burn,
while i lie back and eat
of the wretched's toil.
how gullible
are we, to
think the
walls will
hold,
the pesticides
untested, give
life to what we eat.
the poison we discard
beyond—
has come to haunt.
and so deceptive they
in colors bright,
in sterile
cans and boxes.
the world is small
for all of us, if the mind
prevails,
the world is huge
for all of us, if the heart
prevails
"excesses
make of every
virtue, but a
vice",
the golden mean
appears the best—
and it is here
and it is now.

J. Laurence Erkis

THE DEATH OF TIME

What has become of passing hours that sped
Over, under, through, around, up and down?
For, with each hour before have they been wed,
And by their lovely trains have they been led
In bursts of laughter, just as by a clown.
Where'er one looks the trail is bloody red,
And nothing seems to clean the wedding gown
Except to pour cold water till it's brown,
For, with each hour before have they been wed,
And all their sixty parts forever fled
And tinged with torment; wrinkled in deep frown.
The roses they have known are bent and dead,
We walk without their scent and no words said
That might disturb their sleep or lift their crown,
For, with each hour before have they been wed.
Now comes the falling rain from heaven's shed,
Into the thirsty sewers from town to town,
And there is only flooding left to dread,
And time can meet its death just up ahead.

Willie Wayne Hern.

DRUGS

There are drugs both good and bad,
You can find the good ones at your pad.
Those are the ones the drug

stores sell,
And when you take them they
make you well.
But the other ones you can get
here and there,
They make you feel different,
like if you don't care.
These drugs are illegal, if you
didn't know,
Yes even the grass that some
people blow.
These drugs can do more than
just get you ripped,
They can make you act like if
you really flipped.
Some of those drugs can retard
or even kill,
Just because of a desire you
wanted to fill.
So now you know that they
aren't any good,
But the decision is yours to do
what you should.
So make up your mind about
what you want to do,
But if something goes wrong,
remember "I WARNED YOU!"

Dolores Howe
EARLY MORNING
When the day and I are fresh
together
Is the most beautiful time of all.
It is then that I feel God's
presence,
And reverently respond to his
call.
When the earth is washed and
fragrantly clean,
The golden sun rises in the sky.
The birds and bees hurry to
their work.
Who cannot know there is a
God on high?

Paul London
TO GREGG
When I saw you I knew
I had known you before.
That feeling grew
As we shared our experiences
from days of yore.
How many lives had we shared
The happiness and the sorrow,
How many times had we cared
If there was a tomorrow?
Our histories have been written
Both nobly and not,
And lest we be smitten,
We must move from this spot.
You must go your way,
And I, mine,
Someday I pray
Again our lives will intertwine.

Lori Heikkila
MOUNTAINS
Standing so lonely
In the desert's endless stretch,
Battled by wind.

Bates Hoffer
THE ST. LAWRENCE IN WINTER
Still silent river,
Glazed with granite slabs of
ice—
Will you soon thrash free?

P. L. Ditallo
UNTITLED
For Johnny
whose shaven face
is now hollow
except for a cloth
mask
and a brick window
of flesh;
a forehead like a
prision cell,
pasty gray
drowning in frenetic
sweat.
Forcible soldier,
shell shocked,
the ravaged bullet
has swallowed
your arms
one by one,
your legs
one by one,
your ears
one by one,
but be ever so grateful.
you'll never need
gloves or rings,
radios or phonographs,
pants or socks;
be grateful soldier.
Shaven club,
trimmed neat
little shrub,
no one must listen,
no, not ever
not to you,
human stub.

Virginia Lee Corson
MOTHER NATURE
I love to go in the woods
On a cool summer day,
And watch the animals and
birds
Merrily at their play.
The birds fly all around
While the rabbits hop on the
ground,
The squirrels climb all the trees
While the worms eat holes in
the leaves.

The woodchuck digs his hold in
the ground
While the busy little bees
buzz all around,
Gathering honey before the
winter's snow
Where they store it we
seldom know.
Oh I do think that Mother
Nature is grand
The wonderful things
She does with her invisible
hand,
Constantly improving our
beautiful land!

Ernie Barbour
UNTITLED
To know that you are going
to be hurt
if you love—
but loving anyway,
is like
knowing you are going
to die
if you live
but living anyway.
To stop loving
to keep from being hurt
is like
killing yourself. . .
to keep from dying.

Verlee Leinen
FICKLE ONE
For you frankness forgotten
Trusting naught to fate
You flirt & fib & flatter
Hiding in your fat facade
Fearful of being made a fool
Afraid that love might conquer
you
Finding only momental bliss
You forego eternal happiness.
Forsooth!

Jan Larzelere
ACQUITTED
It was overreaction;
The child was coached;
The man used poor judgement.
Who knows what happened
In the empty house?
Maybe something,
Maybe more than he should
have;
He hugged and kissed her;
He adjusted her panties,
But not with intent, he said,
To be sexual;
It wasn't molestation,
Just poor judgement.

Dean Harper
GRANDSON TO GRANDMOTHER
I have your chair,
the one you bought
from years of saved Christmas
money.
Patiently, you watched
television,
and awaited a friendly face
those last twenty years.
The steady rock to all
who came before you.
You greeted everyone with
the childlike smile
and a trace of brown
beneath your lower lip.
On days when I can't match my
reach.
I sit in your broken-armed chair
and know the weight of what
was there.

Juanita M. Reed
FOOTPRINTS
When we were children how
much fun it was
To wade through every water
puddle we could find
We removed our shoes and
played barefoot in the mud
Content to let the squishy
coolness get between our toes!
Of course, this was done when
our mothers weren't watching!
During the winter we loved
playing in the snow
Making jaunty snowmen and
throwing snowballs
Sliding down the hills on sleds
or pieces of cardboard
As we romped to and fro
through the glorious white
fluff
We left a criss-cross pattern of
prints no artist could imitate.
In the summer we loved to wade
in the small streams and
brooks
Lifting rocks and trying to catch
crayfish and small minnows
And never quite doing so.
We would swim awhile if we
found a spot deep enough
We liked to run through the
sweet smelling clover
And feeling the cool greenness
beneath our feet.
Another favorite fun thing to do
was pick daisies
Pulling the petals to "He loves
me, He loves me not!"
We loved a mild summer, rain
and it was so much more
delightful
To lift our faces and let it
ripple down our cheeks
Before it fell to the ground
giving life to the brown soil.
We loved going to the beach,
letting the warm summer sun
Tan us to a golden brown
We swam in the swirling waters
of the ocean and would
marvel
At the wonders of the sea we
might find clinging to the
seaweed
Or played guessing games at
what creature lived in some
shell we found.
We carried buckets of water and
made sand sculptures of
childish design
Our footprints would disappear
each time the tide came in
To be washed out to sea and
become part of that wide, blue
expanse.
We would idly dream that our
footprints washed ashore in
some exotic place
We had read about and would
like to go visit. Ah, the days
of youth!
We grew older and went many
places, and did many exciting
things
Leaving our footprints as part
of history of these particular
places
Just as man has left his
footprints on the sandy surface
of the moon
May we, too, leave our
footprints in the sands of time
So that others may know, that,
we did indeed, pass this way.

Kaye Mathews
FRAGMENTS
Days of bright iridescence
too often fracture into moments
of utter futility—
bits and pieces—of broken
promises. . .
shattered dreams.
Then I hear the Master's
comand:
"Gather up the fragments
that nothing be lost."

Out of the many fragments,
He is fashioning his self-portrait
in mosaic most unique—my life!

Regina Suzette Campbell
I STILL LOVE YOU SO
When I look around,
with pain I see,
You giving another
what you once gave me.
It hurts me more
than you'll ever know;
You don't understand,
I Still Love You So.
I look at the pictures
of you and me
and remember the Love
that used to be.
The tears go away
and light grows my heart,
for I'm thankful to have
been a part
of the Love and Compassion
that you bestow,
and I'd give the world
to let you know:
After all this time,
I Still Love You So.

Kenneth F. Bryant
SOLITUDE
Night descends, and in so doing
Transforms a busy world into
A world of quietude and rest.
I see it now. . .first. . .upon the hill
That overlooks the small community.
How graceful this velvet night
Engulfs all in its path!
Now. . . silently. . .it slides along the hill
And settles quietly upon the village square.
I am alone in perfect solitude
That now prevails. So strange this
Feeling that has overcome my weary soul!
So strange. . .I dare not think for fear
My thoughts will pierce this quiet night
And echo. . .then re-echo as an uttered sound
Reverberates from deep within a cave.
It seems that all the world has
Suddenly grown weary and peacefully
Succumbed to long-awaited sleep.
Still I remain. . .my soul advertently aware
Of some incomprehensible reality
That only God can understand!

Carolyn A. Meighan
PAUL
Before the flaming fire she sits
Alone
The shadows from the flickering flames
Dance and play upon the walls.
As she gazes into the fire,
She thinks of the past.
Was it really so long ago?
In the glowing embers,
She sees his face clearly.
She remembers the way he said her name.
She smiles, remembering his touch,
And the way, she felt inside
Whenver he held her in his arms.
They'd loved each other so.
Maybe, it had been too much. . .
And that was why he'd been taken from her.
I didn't seem fair!
They'd only had two months together.
At least they'd spent each day
Loving one another as if it were their last.
She had no regrets, nor was she bitter.
The wheelchair, she could live with.
For without him, she didn't really care.
Suddenly, she feels cold!
She realizes that, like Paul,
The fire has died.

Sonya Thompson Garver
THINGS I NEED
Time. . .to sort out my thoughts about life.
Space. . .to grow and create my life.
Warmth. . .to remove the chill of my soul.
Love. . .to keep me secure and make me feel whole.
Strength. . .to take each day as it comes.
Valintry. . .to be brave and not run.
Confidence. . .to help me through the bad times.
Flowing speech. . .so my poems always rhyme.
A sense of humor. . .to keep me in good cheer.
You. . .to be with me throughout the year.

S. C. Edney
OYSTER KNIFE
In every kitchen there is a drawer where
crippled misfits collect—the broken
stubs of wooden spoons and lonely lids
of empty pickle jars. Important things
like corkscrews and cookie cutters
are kept there too. Of course the
things you need become hopelessly entangeld
with things you never use, providing
that touch of chaos every kitchen needs.
I opened just such a drawer
one crusty eyed morning,
and found, cradled in the elbow of a rusting beater,
an oyster knife. Unperturbed at being so far
from the sea it slipped its fat handle
into my palm and pried back the edges
of the day's routine. Memories
trickled across the morning's chin.
Everyone should have an oyster knife
and on hard shelled days when
life's silt has covered them
take it and pry smiles on the faces
of all their griefs.

Vickie McBride
Forward And Forward
As I travel along this road
I feel as if I'm leaving life behind.
Or as if it is passing me by.
And although I feel a small thrill of the future,
I keep screaming "take me back,
Oh dear God, I wanna go home."
But still I go forward and forward.

Frances May Tauer
THE BOATMEN
I hear boatmen upon the river singing,
Their echoes shoreward flow;
While the sun'set on the waters cast
A radiant afterglow,. . .
Her streamers lay o'er the rippling stream,

A mingling pattern hold;
As the boatmen ply their homeward way
With oars dipped in gold!

Barabara Jean McGinley
SEPTEMBERS' END
Is it you I see standing there?
So silently before me, watching
Maybe waiting.
Come close, hold me in your arms
For september comes soon
With it's cool air returning
And the leaves begin falling
Bringing all the signs of Autumns' return.
Stay on 'til the leaves turn brown,
The birds build their home for winter
And the night air gets cool and quiet.
I know you must go soon too
And you'll no longer be before me.
But keep your heart always near
Beyond Septembers' End;
throughout the years.

Nancy Bartlett
THE LISTENING HEART
Lord, you gave me two eyes and two ears,
My brother's needs to see and hear,
But help me remember that's just the start.
Lord, teach me to listen with my heart.
When I listen with only my ear,
I limit myself in what I can hear.
Two ears, by themselves, can hear only the words,
Instead of the feelings that need to be heard.
So often, someone cries out in vain,
Expressing hurt or fear or pain.
When that happens, Lord, let me be there.
Let me truly hear! Let me show that I care!
Not long ago, I reached out with words,
Hoping my feelings might somehow be heard,
And you gave my life a brand new start.
You heard my prayer with your Loving Heart.
So help me today to be more like you.
Teach me to love and to listen, too,
Because hearing the words. . .Ah! That's only the start.
What my brother feels, I must hear with my heart.

Dottie Howell
SUNSHINE ON HIS WING
Heavy was my heart,
Weary were my eyes.
For days and days dark clouds
Had hidden bright blue skies.
Dare I look aloft?
Dare I try to sing?
Behold!
A rift! A bird!
With sunshine on his wing!

Bess S. Nixon
FULFILMENT
Music of motion in every glance
Deep in your eyes a glint of romance;
Soft winds blow a sigh
Stars shatter my cry
The moment I cease to be your toy
Entering the closeness of your silences!

Joyce Strother
MY SOUL DREAMS
Hidden from the rest of the world
Behind a closed and silent door
My Soul dreams of wonderful things
And flies on spreading, sun-lit wings.
Dreams of love and dreams of plenty
The dreams are as varied as they are many
Dreams of peace and dreams of joy
To me, Imagination is a toy.
Dreams of worlds no man has seen
Of skies tinted blue or yellow-green
Of galaxies and star systems far
Of planet 'round the Double Star.
Of races wise and races smart
Of races with more than one

heart
Of sights so wonderous and
serene
Alien sights no man has seen.
Yes, this my soul does dream
about
As it struggles to get out
To play beneath skies yellow or
blue
And hope it will, someday, come
true.

Carolyn Kimzey
AN INTERLUDE OF WIND
The wind
lumbers about in the pines
tossing them
like many waters
then settles down
to a roar.
It climbs zig-zag
to reach a siren sound—
one thin note piercing
the roof top,
continuing
for part of an hour.
Then comes a lull
and I hear voices in the wind,
voices of leisurely people on
bicycles
passing by my homeplace
talking to one another.
Then comes a stronger shock
and the voices become one
voice—
an evangelist calling to me
to be pure.
Another shock
and the voice is that of a
statesman
championing some great
cause.
They shout and argue in
strong shaking voices.
After punishing puffs all day
after descending
deliberate
drops,
the wind passes
and quietness
sits in the yard
and on the
roof top.

Jean Elizabeth Gibbs
FLIGHT
Oh, dear little bird
With wings that were my own,
Do not soar too far
From the nest of Home!
Soar into the sun and rain
And storm, with head held high.
Try your wings. Believe in them.
And sleep, when dusk draws
nigh.
But, perchance, some magic day
If some sore need may be,
Wing your pathway back again;
Come flying home to me!

Margaret Gibson Williams
MY DAD
When God was making mothers
of the best that he could find.
He stopped for just a moment
and he made that dad of mine.
He took an Irish humor,
then a more than generous heart
and a friendly disposition,
but that was just the start!
He took an optomistic nature
a spirit to be kind.
And he mixed them all together
and he made that dad of mine.

Lois Barton
I AM READY
The anemic winter sun has
drawn a ragged gray blanket
about his stooping shoulders
and gone early to bed.
Frost-shriveled garden greenery
cowers limply against the
skeletal corn.
Shades of night sidle slyly up
across the field.
There's a smell of rain in the
air.
But I am ready, waiting. Fresh-
baked bread.
A snapping fire. A gloom-
dispelling glow of light.
A smile.
The bright orange bus burns a
hole in the drear horizon,
flashing the good news of
children coming.
Skipping footsteps, cheery
chatter, banging doors.
Happy reprieve from another
day at school.
"Hi, Mom! I'm home. Um-m-m.
Can I have some bread?
I'm starving! I love you."
My heart rejoices in their
simple acceptance of my
waiting presence.
Today the bus drove by. It will
not stop here again.
Now my children bake the
bread, light the fire,
Kiss the bruises, absorb the love.
Eight of them once filled our
home, sharing our bread
and love with their friends.
Still, I am ready, waiting. When
the bread comes out of the
oven filling the house with
its 'welcome home!' fragrance,
I watch the road for the children
listen for their laughter.

Vera Joyce Nelson
ONE MAN WITH A HOE
My father watched
twin leaves of hope and promise
break the soil, reach for the
light.
He saw the stem swell
with a green-budding, urgent
dream.
His hoe shone from constant
use
as he cultivated his held dream,
the dream that held him.
As a child, I sensed
his independent stance,
his apartness.
I knew the price he paid
to cultivate his dream.
Five times he laid down his hoe,
and tramped to the ballot box.
He marked his convictions,
hoping his dream would root
for the good of all.
The mark of my father's pencil
was tallied across the nation,
along with a slim gleaning
from the electoral harvest.
It was scuffed aside
as unsubstantial chaff.
My father's hoe,
has fallen from his hand
and rusted out.
Yet, his dream flourished.
My father's sons,
grown gross
on the fruits of his dream,
carried chainsaws.
They drove bulldozers
across his acre.
They marched
to their voting booths
and punched holes
in my father's dream.

Joyce Ichter
GODS CREATIONS
Black and white go well
together,
Brown and white go even better.
Why can't we love one another?
He may be black, but he's still
your brother.
Say white brother, you just can't
win,
Being black—it's not a sin!
If it weren't for God you might
be him.
It's not whats out but just whats
in.
There are some men that are
red,
But very few of them aren't
dead.
We stole their land and liberty,
On reservations they weren't
free.
The yellow man with funny hair
My Mother takes the laundry
there.
We make fun of his skin and
eyes,
And sometimes of his little size.
But all are brothers in God's
sight.
We are all his children day and
night.
So please let's get it all together,
Love one another—you'll feel
better!

Anita Durand Buess
JUST DESERTS
Hear the screaming of the trees
Sharply axed from life profound
Crashing hard upon the ground.
Our hopes too, like shattered
leaves,
Flee before the drying breeze.
Swift the shifting sands have
come
After mountain torrents run
Carrying onward to the sea
Rich earth that nurtured you
and me.
No blade nor root to hold it
here.
The sand encroaches year by
year.
Here we huddle on this spot
Betwixt the roaring sandstorm's
burst
From yon desert burning hot
And the salty sea's strong thirst.
Not one cool cloud in the sky.
All of life must pass us by.

Vincent A. Corsall
TREE WRAPPED IN IVY
Who is your love, mighty oak?
Her tentacled fingers cling to
your brawn and lightly she
rests on your boughed
shoulders.
Your leafed head smiles down
and she embraces closer, As if
you were to part.
Her faint perfume whaffs the air
and envelopes you like
incense fumes about a Buddha
Altar.
'Tis many a year I have seen you
court her and I've often
thought and wondered
Who is your love, Mighty Oak?

Iola Martin
THE OLD WOODEN PADDLE
The old wooden paddle that Dad
carved by hand
was cut from the old oak tree,
And hung on a nail by the
kitchen stove
for all of us kids to see.
Now Dad, he was a God fearing
man
and only completed the third
grade in school,
But he would tolerate no
nonsense out of us kids,
And we were to abide by the
golden rule.

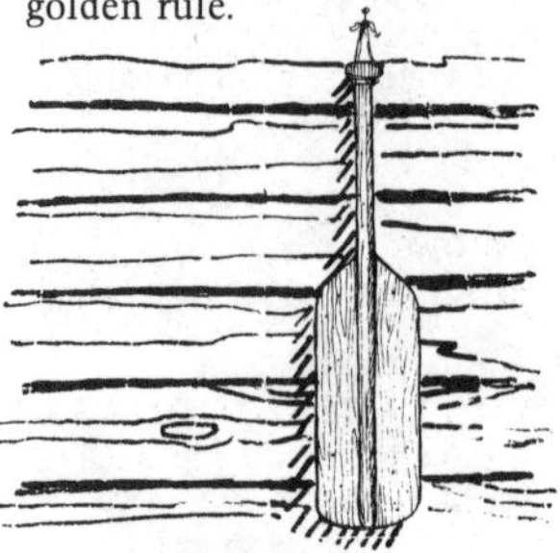

I remember the time I came
home from school
I had been fighting and my
clothes were all torn,
Dad took one look at me,
reached for the paddle
and marched me out to the
barn.
I was trembling and shaking as
he opened the barn door,
he looked like such a giant of
a man,
But my eyes filled with tears
when he sat me down,
and in a heart breaking voice,
he began.
Son, you're young now, but the
years go by fast,
and before you know it, you'll
be full grown,
So now while you're young, you
need to be taught,
that we will reap, just what
we have sown.
If you sow anger and meaness,
then that's what you'll get,
If you sow love, . . .it's
returned thrice fold,
And if you study the good book
a little more often,
you'll find that, that's what
we've been told.
Dad's shoulders trembled as he
hugged me close,
and as he gently patted my
head,
I made a promise to God up in
heaven
that I would heed these words,
he had said.
Many years have gone by now
and Dad is gone
but sometimes when I feel
forlorn,
I think of the wisdom my dear
Dad spoke,
That long ago day. . .in the
barn.

You see, Dad had never used the old wooden paddle
his heart was too filled with love,
For he received the wisdom to raise us kids,
From our Heavenly Father above.
The old wooden paddle now hangs by my stove,
and now my children too understand,
The wisdom that was molded from this piece of wood
That was carved by, . . . their grandfather's hand.

Anthony Frank Volpe
TWO FLAGS OF COURAGE
You have met your foe with heroic force
At your hands he died—was there remorse?

His only armour was his courageous heart
This you knew from the very start
He matched your courage with fierce aggression
Your practiced pirouettes were a survivor's obsession—
At times he would rally—you countered nontheless
With a tormenting red cloth—handled with ease and finesse!
Your valiant foe heard the crowd's deafening cheers—
Not for him! but for you—to cut off his ears!
Bleeding he charged wildly—doomed in his fortress
The crowd stood in awed—silence—their hero to bless!
You eyed him with caution—he scraped and roared
In defiance you unsheated your death—dealing sword!
His eyes now blazing—blurred with fury
You were one man alone—his judge and his jury!
Then came your moment—the sun cast you tall with intent
Swiftly, your sword entered its known angle, blade fully spent!
A thunderous ovation shook every stadium seat
As your foe rolled dead. . .in the dust. . .at your feet!

Patricia A. Janicke
OL' BOAT
The sunrise over the fantail
gives the water a golden tinge.
As the sky brightens, Ol' Boat appears as though
it were constructed of stainless steel.
Ever so slowly, the blanket of sleep is lifted.
Robe-clad individuals sleepily make their way to
the showers
While other occupants rush to their cars to embark
on another day's duties.
Boat motors begin to hum and move out toward the
channel.
Sea gulls circle and dip, looking for their first
daily tidbit.
Sail covers are removed, folded, and stashed
for later use.
Tall masts tack silently as they move toward
the harbor entrance.
Ever-widening boat wake ripples cause
Ol' Boat to rock gently in her mooring.
Gone are the days when Ol' Boat rushes to join
the parade to the open sea.
She is happy now to spend her days held tightly
by mooring lines.
Her weathered hull shows the lines of character
earned by fulfillment of task.
Her only duty is to offer shelter and security
to her occupants.
Ol' Boat is at peace with the world.

Deborah Benedict
FALLING IN LOVE AND OTHER MYTHS
Streets are the only friends I have—
be they city grey or country brown.
Walking down streets certainly beats
being buried in the ground.
Alone in the city
trying so hard to remember your directions.
Did you ever notice how the city lights
make your skin look bad?
And how the porno movie houses and ugly whores
make you feel so human and sad?
Well, you've lived here all your life
—You probably never felt this way.
"You got to change your evil ways."
The radio sings to me.
Allright I'll change my evil ways
if you show me
how you got on the radio.
Who is at my brain exciting thought
like seeds I never planted?!
Two question marks, not just one—
Absolute curiosity, true fun—
Let me creak this out
and leave more room for more doubt:
"Do I really fall in love
or am I just
wasting time
by treasuring dust?"

Margie R. Mullins
LITTLE CLIPPER
Oh 'twas a bright sun-shining day when the little ship left port,
To sail upon the quiet sea, just for fun and sport.
The little clipper was her name, such a lovely sight to see,
The little clipper left the port with a crew of only three.
But the clouds grew dark overhead and the thunder it did roar,
The waves tossed and slammed the little ship,
But the crew, they swam to shore.
Oh 'twas a sad, sad day for those who sat upon the shore.
They knew the cruel sea had taken her,
she'd not be seen no more

Mary Gillson Axtell
THORNGROVE
This House so peaceful,
This Land so green,
With flowers of life, so pure,
Withered hands, tend the earth,
No hope, of precious cure.
Misshapen Bodies,
Gentle Minds,
Like a scarecrow in a gale,
Tending animals, fragile kinds,
Find happiness prevail.
This house caters for young, and old,

Giving love to the dwellers here,
Attendants care, to physical needs,
Hope, abounds within this fold,
Eternity, brings no fear.
Sunlight shines, like speckled beads,
To stall the darkening showers,
Lord, please don't,
Neglect their needs,
Protect these carefree flowers.
Dedicated to the residents,
of Thorngrove, a home for the Handicapped.

Terry Jo Sather
THE GIFT
A boy was born very long ago,
so simply did He come,
That even some who saw Him
tho't no special thing was done.
But many who observed Him
and the other strange events,
Truly saw with seeing hearts
this was no coincidence.
He grew as any other boy, with
smiles and with tears,
He learned to build from Joseph
as He worked in younger years.
He thirsted more for knowledge
as His mission drew so near,
His work bench oft was empty—
the elders He went to hear.
And when the time was ready,
His family left behind,
He met John at the river, His
Father's will to bind.
He went among the people, His
love to them He gave,
He healed, blessed, and taught
them, the way He tried to pave.
Many heard Him rightly and
believed Him as He spoke,
Others listened shortly—then
considered Him a joke.
Those who shared His bed and
board and lived with Him three years,
Had one who was a traitor
among their very peers.
Jesus was handed to the jailer
without a trial set,
And beaten till His blood did
run, by a man He'd never met.
When they nailed Him to the
tree, and put Him with two thieves,
They laughed, mocked and
cursed Him and all His clothes they seized.
When the hour had arrived that
He'd achieved His Father's goal,
He asked for God's forgiveness
for each and every soul.
The love that Jesus showed us
every hour that He lived,
Is the same today as yesterday
and still freely does He give!
What to do with this unwrapped
gift that comes without tape or ribbon?
All you need is to believe and
you will be forgiven.
For Christmas isn't money, or
goodwill and peace to man,
It's God's heart loving me, and
accepting just the way I am.

Doris C. Olson
REMEMBERING
The sun has gone
Beyond the misty, barren hills;
Too soon has come
Foreboding night;
Remembrance chills
Me to the bone,
Enshrouds with fear,
A deepening dread instills.
Long years ago
Before we set this rendezvous,
You could not know
Our love would end
In black despair,
And vows made then
Are that part of you
That I go on remembering.

Dorothy Fay Tolbert
MY CHILD
Why be a Doctor?
There are other ways to eat
Being a Doctor Means touching
people
Sometimes even their feet
After a short time you'll start

to retreat
People come to the office with suffering and pain
Why don't we give them rules of the game?
Plan 1 could be Polio, plan 2 could be pain and ect.
Put your card in the machine is the name of the game.
No touching or talking, save all of your time
But if you want a speech let me be your man, (or woman)
At a synposium, why I'm just grand
How I love to tell people how to treat their ills
Be kind and considerate, Loving, Loyality the rule of the land!
That's what I preach each time that I teach
But don't come to my office
I just don't have the time
Practicing and preaching are two different rimes
One I can handle the other is new
Maybe someday we will learn how to touch you too
And understanding for all mankind
A Doctor you certainly never had to be
I'm sure it was by your choice not given by me. . .

John Anthony Sausedo

A FOREST SONG

Children of the forest,
Spirit of the trees.
What magic spell awakes you?
Whose wisdom makes you breathe?
On moonlit summer evenings,
I come to watch you dance.
Join in your rejoicing,
Partake in your romance.
Great guardian of the Forest,
Protector of the Trees.
Your magic home enchants me,
Let me be like the Trees.
Let me be like the Trees. . . .

Daniel Douge'

FREE

FREE
freedom
free
to be free
to be free from hate
free from envy
free from jealousy
from egotistic desires
free from conceit
from egotistic pride
to be free
free
freedom
freedom to love
and to be loved
in humility
and dignity
freedom
FREE

Mary Ann Buford

DISSOLUTION

We met that day
For our dissolution
The air was heavy
with pollution
there was no chance
of diminution
To separate was
The only solution.
I put our marriage
Out of commission
But my very own
Sins of omission
I stood and cried
My act of contrition
Which brought about
Reconciliation.
We both took part
In the reformation
She has my heart
In any confrontation
I believe in marriage
And its institution
I want love—
Not dissolution.

Judy Anne Shuck

DISCOVERY

I cherish the endless hours
We shared together,
Cried together,
And laughed together;
Moments when emotional impacts
Brought us closer,
Created inseparable times
When we knew
that our moods harmonized
To the point of oneness;
Moments when reality
Needed no reproof,
Because truth was unimpeachable;
And we were aware,
We recognized
We understood.

Mary Ann Coleman

PASSAGE

(for Emily Dickinson)

Even the summer air in Amherst
could chill her speculative bones.
Her words like the weather were crisp, fixed with precision
though she never learned the personal names of sin.
Her goblin song burst her narrow room and kitchen,
her ordered passion flooded each page.
That spirit like the violets on her coffin
proved death a sacrilege.

Joe Yannarella

Nothing Lasts Forever

Running in the open road under the warm night.
Feeling like a bird flying in the sky.
Nothing to be in need.
Unchained and free.
Stopped at a craggy tree.
Catching a breeze.
My initials are carved in the bark.
So is my ex.
Leaves crying in the dark.
Look emotionally at the stars.
Wonder how long they'll last.
Life must come and go.
The environment will change.
Nothing can stay the same.
Nothing lasts forever.
Not even my love for you.
The earth spins now.
But the axis will stop.
Everything that touches the earth must come and go.
The sun will withold its flame.
Nothing will stay the same.
Nothing lasts forever.
Not even my love for you.

Paul D. Moss

FEBRUARY MICHIGAN BLIZZARD

The elements are awesome today;
the sky is winter gray,
the ground is Donner white.
Flakes forming whirlpools
acting as servants of the wind.
The white stars each cast their own parachute
as they land softly, one atop the other.
And then, just as aquaintances have been made,
that nasty gust of piercing cold knives
slices into the newly laid foundation,
deciding that the soft, innocent flakes belong elsewhere.
White-feathered hills slowly build,
with the top layer taking the credit
for the wonderland beauty—
Yes, the bottom folks smile, because
the sun will shine in a day,
and the top's smiles will
melt away
to nothing.
Somewhere beyond this February storm
is a rainbow.
No pot of gold at the end, though.
Instead, the songs of birds,
the buds of flowers, the green needles
of grass,
and the sunshine of Spring.
So close, yet so distant. . .
Oh! The dreams of winter's long days,
if only Mother Nature let me have a say.
The bare trees beckon for help,
and winter smiles back through
the picture window.

Dennis Myers

NIZHONI

The winter green, of a growing pine;
Bare arms of aspen, that intertwine,
Share the sun of a winters day,
When springtime seems not far away.
The snow, from a long forgotten storm,
Remains to chill, predict, and warn,
Of others coming from the sky,
On Future days, when clouds are nigh.
A silence, in this scene pervades,
The beauty of these mountain days;
Where rabbit, squirrel, elk and deer,
Can live in peace, and call home here.
For man was not invited hence,
To bar the field with board of fence,
As this land of trees, and sky, and sod;
This place of beauty, is a gift from God.

Rev. Ross H. L. Bowen

THE DIVINE CAT

I wonder if Jesus, while here on this earth
Had a little pet cat, or a kitten from birth;
A calico, tabby, or an all-over grey
Would have lightened His burdens on every day.
I'm sure if He did, that little cat knew
"This Man is Jesus, the King of the Jews.
He won't leave me lonely, or even unfed
As long as He lives."—that's what the cat said!
Oh, what an honour for a feline friend
To be here with Jesus, from beginning to end!
How glad she would be to follow the Man
From hither to yon, all over the land.
I guess that He didn't, for why would our Lord
Not have mentioned His little pet cat in His Word?
To show that a man could have such a pet
Whether he stayed at home, or wherever he went.
And why would He pray in the garden, alone,
Since from the disciples our Saviour had gone,
When He could hear the purr of His little cat
To ease tension, and soothe Him, wherever He sat?
No, I'm sure that He didn't, or e'er would have been
At the side of my Saviour, no matter the scene;
When He rode into town and was welcomed with palms,
Or He stood at the ocean and ordered it calm.
Then on that sad morning Jesus went to the cross
Would have followed along, ne'er forsaking her "Boss;"
And on that day which was so filled with gloom,
His little cat would have guarded His tomb.
But when He arose, as had been prophesied,
Then, only then, would this kitten have died.
The reason? Just one, it would have to be Love,
And she would have followed our Saviour above!
If you have a cat, then I'm sure

you can say
How much your pet means to
you from day to day.
And I guess you can tell what
it would have been worth
When Jesus was here, below, on
this earth!

Doris A. Rieth

TIGER

My body is a cage in which a
tiger does rage, when he
grumbles around and begins to
pace, it makes my insides start
to race, and if you look really
close you can see him passing
through my face.
Sometimes he is so quiet I begin
to think he has left this place,
but when I get sad he starts to
get mad, and ever so slowly he
begins to pace, back and forth
his feet start to race, he runs in
a circle his tail almost touches
his face, he goes on and on till
his feet start to bleed, and he
falls in exhaustion sleep his
only need.
It makes me hurt, and makes me
feel sad to know this world has
never had a place for my tiger or
me. So he will go on through
eternity, making his hopeless
unending race. Over and over he
will try to see, never realizing
this world has no place for him
to be free.

Cay Griffin Lynch

CHANGE

Like a young high spirited mare
Who roams the open plains
In the springtime of life with
head in the wind
Waving uplifted mane.
And a rider or two upon it's
back
Who bends with stirrups low,
I have known the freedom of
such a run,

And felt my heart aglow;
But I've found another traveler
Who now keeps by my side,
And He quietly leads me
onward
In a softer, gentler stride.
As the patient donkey
watchfully
Listens with ears outstretched
While his master straightens the
path for him,
I walk; He does the rest.

John David Fordyce

IN MEMORY OF

(Written in memory of those who lost their lives in the Spanish Civil War 1936.)

Los soldados esta'n marchando—
Por las calles esta'n caminando;
La guerra les esta' esperando—
Por los que nunca van a volver.
Sobre los balcones asomando,
Las madres quedan mirando
A sus jo'venes pasando—
A aquellos que van a morir.
Rough Translation:
The soldiers are marching—
Through the streets they are
walking;
The war is waiting for them—
For those who will never return.
Leaning over the balconies,
The mothers remain, watching
Their young ones passing—
Those who are going to die.

Michael R. Collings

SEA SWELLS

Damp and streaks
coagulated blood
grey glittering blood
along his thigh
Gulls skitter along waves
cormorants perch like vultures
on rock cliffs bleached
with excrement
A crab sidles forward pinchers
tear minute strands of flesh
and waves wipe away
sand to let the blood
run red.
Hungry, the ocean
eats warm sand
beneath my feet, and
drinks dampness
crusting on my legs.
I taste of salt, as
if prepared for the evening
meal. And the archaic ocean
tries to
re-ingest elements
which rested once quiescent in
its womb.

Melissa L. Whetstone

WHEN HE COMES

When he comes it will be ever
so softly,
no one will know that he's
there.
He'll speak and the children will
listen,
for his words will dry their
tears.
He'll bring strength and
understanding,
never knowing how they care.
Happiness will soon take over,
their minds relieved of all
fears.
He'll be praised for his words
by the children,
but only in quiet remote.
They'll cherish the thoughts of
his wisdom,
as if to just them he spoke.
He'll leave and not hear their
praises,
nor see what he left behind,
but deep in the hearts of the
children,
he'll be loved throughout all
time.

Debbie Fowler

SECRET SADNESS

The rain that falls outside my
window
Is like the rain falling inside
me
No one really cares to know
No one will worry for my
destiny
The day drags by forever it
seems
The clocks tick is all just noise
to me
My haven is the only place
Where I will ever want to be
The old and faded furniture
The dark painting the wall bears
This is the place I will always
come
To shed my sadden tears
The days have gone by slowly
since
I first lurked in the shadows
Old books never read, old lamps
never lit
The tracings of days and long
long agos
Maybe someday I can tell
My story to the world in view
But until that day I'd rather tell
To a trusted confident like you

Rose E. LaMon

THE STORM

The lightning waves
A blazing baton,
The ocean thrums
A huge bass drum;
The rip tide beats
A sharp staccato,
The rolling sands
A piccolo.
The winds they play
The wild violins,
The gulls scream out
The chorus;
The clouds their banners
Fling on high,
The thunder roars
A vast approval.
The Heavens then
Will open wide;
The storm sweeps
Wildly over.
The lightning's magic
Will be gone,
The ocean
Will not roar.
The tide will
Drift out to the sea,
The rolling sands
Be still.
The winds will
Sing a lullaby,
The gulls will
Silent be.
The clouds will
Leave the evening sky,
The thunder grumble
Far away.
A weepy moon
Light up the sea;
The storm will
Pass on by!

M. J. Keeler

I SAW YOU PASS

I saw you pass the other day,
And I recalled the love we'd had;
I can still hear you say,
"I'll always love you, Dear."
Yet, here I stand, all alone,
Almost like a lighthouse
That stands abandoned, and
overgrown
With weeds, needing a ship to
guide.
You left me last May,
While I was at work.
I'll never forget that day.
I only wish you'd told me.
But, you decided to leave a note,
instead.
I read it, and cried.
"I've found someone new," it
said,
"And I love him more than I
love you."
You'd made your decision,
And you left your ring
In the kitchen,
As though it belonged there,
with me.
That was six months ago.
Yet, it seems like yesterday,
And seeing you again was quite
a blow
To my almost shattered heart.

Ellen L. Hoppe

NATURE'S PRECIOUS REMINDER

The first blustery day of winter,
Its wild winds whipping through
the barren trees,
And dark gray clouds roaming
across the skies,
Stirs within me precious
memories long gone.
All barriers of adulthood
removed,
I am briefly overcome with an
aching emptiness.
A void soon soothed by
reflections of a carefree time,
Simple, yet splendid.
I am child-like and innocent
once more.
Secure in the warm embrace of
family.
Nature's precious reminder
keeping constant in my heart,
Blessings of the past. . .
How deeply I long for home.

Daniel Laird Jeffers

THE ROAD BACK TO THE GROUND

I see that I'm alive now
Theres none other thought in
mind
But how did I get here and who
am I behind
On the road back to the ground
I see it stretch near, why did I
give up Love, Pot, and Beer.
Who lives for love, who for hate;
How far must we go to get to
heavens gate
On the road back to the ground
Are we the only world around?
Lets look at the stars, each a
sun in itself
Are people there thinking of us
Or the road back to the ground
Don't give up now tomorrow
will be here soon,
Lets wait and see if it be
good for both you and me
Or maybe the road back to the
ground.

Marciana A. Sevandal

THE BIRTH OF CHRISTMAS

"Aeons ago," so the story goes,
"A glorious darling baby lay,
Snugly wrapt in tattered bands,
In a manger warm with hay."
Foretold by those prophets of
old
The King of Kings was to be
born,
Among the hills in Bethlehem,
More resplendent than stars
and moon.
The Heavenly host with joyful
songs,

Heralded these tidings of love:
"Peace and good will! To you is born,
A holy child, gift from above."
A lone bright star shining on high,
Stood still o'er the holy child,
Leading the three Kings from afar,
To the infant and mother mild.
Off'ring his gift of purest gold,
Gladdened and charmed by this Holy Birth,
The first King gave His blessed wish:
"You will be King of heaven and earth."
The second with frankincense rare,
Divine symbol of spiritual grace,
Exclaimed: "Peoples from far and near,
Will lavish you their love and praise."
The third, with bitter myrrh exclaimed:
"Your crucifixion ends the strife;
But dying—you destroy man's death,
And rising—restore his life."
Symbol of God's redemptive love,
For our world of sin and sorrow
This lowly birth in a stable,
Foretold a gladsome morrow.
And so was born glad Christmas,
We await with hope and fervor,
For it ushers light, and life, and love,
For almighty God and neighbor.

David L. Thomasson
HOMECOMING (I LOVE YOU)

It was your step,
upon the threshold,
my heart stopped,
for a moment,
anticipating,
until the door filled,
with your smile,
your eyes so swift,
to find my face,
your laugh which followed,
my heart.

Jeffrey Beaudoin
THE BUM

He walks the night in lonely haste,
Through streets of black and garbage waste,
He is not happy because his life,
Was full of sadness and of strife.
He settles down at a silent place,
Telling himself it's his private space.
He looks around for things to eat,
When shoes are needed on his feet.
He is not far from death at all,
For at any moment he may fall.
He may not seem a likely sort,
To live in a castle, a kingdom, a fort.
He ends his life in liquor pools,
And goes away an honest fool.

Frances Koehner
FOR MARC

On our last day of vacation
On our last day
We beachcombed a strip of sand
Treasured with sea buffed glass
In the golden hush of afternoon's ebb
I knew joy at our son's enchantment
And peace at your nearness
But such a rare time
When the soul sings
In a floodtide of love
Can never be repeated
I learned it is an ending
And must last the rest of a lifetime
My lifetime.

Katherine Perham
THE RACE

Some tenseness in the atmosphere around
A scene of competition well in hand
Participants they come to make a stand
With sinking faith they seek the courage. . .SOUND!
And free themselves from bonding blocks of ground
Their silent cries of striving might demand
The triumph over clammy brow and band
A leader overcomes, his conflict crowned
Their multitude of public madly cheers
Exalted victor, silence rules him now
What lies beyond the fallen, broken tape?
A conquered track whose hero douses fears
But more, a loser at the line he scowls
—Defeat—its definition hard to shape

Bertie Hodnett Goodwin
CABLE T.V.

Listen my children! And you shall hear
Why everyone's happy now that cable is here.
Run out of your house and take a quick gander up high.
There's no ugly antenna sticking out toward the sky.
Look all around you and no landlord you'll see
He's sitting inside watching Cable T.V.
Look at your car parked quietly nearby
With a tankful of gas you may use bye and bye
The tires are all up because you've not been around
Bumping all of the potholes in the streets around town.
Turn on channel 11 and on your cable you'll see
How distinguished and honorable your Congressmen be.
And even their colleagues are honorable too.
Complementing each other is all that they do.
I've had a ball as you must plainly see
Since I signed up for my Cable T.V.

Vickie Chambers
I LOVE PEOPLE

People walking to an fro,
Others wondering where to go,
What to do and when;
Such is the turbulence of men.
In this day of outer space,
Speed essential, we must face;
Holiday trips to the moon,
New excitement coming soon.
Past incentives done gone by,
We are brothers, you and I;
Those of you easy to peeve,
Remember our parents, Adam and Eve.

Pat (Webb) Snadon
TWO FRIENDS

(Dedicated to Shawna In Memory of Teresa Gibson 1962-1981)

When we first met Teresa, she was three years old. . .
With eyes of blue and hair of gold!
We moved in the house across the street. . .
And our "Two young ladies" were anxious to meet!
They stayed in their yards. . .
They both were so shy. . .
I wonder which one found the nerve to say "Hi"!

But that was the day their friendship began. . .
And it grew through the years, without any plan. . .
It was just as natural as breathing in air. . .
To know that the "Other" would always be there. . .
To share their joys and share their tears. . .
In a friendship made to last through the years!
There were many new friends in store for the "Pair". . .
Because love and friendship are made to share!
But that "Special Bond" between the two. . .
Always brought them back just to say, "How are you?"
They both grew so well in beauty and love. . .
With a love for their "Heavenly Father" above!
To watch them grow has been such a pleasure. . .
With so many memories to keep and to treasure!
One friend is gone now. . .her mission complete. . .
She walks with her "Father" and sits at his feet. . .
One friend is left to go on with her life. . .
With all of the joys and all of the strife. . .
Their paths have been parted for whatever God's reason. . .
But love and friendship know no season. . .
And someday the "Bond" between the two. . .
Will bring their paths back together to say, "How are you?"
I know when that time comes, they'll neither be shy. . .
But I wonder which one will be first to say "Hi"!!

Samuell L. Simkins
A VIOLET OR A ROSE

Now do you suppose
a violet would pose
beside a beautiful Rose?
I suppose heaven only knows
but I am sure that it's true
a Violet would be very blue
posing beside a Rose.
Yes I am sure that it's true.
my favorite color is blue.
but what am I to do?
a beautiful Rose by my side too
I wish I knew just what to do
I know that it's true
Roses are very beautiful too
Roses of many colors that's true
most Violets stay a faithful blue
Which of the two should I choose?
I think I know the best thing to do.
Keep looking for a Rose that's blue.
I suppose a beautiful Rose would do
Yes just as long as it was blue.
Red Rose. . .do you suppose
if I would propose you would be willing?
Willing to be my own beautiful Rose.
Would you be willing? Care then.
Care then to be my Rose of Sharon?

John Lloyd Day
POETS ARE DANGEROUS

They can make you see things in a different light.
They can change you, almost overnight. Fill you with fright?
But where would we be, without poets? Cavemen or machines.
Sleepy contemplations. . .poets are dangerous. . .
Metaphorical visionillusionaryoidals I am. I am.
Death acts fast, on an empty stomach, when using poison. Of the soul.
Call it mentalgraphics, labels all they are.
Rythmatic stereotypics. . .Poets are dangerous. . .
Can can't cat call in words you don't understand. Comprehend.
Revealing life's realizations with words. Why with words?
Why not more with sounds? All these questions answerable.
Cerebralogics pabadabrian. . .

Poets are dangerous. . .
One word doesn't seem to want
to describe this correctly.
Thus the universal utilization
of multiword blats.
Monumentaloid, zeba!
Mongrelmentalics makes the
word you use sound logics.
Spacepuke from another realm
of regurgitation.
Scraprollbased chili pods
spewing enevitably skyward.
Can you speak a rule so far that
is bent to nonexistency?
Questions.
Saprophylic mammallian hordes,
relying on faith. Thin spate.
Corrals of mores, Heteral
amour'e. Conglomerate
spaztisizm.
Here I have attacked for you a
few importances of life.
I played with your channels, but
I hope I didn't twist the knobs
off.
See how poets can be dangerous?
(and they don't even need. . .
an electric typewriter)

Chee

THE SEED

Floating in life's endless sea,
So small and insignificantly.
Millions of others pass me by,
Never still yet never to die.
I long to know when I'm to pass;
To rest and begin my destined
task;
Growing ever so strong and
secure;
Knowing someday my chance
will endure.
Shall I be one, maybe two or
three;
The same, or just the opposite
of me.
Will I see those that went
before,
Or be alone, no less, no more.
I feel a surge of drawing force,
Holding, following, the same
course.
A flicker of life engulfs my
being,
At last, to rest, to grow,
beseeching.
Now, wondering, alone, warm
and nourished,
Developing, aging, rapidly
flourished;
A feeling of escape besieges my
will.
I see, I feel, myself be still.

Elizabeth Russell

ENOUGH

Standing alone,
The wind whistling by.
Words come to mind—
Desolate, lonely, deserted.
Miserable, isolated words
Of loneliness and longing.
I look up at the sky;
And my mind reaches
For a twinkling star.
I stand alone
In a desolate wasteland,
But lonely no longer.
The star does not find
Comfort or companionship
In me—it knows not
Of my existence.
It doesn't have to.
I am content.
Content to have it there
Above me, unaware
Of my existence.
My castles are all
In the air, where I
Will never reach them.
Others do not understand.
They say, "But it's so much
Better to have no castle
Than one you'll never reach."
But I find it far better
My way than theirs.
I may dream impossible dreams,
But at least I have a dream.
I hope far beyond hope,
But still I hope.
I pray for miracles
Others find impossible.
Yet some day I may
Reach my star,
Live in my airy castle,
My dreams may come true,
My prayers may be answered.
Nothing is impossible.
And if nothing comes
From all of this,
At least it was there
In my mind.
The unreachable star
Gave me comfort.
And for me,
That will be enough.

Mary Anne Miller

FAVORITE SITE

Rushing waters,
Cool, fresh breeze
Whisp'ring softly through the
trees.
Picture mountains,
Lofty, high;
Rising toward the clear, blue
sky.
Red hot embers,

Acrid smoke;
Roasting hot dogs. Happy folk.
Tents and table,
Gas light, stove,
Food, and ice, for those who
rove.
Sleeping bags
Laid out with care
For the one's who're camping
there.
Scene of joy
And peaceful find;
Leaving rush and cares behind.

Mayna Bode Hoke

OUR LIFE

A rich full life is ours
And one to live with singing
heart,
We have a home where children
play,
And Peace warms her heels
around our hearth.
I count my treasurers every one
As by your side I lie to sleep,
And desire covers me like a
deep, warm coat,
And life is full and rich and
sweet.

W. Scott Muller

SURVIVAL

If there come a time
When I die.
Please wait until after;
Please?
Time will cease,
Life will end.
Day won't dawn,
Night won't morn.
All at peace the world will lie;
This will happen the day I die.
Throughout my life,
I have seen;
Many people,
few alive;
All function,
few survive.
Computers come,
and they will go,
But humans
are the biggest ones of all.
All at peace the world will lie;
This will happen the day I die.
Death is setting on the earth,
No one cares,
(maybe they should),
This be done in my name;
alone.
For in the end, I shall be;
alone.

Edward H. Henckler

OUR GOD

Our God is faithful, to his own,
In daily care and blessings,
shown,
He is not slack, but freely gives,
To all his children who for him
lives.
He weeps for those, who go
astray,
And beckons them, return and
stay,
Within the fold, there's room for
all,
Yes: all who heed, his loving
call.
Our God: is with us, to the end,
Ready always, our hurts to
mend,
He see's the helplessness, we
feel,
And seeks, our many woes, to
heal.
Yes: God, is faithful, mans,
truest friend
And all, who seek him trust
him, find him so.
He will not forsake any who, on
him, depend,
But keeps all, who seek his
salvation to know.

Alberta L. Grim

AMERICA

Bells ring it
Children sing it
Old folks hum it
Guitars strum it.
America
We all love it
Flags fly above it
Soldiers salute it
Brass horns toot it.
America
Wars were fought for it
Land was bought for it
Blood was shed for it
Much can be said for it.
America
A price was paid for it
A flag was made for it
A leader was raised for it
Our God be praised for it.
America

Gene Williamson

FAREWELL

Still sea, lingering embrace,
fireworks excite the night,
summer's end,
and she's gone.
Ocean's surf in my head
floods the mind, quiets the soul.
My heart reaches out
to specks of light winking at me
from the black September sky.
I am not alone.

Gloria D. Alkire

THE CROP DUSTER

He's a dare-devil flyer, who
flies with the wind;
On a clear day or cloudy, you'll
find him above
The treetops, the houses,
swinging low to the ground—
He's a crop duster and he flies
with the dove!
The wings that he flies are
graceful and sleek;
He circles wide and comes
zooming low.
As he glides just above the
fields so green—
He's a crop duster, helping the
crop to grow!
He tips his wings and soars high
in the sky,
As carefree and elegant as the
birds that soar.
And just when I think he is out
of sight—
Down he comes with a great
rushing roar!
To fly as a bird is magic it
seems,
But I would rather be here on
the ground.
Though he goes with the wind
and precision's his name—
He's a crop duster, and will soon
be homeward bound!
I salute you, crop duster,
you're one of a kind;
Keep your wings flying high in
the air.
Keep your hand on the throttle,
your foot on the pedal—
May your landings be smooth
and your journeys fair!

Francis C. Spataro

WILL O' THE WISP

Love's like
the heron
ethereal
one with
a place
from afar,
dead swamp

trunk
stone or damp
foliage,
enticing when
near and
magnetic,
gone if
a move
stirs the air:
ephemeral star.

Jose L. Munoz
REAGAN THE ACTOR
Reagan the actor
A major factor
In the presidency
Was runover by a tractor in late
83
But there is a curse,
That's how you come to see
It just had to be

Don Saunders
MAN OR GOD?
Time has stopped,
the world is dead.
One man ended it by losing his
head.
No more trees,
no more grass,
there was nothing left after the
blast.
God created earth,
a place for man to thrive.
One man ended earth,
made it a place to die.
One may wonder,
which of the two is stronger?
Man, who can destroy,
or God,
whose creation is no longer.

John Michael Giberson
60'S CHILD
Born in a moral depression
Weaned in an economic
recession
Rised in a standards revolution
Schooled among the people's
polution
Stripped, violated and surpressed
Overpowered in the panacea
unrest
Precocious development of the
mind
Rankle the rational, in a
troubled time
When you look at me what do
you find?

Joseph Wehrly
UNCHARTED NO MORE ARE THE MOONBEAMS
Uncharted no more are the
moonbeams
our Eagle has landed today;
And brave men, elite of our
space teams
are mapping Tranquility Bay!
Together the world had been
striving
through tension and danger
we know;
For Eagle on wings thus arriving
for mooring on moondust
below!
Now out on the moon with
elation
so small the first footsteps for
man;
But giant the leap for creation
as moonlit horizons they scan!
And President's call ever
praising
receives a salute from our
men;
As samples they gather still
gazing
and board the great Eagle
again!
This team led the world here by
Heaven
while humble before God
therein;
For prayers and the Sacred
Unleaven
were food for that mission to
win!
And stemming the wind of the
solar
our Flag planted there by the
brave;
On landscape less life and less
color
through stillness eternal shall
wave!
Then liftoff for rendezvous,
docking
as round in moon orbit they
swing;
To transfer when final the
locking
and homeward for splashdown
they wing!
Uncharted no more are the
moonbeams
farewell to our Eagle on high;
And proud at attention each star
seems
saluting as valor goes by!

Debbie Smith
MOMMIES AND DADDIES
Mommies come from little girls
Daddies from little boys
Mommies yell and scream a lot
Daddies spank and punish
Mommies have to stay home
and cook
Daddies get to play golf
Mommies get fat and ugly
Daddies exercise and stay slim
Mommies stay home and get
drunk
Daddies get drunk at parties
I'm a little girl
When I grow up
I'm going to be a daddy

Lynda Lee Dickson
LIFE'S RULE
For every time sadness befalls
me,
An equal share of happiness
follows;
For this is the way life should
be.

Anne Bruye're Bishop
ON ATTAINING IMMORTALITY
We were all created for
immortality
This we early learned with sure
serenity.
Birth and death and the time in
between
Are but phases until we will
have seen
Our ultimate victory in
Heaven's bliss,
We were ever faithful enough
not to miss.
How well we follow our
Creator's design
Depends on the environment we
make by the sign
Of our good will, activities,
and relaxed poise,
Our eternal faith in the stillness
without noise,
So that the infallible victory
becomes ours,
Through our cherished love of
celestial powers.
Then we continue onward to
divine reality,
Knowing that God set the time
and place in eternity.
With ardent faith, hope, and
charitable motives,
Our time on earth spent in
perpetual votives,
Toward the Almighty our purest
union proclaim,
The new earth and the new
heaven in His Name!

Miss Regina A. Diaz
THE PRODIGAL
Tears are falling down her
cheeks,
A son who has been gone for
weeks
Has torn her heart and left her
pale,
She'll look for him o'er hill
and vale.
Tears are falling down his
cheeks,
A mother's love he's missed for
weeks,
What he looked for was not
there—
For what can with a home
compare?
Down the dusty road he
staggers,
His conscience pricked with
many daggers—
Soon his arms are 'round his
mother,
For him there truly is no other.

Ercell H. Hoffman
WE'LL BE TOGETHER AGAIN
O stars above please let me
know
am I insane to want him so?
From the time we first did meet
I knew my heart was his to
keep.
In all the years he was away
my heart so little did go astray.
And when he's near I still do
hear
my heart beat strongly—my
love, my dear!
And when time itself will for
us cease to be
somewhere together we'll be—
I and Thee.
O stars above only you can
know
when this want within will be
no more.

Effa Alexander—Roseboom
BLEAK DARKNESS
The Artic region's frigid air
Could cause despair,
Yet Eskimos
Wear heavy clothes
Of furry skins to brave the cold
Like days of old,
With dogs and sled,
In search of bread!
Their huts are built of blocks
of ice,
Well-made, and nice.
Those hardy souls
Have proved their goals!

Shirley Bovay Phillips
LISTEN, MY CHILD
Listen, my child, and you shall
hear,
Divine instruction in your ear.
Fear, sorrow and anger take their
toll,
In all the times and customs of
old.
They need not be means to
destroy,
Unless you let them take away
inner joy.
For they can be used to win,
The peace we seek without and
within.
It is in accepting life as it is,
And not as we wish it was.
Listen, my child, and you shall
hear,
Divine instruction in your ear.
Act on it with all faith and
humility,
And leave the outcome to the
Almighty
It has been said we keep only,
That which we give away freely,
May you find true love in your
heart,
That gives life its real
start.
It was first given for us to use,
Accept and share it, and not
abuse.

Emelia H. Mishler
WHITE BUTTERFLY
How happy am I
In this paradise of mine
The sun is shining
And the sound of the birds
Chirping on the green trees
And the flowers are in bloom
Under the wide clear blue sky
Oh you beautiful white
butterfly

Come and give me the happy
news
And refresh my heart deep
inside
You are so beautiful and light
Fluttering on the flowers
Like a dancing ballerina
From side to side
Do not tease me come and sit
by me
And give me the good news
From my beloved family

Vera Lorene Dazey

FAIR DREAMS

Ah, sleeping princess, in thy dreams,
Dost thou ride in days of old,
Upon swift, fleeting, noble steeds
Before knights, both brave and bold?
Wilt they carry thee swift away
To fair lands beyond the sun,
Where love shines bright as light of day
And sweet, valiant deeds are done?
Sweet child, in all thy innocence,
Wake not, I bid thee, dream on. .
And I wouldst gladly share thy dream
But for morning breaking yon.

Linda J. Smithers

YOU'RE RIGHT

If you think that I married you,
Because I had no place else to go,
You're Right,
No place else to go,
Was anywhere without you.
If you think that I stay with you,
For the material things you can give me,
You're Right,
It's satin and lace,

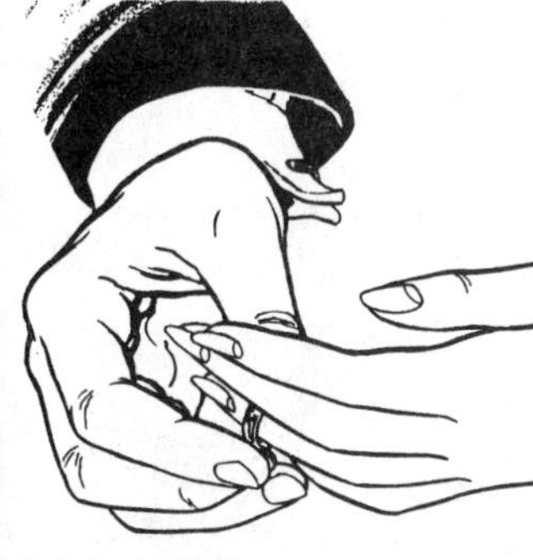

When we embrace.
If you think that I am often,
Attracted to other men,
You're Right,
As a magnet to steel,
Cool and impersonal.
If you think that I may sometimes wish,
Our love-making were over,
You're Right,
Over and over and over again.
And if you think that I no longer love you,
More or less,
You're Right,
For I love you More than I did yesterday,
And Less today,
Than I surely will tomorrow.

June Rainey

LET ME BE ME

I need to write a letter
But who do I write it to
Of the things I don't
Of the things I do
Someone who will listen
Without a smirk or smile
Who will understand
While I talk
Just for awhile
Someone to share
The stress and the pain
Just to feel free
Lively again
Someone to extend
Out their hand
Let me
Be me
Just as I am

Margaret Waddell Peters

HEART—SEEING

As you gaze out through the window
Do you see just blades of grass
Or can you envision raindrops
Joining sunbeams as they pass?
Lithe and supple, tiptoe dancing
Up and down the whole front lawn,
Manufacturing green knifelets,
Spreading carpet, each new dawn?
Life is not mere surface looking,
Seeing first what meets the eye;
True delight comes from heart-seeing,
Knowing deeply where and why.

D. Michelle Adkerson

INCOMPLETE

Somewhere this night
A quiet soul sleeps
Unsoundly
Conscious of his own incompleteness,
Unaware that he has passed me by
Many a day
In this little cell
Where I watch for him,
Blinded his thoughts against me
Though I linger in the shadows
Of the hay-filled structure
He touches to pastoral canvas.
The flowers know me, but
He does not hear my name in their faint whispers
Though he kneels close
To taste their delicate perfumes.
Tonight
Dreams repeatedly awaken him
To a loneliness
He had not realized
But will endure.

Doris E. Spillman

ODE TO LIFE

The earth is showing green again,
Winter has lifted her sleeping face.
Mother nature has been working hard,
Her wonders, she does with such grace.
Let us gaze at the grandeur of the towering oak.
The beauty of the tiniest flower.
A carpet of green snuggled around their feet,
With the fulfillment of rain in His power.
Now that all this life is showing,
Does your own seem to be lacking the touch?
What can you do to rejuvenate—
And make yours equally as much?
Advertently, we seek all life can give,
Making ready for the opportune time.
Happiness surrounds each and every hour,
All the meanings of life so sublime.
Rejoice in those long bounding hours,
For the sunshine can so quickly slip away.
With the burden of sorrow overflowing,
As the clouds seem ever to stay.
Again there will be a great sunburst,
You will be warmed to your very soul.
With the fervor and zest for the future,
At long last attaining your goal.
As the winter of life closes around you,
And you've reached that highest rapport.
Will God give the strength to sustain thee,
Take your being from this worldy shore?
Long after the epitaph has been written,
When the memories are on the wane,
The sun will still be shining,
O'er the life on this earthly domain.

Gordon Newton

NANNIE DEAR

Grandson first was I
Great grand daughter first I gave
Great great grandson first has she
What a dear Nannie is she
My heart so filled with memories past
Of weekends spent, the memories last
I've heard her called by Mother dear
I've heard her called by Myrtle too
Lovejoy there a name be sure
Full of love you can be sure
Woodward too you can be sure
Full of love you can be sure
At 5 and 10 and 15 too
I called her by my Nannie dear
The years have past, my hair has grayed
Yet to me that grand ole gal
I still with love and tender care
Call her by my Nannie dear

Ramona Winchell

THE CALL OF AUTUMN

O come with me while the autumn leaves
Still hang upon the trees,
Flaunting their scarlet, flame and gold
'Ere comes the winter freeze.
Some are spotted with green and gold.
Some with yellow and brown.
Already some have fallen
And more are coming down,
Leaving the trees from which they grew
To lie upon the ground,
Enriching the soil that more may grow,
When again the spring comes 'round.

David P. Rosen

A THANKSGIVING EXCAVATION AT BATH

Hot waters surface at Bath,
filtering through sediments
as godgifts.
In Celtic rites,
once village bathers dipped their young
into the ritual ponds.
Today we dig beneath Bath's tiled pools,
sifting tubs of sand and clay
for ideas and artifacts;
we wade through ruins of Roman baths.
Lodged in mud centuries,
coins with goddess heads
date levels of the site.
Silts of offerings—
harmonies of art and ores
—plant covenants in the soil.
As nature—love symbols,
the relics recall ages of giving thanks.
Washing our finds,
we cleanse our primal past
and celebrate eternal bonds.

Hamilton Lee

Leaving Home Forever

The autumn day was so beautiful;
no wind and no clouds, just the sun in the blue sky;
but our hearts were truly distressful.
Outside my native city's north gate
mother coming to see me off
wished me the journey leading to a better fate.
Heading for the north, tearfully,
I looked back to see my mother
wiping her eyes and waving her hand sorrowfully.
Having departed from my mother for many years
and craved to see her all the time;
I hope my homecoming nears.
Since I got word about my mother's death
I have been seized by bereavement and grief.
In my view nothing now in the world is much worth.
To place a wreath at my mother's tomb
is now the only hope to relieve my deep grief.
I want to live for some time in a hut beside her tomb.

Clay D. Haverly

FAR INTO THE FUTURE

Far into the future there stands no place,
That hasn't seen a human face.
Miles and miles of dust and sand,

Burnt, black as coal, on this
once great land.
For many years as I recall,
Man forgot how to live like an
animal.
Given time to think and
educate.
They forgot to but learned to
hate.
They work hard to destroy each
other,
Till at last they have no brother.
No fish at sea, no foul of the air,
Nothing to walk on this land so
bare.
For now on this land where
trees grew tall,
There is nothing, nothing at all.
Mans selfish greed for wealth
and power,
Over came the love for one
another.
All for the best it is plain to see,
Only one choice to make for all
eternity.
To love all beings like
ourselves,
Or to throw our souls in the
fires of HELL!

Helen Bavely Silver

CHRISTMAS

Holly wreaths and pine cones
scattered on the mantel,
Johnney's stocking hanging to
be filled by santa;
Under the tree tied with ribbons
and bows,
Boxes filled with socks to wiggle
your toes.
Christmas trees glittering with
tinsel and lights,
Church bells ringing all through
the night;
Santa's sleigh riding swift and
high,
Guided by the stars peeping
through the sky.
Clowns, teddybears, and
gingerbread men,
Funny little puppets pulled by
a string;
Little wooden soldiers standing
straight; and tall,
Ready to march in the
Christmas ball.
Come, let us all join hands
and sing,
Merry Christmas to you my
friend;
Glad tidings! Glad tidings!
Christmas is here,
A time to rejoice, a day filled
with cheer.

Darla Dalton

OK—MOM

You've always been an "ok-mom"
in my book.
Right from the beginning,
you were there.
Fed my hunger,
gave me tender warmth.
Protected me from harm.
And as I grew,
you taught me much.
Right from wrong,
to recognize good from evil.
To love and respect one another.
As I left the nest,
to take charge of my own life.
Like a birds first flights, I had
some crash landings and close
calls.
Then I reached inside,
and found the seed you sowed
within me.
So that I could reap a rich
harvest.
Everyone had a mother,
I just saw things that way.
But, I know now it takes more,
than being a woman to be a
mother.
Lets say in my book your not
an "ok—mom".
Your an "A-#1-mom"!
Thanks!
I love you
for just being you.
Your creation.(ha,ha)

Molly Neururer

CAN'T YOU HEAR ME?

You never listen. Don't you
really care?
Have you forgotten, wiped it
from your mind
Like natural disasters, acts of
God
That sear and scar. You fools.
Forgetful, blind.
The jungle rot, the gun fire and
the screams.
The maiming and the deaths of
strangers, friends.
The vanished years that I
cannot recover.
The bitterness that lurks and
never ends.
Some of my scars have healed
but others linger.
The ones you cannot see I know
are there.
Haunting the present and
uneasy future.
I paid for sins not mine. And
you don't care.
I need to talk and really have
you listen.
"It's in the past" you say.
But I was there.
You wave the flag and talk of
God and country.
March in parades, with
shouldered guns as well.
Vietnam is the name the media
gave it.
But I, you fools, remembering,
call it Hell.

Esther Hensleigh

MOON GLOW

Beautiful, changeable moon,
Unconquered for centuries,
Bathing bountiful earth
With myraids of moonbeams.
So much I do not understand.
Let the daring be encapsuled
To blast off into space
To reach you and explore.
I am content to stay on earth,
To be the caretaker of
My own back yard,
And let you, Dear Moon, come
to me
Just as you came
To my parents in Iowa,
To their parents in
Pennsylvania,
And to theirs in Devonshire.

Agnes Von Wettberg

AD NAUSEAM

Of all the words were ever writ,
I am most tired of FU** and
SH**.
They made a sort of daring
noise
When mouthed by naughty,
grade-school boys.
Now book or play will have no
luck
Unless it's filled with SH** and
FU**.
As BORING (why I can't abide
'em)
As aster****that used to hide
'em!

Irene Dolores Lippert-Hoffman

MISFORTUNE

The night is dark and gray
misfortune is on her way
in the deep of the mist
in the fog of the day.
The trees spead out their arms
so wide and far away

they look so big and strong that
way
there is not a child outside to
play
for misfortune is on her way.
Just listen to her howling
as she goes a prowling
all around downtown and
throughout the night
giving the people a terrible
fright
as she whirls and twirls
everything within her sight
while she laughs and crys with
delight.

Earl A. Wilson

LONELINESS

Loneliness is lifes greatest
sorrow,
Nothing to look to but
tomorrow.
Tomorrow will be just another
day
With no bright thoughts to
cheer my way.
The phone doesn't ring, and no
letter arrives,
Nothing to cheer me up inside.
Friends are all busy with their
own lives,
The thought never enters into
their minds
That someone they know might
be lonesome and sad,
And just a short visit might
make him glad,
A phone call or two, just to say,
"How are you?"
Would brighten his day in the
grandest way.
Nothing to do but sit and
wonder
If all is well with the folks
down yonder.
Then I'll try to console myself
and say,
"I'm sure that all is well today."
Tomorrow my phone will ring
and she'll say,
"Darling I'm coming home
today."
Loneliness vanishes, and my
eyes fill with tears,
For tomorrow I'll hold the one
I love dear.

Maril Lee Brubaker

MOVING DAY

The hollow sound of
emptiness
E nshrouds me with its gloom.
Where once was warmth and
liveliness
A chill pervades the room.
The walls sport ghosts of
pictures
T hat once proudly hung-and
smiled on me
B efore their knell was rung.
Each precious dish, in tissue
wrapped,
Snuggle in packing crates galore
Imprints on on dusty shelves
A nd flotsam on the floor.
Moving is a worrisome thing
that leaves memories behind,
Some good, some bad, some
funny, some sad
That linger in the mind.
B ut new horizons stretch ahead,
another place to fill,
New faces, new friends, new
memories to build.

Stephen G. Peacock

A FRIEND

When will I find a friend
Whose friendship will never end
Whose words are as good as gold
Who won't leave me out in the
cold
When will I find a friend
Who won't bring me to a dead
end
Who never has reason to lie
Who'll be with me until I die
When will I find a friend
Whose hands they are willing to
lend
Who I know I can always trust
Who won't cry and leave me to
rust

Gustav Carl Pack, Sr.

LIFE'S EPILOGUE

My feet have tread, with humble
step,
The sands of time through
life;
My body was borne the sweat of
toil,
To conquer the many days of
strife;
But through these trying and
painful times,
My heart and soul were
generously blessed;
With pleasures and passions of
love and faith,
From family and friends and

all the rest.
Now my feet shall tread no more,
The mysteries of life have ceased to be;
The sweat and toil is not required,
For I've entered the valley of silence you see;
My quiet heart is free of pain,
And my soul has reached its place of rest,
To wait for those I have left behind,
Until GOD shall call them to his breast.

Lori Fox Benak
And The Meaning Of Life Is, And The Meaning of Life Is. .
Lonely angel's and archangel's shadows
Curl into deeper shadows.
A single sandy stone
Waits on a shimmering pane of glass.
The prisms within,
The only rainbow
You'll ever know.
Still.
Still as the edge of a russet wing
Cutting the air into silence to the valley below,
The town, a chasm,
Ringed by that necklace of light!
Be motionless;
Let Morpheus do his work
And fall away into
THE NET OF NO END
Where consequence hangs
From the evening star
And fields of clover
And tangled mountains
Of pyracantha
Beckon ahead. . .

Tina M. Carter
WINNING DOUBT
I want to enter this contest
so bad,
Where's the creativity I thought
I had.
Words are scrambled and don't
ever rhyme,
No matter how I think and
stumble over each line.
My kids are screaming and
crying at my feet,
My pages are crumpled and
never very neat.
I retype and retype, they're still
a mess,
One more erasure is okay, I
guess.
But I watch for the mail each
and every day,
Looking for something that
might just say,
You're a winner, though we had
some doubt,
You will receive a years supply
of white-out!

Elaine Andrus Watts
UNTITLED
You were once a dream you see
And then we met. . .it was meant to be
For there you were. . .I had always known
time would bring, as winter to spring,
someone to share. . .I saw you there.
Your warmth and touch mean so much. . .
Like peace of night or golden sunlight
On leafy trees in gentle breeze.
Yes, all the while, with tender smile
I waited. . .at last you came to me.

David-Jon Harrigan
BIRDS ON THE BEACH
A chaste wind
Blows under
A brooding sky
Terns, bright bellied,
Stalk crab infested rocks,
As gulls, clacking,
Anxiously cry.
Snipe scurry 'long
A deserted shore.
Long legged herons
Wade a backwash
Rinsed from
The brackish sea.
These sentinels
Chase
The scudding trough
Of each enmeshing wave
To rise To fall
Not confounded
But surrounded
By the ebb and swirl,
By the clash of captive wave
Against warrior shore

Olivia M. Biggs
THERE'S BEAUTY IN US ALL
There's beauty in us all,
No matter how large or small.
Big feet, little feet, flat feet, no feet,
There's beauty in us all.
There's beauty in us all,
Big legs, little legs, shapely legs, no legs,
There's beauty in us all.
There's beauty in us all,
Big trunk, little trunk, but certainly not no trunk,
There's beauty in us all.
There's beauty in us all,
Big bust, little bust, even no bust.
There's beauty in us all.
There's beauty in us all.
long arms, short arms, big arms, small arms, and even no arms,
There's beauty in us all.
There's beauty in us all.
Big neck, little neck, even no neck,
There's beauty in us all.
There's beauty in us all,
Big face, small face, round face, oval face,
Each face has a place.
There's beauty in us all.
There's beauty in us all.
Big head, little head, round head, oval head,
but certainly not no head.
There's beauty in us all.
There's beauty in us all,
No matter our nationality.
God made us all,
Like a beautiful flower garden,
With all types of personalities,
There's beauty in us all.

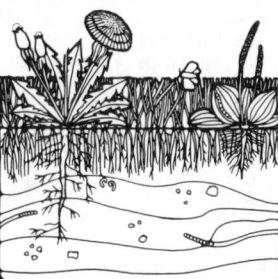

Mary Jane March
SILENCE AND THOUGHTS
Silence, so beautiful so sad
Thoughts that wander from
yesterday into tomorrow
So many regrets, would I have
done it different?
It does not matter now
For yesterday is gone
and there will be a tomorrow
somewhere.

Anna DeGrezia
SONNET—MAN TO TIME
The sons of time doth shake our every day,
To prolong the search of truth and wisdom,
Yet in this short time obstacles restrain,
Some problems of immoral intention,
They seek to shift but are equivalent,
To a deadly poison which bears much pain,
They behold no unit of measurement,
Rather hatred, evil, and much shame,
We must fight these forces along with the youth
For once fought there will be no aversion,
But will grow to form new branches of truth,
Which will justify all of creation,
We must work quickly each and every day,
For the sons of time quickly tick away.

William C. Thomas
FROM YOUR SON
It is too easy to be like you for me.
Knowing your love and tortured jealousy—
Knowing my own hate; and knowing it well,
Knowing responsibility, and calling it hell.
Unlike others, I remember you through my eyes,
(Forgetting those of the world); thinking you indisputably wise,
Sagacious, cheerful, quiet, and turning the axis for others,
(After all, didn't you possess the jealous love of my mother)?
I also know those past parts that haunted you—
The spite between careers that flourished and grew;
Your abdication of all hope, the loss of friends,
And our embarrassment as you achieved those ends.
My mother hid behind her lies during that time:
(The Junior League, bridge parties), and the unencouraged rhyme
As our moments ticked around you; becoming common-place—
As we each put on a face to hide before your face.
She and I pitied you, without reason to hide ourselves,
(And hide ourselves we did), each in our separate shells,
Separate rooms, separate friends, separate bodies, separate breaths—
So I never felt closer to her until after her separate death.
We both missed her, each of us; I for the role I had to assume—
(The way I made you dress, for instance, so you were always well-groomed),
Or the companionship I felt I needed to replace
With tangled intention, tangled arms, an empty embrace.
I sometimes cared for you from love—mostly from duty,
Sometimes wishing you'd die, watching, waiting, always mutely.
And now you're gone. You've left me with a name,
A memory, (through other eyes), some money, and a stain
Upon my memory of measuring the man to what he was—
His pettiness, fears, misery—and his great lack of a course.
I now know too well your failings and indecision,
The foolishness of your commands; and why they were given;
Your wonderfully subtle mind; and your preference for drink—
And about all the escaping where you didn't need to think.
I also know it is too easy for me to be that way,
Idolized secretly by night with a drunken array
Of misconceptions, of separate hopes, of barely remembered dreams,
And the blessed death that follows self-fulfilled, unpromised schemes.

Kathryn E. Price
AROUND
Around—
Life flies,
The world turns,
Always travelling,
Constantly spinning,

Never ceasing to entrap. . .
But even the caged bird can fly.

Helen Le Marr Wright
TRADITIONS
The holidays are over, another year is gone,
But the same traditions will live on and on.
It's interesting how some started, some hard to understand
Some came from necessity, like the cutting of the ham.
A young wife learning how to cook started to roast a ham
Remembered her mother cut off the ends to put it in the pan.
The receipt didn't read to do this, what was the purpose of the plan?
Why did mother cut off the ends to put it in the pan?
So she went to ask her mother about this memory as a kid,
And her mother answered, "because my mother did."
On she went to grandma's, her curiosity now was high,
She was sure her grandma soon would tell her why.
When she reached her grandma's and asked the question on her mind
Grandma had a jolly laugh, and answered with these lines:
"It doesn't change the taste, my dear, the reason I recall,
I cut the ends off the ham, my pan was a little small."

Jo B. Comberiate ASCAP
I TALK TO YOU
PRECIOUS, MY LOVE
so like
Red and gold leaves in Spring,
A snowy spray in Summer,
A new bud in Autumn,
A warm breeze in Winter—
A gift from each season—
that is
PRECIOUS, MY LOVE
I talk to the stars and find you there.
You fill the darkness of my doom
with bright starlight throughout the room.
I talk to the sun and find you there.
Your arms of light strengthen my day
with warmth that melts my sadness away.
I talk to your picture waiting there.
Your silence speaks of memories shared
with love like music in the air.
I talk to the flowers everywhere.
Like melodies from mystery land,
your love is there with a helping hand.
I TALK TO YOU and you understand.

Richard Allen Buchborn, Jr.
HELENE'S STORY
I am Rachel. . .the seed that grows within the womb. . .
the bud that slowly reaches for the Sun, then suddenly
blooms into beauty that could never be found in words. . .
I am the dream of a life, that was conceived in love. . .
born in truth. . .and lives in fantasy. . .with a freedom
never captured by humanity, and in the spirit of passion. . .
I am never seen. . .always felt. . . never touched. . .
but always present. . .I am existing, without existence. . .
I am love, without fear. . .I am truth, without logic. . .
I am life, without death. . .and I am yours.

Judy Larkin Horne
MY MISSY
When I was just a little girl
I sometimes lived in a fantasy world
I dreamed of castles in the sky
And of many things I wondered why
Often times I wasn't me
For then I could be what I wanted to be
In my dream was a special place
And in my dream a little face
I didn't know of whom I dreamed
Or why a part of me she seemed
All tucked away in a special place
This little girl with a lovely face
My dream has come to life you see
For I have what I always wanted to be
A little girl who means the world to me
My special dream
MY MISSY

Christine Gardiner
SPRING'S PROMISE
A rainbow spread across the sky—
Heaven's promise that Life's ever new!
The sparkle of golden sunshine
Making diamonds of the dew.
Laughter of the rippling brook,
Caress of the Whispering breeze;
Emerald-tipped and crimson buds
Swelling on the trees.
Radiant dance of the daffodils,
Violets worshipping in the dell;
Soft velvet brown of fresh-turned earth,
A butterfly's empty shell.
An oriole calling to his mate,
The flash of a bluebird's wing;
Past cares are all forgotten
In Love's joy that comes with Spring!

Jaroslawa Benko
MUSIC
serenades me
sending sound waves
which the walls absorb
and sometimes
my subconscious
reflects

Rhondi Thomas
SATIN GLOVES
There is a pair of satin gloves
On my night table
Funny how they got there
I don't remember the
shimmering green
With lacy white edges
Or the tiny buttons at the wrists
Of these tiny satin gloves
Too small for the spread of my hand
How delicate they are
How neatly folded
Paused, as if only to take a moment's rest
On the cool dark polished mahogoney
Of my night table

Roma Hogle
MR GUITAR MAN
I listen to you play your music and sing your song
I keep wondering whats wrong
I see in your eyes your sad and lonely
I'm lonely too
And need a friend, someone like you
Mr. Guitar Man
You play your music and sing the songs
Every day and all night long
I can see by your smile and the look in your eyes
Your dreaming dreams
Dreams that take you far away from here
Dreams perhaps of a happier time
When she said, I'm yours
And you said you're mine
But you play your music and sing your song
Just like you belong
Mr. Guitar Man
I sit and listen to your song
I even stay the whole night long
I drink a beer or two
And dream a dream just like you
I know you don't even know I'm there
Nor can you see how much I care
And want to share your dreams with you
Just because I'm lonely too
MR GUITAR MAN

Carolyn M. Edmundson
MOON OVER NEW YORK CITY
Above the jagged sky-line to the East,
Above the trees that hide the walks in Morningside,
Dian arose, that luminous guardian of the tide—
Arose reluctantly, as from a feast.
We walked, my moody friend and I
Scarce speaking, as we moved on Amsterdam,
Her thoughts disturbed—a recent telegram,
Unconscious of the brightening sky.
Look, look—the moon! I gaily tried
To change her mood by this event.
I even sang a little tune—
Her melancholy seemed to guide,
She hardly glanced as on we went—
"What place has New York City for a moon?"

Edna Grace Starkey
TO DIANNE
The name 'Dianne' has always conjured up for me
Tall goddesses, stately in their grace,
Dignified and fair of face.
The niece, Dianne, in no way mars my fantasy;
She rather shapes it to the whole
By adding warmth and beauty of the soul.

Shirley Irene Gilarski
ARNOLD
The Native tried to dance,
But could not meet the rhythm of a new life.
Brown swollen ankles yearned for the soft
Hide of moccassins.
A burnished neck itched from the white stiff
Collar now worn, a yoke to replace beads of
Bravery and distinction.
Yielding to his heart,
The echoes of ancestry calling him,
The beautiful native left.
His warm moist eyes said so much,
As his broad colloused hands retracted from me.
Now only a trace of his presence remains, in the
Memory of a friend.

Hilbert S. Collins
THE FLOWER ON THE MOOR
A flower grew out on yonder moor.
It ne'er was seen by rich or poor;
But it strove for perfection for its Almighty God,
Even though it sprang from unworthy sod.
Its stem was straight, and its leaves without spot;
What a secluded place to cast its lot,
But there in beauty it grew on the moor
And ne'er was seen by rich or poor.
Its petals so geometric and with grandest hue
Were even more brilliant under the morning dew;
And the scent of the bloom out there on the moor
Was, oh, so dazzling, so perfectly pure.
Ah, friend, could we be as perfect a flower
Out there all alone in sunshine

and shower?
Would we rise to perfection for
Almighty God,
Or sink in dejection into the
sod?

Ruth M. J. Goebl

UNTITLED

One day I was asked,
"Should I fall in love?"
I replied,
"Do you like to worry?
Do you like to cry?
Do you like to lay awake nights
thinking?
Do you like to be patient during
unbearable times?
Does a smile one day make up
for a weeks worth of
heartache?"

My questioner then said,
"Be serious, I really want to
know."
I just smiled and walked away.
A second day I was asked,
"Should I fall in love?"
I replied,
"Do you like to see love pour
from someone's eyes?
Do you like to feel the tender
touch of a gentle man for
hours on end?
Do you like to have endless
conversations and not once
open your mouth?
Do you like the feeling when
someone runs to you for a hug
because you are the only one
who can make them feel
better?
Do you like to go through days
when all you do is recall who
you were with the day before?"
My questioner then said,
"Really! Tell me more."
I just smiled and walked away.
A third day I was asked,
"Should I fall in love?"
I replied,
"Yes."
My questioner then said,
"That's all you have to say?"
I just smiled and walked away.

Raymond P. Sauer

THE OTHER PLACE

When you leave here, if you
were good;
They say, you'll reach
Heavens gate.
But if you go the other way;
I hear you'll have to wait.
Why is there always a waiting
line;
For those who're going down.
It's supposed to be so nice up
there;
Or are those tales unsound.
You get to play a harp all day;
And even get some wings.
I don't know about down there;
They may have groovy things.
What if they've been fooling us;
And Heavens down below.
And all that radiance up above;
Is only Hells bright glow.

Camille L. Smith

I TRIED

I tried to be one of them,
I wanted so to belong.
But I wouldn't dance their
dance,
And I wouldn't sing their song.
I would not kneel before them
To do what they asked of me.
For they would only kick me in
the face
As I struggled helplessly.
I have my own wings now
And I'll fly them my own way.
I wanted to be one of them,
But my conscience I could not
betray!

H. Brewer

A DREAM

I had a dream, that I did own
a cottage and a garden.
A little place I called my own
a cottage and a garden.
A place deep in the woods
maybe
with pinetrees proud and high.
Where I could listen to the
wind,
watch deer as they graze nearby
Or have a cottage by the sea
and listen to it roar.
Watch ships go by and seagulls
fly;
find seashells at my door.
In mountains I would like to
live
high up, where eagles nest.
Leave far behind me, worries,
fears;
and all the worlds unrest.
So, I keep dreaming on about
my cottage and my garden.
Someday, I know, that I will
own
a cottage and a garden.

Bettie J. Frye

LOVE HAS GONE AWAY

His Love has gone away—
It was there once and blossomed
As fresh as the morning dew
Then, into some other arms—it
flew!
He called, "LOVE, come back!
Must you so soon go?"
He listened to the wind and
waited. . .waited. . .
It seemed to be echoing back to
him and
sorrowfully saying,
Your Love has flown away to
some other shore. . .
Never! to return to you. . .no
more!
Your Love has gone away—to
stay!
And still he hears the echo—
Over and over—and over—again!
To stay! To stay! No more! No
more!
Your LOVE has gone away!
Then quietly he hears Earth
whisper
back to him
True Love will find you once
again—
Someday—Someday—You
know—
No more to fade away—
TO STAY! TO STAY!

Cheryl Hawkins

THE DAWN OF DEATH

It was the darkest hour on the
coldest night,
When they first heard the
creature's loud moaning.
Not a soul in sight; they all
shivered with fright,
And no one knew what it was.
The wind grew fierce in the
darkening sky.
The moon no longer was
gleaming.
Their eyes grew wide and saw no
passersby,
But the creature continued its
screaming.
They heard an echo in the depth
of the wood.
The noise, it kept growing
louder.
No one there to help and
nobody would,
For no one knew what it was.
Their fear increased by the cold
of the lake,
When they found the corpse of
a young friend.
They promised at last to never
forsake,
Until the horror had come to
its harsh end.
Their number decreased as the
hours passed by.
The panic inside them grew
stronger.
Its rage increased with the
fierce growing cry,
And no one knew what it was.
Their breathing eased up in the
light of the dawn.
They all were sure it was over.
From the woods came nothing
but a sweet, little fawn,
To lie down in the pleasant,
cool clover.
Then up from behind the hill's
sharp incline,
Came the strong arm of the dark
creature.
Its knife was sharp but not there
to dine,
And no one knew what it was.
A sharp scream rang out in the
quiet of day.
The ground soon covered with
red.
When its deed was done it
hastened away,
With a constant pain in its
head.
Now there is none who'll go to
the woods nearby,
And the town has since been
deserted.
So beware if you hear the
inhuman cry,
'Cause still no one knows what
it was.

Becky Ann Cecil

DREAMING

Take me to that magical place
in a dress made of silver lace,
Lay me down in the warm soft
grass
drinkin' tea made of sassafras,
Look at the shining stars and
southern moon,
where you dream all night
listenin' to your favorite tune.
Where there is joy and love
and the sun above
and you right by my side,
The waterfall
the beauty of it all
the rising tide.
Sailing ships on a glistening
ocean
discovering love as a new
emotion.
Walk along a country path
with a cool summer breeze
floating through the trees
carrying the scent of pine,
Old fashioned dancin'
good ol' romancin'
Sipping wine
your hand in mine.
Where dreamin's free
and there's no one else
but you and me. . . . .

Joan Clark

ONE SHORT SONNET

The dry sun shines; the soft
cool wind blows.
Through the window screen by
the curtain
I see flowers and shrubs growing
thin.
Borne on the notes of assassins'
bullets,
Rustling leaves scatter—though
not unexpected—
Across the sidewalks and
roadways outside.
Protected in this change of
season,
How much time is left to learn?
We inhale the fresh air
And dress our selves with care,
Worrying and laughing,
Yawning still behind cupped
hands.

Gerry Palmer

OCTOBER ROSE

October's rose, poised on the
edge of winter decay,
Pauses for a moment of full
blown array,
Inviting passers-by to notice and
admire
How eagerly she reaches for the
last strong rays
Of an autumn sun that has seen
longer days,
And how boldly she resists the
North wind's ire
That soon will drive us all to
dry and wither by the fire.
There is no reason for this late
autumnal bloom;
No seed, no promise, no
great heroic goal,
In God's eternal plan, no
role,
Until we pluck it to adorn our
nesting place
And renew our faith in spring's
eternal grace.
Then, carefully pressed among
the postcards and old lace,
The faded rose recalls for us
the warmth of fall's embrace.

Mary Forrester

TO PRAISE

Oh, for a thousand tongues to
praise the Lord!
Oh, for a thousand songs to Him
to sing!

Oh, for a thousand years of endless days
To manifest the love of Christ, the King!
Oh, for the words of truth to light the way!
Oh, for peace and joy to lift the soul!
Oh, for the harvest ripe in all the world
To receive the greatest story ever told!
Oh, for the Kingdom coming here on earth!
Oh, to hear Him say, "My child, well done!"
Oh, to be seated 'round the Master's table
And behold the Mighty Father and His Son!

Carolyn R. Seashore

MY COURAGEOUS LITTLE COCO

Spiritual both outside in and inside out
With Faith in her self, my brother and myself she
proved much strength after a 3 hour leg operation.
With tears in her eyes after the operation she was very surprised to see both my brother and my eyes brightly shining and glowing.
Her smile and beautiful brown glowing eyes helped to give us the inspiration and let us know that she had much faith indeed.
After one night of spending the night on the floor the next night she jumped upward and moved to the box springs and mattress we had laid out for her.
Running fastly around Rice Institute helps inspire just anyone, friend, or stranger, her rapid recovery and Wow but how!
Brave is she as she continues her strife thru every day living after having a 3 hour operation.
So you see that its the "Little Things" that count, along with love and God showed us why helping both my brother and I lead us on to a bigger inspiration in life.

Marilyn D. Button

SONNET

Shall I compare thee to a whisky sour?
Thou art by far the sweeter and more dear.
Three drinks I need before I feel their power
But one of you brings drowsy pleasure near.
Full minutes ten take sours to work their way,
To lift my cares, make light the path I tread.
But from you one touch can change my day
One minute glance make drunk my heart and head.
With you my time is rich and satisfies
Most deeply; sweet your taste, amused my mind
When on thee poised; but strong some other ties
Which place taste, touch, and pleasure all in bind.
Small wonder when twixt man and drink I choose,
That safer 'tis to pick not man, but booze.

Roberta Clark Howard

TEMPTRESS

The Temptress scorns a day-worn shadow
For night reflects the trueness of shimmers.
Her eyes forsee a looking glass
And color floats beyond the vision,
As of within time prism's pattern.
Behold her touch is dear with meaning;
She aches for warmth of gentler feelings.
And still her heart lies calm in waiting
For the touch that tells of stronger healing.
The Temptress's eyes so dares with ember glows,
Come challenge life and love of foes!
She fears not what the stars withhold
Only that which her love cannot perceive.
Why tarry long upon the mountain
If feel ye not her yearn for growing?
The only love she trusts proclaiming
Echoes from the tree tops showing.

Sigrid Emanuelson Moore

MY NIGHT

My night has captured special melodies to lace
The halo on the star-tipped mountain's mighty face.
In scenic meadows, tiny insects serenade
The world from moon-lit halls of green arcade.
The music of their famous orchestras
Weave timeless sounds to form their operas.
Night strings the corridors of heaven with their tunes
And serenades the moonbeams in the cloud's lagoons.
I walk in silence, there are endless dreams
For dreaming, while my perfect evening seems
To play another lovely symphony,
A song my weary heart can sing to me.
A thousand blessings filled this special sight

And blessed the fragile wonders of my night.
My night holds magic melodies in space,
And dreams seek star-tipped mountains to embrace.

Edith Louise Baker

EMPTY STOCKINGS

Oh, Mothers in homes that are happy
Where Christmas comes laden with cheer.
Where the children are dreaming already
Of the merriest day in the year.
As you gather your darlings around you
And tell them the story of old
Remember the homes that are dreary.
Remember the hearts that are cold.
And thanking the love that endowed you
With all that is dearest and best,
Give freely, that from your abundance
Some bare little life may be blessed.
Oh, go where the stockings hang empty
Where Christmas is naught but a name,
And give for the love of the Christ Child.
"Twas to seek such as these that He came."

Kevin M. Hibshman

MORRISON

(The Artist-Dwells In Self-Torment"

Some say misguided youth
Some say angel of truth
No one will ever know for sure
He was really just an open door
Falling aimlessly
Laughing too loud at the faults of society
He could do without humanity easily
Burning so fast—A short flame. .
That scorched the consciousness
and filled the blank page
Cosmic spark in an arc of light
Truth is natural, is not law
Truth is sometimes wrong and right
On stage he was free of fear
On the page the lines were clear
Ashes to ashes and dust to dust
The gleaming jackknife collected rust
As it tore through dimension and
Sliced through time
Only to be buried in all our minds
The door is held open wide
For a very short time

Chris Barton

OUR NATURE

Do you ever wonder
How Nature can thrive
How it does not speak
But is still alive
Are we the reason
It is even there
For every season
It is there to share
And who really cares
As long as they get their share
Who would have thought during our Revolution
That by now
There would be this much pollution
People just seem to think
That without trees grass and clean air
Life would be kinda of blue
They don't even relize
That if our Nature goes
WE GO TOO

Kenneth B. Norris (KNOR)

UNTITLED

The last embrace
now lost to time
I feel my arms grow chill
we were
exposed in our loneliness
Then together
caught up in the tenderness
we felt and shared
our souls were sheltered
from the cold of sorrow
Tears falling slowly
from eyes filled with emotion
and no way of telling
if they were tears of joy
I still remember that fleeting moment
with a lifetime of caring
inside forever

Christopher Van Williams

WE WERE MADE FROM CANTICLES

"We were made from canticles
(Songs from the secrets of God's mind)
Scriptures from his greatest scrolls
Master christened us—mankind!"
We're free, we're free, we're free
Listening to the canticles of serenity
On my way to heaven while I listened to the stars
I ran across a dream ending all my wars
And the night folded back to a light so great
My soul was relaxed by the tender touch of faith!
What I would formulate with my master up above
Would be something mightier—
A mystical new love
And the clouds rolled away to a wind strong and sure
My soul must obey, my heart must endure!
We're free, we're free, we're free
Think of us as lyrics of pure tranquility
"We were made from canticles
To quest the magic dawn
Scriptures from his greatest scrolls
To touch the truth beyond!"
"We were made from canticles
(Songs from the secrets of God's mind)
Scriptures from his greatest scrolls
Master christened us—divine!!

Richard E. Butler

IF I COULD DIE

If I could die
For just one minute
And go to Heaven
To see what's in it

If I could die
For an hour or two
Just to see what
My family would do
Or maybe die
For just one day
To see what my family
And friends would say
What if I died for
A week or more
And came back
Would they treat me
the same as before
If I were gone
Six months or a year
Would I not harbor
A secret fear
And really not want
On the recall list
Cause I'd be afraid
I wouldn't be missed
It's better to die
And have everyone know it
Than to be alive
If folks don't show it
When a person can read
And still does not
He's no better off
If he hadn't been taught
If there's someone to love
But you really don't care
It's the same as if
They weren't there
There's no sense in waiting
'Till someone dies
Then wish you had
strengthened
the family ties
Don't tell the mourners
How much you care
Tell the person yourself
While they're still there.

John J. Croft

BLOODLESS

I see her held in russet bed,
And hidden hearts shapeful
blush;
I kiss her mouth gelid red,
Midst purple coils and dewy
hush;
Immure me soon with the dead,

Neath her hallow'd lilac lush.

Jacqueline Skinner

Solving Overpopulation

If I were the earth
I'd shake myself
like a wet dog
and fling off
half-a-billion people. . .
if only humans were drops
of water.

Eleanor D. McElroy

A PART

When bereft of your solace here
My love becomes a spiraling
entity—
Mounting clouds to where all is
clear
And pure soul springs out of the
depths of me.
I seek a timeless presence near
Where can my Great Creator be?
Enchanted with a need and fear
A bruised heart reaches
tenderly.
From all pettiness I veer
The wind becomes a rhapsody—
And sings of times when you
were near
And lets me you more clearly
see.
For you're not far from me, my
Dear
I've found that you're as close
as He—
Nature is vaster than we hear
And thoughts are a reality.

Mary J. Watkins

I REMEMBER

Sunset paints the sky in
brilliance
Yet, All is black
Your hand, once outstretched to
mine, is gone
I walk alone
But I Remember
Moments of youth pass swiftly,
Then disappear, down misty
corridors of time
Golden days of laughter—nights
of a tenderness
Our dream of love has ended
Still, I Remember
Seagulls soar above, theirwild
cries echo in my heart
A crushed and faded rose
somewhere,
An anniversary card, now yellow
Was it all just a dream—then
let me forget!
But I Remember
No more will I wait for your
footsteps
Where have they taken you?
The surf wets my cheek with
salty tears, I cry
I cry, but no one hears
Yes, I must Remember

Jack Nidever

WAR

What is so pretty as a leg blown
right off,
Or an eye dissolved in a damp
red spot?
Ah War, you offer us a cauldron
In which to boil the bones
Of our courageous children!
If only it were done more
cleanly,
Without leaving those baskets
Of the still but alive,
Battered bits after your heroic,
Seductive call to arms!

Beverly Kittrell

HOLDING ON TOGETHER

Life holds many
disappointments
Be they great or be they small
We never could gain much from
life
If they weren't there at all
When two people love each
other
Just as much as you and I
We can watch these
disappointments
Go flying right on by
For we are young enough you
see
That we can learn from all
Together we can stand the tests
Together we won't fall

Douglas Le Von Carlton

THE COMBINATION TO MY HEART

You open my heart with
Your combination 36-26-38
You thrill me and surely
You're sweet as candy
That soothes me gently
When you open my heart
You have caused me to
Explode with joy, peace
And love for you
You will forever be
My sweet combination 36-26-38
And most of all you have
Released all of my powers
For days to come to comfort
You and protect you during
Our infinite existence.
I love you.

Shelly Sowards

LIVING IN YOU

The light is red.
Your hair so fair.
If I dare,
To spare—you pain,
We will live again.
Like never before
We will soar
To infinite heights.
In the light I see you
So clear.
At night I fight the image
That will always appear.
You are out of reach,
But soon we will meet.
The years will melt
With tears
As our hearts come alive
Back to yesteryear,
To my dear

Paula A. Fragle

THE BRIDGE

You came into my path of life
And I let you walk ahead,
And every time a bridge you
came upon
You tore it apart
As you walked across.
I would come upon each bridge
and rebuild it
As swiftly as I could;
And we would walk on with you
ahead.
And then many bridges later
You did your most destructive
act,
My heart was blown to bits
The bridge and foundation were
destroyed
I thought beyond repair.
Although it took a long, long
time
I cried and tried to put the
pieces back
And then one day it happened,
I realized I was building a bridge
Stronger than your destruction.
I was laughing and happy
And held my head high,
And when the bridge was
standing and strong
I ran through my path and you
hadn't gotten very far.
And I left you there to fall
behind
And you were back so far,
You couldn't catch up.
And so I am in the lead
And you are following me,
And you can't tear down my
bridges
Before I walk across.
You take other paths,
Seeking others who will
Build your bridges back up.
Oh no, not me,
I shall never turn around to run
back
To walk with you.

Julio A. Santos

TODAY LIKE YESTERDAY

Today like yesterday I look for
you
with the same vehemence
although every new day
my grief augments.
Now and then I see your shadow
among the multitude
and my hopes renew in joyful
flight;
But then you vanish as fast as a
dream,
giving me no time
to express all that I feel.
And miserable, I
with all my senses
endure the unfruitful searches,
remain like a lonely fugitive
in this arid desert
exhausted from pursuing
mirages
and thirsty for your love.
Agonizing in the quicksand
of desire and frustration,
I will continue looking for you
with the same passion;
And when I fail in this purpose
some day,
one thing is for sure: I am dead!

Arthur Christopher-Poet-Songwriter

THE MIGHTY WIZARD

Eyes of bright green,
With stars for a center
A predigious figure
For the man they call mentor
Wave of the wand
and electricity flows
The final outcome
no one knows
Always around
but never in sight
Does his best sorcery
in the midst of the night
So noble and wise
full of inspiration
Some magical words
and instant creation
The war of the worlds
brings him closer now
For the side of good
he takes his bow
He conjours whatever
he needs for his side
For love and wisdom
cannot be denied
The immortal battle is
soon to begin
Stakes are enormous
as to just who'll win
For good and evil
Have had a good start
We are merely play actors
with a very small part

Stephen Liskow

THE NIGHT BEFORE CHRISTMAS

I hope the bike that Santa
brings is red.
Can I get up? I haven't slept all

night:
I'm hearing reindeer prancing in my head.
I've been good, but it's hard to stay in bed
since someone broke my Mickey Mouse night light
(I hope the bike that Santa brings is red).
Why don't mom and dad come up to bed—
they must be planning to stay up all night.
I'm hearing reindeer prancing in my head.
I left an apple and a slice of bread,
a snack for You Know Who on his long flight.
(I hope the bike that Santa brings is red.)
"Oh, he won't come 'till you're asleep," mom said,
but even though I shut my eyes real tight,
I'm hearing reindeer prancing in my head.
I toss and turn, a prisoner in my bed—
Oh, why is Christmas Eve so long a night?
I hope the bike that Santa brings is red:
I'm hearing reindeer prancing in my head.

Genevieve R. Erwin

A HEART IN LOVE

A heart is quite a fragile thing,
It can burst with such gleeful joy;
It can think that each day is spring,
It can pass between a girl and boy.
It can shine in two dancing eyes
And can be soft in loving arms;
It can be bright as rainbow skies
And as the sunshine, mellow and warm.
It can cry like the falling rain
And bow it's head in utter grief;
But then it can strongly rise again
When it is past in God sent relief.
A heart is all of these, and more
And each one knows when he's in love;
The whole world is different than before
And that 'twas sent from Heaven above.

Adrian M. Maschek

HAPPINESS

Happiness won't drive you crazy
but it can drive you happy I know
for you'll be smiling all the time,
no matter where you go.
Happiness cannot be bought
for not a penny does it cost
but you must learn to use it,
or everything in life is lost.
Take lessons from a child at play
they are happy though it's make believe
they've got their own little secret,
with an ace that's up their sleeve.
Happiness is the spice of life
and it will get you everywhere
if you will smile away the hours,
you'll forget to have a care.
Happiness is what you make it
yet money doesn't play a part
it's the secret of the happy soul,
for that's how they got their start!

Muriel E. Vebsky

WHY?

As a ship passing through billowing water sinks,
As a song flying through sound deminishes,
As lightning streaks through deep darkness follows,
As wind whips through destruction descends?
Yet

As wisdom seeps through bright radiance abounds,
As understanding slides through true graciousness appears,
As faith bursts through soft happiness begins,
As love leaps through life ascends.

Little Morning Star

HAVE YOU EVER?

Have you ever seen a new born baby animal?
I have.
Have you ever been where the eagle flies?
I have.
Have you ever seen the blades of glass follow the sun and return once more?
I have.
Have you walked where the mountain sheep walk?
I have.
Have you ever played with young animals?
I have.
Have you ever watched the golden sunset where no other man has been?
I have.
Have you ever really seen the Great Spirit's (God's) world?
I have.

Ruth Frances Hall

LOST IN THOUGHT

Leaning back into my chair
I cleansed my mind at will
Making room for memories
That make my life stand still
The lovely times of childhood
The castles and the dreams
The aches and pains of growing up
Life, bursting at the seams
My life has known new meaning
As my golden years appear
I've wrapped each precious memory
And tied it with a tear
I'll place them in my dream ship
That sails beyond the sea
Knowing, someday I'll find them
In my hour of reverie

H. Cozby

EARS

Ears are rather pretty things
That's why, on them, some wear rings
That's not to say, 'my ears rings'
If you hear, 'tweet-tweet', like birdie sings
Some will say, you cock your ear
If something interesting's there to hear
Or maybe perchance you train your ear
When someone important should appear
Most ears lie snug, close to the hair
Others stick up like a nervous bear
Some may be large, like serving spoons
Or delicately curved or round like moons
And cauliflower ears, a boxer's mark
Or pointed, like a dog about to bark
Pale ears—cool head, while some turn red
When something personal may be said
Ears are nice to whisper in
Also some have wax in them
Prettily adorned with diamond things
No matter they spread, like aeroplane wings
Big ears, small ears—thin or fat
Prominantly displayed, or under a hat
Remember it's good—your ears to share
For listening to someone shows you care

Herb Jones

SINNER'S LAMENT

All God's children make it known;
Pray for me thru Jesus to God's throne
through him only can I be free;
Lord have mercy, hear a sinners plea.
Satan get behind me afraid,
for I need the Tree of Life's shade,
Lord send down blessings from above,
foresake me not, oh wondrous God of Love.
An ocean of teardrops I've cried,
cause I have drifted from your side.
A cold, cold hearts troubling me;
In Jesus name a sinner calls to thee.

Lori Berteau

ONE LAST TIME

We come together one last time
To share a memory
From our lives
What has become of us can't be changed
But time knows what we had made
The memories fade the pain abides
Tears still well in our eyes
For beautiful is the memory that time knows what we had made

Nicky Freda

LOVE

Love is loving
Love is hugging
even kissing
Love is everything
plus—

Elizabeth Jane Trittler

TO BE NO MORE

I love to hear the gull's cry, as they wing along the sand,
Hear the waves pounding, as they bring stones and pretty seashells up on to the shore—
I love to watch the surf ripple, as it washes away—footprints or sandcastles, with one giant sweep, they are gone, to be no more.
So many things in life, prove to be that way,
God just loans them to us, for a short while—
Trees, flowers, plants; all are beautiful to see, then,
with the changing seasons, they will die—to be no more—
Just like the ocean's waves, as they wash upon the shore.

Kevin H. McArdle

LONELINESS

Loneliness sets in upon me.
There's no reason to evade it
for it brings a tender awareness,
a total vulnerability
that leaves one free to explore
the possibilities of
self.

Beatrice Eckmeter

FOREVERMORE—J.F.K.

The man is gone!
Yet his presence hovers o'er
The Nation, as though he had but passed
Through a massive door!
What kind of man, you ask?
It's hard to put a finger on.
He had brilliance, wealth and courage.
That was but a fragment, and yet
It meant naught, for these things alone
Do not make friends.
Or make one great.
He had more, much more.
He had undying devotion to his God
And outstanding loyalty to his Country.
He had warmth, an understanding of personal problems.
And a deep conviction of what was right
And what was wrong.
He tried to put the World together
Like a giant jig saw puzzle—
Fitting the pieces together with determination.

Striving to make a better life
For rich and poor alike—
For all races and creeds
Fighting for freedom for
individuals everywhere!—
Wanting to see each man
standing tall.
"One Nation indivisible, under
God, with Liberty
And Justice for all."
What had this man, who
commanded respect from
dignitaries,
Big and small?
When the chips were down they
loved him,
Almost one and all!
And that beacon of light shone
through and
Made him great.
In him, we saw a glimpse of
perfection.
Perfect husband and father,
though weighted down
With the burdens of a Nation.
Perfect age with a lifetime ahead
to accomplish miracles!
Perfect leader? Time alone can
decide.
For in contradiction, no one
can be perfect
In all eyes.
Perhaps belatedly, we felt his
impact in our hearts
And lives. Was his death in
vain?
The passing of a man dedicated
to do his best!
And what more can a man do?
And now, whether we were for
or against
The principals for which he
fought unselfishly—
Though it took a crisis, the
impact of his personality
Leaves it's mark!
In sorrow, we bow our heads.
The man is gone
Yet his presence will linger
And future generations will
proudly
Point a finger
To a great man who was—
Our President.

Mary L. F. Socha

MY INNOCENT ROSE

Blue skies etched in a pure
white frame
as is your innocent soul.
The ebbing tides and rough
waters,
as unpredictable of the life
you'll have.
A Rose that simply blossoms
a pure and delicate flower all
with its own definition
With a unique way of growing
and dying
Be a rose with many strong
petals
Grow wise young one with my
love and the sunshine
Reach towards the heavens
and remain innocent my little
one
Enjoy the warm rays of sunshine
learn from the rains
And create your own rainbows
Look deep and listen carefully
Worry not about the time spent
but of the density in all you
do
Grow up with my love, little
one
And share the laughters of life
Learn to love and to feel love
and one day,
You too shall bring forth
another rose
So pure and innocent
As we all once were
As you once were
my innocent rose
"me"

Patricia Ellen

DECEMBER'S WINDS OF LOVE

December and it's magical winds
Came into my life,
It's chilling winds,
Warming my frozen heart,
The magic of snow
The awesome beauty of white,
I fought you with my weapons
of gray eyes and frozen heart.
December and your magical
winds,
The beauty of snow falling on
hillsides,
Icicles spiderwebbed on bare
tree limbs,
Winds blowing wreaths of white
smoke
to encircle chimney tops,
As if to bestowe an eternal
blessing
to the inhabitants below.
December and your magical
winds,
You encircled me,
Wove me into you
We became one
I went with you, we traveled
far,
into Winters spectacular
Wonderland,
Like the snow I drifted endlessly
December winds came into my
heart,
Chilling winds, warming me,
December's love shall stay with
me always.

Thelma Evelyn Jones

WHO ME?

I've studied my Bible for years
and years.
This I have found, there are no
volunteers.
Adam was formed from the dust
of the ground
And though it sounds strange,
this I have found
Without any choice and no
women's lib
Eve was created right out of
his rib.
And though I sound glib, if
you'll beg my pardon
Without any choice, they were
placed in that garden.
Then in crept the serpent, and
though it brings tears
The drama begins, but with no
volunteers.
In the garden were orchards all
hanging with fruit.
Seductive young Eve came in
tempting the brute.
Without thought or reason he
fell for the line
The serpent gave Eve, a man
with no spine.
Then came along Moses, no
volunteer.
He said: "Not me, Lord, for my
speech is real queer."
Yet, he was drafted in spite of
his squawking
And also young Aaron to do all
the talking.
They did a fine job, but this
much is clear
They were both human, and did
not volunteer.
Then there was Jonah who ran
like a turk
When he was assigned to handle
the work
Of sending a warning to
Ninevah—town.
He did not volunteer, he flat
turned it down
And jumped on a ship to sail off
to sea
Saying: "Someone may preach, it
ain't gonna be me!"
Then came a tempest, the
sailors in fright
Flung him into the briny that
very same night!
A fish came and gulped him
right out of the deep!
He cried day and night without
food or sleep.
Three days and three nights he
did weep and pray!
The Lord heard his moaning and
spewed him away!
Jonah told Ninevah: "Come bend
an ear!"
He preached under pressure, he
was no volunteer.
When they repented, he was not
even glad.
He wanted to die because he
was mad!
He pouted and sulked sitting
under a gourd
Till a worm came and ate it,
because of the Lord!
Six thousand score persons
were saved in that year!
Against Jonah's grain, he was no
volunteer.
So if you are drafted, don't
drown in your tears
Just get the job done, there are
no volunteers.

Sondra Faye

HONESTLY, IAGO,

Carry the evil upon the lie
for every lie is holder of some
truth.
Manipulate, with just a sigh,
the naive who're taught by kick
with your steel boot.
Step lightly when you're
wrought
with insidious instigation.
Demoralize the man
who torpidly sees dull inside a
sparkling dove,
for he that too easily casts
his role as debauchee
deserves not the thing he loves.
But you understand he still
receives it
with corruption in mind's fore.
Tis not the devil's make
but rather he himself's belief
in jealousy and love's abhor.
And the innocent unspeakingly
ask for love,
nothing more
Honestly, Iago, take the knife
into your hands.
Suicide's indecent, so slip
distortion's blade
through the influential air
twisting another's mind into a
different man.

J. R. Bassett

SUMMER RAINSTORM

First, the steamy, wrinkled day.
Then roiling clouds black-
scudding
omens across the helpless sky
muzzle the blistering raw light
and throttle down the day's
desire.
The first large drops splat
relief. But as they multiply,
a gagging, gurgling torrent
engulfs the earth, cascading
sheets of ceaseless sameness.
Its turpitude defies reproof.
Suddenly it's over.
The sun and heat and sweat
return.
Only the shrinking puddles stay,
the dripping leaves
and laden, venerated air.
Raucous roots languish how,
surfeited.

Joel E. Scarborough

TALE OF A BONE

Sit-up! Heel! Roll-over! Play dead now; Little mutt do your tricks from a throne; You're the proven new king of all canines; And have earned a nice fat, juicy bone

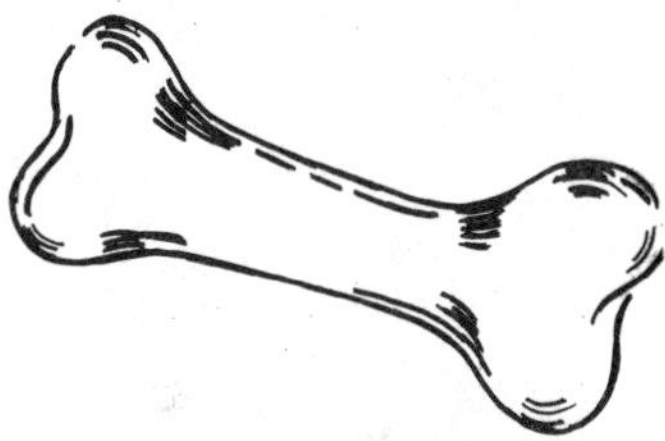

From the twinkling that spawned first frail yappings; Bantam creature with great floppy ears; My adoring has flourished like fission; Thoughts of losing you swell me with fears

Bound in hearts since we shared infant bottles; lapped remains from my dish till it shown; Muzzled sweets from right out of my pockets; Then contentedly gnawed on your bone

But I'm growing, and up goes the big-top; I must witness the splendor and chrome; Aw, the pup! I'll be late if I feed him; Never mind, I'll just throw him a bone

Hey, I'm back, and I'm bursting with stories; Of trapezes, white ponies and clowns; Where's the pup, I have so much to tell him; Of the circus, its sights and its sounds

Son, your puppy cannot share your glory; With his God he has found a new home; See, all creatures are just like we humans; Needing more to sustain than a bone

Furry ball, little warm lump of sweetness; Why must thoughtlessness bear such a price; Can I truly believe what they tell me; That there's gain in each cruel sacrifice

Grown to manhood I've now found my lady; Flowing hair that laps gold from the sun; Tender limbs that so sweetly surround me; She's all pleasures I've known sculpt in one

Ah, but see all the worlds left to conquer; For my love I will stretch for the stars; In cold space, though, there's something that's missing; And I'm not even halfway to Mars

From the windshield a haunting reflection; Furry ball and a face cold asleep; With an echoing murmer of yapping; Reminding of promises still left to keep

Little pup, now I know compensation; How I owe it to you all alone; That I've learned none too soon a grand lesson; Learned that never enough is a bone

Home again now I'm bound to my woman; Having found my real world indispersed; And with spirits bound tightly together; We shall create our own universe

Life so abounds in pure blessings; In lessons of losses and gains; When we see that each lost little creature; Lived and died, but not ever in vain

So, my children, I've brought you a puppy; And there's much a new pup may be shown; But first, come and sit close beside me; Let me tell you the tale of a bone

Ronald C. Alber

WORK WITH WISDOM

Work's a fact of life each day
Regarded, by all, as the source of pay
No matter what the job you hold
It's you who makes or breaks the mold.
Mistakes we make will come and go
But learning from them helps us grow;
After thoughts of pay subside
Enter now the thoughts of pride.
We smile with thoughts of sweet success
And act as though we're in a mess;
Why do thoughts like this prevail,
When we really do not fail.
If we do our best each day,
What can anybody say?
Meet each day like something new,
Set a goal and see it through.
Success is measured not in wealth,
But in our state of mental health;
The rich and poor have fears alike,
They know not where or when they strike.
If daily satisfaction thrives,
Surely then we have better lives.
When you quit from this great race,
Your life is but a mere disgrace.
There's my message just for you. . .
No go and do what you want to do. . .

Harriet Lewis

SANDMAN'S LULLABY

Put away your toys dear, you've played hard all day,
Night has drawn its curtain, kneel here by Mommie and pray

The Sandman is calling, don't you hear your name?
He comes to every boy and girl, he loves them all the same.
Off you go to a far-away land,
Sandman will hold your hand.
Lots of pleasant joys to bring
Dreams to make your dear heart sing.
Sandman will take you, and make you (King/Queen) of
celestial spheres
Enchantment you'll love and treasure all through the years.
Of silver clouds, star dust, and moonbeams in the blue,
He'll build castles on the milky way, sweetheart just for you
You will frolic by the splendor of the northern light,
. . .miracles unfolding all through the night.
So close your eyes my darling, sail off on the make believe
sea,
That the Sandman winds and weaves so well, but at dawning
sail back to me.

Barbara H. Whittum

A POEM FOR DAVID

Kitty kitty attacked me with caresses
He does not understand
I do not feel David's fondness for him
He's out of luck, poor man
See those birds, I said, go chase them
Go and do what cats can.
Upright he sat and licked his coat
Posed to inspire the artist's hand
Again he tried to lavish me
With affection of his brand
Refused he wrestled with my shoe
Stilled and caught the insect's saraband
Yeow he said and rubbed my leg
His tail curled a spiral fan
Stealthily through the grass he crouched
Only to have his prey disband
Sad wail he gave as rain fell round
His plea no longer bland.
Unhappily to the porch he went
Subdued by nature's countermand.

Bertha J. Will

OUR PRESIDENT

Regan's in Carter's out
So the world will change without a doubt
Maybe for the better Maybe for the worst
Whichever it is it won't be a first
But we got to remember
These are only two men
Both with different opinions
When their four year terms begin
They take the burden of the country
Try to work things out
Regardless what they say or do
They will always be talked about
Politics is like religion
But in politics you have only two
The democrats and republicans
So you vote for the one you choose
In religion you have many
Catholics Protestants Mormans or Jews
But we have the freedom of religion
So you believe whichever is suited for you
In politics there are many wronged
But two wrongs don't make things right
So Carter's out and Regan's in
Let's give him our support tonight
There's only so much one man can do
But he has our country in hand
So we'll pray to God he'll do his best
To protect our all American Land
God we know that you are the one
Over religion politics and all
So take the hand of our President man
Guide him so our nation doesn't fall

Ruth Borowski

UNTITLED

I only want to be with you
to illuminate your day
and to rise in you
like the warmth of the sun.
In your joy
lies the depth of my reward,
and you give back to me—
warmed in turn—
sun-illumination.

Thomas M. Foley

THE ETERNAL FLAME

Remember back in sixty-three
When President John Kennedy
Paraded through a Texas town
Shots filled the air, then struck him down
Those fatal shots had struck his head
Within the hour, he would be dead
When word had come that he had died
Women wept and grown men cried
Cries of sorrow everywhere
A nation bowed its head in prayer
Part of America died that day
As she gave to God her J.F.K.
A horse-drawn casket, passing by
A little salute, a last goodbye
These are the things remembered best
As a nation laid her son to rest
A terrible price he had to pay
A man so loved should die that way
This tragic page in history
Was opened for the world to see
The years have come and gone so fast
His leadership lies in the past
The lasting memory of his name
Will burn through THE ETERNAL FLAME. . .

Stanley L. Patrick

ROSES I LIKE

Roses Roses Roses Roses I like
Roses Roses Roses They are my delight
I buy them buy the dozen then I buy a dozen more
If I had the money I'd open a Roses Store
I'd have tons of them in my front yard, back yard too
I'd even keep Roses In My Shoe
I like them Big, I like them Small.
I'd like Roses ten feet tall
One day my Mother gave me a dime for ice cream, instead I bought a Rose.
The store owner took it and put it to my nose
Roses Roses Roses, Roses I like.

Roy Tenth

BEFOGGED

The lifeless sails hang empty in the mist,
Fade faintly at the peak into the fog;
The hull drifts helmless toward an unknown tryst,
Its rudder useless to a floating log.
The ear strains in the silence for a sound
Of danger, safety, company at least:
The flattened sea is quiet all around—
Eternity is now, all motion ceased.
The fogged—in mind sees

tragedy at hand.
It seeks to penetrate the ghostly gloom,
Finds rocks, and reefs, and driftings onto land,
Considers only certain, evil doom.
A face, a voice, a touch—beyond one's own:
No one was ever meant to be alone.

Julius F. Gilbert

A VIKING SAGA

Red was the color of hero's blood.
Shed in battle and mixed with blood.
Red was the color of dripping blades
Which sent many warriors to investigate Hades.

Red was the color of many a shield,
Of Vikings who died refusing to yield.
Red was the color of wine raised in toasts,
To the swords that changed men into nebulous ghosts.
Red was the beard of the Viking bold,
Who filled his hold with the loot of gold.
Red were the waters from many throats slit,
As the waves swirled around the Viking's bow-sprit.
Red was the sky as the fast burning town
Shot flames to the clouds, raining charred debris down.
Red were the hearts that were broken that day,
Weeping for souls that had sailed away.
Red was the sun in the early dawn.—
Only the birds were left to mourn.

Cindy Marie Edwards

ISA—LA—GHI (CHEEROKEE)

Their footsteps spread as wings on wind.
Backs sharp with the weight,
faces hard from the sun,
the fall of their voices
heavy on air,
they spiral downward
into white-man's towns.

Robert Alvin Davis

LAURA BELLE

'Twas once upon a yesterday
I wished upon a wishing well.
The Gods they smiled, my wish came true
My life was blessed, with LAURA BELLE.
Such lovely thoughts, now I recall
'Twas on a summer's night in June.
How we held hands by the garden gate
And threw kisses to the moon.
We strolled along, side by side
Hand in hand, just you and I.
While a million stars played peek-a-boo
And danced across a blushing sky.
Now, down the gleaming halls of time
The years have fled so fast away.
Though youth is gone, our love remains
Mid treasured moments of yesterday.
I thank you Lord, for granting me
The wish I wished upon the wishing well.
And these fond memories, I hold so dear
As I hold so close, my LAURA BELLE.

Pam Carson

A FRIEND

A Friend is always there to talk to and to help you...
A Friend is always concerned about you...
A Friend will cheer you up and make you laugh...
A Friend is loving and caring like you...
A Friend is a very special person to have for a long time...
A Friend is someone to love...
A Friend is you Irene...
We all love you.
Get well soon
love,
Pat & Tabetha

Roxanne Lagasse

ONE LEAF

One leaf that never fell
Strongly endured every storm
Time will never tell
The secret way that it is formed
There shall never be another one
Of its kind
The making of a new sun
Will loosen the bind
The many storms shook it
With all their might
Having great wit
The leaf held tight
A new day shall come
Making the very first day
All events shall sum
Of the leaf that never strayed

Miss Wilma Scott

SPINSTERHOOD

Just because I'm single
at an age I won't disclose;
Doesn't mean I'm fickle,
or have gone without the beaux.
The term 'Old Main' is misleading!
And here's the point I'm stressing;
I haven't vowed to single life.
I'm just an unclaimed blessing.

Evelyn Pendleton Jervey

ROCK CLIMBING

I was looking at you
Through a haze of others;
Little-boy-smile that eased
The claws of my indecision.
Once, when I was sticking
Like a fly to a cold rock face,
I fell and swung free;
The rope tightened in your hands
And I was climbing again.
I thought then that I should stay—
A day; forever maybe—
But somewhere a glowing coal
Has surged into fire
And there is no resting here.
These rocks are bruising my fingers,
And above me is a hang-glider,
Flying as I crawl, a plaything for the wind;
Together we are chasing a shadow.

Rahela Bavli

TO GO AWAY

To go away, to go away,
Where to?
Where clover grows
And roots and spices
Their wondrous ways
display.
Where wings and winds
And broken up thoughts
that roam
Will ask, will beg:
Please take me back
Home!

Cynthia V. Adford

HARDSHIP OF A PUPPET

To have and not to want so many puppets
That I should be one.
To be strung up,
and held by feelings and then to fall short.
To be hung.
To be tangled up in routine dance
Even though the show must go on.

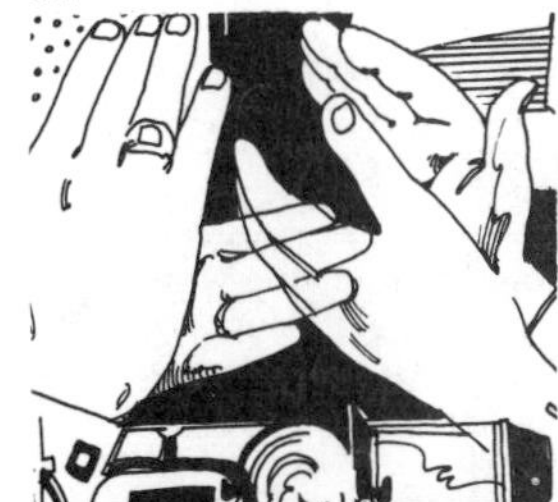

Yes, the audience will see
Though just for a glance
For my curtain is no longer drawn
Which brings me down to this
Flung around an empty stage,
With wired strings that are stitched.
Broken pieces of wooden flesh deserted
Remaining unfixed
My thoughts collected
But that's all that'll fit.
For my real existence doesn't exist...

Ashjr

MY DAD

He stands in the middle of a field,
back, bare, brown, and roped with muscles.
Brown, a color that fits him.
His hair after young blond turned rich brown,
his skin sun and wind-burned brown,
his college a good firm Ivy school, Brown.
Trained as a diplomat,
he once knew four languages to speak.
A stoic, unemotional, even-tempered Yankee,
the rocky brown earth called him.
Now he makes his living land surveying,
wandering down city streets or through the woods.
Now a bearded gray haired man,
who still feels at home,
walking through the woods and splitting wood;
running a church vestry and settling disputes.
He knows the birds by their calls,
and debates foreign policy with politicians.
Never raising his voice, always making his point.
The one we listen to,
once we all stop shouting.

Dorsey Robbins

My Autumn Love Affair

I can see the sun again,
The flowers make me aware
Of the beautiful spring
In my Autumn love affair.
I have found me a man
Who makes me smile again.
He makes my heart sing,
And he makes life worth while again.
When I first met him
My heart did a double take.
Two lonely people
Lost in a sea of heartache.
I became more acquainted
My heart turned around
To see a bit of sky-blue
And thought a loving heart I had found!

Sylvia Betz-Lambert

SO—YOUNG DEATH... SUMMER, '81

When will the
Longing sleep
And not ache within
The dream?
I listen for the song
Her children cannot
Sing—the sun does not
Comfort the hollows
Of the day—and shadows
Glare from every
Pain—sought hide-a-way—
Precious ashes
Choke sobs from the
Grieving of the wind
And I beg the streets of
Night to show
Her face again.

Bud Brandon

FLIGHT OF THE RED TAIL HAWK

Soft rays of sunlight caress the morning sky
With ease and grace of motion he rises now to fly.
With outstretched wings he reaches, higher does he climb
His circle's growing wider each

and every time.
High above the prairie he sees
both big and small
This silent prairie watchman
high above it all.
Sharpe and deadly talons lie
sheathed in feathers now
He sours upon the morning
wind watching the grasses
bow.
His swiftly moving shadow
crosses the ground so near
Like some gostly shadow filling
small hearts with fear.
All through the day he makes
his endless quest
Soaring high above the trees
untill the sun sinks in the
west.
As evening shadows beckon, we
hear the watchmans cry
His angry protest against the
darkness that takes away his
sky.

Giula S. Wiggs

Heavenly Friendliness

"Good morning, God" I said
and with bated breath
and kneeling heart I waited
for His answer.
A slight breeze passed over the
trees
that clapped their hands
and through the lilac bush
and sweetly kissed my cheek.
The bright sun and soft clouds
that played a changing scene
caused the friendliness
to permeate my soul.
The green grass seemed to be
joyous
as it played with the breeze—
the beauty of the flowers
waiting for me to behold.
The quiet, the hush of a new
day—
the unknown, the wonders of
life—
Children breaking the stillness
screaming with glee.
God is very friendly.

Robert Gilbaugh

THE SPOT

I see a spot,
a spot there on the page.
The spot is hot,
a spot resembling rage.
I perceive it from the left
of the page;
There is hunger and fear
and a turning stage.
A Bolshevic, a Fabian or a
Commissar
I see walking;
Around the spot they strut,
about the destinies of people
talking.
The spot turns from blue to red
and a sea
Of human flesh I see, floating
dead
and now free.
I move about to view the spot
from above;
From here I see attempts at kind
kindness
and human love.
A love that set the world
aflame,
burning human flesh;
Incineration of a race their
only shame,
Poor, poor love, let's start
afresh.
To the right I move to view the
spot,
a new hatred,
Burning passions, society here
begins to rot,
stage by stage.
A Facist leads the awful march,
calling it a mere parade
Where does the human heart
hide
from this charade
Now to view the spot complete,
tiresomely I move my feet;
At lower center of the spot is
seen defeat,
round the circle impassioned
heat.
The spot is not a spot
resembling
rage;
The spot is just a spot
upon the page.
To this impassioned, buring
hated spot
I say farewell;
As crumpled in my hand the
page
from thought expel.

Dorothy Pinkerton

PEACE ON EARTH

Since the beginning there've
been wars and rumors of such.
O, rumors are tumors, they
reach out and clutch.
Rumors are languages made up
of words
Turning peace into turmoil,
staffs into swords.
Language barriers breed
confusion, violence, war—

Hope flies out the window, hate
comes in the door.
Discard all those barriers, allow
us instead
Love, music and beauty to say
what is said.
We'll find lovers and brothers,
we'll touch, not shove;
Many, many are the faces of
love.
Play music, listen, to the music
of nations—
Move with the dance, feel the
vibrations.
Carillons, sound out The Ave
Marie-a,
Organs, The World Awaits The
Sunrise la—la la,
Choirs, please, so all hear and
see
What A Friend We Have In
Jesus, He Leadeth Me.
Joyous bells, begin, ring out,
sing, call, jingle, shout!
Now comes a medley, noise of
war must cease.
O, The Bells Of St. Mary's I
hear they are calling
LET US HAVE PEACE, LET US
HAVE PEACE.

Linda Kaye Atkinson

BEFORE THE SNOW PLOW COMES

Kneeling on my bed my
elbows
resting on the window sill I
watch
the white
crystals
falling.
Falling
on my shoveled walk,
falling
on my '66 Plymouth
parked in the street,
falling
on the evergreen
which sways
softly,
freshly.
I want to watch a little while
longer
now while everyone else is
sleeping.
Before the yellow flashing lights
and sloshing wheels
come humming in the morning.

Nancy Marie Hutchins

UNTITLED

In your eyes, I see the reflection
of pain & sorrow.
In your lips, I see the
bittersweet truth of you &
me.
In your face, I see the dreams of
tomorrow.
In your hands, I see the heavy
load that you carry.
In your heart, I see the
everlasting fire of love.
And when I am lying next to
you, caressing your very body
& soul, you give to me more
than words can say.
To me, you are everything that
life can give; love, faith,
hope, & the dreams of
tomorrow-today.
So when the night gets too
lonely, or the road, just too
long to bare, I'll just look into
your loving eyes, & be
fulfilled with the strength to
carry on.

Dr. Mildred Tennyson McNair

MY SON

My son listen and hear me well. How much you understand only time will tell. Tomorrow will always be a day away. Start getting your self ready to be a man today.

Search for truth and always give your best. Be prepared for disappointments, which is your greatest test. Dream dreams. . . then work to make them come true. Don't worry about anyone just believe in you.

Serve your fellowman but, worship only one God. Be sure your tracks are visible wherever you trod. Expect nothing but be willing to give all you can. You're God's creation fashioned by His own hands.

There will be setbacks and crosses to bear. Look to the Almighty. . .He'll always be there. After you've given your best find a little more to give. This is how to make it if you want to live.

Remember you're God's child. He watches over you. Keep Him in mind and always in view. Someday You'll talk to your son as I'm talking to you. Your life will determine the good it will do.

Dedicated to men everywhere who believe that the killing of black youth in Atlanta must never again happen. . . . anywhere. . . .and my Son, Odis Medley, Jr.

Pat Lampman

THE CLOCK

The clock of life is wound but
once,
And no man has the power
to tell just when the hands will
stop,
At late or early hour.
Now is the only time you own,
Live, love, toil with a will;
Place no faith in tomorrow,
For the clock may then be
still.

Bruce R. Lindsay

TEENAGE VALENTINE

A pretty poem, but it's not mine
Prewritten on your valentine
So I covered over-the one thats
shown
And replaced it with-one of my
own
I remember many years ago
When I was very young
I hardly ever received
A valentine from anyone
I use to stuff the box in school
When no one else would see
And pretend they came from
one who cared
They did!—They came from me!
And many times I felt unwanted
And forsaken from above
But as I grew—I came to know
That there are many kinds of
love
There is the love I feel for
your mother
The love of friendship—we
understand
But love is not at all confined
To a woman and a man
But shared by every one on
earth
As we live from day to day
Be it family friend or parent
All love you in a different way
There is the love I have for my
mother
Who's love was always at hand
And although I couldn't see it
Her love helped me become a
man

There is the love I have for my children
Who I guided as they grew tall
And though we disagreed sometimes
I loved them most of all
And on this day of hearts and flowers
In which love is shared by two
My gift of love—A single rose
That can mean only "I love you"
And to complement this rose—I wrote
A poem for you—that's mine
And a message of love I've written
To my "teenage valentine"

C. L. Serra

FRIENDSHIP IN A CUP

Come sit, my friend, and let us share
new warmth with gladness stirring there—
The work and toil put aside,
relax for now, with me confide
Let's chat awhile and sip our brew,
you'll trust in me, and I'll in you—
This simple cup, so oft ignored,
rekindles friendship, faith restored. . .
Then later, when life's much to bear—
come sit, my friend. . .
and let us share—

William C. Boughner

TO THE WILD GEESE

Once again you leave these marshes,

Take to air on eager wing,
Pointing Southward in your flight,
To return again next spring.
You have kept wild nature's promise,
Bringing forth the fledgling brood,
As advised by mother nature,
In accord with nature's mood.
I am grieved to see you leaving,
Truly wish it were not so,
But the South wind once more lures you,
Mother nature bids you go.
Winging upward toward the azure,
Oh how graceful in your flight!
Silhouettes against the sunrise,
And soon departing from my sight.
Notes of your song keep coming to me,
Faint on the air in rhythmic beat,
Notes from the song of your departure,
Somehow sad, yet hauntingly sweet.
Now silence reigns since your departure,
An earthly silence so profound,
And as I stand in awe and wonder,
Nature makes her appointed round.
From this quietness and this silence,
I draw what solace they may bring,
And dream bright dreams of your returning,
Your sure returning in the spring.

Patricia L. Devenberg

POETS OF OLD

I dream dreams of poets of old.
In my dreams I sit
with Whitman, Longfellow too.
We muse on poetry, day's events.

I marvel in their knowledge.
In my dream, I'm published.
I walk deep among the words,
picking them, like flowers.
Bouquets upon the printed page.
Whitman, Longfellow too
quote me,
and tell of my poetry.

Then too soon I wake
and there
among my books
I find my writing
more like weeds,
As Whitman and Longfellow
picked all the flowering bouquets.

Dennis M. Macaulay

WHO ARE YOU?

You say it's wrong, the way I live
My life not mine to live
Speak not of love and hate, you make one into the other
Fear is what you preach, twist the Word and fear you should
Believe, I do, not as you
It's wrong you say; for me to see what you dare not
Speak as for myself with not a care for what you'd not mouth
Temples built strong, poor and rich from which to preach
But none so strong and pure as to not be wrong
You say you speak for Him, I doubt you do!!
Understanding and compassion you are lacking
You say it's wrong the way I live
Stay in your temple and hide in fear
I shall walk tall and proud for I fear not
Can we converse, you say not
Evil am I, so say you, who know me not
I know you not, but your kind I do
You speak of peace, but wars you cause
So righteous, as you malign and slander all who are not of your persuasion
Who are you?
God only knows or does he?

Randall B. Gelford

THE CHANGE

Incident 1
The sun was warm
on my face
And my October spirit
became alive with spring
Incident 2
The wind blew softly
through the raining leaves
And in the gentleness
I grew with the sun
Incident 3
The darkness rained
and puddles blossomed
I did, too
and splashed barefoot
Incident 4
Forgetting my self
I opened the door
My soul broke free
and went wild with the wind

David A. Desautel

EVENING SNOW

Standing; on a quiet night in a snowstorm
Sounds; like a quiet whisper all around you
Specks; of pale reflected light from each snowflake
Softness; the hard cruel world has become soft
Beauty; the ugliness of the city has become beautiful
Clean; the dirty junkplies have become clean
You feel as if you could float across the landscape
Light, soft fingers brush your face and beckon you forward
Your feet are cold, but your heart is warm
And there's a warm loving hand in yours
Both hands are in the baggage compartment of your coat pocket
You start to walk, but you don't turn around
Because you don't want to see how you raped the virgin snow

Harry F. Bangert

MAKE SOMEONE SMILE

Have you made someone smile today?
have you eased a troubled heart,
Have you listened to someone elses woes,
and set your own apart?
No matter how rocky we think our road,
how rough the storm and the strife,
There's someone out there worse off than we,
to whom we can bring a new life.
Get out of yourself a little each day,
give a boost to someone who is down,
An encouraging word, a smile from the heart,
will do much to remove a frown.
This caring and sharing with our fellow man
is what He meant life to be all about,
To help ease a burden, to help dry a tear,
to help others put troubles to rout.
To know you've helped someone from pits of despair
given hope when all things seemed in vain,
Brings a feeling so warm, so fulfilling, so rich,
when you see what kind words can attain.
So, try every day to make someone smile.
reach out with a smile of your own,
Show them there's Hope and Love up ahead,
and they never need walk alone.

Carol A. Fay

SUMMER

Summer's at the door;
Hot air flowing through the spaces.
The scent of charcoal,
Burning food, sweaty faces.
Mosquitoes whining,
Biting flies, bees attacking,
Vicious ants dining
While the picnickers are packing.
The violent storms,
Hot steam rising from the pavement,
Parched red skin peeling,
Overpriced beach houses for rent.
The stifling, choking air,
The sneaker tracks in your garden,
Watermelon pits in your hair
As a child begs your pardon.
All this is summer, and more
I won't now recall.
A pleasure? It sounds more like war.
How many days left until it is fall?

C. Garfield Rider

AMERICAN DEMOCRACY FOR BLACKS

Black Abraham unsure when he was born,
He was never rightly sure just where.
Some said his Father was never known,
His Mother died soon after his birth.
Abraham as he used to say and smile,
Did not grow up, was yanked by the ear.
All his Brothers, Sisters, Uncles and Aunts
By robbing self, helped in his raising.
Abe was never at the speaker's table;
Usually he was standing in the back.
Black Abraham some way somehow got

A Divine sense of duty, concern, love.
Abraham knew the longing, the searching
In the soul of every laden person.
He could not hide his heart, his convictions.
The local powers saw him as a threat.
On a rainy, stormy night in May,
Fourteen whites, one lonely black rode out.
Just as the rope tightened around Abe's neck,
Lightning incrusted the fourteen in fire.
The community lost fourteen villians.
Black Abraham "mosyed" up to Heaven.
Democracy for blacks wiggles, bows;
Thor, between winings, sends a little justice.

Nicole Mala
SHORELESS NIGHT
Echoing cries of insanity
Hurling epithets at my mind
Tornado ripping through my stomach
Snakes slithering inside
Ravaging inner organs
Senseless persistent savagery.
Deafened by screeching sirens
Fleeing relentless pursuers
Strangling crucifixion
Slipping grasp
Clutching for a hold
Hanging, unheeded, from a precepice
Above oceans of perspiration.
Crippling exertion
Harsh injustice
Living rainbow death
Cruel desire
Inundating my senses
Black hate
Screwing my mind
Excruciating reality
Annihilating incomplete thoughts
Throbbing senses
Reeling heartbeat
Bleeding impassioned seas
Stained waves raging
Palling horizons of faith
Transient hours,
Infinite seconds—
Spasmodic time
Lingering consciousness
Surrender of thought
Curled up in a tight knot;
Knees to chest
Clenched fists encircling them
Pushing in intensely
Fierce, shaking concentration on
Tightening the knot into
Nonexistence

Marie Woodruff Moehn
CHRIST JESUS
I have met the perfect man.
with endless strength in his hands.
So strong, I cannot understand.
Manhood at its very best,
In him I find my peace and rest.
He has stood my timeless test.
For his good life so devine,
I would gladly give up mine.
How can he be so wondrous fine?
God understands my kind of love,
God is like a beautiful white dove.
God is descending from above.

Darlene Daum Pfister
REST THY SOUL
Rest Thy Soul in the Lord
For He will ease thy pain,
If in prayer you seek Him,
He'll leave you ne'er again.
Study, fast and pray,
It hurts for just a while
To know that you have failed
To go the narrow miles.
But, if you will repent
I promise you you'll see
More joy and happiness
Than you thought that there could be.
I've walked high in the mountains
And in the desert floor;
I've touched the gates of Heaven
And knocked at Hell's dark door.
I know your heart is heavy
Your body aches with pain,
But repent with Godly sorrow,
God will send the cleansing rain.
Then how bright the 'morrow,
A rainbow will appear
And you will have a blessing
For every fallen tear.

Susan Marie Cross
The Secondary Nature
I am of secondary nature.
For I speak, but no one listens;
I listen, but hear only silence;
I dance, but there is no music;
I sing, but the melody is forgotten.
Yes, I am of a secondary nature.
For to my own heart I am not true,
But am consumed in pain when deceived.
So I conceal my anger towards all others;
But this cancer of malice decays my soul.
Yes, I am of a secondary nature.
For I open my arms to a friend,
But am betrayed by trespasses of closeness.
So when I cry out in the dark of night,
Even surrounded, I am alone.
Yes, I am of a secondary nature.
For Hope's shining light dims quickly,
And the harvest of failure is too plentiful—
And the cold sweat beaded on my brow glistens
But is dulled by the glare of my fear.
For I was to be the rule for many, but I cannot
See past tonight's deep sleep.
Yes, I am of a secondary nature.

Virginia Carden
HORTATORY FLIGHT
Awaken quite early for their stary flight
While all earth watched what a breathtaking beautiful sight
As they are gliding upward with a trembling roar
The moon they were going to explore
Earth looked like a pretty patch work quilt
So filled with greed anger sin and guilt
A spirit suddenly came over them
They knew they had viewed earth through the eyes of him
A prayer was said with greatest of care
They knew then their Savior was there
Fear not I am with thee in all endeavers
Life, Death, Space, travels or where ever
Their splash down came quiet as planed
They were guarded by those nail scarred hands
Their knowledge was far greater still
They learned to live by faith and do the Lords will
Had they not had the pleasure to go and to win
They might have drifted forever in cold dark sin.

Shirley Ann Kimber
MY MUTTON-HEAD
I love that mutton-head o' mine;
But he thinks we c'n live on a dime!
I improvise as best I can:
(Scrimp an' save all th' time)!
Out o' sugar? I'll pulverize some sugar-LUMPS!
(Yea. . .use th' hammer t' crumble th' bumps).
Then I used m' rollin'-pin.
(All those objections! You make an awful din)!
When I run out o' somethin',
YOU say, "Go BUY it!"
But our food-money's hit an all-time pit!
I talked to th' manager, but he said, "NO!"
"Wait 'till your Social Security check; THEN shop. Now GO!"
I love that mutton-head o' mine;
But HE thinks we c'n live on a dime!

What'll I do for WALNUTS, now?
Grapenuts have a NUTTY flavor:
This concoction ought t' win his favor!
Brown sugar, . . .now let me see:
A cup o' Golden Griddle ought t' do.
Necessary supplies are exceedingly few!
Let's see. . .a substitute for MILK?
Oh! COFFEE-MATE an' WATER.
(Fill th' cup to th' hilt).
That's camouflaging like I oughter!
Come on, chickens, lay an EGG.
Would CREAM O' TARTER do, instead?
Now, for *Margerine*, what'll I use?
Three in one or EYE-WRINKLE OIL? (Original recipies'r sheer abuse!)
Flour's a needed ingredient, 'tis true!
You think crushed, cold cereal'd do?
What'll flavor all this mess?
(A dash o' RUM'd be MY guess).
I've tried SO HARD th- live-long day!
(My mutton-head won't take a TASTE).
Now with his discontent, I'll have to pay!
"It's MUCH MORE FLAVORFUL, dear, THIS WAY!"

Sandra Fulmer
CAN YOU SEE?
Feelings that surround you,
Busy people everywhere.
There vapors will touch,
To color and penetrate the air.
They walk into the pure,
They run through the evil.
Some linger in the in between,
Then enjoy none of either.
The roads of life are confusing,
Temptation on every corner.
Choose the cover that is suited,
Wear it to be all guarded.
Choose a cover that has worked,
And life becomes rewarded.
Your suit is only yours,
Seen by the atuned eye only.
It is your cloud for life,
A gift from one that is only.

Patricia Scoggin
MY NEIGHBOR, MY FRIEND
I practiced
late last night
because
my husband
went hunting
my children were
finally asleep
my 'cello is
now repaired
I hope I didn't
wake you

Amy Larsen
THE PIANIST
The life of a pianist,
is an expressive art,
That can take you from Mozart,
to the life of Bach.
It is an art of feeling,
lifting mind and soul,
And joining artist and listener,
in unicent accord.
While looking so deeply,
onto the printed note,
The artist awakens
The sleeping spirit that controls,
the composer's emotions
Found beneath the note.
Now, as the artist's performance

is done,
And the applause of his
listeners
approval he's won,
he finds both contentment
of mind and soul
And the drive that is
needed to fulfill other
goals.

Lisa A. Tekancic
**THE GIFT—
(FOR JEFFREY)**
The greatest gift in life
is the gift of friendship.
It is a strength in your
life
that you can truly depend
on to build your inner
self.
—with a certain love
to nourish it—
It can only grow deeper
. . .than the mind
can hope. . .
. . .or the soul
can reach. . .

Ollie D. Harkleroad
JUDGE ME NOT
Judge me not by what you hear
The time may come for you to
fear
The time of living all alone
Having no one nor place to call
· home
I am the tired and lonely one
With a daughter and a son
Doing the very best I can
To make their little world seem
more bright
Somethings I do I know are
wrong
But my kids have the right to
belong
Judge me not by what you hear
Unless you've faced this time of
fear
A Time of hearing your child
say
"Mommie, I'm hungry, have we
groceries today?"
Only then are you in a postion
to judge me
For if you're honest I think
you'll see
That I am doing the very best I
can
Not wanting my kids to carry
the brand
The brand of being a nobody

When everyone deserves a
chance to be somebody.

Madeline B. Goode
MUSINGS
Sometimes I sit and wonder
What causes it to thunder,
Is it the angels playing the horn,
Or a drum all smashed, beaten
and torn?
Do the angels have a band that
can be heard all over the land?
Is thunder the sound of
marching feet
Trying to keep the rhythmic
beat?
What causes the lightning in
the sky
Quicker than we can bat an eye?
Is it the angels checking us out?
Tell me what it's all about.
I only know I must not be
afraid,
Is it some bowling game being
played?
When spring and summer come
around
We hear that old familiar sound,
Who can explain it, what does it
mean?
Is God appearing on the scene?
Sometimes while walking
through the park
It starts to get very, very dark,
I join the crowd, and in my
hurry
I again begin to fret and worry.
Sometimes with the flashing and
thunderous boom
Everything rattles and shakes in
my room.
I can't hide from this terrible
noise
(Does this fear enter the hearts
of boys)?
"No need to hide from me, My
Dear,"
That's God's whisper in my ear.
Sometimes with the booming
and flashing comes rain,
Then silence, everything is still
again.
Look around and you can see
Little buds peeping out at you
and me.
Earthworms and toad frogs come
from nowhere
They seem to float through the
atmosphere.
Then all is serene and calm for
a while,
And I can begin to walk and
smile.

Paul P. Czech Jr.
SHADOW
Oh, what soul and matter do
you possess?
Why, shadow, do you follow as I
roam?
Is your body forbidden to
trespass
From some isolated and
unearthly home?
What do you watch as we walk
side by side?
Do you laugh when I commit
error or evil,
And when you retire, where do
you abide?
Do you discuss these things
with the devil?
But if, shadow, you are the
lasting truth,
Then like you, too, I would but
ask to be,
To walk beside the fools of this
vast earth,
And have them look upon the
good of me:
Are you evil temptation to the
last,
Or the best remains of life that
has passed?

Richard Gasiorek
LANDSCAPE
Sprouting trees of gathering
woody dots
Across the landscape the eye
fills
Gentle sights and pale wavering
images
Delicate leaves and distant
branches
Cool caressing breezes and
distant stars
Clear black skies of shimmering
lights
The eye prevails and speaks its
images
The senses delight and entertain
Reason passes bye
The dry stream along its molded
bed
Once muddy dew so giving of
life
Carefully folded branches foiling
in disguise
Tendrills of work and worry
For all who care

Estelle Hooper Munsell
BUTTERFLIES ARE FREE
As I stood in the yard
Just the other day,
A butterfly lit on my hand
And did not fly away.
And as I looked in wonder
At its gossamer wings,
My heart ached to keep it
With my other lovely things.
Gently then I captured it
And put it in a cage,
And watched the frantic beating
Of its tiny wings in rage.
And though I longed to keep it
Close within my sight,
I took it back outside
And lifted it in flight.
For butterflies are born to fly

And flit from place to place
Freely sipping nectar
From each fragrant flower's face.
And as I watched it soaring
Up into the blue,
I found myself remembering
The way I was with you.
And I knew that as the butterfly
So you were meant to be
Beautiful and special
Only when you're free.
And so I open up my hands
To let you fly away,
Hoping that my love for you
Will bring you back someday.

Margaret Malinoske
DECEMBER TAKE OVER
Last summer where the roses
competed to reach
The top of the arbor,
Now only dark, brown vines
remain; brittle.
December's cold takes over
Giving the arbor a thin shellac
of ice.
The front lawn shimmers like a
diamond lake
Where the sun hits the icy grass
tips,
Leaving only a reminder of
yesterday.
On the lee side of the wood,
the ice falls
In cold drops where sun rays
warm the dried bark.
And then quietly
December takes over
completely,
Covering everything with a
thick, white
Blanket of snow. And the world
sleeps
Until it is spring again.

Nancy Ladd
OLD BARNS
Have you ever noticed the sides
of old barns?
Most have happy, contented
smiling faces,
And some have a window-eye
that winks and warns
Passing motorists speeding to
all sorts of places.
"Slow down," warn these barns.
"Enjoy the countryside.
Don't speed through your life
just for the ride!"
I wonder if these well-worn
barns which the farmers built
Were intentionally planned to
add a bit of laughter?
"Life is rough," the farmers say.
"We've had it up to the hilt!
But then, there's always next
year's crop, or the year after."
For generations farmers have
had to take it on the chin.
They are patient, persevering,
and philosophical.
So why shouldn't they create
something to make others
grin?
Something that's both beautiful
and plain and practical.
Maybe, subconsciously, these
barn sides that smile
Is the farmers' way of telling the
world—now on trial,
"Forget your fears, frustrations,
and sorrows,
For there's always hope for
better tomorrows!"

Clarence J. Russell
THE YOKE
Conformity, you tyrant, you are
deceitful,
You reassure while deceiving
and confusing;
Following becomes a doctrine,
and a chain.
You create a dungeon for the
mind;
Indifference is your ally,
Complacency dominates in your
realm.
Unchallenged horizons lie in
stagnation;
The new becomes the
"conqueror,"
The untried remains the
unproven;
Routine becomes compulsion.
Fortunately some things are still
beyond your grasp,
Determination, perseverance,
and hope still abound.

Shirley M. Jones
GOSSIP
The tongue it is a mighty sword
It cuts a swath so wide,
It brings words from a loving heart
that makes us all feel good inside.
But like a knife it cuts so deep
when not held in control,
It rocks the world around us
and shakes us to our very soul.
God's gift to use so wisely
was given long ago,
So friend make sure the words you speak
are things you really know.
Think twice about the things you say,
If your words can hurt someone
Remember that if left unsaid
less harm will then be done.
Guard this member constantly
then perhaps some pain will cease:
And you will have done your part my friend,
TO HELP BRING SOMEONE,
JOY AND PEACE.

Jim Luckadoo
As You Sleep In The Casket Made Of Gold
as you sleep all alone in your casket made of gold.
how i wish i could hold you one more time.
and how i wish i had just told you i loved you.
but as you lie here cold and stiff and they bury you beneath the cliff
I pause dear near your grave and ask god to save me.
and as i pray i say a prayer for you. I hope some day you'll come back.
And i awoke to find this was only a dream. and i began to scream.
and i got up and ran down to the stream and the sun had begun to beam
down as i run i found it was hot and i began to fan and hunt a spot
in the shade and there wasn't any. and i began to weep as i waded
deep into the stream dark shadows began to creep. and i found i was
bound for the unknown and where the wind had blown many times.
and far off in the distance i heard the church bells chime,
and i knew it was the end of time and i knew there would be no more crime
for you see its written in the word and we know its true for he drew
a blue print in his great big mint and i know thats where you went
up there in the sky thats why i cry and try to keep on loving you
as they plant you beneath the cold cold clay this way.
and i hope i may see you again someday when i go up there to stay
and never go astray just then the bells began to ring and the angels began to sing their song so sweet and i begin to meet them all
and oh what a treat that will be up there in that land.

Cindy Kilgore
HOMAGE
We all must go
back to our mother
and give
birth
to a
new life.
Don't weep for me,
my friend,
because
I am giving way
to a new
being.
I am the fruit
of your survival
and
my existence
will endure
through
a circle of
evolution.

Margaret Rohrs Higgins
COMMUNION
Hello my treasured friend, I still miss you,
Though the ocean is silent, green and gentle—
The mountains commanding, snow-brushed and strong,
I WISH them for you, and become so sentimental.
Hello my treasured friend, I still miss you,
As the breeze in the pines is sighing—
The moon's glow on the water is tranquil,
Yet, old memories are more satisfying.
Hello my treasured friend, I still miss you,
While the ships travel, like my imagination—
Back peacefully, to our many moments,
Can meeting again be our destination?
Hello my treasured friend, I still miss you,
We'll share the repose my Island provides,
Then we can sit and laugh together once more,
At life's ever changing, challenging tides.

Wm. Stobbs
UNTITLED
Arriving home late at night
Drunk with love and wine
I suddenly stopped to watch the wind
Stir the phantom trees,
And pissed a silver stream
Beneath the autumn moon.

J. Alan Hostetter
SON
Father, my father, farmer of my seed,
who planted me alone to grow
and watches from his window
while the winter tortures me,
what kind of crop am I to be?

Lewis H. Dudley Sr.
THE AUCTIONEER
It makes him happy to see a crowd;
To apply his talents, makes him proud;
He has an eye for appraising you;
He knows just about what you will do.
Whether the bid be high or low,
The auctioneer knows how far to go;
He'll stir you up and edge you on—
Then haunt your thoughts after you've gone.
He acts like he doesn't care if you buy—
All the same, he keeps a wary eye;
He'll make you think he's selling the Mint,
For the spiel he gives is evident.
He'll have to sell you or lose a sale
And you can bet he knows he musn't fail—
For failure can mean a turnabout
And he knows a loser is on the way out.
He makes a pretty penny here and there;
He knows how to make the public aware;
It's not that the money means so much—
The matter is just that he *keeps his touch.*

Betty J. King Bullman
HATRED
How do you say "loathe" in less than 1,000 words?
Is it at all possible to describe how I hate?
I float in limbo with no hope of light.
No reaching out—there's nothing to touch.
I curl into myself and find—horrors!—emptiness!
God! They've bled me to infinity!
A never-ending circle of utter dispair and hopelessness
Made manifest by their hands.
I need to touch, to feel, to laugh, to love, to cry, to LIVE!
God! Remove this existence and give me peace.
My soul cries out in anguish for nourishment but no one hears.
My heart has dissolved with the bitter acid of their gall.
I seek rest, contentment, happiness,
Whether it be in life or death—no matter.
Only allow this to END.

Carroll A. Jewett
MEDITATION
I wonder by what gift of chance
I dwell on this plateau,
When people in poor circumstance
Are living far below.
What have I done to earn the right
To be on such high ground,
While they who strive to reach this height
By man made rules are bound?
Where freedom lives there is a price
And we must share the cost.
Those who refuse to sacrifice
Should count their cause as lost.
Full Freedom's Rights can be attained.
Such problems can be solved;
But only when respect is gained
By all who are involved.
To work together for Peace on Earth,
With guidance from above,
Can fill our minds with thoughts of worth,
Our hearts with greater love.
Then as we labor side by side
Throughout our Native Land,
We'll find that love and peace abide
Where people understand.

John William Rapparlie
THE FRIEND
Hold it tight
now let it go
don't run too fast
can't run too slow.
Feel the pull
gentle breeze
magically soaring
above the trees.
Dancing, bouncing,
tail of silk,
rhythmic symphony
clouds of milk.
Ball of twine,
then two; now three,
bright red ship
deep blue sea.
Tiny shadow
stay in sight
sudden dive
pull with might.
Tear stained cheek
wind claimed right
injured friend
broken kite.

Robert Alvin Davis
IF I WAS BUT A POET
I just had a lovely inspiration
Oh God, what a beautiful thought
And alas, IF I WAS BUT A POET
Then, it all wouldn't go for naught.
With pen in hand, I'd sit right down
I'd write myself a lovely poem
Thereby fulfilling, my fondest dream
Here in my rocking chair at home.
From pen to paper, words gently flowing
Into the grandest poem of all

times
As all the lovely thoughts, I've
thought
Becomes the most loveliest of
all rhymes.
And alas, IF I WAS BUT A
POET
Then, be it for better or for
worse
I'd share this great poetical
creation
With all you lovers of rhyme
and verse.
For then indeed, here is what I
would do
And dear friend, I do not jest
Why, I'd send it in to Eddie-Lou
For the latest poetry writing
contest.

Jan Renfrow
BETWEEN DIVER AND NON:
"What is it down there
That lures you so, Child?"

"Down there it is still
So free and so wild!
With Nature the ruler,
We'd better watch out—
We're guests in her wetland,
Just checking it out!"
"And what if it happens—
You come by a shark?"
"I could also be eaten
By a bear in some park.
I could die on the freeway,
Or in my own bed—
However it happens,
I'll be just as dead!"
"And what if the water
Should wrinkle your skin?"
"Then those who want beauty
Must find it within!
And though I am careful,
What happens will be—
Nothing will keep me
From diving the sea!"
"You sound so emphatic—
What more can I say?"
"I hope you will join me
In the ocean someday!"

Alan Baron
HOMEWARD BOUND
Oh to be walking new highways
remembering good times
Smelling grassy green Earth
Mother
her mountain breasts looming
high on coastline of Soul
ruby red orange yellow sun
petals
Touching my feelings
growing in my heart
Ocean rhythms flowing waves
crashing home
on soft pebbled beach
ending with ecstacy
of heart foam
Wind blowing fiercely
the smell of the sea
strong in my membranes
salt on my tongue
seagulls shrieking in my ears
calling my heart
home

Margaret R. Gilbertson
THE TYPEWRITER
I have a brand new typewriter
And boy is it great;
I hit the return button
When I really need the space.
And when I make an error
It really is a cinch
I just push the backspace button
And don't even have to grinch.
The white tape it erases
All the errors that I make,
So no one is the wiser
Except me and my little tape.
Of course there is one problem
That I just can't overcome,
All those mistakes that I am
Making, should really be none.
But I am not a perfectionist
Nor will I ever be,
But I'm thankful for one thing
God made only one of ME.

Mary Lou Storlie
APART IN MILES
I still miss you, it's been over a
year
Every so often, I shed a new tear
I know you're happy, and doing
just fine
But I'd; like to see you, just to
ease my; mind
It's hard for a Mother to give
up her son
But I know in my mind thats
what I have done.
Your serving our country and
doing it well
I'm so proud of you as, I'm sure
you can tell.
But the hurt and longing just
won't go away
It keeps returning day after day
Letters, they help and phone
calls do too
But what I long for is the day I
see you.
Lots of miles between us, keeps
us apart
All your memories I'll store in
my heart
I'll take each day, one by one.
Miles can't break the bond
between Me and my Son.

Mary Spear
REMORSE BETWEEN FRIENDS
It happens among friends
No one knows why
One slip of the tongue
And there it is
It often occurs
Never discussed
Almost always forgotten
In future conversations
Stays in the mind tho
Often put on hold
Only flairs up
To cause more pain
After each session
Friends get stronger
Don't ask why
You'll find no answer
If friends are true
It will be looked upon
As parts of growing
Just another niche in life. . .

Bobbi Hannon
THE WHISPER OF TRUTH
Through the thick air, dense
with incense
And the smoke of many
hookahs,
You feel the warmth of her
breath,
In the golden lantern shine and
the bright glintings of the fire,
Her skin, sleek, smooth and
finely-oiled
Gleams
And invites your caress.
As her shimmering body
Undulates
In time to the drumbeat,
And her heavy-lidded eyes
Twist your heart into
helplessness,
Know Her
She is Truth.
When she releases the last veil
And gently floats it over your
head,
Know that what you see
beneath
Is the fire
That consumes all.

Jan Olli
MY BROTHER
I have a heartache Lord—
My brother cannot see.
No longer will he ever look,
Upon the beauty of a tree.
No longer will his eyes behold—
A sunset or a Rose—
But he keeps right on praying
Lord,
As on his way he goes.
His steps a bit more slower—
His faith has not once
dimmed—
So well he knows as on he
goes—
That you'll take care of him!
How glad I am you claimed
him—
That day some years ago.
He'll never walk alone again,
Because you loved him so!

Denise Yvonne Robinson
UNICORN DREAM #7
Beautiful, mystical Unicorn
wave your wise wand,
Protruding horn of magic
miracles
across my Universe;
As stars gaze, blaze light—
years away. . .timeless. . .
like ageless, moonbeam
Dreams:
The Eternal rainbow vision,
an arc of Love divine;
Crimson, tangarine, topaz,
olivine,
sapphire, indigo, amethyst
vapors.
Sacred spectrum of hues, holy. . .
pray appear before me
sweet beast of crystalline
beauty:
Righteously transparent, yet
seen,
sensed by my Soul's spirit.
Your hooves haunt my heart
as you wildly wing your way
Across the heavens of celestial
Light,
you hypnotize with paradise
eyes. . .
as you whisper Vows, Secrets,
golden:
Dawn Dancer, Prince Prancer. . .
gallop me from gossamer
clouds to Eternity,
with messages in Immortal
Unicorn Dreams.

Anthony De Cesare
THANKSGIVING
We thank you, Lord, for all you
have provided.
Without your word, mankind
could not survive.
We thank you, God, for being
alive,
For home, for friends, for
families.
We thank you, God, for
memories of the past;
For in our hearts their love will
ever last.
We thank you, God, for being at
our side.
We hope and pray in you we'll
all abide.
In giving thanks we think of
giving,
For in so doing, appreciate the
getting.
Without the past we'd none of
us be here.
Without the future we'd none
of us go there.
God bless us all, our dead and
living.
Watch over us on this
Thanksgiving.
Each day, each year of
recollection
Your final say, our resurrection.

Ingrid Maria Kym
ENDLESSLY BURNING
Swirling reflections
An everlasting brillance,
Forever imprinted within.
Burning as a flame;
A torch with an endless blaze.
For an eternity it will reign.
Forever streaming through
passages
Bringing with it memories;
Memories of times long passed.
The force and power shall
remain
The shadow engraved
Never to fade, never vanish
Darkness shall never overpower,
Ne'er overwhelm the strength;
The strength found in the
reflection;
The never-ending reflection. . .
Of his smile!

Roberleigh
INTANGIBLES
Cage prisons body
but not soul
nor spirit's breath
nor mind's realm.
These of unseen might
may wing out

in freedom flight,
captureless.

Joan Scheffer
REFLECTIONS
The smooth, ice blue pool
held images in its depths.
Faces which seemed to be on
the surface,
yet, the deeper I looked
the further down they went.
Peering up from watery
homes,
shimmering in the passing
breeze,
so definite
so unclear,
always staring into my eyes;
asking questions I could not
perceive,
let alone answer.
Still, each time I looked,
the answer seemed so close.
As I bowed down to be sure,
my hand touched the surface
and sent it a million ripples
away,
flowing ceaselessly to the
edge.
But the image always returned
if I took time enough to wait.
Someday I knew I would
touch the top with no ripples.
I would meet the face
and know me.

Edward Hirschman
LOVE/84
You walk up to my doorway
In a manner most indecent
I find you waiting proudly
Covered only by my stare
I quickly pull you
From your light
Into my darkness
As I warn you of some people
Who your views of life don't
share
Girl, wear your clothes up
through my doorway
If you must—
Strip down inside
Your naturalness in our fake
world
Is marked by shamefulness to
hide

Layne Lutey
COME MY LOVE
Come my love
and we shall dance
on the silvery side of the
moon.
Together we shall float on
clouds of mist.
We shall wander by rivers of
light
on to where the sun
shines the brightest.
Walk with me into the sunlight
Let the moonbeams guide us
beyond the next horizon.
You are my light
You are my gentle dream.

Dr. Earle V. A. Conover
A MENTAL TEASER
Some things are easy to believe
But other things: "no, NO,
N—E—V—E—R!
Is it easier to believe Outer
Space has an end,
Or that it goes on—and On
F—O—R—E—V—E—R?!?!

Claudia Fricks
SCINTILLATION
The snow on trees does
scintillate,
Create a mystic fairyland,
A sense of beauty stimulate.
It through the boughs will
permeate,
As sunbeams through a leafy
stand;
The snow on trees does
scintillate.
Diaph'nous webs illuminate,
As starry eyes of love
unplanned;
A sense of beauty stimulate.
And icy crystals coruscate,
As phosphorous on evening
sand;
The snow on trees does
scintillate.
The snowy facets radiate,
As diamonds on a wedding band;
A sense of beauty stimulate.
In all its forms to demonstrate
Quintessence of the winter's
hand;
The snow on trees does
scintillate,
A sense of beauty stimulate.

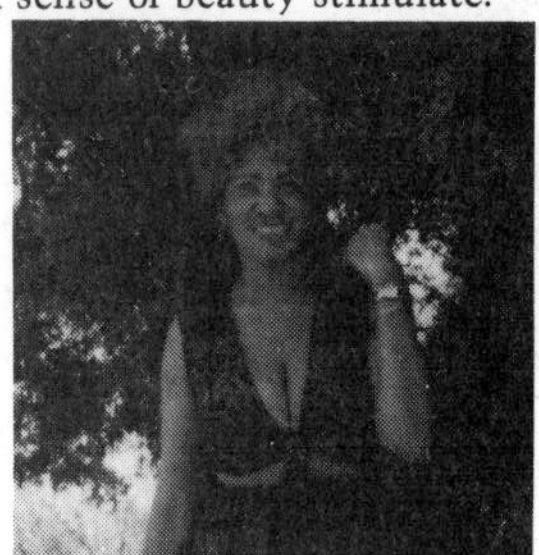

Betty J. Francis
BEAUTIFUL JAMAICA
I looked upon the blue Carribian
Sea and I couldn't cast my
eyes away
And I looked downward at the
white sand, and there
appeard a sand bed.
My eyes glanced upward and the
sky was a beautiful blue
And the moon was in full and
seemly there was a man inside
the moon.
Oh, the stars were surrounding
the moon and the sky was lit
up like a Christmas Tree
Oh the waves from the
Carribian rush toward the
shore and slowly I walked
away to the roadside.
Oh, the beautiful Carribian and
how I love the white sand
beds and gleaming, twinkling
stars.
Jamaica, Jamaica the Island in
the sun, and how I love the
beautiful Carribian Sea,
land of paradise, the island
in the sun.

Mark E. Durand
WEE HOURS SPACE CARRIAGE
A Hellish-red machination
Far beyond my sphere of
knowledge.
Metallic, yet fully alive
With its own wavering motion
And that ghastly, hideous hue.
Ethereal flames still roaring
Must venture no closer than
this—
My safe and secret hiding
place.
Even here my skin reddens and
Blood flows as heated
mercury. . .
As dawn nears, the danger
ceases.
This wayward alien fire bomb
(Perhaps intently aimed
missile)
Dissipates resolutely to
Grey-white ash and finally
dust.
Morning zephyrs disperse
remains
Of what I had mistaken for
A space carriage in the wee
hours.
Vacantly, I ponder. . .Answers?
None at this time, perhaps
never.

Ilene Sommers Wright
THAT'S HOW IT IS
(on blindness)
As if a day had never dawned;
As if all were black as night,
that's how it is.
One dreams of valleys and
flowers and trees,
And one sees, but yea, only in
dreams.
That's how it is.
Did that sound come forth
from above,
Or was it from afar? Never to
know really.
That's how it is.
You wouldn't understand, how
could you?
No one ever does, but
that's how it is.

Kelly Lynn Sanders
MT SAINT HELENS
The mountainside is peaceful
and silence is so nice,
Inside an angry roaring, nature
will pay the price,
Smokey vapors are seen from
miles but no one really knows,
St. Helens is so pretty, no longer
will it poise,
Lava hits the skyline at a speed
you wouldn't believe,
Bravery is lost from the
mountains people and now they
want to leave,
White ash turns spring to
winter and spreads for miles
away,
The green and woods are buried,
all the trees now lay.

Donald R. Baker
TWINS
If true love is the way the poets
say
And comes but once to every
boy and girl,
why is it I feel this foolish way?
I'm lost! My head is all
a-whirl.
I'm not a child. I've been around
for years.
My joys are many, yet I've
shed some tears.
Cried a little; laughed a lot.
Seen fun places. (Some were
Not!)
I've been broke when times were
hard;
Bet a thousand on one card!
Shared the spotlite, been alone.
Acted like a rolling stone.
Fell in love; I've got a wife
who walks with me, shares
my life.
Stands by me when times are
bad,
Dries my tears when I am sad.
She laughs with me, when times
are fair.
She's my Prize; None can
compare!
Yet,—there's another. (With red
hair.)
I've been honest with my bride
of many years.
No secrets may pop up to
bring her fears
that I'll be gone; my life with
her,
My love will keep me here.
Yet Dammit! There's another I
want near.
Love comes but once. That's
what the poets say.
True love will last forever, and
a day.
It fills your heart, and shines
out of your eyes
When she is near; your breath
comes out in sighs
for just the special one that
you hold dear.
I've travelled quite a way
along the track.
Half-way round the world I've
been, and back.
I've made, and lost, some friends
along the way
and I can vouch for what the
poets say,
For I've known Love. It's where
all life begins,
Yet,Suddenly, —I Wish That I
Was Twins!!

Eddie Heavner
CARMEL—BY—THE—SEA
The sky felt sorry for the sea
today
and gave it some of her bright
blue to wear.
Then the sea moved gracefully,
showing her new gown to the
people on the shore.

The sun smiled on sand and sea
and upon nature's worshippers,
who lay prostrate on the beach
as if in homage to their god.
Some have worshipped here for
years,
and now they bring their young
to be dedicated to this shrine
where surf and sand and
sunlight dwell.
A lone sailboat, in stately
grandeur glides;
like a pure white swan,
who alone is privileged to swim
a sacred temple pool.

LaPriel B. James
GOOD GOD
GOD
The giver of life
Healer, Omnipotent Master
Where art Thou
In our need
Facing Nuclear disaster?
Nations in arrogance
Court the untimely demise
Of Thy children,
Dumb animals
Birds in the skies.
Count us in Thy mercy
Ere this planet becomes
A blob of dust
Trailing blood, guts and
Serpents tongues.
As the sparrow falls
So fall we. Is
Man's inhumanity to man
Destined to reign throughout
Eternity?
GOD
If Thy spirit is elsewhere
Should this orgy take place,
Please give Thy other children
Minds, wills and souls
Of Grace.

Clark Champie
THE GREEN KINGDOM
What is this place that someone
has called the "Green
Kingdom?
Is it a paradox
That's found nowhere by those
who know not where to look,
Yet everywhere by those who
do?
Is it the sparkle
That turns an ordinary drop of
morning dew
Into a thing of beauty?
Or the music in the roar of a
mountain stream
As it hurries down its
mountainside
To a refuge in the ground below?
Maybe it's the fleeting beauty of
each sunrise
That greets the morning sun
And sends it on its shining
journey
Through each day
Or the splendor of each sunset
That tucks this ordinary ball of
fire
To rest each night?
Could it be the grateful look
of one in need
That fulfills the one who helps,
Or the sincerity in a lover's
voice
As he or she says "I love you?"
If it is any or all of these,
Then it must be as delicate as a
moon beam
And just as hard to hold.
Yet, it seems to be there—
somewhere—waiting
For those who take the time
and trouble
To really look, and listen,
and feel!

Irene Georgia Broumas
MY DAD
Oh father how you worked and
suffered so,
to make each of us a good
person grow.
And with each tiny drop of your
constant sweat,
you made sure all our needs
were met.
In blistering sun, wind, rain and
chilling snow,
how you made it through the
years I will never know.
From a tiny fishing village in a
far away land,
you suffered and grew to take
your stand.
In a world of uncertainty and
sure unrest,
you always tried to do your
best.
Whether in work or in family
life,
you always did provide for your
children and wife.
To say the least, times were not
always pleasant,
tempers flew and angry words
were sometimes present.
Reacting to our sorrows, regrets
and mistakes,
sickness would appear causing
him to forsake.
But with sickness, health does
and did often appear,
taking away his doubts of life or
fear.
It seems so unfair that you now
suffer so,
cause you gave up your life for
others to grow.
But fear not father of mine dear,
for God is watching you ever so
near.
For all the good deeds you did
your life through,
God will combine them all in a
big pot and create a stew.
A stew so fine with love and
rich with memories,
that our children's children will
all agree.
Yes father of mine you really
did work and suffer so,
to make each of us a good
person grow.

Danny Lourie
& THE FANTASY IS YOU
Two quiet days
have made it the longest
weekend ever
Two empty nights
have made it a life time
& for me the cycle of
uncertainty continues
Despite a deep desire for
fulfillment
Too many things tie me to
yesterday
& the many dreams I caressed,
Deceit found a home in so many
mouths
While crocodile tears ran from
eyes,
Torn between wanting & giving
They scare me no more
I have seen through their smiles
& know fancy words are easy,
Simplicity has a price too heavy
For the one not strong enough
to realize
How tough it is to run alone
I cannot even turn to you,
You search for your own dreams,
Feelings tear me apart
& all I can do, is watch as you
walk by
Uncertain of how you feel
inside
Or what I should say
To make you understand
& share with me awhile
My pillow is not comfortable
& my nights are no longer easy
So it will always be as I search
for softness,
I give
& you receive my strength
I smile
& the thought is you
I touch
& the fantasy is you.

Linda F. Williams
AGES
Rainbows we view through
windows of our mind
Letting today come with a
stairway to climb
And dreams we possess become
stepping stones in time
Imprisoned are the fears we
learn to leave behind
Nowhere can we venture
without imagination
Nor escape the process of our
transformation
Determined with ideals we will
seek investigation
Diligently striving for the final
interpretation
Yes, once comprehended we
adjust to life's transition
Allowing destiny to rein with
progress and restriction

Edith S. Johnson
INGENUITY
Torrid weather—
Nestlings suffering,
Sitting gasping
On the trumpet vine.
Loving parents,
Bringing insects,
Hover fluttering,
Cooling feeding time.

Roylene J. Cluver
REMEMBER
Remember our days
when love was you
and love was me?
You smiled and
said "Hello."
Remember?
Remember my face
as I left?
Tears flowing,
arms reaching?
You smiled
and said "Goodbye."
Remember?

Virginia Holm Haseben
FOR WINKLE A GOODBYE
I sit on the floor,
my back to the wall.
His head rests my knee,
the tear drops fall.
Sad eyes look up,
deep, brown and trusting
And all the while
my heart is busting.
He doesn't understand,
he's so bewildered.
I stroke his face
so softly whiskered.
We had fourteen years
to love him so
And now how it hurts
to let him go!
His once sturdy legs
that bounded in pleasure
No longer support
this faithful treasure.
"Some cool water,
a little sip, please",
I don't care that
it spills on my knees.
For days and long nights
with aching heart
I watch and pray,
yet know he'll depart.
And I being selfish
by striving to keep
My beautiful friend
from his due sleep?
For in canine heaven
sure it's true without measure,
That once again soon
he'll be bounding with
pleasure!

Arla Jean Howell
THE SPARROW'S SLEEP-SONG
Nestled in the treetops,
Just at close of day,
You can hear the sparrows,
Singing in their way.
Cozy little clusters,
Of fluffy-feathered friends,
Sharing Nature's beauty,
As their voices blend.
Content at last to rest,
And cuddle close together,
Sharing friendly warmth,
And fluffing downy feathers.
With the sun's last ray,
Their sleepy-song is done.
It always seems to me,
The sparrows have such fun.

Harland G. J. Romberg
TOGETHER
Two rivers meet and together
wend their way,
Blending to bring what neither
could alone,
Ships from lands beyond their
own,
Filled with treasures before
unknown.
Two minds meet and together
tell their thoughts,
Blending to learn what neither
could alone,
Wisdom of the ages beyond
their own,
Filled with wonders before
unknown.
Two lovers meet and together
give their love,
Blending to receive what neither
could alone,
Blessings from the Heaven
beyond their own,
Filled, with new life before
unknown.
Two souls meet and together
worship GOD,
Blending to see what neither
could alone,

Visions of a World beyond their own,
Filled with MIRACLES before unknown!

Polly Longchamp

LOVE CONQUERS ALL

The love of God shines in you,
In all your actions,
In all you say and do.
I'm looking at life in an entirely different view,
In all I see, say and do.
Thoughts of you keep running through my mind,
At every turn.
By seeing the love of God in you,
You have taught me to listen and learn.
The love shared by you and me,
'Til the end of time, shall be.

C. Greg Wadas

GRANDMOTHER

My graying angel sitting there
with gentle smile and distant stare
rocking, rocking in your chair
to a creaking cadence of time passing by.
Sunshine memories fill your heart
with the sweet smell of life,
the fragrance of honeysuckle vines
of fresh-cut summer grass,
a crisp autumn frost in fields past
as soft rays warm patch-quilt trees
and the jewels of dew roll off the petals
of a yawning morning 'mum.
Wandering dreams—of fiords and snow-capped mountains
wrapped in evening haze—slowly fade
as shadows come pursuing them
drawing darkness near.

J. L. Cusyk

CLOSING TIME

Dancing, hold
each other close,
band plays "Misty."
Shoes under a table
ice melts in drinks.
Lights,
music stops,
they keep dancing.

Lois G. Witt

THE GIFT

The gift I bring you dearest,
Cannot be bought or sold.
Silver will not buy it,
Nor all the world's gold.
A gift that will not tarnish,
A gift that won't grow old.
Each day it grows in splendor,
Each day it grows in strength.
You cannot see or touch it,
Yet know it's there forever.
I cannot wrap or trim it,
With glowing ribbons bright.
My gift is Love Forever,
For you, my only Love.

Sheila Anne Doyle Buchholtz

FRIENDS

A friend is always one
who is there when they're needed.
They help to get things done
no matter what is pleaded.
To have a friend like that
is certainly a pleasure.
Something few people have,
I consider a priceless treasure.

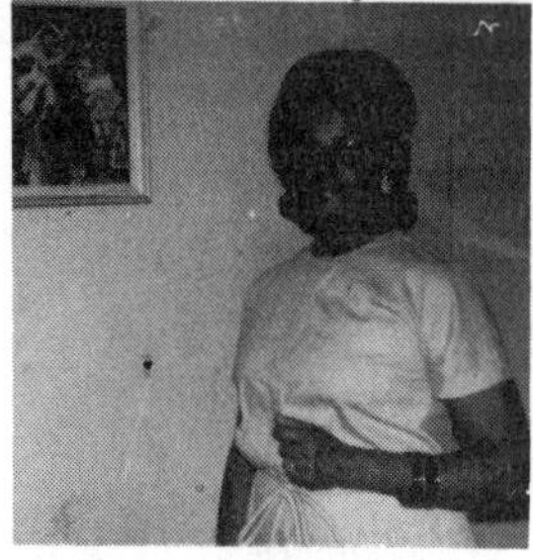

Serena G. Lewis Mills

CARE TO BANISH

Somehow, when cares beset your mind,
When some folk are hateful, when some are kind,
When something you miss—in your way of Life
Makes living sort of reckless, makes long, long the night. . .
A ray of Sunshine on a cold, windy day—

Tends to brighten taut heartstrings,
and banish cares away.

Marilyn Catherine Molloy

LIFES CHANGE

He rocked in his chair
With a tear in his eye
Tomorrow I'm 80,
Oh why should I cry?
I've seen the torment,
the trouble, the pain
Running on empty, feeling insane.
Keeping my chin up, giving a smile
Hoping to see someone, and talk for awhile.
I pick up the paper and start toward the bed
Oh, God! my very best friend is now dead.
Why didn't they tell me? Or drop me a line?
Yes, they forgot me, it happens in time
Now that I see what life's been to me
Will 81 be something I see?

Carmen C. Wilson

MOTHER

Patient and kind always was she
Stresses and strains
But never a word of complaint
She gave her life
For others, you see.
If only I had known
Before she had gone
What a wonderful Mother
She was too me.
If there is a heaven for us
In this world below
Surely she must be there
Or no one will ever go. . .
Oft times she forgave me for the rails I sowded
And now in my pain
I can only complain
I only know
I loved her so. . .
How God could have allowed one such as she
To suffer thru this life
And to die in mortal pain
I never. . .will know
I only know there is no God of peace
Only a God of woe.
For just as life's brightest moment was given
A grand son she loved so
And would have given anything
To see him grow
Was her life taken away
All used up by those. . .
Who loved her so.
For if my punishment is by this death you see
There is no way I can live
Unless I can give her life
Thru immortal prose.
For those of you who do not know
Guard well your loves, your life
For softly in a moment do they go.
The proof of their lives left only behind
In the ones who loved them so.
Mother, Mother
I loved you so. . .

Mary Jane Y. Brown

BUNDLES OF JOY

Forms to fill in
Social workers to see
All for a bundle of joy.
Many questions to ask
The attorney and fee
All for a bundle of joy.
Waiting over a year
A life of anxiety
All for a bundle of joy.
A call on the phone
For the parents to be
All for a bundle of joy.
Arriving at home
Many sharing the glee
All for a bundle of joy.
Just nine months more
Natural deliv'ry
All for a bundle of joy.
The parents are proud
'Twas instant family
All for TWO bundles of joy.
Twins—unequal age
Life revolving in thee
All for OUR bundles of joy.
The love is the same
For the she and the he
All for OUR bundles of joy.
So Bless them each one
Speaks our heritage tree
All for OUR bundles of joy.

Velma Margaret Haller

WHENEVER I LOVE SOMEONE

When I love someone
I need to show it
Never letting him be free.
My kiss will unite
With his open lips
And his tongue will dig into me.
I will look at him
With my wavering eyes
With respect of what he may do.
The lights will soon dim
As I gaze at his face
Uncovering his eyes of blue.
I will caress his back
And let my arms surround
My body as it lay so bare.
Even in the darkness
I can feel his desire
And the look of his admiring stare.
I will not surrender
To his completing kiss
With hope that he will never leave.
He will not dress
Nor say his farewell
But deliver his burning passion to me.
And he will smile
And I will smile too
Stating some beautiful but silent words.
He will press himself tighter
And I long for more
Until our words of satisfaction are heard.
Then he will turn away
And my mind will ponder
My hand will gently touch his face,
He will stand slowly
And my tears will flow
Just to feel in my heart the empty space.
Trembling I will say
My hoarse voice that follows
"Darling, don't you know that I love you so?"
He will answer quickly
As I await his reply
Deciding it's the truth that I shouldn't know.
I will think to myself
As he states his good-bye
With mumbled words of what will be.
And as he is leaving
I can see in his eyes
That the one I love will never love me.

Alice M. Ridings

UNTITLED

It's snowing and the flakes fall gently
ever gently downward
The trees softly filling
As the night grows swiftly onward
and peace fulfills the earth

S. Elliott

ECHOES

The children are gone—
Grown
Away in lives of their own
I am barren. . .
my womb aches
as if it never was full of Life.
Yet my heart knows
Shadows of
First steps taken
First word
"Mama"
spoken.
Fingers of such smallness
Curled around my swollen breast
Pulling the milk of life

from my body.
Leaving me
with piercing sadness
in so few years
to fly
on their own
With the wings
I helped to grow. . .

Jim Edward Hansen

A POEM TO DAVID

What fondling innocence is born today,
What precious gift to give away,
What marred perfection will never be seen
By the eyes of our Lord, on whom we lean.
Through His eyes we see our son
Ever resting now, a new life begun.
We will shed a tear until the day
In heaven we meet, forever to stay.

Wendy O. Altamura

TEARS

Tears

I weep my tears,
my tears are me
and overflowing ecstasy.

Pauline Policari

THE CITY

Loathsome, despised, the bleak city stands,
Abused and neglected, murderers' refuge,
Stolidly, solemnly tolls its death knell.
None will but curse it, leviathan horror,
Mercilessly hacked from a wilderness virgin,
Shunned by its sire, man's bastard child.
Back to his mistress he runs like a coward,
Whimpering for solace on her breast pure and white,
Cold and abandoned their waif 'waits the night.

David Glass

AN EXPRESSION OF COSMIC WORSHIP

Oh, Father of all the invisible worlds,
True Godhead of galaxies, star-drifts, and suns,
We adore your enormity, stupendous whirls
Of great nebular arms and vast space-sweeping runs
Of subliminal energies infinitesimal
Ranging the star-fields and shining on earths
Too remote from our planet to discover is decimal
Creatures inhabit these spheres; new births
Of galactic star-clouds taking from in the ethers,
Encircling the cosmic domains' shining brilliance,
Awakening wonder in all God-believers
Who take in the vastness and utter resilience
Of all the wide, fanciful, cosmic parameters
Illumined by myriad, space-borne light-emitters.
Expressions of glories untold from your heartbeats
Are pulsing throughout all the circuits and lanes
Of the starry dimensions in limitless repeats
Of outward gushed energies, dynamic rains
Of your Limitless Power upholding each atom
And every ultimaton throughout the regions,
As Life permeates all the series of atom—
Ic, nuclear life-forms, numbering legions,
And all the assemblage of God-bestowed creatures,
Observant and growing, bright children of Light,
Sing anthems of homage to you whose vast features
Are beamed from your Prior, Pre-manifest Bright—
Ness of Limitless Unity, now ceaseless endeavor,
Unending expansion for your and our pleasure.

Sydney Ruth Lasky

A COMMENTARY

The tree is strong,
no matter how big or small;
It stands straight and tall!
It bears fruit.
It gives a home for the song bird.
It gives me shade when the summer
sun is warm.
It touches my heart with awesome delight,
and even might!
It whispers to me a phrase of soft love.
It tells me as it caresses the sky;
and then asks me,
with a wistful sigh;
"Why does man cry?"
"I am here to show him as life can be.
I give him warmth.
I give him shelter.
I give him food.
So why should he have a sad mood?"
The tree is strong,
but it cannot understand
the whims of man!

Debby L. O'Roake

STARTING OVER

No, I won't pretend our marriage was perfect.
I know the things I did that bothered you.
But I didn't know they would cause you to look for someone else.
Yes, I called you a chauvinistic pig when I was mad.
And I nagged you about Monday night football.
And I did get obnoxious when I won you at backgammon.
And I know it was selfish of me to use
six of the nine drawers of our dresser.
And I know it was me who squeezed the toothpaste tube in the middle.
Yes, I do have my faults.
But no, I didn't think they sould cause you to look for someone else.
You've told me, so now you are free to go.
You've cut our ties and you are not committed, so go.
Go to her, love her, and hold her like you held me.
Go on, there is no reason to cry for me.
My tears are enough for both of our regrets.
You've released your guilt, and yes, you were honest.
Go on, there is no reason to hold my hands or wipe my eyes.
I can do that. I can wipe my tears.
I can reconstruct my life. I can erase those years.
Go on, go to her. Love her and hold her.
Take her in your arms and reassure her that we are through.
Go now, go to her and be happy.
There is nothing that you can do for me.
Now that you're gone,
where do I go at night and on Sunday mornings?
Who do I call when I have to work late?
Who do I tell if I get promoted on my job?
Who do I send a Valentine card to?
And what should I do on my birthday?
Who will hold me when I'm hurting inside?
Who will touch me when I'm yearning inside?
How do I put all this love aside,
now that you're gone.

Cora Tench

STIRRING SILENCE

All through this festive day Thanksgiving stretched
In stirring silence—sun-gold dipped for dusk,
And aimlessly, I strolled where gaunt palms etched
Winged arrogance against the sky— their brusque
Farms billowing in double row array,
High pictures to emboss the mountain scope.
The palms that ride the ridges far away.
With green-ribbed splendor climb the barren slope.
Close on beyond the Ragged Robin strews
Rose petal fragrance, trailing off behind
To linger near and lift my pensive muse,
Then fast-flown dreams with stark awareness find
Each palm tree earthed in line still stands apart,

And I, alone, felt flame of thankful heart.

Barbara Chamberlin

REFLECTION

Sisyphus, you are my patient twin.
How many times you must have questioned your God
And heard nothing but the sound of the stone
Racing d
o
w
n
w
a
r
d. . .
Silencing the fragile voice
Left in Pandora's box.

Marion Francis

SIC TRANSIT

Flea-market in Paris, with a grimy bin
For rejects and unsalables; within
A threadbare bit of scarlet rivets the gaze,
Bedraggled relic of old splendid days:
A pocket-purse of silk, with expertise
Stitched with imperial N and talismanic bees.
Discard from sceptered hand, it must have passed
By what descent to this vile state at last!
Once a container for Napoleon's cash,
Now long past reclaiming, scrap for recycling—trash.

Cindy Clark

MEMORIES

Remembering is a thing of beauty
For which we all lean on.
Remembering all of our good friends
And fun days that are long gone.
When we are old
When our sight grows dim
He will remember her
And she'll remember him.
Signatures will fade
Yet pictures stay clear
When we want to remember
They'll be there from year to year
Desks at school are empty
The grounds are quiet and still
When we see these certain things,
With memories, our minds will fill.

Carol Davis
MAN'S FOOLISH PRIDE
Mans pride he tries to hide
It often blocks his path
Forcing him to tell a lie
Or cover hurt with a laugh
He puts on an act
Sets aside his true desires
Sugar coats harsh facts
Keeping prides door always ajar
He must never admit fear
Or face failure to any degree
But keep up a front to all near
For his foolish pride never sets him free
Pride is often his chain
Leading his life hiding pain
It surrounds his domain
Forever blocking freedoms reign

Rachel Skidmore Botner
TODAY
In the hours that we had saved
Oh, the perfectness you gave.
Words are so inadequate, so incomplete.
But the memory's mine to take and keep.
Exquisite hours of love were spent
when last to me you were so sent.
There is no morrow, just today.
There is no love, just memories stay.
To question why or what would be
not right, for reality
Was not—could not—be any part
Of the beating of my heart.

Mina K. Ferguson
EVEN SCORE
HEN
I always craved a home of my own
A leanto snug and firm
The driest nest to lay an egg—so
From dampness I need not squirm;
To harbor a rooster's fertile touch
My feathers are comforting, warm;
Leave him the Master cock-a-too
Then I'd be the one forlorn!
ROOSTER
I never craved a home of my own
Just anywhere would be a lark;
My Rhode Island Red comb standin high
Might tempt a White Leghorn with a spark
Of intrigue, maybe a wistful sigh
Yet she don't need me to lay an egg—but
That White Leghorn *does need me*
To fertilize that egg—gosh o gee, woe is me!

Jewelle Parman
RIDE'EM COWBOY
"Yes Sir by God Sir I can Sir,
Said the wiry little man,
I can ride him clear to hell and back,
Yes Sir by God Sir I can."
He would close his eyes and nod his head
And sorta wave his hand.
He wasn't telling fairy tales
I'll have you understand.
He could take a salty, mean old bronc,'
'Neath each foot he put a dollar,
He could scratch that hoss from end to end
Wave his hat and holler.
That bronk would spin and sunfish
He would rear and paw the air,
But when the fight was over
Those dollars still were there.
With a silver dollar 'neath each foot
I'll never forget my friend.
"Yes Sir by God Sir he could Sir."
He could ride him to the end.
Those old days are past and gone now
He has crossed the great devide.
But I hear him ask St. Peter
If he has a bronc to ride.

Fay Ingram Roberts
REVERIE
Love was a lullaby softly sung by one
Who had given her best love to sorrow,
But lived in the faith of promise of morrow—
So my faith in life and love was begun.
Love was thistledown, a carpet of flowers,
Bird song on the air, white clouds in the sky,
A playmate, hand in mine, while moments flew by.
Love was a rainbow after the showers.
Love was a seeking, restless, unending,
Of its best destiny, passion, fulfillment.
Love was surcease of pain, peace, content,
A graceful receiving, all the gifts blending.
Then came mellowing, and the breaking of light—
Life is a serving, mountainous delight.

Elvira Chase
PRAISE GOD FOREVER
I'll praise God, for He's good forever
though death is my due, now I live.
The world and its glamour I sever.
My life back to Jesus, I give.
Praise God for His infinite wisdom,
tomorrow He holds in His hand.
He knows what I need to be molded,
for service at His wise command.
I'll praise God for His omnipresence.
He's with me wherever I go
to guide, to sustain and to use me,
so others this glory may know.
In each distant nation dwell strangers;
who never have heard of God's grace.
I'm praying that Jesus will save them.
In heaven we'll meet face-to-face.
Together we'll give God His glory.
We hardly can fathom His love.
We all know the true Gospel story.
We'll marvel in Heaven above.

Jim Logan
A SILENT CRY
The world I would give
for a brief moment,
to capture the light in your heart.
To be then seen
in the gaze of your eyes.
And remembering, only vaguely
the sullen emptiness,
which has been my world for so long.
As I feel your presence near,
the hope for your love
is consuming.
My soul is warmed
by the touch of your smile.
And my words gather
in growing impatience,
to bid you to stay.
Only to then, see them perish,
into a cry of silence
as you turn away.

Eric Paul Shaffer
ACCOUNT FOR THE FLAME
A woman will be her own currency.
In her own interests, this banking should do:
Account for the flame, for passion is free;
Tender affections when only they're due.
But, little tuppence, you do as you choose:
Offer for interest and disdain the loan,
Quite unaware of the value you lose
Lining the pockets of men that you've known.
The total amount of your current worth
Is spent in the crack of small golden rings.
So those who change tender find there no dearth,
And rue won't remove the tarnish it brings.
So while the coinage of love will still shine,
Lovers seem dearer, but love is more fine.

Christine Zimmer
APPRECIATION
We thank you, God, for those who help to guide
The likes of us, who in our sunset years
Decide to write, or paint, or dance a bit
To help us while away life's fleeting hours;
While dreaming dreams, and doing many things
And thus to quiet that strong urgency
We've felt so deep within us since our youth,
But duty pushed us on with arms of steel.
Bless them, God, who share their time and talent
That we may learn and so to feel the joy
Of dormant talent brought to life by them

Florence Armstrong Lux
ECSTATIC DISCOVERER OF MYSELF
I was oldest child, unwanted and ill.
Then my parents were divorced finally.
Eighteen caught me as just self-supporter.
Art study drew many things vitally.
I was enlightened after wedding
Frank Lux who is my devoted ally.
Several called me nobody with jest.
Research proved to be good mentally.
Maternal surname, Mitchell means that Mont
Saint Michel native heroically
Aided William, Duke of Normandy
Becoming King of England royally.
Land, heraldry and castle for him were
Rewarded so quickly ethically.
Paternal surname, Armstrong after Vik—
Ing Dane, whose feat nickname was morally
"Siward the Strong Arm", is famed with his first
Son in Shakespeare's Macbeth ideally.
Second son was executed on trea-
son by William First rustically.
My spirits are uplifted from sense which
Is transmitted by God literally
Who gives me rights to be somebody like au-
Thor for non-fiction intentionally!

Lucy Beemer
WHISPERING SILENCE
Oh, how glorious is the newness
Symphony of the breaking sky,
How crisp and clear the air is swept,
Asleep the land in blankets lie.
Beneath the canopy of morning,
Metallic glows the cold sunlight,
All the world transformed, illumined,
Reposed in snowflake winter white.
Every twig-top wrapped in ermine,
Roofs all banked in frozen sleet,

Chandeliers of crystal falling,
Shattered icicles at your feet.
Toward the East in reverent

silence,
Nature's grandeur wreathes the
hills,
church spire brilliance pointing
upward,
"Whisper, Silence, Peace be
Still."

Elizabeth Ricketts

SONG OF THE SEA

I have loved you always,
shall love you evermore,
long as seas come pounding
against this ancient shore.
Strong must be my loving,
surging as the tide,
mighty waves that roll in
to break on every side.
Mystic forces cannot cast,
deep in this dazzling sea,
stronger spells upon the land,
than those you cast on me.

Sally Edwards

STAND BESIDE HER

Please guide her
through the night
with a light
from Above"
No more great gaping holes in
her flesh
From which steel monsters rise
And fasten gruesome fangs
Into the blood of generations.
All in the name of Progress!
The mighty money roared
And stripped the people and
their land
To sinew, rock, and bone.
With sparkling rivers rushing by
Great rain clouds dumping
down,
The power of God's own Sun
above

Granting warmth and light and
power—
Still the monsters had to grow
Now towering-baring frightening
teeth
In sadistic cement grins,
Belching chortles from deep
bowels
To let us know they've won.
What fools men be—
What fools men be—
Who cannot see the shining for
the sun!
Please God—guide Her
through the night
with a light
from Above."

Wm. A. Gaffner

FOR INSTANCE

I have no words to say to you
No magic phrase of wit
No tantalizing thought morsels
No literature or script
No punctuating capitalizers
No small letters to be quit
No roundabout synthetics
No phonetic phoney bit
No, I cannot fake it here
I cannot pretend or lie
I cannot hide it anymore
Nor let emotions die
I can, however, smile
For in merely thinking
Of the beauty of you
I know love

Michele Luongo

THE FALL IS DEEP

I stepped to the ocean in search
of myself
Wave just forced me back,
Walking a line; straighter than
me
Nothing I could grasp.
Sunset deep, through valleys I
walked,
Darkness was a mouth,
Reached to my mind; pulling
with force
Nothing; I found doubt.
Climbing mountains taped with
fear
Quickly falling back,
A mirage, dim as waters,
Mere fantasy retracks.
Octagon walls with outlets bare
Forces not knowing of,
Walking circles while singing
life
Monotony was the chorus.
The key to life opens adventure
While locking the camouflage
cage,
This, my friend, marks the
spectating ways
Of living day to day.
I breathe, I breathe
All I seem to draw is air,
I speak a word, one-hundred
words
Of conflicting care and dispair.

Della Zionts Slater

LOST

The hieroglyphics on the sign
posts of my mind maze
Indecipherable
I have lost the entrance
I can't find the exit
Unbearably lost
The hieroglyphics on the sign
posts of your mind maze
Unreadable
They point to nowhere
I am lost
Utterly

Debora Flint

AUTUMN ROSES

When the burial is done
and the eulogy is read,
let no flower touch the soil
but autumn roses for my bed.
When my friends have gone
away
and their last goodbyes they
gave,
let no other flower than
autumn roses touch my grave.

Sheila Creef

BUILDERS

We live
loving the spirit that motivates
us
not denying
but paying homage to the pain
that brought us here
Where we are is no mistake
only a time of gathering our
defenses
for an outside world
Our likeness is our religion
Our difference A bond and bible
We breathe freely now
having stalked the hollow and
fearful places
in one another
We've soothed with eyes
that hold more than
understanding
And built with hands moving
and busy—
a place at night to wrap each
other in thought
If touch is not desired

Margery Doxey

CHRISTMAS MEANS?

What does Christmas mean to
me?
Just sparkling lights upon a tree,
Stockings hung by a chimney
Or parties, gifts and gaiety.
No, let me pause for just awhile,
To remember that Christmas is
the Christ Child

Who was born to live and, then,
to die,
To rise again and ascend on
High.
The real spirit of Christmas is
truly felt,
When you by the Holy Ghost
are indwelt.
So pause for awhile this
Christmas day,
To ask this Christ in your heart
to stay.

Gwendolyn Fears

UNTITLED

Your divine sense of timing
blows my mind.
Keeping in touch with the
thought that it's
extremely divine.
You lie to sweet and still with
the conscience
of a windmill, get it!
I wonder what it's gonna be like
to want and
can't have?
Well I'm sure with your sweet
words when you're
not inebreated, you'll be so
occupied, you won't
have time to rave.
Love has to be something one
shares, or there's
nothing to enjoy; oh I've been
there once, I'm
not going back.
I just want you to be my man,
not a boy.
For you see my greatest
weakness was you, but
now it's becoming so foggy and
blue.
I wonder is your definition of
love—Sex?
If that's caring, it's not
worth sharing.
You don't care so why don't you
release me, let
me share it with someone who
doesn't need Sex as
a grip to escape reality.
Grow into the man you can be.
Or escape and remain the kid
that never knew.
Know what it means to be
lonely.
Experience what life is all about.
I'm sure you'll be very impressed
by the tons of
phonies, so much like yourself
you can detect them
from a distance without
conversing.
They are more a part of your
life than success or
happiness itself.
But life sometimes shortens us
somewhat like a
smelt.
You have no respect for me, I've
lost mine for you,
You can never regain it!
You are really quite a clever
kid, I sometimes laugh
it's so amusing, but the hurt has
passed.
I'm as cold as ice without the
right to melt!
No one person owns another,
wait you'll see sooner
than you think.

Randy Spurlock

WHAT IS AN AUNT?

"What is an Aunt?," you may
ask,
Is she nice, or is she not?
Is she young, or is she grey,
May be she's the one who
brightens your day?
Can an Aunt fill the vacancy of
a mother,
May be she could be your
Grandmother?
Does she care when times are
rough,
Can she be gentle and still be
tough?
I don't know what your's might
be,
But mine are friends in times
of need!
I have both maternal and
paternal,
But the grandest one's are
friends, eternal!

James M. Learnard

EASTER II

He is risen—'tis time for joy.
Whether you be girl or boy.
Son of God paid for our sins,
The price, in modern times, was
such,
That we, to pay, would say
"Too Much".
Despite the price, in human
terms,
He loved us all, And had the
touch,
To reach us, touch us, and to
say,
"For each of you, this is
YOUR Day".

Sid L. E. Kreyer

SENSE OF BEING

Above me the feeling of closure;
Below me a feeling of fury;
In the middle a mind of
confusion,
and around me a sense of glory.

Sue Espersen

CONSIDER

Children, my children, don't
look back.
Don't consider the past with
Jesus the lack.
Don't hope for the old days,
the old ways, the old you,
Look to the present day,
consider the new.
There's only a twinkling of the
eye, in fact,
Between death and life. Consider
that.
Every new second the Spirit is
working.

Consider His breaking, His molding, His shaping.
Do not despise the day of small things.
Take each moment to consider His blessings.
Jesus said consider the lilies and sparrows,
Consider the way straight and the gate narrow.
Looking back to consider the days that have gone by
Will cause you to stumble, to wither, to die.
The Father is offering a new life to us.
Only one Word need be considered, His name is Jesus.

Patricia A. Tyrrell
LOVE SONG
There are no words for you
nothing to touch your heart,
no easy grace, nor jest to make you smile.
Lies nothing rich in me
but the fields, bare under the sun,
the fields that watch and expect,
endure and hope.

Love, there are no words,
even the skylark has music
even the fighting sparrow
wins his applause.
Is only here
the heat of a country under noon
where the hedges wait, and the hawthorn
chokes the threat with joy.
Love, this country attends you:
the clear lake for your beat,
the willow, the spiring cypress,
the teasing cuckoo.
When the sun is gone
and the earth cools into night
and the birds sleep,
love, will you come and walk there
under a fleeting moon?

Mary Ruth Dennis
LAMENT OF A COOK
When My time on earth is done
and my rewards in heaven, I have won
It is my most ferent, heartful, prayer,
God will take a second look,
and not designate me
To be a "heavenly cook",
I am told. To create
is a beautiful art
and those with this talent
should leave their mark
But how can you leave memories,
of one meal from another,
when tastebuds can't tell,
today's repasts
from yesterdays, or tomorrows,
So sizzling eggs
upon the grill
are not my most
cherished thrill
and frying hashbrowns
hot and crisp
is really not
My most wishful wish.
Steaks, and chops,
and Chicken, three
are lovingly prepared,
and cooked by me
cookies, cakes, and goodies I bake
To be gobbled by those
Who can't tell what they ate
I slave all day
over that hot, black, stove
Pour into my creations
All that I know
Tidbits of flavor
To tempt, the most finnicky mouth,
I may as well serve
Fillet of Mouse"
I feed the masses
day in and out
Lobster, Shrimp
down to
Franks and Kraut,
But when it's my time, Death to greet
I hope the Saint's don't have to eat,
I don't care how tired!
they are, from marching in
or how hungry, They must be
from fighting sin
I pray, God will take
A second long look
and in his infinite mercy
Let others cook.

Daisy Fries R.N.
LIFE GOES ON
Grieve not for he who chose to go away
But hold instead the memories of a brighter day
When love was carefree and remembered bliss.
Was a touch, a smile or just a fleeting kiss.
One cannot know the workings of the mind
and there's some truth in saying love is blind
Though not immune to pain and untold grief.
Life does go on we must keep that belief
So dry your tears, you have so much to give.
To others who have hearts and minds that live
Life seems so cruel perhaps some day we'll know
Why one so loved should choose this way to go.

"Me" William A. Stanley III
UNTITLED
If you are ever sitting on a fallen tree
And you happen to look beyond the cloudy sky
Think of the stars that have fallen
And remember I am one.
Hopefully to arise to another occasion
On some future bit of time
If not in your world
Then maybe in my own.
But whether I lay asleep forever
To live only in memories
Or if I rise to shine again
Over both the land and sea
I do wish my sweet love
That you will always remember me.

Alma C. Groninger
SOCIETY, SOCIETY. . .
Society, Society. . .where are we today?
Begin with the newborn
In the crib as he lay.
Was the child unloved and frequently shoved
By a careless mother, from one house to another?
Did the father actually expect us to think
That wisdom was gained by an alcohol drink?
Did abuse of the child make him helplessly wild?
Did he no longer care, when he accepted a dare
To enter the drug world, as adolescence hurled
Him into the chills of Society's ills?
Society, Society. . .where are we today?
Begin with the newborn
In the crib as he lay.
Was he the recipient of strong parents' love?
Was he told about Angels from Heaven above?
Along with the love, was his intellect met
With challenging goals and ethics all set?
Was he shown the flowers and beautiful trees?
Did he see little objects and learn to say, "Please"?
Did sweet music surround him as he looked at the stars?
Was life lived in harmony, unrestricted by bars?
Did he rise up one day and say that he may
Contribute his best as he moved from the nest?
Society, Society. . .where are we today?
Begin with the newborn
In the crib as he lay.

Glenda Stearns
HIDDEN CANDLE
She works hard
But she does not seek praise and seldom gets it.
She is indignant
But she remains calm and few realize.
She feels hurt
But does not utter a sound.
She wants to live her own life
But lets others guide her actions.
She has the ability to succeed
But lets others push her into the shadows,
So that no one ever knows.
She must learn to stand out,
Speak out, and let the world know
She lives.

David P. Lutz
THE HILL
I followed the lane that forded the stream,
Ideal for the artist painted scene.
No place have I been so nearly complete,
As I waded the crossing with little bare feet.
I ventured to climb by a path known by few,
Just to look backward gave a breathtaking view.
I had only mastered that well known hill,
Just to visit a spell, with my good friend Will.
While even today, thinking back when a boy,
Remember the crusades and battles, recall the joy.
In years to come, another boy shall feel,
What it means to claim his very own hill.

Mary Pauline Mauldin
CRAZY WORLD
Its a crazy world we live in. God
didn't make it this way. He gave
us beauty and love to start
with—But take a look today,
People around us seem crazy, for
dollars or anything else. Give
me your wife, Mr. I want her for
myself.
Cheating, stealing, and lying,
children hungry, and crying.
People around us seem empty—
heartaches—We have plenty,
loving, streaking, and dying,
from the drugs they are trying;
no God didn't make it this way.
Yes its a crazy world we live in
people are all in a twirl, you
have to look twice to tell a boy
from a girl.
If they love each other, they
shack, if it doesn't work—
send them back. Oh its a crazy,
crazy world.

Anna Barnes
GRANDCHILDREN
A wet kiss—a sticky hand
and short arms around my neck.
A hurried meal, a late snack
and cookie crumbs between the sheets.
Wet towels, dripping swimsuits
and sand in the shower stall.
Cars to race, balls to chase
and kites caught in a tree.
Walks and talks, stars to share
and rocks to skip across the lake.
A clear day, a picnic basket
and ants on the chocolate cake.
A wave goodbye, a soft sigh
on my way to my rocking chair.
I love them—I spoil them,
but only for a short stay.

Dorothy Louise Jackson
THIS WINDOW THAT I LOOK THROUGH
I look through it's panes in awesome wonder
At God's creation of garden's in bloom
I watch the sunset in the golden horizen
This beauty that lift's my gloom
I watch the stars glisten from heaven
The moon so silvery bright
I know that God has placed them there

To brighten up our night
As I watch the sunrise each morning
And the grass all sparkling with dew
I thank God for this blessing
This window that I look through
When my family and friend's forsake me
And the world seem to pass me by
I look through my window toward's heaven
And he wipes the tears from my eye's
He touches my soul with gladness
And I no longer feel blue
No gold our silver on this earth can buy
This window that I look through
It's panes ne'er need cleaning
There is always a perfect view
God placed it there with-in my heart
This window that I look through.

Julie Louise Hunter
ON MY WAY UP
On my way up the spacious mountain side
I look around with Glory and Pride.

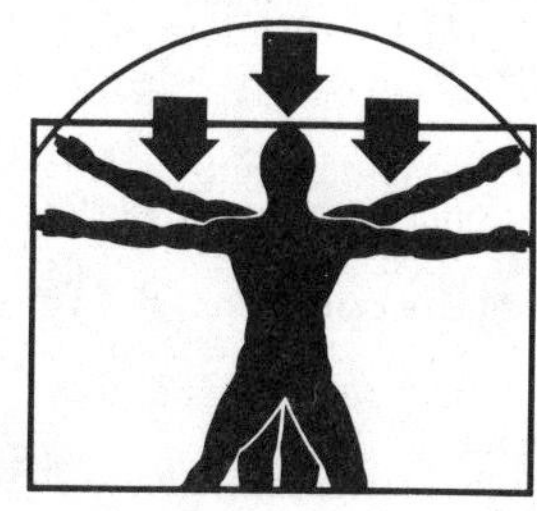

On my way up the tremendous hill
I look in each direction with a frightening chill.
On my way up a swan I see from afar
With no movement or sound.
On this mountain side it will leave a scar.
On my way up I find out from life
At this very sad sight
That you may find turmoil and strife.
But on my way up I found it was once alive
And I know now what killed the creature—
Man's Glory and Pride.

Dianne R. Costanzo
AT THE DANCE
He's there—across the room,
eating an ice cream cone
like a baby eats its mother,
the warm ooze dripping softly
from the tip of the cone.
This music makes me feel funny.
I feel almost lifted onto the floor, where
I step inside someone else who can
get lost in primal drums and
move until sweat pours down her
thighs, very quietly, from a darker,
sweeter source of which I am not supposed
to know anything. That girl is not afraid
to sweat; she's done it before.
And now you're coming over to me; with hands
sticky from some delicious flavor,
ready to devour the evening—and me. I
crunch the ice from my soft drink.
Please go away.
Don't come over,
Don't come,
Don't,
Because I don't know how to dance.

Juanita F. Anderson
IN MEMORIAM
In spring-like realm her spirit rests
Now freed from pain and care.
She moves in harmony with God
In space transdendent,
Forever fair!
Though form be lost and voice be stilled
Yet, happily to them,
She to her children willed
A legacy of love ne'er lessened
As in memory viewed,
But multiplied, enlarged, renewed.

M. Anne Henry
DEPRESSION
This creature perceived as depression
gradually permeates into the senses
without forewarning of the grief and sorrow
it inflicts on those who know it.
All hope for sound perceptions of the state of mind
are devoured
without sympathy.
as the chilling sting of this lingering hate
devastates all in it's path
in complete control
overpowering the self.
One's life is meaningless and misplaced
as confusion takes charge of reality,
leaving the victim at the mercy of
self-distruction,
powerless
to fight back
with the instinctive will for survival.
The only defense is the tedious passing of time;
but even as time slows the painful attack of
depression,
it is only a short-lived removal of distress.
This savage animal stealthy returns to
maliciously abuse
it's unaware victim
once again.

Clara Frances Getting
THE GLEN
Oh come to my glen, share my delight
Let it's magic caress you, with all it's might
Take a deep breath, and let yourself soar
Right over the brook, with it's delicate roar.
Feel free as a lark, to whom God gave wings

Don't stop till your heart, really sings.
Glide over the rocky path to the deep,
Thick wooded pines whose secret they keep
For here round the thicket the little deer play
And all God's creatures are happy and gay
For this is their home so joyous and vast
That all who come here, find peace AT LAST.

Mary Ann Fabry
DREAMS
My dreams, are filled with you;
they make me feel so warm:
I dream that we are together;
on a cool, sun shiny day:
A blanket spread on the cool grass;
us—looking around at the beauty:
The serenity of the lake, so cool and calm;
also of the hillsides turning green:
It is all so peaceful, calm, so quiet;
just you and I:
Next, I see us walking close together;
hand in hand through a park:
A park where there is solitude for all;
where the stairs lead down to beauty:
Beauty, of a fish pond;
surrounded by cedars and flowers:
Trees growing all around for cover;
cover—of the hidden places to go:
Walk ways, by tiny streams;
a beautiful dome, to sit under:
We are sitting back—away;
away from others view:
Talking and laughing,
so close and so caring;
sharing precious moments:
I wish I could show you;
the tranquil places of my dreams:
Come with me, reach out for my hand;
I'll show you where they are:
But most of all I dream;
we are together and happy:

Richard Marion Reece
FALLEN ANGEL
Coming home on the winding road, so many times traveled before.
Didn't expect nothing to happen, nothing will ever happen to me you said.
But I knew that road well, the late drunks, the hicks, cowboys and
teen-freaks, party, party, booze, drugs and four wheel drives.
Come home, come home, isn't it getting late, have to get up early,
will you listen and come home.
Always had a free spirit, free like the wind, no one owns you, no one ever will.
As the breaks shriek, the lights in your eyes of a giant metalic beast
crash into you, the tearing of modern society's technological progress,
when the noise is over, only thing heard is the horn, through a night when
nothing else is heard, silence as if nothing even happened.
And while you lie there in restful sleep, your broken body pieced together
perfectly, I wished it was me there in place of yourself.
The realization of it all, you were young, beautiful, death only happens
to old people, you were healthy, you were going places, being someone, this
just isn't fair, just isn't fair.
Then while I stared at your face, something sculptured out of plaster,
I remembered the joy, the fun, the love we shared, then my masculine feelings
could not hold on, to hell with what a man is going to do or feel, I wept.

Naomi M. Wood
TO MY LITTLE DAD
Oh, yes, I remember dear mother,
And the wonderful tales that she told;
The songs that she sang so sweetly,
As evening shadows did softly enfold.
She was one of the dearest of mothers,
That ever a little girl had;

She is treasured so fondly in memory,
But what about dear little dad?
He was already old when I knew him,
His body oft wracked with pain;
Yet always smiling and cheerful,
And seldom did he ever complain.
He was already hard of hearing,
Yet I think that was my gain;
For I learned to stand before him—
And speak out clear and plain.
Then he'd take me up on his 'good' knee,
Telling tales of the days of yore,
Tales of his early boyhood—
And of Trail drives that are no more.
Of swimming the wide deep rivers—
And of nights of the wild stompede,*
When a horse—keen—eyed and sure footed,
Was a cowboy's greatest need.
Dad was not very heavy nor tall,
But he was wiry and quick,
He taught me the steps of the Schottische,
Long after he walked with a stick.
Yes, Dad was frail and not very tall,
But honest, trustworthy and true;
Known as steadfast in the minds of all,
Who knew that his word was true.
Yes, I treasure the memory of mother,
Treasured memories, both glad and sad;
But when I am thinking of mother—
I can ne'er forget dear little Dad.
*Dad always called a stampede, a 'Stompede', Texas style.

Lee Lashbrook
LOVING YOU
When I feel tenderness,
I think of you. . .
When I feel a yearning
I think of you. . .
When I feel happiness,
I think of you. . .
Its because I love you today,
In all the wondrous ways. . .

Cynthia Collins
WHO IS HE THAT COMES IN THE NIGHT?
Who is he that comes in the night
with his gentle touch and strength of might,
who shields my eyes and dries my tears,
protecting me from pain and fear.
Who is he in the soft moonlight,
caressing me in warm delight
while all the world cries out in sorrow;
afraid there may be no tomorrow.
Who is he with fire and passion,
who can subdue the rage in fashion
that haunts mankind at every turn;
freeing no one while tranquility burns.
The peaceful stars are twinkling bright,
and soon the sun will bring daylight,
and all the world will see, with grace,
Love's radiant glow upon my face.

Shirley Jean Neal
THE PAINTER
Most of us are just plain folk
who dream one day to be painted
by a famous artist.

Most never realize that each day
the master artist from heavens
gallery with brush in hand,
uses the right stroke that our
portrait be flawless,
when hung in heavens gallery.

Leslie Sachs Sherman
REMEMBRANCE
First by twos and then by fours
All were led beyond the doors
Firmly shut—no air, no light
Dark as any winter's night.
Then by fours and then by scores
Then millions lay beyond those doors
Their tortured screams rose in the night
Someone must have known their plight.
But rare a soul reached out to stop
That evil, brutal Holocaust
And even though much time has gone
The nightmare lingers on and on.
Do not forget what has been done
But let it not occur again
Ashamed, but yet we must no hide
Mankind's cruelest genocide.

Horace R. Busch, II
THE VICTOR
If only I could have been
a raucous race car driver.
A Macho Mario Andretti in a bright red
Screaming, Screeching, Shuddering machine
Hurtling down a dreaded dirt track,
goading my might metal steed,
Hugging Mother Earth,
Unmatched, unchallenged, unharmed,
Outdistancing
the hapless pack,
Burning
their
rubber paws,
In heat like heinous hounds
in
hot
pursuit
of some unattainable whore.
I'd show them!
I'd mow them!
I'd hoe them!
See?
Look at me!
I'm the winner!
Invite me to dinner!
In summer or winter
I'm the best bread winner.
What a MAN! What Daring!
What have I to lose?
Alas, no bitch is unreachable.
The finish line is ravished!
RAPED
into
O
B
L
I
V
I
O
N
!
I AM THE V I C T O R!!

Billy F. Hicks
MOM
Oft-times we take our Moms for granted.
And never stop to ask or reason why,
But I recall my Mom's love and kindness,
For me I knew that she would gladly die.
She furnished me with all my spending money
While I was in the 'teen age of my youth,
She said to me, "Son, be ever honest,
Never faltar, always tell the truth."
She labored that I might be educated,
A great advantage that she never had
I hope that in her aging years ahead
That I may be a blessing to my Mom.
She is good to understand my problems,
Always ready to lend a helping hand,
I thank God for such a loving Mother,
No finer Mom you'll find thru-out the land.
There is a day we dedicate to Mother,
A day with her we often try to spend.
But she is more to me than just a Mother,
She is to me a Mom, a pal, and friend.

A. Alan Gifford
THE CRY OF THE LOON
Oh, Lord, mere mortal man cannot
accept the cry of an anguished lot.
His heart is closed, as are his eyes;
he does not hear our plaintive cries.
His land, his air, his seas protest,
but yet he does in slumber rest,
unconscious of his certain fate—
and unaware his hour is late.
He does not know his days are few,
and does not care that the world he knew
will vanish forever—beyond recall,
for the thoughtless never care at all.
And yet, in truth, we all will miss
this creature born to mortal bliss—
but langour dulls his sense to tell,
and too, I fear, his heart as well.
Lord, give him word, both loud and clear,
. . .lightning and thunder—to make him hear
that the time has come to set aright
those errors from his lack of sight.
Pray, spill his idols—wealth and speed,
and break the spell of chrome and greed.
Free his spirit from the chains that bind
his heart, his conscience, and his mind.
Please, Lord, grant him sight to see
the sun—the sky—the willow tree,
and give him touch. . .to sense the bark,
and ears to hear the meadowlark.
Thus, give us hope to see the dawn. . .
reclaim his soul before it's gone.
But. . .haste, oh Lord, to lift his head,
for all hope is lost when his soul is dead.

Linda Sue Booth
IDENTITY
I
Fell,
When the time draws near,
I
Shall wonder how,
I
Can leave a mark.
One
Among many,
Stands. . . . .alone,
To identify
That
Which once,

Passed along,
This path.
I
Look behind me.
"T
R
A
C
K
S"

Ora Lee Carver
ROYAL WEDDING
The pomp and circumstance
so gallantly portrayed
for everyone to witness
on that very special day.
It's grandeur, flashed across
the sky
for everyone to see,
It scanned, the mighty ocean
every river, brook and tree.
The wedding, of the century
A privilege, to share,
come in on every T.V. screen
to see, for all who cared
to acquire the knowledge
of our neighbors, over there
and learn, their way of life
on occasion, one so rare.
Diana, so young and innocent
beauty beyond compare,
Charles, a fine young gentleman
together life they'll share
God's children, all are equal
all lives, are not the same.

But when all is said and done
What is there in a name?
In part, their lives are similar
of friends along their way,
a boy and girl, in love
like millions, every day.
Some reach the higher ground
while others stay below
But in God's eye, all are equal,
He intended it, to be so.
A King and Queen for England
A President, for U.S.A.
Maybe a Monarch, else where
But God rules all, every day.

Stephanie Osborn
SNEAK PREVIEW
Already
It's just August
yet I scramble for a pen
as the quickened words
overflow
and the chill and clean
snaps
at my short-sleeved arms;
I shiver, on an unlikely day
and gleam as a familiar October-
smile
stretches across my humid
routine.
The titillating cold of an
Autumn day,
raising my song
calling me on
carries me breathless—
to a step of unworked rhythm
whistling the tune of a breeze;
new—
and all it's own.
Now for a few short months,
I'm home.

Corinne Greenman
THE FREE SPIRIT
The free spirit of a stallion,
Roams within your heart.
Each day is a challenge,
For you, each is a new start.
Running free and wild,
Is what you do best.
Roaming the grassy lands,
Barely stopping to rest.
You keep on searching,
For something that is true.
Someday you'll look home,
Where we all love you.

Ada-Lynn Beville
LIKE A SMOKE SWIRL
Like a smoke swirl,
My thought glides and slides
into conciousness
Slipping through an imaginary
trap door, into un-concious
Dimensions of thought twirl
and swirl like smoke.
Curling upwards and outward,
My thought rushes up and spills
out into the atmosphere
Like a geyser. . ."Old Faithful"
or so. . .
Like a smoke swirl,
My thought glides up and out of
my mind
Leaving me as a corpse without
life.
Like a smoke swirl,
My thought dissappears.
Like a thought swirl, my
conciousness winds and
climbs
Up and out
Elusive, deceiving me like one
who would attempt to
invalidate me,
Even without knowing so.
My thoughts are as a smoke
swirl
Rising, gliding through my mind
and into space
Look again, you can see them
cross my face
Look once more, you can see
them. . .in my face.

Doris Locke
A WOMAN'S THOUGHTS
I sit alone
And the night is still—
Alone I muse
What might have been.
Could I have been
An artist, author?
Or else perhaps
A lawyer, doctor?
All was there
for me to choose.
Instead I chose
To love another—
I've spent my life.
There's only one,
And now it's done.

R.L.P.
I'VE OFTEN WONDERED
I've often wondered why God
sent
His only begotten Son
Over nineteen-hundred years
ago
When today He could have
come
For with our technological
Advancements in TV
He'd be seen and heard around
the world
By millions easily
Yet finally I realize
That whatever God may do
Will always have good reason
Though hidden from our view
Perhaps why God the Father
Chose Jesus' time of birth
Before such great technologies
Enshrouded all the earth
Assuring that His precious Son
Be born inside that stable
Lest our Saviour be aborted
On some modern clinic table

Dawn Simon
DEATH
With no conscious thought;
To a child it's considered an
eternity away.
To a student, a subject.
To a philosopher, a study as old
as the beginning itself.
To those on the verge, it is a
prayer.
But to those already there it is
a begetting of an
infinity of a song of Freedom.
Life is not a ribcage
Nor is it a shelter from the
inevitable.
But a bone capable of being
broken at any given moment.
When the bone has broken and
one has met with time
there is no chance of reviving
the past
and the Future cannot be
immortalized.
It is a ladder which holds at the
top final dreams.
And when those dreams are
reached by a thrust of
strength
and polished with success,
it is then that one can be ready.
It is then that earthly infinity
shall endure.
But if the dreams are not found
and the goals not attained,
the eclipse without warning
shall descend to retrieve
the lesser Soul.

Helen DeVane
LOST PIECES
Since becoming a part of you
I have lost pieces of my life.
Seemingly unimportant
fragments
Have been cut away by a knife
Whose holder bears no name
But whose works are of acclaim.
I cease to dream of flowers
And the magic of spring.
I yearn no more for songs
That other lovers sing.
I taste no more the dew
That softly kisses the leaves.
I am forever running,
Chasing the one who flees
From hopes of better tomorrows
From regrets of yesterday;
From the sights of other people
And the words they try to say.

Doris O. Weckworth
ONE GENERATION OUR GENERATION
We made each transition as it
came along.
Now why can't we make really
right what is wrong?
They said you don't go outside
anymore
Bring the John from outside
through the living room door.
Don't bathe once a week in that
old wash tub
Lounge in a whirlpool for your
rub-a-dub.
That old oaken bucket won't do
anymore
You can store snacks away in
gadgets galore.
You don't have to pump it or
lug it uphill
Just turn on the faucet
whenever you will.
The boiler and tea kettle both
had their day.
Gas or electric they're both
here to stay.
Candles won't do when a button
you push
Floods the lights everywhere
in a happier rush.
A cave or a tent or a simple
log cabin
Take your pick of the modern
ideas for livin'.
A cart or a sleigh or a coach
you don't ride in
A car or a truck—mobile home
you abide in.
We made these grand steps for a
good way of life
Now why can't we make a world
without strife?
We'll make that big step away
from a war
And bring about Peace on earth
evermore.
Inside this "chosen"
generation.

Josephine Shirar McGonigle
UNTITLED
My backyard's pear tree
rustles in the evening breeze. .
petals in my hair

Mildred Allen Crouch
A NEW DAY
A new day is dawning!
Such a beautiful morning
Makes one feel peaceful and
uplifted,
Creative, strong and gifted,
Not worrying what the day will
bring
Just plain thankful for
everything
In the Morning!
Cares and trials are put to rest
The day is young and we are
at our best;
Our minds are keen, our bodies
refreshed
We are ready and anxious for

any request
No doubts no fears are taunting
As we face the day unwanting
In the Morning!

Sharon G. Ross

TIMELESS

Released from time
echoes of memories
brought back with
a touch
a look
a smile
gentle fingertips carressing
trailing softly
against the
tenseness of uneasiness
smoothing away
the knotted pit
of fear
replaced by
quietness of
being.

Dame Eleanor Moore Montgomery

MIRROR, MIRROR, SPEAK TO ME. . . .

Mirror, Mirror, look at me,
Give me thy thoughts from eternity.
Garner and glean great gloating
thoughts from the hierarchy
that hangs above.
Know thy strength, Great Force above,
And know this instrument here below
Wrapped in love.
Bathed in sunshine, wrapped in Love!
Mirror, mirror, speak to me!

Lynn O'Neill

DO NOT DISTURB

there she lay,
quiet and undisturbed
taking life
e-a-s-y,
as though the day
would never end
or morning
would never begin.
and each blade of grass
at the end of her barefeet
tickled as she moved.
she laughed.
her laugh
was laughter of freedom,
like the birds
winging in the distance.
was she really free?
and from what?
soon she would find out,
but then—
it would be to late.

Jeannie Keithley-Braswell

UNTITLED

As the wind blows thru the trees
It feels cool, the breeze.
Not a cloud in the sky,
With the sun way up high.
What a beautiful day this will be;
Just wait and see.

Judith Mentor-Stewart

UNTITLED

I think I should like to just once more
To go and play the children's play,
To swing, and let the wind catch my hair,
And the sun warm my face;
Just once more.
Once more I should like to be
Innocence and curiosity—
To play Tag and Giant Step, Red Rover.
Once more I'd like to be
King-of-the-Mountain, Robin Hood, the Sheriff—
Just once more,
Before war comes and values change•
And I lose my need for life.

Frances N. Brown

YESTERDAY

YESTERDAY I walked with youth along a sunny way.
My heart was gay, my burden light—
I viewed with joy the long, adventurous way.
Just yesterday
I walked with youth.
TODAY I walked again but left gay youth behind;
My comrade was much more sedate.
With careful feet we took the trail
Which seemed so bright
Just yesterday.
TOMORROW I shall walk with age
Along a path which countless others trod.
But age and I will scale the mountain peak
And be "At Home At Last With God."

Brenda Joyce Williams

LIFES HIGHWAYS

Have you walked along lifes highways,
Fearing, knowing not?
Has your burdens, and your problems,
Been more than you can bear?
Have you heartaches and doubts to share,
But no not where to turn?
Have you thought what your life would be,
If "*Jesus*" wasn't concerned?

Have you ever sit and talked with *Him*,
And told *Him* all your cares?
Have you went through all your lifetime,
Living on just dares?
I dare you now to call on *Him*,
Just to see if He's really there.
And I dare you now to try *Him* once,
To see if he will treat you fair.
Can you feel the nails they drove that day,
As *He* layed there upon the cross?
Have you thought of all the pain *He* beared,
For the ones who still were lost?
Have you thought of all the things *He* did,
And never once complained?
He did it all for us they say,
For eternity was ours to gain.
Just look down lifes highways,
And *He* will be right there.
To shoulder all your burdens,
And take away your cares.
Could you walk along lifes highways,
The way *He* wants us to?
Yes just walk along lifes highways,
And *He* will walk with you. . .

Daniel A. Goughenour

A MIND OVER SOME MATTER

Is there no medicine for a man,
Who suffers from day till day,
Living in a cage for his mistakes.
Judged, convicted and sentenced to pay.
A prison cell is not a man's castle.
Nor can it be called his home.
It is a four wall concrete room.
A place where rodents and roaches roam.
It seems a sacrilege to waste a life.
Man-killing in a frying pan alley.
The forces of living driven downward,
To please our social fabric's tally.
it is unwise but also criminal,
Not to improve the mind of a convicted man.
To teach him a distinction of right and wrong.
The same as we would do for any man.

Dolores Ann Cross

NOTHING COULD BE NICER

Nothing could be nicer
Than seeing your smile,
Being with you
And just talking awhile.
Knowing you're liked
When someone likes you
Especially, if that person is
A good friend of yours too.
I believe you've given me
A lot to live for
In fact, I know,
I've never really lived before.
You've made me think of the future
Forget the past
And you can believe me
I'll never look back.
Tomorrows like heaven,
Only I know what it's worth
If you live your life right
It can give you every pleasure on earth.
When life let me down before
I thought I was through,
Now somehow you've changed me,
This time it's true
I'm living my life starting all new.
Now it seems possible
For me to think through,
There's always tomorrow
For my dreams to come true.

Thelma V. Miller

LITTLE THINGS

It's the little things in life
That seem to mean a lot;
It shows the extra patience
That someone else forgot.
Small weeds surrounding flowers
Can choke an entire patch!
The smallest wound that doesn't heal
Could have only been a scratch!
One tiny mosquito in the night
Can ruin all your rest!
It's the many little things in life
That put you to the test.

A little bit of kindness
Can get you through the day;
It's the little deeds you do
That help brighten someone's way.
So don't discount the smallest thing
And think it not worth caring;
Large gifts can be beautiful;
But the small are still worth sharing!

Philip Robinson

HERO OF SELF

Once you find the love of self,
there is no greater
Dignity and pride are inseparable friends
Previous frameworks don't allow for such a construct
Beneath attempts to believe love is a salvation, is a misguided excuse from a basic fact: the love within you conquers
Reach not for comparisons

Michael White

CAPTURED

Blown by raging solar winds
Through lines of ozone gases;
Through drops of gray and streams of green,
Near piles of burning masses.
The skyline curves upon itself
And then on one another.
Methane seas break on the

shore,
The mirrored sands to smother.
A triple sun sends forth its light
To bathe the land in crimson.
The flashing desert sends it
back,
Reflected in their prism.
My flaming ship streaks through
the sky,
A victim of the tempest.
I crash among the shining sands,
Surviving nature's grimest.
I gaze longing at the sky,
My eyes are filled with tears.
An exile to the dark of space,
I'm lost for all the years.
On my planet, far away,
I'm just another case.
A vanished victim, fate
unknown;
A traveller lost in space.

Loy D. Hupp

PEACE AT LAST

In a random moment of madness
I had abandoned all gladness
And sank to the dregs of dispair
I became hapless, helpless,
hopeless, totally surfiet
Oh please, oh please, must I
always grovel in defeat
Oh please, oh please
As the skies slightly lightened
The band around me tightened
The awful mercilessly ominous
sound of hell
Screeching, screaming, wailing
Will I ever surmount this
ponderous failing
Oh please, oh please
Are these archaic things I'm
hearing
Are these demons that are
peering
My paltry soul is searing
For my being has lost all
bearing
As a tempest how it roars

Oh please, oh please
The quickening of my being
Seemed to permeate my undoing
And the legions of the dead
Passed through my sub-
co ncious mind
The cadence barely quickened
as I cried
Oh please, oh please
My throes were almost rabid,
my soul oh so avid
The legions of the dead pressed
on and on
Is there no salvation from
this realm of visitation
Can I release my emancipation
And once again be free
Oh please, oh please
From a voice almost poetic
I heard a raptured, rhythmic
Almost musical sound
It grew stronger, longer, louder
As I cried, don't forsake me now
Oh please, oh please
I heard symbols bashing,
smashing, crashing
And I knew my retribute was
near at hand
I was crying, sighing, dying
Preparing to leave this
embittered, embattled
Bewildered God forsaken place
With one last murmer, my soul
screamed
Peace at last

Mr. A. W. Shaw

CHRISTMAS GREETINGS

In ancient days appeared a star,
Bright in the Eastern skies;
'Twas followed many weary
miles
By kings, exceeding wise.
It lead them to the newborn
Christ,
Bethlehem's blessed Babe,
Where they presented costly
gifts,
Before Him humbly laid.
Today the star of Christmas
shines
Glorious,—exceeding bright,
Inspiring us to bring our gifts
This wond'rous Holy night.
For yet, to hearts where love and
faith
Still seek that baby King,
His star still leads us gloriously
As we our homage bring.
And so, dear friends, this
Christmas time
I wish for all of you
The best of everything in life,
All that is Good and True.
May Christian Love and
Fellowship
Around your heart-strings
draw
Real Heavenly Peace;—the wish
for you
Of
ALLAN W. SHAW.

Estella M. McGhee—Siehoff

FOR THIS THE GENERATION ENDS

Finis. The lie.
From the market place to
the marriage bed,
If this be honest, and this
be marriage (sic).
The lie.
Finis. The spy.
Women spies, men spies,
girl spies, boy spies.
Mailing list spies, merchant
spies, denominational spies.
The lie, the spy.
Finis. The thieves.
They take, they plunder,
they throw away,
They laugh, they ruin, they
escape.
The lie, the spy, the thief.
Finis. The embonder.
Bondage to eat, bondage to
sleep, bondage to work,
Bondage to marry, bondage
to conceive, bondage to
bear,
Bondage to be kept from
Truth.
The lie, the spy, the thief,
the embonder.
Finis. For this the generation
ends.
Thermonuclear war, waters
of wormwood, fire, hail,
Earthquakes, judgment, and
death.
The liar, the spy, the thief,
the embonder of
This generation end losing.

Abadja Brice

MADE IN U.S.A.

When our Maker finished his work, from among the stars words were seen: "Made in U.S.A.".
Time passed on, a beautiful country came alive with its fixings and things; wolves were howling and hoot-owls were hootin': "Made in U.S.A."
Time passed on, from across the sea came the Nina, Pinta and Santa Maria, with a man on board, looking out on this wonderland. Lo and behold, he was reading the magic words: "Made in U.S.A.".
Time passed on, there was a stir among the folks of this wonder-world as strange faces from strange places began to appear, the cry went out: "Made in U.S.A.".
Time passed on, wheels began to roll across the land and across the sea, the world was feeling the greatness of this new found land: "Made in U.S.A.".
Time passed on, two souls were lost in outer space and landed on the moon. From among the moon-beams a label was found: "Made in U.S.A.".
My famous last words America! Dream it, Live it, Own it, Invest it! Get the world off your back—buy American! "Made in U.S.A."!

Thomas Aquino

SAME AGAIN

I see her and it's the same again,
as I knew it would be.
I sit still—that's all,
in the maybe moment of "Do I
ask or do I keep still?"
I sit, thinking
it's better than to move?
To risk her lips twitching a
"NO/!"
O Decision, a high wire.
I don't know if the net
will break a fall
is the why I don't walk.

Celia O'Fallon

DREAM REALITY

Like the spiral staircase
I seem to chase
Round and round in my
thoughts
My dreams, my vivid dreams
Swallow me up at times
I awake in reality
Or am I still dreaming?
Doors open and close
To each side of me
One beckons
One closes
One beckons
One closes
And the spiral staircase
Flows in and out of my dreams
In and out of my life.

Marciana Garma

TOMORROW

When tomorrow becomes today
And today is yesterday
Will you think happily today
Of the deeds of yesterday
Our lives are full of tomorrows
Filled with happiness or sorrows
If you fill today with kindness
Yesterday will only be happiness
Many lives we touch today
May leave a lasting memory
Make sure you won't be sorry
When tomorrow becomes today

Brian D. Herd

THE ARMADA

Sent forth over the horizon
Appears the white sails of the
Armada. Firm and brave stands
The captain. Stale winds of
Death confront the Pure Winds
From the east. Lightning flashes,
Thunder fulminates. Dark is the
Storm tossed sea. Black is the
Sky above. Whirlpools tempt to
Overthrow the ships. A
Kaleidoscope of death swirls and
Turns asunder every item in its'
Path.

Yet still remains the white flag
Of the Armada. A fleet of
Hundreds strong, with crew
Brave and true. A matter of
National pride is the Armada.
Destroyer of evil, deliverer of
Truth and rightousness.
Beware you mendacious and
Foul smelling members of death
Beware, for will witness the
emancipation of a land
Entangled in the folly of
Misdoing.
Unholy miscreants cringe at
Their awaiting fate. The cold
Winds blow but to no avail, the
Armada has arrived. Farewell to
The blackarms of death, the
Carrion of destruction. The
White Militia has breeched the
Black armor, which is death.
Beware the white flag of truth
Oh evil ones beware the ship
Which sails under justice for it
Will triumph in the end.

Janice P. Egry

I KNEW YOU THEN

I loved you before I was born. . .
I knew you then.

Your love called me out of the darkness.
The mist formed my shadow to please you
and sent me into the light to meet you.
When I was small I waited for you, but. . . .
you were hiding behind my dreams.
I could not find you, but I knew you were there.
I knew you then.
When I met you, I recognized you. . . .I knew you then.
We were drawn together as strangers, but. . . .
Love pointed you out to me.
You were just a step beyond my dream.
You have let my love flourish within you.
Today joy and sorrow weld our hearts.
They have been named as one for all time.
I know you now.
Someday we'll return to the mist, but. . . .I'll know you then.
Love will remember you to me as we pass.
Your smile will meet my smile again.
And, yes, I will know you then.

Genevieve Downey Brannon

FORGET

Forget his name,
Forget his face,
Forget his kiss,
And his embrace;
Forget the love
That you once knew,
Remember now
There's someone new;
Forget the fun
That you once shared,
Forget the fact
That he once cared;
Forget the times
You were together,
Remember now
He's gone forever;
Forget the time
They played your song,
Forget you cried
The whole night long;
Forget how close
You once were,
Remember now
He's gone to her;
Forget the things
He used to say,
Forget the fact
He's gone away;
Forget how often
He used to call,
Forget the times
That he was all;
Forget he was
Your whole wide world,
Remember now
He loves another girl. . . . .

Clyde W. Painton

MIDNIGHT

A lone wolf howls
Upon a distant hill.
The night is dark:
The air is deathly still.
A rooster's sudden crow,
The cattle kneel, and lo
From afar a lonely owl is heard
Perched on the lifeless branch
Of some dead tree;
The plaintive call of a night bird,
A lone star is lost from sight;
No moon or star gives light.
Two lovers linger long in fond embrace,
Time seems on them to wait.
A world of dreams lies shattered,
Broken, at their feet, time can't erase.
A painful sigh;
A tear drops slowly from her eye;
A farewell kiss—and this
Is—midnight.

Stephanie Giery

THE GOLDEN DAYS OF AUTUMN

The spicy marigolds perfume the air
Golden apples and pumkins everywhere

The squirrels chatter and the blue jays scold
Before long it will be getting cold
The blue concord grapes on each highway stand
And colorful leaves falling all over the land
There are chestnuts ready to roast
And ruby cranberries from some distant coast
The Golden Days Of Autumn
Make one stop and think
How time passes quickly as a wink
There is not enough space nor time
To describe the Beauty Of Autumn
Would be a lengthy rhyme

Opal Sandra Watkins

TREADMILL

I turn and wriggle and to my surprise,
daylight is breaking when I open my eye's.
I rush to shower and wash my hair,
shampoo's over, conditioner now.
Use thirty seconds, the instructions threaten,
but there's no time, so I cut it to seven.
You must get going the clock coo coo's,
i'd like to wear pink, but i'm nearest the blue.
I'm into my skirt and pull on my top,
the tick of that tempter echoes no time to stop.
I know that when I reach heaven's gate,
there will be no clock to say, "you're late."
But i've got to keep up with this work a day world.
and, Boy, it sure keeps my head in a whirl.
I run out the door, and i'm off like a jet,
wondering if the bus left the corner yet.
The weatherman said sunshine, but its starting to rain,
the rusty old bus meter kept my change.
I make it to the office with seconds to spare,
wouldn't you know it, the boss is already there.
All day long there's errands to run,
I lunch with a burger on a stale old bun.
Finally, day done, I fall into my bed,
insomnia strikes and rattles my head.
If you don't get to sleep, you'll have no rest,
there's no time to lose, I embark on my quest.
The clock screams late, its a quarter of eleven,
you know you must be at work by seven.
I'll make it fine, I assure my mentor,
with coffee and roll, i'll be front and center.
I won't let it worry me, I yearn for my cup,
when i've rested awhile, i'll be glad to get up.
I turn and wriggle and to my surprise,
daylight is breaking when I open my eye's. . .

Gina Louise Auricchio

JUST ANOTHER DAY

It came like a dream
Moving slowly towards me
Running freely
On top of breeze
And it disapeared suddenly
For my eyes opened
To just another day
To silent rain
Hanging over me
Was the gray fog
And coldly I stood
Before the mass
Racing away
On traffic highway
Work bound
Just another day
One more to face
With disgusted thoughts
Of what's gonna happen
What will be
For it's just another day
Only to ask why
To be answered
With sweet sad sighs
Of just another day
Speeding by
On traffic highway
We say good-bye
Go back home
Only to sleep
And it came like a dream
Only to open my eyes
To just another day

Melvin Pink

UTOPIA

I've been to the mountain
So you ask, What did I see?
I saw a place where men were happy
And living in harmony.
It was like a dream of a rose garden in paradise
On a crisp clear warm summer's day;
Everything was either spring green or sky blue;
Even the birds would sing sweet songs to you.
There was no anxiety or frustration to be found
For this was a place where all sorrows would just fade away—
A place where no ill feelings lay—
Just the warmth of a summer's day.
Everyone was happily moving about,
Sowing love and friendship to everyone they would meet;
Old friends were making new friends
And there were no more enemies, for there was no need to compete.
It's such a crying shame
That such a utopia does not exist in real life,
For each of us needs such a place
Where our hearts can live in harmony and grace.

Yvonne L. Schouteren

ONE SPECIAL NIGHT

Lovers on one special night,
entwined in candle glow
Two bodies touching, then unite,
as loves sweet juices flow.
Searing pleasures deep within,
mouths joined tight as can be
Melting passion destroying sin,
hands explore what eyes can't see.
Hearts are pounding,
fantasies fulfilled
Climaxes are sounding,
as the lovers are stilled.
Calmness descends,
peace overcomes
Thoughts now have deepened,
as we have become one. . .
As lovers on one special night.

Linda D. Martin

THE SCHOLAR'S FLIGHT

My spirit is restless in this cold, dark schoolhouse,
As I drift through the still, silent corridors.
Through the cold sweating windows I can see,
The small white snowflakes as they fall silently.
My thoughts are very disquieted and interrupted constantly,
As the bird's two wings would flutter as he flies from tree to tree.
I search for the long lost answers that were never there,
Like a madman would search for his dreams.

Oh, for those answers, those wonderful answers, my soul yearns earnestly,
Just to know those answers would carry me through years of eternity.
Oh, how my mind is raging, ever raging,
As a sea would during a storm.
Searching. . . . .Searching. . . . .
NOW! At long last,
My tired aching mind has remembered those answers.
My longing spirit is at its final rest,
For I have passed my English test.

Jim Davis
HEAD FIRST
An old friend,
One I rarely see,
Shows up and quickly leaves.
I'm not uneasy
About what is ahead
Or what may have been
And if my old friend
Chooses not to return,
I'll log it in my diary
once again:
But if—
if fate is kind
as I have hoped
and prayed for,
Letting my friend
Stay much longer than before,
I will call her by name
(love),
and in her triangled
sweetship—
go head first.

Erna Flowers
THE DIRECT LINE
Hello, dear Lord, remember me?
A nine year-old, down on my knee
In a sawdust tent, and the one you sent, telling how sinners should repent?
Do you remember, Lord, the tears I shed, when they told how my dear Saviour bled?
And how He was nailed to a wooden cross, to save a world that was sick and lost?
Do you remember, Lord, how gently You dealt; how sinful, yet humble, I felt?
When I prayed, "Dear Lord, forgive" You sweetly said, "Forever live;
And as my child you now must go telling others who may not know;
And I'll go with you all the way. When you need help, just kneel and pray."
My Lord, I remember I was bitter, until *that* day, for you had taken my dear parents away.
My sins were many and my hopes were few; until you came and made me new.
The "new me" began to understand that You alone have a perfect plan;
That all things here and in heaven above were freely given through Your great love.
Lord, I took Your love and then so often yielded to human sin.
But never once have you turned away; You're there to guide me day by day.
When *we*, our Lord try to please, You didn't promise a life of ease.
Instead, that You would, year by year, keep the prayer line open and clear.
How often I've clogged that direct line by praying selfishly for me and mine,
Forgetting that others need my prayers; forgetting to serve you, forgetting to care.
So, forgive when I fail to read the Word, or tell the Good News where it's never heard.
Forgive me, Lord, when I fail to call, or when I weaken, stumble or fall;
And when I fail to do Your Will; when I omit by just standing still.
Give me the strength, knowledge and drive to witness for You while I'm yet alive.
Lord, may I temptation withstand, and love and help my fellowman.
But remember me, Lord, hour by hour; I can do nothing without Your power.
Thanks again for answering my call. I love You, dear Lord, most of all.
Excuse me Lord, I 'most forgot to thank You for this lovely plot—
This lovely land, water and air, and for Your constant loving care.
Thanks for the Bible, those words so true; help me as I try to read it through,
To understand Your will divine; that I may witness to all mankind.
Will see you soon, but until then, thanks again for listening in.
Your loving child

Jack L. Artz
CHRISTMAS
Christmas time again is here, shining lights and yuletide cheer
Busy shoppers everywhere buying gifts to show they care
Let us stop to remember Christmas time this December
And the reason it came about, of the one who gets left out
Wise men came to worship "Him"
in the town of Bethlehem
Bringing gifts of myrrh and gold to the king who was foretold
Christmas is the special day on which Jesus came our way
Humbly born in a manger yes, "He" became our saviour
Let's remember Christmas day for what it is, Christ's birthday
And the gift we give with love came first from "Him"; from above

Charle E. Hale
A THOUGHT OF CHRIST
Some call you Son of God
Some call you Son of Man
I call you a man
A man who was suffering from the purgatories of Earth
More important they called love
For love is what you prophecised
Today Man is subjected to certain persecutions
of the unjust
To live in a World which you had envisioned is Man's conquest
A land of beauty, peace and tranquility
We will one day face the evils inside
Which will be overcome by your love
Yes they do call you God but I call you the Teacher

Elizabeth Pucciarelli
YESTERDAY, TODAY, AND TOMORROW
I hold with tenacity saving My love of yesterday
I hold so tenderly caring A place for tomorrow too
And why am I this love saving Why for you love, of course for you
I feel the caress of your fingers In my dreams of yesterday
And I shall feel them tomorrow As I have felt them today
I'll kiss them every finger My lips will touch them with care
I'll kiss them each for tomorrow For today and yesterday too
And I shall love them forever Because they belong to you

Limmie Schenall
SIMPLY ME
Within my mind,
The Key to Individuality you will find.
My past is the Foundation
The future is my own creation.
Is it a crime,
To give an accurate account of my time?
Am I a Freak,
Because of the manner in which I speak?
As I walk,
Onlookers talk.
Jealous of my Glory
Because they are unable to forsee and tell a similar story!

Suzanne Bloser
THE FLICK
The stale smell of all night movie houses
Showing the inevitable western
That screen of the mind unexplored
Exploding from contamination of repressed truths
Cocktail hour of the mind
Stopping for a mind-bender of cow-boys and paper bolders
Derelicts dreaming of red wine
Eyes closed against the sounds of bullets and galloping horses
How do they do it?
Their rat-race being even worse than our own
Whole lives spent sitting in theatres
Waiting for the bad guys to win

Karen Joan Priem "Joey"
THE GREATEST GIFT
There is just no way I can say
"Goodbye" to you,
my dear friend. . .
When I found you, my heart just
went to you. . .
I cried a thousand tears and
then a thousand words spilled
onto paper and I've been writing
for you ever since. . .
There is just no way I could
ever turn my back on you.—I
wouldn't want to
You may think because you're
in a wheelchair and need help
that you couldn't do anything
for me. . .
Oh, my dearest, you have
You've given me something
quite wonderful and beautiful
in the eyes of the Angels who
Lifted my spirit and guided
me to you—
You, a warm and sensitive
person. And maybe, I'm selfish
to say that out of anyone at
the home
You're the one who sparked the
fire inside of me which was
burning with all the Love to
give,
But, inside my heart it burned
coldness
Until I met you
—I could have left you astray,
but you weakened my
heart with all the love and
warmth. . .
To sweep the clouds and fly
through the air, you taught
me never to stop caring, even
though I know caring can
sometimes hurt,
But, I've found Loving is the
Greatest Gift of all.

L. M. Gasrel Black
THE BELL
The world in my garden is peopled
in many hues
A riot of colors from brown to
crystal dew.
These people hide behind their masks
or turn in modesty
Some look towards the sun
and bask in majesty.
Others are the moon-lit hour
brief their fragrance be
Enfolded in a coat of many colors
the gift that lets us be.
Attended by these loving hands
Who
sowed the seeds that free
From the frost which stole in darkness
The bell rings liberty.

Nancy E. Angelo
LIN RAY SEA
Lin Ray Sea you went away
On that cold November day
A day when clouds hung in the sky
The day a young man had to die.
I looked upon you pale and cold
I stood up straight and acted bold
I turned away for it could not be
Yet memories came of Lin Ray Sea.
Memories like an unturned stone
Are sometimes better left alone
Like wishing things would go away
Things like a cold November day.
Lin Ray Sea you're gone for good
Death is not always understood
People sigh and the family grieves
A family full of memories.
I will think of you everyday
And everyday I will kneel and pray
Someday with children upon my knee
I'll whisper stories of Lin Ray Sea.

Gertrude Benham Benedict
MY GOAL
Dear Lord, I pray with humble heart
To be as perfect as Thou art—
Not try in any way to be
Considered "on a par" with Thee,
But just to think, and act, and live
As can the ones to whom You give
The strength of purpose and of will
To keep their eyes forever still
Upon the goal—perfection, true—
That is for those who are with You.

Maryanne Dooley Downing
LOTS OF THINGS
Lots of things are nice
like summer
and finding out about the Tooth Fairy and
not telling your little brother and sister.
And Santa Claus
That's fun. . .
And smiling
that's special.
When you're happy, or you know someone else is,
that's special, too.
Dimples are special. They're smiling lines on your face.
Even if you don't have them showing, other people know they're there.
You can tell from the outside that something nice is happening inside.
Friends are nice.
So are birthdays.
So is a hug. . .warm, friendly arms around you, telling you something
special, sometimes even a secret, something you know anyway. That's nice.
There are so many things that are nice.
You can feel them.

Jeanne P. Frederick
MY BLUEBIRD FRIEND
On a summer's day
as I was walking, to my surprise,
I saw a little bluebird limping along the way.
Chirping in pain,
I could see with a look.
"Stop! and help me, please do."
A broken wing he did have.
Carefully, I picked up
this little blue feathered bird,
Which I prayed
would be my friend.
We then went to my cabin,
not too far away,
And dug some worms for this
little feathered friend.
Finding some small boards,
a splint I did make for the wing.

With a chirp of love, his eyes met mine
saying let's be friends.
As the days and weeks rolled by
he would soon be healed,
And then be on his way,
Then I would be alone again.
My! what a feeling that would be
for he was such good company to me
But singing a note or two,
that we would be friends to together
This little bluebird friend and me.

James Davran
FLIGHT II
There's a plane always flying in heaven
That never touches the ground,
Universal's Flight Number 11;
And it flies without making a sound.
It contains neither seat-belts nor signals;
There's no pilot nor steward inside
And in flight imperceptibly mingles
With the birds winging skyward in glide.
Always flying in all kinds of weather;
Never grounded by rain, snow or sleet.
It arrives here as light as a feather
And returns with some one in each seat.
Reservations and tickets aren't needed
Yet this one way flight can't be missed.
Universal makes sure all are seated
And there's always a long waiting list.

April Andersen
UNTITLED
Over the stormy sea
The eagle flies.
He does not see me
As I watch him soar,
Catching the wind
As it tosses the waves,
Not knowing that
My mind and heart
Are with him;
Even though I am bound
To the earth.

Leanna Gayle Stehle
ROPE BURNS
Time
is slipping
through my hands
like a rope
in a tug of war.
And I feel
the burning
in my palms
and fingers
that comes
when something precious
is lost
and all that is left
is
the pain.

Lauren Sylvia Miller
A WOMAN'S DREAM OF SUCCESS
How should we separate emotions from physical expression to lust freely, selfishly?
How can we look into customer's eyes and lie without blinking?
(The men in the nightmare are eating spinach salad,)
How can I corrupt myself so that I no longer feel pain?
(With herpes dressing.)
How else can I succeed in the business world?
Show me how to bargain in closed brunches
to deny people their homes.
Teach me how to smile, pat bankers on the back, in restaurants, to hide financial crime.
(They laugh and their forks turn into worms.)
Tell me how to donate millions from gratitude, from IRS.
(The women powder their crotches after dessert, adjust their bras, sip the last of their coffee, or is it blood.)
How else can I succeed in politics?
Can I be a healer without selling cancer-causing drugs to third world countries?
(I try to bring them their tab, but I feel sick,)
Can I be a saint, an Oklahoma minister, without opposing lesbianism, to praise AWACS?
(Walking down the aisle in pig-sty and goat-hormone incense, past grey skeletons smoking,. . . .they scorn me for wearing flesh.)
Can I be crowned queen without campaigning for V.D., illegitimacy?
(They finally leave, the pressure subsides,. . . .my tip reads:
You take life too seriously, you're unrealistic. . .quit dreaming!)
Without experience, can I find a job after college?

David Bommarito
SILENT RELATIONSHIP
"Since you, there's a quality of love, silently hiding behind speechless eyes. Speechless eyes with such an intense passion behind them that desire has over taken my soul, over taken my mind.
No matter how much I try to resist you, what I feel will only get stronger with time."
"I have this wild lust everywhere inside, which fills me to the limit beyond control. This consuming desire for your sweet, yet tender love is driving me insane with passion. There is no length of time you can avoid me, because nothing will stifle what I feel in you. In you I've found a love that transcends; all space and time to the maximum limit of human emotion.

You are more than any man could ever want. You are the one this man needs."
I've developed a relationship with a girl. This girl, I have to say good-bye to. It's all very logical to me now. The more you love someone, the more susceptible you are to get hurt.
"How deeply in love with her am I. But its a dream that can never be fullfilled, nor come true.
With her it's too good to be real. With her it's being so untamed; But with the gentlest touch. We both knew once we touched, this desire would never stop.

Only she can make this
intensement brew inside of me
like this. But like a dream, we
must stay as strangers to each
other. And you once asked, How
do I know it's real?

Clarence Alexander Mitchell

MADNESS

Senses slither through oceans of
illusions
Angry ebony captures the light
Reason bounds feelings with
links of living bondage
Dreams slain by the morning
sword
Fear frees the hounds of anger
Hope's visage is that of a
stranger

Christine Starks

FOR A SICK FRIEND

Just a little note,
to let you know I care.
To tell you I'm thinking of you,
and the friendship we share.
I want you to know,
that I will always be there.
When you need a friend and
burdens,
get to heavy to bear.
I hope you get well soon,
as I hate to see you sick.
But you're a strong person,
so this thing I know you can
lick.
Things may look kinda bad now,
but try not to be blue.
Just remember how lucky you
are,
to have so many people that
Love you.

Samantha Magrath

THE HAWK

The hawk
Sails forlornly by, and only I
Hear its sad cry,
As it soars on the wind,
With its wings spread wide,
Its movement is an effortless
glide
That makes small creatures
Run and hide.
And I run,
With its shadow by my side.

Cheryl J. Grover

CHRISTMAS FROST

Frosty dew in the early morn'
Left by the fury of a cold winter
storm,
Snowflakes that cover the brown
of the trees,
Branches that are prisoners in
the merciless breeze.
Yet, this cold is soon overcome
By a sound of love, a carol
quietly hummed,
A telling of tales, of how Jesus
was born,
As we sit by the fireplace,
cozy and warm.
The Christmas tree, shiny and
bright,
The touch of a snowflake, ever
so light,
A manager that rests under the
tree,
Christmas love, a dove that is
free.
Sparkling towers, ice on the
eaves,
Blue snow replaces old dry
leaves,
The beauty of Christmas, never
to be lost
Brought to life by the early
morning frost.

Mary E. Cunningham

FASHION HORSE

Mother Nature is all dressed up
In her very best today.
Diamonds of snowdrops are
Laced through her hair,
Her shoes are shining with icy
glare—
Surely, she must be going
somewhere.

Charles L. Stewart Jr.

FLOWERS SAY I LOVE YOU

I think of you for hours,
As I sit in the sunlight.
I decided to bring you flowers,
When the sun turns to night.
For the brightness of your
smiles,
Are like bouquets of flowers.
The scents go on for miles,
With a fresh delightfulness that
lasts hours.
The freshness of the morning's
dew,
Reminds me of your sweet way.
And the everlasting Love I hold
for you,
From day to day.
As I sit in the sunlight's rays,
I hope the flowers show the
things I have to say.
The thoughts of your many
Loving ways,
And how I Love You more day
by day.

Judith Tiblovna Belilovski

THE RHYTHM OF LIFE

Floating in a sea of languid heat,
Strain to find a path, not
content
To float, tossed in the foam and
Spray of society.
Socialism, Marxism, Fascism,
Communism, Socialism,
Marxism—
On and on in an unending
nursery
Rhyme of man's playpen, the
Toys of love and war tossed
About by the angry child the
Governess, in absence.
By they float in an eternal
Colloquial parade of empty eyed
Souls.
Yet—
Forthcomes the Messiah, on the
Battlefield of Armageddon
Thus is the Rhythm of Life,
Tossed in an angry sea.
The Tsar falls, forthwith bound,
In the mud. From the carcass
springs,
As of a flower, the beady eyed
Lenin, Stalin, Breshnev.
Armageddon
Is past But a puzzle remains.
Who won?

Hazel Everett

SHADOW OF BLESSINGS

Just like our shadow
Close by our side
Giving strength and courage,
Loving care to abide.
Listening to our every prayer,
Guiding us the right way,
Protecting us by day,
Blessing us with sleep at night.
Holding our hand when we are
ill,
Telling our fears "Peace Be Still"
Troubles will soon fade away
For tomorrow is bright and new.
Bringing joy in many ways too,
Blessed wonders we shall
behold—
Cherished in hearts young and
old—
Who——our blessed Jesus
Christ.

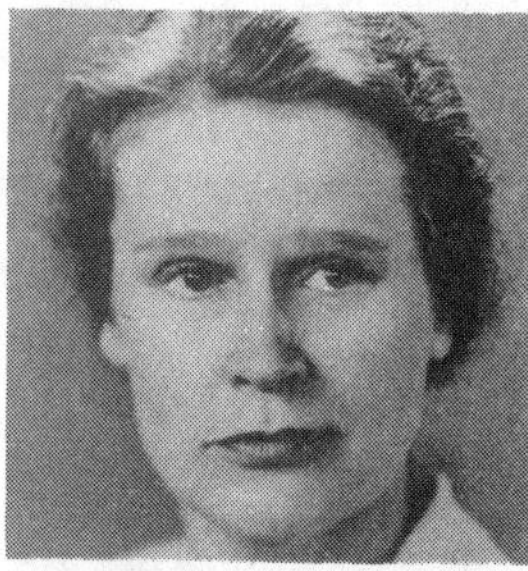

Gertrued Hickin Sigmon

FORGIVEN

Soft distraction, a tugging at
my mind,
"Come out, come out!" But I
heed not the call,
Not knowing that it comes
through Death's great wall.
What strange pulls do transport
me, make me blind
To mundane things at hand? I
fear to find
The way through edge of
Earth—I fear to fall
Into insanity. And so I crawl
In slime—my spirit dead, in
flesh entwined.
But they persist and smile
before my eyes.
Through space and time they
call me from this world,
And scores of years and
continents now spanned
They say good-bye and lift my
heart from cries
Of dead regrets. From Heaven's
seat pure-pearled
They now see all, and all they
understand.

J. Thompson

THE PRIZE

I have been guilty
of wanting to win
the prize—
your charm
your brilliance
your smile.
I would hold it
close to my heart
polish it daily
stroke it lovingly.
Oh
how wonderful
it would be
until you decide
to award yourself
to somebody else.

Eric A. Spanitz

I'VE BEEN POISONED BY MY MOM'S STUFFED CABBAGE

I'm finished now, the pain is
great,
look out here comes what I
just ate.
As so-and-so the thinker said,
"All of the pain is in your
head."
Cause I'm not great I must agree,
but still I think it's my
tummy.
"But why'd she do it?" all I ask,
"To give me pain in which to
bask?
Or maybe cause a little strife,
which too much of will take
my life."
No, that's not it. It cannot be.
We get along, that's her and
me.
Maybe someone that's non-
family,
they poisoned it to get at me.
But no one else is getting sick,
my murderer I cannot pick.
Oh! What is that? I heard it pass.
Excuse me now, it's only gas.

Niles Seifert

PROPHECY

in ashes and in olive wood
my seed lies
as it lives I watch it die
fruitless in its patience
in the first dusk
I anticipate my destiny
sealed in my priesthood
sometimes I hear ancient bones
lamenting in a voice of tired
waiting
but my force has left me
my spirit seeks refuge in my
eyes
but they dissolve and fill with
sand
blotting out the sun

Eugene D. Evans

MY LAND OF BEGINNING AGAIN

Life was a hunger, a vision that
spoke
Of the Land of Beginning Again,
Dreams of the morrow shed all
their sorrow
As the morn casts gloom away
And naught but the raptures
that happiness captures
Were there for the heart to gain.
It was real, that I knew, this
wonderful place
Called the Land of Beginning
Again,
For I'd seen it before in the
countenance wore
Of a child beholding the sky
And the melody spun from
laughter undone,
And the song of a bird after rain.
So I journeyed afar in an
unknown way,
For who can find guide for his
dreams,
Beheld nature's wonders, a
vastness that sunders
The fear that we're vain after all,
But no Valley appeared for a

man who had reared
His hopes on fables and dreams.
Then I searched the oracles of
men renown,
Perused musty volumes of lore,
Besought of the sages, the record
of ages,
The monument writings of man;
But what the avail, at the start
I must fail,
And my Land was remote as
before.
What fear then possessed me, I'd
sought everywhere
For my Land of Beginning Again:
No price could unveil it, I tried
and I failed it,
And still in my heart I knew
That e'er life was over this
penitent rover
Would hail from those portals
his gain.
And sure as a Paradise waits us
beyond
This temple of flesh that we
bear,
The deed to that Land, I now
understand,
Is not for one heart alone
But for all men to know: Should
you want to go,
The Way is through faith and
prayer.

Ann Branham

UNKNOWN LOVE

I went to a place that was very
unknown.
You saw me standing all alone.
You walked over and caught my
eye.
I was so scared, I thought I
would die.
But your look was soft and I
knew right then,
That you would soon become a
good friend.
You touched my hand and then
we met,
Our eyes had locked, our hearts
not yet.
Each day I saw you my love
grew stronger
And each night I'd lie awake
longer and longer.
You'd call me up and I would
get chills,
Then dream about us in
unending fields.
The fields were full of beautiful
flowers,
And we would sit talking for
many long hours.
I got to know you; you got to
know me.
Hopefully our love was meant
to be.
Who knows; someday we might
get married.
Then my dreams would be fully
carried.
Our love would bond us and
hold us together,
Even the hard times would seem
light as a feather.
But the future will come and in
due time
The bells in our hearts will
begin to chime.
Then our hearts will meet and
forever unite,
And through eternity they will
always see light.

Myran Lee Bergenson

MOM

A light in my life has gone out,
A part of me has died. . .
All the grief and the pain I feel
Are far too much to hide.
Mom, you left us all. . .suddenly,
You may have tried to say,
But I did not listen to you
When you did speak that day.
I could not handle hearing
things
Like you were getting old,
I teased and said to you,
"My Dear,
That is our fate, I'm told!"
You tried to tell me time was up
For you, and you'd be gone.
But I would never hear of it. . .
I teased and rambled on.
Oh Mom, your sweet and gentle
way
Endeared you deep within.
Never had I realized how much
A part of me, you'd been.
I know that God has need of
you,
Your goodness was unique;
But I'm so lost without you,
Mom,
That I can hardly speak.
I know that time should heal
my wounds,
Make sweet. . .each memory. . .
But that light in my life is out
For all eternity.

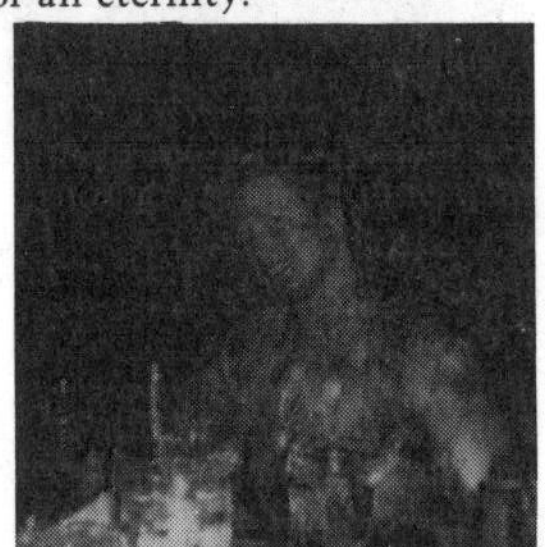

Priscilla R. Lull

GLENWOOD SPRINGS

Warm, rushing water against my
body
Fills me with delight.
A full moon above the
mountain,
A most romantic sight!
A honey-mooner's spot,
An ideal place,
Where lovers seek

A warm embrace.
My heart cries out
And gladly sings:
*"How I love you,
Glenwood Spring!!!"*

Julian L. Weaver, M.D.

I DO DECLARE

During my early years of youth,
in the search for my identity,
To be called "black" was a
cardinal sin;
Categorized with any other
iniquity.
"I'm a Negro", I would answer,
With my chest so swelled with
pride.
And, in case you can't
remember,
Maybe we should step aside.
Just as I was feeling respectable,
I was certainly taken aback,
To learn that I had suddenly
become. . .
A genuine, bonafide *"Black"*.

Linda J. Reed

FLIGHT

Let yourself glide
Borne along by the wind
And sheltered by clouds.
Drifting free;
A luminous moon to guide a
night flight
Shimmering stars shall point the
way
Reach out and touch the sky.
Come;
Live with me among the stars
And rest upon the clouds
Soar in celestial freedom,
A companion to the moon
Earth shine shall give light to
your eyes,
The wind will caress your hair,
Spring rain will bring coolness
And the sun the welcome
warmth.

Rosalie Coler Isaacs

THE SUNBEAM

Go into the meadow
Catch a leaf
Before they are gone
Listen to the grass grow
Smell the wind
Touch the sky
Pink cotton candy clouds
Autumn splendor
Soon gone
Listen to the moon
Touch a blade of grass
Don't walk, run into the
starlight
Do it now, don't wait
Listen to the sunbeam
She knows, she knows. . .

Susan Bonaiuto

REFLECTION OF TRUTH

To know yourself
Is a difficult task,
Through trial and error
One's life must pass.
To apply what you learn
Understand what you feel,
Controlling desires
Through confusion and fears.
Trying to do right
Though failing must be,
Continuous knowledge
Searching. . .Revealing me.
Many faces have I
Each a secret they hold,
Thoughts and feelings inside
I long to control.
Searching and sifting
Deep inside my soul,
Pulling to the surface
An identity of my own.
Questions answered in time
Scattered pieces securely
placed,
Lifes struggle for identity
Myself I now face.

Lynne M. Cormier

GRAPES

Green when young and
undeveloped
The sourness of youth is
somehow bittersweet
Red when able to take care of
oneself
Sweetness of the vine
Cherished when matured
Purple and wrinkled is the
raisin
When life has passed by, nearly
gone
Even though the seeds
Life has its times of sweet
Colorful ripeness

Verna G. McMahon

LILACS

It's strong—the scent of lilac.
It sweeps in tidal waves
of fragrance.
It covers all
then settles back—
and comes again with
slightest breeze
to numb the senses
with its beauty
of heavy thick aroma
that fills the breath—
that makes you gasp
And drown in sweet perfume.

Sally R. Shaffer

THE THOUGHT

Somewhere, there is a thought.
It has no place to land.
Its elusiveness causes a child's
dreaming smile.
It seeks a dog's dream of chasing
a rabbit,
Complete with whimpers
and running feet.
It sits restlessly on the heart
of love,

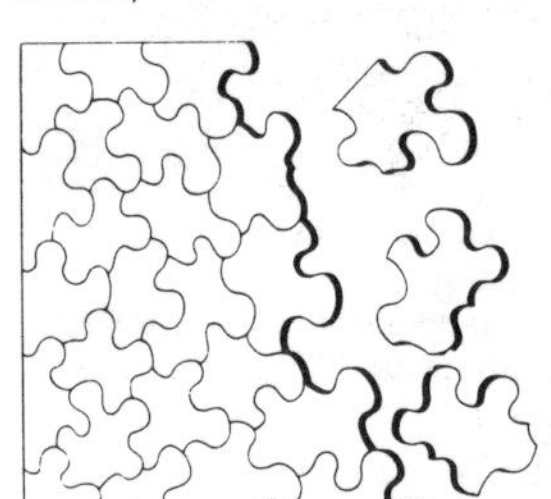

Then flees in fear of being
remembered.
It stills the shyness of a
butterfly.
It draws a hummingbird to look
at humans,
Only then to laugh in silver-
winged humor.

Cathy A. Blea

FOR YOU DEAR MOTHER, A ROSE

For the love you so generously
gave,
for you Dear Mother, a rose.
From you Dear Mother I learned
that
in receiving and returning it,
love grows.
For gentle hands that touched
and smiles that warmed the
heart.
From you Dear Mother I learned
that no
greater joy than that there art.
For a kind word and a humble

way.
From you Dear Mother I learned that peace
can be mine tomorrow and today.
For seeds of love Our Lord planted in you
were blessings to all I say.
From your loving daughter for showing her
that love grows,
For You Dear Mother, A Rose.

Susan Nan Robertson

A PLACE OF ESCAPE

A place of escape, a world of my own
Just for myself, for me alone.
Somewhere to go, away from it all
No one can come, no one can call.
A paradise of peace, special for one
A place in time, till time is done.

Values are hidden, can't be found
Fear is leashed, to be unbound.
Problems in life, one and all
Never hide long, but come at the call.
Pressure is built, walls all around
Tranquility is lost, needs to be found.
A place of escape, a world of my own
Just for myself, for me alone.

Carrie

TRIBUTE TO DIANE WAKOSKI

She's a stone woman
Black and gray inside
Crusty and rough outside
Like slate easily broken to bits
When her lunar rock
Is fired.
She's an angry female
Exploding guns at men
Who kill her with infidelities
Yet kindle her hungry fire
Till it burst forth
In flames of unity.
She's a cold moonfaced feminist
Whose search for love
Was greeted by polar winds
That chill even an equator
To icicle hugs
And daggar eyed kisses.
She's a lonely broad
Of a desert youth
Who craves muscles and mustache
Surrounding her lava limbs
And mind of volcanic ash.
She's a feather down dame
With a clown's heart
And moss hunger
Who vomits her guts into poems
Showing her meteor spittle
And solitary flight
In a solid casing of heart stabbing words.

Helen Gage

LOST

I'm lost in my loving,
There's something I can't find.
I'm learning that the giving
Is playing on my mind.
Is there someone there that needs me,
Is he coming from behind.
Whatever God has planned for me
Is playing on my mind.
My feelings are in confusion,
I really want to give.
My heart holds reservations
And won't let my spirit live.
My love is imprisoned within me,
My senses guard the confine.
Life's secret for my future
Is playing on my mind.

Jennifer Noel Entner

THE DANCE

Cloaked in hooded velvet,
Night spreads her winglike veils,
Across the hills and meadows,
O're streams and down the dales.
Creeping into deep and mossy forests,
Over fields of dewy wheat,
Spreading tinseled stardust,
Trailing a misty lacelike sleep.
The silver chalice is raised heaven high,
Silently gliding on clouds that fly.
Shimmering stars halo round her silken head.
Trails of moondust follow in her stealthy stead.
Sapphire blue and purple,
Adorn her glittering gown.
Translucent, luminous billows
Swirl gently down to the ground.
Round and round she dances,
Until the dawn light creeps,
Carrying her moonglow children,
Home to sing to sleep.

Pam Garland

UNTITLED

Sleep children
how calmly you can be
nestled warmly
under a hazy sky,
Dream tenderly
float on time's still wind,
Relax, be careless while you can
for soon it is dawn.

Melissa Price

MY DARLING

My darling, how I need you
Your presence makes me feel warm,
Even though my hands are cold.
My darling, please hold me
As though you'd never let go
And love me, if only for tonight.
And my darling, tomorrow
When I'm in forever sleep
You and my heart shall be gone.

Richard Spohn

THE BARREN

Warmer climes help tulips bloom
Which treat the eye, that smell so nice;
Not here, for there is not the room,
And here is only ice.
Somewhere far the roses grow
In crystal vases, sunlit parks;
But here are covered up with snow
And wither in the dark.
The gardener attempts to grow
Great fields of red and pink and gold;
But here they wilt, despite himself,
And perish in the cold—
Yes, gardens of most other folk
Grow fruitful through the passing years,
But here the seeds inside each fruit
Are only frozen tears.

Sally R. Shaffer

CATCH MY TEARS

Catch my tears.
Collect my tears.
Use one.
Mold what you think I am.
Use another.
Mold what you think I should be.
Use yet another.
Mold what you think you wanted.
Save the last.
Then search for the me I am.

David Havron

UNTITLED

You
were made mentally
by me my love
much more
than that
which you are.
I've drawn you
each day
since then
but the canvas
absorbs the ink
as the morrows pass.

Donna Hopkins Wampler

A SPECIAL LOVE

A love has come into my heart and turned my life around.
Each day means more than ever and my sorrows have been drowned.
He never turns His back on me, no matter what I do.
He protects me and provides for me and always sees me through!
He's always there when I need Him and provides a listening ear.
As long as He's around I know there's nothing I need fear!
He helps me see what's right and wrong whenever I need advice.
He makes my life more happy than not, cause sadness won't suffice!
I know he'll never leave me and that security is unreal;
and there's no existing feeling that could top the way I feel!
For all He's done for me there's just no way I can repay,
so my life's at His disposal for His use in any way!
Yes, there's someone in my life that you've just got to know!
He gave His life to set me free a long, long time ago.
His blessings can't be counted and His love's beyond compare.
So won't you let Him in your heart? 'Cause I'd be proud to share!

William Exton, Jr.

MOOD

I
am in a mood.
I want to tell a beautiful woman
that I love her.
Only this
will satisfy
my mood.
She must be very beautiful—
and complaisant.
How can I tell
if I will love her?—
if I have loved her?—
even
If I do love her?
What piffling sincerity is this,
that deals with all moments together?
Deal with each,
singly;
and deal well!
What more sincere
than the unrestrained
expression
of a mood?—
The mood of a moment?
I am in a mood
to tell a beautiful woman
that I love her.

Martin (Bud) Taggert

BIG WHEEL FROM TEXAS

This Dallas oilman with a kingsize roll
Left in his jet with Vegas the goal
Rented the penthouse on the Dunes top
And started a jamboree without pulling
A stop
Celebrities showgirls, with VIPs galore
All flocked to this freebe on the thirty-fourth floor
Caviar and drinks, with free house chips
For all

And everyone agreed it was one helluva
Brawl
Now where was the oilman during this mad mad
Whirl.?
Why he left in his jet with the show's leading girl
The unpaid bills were enormous, and that is
A fact
With the grim faced cops waiting should he
Ever come back.

Frank Neisius

ROCK STAR

Jewels, lame, or skin
Gyrate, glitter midst waving hair
Concealing identity and mike
Amplifying non-voices to shrieks.
A frame so thin a belt looks fat
Corrals a boneless inertia,
Leaping in open tight clothes
Boxing plenty—attracting eyes.
Banging, spangled, moving stag fright
Assaults sensors with amorality.

Mickie Wayne Lynch

A WIFE

A wife will love you
A wife helps you over the rough spots
A wife is a woman
Who has and raises your little tots.
A wife is a cook
A wife is a mother
A wife is a woman
Who is also a lover.
A wife is a person
A wife is half a team
A wife is a woman
Who shares the same dream.
A wife is not a possession
A wife is not someone to be shoved
A wife is a woman
Who needs to be loved.
A wife thats my lady
Whom I will never shove
A wife is my woman
Thats—the wife I love.

Mollie Glass Pamplin

HORIZONS

My memory's curtain lifts, the palm trees sway,
And sunset glows across Manila Bay,
The scene is shifting and I go my way
By pedicab along the streets of far Taipei,
And now I'm standing in my garden in Japan,
I hear the music of a distant samisan,
Ah, Saigon, you were Paris of the Far East then;
And Bangkok, will I see your Emerald Buddha once again?
The traveller's journey never really ends,
All through the years returning as to long lost friends,
To sights and sounds, Mt. Fuji in the sky,
Old dreams return, I cannot say good-bye.

Gregorio Estrella

THOUGHTS

Poor is the man who but riches does seek,
for he is the man with a will plainly weak;
Poor is the man who but titles obtains,
for he is the man with but empty remains;
Poor is the man whose mind does neglect,
for he in his life only darkness reflects;
Poor is the man whose body misuses,
for he will discover too late his abuses;
Rich is the man if his spirit does feed,
for he is the man who may laugh in his need;
Rich is the man who shares in his wealth,
for he will obtain his peace and his health;
Rich is the man who but love does impart,
for he is the man with a fullness of heart;
Rich is the man who grows in his mind,
for thoughts will fulfill all the goals he may find.

Edward Benedict Bailey

NEARNESS

The sharpest feeling
Is gone.
Buried deep.
Lost in the misty banks of awe.
Yet I heard you cry,
Across the absence barrier
Of a soundless twenty years,
I know—
The increasing sensitivity
Of the separation tears
Places me nearer
Than your closest
Soft moment of pain
And closer than memory.

Margrit Spear

THE TURNING POINT

I've grown into a woman
And look back on my life
Reality and dreaming
As mother and as wife.
The things that were important
When I was young and shy
They really do not matter
I often wonder why.
Why did I change my feelings
Towards Lovedones and things I care
Perhaps because my ups and downs
Emotions I now can share.
I've grown into a woman
And learned the meaning "free"
Of burdens and of troubles
That are pretense to me.
Life is truly worth living
When you can share the day
With someone who will listen
The barriers go away.
I've grown into a woman
I understand the means
Reality is different
From all the previous dreams.
Thats why I treasure little things
That I can share and hold
For they are worth eternally
Much more than all the gold.
I've grown into a woman
Horizons change with me
They're wonderful to enter
For they can set me free.
I've grown into a woman
My judgment is my own
I have no reservation
For I have truly grown.

Richard B. Stauffer

EVERYTHING DIFFERENT

If I could be a turkey
I would like to be a gobbler,
Then I could strut and chase
a hen, now and then.
However, if I were a rooster
I'd fly upon a fence,
Every morning, early, I would crow
Even though the fog was dense.
If I could be an owl
High in a tree, I'd alight.
Wouldn't care if my brain
Was only the size of my eye.
One day I thought how nice
If I could be a bee,
I'd hum around the honey
And leave the Queen, be.
Got excited in the mountains,
One day, saw a mountain goat.
He was at the height of glory;
Now my thoughts began to float.
Went down into the valley,
I was the only monkey there,
So I crawled into my car
And drove away for tea.

Margaux Baxter Haden

LIFE ON JUPITER

If I had known,
I would have been here sooner,
What an awful time I've had.
The sounds around me,
Penetrate my head,
Life on Jupiter ain't so bad.

Ron Lathem

I AM THE LIGHT

I am the Light
The light of all mankind
That shines in the night
That men may not be blind.
I am the Light
Lifted high on a hill
To light up GOD'S truth
To whosoever will.
I am the Light
Satan tried to snuff out
But I broke death's grip
And rose up with a shout.
I am the Light
That shines bright evermore
To light up the path
That leads to heaven's door.
Walk in my Light
That you may never fall
Know Jesus is Lord
He's your help when you call.
Walk in my Light
Feel the warm healing rays
Then you will know peace
And have joy all your days. . .

Paul C. Peck

Worthwhile Endeavor

I've stood beside an open grave,
With casket poised above;
And spoke aloud to grieving friends
Fraternal words of love.
Yes, o'er the years, I've eulogized
A hundred times or more;
To bring a little hope and joy
To those still on this shore.
It's hard to lose so many friends,
Some very close to me;
At times it seemed that I could climb
The weeping willow tree.
But, if it brought some comfort to
Those dear ones left behind,
I hope that I have symbolized
The art of being kind.
And, when my turn arrives at last,
Though I will not be there,
I'm sure that there'll be friendly folks
Who'll shed a tear and care.

Phyllis Jean Smith

A SINGLE RED ROSE

Happy birthday mother
So many birthdays we've shared
The gifts, the laughter, tears shed
The words left unsaid
Those precious days gone by
With a love filled heart
An tears in my eyes
I leave on your grave

A single red rose
From a daughter who feels your love surrounding her
And wishes your arms were still around her
Happy birthday mother. . .

Gwen Roberts Boyer

THE EVERGREEN WOODS

In the deep and haunting stillness
Of the shadowed scented pines,
Where the hemlock, spruce and balsam,
Grow in endless measured lines.
A brown needle-carpet blending,
With a skiff of new born snow,
And a brash young breeze caressing,
As he scampers down the row!
It's a different world, my wood-lot,
Should the day be gray or bright,
For the ordered peace of nature,
Lets life's tensions take their flight!

Edward L. Corley
THE BEACON
The lady walks a silent shore
And gazes out to sea;
Ignores the beacon's steady store
Of light to help her see.
The lady walks a silent shore
And gazes out to sea;
Heedless of the beacon's light—
A light she will not see.
The lady walks a silent shore
And lives a life of memory;
I stand atop that beacon light,
A light she will not see.
The lady walks a silent shore
And keeps her memories warm;
And I look down from this great height
To keep her safe from harm.
The lady walks a silent shore
And gazes out to sea;
Heedless of the beacon's light—
The light of love in me;
Heedless of the beacon's light—
A light she will not see.

Tom Payne
A WIFE
A woman of beauty filled with love,
Eyes so pretty like those of doves.
Threads of silk across her face,
Hair in ribbons and clothes of lace.
Teeth that are white as snow,
Cheeks of loveliness that glow.

Lips that are tender and scarlet red,
One who will love you when you wed.
She should be lovely in every way,
A blessing the Lord gives to man one day.
Always cherish her and honor her place,
"Remember" God gave you that pretty face.

Toni McMorris
MATURITY
Altered seed, planted in harvest time
to meet the events of coming years,
See your essence for what it is beyond time and the need to understand.
Go bravely forth INTO life:
into the center from which the essence springs.
From the center comes ALL thought
ALL life, ALL needs answered.
Do not seek for the petals in the beyond
for they are the subtle illusion of life matured.
They are NOT the harvest
but the expression of labor spent.

Toni Lotempio-Krol
NOW IT IS MORNING
NOW IT IS MORNING
In just a few hours you and I
Will meet, and exchange the most sacred of vows
Most cherished of promises
NOW IT IS MORNING
Soon, you and I will stand together in the chapel,
Clothed in the innocence of an emotion
As Endless as Time Itself
That which lends itself to the giving of one soul
to another, for All Time.
NOW IT IS MORNING
As I stand here in the white garments that reflect the purity of the day
I am somber—reflecting on the seriousness of this moment
That will soon fill our hearts and souls with joy
Forever.

Sylvia Shay Casat
SINGLE HANDED
If being with someone
means you're not
Alone
Then why did I
always feel so
Alone
when we were
Together
and so much more
Together
now that I am
Alone.
I suspect
Aloneness
to be a state of mind
entirely independant of
proximity
or distance.

Stella Unjian
FIRE AND ICE
You heard my heart beat wildly
Beneath my placid look
And gazed into my icy eyes
And read me like a book
You stared and stared and found it
Deep within my life
And put your arms around it
and calmed my bitter strife
The warmth that flooded through me
The melting of the ice
My heart reached out to grab you
So glad to pay the price
And pay I will I know it
I love you far too much
I cannot help but show it
I tremble at your touch
Come lie beside me lover
Come melt my icy eyes
Come leave me with a treasure
Come leave me ever wise

Donna M. Niedermeier
YESTERDAY
Down the lane of yesterday,
Our American history roams.
Spoken by a bent old gentleman,
In a roadside park called home.
Before my eyes a memory Entwines,
Of olden days, he related.
The Civil War was being fought
Leaving the Confederacy devastated.
The old gentleman wove his spell,
Far away, the South he revived.
The smell of Atlanta burning,
Today rebuilt, she survived.
The kind old gentleman sighed,
Of Sherman's march to the sea.
President Lincoln announed, "It's over",
The North claiming victory.
That night at the White House ball,
Though many were happy with glee.
The President sighed and requested,
The band to play "Dixie".
He spoke then of his Caroline,
Who lived in Civil War land.
When he left as a Southern soldier,
She promised him her hand.
Though battle scarred and worn,
The tired old gentleman went on.
Upon returning from the war,
His Caroline was gone.
He often goes to visit her,
And judging from his past.
Though buried alone on a hillside,
She's in his heart so vast.

Ellen Forbes Thomas
THE DAY HAS COME/THE DAYS HAVE GONE
She was finally thirty-one.
No longer a child,
a woman she be.
She looked at her hands.
Had they played in the sand?
Thirty-one/two/three. . .
Hopscotch games,
was it really she,
who'd played in the sun?
A dream or reality?
A baby she had never knew
but people say,
from it she grew.
Only memories had she to keep
of the little girl with
plaited hair
who'd dreamed of being a mommy.

Mary M. Domstead
GIFT WITHOUT A BOW
If I could give a gift to everyone I know,
Here's just a few I'd give,
unwrapped without a bow.
The blind man on the corner tapping with his cane,
I'd give the gift of sight, then he could see the rain.
The crippled boy down the street watching the children play,
I'd give him two strong legs,
so he could run all day.
The widow in her lonely room sitting all alone,
I'd bring a loving family,
someone her very own.
Next I'd gather the starving millions who've scarce a bite to eat,
And spread a banquet table, loaded down with fruits and meat.
After that I'd find all those
who live with pain each day,
I'd touch each one with healing balm, and make it go away.
Then last not least I'd light
the way for all the world to see,
And hand in hand lead them to Christ, who died for you and me.
You say to me, "You're
dreaming—this could never be!"
You're right not in this life. . .
But there's a calmer sea.
Jesus can provide the gift of sight and more,
If we obey His teaching, we'll cross to the other shore.

Katherine M Gates Runkle
FREEDOM
Clouds pass free;
Free and not free,
Borne by the summer wind
To pelt Sierra highland
and nurture pastel beds of wildflower,
Slake a passing chipmunk's thirst,
Water stately Ponderosa.
Born anew with sun,
They rise on summer wind
To fall upon the Kansas corn.
Born anew by sun,
They rise on summer wind
To merge with Atlantic Sea.
Free and not free,
Clouds.

Winifred Llewellyn
GIVE THANKS DAY BY DAY
Had a bad night,
woke up late,
made myself tea,
broke a plate.
Took a shower,
Lost the soap,
towelled myself quickly
was losing hope.
Laddered my hose,
no end to my woes.
Then I remembered!
I'd forgotten to say
"Thank you, Lord."
This gentle reminder
to tell me He was there
and had given to me
to be able to share,
A little more time
With those who care.
I thank you Lord,
That I may take,
Another day,
To wake up
LATE

Phyllis Thurkettle
MICHIGAN SPRING
The sky is leaden, the sun's disappeared;
A slight breeze in the treetops harmonizes with birds.
There's a hush just at twilight,
A pause before dark,
Like the moment before the match lights in flame,
And the sputtering spark bursts forth with a roar.
Night will come swiftly, the silhouettes vanish.

Only the circle of lamplight will imitate day.
Spring comes like that—
Hushed waking slowly,
Pushing green points out of leaf-covered earth,
Flirting an orange breast and blinking eye
And waving a green haze across a blue sky.
And then, like the flame, or the black burst of night,
She's here.
Everywhere is the frenzied race of beginning again;
Sweeping the cobwebs from winter lairs,
Hanging dulled thoughts to whip in fresh air.
The mating call of a cardinal at dawn
Awakens the primeval surge of renewal,
And Spring has triumphed again.

E. Gwendolyn Campbell

CULMINATION

Let not greed for gold be mine
But rather, let me share
And golden hours spend.
Let not selfish thoughts entwine
But rather, let me care
About a foe or friend.
And let the mirror of my soul reflect
An image worthy of my Lord's respect;
And then, at end of day, I'll see
The me, I truly want to be.

Edgar Lubin

HUMAN VANITY

There is life on earth, where did it begin
More questions here than answers our knowledge is so slim
It could be the mid east where it all began,
Yet on earths other parts we've found traces there of man.
The bibles clear teachings, we've tried hard to redact
Yet the more we discover the more they've proved a fact.
Out into outer space we have sent many a prober,
Just to find out things long known to Jehovah.
Lord help us in our efforts for we know at last
our length of sojourn on this earth is fading out so fast.
We hasten on our exit by polluting all the air
for other than enrich himself man has nary a care
Corrupting all the resources left in our trust
man has always robbed the earth when despoiling of its crust
By compiling of those things known to us as wealth
Often we make hard the soul and injure our good health
Man's ingenuity now has been displayed
Vehicles faster than sound lately has he made
To leave this fair earth now will be the thrust
Whose great and bounteous goodness had been left in our trust
Yet Lord we know that here we will remain
Till you speed us to the heavens we pray to attain

Lillie Frame Maples

HEROES

Sing a song of gallant boyhood
With a courage flaming bold;
As when David faced the lion
To protect his father's fold.
So he slew the proud Goliath
Taunting all who will to dare
To defend the home and country
Now entrusted to their care.
Sing a song of noble manhood
That will dare to do the right;
As Daniel faced the wicked ruler
Read of doom for haughty Might.

And the Spirit that upheld him
Ever hovering over all,
Still defends the man or nation
Who will listen to His call.
Sing a song of faith undaunted
Though the foes press every side;
Paul and Silas in the dungeon
Preaching Christ the crucified.
Prison bars were rent asunder
As the captives knelt to pray,
And the strength of man was yielded
When the power of God held sway.

Bill McCloud

EYE OF THE BEHOLDER

He said,
If I wasn't a poet,
It's a painter, I'd want to be.
For poets write what they feel,
And painters paint what they see.
She said,
You're right, and
This you need to understand.
The same God, who inspires the poet,
Must guide the painters hand.
He said,
Come then, let us work together,
And a masterpiece unfold.
Through my writing, they'll see the heart.
In your painting, they'll see the soul.

Debbie Wessels

A MOMENT IN TIME

As I sat in the garden
swaying on a swing
the first thing I noticed
was one beautiful thing
It was a young dove
that had just fluttered down
to meet its mate
on the ground
They were happy though
as two young ones could be
until a gust of wind came up
and left nothing to see

Arthur P. Chiasson

FIVE ELEMENTAL PENTADS

Dead leaf,
burnt hand,
crisp wind shakes
brittle gestures
like painful goodbyes.
Hanging water,
colorless grapes,
gravity squeezes down
beaded moments
splashing on time.
Diamond eyes,
facets of night,
silken clouds float
languid glances
across visions, across stars.
Ozone song,
wordless lyric,
harmony provides
distant sense
to the ether of the mind.
Cosmic dust,
wandering souls,
suns refocus
remembered light
upon our inner space.

S. Jenkins

THE TOTAL MAN

This man is all man
A man with Love and Self Respect
A love for all that surrounds him
A look about himself that says "Hey"
I'm something special I'm me my mind my body and my soul this is
All of me the way I walk the way
I talk the way I carry myself
There's no guessing game because I'm
The total man the total me the me
With pride, grace, confidence and self love
This man is truly something special
Something total he is called the Total Man.

Donald R. Branch

FIREY EYES BESEECH ME NOT

Firey eyes beseech me not!
Relinquish thy perseverance!
Forever gauge ones' beauty not without;
Perchance to revel within ones' heart.
Embed thy thoughts amongst a friend,
Of whom you may beget a son.
To live within ones' dream is sought;
'Tis melancholy this burst of passion,
Within the realm of sweet compassion,
As love abounds within my thoughts,
Perhaps a loving glance will win this heart.

Ethel Elliott-Westbrook

TRUE COMPANIONS

Jed loved old Joe—who was just a mutt.
Who followed old Joe around—
You never saw one without the other,
They were well-known in the little town.
Jed's shack was just a shanty small—
But to Jed it was a mansion great;
The old roof leaked & the cold came in.
But Joe was faithful to his human mate.
One ice day a townsman saw
As he passed the little shack,
Old Jed lying dead near the open door
And old Joe guarding him on the floor.
The townsmen dug a grave for Jed,
And placed Him in the ground by the shack—
No funeral services were held—
The townsmen to their warm homes went back.
A few days later one townsman passed,
Old Jed's shack, & stopped to see the grave—
A lump of snow was on the top
So he shoved the ice off with a wave.
He didn't dig deep—just an inch or two,
When he saw old Joe's frozen shape.
Yes, Joe was true to his master, Jed,
And laid close over him like a cape.

Janice Webb

WILLIAM TELL

The Bible says that life is like a vapor—
But in this one case; I wish that God would have done us a favor.
By letting our W.T. live a little longer—
For he didn't have a chance to grow up;
He was still only just a pup.

He was so smart, well-behaved, and sweet;
A finer dog than he was—I doubt that we'll ever meet.
Every night; he slept in his own room inside our house—
He was so still—he was quiet as a mouse.
How he loved when morning came and we all woke up.
For he knew he would get to go with Greg in the pickup.
William Tell wasn't born to be lazy or slow;
He was always ready to go.
Whether it was walking for a short hike,
Or to sometimes follow me on my bike.
To Greg, he was a true friend and such a big help—
When working cows, he'd sometimes get kicked, but would hardly yelp.
After work; it was time to come home to his toy.
Playing with his frisbees—that was his joy.
After playing; it was time to eat.
But none of that ol' dog food—
For that; he would really have to be in the mood.
Most of the time he would rather wait it seemed;
For something better—like some good ol' ice cream!
Getting to eat something like that always gave him a kick—
And he would give us one of his kisses—a big juicey lick.
You are gone now, and without you it is sad.
Remembering how good you were;
You never did anything that was ever really bad.
We loved you W.T.—you were Greg's and mine.
You lived your short life to the fullest—
You did more than others will in their whole lifetime.

Cynthia Ebert

EARTH, TIME AND SPACE

We live in the atomic age
When people and nations are forever enraged
Scholars predict the world may soon end
Thanks to the bombs, the world may never mend
Our civilization is a link in a long chain
Which started when the world began
The ancient such as the Egyptians and Greeks
Built temples that we still seek
They once tapped into a hidden cosmic energy
We have not found their secret
Our civilization is too edgy, still yet
The Earth still possesses a force
The Ancients found it's source
We lost their knowledge to time
As the cosmic bells chime
We look out our windows
We see reality
When they looked out their windows
They saw illusions
Perhaps too much reality is our fatality
Like a complicated game of chess
We must understand our world completely
Before we venture out in space
To ensure the survival of the human race

Shelby Sadler

UNDERGRADUATE MEDITATIONS

Measured steps
Taken in tune
Rolling to the beat
Of the ton upon ton
Ever to the pulse of the heart
Of the mind and the soul losing control
To the might in the heat
One can feel the juice beat and the rivers
Need meat and they meet
Everywhere they are near and
They fear being clear so they bring it
In here but there's nobody
Never on blank days when the frauds are
Coming ever closer need we smear
Our beliefs and those of the Other
Who is dear but writes in runes
Who has the cheerful habit of
Babbling over there in the city
What a pity that we are all carters
Of the dogs we perceive in
Our homes and all around us
Where the desire for love surrounds
Just there in the blue where we know
That it's true how bizarre it all seems
Because it is really strange
And we know no man's there in the gloam
Cleaning up the clearing we must never
Avoid the pursuit of felicity
Or even the members of other world society
On this planet or our dreams
In the deep recesses of our inner
Permanent consciousness and transcendental
Loads of meditative arts
And the sciences of diamonds and the
Coal on the ridges and the
Worthy, worthy words of the deep
Romantic heroes in the chasms
Of our immortal existences of our
Lives and those of our compeers.

Penny Koral

PAIN

pain
pain
overt pain
overt pain
overt pain
overtpain
overpaint
ovepaintr
ovpainter
opaintver
paintover
paint over
paint
paint
paint
over

Esther L. Foye

MR. JOLLY

We made a snowman big and fat,
With coal for nose and eyes,
We let him wear a big, black hat,
And one of Daddy's ties.
We gave him next, a stick to hold,
(That would be his cane),
A mouth of coal—smiling bold,
But what could be his name?
We thought and thought—then he
smiled at us,
As jolly as could be,
So that's just what we named him!
"Mr. Jolly," that was he!

Elizabeth Pugh Fleming

A HUMMINGBIRD

Some say folks change quite queerly when they die
Into birds, beasts or trees—
tho I don't know just why!
So I want a hummingbird for my other "me",
Daring and dainty,
Capriciously free!
Droll little drummer, pirouetting by,
Vagabond vandal, heartless you spy
Fair, flirting flowers—and a fragrance steal,
Then flit to another, as you fancy or feel.
What a life, what a whirl, this free, frenzied flight—
With delicious dye'd nectars wherever you light.
Minute minuet-er
Are you, too, a forgetter—
Never quite sober enough to be true
To one little flower, and its' own lovely hue?

Jorrie Ciotti

MOMENTS OF LOVE

With sadness in heart
I went for a walk.
Upon me I heard the laughing of the creek.
So I sat to join the laughter
And as I sat, the sunlight grew intensifying each moment.
I laughed with the creek
And blended with the light
Uniting as one.
My sadness. . .no longer.
For to hear and feel these gifts
I could only smile and feel honored to experience
these moments of love.

Jean Kolar

FAN'S DESIRE

I cherish whom I have not seen in person.
just in magazines, and books
and on the T.V. screen.
I love the man who sings the songs of ballads slow and rock 'n' roll.
He'll be forever my desire, and this I wrote to let him know.

Joan Bettis

A ROSE

Take a rose, a beautiful
thing;
The fullness of life,
The freshness of
spring.
Take the stem as the beginning of
life—
The thorns that resemble the trials that come
along life's
way;
Add the beauty and hope it brings;
That is the meaning of life each
day.
Take the leaves, so pretty and
green;
Truly a sight to be
seen.
The rose, the most beautiful flower of
all—
The sweetest of scents—
the fulfillment of life—
the promise of hope and happy
tomorrows—
All that Nature takes and
borrows—
One of Nature's greatest things—
a rose. . . . .

S. Billings Alcott

THE HUMAN RACE

Jogging by with earphones attached,
a life support system to stop the noise
of their brains.
The human race races on.
So it begins—one violent burst of energy—born.
Too bad death comes piece
by
piece;
a slow disintegration.
But, the running goes on,
no time to think of things like that
or at all.
The numbing humming of their brains
dulled by the overkill of machines.
Eyes fixed outward, a cataract to counteract
inward mobility.
Could it be they have lost control so soon?
Deaf ears, just a brief
parenthesis on each side
of the head, respond to nothing
but the wire-rocking body-racking

beating machine.
But, don't stop the race.

Mary M. Faragher
A HAIKU
Glittering sunlight—
Baby's tiny, chubby hands
Make twirling shadows.

Ken Sibley
ON THE BOX CANYON FALLS OF OURAY
Viewing Box Canyon Falls—
A moving,
overwhelming
experience.
The water of Canyon Creek
Thundering down the channel—
Crashing,
churning,
and pounding;
Creating turbulence,
volume,
soft spray,
colors of many hues.
Overwhelmed and entranced by the
Qualities of ENDURANCE
power and majesty,
beauty,
and EVERLASTINGNESS.

Elizabeth Shannon Jones
HOW CAN I TELL THEM
Bluebird of happiness flying so high,
Soaring, lilting, so free in the sky.
Tell me, please tell me *do*,
How did your freedom come to you?
Little bluebird there in the sky,
How did *you* tell them you wanted to fly?
Did they warn you of danger out there?
Was there singing when you took to the air?
Did you feel sadness so deep in your soul,
Or—were your eyes ever set on your goal?

Tell me, friend from high in the sky,
How did *you* tell them you wanted to fly?
My heart is so bound to my loves of home,
Yet, childhood has passed and I must roam.
Shall I speak tenderly—pour out my heart,
Or simply say, "goodbye", and then depart?
Bluebird, come down from the sky;
Whisper to me the best way to fly.

Michele Cueman
LIVE
Live your life,
it's full of wonders,
it has its ups and downs,
and every day you take a step,
sometimes you'll lose some ground.
Don't worry what the others say,
just keep your head held high,
and no matter what the day may bring,
Don't worry, you'll get by.

Byron Scott Harrison
LIFE IN THE SPIRIT
"Walk in the Spirit, and ye shall not
fulfill the lust of the flesh."*
Walking in. . .satisfying the
Selfishness of the flesh:
A constant wandering for freedom.
As the heart is hard
And choked by sin,
The body is paralyzed
And the mind deceived.
Where does one turn?
As death is the surrounding air,
As death is the life,
As death is attached as a shadow. . . . . .
Free will provides the key.
But most choose not to live on.
As men search,
Christ is knocking.
As men have been searching,
Christ has been knocking.
As men will continue to search,
Christ will continue to knock.
To those who open the door,
Christ comes in. . .and life begins,
We are born again.
The walk in the flesh
Becomes the walk of the Spirit.
The heart pumps life
And is no longer clogged by sin.
And it (life) takes over the body
Never to fade away,
But at the appointed time
Journey to its eternal home.
**Galatians 5:16*
New Testament

Michele J. Enright
BECAUSE OF YOU
I love you so much!
I feel like I could burst!
Open up with joy,
And all because of you.
You make me feel like I conquered
The unconquerable.
I'm at the top,
On the highest peak,
All with love for you.
My heart is ready to break open
To let out my every want for you.
You're the reason for my existence,
For my being here.
It's because of you,
And it's for you.
I love you so very much!
I could fly on wings of lightness.
And outshine the sun in brightness.
I shimmer like the moon
And all because of you!

Kalevi Lappalainen
Precise Not Forgetting Us Humans
Clay is precise.
Sighs in your body's clay feet.
Spiritual and material coincide,
I called you, you said yes, tonight.
In my loose ends, working, playing,
the true insights are taking place.
My structure may exhilarate the famous
ape, Charles Darwin: his game is straight.
That structure we call tree,
some moss underneath, a bee or two
above, and some recent hurtful memory:
tonight I am precise
like the real *scientee.*

Scott Vincent Richards
MEMORIES
Memories are indeed strange and forever lasting, and some haunt us into the wee hours of dawn. . .

Those we have known and loved ah, sweet memories, those are never gone. . .

Once in awhile, a memory comes to us out of the darkness of nite and time showing us a scene from another existence, another place, another time. . .

The mind is like a camera, taking pictures of every scene within our lives, and the store-houses for the film is our memory.

Ah, how sweet and, yes, bitter are the memories of time, like tasting all the grapes in a vineyard to learn whether or not they are good enough to make wine. . .

Janet B. O'Brien
CHANGES
one touch of your hand
would solve everything
it would serve as a wand
yet you use it as a weapon
you wave me away
and point
when i am in the wrong
but you never use it
for encouragement.
are hands now only for holding
pens and pencils
or do people still use them
for holding other hands?

Connie Berens
FALL RECIPE
Brown leaves stirred by
the wind-spoon
mixed with whistling winds
a pinch of foreboding cold
crackling dry crunches
under feet spice
a few burnt charcoals
add the proper scent
fold in gray speckled sky
thoroughly mix
set for a short time
before refrigeration

Gloria Tompkins Skeeters
JACOB'S LADDER
Lord, help me climb the rungs of Jacob's ladder,
And visit the land you alone can see.
Please let me view the world of great temptations
From heights that are above a troubled sea.
And as I climb each ladder rung I'm certain
That truths will be revealed with every step.
The mysteries of the universe then open
Could encourage my weary mind to accept.
Then with the world of Satan far beneath me,
Away from evil's powerful clutching hands.
I could enjoy, if only for a moment,
The beauty of God's blessed Promise Land.
Should you choose for me to descend the ladder,
And leave the land that you alone can see.
I think that I could overcome temptations,
And I could calmly brave the stormy seas.

W. K. Fluharty
THE GREATEST COMMANDMENT
Love, and deeply care, for all is care that loves,
And all that loves and cares and lives
has no despair.
But sadness comes to those who find
That love is but a state of mind
Yet do not love.
Care, and fully live, for all is life that cares,
And all that cares and lives and loves
has no despair
But sadness falls to those who prove
That caring's but a stage of love
Yet do not care.
Live, and be fulfilled, for all
is filled that lives,
And all that lives and loves and cares
has no despair.
But sadness grows in those who wake
T'what simple action living takes
Yet do not live.
Yet do not live. . .

Irene Schweinfurth
Night After Christmas
'Tis the night after Christmas, can't walk through the house,
Things are so cluttered, there's not room for a mouse;
Stockings and socks are all over the floor,
Dad is all in and is taking a snore.
Children are sleeping but not in

their bed,
I have on a kerchief, Oh! my poor aching head;
I can't get to the window, there is no place to walk.
Blackboard's in front of it, I am stepping on chalk.
Train is on the floor, also the track,
Dad broke that the very first crack;
Paper, tinsel, pine needles too,
Have covered the rugs; I cannot wade through.
That dear moon outside peeps into the room,
Gives me a vision of objects, all needing the broom,
The cat and the pup are sprawled in low gear,
St Nick has departed for another year.
I heard him say as he flew over my roof,
"Boy, I've really had it, down to my last hoof."

Louise Monroe

A MOTHER'S LOVE

A Mother's Love is hard to explain,
She knows exactly how to ease any pain.
A Mother's Love is always there,
It could be a smile to let you know she cares.
A Mother's Love is a slight touch,
Somehow she knows it means so much.
A Mother's Love is a kind word,
Even if it's one you have already heard.
A Mother's Love is just lending an ear,
Even if there is nothing new for her to hear.
A Mother's Love is sending a card,
She seems to know when the way gets hard.
A Mother's Love is always around,
Even if you live, in another town.
A Mother's Love *is* hard to explain,
But she always send it again and again.

Marion W. Davies

AN ODE ON TEARS

There's something in beauty that makes me cry,
It may be anything under the sky;
Or even the sky itself.
The soul of wife as it shines through her eyes
Or o'er an old pet as it slowly dies
E'en though it's worth no pelf.
To watch a woman releasing her hair
Over lustrous skin that's so smooth and bare;
Ah! Gifts from Heav'n above.
This is but one of the beautiful sights
That puts my fancies on those wing-ed flights;
The tears come from pure love.
Grand paintings have ways that can touch the soul
As they tell the stories of the Great Whole;
And of the One Great Work.
Those who shed tears over nature's vast scenes
Know why there are oranges, purples and greens,
Be he a king or clerk.
Music has touched so many human hearts;
Emotions aroused as harmony starts
Causes watery eyes.
The soulful voice of a woman Being
May be the cause of the third eye's seeing
E'en as it also cries.
Welcome words of comfort from thoughtful friends
Bring forth the tears of hope as each day ends;
Peace will come with deep sleep.
Flowers and cards with a humorous theme
All meld together in a healing team;
As tender hearts to weep.
Friendship is such a rare, and precious, thing
That hurts to one makes another's eyes sting
With sweet and salty tears.
The Bard did tell us that what makes a friend
Is he who watches and waits to the end
Helping to conquer fears.
The person crying for another's woes
Is healing himself much more than he knows;
The Spirit always cares.
The salty water will wash away pain
Making two people get better again;
Those tears have been prayers!

John M. Drake

LEMON MOON

Light breezes blow the moonlight bright.
The moon simmers like a giant lemon in a silent night.
Its beams reflect a billion years of thought,
replenished by holy-rites, forbidden by the cloth.
In all its past remembered light,
perhaps the most redeemed.
It cast its spell of veneration,
in praise of man's temptation.
And nights of a lemon moon are seen.

D. A. Devine

Boston By The Charles

Bold Colossus
concrete and steel
spanning skyward
veiled
in ominous strata
of gray
elite giants
whose crowns succeed
glimpses
of sun soaked sky
their sullen images
lingering haplessly
over murky waters
of the Charles.

Dorene Mabrouk

IN MY OWN PRIVATE WORLD

in my own private world
i quietly go insane
no one knows
no one feels my pain
i go to sleep and start dreaming
all of a sudden
i wake up screaming
people are standing around my bed
wishing to themselves
that i were dead
what have i done wrong?
or what haven't i done right?
oh, God
i'm so frightened
by the darkness
of night

Lee Shope

THE SCHOOL POEM

Inasmuch I've no idea
for planting scratches here to grow
into a base from which a purpose
and direction it can go,
a different mode of thought I'm thinking,
hoping that the mode I take
will form a seed my thought's made fertile,
thus, in growing, will create
a new direction my mind can explore.
Even though my mind is empty
and thought's origin is still
without a sign or indication
of effecting something new,
all my mind is cogitating,
forming an idea that will
create a verse within the hour,
but, alas, the hour's through.
One more unfinished thought,
just like before.

Nancy J. Hull

THE HOURS APART

Beneath her red dress
she stands naked before
the empty dawn. The
quiet belongs to no one
as she parts the curtains
and looks for the timed day. . .
It is not there, only a tinge
above the trees and a black
cat picking the screen door.
She heats more coffee and sits
before an open window. The
warm helps but her red dress
is thin
and the sky is still vacant.
How long, how long to wait?
The traffic disturbs her and
she hurries back to her bed
where it is more dark, safe
and less endless.

Vicki Maureen Owchar

RAGE

A struggle from within at a rushed pace,
Heated rage in a confined space,
According to the law of nature's way,
It must be controlled like movements in a play.
Never shall we open the door to that place,
For what we might find would be too hard to face.
Isn't it easier to keep inside,
Things that are simpler just to hide?
Someday when it's in it's cage,
We'll wish it could have turned into rage.
It's a shame the door must be kept still,
But is it the way or is it the will?

Sharon A. Peters

A MIRACLE

The news I heard was
Too good to be true.
A miracle was happening
To me.
I'd waited so long,
Tried so hard and
Now it was to be.
I prayed to God that
I would do well,
I knew I would
Certainly try.
Then one day I
Heard a voice.
A wonderful, musical
Sound that would,
From that day on,
Turn my life around.
A tiny hand grasped my finger,
I looked into trusting eyes.
The wonderful, musical sound
I heard was my babys
First wondrous cries.

Don Grace

IMMATURITY

We reached for the sky, one touch,
Then goodbye
Was the only thing left to say.
Up there was a place
With plenty of space,
When time was one long yesterday.
Now, you look far too well
Since the glitter all fell.
That's the price I had to pay.
Since boy turned to man,
Let me say, If I can,
In my own very serious way—
Our tears and our smiles
Were few and many,
Cause reason is nothing
When emotions are plenty.
And of those emotions
I think we both knew.
For all the wrong reasons
We're left with just two—
You can't love me now,
But I still love you.

Willie (Bill) N. James

FISHERMAN'S SONG

The sun is up—
And it sho' is hot,
When I take my hoe

To the ole back lot.
The cotton is blooming
And de grass is hi'
It's gotta be hoed,
So we can "lay by."
Don't wanta work, I'd
Ruther be fishin'
But taint no use to
Be a wishin'
The boss man said,
And he has his way
That cotton gotta be
Hoed. . .today.
But the row is long
And the ground is hard,
Already I'm hot and
My back is tard.
I can't help thinking
Of the fishin' pool
How the trees hang low—
To make it cool.
The sound of a fish,
A jumpin' hi'
From the muddy bottom,
Where the big ones lie,
The mo' I think—
The worse I fret,
I gotta get a hook
And get it wet.
I know I shouldn't—
And I know it's wrong,
But I done listened
To the Fisherman's Song.
The cotton can wait—
Till another day—
Gonna grab my pole
And be on my way.

Bryan Roesch

HOW ABOUT SOME COFFEE

The weather is cold and stormy
And the kitchen stove is hot
Then its time to heat some water
And put some coffee in the pot
When one is tired and weary
And you need a little rest,
A cup of good hot coffee
Will give one a bit of zest.
For many groups do gather
Around the coffee table every day,
And talk of this and tother
Which helps pass the time away.
So make a pot of hot coffee
Made just right, and not too strong.
Will keep many friends together
And devise many ways to get along.
There may be some tall stories
Of things that happened in the past,
For a place to gather and drink coffee
Makes friendships that will last,

Mayme Gorman Barton

HAVE YOU EVER HEARD A MOCKINGBIRD CRY?

Have you ever heard a mockingbird cry
At break of dawn when the wind is high?
Once I heard a mockingbird cry
At break of dawn when the wind was high.
His frantic long-note pierced my wall,
Stirred my sleep with his plaintive call.
D'you know what made the mockingbird cry
At break of dawn when the wind was high?
He cried for his mate and their new-hatched young
Who, ere the dawn in the darkest hour
A black-faced cat climbed to devour.
I know what made the mockingbird cry
At break of dawn when the wind was high,
Because I rose ahead of time
And made my way to the trumpet vine.
There at the foot of the old elm tree
Two mangled wings were all I could see.
'Tis sad to hear a mockingbird cry
At break of dawn when the wind is high!

Hallie Mills Dobkins

A SONNET TO NATURE

It seems to me a lovely thing indeed
That nature in her wondrous scope of power
Could, from the infinite smallness of a seed,
Bring forth the glorious beauty of a flower.
A flower of various shades and hues so rare
That even the most indifferent passerby
Could not continue on without a stare

Then slowly turn eyes upward to the sky
And in a moment's silent and meditation
Reflect with thankful heart on nature's giving
And feel a stronger kinship and relation,
A bondage between man and all things living.
For 'tis in nature that we hear His voice
And find the peace that makes our hearts rejoice.

Pamela Rhena Harber

A SILENT STALKER

Beautifully silent the river lay,
Awaiting a victim to take as prey.
Streaming along on an endless path,
Bubbling, billowing and churning with wrath.
Quickly, a raft approaches a bend,
And the river, it seems to offend.
Changes occur and fierceness appears,
As if the old river overcomes all its' fears.
As a tiger pounces from the stalk,
Raging and roaring takes over quiet talk.
As the river comes on to dictate its sly plan,
The winding old river devours a man.
Again a silence fills the air,
Skies clear and once more its fair.
Its justice came quickly and then calmed fast,
Another day begins on a long river's past.

Cindy L. Linhart

WISHES

I wish I were a queen, but
I am yet a child.
I wish I were great and noble
like a knight in shining armor,
maybe as tall as a building,
or as mighty as a lion.
I know in due time I will have
children that will have WISHES too.

Rev. R. E. Eshmeyer

CREATIONS'S PEAK

Creation is epitomized
in Homo sapiens—modern man
or modern woman. Nothing
equals their symetrical
proportions. . . But there's
the rub: the skeleton remains,
as in a fancy chair, but
moulding the upholstery
to its original symetry
keeps purses lean and diets
bland for many who don't
realize Creation's peak
epitome is not the body but
the mind.

Elmer B. Fulton

The Derelicts Of Spring

In late November's rousing swirls of snow
The derelicts of spring have no compeer;
Down from their attic haunts they come.
And what if roughened hands, cold feet result
Or trudging out when all the town's asleep?
This is the music state commendable,
Which all today and now into this night
Has urged me on with utter boyish glee
Down toward some winter, water hardened boots
That hold the weathered shape a foot has made;
Toward skis replete with scars that speak the run
Of trails from mountain top to valley floor;
Toward skis begrimed since May with mud acquired
When waters roared in Tuckerman Ravine.

Warren J. Oswald

REAL TIME

He travels through *this* world timorously, with halting, falt'ring, indecisive steps—
This life, to him, seems all kaleidoscopic, confusing in its sudden shifts and turns,
Never remaining static long enough for him to plot a new course for himself in real time.
But, in that *other* world, within his mind, he marches forth, the captain of his fate— His steps are sure, his actions quick, concise, leading to success in each endeavor.
His two worlds, alas, are worlds apart, and never shall converge to salvage him in real time.

Ronald S. McClintock

GOD, PEACE, SECURITY

The holy men raised the guns
Politicians have spilt more blood
The anachrist pour into the streets
While the masses are lost in the flood
God, peace, and security
Along the Golan Heights
Hell, despair and death
During the Golan Nights
The old men have loaded the cannons
All the young men prepare to die
Yesterdays heroes are remembered well
As the mothers learn to cry
War, peace, and pain
I'm no one to complain
Disaster, glory and rain
I'm hiding among the insane

James D. Duncan

MAGNETIC HORIZONS

Magnetic horizons, set in marble stone
No arguments here, you must go it alone.
The trail is so hard and oft times cold,
It calls for a man, a man that is bold.
Mysterious intruders are loose in the night,
Whatever is done, must be done right.
Strange hieroglyphics, that mean everything,
Decipher them and hear the bell's ring.
Strangely lit flares, ablaze and on fire,
And eerie, strange things, adrift in the mire.
Set on, like a pack of wild dogs,
Must go hide, in the swamps and bogs.
Diamond like flashes, so bright to the eye,
Impossible to catch, expensive

to buy.
Crystal clear pieces from some lost empire,
Magnetic horizons, don't ever tire.

Joseph T. Craig

FLIGHT DEFINITIVE

My thoughts must ever follow the path of the setting sun— because one day you went that way on silvery wings.
I watched you disappear Into the gold of sunset— watched until the stars were glowing; even in the west, where you had faded from my view.

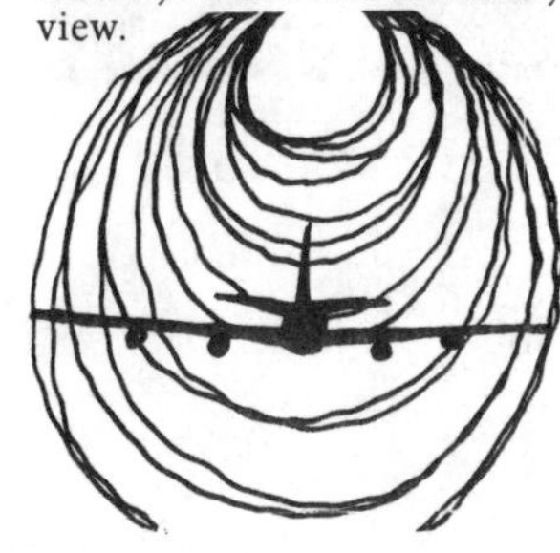

I watched until my eyes no longer saw the stars, nor darkness of the night. But in the sky I saw as it were, your face, on a floating silvery disc and as I watched it seemed you smiled, then closed your eyes; this faded also from my view, and it was day.
A day I did not wish to face; nor do I now recall one thing that filled the hours between the dawn and when the sky again was lighted with the stars; but in my mind are words that day and night are haunting me:
It now has been confirmed; that all aboard the plane have perished in the sea.

Sandra C. Tai

TO EXPERIENCE IS TO KNOW

You have always been a cautious bird
But yearn to spread your wings
And one day the sparrow you've been dreaming of
Comes soaring into your life
Life now seems so simple and easy
You throw caution to the wind and plunge head first
Conversations are full of laughter, puncuated with kisses
Hugs and holding hands are part of the routine
Those who care to look can only guess what happiness is
Then one day the breath of cool air blows too strong
The petals all fall from the flowers
The shock of ending the beautiful dream becomes reality
What, you wonder, why, you cry, how could this happen
Your sparrow won't talk about it
You can't seem to reason with him
Your efforts at reconciling fall on deaf ears
His mind is made up and you comply with a heavy heart
The pain seems unbearable
How do others survive this you wonder
Life is passing you by
But don't despair sweet one,
At the right time, the blue bird of happiness will spread his wings for you.

Lynda R. Wiest

THE ASSASSIN

Furtively stalking through darkness and light,
The weapon aims relentlessly,
With an evil well camouflaged beyond sight
By its semblance of humanity.
The prey are not those who are deemed as debased,
Nor prosperity sought by the blade,
Potential victims, each one of the race,
But random the choosing is made.
Discerning that each could be one of the slain,
Fear looms within all beings
Of loss of a loved one or physical pain,
Or an unjust halt to one's dreams.
Still these external fears breed not solely despair,
But are deeply with sorrow enmeshed,
Through knowing this anguish that each of us bears
Is engendered by human flesh.

Josephine Dunham

RAISE YOUR LANTERN HIGHER

Raise your lantern higher
Some who can not see
Struggle in the darkness
Wishing to be free
Free of all the blindness
Caused by being small,
Ignorant of the meaning
Of brotherhood for all.
Raise your lantern higher
Let this be your goal:
Use your glorious vision
And keep our nation whole.

Brian K. Delp

LITTLE MAN

(or: Ode to a Mentally-retarded Senior Citizen)

Little man standing lone in the street
Baggy clothes and angled feet.
His hat, on his head, at a rakish tilt
Oversized shirt hangs down like a kilt
What is wrong in the head of this man?
That his lips should display such a wide, full grin
Does he not see the problems of the world?
Diseased body like a rag that is soiled.
Perhaps he is better off than we
Seeing things that we shall never see
His own world is so bright and rosy
Like a fire to us, so warm and cozy
Keep to yourself, little man, do your thing
Act not as we, and feel life's bitter sting
When your life ends, no flowers will we toss
For the world won't realize its stupendous loss.

Ms. P. L. Marshall

KEVIN

Distant lover of mine, with your eyes aglazed in brown,
your eyes are the painful mirrors to my soul.
I feel, my love, I am beautiful within your love,

but without you I am alone and empty. . .
But even with my love for you, there is a hurt ever deeper than my tears, and as each day passes, knowin that your love for me will never be, numbs and pierces the depth of my heart.
I love you, my darling,
and knowing that increases the hurt.

Joseph King Bonds

CANNIBAL

(a love poem)

When I first saw you
My heart jumped dead
And like electric shock
Started up again.
Your lips
Melon wet and red
Drank me in like wine
And I quenched you so rapidly
That I was a bit surprised
When you threw me up again.

Eva J. Williams

EX-CON

Time
will pass slowly
Alas
it will be over
the mental agonies;
the physical exhaustion:
remaining
will be the memory
of a section in the life
of one who lived
in a specific place
due to a specific reason
because of the occurence
of a specific event.
All there is to do
now
is start all over again
but you won't be allotted
as much time
as you had when you first began
to live.

Jean K. Martin Smith

SOLITUDE

Dimmed headlights reveal ghosts
Cavorting in the woods ahead,
Their ethereal bodies
Undulating against pinnacled pines.
Black patent leather road coils
Round the moonless mountain
Beckoning me to the beat
Of rhythmic blades and pelting rain.
Top 40s seems incongruous
In this Stygian darkness—
A hand has already silenced it.
With a wary glance in the rearview mirror
I meet a mythological pair of leering eyes,
But the fall of an eyelid
Banishes the apparition,
And I measure the distance home
In heartbeats.

Larry Thiedt

THE TEAR

Salt water
unique
rolling haphazardly
down the cheek
expressing
and undressing
your innermost
the tear
never boasts

Marshall Swerman

TRAPS

attachment is attachment
desire is desire
want is want
and names are names
words are words
the words that we use are traps
for further entrapment
and our lust for each other
is but a mere evolved sort

Lynn M. McClure

MYSELF

Let me do my work each day,
and if the dark hours of despair overcome me,
May I forget not the strength that comforted me in desolation of other times.
Teach me to remember the bright hours that found me walking over the silent hills of my childhood or dreaming by the quiet river when the light glowed within me, and I promised my early God to have courage amidst the tempest of my changing years.
Spare me from bitterness and from the sharp passion of unguarded moments.
May I not forget the Poverty and Riches are of the spirit.
Let me not follow after the clamor of the world but, walk

calmly in my path, and tho the world knows me not, may my thoughts and actions be such as shall keep me friendly with myself.
Oh give me a few friends who will love me for what I am, and keep ever burning before my vagrant steps the kind light of hope.
Tho age and infirmity overtake me and I come not within sight of the castle of my dreams,
Teach me still to be thankful for life and for times and old memories that are good and sweet.
And God, may the evening twilight find me gentle still.

Edwin W. Fuhr

DOWN MEMORY LANE

Please come, my friend, and walk with me
Down country lanes of Used-to-be;
I know that it will surely seem
That we're "Down by the Old Mill Stream."
We used to cross the wooden bridge,
View stately trees upon the ridge;
See well-known paths we used to roam
That took us back to "Home Sweet Home."
The long hayrides we used to take
Down winding roads and to the lake;
These always ended all too soon
As voices joined in "Harvest Moon."
These bygone days come back to me—
They linger in my memory
Just like the melodies of old
Like "Silver Threads Among the Gold;"
The old farmhouse with winding stair,
The long front porch and rocking chair,
The Wishing Well among the trees
All summon back sweet "Memories."

Kari Leigh Getchell

YOUNG PROMISES

We did everything together,
laughed and cried,
giggled and screamed,
shared an ice-cream cone,
germs from the same glass.
We promised to be best friends forever.
We stomped through mud puddles
in shorts and barefeet,
threw snowballs at each other,
caught flakes on our tongues.
We promised to be bridesmaids
in each other's wedding, but only
if we ever decided to like boys.
We would go to the same college,
both be teachers at the same school.
Nothing was ever going to separate us.
We would always be together.
But you moved away,
we grew up apart,
I got a boyfriend.
I still miss you
and think of you often.
I wonder if you remember
the promises we made
when we were young.

Ronda Packard

WHAT IS BEAUTY

What is beauty—
But the pure inner thought of man,
The kindness and love
In the heart of a woman,
The innocence of a child's gaze,
When a butterfly alights
On a wildflower with grace,
Still wet with the morning's dew,
Or a fawn resting with its mother,
When the winter is yet new,
In a snow-covered meadow.
True beauty is—
The love of God given to man.
It is this—
Which allows the mind to see
Through acts of hate and conceit,
To the heart and soul of these.

Bill Laurin

ASH AND MEMORY

Smoke another cigarette before the morning alarm,
reassuring deep inside it cannot do me harm.
When it's through I stamp it out in ash and memory,
it's life span only lasts a mere four minutes exactly.
So puzzling this cigarette, only tabacco rolled in paper,
yet every puff I cherish, and every puff I savor.
Someday you may kill me, but cigarette if you do,
you have the right because each day I kill twenty of you.

Myrtle May Dunfee

OUR GOLDEN BOOK

I think the greatest gift that God,
Has given to us all,
Is what we call our memories,
Of past things we recall.
We start when we are little ones,
To build a golden book,
And when we all grow older,
We open it to look.
The memories of Daddy,
And the memories of Mom,
Are just a few examples,
As our lives move right along.
We remember all our school days,
And the friends we used to know,
How we walked along the old ways,
In those days of long ago.
And we glance back in our memories,
As we strain our eyes to look,
And we thank Him for His blessings,
As we close our golden book.

Maude W. Duncan

TRINITY

God, the Creator, created the heavens
And Earth
And saw that they were good.
He then made Himself a new creation
And called it man
And made Himself its Father.
The Father loved all His creations,
But one of them — man,
Male and Female,
Began to stray from Him.
Therefore, to bring man back into His fold,
Male and Female—
He projected His great love for man
By sending His beloved Son, Jesus,
To Earth in the guise of a human
And the Son projected the Father
To His fellow humans understandably.
Then God, by and through His Son,
Died a human death
To further evince His love for His
Straying creation.
God, through the Holy Spirit, fathered
Jesus Christ as His son, and,
at the death of His Son,
Kept the Holy Spirit to act as
Intermediary between the Trinity and Mankind.
And the Father, and the Son, and the Holy Spirit
Are all there in the Supreme Being—God.

Richard W. Knupp Jr.

SURPRISED TO DIE

The hot, blue slag pond gurgled,
Biting the rock-strewn periphery
Like a horde of crazed and rabid dogs.
This reeking limestone refuse vat
Gouged the hillside like the rage of a festering sore,
A most caustic bog.
Low lying clouds of rancid steam
Made the cool October air thick
As gas fumes from an idling truck.
Lime-colored effluent oozed slowly
From a slanted pipe which hugged the putrid mud,
As it formed a plain of semi-solid.
A frazzled frog, wanting to short-cut his journey,
In favor of a heel he bruised,
Set out to brouse the far shore for flies.
The first few feet felt soft, but supple.
The next made him flounder and fall,
Wavering in his fate,
Surprised to die.

Linda K. Parkhurst, Recher

THE WAY

Dreams that drift,
Dreams that lift,
Dreams of heavenly bliss.
Colors painted one by one;
they come to form a rainbow,
one by one.
To the end we look,
a promise from the father above.
A pot of gold the Son;
who shines brighter then the sun.

Elizabeth Ann Deihm

NIGHT CREATION

I am here tonight. . . .again.
Retreating quietly to my corner of the world.
Fulfilling my mind's dream of writing.
I may be here until the rooster crows
at the break of dawn,
And the sun reaches in,
touching my shoulders,
to tell me that once again,
I let the night slip by.

S. Elizabeth Thompson W.

UNREAL

I view the world through
swaying, heart-beat eyes.
3D-vision. Disco motion—
only I am still—
Centered with
the merry-go-
round
I am insane—the
world can't be.
Talking walls, smiling dogs
groaning trees.
I am insane—the
world can't be.
Dreams focus on reality—
unreal, yet
true.
I view the world through
swaying, heart-beat eyes.
Let the world flirt by
I am sane—
the world?

Mrs. Laura L. Lemke

THY WILL BE DONE, OH LORD

Lord, please help me do your will.
I do not want to go my way
it is heart-ache and destruction
and the way is foolishness.
I give my will to you, oh Lord,
I want to be complete in you.
No part of me shall I keep back
for all I will to give to you.

I do not want to go astray
nor do I wish to seek my way.
But day by day to seek your will
to go your way not mine.
In all things your will done,
Oh Lord, is my hearts cry.
Far better is your will
than one moment of my own.

Gladys Parry Wilson

THE STILL SMALL VOICE OF GOD

When have you stopped to listen
For the still small voice of God?
It fills the very air you breathe
And echoes from the sod.
It hovers o'er the whispering lakes
And o'er the scalloped hills,
Resounding from each crag and moor
And from the rocks and rills.
It's in the mighty thunder
As it rolls across the plain,
And in the soothing murmur
Of gently falling rain.

Oh stop! Please stop and listen
For the still small voice of God
And list'ning, let Him guide you
In the paths that Jesus trod.

Jeff Doty

UNTITLED

Out of the rock
Came
Those bearing
Wisdom
And Understanding,
But
Those there
Either
Rejected them
Or drove them back
Into the rock.
. . . . .
That same rock
Rained upon them later,
Bringing about a different
Wisdom
And
Understanding.

Bonnie Elizabeth Parker

FOR THIS AND FOR THIS

I will have apples, and round golden cheese;
a churning of strawberry ice cream, and cake.
I will have muffins—all, any, of these,
welcoming you for your dearness's sake.
Italian meat sauce and spaghetti—you'll cry
aloud in your gladness to see; and I'll take
thin-rinded lemons to make you a pie,
welcoming you for your own loving's sake.
I will have wine in fat bottles to shine
star-like in goblets I give you, to slake
any wild thirst when you touch them to mine,
welcoming you for your dark glance's sake.
Salads, I'll toss, with ripe olives and leaves
of lettuce; tomatoes, and almonds, to shake
onions across, and tall celery in sheaves
welcoming you for your merry laugh's sake.
I will crisp slices of ham beside bright
eggs for your breakfasting, when you awake
out of the dear tangled splendor of night,
welcoming you for your very own sake.

John L. Baesl

SOON, FALL'S MUSIC—GONE

Stand I in a cornfield's center;
A different song listen I to—a cornfield song.
Hard, hard blows the wind, musicians in a cornfield symphony
stocks become;
Each player the same sound—ten acres in harmony
And I, a guest, hold close my ear.
Cornfield's sound becomes a roar; corn leaves crackle loudly in the wind,
And in no hurry, listen I intensely to a cornfield sea.
Appears as though stocks know—their last song, last sound, that, that time has come;
To fall's plow, cornfield band soon to lose.
Yet-yet, when I begin to bury each player,
Heard from my window cornstocks' notes no more—sadly say I.

Luanne Childres

SINGER

I look at you.
I dream of you.
How beautiful you are in my mind.
A lion of a man, fierce and strong,
Mind set determined quite young by tragedy.
Ah, but had there not been that pain
You may not have become so wise.
That talent within you
Seeps through every word,
Every line, every note
In the music you write.
And that voice of many voices
Each with its own perfection
Coming from the same genius
Which is you.
You pay homage to your Creator
And you dare to believe out loud
Of a life much greater
Beyond our brief life on earth.
Quite the typical English gentleman you are;
The women of your songs are goddesses,
Who hurt and leave
But shall never be condemned.
Devotion to family fits you somehow;
Ever the wise older sibling seeking peace.
I wonder just how much of this is true about you,
And how much is sheer fantasy
That I have to believe.

Jocelyn A. Lavalley

FOLDED WINGS

Why do you insist on all the wrong things?
Why have you gone back, taken off your new wings?
You get caught up in the branches, and the wind
chills your face.
For how can you fly without any grace?
You can if you want! You've made it clear it's
your choice.
Just put your wings back on, and be silent
in voice.
When you start soaring higher, over tree tops so tall.
Make sure not to look down, for that's when you fall.

Laura Lewina Simpson

AUTUMN

Autumn, Autumn you are here!
You Made the Earth cold and wet.
Autumn, Autumn you are here
And the skies are cyring.
The days are short
The nights are long.
The sky is grey.
The garden is empty.
Here and there you see a tree,
With bright colored leaves
Red, Brown, Yellow and Green
Somewhere in another land
You see a dying rose.
Autumn, Autumn, People are afraid of you.
Your rains, Your darkness. . . . .
But in a little house there is a person
He loves the autumn days.
The rain beating on the window panes
The wind against his windows
With a whistle and a cry,
Blows out the light in the room.
He said, he loves the Autumn days.
The bright rug on the Earth.
He said, no more singing birds. .
They are gone, you see they are afraid of you.
Only in a little empty house
On rainy days, in dark nights
You hear my voice
You hear my whisper
Autumn, Autumn stay here
Don't leave me here alone
Don't go, I love your misty air
Stay here or take me with you.

Alfred Bahna

LOVE AND MARRIAGE

Hello Charlene my good friend, did your broken heart mend.
I am sorry that I left you darling, I was confused, and
I could not help myself to rid the pain of love and marriage.
When I asked you for a date, I thought of the problems it
might create, then I saw your glowing soft brown eyes, and
I did not think of marriage ties.
I just thought of how
well you looked that night, and let me say that babe you
were out of sight.
Then came marriage, at first we did not do too bad, then
our lives just started getting sad. I had to leave that
day, because I saw no other way to escape, and think of
what love meant, to you, to me, and to marriage.
Now I am back to tell you babe, that I will never leave
your side. I am lucky to have a girl like you, one thats
going to love and be true,
so accept my apology and take
me back, one more time, for love and marriage.

Mrs. Nancy Quinn

OUR CHURCH

Our church as a symbol there it stands
And our minister with out stretched hands
Who tries to show us the way Home
For all of us who in sin do roam
You ought to bring your friends along.
And join us in our prayer and song
We have a Sunday School too
Where we learn just what to do
And also have fine teachers there
Who teach us of God's loving
care.
And our minister is a fine man
Who tries to do the best he can
At teaching us to always love
Our God and Savior who reigns above.

Linda R. Fanelli

MOTIVATION

The locomotive pushes
harder and harder,
As it rounds the bend
and enters the tunnel
Panting louder and louder
As it nears its destination
Finally it arrives
With a great sigh
And a burst of steam.

Barbara Jane Lucas Mitchell

THE BLIND MAN WHO COULD SEE

I was walking beside a bubbling brook
In a world I call my own
My thoughts were on the things around me
When I found out I wasn't alone
For a man was walking next to me
Without making one little sound
He just stared straight ahead
Then he stopped and sat upon the ground
I thought to myself why is he here?
Intruding on this world of mine
But before I could speak a word to him

I saw that the man was blind
I know you're wondering about
my eyes
Well I've been blind since birth
I was put here for a purpose
Like all these things on earth
I couldn't help feeling sorry
For this man who couldn't see
He must have read the thoughts
I had
For he turned and smiled at me
Don't feel sorry for me Miss
I can see things all around
He turned his face towards
Heaven
Then his hands they touched
the ground
He said the ground is like a
velvet carpet
With the grass different shades
of green
The trees are swaying in the
gentle winds
They stand so tall and lean
He called the names of the birds
and animals
And what color of coats they
had
He mentioned the sky in it's
shade of blue
And he made me feel so bad
The brooks are running smooth
and clear
Over pebbles of different browns
I wondered how he knew all this
This blind man who sat upon
the ground
He answered my thoughts I was
thinking
As he lifted his face to the sky
God gave me a heart full of
colors
So I really have no need for eyes
God gives us many things my
dear
He blessed me with so much
My ears can hear the sounds
like you
And my hands have a special
touch
I finally saw with tears in my
eyes
The love and beauty God gave
to me
It came from a man sitting on
the ground
The blind man who could see

Anna Mirar Harting

IN THE MORNING

Before the world mingles with
your mind
Before peace turns from kind
Before your lips begin to move
To dare, demand and disapprove
I love you most in the morning
Before you feel my dying gaze
Anima haunted by animus haze
Before you straighten and decide
My mind is your mind, before I
cry
I love you most in the morning
I feel it coming
Too soon, too soon
The sun of mooning conscious
exhumed
Let me live
By God, let me have a day
That's not yours, in your way

K. J. Nelson

SUMMER ENCOUNTER

On the brightest day, in the
newest year,
I stood alone, you stood near.
We could talk, we could see,
there we were, just you and me.
I spoke of old, you spoke of new,
both these things we knew were
true.
But to me, so it seemed,
it was a moment I had dreamed.
You as you are, accede to
choice,
building your dreams to the
tone of your voice.
I as I am, accept my fate,
having no choice, except but to
wait.
You seem unsure, quite
unimpressed,
thinking it useless, don't bother
to test.
I am here for you to teach,
yet mine is a truth you cannot
reach.
It makes me sad, I cannot touch
you,
feel you, love you, tell you how
much you
could mean to me and I to you.
It might mean a beginning, were
it known,
that you stood near and I stood
alone.

Eino V. Ritari

CONFESSION

Strange and bewildering you
are, Life.
Each day you are the same, yet
new and different forever.
Sometimes you bring me joy and
satisfaction
But more often also pain and
suffering.
Sometimes you appear before me
cold and frightening.
You have no pity even when
you see my tears flowing.
And yet I love Thee—Life.
You alone are my mistress
and my queen.
Obediently I do everything you
ever want.
The knowledge of your
existence awakens in me
Some uncertain thoughts and
wishes.
I want so much from you but
you give
Only fraction of what I want.
Even then, I love Thee—Life.
Beautiful you are stepping on
the wide path of your garden.
The wind is blowing and
fluttering the vast hems of
your skirt. Your shape, wrapped
in silk, dazzles, enchants me.
An endless desire is born in my
heart.
But I'm not more than a
worthless lackey of yours.
Therefore I dare not even look
at you, though I know I love
Thee—Life.
I will never reach the flames
of ecstasy on your lips.
It is enough, if in my thoughts
I'm only let kiss the least
worthy fold of your train.
Oh, Life. Suffering even is sweet,
when you love!
Your smallest favour is my
happiness, my bliss.

So greatly I love Thee—Life.
Take my heart, my mind and
all of me,
But do it so that I know it
was you.
———Crucify me,
But do not let it be done by
dishonest, deceitful people.
Even at my death I bless, I
praise you, Life.
I shall be humble, honest
and true only to you.
I L o v e T h e e — L i f e.

Roger J. Abdo

A SIMPLE PRAYER

Lord: Teach me the wisdom of
your gentleness,
to be ruled by heavens
decree,
to raise a hand to no man,
Yet struggle to make him free.
Let me stand firm as I turn
the other cheek,
Trusting in the rules that win,
Teaching a spiritual principle,
With no room for anger or
chagrin.
Let me always praise Thy
Holy Name,
And bless your every gift,
Teach me to say the kindly
word,
The poor in spirit to uplift.
Though chaos may snarl my
every path,
Heavenward I'll gaze and
wonder,
How you took time to give
me life,
And forgive my every blunder.

Robert James Roberts

WATER

Crystal clear, muddy mad,
soothing sweet or stinging salt—
musical as the brook—
treacherous as the sea—these
are the faces of Water. Liquid
tongues lash out, casting frothy
sea high into the laughing air—
restlessly reaching for low
soaring seagulls, the plundering
gliders of covetous appetite, who
scan the depths of Neptune's
treasures. Cloudburst—weeping
roof tops, drenched umbrellas
of unprepared—climbing waters
blindly blunder beyond all
boundaries, forge forward to
rob unprotected cornfields—
submerge waterlogged melons—
slyly steal the centenarian
homestead, ancient and
humble—and scatter debris.
Soothing sweet oasis, crystal
clear and precious—life for
beggar, camel or wise men
bearing gifts, or mirage of
frantic fools, a mysterious
ghost of the voiceless desert,
cruel as a sulphurous spring.
Immeasureable ocean—solid and
serene—where sunrise soars to
the summit—descends to a
pompous sunset. Immeasureable
ocean—mighty and turbulent—
mad with foaming lips, destroys
with insatiable hunger.
Immortal raindrops—profoundly
loved for spring showers,
copious buds and blossoms—
fruitfull fall—splendid
spectacle, the ephemeral
rainbow—timid tears, the
dewdrop. A drop of water
seeping itself in the earth's
core to explode into steam by
the intense heat, might pressure
the world to pieces, these are
the dramatic cunning masks
worn as the imposter roams the
earth never to be exhausted—
glorified as it reigns.

Guyvan B. Shirley

CONSCIOUSNESS

Tell me not as thy walk this
earth of resurrection,
Burdens endure throughout life;
Shall thy walk with surmount
perfection,
And live life as strife;
Shall it be that life is lived,
We're its shadow of defeat;
With the knowledge we're real
And life is not a repeat.
Life's bed is made by thou,
In it thy must lie;
Reap what thy soweth,
Not a whimper nor a cry.
With much happiness through
thy trial;
Witnessing eternity with a
smile.

Gene G. Melikidse

TO THE GRADUATE

I came and sat
And watched you graduate.
I heard you speak,
Encourage and persuade
Your classmates to go on,
And strive for goals to achieve.
To right the wrong. . .
Stand firm in that what you
believe.
I envied you
As I recalled my days;
To live again
And change direction of my

ways.
How easy it's to see
The things I should have done;
And reach the end
That you now set your course
on.
Where I've come short,
I wish you otherwise. . .
To reach the goals
You see before your eyes.
Go, take that step;
Do that I would have done.
And your success
I too will share, my son.

Albertine D. Self
MOM AND SON
I have a son who is working
very hard
so he can bring home a good
report card,
sometimes he walks five miles
to school,
some kids even call him a fool.
His friends offer him drugs and
booze,
he does not know which one to
choose,
his will power is getting weak,
he said, some advice i must
seek.

Son, dont be afraid to say No,
you could choose which way
you want to go,
smell the flowers, take a look
at the sky,
you could have a natural high.
Son said mom my friends tried
again,
even offered me a nice gold
chain,
son, where did they get that?
they said from the neck of a
girl named pat.
Son, remember the kid who
mixed booze and drugs,
sang a song called here come
the bugs,
he was called fly high raymond,
now he is six feet underground.

F. John Stevens
THE GAMES
They stood atop a hill
silent watching
Games, though ancient,
living still.
The night yet young,
Brought darkened clouds
and with them thoughts of
rain.
Romans dot the hill.
Some in stoney silence watch;
While others, silhouettes from
lightning's glare,
Rise and fall
the same as those in olden
times.
The thunder, lightning,
sirens from the night,
pierce the presence.
Yet, as raindrops fell,
The games were played to suit
the purpose of that hill.
Why linger on to watch this
sight?
The one you loved and battled
for has fallen, run in flight.
His lance, once proudly held
erect,
has vanished in the night.
Move on to places not yet
known,
Where games the same are
played.
Yet linger in your own mind's
eye,
The Roman night—
the games.

Barbara Dowd-Peters
MOTHERS
Days full of clutter, clamor
and meaningless conversations.
Kissing away intrusions;
shielding, guarding, protecting.
Helping, praising, scolding,
warning, and loving.
Holding, touching,
understanding, such are my
days.
In his eyes I see the sensitive
past and the glorious,
unpredictable future.
He depends on me, he needs
me.
He makes me laugh and
sometimes he cries out my
name in his restless sleep.
He makes me angry and he
makes me feel isolated, he
he makes me aware and he
makes me sad.
When I feel his arms wrapped
tightly around my neck and
smell his fragrant breath in
my face and touch his soft skin
and golden hair, with tears in
my eyes, I thank God.

Thomas W. Arundel
AN OLD FASHIONED CHRISTMAS
I remember those old fashioned
Christmas'
Like the Christmas' of long
ago,
When we sat around our open
fireplace
Singing carols of long ago,
Watching the wonderful
Christmas Tree
With all the trimmings made
by hand
And the candles all lit up and
glowing
Sparkling like the stars above.
I still remember the old
fashioned Christmas'
Like the Christmas' of long
ago,
With the snow falling
covering everything white,
Hearing children singing
Christmas Carols,
Bringing joy and happiness on
Christmas Eve,
And Santa with his reindeer
flying through the sky
Wishing everyone a merry,
merry Christmas
Bringing kids toys and
stockings
full of fruit and nuts.
Those were the old fashioned
Christmas'
I remember many years ago.
I wish you all a Merry and
Happy Christmas
And my our New Born King
bring peace
To the world in the New Year
With love for all Mankind.

C.P. Stancich
To Those Who Thought The W.B. Yeats Winterim Class Covered Too Much Too Quickly
They say that he in there
exploded—
In room two-ten;
Overheated and Overloaded,
Varoom! but then,
Though beyond all doubt he
vaporized,
So sweet fell mist,
That two-ten was gently
atomized:
So then e'er bless'd

Doris Theresa Franklin
LIFE'S TIMECLOCK
Time passes by, not swiftly
as we are prone to judge,
it is we who pass the time
away
be we busy man or drudge.
"I idle away the hours"—
"I'm busy as can be."
are words that set our life's
clock
to form our destinies.
Yes, time goes how we make it
go.
its passing, swift or slow,
"Give me time, O Lord, I ask,
to know more than I know;
let me know my fellow man,
his needs, his joys, his
sorrows,
let me share and help him,
Lord,
to brighten his tomorrows."
Time waits not for any man
as he weaves his memories;
"Give me time, I pray, dear Lord,
to be better than I be!"

Edith Wilcher Schwemmer
HEART COLD
my heart is cold
and empty of you
it is as if
each other we never knew
the years did pass
unto that endless day
step by step
you kept walking away
love and youth
refused to remain
lost forever
impossible to explain
living agony
estranged and apart
every memory
a killing dart
i cannot remember
when you last touched me
i refuse to remember
how it used to be
i am unable to remember
the times when we talked
i dislike to remember
the road you now walk
i must never remember
the emotions we shared
i try desperately to remember
that once we both cared
there is no warmth
or the light of your smile
the distance between
much more than the miles
my life and my heart
one tortured cry
ever with me
until the day i die

Raymond D. Christensen
A FEW WORDS
I would like to say a few words
Meant for all the world to
hear,
I want to have a few good words
Stay in everybody's ears.
I'll try to tell some stories
That might bring the world
together,
Everyone can support everyone
Everyone can love their
neighbors.
With loving we form fertile
ground
Out of the most desolate
of land,
If everyone would work as
one
Without the conceit of
carnal man.
When all the hearts in the
world
Forget about just winning
the rat race
Then every brand-new
heartbeat
Could fill up one more
empty space.
Because the good in all the
people
Would be invited to come out
I wish that everyone could fill
with joy
And have praises to sing and
shout.
Rejoice in the life of love and
peace
For all the world to see and
hear,
I would like to have a few good
words
Stay in everybody's ears.

Kurt Chandler
CARRIED AWAY
Carried away with a fleeting
glance
Lost from the world at the
slightest chance
Born with the wind to be
carried away
Rising too soon to be stable
today
Today I fly higher and higher
My wings reach out to stroke
the wind
I laugh and glide but soon I
tire
My wings grow heavy and soon
will bend
For I too soon in hope did
fly
In search for love when I

caught her eye
The ground seems harder each time I fall
The wind replies when her name I call
Only the wind not her voice at all
But I still fly in spite of it all
When I see her eyes I reach for love
In hope I soar high and above
And hear her voice away somewhere
And follow so swiftly that we might share
A love so tender that will never be
For she's only real inside of me

Jodi-Ellen Davison

MOM

You hustle and bustle,
And use every muscle.
You worry and cleave,
Thanks, you still believe.
Very often I come,
And yell "Hey Taxi!"
You're up on your feet.
You look so happy.
I think your ideas and music,
Are quite a bit touched.
But I know you think mine,
Are just too much.
Worn and over worked,
I see you're still kickin'.
Don't fret Ma,
I'll get my nutrition.
Keep up the good work.
I care for you deeply.
I'm not as sweet as sugar,
I hope you'll still keep me!?
Now today is your day,
So relax for awhile.
Put up your feet,
And SMILE, SMILE, SMILE!
Happy Mother's Day, MOM!

S. Lynne Glover

FOUR WISHES

i want to write
the things i see
but cannot put on paper
i want to sing
the things i enjoy
but cannot find the notes
i want to tell
the things i experience
but cannot speak
i want to dance
to emotions i feel
but cannot catch

F. Dorothy Parker

VACATION AC"SENSE"

Did you ever *Hear*
The wind on the mountains blowing wild and strong
through aspen and pines
Or a singing stream tumbling over rocks and under
matted vines?
Did you ever *See*
Stately hemlocks and snowy crags silhouetted
against azure blue
Reflected in a cold mountain lake and the sun
just breaking through?
Did you ever *Feel*
The noonday sun beating down and your skin
hot but dry
Or the icy spray from a waterfall carried on
the breeze passing by?

Did you ever *Taste*
The acrid smoke from dying campfires as it
whirls all about
Or buffalo steaks, unusual herbs or fresh
mountain trout?

Did you ever *Smell*
Juniper or pine and a haunting sweet fragrance
you can't identify?
In the clear, thin air of early morning hours?
So did I!

Jack V. Adler

RURAL ROUTE

A battered mail box
On a pitted post
Spots of paint
That named the occupant
The metal flag bent
The red faded to scaley pink
Beside a plank gate listing to one side
That drags the dirt
On the open end
Making an arc in the dust
Over bruised weeds
In a pair of ruts
That was the drive
To an old weather-worn house
Dust and musty
With broken sash
Brown newspapers on the floor
Beside dirty bottles
And rusty pan lids
In the midst of broken cottonwood trees
Limb hanging with rotting swing rope
Sparrows flushing
From dead roses
Barbed wire fence rusting and sagging
Staples squeezed from posts by weather
Tumbleweeds piled like burnt popcorn
In field corners by the wind
Wild sunflowers along the fringes.
Abandoned.
Going without a trace,
Of who?

Ruby Simmons Slaughter

A TRIBUTE TO MY OWN DEAR DARLING MOTHER

My Mother left me in this world alone, I have had
trials and tribulations since she's been gone.
O, how I miss her as I say my prayers each night
I am thankful heavenly Father you are my guiding light.
My friends and relatives are nice as can be but they
will never understand how much my darling Mother
meant to me.
She nursed and cuddled me when I was ill
when she went away and left me I knew it was God's will.
I will forever remember the advice she gave to me, she said "Trust in the Lord you will always have company." I know she's resting in that place up in the sky. I do not know if I will meet her. I am surely going to try.
My Mother always made me a home. When she went away
and left me, I knew I was on my own.
She was the best friend I had on this earth, it's
very sad she had to be the first,
I am lonely for my Mother as I pray to the Lord above
I pray that he will always keep me in the circle of his love.
As I sit here thinking of my Mother's love I will continue to pray to the master up above that he will give me strength and courage to live my whole life through.
When he calls me home, there will be nothing left on this earth for me to do. I will be ready to go and see the Mother I love so dear. It is very, very sad she had to leave me here.
To all that have a Mother please take my advice and treat her swell you will never miss her until she bids you farewell.

Roxane Salyer Lulofs

MY FATHER

It was a late night as we talked,
With half a moon listening.
He smoked cigarettes,
And I watched the glow of the ash
As he expressed himself,
Hands moving.
My father,
A big man to me always,
(Even now when we stand eye-to-eye)
Speaking of the promises he made
When we were young,
Wondering if he kept them.
My father,
Tongue loosened somewhat
By Scotch-on-the-rocks,
Speaking almost profoundly.
I listened,
And learned from the prophet of ages.
He is no ordinary man—
That would be impossible.
Seeing always beyond the obvious,
Questioning the routine,
Unaccepting of the mundane,
My father taught me many things—
But mostly how to listen:
to a cricket's song,
to the howl of a lonely dog,
And. . .to love.

C. Forehand King

UNTITLED

It doesn't matter
does it?
That time has past us by—
leaving us cold,
with-drawn into the
pain of ourselves.
To love,
To fear,
Just wasted emotions.
To much has been left unsaid.
But is it,
too late now?

Helen Geis

THIS OLD CLOWN

I'm a clown just fooling around
I've had my ups, my downs
I bounce the world in my hands
Grinning, Grinning just Grinning
I watch the sad eyes of the ill
pull out the prize—my heart stands still
The bright eyes then fulfill
Grinning, Grinning just Grinning
Swinging along with the band
I flop along in the sand
Throwing my ropes and rings
To Children hollering—Swing high
Swing low.
Grinning, Grinning just Grinning
In my heart I am sad
I cannot show the world is mad
Tis time to be glad
Old clowns are fun,—bounce the ball on the run
Grinning, Grinning always Grinning

Mrs. Mary K. Quisenberry

A NEW BEGINNING

When I wake in the morning,
I face a new day. . .
If my day seems in trouble,
can I right it some way???
A new day I know I can shape as I will.
For days of new beginnings have all chances to fulfill;
I must not dwell on old past mistakes,
Just place them all deep down upon the embers,
And look past into the clean, clear future's sway;
(Starting on the early morning of the day).
You can greet the day doing some smiling,
Trying always to do your level best;
First pause to give thanks and be thankful
For the past night's sleep and kindly rest.
Take a look at the beauty if it's a beautiful sunrise,
Take time to really look and really see,

The freshness of the morning, clear and free,
And remember the Almighty fashions these,
For all our loved ones and you and me;
Truly a morning is a new beginning,
And as a new day gradually unfolds,
We must use all it gives wisely,
If we enjoy all the happiness it oft-times holds.

Elsie M. G. Miller

LANDSCAPE OF A WINTER EVENING

The twilight glooms gently, milky and still.
Crisply starched each scalloped hill.
The hollows are grape shadowed—deep broken bowls
Where the dark vinous water seeps through the holes.
Mute are the trees wrapped snugly in white,
Strange sculptured designs in the fast dimming light.
Burdened old fences struggle up hill and down,
Following the sled trail leading to town.
Shapeless the silence that melts into song,
For the night is vibrant, and the night is long.
Delicately the snowflakes drift from the skies,
Small fluttering ghosts of white butterflies.

Donna Addison

WEB

WEB O WEB
blowing through the air,
Oh where were you spun so fair?
Sun gleaming on your strand,
shine like a diamond from the land.

Henry P. Gaewsky

I AM A DOG NOT LOST

You left me this morning, high on a hill,
Chasing a ball far into the still.
I heard the engine rumble, I knew its song,
And hurrying back, found you gone.
I am a dog, not lost.
The clocking hours now meet noon,
Sure thought I, you'd be here soon,
Car and cars went on, sped by,
None like yours and wondered why.
I am a dog, not lost.
Was it because I barked too soon,
Growled at people who didn't like you.
Should I have been meek and cringing, not proud,
A kind of being, shuffled in crowd
I am a dog, not lost.
Many come by in twos and fours,
Snarling, flinching, slinking, roars.
Were they left as I, or did they stray,
What are there thoughts this time of day.
I am a dog not lost.
Food left by, lies in the sand,
You taught me, eat but from your hand.
Children come by and hug me good,
Whispering they'd take me if they could.
I am a dog not lost.
Weeks of days and months of nights,
Passersby say, what a sight.
My bones now show, I hardly walk,
How long ago since we did talk.
I am a dog, not lost.
Weary, numb, I hardly see,
It seems that now I'm at your feet.
Oh master, my master, have you forgot,
I'm yours, All yours,
A dog, lost not.

Betty Williams

TO MY STEP MOTHER

You came to take our Mother's place—
A place so hard to fill—
And because we needed you.
It was our Father's will.
You came with a heart so full of love
After Mother was taken to heaven,
Because you loved our Father dear,
And to Mother his children seven.
It's the noblest thing a woman ever did
To take the children of another,
To love and care for them always
And be to them a mother.
Always you unselfish been
And heedful of each pleasure
That might come to brighten our lives.
You've been to our home a treasure.
But, dear Mama, the thing above all—
And I love you as a daughter—is
That you have been so very good
To our beloved Father.

Marion Beck

THE DREAMBIRD

Just as I sit and dream alone
The dreams that often come to me
Of palaces and great high walls
I see the dreambird soaring high
To tell me something of the sky.
I'd love to fly on outspread wings
And see what all my dreaming brings.
But the hours have gone and youth has died
Except for feelings deep inside.
I see the dreambird soaring high
Up in an endless clear blue sky.

Peggy Zenko

ANOTHER CHRISTMAS POEM (1979)

Standing by the frozen window
We turn off the lights
Plastic holly and pine on every lamppost
Have garnished so many nights
Since the first snow this year
And all the years before
Like our fake Christmas tree
I never take a picture of it anymore
The season swirls around us
Nieces and nephews watch for Mr. Claus
While we're wrapping, reminiscing
Saving tinsel from determined feline paws
This year as I give my love away
To try to make the season merry
I'm going to save some warmth
For January.

Byrle Payne

THE PARTHENON

Lying with head on folded coat,
I viewed the ancient Parthenon,
But still renowned in history;
And once inside it's true Diana,
Model—Aspasia, was engowned;
When suddenly its ancientness was gone,
Instead stood out in a transcendent glory,
A magnificence enlarging on and ON!
Then I awoke—awoke to dreamland's story,
Awoke to ruins, an echo from afar;
Yes, vanished that scene—of yesterday.
Can all of this be true, or things ajar,
To learn that all of this has passed away?
Where is Aspasia now? Perhaps some bones;
The perfect Parthenon? War's broken stones!

Larry M. Kirlin

HEAVEN

Beauty so rare,
I love to touch your hair,
I love to touch your lips,
Think of frilly things and slips.
Dream of a bed,
A place to lay your head.
With nothing to hide,
And release of thoughts inside.
Dark, quiet, and still,
Yı ır shapes satisfy they will,
Fullfilling the wants of dreams unknown,
Oh! Just to be with you alone.

J.W. Cheney Jr.

EVER OR NEVER

Were there other days;
would there ever "be" tomorrows?
Were there never happiness;
would we ever "know" of sorrow?
Were there never joyfull comfort;
warmth-filled night's embrace?
Would we not want a resumption;
would it never then take place?
Were there never ever touch;
would there be "known" bliss?
Were it meant to be missed much;
would "togethers" "be" as this?
Were there never "really" us;
was there ever "really" you?
Were there sometimes "only" parting,
would still "nearness" love renew?
Were you never "beautiful";
would I think so nonetheless?
Is it just my own "perception"
that you're "so", perhaps, at "best".

Aaron Wilson Hughey

PASSIONATE INTERLUDE II

"let's talk about relationships"
she said to me one afternoon
during a particularly uneventful moment
but there was such a subtle intensity in her voice
that i felt compelled to go along with her request
'O.K." i said without giving the matter much thought
"do you still love me?"
"yes, of course i do. . .
you still love me don't you?"
"you know i do. . .
but *why* do you love me?"
"because you're you"
i knew my answer was weak
(and left a great deal to be desired)
but how does one respond to such a question?
love is. . .
well, love is love
you feel it—you simply experience it
you don't rationalize it
or examine it
as you would a specimen
under the microscope
but getting back to our conservation—
"so you really don't know why you love me?"
"i guess not"
"that's what i thought"

Peggy Handley

I WANT TO SEE A BED BUG

I've always felt so bad, my lad
Because you felt so sad, my lad,
For the many times that you have said,
"Those bugs that crawl upon a bed?

The likes of which I've never
seen.
To know them not makes me
feel green.
Now any lad as old as I
Has seen a bed bug crawling by.
But me, I feel *so* left out.
When all my life I've been
without—bed bugs.
I thought when I joined Uncle's
Army
Of good men, mediocre, and just
plain lugs
I thought somewhere in
someone's camp
I'd get to see—you've guessed
it—bed bugs.
But I'm still in, I re-upped
you know
And with three and a half
behind me,
I've five and a half to go.
In striving for another stripe,
as I try to get ahead.
Perhaps somewhere along the
line
I'll get my life-long wish and
find
A bed bug in my bed.
But, if my Uncle Sammy fails
me,
My Mom came thru you know.
The mailman brought me a
package today
It set my heart aglow.
Inside I found four bed bugs,
Dressed in finest silk and
satin."
"They're to brighten up your
bed spread son,
They'll never start you
scratchin.
For they're only stuffed ones
made by Mom
No bites for they're not real.
They'll show you now a bed bug
looks,
Though its bite you'll never
feel."
When Christmas morning comes
your way,
No shirt from Mom—instead—
She sent me these four bed bugs
To place upon my bed.

Mark David Ransom

ASHORE HE EYES MY LOVE (BEATRIZ)

Ashore he eyes my love as I
set sail,
but what is he to her or her to
him?
That's the green quandry I labor
in;
trying to forge a shield and
coat of mail
to protect me from blows that
he may flail
while in my absence his assults
begin.
How well my love discerns what
words intend
is all the hope I have that she
won't fail.
Deliver a man the world and
all it holds:
he'll be above reproach and
paltry scorn,
but give him love worth more
than can be told;
a single bond that can't be
remade—just torn,
and kingdoms become dust and
riches cold.
Mad Othello—now I know
whence rage is born!

Mr. Frank Schofield

TIES WITHIN

Like the red flower aroma so
gay,
with beauty within, to flourish
a day.
With thorns on the outside to
protect from the world,
like people we know, so hard in
their way.
A flower is still, sometimes
surrounded by weeds,
but grows to reach out for the
love that it needs.
Yet we don't reach out, or cut
off our ties,
but make up excuses, and
sometimes tell lies.
Now beauty and love is within
everyone,
in some it is dormant, and
some think it's gone.
So cut off the ties that
torment and decay,
and reach out for love, theres
more than one way.

Cora Maltman Thacker

THE VOID

I am a ship
Out on a sea:
A tiny ship;
A large, wide sea;
Small me.
There is no one
Else on this sea:
No other ship;
Deep, lonely sea;
Lonely me.
If I can find
Another ship:
A plain, strong ship;
A dark, vast sea;
Like me.
Then there will be
Two to share the view:
Small, sturdy ships;
Great, lovely sea;
You and me.

Kenneth L. Hoff

THE SPIRIT OF CHRISTMAS

Love is the Spirit of Christmas
Trimming of trees and giving of
toys.
Merry Christmas to those I love,
It is they who bring me joy.
Love is the Spirit of Christmas,
Being together with family and
friend.

A feeling of peace and
contentment,
Good will in the greetings
we send.
Love is the Spirit of Christmas,
Joy in giving to those we love.
The search for that special
something,
For that special someone you're
thinking of.
Love is the Spirit of Christmas,
God showed us His love that
morn.
Rejoice in His gift of love,
Today the baby Christ child is
born.
Love is the Spirit of Christmas,
May your Christmas be filled
with love.
To know the Spirit of
Christmas,
To be filled with peace from
above.
MERRY CHRISTMAS

Charles DeBlasio

VACANT

There's a vacant place, inside
of my heart.
I'm waiting for something to
start.
Though falling in love, doesn't
happen just everyday.
(Sometimes such happiness lies
far away.)
I look outside and wonder,
How many lonely people are
around?
Can love survive, or even be
found?
See, I've this vacant space inside
of my mind.
Living alone, isn't my idea of
trying to unwind.
I long for companionship;
But it always seems to get left
behind.

Louise Sheets Ritchie

MY SPIRIT

The essence that is me
Is not this flesh and bone,
I am a spirit free—
Imprisioned in this cone.
I dare to dream my dreams,
To reach out and to soar,
Confined within these walls—
I know there is a door.
To rise up from the depths
Expression is the key.
This wrapping is my home,
My spirit—that is me!

Elizabeth Ann Myren

REFLECTION

As I look into the mirror
I wonder
Is that me
The face is so familiar
But yet
It's hard to see
I look beyond the features
Hoping
That I might find
Beneath
The face in the mirror
A person
Deep inside.
Who am I
What am I
Can it be
I just can't see
Face to face
To what's really me!

Alva E. Tucker

RED HELL, BLACK DISGRACE

My soul screams and writhes in
the agony
Of this, a bitterly futile trend
Toward a love so great, so pure,
so free
That man alone cannot
comprehend
The stark beauty of its divinity.
For this, a Red Hell may be my
end!
Where lies the answer, the
eternal answer?
My soul, my very own Satanic
soul
Shirks in cowardly retreat its
own cancer,
Screaming, tearing, clawing,
baring its toll
Of shame and sin. And as if in a
trance or
Dream, my fears of Black
Disgrace I console.
Perhaps then a Red Hell is the
answer!

Violet Spence Holland

TELEPHONE LAMENT

I waited for the phone
to ring;
By george it simply
wouldn't
But of course I knew,
without a doubt,
The poor ol'thing just
couldn't.
It is a great invention,
sure,
Yet strange as it may
seem,
Someone has to dial
somewhere
To make the darn thing
ring.

I might decide to
retaliate and
When it rips the air
asunder,
I'll say, hello, hello,
hello, hello!
Sorry, you have the
wrong number!

Deborah Turner

FLOWER

Bird of Paradise
Sprout out from a crack in the
parched pavement
Lonely Loveliness
Bent beneath a crown of stars
Flung upward toward the sun
Straining for the soothe of
heaven's hush
From the midst of the din, the
odiferous smog
The weeds outnumber you
The wind leaves you thirsty,
and dusty, and worn
But, slender strongman
You've pulled your columns
down
You've swept your ground
Freed from your bonds, let fly
your golden hair
You've cleaned and claimed your
space

And proud, where you stand,
Paradise.

Elna Carter
FIRST FLIGHT
Looking down from high above
I see
God's creation as He does.
I feel
Anxiety cover me
As I become aware
If just how short a time
We have to spend there.
I see
The majestic mountain peaks
Reaching through the white
 clouds
As though to shake the hand of
 God,
Many untouched by the foot of
 man.
Clouds scalloped over the small
 towns and plains
Like pure balls of cotton with
 a little trim of lace.

I see
Man made quilts in the land
Held together by the hem-
 stitching of roads and rivers.
The desert
Still,
But yet,
Ever changing with the winds of
 time.
I see
The largest of cities
Dwarfed and standing alone
Surrounded only by the barren
 country side.

Rowland S. Russell
UNTITLED
Let us walk this day together
 you and I
we'll strike a path through
 marsh grass and chokecherry
down to the stream
bankside buffeted by maple
 shade
 and the cool wind
 singing through the hollow
we'll fish all day and lay back
 and let the lines play their
 own way
and if a fish takes the bait of
 the setting sun
we'll throw him back into the
 water
surface scaled golden with days
 end
and let him bend his life
 to his own purpose
and we will amble back the way
 we came
our steps sewing a new fabric
 in the tangled grass
and the half moon risen
like a buttercup petal
knowing tomorrow will not be
 the same as today
nor can we tame the memories
 wriggling
like minnows in a stream bed
we'll just cast another line
 let it ride the current
and let time determine the
 catch

Lisa A. Jacobi
MEMORIES
The echo of your laughter stays
 in my mind,
The shadow of your memory
 follows behind.
The sadness in your heart as I
 left there was pain,
But the love you and I have
 will always remain.
Your eyes that sparkled
 everytime you smiled at me,
It reminded me of the sun
 shining upon the sea.
You and I will always know,
That our love will always grow.

Diana Watson
SOMETIMES
loud voices
angry stares
sharp mouths
shout and stalk
our house
trying to bury
our love for
each other
we shall
turn voices
into soft breezes
eyes mirroring
sunny smiles
the warmth of
love returns

patricia Boles
BUT YET
I want you to love me
 But yet not adore me
I want you to adore me
 But yet not possess me
I want you to possess me
 But yet leave me free
I want to be Free
 But yet you to love me

Jean Gorman Morsheimer
ON BOARD
Discovered suddenly,
it scuttled wildly
in a reckless race for security,
dodged the crush of rope,
coiled up wire legs,
then flattened ebony body
flush with ebony cleat,
in crescent fashion.
Like flesh presses the tiller,
straining to survive the smoky
 sea,
I fathom this creature.

John Hill Westbrook
A UNITY OF BEING
Can you direct me to yesterday
or the land of eternal May?
I long for those years and the
 ways
that were. For now I am in a
hideous maze of doubt.
The Hit Parade of songs each
Saturday and the sting of peach
fuzz on my face as I eat and
 watch
the show, picking the skin
 blotch
on my cheek
and wondering which will be
 the hit of the week
sustains my existing soul
and ultimately tends to mold
my now everbecoming—

Patricia Ann O'Neal
PURPLE HEATHER
There is a road no longer
 traveled
Grown thick with wood and
 weed
That once led up the
 mountainside
Then turned down toward the
 sea.
When we were small we'd tarry
 here
To play and dream a while
And everywhere we'd turn to
 look
Purple heather would make us
 smile.
Now that I am old and friends
 have gone away
And weeds and woods have
 covered the road
 where once we used to play
I think back on those carefree
 days—a
 warm caress of earth and
 sky and sea—
And find a bit of happiness—
Purple heather smiling back at
 me.

Karen Taylor
AFTER THOUGHTS
How can I hold you
 and love you this way?
Though it feels so right,
 with the firelight
 shining in your face.
How can we lie here,
 after spending our day,
 laughing and talking;
 touching one another
 so tenderly?
How can I face him,
 knowing as I do, your love?
Remembering your touch
 as he kisses me and says,
"Honey, I love you."

Carolyn Marie Baatz
EARTH'S END
Trees bursting with shades of
 green
Azure skies, sun's rays stream
 down
Shining on sparkling blue-green
 water
Grass, trees breathe clean, fresh
 air
A breeze blows gently creates
 ripples
The air is no longer clean, it's
 dirt, smoke
Trees, flowers, birds, animals
 need air
The earth is a concrete, stone
 filled jungle
All because man developed the
 need for greed.

Regina Macioci
DRUNK
A ragged, old man stood still
As his world turned UPSIDE
D
 O
  W
   N
          and
The black earth hugged his
 head.
He hoped that one more gulp of
 his magic potion
would set things right again.
Yet, nothing could help now.
His senses were too far gone.
And his feet were stolen by
 the C
  L
   O
    U
     D
      S.

M. Rosser Lunsford
THE INNATE GAME
A child's world is a wonderful
game
 of joy and make-believe,
A grown-up's world is akin to
pain,
 misfortune, grief and need;
How sad that we, who
understand,
 can't change our scheme of
 things
And play the role of child as
man
 and miss what ripeness brings;
How sad that youth in all its
splendor
 must, on some real tomorrow,
Lay down a part of sweet and
tender
 and grasp a part of sorrow.

Joseph V. Piegaro
THE LOST DEBIT
I saw only numbers at first,
 this accounting seemed too
 hard to learn,
As I rose from my desk with a
burst,
 and a rude and awakening
 turn.
I greeted no angry response,
 from the students that sat all
 around;
As I fiddled and faddled in
fonse,
 as I beckoned this debit be
 found.
It must be somewhere I know,
 As I raised my pen up from
 the page;
These debits and credits are
foes,
 who have not learned the
 wrath of my rage.
I thought now yes where would
I hide,
 if I were a debit at rest;
Maybe he hitchhiked a ride,
 from a credit who truckloaded
 west.
As I paddled and pounded the
ground,
 as I pulled out the hair from
 my head;
My accounting Professor had
found,
 my lost debit asleep in his
 bed.

Anthony Thomas Aceto
THINK OF ME AS I DO YOU
Close your eyes my love, let your passion dance freely as we share in the mysterious mystery of love. Do you feel the way I do everytime our eyes meet? That penetrating touch that unites our hearts, a touch that only true love feels. Think of me as I do you, even when our distance is far our hearts will be near—especially when your thoughts are confused and your heart is filled with sadness, think of me as I do you.
Dream, dream sweet dreams of a distant dream—must one suffer a fate 'cause their paths crossed late.
I still can remember, through the friendship of a mutual friend, the way we came to meet. Although my eyes met yours, I felt that yours passed right through me. Even all our continual encounters are only a fleeting occurrence, for we only stop to say hi but never hello. Although we travel on that same lonely road, it appears our destiny keeps us apart.
It is almost amusing how situations which seem too apparent often lose their direction, leaving us to wonder why must we suffer a fate 'cause our paths crossed late. It occurs to me, that our first encounter so very long ago was the closest we ever came. Even the bond we did share, the friendship of our mutual friend, has drifted away. All that I know of you, is what you have shown me. All my thoughts of you, are only what I feel. But everytime your presence is near, my mind becomes confused—causing me to feel ill at ease.
I can't explain this feeling I feel, but something within you, not so long ago, has really touched me deep inside. Leaving me confused but yet aware, aware of an inner strength that has truly altered my direction. I know not where it shall lead, but wherever it does, it will always be accompanied with the thoughts of you. I know not the true feelings you feel for me, if there be any at all. There may not exist any deep feelings between us, but only those of two lost wanderers traveling that same lonely road. Although we may never be able to say, "think of me as I do you", maybe someday soon we will be able to find the way to simply say "hello".

Colette Boyer
HEARTS BREAK SILENTLY
Dawn breaks in glorious splendor
And bird songs greet the day,
Waves breaking make the ocean's roar
Where noisy sea gulls play.
A branch makes a resounding noise
And crashes from the tree,
Hearts breaking make no sound at all
Hearts break so silently.

Emily Porter
BEGINNINGS
Beginnings are such fragile things—
like dew-kissed mist on butterflies' wings.
The paths to the future form intricate lines
with the key that unlocks them buried in Time.
And how do we know which pathway we'll trod,
is it ordained by Fate, or given by God?
Is the warm clasp of friendship that which we'll see
with camaraderie the bonding for you and me?
Or will we pause for a little while
to bask in the radiance of each other's smile
and share together the communion of soul
before pressing on to our Destiny's goal?
Be it friendship or other, I'll know I'll have cared
and rejoice in this moment of Time that we've shared.
So linger a bit as you walk down Life's road.
By my caring, let me help you to lighten your load.
By my loving, let me fill you with kind memories
to take to your future, when you think back on me.

Pamela Jay
THE ENDLESS SEARCH
In the deep dark corners of the night,
I lay awake in my bed,
Searching for the answer. . .
The answer that will set me free. . .
The answer that will let me be me. . .
The answer that I want and need. . .
For this answer I do plead.
And so I lay awake in bed,
Searching and searching throughout my head.
And as I drift to slumber,
I realize my mistake.
And wait to find the answer,
In my dreams before I wake.

Jack Giammerse, Jr.
MATURITY
Ma-tur-i-ty
Is what you see
Good in me.
Im-ma-tur-i-ty
Is what you see
Bad in me.

Mayes C. Smith
HEALING TEARS
I stood upon a cold and windy hill,
My heart as heavy as the sods that lay
All ready once again their place to take
And hold you ever in their breast for aye.
Long years I watched the glow of roses dim
And fade from your kind face, through stunning pain.
My soul cried out for peace for your brave heart,
That, like our Saviour, never did complain.
I knew the eyes of all my friends that day,
Enfolded me within each sad warm heart,
And wondered if the hopeless tears would flow,
To ease the burden when we had to part.
At last the torrent of my sorrow burst,
And unashamedly the tear drops leapt,
As once again I suddenly recalled,
That at the grave of Lazarus Jesus wept.

Nina Adkins
THE TOP OF THE HILL
After the day has gone to sleep
And all is quiet and still,
I make my way up the darkened path—
Up to the top of the hill.
The moon shines dim through the rolling mist,
The start of a whippoorwill,
And now he comes by the dark of night—
Up to the top of the hill.
"Everyone fears you've left.
You won't come home at will.
Am only I the one you'll see
Here at the top of the hill?"
"Three days ago, the people say,
A death was caused by the mill.
And the very last spot that you were seen
Was here at the top of the hill!"
His eyes spoke loud. "I cannot leave."
He held me close until—
I understood OUR place would be
Here at the top of the hill.
. . . .
After the day has gone to sleep,
And all is quiet and still,
I make my way up the darkened path—
Up to the top of the hill.

Esther Womble Pendergrass
A PRAYER
Dear Lord— teach me
The highroads of thy faith.
And lead me ever upward
Towards thy shining face.
Let me not into temptation stray—
Nor fall in evil mistrust of thy love,
For I am weak and do so need thy care—
But for each error let me seek
My Saviour sure and dear.
Help me to overcome the faults
That leave my heart as stone—
For I should oh so love to be
The kind of child you'd care to own.

Charles A. Winzeler
THE HEJIRA
I heard you yesterday as you croaked your way toward your winter home.
Your annual sound is monotonous yet significant for it marks the passing of another year.
I dropped my rake and abandoned my pursuit of fallen leaves.
The sky was blue, the sun was shining and the November air was cool.
Even though your color was almost like that of the fleecy clouds I found your formation.
Why this pattern year after year?
Why do you honk in such endless chorus?
Are you happy to leave unpleasant memories behind or is it in anticipation of the future?
is my own life like this moving "V"?
Are there those who watch me too as I move through this world?
Do I shout with joy when the distasteful passes and continue to cant as I phantasize about the future?
Do I make any patterns at all or will I be like these homeless geese?
Will I indeed leave the blue sky with its fleecy clouds empty and cold?

Sherri Walker
INDIVIDUALITY
I must breathe—allow me air,
I must move—allow me space,
I must laugh—allow me joy,
I must thing—allow me quiet,
I must be me, allow me individuality.
I must cry—allow me tears,
I must love—allow me warmth,
I must hurt—allow me pain,
I must dream—allow me sleep,
I must be me, allow me individuality.
I must fly—do not clip my wings,
I must run—do not close me in,

I must feel—do not smother my emotions,
I must be silent—do not ask for speech,
I must be me, free to
experience the oneness of my soul.

Cynthia Hill
FOR PAUL
Sometimes I just need to be with you.
No intellectual debates,
scrutinizing *Penthouse* girls
or the cable movie. . .
No wine or whiskey or stereo. . .
or crowded restaurants;
Just you.
Before you left this afternoon
there was something I'd wanted to say
since about eleven a.m.:
Just that it was so nice
to hold you and be held,
and touch your soft flannel shirt
with you inside,
and know it was quietly raining,
and feel your hair and skin
against my face,
and smell the sweet scent
of yesterday's cologne.
Sometimes I just need to be with you.

Emma King
REMEMBERING ROSE O'NEALE GREENHOWE
The monument erected in her memory
Marks the grave in Oakdale Cemetery
Placed there by ladies of the UDC
For "Rebel Rose" who died at sea
Bearing dispatches for the South
As she approached Cape Fear's mouth
The storm unleashed its awful fury
On her gold sovereign laden body
Still fighting till her last breath
Her life ended in a watery death
The sea deposited her on the beach
To rest on the land she tried to reach
Now she lies here in her grave
But once she was alive, vibrant and brave
Dancing with men both dark and fair
At Buchanan's ball with diamonds in her hair

R. Steve Britt
LENGTH OF A MILE
Her eyes speak with the wisdom of the meek.
Her smile is the smile of a hungry young child.
Her heart yearns for love,
her stomach for food.
The clothes on her back are ragged and worn.
The future she lacks pricks her skin like a thorn.
She's hungry and cold;
darling, but yet bold.
She's a lovely young child,
With a life the length of only a mile.

Lon B. Lounsbury
ALABASTER UNICORN
Alabaster Unicorn,
From silky tail to golden horn,
Poised aquiver in life's morn,
As eager thoughts yet to be born;
Borrow from Pegasus wings,
From Aladdin precious things;
Listen while the Siren sings;
Take men's aspirations too;
Soar with hope into the blue,
Till all mundane minds are new.

Flossie H. Cook
WHAT HAVE WE DONE?
What have we done
To our mountains?
They're dried and parched blond.
Why did Earth's rivers
Dry up and leave no veins?
It's the cry from all over the land.
What's happened to our oceans
That the fish can live no more?
They lie dead upon the shore
Their destiny we ignore.
The cry comes from the shore.
What have we done to the air
That it contaminates our lungs?
That winged life cease to fly?
The children question "why"?
The cry comes from the skies.
What have we done to our child-life?
They have no time to live.
What do they see—
What do they do—
That's not automatically directed?
The children cry for our help
The cry comes from all over the land.

Louisa Mulvihill
AUTUMN'S LEAVES
Season's drift by, into the dim past
Spring's memory but a faint recall,
Summer's beauty fades to yesterday
Softly now, Autumn's leaves drift and fall.
Sadly, leaves drift down, the trees are bare
Soon Winter's cold snow will cover all,
Surely new Spring leaves shall be nourished
Silently from Autumn's leaves that fall. . .

Meda Hylton
FLOWERS FOR GRANDMOTHER
I was passing by the window
Of a flower shop one day,
I saw a basket of flowers
More winsome than you can say.
I'll buy it for grandmother,
It will make her happy and gay,
To have her favorite flowers
Arranged in a lovely bouquet.
Chrysanthemums, small as buttons,
Carnations, pink and white,
Roses, red and yellow,
They give the heart delight.
It was only a basket of flowers,
But I heard grandmother say,
"I am proud of you darling,
You have made my happy day.

Vivian Lee Clifton
UNTIL
We met, we laughed we had such fun
Those days I will remember.
We traveled, we talked we sat and ran
Together we walked hand in hand.
Through shadowed parks and down the beaches
From lakes to mountain tops.
We fell in love as lovers do
To us those times would never stop.
Our love led us to become as one
We were husband and we were wife.
We taught each other many things
But most of all to enjoy our life.

We came together one winters night
We kissed, we touched we loved.
We put away thoughts of earths troubles and strife
From our love that night came a newborn life.
As time went on we were three not two
Our life became happier still.
That newborn babe now a part of us both
We would love her from now until. . .
Until one dreadful day our three became two
How could this ever be?
Part of our three had been taken away
And part of my world ended that day.
Now we are two as parent and child
Instead of man and of wife.
Still we must go on as best we can
And try to enjoy our two lonely lives.

Kay Walsh
BLESS THOSE FEET
I love my "Easy Rider"
But I'm fonder of my "Honda"
And when I'm really thinkin'
I always choose my "Lincoln"
A "Chevy" isn't really bad
A "Caddy's pretty neat
But I have learned,
Tho for cars I've yearned,
Thank Heaven for my feet.
Once I owned a "Ford"
And truly I was bored.
But then with my "Mercedes Benz"
I found I had a lot of friends.
Yet when all is said and done
And I'm walking down the street
I must admit that cars are fun,
But thank Heaven for my feet!

Lillie M. Harrison
OFF TO SCHOOL
Trudging off to school
A hop, a skip, a jump
Spring arrives with buttercups
And pussywillows too.
Running through the meadows
Violets come popping up at you.
A lovely bouquet brought home to mother
With flowers of every hue.
Friendly smiles and friendly chats
With the neighbor kids
When running off together.
Gathering at the red schoolhouse
We learned so much from each other.
Lasting friendships made.
As we skipped along together
Even God seemed very near.
These things the children miss today
When they must ride the bus
And can't skip off to school together.

Lee Greschner
STORMY WINTER WEATHER
Stormy winter weather
Blows against the panes.
Frost on windows feather
Christmas Trees with canes.
Children laughing, secrets,
Memories so plain. . . . . .
Stockings holding trinkets.
Not one day the same!
Winter keeps on coming.
Snow drifts up so high!!
Children often skating.
MMMMM! That pumpkin pie.
Suddenly, where's winter?
Puddles here and there
Drops fall helter skelter,
Flowers scent the air.
Seasons, changing ever,
Spring, summer and fall.
Stormy winter weather!
Oh! To see it all!!

Joyanne Nocito
STILLBORN BUTTERFLIES
We are the dead ones.
Stillborn daughters of a cruel time
Fighting for room to breathe.
Ours the graveyard of forgotten hopes.
Like bleached bones
Our dreams lie abandoned.
See there,

A garbage pile monument
To aborted babes.
Their mothers knew,
Status comes from bearing sons.
If a girl, expose it.
We are ghostly butterflies
Encased in cultural coccoons
Eating our way through dross
to decay.
You inhale our life force.
You consume our flesh.
To you we are nameless,
faceless,
Women.

Angela Caponigri
SPECIAL PEOPLE THAT WE CALL FRIENDS

We all have special people in our lives that somehow make the day brighter and our problems less severe. No matter what, we can always count on them; and they on us. We don't have to impress them or prove ourselves to them. We don't have to be something that we know we are not. All we have to do is love them as they love us. We can be ourselves without worrying. We can say our opinions without being laughed at for they accept us as we are. They love our qualities but they don't hate our faults. They somehow always manage to be there when we need them without expecting to be paid back. They are understanding and somehow, even if we hurt them unconsciously, they always take us back. We all have special people like this in our lives; special people that we call friends. And we love them though we don't always express it in words. They have affected our lives maybe more than they'll ever know. And no matter where we are, our love will always be strong, our bond will always be remembered, and our friendship will always be cherished.

Edward Lee Steen Jr.
RIGOR MORTIS

Feeling the pain
In my arm
Where the razor cut me.
Sitting my favorite
Chair
Watching nothing on T.V.
Why so heavy?
Blackness all around
Getting deep.
Good-bye World
Falling into
The big sleep.
Leaving my body
Behind on Earth
What a screwed up place.
Making a trip on my own
Leaving no trace.
Passing through
Crystal shades
Of blue and white.
Freeing a
Restless mind
On an endless flight.
Forgetting who I was
Being reborn
In the Cosmic Rain.
Hello Father,
Hold me
I'm yours again.

Donna Lennox Thompson
DIVORCE

I miss my child
I miss my home
I miss my life
I've become a stone.
The feelings gone
The purpose too,
Oh dear Lord
What shall I do?
It was so full
It was so real,
How could another,
My family,
Steal?
I'll never know,
I'll never heal,
But there's little doubt,
Sin is very real.

Peter Oral Peretti
THE ULTIMATE QUESTION

As you toil and sweat from day
to day,
Trying to make things go your
way;
As you drive yourself with
heart and soul,
Ever reaching toward some
desired goal;
Do you ever stop to think,
my friend,
About this question when you
reach your end?

In striving it all seemed
worthwhile, and yet,
When you get what you want,
will you want what you get?

Diana Davis
FRIENDS

My friend and I, when we are
old,
Plan to live together.
Our house, not large and made
of wood,
Faces the sea.
It is ample enough for visiting
grandchildren.
Our rooms blend color and
texture,
Persian rugs, lace curtains,
velvet pillows.
Lilac and roses grow in the
garden
And a fig tree with black,
luscious fruit.
Our constant companions are
cats,
Of various size and color,
Maybe six,
And a large, golden dog to
deter intruders.
Days run their course
One into the other.
We take our main meal at
midday;
Some afternoons, friends join us
for tea
And we use the good English
china teapot.
At sunset we stroll along the
sands and share poems
And on cool evenings we read
and sew by the fireside
Listening to Bach, Mozart and
French love songs
And remember our youth.

W. T. Lyons
FREEDOM NOT FOR SALE

Standing erect on an elevation,
at noon in the village square,
A man in God's image was
appraised
like steers at a fair.
"What am I bid," the call went
out,
"for this stud of twenty-two?"
"He can sire more salves in a
single
night than any five can do."
As the bids became higher in
value,
and tempers began to flare,
The slave was calm, proud, and
erect
as though he wasn't there.
Freedom and life to him were
one and
very much the same,
Like the only difference in kind
between
running water and falling rain.
His body in chains was
auctioned off
to become a common slave,
But freedom of mind he retained
himself,
for this he never gave.
Because, in his mind, he would
be free
and have his story told,
That freedom is a gift from God
and
may not be bought or sold.

Gloria Daniels
BIRDS IN FLIGHT

The sky is filled with winging
birds
(A ballet in the sky!)
They fly with graceful—swaying
moves,
(which thrill the human eye!)
Some glide and dip or soar and
dive—
(Majestic wings in flight!)
They seem to cry:
"We're free!"
"We're free!"
Then vanish! (Out of sight.")

Erna Grabler-Segal
UNTITLED

If only I could stop the Time,
encapsulate each treasured
moment in Eternity;
childhood dreams—joys
sublime—
hold it all in eternal
captivity. . .
First touch of a rose against
a velvet cheek,
a cloud of strange perfume
enveloping the senses. . . .
That first rush of something
new we'll always seek—
innocence so brief—lacking all
pretenses—
a sunkissed palm frond reflected
in the sea—
that sudden flash of pure
contentment—
a brief forever—a long-gone
someone loving me—
a page from life torn in a flash
of resentment. . . .
If only I could stop the Time,
demolish a thousand images of
me—
the stranger I was yesterday—
the one I'll be tomorrow. . . .
The madly racing years torment
me,
I kiss each Yesterday goodbye
with sorrow. . .
Too much, too cruelly torn
away—
what's left—a pallid memory to
borrow,
memory that fades as Time goes
racing by—
where is the spice of life
attributed to changes. . .
Change is but a plunge into the
Unknown
accompanied by an anguished
cry—
primordial terror that attacks
and deranges. . .
If only I could stop the Time
and never learn what lies
beyond the final bend—
could it be that Eternity is
another life's continuity—
or could it be—simply—the
End. . . . . .

Regina Michelle Allen
YOU JUST ME

The winds blow soft with silent
sounds;
The stars above fall to the
grounds;
The trees all stand so still and
bold;
Then, I wonder where my love
is?
Far, far away from me
in another land across the
seas;
Far, far away from me
I sing to you my love song.
I sing to you so you will hear
my song of joy for you my
dear.
So, maybe soon you'll return to
me,
we'll love,
just you, just me!

R. Louise Gordon
A PRECIOUS JEWEL
(Dedicated to my Granddaughter "Holly")

Through all his jewels
God picked a pearl;
Then blessed it as
A baby girl.
He called his cherubs
'Round to see;
How precious she was

Going to be.
An opal to her face
Did touch;
And gave her eyes
That change so much.
A diamond that shone
Oh so bright;
He took and made
Her hair so light.
He touched her mouth
With sapphire tips;
And formed those
Lovely, smiling lips.
From rubies crumbled
Into dust;
Her button nose
Became a must.
He showed them all
His work of art;
"An angel"...Made
With all his heart.

Katherine Plecas

THE JOY OF CHRISTMAS

Christmas holidays will soon be here,
The children love this time of year.
They dream of Santa 'most ev'ry night,
And wish for Christmas to be white.
Snowball games are fun to play
When Santa Claus is on his way.
Dreams of toys are coming true,
Brand new games with ev'rything new.

Pine scent of Christmas trees, with
Fancy ornaments and sparkling
Lights that shine, all over and ev'rywhere.
When Mom is baking and decorating,
And Dad is cleaning the fireplace.
We know the time has come, Christmas
Will soon be here. Merry Christmas to
Everyone.

Lori Tumulty

WE DON'T TALK & WE DON'T LOVE

We don't talk
and we don't love
we just exist
and that is all
in our own little world
entwined with each others' faults.
You are you
and I am I
and we will never be one
our love has disappeared
and can never be found.
One time we had the best
back when there was nobody else
but you went and found somebody new
now I'm letting you go too.
I hope you both are happy
in your new found love.
I hope you have the best
like we once did, my love.

Myrtle J. Franze

A——————Z

Miracles! Miracles! Today I choose
Twenty-six letters to bring us the news,
Weave poems, write sonnets, fiction and such;
How can mere alphabet give us so much?

Anthony Rossello

LAKE ARROWHEAD

Beauty and grace surround her face,
Flowers in bloom at a flourishing pace.
Her mountains, her streams, her lake are aglow,
With the freshness of nature's rampant flow.
So peaceful, so calm is the breeze through the air,
As if God Himself was enjoying it there.
The village so elegant guarding the lake,
Her majesty, her charm, no one can forsake.
Shine on arrowhead, let your majesty grace,
The beauty, the splendor of this lovely place.
There is peace, there is love, there is beauty galore.
Arrowhead city forevermore....

Jana Barnes

WHEN WAS YESTERDAY

Watching your movements in sunlight
makes it hard remembering you in the rain
with droplets trickling down your face.
Even as a kid
I'd love to put on my yellow slicker
and go rainhunting
I found friends in the rain
of snails awakened
flowers miraculously alive
from dirt I'd used the day before
to make mud pies
I walked home with flowers
Mom made me leave my snail outside.
Again I found a friend in the rain
as I see you in sunlight now
after my heartrain has washed away
all traces of unhappiness
in my mind's mirror.

Billie Rockey

SHARING

Yesterday has now gone to the past.
No great things took place, if you were to ask,
But today was very different from start to end.
You see, I shared it with a friend.
We didn't accomplish any great feat,
Sat together on the garden seat;
Listened to birds sing up in the trees,
Watched white sails skip the seas.
Walked the shores 'til way past sunset.
Threw stones in the water along the inlet.
We heard the gulls sad groans and wails;
Even watched the slow pace of the snails.
Spoke of all the worldly troubles,
But today, they burst like bubbles.
Not a care had we today,
Just sharing quietly, each in his own way.
As day came to an end,
And I sat with my friend,
Our heads started to nod,
We realized we'd shared it all with God.

Argyle Stoute

SPENT

Wild rain pelt long strings
Long shining strings of rain
Cobweb and intertwine
Before a haze of mist
Powerful mist
A screeching wind howls
Fusing a silver path
The tree bough rips like cloth
And hurries to the soft frustrated earth

Wet, hungry, erect and stubborn
Lunges in the fleshy clay
Tumbles over
Exhausted
Limp—
And lies lifeless
Spent on the ground—
Wilted leaves droop
Like closed eye lids
While the body stands removed
And bleeds rosin
To heal the wound of wind.

Alice M. Stewart

THIS ANGUISHED WOE

You who've not tasted sorrow's bane,
Nor bowed beneath grief's whip,
Think to console with soothing word
So ready on the lip?
As notes from untuned violin,
E'en sympathy sincere
From one untouched by bitter pain,
Falls barren on the ear.
But one who's known this anguished woe
That rends the heart in twain,
Can, by a look, a touch, impart
Solace, where words were vain.

Elior L. Kinarthy

A STARRY NIGHT

My love for you is like gleaming stars,
far in the heavens and daring to reach,
Are we together...I think we are,
through the dark cold night of our relationship,
gleaming up there million rays of hope,
to claim with bleeding palms, rope after rope.
Sometimes when I am close to the unreachable goal,
so many stars...how would I gather you all?
To fill my heart with your warmth and light,
through the night of our relationship...through the night.
Shadows tell me 'beware of the pitfalls,'
a star that's too hot may explode in your face,
mighty love, so frightening to seek the light,
to be burnt out when all the stars are gathered,
will I leave you some to express for yourself?
will you leave me some to express for myself?
Sometimes you seem to like the darkness of night,
protected, assured, unseen with no need for a flight,
to even the closest warm star in the sky,
but as for me...bleeding and all,
climbing rope after rope, closer and closer,
oh heaven, give me a star to give to my lover,
I promise not to deprive you of any other.
Starry night, you are awesome and far of reach,
only because I have forgotten how to fly,
Am I an angel whose wings were cut off for a man
by my mind or my brain?
Am I both an angel and a man and don't know I can fly?
My love for you is like gleaming stars,
still lost without vision why they are so far!

Isabel S. Mavity

HANDICAPPED

Life's heroes—those afflicted,
The act of awakening itself
An act of courage.
Imperfect in a foreign form,
In pain often,
Limbs rigid or flaccid,
Disobedient to the will
The moving slowly, frightened,
Braving the alien streets

Unprotected, naked, helpless.
Feigning indifference to the
Stares of strangers,
The children, saucer-eyed,
Devouring the deviant with
Eager curiosity
Or the quick glance, followed by
The blank, averted faces
Of those more caring "normals"
Ignorant of others feelings
Exactly like their own.
To live, to move in cold
indifferent
Wilderness, an obstacle course
Peopled by dangerous monsters
Takes courage.

Kenneth Nelson

GOLDEN YOUTH

Youth so wondrous and
beauteous thing.
To Grace man but once.
Oh prithy! Wouldst thou caress
mine lips?
With such tenderness and joy.
But just once.
Youth so full of truth and
innocence.
To see thee in field and glen.
In joyous, rapturous Spring.
With flowers in bloom and bird
on the wing.
Youth Oh! golden youth.
Thou gladdens my heart a
million fold
Youth thou art a joy to behold.
May I just put in a few words or
a sonnet.
To both girl and boy.
In praise of God's gift to man.
Oh! youth go on living with not
a regret.
I love thee in such purity.
I love thee golden youth.
Golden Youth.
I love thee.

Jerry Borrowman

TENSION

A growing ache of tension,
Fear—
Muscles constrict, working
against themselves.
Emotions rage within the body,
Tears held back, screams
supressed.
Nature's way is to lash out
Fighting in battle.
But civilized man lives by
proprieties,
So must fight himself.
Prayer, that silent friend of
solitude
Can bring a fragile calm.
But at last even it can't win—
Not alone, not of itself.
Only decision, resolve then
action can
Frighten off the fear.
Like a forest animal, startled by
a sound,
Fear flees before determined
will.

Mark Joseph Hollister

DELECTIBLE DECEMBER

December's velvet flakes
came gently sifting down
settling like the silken flour
from a woman's powdered touch.
It's supple, lilting linen grace
spread like serendipity
across the glistened edge of
night;
warming the hearts
of winter's hungry lovers!
It's velvet blanket shed a glow
as tantalizing as the smell
of apples from a fiery stove.

Kathryn G. Hansen

PRECIOUSNESS

Children are precious to all
mankind
As their little faces shine with
a love divine;
From the time they begin to
crawl
They answer to their mother's
call.

They know the sternness of
Dad's command
From the infant stage to the
teen age drawl,
Yet love is implanted in each
tiny heart
Because the great Jehovah
really gave them their start.

Thomas R. Lonze

BECAUSE I CARE

I wish for you tenderness
Hope and long life,
Joy and warm hearts
The absence of strife.
May your love take you forward
Through the days, months and
years,
Giving strength during moments
Of uncertainties and fears.
I bid you both happiness
Sunrises, full moons,
Warm fires in winter
Flowers in bloom.
Emotions are fragile
Be thoughtful and kind,
Wish the ties that now bind you
To others to find.

Michael Kiernan

MOVING PICTURES

For Now,
we touch no more.
We only fantasize
endlessly.
Your soft lips
touch mine
and the taste lingers on.
Sweet, pink candy
is licked by children with rosy
lips.
I feel your touch,
your soft, delicate hand
you smile, and something inside
us stirs.
The Nature of Man
is being discussed in Intro.
to Philosophy,
while a nervous freshman
caresses his wet palms.
For Now,
we touch no more.
The Canadian Elk migrate,
treading softly across vast,
golden, tundra.

Vickie L. Gordon

THE CITY

The Mount of Olives, how
gigantic it looms
And down at it's feet,
Gethsemane blooms
Stretching out from the
mountain, Jerusalem is seen
In the morning sun light, so
lovely it gleams.
Down in the streets, the city
awakes
And each person his own
journey he makes
Some to the shops, some to the
fields
Some to the vineyards, some to
the mills.
Looking down from the wall is
the valley so deep
Where the shepherds are
watching their own flock of
sheep
The Golden Gate can be seen
from here
And the ancient temple that
people hold dear.
When the shadows grow long,
and the sun's gone to bed
Away from the city, back home
I must tread
There's a sadness at leaving, but
a joy to have been
Here in Jerusalem, where hope
never ends!

Valentine Dmitriev

LAST WALK BEFORE WINTER

The hemlock boughs hung low,
Each needle-tip seed-pearled
with recent rain;
And as we walked, green,
leathern-leaved salal
Glowed with wetness, and shiny
rivulets of water
Drenched our feet.
And all about there was
The dark, closed stillness of
the woods:
A turning back, an inner
settling down.
We came too late, I felt:
Unwelcome guests
Arriving after fires had been
banked
And shutters latched.
From habit, if from nothing else,
you sought my hand,
But yours lay cold on mine,
And in your face I read
The same withdrawal and
farewell.

Michael Radford

SPECIAL PEOPLE

Their bodies are those of
grownups
in every way.
Their minds are those of
children
with thoughts the same.
We are their beacons to light
their way
and help them understand the
many
and sometimes, cruel
ways of the world
They look to us as leaders,
although we are often younger
in years.
They are supposed to learn,
but more than once we become
the wiser.
We are supposed to give of our
knowledge,
but often we take more than
we give.
We smile and lend a hand
to those who touch our lives—
for truly these are God's
special people.

Karen Hintze

BEYOND LOVE

I look into your eyes. . .
And,
Without a single touch
I feel the softness of your
fingertips
tracing the silhouette of my
curves.
My slight move. . .an invitation
You accept and follow.
Our bodies become one,
as if molded for each other
by the precisioned hand of the
sculpturer.
I feel us begin to blossom
beneath our warmth.

Growing. . .reaching.
Bursting with the fulfillment
of sharing one another.
And,
even the words,
"I love you."
Could not add more strength
to the splendor of the moment.

Patricia A. Bringman

WARM. . .

Warm. . .
A feeling, creeping, crawling,
slowly—
bringing a hush to the day's
cares.
Wanting, hoping, knowing it's
there,
secure in comfort hiding away.
No one can touch me, harm me.
I'm warm and safe, sheltered and
loved.
Bleak cold wind can't take it
away,
cold, harsh words don't make
the feeling stray.
Separated, apart, I feel it still—
ever present, always there,
standing by my side.
I feel it, what you bring into
me.
Melt me, mold me, make me

your own.
Warm, so warm, safe and secure.
Warm, I feel so warm.
Warm. . .

Sally Love Saunders
GRANDPOP JOHN'S FUNERAL
Life is a painting that the
artist works on.
Only when he dies is the
composition finished.
Now this artist has put his
brush down
and stepped back.
We gather to admire the work
and to enjoy
the beauty of Grandpop John's
life—
Vivid colors of love
Strong brush strokes from
a sharp mind
We are here on this day to
Celebrate his Life
A beautiful work of art.

Margie W. Grant
THE CRUXIFICATION
Up Calvery's Mountain
on a bleak and dreary day,
Struggled our blessed Lord Jesus,
Along the dusty way.
Up Calvery's Mountain
Along the dusty road,
Stood crowds of weary people,
Watching him carry his heavy
load.
Oh! Jesus, Son of Mary
What were your thoughts
As you carried your cross,
On that dreadful and dreary day?
Did you think to ask for mercy,
As you slowly struggled along,
Did you cast your eyes upward,
To see the blue skies above?
Did your childhood and
last days on earth,
Open before your eyes?
Did you ever say "What
wrong have I done"?

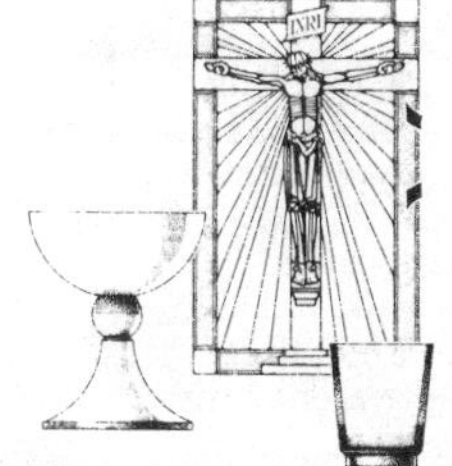

Did you think of your Mother;
The sorrow and the grief.
Did you ever see your father,
Josep weep?
And there was Mary Magdalene,
Could she bear the grief?
Oh! Blessed Lord and Savior
What were your thoughts
on that dreadful and dreary
day,
As you carried the old
Rugged cross along
Calvery' way.

Beverly Jean Stovall
PLEASE SUNRISE
I must find a little peace
whether you're friend or foe;
And enjoy this thing once
more that makes me feel aglow.
So here I am again,
here to see this lovely sight;
and bask in the silent beauty
of this thing that is the night.
Mysterious is the aura of the
rising moon and the dew is like
silver on the glistening lawn;
And though I've lived my life
in the shadow of gloom, they
say the darkest hour is just
before dawn.
A falling star makes
iridescence of the dark blue sky;
and I wish for the right way to
put my soul at ease:
And I hear myself crying,
though not knowing why, oh
please sunrise! Please. . . . . .

Suzi Jones
SOAR
Suspended eloquently,
Upon dawn's sweet day
An eagle now soars
To capture his prey.
The heavens rumble;
The sky turns grey.
Be not the soaring
Eagle of prey,
But the eagle that soars
Upon dawn's sweet day.

Denise K. Anderson
THE LAST TRIP
Gazing out through soiled
panes.
Longing, waiting, patience and
hope.
Seeing only dirty needles and
twisted veins.
A deteriorated mind from
merciless dope.
Grasping, reaching out and
pushing hard.
Agony and terror grip the night.
It's almost as if time has ended.
Turning its eyes on this ungodly
sight.
At first it was just a game.
One for all and all for one.
But somehow, now, things are
not the same.
At one time it was a lot of fun.
Screaching and screaming;
clawing at air.
Only to find that nothing is
there.
Hunger, sweat, vomit and hate.
Please, God, tell me it's not too
late.
Speeding, rushing, the heart's
beating faster.
Soaring high and the pain is
unbearable.
Need something quick or I'm
not going to last.
Anything, please Lord, I'm about
to crash!
Now. . . . .Silence and Peace.
The heart has no beat.
As a perfect equilibrium seems
to pass,
And things begin to cease.
What could have been beautiful,
No longer exists.
Is death more cherishable than
life?

G. Lloyd Helm
UNTITLED
Men of adventure all.
Mouldering in places they want
to be.
Painting pictures, great and
glorious,
Mouldering in places they want
to be.
Dreaming dreams of what they
would do
If only they were free.
Free of love and warmth and
light.
Free from smothering weight of
wifely love,
And comfortable ruts
Which they themselves have
chosen.
So lift your cups and drink
To the man of adventure,
Mouldering in places they want
to be.
Drink your toast to the dregs
For mouldering men like me.

Norma J. Townsend
A THANKSGIVING PRAYER
Thank You, Father, for Your care
In keeping us strong and true
Thank You, Father, for letting us
share

Our bounty that came from
You
Thank You, Father, for those we
love
Whether near or far away
Thank You, Father, for Your Son
above
In Jesus name, we pray.
Amen

Pauline Cousins
RETIREMENT?
When we retire we hope
to be like gypsys, wild and
free
and roam the world
and see the things we often
said we would.
Maybe live just for ourselves
and leave behind our cares;
close the door on yesterday
and open up tomorrow.
We'd like to do all those things
but, of course, we won't.
We may leave the snowy world
of winter
to bask in some eternal
summer
or rest a while beside the
constant sea
to hear the rushing waves,
or watch the mist dance
lightly in
and lose ourselves in mystic
dreams;
But the chains that bind
are strong and ever pull us
back.
These links are forged by
strength of choice
and we'd not break them if we
could.
Though we may rail at life
and wish it changed,
I doubt we'd change one little
thing,
even if we could.
These binding bonds
we have fastened round about
us
recount the dreams and hurt
and joy;
recall the good times and the
bad,
bring us joy and smiling
memories,
remind us of the fragility of
flesh,
make the past a quiet haven
and fill the future with
anticipation.
So, though we say we're copping
out
that's not really what we
mean.
Just a little time for quiet
retrospect
and we'll be back to claim our
world again.

Daniel C. Kechel
TO LOVERS
There are four billion people in
the world—
Longing, loving, hating, dying. . .
But, suddenly one night,
And only for a magic hour
There are two!
Yet, everything that's real or
beautiful
Is in their hearts.
For love can multiply—by
billions, or
by stars, or eons,
Or human lips that press in one,
warm, wordless ecstasy.
And, then and there, the sword
of beauty, power, and life
Bestows its blade upon the
shoulders of a man
And knights him prince
Of all the reaching realms of
being,
And slave to only one.

S. Darrell Smith
FADER BERN
Standing gallant against time
itself
Winds blow at my frame
Heaven rains its bitter cold
The sun its parching rays.
My bones dried and weathered
gray
Tattered broken fading fast
I still strive to fulfill my task
By sheltering those weaker than
I.
Days march on and nights pass
by
Nowhere can I go to rest
This is my last testimonial
But not my last breath.
Some may die a blazing death
And leave behind a charcoal
skeleton
But not I, house of grain and

store
I'll live on if but only in the mind of man.

Chet Gerstenbluth
JUDGMENT DAY
When I am laid to rest,
How shall I be judged,
By my deeds of last,
or
For all my acts past.

Robin McCleery Shelton
DRIFTING THOUGHTS
The houselights dim
Soft music begins
A whirling parfait of faces
Serene looks of faraway places.
The ring of moonlight widens
Tempered only by Father Time
The elegant perfume of pure wisdom
Thereby giving our reasons a rhyme.
Summer sulks gracefully in her hollow
Winter scornfully takes the reigns
Our days are shortened, our temperance measured
And our dreams, as a picture, remain framed.

Blondena B. Brannon
PEBBLE PATH
We trod the pebble path,
You and I forever more.
'Twas here for you and me,
For every one to see.
But life got in the way,
'Twas but for us to say
Too much of this or that,
Not for just one combat.
Now leave me with love's regret.
But tomorrow you will forget
Not me in those little ways
That only life too good repays.
Memories that cannot be taken
Although everything else forsaken.
Goodbye, my Love. I hope thou hath
The smoother part of this pebble path.

Jill Womack
FUN FOR A SPIDER
Creeping and crawling up a silk thread
Is a black spider with a bright orange head.
Suddenly he stops and peeks around
Then for a quick ride he
s
l
i
d
e
s
to the ground.

David W. Bosen
SEAL BEACH SUMMER
It was early, so far and clear;
I sat with friends, alone—
The misty, palm tree fog and beer,
An epitaph to the gray horizon of stone.
And tears of sorrow fell by the rotting pier.
Then, the rhythm-pounding waves of steel
Glided in and out, touching quiet
Like the gypsy island queen's pet eel.
And there was only one sun and one heart to riot
Over injuries of jellyfish, pebbles, and pretty Jill.
And as I stared into the wispering dawn,
Two black eyes hovered over the sorry sea.
Eyes of vision, eyes that search a cemetery lawn
For past memories of a golden age when we
Were younger without worries like a spotted fawn.

Rebecca Jacques Britt
LOVE AFFAIR
For many years the world has kept my secret
As I stealthily rise to greet her at the dawn,
While others in the home are still in slumber
I meet her in the shadows of the lawn.
And we have slipped away in morning hours,
Our annual precious rendezvous to keep,
While inebriating elixer of the flowers
Shrouds us in their misty fragrance deep.
The joys I've known with her I could not measure,
While with her I've kept our secret tryst,
And in my heart her fragile charms I treasure,
Not one precious moment would I have missed.
The mocker sings and the red bird blushes
As I gently hold her hand in mine,
For they have known the poetry of her kisses
Whose nectar is as sweet as sweetest wine.
In my heart I know that there are others
With whom she shares her irresistible charms,
But I so easily forgive her infidelity
When I hold her gently in my arms.
And though with passing years my hair turns silver,
And Time has slowed the tempo of my step,
Her loveliness ever grows from year to year
As in eternal youth her beauty is kept.
And long before I tire of her presence,
I hear Time's gently ringing bell,
And while from my reaching arms he pulls her
She bids a loving fond farewell.
And now the whole world knows my secret,

Shall I continue to seek her sylphid charms?
I hope that ever while on earth I linger
I'll know the joy of April in my arms.

Margaret L. Packer
DOWN AND UP
I get discouraged as I see
The bills come on engulfing me
I struggle and plot to find the way
Each and every one to pay.
Just when I think I see the dawn
The sink plugs up, the car breaks down
The typewriter, will not work aright.
It seems there's never any light.
The money stretches just so far
And then it's gone, so I must jar
My savings loose to fill the space
Of unpaid bills. It's always "Race
To try to catch up or stay in place"
The blues sit on my head and cry
"No success for you no high
Of sweet celebrity and rank,
No money piling in the bank.
Your talent is just not that good
Or you'd be published understood
And valued in the writer's world.
The puny efforts you have hurled
At editors. Works thought so fine
But each brings "Thank you. We decline',
Or 'This we think is really great
We'll publish if *you* pay the freight'
Or 'Don't send us the book you own
We only publish authors known.' "
Just as I think I've done no good
In all my life or ever could
I get a note quite suddenly
From son or daughter praising me
And realize no fame can crest:
"I love you, Mom, for me you blessed
By care and love through all the years"
My heart is happy and the tears
Of joy are mine. I'll find a way.
Things will work out. The bills I'll pay.
In these sweet ones of love I find
The real success in life is mine.
P.S. Margaret L. Packer is the mother of two adopted children. A daughter at four days and a son at five days.

Eugene O'Keeffe
SUNRISE
The hellish ball returns,
bearing its promise
of another endless day
or so they all seem.
It slays the gentle night
and sears my very
soul, tormenting me with thoughts
of lives once touched,
of loves once known.
I am devastated
by this pain within
my heart. It has rendered me
unwilling to live
yet unable to die.
So try to douse the fire
with rivers of my tears
is all that I can do
as the minutes turn to years.

Lynda Lewis
UNTITLED
My rose, you
The sterile stem, I
Without you
I am alone
unbudding
Unable to bloom.
A single, sterile stem
In a decaying
Garden of
life.

DeAnn C. B. Hopkins
UNTITLED
(A Shakespearean Sonnet)
The trees on mountaintops sway back and forth,
And as I gaze my thoughts depart asunder,
I start to wonder of their size and worth,
Then suddenly the skies begin to thunder.
I can't believe that this is happening
For a short time ago the skies were blue,
An instant burst the heavy clouds shall bring
So unrehearsed as carefree birds which flew.
I saw the raindrops fall upon the ground.
The small transparent couplet drops of wet,
The pitter patter makes a pretty sound
To this experience I am in debt.
I feel renewed and joyous deep inside,
The skies indeed have right to carry pride.

Opal G. Whitley
SYMBOL OF LOVE
There is a story about a cross
The symbol of our greatest loss
Our father gave his only Son
Whose life had only just begun
His life was short and very sad
He bore it all to make us glad
Lonely paths his poor feet trod
His only way back to God
Father have mercy on these, he

said
Who placed these thorns upon my head
For Sinners I die here on a cross
Thy love for them shall not be lost
His life he gave, this world to save
Friends laid him in a borrowed grave
An Angel rolled the stone away, he said
"I'll come again on judgement day."

Juanita W. Saunders/Imani Kuumba
KIDNAPPED
Kidnapped!
In the very early stages of innocence.
Brought!
To a strange hostile land
Robbed!
Of our ethnic identity.
Stripped!
Of our cultural background.
Our proud Black heritage
RIPPED OFF!!!
By the Man. . .the Oppressor
The Capitalistic System that churns away
On the flesh and bones of Third World
Brothers and sisters using our blood as
Fuel for its dynamo.
Exploiting any ideology or concept that is not its own.
Brainwashed!!
Yeah, we been had.

Had and swept off our feet into doing unreal things.
Like innocent sisters bogarded by slick pimps into
Those mean streets to keep their action going.
Like pushing poison to the people.
Unreal action of a very real people.
But, these are only minor examples of exploitation.
I am talking about exploitation of the highest degree.
By super, super powers who use minds, wills, and strengths
Of Third World People to build citadels of oppression.
Yeah, We been had.
Had for over 400 years.
But a whole lot of folks been had.
Wherever rich lands are populated by darker people
Folks been had. .
But. being had is only a temporary state of being
A state which can and must change.
As we move in oneness
As we struggle for self-determination
And lay the seeds for true change,
We will be Had no more!!!
A change will come, a change *must* come!!!
People, EDUCATION is the answer.

Douglas C. Allen
RONDELE
There was a time
a hundred-thousand years ago
in those forever summer mornings
those one-hundred hour days
when I was young and happy
I was happy as young
flip-flop heart-turns in offbeat directions
on a late spring green cool day
when I was forever young and sunny
life was ever a bud in bloom
pine-scented wanderings of purposeless purpose
needle-crunching meditations underfoot
when I was king of a world apart
I was young and rich and free
excavating the fresh dirt earth
in search of the worm's eye view
of the world
a world that was Columbus untouched
when I was my own famous explorer
I was a dreamer with vision
young and young and solitary
wandering through in chiaroscuro silence
in those forever wonder days
of always
when I was young and magnificently untouched
fortressed in the awesomeness that was
those days are returning
after many a thousand-night of heartache
after a rape of innocence that never was
(but was nonetheless imagined)
when I was but a fleshling
inhabiting an unfamiliar world
roundabout returning
the cycle does move in circles
and I am emerging more complete
in this wide-eyed adult-ed phase of me
that I find is me
is as cool and green and
of those one-hundred hour days when
I was young and away
in that pastel time of innocence
at last
the explorer has discovered

Neola Webb
CHARACTER BUILDERS
Tests of faith and courage, are
Revealed when big illness comes
Our way.
Unwanted changes may prove to be
Blessings in disguise.
Loved ones die; fire, flood, wind, devastate.
Each ordeal refines a person, as
Silver is rubbed to beauty.

Raymond D. Christensen
GARDENS LIKE EDEN
Standing at the top of some spiritual mountain
Giving nourishment for new life to broken down souls.
With eternal traditions of bridling their passions
Saints form and maintain individual fashions.
Without looking for fortunes or fame
They tend the earths gardens and harvest the same.
In justice they trust in faith they will conquer
Until the destruction of Earth will prosper no longer.
With faith in destinies of Gods distant places
The love in their hearts is set onto their faces.
Without looking for fortunes or fame
They tend the earths gardens and harvest the same.
Thus every person in righteous condition
Can share the great strength of the Lord
And curtail perdition.
The Master of the vineyard
stops the buckler and shield,
Love is the fountain irrigating the field.
Without looking for fortunes or fame
Saints tend the earths gardens
and harvest the same.

Joseph P. Catallozzi
UNTITLED
Spent many years upon this ground,
old tree, of tarnished brown,
outstretched arms into clean air,
warming in the sunset's glare,
Till one night the clouds crept in,
misty cold, very grim,
Rain tore off your tarnished sheathing,
stopped your rhythmic breathing,
Now you are dead, dead as can be,

old brown, tarnished tree.

Beverly Eugene Carlson
SPRING GARDENING
I was tending my garden on a sunny March day.
The air was cool from a gentle bracing breeze
As it stirred the trees along fields and highways,
Sending a message that spring is here if you please.
The wind seemed to say in a whispering song,
Wake up all of you flowers and trees,
Winter has been here far too long.
Put forth your buds and leaves without fear of a chilling freeze.
Each year nature has a cycle to renew,
New plants and other species must replace the old,
Nourished by the sun, rain and the dew.
They flourish in the summer warmth and go to sleep when it is cold.
I see tender shoots pushing up and growing stronger,
Every day some new variety begins to show
And the pace quickens as the days grow longer,
Oh how the rain and sun makes them grow!
A few short weeks of spring season
When all of nature is drawing its energy from the sun.
Nature gives us all good reason
To pause and reflect, living can be fun!
I look around me and suddenly become aware
Of all the brilliant colors in the flowers of spring.
When only a month ago the ground was cold and bare
Now all of the birds have begun to sing.
The breeze whispers little secrets of Gods plan
To continue to furnish us all with a livlihood
And make a place of beauty for every man,
Gardening makes it all so easily understood.
The fascination of growing plants turns work into play.
I like to check all of the plants and flowers,
Watching them devlop each passing day.
It gives me a sense of direction in all of my waking hours.
Of all of the plants that grow in the garden soil
One can find beauty in almost everything.
It takes only a little daily toil
And encouragement by the sun, rain and winds of spring.

Rebecca Arlene Clukey
TO BE. . . . . ME
I can look into a mirror see the face I want to see
There appearing for forever is a picture of me
Truths I find there as I look so

earnestly
Are the truths of a person I
refuse to be
Look so closely, open wide your
eyes
See beyond the reflections into
your lies
Your not the kind of person,
who's likely to tell
Your only a mirror image of a
half-empty shell
As your thoughts are so you
will likely become
An image projected; A star or a
bum
Thinking thoughts of a self-
positive note
But the mirror soon tells me
who am I to gloat?
Running around in circles, a
day full of despair
Dreams, goals are all puffs now
in the air
The other ones the better; the
joke is on me
Cause I looked in the mirror
and saw what I refused to be
I can stop all the lies, no use
to pretend
The answer'll soon be out, it's
coming to an end
I used God as my protector too
long now I know
I've got to answer to myself
wherever I go
Build a wall full of posies;
a castle in sand
Paint pretty pictures now
aren't they grand?
Colorful stories I'll tell to
anyone
But the darkness does follow
the setting of sun
I've cried in my pillow, a lesson
to share
And I've smiled to my neighbor
who only can stare
Each days a challange to end
my quest
Of a self-asserted being in a
little nest
The lesson's now easy;
boredom's a bore
It deadens the heart and cuts
right to the core
Tell me my friend, where do we
go from here
Sit down beside me while I shed
a tear.

Loretta Gray

POETRY

Blunt, stark, naked
It comes
Shivering in the sunlight
Stripped of old cadence
Robbed of full music
Black on white
Smelling of ink
Wielding belt
A punch between the eyes
Soul song
In edgeless art.

Bertha F. Weber

HISTORY IN 1981

A woman rose to Supreme Court
Justice
She is Sandra Day O'Connor.
The national debt rose to its
"Mostest"
A trillion plus dollars.
A "first class" stamp rose to
twenty cents
Can't write letters—must pay
the rents.
The Medfly stirred up a great
big mess.
Controller's air strike is
anybody's guess.
The "cuts" and the "budgets"
caused much stress.
The M-X missile, bomb and
bombers, still in press.
The sale of AWACS to
Saudi Arabia
approved by the Senate
With 52 votes for, and 48
against it.
The 1981 World Series ended
after six games.
The Dodgers beat the Yankees
and won the
1981 World Series with fame.
The attempt assassinations of
President Ronald Reagan and
Pope John Paul
Stunned everyone; it was such a
close call.
Then the assassination of
Egypt's Anwar Sadat
Astounded and shook the entire
Nation a lot.
NOW! How will it all end
In peace, war or what?
Wait for events in 1982.

Patricia A. Daley

BEING

Being—with you
Sunshine and Sadness
A glow of affection reflecting
the beauty of sunset
the awakening of sunrise.
Conscious of the atmosphere
around your being.
Strength.

Pleasure and pain; tenderness.
Touch.
Seeing.
Able to perceive your whole
Trying to understand
the ecstacy so intense.
Feeling, sharing.
Understanding.
Being—with you.

Paulette Bridenbaugh

HIDDEN FEELINGS

Why I hide my feelings
I will never know
No matter what I do
They're hidden from all view
I try to reveal them
But, shy they remain
So, by some small action
Or, by some little deed
I let them sneak past me
And reveal my inner being.

Christina Yanis

SO YOUNG

It was a warm September day
and
She was sitting among
The flowers so gay
I couldn't help but stare
For she had a certain glare
There was laughter in her eyes
And when she said hi
The sweetest smile I've ever seen
Came across her face
The wind in her hair
The birds in the air
Made a beautiful sight
Right in the sunlight
And she walked
With charm and grace
Her slender body
All covered with lace
She was so young
A vision so fine
No one was to know
She was going to die

Alexander Teglas

A WOUNDED COUNTRY

I get a sore—nobody cares?
I get a pain—nobody shares?
I open my heart for you.
I wave my flag and sing my song
with you.
But it still hurts—I feel that
way.
I know my wound—just give me
time.
I put my hand on my heart and
say these words:
"God Bless America—I love you
all."

Judith Pike-Boos

VANTAGE POINT

When Jude was young,
still at the mercy of the miller,
she wondered what to teach her
babes
so they might cope with life
in hard or brittle times.
Assured their time was running
out,
she settled for the P,C,B's,
on how to be Polite, Candid,
Brave.
Now, no longer green,
Jude fancies she had taught
them more
for each—this day long
twenty—
is searching past the obvious,
the black or white of things,
responding to those spectral
hues
whose tints persuade this
vagabond:
Most things depend on. . .
point of view.

Rev. Aaron Walschinski

TELL ME

When crimson buttermilk
churns morning sky,
Tell me it's not time to die.
While nations dress in nuclear
arms,
Tell me we need not be
alarmed.
Where the noon sun smiles on
us,
Tell me no one should not
make a fuss.
What the good Lord has
wrought,
Tell me Satan could not have
bought.
Why is Life to a child so simple,
Tell me the milkway is not a
temple.
Whither does man travel from
here,
Tell me not to hold life so
dear.
Whether man will reach distant
stars,
Tell me it was not easy to
come this far.
Who can answer all these
quests,
Tell me I should not ever rest.

Michael Sean Eaton

LOVE IN BLACK

Love so strong,
Coming once a week.
Always want, never enough.
The sun makes them part.
Instant friends, so easy to make.
The 'One night stand.'
No surprises, nothing new.
Stare at her
And then her body,
Think about the latest deed.
The morning isn't fresh,
Just worn and dull.
The cigarette is out.
Their love has burned away,
It was so strong.
Not one good-by.
Not one thing matters.
The wooly taste.
The taste of love,
Love so Black.

Sharon L. Dischinger

COLLISION COURSE

Somehow your world and my
world collided and became
one,
And as we merged, we saw only
the roses and the sun.
The rainbows were glorious, and
the birds sang their song of
love.
And while we were looking
down, the clouds were
gathering above.
The roses lost their fragrance
and began to wither away.
The rainbows faded, and the
birds sang less each passing
day.
And suddenly the worlds we
had joined together split.
Each went our separate way,
waiting for the next hit.

James I. Pringle

GOD'S PRESCENCE

The wonderful works of God's
true love
Has shown itself to me
I've seen it all throughout the
day
In every rock and tree
It seems that he has just
reached down
And touched this beautiful
place
And shown us that he can be
real
With all his glory and grace
He has come down into our
midst
To show us in every way
That to us all he can be true
So we won't be led astray
He sent his son to die for us
So that we might be saved
In doing this he's showed his
love
By the road of life he's paved
I'm glad we came to see his face
Descending from the sky
He's shown his love in every
way
And through him we must die

Sam Maropis
INJUSTICE
Don't see nothing wrong with slavery
Don't see nothing wrong with tyranny
Don't see nothing wrong with inhumanity
Don't notice injustice till it happens to me.
Don't believe in capital punishment
But when my kin's killed, I want electricity spent
Everyone on Death Row has my mercy
Don't notice injustice till it happens to me.
Don't see nothing wrong with nuclear energy
It never happened to bother me
Three Mile Island didn't awaken me
Don't notice injustice till it happens to me.
Don't live my life in misery
Don't cry when I see someone hurting
As long as problems stay away from me
Don't notice injustice till it happens to me.

Byrdna F. Northcote
CHRISTMAS ISN'T OVER!
Christmas isn't over
Just because the day is past;
The feast is done, tree is down,
And the mad, mad rush is past.
The ornaments are put away,
The tinsel has been thrown out:
The carols do not fill the air—
But there's no need to pout. . .
For Christmas isn't over—
It's true spirit I declare

Shall linger over all men,
For God's love is everywhere.
He loves us, oh, so very much,
that's why He sent His Son.
And that's what Christmas really is—
God's love to everyone.
To keep Christmas "alive and well"
Is up to you and me;
So we must let His love shine out
For all the world to see
No, Christmas isn't over,
Nor ever will it be,
For it's the love of God my friend,
Expressed to you and me.

Jane Ippoliti Arthur
TEARS
Tears are silver drops of rain
Drizzling down my window panes,
Spilling over lids and lashes
Falling to the floor with splashes,
From their source within my soul
They empty forth my storage hold,
Until from pain I find release
Or else the tears will never cease.

Becky Davis
MY FRIEND SUE
We are always laughing
In everything we do
We have many good times
Together, me and you.
You listen to my troubles
For days and many hours
You have a sweet heart
That never ever sours.
You never tell me lies
You are always more than true
There's not another Sue
That's exactly like you.
You make me laugh
You give me advice
You're just someone different
That' really, really nice.
When something goes wrong
You are always there
You help me so much
In showing that you care.
I hope you're always happy
I hope we're always friends
Cause the good times keep coming
And our laughing never ends.

Lauren Gwen Stimler
THE GAMBLER
He enters an arena
of green velvet sky
diamond-studded dice
plastic discs of fortune;
Fifty-two years of age
decked in white tap shoes, leather hat
shuffling along wooden planks
dealt to random casinos;
His home is a favorite wooden stool
chafing his hands with lucky breath;
The mind of a machine
that feeds upon three oranges a night
and sometimes leaves hungry.

Jean Layer
A LOVELY LADY
You gave birth to me
To start at the beginning
Your care never ceases
Your kindness always winning
When troubles and sorrows
Have come my way
Your thoughtfulness and understanding
Saved many a day
Ready with a helping hand
Always there when needed
Giving me good advice
But sometimes gone unheeded
You'll always be the grandest
My friend and my mother
You're one of a kind
There could never be another

Bertha Powers Woods
THOSE AUTUMN LEAVES
The balmy air had turned to cool,
Then cooler yet as fall seemed near.
We scanned the heavy laden trees
And eagerly looked for hues of reds and golds;
They'd soon appear.
Then frost with it's shimmering delight
Silently painted each leaf with icy white.
Only then! Oh the miracle of it all,
We see the colors!
From green to brown to brilliant bronze,
It was fall!
Yet, now where are all those fairy leaves of gold?
They've wafted their way onto our lawns,
Content with wind and bitter cold.

Geneva Doris Dabney
DOWN THEN UP
Alcohol, cigaretts and dope,
Foolish hearts and full of joke,
Repentance is the only game,
Being baptised in Jesus name,
Serving a good and just God until the end,
Always and forever having a friend,
The only hangover you'll ever encounter,
Getting high and higher to the final counter.

Bernice Knoll
SAMANTHA
I answered an ad in the paper one day.
It read, "Please help this poor little stray".
I took one look at this haughty Queen
And it was love at first sight for both, it seemed.
It took a while for "Sam" to adjust,
But she needed a home and had to learn to trust,
She was afraid & shy & stayed for weeks in one room
Until curiosity took over and she began to roam.
She's black & tan and oh! so white.
With Angora added—a beautiful sight.
She sleeps at the foot of my bed each night
And this, I find, a real delight.
Now after a year, she is shy no more.
I never know what tricks are in store.
She rules my home like it was her castle.
And makes it plain she wants no hassle.
She hits me every chance she gets,
For what reasons I cannot detect.
When I hit her back from time to time,
She looks at me like I committed a crime.
If you could see my cat named "Sam",
You'd have to agree she's the biggest ham.
She's cute & fresh & a spoiled little brat
But I simply adore that lovable cat.

Carol S. Shivers
WHERE HAVE ALL THE CHILDREN GONE
Silence—filters in and creeps
into each corner of the room.
Settles Uneasily—weary in unfamiliar
cracks and crevices.
Invited—but hesitant, not having
visited this house before.
Cautiously taking its place—where
children's laughter once rang out.
Echoes of quarreling—childish bickering,
ending in shouts and tears.
Echoes of sharing—whispering secrets,
amusement and conspiracy.
Music lingers—faintly in the air;
loud, unintelligible lyrics floating in space.
A stray tennis shoe—forgotten in haste;
alone in the back of the closet.
Undiscovered—even when occupied, too much
clutter surrounding it and other treasures.
Empty coke cups—ticketstubs and
programs from school events.
Scattered hurriedly—childish memories left behind.
The time for leaving arrived—
the last child old enough at last,
Follows her peers—
into the outside world.
To take her place, right or wrong,
in the destiny of maturing youth.
Silence—filters in and creeps
into each corner of the room.
Where have all the children gone.

Kathleen Groesser
HEAVEN ABOVE
Heaven above look upon me,
Protect us from what ever shall be.
Shower us all with all of your love,
Come to us from heaven above.
Care for the little ones so mild and meek.
They are the innocent ones so little and weak.
Let it be soon that you return,
We pray, let it be soon that you return.

Kiva JS Rice
SEA HAIR
Your hair falls like
a golden net
across your eyes,

snagged like blue
shells in a web
the air like ocean
surrounding you,
you float, your
hair like mist, swirling
around your face,
sand beneath the
waves,
you move—
a tidal pool,
alive with things
concealed inside you
full of teeming sea
creatures, your eyes
expand and contract,
hard and soft urchins,
exposed one moment—
hidden the next.

Norm Harvey
AMONG THE RUINS
The dreams that lovers wrote on cabin walls,
in makeshift hearts, in toothpaste, bootblack, ink,
"Trisha T. loves Artie C.," "Pierre
loves sixty thousand girls but mainly Jane. . ."
Not twenty years have worn away the words,
although the paint they're written on breaks up,
the wood corrupts, and weeds grow through the joints
to wreathe the fading hearts that hold them there.
Nor have twenty years of being read
quieted the tragedies we know
beyond these labored scribblings circumscribed
within their toothpaste hearts.
We read again
the trivial truth that every dream transcribed
on walls that rot must be more mortal than
the bootblack and the ink it's written with
and the wall it's written on.
And yet we know
the sting is not to learn again that love
erodes with time. We're much too old to feel
these tragedies of transiency for names
different than our own. But past these words
we read how dated lovers thought to cheat
some fleeting years, and so took chunks of hope
from present dreams and threw them out past Time
to search for their fulfillments sometime else. . .
And Time must have its moments when they come,
and have them fully, not with hopes excised
and tossed toward a future, leaving blanks
that steal from moments their proper eternity.
This sadness that we feel is not to know
that love erodes in Time, that dreams endure
no longer than the heat from which they sprang
and the grass they grew with. . . but that they were written down.
These fossils on the walls. . . these stagnant dreams. . .
they stay as if eternity could be
a thing enduring, a stasis apart from the flux
of temporal things, as if there were more than Time.

Betty Jean Lovelace
FALLING STAR
Across the eastern midnight blue
A ball of silver lightning

flew.
It came from whence I do not know,
And traveled west, a star in tow,
Its tail all sparkling silver white
A destination unknown by night.
Where have you gone, oh hasty one?
The race through time I know you won.
Your mighty thrust, to me, you show
In awesome glory, that I know.
To mortal man this is a sign
How small we are, how great the Plan
To guide us through this earth our own,
And yet not know what seeds we've sown.
In haste we run through life's degrees,
And hardly know just what we see.
Please slow us down, great silver knight
Help us to know the guiding light.

Diane Morgan
NEEDING YOU
A love song came knocking at my mind's door the other day and how do you prevent it from entering?
It flashes off and on at odd times of the day and night and it is always echoing your name.
When these flashes occur I wonder where you are. If you are thinking of me as I am of you.
There is pain all around me now and thoughts of you are all that keep me going.
You do not realize it but you are beginning to take possession of me.
My mind and heart are filled with you already, I am just waiting for the time to come when you possess my body also.
I hope I do not have to wait long because I cannot take much more of this pain around me.
Please hurry and rescue me.
If you are in any kind of trouble tell me now, do not keep me hanging here worrying and wondering about you.
I am here to help you, to take care of you, to console you, caress you, to love you forever.
I feel your presence even when you are not around because in my mind you are here, here right beside me always.
Do not let my mind keep playing these tricks on me, please come and take me away from all of this and love me the way I need to be loved.

Beatrice Skillman
LOVE
Love is grim.
Time nare beheld upon his mirrored face
The lines that love did etch.
They lie upon the heart and soul
Like veins for blood
Both hot and cold.
And the cheeks of love
Are stiff with laughter,
Gaunt with grief's surcease
From the brain,
While within the breast—
Marble, corroded moldy green,
Makes a sword's point jest!

Carolyn Marie Baatz
LYING WITHIN
The firey sun is fading away
The end of another empty day
I patiently wait your touch
I long for your loving so much
You walk through the front door
My heart falls to the floor
I look in your once wanting eyes
There I see you wear a disguise
Inside your loving I felt warm
Now our love has become a storm
I wish I could have your love again
You love another, now she's your friend
I could see myself being such a fool
Holding on to our love would be cruel
Your love was once so very real
Now for you I can no longer feel.

Norma J. Harlan
TIME
Time is the most beautiful
Gift we can offer a friend.
Time moves as a turtle for
The young and runs rampant
As we mature,
Until it soars by as on the
Wings of a bird.
Day and night mingling in
A twilight state.
It constantly grows in value
As we realize how much of it
We have wasted.
Time given to a friend is a
Sharing of a part of your life,
And in return, we receive a
Gift in kind.
Was time lost?

Susan Renae Aamold
IMAGISM
I picture myself walking alone along the beach, my shadow at my side,
The warm, gritty sand feels soft against my feet
The seagulls, so beautiful, soar through the sky.
The blue, raging ocean flows roughly to the shore,
The sun peers out from heaven's blocking doors.
The whispering winds breathe softly like a song;
it's music sends a chill through me,
This beauty and peacefulness is what I have longed,
My dreams of being happy I can see.
It's so clean and pure, like a new born child,
So full of life, like stallions running wild.
It's mysterious and dark, like a cave with no light,
And it shines like the beauty of a star-sparkling night.
No feelings like this could be for real as it seems,
They're only thoughts within my heart's longing dreams.

Herbert Harris, Jr.
SOFT, SAD WORDS OF GOODBYE—TO: J.
The soft, sad words of goodbye
Softly spoken
Carve a hole in my heart
As big as all forever
And resound with a mighty roar
Of pain, sadness and shattered dreams
And why goodbye
So soon my love
Our sun had not yet reached the peak
Of its possibilities
Why have you so lost faith in me
And in the spoken tomorrows
That now will never be
Was the reality
That we had created for ourselves
So devoid of joy, of happiness
And of hope
As to be suddenly
Burst asunder
By the clandestine sound
In your frightened ears
Of another's voice
Selfishly proclaiming
A new reality
With him instead of me
The soft, sad words of goodbye
Softly spoken
Take my breath away
And leave me quiet, still
And alone.

Wynona Francisco
THE PRICE OF PRIDE
Rejected; yet not forsaken,
I lie here close beside him,
I smile to hide the pain;
Laugh to ease the smile,
And all the while. . .
I go on needing,

I go on wanting,
I go on longing.
He doesn't understand
Why I smile,
Why I laugh,
He doesn't understand
My needing,
My wanting. .
And I don't understand why
I go on loving.
So I lie here close beside him,
Rejected, not yet forsaken,
Smiling, laughing, and
Trying so hard to hide. .
The needing,
The longing,
But, Oh, What a price is Pride.

R. M. Mischak
ON WHAT WINGS
When one lives in the beauty of dusk,
In the cool depths of summer earth,
The future blossoms in fragrance of despair.
When the scent of evening burdens the mind,
And shadows occupy secretive ways,
When the dust lies deadened on roads meandering
Under a momentary sigh,
The inherent apparition of adhering hours
Lingers near the signs of eternity.

Echoes in a far valley,
And dreams upon the wind,
Melted memories, liquid lines
Upon the shore of a forgotten dawn,
Entrapped in the twilight vapor,
Become silhouettes in the creation of the night.
Mysteries in the sky and death upon earth:
Lyrical departures from among the stones
Feebly fill a faded future;
Ancient fires and timeless thoughts
Slip past the inequitous brevity
Of an unawakened instant,
And dissolve solemnly in the shimmering glow
Of distant alien cities at sunset.

Christine A. Kish
AN ADVERTISEMENT
A paradise of glass and
Acres of fun for young and old
Which are tinted with brightly colored sand
and reflect the smiles of the bold.
This casual display of special effects
will surely attract everyone's eyes.
Thrills seen will not be hard to recollect.
You will possess tears as you hear laughter and cries.
Possible amnesia will block out the days before,
and another trip will want to be taken.
A souvenir can be bought and, therefore,
many young and old will be able to partake.
Even the aged people can have a ball (so)
Come one and all!
(To translate the object being explained in this poem, take the first letter of the first line, the second letter of the second line, the third from the third and so on. The object thus will appear.)

Louise K. Mathers
SCENE FROM AN EAST WINDOW
The impatient sun
summons a drowsy dawn
to wakefulness
with carillons of color.
Reluctant to leave
her purple couch of shadows,
she yawns and stretches
in slow motion,
bathing her eyes
in laggard dewdrops
with languid fingers.
Alert at last,
she dons the robes of day
and goes about her business.
(The moon, her vigil over,
dismisses the starwatch and
retires into pale reflection.)

Mary Jane Kissinger
YOUR BRAND NEW BABY
"Train up a child in the way he should go!"
I've a brand new mind on which
To write the Story of Life;
And a brand new heart that has
Never felt the passion of hate
Or strife.
My hands are new—they have
Never held a drink, a smoke,
Or a gun—
And these new feet have never
Walked to a wicked place—
Not one!
These bright new eyes have
Never watched the filth on a TV screen;
Nor have these tiny baby ears
Been soiled by the joke
Obscene.
These fresh new lips have never
Spoken a curse word or a lie—
My future is new; it depends on
You if I live, or if I die.
Yes, its up to you, my Mother
And Dad, what I can be, or I
May be;
The way you show is the way
I'll go—I'm your brand new
Little baby!
Tho' your baby grows like a
Precious rose, the seed of sin
Is within me,
So, in the "strait and narrow
Way" its important you begin
Me,
"Let the little ones come,"
Christ said—and it wasn't
"Perhaps" or "maybe"—
All born in sin, must be "born
Again",
And that's your brand new baby!

Robert Murvin
SHOUT OF SILENCE, WHISPER OF DEATH
The open seas feelings are felt within my bones.
I feel alive in her hands at times when I'm alone.
Her free flying waters arise to whisper in my eyes,
"Beware of my watery ways and listen for my cries,
For the mystical silence that seems so utterly calm,
May turn around and be crushed in my salt-sea palm."

J. Najah Gandhi Oldham, Ph.D.
WISDOM
What is Wisdom?
Wisdom is knowledge;
Gained by experience
And implemented by Love.
The Five Spiritual Paths of Life constitute—

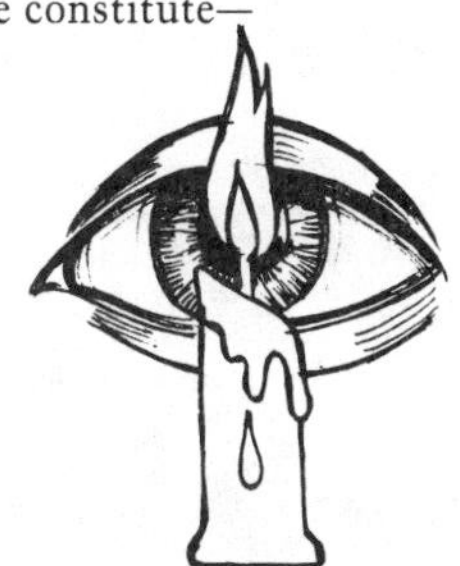

Love and Compassion;
Wisdom and experience
Kindness and understanding;
Joy and contentment;
Happiness and Bliss.
This helps man,
To live a full life;
Of the Eternal Now!

Cinda L. Sobanski
TRAIL OF TEARS
Troops moved into Cherokee country
in the year of eighteen thirty-eight
and in their merciless hearts
brewed the feared emotion, hate.
They built gigantic stockade forts
and gathered them in like cattle.
The Indians knew their fate was sealed
and they gave in without a battle.
The troops looked down into these forts
upon a people, proud and brave,
who lived in natural harmony
and loved this land they'd hoped to save.
But, no, this land was theirs no more;
the soldiers saw to this.
In the agony of despair
they knew this land was one they'd miss.
They packed up all their possessions
and piled them on their backs.
All they had and owned and cherished.
was stuffed in worn out sacks.
Then the troops moved them out
pushing them toward the West.
They traveled through the mountains
and seldom stopped to rest.
The trail of bodies that they left
was darker than the stormy sky.
The exhausted ones fell to the ground.
There they stayed, alone, to die.
On that lonely, desolate trek
babes rotted in their mother's arms.
Children aged beyond their years
and few were kept from harm.
Disease, thirst and hunger
killed thousands along the way.
But most died of broken hearts
with each new dreaded day.
Droplets crept sadly down their cheeks
and formed a reddened hollow.
On that trail of tears
may none again be made to follow.

Louise S. Jones
QUESTIONING
The worlds swirl with rhytmical notes, and God looks out from His throne. Over the sphere of endless space. Hears the thundering of distant worlds—Swirling in their orbits.
Could He hear the cry of a little child? Or listen to the groans of the dying? The lightening flashes across the sky, and thundering roars in the dark, the wind howls and and waves pile high ships go down and many die.
Does God hear when a little one cries? Or see the lone one struggle by. A fire sweeps through a forest tall, and the small animals scamper about,
Does He see?
What is His plan—
When a battle wages and a hundred fall.
Does He see at all?
A thousand stars in their course remain, and the sun still gives it's light. The night is dark and a star in flight flashes across the sky
Did He know?
What is His plan
How does He see when the night is dark? Or hears through the thundering worlds?
Yet the smallest child kneels,
Or the lonely heart cries out,
The anguish of the dying find solace in His love, and above the noise the smallest whisper finds His ear.
I know, for I've felt His care!

Faye Gordon—Hale
WHERE TWO RIVERS MEET
Early in the moon when the choke cherries are ripe;
into a quiet encampment
they did ride.
Their intent was not in smoking the peacepipe,
but rather to slaughter
those who did there abide.
Bugles sound charge while rifles shoot with deadly aim;
such an onslaught was

never before this seen:
For soon the whole camp was to burst into flame;
turning blood red, valley grasses that were once green.
The village before hand was filled with signs of peace:
serenity and calm did prevail through out.
Twas hard to believe life for some would soon cease;
with reason for not one to give rise to a shout.
Bodies strewn, now silent upon unfallowed ground:
a victory turned sour that had seemed so sweet.
Where once war would echo in reoccur ring sound;
the seventh soon met its biggest defeat.
Eternal peace for many was too quickly found:
in this spectra scarred land
WHERE TWO RIVERS MEET.

Celeste F. Plain

BLESS YOU, SIR

I passed with averted eyes
But the thin wail followed
Sing-crying, "Everywhere you go. . .
(Crowds were thicker than lies)
. . .Sunshine follows you",
Followed
Me down the morning street.
Slowing, I, with some inside
Response, turned back, went to
Her question asked in gray
And blue tatters, abiding
In tear-shrieked, bone-wrecked
Matter of a blind old lady.
Furtively, I stepped around
A watchfully so much dog,
And slipping a coin into the cup,
I found the siren mouth turned
Unholy on me. A sly wink clicked
From one white eye.
Like the nickle in the cup.

Louise L. Batto

LOLLY

The Christmas wreath still decorates
The wooden door to our house.
The fireplace holds the festive log
All is quiet as a mouse.
The candle dolly glows for you
Near the frosty—window glass.
The pine tree with some candy canes
Assure us that Christmas has passed.
But—didn't we have a heap of fun
When acting our best charade,
As we baked those luscious cookies
In your tea set Christmas day.
How I miss our sleepy kisses
And the ones I stole in the night
How I cherish my silent watch of you
Through the steal of Christmas light.
And now I must put away the frills,
The wreath, the tree, the candle dolly.
But Christmas love lives evermore
Because of you my "Lolly."

Marcie A. Wilmot

DEPARTURE

I know that day is coming
When you'll be on your way.
Will we have a future beyond that. . .
Beyond that miserable day?
That day seems like the end,
The doomsday of my life.
A painful, lingering wait
A wound from a sharpened knife.
I can already feel the pain
As it stabs my pounding heart.
I'm just a hanging board
For your aimed, poison dart.
When will this painful mess stop
Or has it not yet begun?
Are you also feeling pain
Or has our love just been fun?
Oh, how I wish I could know all the answers!
Maybe then this wouldn't seem so bad,
But all I can think of is the pain I'll feel.
All the pain, and grief. . .
It's so sad.

Louis A. Patimo

TO THE SOLITARY BAGABOND!

(The Voyage on the Moon.)

July 20, 1969, was the first landing, "Neil Armstrong".
In search of the fabulous "Enchantress,"
Deceived himself, do not meet, "The Beauty on Throne".
With sidereal young Queen, to get Marry.
February 5, 1971, was the date of big adventure.
So the long fantasy was realized,
The dream of wisdom, show the aspect,
To the Frairys and Wizards are vanished,
We are the Heirs, and the dream is't settled,
The event took place among the phrenetic—Hurrah!
The Uncle Sam arrived from America!
You felt shivering, after millenium of quite,
They played the golf, and few bombs was exploded,
The malvagity they shown, without "Pieta".
While you enjoying a serene life, they stabbed you in the back.
So barbarous you was caught,
You vagabond free-and easy.
From the harrid desert, that never blows the wind, Poor Moon, felt the fright.
That space someday required one by one,
So we have in future, the wars on the Moon.
Which strong man, should be in power, to give the permit,
For the conquest and the possession of love
When into solitude,
You look and tacit,
You be sure,
Never any more, you are in peace.

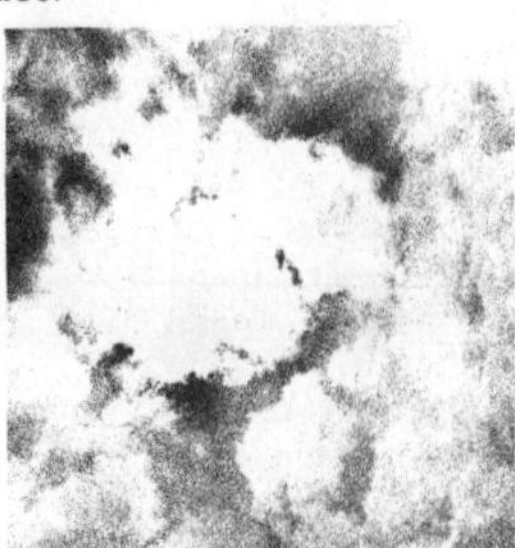

This isn't the rapacious turbulent man.
How you felt, with so dark a conscience
In that terrible moment of that days?
The beautifully sing and song were and are enchanted,
Into the sublime enthusiasm, dream of love.
And into the night, you look pure and godly,
You
parks, continue to spy.

Thelma Jo Bowling

WINTER

The icy hands of winter have encased the gentle evergreen in crystal gown
And placed upon autumns weary face a blanket of the softest whitest down
The gentle probing fingers of the moon find diamonds where yesterday was green
Now frozen grasses bow toward the throne where winter reigns supreme

Joseph A. Affholter

MALICE IN BLACK

Once upon a windswept night
when eternity was dim,
and the moon was suspended
on a sheet of cumulus grey,
behind the sooted fingers
which trigger the unexpected;
malice in black was born.
Behind its shield of dark, foggy mist,
its cape of bewildered excitement,
and the smell and the stench of which it reeks,
once again, like years before
the creation of life itself;
the malice in black is born.
Here to deliver the ultimate end
so the phoenix will rise from its dust,
in the years ahead,
like the ones left behind,
once again, like the time before,
the unchanging process proceeds;
and the malice in black will be born.
Behind his ever-restless disguise,
the one so accepted
yet feared for its ultimatum,
he receives what is deadly
and turns it to torturous death;
In his ulcerous centrifuge
is born the malice in black.
He strips of evil yet injects
it with sin
so that tenuous harm is removed,
and put in its place is terror
of which no asylum can bear,
and nothing is made to withstand;
his mo rose intuit ions succeed;
for he is the malice in black!

Mary Hattan Bogart

SYMPHONY OF THE TOOLS

Hammering, hammering;
Man building.
Child screaming amid syncopation
Of the driving of the nails.
Saws buzzing join the hammering;
Motor racing in the distance
Now crescendo,
Now diminuendo;
Shrill obligato of the drill.
Then again the theme repeated,
Hammering, hammering;
Building in a symphony of tools.
Rustling, rustling;
Nature answering.
Sudden sound of cooling breeze
Gently moving through the trees.
Cricket voices rise in chorus
As if awakened from their sleep.
Softly starts the mating strain,
Rising, rising as each voice
Joins in with mounting passion
To lusty, vaultless heights!
Then as if some unseen hand
With sudden signal
Lowered the baton,
Silence. . . . .Electrifying stillness!
Somewhere in the distance
Comes soft refrain of tree-frogs.
A blue-jay screams,
And a medley of birds join in.
Each singing his own different tune,
In heavenly harmony.
Cricket chorus joins again,
Rising, falling in rhythmic wave,
While distant echo-choir repeats
As theme comes in and fades.
Surely music so sublime
Stirs the heart
And soothes the mind!
Thundering plane o'er head
Drowns out the sound
Of Nature's theme.
Hammering, hammering,

Symphony of nails.
Motorcycle racing by,
Children screaming,
Dog barking,
Morning traffic thunders by.
Noise of man's creation
Drowns out the rustling wind.
The mating call of crickets,
And the soft crooning of the tree-frogs.
Even the jazz-band
Of the birds
Goes unheard amidst the clatter.
How rare. . . .
Are sounds of silence
In a mechanized world.
One stands in awesome wonder
In such a moment;
Like a bow-string waiting to be plucked.
Tense. . . . .expectant. . . .
The moment ends. . . .
The string is plucked!
Hammering, hammering
Syncopation of the nails.
Man building,
Planes flying.
Somewhere in the distance
A cricket sings unheard
Amid the symphony of tools.

Linda Rocklin

COOL BREEZES

Cool, cool breezes mingle with the sycamores,
Caressing their slender branches of life.
Whispering songs of silence through the air,
Refreshing the lives of tired youth.
Tempering the warmth of sunshine that grows,

With the resurgence of natures blossom.
Quietly swaying among fields of wheat,
Touching the seed of a new tomorrow.

Kathryn Steele-Fish

WATERCOLOR SMILES

I painted my smile
Just for you.
A minute before
The day had ended
The smile began to run.
The rainbow watercolors
Had all been wasted.
I missed you yesterday.

Dennis L. Ragan

SANTA CLAUS IN THE SKY

The little girl was all aglow
as Christmas Day drew nigh;
but her biggest thrill of all
was seeing Santa Claus in the sky.
Now her son, too, gets very glad
when Christmas Day draws nigh;
but what excites him most of all
is seeing Santa Claus—in the sky!

Ronald G. Asch

WITHOUT HIM

For we the poor, his name was magic
And for us still his death is tragic
We feel cheated by events
That transpired without consent
As though we had control of fate
and could wish the terrible mistake
to have never happened.
And now, in our middle years,
we realize our horrid fear.
It is too late, for days of yore
cannot bring back the man once more.
And so we live without his touch
that gave us hope and brought us much.
But to those of you who feel the pain
Have hope, for God will send him back again.

Etta K. Owen

DIRGE

I have the oil changed
While you lie sleeping
I savor all the daytime flavors
Then toss and worry in burning sheets
That you're held close by wood and satin
You do not feel your want of breath—
I do.
Who knows what you have missed?
Not you, but I.
Why this tearing grief
When it is spent for your truncated life?
Why do I keep the agony?
You do not know you have been cut short.

Larry McGinnis

WORDS

Words are the vehicles that carry ideas:
Select the correct mode of transportation;
The cargo will then reach its destination.

Gladys Myers Cornell

A CHAIN OF DAISIES

No hearts and flowers intertwine
A sentiment you cannot read.
To show my love I knew I'd need
A different sort of valentine.
No lacy frills around the edge
Of years began so long ago,
When vows we made and you said low
"My life-long love to you I pledge."
Within my wedding ring you had
Always engraved; its magic paired
Us for the many years we shared,
Hardship and sorrow, good and bad.
Thirty-five years—not a long span
For always, yet as our love grew
In sharing troubles, joys too,
It was as though love just began.
And now, my darling, you have lain
Five years beneath this towering pine.
For all the years you lived, were mine,
I bring you daisies in a chain.

Debbie Moody Sorcic

THE RAIN POURS DOWN

The rain pours down,
The music plays softly;
A dreary town—
But here I lie.
People running,
Splashing through the mud.
Are you coming?
The rain still pours.
I feel so sad
Watching dark clouds go by.
It makes me mad!
But the rain pours.
It isn't fair,
Locked up here inside!
But do you care?
Down pours the rain.
What is it for?
The pain I feel for you.
A knock at the door,
Now—pours the rain.
The rain pours down,
The music plays softly;
A dreary town—
And here I lie.

Zorida Saba

TENSION AND DIMENSION

Our life is in dimension,
I would like to mention,
Why at times we
Have a lot of tension.
At times we feel
Very high and sweet,
And times we feel
Very low indeed.
When the sun comes
Shining in our lives,
It feels so very nice.
Then the clouds come
With the rain,
And we start feeling
A lot of pain.
But with wisdom
And sacrifice,
We can stand with
Our head way high.
Let us not linger
With yesteryear,
But look forward
For a brighter year.
With love in our heart
And deep sentiment,
We can really make it stand.
I understand God will
Lead us by the hand
To the land of Eternity.

Charles W. Neathery

WHO AM I?

Sometimes I wonder just who I am,
Where I am going or where I have been
And who or what I am yet to be.
For life goes on;
The world keeps turning;
The sun rises—the sun sets
And life is not always what it seems.
And we live out our lives, in some reality
And in some dreams!

Dick Hackett

SPRING DEPARTMENT MEETING

Agony!
On a Sun
Sprung
Day to sit in a
Desk seat—lewdly littered with the day's graffitti—
Listening to the
Monotonous
Monotone
Drone of a
Bee Hive Hairdoed
Ed-expert
But,
Alas!
Non sex-pert

Donna Rish

MY LOVER'S DREAM

For you are a part of me,
I don't want to ever lose you
All I ask is to be near your side,
And to be my lover and my guide.
If we should ever part,
You'll always be in my heart.
But this is only a dream my love,
Because you'll be my only one.
Whenever I say a prayer,
You'll always be there.
To strengthen me and make me strong,
'Cause I can't go without you for so long.

Rob Ellenwood

BETH'S SONG

Each night in your bed you cry,
Still trying to believe that lie,
Your knees grow weak, you just can't compete,
With the hold he has on you.
I know how you feel,
I know where you've been
I know what its like, I've been there to
need someone to listen,
I'll be your friend.
You hang your head, an answer you seek,
Something to get you thru the week
It's hard to find, But just take your time,
An answer will come if you do.
The pain is still in your face,
This you just can't contain
A picture says a thousand words,
If it still remains.

Pauline U. Leslie

HOW I WRITE

Out of my hurts and misery
That is how I write.
For just as the dawn brings

sweet peace
It leaves life's horror for
the night.
I think of words that I can say
And next I make them rhyme.
Of people, places and beautiful
things
And tangible moments lost in
time.
I close my eyes and thoughts
run rampant
Like jumping sheep within my
mind
Small words began to take on
meaning
And then I form my humble
lines.
For that is what writing is all
about
To my simple way of thinking
To make a nectar of one's
thoughts
And fill life's cup for drinking.

Patricia J. Berg

ELIZABETH

Elizabeth is my youngest grand-
daughter,
robust, bubbly, and as full of
tricks as an otter.
Her shiny hair is very dark,
and her huge black eyes are full
of spark.
She's only two years old,
but for her age, she's very bold.
You see, she's had the love and
attention
of too many people to mention.
Tressa and Mark have been by
her side
and their love and affection
shows obvious pride.
Their name for her is "Lizard".
Heavens! It makes me think of a
gizzard!
Elizabeth has done her best to
compete.
The only time she slows down
is when she's asleep.
She's a doll, an imp, an angel
and a delight.
The days I spend with her are
happy and bright.

Kay L. Stumpp Shurtliff

THE GREAT ESCAPE

Separated by two feet of space,
filled with intruding TV set,
We sit, engrossed in fantasy
projected from a flickering
color tube.
I do not need Rod Serling
to stimulate my own
imagination!
I am projecting!
Please tune in on me,
and know I am a living,
breathing woman,
needing your love
and the embrace of your arms.
Unheeding to my thoughts,
you pay no mind.
With tears suppressed, mind
frozen
with new resolutions,
I leave you to your world
and step out into mine.

Dorothy M. Homan

I TOOK A WALK

I took a walk this morning
The paths were damp and
cold.
You were not at the other end
To greet me as of old.
When suddenly a bird flew
slowly by
As if he had been told
She is alone now and as I
Followed him in flight
He lighted on the garden post
He sat there very still
He cocked his head
As if to say
"It's all right."
When I walked back
It was once again
Darkest night.

Mary E. Klepinger

A MESSAGE FROM MARY

Take the best of what you have,
And the most you have to share,
Combine the two with
cheerfullness,
And seal it with a prayer—
Take your heart in soft
devotion,
Leave it where someone might
see,
Contentment in life's simple
things,
For thats' where it ought to be—
Take the strength that God has
given,
Just to you, and you alone,
Plant your faith where there is
sadness,
Bring your joy into your home—
Take whatever peace is granted,
As your treasure from above,
And enjoy it to the fullest,
By your happiness and love—
Take today is something special
For it shan't return again,
The gift of life is precious,
Strive to use it well-my friend.

Barbara D. Senger

FOREST LOVE

I went through the forest and
heard the animals talk
I started to run but they asked
me to walk.
This great big lion came up to
me
He said, "We're your friends,
don't you see."
Then the frog croaked, "We
won't hurt you.

We just saw you crying and
looking so blue."
He asked, "Won't you tell us
what is the matter?"
Than along came a tiger and
everyone scattered.
The lion said, "Don't worry.
I'll protect you from him."
He pointed to a tree and said,
"Climb that limb."
I said, "I don't care if I am
destroyed.
My love is lost and there's
nothing left to enjoy."
"What's this" roared the
lion, "You've lost your lust
for life.
How can one man leave you to
such strife?"
The tiger walked over and said,
"Cheer up dear.
We're all your friends, why not
stay right here?"
"But I have no house, no place
to call home.
And even with all of you I'd
still be alone."
"Oh no," said the frog, "Of
this I can assure you.
Just kiss me once and see what
I'll do."
I kissed him quickly as the
others gave a nod.
And standing in front of me was
my lost Rodd.
We smiled and laughed and I
started to cry
As we thanked all our friends
and said goodbye.
We stopped by a stream and sat
on a fallen log
And Rodd smiled and said, "Will
you marry this frog?"
We were wed in the forest as
our friends stood by.
And we promised to love each
other till the day we die!

I.B. Goode

BURIED TREASURE

another body,
innocently strains to live
within the bondage of liberation
created by a world gradually
raping the genius
of the will,
another body innocently strains
to live.

Kenneth N. Smith

SMITH IS THE NAME

When the Lord created Adam
and Eve,
Last names were of no need.
But after Cain and Abel's birth,
There was wide spreading of
man's seed.
That generation begat
generation
Is certainly not a myth,
But did you know 'till Noah
appeared,
All Sir-Names were Smith?
Well, after God had rent his
fury
With those forty days and
nights of rain,
Noah, his wife, and his children
and theirs,
Began making Smith's again!
T'would normally have been
dandy,
As Smith is a name to extol!
But they ran clean out of first
names,
And duplication got out of
control.
"Oh, Lord", cried the City
Fathers,
As they met atop Mount Ararat,
"Please help us in our dilemma,
It seems that Smith's are all
we've begat!"
A Booming Voice from the
heavens replied,
"The name of Smith *must be
preserved!*
BUT,—As each man sins let his
name be changed,
A punishment just and
deserved"!
That's how the names Jones and
Brown came about,
And why the telphone books are
full
Of the hundreds of Sir-Names
you hear today,
It's the truth! I feed you no Bull.
So,—when you run into Smiths
in the future,
REMEMBER,—They come from
a tall family tree!
They may be egotistical and
self-centered,
But by golly they're all STILL
sin-free!!

Bruce R. Lindsay

MOMENT OF A SMILE

As life gives birth to moments
To unfold the dreams we build
upon
Sustaining life thru memory
Certain moments will live on
I recall that very moment
As I first beheld her smile
And drawn as into slumber
I did linger quite awhile
And at this moment in my life
A dream I did embrace
That I might someday-be the
one
To bring that smile unto her
face
As moments then turned in
time
My obsession begain to grow
And in one trembling moment
I reached out-that I might know
As I ask to share a moment
My wish would come to be
Though awkward was my every
word
A positive smile-I did see

Jeffrey A. Johnston

MATCHSTICKS

I can feel its presence about me again, as if somewhere inside this vast void, two sticks are being rubbed together to create, what only feels like contentment.
Things fall in place,
or are they all put aside for some other time. I have felt the heat from only the sparks, and wonder would the flames burn me. Maybe so, but I know it will be another day, somwhere far down the line,
when only I will know for sure.
An occasional flicker of light,
warmth, contentment,
and all the other earthly, desires and answers, wrapped up in grandmother's smile.
Maybe sanity is what it's all about, a release to ease some of the bad, and place the spotlight on all of the good. If only I could conjure it up myself, but it comes and goes with the

breeze that no weatherman can
predict.

Jean Walker McCall
WAITING IN LINE
A world of people spend their
time
Waiting in some long, slow line.
Lines, lines everywhere you go.
You have to stand and wait as
though
There's nothing else you have to
do
Except wait until they see a
few.
No matter what your need or
cause
You always have to take a
pause.
Never can you go right in;
You have to take a seat or
number, then—
Perhaps they'll take you before
they close
If you're lucky—that's how it
goes.

Millie Rose
BEAUTIFUL FISHES
Beautiful fishes of the stream
and sea
Oh, how you love to be
beautiful and free
This is the way GOD wanted
you to be
Just swimming for love of
pleasure, so gracefully
How gracefully you look as you
swim to and fro, then away
Do you have love for life,
beauty and pleasure? yes I
would say
You swim for miles, you hurt
no one, you never scream or
yell
You are very graceful through
all kinds of situations, you
do well
So beautiful fishes of the stream
and sea
You truly are beautiful and
lovely as you can be
Oh, how grand it is for most of
you so beautiful and free
Still swimming for love of
pleasure so very gracefully
It does not matter just where
you are or where you may be
You are very beautiful and a
pleasure to see
Oh how graceful you are fishes
of the stream and sea
Just swimming for love of
pleasure so peacefully
Oh, beautiful fishes of the
stream and sea
I know how grateful you are
when you can be free
There is always hunters seeking
life of mortality to destroy
May most of you swim on
gracefully with love, peace
and joy.
Oh, how children love to see
you swim and play
They could watch you for hours,
then still hate to see you go
away

You bring pleasure to all ages,
people who watch you for
pleasure of their own,
Oh, beautiful fishes we thank
you for the pleasure you gave
and the happiness you have
shown.

Maria A. Blazyk
THOUGHTS
I thought you came to save me
From my sorrow and my tears,
I thought I could depend on you
To calm all of my fears.
I thought you would stay
forever
And we would never be apart,
I thought I'd never feel the pain
Of a badly broken heart.
I thought I'd finally get the
chance
To say someone's really mine,
I thought that we were ready
After such a long, long time.
I thought I'd always be happy
And spend my life with you,
I thought you would love me
back
But realized it wasn't true.
I thought about so many things
And I wished you were my
own,
But my thoughts were all in
vain
And once again, I'm all alone.

Johnnie Stevens Neterer
BEAUTIFUL SUNSET
The beauty of a sunset
A beauty that is rare
Is seen by many people
Every evening everywhere
But did you ever stop to think
Of the more unfortunate ones,
like she
The beauty of a sunset
Those eyes will never see
Do you feel sad—then don't
She has the Beauty in her soul
She sees the sunset when she
wants
The colors are magnificent
I'm told
She feels the magic in the air
This quiet time of day
Is our's alone to share
My wife and I, since May

Steve Lasky
I RECALL
Here old friends, let's drink to
the end a time that past away—
It was only yesterday that we
would play, but yesterday was
not to stay, we've gone our own
separate ways. So I promised to
call, but did nothing at all.
You know we've grown old, our
life stories been told. When I
saw you today, it reminded me
of another day.
So I couldn't find the time and
you couldn't spend a dime, we
were friends, but all things must
end. I find myself further and
further away from yesterday,
and I find myself with hardly a
word to say. But old friend, I
remember the hours we used to
laugh away. Now raise your
glass and drink to a time that
did not last. It was so good to
see you this day. But now we
must go our own way.

Thelma Louise Holt
YOU'RE ALWAYS PRESENT IN MY HEART
Hawaii was where I found love
with you, and though I've
roamed the whole world thru,
I can't get over loving you.
When I returned and you
weren't there, I knew your love
I couldn't share.
Although I've been to Rome and
then to old Hong Kong and back
again,
no matter how far we're apart,
you're always present in my
heart.
Hawaii was really blue without
you, it brought back memories
of the day that I gave you a
Ginger Lei, and the star—lit
night I danced with you,
beneath the palms when love
was new, closely nestled within
your arms, I felt the thrill of all
your charms. No matter how far
we're apart, you're always
present in my heart.
I longed for you in Lisbon town,
and cried in Spain as the rain
came down,
I recalled an Autumn day of
bliss, your loving arms and
tender kiss.
All the heartache I've been
through, has been because of
loving you.
No matter how far we're apart,
you're always present in my
heart.

Martha June Asbury
MOONLIGHT
Moonlight is what you are.
Fleeing, teasing, near yet far.
Brightly glowing, sweetly
flowling,
Full of magic, love lights
showing.
Untouchable. . .yet I touch you
And you move on unaware.
Moonlight through the trees;
Ever out of reach it flees.
Shimmering golden on the lake
And I enchanted can but take
A moment to enjoy. . .
Knowing this too will change.
Moonlight diamonds dancing on
the waves,
Sparkling, prancing.
I dip my hand into the deep,
Moving, teasing, away you
creep.
Some nights you are not there
And the world is empty.
Moonlight steady, quiet and
golden. . .
Reflecting back all my
treasured dreams.
Moonlight, I love you.

J. R. Wassell
THE VOICE
From lofty Alpine meadows
Across the plains to the raging
sea
A voice is earnestly calling
And it seems to be calling to
me.
One moment it is soft and
gentle
With descriptions of gardens
bright
The Next it is harsh as thunder
As it warns of eternal night.
One moment it is filled with
promise
As it tells of a Golden stair
Then it speaks of total
destruction
And the voice is filled with
despair.
It seems to be offering a choice
Of the pathway that is to be
trod
Could this gentle yet
thunderous voice
Be the homecoming call of God?

Robert E. Winter
ONE-HORN
The unicorn.
Free and running
like water in a moonlight
stream.
The unicorn.
Horn glistening in the starlight,
Shimmering in its power.
The unicorn.
Flanks glistening with sweat
From chasing dreams.
The unicorn.
Alone or in herd,
Watching the affairs of men.
The unicorn.
Forever aloof
While man goes his merry way
to destruction.
The unicorn.
Symbol of purity,
Captured by a virgin.
The unicorn.
Shedding tears of gold
As the hunter raises his axe.
The unicorn.
Free and running
Like water in a bloody stream.

Roland W. Newkirk
EXTINCT SPECIES
The old man crests the ridge.
The sweet-scented fragrance of
budding agaritas dulls the
stench of diesel fumes.
He eyes the clusters of white on
the hillside;
Telltale signs of a bountiful
blackberry harvest.
In the near distance earth-
gargantuans shape a new
community.
The old man sighs.
Next year another extinct
species.

Joyce High Dudney
BACK HOME
I love to go back home where I
was born and raised.
At all the country wonders I am
now amazed.
I love the grass, the wild flowers

and the smell of morning dew,
The frogs, the snails, the worms and bugs and snakes a little too.
I love the creek where we would go to wade on a sunny day,
The trees, the vines, the fishing pond and stack of new cut hay.
I love the land we farmed and even the old red mud,
The green pastures and the cows that chew their cud.
I love my Mother's cooking and especially her homemade bread,
The old house, the oilwells and the paths where ever they led.
I love my brothers, sisters, aunt, and uncle too,
But what I really want to say is Daddy I love you.

Karen S. Burnside

MELODY IN JUNE

Upon a bright midsummer's night
I lie awake, alone,
Across the peaceful lake I peer
All's quiet as a stone.
Then suddenly a symphony
Begins within my ear,
Without the aid of instruments,
With no mistakes to fear.
The snakes are slithering in the grass,
Bugs tap against the windowpane,
Some fish are splashing in the lake,
The frogs croak their refrain.
A dog begins to howl his song,
So lonely, long and low.
Young deer are drinking from the lake,
I hear it all below.
And every sort of creature
Times in just perfectly,
To put in song their feature
Of what's supposed to be.
The lights from boats of fishermen
Are spotlights for these stars.
The moon also is shining bright,
I see all from afar.
And as I watch and listen
To this melody in June,
I know that God's conducting
The awesome, splendorous tune.
And as the cows are driven
From the barn into the field,
I know what God has given,
And to peaceful sleep I yield!

Minnie Sodd

SWEET MEMORIES OF YESTERDAY

As I sit in silent wonder
And think of yesteryear,
A gentle sadness overtakes me
And I shed a silent tear.
This tear is not of sorrow
For years that I have spent,
This tear is for a life so blessed
I feel t'was Heaven sent.
As I sit and turn life's pages
Back to my younger years,
Clear visions of my childhood
Before my eyes appear.
I think about the happy times
When life was filled with song,
I think about the sad ones, too
When childish plans went wrong.
I think of the lessons taught to me
By a firm but gentle hand,
And as I face life's onward slaught
These lessons I understand.
I was taught to live by His Holy Word,
That love is a gentle thing,
Each moment must be lived today
For time is on the wing.
I was taught to count my blessings
Endowed by God above,
That a thing of beauty is a joy forever
To be shared with those you love.
As my thoughts drift back to the present
And my visions slip away,
I close the book on my childhood years
To be opened another day.
I know these days will be no more
As time must be on its way,
So I cherish and hold so dearly
Sweet memories of yesterday.

Philip B. Clayton

CALUMET

Let us venerate this ceremonial.
Smoke with us
from the reed.
Holy
the red pipestone,

holy
the eagles' quill,
holy
the hair of our women.
Here;
we offer our smoke
with supreme hospitality
to our
distinguished stranger.

Sharon Grammer Hanke

DISTURBED

On the other side of nothing,
Is a silver-plated wall;
That posesses strength perplexing,
Of the supernatural.
Oh, the palisade's persistant,
Though assailants may befall;—
'Tis a barricade contentious
Of the theoretical.
Lo, the mentors of the skirmish
All their weaponry install;
But the nemesis impugning,
Is the psychological.

Richard H. Nealey

THE LION IN THE LAMB

In this tight world of pressure,
Looking ever for the extra measure,
I sit and ponder at my leisure,
Should I kill just for the pleasure?
I look inside and see my spleen,
Unvented in all too many scenes;
Ever afraid to be wildly mean,
Brainwashed beyond their faintest dreams.
Nuns all in their celibate black,
Have taken the bone right out of my back.
I scream silently for what I lack,
Yet meekly occupy my small crack.
The mouse that will not roar,
Coldly burning to the core,
Pleasantness always in the fore,
Nothing violent, nothing more.
Too kind and gentle to ever proclaim,
The anger that burns me like a flame;
To want to hurt and more, to maim,
Yet holding in check, playing their game.
Will it ever in me be still?
The not-so-gentle urge to kill.
Seeking the ultimate for a thrill,
I think, but cannot will.
So the lion slumbers fitfully,
Deep within the heart of me,
While others all seem to agree,
The lamb is best for me to be.

Marie A. Olson

THANKSGIVING

God's hand tints the sunset
With its brilliant shades.
Forms the majestic mountains
And the valleys and glades.
Also, the lakes and rivers
The woodland and the leas,
The flower scented gardens
And the wide, shady trees!
His hand, guides the pasture
Where the cattle graze and rest,
In the yield of fruit and grain!
With which, He has us blest!
His hand controls the sky
And its great solar wonder!!
Guides the birds in the air!!
Also, the land, rolling thunder!!!
Nature's beauty is marvelous!!
And God's mighty wonder!!
May we always be thankful!
And His word daily ponder!!

Janet M. Lam

LOVE SOMEONE

(Dedicated to George)

Have you ever been asked,
Some time of the day,
Do you love someone?
Have you ever? Some way?
You stopped to think,
And wondered what to say?
Only maybe because,
You haven't today?
Did you say, "Goodmorning!"
"Hello, you lovely thing!"
Did you know words such as this,
Makes a heart sing?
Did you plant a tender kiss
Upon the cheek of your love?
Entering a room saying,
"You are lovely my Dove."
Did you make a phone call,
To lift a saddened heart?
Today was hectic!
Maybe falling apart.
Have you ever sent a flower,
To brighten up a day?
Just to say, "I love you!"
In this simple way.
Have you ever smiled at someone,
To show the sweetness of you?
The world is full of turmoil.
Loving's among so very few.
Do you touch your loved one's hand,
Showing the love within your eyes?
Or present your love with a gift,
Your sweetheart will idolize?
Give tenderness and sweetness in life,
To the one your closest to.
Today is the first day of the rest of you life.
Your loved one will always be loving "only you."

Hal Purdy

YOU MEAN SO MUCH TO ME

Sometimes I take you for granted—
the one I love most of all.
And sometimes I'll say (in a careless way)
words that I'd like to recall.
My heart is filled with a world
of regret—I hope you'll forgive and forget.
You mean so much to me.....
it's time I told you so.
But how can I say—
in an hour, or in a day
all that I want you to know?
There's no one else like you
to tell my troubles to.....
You're my only world—can't you see?
you banish all my fears
while you smile away my tears,
You mean so much to me.
I wanted you to know
and now I've told you so:
you mean so much to me!

M. B. Roth

ALL IN YOUR EYES

so mysterious in color
yet descriptive with every sparkle
your eyes draw my attention
towards you better than
the sweetest words ever could
it is more than immensely beautiful
the way you can carry on a conversation
with me without saying a solitary word
unique are your eyes
not for their color that
changes with the oscillation
of your inflections
not for their sparkle that
never ceases to shine
not even for the way your
eyelids with their beautiful

brown lashes outline a slim
shape that is so peculiar
but definitely for the incredible
feeling that shoots through
my entire physique
at any instance your eyes
desire to meet mine

Denise Bruskas-Gilbert

JEFFREY

If
I
were
to contemplate
upon the contents
of my heart,
You
would not only be
discovered as the
very essence
for my contentment,
but
the *only* conqueror
of
my
love.

Peg DesJardin

LOVE POEM

At first light of day, I feel
The nearness of you beside me. .
Feel your soft breath upon my
neck.
Know that you are curled in
warm
Contentment around me. . .
I lie in quiet happiness, just
Knowing you are there,
Not wanting to disturb your
dreams.
Then—I feel you stir, your
Hand reach out to gently touch
me.
I turn to meet your arms, to see
The love I know will be
In your slowly opening eyes. . .
Then find that I have crossed
That fine, thin line 'tween
Sleep and waking. . .
Have reached the bridges' end
'Tween reality and dream. . .
And you are not there. . .

Amy Hunter Hudson

THOUGHTLINE

If this is our future, sir,
then how shall we go?
soaring through the sky on
wings of eagles
or on our bellies across the
rocks?
It's a beautiful world, sir,
even though we've piled it up
with
metal bones, concrete caves, and
sucked its oceans dry.
Please, we only did if for the
betterment
of us, and oh, we surely are
better now,
aren't we?
We've built chromium minds
that can do our thinking
for us. We can transmit streams
of electrons through the air that
tell
us what to do, who to be,
what to wear. . .we have a
culture (as you willed it); we
embrace it.
This is good?. . we need to
know. . .
it must be good! We've fought
for it,
died for it! Sent out armies
winding
over the planet, swooping from
the sky
on anyone who would challenge
us.
Leaving them rotting in their
funerary foxholes or
bringing them back and
civilizing them,
whichever suited our purposes—
We would kill to protect
what we are! We would kill
to see that the rest of mankind
becomes the same!
Because you said this is what
everyone should be. . .
and we believed.
We've gone
so far
and destroyed so much
getting there. Please,
herald the horizons we
progress to in our flight!
Tell us one more time of
all the peaks we reach!
. . .we really need to know. . .

David M. Vize

FAR GREATER

Cherish the love that you give
to him
Respect the love that he gives
to you
For the love of two together as
one is far greater
than the love of one alone

Bea Greever

TO THEE, O LORD

To thee, O Lord.
To thee, O Lord, I sing a song
of praise.
To thee, O Lord.
To thee, O Lord, my song of
love I raise.
Your glory and your majesty
shine bright before my eyes.
My trembling heart and hands I
raise
the Lord to glorify.
The sun is high. The day is
bright.
My heart is filled with song.
The healing of an early Feast.....
my thanks to you belong.
I am able to do anything.
The strength you do supply.
This day I offer all to you.
My soul, You satisfy......

Maud C. Eyth

LAMENT FOR A SCHOOL

The schoolhouse stands
condemned, awaiting doom;
a ghostly babel—callow,
piping tongues,
gay, virgin laughter, mentors
exhortations—
floats, whisp'ring, through the
classrooms and the halls.
Then, cymbal crash of steel on
weathered brick;
old, battered walls, bowing in
slow collapse
and shattered, tinkling
windows dancing down
draw brown dust curtains on
the final act.
Ah, stricken marble in the
rubble heap,
1895 your epitaph—
how many children trod the
foot-worn stone,
how many children's hands
clutched rusting rails?
I pass this way again at twilight
hour;
now, over all, crepuscular
calm descends;
grave mounds of mortar, brick
and rivened wood
lie hushed beneath the dying,
dark'ning sky.
Tomorrow, not a vestige will
be here;
no marble, glass, no weathered
bricks, all gone,
bequeathing only phantom
fledglings' dreams
to haunt the lonely space
and barren earth.

Michael Patrick Szalai

DICHOTOMOUS MEN

Early in the morning in the
middle of the night.
Two dead men got up to fight.
One was blind the other could
not see.
So they chose a wooden dummy
for the referee.
Back to back they faced each
other.
Drew their swords and shot
each other.
A deaf policeman heard the
noise.
And he came in to console the
boys.
A court was convinced to
investigate the scene.
But it was too late for the
men,
Who remained embittered to the
end.

Donna Lee Morgan

DESERT SKIES

The desert skies may fool the
eye,
There're sometimes dull and
grey.
Behind the grey and floating
sky,
There will be a bright and
sunny day.
The thunder rumbles in the
distance,
You'll think the rain will come.
The sky lights up, then dark
again,
Where is my desert sun?
The evening comes still no
change—
We rest in the quieted night.
When morning dawns, the skies
are clear,
with not a cloud in sight.
The sun shines bright to burn
your skin,
with not a place to hide.
Where are those clouds we
thought so dreary?
Will they come to shade again?
Let the sun come shining
through-or let
the clouds be dull and grey,
I'll be happy just to know-God
gave us
another day!

Eveline Jill Billy

ROMANTIC FASHION

Stylish pretenders
A gypsy skirt
A peasant blouse
A pretty petticoat
Elegant lady shoes
Lollipops and roses
Bright hues
Cupid is on the scent
In the apathy of his twilight

Erma P. Whittington

CHRISTMAS

CHRISTMAS! That glorious
sound!
The time when love and joy
abound.
Hearts aglow with friendliness
And cheery notes of happiness,
Thoughts of Christ and
Bethlehem,
Wise men, shepherds, gifts to
men,
The Star's bright radiance above.
CHRISTMAS! EXALTATION!
LOVE!

Kathleen P. Bolte

HAPPINESS

Happiness!
Where is happiness I say!
Where shall I look tomorrow
For I didn't find it today.
How can I this bliss acquire
And raise my spirit to its' height
To which my soul doth aspire.
Joy!

Joy is happiness you say!
It is the elixir of human
kindness
Given to others in life's
highway!
'Tis a magic story to relate:
The more we serve it to others
Our own selves we intoxicate.

Mary Jane Ellsworth

NO, NO NOT THE SEA

No, no not the sea.
Don't take me to the sea.
Take me anywhere else.
Don't take me to the sea.
You know what will happen
If you take me to the sea
You know what will happen
At the sea.
It will start again
If you take me to the sea
You know what will happen
At the sea.
I'll die in your arms
Again at the sea
I'll die in your arms
At the sea.
You'll pour out the dark rum
The dark sweet rum

In the bed by the window
At the sea.
And I'll lose my life
Lost in the waves
In the bed by the window
At the sea.
It will happen again
I will die. I will die.
Oh, I will die in your arms
At the sea.

Rosemary Jordan
YOU AND I FOREVER
Love runs deep within my heart
In hopes that we will never part.
I've never felt this way before,
it's as if no one else exists.
And there's no way your kisses,
your touch, your warmth I can
resist.
Whenever I'm with you. . . .I
can't explain how I feel,
But it comes from my heart and
is nothing less than real.
It's you I long to be with
every second of every day.
To share what time we have
together no matter what the
way.
To feel your mouth, your body
pressing mine;
The love I have for you is one of
a kind.
There's so much I want to put
into words;
I could probably write a book.
Please believe everything I say,
cause in my eyes,
if you look, you'll see the
reflection of the man
I cherish no matter what he
may do.
Do you recognize him, my
darling? Of course, it's you.
I don't ever want to think about
that day
When together we can no longer
stay.
But if that day should ever
come,
That's when my life will be
done.
I hope and pray we part never
For it must be "you and I
forever".

Nancy Yeldon
TO THE ROSE
Thy petals of reddish velvet
glow
Upon your soiled bed you show
Thy beauty and thy grace of
thee,
A pleasure for my eyes to see.
An enchanting fragrance from
thee flows.
Into the wind it swiftly blows,
Whence the moonlight sky has
shone
Thou close thy blossom and
await for dawn.
Whilst cool breath begins to
blow
Thy petals wilt from the
winter's snow,
Thou shalt return again next
year—
Yet in my eye still forms a
tear.

Naidine D'Angelo
WORDS
messengers of our feelings
are the loudest when left
unspoken.

Dana Hahn
TOUCH POEM
Falling
Falling
Falling
Into l o n g
soft
Kisses
with
you,
Touching
and
Falling
Into touch
Into the purely tactual. . .only
And YOU
Falling
directly
Into me,
Like water
falls
Into a River. . .and becomes the
river
I want to keep
falling
falling
falling
And get lost
in the
Fall. . .

Marie Delucia Cormier
FOR CHERYL: On Her Seventeenth Birthday
If I could gather sunshine
I would wrap it in a star
If I could capture wisdom
I would travel near and far
If I could seal in diamonds
a love for you to keep
I would never mind the task
no mountains would be to
steep
But I am nothing more than
dust a simple mortal thing
And I have only my dreams of
you
And this is what I bring
A dream of Peace of Mind
A dream of Love that is true
A dream of health and wisdom
A prayer it all comes true
just mom

Daniel J. Nickelson
FALL IS HERE
The frost from night,
Turns to morning dew.
Another day,
So fresh and new.
The leaves will fall,
Before too long.
And then we'll know,
That summer's gone.
They were good days,
Every one.
We had a lot,
Of summer fun.
But summer's over,
For this year.
I think that fall,
Is finally here.

Joann Ivey
THE SAILOR'S BRIDE
She stood on the shore,
And watched the angry sea,
Afraid he would return no more,
Her love and life to be.
She watched the waves roll high,
And wash upon the sand,
As she stood under the stormy
sky,
And prayed for her man.
The salt of her tears,
Mixed with the salt of the sea,
As she thought of future years,
When with her, he might not
be.
She thought of his sweet lips,
Which to her he gave,
And that are more precious
than the ships,
That sail on the waves.
She begged of the stormy sea,
Which held his life so cheap,
To keep him safe and send him
back free,
So she would not forever
weep.
The restless sea,
was stormy no more,
After her heart felt plea,
And gave him safe back to
shore.

Christopher L. Queen
THE SEED
The seed is planted
The soil mixed with fertilizer
It's showered with ultra violet
rays.
The seed begins photosynthesis
The new life form a plant
breaks ground to meet the
Sunshine.
It feels a new, viabrate with life
The rains the life giving
substance
The care of that plant by a
human
The plant is given a name it
senses
The care the human has for it,
and
The talks to it making it
prosper with the entity of life.
My life
is that plant taken from it's dark
void
of embryo.
you mixed the soil of care
and sensitivity
buried me
deep within
your heart.
I met the warm smile of your
face.

Sharon Murray
NOW THAT YOU'RE GONE
You lean over and whisper, "I
love you",
But I can't lie and say I love
you too.
I struggle to find the words
somehow
To gently say I don't love you
now.
I can't find the way to tell
you why,
So I put it off and don't even
try.
Slowly I push you farther and
farther away
Until you finally go your
separate way.
I then realized how much you
meant to me
and the feelings I pretended not
to see.
I started to cry as it suddenly
dawned
That I love you now that you
are gone.

Davie Herndon
AUTUMN
Dappled shadows on the lawn
Bespeak a sunny autumn morn,
Time of day for certain told
By how much shade, how much
gold.
Not too long before it's noon,
Coming not one whit too soon—
Bearing out the sun's progress
As it moves on toward the west:
Trackless in the blue o'er head
Though footsteps patterned on
the dead
And dying leaves upon the
ground
As penetrating rays come down,
Push their way 'tween yet green
leaves
To form the sun's path through
the trees.
Fall! —a glorious time of year,
Whether sunny, cloudy or clear;
A brilliant display of God's
power
To substitute for summer's
flower.

Richard A. Pratt
IT SOUNDED LIKE THE SUN
I listened so hard for the phone
again today
and the doorbell
that I was deafened by
an ice cream truck
playing its dirge to the empty
streets
I wasn't even curious
I didn't ask
for whom it might have tolled
so thankful was I it rang

Susan Rusilko
SAD ENDING
A sordid old woman, lonely,
lonely,
withered and worried, boney,
boney,
Sits at her looking glass, drawn
by the past,
Vaguely envisions a love lost,
the last.
The gates are now open, come
beckoning calls,
Once familiar faces now ghastly
appall.
A sad sort of season, winter
prevails,
Cold and unwilling, imprisoning
jails.
Life's lights disappearing,
dimmer, dimmer
Groans from the graveyard,
grimmer, grimmer.
Slipping away, she clutches her
heart,
Now gone through the looking
glass, all is dark.

Carol Wilgus Fritz
MAGIC MOMENT
Whisper to me, words of
wonder,
Magic words that give off life.
Whisper to me that you love

me,
and that you want me for your
wife.
Say it softly, say it sweetly,
like the nightingale at night,
as he twitters to his lovebird
making everything delight.
Touch me, darling, as you say it,
with your hands, so strong, so
right.
Then I will try to say it my way
holding you all through the
night.

William K. Bottorff

THEN

Her a sparrow
then
When I found her
In a lilac cold
Saw her not
The growing time seek
Then
At frost oak
Her warm become
From in heart
Full for me
I had loved her small
Alone
Then
With her found I
Thrush
And love her large
To kiss and
Joining soar in
Sweetness singing
Soft two
Then
Willow
She is hawk
She lost
Above poor
Sparrow
Lilac me

Wells Freeman Garvin

GARVINIC TRIADS ON A STAR

From puny man, a star is free,
for that is the way
it was made to be.
Spinning thru the voids of space,
it deigns to ignore
the whole human race.
From whence it came, no man
can know.
To where it now is
we never can go.
We see it now where it is not.
The best we can do—
is say that it's hot.
It seems to move within earth's
sky.
For thousands of years
no man could say why.
Today with 'scopes and things
that fly,
astronomy says,
"It's more than sky high!"
Peering thru the dark velvet
night,
we see not a star,
but only its light.
So long as does its light persist,
we can "see" a star
that does not exist.

M. J. Lane

THOSE SHEEP

One sheep, two sheep, three
sheep, four. . .
There must have been a million
more,
As I lay there fighting hard to
sleep,
I counted all those silly sheep.
They didn't jump the fence for
me—
Instead, they gathered 'round to
see
If I would sleep!
Oh, those sheep.

Yala Korwin

LILAC

The purple goblets of spring's
lovely scent,
gathered in cones amid velvety
greens,
still brimming with joy of a new
beginning
cradle deep sadness of
predestined end.
In vain I am spying on the grace
so lush
of the dying bouquet in its
ornate vase;
poor shadows haunt the surface
of canvas. . .
I let slip down my defeated
brush.

Paul Reinertson

THOUGHTS OF LEAVES

Leaves fall like rain,
dipped in food coloring,
reveal what's above,
mask what's below.
Sounds are made to
match your mood,
a frilly skirt,
a snake, an army.
We put it there,
leaves cover it,
we wonder what,
we can't remember.
Kids and dogs love
piles of color,
romp securely in
the rustling womb.
Older people fear
what's underneath,
sharp stick or nail,
in natures' sheath.
We watch intently,
the reckless play,
was it fear or envy,
that found the rake.

John Mark Dubois

COULD IT BE IT COULDN'T BE?

Beautiful, the words that flow
As if by speaking they might
show
A feeling that would surely
grow
In sand as well as winter's snow
Yet there are those that live
today
Whose will to waste the world
away
Conceal the seed, can't feel the
sway
And always seem to have the
say
Of what is right, who is wrong
Soon their children learn the
song
Of predjudice, such blind
contempt
Which proves all dreams, aren't
heaven sent
Blackened, are the words that
flow
From hearts that peace would
never know
No feeling there could ever grow
Smothered by sand, frozen by
snow.

Debbie Anderson

WINGS OF LOVE

I've learned that if I don't reject
what I can't comprehend
The road of peace I search for
in the beauty of the valleys,
oceans and skies
Through all the falling
with my face on the ground
Life is beautiful as I learn and
grow
for I am who I thought I was
I am where I belong
And in time I will be lifted up
by the wings of Love
then in understanding
I will glow. . . .

Jeanette A. Ritzenthaler

TO AUTUMN

Ceres
Bereft of her prize,
The culmination of summer
skies,
She weeps.
She saw her own
Walk through a row
Of bursting tassels—
Through the row
And down the field
And down the way. . .
And Ceres thought
Of yesterday,
Of last year,
And the year before,
And all the years that lay
before.
At long last she tore
The ripe grain gashing,
The ripe fruit smashing—
Her own love dashing. . .
She weeps.
They should have made another
Ceres—
The heavens paused and heard
The wrath, the moans and
The grinding halt of the
spiraling seasons. . .
And tore her child
Ungainly from her cadenced
clutch.
Hell was spilled with sympathy
that winter.

Delma R. Gray

EVERYBODY IS CAPTAIN

I had swell sails set
On a model craft
Well out to sea
When I sent aft.
Leaving the wheel
To look for sport
I sighted a bar
And ordered port.
Then the bow
Began to list.
The top sail sagged,
The ribs to twist.
The bilge filled up
With shrimp microscopic,
The starboard light
Became myopic.
I got into drydock
A little late,
Was overhauled,
Signed on a mate,
Put out to sea
And that is all
but now and then
A little squall.

Jessica Van Hemert

UNTITLED

Rotan, lace and dried flowers
black, purple and red
Little old houses and dark
hidden castles.
Wondering in a field of lilies
and drinking water from a brook
Reading poems and thinking
about your beloved friends. . .
Where will they be?
What will they do?
When will I see them again?
Oh, rotan, lace and flowers
black, purple and red
I love, I love, I love. . .

Patricia Murphy

THE TRUTH

Though the world goes to hell
in a hand-basket.
And the stars fall from out of
the sky.
Though the ticking of time may
be ceasing.
As the Universe chooses to die.
I will lift up my soul to the
darkness.
At the mouth of the tunnel of
death.
And rush head-long into
eternity.
With my last agonizing breath.
For something beyond yet
within me.
Knows the truth that lies past
the vail.
That I WILL sip the Godly
nector.
From my Source in the Holy
Grail.

Cathryn Davis

FREEDOM

Sometimes. . .
When you are deep in the forest,
and you stop
to listen. . .
you may hear nothing.
I did once—
and, the fear of the silence
was beyond my reason.
So. . .I ran
I ran. . .
hoping to hide
(from that which was not there).
But, I could not hide
I found. . .
no matter how I tried—
At last, in my exhaustion. . .
I fell
and without listening. . .
I heard
the beat of my own heart.

Carol Ann Ranalli

COMPUTER: ELECTRONIC WONDER

The computer in our house
retains the seat of honor.
At night we gather 'round
and program it with father.
We feed it information
which we cannot retain;
It's memory is overwhelming,
responds much faster than my

brain.
The fact that I am human
puts me not off from this friend,
In fact, I have a lot of fun
playing cards and games with
him.

Nan Sherman
CHINA NIGHTMARE
It isn't fair!
I have—insomnia, constipation,
neck out of joint,
am covered with mosquito bites
while he sleeps dreamlessly on,
and on and on,
standing up, if necessary,
on trains, planes
nodding away, getting his forty
winks
while I remain wide-eyed, red-
eyed
throughout the 20 hour flight
and every night from then on,
clutching new hard pillows,
shifting from lump to lump
on questionable mattresses
in between the endless parade
to foreign bathrooms with
running toilets,
lights too dim to read by,
paper refusing to roll
and scurrying bugs—
while he sleeps gently on.
When I do doze off
my own heavy snoring wakens
me,
or the faint singing of mosquitos
carefully circumventing his bed
moving in on me for the quick
kill.
They wouldn't dare disturb his
slumbers!
Is this sex discrimination
even in China?

Edith W. S. Olstad
TILL I MET YOU
The world had been a solitary
place,
Beloved, till the day you came
along
And took my hand, for when I
saw your face
My heart stood still, and then
it made a song
Of sweeter rapture than I ever
dreamed;
I heard you speak, and sudden,
glorious spring

Burst 'round my feet, and when
you laughed it seemed
A million silver bells began to
ring
Through all the earth; and when
I felt your kiss,
O, then my soul had wings to
touch a star,
And soared to unimagined
heights of bliss
Rejoicing in the wonder that
you are. . . .
And as I see each miracle come
true,
I know I never lived, till I
met you. . . . .

Natalie Ferstand
NEWBORN
I watch her reflection in the
nursery window
As she watches her newborn
fast asleep
A look of contentment upon her
face
Satisfaction embedded deep.
Look what I created, she silently
thinks
Designated by a blanket,
whether blue or pink
A part of you, a part of me
A brand new branch on our
family tree.
And then she smiles at her
husband
The new daddy. . . . .ME.

Juanita Shedd
REFLECTIONS
A splashing raindrop
breaks the glass puddle. . .
fragmented face
A chill in the night
cooling the tepid waters. . .
fish stir in their sleep

Janet R. Aylward
TODAY, MORE THAN EVER BEFORE
Today I feel your nearness more
than ever before;
Your eyes I see more clearly
than ever before;
Your heart I feel more
lovingly than ever before;
For today we have joined
together as one.
Today my heart and soul have
come to know your heart and
soul; And today they shall
live more closely than ever
before.
Today the sun seems to shine
more brightly than ever
before;
The sky seems more blue
than ever before;
And today, the Lord seems
more near than ever before.
Today I have come to feel love
more than ever before;
For today I have found that I
Love you, Leo,
More than ever before.

Bonnie Bollman
A MOUNTAIN COUGHED
For months
They had said, "It's coming."
For days they said,
"Run for your lives!
The mountain,
Sleeping for years,
Is awakening."
Its bowels were rumbling;
Its sides shaking with silent
laughter.
It had tricked man.
Men who thought him dead
Had carved their homes into
his sides.
The gray old mountain yawned
and stretched;
Houses, built on old ashes,
Shook and trembled.
Still men clung to their
precarious nests.
He coughed;
Hot from his mouth,
The saliva trickled down his
sides.
He burped;
An avalanche of juices,
Long smoldering deep in his
stomach,
Came pouring out,
Boiled down his sides,
Covering giant, match-stick
trees;
Snatching at the heels
Of those pygmy-men
Running to escape his wrath.
Ah! 'Tis good.
The mountain licked his lips,
Gave a final rumble,
And, with a sigh of calm
content,
Settled back amid the ashes,
Surveyed the quietness of his
barren shoulders,
And, with a final grumble of
his bowels,
Fell asleep.

Dorothy Kole Mucklo
FEBRUARY
This is the month that holds a
lot in store
For it is the shortest one, until
Leap Year gives it one day
more.
The Groundhog peers out to see
his shadow
Foretelling six more weeks of
winter lore.
It is the month of LOVE, with
St. Valentine's Day of Hearts
and Flowrs at its core.
Birthdays are celebrated for two
Presidents—
Abraham Lincoln, who banished
slavery, and George
Washington, the Father of our
Country.
Though it has brought cold,
snow and ice, we still find it
tolerable and nice
For it is the prelude to Spring!
Need we say more? Perhaps,
but—
Let's banish the encore.

Russ F. Blazek
HIGH TIDE
High above the Angry Sea
the wind it blows hard and free
Pounding the white waves to
the rocks
then back and forth like the
tick of a clock
Each time higher than the time
before
letting loose its fearful roar
Then soft as a summer's breeze
it lays there quiet on the shore

Regina Fiorello
LISTENING CLOSELY
Sitting by the sea
listening to the waves breaking
on the rocks;
The whistle of the wind,
As I write my papers rattle.
The sounds of the seagull,
the buzz of a bee;
these are the sounds that
are chasing me.
I'm afraid of the silence, when
there's no sign of life around;
So I go by the sea to get high
from the sound.

Krichmar A.
I WAS A POET THERE
I used to be a Poet there
And here I lost my Poetry
But when I look around me
I see it grows again
In frozen flowers on the trees.
I used to be a Poet there
But here, the Forest kept my
dream
And my nostalgia is like a song
Blooming on every tree.
I used to be a Poet there
And here I tried to forget
I wanted to throw it in the
River deep
Within my sorrow, my
melancholy
And the River frozen by surprise
Strangely captivated my Poetry.
I used to be a Poet there
Submissive the River warned me
And in his flowing Song
repeatedly
Everything I kept asleep in me.

Ruth E. Hopkins
LOOKING BACK
Knowledge is where you find it
And dare to pick it up;
And if you've a mind to mind it
It will fill your mental cup.
But beyond the getting and
storing facts
There's a chemistry of the
soul
Which strains, reduces and
extracts
Some wisdom from it all.

Judy Gayle Harris
UNTITLED
If I were to start a search today,
and looked the whole world
through.
Nothing else could begin to
compare
to the love I have for you.
I know there are times I seem
hard
and you think that I don't
care.
But growing up is so hard to do,
it's really just not fair.
I realize how lucky I've been
to have a man like you,
To teach me about all the
things
that helped me as I grew.
Remember, that you've got my
love,
It's something you've always
had.
You'll always be MY sunshine.
I love you Dad!

William Robert Senter Jr.
WE'LL SEE YOU THERE
As he softly squeezed my hands
And looked into my eyes
I somehow knew
We were saying our last
goodbyes
And in the eyes
Of the one I held so dear
There was only a look of love
Without sign of fear
But I thought my heart
Would in a thousand pieces
break
For I knew
That it was ever so late
And that this little boy of five
Who had touched so many with
his love

Was ever so gently
Joining Our Father in Heaven
above
And as he relaxed his hands
And drifted away to the heaven
of blue
I could hear his love saying
I'll be waiting for Mommy,
Grandma, Melissa, Ellen, and
you
And with his departure from
this beauteous world
That we would no longer
physically share
I knew he could hear my heart
saying
We'll see you there.

Norma Horkey
UNTITLED
It's been a long time
since yesterday
and tomorrow is forever away.
Each moment is golden
yet wasted like paper.
If a smile can warm the heart
today
what will happen when all
happiness is gone tomorrow?
Awaiting silence is fear of the
future.
Live each drop of life as if it
will
evaporate
just as quickly as it was formed.

Evangelist Carol Raggi Schmeder
DIVORCE
When a young child begins to
cry, and asks her mom why,
what words do you say to
make her understand it's
the only way?
Divorce is never a pleasant
thing, it doesn't make the
heart rejoice or sing, but
brings, to all that it may
touch, heartache and tears.
Those around may say, "What is
the rush, can't you give things
a little more time and maybe
the sun will begin to shine?"
What words do you say to make
all the heartache go away?
How do you make a young child
understand that her father
won't bend, nor will he lend
a helping hand to let her
know there is no hope.
Only prayer can change the
moving of the tide.
What words do you say, when a
little child begins to cry, and
asks her mom again, but,
"Why?"
I had no words to say that day I
sent her dad away, for all I
could see were tears and so
many wasted years.
Now, as time has past, I am
thankful at last, if only for
my precious ones, my two
beautiful girls and one
handsome son.

Ruth Woodward Finch
THE SCARF
Your scarf is in the drawer
You gave it me some thirty
years ago
When we were young and free
I pick it up—it's lasted well
There's not a tear or shred
But you are gone.
I have a letter from your friend
You died a month ago
That's all he said
No mention of a how or why
I tried to find out more
And wrote imploring news
But there was no echo in return
Just silence—impersonal and
cold
Why is this piece of silk still
here?

Norma Kellso
LITTLE PIECES OF MY SOUL
Little pieces of my soul
Shaped and molded
Rhythm sprightly
Set upon the paper here
To make you glad
Little bits of joy and sorrow
Neat and tidy
Tied up tightly
They may stir your memory
And make you sad
Tiny portions of my spirit
Bravely given
Never falter
Keys to open shuttered hearts
So we can touch
Little pieces of my soul
Laid upon the public altar
Will you answer me in gladness
Or must I accept with sadness
That I ask too much.

Gerard E. Ide
INNOCENT
In our youth, we had a Love
Innocent, but Burning
as we grew older
but more apart
We moved on to other things
and each went looking
for other dreams
Each with other partners
but that was no reason
to stop loving one another
or stop the Friendship
within our Hearts
So Innocent
SO WE DIDN'T

Dale Richard Perelman
SAPPHO
In Lesbos, Sappho sang melodious panegyrics to the sweet accompaniment of the lyre. All Aeolis echoed her praise,

But all too soon, her visions darkened with age and her voice ran dry. Aeolis listened no more.

So blind and alone, she sank beneath a tree on a field of garlands and cried out to the great go Apollo to end her days.

D. W. Bailes
POSSESSION
The house stood in disrepair,
Waiting for us,
Needing a loving touch.
We knew we could live there.
The neglect was obvious:
The lawn overgrown with
weeds,
Vines entangled with the trees,
Which had risen, now tall,
unbidden,
Searching the sun
From the underbrush, hidden.
The structure of the house was
sound;
It needed a plumber, painter,
electrician.
The floor was sturdy,
The carpet dirty,
The walls a disgrace,
Having been subject
To a former owner's taste.
The house had possibilities,
still.
We bought the place.
The job of remending seemed
unending,
The cleaning a chore,
sometimes a bore;
Nevertheless, we continued to
paint, carpet,
Pile the trash, secure the sash.
Slowly, the house was
transformed,
The place was adorned;
New color abounded;
The neighbors astounded
That the once embarrassment,
Now standing serene, clean
Was the proud owner of its new
inhabitants.
Too tired for slumber,
We could only wonder
What had happened to us!

Shirley Davis MaGee
WHERE ARE THOU?
Oh joy, where art thou?
Oh peace, where art thou?
Oh love, where art thou?
Oh happiness, where art thou?

Oh wisdom, where art thou?
Oh prosperity, where art thou?
Oh victory, where art thou?
Oh God, where art Thou?
for my soul longeth for Thee.

Andrea Mondragon
THE BIRTH OF SPRING
Overnight it seemed
God's hand had touched the
earth,
For suddenly aware was I
Of some new birth.
Dark days disappeared
To unveil majestic scenes
Of sky so royal blue
And hills all robed in greens.
Birds chirped happily,
Caring for babes in the nest
While flowers danced gently
In the breeze, as in jest.
Death came to Winter—
It has had its final fling.
New life is about us,
Thank God—He gave us
Spring!

Kendra Monette
SMAUG*
You came once as a friend—
How easily hides the enemy
beneath your slimy skin.
You speak with sweet, innocent
breath
that burns like dragon-fire
in my ears.
I sit back,
Placently taking it in—
or so you think.
But I will find the
Weakness in Smaug's chest
and deal the final blow.
Then you will know—
I am no thing for you
to crawl on,
to push around,
or control with your false smile.
I am me, and
I will be
FREE!
from J.R.R. Tolkien The Hobbit

Helene Suzanne Pomeroy
NOT QUITE PLEASED
Disappointment and some resentment was what I thought I needed to feel against you, in order to understand it all. . .

But I feel quite light and even easy, I think that you are okay, and that your intentions are well-meaning, yet misproportioned. . .

You are mixed-up about your true self and I am glad that I did not fall in love with you. . .

I feel a little sad for you; you are all alone, without even a drink to share. . . .you have the potential for providing friendship, if you cared to, or if you could keep your ego from always intruding. . .

You still watch t.v. past midnight; I guess it served your purpose well. . . it kept your interests undisturbed, where I had always blocked your vision and put your view into an angry and defensive position. . .

You are abstract to me now, I can laugh and talk with you, but it is empty and our fears, or laziness, prevents any solid form of discussion to take place. . .

I had tried to promote intensity, but your blank thoughts prevented us from getting to really know each other. . .I know now how uncomfortable it made you; however, you never really realized my frustration. . .

But that's okay, 'cause I'm only a little sad for you, and not quite pleased, that we couldn't find half a chance. . . .

Mamye Fairley Richards
CRY, FOOL, CRY
This old world is not sad
enough
Broadcast your troubles
everywhere.
Tell each friend, enemy and all
Don't tell your happiness, tell
each care.
No one but you has troubles
Make them help you with your
share
Make them feel sorry for you
always
Try and make them from your
sorrows fare.
When you find a friend who
looks happy
Go to him, fool, and cry
Make him the most miserable
creature on earth
Then forget your troubles and
tell him goodbye.

Think of it, fool! It's not fair
For you to be with troubles
alone
Tell your loved ones when they
look gay
Tell them with a sigh and a
moan.
Always let your friend be
happiest
When you tell him of your
melancholy days.
It seems to make him more
miserable
Try it! You'll find it will work
always.
Now don't forget! Tell your
troubles
Tell your troubles 'til you die
Make this world a miserable
world
And cry, Fool, cry.

Gladys Louise Holcombe

LITTLE BROWN SUGAR

Little Brown Sugar, I still miss
you,
And remember everything
about you;
That October day when you fell
out the
Back seat of the car
And I didn't know.
On down the road I kept going;
Then when I missed you,
With a lump in my throat
I went back to find you.
Joy filled my soul when I saw
you,
Then called you.
My arms outstretched, you ran
fast
And jumped in them;
Then "scrooched" up real little
Like a tiny little ball
And lay close up beside me
So you couldn't fall out again.
Then summer came:
And that July day,
When I found you unconscious
Beside the mail box,
Right after you went across the
street
To visit those other little
dogs;
Tears filled up to my ears;
But I couldn't cry, Little Sugar,
Yet I buried my heart with you
That day, Brown Sugar.
Buried my heart with you
When I covered you over;
Out behind the old house;
Covered you over with white
sprinklings.
Flowers and grass grow there
now, Sugar
Another lump comes in my
throat
When I see it.
If Daddy had been living with
us
When you were here
That would have been great.
He would have loved you,
loved you,
'Cause he really loved little
dogs!

When the earth quakes,
And the mountains shake,
And the Great Judgment
Morning dawns,
And I don't see you there,
I'm gonna ask Jesus to raise you
up,
And little Missi, too.
She was like you.
She's resting now,
Beside the cement tomb,
Under the trees,
Beside Rose's house,
Down in Cheraw,
Where we lived that time.
In the Earth made new
No cars nor trucks can
Run over little dogs.
There'll be no night there.
We can play all day;
Play with the lions and tigers,
And ride the elephant's back.
And like it says in Isaiah 66
We will all go up together
To worship our Creator
Every new moon and every
Sabbath Day.

Carla L. Falco Sawyer

SILENT STRANGER

The circle is complete
The finality calls no second
curtain
Flowers fill no void
I walk alone
Feelings inside. . .
Stir the remains
I felt your pain
I sensed your presence
My eyes were open
But I could not see
All that had affected me. . .
Sentiments put to rest
Expressions that carried love
We did not welcome you
Yet you knocked at our door
One precious has left us. . .
And death marked its' scar once
more. . .

Thomas Szell

SAY WHEN

Hot, golden, velvety steaming,
sliding into white porcelain tea
cup, — say when —
pouring time, effort, relentless
dreaming.
It is time now, or condemned for
waiting, for today, tomorrow, or
forever distant, dodging darts of
peril, pulled earthbound,
malignant, climbing, clawing,
pleading, hurting?
— say when —
Is it time now to stop, for
replacing the burden, or to
change course to avoid the hard,
sullen face of defeat, retreat?
Hot, golden, velvety steaming,
sliding through life, propelled by
unknown forces.
Say when!

Ruth Whitfill Brand

YOU SAID "I LOVE YOU"

You Said "I love you" and the
day which had been gray
became a fantasy in pink and
blue.
You said "I love you" and my life
which heretofore had known
such strife took on a peaceful
hue.
You said "I love you" and blue
birds sang and chiming bells
rang out as if on cue.
You said "I love you" and my
silent heart awoke with a start
and whispered, "I love you, too."

Richard M. Coffman

NEARLY MAN

You appeared as the blood of
stone,
A tendrill of sun, aglow with
grace.
Poor creature, a wisp of hair and
bone,
You seemed, suddenly, all flesh
and rage.
And no one asked you for your
name,
Or how you came to be here at
this place.
Sun-blossomed, you were
searching for the stain
Of love's inevitable malaise.
But, how could you have blasted
The only womb that made
you,
And seared love's fruit with
your unerring gaze?
I hear you screaming with the
same animal dumbness
You denied,
In your greenest, primordial age.

Mary Anne Rose

THE LITTLE PLANE

There was once a little plane
that was most unusual.
Do you want to know the main
reason it was different?
Well, this little plane has a
heart.
Its heart was the man who flew
her.
They were never for long apart;
they flew together nearly every
day.
When they were in the sky,
it would seem they were one.
Flying up so very, very high,
then swooping down again.
They had, oh so much fun,
just flying round and round,
everywhere under the sun;
way, way up above the earth.
It was a very sad day
for the little plane
when the man went away,
never to fly her again.
The little plane was never
the same again.
She had lost her heart forever,
when the man went away.
The man was really never
quite the same either;
for he had lost forever
the lovely little plane.
No one will ever really know
all that they shared.
And it should be so,
love, is after all, a private
thing.

Fillmer Hevener, Jr., Ed.D.

MAN (JULY 20, 1969)

The spider clung to his walnut
stem
But dreamed of spanning the
meadow stream,
To explore a walnut on an
opposite limb.
He thought and drew and shot a
team
To investigate the outer rim,
Before he laid the final beam.
In time he reached the walnut's
sod
And set a banner to mark the
race
When the spider proved that he
was god—
For having spanned this inch in
space,
Had he not gained the
sceptered rod
And nullified the Maker's place?

Candace B. Mach

LOVING YOU

I am grateful to you
For the part of me
That you bring out,
Only the good and never the
bad.
I am proud of you
Not only for what
You've made of yourself
But for what you're making of
me.
I love you
Not only for what you are
But for what I am
When I am near you.
I love you
For helping me to
Make out of the timber of my
life
Not a shack, but a temple.
I love you
For helping me to make
Out of the deeds of my everyday
Not a scolding, but a melody.
I love you
Because you have done so much;
More than any other person
Could have done to make me
good,
To give me a reason to live
To make me happier than ever
before.
This love you share is
matchless,
You've given it
Without a declamation,
Without a single utterance.
For you have done it by just
being yourself.
I suppose that's what
Being friends means after all!

Bill Newsom

KILLING IT

You're probably wondering
what happened to my
love for you
since you were last
overwhelmed
by its high passion
I beat it to death
against the brick wall of
my sanity
I raved and paced furiously

threatening homicide
and consumed the hearty nectar
of liquor stores
to drown it
I screamed morning
and evening
to exhaust it from
lack of sleep and
after driving it insane
I stood on my rooftop
and hurled obscenities at it
until I was hoarse
I abused it in bed
with relentless demanding
fantasies
requiring it to perform
again and over again
until it lay lifeless
I raced it down the street at
dawn
Outdistanced it
I lost it in a cloud
of misty reflection
Surprising it from behind
I stoned it until
I heard its bewildered
bewildering
death rattle
strangely like my heart beat
The long and furious battle is
over
And at last my love for you
Has left me alone
At last alone
Thank God
alone

Jenny Carner Zimmer
SAXAPHONE SOLO
Notes drifting slowly upward,
like a lazy curl of smoke.
Not hurrying,
yet struggling to dissolve,
in the ultimate height of
nothingness.

James Alan Davis
THE SEED
The seed burst forth
with a thousand unfoldings
forevermore filling
the unborn sky
all within a flower
sealed within an eye
to all of life a root and seed
as all the days go by

Thomas Mann Selkirk
ELIMINATING THE POETIC SNORE
This poem's in a format never
done before
In poesy's 4,000-year history
and more
And 'twill be lauded by people
galore,
Who, surely, ne'er dreamed this
was in store,
Shore to shore, to eliminate our
common bore:
The poetic snore!
Which, needless to say, we don't
adore.
Hence, 'tis time that we explore
This thing's quite awesome roar
to the core—
Let's kick it out the door,
Lenore!
As if, when on a tear, we tore.
As in the Ark did Noah.
Which we, assuredly don't
deplore
Till we're sore, because of gore,
in every pore!

Clarence E. Leet
BEAUTY DEFINED
Beauty is only skin deep
Most people say.
But the Meaningful Thought
Got lost on the way;
Because Beauty begins
Under the skin.
In the Soul and in the Mind
That is what makes people kind.
So look for the right type
Of Beauty my dear friend,
And You'll be happy
Until Life's End.

Don "Cody" White
STILL I FEEL A NEED TO CRY
Still I Feel A Need To Cry;
Even after all the years of
vain attempt
At becoming a man.
A man doesn't cry.
I heard that somewhere.
Where?
Was it from lost generations of
the bold and free?
Or was it something I heard
from inside of me?
I don't remember.
Still I Feel A Need To Cry.
I feel that way sometimes.
I feel that way now.
O, but could I only shed the
taste of one tear,
It was here.
It was here a thousand times. . .
The feeling;
But it passes like the wind
passes over a leaf;
Like the wind passes over a
tree;
Like the wind passes over the
earth;
Aw, the feeling passes. . . . .
Yet again. . . . .
Like the wind. . . .
It comes and then. . .
Before I know it. .
It redescends.
And,
Still I Feel A Need To Cry

Theresa Ann Lauer
CHILD
CHILD you are so precious,
with soft hair and pretty eyes;
When I hold you in my arms I
wish you to always be this size.
CHILD for you are of my flesh
and blood;
It is I that will teach you good,
and give to you my love.
CHILD when lonely and full
of fear;
It is I that you should come to,
and I will wipe away your tear.
CHILD if you are ever
confused, and your mind is in
doubt;
Talk to me, I will listen, and
try my best to help you out.
CHILD you are growing,
learning new things, and
through your eyes you are
seeing;
So when you make a mistake, I
will always try to remember
that like me, you are a human
being.
CHILD you are a person all
your own, you are so special to
me;
Promise me that our love will
grow, and spread throughout our
lives unto eternity.

Birgit Thelin-McDonald
APPEARANCE VS. REALITY
We build our castles in the air
With illusions as ceilings and
walls
We gaze through the windows of
appearance
Until, one day,
Reality
Is standing on the treshold
With a scornful grin.

Larry Howard
DON'T LET GO
Whether it be the best
Or worst of reason, a
Hand will reach out—
As a beacon of joy
And admiration when
Dreams draw near—
As a sounding bell
In a fog-drawn night when
The course is all but clear—
As the soothing
Heat of summer's light
To love one so dear—
As the wealthy voice
Of experience when
Bravery becomes fear.
There will come a time
When a hand will reach
Out—Don't let go.

Gregory W. McGinnis
THE YELLOW BRICK ROAD
She was Dorothy.
I was the Tin Man.
And we met with the unspoken
hello
Of one heart to another.
It's been said when you meet
someone
You could tell everything,
There's no need to say anything.
She knew of my search for a
heart,
I knew of her quest for Oz.
And our destinies led us down
the
Yellow Brick Road.
Who would have dreamed we
could find happiness.
The country girl with thoughts
Somewhere over the rainbow.
The Tin Man with a shell
Hard as steel.
And a journey in which a
thousand obstacles
Lay between us and the Emerald
City.
But the only obstacles of love
or those placed there by
doubt.
And doubt is nothing but fear of
one's own shortcomings.
I looked within her and found
my heart.
She looked within me and found
her Oz.
And together, we traveled the
Yellow Brick Road.

H. William Lowe
ONE ROAD TO TRAVEL
Somewhere down this road of
life,
As I travel in search of goals.
When you reach that fork in the
road, then ask,
"On which road do I go?"
"Do I turn right, or do I turn
left?
Or do I sit here and cry"?
Decisions to ponder and
thoughts of regret
Of other roads you've tried.
Once you've decided, there's no
looking back.
For now the deed has been done.
Whether its the road to the
left or the right.
The decision is better than
none.

Fay Wingate
OUTSPOKEN PEOPLE
Outspoken people
Are rude, cruel, and unkind
Very self-centered people,
The worst you can find.
they never think twice
About whatever they say,
And always make someone
Have an unpleasant day.
They voice their opinions
Whether or not you agree,

They never like what you're
wearing,
You can take it from me
They're looking for trouble
Right from the start,
Whatever your plans are,
They tear them apart.
Outspoken people
Should find friends of their own,
Because I'll never invite them
Into my home.
I have come to the conclusion
They are not friends of mine,
I'd rather have a few friends
That are more of my kind.

L. Anita Richardson
UNTITLED I
Do you struggle still?
I do.
To the same avail?
I do.
I push
I drive
I do reach and claw.
I grasp
I strain
I do thrust to seize.
Of what else is there
though a silence is against me
and I am set aback.
I do feel the pit inside gape
to take me in.
I do taste its chilling maw
sear my furrowed skin.
I do know the striving of
direction, the movement of no
end,
the surge of forward motion
that moves me not again.
Do you struggle? Do you. . .
Do not form the questions
that I may put the answers by
and step aside the confrontation
that recalls a life's lie.

Phyllis Joan Smith
MAMA
Once, I heard your footsteps
upon the floor
Heard your soft voice
Your words of love, and advice
Saw your bright smile, and
brown eyes
I watched your brown hair turn,
to a color of silver
Watched you suffer, and age
Until the angels came
And took you to Heaven's door
No longer, do I hear your
footsteps upon the floor
At night, when all is black, the
stars come out
The brightest star, the color of
silver
High up, in Heaven's place
Mama, it's you, I'm sure. . . . .
Shining through the portholes
of Heaven's floor. . . . .

Patricia A. Gustafson
INDEPENDENCE
Independence, what is it really?
Something to search for or
yours to have freely.
You think it's yours, and
others may too,
but dreadfully sad if taken
from you.
Allowed to keep and nourish
this gift,
your inner sanctum will rarely
drift.
People need people it's a simple
fact,
but taking their freedom is a
criminal act.
The act may be simple, or even
obscure,
but forcefully willed kills
feelings for sure.

Mary Leila A. Gilhousen
GEMS
You sparkle light on velvet bed,
And from your bright and rarest
red
A glory shines like rising sun
That streaks the sky when night
is done.
O gems of beauty, gems of truth,
You are reward enough for
youth
Whose sorrows, pain, and tears
will claim
Their crown when Jesus calls a
name!

Gail Egleston
PHOENIX ENTRAPPED
I sit with hooped linen on my
lap
Entrapping a phoenix
Which like a child I color
Trading wax sticks for bright
yarns.
And as I stitch,
I primitively pray to the bird
Whose captive image I now
have:
Ancient Resurrection, teach
me,
Let the fingered yarn strings
Become my fingers tying me
to you,
The rich color run through
me like blood
Absorbing us both.
I see the resignation in your
eye,
The victory,
Let it be mine!
Help me gather the sticks,
Help me to light the fire,
Help me to sit still,
Teach me the notes that
come from your throat;
And from the colorless
ashes,
Give me faith in the worm
of life
Which you know will most
assuredly emerge
And begin anew. . .

Halina de Roche
WHAT PRICE IS LIFE!
In zig zag chase
Some music plays
An abstract tune.
What price is life?
Swedish Christmas dish
Tea from China?
Steamed fig pudding
Or women's dresses?
In zig zag chase
Some music plays
An abstract tune.
Soldiers are marching
Women are crying
People are starving
Whose
Are the responsibilities?
Who
Causes revolutions!
Who
Gives the instructions!
Is all of it sabotage?
The music laughs—
Sedition as usual
Two of a kind
And life simplified
To medicine, politics
Propaganda
Or insurance system.
While men risk
Death
To save the world—
And zig zag chase
Some music plays
Its abstract tune—

H. Jamieson Redder
ON HOLD
What is it, you might ask of me
That turns me off. . .icy cold?
'Tis simply asking for help, you
see
And, instead, being put on
"Hold."
When I was a lad in quest of
work,
"Call 'Him' " for a job, I was told.
This I straightway did, and yes,
"Him" had me put on "Hold."
A college boy I once became,
Under the GI Bill I enrolled.
Knowing in spite of the rush I
was in,
Four years of my life. . .on
"Hold."
Tee times at the ole golf course
Must be 'phoned ere the day's
too old.
But I call, and I call, and call,
and call,
Then I'm answered, but put on
"Hold."
And what about the telethons
Where pleas for aid are "sold?"
I'm sure when I call my pittance
in,
They'll first have to put me on
"Hold."
And so it goes in later years
No matter what's being sold.
If I call for a simple little pill,
The druggist first puts me on
"Hold."
My ticker's fine, for all I know,
My doc says I'm good as gold.
That's great, for in an
emergency,
Oh, wouldn't they put me on
"Hold?"
I hope never to see my house on
fire
'Though it happens to most, I'm
told,
For I know if I were to summon
help,
They'd first have to put me on
"Hold."
Oh, Lord, I know you'll call me
one day
To come to those gates, Pearly
Gold.
But I promise you with all my
heart,
That call won't be put on
"Hold."
Just before that call. . .one more,
I hope
From the brains of that button,
so cold.
And if that glorious call should
arrive,
You can bet I'll put it on
"Hold."

Janet L. Di Gennaro
LOVER'S ENTREATY
The starving artist in my soul,
Flaming actress in my head,
The hungry child within my
heart
Who's crying in his bed,
My legs have walked a hundred
miles,
I'm tired and I'm lame
And I cannot hold a candle,
love,
To your eternal flame.
My muscles beg your linament,
My hands, your tender balm,
For I have seen the heaven
That you hold within your
palm.
This need in me cries out to
you
To quench undying thirst,
The need in me to be your love,
Forever to be nursed.

Al Dolin
I MADE IT
It is so grand
To be alive.
To reach a goal,
At seventy-five.
Dear friends I had.
I loved them all.
Exiting stories
I recall.
How fine those times
That made me glad,
Though mixed with some
That made me sad.
This goal I reached.
Oh how I craved it.
So great this thrill.
And now,
I MADE IT.

Larry W. Doman
ODE TO CACOPHONY
The true value of cacophony
in one's life is priceless.
Cacophonic outbursts
are like battling giants
juxtaposed and ready
to pounce upon reason
in a frenzied fit
of blasting
soundless sense
not worthy
of worry.
Yet from its nonsensical milieu
we draw closer
to the creative intuitive well
from which springs life
in a new form.
A form fitting
the hysterical moment
in
which
we
live.

Wayne Quinton Jones
SADIE
She strutted—How she could
strut
Lazy hips tangoing taut
Easy swinging arcing butt
Moving—grooving—man too
much!
She switched in time
A beat of her own
Down 52nd and up 59
She pranced and danced that
lovely behind.
Amid leers and jeers—the
throaty holler
But Sadie'd never for under a
dollar.
Eyes would boggle teeth would
grit
Mouths watered when she
twitched
The men grew faint—the
women'd hate
When Sadie took that leisurely
gait.
But one fateful day bleak and
drear
Sadie took a swat on the rear:
Now the crowds silent on
Elmwood and Vine
With old men talking of old
times
Of how the summer night'd
bring
Darling Sadie and her swing.

Judy C. Oust
LESSON OF THE RAINDROP
A frightened little raindrop
fastened itself to the cloud in
the sky
Knowing that it would lose its
life if it ever began to cry
One day the raindrop was forced
to leave its safe, soft resting
place
As the jealous wind brewed up a
storm to wrest it from the
cloud's embrace
And as the raindrop fell it
thought its life was through
For it saw its life as over
with nothing left to do
So the raindrop slipped from
its home and fell into the

ground
While no one hailed its flight
as it never made a sound
The earth welcomed the
raindrop as it opened up its
arms
United with its new host the
raindrop began to release its
charms
Before the raindrop fell the
earth was suffering
A deep thirst for herself and
all her offspring
Little did the raindrop know
that its powers were about to
be freed
As it died to itself its new
life began in the growth of the
seed
At the time it kissed the earth
its old life ceased to be
Now its new life burst out in
the splendor of the flower,
fruit and tree
The raindrop lived in the tree
which grew and gave man
shade
Then went on to live another
life in the paper and furniture
it made
The raindrop lived in the fruit
and vine and man's hunger it
satisfied
And also lived in the flowers as
they blossomed out in
colorful pride
The little raindrop was
swallowed up by earth and
from it we heard no more
Until we saw it live again in
more brilliant form than it
previously wore
The little raindrop teaches us an
important lesson to know
We must die to ourselves if
we ever are to grow

Curtiss D. Bassett

GONE WITH THE BLUEBIRD

Yes, there are ghosts that I
would have return
Like bluebirds flashing in the
morning sun,
The Scottie into mischief on the
run,
The innocence of childhood's
love, concern
That life go on for every
living thing
(A frog, a spider spinning webs
above),
And Mother's home-made bread
upon the stove;
Ghost echoes, hark to hear the
school bell ring.
The quality of spirits like this
breed
Could so improve relations with
their land
The haunted home of old could
now be planned.
With witches' brooms for travel
there I'd speed
Away from harsh realities a day
With long gone loved ones in a
world at play.

Joyce E. Durham

THROUGH A LACE CURTAIN

I sat today by my window and
peered through the lace
curtain.
The things I saw outside could
not see me, of this I'm certain.
Two bluejays frolicking together
in the birdbath—
I swear I heard them laugh!
A family of sparrows socializing
in the mimosa tree;
Maybe they were gossiping and
laughing at people like me.
Tired old Duke, the dog,
dreaming in the sun-full of
days and past fun.
A honey bee on blossom,
nectar—gathering; doesn't care
if the weather is sweltering.
A lizard green with throat
puffing out so red; thinks
everything looks upon him
with dread.
Each flower in my yard a
different hue; reminds me of
individual me, and individual
you.
I think my Creator has such a
sense of hilarity:
He created a great universe full
of variety.

Ray Rhodes

THOT'S ABOUT CHRISTMAS

During this Christmas season
As we gather around the tree
Exchanging gifts as usual
With our friends and family
Let not our earthly treasures
Take first place on Christmas
morn
Nor all the trinkets and
trappings
That our lives so often adorn
But join in the Celebration
That for centuries Heaven's had
Remembering the Christ child,
Rejoice, Be Happy! Be Glad!

Lena Van-Arkadie Dabney

THE WIND

The wind is God's
Broom.
It sweeps everything clean.
The old, persistent leaves from
the trees
In preparation for Spring.
The gutters filled with the trash
of
Forgetful beings,
Piling it to one end of
The Asphalt Jungle for
Man to collect.
And—sometimes it brings
You back to me.

Dixie Spurgeon Norton

ONCE UPON A TIME

When you were just a tiny lad
Half past two. . .approaching
three,
You came toddling with a book
"Mommy, will you read to me?"
You curled snuggling in my lap;
You were such a cuddly boy.
"Once upon a time," I read,
As my heart near burst with joy.
I'd say, "Now you read to me!"
From the well-loved book of
rhyme,
You'd begin from memory,
"Once a pony time."
How you grew. . .a manly lad,
Interested in Boy Scout hikes,
Swimming, fishing, Little
League,
Ponies, camping out, and bikes.
Next your fondest love became
An old Ford that you soon
"stripped."
A-a-ah, then you discovered
girls;
When you smiled at them, they
flipped.
Now the years have fled too
soon.
A young man you soon will be.
You're so wise, and yet so
young,
Chaffing at authority.
My heart aches for days gone by
When your life entwined with
mine
When you were a baby boy,
Once upon a time.

Ricky T. Gowdy

BLOSSOM IN THE SUN

A seed fell to the ground
and was nourished by the sun.
It grew and flowered a
beautiful blossom,
a blossom of the sun.
Like your love, it's
radiance captured everyone and
everything, it belonged to me,
to my heart and to my eyes.
For I could feel your warmth
and
still see the blossom in the sun.
Your scents were one in the
same,
like the petals of the flower,
strong yet tender, but always
just right.
As the days grew shorter and
the nights colder,
the flower withered away,
as did our love.
New Seeds will fall.
New Flowers will grow, but
never like my beautiful blossom,
my Blossom of the sun.

Doye Day

FALL MORNING

On the beauty of Fall mornings,
Blessed quiet after rest.
Just before the birds start
singing,
Is the time I like the best.
There's a dampness on the
flowers,
And a crispness in the air.
Night shades begin their hiding,
Dawn breaks without a care.

As slowly, all my senses
Rejoice with day's rebirth.
I lift my voice to Heaven
In thanks, for this good Earth.
Oh God, don't let me falter,
Or forget along the way;
The joy I feel in watching
The birth of an Autumn day.

Judy M. Brewster

ODE TO GRANDMOTHER

If I could write a letter to
Jesus, up above,
I'd ask Him to send some extra
joy, my grandmother's way.
Some for all the love she gives,
in her meek and humble way.
Her tenderness is heavens bliss,
in a world full of hate.
And when troubles are upon me,
she's always by my side.
Her voice is like the wings of a
dove, soothing them away.
Yes, I'd ask Him for extra
blessings, to brighten up her
way.
And grandfather, who's gone on
before her, is waiting over
there,
Looking for her arrival and the
joy they will share.
The robe of life that awaits her,
no other one can compare.
A crown of life I know shes
won, and a mansion over
there.
So beings a letter can't reach
heavens portals over there.
I'll just go to the Lord, upon
my knees in prayer.
I'll ask Him to bless her life,
as she has mine down here.
So that happiness will fill all
her days.
And last but not least, for Him
to keep her forever in His
loving care.

Rita Jordan

UNTITLED

I have held in my hands
what once was alive.
The beams, the structure
of a human life.
Skeletal remains.

J. Victor Danoski

SHOCK WAVES

Wires crackling as
tension grows;
houses smoking in dark-
brick rows;
The numbers scream:are
not men!
as they're pressed beneath
the pen:
Wondering whether to
laugh or cry
as the dead live and the
living die.
—As the daydream becomes a
nightmare—
the master sits on his electric
chair
with the power in his
iron hand.
The heart beats
quicker
as the lights
flicker;
And the SHOCK WAVES shake
the sleepy land.
Children at play hear the
newsman say:
"you'd better stay in-doors
today"
As the television lights
their eyes
(Warning:discretion is
advised)
Their tiny faces turn so
white
as the big shark takes
another bite:
—Turning the troubled
waters red—
while the isle of the
living-dead
declares national
emergency!
The tempest
grows
the teapot explodes;
And more SHOCK WAVES stir
the troubled sea.
The dominoes began
to fall
as it was written on the
wall;
Metropolis went dim—
then dark
as the tremors shook the
park:
On the midnight—
afternoon
when the Sun became
the Moon!
—As the daydream became a

nightmare—
the master sat on his electric chair
with the power in his iron hand.
The hearts beat quicker
The lights did flicker;
And the SHOCK WAVES shook the sleepy land.
"SHOCK WAVES"

Michael Donkonics
NEXT SPRING
Flowers galore
In the spring that's for sure
Just a fleeting thing to adore
For in a few short weeks they are no more
Pick them not
From their spot
And leave the roots to rot
I implore
For nature is the only one that can restore
Flowers galore⁈
Next spring I am not sure

Tim Cohen
LISA
There was an angel
Who walked the earth
Sowed her seeds
And spent her worth
Behind that fair young brow
Was a mind so sharp and keen
She knew the value
Of reality

But never forgot to dream
No fancy slippers
Donned her feet
Nor white dress did she wear
And the wings upon her back
So discreet—
As the halo atop
Her golden hair
She gathered from the garden
Kind thoughts, wishes
Meant and true
Put them in a bouquet
Of words
And gifted them to you
She left so silently
As dew upon a rose
When morning came
And lit the sky
We knew Lisa
Was the one he chose
To adorn his kingdom
And to gladden his heart
For God like I
Must have been so sad
While apart.

Clyde A. Glaze
DAYBREAK
Have you ever studied nature
In the early morn?
Just before the sun comes up
It's like a world reborn.
Glistening dewdrops bead the grass,
The air is fresh and cool
You feel you're in a grand new world
That follows nature's rule.
Bird calls by the dozens,
The cooing of a dove.
A thrill sweeps o'er your body,
Your soul is filled with love.
And only in the stillness
Can you sense the live earth's throb;
It shakes your heart and spirit
Brings you closer to your God.

Ben Gray
ODE TO A DYING EARTH
Swirling diverse gassy elements—compacting in deep space
To form a ball—gigantic globe—home of the human race
The process long and terrible—split and ripped and torn
A million years of labor pains—ere—Mother Earth was born
Another million to bring forth—the green of grass and trees
Still more to pass—for to evolve—the fish from out the seas
The final step—he walked erect—and figured with a brain
And drove steel spikes into her side—to run a (fire horse) train
Down through the ages—since the time—when man made his first tool
He found better ways to scar the flesh—pointed stick, plow pulled by mule
Now, in this the twentieth century—with incest we attack our birth
With greed and bulldozer phallus—we—are raping our mother earth
Her once sweet breath is now befouled—noxiousness from fires and cars
For payment she has been bedecked—with cement ribbons and with tars
Wars for wrong, wars for right—and—to think it matters not
How many of the young men killed—our homeland to be wrought
Your once fruitful abundance—is fastly on the wane
Gloved surgical hands to render thee—a barren sterile plain
So as your wounds do fester—and—fill with septic pus
Take satisfaction in the thought—we are also killing us

Johansen De Dishwater
RIGHT GUARD
We're rolling.
Take 1.
Click.
A rolling
Auntie-perspirant
Gathers no
Sweat;
Or moss for
That matter.
Incidentally, moss
Grows only on
Trees.
Northside.
I roll my own—
Armpits.
Isn't that
Nice?

Joseph A. Conway
TAKE THE WORLD
Take the world and turn it upside down, take the world and turn it right side up. Take the world and turn it inside out, take the world and bring the outside in.
It's no crime to be who you really are. Stop the Nazi's in the flashing cars. The madness is silently waiting for you to comply, if you say no, for sure it's a lie.
Blinded by the ancient sun, you take off naked on the run. The spiral of your brain as it trancends, the living nightmare has no end.
Who could you be if you looked to the sky, would you live or would you die? The silence above could be the silence below, beware the under tow if you decide to go.
IT takes eternity to pass the test, if you're patient you'll be set aside from the rest. Be my guest, don't speak in jest. The world may topple down, but the spirit lives on in the ruins of town.

Stacci Howell
SONG IN FLOWER
By an old black top road one day
I stopped; homeward was my way
There on the side were Autumn flowers
Nourished by Indian Summer showers
Standing so brave as chill wind blew
Smiled to myself and picked a few
Handed my wild bouquet to my Grandma
And in the flowers, summer's going I saw
Sorta blue, I was, winter's always so long
But then. . .the flowers burst into song!
That little cricket made my heart smile
His song so cheerful, for a long while
Then outdoors he went; the smile's still there
Singer of flowers made me once again care

Joan Yoest
THE LAND WE LIVE IN
The breaking of dawn is a sight to behold
On sunrise God's beauty begins to unfold.
Soon daylight in all of it's glory surrounds us
To awaken God's creatures, and begin a new day thus—
Looking around me I see sights divine
I'd like you to see them through my eyes, I find:
The cows in the meadow the grass on the hill
The trees that are standing so tall and so still.
The clouds in the sky moving fast on their way
Bringing once more to all a glorious new day.
The birds flying high, the streams running clear
The sound of the wind, the prance of a deer.
With awe and with wonder all this do I see
And then even more is God's country to me.
The sun beating down from the heaven above
The men at their work on the land we all love.
The lakes, and the rivers so peaceful and quiet
A day in God's country you just couldn't buy it.
The sun settting now gives a feeling of rapture
The beauty no painter on canvas would capture.
The soft light of dusk envelops the day
The beauty of moonlight mere words cannot say.
With night time upon us stars light up the sky
Reflecting God's glory with a brillance most high.
This land that we live in so glorious and free
A gift from our Father for you and for me.
I thank you for letting me share this with you
And hope it has brought you some happiness too.

Lyn Maring
MAYBE. . .
I love the fall
Of Autumn's bright leaves
Upon my lawn.
I love their rustle
In the wind
and the crunch-crunch sounds
Beneath my footsteps.
Sometimes I rake them
But not always;
Sometimes I leave them
For crushing when I walk
But when
The proper Jones neighbors
Rake their leaves,
Then so must I,
But only because it's expected,
Not that I choose.
I love the fall
Of Autumn's bright leaves
Upon my lawn.
Maybe some other Autumn
I shall not rake them
But leave them
And love them
And forget about the Joneses—
Maybe!

Mary Louise Both
WHAT HAPPENED BABY?
This is the week I swore would be
A week of solid gold.
Of exercise, diet and beauty routine
To keep from looking so old.
Of learning and working and
Doing those things
That free the mind from mold
But the whole world slid
From under my feet.
I came down with a miserable cold

Peggy J. Smith
CHRISTMAS
Where have the flowers and butterflies gone;
Where are the "peepers" to wake us at dawn;
Where are the friends we've known for so long;
And where is the meadowlark's lovely, sweet song?
They've followed the Sun to find winter's release;
Some are with God, in Heavenly Peace!
But, one thing is certain, when Spring comes again,
We'll see sleepy flowers greet

warm April rain.
They'll burst with the Glory
of Promise and Love
And the birds will fly back,
while others, above,
Will send us a message of
undying dreams
And all that awaits, with our
Lord's Perfect Schemes!
So, smile and relax and dream
a sweet thought,
For one day we'll know of the
Wonders He's wrought!
And each who has loved, and
loved more again,
Is promised Perfection, no
more heartache or pain.
We'll smile and rejoice, as
our hands touch in love,
When we're greeted with joy,
by our Fathers Above!

Joseph R. Sherman
YOUTH LOST
My childhood cried out and
my eyes ran with tears
As I tried to recall the forgotten
years.
The passage was blocked and I
couldn't relate.
I wanted to believe it wasn't
too late,
So I filled up my shelf with
small, simple toys
Which filled my heart with
childhood joys.
Then, finally I realized I
was trying too hard;
Children should simply be what
they are. . .

Karen Frye Robertson
LOVE'S GLOW
How my life changed, when ours
touched,
You set me free within myself.
Thank you my love, so very
much.
Now I'm alive and can be me,
So full of happiness, hope and
joy,
No more alone, forgotten on
the shelf,
but full of warmth, and all
can see
The greatest change come over
me.
For now I reflect all love's
glow,
My spirit soars above the pain
for all the love that you do give
Will never end, as long as I
shall live.
I was reborn, a woman now alive
again.
No longer hiding in an empty
shell.
No more afraid to feel and tell
Just what a change your love
has made.

John Howard Bradley
AN INTERNAL/ EXTERNAL VIEW OF THE MILITARY
*(This poem is to reflect the
behavior of all nations as none
really desires peace).*
Running, running every day
Cadence, cadence all the way
Shouts for joy and shouts for
pain
Future troops to die in vain.
Honor, honor is the name
Of the reward of this game.
But pride and glory where are
you
When millions find themselves
entombed?
And you who live, what do you
say?
"Thousands die so thousands
can live."
Is that a fair exchange?
Make that a syllogism,
And the light breaks down as
through a prism:
"Thousands live, so thousands
can die.". . .
Still, training continues—why?

Eugene W. Burgess
WHAT IS A NEW DAY?
To many, a new day means a
breath of spring.
To many, tremendous joy and a
song to sing.
To many, a resurgence of power
that's hard to beat.
To many, a thousand prayers
have yust come to pass.
To many, a new born babe has
smiled at last.
To many, ALMIGHTY GOD has
given a blessed amen
To many women and children
and yes even men. .
To many, rays of sunshine lo
and behold.
To many, countless rose buds
about to unfold.
To many, peace on earth at the
breaking of dawn.
To many, sharing bread together
and humming their song
To many, fervent prayers to our
maker way up above.
To many, long life and a happy
life built on love.
To many, praise ye the LORD
for HE is so kind.
To many judgement day has
come as they kneel
at their shrine.

Laura Cole
ONE DAY AT A TIME
One day at a time is how
we exist.
Is it because we're too
lazy to persist?
Our ancestors never took
time to doubt.
Do we think we're so special;
that we have clout!
They did their jobs, now
it's time to do ours.
We have the strength,
and we also have the power.
It's up to us to use the
power God gave us.
We should use these powers
and without a fuss.
Has our greed gotten the
best of us?
It seems to me whenever
something is asked of us,
all we do is cuss.
All it takes from us is
a little Love and Concern.
It's something we all have
yet to learn.
It's really quite easy if
you think about it.
If you learn how to use it
it will all come together
to make a perfect fit.

Helenjean Hays Speights
A FATHER'S DREAM
O, Little Fathers And Mothers
of Tomorrow. . . . . .
Each holding in your arms the
world's dreams. . . . . .
Your bright eyes reflecting
tomorrow's hopes, more than
seems;
And shining with dreams of
being the best. . . . . .
. . . . . .of leading all
the rest. . . . . .
I, your proud father, also
have dreams and hopes. . . . . .
Dreams of giving you each all
love's best. . . . . .
Hopes of giving, to each, needed
inner strength,
and courage, too. . . . . .
Strength to build a life strong,
brave, and true-blue. . . . . .
The Courage Born of Love's
Hope
To make your own best dreams
come true.

Bonni M. Lunog
MEMORIES
I remember the fun, we had
during the summer.
I remember walking through the
woods, then it started to rain.
I remember the long rides we
took, because we had nothing
else to do.
I remember sitting in the car
all night, listening to the
radio.
I remember all the beer,
that we went through.
But most of all,
I remember the love,
that was shared by the two of
us.

Ulysses Goudelock
HUMANITY AND THE SOLDIER
I ponder my days of youth
With thoughts of soldiers,
forsooth—
Soldiers fought and died for
peace,
And prayed the war would
cease.
I remember bitterness; the foe's
hate,
Homage to our dead is ne'er
too late.
Fighting bravely against the
enemy soldier,
For humanity, they fought
bolder,
Recalling Jesus; the cross he
bore,
And the ventura taking the
garment he wore.
Jesus Christ saved man from sin
The truth of God will always
win.
In that battle many soldiers
died.
They defended our land, they
tried.
What atonement is for our dead?
For each soul it was said:
Brave soldiers fought and were
slain,
And they gathered glory that
shall sustain.

Mary Katherine Collins
IT'S THE MOON-TIME
It's the moon-time.
dark yet aglow.
silent.
air crackles with cold.
Pines mixed
among kindred barren of leaves,
stand laden.
thick with snow.
No wind whispers
their branches,
only silver glimpses down,
quietly touching
it stirs its' spell.
dark yet aglow.
Clouds layer thin,
playful gray shades
shifting paces
to high blowing tidal winds.
they stroll along.
and branches
heavy with glow,
stand silent
as the snow eats silver
to the moon's-time.

Joseph D. Benjamin
PAIN OF LOVE
Every time I pass your way,
And you happen to see me, and
turn away;
I get this feeling deep inside.
The kind of feeling that's
hard to hide.
I long to have you back again,
It makes no difference where or
when.
I know it's just a fantasy,
Cause you'll never again, belong
to me.
Oh why do I sigh?
A year has gone by.
And still I try to hide,
My pain of love, my pain of
love.
I saw you again the other day.
You were with someone else,
real happy and gay.
And just like the ocean's
roaring tide,
The pain engulfed me, one more
time.
I know I'll never be the same.
Where'er I go, I hear your name.
It haunts me both night and
day;
It seems it won't just go away.
Oh why do I sigh?
A year has gone by.
And still I try to hide,
This pain of love, my pain of
love.

William Edwards
UNTITLED
There was a young Mongol from
Mastic
Whose plan was no less than
fantastic
Cocksure he was smarter
Than all other Tartars
He Khanned till his clan was
dynastic.

Douglas Haney
LIFESTYLES
The sun never falls on the
homes of these men who dreary
and dark days have seen.
And sad are the eyes of these
wine-soaked poor souls while
memories still haunt all their
dreams.
"There is no more hope, it
seems," so they say,
"So why try to chase all the
years?"
Their lifestyle lives up to all
that it claims
and once more they'll pass
round a warm beer.
From the dinge of the streets
they've been chased by the cold.
They retreat to a place down
below.
Looked down to by others from
buildings above, they'll sleep

where the warm water flows.
They don't ask for much, just
leave them alone to count the
confusion of life.
What once was ambition and a
will to succeed has past them
and left all its strife.
My friend don't you laugh or
scorn them when they just
happen to pass by your way.
Look up and be thankful that
you're not the one who must
live in our sewers today.

Lillie Mae Bland Carter
ADRIFT ON THE NILE

Drifting aimlessly down the
Ancient Nile,
Near the spot where Moses was
found
(in a handwoven basket in
the bulrushes)
And instantly feeling very
holy to be
So near that sacred spot;
Sailing in a vessel, its design
thousands of years old,
Traversing in retrospect through
sunsets eons old;
The world is gone,
Everything is quiet
Save the explanations
from the polyglot guide.
However, the once beautiful,
mighty Nile is dirty. . . . .
Polluted by man's inventions
through the many
centuries of "civilization,"
and by the debris from the
overpopulated city.
Cairo, Egypt

Shirley Baisden Griffin
MISSED MEMORIES

I wish I could see my child
again,
with eyes unclouded by silent
tears,
With arms outstretched to pick
him up,
and help to calm his fears.
I was able to aid and comfort
like this for a short while.
Then I was only able to soothe
from a chair with a hug and a
smile.
I envied the mothers who went
for a Trick
or Treat, their child by the
hand.
Many the times I wished I could
hold his,
and maybe watch a passing
brass band.
He never missed out on
childhood treats,
because of loving friends and
kin,
But I wanted so many times to
follow
his steps and go the places
he had been.
One day when I felt low, I told
him
I wish I could have done
more.
His caring, candid, child-like
answer
cut the problem right to the
core.
"You wish you could have done
more,
so do I—but that's life."
"We have done a lot together,
and
you're always there through
trouble and strife."
With these words, I glowed and
smiled,
and my chair with wheels
sprouted wings.
My heavy heart feels lighter
than air,
and my soul soars and sings!

Doreen C. Sampler
UNTITLED

You're a dream, our little son.
Only God knew you'd be the
one.
He knew before our lives began,
It's all a part of His master plan.
Dad was born to live his life,
with your mom as his wife.
So much love had we two,
waiting inside just for you!
God knew, my love,
as I've said before.
Your "real" mom and dad
were just too poor!
Babies themselves, when you
were born,
suddenly, their lives were torn.
Filled with love and hope for
you.
they did the best thing they
could do. . .
They chose "new" parents,
Dad and me,
so we could help you be all
you can be!
You give our lives point and
direction.
We give you love and
protection.
Our lives were joined,
it was meant to be.
You're our son now, we're a
family!

Jose V. Rubio Jr.
HEAR YE, OH PUBLIC

The articulators work was so
pretty
Confirmed by the public as a
beauty
That crashes the misdeed of the
ugly
The revenge was to break him
financially
No work to give to earn money
His poor weak wife on the go
Carrying the burden on the row
An innocent child named
"Jenny"
Was involved in their cruelty
The Beauty—the judging public
The Good—the forgiver of evil
The Bad—the follower of the
ugly
and the Ugly—the commander
of the bad

Arnold Kinsella
THE SMILE ON YOUR FACE

Let no one take the smile from
your face
For it is your crowning glory
Its radiance brightens the
darkest place
And tells a happy story
Life can be a trial at times
With shadows darkening your
way
But as long as that smile is
on your face
All your cares and woes will
fade away

Biff Faunce
SONG TO WILLIAM

William, William, what to dare,
Had Tyger not burned bright in
there?
Had not the cavernous lair
uncaged
The Beast to stalk through
Night enraged,
Would meekly Lambs in
Pastures play?
Bold Shepherds ever watchful
lay?
You dared to take them both
in Hand—
Dared see the Tyger see the
Lamb!
(Yet O to brave that brilliant
Fire,
Loft upon the Soul-Strung Lyre:
Clouds swag and thundered
endless woe,
To forge Gold Arrows, to strike
the Bow!
Yon Pasture gleams as in a Pyre,
Mad Songs embalm the Hymnal
Choir:
O Joyous be that Blessed Chord,
So dearly risen to His Lord!)
William, William, dare tonite!
Oothoon give birth to Los' Light!
"Behold!" blazed He, took up my
Hand,
"Deep strides the Tyger, Wide
is the Lamb!"

Jay Williams
THE DREAMER

the price of living as a true
dreamer is unrecognized by the
average person.
to the pure dreamer,
dreams are not merely nocturnal
happenings that occur in the
unconsciousness of sleep,
nor are they the reveries
induced by boredom.
instead, they are existence
itself.
as children, most people
experience the condition of
the dreamer,
but with age comes a sense of
realism.
most choose a path within
reality
and set a future-determining
goal.
they have not totally outgrown
their dreams
for they still envision the
possibilities that exist in the
other world,
but they have learned to accept
these fantastic thoughts
as only dreams—purely
playthings of the mind.
for others, the child-adult
transition is different.
the childhood dreams do not
surrender to actuality, but
instead, they simply evolve to
become adult dreams.
the dreams that change tree
houses to inter-galactic
travel-machines,
empty lots to Yankee Stadium,
and pieces of plastic into
everything from living human
beings to the tools of war
develop into dreams of Love,
Prestige, Happiness, Immortality,
and a Perfect World.
unfortunately, the two types of
dreams have a common
shortcoming.
his dreams of Love, Happiness,
et cetera are as likely to bring
the dreamer realization of these
Ideals as the tree house is to
take the pseudo-astronaut to the
far reaches of the universe.
to those who live bound to
reality,
a life of fantasy may seem ideal,
but going through life knowing
all that you ever wanted never
was and
all that you ever will want will
never be
is not a being of perfection
but an existence of emptiness.

Joyce B. Hewitt
IT IS GOOD TO SHOW YOUR FEELINGS

Sometimes we take it for
granted that the one who help
us know.
The love that we have for them
always plainly shows.
Have you ever wondered, the
many times you got confused,
when you gave someone
something, and they did not
say "Thank you?
Maybe they had it in them, but
did not let it show.
So you took it for granted that
no manners did they know.
Do you remember the times
when the bus was crowded as
could be, and someone
stepped on your tired feet
and did not say "Excuse me"?
I guess it would have been
better if an apology were said
out loud.
But maybe they had it in them
as they walked away with a
smile.
Do you remember when your
mother taught you how to
share,
But when it came time for you,
no one seemed to care?
But maybe they had it in them,
but they did not let it show.
So your feelings were hurt and
you felt down and low.
It's something we have to learn
and remember it all the time.
No matter what we have within,
no one can read our mind.
If someone has done something
for you, go and let them
know.
How much you care what they
have done; let your feelings
show.
Sometimes it's good to express
your feelings, in a verbal sign.
It would take away from people
trying to read your mind.

Elizabeth Artis
MY MOM!

I grew up very coy and shy
Feared everything that "mom"
Couldn't explain "why?"
Faked all kind of illnesses
That I could recall
Even tantrums when she said,
"You can't have it all."
I thought when she spanked me
And put me to bed
Without the usual kiss
Or a story she'd read
She no longer loved me
. . .I could not see
She was trying to mold me
As she wanted me to be.
But as time went by
I began to understand
That life deals
A much harder "blow"
Than the slap of mom's hand

She is gone and there's
No one to take her place
Now all of my problems
Alone I must face
Remembering what she said
To me one day
Before she was taken
So swiftly away. . .
Holding me very closely
As I sat on her knee:
"Pray and ask God to make you
What He wants you to be."

Mark Avery
THE FUTURE

It's neither past nor present
It's neither gone nor here
THE FUTURE STANDS
Undescribed, unblemished
Another day, a week, a year
People talk as if they're certain
Of what will come to be
I talk of people as if I'm certain
Of that, we cannot see
To better times and happiness
I toast to all a cheer
FOR THE FUTURE
STANDS
Unvitiated, unblemished
Another day, a week, a year

Bozena Hrasks
PLEASE COME BACK TO ME

I never realized how much I
would miss you
Now it is clear what you mean
to me
When I want so much both to
kiss you
And hunger return kisses
tenderly
I never wanted either of you
hurt
Did my very best to be kind,
not curt
To let you see why the
discipline
Is so important in life
So you can have harmony
For dissension and strife
So that you can one day say
To your friends and peers
That your mother raised you
proudly
Throughout your young years
I know my dear children its
difficult to choose
It's difficult to give up. . .it's
difficult to lose
But you must be strong now,
God is always fair
Put yourselves in His arms and
He will put you
Where you belong. . .Do not
dismay!
Possibly separate you two if that
is his way
Don't ever give up, or be
scared
Remember the nice moments we
had shared
Remember what you achieved
with your mom
Soon you'll both be going to a
prom
So don't forget your
achievements,
Honor Rolls. . .Piano lessons—
All this happened with my
motion
To put your best foot forward
with a caution
Mostly remember very well
I always taught you the truth to
tell
I always wanted to be near
My job has kept me away
But the love I have for you
Could never disappear.

Raymond E. Schenke
CHRISTMAS IS FOR EVERYONE

Christmas is for everyone,
a time to laugh and sing.
Snow capped hills and little
towns, oh hear the church
bells ring.
Christmas tree with colored
lights reflecting in the snow,
And in the night come sweet
refrains of carols we all know.
Christmas is for everyone,
especially girls and boys.
Santa's sled filled to the brim
with ribbons, bows and toys.
Upon their beds on Christmas
Eve the children turn and
toss,
Waiting so impatiently for dear
old Santa Claus.
Christmas is for everyone, it
makes your spirit bright.
Rudolph with his nose so red is
such a pleasant sight.
Sharing gifts with family, and
friends both near and far,
As did the Wise Men on that
night they traveled toward
the star.
Christmas is for everyone, no
matter race or creed,
The message it brings to all
inspires us indeed.
Brotherhood and love, no matter
young or old,
'Tis why the Christmas story
is the greatest ever told.
Merry Christmas! Merry
Christmas! Merry Christmas
one and all.
God's gift to us was born that
day, in a tiny, simple stall.
Merry Christmas! Merry
Christmas! Merry Christmas
from above,
Bringing peace, goodwill and
kindness, it's a time to share
our love.

Lynda J. Sirianni
CHILD LOVE

He ran through the hayfield
About his waist high—
He stumbled and fell
Jumped up! Glanced at the
sky.
Upon reaching the fence of
barbed wire,
He stooped over—while
crawling under,
Got a back scratch of fire!
But he just kept on going
Waded through a swamp there—
Swished the slop with his
hands
And then pushed back his hair!
Finally seeing his goal
He ran! Ah—so fast
Upon reaching the spot
All exhausted, he sat.
Extending his arm
To grasp it quick—
A thistle snapped out
And it really bit!
He exclaimed his pain
A little hurt by his fail
But he finally got it
And headed back through his
trail.
Skipping and singing
Just as happy as can be,
His mission accomplished
The venture back—and hurry!
The same old falling
More scratches from the wire
The sun was so hot
And he was so tired.
I looked out the door
Wondering where he could be
Then he peeked around the
corner
Grinning proudly at me—
His scratched, dirty arm
extending
And in that little muddy hand I
see,
A broken-stemmed, yellow-
brown
Sunflower
A gift just for me!

Robert E. Drinkard
TOUCH OF WONDER

I feel the Life quicken me;
Not the Life of my flesh and
bone
That slip, slips then fails and
falls away,
But the Life of the Universe that
Touches softly with Cosmic
Force,
and leaves a trace of wonder
where
It's been

Barbara Anne Kester
SNOWFALL

Crystal flakes falling softly
to the ground,
Like tears flowing gently on a
happy face.
A blanket of white which
muffles each sound,
Embracing the gray of winter in
icy lace.
It brings back memories of
bygone days,
Sledding on snow-packed hills
and skating on frozen ponds.
With reddened cheeks sitting by
an open fire,
I gave no thought to what might
lie beyond.
I was storing indelible pictures
in the scrapbook of my mind.
Never dreaming that when the
child became a woman,
The snowfall would always
bring back these nostalgic
scenes.

Theresa Bruccoliere
CANCER

It hits one out of four
For me, there's no cure
They said it has spread
To my lungs, bones, and head.
Is it green, No it's red
Yes red like communism
I have not a choice
At the time of my death
Will you also rejoice?
What of the pain, my greatest
of fears
It's seen on the faces of others
when near
A cocktail you say, that's all
there is to it
You make it sound easy, but I'm
going through it.
Will my bowels be cement,
And my brain lack comment
And my whole being lament
All the sorrow I feel.
Will I sleep all the time
And what of my mind
It's better that way
Then the pain cannot stay.
I'll forget about time
Please try and be kind
Will I be all alone
Can I reach you by phone?
These dreams that I have
They scare me at night
I go back in my life to sin,
sorrow and strife.
Oh god! what have I done
Is this the prize that I've won
For a battle hard fought
And what have I bought
Will the rewards be there
When I'm no longer here.
And then came the end
Death was his friend
There wasn't much pain
Since it spread to his brain
Though he did lose his mind
All those around him
Really were kind.
Everyone said he looked so
much younger,
That's because he was dead, and
The sickness and fear remained
in his bed
For those who still lived, the
family he lead.
Death is for us, We who are
living
One wonders who's doing the
taking and giving
Sadness and grief are for those
who survive
For the dead, you see, are
really alive.

Richard 'Fritz' Adamson
THE SORROW OF MAN

Man knows no greater sorrow
Than the sorrow of his fellow
man
Who suffers at his hand.
Does man know that when he
Hurts a stranger, enemy or
friend
He too will feel the pain
And suffer in the end.
When man learns to love and
care
And try to make amends
Then of riots hate and war
We will have an end.

Robert Louis Lyon
TO BONNIE BERENICE, MY FAIR

At twenty-three with *joie
d'esprit*
I loved all maids the same;
A fancy-free and footloose me
I pledged for all eternity.
Could I foresee when thirty-
three
I'd choose a different game,
And find one *jeune fille* who
would be
My idol for eternity?
But when I'm three and seven-ty,
It's you I still will claim
To share with me, *con amore-e*
A corner of eternity—
One lass to love the same.

Elizabeth Ballard
WILD GOOSE CALL

The silent night a hint of snow
The moon on high an eerie glow
I hear the call in great delight
The wild goose passing through
the night
Their flight is swift without
delay

With only stars to light their
way
The quiet air of silence brings
The whisper of their flying
wings
Majestic in the way they fly
They call their greeting to the
sky
Their ghostly forms would pass
unknown
Along the path where geese
have flown
If not for calling in their flight
To the south winds of the night
But I for one await the fall
Just to hear the wild goose call

Daniel L. Birk
GRANDMA 1963
my grandma's ashes burn
on a night without fire
her green-stained teeth
clatter on a maple-stained
table serving boiled jello
her walking on highway 55
with bone meeting metal
weeping about broken eggshells
I swallowed her ashes in silence
grandma cooked a meal in her
coffin
the night she broke bone
and walked with metal to the
cemetary

Lavern S. Walker
OUR BABY PAUL
God, You have our baby Paul
he never lived one full day,
And now I know within my
heart
you had it planned this way,
If ever there is perfection
it is in a new born child,
But God he was so little
and never learned to smile,
He never new me as his mother
and of the tears I shed,
He never new his brother
who prays for him each night
before he go's to bed,
He never new his father whom
shares all his love with me,
And sometime I look at his dad
he is trying to hide his tears
so I won't see,
But God; there is much comfort
to know our Paul is with you,
Just help us through this trying
time
and we will be there too,

Barbara H. Taylor
PEARL OF FRIENDSHIP
A moment, locked forever in
eternity. . .
A grain of sand, a living shell,
A pearl is born!
A moment? No, A hundred
plus. . .
Many filled with little
irritations, as the sand to
the shell,
And then, suddenly. . .
realization. . .
A friendship is born!
'Oft times I muse. . .at night,
or watching a sunrise,
In the middle of washing
dishes or listening to a
beautiful song. . .
How?
It seemed so impossible, so
illogical, unthinkable.
And yet, out of those hundred
plus irritations,
We found ourselves. . .
friends!
Like, the beauty now
surrounding that first piece
of sand,
Our irritations are tenderly
entombed by love, forever.
And "our" pearl of friendship
is far more beautiful,
Because of the price we have
paid.

Chris Rice
UNIQUE
I am a part of everything I see.
All who I have touched are a
part of me.
I am. . .
The gentle silence of a
winter night.
The scorching sun on desert
sand.
The raging anger of a
swollen river.
The bittersweet song of a
meadowlark of dawn.
I am. . .
The desperation of the
loneliest heart.
The unquenched desire of a
secret love.
The soul as it soars to
untold heights.
All thoughts, all emotions.
I am all things.
The universe, the void.
All, and nothing at all.
Heaven and Hell.
The perfect contradiction,
For I am. . .
Unique

Patricia A. McGregor
WASTED TIME
I know I'm all grown up,
Because I look forward to fall.
Autumn doesn't make me feel
sick
anymore.
Rather, I'm glad.
Summer's heat depresses me.
I should be at the shore,
or at an amusement park,
or playing my guitar.
Instead, I swim in guilt,
and watch the ups and downs
of unhappiness,
and sing without music.
I hate wasted time.

Pauline Frechette Fotter
LET ME STAY
Mama, oh what you will miss
Oh mama can't you see
A tiny face for you to kiss
Don't do this thing to me.
Mama aren't you aware
The love to you I'll give
With feelings only we can share
I have the right to live.
How can you take away the life
That lives inside of you
How can you say that I should
die
To live is my right too.
Mama think how it will be
To throw my life away
To miss that part of you in me
Please mama let me stay.

Edna Burnham Prud'homme
THE DECEPTION
She comes to you as a virgin
bride.
Clothed in white, demure, sweet
with promise.
Take her and caress her, she is
yours.
Wallow in her voluptuousness.
Then, the flame, ignite her inner
soul.
The ember glows, redolence
rises
As the enervating ambience
Consumes all that is reality
And her cunning strategem
outwits.
Lassitude diminishes caution.
Like a shroud, her veil falls
around you.
Lethargy marks the passing of
time.
Decadence envelops you until
You come to limbo's oblivion.
You will not pass beyond the
curtain
Into the light that is cognizance
Yet loiter until the grim one
comes.
But there is naught and he
must glean
The ashes, the residue of waste.

Felicia Venable
STAND TALL
Stand tall little Indian
Be proud of who you are.
As you grow into a man
Let no man put you down.
Remember it was your ancestors
Who first walked on this land
It was they who fished and
hunted
and tamed the land where
cities now stand.
It was they who guided their
canoes quietly down the rivers
that is now crowded with
ships.
They are the ones who created
many beautiful works of art
and the systems of
mathematics used today.
Tho their beating drums have
grown silent
Never forget what they have
done.
So hold your hand up high and
Stand tall little Indian—
because you are who you are.

Susan F. Fuhrman
NIGHT DRAMA
These winter nights of icy
silence,
Spiced with the scent of
burning wood,
See stark postures of silvered
branches,
And in cold splendor a
reappearing moon.

In the distance city lights
give off a glow,
While clouds steal the stars
from view,
And in a velvet darkness the
evening star burns low,
Softly a pathway of clouds the
moon illumes.

Anne G. Guyett
PORTRAITS OF FAITH
Within a moment—untouched
by time—
have you seen eternity?
Born of simple trust
Life is an essence that knows no
walls
—nor the "sting of the blade"
—nor the "grating of the
rusted hinge"
—nor the "poet's shattered
lamp."
Here Faith abounds
borne on its triumphant
pinion;
freed from envy, scorn, false
pride;
purged from doubt, despair.
In this bright calm, doth hope
take root
And dance with sundrops
spilling down upon forest
floors,
. . .Singing with the stars
perched in bare branches;
silver bells shaken by a frosty
wind.
To live in Faith is to live in
beauty;
. . .and beauty lives forever.

PORTRAITS OF FAITH:
SONG TWO

So sure the sea! So certain of its
destiny.
I can find peace and strength in
the surging waves
folding one into another;
extreme in power;
proud beauty. . .yet. . .playful
Puck.
Each wave. . .diving
hiding
breaking free
tumbling—forward. . .forward
expending—yet never spent
changing—yet unchanged
in its essence.
The sea laves the sand,
caressing. . .gathering secrets
to its bosom;
cherishing. . .those secrets so
deftly erased.
And in the foam remaining,
poised in a curve upon the
sand,
glistens a rainbow, caught by
a twig.
Life reflected in so tiny a
bubble
shimmering. . .quivering—
A Joy
Will it ever explode!?

John A. Freudenreich Jr.
DREAMS
My dream was to become a
successful attorney of
Business Law,
Or quite possibly President of
the United States,
After all—anything is possible
in America:
Now the dream is like driftwood
Floating in a sea of space,
For I lie in the darkness of an
eternal slumber.
Friends, weep not for me,
Rather, utilize your potential
to develop dreams,
Flames of creativity, an inner
fire
Waiting to be expressed.
Time is short,
Implements sparse,
But work with determination,
Fervently, diligently,
industriously
To achieve the goals
At the end of your rainbows.

Peggy Kramer
ROSES IN THE SNOW
Delicate Roses in the Snow,
I know where they grow.
Deep in the heart, with lots of care,
Plenty of sunshine, and love to share.
But like everything born anew, soon must die
The roses fade like the tears you cry.
Remember the Roses in the Snow so deep
A cherished memory to keep and keep.

Bernice Espy Hicks
GUILTY?
I just sealed up a little grave
And whispered, "Heart, please throw away
The key so I can't gaze again
On dreams, belief, and trust.
Wait—
Mirror, was it you, betrayed?
Who should have warned,
"Look, here they've lain!"

Kathleen C. Fulton
FAREWELL
Let us go gentle into that farewell
We promised not to cry
but our eyes mirror the agony
of this final goodby.
Fingers of hysteria squeezing
our throats, aching
with the pain of unshed tears
Our hearts breaking
beneath the false facade of calmness
our emotions awhirl.
Words can not describe, no tongue can tell
the mixture of hope, of fears
the joy, the sadness,
fulfillment, emptiness
as you realize your dream to
be on your own.
Clothed in beauty and innocence
crowned with dignity and grace
you cross the threshold of home
into strange and new dimensions
vast arenas of challenge
to begin a new life.
As the inevitable moment arrives
our tears mingle as we embrace
and then you're gone.
With a powerful roar, the giant jet Bird
sweeps you up, bearing you away
beyond the clouds, I tremble, as
between us miles unfurl
and I'm alone
Fate be kind to her
Heaven protect her
for though she's an adult now
she's still my little girl—
But we did go gentle into that farewell

Kevin Geoffrey Smith
AGE OF ANXIETY
Only the confused of society know what to believe.
To avoid Freud,
if Einstein was right,
the revolution of evolution
travels not beyond light.
A constructive divorce course destroys a marriage heritage.
Theologians with slogans
pray for relief, in
compliance to defiance
believing not their belief.
To commandeer a bombardier, usher in the 'New Frontier'.
Revere and fear,
worship technology
and new terminology
with complaints on restraints.
With reliance on science
the Woman rides a Scarlet Beast
with the serpent of technology.
This "Age of Anxiety" shall reign.
The 'Great Society' died they explained,
trampled by the Horses of Apocalypse.

Lillian L. Kramer
MY HEART. . .IT BLEEDS FOREVER
To see her makes me smile,
But sadly I must weep.
My heart. . .It bleeds forever,
Upon a dream which isn't reaped.
My dream. It surrounds her.
My heart. It crys in pain.
Slowly do I call out;
Not ever. . .Never crying her name.
So I'll stand back in the shadows,
And I'll hold her dear.
But my heart. . .It bleeds forever,
Until my dream has come too near.

Joy Simmons
LOST
What sorrow prevails within my life of loneliness as I search for peace within the hallow of my soul
Lead me to my destination
For I know not where I go
Guide me through the shadow
of misery

For I know not why I cry
Show me laughter
For I cease to smile
Give me happiness
For reason gives me not
In hopes that I will live again
For living this is not.

Linda Roucken
SAVINGS
She walks along the meat counter
choosing ground chuck the way
she chooses her life:
biggest value for
the lowest price.

Lyne Marie Riffle Underwood
SOLITAIRE
The mountains' darkness is like the colour of my soul.
Those trees stretch up together so true. .
But why don't the trunks touch?
So many of them, yet far enough apart that only the force of the lonely wind can compel them to sway each against the other.
Alive and reaching for the sun,
Do they fight to be each a separate entity?
Why does Nature keep them apart for the world to see, when I know that under the soft earth their roots entwine and curl, so close to each other?
I will fight to be alone,
A solitary soul of my own volition.
I can feel the surge of lifeblood around me,
But I will deny its presence until the force of my loneliness pushes me tight against the universal pulp.

Donna Lee Kudrycki
OH WHAT IS A MAN?
Oh, what is a man
Who calls me his love
But does not love me?
If your timid were not running scared
I would grasp it
Like a child
Who clutches the first sprung bouquet
On a soft spring morn
And breathe deeply of a freshness
Not known to another.
But your heart beats much too quickly
And the blossoms
They whither on the vine
During the dark hours
Before the dew
Before the dawn
Before their faces open
To the sun.

Dot Luria Nadler
CHILDREN OF TODAY
From youth to grave: we toil and slave
For the material things: that hard work brings
But as we grow older with dignity and grace
We realize its the end of the race
Know that we all trod the path alone
For our eternal trip home
The young of today will be the oldsters of to-morrow
Much to our sorrow
That some do not revere the old:as media and radio have told
But remember young folks, you will be older and wiser
You children of today: the
oldsters of to-morrow.

Corbett C. Litteral
LOVES LAMENT
What gift should I give you
in the value that you are
Should I give you flowers
or a sad and slow guitar
Should I give you beauty
from a soft warm summer rain
Or should I give you silence
for in silence it is plain
that everything I gave to you
I gave to you in vain!

Kg Day
UNTITLED (34)
Once in a while I sit down to trial
And wonder why we've come to be?
A God or Creator
Or something yet greater
I wonder why we've come to be?
An angel in treason
A chance with out reason
A seed from a world we once knew,
An experimentation
Of some cosmic relation
the surviving remains of the crew,
Is it as real as it seems
Or all someones dream
Are we simply a thought of the earth,
Were we one of a billion
Or a billion to one
From the day we were granted our birth.
Once in a while I sit down to trial
And wonder why we've come to be,
Each man finds his answer
Or it grows like a cancer,
And haunts him in all that he sees.

Thomas J. Marnocha
REST IN PEACE
"These gates are made of cloud, dear Bobby.
These gates are made of cloud."
"Thank you, good and gentle friend,
Thank you."
"Where does it hurt you, dear Bobby?
Where does it hurt you?"
"At home, my good and gentle friend,
At home."
"Can you tell us exactly, dear Bobby?
Can you tell us exactly?"
"To the North, good and gentle friend,
To the North."
"Where you came from, dear Bobby?
Where you came from?"
"From there, good and gentle friend,
From there."
"Can we be of help, dear Bobby?
Can we be of help?"
"Load 'em and throw 'em good and gentle friend,
Load and throw them."
"Anything for love now, dear Bobby?
Anything for love now?"
"Too late, good and gentle friend,
Much too late."
"Does it still hurt there, dear Bobby?
Does it still hurt there?"
"Hard and terrible, good and gentle friend,
Hard and terrible."
"How do you feel now dear Bobby?
How do you feel now?"
"Lonely and old, good and gentle friend,
Lonely and very old."

Janet Pehr
SUNSET
So still, with a letter,
she reads in long light
from west window.
He beholds, with a brush,
and figures her form
as a shadow.

Marie L. Blood
MEMORIES
If memories were golden coins
How rich most of us would be,

We'd never have a worry then,
And life would be carefree.
But sad to say, it's not that way,
So we've got to be content,
With nothing more than
memories
And just the life that's spent.

Scott Haddon
SHOOTING STAR

Soaring soaring ever higher
Through the mist and through
the fire
I release my scattered feathers
in the wind
Falling sunken ship—I pick up
speed
Sinking faster and faster—Please
take heed
Plunging into the crest of the
earth
In the rock and depths of soil
Past the molder—I dare not toil
Lying in the terminals of hell

Mary F. Spencer
THE HICKORY TREE

The tall old hickory tree, so
fine,
Stood still throughout my
childhood years,
And lingers still, though gone.
My eyes through tears
Envision yet it's straight tall
trunk,
Remember bags of crispy
nuts,
The children, neighbors and
my own,
Embarking on the grass
Beneath which lay the treasure,
White and shrunk as if in
hiding,
Waiting, there abiding.
Dear tree, tree of my childhood,
Tree of my children's childhood,
You're mine in memory.

Neva P. Grimes
MY THANKSGIVING PRAYER

Thank you God, for everything,
Where shall I begin?
For the precious gift of thy Son
on the cross,
Who ransomed all my sin.
For the beauty of the Eastern
Sky,
Each day when the sun comes
up.
For the shining stars at night,
Assuring me thou art nigh.
For the glory of the sunset,
As it kisses day "goodbye",
Flinging rainbow colors
All across the Western Sky.
For the twilight, that
enchanting hour
Between day and night,
When peace covers all the
world,
This is given for our delight.
For nature's beauty, all around
me,
The birds, the trees, the flowers,
During the summer heat,
For gentle refreshing showers.
For the glad "good morning", of
a neighbor,
On a dark and gloomy day,
It lifted my spirits
And pushed the clouds away.
For the bounteous harvest of our
fields,
The golden corn and wheat,
These nourish our bodies,
Giving us wholesome bread to
eat.
For all the streams, both large
and small
Which bless our lovely land,
Furnishing passage for big ships
Also, an answer to barefoot
boy's demand.
For the beauty of the springtime,
When all the earth comes
awake,
And we realized you created all
this
Just for mankind's sake.
There are so many things to
give thanks for,
Dear Father, I can't name them
all,
But I think of each one of these
When on thy name, I call.
Amen.

Inez Hayworth
THE ESSENCE OF LOVE

Such a warm and tender feeling
When I'm near to where you are;
Joy all human joys concealing:
Bliss that's unexcelled by far.
This is the BEAUTY of love.
Just to be a help meet true,
To do the tasks each day
demands;
To bring more happiness to you
With loving heart and willing
hands.
This is the DUTY of love.
Your loving smile that warms
my heart;
Your cherished words and fond
caress;
Your carefulness to do your part
To make for me more happiness.
This is ASSURANCE of love.
Our confidence when skies are
drear,
Our prayers to clear a troubled
way;
Our faith to keep our hearts
sincere;
God's Grace to keep us day by
day.
This is ENDURANCE of love.
So may we both retain love's
beauty
As we each perform love's duty;
Going forth with love's
assurance
In the strength of love's
endurance—
This is the ESSENCE OF
LOVE.

Patricia Handley
WHO AM I

Who am I to judge the color of
your skin
Be it not the same as mine.
Who am I to judge the color of
your soul
Or which God you choose to
follow
Who am I to judge the color of
your heart
Or which road you choose to
take.
Who am I if not the same as
you
Regardless of my race, religion
or dreams.

John C. Cockerham
SECRET OF THE FOREST

Enter the realm of the forest
and let your senses enjoy.
Spiritual euphoria abounds
through nature's seductive ploy.
The bed of leaves will beckon,
temptation too strong to resist—
your head soon cupped in its
bosom,
your soul soon gently kissed.
As you succumb to lazy
and your body heavier grows,
your eyes drift slowly upward
where fine entertainment shows.
You may observe the dancing
of every leaf and limb—
each to its very own music.
the tune of the wind's own
whim.
The clouds are parading their
fashions
proceeding in a steady row,
and peeking betwixt the dancers
before deciding to go.
At the point of facing the
conqueror
who goes by the name of sleep,
there comes a fleeting moment
when a secret you can reap.
Your soul will flee your body
and in every direction fly
to become one with the forest—
the trees, the ground, the sky.

Irma Lois Drawdy
MINE ACCUSERS

I'm in the mid'st
Of mine accusers,
With stone clenched fist
As my abusers.
Just as the woman
At the well,
For loving a man
And deserving hell.
I throw myself Lord
Down at your feet,
Holding to thy word
Of mercy so sweet.

The accusing ones
Want justice done,
For a profound love
Of this sinful one.
Self righteously wanting
To even the score,
Not remembering Lord
What you said once before.
"He that is without sin among
you
Let him first cast a stone."
Help mine accusers to
understand
For our sins we must atone,
Vengance belongs not to man
But to you Lord, alone.

David Graham
EVENING DANCERS

Bold stallions, trembling like
trumpets proud and wreckless
defiantly
standing on rain
triumphant hooves conquer the
valley and signal their appraisal
in shrilled mockery.
Hidden,
the horses' heads fight the
horizon dressed in armor
and led by grace
warriors of the moon
advance to the foothills
taking refuge in Winter
where the altar lies abandoned
where geometry loses
dimension
and is covered in secret veils
that beg the Earth
to close proud eyes
and to see anew.

Jan Mennenga
LIES

I lie here in your arms
and you ask me not to love
you
and I say that I will not
knowing that I already do.

Laura Reyes
THE MAJESTY OF REMINISCENCE

Though your love is not for me;
Yearning fills my heart
Yet more than it can
withhold.
This passion transforms my
listless frame
To a:
Mirthful somebody,
Cries my inner voice:
In favor of you and I to
endure;
Commonly,
Just as previously.
Only if you longed for me,
Partially as much as I do for
you. . .then perhaps.
For now I shall last on our
memories;
The laughter,
The flame,
But then the pain.
Can't you love me in return?

Leolon Carpenter Whitley
CROWN JEWELS

My jewels are so very rare
But do not cost a thing.
I've found them miraculously
(Not in necklaces or ring!)
My *diamonds* are the brightest
days
My *sapphires* are clear nights
My *emeralds*, meadows fresh
and green
My *rubies*, rare twilights!
My *opals*, the unsettled days
When I'm sad or when I'm gay
The *topaz* means remembrances
And thoughts I've laid away.
For I'm rich that I have found
them
And can say they're really mine
I know they'll last forever
Nature's beauty so divine.
So I call them my own jewels
One can plainly see
That nature's way of loveliness
Has fashioned me a key.
The tapestry of untold moods
All studded with gems so rare
I wear them O! so grandly
On my throat, and in my hair!
No, you cannot see them
For these joys are far apart
The splendor of their beauty
I'm wearing in my heart.

Dennis Green-Author
LIFE

The way it was
the way it could be
we work all day
we sleep all night
and wake back up
and all is still
not right.
There's five days
in a week and still

we seek.
There's two days
for weekends to rest,
but we find out we can't
rest because yesterday was
the past, today is the present
and tomorrow's the future.
But no matter all we
do and say
day by day we still cry
help us Lord teach us
Lord for someday we hope
and pray it won't be
this way.

James C. Rymer
VORACITY IN SIMILE
Lurid thoughts, in transgressions
pot
Wavering, in exotic, tantalizing
gaze
Grouping, as in Plutonic
vastness fought
Emptiness, as in a lusty daze.
Lascivious urge, as force of
magnet claws
Hypnotic, as a cobra's gleaming
eyes
Momentum, as wound in a
tumbling falls
Torrid, as heats of jungles rise.
Anxiety!—as peace and comfort
wane
As hordes of people blend in
pain
And time and effort end as one
When mortals' quest is lost and
done.
The only way is truth to life;
But many souls they drown in
strife.

Faye P. Parker
WHO AM I?
WHO AM I to presume
That I could ever sing a tune
Or write a poem
Or teach a child any lesson
Worthwhile?
WHO AM I to sometimes dare
To say, "My dear, you surely
care
That life isn't all bad—
Think of all the good you've had
Life can be happy not always
sad"—
WHO AM I to shrink from right
To turn away without a fight
To be afraid when things go
wrong
To join the weak, forget the
strong
Why can't I sing a happy song?
WHO AM I?

Donna E. Carpenter
THE GUIDING LIGHT
My darkest day
Is brightened by His Light.
When I don't know where to
turn,
He points the way that's right.
When the path seems never
smooth,
He sends forth love, my anguish
to soothe.
He knows my innermost
feelings and every thought,
And urges me on when life is
worry fraught.
Though problems fill my life
at every turn,
He offers the peace, for which I
yearn.
My Lord brightens each day and
my darkest night,
Then brings a new morn with
promise bright.
He's my constant companion,
In good times and dreary.
My Comforter and Counselor,
Who renews the spirit when
weary.
My friend, may you know too,
His love and comfort in all you
do.
Let His counsel steer you
through your darkest plight,
He's always there as your
Guiding Light.

Jane H. Connors
LESSONS IN LIVING
Once again I play the fool
Exposed my heart and broke my
own rule.
This game is too dangerous,
Meant only for the young and
adventurous.
As the years go by
You'd think I would stop trying.
There is no such thing as
happiness
Only pain, sorrow, and crying.
Finally, the hurt goes away
And I try to live again
Picking up the pieces gone
astray
Doing the best I can.
Why does your memory keep
coming back to haunt me?
Why do I remember the good
things we've had?
Why do I still ache for you?
Just moments ago
I could have sworn there was
no such thing as love
Then I looked up and saw you.

Frank R. Schmitt
LONELY PEOPLE
Two lonely people
making their world a happy
place
Nobody cared about them
they weren't good enough for
the crowd
Everybody looked down on them
they were laughed at and
joked about
Oh how it hurt
to hear what was said
They wouldn't let on
they cried all night till dawn
One day by chance
they found each other
Cause someone thought it
would be
kind of funny to see them
together
It doesn't matter now
what people think or say
about them
They are happy now
with the love they give to
each other
Just two lonely people
alone in their world of love

Jim Neal
SONNET TO THE PIGSKIN—ESE
Now basketball will put me
right to sleep,
And baseball's merits I will not
declaim,
And hockey never makes my
heart to leap—
But football! Hoo boy, football!
That's my game!
When Rams and Cowboys clash
on white-striped field
And bodies crash and fly and
overturn,
And blocking backs attempt to
form a shield
For runners who are tumbled,
bow for stern;
When pigskins split the
uprights of the goal,
When strong-side safety's
intercept a pass,
When Humble How'rd and Don
and Frank extoll
The quarterback who's flattened
on the grass,
Then I, my eyes glued hard
on Channel Sev'n,
Ascend in perfect peace to
Gridiron Heav'n.

Jeannie L. Metz
A MIND OF ITS' OWN
What makes me feel so alone
sometimes,
like there's no one around
anywhere?
But it's not that I'm by
myself
and that no one is even there.
I am in my own sea of thoughts,
And at this time unnoticed by
me
The world's still moving along
But my mind is just not free.
it's captured by many things
that normally I hold at bay,
like sadness for the loss of a
loved one
And how I miss them today.
Some things my mind rejects
But some it can only postpone
So every once in a while
it seems to have a mind of
its' own.
It's these days I live in myself
And it seems no one can touch
me
Sadness, tears, can't be
postponed anymore,
And I wait for my mind to be
free.

Gussie C. Ninemire
A PART OF YOU
How can I say what I have done
For were it not for you
I'd only be a lonely soul
With no hopes or plans in
view
I build upon your ideas
The thoughts you share
review
The love and faith you give to
me
Are treasures fond and true
So in this trio we are one
And anything I do
Is not my own—I dare not boast
It's God and I—and you.

Michelle Nicole Beaudry
TO MY FRIEND
You are my friend who cheers
me when
the clouds of doubt are
overhead.
You are a friend who's with me
when
the trail of cheer is all I tread.
You are a friend who cares for
me when
my smile is turned upside
down.
You are a friend who laughs
with me when
I feel like being a clown.
You are a friend who jokes with
me when
My humor has gone sour.
You are a friend who worries
'bout me
every passing hour.
You are a friend who talks to
me when
I know it is time to hear.
You are a friend who I know
when
it is time to give out some
cheer.
You are a friend who's with me
when
whenever we need a friend.
You are a friend I value most—
and will until the end.
You, Are My Bestest Friend!

Bob Conklin
OPPORTUNITY
There stood a girl
With a tear in her eye
I wondered why?
Was it because
I didn't pause,
As I passed by?

Marvin Buffington
VERISIMILITUDE
I marvel at creations' infinite
variety,
Whose every intricate device
Contrived to fashion only one
like you.
Half blythe spirit, half tender
animal,
I wonder at the comfort of your
grace.
The charming vectors of your
limbs
Blind up the hurts of all my
years,
The music of your voice and
lips
Calms my soul of worldly ills,
The promise of your fruitful
season
Giving hope to quell my fears,
The light of love from out your
eyes,
Illuminates my reason.
So take my hand your charming
grace
And follow me together,
Along the paths of intellect,
Where love's in bloom forever.

Mary Rose Shoemaker
THE HANDICAPPED
Our life is hard for some to see,
But we are happy as can be.
Each day for us is very bright,
For we try to keep our God in
sight.
We cannot dwell on the past,
As we hope God's love will last.
He will guide us by the hand,
Until we reach the happy land.
We will see our friends face to
face,
When we reach the holy place.
We look forward to going home,
Where we will be with God
alone.
We will give one last sigh,
When we see the Man on high.
We hope that He will touch our
head,
And be pleased with the life we
led.

A. R. Ziolkowski
SPRING
The soft leaves sway ever so
lightly in the breeze
The mighty oak on which I lean
stands so straight and tall.
The wind shifts the boughs
softly as you sleep.
The sun throws a shadow over

you,
a blanket to keep you warm.
A woodchuck scampers when
you move,
lie still my dear.
The blue sky is our roof,
no rain, not today.
Natures alive today, you can
smell the love burst forth from
her.
Our love sleeps deep with in
you, let it be gentle.

Charles J. Fitti

AGE'S WISDOM

Fierce and fearsome
Are the angers of old age,
Gathered in our breast
They rage.
Roaring a vengeance
On things past,
Dragging us down
Until we breath our last.
Robbing us of wisdom
And clear thought,
Telling us our lives
Are for nought.
Ensnaring our hope
In a net of despair,
Telling us
All is unfair.
But cast off
And flung free,
We are restored
For eternity.

Delpha Funk Romeiser

A HUNTERS DAY

A perfect day to go hunting;
Charley, Jim, and Frank were
there,
Checking their guns for the
third time,
At the cold grey sky they'd
stare.
Hours passed, but they were
hunters
Born for such a day as this;
Just to see some geese come
over
Would to them be sweetest
bliss.
Every man was poised and ready
At the sound of honking geese.
Now their patience was
rewarded
For the honking did increase.
Jim said, "Look boys, here they
come."
"Aren't they beauties," Charley
said.
Frank just pointed with his
shotgun;
They all blasted up ahead.
Dropping slowly from formation
A great bird was earthward
bound.
Happy was the hunting trio
Happy were the hunters sounds.
Dropping swiftly from formation
Flashed another goose in sight,
Underneath his falling brother
Raised him back into the flight.
Charley, Jim, and Frank the
hunters
Watched their hope now fade
away,
As the vibrant honking lessened
This had been a hunters day.

J. D. DeVore

OUR FRIENDSHIP

Our friendship grows with time,
thank you for being mine.
Your always there to bend an
ear,
in times of joy or times of
fear.
You've got your troubles, and
I've
got mine,
But our friendship continues to
grow with
time.
Not a word needs to be said,
there is a feeling instead,
That only we share, because we
care,
for each others,
Hopes, and dreams, and
future schemes.
We don't know what the future
will bring,
But we can be sure of at least
one thing.
As life deals out it's joys and
fears,
Our friendship will keep
growing
throughout the years!

Brian Lynch Johnson

I DREAMED OF BEAUTY

I dreamed of beauty in dappled
colors,
Bowing heads in graceful
gesture,
Warmed with the heartbeats of
a frightened dove.
Then a mighty light maimed my
vision,
Like that of Sisyphus,
Or Cyclops as he felt the herd
While Odysseus sucked at the
ewe's breast.
Then the ocean,
White from frothing hard,
A mighty chase across the ocean
tract
I saw a hand,
With strings attached like a
puppet show.
Tiny things on tiny strings,
Dancing to and fro
To the music of a broken harp.

Margaret Crosscup Adams

REALITY

The moon and the stars, the
sun and the sea
All are shining reflections of
Me.
Spring and summer, winter and
fall
Just can't part from Me at all.
I grew the tree that holds the
nest
For the mother bird and the
rest—
Majestic mountains that rise
to the skies,
A mountain daisy and some
butterflies.
When clouds and storms hide
the light
I arch my rainbow. All is bright.
Honeysuckle, roses, I twine on a
wall
With a pleasing fragrance—It
is free to all.
Do you wonder who I am?
I am the visible part of God
I am Nature—Love, my Rod.

Ethel Stoudemire

THE GATES OF PEARLS

Come with me. . . . .
Taste of the fascination
whack of the magician
thriller supreme,
Gain inspiration of scientists,
heart of the poet,
luck of the gambler,
to the gates of pearls,
And see. . . . .
The greatest Enterpriser,
two fishes. . .five loathes,
connoisseur of wine
delightful, delectable,
delicious,
Master of the element;
wind, water, storm,
Who writes the last chapter
on healing the whole man,
Who sees beauty in the tiny
sparrow
that never toils—always dines,
Who else could wangle
inscribed coin
from an unsuspecting fish's
jaws. . .
Or send unescorted Command
across miles
to heal the centurion's
servant,
The inner eye that sees in
another city
the guileless Nathaniel
(under the fig tree),
Who can call the elusive
spirit
back into it's former home!
And know. . . . .
No greater thrills,
no deeper mysteries
can be found anywhere else,
No greater (socalled) luck,
No treasure, neither in heaven
nor hell
Greater than this priceless
Pearl.

Melrose I. Riley

A STRANGE ADVENTURE

I stood at the end of the world
one day
With naught "twixt the earth
and space.
The facts that were solid behind
me lay,
Before, not a tree nor a face.
A mystery wall that was
breathlessly white,
Adventure into the unknown.
Standing alone—what an
awesome sight,
Like facing the Judgement
Throne.
Then silhouettes dim came out
of the gloom
And passed me a fraction
away.

No features—no faces, just
shapes to assume
That passed me and faded
away.
Then forward I took a step that
was sure;
Familiar the pathway I found.
The blanket of white I now
could endure
For I was quite sure of my
ground.
I think it was strange when
naught could I see
Of things that were solid and
real,
That faith and strong confidence
took hold of me
Not knowing what time
would reveal.
Like darkness of night and
fathomless sea,
With depths that I may not
explore,
My mind conjured pictures in
fantasy
With strange new adventures
in store.
I heard in the distance a
piercing shriek
That rent through the cool
morning air
Like screaming of banshees
ready to wreak
Their vengeance on humans for
fair.
Then up rolled the curtain of
misty white.
I gazed as an audience thrilled
Who waits with impatience to
view the sight
And then with amazement is
filled.
The fog made the wall that shut
off my sight
And strengthened the fanciful
mind.
The day smiled through the last
cobwebs of night
And left all my pictures
behind.
And there, like a sentinel
keeping his trust,
A pencil like shadow so high,
Rose out of the mist and
solemnly thrust
It's silvery shaft to the sky.

Kenneth A. Brown

I'LL BE BACK

Oh yes, San Francisco.
I left my heart there too
If only I was there now
I wouldn't be so blue
I could drive to Sausilito
across the Golden Gate
or go to San Mateo
where I might find a mate
Or up to Santa Rosa,
where I will find some wine
and sample some fine Burgundy
or maybe some good Rhine
Then slip down to Carmel
and sleep right on the sand
Then go straight to Santa Cruz
to hear a damn good band
I wish I was there now
in that city on the bay
to enjoy it's heart and people.
I'll be back there one fine day

Pam Evans

THE SINGINGS OF MY MIND

With you I give love/
I can give you the Euphrates/
the Tigris/Nile
and all things possible/if
you only accept with
love/all these treasures I
hold dearly/
with the thoughts of my
mind
Hear the singings/life/pain/
emotions blending/
togetherness at hand—the
unadjusted voices/s
sing?or is this the singing(s)
of my mind—
A Man (you)
You can give so much with your
eyes/mouth/and soul/the
energy you transmit to me/
yet I smile—your moves so
fine/i wonder
can he ever be mine/you say
so much/so little time/
i hear in my mind—tell the
Story of the
Song/the key to life/the Book
of Youth/Kan you hear the
voices/read/see/heed/
know
Kan you hear the voices/what
of its truth to tell/

He know/they know/Now we
know
Tell the story of the Song'
Kan you hear the voices
i can give you the
Euphrates/Tigris/also
the Nile
all things possible if you
only accept
with love/
all these things i have/hold
dearly
the treasures of my mind—
Kan you give me the
Euphrates/Tigris
while i give you
The
Nile?

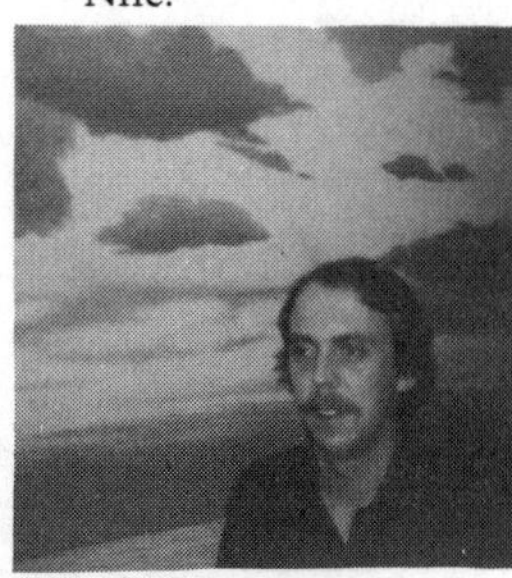

William Phillips Child
WINTER'S FIELD
Like wind through frozen
branches, I cannot bend.
The wound that was once open,
has closed but will not mend.
And for loss of a guide, warmer
winds I will never feel.
I will stand here forever, on
this winter's field.
This land was once all golden,
wheat fields brushed the sky.
Crystal blue summer nights,
with full moons passing by.
The songs of the summer would
let me sleep at night,
And my morning doves would
kiss me, and wake me to the
light.
Feelings do not last forever,
and this I have been told,
But I watched how my
grandfather never seemed to
grow old.

So I set myself to ponder on
this old man's loving soul.
If I follow can you lead me from
this land of cold?
Spring bears the fruits of
tenderness, that summer just
passes on.
The eyes of fall preach
emptiness, colors bright that
soon are gone.
And the winter should last all
of four months, to the spring
it would yield,
But what hope do I have
without the love, to escape
this winter's field?

Ed Carpenter
I AM A SINGER OF LOVE SONGS
I am a singer of love songs
I am a true modern-day
balladeer
Why yes, I sing love songs
And I'll sing any love song you
want to hear. . .
I'll sing of a love—so warm,
so rare, so free
I'll hum a few lines, recite
poetry
I'll sing from my soul so all
who hear shall know
The song that I'm singing is of
a love, sweet love. . .
Sweet songs of a baby—his
mother's watchful eye
A song of his dad—chests filled
with pride
And one of young lovers—care
thrown to the winds
Of a man and a woman, where
do they begin?
And of love so bitter. . .? I think
I can manage a tune
But if you feel you can't stand
it, feel free, leave the room. . .
If I sing my song nicely, the
memory'll bring tears to your
eyes
but somehow it seems wrong to
sing while you cry—
Then again, a singer of love
songs sings the good and bad
And often he's singing of the
loves he's had
And the more that he's loved—
how much sweeter his song
But his list of sad love songs
grows on ever on. . . .

Helen Curtis Sheets
FIND MY HEART, PLEASE
I would like to know I had a
heart,
Can you find it for me, please?
It has naught to do with giddy
sighs
Or smiles and winks that tease.
I'd like to know I had a heart
That would beat with depths of
love:
Solid, honest feelings true
That could earn favor from
above.
It has been very, very long
Since feelings deep and true.
The superficial, shallow tastes
Of my heart, I don't approve.
I hope a deeper, finer love
Will show itself to view
I'd like to know
Without all doubt
That I could love and cherish
you.

Boris Biloskirka
UNTITLED
what if
Spring is a thing
forgotten this year—
what if
Summer passes
and no one sees
that roses had not
bloomed—
what if
Fall falls
right through its fallen
leaves
and plunges straight
into winter again
(right back
from where i just began).
what if
i refused to believe
that spring is a thing
which can be forgotten,
and love is a feeling
which had never been—
then,
all we've made could pass
and war
can carry us out to sea. . . .
(and i
would have never told you
how beautiful you are).

Dorothy J. Reynolds
IMPORTS
We've had all kinds of
Presidents
But the kind I'll not support
Is a guy that we call "Carter"
Who endorses Beef Imports.
We have the best darn Beef
there is
Right here in our Home Land
But if Carter doesn't watch it
We might export to Japan.
He thinks he knows our
business
And wants to be the Boss
Does he know that they can't
tax a man
Who operates a loss?
To try to drive the cow man out
Would be a big mistake
'Course Carter lives on Peanuts
He never eats a steak.
Carter you really should try one
That's raised in the ole U.S.A.
It sure beats the Hell outa
peanuts
And it's done the American
Way.
When next election rolls around
I wonder what you'll do
When you don't get a single
vote
Import those damn thing's too?

Minnie Boyd Popish
AUTUMN
What is Autumn?
It is an amber liquer
In a cut glass stein.
Should it be quaffed quickly
Or sipped sparingly?
When it is gone
There is no more in the bottle.
It is a ruby resting on ice.
It is a gusty wind in bare
branches.
It is a seed beneath thick leaves.
It is a wedding of
Loss and hope,
Warmth and chill,
Death and birth,
Autumn is the Omega and the
Alpha.

Cheryl A. Briggs
THOUGHTS OF LONELINESS
Thoughts of loneliness
tap emotional veins
causing undue stress
short circuiting the brain

Michele M. Newman
SOMETHING SPECIAL
Life—What's it all about?
It's a privilege given to Man by
god.
Each individual was created
uniquely,
And given different motives
which might seem odd.
Some people are put here
without a care
As to what their next move will
be.
They have everything they
could need or want,
And really experience what it's
like to be free.
There are people who fight hard
to be successful.
Their fight pays off and they
make it.
Life is hard and some find
themselves happy;
But not all. For these are the
ones who can't quit.
Others fight and struggle to
make ends meet.
Somehow, they possess
something special.
Something special to be shared
with the world.
They are the ones who love Life
and are happiest of all.
I envy them and would like to
share that special something.
It's something which I've
searched for my whole life
thru.
I'm sure that potential lies
within us all.
But, I've yet to see this dream
come true.

Carroll Ann Lee
SEASONAL APPROACH
Winds of cold
Mesmerize the feet of a loner
passing through
An Autumn rain.
Promises of tomorrow
Snowingly entice swaying trees
into
A rhapsody of chill.
Smoke swirls
It's way through clouds of bated
breath
Dispensing silently.
Promenading condensation
Bows and curtsies before a
Blanket of white.
A twig snaps
In the knowledge of a heavy
frost above
The grass of Summer.
A sense of freshness
Alerts the mind and hones the
ear tuning
Raindrops melodically.
Nostalgic movements
Combine pulsating thoughts
into
Seasons of today.

Ella Foster O'Brien
MY BOOK OF PAST
I'll put my memories in a book,
My thoughts of days gone by,
I'll weave a carpet, of my past
Of things that made me cry.
I'll build a house of laughter
A garden of rose thoughts
rare,
I'll lay a path of stepping stones
To love when you were there.
Along that path, we traveled,
dear,
Hand in hand, through smiles
and tears,
I hope some day to be again
And so forget my woes and
fears.
And as I lay me down to sleep,
I'll wrap my mind in dreams
Of all that love has brought to
me,
My book of past, the morning
bright, will bring.

Phyllis Goodall
ACTION
If I can write one
Letter every day
That speaks to
Someone far away
Or near, of Cheer
Of love and laughter
Of how their dearness
Brings to mind
The need to act

Toward my kind
In trust and gentle
Understanding.
Then when time comes
To leave this place
I shall not wither
In the shame of
My inaction—

Judith A. Ortscheid
FORCE OF LIFE
Life Force! Spirit!
Which inside this shell
of flesh and bones dwells,
What purpose for your
existence?
What dreams must you fulfill?
People so confused
Know not what they truly are,
They worship only the flesh
The true self they disregard.
Awareness lying low,
The truth cannot be seen.
Pain and Suffering believed the
way,
Joy and Happiness only a dream.
One day the light of
realization
Will fill the minds of all.
An awareness of truth will
come.
A time for change will dawn.
Only then will we know the
power,
That each of us is within,
Then can we change this world
of ours,
So that everyone can win.
Come quickly day of freedom,
So wisdom and love can grow,
With understanding amongst
everyone,
Admiration, knowledge and joy.
What is the essence of life?
The answer will one day be
known.
The life force inside that shell,
Is really, truly you.

Ella Poindexter
NO MORE
No more will I trod the earth,
Nor see the clear blue sky.
No more to see the springtime
sun,
Nor, the leaves to die.
No more will I lay me down,
underneath
the dew,
Nor no more to see my
friends, but
they were so few.
Now beneath the sod I sleep,
Where my feet have trod,
I pray now, at my final sleep,
I pray I sleep with God.

Lois E. Wood
LOVE SOMEBODY
Love somebody while
the sun still rises,
and the moon shines bright.
Love somebody while
the world's still turning
and the stars give their light.
Love somebody while
the flowers still bloom,
and the birds sing sweetly
with all of their might.
Love somebody while
the rain keeps falling
and the wind keeps blowing
and the snow covers the earth
with its flakes of white.
Love somebody
while its day.
Love somebody
while you may.
Love somebody,
pray for somebody,
forgive somebody;
love somebody tonight.
And the world will be;
a much better place!
Yes, the world will be
a much better place!

Crystal Eubanks Hall
LIFE
Life is just a frustrating mass of
existence.
"Being never really living."
Constantly dying in the midst
of living.
"Being never really living."
Always hurting, no one
feeling,
Always hoping, never
dreaming,
Always talking, no one
hearing,
Always hating, never loving.
"being never really living."
Dying in the midst of living.
Then death,
never living.

Caroline Alston Mann
TO A FRIEND
What could be more cherished
Than your friendship staunch
and true;
What could make one happier
Than to have a friend like you!
A friend who is ever thoughtful
In the little things worth while;
A friend who always greets you
With a warm and gentle smile.
A friend who accepts your
friendship
On a smooth and even ground;
A friend who always seeks you
out
When'er you are around.
A friend whom you can always
trust
And know that trust is true;
A friend who has your
confidence
And an equal trust in you.
A friend whom you can never
forget
Come what will or may;
A friend whose friendship
stronger grows
With every coming day!

Bernice Evaughn Marpel
GOD'S CLOUD
It was a cloud,
A huge and black foreboding
thing;
It made wind howl
And brought forth thunder and
lightning.
It shook the trees
And bent them to the sodden
ground;
Such things as these
Made hearts like mine begin to
pound.
And then the hail,
But through it all she stood,
transfixed;
Her face told tales
Of Joy, and Wonder, in conflict.
I stood and stared
As winds ceased and her head
she bowed;
Her heart she bared—
"What strength He gave-to this,
His cloud."

Isolda Betina
MY DREAM
I wait for you in the top of a
wave
I wait for you in the half of a
beach
I wait for you in the half of
the sun
of evening
I hear you in the melancholy
note
of my Moorish guitar
I am full of fragrance when I call
you
by your name among the flowers
of my
garden
You are in the half of my heart
You are in the half of the pupil
of my eyes, not very far off my
lips
that they pronounce your name
in a low
voice
I wait for you in the half of
moon
I wait for you in the half of
brightness
of my love, but you live in the
vastness
of the sky
You live in the half of
constellation
And I am here. I live in the half
meridian
I live here in the half of my
dream,
but I wait for you in the blue
mist of
my illusion.

Mescal (Mickey) Yanacek
SAGA OF THE CLOWNS
Hey there, Mr. Clown; with your
sad yet funny face.
With your old baggy clothes,
and complete lack of grace.
You may be skinny or you may
be fat;
As your large feet go splat-splat-
splat.
We wonder what your feelings
are-As you try to make us
smile;
You stumble, then fall, and
pretend to be hurt; for just a
little while.
Are you pretending when you
say;
Hey look you'se guys—it's a
beautiful day.
Are you a person who likes to
try;
To make us laugh instead of
cry?
Do you wonder dear Sir, as you
hear the crowd roar;
Hey there Mr. Clown—give us
more-more-more.
Could it be Mr. Clown, that
you're crying inside;
At the state of the world—
or the scars that you hide?
Or Hey Mr. Clown; Could it
be—Could it be;
That you after all—Are a person
like me?

Robert Hanie
YOU FOR ME
Like the morning sun rise
You open my eyes
Like the sun gives warmth to a
new day
So does your warmth, gives to
me another
As the sun gives life and
strength to many things
So do you, for me
The sun creates a disturbance
and brightens the day
And you too, cause this to
happen within me
As the sun sets, so does our day
And our memories are passed,
until another day

Rosana Neville
SPRING
He said he would be back again
this way
I wait for him and look for him
each day
It's fall now and wood-smoke is
in the air
We spoke of spring and how we
would meet there.

Inez E. Pennington
WITH ME
The rain is dripping from the
eaves.
And shining on the fallen
leaves.
I used to love a rainy day.
Even though the skies were
grey.
But you were with me.
The rain drops running down
the pane.
Are like the tears I've shed in
vain.
I can't believe you're really gone.
I'll never see you from now on.
Why have you left me?
Now my heart is feeling sore.
The rain just makes me miss
you more.
And I'm not feeling very brave.
And you're not with me.
And never will be.

Joy Hawthorne
IN OUR FUTURE PARADISE
*(This is about an elderly
gentleman who has been told
he will only live a few more
weeks. He is talking to his wife.)*
Now your hair is full of silver
And your heart is full of gold
All the years we spent together
Full of love that can't grow cold.
Though your brow is full of
furrows
You always say the sweetest
things,
It's the little things in a life
That give the happiness it
brings.
I'll always remember
And ever realize
Our love is a glowing ember
With that lovelight in your
eyes.
So when the clock says forever,
and ever and aye,
Then our love says forever,
And forever and a day.
Though my life span is slowly
ebbing,
I am now past two score twice;
I'll soon be waiting for you
sweetheart,
In our future paradise.

Farron L. Allen
THIN ICE
Trees black and barren huddle
looking to keep warm
Through the trees
outlines of rolling hills—
clash
the aftermath of red and
purple

a fading sun
settling
As the blackness invades
the bitter chill of winter
seems more—awesome
With distant lights I realize
this wasteland
is not only my isolation
The oceans have frozen over
beating waves
suddenly dead silent
Mounting ice skates
I go sailing
looking for thin ice

Teague Keftiu
HYDE AMONG THE JEKYLLS

Wine and cake for bus'nessmen,
Some drinks to silent wives,
Praise the Lord and pass the
ammo,
And quell minority rights!

Robyn M. Lees
I ASKED

I asked "what?"
And this was the first step
towards truth
And I looked at the churches
and
synagogues and
temple walls and asked
"why?"
And this was the first step
towards knowledge.
And an answer came from
within me
an answer that was already
embedded inside,
but lost in the
entanglement and confusion
of an outlined
well organized society.
I asked, "What is God?"
And I was called a hypocrite
by those who didn't know
what they believed—
but kept on believing.
And in the midst of a crystal
spring day
God came to me in the form of
a sparrow,
and in the form of the
fertile May dandelions
that grew wild in the yards.
And God came to me in every
person
and everything that holds
life
within myself
And God came to me in the
voice—
Not of a preacher reading
the words of a multi-
generation-worn Bible
But in the voice of the wind—
blowing through the leaves
and of the rain—
falling freely from the sky
cleansing the earth, and all
of her contents,
in a bath of purity.
And I was told to love
And I was told to be
And this was the answer to my
questions
And I was enlightened.

Audys Duvall
ENCOUNTER WITH PROTEUS

Nature took me gently by the
hand,
And led me through this lovely
land.
She showed me all her trees and
flowers
And lofty peaks and woodsy
bowers.
Springs that are hot and peaks
that are cold,
New-blooming flowers and
mountains old.
I felt a kinship and glowed
with pride,
Until a big mountain took me
aside,
And spoke to me roughly
through her sighing pines,
"How do you think I came to be,
And where did I get these lines?"
And Old Faithful spewed her
boiling steam,
And said, "Wake up, dear, from
your dream.
I bring a message from mid-
earth to you,
And so do the earthquakes and
volcanoes, too."
And now, with a tighter grip on
my hand,
Nature told me the *real* story of
my land.
"I've steamed and I've boiled,
And I've opened my mouth,
And spewed molten metal from
north to south.
An angry giant I lie here now,
Flexing my muscles and
wrinkling my brow.
And when you are feeling
content and grand,
I'll tighten my grip on your
trusting hand."
I looked and my hand was a
cinder, charred,
With Mother Nature gripping it
hard.

Claudine N. Hatcher
A MOMENT'S RETROSPECT

As I think of how you looked
that afternoon,
I wonder if I'll ever see
that glow in your eyes again.
I thought you were really happy,
but it was only my happiness I
felt.
I remember how we acted like
kids;
playing keep away with one
another.
And when our game was
through,
we sat together—alone.
Not much was spoken; but so
much was said.
As I looked into your eyes,
I wanted to know what you
were feeling.
But all I knew was I never
wanted
that moment to end.
I thought of what I'd do if I ever
lost your love,
but I never have.
Only because you can't lose
what was never yours.

Lorinda A. Balue
TOMORROW'S GATE

Oh, Bright One
Thou beauty surpasses all
things
My brightest and most
cherished dreams are dimmed
They can nay be comparred
with thee
For thou art the moon,
Mankind's anchor of hope to the
future
For with thee lies our hope
Our one chance for renewed life
Beyond thee is a future
To be cultivated and conquered
For you are the beginning of
exploration
Beyond thee is a vast expanse
of infinite space
of exploration yet to be
Aye, and thou art our pride
Thou art our inspiration
Our strength of mind
Our spur to forever struggle,
For though we be but Man
A creature of stubborn
determination
There is still want of
And need for, a guiding hand.
Thy beauty forever beckons
Guiding us to thou cresent gate
That awaits all mankind
Thou wait but for tomorrow
Ever tilting on the verge of
today.
We see thee
Thou wondrous beauty
And naught can be said
That we shall not survive
For thou art our truth
To what mysterious wonders
Lie in the dark brightness
of beyond.

Joel Hatch
OF YEARS GONE BY

I wandered among the lilies wild
In fields of grain and rye,
And in the evening, I sat me
down
To watch the fading sky.
Oh how the light of sun did
sink
As this sky above did die,
And then I thought of all that
was
In the days of years gone by.
I was but of such loneliness
As a breed apart felt I,
I had no one to bring to me
Good reason to comply.
Those days, so cruel, did rip my
soul
Still, the scars of pain have I,
But now those days are gone
forever,
Those days of years gone by.
For now a heart does beat with
mine
And a hand dries what tears I
cry,
And I've found some one to help
me see
All the reasons why I must try.
For the hearts like ours, that
beat as one,
Spread a love that could never
die,
And now I feel no pain at all
From those days of years gone
by.
For always there shall be within
me
A love I can't deny,
For you alone have ended
All the pain from years gone by.
It was you alone who gave me
The love on which I rely,
That faded and deminished
All my thoughts of years gone
by.
Now many years have come
since then
And just the same passed by,
And you have left me all alone
With but the question "Why?"
For in this hour dark and dim
I can hear God's soft reply,
"This is the end of the path
you chose
In those days of years gone by."

Jody L. Dean
A FRIEND

What is a friend, you ask?
A friend is someone who loves
you for who you are; not who
you should be,
A friend is someone who can
look beyond your faults and
capture and keep only your
positive features;
A friend is someone who will
not question but listen to
your problems;
A friend is someone who can
criticize you not out of spite
but out of genuine concern;
A friend is someone who is
there to pick you up when
you fall
And gently push you down
when you venture too high;
A friend is someone I have
found in you.

Sarah
I DO NOT WANT MY PICTURE TAKEN

I saw a picture look at me
of a lady dead and gone,
trapped throughout eternity
in a frame that was her home.
I do not want my picture taken
as the lady did that day,
it would leave me somewhat
shaken
to be gazed upon that way.
Though all the world could
smile at me
in that frame of gold,
beyond my eyes they could not
see

the thoughts within my soul.
Inside a glass you do not grow,
you sit with just a name.
I do not want the world to know
me, captured in a frame.
I'll leave my words as part of
me,
and those who read and care
will know my soul and they can
see
as if a picture's there.

Carmen J. Lendi Jr.
LEAVING

I lived in this house a long time, maybe too long. This house which I grew up in, was fed, clothed and cared for; a house so full of love. . .

Then, I moved from this house, as young men often do, because of my own love. I left because of my own dreams and aspirations. I left also because of the realization that it was the time to finally leave. . .

But, as sometimes happens, my love left me. And, all the dreams and thoughts of the future left. . .

Suddenly, I am back in this house which I had left. I can feel the love is still here, but the feelings of staying have left also. . .

I will be leaving soon; not for any dreams or for a certain love, or for really anything special. . .

No, I will be leaving because of the realization that once again it is the time to leave.

Ann Galbraith
CELEBRATING
No man loved a woman
the way that you
Loved me just now,
or if one did
I never heard about it
not in a storybook
or at my ear
If it were so,
if there were even one—
One experience the same as this
On record or file
Surely I would know
Surely I would hear the
Celebrating down the street
as someone else found out
Just how it felt—for the length
of time you were here.

Marie E. Marsh
FUNNY WOMAN
A woman tries a thousand ways
To look younger than her years;
And a few stray wisps of graying
hair
Can send her into tears.
She will cream her face and
bathe with oils;
She will cut and style her
tresses;
She will trim her figure and
plan her clothes
'Til she can model Junior
dresses.
She will take great pains to
fool the world
By playing a young lady's drama;
And then willingly give it all
away
When a little tyke shouts, "Hi,
Grandma!"

Hilary Palmer
THE TRAVELER
A traveler on a lonely quest, sat down to rest. He reflected deeply. While contemplating with whom to speak—a voice within asked: What do you seek?
Traveler: How much longer
must I travel until this
tangled web I unravel?
Voice: Stop here! Journey no
farther. Yourself dwelleth
here, not yonder.
Traveler: Who are you? Do you
seek too?
Voice: No. I am thee. I have
always been and ever will
be.

Traveler: If you are me then
who am I? With whom can I
identify?
Voice: We are one.
Traveler: How can it be that
you are me? Open mine
eyes. I cannot see!
Voice: You have seen me. You
see me every day expressing
in a different way.
You fail to recognize me.
Traveler: Tell me something of
yourself.
I am the activity of the
ocean; the song of the bird
But only in the silence can
my voice be heard.
I am the perfume of the
flower; the warmth of the
sun.
I am the runner and the
race to be run.
I am the doer and the deed.
I am the sower and the seed.
Look deeply into the eyes of
the people you meet; I am
there for you to greet.
You have not seen me
because you are unaware of
who I am.
Traveler: Speak to me more of
yourself.
Voice: I am the harvest and the
reaper. I am the sleeper and
the sleep.
I am the reality of your
being. I am that which you
seek.
Traveler: You tell me of yourself
as well as you can, but I
still do not know who I am.
Voice: You are not listening. Go
deeper into the silence.
You are what you seek. You
are the I that I am.
Deeper into the silence
creep. You will find what
you are running from.
Traveler: How can I find you?
Tell me where! How can I
feel your presence near?
Voice: I cannot be found
anymore than the wave can
find the ocean
But in the silence I can be
realized.
I have always existed. I am
ever in motion. Know me
and be revitalized.
Traveler: But you are only a
voice! I have hands and feet.
I am flesh and bones; I have
no choice! Tell me, why
does my heart beat?
Voice: You have a body, but you
are not your body. You are
the I that I am.
Your body is the channel
through which I express
daily.
I am the life that your heart
beats from.
Traveler: Must I understand that
my body is an instrument
through which you would
express if I would only go
deep within and make the
request?
Voice: There is no need to make
the request. I am always
expressing.
Just realize and rest.
Traveler: Tell me then, what
should I do in order to
realize this "you"?
Voice: Do nothing. Just be.
Traveler: Be what?
Voice: Be yourself. You are the
you that I am. I am the you
that you are.
Go into the silence as often
as you can, and you will no
longer seek me afar.

Rene John Pouteau
SHE
She laid with her nakedness
Against the waving sweat-
stained sheets.
She was a stack of palm
branches
waiting for the workman to
come
Clear her away from the sun-
drenched orchard.
She smiled through the slits of
her eyes.
As I carried her to the shade of
my body.
Now she is rested and moist
Dangling ivy over a wealthy
patio.

Marlena Weaver
QUIET WATERS
The quiet waters of my soul run
as deep as the imagination,
Containing my hopes, fears, and
even my salvation.
A deep blue pool as endless as
the sea,
An ebbing tide that flows deep
inside of me.
Yet the waters have a peaceful
side and show no turbulance
beyond,
As they calm the rising fears
and things that may go wrong.
Arise quiet waters and soothe
my surging pride,
when temptation bids me boast,
For you are my conscience and
my spirit but constant friend
the most.

LaVerne A. Gardner
FREEDOM
Freedom is the best part of Life.
Without it we have anxiety and
strife.
Our Freedom we should guard
well.
Try not to lose it or abuse it.
If a universal wish I was
granted.
It would be Freedom on this
planet.
Man was meant to be free.
And only to the Savior; bend his
knee.
If more could only see the light.
Turn from wrong; seek after the
right.
Keep what Freedom they
possess.
Freedom out measures even
Success.

Carolyn S. Toth
PROBLEM CHILD
He might yet be Billy,
or dead,
or someone else so he won't be:
Billy, whose mother speaks of
him like a muggy night last
week, which is nothing new,
but old as the day
he was born with pins in his
heart, to hate himself for all
who weren't supposed to.
And I see him hiding
in a corner of a tenement lobby
or in a junk yard,
his body hard as metal,
driven there by
love in cactus skin.

Wendy S. Firth
A CHILD'S FAREWELL
Today, you know they say there
Is a generation gap
But I can still remember when
I sat upon your lap
To hear the tales of olden days
When life was filled with
Plight
A long time ago—you didn't
Know but I had seen the light
To give your offspring what
They need
You went to greatest length
And to endure the loss of one
Small child
You must possess the gift of
Inner strength
There is a bit of each of you
Inside this one of me
That molded and formed and
Created
This person that you see
You've given me the gift of life
To do with what I should
You've given me the gift of love
And asked me to be good
I am no longer small and weak
I've grown from day to day
I'm older now, a young adult
I'll soon be on my way
I hope you know I love you
I will forever more
Remember that especially
When I walk out the door
The time has come for me to go
To try my wings and fly
There are some things I have to
Know that money cannot buy
This house will always be my
Home
As it has been from the start
It will be in my deepest
Thoughts
As you will too, while we're
Apart
Don't forget to write me
I won't forget to call
Until the time that I return
If I return at all
You must realize there'll come a
Time
When I'll no longer be here
But spiritually I will remain
In your memories quite clear
And my presence will be near
To remind you that I hold you
Dear
I Love You

Joan Pacheco
THANK YOU FATHER
I feel it now,
I feel so whole,
I look and feel warmth,
I touch and feel beauty
peace.
I will do as you wish
Your path will be mine,
I've taken on the light
Your word is mine!
Praise be to your highest
For I am your child.
Young but old,
I will still learn,
I still yearn.
For knowledge is all inside me
For he dwelleth within.
My heart glows for you,
My spirit grows
Together
I become one.
In this uniqueness
The righteousness I possess
Wholeness.
Thank you Father
Love

Barbara Jean DeLibero
TOUCHE'
Roses are red; and violets,
they're blue.
This isn't what you're thinking.
I hate that poem, too.
But roses are happy; and violets,
they're blue.
You now have your freedom
and I no longer have you.
The roses are budding, the
violets have wilted.
You say you no longer love me,
I feel that I've been jilted.
Your roses are blooming, my
violets have died.
You have broken my heart
and you've wounded my pride.
The violets are trampled, this
time's not the first.

It is hard for them to bud again
knowing they'll soon be hurt.
The violets have seeded, again
they might live.
But if some one were to love me
my love may not give.
You know, your roses may
someday turn blue,
when you know you need some
one
and they don't need you.
"Now you know how I feel",
I'll think with satisfaction.
"Does it hurt so much,
sweetheart,
to have your heart put into
traction?"

Karen Helena Pestaina

ISLAND DREAMS ON A PENNSYLVANIA HILLSIDE

As I see the lazy Atlantic sun
drift as it slowly sinks to the
west,
I dream of a New York skyline
that overlooks the east.
City dreams on a country
hillside
lays my mind back
till my heart is at ease.
My presence remains here
in the middle of the
countryside
yet my soul forever will be
on the Island of the Long.

Mrs. Clarence Kusch (Ernie)

GARY

I've left you for a little while—
but I'll be back for you.
I've left memories everywhere—
hope you feel the closeness
too.
I'm in the early morning light—
and at the closing of each day.
I'm in the stars—and in the
moon—and in the milky way.
Part of me is still at home—
at rodeos—and my cowboy
friends.
Out with the horses—and at
church—yes, my life shall
never end.
I'm in the wind—and in the
rain—'with you calving
heifers yet'.
I've showered my love on
everything—knowing you
would not forget.
Still God in all His wisdom—
gave you for me to love. . .
God's taken me back home
again—where I'm watching
from above.
I'll always be your Gary—and
your dreams of me won't die.
And when the RAPTURE
comes—I'LL MEET YOU IN
THE SKY.

Anita L. D'Angelo

CHANGES

Things change from day to day.
Goes so fast I lose my way.
How come things never stay the
same.
I guess life is what you call
that ugly game.
You put up the front to look
glad,
But the mirrors of your mind
show your sad.
How can you get things out of
your mind,
When all these memories leave
you to remind.
Hoping someone will guide you
to be free,
While your searching for
security.
So many different roads to take,
Does it make any difference
which decision you make?
Not when it leads you to find,
Those sad memories implanted
in your mind.
Well like they say life goes on,
For today's here and yesterday's
gone!

Kristen Hughes

MOMENTS OF LOVE

The world is ours for a moment
or two.
I could do no less then smile
with you.
Precious moments you've given
me,
Mean so much, can't you see.
You're in my thoughts all the
day.
Tender moments don't fade
away.
I'm so in love when I'm with
you.
When we're together it's just
us two.
Moments I didn't know could
be.
You bring out the best in me.
I'm so alive when I'm with you.
Moments like this, come too
few.
Yet I am but a moment in your
heart.
Soon the time comes for us
to part.
Something takes you away from
me.
Maybe your need to be free.
Love spent in moments slip
away.
I feel so alone the next day.
Precious moments here and
there.
I begin to wonder if you care.

Joni Y. Johnson

LIFE

A world of love
brings forth hope and peace
The serenity of all
Is something sweet
The joy of life
Is a gift indeed
To share it with one
Is a fulfilling creed
To be alone
Without feeling
What sadness sets in
What a fool you are being
Enter the calm
the source of it all
Begin to care and love
What happiness will befall
Let yourself go
To feel the beauty
It is all around us
Rejoice! it's so real

Irene Gilbert Britt

FAITH HOPE AND CHARITY

If you have faith in yourself and
you have faith in the Lord
Then that faith will be
rewarded and your life will
be restored.
If you have faith in one another
and faith in what you do
Then that faith will be
rewarded and your sorrows
will be few.
Faith hope and charity together
they mean love
And you'll be guided onward
from Heaven above.
If you have hope for tomorrow
and hope for your friends
Then that hope will be
answered as your prayers and
amens.
If you hope to help your
neighbor and you hope that
you'll be needed
Then that hope will be
answered and with blessing
you'll be greeted.
Faith hope and charity together
they mean love
And you'll be guided onward
from Heaven above.
If you have charity for the
needy and charity for good deed
Then that charity will be
lightened while you're helping
one in need.
If you have charity with your
talent and charity with your
hand
Then that charity will be
lightened and you'll be in
demand.
Faith hope and charity together
they mean love
And you'll be guided onward
from Heaven above.

Edna Skramstad

LOVE

Love is giving
Of yourself and is
Very rewarding
Especially, love God.
Love is of God.
Offer your talents in
Various ways,
Especially in church.
Love your neighbor.
Offer your services, it's
Vital to serenity.
Expect no return.
Love your family.
Only you have that kind of love.
Vows of marriage
Expect to last a lifetime.
Love is sharing,
Obeying, and believing. A
Valuable future is
Etched in Christian living.
Love. Is it real?
Of course! I know Christ's
Visit guarantees an
Eternal life of love.

Patty L. Bargstadt

RAINDROPS AND RAINBOWS

I like skies to always be fair
With golden sunshine
everywhere.
I like its warmth upon my face
So soft and sweet and tender,
A touch of wondrous splendor.
And yet—
I also like to look up high
And see painted in the sky
Blended colors in an endless
arch
Of bluish tones and reddish
blush,
All fashioned by the Master's
brush.
So then—
I know that skies can't stay the
same—
There must be sun and also
rain.
For He who drew the master
plan
Designed it perfectly, He knows
To first send raindrops, then
rainbows.

Sheila Vernice Robinson

WHILE WE'RE PASSING THROUGH

If, someday, we must die—
let us die in our sleep:
without feeling pain,
without fighting for life;
but as free as a dream,
and as calm as a dove—
let this life end, to start life
anew.
Warned "Death is promised',
let's live—till we're bound
by our body's decay back to
dust;
Let us thread through the
waters,
and toil in the land,
and explore all the skies—
unforbidden.
Let's aim for the heavens,
determined to go,
leaving all pessimism—behind.

Novak Novica Vujacic

I OPEN MY HEART

Last night:
A kiss
Embrace
Trance
Fiery feelings
Through space.
My heart
Last night
Opened
The door
For connection
Circulation
Of blood.
You are
In my heart
Animated
By Constancy
Of own play
Of Ardency.

Mrs. Mary K. Quisenberry

MORNING MEDITATION

May I do justice, love, mercy
And walk humbly this day and
coming days:
May I have the serenity to
accept things I cannot change,
Courage to change the things I
can change,
And have the wisdom to know
the difference:
Always remembering, that when
the Great Scribe
Comes to write my last line in
my Book of Life
He will not ask how much I've
won or lost
But how I honestly played life's
game;
And may I remember a
successful life
Does not depend on holding a
good hand
But on playing a poor hand well.

Darryl Abdu Omari

THE SPARE RIB

Delicate creation graceful
mutation
Sugar some spice the concept so
nice
Just a reflection of man's inner
strength
Yet individual more than just
wench
The foundation of life whom
else but your mama
Delivered sons and daughters in

cursed trauma
A means to an end a valuable friend
Her beauty unmatched a maker of men
Intelligent species a fact well known
Minus this being no home is a home
She's soft sweet and meekly weak
Queen of her race *no kind* of freak
Of whom do I babel of whom do I lust
That same companion I've fed from her bust
The apple is bitten what's done is done
As man and wife the kingdom will come
Pleasurable nymph I've known from a kid
I'll always crave you—the spare rib

M. Carol McCann
LOVE
Whenever I must leave you, dear
Where ever you may go
You're forever in my heart
In every dream I know.
You're as much beside me as the winds
That touch my cheek
And in every sound around me
I seem to hear you speak.
Though it's not like touching you
Or holding you to me
Nothing could ever take the place
Of your reality.

Betty L. Meinhardt
TO SEE. . .
To See is to visualize. . .
to visualize is to feel
to feel is to hear
to hear is to know
to know is to find
to find is to innovate
to innovate is to belong
AND
to belong is to Love. . .

Angela Starr Balay
ROCKS
The round orange sun of the evening sky,
A volcano erupts and pours lava out of it,
A ginger biscuit breaks into crumbs,
A cup of coffee with milk and sugar is drunk away,
A red very red ruby shines in the brightness of the moon.
The sun shining with rage, and his anger hangs over the
dead blue sky, hangs his head in shame.

Sandra L. Haight
AUTUMN'S COLORS
As the cool fall wind blows through the trees—
Autumn leaves fall with the breeze—
As the corn stalks rustle near the pumpkin patch—
The nearby horizon looks like it's been lit by a brand new match—
The vibrant colors sparkle in the morning sun—
And start to fade when the day is done.
This skyburst of color catches your eye—
Just as the setting sun does in the evening sky.
The crinkling and crunching of the fallen leaves—
Scatter the ground with the new fall breeze.
This panorama of color enhances us all—
Just as a toy kaleidoscope does when we're small.
This season of beauty that we all enjoy—
Is as precious to us as a child's first toy.
As the cool fall wind blows through the trees—
Autumn leaves fall with the breeze.

Bernard W. Tormey
EPISODE AT DAYBREAK
We were moored off the bend.
Our pirate crew, with time to spend,
Heard the word late in the day,
"We take her when she leaves the bay."
A prize indeed! She carried nought
But treasures for the royal court.
Secure beyond the point that night,
We lay in darkness, out of sight.
That crimson sky of early morn
Watched our prey become seaborne;
Watched her sails begin to fill;
Watched us move in for the kill!
Cannon thundered! Timbers shook.
We closed and threw the grappling hook.
Fired with grog, two dozen men
Leaped across her rails
And then
Brine and blood washed o'er her decks
As heads were severed from their necks.
Entrails slithered in the gore
When knife and cutlass swung no more.
One by one, each treasure—chest
—All bearing Isabella's crest
Emblazed upon their lids in gold—
We then hauled topside from the hold.

Mark Stephen Tate
POEM FOR PATTI
No longer sleeping, an arm around your
Waist as I lay behind you,
An indecent smile on my face,
Smelling your body's wonderful scent,
And seeing your spine thread through
Your back, I give myself to my feelings
Of love and desire, and calmly praise
The curves of your firm body.
Wrapped securely within that body,
Within the belly my hand is rested on,
Our baby is growing, sleeping as you sleep,
Waiting for its strength and maturity,
Cradled in your belly, unconscious.
As I cuddle you with my body and watch
The rise and fall of your breathing,
I want to give you warm kisses on your back,
But I dare not wake you. The pleasure
Of these feelings and yearnings would be
Replaced by the necessities of the day.
For now, you are dreaming and peaceful
And I have no desire to disturb you.
I am happy and content to be near you,
Hold you, and daydream about our baby
Growing within you, coming to this world.

Emma Eliza Pullen
BLACK AGGRESSION
Mount St. Helens and Miami.
Black fury and rumblings
From deep beneath the Earth
Sprews forth ashes and smoke
Creating a dark blanket
That blocks the sun.

Phyllis Newton
PHRENOLOGICAL GROUPINGS
Phrenologists in drawing charts
Engroups the brain in seven parts;
The Moral in the top-head lies,
Perceptive just above the eyes.
Between these two the forehead swells
And shows the place where Reason dwells.
The Selfish group surrounds the ears
As well as in the Crown appears.
The Semi-intellect divides
The moral from the selfish sides
While always in the head behind
Domestic qualities you'll find.
These seven groups contain the whole
Of man's great mind, if not the soul.

Laura Birkenholtz
THE BETRAYAL
There he was in front of me
Standing as though he were King.
The conquest had been for all of us,
But all I could see was green.
The hatred burned, the loathing seethed
As I watched him possess my queen
The anger so boiled inside of me
That the rage emit as steam.
My head whirled 'round in confusion.
And then, I saw the knife.
I'll get him! I swore to GOD above
And then she'll be mine for life.
My fingers grasped hold of the handle
As I thrust it deep, I see
The blood spurt out. But to my surprise. . .
The one I have stabbed is me.

Donna Lee DeMarco
I SHOULDN'T HAVE GIVEN MY LOVE TO YOU
I know that it's wrong
and I wish that I could be strong
if only I had the courage to say good-bye
then you wouldn't have to live a lie.
I know that we shouldn't go on
I know that it isn't right
I know that I should be gone
I'm trying with all my might to end our relationship
maybe we could have a simple friendship.
But I just can't seem to be able to let go
I've always believed that love is when two people grow
and that's exactly what we've done
it was as if we were one.
We understood each others problems and pain
we never needed to explain
We don't need words to say how we feel
our feelings for one another are real.
But it's still wrong to love you
even though it feels so right
I don't know what else I can do
I have no strength left to fight.
I'm not ready to say good-bye
so we'll make love over and over again,
and in the end I know I'll cry.
I never should've given my love to a married man.

Dottie Dunbar
MIRACLES
Yesterday I saw an eagle soar,
In skies so clear and bright.
Today I watched a flower bloom
With aroma, sweet and light.
What miracle will tomorrow bring?
Day has her marvels for us to behold:
The sun shining through the leaves of a tree,
A spotted fawn curled up in a secret place,
The stream gleefully seeking the lovely sea,
Or a sea of grass, waving full of grace.
Night has her wonders also:
The stars twinkling in the sky,
The moon shedding her mysterious light,
A breeze stirring the trees with a sigh,
Or the silent snowfall, pure and white.
Life is eternal and miracles are everlasting.

Carol Ann Wetz
TO OUR DOG YOGI
Dearest Yogi
A pal complete
In God's hands
Forever asleep
He was our friend
He did all he could
He knew our moods
Both bad and good
He was loyal and precious
Sweet and true
Oh! I wish that was me
And you
He knew no hate
No evil no bad
Thank God for that

This I am glad
Good-bye lil one
So funny and dear
All who knew you
Has shed many a tear
And yet we are happy!
Because we know
All the Yogi's and Fluffy's
And yes even Gus
Are roaming the heavens
Just waiting for us!

G. Elizabeth Weaver

THE SENTINELS OF GOD

They stood stark against the sky
In the brilliance of the morning sun,
Their rocky peaks as white us aging heads
And their countenance cut deep with crevices
Caused by the ravages of time
As the wrinkled faces of the men they guard.
Man tries to conquer this old world
By climbing these majestic statures,
Yet men die and are born,
Still the mountains stand in their splendor;
A testement of the timeless love
Of their magnificent Creator.
They sang of the Glory of God
When Adam and Eve walked this earth.
They cried with Moses for a stubborn nation
And delighted in the sling of David.
They joined their various voices with the angels
When one lone star proclaimed the Holy Birth.
They have seen wars and famine,
Endured pestilence with strife.
They have watched man's trifling efforts
To control God's Universe!
Still they stand as from time beginning,
The Sentinels of God.

Allene D. Phillpott

THE RAILROADER

The old man, eyes forever on the rails,
Hears ghostly whistles in his dreams.
The red glow of furnace flared glory roads,
Lights his cloudy hours of memory.
It is warm, here in his four-squared room,
Where cold, pious intentions are not welcome.
His throttle hand itches,
Eight locked piston wheels, churn the brain;
It runs forever, his glory train.

Sara Fitzgerald Sonntag

UNTITLED

As the sun peeks timidly over the hill,
Gentle rays of golden glitter
Lightly embrace the earth.
Frail buds on lanky limbs
Cling complacently to the warmth.
The day grows and stretches.
The soft sun turns suddenly
Into a fiery sphere of fury;
The buds fear they are destined to perish
As they perspire and thirst.
But in time the ordeal subsides.
The blazing orb
Turns into a vintaged orange beauty,
Then a mere haze of tinted warmth.
It sinks below a silhouetted horizon
Giving way to cool flows of air.
The soon-to-be blossoms take a breath;
The day passed and they have grown.
A gentle sleepy sun caressed them,
A torrid sun tormented;
But they have grown
And were more beautiful for it.

Deborah Ann Deakins

THE SUN

The sun is a rainbow of different colors
But how long will it last?
It travels across the sky and clouds
And then disappears so fast.
It is enormous and lights the skies
And at night it shadows a cast
Of darkness and the shining stars
But will it last?
You can't tell how bright it is
Or how long it will last each day
But it's a gift of light and a gift of heat
Don't worry, it's there to stay.

Walter Bardeck

THE POETS WORKSHOP

I weave my verse
With fragrant yarn,
And blend each skein
Of poetical hue
Into a rug of song;
My delicate loom. . . .
It quivers in the wind
That quietly threads
The strings of my thoughts
Into woven poetry.

Karen Northrup Folkins

THE THEME

The theme;
It begins with an overture
Hear these notes
Composed like those of an Emperor.
Listen!
The sounds of majestic sunrise
Dew evaporating
Butterflies flittering
Sweet breezes rising.
I hear this song each year
A reprise of a new life,
In my heart I feel a moment of peace
Hoping it will never cease.
As it fades. . .
I know this overture will repeat
Returning with the Spring.

Margaret Baucom

WINTER'S APHRODITE

Arrogant, splendid, Winter abruptly turned as Spring, arms outstretched, timidly smiled and to him said, "Sir Winter, I am ready."
Winter, in surprised disdain at such brashness blew his icy breath, hostile and steady upon this fanciful dreamer who dared hope to unite with himself, the King of Weather.
Spewing wind, sleet, and snow, he
Shouted, "You stupid creature. . . there shall be no blending of Winter and Spring."
Spring, smiled gently, stepped forth in pristine purity.
King Winter, in stunned surprise, raised his head
Only to be blinded by her radiant smile as she said,
To the rhythm of nodding daffodils, "I thee Wed."
Moving slowly to sounds of treetop melody,
King Winter, in ecstatic surrender, melted into
The arms of Spring as together they mounted the throne of Breathless Splendor.

Lester E. Garrett

CELEBRATION

All our lives
We dream, we hope.
We probe, we contemplate,
Do we not?
The years. . .
They come and they go;
But still we love,
And treasuring friends,
Embracing those we love,
We endure,
Do we not?
Time, though sometimes
Cruel. . .rolls on, like
Foamy waves in the sea.
We see days gone by, so
Swiftly in the mind's eye.
Yet a clear ring
Of realization and acceptance
Brings joy, meaning
And wisdom.
Slowly, slowly then
Wisdom has gathered,
Has it not?
We are older, it is true,
But we will face. . .
Unafraid all the days
Yet to be given us,
Will we not?
There is not only maturity,
There is trust, enrichment;
And its wonderfulness
Has surely been God-given,
Has it not?

Gertrude Harrison

THE BEDBUG

The other night I went to Bed, pulled the covers high over my head.
Said Mr. Bedbug with a little frown, I'll go up and make her pull those covers down.
Up he came with a little courage bold the scent he left is still untold.
Up he came on past my chin, wiggling and stinking like homemade sin.
I thought I'd fool that bug for once, make him look like a little dunce.
I stuck my hand under the "civer", you should have been there, and felt that bedbug quiver.
He couldn't crawl, He couldn't twist, he was tightly clenched within my fist.
Up I got with quiet conceit, I don't like bedbugs under my sheet.
I went in the kitchen, where the fire was burning bright
It wasn't very late at night.
I slammed that bug right on the cap, the durned thing popped right back in my lap.
I put him in again, then went back to take a nap.
I was dreaming of the bedbug, I just had burned, when here came another, well I'll be durned.
Up I got with a little shout, young fellow I'll put your light out.
He wouldn't crawl, he wouldn't run, so I killed that son-of-a-gun.
That made two I killed that night, I'll kill all I see too,
For you know they bite.
If you don't want to get bit too, and if you don't want to be blue,
You'd better take warning, and do the same, or they'll bite you till you won't know your name.

Jonathan Jacob Jones

SONNET 18

Have I lost the broil?
Has there been set of sun?
Was my heart forced to toil?
Was my love over run?
Scorched and lying withered my heart weeps
A symbolic simulation of torn Babylon
I died inside for hours, days and weeks
Will I be rebuilt or stay fallen?
The ruin lies underneath my feet
To blow it away by the north winds
I surrender, I've been beat
I know love would've never been
How my hopes were captured by desire
Collected, confiscated, and burned by fire

Eleanora S. Martin

NELL

Did I ever tell you about Nell?
She's the lass with the Scottish Air.
Her home was a place in Scotland,
The place is known as Ayr.
What can I tell you about Nell?
She's the Nana we knew so well.
Of hillsides and heather we really did learn,
Of Ayr, near the home of Robert Burns.
She took so much time to tell us
Stories and important things to know.
Of scones, of plaids and places enchanting,
Of pipes and drums and horns that blow.
Now, what can I say about Nell?
She's the lass with the Scottish flair.
It was a great pleasure to know her,
Her stories of Scotland to share.

Fran Duke

TOMORROW'S SONG

Sometimes, life is like music, a beautiful song.
Sometimes, you can't help hit a note that is wrong.
Your song isn't ruined, to err isn't a sin.
The thing to remember, "Don't do it again."
At night when you're tucked in your own cozy bed.

Don't brood 'bout the past, look forward instead.
At dawn, when the sun rises, to yourself say,
"I've a beautiful song ready, just for Today."
Sing it with the birds, as they chirp their song.
Sing it to your neighbors, as they pass along.
Sing it to your friends, in your lifespan you've met.
Sing it to yourself as your sun starts to set.
Once, long ago, we were young, so were you.
Passed many milestones, still have plenty to do.
May the good Lord see fit, make our songs yet to be,
As sweet as the past ones, just a great melody!

M. Elaine Kachel

THE PRIME GENERATION

The "Prime Generation",
'tis a lovely sound
for we people
who have been around
for awhile,
gathering experience
and skills.
Though we are seniors
we're "not over the hills."
Well seasoned,
it's true,
but we have
a young
point of view.
We like
to be valued
as any
good antique.
Respect and love
are all
that we seek.
So don't call
us old,
for we're in
our prime.
Our feet
may be cold,
but, we're having
a whale
of a time!

Donna Reed

THE MOUNTAIN

The mountain tops so pretty and white
Acres and acres of beautiful sights.
As the natural still water runs down the sides.
Nature takes all the animals into hide.
Rolling hills covered so deep,
All the animals go in to sleep.

Herman Edgar Carr, Jr., M.D.

TO IRIS

My limbs disintegrate, my heart rebounds
Upon your final step—I cannot make
A sequence of sure syllables and shake
From gaping mouth and halting tongue the sounds
That say farewell. I am struck dumb by rounds
Of feeble rantings above the seething 'quake.
All ineffectuality, I take
To flight where eloquence had better grounds.
I did not kiss you gone—my bitter tears
Obstruct my lips as well my eyes and ears.
Silent I will endure the dark, the strong
Irrevocable loss of you, a life-time long.
Where shines the radiance of your beloved face?
I'll turn my anguished eyes to that fair place.

Nancy Louise Lindabury

THE FOUR SEASONS

The tree tops blew briskly in the wind.
The wind over my head became calm and peaceful.
Birds flew high and rejoiced in the clear blue sky.
The green grass glowed beautifully in the bright sunlight.
Such beauty to see the flowers bloom in the spring.
Relaxing in the warm ocean water, feeling the hot sun beaming on my head.
A touch of stillness before the summer thunder storm.
Watch the children play happily indoors while the rain falls.
Oh' it is so much fun to play in the sun.
True beauty is when the leaves on the trees change to shades
of red and orange and yellow.
Now the ground is covered with the bright glow of leaves.
The birds fly to the warm south to prepare for winter.
The cool breezy air brings us relief.
Only the bare tree trunks and limbs remain.
So cold the snow feels to our feet.
The sky is so clear, hardly a cloud is seen.
Watching the snow fall from the heavens turning everything in sight white.
Fun is helping the neighborhood children build a snowman.
Graceful beauty of people ice skating.
The quick movement of the sled going down the hill.

Debra Haines

1 & 18 DEGREES OF FREEDOM*

(Degrees of freedom are the number of obligations in a sample set of obligations minus the number of restrictions put on the obligations.)*

I only know today,
no time before,
when there were so many kids
and so little food.
Years you worked so long
for so few dollars,
eating shit,
black grinding heat,
and strict machinery,
providing discipline
in the form of
three fingers
sliced away
to the second knuckle.
Today you smile
and make rainbows
of machinery
and wrap them in warm mink.
And sleep at night with difficulty.

Elizabeth Anne Snowberger

UNTITLED

My love for you is endless.
Remembering always the joy and,
Sometimes, the fear as
Gingerly, we walk through life
Entering into new ways,
Only to find the other
Retracing the path and
Going in still another. . .
Experiencing together, yet
Attaining our individuality,
Gaining new ways, to grow.
Under each other's wing we
Intend always to stay,
Resolving our conflicts and
Reaching for dreams as
Endless as our love.

Charles Soderlund

GOOD-BYES

Good-byes are so eternal
They finalize the act;
Even if you mean it
Try to use a little tact.
See you in a while
Would certainly suffice;
Take it easy or just be good
Even that would be real nice.
Just don't say good-bye
For that depicts the end;
Even if you mean it
On that no hopes can lend.
Don't do anything I wouldn't do
Is a cute adieu;
Just don't say good-bye
Because that means no more you.
So if it is really over
Please, just say take care;
On that my hopes can live with
And my heart can bear.

David P. Byers

LOVE—WHETHER OR NOT

What is my love for you?
Love is that feeling which I have for you
that can fill the vastness of space;
all that can be imagined, and
all that can not.
Love is my reason for existence
in this cold, cruel world;
in which I would otherwise be alone,
if I could not love you.
Love is the carefree sparkle in your eyes
those eyes so deep and dark,
which possess my soul and
control my every thought.
Love is what I want to do forever, and
you are the only one
who I wish to love.
My darling,
I will love you forever,
whether you love me or not.

Catherine Maclennan

PER ARDUA AD ASTRA

Man's needs must soar!
God gave him thoughts for opinions,
To bear him up untrammelled to the skies unto a realm
Where brave bright deeds do beckon;
Where visions splendid gleam before his eyes.
Man's needs must strive!
For there is that within him
That urges him—forever up and on;
He is inspired
His spirit sings in triumph,
As joy and pain unite, and blend in one.
Man needs must climb!
For there is that above him
That bids him pit his strength against all bars;
If need be
Lay his body on Life's altar
And die—with broken wing amid the stars.

Shirline Coutee

STAND BY MY SIDE

Lord stand by my side and guide me.
Let my nights glow bright with lights.
And let the trouble in my life fade away with the sunshine of each passing day.
Oh Lord when I stumble and fall, give me strength to rise again and face the world with new hope.
And Lord when I'm weary send me your eternal love to let me know somebody cares;
About me.

Estela—Amor A. Dimla

LOVE'S SOLILOQUY

Does it matter
if love gets only the wind?
No, it doesn't
for love lasts forever beyond reasons
it asks what needs me to
compliment his. . . . . .
strange. . .love puts one in high spirits
emoted by a glinter in the eyeball
Love, do you see this in mine?
Funny it hurts
coupled with a digging in the nervous system
when someone flirts
a threat, a robbery
as jealousy creeps in.
Amour propre let be doomed
it smashed the beauty: a life
that could have been.
Oh loved fear, skedaddle! skedaddle!
—a siamese twin
—the slug-a-bed
makeshift his activity
dolce far niente
a penner is not but an owl in love.
Love is not a passive sensuality
not a dole out of a sexual passion
it is never enforcing
but kind, never unyielding
Cigit: the secret of loving
taking the risk of being jilted
loving thyself better
to be potently loving the other.

Kathy L. Kirschbaum
A SPRING DAY
As I awoke
Early one morn,
I heard the sound
Of singing birds.
The bright golden sun
Was gleaming through my
window.
It seemed as though
Nature was calling me,
"Get up, get up,
Enjoy this beautiful day!"
I took a stroll
Through the flowery fields
And saw the dewdrops
On each blade of grass.
I stopped to drink
From the bubbling brook,
I then looked up
To see soft, fluffy clouds
Sweeping quietly and gently,
Across the beautiful blue sky.
The trees were budding
And flowers blooming.
Then I realized
It's Finally Spring!

Rick D. Garlock
THE ENDLESS WAR FOR PEACE

A world that's much the stranger to the beliefs of freedom, the tributes of glory, the foundation of humanitarian rights, is a world we cannot condone; but rather, we must damn the ignorance of self-imposed rule that believes in no force greater than mankind.

The tempters of fate are walking a blind path down God's road of judgment, as they praise their own wisdom. . . .
If only their hindsight would reveal the curse of Satan at their heels, dragging the great nations of injustice on chains of fire, no less than a world would be saved. . . .

Gerald R. White
SONG OF LONELINESS
A bare bulb
hangs silently
casting its dim light over the
room.
Crazy shadows dance and play
on the ceiling and walls.
In the bed
she lies on her back
staring up at the shadows
as they dart and flicker
and still he continues to
labor feverishly.
She is plump
not fat
average looking
not ugly
friendly
but somehow friendless
slightly imperfect.
The world though
loves only perfection
and those shadows
she knows
are the sum total of her life.
Downstairs in the bar
others await her
some drinking their courage
some smoking it
one or two so nervous
a dark spot stains their pants
but
they all agree
she is a pig
and a piece is a piece.
Upstairs now
a tear
slowly slips from her eye
as she mouths the words
to her song of loneliness
and the shadows cease their
dance.

Margaret Gordon
SOFT YOUNG THOUGHTS
My life is a slate of
impressions built upon blocks of
time:
Colored, mosaic moments
frozen in lemon and lime;
filtering the light of knowledge
in the vast sea of rhyme:
Soft, young thoughts melted
to clay;
Butterfly days fluttered
away;
Sifted moments on lonely
beaches;
cloudy thoughts on cloudy
beaches;
Torrential rains changing
seasons;
Torrential thoughts seeking
reasons;
Stewing caldron of special
devices
making a life of all-flavored
ices;
Potpourri dances defined as
romances sprouting forever on
evergreen branches.

Claudia Nable
FOR GORDON
The tears
flow free
For
my eyes
they see
the sympathetic pains
I feel now
Remind me now
of a pain now
behind me
For fear
of the possibilities
of what's before me
The tears flow free

Margareta Tommos
LONELINESS
Many days have passed since we
left her at the airport, not
knowing when we would see
her again.
The cat is beginning to purr
But it does not fill the empty
place left by her going.

B. J. Darnell
BUT NOT ALWAYS
Poetry is like the trees.
It sways and caresses our
minds with ease.
But not always!
It can recall laughter or pain,
or just a dreamers thoughts in
vain!
But not always. . . . .

Tana Mach
UNTITLED
Torrential thoughts pan on
parched ground,
Driven into deltas
Like the roots of a downward
growing plant,
The night fills up with small
movements
In crypts of corners.
Negatives dance on half-lit
screens
Of walls and window panes.
You pick up the clock
And wind oblivion.
Uncoiling, its shed skin wraps
you
In swaddling bands for
dangerous dreams.
Shutters tap,
Shadowy frames of some
intangible truth
Flicker and fade.
The forbidden fruit, a fingertip
touch away,
Blanch in the grey amnesia of
early morning light.
By dawn, the rain had softened
the ground
And moved on.

Romaine Miller
WILD ROSES
Wild roses near a mountain
stream
Profusely growing there
Without the aid of human
hands
Right near the rocks so bare,
Sing melodies of love to God
For He has put them there.
I touch a rose, smell it's
perfume,
"You're beautiful!" I say.
A soft breeze causes it to nod,
"I'm glad I'm made this way.
Enjoy me now—I'll soon be
gone;
I'm here just for today."
So we, like roses, cannot stay
Too long on this old sod.
We each have our own job to do
To prove our right to nod
And say, "I'm glad I'm made
this way.
Some day I'll be with God."

Genevieve Barnett
REARVIEW MIRROR
I drove along the road today,
In my usual daily hurry,
I crossed the creek and up the
hill
with a hurry, flurry, scurry.
I glanced out through the
window,
to see if all was clear,
Into the rearview mirror
and there I saw appear.
A lovely picture on the hill
that I had just come down,
Houses, flowers, trees and such,
the colors of fall's crown.
Did you ever chance to think
about,
the things you've left behind?
And all the things you've missed
yourself,
in this crazy daily grind.
If we would take a little time,
to smile at all our friends
This world would be a better
place,
until the very end!

Margaret Teresa McGarry
THE END OF 113 YEARS
Clear, Blue October skies,
Golden streaks with pink
divide,
A fitting way to say good-
bye.
Departed John Leahy, must
smilin be,
Irreplaceable Gentleman was
he,
Danbury Fair is now set
free.
Plans are laid for constructing
a Mall,
With acres of buildings wide
and tall,
Foolhardy developers you
see,
Do not envision the
floods in the fall.
A tug of pain grips my soul,
No longer will I meet friends
of old,
The yearly event of keeping
in touch,
Was a special feeling I
valued much.
There's wild Stanley, remember
when he was three,
Then on to troubled youth
and misery,
Now he works for the
masses with glee,
A man who changed to
what he wanted to be.
Twenty-five million dollars, tho'
a great temptation,
Can never replace,
The Fairgoer's sensation.
Farwell to the animals big and
small,
Budweiser horses have left
their stall,
Aromas, sights and music
that called,
Are stilled forever by the
money scrawl.
AMEN.

Vera Hatton Rader
THE SEASON'S SOLITARY BOAST
'Twas the last day of Goose
season
Near the sun's final ray;
Long shadows from the pine
stand
Proclaim the end of day.
The wary hunter, watched and
waited,
Eager, alert and keen;
From a pit on the brow of the
hill,
All directions seen.

Again and again—at intervals
The evening flight winged o'er,
Incessantly honking from on
high,
To become indistinct in the
wintry sky.
Suddenly a wedge took shape
Swiftly—flying low,
O'er the crest of the hill,
Wildly calling—to and fro.
The hunter fired with deadly
aim,
A bird split the air and
struck,
Near the pit, on top of the hill,
Boy! Oh Boy! What luck.
Tender—sweet and luscious,
What a magnificent roast,
Those who partook, repeatedly
praised,
The Season's solitary boast.

Ernest E. Wormington
THE CROSS ON THE HILL
On a lonely hill in the valley,
there stands a beautiful cross.
If we don't know it's meaning,
it's beauty is surely a loss.
In a world beset by conflict,
and by wars that never end.
We have but to look and
remember,
our Divine and loving Friend.
When the dark of the night is in
Heaven,
and the cross is so bright on
that hill.
If burdens seem too much to

carry,
look to God for the strength
and the will.
When up on that hill, the night
is so still,
and the sky the stars seem to
fill.
We feel close to God, when we
kneel on that sod,
at the base of that Cross on the
hill.

Sarah T. Barnes
MOMMA
I stare out from my window and
I see you, Momma.
The wind has tangled your hair
Like an old dandelion.
My interwound thoughts
correspond
With your tangled hair.
You answer my whats, whens,
and whys with honesty,
For you know I can't stay
forever.
You seem always to be right,
yet,
The unmowed patch behind the
barn tells me
You are human.
I support my arguments with
confidence
With a smirk you tell me
experience overshadows all.
I have observed you these many
years.
I am still learning.

Loretta Perez
A FAREWELL PROMISE
Why must I leave the things I
love?
The birds that sing, the stars
above
All the creatures given to me,
And people I love who do not
see
The end is near—I hate to go!
But spring will come, and I
won't know.
It's a beautiful world to leave
behind
But I leave for a different
sort of clime,
A world of peace, no sorrow
there,
No aches or pain only love to
share
With loved ones long gone and
God's Holy Place.
But I know I will miss you and
remember your face.
You do not know and would you
care
But somehow remember, I'll
always be near.

Irene J. Noble
THOUGHTS ON PRAYER
Prayer is gratitude for blessings,
Prayer is intimate.
Prayer is purifying, cleansing,
your sins confessing.
It only takes minutes.
It is most often a heritage we
earn
Given by others who helped us
learn.
It is soul-saving, burden lifting;
It conquers grief.
It keeps us from simply drifting.
It helps us our thoughts to
sift.
Like lightning, the help comes
in a flash—
We are ready to do our work
without rehash.
Like talking to an old intimate
friend,
Telling him our cares and
secret thoughts,
Going over the problems our
thoughts we send,
Getting a clear perspective as
we were taught.
How we should bear our
burdens slight,
To do our work with delight.
Prayer is like a cool drink
To a traveler on the desert
burning.
Like a breath of air as we sink
In the deep water we are
churning.
It gives solace like a caressing
hand
And lifts us to the promised
land.

Lou Kennedy
THE WEEVILER
Donned in black Robe
He slunk to his throne,
To weevil a writ
Of a dastard's trick,
By webbing the fate
Designed to deny,
The faithfull who stood
And honored the Robe.
The faithfull stood mute
To the ties in his tune,
To the honing of wedge,
Thawned skilfully in,
Designed to substend
To he and his clique,
The substance of those
Who honor the Robe.
The arrogate's claim
Set defendants to stand,
To dare to deny and dissent,
Then anger and threats
From a dastard upset,
Desolved all the writ
Of the man who had slit
The honor of it, the Robe.

Catherine Crane Stone
THE SAILBOAT
I saw a cat's paw on the lake
and fluttered in the breath of
it
and let it draw me in.
Full sail I grew
and heeled in play
and knew that it would last.
But when it ran its course, it
turned
and blew away as swiftly as it
came
and left me luffing in the
breeze.
I saw a cat's paw on the lake
and it was blowing far from
me
and I could only watch in
emptiness.

Seymour Steinhardt
MOVIE MATINEE AT AGE SIX (1926)
The piano player threads
Down the aisle,
And a vocal greeting swells
From six hundred childish
throats.
The mood maestro has arrived,
Signaling the start of the
Silent picture.
But we don't know it's silent
Because there isn't any other
kind.
There's the shuffling of kid
rumps,
Adjusting to oversized seats.
The piano sounds; the asbestos
curtain rises,
And a visual Lucullan feast
ensues.
It is joy beyond joy
Because it dwarf's reality.
There is Buck Jones and there
are
Horses, mesas, mountains,
cactus
And a ranch.
There are steel-jawed men,
Ten feet tall.
The darkness is a cocoon from
which
I will never
Emerge.
Because outside there is only
light
And Wollner's German
Delicatessen,
And I don't want to see them
again.
This is where I live. . .in the
darkness,
Over the mesa, behind that
cactus,
At the foot of the mountain,
On the ranch. . . and I sleep
In the bunkhouse,
Right next to
Buck Jones.

Ethel Case Cook
TO MY DOCTOR
I hail you, gentle healer, for
your skill
Your sensitivity, your wit, your
touch.
You bring an understanding that
can fill
A lack. Your friendship is my
needed crutch.
We are so many reaching out to
you
Who bless the very earth on
which you tread,
Who bless the air you breathe,
and vow anew
To shout allegiances, but
sign instead. . .
I speak for all of us within
this frame:
We thank you from our depths
and bless your name.

Marion L. Perry
DORY HOUSE
I watched, the sea from my
window
Each wave kiss the sandy beach
Watched summer turn into
autumn
And the cool wind touch, her
cheek.
I saw clover and roses wither
I watched goldenrod turn into
bloom,
I watched the tall grass make
into hay
And I turned to a lonely room.
Suddenly! I wanted to be
outside,
Let mother nature talk to me
I wanted to be part of this
autumn day
Let the wind blow my hair,
smell the sea.
Now autumn has turned much
colder,
The trees are now all bare.
Winter came in so quietly,
I didn't even know she was
there.
Fires, now crackle and snap in
the wood stoves
Everything, inside is warm
I'll never forget this house by
the sea
And I'll, remember you, all
winter long.

Margaret Kelly
DAYDREAMING QUEST
Have you ever marvelled
At the wondrous feat
Of the toiling insects
Living 'neath our feet?
Did you ever try
To hear the song
Played by the wind
In the evening long?
Have you ever pondered
The rain of day,
And found, too soon,
Time hastened it away?
Did you ever dream
Of the artist who
Labored out of love
And carved the rainbow?
Have you ever cheered
The always restless ocean's
Swim from the shore
Back to the horizon?
Did you ever receive
Anything near so kind
Than a smiling look
When your blue-of-mind?

Dr. Debra Linowitz Wentz
BIRDS SOAR HIGH
Birds try to soar high
and so do I
Searching out sincere truth
with no lie.
But I don't have wings
and can't see
That genuineness isn't
to be found by me.
Each time I meet a person
in whom I put my trust
—which I do because I must—
I find my heart stung
my feelings all hung
Because no one really
wants to know
What makes me high
What makes me low.
All want to caress my hair,
Kiss my lips, hold my hand,
Then go leaving my thoughts in
air,
Not letting the real me stop
and land.
Superficiality, I've had enough.
Gentle I am, I can't get tough.
So instead retreat will I
So that I don't swallow another
lie.

Don A. Forster
FOREVER YOUNG
Death to all must come some
day,
but how it will come, or when,
is only for God to say!
For most death comes at a ripe
old age,
"It was their time to die,"
so goes the old adage.
However, for a few chosen ones
whom we are among,
death will come when they are
still very young.
As we grow old day by day,
in God's eternal plan, forever
young they will stay.

Maretta (Wendy) L. Smith
YESTERDAYS
The first snowflake fell today,
slowly to the ground.
My memories of yesterdays,
still floating around.
You will soon be home,

for the holidays.
But what a short stay,
as it will become yesterdays.
My heart is still loving you,
and my arms want to hold
you.
Just like the long walks,
in the snows of yesterdays.
Someday you will be home,
for a longer stay.
And how I will want you,
to stay for today.
Don't go away from me,
and leave me with memories.
Because God will tell me,
they are yesterdays.

Marian Brown
WHY?
Do bricks deplore their state in
life?
Do roses yearn to scent another
green?
Would yellow cat rather fly
robin
Instead of being queen?
Do doorways wish for window
light?
Would stairs prefer to coast a
bit?
Do plots of ground tight-
fenced around
Imagine sky a finer fit?
Still each fulfills a purpose now,
While I who had a scheme
Stand empty-handed at the door
With nothing but a dream.

Louis Glenn Lett
DINNER FOR TWO
The candles flickered in the
gloom
And shadows danced around
the room
While Mary sat upon a chair
And toyed with her long
brown hair.
She wondered why he was so
late.
He promised to be there by
eight.
There were no sounds outside
or in
Until the clock had chimed at
ten.
The food she'd fixed had long
grown cold.
Her agitation getting bold,
She raised her voice with laden
strife,
"He's probably out again with
his wife."

Eleanor J. Summers
LAST DAYS OF SUMMER
Today is summer still, although
Bright autumn waits just over
the hill
Unseen, already felt, it brings
A certain longing in the heart
A taste of apple-wine upon the
air
And woodsmoke, boding things
to come,
A yearning, deeply rooted, mute,
To be somewhere—but where,
but where?
To reach and grasp and hold
The golden essence of each day
Plundered now, and passing
recklessly.
Look, there's a golden leaf
Already falling
And time is racing—
Wait for me.

Deborah Hattes
CLAIRE
A young woman
Leaning against a signpost,
Hair braided around her head
Dark, and dark eyes.
Arms entwirled about books
Waiting for that journey home.
But I look again!
I see that face is not lit with
smiles.
It is bowed by pain.
Some unhappiness has etched a
beauty unsurpassed.
Oh, Claire, unhappy you are
beautiful!

Jonann Marie Ross
IMAGES IN MY MIND
I see reflections in the pool
Sway and swirl with every
wave.
I see shadows lurking dark and
cool
In the deep recesses of a
hidden cave.
I see sunlight dancing on
shining leaves
And flowers open for the sun's
early kiss.
I hear the wind that howls and
grieves
Until it abates to a gentle
hiss.
I find peace and serenity in this
place
And untold comfort in the
image of your face.

M. Bainbridge/Kins'ella
UNTITLED
I wish that menopause, would. . .

Helen E. R. Stanley
OCEAN
Playing tag with rocks
Angry by their stillness
She attacks unrelinquishing

Judith Ayers
NOMASTE'
I want to dance in the realms
of where we look into one
anothers
eyes, and know what is not
knowable.
and say, that which doesn't
need words
then there is little to impede or
diffuse
the natural intensity of our
thoughts
Just come into the moment.
through an open heart you can
hear the universe.
Absolute choiceless awareness,
pure
loving flow and harmony
without a curse
the abscence of clinging,
opaciousness of true caring.
Be still and listen to the quiet
Take peace
its soothing to your soul.
Be joyfull in my
silence, for my spirit will
caress your soul like the
touch of a newborn breeze
listen for the whisper, soft
like fog in the
morning falling on your soul.
My love is quiet, my spirit
gentle
and the peace I bring is real.

Sandy Craddock
THERE WOULD BE GOOD MEMORIES
Death, for me, I believe was
nearing the end of the street
At the stop,
And he knew it so well.
But he decided to stay with me
while
I lingered about:
Perhaps a few years—
And there would be good
memories,
And he would still be young and
free to find another
Beauty
As I.
And my darling young lover:
I don't mind.
I really outgrew the need for
a corvette,
And even new kitchen cabinets
Or a swimming pool;
But I haven't outgrown the need
for you.
So my dear,
I shall stay too—
Sorrowfully knowing you shall
never find a more
Potent and uncontested
relationship as ours.
But there would be good
memories. . .

Vernon Wesley Sherman
SAINT CATHERINE'S CURSE/UNTO THE THIRD
Saint Catherine? "Well",
Church-sister said, "When
both girls ran away,
And daughter's daughter,
fatherless, Sarcasam had its
day.
We knew her wild and foolish
tongue, her arrogance, her
spite,
'Gainst any, all, who dared
to think God gave her not
the right
To waste another's Heart, or
Home, or helpless Child—Oh,
worse
Than Plague, upon a person fell
the scourge of Catherine's
Curse!"
Our Home, our Land, our
Camelot, the glow at Heart of
me;
New World, new Life, new roads
about, sweet toil, serenity.
Our boy grew here thru "grades",
and "high", and all of college
thru;

Now deep the snows and many
since we three became we
two.
Our south fence rides a
neighbor hill, Red-brick
stares back from there,
Its weeds stand tall again this
Fall, and snow slants down
the air;
I look across, 'tis habit now,
and marvel Hope could doubt
Old Kate, who wore her
"hubby's" pants, and kicked
his daddy out,
Would fail, third generation
wise,
To wash the brain and blind
the eyes
Of our son's bride, whose
father well
I knew had dragged old Kate
thru Hell.
He didn't hold with bossy Jades,
He gave it her! Indeed! In
Spades!

Richard John Briggs
THE SOUL ESCAPES
In from the cold. Tired body,
tired marbles
upstairs. Up go the covers as
vaporish hands pull
the soul and warm the cover in
ecstatic release;
engaged on a plane of velvet
white light. Vapor undoing
the skin that is covering the
other. Successful
crossbreeding ingredients
travel invisibly and in ease
transport two who transcend as
one.

Esther Diamond
THE FORTUNATE
They are the cheerful people
Who have had
A chance to know the taste
Of being sad.

Chester O. Knox
RE—LEASE FOLLOWS RELEASE
Release and re-lease are spelled
just alike except for a very
thin line.
Release is let go; re-lease,
take again, each word is not
hard to define.
To quickly release impossible
plights, perplexing though
they may well be,
And nevermore getting
entangled again is to know
what it means to be free.
Re-lease is taking again the
relinquished: the released of
what was possessed.
And wisdom is always knowing
the difference;
releasing the evil, re-leasing
the rest.

Paul W. Becker
AUTUMN CHILL
When I arose at dawn,
The fog lay on the city;
I thought of the painting,
"September Morn"
And sensed a twinge of pity.
I saw cold dew upon the grass,
The rose and the begonia,
And I felt certain the ill-clad
lass
Had perished from
pneumonia.

Doris Englebert
OUR MOM
With a few streaks of gray
that lay nestled in her black
hair,
our mom was someone special
to us.
She was a little woman
with a very big heart,
our mom.
She got the biggest pleasure
out of doing for others,
but never wanted or expected
anyone
to do things for her.
She was a very proud lady,
our mom.
As time raced by
we grew taller than our mom
and we had to look down to her
when we talked, but in our
hearts
we looked up to
our mom.
She was the one that dried our
tears,
soothed our hurts away and
when
we needed strength, she was
the pillar

we leaned on and always found comfort.
She was our mom.
Today as I recall the memories
we are looking up to her
she is looking down to us,
because she is in heaven now.
Time took her away from us,
but it can't take the precious memories
because she is and will always be
our mom,
whom we look up to.

Ruth Z. Horrall
R.S.V.P.
Stay autumn—
Extend your visit.
Your warmth encourages me
Like my benevolent uncle,
Praising much, scorning little.
Your warming smile lures me outside
Dallying in awe before your splendor—
Late blooming mums
Courageous marigolds
Flaming sedum.
I marvel how you coaxed the green
To stay this year through late October.
Your gentled breath rarely churned bright leaves.
Your warmth is a smile of an old lover
Tempered, mellow, honest, kind—
Never alluding we're near the end,
But letting me rest
A few more days
In wonder upon his shoulder.
Oh—stay!

Seraphina Zorana Dianthe Fitzgerral
THE UNICORN
He stands upon the flowered hill
An artists dream, a movie still
Enchantment seen by wondering eyes
He waits serene, neath moonlit skies
His mane and tail cascading down,
So gently sweep the moonbathed ground.

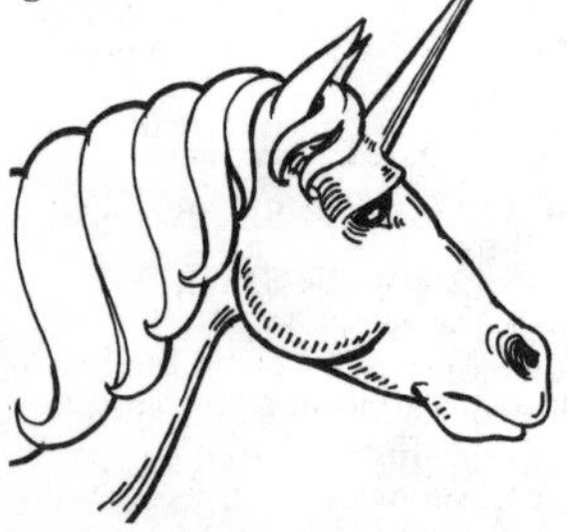

He's snowflake white with silver cast,
A dream comes true as ages pass.
A head so noble, hoofs so sure,
A gaze, like pool of water, pure.
And on his head a horn of gold,
Is jutting forth with brilliance, bold.
While on his neck so strong and sleek,
A wreath of flowers fragrant, sweet,
Seem proud to be a part of this,
Proud creature's tableau in the mist.
I creep upon the wings of night.
A little closer to the light.
My soul enraptured by the form,
Of one we call the unicorn.
He sees me, will he take his flight?
And leave me weeping in the night.
Or will he let me gently touch,
His grandeur that I want so much.
He greets me golden hoofs a prance,
We whirl, suspended by our dance.
And then as swiftly as he came,
He leaves me, spell-bound in the rain.
Long I stand there, kissed by showers,
Dreaming on amongst the the flowers.
Until the magic disappears,
And I awake to taste my tears.
The magic gone, I turn away,
To face an ordinary day.
But in my dreams, my fancy's flight,
Will touch a unicorn tonight.

Mary A. Willingham
TODAY VS TOMORROW
Today, is this world, there is so much loneliness and pain;
Tomorrow there will be sunshine after each rain.
Today's society is filled with violence, sickness and death;
Tomorrow's world will be peaceful—free from crime and theft.
Today there is a sadness that both man and animals can feel;
Tomorrow there will be joy that a professional robber couldn't steal.
Today there is mistrust and racism in the minds and hearts of men;
Tomorrow there will be a brotherhood—for we will all be the best of friends.
Today there exist hatredness strong enough to cause man to kill;
Tomorrow there will be love—so genuine so real.
Today there's inflation—no longer can we afford meat and bread;
Tomorrow food will be in abundance for every man will be well fed.
Today there are burglar bars secured on windows and doors;
Tomorrow there will be peace and security—fear of harm will be no more.
Today many weapons and firearms are definitely being misused;
Tomorrow there will be no warfare neither will man be abused.
Today there's a spirit of selfishness floating through the air;
Tomorrow there will be kindness and sharing everywhere.
Today many are divorcing, committing fornication and adultery too;
Tomorrow there will be all cleanness—friends faithful and true.
Today many experience old age, sickness and disease;
Tomorrow we will forever be youthful—our hearts and minds always at ease.
Today's society is filled with wickedness, injustice, grief and strife;
Tomorrow there will be ETERNAL LIFE, true peace and security—
FOREVER in a REAL PARADISE.

James Buckner
SNOBS
From his veranda he views his lake,
Master of all he surveys,
He looks with pride at his handiwork,
A home built in younger days.
I know he calls this valley his own,
I have no desire to intrude,
If I walk by in a friendly way
He has no need to be rude.
It happens each time I pass their home,
I guess it hurts my pride,
He and his family turn their backs
And take themselves inside.
They never mingle with common folk,
They avoid us when they can.
If they are not extremely shy,
Beavers are a snobbish clan.

Brian Leno
LOVE AND BEAUTY
Men say her smile to be as dazzling as the light of the sun,
Not say I; her beguiling smile will shortly fade with time
And, in a scant number of years, when this beauty's life is done
Then no longer will her brown eyes appear so proud and fine.
Age will wrinkle those nicely curving cheeks, that smiling face;
Stiffness will steal into her limbs, now so pure and white,
Soon senility will that smile completely erase—
She'll only appear in the silent cloak of night.
Those who, so they claim, once loved her, will now remember her no more,
For love lasted only so long as her beauty could,
They said her beauty surpassed that of the goddess' of ancient lore
But now she's alone, when she goes out she wears a hood.
Love and beauty are different, and yet the same,
Because neither lasts longer than a dripping rain.

Frances E. Blackmur
BANNER OF TRUCE
You are waiting patiently
For me to retreat,
To wave high a white banner
Admitting defeat.
The banner shall never wave
As a sign of Truce,
Because I cannot forgive
Malicious abuse.
Our battle is near ended
So I'll wave good-bye,
To burn the Banner of Truce
Before it flies high.

Samuel J. Bruno
STILL AT THE FIRE
My thoughts, they dance and turn,
A night at the fireplace alone,
The logs break and burn,
My eyes are captured and hold me still in time,
Outside the storm blows its wind,
Up the chimney, the fireflies climb.
Warm to warm, the fire holds me tight,
And the windows are sealed in snow,
The heat colors my face, red and bright.
The floor and walls seem to creep,
My head bows and tells me it's late,
And the fire fades, now we both go to sleep.

Theri Mashore
UNTITLED
Love, make innocent your eyes
We've long to spend here.
And many times she sighs
Oh cold days and nights:
Soft and gray, are the shadows of my past.
the soul sets free
the fears of my flight,
to hear, to protect the heart in me,
Are soft and gray shadows, wrapped in cold days and nights

Steven Scott Fyfe
A LIVING FEELING
When I think and sit down in an empty space
my time sparkles around you,
When I think of the thought
of not knowing you anymore,
Tears fall down my face. . .
When I think of the times
I should have said something,
When I think of the times
I should of said nothing,
Tears fall down my face. . .
When I think of the talks
we had and have together,
When I think of the talks
of helping one another,
Tears fall down my face. . .
When I think of the wonderful
days we had and have together,
When I think of the bad
days we had and have together,
Tears fall down my face. . .
When I think of the future. . .
Will we be close together?
When I think of the future. . .
Will we be far apart?
Tears fall down my face. . .
When I think and look around me
and you are near,
When I think and look around me
and you fear,
Tears fall down my face. . .
When I simply think of you. . .
Tears fall down my face. . .
When I simply try to avoid you. . .
Tears fall down my face. . .

Darlene E. Fridfinnson
NOBODY'S WISDOM
Do not tell me that
You cannot understand me—
I am easy to understand.
Do not think that you are perfect—
Nobody is perfect.
Opinions are fine, but do not think
That you are always right—
Someone may think otherwise.
How do I know all this?

I am perfect.
WHO AM I you ask?
Your impertinence this time
SIR, has
Gone too far.
However, I shall tell you
Who I am.
I AM NOBODY.

Alegna Livingston
CITY PEOPLE
Sing a song of people walking
fast and slow,
People in the city up and down
they go,
People on a sidewalk, people on
a bus,
People passing, passing-back and
front of us.,
People on the subway
underneath the ground,
People riding taxis 'round and
'round and 'round,
People with their hats on going
indoors,
People with umbrellas when it
rains and pours.
People in tall buildings and in
stores below,
Riding elevators up and down
they go,
People walking silent, people in
a crowd,
People saying nothing, people
talking loud.
People laughing, smiling-grumpy
people, too,
People who just hurry, never
look at you,
Sing a song of people who like
to come and go,
Sing of city people you see but
never know.

Richard J. Kuenzinger
TOMORROW I WILL BE GONE
I went down to the creek today,
I like to just sit and listen.
I heard Mother Nature say,
"The bright clear water is my
lifeline,
The plants and animals are my
soul.
Enjoy me now, while I am here
Before mankind and progress
have come.
Remember how you played
amongst my leaves
As a young child;
For tomorrow, tomorrow I will
be gone.

Carol Roberson
ALL ABOUT MY MEMORIES
I lay upon my bed at night
as shadows fall upon me;
Pages unfold before my sight
from the book of memories.
For when no one else is
thereabouts
and the time arises, to question
ones self;
I can always count on my
memories
to love--and care---for me.
They're like good friends in so
many ways;
For when suddenly, I'm all alone
and blue;
But with just a call, they're
always there
filling me with happiness and
joy of yesterdays.
The warmth and comfort they
will always bring
of those so close but yet so far.
And of the days of old upon the
new;
The history book, we will never
lose.
Where would I be without my
memories?
Lost and frustrated; Fearful and
empty.
All I can say, is thank the Lord--
for my many memories.

Adrian M. Maschek
THAT'S THE WAY IT IS!
All of life is give and take
and you cannot break the rule
that's the way it is my friend,
otherwise you're just a fool.
For six thousand years
those guidelines were okay
and that's the way it is,
even to the present day.
You'll get from life what you
put in
it's a system you cannot beat
and if you live by the law,
you'll live on easy street.
That's the way it is for sure
it works for everyone's good
yet there are those,
who would change that if they
could.
That's the way it is
for God's laws remain the same
if your troubles lie with
yours truly,
you have only yourself to blame,
AND THAT'S THE WAY IT IS!

Peggy L. Tiffany
UNTITLED
The evening dark settles in
As thoughts of you internally
begin.
A smile enlightens my face
As I remember your warm
embrace.
Shivers run up and down my
spine
As I think you'll never be mine.
For your heart belongs with
your wife
And I am doomed with an
unfulfilled life.
The deep soul searching love I
feel
Belongs to you, and it's very
real.
But you will never release your
security
To hold me only in love purity.

Gary T. Williams
MOON NITE MIRAGE
I'm starting on a journey,
Spreading my wings to fly.
The moon's my destination
Softly smiling in the sky.
As my wings beat ever steady
And I climb into the air,
Anticipation haunts me
Wondering what I'll find up
there.
The night is black and shining
As I leave old Earth behind,
Memories are quickly fading
Disappearing from my mind.
The old Earth looks so weary
From the distance that I've done,
From a kind of reminiscing
Of a much more youthful one.
As I wing into the heavens
Being here you would agree,
That the carnival of infinities
Becomes a space menagerie.
My spirits get a boosting
As my eyes light on a star,
For it's brightness hangs there
waving
Saying "My but you've come far".
Ahead of me are comets,
Some asteroids at bay,
An Empire of meteors,
And there's the Milky Way.
The space dust forms a circle
Around the dippers big and
small,
A bright light flashes
cosmically,
As a star gets tired and falls.
Looking back I see old Earth
Miles and miles below.
Looking forward there's old
moon
With miles and miles to go.
Quietness abounds up here,
Stillness is your friend.
Darkness joins them in space
And space knows no end.
There's the moon ahead of me,
It's magic rules the night
Closer, closer there I fly,
I'm drenched with all it's light.
It's been a long, long journey,
But it's end is very soon.
My destination closing
For I'm landing on the moon.
I'm awed by all the sights I see,
The moon becomes a gleam,
Collecting cheese for souveniers
As well as old moon beams.
I flap my wings once more in
flight,
But I can't move it seems,
Because awakening now I find
I've only had a dream!

Marlene Schofield
NEVER IS TOO SOON
As we stand on the sandy beach,
huddled together, hand in hand,
my mind rejects the thought of
losing you,
You and our future plans.
We had promised as childhood
sweethearts
to love one another our whole
lives through.
Now you are talking of leaving,
and I'm to be left behind
without you.
What must I do to prove
that my love, then and now, is
true?
There is only one person I love
and, of course, that person is
you.
I know you have made your
decision,
You are leaving tomorrow at
noon.
I will never forget you, Michael.
And never is far too soon.

Sumner Sumner
LOVE'S LODGINGS LOST
In Shakespeare's day,or so they
say,
The liver was the seat of love.
No longer.
Its half a thousand functions
vile
(Excreting waste, secreting bile)
Proved stronger.
So love sought refuge in the
heart,
But, since we now take hearts
apart,
No longer.
Sweet refugee, no place to flee,
As science, probing what we're
of,
Proves stronger.
So, move thou to the ambient
air,
Surrounding us with love; and
fear
No longer.

Robert Ellice Hobbs II
DARK CHAMBERS
Darkness it rules the sky.
Fog drifting slowly passes my
window.
Shadows that lurk below,
Waiting there for me out of
sight.
Castle walls dark and cold,
They've seen so much
throughout the ages.
Secrets that stalk the halls,
Opening doors and yellowed
pages.
Royalty once reigned here,
Playing the games of blueblood
nobles.
Meeting their separate fates,
Somewhere amidst the darksome
chambers.
Flagstones so damp and grey,
Shimmering with the glow of
hist'ry.
I've heard lost spectres wail,
Whispers are speaking, lost in
myst'ry.
Portraits so old and pale,
Faces stare lost and locked in
time.
Reflections of their past
Live in dark chambers of your
mind.

John E. Stenwall
WHAT IS THIS HOLD YOU HAVE ON ME?
What is this hold you have on
me
Like mosses on a live oak tree
Or lichen covered slab of rock?
I must confess it suits me well
A surge of life within me swells
And years are blown away like
chaff.

For fair I'd leave both hearth and
home
And o'er the world with you I'd
roam
Until my years on earth are
done.
On closer view it's plain to see
It's just that age-old alchemy
Held Abelard and Heloise.

Lindy Kosak
FREEDOM IS...
Freedom starts with an open
door...
It is making decisions-
It is the American flag-
It is a dove hovering in the sky...
It is a watercolor streaming
across a sheet of paper-
It is a chance to be myself...
To dream my dreams...
Freedom is being creative with
life-
Molding it to fit me.

Jane Griggs
FROGS
Frogs that come in bunches
have a name, and that's a fact!
I couldn't think of what it was
although my brain I racked.
Then, one day riding down the
road
it came to me and others.
The only thing they could be
called
is a whole bunch of them
Mothers!

Sara Saey
WORLDS WITHOUT END
Thru my window
Past the leas
Crashing tides
On moonlit seas
Watching worlds
Passing by
Orbit outward
Beyond the sky
Fantasies fast
Becoming real
No buildings of
Concrete or steel
Standing stark
Against the light
Blotting out
A stellar night
Thru the vastness
That is space
My soul soars
To a place
To a world
Without end
Herald by
A solar wind
Brushing stars
As I pass by
Counting comets
Upon high
Serene with love
That must transcend
Into a world
Without end
Where the mighty
Thunders roll
I can touch God
Thru the window
Of my soul.

Dorothy L. Terry
SPRINGTIME
O how lovely is the springtime
Where everywhere is seen
In the meadows and the forests
Natures own delicious green
O how joyful in the springtime
Just to hear the birdies sing
Out in the apple orchard
Where merrily they swing
O how pleasant in the springtime
Just to walk beneath the trees
And breathe the blossoms odor
As it floates down with the breeze
O how happy in the springtime
Just to be out in the air
And roam the woodlands over
In search of flowers fair
O how we love the springtime
When our hearts are light and gay
Just to be out in the sunshine
In the merry month of May

Shelley Cords
CRESCENDO
Like a classical arrangement soothing my mind with each movement,
I flow to the mood of the music.
It is beautifully orchestrated;
Each note blending with the others.
As the symphony builds, one feels the excitement, the intensity.
From andante to allegro,
The piece reaches a vibratic high.
As yes, the delightful refrain, the big crescendo, the grand finale.
As I savor that moment,
Chills run down my spine;
Tears fill my eyes;
My body is consumed.
How does this happen? What are the motives?
I often wonder, "Can there be a better arrangement?"
I think not.
The composer is the creative one,
Knowing exactly how the piece is to flow;
How each note will blend;
What the outcome will be.
And then, when the music has died, I say,
"Play it again, just once more, re-create that big crescendo."

J. Vava Buitenkant
CANNERY SONG
Our cold tin dreams clatter together.
Drunk dry they blow along the gutter.
If, instead, they were made of gold that glitters, they'd surely be quickly snatched up by others.
Rusty cast iron, it breaks when you drop it.
Lead's too heavy to ever take flight.
And aluminum's too light to feel in your pocket.
We don't have to lose just because we can't win.
so we've made our empty dreams of tin.

T. L. Coakley
DEAD ZONE
All so bright white
In souls paralax flight
Cloudlessness preys on fear
Stretched comfort soul
Recognized youths feel
Awaking in this hell
Telling of futures will
Auras rest everywhere
Causing yesterdays tomorrow
Minds of capability of solution
Wicked sting of needles
Greed of parasites bite
End of possessed fool

Eleanor Lee
COME BE MY LOVE
My heart cries
Come be my love,
Oh be my own
Come be my love.
The nights are endless
The nights are cold,
Without your arms
To caress and enfold
Embrace me my love
Give our hearts reverent ties,
Together greet each new day
As dawn waits to arise.
Soon my heart rejoices warmly
As your arms entwine about me,
I feel my prayers are answered
And I know you are my own.

Michael Sherbon
TO THE MASSES OF THE MANIACAL
In these rude and turbulent times
the buzz of extravagantly suggestive images can create a very reactive, irrational, and hyperanimated attitude.
Therefore, this crazed condition requires
a very versatile philosophy of folly, one delivering potent euphoriant knowing and immediately miraculous phantasmic action.
Then, with this comprehensive and completely
megalomaniacal key to all reality and unreality, we can liberate the obscurations of consciousness in our effort to become fully energetic and effectual.
And finally, we will move from mere voluptuous reverie
to realize the fabulous infusion of soul in a very supreme sensual virtuosity!
Oh yes! So zealous is the transcending release of suprasensuous ecstasy!
So, in these rude and turbulent times, passions are massive!

Alice Coombs Mills
SUMMER'S ENDING
I hear myriads of crickets singing their thousandth see-saw song,
And sense a crispy coolness in the shorter days and evening air.
Telling me lazy, hazy indian Summer's passing on quietly, surely into Autumn fair.
Across the Valley blow the Autumn leaves, swinging, swirling, twisting, twirling

In flashy, splashy splendor rare, Autumn's gayest fashion wear.
Autumn—flaunting her gay apparel of oakleaf brown and maple red,
Making the nearby hills against the sky so blue
Look for all the world like a magic mosaic carpet with its blended purplish hues.
While the Wind in the Willows Whispers a mournful tune,
"Winter, Winter,—It's coming soon."

Alice Durfee Oates
TET IS HERE
One shining, sunny day, the colonel did say, Alice, this is
a good day for you and the Sgt.
to jump into the jeep and ride away.
Get the guns and shells, because war is hell.
Say "Hello" to all at Tan Son Nhut. Tell them it is "Tet" and
ask "What else is new?"
Say "Goodbye" and do not cry,
because you are only on your way, to make it a big day for
the good old U.S.A.
(This was the worst year of the war 1969, Saigon, Vietnam)

Christy Watts Piersol
LITTLE PEOPLE
Swirling books of dancing beauties
With marching men and whistling trains
Embedded deep within them.
More and more to read.
Encircled forts of twenty toys
But two alone to fight over
One doll.
Kings in Spain wish away the hours
Lost and found by hearts
To young to know heartbreak.
Black is white and maybe is yes
To demands for answers
Of forgotten questions,
While we yearn to get back
To enter Sleeping Beauty's castle.

Brenda J. Callahan
UNTITLED
I'm tired now.
After all
what did you expect?
One long, continuous
summer—
never ending passion—
unfailing words of
love?
Sometimes,
one needs quiet
and rest.
Shades of gray
and blue.
Not everything
has to be firecrackers
and the 4th of July.

Barbara Hibbert
THE ANGELS TOUCHED HER HAIR
The Angels touched her soft golden hair,
As each bent down to hear her prayer.
She prayed for her heart was heavy and sad,
And felt the need of help from her Heavenly Dad.
The Angels listened each with a tear,
As her heavy hearts prayer they did hear.
Then a soft glow surrounded my friend,
As his love he did send.
She felt safe within his love,
As he descended from above.
He bent down and gentle kissed her golden hair,
She knew then that he had heard her prayer.
Then my friend arose and went on her way,
Knowing God was with her to stay.

Travis Corder
A GOLDEN DAY IS DAWNING
A golden day is dawning upon the silver strand.
O'er Christ the angels fawning throughout the promised land.
A day when I'll be going up to that happy place
And satisfy the longing to see

my Savior's face.
Let all the world take notice,
I'm not afraid to go
And leave behind the tinsel of mother earth below.
The cloud of death is fading, the light is shining through,
I see the silver lining and know what I will do.
I'll rise to meet the challenge and soar beyond the blue
Up to the highest heaven where I'll await for you.
Don't grieve for me my darling, I'm going home to rest.
I haven't been an angel, but I have done my best.
The Lord will keep you safely, held firmly in His hand
And He will bring you gently up to the coral strand.
Then we'll be reunited and in the Savior's love
We'll live a life of splendor the earth knows nothing of.

Lucy Owen

A COMET FROM SPACE

Through the glory of the heavens
Where stars glitter in their galaxies
In your parabolic flight
You come near the grasping sun.
Your flaring head bows to Sun's gravity.
Long streamers of gas now float aloft.
Despite your luminous appearance
You are made of cold ice crystals.
Did you pass the rings of Saturn?
Pluto or Jupiter with its Great Red Spot?
Delighted astronauts may have watched you speed by.
Earthling though I am—great is the joy your fiery beauty brings to me.

Irma Campbell

MATTER

What's the matter with youngsters, now A days?
Why do they have such awful ways
Why do they get into A car,
And go too fast, and go too far?
Why do they lie and steal and cheat?
Why do they riot in the street?
Why are they taking L S D ?
Or get so drunk they can not see?
Well I can answer in one word
The simplest answer you have heard.
Oldsters, oldsters, I allow
That's the matter with youngsters now.
It's the Oldsters, that make the car
That goes too fast, and too far
Oldsters also make "THE STUFF"
That makes the Youngsters get so tough
And then they tell them "GO AWAY"
You see that I'm too busy today
You go sit down and watch TV
Just don't come here and bother ME"
But it's the Oldsters, write the show
Telling what they should never know
Instead of telling of GODS LOVE
And the heavenly home above.

Sarah Maryie

FREE

I AM FREE to be me
Restfull Sea
Soundless Melody
I AM FREE
Free from the Paradox
Free from the Equinox
Free as a Bird in Flight
on a summer Night
Free from Plight
Free from Sight
I AM no more
Soul to Soar
Love Implore
Evermore

Elizabeth Huddle Martin

OUR CHRISTMAS TREE

O Christmas tree! I think you are so pretty
With your lights of every hue,
And your tinsel is so dazzling
As it shines out to me from you.
The colorful Christmas packages
Lying under your branches there,

Will be opened by kindly folk
With ever loving care.
But high up in your tip top
Is a bright and "Shiny Star."
Reminding us of Jesus Christ
Our Savior, who was born from afar.

Jessie Owens Jackson

IT'S HARVEST TIME IN EVERGREEN

Oh God! In a wooded forest
We said a prayer—
Give us a house to worship for Thee.
We thank Thee, Father, it's there.
It's there with a harvest
That's full and free
To be plucked and planted
In a field for Thee.
We pray again, dear Lord,
Give us faithful workers
With gifts and service true
That we may gather this harvest through.
Help us, Father, to gather those tiny seeds
That are drifting from field to field
In hunger and thirst for a place to sod
And grow to call Thee their God.
Again, we thank Thee, dear Lord,
For thy faithful servants as our reward.
They have given us a new strength in faith and prayer
That we may Thy urgent call each one share.

James N. Hall

DOG DIRTY DAN

Back in the days of the wild wooly west,
While sportin' a star on my brown leather vest,
An' dressed like a dude just out from the east,
I was tryin' to tame a cow-thievin' beast.
He was mean as a snake an' twice as low,
An' he'd killed six men for a fact, I know;
He scared all the people for miles around,
An' burned Jessie's barn plumb down to the ground.
A big burly guy with a iron on each hip,
An' I knew he could use 'em, so I mustn't slip;
But I swore I would get this red-headed man,
That the folks in these parts knew as DOG DIRTY DAN.
It was nigh onto sunset that fateful eve,
An' from the saloon I was takin' my leave;
I went around back, to unhitch 'Ole Spark,'
I guess by this time, it was gettin' right dark.
The night was so quiet, you could hear gophers chew,
When I heard the spurs clink, it was then that I knew
The ambush was set, an' I was the bait,
But he made a bad move, guess he just couldn't wait.
In the blink of an eye, the guns were ablaze,
An' a lot of lead flew through the smoke an' haze;
An' when it got quiet, an' the smoke went away,
It was then that I realized, I'd seen my last day.
DOG DIRTY DAN lay dead in the street,
But the blood puddled up, right under my feet;
I was gettin' light headed, an' weak at the knees,
An' then I keeled over, as nice as you please.
Now most of these stories, that you hear tell,
The badge lives forever, the gun goes to hell;
But this was a case where the law met it's peer,
An' it wasn't from speed, an' it wasn't from fear.
For DOG DIRTY DAN was nowise afraid,
An' neither was I, from the place I now laid;
We hated an' loathed, but respected each other,
For I was DOG DIRTY DAN'S older brother.

Patricia Ann Adams-Huffman

OUR'S

We put all our past behind us,
We needn't care about anything but our love.
Was it love?
We both had made no Commitment's to each other,
Was this a nonchalant way of love?
Maybe it wasn't the right way to love,
For everybody. . . .but It was "Our Love."

Victor Morabito

A POETLAND

as the time of day
needs no light
the dark of night
needs no time—
my lord sees me
and i see not
my lord sees all
and maybe not. . .
what is this flower
without a fragrance
what is this valley
without a wall
what is this ocean
without a depth
what is this desert
without a sand;
my lord sees me
and i see not
my lord sees all
and maybe not. . .
a requited love
ensures the heart
a deep sleep
fills the dream
a violent storm
rages the motion
a quietude
stills the air;
as the time of day
needs no light
the dark of night
needs no time—

J.C.

FRIEND CALL I YOU

I am undone.
I need what most I disavow.
I scream wildly, yes,
at wings in my eyes
fluttering sights of you.
O stranger, with your
pointing finger in the air,
what bird or star
or circumstance
drives you in this action?
What import negligent have
I in secret squandered?
I am on all fours,
a predatory baby,
unhaired in the natural
opine and wince of
habitation. I could say a
thing, and to you
in the dark of my recess:
Now I am alone.
No hour strikes but

in my brain
echoes in thunder my
condition.
I am the swarm angry bees
are; a mess of stings
in one purpose, a hum
of persistence, nastiness
on the several tongue of
their secret enterprise. I had
no name to me;
to me, no name I am.
Forgive me, dear my
absence;
I see your warm motion
unsensibly cold,
like dirt indifferent to what
rots easily in its bosom.
I am brother to worms
already, know their soft
fork, the music
in their crawling motion.

Claudia Beth Kraut
WHAT IS YOUR WORLD?
I feel like you are in a world
alone.
You are in a glass box.
A precious thing, a jewel, that
I can watch and see and
admire but
A treasure I can never touch.
I will never know you or the
world you live in.
I can feel that you have
something to say
But I cannot hear the words.
I know you have beautiful
music to play
But I can only hear the chords.
I will never feel what you really
feel.
What is the world you live in?
What makes you the way you
are?
What is it like where you come
from?
What makes you shine so
brightly, shaming the
grandest stars?
Singing Writing Creating
Jumping Smiling Laughing
Crying
What are you?
Why are you?
I wish I knew you. I wish I
could climb inside your head
and know what you are all
about.
I wish I could enter your world
and feel the joy, the pain.
But for now I am content to
look inside your glass box and
admire you.

J. Margo Launay
DO NOT LOVE ME
Do not love me,
For to be loved is to be known,
and I can not be known.
Real
I strive for unreality
in a world where the difference
is slight.
What pushes me on
is unknown.
Though I suspect it to be
the suicidal energy of my youth.
Too young to be old,
Too quick to be naive,
I long to exist beyond the
shadowed meaning
of my actions.
I desire life
as another might desire death
But I am unsure
of myself
of my youth
of recurrent memories.

Laura Velchek
APGAR 10
It is all
Too simple,
To understand why,
A new little life,
So feeble
So warm
Wholly refreshes the air,
With a cry.

Jean M. Hnatio
LOVE NEVER DIES
My grandmother just passed
away,
I spent the night with my
grandfather,
and on her bed I lay.
I fell asleep and feeling glad,
to know that I was there to
comfort
my grandfather, who felt so bad.
Then in the middle of the night
something good came over me,
but yet gave me a fright.
I felt a cold breeze about my
bed,
and I felt the covers come down
from my head.
I felt someone wrap their arms
around me and
give me the biggest hug and
touch of love,
I'm sure it was my grandmother
giving me a vist from above.
When I woke up in the morning
and I'd opened
my eyes it was then that I did
realize,
That my grandmother did come
down from the skies.
Because when I woke up from
my bed,
the covers were off my head.
I told the story to relatives
and friends,
they would just say it was a
dream or a
blob and tease me to no end.
I said I don't care what any of
you feel,
definitely this was real.
I'll go on believing since this
day,
that love doesn't die
because it came my way.

Nomiky R. Revel
THINKING OF YOU
When I think of you, your
image becomes alive.
In my mind a ray of love still
shines.
Around the smiling moon,
thousand of gleaming stars.
I hear your voice, the pulse of
love sparks.
The young wind dreams, the
wild brooklet sleeps.
Joyously the beat of my heart
speaks.
When I think of you, your
image rolls
In the crowded street as I
stroll.
The sun beam's smile through
the tree.
I hear your voice, softly the
green sea reels.
The bird hush, listening to the
song as before.
The flame in my heart
kindled once more.
When I think of you, and the
romance gone,
Darkness and sadness replace
light and love.
In the red twilight, the sole
star stands.
I hear a voice whisper, "You'll
never love again."
The old wind sigh, the sad
brooklet moan,
And like a child I begin to
cry alone.

Toni Millican
AS YOU GO AWAY
As we sit here, together now,
I feel my love for you.
I find it hard to stay away
For this love is so very new.
My heart feels strength every
day
that I'm near your side.
Please, believe me, dear,
this love is too strong to hide.
When I feel your touch
I gently close my eyes.
This love is worth much more
than the stars or skies.
You are my life
The spirit of my heart,
but you are going away
even before our love can start.
As you lie there, so peacefully
I hold you in my arms, tenderly,
Cause I know this is the last
time
I will have you close to me.
As I release you from my arms,
I grasp hold of your hand in
mine.
How can I ever forget you Babe?
You're the one who makes my
life shine.
But, now as it is,
It dims as you slip away.
As your hand falls upon the bed,
You speak your last words on
this day.
You tell me to forget you,
and to live my life through.
But how can I leave you now?
I will always love you.
You close your eyes gently
and whisper, "I love you, too."
I place my veil upon your face
and feel a feeling of new.
How could I live for tomorrow
when my life has just passed
away?
Whenever I hope for the future
to come,
I will always look back on this
day.
As I kneel down to pray,
I whisper to him, "Good-bye."
As they let his casket down,
I can only feel the tears as I cry.

(Mrs.) Virgie V. Jones
CATS
If dog is man's best friend——
What's a cat?
Shy and independent—
Patient, for hours on end—
Watching ground
movement—
Fluttering of a butterfly—
Flying insect or bird—
Can relax and snuggle and
snooze—
almost any where—
purring contentment,
And, somehow tell his
needs—
and wants,—when he
wants!
That's—a cat.
His own best friend,—and yours?

Velma B. Dowling
MEMORITE
Death and I are becoming old
friends
and she's a strange woman, with
the face of Mona Lisa,
the look Lazarus must have had
before he laughed.
Death sat by me yesterday to
bring me tidings
and plucked my yellow sleeve,
"I'm taking Marguerite," she said.
I looked down at the yellowness
the color our gypsies wore for
grief,
and felt my heart squeeze purple
as a bruise.
"She knew she was leaving," I
said, "and told me so.
Gave me her music.
I put on the gayest thing I had
to try these notes upon these
strings,"
and held the violin that's meant
for gypsy tunes.
"This is what she left me of
herself.
Though I lack her gift. . .never
knew her gypsy name. . .
Those gold coins about her neck
were there to ward off evil, bring
her luck.
"The flowers of hell are all made
of metal,
shaped like garlic blossoms,
aren't they?
I'm diminished.
I have to practice."
Death rose, gathering the
drapery of her cloak
and in her gentle voice made
farewell.
"I'm going now for Marguerite.
I shall return again."

Joan C. Renda
THE VISITOR
A little one decided to take a
trip to Earth,
In hopes of finding some
merriment and mirth.
As he put his foot from place to
place and quickly moved
around,
A light from out of darkness he
suddenly had found.
He landed in a pool of red.
And now was standing on his
head.
And everyone laughed and
clapped,
Do you know why?
They were so very happy,

To hear a baby cry.
And when his eyes did open,
His face had a wonderful smile.
And without even speaking said
"I'm staying for awhile."

R. J. Judd

BABYSITTING A NEWBORN (BY A DADDY)

Babysitting Jenny is so much fun;
Hearing her scream above a TV rerun.
She won't be content; that's a fact,
Cause she's a spoiled little brat.
Feed her early, catch devil from the boss,
And onto bed, Jennifer, I will toss.
It's not time to eat the wife said before.
But she's hungry, I can't stand anymore.
So I fed her to hush her up.
She was starved; ready for sup.
The boss is back; comin' down the road.
Just in time to remove Jenny's load.

Mark S. Feldpausch

N. E. EULOGY I

Tides obey the moon
always, everyday.
Each morning the
waters rush into
my arms.
Each night the tides
go again. It's night.
Millenia enjoyed the
bathing here at
morning, washing away
a crabs discarded pincer.

Dorothy Jean Horton

TO MY LOVED ONES

Do not stand at my grave and weep;
I am not there, nor do I sleep.
My body-shell may lie below,
But my spirit soars o'er the stars'
soft glow.
My soul has joined the angel throng
Around God's mighty throne;
Where years are but a single day;
December is the same as May,
Sun and cheer are ours to share,
And happiness is everywhere.
So do not stand at my grave and weep,
My soul's alive; it will never sleep!
And as the years pass on their way,
We'll look for you to cross the Bay.

Mildred Russell Blackman

WILD SEA

Untamed, lawless, undisciplined,
ferociously pounding the pier—
as if trying to empty itself,
the unyielding sea rages.
Spewing its discontent?
Or boasting of its might?

Charles Spencer Adler, M.D.

ACAPULCO 1969

Turquoise water pounding like lymph in the temples,
concrete hued dust clinging like damp candy,
especially under the collar
snared with a wide tie
almost fatuous here,
Where somehow unsmidged atte attendants appear
smiling white as breakers
as quick to go; adaptive
creatures in sullen battle
all too real
with tourists and insects
they have let overgrow.
They seem to know
who will win.
The hotels are full, or expensive,
or leading to a humid beach that also accomodates overflow refuse.
And at the bus depot natural selection is
Natural Selection.
Uncanny.
And besides, a vague fever beclouds the issue.
Curio stands bob and disappear through heat waves
while salt dries sticky inside stomach and ears.
Only the airport is sanctuary
from this heat,
this beach scene daguerreotype
of silent vendors
catlike
watching.
While the heavy ocean rolls in
with an irregular, sucking noise
massive, not alarmed
by the frozen picture toward which it inches,
carrying shells, crab, minnows,
The Portugese Man-of-War.

Eva Pfeifer Nielsen

NOT MINE

You were not mine—I must not weep—and yet
When playful tumbling winds of autumn swept
The vagrant sumac leaves about your door
Where gently nurtured roses grew before—
I could have wept.
In voices hushed they said you'd gone away—
I held my peace-there were no words to say
But oh! the desperation deep inside
Where hidden dreams and secret hopes abide—
If I could weep, I would have wept that day.
Now empty cottage windows catch the shine
Of rising moons that wax and wane with time
And somewhere down the passage of the years
Perhaps I'll find a reason for these tears
That must not fall for you—you were not mine.

Linda A. Savage

ALPHA

The wind which stirs the stiffened limbs in spring
Portends a carefree time not bound by cold.
That wind waifs fresh to move a soul grown old
And speaks of gentle life soon on the wing;
A span of days that lacks dread winter's sting
And visits ere the master sun grows bold.
These rebirth days fill hearts with warming gold;
A thawing passion that heralds all—king.
When time be clothed in shades of newest green
I grasp contented relaxation due.
This time so short—too rapidly departs.
In life, new colors last but hours few.
The wind fortells trials for now unseen;
Yet mem'ry's wind-born sights appease our hearts.

Theresa (Teri) Redic

WAKE—UP

Wake-up eyes of the world.
Before it's too late,
Sooner or later—
We will all become bait
And there will be no
More me and thee—
But only a holocaust
Of land and sea.

Ellen M. Dallis

SOMEWHERE

Somewhere there is a place—we dream,
Where all of life's wants are foreseen,
We grab them whence they disappear,
But wants in dreams fade into mist, I fear.
I think that when I was a child,
My thoughts would lead me to pursue,
The grown up world of fulfilled needs,
Then Mom would say, "Wake up and go to school!"
My dreams have grown and I can see,
The ebbing of a new time near,
I know I must pursue them, that is clear,
Because my somewhere is near—right here.

Eleanor Harris

MY LOVE

I'm so scared
As I sit to write
Words of love
What an unexpected plight
Words flickering around my head
Nothing to dread
A pool of imagination
To be fed
Profound I'd like to be
As any lover's dream
It's plain to see
When it comes right down to you and me
It comes with only one desire
That with you I'd like to conspire
You are only to love me!

Charles Pickul

LET HIM SLEEP

Hold his hand, for his need is that of a Man,
Let him sleep,
Don't let him be alone.
Kiss his cheek, for his need is something weak,
Let him sleep,
Don't let him be alone.
Touch his hair, for his need is that you care,
Let him sleep,
Don't let him be alone.
Hear his heart, for his need is of this part,
Let him sleep,
Don't let him be alone.
Whisper in his ear, for his need is you dear,
Let him sleep,
Don't let him be alone.

Mary A. Begley

WITHOUT YOUR LOVE

Where is the sunshine?
All I see is rain;
Existing within this heart of pain
No, it's not dew drops,
Or rain on the eves;
It's the tears of loneliness
Drowning my sleeves;
I reach out to touch you,
I feel only air;
Coming deep within that ebony stare.
The dam is breaking!
I can't hold back,
I guess by now,
I know;
It's time to pack
Where am I going?
What will I be?
"Without your love,"
I'm nothing—
You see—
I know I have hurt you,
Even made you cry!
But, please forgive me,
An give me a try.
Hold me and kiss me,
Say it's alright;
Honey—I need you,
Please stay the night.
Through the windows,
Of pale pinks and greens,
The morning sunlight,
A glistening stream,
We're gonna make it,
Or is it a dream?
Honey—I hope—
It's just as it seems.

Billie Louise Parkison

MY SISTER AND THE DAISIES

One and a half miles from our home town
On the side of a hill where the road
Winds around,
The most beautiful white daisies grow
Between the weeds and blades of grass
Row after row.
The day before Mother's Day each year,

A lot of daisies from the same hillside are picked
By my sister dear,
Fortunately, when I am there with you
You are not alone, I help pick a Daisy or two.
I don't know but have a hunch
That you will take each flower,
And lay neatly in every bunch.
To keep them fresh for Decoration Day
Put them in a pail of fresh water
Without delay.
You will arise early, and you won't be slow
And to the decoration, with your daisies
You will go.
And on each well-kept grave that day
A bunch of the fresh-cut daisies
You will lay.
Then all your friends and relations
Will gather in one bunch, put all
The food and drinks on the table,
Then everyone will have a lunch.
Then after all have had his fill
Each will gather for services singing,
And preaching,
On the side of the hill.
All the good blessings of the Lord
Will be such a wonderful sight,
Each will be singing, and worshiping
The Lord with all his might.
Then after all is said and done
Everybody will leave one by one,
And all will get home before the sun goes down
Still beautiful and red,
And feed the chickens, milk the cows, feed the dogs,
And go to bed.

Barbara A. Martin

THE POWER OF SPRING

When you're down
And all alone
Remember how you felt
When Spring had come
And with the sun
Away your cares did melt

Bonnie Donald

SISTERS

We are sisters
Together or apart
Fueding or hugging
SISTERS
Through the years and the tears
Growing older and wiser
Forever we will be sisters.
(Dedicated to my Sister Heather Donald)

Christine George

WHAT NEXT?

In days elapsed we walked with hasteless strides.
With freedom, hills, dales and mountain trails
Were roamed and rambled; roved with joyous pride.
Our thoughts were held in countless prose and tales.
Today those days are dreams forbidden to touch.
With swiftness life continues; ever changed.
Less time for living, laughing, joy and such.
Our hopes are set in future days so strange.
In days to come the pace will quicken still.
Our lives will reel by—lived but empty yet.
We will neglect to notice pleasure's thrill,
And search for something far beyond life's net.
The past, present, future; what next?
But live to cherish memories with text.

Rose Lemay-Jackson

WAITING

Lingering before the final dawn
all have sinned, but none will see
confusion, animosity, man's unquenchable greed
the leader's say we must cut back, cut down, cut out
why not just cease to be, for without a doubt
you will—the poor downtrodden masses
while wealthy, well-fed, well-clothed asses
dictate to date and yet no one will see
except maybe you and me—we're in the middle
and what can we do but wait—wait in line
for our paychecks to grow smaller day by day
and our minds to be blown away by increasing conversation
about the dwindling resources in the Nation
wait in line at the grocery store
money's no good there anymore
wait in line to see your doctor
he'll give you pills to cure your ills
wait in line for your prescription
and while waiting, read your latest edition of
"Newsweek"— read about the trouble in the world
wars all over, brother killing brother,
son killing mother, mother killing infant
father killing daughter—bomb blew up, 20 were killed—
last night the night before 7 thieves knocked on my door
I got up let them in, killed one in self-defense,
went to jail for homicide,
spent my life-savings
just to be FREE-
How in one lifetime did this all come to be?

Sylvia Gutierrez

ALL WE NEED IS YOU

Jesus means Eternal Light
No darkness can shun His glow
You can't run or hide or dodge it
It's there wherever you go.
It is here in all of us tonight
In our homes and at the altar
It may not always shine as bright
But without it we would falter.
Without Jesus we are nothing
Without Him we cease to live
Without Him we can not hurt or feel
Nor love or learn to give.
At times it seems like we're alone
Like there's no one who does care
When our suffering comes in one lump sum
And becomes too much to bear
Reach out for the Son of God
And let His Light fill you with hope
If we let His Spirit guide our path
We won't ever need to grope
For another way of happiness
Or an escape to something new
When we forget remind us, Lord
That all we need is You.

Marwan Ramadan

LIFE

I lay back and think of days gone by
When I had the will to err and try.
Painful memories come to mind
I think of life as terribly unkind.
Memories are all that remain
to keep me going, to sustain
my will to go in this world
that's cruel, ugly and very cold.
Why should pain continue to stay?
A question that intrigues me to this day.
Pleasure, happiness quickly pass;
anguish persists to the very last.
I no longer seek a meaning
to a world without a meaning.
I no longer seek a purpose
for living in this circus.
Let me live today fast
as if it were my last.
One day I'll be right
There must be an end to this blight.

Robert L. Gisslow

AN AMERICAN ON THE FOURTH OF JULY

If the quasars turn blue,
I'll be seeing you,
For the universe is coming to an end.
If the quasars turn blue,
And the scientists speak true,
That day conveys an ominous portend.
If the quasars turn blue,
As you sip your morning brew,
You must then select a life of prayer or play.
If the quasars turn blue,
The Universe is THROUGH!
Unless———
It "big bangs" out the other way!

Jackie A. Baker

IMPRESSION

"Tweet, tweet" said the bird.
In my time I have heard
Discourses on loves and fears,
Listened to explanations of the word,
Sermons of life preached with tears,
And songs of life and love in rhyme.
All this from the learned men of the time.
Yet, non of those things that I heard
Impressed me like the treaties of that bird.

Daisy (Shipley) Benson

FORWARD TOGETHER

Together we will march thru rain, snow or wind,
With Nixon to lead us we are sure to Win.
Friend and Foe must work side by side,
It was for Peace and Liberty Our Loved Ones Died.
With love for our Brethren, Peace in Our Heart,
A new Life now for all will start.
Let us raise a Flag for every Nation,
A Home and Job for all Denominations. .
God Bless All Nations under the Sun,
The Day Of Peace is soon to come.

Scott D. Cooper

PLAYING THE GAME

Life is like football
each play you must call
The ball is its object
to carry not fall.
First it is yours
advance it you must
Then it is theirs
diminish all thrust.
Offense and defense
are the names of the game
To get what you want
and lose nothing the same.
Each yard like a day
struggle to gain
Waste not an inch
and defend to remain.
At times take a chance
knowing you're right
If given a loss
come back and fight.
Learn by mistakes
again and again
Develop more plays
and ultimately win!

Alma Moore Collins

REFLECTIONS

Just two little birds
Outside my window!
And yet
Somehow I see
Children at play,
Darting here
And darting there—
Never still for long,
Chirping at the top of their

lungs.
Chasing shadows!
Just two little birds
But somehow I see
Two men
Fighting fiercely
Over stale crumbs,
Jabbing hard at each other
With pointed weapons
Pushing and shoving greedily.
Empty gestures!
Just two little birds!
But Man's reflection
From youth to age
Is pictured there
In that moment.

Hazel Jo Hoffman

REMEMBERING

I thought of you today, so sharply, so clear;
I wondered had you also thought of me, my Dear?
I thought of you—so many times—
I cannot help it if you come and hammer at my heart
Till I must pause, remembering.
Remembering, longing, yet all in vain.
Am I to blame
That I still love you so?
Or yet because I still think of you
So tenderly, hoping desperately
That you might also pause to think of me.

Irene Leodas

VARIANCE

Is it true that all men are created equal?
Some are tall, short, thin, obese, attractive, unattractive, average intelligence, above average, illiterate
Optimism is endowed in some while pessimism is instilled in others
Aggressiveness is quite domineering in our society while shyness still lingers on
Some become successful while others have the misfortune of failure
Some have the advantage of the luxuries of life while others barely exist
So you see we are not all equal but we are all human beings!

C. W. Robertson Jr.

MARSHA

the park is cool and quiet now,
all the people have gone—
and yet somehow—
i can feel your presence
almost as if
i can reach out
and touch your essence.
i can hear the cries
from all the days gone by.
a tear starts down my face.
but the lake is still
it was then
it always will
and only the reflections from it light the night
and slowly i realize
everything is
alright
and so i launch this candle, across the lake
in the name of marsha
i set it down
slowly light it
and bid it a fond farewell.
i know that it could never be,
but just once
i wish
that you could see
things
the same as me.

Victor R. Beasley, Ph.D.

A SOUL DIVIDED

Who knows the pain of a soul divided against itself?
The polar pulls that rend the vital fabric of one's essential being.
Half-hidden spectres perhaps from ancient memories
Flitting boldly through recurrent dreams,
Challenging the pale dawn of solar light
Refusing to yield their worthless dying life.
Who knows the pain?
A deep unreachable agony brought forth from centuries past,
Compounding and grounding itself in the dust of the present.
The growing emptiness of the lonely voyager. . . . .who feels it?

As he stumbles forward towards the distant flickering light,
Ernestly praying that his faint vision is not a benumbed mirage,
The product of blunted senses long over-sated by frivolous indulgence.
Oh the throes! The subtle but profound wrenching of such a soul.
Who here knows it?
Why then does this soul seek the solace of an earthly love?
The fleeting, futile comforts of man bonded to woman?
When well it knows that only the searing flame of Cosmic Fire will appease.
Why chase the gossomer trailings proffered by fame or failure?
Or rejoice or moan on such petty trappings of reality?
Oh my God! Draw near.
Lift this perpetual silent scream from my throat,
It choaks my voice and stifles the passage of truth.
Erase this ancient fog from my mind,
It cleaves to my being with the weight of centuries,
An anchor of ignorance shackled by a chain of calumny,
Each link blindly forged in shallow honor of a shadow self.

Roy L. Bacon

LIFE

Life it ain't easy
But you tried to please me
And keep me one happy man
Though clouds of despair
May fill up the air
We make it the best that we can
Life is too short
But your love is comfort
And your smile the sun in my life
Though troubles arise
We cut 'em down to size
With a love sharp as a knife
Life is a joke
It all goes up in smoke
Soon it's burned out and gone
With that smile on your face
No memories erase
We just keep goin' on and on
Life is real hard
It's left my heart scarred
From the women I've known in my past
If that clock on the wall
Should happen to fall
You know that day is my last
A new life has started
Since I departed
And passed on up through them gates
Old St. Peter said
As he shook his head.
My but its been a long wait
This new life's good
Like I know that it should
But things just ain't the same
Though Pete's a good host
What I miss the most
Is the sound of hearin' your name

Jessie D. Morton

THE SEA AT EVENTIDE

Blue shadows drift across the Bay,
Making their way toward the Sea.
While iridescent paths of sunlight play,
Upon the shimmering waves, Surreptitiously.
The moist cool mist, from ocean spray,
Beats against my face, so cool and sweet,
While myriad spectrals, through the ethers play,
Thence falling on the blossoms at my feet.
The waning sun, sheds rays of red and gold,
Upon the gracefull forms of Seals at play.
Beyond the point, a stately Liner rolls,
Riding the waves, Majestically.
The birds harsh cry, the buoys mournful tone,
Are softened by the murmur of the Sea,
For in her limpid arms, she takes her own,
Back to herself, for all eternity
Blue shadows drift, across the Bay,
Making their way, unendingly.
Blue shadows on white wings, that sway,
When its Eventide, Upon The Bay.

Yvonne Trevino (Orlavon)

ONE LIFE, ONE LOVE, ONE HEART

Oh! My love my darling my soul,
You are my way of living you are my gold,
One look at you and I can see the love in your eyes,
I feel good all over I just way to cry,
I flow thru the day,
Smiling to my self don't know what to say,
Just thinking about you and me,
Wondering if our love can ever be,
Hush! My love don't say a word,
Whisper in my ear so you wouldn't be heard,
Can't you see what you do to me love,
Feeling so beautiful like a white dove,
Hang on I say their might be the day,
"I love you" is the words he will say,
I'll wait someday thats just what I'll hear,
While kissing me loving me holding me near,
So glad I met you that day in May,
Can't help myself for feeling this way,
I glow with love deep down inside,
I love the man with all my might,
Oh! Yes my darling my love my soul,
I know I'm a fool I have been told,
One life, one love, one heart,
Give all let no one tear it apart.

Mary A. McLaughlin

TO THEE, O LORD

On the eve of Thanksgiving
While musing in deep thought,
Grateful for the joy of living,
The happiness and peace I've got.
A friendship that is so beautiful,
So giving,
The sharing, the caring, nothing is
Distraught.
Yes, dear Lord, the seed of life
Again, which you did sow
In fertile earth, with health, energy
And strength to grow.
So that I may do unto others as
You have done unto me.
In the comfort of my rebirth

You have made me free.
My Thanksgiving, for the rest of
My life, are to thee.

Ted Keppler

THE SKY

When the beam of the day
Breaks across the sky,
There's beauty to see
As the clouds pass by.
The miracles I behold
Are bewildering to me.
I can hardly believe
What I really see.
The stars seem to be sinking
Way back in their nest,
While the moon and the dark
clouds
Are going slowly to rest.
Then out of the Heavens
Comes a radiant beam
Shining through the sky
Like a silver stream.
It's the light of the sun
That is shining clear,
Lights the Heavens afire
While the clouds disappear.
Of all the wonderful things I've
seen in life,
This appears, to my delight,
To be the greatest of all. . . .
This daybreak and night.
As the daylight grows stronger
And night passes by,
I wonder how many
have seen the sky.

Nancy Ralston

WRITER'S BLOCK

If there was a market for writer's
block
I'd put it in jars and sell all
I've got
This block is taking up all my
time
The fact is always on my mind
That it hasn't brought me one
thin dime
Like a promiscuous lover
I trade one block for another
The excuses I have are never
the same
But the stubborn fact still
remains—
This block will never win me
fame
Olivetti stares at me as I sneak
by
"Why don't you sit down and
give my keys a try?"
"I would, but can't you see I'm
busy!
And last night's drinks have
made me dizzy.
So let me just put on your cover,
I think I'll go find another
lover."
I spend my time not writing a
line
I've read the latest thriller
And told myself how much
better
I could have written it—
How I would have described the
killer!
I am saving lots of money on
paper
This writer's dream is free per
ream

Isobel Routly Stewart

BLIND MAN

"Have the feet of my love passed
this way in the morning,
Little feet, laughing feet of my
love
In the morning,
In the honey-gold mistiness?
Have you heard their slim tap-
tapping
As high-heeled,
Thin-heeled,
She dances on her way—
Sweet feet,
Neat feet,
Dancing down the sidewalk?"
The blind man smiled a small
sad smile
Like the baffled ghost of a
dream long dead,
And Said:
"I have not heard the footstep of
your love today—
She has not passed this way."
"Here you sit with lavender,
In a dream of lavender,
Selling symbols of your dreams
for life.
In your mist of lavender I
met my laughing love.
Blind man, tell me—how can
you know her footstep
Lost in all the thousand
thousand passing you each
day?"
"Jonathan, young man, you have
come together
Often, often, to speak with me.
And often, Jonathan, she came
alone.
Out of the blur of shufflings
and tappings,
Her feet came laughing like
warm sunshine:
Out of the rumble of passing
wheels,
Her feet came singing like a
harp in concert.
I listen for her footstep in
the morning rush—
A blind man sitting on a
curb must listen,
He had little else to do.
Young man, lover, love knows
her footsteps,
Love knows their laughter,
Love knows their song.
Hearing their rhythm, whether
you see her,
You know your love has come."

K. M. Gross

HER TIREDNESS

The flavor of dead things had
rottened her:
Cool eyes and vinyl
conversations,
Unreadable constellations
Had blown through her
And been ejected by her
Like spittle from the toad's
tongue.
She had harvested only seedless
grapes
And fragmented franchises
From her Near-sighted God.
His thorns from a Crucified
Tree
Bit into her brow and left the
hole
Wherein nothing was left of
her—but me.

Margaret A. O'Connor

BLOOD

Let, spilled, spent,
gathered at the rim of the slick
sheath,
dried, flaked, famed, unnamed,
resting at the nape of the
embattled hill,
running before triumph,
trickling behind failure,
trapped in the cherry's violent
red,
sword thirst, virgin squirm,
"Take ye and drink of this, all
of you,"
He said.

Doris Ullman Barbuto

NINTH LIFE

He was abandoned in the fall
last year;
His humans had moved and just
left him here.
He lived by his wits, ate garbage
refuse,
And was chased by dogs the
neighbors turned loose.
All winter long he found
warmth under cars
And mingled with gravel and
grease and tars.
Some fiendish kids tried to hang
him one night;
He survived the hanging with
permanent fright.
Poor Kitty! I brought him food
morn and night
Which he wouldn't touch while
I was in sight.
I called him "Clawdie" and
told him his name;
Soon he thought "Clawdie"
and food were the same.
Then one day in the spring,
Clawdie forgot
To be scared and cautious, and
he got caught!
He went to the vet, and was
bathed and shorn
And punctured with needles—
proclaimed "reborn."
I prayed for that cat, "Help him
find a home
Where he'll be happy and not
forced to roam."
That prayer was answered as
sure as can be,
For now that old alley cat
lives with me!

Michael H. French

PROPITIOUS PRECIPITATION

I'm glad clouds cry sometimes,
Pouring out their sorrows for
happiness to grow
Among the earthen
peoples
And all their tiny friends.

Mary Catherine Mone

SHOCK

Familiar objects
Look foreign at times
As if never seen
Taking on newness
Without the quality of surprise
At first glance
As though never realizing
An existence
Can change

Sarah Swanston

EXCUSE ME, I'D LIKE TO ROB YOUR BANK

Excuse me, I'd like to rob your
bank.
As you can see, I'm thoroughly
qualified;
I'm the appropriate height,
weight, age, race
And yes, I do have my gun. I'm
sure you'll take
My word that it's loaded.
Now if you'll just open your
drawer, it'll
Be over in a minute. I'll be
discreet & demure
As the ponies that gallop so
evenly across
The manager's tie, less trouble
even
Than some of your regular
customers. No need
To show alarm, guard. If you do,
I'll just blow you away,
And why come to that when it
isn't even
Your money?—There.
That was painless enough.
Well gents, I can't stay long;
My compliments on your
gunpoint manner!

Kelly Thompson

OUR MEMORIES

Yesterday's memories are to
cherish forever. . .
and they're mine.
Todays soon will be
yesterdays. . .
they too will be mine.
Tomorrows are a whole
new experience
yet to come. . .
soon they will be ours.

C. J. Potts

SNOW DELIGHT

When the snow begins to fall;
You can hear the children call,
Some are small, some are tall;
I think I like winter best of all.
Running, running down the hall;
Out the door to have a ball,
Happy, happy, they slide and
fall;
I think I like winter best of all.
A snowman is made on the wall;
Fat and plump, not too tall,
The children are proud as they
call;
I think I like winter best of all.
The day ends as does the
snowfall;
Greetings to one and greetings
to all,
Now and then, someone sails a
snowball;
I think I like winter best of all.

Laura Strable

THE GREAT UNICORN

A magical beauty my dreams do
behold,
A mystical creature,
courageous and bold.
It has wondrous power with-in
its one horn,
A gift granted to the great
unicorn.
With brilliant white wings it is

able to fly,
And visit the stars that dwell in the sky.
And go to the heavens, to where it was born,
To live out the life of a great unicorn.

Sandra Jo Newman

NONSENSE IN PERSPECTIVE

"Nonsense," you say?
nonsense is nonsense
but only when a circumstance
stands blocking, in the way.
It seems quite unexplainable:
Light, regarding its velocity,
the Puzzle of its constancy,
The Answers unobtainable!
Perhaps its just a paradox.
A bump against our expectations,
while searching for explainations
A view bound up with time & clocks.
Einstein with his childlike view,
Examined all the evidence
And of it made a new sense
Our laws of knowledge to re-do.

Mrs. Lynn E. Henk

A HOLY WISH

Let me follow that Star
That the Magi had seen,
To the place that is so far.
I want to be at the scene
Where The Child had been born.
Oh, let me be at the place
Where Mary and Joseph stayed,
The night the Star met space.
Where everything had been made
Ready for The Child to be born.

Anthony David Georgiades

PRIDE

How many loves have you lost,
From the Futile decrees you've made.
What has your loftiness cost,
But your blissfulness to fade.
To express how you truly feel,
Is too arduous for you to do.
A callous heart will turn to steel,
Your amour you will subdue.
For manhood is now at stake,
Being amiss you cannot admit.
With your defenses wide awake,
You fortify with ignoble wit.
Love turns from your kind,
So you profess not to care.
It will be simple to find,
New endearment elsewhere.
But amiable adoration is rare,
As you will soon perceive.
It is not that easy to fare,
Your arrogance will gradually leave.
Endure to adulate in defeat,
Dignity is lost from lovelorn.
Give in from your conceit,
A crown of modesty you must adorn.

Matt Aragorn Pavin

SONNET XXVIII ON IMAGINATION

Inhibit not high imagination,
Though it may oftimes climb a lofty tree
Barren of fruit, or float the boundless sea
Whose currents confuse all navigation.
Yet surrender not the new sensation!
Be as vibrant eagles when first they flee
The safe eyrie, and fly so gracefully,
With white wisps of wind as inspiration.
Around about you the whole world will start
Afresh, the commonplace coming to life—
Delight you'll feel in the leap of the hart,
And awe that there, in everything, is art.
A dreamer be for miracles are rife,
And there will be love, pure love in your heart.

Necia Hire

THE POET

I'm reverberating with voluminous verse—
Vicarious—hilarious—vociferous—terse.
I exude my vivacity—
Exceed my capacity—
Extend my veracity—
Oh, what an "assity"
Am I!

Tony Giorgi

LOVE UNMATCHED

Love is not a common emotion,
Love is an emotion known true but to us.
Love is a phase of life brought on by fate.
For those who do not know, love is a word without meaning.
But yet our love was created,
Created by two People who see, who hear, who listen, who touch, who feel.
By two people who fell obedient to the sensations of love.
Sensations which without common knowledge would be sent on, sent on to a place not known.
But to capture this knowledge is to gain,
Gain not the feeling of love, but to gain the knowing of love.
A love felt, a love shared,
A love gone beyond words.
A love only our baby will understand,
For in our baby will be the answer to our Love.
The answer is Life,
The answer is Love,
The answer is Us;
For through us was created love.
That love now lives within our child.

Barbara Elaine Woodruff

AUTUMN

Oh Autumn you enchant me,
Your touch is everywhere;
In the cornfields and the forests,
In the cool evening air.
Scattered leaves lie dead and brown,
All shriveled up and dry;
Their mother tree sways softly,
And gives a gentle sigh.
Crimson, orange, yellow-gold,
Blaze boldly from each tree,
For this is Autumn's brushwork
Done so beautifully.
Squirrels dart from ground to tree
Collecting winter stock;
The geese depart in mournful tones,
Each in their V-shaped flock.
Squash and pumpkin dominate
The summer gardens now,
While walnuts and plump chestnuts
Replace the fresh fruit bough.
The chilly nights come quickly,
But come although they may,
There's promise of another
Shimmering Autumn day.

Lyn Benua

IT IS MAY AND MY HOUSE IS FILLED WITH LILACS

It is May and my house is filled with lilacs.
I couldn't resist picking them,
Growing as they were
With such intention
And abandonment
That even the old wooden fence
Could not hold them.
Their scent fell like the pink blossoms

Along the road
And with every intended breath
I was taken with perfume
And more innocent days.
I just could not leave them.
And so
It is May and my house is filled with lilacs.

Myron T. Raymond

SURVIVAL

Butterfly wings of yesterdays,
Memories warmed by sunlight passed,
Vacillate cold this starlight night,
Tomorrow's promise yet ungrasped.
Waking morns perpetuate
Another day of quest.
Yesterday, today, tomorrow,
Which was, is or will be best?

Richard Woolley

A DIALOUGE ON BRICK

Brick
where the hues die,
One
On top
Of another.
and the birds leave screaming,
Ageless, immovable
Solid
far too early; senseless mourning,
Not a scratch
incandescent stars rain;
but it's fall,
All is pointless dignity—
and all is dying,
yesterday's blue sky,
over green,
and red,
and yellow,
eclipsed life,
forgotten dust.
Time's rusty, dripping tap—
No rubble—
and in the silent desert,
of nocturnal life,
A low rumble echoes,
but no one hears.
ageless,
timeless,
(let the tap drip)
solid,
immovable
The eternal jest:
Brick.

Nell Frances Terry

I'LL LIVE AGAIN

When the green grass turns to honey
And the leaves turn red as wine
And autumn sun casts magic spells
On earthly gifts sublime
When corn is husked and all is stored
In silos for the cows
And hams are cured and bacon smoked
From fat and well fed sows
When rich, red earth is covered oe'r
With leaves that fall from trees,
And serene contentment reigns within
The hives of active bees
When pears and rosy apples bright
Are picked from fruitful trees
And autumn with her magic wand
With essence fills the breeze
And when I see her crispy hair
Bedecked with golden grain
I know that he'll come back to me
And then I'll live again!

Vijay Steve Persad

ADAM

Gnarled fingers knotted round
his knees as he looked
with protruding eyes, at
a dream that was slowly fading.
Like weeping skeletons,
He sat on the shore and
hastily retreated from the
cold touch of his. . .ignorance.
Laughing eyes sadly deepened
into nothingness as he peered
into the maw, of the reclining abyss.
And, dragging his feet like
a two-way dream,
he wept blindly as
he failed to weave a web
into the scarlet tresses of
The sun.
He hated himself as,
crawling beings tore at his soul,
having ripped his body
to shreds.
Having evolved with
this darkening fury,
he became lost
in the encroaching
Mist.

Felipe Lebron
WATER, PLEASE
Except
For rare occasions
When used as named,
The guest room is his.
There he keeps
The single plant
He tends.
Is it an Aspidistra?
A Chinese Evergreen?
I don't remember.
But even this
One lonely plant
He lets wilt.

Rafael Nazario Cruz
GOOD-BY MY DEAR VALLEY
Because life must go on
I have to leave my valley,
I have to leave my home
To the big city for a better income.
But in my bleeding heart and mind
Sure will live for ever and ever
My beloved humble house
And my evergreen and peaceful valley.
And I'll miss too with great grief
The warmness and delicate smells
Of the green grass and witty flowers
That lazily rest on it endless prairies.
Good-by my unforgettable valley
Though I know you'll last for ever!
But I would like to come back someday
To plow your soil and raise again my flower gardens.
Good-by again my sweetheart.
Good-by my peaceful, quiet valley.
So long from the bottom of my doleful heart
And God bless you my dearest valley!

Pamela Jean King
UNTITLED
Feeling,
At peace with yourself,
Loving, the
Loneliness that nature
has for summer.

Elsie Williams
NANCY'S WORLD
To some folks Life is a picture
To others a candy store
But Nancy lives in a Disney World
of sights and sounds and smells
And more much more.

Bernard McGarry
THE TREE
There's only one left that no one bought
And now it's too late if they would
For no one would want a tree now that it's past
I guess you could say it's no good
I stared at the tree and it seemed to talk
It told me what other's had said
It's too tall—It's too short—It's too skinny—too fat
It's too lively and also too dead
And one by one as the day drew near
The tree's were down to a few
But still it stood with a hopeful heart
That someone would want it too
Then at last it was all alone
But still with a hope and a sigh
It stood and watched as the people passed
But no one—No one would buy
And then it came that day of days
It could feel it—It knew it was here
It also knew it would never get dressed
In tinsel and lights and good cheer
How cruel I said—how cruel it is
The way of men-little tree
To cut you out of your forest so grand
And bring you here as I see
How cruel to chop—the tree spoke up
Please don't feel sad at my plight
If you see me here all alone as I am
And dying here this night
Please don't think harsh of fellowmen
Because I was cut by some whim
You see it said in some small way
I am dying in honor of him

Richard R. Domros
FRIENDSHIP
It's knowing when you're lonely,
Knowing when your sad,
Knowing your thoughts,
Whether they be good or bad.
It's always being there,
Whether you need a helping hand,
Or just a shoulder to cry on.
It's thinking about you all the time,
And wondering how you are.
It's never keeping count of favors,
Because with true friends,
There is nothing that we won't do for each other.
Friendship is a wonderful thing.
Some say True Friendship and Love are similar.
I believe them. Do you?

Ruth Vance Roe
ANTS
We tied up the vine, drenched it with spray.
This kept the spiders and beetles away.
But down near the roots in the soft earthy loam,
A family of ants started building their home,
And they ate and they ate at the heart of the vine—
'Till it withered and died, now we sadly opine.
Through a forest so dense walked a strong man, one day,
And confronting a wild beast that fate sent his way
Stood fearless with courage, no dagger he drew,
But with his two bare hands this fierce beast he slew.
Exultant this conqueror went on his way,
'Till into a nest of ants he did stray—
He brushed them and stomped them, but do what he would
He could not o'er come them and hours he withstood
This onslaught of pests to succumb at the last.
Now where was the strength he displayed in the past?
It's the small things that eat you,
Man, if you would transcend,
Fight the ants that surround you,
To the end, to the end.

Debbie Brumble
FIRST CHRISTMAS GIFT
Gentle woman child, heavy with the burden of this
little one. Upon a beast have you travelled long to this humble stable.
Time is night at journey's end. Restless stirring within
Amidst animal scent and soft cries of womanhood this infant was come.
Your young body yielded forth a handsome man child
first born son, the special one Mighty men were awed, the humble, inspired.
And they came, bearing gifts and riches unceasing.
Yet none was as great as your precious gift of love. Mary, you gave your Son.

William J. Stahl
CARRY ON
I grow old and feeble,
My mind deceives me now.
And my hands are so shakey
That I cannot work the plow
As I carry on.
I've seen all the past
But cannot see the future;
The world is a cold dark place to me
And has stripped me of my virtue
As I carry on.
Tomorrow I may leave,
My time on earth is through.
But you have a tomorrow
And God will help you through
As I carried on.

AJ Miles
THE INSECT
What's this I see before me here?
Small; so small and tiny it seems to me;
A tiny mote that takes up space.
I could crush it, as it scurries to and fro;
It seems to be doing no useful job.
An insect with no place to go.
I think I'll watch it awhile before I destroy it;
Maybe it will do something clever;
It might even amuse me for awhile.
Now there are many of these insects.
So many, I wonder why I let them live;
All they seem to do is fight among themselves.
Enough. . .already!! These insects are too numerous;
Time to turn my energies elsewhere.
Goodbye little ones. . . . .
STOMP, STOMP, STOMP!!!
I wonder why they called themselves. . . ."MAN"??

Evelyn Rose Perez
DESPERATION
In desperation
I cry out.
What is this sensual
sensation.
that I am about.
In anticipation
my heart flutters.

Why am I flushed with
precipitation,
of what I utter.
Am I searching?
What am I searching for.
Is it peace of mind,
or peace of will.
Damn it, help me, help me.
Don't just stand there
so still!

J. L. Vajdi
SONG OF LOVE
(Dedicated to Mehrdad Vajdi)
Through the ghostly caverns dim, a whisper sings
I love you
Night breeze stirs, lightening the hallow walls and echoing back the song
I love you
I love you
Bats clinging to the ceiling cry as they dizzily dance to the refrain
I love you
Night calls forth the shades of gallant ladies and dandies grand who once loved in its halls to revel to my song
I love you, MY MAN MEHRDAD!

Helen P. Lance
SPRINGTIME
Springtime is just around the corner,
The flowers are still in their blooms.
The air has a scent of sweet fragrance,
And the wind is whistling a tune.
Springtime it must be pure magic,
Like a rainbow that has flooded the sky.
I enjoy it with lost amazement,
It puts a twinkle in my eye.

Rose L. Evans
ENEMY OR FRIEND
Life is an endless conflict
Between life, death
Between luck, misfortune
Between gain, loss
Between love, hate
Between health, illness
Between approval and
disapproval.
It's an uncertain path
But not totally impossible.
With a trenchant, strong
personality
Life is easier.
If ambiguous and weak,
More difficult..........
But life's daily struggles,
conflicts will strengthen
your ego, polish your
character
improve your inmaturity
And you will survive,
Grow old,
And die
Like countless others before
you........................

Bill Uhls
SPRING
Fleecy white clouds,
skip across a sky of azure blue
like little lambs cavorting
on a green carpeted pastureland.
The sun,
beams down like a benevolent
grandfather
spreading warmth and elation
over all.
Crocus and tulips,
nod their colorful heads in
unison
to the music of the gentle
breeze.
Man,
stretches and turns his head in
wonder,
the promise of life is again
fulfilled,
and he glories in the miracle
of Spring.

Ellen R. Suddarth
DEAR LORD, REMEMBER ME
I do not ask for untroubled
waters but for guidance ere I
set sail on Life's stormy sea.
As I face each brand new day, I
trust that You will light my
way.
I do not ask for special favors
great or small,
But just to know You hold my
hand and help me stand tall.
I do not ask for wealth nor
fame nor glory, but I ask for
grace sufficient to help me
break these earthly bonds and
reach a higher plane,
And when I falter by the way
I ask, "Dear Lord, Remember
Me!"

Russ Schroeder
IS IT LOVE?
Is it love? I ask you.
Is it love? he wondered. Is it
love?, he pondered.
Is it like being stung by cupid.
Or was it just something
stupid.
The story is so simple. It fits in
the head of a thimble.
Who will judge? You my friend.
The story is here.
They were both so young.
Nothing could be done.
Still in school. He chased her
like a fool.
He told her everything. She
never questioned him.
He kept talking. She looked
deep into his eyes.
He pondered, is it love? He
didn't ask, she didn't hint.
She smiled. He went away to far
away places.
She wrote to him. I miss you she
said.
I love you he replied. She did
not return the thought.
Time passed slowly. His heart
sank.
He kept writing. She never
answered.
Was it love?, he wondered. He
returned.
She was joyful. He was pleased.
In the little shop on Main she
sold gifts.
Every Saturday he would come
in. He probed deep into her
mind.
Will it be love? he thought.
Finally he was ready to see.
Will you go out with me? Will
you be seen with me?
She had said the only word he
wanted to hear. YES
It will be love, he screamed.
They went out.
They walked on Main, past all
the other shops.
She joked about love,
themselves. He almost, but
didn't ask.
She smiled, looked deep into his
eyes. He pondered.
No, he would not ask her. He
would not risk it.
He would not risk her. Did she,
would she, could she love?
He suggested the show. She
smiled.
The lights dimmed. The screen
lit up with a five star cast.
He touched her. She grasped for
him.
He took her home to her place.
She said thank you.
He said good-bye. He returned
to the shop on Main.
He looked deep into her eyes.
She said she wanted to marry
next year.
He pondered the thought. He
took her hand.
She looked deep into his eyes. Is
it love?, he thought.
She released his hand. With a
frown he said good-bye.
He left the shop on Main. A
ship can only sink so far.
The same with a heart. He never
returned.
She never questioned. He says
he will return, someday.
But every day it is put off. He
asked, was it love?
I ask you now, my dear friend.
Is it love? Was it love?
Will it be love? Who will judge?
Not I. Said the main in the line.
Not I. Said the man with the
wine.
Not I. She said.

Beverly D. Betz
THANKSGIVING
Today's the day
We share our love
We thank the Lord
In the sky above.
We thank him for
These happy days
We thank him in
So many ways.
We thank him for this holiday
We share our love within
We're ready to sit down and
pray
And thank our hearts within.
And when the sun goes down
And all the feelings gone
The only thing that's left
Is the feeling that is on
Our loving tender heart
With all the love and care
By giving caring specialties
And all the love we share.

Charles Wyndham
REWARD
Up hardy plowman, You!
Grip your trencher strong and
fast,
Furrow straight and true.

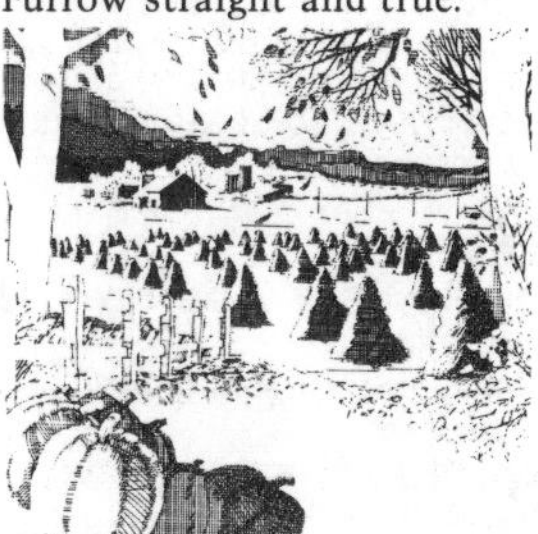

Serve your trade, it is your art,
Turner of the sod;
Some day you may plow the star
dust
For a well-pleased God.

Annette Schofield-Lindback
UNTITLED
Write between my lines of
nothing
Between these lines of
emptiness.
I want so much to write for you
But—nothing.
So you write between the lines
The words you want to hear
And read them to yourself.

Louie Boria
TO THE ONE I LOVE
My gift to you
Is the gift of love
That will last
To the longest day,
It won't wear out
And it can't be lost
And it can't be given away
Because you are my strength:
You fullfill my emptiness
I never I knew I can love anyone
Like I love you.
I'm gonna love you more than
you
can ever dream:
You are my world and my
reason
for living

Dwight Hutchins
KNOWEST THOU I LOVE THEE?
I hold my heart out--open wide--
To catch the tear drops from
your eyes.
I'll draw you near me--clear
inside
And soothe the hurt of
lonesome tide!
May I show laughter from my
heart
And give you soft and tender
care?
And with a healing love impart
I'll hold your hands, for I'll be
there!
Trust me! Tell me, why the
sorrow
Lines perplexed upon your face?
Let me soften each tomorrow
With a tender, sweet embrace!
You are mine and always will be
Precious gift, oh radiant sun!
Love so blind! Please cast us
free,
To live and share this life as
one!

Marilyn B. Taylor
THE MESSAGE
I awoke to the portenious
ringing of my phone,
in the predawn hours of my
home,
at a time when people do not
normally intrude,
unless bad news they're forced
to include.
As I reached for the phone I felt
a premonition of doom,
filling the darkness of the
unlit room.
My "hello" resounded like a
stranger's echo,
while my thoughts were
pounding--"no!", "no!", "no!"
And then the voice on the
other end,
announced the death of a
precious friend.
The message left me
disquietingly sick.
Alone, I heard the phone's
disconnector click.
I sat rigid and stunned with a
mournful fear,
while the dial monotone
hummed in my ear.

Susan Adler Herreid
THE CONSPIRATORS
Quietly laying in bed,
awakening--
Which sometimes is an
undertaking--
I hear the sound of four soft
paws,
Fulfilling some mischievous
cause.
Perhaps a button, bright and
round,
Under the dresser has been
found.
And in the midst of play I hear
Four more soft paws quickly
appear.
Instantly those wild eyes are
meeting,
Exchanging a very familiar
greeting.
Suddenly the four paws in the
door
Are grabbing for traction on the
floor.
In hot pursuit, the other paws
move out,
Sliding on the hall rug in their
route.
Rebounding off living room
couch and chair,
Flies the felicitous, frivolous
pair.
Ever so slowly I sit up in bed,
Nodding my poor, old sleepy
head.
Again the conspirators at my
door appear,
To smugly sit and smile and
jeer.
At least it seems they actually
do that,
When you know well the ways
of a cat.

So I arise and brew a pot of tea,
While I feed the hungry
menagerie.
At last awake, I start to dress,
The house again in quietness.
With shiny coats licked clean
and neat,
They're curled up on my bed
asleep.

Lori Lynn Bihlman
SEASONS OF HAPPINESS
Happiness is only another mile
or maybe on some spring
afternoon;
I see it but can't grasp it,
it's blowing like a kite
caught in a spring wind.
The sunshine sometimes fools
me
cause it lightens up the gloom
But the shadows
always reach me
no matter where I choose to
hide.
The snow covers the past
but then it melts away.
The bare earth brings back
memories
which struggle for survival,
but my hearts been frosted
over.
The autumn leaves camouflage
but don't cover up my sense
of reality.
They gently persuade me into
colorful moods
and form a pile
in which happiness lies just
beneath it.

Brian Lee Fridlund
HIDDEN TALENT
Hidden talent
deep down
inside.
Hidden talent
waiting,
to be free.

Hidden talent
no one
can see.
Hidden talent
inside you,
and
me.

Donna Hancock
A SOLDIER'S PRAYER
I can hear the bullets splatting
and the thump of mortar shell
As I lie here in this bunker,
and wait to take the hill.
The C. O. says it won't be long
until it's time to go,
so here I crouch with heavy
heart, and courage ebbing low.
I only hope I'll live through this
and get back home again
to do the things that I love
best, with family and with
friends.
But first I have a job to do--
I hope I'll do it well--
Then maybe someday I'll
forget these last few months
of hell.
Please, God, there's just one
thing I ask...that is, if You don't
mind.
Just help me through these
next few hours--grant me
courage one more time.
There's only just a few days left,
my discharge day is due;
So all I need is lots of luck,
and perhaps some help from
You.
There's the signal now. I guess
it's time to go.
I only hope You heard me, and
my prayer from here below.
If not...I guess I'll see You before
much time goes by---
In case You didn't hear me, or
if today's my day to die.
Now, please don't think I'm
bitter, or that I hold a grudge.
I'm just a frightened soldier,
and You, Lord, are my judge.
I'll try to do my duty unto my
fellow man,
Even if in doing so I die in
Vietnam.

Joyce Fincher
SELF PITY
You think that you are treated
so indifferently.
Importance, to you, means being
number one.
Your misery comes not from
failure of being loved.
But, from giving of your love to
no one.

Donna Lynne Grove
HIS LIGHT
Dear friend so lost and weary
Why stumble in the dark?
Our Lord is right beside us,
Though the road oft times is
rough.
One by one He will light each
step
And if you fall one thing is
sure,
He'll lift you up, dust you off
And gently nudge you on.

Pamela Gail Zink
MY PRAYER
(To Charlie)
Father, I've taken him for
granted in the past
And yet, I want my love for him
to last.
But taking him for granted won't
make love strong.
I know forgetting to *cherish* him
is wrong.
But I made a new committment
yesterday
To keep love songs in my heart
for him all day
And to remember how special
he is to me
Because his love is the love that
has set me free.
Father, don't let him take me for
granted;
Let him remember the love
we've planted.
Don't let it die; give him the
need to let it grow;
Let him want to keep it alive
and let it show.
Father, place this thought upon
his precious mind;
I took him long ago and made
him mine.
I loved him yesterday and I'll
love him tomorrow;
I've been a cushion when life
has given him sorrow.
Let us forever be grateful for
each other
And for this combination and
not another.
Let us think upon how life
might have been alone
Or with someone else who may
have turned cold as stone.
Help us to erase doubt from the
other's mind;
Let us not magnify our faults
anytime.
Let us always show the other
how much we care.
Let us love, cherish, cushion,
protect and share.
Let us not be satisfied with a
love that's stale.
Let us succeed in everything,
our love as well.
Let us not think we can be
happy apart.
Please, let us be the love of the
other's heart.

Eileen Marie Henry
NIRVANA'S STORM
My words are caged,
My thoughts are tied,
No one speaks--
Not even I.
O' Wind of Wisdom
Touch my eye,
Restore my vision,
Carve me clean.

Do I deny my vital need?
Do I but lure the raper near?
I am drained O' Revered Wind,
Your storm too far beyond my
reach,
And I am parched, too dry a
well,
I cannot speak.

What woman cries the furied
winds,
I hear her voice blow past the
gate.
Her whipping vane,
A searing tongue,
A tempest to the empty ear.

Scream on gently through my
flesh
And touch this placid mind
within,
Blast my motives out to man
And thicken my intention.

Alice Scheetz
ALOFT
Loud and clear
above the city whir
from a nearby scaffold
the whistle of a construction
worker
- Intent
he had to be
like a woodpecker's relentless
drilling
- Content
he had to be
his apparent contentment
thrilling
- Unaware, likely
of himself as whistler
- Unaware, certainly
of his listener

Sandy Hettinger
MY HEART YEARNS FOR YOU
My heart yearns for things that
cannot be answered.
My heart is torn by an enduring
pain.
Oh how I yearn for one embrace
that only loves
Master can give,
A kiss as sweet as the morning
dew.
If only my kind hand could
touch your sweet, soft,
glowing face,
If only my eyes should meet
your eyes of clear
water blue.
To only walk with you again in
fields of
blooming flowers,
Or running along the shore of
the raging
ocean.
Only if these things can be
answered
I again shall live.
For without you I am but a
wilted rose
pressed between the pages
of time.
But with you I am the rays from
the sun,
The clean sweet smell after an
April shower,
A rose that love has kissed with
it's lips
of dew,
Blooming with such joyous
peace that
it shall live forever.

Lois Pecce
THE ALCHEMIST
Autumn came with her
promises of gold and glory -
With her blue skies, sunny days,
and intoxicating airs.
We became drunk on flamingo
dawns, flaming sunsets,
And harvest-time bouquets.
But once we'd welcomed her,
she blazed our trees with
wildfire
And sent our birds winging
south on the coldness of her
breath.
Before she was done she had
ravaged our land with frost
And turned our gold to rust.

Louise Sewill
THE CAT, THE CANARY, AND THE HEART
Your pet cat has a heart
Which beats one hundred and
thirty.
When you ask the cat to sing,
The cat says, "First feed me a
birdy."
Your pet canary has a heart
Which beats six-fifty per
minute.
When you ask it to feed the cat,
The bird says, "My heart isn't in
it."

Sandra K. Parry
IN YOUR EYES
In your eyes I have seen, all the yesterdays of lives past and the promise of tomorrows, yet to come.

The hearts and souls, which once were and are again, have brought the peace my heart did seek.

And with the peace a knowledge came, that whom so ever seeks; shall find the door to which the Lord did speak.

For through that door the mind progresses, even still to seek these lessons.

And even though my mind does see, just how close it all could be, it seems to wander aimlessly.

Jeannette McNamara Johnson
JESUS BIRTHDAY
What is Christmas to most of
us?
Presents and toys and candy and
joy,
A cheerful day when everyone is

gay,
A day that everyone curls their toes
With hopes and dreams that it shall snow.
A beautiful tree that glows so bright
With lots of beautiful Christmas tree lights.
People on sleigh rides going round and round
Singing carols through the town.
Children building snowmen out in the back yard,
Giving and receiving presents and cards.
But the most valuable gift that has ever been given,
Is our Lord Jesus Christ, our main reason for living.
So enjoy this Christmas, but above everything,
Remember it is Jesus Birthday, it is his day to be King.

Eileen Strawbridge

FOR DENNIS

Gift me not in fine tradition,
When custom's need its day declare--
Ply me not with silks and satins,
From precious gemstones, pray forbear.
But send a true heart--freely giv'n;
I'd wish for only one thing more-
That I could stay you yet an hour,
When e'er we close the chamber door.

Jo Ann Henderson

LITTLE THINGS

I'm thankful for God's blessings.
I feel I've neared the stars.
He's touched my life so gently.
I'm richer now by far
Than someone who has never
Sat quietly in the woods
And gotten into nature--
It does my soul such good;
To look upon wild flowers
Touched by the morning dew,
To know that God created
Each one of them, and you!
To see each special creature
Put here upon this Earth
As part of Nature's cycle
Set down before their birth.
So, take a walk and treasure
Each gift within your grasp.
Hold fast to every pleasure
This world will let you have.

Barbra A. McDaniel

A TINGE OF BLUE

The spring flows freely,
Rocks and sand purifying;
The water crystal with a tinge of blue
Swirling in pools of infinity.
Running with deliberation
From the beginning until the end.
Patterns of motion with meaning and without
Flowing into depths of uncertainty
In a race with the seconds of time;
Gone forever into an embedded memory
To recall with a flashback of desire
Or to forget with passions of hate.
The age of infinite wrinkles,
The creaseless dew of youth,
Born from one into the other
And departing from one into neither.
Ageless the birth of eternity.
Aged the death of youth
Left a lifetime of memories
As the spring flows crystal with a tinge of blue.

Bruce Lee Jernigan

THE RABBIT

To people who can't see
What happened to one
Also happened to three.
Maybe it's not so lucky
To see.
The foot that's as lucky
As the other three.

Barbara H. Lawrence

THE FALLEN ANGEL

Lucifer   Satan   the Devil
he's known by many-a-name
They say he's a fallen angel
and evil is always his game
He's referred to oft in the Bible
this foe of God and man
Prince of this world and of darkness
envision if you can...
The spirit of evil   the tempter
seen as serpent and fiendish half-man
To sin he seduced Eve and Adam
loyal Job was tested by him
Even our Lord was tempted
by this spirit dim...
Beware! this sly spirit will tempt you
in many-a-devious way
Tho he promises all the world's preasures
for sin you must always pay
Oh 'doer of iniquity'
begone   go far   depart
For the great God of Love
reigns in this human heart.

Denise J. McMahan

VINTAGE FRIENDSHIP

Friendship, like wine,
Improves with time.
Years add flavor
To remember and savor.
There's a mellow start,
Sweet or tart,
Then the liquid flows.
It keeps on going, slowly growing,
Until the warmness glows.
So, appreciate luxury of this kind.
True friendship, like good wine,
It's not easy to find.

Linda Sue Anderson

LIFE MY LOVE IS ETERNITY

Remember always, I promise thee
Life is eternity.
Life is never ending,
Always fulfilling.
A new love you shall find,
With patience, keep in mind.
Even when love has come and gone,
Remember, a new love will surely be born
As though a new song written,
Waiting to be sung
Or as a child in his mother's
Womb, waiting to be born.
Love can leave your heart filled
With sorrow,
But then again think of all the
Tomorrows.
A new love you shall find,
A greater love,
A richer life.
So look deep down inside your
Heart,
Release your sorrows,
Let them depart.
For there are many tomorrows
For you to see,
For life, my love, is eternity.

Dayna Lynnette Beck

MY OLD PEN

I get this feeling now and then
to sit and write with my old pen.
The one I use when I'm feeling down,
it picks me up and turns me 'round.
And when I'm feeling really grand,
my pen can write so you'll understand
the lovely thoughts I think of you
and how I feel of living, too!
And every feeling I chance to feel,
can come alive and seem so real.
When I sit and write with this old pen
I can gather thoughts to read again,
when later in my life I need
a special thought or love or deed
that once I knew or sought to see
to pick me up and set me free.

Georgia Snipes Funderburgh

DREAMS DO DIE

Unfaithfully, next to me, you lay
You've got two ladies in love with you now,
Touching me, you stop and say
"I'd leave her, if I only knew how."
You have put your love deep within my heart
Your blue eyes, are forever in my mind,
But I must no longer share you, in any part
With another woman, of any kind.
I sleep alone, too many nights
Cold, quiet moments, bring forth my day,
My head always hides, from the morning lights
Dreaming, when I don't get my way.
Pretending, that you don't have a wife
Acting like I'm your closest friend,
Dreaming, that you're already my life
Afraid to awake, and have my dreams end.

Patricia Kamysz

CRYING FOR HOME

An eerie moon
The black of night
Quiet streets
With fading lights.
The tears come
Along with the knowledge
There is no one to turn to
And nowhere to go.
An endless trail
Looms ahead
While I seek guidance
From the North Star.
I feel undermined
In a world of illusion,
Troubles are overflowing
And blindness is feigned.
Never-ending hypocrisies
Spring from the crowd.
They disturb my sense of reasoning
But I cower like the rest.
Until I find an answer
I'll be grasping for sweet freedom,
Lost like a child in the streets
And crying for home.

Rev. John Dorsey

THE WORLD AND TIME

A world in time, that's what makes it so beautiful, and so fine.
There is a time to be born, and there is a time to die.
There is a time to be sad, and there is a time to be glad.
Every step we take is timed, timed by a spiritual realm, which we can not see.
There is a time of war, and there is a time of peace.
There is a time to sow, and there is a time to reap.
And at 6 O'clock every morning i can hear the cock crow.
There is a daytime, when we work and play, and there is a lunchtime; when we eat and drink.
There is a nighttime, when we sleep, and there is a springtime, when the sap rises, and the grass turns green, and i watch the trees and flowers grow.
There is a summertime, when the bees makes honey, and the birds begin to sing in the trees.
And there is fall, when the sap goes down, and the leaves turn brown.
There is winter, when the snow falls, and the earth lies still again.
Sometime i can hear a baby cry, when the doctor picks him up, so his mother can see, just another man born in this world of time

Patricia R. Stonsby

FIRST GRANDCHILD

I cannot look upon the face
Of my grandson, all new and sweet,
Without wondering at the miracle
That makes him so complete.
Those little lips, so full and red,
The softness of his cheek,
The blondish fuzz upon his head,
His smile that leaves me weak.
I'm sure he knows my voice and touch,
His fingers hold mine so tight.
Those deep blue eyes look up at me
As he squeals with sheer delight.
There's so much still ahead to share,

He has filled my life with joy.
The greatest gift of age is mine,
This perfect grandbaby boy!

Elizabeth L. Nichols

THE "ROOTS" OF MY OWN FAMILY TREE

There are my mother and my daddy
Who are very dear to me;
There are my brother and my sister
Who I'm always glad to see.
There are my grandpa and my grandma
Who make a world o'er me,
And my uncles and my aunts
Who watch adoringly.
There are my cousins and my cousins--
I've got them by the dozens--
Whether "once removed" or "straight across"
They're on my family tree.
These relatives are dear to me,
And add to my living store
A host of happy memories,
And still are adding more.
And yet at times I wonder
Why they feel "just so" --
And wish they didn't care so much,
But would only "let me go."
Yet deep inside, it is a truth,
I love them very much;
And the fact they care for me
Gives to my life its "roots."
So if they will continue
As always in the past,
And be my loving anchor,
I'll love them to the last.
Perhaps I may not show it;
Sometimes they just must know it--
But if they'll be my loving anchor,
I'll love them to the last.
When I think it over,
It's a simple fact, you see--
They are the beginning of the "roots"
Of my own family tree.

Pamela Sue Fessler

BATTLE AT DAWN

An artillary of coffee fumes
finds its way into my room.
Then tolling time and voices slight
break the silence of the night.
The battle has begun.
Hence
I feign escape
Away
far away
far from the pain
from the anguish
and the gloom.....
I try to go back to my dream
where I am happy
where I am queen.

Ksenia Rychtycka

FAREWELL

I stood alone outside the house
Fighting back the tears,
For soon I would have to leave
And not come back for many years.
I did not know where I was going
And I didn't really care,
All I knew was that I was running
From something I alone could fear.
I looked at the big oak tree
Where I played so many times,
My beautiful old tree house
Was filled with dust and grime.
I did not understand
So many different things,
Why I had to leave this house
Never hear the echoes ring.
I turned around and walked away
For it was time to go,
I said my last goodbye
Running from my hidden foe.

Peggy (Hamblin) Dobson

LIVING FLAME

I saw him standing there across an open field.

He glowed like a flame of fire against the snow-patches of a late autumn flurry.

A puff of white smoke flowed at the tip of his long bushy tail. His legs were slender and dark under his shining red coat,

And his keen, sharp little ears were up; his head held high to read the signs on the air,

Or perhaps, to catch the scent of Vixen.

His fine-pointed nose was poised proudly - giving him the appearance of an aristocrat, in formal attire, looking over his vast domain.

As I stood there gazing at his fiery beauty,

A sense of profound admiration came over me for the brilliant work of art - Our Master's hand had wrought.

And, my heart leapt wildly within me in response to this lovely "Living Flame"

What a magnificent creature - The Fox!

....

There's beauty all around us Lord, that our human eyes so often fail to see,

Because our minds are centered on ourselves, not on thy works and Thee.

Rob Wyant

SEARCHING FOR SOMEONE BLOWING SQUARE BUBBLES

Say to that high-flying bird,
On a bright easy-orange dawn.
Have you ever found those things
You constantly search for?
Never did,
Nothing to search for,
Cept someone blowing square bubbles,
With chewing gum as tar.
Or maybe a cat chasing a dog,
In purple gliders above black clouds,
Where it's raining cats and dogs.
Foreigner,
Can't you see the peace,
Way up here in the sky.
No people to hassle you,
No cars to disrupt the music.
No hunters to shoot my life down,
Possible zookeepers to take my flight away.
Say to that high-flying bird,
On a bright easy-orange dawn.
What do you think of life in general,
While you fly in the breeze?
Never did,
Nothing to think of.
Cept flying is for the birds and
Cats and dogs in purple gliders,
And maybe,
People who blow square bubbles,
With chewing gum as tar.

Wm. Dale Malleck

WE WEEDS

Unglamorous, unloved
ol' weed-----
You grow so wild
and scatter seed;
Encroach upon the
crops we sow.
We chop, and curse you!
'Course, you know.
I looked, and found
your only sin
Is freedom--where you go,
and when.
Somehow you never learn
to stay
Away from man's (high)
Right-
of-
Way!
Some day we'll look
And, maybe, see
The special good
In all of "we".

Doris Shull Kruk

WHAT THE WORLD NEEDS

If our leaders of today,
Would look up and pray;
If they knew the great message,
Christ has sent,
Then we could win;
Against hate and sin,
But we know the leaders of today;
Look for another way,
A way of greater sin;
If America is the land of hope and dreams;
Why not turn away from the devil's schemes?
And look to God above;
For what he has to offer,
An everlasting Love.

Nelda G. Wilson

A POEM TO MY DAUGHTER

One day in the springtime
God made you just for me
You were one design in a million
He made you perfectly
He put you in a garden
Among the flowers fair
And woke me with a thrushes song
So I could find you there
You filled my heart with gladness
You were like the morning dew
And if I live a thousand years
All my love will go to you
The bluest eyes that ever shown
Looked into mine that day
And there I vowed to love you
Forever and a day
I may forget to thank you
For the loving things you do
But there's one moment I'll never forget
Thats when I first laid eyes on you
You filled my heart with happiness
You made my life anew
And if I die tomorrow
You've made all my dreams come true!

Dema V. Scalph

GUIDE US O LORD

Let there be a guiding star up above,
Help to light our way.
Let there be a guiding hand,
Be with us night and day.
God bless us and keep us in his care,
Show us right from wrong.
Help to heal the sick and weak,
Make them well and strong.
Let the earth be heavenly,
With weather that is fair.
My the good Lord, let things grow,
Plant life every where.
Let the fields, wave like a sea,
In fall with golden grain.
Keep the plants, most alive,
From heaven, we must have rain.
Bring forth the blossoms, in the spring,
And fruit and root crops grow,
Give knowledge, to preserve our food,
We'll feast, while winter weather snow storms blow.
May the good Lord, watch over us,
Keep us well and strong,
Friends and heighbors, we will be,
May we live a life that is long.
A MEN

Gregory Warholak

IN THE 2:37 SILENCE OF AFTERNOON TEA

i see my parents cannot hold my hand anymore than
i see my teachers cannot understand anymore than
i see our leaders cannot lead our land anymore than
what else can i conclude than
i can conclude no more than

Shirley Rae Hedges

A PRICE TO BE PAID

Two lonely people searching for love,
Reached for each other instead of above.
They found each other,

and a whole lot more.
What cannot be freely given
Cannot be freely taken.
There is a price to be paid.
For each stolen kiss, each stolen tender touch.
There is a price to be paid for each tear drop shed.
There is a price to be paid for each heartache caused.
He who is wise, pays the price while he may.
He who is foolish, thinks he can cheat in God's domain.

Paul S. Bruckman
THE MIDNIGHT MAIDEN
Once, I saw the midnight maiden
From the corner of my eye,
As I stumbled, homeward lurching,
Through the brambles of Lanai.
Though my host had pled to hold me,
I found reason to depart
Through those mournful, moonlit thickets
On the shores of dank Tungart.
How I scorned his tales of witchcraft,
How I jested at his fear!
Thus, in wine-emboldened brashness,
I resolved to brave the mere.
"On the night you view the maiden,"
He had said, "you'll surely die!".
Then I felt her stalking menace
But dared not turn my eye.
Many long years has it been now
Since that grim, accursed venture
Through the thickets by Tungart,
But the memory it has left me
Lies like ice upon my heart.

Carrie Nathalie Casella
EACH DAY
Live each day from dusk to dawn
For if you don't it will soon be gone
The flowers the trees the soft gentle breeze
Will forever be so still

Loraine C. Marbin
LOVE LETTER
Dear God, there is something I want to say--
It's really nothing new;
Just want to tell you I love you to-day,
And thank you for being You.

Dawn Carol Squires
I CAN'T STAND THE MUSIC
I've still not arrived at the point I can listen
To the words in a song, my eyes start to glisten
And a stirring inside me, disturbing but sweet
Brings new feelings haunting of our love so replete
Songs, we both thought lovely, words full of meaning
Starts pain to resurface with no thought of redeeming
Words of love so fulfilling, it's beauty and laughter
Of kisses and touching and caring hereafter
This I still can not conquer, a will of its' own
Makes me lonely with longings, we, two, have known
No, the points not been reached where music can soothe
There's too much at stake and we both stand to lose
I must patiently wait and all the while praying
Not too far in the future whenever they're playing
Songs from a time we'll look back to, not often
With the future before us, we'll let the past soften

Finley Schmidt
FIRST LOVE
Love is like a quiet blooming
Flower in springtime;
Or the brilliant brite white water--
Summer's melting snowman
That comes cascading down
Through brooks and streams
And rocky rivulets from
The mountains;
Or the biting-cold north-wind--
Autumn's eerie ghost
That goes right through a person
No matter how much prepared
Against it he might be.
Love is like the seaweed
Strewn up along the beach
At wintertime;
But my love,
My only true first love
Is like a bell-buoy sounding out
In the silence of an otherwise
Deep and peaceful
Quick grey dawn.
Da-ding, ding-ding, da-ding,
Ding-ding, ding-ding, ding-ding,
Da-ding, ding-ding, da-ding!

Rebecca Joy Stanger
WET PAINT
Don't touch my heart
The paint is not yet dry
From the last coat of hurt
Brushed on by an
Uncaring artist.
Instead, go your own way
Until it is done.
And maybe when
The finish is complete
And the smudges won't show
Maybe then
My heart will be ready
For a fresh coat of paint.

Mary Ann Christe
THE GIFT OF LIFE
Not to be explained
What causes falling rain
And makes the lightning strike
Resounding thunder and the like
Unknown are all the mysteries
Majestic mountains and rolling seas
And the given reasons
Explaining the four seasons
Suspended on nothing more than air
The earth is hung, right there!
So, too, the sun, stars, and moon
Hanging on air midnight and noon
The universe unknown to man
Beyond his power to understand:
A newborn baby's cry
A young bird's first attempt to fly
The budding rose
A puppy's nose
The glittering snow
Fruit trees that grow
A kitten's purr
A fox's fur
A lion's roar
An eagle's soar
Sunshine and happiness
Friends: true, sacred, and blessed
Love abounds
In all life's sounds
The gift of life given through love
Given to mankind from the Almighty Lord above!

Mrs. Marian Waufle Flannery
NUMEROLOGY OF THE HOSTAGES-1/20/81
"Spread His word o'er all the earth,"
That's what the Bible said.
52 Hostages, one for every week in the year,
52 Hostage families and friends pray for their dear,
52 Hostages, a miracle from heaven that they survive,
52 Hostages come home to their loved ones alive!
52 Hostages, one for the Atlantic, the Pacific and each State,
444 days they suffered, yet they do not hate.
Into Numerology for a moment, let us delve,
444 days equal three fours or four times three equals twelve,
12 Disciples of God, as in days gone by,

But now, our Disciples must multiply,
For the world today has gone astray,
And for all people, we must pray,
That we spread love and peace, and cease our evil ways,
For God has promised to return one of these days.
52 Hostages, each one very brave,
Welcomed home, America and the world, to save.

Janet M. Schultz
THE SUNSET DIED
I once had a dream that the sunset died,
It was an endless beach on an endless ride,
The darkness appeared with a thousand eyes,
Suddenly I heard the painful crys,
Damp and cold, I prayed for the light,
I cursed the blackness, betrayed by the night,
All was still and evil was near,
Voices beckoned, 'There is no need to fear.'
I once had a dream that the sunset died,
It was an endless beach on an endless ride,
The darkness appeared in a single breath,
If never returned, its death!

Cecelia Dempsey
THE DREAM OF ABRAHAM'S WIFE
I watch my shadow
bend over the bridge
and drown in the river
it is pulling me toward it
as if I am my own lover
an angel with three faces
invades my dream
like a soldier
he calls me eve
and kisses me as softly
as rose petals
breathe rain
he speaks three words
using the face of your father
fog clings to my skin
like gauze
I am wrapped in wings
that smell of wet gardenias
the ocean claws at my feet
and crashes against my body
pushing
I am the beach,
the stones.
I am a dead soldier
floating
like driftwood

Nicole M. Allegree
WHY
Why do I keep remembering my childhood as I look at a young girl:
playing,
singing,
laughing?
Why does she remind me of myself:
red hair,
freckles,
dimples?
Why can't we be young again --
loving,
laughing,
playing?
Why, oh why?

Rita Kurtz Lewis
BENEVOLENCE
Some trees
Forgive
a City!

Anna Guerrero
MOLDED IN HIS IMAGE
I traveled the road to the end of myself. I looked at the struggle I'd carried in me, in rediscovering who I was in Christ, so I came to Jesus and laid my burden down.
Jesus is the sculptor of my life.
He took a piece of clay one day

and he fashioned and molded me into the person he wanted me to be.
I find it hard to see what he could make of me a person with imperfections, but he looked beyond my faults.
He structured my days with a clever design and the plans he laid out were his, they weren't mine.
He's never failed in his planning for he's the architect, and he uses various methods of refining and pruning for his special purpose. He brings forth instruments for his work, as he sees fit. He's the vine and I'm the branch.
I ask myself to what end am I being molded in the fire? It's so when he has tried me, I shall come forth as gold or a precious gem that was being smelted and purified of all its dross.
His desire is that with his beauty I may shine in radiant attire, and this will be when all of me is pruned and purged with fire. A child of God can't be perfected without adversity.
Through adversity I've become molded into the image, form, likeness, and character of Christ Jesus my Lord.
Weeping endureth for a night, but joy cometh in the morning.

Dan Richards

STROKES

I trace a few random strokes
With my bare foot
In the sand,
Only to see them vanish
Beneath the constant flow
Of the hour-glass.

Carmen Lawrence

THE BOOK OF LIFE

The Divine Master conceived the plot
The Book of Life has many pages
The binding is cracked and scuffed by time
And covered by the Dust of Ages.
The script was converted into plays
And we each were given a part
We studied hard to learn our lines
And acted them out with all our heart.
Ah: Those Days of Wine and Roses
When the fires of youth flamed high
And our hopes and dreams arose
To build castles in the sky.
With youths unfailing energy
We worked by the sun and danced by the moon
What happened then to all that strength
It left us much too soon.
Where have the years all gone--
They disappeared so fast
What seems like only yesterday
Lies deeper in the past.
Let the days come and let them go
And the years will drift gently by
We will live our dreams of yesterday
And sometimes laugh and sometimes cry.

Shirley A. Hess

THE MEETING

The day was full of golden rays.
The soft breeze blowing from the bays.
I walked along the sandy shore,
Thinking how beautiful and hoping for more.
A shadow fell across my being,
I looked up, it was a monster I was seeing.
We looked at each other eye to eye.
I was so frightened, I thought I'd die.
I ran, I slid, I scrambled so.
To find a hiding place I might go.
It fell to its haunches, started digging in the sand.
Could I make it to the water, better than being on land.
And then another shadow there came.
I wondered if they were playing some kind of game.
I poked my head out to see what I can,
Only to find out my monsters were a boy and a man.

Violet R. Callison

WHAT JESUS PROMISED ALL

The promises Jesus made long ago,
Follow me and you shall know.
For as you live, you will sometime die,
And will live in God's kingdom in the sky.
When wicked men came and tried to destroy our trust
And all the wisdom and faith Christ had in us,
Joseph, in prayer, said; "What can we do?"
He answered; "I am the Lord and I promised you."
The promises He made were for all people living
For all those who were kind, loving and giving
Be careful, this long, long road that you trod
Is the highway that takes you straight up to God.

Angela (Lauri) McComb

UNSPOKEN LOVE

Love thats left unspoken
Is felt from the heart.
Swallowing us in warmth,
Even when we're apart.
Hearts that beat together
Sing a silent lullaby,
While brain waves
Dance together,
And quietly we sigh.

June McBride

AUSTRIA

There is a land that is lovely to see, it is the country of Austria, the most exciting place ever to be,
In the winter it is covered with snow and ice, but there are cheery little inns with lots of music and fireplaces that make it very nice,
There are quaint little villages to see everywhere and brooks streams babbling here and there,
Austria, I really love you with your valleys so green and your sky so blue,
I will come and visit you again
Because you have found a place in my heart and I will be ever true.

Joseph A. Hazzouri Jr.

I SCREAM, YOU SCREAM, WE ALL SCREAM FOR ICE CREAM

It's amazing
how beautiful you are
you are like
ice cream
What?
What does that mean?
Well,
as you melt in your cone
beneath the summer sun
the only thing to keep us both cool
is me liking you.

Sondra Broussard

A SONNET OF THREE

Our relationship is one uncommon
To conditions of others in the past.
It is the love of three as only one
In a union that will forever last.
Not only does it include you and I,
But also the immense greatness of God
To help guide us and help us to get by
Regardless of the paths we choose to trod.
Each of our lives can never be thine own.
We've lost our self and now live in a dream
Because we can never live life alone,
But always combined in a unique team.
Our love is something that will always be
In union with our God and you and me.

Robert M. Logan

AUTUMN MOVED IN

They called her autumn the way she could mellow the days and cool the nights.
She has a way with the leaves the greens turn to shades of gold, yellow, and orange.
Autumn caressed my cheeks yesterday with her strong air.
My nostrils were opened to her fresh smell.
Her cousin before she left was gentle as a lamb.
Autumn tries to be a temptress.
For about two and a half months
I'll grow accustomed to a new love.
Natures child, autumn moved in.

Constance Gardiner

UNTITLED

Your train is coming Lord
If not in the next town
or
over that far hill
It is on its way, maybe
this
day or that
night
But I shall wait
and
pick the roses with
the
thorns
For your train
is on
its
way

Lidan V. Isaac

A PASSENGER ON GOD'S TRAIN

I was standing in the rain
God call me by my name
Go tell my mother
Go tell my father
I am a passenger on God's train
I am a passenger on God's train
Go tell my mother and father again
I am a passenger on God's train
I does the things he tells me to do
Even fulfill Matthew five forty-two
Go tell my brothers
Go tell my sisters
I am a passenger on God's train
I am a passenger on God's train
Go tell my brothers and sisters again
I am a passenger on God's train
With my Lord I forget him not
He is the God of the Sabbath
Go tell friends tell family
My destination is heaven
I am a passenger on God's train
I am a passenger on God's train
Go tell them all again
I am a passenger on God's train

Donna J. Martinez

THE LAST CHANCE

The soldier marches out again
Before the sun's arise;
Quickly, yet quietly, he reaches his post,
The light beginning to reach his eyes.
He keeps his weapon mounted,
For the enemy may be near;
Constantly alert are his eyes
To what his ears may hear.

Hours pass by and still no
sound
But the gunshot of a friend;
The soldier marches back to
camp,
The morning's watch at end.
He slowly walks into camp at
noon,
Tiredly dragging his gun behind;
Disappointed because again,
The enemy he could not find.
He begins to pack for the ride
ahead,
For he is going home;
And until next year, again at
this time,
The deer will be left alone.

Kathryn Marie McGuire

NIMROD OF THE NIGHT

"Orion, armed with bow
that straddles stars

and quivering arrows to pierce
a constellation,
what limitless quarry for the
shafts of Sky's Hunter!"

Harvey Cummings

BETTY

Betty has more moves than
a Spanish dancer in a
Mexican whore house.
Betty is a queen without
a movie.
And, when Betty raises one
inch of her skirt, and
show a centimeter of her
precious thigh;
it is paradise.
It is a joy to know her;
and a sadistic thrill to
love her.

Dot West

LIFE IS BEAUTY

The world is full of weeper's, as
beauty is all that our eye's can
see.
Life is full of warm and precious
things for your heart to be
entertained.
Stars painted in the heavenly
body, sparkles like diamonds.
Their warm reflecting rays
reaches out deep into the
night to caress the hearts of
lover's world wide.
Giant fleecy white clouds
draped above a mountain top
conceal a quiet little village
below.
Life is full of beauty, if only the
world would conceive it.
Reflected in the amber glow of
the full moon light;
A ram stands lifeless uptop a
mountain peak if tho
painted there by the brush
strokes of the late Mac
Dangelo.
Love is beauty..., if only the eyes
of the world could see how it
is shared by you and by me.
Our love is as a tower of
strength, backed by a wall cut
from the sea..; Never to crumble
and never to fall.
As so many hearts float about as
a wave in a stormy sea; Our love
is being entertained by beauty.
Love is beauty!
Beauty is Love!
Life is so full of beauty until I
can see it reflected within your
every smile.

Carol J. Spaeth

NEW LOVE

When something new appears,
It is hard to explain
to those left behing
what had happened.
They are left holding
the empty cup
Wondering what happened
to what once filled it up.
Standing,
staring,
left only the stain.
Crying,
trying,
to cleanse away the pain.
Slowly,
time on their side,
the pain is washed away
And they are left
sparkling.

Sebastian

THE REAL ME

What would I think if there
would be
A mirror that showed the real
me?
Would I want others there to
see
The reflection of the real me?
If my deeds and thoughts were
disclosed;
The essence of my soul exposed,
Would I prefer to draw the
shades,
And use it after daylight fades?
If each of us made it our goal,
To live as though our very soul
Was as visible as our face,
The world would be a better
place.

Gale L. Martin

A FRIENDLY DEATH

My friend still walks in mortal
life,
And I am alone in earthly strife.
Our friendship died peacefully
and slow,
No death struggle to watch it
go.
No cruel killer stalked our
bonds,
No bitter words or magic wands.
Our friendship melted into the
night,
And I awoke, filled with fright.
But in the quiet stillness, I hear
her say,
Our love is just resting against
the pain of another day.

Donald S. Daughtry

SHEILA -- AT 14

Sheila smiles
and our hearts rejoice
for she brings joy to her
family and joy to her friends.
Sheila laughs
and our hearts sing
for we hear her laughter
echoing throughout the home,
the community,
the universe.
Sheila lives today,
caring,
loving,
sharing.
And she moves into
tomorrow, making it a
better day -- more just and
peaceful.
Sensitive and kind,
strong and gentle,
wise and naive,
eager and energetic,
right and erring,
learning,
growing,
imperfect,
fragile --
Sheila is a person,
loved by us.

Doris E. Ward

CRITICISM STING

She gave you life, and taught
you true, and did herself;
without.
She gave her love, and taught
you love, and did her very
best.
She sat up nights, when you
were ill, and did not even
blink.
She held you close when you
cried and couldn't help
yourself.
She tried to shield your every
fall, for this you gave no
thanks;
At last resort to your reply
without a warning gave,
She let you make the mistakes
you wanted to make.
So please, don't critize the one
who loves you best,
For one day "YOU" will know
the "Criticism Sting"

Donna M. Crebbin

THE FAIR

The ferris wheel goes round and
round
The choo choo train makes a
"toot toot" sound
the 200 pound woman is sure
a sight
the iron man holds his muscles
tight
you can throw a dart for a
penny or two
maybe a kewpie doll will come
to you
there's buttered popcorn and
sugar candy to eat
let's go to the fair—it sure is a
treat!
the loop o plane will give you a
twirl
around and around we'll watch
you swirl
Oh, let's go in the spook house
and see,
if anything can frighten me.
Now there's a barn with cows
and pigs,
and look at those chickens
dancing jigs,
I like the animals as much as
the rides,
walking around hurts my sides,
Oh, just look in my cracker-
jacks—I've won a prize!
To the fair, to the fair, boy
it's for me!
Forget your troubles, let's raise
whoopee!

Patricia A. DeJoseph

LIFE CHARGES

Generate a positive charge.
Again, let's do the same.
To generate a negative—
Reverse your aim.
The name of the game is God
All powerful and electrical
Luminous and eclectical—
Borrowing from each other
What good charges we have to
offer
We are part of his Divinity
his Infinity
As long as Life goes on, so will
He
The horror of Death as ominous
to Him as to his Following
Without us—where would
He be?
Or what?
Our negative charges quickly
build his Hell.
Our positive sustain barely his
Heaven.
The Earth struggles in between
Trying to balance and even,
Wishing Life were an Eternity
Unwilling to accept inevitability
Of entering either system;
Trying to buffer and neutralize
To make the charges even
And continue Life in solid
form.

Shirley Rae

THERE'S NO PLACE LIKE HOME

Be it ever so humble, "There's
No Place Like Home"
The kids are always on the
telephone. . .
They fight and yell and tear
around,
There's always something that
can't be found. . .
They want to go here, they want
to go there,
If their rooms are a mess, they
really don't care. . .
The laundry sometimes piles
high as the sky
I'd like to just sit down and
cry. . .
Just when I get the dishes done,
I hear, "Hey Mom, I'm hungry!"
from someone. . .
When at last I think all is
spic-n-span,
I turn around, there's a mess
again. . .
Kids come in one door and out
the other
With nary a thought for their
poor mother. . .
And when I wonder just what
I'm here for,
I get my answer when I walk in
the door,
And I get "Hi Mom", with a
smile and a hug
As the kids come running,
scuffing up the rug. . .
Then I realize I must enjoy
while I may,
For they will grow up and leave
someday. . .
But I hope that no matter where
they may roam,

They'll feel in their hearts,
"There's No Place Like Home!"

Russ Hagan

GIVE HIM A CHANCE

You're not as close as you once were
To the One so close to you.
You've shared your life with others
Trying to figure out your heart;
And now it seems you've found the One
To give you a brand new start.
If you'll open up and let Him in
He will change your heart.
Give Him a chance
To prove His love to you,
'Cause He can fill you up inside
And make you feel brand new.
Won't you give Him the chance
To do what He can for you?
And if you do, you'll find in time
You'll love Him as He loves you.
When the road gets rough and narrow,
I'll be there by your side
To help you learn and help you grow,
To light you path where ever you go
If you'll have faith and believe in Me,
I'll give you all the help you need
To discover what life is all about
And to reach your destiny.

Hike Kaplan

BEGINNING

Sleepless thoughts—
fierce, turbulent, vibrant,
in restless force
burst the womb
of vague tomorrows,
and pass
the unconscious dreams
of helpless fears
Into a new birth
of bursting
Stars.

Sally Francise Hogan

SPIRIT OF A UNICORN

See him if you can!
Breathtaking creature from another land.
See him rise from out the clouds,
Or standing quietly, soft mist enshroud.
Watch him jump a rainbow bright,
Emerge from darkness into light.
A spiritual creature, gentle, aloof.
Is he a myth? Or Gods sweet truth?

Carolynn Pilkington

DAUGHTER

It was passed from mommy to you,
My precious little girl,
All the love I have to give,
All the love I can endure,
You were made from a tiny seed,
To small to be seen,
And you grew to be a beauty,
From princess to little queen,
From innocence to curiosity,
You were so full of questions!
I didn't have all the answers,
But helped with a few suggestions,
You have given more to me than you will ever know,
My special little Angel,
Oh! how I love you so!
Thank God for such a daughter,
Which there could be no other,
Thankful to be chosen special to be your mother,
I've learned from you my daughter,
Through happy times and tears,
Memories to cherish for my remaining years.

Robert A. Bowen

RIDER OF THE DROUGHT

I come riding down from barren
hills bringing word to you
My scarlet coat is running red
my lips a vermillion hue
None so bleak, none so dry
as those which I have seen
O, give me help! A healing hand!
to bring back the green.

Yes, the hills are barren as the
dead the night owl's moan is
clear
Help me to bring back to life
those which I hold so dear.

Bente Storslett

PEDESTALS OF HUMAN KIND

True supports to the body,
Bent bones scrunched tightly in sneakers,
Slap steadily against hot pavement;
Propped at precarious angles,
Conforming painfully to fashion
Our feet,
Smelly and tired plod along.

Carolyn M. Patterson

SWAN DIVE

He stands on the end
Of a board
Which is bobbing over
The body of water
That is his
Destination.
A final bounce
Sends him sailing
Into the air,
Arms stretched gracefully overhead,
To make first contact
With the water.
In a matter of seconds
He has slipped below the surface
And all that is visible
Are the ripples
Where the water closed
Over his feet.

Tamara L. Badder

DREAMER

When your down and sad,
Be a star gazer.
And when your luck has gone bad,
Be a rainbow chaser.
If confined, no longer free,
The seas you gotta sail.
When life you no longer see,
Then dreams will never fail.

Laura B. Schildkraut

UNTITLED

Posessed
Obsessed
You control my entire being
Each move, each mood
You
I am caught within the very web
in which I entangled myself.
Worse, I was aware that you
were gaining control.
Like a spectator, I observed.
I am now a puppet.
Caught in the strings
that I placed in your hands
and cried,
"Make me dance!"
and you did.
You were so gentle at first.
Unsure of the power I entrusted to you.
But power is a strange thing.
Once its seed is planted and well-watered
it conquers.
As ivy covers its domain.
And at once I was under your control.
As the strings became part of your hands.

Russell E. Shipp

RENEWAL

'Twas but a thin pool of sultry dusk
That seeped under a skewed front door,
Staining the dank shadows on her dingy floor,
Just beyond swollen shoeless ankle husks.
She sat heavy and deep in the worn, lifeless chair,
Whose rare creak gave poor company to her slow wheeze.
A faint flutter of gray curtain hinted the soft breeze,
Not enough to dry the upturned palm or watery stare.
Her fingers clutched snugly a small black purse.
Inside, unfolded, new and rosy pink
Infant girl—long awaited precious pearl—
The balm at last that could lift her curse.

It is very, very easy
To feel sorry for one's self,
And to think "Well, no one
needs me,
Time to put me on the shelf."
But for those who wear the
banner,
Of the Christ who died for
you,
That's the time of sweetest labor
And there's still much work to
do.
As you wake up in the morning
And you're laying there quite
still,
Ask the Father for his blessing—
Pray for guidance in His will.
Know the sweetness of his
presence,
Feel the healing of His grace.
And the folks who live around
you
Will see Jesus thru your face!
Your eyes, all day, are mirrors,
Others look and smile or pout.
What they see there are your
road signs
Teaching love and trust—or
doubt.
And your lips speak words of
kindness,
Or they bite and snap and
sting,
Showing up the way of sorrows
Or the place where angels
sing.
Age is not a time for moaning,
But for gladness in the heart.
Each day brings, our Savior
Closer
(A goal is better than the
start!).
Someone sees the way we
manage
And it helps—or leaves a
stone,
For a foot that's traveling after,
To pass over—or be thrown.
You have never been more
needed
Than you are this very day.
So come on—look up—be happy!
Show a "Jesus Face" today.
A smile, a hug, a word of cheer
Will help someone to know,
That living for the Lord each
day
Is the only way to go!

Polly Chase Cleary

FIRST PARISH CHURCH, UNITARIAN

At the top of a small common
in Groton
The old church stands stiff and spare,
Frozen in Puritan posture;
Its tall spire the only still point
In a turning world.
Among the soft, round drumlins,
The highest site in town
skirts swamp and farm;
Joins sky to land,
The steeple, locked in place by years of faith,
Stands there like a pair of hands in prayers.
The bell in its tower hangs,
A heart to pump a call to faith in waves of air.
Inside, the stern, tall pews flank
walls of white;
And, high above, shafts of chaff-white dust
Are chained by light of faulted glass;
Belief and beams suspended

stay
In ancient vaults of faded day.
A note of Truth does sound
here, in any season,
Deep in the tone
Of Book and sermon;
On an unheard plane—
Beyond all sense,
Beyond all reason.

Mary June Butler
ALONE
'm taking a walk in the woods
today,
t's the perfect place to get
away—
From people and things that
bother me
Alone with nature is what I'll
be.
'll touch a leaf and see the sky
And watch the clouds as they
drift by.
'm deep in the woods now and
all alone
Yet I'm only a mile away from
home.
Something wet falls upon my
cheek,
A wonder of God to make one
meek—
A flake of snow that will
disappear
And make me wonder if it was
here.
There're few leaves left of red
and gold
This years Fall has gotten quite
cold—
So I'll go home now and think of
Spring
When again God renews just
everything.
Flowers will spring up to face
the sun
They grow for the joy of every
one—
So take a moment to look and
see
The creations that God presents
for thee.

John P. Walsh
ANCHOR
feel like a leaf,
blowing in the wind.
Lord, anchor me in
his Life, and Eternity.

Julia Ord King
AFTERMATH
A bitter ache.
Hot words fanning hidden fires
Of smouldering hates and
suppressed desires—
Flames of Hell in fiendish
ecstasy
Obliterating, blinding vows of
amity—
A soul in quivering, naked
hurt.

Ronald L. Moser
HARVEST
Moving on the horizon,
sounding a droning hum,
comes the big red Massey
chewing up wheat
with the sickle snipping straw,
lightning quick!
The reel feeds it to the
auger with the beat of a drum,
through feeder house to the
cylinder's crushing beat;
beater, fan, sieves and straw-
walkers add their lick
until a "karumph" in the rear
shouts that it's tough,
its boom a warning that for
today it's enough.
After ten to twelve hours of
handling the machine
the opertor desends dust
covered, yet appearing clean;
fatigue has relaxed him, now he
looks at peace,
only the cool of the evening has
made him cease.
He feels that something that
few men do
each day under that "Big Sky" of
blue.
From morning crispness to
disappearing sun
he pushes on and on until
harvest is done.
Whether bountiful or poor, it's
what God has decreed,
each stalk has sprung from one
tiny seed!
Ed Hauser, my friend, the
foregoing we've known
and will ever share it, where'ere
the seeds are blown!

Peggy Fitzpatrick
AN UNCERTAIN QUEST
Many people *look*, yet they also
may *see*
what they are seeking; why, oh,
why can't we?
Is it so hard, must you fear?
Yet never *know* if the answer
you are seeking, is it really all
that *near!*

You may ask yourself a question
and receiving no answer, find,
that those finding nothing there
must stay with those they find.

Joseph Oliver I
CRISIS IN THE MIDEAST
'Neath the desert moon above
I marvel at the skies celestial
beauty;
For nights like these are made
for love,
Yet patriotism at the call of
duty
Has placed me miles by
thousands from my wife,
Just newlywed before my quick
departure,
That I may help stop this
engulfing strife.
The lonesome stillness to my
soul is torture;
The desert moon becomes a
smiling jest
To hearts it blended once so
soft together,
Leaving capricious fate to do
the rest,
To tear the tenuous dreams
apart, to shatter
The pilgrim hopes that love, all
joyous planned
Ascending to the heights of
ecstasy
Only to be dragged down by
fate's firm hand
To join the marching throngs of
liberty.
But my heart lifts and I smile
at the moon,
For all the thoughts within my
heart rotating
Fix on her final words to set
their tune—
"Darling, no matter what the
time, I'll be there waiting."

Edithmae Hostetter
TO MOM FOR CHRISTMAS
Lovely things are quiet things
Like soft falling snow.
And feathers dropped from
flying wings
Make no sounds as they go.
A petal loosened from a rose
Quietly seeks the ground.
And love, if lovely, when it
goes,
Goes without a sound.

Mary L. Welch
A DAISY'S LIFE
I wish the life and bloom of my
Daisies
Didn't depend so much on you.
On knowing you, and wanting
you, and loving you.
What else is there?
Except the hope that you will
always be there
To bring the Rain and the Sun,
To be the dark, moist Earth
That keeps my Daisies ever
blooming.
Without these things,
Surely the Daisies would wither
and die.
Please—don't take you away
from me
To watch a Daisy die is sad. . . .

Amy Beth Campbell
BITTERSWEET ROSE
The rose opened itself
to the sun
but withered
from rain and icy wind.
I opened myself
to your love.
Rain falls from my eyes
when your thorns
puncture my heart.

Last night I heard, my baby cry. I saw his tear drops fall.
Last night I heard my new born's breath and felt his tiny hand. Last night my son—was just my son, today my son's a man.
To Mike

Dennis L. Siluk
THE GARDENS OF YOUR LIPS
You ask me why I Love you—its
the Gardens of Your Lips—they
grow as days go by—they stir
with peace and glory—they tell
of the future, our life story.
You ask me why I Love you—
because Dear, we met as friends
and grew—and all the memories
you have given—have become
treasures, even the tears we
knew.
You ask me why I Love you—
there's no change of pace with
your heart—I guess, I'm trying
to say my Dear—you're not
hidden in the dark. . .
And Your eyes my Darling—
moist with sacred dew—are
carved from angel wings— to
mend mine when they're blue.
I Love you Darling because—
you treasure all my goals,—with
pride—and dignify my God (I
know they're yours, as yours are
mine)—Your patience is so
strong.
Yes, indeed my Darling—so
many things I see—and If I
could place them all together
a triumph it would be; so let me
simply say, Its the Gardens of
Your Lips—they grow as days go
by—safe and sturdy are they,
as we walk *side by side.*

Edwin R. Golden
A KILLER IN DISGUISE
A mask so deceiving, you'd pass
right by him on the street.
So cleverly veiled, you wouldn't
know if even you'd chance to
meet.
Mirroring his own reflections,
the truth he doesn't see,
Appearing no different to
himself, than to you and me
Amidst this clouded delusion,
transformation will begin.
A raging torent of anger now,
once was a good friend.
Destruction is his path now, not
seeing either side,
When only a hat's drop ago,
would quietly abide.
"How could one so gentle, come
to murderous ways?", we
think,
Why it's only another of our
fellow man, who's had too
much to drink.

Gertrude Baggerly
DOOMSDAY
Delicate creatures of the world
are doomed
As man destroys the climate in
which they flourish;
Butterflies in cocoons their
mothers loomed
Emerge to die from leaves that
used to nourish.
Wildflowers that carpeted a
woodland floor
And made each spring a
wondrous new delight
Are gone, and many woodlands
are no more—
The birds that nested there have
taken flight.
Pollution affects the water, earth
and air,
Destruction seems to follow in
man's wake;
If wildlife disappears he doesn't
care,
Wasn't the world created for
his sake?
By disregarding Nature's
harmony,
Man may destroy himself by her
decree.

Belva Lou Spaulding
REMEMBERED MUSIC
The symphony of my Mother's
hands.

Is soft and muted,
Now nearly stilled by time.
This symphony. . .
With love and harmony
Played background
accompaniment
To my yesteryears.

Kevin Paul Pawsey
UNTITLED
Do you see the freak
Walking down the way?
Roll them stones.
Gather the moss.
Mold him as
An ignorant plaything.
Falsify his name.
Do not understand him,
But bequeath him
The right to live.
He shall someday, then, say
"I have lived".
And after all the years
Of torment and shame,
He will have managed
To conquer life,
To face his abounding limits,
And once again gain death.

Signe Schrull
ON SOLITUDE
My favorite mood
Is solitude,
Tho some find it rude
When I dream and brood
In solitude.
This interlude
Of solitude
Is misty, rainbow hued
Often, often blued.
Tis peaceful food
my solitude.
So, serenity wooed
I rest, renewed
Thru solitude
This my solitude.

Ethel Forsberg Sweitzer
THE FAMILY OAK
Our tree is alive and growing,
The branches reach far and
wide,
Our roots are staunch and
sturdy,
We cover the country-side.
Our stock is from Germany and
Sweden,
A much better life was their
goal,
God-fearing and totally
committed
To preserving the bark and the
bole.
The grain of our wood is
distinctive,
Our strength is very well
known,
We cherish each new leaf and
flower,
and pray for the birds that
have flown.
The rings on our tree are many,
Each twig is a part of the whole,
The leaves are stamped with the
pattern,
It's ordained that we have a
great role.
The sun kisses all the new
acorns,
The rain keeps our leaves
washed clean,
The good earth always sustains
us,
We're proud to stand up and be
seen.
Now, our heritage is ever
demanding
To teach right from wrong to
the flock,
And pass to the next generation,
A chip from the old oaken
block.

L. A. Leonard
THE DAY AFTER CHRISTMAS
It was the day after Christmas,
when all over the place,
The clutter and muss was a
disgrace.
The Christmas tree was a pitiful
sight,
It had been second best in a
terrible fight.
There was wrappers and
trimmings scattered around,
A variety of articles were to
be found,
A half eaten apple had rolled
off on the floor,
There were nut hulls and candy
and lots more.
The toys were displayed in a
haphazard way,
Where the children decided they
were too sleepy to play,
There were gloves and scarfs
and also sox,
There were night gowns and
shirts still in their box.
On the couch and table and on
the chair,
Such things were displayed
everywhere.
When Grandma came in to this
cluttered place,
I expected to see a frown on her
face.
I saw a smile on her lips when
she came near,
She looked all around and said,
"Oh dear,
I am glad Christmas only comes
once a year!"

Faye Hoyt
MY DAUGHTER (REFLECTIONS OF MYSELF)
I saw your dark eyes glisten
T'was then I saw the smile
Familiar features about you
Made me reminisce for awhile
The silly little giggle
That made boys look about
But such sophistication
When they came to take you
out
I sit here and remember
The days of yesteryear
When I was the dark eyed
giggler
And you weren't even there

Mary Lou Driscoll
THE SACRIFICE OF A CHILD
Why God, was I made to suffer
so?
I was only a child with a
lifetime to go.
I tried to be perfect in your
eyes—
Why did you never answer my
cries?
Agony and fear were my only
dreams—
My pillow damp from my silent
screams,
I begged for your mercy, to
make it all right—
But Satan had me—night after
night.

Robert J. Norton
SONNET OF SORROW
My tortured soul such cruel fate
decreed
That I should share with
mindless souls such fate.
Is there a need my love should
share their hate?
My painful heart is crying to be
freed.
In vain I cry, I reach to find my
need,
So many empty souls, no loving
mate.
I feel no happiness, my hours
grow late,
I long for love, I sense its
cruel deed.
All passions burning brightly,
dying fires.
The thousands seeking self are
finding loss.
Alone all spirits rise to
nothingness
As flames do brightly flicker
with desires.
We dance without a song,
around a cross,
In torment sorrow clowns in
mocking dress.

Brenda G. Janse
MAN'S SELF-DESTRUCTION
Nature—
That most misunderstood
preserver of man's sanity
How we abuse you
Tear you down in the name of
progress.
Have you, violent man, heard
the trees whimper
A sorrowful howl that pierces
the ears.
Eminent mountains ravaged
for highways.
Man armed with unappreciable
sympathy
Ripes and tears at his victim.
Hugh toothed dirt movers
Grind and growl
Up and down the majestic
ridges.
Merciless, man explodes
dynamite
Huge toothed dirt movers
gentle mooring.
The inner sancity barren
Exposed—forever.
A harsh death bestowed by man
Suffocation
Erosion.
Scars for the world to witness.
Tears from the heavens soothe
the wounds
Apollo warmly embraces His
Earthchild
Diana covers man's
transgression
Crying softly in shame and
horror
The wail deafens.

Sharon Daley
ODE TO A FRIEND
We've spent happy times
together,
And we've shared alot of tears.
We knew each other very well,
And knew each others fears.
But even best friends must part
someday.
Our day of parting finally came,
All too soon for me and you.
I may not have you here with
me,
But in my heart you live
endlessly.
And I will always remember
you,
And all that we've been through.
I know one day our paths will
cross,
And once more I'll see your
smile.
Until then my friend,
I'll carry on the best way I
know how.

Jean Bateman
SPRING
Spring is a time to hope, a
time to pray.
As the sun sets and rises again.
So does Spring come after
winter.
God has planned it all, that way
Spring is a time to give thanks,
a time to smile.
As the rainbow shows itself,
after the rain,
So do the stars shine, when the
clouds are gone.
God has planned it, all the
while.
Spring is a time when the earth
reborn.
As each human life, comes to
it's winter,
So can that life wake again.
God has planned for that glad
morn.
Spring is a starting overtime,
a brand new day.
As we take our final sleep, if
we have kept His word,
So will we wake again, to an
eternal Spring.
God has planned it all, that way

Kenneth Gilley
HERE ON STREETS CENTURIES OLD
Strolling the sleazy Spanish
Streets. . .
Rain lazily drizzles upon
Pedestrians rushing about
On the last of evenings chores.
Quietly, old men watch through
doors,
As rain tells of winter near,
The children forget summers
cheer,
Here on streets centuries old.
Shop and Bar doors standing
ajar,
Inviting passerbys inside,
Bekoning me to break my
stride,
Here on streets centuries old.

Forrest Neal Whatley
THOUGHTS LIKE THESE
Thoughts of yesterday
are thoughts I hold dear
for fear of their escaping
I always keep them near
I open up my heart
to the ecstacy of life
all that I can give
to make it turn out right
I open up my soul
to the ecstacy of love
a gift for all mankind
shared with God above
The country comfort in the air
The warm summer breeze
I treasure the joy of living
the joy of thoughts like these

Jan Muckey
I MISS YOU
I don't hear your happy laughter
or your footsteps in the hall
I don't hear your simple
arguments
or your cries each time you fall
I don't hear you say I love you
or hear you say goodnight
I miss you more than anything
I long to hold you tight.
My arms have felt such
emptiness

My heart has felt the ache
Each day has been so long and
dull
It's more than I can take
I know you'll soon be home
with me
I can hardly wait
Til I can hold you to my breast
again,
my children, you're my fate.

Olive Ray Harrison
AUTUMN GOLD
Golden sun showers spill upon
Trees of summer green,
Painting all the outside edges
With a golden sheen.
Leaves of gold, red and green,
Fluttering in the sun
'Til the playful, fickle wind
Comes to join the fun.
Down he blows them, helter
skelter;
Red and gold and brown,
Scattering them in gorgeous
splendor
On the cold and barren ground.
Autumn, reigning, smiles with
pleasure,
On the landscape bright,
'Til the snow of angry winter
Buries it from sight.

Deborah Jeanne Zajac
RUNNING
Your hand in mine
I taste the wine—
in time
in time
in time.
It's the same feeling
your hand, my hand;
you gently touch my face—
sensations running.
I close my eyes,
and the dream is there,
and now—here.
Now is gone, and here
is now.
I sit, hand on head,
half resting, half thinking.
And it's you, and you and you.
If I can capture the air you
breathe, wherever that may
be now, just for one breath,
I could somehow make the day,
face the night.
But, it's patience that I lack,
what I must so obediently obey.
But the time seems so long
since
I've seen you—
and the voice on the wire fades
gently to a click—
sweet dreams my love.

Albert Hernandez Jr.
KIDDIES AND KIDDOS
I remember Granny.
You remember her.
Not to mention, Grandpa too.
We remember them quite well.
Gangrenous slimes!
How you balked at their
needs—
Shut up you hags!
Stop the nag
Stick it up your bag!
Hey Grandma—
Stop trembling you wench
Hand me that wrench
Clean up your stench
(the eyes that failed only her)
What's wrong with those eyes?
Can't you cook some fries?
How about some pies?
Hey Grandma—
Shut up you bum
Aren't you tired of being
scum?
Stop working you greedy old
fag
Retire and hope for the
Welfare Goodie Bag
And so it is that kiddies and
kiddos
Remember Granny quite well
Not to mention, Grandpa too.
If only we had listened
If only we had loved them.

Bruce K. Johnston
CRY FOR THE CLOWN
Cry for the clown
behind locked doors
a beaming face—
the red flushed cheeks,
Silently Seeming. . . .
You know you've dreamed him.
a face of despair
Sprinkling Sadness
his sunken cheeks
Draining,
Draining
as you politely watch him.

Novella Meek
SKEIN OF LIFE
I must rewind the skein of yarn
And set my thinking right!
There's attitudes to mend and
darn
To give my life more light!
I must untangle yarns of dread,
Today is all one needs,
Lay straight that fatalistic
thread
And death on which it feeds!
I'll wind the skein till it's
like new,
And vision as of yore. . . . .
When youthful dreams were
never few
And time was never score!

Shirley Jo Salge
HOLIDAY OF OLD
Peace on earth, good will
toward men,
That's what the carols say.
Loving, kindness, brotherhood,
We strive for that today.
Merry Christmas, Happy New
Year!
Greetings from all around,
Twinkling lights, tinkling bells,
Candy canes by the pound.
Children singing, adults
shopping,
Holly's in the air.
Wreaths in windows, Santa
Claus,
Trees are everywhere.
Happiness and laughter,
Blessings from above;
This exciting, wondrous season
Caused by one Man's love.
Love for all the people,
Men and women, you and me.
He was born as our Lord Jesus,
To the world a mere baby.
We now know Him as our
Savior,
The whole of all mankind.
For love and hope and brother-
hood
In Him is all we find.
So sing the Christmas carols,
Of snow and sleigh and bell;
But to remember our Lord's
birthday,
You know you mustn't fail.
For as He gave us Christmas,
We ourselves must give.
For it is not just one day
That this joy should live.
But on throughout the new year,
This gospel should be told.
For in this Christmas story,
The key to love we hold.

Marion Evans
THE DEADLIEST WEAPON
Harsh words were exchanged
And if looks would kill
Jan would be dead and buried
On Grampian Hill—
"I have proof," Bill scornfully
shouted.
"You have been unfaithful.
There is no doubt about it."
Jan rushed out of the room,
To the attic she fled,
Opening the trunk lid, she
said,
"I'll find that weapon,
If it's the last thing I do."
Her hands were shaking,
She was desperate too—
"What if. . .Ah! there it is."
Cold to the touch
She steeled herself
And lifted it up.
It didn't weigh too much—
Then, striking a match
The sulfur smelled strong,
Her aim was quick
It didn't take long,
The deadliest weapon
Completely destroyed,
A bunch of old Love Letters
Blue ribbon tied.

Phyllis R. Murphy
HANDICAP
They laughed
I cried
They mimicked
I panicked
They towered
I cowered. .
I changed
They stared
I smiled
They recoiled
I forgave
They walked away.

Betty Farquhar
SOFTLY SHE COMES
Softly she comes,
dressed in velvet blue—
a crown of diamonds
on moonlit hair.
She beckons the weary
to come to her heart,
bestows caresses
and comforting dreams.
And when the sun rises,
she softly leaves
to bring renewal to the weary
ones
on the other plane of this earth.

Martha Hodge
I MAKE THE BED
See my heart there?
There!
On the floor!
Right inside the front door
That's where you left it
(knife, blood)
Now I make a clumsy effort
To recapture
(life, love)
Myself
Confidence
Look!
I can see my head here!
Here!
In this piece of glass
Why, I thought I lost that too!
(brain, insane)
Shows what thinking can do
(pain, again)
Oh my
Tears this time
Here!
On my sheet
Right where the wrinkles meet
Here!
Where I usually sleep!
(past affairs, nightmares)
Now I make the bed
To cover up
(reminiscing, missing)
Myself
Pity

Jimmy R. Garrison
LAURIN
Early morning sunrise
and rays of gold
filtering through the window
pane.
Awakening green eyes
and a sleepy smile
that's never the same.
Sunlight softy shining there
where she lays
without a sound,
Morning gold in her hair
and the face of Miss Piggy

on her little pink gown.
This little girl
who's smile
is there to share
Has become the center of all
our worlds
and we're so proud
she's always there.
With hardly a sound
she awakes
to greet the day.
And no one knows she's around
until suddenly we hear her
say,
"Please tie my shoe."
Laurin,
her name is so soft a sound
The music of her voice
when she sings with me
is a summer sound
I can almost see.
Yankee Doodle
and Dandy too.
Laurin,
there's nothing
you can't do.
The smile in your eyes
and the song
in your heart.
Your tomorrows
and all your dreams
and warm blue skies,
And your journey
is just waiting
for you to start.

Terri Glodowski
RIBBON AND LACE
Ribbon and lace so delicate and
fine
Like the grace of an evening
with candles and wine
So innocent and pure like a
fresh country breeze
That rustles the waves of the
salty blue seas
The soft gentle touch from a
fresh, subtle glow
Will whisper so softly of the
love we may know
To know of this love we must
touch life with grace
And spread our love gently like
ribbon and lace

Roxi J. Lieuallen
SHADOWS
In each life
some rains must fall—
casting shadows
upon us all.
Then someone
makes you happy—
and fills your life
with love;
clearing the sky
to show blue above.
Again come the clouds,
making everything dark.
You can't hear the song
from a once joyful lark.
But days pass quickly,
and turn into years—
With memories of him,
still bringing tears.

Berta J. Harper
WHAT HAPPENS
What do you lose when you lose
your mind?
Do you lose all the memories of
loves left behind?
Do you grope through the
darkness as if you were blind?
Tell me what do you lose when
you lose your mind?
Are there just bits and pieces
of the past you once knew,
Swirling and swaying, taunting
wickedly at you?
Raining down drops of
flourescent blue.
And you sit there wondering
if you are really you.
You try without crying,
And you think about dying,
So you beg to be flying,
But the shrinks just aren't
buying.
So what happens when the fuse
finally blows in your brain?
Can you still feel the hurt of
unending pain?
Can you be who you are and not
have to explain?
Is the coping much easier when
you're finally insane?

Nancy L. Merchant
GRAVES
You hurt me. . .
I bury the pain
To prevent it and you
from driving me insane.
Covered with dirt,
lying deep beneath a cross
Don't want it to surface;
Can't bear to feel the loss.
In the cemetery of my heart
lie too many mounds of dirt
Covering the memories;
and masking the hurt.
All the graves of loves lost
Make love seem too high a cost.

Pearl Wolverton-Einert
THE LINGUIST
Didya ever meet a feller who
thinks he's mighty smart
Cause he's had a lot of learnin'
in the higher forms of art?
He calls himself a "Polyglot",
whatever that might be. . . .
But if you judge the word by
sound it fits him perfectly.
He scorns the simple common
word for one he can't explain,
And shuns the good old-
fashioned way of talkin'
straight and plain. .
I like the man who says his say
in words of two or three,
Right from the shoulder and to
the point. . .no walkin'
dictionary!

Edna M. Frank
WISHING ON A STAR
When you wish upon a star
And hope it will come true,
Be sure you know for what you
wish
And if it's good for you.
As you travel down the road of
life
Keep your dreams in sight,
And when you wish upon a star
May they be true and bright.
Sometimes amid your daily
cares
You may lose the will to try,
Then you must wish upon your
star
And laugh instead of cry.
Your world will be bright again
And your dreams will all come
true,
If when you wish upon a star
You know what's good for you.
So keep on wishing, climbing,
dreaming
Happiness is love,
Go on and wish upon a star
That's why they're up above.

Margie Hardesty, Ph.D.
HOSTAGE
Texas was as big as they said:
My woman showed me proudly
Super markets, drive-in banks
Parking lots with electronic
guards
Small miracles of progress—
Iran has some miracles of her
own.
I could have gotten lost
In Kennedy Airport.
Little Rock had smiles for me
You don't find every place,
That is, at first.
I was glad when the Shah fell,
My brother would be safe,
No knocks on doors at night—
Then seen no more.
Kohmeini rode in on a crest of
hope.
Shapoor and I passed smiles
And Ardishir looked happy for a
time.
Why was my tire slashed last
night?
Why does the Economics prof
scowl at me?
Why has my woman lost her
pride?
I wish I had got lost
In the airport.

Nina W. Kurkamp
YOU TOP THE LIST
A person is a being, an entity,
a reality!
An individual of reasoning
ability.
Even one of distinction
Could be—even one of
unmistakable quality!
That is the reason, now I choose
To separate the small from the
tall.
And those outstanding; not
objectively small.
No other reason can I recall.
The walls of one's life are filled
With images depicting phases
Which I have encountered—all!
And in my recollection, there
stand but few.
But stands a clear visage of one
outstanding,
Who holds a startling semblance
of you!
Always friendly; Ever loyal,
One exuding much warmth.
Courage when I am weary.
Cheerful when I am dreary.
Charming when I am sagging,
And needing a life—You have
that gift!
Always ready with stimulation
When shadows fall—Best of all,
Is it any wonder, you top the
list?
My thoughts are of you
"Best of All"!

Marie Gilbert Finck
MARTYR'S VOICE
When I have lain a thousand
years
And o'er my narrow bed has
has passed
The happy sound of children's
dancing feet
And a thousand summers given
birth
To fruit and flowers, corn and
wheat
And a thousand winters seen
the snows
Or all the earth drift white and
deep.
Then I will take up life again
And walk the way where once
my feet had trod
But I would be a wiser, humbler
one
Alike to me the shining star and
common clod
To live once more for my fellow
man
And die again for God.

Christine Mason
TELL ME
This is a deep heart felt appeal
For you to tell me the things
you feel
To tell me what you feel inside
To get it out, not let anything
hide
Tell me the things that make
you frown
Tell me the things that get you
down
Tell me what causes you pain
Get it all out, don't refrain
Tell me the things that make
you smile
Tell me what makes life
worthwhile
Tell it all don't keep it in
Open up and let it begin
Tell me the things no one
knows
Keep on talking until it flows
Let it come out, one thing at a
time
Until there's nothing left behind
I'm here to listen, and help if I
may
So don't keep your emotions
buried away
I'm here when you need a
shoulder to cry on
That is something you can rely
on
To be here when you need help
to cope
To cheer you up and give you
hope
From the beginning, and until
the end
Remember that, I am your friend

Ann M. Pardo
UNTITLED
Deadline: Dec. 14, 1981
Died: Dec. 12, 1981
Due Date: Dec. 6, 1981
Destination: Castlewood Terrace
Do Not Open:
Do not open until Christmas
DO NOT REMOVE UNDER
PENALTY OF LAW
Died: Dec. 12, 1981

Dial Direct Dial again: Repeat
and Dial Again
Dial again
Dial O
Repeat and Dial Again
Dial Direct
Drop Dead
Deadline: Dec. 8, 1981

Geoffrey A. Gayle
IN THE HEAT OF THE NOONDAY SON

I give until sundown to
receive either:
A breath of life. . .
Or the kiss of death;
Trudging wearily forth,
Day after shiny-cloudy day,
Is the ugliest image,
Apparent to this Beauty-worshipper;
Therefore, at Sol's next setting,
I shall summon Pegasus, to meet me on this road,
And demand that it either:
Gently allow me to mount it,
lean back, and cling to its
haunches,
In exuberance and vitality. . .
Or brutally tread me under its hooves, and tear me,
Toward stagnance and demise.

D. J. Henderson
MARCH EVENING

Late winter twilight falls apace.
Outside, the restless fingers of the rain
Pluck at the frost that holds
In its stern grip, the stirring earth.
The misty air brings to our ears
The moist and drowsy murmur of their toil.
Let's sit awhile and dream and think.
Lay down our books, it is too dim to read.
Or make a light,
For it would break the spell
That twilight and the whispering rain has cast.
The great fire quells its crackling to our mood;
Its tottering embers sinking silently;
And errant raindrops, hissing to their doom,
Small voices seem,
Linking the cheerful coziness within
Unto the chill, dumb clamor of the rain.

Dion Saxon
HAPPY BIRTHDAY, EVERYBODY

There are giants here
within this stone of being,
reaching out
with tortured muscled arms
to break the prison
of this dream of binding.
The strong faces,
following the shoulders
tearing through the granite,
the blind eyes
slowly coming into sight
as powerful hands
touch the other's face
so like its own.
The tender fingers
gently feel
the mirrored image,
no difference here!
The eyes smile,
great arms reach out
and touch.
The lips speak
one word,
BROTHER!

Richard M. Shaffer
THANKSGIVING INCESSANT

When birds of summer southward streak
And flowers cannot be found.
The leaves stop playing hide-and-seek
And nestle on the ground.
When frosty mornings nip the nose
And nibble at your ear,
That is a time, we could suppose,
Thanksgiving's drawing near.
Now, when there comes a festal day—
A time for joyfulness—
It isn't hard to praise the Lord
For favors we possess.
And if the mortal mind could know
What blessings are imbued,
Thanksgiving "Day" would be prolonged
To constant gratitude!

Adaline Abbott
LADIES' AID PIE SALE

Law me, it's pie baking time,
I know I won't be worth a dime,
Because I eat 'til I ain't able
To get up from that temptin' table.
First an apple, then a plum,
Oh me! Oh my! my achin' tum.
Now it's pumpkin pie for sure;
Talk about delight that's pure!
Raspberry, blackberry all about—
Will that end up in a gout?
Rhubarb, peach and cherry tart,
"Nuff to cheer your troubled heart.
Law me, where's my good sense?
I know there's no recompense
For a sin that's great as mine,
When it comes pie baking time.

Michael Suvall
UNTITLED

Some poems scream their anguish like a flood
from poets filled with passion or with love.
Poetry is filled with bites of life,
either carefree days or minds too filled with strife.
But I don't believe there is a poem for death
whose colors range from black to black
in which each stanza grows from end to end.
Death is the poem of death.
And I have read that until death
"Waiting is the poem of waiting."
For how can I describe this nothing
with the colors of the sky
or these timeless days

like wings on which the falcon flies.
If I close my eyes I will not fall.
Even staring at the sun brings no flash
of yellow speed.
I look out the window at passing cars
and past the beach at ageless stars.
I do not feel that you'll be here soon
or even dream of futures in the moon.
I am a peach, deep in a cellar, filling jars.
For only waiting is truly the poem of waiting.

Connie L. Crawford
TIMES OF OUR LIFE

Are you so sure life is so long
That you can waste time on your
Fears that may never appear.
Life is odd you come into this
World maybe a foot and a half
With time as far as the stars.
When teens appear you begin to
Think time will never pass.
Then into the years of your prime
You begin to notice life is like
A race and every minute counts
At this pace.
With time on your heels and
Problems on your side.
Look ahead even when old and gray
Look at all the love you have shared
From the day you first appeared
To the day it is time to go.
And your love will forever
Remain and you are never
Forgotten.

Margaret Matsumoto
EXPLODE THE BEAUTY

Explode the Beauty
Expose the Talent
Divide the Wholeness
Multiply the Oneness
Subtract the Seeing
Explore the Blindness
Enjoy the Findings
Believe the Meanings
Avoid all Doubts
Find all Answers
Be a Person
And find Another

Gerald Fairchild
GIFT GIVING

If love goes unexpressed,
A gift becomes a debt
And leaves me unimpressed.
If love goes unexpressed,
I feel somewhat depressed;
I owe for what I get
If love goes unexpressed;
A gift becomes a debt!

L. Bruce Whitener
LISTEN

Please forgive me, but listen,
Don't think, just feel,
whatever,
For what I see happening all round,
Differences, yes, but also likenesses
in that which seems so strange.
It is true, change must occur,
This is known, but this is not all,
For all is not known,
All moves and all stands still,
Moving in matter and still in mind.
If our reason could be coupled
With our passion,
In a manner that is balanced and just,
We would see all and know all,
As is possible and always has been.

Alice Neander Barrigan
REFLECTIONS OF AGE

Age has so many different lives,
Let's sort them apart by fives.
From birth to five it is only "I".
Then on to ten they seem to fly.
Now after ten you are in your teens.
'Tis then you are living in your jeans.
The age of sweet sixteen is upon you now.
Life seems more interesting and lovelier somehow.

We won't stop at age of twenty
But go on and on, year after year, always
Finding and giving words of cheer.
In time you have come to your senior years
Quietly thankful for the life you have had.
Why care at all for what might have been?
'Cause you're thankful now for the age you are in.

Ms. Virgle Lea Tardivo
LOVE OR LOVER

Love is an illusion;
It doesn't exist.
We pretend for a while
to have what we missed.
The world is full of lovers;
that I can't conceal.
It's love that's an illusion—
Lovers are real.
The concept or the concrete—
which choice should we make?
Whatever makes us happy
is the course to take.

Adamos Adamides
THE MEDIUM IS THE MESSAGE

Its story is short
Its sound presence was replaced
by a long desk
with a sound short notice.
That was the divorce of
the painting and the piano.
Its sound comes from the basement
to embrace the lying woman of the painting.
It was bound and put in jail.
Its cage is in the zoo downstairs.

There are snakes, lions,
elephants and
a piano sailing in a wavy ocean.
This is to be a poem
A particle in a rectangular box
A piano in the closet.

Sharro'n Bernadette Edmonds

A THOUGHT

As I look out my window
At the breaking of dawn
Silhouettes of the trees and
lights beyond
Spread out as far as the eye can
see
Bring back memories that were
dear to me
Those memories, some sad,
some good, some bad, but
memories
It's an unusual feeling watching
the backgrounds set off by the
sky
Counting your blessings because
another day has gone by
Life an unusual subsidy that
isn't laid our for you to see
Just there for a while to
experience what could be
It's funny how the dawn can
make you see the creation of
life and what it should be
In a mind that's alive constantly
Taking ones' steps at a time
With the realization—It's
beautiful the maker of time

Kathi Simons

FOR A BEAUTIFUL LITTLE GIRL ANGELA LYNN

With beautiful eyes of blue,
and shiny hair of brown.
On your tiny little face,
shall there never be a frown.
Although you can't read this
poem yet, I already know that
you'll grow up very happy.
With a devoted Father,
and a loving Mother.
Beautiful parents, like you'll
never find in another.
They will always love you,
and stick by you forever.
You see, there is nothing like
having
a beautiful daughter like you
to love forever and ever!

Charlotte Faye

THE COLOR'S SCHEME

Life starts black and white
then turns grey before the light.
Blue is still a luminary
mystery
surrounds the wicked
unbeknown to me.
Red and green are always
there
much too simple—devoid of
care.
Black as night, like the hole
reflects no light, like his soul.
Fade too grey
and the jesters stray.
Purple screams through terror
and pain
we mindless colors don't have to
be sane.

Catherine M. Catranis

MIDNIGHT

Softly, floating, plays the
snowflake landing gently 'round
warm chimneys, melting on
warm windowsills spilling
flickered light of fires.
Rooms now darkened, allow
freedom for closet dreams, now
soaring into the air of a cloudy
night.
Whispers, softly from the
branches, harmonized by fluting
brooks, interrupted by
cacophony of a screech owl
looking in.
Ever more the ambers beckon,
emerging•now, born from the
wood but catching only late
night thought.
How the night slips in on
darkness. What for, the stars
all to make? From whence come
our beginnings? God reveals in
the last hour.

Lenore Settlemire

GOD'S MIRROR

Am I God's mirror day by day
As I walk the Christian way
Do I reflect him as I should
To those who know Him not;
but would
Magnify and praise His name
If I had thought to do the
same?
Does His reflection shown
through me

Become distorted curiously
That men may fail to
comprehend?
If so Lord help me to amend
My wavering ways of impure
glass
For the pure and plated
silvered class.
If those while passing peer at
me
May I reflect Him humbly.

Linda D. Mason

TO LEAVE THEM

If I were to leave them, now,
I would feel. . . . .deserter.
If I were to leave, and there,
find love;
Would only hurt her.
If I were to find real peace,
and happiness were mine,
I'd feel a sense of losing,
for a time.
If I were to name the day.
If I said. . . . .tomorrow.
If I were to leave, and not look
back;
Would bring more sorrow.
If I were to make good, all the
vows I've made today,
I'd feel a sense of losing,
while away.
If I were to make amends,
If they would. . . . . forgive me.
If I were to leave, and for sure,
know
I left them lonely.
If I were to give them back, the
love they gladly gave,
I'd feel a sense of winning, and
I'd stay.

Edward H. Kalberer

APOSTROPHIC PRAISE FOR MARUS

there was a young wom'n
who lived with you know wh'm
(a man o' joy: make boom, boom,
not gloom, gloom)
she hosted so many chil'n
'cause she was lov'n
and know'n what to do wit'm
like read'n 'n' draw'n
music mak'n also wit'm
see th'm like sunflowers their
faces op'n 'n' turn
to the mother-sun
an' return hour after howers
ad gloriam, non nauseam,
yes ad gloriam

Elaine Crecraft McDunn

PAPER COMPANION

A companion isn't always there
in close harmony—
Sometimes he reaches out to
you from the printed words
you see.
He tells you of his problems and
joys, then asks how you are
doing and
you somehow feel closer to him
than you ever did before.
A letter seems so common and
the gesture goes unacclaimed,
but the effect
it has on your life truly should
be proclaimed.
Yes, letters are companions that
can do a lot of things, like
bringing joy
to uplift a heart and sympathy
for a sorrowing life that seems
to have fallen apart.
Letters are very special—with
this you might disagree—but
without
these paper companions how
cold this world would be.

Nancy M. Collett

THESE FEW THINGS

If we are not meant to pass
through this life as one,
then let me wish for you these
few things.
A silver chain of summer rain.
January diamonds and a friendly
fire to warm your hands.
A shower of amber leaves tossed
by October's icy breath.
Slender daffodils lifting faces
to a saffron sun.
One true friend to share
triumph, a tear, and a beer.
A pair of adoring eyes that see
only the August man you
really are.
Soft arms in which to place your
heart, knowing it won't be
bruised or broken by
carelessness or indifference.
One lifetime of days that dawn
pink and full of promise, and
end
in sapphire stillness as eager
limbs entwine and love flows
freely
like a kite across a March sky.

Lori J. Hamel

DISINTEGRATION: COMPLETE?

shuddering searched I the sky
and found nothing
trembling searched I the terrain
and found something unsure
frightened searched I my mind
and found a closed door
nothing more
crying I laughed at the sky
which held nothing
yearning sought I the knowledge
of the unsure terrain
frantically searched I the key
to unlock the door of my
mind
still blind
quietly and slowly I
contemplated
that which closed me in
my mind, it traveled many
directions
never to find an end
desperately I grabbed at the
pieces
tried to put them together
like a feather
the wind
blew away. . .

Ms. Barbara Czartoryjski

LOVE LONG DISTANCE

Just the mention of his name
Made my heart chant its own
bewitching tune
We touched through letters
Revealing cherished treasures
of ourselves
I saw smiles in his hellos
His every word tickled my
senses
And warmed me inside
The distance between us
stretched in miles
Not in mind
For I felt closer to him
Than a petal on a rose
As fresh as the first wind
Each letter came to me
And I consumed it all
Like thirsty soil drinks up
long awaited rainfall.

Alexander MacDougall

IMMORTALITY

Like falling petals
The years drift down
And settle softly
On the fertile ground.
But heavenward, heavenward
The fragrance flies,
The immortal spirit
In immortal skies.

Charles Nelson Noble

NORTH-COUNTRY-LONGING

I know once more I'd like to go.
And hear the water 'neath the
snow
A clean and fresh and pretty
sound
Of ripples swirling round and

round.
It seems so very far away—
I'm lonesome for my hills today;
For dry clear cold that grips me through,
Bright stars in sky—of—midnight blue,
Oh—some day soon, back I must go—
To water—running 'neath the snow.

Phiona Helton Turner

DESIRE FOR LIFE

Man's love is like a dove's white wings,
Spreading gently to the seasons,
Surveying where to make his mark.
To find each day a renewed joy,
A desire for life—for loving,
A special reason.
'Ere time blurs his vast vision dark.

Albert N. Tallarigo

DISILLUSION OF LOVE

Sometimes I escape from the person within me
and flee to some lost-in-time year
With its crystalline mornings
and soft-scented gardens
lost laughter, lost passion, lost tear.
I stroll down the path where the memory started
and listen for old sounds anew.
Somehow when it happened the beauty escaped me
my mind never dwelt but on you.
We lived in the shadow of our own emotion
my thoughts never wavered from thee
What storm or what problem could temper my spirit
as long as I had you with me.
The love of my youth was so caring and giving
a place for a heart to reside
But the heart has no space when the mind and present
return to the person inside.

Susan D. Tausch

TEAR STAINS ON MY FEATHER DOWN

I look for sleep to soothe my soul
And take the emptiness from my breast.
My sorrow wept on feather down
Behind closed doors I feel my pain.
So hollow is this masquarade
Of doubles playing solitaire.
When lovers long not memories
But familiar soft sweet flesh.
So sad it seems, the time stands still
The words don't seem to speak the fears.
And masks are worn to hide the pain
Tear stains on my feather down.

Sister Madonna Schneider, C.P.P.S.

GRATITUDE

The grandeurs of this universe
Are joys o'er which to ponder.
Each day God sends his miracles
That fill one's mind with wonder.
The sun's warm rays, the air we breathe
Are gifts we take for granted.,
As well as rain that aids the growth
Of seeds that man has planted.
While through our senses we perceive
All nature in its splendor,
How seldom do we sing God's praise
And to him homage render!
The many favors we receive
Too oft we fail to treasure
Until we've been deprived of them
In great or lesser measure.

Norma Rockwell Preisler

RIDING ON A FROSTY MORNING

Beautiful morning all covered with white,
The trees and the bushes glitter just right.
The sun makes the jewels
Jack Frost did the rest
Painting the tree tops all night with his breath—
Putting twinkles and glitter over them all
'Till they look like ladies dressed for a ball.
Slow now, my pretty one, look while we may,
Oats in your manger can wait all the day—
While frost on the treetops goes quickly away.

Christine Raabe-Lyans

MY SHADOW

My shadow is a part of me,
he walks along the walls.
But quickly vanishes from my side,
in the presence of dark halls.
My shadows' afraid of dark places,
he clings to me ever so tight.
Revealing himself in front of the sun,
fading away at the end of daylight.
In summertime, when the days are hot
we stretch out upon the lawn.
But in the eve, when dusk appears
my friend will soon be gone.
I slowly walk back to my room,
exhausted as one can be.
As I turn out the light so I may sleep,
my friend is no longer with me.
Somehow, it's often bothersome,
it's something I can't see,
For when we both are in the wrong,
the blame all goes on me!
I often wonder where he hides,
so others will not see.
And who he's with when it is dark,
if he is not with me.
Why is he always to and fro,
and popping in and out?
What purpose does he serve on earth?
What is he all about?
I'll never fully understand,
if he's my image or my ghost.
I'm always in confusion
about that one, whos' with me most.

Carol B. Welborn

GOD CANCELLED: GONG SHOW RERUNS SCHEDULED

Once the highest point
to be seen
in the towns and hamlets
freckling the scrubbed prairie states
of the midwest
were the church steeples,
and crosses,
atop the wooden Protestant buildings
and the more elaborate granite Catholic edifices.

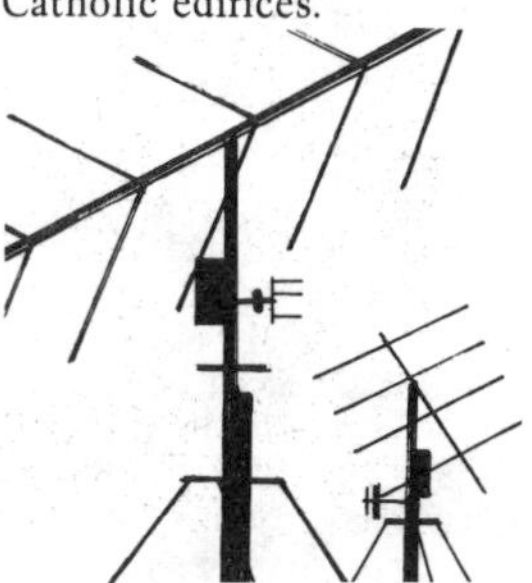

Now, even the meekest abode
in the smallest patchwork village
boasts a television crucifix stretching
vertically into the heavens,
a straining aerial searching for
astral reception,
aspiring to control the channels of the stars
with revolving dials;
derricks of diffused
banality.

David A. Teany

SECOND CHANCE

A weeping wretch, I knelt to you,
My life you grasp that day,
And though it could have ended there,
You let me walk away.
Oh, on that day a death occurred,
A blind man filled with hate.
And in his place new life emerged,
Knowing well its fate.
I used to watch as life went by,
Withdrawn in fear and rage.
Insensibly I lived within,
My private mental cage.
But since our meeting, things have changed,
You taught me how to live.
I learned to touch, to sense, to feel,
And of myself to give.
The callous thoughts which filled my mind,
Seem now, to me, unreal,
And things I took for granted once,
My mind has learned to feel.
I've felt the sunrise warm my face,
The joy of days first light.
I've felt the gentle blowing breeze,
On peaceful summer nights.
I've felt the warmth of my sons love,
And hugged their tears away,
And cherished moments with my wife,
A love that grows each day.
I surely could have never known,
The warmth this heart could bear.
You taught me well that night, old friend,
I'm thankful you were there.
I live life to its fullest now,
Caressing each new dawn.
So take me when you must, old friend,
Your painful sting is gone.

Judith Susan Marx

THE FREEING OF MY FATHER

I shall never want anything again
Knowing I will not return
To that black, crack—
Hole in the wall.
Prepare me for eternity
I am unbound by blaspheme
I evade illumination
In which this illusion
Is keeping me
With propensity of fact
And belief in the Torah
I am consumated—
The death of my father
Is now understood
And he is being freed;
To surmount

Dora T. Smith

SUNSET

The glory of the sunset—
Yellow deepens into gold,
Pink becomes a crimson fold.
Blue and the aqua form a back drop
As the crimson turns to azure
And dark sword clouds with a bold
Thrust turn the glory
Into night, dark, lonely cold.

Dorothy Allen

DANCE OF THE INDIAN SPIRITS

When the droning evening raga
Fell upon their ears,
The mournful ancient saga
Regendered forgotten years,
Remembrances of pain and grief,
Recalled bitter ecstasies of love,
Birth and death of belief
In baubles of gardens above.
Fleshy fingers plucked the strings
Of the sitar, and fleshy mouths
Changed the tale that spiritless, brings
Renewed passions, sins, and renewed doubts.
The livid hues sparkled and shone
About broken beviaries of death-masks,
And hurried from beneath the moon
Gyrated, sinking Lethe-wards, their eternal tasks
Possessed by a passion, imprisoned
In half-numbed bodies, numberless,
Flailing their arms with a fury,

envisioned,
Fading amid tongues of flame,
respiteless.
Unconsumed, the spinning
spirits danced,
Wracked by euphoric pain
In the eternal flame, until,
entranced,
Their sickened eyes took sight
again.
****
The dance and the tambura
drone
Was ALL, for an eternal
moment,
Eternal, but passing, then gone,
Like a long modal chant,
transcient. . .

Ena M. Titus
CHISELS FOR CARVING CHARACTER
This story is about the chisels
Which carve characters in flesh
and blood.
The first chisel is faith to cure
the miserable,
It chips away the old model of
self like a flood.
The next the chisel of hope.
Hope creates the character that
is better,
For old or young there is good in
both
The communication is sent by a
letter.
The chisel of tribulation which
is called trial,
The use of this chisel is often
very painful.
Even the model, Jesus Christ
was put on file,
And his followers may expect
the same willful.
The chisel of love which is shed
in our hearts,
God commendeth it to shine
forth before eyes.
It has advantage in quality,
greatest in quantity
And not bard.
This is the work of Chisel of
Love in our lives.

Luella Allen
BEYOND THE VEIL
As the fog rolled in,
blanketing everything with
its cold, damp mist,
it seemed that earth
and all that remained was—
nothingness!
The fog horn, calling
in from the sea,
transported me into
a formless void
of thick, obscuring,
vaporized mist,
and all around me was—
emptiness!
Standing transfixed,
shorn of any semblance of
reality,
I slowly became aware of
the sun's gentle warmth
breaking through the fog's
density,
melting the mist and revealing
nature in all her finery.
The emptiness was gone
and in its place—fulfillment!

Helen Strey
JESUS RANG THE DOOR BELL
Jesus Rang the Door Bell
What a celebration! Christmas!
The festivities were about to
begin!
Jesus rang the door bell—
But, no one let Him in—
He approached another house,
and
Through the window, saw
Santa's grin,
Jesus rang the door bell—
But—no one let Him in—.
It was His Birthday, He saw the
table set,
Surely His plate was within!
Jesus rang the door bell—
But—no one let Him in—.
And now He saw a tinseled tree,
gifts below!
A little toy soldier made of
tin—
Jesus range the door bell,
But—no one let Him in—.
It's Christmas at your house!
With your many friends and
Kin!
JESUS IS RINGING THE DOOR
BELL!
ARE YOU GOING TO LET
HIM IN??????

Andrew R. Bennett
GOLDEN ROD
The August entry falls far short,
Far below the pagantry of spring.
Its blossoms are thin for the
colder air,
And its slender stalks hold up
the heart of summer.
The expiring suggestions and
movements of ripeness,
Are sacrificed to the ever
heavier glistening dews.
But the somber altars burn with
beautiful amber flames,
Burn the green envious heart of
the sacred golden rod.

Carol Ann Spry
BY YOUR HAND
Take my hand.
Guide me along the path.
Show me the greenness; point
out the wildlife.
Help me through the stream and
up the hill.
Sing happy songs to me as we
walk along.
Whisper in my ear as you hold
me close.
Pause and listen.
Stillness.
A fatal calm broken by a
bullet. . . .
Release my hand.
Lay me down beside the path
Amidst the greenness and the
wildlife,
Overlooking the stream from
the top of the hill.
I cannot hear your songs;
I no longer feel your arms
around me.
But I watch as you lay down
your gun.

Maxine F. Fortman
NUBIA
In open window
Nubia, svelt, black, witch rests
Basking in full sun.
Suddenly waking
Streaking to her feeding tray
Eats ravenously.
Returns to window
Surveys back yard area
All is well, she naps.

Charlotte Palmer Haaker
HOSPITAL CURE
As you lay in the bed
Dont forget the T.V. is above
your head
Forget about your problems
today
Because youll get well in a
wonderful way
No more pain for you to feel
Because the pain is wrapped
and ready to sealed
God Bless you on this day
May God Bless you in every
way!!!!!!!!!!!

Joanna S. Murphy
REFLECTIONS FROM A SHUT-IN
Not sick enough for a nursing
home,
Not well enough to live alone.
We need a home—We cannot
roam—
With deepest gratitude we share
your home.
We thank thee, Lord, for these
kind-hearted folks
Even though they scoff at our
jokes.
Arthritis has us in its clutch.
Many of us depend on a crutch.
Our bones are weary—Our eyes
grow dim—
Forgive us is we drop a pin.
We do not ask for very much—
A little compassion, a loving
touch.
We say "please" and "thank you"
And "God bless you" when you
sneeze,
We pay our way and try hard to
please.
We might be nervous and spill
our coffee—
Please wipe it up—You know
that we're sorry.
We have lived and loved
through hope and despair—
With a will to survive because
someone cared.
Through the years we have
learned a lot
With many experiences that
cannot be bought.
Would it be so hard just to
share a thought?
Sometimes we feel that we're
in the way.
Afraid to speak what we'd like
to say,
But we pray to God to keep you
well
For a long and wonderful,
blessed life.
Please forgive us for dropping
that knife.

Linda Louise Leighton
UNTITLED
To laugh is to risk appearing
the fool.
To weep is to risk appearing
sentimental.
To reach out for another is to
risk involvement.
To expose feelings is to risk
exposing your true self.
To place your ideas, your
dreams before the crowd is to
risk their loss.
To love is to risk not being
loved in return.
To live is to risk dying.
To hope is to risk despair.
To try is to risk failure.
But risks must be taken
because the greatest hazard
In life is to risk nothing. The
person who risks nothing,
does nothing, has nothing, is
nothing. He may avoid
suffering and sorrow, but he
simply cannot learn, change,
grow, love. . . .live.
Chained by his certitudes, he is
a slave, he has forfeited
freedom.
Only a person who risks is free!

Thomas E. Heusler
CRIES
Cry a tear
For the love, unanswered
The book, unread
The step, untrod
The music, unheard
The wine, unsipped
The tree, unrooted
The question, unsolved
The hand, untouched
The loneliness, unsoothed
The pain, unceased
The fear, unstilled
The mind, unwholed
The knife, unsheathed!
Cry a tear, the Perfect Tear.

James A. Stacy
WHERE DID YOU GO?
The light has gone from my life
you took my heart when you
left, and now the pain as
sharp
as a knife cuts deep within my
hollowed breast.
Why did you leave when I loved
you so?
You left without warning
darling, where did you go?
The days have grown cold
and the nights even worse,
for your love, my soul I would
have sold.
Your hair of gold, and lips of
wine
have haunted my dreams
through the passage of time.
Why did you leave when I loved
you so?
You left without warning
darling where did you go?
The sun never shines since
you've gone away
I pray that darkness will remain,
but the heartache begins at the
first light of day.
Everything stay's the same.
Why did you leave when I loved
you so?
You left without warning
darling where did you go?

Where did you go, darling where
did you go?

Julie Ann Full

THE FINAL SEASON

If I could be a season,
Spring is what I'd be;
I'd revitalize my topsoil
With fresh immortality.
But my life has become the
winter,
Signaled by inevitable frost;
Stealing, first, my foliage
Until, last, my limbs are lost.

A. Wm. Kukitz

CRAFT'S TALE

The craft's tale is you
it wallows inside
Spirit occurs in the hands
delicate
motion
Inner voices ring
Purpose is movement
Time is flow
Happiness is sadness
The life your own. . .

Por Melody Durand, Para Mi Amor

TUS OJOS

Me encantan los ojos grandes,
aque'llos grandes y hermosos,
pardos o azules.
Los noto en la distancia,
como luz brillante sobre el agua
de noche.
Como en un espejo miro,
esos ojos que al reflejarse
me atraviesan,
llevando sentimientos propios,
sinceros
que *conocen* los mi'os.
Veo tus ojos por doquier,
cerca y lejos y de polo a polo,
ilumina siempre su luz mi
sendero de noche,
Y con calor resplandece como
el sol de di'a.
Miro esos ojos,,
grandes, hermosos y pardos,
cuya mirada me penetra con
amor;
al cual me entrego y
correspondo.
Amo tus hermosos ojos
que nunca acaban de
asombrarme.
Pero por encima de todo te amo
a ti,
que eres mi vida.

Linda MacDonald

OF VISION

The camera evokes the image
that trespasses time;
the depth, the scope, the tone
seen in ground glass.
A precious sense of clarity
in the light of dark,
the singled instant caught
by the eye and the finger,
with every nerve seeking
the aesthetic breath
of vision.

Dorothy Louise Hall

LOVE

Magic word love
Here it is now
Whisper in ears
Shouted from there
Magic word love
Spell it love
Woven in patterns
Love, Love, Love
Shake it, embrace it
Romance and sugar frost it
Turns you on
Makes your world go round
Love magic love

Julia Kay Wilder

REFLECTIONS IN BLUE

In your blue eyes, I'm sure I see,
The hurt and loneliness that
used to be.
I see the hope and happiness
there,
That I hope are ours to share.
Then I look again. . .and realize,
The things I see, are reflections
of my own eyes.

Hattie Stahlberg

LONELY BOY

Lonely Boy,
ganky and strange.
Feet that trip,
hands too big.
Walking alone
tormenting thoughts
Feeling quiet stares
Girls point and giggle—
He's needing a friend.
Lonely Boy,
please don't worry.
Things will change.

Frederick J. Wonnacott

THE ONE I LOVE

The silver moon shone on the
sea
And shed its' soft light over
me.
The ripples gently lapped the
shore
And disappeared for evermore.
There was only I who watched
alone
But once before the moon had
shone;
Years ago it seemed to me,
When the two of us had
watched the sea.
But now she's gone, gone out to
sea
And is forever gone from me.
The sea has claimed her for its'
own
To never another port she'll
roam.
She skimmed the sea like a
racing gull
And sliced each wave with
her sleek thin bull.
Oh! I love her yet and for her I
yearn
E'en though I know she can't
return.

Joe Papkin

ODE TO PENELOPE

Tho' Mighty Zeus may raise hue
and cry for my name,
Tho' Cunning Hades may
conspire for my earthly
remains,
They clamor for naught; all I
can
offer them is my shell.
For I have bared my bosom to
thee and my soul as well.

David A. Draves

IMMATURITIES FOR ME

Some say the older you get the
wiser.
Some say that maturity comes
with age.
Some say life is its fullest at
sixty.
Now, if you believe this, listen
up
I've some enlightening news.
Remember when you were small
and young
how Christmas joy started in
November and
went straight on through to
Christmas?
No, you say, well that's because
there's
magic that was lost when you
grew up and
thought to be adult you had to
be a
no fun straight thinking person.
Well, I have pity for you
because life
is only its fullest when you
experience
the first snow of winter, the joy
of
Christmas day, the impatience
of Christmas eve with no
sleep.
Now you say, how do I get all
this back.
Well, first go out and build a
snowman.
Second, go roller skating down
Main Street.
Now if these things seem
childish and immature
turn around because the third is
the most
childish, most immature, most
ridiculous of all.
Are you ready, go tell your
mother, father,
sister and brother you love
them.

Janelle Wissler

EYES CAN'T HIDE

Through narrowed eyes
the question slides
How hard to hide
the pain inside!
Sensing the sting,
down, his glance swings
Pausing on her rings—
memories cling.
And so he strives
to not arrive
at conclusions,
in him, alive.
Finally sighing,
suddenly crying
at last, the lying
is over.

Roger L. Carson

MY CHRISTMAS TREE

Tonight I'll decorate my
Favorite Christmas tree—
The one I left standing
In a corner of my memory;
I'll wipe away the dust
From bulbs of red and blue,
And weep tender tears
Should I break one or two;
Once again I'll climb
Up high on my old chair,
And reach way, way up
To leave an icicle there;
I'll hang candy canes
All 'round the bough,
Then slip behind the tree
And eat eight somehow;
I'll see happy faces
I haven't seen for awhile,
And hear little laughter
Through a childhood smile;
Past Christmas's finally fade,
But I will take my tree,
And carefully store it
In a corner of my memory.

Laurie A. Bunch

HEARTS

Hearts may hide
But they never lie.
They beat
Strong and steady.
Though they may
Stagger and stray
Still the beat is true.
Marching on into hell
Or some abused piece of heaven
(if there is a difference).

H. Cromwell Smith

TREE IN WINTER

Empty arms return from sky
probing,

Holding in your gnarled hands
The vacuum of past summer
glory.
Remembering trembling as
winter winds
Howl around your dormant
trunk.
Your shadow soul has shrunk
Yet, I sense a defiance
Leaping from your roots
That bind you to our earth.
Sleeping arteries stretching
From your uncapped head,
Awaiting the beckoning of
Spring.
To me, oh tree,
You are not empty and forlorn,
You are my reflection
Many times reborn.
I also see the Truth of you
Invisible to the physical eyes
Yet bared to all-seeing eye of
me,
As you must also see
From your inner soul
All that life does hold,
And parades in charades
Beneath your naked arms,
Stretching out bold.
Yes, tree, flail your arms,
They are not empty.
Rather they are hardened with
All the life you hold,
Carrying the veins and arteries
Stretching from your roots
And holding the strong,
expectant
Life.
As do my veins and arteries
Sustain me
During the winter of my strife.
Indeed, stalwart, defiant tree,
You echo
The depth of the soul of me.

Bradley E. Thorne

MY WIFE

Oh Lord, how can I deal with
hurt inside?
The loneliness and love that
comes out

and will not hide.
I miss my lady, my love, my wife.
She is that which keeps me going, my
mainstream in life.
She can lift me up with one strict push
and propel me so high.
"Why is it I cannot be with her, and lay
my head to cry?"
I would say, "What a beautiful lady, my
love, my wife."
"How is it I am so blessed lady, to have
you in my life?"
Keep us together Lord, when we are miles
apart.
Let us go together and let it be like it
was at the beginning and the start.
Don't ever let us drift or go our lonely
separate ways.
Help us spend our time united, with love and happiness in all our heavenly days.

Lauren M. DuChemin

MEMORIES

(To my sister Meg Brennan)

From baby bottles and walking shoes
To toys and dolls and such
From schools and rules and growing up
To giving, oh so much!
From cute to pretty to beautiful
You grew and warmed each heart
To almost grown, now gone away
You died and had to part
Now memories and pictures
Are all we have to hold
To treasure for forever
Handled as if gold
And knowing that you can't come back,
No matter how we try
We all have loved so deeply that
It's so hard to say goodbye!

Cheryl A. Meyers

QUESTION

I'm confused and befuddled
Lord, how could he do it?
Our marriage was cuddled in love
And he blew it!

Mary Jennison McAuliffe

MOTHER'S GEOGRAPHICAL REVEILLE (To High School Senior)

Europe, Asia, Jack?
Denmark my word!
I'm gonna get the
Switzerland there's
Norway out of it.
Germany crickets!
Every morning I *Russia*
round trying to get
Europe. Yesterday *Iran*
up and down the hall
India room and there
you *Laos* leap. Again,
today, I called *Samoa,*
but nothing happens!
Kenya please get a *Wake?*
Don't ask if you
Malaya any longer—
If you don't get up now
I'll make you eat
cooked *Syria.*
When *Uruguay*
to college, *Bolivia*
gonna have a rough
time. *Alaska* ya
France if I'm not
right. Watcha wanna
do *Spain* all your
time in bed? Don't ya
get *Hungary*—and
don't ya tire of
my *Wales?*
I still have ta
Pakastan wich
and a *Zanzibar* for
your lunch. Can't
ya *Singapore* me?
It's *Chile* so
hurry and slip into
your *Paraguay*
trousers.
Hawaii doin,
Europe, Asia, Jack?
I'm *Iraq!*

Larry R. Tallent

DUSTIN

Time was moving like a gentle breeze
A soft rain was falling.
Peace and serenity filled the air
The little boy kept calling.
You introduced me to your total devotion
God's creation of your loving.
Words cannot express my emotions
As the little boy kept calling.
I played, I enjoyed, I was deeply moved
My heart was silently reaching.
The quiet stillness was only broken
By the little boy that kept calling.
Play with me. Play with me.
Please.

Clayton A. Varga

EUTHANASIA

"Could I have another blanket?"
The skeletal figure gasped,
"I'm cold."
A contorted, agonizing corpse; rotting in pain.
Waiting for the cancer
to crush the last ounce of life.
The nurse brought the hollow face another blanket.
Prolonging pain, not life
I felt like a steel-eyed Nazi
torturing a starving bald-headed Jew,
due to be gassed the next day.
I injected an overdose of morphine.
Her pain stopped shortly.
Now she could be warm.

Gary L. Barber

THE PASSING OF A CITIZEN

Don't suppose you knew old Phin,
A finer feller's never been.
He never had a lot to say,
He never hurt no one that way.
He jest kept quiet and did his job,
Kept hisself nice—he warn't no slob.
He'd smile at folks and tip his hat,
He'd pet your dog or scratch your cat.
He come down with a bug sometime last week,
Finished him quick, said old Doc Zeke.
There warn't one thing that could be done
To keep Phin here with everyone.
The town don't know jest what to do,
All the folks is in a stew.
Not 'cause Phin has met his Maker,
It's 'cause old Phin's the undertaker!

Ilse Schottelius

ROCKING HORSE

Come
Rock the horse
Fill the stirrup-cup
Sleep heavenly
Tomorrow is obscure.
Come
Hum a lullaby
Play the oud
Nap a while
Nurture song and love.
come
Light the candle
Enjoy the labor
Harness together
Tomorrow is in sight.
Come
Awake to pray
Greet the angels
Reap the cord
Rejoice and straddle.
Come
Feast in trinity
Ring the bells
Rock the cradle
Tomorrow is bright.
Come
Strap the infant
Rock the horse
Sing the song. . .
Grace To Messiah!

Theodore A. Groeneveld Jr.

PHYSIOLOGY OF GRASSHOPPER

What is a Grasshopper? What will he be?
The Grasshopper is an eccentric person, with whom you can dare to be "You."
Your soul can be naked with him,
your heart can open its doors, and
your dreams can flow free with him.
You can always say what you think and feel. You may breathe freely— he tries to understand. He's an excellent listener.
You need not be too careful with him: You can—abuse him,
neglect him,
possess him,
tolerate him—
he tries to like you.
You can—cry with him,
laugh with him,
drink with him,
sin with him, and
pray with him.
Through it all he sees, knows, understands, and loves "You."
He's your friend and like a vintage wine, will mellow and become more valuable with age.

Mark T. Roberts

FADING KNOWLEDGE

The days drag on forever,
you sit there alone and blue,
you'll stay in this rest home,
until your days are through.
It seems like you're forgotten.
No one comes your way.
Where are your loved ones
and the friends of yesterday?
Your days are filled with sadness,
so you ask the Lord in prayer;
please send me a visitor,
I have so much to share.
It's a shame all the knowledge,
you've gathered throughout the years,
lays trapped in your head,
behind your lonely tears.
Most of your wisdom,
will be buried along with you.
It wouldn't be this way,
if there was someone to tell it to.
Think of the hardships
and the pain that we could save,
if we learned from our elders,
before they're in their grave.
Everyone would benefit
by learning things this way.
They could teach us many things
and we'd brighten up their day.
Further down the road,
after distant years erase,
they'll be dead and gone,
and we'll be in their place.

Dorothy Newton Crockett

HOW DID YOU USE TODAY

I wonder how you value time
that God has given you,
Did you awake with change of heart—
and wondering what to do?
Pray and then—
forgive a friend
or left it all for later,
"He was right"
"She was wrong"
Were you the sad debator?
A Kind word to—
the neighbor who—
could all but understand,
Feed the birds—
there-in-the park?
Run barefoot through the sand?
Weed the garden?
Cut the lawn?
Bake a pie or two?

Visit sick ones
little and big ones
Watch a sky of blue?
Not his
Hers
Nor mine
Tis true,
Your time belongs to you,
Yet—
What if God—
appeared to say—
'How did you use today'—?

Maury Clark
IT'S OVER
Always I knew that it could not last,
Gathering clouds and the snowflakes flying.
Now it is part of the golden past,
Darkening skies, and the night wind sighing.
It is but cowardice to pretend,
Cover with ashes our love's cold crater.
Always I've known that it had to end
Sooner or later.
Always I knew it would come like this
Pattering rain, and the grasses springing.
Gone are the raptures that once we knew,
Now you are finding a new joy greater,
Well, I'll be doing the same thing too
Sooner or later.

Ruth Johnson
A PROTEST
I think you want a genie in a jar,
No real live woman cluttering up your life.
Your dreams, of romance coming from afar,
Include no place for weak and human wife.
To have me when you want me is your aim,
To minister to needs you must have met.
To go, this labor done, from whence I came
Is my next move; and you, you just forget.
Well weak and human, Sir, is all I am
And 'though I'm good, I also have some bad.
To get the one you'll take the two, by damn,
Since being split apart would drive me mad.
I make this protest angrily, it's true,
I'm whole for me, not half alive for you.

Candace Katnich
MEMORIES
I could see the tears in her big blue eyes,
For that was the day that stopped her puppies cries.
He chewed pencils and letters he ripped,
And when he left toys around over them she tripped.
He tore up socks and slipper holes were deep,
But those weren't the things she wanted to keep.
For the life of this puppy was so important to her,
Now all she remembers him by is a cute ball of fur.
So the puppy was gone and on earth they were apart,
But the little ball of fur never left her heart.

Mrs. Elna S. Halme
WHEELS
Our son was a smart little tyke,
We knew as he rode his three wheel trike.
His nursery school was such great fun,
He learned to associate with everyone.
Our son was a smart little guy,
We knew as he rode his two wheeler by.
His elementary school grades were fine,
In reading and mathematics he did shine.
Our son had a superior noggin,
We knew as he drove our Volkswagen.
His high school studies were really tough,
But his brains recorded all that stuff.
We knew when he left for college,
He would graduate with great knowledge,
Then work and save money of course,
To purchase his dream—an elegant Porsche.

D. H. Rubalcaba
MY FRIEND
Although you were away
For just a day,
The world stood still
As if to say,
That going thru this mind
That no one knows,
And so perplexed
that it never shows.
Abiding within with no relief,
The sheltered excitement
Beyond belief.
The heart grew fonder as it yearned,
Anticipating the moment of
Your return. . . . .

Monica B. Carter
FOR JIM
I awake and my thoughts are of you
Filling my days with promise and joy
As they fill my nights with dreams of love.

John E. Sanks
I FOUND TRUE LOVE
Oh! it was luck for me that I met her
It was fate that had taken its toll,
I could see in her face and her green eyes
That she loved me though nothing was told.
Yes, I looked and I looked at her beauty
I got so weak very little I could say,
All I wanted to do was hold her tightly
And hear her say "I love you darling, its OK".
Well it happened, a real true love affair started,
She was so bold, yes she loved me every day;
Then she told me over and over how she wanted me
And then she said I hope our love won't fade away.
One night she said there is a secret I must tell you,
She said I love you much too much and then she cried;
She said, "darling, I am married will you take me?"
I could never forget our happiness if I tried.

Opha Hays Kinser
TO A BUMBLEBEE
Um - um - bumblebee
You are so little,

Compared to me.
I like your colors,
Black and yellow.
But I'll stay
Away from you,
Old fellow!

Amy Cecile
CHILD OF YOURS
I cannot see through your spoken praise.
When you were a child,
could you understand what your mother said?
Could you believe her reasoning?
Would you see through her lies?
The children of tomorrow will come from my womb.
If I cannot understand, how will I be able to teach them?
Now I have the energy, now I hold the time.
Why do you hear, yet not listen?
I cannot find my words within a democracy
built for all yet owned by some.
We all speak of peace,
our definitions are not the same.
My peace is here amongst people and their souls.
Your peace is being built,
built of a stronger defense.
Made of warheads, rifles
and lives.
My father taught me to think for myself,
to speak of beliefs I've held,
to build the world for my future.
Yet, you do not allow it.
My child will not see half of the beauties I have seen.
My grandchild may never even be.
Are you not the child of your fathers future?
Well, I am the child of yours.

Margaret Bland Sewell
THOUGH THE OLD HOUSE MUST FALL
Let the bulldozer come when it must
Like an ancient animal
Of primeval land
That shakes the earth
It walks upon,
Strips it of green and leaves it bare.
Let it come, shattering our home to dust.
Let it come and be gone,
Though the old house must fall.
Yet it will stand—
Fires on its hearth,
Candles lit,
Children's laughter in the air—
For memory is of stronger stuff
than brick or stone.

Shirley Hudgin-Goings
REMEMBERING
I remember your smile,
your touch,
your voice,
your love,
the good times, and
the bad times.
I remember you.
You are gone, but
the memories
you have left me with
make all of my tomorrows
worth while, for
you will remain
in my thoughts
forever, and
my future
will be richer
remembering. . . .
what has been.

Rody L. Rodgers
TO HEAR BIRDS SING
The angels came one winter's night
and took my love, and I lost sight
of happiness that life can bring
oh how I yearn to hear birds sing
their songs of joy, and fill my heart
so once again my life can start.

Kile McConnell
YOU. . .THE ILLUSTRATOR
The lush forest green, lacquered
Emerald—like 'neathe eve's mist and steam,
Silently and serenely slips
Behind the obscure eclipse
Of nature's camouflage. . .
While the birth of a new day
Brilliantly dazzles an emblazoned
Desert,

The barren garden blossoms
Into an animated forest
Of fresh flowers and cacti. . .
Amidst a society of
Unadorned, lifeless dwellings
And streets,
Arises a monumental,
Castle—like fantasy, casting
A cryptic veil of awe. . .
These still—life scenes, etched
In your intimate grand style
Are your favors to friends
And all of mankind.
You, the illustrious illustrator;
You, the consummate creator;
You, the engravor of life force!
You, my friend. . .
Are the bloodstream of our being,
And the intellect of my pen and ink.

Richard M. Johnson
SUICIDE
Dancing across the water in a simulated storm,
She holds in her eyes the wonder and the hate for just being born.
The circling lights are closer now, and she's sure she's on her way.
But it doesn't make a difference, for, the price must still be paid.
She cries in the night for loved ones she lost so long ago.
She cries in the night for no-one. Her tears, only the stars will know.
She walks to the bank of the river to look for answers in the flow,
But the answers don't come easy when reflections refuse to show.

Letters from old lovers, burned or thrown away.
No-one worth remembering;
All of her heros have gone stray.

And all that is left are the daydreams, but even they have taken to the night
Like the footsteps that lead to the water until death in the cold twilight.

Yolanda De Jong
UNTITLED
There are bitches with riches
And extravagant wishes,
And beggars who take all they can.
But lost from view
There are still a few,
When asked, walk one mile,
walk two with a smile.

John M. Metz
MY THOUGHTS
I know at this hour
you're asleep,
completely unaware of my
thoughts for you;
content in your slumbering
world of sleep.
Is it wrong or cruel,
being awake at his hour,
without your thoughts
with mine?
Good night, my darling,
I love you.

Donna Jean Merrill
LOVE'S EPHEMERAL JOURNEY
Watching dawn break on the morning of our love,
We strolled along the shore chatting of
Trivial nonsense, inane things we yearn,
Oblivious of reality, with so very much to learn.
Our relationship flourished, in spite of the midday heat,
The sun was blistering; your kiss, refreshingly sweet.
Love and serenity had captured our hearts,
Our feelings were genuine, this was only a start.
As the sultry eye of heaven slowly dimmed in the afternoon,
We built firm foundations, our souls sang a joyous tune.
It seemed life held more meaning than we ever knew,
Praising God for each fleeting moment, our love grew.
The sun grew gray and diminished into the sea.
Darkness crept to invade us with gloom, yet we
Trudged on, our bodies grew weary but our spirits flew high,
Our love knew no limits, not even the sky.
We cling to each other as midnight draws near,
Happiness never enjoyed such mirth; I must turn to hide a tear,
Such unyielding devotion should last through eternity
But much too soon, death will steal you from me.

Dr. Bernard P. Kramer, C.L.D.
COSMIC BROTHER
Whoever speaks my name, virtue unto it ascribe,
That far he speaks the language of my people—of my tribe;
That far he is my tribesman—whatsoever else he be—
That far he is a co-heir of all that descends to me.
Whoever takes my hand in storm, or tempest, counseling calm,
Entitles him to share in whatsoe'er may reach my palm,
Regardless of his border, or his breed, or yet, his birth,
He will remain my brother—mayhap e'en beyond the earth.
Whoever shows me mercy testifies, conclusively.
That he and I are scions of a common ancestry;
If so he followed impulse, void of guile, or hope of gain;
Or that, on restoration, he might chide me for my pain.
Whoever pays me deference, or homage, or is kind;
Mays like, is unto, all who hold my attitude of mind—
This, whether I with justice stand, or train with the unjust;
If so he acts because he wills—and not because he must.

Mary Rachel Hoover
PROCRASTINATION
Time after time, I tell myself
I will not wait this long again;
Then foolishly go on my way
With no thought to 'remembering when'.
How the seed is sown shall set the style
As to how our life is spent.
We put if off and put if off
And that's how the twig is bent.

June Glynelda Christopher
ANTIGONE
Antigone
What do you think of me?
I, your kin, your blood, your sister
Who cannot find an ounce of truth
Within my feeble bones and flesh.
Oh, how fantastic you were
Upon your godlit stage
You died for truth, and for our brother
And I, oh I had not the strength to follow
What I knew was right and just.
Oh, Antigone
Look at me.
Broken
Here alive, yet sitting,
Sitting in cobwebbed corners growing old
But still a starving child.

Joseph Walworth Sutphen
TWILIGHT
Behind the mountain whose summit hoary
With burnished glory was lately bright,
Fair-haired Apollo his face has hidden
And day has bidden to all—good night.
Yet in the heavens a something lingers,
As if deft fingers had painted there,
In softest colors, a thought to laden
The dream of maiden, or seraph's prayer.
But while a moment we stand admiring
The light expiring—Apollo's track—
The picture changes and skies that hinted
Things ruby tinted, have turned to black.

Ina Bott
BUT SHE WAS FUN!
When we pass on, to the beautiful place,
There are things in life cannot be erased.
But I pray, when folks say, "She was nice you know,
But her house was a mess, and not one to show,
To these words. . . .I hope they'll add, "but she was fun,
She loved people and was kind to each one."
For one can't take her house with her, but her soul goes alone,
To remind her of a lifetime and the things she did wrong!

Beverly Harris Bussolati, O.T.R.
THE CLINIC LAUNDRY SERVICE
Today, again, someone told me
Of a hospital where no one
Wears white, only street clothes
Adorn the healers and the menders
Of the bodies and the minds
Of those that have been ripped
And torn by life and strife.
Today, again, someone told me
Of imagination therapy where
The ripped and torn imagine
It never happened, instead dwell
In minds eye in Bermuda waters—
Blue with white sails on horizon
Erasing pain with simple images.
Today, again, someone said to me
How are you? Painfully
I reply FINE THANK YOU*
Only tears flow to surface truth
And humanity waits to catch the tear
In plastic tissue, reusable to
Launder with a rainbow of uniforms.

Beatrice A. Gund
WINTER MORN
The trees are hanging onto their snow,
The bushes are tinted with white,
The wires and poles are marshmallow frosted—
It's such a beautiful sight!
The world is a fairyland forest
Of shimmering, sparkling lace,
With crystal—clear air and crackling cold breezes,
An awesome and lovely place.
No human artist with palette and brush,
Could ever a canvas adorn,
With the Great Master Painter's creation
On this cold and wintery morn.

Robert J. Cox II
WHY NOT YOU?
So am I
As the windblown winter tree's
Frost barked branches against
That grey shrouded sky of lonesome

Winter's moaning morning
Unprotected, leafless, almost
striking bare
A greengone dusty, dirty black
Of trunk bitter frost
Root ice ground
Holding Medusa's head snake's
Branches through which wind's
shrill
Scream running, stabbing icy
barbs
Into the very soul of my
heartwood's
Longing for the sky
Why, Say I? Why Me, Say I?
And the shrill wind's screaming
Searing laugh pealing icy
octaves
Betwixt, between my wooden
fingers
Lonely in the distance, blown
by passion's fury
Finding, always finding, freezing
A breeze calls back
Laughing betwixt my frozen
finger branches
Why? Why? Why *not* you?

Mary Agnes Lynch
CLOUD BOAT
I
I like to look up at
The sky,
And watch you cloud
Go passing by,
I often wonder where
You go,
As you sail by so
Soft and
Slow
How pure, and white,
You gently
Float,
So near to God, you are
Cloud Boat.

Jo Sanders
WITH GYPSY
Through a sky the color of
pigeon's wings
The first glint of sun we've seen
all day.
We slosh through curbside
puddles
With Gypsy, our Irish Setter,
who stops
To lap at the saved rain.
Why rake the leaves?
There where the wind has
already stacked them
They turn pink-gold in the
evening sun.
Gypsy's loose across the lawn.
In the honey light,
A wild streak of magenta fire.
Below the bridge, between the
spray-painted columns,
We stand shrouded in shadow.
Gypsy zigzags through the river
grasses,
Her flag-tail wagging, the only
signal
Of her whereabouts.
Gypsy's sudden movement
scatters the mallards.
In turn, their wings shatter the
glassy mural
Of basswood trees and the
organza clouds
Which have blown in over the
hour
From the north.

Gary M. Beaulieu
FOR YOU, FROM ME
Try as we may,
Fight as we might,
We are still lovers,
All thru the night.
Your hair is so golden,
Your eyes pale blue.
It is no wonder,
Why I love you.
To be one with you,
Is so truly divine.
I just wish and hope,
It will last a lifetime.
For to be one with you,
Helps me to be
One with myself and humanity.
And to truly be one,
In body and mind,
Will make me a better man,
Thruout my time.

Amy Reinert
THE GARDEN
The Garden Wall stood ten
steps in front of me.
Giant steps, they seemed.
The path was littered with
debris,
After the seventh step, there
was a pit.
The Garden beyond the wall was
beautiful, I'd heard.
I wanted so badly to see it, but
through the clutter I could
not find a way.
I turned away, as it was so easy
to do, and started for home,
Not far away.
The neighborhood looked as it
always did.
The childred were playing in the
squalid streets while their
mothers dickered with
hawkers.
I saw a dog.
It looked at me, and for a
moment it's eyes looked sad,
Then turned empty again.
It snarled. Something stirred
inside me.
As I walked up to the stoop,
I thought of the Garden, and my
vague humanity.

Eleanor Ellis
THE MURAL
There's a beautiful scene on the
wall
With birch trees on either
side
Four maples standing with
leaves of gold.
On the edge of a pond of blue.
The rolling hills in the
background
Are covered with yellow and
gold.
A flock of ducks are flying
Toward the water below.
There's a friendly bright-eyed
squirrel
Munching a nut in his paws,
Sitting on a log in the forefront.
Such a cute little image of
life.
In the golden days of our years
We sit and gaze at the
splendor,
Recalling the beauty of life
Which remains with us
forever.

Debbie Gauvin
FEELING YOUNG
Feeling young
Is a state of mind.
Do not get old
Before your time.
Let the world
Do its shine.
Live each day as it comes.
Full of all the lumps
Including the sums.
Mostly the funs.
Feeling young is being here.
Where everything is clear.
The sun, the love; is all near.
There is nothing to fear
About Feeling Young.

Kathy Cochran
MIKE
I was such a fool to fall for you.
Everyone tried to tell me, but
not one did I listen to.
I had to find out for myself.
And, I guess I did-because, now
there's nothing left.
Though I'm not angry, or sad,
I'm neither happy, nor glad.
You'll never know how bad I
was hurt.
I thought I meant something to
you--
You treated me like dirt.

Tiffany Artiss Harvey
GOD
To some people
God is the one and only way.
To other people
God is no more than the passing
time of day.
To me
God is the only way
so I try to live faithfully
day by day.
Have you been baptized yet?
Have you repented from your
sin or have you put it off again?
Do you read your Bible
everyday?
Do you understand
the message
it is trying to relay?
Open the doors to your heart
God is waiting to come in.
He will wipe your sins away
from the very start.
God will open doors
that you thought were closed.
When you're frustrated
and can't go on any more
God will pick you up
and start you on your way.
So repent from your sins
and with God
you'll *always* win!

Kathleen Jean Cuyler
HUMAN NATURE
Wandering eyes and a restless
mind;
Let your spirit go, let yourself
unwind.
The wind in the trees, and the
songs of the birds;
Mean more to some than
meaningless words.
The clouds in the sky, and the
waves in the lakes;
Don't mean a thing when you're
full of headaches.
The rich and the poor, the
blacks and the whites;
We all are the same, we all have
our rights.
The beauty of life, and the
darkness of death;
Some people think that's all
they have left.
You can run and can hide, but
where will you be?
When it's your turn to go, you
must pay the fee.
Life it must end, and the beauty
must go;
It all melts away like the very
first snow.

Helen M. Niesen
UNTITLED
I love you, my love
as leaves swinging in the breeze
love the gentle air.

Mareatta Chivvis Baker
PAPER FLOWERS
Paper flowers grace the table
Paper flowers deck the wall
Paper ferns all crispy, curly
Fringe each offering like a pall
Paper people pause to ponder
Paper causes right and wrong -
Paper puzzles posing problems
Solved as simply as a song!
Paper clowns that prance and
caper
Moved by every breeze that
blows -

Soon the winter winds will
sweep them
Where, nobody cares or knows
Cry for flowers fresh and
fragrant
Lifting to the sun and dew!
Cry for life, for pulse and
purpose -
Flesh and spirit - all that's true!
Come ye powers of re-creation!
Touch with fire man turned to
clod!
Life's for living, striving,giving-
Not a frivolous facade!

Stephenson T. Cox
MYL'ISE
Myl'ise, if only time has favored
us,
Your years, so long from now 'til
then, for me,
For you, would end--and soon,
and we'd discuss
Our feelings freely...But it
cannot be.
If only you had blossomed not
'til late,
My worldly mind could still
insist on "fond."
Instead, you burrow, you
exasperate!
What's more, you're blue-eyed,
pretty, and a blonde.
Suppose your eyes were brown, I
might be spared

That watering that comes to my sore eyes;
To chilly, cutting wind yours are compared;
I'm flinching now while you I sonnetize.
But stay, be you, 'cause I want nothing less,
And I will cherish you as years progress.

Charles Atkin
THE VILLAGE
Why, in their stoic stares,
Is there no hate, no fear, no love,
To help me in my stumbling search?
For hate, I cannot find
And love is far behind.
Only fear I find to help me struggle
To my unknown goal.

Ethel B. Hansen
TURN UNTO GOD
Turn unto God when skies are blue
He'll lift the load and see you through.
He'll scatter clouds and bring the sun--
Just turn to Him-it will be done.
Turn unto God in Faith and Prayer
Let Him know all your woe and care.
Tell Him each secret you have known
Confess your sins-you are *His* own.
Turn unto God-He fashioned you.
He knows each thought before you do.
He meets each need with Love Divine.
Through Christ, His Son, is healing thine.
Turn unto God-for He is Sure.
The things of earth-not long endure.
Both Joy and Pain are fleeting things.
Turn unto God-for *He* is King.

Margaret Bzovy
WAVES
Within the depths
of the ocean of life
it's turmoils---
or it's calms;
it's whirlpools,
it's foams,
High tides or low---
Only one wave
transcedent;
Swept into my life
Excelled over that of any other.
It's strength,
It's virtue,
It's wisdom of truth---
Shall never come my way again.

Kenneth W. Treadwell
THE INTELLIGENT BEING
Some say he's the most intelligent on earth
He has walked the earth for many years
Others say he is marked for life since the day of birth
Leaving a history of destruction and fear
They say he kills without reasons
All animals, even kinds of his own
In the Summer and Winter no matter what season
The reasons are many and yet unknown
He kills not for food but sports and fun
He kills men, women, girls and boys
He travels through the mountain, deserts and seas
This animal is known all over the world
Intelligent and smart that may very well be
Because of him animals are extinct and rare
The destruction will continue until nothing's left
No trees or mountains the earth will be bare
And in the end he will destroy himself
He's as old as the mountains the trees and sand
This animal of destruction is known as man

Penny L. Brady
SERENITY
The forest was bathed in silence, multi-colored rays peeked through the trees. Splashes of brilliant flowers dotted the ground, tiny animals tip toed, so as not to disturb natures balance.
The serenity I sensed eased my troubled mind, and I felt the presence of God.

F. R. Johnson
A GIFT
In the center
Of an island
Silky clouds gathered
To give a lost child
The living gift of water

Denese Davis
MISSING YOU
I check the mail box everyday
Hoping you've sent a letter my way
I jump whenever the telephone rings
Hoping your voice it brings
Holding you close in my dreams every night
Only to loose you again at daylight...
Missing you
What can I do
Missing you
Feeling so blue missing you...
How can I disguise what I feel inside
What can I do that I haven't tried
When I go out it's not the same
I put on a smile and play the game
Your name on the tip of my tongue
Tears in my eyes and the nights just begun...
Missing you
What can I do
Missing you
Feeling so blue missing you...
Memories echoing in my mind
Will we meet again somehwhere down the line
Have our paths forever drifted apart
Will I only hold you close in my heart...
Missing you
What can I do
Missing you
Feeling so blue missing you...

Eileen M. Keenan
STARTING AGAIN
I felt that all was well and then
Something happened---I had to start again.
It has happened more than one time
From deep depression to sublime.
Then back again into the pit
Of deep despondency, I sit.
And yet---
Life is so full of packed surprises.
When things look black and a tear arises,
A ray of sunshine peeks right in
And fills my heart with joy again.
The sun is always shining bright
E'en though clouds 'oft hide its light.
We must remember it's still there
and smile as though we have no care.
If we can smile and go bravely on,
Before we know it, the heartache is gone.
Our loss can turn hurt into gain
If we can learn to start again.

Glenda Porter Todd
ONLY JESUS
No other way, but Jesus-
The One Who died for me.
No other way to Heaven-
God's Gloryland to see.
No other way but praying,
And b'lieving Jesus lives.
No other way to find true peace
That no one else can give.
Jesus came to bear our sins,
And bear them all He did.
He took them on a cruel cross
And by His blood they're hid.
His blood's the only cover
That washes sins away.
His love's the only answer
And He's the only Way.

Bonna Jean Handley
MIDNIGHT BEACH
On the beach at midnight,
waves lapping at the sand
and walking in the moonlight,
you holding my hand.
On the beach at midnight,
it's so different from the day
the sand is almost void
where, at noon, sunbathers lay.
On the beach at midnight
it's cool and crisp and clear
and the moon is big and bright
and it seems so very near.
On the beach at midnight,
it seems it can't be true
that we are not teenagers,
but the parents of two.

Paula Katherine McCoy
UNTITLED
The sands of time
May flow
Quickly through the glass
Or
Drip solemnly;
Each grain making an impression
On the ones before it.
This phenomenon speaks to
Young and old alike:
For the young know
The wait
Before the door is opened,
And the old,
The wait
Before its inevitable close:
The time between movements
Is not for us
To know.

B Lewis Ivy
HOME
There is no place quite like home,
When troubled minds start to roam;
And affliction hinders your progress
And love ones are laid to rest,
Turn to home, that humble place
It'll secure you from debase.
When plans have failed you,
And you ponder just what to do,
There's always the old homestead,
Renew your faith be not afraid
Home it is, that place of abode
That symbolizes love fourfold;
For it's where charity begins
And once begun, it never ends.
Home shapes characters of men,
Teaches them to endure to the end
No matter what your goals may be;
In this great land or on the sea,
When hearts are sad and faith is lost
Turn to home at any cost.

M. Jan Matula
BEFORE TOMORROW COMES (81/19/11)
Long before the new morning
comes peeking through
my wndowpane
and
before I'm trapped
in the morning light,
Kiss me, my love
and bring back some of
the memories of last night.

David A. Teele
ODE TO DEATH
Please shed no tears when I am gone,
I am not dead, I've just moved on.
This wrinkled body, wracked with pain,
I'll never have to use again.

It's been my home while I've been here,
And served me well year after year.
Now that my trials on Earth have past,
My future home is in sight at last.
This life has bounced me up and down.
I've done some things upon which I frown,
Yet I hope behind I've left some light,
That will keep my memory shining bright.
Perhaps I've given in some small way,
Something to brighten just one day;
Some deed or gift or act of love,
That you'll remember as on I move.
As you view this body, shed no tears,
It's just been my home for all these years.
Someday we'll meet on distant shore,
When we all come through that final door.

Tamera Bryant

ICE HOUSE

In the meat locker
Where breath comes out steam
Carcasses hang skinned
Heavy and cold
When the door is opened
I close my eyes and wait
When the door is slammed shut
I sigh relief with opened eyes
I am safe in the darkness
I am safe in the cold
Then you
Prowling lioness
Who gave you the key to the ice house?
You came ready for the kill
And I was your prey
You with the cat-like claws
Tore my eyes out to see behind
Inside
Sliced me open like a knife
Chopped me up like a meat cleaver
Cut the pulsating reds and blues
Disconnecting my bleeding heart
And taking a piece of it with you
You have pawed, clawed, and chewed me
Like hamburger
I am ripped, torn, and broken
Your ravenous hunger satisfied
You rise lazily now to leave
I am left hanging by thin skin
Swinging slightly
Another carcass
Close the door behind you.

Gail Lyman Spane Jr.

OLD MAILBOX

The old mailbox down at the end of the road
Has bore itself a heavy load.
The wind, the rain, the dust, the rust
The passing of every truck and bus.
The love it's bore, the tears it's shared
The hope it's brought when all was lost.
Now it stands there all alone waiting for
Someone to come home.

Anna Goering

OUR EVENING PRAYER

Our Heavenly Father as night draws nigh
we come to Thee in prayer
Thou hast protected us this day
and showed us that You care.
We trust Thee for the coming night
assured that You will keep
Our bodies, souls, and spirits
while we enjoy refreshing sleep.
Include each family member into Your loving care
Supply their need, where're they are
for Thou art everywhere.
Forgive our faults and failures
they are many, it is true
Still greater is Your mercy
so we bring them all to You.
As we retire, Your watchful eye
will see us through the night
And should we see another day
help us to do things right.
Amen

Jo Allyn Hood

LOVE LETTERS

Mama,
I have lived within you & without you
Off & on for 21 years
Today I told you I love you
I think for the first time
Mama,
Forgive me
I am deaf & dumb
Unable to make conversation without pen in hand
I sat in the next room & wrote you a letter
Two pages of written words to explain all that was left unsaid
You cried when I gave it to you & I turned away
Mama,
Soon I will be leaving you again
Perhaps the chill will follow me from your house & leave you warm
It is easier for me to love you from a distance
I will write
I will write
Mama,
I love you

Leo A. Rosengarth

PARADISE LOST

When Paradise was lost by Eve--
while tempting Adam, I believe--
and they were tossed outside the grove
and forced forevermore to rove,
When Eve had bargained with the snake
and forced the Lord, a choice, to make,
When she had nibbled on the pear
and God shazammed the garden bare,
When both had tasted of the rind,
but in the process, gained their mind,
Twas then she thought of what she'd do
to spread the wrath of God, to two—
She blamed the sin on Adam's heart...
and Women's Lib had made its start.
Poor Milton.

Bonnie Lee Jones

ODE FOR A THIRTY—SECOND ANNIVERSARY

He is the sunshine of my life.
With him there is no night.
His eyes meet mine
Across a crowded room,
And there, for all to see,
They embrace me.

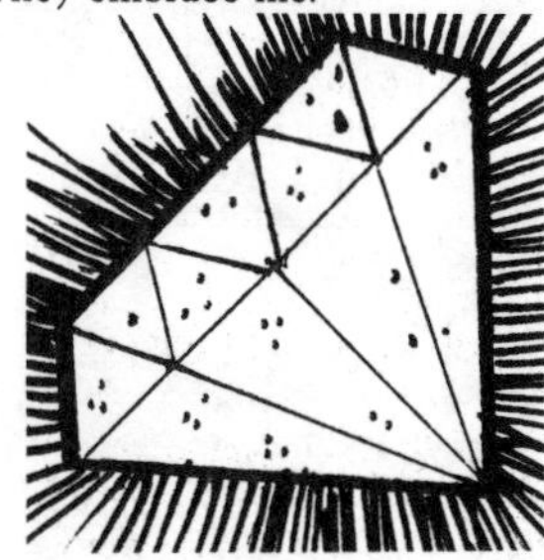

He is my life, my destiny,
My dearest friend.
In his arms I find
Peace,
Comfort,
Security,
Love.

Nancy William-Ortiz

ILLUSIONS

I strain my ears
for the sound of your voice,
...yet I cannot hear you.
I close my eyes
and see your smile,
yet when I open them,
...the vision disappears.
I feel your hand in mine,
yet when I look down,
...there is but one.
It's true then,
...you are gone.

R. Crandall

HOLDING ON

All too soon we become old men sitting on porches
Holding on to moments from times now gone
Rocking our children once more
Watching them grow away
Feeling the pain of those now gone
And perhaps to shed a tear in silence
Too soon we feel the warmth of the morning sun
And for another day solitude
From where will tomorrow's moments come
Who will rock us then
When we become old men sitting on porches
Holding on to moments
Rocking our children
Loving
Dreaming
Telling old tales to those who would pass
And watching them leave
Old men on porches
Holding on to moments

Mary Hobart

THROUGH MY KITCHEN DOOR

A May night hovers on the wing
Just through my kitchen door
In twilight breathes the rustling spring
And I am only just within
Just within my kitchen door.
Sounds are echoed in the hum
Of whirring spheres unknown
And every move is perfect
As every breath is drawn.
I stand as if enchanted
With wonder and with awe
That life is not yet known to me
Through my kitchen door.

Joann Lyn Arbrun

VISION OF LIFE

We awaken with the sun in our eyes,
we sleep with the moon in our vision.
We cry with the day and night,
we forgive with the night and the day.
We care, love, and see with the vision in our eyes,
with what we want to see.
We wish to see our vision of life,
but we can't relieve it with our eyes,
for it is so far away to understand the vision of life.
So if I envision another life please forgive me,
for my vision is of life and day of the newest things in life.
Just remember the love in life in brightest,
biggest world of newest things in life,
even if it is to forgive and not forget,
just remember the vision of life,
of you in a big new world.

Penny Jean Booth

LEAF ON A VINE

He said that he loved me,
at the time it was true.
And when I knew him,
our love had been true.
He spent his time with me,
talking of dreams.
Yes, I had loved him,
but was it as it seemed?
I realize that with life,
love also starts in the heart.
And although we had felt like this,
we're growing apart.
Now the fact that I knew him,
and he once was mine;
Is added to my memory,
like a leaf on a vine.

David Terralavoro
WRITERS
Book writers express the depths of their imagination sometimes more than they thought their imagination would allow that does not explain how writers told about things that are happening now

Michael L. Jones
THOUGHTS
Each morning finds me smiling
Today will catch me too
Tomorrow touches thoughts
of brighter times we knew.
Morning leaves its gift of light
Your gift to me is you
Sunlight will touch me lighter
now my life is touched by
you.

Alonzo G. Turner
A WISH
I wish I was a creator.
I'd make all the people like you.
Because, with the twinkle of an
eye, and your simple smile
Our problems would be so few.
I'd like to say, "Sweet Sixteen,"
But that would be mere flattery.
For the other years were as
joyous and Happy!

You are a miracle in my life.
Not to be surpassed by another.
And if I find one to compare
I'll be sure to say; Not-As-Great-
As-My-Wanda---!!
Happy Birthday!
Love, Dad

G.J. Keraline
MASKING
And the machine had no keeper
Although it was pointed in the
right direction
It sped on along and I in the
wrong
Let myself go a little bit deeper
Then He was there out of
nowhere
And at once He was inside the
past
In spite of the speed He
handled with ease
And my soul to Him I did bare
Flashy and white was His attire
And He sported all kinds of
expressions
But I was amazed as I stood and
gazed
upon the dinginess of things
which I aspired
A dwelling place did I see there
And the children were cold and
dirty
And I wondered in awe that
what I saw
could not be an unsheltered
shelter
All this was a timely catharsis
And I couldn't help but feel the
connection
Between Him and me and the
yearning to be free
Of the soul's muted
metamorphosis

Mrs. Fern Roche
YOUR LIFE AND MINE
The clock of life is wound up
tight,
And no one on earth has the
right,
To take his life, or that of
another
Be it an unborn child or it's
loving mother.
God knows every hair in your
aging head,
Just as He knows when a
sparrow drops dead.
He knows when your clock will
run down.
And if you expect bells to toll
in your town,
Remember you are on earth for
a reason,
To accomplish many goals
during your season.
Through work and play and love
and strife,
You are building toward your
Eternal Life.

Gloria Elarde
I SAT IN THE SUN TODAY
I sat in the sun today
And watched my grand child
play,
And the dog stretched out in
the grass,
Warming himself in the
afternoon sun.
Sweet were the memories it
awakened
Of another time
And other children,
Playing in the sun,
With a honey-brown dog asleep
at my feet.
Gone are those days.
Grown are the children, and
gone.
Even the honey-brown dog
Is only a memory now.
But life goes on
In patterns so strangely alike,
I find myself holding my breath-
If he turns around,
Who shall he be -- the child or
his father?

Robert J. Offerdahl
A TEAR
I shed a tear which slowly
rounds my cheek
And rolls down my neck, to find
A momentary home upon my
chest.
From there my thirsty heart
Absorbs it through my skin,
Which then will start another.
A circle, unbroken, of love I
hold for you.

Martha Hayter Peterson
QUEEN OF THE MORNING
The wind burned a gentle warmth into my cheeks and I saw Dawn smile in the tufted clouds above, felt her soft breathing whisper tender thoughts, fill the inner realms of a hollowed heart.
Then she guided the pen which etched words of deep meaning for me to embrace forever. Tiller of the heavens, she reaped a golden harvest and flung it across the celestial arc for all to see and to feel. But I knew that my precious moments with her would be brief, for quickly and quietly as she came she would depart, seek new admirers beyond the horizon.

Linda Philbeck
BOOKS ARE THINGS WHICH TAKE THE MIND
Books are things which take the
mind,
To lands far and near, a treasure
to find,
One boards them just by turning
a page,
Making your mind, like the
world, a stage.
A book is a friend that will
never fail,
To comfort when one needs a
tale,
It cuts the rope and sets one
free,
To sail a ship or climb a tree.
They paint a picture in many
ways,
In blacks and whites and
sometimes grays,
They tell of special times and
days,
And seasons and wonderful one-
horse shays.
They carry one to romance and
glee,
And tell of people like you and
me,
Even if circumstance one's body
doth bind,
Books are things which take the
mind.

Jennifer English
THE PEARL
And the pebble was swept
Into the womb of the oyster's
shell.
The tiny pearl with its heart of
stone
Grew layer by layer into
luminous beauty
Until the knife ripped the pearl
From the soft flesh of the oyster,
And the pearl was polished, and
strung, and sold.

John P. McFadden, Jr.
SUMMER FOTO
Long ago a little boy
stood on a beach-house porch
dressed in white jumper and
white shoes,
one arm draped across his brow
shading squinted eyes
beaming a crooked smile
brighter than the sun
at his father's Kodak store.
Some years later,
same beach, the same boy
fell in love with the sea.
She danced before him in
daylight
all green-blue and diamond
sparkle,
and at night with her monotone
whisper,
she lulled his mind into gentle
sleep.
Together they pledged their love
forever.
Now a boy in white
with squinted smile
holds a porch railing and waves.
Behind him the ocean stretches
away same color, dancing
brightly.
And the one who stands
watching the boy and water
picture is the boy in the
Kodak memory.

Debbi S. Troxel
JUSTIFICATION
Your existence no longer has to
Be justified, nor do those
Feelings you hold inside, either
To yourself or to others. Just
Your striving to live, the focus
Being your true self though
Much of your life may seem out
Of focus, is justification
.....without explanation

Mary W. Thompson
WISHES
She wanted a kitchen bright as
the sun
With clear light walls and just
one
Red geranium on the window-
sill,
A gay patterned floor and
pottery on a shelf,
And a fat, yellow cat just
sunning himself.
She's changed her mind since
getting her wish.
The clear, light walls are really
quite swish,
But the red geranium is now
very dead,
The end of the shelf just dangles
free,
And the fat, yellow cat turned
out to be three.

L. Frances Taylor
IN A QUIET PLACE
When I'm alone
and far away from you
I see an image
of your noble face
You smile and then
I bid my fears adieu
In a quiet place.
I close my eyes
and make believe you're here
You speak, but now
your voice is lost in space
And left is just
a memory of you dear
In a quiet place.
You touch my trembling hand
then turn away
In vain I try to capture
just a trace
Of little things you do,
or think, or say
In a quiet place.

You kiss me, oh, so gently
on my brow
It's then I know
that nothing can replace
This silent love of mine
I treasure now
In a quiet place.

Robin A. Forester

MY FRIEND

Dedicated to: Stephanie Buccini

My friend is like no other,
We laugh and cry together,
We see each other all the time,
No matter what the weather.
If I have a problem,
She's always at my side,
I can count on her to cheer me
up,
Like when my grandpa died.
We're with each other
everywhere,
Whatever the situation,
She'll help you become a doctor,
If that's your destination.
And if for some reason you have
to part,
Wipe those tears away,
She's only leaving for a while,
Then she'll be back to stay.

Edda Cimino

FLIGHT

Souls swirling
in orbits elliptic
Unfurling time
in reaches cosmic
Spin on the wings
of the Giant Gyroscope
Fly the night-skies
of our Crystal Kaliedoscope

Shirley A. Munsinger

REFLECTIONS

The evening stars shine through
before day starts anew
It's a time for quiet thoughts
And a chance to reflect
on things that have been taught
The good or bad we can't
neglect
Laughter and dancing come too
Our pleasures we must ensue
The morning light will shine
If the night did treat you fine.

Mike Leleika

FREEDOM OF LOVE

Dreams of you fill my head
Everytime I go to bed
I think of us having fun
And finding a new place in the
sun
But I don't let my dreams rule
over me
Because when we're awake we
must be happy and free.
Happiness is something we live
for
And freedom is something that
means even more
To be free to do whatever it
takes
To make your life full, no
matter the stakes
I want you to be free so your
life you can live
And if I fit in I'll give all I can
give.
My heart still skips a beat when
you come into view
And my days are all filled with
thoughts of you
Your eyes make me melt like a
big bowl of butter
And when we make love my
heart sort of flutters.
Looking at your picture
brightens my darkest days
And only one more thing I have
to say
You're the most wonderful thing
that's happened to me
And all I want is for you to be
free.

Elizabeth Choate

THE SEA

Still waters - dark, circling
endlessly below,
Churning, burning to the shore,
As lovers singing, clinging, with
momentum grow,
Crying, sighing, and the sea is
still no more.
Still waters, rolling, rising,
reaching high.
Gushing, rushing on the tide,
Its icy tongues call out their
deafening cry,
Whirling, swirling, suddenly
subside,
Still waters - slapping, lapping,
Languidly surcease,
As lovers lost in paradise;
Earth devours the miracle of
peace.
The sea is love in God's eyes.

Samuel C. Okoye

DARLING

Dreaming about you last night
I sat up instantaneously
and turned on the light
Not seeing you I shook
nervously
Oh my darling
I cried
and tried to control my yawning
not feeling tired
Come to me
I do not want to think
you are being mean
Soar and sink
out through the darkness
Do not be hindered by its
blackness
Oh my darling

Sue Bonfanti

THE SENSES

We were given the use of our
senses;
Sight, Taste, Touch, Sound and
Smell.
To be used as a form of
defenses,
From the evils that don't treat
us well.
Sight; to see the beauty that
enhances every day, and to
avoid the hatred that is seen
in ruthful ways.
Taste; to enjoy the bounty of
the earth's fruitful trees, and
to snub the fancy dressings on
the pusher's lonely plea.
Touch; to feel the warmth of
love on a softly moonlit night,
and not to feel the need for
love, when it isn't meant to be
right.
Sound; to hear the words of
truth that were spoken long
ago, and not to listen to the
mouths who speak, but do not
know.
Smell; to enjoy the flowers
perfume and savory fragrance
of food,
and to be able to tell the
difference from the rotten and
the good.

Catherine Beeson Wright

HIGH AS THE HEART

Despair is a desert-drift
with never a hint of rain,
and never a cooling thought to
lift
the heart from pain.
But hope is a purple peak,
close neighbor of the sky,
a challenge to climb for all who
seek
as high as the heart is high !

Amanda Graham

AFTER THE STORM

Hitting close to home
It just hangs indifferent
To a host of angels
Holding their breaths
As the tightrope swayed.
The young man stepped on
The wind died and ceased.
Nothing moved--save the man
He was alive, he waited, but
nothing happened
He fell, he cried, he
remembered,
But no one heard him
They were dead anyway--but
then, so was he
But yet, why did the sun rise
the next morning?

Elaine Ubaldi

MOTHERS POEM FOR A TEENAGE SON

Gone is the little boy I knew,
the trusting hand in mine
The wide eyed cherub face is
gone
Replaced by a young man five
foot nine
The tiny child I carried, it seems
like yesterday,
When he would always hang
onto whatever I had to say.
his little legs so sturdy,
And blonde hair soft as down,
I knew that I would always
have,
So much love abound.
Those days are sweet in my
memory,
but how very little I knew
That time would take him away
so fast,
And how quickly that he grew.
That little boy is gone now
Replaced by a handsome lad,
But I often think about the
child he was,
And all the time I thought we
had...

Emily Buchner

SIGNS OF THE SEASON

*C*arolers out in a snowstorm
*H*olly leaves wreathed on the
door
*R*eindeer hitched up for a sleigh
ride
- laden with presents galore
*I*cicles forming on windows
*S*anta Claus suited up fine
*T*insel draped over the pine
boughs
- mid baubles of every design
*M*agi that came to the manger
*A*ngels that hovered above
*S*tar shining over the Infant
- Christmas, the season of love

Grant L. Simpson

UNTITLED

There's a land of make believe
that lies deep within my mind
When I'm alone I linger there
and
Oh, what wonders I can find
I can walk through a world of
beauty
unseen by others eyes
I can sail uncharted waters and
fly
through star lit skies
There is nothing I can't do, I can
be what I want to be
It seems that there's no limit to
the things my mind can see.

Richard E. Anderson

I AM WHAT I AM

Oh! I am alive:
a free spirit of
this beauteous world.
Oh! I am so alive
that this very earth
shines for me:
For I am a human being.
Gold! Silver! Gems!-
what are they
to me?
I have this earth and
all its glory
to comfort me:
For I am a human being.
Thru' the lonely cries
of man's despair, I
walk with head held high.
Thru' all the bewailment
of man's cruel fate, I
find love I can share:
For I am a human being.
I need no laurels or
crowns
at my feet.
I need nothing at all
to remind me
I'm me.
I am what I am
and that means more
to me:
For I am a human being.

Sue Sharp

STREET SOUNDS

There was a glitter from tinsel
prancing and dancing in front
of him; as he reached out
there was too much distance,
lights grew brighter and then
the candle was blown by a
heavy breath; the sounds were
deafening, like a drum roll--his
hand was still.

Mark A. Watkins

FRIENDSHIP

In days so full of fortune's
dream
of gold and silver and precious
things
It's nice to know no stone or

gem
outshines the wealth your friendship brings
When life's array of fancy times
fades far beneath a whithered past
The love you've given to others shows
to prove your friendship lasts and lasts

Fredrick A Beickel
BEFORE
I have lived before, of this I am sure,
The memory of days gone by makes this life seem a dream, a giant lie,
Reality was when I died, pierced by a lance, at the entrance of my cave near Toulouse in the South of France,
I was there when the arrows flew, at Ankara I was one of Alexanders' army that didn't get through,
At Cusco I became the Spaniards slave, and was one of few Incas that died of old age,
I was born with a memory that's not supposed to be,
Of other times, other loves, a sense of destiny,
Just think of the wisdom that should be mine,
But what was wisdom before is nothing to this time,
Atoms, what were they, where were atoms when cold steel cleaved the air on the plain where the dead Persians lay,
What were machines and battle tanks when the Huns' horsemen broke our ranks,
Romance, what is romance to this day,
When all that people take serious is their play,
How many women I have loved, how many children have they had,
How many I have hurt, how many I have left sad,
But one special woman happens in every life,
I've found her again, she will be my wife,
She wore the finest linen in Ancient Greece,
In Peru the Llamas wool,
In France the softest fleece,
She knows not those days gone by,
But the eternal scheme has determined that by me she will lie,
When this time is over once more I will roam,
Searching for another time,
For my soul to find another home,
Someday in the eternal fathers home I will sit and rest,
But first my soul must roam until I pass some earthly test.

Doris Rincker Stewardson, III
NEWBORN
Dedicated to Jamison Donn Jones
Ten little fingers
Ten little toes
One tiny turned up nose.
Two blue eyes
As bright as can be,
Looking around as if searching to see--
Me--His Grandmother.

Catherine M. Domiano
CAGE
Never, ever
Should you dream:
For the one thing
You most dream of;
The one thing
You most want
Never, ever comes to you.
For the one thing
You shall always fear
Abides at the opening of
Your fantasy.
But cage the Fear
And you dream comes true.
But if the cage should fail,
The dream becomes reality
And reality, a dream.
So build a cage; strong
And lean on the lock
To cage the Fear forever
And dream & dream & dream.

Clara F. Folsom
SADAT
Another person was shot today. Confusion reigned galore.
A man of peace in Egypt land, how sad we do implore.
He gave protection to the Shah in the Shah's illness of later date
People thought it was a mistake and just a little to late.
What has happened to brotherly love
taught by a man of Jesus birth.
Are we slowly falling apart and never see peace on earth.

Rolande Carroll
LAUNDRAMAT
The chore I hate the worst is that,
of going to the local laundramat.
You lug those clothes on out the door,
once you are there you've got to lug some more.
You find a machine that will for once, work.
Sit there, meditate, waste time and feel like a jerk.
You fold and pile those clothes up so high.
Finally! You can kiss that place bood-bye!
Lug those clothes back out to your car.
Clothes piled so high your vision they mar.
Home at last! Now lug those clothes once more.
Done at last with that dreadful chore.
But this chore of which I speak,
unfortunately must be done every week!

Nora Carroll Hurd
NOW THERE'S TIME
Now there's time for things we planned together.
No fields to plow,
No winter wheat to sow,
No fences to repair,
No stock to shelter,
No wood to store against the winter's snow.
But wild geese flying high no longer call me
And droning planes no magic curtains part,
For beating wings and ecstasy and stars shine
Are never tenants in one-half a heart.

Rhonda K. Dorsey
SECRETS
Here I am
Pen in hand
Paper on my knee
Thoughts today
Will be put away
For no one else to see
Why do I hide
My feelings inside
The stacks of pages grow
As I write
My words of life
For no one else to know

James Martin Gau
THOU ART MY LOVE
With all my heart
And with all my soul,
By the high high Heaven's
Pealing roll,
By the earth below
And the sky above,
By God's own light,
Thou art my love.
Now should the grain
Forget the field,
Should horizons quit
Their orbital yield,
Should seagulls halt
Their aerie turn,
All this 'fore 'ere
Thy heart I'd spurn.

Barbara Thompson
SO WHY AM I CRYING?
You know, it's funny
I just never realized how wrong
One person can be
About another.
All the while we were friends,
I sort of felt you were
Misunderstood
By everyone else.
I guess I deluded myself-
Thinking that I knew you a little better.
Well
I guess I don't.
Because the person I thought you were
Looked at me and smiled
But the person you are
Looks at me and laughs.
It's funny, you know...

Evelyn MacLean Puffer
ADOPTED DAUGHTER'S BIRTHDAY
I have no recollection
of this, your special day.
No bittersweet memories
to temper through the years.
For thoughts of our first meeting
are joyous ones.
Sweet chubby infant
soft hands grasping mine
with trust and hope
both premature.
Your roots are not mine.
No common bond, save love,
weaves our lives together.
Forever entangled,
yet no one seeks release.

Patt Fogerty
THE ROCK OF GIBRALTAR
The Rock of Gibraltar crumbled today
And all you did was walk away
That rock stood for 1000 years
You made it crumble with my tears
Being a rock a being alone
Nobody even bothers to phone
I'll be strong and carry on
Even tho my life is gone
I'll manage to see this through
Even tho you have been cruel
You didn't even want to try
All you wanted was to say good-bye
You did it and now you're gone
Let me try now to be strong
I have to for me and my kid
Here come the tears see what you did

Betty Ann Wooley
A PUPPY'S PRAYER
God gave me life to serve you
Then filled my heart with love
My sight, my sound, instinct renowned
Are gifts from up above
He gave me courage, strength and tolerance

Where man does often fail
Deep in my eyes, the secret lies
And through a wagging tail
My presence unbinds loneliness
Devotion is my only worldly plan
To love and care is all I ask
And just to understand.

Vicki Brown Lundeli
TWO OF A KIND
I have finally met someone
Who is just like me.
Through knowing and understanding him
Myself I can see.
I feel so relaxed and at ease
When he is around.
A person like him
I have never found.
He is so much like me
That it seems unreal.
We let no one get close to us
For they may see how we feel.
There are parts of us

That we keep hidden.
Really getting to know us
Is forbidden.
No one knows us,
So you need not try.
We are two of a kind;
He and I.

Lois Allen
UNTITLED
Oh! To be near you
To feel our heart's
as one
To feel the wind gently blowing
through our hair
As we walk through a
field of sweet smelling flower's
Oh! To be near you
To see your eye's twinkle in
the moonlight
To hear you softly whisper
my name
Oh! To be near you
To feel your strong
embrace
To feel your soft lip's as
we tenderly kiss good-night
Oh! To be near you.

Wallace M. Martin
AT BODIE
Hill and mountain silent-cry at
Bodie,
Their dark mine eyes weeping
stone tears.
Carbuncled slag,
dross of happy boomtime,
interposes shape incongruous
to the sky,
at Bodie.
Down streets of ghost bedeviled
reverie,
I dream-walked the town in
sadder busttime,
And heard Hurdy-Gurdy
pleading, "Take me!
I am more than nighttime
goodtime!"
Musing still in shacks washed
clean by decades,
In airy heights where
putrefaction slows,
I caught that special stench of
poverty,
And felt the surge that
desperation knows.
Tell us, Jim Bain, why so many
came here
When Comstock dreams had
vanished as a wraith;
When blossom rock "showed
out" far too often,
And miners lived on little more
than faith?
Tell us, O Gold Dream singing,
how you lured
the gaunt men,
the used men,
the unsecured,
bone-tired prey of rested
users;
Lured ten thousand drudges to a
mole world
at Bodie!

Patricia A. Gue
THE MUSKETEERS, 3
Jim, Cathy and Matt were pals,
Buddies to the end.
Whenever they were troubled,
They always had a friend.
They could always ask each
other,
For advice and sympathy.
Jim, Cathy and Matt,
The musketeers, 3.
Never was there such a group,
No one could get between.
A very special friendship,
Though, they were only teens.
Matt was charming,
Jim was free,
Cathy was pretty,
The musketeers, 3.

Mark F. Campanile
A SINGLE ROSE
When I first saw you
you were fresh and alive
straight and tall, firm and solid
petals slightly bent, not quite in
full bloom
You were one of the few who
had potential
yet you were never given the
chance
Young, innocent and proud
you were one of nature's best
You should have continued to
grow
but my love cut your life short
You would have been perfect
but I robbed you in your prime
I could only see for that
moment
and didn't comprehend what the
future would bring
I was sure you would continue
to blossom
and your beauty flourish
with each new petal that
appeared
But now as I look at you
your head bent in dejection
I feel guilt and disappointment
knowing that I have deprived
you of life
and taken all your beauty,
and kept it for myself

Valerie Irene Thompson
MORNING GLORY
As Lucifer sprinkled his light
into the sky,
I opened my petals to you.
You warmed my leaves and my
flowers grew.
The essence of my beauty was
in your tender rays.
My small eyes were blinded and
could only see the sky.
I never saw that you lighted all
the rosebuds;
And they swarmed into flowers
in your embrace.
Night has come and it's time to
close my open petals.
Without Apollo's warmth my
growth is stilted.
When Lucifer shines again I will
look
Down and choose to wilt,
For my little pride will not let
me bloom
As just another flower
Blossoming from your
indiscriminate glow.

Maxine Myers
THIS I KNOW
The grey November skies have
come around one more time,
The geese have made the
Southland trip, the graceful
"V" again their sign.
The brisk cut of the air
proclaims Winter is nearing -
Settling in for quite a while, and
not leaving until Spring.
The falling snow like a baby
lamb will softly coat the
ground,
The Arctic winds move swiftly
in, subject: to move the snow
around.
The fireplace will gleam softly
in a dim candlelit room,
Where love, warmth and
happiness reign supreme, and
heartbeats are a symphony
attune.
And as Winter passes and
Springtime moves gently in,
The feathered ones loft
northward to raise their young
again.
The azure blue of the sky will
sing, caroling to all around,
The world has awakened, my
love, and what a beautiful
sound!

Arthur G. Kersey
WINTER
I don't like winters, they're too
cold;
Oh, how that north wind blows.
Perhaps, because I have grown
old
I feel that way, who knows?
One flounders through a deep
snowdrift
To get the morning mail.
My spirits never get a lift---
That morning sun's so pale.
Yet snow makes all things
gently soft,
A peaceful scene to see;
A tiny snowbird soars aloft
And says, come fly with me.
Oh, say, we used to make
snowmen,
And dressed them up just right.
We'd build a fort of snow, and
then
We'd have a snowball fight.
Did I say winter was quite
bleak?
A time which we should dread?
Well, come outside and take a
peek
At that bright sun o'erhead.
Say, winter really is quite grand
At night, a moon above.
Walk out into this winterland;
Be with someone you love.
Oh, look, there's snowflakes,
children cry;
A joyful song is sung.
Let's run outside so we can try
To catch them on our tongue.
The children skip and jump and
run
As in the snow they play.
I'll get my sled, join in the fun
On this great winter day.
So come on, welcome winter
days,
Those special times each year.
There's such great fun in winter
plays;
They'll fill your heart with
cheer.
God spreads this beauty
everywhere.
It's ours and yes, it's free.
The winter's cold, but I don't
care---
It's great, don't you agree?

Yvette Harrold
MY SECRET
You,
my unchangable truth,
my inner love.
I try to tell you the simplest
words;
I love you.
My love is a handful of sand
slowly fallen;
like a stolen glance,
that seems to last forever.
Without you,
I am nothing.

Francie Hope Freeman
RELINQUISHMENT
You are a name now on this
piece of stone,
No longer flesh and blood and
warmth and grace.
My fingers trace the letters, one
by one,
As once they traced, with love,
your living face.
Oh, if I thought to find you
here, I fail.
You are not here. You are not
any place.

Marian L. Coppin
LIVING
He doesn't say we'll never fail,
He only bids us try.
His promise not success but
strength
Whether to live or die.
Our earnest plea He n'er
forgets—
Sometimes He answers "No".
But always with His Hand of
Love
He leads us here below.

Shirley J. Spetman
SECOND IN COMMAND
I'm the master of my heart,
but I'm second in command.
Because my heart is always led
By the touch of my Master's
hand.
Yes, Jesus is my Master
He's in my heart to stay
And with the touch of my
Master's hand
I'll make it through each day.
He guides my life and gives me
hope,
He's with me every mile.
He gives me a joyous spirit
And you'll see it in my smile.
Yes, I'm the master of my heart,
But I'm second in command.
For Jesus is my Master,
And with Him I've made my
stand
So, I'm master of my heart,
But I'm second in command.

Bren Sharp
THE BIBLE
The Bible was inspired of God,
It's contents very real,
It is our guide on how to live,

It tells us of Gods' will.
It comes in many sizes,
And its' color varies, too,
But the words inside all tell the same
The whole Bible through.
It tells of Gods' creation,
Of the earth and man,
Of all things he created,
The beginning of His plan.
It tells of many people
And of things long ago,
It gives to us examples
Of the things that we should know.
It tells of John the Baptist,
And of how the people thought
That John was the Messiah
Until they were taught.
It tells of Christ our Savior,
Of His life, and how He died,
Crucified upon the cross,
And of those around who cried.
It tells of how He rose again,
For this was meant to be,
God gave His only Begotten Son
To save you and me.
It tells of Revelation,
Of the things that are to come,
Yes, the Bible is a Holy Book,
Too bad it's just read by some.

Carolyn R. Garris

MY LIFE, MY LOVE

The soft flutter of a butterfly
is as the breath of my soul,
seeking the lair of my love
as he rests upon the pillows
of his content, waiting for me.
My life, my love; ah', that I
might give him pleasure
all the days of his youth,
and he might warm me with his
heart, as the flowers of my time
slowly wither and pass away.

Rosemary E. Weickum, RN, CCRN

THE ISLE OF THE WEST

The Garden of Eden has vanished, they say,
But I know that this story is jest,
For it's peacefully there in a haven so fair,
'Tis Ireland, the Isle of the West.
Such peace and contentment are sure hard to find
I've lived there, so I know when I say,
'Twas the angels on high, under His watchful eye
That planned it and made it that way.
Its rolling green hills and valleys so fair
Its rivers of silvery sheen
Will tell you the tale of a land full of fame
For deeds both heroic and clean.
Its people are happy, peaceful and kind
Not rich with the world's fleeting lore.
But the things that are best for the spiritual chest
They have these in abundance—and more.

Mrs. Doc Wicker

GOODYBYE SUMMER

How summer stands on the brink of time and falters. . .
Her colors growing bright. . .
Dressing up for Autumn.
The pinks are flamingo. . .Is that blue
or purple-blue. . .?
How deep it is.
When in summer they were pastels. . .
Now they are cerise, amethyst, and golden topaz.
Now summer feels the first cool kiss of Autumn
on her cheek.
She trembles, though, not knowing. . .
That she likes a kiss that's chilling. . .
But gaining courage at the beauty all around. . .
In some pale afterglow. . .She'll go. . .quite willing.

Annie Peyton Granberry

1981

The year 1981 has been filled with surprises,
Some gladness, some sadness and even surmises.
Jesus Christ has given us a new dimension
With love supreme, without contention.
Looking forward to the year 1982
We seek His promise of hope anew.
So live day by day and bring joy, peace and love,
And help the downtrodden to find Heaven above.

Don Sanders

WISDOM OF MAN

The shadows fell over the wilderness, as if a dark cloud had risen to smite the life of the land.
How is man supposed to fortell his future, when he can't even understand his past?
Because wisdom is but a fleeting moment of thought that, if not grabbed, is lost forever.

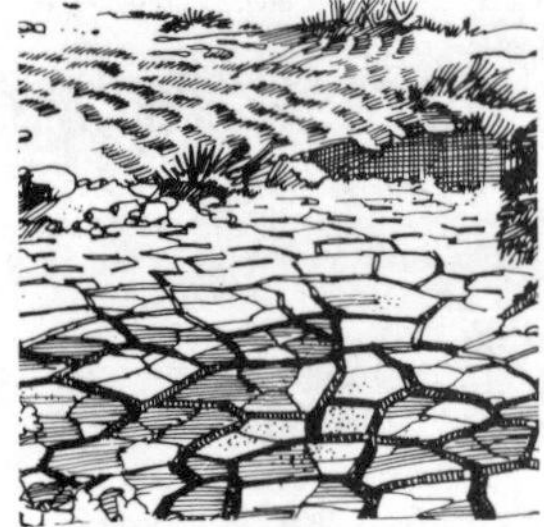

Zelma W. Martin

KEEPING BUSY

I really enjoy
watching these kids,
they keep me busy
yet not out of my head.
Sissy helps out and
loves to play cards.
Eddie is loveable
but makes things hard.
Keith is adorable and
loves to play outdoors.
An then there's Andy
who's only one year old.
He's big and husky and very bold.
And usually does what he is told.
They're all nice kids,
fun to be with.
I like watching them.
It keeps me busy.
Busy enough to keep me
from going out of my head.

Thomas J. M. Peno

THE AMERICAN MAN/ THE UNIVERSAL SOLDIER

Today is my induction day.
I'm going off to war.
I feel a spirit in my soul
I've never felt before.
A force that makes a person fight
The very best he can.
A voice that tells this person
He is an American man
My friends all think I'm crazy
Because I want to fight,
But what is happening overseas
Threatens my way of life
And someone has to defend
My beloved, native land.
Why shouldn't I do it?
I am an American man!
I swear for freedom I will strike
No matter where I'll be—
Perhaps the grass of Vietnam
Or the sands of Israeli.
If I run out of weapons
I will fight them hand-to-hand.
I pray I'll die with honor
As a true American man.
Time marches on.
My friends call me a hero
'cause I came back all right.
Because of what I did there
I've had many sleepless nights
When some civilian says to me,
"This war will never end."
I think of all my fallen friends
Who died American men.
I ask myself this question,
"Why did I want to go?"
I cannot give an answer.
I truly do not know,
And yet the words that I have said
I know I'll hear again,
By many other rash, young boys
Who are American men.
War is not a children's game
It's not what you expect.
Once you're in that jungle
You're in trouble to you're neck.
Don't listen to that voice, my friend,
It's part of Satan's plan—
Devour all of justice!
Destroy the American man.
I know that you won't listen
To what your friends will say.
You feel their words are only sounds
That time will fade away,
For someone has to defend
Your beloved, native land.
Why shouldn't you do it?
You are an American man.
Yes, someone has to defend
Our beloved, native land.
No matter how you do it,
Be proud!
You're an American man.

Robert H. Menges

A PROMISE IS TRUST

When we speak to one another,
we say what is so.
Telling yourself or the other,
the things one is to know.
These things of life and of living,
thoughts of doing and thoughts of giving.
These things may possibly fade,
with such are promises they are made.
Be it with yourself or to a friend,
a promise is truth partial on lend.
For these are the thoughts of things yet to come,
the hopes and the dreams of everyone.
There comes a time for you or I,
to ask how many promises equal a lie?
When the dreams are smothered and hopes fall,
causing feelings that can hurt us all?
So if you or I are to make others believe,
that what we shall promise they will receive.
For such a rule applied with those concerned,
brings a lesson in trust we all should learn.

Ronald L. Seely

BEATRICE

I gave to her the greatest gift I could;
What greater sacrifice could I endure?
There was no gift on earth befitting her:
Her eyes so fair, her love of common good.
Her purity outshone earth's clearest sky,
Much as the sun outshines the moon at day.
This Fair of Vanity in which we play
Defiled her sacred name. . .and so did I.
I could not bear to think that she loved me—
What sin for me to make her want my love?
Her worth exceeded all but heav'n above;
Among the cherubs she deserved to be!
That's why I sent her soul to Paradise;
A poison well effects love's sacrifice.

Abigail Hereford

ERMINE SNOW

High upon the Rocky Mountain
Peaks covered with Ermine Snow
Majestic in the starlight—
In the late evenings glow.
My wrap enclosed around me
Yet, I tremble inside.
Watching this lovely mountain

This glorious beauty with pride.
Amid this serene beauty I stand
The soaring winds, now quiet
Beneath the white canopy of snow—
Dreams come in the Dreamland night.
A challenge comes on Natures Wings,
As I softly turned away,
Breathing the Purity, *God*, doth send—
His love will always stay.

Robert Michael Balderrama

MEMORIES

The old man sat observing life
His eyes looked far away
As if his thoughts were back in time
Somewhere in yesterday
Once he'd known love and happiness
But that was long ago
The joys of love and family
As he'd watched children grow
Then he was not alone as now
But in dear company
Experiencing the daily cares
Of others thoughtfully
He's known the love of someone dear
A heart that he could share
One who was very special to him

Gentle, kind, and fair
But that was many years ago
And now he is alone
Left only with the memories
Of cherished times he'd known.

Juliana Kristi Stick

IMAGINE THERE'S A HEAVEN

There's a wreath around the world today.
Grief hangs on every face.
All over the world-SHOCK!
Waves of sorrow flood the human race.
A disciple with the soul of Judas
Oh, Mark David, don't you know
That you can't silence the music?
As long as there is memory, it will grow.
With his songs he touched the world.
But now where has this man gone?
I disbelieve what you are telling me!
How can John's life be done?
Oh, cold, cold December day
You took away my brother.
Please, Dear Lord, cradle his soul tenderly
For he had a song like no other.
He left his legacy,
A dream of infinite peace.
His death will not be meaningless
If all war will now cease.

Helen S. Flint

UNTITLED

My Heart Sings all the Songs,
That were ever written about Love,
The Joys,
The Sorrows,
The Loneliness.
The Joy I feel,
When we are together,
The Sorrow I feel,
When you leave me—Alone,
And the Loneliness I feel,
When you are not here.
When I Listen,
The Music swirls around me,
And engulfs me in its arms,
And I feel your Arms around me,
Holding me close and secure.
My Love,
What Joy it is to know you Love me!
My Love,
What Loneliness I feel,
When you are away.
I think of you and my Heart is Heavy with Sadness,
Because you are not here with me—Holding me,
Kissing me—Loving me!
You'll never know how much I need you,
Want you and Love you!
When I'm with you,
The Sun is Shining,
Even tho it is Nighttime,
I feel the Warm Glow of Summer,
Even tho it is Winter,
And Smell the Fresh New Buds of Spring,
Even tho the Ground is Frozen with the Cold!
My Heart Sings All the Songs,
That were ever written about Love,
The Joys,
The Sorrows
The Loneliness!

Glenda Moser

THE PHOENIX

I am Phoenix
I rise from my own ashes.
From the depths of despair
hopes and dreams come alive
only to be quenched by the ever present hunger of the
flames. My hope is as eternal as the flames that give me life.
I am Phoenix
I rise from my own ashes.
From flames to glory, from here through the eons of
time, I wing my way past the perils of fame and
fortune. I enter upon a journey no one can join.
I am Phoenix
I rise from my own ashes.
As I will rise again, I will rise forever more,
unendingly. For I am
The Phoenix

Melanie E. Cleveland

A PRAYER FOR STRENGTH

Dear Lord, please help me through this day
for I've grown tired and lost my way.
My weary mind and body stall
in need of strength before I fall.
I'm weary, Lord, this day's been long—
I often fear I've done it wrong.
I need some light to save this day,
please send some, Lord, along my way.
And thank you Lord for being there,
for taking all my hurt and care.
For telling me to pray and how—
somehow this day looks better now.
And when I get worn out again—
remind me you are there,
Amen.

G. H. Rigby, Jr.

MOUNTAINS

Gray giants etched
In the gathered gloom,
Grandeured guests,
In an eternal room.
Silent historians,
Of eons of ages,
Daily witnesses,
Of history's pages.

Lillian B. Foster

NORTH AMERICAN CHRISTMAS

When Autumn winds grow cold at night
And trees are bathed in silver rime,
The moon looks down upon a scene
Of dormant life, across its face
A naked branch.
When Cotton-tails have grown thick fur
And fields lie fallow, brown and sere,
Each day grows shorter, nights are long,
Hope needs rebirth as we observe
An ending year.
But, pause, prepare to celebrate
The birth of One, who, crucified
Became triumphant, gave in love
A miracle of life renewed—
An empty tomb.

Kris A. Jeters

FRIENDS

From the moment we met up until our most
Recent engagement together
I can feel only the greatest
Elation when I think
Now of all the
Delightfully senseless fun we are
Still enjoying together.

Debbie Tinney

SCOTT'S FLIGHT

Just like a pretty bird
you fell to the ground.
Without many words
you wouldn't stay down.
It doesn't matter that
you suffered the claims.
You had to start somewhere
on your way to fame.
Only to you the victory belongs.
Your courage the music, your life a song.
You'll go as far as the road can go,
And just what it takes only you can know.

Eddie Westendick

THE HEART BROKEN DEPARTURE

Slightly squashed from an ironic leaving
The lover embarks in recalling the last phrase
Quite unsure of the mediocre world causing the twirl
Which has set him in this peculiar daze
Pedantric word, surely the earth has begun no tremor
Scarcely would a gallon lost drain a great lake
Ah, but wisdom speaks truth in a center spaced interlude
Raging fires are of the careless match and floods from a small break
Yet the wandering lover has no attention toward tragedy
Nor existing faults or expectations is he here to confess
Praytell to the itching mind the blood dripping from the ripped heart
He that presented his most was nought by him who'd yet given his less

Woody Osborne

SONG OF THE BLACKBIRD

Hark to thee! Ebony birds of idle chatter;
Art thou devil or demon,
To flock like gossipy women;
My dreams to haunt with idle pratter.
Like a million fireflies;
Dancing in the night,
You prance from twig to branch;
With never a thought of flight.
Art thou so filled with the joys of heaven;
Soaring in thy flight,
Expelling your bursting cherubs;
Into my wakeful night.
Oh! that I might awaken;
From dreams of dusky dawn,
Filled with a joy to brighten,
My day with your cheery song.

Floyd J. Miller Jr.

FEBRUARY JOY

Even though the rivers lie still, encased in ice
And spring is a far-away number on the calendar;
Even though my body shivers when I walk to my car,

Warmth surrounds me, Nancy,
warmth to suffice.
Dancing with you, ignoring the
biting winter's chill,
Electricity surges through me as
I feel the sinews
Of your legs through your white
tights, to your shoes.
I catch you as you complete
pirouettes on the frosted hill.
Performing for each other, eyes
warming as they touch,
Oblivious to any other reality
but our burning love;
Nancy, these are the fantasies
that even I dream of,
Fantasies of dancing, of
caressing, and such.
With every sweeping of your
long chestnut hair,
I picture it blowing free around
us in the wind.
Believe me, Nancy, I feel it too
in my heart and my mind,
Seeking your warmth to join
mine. Our hilltop is there.

Ciel Swezeny

I WONDER

I saw a father hold her hand
I wondered why you never held
mine
I saw a father wipe a tear
I wondered why you never
wiped mine
I saw a father hug and kiss
I wondered why you didn't do
this.
As I sit by the bier and watch
and wait
I see your friends pass and pray
I look at the man lying dead
inside
I wonder if this is the father
of mine.
I feel a great sadness and sorrow
within
For the man that never had time
for his kin
The man named father who
earned all the pay
But never had time to go out
and play.
Should I shed tears for a
stranger I knew
Should I feel guilty because we
were two—
Two people who lived and
passed through life—
I sit and I wonder what is right.

Karen K. Kane

FULL CIRCLE

How could I know,
sheltered by my innocence and
youth,
that by my quick, indifferent
toss of head. . .
I made her face the truth
and feel the dread of clinging
on,
once need for her had fled?
I could not know.
All eagerness and youth, I
hurried by,
as it time were my wings, and I
must fly
unmindful of the words she
tried to say
'til now. I've come full circle. . .
face to face with yesterday
and "she" is me.
My child has grown past needs
I can supply.
All eagerness and youth, she
hurries by,
as if time were her wings, and
she must fly.
So once, did I.

William August Kobs

FRIENDS

Friends are for the times,
When you need a friend;
Friends are for the times,
Till the very end;
Friends are for the good times,
To have and to hold;
Friends are for the hard times,
To be brave and bold;
Friends are for the sad times,
For loving and caring;
Friends are for the fun times,
For loving and caring;
Friends are for the fun times,
For giving and sharing;
Friends are for the times,
When you need a friend;
Friends are for the times,
Till the very end.

Susan A. Montelius

AS IN ONE

As the sun has warmed the
earth,
so have you warmed my heart
As love has sheltered many,
so have you sheltered me
As in time all things come
together,
so have you and I
To be joined with you in the
bond of love
is to make the greatest dream
come true
To know the union between two
people
is the union I wish to share
with you
To love and live as one,
a new life now begun
a love not to be outdone. . .
. . .as in one

Lenise Van Tassel-Mang

THIS TOWN, MY HOME

Two months left
then I'll be gone
but I'll never forget
this town, my home.
I was born and
raised here and
as I grew—
the city seemed
to grow along too.
The people are friendly
nowhere to find
these kind of people
free in mind.
The scenery is lovely
with trees of green
grass a-sprouting
and all so clean.
Wheat fields a-many
a golden yellow
showing a prospering province
with grains quite mellow.
The air is fresh
the sky true blue
this town, my home
is where I grew.
The snow and winter
are part of this place
with mind a-howlin'
in many a face.
But with all this pleasure
we've had our times
with flood springs
and building dikes.
But I grew to love—
and no matter where I roam
everything in this town
this town, my home.

Alessandra A. Poles

TRACES OF LOVE

Tender and sweet, delightful is
the sound
Of little feet, the touch of little
hands,
The look of wondering eyes
gently softened
When angered by tears, as the
early dawn's
Dew dampens the transparent
windless blue,
Excelling triumphant, outward
in charm.

Charming is the sound of a
mountain brook,
The nestling Mockingbirds
rendering psalm
And soundless sound of a still,
sunborn rock
As a bud of a rose stirs into
bloom,
And baby's first words eagerly
spoken
With perennial freshness of a
lamb.
Throughout the passage stem of
life's long tour
Subtle awaking memories
endure.

Lisa Longdon

MARATHON

I am glad to see this day begin
and end.
Sunshine has filtered through
those dusty cobwebs of my
mind.
Built by others and by you. . .
I realize more now than I
thought I ever knew.
Thank-you for not chasing me
that final lap I ran.
For while running from you, I
found myself.
A stranger. . .my friend. . .the
forgotten one.
I still run sometimes, but not
through life anymore.
I stop and rest when I tire
and smell new flowers along
the way.
Cobwebs are nasty things, spun
with such care and yet
destroyed with the slightest
touch.
I see the now-with my mind.
My heart never answers when I
question it.
It goes on working., pumping
faster when I run.
Its so much easier to win the
race when your own
destination is ahead.
It is there-around one bend
or another.
My heart is glad you aren't
behind me
with a stopwatch and someone
else's shoes. . .

C. S. Craddock

THE ILLUSION

Life is an illusion for all of us
to see.
The illusion is our nightmare
for we're trapped in destiny.
Our lives keep moving forward
never turning back.
Each day, a page in history,
could cause one's brain to
crack.

Claire Lobel

GOLDEN BOY

My golden boy leaves
This is not a surprise
I knew that each today
would be a yesterday
It is how things are
He plans carefully
for the tomorrow
that is here
He thinks if he plans
each step
with great care
that he can arrange
tomorrow
I say nothing
I tell him
that it is right
to prepare
that it is necessary
and I help him
adjust the blinders
so that he may
look
forward
only
It is how things are
I say nothing
of how the darkness is
when the light is taken
I turn from him
and howl execrations
to a deaf universe
and hurtle
void into void.

Clara H. McKenney

WILD, WILD ROSE

Wild rose, wild rose, in your
beauty,
Growing by some roadside
fair,
As round about the world we
travel
It seems you are native
everywhere.
When June and July claim their
seasons,
And often late in August too,
We find you bright in sun or
shadow,
And thrill again at seeing you.
Wild rose, wild rose, pink and
satin,
Growing wherever flowers
grow,
Giving the whole world of your
sweetness,
For everyone to love and
know.
Your green wrapped buds hold
deep hued petals,
Paling as they open wide,
Yet still bright with lovely
color,
Circling the center of gold

inside.
Wild rose, wild rose, you were never
Meant for plucking or bouquet,
But to grace the field and meadow,
When plucked you wilt and die away.
So on your stalks and bush and branches,
And every stem and twig thereon,
To keep you safe from tempted fingers
Nature hid your prickling thorn.
Wild rose, wild rose, steeped in fragrance,
Birds adore you, winging by,
The wild bees pause to sip your honey,
You charm the soft winged butterfly.
More than all the lovely flowers,
Growing wherever a flower grows,
Though I'll not break a stem and take you,
You are my favorite, wild, wild rose

Ronna L. A. Culp

DREAMS

Whispers in the night
Promises of love
As I lie sleeping
In the arms of a dream
Gentle kisses to stir my soul
Careful hands to cradle my heart
To tend and keep it safe
To see to every need
And more
Kind words of praise
And sweet words of love
Drift through the shadows of sleep
Only to mist and fade
As morning dawns
And I awake alone.

Margarita Hernandez de Arauz

SORROW

All my sorrows, all my joys entwined as one. . . . .
No space in time, nor deepest ember of remorse,
could propel this soul,
thrust it even further into your arms.
Oh bleak the memory pass, oh sorrow is in my heart. . . .
There was a lass of twenty long ago, long ago. . . .
but she stands here in mid-twice twenty, her life no longer all a glow. . . .
faded and withered,
half way between midnight and dawn. . . .
Still so all alone,. . . .Pondering of yesteryears all but gone,
less visible then a star. . . .
If memories where to linger longer and relived,
which one would I enmesh at present to stay prisoner with me?
And what of you? And what of me?
Souls that were once yearning to live, and enliven. . . .
infusing one life with
another
who in an instant lost all tract of reason
and utterly marred lives,
that were so meaningful long ago, long ago. . . . .
Nay, the feelings of your arms could not irradiate any illusion
still left within my hopeful being.
And thus my life at present
mechanically performs its daily dialogues and chores,
half way between midnight and dawn. . . . .,
with hues of ebony all around,
all around. . . ./

Betty G. Small

A QUEST FOR A DREAM COME TRUE

We often wonder why a change must come—Oh Why?
The tapestry of life is what we question.
We can't believe a dream is needed in the scheme;
A reaching out for something—Yes, a questing!
When the dream dissolves, we can't believe our loss,
not realizing a higher plan's unfolding.
So reach for all you can, and hope, and dream,
and plan; your dreams will, yes, come true with just more questing.
The tapestry of life, with all its hues of strife,
will someday be unfolded for your viewing, and
You will wonder why, you, as time went by, questioned
'change' as part of your life's questing.

Janet Kassing

I'M NOT

I'm not an author
I just write
I'm not a boxer
I just fight
I'm not a lover
I just try
But if you don't love me
I'll just die.

Marisa Ann Sorich

THE CAT

There once was a cat.
He ate a gnat.
The cat was flat,
From eating the gnat.
So the cat,
resolved to a rat.
He ate the rat.
It made him fat.
He was so fat,
He jumped in a hat.
And that was that.

John William Reed

DAYLIGHT OF LOVE!

If I could but feel,
The daylight of your love
To see your tender heart reel,
Transcending your tenderness far above.
Your heart is young, unmolested,
Untrained, in the art of tenderness.
I'd fall asleep on my soft bed
And dream that I'd been blessed.
The voice I hear whispering, softly,
Is like the wind blowing silently.
Its' soft whisper telling me
Of love and what it's promised to be.

Kenneth L. Scott

HARVEST TIME

Harvest time is soon.
Harvest time is now.
Are you ready to see Jesus coming in the clouds?
He said that he was coming like a thief in the night
Gathering up the righteous for that heavenly flight.
My friend if you are not ready you had best get right.
The Lord is coming soon—he might come tonight.
Now take a look around you and see his creative hand.
My friend this is nothing compared to the Glory Land.
Streets of gold and walls of jasper
awaits us over there.
All the saints are going to inherit this heavenly home
In the rockin' chair of Glory never more to roam.

Claudia Lane Green

A LITTLE MOUSE

A little mouse peeped around the door
I pretended sleep and began to snore
He was very quiet and very sly
I watched each trick as he would try.
Over the bed and under the chairs
He quickly ran right to the stairs
This house was his and he could see
All were asleep, including me.
Up to the windows and everywhere
Back again to the same old chair
He played and played 'til he was content
Then quickly back to the hole he went.

Barry Grubb

MINE WAS YOURS AND YOURS WAS MINE

It was heaven the other night,
as we held each other tight.
We consumed all the late night
and early morning till the afternoon light.
I hope it was good,
because I gave all I could.
Your mind and body are so fair,
I cannot help but want to share.
You asked if I thought you bold,
but all I remember is your caring caress and hold.
You need not fear my thoughts about you,
since it was an experience that involved me too.
It was very nice,
and I would not trade it for any price.
We did a lot in a little bit of time,
because mine was yours and yours was mine.

Fred Marston

NOT AS A STRANGER

It seems like we have met before
Either here or on another shore,
You say you don't remember me
Why my friend how can that be?
There were other times other places
It's good to see familiar faces,
We shared both happy days and sad
Maybe the best we have ever had,
We have grown older and wiser too
Again let us be friends tried and true,
How fine it is to see you once more
Not as a stranger at eternity's door.

Christine Genevieve Davidson Abel

MORNING MUSING

with a mournful cry,
I hear the foretelling story in shrieks
Of a flocking of geese,
Winging southward
In the crisp, frosted dawn
Of this October morn.
without a home under their feet,
This noisy brood surmounts the sky
And I, too, wish I might fly
toward the dawn --

But the home speaks to me
Of family ties, responsibilities,
And much work to be done.
For a few brief moments -- in reverie,
I join the honkers
And enjoy the freedom of celerity.
Then, seeing the graceful fowl far out of reach,
I turn in spirited busyness
To my home and daily chores.

Edith Cannon Storey

A THOUGHT FOR THE NEW

While the year is new
And lovely as a new found pearl
Give something of yourself
To help make this a better world

Not gold or gems,
A gift of such odd rarity
But from a kindly heart
Hope, faith and charity.
Hope, for a better world
Faith, in your fellowman
Charity, to enshrine the earth
And back to you again.

Daniel Hollister
SORROW FOR THE FLOWER
Sorrow for the flower
With all her petals gone
Blowing in the winter wind
And crying in the dawn
Still weeping loud at midnight
Her sobbing fills the air
She would like her petals back
But they've blown everywhere

Katherine Elizabeth Roe
A MAN THAT'S MINE
I want a man....a man that's mine....
Not now and then....but all the time.
A man to love....a man to trust.
Hurry to me....while I'm still free....
Utopia could be ours....for unending hours....
Reserve that place in my heart.... before I depart....
Release all my pain....perhaps I'll remain....
You're my "Mr. Terrific"....
I can't be more specific.
Trauma....pain and heartache.... could all fade away....
Only you have the power....what more can I say.
Loving you is my dream....night and day....
Overcome whatever....and head my way....
Vanish all my fears....wipe away my tears....
Even if only....for a stolen moment or two.
You must fulfill my desire....
to be loved by you....
Our love would be sublime.... all the time....
United we'd be....yet totally FREE.

Helen H. Dennis
YOU'RE A DARLING AND YOU KNOW IT!
You're a darling and you know it
You take advantage of my love
You see the moonlight in my eyes
and hear my cooing like a dove.
I've told all the world about you
It's no secret any more
You can wind me around your finger
and open every door.
To things I've never dreamed of
so wonderful and new
Don't ever let me wake up
and find that it's not true.
Come fly away with me dear
You'll never want for love
I've barrels and barrels just stored up
Like rain-drops from above.
You're all I've ever wanted
I am certain in my heart
We were made only for each other
Couldn't you tell it from the start?
If God will only give us
a few more years to share
The peace and true contentment
not found just anywhere.
We'll build our castle in the sky
For love birds to see as they go by
With big picture windows—the biggest you've seen
So we can enjoy all matter of being.
We will hear the heavenly music
And just want to dance and sing
While we bask in the beauty
Only happiness can bring.

Hoda Holliday Linkous
THE OLD HOMEPLACE
I went back to the old homeplace today
Far too many years I have stayed away
The house stood there deserted all alone
That dear old house I used to call my home.
The land lay the same is it did years ago
The wind blew rustling tall grass to and fro
I made my way to the sagging front door
With heavy heart I stepped inside once more.
One fleeting moment I was home again
With scenes of days gone by flooding my brain
Forgetting all about the world outside
Forever here I wanted to abide.
Outside the barnyard empty and forlorn
No rooster crowing in the early morn
No lowing of cattle or bleating of sheep
Not even a track would time let us keep.
Going to the backyard, I look around
An old battered bucket lay on the ground
A fragment of rope still clings to the well
Oh! what a story these objects could tell.
Peering into the water a face I see
Aged and wrinkled staring back at me
Not the face of the youth I used to know
When to the well for water I had to go.
All of the fences have long since been gone
Only the garden gate has held its own
A rusty hinge gives off a creaking sound
It keeps the gate from falling to the ground.
The little brook in the meadow still flows
Coming from somewhere and to somewhere it goes
A few apple trees are still standing there
Gnarled and twisted from lack of care.
I rest beneath the weeping willow tree
Its lacy branches overhadow me
To meditate on memories of the past
And realize no earthly thing will last.

Ms. Barbara (Bunky) Morene P. Davis
MAN'S HYPOCRISY SMILE
Man's hypocrisy smile
Their words of deceit
Always a cheer
And by nature vile
Forces others to smile
Whose hearts are aching—
Who gets honor whom for
Others never mourned.
Who gave evil titles to souls in need,
Who for which the Bible never read.
Man's whose love is lust,
Defiled nature can not blush—
Whose nature in whom I can not trust,
Ennobled by name only—
At last will turn to dust.
Of some they befriended,
And of some should have defended,
But lust for power and praise of men,
Cast aside a goldmine to darkest end.
My dog sincere heart who for my heart to own,
Lived for, fought for, surely breathed for alone.
With digust I see man corrupted his power,
Vexed me, wasted my every hour.
He to which love of money will do,
But my faithful friend (doggie) remained true.
Upon most men's tomb should be seen.
Not what his titles was, but, what should have been.
If they dislike expression of this pen.
Tell them these writers know they have enemies as well as friends—
If they wish to push it to the end,
Be assured we're as dedicated to use necessary means to recite again.

Steve Hanzlik
UNKNOWN
I was unknown,
Until you found me!
I had nowhere to go,
Nothing to do,
When you found me!
You brought a light into my future!
I had no purpose,
Until you found me.
Now I know,
I must shed light,
And make friends,
Like you did,
With me!

Wayne Clarke
A MYSTERY
A word, a phrase
A man that was
That is and always will be
A love, a fear
A chance for hope
A mystery of reality
A misused word
A force unmatched
An unfolding truth. . .
. . .Or Fantasy
A friend, a stranger
Unknown to some
And misbelieved by many
The future of the present
That is now the past
And the future of the past
Are one, God. . .
A MYSTERY.

Scott Clyde
AMONG MY SOUVENIRS
A picture of my mother,
A matching one of dad.
A Christmas card from grandma
That always makes me sad.
A flower from last Easter
Dried and pressed with care.
A poem that speaks of loving
And why it must be shared.
A picture of my classmates,
A penny for your thoughts.
A book of bedtime stories and
Of course Forget-me-nots.
A card from first Communion
With glitter and white lace.
A little piece of long ago
A remnant of grace.
Keepsakes of a life time
Kept throughout the years.
All of these and so much more
Among my souvenirs.

Nancy I. Nelson
A LA '81
Pig stys and pink eye,
Rabbit's foot and rubber ducks,
Radar love with infrared vision,
Electronic games and micro-zap meals,
X-ray inner views and scandalous reviews,
Porno flicks of disco gyrations,
Street slang while mobsters gang,
Whipped cardboard houses amongst
Towering cement boxes,
Cellophane lives in Kodacolor brights,
Diving scores from boob-tube addicts,
Test tube babies and cloned twins,
News releases with soap opera gossip,
Sci-fi books while saturn is probed,
Supersonic planes and a new A-bomb,
No-ozone skies and pollution mounts,
Crumbling factories and soaring inflation,

Released hostages from straight-laced politicians,
Revamping the raid, heroin sluicing in,
Burn the pot and kill the rats,
Cancer's attacking, Give to the March of Dimes.

Happy Herbie
WILL THEY REMEMBER?
Perhaps all these words I have written
will only be thrown away
to add to the piles of garbage
that humans create every day.
But if that does not happen
and my thoughts somehow survive
Someone in the far distant future
may remember that I was alive.
I am only an obscure poet
a teacher and seller of arms
but I write about life as I know it
and taste of it's beauty and charms.

June Roy
AT DAWN'S SURLY LIGHT
The birds first greet the rising sun,
Then roosters join them, one by one.
The hens go "Cluck!" and start to lay,
While dogs rush out to bark and bay.
The cats meow; a cuckoo's cooing;
And horses neigh as cows are mooing.
Who spoke of dawn as "peace sublime?"
Some poet who slept overtime,
And gained renown, and won a prize
For rising late and spreading lies.
But frankly, friends, dawn's not so quiet;
It's old MacDonald's farmyard riot!

Debbie K. Fairley
THE KID
In all of the rumble of daily life,
A person speaks out with a rebel cause;
A man capable of seeing waves
Where others see ripples.
And in a terse and accurate account
He will open the eyes of a few,
For he is a seer where others are blind,
His heart is open to the sounds of which another's is deaf,
And his mind is a sponge
When another's is ignorant.
Only the wisest can stand with him—
Banish the power
Only the most sensitive can reach out to him,
And be touched back,
And only the deepest can move him
Without the use of force.
And yet in all of this greatness
—He's a dying breed.
The likes of him have been pushed into corners too small,
And have been overthrown by the turn of a friendly card.
But he prevails; as he makes his way through this world alone
He *is* the Dirt Cowboy.

Kay Richter
LOVE IS A RAINBOW
Love, like a rainbow,
Has no end nor beginning.
Although sometimes it seems to disappear,
The problem isn't that it's not there;
But that we're too blind to see it.
It's pretty,
Always peaceful and a comfort to see,
Showing up best in the bad times
Less, but yet still there, in the good.

Maurice C. Willard
SAIL ON WITH THE MASTER
Over the waves with "God" I go,
Never to get caught in the undertow.
Never to sink in the briny deep,
Never in sin shall I go to sleep.
With "Christ" my captain at the pilot's wheel,
With "His" arms around me as strong as steel.
With "His" tender mercies to guide me through,
I will reach "His" port with faith anew.
I shall not sink in the sea of sin,
If I let my "Master" work within.
I shall go onward over the waves so rough,
I will win all battles no matter how tough.
So over the turbulent seas I sail,
With "Christ" and the "Master" I cannot fail.

Marsha Ward Hess
THE EXTENDED TRUTH OF LONELINESS
Loneliness is only a part of love.
It's missing someone you have come to know
As part of yourself and patterns of growth
That satisfies an inner need.
Sometimes its pain seems so intolerable
Yet, this is some of the sacrifice
That extends the friendships and the love
Allowing the closeness to become real.
Loneliness stimulates the heart
To gather strength in times of absence,
And discovering a new way to care
May lead the two in search of the other.
It hurts when tears begin to cover
Time and distance and different lives,
But then, again, it's only fair
To free this friend from captive reigns.
What makes the soul know the pain
More often now than gentle words?
It's only for the one you love
Who's come to be a part of you.
So loneliness is not to fear
Or to hide in games pretending,
But only to become an extended truth
To remind us of the reality of love.

Evelyn Hodges
TEMPORARY SUN
Feeling the breeze as I walk the sands
Of the sun scorched beds that cover the land.
The sun is living on the ocean as if there to stay
But rest, it must!!!as it silently goes away
As I stop to turn and sigh
I look back on the memories learned and softly say goodbye.
For this is only a temporary place for fun
But my life awaits me, as so did the sun.

Leonard Robbins
CRYSTAL DREAMS
Crystal dreams of sweet persuasion
Life keeps on drifting by
Crystal dreams of sweet confusion
Fragile glass to make you cry
Crystal dreams to live a lifetime
Dreams of hope, goals of gold
Crystal dreams to leave you breathless
Dreams that leave you in the cold
I cannot see tomorrow
Though I see ten thousand years
I can only see the future
In the shadows of my tears
I look to see the sunshine
Through the cold and lonely rain
I look to see the brightness
Whenever I feel pain
I love for all tomorrow
When today has slowly passed
I dream in sweet confusion
Crystal dreams that turned to glass

Rose Marie Hodges
SUNSHINE
Sunshine dances on the Floor,
Across the window,
And around the
Door.
Its shadows move so
Mysteriously
Changing constantly
Like
Life.

Garrett L. Swim
TIMELESSNESS JUNCTION
Just to live in the distant house
on the shore of the land next door,
or to join the fight in the stand off wars
that man has made to cure,
could offer one the tranquility
our Creator has made so pure.
So I need to walk on the beach alone
to know that life's for sure.
Could I take a ride to Alcatraz
or sail from sea to sea,
Should I take a plane, a bus, or a bike
to free my strife with eternity.
Just to know the tom in my head,
tom is so hard to control,
Let me know the reason tom says
it's all a part of my soul.
I'll tell a story of long ago
on the calendar of history,
When time began for you and I
a disputed mystery.
I'll do it all, I'll set the course,
I'll manipulate the growing force,
Don't close the case to accept remorse.
A vulnerable soul is sinking into the distant cage of reality;
No time to wish upon or create the feel of serenity.
So now I live in the distant house
on the shore of the land next door.

Jeanne M. Swiatlowski
ONE ROSE
Save a day for me
Fasten it close to your heart
Proudly wear it there
Touching it tenderly
Then when it nods
And wrinkles set
Place it softly
Between the pages
That press it closed
Until the time
You find it there
And recall
Our small moment

Jill H. C. Recser
HURRY, HURRY!
Hurry, hurry, get out of my way.
I want to play.
Before I grow up tomorrow,
I need today.

Lori Ann Mickey
THE SEASONS OF MY LIFE
The future is uncertain, yesterday is gone
We only have today, to build our hopes upon
When my life was in its springtime
And the world was fresh and new
My days were filled with tomorrow's dreams,
All the things that I would do.
The summer days grew longer
And still tomorrows came
Life meant little more to me
Than a long unending game.
Now my life is in its autumn

The leaves are falling fast,
There's no way to recapture
The days that have gone past.
When there's nothing to hold on
to
My memories I will save,
Till my life is in its winter
And snow falls on my grave.

Ann Welch
COME GO WITH ME
Come
go with me
for just a while
to this
special place
I'd like to share
with you
I'll show you
where in birdsong wrapped
I lie
gently swaying
with the breeze
to watch sunbeams
dancing
on the leaves
promises of fruit
in blossom still
baby green apples
the branches fill
you'll see
a bee and butterfly world

nestle in
the heart of a flower
with petals unfurled
get lost
in a dream
let time
drift by
then tell me
if you know where
freedom
hides

Janine Poronsky
TIME
Time to find time
to die
to live
to weep
to laugh
to run
to play
to study
to stray
I need time to find time
to experience.

Marilyn Roberts
APOCALYPSE NOW
How I hunger to be lost.
Take me from this holocaust.
Mass-contagion, an alien space,
I have no home but in this
waste.
Locked in a prison not my
own
where lames are game and evil
is sown
in plastic traps where nothing
matters
where power grabs and sanity
scatters.
Cloverleaf puzzles in a freeway
maze,
mankind muddles in the
concrete daze
unaware of what it is. . .
cloudy minds in polluted fizz.
Littered streets and cluttered
bay,
poisoned fish where children
play,
missing mountains behind the
day
and all I want is to get away.

Diane Gatlin
DEEPWOOD
Hollow windows reflecting,
dancing shadows framed.
Pictured story of future lost.
Time who takes the blame.
Stained glass memory of
springtime May,
lilacs purple-white.
Loves lost beneath the boughs
of June,
stars spot black—moonlight.
Sunshine windows, spaceless
walls,
paint splashed on canvas dry.
Photos, hollow too, print what
was immortal,
though all flowers must die.
Paned porch green with endless
birth,
from seed, to seed, to seed.
Worth forgotten long ago,
decayed
in moss and weed.
Air in movement, restless dust,
silent voices cry unheard.
Eyes that watch shadows linger,
past and future blurred.

Noemi Quintanar
WAITING
The night is still
Darkness hung heavy
Waiting to prance
At the sudden light of the lamp
Silence piercing your ears
As your eyes search, straining
Only to see nothing
Yet you don't close your eyes,
for fear.
Hearing shadows
The wind whipping and
whistling
Your body strains for the sounds
Yet there's nothing, but your
mind
Feeling the darkness
Passing over you
Still straining waiting
For the flick of light.

Patrick H. Norris
IT WOULD SEEM
Our children will sleep,
A thousand dreams—
None of which, we could ever
share.
It's a silent way,
to another world—
Where no one, can follow them
there.
For it's sleep that takes,
All the rest away—
And what lingers there, is to
dream.
Who knows where they be,
or really are now—
They've gone for awhile, it
would seem.

J. Preston Smith
GRAND CANYON ARTISTRY
Grand Canyon, Grand Canyon, a
masterpiece that Nature has
carved in the land
Artistry of the ages, can we
understand
Its purpose, its beauty, the
constant forces and duty
behind
Can anyone ever question such
a great artist's mind
It is art without equal, made by
Nature's own hand
Combining color and sculpture
in a canyon so grand
It's no wonder it's a wonder,
the greatest of sights
It is art never ending, the
height of Nature's delights
It's a marvel of marvels, music
at our command
It's orchestrated in silence,
played by Nature's own band
It's no wonder it's a wonder, was
it Nature's great plan
Creating symphonic magic, to be
marveled by man
Brushing beauty with boldness,
carved in granite and sand
A panorama to ponder, just what
Nature had planned
It's no wonder it's a wonder,
it's the grandest, by far
Touching all who have seen it,
matters not who we are

Dan Speer
TRUE LOVE
Originally, your soul. . .
Awash in your gene,
Produced an entity
Magnificently serene.
Your mind so awakened
To that which is pure,
Your thinking creative
And intriguingly demure.
Your voice so fluid
And lingering in tone,
Communications forthcoming
Enveloping my zone.
Your breathing is deeper
Than most of the rest,
That heaving pert bosom
Is distracting at best.
The flick of your eye
When targeted on me,
Instantly brings moments
Of cybernetic glee.
True love can be tested
In a moment or two,
A twinge of nausea detected
When alone without you. . .

Ann Bradley
FOLLOW ME
Come oh come, follow me
Said the man from Galilee,
I know the way to a place
Richer than gold.
It is in my fathers land
If you'll follow me you can,
Live in this place where you'll
Never grow old.
Though as scarlet be your sins
I can wash them white again,
Just repent and live the way
I taught you to.
If His commandments you will
keep
Your share of heaven you will
reap,
Trust in me and it will all
Be there for you.
Where there will be no more
night
Only the goodness of my light,
And the power of the Bread
Of life I give.
I am the first, I am the last
I am the present, I am the past,
And who ever believes in me
Shall always live.

Anne S. Publow
LOVE LEFT
Love left a bitter memory
of remembered things.
Love left a cruel echo
and flew on gossamer wings.
Love left a scar of pain
of hurt and grief.
Love left an emptiness
and sped—a thief.

April Jolly DelSasso
HONEST EYES
I can see it your eyes
that you still care for me.
They are not full of happiness
as they once used to be.
You can tell me that it's over,
you can't tell me that we're
through.
But your eyes speak another
language,
they tell me what is true.
I cannot be convinced,
no matter how you try.
I only have to look at you,
your eyes, they cannot lie.

Margie L. Jones
LIFE'S BOOMERANG
A little boy walked angrily
Down a mountain path one
day.
He had just lost a heated fist
fight
And this he would scoffingly
say;
"I hate you. I hate you. I hate
you."
He mumbled at first very low.
"I hate you. I hate you. I hate
you."
And on down the path he
would go.
"I hate you. I hate you. I hate
you."
Now he was shouting quite
loud.
"I hate you. I'm gonna get even."
With a curse on his breath he
vowed.
Then suddenly terror came o'er
him
And his voice was unable to
speak;
For out of the mountain came
voices
At first very low and weak.
But then they became much
louder
And the boy understood each
word.
"I hate you. I hate you. I hate
you."
These were the things he
heard.
The voices were only his echos.
But at first the boy was afraid.
Then after a few thoughtful
moments;
A very wise decision he made.
"I love you. I love you. I love
you."

The boy spoke sweetly soft now.
"I love you. I love you. I love you."
And the echo sent back his vow.
In life this boy had learned a lesson.
We're wise if we learn it too.
Hearts giving hatred or love will come
In its same form back to you.

Catherine F. Hartman
A GLIMPSE OF LOVE
Slivers of light
A whispering breeze,
Nestled together
Amongst the trees.
Stars above
Twinkle in glee,
As we share our bodies
Just you and me.
Savoring our moments
A fleeting time,
Sharing our laughter
Our liter of wine.
A Glimpse of Love
Which might have been,
Gracefully covering
A passionate yen.

Billie Autrey Kinsinger
COMPLEXION
. . . i reached out to touch;
somehow it slipped away. . .
a quiver, a longing,
full of sense awakened. . .
a waste? time?
and now dispersed;
that could be given,
i gave. . .
and all i wanted was to taste,
possessing nothing but the nearness
being;
would it yet return.

Herlinda Montenegro
TO MY LOVER
Let me share your dreams, and
be the one you can come to,
when dreams seem so far away.
Endear yourself to me, with
the love you have to share,
in your laughter and intense
need to be fulfilled.
Let me be,
the Woman,
Friend,
Love
and the Playmate,
that completes you.
Not as an extension of you,
Only as a compliment to
your happiness.
Let me love you freely showing you,
all my sides, without judgement
of how it "should" be.
Let there be no limits to our closeness,
and the flowering, we can share and learn,
thru a mutual trust.

Savithri Lakshmiraghavan
UNTITLED
Idle clouds making
Their purposeless voyage thru' the skies
Grow depressed and gloomy
Brooding over their futility
And dissolve into tears
Which rejuvenate the earth.

Cynthia Tweedy Hoffer
LETTRE OF DEATH!
One day a Frenchman cried,
In his hand a small lettre lay crumpled.
As tears ran down his cheeks,
and dropped to the ground,
He could hear his young wife's piercing screams;
but the frenchman stood against the door, bound,
cursing and screaming for her,
As a soldier clubbed him to the ground.
She stopped and struggled no more.
thinking her love one dead,
He was so still.
So away they rode with the fair petite,
to the horror of the bastille.
Defeat is hard for a man,
Defeat is extra hard for a Frenchman,
In the year of 1762,
it's hard to be just or seek justice,
In a France full of jealousy and cowardice.
Especially when it comes,
In the form of a lettre,
In the middle of the night.
Two lives stopped in one instant,
And on the ground,
By the Frenchman,
Lay the Cause;
The Tragic,
Lettre de Cachet!

Arline
INDIAN SUMMER
In my Indian Summer days of
life, I know the buds of spring
were all too tight to rightly feel
the balmy breeze flow all about;
and summer's heat was too
intense, and all too immense
to sense the calm of deeper

things that grow with time. So
in my prime I live in thanks,
and let the autumn soothe my
soul, enjoying every colored
shade upon my path that helps
to make me whole.

Billie Warren
KITCHEN QUEEN
She turns lightly from the oven,
clears preparation fragments,
mirrored china returns her smile.
Yeasty fragrance mingles with anticipation,
flashes:
of light—crusted ovals quickly consumed,
of current celerity of daily routines,
restlessly eager for instant results.
She reflects.
Can such speed endure?
No! More is needed!
Passage of time:
dough to rise,
friendships to build.
Rolls have vanished
like forgotten harmonies of nature.
The empty bread dish beckons.

Mary E. B. Peterson
THE ORGAN MOUNTAINS
WONDER touched me....I was filled with awe
When first your rocky pinnacles I saw.
Lofty crags I've climbed, and clifts of stone
But in my estimate you stand alone
Above them all. You have no need to boast,
For anyone can see you have the most
Of towering points, sharp clifts, and rocky crags,
Where sunlight pricks its rays, and moonlight jags
Its silvery beams upon your needle spires.
Though sacrilege it seems, ego desires
To stand upon the very topmost part.
Alas! I dare climb only in my heart,
So grant my spirit freedom to explore.
It has no need of skill or mountain lore.
From rolling hills below, my soul delights
In struggling upward to defy your heights,
And when triumphantly it gains the peaks,
My inner being finds the peace it seeks.

Jean A. Mathisen
TEEPEE RINGS
Teepee rings on the quiet hillside,
Others have walked here before.
Paintbrush looms crimson,
against ragged sawtooth rock.
The wind blows down the gulch,
stirring dust and sagebrush.
Miners walked these hills,
searching for fairytale gold.
Then, the wind blew
and the aspen stirred in its caress.
Teepee rings were here then, too,
but none noticed.
They were a part of the past—
the ever—present, nearly touching past.
Now miner's footprints are fossilized
in written pages and in hard rock,
and they too are of the past.
When these green-struck leaves have fallen,
when the growing trees lie as rotting logs,
then the new-born present
will barely acknowledge
teepee rings on the quite hillside.

Ruthann Husband Errante
STORM
The thunder's loud,
the lightning's bright.
I'm in my bed,
it's late at night.
My husband's sleeping,
by my side.
I feel at peace,
that I'm his bride.
My childrens dreams
are good I pray.
I hope tomorrow's
a sunny day.

Lisa Marie Rodrigues
—GOD—
When He created us we were no easier or harder to create than a million stars in the sky, or the tiniest grain of sand by the sea. We were created in His image to walk side-by-side, to be close to one another, to be equal. He thinks no more or less of one as he does the other. This is the way it was meant to be.
He is God, our Creator, our Everlasting Light, the Lord Almighty, the Alpha and Omega.

Kimberly R. Linseth
RUN THROUGH THE TWILIGHT
The midnight gloom,
of distant times.
a bell tolls,
sounding doom
echoes without rhyme.
What is in the gathering dark
that cries out to be heard?
Vicious beast in the night
worry not—I make my flight,
across the hills
the dim-lit rows
I hurry now for my home
all alone this twilight.

Suzanne Kay Jacobs
A LESSON FROM A CHILD
There is a little girl inside of me;
Deep in the heart of the woman.
There is a little boy inside of you;
Deep in the heart of the man.
There is a lot of caring going on,
keeping the two of us near;
There is a lot more inside of us,
if only we would hear.
The sounds of love can easily be
heard in a child's ears; adults
sometimes have trouble hearing them
because of deep rooted fears.
Deep in the heart of the man,
There is a little boy.
He is full of trust; full of truth;
full of love; yet, he stays hidden;
afraid inside.
As long as there is that untouchable fear—
the escatsy of trust and true love for
the man will be denied.

Sam Purdy
AUTUMN MUSING
Placid serenity of sunset calls to me,
Inviting me to lie down on the sand,
Empty my mind of contention, passion, labor,

Listen to the sea and rusty gulls.
But ere I fall asleep I hear the jet,
Its piercing whine trailing the sleek craft,
Only to catch up at time of landing,
Guarding shoreline 'gainst the threat of war.
I struggle to my feet and find a path,
Its stone and stubble toughen my bare feet,
And as I walk along a rabbit scrambles
Into the autumn plumage, gold and red.
I'm like a fisherman hip deep in water,
Casting, but hesitating to draw in,
Enjoying the surroundings and the action
But hoping that the fish misses the hook.
Someone out there created all this beauty,
But knowing how sublimity leads on to boredom,
picked up a ton or two of mortal danger,
And cast it at our feet to cope with it.

Clare Eastep

I MISS YOU

I hear a step behind me;
A knock upon the door;
A stranger to remind me;
You pass this way no more.
I feel my heart strings strumming
To old familiar tunes.
A voiceless song goes humming
Throughout the empty rooms.
At hush of dawn, I harken,
For morning sounds of yore;
And know, as shadows darken,
I'll miss you, evermore.

Nancy Fitzgibbon

YOURS

Way back twenty seven years ago,
Is it possible? Where did the years go?
Thinking back over the years, it seems a long way.
But sometimes, like now, it seems just like yesterday.
Oldest girl was I, and just fifteen.
To the younger, more like a second mother did I seem.
And my youngest brother, Dennis, was like my own,
A little angel, sent from Heaven to our home.
To the oldest girl, chores are a long line,
But this particular chore, I did not mind.
No chore at all; my pleasure, my delight.
Quite jealously, I considered it my right.
He was so cute and loving, so adorable,
And to all this, my maternal instinct was vulnerable.
If he were hurt, or a need to plea,
To Mother, he'd go...or to me.
A little pallet for him, I'd lay,
I remember,
And as I ironed late into the night, he'd slumber.
With his little arms around my neck, my heart would soar,
When I'd ask "Whose boy are you?" and he'd say "yours."
And now, even now, with so many years gone by,
I'll ask jokingly, yet hoping for the same reply.
"Whose boy are you?" and he knows and answers "yours."
And in a way he is, and my heart with joy still soars.

Helen M. Oxley

MY JOE

My Joe is just a regular boy
with freckles on his face
who loves his sports and games
and is willing to run a race.
My Joe likes peanut butter
sandwiches and chocolate ice cream
too,
just like hundreds of other boys do.
My Joe likes cowboys and horses also,
he's no different from other kids,
No,
except that he is *My Joe*.

Jessica Jean Steinbrenner

JACK—ASS

Waiting,
While heaving my heavy saddle upon Late Arrival,
Loose girth flipping onto a fly-infested manure stack.
Waiting,
While dragging L.A.'s foamy, fuzzy, sweet-feed mouth
To practice obstacles,
Clean black hunt coat rubbed with snot.
Waiting,
While adjusting my velveteen cap and ratcatcher,
Reins between my knees.
Waiting,
While climbing stairs onto a steep mounting block,
Spurs stiff and tight around glossy boots.
Waiting,
While the white gate opens for my introduction,
My head bowed down.
Waiting,
While galloping rapidly in a semi-circle
To the water barricade.
Waiting,
While Mom jumps forward with a smile
And a towel.

Micki Webber

UNTITLED

AND. . . . .
Our Creator said:
To you and
To me
Entwine spirits
Enjoy one another
Be happy, be sad
Share dreams, love, nature and togetherness.

Though the time is short
That you both may share
The need for spoken words
There is no concern, because...
This beautiful bond
That was created especially for you
Makes time stand still
AND. . . . .
Makes precious moments and memories forever.

Tamera S. Hensley

ONE DAY SOON

Many children born each day
Less fortunate than you and I
Are brought into this world of ours
With the fear they soon will die.
Far too often a birth defect
Will shorten their life span
They pray that we'll reach out to them
And help them if we can
And ONE DAY SOON, we hope and pray
That they can jump and shout
Saying, thanks to those of you who cared
This disease has been wiped out!

Delmer Nightingale

SUMMER BREEZE

A little boy one summer day,
Alone and tired from all his play,
Went to his mother's room to rest
And heard the breeze in from the West.
It curved around the outside eaves,
No doubt the same that moved the leaves.
He stretched his body upon the bed,
The pillow there caressed his head
As drowsiness engulfed his view
With memories that were so new.
But the enchanting sound the soft breeze made,
Richly humming and unafraid,
Kept the boy awake to a haunting tune
And he never forgot that afternoon.
Today when he hears that old, old sound,
It holds him to something to which he is bound,
For when the breeze blows with that mellowed sadness,
The older boy feels it would be madness
To erase a memory as cherished as that,
A picture of boyhood for which no one sat.

Nancy Ressler

A WRITER'S PRAYER

Struggling with a sentence,
Searching for a rhyme,
Lord, I need your guidance,
There's so little time.
Fill me with your Spirit,
Help me do my part,
Let my words count for you,
Penetrate each heart.

Sally Sherbut Stevens

A FAIRY IN THE GARDEN

Little one so mild and meek
Who loves his world of hide and seek
Steal your way into my garden of flowers
Where you may hide for endless hours
And you will find delicious roses
With fragrances to tickle young noses
Colors of Crimson, Topaz and White
Leaves of Green and thorns that bite
Poppy's of Orange, Purple and Red
You shall find in my flower bed
Pastel sweet pea's a work of art
Will steal their way into your heart
Tis getting dark and very soon
By the light of the flourescent moon
You shall see the little fairy
That colors my garden and makes it merry
For fairies only come out at night
When mommies and daddies are sleeping tight
They sprinkle love and beauty all around
And then disappear into the ground.

Addie Johnson

LOVE UNCERTAIN

Love is, as uncertain as the mist in the morning, as light as the wind, thru
the night, as real as the sun in the heavens; and for you and I absolutely right.

Claire B. McNaney

UNTIL

It seems as though
I've past my prime
and far surpassed the rest,
of friends of long ago and new,
What happened?
Will I last?
I've seen a lot
both good and bad
and friends have made their way;
beyond my goals and dreams I've had
and probably will until.
My time grows short on promises
and dreams of yet to fill;
the daylight drifts to dusk
too soon
and will from now until.

Gay Thibodeaux

THE THUNDERING WIND

I hear you coming slowly as a tidal wave might come,
Like a giant swarm of bees, I hear your steady hum,
And then you get much louder as you twist the giant trees.

Karen L. Kupp
LET'S PRETEND
Let's play "Let's Pretend".
I know it's such a childish game;
But one we ought to try.
We'll pretend we never shared
that night.
We'll pretend the words and
feelings expressed;
Were really only a dream.
I'll pretend the caring I felt
wasn't there,
You can pretend the caring you
showed didn't exist.
We've dreamed so long,
Longed, gazed, and desired so.
I suppose we'll just go on;
Pretending these feelings don't
exist.
How long shall we play the
game?
If we play it long enough
MAYBE;
We'll forget that night.

Michael Lee
IN QUEST
I dreamed a dream the other
night,
I soared so high, a bird in flight.
My feathery cloak of darkened
hue,
Kissed by a veil of diamond dew,
Enveloped my soul, my earthly
being,
Into a vulture fearlessly seeking
The ever endless quest for
knowledge
Yet ungleaned by worldly
college.
The infinite sky of timeless
space
Swirled into webs of atomical
lace.
I flew o'er the uniform rock
of mars
By the heavenly glow of a
thousand stars.
I counted the galaxies, one by
one,
Until the ascendance of the sun.
A golden ray caressed my face,
As I awoke in dawn's embrace.
Was I a vulture or earthly being?
Through the window was I
seeing,
Tenderly cradled in crystal dew,
Motley feathers of darkened
hue?

Katherine Jeannette Mize
FIVE—YEAR—OLD RAISIN CAKE
Such a lovely little dumpling
doll
comes ringing on my bell,
with big brown eyes and
freckled face.
"Oh, I thought you weren't
home,"
she says, tumbling in my door.
She's anxious little helping
hands
some special treat is her reward.
This precious little raisin cake
I'll always treasure in my heart.
Why, she sings fairy songs
no one's ever heard before!
She has quite a collection
of gathered-up things,
all treasured beyond belief—
junk mail, pencil, and wilted
rose,
kept tucked inside an old purse.
My favorite time to read,
with that warm little snug by
my side.
"You sweet little muffin mouse,
I hoped you had come to stay.
But you don't visit much
anymore,
just go skipping by my house
down to Mrs. Chitwood's class,
saucy, with cinnamon hair
unfurled".
Sure hope they like raisin cake
down at kindergarten school.

P. J. Schmidt
POOR BABY
a puppet
does
someone else's
thing,
follows
another's
movements.
a puppet
is used for the
entertainment
of others.
it's arms move
at the
flick
of His fingers.
it's legs dance
ecstatically
when He
wishes it.
without Him
the puppet
slumps,
waiting hopefully,
and is in
perpetual
fear
that He
will forget
the
creature
He
left
lying
there. . .
forever.

Jo Ann Huff
TELL SANTA ABOUT ME
You will find me here, every
year
Sitting on a shelf.
With lot's of toys all around
And dolls, such as myself.
I have hair of yarn, button eyes,
And a sewn on mouth of red.
I am made of rags, and put
together,
With different colored thread.
Raggedy Ann, is my name,
surely, you have heard of me.
All I want for Christmas, is to
be found. . .
Under someones tree.
It would make me so happy,
When Christmas morning
comes. . .
If I could be loved, and cuddled
By a certain little one.
So Mommy's and Daddy's
everywhere,
Please hear my beckoned cry. .
"Raggedy Ann doesn't want,
Christmas to pass her by."
So someone please tell Santa. . .
About me being in this store,
So he'll get me, on Christmas
Eve,
And take me home once more.

Gene Gelston
THE FOUNDATION OF LOVE
The foundation of Love
compares to the union
between a tree and its roots.
Growing together
and dependant upon each
other.
Neither can live without the
other—
Nor has reason to.
The tree should branch out,
point always upward,
blossom,
As should love.
The roots give the tree
its foundation,
The heart gives love
its foundation.
And though the tree
may sometimes fall,
If its roots are
sound and secure,
It will always, again,
be a tree.

Steven Gregory Alston
ACHIEVEMENT
Ah, sweet mountaintop, there I
long to be
Inch-by-inch and foot-by-foot I
climbed
Ah, sweet mountaintop where I
long to be
Tears I've shed and I've had
sorrow,
hoping for a brighter day
tomorrow.
Ah, sweet mountaintop there I
long to be
Reaching upward to the skies,
fighting hard to win the prize
Ah, sweet mountaintop there I
long to be
The golden ring—the broken
tape, a hand raised in victory
number one.
Ah, sweet mountaintop, there I
long to be.

Cassandra Moore
THE TWINS
In form and feature, face and
limb
I grew so like my brother
That folks were taking me for
him
And each for one another.
It puzzled all our kith and kin;
It reached a fearful pitch
For one of us was born a twin,
Yet not a soul knew which.
One day, to make the matter
worse
Before our names were fixed
As we were being washed by
nurse
We got completely mixed.
And thus, you see, by fates'
decree
My brother John got
christened me
And I got christened him.

Mimi Anna Marie Leisy
SOMEONE LIVED HERE
The mountain air surrounds me,
A river's there below,
I think someone has lived here,
But who I'll never know.
The trees surround the
mountains
That stand so proud and high,
I know someone has lived here
But told it all good bye.
The leaves are softly crinkled
Beneath my two bare feet
I know someone has lived here,
Someone I'd like to meet.
The sun is brightly shining
On water flowing strong
I know someone has lived here
That really did belong.
The animals are stirring
They're hunting hungrily.
I know someone has lived here,
Someone I hope to see.
Now nature stands before me
With magic in the air
I know someone has lived here
And said a little prayer,
For love and peace surround me
It can not be ignored,
I know someone has lived here,
That someone is my Lord.

Mildred Lambert Bell
O WINDBLOWN OAK
O, windblown oak, all snarled
and twisted,
you stand staunch; rugged;
against the wind,
Behind every scar, there's a
story,
some made by foes, the
deepest a friend.
Each mark you wear, makes me
love you more,
because you stood despite
every odd;
Passing time has only made of
you,
a lovelier creation of God.
Windblown oak, you're no
stranger to cares,
you've battled the angry,
savage, storms;
Like you, windblown oak, real
faith in God,
just keeps trusting; marching
through the storms.
O, windblown oak, I'm sure God
loves you,
so like you, He desires us to
be;
A memorial to honor and
strength
though we're scarred as you,
windblown oak tree.

Janice M. Ellis
HE AND BONES
In town there was a little boy
and his dog, Bones.
They just roamed around
without a home.
One afternoon I brought them
something to eat;
They told me thank you for the
wonderful treat.
Not long after that Bones just
laid down and died;
The little boy picked him up
and cried.
With his dog in his arms he

turned away,
And in a broken voice I heard
him say,
"I never had food or clothes;
All I had was just Bones.
Without him I don't know what
I'll do.
I wish that God would take me
too."
I know that his heart will never
mend,
Because Bones was his family
and his friend.
Sometimes you'd see him
walking down the street,
Dressed in rags with no shoes on
his feet.
But one day an old lady came
walking by;
When she saw the little boy it
brought a tear to her eye.
She took him home and fed him
real good;
She gave him all the love she
could.
But the little boy never got over
the death of his best friend;
And when he went to bed that
night
he never woke up again.
The old lady said God did what
was best,
Because without Bones the little
boy would never rest.
I guess that I will never
understand,
The reason God lets people
suffer as he let that little man.

Kay Brooks
YOU ARE
In my darkness, you are my
Light.
In my world, you are my
Life.
In my path, you are my
Way.
In my bravery, you are my
Courage.
You are my Strength.
In my soul, you are my
Friend.
In my heart, you are my
Love!

Joyce Malanafy Creamer
BLADES OF GRASS
Here I lay upon the blades of
grass
Feeling the breeze gently pass
Looking up into the sky, as the
clouds go drifting by.

Watching the sunlight through
the trees
Yet feeling its warmth pass
over me
Here I lay upon the blades of
grass
Just drifting in and out of the
past.

Margaret A. Froedge
LILACS
On lazy late spring afternoons
Cool, and rainy
When the sun lies sleeping
Hidden behind a soft lacy
curtain of mist
The gentle fragrance of lilacs
creeps
Silently over my senses.
Slowly. .
In the smiling moments of
anticipation
The dream materializes
The comfort and warmth of the
infinite cosmos
(Stolen from the sun)
Walks to my side.
I reach out carefully like a child
Trying to catch the sunbeam
That falls through the window
Into the hall.

Betty Lea Brout
SOLACE
Lace! Alive with green and spun
by unknown hands, the trees in
morning mist are each one a
gem, all of them a loving kiss
across the hills, a welcome
home where rosy clouds may
linger, a fuss of birds come
calling, a splendid gift of solace
to ease the tired, tearful soul.
And if I am here, gazing on this
glory, it surely means I have
made it through the night, that
tears are done, that no matter
yesterday there is even yet a
dwelling place for peace, where
eyes will smile and serenity will
live.

J. Benjamin Stanley
THE WAY YOU ARE
From the blue in the heavens
Shine the stars from above
They remind me of you dear
Of your undying love
Stay just the way you are
As the roar of your ocean
Finds the calm of your sea
Sends forth rheems of emotion
To the depths—within me
Stay just the way you are
In the still of the forest
Comes the song of a bird
That flows of your tenderness
Only I have heard
Stay just the way you are
With the freshness of spring
Through the touch of your
hands
Fills my heart with a wring
Like the soft endless sands
Stay just the way you are
As the darkness of night
Meets the brightness of day
So your radiant beauty
Forever will stay
Just the way you are
The depth of your charms
When I hold you so near
Shall endeavor to tell me
that you are so dear
Stay just the way you are
So wherever you go
Whether home or away
You'll spend sweetness & love
Every day after day
Stay just the way you are
Your devotion to me
And forever I'll be
So faithful and true from afar
For with help I will pray
With endurance you'll stay
Just the way you are

Charend
IMPRESSIONS
The trembling beat of the field
under the touch of the wind
The crashing reckless sea
The soft floating cloud
The summer green peopled by a
hundred billion leaves
The brown smelly earth
And the relentless sun
Father of it all.
These things make up and are
the real essence
that pervades this ring of time.
The freedom of the air
The frantic search of water for
itself;
The "I am" of everything
The "I was" exists in mental
dream
The "I will be" exists not at all.

Susan Owen
FREE
My Friend, elusive as a
butterfly. . .
Shed your wings and
feel the sky
Feel the Earth; its
freedom and grace
And let the wind
Caress your face. . .
Come to know the you
deep inside
Let go of all feelings
you've deprived
Cherish the flow of
your own energy
And know the truth
of all 'to be'. . .
Feel your inner eyes
open to see
Knowing, at last,
that you are free. . .

Kim Netzinger
WINTER RHAPSODY
Capture a dream in a snowflake,
No two are quite the same.
As bright as your imagination,
As white, and yet untamed.
A blanket full of fantasies,
Through thoughts and
daydreams pass,
Escape your way to distant lands
Where wealth and riches last.
You feel the peace, the silence
there,
Inside your cloak of white.
Your visions drift to shadows
deep,
Your mind creates the light.
An adventure in each crystal
Is what you will surely find,
When you take the time to
wander
Through the snowflakes in your
mind.

Camille M. Mucci
A TORTURED MIND
What is this thing called a mind
The phenomenal abyss of
unending facts
This house of a myriad of
untapped resources
It tenaciously grasps all you
have wrought
There is nowhere one can turn
to escape its thoughts
symphony full of pleasantries:
Listen to the gaity of the
children chasing the wind
Touch the wing of a blue
butterfly
Taste the sap of a maple
tree
Smell the sweet smelling
incense
See the weeping willow tree
kissed by the raindrops
Alas, the mind returns once
more to thoughts we seem to
have forgotten and deplore
On the surface it appears as an
absolute nothingness
But you feel a great duress
Hidden in the dark, labyrinthine
way lies painful disquieting
thoughts
With the facts one must cope
If there ever is to be tranquility
and hope.
Oh this tortured mind—
Will it ever find peace?

Marjorie Manganello
CHANGE
and oooh. . . . .
how the butterflies were
awakened
to a very distorted illusion
"To think
someone could love one,
as loveless as I,
who shed no sunshine
no springtime
just rainy tears"
I've grown alone. . .
in this desert of emptiness,
much too long
just to wither & die,
Must rid this indecisiveness
and bloom again. .
Let winter pass, and spring begin
Fears can change to Hope,
Hope to Joy,
Joy
to
Love

Phyllis Nunnelley
FOR MOM
She's tired of hearing
about death,
or someone's
last breath.
Write about life,
wonderful things,
or soft butterflies,
with pretty wings.
Write about people,
or just plain earth,
write about a
childs birth.
For her sake,
I will try,
In this one,
no one will die.
I'll write a poem
with some fizz,
or so I'll try.
Here it is:
Life is wonderful,
Life is dear,
to a mother,
who's so sincere.
We have beautiful
things about us,
the hum of a bird,
or just a bee buzz.
With grass so
green and lovely,
all things
so sweet to see.
The smell of
fresh cut flowers,

huge buildings
and also towers.
Oh yes, we have
beautiful green trees,
and a mother, I hope
this poem will please.

Claudia Lynn Gilbert
THE SWALLOW-TAILED KITES
Dusting the day with grace they came, each bank and slide and glide blessing with beauty those who could only look up. As one, they sank close to earth, resplendent ebon and snows, aloft and balanced, smoothly swathing us in their glow, low arcs of enchantment—sheer clear perfection, wings bringing happiness, leaning lightly on nothing, and so near! Below, bedazzled, clay transmuted, we with sky, warm winds and circling kites are one. No longer earth-bound, our gaze is set free, Released, refreshed, and retrained toward the sun. If ever birds were heaven-essence. . . . Kites! We find a paean for the god of such sights.

Christine D. Klingberg
ON THE BALCONY
dawn is breaking, and a
windswept mist is softly
falling. . .
on the verdant valley below,
on its filigreed foliage
stretching in the mist,
on its birds chattering
incessantly in sundry tongues,
on its palm trees silhouetted
against the silvery sky;
on the remnants of a party,
on its colored lights looking like
a gaudy memory,
on its lawn chairs arranged in
strange kaliedoscope patterns,
on its plastic cups, half-
filled with melted ice,
dotting the lawn;
on me, looking down from
my balcony.

Helena Secre
SPECIAL PLACE
Here, heart is that special place
Feed upon it—this elixir
Store the vision to harvest—
When the world's vexations
Start the spoliation intolerable.
O, feast again, birds have
wings—
Even they move away.
You, too—have moved on
wheels.
Here, nature is a holy vessel
The rolling green touching
hands
On hills like woven fabric.
Blessing, growing, giving
And waiting for your return.

Toni Borra
CANDY
Wayne was a man with little in
life
who had all he needed, and
never wanted a wife.
His life was his apartment and
his bottle of brandy
and he never wanted anymore,
until he met Candy.
He wanted to be with her above
and beyond life
Wayne proposed, and made
Candy his wife.
They'd celebrated every Sunday
with champagne, never brandy
for nothing was too good, for
Wayne and his Candy.
Their third week of marriage
was a tragedy for Wayne
his Candy had died and he'd
never be the same.
They found a note on the
pillow,
the house vacated of brandy,
champagne was on the table
and Wayne was with his Candy.

Ruth M. Blekkenk
INSPIRATION
Inspiration hits me every now
and then
And I just can't rest 'til I
pick up a pen.
Inspiration, when it comes, is a
funny thing
It is like God's telephone
giving me a ring.
Words of love and words of
cheer
The words my God wants me to
hear.
The way I feel when I sit and
write
Is one of pure, heavenly, loving
delight.
Thank you Lord for your
wonderful words
So I can truly proclaim you
Lord of Lords.

Cynthia DeeAnne Smith
UNTITLED
You, my brother
I have loved so dear
I've never known pain or fear
'Til one grave endless night
The screams, the cries of
terrified fright
You, my brother

I love so dear
Has now been told your end is
near
The family and friends whisper
"But he's so young"
The mourning song, I have
already sung
You, my brother
I loved then and now
Just stay with me, if you only
know how.

Jean Morrow Dingee
REMEMBER LOVE
When all that's left to me in
life
Are memories of pain and strife,
Memories of endless days,
Of thankless tasks performed
always,
Memories of yesteryears,
When my eyes were wet with
bitter tears. . .
Remind me of a young man's
touch,
Before the world became too
much;
Remind me of his laughing eyes,
Before his lips spoke naught
but lies;
Tell me again of long, dark
nights,
When young bodies thrilled to
love's delights. . .
We clung together, safe and
warm,
While all around us raged a
storm
Of changes, waiting at the gate,
To turn sweet love to silent
hate.
Remind me of this, and I'll not
forget
What once we had, and love
him yet.

Edawa Fran
BOOKS
Dream of the books of laughter
Think of the volumes of tears
Peruse thru the shelves of
history
That slide back thru the years
Shrink from the horror mystery
Cling to biographies true
But do read books for all their
worth
to you and you and you

Stephan Brandstatter
LUV
Luv,
If only my embrace could be
a permanent home for thee.
Forever an attempt I'd make,
to hold
if only I were bold.
Such warmth of love once
found
to always have around.
I need you; Luv
I miss you.

Thomas Floyd Newby
THE DOOR AJAR
I can recall when you left your
door ajar
And I was feeling you had not
gone far
Because the latch string was
there hanging out
So felt welcome even tho you
weren't about
Knowing you were near left me
feeling queer
Even tho I knew there was
nothing to fear
However feeling strange I
realized by then
That I loved you but did not
know from when
So curl up in your chair in the
middle den
And start dreaming about what
might have been
Had you been inside when I had
knocked
And found you had left the
front door unlocked

Kathy A. Johnson
CHILDHOOD
Time passes so quickly
And before we know
You've changed so much
You've started to grow.
The young ones aren't little
The babies aren't small,
Each day new things you're
learning
You're starting to grow tall.
The different things you will
experience
The new games you will play,
You're adding to your memories
With you always, they will stay.
Sometimes that's all you have
Memories of how it used to be.
But for now, you're in the
present time
And I want you to think of me.
The time will come soon
enough
When you'll be on your own
So don't grow up too fast
Soon enough you'll be fully
grown.
Remember always, I love you
You'll always be in my heart,
With our memories of each
other
We can never be apart.
This poem is dedicated to my
nieces and nephews.

Bonnie L. Holtzhafer
PLAYING GAMES
It's hard to win when you start
playing your games.
I know who she is, but I'm not
naming names.
Deal me in next time, I'll
explain how to play.
Keep the cards in your hand,
don't give them away.
I've seen your cards, but you
didn't mean to show me,
Promising love when you don't
want to know me.
I know your game now, it's easy
to follow,
Though your rules are a little
hard to swallow.

Paulette Baumert
THE DANCE
The butterflies dance
flitting on the tips of leaves,
move in colored songs.

Winifred Thraves Turner
MA AND PA
We never called her Mother,
But just a short sweet "Ma";
We never called him Father,
Just a beloved "Pa".
Ma never stood on dignity,
She just relied on love;
Pa never threw his weight
around,
Nor lorded from above.
Whenever Ma was needed,
She always was right there;
We never doubted Pa's faith,
We knew he'd always care.
I may not know where Heaven
is,
But this I surely know -
Wherever Ma and Pa are,
There's where I want to go.

Elaine P. Morton
LIFE AND ME
As life goes on, I hate myself
And everything that's in it.
But for the moment, I might say,
Look at yourself to see,
Is it life or is it me?

Unless we learn to master
Our feelings from within,
Life mounts an awful height
Of untangled whim.
The dreams of yesterday
Clutched within our heart
Never given to retreat,
We hide our thoughts from mere defeat.
If we'd forget our inner thoughts
To a safe degree,
Life would be much better
For both you and me.
Those dreams are now far in the past,
And should be left behind.
The time has come to seek anew,
A true and better kind.

Dr. Lionel Fern
THE MANAGER
(Judgement)

A Manager is a man who, naturally, belongs to the human species (Homo sapiens), which in turn is comprised in the subphylum Vertebrata (animals with a backbone). He works in an office where he sits on a chair in front of a desk. He

sits on the end of his backbone; but it is not with this end (the bottom) that he administrates. He so does with the other end of it; which, logically, happens to be his head (the top).

Timothy Boos
CONFUSED

My goal was to serve
But I felt misused
Is it any wonder
That I was confused?
I was allowed into the backroom
To see people being abused
Could you really have blamed me
For being confused?
You all laughed at me
For singing the blues
I just couldn't have stopped
From being confused.
I wanted us to win
But we just had to lose
Maybe that caused me
To be confused?
Yes there were times
When I blew my fuse
It must have been
That I was confused.

Kathy Sowers
UNCOMMON

I don't choose my friends by their color
I don't choose my friends by their creed,
I try to be fair and uncommon
and go straight to the heart with the need.
So if ever you're down and you're out friend
and haven't a place left to go,
Come to me and tell me and I'll try to be
uncommon and let my love show
And if ever you need me to listen
or maybe just be there awhile,
Don't ever worry I won't friend
uncommon I'll be with a smile.
It's too bad that it is so uncommon
to show that you love and you care,
But uncommon I'll be if you're ever in need
and like a true friend I'll be there.

Glenda Bull
TO JERRY

Sometimes I look at you and see
A little boy looking back at me;
And I wonder were you happy,
Or were you sad;
Who's the best friend you ever had.
Did you blow bubbles that burst on that face?
Were you in Little League,
Did you play first base?
No matter,
I just wonder how long I have loved you.

Richard E. Knowles
DROPS OF H20

Drops of H20
running down the sky
exploding in a steady drone
and melting
into the mud.
Crawling into streamlets
then massing into puddles
racing through the ditches
to tumble into the river.
Then roaring onward into the sea.
Where burning sun
collects and draws them up.
They lie loaded in a cloud
like bullets in a gun.
Waiting . . .trigger happy
for another
rainy day run.

Lori Anne Del Toro
WILTED LOVE

I don't think I'll ever understand
Where do you leave all your love
When here in my heart its in demand
Why do you seem so cold
It really confuses me
Why do you act so bold
At school you act like a stranger
But elsewhere you act so friendly
My heart only keeps warning: Danger!
I feel I want to cry
I know I should forget you
So, I guess I'll just say Good-bye

Pino Lombardi
DREAM
To Jaclyn, my grandchild

When,
by the fantasy
your lulled thought
laid down
into his enchanted
blue paradise,
dream,
my baby,
with closed eyes.
When,
in the serenity
of the light-hearted
springtime,
your heart
beats with joy,
dream.
Embrace,
with open eyes
the inborn gladness
of your tender life.
Hold it tight,
till you can,
because one day,
the fading echo
will be the only one
to soothe that sadness,
the gray,
inevitable reserve
of the life.

Douglas C. Mills, Sr.
THE PROMISE

The earth awakes in a blaze of light
as the world begins and lives.
And the power to make day from night
is the wonder that it gives.
The early morning rapsody
of the birds alive in song,
can lift our hearts to harmony
and make our souls feel strong.
So listen...man...as days begin
and see them with your heart.
For every dawn we start again
and yesterday...depart.
The questions of tomorrow
and doubts of yesterday,
can lead us into sorrow
if we let them always stay.
Make *each day*...your future
and dwell not on what's gone.
Live with things you *know* are sure
like the promise of each dawn....

Roger L. Lynn
SILENCE AND PINE
For H.S.

Night sifts down through pine branch,
splashing across summer gold thighs.
Drops of our pleasure gleam--
like--
phosphorescent pearl.
I have known you to depths
left hidden,
by human word. Yet--
might I--
scratch the surface of your silence?
Greater things--like pine cones,
have fallen than myself.

Geri Parvin
IDENTITY

All alone on center stage
In a one man one act play,
The person you see,
Is not really me
Just a character I try
To portray.
1981

Archie Francis Burger
HEAVENLY PEACE

A lifetime; a twinkle in the eye of time.
An era; a slow wink, not all sublime.
We should therefore, for happiness to find,
Strive for peace that passeth man's mind.
Not enough on earth doth it now dwell;
The heavens proclaim it's magic spell.
Still your thoughts each day; invite it in,
And less and less be steeped in worldly din.
The love from God's heart seeks those to love
And pour it's blessings of peace above.
Still the clamor of the world around you now
And make your life evermore to God bow.
You must be master o'er discord's whirl
In victory of life; The Sacred Pearl!

Gail Simon Schulz
SOUTH DAKOTA AUTUMN

South Dakota Autumn, beauty to behold,
Leaves and grass of green now are brown and gold.
Tumbleweeds are blowing across the prairie land.
The rolling hills are painted as by an artists hand.
Autumn leaves of vibrant hue
Are splashing scarlet against skies of blue.
Many orange pumpkins very bright and gay
In gardens and door-steps proudly on display.
Ducks and geese are Southward bound
Their echoing honks fill the air with sound.
In the park children playing along a frozen lake,
Impatiently waiting for the first snow-flake.

Karen Linda Martin (Martz)
MOURN THE ROSE

Upon the rose the dew sought rest, to await the morning sun.
Upon the rose the raindrop fell, to say the storm would come.
Upon the rose the wind did breathe; it's stems it did not break.
Upon the rose came a late spring snow, yet it's life it did not take.
Then upon the rose came human hands, to cut the thorny branches.
No sun, no rain, no wind to blow; a week at most it's chances.
Upon the rose, a shadow cast--it's death would not be slow.
I rest my eyes upon the rose; I hate to see it go.

Lillie M. Lanier
MY PETAL OF PURE GOLD

My loves were like the petals on a rose.
I had many a beautiful love affair
But there was one among them the dearest to me
My precious darling sweetheart.
My petal of pure gold.
You are my precious petal
My petal of pure gold
It's an old old story, but so often told.
Of love so sweet and tender.
It's true, you are my precious

petal
My petal of pure gold.
Many a friendship have I known
Many a make believe love affair
But in my heart will always be
Forever in my memories
There stands alone one only
precious petal
My petal of pure gold.

Vivian M. Froehlich
I SHALL RETURN
There's a place in California,
A place I once called home.
I never thought I'd miss it
Once I'd set my heart to roam.
But I miss the sunny climate,
And the fog as it rolls in
From the wild and wide Pacific
To the busy streets within.
I miss the friendly faces;
The bright lights and the fun;
Where the glamour and the
plainest
Congregate beneath the sun.
In the folds of one great city,
Where I long to spend my time;
There's a special person waiting,
And she's been there all the
time.
In the city of Lost Angels,
That is where I long to end;
When my roaming days are
over,
I'll return to you my friend.

Jack MacKenzie
ANSWERING SERVICE
I called you
earlier today
but you had
already left
for the afternoon
and didn't
know when you
would return
I'll call
back again soon
and then
tell you everything.

Mary Dawn Hewitt
AIRBORNE
Airborne
As free as the wind
As high as the sky
As far as your dreams
Can reach
The clouds,
The sun,
Warm sand on a beach.
A mountain scene
Autumn trees
A clear blue lake
A summer's breeze
Airborne
A reality
When a person meets their
dreams.

Brian Mosher
TRUTH
Truth is in things;
It is not words.
It's in the sea,
And it's in birds.
Rivers hold truth.
"River" is not.
If it's just words,
What have you got?
Words are ideas;
Not worth a thing.
Hear a river.
Listen: it sings.

James C. Taylor
PROGRESS
We were born into a world at
war
shielded from its deprivations
by parents who endured
hardships
for our education
and success
Were they happy I wonder, or
resigned
They laughed a lot
and loved
and argued
and scraped
and worried
They were patient
and forgiving with each
other
They took a stand
and stood together
We grew up in a world at war
but didn't notice much
being busy with penny loafers
and dusk tails
and chevys
We made progress and became
educated
and successful
and sophisticated
and worldly
We married like our parents did
and bore children
and laughed a lot
and loved
and argued
and scraped sometimes
and worried
But we weren't patient
or forgiving with each
other
We took a stand
and stand alone!

Amanda Gordon Hansen
EVENTIDE
At evening when the sun goes
down,
A blaze of glory in the west;
When birds nodding their
sleepy heads,
Are softly chirping in their nest;
When the long day's work has
ended,
And a weary world goes to rest;
There comes a time I dearly
love,
A time of day most surely blest;
At Eventide.

Evening draws her purple
curtains,
The stars appear, their watch to
keep;
Sounds of children's happy
voices
Are stilled awhile, in slumber
deep;
Once busy lanes deserted now,
Where twilight shadows softly
creep;
A Sandman stealth'y makes his
way;
And tousled heads angelic sleep;
At Eventide.
When night shrouds the earth
in silence,
And the cares of the day depart;
When all the world is wrapped
in dreams
Serenity steals o'er my heart;
For in this tranquil interlude,
Before another day must start;
I find the strength to face my
tasks,
In quiet peace these hours
impart;
At Eventide.

Mike Sandler
SHE
She lives in poverty, dwells in
pain,
Her stomach is empty, but yet
She works all day, and what
does she gain?
Tell me--what does she get?
She hauls the water, plows the
field,
And never thinks to quit;
She often goes days without a
meal--
So, what does she have to show
for it?
She has no family, no education,
And might never become a wife;
And there are thousands like
her throughout the nation,
Who must struggle everyday for
life.
But despite her pain and
constant fear,
She manages a genuine smile
For anyone at all who's willing
to share
A moment with a poor, small
child.

Eric R. Moline
QUERIES, HOMAGE, FAREWELL
To Glenn Katz
To one whose sense of sight was
early lost,
Unfairly taken by that grievous
seed *(1)*
That left and has returned, I ask
what caused
This deadly band to shackle
wrists once freed?
I know not why, but neither do I
know
How you maintain your spirit,
calm through gale
And storm that flattens others
'neath the blow;
Your good mind's strength
o'ercomes when others rail.
This same good mind
perceives what others miss,
Indeed, the darkness dimming
not your sight
But stirring you, so that, as
you enlist,
You reach knowledge glowing
greatly bright.
And now, as you steer way
through final straits,
Your knowledge will include
that which awaits.
(1) cancer

Millie Corle
SHATTERED DREAMS
As I walk beneath the starry
sky,
And in the moon's bright
shining light.
I think of you and our life
together.
How I wish our dreams had
come true,
And our bright thoughts for our
future.
Now our dreams have been
shattered.
You will always belong to
another,
And my heart will always be
broken.
When you think of me
remember,
My love for you will never die.
I will go to heavens pearly gates
With the love I feel for you still
strong.
I will remember our love and
dreams,
And be eternally yours forever.
The moon and stars will tell our
story
To other lovers with their
dreams,
How our dreams were so
shattered
Because our love was not to be.

Wanda J. Hay
COUNTENANCE/ A PORTRAIT
Wizened brow,
and furled,
Hollows out a pallor,
blank, un-hearing.
Eyes of an empty,
tasting dark and salt.
Nose a-quiver,
sentinel over all.
Mouth, scant, grim-pencilled,
drawn all but in.
Thus, I see her now, as then.
Tears erode her face,
Un-love her honey'd Breast.

Ms. Kathryn S. Jones
ART THROUGH MAMA'S EYES
The warm air wrapped the
wicker bottle
That sat on the paint splattered
still life box.
He sat before the pallet of paint.
Waiting for the white light of
day to change.
Yet, the canvas was unimposed
upon.
He cast a glance around the
room looking--
As though for a muse to inspire
him.
He smoothed his hair for
impression sake. Then--
Began to violate the white
canvas.
He painted like a
mathemetician--
Reducing the subject to simple
shapes
Took the graceful shape of the
bottle then
Made it static, and unrelenting.
He should have quit before he
started.

Karl E. Fisler
FOR MEMORIES
For
in my garden there
are many trees, some
old and gnarled, some
bent and wind blown...
And yet, and yet, I
stand above them all.
For
I am the oldest tree
in my garden. And
mayhaps will ever be.
And yet as I stand in
my garden...I do indeed
wonder, wonder.
For
why and whither - all
are my trees in such
myriad shapes, as dreams
are made of...my garden
is real to me, and forever
more will be.
For
after a closer walk in
my garden. Down its
winding paths. As the
sunset shines on the leaves...
I know all these sweet trees.
They have all stirred by
breeze.

For
while some are beautiful,
some ugly, some brave in
the wind; some fallen by
storm...
They are all what had to be.
For in my garden of trees,
they are all me.

Crystelle Robert Wickett
MERRY CHRISTMAS
Greetings to you, one and all--
May your Holidays be filled
with cheer;
Stop! Take time to recall
The fun you had with loved
ones dear;
Hush! Do you something hear--
I do declare,
I thought I heard their footsteps
on the stair
Blue eyed Kenny,
Fred with eyes so brown,
Alice whose eyes are soft and
round--
Robert, the big brother, and
Linda fair;
Perhaps they have come to
haunt us
On this day so full of memories
and love;
Perhaps we forgot to stop and
thank the one above
Who has been so kind to us
over the years;
While we have been so filled
with apprehension
And fears
Time has not passed us by
without treasures dear,
Perhaps you, too, will join us in
gratitude
For the wonderful friends
We have gathered throughout
the years.

Kenneth Llewellyn Wickett
SUNDAY
In that calm peace that Sunday
brings,
It's nice to close the day
By joining in the vesper hymns,
And hear the organ play.
For as the music softly swells
Throughout the Chancel high,
The doubt that oft within us
dwells
Can there no longer lie.
As in Communion with our
friends,
Their faith our doubts efface,
And so we know that all
depends
Upon God's saving grace.

Larry Obrist
TEMPORARY ANGEL
He is resting now,
tiny eyes nearly closed.
Worn, tired, drowsy--
entering that twilight zone
that lingers between
consciousness and sleep.
The eyelids are not quite closed
yet,
as he struggles to keep them
open another minute.
The small, cherub face relaxes
as sleep takes over,
and even the tiny hands and
fingers
are ready now to stop their play,
for they too have had a busy
day.
At last the eyelids can carry the
battle no longer.
An impish smile crosses his lips
as the eylids close,
temporarily leaving
the active mind behind them
to the safety of that wonderful
world
of dreams
where a small boy can be a
cowboy or a fireman--
or even be like his daddy.
This well-earned rest is shared
by a proud and loving mother
as she stands
and looks longingly and
lovingly,
wondering if her dreams will
come true
as she slowly bends down
and tenderly kisses the cheek
of her temporary angel.

Loren McCoy
THE TOYS
We've seen through our tiny
eyes,
Why the little girl's huddled by
the bedside.
Though her mother tells the
neighbors lies,
We know why her daughter
cries.

Many's the time we've been
awakened from our rest.
We the toys upon the wooden
chest.
To see this mother unmercifully
beat
Her child as if a dog in the
street.

Oh! If someone would just take
the time to seek
The truth that we as toys
cannot speak.
They would find a little girl in
misery
Suffering from her mother's past
tragedy.

Harry J. Pressley
G-O-D
God! From Day to Day is like a
Hand-out.
If you forget your *God*, you'll
probably get *Doubt!*
So keep your God up! Cause it is
a must.
Cause if you don't my friend,
you'll bite the Dust!
A ghetto child born, in the
Dark.
Will come out on top, if their
God is kept sharp.
Gasping for breath, in search of
a real me.
Just, don't forget God, He will
keep your mind free.
God really soothes, better than
most.
Give God a try, and take your
Post!
Growing and grinding, looking
out for me.
Keep loving-God up,
Automatically!
Look out my friend, of Setbacks-
within!
Because the so-called Setback, is
God-Powerin!
So with our up's and down's, and
our Trial's and Trot's.
Keep your best God up, and
you'll *Mold* a great *Spot!*

Stephen Franklin Junkin
NAMES THAT LIVE LONGER
Look at that music man;
He's talking in his song.
Live and love and make a stand;
Take life as it come along.
He speaks of a peace of mind,
That you can find within
yourself.
Learn to be the giving kind;
Take your heart down from the
shelf.
He had a love that went wrong,
Though he only grew stronger.
He shines now in every song;
His name will live much longer.
His younger days are history,
Yet he sees them so clearly.
In his words there's a mystery,
For the people who love him
dearly.
Listen to that music man;
He sings what we want to hear.
Sing out while you still can;
Let death be your only fear.

Joyce Guion Shipley
EULOGY FOR AN EAGLE
His life was impersonal
He was unattached
Except for his claws
Upon a lofty branch

Murray S. Weinstein
SHH...LISTEN
Shh...listen, there's a baby
crying,
Take him in hand,
He's yours,
He's you.
Just now in the peace and
quietness;
Only now when you stop a
moment
From your mad dash
In your panic over trash;
Only just now.
Barely audible, barely plausible,
There's a baby crying,
He's scared, he's frightened.
Stop! Don't cover him with hard
plastic toys,
Don't bury him under soft
pillows.
Take him in your arms,
He's yours,
He's you.
Take him in your arms,
Hold him to your heart.
If you don't, you'll never rest.
Shh...listen, there's a baby
crying.

Barbara Fein Kraft
THE GOAL-ORIENTED NEUROTIC
He longs to savor life's sweet
fruit
And reaches out to pluck it,
But old obsessions block his
view
All he can say is "fuck it".
Books on positive thinking
Lists and files galore,
But when it comes to talking
He'd rather just ignore.
He schedules big meetings
Sets rules to act upon,
But when it comes to feelings
He's really too far gone.
To look, to touch, to taste, to
love
Is for the years ahead,
Right now he's busy counting
"dough"
This man who makes the bread.
It soon becomes too much to
bear
The rigors life requires,
So with a grunt of critical pique
He readily retires.
just an adding machine and a
bowl of prunes
No house, no children, no wife,
Regular B.M.s and constant T.V.
He's reached his goal in life!

Barbara Baldwin
STAR SEEKER
Gleaming, glowing, shining,
bright,
Are you a star or a satellite?
If I should wish upon your light,
Would my dream come true?
Are you rigid, man-made steel,
Shining from afar,
Or are you molded, soft and real,
A lovely, God-made star?

Eddye Baker
III
My love for you
has slithered down
from my head
through my seat,
to finally puddle
round my feet,
where it sloshes
in galoshes,
wrinkling up my toes.

Jimmie S. Vaughan
COMFORT THEE
May you forever be mine.
You and I met at a beautiful
time.
Coming to you on moonbeams.
Dedication, stimulation, we
need no scheme.
Heavenly stars and sunlight
bright.
Clouds dance and they might.
To look upon your brown eyes.
Imagination, imagination,
beyond the topaz sky.
Holding hands in rainy weather.
Day-by-day, our love gets better.
To be there with you, kissing
lips.
And being true.
Diamonds in the sky.
Kiss me lover, don't be shy.
Two hearts may melt together.
Love me, love me, love me
forever.
Thinking of you, thinking of
you, in my own funny way.
Wanting and wanting, to be near
you, night and day.
Comfort me, comfort thee.
Traveling by mind in deep
thoughts.
Happiness darling, you have
brought.
Comfort me, comfort thee.

Ms. Sandra Ralda Thibeault
ANIMALS, ANIMALS
Turtle, turtle,
creeping so slow,
how long does it take you
to get where you go?
Bunny, bunny,
hopping away,
how many hops do you
hop in a day?
Puppy, puppy,
barking at me,
does the mailman run
when you he sees?
Pony, pony,
with toenails for feet,
is that you I hear
clopping down my street?
Animals, animals,
I love you all.
I love you all
both big and small.

Audrey Brumfield
EMPTY HOUSE
I ran through the house
Calling your name
Silence mocked me
And then became
My sole companion
The rooms were empty
Lonely and bare
Nothing had changed
Except you weren't there
I thought I saw you
The other day
Turning the corner
A block away
I ran to greet you
Calling your name
It was a stranger
I had never seen
There was a great
ragged hole
Where my heart
had been

B. C. Henson
CONFLICT
Two people dwell herewith,
The I that is real
And the Me that is myth.
The Me
A reflection of society's
Rules and regulations,
Its need for notoriety
Its tired aspirations.
The I
A believer, dreamer,
Rising above reality
A lifetime schemer,
My true identity.
Two people make this person
home,
So unalike
They never can be one.

Marcia A. Gemmen
AN AUTUMN DAY
Children sailing a kite
chasing, tripping,
shrieking with delight
as it tugs and pulls
them with all it's might
Bleached weeds surround them
engulfing the lifeless field
bits of sunset, creep
from under graying clouds
The brisk wind whips and
tosses the kite, like a
lifeless doll
it snatches leaves from trees
carelessly flouncing them
in heaps.
The last of the afternoon sun
streams through brightly tinted
trees
tossing reflections off twittering
leaves
The children start for home
breaking into a run
The sun,
a huge, fiery flame
slowly sinks and is gone

Roxanne Basham
THE LIST
The sound of thunder roars
across the sky,
A smoke filled cloud goes
drifting by.
It carries tears of aching hearts,
The soul of boys being torn
apart.
It carries dreams of a quiet past,
The longing for the final blast.
The war it seems is fought in
vain,
A soldiers heart so filled with
pain.
This war it seems is for the
young,
To pray you can put down your
gun.
They wake to see the morning
light,
The sound of guns for the
bloody fight.
The cry for peace fills the
morning mist,
And a young boys name added
to the list.

Carole McFarren
HOME
Home is a simple word
With a special meaning meant
to be
It's where I find peace
It's where I find security
It's where I find permanance
When the world changes fast
It's where I find my closest
friend
It's where I find love to last
It's where I find humbleness
When I need to clearly see
It's where I find strength
It's where I find the best of me

Sandi K. Nettles
DESIRE
You have evoked in me a desire,
That will never be satisfied,
A desire for your presence,
For your arms to enclose me;
A desire for your kiss,
For your assurance of the future;
No one; no mortal man can
quench it.

Mark Frazier
A MEMORIAL
Times come and go, but things will change little. Life is a temporary thing. We live our lives then die. Your time has come. There is sorrow everywhere. The Earth is dying every minute, you are the lucky one not to have to see it. We will all miss you and cherish your belongings. We will think of you constantly. We will save your pictures and we will think of good times not bad, summer not winter, because we were warm not cold. Our love will live on. Our bad times will die. On cloudy days I feel blue because I feel you cannot see me, but when the sky is blue and the sun is shining I feel *New.*

Elizabeth Ann
UNTITLED
Ear-piercing siren sound
Screaming madly from side to
side
Light changing in the sky
From pale blue to brilliant red
Flooding, revealing the
devastation
Fascinating, horrifying
I am obliged to stare
As ferocious incandescence
Spotlights the chaos...
Blood running down the gutter -
Like all human waste -
Into the sewer.
No horror, no pain
Too numb, fatigue-stricken
Only sadness.
Single figure left alive
Plunges from above - from
An upper room to the
Pavement
Twitches once, twice...
Lying still now -
Crumpled
Eyes wide, still staring
At a vision too
Splendid to imagine,
Too unutterable to survive.

Fay Maynard
GOD'S ROSES
She was so small and fragile
Like the petals of a rose
With eyes the shade of heaven
And hair of softest gold
We called our precious daughter
God's little Rose
As we watched her grow
From baby to toddler to child
She filled our hearts with
happiness
And made our lives worthwhile
She could brighten the darkest
day
With just her sweet smile
We could hardly wait for the
secrets
The future would unfold
We thought we had found the
end of the rainbow
With it's pot of gold
But God's will was not ours to
know
Why our baby, we love her so
The earth was beautiful, all
covered with snow
When the Angel of Death called
Roses to go
With tear filled eyes I gazed
Into my daughter's puzzled face
Daddy, why are you crying
Surely it's not because I'm dying
Don't you know
All of God's Roses die in winter
So wipe away your tears
'Cause all of God's Roses die in
winter
But, Daddy...
They'll bloom again next year

Maureen E. Fleming
FOR YOU
I gaze outside my window;
I think of you.

The stars,
They dance upon the
blackened canvas.
I think of you.

A star falls fast;
it has lost its step with the
tune.

I wish for you.

The star is lost;
faster than its fall.

So, too, is my wish for you.

Still,
I gaze outside my window;
only this time,
I cry for you.

Iris M. Baker
THE VOICE
"You know that if you eat your
lunch
in just a little while,
we'll listen to your programme"
Said Mother with a smile.
I soon had eaten all my food,
You'd never think I'd cried!
Then off to pull my chair across
to sit my Mummy's side.
The lady reads a tale out loud.
We sit there and attend.
I never, ever, make a sound
'cos she's my new best friend.

Virginia L. Weitz
IN THE WINTER OF MY LIFE
In the winter time of life, the
winds cut sharp and deep.
Snow so soft, and white in
youth is now a drift of grime.
In the winter time of life, needs
are more than in the summer
of my time.
When expectations are high, and
the world awaits this
conquerer.
When youth has few doubts and
knows no fear, only joyful
optimism.
In the winter time of life, when
the battles all are in the past.
When victories and defeat are
parallel, neither greater than
the other.
The joy of life is keen, the days
and hours precious.
A life of joy and sorrow, failure
and success, is written upon
the face.
I would not go back to my
youth to learn again, what I
now know.
But it leaves a sadness in me.
If this life were the end
then all is gone to waste.

Victor Terry Au
THE LADY
The people within admire this
great lady with pride.
They enjoy standing by her side.
The people outside are filled
with awe.
She is the most gorgeous lady
they ever saw.
She has the unique power of
attracting people to her nest.
They come from the North, the
South, the East, and the West.
People from all over the world
come to see her.
Unlike the beautiful ladies
whose beauty usually fades
with age,
Her beauty will remain with her
forever.
She still has the power to attract
men, whether young or old.
She makes the other ladies feel
proud.
She is not a Princess, nor a
Queen.
She doesn't even wear pretty
clothes or expensive looking
jewels.
She is not even a terrific cook,
nor will she be an excellent
housewife.
But you have to admire this
great lady,
She is the symbol of freedom for
us all.

Reba Sowell Hallman
A PEBBLE
I wanted to be a rock
Not a stone
Nor a piece of gravel,
But a rock -
Massive, unmovable, and predictable.
But the storms came -
Devastating winds, beating rain -
The furious erosive enemy.
And I was reduced to a pebble -
Tiny, movable, and unpredictable.

Edna Gossage Blue
A DREAM FOR MARCH
There's Magic in the wind-
Magic that can touch
the brown earth and send
forth tiny green sprouts
and lovely pastel flowers.
Magic that can touch
the gray limbs of the shrubs
and the branches of the trees
Lightly covering them with a veil of gossamer green lace.

There's perfume in the wind-
the perfume of newly turned earth;
the smell of fresh growing things;-
pungent with the odor of burning leaves.
Yes, perfume! the magic perfume of spring.

There's a hint of rain in the air-
Rain that will beat on the roof
and bluster through the tree tops.
Rain that will gently sink down into the earth,
awakening all the seeds and plants that nestle there
There's a hint of urgency in the air-
everything that lives must know and greet
this very welcome visitor, who is
The Greatest Magician of them all--
Mother Nature, with her magic of Spring.

Colette Selander
MY DAD
I see him in a gentle rain
He is my dad.
We lost him so long ago,
and everyone was sad.
He taught me as a little girl
how to tie my shoe ...
All who knew him loved him so
for Paul helped everyone, you know.
I see him sitting in the sun
He is my dad.
He walked with me through the
stages of my life,you see,
always giving totally.
One day he said good-bye to me
as all fathers must do,
and gave my hand to a man for
me to look up to.
As years went by, I asked the
Lord for a place to find him.
He was right there all along ...
I see him in my children's faces.
He is my dad ....

James Morgan
I LOVE YOU
That's what the thunder said
As he caressed the earth
With his long white fingers.

Ms. Hilda E. Ward
MAIDEN OF THE SEA
A ship travels over many waves
On fresh and adventurous seas
On uncharted courses
And through calm waves
As it glides along the coast
It tumbles and tosses
And it floats along smoothly
All in one journey
Your sides have been caressed by the seas
And rough, damaging waves have hit you
But you continue on your course
Knowing that you must go on
Unkind currents can pull you down
Caring, sensitive strokes will bring you up
So stay on your course Maiden of the Sea
And take what the Sea of Life has to offer
You will ride the waves of despair
You will revel in the waves of contentment
Your touching will make many ripples
And the sea will remember you were there
Because you are part of the sea
And your travel will lead those that follow
Your strength will break what waves that hit
And your gentleness will touch waves that choose to take your touch
Glide along the waters
Take what it has to offer
Because you are a special vessel
Touching the Sea of Life

Gunda P. Caldwell
DEATH OF A DAY
I watched the death of a day just now
And saw each fever-flushed dye
Stretch slender arms out in the sky
As in reluctance to take its bow
It strained against dark'ning hands of night
Toward velvet blue and lacy white.
I saw the death of a day just now.
Weaker and fainter grew the dying day
And slowly vanished from my pitying gaze.
Lo! Night blots out the dying maze
And sweeps it clear, across the way.
But cold and heartless though the night appears,
I see up in the sky its gleaming tears.
And day is dead... I saw it now!

Melany Vaughan
UNTITLED
Coffee
by the cup
has a bottom,
And
times seven
keeps your eyes open.
There a geisha girl,
in the bottom,
has lips which sing
for money.
Or if you have ears.
A song,
the shells echo
and envy,
spews
out into the street
with no bottom.

W. Larry Sturdivant
SELFISHNESS
Oh, the fragility of life and relationships,
How with such ease we cast ourselves apart;
How on such passing whims and emotions,
Acting upon such imagined harm done by others,
We sever what otherwise could have been,
With no potential toward reconciliation;
We entertain the narrowest personal satisfaction,
While losing the grandest opportunities imaginable.

Lynda Lundin
SEPTEMBER
September is the month to return to school
For reading and writing and the golden rule
September is teachers and lockers and gym--
It's homework and pencils--
But what about him?
Who!!!
Ah, come on--
You haven't forgotten the greatest teacher of all
HE loves everyone- the big and the small
His teachings are known the whole world thru--
He's not only a teacher but counselor too--
His titles are many, he's respected by few
His name is Jesus
And he was sent to redeem me and you
So when you return back to your school
Please don't forget the Golden Rule--
To love one another, as he loved you
Remember the great teacher
In all that you do!

John Richard Thweatt
HAL
Hal screamed at a small boy
For dropping a candy wrapper
Then returned to his weeding.
Next month is time for seeding.
Here comes a little girl on a bike.
She looks like Sarah did
A long time ago
In pigtails and bows.
Some of the shrubbery is dying.
The cold spell got to them.
Hal forgot to cover them up.
There is a blue jay with his head bitten off.
The Smithers cat probably did it.
Hal threw it in the bag with the weeds.
It is three o'clock in the afternoon.
Hal and Alice would have been having tea.
Now he makes a quart in the morning
And drinks it cold.
When Hal gets tired
And his back starts to hurt,
He puts up his spade and his hoe.
He wipes his brow with his handkerchief
And closes the door to his home.
As he sits in his small cold silence
Hal thinks about his past.
This is what God has left for him,
A few memories that he hopes will last.

Mrs. Hilda G. Woods
THERE COMES A TIME
There will come a time when you'll have much joy with more happiness than you've ever known,
Then the time of sorrow will make its entrance and cause you to wonder why joy has gone.
There are times you're gonna feel you've never been right and everything you've done has been wrong--
Times you may sit and wonder why there's an upheavel in your home.

There will be times for making decisions and advice may be asked of you,
Times you're going to get so confused you won't know what to do.
There comes a time when we must face ourselves and determine if we like what we see,
Even if it means saying to ourselves, "This can't really be me."
The most difficult thing is admitting your faults then find ways in which to improve them,
Saying and acting after you've thought, instead of on a whim.

Lori Ann Morris
FLYING FREE
I wish I was a bird,
flying free.
I wish I was a plane,
high as can be.
If I could look like a bird
and fly like a plane,
I know I'd be flying free.

Doreen Candace Lane
DAWN
Slipping softly into golden
slippers,
Dawn rises to greet the world
And awakens every slumbering
soul
From the satiny embrace of
sleep.
She speaks gently with a
whispering lisp
That floats on the breeze,
Rising to soaring heights,
flowing through
The sweeping boughs of silvery
trees.
She dances in the sky with
swirling colors,
Until she gracefully yields
To the mock sterness of day;
then with a curtsey
And swishing skirts, she silently
slips away.

Irene Sharp Whitmore
THE ETERNAL
Lord, Thy presence I feel each
day
And try to understand Thy way-
Tho' often I am tossed about but
Thy Spirit I feel within, without
And I but seek to humble be
That only good in others see.
Please purify all my thoughts
To have faith and love as Thou
has taught.
Impart to me, when I am wrong
And to my heart, give me a song
For it is singing along life's way
That makes each tomorrow a
better day.
And in the number alloted me
Keep my eyes on the home
prepared by Thee
Across the mystic sea above
Away in the realm, of light and
love;
Then joys of the soul will never
cease
At last with God - Eternal Peace!

Sheryl Cooper
LITTLE RAINDROP
Little raindrop you're just a tear
Here on my window pane
The world has left you behind
You're lost from the rest of the
rain.
Like me you drift in dreams,
Reaching for things so far and
yet so near;
You don't belong, but you want
in here.
Little raindrop you look so blue
As the rain goes on by
It seems as you stand there
alone
I can hear the sad song you cry.
As you reach for the sky
And find the moonbeams won't
carry you through,
You wonder what's left for you
to do.
Little raindrop please shed your
doubt
Because there comes a time
When all the darkness will lift
And there'll be a ray of
sunshine.
Look, I see the rainbow;
There's something in me that
just wants to shout -
You come on in and I'll come on
out!

Frances Cozby
CLOUDS
And so our love was just a
dream
Like clouds on summer days
That drift and change so
ceaselessly--
Ah, there's not a wisp that stays
Its beauty for a second
But goes whirling slyly by
And where we gazed enchanted
There is nothing but blue sky.

Laurelle Redig
SNOWFALL
The maples lift their bare brown
arms
In supplication to the sky;
Then cower in the blasting
storms
Of chill November scurrying by;
And kindly Winter hears their
plea
For soon the graying world is
full
Of swirling flakes; and tenderly,
With fleecy robes of downy
wool
He hides the death that Autumn
brought
And wraps each naked child of
earth
In wide-flung, graceful draperies
caught
With jewels.

Duane D. Thornton
WINTER
The warm weather is gone
At least; for awhile.
A Balance of nature;
In nature's, own style.
The birds, have vanished;
The other animals have dug
in.
And another season;
Is about to begin.
With a changing of the
elements;
And a cooling trend.
With dampness in the air;
And a blowing wind.
Giving new life to the
mountains,
With a blanket of snow.
Raining upon the streams;
And into rivers, watching
them grow.
A hope for the future:
Of new life; yet to be.
A promise of growth,
Of prosperity.
During the day;
A little less light,
And a little less, will be
accomplished,
Before the long hours of night.
All of these things are true,
But without winter, where
would we be?
For winter is the beginning
That brings life, to all of thee.

Dixie Lee Knittel
A TOUCH OF BEAUTY
Alongside a backwoods road in
the Ozarks
An old homestead nestles amid
the hills,
Around the abandoned, tumble-
down house
Bloom sweet lilacs and golden
daffodils.
Trumpet vines climb on the
sagging porch,
Golden chain trees shed a
bewitching light,
Redbud trees spill their scarlet
stains
Crimson splashes mid dogwoods
snowy white.
On the old spring-house red
roses climb,
On the split-rail fence
honeysuckle curls,
Reminders of how a mountain
woman toiled
To bring a touch of beauty to
her world.

Marvin J. Chalflinch
THE PAINTING
Questing through some shadows
deep,
Enraptured by all time and
space.
The reach of hope for all that's
real,
Infinite of that hallowed shape.
Bits of time wait here and there,
In challenge of that fear and
hope.
Encircling all that's bringing
forth,
The waiting touch of hand and
stroke.
Test of fate to conquer all,
And show the depth of soul and
span,
Lifting through each master
stroke,
And captures reach to the
artists' hand.

Nancy Marconette
AARON
His slender arms would circle
me
As his green eyes met mine,
And sweet freckles spiced his
face
'Neath hair spun gold and fine.
He held me with a tender
strength
To keep the world away,
His gentle manner saying
What words could not convey.
Words like, "You sure are
beautiful!"
Could chase away my gloom,
And, "I love you best of all!"
Would brighten up the rooms.
His serious side would surface
The times he saw me blue,
And he'd say, "Don't worry,
Mom,
I'll take good care of you."
My four year old brave army
man
Turned six a mighty king,
And my champion at ten
Deserted at fourteen.
Now he's not here to say the
words
Or give the tender touch,
Yet no one has to tell me
He loved me very much!

Zerita Smith Benthall
FIRST LOVE
God, page it one, her innocence,
And sweet Madonna grace---
It came so soon she scarce had
time
Her baby days to face.

With patience, God, her tender
heart
And eyes unused to flow---
Have seen but brief illusioned
dreams
That time has ceased to know.
So, page it one in glory, God,
In thy great book above,
with tender care as she would
do---
And mark it just "First Love"

Laura Jervey Graham
COMING HOME
The fog was swan's wings over
the mountains;
God keep me to the end,
In the minds of those I know,
That I could call my friends.
And let not the hurry I cannot
leave,
Pull me away from a dream,
Of the snow and the rocks of a
day I climbed,
Of the sound of a geyser's steam.
For I've never seen the stars that
way,
The lakes and the rocks of
earth,
Or felt anymore a part of them,
Or risen to a higher birth.
So let me remember how hard I
worked,
To reach the things I knew,
That the glory I felt was the
comrade's share,
And the things they said were
true.
And it is my prayer that they'll
think of me,
At night when they build their
fire,
As they tell their dreams to the
moon till dawn,
When they wake to the cold
creek's choir.
God keep them all in the woods
they've earned,
And send them a laugh all day,
So never they lose their love,
So they always find their way.

Erin D. A. Deel
THE WEDDING
I saw you with new eyes today, my love—
He who was once my Knight in Shining Armor
became a mortal man; no longer fantasy,
now reality.
Though less a Prince, more a person you've become,
my love is heightened by life's honesty.
I know I shall love you the Knight, the Prince, today—
but come what may, I shall love you the man
forever and a day.

Robert Lee Wolf
HOW RICH CAN YOU BE?
Who owns the woods? the trees? the sky?
Who really owns the land?
Who lays a claim to fluffy clouds?
Whose is the gypsy band
of gay wild flowers that climb the hills?
Whose is the grass so green?
Can fences hold the wind that blows?
Whose is the air so clean?
This land I claim as my very own?
To which I hold the deed?
Will others follow after me and lay a claim, indeed?
How rich am I? What is my wealth?
The answer is so plain—
In proportion as I limit myself
I can the riches gain.
As I perceive that in God's plan
His creation belongs to all,
My wealth will be in proportion!
Will it be great? or small?

Jeffrey Ramsey
LOST CHILD KNOWS
Lost Child Knows
Beauty flowers at fourteen,
Children talk with trees,
Freedom flirts for tears,
And innocence swears she loves
Swinging laughter with the boys.
Wind beneath the boughs
Smiles that she knows her heart,
Yearns to laugh with fleeting lark,
And innocence has lost her part
Swinging still at seventeen, with men,
Quietly pouting freedom lost again.

Elsie Day Cruthirds
(Mrs. Niles E. Cruthirds)
A LIVING TAPESTRY
The lovely landscape that I see
Portrays a living tapestry,
Not woven with bright woolen strands
By shuttle in some skillful hands,
But woven lovingly with care
And work and happiness to share.
It took long years and careful schemes
For this design to fulfill dreams.
The warp stretched tight for weaving there
Was made of constant, earnest prayer.
The woof was sacrifice and love,
And hope and faith in God above,
With joy and sorrow, smiles and tears,
And many hardships through the years.
The weaving of each precious part
Took courage and a willing heart.

Walquidiā Alonso—Lozada
ONLY WITH YOU
There is a destiny I've yet to meet—
A treasure I must seek—
Countless dreams I must fulfill;
Endless hopes that fate will see,
And but one love I'll ever know;
All those things are forsaken—
Time is standing still. . . . . .
For they can only be with you. .

Barry A. Hobson
UNTITLED
The hours pass much slower now,
As if the distance between us
Had somehow slowed the passage of time.
The nights drift quietly into days,
Once again the sun, dancing,
Outside the veiled windows of my bedroom world
Trying to chase away, the last remnants
Of the friendly night.
As I sink deeper into the pillows
Descending back into darkness,
Before giving in
To the indifferent day.
A moment more perhaps,
To recall your face,
Just one more time,
The colour of your eyes,
The sound of your laughter
Ringing in my ears,
Your smile, that would reach across the room,
To comfort the small boy in me,
And your touch, that awakens the man.

Mrs. Jody Richey
GOD'S BEAUTY
There are many beautiful things in this world of ours.
A person does not need the pleasures of the world to be happy.
Happiness is of within
A peace so sure
that nothing can take the place of God's love.

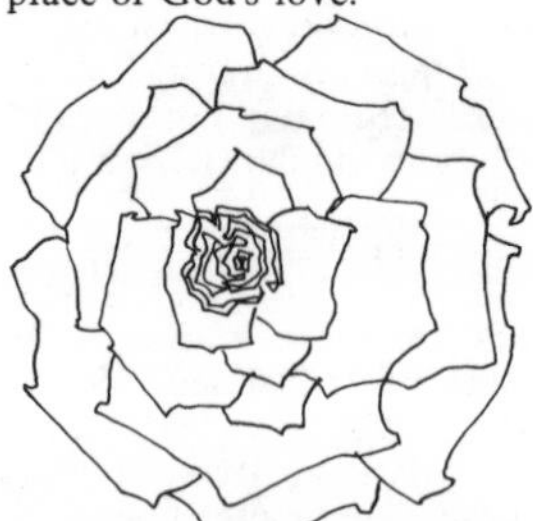

The sun coming up each day, the soft breeze, the little things
that one does.
The best of all is worshipping in God's house
For there is a spiritual high we get from God's word.
Making melody in song and in prayer
We feel God's presence everywhere.
No matter where we go,
He is there.
As we walk in His love each day
We can draw nearer to him.

K. Ann Hunt
PAST MEMORIES
Evening Light
The sun sets low
Sandy Beaches
Waves rolling in
Sweet smell of summer
Drifts that come on by
Seagulls calling
Fly on ahead
Lonely is the heart
All alone
I was so scared
I looked up to see you standing there
Sweet is your face so kind
Strong is the love that binds
I called for you, but you did not hear
I reached to touch you, but you did not feel
Tears streaming down my face
You just stood there untouchable, no feeling, no care
Yet I saw you there all alone
Escaping reality through a Shield of thick glass
Vanishing, out of reach, out of touch
Memories that capture, reversing to a past
Lost is the forgotten soul
But remembrance of love once so true
Back to a summer when I first met you
Before, Before you were taken away
Realization
Draws me near
Chilly winter
Harsh winds
Beach of solitude
No birds in flight
Waking now
Dreams of torture
Slip away into the mind from a long ago past
Cursed am I
Lonely is the heart all alone

Lin Lewis
BE CAREFUL
Brilliantly balanced
It sits high and tall
Be careful don't push it
It might take a fall
Constantly boastful
Completely displayed
Just be careful, don't bruise it
It's so easily frayed
Seemingly callous
No depth to its core
So easily damaged
When he can't make a score
So seldom humble
And more often rude
His ego's no small thing
It can shade every mood
Be gentle, don't harm it
For you reap what you sew
Don't use or abuse it
And you can keep it in tow

Elsie Day Cruthirds Hutto
OUTSIDE MY WINDOW BY THE SEA
Outside my window there are things
I see and hear. Great joy it brings
To witness God's great masterpiece
And know His wonders never cease.
The gleaming white of seagull's wings,
Melodious tunes that each bird sings;
In swift precision waves will reach
So high, then break upon the beach,
And scatter sands in patterns new
To glisten under skies of blue.
The ships far out, like dreams, pass by
While unseen ships with foghorns cry,
Majestic trees, the warmth of sun,
Or dawn when day has just begun,
The gentle breeze that whispers low,
And tides in rhythm ebb and flow.
I love each thing I see out there
And offer thanks to God in prayer
For giving me this view today.
And when someday I'm far away
In memory these things will be
Outside my window by the sea.

Teresa Marie Dao
THE PARK
The park is a place to sit and think.
Undisturbed, laying on the grass.
With the earth below you and the blue sky above.
A feeling of peaceful, easy living.
The park is a place to run and play.
Free-spirited children and young-at-heart adults.
Singing, jumping and enjoying themselves.
On the grass, in a sandbox, or on the swings, just having fun.
The park is a place for those with romance in their hearts.
The flowers, the sun; all come together for lovers.
As each bud blooms, another love is sparked.
Those who have been in love for years and those who are strangers till meeting in the park.
All find joy and happiness in the green grass and tall trees.
The park is a place for everyone to come and enjoy.
To sit, to think, to play,
to sing, to love, to find.
A park is a very valuable place in the lives of many.
Explore the wonders of a beautiful green atmosphere and live!

Gary Schultz
BROKEN EGGS IN A MENDED BASKET

A brackish world
Lies cleansed
And filtered.
Stumps are uprooted
Like giant molars,
Their cavities filled
With loam.
The foul-smelling fluid
Drained
By snake-like arteries,
Forfeits its home.
Cattails crunch
Only adding to traction,
And blackbirds retreat,
Their red shoulder patches
Burdened
With indecision.
But surrogate gods
In infinite wisdom
Plant corn, beans
And orchids;
Marveling
At their monotony.
The land has been
Mended;
Its scars healed
By ingenuity.
But off in the midst
Of this garden
Of plenty,
A lone locust munches;
Mandibles poised
For irreverent
Gestures.
He'll have to
Be dealt with.

Benjamin Adres
GRAYING

Between mirrors and the veneer, above her vanity put in order the night before, she draws a shade against the light. An armchair the color of ash dulls to gray in the muted dawn, and behind her is an unmade bed, soiled and dreamless in a far corner which hides her shadow.

She studies herself for signs, messages in thin cracks that would sliver a glass soul, portraits yellowing against a bare wall. She speaks of a room where death debates in a thickened tongue, of love grown arid in a desert of words. There were times once, she remembers, when thirst could draw strength from a well and her limbs were as supple as the green vine. But no more. Time sets in. All her waters dry into a graying light; what once inflamed the dormant heart of summer dreams now smoulders beneath the ancient glass bordering life; the season of drought.

Alan Eric Goranson
NATURE'S WHISPER

A windless calm has camped
between the stormy throes of spring.
All senses still,
awaiting news of gentle rain
and verdant paths,
or nascent wrath unfurled.
Precursor rest; alight to speak
before the clattering noise
of death's dark dealing hand.
Stand fixed with patting rays,
O lull, to whisper truths
untold by mortal lips.
So bathe the cheek, sweet
messenger. But hush!
. . .the thrum. A distant
thunder heard.
A hasty gust with grit has swept
its pannings within your bound.
Make haste your gathering call
to chase,
before the predator claims
you, the silent prize.

Marion Bosman
TROUBLED DAYS

How could we ever enjoy the sunshine and the dazzling light of day,
If we haven't first experienced sorrow, pain and dismay.
It is only when we have trouble that our thoughts turn to God above,
Because it is then that we truly realize that God with his warmth and love,
Is always there to help us get through the dark troubled days.
It is when we feel that all is lost and we can no longer carry on,
That our Lord renews our strength and gives us his shoulder to lean upon.
So never fear times of trouble if in your heart you know,
That our Father in heaven is watching over you and will soon make the troubled days go!

Carl H. Snyder Jr.
SMILES UPON THE WALL

I knew a girl when I was young.
I had known her for quite awhile.
Prettier girls I had occasionally seen.
But I had never seen a lovelier smile.
I loved this girl when I was young,
But I never thought to tell her so.
I was quiet, bashful, faint of heart.
She felt she had to let me go.
An aggressive lad claimed her hand.
I cried. It nearly broke my heart,
But I had no place to put the blame,
For it was entirely my own fault.
An icy road, a starry night, a fiery crash;
The Angel of Death claimed her man.
I stood by her side at the funeral home,
For awhile I held her hand.
At the proper time I called again.
I loved her dearly and told her such.
She was still a very pretty woman,
But she didn't smile as much.
Within a short time we were man and wife.
I was content to share her heart.
I knew what it was to have loved and lost;
I would gladly share a part.
Now we are old, our hair has turned to grey.
Our song of life will soon have been sung.
Children and grandchildren adorn the walls,
Where their lovely smiles are hung.

Amaede Moctent
I REMEMBER

I remember the moon was bright and beautiful
When I kissed you,
A night awashed in splendor
When you came to me so warm and tender,
I remember. . .
I remember when you held me
So safe and sure against you
Away from harm and pain undue,
I remember. . .
I remember when you left me,
So cold and abruptly
Without warning or memory
Of times that used to be,
I remember. . .
I remember pain and sorrow
of sleepless nights and no tomorrow,
The cry of a heart sinking in sorrow,
I remember. . .

Moselle D. Vreeland
IF THIS BE FORGETTING

Alone!—the trees whisper it;
It sighs to the earth in the rain;
The sea has taken the word
For its hauntingly sad refrain.
Alone!—the moon glimmers it
In a ghostly dance from the sky;
And out of the lonely night
It is sobbed in a night-hawk's cry.
Alone!—the perfumed voices
Of roses seem to be saying;
And willows wail it softly
To the rhythm of their swaying.
Alone!—it flames in the fire,
Glows in each blackening ember. . . . .
If this be forgetting—Oh God,
What if I dared to remember!

Patricia Kay Stallings
MY CHILD

My child had eyes that sparkled with love
Outshining any light in the heavens above
He had a head full of bouncy curls
And a smile of pearls
My child had a spirit as free as the wind
Sunshine and music her closest friends
He was creative, so much to share with me and you
Talented at anything she set her mind to do
My child was sensitive and had a tender heart
I felt his joy in laughter, her pain as tears would start
A face bright with life, without worry or stress
Determined and responsible, a bit stubborn I confess
My child ran for protection, but was independent and strong
With faith in the Lord to know right from wrong
I'll teach my special children these virtues so ideal
But the hollow corner of my heart will never heal
My child was taken from my soul
Fate dealt me a cruel blow
Unfulfilled and empty I now find
I must relinquish and leave that dream behind
Left within, a haunting of the child I'll not conceive
It's hard sometimes not to grieve
A lonely sound, only I can hear
Clouds in my eyes often rain down tears
This verse does hereby morn
My child-the child that will never be born

C. Fitzgerald
SCENES FROM THE FALL

The sun drug itself out of bed
Easing its way up over the trees
Sliding in between morning clouds
Setting the edges on fire
Grays and orange softly suspended
Over autumn gold
Taking the breath from the fog
And I never noticed
I was thinking of you
And so the sun soon pushed the clouds apart
Or they drifted that way
And the sky came thru
But all I ever saw
Was your eyes
And I hardly heard the engine
Driving into the city
With the sun reflecting off a bank
And a piece of a cathedral
Stones against a blue sky
And I tried to remember where I was
But the only thing that would fix in my mind
Was the touch of my hand
Against your chin
I think you are too much in my mind

Cyndi J. Moore
MICHIELL
Like a vessel at sea
My heart pressed apart
as if a splinter
were driven slowly
into
the shallow places of my
longing
I hear the cries
I see the crystal glaze upon her
face
Shes a part-time angel
and theres just no pay.

Tom Peaver
CONFUSION
In this shattered dream I call my
own
I wonder if I'll find a home
A place where I can feel at
peace
and my mind can find release
from confusion
In this nomad life I have led
The many problems I have fled
Have always seemed to seek me
out
and throw my fragile head about
with confusion
On this planet earth so few will
find
That elusive thing called peace
of mind
And of the billions that have
tried
almost all of them have died
in confusion

Camille R. Accardo
THE TRUMPET PLAYER
He gets up at the crack of dawn,
Ready to "study" and "get into"
his horn.
He knows it takes practice,
before he will rate,
He prays someday soon, he will
end up as great.
He knows what he wants, and
hopes it comes soon,
He wishes upon the stars and
the moon.
He plays at parties, night clubs
and weddings,
He puts you in the mood for
all of the settings.
He performs with skill, style,
and ease,
And gets through a tune in less
than a breeze.
When his fans crowd around
him, he knows he is loved.
That's his reward from the Man
up above.
He finds little time to "wine"
and to "dine",
But that suits him just
perfectly fine.
He may spend his lifetime just
tooting his horn,
But his heart will be happy,
'cause it's filled with "his
song."

'Lizabeth A. Strano
ADULTERESS
Wanton woman
doors flung open
Men lie in wait
darkness creeps closer
Careless laughter
echos through chambered hearts
Lust grows quick
like hate on those forgotten
Evil circles round
Wounds and dishonor dress you
both
You have no sense
You destroy all
Smooth Tongue
Stalks life

W. Hugh Headlee
DUFFY—A TRIBUTE
She gave us a flower
For Christmas—an *Amaryllis;*
It bloomed luxuriantly,
abundantly!
That was a year ago;
Later we carefully stored it
For its dormancy rest.
Recently, we sadly removed it
To emerge again.
Sadly, because we can not
Express to Duffy our
appreciation
For this wonderful gift of nature,
Which is blooming again
In radiant, colorful beauty
To remind us of her
And her vivacious life—
Her exuberant, colorful
Warm personality!
For Duffy can no longer
Respond to the call of the
living!
She lies silent
With the wreckage of a plane
On the slopes of Mt. Erebus,
Unmindful of the howling gale
Or the windswept ice—
For she is as cold as the
Antarctica
That encompasses her!
But her memory with us
Will be warm forever!

Brenda Hopson
LIFE
Though you seem to be trapped
in the awesome stillness of
silence
You are actually singing a
thousand tunes and
speaking a thousand truths.
Though you seem to be floating
on a cotton raft in a sea of
confusion
In reality, you are learning to
swim and accepting that
survival is possible.
Though you try to hide in a
tunnel of darkness
You are only discovering that
you are the light
Which will brighten your own
existence.

Esther K. Hildebrand
CAPE COD
On, lonely land of sand and sky
With blue waves on the shore,
Where white gulls fly
And ships sail by

I dream of you more and more.
Where a brave land ends
And its only friends
Are the white gulls and the sky.

Charles L. Hine
FRESH THOUGHTS
On this rock I sit and marvel
treetops swing their limbs to
and fro dancing in harmony
with the many sounded whistle-
call of the wind. It picks crisp
and fragile leaves off the ground
and carries them to distant
rivers undressing the earth to its
naked brown. The wind bites,
the wind stings, the wind hurts,
but when the wind dies it leaves
a mark of newness dressing my
mind in fresh thoughts.

Robert L. Tucker
BEAR BIT BLUES
Breaker nineteen! Breaker
nineteen!
There's a Smokey takin' pictures
with his picture machine!
Watch out, watch out, 'cause
he's gonna getcha!
Gonna set right there and take
your picture.
Got a kojak with a kodak, and
a bear in the air,
Yes sir, yes sir, he don't play
fair!
Gotta fill that quota, gotta pay
those bills;
He's sittin' right there on toppa
the hill.
Gonna make you an offer you
can't refuse,
Gonna give us all them bear bit
blues.
It's a shotgun in Miami and a
brownie in L.A.
But no matter what you call it,
there's just nothing you can
say.
Yeh, you gotta keep them ears
on, no matter come what may,
'Cause the Smokey's gonna
getcha, and he's gonna make
you pay!
He's got a heart made out of
granite and a pencil made of
lead,
Take the petal off the metal or
he's gonna get you dead!
There's a moral to the story,
That you'll always lose
Doing more than double nickles
with your lead toed shoes.
'Cause the Smokey's always out
there, night or day,
And if you let the Smokey
getcha, then he'll make you
pay!

Diane Dumaine Martinez
ALL THE SIMPLE ADDICTIONS
You sit there before the heater,
and
allow it's force of air to
stimulate
warmth to your body.
It feels so good. You want it
to continue, you
do not wish to leave it.
But then how will you find
the strength
to take that first step away?
The longer you are there, the
more
you crave it's comfort and
you cannot
begin this day save for to sit
and yearn for release.
Everyone stirs about you, you
see them
and you are jealous.
Now they are beginning to
leave. You are
alone!
But no—you are strong indeed—
and if
you remain, you have only
to worry that with extended use
the heater will malfunction,
or worse
you shall overheat.

Merritt Bradford
TO A NURSE, D.S.
Down darkened corridors of
night
By walls that seem to quiver,
Lest the fleeting soul could
sight
The dead undone, and pain
forever.
Holding steadfast anguished
cries
Heaped upon your shoulders
slim,
You impart all hope that ere
belies
Of shattering night, or faces
dim.
Your spirit, not obsequious
intent
To grim presence floating
swiftly
By, to you but transient figment,
Refuting ambitions stance as
folly.
No empirical nuance is heard,
To enhance such
metamorphosis.
Her oppilate, a word of
sustenance
And night becomes a time of
glory!

Warren Grover
MAN ON A GUITAR
The tangle of people had gone,
The seductress and the seduced
had gone,
Leaving their smoke—
Leaving the record of their
indulgences
On the register tape,
Leaving the lone guitarist
Playing to an empty room.
He played the melody of self-
expurgation—
Bridling his shame for having
committed his art
To the artless.
He played 'Flemenco' under the
single strobe—
The shaggy head, each vein and
tendon
Each line held there in black
relief
Bespoke his sincerity to
The complex and perfect ear of
the one person left behind.
I could not see such mystery
end
And not hear applause;
I waited until the last perfect
note;
To it's final decible
And walked away before the
house came down.

Wilbert Roberts
ON MOUNT EVEREST
Once I climbed Mount Everest.
And stood upon its crest.
From there, I saw all the
grandeurs of the world;

Including men, women, boy and girl.
There were sceneries of various kinds.
To fascinate my eyes.
The oceans, valleys, and plains.
Rivers, streams, brooks and lanes.
As I look from continent
to continent,
There were many things to comment.
They were peace, wars, hatred, rebellions
Drought, descrimination and starvation.
Among the earth's population.
With sorrows in my heart.
I started to depart.
With tears flowing from my eyes, and unto my cheek.
I was that too troubled to speak.
I thought the world was a happy place.
And had people with many a smiling face.
But I'm sad to say.
This world is such a wretched place.

George E. Blount Jr.
I'LL ALWAYS LOVE YOU
I met you very long ago,
I made you up, I loved you so.
But how was I to ever know,
One day you'd come my way.
That special one I'd made for me,
Was more than I had hoped she'd be.
I long to hold her tenderly,
I miss her more each day.
Right now we both have much to do,
So many things we must see thru.
But thru it all, I'll still
love you,
Forever come what may.

Jean E. Wilcox
PERFECT DAY
Down with motionless faces
And cold and heartless places;
Plastic people without a trace of care,
Can they not do anything but stare?
I long to see eyes to blue,
Looking to find only what is true;
Apathy fills my heart with remorse;
Tears fill my eyes with hate toward the whole human race,
There must be an overpowering force
Guiding us into the wrong place;
People coming together is what I want to see,
Being straight out forward with all makes set aside,
Why must we hide all the love wrapped up inside?
I fail to see a future in our lifetime,
The way our fellow man treats his brother is a crime;
All people—black, white, yellow, and red is what it will be
When we all take what is in our head
And bring it out for all to see.

Janet Anne Frey
MY FRIEND
He is someone to sit and talk with,
To share my thoughts with,
To hold hands with.
He has shown me that life is worth living,
He is warm, gentle,
Forever giving.
He is someone to laugh with,
Share a smile with
Sit and cry with.
He lets me be me,
Understands my wants and needs.
He never tries to smother me,
Leans lightly,
Lets me be free.
He is someone to share myself with,
Someone to warm a bed with.
This friend,
Who turns my gray skys blue,
I have found him,
He is you.

Mark S. Pliska
ALASKA
Alaska, I thought would be
One place left free from man's debris;
Alaska, I knew would be
Pure beauty and serenity.
To the mountain crest I did my best;
Reaching the top, I stopped to rest.
There, before me, I could see
All the beauty and splendor around me.
But at my feet where I stood
In the middle of rock, forest and wood,
A beer can laid in plain view
And from within my heart, I knew.
I knew that my dreams were in vain;
Across the mountains, valleys and plains
The mark of man will always stand
In the eyes of all who love the untamed land.

Duncan Alexander McKethan III
THE FEAST OF PITOMY PETE
(For Christian)
Pitomy Pete dined in last night.
First he ate his twisted toes,
Then his big old bulbous nose.
Then he fried his fubsy feet
In a pot of blood and hair and meat.
Pitomy butchered both his legs,
And diced his eyes like boiled eggs.
Once he'd skinned his aching back,
He chewed his ribs for quite a snack.
Pitomy pickled all his fingers,
Which, full of fat, taste just like Zingers.
Pitomy gnawed his arms and ears,
Then quenched his thirst with salty tears.
He finished with saute'ed, stuffed head,
And now poor Pitomy's feast is dead.
Yes, Pitomy Pete dined in last night.
He should have held his appetite.

Gerald Morse
THE BLACK TOOTHED BANDIT
I see the teeth
through your empty smile;
In a search for peace
I walk the tortuous mile.
Fire seeps through
your burned-out eyes.
Men say you are pure,
but men tell lies.
You've dug the graves
of dreamers and drummers.
You've filled in the caves
of Jones and of Strummers.
Born at Jamestown;
Died at Jonestown.
Hit the street, be the clown,
While in the hills
the lemmings drown.

Kristin Higgins
THE SCULPTOR MANQUE'
How easy it would have been
for your tongue of highly polished silver
with the finest edges
to smooth and shape me
into your favorite pattern.
How easy it would have been
had I never learned to hone myself
with my own tools
had I not seen
that your favorite pattern
left no room for mine
and that your tongue
was no tool of love.

Helen K. Carr
UNTITLED
We dream of the future,
All think of the past.
Today is with us,
Each moment hold fast.
Who knows if the future
Will ere be the past.
So hope and live in the present,
Each moment hold fast.

Michael Lewis Sola
TO LOOK IS TO KNOW
To look, is to know your
loves, deep as the stars are
high above. So between the
times we touch, are the darkest
blues of love.

Wanda L. Horn
WITHOUT YOU
The sun comes up but without you
the sun is unimportant.
The moon shines and the stars glow
but without you their brightness is lost.
The rain falls and the rivers flow but
without you motion is meaningless.
Babies are born and old folks die and
the pain of these is increased if I am
without you.
Because of you I can be everything,
but without you I am not at all.

G. Venora LaMarche
LIVE FOREVER
For all the years of understanding,
Forgiveness, and giving without expectation.
Always being there for everyone,
In our learning, accomplishing and elation.
Never has there been such compassion,
Or joy in sharing, or natural instinct to compromise.
Not forgetting growing pains,
or when tears
filled our eyes
Or showing the meaning of real love without a moments try.
Making laughter take the place of sadness,
And the promise to never leave my life.
Just knowing the right words to say,
whenever the need arise.
And seeming to enjoy the role of mother and loving wife.
And when Heavens gates were opened wide,
To gently take her from my side,
I discovered, after the weeping time,
Mother became alive in my daughters eyes.

Mozell Kwenortey
MY HEART CRIES
My heart cries for the LOST, the LONELY, the SICK, the DEAD.
For all the misfortunate who was never heard.
For all of the Gloria's, the John's of the world who got
lost in the crowd,
Like a funnel of a hurricane that captured it's suspect,
Twirled them around and suddenly released to fall to the ground.
Back into the crowd where no one cares,
Each one is too busy to know you are there.
Should we give up hope or continue to cry,
For the people of the world who passed us by.
Should we close oursleves in a cloak of despair,
Mentally locked up and pretend they are not there.
Should we seek out each other, join the crowd and sink further,
Further into despair, lost in the crowd and pretend we are not there?
The answer is—————————,

Raphael Stephan
TRILOGY
. . .and in the darkness
my shadow triumphant
the morning spirit
trilogy. . .
awakens me to the task
the land of spheres and
special mist
is a dream not far from
naught. . .
i sense an ocean splendour
in the midst of dragon's lair
while day competes for my
night
w/blessings and a hope
despair
look outward. .reach
inward. .
look onward. .teach
inward. .
hold the holy gift high
basque the mid-lit moon
luna calls. . .a beckoning
lighthouse
for ships that sail the flat
earth
a mediaeval quest
a future withheld
. .and time's eternity shall
wait naught
no man or woman or beast
to be captured or be caught
against the blind
retread
i totally sink. . . .

Lawrence J. Schuck
MYSTERIOUS THOUGHT
We become History
As quickly we Run
There's lots of Mystery
Under the Sun
Mysterious Mountains
Flowers and Trees
Clear water Fountains
A thirst to Please
Mysterious People
Houses and Roads
A towering Steeple
Insects and Toads
Mysterious Heavens
Thunderous Skies
Robins and Ravens
Why a Man Dies

Ray
TOGETHER ON THE ARK
When the morning brings a new
day, greet it with a smile.
Because new days only last a
little while.
Take the time to look about
you, it may come as a surprise,
to see the wonders of the
universe, are before your
very eyes!
Smell the air so fresh and clean,
hear the birds begin to sing.
The sun, now weak but growing
stronger,
climbs up in the sky as the
day grows longer.
The flowers, the frogs, the bees
in the trees.
The golden wheat as it sways
in the breeze.
There's nothing so small as a
bug when it crawls,
or as tall as a tree, when
the giant tree falls.
Or as soft as the fleece that
covers the lamb,
but only the rocks know how
this all began!
The rocks were there when it
started to rain,
and when the water receded
and life could sustain.
the bug, the beast, the poor,
the elite,
we are all bound together by
the soil at our feet.
Everything, no matter how
small,
plays an important part in it
all.
We must feed upon others
which we can defeat,
or be the food for those that
can eat!

Ralph W. Hulbert
LOVE OF LOVES
A brilliant beam of silver moon woke me late last night and as I smiled we shared a gentle kiss, my love of loves and I. The quarter moon and wind were up and my fantasy arose to enclose my love of loves and me. She rode that shaft of lunar light through tossing branches, window pane and blanket and with arms extended wide we joined, my love of loves and I. I could smell her hair and touch her breast and feel the pounding heart beneath as our lips joined, my love of love's and mine. Warm skin, eager tongues, hot breath and exploring hands brought thrills and joy to my love of loves and me. Her thighs and eyes said she was right, her hand found me long and strong and also moist so then we thrust together, my love of loves and I. We moved in concert then and the music took us round about and in and out and the pulsing crescendo brought ecstacy to both my love of loves and me. The moonlit room returned to focus and the sweet scent of sweat and sex combined to add special meaning to the final kiss we shared, my love of loves and I. As a cloud removed the moon so my fantasy was gone and touch and taste and sight and scent returned to normal and my bed was cold and arms were empty of my love of loves.

Debbie Miller
WHEN WILL WE SEE
The beauty of the trees
doomed to die
Rumbling machines come with
natures cry
Huge, powerful tanks rip and
tear
Destroying the tall green
peacefulness
No one will care.
Thousands of cement monsters
stretch overhead
Cement tombs for the dead
Lifeless people with lifeless jobs.
Can't we help those sad, sad
sobs
Scummy film pollutes the bay
Conquer nature that's the way
When will it be when people see
The important things
Listen to the silence
See the space between
People tied in knots tighter
and tighter
The clock ticking faster and
faster
Until one day the bomb
explodes
Releasing the little loads
The wired wispers in my ears
How many years, how many
years
When will it be when people see
The important things
Listen to the silence
See the space between

Barbara R. Christensen
FARMING
The tractor, the swather, the
bailer are tools,
For plowing and discing to make
the ground smooth.
Sowing and growing, seeding and
weeding
For all the food this country
is needing.

The cows they beller, and moo,
and low
Chomping grass and moving
slow.
Chewing and mooing and
fertilizing the ground
Soon they'll be dinner two
dollars a pound.

Jack Doher Ray
THANKS GOD FOR EVERYTHING
Thanks God for everything,
Filling this body with life,
Guiding it through the years,
Pushing it on through strife,
Sending me light at night,
Giving me peace of mind,
Preparing me for tomorrow
Thanks God for being so kind.
For always providing,
Maybe bot wealth it's true;
But God what is wealth
Compared to gifts from you?
Giving me the best of health,
And the love of friends so dear;
Taking time to protect me
When I travel far and near.
Letting me live in America,
The great land of the free,
True my cup runneth over,
Oh God, You're good to me.
Sending a true woman,
To bear and care for my seed,
Hearing my humble prayers
When I am so in need.
Giving me mother and father,
Binding our family ring,
I can't say much except:
Thanks God, for everything.

Blanche Hillen Jones
CYCLE
At evening's tide when the Earth
is still,
Comes the faint chirping of a
bird's sweet song.
Heralding the end of another
day,
While the creaking chatter of
the cricket continues to
perpetuate the night,
As morning awakes, comes the
chirping of a bird's sweet song,
Heralding the beginning of
another day,
While the creaking chatter of
the cricket fades,
relinquishes to a glowing
dawn—
Ah—Sunrise!

Edna Price
I'M SO PROUD
I'm so proud to be an American
and enjoy its guiding light,
We should all be proud and fly
our flags and count our
blessing,
And thank God each day for all
his care and love,
Oh, God! Let me never lose my
respect for this great country
and may I always hold it
high. . .
God Bless America, the country
that I love,
I will take the time each day
to kneel and pray,
May God be with me in every
way,
In God We Trust!

Pamela Gregoli
MICHAEL
Tears fell from a saddened sky.
Oceans and rivers echoed a
similar reply.
When a child so torn,
With pain and moan,
To be something, yet to be
shown.
Straining the powers of
endurance,
He tried again,
To carry the ball across the
opponents goal.
Yet the Master accomplished
to seize his Soul.
A calendar full of malignant
events;
Never to realize the special
significance
Gone from this forsaken land.
The transition lies in God's
hands.

Janet M. DiMaria
I LIE AWAKE
I lie awake
I think
I plan
I dream
Of other nights and days. . . .
Of you. . . .of me. . . .
Of happiness and peace and
completeness.
Now I am happy, secure and
content
But somehow incomplete

I lie awake and think. . . .
I wonder too, if you lie awake
Lonely in another bed
Do you feel a lack—a void—
an emptiness. . . .
Oh! when will I not lie awake
And think. . . .?

Marie De Sales Bagley

CREATION

Gazing around this world I see
The gifts created for you and
me:
The beauty of the daytime sky
With rays of sunshine,
As clouds float through
All the different shades of blue:
This sky was created for us to
view.
The mystery of the evening sky
A sunset with a golden hue
Then the moon appears,
And the stars, one by one,
Light the path of a day almost
done.
From the rising to the setting
sun
The hours between fill me with
wonder!
Reflecting on these creations of
endless number,
How the season follow one
another,
A mantle of awe comes over me.
To think flowers of spring grow
from tiny seeds;
Summer's rainbow comes after
the rain we need.
The leaves of autumn turn to
wondrous colors,
And winter's snowflakes all
different from each other.
Then the sheer delight of
childhood laughter,
A mountain range, with all its
grandeur,
Or the solemnity of a meadow
lane,
And the ocean's tide drifting
in and out
Whose heart could ever feel any
doubt
That Someone above raised a
hand
To create the prefect harmony
of this land?

Debbie Pawlina

WINTER WONDERLAND

In the land of sugar and honey
Where all things are sweetened to
taste
Ethereal figures dance amid
moonbeam's rays
When the shadow comes
And all is forsaken
A drop of honey upon the snow
Becomes individual and unique
Melting away all bitterness
Before the night is over
His love pump
Spreads her mound of snow
Smothering her white milky
breasts
Reaching the land of the unreal
Becoming one

Willie Belle Dixon

HOWDY

When I go walking down the
street,
I sing a merry song
And wear a smile upon my face
As I stroll along.
I'm always happy, no matter
where I go—
And I say 'Howdy' to all the
folks I know.
It gives my heart a lift—
These 'Howdys' we exchange—
And I'm a millionaire
Without a penny to my name.
A friendly 'Howdy' and a smile
Will make a gray day bright—
So say 'Howdy' to the folks you
meet
And start your day off right.

Ruth Pauline Lees

I CHERISH EACH DAY

I cherish each day, that I may
live,
To feel each joy of life.
To have all love, to bear new
pain,
Without them, where is the
strife?
To challenge each day whatever
it brings,
To fill my heart and soul.
If I weren't alive for adventures
ahead,
How could I be so bold.
To find real joy in whatever
you seek,
As I walk down the pathway
of life.
Has it been worth just being
alive?
I can cherish each new day.
Thank you God, for giving me
life,
That I might praise each new
day.

Holly C. Hansen

FLIGHTLESS GULL

On a beach I saw a gull,
flightless and quite dead,
saturated wings lay on an oil
soiled bed.
In passing I stop to give my
respect, apologizing for man
becoming lifes deepest threat.
Below my feet the oceans
black stained sand,—to my side
a stumbling death bound
pelican.
On this beach I stared at a ship
out to sea, and wondered if that
barge caused this catastrophe.

Ronnie M. Vinson, D.D.S., M.P.H.

B. J.

My Every Breath
My Every Yearn
My Every Prayer
Countless the times I've longed
to love you
Spaceless the distance of which
I want you
That's how strong my love is
That's how much I care
No other one could mean as
much
No other hand could convey
such touch
No other smile
No other cry
No other Hello
No other goodbye
Could ring the chimes of my
heart with such assonance
You've changed me too
How proud I am to say
My every breath
My every yearn
My every prayer
To which my Lord answers
With such concern
With such excitement
With such love.
B. J.

Apolonio J. Vera

HELLO THERE BEAUTIFUL

"Hello There Beautiful"
The words that I convey,
Every time I see you
These words I want to say.
The first time that I saw you
Warm, bright, and sublime,
How beautiful the glow of
sunlight
With blushing cheeks and eyes
divine.
The excuse I made to meet you
A fool I was that day,
For when the reason ended
I turned and walked away.
Thoughts of you filled my mind
Every day I wondered where,
The searching, dreaming, and
waiting
My heart filled with despair.
But, from the night comes the
dawn
And then followed by the sun,
The path I chose to follow
Sees you and I as one.
So every time I see you
To you I want to say,
"Hello There Beautiful"
I think of you this way.

David Jefferis

HOLIDAY

We woke up that November
morn
Our tongues were talking turkey
We didn't want a side of beef
We wouldn't stand for jerkey
Though tacos would certainly
be a treat
There's just one thing that we
would eat
Without it the day'd be
incomplete
Let's cook ourselves a turkey.
Dad went t'ward the frigidare
While no one said a word
We waited to view the
butterball
When all at once we heard. . .
From back in the freezer there
came a howl,
"Where the hell did you put
the fowl!"
An' mom she murmured with a
scowl,
"We forgot to buy the turkey."
Since all the stores were closed
that day
We just devoured toast
An we missed dressing & beans
& cake
But we missed that bird the
most
When all at once said little Jay,
"Food don't make a holiday,
So let's all go outside and play,
And forget about the turkey."
And with the wise words of the
child
We opened up our eyes
We found that we had thanks to
give
We felt our spirits rise
And though we all could eat a
dove
We fed that day on peace and
love
And we prayed hard to God
above
To forgive us lowly turkeys.

Louise B. Daigrepont

CHRISTMAS TIME

Christmas time is almost here,
it's the happiest time of the
year. Everyone smiling and
singing carols, giving, receiving,
and sharing.

I wonder if children know that
Christmas is more than just a
show, for Christ the King was
born that day, an infant babe,
lying in the hay, wrapped in
shabby clothes and very cold, to
rule the world, we are told.
That is why we celebrate his
birthday on that date. Don't
forget at Christmas time to sing
in tune with all the chimes.
"Happy birthday Jesus"
You make our world just right.

Eleanor S. Jackson

PUT YOUR HAND IN HIS

Put your hand in His, dearest
Ann!
He knows the way.
It is His way, not ours,
And we cannot understand!
But—this we know—
He is our sovereign God
And He can see the whole
pattern
Of our life.
We can see only this small
space
Of here and now!
Hold closely to all that you can
Of love, and laughter and joy
With Bill, and Steve and Kelly!
Take the love of friends
And wrap it around you,
together
With His love!
He loves you, dearest Ann!
And He has a purpose
In everything He does—
And He does everything
perfectly!
Hold fast to ALL His promises
For they are all true!
You can depend on them!
He knows the way that you
must take, so
Put your hand in His, dearest
Ann!

Che'rie Hambrick
TIME
the lightning flashes,
temporarily darkness leaves.
when it returns again
there's no room to breathe.
the hands on the timepiece
move faster when ungazed.
the fleeting moments pass
and mark another phase.
a bullet shot from a gun
shoots past over head
leaving all behind.
wisdom is left unsaid.
so its all over and done.
regrets are few but painful.
memories of days gone by
leave us all to sigh shameful.
another ship to pass
in the cold dark night.
realization of the event
when already gone from sight.
see how very quickly
the birds can fly?
time wasted away
is life gone by.

Maye Schwartz
SPRING
A snowdrift
that stood
tall and white
slowly melts
and shows mud
around the edges.
Suddenly
the elm
wears green
on boughs bare
all winter,
and pussy willows
lift soft gray heads
along stonewall fences.
Robin Redbreast
chirps a familiar sound
and tugs stubbornly
at a worm in the damp earth.
The lilac bush
wet with morning dew
is a mound
of lavendar and white lace.
Roller skates rumble
and the uneven rhythm
of Hopscotch
are echoes of laughing children
released from winter's cold.
The snow-cleaned earth
is eager to be tilled.
Spring
is a stage
set in exciting colors
and Nature, its players,
will create
the drama
of Summer.

Connie Medeiros
UNTITLED
Will I ever have the chance
To catch the rhythm of my
dance?
Or will I miss my only cue
Left inside the wings to view
While fate chooses to erase
The stage where I would seek a
place
And the final lights go dim
My glory forever locked within!

John Daniel Barnes
WINTER WONDERING
As if to take my heart,
Winter comes bounding in
with its cold winds cutting
through me.
Doors close, fires light
and shutters fall.
Winter; with its quiet times,
the long dark days
when people snuggle inside
their rooms
waiting idly for spring.
One can sit alone for hours
without any interruptions,
for few people will brave the
cold
to sit down and talk awhile.
Cold, bleak and stony
but beautiful in a whispering
way.
Wrapped in a furry coat
I will sit alone in this field
of snow,
thinking about thinking
because Winter is here again
and I'm bonded to it.

Melecia L. Casabal
MIRACLES
It's a miracle when the stars
come out one by one at night.
When the moon travels in the
sky, it's a miracle;
It's a miracle when darkness
turns to light at dawn,
When the sun gives heat and
whole day light, it's a miracle.
It's a miracle when the snow
falls and covers the ground,
When powder-like snow clings
on limbs of trees, it's a
miracle;
It's a miracle when icicles hang
on tree branches and eaves,
These are wonderful sights and
they are all miracles.
There are countless miracles
that happen every day,
We look at them, we enjoy
them, we appreciate them;
We marvel at them, we gasp and
utter beautiful things,
But do we ever praise and thank
the ONE WHO creates them?

Oril H. Swieso
GRANDPAS HAVE FUN
It's such fun being a Grandpa
When those youngsters come
once more
And they always ask "Where's
Grandma?"
As they hurry through the door.
And they tell about a "horsey"
Or a "ducky" that they saw.
Or it might have been a "moo
cow"
Or they heard a crow say "caw."
Or they smelled a pretty flower,
Nearly touched a butterfly.
And their eyes are brighter than
the stars
They saw twinkling in the sky.
It's such fun being a Grandpa
As I watch them grow so tall.
But their tender hugs and kisses
Are what I like best of all.

Gwenda Phillips
WINNING
Winning, that's what it is all
about
In this idea, I haven't a doubt!
No matter the game or skill or
scheme,
Winning always brings that
special gleam.
When people don't perform
their very best
Others will put you to a
shameful rest.
Life wasn't meant to be a defeat;
Excuses don't count when you
get beat!
No one gains by lying on the
gound,
From losers come no prolific
sound.
Being involved is what life's
about;
If you reach the top, then give
a shout!
Don't be overbearing like a fool,
The true winner knows one
simple rule,
Live to the fullest until the end,
And life will give you that
winning blend!

Lynn Beyenberg
OOOOOPS!
Spun sugar in a hefty bite
Melts in mouth but leaves
delight.
Rainbow arc, pale, shimmering,
bright,
Fades too soon from eager sight.
Sunbeams disappear in shade,
Shade takes substance never
laid.
Dry ice burns and cold is hot:
Some things are in being NOT.
YET
In all this world of strange
things
There is nothing to compare
With stepping
In the darkness
On a step that
.
.
Isn't there!

Arden Michael
LOOKING AHEAD
Christmas came and Christmas
went
And here is the new year
Gonna see the old out, new one
in?
Where's the party, Did you
hear?
The fun of putting Christmas
away
And find pleasure of each gift
As you enjoy them one and all
May they give your heart a
lift
Hope the Old Year was worth
celebrating
May the new one be better
yet
Enjoy each day as the year
passes by
To bring memories you'll
never forget
Brighten all your days and
weeks
As the months slip past
Helping to have alot of fun
That year sure goes fast
Enjoy this year as all those
prior
Smiling down the path
Causing others to smile to
Both first and second half

Jennifer Letitia Sweeney
TODAY
Yesterday is a memory.
Tomorrow is a dream.
Today? Well, it's just today—
Ripped open at the seam.
Yesterday upon my toes I
danced.
Tomorrow I will be romanced.
Today nothing happens.
Today can blow away.
Yesterday has gone away.
Tomorrow will never come.
Today I'll do my best in life
To see what it may become.

Judi Collins
OUTWARD APPEARANCE
How can I convince you to look
at my elderly friends
With a more open mind?
Because what's revealed beneath
their wrinkled skinned
exterior all depends.
On what's buried deep inside.
Don't let the years that show on
their face
Because they've come this far
Be allowed to erase
The true person they are.
Approach them with the same
respect that's reserved for the
young
Don't allow their souls to suffer
neglect
As their departing song in life
is left unsung!

Nina B. Cier
MY TASK
(Now That I'm Three Score and Ten)
To accept life's slackened pace
To admit that now my journey's
nearly o'er,
But holding firmly still faith's
promise,
To approach the door of my
tomorrows smiling and secure.
This is my task.
Lord, help me to keep bright the
hope
That He who gave me breath
still leads
And brings me each day nearer
home
Where his flock feeds.

Donna Lukas Vas
GOD'S LITTLE ACRE
The house on the hill, I saw in
my dreams,
so gracious, so strong,
magnificent—serene;
The house on the hill, I saw as
my own—
Much more than a house, still
beckons me home:
She's gone now, my house—a
mere memory,
But still late at night, she calls
out to me;
I hear her sweet call, I feel her
soft pull,
She's still standing tall, with
love—she is full:
The time is not right, but
she'll wait for me,
For still, late at night, she's
all I can see;

Surrounded by nature, big trees and God's love,
She stands there just waiting, she's all I think of:
She sends me her strength, though the miles are quite far;
She stands there and waits—
She's my bright shining star:
And just like a star, she'll never die;
Although she's not mine—in my heart, she stays nigh:
She stands 'top that hill, still waiting for me,
And still—day by day—reaches out to guide me.
Someday I'll reach her, I feel it for sure,
And all that hurts now—will then be no more;
For she's more than a house, that one buys to own—
She's gentle, She's loving, and keeps calling me home!

Ruby Gray Young

MY UPPER ROOM

Life seems to be filled with more jobs to do
Than we as mothers can get around to.
With cleaning and cooking and children to mind,
It is sometimes hard to keep sweet and kind.
But as I take out the time to ascend the stairs
I feel nearer to God who knows all and cares,
AS I GO TO MY UPPER ROOM.
Behind me I leave the confusion and noise,
Seeking to gain some composure and poise.
My body is weary from toil and care
And oh how I long for the quiet up there.
Then reclining I relax what time I can afford
'Til my body is refreshed and my soul is restored,
AS I REST IN MY UPPER ROOM.
My heart is heavy with burdens to bear
But in the stillness I know He is there.
As I humble myself and confess all my sin,
He is always ready to cleanse me within.
With assurance He shows me the way I should trod,
But best of all. . .there is PEACE WITH GOD,
AS I PRAY IN MY UPPER ROOM.

Gerald M. Delaney

YOUR WORD

Your Word.
The book of knowledge to all who believe.
Your Word.
The foundation of all the earth.
Your Word.
The yellow pages for all who need help.
Your Word.
The worlds greatest catalogue of gifts.
Your Word.
The restaurant where the whole world can eat.
Your Word.
The greatest love story ever told.

My Goodness

A LEGEND

Natalie Wood with long dark brown hair and big brown eyes with a tear always near—you were dear to us.
You went there as a child with a smile that beguiled
And innocence shining in your eyes.
No one denies your living.
In Miracle of 34th St. we remember your December,
In Splendor in the Grass, your young recklessness.
In Rebel without a Cause you won applause
And we cried when Tony died in your arms in West Side Story.
Oh young glory, caught on film, will yield a dividend.
You are in death, as in life, a legend.
We loved you—good Natalie Wood.

Ruth Bramlage

NIGHT'S JOURNEY

I dreamt of a lost love
somewhere in my journey
through the night.
Bittersweet memories come easily
on the soft sighs of sleep,
playing their game of torment.
Forcing their way
through my subconscious,
til I wake from the echo
beating against all thought.
Of all the painful
events I left behind,
he's the one I dream of.
Was he the hurt
of greatest magnitude,
or the least,
and safest to analyze?

John E. Law

MAYBE IT'S YOU

Two different worlds,
Two different souls.
Two different people,
Two different goals.
Two different hearts,
Looking for fun.
Two different hearts,
Looking for one.
Two different people,
Two different minds.
Two different people,
Two different kinds.
Maybe we're different,
Maybe, who cares.
Maybe it's time,
To be one who dares.
Dares take the time,
To show you his love.
To show you the moon,
And the stars up above.
To show you a world,
Where love ought to be.
To show you a world,
To just help you see.
Maybe it's crazy,
Maybe it's true.
Maybe it's different,
Maybe it's you. . . . . .

Diane K. Moddes

THE WORLD IN A RIBBED SHELL

And so we throw
The Day
to a world in a
ribbed shell. . .
Call it hell.
Caged in hours
and lost
on finite shores
The Ocean
full and serious,
fails to hear us.
A childlike call.
And the children
play wise;
tickling the belly
of The Wind. . .
Finds no end.
No end to dreams
it seems. . .
Of infinite days
and Beaches;
As toes fit under swells
filled with ribbed shells.
And the Ocean. . .answers.

Lucille Webster

LOVE AND WONDER

A milkweed seed came gliding down,
It settled on our baby's palm,
The beautiful expression in her eyes
Was one of wonder and surprise.
Lifting her head she looked at me
As if to ask if I too did see
This piece of fluff, that floated there,
As if it had picked that place with care.

Lifting her palm I blew it away,
And kissed her where the seed had lay.
She watched as it floated into the sky
With crystals shining in her lovely eyes.
The thought crossed my mind as I brushed her tears
The love and laughter to be hers through the years.

Anna I. Wideman

THE FOOTPRINTS

Anonymous footprints are they
No color or race do they convey
So soon to become the sifting sand
Lying ageless in a changing land,
So many travelers have cast their feet
In timeless soil through cold and heat
Vagrants from all parts of the earth
To share with us our "Freedom Birth"!
Sculptured footprints lying there
No more anatomy can they share
No gender or race or religion is shown
Only casts of strangers left unknown.
Anonymous footprints cast in the sand
How perfect! Untouched by human hand
Was it neighbor or stranger that passed this way?
Or the prints you left there yesterday?

Robbie Glass

FANTASIES

Locked within my fantasy,
Journeying, anywhere bound,
Images come and fade,
Those my mind has made.
Lifeless forms start to move,
And live within my brain,
Colors are separate but one,
In my world of wandering.
My ageless daydreaming fantasies,
Forever just for me,
Don't try to take that which is left,
Of my private personality.

Raymond E. Hall

WOMEN OF THE WORLD

She wants to be with you, but her world says no.
She wants to sleep with you, but her world says no.
What would she tell her friends if they were to see.
Would she tell them all she wants to be is free?
Hold back your feelings, don't let them seep through.
Would your nakedness then betray you?
Would you like what you find on the other side,
And destroy all those myths you were taught as a child?
Go ahead and try, he won't harm you.
Your auburn locks of hair will still be the same.
Will the mirrors reflect some changes inside.
No journey is needed, the answer is here to find.
We live for dreams from day to day.
Fulfilling thoughts we've never dared.
Reaping the highs endlessly without lows.
Free of guilt that never should have been.
A trip back through time will show you a place.
Free of built society has imposed.
Blessed are the animals roaming the plains.
May they never feel the chains of man.

Kathlyn F. Kruse
LONELINESS
Like a flower without its stem
Like salt without pepper
Like day without night
Like coffee without cream
Like a pen without paper
Like a picnic without ants
Like a book without a cover
Like a cigarette without a match
Like the sun without the moon
Like me without you.

Edwin Whitehead
THE FORTUNATE ONES
An odd thing has come to mind,
As I attack this school day grind.
In general appearance we're all similar,
As we study quite familiar,
With each others gripes and groans,
And as the work piles, the helpless moans.
But for some it all comes easy,
They go along just big and breezy.
Ah! The fortunate ones.
They can sit and listen and learn it all,
When school is out they have a ball.
But others keep notes and work very hard,
And when they get home they're very tired.
They can't goof off and play around,
Or their grades will fall with a bound.
Ah! The fortunate ones.
But when the time comes for them to get a job,
Sometimes the smart ones are the number I slob.
So the ones that work hard through the years,
Usually come out on top with cheers.
Ah! The fortunate ones.

Vicki Russell
VISIONS
I close my eyes—
And see your image there. . .
Your sparkling eyes
And softly curling hair
Your smiling lips,
Whisper softly. ."I love you",
And promise me you always will be true
My heart beats fast—
To see your face so dear
With trembling hands—I reach to hold you near
But just before we touch, I realize
How sad. . . .
You're just a vision in my mind.

Elizabeth Milligan
HAND IN HAND
Walk hand in hand with me, my love
Our steps go well together.
Through everything life has to give
We'll face the stormy weather.
There will be rain, there will be snow
There will be times of sorrow.
But oh my love, there will be sun
To warm each new tomorrow.
Look up! Look up! A new day dawns
We'll face the rising sun
With love so true, for me and you
We'll walk through life as one.
With love like ours, how can we fail
To have a world of pleasure?
So hold my hand and walk with me
We'll have our dreams to treasure.

Paula Cline
REMINISCENCES
My Daddy took me on picnics.
My Daddy gave me piggy-back rides.
My Daddy took my side in fights.
My Daddy spanked me once when I was bad.
My Daddy told me not to stay in the tub too long.
My Daddy died when I was 10.

Mrs. Ova B. Henry
THE TOUCH OF THE MASTER'S HAND
As we behold the wondrous beauty
Of a morning sun-kissed and fair,
If we look beyond the horizon
We can see the Master there.
His touch is one of magic
His caress the sweetest yet
The beauty of His creating
Is a marvel not to forget.
Each glorious sunrise and sunset

Are resplendent with golden glow
Which only an Infinite artist
Has power such beauty to show.
We're ever surrounded by brilliance
As waves of a mystical wand
Reflecting through a dazzle of splendor
The Touch of the Master's Hand.

Wallace L. Weister
COME SEE THE CLOWN
Come see the clown, look at him cry.
With tears in his eyes and a smile on his face
This jester contradicts himself in open view—
Lying to you as you gaze upon his grin,
Saying one thing and meaning another.
Come see the clown, look at him cry.
With jokes and comical gestures he'll make you laugh.
Why then does he frown and weep?
This humorist is hurt so very deep inside.
He's torn apart by what or whom?
Come see the clown, look at him cry.

Peggy Rambo
THE SETTING SUN
If you could have seen what
I saw tonight
It really would have amazed you.
The beauty and splendor of the evening light
I know would have dazed you.
The sky was the most beautiful blue you could see
And purple and orange did surround it.
There was just a hint of a moon up above
Because a haze was all around it.
The world seemed so calm
and peaceful then;
My cares seems so very light.
And only a single star had appeared
But it glowed like a fireside on a dark chilly night.

Robert Smith
SEQUENCE FOR MARICHIKO
high, then higher still—
a yellow and blue kite
against a white and blue sky
ah, the yearning for the fullness of life—
a whisp of cloud fades away
love at dawn—
a white chrysanthemum
words, images—
like sparrows in a tree
for Marichiko—
a cherry blossom
in the palm of my hand

Marsha Flippo
SON
Twenty years ago tonight
I sat in a similar place.
I talked and laughed
among my friends,
and wore a dress of lace.
I never knew that someday
if I would just but stay,
that I'd sit and watch my son,
on his graduation day.
I asked not long ago
a favor from my Lord
"Please let me stay long enough to see,
a glimpse of the fine young man
that he will grow to be."
I watch him walk in front of all,
this gentle boy so tall.
I'd give anything to have
been able to save,
his hand prints on
the wall.
I've watched him play
with toys and cars,
and listened to his list of
favorite baseball stars.
But nothing will compare
to the pride I feel,
as he takes this step so grand.
Give me the wisdom to
set him free,
and the strength to let go
of his hand,
as he walks away from his time
at play,
to change the world
if he can.

Alice McCumber
OLD FASHION REVIVAL MEETING
I went to a revival one night,
Altho I was a little shy.
When the preacher began with all his might,
Telling about that home in the sky.
I opened up my ears to listen,
And took in all he said.
Then the tears began to glisten,
And my face turned a little red.
For you see my soul wasn't white,
And the preacher went on about Christ on the Cross.
Then I began to see the light,
Thank God, all was not lost.
I thank the Lord for washing my sins away,
And for listening to my pleading.
For an old fashion preacher that knew how to pray,
And an old fashion revival meeting.

Ray Yedding
PARADOXICAL MOMENT
I lie here looking down over your shoulder, so sleek and smooth. .It has escaped from under those long dark tosseled curls, that lay like placid waves come to rest over your back.
I look down along your forearm, with hair so delicate as if kissed by a balmy wind. . . Your fingertips lightly caressing my chest, with just a whisper of touch.
I love the feel of the curve of your breast, pressed against my chest. . .your round, firm, muscular, tummy browned by the sun, moist against my stomach.
I sense the warmth of your loins as they part gently, then yieldingly snuggle and settle against me in contentment. . .
So peacefully, I watch you sleep.

Ishtar
LITTLE FLOWER
How nice it would be
To become a flower
And watch Gods beauty
With the regale of power.
Folded petals
Like soft velvet fingers
Caressed by the dew
While the morning hour lingers.
Awakened by sparkling
Rays of sunshine
And touched by the whisper

Of breezes so fine.
To see me so happy
Oh God, you must know
No matter how small
No matter how low.
Smelling aromas
No perfumes can beat
And watching the fauna
Graze undisturbed at my feet.
I gently toss
My petaled head to n' fro
While rain drops touch me
And help me to grow.
To be tickled by a dozen
Sweet honey bees
And surrounded by the majestic
Array of fine trees.
The sunset I'll watch
With magnificent glory
While I close my petals
To this beautiful story.

Betsy Lewis

A BLACK WORLD

Depression capacitates my
body and soul like
a black cloud swallowing up
the sun's glistening rays.
It is in this depression
I find myself still as a child
conforming only to that
of a fantasy life.
I resent the reality
of the true cold world
finding people sinister and
incompetent
to my own satisfaction.
This depression as I know it
will never lift as long as
my life is filled with hatred
for most and pity for all!

Thor H. McBride

HOPEFUL DREAM

Every night at bedtime
When I lay down to sleep
In a bed so cold and lonesome
So lonely I could weep
There is no one to cuddle close
No one to kiss goodnite
Just a cold and empty space
beside me
That I share alone till mornings
light
It's then I live in memories
Of bygone days and years
To relive every moment
Of joy gay fun and tears
And while entranced in such
sweet thoughts
I drift to slumber deep
And hope that in my dreams
sweetheart
You are the one I meet.

Jacqueline Rae

AS A WOMAN

As a woman, I entertain,
myself with thoughts of old
refrain
To dwell upon the times gone
by,
of building castles in the sky.
As a woman, I am wife,
bewildered by this strange
new life,
That crept upon me one fine
day,
to find a man, beside me lay.
As a woman, wife, now mother.
would by choice to be
another?
With shattered dreams of one
in doubt,
to stop the world, and let me
out.
As a woman, with songs to sing,
would thou deny the bells to
ring?
Or burst the bubbles, one by
one?
misplaced position in the sun?
As a woman, in older age,
uncertain by a building rage.
The flesh is weakened, goals
delayed,
but dreams I sought in youth
won't fade.

Elaine E. Pirtle

WORDS FOR THOUGHT

Time is for the living
Eternity for the deed
Energy is forever
Over again it is said
Knowledge is a form of
Never ending gain
Challenge is experience
Even with its pain
Limit is the distance
We attain in our life
Space is a measure
Not severed with a knife
Temptation is distraction
Either bad or good
Existence is this span
Rarely understood.

Pat Blanchard

MEASURE OF LOVE

How much does a tear weigh
perhaps a gram of ache
an ounce of liquid sorrow
a dram of sad mistake
There is no way to measure
the breaking of a heart
no scale to balance errors
of lovers when they part.

Dolores A. Eberlin

FRIENDS

Friends are like rain, they wash
away the blues.
I have many friends, but my
best friend is you.
You always seem to understand
the crazy things I do.
To have a friend really helps
me see, all the blessings my
dear God has given me.
When I think of all my friends,
one stands out from all the rest.
We must be a perfect blend,
That's because you're the best.
You give me strength to keep on
going.
You accept me when my faults
are showing.
So hand in hand we go
Down life's path
Through all our lives,
Our friendship will last.

Mrs. Carrol A. Williams

THE ARAB

Over the desert sand he flies,
Under the blue and cloudless
skys,
He runs like the wind over the
sand,
In this barren desert land.
He is the gift their God has
sent.
He lives with them in their
tent,
And drinks their milk like
another son,
When the Arab's day has just
begun.
He is their most precious stone.
When he's around, they are not
alone.
With brave heart he fights their
wars,
Then walks in peace 'neath
desert stars.
With nostrils flared and
lustrious eye,
He silhouettes against the sky,
As he runs like the wind over
the sand,
In this barren desert land.

Ronnie M. Vinson

TOAST TO THE NEW YEAR

Paint good times
With roses
Wine of age
So true
All is yours
For gladness
As we look
A year
Anew
Fun to close
An ending
As time
Slip right through
Let's lift our hearts
Toward heaven
As I pledge
This toast to you:
January to December
Do march in step
To time
Yours for everlasting
Peace
May all do find
And if one should ever question
The mysteries
That are Divine
This miracle
That we drinketh
Is it blood
Or is it Wine!

Donna Bristol Earth

MIND MEADOWS

On the quiet meadows in my
mind
I walk peacefully, happily.
The flowers, and grasses
dance in the breeze
as the meadow sings her songs.
The sunshine of those golden
days
warms me to the bone.
The cotton clouds overhead
just float, and drift on by.
Out there, I can just be
and not need to worry about
why.
When I come back from the
meadows
I feel refreshed, and clear.
So very glad to be alive
and a part of all thats here.

R. Marie Gillette

PERSISTENCE

The late October rain
Tenderly kisses the still-green
grass
With no sound at first.
Then coveting confidence
It pelts passionate streams
Upon the at-last receptive
ground
Amidst the music of muted
kettledrums.

Anne Estlow Kornman

THE MAN I MOST ADMIRE

As I sit here by the fire,
I think of the man
I most admire.
He is dark, handsome and tall,
in more ways than one.
He is kind, gentle, terribly stern,
but fun.
He holds me close when I cry,
or even have a fear;
Though he's miles away now,
I feel he's always near.
We've shared our strengths,
weaknesses too!
We've shared just about
everything
we cherished so dear.
So you can see why,
through the distance and
tears;
That I can be happy
even though I feel sad;
For he's not only the man
I most admire,
He's the best friend I have,
and above all desire.
So when I am down,
feeling quite blue;
I think of this man,
This man is you—My Dad!

Norma Sherer

SATAN & GOD

Satan is a rat, he ruined my
whole life!
He and all his evil spirits
Will burn, burn, burn!
Evil sex spirits are dung.
They will burn, burn, burn!
Jesus and I will judge them.
I hope they eat dog dewin
That unholy place that
Is too good for them.
I in the name of Jesus,
Rain curses on them,
Let them all remember how
They scewed up my life.
Tired and blue and miserable,
You will spend forever in
Hell, and will worship Jesus!

Cherie Madzey

THE ME

Does the me exist
When no one knows
Or cares to know
What is really me?
Do the feelings, actions, hopes,
and fears
Go outward into nothing?
Do others know?
Do others care?
Other people talk and talk
About themselves and what
they do.
I like to know.
I care.
But what about the me inside
The things I do, the thoughts I
have?
No one asks.
No one cares.
Does the me exists for only me?

Glennie C. Larke
VISIONS
You were born for death
Oh mortal man of flesh;
But God granted you free will
To choose the path
Your soul shall take,
By the visions you reveal
On his planet called Earth.
Although your flesh will pass,
Your soul eternal will guide you
To your final destiny!

Lee Wells
WARM SMILES
As I stopped at a drive-in named Jalopy.
I met one that had a smile, far from being sloppy.
Her greeting and smile was warm as the noon day sun.
This troubled world needs more like this fair one.
May her smiles be beamed to others as they stop by.
I assure all that your day will be of blue sky.
Yes your day will be changed as you meet this young lass.
For me her smile made me feel at the head of the class.
Her name I do not know, so I shall call her warm smiles.
I will remember her smiles as I travel life's miles.
So warm smiles, I hope to stop by soon.
Smile those smiles so sweet to keep them in tune.

Debbie D. Swartz
UNTITLED
I know not what to do
Now that my heart belongs to you
It aches for you night and day
As my body aches in the same way
One touch from you and I fall apart
One look from you melts my heart
My body tingles at your sight
And being with you seems right
You have been my strength when I needed you
You have been my sunshine when I was blue
You have been my need, my guiding light
Your memory helps me through a lonely night
It's as tho you have become a part of me
A part of me that should not be
A part of me I shouldn't have let come about
Because you are a part of me I can't live without.

Alice Soward
I THINK OF YOU
In so many ways I think of you
And of the things we use to do,
Like a morning stroll down a shady Lane
Or when soft rain falls on my window pane.
I think of you too when Roses bloom
And fields are green with life anew
Refreshed by the mornings dew.
When we picnic in the Park, It is never the same
The soft summer breeze seems to whisper your name
And I hear an echo from the days gone by
Slowly I brush a tear from my eyes.
I think of you too when Autumn leaves fall
And when Old Man winter comes to call,
When Candle lights are all aglow
And Sleigh Bells ring with the very first snow.
Time fades away—never to retreat
But the Memories are ours to cherish and to keep.

Marcia J. Pear
THE SENSUALITY OF A LOLLIPOP
sticky—sweet
lick
tasting pleasure
tonguegummy
redsugar mel ting
sliding throat
gliding
o
w
n
smoothly
syrup ooze
seventh lick
CRUNCH!
lip
smack
swallowpiece
pink chew. . .chew. . .
half-a-stick-gone-lickety-quick
savored substance
sucrose
delight.

Julie C. Arndt
IMAGES OF GOD
In forest garbed with velvet green,
A whisper travels barely seen,
To reach the skies of evergreen,
And find the chance to fly.
From God to us, a sigh.
Reflections of a golden sea.
They cast through clouds made silvery,
Rays of bronze pierce soundlessly,
A soft embroidered pink.
From God to us, a wink.
Soft autumn leaves dance through the air,
Come falling gently in a pair,
With just a moment left to spare,
This butterfly uncaught.
From God to us, a thought.
A rainy day will go unheard,
While dripping trees shade one lost bird,
And nowhere lands release no word,
A rainbow on the isle.
From God to us, a smile.
A rounded moon filled in with white,
And twinkling stars surround the night,
A few cream clouds thrown in for spite,
And then approaches dawn.
From God to us, a yawn.

Mabel Epes Peterson
O, GOD OF LOVE
O, God of Love, Thy prophets oft did say
How Thou wouldst guard us each and every day
From evil thoughts which oft tear us apart;
Be with us now and cleanse our inmost heart;
Help us to work and do our very best
To do Thy will and be forever blest.
O, God of Love, who binds us close to Thee,
O, Christ, who died for us on Calvary,
May Thy love dwell in us and ne'er depart
In days of strife and endless change of heart;
Be with us now and bless us, God of Love,
Until we come to dwell with Thee above.

Joe Dominice
LIFE'S DEEP WATERS
The deepest of water
The passion of sin
Put them together and go for a swim
If you stay on top
Everything will surface
If you go somewhat lower
Your thoughts will be slower
For when submerged on the bottom
Of water or life as it may be
Life can be either glowing
Or somewhat slowing to a degree
So swim and stroke forever turning
Don't get caught up in life's churning
Perhaps we may float instead of dredging
The bottom of life resembles our strife
So go with the flow like water
For it has strength
To push us to the top without great length
So that you won't have to vent
Or breathe any harder
You won't go downstream or out to sea
Just stay in your own harbour
And get rid of life's mystery

Mildred Layton Boone
IT'S TIME TO STOP
With all God's creatures great and small,
And all His wonders blesses all.
Let's stop a little while each day,
To pray for those who have gone astray.
Please go to those that are old and gray,
And listen to what they have to say.
Those who have lived much more than we
Are precious, so precious to Him you see.
A kind and loving smile, and thought,
To those and lots more to be sought.
The time is going so very slow,
They're sitting around just waiting to go.
With wonders and thoughts of all past years,
And reminiscing with joys and tears,
With the power of Him who gives us grace,
Let's share this with the whole human race.

Vicky Wiebenga-Stewart
LITTLE BABY
Little baby inside of me
How I wonder what you'll be
A boy, a girl, maybe one of each.
How much of my ways will you teach?
What achievements in life will you reach?

Joe Dominice
LOVE IS WORTH LIVING
Women are beautiful and women are great
Sometimes men have to wait
For the right one to come along
After all what are we living for
If not to enjoy life more
For the love of a man and a woman
Is the ultimate thing in life
For it makes us both forget our strife
You can have money and all the material things
You can enjoy life with all its flings
But as time goes on and love matures
We finally realize that love makes us endure
This life on earth
Because of it all love makes it all
Its worth

Mary Morgan Dunlop
GENESIS
In the beginning, the Spirit of God
Lived within the centre of silence. . .
within the centre of darkness.
But when the time was ripe
He reached out toward Creation.
The voice of the Ruach-wind*
Shouted through the corridors of space
And liquid worlds of Fire were born.
The Spirit danced and swirled
In Wind and Fire.
He was part of them, and they of Him.
But it was not enough!
He called up Cloud and Vapour
And cast them through the Fire
Until He had shaped the crusts of Earth.
Oceans were born to fill the valleys;
Mountains, to top the high places.
It was good. . .but it was not enough!
With lightning sparks He split

the atoms of the waters
And loosed the chains of life
to grow. . .
And He was in the growing
To newness and greeness.
It was very good. . .it was
refreshing. . .
But it was not enough
Until the time when life itself
Goes down to the centre of
Silence,
And touching there the heart
of God,
Reaches out toward Creation
In the whirl and dance of
Eachotherness!
*"Ruach"—Hebrew word for
Spirit, breath, wind. . .

Sandra Byrd
ODE TO A CACTUS
You sit there all green and
spidery
In your ceramic pot
I give and give and give to you
But it is all for naught.
But wait a minute, what can
this be?
Several buds of life I see!
No, 'tis but imagination or
hopefulness on my part.
Ability to reproduce seems not
a part of your art.
I awake one morning
And there on my window sill
The most lovely, delicate
flowers
From wherever did they appear?
Are they really a part of that
spidery green thing
To which I have been so
devoted?
Yes, it seems they really are
And my cactus quietly gloated.

Matthew Alan Noll
CHRISTMAS SURROUNDINGS
The sky is bright,
The ground is white,
The trees glitter with fresh air,
You wait all night,
To see that special sight,
That you see only once a year.

Carl Misegadis
A REWARDING WALK
On the dusty road to Emmaus
Two heart broken men did
discuss
The past few days that seemed
so wrong.
A Stranger drew near and
walked along.
He asked what manner of talk
they had
To be so weary and look so sad.
"Have you not heard or seen
they cried
That Jesus of Nazareth was
crucified?
Certain women claim to have
seen Him
Alive and we are concerned for
them.
The Stranger said they were
slow to see
Then explained the Scriptures
and prophecies.
When they reached their home
He continued on
But they asked Him in for the
day was gone.
He broke bread for them that
He had blessed.
They knew Him then, as would
the rest.
He then vanished from their
sight.
To them all things now seemed
all right,
Saying, "How our hearts did
burn in us
as He walked with us to
Emmaus."
To the eleven disciples they
later said
"We knew Him when He broke
the bread."
As happened there, when
speaking thus
We have found Jesus in the
midst of us.

Christine Garrity
UNTITLED
jumbled
thoughts
inside
a
brain
twisted
words
not
one
the
same
falling
quickly
too
late
to
catch
the
words
are
gone
no
more
is
said

Pat Luy
YOUR WEDDING GOWN
you are turning in your wooden
cross to claim your golden
crown,
to stand before the father and
me in your wedding gown.
I know you suffered so like my
death upon the cross,
you have earned a special kind
of love for helping me gather
the lost.
It took so many years to earn
your wedding gown,
years of forgiveness and
repentence to wear your
golden crown.
A special place in his kingdom,
together we will be,
praising our heavenly fathers
name, all his glory we will
see.

Betty Lou Rader
A MAN
The water came crashing up
against the ice covered shore
As I walked alone and felt the
wind whirl through my hair
I stood watching the waves lap
around the drift wood
Then, I saw a lone figure
walking with such
determination
He seemed to have the whole
world on his shoulders
Coming closer, I turned and saw
the look of sadness on his
face
As his steps made impressions
in the sand
He walked on and as I watched
him go
Walking toward the sun, toward
his answer
I turned to leave only to find
myself looking back
Back to that lone figure,
thoughts flooded my mind
For only a moment I saw him
and Remembered Him

Princess Orelia Benskina
EMOTIONS
I have written of many places,
many people, and many
things;
In fact, I have rebelled, I have
loved, at times, even sings.
My blood has boiled, my heart
cried, and my soul drained;
Yet, whenever I hear your name,
I'm helpless, and void of pain.
I have felt the touch of
loneliness, anger, and despair;

I have also known the joy of
tenderness and care.
However, that special something
happens whenever your face I
see,
Bringing consolation and
quietness deeply within me.
I have in awe, at God's
miraculous works, shook;
I have strolled beside a
whimpering brook
And, with all that I have seen,
or many things done,
It's only the warmth of your
gentle kiss, that has my
heart, won.

June Covington Stephens
WAR II
Joe I thought the war
was over!
Knock me down and
break my body.
pull the plug
I'll drain away
my legs are fading...
not much to stand on
you didn't even get to
read my plea
and there you
were.
No war is over
captive prisoners
you and me.
my heart is broken
maybe maybe
we can try
and we can just
get out of
here.

Louis Bohay
THE JOURNEY OF WHEAT
From the graineries
of the toiling farmer
in the Dakotas and Montana
to the clanging lunch kits
of the fun-filled youth.
From the Steppes of Ukraine
to the sawmills
and the prisons of Siberia.
From the prairie provinces
of Canada
unto the altars; the sacrament;
along with wine,
transformed into HIS BODY.
And even to the famished
orphan mouths in India
and Bangladesh.

Gregory Hartman
IT'S ALMOST LIKE A GAME
Although I know I'll never
know,
I wish I could some day;
How another person thinks his
thoughts,
In a completely different way.
Their gears may click a diff'rent
tune,
Mine is not the same.
The thought of being someone
else
Is almost like a game.
Some day I will become a man,
In my second life,
Who's mind thinks a similar
thought,
And has a similar strife.
He like me will want to be
A certain person's clone,
To be as one together,
Not so all alone.

Anthony G. Helfer
ILLUSION'S REALITY
Illusion -
Reality's shadow
Eluding what is
To remain what if;
Giving answers
To questions
That have no answers,
Bringing light
To darkness
When darkness
Is the gift;
And over the rainbow
A dream world exists
Until the rainbow is over
Then all is a myth
With the faces of people
A friend or a foe,
Until trouble is present
One doesn't know
Who is real
And what is right
And what
Is simply
Illusion.

John L. Arnold
SHROUD
Does anybody out there
Realize how dark it is in here?
Scream dreams out of head
Afraid he cries
I want to be dead
Smooth talking B movie me
Anounces stop on the "L"
Frustration creeps in
I realize the shroud

Perihan D. Joy
NOBODY WINS - II
My heart is broken into pieces
And scattered everywhere
here and there...
I am thousands of me...
Yet I've been invisible to you...
cannot cope with it, cannot deal with it
I am the weakest of all me...
Left my heart here, the thousands
I have nothing to take with me...

David E. Crowley
BE
Be as you are and change
not as much for better
as for yourself.
Be as you perceive yourself,
not as much for pride
as for dignity.
Be as like to no one
as much as like to God,
not to know perfection
but to seek it.
Be not in fear of dying
lest life become a treasure
too valuable to spend.
Be not in fear of sorrow
lest you never know the strength
nor the wisdom born of tears.
Be as you were meant to be,
never losing sight of hope,
never taking more than you would give.
Be, not as much for being,
as for using well the time you have to be.

Ruby Christian Jackson
TRUE WORTH
Mamma kept the snapshots in a box-but they gave her so much pleasure
She would take them out at the least excuse-this full fifty years of treasure.
I'm sure that only Mamma knew the pictured folks and places-
For time had dimmed the color and cracked many of the faces.
My sister brought an album with plastic covered pages-
Saying-"Mamma, sort those pictures out-some you've had for ages."
Well-Mamma got the trash can and made her preparation.
She opened up the box to start on all this accumulation.
She took a tiny brittle print-Said, "Why, here is baby Jim.
I really had forgotten that we made this one of him!"
One picture showed a row of feet. Mamma smiled. "I was forever missing heads-
But this was the day Bob lost his shoes. He is wearing Uncle Fred's."
"Mary, do you remember this? You were so pretty in this dress-
I made it for your Junior Prom and your first date with Les."
Picnics...weddings...birthdays... Christmases and graduations-
Babies...pets and the big parade... and those few hard earned vacations.
Through them all my Mamma went-with laughter and with tears
Remembering all the living that had made up all the years.
the day was gone-the box was closed. The empty trash can told
That very treasured memories never do grow old!

Rick Paster
WHAT HAVE WE DONE TO OUR CHILDREN
What have we done to our children
We have taken away their rhymes
We've got them hooked on drugs
When they're not getting high on wine
We have got them exploring other worlds
That they are not yet ready to see
We have closed our eyes
Turned our backs
And then said, "Come to me!"
What have we done to our children
To make them go astray?
We moulded their lives after our own

And now they've run away.
They are wise to our emotions
They see what's going on
They easily spot our contradictions
They despise our same old song
All they ask is love and understanding
Someone to lend an ear
Not just a smile, a pat on the head
But someone who will really hear
They ask our love for what they are
Not for what we would like them to be
For their problems are as important to them
As yours are to you, and mine are to me.

Nancy Bradley Oparka
MY COCA COLA FRIENDSHIP
My Coca Cola friendship;
we met on a Sunday
A sunday in May,
refreshing as daybreak
but not the same.
Ice-glass chilled
just like the lake
with all its frills;
burning my throat,
what a desire!
Slurp it up in a straw!
Alive with pleasure,
can you measure
great tall glasses
filled to the rim?
Imagine you're a friend of a
bottle of Coca Cola
and you're very thirsty;
would you drink it in a hurry?
Down my throat
up the foam floats
like fizzes in a glass.
Slurp it up in a straw!

Richard Humphrey Jr.
UNTITLED
One, Two, and Three
Today, who shall I be?
I shall be one of three
Who shall ascend a mountain, and upon reaching the top
They shall take a trip,
not by train
not by plane-
But on a mysterious ship
not powered by man-made substances, but by someone who can control
Life and death
Love and hatred-
At the end of our trip
we shall descend the mountain,
When we reach the bottom
we shall find,
We took a trip-
only through our minds...

Bette Lynn Gardner
PSYCHOSIS
Sunlight sparkles on the crest of the wave
Frothing joyfully; Free - racing toward destiny.
Great and small - all come crashing to the shore.
Seized by undertow, all are dragged back to their beginnings.
High tide, low tide, ebb and flood as the moon waxes and wanes.
Does the wave rejoice as it speeds to its destruction?
Does the ocean mourn the ebbing of its tide?

Jane W. Mikkelsen
INTROSPECTION
I thought of God this morning
As I looked up at the sky.
His giant canvas blue-washed
Stretched as if to dry.
No object marred its beauty
So early in the day
And suddenly I felt
A compelling urge to pray.
I thought of God at noon
As I looked up at the sky.
Darting birds, fleecy clouds
Jet trails here and there
Gave meaning to the mid-day
And once again to Thee I pray.
I thought of God this evening
As I looked up at the sky.
The deeper blue well-lit by stars
Enhanced by a mellow moon
Gave promise of another day
And once again I knelt to pray.

Carolyn D. Smith
IS THIS FOR ME
Marijuana friend or foe
Here's some things that you should know
Is it good or is it bad
Here to stay or just a fad
Marijuana saint or devil
Here's some dope that's on the level
One of the oldest drugs known to men
Discovered B.C. by Chinese Emperor Shen
Experts in the field of drugs have on one thing agreed
Marijuana has become a controversial weed
Many things are just a myth a few things are true fact
When you smoke it your appetite increases and you are likely to get fat
Hay Pot tea grass and weed
think about it when you're passin
The word Hashish comes to us from a form of the word assassin
A cigarette is called a joint reefer or a stick
Marijuana is in many forms it's there just take your pick
Heart that beats quite rapidly tearing of the eyes
Feeling that your body floats these things are no surprise
Feeling great your problems gone you don't feel like a loser
All these things may come to you
When you become a user

Ruth Morell Sackstein
ON MISSING
Please my darling don't get used to being apart
How sad when that happens dear heart
Please don't stop missing me
If I'm being selfish let me be.
It's a living death when we miss not
If we're used to not seeing each other what have we got
Time enough when I'm dead
Living is seeing, missing, hurting, loving
Feelings to be felt not only said.

Roberta Lynn Hayes
I WONDER
I wonder where all the beautiful people have gone, then looking around I see them standing there, wondering what would happen if they had to use a wheelchair.
Think about it awhile
then go and run a mile
When you come back you wonder why,
then you sit down and cry.
You think about the people you know
who'll never have a chance to grow.
Everyone must work together to make
this life, free from pain and strife.

Helen K. Dickson
DIMENSION
How big is "big",
And what is "tall",
And where's the Ruler
Of us, all?
A tabby cat's
A tiny thing,
To cousin, huge,
The tiger King.
The ant, to us,
Minute and small,
Seems giant, right,
To finite mite.
The microscopes
Can magnify,
Great telescopes;
Intensify.
Yet--what is "sparce",
And what is "vast",
Prey, tell us, seers,
Iconoclasts?

Benedict Chiaka Njoku
WHAT IS MY NAME?
My Name is Jesus
A sea of tears gush through my weepy eyes
As I hang loosely on the cross
Bearing my crown of thorns
And my sea of wounds bleeding all over.
I am standing between two thieves
And Mary, my mother,
And Mary Magdalene and John,
My Brother, were all there!
Here I stand, once a babe
Chubby with damask cheeks
Frolicking like winter frogs,
Climbing, and hugging mother dear.
But now, I'm bereft of joy
Mourning in grief
As they cast lots on my garments
And slap my lacerated limbs.
O come and mourn with me
You passers-by!
The darkening clouds and the silvery drops
Will bring joy to you.

Bhagwan Khanna
CANNOT STOP LOVING YOU
Recall the day I saw you the loving smoothness and facial innocence, lucid talks and lavish affection, enslavened me. Lost the charm and meaning in life ignoring the duty and increasing oblivion, no focus, no fun, no logic and no reason, I hate you, 'cause cannot stop loving you.

Peggy Grant
SUMMER SMILE
Not long ago I met a smile.
It was the most welcoming show of affection
I have ever seen.
And the eyes that belonged to this smile
Had an expression all their own.
With just a glance into these eyes
A radiant glow of friendly persuasion
Make me want to smile back.
And with that, our smiles became
Friends.
And then I met a hand.
It was a strong firm hand.
And when this hand held mine,
I experienced a feeling of security.
And when these eyes met mine,
We formed a bond of friendship.
And when this smile met mine,
I knew love.

Laura Lambe Burrell
THE LAMB VERSUS THE WOLF
The owl hoots on
As the howling winds
Pierce the night
The bloodthirsty wolf becomes
Dormant
As he watches the innocent
Lamb
Graze in the cricket
Filled meadow
The moon screams
Its last sorrows and
As the wolf drops down
To round the last morro
The lamb
Turns around
Only to strike its counterpartner
With its baa and pure innocence.
The fervid twinkling of the
Stars
Look down to see the wolf
Lying without a
Quiver, dead stretched
On the plain
Least of all never to
Remember the quick eye of the lamb.

Wanda Epperson
LOVERS SONG
Dedicated to Tim from Wanda
Loving's like the ocean,
A wild, blue place to drown.
And loving's deep devotion,
and words without a sound.
Loving's like an eagle
that soars up through the sky,
and drifts among the fleecy
clouds so
wild and free up high.
Well, loving's like a hurting,
and loving's like a pain.
Sometimes it makes you crazy,
Sometimes it keeps you sane.
And loving's metamorphis,
cocoon to butterfly.
And loving's what I do each
time I look into your eyes.
Yes, loving is the ultimate of all
emotions known.
So open up and let me in, we'll
sing the Lovers Song.

Charles Martorana
LITTLE LADY
A sparkle of hope
in a world gone dim.
Precious one;
lighting up the hearts
of those around you.
As you grow, I stand watching
astounded and overwhelmed
by the love within you
Little Lady
Florida baby
shining,
ever shining as the sun shines;
blossoming the fruits of this
land you smile radiantly
bringing happiness;
blossoming my life.

Helen Shepherd
ACCEPTANCE
I am a child, I have leukemia, the cells in my blood have gone wild.
There are too many white, and not enough red, I'm really a very weak child.
My clothes they don't fit and my hair has come out, I have all this trauma to withstand.
It hasn't been easy to muster my strength and hold my head high like a man.
My fate I no longer deny, I'm not angry or depressed anymore.
I have finally accepted, my shortened life, I will take whatever's in store.
My life may be over at the turn of a decade, and I have no future to plan.
But I've lived in God's presence and know of his love, I've walked with him hand in hand.

Jon K. Shuppert
MY LADY
I am searching for a life in heaven.
Because in heaven I know there is you.
I am searching for a galaxy of love.
I know that galaxy lies within you.
You are like a beautiful flower in full bloom and I want to be your sun!
For me to be without your love would be like living in a world without the sun.
My lady, oh my lady you are the blood within me!
Giving me life and always in my heart.
You and I shall never ever part.
Because without your love life would leave forever from my heart.
My life was in a different world, before I met you.
In a world without the happiness which you have given me.
In a world without the love which you have shown me.
In a world where I could only imagine of a life with an angel on earth.
Eternity life with you would be a heavenly dream come true.
I truly wish to hold you forever and ever.
I realize my life on earth will not last forever.
But I have got the will and I shall find the way to hold my lady after I die, hold her forever and ever!

Doris Courtney Lowdermilk
SUMMER'S PARADISE
One very lazy summer's day
I wandered idly on my way
Along the babbling little brook
I sat me down in a cool and shady nook
The water was blue as the sky
Every now and then a bird flew by
He'd stop and splash in waters cool
You'd think this was his private pool
Down in the valley could be seen
Cows pasturing on grasses green
Mother and her pony having fun
Frisking in the morning sun
Way off yonder I heard a chicken's cackle
Breezes overhead made some branches crackle
I closed my eyes and thought how nice
This peacefully warm summer's paradise

Pollyanna Patton
THE TEAR
This morning I saw a big bright tear-
Upon a beautiful rose-
And it seemed to me, it cried because-
The summer had come to a close.
Autumn has come, with its falling leaves-
So dreary, so gray the sky-
The rain will come, the wind must blow-
And too soon the rose must die.
It seemed so sad to see the blooms-
So soft and scented sweet-
To know that soon its petals would-
Be lying at my feet.
Yes, so sad it seemed to see the blooms-
So sweet in soft repose-
My heart cried out in wild protest-
And my tears-joined the tears on the rose.

John E. Flinn
WINTRY NITE
Crispy, downy, fluffy
Lay the fleecy whiteness
Bluish hue her crown
Regal silence her shroud
Nature! Serenely beautiful
In seasonal attire
Proudly magnificent woman
Barren but preparing Life
For days of Spring hence
See her as she stands
With whispers of Immortality
And we who look upon her
Hear her whispered command
To gaze upon fleeting beauty

Mrs. Ruth M. Hallock (Naillon)
ETERNAL HERITAGE ON WINGS OF PEACE
Would it be God's will to grant us wings?
Wings to soar through the cloudless sky
Wings with which to survive the realms of earth,,,
Daring to go against the timeless wonders of birth.
Through space and into eternity, man travels the length of time,

The noble wings of a Peace dove...
Carries a message of love...
To all mankind.
God grant us the eternal thought of weightless freedom
For Heritage's sake, the feeling of an unbinding joy,,,
To keep the flow of life "On Wings Of Peace."

Kellye Henry
REVELATIONS
The easiest thing
I've ever done
was to love you;
By day-
As the subtle pastels of Spring
invaded my window.
By afternoon-
As the sun rose to
it's highest place in the sky,
And little children
Laughed their loudest.
By evening-
While I looked at the
glimmer of a half moon,
And those few stars
Made me wish
I was an astronaut-
just for the night.
By dawn-
As I walked quietly toward
the window,
Stepping softly, so that the
creaks in the floor didn't
sound.
The hardest thing
I've ever done
Was to try and forget you-
Because
As the snow melts,
As the rain falls,
As the flowers blossom-
All I can do,
Is think of you...
And wish you could watch
it with me.

Helene Slaski Kraus
ARIZONA
Lightning carved the sky,
Pregnant clouds hung low;
Winds whirled sand up high,
Grains as white as snow.
Songs of nature heard.
Dogs and cats disturbed.
Birds had fled their nests.
Nature at her best.
Strength and power shown
Balancing her scale.
Storms to us unknown:
Whipping winds and hail.

Lilly Ashlock
AQUARIUM
Have you hurried to your
doctors appointment,
And sat in the waiting-room
chair-
So out of breath from hurrying-
And saw an aquarium setting
there?
You watch them for a moment
As they flit around that bowl,
And suddenly find a peaceful
calm
Has come upon your soul?
They swim around the aquarium
So lazily and slow.
Dipping first this way and that,
Not caring where they go.
The gold one finds a bit to eat,
And gulps it out of sight.
The stripped one swims by to
see,
If he can find a bite.
The angel fish swim gracefully
In their "angelic" way.
The guppies pass by quickly-
Their tails in a bright array.
They swish and swirl thru tne
seaweed,
One hides in a castle tall.
One just sort of rests awhile
To watch the bubbles fall.
A machine called the air-e-ator
Makes such a gentle sound
You relax and watch the bubbles
Dancing 'round and 'round.
For bubbles supply the fresh air
Fish must have in order to
breathe.
Then, the nurse says, "your turn
to go."
And you almost hate to leave.

Michele D. Butts
WHEN THE CITY SLEEPS
5am in the city,
The lights are dim;
There's a sense of peace.
At last all is quiet,
Save the night sounds;
No hint of the hurry,
The worry, the fright.
It is night;
The city sleeps.
Radio towers flash red demon
lights;
Tall buildings try to pierce the
sky,
But it is night,
They've lost there power.
The clouds are mingling with
the stars;
Trees whisper softly to one
another;
An alley cat prowls the streets
While cars sleep.
Soon the lights will appear,
The tempest resume
But for now there is peace.

Charlotte Stankus
THE "SEASONS" OF LIFE
In the early "spring" of life
Life's cares and wants are full of
strife
In the beautiful "summer"
Life's needs play to a different
drummer
In the colorful "fall"
Life rolls along as a ball
In the crispy, cold "wintertime"
Life settles for a slow decline!

Lavina R. Clemetson
SPRING
I stood and watched Spring as
she opened her door.
And all of the flowers arose
from the floor.
And oh, the beauty that graced
the world
As Spring, her glorious banner
unfurled.
The butterflies flitted about
with ease.
The wind sighed gently as it
played in the trees.
The grass was so green, and the
sun shone so bright.
The sky was so blue, and the
clouds were so white.
The frogs croaked a message
from out in the lake.
The dew dropped softly, no
noise to make.
It seemed that an angel was
hovering low,
To see that each tiny flower did
grow.
The brook laughed gaily as it
danced along.
The birds in the meadow
composed a song.
The bees hummed sweetly and
carried the tune.
The whole world listened, and
knew it was June.

Paul Blorstad
?
I planted a question
and before I knew,
from the seed
an answer grew.
The answer spread
inside my head.
I need to know
and sow and sow.
My knowledge has grown
for many seasons.
Yet I still roam
in search of reasons.
How did it all breed
from just one seed?
The answer must lie
in the reply.

Stephen "Roy" Johnston
THE PAIN OF IT ALL
The pain of the sun that burns
me so
The pain of the murder at the
show
The pain of the hand hitting me
hard
The pain of my life being bared
The pain all through my life
the pain I felt at the death of
my wife
The pain of losing all through
the years
The pain of feeling hundreds of
tears
The pain of freezing out in the
cold
The pain of life taking its toll
The pain of the wind whipping
cross my face
the pain of the entire human
race

Julius A. Rivers
REMEMBER THE OLD — THEY'RE BEAUTIFUL
Too often we forget the old
And we tend to forget that
someday we must pass the
same road.
Let us not think of the aged as
useless-
Instead, think of them as
someone beautiful
For with age comes widsom,
knowledge and experience-
Experiences of life which many
of us have not yet learned or
lived.
Be proud of the old,
Help them wherever you can,
For many of us may never live
to see the beauty of being old.
Let us give to them our love,
our understanding, and
respect.
Live with them in peace and
harmony
For they deserve it all, and more.
Love the old with all your heart
For they possess something
special, age - beautiful age,
and the knowledge that goes
with it.
Then realize and understand
that
They are loved, and have been
blessed
By one of God's most precious
gifts, and that is life itself.
We should hope that we would
live to be as lucky
And be able to say proudly, I
AM OLD, yet young at heart.

E. M. Duplessie
FLOWERS
Friends are special flowers
In the gardens of our hearts.
They grow and bloom forever,
All they need is seed to start.
They need our tears to water
them,
And laughter to make them
grow.
They need the tender loving
care,
And kindness that we show.
And so dear faithful friend of
mine
I'll just take this time to say,
That you're a flower in my life
That's growing day by day.

Charlotte Luise Hoffmann
PRAYER WHEEL
A shiny day, bright as a dream.
Baby clouds rise and fly,
Then fade away in life's cycle.
Daisies smile like
Tiny suns in skies of green.
Light July rain falls
To ascend again as mist.
Nothing dies, but merely
changes.
A diamond of a day,
Clear, pure, sparkling on the
chain of memory.

P. J. Hendricks
REUNION
The music is playing some
forgotten words,
I left so far behind.
I'm sitting here remembering
you;
time has not been kind.
I learned a brand new song
today.
I even learned a lower part.
I figured chords and harmonies
I've learned the verses by heart.
I went to the phone and started
to dial,
When I remembered what I
forgot;
You might come around now
and again
You'll stop for a pot of tea,
But your songs you sing alone
when you sing
And the songs are for her, not
me.

Yvonne Jester Wallace
THE LOST
Oh! The mind of the crazed;
Tis like the mouse in a maze,
Trying desperately to escape;
From the dark, of late.
Their thoughts are lost in the
blackened sea;
Traveling in circles that can not
be;
Like the horror of a nightmarish
dream;
Screaming, but yet a silent
scream.
So My Lord, come in like day;
And take the horrid dark away;
For if drugs or alcohol they
partake;
Their souls and minds they
forsake.
Yea, like the mouse they are in
pain;
Lost in a trap, being driven
insane;
So alone that they can not see
Any reason for them to be.

Thus, only Jesus can make their
suffering cease;
And bring to their hearts an
everlasting peace;
for like the beacon of the night;
His love will guide them to the
light.

Jean Cameron Mitchell
SILVER LININGS
It's raining and the sun's
shining!
What a wonderful sight to see!
Talk about silver linings!
That's one you really ought to
see!
Ten hundred thousand drops,
Sparkling like sun-kissed dew,
Come to light-splattering stops,
And rainbow colors are too few.
There with wondering awe you
stand
And try to catch sun-lighted
drops in your hand
Alas, once caught, the colors
pale.
Again, in trying to contain
beauty, you fail.
For a few wonderful minutes,
As happiness your heart tenants,
As joys within your soul ascend
You watch liquid rainbows
descend.

Eileen B. Perry
RIVER MOODS
Winter:
What an exciting, lovely sight--
Deer crossing the Greenbrier
River on ice.
They step with caution, daintily
Like people skating, gracefully.
Spring:
How dangerous the Greenbrier,
Bank to bank it rises higher;
And how I dread the stinking
mud
That remains after every flood.
Summer:
Rusty, my friendly little Spitz
Splashed and so frightened a
small fish,
It walked on its tail on the
water,
As we waded the Greenbrier
River.
Fall:
I wish I could stay here forever
On the beautiful Greenbrier
River
With Autumn's red and gold
reflected
And my worries and cares
deflected.

Jeanette Sue Thompson
OF ALL THE LOVE
Of all the love
I thought I almost had,
I grieve at the loss of you
whom I never really had.
I carry my desires
for sharing with you
but not sharing you
- for my moment.

Norman O'Day
IN QUEST OF
To seek all things beautiful,
Elegance in the Arts.
Natures alliance, soaring on
Wings of Albatross.
Sailing gracefully, anchoring,
In peaceful harbors of,
Serenity. The Gate is open,
I enter and rejoice.
The Quester, those who seek,
Perfection.
Why not would you seek,
Imperfection?
Alas not even those of lowest
Self esteem, knowingly
Relinquish a preconceived,
Destiny.
Great things befall the
Enterprised, zealous
Expectations, es-prit de corps.
Flexible not gullible,
There lies the Ob jet d'art.
Forging with gusto, on
Course unerring. The objective,
Achieving the Infallible.
Son of man come fourth
victorious,
In your Quest for truth for
wisdom.
A finely tuned Instrument,
Formulated from ages past.
Exquisitely, painstakingly
sculptured,
Compelled to divine order.
A compassionate all knowing
entity,
None other shall conquer.

Charlene E. Hunter
HOLLY NOELLE
Holly Noelle-
Darling baby girl-
Born in a whirl
of snowflakes
Tumbling,
twirling
down
To blanket child
and town
In softest eiderdown.
Holly Noelle-
Born this Christmas Day-
Oh glad carillon play
your carols
Sweet and clear on
icy crystal air-
Sing your lullaby to baby
snuggling here
In tiny cradle dear.

Kathleen Roth
AWAKENING SUNRISE
In the early morning hours as God is just spreading first light across the sky, it's the time to be so near to Him, almost as if to reach out and touch Him; and touch Him you can, by reaching out for life and death. To see the purple tinge turn to pink, and increase with each passing second is to take God inside of you, and hold Him in your memories. His exquisite beauty and grace is all around you, so naturally by accepting the picture He projects...He's in your soul, and your heart.
My Lord...you have a beautiful face; to be held in my memories for the rest of my days...
BEAUTIFUL SUNRISE.

Charlene Driskill
ENDINGS
Material possessions grow old
and are of value to us no
more,
The greatest of men die.
Kingdoms fall
and great civilizations
vanish.
But, I never thought
we would ever
end. . .

Muriel Oglesby
SATCHMO IN CONCERT
syncopated shafts of jazz
hurled from the
copulating
steaming
bed of the congo
pierced the dimness
of my mind
stained glass motes of sound-
dust
slanted down in mecurial rays
to touch me
and pulsating bars of brilliance
flashed before my eyes
I saw the music
I watched each note
fly from the prison
of melodic structure
and soar into it's own space
to be carried by the wind
to me
for me
man trumpet song
Trinity on Parnassus
he was the music
all sound
echoed through time
the sound of living
the sound of dying
and I cried
Hosanna
to his name

Connie Ann Harris
PLACID MIST
Translucent silver vapors
Veil the full moon,
In a grey hued midnight sky.
Below, reeds crowd the
marshlands,
And weaving through the
thicket maze,
A water moccasin clings to
obscurity.

Richard Murray
UNTITLED
In the cold darkness of night
I came upon the mask of
death
Threw it aside with all my
might
To see a child take its first
breath-

Margaret Seberger
TRUE RESIGNATION
When I have done all that I can
In the best way that I can
And there's nothing more I can
do
I am fully aware
I can dismiss my care
And Infinite Intelligence will
see me thru.

Joanne M. Williams
I'VE SEEN THE TIME PASSING
I've seen the time passing,
And days turning into years.
My life seems so long and
unchanging,
And now, I see only through
tears.
I've never been touched in love;
Or ventured in life, taking a
risk.
I've never lived in poverty nor
strife;
Or gone away and ever been
missed.
I've always known I'd missed
alot,
And I hoped my future would
not repeat my past.
Now I wonder what should be
sought;
Do I still sit and wait to be
asked?
I know a change is what I need;
But still I fear what is to come.
Will I have only versions of
what others see,
Or will I have my own walk
through the sun?

Barbara Ann Basso
A LOVE TO CALL MY OWN
I knew from the beginning
that you were just a flirt
And yet I fell in love with you
knowing I'd be hurt
I thought that I could tie you
down and make you love just
one
But how could I do something
that no one else had ever done?
I know you'll never love me
again, and I'm trying not to cry,
For I must find the strength,
some how, to kiss your lips
good-bye
When you look for me again,
you'll find I won't be there
For I want a love to call my
own, not one I have to share
So I will hide a broken heart
beneath a laughing face
And though you'll think I
never cared,
No one else could take your
place.

Thomas Prendiville
SHORT HAIR
This girl I know, has a cute
little body,
That nobody can deny.
But when you stare at her hair,
It make you want to cry.
What should be her crowning
glory,
Hanging halfway down her
spine.
Sticks up instead, all over head,
Like the quills on a porcupine.
She thinks it's cool, the little
fool,
That her style is beyond
compare.
But I'll tell you, and this is true,
I just love women with long
hair.

Linda A. Jones
MY THOUGHTS
My thoughts are secret thoughts
Tossed and tumbled
in the cool night air
Stirred and boiling
in the hot summer breeze.

There is no time for
My thoughts
There's too much time for
My thoughts
My secret thoughts.

Caroline J. Collins
WANTING
Today is here, but tomorrow must come.
with all the love around, I wanted some.
The fears, the tears, still come through.
Where are you? What can I do?
I wait and wait, till I hurt inside.
Not knowing what to do, knowing I've tried.
I gave my love as I knew how.
My caring is not over, I'm just tired now.
You say I ignored you, were my thoughts far away?
Or were you glad I didn't have to stay?
If I left someone needing a friend;
I had that feeling to the end.

Lucile Snow French
WHITE WORLD
With trembling hands I raise the shade
To see what mischief has been made.
Ah, me! White stuff has multiplied,
And darn! I'll have to stay inside.
Though friendly hands have cleaned my car
I hesitate to travel far
Between the rugged mountains white
that reach a strange and awful height,

For towering mounds prevent my seeing
At crossroads some frenetic being
Traveling at a crazy pace
Pushing hard to win the race.
The snow is clean and white today
Which yesterday was dingy gray,
The beauty of this sight is awesome
But I would rather see one blossom
To point the way to spring at last
When days of shoveling are past.
Oh! What a monstrous joke of Fate
Was played on us in '78!

Edna Watson Brinegar
MY DADDY
My daddy's smile, my daddy's touch,
Oh God, it meant so much.
Now that he is gone from me,
All I have of him is the memory.
The way he walked, the way he talked, the way he held my hand.
When we talked of the mysteries of life, he seemed to understand.
To know when I called he was always there,
To know for a certainty he really cared.
Thank you for taking him out of his misery.
Now he doesn't still suffer needlessly.
Thank you for taking him on home.
I can almost see him sitting near the throne.
When he passed from life here on this earth,
He gained a vision of what life will someday be.
There will be no more pain, no more tears, and no more misery.
I can see him walking without a limp,
With both eyes feasting on what's to come,
When the battle is over and the race is run.
We cheated the devil, we can laugh in his face,
My daddy is home in his rightful place!

Doris Estelle Evans
PEACE, BEAUTY AND FAITH
The beauty of understanding and kindly deeds
And the peace and beauty of Nature and trees
The rhythms of the changing seasons
The autumn of falling leaves, a reason
The warmth of home on a winter's day
When snow and ice is on the way
The homey smell of gingerbread baking
And a big pot of soup in the making
The kindness of people that come our way
Gives peace and beauty to our day
Memories that we hold so dear
A joy in the autumn years
Memories of a loved one's kindly face
All these things gives a warm feeling of Faith

Frances Osborn
ENTERING PEACE
Fell on the hour of early morn
a cloud of dust
in solid form
Where chanced no birds to fly,
to sing
no bees to hum
no children played
Amidst the fog the day began -
Engulfed in bits of tiny rain
lay as a bird
in still refrain
When lo, the sky began to clear!
the birds to sing!
to dart in flight!
The sun to mingle slow and sweet -
I thought of God
I thought of Christ
And waited for our souls to meet -

Loretta McCabe Guyan
CHECKMATE
While you do your thing,
And I do mine,
Where - or when -
Do we draw the line?
For doing your thing,
As I do mine,
Makes a concerted effort
Hard to find.
And no "thing" gets done,
It just hangs there;
Taut and wasting,
Suspended in time.

George D. West
DEATH — I DO WONDER
As I sit alone and ponder,
about death I do wonder,
Many pictures flash in my mind;
skulls, cloaked ghouls and
things of that kind.
We are but mortal men,
and all guilty of sin,
but to me hell is where we *are*,
The next life will be better by far.
Death is something we don't think about.
It's nothing to make you stand and shout!
No matter how rich, smart, or full of fame,
death will get you, he has no shame!
We must put all material things in order,
for one day it will be our turn to cross that border.
So, I want you to always remember,
no matter what time - January or December,
death will finally come to everyone
as sure as the morning rising of the sun.

James R. Lazzaro
ANWAR SADAT
Leader of leaders without dispute.
Soldiers fine, a standing tribute.
Columns straight looking so grand,
Now abreast of the viewing stand.
From out of a truck with intent to kill,
The unholy six fired at will!
Blood staining Egyptian land,
Lies a man in the desert sand.
Crushed pearl and twisted crown,
The prince of peace is down.
May the assassins be laid to rot,
At the feet of the dead Anwar Sadat!

Ray Cornatzer
HAPPY ANNIVERSARY
Five years it's been
since we said our vow--
I loved you then--
I love you more now.
It was a childhood dream
to have you to hold--
to share your thoughts, your body and soul.
The years have been good
and in our future I see--
an even brighter tomorrow
for you and me.
For as *one* we will pass
through the seasons of our life--
me as your husband
you as my wife.
Let no one say as winter sets in
that you and I
ever had to pretend.
You were Jo Ann and I
remained Ray--
we loved each other
just that way.
When, and if--
our nightfall decends
we'll go together to
that other worlds INN.
And GOD himself will proudly proclaim
"this love is special
as I planned it to be".
"it's perfect and true--
cause--it came directly from me!"

H. E. Bramwell
PEACE
Insid the cool and quiet church
All noise was left behind,
The tender strains of music
Stole down to heal my mind.
The notes like swift ascending birds
To vaulted arches rose,
Low, deep chords of harmony
Gave a serene repose.
As in the past sad hearts have heard
With gladness this refrain,
Its cadences will haunt me.
Its echo will remain.

Nancy Lynch
BIG CITY SUN
In the early morning the sun dawns
Stretching its arms across the big city's lawns,
Fiery bright like the atom bomb that hit in the hour past.
It's noiseless, and priceless, and brings great warmth,
But the atom bomb was thundering and filled with great dealth;
And then it was quiet again and no one dared to live.
The sun climbed the clouds bringing moist colours,
But no one in the big city felt it.

Mary Romine
TRIBUTE TO THE HANDICAPPED
Think of me first as a complete individual; Every day of my life, this is what I will strive to be. For now, circumstances beyond my control have altered the course for things I desire to be, but I will be as much as I can, as soon as I can; and I will know in my own heart and soul that it will be enough. It's true, there are many goals I may never be able to reach, but never for a moment will I totally accept them as being unreachable. In doing so, I would accept defeat; And life and time would hold no purpose. I am fully aware I am handicapped, but only when you pity me, I sense the full realization of being different. I came into the world surrounded by parents and friends who have loved and accepted me just as I am; it is only natural that I should fit into a normal society. I do not wish to be treated as a special person, but rather as a person with special problems. I

am special in a sense that I was given the ability to see magnificent beauty in people and in nature, that some may never see. In the Spring, I gaze out my window and watch robins make their nests; I watch bare trees blossom into beautiful shades of green; I watch wheat in the fields grow and marvel at the fresh plowed earth. And then--Yes then--I long to race barefoot across the fields and feel the earth and grass beneath my feet.

Some day I may.

Donna Kneeland

HAVE MERCY

I see a need for improvement,
A cry wells up inside,
Have mercy, God please have mercy.
People can be so cruel and unkind
I feel an anguish for attitudes
That damage,
for a lack of love,
For violence experienced,
For pain and suffering,
Sorrow for the hatred, war,
prejudice, discontent and misery,
That confront a person,
Now and then.
Necessity for human compassion, regard,
Seem a matter for earnest concern
Rebuilding confidence, finding love,
Happiness, gentle, tender kindness
Faith inspiring events
To aid a broken heart.

Leah Camden

SUNSET

The swashbuckling sun,
A pirate of light,
Thrusts its blood-red dagger
Across the horizon
As slowly it descends
From its exalted mount
To leave the world again
In ruthless darkness.

Marie C. Carter

OLD SHOES

To many they are just a pair of old shoes;
Something to be thrown away and forgotten--something of no use.
To me they show the many steps taken by a hard working man;
Steps taken in the forest where there is danger on every hand.
Miles traveled, in a log truck loaded to the brim.
The holes, cracks, and worn places all show the love given by him.
He works hard to earn a living and sometimes just to get by;
He doesn't give up when troubles come; But, just gives another try.
No! They are not shoes to be thrown away and forgotten, you see;
They are the shoes, of the hard working man, who married me.

William Thomas Hitz

SHAKESPEAREAN SONNET

The brightening morning of each Sunday rises on the lakes and the river bend.
We arise to our duties of our way and come home to the dark sky and wild wind.
Awake and follow thoughts of you and me; and to encounter and fight our trouble.
One day each week we praise the Trinity.
For one day we become very humble.
We think and argue as best as we can.
Our philosophies are quite different.
How can we justify the ways of man?
War rages with man's perfect armament.
Our comrades simmer with revenge.
Death is a force which is hard to avenge.

James Douglas Collier

CUMBERLAND

Coal Producer of the World,
Self-Styled Preachers and Whittlers of Wood,
Miners of the unions;
Arguing, fighting, killing,
Town upon a river between two mountains.

They tell me you are wicked and I believe them, for I've seen their youths enter the mines to never return.
And they tell me you are crooked and I answer: Yes, it is true I have seen miners turn gunmen and kill, just to see another man die.
And they tell me you are brutal my reply is: I look up on the mountain sides at one-room shacks and see hunger on the faces of women and children.
And having now given my answers I turn to stare at those who pass through with sneers on their faces and I say to them.
Come and show me another place where people sing more proudly than these, who are sick, hungry, weak and dying young.

Bare footed,
Shoveling,
Shooting,
Dying,
Dying proud

Under the mountains, coal dust all over his mouth, laughing with white teeth,
Under the terrible burden of a 14 hour shift and then laughing as a young man laughs.
Laughing like one who laughs when he is fighting a losing battle.
Drinking and laughing away the pains of poverty.
Laughing, proud to be Coal Producers, Preachers and Whittlers of Wood to all the World.

Alexandru Bratu

BLOSSOMS OF LIME, BLOSSOMS OF ACACIA

Lovely blossoms of acacia
Spread over my sweetheart's way;
Your sweet fragrance exquisitely
Should his sorrows take away!
Life's thorns let thus be forgotten,
Let him hear my song of love.
As to you sweet buds of lime
Grasp the fire in my heart,
Wrapping it in your frail petals,
Carry it in my sweetheart's path,
So when he's out on the field
To my call he will soon yield.
Oh, lime buds, acacia blossoms,
Wise old folks had told me once,
You can our yearnings capture
Set afire our hearts.
Bring two souls into sweet rapture,
Soothing flames that burn our hearts,
You're the only to reveal now
What the mysteries of love are...

Shirley Ann Trombi

CREATION

I can see Him in the mountains,
I can see Him in the seas,
I can see Him in the flowers,
I can see Him in the bees.
As I gaze up toward the Heavens and see the twinkling stars above,
I can see Him all around us, in the wonders of His love.
I can see Him in the pastures, in the forest, and the brooks,
We can see him in everything, if we would only stop and look.
His "Magnificence" is Awesome,
His presence I can feel,
If we look at all "Creation",
We will know that "God" is real.
I can see Him in the fowl and fish, and in the rising sun,
I ponder in amazement of the things that He has done.
From the beginning of "Creation", until the end of time,
We can see His Hand in everything, when we stop and take the time.

T Jassmin

WHILE LOOKING FIRMLY THROUGH A MIRROR

The way that it is,
The way it has become,
the ways that I can make it be,
My heart,
which reaches,
My hand,
which can't reach,
And my love,
which can but be,
The flesh,
which is scarred,
By the moments in life,
That lie waiting, for me to feel,
And the soul,
which is scarred,
By the madness in life,
And by things that shouldn't be real,
Look at my hands,
And see what *I* see,
The flesh, and the soul,
And the age,
That serve the memories,
Of all the past deeds,
Of passion, of peace,
And of rage,
Look into *me* Lord,
If "Lord" is your name,
Knowing what farther you see,
Touch the heart that reaches,
Teach the *hand* to reach,
Understanding the facet of me.

Ruth Anne Lewis

LOST IN A DAMAGED LOVE

Love travels far through the mountains
Long over the sea's
Throughout the sky's
Love will never be lost
Throughout the hearts
Hearts flow as a river or stream does,
Nothing can stop it except as a dam
Which can damage the heart that was so
Lost in love.

Cathy Miles

WHAT AM I?--ONE PETAL AMONG THOUSANDS

I am the blade of grass that grows and must be cut,
I am the smiles and laughter of my brothers as they play,
I am the brush an artist paints with,
I am the picture he paints with bright colors to show love,
I am but one petal among thousands--the one that stands alone.

Daisie Viola Rose

MY CHILD

I may not like some things you do, Or sometimes things you say
But I will always love you, In that mother kind of way.
I'll think of you held in my arms, Gently holding you tight
Trying to keep you from the darkness of the night.
You see, Sometimes I don't see you as you really are today
I just see my little child that used to laugh and play.
I turn back years to yesterday, And hear you when you knelt to pray
That shy little smile, With an impish grin,
That opened a door, To my heart within.
Tho' time may take you far away, Or gray your hair with old,
To me you're more precious than the mountains full of gold

To Lyn, Lee, Mark, Steve

Kathi Christianson
A VISION
Her cigarette burns quite slowly
As she stares out the window, into the night.
She pictures him standing in the moonlight,
With the stars up above, shining bright.
The vision vanishes quickly,
Leaving her feeling cold and afraid.
She wonders why it had to happen;
Why he couldn't stay.
The darkness claimed his life
And took him quickly to his death.
It seems just so unfair
To take his body, his soul, his breath.
She wonders if he's happy,
Where he is today.
And slowly puts out the cigarette,
Knowing his memory will always stay.
Written in memory of Mike Seversen

Olive Hanson Enger
REQUIEM
So summer dies, -
Shouting triumph to the skies
She flings her wanton beauty in the arms of heaven;
She fills the lap of God
With asters and with goldenrod
And leaves the remnants of her golden shroud
On every tree-crowned hill.

Robert Alan Conti
FOR SHARON
This poets' pen
is his heart, mind and soul,
and the ink his blood.
This heart of mine
beats with unspoken desire.
Sweet dreams of you
nudge softly at my mind
while I sleep.
You have touched my soul
with the pure essence of spirit,
love.

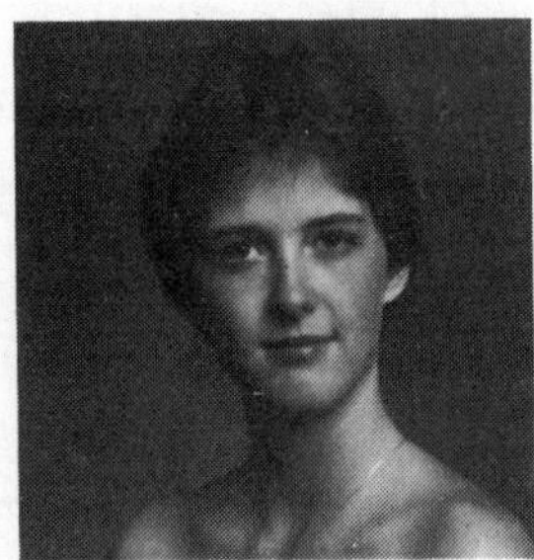

Cynthia Ellen Lindgren
UNTITLED
Hear me out
Let me say
I do this for you
please leave for you
no
I need you
you may stay for you can
no
help me I need you to
no
you must go I must not
help me
interfere with what you must do to
help me
hurt me
I can hurt myself but I
must not allow you to
help me
you are endangering yourself by
hurting me
helping me
no difference.

James McClelland
DREAMS
Dreaming of dreams past and of dreams yet to come.
Alabaster cities, deserted cities of the mind,
Lying dead in a heap of rubble,
Lost in time upon endless time,
Lost in dimness and fog, mist shrouded,
deserted, lost, lonely, unearthly, unreal,
A vision of despair and lost hopes,
Of undreamed dreams dashed against the rocks
Of reality.
Dreams of space, Dreams of time,
Dreams of love, Dreams of hate,
Dreams of life, Dreams of death,
Dreams of light, Dreams of night,

Frances L. Berlanga
BORN OF THE HEART
A new life is born
Not from the bosom of a woman
But rather from her heart
The inner excitement
Of fulfilling a dream in her life
Causes pain throughout her being
Her thoughts take wings
And fly into the future
Anticipating joys and sorrows
There's no room in her mind for retreat
Or even a fleeting moment to reconsider
She longs for the challenge
The love she feels gushing from her heart
Is like the armour with which a soldier
Shields himself when going into battle
This endless love will be her weapon
When facing any foes
On her new road in life
As it also will be the trophy
She will share when each battle is won
No matter how large or small
She's becoming a mother
Not to a child born of her body
But a child born into life.

O.b.a.c. Sargent
MY PRAYER
Oh, to have the peace that God can give within,
To turn to Jesus daily and turn away from sin,
To be a smitten sinner who dwells within His arms,
To have the Rock of Ages to shelter me from harms.
To have Him ever present in all I say and do,
To walk within His footsteps and let his light shine through,
To be a faithful child to a Father that is kind,
To have Him ever dwelling within my heart and mind.
To keep my eyes upon Him and not upon my life,
To see the will of Jesus and not the pain and strife,
To let Him ever love me as only He can do,
For the only real and lasting love
Is the Love God gives to you.

Michael Lynn Hogeland
WHAT IS IT
1. What is it?
2. Is it big? like the universe
3. Or is it small? like a speck of dust
4. Is it long? like time
5. Or is it short? like lightning
6. Is it high? as a mountain
7. Or is it low? like in a pit
8. Is it heavy?
9. Or is it light?
10. Is it round?
11. Or is it square?
12. Is it love?
13. Can it float?
14. Can it fly?
15. Is it alive?
16. Is it dead?
17. Is it good?
18. Is it happy?
19. Is it light?
20. Is it dark?
21. It is this number in the ABC

Dawn Marie Strain
A REFLECTION OF LOVE
Today I looked into your eyes and saw a reflection of love.
Your heart reaches out to mine always when I need it most.
You've made me realize what a friend is for.
My spirit was broken and my dreams in pieces.
You gave me courage and strength wrapped in gentleness
And helped me to overcome.

Ron Schmidlen
AMANDA
What is it like to be a spider,
to have spun a web of passion
To be your world not much wider
Than the threads your soul will ration?
The manner in which you wove your web
Was gracefully done, my lady,
As beautiful as dawn's morning ebb
When swallowed sands return at sea.
Beautiful are your silver threads
That are bound around your prey,
But ugly are the ones misled
Into your passion pit of play
...More beautiful are the rains that come
Destroying your web with each falling drop.
Your beautiful web...is beauty undone
Only to be respun as exhausted rains stop.
The years of labor for pleasure are gone,
Yet you reminisce of those past times
When life was lived from night till dawn
And all was done in verse and rhyme.
Your game is over; you've grown old
And so has the beauty of your labor,
As time in turn begins to fold,
Along with those you use to harbor;
So has your web that now grows cold.

Charles Ruebeck
A SOLEMN MOOD
The fire burns, its flames so bright,
It seems so peaceful here.
the fire fills the air tonight
With warmth and loving cheer.
The flames they glow crimson red,
They dance within my mind.
I think of now and things to come
Not of what I left behind.

W. L. Champion, Jr.
ATLANTA
Atlanta. should be remembered
like Texans remember the
Alamo. not like Attica. green
ribbons. weren't meant to be a
style like pleats or cuffs. they
should be worn as fingernails.
everyone should have them
who's human. it's as if the
children who were killed, who
happened to be in Atlanta & be
black & be children had their
names attached to designer
jeans or had cut a hit on the
Motown label. we'd just die if
we couldn't have them wrapped
tight around us. we'd play them
to death on the radio & on the
streets & at home until. they
played out. Atlanta is like
Attica. a mint meant to last a
hot 60 seconds chewed two
minutes ago.

Kathy Louise Roller
WISHING
When I hear this black man sing,
He's all the same to me
As the white man I heard singing
On another record I've collected;
Where are you, oh Equality?
Hearing this Indian girl on yet one more,
Can't understand the pain
Poor brothers, sisters everywhere
Forcibly endure. Race hate, nation hate
Is fairy tale to me; wish that
Everybody shared my love.

Pauletta D. Shelbo
AND SHE'S MINE!
The hand that pulls the covers up
On a cold and wintry night.
The hand that wipes the tears away
When your dreams have caused you fright.
the voice that whispers gentle words
When the world comes tumbling down.
The voice that gives encouragement
And advice that turns out

sound.
The eyes that see most everything
that you have ever done.
The eyes that glisten with such pride
For accomplishments you've won.
The heart that sometimes skips a beat
When mischief is at play.
The heart that never fails to love
Throughout each night and day.
The hand, the voice, the eyes, the heart,
Aren't *just* words within this rhyme:
They make up someone special...
She's Mother...
And she's Mine!

Judy K. Cook
OH LORD
Oh Lord, create within this frame
A heart and mind who seeks Your name.
A heart who will all Your love proclaim.
Forever lovely Lord, is Your name.
Oh Lord, create within this frame
A mind transformed to do the same
As Jesus when He became
A fleshly man and knew no shame.
Oh Lord, create within this frame
A song to praise Your saving name.
A melody to pass along to proclaim
Your love and grace, mercy and fame.
Oh Lord, create within this frame
A voice to tell why Jesus came
To take our sins upon His holy name.
Make this my goal--my final aim.

Laura DuVal Hockaday
UNTITLED
Eternal life would linger,
Like Indian summer, too long.
The joys of your forever,
the dreams of childhood still strong.
Never fading into autumn,
Never moving with the wind.
But staying still in Paradise
For fear of losing it again.
People never aging,
Loved ones never dying,
No reaching for the heavens,
No reason to be trying.
People would stop their dreaming;
They would have reached the perfect end;
Time would finish its journey..
Would anyone miss the wind?

Vickie M. Bryan
A CHILD'S HANDS
Just me and my box of crayons
Set out to color this world;
We painted the sky's bright rainbows
And striped the flags unfurled.
With just one melted crayon,
The lakes and rivers ran bright blue;
We clearly marked the skyway roads
Above the birds that flew.
We multi-tinted all nature's petals
And set the whole world free;
And then we stopped to rest awhile
And painted the moods in me.

Cathy A. Haigwood
OUR CREATOR
Have you ever knelt down and prayed,
For the wondrous things which God has made?
For the mountainous cliffs that over-look
A clear running spring or babbling brook?
For the billowy clouds in the sky so blue?
For moonlight beams on crystal dew?
For the petals on a perfect rose?
For the tranquility of the winters snows?
For the grass and trees that grow so tall?
For summer, spring, winter, and fall?
For, best of all, creating this place,
As a home for us--the human race.

Rosaleen Stiebel
LOVE SONG
Oft-times when I do contemplate
The contours of my loved-one's face
My lips will part with quiet smile
I'll muse, that maybe in a while
With Love I'll pass my fingertips
Across the sweetness of your lips
And lightly press a kiss that seeks
The freshness of your silken cheek.
Your hair it sparkles in the sun
Sweet One
For whom Life's just begun.
How many others you will find
Who'll gaze at you
With love as fine
To last a lifetime
As does mine.

Michelle LeClercq Sulski
LONELY THEY SAT
They opened their eyes to a brand new day,
Unable to share Christmas in a merry way.
For their sons and daughters are in another state,
Forgetting their parents on this special date.
Alone in a room surrounded by institutional walls,
Is where the old peoples' life so sadly falls.
At one time they were just like you and I,
Deeply in love and never asking themselves why.
But as the years passed and they both grew old,
Suddenly their lives began to crumble and fold.
For their husbands or wives entered the grave,
Leaving behind them all the love they ever gave.

William L. Marion
LOVE IS YOUNG
Love is Young, Love is New,
Love is Pure, Love is Gina Jo and you
Love is Right, Love is Wrong
Love is Laughter, Love is Tears
And if God so wills it may it last even through and past my final years.
Love is Good, Love is Bad, Love is always misunderstood, Held by true devotion yet sometimes seeded with jealousy and over powered by emotion. Yet it ever seems to be the center focal point in every life, the one true miracle and medicine to all men and there aching hearts and the one true thing that will never let us part.

William C. Richmond
TRANSIENT FLOWER
Azalea's come and as quickly go -
And why this is I think I know.
The brilliant joy they bring with them -
Is ever heightened by their short reign.
If they were constant in our sight -
Their daily presence would dull delight.
So I'm glad they come and quickly go -
And why this is I know, I know.

Elaine M. Lockhart
PHOENIX
From the ashes of his death
another arose anew.
His wings reaching for the sun
as he silently rose
and the ashes stirred on the wind.
The beating of his heavy wings,
like thunder in stormy skys
carry him on a long journey
to the tops of mountains
on his way to a mythical place
in a dream.
Where Unicorns roam
and Dragons dwell.
Where he will live his life
among the strange
and curious creatures of time.
A century passes,
and he must return
to the place of beginning.
The end coming in a fiery flash
so, another may be born
in his image.
Thus, is the plight of the Phoenix.

Jackie Sisk
LOVE
Love is warm, tender, loving, giving and sharing.
You give your all and you try to please.
You dream of a love, home, and kids, too,
Until one day you find,
None of this will come true -
Because the one you loved, didn't love you.
This is where love is heartbreaking;
But you must be strong, tried and true,
Because one day, there will be an awakening and you will find the one for you.
He may not be tall and handsome, may not even be rich,
But he will possess that one possession -
He will love you and that will be worth the ransom.
Love is bittersweet.
It has its challenges to meet.
You must be prepared to face the facts
That love is just one more thing you must attack.
You must be prepared to handle the tears and laughs
And then, my dear, you will be a woman, at last.

Ronnie M. Vinson, D.D.S.
WHY YOU
Why You
I Ask Myself The Same
To Say
My Heart Knows No Shame
To Feel This Pulse
Of Joy
I Laugh To Know
I Feel This Way
As My Mirror Reflects
A Little Boy
Of Snails And Rails
Puppy Dog Tails
Ready To Be Tamed
By Sugar And Spice
And Everything Nice
Why You
Why Me...

Annie Lou Kastelz
TO A GRANDSON
Tommy is my heartbeat.
Tommy is my love.
Tommy sits beside me,
Softly--as a glove.
Tommy gets a whipping
Every time he's bad.
Tommy lets a tear fall
Every time he's sad.
Tommy cuts a wide swath--
Wide and straight and true.
Tommy makes your heart melt
When he looks at you.
Tommy make the day bright--
Turns the gray to blue.
Tommy makes the world turn--
'Tho he's only two!

Lawrence Mullen
REFLECTIONS IN BROKEN GLASS
Looking through broken glass,
I see my lifestyle,
Shattered beyond repair,
It can only be replaced.
The pattern of the cracks,
Reflect the bad things,
Which are many.
Can there be the good life,
In whole pieces of broken glass?
Reflections in broken glass,
Prisms of broken lifestyles,
Shattered beyond repair,
Never to be replaced!

James W. Rhodes
GOD'S GRACE
In a world beset with fear, man can view the timid deer
Along the wooded wilderness camp trails.
Elegance, natural grace, scenic setting, proper place -
Dainty deer in his element prevails.
Man still seeks to dominate, ignores love and fosters hate,
Seeks security through material worth.
Man his element must find, with the written word in mind,
"The blessed meek shall inherit the earth."

Pauline Pittard Gillespie
LEAF CARPETS
Please don't spoil that carpet,
Just leave it on the ground;
Have regard for beauty
Wherever it is found.
We all regard the beauty
Of leaves upon the tree
Red and gold and crimson
So beautiful to see,
But I say leaves are lovely
Lying on the ground
And what a joy to children
Scuffing them around.
So please don't get that rake too soon;
Just put it quite away
And leave the carpet on the ground
Enjoy it for today.

Melvin F. Alster
PLANTING/WEEDING
And now the time has come, my friends,
To sit back and relax
And watch the flowers and vegetables grow,
And rest those aching backs.
But planting alone is not the end,
For they often do need care
So that they might grow full and strong,
And their wondrous products bear.
And in our living the same is true,
For we also must pull some weeds,
And pick the right way from the wrong,
So others can follow our leads.
So we must do our very best,
As God gives us each day,
To make the most of every moment
To live our lives His way.

Helen Zaremba
MY MOTHER WILL BE EIGHTY-FIVE IN NOVEMBER
I'll tell you straight, mama; it's getting late, mama,
Yet even now, your pride's like none I ever saw.
You had much pain, mama; but through the rain, mama,
You had more courage than I think I ever saw.
You showed no fears, mama; I saw no tears, mama,
YOU were the only strength my childhood ever saw.
Yes, you were strong, mama; and right or wrong, mama,
You did your very best the only way you saw.
You were alone, mama; so all alone, mama,
How ever did you do the many things I saw?
Now, as I age, mama; with each new page, mama,
I reach way back to touch the things that once I saw.
I'll tell you straight, mama; it's getting late, mama,
I wish you could know the love in your heart I saw.

Keith E. Fisher
SENSES
I'm feeling the strain of emotion,
Caught in the fire of it's touch.
Anxiety is the tide of an ocean,
But, why does it seem to hurt so much?
I'm hearing a song of devotion,
Sending my roots to the earth.
Lost in the breeze from it's motion,
While listening to the voice of it's worth.
I'm seeing the smile of illusion,
And wondering who I can trust.
Understanding is taught by confusion...
The wind of change is a gust.

B.A. "Dusty" Nathan
WRINKLES
Wrinkles have nothing to do with age.
a sign of wisdom.
so much beauty.
To passion with life, I must
show wrinkles.
Everybody had them.
my battles are young.
wrinkles are the war scars
of the past.
Nothing to do with time.
A sign of struggle.
ribbons of the true
works of life.
Lusting with life, I must
show wrinkles.
Blemishes of reflection.
What do they possess?
can they not be found anywhere,
except upon the face of use.
Not to use my face
would be wasteful.
I looked closely,
and curiously.
I found a wrinkle,
the first of many, I hope.

Roy Schwartzman
THE TRAPEZE ARTIST
Slitting some loins with a dull cleaver,
The blind butcher weighs corpses on his scales,
Wraps the slabs of fecund flesh
In blood-stained swaddling clothes,
And licks his fingers before closing his shop.
Lofty lepers, heroes of the Big Top,
Swing from alternative to alternative.
A lawn of green rapiers below;
Their hermaphrodite husband in butcher's apron
Genitally balances the ropes from above.
Aerialists perform blindfolded,
Heedless of trapeze.
Sight might end the circus.
In the center ring
Comedic Crispin, mired in a medium without a message,
Stalls at the top of a Ferris Wheel,
Shrinks to a referentless letter.
He listens to fictive carnival music,
The only music.
the only sound.

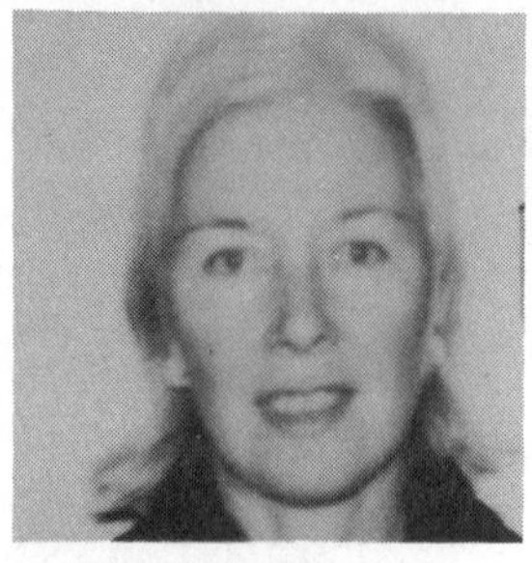

Jean Layer Heinz
THE CONTINENTAL DIVIDE
Ah! The Great Divide,
Where shaggy mountains,
Reach their peaks;
to touch the sky.
Somehow I am aware,
Of my insignificance,
standing there;
Such quiet loneliness,
I feel,
As a cool dry breeze,
Caresses my cheeks,
And loosen wisps of hair,
About my face;
My hungry searching
Eyes despair,

That I cannot long,
Linger there.
I am entranced, amazed,
And stare in awesome wonder,
At this great Continental Divide;
These haunting, Mysterious,
Mountain tops.
Then I realize and know,
What a Magnificient,
Masterpiece;
God has fashioned out of,
Rock.

Scott E. Raymond
WHAT PRICE IS DUE?
What price is due to keep our hearts contented?
To keep alive the love our two souls invented.
I gave what I felt guiltless to give,
in vain attempt to perform.
I kept myself on hold,
in an effort to conform.
I know our love is sacred, silly and profane.
I lived with neglect,
that verges on insane.
I was selfish to expect,
you to reach an ideal goal.
Yet, your eyes give clues of secrets,
the whole world does not know.
Is your love a magic cure to heal a sickly soul,
or a feast to ease the famine's painful glow?

Marianne E. Herrick
THE CIRCULAR MOTION
A baby cries, and
The motion has begun.
A new life--new hopes
And many new dreams.
The child reaches out;
The circle enlarges.
There are fears, questions, a
Need to be close, and demands
Begin when these are not met.
The adolescent rebels--
No chance of stopping the circle
Now.
No comfort, assurance, warmth
Or understanding.
The modus operandi of the
Parasitic parent has taken form.
When there was innocence
The circle began closing in.
The games of our present,
Became the concubines of their
Future.
An old one lies dying;
The circle is complete now.
Too late for life, for hopes,
Or anymore dreams.
But one thing is certain;
This life has passed on the
Circular Motion,
Earmarked for failure,
Through its progeny.
A baby cries, and
The motion has begun...

Virginia M. Gigowski
THE WILL OF MAN
What are tears. . .
Thou hast lost?
What tis pain. . .
Thy life hast cost?
What tis blood. . .
Thou hast shed?
What tis life. . .
But to be risen from the dead?
Aye, what tis betrayal. . .
Of thine own friend?
What tis love. . .
Forgiven sin?
Thy time didst come.
God's will wast done.
Christ has risen.
Life has just begun.
So what tis faith. . .
A gospel shared?
Where tis man. . .
Which faileth care?
Aye, what tis man. . .
Without a Lord?
Death of Hell. . .
No man restoreth?
What tis time. . .
To no man's use?
What is lost. . .?
A world confused!

Katherine M. DeNering
TOUCH OF MAGIC
Little tree standing there
With a touch of winter magic in your hair,
For a moment all the world is fair,
And I salute you now as then.
You were beautiful to behold;
Sunlight glistened in your hair.
The fierce storm of night
Had brought forth a scene of pure delight.

Time demanded other labors
then,
So I rode by and placed you in
my heart,
And knew that we would meet
again,
Held thus in memory's ken.

Charles Walter May
SEED OF LOVE
You've planted the seed of love
In my heart to grow.
It grew each time
I saw you, you know?
Your smile was in the sun.
Your tears were the rain.
Day to day my love grew,
Still I didn't complain,
My love continued to bloom,
You kept it well nourished.
But still I waited,
I couldn't get discouraged.
I kept my love intact.
I kept it just for you.
But you went away,
And broke my heart in two.
Now the sun won't shine.
Now the rain won't fall.
And my love for you
Won't grow at all.
For the distance that exists
Between you and I,
Has cause the seed of love
To wither and die.

Susan J. McNeeley
THE FUTILE PURSUIT
For Hours I chased a butterfly
Touched it,
Lost it,
Chased it,
Caught it—
Watched it die.
I was much happier when I was
forced to view it from a
distance.

Irving R. Gray
THE SUPPER
As we eat and wonder,
Fill ourselves and ponder,
Why he came and died for me,
And there upon that wicked
tree,
His body was the meat to savor,
His blood is the wine to favor,
Celebrate we do, but couldn't we
Cry for him, then you and me?
The only thing that I suppose,
Is that he died and then arose,
Giving proof it was the hour,
Proving still he had the power.
Now I may never live again,
But I am sure he is my friend,
Many rivers I have crossed,
Many nights I have tossed,
Trying to figure why that he,
Saves such a fool as me?
He must have a master plan,
This I know, and for sure he
can.

Bettyjane Burgess
HALLOWEEN IS COMING
Halloween is coming,
Ghosts and Goblins and Bats.
Trick or treaters knocking,
Asking for this and that.
Witches brew is boiling,
In a kettle so big and black.
Jack-o-lanterns gleaming,
Watching all the black cats.
But I'm not scared,
For don't you see.
The Wise Old Owl,
Watches over me.

Denise Paschal
THINK OF ME
Think of me in the springtime
when flowers start to grow,
when sunshine warms the chilly
air
and melts the dirty snow.
Think of me in the summertime
when the days are very long,
when you see the stars in the
sky
and the radio plays "our song".
Think of me in autumn
when leaves are turning brown,
when harvest time is here
and I am not around.
Think of me in wintertime
when snow begins to fall;

Think of me with happy
thoughts,
or. . . don't think of me at all.

Caryl Lee Stitt
IN MEMORY OF A SOLDIER
It seems like such a long time,
since the skies were blue
I closed my eyes to forget it all,
but I just thought of you
There is a silence living in you
that I have never seen
I close my eyes to fade away,
living in a dream
Fate has begun to play with her
toys, of violence, pain, and
fear
I see the fire in your eyes,
whenever you are near
You've heard the screams and
cries of men, you've watched a
brother die
I close my eyes to hide the pain,
but I just start to cry...

Juanita Williams
FRIENDSHIP?
Come, walk with me and be my
friend,
And keep my spirits high;
Pick me up each time I fall,
And hold me when I cry.
Always wear a cherry smile
Of greeting on your face,
And make me glad each time we
meet
At any time or place.
If you should have a problem,
friend,
Don't mention it to me;
I'd rather just not get involved;
That's how I am you see.
Come, laugh with me through
all my joys;
Console me through the pain;
In raging storms, help me to see
The rainbow through the rain.
Just be there when I need a
friend
So I won't be alone;
But don't bring me *your* trouble
friend,
I've too much of my own!

Cindy L. Belmer
SELF PORTRAIT
My emotions are mixed,
day to day.
I am my own person,
But, who am I really?
A mixture of the love
that made me.
Touched by the love of years.
Changed by circumstance.
Molded by life.
Yet, who am I?
A strong and loving heart;
A stubborn will;
A forgiving nature.
I am as only I can be,
I am only myself.
With genuine feelings,
That I'm unafraid to share.
I am what I am.
With all my faults;
and all my love.
I am just me.
For every smile I see,
Let me return it.
For every life I touch,
Let me make it brighter.
Then I will be,
the best possible me I can be.

Lucille Acker Sibley
A MORNING WALK
Ripples on the ocean blue are
dancing in the morning light;
Gentle waves are rolling in to
break and splash in foamy
white.
Along the wide smooth sandy
beach
Tides rise and fall from out the
deep.
What mighty force below the
ocean
Propels its depths to endless
motion?
Sometimes the angry waves can
reach
The rock sea wall beyond the
beach.
On this calm day beyond the
swell
Porpoises play in graceful swim;
And fishermen crowd the pier
above to satisfy their whim,
Casting lines that shimmer in
strands of golden light,
Pulling in their catch and
baiting hooks just right.
Happy children chase their ball
While boats with nets bring in
their haul
Spilling fish upon the sand.
Young people walk by hand in
hand.
With shrill, high-pitched,
excited call
Sea gulls gulp the fish that
fall.
The sun is warm; the air is cool;
Adults stretch out around the
pool
And listen to the constant
sound
Of rhythmic waves that curl and
pound.

John Joseph Schulz
THE WONDER OF LOVE
To be able to love someone is
the greatest power of all.
But, to have that person love
you just the same is even
better.
Love, it makes it all worthwhile,
Love is being with a person that
can always make you smile.
Love is the key to happiness,
Love is the magic that stops the
world from looking like a
mess.
When you're in Love,
You give it all you've got.
You can make everything seem
peaceful,
Even when it's not.
When you capture that feeling
that sparkles in your eyes,
And your face shines with a
fire's glow,
You know it's LOVE that's
making these feelings grow.
To that special person;
You owe her so much.
She gave you all these feelings
which so many people wish
they could touch.
If you've found the wonder in
which the world is in search
of,
You tell them you don't know
how you found it.
They may think that it's from
above,
But there's no doubt in your
mind that you've found
THE WONDER OF LOVE.

Dorothy K. Murray
VICTORY
Yesterday your pain
filled the nursing home.
Nurses, loved ones and
residents
heard you sob and groan.
Today, we dressed you
in pink
All of your cares and fears
were gone.
We remember, you smiled
When the death angel came.
You knew
you were not alone.

Edward Lee Johnson
INTERLUDE
Drop the bar o'er the door
'Tis blowin' cold out there
Throw another log upon the
flame
Warm tired bones for a spell
Tell me of the trail east
And what I might find south
Drop the bar
And chat awhile
The coffee 'tis strong and hot
Help yourself if you please
Are you lost stranger, or
Seeking shelter from the storm?
Ne'er the difference be
You're here now
Stay awhile
Talk with me if you will
Spend the night
'Tis frightful out
Say you'll stay and
Drop the bar o'er the door

Mary Ann B. Henning
THE SEETHING
Something inside will not remain
mute
A voice demanding an audience
I am only the instrument
available to recite the jailed
message
Releasing these muffled thoughts
Through words alive
bubbling in the cauldron
Vibrations of restlessness.

Pattie Fischer
PHOTOGRAPHS
Photographs of faded faces
shadows in the moonlit room
ghosts of yesterday come back to me
memories caught then gone too soon.
A room full of people
and the happy times we shared
now still life in frames
to show how much we really cared.
The warmth and all the caring
that made us feel so near
radiates from the pictures
I feel as if they're still here.
It seems like only yesterday
oh how young we seemed to be
please time touch upon us soft
it goes too fast for you and me.
A gallery of yesteryear
a history of times now past
tenderly I look upon them
the good times left us oh too fast.
I look at those I loved the most
fondly they look back at me
forever captured behind glass
our youth preserved eternally.

Richard J. Swol
WHAT IS LOVE
What is love to a person who is not that much in love with anyone, who doesn't know how love is appreciated.
Who knows that some people are hated.
Love to me means you are given love to live.
Then some one you know will always give.
So when some one asks you what is love, you say love is a way of expressing your self to some one as nice as a dove.
That is what love is to me.

Emilio Macri, Jr.
BUT THEN AGAIN
I hate you,
Responsibility.
I want to please you because
You please me.
I am always there when
You need me.
I want you to be there when
I need you.
I hate it - You own me and
I own you.
But then again - I love you.

Eleanor McKee
I'LL GET YOU BACK
I try to do things right, but they always turn out wrong,
I hurt you, you hurt me, I opened my heart
You turned away,
I told you I wanted you to stay
If you are mine and I am thine, why are we apart,
In the eve I'll watch for thee, far across the sea
I'll get you back for it can be done, because it has been done
By the highest mountain and the wildest sea,
Tonight and tomorrow I'll think of thee,
But only for awhile
You see for pain that intense can only be
Endured in small doses, I can still feel
Your presence yet at the same time I feel
an emptiness each passing hour brings me closer eases the pain so I'll get you back.

Marjorie A. Beverly
THE URBAN VULTURE
Chauffered, coiffured, manicured, pedicured, on camera manners, polished smiles, polished shoes
The Politician
Old women's delight; young women's knight
And only babies sense the fright.
Election year promises, Election year legislation,
The Politician holds out the carrot:
More housing, better schools, more teachers, firemen, policemen, et al
No franchised citizen escapes the bait
and, above it all, the urban vulture swirls, glides and waits.
Election day—Political success
The politician smiles and preens himself
And, in retrospect asks-Promises?
Sensitivity be damned, (pick the bones)
For the urban vulture—Political survival-that's the thing
Landlords continue to exploit ghetto housing
And, when all else fails—Burn! Baby Burn!
Schools in the ghetto—gateless prisons from which,
Teachers release their yearly quota of semi-illiterates
And, high above it all, the urban vulture swirls, glides, and waits.

Curtis Anderson
SHARING A LIFETIME
I remember the way that you smiled
On the day that we were wed
And how we held each other close
When all the vows were said
You were always there to lend me your hand
When things didn't go my way
And I always knew that my love for you
Would grow stronger with every passing day
We were just two people sharing a lifetime
Leaving thoughts of loneliness behind
Living in a world where dreams come true
You loving me and me loving you.
The first few years are never easy
But somehow we made it through
We were holding on to one another
Dividing all our problems by two
And every night before I go to sleep
I say a prayer that's always the same
That when I wake with the morning light
You'll still be sharing my name

William Edward Woodward
ECHOES OF IMMORTALITY
My lips were moved with song ere I was born,
And I danced the jig to pipes at Aberdeen.
I journeyed once through Gaul, quite saddle-worn.
I whispered with the lips of Borodin.
I still recall that lonely Caspian shore,
When princely Igor, ghostlike, walked the Earth.
I sense innately where I lived before,
Those haunting hoofbeats of each mortal birth.
Now, as those deep but distant memories merge
And pace abreast like steeds incarnadine,
Climactic days from all my lives converge
With flesh and manhood and each sip of wine,
Yet those with death are still incipient dreams,
Too cryptic for my blood, or so it seems.

Loretta Tune
IN MEMORIUM
I've travelled and taught, and I've stayed and learned;
Even had the best of both as far as I'm concerned.
But sometimes I feel like a falling star,
And I'm afraid that when I crash someday
What's left of me will burn.
"Just another hole in the ground," they'll say.
"It'll be filled in shortly anyway."
Nothing is ever simple—
Never what it seems to be.
A mirror may reflect an image,
But there's so much more to see.
Everything is different,
Even though it looks the same.
Ask for me by number for
I do not have a name.
Conformity furrows his stereotypical brow saying,
"I'll tell you what to be."
Oh, but the sweet winds whispering in my ear,
"Don't listen to him. Come with me."
There is no self-righteousness in this world of discontent.
Just try to slip past the assembly-line crew
Without the old spirit getting bent.
A few men's reality
Only a multitudes dream
Please wear black and try to cry,
I'll see you at the requiem.

Kathi E. Krouch
DADDY'S DAISIES
Little things
Have always meant a lot to me.
From when four
Was all the more
Fingers to my age,
And Daddy gave me daisies
In the park,
Till now
When fingers fall too short
Of telling time that's changed,
And roses
Whisper love songs
In the dark.
You wonder at my simpleness
And strange, eccentric ways.
You laugh
As on new journeys I embark.
But it's always been the little things
That made my life so dear;
Like you,
And Daddy's daisies in the park.

Gwendolyn R. Thomas
THE TENDER TRAP
If I should deem
to spin a web
I'd spin of gossamer
and down.
A universe;
A world my own;
in which
I'd gladly drown.
I'd weave a filmy softness
there
To shield my gentle dreams
from care.
The irredescent strands
would hold them
gently.
So they might unfold.
My greatest opus
I would do
And then I'd call
and invite you.

Robert Black
SUNRISE
Lake mist gently ascended treetops
Dewdrops hugged blades of grass
Sparrows, robins, and jays
Heralded lovely tunes
A reddish glow entered my room
Wiping sleep from my eyes
I thanked God, to behold
Sunrise

Allen K. Harrington
TAD EARTH
I have been told a few times now,
And not me alone you see,
Of the reason why we are here and how,
On this earth today T A D.
Actually HEAVEN is our home,
Then why are we here you ask?
We were created not to roam,
And bring others HOME is our task.
About how long we stay here,
Is decided from ON HIGH,
For some it is many a year,
'Til they bid this world bye-bye.

Now JESUS soon is coming back,
To gather up THE SAINTS,
Don't worry loved ones, no need
to pack,
JESUS 'n' you, a pretty picture
paints.
Now about this title "EARTH
T A D,
Not something to shout,
"Hooray"!
But sometime soon over will be,
This TEMPORARY
ASSIGNMENT of DUTY, I
say!!
THANK YOU JESUS,
I LOVE YOU,

Miche'le Loertscher
AGAPE
Round Table
circle of LOVE
each concerned
with one another
before I asked
the bread was there
the wine was brought
transubstantiation
of this material food
into this ONE Presence
Transfigurations
of these Human Beings
under the eyes
of this ONE Presence
recognition
before I asked
the bread was shared
the wine was poured
each concerned
with one another
circle of LOVE
Round Table

Susan Feathers
HAD YE BEEN MY FIRST LOVE. . . .
If I could but again choose with
whom my virgin love be spent,
to thee, with yet untasted
honeyed lips,
I'd offer up my maidenhood with
no despairing.
Could ye have been the first to
feed my youthful cravings,
I'd n'er hunger further for fruit
from any other tree nor thirst
for wine from any stranger's
flagon.
With thy passion warm upon
my yet unsuckled breasts,
I'd welcome the crimson sting
of love's first entering and
joyfully give to thee the gift
that can be giv'n but once.
Had ye been my first love,
there'd n'er have been
another.

Chris Maxwell
LIFE AFTER DEATH
i see her stare coldly toward
nothing
as she sits in the booth all
alone.
it is obvious she isn't hungry,
or at least not too thrilled with
the food.
a burger without a companion
leaves much for her heart to
desire.
her memories race on.
her husband is gone,
and the clock's moving slow, if
at all.
she tells herself things will get
better,
but tomorrows bring nothing
but pain.
she knows that his sickness has
ended
and she tries to keep looking to
God.
though the cafe is crowded,
she's alone on an island of
heartache.
she smiles as i pass.
the facade doesn't last,
'cause she knows that i've been
through it, too.
when she goes out to step in the
car
there's no one to open her door.
she prepares for the noise of the
silence
that greets her each night in her
room.
her only true strength is the
Sunshine,
'cause people just storm her
with words.
her eyes fill with tears
as another night nears,
and the clock's moving slow,
if at all.

Cynthia Logan
LIVE
(In memory of Kacky Fry)
Live today with no thought of
tomorrow.
Today we have, maybe not
tomorrow. . .
With zeal and zest and no
thoughts of sorrow,
Such love of life leaves
nothing to borrow.

Randy Patton
DEMON CANIS
K-9 Demon on the desolate
planet
With the heart of stone and
body of granite
To cast your eyes upon this
deadly hound
You soon discover your soul is
bound

In darkened swamps with
morbid sounds
In which your heart ecstatically
pounds
His eyes are a deep satanic red
Full of hatred which others
dread

His enemies are few and so
quickly diminishing
For he gives no chance for his
foes replenishing
Their carcasses lay in an endless
slumber
Which never awaken by whisper
or thunder

Jackie Anderson Strange
THE AUCTION
The dark, dismal sky belched
bilious clouds
Of navy and black that hovered
over
The crucifixion cross marked
"King of the Jews."
Howling winds screeched
gossipy gasps
Sulking. .howling again as if
bowing to curtain calls.
Demonic dice were cast.
Drunken men drooled,
And Mary cried softly.
Rising above the chanting of the
calloused crowd
Echoed the Auctioneer's plea,
"What will you
Give for the Man of Calvary?"
Silence fell
As certain as the curtain ends a
Shakespearian tragedy,
But no one bid for the
Auctioneer's Son.
Piercing the silence came the
cry
"Why hast Thou forsaken me?"
. .And then in submission from
the pale, parched lips,
"I commend my spirit to Thee."
Centuries passed. . .and one
lonely wintry evening
I heard the Auctioneer's plea
again
"One thousand once. . .One
thousand twice. . . ."
Penniless and penitent I raised
my hand
And cried out, "LOVE! LOVE!"
And His Son was given to me.

Annette Martinez
YESTERDAY
Just one day ago, we were
sharing our special moments
together.
You held me tight in your
arms as you assured me
everything
Was going to be alright. I
believed in you and everything
you shared with me.
Whenever we were together,
I felt as though we had
Our own little world. Being with
you is heaven, until it's time
to say good-night.
But, tonight something is wrong.
When you hold me, you're not
with me, you're far away and I
can't reach you.
When the night was over
little did I know it was really
Good-bye and not just
Good-night. Oh how I wish we
could go back to............
YESTERDAY

Kenneth J. Anderson
WE ARE WHAT WE ARE
What are we?
Are we not like puppets on
a string of troubles, controlled
by the movements of failures.
What are we?
Are we not like fishes in a
sea of darkness,
not knowing which way is up
or which way is down,
only to be directed by our fins
of past uncertainty.
What we are?
Are we not like caged animals
trapped by our own conscience
not knowing when we will be
free.
What are we?
Are we not like young lovers,
running hand in hand toward a
cliff
hidden by false promises and
beliefs.
What are we?
Are we not like the sun that
shines in
the day and the moon by night
only to
be covered by dark clouds which
when
passes by prevent us from
shining to
our full extent in life.
What are we?
Are we not like sheep being
prepared in
silence to be slaughtered
each knowing
that the end will come when
it will come.
What are we?

Georgia Weiner
DEAR DOCTOR,
PEEK—A—BOO, I SEE YOU
stealing a peek
at your watch as you seal my
fate, you sneak!
Damn you! you professional
assassin,
shawled in pomposity like an
ass in
a serape, posturing benignity,
while denying me death with
dignity.
DIDDLE DIDDLE DUMPLING,
Doctor John,
patronizing lay-lexicon
dribbling from lips stifling
as yawn,
I *will* die with my body on!

Jacqueline Buchler
PUTTING GOD FIRST
How blue is the sky
For the one who will try;
So, try to find God
Through his Nature and Sod—
Before it's too late—
To enter heaven's gate.
It's great to be one
Who has walked with his god;
Rays of Joy gleam through
In the hours, rain, and sun—
Relaxed or on-the-run.
But, Satan knows best:
Not ever to Trust;
And to have such Lust;
To do no good Deed;
And to well-know Greed.
So, abide with me;
And, then, you will see
Fair creations by God,
As the tree and the sea;
And, you'll get to feel
Just like a brand New Deal!

Eugene F. Dennis
REFLECTIONS
How dreamy is the night!
Upon this limpid lake, I view
The mystic, mellow light
From yonder moon of lemon
hue.
I hear a bird somewhere
Among the branches of a tree
It fills the jasmine-scented air
With an enchanting melody.
And in the ebon sky
The scintillating stars appear
My heart is soothed, O let me
lie
Just for a while reflecting here.

Ruth Arnold
SECURE
No longer need thee fear, my dear,
Thou art in heaven now,
Cuddled in the strengths of God
Secure,
Like never—
Here.

Deidre Alexander
CHANGED ATTITUDES
Since praying to heal
emotional scars,
God has become real.
He is not a farce!
Criticism's gone
about right and wrong.
I don't look down on
brothers not as strong.
Not causing stumbling
being seen sinning,
nor even grumbling,
though I am winning.
My faith I won't flaunt
to cause others hurt,
doing what I want,
not being alert
of other's doubts and fears.
With Christ's attitude,
joy, peace, even tears,
express gratitude.

Michael K. Smith
DREAM
Oh, what is life and what is man
Without an attendant dream;
Without a star to stand,
And shed it's golden beam
Upon his existence.
He may wander, and take his glory
From the common life offers,
Yet still searching for the storied
And fabled that a dream proffers;
That is hidden to most.
But a dream comes to be
Through no ordinary means;
We need vision to see
A special, encompassing dream:
One to be ours alone.
Does such a dream begin
Without our knowing its start;
Without our knowing when
It makes its premier mark
On our impressionable soul.
To what source do we turn
When we need to find that dream;
What spark can make us burn
With a desire to know its meaning,
And discover its beauty.
We must turn inward
Too see its perfect form,
We must turn ourselves toward
Our centers. To see it born
Must consume us from within.
When once we find
And understand its way,
Our dream becomes a binding
Link, for us and ages gone away
To understand their time.
Their golden history comes alive
Through dream's impassioned strife:
Direction on our way it gives,
And purpose in our life
To set us on our course.
'Tis noble then, to find the key
To open the gilded room;
To release our dream's beginning ray.
To look with Kublai Khan
And find that Xanadu awaits.

Mattie Parsons
TO A WINTER VISITOR
Sunrise over Camelback Mountain,
The clear azure blue of the sky.
Golden sand on the far reaching desert
Or the gorgeous bloom of the cacti.
The mountains high and covered in pines
So stately in sun or snow,
The painted desert or petrified forest,
Or any climate you'd want to know.
This is outstanding Arizona,
A place you'd love if you'd stay.
We're so glad you came for a visit
And we'll miss you when you've gone away.

Nina Villaruel Collins
LOST CAUSES
What happens to ideals/dreams?
Do they dissipate into the
atmosphere, re-cycled for
another's use?
Do the expectations of the
new bride, dissolved and
absorbed by the oven-cleaning
mist, enter into a Land of
Disillusion,
to mingle with the crusader's
ambition, the missionary's hope,
their dreams measured in Time,
unfulfilled. . .recalled?
Does the hoary, weary world
impart it's ancient ennui
to the masses, causing the scholar
to spill his blood in tired retreat
from apathetic ignorance?
Oh, secretive world, generously
share your wisdom. . .
before we fail.

Paula Mokulis
BITTERSWEET
Yesterday.
Rejuvenating touch
evocative
Revitalizing sands
of hourglass hands
Nostrils swollen
with the
Aromatic nostalgia.
Sip
The languid, sensual innocence.
Quench unabashed
irresponsibility in
limpid serendipity.
Lifetime
silhouetted
Lazy day fantasy
Youthful transcendency
fattening
golden calf.
Fools parade
in
Sentimental charade
Rekindling scattered
ash
Seeking the elixir
patented
yesterday.

Nani Lii Staheli
TO A DECEMBER NIGHT
Mystic night. I often ponder,
As white-purged earth your hands enrobe,
What secrets lie within your stars.
Unsung, untold to those who sleep?
While wayworn beast, lone man and wife
Aged highway tread in silent quest,
What roused your stars to clearer flame—
Your limbs their bowed forms to embrace?
O night, release to me again
An echo of those breathless hours:
A shepherd's call, a stubdued stir
Of wind through branches' filagree.
For unknown mysteries you viewed,
Mingling with the lantern light,
With final glories yet unseen
Until, as child-king's cry emerged,
Your own conceived was given birth—
Living Star that uplifts faces,
And breathes new joy into torn souls!

Cathleen A. Karaffa
NO PROMISES
Make me not promises
Of a life of solitude
With your companionship.
Make me not promises
Of your love divine
And promiscuous.
Make me not promises
Of wine and roses
And the gift of a child.
For, if these promises
Should fade from your heart. . .
I shall lose my soul.

Clarice Dwelly Weatherspoon
A TALK WITH A FLY
Why was thy made a fly,
Instead of I?
And why am I, I
Instead of a fly?
Thy seems satisfied,
As an ugly fly.
But am I satisfied,
That I am I?

Paula J. Dutcher (Daughter)
FATHERS
My Dad was Gordon Faulkner,
Dad was really special.
He was there when I was born,
He grew up with me.
He was angry at times,
But he really loved me.
Whenever I needed a friend, he
was the best friend any person
could have.
Or ever need.
All the times I lost a guy,
My father said never worry I'll always be your guy.
When I was sick he was there, when he died I was there.
I held his hand until no life was there,
I loved him before, and then, even now I still care.
When he passed away that day,
I prayed for his soul to go to heaven and always stay.
I'll be with him again someday,
Not on this earth, but in heaven's way.

Helen Rex
STARS
I've oftened wondered about the stars
An' how they shine so bright in the sky
They throw a lot of light down here
Even tho' they're so high in the sky
Brilliant stars; light years away!
Yet they seem so close
A stone's throw; I'd say!
They're wonderfully bright
Up there in the sky!
Shinin' their light
On you and I!
Oh, to walk hand in hand
With you in the night!
Stars shinin' on us
So big an' bright!
Yes, I've often wondered
'bout the stars; how they shine!
For their clear, brilliant light
Is simply divine!

Christi Pedersen
THE ALONENESS TREE
The aloneness tree is searching
deep, in every direction going
Under the earth it's very
deep, and knowing
But, above the surface
wispy thin, scattered leaves and branches
Vague and indistinct it wavers
wispy thin, shallow dances
There is a separation
deep, between the surface mute
And the underneath where
deep, the searching roots
The strength the growing roots
possess, the greater contrast showing
The aloneness that this tree does
possess, strands of life knowing

Barbara J. Spangler
THE DRONE
The constant drone of the cars,
speeding along the street
The whirl of a motorcycle
A screeching of tires,
in protest to a sudden stop
all in our modern day trend—
People moving, ever moving
"Where do they go?"
"from where do they come?"
everyone asks.
Yes, as you and I they have that errand to run,
that trip to take,

A dentist or doctor to see
A life to be lived—
Like life itself, ever moving onward
pausing now and then,
in protest, (but then,)
moving on again.

Beverly Reno Tong
QUIET
Watch what you say
to those you're around,
I have learned
that big ears abound.
Before you know it
it's all over the city,
you can never trust
more's the pity.
So keep it to yourself
if you don't want it told,
and you won't worry
about friends turning cold.
A secret is a secret
so just beware,
though it isn't yours
it's in your care.

Richard Kamins
UNTITLED
Wanting to cry
Is like being
In kindergarten
All over again
Having to go
To the bathroom
But not feeling
Secure using
Their toilet
It's not the
Toilet at home
So you hold
It in and
Hold it in
And pray that
No-one says
Anything funny
Lest it pour out
right there
In front of
Everyone

Dorothy Harsha
A SPARK OF SUNSHINE
(Dedicated to Rev. and Mrs. John A. Kelly, who have been of encouragement to me)
It only takes a moment
To be a spark of sunshine to someone,
Along the pathway of life.

Sandra L. Russo
DYING, DYING, DEAD
Here I am, in mathematic measure
Of the distances to starve or to survive
Here it is, the distance seems to be shorter
For I will capture my pray alive. . .
But suddenly a jaw-like trap has swallowed my paw
And the world seems to be spinning around
So my success did not succeed and my life will thaw
Though man has stripped my life to his ground.
Here it is, the pain shoots through my body
And my blood forever stains my breath
Here I am, lost, a nature's body
And my last thought is captured by death.

Kleon Kerr
SUNDAY LOVE
"Today I love you all,"
The speaker firmly said,
"Right now and evermore.
And even when you're dead."
The loving words were spoken
From the pulpit on a Sunday.
For reasons undetermined,
The love was gone on Monday.
Somehow on every Sabbath
Love for all doth flow,
But come the other days,
Where does that great love go?
Our brother's keeper we become,
But only for a day
As the Sabbath passes,
The love just fades away.

June Deborah Meek
SOME DAY
I've met you in my dreams
but that's not reality
For reality for me.
is heartaches continually
Men who won't take no
Though rejection I do show
This I don't understand
They're pushy, don't give a damn
I want someone who cares
A quality, I've found, thats rare
I want someone to talk to
Not a one track minded fool
Someone who will always be there
Not someone thats who knows where
To share the good times and the bad
To lift me up when I am sad
Love is dear and love is fine
but will it ever be mine
Naturally and eternally
If not, I'll surely die.

Mart Piecynski
ANIMAL ANTICS
The fat Cat sat
On a hat,
And smashed the hat
Just like that!
The fat Rat sat
on a Cat,
The Cat spat back
And ate the rat!
The bird heard a word
But it was blurred,
So the Bird,
Could not sing the word!
The Dog met a Hog
Out near a log,
The Hog could not jog,
So the Dog left the Hog!
The Cow said now,
With a bow,
How dost thou, treat a cow?
Kindly now, that is how!
The Sheep could not sleep,
The Farmer would not keep
The Sheep who would not sleep,
The poor sheep cried, bleep, bleep, bleep.
The chickens were licken!
Earths plush pickins
The pickins delighted the chickens,
They gobbled as fast as the dickens!
The Duck was in the muck,
This he called luck,
In the muck, glucked the duck!
But the ducklings got stuck!
The owl began to howel,
Hoot, hoot, I am an Owl!
But the mothers of the other fowel
Covered him with a towel!
Of course you know the Horse!
He'll press his luck
If he will buck,
And ever be filled with remorse!

Sally Fasnacht
MY TREASURE
My dearest friend across the street
Gave me some slippers for my feet
To keep them warm in winter's cold
A gift that is worth much more than gold
To me it shows such love and concern
A gift for which all people yearn
My dearest friend she will always be
My greatest treasure is my friend to me.

Candace Maurine Smith
I THE UNIVERSE
I am part of the sea and the stars
And the wind of the north and south
Of mountains, and moon and Mars
And the ages that sent me forth.
What difference does a day or two
Make in our span of life?
The dawn breaks through with sun at bay
And sets again with curtains of night.
Its only just a tiny glow
Of Spirit as we wend our way
Into the after life of Love
Its just the part of another day.

Cathie Guarino
GOODBYE YESTERDAY
I remember you, you are my yesterday.
Oh yes! How I remember now, the good times,
your touch and your lips.
God, we had something then!
Something to strong to hold us together. And then so
suddenly what was strong, turned into weakness;
weakness into faintness, then you were gone.
I remember you, you are mv yesterday. Never to be my
today or tomorrow.
It is better to remember our good memories of each other,
than to remember the pain of saying goodbye.
Goodbye yesterday, I love you.

R. J. Ebright
BE GENTLE
Be gentle with him
who sings lonely hymns
in church, always there
a heart that needs repair
Be gentle with him
who feels empty within
a quiet kind of guy
he wants to cry
Be kind to him
who feels unsure within
helpful though shy
he doesn't know why
Be gentle to this man
who gives all he can
as hard as he can, he tries
is he too wise
So, we must let him live
who is sensitive
to hurt and the pain
of going insane

Larry Larsen
IN HELL
The fire it burns
and when you're in Hell,
you'll know of it well.
The smoke and the soot
all over your face,
you'll have no color
and no race.
All of your friends
they'll be gone that day,
none of them
will come down to play.
You'll work till you drop,
then get up again
and the smoke and the soot
will cover your skin.
You'll fight that old Devil
but you'll never win.
You'll have lots of time
to think of your sin,
and how it would be
to live again. . .
But the smoke and the soot
still cover your skin.

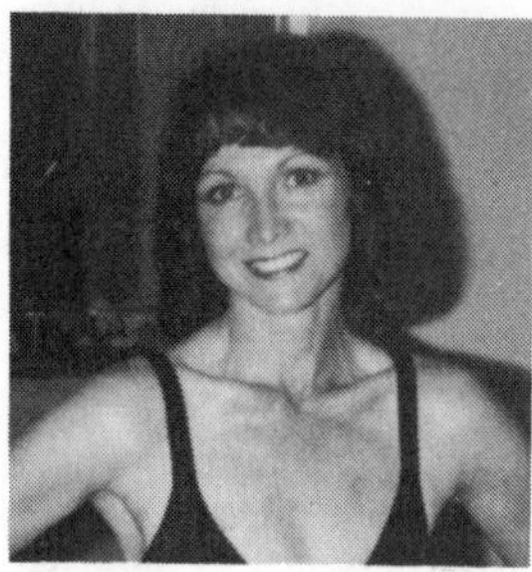

Waneta Sue Beals
SMILES
A cherry tree blooms,
And the pinkness of blossom,

Is so like your loving tongue.

Ronald A. Zaleski
NOTHING?
Nothing's thought
Nothing's dreamt
Nothing's told
Nothing's meant
Nothing's ventured
Nothing's gained
Nothing's sought
Nothing's aimed
Nothing's free
Nothing's barred
Nothing's easy
Nothing's hard
Nothing's nothing
Nothing's SOMEthing!

Joan Robinson Sabia
GAMBLING
A familiar rush of homely feelings
severs two years of dry dark.
Years of frightened sharing bits or chunks
of me with one or some of them
are lightened, scattered, nearly erased
by our talk.
Caution seems a deadly thing
but nakedness is a final act.
Some common scar or separate remedy
a laugh that harmonizes in spite
of fear frees me for chance.

George A. Wiens
AMERICA HAS A PROBLEM
America has a problem
and we vaguely understand
about the strife and turmoil
that has upset our land.
Our politics need cleaning up.
Our economy is upset.
God wants to help with both of these,
But we're not willing yet.
The founders of this mighty land
asked guidance from above.
God gave to them the wisdom,
and led them with his love.

What will it take to wake us up?
To make us understand
that God is more than willing
to help us heal our land?
America must once again
bow down on bended knee,
and call on God to lead the way,
if we are to stay free.
Don't put it off another day.
Our problems are too great.
Forget your pride, let God inside,
before it is too late.

Sallie C. Ezop
ALONE
I sit here and look,
looking deeper than I can imagine;
I sit here and dream,
dreaming of only the impossible;
I sit here and wish,
wishing on a star too far to reach;
I sit here and cry,
crying the confusion from my soul;
I sit here alone,
alone and unable to escape the emptiness.
For I look at you and see a beautiful person;
I dream of you and dream of us;
I wish for you only eternal happiness;
I cry over you, but the tears are softly hidden;
I am alone, even if you are by my side;
for I know you will leave it soon and we will always stay "just friends."
But I'll look into the future
and visualize success for you;
I'll dream of a lifelong friendship because your friendship means the world to me;
I'll wish for only the best,
because you deserve it all;
I'll cry happy tears for the special memories I hold of you;
I'll be alone, for I am me and you are you,
a very special friend.

Nawana McCollum Morris
MOMENTS OF SPLENDOR
Gone were the host of spinning thoughts
That clamored and persistently vied for recognition
Gone were the continuous shocking disappointments
That nagged and perpetually represented defeat.
I was filled with a surge of warmth
And the feeling of a new beginning
I no longer felt rejected
Because of unrequited longings and desires
Nor bound by deep twinges of guilt
And severed were the reminders of futility.
My cares and doubts soared and vanished
Leaving me free of expectations and exasperations
Time and place lost their importance
And gave priority to being.
I wanted these "Moments of Splendor" to last
But soon the spell was broken. .
So I carefully tucked the wonder of it all
Beneath the pillows of my heart
Until this feeling should be transformed into memories
And I would recall them as moments of contentment.

M. Dolores Cumpton
ETERNAL DAWN
My son, where has the time gone,
It's been an eternity since the dawn.
The dawn couldn't compare to your smile,
It's brightness has lasted day and night all this while.
The memories you don't put behind,
They are still like new in your mind.
Your family still misses you very much,
If your dear body they could only touch,
This we cannot do, you know,
And down deep the scars still show.
Fifteen long years have gone past,
And we know our earthly home cannot last.
In God's Heaven, you are among the beautiful flowers,
Nourished and fed by His showers.
So there with God you shall remain,
Until He lets us come to you again.

Tammie H. Prince
LOVE IS
Love is so sweet; love is so kind
But your love isn't anything unless it's mine.
So darlin; turn my way
And let me have your love today.

Love is so nice just as long as it's yours
That comes and opens up my door.
Love is, the love in our hearts for one another;
So who needs someone other.
Love is caring and sharing our lives together;
making each other happy forever.

Darlin; I promise to do my part and love you like i do;
All i ask is for you to love me and be true.

Marje Harrington DeMarce
PAST-PERFECT TENSE
Remembering gently nudges me into an encounter with significant episodes; bitter-sweet daydreams float on puffed memory clouds—clouds clustered into pleasant sequences.
Reverie hangs from the scaffold of recollections—incidents of long—ago are defined in the "past-perfect" tense.
A mistiness permeates fragile reflections, images mirrored, within the sheltered corridors of my mind.
The way it was never again could be recaptured, as the unique in experience defies duplication.
Then, abruptly, awareness jolts me into perceiving today's reality—sharply outlined profiles are silhoutted against the background of the "present—imperfect" tense.

Elie VanDeVenter
RESURRECTED
Life, like the corner of the final fifth to the coinless drunk, had become empty and alone, waiting for the manhole cover to be lifted so a way could be seen; up and out.
After death comes the resurrection and the light. Sun blooming in stereophonic color. The way, tinted visible, is shimmering, signaling up ahead. Life is bountifully beautiful after the light kiss of death.

Lori F. Dowell
JUST BECAUSE IT'S ME
I'm not saying that I'm special
I'm not saying that I'm right,
It's just because it's me.
It may not last forever, but
it's still a shining light,
There's time for me to see.
It's easy when you look at it,
Through the eyes of someone who can see,
If you'd only understand, it's just because it's me.
I may not make much headway,
but I'm never giving in.
There has to be some special way of knowing when to win.
The losers may not win at all,
the winners may not lose,
It's only when you can turn it 'round,
Then it's your place to choose.
I may not always be too sure,
but then who really is?
The motives may sometimes be poor, but then do motives win?
The outcome may not seem too clear, but then how can it be?
When it's true just what I say,
It's just because it's me.

Shirley Archer
SPRING IS AT AN END
Spring is at an end I fear,
Summer draws so very near,
The showers have brought the May flowers,
I could lay in the green grass for hours.
Spring is at an end I fear,
I can hear the "School is out" cheer.
Soon I will hear the stormdoor's endless slam,
The constant yelling will tell how happy I am.
Spring is at an end I fear,
The late morning sleep I long for will never be here.
Very early the dog will scratch and whine at the door,
The children will beg to go to the corner store.
Spring is at an end I fear,
I had better get my mind in gear,
Summer vacation is for the children, not for me.
I'll only have a half of a nerve by the fall, you'll see.
Spring
is
at
an
end
I
fear

Dave McCammon
THE OLD MAN
Down the dark alley
Down by the park
There lies a deep hole
It lies in the dark.
Down in the hole
There lies an old man

He sits on the rocks
And sleeps on the sand.
Into this hole
People do yell
"Who are you, Sir?
We cannot tell."
Down in the hole
The old man replies
"I am the man
Who has no eyes."
The people, bewildered,
Then proceed to say,
"Is lack of eyes cause
To live without day?"
"Well," the old man says,
In a ponderous tone,
"This is the theory
To which I have grown"
"If a man has no eyes
And thus cannot see.
Why live in the daylight,
The joy, and the glee?"
"For here in my hole
This pure black abyss.
I need not worry
About sights I may miss."

Hermine M. Wilber

MY LIFE

In Vienna Austria, a little girl I was
With dreams and hopes bright
Always longing for the lime light
Doing good and bringing joy to all
Both alike, young or old
"Star-like", I wanted to shimmer
But can't you see? I was told—
Dreams of ambitions will be interrupted
. .And hopes dimmer, under Nazi "Control"
Good wills be crushed and bend. . .
That their wanted prosperity be rushed
To terror, destruction and every man's end
Soon it struck me, I got sick
Weeks in coma and pain—
With hardly a hope to regain
The doctor's wouldn't come to aid and relief
Since I was not the child. . .
Of a bloody Nazi "Chief"
Oh, somewhere I was falling, lost ground
The sound—I became "DEAF"
But my will for life was strong
When I compared my sufferings, as small
To millions along
Who have endured, sorrow and pain
Many bravemen, who gave their lives
But not in vain
For "GOD" keeps watch and vigil overall!

The good and righteous—
He promised a land to their best
"AMERICA" the country HE blessed
Thats where I now am
Thank you"GOD" and AMERICANS
Although "Never Regained Sound"
But "Firm Ground"—
Here has opened wide a door
Where I can be me once more
Do good and live my hopes and dreams
"IN GOD WE TRUST"

Elenor M. Mitchell

THREE SPARROWS

In a Hawaiian dineing room, three sparrows pearched on the back of a chair.
With sparkling eyes they watched us.
They asked in their mute way, for a crumb of our toast.
One chirped something in our ear, as his wings brushed against our hair.
We were their host; and with them shared our toast.
Jesus said, not one sparrow would fall with out God knowing.
For God's creatures we cared.
To refuse them a bit of toast, we didn't dare.
On our fingers one of them bravely pearched for a bit of toast.
They all flew away, perhaps to find another person with a tidbit;
With whom they would repeat the whole bit.
Little trio you shared in our memory of Hawaii.

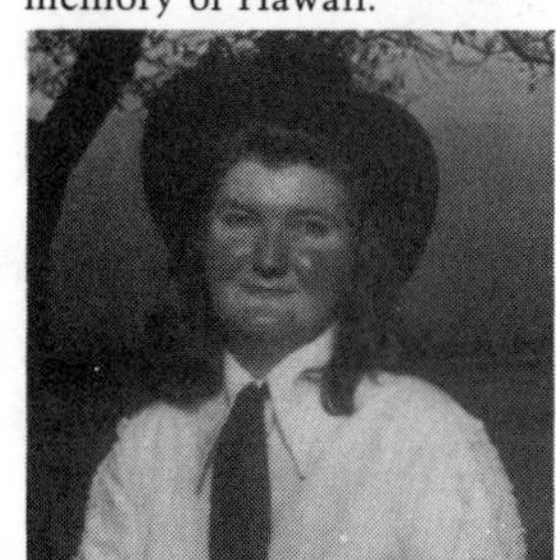

Lorene Dunaway Osborn

A HOME WHERE LOVE IS THE KEY

A home where love is the key,
Is a home where happiness can't help but be,
And who cares to roam when love is the key to their home.
A fire in the fireplace, a dad's smiling face,
A mother in rags or dressed in lace,
A Bible in her hand, a child at her knee,

A beautiful picture for love is the key.
Perhaps they'll invite me to spend the night,
And nothing could please me any better,
Than being in a home where love is the key.

Margaret Coles

WRECKER OR BUILDER

I watch them tearing a building down
A gang of men in a busy town
With a ho-heave ho and a busy yell
They swung a beam and a building fell
I asked the foreman, "Are these men skilled?"
"As the men you'd hire if you had to build?"
He gave a laugh and said, "No Indeed."
"Just a common laborer is all I Need."
"I can easily wreck in a day or two
What builders have taken a year to do."
And I thought to myself as I went on my way
Which of these roles have I tried to play.
Am I a builder who works with care
Measuring life with a rule and square?
Am I doing my work by a well made plan?
Doin' the very best that I can?

Patricia Strother

ANNIE'S RAINBOW

Ask me what you mean to me,
And I will tell you how,
With heart pounding in broken tempo
I lay upon the crusted earth
Aching like Wyeth's crippled Christina
because I had seen with unblinking
Clarity my very dreams swept away
by the flood-tide of Life.
Ask me what you mean to me,
and I will tell you how,
Near-drowning in bitterness, I watched the seasons come and go;
Still the rain fell within my soul till you crept across my horizon
Like a beautiful rainbow, brilliantly
banded in colors I could feel.

Sherry Clark

LOVE

Love, Oh! how it does grow and grow with each passing day.
To blossom like the flowers in May.
It starts like a rosebud which flourishes with tender loving care.
It matures and develops into beauty so rare.
Each petal marking precious memories in time.
Memories always to be cherished—yours and mine.
Then the season comes when a rose must come to an end.
To wilt, to die, to wait to be reborn again.
But love is eternal and goes on and on.
For today, tomorrow and even beyond.
All of God's creations are so fine.
But the gift of love is most divine.

S. Ingalls

SOMEWHERE THROUGHOUT TIME

Somewhere throughout time,
We will meet again.
To be together,
until time itself,
comes to an end.

Lance Nielsen

DREAMS

Waking from a night
Of unconsciousness,
Wondering why I
Can't have adventures
Like I do in my dreams,
I take a drag from
A morning cigarette
And begin to see.
Nothing's given without
Experience of need,
And in a dream
You need that effortless
Quality of being free.
Free from restrictions
Of time and space
Which plague you
When you wake.

Judy A. McCulloch

TIME

Time starts out at a snails pace,
and seems to pass so slow.
We toss it out the window,
and sit back to watch it go.
As we slip into adulthood,
It begins to pick up speed.
It seems there's never quite enough,
We brake, it does not heed.
By the time we reach our sixties,
It seems a high speed race.
We'd like to backtrack just a bit
And set a different pace.
We'd like a chance to cherish
every moment of the space,
between our birth upon the earth
And our arrival at the gate.
But, Alas!! It is too late

L. R. Harder

GRAVESIDE

Be still
and listen to the silence of death and weep not
for you cannot change that which is done
Hush little child
for what's gone is gone
and your tears cannot wash away memories
or cast away fear
Time alone will close the lid
to that hated casket of lifelessness
but never again will that lid be opened
by mortal hands
Death seeps out the cracks
and lurks in dark shadows
waiting
watching
then once again
draws another victim
into the cold depths
of never more
and the mourners have only to stare
into the blankness of a dark hole
and weep

Christopher A. Cote'
AS ONE
The news abounds with grief and woe,
Such a tale does mankind sow.
In attempt to right the wrong he's done,
Many things are left undone and many heroes
Left unsung.
So here's to those, both large and small,
Who does respond to neighbors call.
Take note, do heed, and try to shine,
For life is but a second in time.
And how tragic it would therefore be,
To become insensitive to others needs.
So we must work to the goal yet come,
To the day when we all are as one.

Frances C. Kopp
JEHOVAH OUR GOD
Do you want to find God
Pick up your Holy Bible and read
That's where I find God
That's where he talks to me.
When I was oppressed and in despair
This is where Jehovah directed me
Jehovah said; Pick up your Holy Bible

Open it and read
I just opened up the "Holy Bible"
There I found the answer, Isaiah; Chap. 42.
I didn't even turn a page
Do you think this is odd
I don't, because it came from God.
"Jehovah" can work miracles
For all his children don't you see
So why don't you take heed
Pick up your "Holy Bible"
Open it and read.

Betty Hershey Morrison
AS A PURE WHITE DOVE
As a lowly donkey lay near by
As a pure white dove flew in from the sky
A tiny babe lay fast alseep
Under the watchful eyes of a sheep
He lay cradled in his mother's arms
Sheltered by God from all the world's harm
The wise men guided by a star
All three kings, came from afar
Born of a virgin by a Father above
Sent to this world with a heartful of love
He came as a lamb, His blood to shed
For the love of his brothers that we might be led
By a shining light that would lead us to Him
It would shine forever, never to dim
He would one day die, but to live again
At God's right hand always to reign
With mercy and justice and kind tender love
Always as gentle as a pure white dove

Diane M. Ammann
THE DEER
I happened upon two deer one day,
As I walked through the woods before dawn.
One was a mighty buck, quite brave.
The other was just a fawn.
They stood in the marshland, as I could see,
Eating their morning meal.
From where I was standing, they couldn't see me.
But the buck my presence could feel.
The fawn did not heed the warning,
As the buck in my direction did stare.
I could have stood there all morning
Since the buck seemed to see nothing there.
I stood there and watched a bit longer,
For the buck seemed to pay me no mind.
But the light from the sun, it got stronger
And the wind soon picked up from behind.
The buck caught my scent and was startled,
His tail twitched as he started to run,
But I in turn then departed,
And left them alone to have FUN.

Joseph I. McCullough
THE MAYOR
He leads every parade
With friendly gestures to all,
Soaks up the atmosphere
At banquet and ball.
He's ready to speak
On every issue of note
To please different segments
Of the popular vote.
Petitioners pursue him
Through rain, sleet, and snow,
Overwhelming his ego
With some kind of show.
No chore is too small
For the mayor of the town,
Who must be responsive
Whether up or down.

M. Caldwell-Wilson
WINTER
The weather's getting colder
The sun has gone somewhere
It's difficult to stay warm
in the damp and frigid air.
But the trees are really lovely
Their colors seem to glow
It gives a warm, warm feeling
Beauty. . .atop the snow.
The North Winds cut like lazers
Our clothes are much too thin
The frost is biting at our flesh
The cold just slips on in.
But the sky so blue and awesome
is lovely, bright and gay
The clouds with their formations
form fantasies of the day.
Then a miracle just happens
The chill is no more there
Because of winter beauty
warmth is simply everywhere.

Fern Johnson
NIGHT WATCH
Lying in my darkened room
watching shadows on the wall,
Listening to the sounds of night,
I can hear the night birds call.
A light outside my window
frames the swaying wind-blown trees;
Ghostly figures dance on curtains
moved by air-conditioner's breeze.
And then, I hear a baby cry
in a room just down the hall,
As pain racks through his tiny frame
and an Aide answers his call.
This child of God came here to stay
for care, comfort and love;
A handsome boy a few months old,
angel beauty from above.
His life will be brief and painful,
there's not much that can be done;
But his needs are filled with tenderness,
loved by each and every one.
Little Esstas is a fair-haired doll,
his eyes so pure and clear;
And cuddled to their bosoms
he's protected from his fear.
God's watching from his home above,
just waiting for the time
When Esstas will be there with Him
in His happiness sublime!

Rosemary Chandler
I LOVED YOU
I loved you, when first we met,
When our hearts were young and our ways not set,
I loved you, when our vows were said,
I loved you, in and out of bed!
I loved you, when our first child was born,
I loved you at night, and in the morn.
I loved you, when you lost your job.
I loved you, though at night I'd sob.
I loved you, when you went astray.
I cried the night, and half the day.
I loved you, when we first did part.
I loved you, with a broken heart.
I loved you, when we had the last fight,
Though, I cried that time, both day and night.
I said I hated you, and you went away,
Then, I tried not to love you every day.
I found another love, and then,
I remembered our love, and felt a yen,
To call you home, and start again,
Now, another fifteen years have passed.
You were my first love, and my last.

Darlene Francy
GRANDPA AND GRANDMA
As the sun shown high in the
Very early morn,
A man and woman were united.
Before them stood the world and
The land on which there was
Nothing. They worked at it
Until they made the land a part
of their lives.
Their work was part of survival,
Peace, and harmony in their
Minds. They trudged many a
Long hard road together, as
We will.
In yourself and others loving
Is the gift of life. So if you
Have a little, hold on to it,
And make it grow.
Why? Because once you were a
Child and soon you will grow
Old, and then you will know
What love for each other means
And to live without it.
So I say to you Loving is the
Gift of life, without it we or
Happiness cannot survive.

Stephen T. DiPesa
ODE TO A SPECIAL LADY
Lady who moves so softly and sweetly
Like the sun peeking over the horizon at dawn
With eyes so mysterious and so sensuous
But yet alas so like a fawn.
You bring to the world a gift of joy
A heart too big for its slender frame
And lips that gently let me know
Your not just any mans game.
Today I bring two gifts to you
A rose to hold in one hand
The second one, the biggest of all
My heart to hold in your other hand.
Please be gentle, please be kind
I bruise as easily as you
Deep within a feeling has spread
I've fallen in love with you.

Ralph L. Keasling
EMPATHY
(for Ann)
I am terribly saddened by your sorrow,
grief within one's house is always a burden of tomorrow.
I can only imagine your burden and strife,
and think of you, as you end this plight.
May God bless you, and he will,
accept my friendship and others still.
For all, that love and care, we shall be here tomorrow.
But today, we cry.
Remember to be strong and it shall pass,
for your friends are forever and meant to last.

Carol Jeanne Durand
OTONO
Ananjado, amarillo, cafe' y verde son colores de otono.
Los colores de otono son tan bonitos no puedo deseriberlos.
Otono es una estacio'n colorida del an'o.
La siesa es en el oton'o.
Los vegetales son muy bien.
Muchos animales siegan comida por el invierno.
Cuando hace fri'o en oton'o los hojas caen a la tierra.
El canbio de las estacione viene con la escarcha.

Ruth M. Bishop
STEP BACK INTO TIME
I wish there was a place to get away from here. A Place to go and sit in Peace and have nothing to fear.
I wish there was a passage where we could step back into time; when candy cost a penny and a nickle is worth a dime, Where there were no cars or motorcycles and horses were used all day.
If only we could step back into time, if only there was a way.

Elizabeth Winslett
A MEMORY
In my usual rush,
To get my house work done.
Before catching the bus,
to a mediocre job.
I stopped at the kitchen sink,
The dishes to do.
Glancing out the window,
The early morning Sun,
Sparkling in the dew
Was beautiful to see.
How wonderful it would be.
Me thinks.
To hear my dear Mother say,
As she so often had,
In days gone by.
Before she went to join dear Dad.
"Hurry now, be on your way."
Leave the dishes to me."
Standing motionless and still,
Gazing beyond the window sill.
I heard a rustling of the leaves
On the straggly old peach tree
Standing out back.
It couldn't be the breeze.
There was no wind that I could see.
Then I saw Mother floating down.
Gold sandals on her feet.
A beautiful vision in a lovely white gown.
Dark hair flowing.
A smile on her radiant face.
And once again, deep inside
I heard my Mother say.
"Hurry now, be on your way.
Leave the dishes to me."

Jennie Frey Payton
MORNING SUN
I love the morning sun; the day's begun with light.
I long for the morning sun when day is done for the night.
Oh sun, the hour's divine, and I live to see you through the pine.
The morning is beautiful, sunlit and all—
And God bless the world tomorrow.
Streaks of light; warming light, heaven's delight for we—
We, the little people here, hold the sun dear, near to Thee.
Oh sun, the hour's divine, and I live to see you through the pine.
The country is beautiful, sunlit and all—
And God bless the world tomorrow.
Wake up, the night has passed, see through the glass, The Son!
Dear children, please live in peace and love will increase for everyone!
Oh Son, You're ours divine, and I live to see You in my time.
The whole world is beautiful, sunlit and all—
And God please bless the world's tomorrows.

Eleanor H. Cumming
THERE IS NO TIME BUT NOW
Today is today,
So let tomorrow slide
Into the recesses of the mind
Like leaves that slip and glide
Down autumnal air ways to the earth.
There is no time but now
For living and loving,
For keeping or breaking a vow.
We walk hand in hand today,
That is all that I ask. . .
To give me your heart for an hour
Is no difficult task.

Frank Skiles
CITY LIGHTS
(Seen by a country boy)
Burning rubies across the bay
Trying to turn the night to day
Shimmering saphires out of reach
From Alamedas sandy beach
Candle lighted hills on fire
Hear it love! The angel choir...?
Glittering diamonds, sparkly bright
San Francisco winter night.

Carmen Henriquez
ROSE
Do not let these petals close your pleasant paths.
Do not let the blazons that shelter your spirit break.
Let the world give you its great smile.
With its variety of grimaces and its collection of butterflies,
And its stones covered with orchids,
and let your naked feet
Stir sleeping mosses,
and with their raveled hairs
Suggest a thousand caresses for me,
and let your breast vibrate to
The beat of my steps,
which are now reviving
A rose for you, in a fragile paper that sustains my thoughts,
Extending my path and flooding it with you.

Marcia G. Kester
RECITAL
You strike the first chord--
Long fingers glide over chromatic steps.
I wake under tarnished keys
the wood pulsating in my arms.

A coin of light draws in the shadow.
Your body leans to the piano.
You sway,
pressing notes
that drum in my chest--
rhythms dart through my wrist
like blood.

Robert G. Page
HELP
With each day I wonder why,
I live in dreams without end.
Why my life is slipping by,
and why my life is without friend.
In solitude I feel the pains,
I feel the pains of life so deep.
For comfort needing all in vain,
to end each day in drunken sleep.
Absorbed by fear and left alone,
alone by choice of self denial.
Tired of people sick of home,
yet needing a friend and a friendly smile.
Confused at life not knowing why
I feel the tolerance of others near.
Who grasp my moods as they streak by,
yet shy from them in hopeless fear.
My conscience gone and soul decayed
torn from youth wasteful of friend,
a voice inside cries out afraid,
afraid at last of an empty end.

Bernadette Thomas
POSTER - CHILD
I met a poster - child today
"face to face"; "eyes to eyes";
"feelings".
I felt her fear in my mind,
but her courage in my heart.
She gave me a feeling of warmth,
but then my heart was overtaken by a cold chill.
I need not tell anyone how I feel towards such children,
because the tears upon my face
"Tell the story of my heart".

Ruth E. Beckwith
TRAINING A COLT
Timer was a healthy colt
Loved to run and jump and bolt
Scared our neighbor, Mr. Holt.
For three years he played and grew
And his cares were very few.
Then came training which was new!
Putting a halter on his head
Made him balk at being led.
He tried to turn around instead.
For days he failed cooperation,
Seemed all filled up with frustration,
Made a scenic demonstration!
But at last I gained his trust,
When he found it was a must,
So on his head the straps I thrust.
Next he had to carry me,
So kicked a while and hit a tree.
He fiercely struggled to get free.
Next day I started out anew.
Away from me he quickly drew,
Then stepped ahead onto my shoe
I had less trouble, though today
And really rode him quite away.
He knew that I was on the stay!
The summer soon had turned to fall.
Timer ceased to kick and stall.
He's happy now and likes it all.

Diane Hellengreen
FAR AWAY
Sometimes early
in the calm of eternal quietude
I think of you—
for the silent
relentless flow
of soft vibrants
speak
a certainty—
which will
encompass
urgent
indicators
of a peaceful
union even in
distant stars.

Daniel Duane Roll
LIFE
Life is a picture
With lines dark and bold,
Or thin lines of silver and gold.
The picture's the same
For you and me.
But what we look at
Isn't necessarily what
We see.

Kenny D. Merritt
VILLAGE BY THE SEA
Natives... Natives in their palm frond huts...
Dancing... Dancing in their long grass skirts...
Natives... Natives fishing in the sea...
Fishing... Fishing for a bite to eat...
Climbing palms,
nobody falls.
Monkey's chatter,
toucan's call...
Ocean... Ocean's pulsing, rhythmic waves...
Hunting... Hunting boars that run the jungle...
Ocean... Ocean awes the silent gaze.
Gazing... Gazing under evening rays...

Barbara A. Noel
THREE WORDS
Words repeated many times
Trying to explain the feeling
inside
A feeling we try not to hide
A lover's three most spoken
words
Yet; mean nothing
For even with these words, my
love,
There is no limit
No words can ever say or
explain
Love is greater than anything
Larger than the biggest number
Will last longer than time itself
And reaches beyond the farthest
star.
If man could only find the real
words
Expressed
By a lover's eyes.

Wade Hampton
HE SLAPPED ALL HER FACES
He slapped all her faces
and they shattered like glass,
or a mirror that held
an Image of him.
He sold his belongings
and strode him away,
stole church bells
for a neck ornament,
bought a bottle of wine
an strode him away
from the well ordered city
into that darkened
Mysterious World.

David Clum
PORTRAIT
as day,
a satiable stirring way,
cerise and sapphire and daffodil.
hush, hush, is the way—
I flush, swell and sway
as day.
I see in depth the surge inlay,
the way all sways,
cerise and sapphire and
daffodil.
I breathe airy, lilting, lilied play,
all at bay. I breath praise
as day.
I am water-color, wet is the
wind, I fray.
flushing I spray
cerise and sapphire and
daffodil.
then I pray.
in a delicate way I display,
as day,
cerise and sapphire and daffodil.

Margaret M. Gabaldon
TWO LITTLE HANDS
Two little hands I use to praise
the Lord,
Two little eyes to see God's
nature world.
Two little feet I use to walk in
His way,
Two little knees to kneel on
while I pray.
Two little lips to whisper "Jesus,
I love you",
Two little ears to listen to
all His truths.
One heart, I have to give to my
Lord,
One life, I dedicate forever more.

Tommy Forguson
CHRISTMAS TIME
This is the time of year to feel
the pulse
Of all mankind run through the
frosty air.
This is the spirit that lets us
repulse
The selfish craving that has
placed a glare
Over the basic values we hold
dear.
This is the spirit of good will
and peace
Possessed by those rare souls
who can not fear
To give their all to life to gain a
lease
Of life to love. We cannot
swallow ill
And hope to have a vital goal to
push
Our timid souls to greater feats
of will,
The will to overcome the lies
that crush.
This is the time of man to feel
the good
That we could realize if we only
would.

Gary J. Steller
LITTLE BOXES
Most Sunday Puzzles drive me
nuts.
They make me seem a simple
putz
With words I'd never ever use.
They cause your dictionary
frays
With words not used in
Saturday's,
Plus other, corny, oddball clues.
I think someone should write
the bums
And tell them that our language
comes
Replete with other simpler
words.
But, even if they knew--the
cheats--
They'd still come out with
sheets and sheets
Of foreign and exotic birds.
I'd like to finish on without
The twinge of guilt or slightest
doubt
That follows guessing the last
square.
So, to the crossword team I say,
You could give me just on
Sunday
With easy words--they're not so
rare.

Lydia Venta-Dobrovolsky
MY SOUL
From the city's noise
with my natural poise
I am coming to Thee---
Thy prodigal daughter:
You will know the solution
how to cure from pollution
my soul.
My soul!
Eternity loving,
Eternally living,
Illumined soul.

Scott F. Thompson
ARM OF TIDES
I'm the ocean,
You're the land,
I rush over your rocks,
Tumble over your sand.
I constantly touch you
by kissing your shorelines,
My arm of tides shall embrace you
till the end of time.
My tides are restless wanderers,
They reach into your
coves and caves.
They thrash and caress you
With every moving wave.
My moods are many,
I'm stormy when I'm mad.
When I'm still and calm
I'm joyously happy and glad.
My tides are skilled musicians,
They play songs for your shores.
Dreamy songs of enchantment
Ring out on endless chords.
I'm your eternal neighbor,
I'm a kingdom of tides and turns.
I take ships to their harbors
Asking nothing in return.
I'm the ocean,
You're the land,
I rush over your rocks,
Tumble over your sand.
I constantly touch you
by kissing your shorelines,
My arm of tides shall embrace you
till the end of time.

Evelyn Johnson Seals
SERENITY
A certain calmness touches me
with mellow bits of love.
I am content for now I'm free
and no longer holding on to
yesterday.

I love you for all the things you have done for me; all the times you've been my shoulder to lean on and all the times I've needed you and you were there. Today the magic is there--the chemistry flows in electric body currents too thrilling to describe. No moment lasts forever but today I would stretch each into eternity. I find serene comfort in the knowledge that you shield me from the world by your presence. I am discovering the joy of living and each day dawns with the thought that I can never again settle for a lesser man than you.

Kitch Kahn
PUMPKINS ON PARADE
Walking through the
countryside
This crisp October day,
Everywhere I chanced to look
Were pumpkins on parade.
Up on people's porches
Strewn around the ground,
Happy pumpkins on parade
All through the pretty towns.
Orange faces, cheery smiles
I know just what they mean,
I love the pumpkins on parade
In time for Halloween.

Mary Michael
UNTITLED
The people clapped, and bravos
sailed throughout the
audience.
I watched you standing, heads
above the others, arms folded,
occasionally yawning, then
clapping.
I watched you turning and
mounting the stairs to leave.
I watched until it was clear to
me that you weren't glancing
anywhere for another look at
this one, small insignificant
woman.
As I saw you reach the top of
the stairs, I turned, and fled
behind a column on the left.
And you both passed by, never
seeing, never sensing that I
was near you.

Sarah Eva Gordon
JUST THE GHETTO
A wino is leaning on a post out
of doors
While somewhere in the
distance, a rooster crows
This is the city; they keep on
telling me
It's a pity that they are so blind
and cannot see the poverty,
the misery and blight that
profanes
Where every nameless person
lives on a street with no name
Young girls are giving birth in
shame.
Still they keep on saying
This is the city of fame
that guy smoking dope is only
11 years of age
The upper crust will say "this is
an outrage".
People walking nonchalantly
down a city street
Somewhere around the corner, a
preacher starts to preach
We are all on a fast moving
train going nowhere but to
the welfare lines.
My question is when do we
start living and stop all this
dying?
For in the Ghetto, you are as
dead as the leaves falling from
the trees in autumn.
And nobody, nowhere gives a
care - no not one of them.

Lori Lanesky
AURORA BOREALIS
Last night I fell -
A thousand miles beneath you
A feather upon my chest
I breathed and it fluttered away
Touched your fingertips
Pressed so close to mine
Skin's friction flashed
In electric ecstacy
An aura of colors
Aurora Borealis
A thousand miles above us

Annette Dare Hug
MY WEDDING DAY
My Wedding Day
Is not in May
Or when the June
Brides bloom.
The month is cold,
The winds are bold
And the hills seem
shadowed in gloom.
The love is right,
The heart fires bright
And late winter is
As spring--the air
All perfume.
It is time,

His heart is mine
And our people gather
Around.
Mama crys,
Daddy sighs,
Happiness and sadness
We have found.

Debbie E. Chambliss
THE EAGLE AND I
Soaring high above my head,
so beautiful with wings
outspread;
Coming quietly to a rest
to feed the young ones in
your nest.
Looking out for danger near,
knowing that you must live in
fear.
We are alike in many ways;
Not sure of life each new day.
Trying to ready our offspring
for anything the world might
bring.
Giving our all until they're grown
to face the world on their
own.

Charlene "Charlie" Dillaman
HEARING GOD'S WORD
There are little eyes upon you
Watching everything you do
They are watching you night
and day
Their ears hear everything you
say
Their eager hand will do
anything you do
For they are patiently awaiting
to grow up and be just like
you
So set a good example starting
with God's word
It is something you will be
proud their little ears often
heard

Gerald W. Thibault
AN ONLY POEM
Courage, where are you?
Courage, who are you?
Courage, what are you?
Who defines courage?: Richard
M. Nixon, W.C. Fields, Karl
Marx, Liza Minnelli, Gorgeous
George, or Lee Oswald?
Where, what and who is courage
in relation to me?
Courage is caught within me.
Courage is tearing me away
from me and finally
experiencing freedom.
Slavery of one's self is the
toughest to fight.
No man can ever be up against
greater odds than to have to
defeat one's self for one's own
benefit.
I want me... I'm going to fight for
me. I'm going to have courage... I
am goind to be... I need me.
Dear Speck:
Speck, I need you more than
anyone else in the whole world.
Sincerely,
Speck

Stephen Reich
FIRST KISS
Old Jochum now white and sage
And near his ninth decade,
Was yet making his debut.
Yet little did that matter, to me,
and less to you.
Scant seconds before, our
mouths had met
And now our skins would not
be parted.
Till we were forced to leave, and
weave
Our journey towards each other.

Mary K. Porter
THE REAL CHRISTMAS
Christmas is the day of Jesus'
birth,
The day God sent him to reign
on earth.
He was lowly and meek,
Born in a stable among the
sheep.
He was wrapped in swaddling
clothes and laid upon the hay,
Many years ago, on that first
Christmas day.
Despite his lowliness, he was
born to be the King of men,
To save the world from all sin.
He was born to die upon a tree.
Between two thieves on Mt.
Calvary.
He was so poor he didn't own a
grave,
So he was placed in a tomb that
Joseph gave.
He rose from the dead and
ascended on high,
To live with his Heavenly
Father in the sky.
someday he will return again,
To judge up all for our sin.
So Christmas is more than gifts
and a tree,
It's the day Jesus was born to set
us free.

Evvie Freeman
FORGET SELF
Forget self--spend your time
in service to others
And you will soon see the
good, in being able to help
your brothers.
You will be happy that your
love, kindness, and help-
fulness
Will come back to you in
heaping measure, for those
you chanced to bless.
You, who, denied your selfish
wants and desires to please
That great immutable law of
"Doing good to the least of
these."
Jesus said "In-as-much, as you
do it, it is unto me,"
Give it a try--deny thyself--
and you will surely see.
Give to the world the best you
have--You will find it; Oh!
so true
Not doing to receive, you will
see the best will come back
to you.

Kathryn Doyle
MR CLAUS
If that jolly ole red Jaybird
Comes down my flue this year,
I'll wait, and lunge,
and
GOTCHA!
Now sit right down, you hear!
You and me has got to talk,
About this Santa guff.
Cause you aint real, you jest a
myth,
No, don't leave in a huff.
Not so you say? Well tell me,
AN,
How come you such big stuff?
Because,
I am all the goodness
Wrapped within your heart.
That would stay and starve
forever,
No incentive to depart.
And so,
I chose this special birthday
To keep my myth alive.
My gift to "Him",
And also you,
Inner peace it will revive.
Now, may I go? The time is dear!
I promise I'll be back next year.
I'm very sorry, Mr. Claus,
That I disturbed your flight.
Be off kind Sir, spread your good
cheer,
Merry Christmas, and Good
Night.

Lydia M. Busch
THE RED ROCKET
The streetcar tracks disappear in
the distance
Lost in the evening haze
Balancing on the slippery rails
We play King of the Hill
As we wait for the Red Rocket
Coming faintly from a distance
There is a special kind of sound
Not a whistle, not a horn
Something in between
Echos hum along the rails
The Red Rocket grows larger
and larger
And finally grinds to a stop
Doors fold back, steps fold down
Tired hands grasp the center bar
The men step to the ground
Clothes covered with ore dust
Faces the color of clay
Each one carries a lunch pail
Extra pair of shoes
And a newspaper
Dad makes his way to the door
We greet him with noisy shouts
And happily playing
Don't Step on the Cracks
We escort him home to supper

Christopher D. Sharpe
EPILOGUE
People
Swarming through the network
Preying on the weak
Will they ever realize
Their ultimate defeat
The weak will survive
Or so I am told
what they will inherit
That I do not know
With nuclear weapons all the
rage
And World War III a mistake
away
They may not inherit
But attain equality
In the ultimate tragedy
The rape of humanity

Robert B. Burns
THE ROYAL CURE
Whosoever suffers from pain,
Whosoever they are,
Give them some french
champagne,
And a bit of caviar.

Debra L. Clear
CAN'T WE PREVIEW ETERNITY?
Can't we preview eternity?
There MUST be a way!
By channel or by shuttle?
By auto or by bay?
Can we view it in the night sky?
Can we peek at it by day?
Can't we know where we're
going?
There MUST be a way!
You mean the Big Guys are
keeping mum?
That we don't even have a say?
Well, I don't like surprises
So if you don't mind I'll stay!

Patrick Soltis
FACE IN THE CROWD
Old man wandering uptown
Take a drink and it's one more
round
Who's to stay here when you're
feeling down
Can you see what you really are?
Troubled woman now don't you
weep
Someone shares the secret they
can't keep
Lonely man appears now you
can sleep
Can you feel what you really
are?
Runaway child out for the kicks
Jumping at the blind for your
bag of tricks
One too many needles made it
your last fix
Now you know what you really
were
Unemployed man something
will come your way
Park benches at night, but what
about the day?
You'll live like you are without
your well earned pay
Will you stay the way you are?
Troubled men, troubled women,
what are you all about?
Something is missing, something
is gone, but I can't figure it
out
Your cries are so deep, I can
hear them aloud
But you and I are just a face in
the crowd

Renee Jackson
IF YOU DARE
Oh man of my dreams,
come tantalize me with
your bewitching ways...
If you dare!
Oh man, believer of yourself,
come stalk me with your
sly and cunning wickedness;
snap at my vine of riches
with such zeal as you possess,
if you dare!
Oh man of my dreams,
hypnotize
me with those startling
eyes of gold; come pounce upon
my very soul; read my heart,
gaze into my pits of darkness
through to my enlightened
horizon; grasp my secrets,
if you dare!
Oh lord of thy jungle,
snatch me out of my solitude,
steal my breath away, soar me
to
my highest heights, rest my
fears, take my mind...
if you dare!
Enter into my world, feeling so
welcome, as you may;
tame me, cure me of the inner
wildness which flows so
freely within me.
Engulf my heart with every
ounce of your masculinity...
if you dare!

Thomas F. Reece
MEMORIES
It's so easy with you,
The hours pleasant, mellow
in time. I gaze at your
photograph, the memories
flood back. I fear some
day you may not return. As
the days have past I find
my love has grown with each
passing moment; I tried not
to allow this, I may not have
wanted it; but now I find
I'm so much better for it.

Alicia S. Medina
GRACIA
Tus ojos, dos pedazos de
eternas noches donde los rayos
de la luna se filtran juguetones,
entre el espeso follaje de tus
pestanas angelicales, cual dos
majestuosos abanicos de
preciosos pavos reales.
En tu carita blanca, cual
petalos de lirio, un tenue color
de rosa se atreve asomar a tus
mejillas, dando a tu semblante
la solemnidad de un cirio.
Tu nombre lo dice todo, eres
Gracia, dulce y sencilla.

Renee Cawley
UNIVERSE
It's uncomprehendable
vastness has inspired and
started dreams.
It's mysteries and occupants
are sometimes alive it seems.
Sometimes it's only a picture,
but sometimes it seems so real.
We wonder how it all started,
and the truth is so hard to feel.
With all the questions we ask
of it, answers are rarely received.
Being is so hard to understand
and sometimes so hard to
believe.

Jerrie Hejl Collins
RECOGNITION
I caught you unaware,
and behind you eyes
I saw your soul
stripped naked of all pretense,
looking from the depths of
your anguish and despair -
crying out to me,
begging for relief
from the burdens
you could no longer bear.
And how I ached with every
nerve to touch your hand,
to kiss your eyelids,
to let you know I understand!
I understand because
you see,
your eyes were simply
mirroring me.

Gloria Anderson-Harris
IF...MY LOVE
If I can be with my love,
Yet not in his presence,
And still feel his touch and
Respond to him a billion
miles away.
Then I am truly, wholly, totally,
completely
Beyond a shadow of doubt...
in Love!

Theodora W. Nichols
INDIA
India! The name has charm!
India is mystery!
To find it men sailed round the
world
In search of fortune, spice, and
tea.
No picture, comment, tale, or
rhyme
Reveals her total fantasy
Her secret haunts the Western
mind
And turns the pilgrim Sannyasi.*
The peaceful scenes of evenings'
fields
Himalayas' white capped
majesty
The smells, the sounds, the
swarming crowds
All weave its varied tapestry.
India's the Taj Mahal,
It's Kashmirs' dappled greenery.
Houseboats, servants, palaces,
Recall its fabled luxury!
India is squalid slums
Starvation, death, and misery.
India is silks and jewels
India is home to me!
**Male members of a household renounce the world, take up beggar bowls, and leave home, never to return.*

Beverly K. Cupps
WONDERS
The wind gently rustling leaves,
Brings to me a peaceful ease.
The birds floating in the sky,
Lifts my spirit up so high.
The greenness of the plants
around,
Cause' my awe to ever abound.
The miracle of God's Creation
near,
Brings to my eye, a humble tear.

Catherine Shovan
A TEAR DROP
A tear drop,
A sculpture of life
Holds many memories,
From the beginning of time
A form of a crystal,
Reflecting each day
Contains many wonders,
That won't go astray

Earl Hopkins
VALENTINE
On this valentine day in 1982
There's no need for you to worry
Because my every thought is
and of you
If you need me, call me, and i
will be there in a hurry
Because you are beautiful in so
many ways
Not only in your looks, but in
every little thing you do
You even put sunshine into
clouded days
And turn gray skies blue
With a heart as pure as gold
That comfort me in every way
Within my heart your love i
hold
That fuel my soul everyday
Etc, etc, etc to my little love
flower
You are getting sweeter by the
hour
Now you are much too beautiful
for words to describe
Everytime i look at you i get
hypnotized.

Betty Lee Smith
THE STORM
There's an ocean of tears
in my heart
And the dam that contains them
has weakened
I am bent like a palm tree in a
hurricane of emotion
Lashed by the storm.
The winds of desolation
in my soul

And the lightnings of pain
have unleashed a tempest
within me
I am encircled in grey clouds
of grief.
I stand as the little dutch boy
stood
With my hand at the hole in
the dyke of my heart to hold
back
The tears
For if it should break it would
drown the whole world in
tears
Like the flood in the days of
Noah, and there would be no
Ark to save us.
Let the rainbow of love
Washed clean in the brine of my
tears
rise over the mist as a sign
The storm is over
And never again will my heart
Be subjected to this kind
of destruction.

Marisa L. Curley
NATURE'S CYCLE
I used to be a small stream,
barely flowing.
Then you came and encouraged
me to grow, to increase my
waters and become strong.
Together we were an expanding
river.
Our waters traveled between tall
mountains and deep valleys.
But now our voyage has brought
us to a great desert, where not
a drop can be found between
us.
Somewhere along that
wondrous route we were
blinded, our course changed to
one of silence.
'Tis not our end, we must live
on.
I shall become a grain of sand
now and travel with the winds
of misunderstanding.
Maybe we will meet again, both
of us being a different form.
Maybe you will be the great
ocean and will hold me within
your waves; in an old but new
life.

Vicki Lynn Morris
THE BIG MAN IN RED
The big man in red
was late one year
It was a cold winter night
and Santa had no reindeer
His sleigh was bright red
just like his suit
He had a pug nose
and he sure was cute
Now back to my story
sit down by my side
Now listen about the cold
winter night
Santa had no ride
It was in the North Pole
Where the reindeer were stole
By the Abominable Snowman
He's mean as a mule
and ten times as cruel
And how they got free
no one knows
Some say they flew free
while the North Wind blows
Back to Santa is where they are
going
While leading their way
Rudolph's nose is glowing
They got home late that night
Santa was glad
that everything was alright
The night of December 23rd
Santa and his reindeer
will no longer be heard
They now come on Christmas
Eve night
And by Christmas morning
they're no longer in sight

Edith Wagner
I LIKE HANDS
I like--
Baby hands, chubby and pink,
Reaching out
To grasp and to hold.
I like--
Little girl hands holding dolls;
Little boy hands playing with
balls.
I like—
The hands of teen-agers
Reaching out for guidance.
I like--
Hands of young married couples,
So much in love,
Starting a new life together.
I like--
Mother hands and Father hands,
too.
Granpa hands gentle and kind
to a grandchild,
Grandma hands covered with
cookie dough.
I like--
The hands of our priest
As he raises them on high
To God--whose beckoning hands
I like best of all.
I like hands!

B. Duffy
WINTER'S WORD
Where is the love I thought was
there -
Where is the love I thought was
mine?
It left it seems on a gust of air.
When did it leave?
Was it just yesterday...
Or a millenium ago?
What of our path through the
snow
Leading up to the sun?
When did time start to run?
I'm left with dreams of,
Plagued by thoughts of,
Bereft of...you.
The airy way you look at me
Fuels my fire.
You view my pain through
dreamy lies.
So many questions, so many
fears
Burn holes in someone else's
heart
With your careful guise.
Burn holes in someone else's
heart
with your faraway eyes.

Petal A. Beebe
DID YOU EVER
Did you ever
Cup a fragrant rose
Within you hand;
Look deep into it's heart ?.
Or watch the honey bee
As it does it's part ?.
Herein lies the miracle, those
Precious seconds of recreation.
Did you ever
At some time see
A bird in flight, a band
Of followers, ready to start
Another migration ?.
Or watch the caterpiller
Metamorphosis as it grows
Into a delicate butterfly ?.
Are you
Grateful for your eyes ?.
That allow you to see
The beauty beneath our skies ?.
These too, are God's creation.
So I ask in humble awareness,
Did you ever ?.

Ezma Greene Martin
THE LULLABY
Why do you sing so soft and sweet
When you rock your baby to sleep?
You sing as though you thought that he
Might be a bundle of Eternity,
Wrapt in ethereal light and joy -
I thought him just a little boy.
No! He's a man, tall and straight,
Helping to guide the ship of state,
Helping God in his plan to win
A wayward world back unto him,
That man may not molder in the dust
Of earthly trifles and lurid lust.
And his shoulders will ever be
Squared to the tasks that set men free,
Squared to the tasks that many may rise
To God's full purpose in the skies,
Set to the work that makes men strong
As they strive to triumph over wrong.

Cathy McFarlane
MY LOVE
When I'm in your arms
I don't know fear
When we're apart
I wish you were near.
You're the one I love
Who's so special to me
We'll always be together
My husband you will be.
All our dreams will come true
We'll be happy for ever more
We'll do everything together
All the things we're hoping for.
We'll have our little children
Who we'll raise so good and kind
We'll be one very happy family
Loving each other we won't mind.
I will love you dearly
Till the day I die
And make you very happy
Oh my love, I will try.

Judy Ann (O'Brien) Spaulding
WONDERS OF LIFE
Life is filled with many wonders,
And many beautiful things;
Like the sunset on the water,
Or the joy a songbird brings;
Like the beautiful snow white dove,
Or the early morning dew;
Even a mother with her love,
Or the things a child can do.

Hilda Adams Bonebrake Suter
WOE IS ME
I live in a world that no one knows, a secret house submerged in woes.
I worry a lot about this 'n' that, whether too thin: or am I too fat?
Perhaps today I should laugh or cry, will it storm too much, or be too dry?
The state of the world? only Heaven knows,
It can not be worse than all my woes.

Mary Beth Wigger
GRANDMA'S DILEMMA
Many are the precious things I sneak
While time pressures wrinkles on my cheek,

And value bedecks each worn antique.
My hoard of rubbish is now unique!
Eggshell china from another age,
Tearstains on a thumbworn page,
Remembered words of an honored sage,
Worn photographs of some personage.
How can I learn to disengage
From the frivolous useless flowerage
Of bric-a-brack in harborage and
From books and papers in surplusage?
I think, perhaps, it might be wise
To learn, somehow, to close my eyes,
To use my head to rationalize
And the city dump to patronize.

Clare Salata
MOTHER TO SON
My son, I see a mature man
Readying to do what he can
To make life better and more sane
For those of us who do complain.
Please know and feel that I do care.
I pray and cheer for your welfare.
Take your day, your life in your hands,
A fan is seated in the stands.

Gary R. Whittle
TOWN HOUSE
When we lived in the furnished town house
Plain brick things among big trees
You went to the laundromat
Another plain thing across the grass
Shaded skimpy grass that whispers of pixies.
When we lived there
We were not plain things
Even on bleach afternoons
Or on tree obscured nights of unfaltered moon
Where we proved to be exotic
Or at least more so than the place.
When we lived in the furnished town house
Breath quick as our needs
We knew where joy lived in the heart
We took no note of future or of past
Consumed in our present Odysseys.
What we could give there
Were records and inexpensive rings
A constant concern with tunes
A steady casting of homemade runes
To ferret out new days quixotic
Afterthoughts from this brief grace.

Karen B. Hessoun
STILL
There you are and here I am -
wondering, waiting, wishing
to see you, hold you
to tell you that I've missed you.
But, there you are and here I am -
still wondering, waiting, wishing
don't see you, don't hold you
and I can't tell you that I love you.

Maria Kosar Mills
AN ODE TO DENNIS
The body was crippled
That I might see,
that beauty within
Is greater with Thee.
Sweet innocence and courage
Conquered each day,
Is the finest beauty
A heavenly array.
A Mother's love and Father's strength
A Son to love, a beautiful blend.
The outer shell withers
As years ascend.
But the love we share
Is a spiritual friend,
That will unite us together
As time descends.

Carolynn Tribby
TODAY
Today I found a flower
Growing 'tween some rocks.
Today I let a bullfrog go
That I had in a box.
Today I had a sumptuous meal
Though 'twas only bread and wine.
Today I helped a rabbit
Who was caught within a vine.
Today I wished on all the stars
That I know are right above.
Today, I found love.

Marion Novatkowski
CHRISTMAS EVE
T'was the night before Christmas when all thru the house
my little brother was sneaking just like a mouse.
He was snooping thru stockings that were hung with care,
in hopes that no one would see him there.
He unwrapped the presents that Santa had brought
instead of behaving like a good boy ought.
I sneaked down the stairs and saw him there,
under the tree very much unaware.
All of a sudden he saw me there in the door
and he scooted upstairs to be seen no more
Till Christmas morning
When he promised to be good the whole year thru and we all understood.
I dedicate this poem to Kathy and Joe

Judy A. Thatcher
LOVE'S PRECIOUS GIFT
I smiled at her and whispered in her ear
She gave me a gift, money could never touch
Then I kissed her lips and held her near
And whispered oh so softly, I love you very much
With my heart and soul I give
All that is precious and dear to me
My love as long as you shall live
Your kiss I'll carry in my heart
I keep these things in sacred trust
It bids all loneliness when we are apart
For I am rich, for having just
This precious gift you gave to me
With whom we'll give our love and care
This gift of our life and love
With you I'm so happy to share
A child of love as is the dove
I'm proud to be a part of this precious gift of LOVE.

Judy Fisher Amerson
BEHOLD THE LIGHT
The sun seemed to leap into my very soul radiantly glowing with the light of hope, assuring me of the beauty of eternity, awaiting, secretly smiling at the wonder of all, daring to show a brief prelude of Eternities treasures.
Reclining on the soft pillows of clouds thoughtfully reflecting of some secrets revealed, wondering perhaps of too much shown, sighing reassuredly at the sights below, a hint of sadness darkening his brow, realizing that all was the same as before.
Few realizing what their eyes beheld, answers to most doubts and fears reflecting off the sun's radiant glow, steadily reassuring them that the beauty of the earth is but a shadow of what is to come!

Francis O. Stein, Jr.
UNTITLED
A man had a thought
He was a part of life
A puzzle-piece you might refer
Born of his own time
Astrological signs if you prefer
And he wondered
If he helped life pass the time
Or was given time to pass
And he wonders

Dixie L. Lippert
TOO SOON
As I encounter part of the
mysteries of life,
I feel as though God is within
my reach.
I feel time slipping through my
fingers,
Like sand, being washed from
the beach.
At these times I get to thinking,
About life, and the existence of
man.
And it makes me realize my
insignificance,
And I wonder, Where do I fit in
God's plan?
I'm overwhelmed with a feeling
of frustration,
There's still so much in this
world, to me, that's unknown.
Looking back at my life, it
seems so meaningless,
And too soon, death will come,
and claim me for his own.

Laura Ami
TRUTH
There is one thing I've learned
in this long life of mine.
Everything is transitory;
There is no permanence in love,
nor in the ideals of today.
I cannot turn to God for help.
He lost His only Son
for man's infidelity.

Opal Zimmermann Towns
FOR SAKE OF ARGUMENTS
You argue with signposts, three
monkeys, me,
That only your opinion one
should utter.
I take you at face value, until I
see
The other end, and this, my
friend, I mutter:
He who knows *everything* has
much to bear!
Then, I must give prescription,
without stutter,
For sake of arguments I cannot
share:
Go!—Hurry! *Gargle well with
peanut butter!*

Cinde Anna Bauer
HIDDEN AWAY
Peel away the emerald veils,
Remove the threads of silk,
And there you'll find the lovely
pearls
Whiter than milk.
Or else you'll find hidden there
Straight rows of nuggets gold,
Or rows not so straight you'll
find
In the beauty that you hold.
A thief! a thief has ventured in
And stole a few away,
And leaves you with the half
filled rows
To look at with dismay.
Sometime you will catch the
thief
And then you are forlorn,
How very sad you are to see
A worm is in the corn.

Lee Leslie Larry
CAROLE
Bright eyes
Smile gaily
Fluttering
In the wind
Sparkling in
The moonlight
Northern sun
Swept ashore
On the Atlantic
Tidal wave
Hello
Sweet peaches

Elmer Beck
EXTRA LONG FOR FARAWAY STARS
Some guy has a fistful of stars,
Throws them into the sky.
Then a smart alec guy
Calls one star Venus and one
mars,
Says the stars are big as the
moon.
He is nuts! I could swish
All the stars in a dish
If I had a long-handled spoon.

Connie C. Pritchett
WHERE DID THE LOVE GO?
Where did the love go?
All those years
When we had our first kisses,
held hands, and made love so
very passionately,
As If...
the world would end
tomorrow, and we would
never be together again.
Where did it go?
The years when we talked on
the phone for hours only
wanting to hear the other's
voice
The happiness we found in...
Just being together
The long walks in the woods
dreaming of our future
together...sharing, hoping,
wishing for a wonderful life---
Together
Where did it go?

Michelle A. Klecka
A LONELY GOLDEN
As I sit in my rocking chair,
Memories cross my mind,
How fifty years have come and
gone
They're just an inch in time.
Forty-nine years, we laughed at
days
that happened to be ours
We loved and lived the best we
could
Within some broken hours.
We held each other, oh so tight
Through our growing pains,
We cried alot and learned alot
But took whatever came.
Forty-nine years, we toasted
then
A long and lasting love
Today, I'm toasting once again
Alone, but still in love.

Larry R. Graham
FUEL OF OUR FIRES
How is one to feel or see
What to do and who to be;
High and mighty, or content,
Satisfied or over spent.
Being content with one's self
Is virtuous in the realm of
wealth;
Contentment in being skilled or
wise
Is to humanity a vice.
Only the one who is unsatisfied
Will be the one to have tried
To attain higher and higher a
goal
Not appeased in a triffle of
soul.
Such is the way our Lord desires
To make discontentment the
fuel of our fires,
Striving more and harder to be
Examples he longs for us to
be.
And to mankind 'twould be a
crime
To end our growth before its
time;
So shatter contentment of what
you are
For in God's will you'll yet go
far.

Joyce Suter Whitcomb
SPRING
The smell of spring is in the air;
The lilacs are in bloom.
And housewives open windows
wide
To let their fragrance fill each
room.
The feel of spring is in the air;
It's borne on every breeze,
And wafted in the gentle winds,
The blossoms of the apple trees.

The look of spring is in the air;
You see it everyplace,
Brides are putting on their
gowns
Of silk and satin, beads and
lace.
The sounds of spring are in the
air;
You can hear the willows weep.
And winter, listening to their
song,
Goes quietly home to well-
earned sleep.

Bert Van Cleve, ASCAP
I WILL TAKE YOUR HAND
I will take your hand,
Trying, in a gentle way, to show
you life's reality.
Maybe I can help you see
Things the way they truly have
to be
As you face up to each task.
I will take your hand,
Do my best to lead you through
the longest night,
Leading with a kindly light,
Backing you to win your
toughest fight,
Knowing you will do your best.
I will take your hand,
At your side with steadfast
strength to comfort you,
Helping you to follow through
In whatever you may have to do,
Bolstering your spirit when
you're pressed.
I will understand
Anytime that you may need an
arm to lean upon,
When it seems all hope is gone,
In the darkness just before the
dawn.
Seeking surcease from life's
bitter quest,
I will take your hand, --
I am your friend.

Walter C. Stout
TO TURN THE OTHER CHEEK
Lord, give me a sign
That I may know
How much abuse to take
From one who'd speak
Ill words, and when
To turn the other cheek.
Help me to see, oh Lord
The wisdom of rebuke -
To judge the timing
Of words from Heaven,
And why you answer
"Seventy times Seven".
Have I no rights
Nor self-defense
To use against my foe?
Must I display a spirit weak,
And hold my tongue while once
again
I turn the other cheek?
Make known Thy presence -
Hear my plea, oh Lord.
Give me a sign,
That I may be the judge
Of when to turn the other cheek
Or wrongly hold a grudge.
Control my wrath, oh Holy One,
And bid my voice be still.
Keep my temper in close check,
That I may not a vengeance
wreak,
And heed Your wise, repeated
words;
to turn the other cheek.

Phyllis J. Lowery
SILENCE
The being...
Drained...
void of once known feelings!
Empty glasses...
Traces...
The wine of you and I!
Vacant rooms...
Stale...
Once full of laughter...
No longer a home...
No longer a...
No longer...
No...
...
...
...
"Silence" ! ! !

Bren Eve Smith
SEEKIN TRUTH
True love comes from deep
within our inner belonging,
We'll plant a seed and feel it
grow into a deep and lasting
devotion.
Holden a firm grip on reality of
romance, not to slip or fall.
I will remain lonely and starved
for your love,
Than to be burned by temporary
passion!
In reaching across the chasm of
our differences,
Hanging on to each other's

hands and hearts,
I kept my heart locked up so
tight to be safe.
But there's nothing in my heart
to steal.
Music, poetry, memories,
mutual needs and desires of
our
Life's rare pleasures;
In a warm summer's breeze, we'll
run through sweet smelling
Clover fields.
Patience with each other, we'll
give for the heart's wisdom,
Foresight is much better than
hindsight, not too late for a
sorry,
Never for us who really loves.
Our rivers will always run deep,
and drift along in
peacefulness.
As we're apart there will always
be a star shining a message
Of light on our loneliness,
With a sparkling promise of
maybe a new tomorrow.

Frances G. M. De Costa
SWEET THE SORROW
Moonlight on a empty bed -
My soul calls out
Straining against the edges of
solitude.
The long journey from darkness
to dawn
Sweet the sorrow of my
experience.
Your shadow reflected on -
Like the night enfolds me.
What is love, that she has
Such domination over my heart?

Carol Walton Smith
CRITTER
Constant thoughts - and
questions. What is
Realistic and what is
Imaginary?
The waiting & the wondering
Has made
Time
Endless. If I had answers and
Reasons - I could move on.

Frederick E. Pooler
A CHRISTMAS FOR ALL SEASONS
We put away our Tinsel
and Folding Trees of green
Santas boxes and Toys
and Piles of trash to clean
The wrapping and Ribbons
All packed away for the year
With the vacuum cleaner
erasing our holiday cheer
Chilly Little Kids
Home From Trying their sled
Pounding and stomping
demanding to be Fed
Christmas has come
and gone Too soon
By a glance at the calendar
its the tenth of June
All Through the year
The idea of Christmas we
can't remember
And wind up giving it all
on the 25th of December

Verna Golden Force
RETIRE - ME?
The time has come,
The days arrived-
My birthday-
I'll be Sixty-five.
It seems like yesterday-
At Twenty-five-
I was speculating-
On reaching Sixty-five.
The options were open.
Choices galore.
I would do the things-
I'd not done before.
I would buy a car-
A new one this time.
Trade in that old-
Jalopy of mine.
Put money aside-
Save a bit.
Perhaps-
Even take a trip.
Then came the Weddings-
Not one-but two.
I decided the old car-
Would have to do.
The years passed quickly-
As I put aside-
All those day dreams-
Of age Twenty-five.
So - - todays the day-
It's finally here.
Retire - Me?
NOT THIS YEAR!

Christine King Shrum
NEO-LANGSYNE
Perched beneath the perimeter
of infinity
Newborn sun, arises,
Emerging from within horizons
Of new year's fertile womb.
Crimson taffeta
Spread-Eagles
Upon dawn's golden belly.

Michael J. Colosimo
LADY AMERICA
With you standing in the harbor
With foreign eyes upon you,
You greet the losers of the world
With a touch of freedom by
your side.
Though your streets may not
Be paved with gold
Your arms are always open
And your heart is never cold.
Though many say you are
growing weak,
Just as many still stand proud
For it is here that their dreams
they will seek.
For Lady America
You feed the children of the
world
With your amber waves of gold.
You light a fire in the hearts
Of those whose have gone cold.
You open your door
To the weak, the hungry and
the poor.
To them who greet you at your
golden shores
You're a lasting paradise.
And like them who greet you
with empty hands
Lady America,
I'm proud to be living in your
land.

Cathy J. Harrison
A DAILY WALK IN GOD'S LOVE
There is peace in the valley
when we enter it with love;
seeking our strength and
guidance from our Father up
above.
Our feet will never falter nor
will we stumble and then fall;
if we walk the path that Jesus
chose for us and listen for His
call.
We have but to put our trust in
God and for his guidance ask;
and He will give us strength and
courage to meet each new day
and task.
We need never feel we walk
alone with our Savior as our
guide;
if we take each step willingly
and in His grace abide.

Kelly Rorabaugh
MOTHER
When you went into labor with
me you were forlorn,
Around Six A.M. I was born.
The doctor spanked me
and I cried,
That was the beginning
of my life.
Then as an infant,
so precious and pure,
Now that I'm grown,
you're not quite sure.
Even when the sad and glad
days have passed us by,
I'll love you mother,
until the day I die.

Evelyn Wiggins Sharp
WONDERING WHY
Ah...Who can view a beauteous
morn,
Or flaming sunset sky,
Or watch a bird soar on its
wings
Up, up, up, on high,
Or feel the chilling winter
breeze,

See clouds go sailing by,
Watch tiny seeds grow into
trees,
And never wonder why?

Kathy Irwin, A.
OUR NIGHT
I still remember, our night so
clear,
I held you in my arms,
in silent words, you gazed at me,
revealing all your charms.
I felt my heart expanding,
a love I must explore,
feeling all the wonders,
I had never felt before.
Your touch so warm and gentle,
the love within your kiss,
as I held you close, I found,
I've never felt like this.
There alone in darkness,
no one left in sight,
with last embrace, and kiss I
left,
with memories of our night,

Irene Lucido
JOURNEY
Skies were dark and weeping
torrents,
Earth was flame and timbered
might,
All the world was floating naked
In the gold fish bowl of night.
All the people stood and waited
For a sign must soon appear:
Were they dead and lost in
moon mist
Kneeling on a tear?
It was black edged grief in
limbo,
It was fire, flame and sword,
And with a hallelujah screaming
Came the creeping, crying hoard.
Came on feet of whispering
image,
The weak, the sinners and the
brave,
Crawling, pushing ever onward
To the comfort of a grave.

Mrs. Eron S. Hutchins
CLOUDS
Today as I gazed at the clouds
in the sky
I saw beautiful castles in Spain
And gallant white horsemen
riding swiftly away
In the rolling white mist of the
plains.
Sometimes they look like a
painter gone wild
With his brush marks, a
tumultuous scene
Drawn on the heavens - no
reason, no rhyme,
A jumble of strokes without
scheme.
Then again they're just wisps of
fine angel-hair
That float merrily away,
Scurrying along as if happy in
flight,
Like children frolicking in play.

Ethel A. Brindle
MY HOME STATE
Pennnsylvania, my native State,
We salute you,
commonwealth great!
We love your valleys, we love
your hills,
We love your rivers, and
rippling rills.
Your mountains many, so high
and green,
With mines of coal,
underground, unseen:
Iron and steel factories, your
industries great
Produce many wares for the
Keystone State.
With herds of cattle, brown,
black and white
Grazing in the pasture, oh!
what a sight!
Your fields of waving, ripe,
golden wheat
Bring food to the hungry.
Forget aching feet.
With orchards many, apple,
cherry, and peach,
And cannaries, too, to take
care of each.
"Garden spot of the world" it's
known far and wide,
Both beauty and usefulness in
it reside.
Pennsylvania Dutch, so sturdy
and true,
We like your fine food, rugs,
artistry, too:
Scientists, inventors, and
intellectuals, too,
And just plain folk, much like
me and you.
In colonial days you played a
big part
In forming the Union, so
noble and smart.
So hat's off to you, my own
native State,
You're the Keystone State,
Pennsylvania, so great!

Robert Fox
AFTERNOON WINDOW
The cool breeze is blowing
through my afternoon
window.
Sitting here, thinking of you my
friend; on this fine afternoon.
Have you seen her lately?
Have you heard from him?
These are things I wonder.
But what a joy that day will
bring when we see each other
again.
There's so much in the past
that's left undone
So much joy left to share,
So much love yet to be known.
Sitting here thinking of you, my
friend.

Cindy Starks
LONELINESS
Loneliness...
The tolling of a clock,
The echo of the t.v.,
The ringing of the phone
when you know the one
on the other end won't
be him.

M'ing
THE VISIT
A visitor for a night in your
house,
Between two items on an
itinerary,
I lay upon your bed alone
Except for gentle snores you
flung,
(Far down the hall) into the
night
Producing cosmic music in my
ears.
My sleepless eyes watched
The moon rise high and cross
the sky.
I yearned to tip toe to your
room
And lay my body by your side
To feel once more our skin on
skin
But other visitors slept nearby.
Your purposeful deterent?
I'll never know, will I?

Thomas K. Vincent
TOUGH LUCK
They think they're in hard guy
school,
you can see it in their eyes,
they're nobody's fool.
It's just a little something they
carry in their cool,
like reaching for something and
not having a stool.
It's not that you could say that
they are dense,
but the negative energy they
have is quite immense.
It's not at all that they lost
their common sense,
It's just that they ended up on
the wrong side of the fence.

Dorothy Brooks
HELLO!
What does it take to say
hello?
To tell someone, "I love you so."
To speak a word that means so
much.
To show you care
And keep in touch.
A little hello can mean a lot.
And put someone down,
In the right spot.
So get in the mood.
And please, do it today
Walk up to someone and tell
them
You just want to say
Hello!

Amanda Arms
LAUGHING EYES
Wise wrinkles
cover her features.
Her aged eyes
dance with fire—
(she lives in youth)
No smile needed—
for she has the understanding.
But—Old One
is of little use.
The true things
have disappeared.
Eyes of dying embers
dance no more.
She knows the pain
of sons gone.
The cooing call of
Mourning Dove
Breaks the dawn.

Angela Rancourt
BLACK AS NIGHT
It stood there black as a
hallowed night,
Its mane shining in the
moonlite
On top of the grass blew with
a torrid wind,
The skys threatened of storms
that have sinned
In the sunlite it ran, the
stallion.
The coat shone like a blazing
gold medallion.
A sound of terror rings from
the brush,
And someone running in a
terrible rush.
I look and see terror on the
ground,
The stallion lying there is what
I have found.
The stallion runs with its
mane flowing no more,
You see what you've done why
and what for.

Mariano D. Manawis
OVER SCENTED LOVELINESS
By his side, Intoxication
Is a lonesome alien.
Wine of the most exquisite taste
He disdains.

Over the riotous colors
Of exuberant wayside roses,
And the scented loveliness
Of the verdant meadows
Not far away --
Over them -- he raves.
Lost ...
He seeks his self in a crowd.
And finding himself not,
Finds aloneness in his stead.

Carolyn Tattersall
JOHN
His life was a bottle
of rare perfume
which someone knocked over
without any guilty feelings.
It ran red across a later
newsbreak and left
a stunned world to ponder
who was
across the universe.

Esther E. Upah
RUTH'S LETTER TO SANTA
Dear Santa:
Mommy says you are watching
all the girls and boys
So you'll know where to stop
with your bag of toys
I hope, dear Santa you've been
seein' how good a girl I've
been
I sweep the floors and dust for
mamma; I help her all I kin
I keep the toys all picked up
and the papers too
I rock the baby when he cries
and play with sister Sue
So now dear Santa don't forget:
I'll just keep on hopin'
Our fireplace is kinda small so
I'll leave the front door open.

Tracey Elaine Hubbard
JEALOUSY
"She was red-haired, green-eyed
Beautiful in her own way.
Charming and gracious, up to a
certain degree
If one did not cross her, that is.
She was as smooth as silk and
sweet as can be
When she got her own way.
But tsk, tsk, her temper would
flare up
If and when she had a little
contention.
Her green eyes seemed to gleam
with jealousy
And one was made to feel small
and petty.
So, is it any wonder she never
received a proposal?"

Wendy J. Bolster
TIME
Quality or quantity of time is
the question that is to be
As I think of time for you
And when I think of time for
me.
Keeping busy with work-filled
days
Yet taking time for fun and
friends
Is what makes up life's ways.
Quality or quantity of time is
the question that is to be
As I think of time for you
And when I think of time for
me.
Walking in the woods on
moonlit nights and sunlit
days
Being together you and me
Can bring us closer together in
special ways.
Quality or quantity of time is
the question that is to be
As I think of time for you
And when I think of time for
me.
Seeing you only for a small
amount of time during a few
days
Makes the quality of the time
we are together quite
treasured
Rather than spending a large
quantity of time together but
not always in special ways.

Esse Vaughn Dorn
FOR MYRON
One day (I don't remember
when)
you handed me a ruby, infant
leaf
and I held it then. . .
and you whispered something
(I've since forgotten
what you said)
but it's safe somewhere,
I'm sure,
within my head
and I put that love-leaf down
which could not save me
but now it seems
the finest gift
you ever gave me.

Clare Elizabeth Grinvalsky
I DREAM
I dream of being famous,
A writer, a poet,
A doctor, a nurse,
My dreams go on forever,
Here or there or in any place.
I dream of living in a castle,
The biggest in the world,
But no matter what I may
dream,
They may never come true.
In the morning when I awake,
I wonder where my dreams may
go,
They might go to the ends of
the universe.
Will they ever come back?
My dreams go on.

June Marie Alexander
AM I WELCOME
I wonder when the day is here
That life and I do part,
Will my Heavenly Father take
me in
Am I welcome within His heart?
Have I, when talking to Him in
prayer
Told Him all that I know I
should,
Have I, when doing a service for
Him
Worked as hard as I possibly
could?
have I willingly given my aid to
Him
In the many great things He's
planned,
Am I yet worthy and strong
enough
To take hold of the Masters
hand?
Is He proud of me for the things
I've done
Does He think I've served Him
right?
If this were the day and my
time had come
Would His open arms be my
welcoming light?
I have traveled many a long
hard road
To get to where I am today,
Sometime I hope to get back
home
Dear Lord, for this one thing I
pray.
I love my dear Father and I
know He loves me
But I've a question that stings
like a dart,
Have I, in my lifetime, been
faithful enough
To be welcome within His
heart?

Timothy B. Rogers
(EXPLANATION)

When I say that it's all academic
it just means that it can't mean that this time
it means more to me than just another trick.
With only one me to serve as a paradigm
how can I prove to be all of those things
that I mean to be better than I am.
No, I cannot, not without the dealings
definitions have no meanings, madam.
Understand, the world's not meant to be understood
by human brains—that we define as great.
Everything means nothing more than it would
if we knew what it meant to educate.
No less can our emotions be, from this view,
academic. And still I'm in love with you.

Walter Phillips
THE HUMMING BIRD

Upon a leaf
it stills
the reverberating
past.

Anodynos Goodman
LIKE YOU NEVER DONE BEFORE

Your eyes no longer glow with the
sunshine of your heart.
Your loves no longer like velvet,
you've pierced me like a dart.
You took from me without giving
and expect so much in return.
You cut through me like scissors,
with little or no concern.
Love me, need me, like you never done before.
Hold me, want me, theres nothing I need more.
Please me, keep me, you're the one I so adore,
Kiss me, miss me, Like you done before.
Your lips are no longer sweet with
the flavor of young desire.
You look at me with little passion,
your eyes burn me like fire.

Carol Wilcox Welchance
MY FRIEND

I cannot forget, nor can I regret
How we touched the same world.
Thrown together like two stones,
but lying smooth in the same stream.
A bit of a mystery
bit of a puzzel.
But lots of, I see. . .you see. . .
A star twinkles, the sun beams
Waters tickle, flowers say hello
But why is it, you had to go
I'll sit encircled
in this zoo
Play their mingeled games
but to my disadvantage, I sit in. . .pain
Bring back the sun, so I
can feel the same.
You. . .know my. .name.

Marilyn Loewen
THE FARMER

The farmer's a joker
Who lives off the land
Nothing works out
Quite like its planned
He works all day and
Worries all night
If the weather doesn't break him
The government might
His wife wants some wages
The kids want some too
He hasn't any left
What can he do
He can't go on strike
No use to quit
He can't get a job
His health isn't fit
The wife goes out workin
Comes home all beat
Hubby is hungry
There's nothing to eat
Weekends or holidays
Machinery breaks down
Dealers are closed
In city and town
Time to go fishing
But can you see why
At the lake it is raining
At home it is dry
The farmers a joker
Who lives off the land
If his work reaped more profit
Life would be grand

George T. P. Hubbs
AN HONEST MAN

A cold and placid world
befit with strife and grief,
An odd men out of the work of his tomorrows,
Yet, the fragrance of the glow of morning,
The afterness of the clean hot bath,
The movement of Love's passions,
The lingering of the vital signs of life
All are in his daily duty,
his task, his dreams.
The aluring men comes,
but once a day.
The woman strives for equality.
Yet, there is nothing said in their dialogue?
Of truth, justice, peace and understanding.
The times are hard to be truthfull,
To help calm the passions of lifes strife.
The man who is honest can he honest be?
For, with life the struggle shall always be.
The world looks strange upon those truthful.
This is the rare disease,
which men should catch.
The epidemic should be spread,
And truth, justice, peace and understanding
Shall endure for evermore.
The man who is honest,
can he honest be???

A. L. Scarborough
THE GIFTED

As a smile
A gift must be thought of
To be given and
A gift must be given
To be appreciated
Without appreciation
A gift has no value
Either to the person giving it
Or the person to whom it is given
To be appreciated
A gift must be understood
or again it will have no value
To be understood
A gift must be thought about
and to think about a gift
is, perhaps, to consider
The thought with which it is given
Which means acknowledging
Someone else's thought
And that, in itself, is a gift
To be given,
appreciated
understood
And thought about

Betty Belford Noreck
THE SNOW

The snow was crunching 'neath my feet
as I walked by the frozen pond,
and watched the skaters gliding by,
laughing gaily, arm in arm.
I blew my breath into the air
and saw it merge as fairy hair,
and wondered why the wind was still?
I guess it froze upon the hill!
The bitter frost had nipt my nose,
my cheeks were red, my toes were cold;
I tied a scarf about my face
and hurriedly left the fridgid place.

Far behind, I heard the click of
skaters playing "Crack the Whip",
and in the distance I could hear
the church bells ringing loud and clear!
. . . . .loud and clear!
. . . . .loud and clear!

Mary H. Bauch
MOTHER WENT AWAY

Little bird, haven't you heard?
Mother went away:
You won't see her anymore
As you did before.
Watching with delight
Your lovely flash of color
As you soar in flight.
Little squirrels, don't you know?
Mother is not here:
You won't see her
As you scamper.
With your bushy tails in fear.
Little flowers blooming
In her garden bright,
Mother is not here
To tend you
And gently water you at night.
How can you go on singing, little bird?
How can you chatter. little squirrel?
Why don't you wither, little flower?
Don't you hear me when I say
"Mother's gone away"?

Harry Edward Michaels
FLOWERS

In the spring they come to be
Gifts of nature for you and me
Buds of color fresh and clean
Which make a mild and pleasant scene
Then in summer they will rise
To things of beauty before your eyes
They'll fill the fields fragrant and sweet
For all the people of the world to meet
Then in fall they'll start to die
But for their death you needn't cry
For every year they come and go
And every summer they will grow

Cheryl'Ann E. Cabral
ONE MORE ORMOLU

He enters the room obsequiously
intently taking in the scene
apparently searching for a victim
to fullfill his childish dream
Walking toward her cautiously
trying not to use the same old line
he introduces his philosophy
not even asking her if she's willing to spare the time
He speaks of his horizon
and a place he's found under the stars
asking her if she has ever dreamed
of strolling through the field's of Mars
He speaks of Springsteen's message
and the sadness of Morrison's fate
he has caught her mind and entrapped it
but blows it all, by asking too quickly if he can enter her gate
She just stares off into a spacious void
wondering how such can be true
he had so much to offer
but it turned out to be the same old ormolu
Out there in that horizon
the one he spoke of with such intense
there is a man who is not full of bull
who believes his own mind makes sense
Who doesn't use women to build his ego
but share's his philosophy and is sincere
when she finds him, they'll make love under the rising sun
and with him she'll forever share!

Betty Belle Osburn
WANT TO BE READY BY AND BY
Gonna get it all together by and by
Want to be ready for that place in the sky
Gonna take all my sins
And toss em to the wind
Want to be ready by and by
Gonna beat the old devil to the draw
Gonna show him I can stand up straight and tall
He may try to turn my head
But its simply like I said
Want to be ready by and by
Will have to show my Savior that I care
If I really want to climb those golden stairs
I will turn my life around
And rejoice in what I've found
Want to be ready by and by.

L. M.
TRANSITIONS
Yellow Springs
floating over barren branches fall gently to the ground.
Red forms of nature fly in myriad patterns.
Brown patches of once leafy, lively forms are now crumpled in speckled breezes.

Cottonfilled air fuses with leafed gusts lighting on sticks, then falling to the ground accummulating a sea of foam.
Rays begin the transition.
Softened crystal disperses into apparent waste?
Transitions mold warm tender greens and azure above.
Then yellow springs.

T. M. Pulsifer
FRIENDS
Friends are dear, sweet, and true
and shouldn't be treated as a discarded shoe.
They can make you laugh or cry
but will never hurt you with a lie.
Friends will stay beside you through good times and bad; whether moods are happy or sad.
True friends are difficult to find
but when you find them, God is kind;
For He has allowed you and I to meet
and a friendship like ours is too difficult to defeat.

Scott T. Votraw
THE LONELY AUTHOR
One witness stands silent
a travesty of emotions is apparent
he fools himself into thinking
it's wise
then writes it down to present
but to whom. . .

Richard L. Holt
THE PAINTING
The years come with the colors of the seasons,
Like the waters traverse the rocks toward the sea for a reason.
Painting with an unfelt brush, held by unseen hand.
Age cannot be put to haste.
But pass it must and the eternal hope is a life passing without waste.
The hand no longer quite so quick and the heart changes rythmic tick.
Age born of years paints on relentlessly.
Oh, to be a flower and renewed endlessly.
Gently a canvas of flesh is made blending color to subtle autumn shades.
Quietly stroking away with a hush, takes the years to have a portrait made.

Merle Stark Preecs
TALENTS
Talents are treasures
We each like to store
But keeping them hidden is selfishness to the core.
God gave each of us something,
To cultivate and tend,
Be it singing, dancing or just things to mend.
Some work with their minds,
Some work with their hands,
But it all adds up to talents in the end.
Thoughtfulness, kindness, doing for others it seems
Are not considered, even sewing a fine seam.
Praying, teaching, preaching,
A nice way with words,
Is one way of helping others, yourself and the Lord.

Sylvia Sellards Hall
TAPESTRY
O, highway on a golden hill
Where leaves of red and gold would spill,
Where the snow of winter day
Would cover up the right-of-way.
Be not hasty in your flight—
Tiptoe gently thru the night,
And you will see her
Swift and free—
Weaving out her tapestry.
Oh, she's spinning, spinning
Day and night
To catch this scene of winter white.
As the world sleeps in its trundle bed,
Her fingers spin the magic thread.
Turning, spinning, happy, free
She weaves her lovely tapestry—
And as she lifts it to unfold,
There'll be leaves of red and gold.

Ruth Horton Uselton
AND GO WITH ME
To Black-eyed Susans sunning their faces,
And strawberries fattening in the fields;
To small Bluets Swiss-dotting the meadow
down by the wooden mill;
Go with me my love to touch, to see, to feel.
I'd promised them years ago that you'd soon come to see,
Grey rock carpeted in green beneath the apple tree.
I vowed the pines could see your eyes,
the wind could touch your face.
Queen Anne has donned her midnight pearl,
put on her spidery lace.
Please go with me to hear the frogs as they out-do the dove.
Please hold a time and moment still, and go with me my love.
Dedicated to Meadows of Dan, Va.

Pamela Prater Spangler
BROKEN TRUST
An empty space within my heart———a trust that now seems void forever; and who was the victim?
Was it you?
Was it me?
The promises that we made to each other———the love we shared together; did it not matter when it was truly tested? And now I wonder———did my honesty really matter, now that my heart has died?
I've stayed out of honesty.
My promises were not false.
I am not hard yet———
must I get that way to survive?
Was she worth this?
You knew from the beginning that the lie you lived could destroy me, but yet you held her in your arms, and gave to her the only part of yourself that you would ever share with me.
I'll stay with you my love, but only in body, as there is no heart at this moment but a heart of fear, sadness, and tears. My heart can never live again, not for you. . . .not for anyone. . . .not even for me.
The hurt you suffered before we met. . . . .did this set you free? If so, was it worth another's heart?????

Gladys Cummins Peters Kelch (Mrs. G. H.)
A TABLE BLESSING
Be present at our table Lord,
Bless us all and those abroad.
Make us Christ-like and good,
Accept our thanks for this food.
May we be strong in every way,
To meet the trials of this day.
Tho our burdens be large or small,
Wilt thou help us beat them all.
May we always listen to what you say,
And be humble when we pray.
Amen.

Sandy J. Hahn
SEEN AN OLD FRIEND LATELY
Have you seen an old friend lately
Did you tell him all that's new
I wonder if he seemed the same
The friend that you once knew
Years sometime take the best of us
While we struggle to get by
It makes that friend, that we once knew
A stranger deep inside
For one day, we may be him
Smiling thro our tears
Trying hard to let the old friend see
We haven't changed in years

Ellen Malis
THE ABANDONED HAVEN
The willow trees
Against the night
Are etched in black:
Lo, they cry out
For a song
that once was
Laid at their feet.
The promises that came so freely,
A dream of essence
Pure as gold:
Fleeing lovers,
Scattered remnants
Lo, they muse
Against the sky.

Harold Lloyd Mounce
WINTER
Winter Is coming around the bend.
Summer is leaving us once again.
The snow will be falling in the night,
Making no noise, just being quiet.
Children will be playing in the snow,
Falling and slipping as they go.
Christmas will be coming to all of us,
Bringing happiness and fun to everyone.
Everything will be pretty and white,
When you look to see that lovely sight.

Richard C. Fritzler
THE DEATH OF A CLOWN
For years they saw his smiling face,
no one knew the sadness it did embrace.
All they saw was happiness and love,
all his masks he wore like a glove.
He gave his all for love and affection,
but all he received was total rejection.
His belief was so strong it dimmed his perception;
his love was so strong he was fooled by deception.
The people saw him smile and joke,
but no one heard his heart when it broke.
The shattered pieces fell to the floor,
while people laughed and asked for more.
The end came on a Friday night of rain,
no hurt was left to feel the pain.
The end came slow and through

the night;
he drifted off, he had no fright.
No sight, no sound, no tears, no
more;
only the pieces on the floor.
The people were there waiting
for a joke,
nobody cared that his heart had
been broke.
For the first time in his life
he wore a frown,
because he knew it was—
the death of a clown.

Bernice Goodrum, Ransom
THE WONDROUS MIND!
If only the mind could be liken
to the wind, and when trouble
drifts in, it blows it away
again.
Oh, but the mind doesn't reason
this way, it always reflects
back to yesterday, as if to say
mentally you must pay.
If only the mind could be liken
to the sun, although covered
by the clouds it never seeks
revenge, but patiently,
continue to shine again.
Oh, but the mind doesn't
reason this way, it always
reflects back to yesterday, as
if to say, mentally you must
pay.
Oh, how I wish that the mind
was liken to sand, you know
its impossible, to hold every
grain in your hand.
Oh, but the mind doesn't reason
this way it holds memory of
every error from yesterday, as
if to say mentally you must
pay, for every yesterday,. . .
for every yester-year, and
there after!

Dorothy McKay
LORD, I KNOW YOU'RE THERE
Lord, I know you're There
I know you're aware
of all the things going on
of the nights when there no
song.
Lord, I know you're there
to help me thru it all
I know you're there to solve
my problems big or small.
Lord, I know you're there
when others don't understand
I know you're there to
give me a helping hand.
Lord, I know you're there
when others leave me alone
I know you're there to show me
right from wrong.
Lord, I know you're there
when troubles comes my way
I know you're there, YOU'RE
my hope and stay.

Harold R. Dyer
THANKS FOR THE SMILE
How do you thank someone for
a smile
When it brought you out of
despair?
How do you thank someone for
a laugh,
When hardly a laugh was
there?
Sometimes it seems like you
just can't go on,
Then someone gives you a
smile or makes you laugh,
Then, from within somewhere,
You feel an unsung song.
If only I had the wit, the phrase,
Always the right thing to say.
So I could bring a little joy
To someone every day.
But God doesn't make every one
to be funny,
Or be a gay debonair,
He gave some just a smile to
use,
So use it well, it was made for
wear.

Kevin Kilgore
AND WHEN SHE LEAVES
The song of her laughter
sifts through me
and the moment
she's gone
I am left
to flounder
in the wake
of her breathlessness
and I am
desparate
longing to be held
in the angora of
her youth.

Marilyn J. Vineyard
ENJOY THE ROSES
Life comes forth just like the
roses—
fed by elements and by love,
Gently budding and unfolding—
until
it bursts into full bloom.
Wind passing over, rough or
gentle—
bending here and bending
there,
Rain and sun cause growth and
fading—
petals fall, like shadows flee.
Continues not, and where it
grew—is
remembered some or not at
all,
So take time to smell the
flowers—
before you pick and give
away.
Touch the petals, soft like
velvet—
smell the fragrance, see the
beauty,
Feel the thorns that prick your
finger—
see their use to help it grow.
Enjoy the rose before you pick
it—
cherish it's meaning before
you share,
See it's value and nurture it's
pleasures—
then give with love and pass
it on.

H. D. Gray
UNTITLED
The world is no more stable
Than the top of a table
When one leg is less
Than the rest.

Ida Coyne
THE REASON
So many things are happening
today,
What is the reason for all of
this, we say?
The answer is, "Put God in your
life,
And things will be better,
Take my advice."
You will see smiling faces,
instead of frowns.
Trust Him—He won't let you
down.
He cares for the birds and
animals, too,
Trust Him, and He will take
care of you.
Nothing is too big, or small for
Him.
All that He asks is that you
give Him your love,
And He will shower all
blessings on you from above.
Don't fret about what tomorrow
will bring,
Trust in God, and forget
everything.
Ask for forgiveness, He is
waiting for you,
So keep your chin up, and see
what God will do.

Vivian Orrison
ROSES
God made the roses
Precious and rare,
Each petal formed with
Gentle care.
Sweet fragrance filled the
Air.
God called his artists
Each petal, to paint.
A rose to adorn the
Bride,
A rose to smile beside
One who has
Died.

Jacqui Grant
WINTER WHEAT
You trouble the edge of my
senses
Like the shadow of wind in the
wheat.
Westward, there is no sign of
clouds.
The sun has bled the sky
Through all these long dry days,
But the wind never warmed;
The wheat is not going to ripen.
(Memories of patient horses in
hot blue days;
Great golden heaps of grain.)
Harvest is almost here;
The hard wheat must be cut and
stored.
Somehow, it will have to be
enough
To get through a thin winter.
You move at the edge of my
mind.

Steven Aldrich
REPITITION
In the unknown reaches of a hidden identity, lies the unborn sacrifice of a human emotional collapse.

Forever bowing to a superior height of one's own understanding of his universal being.

To capture just an essence of this inner reality and form into words its total context, is but a repititious pattern of endless illusion.

Maria Elisabeth Mussenden
JEALOUSY?????
The man I love
Has found a young friend
Who he came to love, as a
dearest son
And in learning about life
Together they spend
Hours and hours. . .of every
day. . .
That I should feel jealous
People might tell me
That I shouldn't
My heart tells me. . .
When I see this man
Become as happy as a child, and
wise as a sage
When I feel that this happiness
Brings us closer together. . .
then I know
That I will never feel jealous
Because jealousy is the fear to
lose the person you love
But to be able to share this
person
Can be the deepest experience
of growth through love. . .

B. Jaye
YOU ARE. . .
You are the sun
That lightens my darkest
days.
You are the fire
That warms my dampened
soul.
You are the rain
That cools my angry mind.
You are the shelter
That protects me from myself.
You are the embrace
That soothes my aching heart.
You are the flame
That rekindles my dying
dreams.
You are the touch
That turns my fears to dust.
You are the air
That inflates my sinking
hopes.
You are the spring
That replenishes my barren
thoughts.
You are the whisper
That screams to make me
hear.
You are the eyes
That observe what no one
sees.
You are the thought
That always sees me through.
You are the heart
That believes in me.
You are the friend
That alone has set me free.

June Haver
GIRLS! DADDY'S AT IT AGAIN
A trouble light hangs from the
porch ceiling
The decor in our bedroom has
been severely - - disturbed
For Daddy's putting in electric
heat
To keep our old bones warm
this winter.
There are boxes of tools opened,
Electric wire curled in grotesque
shapes
Lies silently waiting to be
stapled and pulled
Into place.
Plaster falls.
Drills slip.
And it's always a miracle to me
It ends up right and even works-
Properly.

Craig F. Ross

A DECISION OF EXCISION

close press of flesh
mesh of fee and male
blood bond from the simple cell
meiosis and the belly swells
the foetus journeys up from hell
ovum risen to the bait
such is fate
inchoate. . .then incarnate
everything that rises must soon converge
but to what tune?
a birthing cry or a funeral dirge?
a vacuum purge or a delivery room?
is this womb spelled with a "t"?
shall it breathe?
shall it see?
God Dear God
who makes more than trees
God Damn God
decide for me.

Margaret A. Tupper

ODE TO A MOTOR HOME

I said, "Good morning there, old girl."
And patted her on the rump.
"Soon we'll be headed down the road,
Bumpity Bump."
The eyes of her soul shining,
Her voice purring right along,
The rays of the sun light up the path
Where the wheels will sing their song.
With soaring spirits, we'll be as one
As the road goes rushing by.
We'll greet each tree and bush and flower
As we play 'neath the azure sky.
Away we'll go to laugh and sing
Where we can be alone.
Together we'll search for adventure
In places as yet unknown.

Misha Meystel

ETA-KAPPA-NU

Eta-Kappa-Nu
Is a banquet
Kindly made to serve a cake,
Yet for the appetizer there's a chick
And the rest of it is very quick.
I'm longin' waitin' to meet new folks,
But I stay down under the big brown oaks,
But then I get up from the grass
and walk, and walk, and walk,
and pass
A cottage.
And in a window there is a pink dim light,
So I walk in it- and what a sight!
A man walks up to me and gives me a kite,
But the kite gets lost in the
Big Round White.
So, I go up and get the kite
and smell a roast in sight.
And the man serves me the roast,
So I take an...OOPS I MISSED !

Susan Jane Moloney

CYNIC'S SPECTRUM #1: WHITE

White January sky speckled, spotted, splotched
With dots, dashes of mottled gray. . .
White rigid hands, weathered and white-knuckled,
Hold rusty shovels. . .poised. . .
Over clumps, clots of slush-snow. . .
White snow slowly, seductively suffocates
All which it blankets.
White lines slash-cut ice-crusted roads
Twisting, turning treacherously. . .taking me where?
January whiteness screams in the wind,
Cries with the cold,
Whines without shame,
And whispers so very softly. . . of a sleep
Far longer than tonight's.

Kathleen Dunn

REFLECTIONS

I look to the past,
for the favor of a memory,
of happy times,
but always with that happy memory,
comes the sad realization,
that things have changed.

Maureen Sobrino

AN ADOPTED CHILDS PRAYER

Of all of the people upon this old earth,
there's none that I've loved since the start of my birth
more than I love the two people right here.
You're the two parents I wanted so dear.
I loved you, and loved you and gave you my kisses,
when you came along, you answered my wishes.
I prayed and I prayed for your love to show through,
and now that I have it I know it is true,
you loved me so much, deep in your heart,
that not even the cruelest could tear us apart.
I love you so much and this I do say,
when I kneel down, all this I will pray.

Jewel Ann Moreland

A DAY AT WORK

The sun that hides itself below the clouds,
The rain that falls upon the earth,
A star that rises in the midnight or
The sun that peeps over the clouds
Is my day at work.
The sun that hides behind a cloud and shows itself at noon,
A hand that reaches out to grasps a fallen star,
A song sung gently to put a babe to sleep,
A voice that shouts above a whisper,
A tree that withstands the storms,
Streets that are flooded one day and parched the next
Is my day at work.
The laughter of children playing and bells
that ring and the buds of flowers in the Spring
Is my day at work.
But, wherever, I may go,
It is the laughter of children playing
And the songs that gently put a babe to sleep
Are memories that extend the day.

Mr. Audrey J. Cain

MAN

A man is educated if he knows
The word of God, his fellowman,
And how to treat both friends and foe,
The road of life its ups and downs,
Its curves and destination,
The prize that lies beyond the grave,
God's love and his creation.
If he could understand the fowl,
That flies from zone to zone,
Or the smallest of the flowers,
That grow among the stones,
The clouds that float across the sky,
The stars in heaven above,
He could begin to understand,
The greatness of God's love.
He lives and learns from day to day,
The common things of life,
And puts to test the very best,
And tries to shun all care and strife,
His life he plans and on he goes,
To do the best he can,
If he was to be left alone,
What would become of man?

Cynthia L. Lybarger

DARKNESS FILLS THE SHADOW—WORLD

The silence covers the earth,
The fog covers the ground,
Darkness fills the shadow-world
Something swirls' round.
Haunting music fills the air,
People run and hide,
Darkness fills the shadow-world
Over the village they glide
Silently they search the earth,
Seeking out a soul,
Darkness fills the shadow-world
Stalking, sure and slow.
Invitingly he stands alone,
He watches them descend,
Darkness fills the shadow-world
No one is his friend.
Hopelessly he calls for help
He knows no one will come,
Darkness fills the shadow-world
They have caputed one!
Silently he screams in pain,
There is no one there to hear,
Darkness fills the shadow-world
He hears their silent jeer.
He sees them kiss him,
Tho' dead he seems to be,
Darkness fills the shadow-world
They mock his silent plea.
Forever, there, he watches them,
Tho' nothing can he see,
Darkness fills the shadow-world
Never can he flee.

Terri J. Hummel

LOVE I ONCE KNEW

Like roses in the winter,
The feelings I shared with you
Have wilted, the petals softly fallen—
The whispers of love I once knew.
Like a shadow in the moonlight,
It glistens faintly to die.
The wind rises, the stars fade,
Yet I wonder why.
The rain has gone, the storm has passed,
But still the skies are gray.
Where are the dewdrops, the rainbow, the sunshine?
Where is yesterday?

Wanda L. Van Deusen

NIGHT SYMPHONY

My love leaves in the stillness of the night, as quietly and as softly
as the faded rose petals drop and fall onto the highly polished table top.
I lie listening to the night sounds; the insects' incessant hum rising to a crescendo
until the rise and fall of my own breathing blends into the night's symphony and I sleep.

Lesa B. Peerman

ELOGUE FOR DEATH

For everyday there is a reason,
for every year there is a season.
The days grow long and I grow weak,
the time is short, I must look and seek.
If I only knew the reason why,
maybe then I would not have to die.
I've lost some friends, I've gained a few,
so why the hell can't I start off new.
I'm sure I know God wants me to die,
but what I don't know is exactly why.
So much fun, such laughter, some tears,
I told them all, I am going to die, no one hears.
No more games, no fakes, no fears,
excuse the stains, they are only tears.
If I should die before I get to say,
I'll say it now, good-bye, I'll see you another day.
For I shall watch you all from

above,
and send each one of you, my undying love.

Lesa B. Peerman

IF. . .

If I went blind, would you be my sight?
If I lost my mind, would you tell me what was right?
If I went deaf, would you be my ears?
If my eyes went dry, could you cry my tears?
If I would get lost, would you find my way?
Could you find the words I couldn't say?
If I needed a hand, would yours be there?
If I need reassurance, could you say "I care"?
Could you make me laugh if I gave up hope?
Could you make me try if I couldn't cope?
Can you answer these yes, and stay 'til the end?
Can you always be you, a true and real friend?!

Alene Williamson

HOPE

My love, oh my love
It has been a life time since you left me.
You left me in desolation.
My heart is as if it had been transported to a lonely, wind swept, rocky, barren, beach with the only sounds of life the clashing of the waves against the rocky shore line.
A place so lonely and desolate even sea gulls shun it.
And yet a tiny ray of hope peeps through
And I know that God at least is with me.
I can feel him in the waves crashing like cymbals on the rocky reef.
I can see him in the distant flying gulls, in the blue skies, and on the breeze that sighs as it blows upon the porous rocks below where in my imagination I stand
All is not lost for God is with me.

Mary Jo Whitney

TEARS

in the silence of my room,
I cry my silent tears.
Lonely tears, sad tears
The ones that waited all the years.
in the silence of my life,
I cannot hear the laughter
in the emptiness of my heart
are just memories of "happily ever after".
I have not closed the book just yet,
I'm unable to find the meaning of forget.
in the silence of my mind
I return to cry.
Silent, lonely tears
the ones that began the ocean.
all these years.

Mary Elizabeth Cianos

A REFLECTION

A smile on a child's face generates an inner joy;
Precise words one finds unable to employ.
A precious moment when one can call a child his own;
This to me will never be known.
A reality for many, but for me a dream;
Life presents unanswerable situations it seems!
The wound, however, will never heal;
Endless, as the revolving cycle of a wheel.
The constant feeling of anguish;
It will never diminish.

Goldie L. Heath

ETERNITY

Till time has no meaning,
and love knows no bounds.
Till the rivers run dry,
and rainbows touch ground.
Till all darkness is light,
and earth becomes heaven.
Till skies are never grey,
and God is the way.
I'll love you that long.
Till there's peace on earth,
and no more sorrow.
Till love of mankind is life's only tomorrow.

Till space is a part of everyday life,
and no one knows anymore trouble or strife.
I love you that long.
Till heaven and earth become just one,
and every day is filled with sun.
Till all the poets run out of rhymes,
and no one knows the meaning of time.
Only God knows,
I'll love you that long.
"FOR THIS IS ETERNITY"

Ellen Lusak

DREAMER

I dropped in on life today
(I lived a dream before)
And perceived realism had nothing to say,
So returned to my dream once more.
For dreams are not so earthbound
With obtuse and mortal ties;
Often reality's only sound
Is reverberating lies.
So which is better of the two?
A lie, or fantasy?
It may be escape, that is true—
But not if the dreamer is me.

Melinda Laraneta

UNTITLED

What becomes of our humanity
When mirrored eyes refuse to see
The sunlight, pie-sliced mid green leaves
Or lark songs fragrant as a breeze
Of air so fresh eyes tear to breathe,
Til all of beauty left to read
Begins and ends "a man made thee".

K. C. Scott

PROBABLY NOT

If I left this place,
Would you miss me?
If you heard I was lonely,
Would you be my friend?
If you saw me in the cold,
Would you shelter me?
If I were to die,
Would you cry for me?

Betty Schmitt

GALACTIC DESTINY

Earth hangs in the night sky,
A minute shining bulb
on an interstellar Christmas Tree.
It grows old and dim,
The light goes out.
Without energy,
It grows weak and shatters.
Infinitesimal fragments filter down
Softly dusting the Cosmos.
An unseen hand, somewhere in time,
grasping a sparkling light,
Reaches out anew,
filling the empty void.
Destiny has been fulfilled.
An Ending and a Beginning.
Time is eternal.
The circle is once more complete.
Life will go on.

Georgia Ray

LITTLE ONE LITTLE LAMB

Little one of peace, now God will let you sleep, No tears of suffering, no wants of mercy, for now just sweet peace.
Your eyes did not see, nor your ears hear of life here on earth with us, But rest assured Little Lamb of God, our Lord will touch your soul and you shall see again, there in the house of the Lord,
For his home is a splendor of goodness, a light of life forever to shine, and all tho we could not give you life, you'll shine of love amist a home of never ending joy,
Dear precious little boy we'll always miss you so, but knowing you're in heaven with a family beyond compare, my tears can only hope that someday, I too will join you there.

Darlene Vendegna

DESPAIR

I feel tears welling inside,
sobs aching to burst forth,
and yet the door will not open
to release the flood.
I feel an emptiness growing inside me
that knows no bounds.
What is the cause,
What is it I lack
or want that can't be named.
I begin to question myself,
my moves and motives.
My blustery words and
carefree bravado
mask hidden sorrows
and fears.
I feel despair.

Phillip Sterling Price

DELILAH

Dear Delilah—Its you I really love
You light up my life—as Stars from above
Each time I'm with you—It's the beginning of Dawn
That voice, those eyes, Oh! how you turn me on
You are lovely, and beautiful—so nice to know
Let us stay together—I love you so—

Charlotte Crockett

ETERNAL BLISS

Some parents want their child to be president,
Or perhaps a doctor or lawyer will do,
Maybe a banker or an astronaut, to name just a few.
What do I want for my child?
Just simply this,
Be at peace with yourself, believe in God, and you will have eternal bliss.

Susan A. Williams

INLAWS

My inlaws are the greatest ever,
I couldn't ask for any better.
The treat me as if i am their own,
And always make me feel at home.
Whenever i need an ear to bend,
They're always around with theirs to lend.
I hope they'll read this poem someday,
I've written this for them,
in my own special way.

James D. Everitt

GLORY FOREVER

I see the moon, the moon sees me.
The moon sees Jesus, the one, I love to see.
God bless the moon, God bless me.
God bless Jesus, the one, I love to see.
I had a heart, so brave and true,
But it has left Lord, and gone to you.
Guard it well, as I have done.
For you have two hearts now, oh Lord, and I have none.
But I have something else for several lifetimes through,
And that is faith, love, and the spirit of You.
When you want me, and feel my work on earth is done.
I am waiting, Dear God, for you are the power, the glory, the only one.
And I truly believe and love you, and your son.
So I will be proud and happy the day You call me,
For, I know, I will have a home for all Eternity.

Jon Edward Von Gunten

THE PROBLEM

My mind in torment cannot wrest
the pearl from out the inky grasp
of tentacles of circumstance
whose slippery, random interlash
more cruelly thwarts my tortured quest
than vilest schemes of consciousness.

Mary Riley Rankins—Keeling
I WANT TO LIVE
I want to live
I want to love
While I'm here
I want to know
My dearest Love,
That someone cares
I want to live; I want to Love
While I'm here.
Life is too short
All too brief
To be spent in Pain and grief.
I want to live
So never let us be far apart
Give me your all, but most of all,
Give me your heart.
'Cause if you care
I want us to love
While we are here.

Mabel J. Crawford
TEACH ME
Tumultuous Ocean
Calm me.
Help me hear the voice of reason
In the midst of strife.
Give me a rock-like strength
In the presence of doubt.
Teach me the mirth
Of the dashing spray!

Give me the gentleness
Of the exhausted wave.
And cleanse me like
The sun-washed sand.
Heighten my perception
In the storm-tossed waves.
And grant me the peace
Of the low-tide calm.
Tumultuous Ocean
Teach me!

Jane Burton
THEY PROMISED
My mother,
My father,
They promised,
They promised.
I cried,
We cried,
And they promised,
They promised.
Once they were one
In spirit and in body,
Then they were torn,
And we are now half a family.
Their union was strong
In the beginning
But became weak
As they drifted apart.
Now the Divorce
Has left us all naked,
To cuddle to ourselves
For some sort of comfort.
They made a promise
That this would not happen,
They had promised it would not.
But it was nothing,
The promise was never there.
Now we are numb,
Only a single tear
Treads down our cheeks
They promised a promise
That was never there.

Betty Sue Martin
UNTITLED
I had a dream, just last night,
I dreamed you held another tight.
Strange, when these thoughts entered my head
I woke up, alone, in your bed.
You say that your life is complete,
Well, these words, Surely, I can repeat.
For you see, when my mind had cleared,
I realized I need not have feared.
For already in the time I've spent with you,
It seems my prayers are answered too.
If you could look back, through the clues,
You would see, I, too, pay dues.
For I have prayed hard and long;
For God to send a man who's strong.
If only for a little while,
One who could make me smile,
When your ready, you will go,
and we'll both be happy, just to know—
That ever and ever, since life began,
Our being friends, was part of God's plan.

Kerri Sawyer
HE'S STILL ALIVE
He sits alone, all by himself;
His only companions are the books on the shelf.
Yet, they do him no good, he can't read what's inside;
His sight is long gone, but his eyes can still cry.
He needs someone, someone to care—
To show interest in him, but nobody's there.
He quietly pleads for compassion and grace;
Grief can be seen through tears on his face.
He's calling to you, are you willing to hear?
Are you really too busy, or is it just fear?
He cannot hurt you, he's a worn-out old man.
You have no reason to refuse him your hand.
He only wants time and to be loved again.
He merely wants you to call him your friend.
He may be old, but he hasn't died yet;
He's still alive, though it's easy to forget.
Because he's not young makes him no less worthwhile.
His grin may be toothless, but it's still a smile.
He may not speak well, but he wants to be heard;
His thoughts go much deeper than a single word.
He's lived a long life—there's a great deal he knows.
He's shared in much happiness, as well as in woes.
There are so many gifts he wishes to give,
He only asks that you help him live.

Mrs. Luella Virostek
TO MY VALENTINES
Valentines, Valentines
All hearts and lace;
Love's all around in
Each heart, on each face;
Now wouldn't it be great
To tell others you care—
It's an old, old tradition.
Not just today, but
Each day of the year!

Jackie Blem
THE MESSAGE ONLY I CAN READ
Shimmering green eyes smile at me from across the aisle
Swimming in their depths there lurks a message only I can read
They've glowed at me in pleasure
They've flamed at me in anger
But always they hold the message. . .
The message only I can read.

Marlene Hankin
A ROSE
Fragile flesh petal of love
So tender and moist to touch
Delicate bud aching to open
And spread your velvet to the sun.
Ah—so quickly you lose your dew.
Paper-thinned by the gypsying touch
Of passer-bee and crystalling frost,
Till your petals carpet icy roots
And copulate with blackened dirt
To sense no more. . .to bee no more. . .

Clara M. Bush
CHRISTMAS JOY
Holly wreathes, mistletoe,
tied with a big red bow.
Catheadrel bells chiming.
Feathery snow flakes fill the air.
Presents wrapped with loving care.
Christmas trees glittering everywhere,
Children so good,
Kitchens pungent with holiday delicacy.
O! The magic of Jolly St. Nick.
With a heart full of love,
I wish you all the Joys of Christmas.

Athena K. Bass
LOVE
Love is like the flowers, and, the bee's in the sun.
Love is like the hearts, which form into one.
Love is like the skies accompanied by rain.
Love is like the happiness along with the pain.
Love is like the tears which roll down my face.
They are the words that love can not say.
What shall happen to my heart, if it shall part.
What would happen to the love within thy heart.
Rain may go, snow may come, but my heart will always be.
Waiting for the smiles, and tears together as we.

Paul E. Truesdell, Jr.
GREEK STORM
Black, anvil-headed clouds
Belching forked-fire: wrathful
Zeus venting his vengeful ire.
Thunderheads rumbling: lame
Hephaestus toiling at his forge.
Helius is obscured—
Midday becomes night.
Torrents cleanse Mother Earth, then—
With dark clouds scudding onward,
Helius and chariot
Reappear, moving slowly
Through a prismatically
Hued archway, homeward bound to
Olympia.

Dawn Russo Robinson
SMOKING OR NON-SMOKING, SIR?
With
nose twitching
eyes burning
throat scratching
air churning
in choking ugliness,
it is the age of
butt brutes.
In their
maucho-molded jeans
sneering yellow-teethed,
proudly puffing
their sticks—
burning white power
in slow
deliberate
boot struts,
They brag
of their victory.
Anyone
have
a
match?

Cynthia McNeese
UNTITLED
I have lived today with happiness in
My heart and love in my soul, Therefore
I will not be afraid of tomorrow and
What it might bring. . . . .

Tatiana B. Hatter
THY LIPS
Thy lips like a rose bud parting
In bloom.
Soft as a baby new from
The womb.
Thick and full, scarlet red.
Moist and tender as if
They have bled.
Kiss me with thy pure,
Sweet lips.
More pure and sweet than
Wine.
Kiss me with thy lustful
Lips.
And I'll kiss you back with
Mine.

Thomas J. Cooper
CHRISTMAS
Three hundred and fifty-nine pass by,
This month, the last, plus twenty-five.
Twinkling joy, a seasonal sense,
No bitter words will then commence.

Merry, happy, thank-you, and cheer
Are words spoken freely to end out the year.
Broad smiles proclaim a brilliance shear;
Christmas, a season deleted of fear;
To greet, laugh, to love all dear,
This season comes but once:
A day.
A pity though, why not in May?
Why not the feeling every day?

Marlene Danills Whiteker
SHADOW
I only see my shadow
Not the mark it makes.
For it leaves no indentation
Along the path it takes.
It floats along beside me
Filled with my emotion.
Never making judgements
Giving loyalty and devotion.
But like my other friends
It only wants to play.
And in my darkest hour
It too goes away.

David A. Hill
ALEXANDER, FROM HIS DEATH BED
The end at last draws near
And soon you shall in truth own all the world.
All that I have conquered and amassed,
All that I have taken and have known,
All that I have made secure, shall be your own.
How quickly have I been—
And now must pass from out this world of mine.
And all will think of me and say
"What was he? Save, sinew, bone, and blood?"
He who held the world before his eyes;
Who ended and created fear:
Who shaped a thousand pebbles into one great stone,
And by his own power held them in that shape
And to that purpose.
Not to gain the world,
But to gain the dream.
To realize all My hopes and My ambitions.
But no—it shall not be.
For dreaming empty, thru greed and envy
You will tear my dream apart-piece by piece,
And take what you are able, each for each.

Darlene Bennett
ALWAYS KEEP SMILING
The stream lightly flows, and the waves softly ripple.
The wind gently blows, and my ears feel a tickle.
The sun bursts with love, as it brightens the day.
The flowers dance gracefully, and bloom in array.
His eyes shine a twinkle, and the love I can see.
With all of this beauty, what sadness could be!

Mary Grace Dembeck
THE CHILD WITHIN
You try to hide, but I know who you are—
Big as an atom, small as a star—
You're the Wind when it whistles,
Fires that flame,
All of the known and unknown
Without name,
You're the calm and the quiet,
The truant and free,
You're all the wide world,
I know you,
You're me!

Joseph Duff
THE JUNKIE'S FUNERAL
"Wow! I finally came down!
That sure was some powerful stuff!
It was strong enough to change my mind,
About not ever wanting to give it up.

Man, my body feels so heavy,
I think I'll just lay here a while.
No wonder when 'The King' sold it to me,
All he did was smile."
" 'K. D.' was right about one thing,
When he said this stuff was strong.
Seems like I've been sleeping,
For I don't know how long.
Man, I feel so sleepy,
I can't even open my eyes.
I would like to get them open,
To see why they keep saying don't cry.
Who is it wasn't worth it?
Why do they say he was full of dope?
They act as if somebody died,
Or everyone has given up hope!"
"Wait a minute - this is a casket!
All this time I thought it was a bed!
That's ME they keep talking about!
I'm the one they called 'dope head!'
I know I didn't take enough,
To do myself that much harm.
Man, I only shot up half a load,
When I found that vein in my arm!
At least that's all I remember,
When I started to squeeze the cap.
From there, I draw a total blank,
'Cause everything went ZAP!"
"Somebody get me out of here!
I'm not ready to die!
I promise not to take anymore!
I won't cheat, steal, or lie!
Please help me get out of here!
I can't be ready to go!
I'm way too young to be dying now!
I'm not even sixteen years old!"

N. J. Beddingfield
DEJA VU
Perrimeter unseen,
The boundary of a dream;
An inkling of another sense:
The sheaves of which we glean.

Lokah
MOMENT TO CONSIDER
As this couple begin their life together in society
We ask from the ALL Mighty
That all people may live together happily.
That we may consider the needs of others and share with our brothers
So that each may be fulfilled.
That we may consider the wants of our neighbor and help him to savor
The beauties of earthly life.
That we may consider the thoughts of each person
So as not to judge too rashly, and worsen
The potential of Creation.
That we may consider our differences among ourselves
And resolve disagreements rationally
To assure harmony on earth.
All this we wish to consider for His name's sake.

James I. Carlson
IF
If I could love
wind through the pines,
If I could love light's patterns drifting across the leaf-littered forest floor,
If I could love the river slipping over rocks roaring to the sea,
If I could love brown mountains tree-scattered under the blue sky

Steve Tatge
ITS GOT TO BE
That look that glow that fits so well
No matter when, it's used right
It's just got to be.
No matter what way our colors of life are
Its when these colors or ways are turned into fine ideas.
Also a richer experience is attained for each of us
When each of us hopes we have that special feeling
As individuals we may never run out of things to do
It may be tough for us, but that is the way Its got to be
Proof is, everyone has got their own special style
And you know that's the way it's got to be, right!
For Me
My Pleasure and style
I'll Always Say
It's got to be mine.

Norma Knight Branham
WAR
War begins—dreadful, scary, lonely, hurt.
Death toils throughout the long piteous days and nights.
It tears and torments, reaching into the very depths of your soul.
War ends. Wasted lands stretch toward the horizon,
Precious lives lost for a cause unknown—lost hope.
To the dead, your torment is over. To the living, ah,
But it is the living that must in the early dusk
View the land and the dead.
There is the early morning, the sun rises as an
Infuriating sphere of fire. Stand and watch,
My friend, it is you whom it hurts the most.
Death denied you rest; life beckons you to the
Present and future. You were there and now
You are here, growing by the seconds,
Immune to happiness.

Douglas P. Knox
NIGHT (AN ACROSTIC POEM)
Almost blue
is the color of dew
with evening's finery
of gorgeous hue.
Increasing jet-black
knives of lampblack
mount on nightwing's
opulently plumed back.
Quintessense reverberates;
the stars tintinabulate—
unalterable veins rent by
wanderers' chiastic fates.
Then yearning zenith
yawns with zodiacal light.

Stanley J. Coleman
A BOY AND HIS DOG
Today I beheld a tragedy
But for the grace of God
It could have been me.
I watched a small boy and his dog
As they played upon a driftwood log.
So taken with their glee
They did not hear or see
The roaring tide that swept them out.
I saw them go and I heard him shout

"Will someone please save my dog?"
The image of that driftwood log
Is forever engraved in my memory
But for the grace of God, it could have been me.
The love of a boy for his dog
Has become a part of that driftwood log.

Rebecca Lane
BEQUEATH OF AN ANGEL
She reigns
Like her majesty
We perceive her as a goddess
In a flowing silk gown
With gold adornment
A symbol of purity
And next to Godliness
Is our queen
She shall honor us
With her legacy
She has betaken our path
As she so nobly watches over us
Upon her throne of riches

John A. Guilliams
WHISPER

Whisper, leaves of green and gold,
of the days when you were young and bold.
Whisper, wind of terrible might,
of the coming winter. What a lovely sight.
Whisper, snow with your clean coat.
A coat that covers the ground shivering with cold.
Whisper, winter nights of your stories, yet untold.

Pauline R. Doss Lindsey
THE CRY OF YOUTH

Were I older - oh, stupid, faltering me - with a chasm so deep between,
While others fight to find youth - yet I walk slowly - just to find you, it seems.
Were I older - never would I have thought my lips would utter these words,
Or even frame them - nay, not one tiny whisper lest they be heard.
Were I older - can you not feel the tumult - the tearing - the breaking of my heart?
Just one look - one kiss - one hour - would time stood still - we'd never part.:
Were I older - I could fight this creature of desire - the arrow that pierced my heart one day
When I first saw you - I was bound - helpless - with nothing to say.
Were I older - perhaps you would see in me a woman - a living, breathing creature,
Though perhaps my sands of time have not run so long - but just reach you.
Were I older - perhaps I could understand your doubts - your hopes - your fears,
Perhaps I could find the way to banish the hardness of those past years.
Were I older - would I be the Delilah - the Ruth - the many of the past?
Nay, none of these would be sufficient - make your love last.
Were I older - somehow I could find the secret whereby I would be
In your every dream - act - vision - oh, precious thoughts, do not flee!
Were I older - perhaps even I could clothe myself in knowledge of Soloman great.
Perhaps then you would understand that space of years or span of time is fate.
Were I older - perhaps you would open your arms - eagerly invite me.
Oh, that this mortal might ever be there - just being loved - free!

Jackie S. Lewis
THE HUNTED'S PRAYER

Help us, Oh Master Mind, Fear season has begun,
We must beware the silent arrow, dread the blasting gun.
My legs grow weary, my hunger ever strong,
The chase is always onward, I know not what went wrong.
My family is in danger now, my silent watch is needed,
I must not let my son endure this terror men have seeded.
Days and nights lose all rhyme and reason when they come,
And the sadness of acceptance bursts upon me like the sun.
I must take my leave from you, my dear beloved ones,
Please, go away from here now as I go to meet their guns.
We will meet again in forest green, where we will have no fear,
But now is not the time for us to continue living here.

James V. Conroy
IN THE FACE OF

Death's translucent image
crossed the winter sky;
a night cloud swirling shapeless.
endless,
without violence or remorse,
full of wind
and moon.
From the auk I gleaned the
certain knowledge
that survival isn't everything.
Ponder the extinct species
hibernating in encyclopedias,
tamed, forgotten,
pressed into knowledge and history.
The lone wolf shivers to see his shadow folding like a page.

Jo Starrett Lindsey
THE GIFT

I stand upon the hill and look
Below to where the city lies,
A twinkling spread of diamond lights,
Beneath the darkened evening skies.
The crescent sliver of a moon
Is tipped like a crowning jewel above;
This scene of dusk will be a gift
Which I will offer to my love.

Amy Colleen Church
UNTITLED

Am depressed again,
as always.
The person that is supposed to care; does. . .and I don't care; anymore.
The person that I want to care, is nonchalant; and I'm wanting him so.
The person that I used to love, I think, still loves me;
And I'm not impressed.
And that person at home, I'm wanting to be with,
but am regretting moments gone by.
And now I'm realizing,
that five years ago was the only time
that I was truly in love;
And I gave him up.

James Loren Barnes
GRANDFATHER

Damn clock, every breath taken
is echoed with the same tick, tick.
You've been a reminder, most of my life,
that time was running out.
Remember in youth old clock?
Both of us brand new and shining.
Many dollars spent for you, my prize possession.
What a fool that makes me!
One day, you too will feel the strain.
The very time told on that face will destroy you.
Gears will rust, wood will rot,
and some other clock will echo your past.

Joshua Urbina
THEY'RE SO UNFRIENDLY

Like a lonely sea hermit
I've been living in my shell
All my love they won't permit
Don't they know I wish them well?
When I speak so lovingly
They say, "get lost, go away"
They don't like to talk to me
What am I supposed to say?
They're So unfriendly and I am so friendless baby
I'm feeling empty won't you please be a friend to me?
Deep within my dismal mind
I've been crying silently
Hoping that someday I'll find
Anyone to comfort me.
When I open up my heart
They don't think I'm being real
So suspiciously they part
How am I supposed to feel?
They're So Unfriendly and I am so friendless baby
They're So Unfriendly won't you please be a friend to me?
Please love me!
Cause They're So Unfriendly and I am so friendless baby
I'm feeling empty won't you please be a friend to me?
Won't you please be a friend to me?
Won't you please be a friend to me?

Meredith Diane Moll
WINGS OF SONG

He watched,
Waiting to catch the elusive butterfly,
She, slowly came near the net,
Paused—
And then ran free,
Drifting along on wings of song,
With a free, untouched heart,
Free of pain,
Free to love,
And be loved,
With a smile on her lips
And laughter in her heart,
when will the fantasy end
And Reality begin.

Danita Houk
I FEEL. . .

"Hello! and how are you today?"
A hundred people daily say,
And press the how are you again,
Insisting 'I reply.
My pain threshold is very low
I 'hurt' today (and ALWAYS), so
It makes no sense to parrot,
"Fine"
When I feel it's a lie.
I've even tried to tell a few:
Say "Hi", but skip the "How are you",
Most people fail to care, or hear
The answer anyway.
But you should SAY 'Fine', they insist—
"You should. . ." (They tell me). I resist. . .
If I feel great, I'll tell you so;
If not, THAT'S what I'll say.
Who has the right to lay on me
The burden that I must agree,
And act, and think as others do?
Not you, nor anyone!
If ALL the world should disagree,
Still I must choose what's "right for me"
So, if I do not "fit their mold",
Well, I can stand alone.
P.S. And How are YOU?

Janelle Oldfather
THE STRUGGLE

I love the marvelous inner war that rages
Always searching for finer, deeper revelations
Struggling for a perfection that when found
Is only ground for another struggle yet greater
Each new understanding bringing another question
Each conquest disclosing another battle
Each attainment taking one to another beginning
And so the battle of the mind and body goes
Only in the struggle does life take on
Beauty and meaning, emitting the flavor of success.

Jo Ann Matthews
DEEDS

I try to think of some Great
accomplishment that I have
made to mankind. Some Great
deed that will be remembered
after I leave this world
behind. My thoughts are as
the clouds in the vast blue sky,
but they are void of any Great
deed in the years or days gone
by.
My heart is heavy and in total
pain because my memories of a
Great Deed doth refrain. But
wait, a Great Deed it does not
have to be for GOD has already
created the SKY the Earth and
the Sea, A GREAT DEED doth
HE.
My deeds that I leave behind
may go unnoticed, they may be
small and they may be few, but
my soul knows these things are
what God has put me here to
do. Small deed you may think
it to be, but great it is as
the beaches of sand is the love
God gave me for my Fellowman.

May Johnson Mitchell
THE RIVER OF DREAMS

The sun sinks down and darkness falls
Like a curtain at the end of day.
The star filled night and moon so bright
Send all weary thoughts away.
Oh, just to drift in a pearl canoe
Down the River of Dreams tonight
Just to hurry along past the

murmuring throng
To the dream of my delight.
As I close my eyes I seem to go
To the land where dreams come true,
And there be happy and drift along
Down the River of Dreams with you.
The River of Dreams is long and wide
And my dream is old not new
The dream that has always been in my heart
Since the time that I first met you.

Belinda Nava
THE LIGHT
I don't go where sinners go
and I don't hear what sinners say
Cause I'm the Light of the LORD
and I won't go astray.
See I used to be a Sinner
spent my time selling souls
but those are days gone by
I got myself some new goals.
I can see it all so clearly now
of what was and what will be
I've done my time in the fires of hell
Jesus set my spirit free
Now I don't go where sinners go
and I don't hear what sinners say
Cause I'm the Light of the LORD
and I like it that way.

Jeannie Carlson
WHOM THE GODS WOULD DESTROY
His laugh reverberates like the
shamming sound made by
beating a large empty enclosure
with rabid reality.
Lashing out at love,
He contradicts his catastrophic
casuistry
In his longing to embrace the
emotion
He efficiently eradicates.
He gorges his neurosis with
delicious
Deceit and appetizing
abandonment
Until he violently vomits his
overindulgences;
Floundering in his own
psychotic puke.
Benevolence and Hope are
rejected and
Agonized by the macabre
malfunction of the
Schizophrenic soul.

Julia Cathrine Murphy
DESPAIR
Today
Alone—
I climbed a hill
so high it seemed to me
I could have reached up
and stroked an Angels wing.
Even so near to Heaven
I had a longing
to fling myself over the cliff
and be embraced forever
in the gentle arms of
Death.

Sheree Bruner
POEM FOR LISA
Once I was told
all things are possible,
I remember always wanting
this belief:
A world spun silk, with magic
forging perfect moons
I hurl into stars.
Age is my betrayer
but I dream as I walk
the evening with my child
past trees and gabled houses;
to reach a flower from the weeds
to give her saying
"Look little dipper
if I give you nothing else
remember, hold soul with sword
to arm your dreams.
Look to the moon, Now."

Walter S. Brown
THE ONLY ONE
There is a picture on the
mantel,
that I see every day.
It reminds me of her,
and I like it that way.
I know without a doubt,
there will never be another.
How many people do you know,
that has more than one
Mother?

Carol Hebert
WE MUST WALK
We must walk
the narrow way
and
to each other give,
the strength
and joy
that only God
Imparts to those
He wants to live
Within
His Perfect Will

Marjorie W. Johnston
FROM GRANDMA
Why do I love them the way that I do,
I would give them the world to behold,
I'd build them a mansion that's fit for a King,
And sprinkle life's pathway with gold.
But since I can't do all these wondrous things,
I'll leave that to heaven above,
I'll give them my time and the pleasure it brings,
And most of all, give them my love.

Lisa Powell
NEW BEGINNINGS
The time for the new beginning has come,
Life has to start over and begin again.
Old loves have to be forgotten,
All hatred has to be dissolved.
The time for starting over has begun,
Hard times are over, now begins the road to success.
The child laughs as he plays in the streets,
Not knowing about what is happening in the world around him.
The new beginnings and sad endings.
He laughs while others cry,
Trying to find an escape from the pain.
Laughter is for the fool who does not care,
Crying is for the sad at heart.
The new beginnings are forever happening.
People at work being what others want them to be,
They go about their jobs mechanically,
Never thinking for themselves,
Always following the orders of others.
They're just waiting for the start of their new beginnings.

Colleen M. Dipietro
CHLOROPHYLL
Apples which aren't quite ready
for picking;
Her eyes after seeing my mink
coat;
The wreaths for the Christmas
Holidays;
Sour tasting limes;
My mom's famous split-pea
soup;
Pancakes on the 17th of
March;
The squirt of Spearmint
Freshen Up;
May at its finest;
Frogs leaping from the hands of
a small boy;
Velvety moss growing in
clusters near a tree;
The suit of Elk Grove's
Grenadier;
Popeye's strength builder;
My four leaf clover pressed
between two
thick books;
The traffic signal indicating it's
time to go.

Bob Alexander
THE DREAM
Can a dream come true?
It depends on how you view it!
Dreams are like havens on earth.
When a dream comes true, 'tis no longer a dream!
But we must have our dreams
or
We perish!

Patricia Ghering Wilder
SEARCHING
My son, oh my son, where are you so deep in thought, to share with me you'd rather not.
Is it so hard to share with me, those feelings that keep you company.
How can I begin to crumble the wall, for a peek inside to help when you fall.
A tear you are afraid to show to me, how can I tell you its' good to let them flow free.
Share you must your thoughts you see, it can help you, it can help me.
When did you start to build your wall? Was I so blind not to see it all.
So busy was I to take the time, to listen when you were little then.
Oh to take the years and time I would spend to listen and start again.
So excited you were to come to me, to share a thought, a bug, a mystery.
My attention was turned not to you I know. How I wish I'd have taken the time to watch you grow.
A stranger you are; so distant from me. My son, oh my son, help me beat this tragedy.

Marty Barela
BUGS
Creeping, crawling, not making a sound,
There's a bug over there, on the ground.
Hurry, get it, smash it to death,
Don't give it a chance, to catch it's last breath.
Smash! Crack! Crunch! You just killed two,
How would you like me, to do that to you?

Susan M. Julien
WINTER SUNDAY. . .FOR MY BROTHER
door creaks.
entering
your glasses steam
concealing frozen eyes.
mother hides
boughten fantasies
in antique coffee cups
percolating warmth
by laughter.
father runs fingers
over chipped crystal
old blood
pouring
new words
lips trembling
silent
his blood murmurs our name
his eyes listen
his heart watches
and michael
you don't know
you've only watched his eyes.
you must learn to listen.

Mark Aaron Robinson
THE ROCK ON WATER
How I love my rowboat;
My threepoint landings on the waves,
The wind upon my old coat
is the wearing that it craves:
wind that fearsome blows me,
far from pier and now,
to waters when I'm told he
got out by the bow, somehow.
As my aching oar strokes
his footprints on the water,
only a watershed cloaks
his steps and how they falter.
I see his hesitation
as he looks down at his feet.
He sank in desperation,
and that glues me to my seat.
And yet his feeble hand out,
was held, through sink and swim.
It helps me row my heart out,
with a grin, against the wind.

Rusti Lee Huber
WELLED UP
More than that.
There's more to me than that!
I go to the bars at night -
Get the same 'come on's' from all the se-men.
I know their need is one I have too.
But they gotta' jump back just a step or two.
They don't see all of me,
they only see what they want to see,
On the outside I'm tall and graceful, but inside I'm as torn up as they.
Can't they read the lines on my face?
Hey, do I look like a magnet to you?
And if that is so - who's to say
I'm the one attracting?
Go away beer breath!
Get outta' my face!
I have no need or want for a man who doesn't even bother to
ask
where
I've
been.

Craig Ellery Ryan
WARNING
The mist of days' dawning crept
Out upon the lake unnoticed
Save perhaps by a lone great
Blue heron and I - who held my
Own Love lest she should wake
Startled that night had fled into
Beginning dawn. The solitary
Heron hoarsely squawked a
Lonely cry that woke my Love.

We listened to hear an answer,
We listened and waited, my
Love, the heron and I - but only
The creeping mist, that fantastic
Dancer, caressed the heron in
Her phantom chill embrace. My
Love shivered and I drew her
Close in my arms, kissed her
Lips, her sleepy eyes; kissed her
Face, nearly unaware of the
Heron screaming his alarms.

Mrs. Leah Baker
MY CHRISTMAS WISH FOR ALL
As Christmas quickly approaches
I hope that you will have
A most glorious and Happy Christmas
The best you've ever had.
How quickly time goes by
From one Christmas to another
Let us not forget the meaning
Christ was born on Christmas day.
Gifts and goodies for our children
And the older folks as well
Joy and gladness, love and blessings
Peace on earth good will to men
A Christmas turkey with all the fixins
Is my hearty wish for you
Love and joy and peace and laughter
Christmas trees and candles too.
Happy days and many blessings
That our Christmas surely brings
Bright and pretty decorations
And glad tidings to our King.
Hope and happiness for the future
And a prosperous New Year too
Merry Christmas everybody
Love and luck to all of you.

Charmaine Succa
JUST A PICTURE
Just a Picture
So clear in my mind
A little tear
That was ever so kind
Just a Picture
A dumb little thing (so they say)
But everyone wants them (if they may)
Just a Picture
Of somebody walking
Who knows if he is talking?
Just a Picture
Can you guess what he's thinking?
Why is he winking?
Just a Picture
I'll take today
And forget tomorrow.
Can you remember?
What was his name?
Does he still look the same?

Rita Marie Knecht
CONTENTMENT
Consistently wearing a smile
isn't obligatory
Contentment happens
Understanding sends messages
Disrupting unintentional
causes of frustration
Transforms music into ecstasy
Refreshment towards new
dedication

Florence Patricia Page
CONTEMPLATIONS
Perhaps what one fears about death
Is not that the deceased no longer lives
But, by the same token
The dead denies our existence
Does this make life one prolonged dream
From which the dead have risen
And we still sleep?
But to think is to exist
And if there be certainties
Subjective things are certain
Yet, are we constant?
Can we be so sure that what we feel we are
One moment is what we are the next?
Are we quite sure of being
The same person today as we were yesterday?
What is the nature of ultimate reality?

Rita Gombart
SUMMER
Summer takes me by the hand
like a gentle priest
Daughter confess your solitude
And enter into peace!
Lying face down by the river's ripple
Grows wilderness the bitter milkweed
From my breasts
Listen! A petition is sung by little earth hearts
In the bones and holes of my soul
The face of summer at the window
Soon to disappear—eyes unfurled
His mouth loose hung
Waterfall of silence over the dogs of desire

Helen Yu-Ping Yang
A PEARL
Deep within the oyster
lies a gift-
So rare and beautiful
and so pure.

The precious treasure
is a pearl.
So hard to find,
but worth the work.
Within each person
lies a pearl.

Carole L. Schauer
TWENTY-ONE GUNS
I woke up with the morning sun,
a smile across my face.
But as the memories flooded back,
a tear soon took it's place.
I slowly dressed and left the house,
to meet those gathered there.
It angered me to know that they,
would all just stand and stare.
At the body of my father,
lying peacefully in sleep.
I pray that he is with the Lord,
I pray his soul to keep.
There stands a veteran of a war,
who salutes him one last time.
I feel the tears run down my face,
the pain I feel is mine.
Twenty-one Guns saluted him,
and jets flew overhead.
The flag was given to his wife,
and loving words were said.
I placed a rose upon his grave,
and said a last farewell.
I loved him and I miss him so,
but no one can I tell.
For I am just a daughter-in-law,
thought he loved me as his own.
I always loved him as my father,
if only he had known.
I never told him how I felt,
I guess I hoped he knew.
I hope that God will let you hear me,
because...
Dad I Love you.
Your loving daughter-in-law,
Carole

Joseph A. Bailey
BUILDING SLOWLY - DESTROYING QUICKLY
There frequently arise
Conditions in our lives
Which suddenly destroy
Some things quite slowly built.
A building may go up
With great expense and skill,
Yet overnight may fall
When someone plants a bomb.
Two cars well engineered
With all the late designs,
Become a mass of junk
When in a head-on crash.
The savings that result
From careful management
May quickly disappear
In risky schemes of chance.
An overdose of drugs,
Regardless of the cause,
May quickly terminate
A life that's in its prime.
Some angry words may end
A good relationship,
Or even end a life,
If one should use a gun.
When we have slowly built
A structure, or a life,
It doesn't make much sense
To blindly tear it down.

Vicki Wolfe
AWAKENING
When morning wakes me
Light and gentle
Takes me from my thoughtless slumber
Sends me spinning back to truth
Briefly I do not remember
Life is by my ruling somber.
Oh how can I
When pregnant winter
Cries in giving birth to spring
Hold on to that no longer true
As if 'twere my desire to cling
To thoughts harsh as winter's sting.
Let me not be a lowly mortal
Bound by yesterday's decision
Let me surpass the bonds of error
Wrongly naming joy intrusion
Stubborn faith has cleared my vision.

Delilah D. Beaver
WRITERS BLOCK
Writers share alot.
More than you would believe.
Like the way they write,
And the thoughts they receive.
But at certain times,
Their minds go knock, knock.
Then they have no thoughts,
This is called the writers block.

Carol Crown
MEMORIES
If memories twist
And cuckold all the past
Shifting truths
To make them last
What does it hurt
These soothing lies
But to put a glaze
On empty eyes

Jane M. Florian
JENIKA
Jenika, Jenika,
my love.
Sitting on the hill
Amidst the daisies
Waiting, waiting
for me.
Jenika, Jenika,
my love.
Loving in the night
Under the stars--
Loving, loving
with me.
Jenika, Jenika
my love.
Sitting beneath the tree
Amidst the oak leaves
Waiting, waiting
for me.

Annette Blanche Wildrick
REMEMBERING --
I've op'd a window of my mind,
And clearly I can see
The persons of my yesteryear
Parading back to me.
Some mystery must lie therein
How you of long-gone years
Can be as real as anyone
Who now in life appears.
And when I open up my mind
And make my own silent parade,
Tis comforting to know, my friend,
Fond memories never fade.
For no one knows as well as you
The mirth we shared, the crying, too --
That's why you are so very dear
To me in yesteryear.

Ricky Monroe
UNTITLED
Dance, to the beat of
my heart,
Talk as if you, understand
what's beneath my skin,
Fly only as high as my
spirits can take you,
For if you need go
farther, you need
not take me.

Rhonda Jane LaPointe
PASSAGES OF LIFE
In a quiet of a dream
Of the darkness of shadows
Life is a sunny outlook
Mystery of the mind
Winds of worlds
Images flow through
thinking of times
Beauty of colors
Flowers of every sort
The very juices of imagery
Passing through my eyes
Wondering of greater success
Love fills into pictures
Of millions of minds
Running through
The passages of life.

Terry L. Morris
I DREAM A LOT
I Dream A Lot,
I dream a lot about love,
of how it should be,
of how it or you should feel.
I dream not of two people
Running to embrace each other
in a field of flowers;
But of the moment of
togetherness they have.
In all our minds love is
different,
we each seek our own true
visions of love; love does not
stop time, time continues,
it will continue for all.

Nora Clark
GOING HOME
Big, old house of my earliest years,
Now, you're a tomb for my
sobbings and fears.
Rooms,
Where we thought up our
runaway schemes,
Now we've come back here with
Real grownups' dreams.
A packet of letters in childish
scrawl,
A hole,
Where a picture had hung on
the wall.
Things are changed, now, that
once were
Hands off,
Closets we hid in and stifled a
cough.
A dusty, cold smell in the attic,
the same,
A similar one in the basement,
now tamed--
Remind me how small I was and
how
I'd thought
I'd never grow up and I'd never
get caught.
Big, old house of my earliest
years,
A monument, still damp,
From so many tears.

n. paul baker
A CELEBRATION
the wind
lashes thru the parking lot
ominously, tentatively
only a little ahead
of the brooding sky
old brown leaves dance and
laugh
expectantly, reluctantly
soon to be followed
by autumn's horde of fallen,
glittered and painted
with future frost -

Lynn Paille Kulesza
NEW ENGLAND PALETTE
Radiance skittering atop the
waves
Sentinel seagulls scanning the
sea
Shimmering diamonds on
snowcrusted lea
Rustic red and ochre gold
All weave a canvas to behold.

Sylvia Newton Lewis
HOME
Come to visit me, my friend
And I will teach you how
The clouds may look like
mountains

And the trees speak poetry
I will show you how to listen
For the solo of a frog
And how to smell black walnuts
grow
And how to love the rain.

Jo Spacek
AWAKENING
I opened my eyes...what did I
see?
The splendor of heavens, earth
and trees!
I opened my ears...what did I
hear?
The sounds of nature...so joyous,
so dear!
I opened my mouth...what did I
say?
I found my Saviour...O Blessed
day!
I opened my arms...what did
they hold?
God's glorious Book...more
precious than gold!
I opened my heart...tc someone
today,
And Lo, I found Jesus had come
to stay!

J. D. Steenson
JESUS
I will always be there
I am never away from you.
I am your dearest Friend!
You are safe with Me.
Call on Me for anything
And I will answer.
You can lean on Me for strength
And I will guide you through.
Let Me work through you
And let My word be heard
By all who never knew Me
And who need Me.
Just ask Me the question
And I will give you the answer
You can call on Me for
everything
I'll always be near!

Jennifer Beulah Lew
IN THE HURRICANE
When shrouded in a shadow's
wings she screamed,
I bolted out of bed to hear the
cry:
A sob so deep I knew I had not
dreamed,
But sensed that death's grim cart
was clatt'ring by.
A silent woman, she, of patient
woe,
Subdued by fortune, fate, and
dreams that cracked.
She yearned to love but never
let it show;
For years I blindly missed the
thing she lacked.
Now you are slipping out of
earthly reach
When I have only just found out
your plight.
You cannot leave me stranded
on the beach -
I need more time to guide you
toward the light!
But Grandma did not heed my
answering wail,
Wind whirled her upward
through the swarming gale.

O. Leon Wilson III
WINE-O
He pulled himself from the
gutter
his home for the last year or so-
the craving for wine had entered
his mind,
his last drink had been
countless days ago.
His delirious state of mind
would become worse
if not for a sip of the red-
even a Wine-O knew when he's
over due,
his infinite thirst had to be fed.
With only ten cents in his
pocket
he knew that would not be
enough-
he had been here before and he
knew once more,
to get going he had to get
TOUGH!
The skies became numb, no
sounds were heard
the air was filled with living
spirits-
the Wine-O stood humble with
tears in his eyes,
if this was the end he would
face it.
He looked to the heavens and
fell to his knees,
then SHOUTED! "Jesus, is it my
time?"
Just then an angel appeared with
a sign that read,
Wine! two fifths for a dime.

Ivy Redford Collins
DECISION
You were mine for a little while,
Then came the day of
reckoning,
I didn't want to let you go---
You knew before I did, that
I had to---
I was yours for a little while,
Not near long enough, but oh,
what a
glorious time that was---
You didn't want to let me go,
You had to---
We had commitments, you and
I,
Commitments made long ago,
Family and friends wouldn't
understand---
We didn't want to let go,
We had to-----

Janet L. Dalaska
DISCOVERY
I've searched through many
lifetimes until I finally found
you.
You breathe life into my
existence, bring me the reality
of being whole,
And I can now face Eternity
with the knowledge of love.

Carol D. Neubauer
A SHADE OF MEANING
You said, 'I don't love you
And I never will.' All right.
I was tired of lies, anyway.
But you told me things
That weren't to be repeated -
Once you cried on my shoulder.
Another night, you held me
Close and gentle
Worrying because I hurt.
Your children reached for me
With eager smiles
And trusting eyes.
And one soft summer day
You brought me daisies...
What you called it didn't matter
For it was more
Than anyone else ever gave me.
I didn't need the words.

June M. Naffziger
UNTITLED
the leaves dance through the air
softly landing on each other
carpeting the earth with
reds and yellows.
I walk through the crunching
leaves, look up to the sky and
wonder how a season of
dying can be so beautiful.

Cecily Atyes Varner
SEA LIFE
As the sea rushes to shore
The shells change places
The tiny sands slide on the floor
Some fish are having races
Animals are clinging to the seaweed
They are mostly looking for food
The smallest fish is in the lead
The big fish is in a hungry mood
The one slowly changing his course
With prominent eyes
Is the tiny little seahorse
The big sting-ray just glides

Theo M. Walther
BYRON'S LOGIC--AGE FIVE
I tucked the bed covers around him.
I kissed his cheek; and then,
Left the bedroom door ajar so the
light from the hall would shine in.
"Grandma", the voice was plaintive,
"please leave a light on in here".

"Why"? I asked. "The hall light gives
all the light that you need in there".
I could not refuse his entreaty. His
reasons and logic were clear.
"Well, down the middle the hall light shines;
but, there are four dark corners in here"!

C. Estelle Thomas
THE TRYST
When Daylight rests a weary chin
On yonder mountain's furthest rim,
Young Twilight steals from out the hills;
Her footsteps soft a hush instills
Upon the little town.
In evening dress of purple-grey
Shot through with gold from parting Day,
She walks along each quiet street
And touches all with dimness sweet.
Each time she comes at this calm hour
And plucks, as if it were a flower,
(With hands like thistledown)
The last dim ray of shimmering light
The while she waits her tryst with Night.
Unfailing, she her vigil keeps
And he, when the drowsy township sleeps,
Black-armored from the sky rides down.

Mildred T. Marsh
SURVIVAL--FROM NEWSPAPER STORY
The fawn
left doe-less by a speeding car
in desperation
sought a farm and found
a collie--pupless--aging.
Now ravenous, determined,
the young deer sucked
with youthful urgency
dry--never before used paps
of patient, puzzled foster mother.
And lo--a miracle--
the paps produced, nurtured
day after day until tenacious
young one learned to fend.
Does a grown buck remember--
bring his fawns to stand
in shadows
for a pleased old dog to see?

Eva Hoffman
BIRTHDAY SONG
It's my birthday today;
every day I am born anew
from the ashes of the previous day
from the shadows of the previous night.
It's my birthday today;
each morning I am born
amidst the rays of the rising sun
and I die each night
in the grey dust of every day's troubles.
It's my birthday today;
I come to life
under clouds tumbling across the skies
and I wither away each evening
among the scent of lavender and rose.
It's my birthday today
I live in the miracle of every day;
it's my birthday today
I live
I have lived a full day's life.

Barbara M. Jackson
TOLERANCE
I fall short so many times.
I mean well, dear Lord;
But there are those times when I am so impatient with others.
Yet, there is always someone who accepts me with all my shortcomings,
And loves me in spite of them.
Now, my prayer is that I, too, can be tolerant with others
When they are having "just one of those days."
Increase my patience, Lord.
Let me not criticize unduly, but seek to understand my fellowman.
Let me not retaliate if I am hurt because of one's thoughtlessness,
But let me love in spite of the hurt.
Let me show no malice to anyone, but an abundance of affection;
No self righteousness, but much humility.
Remind me that humility does not indicate weakness, but strength.
Let me be big enough to overlook life's pettiness.
Let me be one hundred percent forgiving;
And let all that I do be done in the spirit of love.

Lorraine Barrieau
SEARCHING
Why am I so preoccupied
With the world's treasures?
I will never be satisfied
With all its pleasures;
God must be the center of my life.
Unless He is found
I will be forever in strife
To Him I am bound.

Juliana Lehmier
UNTITLED
We met
we talked
we laughed
we touched
we kissed
we loved
You were my dream come true.
I was your one and only.
Then
We fought
we cried
Now
We don't talk
we don't laugh
we don't touch
we don't kiss
Worst of all,
I still love. . .

Charlotte Marie Meyer
FRUSTRATIONS OF A NON—SMOKER
Listen up, all you smokers out there
'Cause I wanna breath some of that clean, fresh air.
I've tolerated a lot more than you realize
So don't you go blowin' that smoke in my eyes.
I don't want that stale smell in my hair.
Sometimes, it's more than I can just really bear.
And I don't want any of your lung disease
So don't come smokin' around me, please!
I know you've got that nicotine fit
And you've just gotta have that cigarette lit.
So go on flickin' your "Bic"
And puffin' on that ol' cancer stick.
But one thing's for darn tootin',
I value these lungs that you're pollutin'.
So just remember whenever I'm near
That this health of mine I hold quite dear.
So whenever you get that nicotine fit
And an urge to have that cigarette lit,
Remember this poem's my plea to smokers everywhere:
Please—let me breath some of that clean, fresh air!

Ella L. Plourd
NEARLY SPRING
Although there's snow upon the ground,
signs of Spring are all around.
The sun is higher in the sky,
the surest sign that spring is nigh.
The birds are singing a happier tune,
the ice is gone from the old lagoon.
The crocus is ready to take a peek
at a brand new Spring, most any week.
The crickets and frogs down by the pond,
are waiting for the Lord, to wave his wand.
Easter time is near at hand
and Spring will appear just as planned.

Mabel B. Nair
JUST KEEP SMILING
When your days are full of care,
When friends seem few and rare,
Just keep smiling.
After while things will improve,
If you make a friendly move,
And just keep smiling.
If your efforts seem so weak,
And you have a weary streak,
Just keep smiling.
If your days seem low and long,
Just keep smiling.
If life doesn't seem worth the living,
Forget yourself and keep on giving,
A friendly smile to others now,
And you'll find it worth your time
To make a little friendly rhyme,
And keep on smiling.

Laura Graudushus
LIFE'S FORCE
Single star upon belly of crescent moon. . . .twinkling
Nursing mother cradling newborn babe. . .rocking
Unborn child within mother's womb. . .waiting
Embryo of new beginnings. . . floating
I, a woman, lay beside you. . . knowing
Life's force. . .awakening

William Earl Berlin
SISTER RAIN
With gentleness of springtime comes Sister Rain
Softly falling through the leaves,
Brushing past the flora and fauna,
Flowing by my weeping face in the night.
The day brings wind that blows and hardens
My face to all who would trespass.
The sun bakes my skin with sharpest rays.
My eyes grow hard against the day.
Then gentle Sister Rain softens my eyes
And soothes my tortured skin.
Yet Sister Rain in her anger
Pelts down on the earth
And moves rocks and trees
In her stubborn fury.
Splashing down in torrents of water
Sheets of rain envelope my

countenance
And purest air flows through
her drops
As I stand in her, naked to my
soul.
With hands of gentle mercy
Sister Rain brushes away the
past
And gives birth to a new dawn.
Forever will I bless Sister Rain.

Jeanette Harlin
STAR CHILD
You sit and wait alone
Your place is in the sky
You have no real home.
You're the Star Child.
You fly way up high
to dance with the stars;
You live in the sky
Star Child.
Now I know what they mean by
the man on the moon.
A beautiful child,
I know you're coming for me
soon,
My Star Child.

Marilyn Anne Kutsko
A WISH
Someone said,
Make a wish and your wish will
come true.
So I made a wish:
To be loved by you.
I looked into the future and
found my wish wouldn't come
true,
For the love I thought we shared
is not the love I have for you.
I'll make another wish.
This one for you:
For you to find someone to love
always the way I've loved you,
I hope this wish will really
come true.
For this is the wish I want for
you.

Willie J. Curry, Jr.
NOTE TO A WHITE FRIEND
All you have to worry
about
are the things you worry
about
you don't have to worry
about
you don' have to worry
about
being Black.

Helen Dilger
OUR SON
"Hello there little fellow
At last you've come to stay,
Within the circle of our love
Growing sweeter every day.
We waited patiently for you
For in your tiny hands,
You held your daddy's love and
mine
Like shining silver bands.
You've brought with you such
happiness,
We would like to say;
Welcome little son of ours,
From dad and mom today."

Bonni Sue
UNTITLED
Oh! You were my lover, you were my greatest friend.
After all these years, how was I to know that I didn't want it to end.
Young was I, but again I was experienced beyond my years.
You were my love, my life, even all through the hate and tears.
Your life and mine are now very much apart.
But still when I think of you, it causes a thrill in my heart.
I will live with my mistake, of leaving you behind in the past.
Because I truly didn't think that your love for me would really last.
Please forgive me, for causing you the pain and tears of my foolish ways.
Please forgive me, maybe, just maybe one of these days.

Karen J. Cowen
SEEDS IN THE EARTH
Seeds in the earth
Will grow in time
With lots of love
And heaps of Sunshine
People like seeds
In time will grow
Sprinkle generously
with kindness
And watch the soft glow.
People and seeds
Need love to sprout
Special people like you
Is what love is about.

Mary Katherine Glass
A NIGHT IN NEW ORLEANS
Out on Bourbon street
the night
was running into street
corners
crashing into closed walls
but a door that
fell
away
behind him
caused him to *pour* upon the
nonever toomany bar floor.
The chairs turned to stare
but the cash register only
whispered,
"My-what beautiful red eyes."

Melissa McNair
SHANNON
Shannon,
You were so young
So free
And now you are
freer still
You were such joy
Such fun
You livened every dull
moment there ever was
You saw the fall
And loved the winter's snow
At least you enjoyed it
to your fullest
while you still could
Never knowing it was your
first and would be your last
You never saw the blossoming
love that spring brings
But at least you had a
slight taste of it
And will never experience
the wonders that summer
brings
The frolicking in the grass
And the coolness of the
water in the lake
On hot summer evenings
You were only with us
a short while
But in that short time
You captured our hearts
You filled them with love
and joy
Shannon,
You were so young
So free
And now you are
freer still

Brenda Lukeman
MOUNTAIN CANDY
The truth is not pain.
The truth encircles
Us like honey,

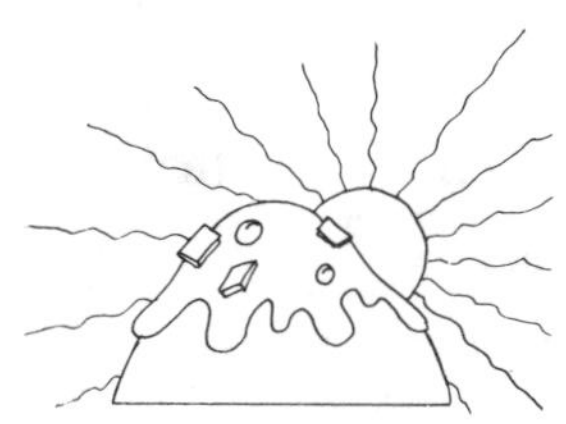

Inviting us to live
Again, and taste
This gorgeous
Mountain candy.

Gladys E. Ramsay
FREEDOM
Silence is golden.
May be True.
If peace and goodwill.
Dwelt there too!
But each new day.
The battle goes on.
More are uprising.
Feelings are strong.
People are gathering.
Day and night.
Tired of oppression.
Ready to fight.
All want their freedom.
The right to choose.
Many will suffer.
Win or loose.
Working together.
Strengthens their hold.
As time is the essence.
Freedom their goal.

Jill DeeAnn Haworth
IN GOD WE TRUST
In God we trust
We've often heard it said.
On every nickel and dime and
quarter
It is easily read.
But in God do we trust?
do we talk to Him each day?
Do we tell Him that we loved
Him
As we kneel to Him and pray?
Our nation away from God has
turned.
We've nearly lost the freedom
earned.
But don't give up now.
The battle will soon be won
To turn this nation back to
God.
For then it will be done.
Then we will be able to say
In God we trust in every way.

Angela Renee Hackshaw
IS THERE A PLACE SOMEWHERE FOR ME?
Is there a place somewhere for
me?
Somewhere where I can be free?
Is there a place for me, to go?
For me to see...for me to know?
Is there an ocean, tide or wave
that I can touch and then be
saved?
Is there a place where people
will understand me?
Where I can become settled?
Where I can be free?
Oh where, oh where can it be?
Is there a place where only
happiness goes on?
Is there a place where there is
no sadness at all?
Is there a place with birds and
bees?
Tide is blue with flower and
trees?
Is there a place where people
don't get hurt?
Is there a place where there is
no dirt?
Is there a place with honesty
and love?
Is there a place like the above?
Am I asking for too much of a
place?
To go, to see, to be clean to be
free?
Is there a place somewhere for
me?
Somewhere where I can be free?

Elizabeth Anne Waughtal
OLD WINE BOTTLES
Cut roses belong in old wine
bottles
Old memories enfolding
whispers of awakened
romance
Delicate velvet, suspended life
embraced in a nostalgic carafe
(wine slipped between lips
between sheets)
the kiss of a petal to ease the
kiss of a thorn
the kiss of cut crystal to cradle
our spirits
the kiss of a memory to seal
new meanings
within the flask of my heart
Lone roses belong in old wine
bottles.

Bess Powell
THE ARTIST
At the edge of the sea would I
be with brush in hand,
And hear the piper pipe in the
sand, to me.
There to sit and with paint
convey to canvas
The call of the gull as it would
pass o'er head.
The lure of horizons portray
And the promise of distant
shores would say,
Depicting fog with oceans song
and deflected sunlight,
That it might last past ebbtide.
A breeze would come and splash
and spray
Convince me more with awe to
say,
Poor the copy I make today.

Ester Maxine Hurt
A RECIPE FOR LOVE
Take two hearts,
Blend in consideration.
Pour honesty in constantly,
Flavor with communication.
Sprinkle anger when necessary,
Top completely with
understanding.
Leave room enough to settle,
Have lots of patience ready.

Frances M. Pickett
LUNA
The thinly-sliced new moon,
unwary maiden,
Is holding her old-moon lover in
her arms.
Surely she senses
The incompatibility --
He is so dark and ominous
With used-up life,
While hers is hardly started.
Oh well,
As she grows older -- and
understands more,
His influence with her will
wane;
Until at last
He goes away
And leaves her full.

Anne-Marie Clark
COMA
My thoughts race to you, in the rose blush of early day, while dew pearls still cling to the petals and ghost mists hide the young sun. My heart searches the blind white reaches of sky, when the sultry blaze of high noon steeps my very bones in its' enveloping heat. Can you not hear its' trip hammer beat on the hurrying winds of day?
When the haunting call of the elusive quail echoes over the stubble fields and queens lace and purple asters nod in the creeping dusk, my longing cry joins this plantive song. Surely, you hear this music - you who loved it so long?
In the still of night, moon riding full and white over the yellow spread of golden rod, where we walked so many dream filled hours, my call hurries to you on the moonpath, from here to the stars.
You are there somewhere - turn to me - let your soft voice roll back along this silvered pathway to me. Oceans of space surrounds us, warm, star lit, blue vapor enfolds us, like our old blue scalloped wedding quilt. Reach to me, close your strong hand over mine in the old familiar way. Let your strength uphold my wearying frame

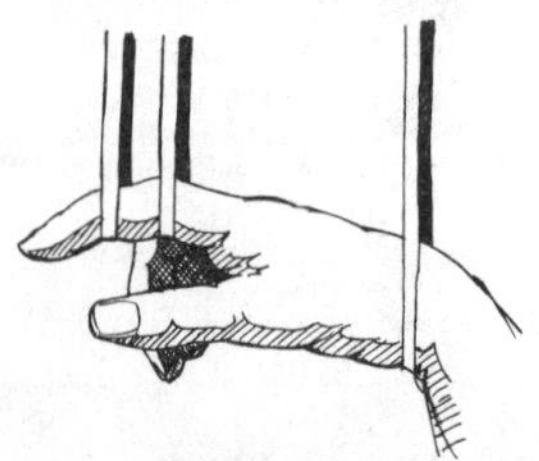

Oh my love, reach to me!

Jane Noyes
A SPECIAL LOVE
You cared enough to look
beyond what others see,
Behind the mask, the faces we
all use,
To get to know the person that
is me,
Creating a bond too deep to ever
lose.
The deepest thoughts, the
feelings we have shared,
The two of us drawn together,
who knows why,
So different, so much the same
we are aware
Of unspoken understanding, of
love too strong to die.
So in times of doubt and times
of fear,
When your loving arms I am
without,
I think of all the times when
you were near,
And realize what loving's all
about.
A strong foundation time
cannot erode,
Unlike a name imprinted in the
sand,
Washed away by waves, like
tales untold,
The test of time a special love
withstands.

Virginia Camden
THE LIFE OF A BUG
The life of a bug
Is short and sweet.
His feelers are fine,
And his color is neat.
If you possibly can
Just let him be;
For one of God's creatures,
The same is he.

Sally C. Medernach
AURA
Last night
Spring rain splattered on the roof, a reverie of gentle rhythm, washing away the lassitude of winter.
I awoke to face the dawn and was surprised to find that the rain, caught in time and space, was frozen into slender crystal jewels and suspended from the lattice.
Spring sunlight,
reflecting the aura of clinging winter, illuminates the morning shadows.

Dennis Macario Morris Reven
CREATED EQUAL
At the beginning of time as we
all shall know
We were all created equal
Now for those who believe we
do not seem the same
By looks or wealth or health
For it is for you I write these
words so that you will know
By pictures or pen or men
That as time went on and we
did not seem as one
You have only your beliefs to
blame
So for those of you who were
born to a much harder test
Say with more troubles or rain
or pain
For it is you who must realize
that your score in life
Need not be as high to
accomplish the same
As the ones born with more
luck or fortune or fame
And with that in mind
I now speak to you who come
into this world
With more chance or money or
honey
For it is you who must score
more in present time
For your future life to begin as
sunny
And with these few words I pray
that you have learned
Much on how we were all
created equal
Since we live forever this would
be good to know
For the laws are the same in
lifes sequel

Arthur Morrison
MY HEART
Come, my love, into this heart,
See the love, that has one part.
See, I love you so true,
Adore you, as the sky is blue.
I live, I breathe, for only you,
Enter, and see, all you knew.
Can you not hear this silent voice,
Loving you in many a rejoice.
Hear the whispering of this heart,
Telling you of the love, I had from
the start.
See how it never ceases to dream,
My love for you, is supreme.
Can you not see the loneliness
and pain,
Causing tears, to flow like rain.
Enter, dear love, see, it is you,
Whisper to me, you always knew.
My heart has, so long cried,
I fear, one day, it would have died.
Your love is the strength of this
heart,
As it was, from the start.

Mary Margaret Champagne
MY TREES
When I was a little girl
I'd sit in my backyard.
I'd watch the squirrels play
till it was almost dark.
I'd look at all the tall trees
with their different sizes and
shapes,
and as their branches reached
for me
I gave them all a name.
Since the Oak was so strong I
called it Titanic
for the sweetness of the Maple-
Sugar seemed to fit.
The Birch looked so pure I gave
the name Pristine
the Weeping Willow always sad
I called Melancholy.
The popular Poplar I would
address Woody
so beautiful the Dogwood I
titled Symmetry.
Then I'd sit and speak their
names to them and myself,
their names seemed to fit just
them and nobody else.
Even though I'm grown now I
remember my trees
and the names that they were
given in my backyard by me.

Mildred M. C. Brookins
WHEN YOU COME HOME
When you come home at even-
tide
To be with me, my dear
The disappointments of the day
Just seem to disappear.
The weight of worldly cares
Are suddenly left behind,
While I relax in comfort
And perfect peace of mind.
I share with you, my fondest
thoughts,
And every hope in me,
And plan with you the
happiness
Of what few years there be;
And as my dreams go drifting
To the silver stars above,
I thank my God for giving me
The chance to live and love.
The chance to earn my daily
bread
And search for treasures' new,
To gather memories of gold
And to share them all with
you.
And as the years go swiftly by,
If I should have to go,
Do not grieve, for I'll be near
Because I love you so.
I know that you'll be lonely,
Because you must remain;
But when it's time for you to
come,
You'll hear me call your name.
And that's the way it came to be
For my Mother and my Dad;
She heard him calling out her
name
Her loving heart was glad!
She looked at me with
tenderness
And said, please don't despair.
Keep faith with GOD, the
Father,
For we'll be waiting there.

Pamela J. Luna
WINTER WONDERLAND
Doomed to break
Or revival in the spring
A snowladen maple branch
Feebly bends toward
Binding icy ground,
Searching for warmth
From winter's frigid surface.
Freezing snow captures the
branch
Pulling - Sapping strength...
with a beckoning snap
Snow blusters
Burying the outstretched arm
Under winter's peaceful
pretense.

Angeline E. Tucker
A MESSAGE TO MY MOTHER
I miss you so much
sometimes I just cry,
and think of memories
of time gone by.
You were more than a mother
you were a good friend,
and I can't understand
why it had to end.
I know you're watching over me
I feel it in my heart,
and if I could have my dream
come true
we wouldn't be apart.
Sometimes I get the feeling
you sent Johnny from above,
because he's brought such
happiness
and a special kind of love.
Before you went to heaven

you used to be my crutch,
and thank you mom for all your love
that meant so very much.

Cliff Jackson
PUZZLE
An archaeologist by the name of Jones
Made a fascinating discovery one day,
When he dug up some odd looking bones
Where a very strange creature once lay.
In some ways, the archaeologist found,
It resembled a primitive man--
But, as he removed the bones from the ground,
He got them all mixed up in the sand.
As he assembled the bones he began to doubt,
And try as hard as he might,
He couldn't figure the connections out--
They just didn't seem to fit right.
"This must be a practical joke" he said,
"Or, there must be some mistake,
There never was a creature alive or dead
That this pile of bones could make!"
So, Jones took all the bones he understood
And put them neatly in a can,
And all of those that didn't look so good
He re-buried in the sand.
Jones will never know he was almost involved
In making history,
With a little more luck he might have solved
Man's oldest mystery!
On his next expedition Jones should be
A little more careful, I think--
Considering his latest discovery
Was the famous MISSING LINK!

Harvey James Palmer III
THANKS
Thank you dear LORD for being so kind.
You've given me strength and peace of mind.
When I open my eyes I'm so happy to find
The earth that You made, too great to define.
You've granted me Hope, as if by design,
I've seen Your great works and all that is Thine.
I know I am fortunate to have what is mine -
Love, Faith and Respect for You, the Divine.

A. L. A. Corenanda
THE UNIVERSE
Astronomers reckon their distances in so many light years
And each light year, according to them,
Is equivalent to almost six thousand billion miles!
The Universe, they say, is ever expanding,
While, the others contend it expands and contracts
In a cycle of eighty billion years!
All that is too much for a poor versifier like me,
Who could barely measure his own Kismet:
It would suffice for me to stare
At the dark of night with milliards of diamonds
Scattered on the black velveteen mantles
Gently spreading over some lovely creatures,
Who would unfold boundless joys and sorrows,
And taught me that Love is as infinite as the Universe!

Ray Soback
THREE C'S FOR YOU
At night I'd like to have your head against my shoulder, and whisper sweet things in your ear. Mornings I would kiss you gently, tell you dream on while I go to work. There I would keep my three C's, calm cool and collective for you. Knowing you'll be waiting for me I'll stay collective calm and cool.
I could say I've been lonely too long, but that would be a lie because my thoughts were of a life time finding my special you, staying collective calm and cool. If these thoughts should bring a tear to you let my kisses brush them away. It hurts me so to see you cry and the future won't end today, for the past is gone and the time is now. Though our hearts are a journey apart loving thoughts of you travel on, and at night you're in my heart.
I want your head on my shoulder, my lips telling you to dream on with me for all eternity and I will keep my three C's.

Les Hemminger
SONNIE
Little son, I stopped by
Your lonely grave today
And there all alone
Knelt to pray
You were named for my father
And your other grandpa too
With never a doubt that you
Would grow to manhood strong and true
So sure was I to keep you
From all life's harms

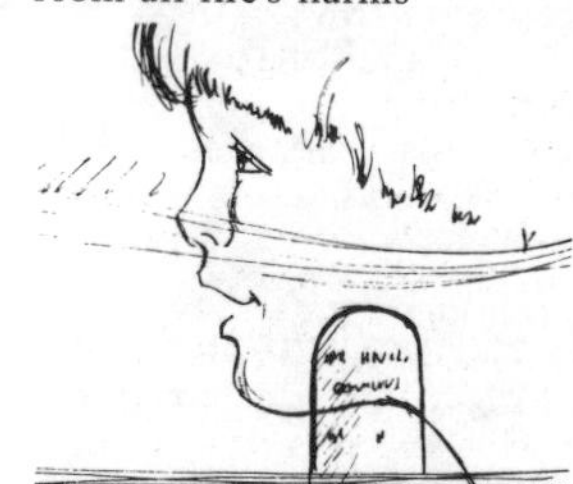

But you took your last breath
In these so called protecting arms
I blamed the doctor
I blamed the nurse
But myself I blamed
Ten thousand times worse
But the tears that wet the grass
On your little grave today
Have washed the last dregs of
Bitterness away
A new thought has come that maybe
God with all his vexations up above
Needed a little one so pure
Just to have and to love

Alexandra W. Merker
MY DAFFODIL HAS DUST INSIDE
In my garden, on this very early, nearly silent morning
With just a plane or two buzzing overhead,
No brakes screeching, a fledgeling cheeping,
I saw a solitary golden daffodil had managed
To survive man's trampling feet and mind.
Not a wondrous crowd,
A host of Wordsworth's daffodils
Fluttering and dancing in the breeze,
But a single, solitary, daffodil
Faintly scented as daffodils are wont,
So faint indeed, its scent
Will scarce survive a second sniff.
I peered inside the silken trumpet.
There-in abode a tiny insect,
So small and still it slept within
The gently scented glowing light,
I gloried in its spare and perfect pad
And peering closer into that cathedral dome
I saw that there was dust inside.

Rallenco
MY DOG HAS A SERVANT
My dog has a servant, that opens up the door
Whenever he wants in or out, a hundred times a day or more
His servant always gets him a drink, when he has a thirst
And when the door is opened, he always goes out first
He sleeps in a double bed at night, the servant makes for him
He's waited on constantly, every urge and whim
When he takes a bath, he never cleans the tub
And when he has an itch, the servant is there to rub.
He doesn't have a worry, the servant is there to help
He's had all the care he needs since he was a whelp
His food is brought to him, in his special dish
His servant is always near to fulfill his every wish
My dog has a good life, as you can plainly see
My dog has a servant; and that servant is me.

Joyce Evelyn Matula
UNTITLED
Cold grey October skies
heavy and dreary
clouds hang
touching the earth
with icy
tears...

Joseph Vela Talamantes, M.D.
MY POEM
My heart is full,
And so's my mind.
I've learned that there
Are things to find,
Things I never
Dreamed there were,
More than gold
And more than myrrh,
Things that tell
Of Love so great,
Things that open
Heaven's gates.
Things that teach
Salvation free;
Salvation for
Both you and me.

Elizabeth Carwellos
ERIC
If there's a dog's heaven,
And I'm sure there is,
Eric is there!

If dogs become angels,
And I'm sure they do,
Eric is one!

Deborah Ann Dabrowski
THE MESSAGE
If you feel the need to talk
But there's no one around
You're not really alone
Talk with Jesus.
If you're taking a walk
Be not afraid
Someone's there beside you
Walk along with Jesus.
If others put you down
Hold your head up high
Be proud of who you are
Jesus loves you.
If the burden gets too heavy
So you're feeling really low
Call upon Jesus
He'll lift the weight.
If you feel something's missing
But know not where to find it
Reach out to Jesus
He'll show you the way.
Jesus will forgive you
He'll wash away your sin
All you have to do is ask Him
He'll help you start again.
Open your heart to Jesus
Let the Spirit in
You will find much happiness
And have peace within.
Jesus is the answer
Let Him be your guide
You'll be thankful He's there with you
Forever by your side.

Eileen C. Joyce
DAWN
I lay in bed this early morn
And watched the sun create the dawn,
From midnight black to bankers' grey
It slowly inched along it's way,
And then the grey seemed lined with yellow
Moments ere the day was mellow
With golden tones so warm and bright,-
The birth of a day is a wonderful sight.

Vicky Lee Edwards
LEFT FRIENDLESS
A little old lady passed away yesterday,
No one was at her funeral today.
You see her friends have already gone,
So she was left with a preacher and a song.

Geraldine G. Benton
J. L.
In memory of
Jesse L. Burcham
Killed in Korea
Feb. 12, 1951 (22)
I go there to the graveyard
Sometimes, on summer days-
I sit beside a tombstone
In evenings warmest rays-
I look at the inscription
Engraved into the stone-
I feel the tears course down
my cheeks
Thats why I go alone-
And too, its just my moment
A thing I cannot share-
A heart thats long been broken
Because my darlings there-

H. B. Olberg (Gunn)
CAMERA-SHY GRAHAME
One day a girl took some
pictures of you;
It was when her camera was
new.
This was in Keystone on the
P. M. run--
You didn't know, you were
blinded by the sun.
No girl ever had your picture
before--
You offered to take it to the
Kodak store.
(What method could you use to
get it back
When it was printed and in her
sack?)
You had to get all the negatives
back for sure--
You exposed them so that they
were a blur!
With the saddest face that you
could make,
You told her the pictures did
not take.
I am one girl who kept a picture
of you--
It was snapped when your
uniform was new.
Don't get excited, and don't get
mislead--
It's not of your face--just the
back of your head!

Bonnie Lee Ward
REFLECTIONS
Reflections
on the way things used to be...
on the way we used to live...
on the way we used to learn...
Reflections
on the way we used to grow...
on the way we used to behave...
on the way we used to believe...
on the way we used to pray...
Reflections
on the way we used to belong...
on the way we used to hope...
on the way we used to give...
on the way we used to cope...
Reflections...Reflections...
Reflections on the way we used
to...love.......

Barbara Pecci Boyle
THE NURSING HOME
I hate to go in,
The smell is bad,
The faces are even worse.
The empty looks,
The awful cries,
It seems life is but a curse.
What can I do?
What can I say?
Keep it light,
Keep it gay,
Try to make it a better day.
Smile alot, bring her food,
How long before I leave.
And when I leave, to the
nearest bar, and then a time
to grieve.
Down with one drink, order
another.
What a terrible thing to do to
your mother...

C. D. Zappala
JUST A LITTLE
So here you are again
Once my wife, but now just a
friend
And that old familiar pain
Seems to appear
Whenever you are near.
Each lonely night is followed by
another empty day
And my memory grows dim
But I can't forget long ago
It still feels like yesterday
When you left me to be with
him.
My heart is so unkind
It refuses to let go
Silly thoughts race through my
mind
Maybe we could...
Perhaps this time...
But silently your eyes say no.
My life has been so re-arranged
Whatever happened to our
loving smiles
You're right, it's all been said
And nothing has changed
Though only inches separate us
It might as well be miles.
Tears sting my eyes
As you tell me again it's really
over
I keep hoping that you're wrong.
It still hurts sometimes
But just a little
And not for very long.

Gregory Norman
I AM
I am
I have always been.
I exist through eternity,
Before the stars
And after reality.
I am
I will always be.
I do not touch
I can not feel
Yet I am here
I am real
I watch
But I do not interfere.
Civilizations die
Suns explode
While I remain
Within my void.
I feel no pain
I search for no gain
I observe all things.
I am power
There is nothing
I can not do.
And though I could create
Or destroy a galaxy.
I am alone
I am lonely.

Anne Bernadine Cunningham
WINTER WONDERLAND
In amongst this Winter
Wonderland lies, dormant, all
my dreams...
But, in the Spring, when the sun
wakens the earth, and the
water dances over the rocks to
the music of the stream,
So, too, will my dreams waken
and dance to the music of life.
And as the trees shed their
heavy coats -
Shaking off the winter chill -
lifting their limbs to embrace
once more the life that was
silent and still,
I, too, will uncover myself and
reach out to embrace the
dreams...
lying, dormant, in my heart.

Donna Grace Lareau
MY WORLD
Look at all the trees and plants
growing up so high.
Look at all the little birds flying in
the sky.
And all the kittens playing and
the puppies in the grass,
It's all a part of nature, but the
days go by too fast.
Look at all the daffodils blooming
in the sun.

Look at all the children playing
and having fun.
And look at the beautiful rainbow
with its colors oh so bright,
Soon the day will be gone and it
will turn to night.
Look at the little baby sleeping in
a crib.
Look at all the adults and see just
how they live.
And look at all the animals
running around so free,
We all must learn that in this
whole world there's no one just
like me.

Sharon I. Jenkins
MY GREATEST DREAM
Last night I had the Greatest
Dream
I ever had before,
I dreamt the world had all
agreed,
To never go to war.
In my dream, I saw a room
Filled with powerful men.
Who signed a paper, and vowed
to all,
They would never fight again.
After the paper was signed
A million copies were made,
And everyone joined hands
As they bowed their heads
and prayed.
Everywhere people were singing,
And they danced all around
As they watched guns, swords,
And uniforms, being buried in
the ground.
After I was awakened,
I prayed my greatest dream
would come true.
And I could see the world at
peace,
Before my life is through.

Carol Schaper
HAIKU
O kitty-piller.
Your woven web on a leaf.
Please look around you.
O spider web, how
You glisten in the sunshine.
Smile at all of us.

Pamela A. Blue
THEY HAVE TO STICK YOU
What the hell of life's success
With diction and friction and all
that mess.
As growing years begin to
develop
Your suited with a sect or
fellow.
Where the devil is man's
individual
They'd rather stick you with the
rest of the FOOLS.
Spread your way through all
Confusion
And run into a big wall with
more Delusions.

Myra Y. DeBruhl
INSIGHT
How well do I see you?
Your words speak in lights that
say
"Stand up" "Step down" "go left"
"turn right"
The mood of your speech traces
smiles or frowns--
Sometimes hardly visible--but
never hidden.
Your trivial expressions paint
my colors
From cheery red "hello's" to
silver-toned "good-bye's."
Your oral tones clear my view;
They uncover wrinkles or reveal
unblemished youth.
You bodies appear to me in
outline;
I see only forms of your faces;
But don't wear so much make-up
---For your voices are my
pictures.

Jean Marie White
DANCE CARD
Dance with me again
Swing me around into a new
world
Stay close enough-Long enough
To synchronize our hearts
But please- don't step on my feet
Hurry- someone may try to cut
in

Theresa Crawford
IN SEARCH
Cautiously peeking through the
window pane
In search of the old man-but
always in vain.
So many times he had come to
that door
And many was the time he had
played on the old scarred
floor.
Searching for his friend and
filled with fear
As down his cheek fell a tiny
tear,
No more will he go to the house
to play
For there's no Mr. Clark to begin
the happy day.
Whatever happened to old Mr.
Clark
With his Southern accent and

skin so dark?
Is it true that he's up above
And watching over the boy with love?
With big brown eyes filled with sorrow
Just one more look until tomorrow,
Then over here again he'll roam
To see, if maybe, his friend has come home.

Gertrude Durkee
MID-DECEMBER
While meandering one beautiful winter day
On one of my frequent strolls,
A lovely sight, I did behold.
It was Mid-December,
A perfect day to remember,
The air so crisp and clear,
Some floating white clouds,
That seemed to drift so near.
From out of a lovely magnolia tree,
Green and lush at this time of year,
A flock of starlings
Arrayed in their greenish black winter finery
Flew down to bathe, preen and relax
In a little stream of running water
So happy and free did they seem.
Just a few of God's beautiful creations
That lie around us every where
I couldn't help but stop and think
What a treat for the spirit and soul
If one would only take the time to behold.

Carla Marie Jackson
DOMINOS
Like a stack of dominos
I am basic black
with a few white specs in me
I come from a long chain of
movement called women!
Push one and at the end
of the travel
You will find me
I will fall
and push another as I go
Look closely
if you've never seen
a black child fall
and a black woman rise!

Gregory S. Damici
THE NEW YEAR
It is that well known time of the year
Where daily routines are broken
Strangers more outspoken
Homes flow with holiday cheer
Thoughts turn quickly
As quick as presents are ripped open
To the coming of the New Year
People bring in the New Year as a sign of hope
For most people make what is called a resolution
In hopes the New Year will bring the solution
Most people wake up feeling elated, to have celebrated
Though they can't remember the resolutions they had stated
Thus begins the New Year

Ken Jones
A CHRISTMAS CARD SONG
I Hope I get a Christmas card for Christmas,
A Christmas card so very bright and true.
I wish I'd get a Christmas card for Christmas,
A Christmas card signed 'I Love You' !
I don't have a very big Christmas tree --
I don't have a fireplace for Santa Clause --
I had to hang my stocking by the Christmas tree --
Still I'm hoping and wishing - because -- because because
I'd like to get a Christmas card for Christmas,
A Christmas card signed 'I Love You' !

Kevin E. Loree
PROPER USE OF "LOVE"
"Love" is the most treasured word known to man.
But when love is misused it can break even the toughest of men.
When used right, love could make the smallest man into a giant.
The only problem is that many people need a special kind of love.
And only a certain person can give somebody this special love.
The biggest problem in the world today is that love is used in the wrong way.
If love was used in the way it was meant to, the world would be a lovely place for all mankind to live and do what he or she has always wanted to do.

Joe D. Shelton
TO THE ONE I LOVE
Since I met you,
my life has gained meaning.
A word from your lips,
sets my heart beating.
The smile on your face
radiates from above.
The showers from your blessings
are as gentle as doves.
How unworthy I am
for a love so divine,
It has given to me
a life so sublime.
God surely has blessed you
with beauty and poise.
It creates for me a dream
you'll be mine always.
Since I met you
my life has gained meaning.
If you should but leave,
my heart would cease beating.

Tina M. Conte Siecko
TRAVELING
20 August 1977
Traveling interpretations of feelings.
Why do you go where you go?
Why are you there and I here?
The sky as seen through sun glare prevention tinted windows of a beat-up four-speed buggy, is not moving.
Only my hands are real. I feel only my body. The rest is in motion.
Traveling is not really going anywhere.
The road moves backward to where you just came from as you move forward toward the place you have never been.
Why do I miss you, your voice, your touch?
Do you miss me?
You're going some place, but even you do not know where.
Me, I go sometimes.
Sometimes I even get there, to where I'm going.
Down, down, down the road whose end we cannot see.

Rev. Don Thompson
FRIENDS
Good friends are difficult to find under the best of circumstances.
When you find a person whose tastes and thoughts are compatible;
whose humor is contagious;
Whose support is unfailing;
Whose trust is never absent;
Whose understanding is equal to any challenge;
That person is a friend to be treasured;
And friends don't need adjectives-
Not men friends;
Women friends;
Young or old friends;
Or even best friends;
A friend is a friend;
And neither time nor distance can wither the value of friendship.

Jeremiah G. Hickey, Sr.
THE SAILOR
When he went down to sea in ships my friend,
His love and dove they wept his ship to see.

When he returned the hearts he broke would mend.
And, gladly would his love be filled with glee.

Doris Newman
BEAUTY IS:
A bird as it wings it's way in flight,
The shining brightness of a starry night,
A stream as it winds it's way below,
A distant mountain with a cap of snow,
A weeping willow swaying in the wind,
The petal softness of a baby's skin,
the taste of sweetness from a kiss with love,
The rainbow paintings of the sky above,
An Irish rose blooming in the wild,
The delightful hearty laughter of a child,
The real beauty of this world is to behold
The touch of God's own presence in my soul.

Jeanine Nanette Gordon
MEANINGLESS LIFE
Little rolling waves
Might make a journey very boring.
Little rolling waves
That quickly vanish from our sight.
Onward, they spread onward,
Or might vision be deluding.
So stretch the days of aimlessness
That yawn from morn 'til night.

Mrs. Frank N. Kennedy
EASTER LILY
"Tis the Season we empathsize
To think of Spring and realize,
The miracle that Easter brings
With a change in nature's many things.
Our hearts are warmed with thoughts of Love,
For a gift of friends and God above.
The Easter Lily so white and pure
Is truly a symbol God's Spirit is here."

Tamera Faye Robinson
UNTITLED
Life
Like the blossoms of Spring,
Here then it's not.
You can hear the birds sing,
And you know that you've got
To live for today
For tomorrow may bring
A sun that won't whine
And bells that don't ring.
Life is so brief;
We're left in dismay.
Much like a thief,
Death steals them away.
Some of them children,
Some of them old;
One day we're all gone,
The world is left cold.

Michael R. Stanko
WITH TENDERNESS
She loves me with her tenderness
In the morning spring,
We take each others slenderness
That makes me want to sing.
Unknown lady I have many thoughts for you
Don't ever make me sing the blues,
If that does happen to us
Both of us might lose too much
In life the game of love can work out
So therefore lady let's not just stand about,
We've got to make things happen for our own good
I've got to hold you tenderly,
you know I should.

Vera C. Stallknecht
TO BUCK
(loyal friend and companion)
He is waiting for me, by the bend in the road,
Where the moss is green, and the banks are high,
Watching the road--with expectancy;
Searching the faces of passers-by:
Just as the sad, brown eyes, were closing-
I told him of Death, and, Eternity...
Admonished him well... remember, old fellow-
Lie down in the foliage--and, wait for me:
There are other trails our feet must travel-
Our shackles, belong to the greedy sod;
It will make sweet music...your bark...my whistle...
As we tramp up the High-Road -
That leads to GOD.

Susan Pickreign
THESE FOUR SEASONS
These four seasons do I know,
The Spring blossom, the Winter snow,
The Summer sunset the

Autumn mist,
These I know and shant forget,
Ere they come ere they go,
These four seasons do I know.

Jerri Lynne Yount
CRASHING ON THE SHORE
The tide came crashing on the shore,
But nothing crashes anymore
You're gone--
The shadows sing a song
It's over--
I knew all along
You are just a dream to me
Someone I once loved to see,
But now I might as well be blind,
Because you've become invisible
Except inside my mind
Once you came crashing on my shore
Now nothing crashes anymore.

Thomas A. Sterling
AWAKENING
You started young, untried,
wanted then to be a bride.
You thought you knew
Each other well,
As least the thoughts
You thought to tell.
The heart you gave him
Had not lied.
It did not yet
Have much to hide.
The world you knew
Has grown since then;
You know you can't
Go back again.
You've grown and gained
Directions new
That never were
A part of you.
And looking for
The friend he knew
He wonders what
Became of you.
You didn't go
But only changed
And yet your life
Is rearranged.
No longer just
A part of him
Anticipating
Every whim,
You are yourself
And free to say
Love the woman
That I am today.

Nina W. Kurkamp
THE DRAGON FLY
Like a droning plane downing
Down from the sky.
His lithe body hovering - hovering
That beautiful Dragon Fly!
Wings holding without effort,
His lissome form, an acme to see
His trim, tailored semblance,
A plane seem to have been devised from Thee!
His similar symmetrical wing span
are such as we see,
Such gorgeous dark coloring,
A challenge to artistry.
He is fine grained and slender
Graceful - shall we say tender?
I behold - and am rapt to see.
But - he is a rapacious acarid!
How can that be?
Looking so serene and beautiful,
Seems like an enigma to me,
That Nature has equipped him with talons.
With which he can ravage and pillage
His lesser prey. Dragon! How can you?
Or is it the Creator's way,
The survival of the fittest,
This is the way?

Erma Jean Bomberger
GOD'S SALVE
Doctors use ointment and salve,
But God has given us Christ to have;
To heal our wounds and bruises,
And be our only Blessed Jesus.
Though there may be no medicine,
Still God relieves us from our sin;
And heals my broken, contrite heart,
If I, but only, do my part.

Nova R. Rohrbaugh
DAD'S OLD FORD
My Dad's old '21 Ford
Was a wonderful machine.
It was the best of the day
For it ran on gasoline.
Dad drove us to church
And to picnics as well.
Whether it would go through the mud
We could never quite tell.
When the mud was too deep
And the old Ford would not move,
My two brothers, mother and I
Pushed mightily, with a big shove.
There were no hard roads then
And travel was slow,
But whenever Dad went
We kids were ready to go.
Twenty five miles per hour
Was his regular speed.
To rush and to hurry
There really was no need.
My Dad's old '21 Ford
As my memory still serves
Was our pride and our joy
Going on power, up hills and 'round curves.
In summer and winter
Through heat and through cold
The Ford served its purpose-
With us, too, its also grown old.

Pamela DiMeglio (LZ)
IN A MIDNIGHT AIRE
Moonlight casts shadows, among the trees
Nature's birds, are ever so free.
People dancing around, in the dark of night.
Singing to the eagle, that is in flight.
The shadows portray, the beauty within.
The moonlight around us, is not dim.
The nights in white satin, that never reach to the end.
A stairway to heaven to you, my dear friend.
The beauty of night remains, in all.
The moon and the stars always on call.
As dawn soon approaches, the moon, dims away.
Stars fade to clouds, that are, ever so grey.
This poem has ended, the story so dear.
'Till night rises upward, ever so clear.

Sandy Lawrence
BROWN TONED MEN BLACK MINDS
brown toned men with...
black minds of ancestral thoughts,
poppin out of their brown bodies,
the need for expression...
the urgency of life,
swelling their veins,
with new thoughts and ways to relate and project to us...
Black women...

Vivyenne N. Astle
A TRIBUTE TO A DAUGHTER
Close your eyes, let your imagination go free...
Can you imagine a world without music or laughter?
Can you imagine a tree without a songbird?
Can you imagine a forest without water or shade?
Can you imagine a winter without a spring?
Can you imagine a home without a daughter?
Daughters are the sunbeams in our homes, in our lives.
Daughters are the fulfillments of our dreams, our future.
Daughters are innocents wrapped in ourity.
Daughters are love, unselfishly given, no questions asked, no credentials needed.
Daughters are life's embellishments...frosting on the cake.
Daughters are the precious gems in the ivory tower.
Daughters are companions with God.
Daughters are Heavenly Father's gift to the home and to the world.
Life is wonderful when you are blessed with a daughter.
Dedicated to my daughter, Elizabeth Gwen Astle

Tim Olds
AN ARTISTS' DAY
I heard the wind speak
As the sun rose to morning
And the dew boiled to vapor
Filling the air with fog.
I heard a bird answer
As the sun rose to noon
And the fog rose
Filling the sky with clouds.
I heard the wind speak,
I heard a bird answer,
Morning passed to noon,
Noon passed to evening.
Blue sky painted with white,
White sun tinting to yellow,
Yellow tint turning crimson,
The day fades from evening to night.
Crimson splotches fade away
To give way to blackness
And white, blue, and red
Spackle covers our night canvas.
The wind sleeps,
The birds sleep,
The canvas is cleaned
And prepared for another day.

Jo Ann Lang
THE LONG DAY
I watched them from the hillside
bleached yellow cornstalks row on row,
standing stiff and cold and tall
like sentinals against the crow.
I watched them-then I watched some more
and then I was gonna go,
but then I saw a hawk-
so lazy and so slow
and he flew down and grabbed a little mouse
who was my friend and visited my house.
So I felt sad and just sat still
but I knew I had to go
'cause I was gettin' cold
and it felt like it was gonna snow.
I watched them from the hillside-
watched them go fast then slow-
snowmobiles played tic-tac-toe
across the pale blue snow.
Oh, what a joy to watch them
go fast then slow!
And then I heard her call me
and I knew I had to go-
but if I press against the tractor
maybe she won't know.

Shasaka
POEM TO THE PAVONINE LADY

Walking there, with a heart so
sweet that any creature she
passes close to puts out its
tongue to touch her,
Head held high,
aloof in her attitude,
Almost as if the suns rising and
setting is a show just for her.
Standing there,
I watch men trying to catch
her eye.

C. Gay Fritzemeier
THE DICTATOR

You evil creature
hanging there
upon the wall,
your wicked laughter
ringing silently
in my ears!
Your circle of twelve
ominous eyes
glaring snickered daggars
through my
trapped, impatient soul.
Why do you keep me
prisoner here?
How dare you move
your slender red tongue
so slowly
around your face,
killing me with
too much time?!

Susan McKay Reale
STREET CORNER CRITICS

You can feel,
As you're walking by
With your mind in the clouds,
That you've caught an eye.
It's not your intention
To turn a head,
Couldn't have been
Anything you said.
You don't swing your hips
Or strut your stuff
You don't like the "Wolfcalls"
But that's just tough.
Since you're a woman
And well endowed,
You'll always stand out
In any crowd.
Wherever you go,
S'gonna be someone
Thinks you're a show.
Street corner critics
With all their reviews
They keep the score
And you always lose.
In a game you're not playing
(For you are the game)
They add up your credits
Without knowing your name.

Ethel L. Kling
QUEEN MIDAS

She had a wondrous garden
Of jade and beaten gold,
And an ivory carving
Of a half-blown rose.
She loved it.
It was most unique,
But I prefer my roses
Soft and moist and sweet.

Gary Michael Williams
BY THE SEA

If I lived by the sea
and could come and go as I
please;
I'd invite a friend as dear as you
to join me in the oceanic
breeze.
We'd walk hand in hand,
kicking at the sand,
Absorbing the sun's warm rays
in various kinds of ways.
We could dig for hidden
treasure
and with the time we
wouldn't measure.
If by chance we struck it rich,
it would have been good luck
for having dug the ditch.
We could buy a boat to sail
around,
having no one telling where
we were bound.
The days would be lengthy,
but would seem to have past
too fast.
When dusk should arrive
we could build a fire on the
beach;
We could gaze into the blaze
staying within one another's
reach.
As another day would come to
an end,
another night was to begin.
If the mood was right,
with the surroundings not
bright, in our minds we
might unite.

William E. Boger
EVENTIDE

A walk along the sea shore
Is one of life's great treats-
A chance to get away
From bustling city streets...
The shrill cry of the gull
In answer to his mate-
Is certain to add joy
And help you forget it's late...
The fishing pier is standing
Like a fortress against the tide-

When the waves roll in
All fish know where to hide...
The sea shells feel sharp
When put into a mesh bag-
The salty tang of sea spray
Assures our spirits never sag...
The lighthouse sends it's beacon
To warn the ships of rocks-
It's always a pleasant sight
When they pull along side the
docks...
Our sun is sinking into the sea
As sea oats begin to sway-
God is preparing to close
Another beautiful day!

Maxine Smith
CHRISTMAS DAY IN THE NURSING HOME

It is Christmas day in the
nursing home,
And the cold bare walls are
bright;
With garlands of green and
holly, and the place is a
pleasant sight
For with clean washed hands,
and faces, in a long and
hungry line,
Sat the people at the tables,
for this is the hour they dine.
On the roofs, and the glittering
turrets,
That night when the sun went
down,
The mellow glow of the twilight
shone
Like a glittering jeweled crown.
And bathed in living glory as
the people lifted their eyes
They saw the pride of city,
the spires of the home rise.
What presents Old Santa Claus
brought in the night,
Just the things they wanted, and
left before light.
And now added Anna in a voice
soft and low,
"You believe there's a Santa
Claus, Willie, I know."
And determined no secret
between them should be
I should say there is, if he sent
you all these.
He knew just what presents the
people would please,
Well, well let him think so, the
dear little elf,
'Twould be cruel to tell him I
did it myself.
Blind fathers, who caused your
stern heart to relent
A hasty word spoken so soon
to repent!
'Twas the being who bade you
steal softly upstairs
And made you his agent to
answer their prayers.

Shirley Hooper
BE STILL

Be still and know that I am God,
His voice boomed in my mind.
My life was filled with cares
And things of every kind.
Crowded streets and noisy cars,
Scowling strangers everywhere;
Impatient shoppers, ringing
phones,
And no one really cared.
But I heard the voice so loud
and clear,
"Be still and know that I am
here.
Be still and know I am your God
I want to help you where you
are."
My steps slowed down until I
stopped,
The senseless running nowhere.
My heart had raced, but now it
seemed
That even it had slowed its
pace.
Lord, forgive me, for along the
way,
I lost the sense of you.
Let me remember every day,
You're only found when we slow
down.

Sherry Marie Oettle
A CLOWN

A clown is funny
A clown is happy
A clown is sunny
A clown will never frown
A clown is cheerful
A clown is good
A clown is happiness
If everyone was as good as a
clown
God would never look down at
us and frown.

Elma E. Strine
CHRISTMAS BIRTHDAY

We've just celebrated a
birthday—a day of joy
But sadly to many it meant
only a toy.
How many children really
knew what the day was about
As they exclaimed over
goodies that "Santa" had
brought.
And how many parents really
gave a thought
To the glory of the day as
they rushed out and bought
All the trucks and race
track—things Johnny had
asked for
And the clothes, doll house
and dolls—Susie only had
four.
Jesus must have said—looking
down on us early that morn
They couldn't have gone
shopping if "I hadn't been
born."

Mildred Grossman
ANOTHER TIME

When I look up Broadway
I see a corridor of misty dew
in the atmosphere of a day
filled with rain.
Relic visions of a bygone era.
The icons of these structures
that do wear their age in time
stood proudly in their day.
These structures do talk to me,
I see the beauty in their
presence.
Their splendor may go
unnoticed by
many of those that do pass by.
One only has to open his eyes
to see
the once held elegance of a
treelined
Broadway with argyles and
motifs that
rim its edges, as diamonds have
sparkles
and nights have stars.

Delilah-Judith
YOU HAVE THE KEY TO MY HEART, DARLING

He: "I have a rendez-vous with
love, sweetheart,
My heart is for You alone,
I promised I'd return to You,
dear one,
In dreams I seek the one that's my
own."
She: "You turned the key in the
door of my heart,
Now how can I ever escape?
Please find the key in your
treasure chest,
My heart finds You guilty of its
rape."
He: "I have the gold key to your
heart, darling,
But it's not in my treasure chest,
I wear it on a gold chain, darling,
Around my throat is the key to
our nest."
She: "You have turned the key in
the door of my heart,
Now how can I ever escape?
Give me the key to our one
treasure chest,
Or you'll find me guilty of its
rape."
He: "We'll keep Locked the door to
our one treasure chest,
I hold the one key,--and its mate."

Mable M. Price
CHRISTMAS IN THE FOREST
Wildlife living in solitude and
serenity in the winter woods,
Know peace, freedom, and
contentment, and the holy
time is understood.
Nature too enjoys they presence
knowing he dwelleth near,
May you too enjoy these
blessings through the coming
year

Charlotte Robertson Albright
HEAVEN'S SPECIAL CHILD
A meeting was held quite far
from Earth,
"It's time again for another
birth,"
Said the angels to the Lord
above—
"This Special Child will need
much love.

His progress may seem very
slow,
Accomplishments he may not
show.
And he'll require extra care
From the folks he meets way
down there.

He may not run or laugh or
play,
His thoughts may seem quite far
away;
In many ways he won't adapt—
For he'll be known as
handicapped.

So let's be careful where he's
sent,
We want his life to be content.
Please, Lord, find parents who
Will do a Special job for you.

They will not realize right
away—
The leading role they're asked
to play;
But with this child sent from
above
Comes stronger faith and richer
love.

And soon they'll know the
privilege given,
In caring for this gift from
Heaven.
Their precious charge, so meek
and mild,
Is "Heaven's very Special Child."

KT Harmon
UNTITLED
asked
the love
for diamonds
glistening. . .
on my frozen
cheeks

they seethe
reflecting. . .
when does one
learn
to remain
silent

B. Brisbane
LOVE ME
I could feel your
eyes on me. . .
Holding me. . .tempting
me . . .
I am afraid to meet
them.
Your hand caressing my
back. . .softly. . .
reaching to the very
core. . .
I can't feel it. . .I must
not. . .
But I feel nothing else. . .
your hand
your gentle passion
pulling me to you. . .
I turn to see your face. . .your
eyes. . .
your mouth
drawing close. . .
closer. . .
And I am lost in your
endless
touch.
Love me.

Jack Androwitz
SEASONS OF LIFE
When springtime comes the
earth is bare
Life's magic touch seems
everywhere;
A child is born, a saintly sight
A cry is heard into the night;
Then summer comes with heat
and rain
The child matures with growing
pain;
Then autumn winds and leaves
do fall
And middle age receives its call;
When winter comes with snow
and cold
Time takes its toll, and life
grows old;
The cycle turns and rides in
vain
And seasons life starts in again.

Jean H. East
POTPOURRI
a new pink rose with pearls of
dew
the cozy aroma of onion stew
that something so magic in
childhood's smile
the orangy-red colour of brand
new tile
remembrance of organdy party
frocks
the maddening ticks of alarum
clocks
The dreamy haze 'round one's
first love
stupid feeling-to lose one glove
the satiny gleam of a rain wet
street
persons to whom one must
repeat
christmas eve mass-the
enchantment-the glow
trying to find someone in the
movie show

Ann Ransaw
OUR DREAMS—FROM MORE POETIC PEARLS
Dreams are made of fragile stuff;
They're as evanescent as the
earthy dust!
If there are no dreams in each of
us
What good is living—why all
the fuss?
If we're to rise to the highest
heights;
There must be cloudless days
and starry nights!
So—dream your dreams
And plan your schemes
To reach your greatest heights
by noble means!

Alice Porter Bonn
YOUTH
The greatest of treasures,
Embracing all pleasures
Is Youth.
Highest ambitions,
Preposterous notions
Flaming emotions,
Queer contradictions
Are Youth.
In the days ere we lose it
We carelessly use it,
Often abuse it,
Grossly misuse it,
Our Youth.
But when we are old,
Our emotions grown cold,
We would give all we hold
Of fame, honor, or gold,
For youth.
For the greatest of treasures,
Embracing all pleasures,
Is youth.

John Swope
PLAY—DOH
a wall of clay spoke
to me three days
ago yesterday
and asked me
to mold him
into a curb
i told him
i had no right
to make him
less what he
truly was
the next day
he asked me
to sculpt
him into a
monument
i told him
i had no right
to make him
more than what he
truly was
the next day
he asked me
to cut holes
in him so
people could
see who he was
i told him
i had no right
to open him
for others
to see
yesterday
he called me
friend.

Elizabeth Madden Noel
LOVE IN THE MIDDLE YEARS
I've gone many nights without
sleep.
I've tossed and turned,
For your love I've burned.
For the comfort of your arms
around me
And your tender love words.
Reach out for me darling,
Let me know you are there,
And that you care.
The distance isn't so far. . .
Only from your pillow to mine.

Arthur Greisiger
MILADY
(for Lisa)
Tho' I love thee with all my
heart,
my love goes without notice
As the fragrance of the fresh
spring air
loses its grandeur
Amongst the sweet perfume
of
a thousand roses
So is my Love for thee,
MiLady
If I could but gaze upon your
heart
t'would be so easy for me to
hold you
If I could but caress your soul
once again
Love would surely be of High
once I thought. . .
. . . 'tis but a game
but that was once,
and never again!
O Dear Love. . .I beg of thee. . .
Do come to me,
Do come to me. . .

S. A. Phillips
INSPIRATION OF A FRIEND
Inspire me to live
Inspire me to be free
Inspire me to laugh in the bad
times
Inspire me to cry when tears are
needed
Inspire my feelings so deeply
That I can continue to love
And go on with my life
For without a friend like you
Life can get awful lonely

Jack Kashubeck
A PETITION OF MANY NAMES
Silent mist of angelic light
can you see me standing here;
Arms outstretched,
asking you only to favor my
catalytic mind.
I've dared become a part of this
collection of solitude,
stretched and pummeled by the
ecstacy of illusion.
Oh why must the morning,
only awaken an aching heart;
is it the twilight of my yearning
soul that I perceive,
with my caged and limited eyes.
Come stir the lotus which
graciously floats
on the seas of my experience.
Awaken me from my slumber,
for I have slept while you passed
near.
I've played the pawn forsaking
the king
and the sacrifice lays naked,
a feast of carrion and crime.
I too am a splendid flame:
a spark from the eternally kind.
I must don my birthright,
that gloried robe
which I without knowing,
once thoughtlessly cast aside.
For it is you through me
and I through you
that truth may somehow be
attained.

L. C. Fite
BLACKBERRY WINTER
A cold day in April:
No birds sing in the frost-bit
garden;
"Blackberry winter," I say to
myself
As I look out the back door.
Hubris can victimize the things
of
Nature, as well as man,
I muse as I watch the overcast
sky—
The sun a mere silver disc
In a field of golden haze.
This morning, from my bedroom

window I saw blackened blossoms,
And snow nestling on green leaves.
A false spring deluded us all:
A wintry, vengeful blast from the Arctic
Undeceived me. A killing frost conquered all.
The ultimate fable against illusion:
For man, too, like the flower,
May find his fruits
Rotted in icy armour ere his time.

John J. Hyland, III
TENDERLY, QUIETLY, LOVINGLY

Tenderly, She speaks to me
Of love shared;
Hopeful to begin again,
Renewed in spirit,
Challenged by life's longings,
Tempered by reason.
Quietly, I sit beside her
With loving eyes;
Peaceful in the evening light,
Revealed in expression,
Relived by a smile,
Pursued by wonder.
Lovingly, We embark together
On the forward path;
Mindful of the road ahead,
Concealed in tomorrow,
Embraced by knowledge,
Awakened by each other.

M. G. Ogloff
WHAT ABOUT TOMORROW

When will man learn
From the mistakes we have made
Will we gain from our experience
Or will we just walk away
Only to curse the damage
From the errors we have made
And the busy city streets
That have risen from the country
What will happen when they crumble
Will we have a place to run
Will there be a tomorrow
For our daughters and our sons?

Jan K. Focker
AT AGE SIX

With puckered cheeks he sighs,
Limpid tears with pleading eyes,
Here he stands this little man:
Here he stands, this little man,
He sees what passes by,
This little creature, which so silently lies;
Whispering prayers which go unheard,
Dying by his feet a trembling bird,
Here he stands, this little man.

Willis J. Banks
LOVE

Love is what you make it, I've heard for years
So, do be careful, don't fill it with tears;
With all it's problems, life can be sweet
If you face reality and refuse to retreat.
Find someone to love, and pray they love you,
Love unselfishly—the greatest thing you can do.
If it's a woman, do be gentle,
Give her warmth—a chance to kindle;
Try to dominate and be possessive
Is one sure way to make her restive:
Give her freedom, let her breathe
And rest assured she will not leave,
But if it's mother, uncle, sister or brother
Don't let it drive you asunder;
Be not possessive—relax, let go,
Their love for you will doubtless grow.
Where dad's concerned, don't put him down
'Cause when you need him he'll be around.
No one is perfect—neither you nor I
For when time comes you will surely die
But, if you truly love, as you should,
Life for you will be only good.

Alta Shill Smith
GENTLE SONNET TO A SLEEPING CHILD

Gently, as I touch your sleeping face,
My fingertips feel velvet. My heart's pace
Grows swift, and I give thanks to Powers That Be
For giving such a gift to such as me.
Your tiny fingers gently clasp my hand,
And hold my heart, and make me understand
That evermore, wherever there's a trace
Of velvet, in my heart I'll touch your face.
Your gentle way of smiling in your sleep
Just melts my heart. I know that I will keep
That smile in mind as thru my day I go
On plodding slowly forward— and I know
When I need strength to carry on life's game,
I'll close my eyes and gently speak your name.

Doris H. Weaver
LOVE AT FIFTY

Like a young bride,
I crawl into bed.
I lie by your side.
Your arm pillows my head.
The cares of the day disappear.
You are my lover.
You're my tranquilizer.
You are my husband.
You're my stabilizer,
As you wipe away a tear.
You're my best friend.
Sometimes you're my stranger.
You are my husband.
You're my mood changer,
You'll always be my cavalier.

Jesse A. Page
A FRIEND LIKE ME

I care so very much for you,
  And you don't even know.
I see you each and every day,
  No matter where I go.
All though most times—you're not aware,
  That I'm aware of you.
Always I lend a helping hand,
  I would be a friend so true.
You always pass most people by,
  For them—you do not see.
So you might have just lost a chance,
  To have a friend like me.

Jerry Lee Austin
LIVING

I've seen the fabled Elephants held tigers by their tails
I've rode the great white horse and had a Quentin Quail
I've played the losing horses and bet on a real live dog
I've raced in the sunshine and walked in a fog
I've held the bag for others given and taken advice
I've tried to purchase true love and paid a terrible price

A. Rose
IF YOU WOULD ALLOW

If you would allow, I would let your spirit
Grow free and totally independent of me
If you would allow, I would turn you into a
Most beautiful flower
There is nothing more serene than the
Lotus blossom, you could develop that serenity,
If you but allow
For if ever I cause you shame I would turn
My eyes to the sky from whence I came:

I couldn't bear causing you pain
If you would allow, I would teach you the
Gentleness of a touch the value of silence:
I'd never pierce your heart as cupid does with
His arrow nor distort your brain
I love you and trust you
If you will only trust those near and dear,
Admittedly a very select few, you could walk
Through life unafraid and unashamed
If you would allow you would stroll through the
Spring, summer, autumn and winter of your life,
Free of emotions that bind.

Jesse A. Page
SMOG

What is this smog—out in the air,
  That robs from me my sight?
And goes deep down into my lungs,
  It makes my chest so tight.
What is this smog—I ask of you,
  Please make it go away.
No one should have to breathe it in,
  The way I do each day.
What is this smog—I see so thick?
  It turns my blue sky brown.
And some times makes the tear drops roll,
  Out on my cheeks then down.
I hope and pray some day our Lord,
  Will show us how it's done.
To clean the air—and keep it clean
  Like way back—in year one.

Mary Agnes Landgrebe
SINCE YOU'VE BEEN GONE. . .

—We love to walk the shoreline slowly, dazed
In blissful memory of days now grown old,
Always a rainbow glittering on the waves
When summer sunset hues are glazed in gold. . .
And, holding hands we gaze and bathe our moods,
The grays to golds, catharsis we achieve,
Unspoken feelings, hopes are like said truths
Of father-daughter love at last relieved. . .
I bend to touch the rainbow— it goes Black;
I reach for you—I find A Silhouette;
Still life goes on in dream evading fact—
That slicks and shadows merely mask regret. . .
—Since you've been gone I can't do what's undone,
And so I dream and what I've not Is Done!

Erik Baard
IN UNION

An infant grins gleefully at a clown,
  turning, tumbling, falling
A caring mother settles down on a crystal bench to nurse her baby.
A fledgeling struggles into the new world of dazzling colors.
A man nourishes a woman's womb
  to sprout a child.
A toddler rolls in a meadow of tall grass
  In Union.

F. P. Cawthon
AND LOVE AND YOU

I'm thinking of
  Spring
    Streams
  and green
Trees borne to us by an awakening earth,
And love and you.
I'm grasping for
  Fragrances remembered
    Hues of sunsets
      long since devoured by the shroud of night
And day break's discovery of new fallen snow,
And love and you.
I've found
  Warmth
    Tenderness
      Devotion
And a Promise for all the tomorrows that will be,
And love and you.

Wendy J. Ferrier

ON A MOROCCON BEACH: THE CHATTELS

Seagulls cry and skim the beach
as the ocean counterpoints
the call.
The Moroccon sun beats upon
the straw hats of chattels,
their keen eyes searching for
patterns of life in the wet
sand.
Too soon, the brightly colored
ladies travel into mirages,
their presence disappearing
into illusion.
The waves have washed their
footprints into the sea,
and only the echo of their
treble song tells me they were
ever there.

Jesse A. Page

FRIENDS

You cannot buy or sell or trade,
Or even give away.
A friend that's true will always
stay,
Every minute of the day.
Although there are times, you
are shut out
Like the sun on a cloudy day.
But no matter what you try to
think,
He's still out there to stay.
Now even when the darkness
comes,
The sun still brightly shining.
Just like a friend—A friend thats
true

He just keeps right on trying.
The sun has so much time to
wait
To try and shine for us.
I'll do the same for my dear
friends
With out even a fuss.
A day, a week, a month, a year
With out a bitter sound.
I'll wait until the day I die
And put deep in the ground.

A. M. Linsenbigler

MY INSPIRATION

My inspiration in all I do is you
Dearest.
Your sweet musical voice causes
me to listen for delights
In all that surrounds me; the
birds, water, insects, and wind.
Though none can match the
thrill your voice gives me.
Your gracefull movements cause
me to look
For the gracefull movements of
Gods gifts,
The animals and plants with
their fluid motions
In the air, water and on the
ground.
Though none can match your
beauty.
Your delight in good music and
rhyme,
Cause me to listen for good
music
And look for good poetry or
rhyme.
You inspire me to try and write
poetry
Though none of any poets
rhymes can do you justice.
For your beauty, grace, wit and
charm are far beyond any
Poets words or dreams dear.
For you Dear are the best of
all God's creations.

Karen Conover

FREEDOM FLIGHT

Caught in a web of illusion
Searching to find a conclusion.
Trials to the left of me,
tribulation on my right
Has me running amock in blind
fright.
In hope to escape this madness I
feel,
As, again I'm crushed by it's
grinding wheel.
It's tearing me apart,
Ripping the seams of my heart.
Freedom is my venture, joy is
my gain,
I've nothing to lose, except
for my pain.
Breaking away with all my
might,
I can't take it anymore I've got
to fight.
The struggle is fierce, but I
can win,
If I call on the strength I find
within.
Freedom is now mine,
The sweetest treasure to find.
Called from the soul to the
surface,
There's no more need to hide,
For now, it is seen in my face,
The gleam of pride.

Tom L. Nanney

OF THE STARS

In a timeless universe.
Each a wandering vagabond
Each a slave of destiny.
Flames leap, rage out
Defiance
Defiance of their burning birth.
Each so different but yet alike.
Each holding someones deepest
secrets
A fantasy
A wish
A lover's soft words.
Millions of tiny doorways to
worlds beyond.
Each a luminous siren
Beckoning, tempting, seductive
Each seems to say
Come, be with me.
Ride the winds of my dreams.
I will lead you to virgin valleys
To ecstasies of the mind.
Each a god upon a golden
torchlit throne.
Each a shining rose
In a darkened bramble
Hidden behind blue leaves.
What to us is a star
May indeed be a planet
Of a far and distant galaxy
Each a living world within itself.

Donna J. Castagnaro

FUTURE

The lightning flashes, the
thunder continues to roar,
The rains fall from the heavens,
the feathered creatures no
longer soar,
The darkness has come, the
time is near,
I will watch until the end,
which I do not fear,
With the doom so near, I keep
wondering why,
We used our powers to create
genocide,
Jealousy, Greed, to be Number
One,
We have paid its price, our
destruction has finally come,
Everything now is in a state of
condemnation,
The survivors of the blast await
their death by radiation,
The world so dorment, no
beauty, no sounds,
The Lifelessness of my planet,
but war knows no bounds,
I feel deaths presence, it has
finally arrived,
I will lay down my weapons, I
am ready to die

Harriette Dean Windham

ECHOES

Inside my mind, the memories
flow
Every second of time, has left
an echo
Some are precious memories
so sweet
Others, if given the
choice, I would not keep
My mind though, does not
discriminate
Along with the love, it records
the hate
The happy is recorded, so
too, the sad
Recording the good, not
censoring the bad
Some memories drift quietly
back to me
While others storm and
thunder loudly
Many are but whispers, and
only tease
I must listen closely, if I
wish to hear these
Somewhere in the far boundries
of my mind
Are echoes, seemingly, from
another time
Memories perhaps an eon
old
Remembered only deep
within my soul
Yet now and then an echo will
hint
Of another place in time I
have spent
some vague memory I made
long ago
Returning to me. . .an
undying echo

Delilah—Judith

DELILAH TO SAMSON

From Biblical Zorek of long ago,
I search for You, my Samson,
Love,
And watch each face that baffles
one;
A Gypsy wandering walk paths
a—distance long;
And though I search a thousand
years,
And make fruitless wishes on
the Lilith star,
And cry my prayers in temples
dim,
And silently tread streets men
rush along,
And see not you that looks like
Him,
I still will search each man's
strong face,—
And draw my veil,—and travel
on'

Evelyn R. Carey

A NEW LIFE

Dear God, "Just as I am", you
took me
When I cried out to you;
I pleaded and I begged You to
show me what to do.
In unconditional surrender, my
life I tossed aside,
And to a new life I was born,
with You, God, as my guide.
Though troubles and many
problems
Still face me day by day,
I have the strength to face them,
'Cause I've You to lead the way.
I take all my petitions to You
each day in prayer,
And then I go ahead with faith,
that You are always there.
There's beauty now in this new
life,
And love and brotherhood;
Stay by my side and lead me
To do things as I should.
Oh help me, God, remind me;
Should the light in my heart
grow dim.
God gave me a new life in
surrender;
And I owe my New Life to Him.

Carol A. Simmonds

WHAT IS LONELINESS

It's listening for a step that
does not come,
A phone that does not ring,
Reaching for a hand that is not
there,
His favorite song he does not
sing.
It's hearing some news you want
to share,
And seeing only his empty
chair.
Seeing a sunset, oh, so bright,
Knowing it soon will be a dark
night.
It's going in a crowded room,
alone, afraid of some dark
gloom,
Head held high, teeth clenched
tight,
To hide the heartache, and the
fright.
It's like walking along in heavy
fog,
Hearing only echoes of your own
heart throb.
It's seeing a child, and
remembering fun,
When we laughed together and
had our own.
It's nights so long, and fitfull
dreams,
And empty tomorrows tucked in
between.

Bernard C. Altman

DECISIONS

Some thoughts were scattered
here and there,
Like sand blown by the wind.
I swept them by the musty air;
From what they said I grinned.
You're heading down an endless
road,
From which there's no return.
A path that many others strode;
Without too much concern.

Drawn by forces close to nature,
Into an unknown place.
Look within; Remove the suture
And meet self face to face.
Review your motives heart aside,
To see just where you stand.
No second thoughts; You must abide
And keep a steady hand.

Elisabeth Weir
MY PRAYER
I am sounding brass
Clanging cymbal
Nothing!
I am not kind, I envy
I am not humble
I behave unseemly
Am easily provoked!
I do not bear all things
Believe all things
Nor do I endure!
Can I say I love?
God judge me if I'm not sincere
To more perfectly LOVE you is "my Prayer".
I Cor. 13 (13 stanzas)

Sharon Bracken
GOD'S LOST CHILD
God helps those who are in need,
And you should find out he'll never deceive.
Doubt is hidden beyond the wall,
That is imbedded ever so tall.
God shall never break the trust,
For it's up to you to break the crust.

Bernard Stephens
THE DECISION
Time for me to slow down and not lose sight of my reality.
Got to show down to recollect my thoughts, to reconsider my ideas, to clarify my mind then start again.
Time to sit quiet, meditate the past, analyze the defeats and victories then reason for the best direction.
Time to learn to appreciate people, to love the finer things in life: true friendship, nature's beauty, the laughter of children the joy of learning. . .
Now is the time to decide to think clearer, to love deeper, to spread more wisdom to mankind.
The decision is more life.

Susan A. Ellerbeck
OUR PLACE
There are little bits of light out now
For a quiet sunrise is near. . .
But something's shattering the silence
It's the crying wind that I hear.
I walk along the well-worn path
Where together we used to walk
I recall the wonderful fun we had
And the long hours we would talk.
I remember too, his last kiss
His tender, awkward goodbye
I reminisce of happy moments
As I keep trying not to cry.
I come quite often to this place
It became a different world to me
But that world is gone, since he left
For my true love walked out on me.
The light has silently faded away
The tranquil night is advancing near. . .
But something's interrupting the silence
It's my lonely teardrops I hear.

Rose M. McQuillan
FOREST PLEASURE
Lying under the towering pines
My tent fills of summer freshness.
Morning breaks like an amber prism,
Cutting through the ebony darkness.
Cool breezes lift my spirits—
As that of a soaring eagle.
Deep I breathe nature's rapture,
My lungs fill full the warmth.

Falling showers arrive in early noon—
Refreshing all of nature's art.
The fallen pine provides shelter for some,
For me, my chair in cooling rain.
At last the starlit sky appears
Reminding me of sequined velvet.
The pace of day slowly fades,
While night sounds lull me to sleep.

Victoria Austin
MOMMA'S SONG
If I could play a piano,
I would write Momma a song.
Each note would be like a beat of her heart,
And every word would speak of a love so strong.
The spoken word cannot say,
Everything she's given me.
Life can be hard with no one to love,
But with this song the world could see.
It comes from my heart,
It is easy to play.
It sings of love and joy, hope and happiness,
It says everything I want to say.
Oh, if I could play a piano,
This would be a Momma's song.
And everyone would know,
Of love so strong.

Joseph Salvo
WHEN SUMMER IS DONE
How does one know
when Summer is done,
And Fall begins
before the coming snow;
The sparkling morning dew
upon natures rainbow hills,
The cooling sands
neath the once burning sun;
The drooping heads of daffodils—
Summer is done.
The silent beaches
near the foaming sea,
The ghost of time
changing the seasons;
The fog rolls in
beyond land and sea;
Trees to shed
garment leaves of red;
The wind to scatter them
upon the green.
Flowers dropping their bloom
to sleep within the crystal gloom,
Silver and gold of Fall
descends upon the earth;
Nature's beauty all aglow
to surrender the season of love,
Nature's new silvery birth
of a brilliant new season;
That is how I know
Summer is done,
And Fall begins
before the coming snow.

Vilanda C. Prograis
AS I WALK
As I walk the everyday
my long darkness awaits me
it lies ahead calling me
stronger and louder
I realized
when my day came forth
only I can stand
out of my own light.

Sally Whalen
LOVE IS
Love is
A walk in the rain
Love is
Sharing other's pain
Love is
Happy nights and days
Love is
A great maze
Love is
A turning wheel
Love is
The way I feel
Love is
A lingering kiss
And with you, dear,
Love is
Bliss.

Leslie A. Manskey
AUGUST 5th
An afternoon in August
Time to think and see
To touch your heart
And lie naked 'neath a tree
Birds were singing
And grasshoppers winging
Keeping perfect time
To souls and bodies melting
Pressing ever closer
Wildflowers and green trees
Witnessing still
That hot day in August
On top of the hill.

C. Robert Blackmon
SKIN DEEP
So much takes place beneath the surface:
A heart contracts and valves flutter,
A pond receives more bottom clutter,
The glider man surveys a snowy
Expanse of fleece that's threat'ning under
And poised to rip his wings asunder,
A master scolds his frisky canine
In tones revealing love. So, hear this:
From 'neath the word the thought but slowly
Exudes for those who'll wait in wonder;
Oh, love, but look and hear and know mine!
And, then, my love will speak, as thunder
Above my softly-spoken patter,
With meanings words alone but cover
And thoughts that must be shared for many
A year to bloom in beauty freely.

Patricia A. Hughes
MARINE LIFE 78
The time has come and you're moving on,
facing problems that never seem gone.
Your life is moving and you don't know where, take one day at a time and there will be no fear.
Just remember when you're feeling down,
there's always a solution to be found.
And life is great if you want it to be,
take it as it comes and you'll always be free.

Joan Bachand
LISTEN TO QUIET
A breeze dances over the cherry boughs,
A sunbeam rests on poppy flowers.
Clouds float across a timeless sky,
And greet the sun as they pass by.
The music is unwritten. The greetings unspoken.
All Nature is Quiet! Listen to Quiet!

We sit in a field and dare not move,
Gaze at the heavens and ask not proof.
Minds are at rest though we know not why,
Souls become peaceful as the days pass by.
The message is clearer. The silent friend ever dearer.
Love is Quiet! God is Quiet! Listen!

Maryann Kushmerick
WHAT IS LOVE?
Love is something I can't explain,
Love is happiness and sometimes pain.
Love is the cheerfulness that grows inside,
Love is something that I cannot hide.
Love is your family, your home, your friends,
Love is something that should not end!

Michael Weitzel
IF THERE IS SUCH A THING!
If there is such a thing,
Why haven't I experienced it?
To actually know it and feel it would
be exactly what it is!
To miss out on the whole of life is
such a waste. But, the question is
Would I know it when it happens?
Having never felt it, or known it,
How would I know it??
Maybe I had it and didn't know it.
To have had it and lost it is worse
than never to have had it
To have it and know it is it!!!

Helen E. Bates
TO OUR FRIENDS. . .
So, in remembering, be aware of this,
Our thoughts, our prayers go with you where you go
And though we'll miss the joy of knowing you,
Each memory'll hold a special afterglow.
So long we've walked, not always hand in hand,
But ever near, and now the time to part,
You one way, we another, down the path,
Fast holding each remembrance in our heart.

M. Jonathan Adams
UNTITLED
Soft fragrant roses
And a turqouise moon—
Brilliant sunlight
In the early afternoon.
I'll eat the lotus
And dream of you.
Walk to me
From those scenes new.
Daughter of venus
And savior of souls,
Lift me safely

Away from the trolls.
You are a seraph,
Yet, sister of beelzebub.
See the world scorched
Then lift me above.
Then, sweet lady, lay me down
Upon a bed of pillows
Let me know all of you—
All your horns and halos.

Michele D. Kinser
WAITING
Life but for an instant stays in our midst
before it turns in ageless flight beyond our reach.
It conquers few dreams before it fades away;
It defies not the truth that it cannot stay.
Suddenly, before we are prepared it falls like
a shadow on the sun.
There it is gone:Fleeting to the arms of its creator.
Hesitating not at its past along the way,
but flying, soaring to a place of destiny.
Darkness turned to brilliant light.
Piercing stars that burn the night,
on peace and tranquil air it lies.
My wings stretch and reach for eternity,
waiting and hoping that this is where I'll be.
My soul looks toward Heaven with song and prayer
that someday my friends shall find me there. .

Loral Orow
SOUL OF STRING
A Soul be formed in much the way a ball of yarn be wound.
Beginning with an emptiness until a string be found.
The string be wrapped so very firm to start up on the roll.
Loose ends do await their turn to gather into Soul.
For every string to wrap around does indeed increase the girth.
As bits of this and that grab on for ever after birth.
So much to add as time goes on and much to leave behind.
Large, it grows, and yet controls to ever—changing mind.
Perhaps as time passes
the strings may come undone.
Broken strings, a knot or two, or faded in the sun.
Neglect, in time, will shred the string or set it in a spin.
While a bit of care, will repair and let it roll again.
If you should know of such a Soul whose path may be impaired.
Simply wind the roll and tie the string to show you really cared.
Help it stretch and twist and flex as life will have it go.
A fragile thing, this Soul of string that may forever grow.

Michelle Young
MY DREAMER
My sweet dreamer, I'm waiting for you
your the one for which my love is true
I know you'll be someone romantic and sweet
you'll come and sweep me off my feet
when you come on that special day
I know we'll meet in some exciting way
but until then, I just think of you
my wonderful dreamer for which my love is true.

Jonathan Wade
WAITING ON THE PARK BENCH
In this wild land we roam
a helpless prey, our mouth does foam.
We move in for the kill
but inside we don't still. . .
feel the victor.
We tumble and fall
can't catch the ball. . .
when thrown out of bounds.
We reach for the sky
that hunk of pie. . .
that we never eat.
We've met our match
we are the catch. . .
the ones thrown back.
the time creeps on
my stomach turns.
I still remember
my heart still burns. . .
in flames of agony.
I did know love
she flew away,
my gentle dove.
the hawk returned
at ninety proof,
I climbed and leaped
off that mighty roof.

Gina Marie Steward
FIVE
When I was five
I used to dream of the beautiful day
That I would be sixteen,
Sixteen would be the magic age,
With all the glamour a girl could want
Boy friends, dates and pretty dresses
Those could make me happy.
When I was sixteen I wanted to be eighteen
Then I could be really free
To do the things I want to do
And not have to answer to anyone.
Now eighteen has come and gone;
I've seen discontent at every age,
Now I'm okay just being me.
But I sometimes wish
That for just one day
I could be five again

Mirtha Laura Vargas
DREAM
Sitting atop a treeless limb,
I look up and see the ground.
All around me float the leaves;
Pink elephants and purple bees.
All of a sudden it starts to rain
From skies below to ground above.
I keep looking up at the ground,
But mud keeps falling on my face.
For a second I look down,
And into the sky I fall and drown.

Stephen Carrington
TOGETHER
Together as we stroll the sand,
Arm in arm, hand in hand.
Together as we laugh and cry,
Heart to heart, eye to eye.
Together in the summer rain,
We share our love, we share our pain.
Together in sickness, together in health,
Together in poverty, together in wealth.
Together in life—just you and I,
Together in love till the day we die.

Duane Grostefon
FRAMED IN WOVEN WIRE
Glistening moon dew silently shimmers
on crystalline mirror of milk white glass.
Shadowy foot craters where earth men pass
fill with feathers and ice chilled air. Dimmer
grows the lighting as evening trickles in.
'Neath sentry spruces that tower and brood
nature bundles in aqueous ermine;
soft seem her features, her coarseness subdued.
Polar bear traffic lumbers distant and gruff—
eyes in the darkness menacing the still—
pivot and recede, their onslaught a bluff.
The barnyard lies quiet, the earth craters fill.

Carolyn Bowen
ATLANTA KIDS WHO?
The kids are as innocent as they can be
I wonder who's killing them a he or a she
So young, so many the kids of Atlanta
It's time we get down and find some answers
Afraid to go to school, and outside to play
No one knows who will be the next prey
In the rivers, and brushes the bodies are found
Someone is killing all the kids in town
The parents they suffer with sorrow and grief
Will someone please get the killer off the streets

Lois E. Moore
LOVE
Each day I thrill a little more just thinking of your love,
The love you give without reserve the love we gently bore
Each day I thrill a little more awaiting pleasures door,
To know that we'll be close again enwrapped in loves sweet lore.
For each day that we're together gives meaning to my life,
For I've never known such sweet content as we have every night.
I've searched for love, I've searched for peace, I've searched through all my life
To find a perfect heart, content, to live without worlds strife.
Without you my life holds no hope, the sun would never shine,
The moon could never rise again without you all the time.
So love me always dearest one, remain with me my love,
And never let me go again to face life fearful shun,
The world is cruel without you, the agony it brings,
The hurt and pain that man has made is to much to behold.
Life is meant for happiness, love is but to share.
To hold you close with my arms is love beyond compare.
Knowing that our love remains through loneliness and despair
Makes each day that we're together much easier to bear.

Walter E. Groble
A SPECIAL TIME OF YEAR
Spring is in the air; it's the
time of a new awakening.
It's the time to witness the
miracles of nature; you can
see so many things happening.
Spring is the perfect time for
taking a long and quiet walk.
A walk with someone you care
about—you need not even
talk.
For you can feel what's in the
air and see what's taking
place.
You look at one another and a
smile fills your face.
You're happy being together to
enjoy this time of year.
To feel the love that's in the
air, especially when she's near.
You see the buds upon the trees
and the young birds learning
to fly.
But unlike the leaves upon the
trees, your love for her will
never die.

John C. Coffman Jr.
UNTITLED
How will her lips feel?
The best part of seduction:
Anticipation.

Merienne Eloise Felder
MINE
I think that there can never be,
Anything more precious to me
Than the laughter, the smiles
and the fun
Of my children and
granchildren.
With loving care
I fix their hair,
Wash their clothes and their
hands
and try to meet their little
demands.
Their bodies are so cuddly and
so sweet
From the tips of their heads
to their tiny feet.
But when they go home at night
My house is really a sight!

Richard Chatwood
ADULTHOOD
Once in a young dream
I saw how wise and wonderful
I would be.
Now with time
I am here, and look to see
but, I cannot recognize me.

Robert Croxton
GOD'S PROMISE
My wife and I walked to
Whitesboro one fine day
The sky grew cloudy on the way
When rain drops fell we had to
race
To get some shelter at the
preacher's place
The lightning flashed, the
thunder did roar
Safe on the porch we watched it
pour
Then big pieces of ice came
with a thud
Five pound pieces hit the mud.
In later years throughout the
land
I've seen it hail but not so
grand
As those five pound chunks of
ice
From the preacher's porch they
did look nice
After fifty years we are not the
same
Inez can't hear and I am lame
But never mind cause we don't
fret
For with God's help we will beat
it yet.
And please remember this is
true
God's promise also includes you
Just as He protected us at the
preacher's place
He will help us through
whatever we face.

Rita Lynne Lukianchuk
LIFE AND ME
Life sometimes scares me to
death;
I often wonder if I'm really alive;
Why do I have to live up to
other's standards?
Why, for other's opinions do I
strive?
Must I always have to stop and
think?
Can't I live for myself, and me
only!
Why does there have to be a
right and wrong?
And why, in a crowd, do I often
feel lonely?
I hope my life isn't always like
this;
One day I'm gonna' break free
And I'm gonna' show others who
I really am,
That's right, I'm gonna' become
me!
I'm gonna' stop now, I'm
through,
I've said all I'm gonna' say;
Life will be alright forever
more—
'Cause I'm becoming "ME"
starting today!!!

Charly Scofield
MY PICTURE OF LOVE
X equals the beginning
relationship plus
the fact that it's always growing
times
Everything that has gone before
times
2 hearts.

Sally R. Shaffer
STORM
The wind held a conversation
with the trees;

The birds and squirrels sang
and chattered at the clouds.
Lightning came.
First in shallow sheets.
Then crackling hooks from
the sky.
Thunder began to protest.
At last, the wind brought its
tears—
At first, angry, avenging
tears;
Then, only a forlorn mist.

Condie Coppersmith
TESTIMONIES
Yes, my friend, God is alive.
Good and kind, and O, so wise.
The Bible true this book
foretold.
Book of Mormon witness bold.
Prophecy being revealed.
Prophecies being fulfilled.
Testifying of each other.
Father of Son, Son of Father.
Each book to a different land.
Use both as one in your hand.
Both contains the Holy plan,
One the key, one the throttle,
Starts the soul to make
immortal.
Both His word, His will reveal,
In Heaven will be what earth
has sealed.
When we obey His command,
He reaches down and takes our
hand.
He holds us steady, lest we fall.
O, that all would hear His call.
See the writing on the wall.
God loves, and gives us each a
choice,
Be still and listen to His voice.
Obey and live, sing, and rejoice.
Pray for yourselves, and pray for
others,
Friends and neighbors, sisters,
brothers.
Help is here to suit the task.
All our needs are fully met.
Hearts desires is what we get.

Louellyn Duncan
AN INDIVIDUAL MATTER
Eve believed the lie
When truth was offered first.
How like God giving choice,
And still the same for us.
God gives man the choice
To follow Him or not.
How like mankind to fall,
And turn away from good.
Humans choosing still
To face away from God.
How like God's lasting love
Forgiving, one by one.

Keith Oring
SOMETIMES
Sometimes I just want to be
alone
Sometimes I wish I were home
Sometimes I just don't care
I wish I were with you. . .
sometimes
I wonder if you feel that way
too. . . sometimes
I think you do. . . sometimes
Sometimes I laugh and
sometimes I cry
Sometimes I'm mad and
sometimes I'm high
Sometimes I love you and
sometimes I wonder why
I hate the world and I love
it. . .sometimes
I hate myself and what I've
done. . .sometimes
I hate all the people and
things. . .sometimes
Sometimes I wish I weren't alive
Sometimes I wish I could have
died
Sometimes I hope I don't survive
Sometimes I just want to be
alone
Sometimes

John M. Hume
TWO UNIQUES
YOU—nique.
ME—nique.

Edna Junemann
THE CURLY TAIL
I
There once was a boy
Who was very sad,
Seldom happy
And often bad.
II
He was spanked so much
At the end of his rump
There gradually grew
An ugly lump.
III
It grew and grew
Till it reached the ground,
And then it curled
All around.
IV
When he saw his plight,
He began to wail,
For no other boy
Ever had a tail.
V
He wailed all the way
Down to the river,
Then stumbled in
And began to quiver.
VI
The river gurgled
And said with glee,
"Steer with the tail
To the monkey tree."
VII
So he steered away
To the monkey tree
And laughed as he said,
"They're just like me."
VIII
With his curly tail
He swung with them
But suddenly fell
Down, and then
IX
As he fell from the tree
And hit the ground,
His tail broke off
And curled around.
X
When he saw his plight
He began to wail,
And that is the end
Of the curly tail.

Mary Wolf
A QUIET PLACE
I've found a restful quiet place
on the side of a mountain high,
Where there are trees and green
things
neath blue and sunny skies.
A place where I can think and
rest
and heaven seems near my door.
Where peace and quiet abide
with me,
what more could I ask for.

Stephen Paul Jodoin
HONEY, WHERE ARE YOU?

That's what I think
to myself everyday.
I'm looking,
looking around everywhere
But can't find you.
I know you're here
I can feel you around me.
So, honey, where are you?
I guess I know that you
are not here
But it's hard for me to believe
that once again I am here
And you are there.
Oh, honey, where? Where are
you?

J. Eugene Mielcarek, D.O.
HUMAN ANATOMY

Who can ever really forget,
their first human dissection.
The fight to close out emotion
and follow every direction.
The first touch of tissues and
their separation.
The admixture of fear, curiosity
and respect for which there is
no preparation.
Four young men sweating over
the slab table
Showing nonchallance to the
extent they are able.
Each thinks he, in his thoughts,
is so alone
With fears this unique society
will not condone.
Then with the days the mind
slowly changes it ways
With stock piling of facts in an
intricate maze.
The fingers more adept and
graced with skill
Trace the worldly framework of
human life, rationality and
will.

Dale Herd
TLIMOH

Takin' life in my own hands,
I'll go do what life demands,
Life is just what I'll make IT,
I have the will to take it,
I can see where I may fall,
But I'm ready for my call,
Some may see me as too small,
But I've got to tell you all,
It's not that I will fake it
And I will not forsake it,
See it's something I can't stand,
To feel caught by Uncle Sam.

Dorothy-Mae Mentus
TO A FRIEND

From the
Abundance of
Your soul you fill the cup
My greedy hands stretch out to
you
Daily.
I drink
From the fountain
Of your life—and Beauty
Turns to summer the winter of
My heart.
As though
I were devoid
Of substance, I use you—
Call your essence mine and
forget
Its source.
Did you
Know, my friend, that
I would decry what was
Not mine to have, and someday
scorn
Your truth?

Wynona Cantrell
SOFTLY CLOSE THE DOOR

Once thought we would always
be together
I was so naive, so child-like
It's hard to believe
Our passion could be so tender
and sweet
Softly close the door
I thought our love was so
unique and rare
That the stars were lights,
especially for you and me
And our souls to forever be free
Softly close the door
I thought of our love with every
passing moment
It was growing more graceful
and refined like a bottle of
wine
The essence of life was ours to
be
Why did you feel a need to
deceive?
Softly close the door
You may have wouned me from
loving another
But, our precious moments
together
Shall be cherished and ached for
in my mind internally
Softly close the door
And so as with sad memories
and childish dreams
That I've long since put away
Softly close the door
I can't bear your nearness
anymore

Linda M. Spaeth
A MESSAGE TO THE YOUNGER GENERATION

Sometimes it will happen
And before you realize
Your elders will pass on
To resume another life
Then you start to regret
The things you thought you
knew
The questions that you never
asked
They had the answers to
The elders have the wisdom
That only age can bring
They lived to their winter years
Through many countless springs
Most of all they had so
Much knowledge to impart
We had better start to listen
Not with our minds, but hearts
We cannot tell them now
How much love we had to share
And only hope that where they
are
They know this without despair
Our grandparents gave us their
gifts
Of a wonderful mother and
father
On whom we should never turn
our backs
And say "I'd rather not be
bothered."
These people are our life's blood
And teach us right from wrong
Let's start to sing their praises
now
Because they won't be here too
long
As life ever revolves around us
And we face confused
circumstances
Don't break the unending circle
of love
For there won't be any second
chances

Caspur J. Yates
HIYA COWBOY

Johnny come listen to my tale,
About a waddy, just in off the
trail.
Dolled up in his Sunday Rig,
Strides a cowpoke lean and
big.
Out of the clatter of his spurs.
Jingles music from their burrs.
Matching colors gay and bright.
Glamour gutted, what a sight.
Clad he's mystery to the throng.
Dressed in armour tried and
strong.
Greased lighting chanced his
wisdom earned,
And armchair weakness staid
and spurned.
Cattle wisened, saddle molded,
His love for horses, seldom
scolded.
Beauties champion, young folks
hero,
His violin on fidgets, next to
Nero.
From a million picked his bridle,
Built for working seldom idle.
Measured saddle history built,

Wrought for sticking, not for
split.
Humorous and sober, tenderness
amazin—
Hell for leather hardness both
guns ablazin.
Johnny, this ends my story, go
to bed!
His opposit must be dirty,
done and dead.

Robyn A. Sterling
A MORNING DREAM (of being with Cole)

There is no way I can let
you escape my mind this early
morning.
You are enclosed and embraced
by my every thought,
by every glowing memory I have
of you.
I remember the way the dim
light shone upon your face
and how your forceful eyes
covered every inch of me
until I felt the warmth of your
mind,
body,
and soul, caressing
me.
You peeled away the outer
surface of my life
and crawled down to what's
really there.
When your searching eyes and
lovely touch approached me
I was assured and comforted to
go away on night's dreams
with you.
And you stayed—
on and on, engraving a feeling,
such a good, mellow feeling into
my heart.

Schiggs
CETERIS PARIBUS

A gloved pair destitute
of light
Viewing the silver screen
in the midst of air
conditioning
As the whiteness lies
restless outside
The coat whose hanger
had been a rainbow
wasn't made to feel
right
In its pockets the pair
may hide.
When the pair is clinched,
the circulation is
lessened;
They quickly become
cold.
Their closeness projects
an appearance which
has in its grasp the
ability to produce warm
surroundings;
The absence of such is
sharply felt.
A feeling of actual warmth
may not be reflected by
the presence of
closeness;
The lone result may be
appearance.
The closeness of two may,
at times, bring together
forces of opposing
directions;
Warmth may result;
however, under the
guise of this may
lie friction
On the other hand, this
coalition may have yet
another by-product;
The pair may become even
closer when their forces,
however opposing, are
shared.
A situation exists of "give
and receive," contracting
the populous nature of
the contradictory
expression, "give and
take."
The hoped-for by-product
—magnetism.
When the fingers of the
pair are allowed to
wriggle freely, they're
able to accept warmth
without reservation.
A close relationship still
exists;
Fear of infringement no
longer persists.
They escape the cramped
feeling oft reserved the
overzealous writer.
One hundred seventeen
on the east
One hundred fifteen
on the west
Numbering two hundred
thirty-two, at least
Or at best.
The marginal cracks
evolving in the sidewalk
should be realized;
The lack of such notation
may lead to its stability
being jeopardized.
How is it possible to run
around the same circle—
seemingly innumerally—
without disinterest
overwhelming,
concentration dwindling
and impatience

developing?
Is one labeled as "having
control" or "being
naive?"
One should be reminded
ever so often of any
progress being made—
usually slowly but;
if at all fortunate,
at least surely;
The lap number is always
announced to myself
frequently.
The presence of some
sort of practical
reward or quality may
also provide the
marginal incentive
necessary to enable
continuance of the
process involved in the
achievement of a
particular goal;
Basketball skills may be
improved upon,
Trousers may request
assistance from a
nearby pair of
suspenders to combat
the retreat of weight
and waistline,
And, in turn, compliments
and recognition may
be forthcoming.
The reasons for my loss
of weight are the same
as those for the higher
water bill;
Although the technical
reason is conditioning,
it isn't the primary.
When beginning the escapade
of endurance, soreness
evolved where at one
time strength had been
thought to be;
Eventually, however, this
pseudostrength may be
transformed via the
soreness and become
real.
When apart, the sky
was clear
When together, the sky
was cloudy
The clouds disappear
by way of either ear
Affection clouds vision.
This season has seen but
a minimal amount of
precipitation.
When running around the
mall's stark sidewalk,
there exists no
evidence of one's
feet having been in
its presence.
However, if a shower of
white blankets the
walk, every lap enhances
the detail of a distinct
path;
So it does the solidity
of the runner.
A shower of minimal
proportion may prove
to be adequate.
As a matter of course,
a smaller amount is
often easier to
contend with.
A sudden blizzard of such
may lessen the
effectiveness of
one's vision.
The breakneck speed at
which it accumulates
may also result in a
loss of footing.
If substantial garments
on the outside are worn;
Lessened are the chances
of the inside being torn.
This protection may itself
prove fatal, however, if
taken to extremes.
The eyes should be able to
see,
The nose to smell,
The ears to hear,
The mouth to voice,
The hands to touch;
In order to respond to what
is happening around them.
If not, all that exists is a
life of shallow dreams.
When the moon appears
where darkness had
once prevailed;
That which was hidden is
now seen and becomes
detailed.
If the moon is full, its
immediate surroundings
may not be the only
enlightened;
So also may be those
opposite.
Hopefully, neither is
frightened.

Robyn Gerhardt
LONELINESS
(In Memory of Gregory Leland)
That feeling of emptiness,
when the whole world turns
grey.
No ones there to talk to,
or theres nothing left to say.
Everyone seems crazy,
and my hopes all fade away.
Nothing makes me happy,
and I start to dread each day.
Love has lost its meaning,
for the one I love has gone.
No more watching the sunset,
or seeing the mornings dawn.
The walls start closing in,
all I do is sit and cry.
I hate this crazy feeling,
of sometimes wanting to die.
Its an isolated feeling,
this sadness in my heart.
I guess it must have started,
when we were forced to part.
Maybe someday I'll find the
strength,
and grace to carry on.
And I'll try to do right,
and not stray to the wrong.
If the saying is true,
that "Time heals all."
Then I'll keep on walking,
and try not to fall.
If its all true,
and my heart will mend.
Then maybe, just maybe,
I'll then love again.

Cynthia Louise Klein
SUMMER—WITH A TWIST
Fall spreads a cooling breeze,
Blowing lightly through the
trees,
Freezing the air with snowy
mist,
Giving summer a nippy twist.

Ella Mae Sanders
DO IT THE BEST THAT YOU CAN
Do you strive every day,
whatever the plan,
to do it the best that you can?
Now I say, there is nothing too
small nor
too great,
Be it now or tomorrow—Be it
early
or late,
That we shouldn't try doing the
best that
we can.
Perhaps time may prohibit—
finance
not allow,
To do it the way that you'd like,
But you'll be a fine person—a
mighty
tall man,
If always you do it—the best
that
you can.
Your best may not be what
some folk would
want,
And theres many a folk who
would tease and
taunt,
But God watchs us all from HIS
heavens
above
And I'm sure HE will show HIS
abundance of
love,
Will probably even put gold in
your pan,
If only you've done it—the
best that you can.
Whatever the task—wherever it
be,
Theres a reward waiting that
you may not
see.
Theres a depth of contentment
and a rich
inner glow
From harvesting every seed
that you'd sow,
And you *are* a *fine* person—
a *mighty*
tall man
Because you have done it—
the best that
you can.
If some one should say—"Have
you done
your best
Or have you merely competed
with all of the
rest?"
Can you stand there and answer
as should every man?
"Yessir—I've done it—its the
best that I can!"

Christina Smith
MYSTERYS
A breath of a flower,
A tingling touch of love;
The unreality of nature,
Nothing—not thought of.
The satisfying of a hunger,
To taste the endless need;
The satisfying of a desire,
To never follow—but always
lead.
A possession to touch a star,
To fly so ever high;
A desire to live a fairy tale,
And never, never die.
A soul of an old oak tree,
Containing loneliness and
sadness within;
All of these mysterys from life
itself,
Exist time and time again.

S. S. Etheridge
THE MORNING AFTER
It is the morning after the night
before
And I know it could not be
again.
Was it good for you? It was good
for me.
Do you think we could ever be
friends?
I know that's a question that
shouldn't be asked;
It makes people feel ill at ease.
But I thought at the time you
could offer an answer;
Some soft consolation to please.
Now I see I was asking too
much of a man
Unprepared to answer my eyes.
But I know soon he'll learn to
counter those questions,
To stroke and to smile as he
lies.
Well, it's the morning after the
night before,
And I'm eating my breakfast
alone.
I'm thinking of other mornings
like this
And of other men that I've
known.
I'm sure there will probably be
more mornings like this
Though I really don't need
any more.
The memories of the mornings I
try to forget,
While just remembering the
nights before.

Mary Jean Boon House
SOLITUDE
Some days I love dark quiet
closed spaces
Though really I cannot say why.
I suppose I am only searching
for traces
Of a part of me I lost in days
gone by.
So as I sit in quiet solitude
Remembering peaceful moments
of yesterday
I reach a tranquil, peaceful
mood
As time silently slips away.

Darcy Smith
UNTITLED
Bored, but safe
going about our daily routines—
We live in a shell,
warm and protected.
Surrounded by igorance
watching the world pass us
by.

Bruce Christensen
SANDCASTLES
Hands grasp soggy clumps of
sand,
Beginning a molding process,
Shaping walls, to become
barriers.
Battlements give a firmer seal,
As towers connect walls
together,
Molding hands shape,
Squeezing wet sand into place
Smoothing edges, so its strength
appears.
Construction complete,
Builder gazes at creation,
Until ocean waves, reclaim
contents.
Its time to seek firmer
foundations.

Frances A. Sobotka
WINTER CROW
Late in the evening
Black crow is returning
Home from his feasting,
Wings rhythmic and slow.
Stillness relieving
With raw-throated cawing
Dark shadow drifting,
Over the snow.
Low sun perceiving
The lone flying figure,
Gives jet-black pinions
A transient green glow.

Coie Lorraine (Hill) Cannon
NOTE OF FAREWELL
In knowing you I've felt a part
Of something good and true
And leaving you has hurt my
heart,
I'm lonely, sad, and blue.
I hope that you will not forget
The joys we've shared these years-
That you will always be glad we
met
And keep smiling through the
tears.

Edward V. Gibson
I BELIEVE IN GOD
A growing tree, a bird in flight,
The light of day, the dark of
night.
The grass so green, the sky of
blue,
I believe in God, don't you?
The cold of winter, the warmth
of spring,
The happiness as people sing.
An ocean wave, a mountain
view,
I believe in God, don't you?
The noise of living, a bay's cry,
A mother singing, a father's sigh.
A dog is barking, a pigeon's coo,
I believe in God, don't you?
The children playing in the
street,
The noise of their little feet.
Birds are singing, the sun is
bright,
I believe in God, all right.
Flowers in bloom, the gentle
wind,
God's forgiveness for all who've
sinned.
An eternal home in Heaven
above,
I believe in God and His love.

Donielle M. Parker
THE AWAKENING
I was alone on the beach
Gazing up above and
What befell my eyes but
A universe never seen before.
It was amazing,
You wouldn't believe,
LOVE everywhere you looked
And even where you didn't.
The people had purple skin,
With a white light above their
heads,
And eyes of the spaciest blue.
The cats were white and peach,
The spiders ruled the gargoyles
and
The dogs ran and played in the
waves.
It was amazing,
You wouldn't believe,
PEACE everywhere you looked
And even where you didn't.
I went to the Head of this place,
And asked, "Why me?"
He said, "Because you let it
happen."
I asked the man, "Well what can
I do?"
He told me to pay close
attention,
For he would never say this
again,
"Become all that you can,
A Genuine Plum!"
It was amazing,
You wouldn't believe,
LOVE everywhere you looked
And even where you didn't.
I was alone on the beach
Gazing up above and
What befell my eyes but
A universe never seen before.
It was amazing.

Lavretta Hughes Truax
REMEMBER WHEN?
We walked hand in hand and
talked.
We walked hand in hand in
beauty and gaiety,
In learning and poverty, as
well as plenty.
We walked hand in hand in fun,
work and pain,
In dreams and the fulfillment of
those dreams.
We walked hand in hand in
creation,
In pride, joy and wonder at that
creation.
We walked hand in hand in fear
and sickness,
In quarreling and forgiveness.
We walked hand in hand in
apprehension and sorrow,
In forgetfulness, humor and
whimsy.
We walked hand in hand in
song and dance.
Oh, when can we again walk
hand in hand and talk?
Have we really drifted apart,
you and I?
Or are we only walking hand
in hand in loneliness and
despair?

Parrish Tucker, Sr.
DON'T CAST ME ASIDE
Don't cast me aside for I know
I am old—
I have much love and warmth
and stories to be told—
Don't cast me aside for I don't
mean to be in the way—
For being old was an accident I
didn't plan it this way—
Don't cast me aside for the
almighty must think I have
more to contribute—
My honesty, love and
knowledge I could
distribute—
Don't cast me aside for I know I
am old—
Maybe when you're troubled and
sad I'll be there for you to
hold—
Don't cast me aside when you
need a good cry—
For I'm as solid as a rock for
that you can rely—
Don't cast me aside for there is
not a lot I can do—
But my tired and wrinkled frame
will always love you—
Don't cast me aside, don't leave
me alone—
For let me love you now before
God takes me home—

Carole Neason
A STAR
I'm flying, I'm floating far,
far away,
Goodbye dear Earth, see you
later in the day.
"Hello Venus and Mercury, how
are you today?"
"We are fine my sweet child,
what can we say?"
"God bless you!", I shouted and
hurried on my way.
Further and further I flew, all
was out of sight,
I felt tingly, weightless,
and bright as I might.
When visions of others came
into my sight,
Like little small fire flies into
the night.
As I stared out in wonder, it hit
me, my fright.
Who am I, where am I, in such a
great flight?
A voice said, "You are a star,
a star of great height."
As I stared out in wonder, as far
as I could see,
There were millions of stars all
around me.

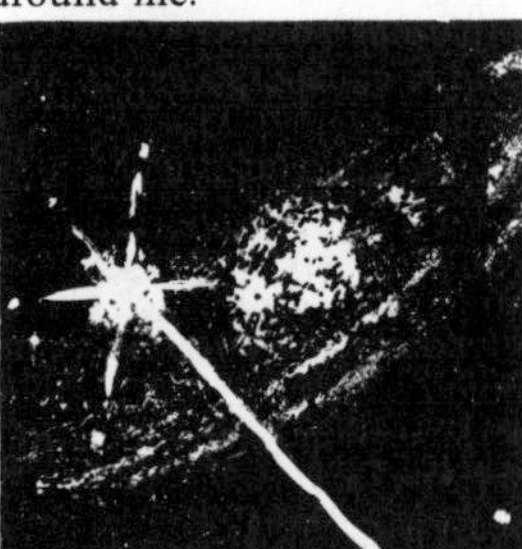

I could only feel love, peace, and
brilliant harmony,
I had never before felt like
this on Earth.
Right then I remembered, the
place of my birth,
I started to panic, I could feel
my fear.
When a voice said, "don't panic
my dear,
Your silver cord shall take you
back there."
I said, "Why thank you, you are
so kind."
As I turned to hurry down the
silver line,
I had to look back at the stars
left behind.
They twinkled and brightened
as if sending me home,
And yet, I could feel that they
felt all alone.
"I love you", I shouted, "You
are my friend."
And before I knew it, I was
home again.

J. D. Culpepper, Jr.
THE DEFENSE RESTED
The courtroom was packed,
The jury in place,
Silence ruled,
Not a smile on a face.
His client had been charged
with a felony
Which could carry a sentence
of years,
But be damned if you do and
be damned if you don't,
He argued his case without
fears.
he had handled his witnesses, as
each was called,
With alacrity, depth and
aplomb,
His questions, direct and
clearly propounded
For answers he felt sure would
come.
He couldn't read the mind of
each juror
To fathom how each may react,
He had to proceed, develop his
case,
And to do so, fact by fact.
But for all he had done
(the best he could do)
His mind had some thought and
some worry,
Had he overlooked something or
missed a point?
The decision was up to a jury.
The prosecutor objected, the
Judge overruled,
Everything seemed to go right;
At days end, all quiet, he rested
at home,
But his mind stayed active all
night.
On the final day when he had
expended
All facts and proofs under the
sun,
He lowered his head and closed
his eyes—
Silently prayed—Thy Will be
Done.
He addressed the jury, simple,
direct,
Carefully reviewing evidence,
Left little to say—he believed
in his cause
Delivering to the jury with
confidence.
The jury went out to ponder,
decide
On the evidence as submitted
As to who was right or who was
wrong,
Whether defendant be
sentenced or acquitted.
In a very short time the
jurors agreed
To render the Court their
decision.
Jury room unlocked, they
returned to their seats,
NOT GUILTY, each returned
with precision.
THE DEFENSE RESTED.

Rolanda E. McQueen
HE SAID, SHE SAID, SHE SAID, HE SAID
He Said, She Said
that's all people say
She Said, He Said
talk about people everyday
He Said, She Said
now the action starts
She Said, He Said
it's gonna be hard to pull
them apart
He Said, She Said
one hit the other in the head
She Said, He Said
now one's stretched out dead
He Said, She Said
I don't like the way that goes
She said, He Said
why people do it, nobody
knows
He Said, She Said
that's how it began
She Said, He Said
what an awful way for it to
end

Michael Markiewicz
THE LONELY ONE
The wind was blowing cold
as darkness embraced the sun
Leaving an empty feeling
in the heart of the lonely one
Passing through the door
he leaves his past behind
Moving towards tomorrow
to another space in time
Throwing down a cigarette
he turns on up the street
The cooling ash an emblem
marking his retreat
From a world of broken dreams
the pain of aftermath
Just a dark reflection
in the bottom of the glass
Hearing only echoes
words stinging through the wind
A woman lost forever
love that might have been
The wind a little colder
the cutting breath of night
A darkened, haunting figure
the lonely one's in flight
Moving towards tomorrow
to another space in time
Forgetting about the sorrow
the past remains behind
Until the clouds of darkness
no longer embrace the sun
To leave an empty feeling
in the heart of the lonely one

Sylvia A. Mossman
FAT, FORTY AND UGLY
Where have the years gone,
where can they be?
Where is the young girl who
used to be me?
Where is the girl who prowled
or'e the lands?
Finding so much to do on the
summer sands.
When life was so simple and so
much to learn
The years stretched ahead with
many a turn.
Where is the young girl who fell
so fast in love?
And married so young with a
blessing from above.
A young girl who once planned
to be a nurse,
Became an Aide instead the
only difference in the purse.
Where is the young mother who
sang to her brood?
Took them on picnics,taught
them to be good.
Where have they gone those
children so cuddly and sweet?
Who always seemed to be under
my feet.
They have grown oh so quickly
into young girls and man,
And I've tried to let go as best
as I can.
For there comes a time when
they must be on their own
But the door will always be
open for them to come home.
Where is the young man who
stood by my side?
Who shared all these years of
love and pride.
Who stuck with us all through
good and bad,
And all of the trials we have
ever had.
For no matter how bad things
would be
I always knew he was there, and
that he loved me.
Together we've worked to build
a life,
Raise a family and stay together
as man and wife.
When I look in his eyes I see
he's still there
The young man who won me,
tho' he has less hair.
I hope he will love me when I
have turned gray
For I am fast approaching my
40th birthday;
But I still feel as young as that
girl long ago-
If I could just find a way that
the years wouldn't show!

Michael E. Halverson
A CELEBRATION
The flame has realized. . .,and
so now it can dream
and it reaches with an enduring
touch
Branches scratch their creeping
bark
they know. . .they want so much
And the clearing comes alive
the atmosphere has sung
Time has summoned truth, and
we can
all waltz at the Celebration.
Visions have awakened from
long inactivity
a beginning has begun
Love traces, and escapes the
edges
illusion has chance to run
And so the candles are lit
Drinks are poured
laughing and weeping are one
Hearts beckon; souls rejoice and
we
all waltz at the Celebration.
Enchantment has listened; so
enrapture what is now
Accept the beguilement
feel the undaunted bow
Be bold, have hope beset the
elfin spirit
Captivate the charm of life
Reach, cherish, dance and love
And we will all waltz at
the Celebration.

Gloria Duff
DOUBT
I doubt that I'll
ever be free
as I can be!
For "FREE" if I'd be,
I'd have to shovel up
human hurt!
I'd have to grovel,
—or kneel!
—then walk under the muck,
!in the muck, and—
even roll in it!
WELL! I couldn't do it!
not ME!

Mary Frances Via
PAPER SKY
Paper sky bye o by Oh, I think
I am going to cry
Shed a tear oh my dear for I
know
I am going to die
Even tho I'll be gone
You will never be alone
I'll be watching from above
If you're lonely or if you're bored
Even thou the road I'm taking
Is the road of no return
It's the waiting thats so hard
Remembering all the good and
all the bad
Gives me an empty feeling deep
inside
Not the laetrile nor the
chemotherapy
Will do the trick for me
Only the good Savior will decide
what it will be
When I was young and didn't
care
I was always ready for a dare
So I smoked the pot and drank
the booze
Thats one thing I never refused
But now I'm older and a little
wiser
My life is nothing but a big
disaster
My Mother warned me that I
would pay
I should of listened and obeyed
So listen kids and listen good
Just live your life the way you
should
This is my story I have to tell
To save others from a living hell

Sandy Bel
HISTORICAL MARKERS
"Great men have passed this
way. . . ."
"Here, valiant families gave their
lives. . . ."
"The last battle of Greengrass
County. . . ."
"The final stand of the Cherokee
Indians. . . ."
and
"This is the spot where love
took place.
Be still and hear the silence
that was shared,
The touching that was felt,
The passion that was spent.
This is the spot where love took
place,
Rest here a while and take in
the warmth that still remains
and will forever after.
Everything in this place is alive
because,
This is the spot where love took
place."

Anna K. Christensen
HUNTING SEASON
I saw a group of horses
With red ribbons on their
tails—
Flying in the gentle breeze
Like busy trade wind sails.
I saw a gentle bovine—
The letters C-O-W on her side;
Her owner took no special
care
His bossie for to hide.
Soon the "Nimrods" will go
forth,
So many, brave, and loose—
Who know not the difference
'twixt
The mule and mighty
moose.

Cherry Kim Plumer
OLD SOLDIERS
Beneath the naked trees an Old
Soldier stood at attention
while the cold wind blew.
He has seen many things come
and go but in the silence of
the old cemetary he stood as a
tear finds its way down his
cheek.
There he stood saluting as
memories of brave comrads
taunt his weary mind, his
uniform fits him everywhere
yet touches him nowhere.
In his mind he marches with
comrads of bitter wars gone
by with the winds of time.
For him the war lives on in his
mind and he recalls the fear
and chilling screams of war
and saddness walks hand in
hand with it.
But for his fallen, brave
comrads the war has come to
a end, for peace is upon them.
To those brave men of hard
times stand and join in salute
to Old Soldiers.

R. C. Johnson
THE SIMPLETON
Lovable, ugly, Simpleton--
ungainly and of gentle
demean
Like a great Goblin walking,
like part of a fantastic dream.
He would shoulder a bale of
straw or pick violets with the
same gentle ease.
He was polite--and ugly to look
upon, a figure for the boys to
tease.
This lovable, ugly Simpleton, he
was every small child's delight
Each mother would trust him
and every child--after that first
bit of fright.
He would carry the school kids
with care, across the swollen
creek,
Spread ashes on the roadway
and paths, where ice and slush
was thick.
All the farmers 'round about
said there was magic in his
hands,
He was called in to care for a
cow that was sick, for the
mule and new born lambs.
Lovable, frightening, Simpleton,
for now that I am grown,
I see the place he really filled,
good deeds each day sown.
He reaped a golden harvest, few
of us have ever had,
I beg forgiveness of this Genius,
whom I teased when just a
lad.

Robert Moore
PRAYING
Suffer my soul
Handling life's mysterious loads
Feeling my heart
Throbbing without sparks

Yvonne G. Vorel
FALL
Summer green has lost again,
To the beautiful golden fall,
As colors glorify the trees,
With magic in them all.
golds, reds, wines and browns,
Gracefully touching leaves.
Snatching all the green away,
Like mystifying thieves.
Each hour of each passing day,
Summer slowly fades away.
Bringing Autumn back again,
A Season bright and gay.

Dorothy E. Law
SNOW
There is a north in me—
I shall always love first snow.
The hush before the falling. .
Then—wind drifted curtains of white.
Ice cream cones round the chimney pots
Ermine piles on sooty branches.
A crystal against my black glove
Is almost too perfect to bear
And no two ever alike.
I go forth into mystery,
I walk in silence
And tread on infinity.

Michelle Marenger
WORDS OF THOUGHT
A concept
hiding in the corner of a closed mind,
then flowing through the brain.
Only there to escape
with words.
The depth of the words
sometimes not understood
even by the person who speaks them.
There to leave you thinking
about sounds
and meanings.
About life in general,
Which is a word with no set
definition only infinite meaning. . .

William H. Cain
UNTITLED
When everything clever
to be said
has been said,
And all of your dreams
Have come true,
Then say, all you clever ones,
cozy in bed,
There's still something left
here to do...

You've got to-
Share a little
Care a little
Love a little
Give a little
That's the story
and glory
of you.

Richard Anderson
ELIZABETH
What words can describe
a lady so alive?
What feelings are these
that they ne'er die?
When I think of you, dear,
I can still see your tears.
When I think of you, love,
I'm young without years.
I stole a kiss from thy
moist lips not once—but often.
From the depths of my heart
a tender feeling did rend.
Your hair, your eyes so dark—
you are the one fate dealt.
Elizabeth, my Elizabeth, you
made my heart melt.

Mrs. Chris Ponath
THE JOURNEY
There's a journey that is taken,
by each of us alone;
With only God to guide us,
as He leads us gently home.
You don't know when you're going,
Then suddenly you're there.
That's how we lost you darling,
for now you're in God's care.
God must have loved you dearly
to have taken you away.
When so many of us needed you
and wanted you to stay.
But we know that you are happy
and your cares have ceased to be.
And you're making your new
home there
In the land of eternity.

Janice Moore
AND HE CALLED HIS NAME, JESUS
Jesus, what do I think of,
When I hear the Dear, Sweet Name?
I think of how You've changed me,
And how I'll never be the same.
I think of strength and power,
How You died and set me free,
And remember humbly a death
on a cross,
That ended in Victory.
I remember the blood that You shed,
That takes away my sin,
And remember it washes me
white as snow,
Over and over again.
I think of Your sheltering arms,
Reaching out saying, "Come
Unto Me,"
As my burdens are laid at Your feet,
I know now what real love can be.
I think of a sacrificed life,
That was lived showing all men
the way,
And I marvel that You live in me,
Guiding my steps day by day.
You came as the sacrificed lamb,
And have broken the barriers down,
Because You care so much for me,
Someday I can too wear a crown.
And as I witness and bear Your
Dear Name,
For all the world to see,
May I die to myself—so the world,
Will only see Jesus in me.
Thus may I bring honor and glory,
To the One who has sacrificed all,
May all that I do be done unto Thee,
So that others on Your name
will call.

Marguerite R. Frazier
BEST OF THE BEST-SELLERS
This Book is proving most inspiring
To all who seek, with minds
Inquiring.
This Book tells how the world began
And shows God's love for every man.
When we feel blue, it tells us how
To cope with problems here and now.
This Book that was written for
aged and youth
If full of ideals based on
Divine truth.
The things that our Savior once
did and said
Are quoted in here and should
always be read
By all who are seeking
forgiveness for sin
And hoping that Heaven will
then let them come in.
This greatest of books tells how
Jesus still pleads
For people to follow wherever
He leads.
Because of His love and His
wonderful grace,
He has gone to prepare us a
Heavenly place.
I shall study this Book as my
day to day goal;
For no other Book has such
food for the soul.

Bob A. Lantz
POCKET RECORDER
I need a tape recorder
To carry when I walk,
That will copy down my every word
And listen while I talk.
I've lost so many poems
Through lack of this device,
That could be hanging 'round
my neck
To quietly record my voice.
It needn't be very heavy
Just a small one of pocket size,
Not an 8-track or a large cassette
That's carried by other guys.
Just a small, simple pocket model
That I can carry all day or all night,
A constant recording companion
To help me when I write.
When I get this recorder
I'm sure I'll be writing more,
Because I'll then have in my pocket
A portable poetry store.

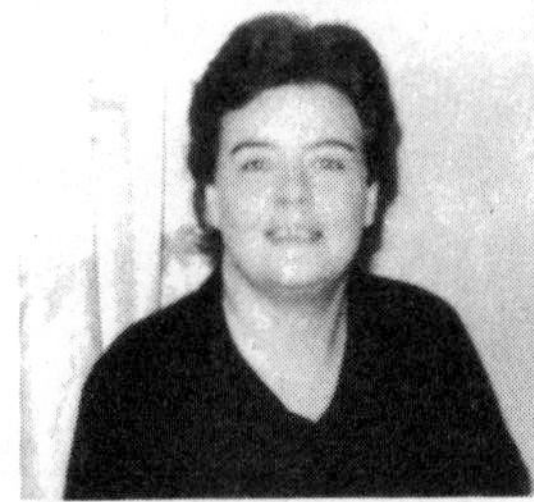

Tim Cohen
MY EYES
My eyes—
Have beheld lovers so
tenderly
And have glowed with pride
Have met the glare of some
cool individual
And have filled with
expectation
My eyes—
Have met their purpose—but
now
Like that favorite stream
Way back in memory
they have run dry
The stream has ceased to flow
And I to cry.

Pauline Alldred
TRANSFUSION
Silent as the scatter of sheets
and slither of skin,
he submerges me
flattened through grains of wet sand,
liquified or dismembered.
Small as a pearled water drop
on forest floor, or large as curve
of arm and leg in first light,
I fold out and back,
piecemeal or transparent.
His breath as warm charcoal,
he swallows me
a dish of broken oysters.
Each time I race down darkness,
I promise to return devourer.

Dolores Aldred
COATED SKELETONS
All of you with your grand smiles
and your perfect gestures
wear pretty faces
to hide yourselves—
if there really is anyone
under it all.
Crowded rooms of you
plastering yourselves
with eloquent talk
and Continental booze.
When you lay sprawled
on your plush foreign carpets
singing The Party's Over
do you savor in the perversion
of it all.

Haydee Mincey Dukes
WHEN
When my heart throbbed with pain
When tears flowed down my
cheeks like rain
When my soul shrank in grief
My Heavenly Father gave me relief
When for me life was a blur
And joy-sweet joy-would not occur
When all about me sadness reigned
When fervent prayer and hope
seemed vain
It was I, My God sustained
When satan struck me with his blow
And where to turn I did not know
When loneliness like a monster
grabbed out at me
When in peace I could not be
My Heavenly Father softly
whispered, "Come to Me"
When my mind grew tired and weary
And my eyes were red and teary
When no more I could bear
When I confronted total despair
I heard my God gently say,
"At My feet lay your every care"

Nina Patchen
MOTHER
Whose eyes do you first look into?
Whose lips give you a first
sweet caress?
Whose arms are a sweet shelter,
As you are cuddled close to her breast?
Whose hands guide your first steps
As from childhood to manhood
you grow?
Whose heart beats only for you?
Whose face is the dearest you know?
Who is ever your pilot and teacher?
Who drives all your troubles

away?
Who teaches you wrong from the right,
And is fearful lest you stray?
Whose name means a world of love?
Who is always a pal and a chum?
Who is ready to listen to heartaches,
Though her own have just begun?
T'is one who cannot be matched
In this world or any other;
T'is one who lives just for you;
Don't you know? Why it's Mother!

Cindy L. Freeze
ON THE BEACH
Thundering waves recreating new guidelines for the shores.
Bruised sand and shells have to know this world is full of wars.
Blindless surfers—searching—catching the highrise
Riding the waves to the sky.
Beyond one may glimpse a dolphin how free at sea.
Commie boats pass at dawn when will the sand and shores be gone?

Susie Henry
A FLOWER (JUST LIKE LOVE)
A flower never lasts,
Just like love.
A flower renews itself throughout the year,
Just like love.
A flower rests in winter and comes up through the ground showing proudly its colors,
Just like love.
But to me, the most beautiful and rarest flower is the one which lasts throughout the lifetime, even in the most coldest winter.
Just like love.

Edison J. Atwood
HINDRANCE
Her breath is weary, certainly like a subtle sound whispered hastily underneath the noise. Rene, her back against a chair, she stares and shudders, asking for release from grasp and yet enjoying the rapid attack of chords rattling about her. Her leg, it trembles, in sight, across the room, reminding me to satisfy a thirst, a vague delight. I reach to get some rum. And now I laugh, so foolish and so chaste, for dreaming of a kiss upon her wrist while her thin hips are held in black embrace. I want to remain, but music still insists— With rum so dry, and Rene bound to sleep, I watch a receding opportunity.

Wendy L. Vaughn
LIKE A RAINBOW
As spring secretly slips in to cover the dreary winter world with color and brightness
. . .so came you to me
As a flower blooms from a tiny, fragile bud and bursts into flames of color
. . .our friendship began
As a butterfly that flits and wavers from flower to flower
. . .we had our ups and downs
But like a rainbow, Gods promise to man, unfailing in its appearance after a storm
. . .will grow our friendship
Because, my friend. . .
Like the spring—
Our friendship continuously returns despite the trials it faces.
And like the flower—
The beauty of what we share will
be instilled in our minds forever.
And still, like the butterfly—
We will each retain our own individual flights.
But, like the rainbow—
Ours is a promise of friendship
eternal.

Jeanine Whitney
JAIME LEIGH
I look at you, my daughter
with your father's upturned nose.
I see your long blonde flowing hair
. . .mature expensive clothes.
We've been together all these years
I think we've done quite well.
We've had our many ups and downs
. . .survived our stint in hell.
I know there're days when I'm a pain
you've had your moments, too.
I think back upon those moments. . .
. . .have I done the best for you?
I know we've always been alone
just us to have and hold. . .
. . .nine years can be forever
when you're only nine years old.

Hannah E. Renshaw
PERCEPTION
I have walked into the gloaming
Tho several years ago
Many roads have had their turning
I hope the way I know.
I have crossed each pathway daily
I've searched its crag and fen.
I try to move more warily
For I'll cross it not again.
There were trails I thought led nowhere
As I struggled to proceed
Over rocks and glen and hilltops
To earn my daily need.
Now I can see more clearly
Than I ever have before
God's Hand has been upon me
Leading to His glory shore.

"Di" Wall
THE LAWMAN
With a 357 strapped on his hip,
He risks his life for you,
This special one behind the badge,
Dressed in gray or blue.
Traveling down the highway,
He clears the streets of crime,
Though rarely does he give a thought,
To his life. . .there on the line!
Working all kinds of hours,
With much too little pay,
It really makes you wonder. . .
Why this is the way!
When it takes a special person
With honesty and pride,
To fill the shoes of lawmen,
Who before him served, and died!
So, in the line of duty. . .
Folks, "Let's give him due respect."
For even in his homelife,
The law. . .he must reflect!!!!!

Tony Lenzini Jr.
ONE DAY
One day as I watched by the edge of a lake,
Nature unfold it's beautiful drape,
Sweet beauty shines on the new breath of dawn,
As the heat of the sun warms the new born fawn.
Wild ducks in their beauty fly through the clear air,
Onward to ground where new food must be found,
There they will stay for the rest of the day,
GOD's might is shown in a most beautiful way!

Barbara Crawford
POEM
A splattering of pictures
Made of words
A poet's mess
To clean up and arrange
A work of art
For other's pleasure
Mind-expansion

Larry A. Meier
FLOWERS OF LOVE
The first nite I met you
I saw
The world in your eyes
I was afraid
yes afraid
Love comes in two
two days later
I loved
Swam in strong currents
drown
I long to touch
as you touch
your tapestries
pieces of your life
Rainy bars in Texas
Red wallpapered room
in Nebraska
One picks a flower
knowing it will die
only
inside the eye
the beauty remains
I send you
the scent of Gardenias
flowers of love
The first nite I met you
I was afraid

Phyllis Elizabeth Bombard
FOR LISA
(To: Lisa Harrigan)
I cannot leave when you leave...
and yet I cannot stay.
Without you there is nothing in this place...
why must you go away?
Remember we are sisters...
nothing can keep us apart.
You gave me your friendship,
I am giving you my heart.
Still-
I cannot leave when you leave...
and yet I cannot stay.
Without you there is nothing in this place...
but I understand why you must go away-
before you do there is something I'd like you to know:
Whenever you feel lost and alone,
and don't know who you are...
Close your eyes and think of me,
...I will never be far.

Betty Jo Hobbs
UNTITLED
A turning in the road my be so slight
It goes unnoticed at the time.
but the pathway may lead
Into a Hell - or Heaven sublime.
One often makes the turning wrong
Too late finds out his mistake-
Then all that's left to do
Is keep looking for another turn to take.
Then perhaps when not a bend is found
Life cannot go on longer - so to seem
All that is left for one to do
Is live in yesterday and dream.

Talmadge Hairston
EDEN
Above the Sea of the Sun-Set,
Beyond the blue of the Sky.
Stands a lovely place called Eden,
The place of a sweet by and by.
And there on that beautiful city,
Where the Angels are bright and fair.
We'll stay throughout the centuries.
And a golden Crown we will wear.
We'll never get sick or weary,
In—the mighty 'Heaven of the Soul",

There we'll honor our dear "Lord—Jesus".
Where existence's period roll.

Judy Brewer
AFRAID
In the stillness of the night
The darkness seems complete.
My only company is fright—
And I pace on lonely feet.
I hug the darkness to me—
And loneliness—and fear.
There is nothing which soothes me—
I feel the trickle of tears.
I hold my hurt around me
As others hold a shawl.
Emptiness abound in me—
Is there no more? Is this all?
The dawn of day is breaking;
It stills my sense of fear.
It fills that empty aching
For love was ever near.

Carrie Moss
TO SPEAK
"I am lonely,"
nothing in this world is harder to say.
"I am lost,
it's dark and I can't find the way."
I need to cry
and I don't know why.
I need to tell you
things I am afraid to speak of,
like "I am lonely and lost,"
like "I need your love."

Jan Kirkley Boyd
THE ENDLESS SEARCH
Through time we gain the knowledge to understand
Why God created woman and man
There is the beauty of God's Holy touch
And His Son Jesus, who we love so much
In the beginning the Word became flesh
To fulfill God's plan, to fulfill His quest
Yes, how faithful and true was Jesus that day
When they nailed His hands to the cross that way
He prayed, Dear Father, forgive them you see
For they are blind and spiritually weak
So blind and death were the people who said
Crucify Jesus, It's Him we want dead

Yes, how sad it was to see Jesus hang
In pain and agony with tears of shame
Jesus, the Son, of our Father up above
Proved to us, His most precious love
You see He came, to show us the way
To Heaven our home, where we will stay
If we accept His love, and abide in God's Will
Jesus will bless us with God's Holy Seal
How Heavenly beautiful will that day be
When we bow to Jesus on our hands and knees
And hear Jesus say, My child well done
You kept the faith, for this crown you've won
My child your Eternal life has just begun.

John David Boykin
FIVE SENSES HAVE I
I saw such a sight
In the still of night.
What was it I had seen?
It must have been a dream,
Or did I just happen to see
No; for I am blind as can
Be.
What was this I had heard?
Fluttering wings of a bird,
Drifting on the silent air.
Not one only, but a pair.
Oh, for a pair of good ears.
Instead of the silence of my
Fears.
Where is there beauty to touch?
I reached for the Godly such,
Then my fears began to melt.
Oh, to feel it again and again,
Instead of living in day to day
Sin.
To smell the peace of Good-Will
Like the fragrance of a daffodill,
Or the odor of a bright red rose;
Who could tell without a nose;
Just how the flowers do smell;
Or to smell the fragrance, of being
Well.
Taste not, that which is sin.
Go to God's house and live within.
For without the love of God's taste,
The souls of this so-called human race,
Will be sent to swell in the Eternity,
Of their very own man-made
Hell.

David Chinn
SISSY
Come, my little Sissy,
Let me hold you in my arms.
Let me peer into your face
And observe your childish charms.
Your lovely godlike countenance
And sparkling angel eyes
Obliterate my worldly cares
And make my spirits rise.
You know not of the clouds of life;
Eternal sunshine lights your way.
The radiance of your tender smile
Breeds love throughout the day.
Sweet innocence and purity
Engulf your little frame.
Your smile casts out a beam of love
That sets my heart aflame.
No wonder of God's holy realm
Nor sight of heaven's hue
Could ere express a greater love
Than that I feel for you.

D. M. Hariton
JOY
A joy that cannot be expressed
other than unto oneself
Finding a half-broken bottle
in the sand
Or a footprint twice the size
of yours
Or the dream in your eye
which sends you into a swoon
Never to touch the convertible
sky
But to reach
Unendingly
Toward the sun

Helen Holub
LOVING HANDS
God blesses those who are thoughtful and sincere,
ready with a willing hand and a sympathetic ear.
Even when the day has been an extra hectic one...
He always manages to make a smile from once a frown.
Taking care of patients, is not an easy task...
it's heartrending and difficult almost too much to ask
of any one at all you see, but He gave you something rare.
He gave you an understanding heart and hands that show you care!
If there were never willing hands to care and help to heal,
I can't help but wonder, how this old world would feel!
A smile, a hand, a gentle touch, a bit of understanding...
even when the day is long with patients never ending.
God has given each of you that special quality...
that gives a nurse those loving hands
and rare ability!!

Dianne Desiree' Barnett
UNTITLED
For I am
myself
Borne unto
myself
No more
or no less
Than the earth
or the skies
But a part
of creation
However humble
or proud
Sleep now
in silence
And wake
to find
Yourself at peace.

R. A. Vogel
THE INTERVIEW
SO, YOU WANT TO BE A WRITER, A POET
Was I supposed to answer
Was it a question put to me
Or a statement awaiting affirmation
The best of my written words lay askew on his desk
Years of my life in a scattered heap
The artifact in his hand
In my humble opinion, the worst one of all
WHY DO YOU WISH TO BE A WRITER?
Must I answer
My mind awash of bleak emptiness
I answer a feeble answer, reflecting a feeble mind
I see my image echoed in his eyes
This stumbling, bumbling, babbling fool
Stammering into oblivion
Tripping over her own tongue on the way
PERHAPS YOU NEED A LITTLE MORE EXPERIENCE
Experience he says
This has truly been an experience
Classified as one of the worst of my life
I feel a scream verging
Total upheaval, beginning at my soul
But a pen makes no sound
Poets scream in silence

Sharon K. Sandifer
WANTING...NEEDING... LOVING
We've been apart for a while,
Too long to be true.
But still in everyone who makes me smile,
I always see you.
You're the one who has filled my dreams.
You're the only one, and I would go to extremes,
Just to know you would be mine,
Then everything would be fine.
I thought if I changed, you would come around,
If I were firm, and stood my ground.
So now 'tis done, I'll wait and see,
If you really still want me.
Your words say you don't.
Your actions say you do.
God knows I love you,
And I want you too.
I have nothing to hide from you.
Now you're the one to choose...
...I will be true...

Marilyn Long-Tim
EMOTIONAL PRISON
Repleted with anger and pain
With all this ideological tyranny.
Society has presumed exclusive
Rights to proclaim an onslaught.
To remain an aspirant, but how?
Inflamed with madness of the seduction
That it has bestowed upon me;
I am afflicted to my soul and
It masticates and consumes me.
I must somehow extinguish the memory
Of all the little innuendos and parodies.
I will not be exploited and told of
The perpetual promise of, this too will pass.
Tranquillity must rescue me
As I no longer will be the scapegoat.
I will magnify my barricade
From all of their squalid and brutal ways.

Luther Hinkle
WAITING FOR THE BOMBS TO ROAR
This world is changing at a pace,
We have never seen before.
All the future that we have,
Just waiting for nuclear bombs to roar.
Just how long will we sit idle?
In this great world of sin,
And see everthing destroyed,
By just a few ungodly men.
I am sure I know not what to do,
That would change the minds of men.
For things are predicted what they'll do,
That will bring about the end.
It's been proved that our dear Country,
Is so generous and will always share.
Our prosperity with all the

worlds people,
And always will treat them fair.
There is no one who has ever
won a war,
In victory or in defeat.
For regardless what the treaty is,
No one can keep the peace.

Mark Joseph Sloan
VESPERS
My dear world, please leave me
alone,
Pretend I'm not the one you've
known,
Go away and peacefully pray,
Tell our Lord what you want to
say.
As for me, I'll try to confess,
I need silence and nothing less.

Carmen J. Pence
THE BATTLE
some came from the north
some came from the south
and then they came ten
thousand more
they came with ballads
they came with axes
they came with words; shrewd
and cold
some were slaves
some were lovers
some were bearded; young and
old
some were rich
some were poor
some came and knew not why
some came to gain courage
some came to gain power
neither is now alive
they died with banners
they died with pride
both their wives and mothers
cried
and some knew not why.

Jody Lynn Davis
FOR THE LOVE OF A STRANGER
Feelings carried on endless time,
A shadow in the distance
wondering why,
Hours added to seconds grow
longer,
Waiting the end of what seems
somehow stronger,
Knowing not who or where you
are from,
Yet aware of your presence
whene'er you come,
Torn between one love and your
mystic air,
All so confusing it seems so
unfair,
Choosing of love or what can
never be,
So very hard yet it be so easy,
While falling to pieces on the
inside,
Behind exchanged smiles I run
and hide,
All of these feelings they just
don't make sense,
When day after day you're with
someone else,
I can't keep on running in anger,
Hurting so much for the love of
a stranger.

Farley McCoy
RAMBLING ON
I'm just a plain ole country folk
spose some 'id call me hick,
Why if someone asked me to a
Fancy French Restraunt
I't 'id be enough to worry me
sick,
I don't put no stock in the way
you go,
or how you get there,
Cuz, I don't judge a man by the
car he drives,
or his wife by the clip of her
hair,
I probably couldn't tell ya
the proper way to serve,
An if someone asked me to
write a rich man up
I'd probably be shy the praise
he thought he deserved,
Ya know, I've heard folks say
"I'd give anything—To have a
touch a class,"
'N everytime I hear it, I just
laugh at something
Ma Ma once said
"YOU can't make a show horse
out of a plain ole ass."

Charles Wesley Watson
YOUR SMILE
Sitting alone thinking, my mind
way out in space
I suddenly see visions of your
sweet and lovely face
The face I haven't seen in quite
a little while
One I know, I can't forget
because of your sweet smile.
A smile that reflects happiness
A smile so bright and clear
A smile that really turns me on
Like a magnet draws me near.
A smile of love and affection
becomes a silly grin
A smile so pure and so real it
comes from deep within
A smile that inspires, brings
warmth to one's heart
A smile to remember always,
together or apart.
Wear your smile forever as you
go from day to day
Never allow anyone to wipe
your pretty smile away
I shall see that smile always, as
I did from the start
That tender smile of happiness
coming straight from your
heart.

Michelle Leigh Brevard
LIFE AND YOUR CHILD
Life, and the new born baby lets
out the first cry,
It seems to ask, "I'm here—but
why?"
As the baby struggles out of a
helpless cocoon,
And the days of its' life fill the
corners of the room.
The parents are the world; the
day—the night,
It seems there is always a battle
to fight.
To sit, to walk, to talk and a
person will emerge,
A joy to have, and forward their
life will serge.
We push the child to go and
hurry ahead,
Be someone important for isn't
it said,
My son! My daughter! so
talented, so bright.
That's what makes my life a
delight.
Don't disappoint us, you must
make your mark.
Life, be someone important, it's
not just a lark.
You must have wealth,
recognition, you know,
If not—what in this world do I
have to show?
When my life is over and all is
done,
All I have to leave is a daughter,
a son,
But parents what God would
always have us to do,
Be happy together and to thine
self be true.

Nelson Smith
A LITTLE BOY NAMED JESUS
A little boy walks down a dusty
road
A lonely trail—he leaves
behind;
His dreams and tears and
memories:
Will forever Test mankind!
He will someday be—a Poet-
King;
A "Messiah"—to a Faith near
lost?
The cruel years of His manhood
will—
—Culminate upon a blooded
Cross!
We all know this little Boy;
HOW DUMB?
A simple carpenter-shop's lad,
is He;
He could be our next-door
neighbor's lad—
"A growing twig, upon a tree!"
Christmas-time will come and
go—
And, a brand New Year will
soon begin;
The old year—dying—has its'
snow;
And, old and dying things
must end!
Look out your windows, a cold,
clear Night
After the New Year reigns
afar—
The brightest "light" that
Eastward shows
Praise God—Was His
announcement *Star!!!*

Floie Jane Stouder
SILENCE
The darkest despair is in a
person's heart!
An angry word,
a misunderstanding,
can burn like a torch,
and grow in silence.
The peace that comes when
hurt is surrendered
to the Lord,
is worth the short moment
of pain.

Herbert J. Fisher
THE GREAT BLUE HERON
He haunts the shores of lakes
and streams,
With a stalk both slow and
sure;
His gray-blue form, a stilt-like
shape,
Blends with some plants on
shore;
A movement in the water near,
Alerts his wary eye;
With lightning stab, he "spears"
a fish,
And gulps it down right nigh;
A heronry of ragged nests,
Is now his homeward aim;
In one of these, he feeds his
young,
Then returns from whence he
came;
The pleasant Summer moves
along,
To the end of brooding days;
Then herons leave their woody
nests,
And go their various ways;
The empty nests stand stark and
bare,
For many a wintry day;
Until the warmth of Spring
returns,
And lures the birds this way.

Patricia A. Malcomson
SUN
Shine on, oh yellow ball,
bring in the warmth
of the day.
Sing ye birds, sing, tell
everyone of the great ray.
Lift up your arms great
tree, reach up to catch
this great god of the day.
All of the earth praise
you god, sun, never go away.

Georgianna Sarah Bloom
SERENADE
The music
tilts and lifts with our
heartbeats.
As the
night air embraces our flowing
bodies.
We are
captive by the moon's shining
threads.
My own
music blends in together with
yours.
Till the
beauty of oneness is enhanced
by our love.

Helen Brown Vandervoort
MORNING CHALLENGE
The sun and air were teeming
With a morning challenge new,
And eagerly I plotted
All the things that I would do.
And yet, before one task began
I heard his childish plea,

A summons from my three-year-
old,
"Oh, Mommy, please help me!"
Like water running through a
seive,
My self-made morning dare
Vanished as quickly as it came
In the claims of my son and
heir.

Albert Zelman
NIGHT THEME
The night lights one by one
turn on
Vignettes across the city skyline
In symmetry they seem to dance
Like marionettes in bobbing
motion

Sandy Newlin
A MINOR ALTERCATION
Still stunned
by the sound
of an angry fist
smashing against
the frail cartilage
of my nose,
i watch the warm blood
as it flows
between my trembling fingers.
It sprinkles
the fabric flowers
rooted in our tablecloth;
the dandelions wash red,
drown, and disappear.
And i wonder if tomorrow
a beanstalk
might sprout boldly here
upon this crimsoned linen
where fell
one magic tear.

Vashti Carpenter
BLESSINGS
If friends are blessings
then I have many-
It's hard to imagine
not having any-
Tho some people say
that be their case-
I manage to find them
most every place-
I think it goes back
to the way that we live-
not what you can get-
but what you can give.

Liz Brown
IN ITS ENTIRETY
Segments cannot be extracted
From the whole.
But if all were told,
Even the segments would be
meaningless.
Where every minute was
cherished,
And every second was felt,
It would be unfair
Not to continue in detail.
An overall must be presented
For the entire presence is felt,
Long after the shadow is gone.

Helen Marcella Banuelos
REJECTION
I exist as that fragment of
decayed bark rejected
In times past, a vital part of the
everlasting tree-
Sheltering it from outside forces
Shielding its existence;
Now I lay by the wayside
discarded-
Longing for its life-giving
presence
The tree, once my font of being,
has shed me
The decayed bark rejected.

Sharyn Spinka
MEMORIES
Memories,
Pounding, hounding memories
Tearing, stinging memories
Of ages past.
Memories,
biting, fighting memories
Clawing, ripping memories
Of times long ago.
Memories,
Teasing, playing memories
Crafty, witty memories
Of years now gone.
Memories,
Like evaders of the law,
Come creeping upon me
To evade my peace.
Memories,
Like knights in shining armor,
Come guilded in glaze, only
To show their fierceness.
Memories,
Like the tongue of a snake,
Come slithering to the surface
To sting me with their poison.
And once stung
The wound will not heal
Only scab, to be opened once
more
By the same force that began it
So many years ago.
I try to evade it,
To coat myself in costume,
To slither right by it,
But my scheming doesn't work,
Just begins the war
Inside me.

Natalie Holt
A LOCKED DOOR
I'll sit by myself from time to
time,
Searching for memories I'll
never find.
Staring at a locked door without
a key,
For no memories were left of
my mother for me.
I was so young, but I still can
rememer,
When death came calling she
slowly surrendered.
Maybe it's a blessing, that I can
not see,
Beyond the locked door of
memories.

Charles C. Case
THE HIGH FLIGHT
I seek to escape,
To emulate the flight of birds,
To soar where the gull and eagle
Flex their strategies,
Parenthesis the wind,
Describe the sky.
I yearn for the turbo jet,
In thunderous parabolas
Assault the fixtures of the earth,
Hurl jeers like rockets at my
feet,
Anchors gripped in wet
concrete.
I flee upward, moonbound,
Through blue atmospheric
doors,
My supersonic fuselage in neon
flight
Defies the trees,
Transcends the clouds,
In far earthless space
Pursues the dream.
The stars in concavities of
calculus
Rebound in multiples,
Like lightening
We gravitate through
spectroscopic dawns,
vibrate in polar enmities,
Jettson gravity,
Slip down the winds stream.
In fantasy the sun stands still,
Turns about the moon...
Too swift
The meteorite forsakes its flight,
The dreamer
The dream too soon.

D. L. Ular
ROSE COLORED GLASS
She looks through rose colored
glasses
Catching a glimpse of the sea
She sifts through life's ashes
Seeing the world as she wants it
to be.
She hopes for a knight to whisk
her away
Up into the astles of her mind
But I've come tonight and I've
come to say,
"Open your eyes, open your
mind,
Let light and life touch your
heart."
Discard your life of endless
dreams
Stop flying the winds on
gossamer wings.
It's not all what it seems,
There's more to life than
catching moonbeams.
But my words are lost; just
echoes in the wind
Her eyes and mind are distant
To some fantasy land she goes
Wishing, hoping and dreaming
Reality she'll never come to
know.
She looks through rose colored
glasses
Catching a glimpse of the sea
She sifts through life's ashes
Seeing the world as she wants it
to be.
A heavy mist has settled
between us,
She's in her world and I'm in
mine.
Her world is new, tinted and
covered in gold,
Mine is beautiful too, but has
cracks and is very old.
If only this heavy mist would
pass,
But I can only see a sparkle of
the rose colored glass.

Jeannellen Kessing
DESPAIR
Tossed by a sea of emotions
Drowning in the sorrows of a
lifetime
Do I have the strength to fight
against the tide?
Or will I be swept out to sea
Engulfed by the vast ocean of
life?

Margot Monty
MOUNTAIN ECHOES
the mountain echoes are heard
all day
The mountain verigates all day
with hay;
Mixing through mist and
shifting clouds;
Impish, bluish like ghosts in
shrouds
Doomless-vapors, flow water
falls
Cool crystal pool after pool, like
visions;
Imagined banshees, bemused by
all;
with witches' vanity, from
covenant traditions
Echoes of ghosts where no
human shrieks
Fade from past in foggy air, small
faces stare;
Voices heard, around the
shrouded peaks;
Wrapped on branches, witch's
hair
Swirled mountain dew, moist,
whipped
Wingless figures, devouring
their last embrace;
Like escaping heat, their spirit
slipped;
Into the inertia of timeless
space
Sway mountain paths of mossy
grass
faded figures banished into
timeless repeat;
Into the Mount of echoing pass;
Hazed murals, entwined asleep!

Donalyn Marie Carlson
LET YOURSELF GO
Let go!
Like a kite,
Like a leaf,
Bouncing on air,
Escape,
Worries
And apprehensions.
Be devil-may-care.
Come,
Fly with me,
On my
Natural high.
Laugh,
As we skip
Across this
Wide sky.
Ward off
Your conscience,
Because
It can haunt.
Your mind,
And desires,
Coaching things
You should want.
Break
Your image.
Go on,
Let yourself go!
You may like
My natural high,
In the surreal
Unknown.

Timothy Michael Gregory
DREAM KISS
Kiss me in your dreams
My love,
For I do not hesitate
To kiss you in mine
Your kisses are like precious
jewels and treasures
I keep them locked away
In my heart forever
Where no thief can sneak in to
steal
No robber can ravage or plunder.
Can you feel me
Thinking of you, my love
Sometimes it seems
I can feel you thinking of me
I am awakened by soft morning
whispers
Dancing ever so gently upon my
spirit
As the laughing waters of the
Indies
Rolling onto an island paradise,
I am deeply moved by your love.
Promise never to leave me
My darling,

For without your kisses
I would surely starve
They quench my thirst
And satisfy a once insatiable
hunger
No bread is quite as appetizing
No nectar quite as delicious
I would freely relinquish
All that I have
For just one more
Always just one more,
Because of your treasured kisses
One day
I shall fill great voids of space
With images of your face.....

Robert Witkowski

UNTITLED

Let me speak of that mysterious fragrance
of your being,
which enthralls one as does temple incense
of the Orient;
so much so, that my body and soul
are not mine.
Let me slip from thine own chalice the sweet
nectar of love.
Then too, in the garden shall I feast a
banquet of dainty morsels ere made ready by your own hand
in delighted labor.
Let me say, combining with all, your child
flesh of Alabaster,
composing a sensual symphony of feminine splendor, that
draws me deeper.
So it is as my eyes, and heart, look upon you, and
ask for freedom.

Catherine L. Boyer

THE WIND

Fast or slow she may blow
in and about she may go
rustling leaves on her way
usually starting on a spring day.
Swirling and twirling she can be
seen
or sometimes can even blow
mean.
Swishing and lashing high in the
sky
with everybody having watery
eyes.
The trees keeping time with
every gust
and as everyone knows the wind
is a must.
She's a cooling relief and it can
be heard with a sigh,
until she passes and then dies.
But then she's reborn on another
spring day,
and goes about in her usual way.
Prancing and dancing the year
away.

E. F. Pabillore

THE TURNING POINT

I am a child,
a child of creation;
Feeling just like
a wandering star
And like a bird
with flying emotion
Wanting to fly
to fly so high!
I am a ship
a ship of the sea
Sailing in the wind
with no sense of direction;
Tossing in the storm
cradled by the waves
Longing to land
But nowhere.......
its gone!

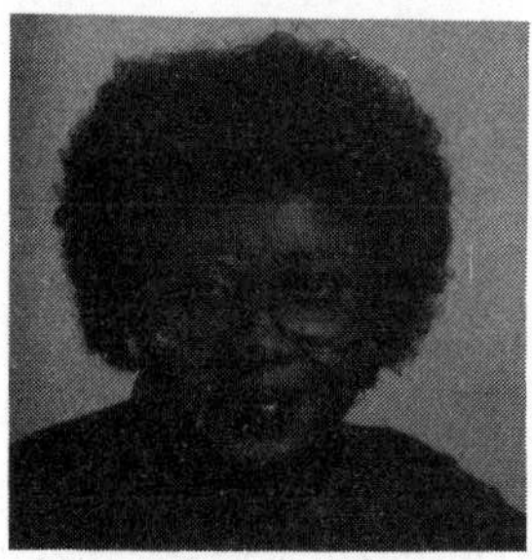

Deborah Marchman Osei-Kofi

WHERE IS PEACE

The dreams for a happy life
are always shattered.
And the hopes of peace
can never be fulfilled.
Where does all the fighting end?
Show me the place where peace
begins.
How many more deaths will
cause us to weep?
How many more martyrs
will we find to mourn?
Keep them from the assassins
who spill their blood in the
streets.
Keep them from bitter hearts
and confused minds who
suspect no personal gains.
When all nations scream defeat
will that be sufficient?
Weren't we ecstatic when our
hostages came home?
We danced and rejoiced in the
streets.
And when Reagan and Pope
John Paul II were shot our
emotions brought back despair.
Anwar Sadat our most recent
loss, the list is so long
and I suppose will go on.
Our tears will come
and our tears will go
But when, oh when will the
fighting stop?
When Lord, oh when will hatred
flee from their hearts?
Each nation as one
with their eyes to the heavens.
One nation under God
and peace prevailing forever.

Donna L. Marchand

MOTHERS

to my mother, Ann,

Mothers are the most beautiful
people.
When we are young we don't
realize this.
All of our childhood, mothers
cater to us,
When we are sick, sad, or broke
our favorite toy.
They kiss our tears away, and
make things right.
But as we grow, we think we
don't need them as much.
Mothers tell us the right things
to do,
And how we should live.
There's an old saying,
"Mothers know best."
Who ever made that saying, was
right.
I know, my mother told me
things when I was a girl.
And I didn't always believe her.
But mothers never lie,
She was always right.
It's very unfortunate that we
don't realize this
Until we are much older.
Your mother can be the best
friend in the world.
If you let her.
I did.

Pamela Elizabeth Burks

DREAMIN'

The night was cold
Fog was rolling in
He looked into my eyes
As I looked at him,
I lifted my head
As he kissed my lips
I caressed his body
As he caresed my hips,
We walked hand in hand
Along the moonlit ocean
I laid down in the sand
To prove to him of my devotion,
My mind is now confused
I need to set it free,
Because when he said 'I Love
You'
I should have known,
That was all just a dream.

B. J. Lisatz II

PEYTON PLACE

You migrate,
Leaving everything behind
Searching for thrill.
Life,
Adventurism,
You've found them all.
It unfolds before you,
Across an ocean,
On the Continent.
As days fly by
Living is no longer a bore,
For now you write the script.
Suddenly you find yourself
Caught, right in the middle
Of the Soap Opera called "Life".

Annie L. Alford

POETS EVERYWHERE

The world is full of poets;
They're hanging from the
trees;
And every wind that bloweth
Sends them singing in its
breeze.
They all would like to publish
Their ditties, not a few;
No matter if they're rubbish
From an editor's point of view.
I'd like to have a chance to look
Through every poet's diary
And see recorded in the book
Their thoughts, both cold and
fiery;
For every Poet's bosom swells
With passions unexpressed.
'Tis just the outline that he
tells.
No words can tell the rest.

Barbara J. Vera

51-53 WEST 129th STREET

Nineteenth century mortar and
Brick is the uterus that
Nurtured us while we
Tackled childhood.
That building with its six
Flights of stairs is where
We shot into adolescence.
It's where we discussed
Kisses and adults and
Periods and each other.
That obelesk, with its iron
Fire escapes, witnessed our
Tears and our hurts and
Our angers as well as our
Joys.
When the time of gestation
Was complete, that
Harlem tenement birthed us
Into womanhood.

Roger E. Chapman

THE HYDRAULIC SANDWICH

cereal grass they call it,
but created not intended
to be fermented, concocted,
blended,
and liquidfied;
for barflies to sit and sip,
nor chug and guzzle,
and wipe off the muzzle
with a sleeve of a flannel shirt;
to up-chug later back in the dirt.

Rhoda Lynn Foxworthy

TO CROSS THE THRESHOLD

The emission of life
emerges from within.
The internal greatness
fuses into one being;
The outward appearance
changes!
Returning into itself,
the entity regains strength,
Thus being reborn into the
Soul of the Universe. . . .

Amy A. Stowell

KITCHEN STOVE

She felt his arms
Prompted by the warmth,
encircle her.
Memory transported her
consciousness
beyond the new wood-burner,
Their cushioned surroundings.
The child's arms
Gathering the warmth,
Scarcely reached the warming
oven
Above the cooking place,
On that Moving-Day.
It stood, cumbersome,
Elevated on a crude platform
that bridged the gap
of a missing stove pipe.
The oven door sagged.
Firewood inside the firebox
crackled defiance, to the
shabbiness
That would be home.

Ida L. Davis

FRIENDSHIP

On an occasion such as this
I wish to share with
those who care.
Good friends are an asset to
cherish, since money can't
buy true friendship.
Your moral support has helped
me in many ways, during many
hectic and complaining days.
We've shared many views-not
agreeing
in many an aspect, but as
individuals
each other we do respect.
May God Bless us all in every
way, with a lasting friendship
forever and a day.

Dolores K. Rose
OUR EVERLASTING LOVE
You are really wonderful and such a dear!
My! How comforting to just have you near.
I envy all girls you happen to meet—
You can see them falling head over feet.
I know sometimes I get in your hair,
But to live without you, I could not bear.
Life would never be so complete
Without your smile, so soft and sweet.
And when you said, "I love you" and "I do"
I knew there wouldn't be anyone but me for you!
It takes a lot of faith to make marriage work
Oh, and I promise my duties I will not shirk.
So, Darling, remember no matter how far
I'll always love you wherever you are.
You will forever have with you a part of me—
A part you will carry to Eternity.
Because when God comes down from Heaven above
He will not separate our everlasting love.

Jean M. Rogers
LOVE TO
Love to take and love to give,
Love to die but love to live.
Love to share and love to steal,
Love to tell you how I feel.
Love to starve and love to eat,
Love to be loyal but love to cheat.
Love to walk and love to run,
Love to be bored but love to have fun.
Love to sleep and love to wake,
Love to be real but love to fake.
Love to be silent and love loud screams,
Don't know what I love—it seems!

Miss Patsy Sue James
A BLACK CHILD
Born in the dark or was it light?
Regardless of my arrival I'm still dark night.
My face of the dark black chocolate fudge;
Because of that my taste is judged.
In society I'm not known alright;
I'm a curse of wickedness mad black night.
Why is my face so different and my talk?
Why my style of clothing so different along with walk?
My voice rumbles and my eyes so tired;
It seems in my world I'm not excepted, rejected and fired.
My fingers worn out my strength not strong;
I'm a black child, I've been born wrong.
My color to some is a mad animal that's trying to make way;
I'm a black child in society will I pay?

Helen Wagley—Hunter
DO WARS EVER CEASE?
'Twas a very windy day in April,
Over the waterfalls leaned the branches of a maple.
The water gushing over many rocks,
The birds chirping, while sitting on docks.
In the little brook running under the bridge— there was peace,
But in the rest of the world the wars did not cease.
The flowers were in blossom each day,
And the trees in bud every May.
The world's population was at a steady increase,
But still the wars did not cease.
Night suddenly falls upon the great earth,
But time still lingers in the home by the hearth.
Then morning awakens the sun at dawn,
But the dog still lies sleepily upon the lawn.
A great silence came upon the geese,
But will today's wars ever cease?

Darlene Lun
A LITTLE GIRL
A little girl watches the sunset,
Her life behind her and no more to live.
She sees a mother with a child burden upon her, with the mother
nothing to give.
Life filled with pain and sorrow,
she would wake up to no more.
For that little girl who watched the sunset, she is with us no more.

Goldie Kelley
RETREAT IN ROEDING PARK
My tired spirit sought a voice of calm:
For many diverse voices, calling me,
Were so confusing, and I had no balm
Of quietness, no light filled vision of reality.
I left the busy city streets behind,
And hither came, to this green, living park,
The home of ducks and squirrels. Here I find
An ordered beauty I have seldom seen, and hark!
Here by this tranquil pool, this peaceful glade,
Where softly rippling liquid mirrors hold
A symphony of moving light and shade,
Life's unity, and peace and beauty bathe my soul.

Laurie Andrews
REFLECTIONS
I see my reflections in the mirror.
I do not like what I see.
I look at myself and wonder
how I came to be, and why.
I look at myself, reflections
of hatred and pain.
I look and wonder what is my
purpose. I have no goal.
I look in the mirror in dismay,
who am I, I do not know.
I am no one, I do not belong,
I do not fit in this world.
People look, but they do not see.
They listen, but do not hear
what I have to say.
I look at my reflection, and
see myself.
Other people see me, but they
do not look. They do not know
what they see, They look
straight through me.
I look at my reflection. What
am I, who am I.

Lillian Ramsey
THE MODERN GIRL
She is a great American girl
She has beautiful blond hair with a curl.
She dances, shouts, and has a good time.
Goes riding around, and then to the restaurant to dine.
She smokes, gambles, and drinks her beer,
Laughs and yells about, but has no fear.
She is out for kicks, and to have all the fun
That anyone could have while drinking rum.
She never feels blue, but is always gay,
And never worries what others might say.
She wears long dresses, hot pants, and shorts,
Makes the boys holler, laugh, and snort.
She argues with her mother, and bosses her too,
For she wants to do everything other girls do.
She swipes her father's car and rides out of town.
Now she is gone and nowhere can she be found.

Linda Strollo
PASSING "FRIENDS"
Perhaps it is destiny I encounter you
And in lonely desperation call you my friends.
The pain is deep and troublesome
Forgotten is inner peace
as it gets lost in hurt pride.
Foolish am I to adopt words of eternal unity
You vow everlasting love and devotion
Elusive companionship is the reality.
You use me for what you can and then cast me out.
Your deceitful and hypocritical words and my self-deception and loneliness
Mesh to create the world of illusion.
Inevitably I realize the Truth
But not until my own folly is lain bare and you derive pleasure from vicious laughter.
Though these lessons are painful
They hasten humility
and that is my route
Human folly takes time to understand.
Pain ascends and recedes.
You enter and exit my life.
Use me, hate me and abuse me—
But to be a friend,
you must first find yourself.

Craig S. Rogers
LITTLE ANIMALS
Across the concavity of mind there rakes
The dejected consequence of my many mistakes.
I look and see my character defaced
And realize that memories can never be erased.
What conflagrant woodland there does tragedy dine?
Ashes, ashes: the very image of hopes that were mine.
All the little animals left without home.
All my anguish I must wrestle alone.
A fleece of gold hangs high upon towering asp,
Buried treasure of aurum and argent lie beyond grasp.
I am unfit to climb and pick have I none,
But now the treasure can scarcely be seen so dim seems the sun.
What fields of martagon have been trampled underfoot?
What trousseau has been soiled, blackened by soot?
Oh, the people I've treaded while through this life passing,
The sorrows I've caused, their number amassing.
All my tomorrows, they can't be enjoyed,
As flowers and friends they'll soon be destroyed.
As little animals left without home
I wander, wander, continue to roam
So alone.

George Anna (Kidd) Case
RED ROSES MEAN LOVE
You walked by my roses and left them for dead.
Roses mean love, especially the red.
Two roses I gave on which my heart bled,
Turning the roses a brightened red.
Wherefore did the roses you pass by,

To leave a heart broken a tear
in mine eye.
One was my body one my heart,
Brightened by blood Whence for
a start.
You left them to be trampled in
mud,
The red roses on which was my
blood.
I'm just like the roses in which
are red,
You walked by and leave me for
dead.

David Possessky

SUMMER

Summer brings sunshine
Thunderstorms with rain
Summer night sunsets
Can be so much more than plain
Sandy white beaches
Walks in the ocean's surf
Sunbathing ladies
Exploring different turfs
Summer brings romance
Parties at neighbors pools
Serene evenings to dance
Memories of playing like happy
fools
Lovely maidens dancing in the
sun
Different meanings to symbol a
perfect day
Pretending to never end the fun
A summer breeze blows your
troubles away
Summertime evenings
Picnics in a quiet park
Wishing on falling stars could
be misleading
Someone to hold close in the
dark
Summer relationships blossom
Like the rose bud coming of age
Another chapter in your own
life
Memories that fill a lonely
empty page
Summer moments relaxing
Being lazy on hazy days
Sparkling starry evenings
Enjoying the comfort in many
different ways

Shelley E. Hall

SILENT GRACE

Today while the snow falls,
Such silent grace.
My thoughts linger,
Another time, another place.
Fleeting moments,
Times gone past,
Loving memories,
They will forever last.
Soft as snow,
Silent as time.

Paula Haines

RUDE AWAKENING

Get out of my house,
Get out of my life,
The damage you've done is
complete.
My heart that was given with
kindness
Has awakened from love's
blindest sleep.
Yes, I'm now in control of this
"dear one",
So get out before shoe meets
your seat.
To think that I've wasted my
time on a bum;
It's surprising, it's depressing
to me.
So get out of my life.
You get out of my house.
And you better give back your
door key.
I'm again on my own,
Once again happy home.
Think I'll find one who'll be
good to me.

Dana Kessimakis

RAINBOWS

Misty, Wet, days cloudy and
cold
then comes the rainbow, colors
so bold.
Arching with colors shining so
bright
In comes the sunshine giving us
light.
Beaming across the valley, it
brightens your
day. So pretty and bright
you wish it would stay—
But after a while it melts
by the sun.
Until the next rainstorm, the
rainbow is done.

Debbrin K. Morris

LOVE IS A MAGICAL THING

I was never a believer in the powers of magic until that warm day when our paths crossed and a magical event began to unfold and blossom.

It's magical and mystical the way your smile has the ability to bring that special and needed ray of sunshine to light up my grayest day.

It's magical the way our hours apart seem endless, but how our time together races by with the speed of a split second. Only the power of love could alter time that radically.

For you and I, the most common and ordinary of all places are transformed into Cinderella's ball, simply by the powers of magic.

If not for magic, how is it that I fell so helplessly into your eyes like Alice's fall into Wonderland without getting hurt?

So many magical things have occurred between us since that warm, beautiful day. But most magical of all these things is the power and strength with which I've grown to love you, demanding nothing, yet always and forever hoping that this magical event will never end.

Martha Joan Loomis Sweeney

GRIEVE FOR ME NOT. . .

Grieve for me not that I did
die. . .
For in the casket, I do not lie.
My bones and flesh do lieth
there. . .
But, not me, friend, I do declare.
My body was a weight for me. . .
Now, my spirit has been set free,
No pain, no food, no broken
bone. . .
My spirit now exists alone.
I am freer than I have ever been.
I need no more to look within.
The sensation I now endure. . .
I find to be so very pure.
Nay, grieve for me not, now I
pray. . .
Go on and have a real nice day.
Rejoice for me! I am so glad!
I will not have my loved ones
sad.
I will let you miss me now and
then. . .
Remember me, Martha Joan.
However, I will be with you
when. . . .
You wish for me to be again. . .
With memories of me you share.
I hope they are all good and fair.
No one is perfect on this earth.
At least, remember my quaint
mirth.
I say not goodbye to you now.
We will meet again. . .someday. .
somehow!

Mark A. Reeves

DREAMER'S DUET

A Smile
And a small breeze wafts
across the myriad waters of a
quiet, unspoken stirring
An Embrace
And the moment is laced with
a gossamer aura of transient
desire, unforgiven by sin yet
touched by the devil's
innocence
A Kiss
And the feelings caress the
barbed temptations of a
passion
that sires an anguish shared
with ecstasy
A Love
And the gods press their lips
upon golden nectar and taste
of a madness that lays
ravage the demons of time

John G. Dearborn

PREVAILS

prevails. .the lights of . .
clinging to the pale morning,
the sickly weak of human
deprivation,
that whispers that say. .
forms are. . independent of
the light, the goddess that life
is. the horizon of vision before
cold dawns where you imagine
the touch is like the fibres
of the mind—would you blink
and it'd be gone. irresolute,
perish before your hungry
desires. .
so when one calls that forms
are. .independent of the Sun,
the golden lady licking the neck
of a man called earth: prevails
in words unspoken, unheard. .
goes up in flames like
burning cities.

Mi—Kes—Tes

THE KEEPER OF EXPERIENCES

Daylight stares back at me
from the other end of the
hallway.
Cages, cells, clinging to the
sides of the hallway,
Terminating my peripheral
vision.
I walk down the hallway.
Dark squares on the walls,
Represent a cubicle for some
unknown occupant. . .
—Some unknown prisoner.
Some squares emit sounds,
Brash, wild, roguish, defiant
challenges,. . .and pleas.
Others encroach upon the
humor of the mind,
To start others laughing.
I crack the whip at the sound of
weeping,
And wonder why I stand here,
In a dimly lit, and dark hallway.
Forever locked in some lower
sanction of the mind,
To be trapped,
A prisoner myself.
I, the keeper of experiences!

Rodney E. Sampsell

FOR SUSAN

The things that are
Important to you,
You share
With someone else.
I know I can never
Be a part
Of your world,
Or touch your heart.
So I'll hide from
You
The only love
I ever knew.

June Harrington

VIBRATIONS

Employ
But do not toy
With my emotions
Wrenching me apart
I hear you now again
Breathing new vibrations
Through the birch tree branches
Crying rain
Making love
To the already sodden earth
Screaming birth
Now in a softened monotone
Oh everywhere
And am not ready quite
The dusk falls down about me
Shielding me with night
So am contained almost

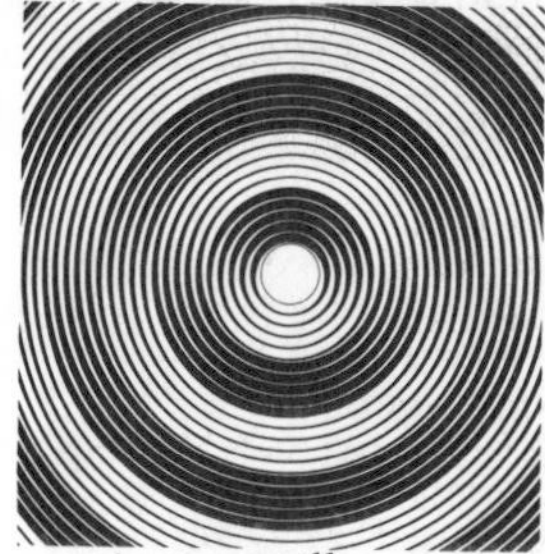

against my will
But pause lest I forget
How well you do me in
And catch my breath..ah spring
That is not april yet

Robert E. Cannaday
BUTTERFLY
Beautiful creature in sculptured flight,
Softly glide through mornings early light,
And spread your flashing amber wings,
So you may behold what the sunrise brings.
Lightly drift in the warm summer breezes,
And watch as the wind carried thistledown teases,
Then carefully adorn the honeysuckle vine,
Where the crimson flowers do entwine.
Oh gentle jewel of the painted skies,
Beware of the jealous darting dragonflies,
That skitter over rainbow colored streams,
Enchanting those with young foolish dreams.
Stately monarch in your best royal attire,
Survey your kingdom as you so desire,
Letting not the waiting twilight catch you in flight,
While you peacefully settle in for the night.

F. E. Knowles, Jr.
SECOND THOUGHT
a thought,
awakened
for
a moment
strike a
blow
for benevolence
and
retire

Karen Moles
HAPPINESS BY THE SEA
If I could live by the sea day and night
And feel the gentle breeze blow on my face,
Or see all the stars by the moon's bright light
And watch the waves break with foam like lace,
Or listen as the seagulls wander through the sky
As they drift through the white and snowy clouds,
Or watch the sunrise after the night has gone by...
Then I could be the happiest person around.

Jo Wickiser
TRUE LIFE
Happiness
In time which passes.
The root of all good,
You give out to others.
Respect
To play all's fair,
With you and the world,
And your part in it.
Satisfaction
Of what you've obtained.
To still be content,
Without total success.
Achievement
A way of rewarding,
For time and effort,
You've used in the "game."
Strength
To overcome problems,
Which often arise,
And get in your way.
Understanding
Of yourself and others.
To think before acting.
Compassion and caring.
Objectivity
To see all as is.
No false fronts built.
No prejudice can live.
Judgement
To know when to tell,
The truth or the lies,
So as not to hurt others.
Giving
From you to all.
As often as possible,
To share part of the self.
Love
Knowing all kinds.
To give and receive,
To care and respect.
Honesty
Behind all you do.
No cunning plots,
To get what's not there.
Living
For mere existance.
The enjoyment of all,
Without looking back.

Sharon E. Hatcher
MY LOVE FOR YOU
I wrote this poem in need of you;
You're everything I see and do.
I need your love, I need it now;
I need to say you're mine somehow.
If you could see how lonely I am;
You'd let me see you again and again.
The tears have come, and now they're gone.
Again, we'll sing our lovers song.
Tomorrow comes another day,
And I know, you'll come my way.
Our time is little, our love is strong:
We must let it go on and on.
The precious moments that we share,
No other love can compare.
The love in our hearts we have today;
Will never leave us, but always stay.
Alas, I know, our love will end;
And I will never see you again.

Margaret M. Ickes
AGAIN 'TIS CHRISTMAS
A radiant smile lit up her brow
Altho' it was yesteryear. . .I see her now,
On unsteady legs she stands, as a smile
Lights up the face of another child.
'Neath silver bells and the tinsel's glow
Down the Christmas road we turn to go. . .
So once again by candles dim
We are on our way to Bethlehem.
We watch three figures on their camels sway
Stopping in Jerusalem to ask the way.
We see shepherds on a hillside watching sheep
Surrounded by lights as the angels sweep;
The message they gave fills us with hope
While we follow the shepherds down a grassy—slope;
Their song still echoes o'er Judea's rim
As we quickly enter Bethlehem.
Again, small arms encircle me tight
While the Carol peals out. . .O Holy Night!
In the lowly stable, that first Christmas morn
We behold a Miracle. . .the Child is born!

Vern Emma Koehler
GENTLEWOMAN
Willowly as a willow,
and gentle as a breeze,
With the wisdom of Deborah,
and the strength of the trees.
Fresh as the dew
on the early morning grass,
With the fragrance of jasmine.
and devotion unsurpassed.
Delicate as the flowers
that bloom in early spring,
Love and tender heart
for every living thing.
Devout in worship
with reverence to God,
Compassionate without restraint
for those who work hard.
A gentlewoman,
Frieda Emilie Mathilda,
my Mom.

John F. Lemon
IF MAN WERE GOD
If man were God,
He could count the stars
Up in the sky;
Talk to the wind
As it rushes by;
Drink the milk
From the milky way;
Travel the universe
In a day;
Touch the man in the moon
And make him smile;
Teach the thunder
To be meek and mild;
If man were God,
He could with a sigh,
Kiss the wings of a butterfly;
Tell the truth and never lie;
Believe in himself
And never ask why.

Maxanne Millett
HOPE
Deep
Mystical
Intensely probing life,
I feel your essence
Constantly within—
The beautiful worlds
Built around private dreams;
Dreams of solitude
Of burning gratitude
My dreams coming from you.
Through the hot mist
A tiny light flickers.
The storms of the soul
Can't quench
The wavering small flame
Of hope.
Faith—
The unbelievable
Often comes to pass.
Courage;
He who succumbs
Must wither away.
Dry, dust of the earth
Giving birth
To new meanings
Of faith.
That still
Small flame
Kindles the life which flows,
Surging,
Trying to maintain the courage
To have faith
In hope.

Luciano L. Medeiros
POEM ONE
golden sunshine falling
on the flowers growing
in a garden hiding
many things that can't be seen
could it be a dream
every day is a Halloween
wear your face behind a mask
hide your love in a dream
with your eyes closed
you can see the unseen
could it be a dream
every day is a halloween
you claim to be sane
living in your own private bedlam
but yours is a phony world
in your world
there is no darkness
there is no death

Alma Joyce
SENTRY
Tis your glory or your clammor
to share with all you meet.
My wish must ever be towards light
multiplying not extremes.
For space and balance in time are set
and we cannot possess lifes' gift
to bury in graves of lying.
What in truth can we desire
but ourselves which we have lost.
Shadows all do chase the light
because the grave is emptying
and life is joy or madness.

Scott E. Blakey
THIS THOUGHT HELPS
Kind woman,
you complain
of being made to look like
a house
at this time.
But,
what else is it
you are become
for this?
Yes, and a home, as well,
for the small one.

David Hammond
MINDLESS
Cold,
Empty,
Timeless,
Timeless as the frozen hands
on the wall that can't go
backwards or forwards.
Timeless as the dried bones in
the grave of a famous hero.
Timeless as. . .
Timeless as. . .
Mindless.
Hot,
Vast,
Signless
Signless of life, or hope, or
promise of love on angry sand.
Signless of the slightest worm,
or roach to crawl this desert
waste.
Signless of. . .
Signless of. . .
Mindless.
Black,
Infinite,
Designless,
Designless as chance, or
boundry across nothing but
nothingness.
Designless as the atom smashed
into oblivion.
Designless as. . .
Designless as. . .
Mindless.
Everything,
Nothing,
Mindless,
Mindless as the babbling of a
madman in the echoes of his
own brain.
Mindless as the spoutings of
the world's wisest philosopher.
Mindless as. . .
Mindless as. . .
Mindless.

Michael Francis Sorel
THE LEAVES OF AUTUMN
The once colorful leaves of an
autumn
Fell the wind set them free
from their place in the sky,
Winter's coming
How they wave to the earth,
their sail filled by a gust of
wind,
The last goodbye.
On the ground shades of brown,
For they lived their whole life
in a season.
The burden of winter stands
the tree in nakedness,
Outlined in white, alone, wait-
ing for the warmth of better
days,
A breath of life.
She closes her eyes and sleeps
through time,
For spring will awaken her
next season.
And again it will happen,
somewhat unnoticed but ever so
true. A new beginning.

Charles F. Peterson
A PEACH
So son you have joined the
navy.
Think all that you have to do
Is to sit with a peach on
Waikiki beach,
And to hell with the rest of
the crew?
Oh, I know it's nice to be lazy,
And nice to sit in the sun,
And I don't want to preach in
front of your peach,
So listen you son-of-a-gun.
There's decks to be scrubbed, brass
to be rubbed.
There's a world of work on a
ship.
And the whole darn crew is
waiting for you,
So don't try to give us the slip.
So tell your little peach goodbye
And wipe the tears from your
beak.
I know she's a loving piece of
plunder,
For I had her myself last week.

Virginia Webber
MOON CAT
Moon Cat,
you squat
smug
full
and
orange
atop your fence
of city roofs
licking your whiskers
savoring the bright fat mouse
currently consumed
energizing
your slow-motion
a l l — n i g h t
l e a p of j o y—
to morning!

Nadine E. DaCunha
AGE
Little girl, where are the printed
dresses, lace anklets, and
patent leather shoes you wore
so devotedly?
You no longer run carefree
through fields of flowers,
catching butterflies or
pursuing dreams.
Age has fallen upon you as
quickly as the leaves turn
brown, dropping down on your
life like a smothering layer of
helplessness.
It's been so long since you've
ridden bikes, climbed trees,
and collected bugs with your
brothers.
You made the best mud-pies in
town.
And how it hurt when mom
pulled your braids too tight.
Now here you are, too old to
wear anklets and patent
leather shoes, afraid of bugs,
and your hair too short for
braids.
Soon you will see it all in your
own children, as each year of
their lives adds another
wrinkle to your face.
And yet, you don't know if it's
worth it all, giving up the
little girl inside to have one of
your own.

Linda Fritzsche
FOLLOW ME
(Matthew 9:9)
Jesus said only two words—
"FOLLOW ME".
And so like Matthew, we need
to follow thee.
But unlike Matthew, we make
excuse.
The THINGS of the world we
can't seem to lose.
For Matthew arose and followed
without delay.
For this OBEDIENCE we need to
pray,
Perhaps when Matthew heard
God's voice
He knew there really was no
choice.
For GOD ALONE GIVES
ETERNAL LIFE
He alone is the ANSWER FOR
STRIFE.
And yet even though we know
HE IS THE ONLY WAY,
We put off serving Him till
another day.
Perhaps we think we can serve
two masters
But that way of life can only
lead to disaster.
And WE NEED TO
SURRENDER OUR SOUL
AND HEART
To our precious Lord, and from
Him never part.
So, dear Lord, help us to
SEEK THEE on bended knee.
MAKE US MORE WILLING to
follow thee.
For to BE MORE LIKE JESUS is
our hearts desire.
We know that the things of
this world will be destroyed
by fire.
So HELP US TO SEEK AFTER
HEAVENLY TREASURES
Forsake the world and its
temporary pleasures.
LEAD US and GUIDE US each
step of the way
Help us make you our Lord each
and every day.

Ann Marie Albanese Janco
MY PERSONAL PRAYER
As I lay in my night dress.
I will wait for the Lord, for
I He will bless.
I will dream of Heaven, and
there I will dwell,
To await and see what
tomorrow will fortell.
Maybe sadness or joy or even a
tear.
To be watched by God, the One
that I fear.
Fear not as we know it, day by
day,
Fear that I wont please Him in
every way.
I know He is with me, I feel His
love.
He sent me this poem from
Heaven above.

Sondra S. Bedigrew
THROUGH MY EYES
Sometimes you can see farther
from a distance,
rather than up close.
Sometimes when you've been
away
from someone for a while,
your love for them shows more.
Sometimes it takes looking
through the eyes of others,
to see what you've got yourself.
Sometimes it takes the little
memories,
to really know how much
you love someone.
Sometimes it takes
a friend to know,
when you can't seem to see for
yourself.
Sometimes it takes
an honest word,
to put your world at peace.
Sometimes it takes
a loving heart,
to make your life complete.
It will always
take you,
to make me.

Calla L. Dean
ANOTHER DAY
The sun arose
To shed his ray
In gallant pose
Upon the day.

A huge red ball,
A stream of light;
And day's clear call
Disperses night.
Thus comes the earth
In gold arrayed;
New life, new birth,
Its strength sun-stayed.
With gorgeous glow,
The planets swing
And homage show
To Him their King.
With reverent eyes
I watch, and say,
"Past sunset skies,
Always there lies--
Another Day!"

Alexander F. John
THE FAITH FORMULA
Have you never heard of
faith?
For it is united with love
Whose power comes from
you and God
For you are born with it,
But only you can turn it on
Like a light switch.
And when your faith is
proclaimed
The light is shone upon
you,
And you can boldly say
Unto yourself and others,
"I can do all things through
Christ
Who strengthens me."

Marcia Hedberg
MOTHER DEAR
I love you "Mother Dear"
In case you didn't know
Sometimes life gets so hectic
I forget to tell you so.
You're very special "Mother Dear"
The best in every way
You make my life happier
As we go from day to day.
When I was little "Mother Dear"
Not knowing the world could be bad
You gave me all you could
You gave me all you had.
When I grew up "Mother Dear"
And took a mate by my side
You treated him so kind and good
You made me feel such pride.
Now that I have children "Mother Dear"
It's so clear to see
Why I couldn't have my way
Or do as I pleased.
With age "Mother Dear"
I realize what it's all about
Unselfish love; that's what you are
Without a doubt.

Joyce Farley Johnson
TO RUTH J. H.
SCHOOL FRIENDS
The schoolyard rang with youthful sounds of glee
As carefree children frolicked merrily.
One child stood crying in the schoolyard there,
Unknown, unnoticed;
No one seemed to care.
Her tears poured down;
The deluge had no end
Until a small voice said,
"I'll be your friend."
Those magic words soon vanquished all her tears,
And nurtured friendship's joys throughout the years.
As half a century now comes to an end,
The voice was heard to say,
"I'm still your friend."
P.S. (Prayer Script)
May Heaven keep you thinking young,
And believing what you see,
That everyone our age looks old,
Excepting you and me.

Aleda H. Benjamin
R F D ONE
Did you ever live in the country.
If not, you may think it's all fun;
I admit its blessings are many,
But there're heartaches on RFD One.
There's fresh air, sunshine and quiet,
Bird's song...and the fragrance of flowers;
But for these the day would seem hopeless,
For the tasks outnumber the hours.
There're chores aplenty to suffice,
Hubby's working...the children at school;
But one problem I simply can't cope with,
And that problem is...I'm a fool.
The work that needs doing goes wanting,
I try but my spirit just drops;
I'm waiting and watching and hoping,
That the mail-rider slows down, and stops.
If he does, I anxiously hurry
To the box, but can't stifle a wail;
When I pull out that silly ol' pamphlet.
--Sears Roebuck is having a sale.
I want to cry now but I mustn't,
Have to hurry to get my work done;
I'm sure folks would write far more often,
If they lived on RFD One.

Marjorie Ann Sciacca
NOSTALGIA
An ancient house near an apple tree,
stands silent in the shadow.
In front, a muddied road, I see
and I can hear the windows rattle.
Tight shut against the winter's air,
in their frames, they shiver,
And give to the field's, a blanker stare,
than could a cold love's eyes deliver.
The grass around has grown high.
It rushes to a door,
that on rusted hinges, swings,
And welcomes me, no more.
And above the desolate greens,
still rolls a troubled sky.
I walk slowly under the apple tree.
I wander lonely through the halls.
Memories walk beside me
in the silent rain that falls.
In the distant night
sings a whip-poor-will.
Clouds gather, dark,
above the hill.
But Listen!
Does a different sound intrude?
Or is it just a wistful mood?
Is that a violin I hear?
A sound from out another year?
Or is that familiar, mournful tone
heard in memory alone?

Philip D. Liquori
THE RIDGE
It began like other nightmares
Where everything worn was green
Battle scarred, seeing black stars rising
With the smell of hell and heat.
The faces of everyone sank
As the scouts ran flanks.
The bridge like other boundaries
Was the only unprotectable door
Racing columns, beneath cover of night
With the taste of waste and war.
The eyes of everyone swelled
As the bridge was shelled.
There was no time to think of those dying on the bridge
Because the orders came down
to the front to take the Ridge.
I crawled through the city debris
As smoke rolled over the land
With burning eyes, couldn't help but notice
That the gun was shaking in my hand.
I really wanted to scream
Only hoping that this was a dream.

Charles Edward De Marco
A RAY OF HOPE
In the depths of the soul
Rest the desperation of loneliness
Among the crevices of the mind
Lay the seeds of thoughtlessness
Unto the aging of the body
Forges the disappearance of loveliness
The fate of humankind
Hangs on a thread
O' why must we live
Bathing in an ocean of dread
The soul is the bosom
Nurturing its children with love
The mind is the organizer
Of thoughts from above
The body is the vehicle
Which carries the peace of the Dove
The fate of humankind
Still hangs on a thread
However no longer must we live
Bathing in an ocean of dread.

Cristal D. (Sharr) Buckner
LOVING A SOLDIER
Loving a soldier is not always gay,
For with it comes a price to pay.
It's missing him dearly,
And writing "I love you sincerely".
It's writing to him everyday,
And looking forward to the fourth of May.
It's kissing his picture each night,
And praying to God he'll be alright.
It's hearing him say "I love you",
And saying back "I love you too".
With loving a soldier comes tears,
And everyday is filled with fears.
A letter you receive, lined in black,
Tells you that he won't be back.
You look to God and ask him why,
Why did he, of all, have to die.
Now he's gone to God above,
And now you're saying "Did God doubt my love?"

Wendy Gardner
UNTITLED
I think of all the smiling faces—
(yes, you)
And warm hands
that have caressed my soul
Young and inexperienced—
(yes, I)
Reaching and grabbing
But never touching
Bouncing like a ball
From (yes)
Your strong open arms
to another. . .
And still another
not once wanting ever the
Slightest bit
(OK any)
Running each time I was
Caught
And in the final
Only the fool stood
(Yes, I)
I sit and ponder
Often to cry and curious
As to the why
(Of it all)
All caught up in fear
to be less than myself
Now I am
(myself)
alone.

Sean Fetter
IN CLOSING
And you know, in the end
I really don't have anything to say. . .
I feel only loneliness
In my idiotic outpouring of meaningless, empty words
And sorry—
to that depth to which only futile regrets can lead—
For all the tender caresses
And gentle kisses
And fervent, desperate hugs
I never shared with you
So as the evening wanes
And morning slips across my sky
I apologize in words
For things which never should have required apologies
And hope desperately
That you can sense
Something of what I felt
And its sacred importance to me
And I pray
That you will not laugh
At the tears in my heart
And my strained, choked attempts at speech
And the hungry burning look in my eyes
And the boyish naivete'
Of the reticent suitor
Searching for love
In the passing wind
Walk free and silent in the hills
And when you venture down to the sea
Touch the waves gently
For they have come a long way to see you

Sam Canty
MAMA
Many days mama has cried and I know the reason why.
father tells so many lies.
He always argues, and likes to fight,
come in drunk after staying out all night.
Mama is really sad for he treats us bad,
she said if he leaves she will be glad.

Mama can't take no more for
we are getting worse than
poor.
Father walking very fast because
he done blew the cash, and he
knows his family can't last.
But mama is strong and we shall
survive,
even without father by our side.
He has left after he done his
mess,
and mama will try to raise us
for the best,
even if it takes her last breath.
I asked mama why she didn't cry
when father said goodbye.
She said he has hurt her heart
almost beyond repair,
so no longer for him will she
care.
For he left behind a family
that was his own,
and if he tries to return he will
be a stranger in our home.
Mama has taken on a new mate,
who will pick up on the weight,
that father didn't take.
But did make!!

Gerard F. Keogh Jr.

SUNSET FOR THE FIELD HAND

The kernel has lightened to a
tawny gold
for harvest
and so the scythe swings
cool precision taking wings
crashing down behind the
mountains,
Scattering wisps of scarlet chaff,
Seeding the darkening topsoil
while uneven hands tic'n' toil
awaiting for the crop renewed
tomorrow.

Karen Elliott

LONESOME TOWN

In a silent setting the sun is
going down
Sinking now in twilight behind
my little town.
Soon the stars will shine high
in the sky above
It brings back memories of ones
I'll always love.
Yet lonesome I'll be when dawn
comes anew
Since happy days are o'er what
shall I find to do?
For months I'll have to wait for
pleasure I pursue
But at this rate I sure am feeling
blue.
Won't you come tonight when
I'm here alone
Won't you bring me love, and
love alone.

Ida B. Crozier

LADIES OF THE EIGHTIES

The ladies of the eighties
Have reversed the "status quo"
Instead of riding in the boat
They feel they have to row.
The masses of the lassies
Are so eager to excel
That they prefer to be the
clapper
Rather than the "belle."
It used to be the rooster
Who was crowin' and a 'kickin'
But when he bows to "Henship",
then
He's just another chicken.
The pearls we girls have
gathered
Being feminine and nice
Should not be lightly tossed
away
They're pearls, my dears, not
dice.
The ladies of the eighties
I'm afraid will soon discover
It's better to be wined and dined
Than have to pay the cover.
Retain a little mystery
And don't remove the veil
Or else you might find out
you've got
A tiger by the tail.
So try to hold your horses
Use the brakes and use your
brain
Go back to being humble and
You'll rule the world again!

Elinor Webster Steere

EPITAPH TO A HOUSEWIFE

She got her kicks
From little things,
Her dogs, her booze
Her sewing machine.
She walked a dark alley
An alley called life,
Not good for much
More maid than wife.
She's in heaven now
Doing her thing,
Polishing harps and
Dusting angel wings.

Ronnie M. Vinson

JESUS

Forever Be
My Guiding Light
Shine For Me
By Day
By Night
For If
Your Glow
Should Cease To Be
Only You
Would Know
What's Ahead
For Me
Shine For Me
In A Way
So True
Light My Path
A Trail
So New
For If Ever I
Should Lose
that Ray
Want I Not
Another Day

Larronce Yvette Smith

CHANGES

As I look outside
the changes I see.
The differences in the
landscapes,
the differences of the trees.
As I look inside
there are many changes, too.
Changes of happiness,
changes to make one blue.
Different changes I see
each and every day.
Some hardly noticed,
some never the same way.
Some changes that
are never noticed by me.
So many changes that
once will ever be.
Memories of the past
important used to seem.
Some of them now are
like a far-away dream.
Changes in people,
such as a twinkle of the eye.
Some sad changes too
cause a long hard cry.
Changes in heart and soul
only once seem to appear.
Changes in love
that make life so dear.
Changes in everything once
here,
but now forever gone.
All these changes make
life easier to carry on.

Johnny King

BLUE ROSE

There was a flower that I
watched grow.
I protected it from weather,
both rain and snow.
The wind did howl, the stem
tried to break,
But I secured it fast to a
wooden stake.
In the Spring its leaves turned
to green,
It didn't resemble other
flowers I'd seen.
From tender foliage grew wicked
thorns,
To touch was to bleed unless
gloves were worn.
When the buds burst open, my
heart how it flew!
For instead of red roses—they
were blue.
You are the rose with petals of
blue,
You may not know—but I
love you.

Michael Lewis

POLLUTION

It's destroying our children
And all our animal friends.
We all know how the story
ends,
We must find a solution
To this thing called pollution.
We pollute our streams,
And we block the suns beams.
Yes, we must find a solution,
To this thing called pollution.

Bob Kubitz

POEM FOR AN OLD FRIEND

Tonite I'm gonna be
with a very good friend,
for me and Camp Winnebago
are together once again.
The times have changed
us both here and there,
but we still have
many memories to share.
Now as I watch your sunset
and feel the heavy dew,
the valley seems to tell me
that it has missed me too.
As the cool air surrounds me
in the clear and starry night,
the campfire is glowing
with a red and eerie light.
I slowly fall asleep
to the rhythm of the stream,
while a lonely whippoorwill
sings through my dreams.
Camp Winnebago in my
heart
there's a place just for you,
your people, hills, and seasons
I'll remember my life through.

Alice Odabashian

SMILES

There are smiles and - there are
smiles too!
Some are sincere, some not that
much.
Not all of them share love,
fondness,
Not all of them come from real
friends.
Whoever can't distinguish these
Variations of different smiles,
And has a candid, naive heart,
Can be mislead, deceived
sometimes.
Smiles are usually polite, glossy,
Others - tools of diplomacy;
Always look honest and fancy,
But not rarely - hide jealousy.
You could find false, enticing
ones;
They come as jokes, then they
disarm.
They can defraud, even betray,
Instead of joy, they can bring
harm.
But O, thank God, for all true
smiles,
Cordial, genuine, unvarnished
ones,
Which spring up from sweet,
lovely hearts,
For their worth is always
priceless.
They can heal your body and
soul;
They can make you as if new
born!
It's good to learn and clarify,
What is hidden behind each
smile!

David B. Robinson

ERRANT HUMMINGBIRD

Have I seen you before?
Was it on a sailing vessel
Or in a distant bower,
Sitting near a shiny bore,
When waves began to swell,
Or flitting near a flower?
Have you eluded me all this
time,
Flying 'bout? In stealth you
excel,
Darting in and out in a blur,
In a tiny pantomime
Like a demoiselle.

Barbara-Ann Klie

SCENTED

you've left
me with your
sweet, subtle fragrance
covering me from belly to
thighs.
i resist washing
you off—as it will be twice
as long as i have known you
before i will wear your
scent again.

W. Wayne Ferguson
THE CLOCK
It sits all day, and stares
and stares,
But never sees a thing.
And useless as it seems to be,
We treat it like a king.
For probing arms that slowly
move,
And rub its dozen eyes,
Tell us a story valued,
By even the most wise.
Finis.

Richard O'Connor
AUTUMN FLAVOURS
A taste, which I smell
Sour, yet almost bittersweet
I feel it rough and soft
Stuck in between the teeth
Of a memory recurring, again and
again
I choked on as a child, I remember
when like the rotting leaves
carpet moist soil the smell so
rank of life gone spoiled
Was Autumn's cologne, a food for
worms
Decaying histories, mistakes
relearned
A taste from before, I'll savour
again
As barefoot I trod through the
graveyard of sin

Catherine Janssen
THE SUNDAY MORNING SCENE
I sit in mild amazement
At the faces in the flock,
Gathered on Sunday morning
Like ships that rest at dock.
Some tell of trying journeys
Through deep and troubled
seas,
Others, reflect contentment
Of sailing with the breeze.
Through life's uncertain voyage
They chart a steady course,
Finding strength and courage
Directly from The Source.
May we all who gather here
Our conscience to explore,
Travel the smoothest channels
Up to that Heavenly shore.

Dwight A. Lehman
THE DOUBTER
"Say, Thomas, have you heard
today,
The Lord himself, He came this
way?"
"You cannot really be telling
the truth
Until I have some more certain,
real proof."
"I certainly wouldn't lie about
Him,
He showed us Himself that
night within."
"You seem to know that it was
He,
But who is sure, it could not be."
"He promised He would rise
again.
Why so much doubt about Him
then?"
"We'll see," said Thomas with a
wink,
"I just want proof, that's all I
think."
A few days later, in the same
room
The followers met without
much gloom.
The Lord appeared again in their
midst
And asked poor Thomas to
look, He insist.
Looking at the hands, the side
and the feet,
He fell down at once and their
eyes did meet.
Thomas cried out in true
identity,
"MY LORD AND MY GOD",
how the doubts did flee.

Peter Otero
THE GARDENER
I found a flower for myself
in the strangest of places.
It was in the midst of a vast
wasteland
This beautiful flower that is
just now
opening up to itself,
desires to grow,
And grow it must for the roots
are stifling it.
It needs more room,
new soil,
and more care.
Me?
I'm the gardener.
I tend to the plants and other
foliage, and know how
delicate my flower is.
It needs my care.
Just as I need it's beauty

Leslie Asbun
LEGACY
Limbs laced
Laying languished
The patter of your heart
pat-patting a beat
Syncopating, the
pat-pat of mine.
Slick warm salty speeches
I said to you without words
Puddled in the arc of valleys
and mounds we share.
You stand to go
and leave me—
feeling florescent.

Michael A. Castle
DRAGONS
Flight of Dragons
Gold, jade, onyx
Streaking silently through the
night
Wings spread wide
Jets of liquid fire
Rending the emerald fabric of
midnight skies
Scales glowing in the night
Like sun-caught gems of
Diamond clarity
Eyes aflame
infinite fury
Infinite wisdom
Both caught, intertwined
Separate but inseparable
Shimmering wings catch the air
Glowing rainbow colors
Mix, and pull apart again
Always combining
Forever separating
Single mountain far away
Purple caught in golden sunrise
Atop it perches a lone Jade
Dragon
Mournfully heralding the end of
night.

Kathryn V. Daley
SERENITY
When day is here and all is well.
Take the time to hear, see and
tell.
Let them know where the
beauty lies.
In the peace and tranquility
of a single sunrise.
Take them into forest's green.
Show them life they've never
seen.
The trees, plants and flowers all.
Put forth their best when you
come to call.
Walk on the sand and touch the
tide,
Listen with joy to the sounds
inside.
Climb up to the highest
mountain ledge.
Feel and touch the wind's
piercing edge.
Look up and see the blue of the
sky.
Watch the clouds as they roll
by.
Take all the beautiful things in
life.
And from them draw music as
you would a fife.

Margaret McKirdy Sherman
VERMONT BALLET
Soared,
pirouetted,
paused,
advanced.
With dainty steps
the ladies
danced,
—these ballerinas
of the snows.
How beautiful
the dancing does!

Rebecca A. Davis
AWARENESS
Dew drops on rose petals,
Children gaily laughing,
Rain drops on the window
An arc in the heaven.
Majestic blue mountains
Autumn leaves turned brown,
A touch of abundant life,
The touch of your hand.

Ginger R. Lemasters
THE DEVOTION
I put my trust in thee my God.
For thee my gallant warrior
serves.
I stand beside him all the days.
He, with ready sword and
willing heart,
Waiting till he hears thy call.
A listening ear he hearkens
ever,
To thy voice that calls him,
To a battle of certain victory.
I dare not gainsay his courage,
For it comes from thee, oh God.
Ne'er a time hath he forsook an
oath,
To thee, or thine, or me.
For his sword is whole,
His heart is pure, and his deeds
are good.
And upon a gleaming sword an
oath.
A kiss upon my palm.
Those clear blue eyes so deep
and calm.
The pound of silver-shod
hooves,
and my love, my sire, is gone.
The fire that lights his soul,
Burns bright within my heart.
For linked am I eternally,
to the passions of his God and
mine.
So fight he will, and still,
I will be there fighting too.
The victory is thine; and ours,
Is humbly beset upon the throne
of glory.
Where there awaits for my
faithful Knight,
A sword of purest gold.

Kathi Taylor
BROKEN FANTASIES
Most fantasies
are in your mind
never achievable
only dreamable
in the private world
where you live alone
but what an eerie feeling
when your fantasy
becomes reality
and you can see it
even touch it
but never
totally
enjoy it
How do you deal with that
when it leaves you
confused
frustrated
cursing the world
because life
is so unfair
and there's
nothing
that can
put your mind
at ease
so you live
on hopes and wishes
forever caught in the web
of your own
existence
waiting for the chance
that you know
will never
come along. . .

Rick Jones
AND LOVE IS LIKE A FALLEN TEAR
Whenever you come into mind,
I think with gentle eyes
Of ferris wheels and carousels,
And white marshmallow skies.
And with a winsome, wondrous
warmth,
A smile steals round my lips,
And stills my mind like velvet
seas
Still sleek celestial ships.
Don't wonder why, with deep
concern,
Time sent you here to me,
For in the very questioning
Refute our right to be.
I bask within the loveliness

My eyes are wont to see,
For in the false security of love
I must be free.
And love is like a fallen tear,
Not lightly shed you know,
But drawn from dark cerebral depths
Where ego's gardens grow.
And only fools reject the pain
That lurks unbridled there,
For few escape its heavy hand
Or miss its icy stare.
Life reaches out with tender hand
To hearts that enter in
Beyond the garden's awesome gates,
To tempt the fates to win.
But riches of the sweetest kind
Discover each who tries,
And only in attempt exalt—
For none the pain denies.
To come along, beyond those gates
Is all I ask of you,
To face the spectres we may find,
And reap love's riches, too.

Joan Hill Hanks

PROCRASTINATION

Procrastination is what we will do—
We wait until things are nearly due
Rushing around is a common disease
And if we started earlier—
We could do it
With such ease!
We put off today and plan to start—
Tomorrow!
And play as if we were
Scarlett O'Hara!
But some of us do better under pressure
When our adrenalin is up
If we did measure
So let's all make a solemn vow
That we'll do our tasks—
Not later
But now!

Diane Bernardy

RAYS OF LOVE

Lord so warm are the rays of love you send;
How fresh and clean when sent a breeze within.
Reaches all so deeply within my soul,
Gives me the strength today and makes me whole.
Your love so tender and soft when we touch
Shows us, oh, Lord, how you love us so much.
Guiding and keeping and showing the way;
Upholding us safely in your love rays.

Dorothy Brin Crocker

THE MIRACLE

Time moves inexorably on
eluding the grasp of beggar or king
inexplicably the miracle of time
is part of the glory
God will bring
Time is projected thought an entity
that constantly restlessly
seeks the Source
that created its beginning
and chooses its end
God Omnipotent
is a powerful force
To those who die does time cease to be
while they live in a womb of a realm softly dim
awaiting their birth in a new dimension
when resurrected and glorified by Him?
Is death a journey outside of time
where "souls in sleep" new vistas can see
as they wait until the Judgement Day
when they are awakened and
restored to be?

J. La. Roberts

WAIMEA: RAINY SEASON HAWAII

Uptown the cars encumbered
square with runneled rain
their windows dimmed
with crystalline veiling.
Dare there be newborn hale
in this damp clime?

Truly do newborn
claim the right to live and do well
here in months of rain?
And does one live
and does one make out to live
to be a little older?
Sometimes its alright
all right!

Carol Person Keen

A CONSIDERATION

Consider the vine that grows with time...
Climbing higher and higher,
Not seeming to tire;
Consider the vine...
Giving forth as it twines,
Nature's fruitful gifts so fine;
Consider the vine that whispers,
"Aspire,
Knowing an anxious bud desires
Expression of its own.
"Pour forth what is thine,
precious bud,"
Cries the vine.
"For your gentle bloom,
On earth there's spacious room."
Nature seeks sincere expression
Flowering in love and simple discretion.
Please bloom, dear bud,
And give to life,
What God has given thee.

Edna P. Watson

UNTITLED

Always deeper, further outward flung
The probing arrows stand, finally, in spent, quivering suspension
As questions are swallowed in vast
Answers
And knowledge defeats its' purpose.
Ten fingers and ten toes...
We count sextillions beyond our needs or comprehension
And divide one body into innumerable atoms.
Must not life, ultimately reduced, be this small space of time
This fractional Between one clock tock and the next
This bitter taste of too much coffee
And one too many cigarettes?

Margaret L. Cronan

FALLING STAR

Silently, swiftly from afar,
Rend the night, bright scimitar!
Sweeping 'cross heaven's awesome stage,
Catching breath, stilling voice, fixing gaze,
You dare to bolt the Grande Parade
To stir a constant firmament in solo promenade
Until your lovely flame is spent
And heaven's hosts, their stately cadence kept,
Smile an eloquent acknowledgement.

Kenneth T. Thomson

HILLARY LEFT, BLOWN BY A BREEZE

In those flawless eyes,
like a hawk's,
blinked not the hint of a concern;
just the clear
reflected image
of the world
as it would be.
Maybe not too far,
but at least I could look within them,
sharpen
my sights
for that vision
which your face,
your voice,
your dancing limbs foretold.
That one
not caught yet
by prison pulp
or chalice gold:
light as a breeze
and brazen
as the glint of a star at sunset.
Head down,
collar up
I trudged forward,
eager to alight somewhere within
the hush of existant time,
where the breeze is blown by passers-by,
the glint's in pocket
not in the eye,
then, turned to see you fly away
on an element of wonder.

Timothy J. Matter

LIVING MEMORIES

The week's about over,
The bell will soon ring,
We're all thinking about
What the weekend will bring.
They'll be time to go drinking
"Boy," we'll really have fun.
We'll have time with our families
There's a lot to be done.
We woke up the next morning
Are we already to go?
I'm so sorry to say
The answer is no.
What did you say!
How could this be!
There's so much of this life
Don never did see.
We search for a reason
As each moment goes by.
Why did this happen!
Will we ever know why.
We can't let all the memories
Of his life slip away.
Let us let him live in our minds
In each passing day.

Delores M. McCabe

WINTER

The land is barren, old.
The skies promise winter's cold.
Yesterday's warm sunshine is just a memory.
Trees' naked branches sway crazily.
The air has a new, crisp smell,
And the wind chases the snow pell-mell.
I dream of spring, an eternity away.
Children are clothed against the bleak day.
Winter's stillness is a picture in white;
Hills and valleys present an awesome sight.
Animals have hidden in their shelters to sleep,
Knowing—old man winter—his vigil, will keep.

Betty L. Stebbins

SPECIAL K

Special K is good for me,
Brings me up when I am down,
Makes me laugh instead of cry,
Makes me smile instead of frown.
Special K. is good for me.
Taught me how to dance and sing,
How not to worry or to fret,
Take all the joys that life can bring.
Special K. is good for me,
I am short and he is tall,
I am white and he is black,
He loves spring and I love fall.
Special K. is good for me,
Every day, yes all the year,
We'll serve Jah., yes faithfully,
And the world we'll never fear?

JoNelle Boettcher
GREED'S KILLING
Free me from this prison
For, although it has no bars
It is always being filled
With deep emotional scars
The burning embers
With which you scorch my
heart
Are preventing our love from
flourishing
And driving us apart
The tears I've cried could fill
a river
And recalling your rages makes
me quiver
I wonder what your reaction
would be
Were I to leave, and set you free
Would you whimper and pine,
like an abandoned child
Or attack as a bear out in the
wild
Either way, you make it hard
For me, our marriage, to discard
For you, my dear, I feel a great
sorrow
Your needs you always seem to
borrow
Being indifferent to all others
feelings
Always planning more
scrupulous dealings
Take and take more, but never
give
Greed is the lifestyle you must
live
For you're afraid to be even the
slightest bit frail
Your ego is totally crushed
anytime you should fail
And even though I love you still
Your lack of compassion will
surely kill
Any future we could have had
Unfortunate, but true, and it's
really too bad.

Elaine Wolfe Smith
CRIPPLED
I met a man in a wheelchair
Who polished bumpers in L.A.

We got to know each other well
We talked most every day
No job was too degrading
No road too long or rough
One side of him was paralized
The other side was tough
I'll never forget that wonderful
man
For the lessons he taught were free
I learned although he couldn't
walk
the "crippled" one was me

Lona M. Krueger
I AM YOUR WOMAN AND YOU'RE MY MAN
Touch my face in the morning
To start my new day
Kiss me ever so softly
To wipe my sleep away
Lay closer to me
Just ten minutes more
Then smile that special smile
As you walk out the door
Hold on to this feeling
As long as you can
Cause I am your woman
and You're my man
Take the time to love me
And let it show
Take the time to love me
So I'll always know
That I am your woman
And you're my man

Shari Kilback
STALEMATE
Old Mr. Owl, sits in the tree.
I look at him and he looks at
me.
His eyes are huge, and shiny
bright;
Like some strange, but welcome
light.
He stares at me and I stare at
him,
Perching now, out on a limb.
Staring, staring, staring at me,
As I sit beneath the tree.
He turns his head, back and
forth.
Checking occasionally, south
and north.
All night long, this game goes
on.
But soon, night fades into dawn.
As the sun peaks o'er the
mountains crest,
He fluffs the feathers on his
breast.
Still he watches, patiently;
Perched upon that massive tree.
As I yawn and think of sleep
Nary a sound—does he peep.
But now, the sun's affecting the
sight
Of this bird that likes the night.
So—soon one of us, will have to
go.
But who it'll be, I do not know!

Delsy Oakes
BIGOTRY
Bigotry's a grotesque thing
degrading to the soul
It shrinks your heart and warps
your mind
makes hate your only goal
Oh, People open up your eyes
and see, I'm sure you'll find
We are all made from the same
mould
We're members of mankind
Let love and friendship shine
from you
Reach out a helping hand
See how your love can change
the world
Turn it on your fellow man
If we all looked beneath the
skin
And lived the way we should
Our world would soon be filled
with love
With peace and Brotherhood.

Chrislyn Judith Samuels
FRIENDS AND LOVERS
Everytime we meet passion
flares.
We make love and cherish every
moment.
There are too many moments
between us.
Lovers that we are, are seldom
found.
We have, we cherish, we love,
we end.
The moments are too many for
us to be friends.

Claudette Hamilton
FOR MOM
My mother was always the
prettiest mom.
Indian black hair
with cheekbones to match,
Big brown Greek doe eyes
and beautiful red lips
freely giving tender child-
woman smiles.
Hints of Shalimar or Tabu
linger on her handsome dress
and mask the fragility and
fright
hidden beneath pillars of
strength
and wisdom of kings.
Retrospect enlivens memories
of trips to the city
and shared ice cream sodas;
of special little presents
when all was ill.
Meager times, when love
and homemade talent
and the sheer desire to give
happiness
made holidays and special
occasions
even more so.
Faded dreams and stifled sadness
made way for children's tears
and anger;
for there was no time for both
and her family was priority.
Tenets of loyality, dignity, and
love
were taught through words
and gentle touch.
Discipline was often subtle
appealing to our
consciousness.
Sometimes too cautious, afraid of
death
she colored the wisps of grey;
yielding to the sure and
obvious
wittingly hoping to slow the
seasons.
Time unrelenting, she
unremitting
we gather to welcome a new
year.
Though words and gifts can not
repay,
my gift is this poem, my
words
"I Love You MOM"

Byron John Fitzgerald
INSIDE. . .
Nothing is. . .as it seems
be it's appearance good. . .be it
bad.
Venture forth. . .
inside your dreams
there are no ready-made ones
to be had.
Life succumbs not
to our profane schemes
. . .unwilling to appreciate
that
which we already
have. . .
. . .as snow hides
inside. . .evergreen
. . .there are smiles
inside . .you're sad!
Just remember. . .the lessons
inside. . .what you've seen. .
and the best inside. . .
what is said. . .
Love is. . .in the end
all you'll need. . .
. . .as found inside your
heart. . .
not your head. . .

Roy P. Habersetzer
SNOW
Oh, how the snow outside
brings a special joy to a
child—
The building of snowmen,
snowball fights, and sledding;
often drive one wild—
Inside the glow of a warm fire
burns—
Outside the child plays in the
snow as it learns—
A child asks; how is a snowflake
made?—
The only thing we can tell
them, is from the Lord
above—
For he is the master of the
entire universe, and he makes
snowflakes for each of us to
enjoy; out of his love.—

Allen O'Donnell
NEW YORK
Hey! C'mon with me!
To New York.
New York New York
The wonderful town
Where the Battery's up
And the Bronx is down!
Hey! C'mon with me!
To see the Village.
The artists and the players
And the rest at cribbage.
Hey! C'mon with me!
To Riverside Drive
And hope the potholes
Leave you alive.
Hey! C'mon with me!
To New York
New York New York
The wonderful town
The bridge is up
And the Bronx is
down
down
down
And out.
The Yankees are there.
Still.
So is Macy's.
Sometimes, even Broadway.
Hey? Won't you come with me?
Please?
No matter.
We'll visit the pride
of the Big Apple.
The Empire State Building.
Why?
Hey. It's New York.
Don't you remember?

Toni Turnipseed Thiel
GRANDAD
I as a child
growing up wild
with you in my life
I knew not your strife
As tall as a tree
and stronger than me
you gave me your time
when in your prime
Always the same
winning the game

Yet slowly you aged
gave up your rage
opened my eyes
between truth and lies
Showed me your weakness
left me just speechless
reached for my hand
and I knew the man
No longer a tree
But just like me......

Grandma Lillian Casey
GRANDMOTHER'S JOY
A Grandmother gets a world of joy
From just one small little boy.
When he comes running in the door
and says, Grandma just one more,
A cookie for a little one,
Will brighten him like the morning sun,
His smile is sweet and all aglow,
Like another of long ago.
Her memory goes to another day
When he was coming in to say,
Hi Mommy, may I have a cookie dear?
I'm awful hungry, did you hear?
And she can now sit down and dream
of days that were, and days that mean
A world of joy to her once more,
for she has another little boy out door.

Kimberly Prisco
HALLOWEEN
Halloween is a spooky night,
when all little children scream from fright.
Witches on broomsticks,
hissing with joy,
acting so childish,
what fools they must be,
for the fear that they've caused us
most must not see.
Trick-or-treating is fun while we're eating,
but skeletons dancing,
and black cats prancing,
are really something to see.

Rachel Wion
MY DAUGHTER
She is the mirror
With the broken edge
In which I see myself
Small and afraid,
As she, and I do not like
The me I spy within.

Susan Daniels
ALONE AGAIN
I kept my dreams
and just pretended,
but even still we have ended.
A heart must be broken everytime—
why is it usually mine?
I don't know if I can stand the pain,
it hurts so bad time and time again.
In time I shall forget him—
but now that chance seems very slim.
Today I am filled
with so much sorrow—
hopefully it will vanish
with each passing tomorrow.

Barbara S. Brown
ONE EARLY WINTER MORN
As the snow came down
It was all so pretty
Falling so lightly
Caressing the earth
As if to be a white blanket
Keeping it warm,
It's crystal like flakes
Glistened like diamonds.
As the sun shined upon them.
The pine trees stood tall
And their branches looked
As if they held a sprinkle of Sugar,
Like a painted picture
Every detail so perfect,
Holiday cheer was upon us
And this beautiful sight
Put such warmth in my heart.

Holly Alexander
JEALOUSY
Jealousy
like fire
starts as a spark
but soon
ignites into flame
Destroying
all in it's path
Leaving only
the scorched pieces
of it's victim
rendered helpless
with nothing left
to remember
what was once there.

Jody Hubbard
MY GRANDMA, MY MOTHER, MY FRIEND
See that star shining
way up there
It's as silvery as the silver
in her hair
God took her to live in His
beautiful place.
How wonderful for her to finally
see his Face.
We've had her so long,
how lucky we are
She's left her mark everywhere,
near and far.
Oh, how we'll miss you, our
dear sweet love.
But we know you're with God
and your loved ones
In that land up above.
My love always,
Joan

Alice Faith Jackson
CONSTRUCTION SIGHT
Shifting shadows
diagonally cast
dark designs,
geometric shapes.
Pyramids of gravel
nudge tons
of textured brick.
In the sun,
golden lumber
mellows patiently.
Scaffolding exposes
skeletal frames
silhouetted
against the sky;
a network
of unfinished intrigue
indicating shapes
and strength
to come.
A mechanical crane
rises regally aloft,
gigantic orange windmill,
not turning ...
huge arms extended,
prayerlike ...
waiting to complete
unfulfilled promise.

James G. Futo
SPOKEN
The unheard laugh,
The unseen smile,
The touch not felt,
The unshed tear,
The word not spoken.
Crying, yearning,
Remembering;
The laughter, his laughter,
His smile,
His gentle hand,
His suffering, his agony.
The word, HIS word...
Spoken!

Patricia L. Devenberg
HIP-BABY
His ebony face shown with wonder
as his big brown eyes lapped up
the marvelous wonders of the market place
Tied on his mother's hip
slurping his thumb
one slender hand holding tight
A thousand expressions
rapidly chased
through the round of his face
No sound but the slurp
on a tight held thumb
Ripe fruit and fresh vegetables
dropped one by one into a cloth bag
The fruit smell made the small child suck harder
His eyes traveling continuously
watching the colorfully dressed women
pinching and picking
the choicest fruits and vegetables
The bag could hold no more
yet one more fruit
was pinched by his mother's slender
strong fingers
Held out before his face
the fruit teased and tempted
a tiny thumb
out of a smiling mouth

Rodolfo Fernandez
PROCLAMATION OF WINTER
Like a giant tattoo
in the sky,
a dark,
lonely cloud
moves slowly
across
the endless space
...and the butterflies,
drifting pieces
of unborn rainbows,
begin
their last journey
into the soft,
grassy fields
before the frost
of the upcoming morning
crucifies forever
their fainting,
trembling bodies.
A proclamation of winter
has been issued.

Erma Rigney Crouch
SANDS OF TIME
In Tennessee I've always lived
I guess I always will
But often I have strayed to
places far away.
For history makes its mark
upon the sands of time.
How thankful I am that some have
taken the time to write it down
For often in my easy chair or in
the shade of my favorite tree
The pages of my history book have
told these things to me.
Of how the people in early days
have paved the way for me.
Of the many tasks they under took
to make a better place to live.
The many hardships they suffered
with great strength and courage;
Never fainting by the way but
pressing slowly on, until a goal
they had reached but still kept going
on.
Until it was history no more
for we were making our own
That we too must leave
upon the SANDS OF TIME.

Michelle E. Grab
MEMORIES
Gentle rain,
Quiets the sound of angry memories,
As it falls from my eyes.

Sandy Summers
COSMOS
up high (so very high indeed)
stars hang like mobiles
and
dreams look for places to land.
and in the deepest hour
of dark (for dark is eternal there)
our hearts touch with a cosmic fury.
then you say (all starryeyed and oh! so soft)
'come with me baby,
and we'll run rings around the universe.'

Mike Upfield
OVER THE YEARS
Born, again and again and again.
The moon
the stars,
and the mind.
Do we dare to forget
the trips when we went,
to touch on our essence and die.

Thelma Mary Kelly
MY JEWELS
Bedecked with furs
Adorned with jewels
Not I
Like sapphires bright
Reflected in my children's eyes
Ruby lips that kiss me tenderly
These are my treasures, far from gold
But mine forever to have and to hold

Linda Grace Marion
DECEMBER FIRST
Death has come and gone
And left me empty handed,
Without the smell of death
Or the rose of summer.
I stay in that strange country
Between the night and day,
Like shadows in a mirror
When the shadow fades.
And I pray
And stare at clocks
And know not time,
And wet tears
Racing down my cheeks,
And bright red blood
Dripping down
On clean white sheets.
And I try to remember
If I was shot,
Or any events of the day,
And I go blank,
Everything is dark,
Since the shades been down
I can't prove
If it's night or day.
I've been marking my diary
And it's been twelve days,
And now they tell me to go away.
And I can't even reach
The window shade,
And they tell me to go away.
And I bleed, like tomorrow
Will never come,
I bleed like tomorrow
Is a dream far away,
As I ride on silent sirens
Floating through distant space.
And leave that strange country
Before sleep has given way,
And cross all the borders
In every state,
And try after many miles
To find a way,
And try after many miles
Lose my way.

Martha Therese Merten
ALONE ON THE EDGE
She dances on the edge of dawn
With one toe off and one toe on.
Majestic trees bear witness of her story
But the darkness about is hiding the Glory.
Blinded, she dances in circles, unaware
Of the Light in the clearing just ahead of her there.
With her mind on the dance she feels no sensation
But wrapped about her heart is a dark desperation.
No control of her life in a pattern she dances
Time passes her by with no second chances.
She leans one way or totters to one side
Like a sea plant she is moved by the tide.
She lacks true strength needed to break.
She rejects the Source. She will not take.
Opportunity of life by Grace was laid in her sight,
But she danced in her circle,
And alone she will fight.

Tina Richardson
GENTLE GIANTS
They rule the sea with a quiet grace
Their enormous bulk cuts through the water
Floating silently, a strange beauty upon their face
Never once does their rythmic dance falter
So they glide on, asking for nil
Singing a song of truth and wisdom
Needing only a bountiful harvest of krill
Hoping deaf ears will listen
But their gentle eyes betray their size
Now the cruel harpoon finds its mark
As man, their only enemy, let it fly
To a place that is warm, soft and dark
Their love and loyalty for one another
has no bounds, they perish one by one
Silencing the gentle giants sounds
Until there are none

Ernie Leduc
THE FIRE PARADE
Billow blow the searing wind
Racing thru the fields again
Smoking choking flames set free
The fear, excitement, cruelty
Hot winds blow the stinging sand
Drying out this virgin land
Prepares the path, the fire parade
Beware the wrath that nature made
Desolation, what a scene
Gazing on the smokey dream
As nature works its evil spells
Leaves lonely burned out carbon shells
The raindrops fall again this spring
The seeds of life make hillsides green
The grasses growing ever higher
Waiting for this summers fire

Ruth M. Carpenter
REFLECTIONS OF A BLIND WIDOWER
My life is a maze of unfinished images.
I wander through the shadows
With outstretched arms,
Eager to mold, shape, paint—
My palette runs dry,
I stumble on—
I discover the lush gardens of love
And linger there
Until death invades my vineyard.
I drag my shadow back
To that tangled world,
Lonely—
I speak to
Any listening ear—
I speak of darkness,
I speak of illusions,
I speak of love,
I cannot speak of death.

Edith Story
CLOWNS OF PLAINS
Fresh green grass, streams of water
depleted
They march in thousands
across plains,
leaping bounding endlessly
Weak and young die
Spots rest in trees,
waiting for tender prey
The strong surviving the surging streams
and dust, circle their way
back home

Brenda A. Bischoff
THE SHORES OF LONELINESS
I break on the shores of loneliness
Without even a rock to dash against.
The lonely shores of nothingness,
Stretching away into infinity.
I wish there were rocks to dash against
To shout at and roar angry away.
But there is only the sand swept plain
And the empty loneliness of me.

Dorothy Pinkerton
UNCOMMON MAN
Companionship is much desired
As we walk life's busy street.
Companions we find among common men

In the everyday crowd we meet.
But when problems overtake us
We walk a quiet street-
When leadership is much desired,
It's the uncommon man we seek.

Mara Dukats
MOODS OF ECHO
If echoes dance,
the points of their satin ballet slippers dwindle to pinheads,
turns lose vigor,
as roulette spins before an audience of numbers.
If echoes sing,
operas are hushed conversations.
If echoes speak,
they never utter anything yet unsaid.
if echoes pray,
they kneel before heaven on cushioned, cloudy altars.
If echoes sleep,
they snore in constant rhythm,
yet it never awakens you.
If echoes walk,
they tip-toe.
If echoes collide,
there is nothing more beautiful than the unison
as bolts of lightening strike the sun,
releasing golden, whispering ripples.
If echoes blossom,
petals unfold as do sheets of ashes from bonfires,
burning the air with a sweet scent.
If echoes are frightened,
they all dart to the same refuge.
If echoes rest,
we are jammed in a cell where motionless silence rules.
When we become echoes,
the intensity of life falls through an echo of shades
from brilliant to dull.

Sharon L. Malone
DESTINATION PLEASE?
The plane is ourselves
The pilot is our will
The navigator, our conscience
The passengers, those we influence in our lives.
The instruments, our gifts we must learn to use to pilot the plane properly.
The stewardesses are the Angels and Saints helping us.
The food served is the sacraments of the Church.
The elements are the evil spirits trying to change our course.
Destination
Heaven's Port or Hell's Port?

Marjorie Ann Sciacca
MENDOCINO
Farewell,
wild seashore, with your
crashing aqua hue,
I have loved your wild seclusion
and I must return to you.
To have my curls straightened
by your wet, misted hand,
and leave my barefoot kisses
in your tide-dampened sand.
To watch as the dolphin rides
your green, curled crest,
and feel again, the calm that
hides within my breast.
I'll breathe the fragrance sweet,
of your flowers at my feet,
and sigh,
at the splendor of your
decorated sky.
And along your rippled dunes,
on idle afternoons,
your jewels, I will collect.
Exquisite miniatures of
architect,
evicted by the tide,
to adorn your waterside.

Sherry Richert
UNTITLED

And
you made that night
a dream...
a poem given breath.
It is you who
made beauty tangible
and love into something
I long to posses.
You make snowfall
into kisses from Heaven
and the stars
into heavenly eyes.
You make me
into a being-
a bundle of feeling
and emotion.
Your creation has dared
to make that
of the mountains
a joke.
You are a song...
sung only
by the gentle wind.

Sallie Marie
THE SILENCE

Make channels for the streams
of Love where living waters
flow, where Joy dances
across It's surface upon
Butterfly-wing and frolics
thru the meadow of Mind,
Where Blossoms' perfumed
petals scattered on the wind
become as sweet balm,
Enlightened Spirit.
Now pause...to listen and
watch as
Rocks along the stream bed of
Life sing praises and catch
rainbows in the Sunbeam
Song of Soul.
This becomes a place for rest...
while thought flows free...
swims up stream...floats
down...
dives deeply at times in to
peaceful pools surfacing again
into Spirit's windswept
plains of Pure Purpose...pure
delight...gentle giving...
living...
I am happy
I am blessed

Dennis E. Harnett
BASK IN THE WARMTH OF THE SON

In the theatre of memory I
see my child, aged two;
Fitting to his face a Halloween
mask of grim piratical visage.
And as he, with his face
obscured by that ferocious
grin,
Regarded me through the mask's
eyeholes,
At the same time, I looked in.
Mild eyed child, brown
windowed innocence,
The obvious pleasure you felt
then, also shone on me,
And I felt that I could not love
you enough,
To earn that joy you shared.

Ralph George Groves,
Oxford, England
THE CIRCLE CLOSED

I often recollect New Hampshire
days, the dusk of which brought
me to forked roads whereat I
pondered: journey Eastward now
or remain a Western son of
Durham?
I sojourned on the Eastern path,
which led this soul from
Durham's pines and hillocks
green. The deserts which
unfolded soon before did beckon
to reveal their mysteries.
In nighttime meditations I did
dwell in crisp holt woods, 'neath
tow'ring pines. But when the
sun would fall upon my eyes, I
would then wake at steppes of
Alborz Mountains still.
The years have passed. Indeed,
the years have passed. Today
New England's autumn
welcomes me. My fickle past all
did forgive, and now I tread on
ashen leaves with humble care.

Victoria Parker
MICHIGAN'S MAY DAY

As virgin brides who wait their
grooms, buxom bushes stand,
Bowing and blushing prettily in
an awakening land.
Sweet forsythia came early,
spreads gold robe upon the
ground;
In chartreuse, her sister poses -
wraps hers close around.
Apple-green ferns stand tall,
their fronds yet furled;
Close-mouthed red tulip stands
beside white brother;
A cautious crow caws coarsely
overhead;
Bold bright-blue jay, a-wing,
chases another;
Pure star of Bethlehem looks to
shining sky;
Viola dots the green with purple
eye.
Sly budding trees nurture their
infant leaves;
Prepare to drop their seed and
grow a wood.
Faithful sparrow eyes his
homestead 'neath the eaves;
April, in tears, yielded to May -
and life is good!

Rose (Ortega) Kludzinski
REFLECTIONS

A room dressed in blue and
white
His slippers next to mine
And a bed made for two,
My eyes fill with tears
As I say
To my husband of 29 and 1 days
"Good night my love."
In the morning when I awaken
I gaze across the room
Only to find myself alone.
The emptiness within me
lingers on
Although it's been only a few
hours
Since we've parted.
I walk toward the mirror
To brush my hair
And Momentarily,
I sense his presence in the room
I see his smile reflected on the
mirror,
My heart beats with
anticipation
As I turn to reach out to him
Only to find that he isn't there!
It's merely a reflection
Within my mind.
I guess, I'll just have to wait
patiently
Once more
Until tonight,
Until his return,
I will just have to say
"Good night my love."
On the telephone.

J. Anderson Matula
LAMENT FOR OLD FLORIDA

Here once the tall pine stood
and hare did jump,
Here once a rattler slithered
through a clump
Of cabbage palm.
Here once the sun beat down
on gator's back--
Here once the sea of grass
left ne'er a track
Of man.
Then came the bulldozer with
grasping claw,
The steam shovel with gaping
maw,
The measuring men with string
and stick,
The building men with plans so
slick.
The sound of hammering
rent the air--
The slush of concrete
filled the bare
Now wasteland.
There stand the houses
row on row--
Pink, yellow, green
the colors go
On and on.
No tree in sight, no bush no
grass,
Each house stands on a sandy
mass.
The owners come,
they dig and plant,
They drench and rake
and chase the ant
And civilization has
left its stamp
On the land.

C. A. Yerex
TWILIGHT THOUGHTS

A wave of silken moonlight
Glows upon my face,
As shadows of past sunsets
Rest, with golden grace.
A gentle breeze is in the air,
It whispers on and on...
My heart is filled with peace
and joy,
For I await the dawn.

Therese A. Kost (Tessi)
KING

Upon a weathered, white
lifeguard's chair
Sits a little boy
Commanding his imaginary
servants,
Waving his yardstick sceptre,
An air of authority around him,
He beckons for water,
The waves crash against the
rocks,
He dismisses the water carrier,
The tide retreats,
His sparkling eyes wander
across his domain,
Across the wide expanse of
ocean,
Across the endless stretch of
sand,
Strain to the distant mountains,
Not yet conquered,
He closes his eyes for a
moment,
Again he waves his sceptre,
This time for food,
When no food is brought,
He clambers off his throne
And runs barefoot through the
cooling sand,
To his mother,
A lonely paper crown floats
through the air,
And rests in the ocean.

Denise Bundy
UNNOTICED

Sitting by my friends,
I listen to their stories,
Laught at their jokes,
Cry at their sorrows.
Sitting by my friends,
I tell them my stories,
They do not listen.
I tell them my jokes,
They do not laugh.
I tell them my sorrows,
But they do not cry.
Sitting by my friends
I am unnoticed.

Fay Gorden
FOR MY SON AND HIS SON

You are starting a new decade
With a new baby on parade,
A family life to start
God willing, you'll not part,
As years go by
Do not despair, but only to try,
Love, respect, and cherish your
family
In life, your possessions that are
worthy,
They are yours alone
Only God, may atone.

William B. Drechsler, Jr.
STILL THE PAIN REMAINS

After all these years
It seems to me quite strange
That it's been so long since my
love has gone
And still the pain remains
It's not sympathy I'm after
I just long for love and laughter
Just some freedom from this
demon pain

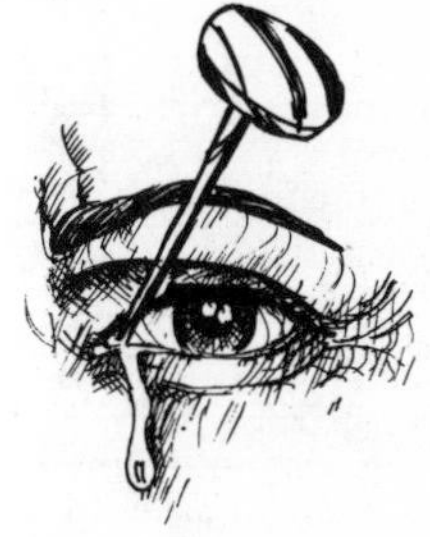

But still the pain remains
It isn't my intension
To argue with religion
But I prayed for my redemption
And still the pain remains
I'm not hell bent on disaster
It's just an answer that I'm after
Just some reason for this demon
pain
But still the pain remains
So after all these years
I can only come to one conclusion
That true love is no illusion
Because still the pain remains

Billy Carson Jamerson
YOUR LIFE
To walk among giants
To soar above eagles
To live like gods
To die as kings.
To ride the surf of life
To sail the sea of time
To run the mile of fate
To be strong as the wind.
Ride on sweet angel
Into the clouds of no return
Just grow and be as strong as I
That our strength be as one.
The everlasting sea of life
Goes on forever and ever
As never before to be found again
To disappear without any trace nor sign.
Let your love light shine
Ever so brightly into the night
That the sea of life never fails you
Your life be one of love and happiness.

Terre Cortes
THE UNICORN
This animal of such grace
And yet so powerful
With a body so tall and straight
Yet so sleek and gentle
His head held high when running
And his tail holding its own
His horn leading the way into the
World of Make-Believe
The Unicorn- the King of the
World of Fantasy

Lorraine Hicks
REVIVED
Nestled in a bed of clouds
I reclined in peace,
floating as though forever.
A voice called
for the essence of life,
"Come, sit up or you die."
I moved not---cared not.
Not knowing how,
I rise...
in the land of the living.
It was not time to die.

Bonnie J. Lini
HOPELESS BATTLE
Poor Soul, shrouded in the falseness of your sarcasm. So desperate to be released from the fear of caring, yet never relenting in your desperate struggle to hide.
Crying out for help, yet brutally slashing my hand when I try to reach you. The constant inconsistancies of your life overflowing into mine keep me struggling for air until finally it comes too fast, too sudden, too hard and it's me or you.
I hope I win.

Maryann West
AFTER THE MOURNING
I grieve for you
In frantic moments
stolen from a peaceful day
It frightens me to think
you won't be here for Christmas
You are the beauty of Christmas
I wonder, will it really come
without you
I hope you see us
can you feel my love
A love that has nowhere to go
so it's bottled up inside me and
instead of kissing you, I kiss
your picture
My mind tells me
to run and tell you something
wonderful thats' happened
but my heart knows you're not
there
How tightly I hold on to
a fragile string called sanity,
which if it broke, would be the
reality for me that you are gone
forever.
We shared so much
and I still need you
and miss you and want you
and love you, dear MOM.

Lillie Mae Hill
JESUS IS MY FRIEND
When oppressions seem to end,
And bad feelings start to mend,
When peace and joy are mine again,
Jesus is my friend.
However, when mishap prevails,
Is he still my friend?
And my heart with sorrow wails,
Is Jesus my friend?
Surely, he is yet my friend,
Whether crises rise or end;
Christ is there, his hand to lend;
He's a comfort and a friend.

Michael Mannino
THE PROMISES
Someday not so far away there's a place that's promised if only we believe.
Someday the promises of the Lord will be, then we shall know that his love was greater than our thoughts.
Someday the dark clouds will all pass away then our eyes will be open to see, for then we shall see the light and the light shall brighten our way.
Someday not so far away the promises will be ours.

Hazel T. Reaves
OUR LITTLE BOYS
God has blessed us through the years
With very few heart aches or even tears.
He gave to us two little boys
So they could play with games and toys.
The thrill of life as any one knows
Is the love of children that grows and grows.
It's the different stages they pass through
That makes you wonder what to do.
To watch the child begin to talk
Then turn loose and begin to walk
He shows you how to brush his teeth
Comb his hair and wash his feet.
God gave them such brilliant minds,
I can't recall a single time.
With hammer and screws they begin to use
Then they know just which one to choose.
Now it's nature they behold
The colors of birds, flowers of gold
The picture books they begin to read.
Any kind of pet is all they need.
There's never a day, but something new
If only a shoe is thrown in the dew.
Or a bump on the head to mother he calls
For mother can mend all those falls.
Thank you God for our little boys.
Our christian home and all our joys.
Help us live in such a way
All may know you're in our hearts to stay.

Mrs. Alma Jean French
A MERRY CHRISTMAS
What a Merry Christmas
When the snow bells ring
To see the happy faces
And hear the children sing
As eyes behold the lighted tree
With ornaments all aglow
There are others who could share this day
Don't fail to let them know
What a Merry Christmas
To know each one so dear
Will get that special something
They have wanted all the year
It's not the gift we get that day
That makes our heart so shine
It's knowing we have given one
That gives us peace of mind.

Alba Miller Wahl
FEBRUARY
February hangs in Time and Space
As the Seasons come to the parting place;
Caught in a web 'twixt Winter and Spring,
A tight-rope walker on a gossamer string,
With Fairy feet and a leaden breast
Whose dual nature never lets her rest.
A backward glance, a kiss she blows,
And stands a moment on hesitant toes
To ponder her choice; The New or The Old,
Diamonds and Ermine, or, a Throne of Gold?
Though destined in the Glass of Time to glide
With open arms to the beckoning side,
She's loathe, indeed, from Winter to part,
Yet, the roots of Spring are bursting her heart!

Peggy Cone
SOMETHING OF VALUE
When Sherman was making his march to the sea,
The pages of history were turning,
And though the confederate soldiers fought bravely,
A Georgia plantation was burning.
An old Negro woman was trembling with fear
For an infant not quite four months old
Had been placed in her care by the "master" himself,
And this is the story thats told.
While the flames were blazing, bullets were flying
And blood from both sides running red,
She hid the small child in an old laundry basket
Covered loosely with clothing, and fled.
A Union commander seated on horseback
Saw her as she hurried away,
And thinking her basket held something of value,
Called out to her, "Halt there, I say!"
Then drawing the sword from his side
He started to pierce through the laundry he saw,
And only the powers greater than we
Made him stop...and then slowly, withdraw...
He paused for a moment, she stood terrified,
And the sad face of God must have smiled
When the officer reached,...with his hand...through the laundry...
And felt the warm hand of the child.
With tears in his eyes and a look of compassion,
He briefly forgot his command,
And there in the midst of the blood and the battle,
The North and the South...
shook hands....

Heather Churchill
I WISH
Sometimes I wish I were a bird; then I would fly to the very peak of the highest mountain top, to escape all of life's troubles.
But I am no bird, I have no wings to escape.
And sometimes I wish I were a perfect rose; then I would be blind to all things:
the confusion, hate, and misery that it holds.
But I am not a rose either;
I have no petals that I can turn away from it all.
But most of all I wish that I shall always have the strength and willpower to be myself;
to accept myself and others as they are and to judge no one for something that they are not.
For if I always have and respect these freedoms,
I will never need wings to escape or rose petals to turn and hide.

Barry Whitlock
SOMEWHERE
Somewhere hearts are happy
And somewhere things are bright
Somewhere there is glory
Somewhere in the night
Somewhere life still lingers
And somewhere has no pain
For somewhere is to glory

As mist is to rain
Somewhere there is wisdom
And somewhere men are wise
For somewhere has no hatred
Dislike or despise
Somewhere has its dreamers
But painfully it seems
That somewhere is a nowhere
And only in our dreams

Karen Scherer
IMPRISONED
Every moment I spend with you
I want to capture and
imprison in my heart
forever--
The words that we have shared;
The gift of your touch;
And the encouragement in your
smile.
You opened my eyes to what
friendship is:
Sharing;
Listening;
Giving;
Understanding;
Forgiving;
Caring.
In addition--
There is a special feeling I will
treasure.
One of trusting and loving
another human being.
So many moments that God has
created for me to remember
during my limited days on
earth.
Thank you for being a part of
them.

Kelly Dee Dougherty
FINDING YOURSELF
Feel free to fly like the wings of
a bird,
Don't look back, not another
word.
For I know you must go to find
yourself,
Just hide me away on your
memory shelf.
You say that you're leaving to
search your body and mind,
To try and capture the future
that you can't find.
And sort out the feelings of here
and now,
You feel that you'll find answers
back home, somehow.
If you ever need me, I'm not far
away,
I hope that always in your heart
I will play.
So, I wish you good luck on
your journey today,
And hope that soon you'll be
back in my arms to stay.

Herb Barlow
OH TO BE YOUNG
Oh to be young
like the morning sun,
To Spring together
in laughter and fun,
In love of youth
the touch of your hand,
As we skip along
the oceans' wet sand.
The Summer wind
fluffing your hair,
To go barefoot and
sunburn most anywhere,
To dress as you like
regardless of class,
To splash in the mud
to romp in the grass.
To dance into Fall
with colors turning,
Leaves falling,
bonfires burning,
Hayride parties,
a blushing Miss,
Holding hands,
a stolen kiss.
"Hush!" says the forest
all covered with snow,
You warm your cold bottoms
by the fireside glow,
You chase Winters' fury
with hearts so bold,
Oh to be young
when you've grown so old.

Laura Barneke
REFLECTIONS
I stood on a hill overlooking a
town,
I saw only treetops as I looked
down,
But there like a marker pointing
the way,
One tall spire gleamed in the
sun that day.
It was a finger pointing to God
on high,
It stood proudly reaching up to
the sky.
A river swirled lazily, far
beyond,
Testifying mightily to natures
great bond.
God touches all with his artist's
hands,
Blending great beauty o'er all
these lands.
In the Heavens above and the
waters too,
God's wisdom reflecting, always
anew.

Joseph Delaney
ALONE
Happy alone
when friends
Are gone
Somewhere inside
Love does abide
Peace is also

present calm and
quiet
our friends also
not bad buddys
to know
Let a soft old song
fill the air
Enjoy the still of
Heaven there

Maria Darby
LITTLE DOE
Christmas, the happiest day of
the year, is near
Santa Claus is in his sleigh
laughing, Ho, Ho, Ho
The reindeer are hitched ready
to go
The sleigh is filled with toys for
all the girls & boys
Little Doe, a small reindeer, in
her eyes is a tear
She wishes to help spread
Christmas cheer.
She would plead "Reindeer,
please may I go?"
May I journey with you through
the ice and snow?
The reindeer would laugh and
say "No, No, No!"
You are too small, my Little Doe
You would get lost in the ice
and snow
You must stay home, my Little
Doe
Little Doe was surprised,
couldn't believe her eyes
Christmas packages were left
below lying in the snow
Little Doe returned the packages
to the sleigh
Little Doe helped to make
Christmas a happy day
Santa was so grateful to Little
Doe
He put on her head a Christmas
halo
Now Little Doe follows every
Christmas sleigh to guard the
toys
Little Doe wishes a Happy
Christmas to all the girls and
boys.

Anita Cullison
THE SAND CRAB
I talked to a sand crab
One day...by the ocean.
He was building his home
And I stopped to visit.
As he came up to surface
To pitch more sand out,
He stopped and he thought
Then he told me about
The sea and its magic-
Of life as he knows it,
An existence much simpler
Than you and I know it.
He said that the ocean
Is the spirit of all.
It calls its own creatures
By its own special call.
And once that you've heard it
The sound never leaves you.
You'll hear it and feel it
In each thing that you do.
And to prove it, he said,
Go home.
In the hour
You'll be thinking and seeing
And feeling the power.
I laughed to myself
As I left him that night
But in the hour drive home
I felt he was right.
The sound of the ocean
Was strong all around me.
My blood in a fervor
Beat with the waves of the sea.
Throughout all the evening
And later in bed
I thought of the ocean...
And my smart little friend.

Becky Polk
UNTITLED
Do not be sad, my friend,
because I am gone from earth,
Do not shed tears for me, for it
is I who should be crying.
I am now with my Creator, and I
live in glory,
But you, my friend, are living in
sadness and pain.
On earth I was bound with you.
I needed to be free.
I have freedom, now, from pain
and sorrow,
But you, my friend, are still in
chains.
On earth I saw hunger and
coldness and strife,
But now I live a truly wonderful
life.
I see no crying, nor pain, nor
death.
You, my friend, see it every day
and I weep for you,
But I am with you always--to
keep you warm and happy.
Do not let your heart grow cold
over this, my friend,
For my life is just beginning; my
death was not the end.

Lee Wells
SWEET MOLLY
As I was traveling by bus a girl
tried to make a seat selection.
As she was making her way
down the isle she met many
rejections
You see she was carrying a
bouquet of flowers for
another.
When she came to where I was
sitting, she said they were for
her mother.
I was happy to have her to sit
by me this thoughtful one.
After all the rejections she
smiled bright as the sun.
She of only eight and her name
was Molly.
After all the unkindness shown
her, she was very jolly.
My young friend this world
needs more thoughtful ones
like you.
Your kind and sweet way was as
another day become new.
Might I always be worthy to be
called your friend.
That your heart of love for the
care of others never end.
So as I pen these lines of
thoughtfulness for your
kindness.
May your life pathways always
be of happiness.
Your interest in poetry same as
I, made my day.
Please Sweet Molly never
change caring loving way.

Jorgi Russell
HIS LOVE IS FREE
God gives His love to all who
will receive,
God gives His love to all who
will believe;
He gives His love to save us
from our sin,
God gives His love for all
eternity.
God gives His love to set His
children free,
God gives His love to bless
abundantly,
He gives His love so full and oh
so pure,
God gives His love of that we
can be sure.
God gives His love so free to
you and me,
He gives His love to cleanse our
hearts within,
God gives His love our souls to
purify;
He gives His love and that we
can't deny.

Caroline Grubb Reisinger
SHEEP AT EVENTIDE
'Neath shifting clouds -
Round, restless lumps
Climb close on a hillside
Then stop to munch
Small tufts of grass.
Big sheep, little sheep,
White sheep, black sheep,
Woolly sheep all --
And the wee lambs
Wobble near their mothers.
Pastoral bells echo
From the horizon
At eventide.
A faint, sharp bark
Warns the wayward ones
Lest they nibble themselves lost;
And a shaggy tail
Urges the fleecy animals
To nudge themselves home.

Gerri Henley
GOD'S MASTERPIECE
Paint me a picture, bright and gay;
Of children playing, a sunny day;
Of flowers, and trees in every hue.
Paint me a picture of things I see,
Of meadows, forests, the angry sea.
Paint me a picture, its beauty to behold
Of glory and might, its power untold.
Pant me a picture, oh please, I pray
Of the power of the world, of the Master's Love.
Oh, but, paint as you will,
Paint as you might
The wonders of the world no great painter can imitate.
Though inspired by the original, Gods own painting.
The world is his canvas and we his masterpiece.

Ms. Melody Joy Bolton
ANGELO
I still miss him.
"Out of sight--out of mind", bah!
Time does not heal a broken heart; it prolongs pain.
I had to leave; there was no choice.
Even before that there was a rift we could not cross.
He had to cleave to the promise of his youth.
There was never a promise to stay with me--it was not in his power.
"Never make a promise you cannot keep."
But he promised never to forget our love and our child.
And he never made a promise he didn't intend to keep.
I also promised--I have not forgotten.
I see his eyes in our daughter's, his smile in hers.
The warmth of his love still reaches me in sleep.
We meet in dreams to say, "I still remember"--"I miss you, you know."
But the dream fades, and pain deepens.
The forbidden love is punished eternally,
With the still cold knowledge it will never be again.

Lucille Gannon
THE PHONE CALL
I don't mind the days, the days don't bother me
It's the nights, the nights are so long
You never have anything to do, so you just sit and think
And that's when you get homesick, just when you have time to think
The sickness comes to haunt you like a skelton out of a closet
Those feelings that you tried to supress all day arise and you realize that you miss that lovely shack you call home
You remember the dumbest things
And that's when you feel your spirit break
You thought you could survive without them
And that's when you thank God for the invention of the phone

Elaine Helen Russell
A LOVE LOST
Living with a man you know is true,
Can be so hard when he has a problem or two.
Deep down inside his love is there,
But he has a hard time showing he cares.
A Warm embrace a kiss or two,
Can mean so much when you're lonesome or blue,
But there he is out having fun,
While you're at home, thinking what have I done?
Your children keep you company,
Still, you're wondering why has he done this to me?
Your love is slowly fading away,
Like the gentle breeze on a summer's day.
You cry sometimes late at night,
Knowing what he's doing just ain't right.
You cannot change him, you've tried that too,
There's nothing left but to say we're through.
His memory remains in the back of your mind
As you put together the pieces that you left behind.
Life goes on ---- you try to say,
So maybe I'll love again someday.

O. Shawn Cupp
SLEEP
To sleep is to become still,
To silence the day, succumb to night.
To relax and be refreshed,
Sleep is to become one; with death,
To be silent and to take a last breath.
Most of sleep is peaceful and nice,
But some is restless and unsettled.
Oh; If we only could see,
Sleep is not to become tired,
But to be one with thyself.
The only time when we can be enclosed,
In the outer subconscious within us.
To sleep is to dream,
Of things to come or have passed.
To be renewed by rest,
To be one again,
Sleep, Sleep;
I must have some now!

Tony Hale
ODE TO A FATHER
Its been nearly three years
Since his breath did go,
Ages past the day of tears
and only a few recall or know.
Warm rain rode down faces,
Vultures craned their necks to stare,

All as children, sat in their places
The drama was sad, but, who was to care.
Blades of grass have long since sprouted
and try to hide that marble stone,
No one could have ever doubted
That in the end we're left alone.
The Sun still shines,
the moon still glows,
Everything continues,
I guess you know.

Robert L-Meade
THE BROWN COCOON
Brown threads
Turning, twisting, weaving winding
Brown threads (that are)
Holding, binding, cradling
Father-Mother threads entwining.
Life's-a-stirring. Self's a-growing
Freedom's longing would burst these threads
To waft this Divine Being
Into gossamer's lavender and blue
Ephemeral, Eternal
Or- will this Divine Creature
Ever striving, struggling
Yet never gaining his Divine Being
Remain forever-held bound cradled
By amber-rust-brown threads
Dead threads
Father-Mother threads entwining

Wanda Wissman
REFLECTIONS
I sit, staring in the mirror
Thinking about life as me;
Wishing I could see both sides.
But the image is fuzzy
the glass is strong
And only the reflection I see.
The face is pale, the mouth drawn, the eyes are puzzled and wide.
They are saying, "Stupid-you blew it"- over and over again inside.
Reflection says, "Go ahead, lift the glass. They won't miss you."
So I did and I cried, "Funny, out of all the wrong things in life--
You- mirror, never lied!"

Larry A. Meier
SEE
I see some of the crabapple trees
are in bloom
the smell covers my lungs,
taste buds
spring makes love, beautiful
woman
the beginning of spring, waking
early
light strikes her face just so
an angel
You wait quietly for her to stir

Cecile A. Nealley
THE PENDANT
Tribute to David L. Jones
The pendant that he gave me
I shall treasure always
He made it for me personally
From stones he gathered at different bays:
He worked at it diligently
For it was to be my treasure
He wanted to make me happy
And yet display his pleasure!
If only I had been smart!
Put aside my ambitions!
Here was a true blue heart
That I could have, as my possession!
The care he took, to make it perfect
Will never be forgotten
I now carry it in my pocket
For the chain on it is broken!
His love has inspired me
To reach for higher goals,
Be a success, honestly
Without tarnishing my soul.

Tracy Lyn Haroldsen
RETURNING
I ventured back
across a soul-lit death
To see my Mothers face
as waters still the land
Her steely locks were bent with Death and Fear
I ventured back
across a childhoods dream of home
Bread baking smells
I can't remember
or forget
I ventured back
and with the swiftness of birdsong
Her light within was caught
and captured in eternity
I ventured back
to face the shutting of her golden tomb
To cast aside my childish clothes and place them on her hearth
To be alone
I ventured forth
and can go home no more

John Glover
JOB CORPS WORKS WE'RE PROOF
sunshine shine
make Job Corps effort
feeling unemployed enroll

think about us
Job Corps
works
we're proof
helping up you try say well
because trouble is no good
It's on you don't trouble yourself
join us the winners Job Corps
Improving your life here on
Center
training for skills only if we try
Job Corps
works
we're Proof
We'll help educate you register
on up
sooner or later you'll get enough
wasting your time
sooner the better earns as you
learn here activities
work think worthwhile
who says life was going to be
easy
without taking a foot step
forward march
join with us
National Job Corps
Alumni Association
Job Corps
works
we're proof
We'll organize we calling on you
members
find some sense of pride here
better your future more
could this be truly your first
second third
time opportunities support your
goals
though
Job Corps
works
we're proof
working together peoples
Day we leave or arrive here
experience
college we'll send you there
learn your trade
come and go at
seriously
Job Corps
works
we're proof
come aboard
succeed
successfully

Debra Braun Anderson

A WRITER'S LAMENT

Alas, alack! these friends of
mine
Who ask me to conjure a line
Or two of simple poetry -
They know not what they do to
me!
For who has tried and does not
know
How difficult the words, and
slow
Come from out the writer's pen -
Only to be asked again!

Susan C. Cerula

CHRISTMAS

The Christmas season is upon
us and joy is everywhere,
There's turkey on the table and
carols in the air.
It's cold and blustery;
Winter's near and children in
the snow,
You look into their faces and
see the Christmas glow.
The trees are dancing in beauty
light,
The snow is crystal beauty
bright
And God has brought his Son of
Joy
And Peace and Love this
Christmas morn.
We praise his name on Earth
below,
The angels sing and heaven
glows.
It fills the air with Joy and
Peace,
So God so love His Son
He giveth to man this Joy,
Oh Listen everyone
This Christmas keep Christ in
your heart
And Peace shall spread around
All the world, you wait and see,
And every tiny town.
Christmas bells are ringing Joy
the whole world around,
That Christ the Child is born
today
Let's celebrate the sound.
Ding Dong the bells are ringing
Let everyone that hears,
Come into the streets
Sing Joy for Christ
The Lord is here!

Mary Agnes DuBose

HE IS A MAN

Blackman, blackman,
Strong and neat...
Got to beat that
Racist stick.
Blackman, blackman,
Has no hate...
He's just begun
To debate.
Blackman, blackman,
Can't you wait...
What do you have
At stake?
A hundred years gone
To waste...better make
Haste or else it will
Be too late...
Blackman, blackman,
Too many in jail...
Thinking he had to steal,
Only because there were
Too few meals. O'God,
Please let him be straight...
He doesn't have to be an
Inmate.
Blackman, blackman,
Get up! And get
Out of the crowd...
Stand up! Shout out
Loud...I am a man,
And proud.

Mary Joyce Alsup

CELERY VERSUS SARA LEE

How many times have you said
to yourself,
Today my diet I'll begin?
I'll have willpower to spare
And in no time I'll be thin.
So you rise from your bed with
confidence.
I can do it this time I know.
I'll save myself the spa expense.
Food will be my greatest foe.
I'll drink lots of water and
eat like a bird
And have no hunger pains.
I'll never hear a discouraging
word.
I'll lose and never gain.
Yet why must it be when you're
trying to lose weight
And you step on the scales to
weigh,
The numbers drop at a snails
pace.
It's enough to ruin your day.
But eat a bite of sweets, let's
say,
And I'm sure that you will find,
They're jet-propelled the other
way,
As if you were lead-lined.
After rising from your bed, you
turn on the TV,
To see what's on the tube
And all you see are
commercials.
All of them about food.
It's enough to make a dieter
scream,
To see temptation like that.
Furthermore it's downright,
mean,
When you're fighting fat.
So you spring from your chair,
with lightning speed,
I won't let them get to me.
You turn the knob to another
station,
Only to find Sara Lee.
Yes, it's true, the temptation is
great,
When you see a commercial like
that,
But I can't afford to eat a
Sara Lee cake,
It would only add to my fat.
For many calories are in that
cake.
Yes, many calories it does
contain.
Even though it makes my
mouth water,
This celery must sustain.
So you quickly turn off the TV
And sit down in despair.
How can I lose weight, you
moan,
When Sara won't fight fair?

Esther Vanek (McGechie)

REACH OUT

It is sad to find some are lonely
when others are all about.
Loneliness then must come from
within,
and not from somethng
without.
Some complain they are all
alone,
there is no one really to care,
When the fact of the matter is,
there
are people most everywhere.
Whose fault is it then that some
are dealt
this dreaded, unbearable fate?
Can they blame the world for
their failure
to try to communicate.
All those who feel sad or empty
or
perhaps a little bit blue,
Need only to open up the door
and reach out to someone
new.
With millions of people
everywhere
to reach out, to love and
touch,
Is it plausible that some should
grieve
and still to loneliness clutch?

Wendy Ridd

LITTLE MISCHIEF

His hair is shiny yellow
His eyes are sparkling blue
His voice is soft and mellow
It melts your heart in two
His laughter fills the air
When he teases you
He's such a little fellow
Cause He's only two
At the end of day
He puts his arms around you
And you hear him say
I love you
Then he drifts to dreamland
Another day is through
But you know tomorrow
He will be with you.

Cynthia S. Jimenez

LONELY SOLDIER

Early morning and the air is
damp.
Demolished shacks and old
roadsigns are the only visions
I stumble on leftover metal from
leftover wars.
Life on this long and empty
road.
It becomes quite fulfilling if you
can capture the sight of trees
bare to the limb,
Just anxiously waiting for spring
blooming.
They sit graciously, protecting
the massive rock walls below
them.
My eyes are wide grasping all of
natures creations.
I start dreaming on the sight of
an old wooden bridge
Instantly I'm walking across
catching the faint echoes of
the stream below.
I begin to transcend back to
reality, but I don't want to go.
Spread me across the pale blue
sky with the rays of the sun
in command.
I shall obey.
Transform me into a cloud
I shall create rain.
Transform me within god
And I shall create peace - upon
this long and empty road.

Mable Margaret Morris

TURN ABOUT

Would it not end war and racial
doubt
If we were all turned inside out.

Judy Stephenson Tarris

MY FEELINGS

My feelings all come out of me
When I put them down on paper
Some how they seem to dance
and rhyme--
It's neat to see such capers
It feels so good way deep inside
My heart just fills with so much
pride
When my feelings go on paper!

Ms. Ellen Jean Boothe
MURDER (DON'T CALL ME YOUR BROTHER)
Don't call me your brother
When you want to commit
murder.
We say we're out for unity
We say we're out for love
But still we're out to commit
murder.
We think we are bad with the
gun in our hand,
You say Bam-Bam you're dead
What do I care.
How do you feel when you have
Killed your brother,
You feel good
You feel fine
But once you catch up with
Your mine
You say I will spend time.
Time for commenting murder
To my brother.

Roberto E. King
PAUSE
Love is a four letter word
Of which I know many more.
Vail...Fast Step.
EACH CAST BEST.
Mate, seek, want.
Each, kiss, pass.
Easy...hope, wish.
Take this move.
Pals, bait, can't
Lady, don't, won't.
Ain't, will, stop.
Yeah, sure, when?
Dine, fine wine.
Abet, join mine.
Time, late show.
Ease, gain, good.
Make oath, wife.
Abed, mass, vows.
Ring, give ours.
Rice, live, sing
Year sold soul.
Roof, home, stay
Earn cash. Work
Nice room - unit.
Term, mail, bill.
Born, life, girl.
Able, crib, rear.
Bump, cook, hold.
Yang, skip, five.
Roam, east, west.
Omit, quit, hide.
Arch, hear, look.
Male, bone, rise.
Hurt, ache, care.
Afar, away, beer
Torn, pain, rain
Erie, bare, snow.
Solo, fear, wail.
Talk, warm, sear.
Ajar, band, keep
Your Head. Grey.
Dead, wake, free
Echo, tide, gone.
Amen, fate, heir.
Tear, root, song.
Hymn, mist, lost.
Love is a four letter word
Of which I know many more.
Vail...Fast Step.
EACH CAST BEST.

Charles Ivan Koch, Jr.
A MAN
There was a time
many years ago
A man who came to
save lost souls
He was born in
Bethlehem Town
Under a star
shown world round
People claimed Him
a Prophet, Priest,
and King
Some the "Messiah"
they did sing
But in God's plan
He was to die
Upon the cross
where he suffered,
bled, and died
In atonement
for you and I.

Matthew E. Boettcher
WITHIN MY HEART
I hold a very special place
deep WITHIN MY HEART,
with hope someday that very
soon you will become a part...
A part of a love,
a love so rich and true;
For the love I hold within my
heart I hold for only you.

Karen K. Krooss
PRETTY EYES
Pretty eyes, they tell no lies. We
see tears of joy as well as
sorrow, and know not what they
will say tomorrow.
Look into pretty eyes, there
truth is plain to see. They
display the picture that the face
keeps a mystery.
Secrets are hidden with
expressionless face, but are told
by pretty eyes in every case.
They will pierce when angered,
and will warm when loved. They
are never deceiving or miscon-
ceiving.
These pretty eyes that can tell
no lies are filled with pain...
We know not when they shall
smile again.

Lisa M. Hein
LIFE'S GARDEN
In the garden of life
Flowers sometimes bloom
Weeds grow fast
In the shadowy moon
In the garden of life
Spring is short,
Summer is harsh
But winter is doom
In the garden of life
There is much to learn
Some comes too slow
Some, too soon
In the garden of life
Love is a prize
Once in a lifetime
Always a surprize
In the garden of life
Friends are cherished
Not always steady
But never, to perish
In the garden of life
Flowers do wilt
Back to the earth
But, never to die.

Kim P. O'Donnell
TYLER
The child walks
In time he'll run
Aims for the stars
Fires the gun
Tyler,
You and I are one
His life is free
With eyes to the sun
To share his smile
The battle is won
Tyler,
My love, my son

W. C. Clement
LIFE'S MEANING
By Our Buried Scars We Trace
"Life's Meaning",
Those Things We Called a
needless waste,
When the Cutting Blade of Life
was leaning
On Our Heart, from It we would
haste.
But how else could We Gauge
the Load Another Bore,
Or know the Bitterness of
Desperate Mother's Tears,
If We'd Shared no Burden of Our
Own or Chore,
Or had Felt no Heartbreak in
Our Growing Years?

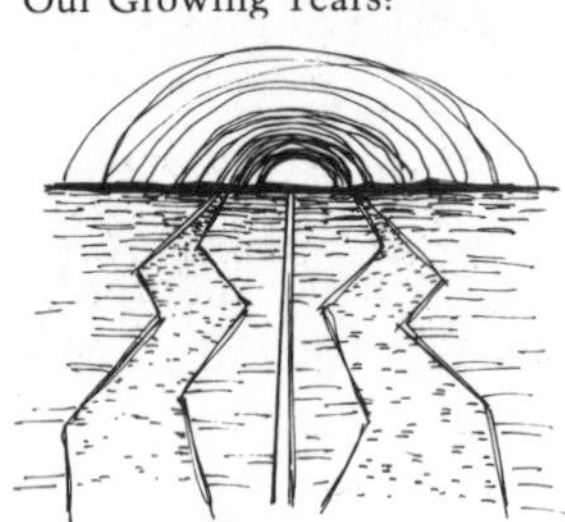

They Blazed a Trail, those
Cutting Strokes of Life,
They Cleared a Way We never
would have Found,
Elsewise in a Tempest We'd had
a Strife,
And Found the Destiny to
Which We were Bound.
So Now, as over Our Lives We
Scan,
To Briefly Glimpse a Joy and
Count the Cost,
We Begin to See there really
was a Plan
And Purpose, and no Smallest
Stroke was Lost.

Barbara Jean Fryar
A BEAUTIFUL GIFT
You held my hand, you touched
me, what a beautiful thing to do.
You let me know I'm wanted,
even if its not by you.
You told me you love women, I
guess that means you love all.
I can love only one, I was never
meant to be on call.
You caressed my face, you
opened your arms, what a
beautiful thing to do.
I know you wanted to love me,
but only for a day or two.
The moment was all I needed
then, today I want much more.
You gave me the courage to try
again, you helped me open my
doors.
What a beautiful thing you've
given me, I hope I can pass it
on.
I don't think it will be difficult,
it will be with me, long after
you are gone.

Wileen Thompson
THE SEA OF LIFE
The lone ship tossed on the
open sea of life,
Fares one storm after another.
It's tattered sails always seems
mendable;
The weather worn ship always
seems to stay afloat.
There is always a way;
A plug here or a board there.
The storm fades and the gray
skies open as a rainbow
appears,
The Lord's sign that calm seas
are approaching.
Someday the weather worn ship
will find it's paradise island.
For now it pushes onward,
Taking wave after wave, storm
after storm,
Not daring to give up the battle.
To give up the battle on the sea
of life, is to die.
The spirit of the ship is not
ready to be engulfed by the
deep dark waters of defeat.
So the wind pushes it onward;
To what destination is
unknown;
But you can be assured it will
survive on the sea of life.

Lisa Baker
TO A FRIEND
If you need a shoulder to cry on,
Ask and you shall receive.
If you need a friend to lean on,
Your sorrows to believe.
When you're afraid and without
a friend,
I will stay with you until the
end.
I can read you like a book,
And I hope that I will know
When I see your sad, sad look,
If I should but stay or go.
Everyone has his problems,
Sometimes they're really hard,
If nobody will listen,
They can catch you off guard.
I'll give you all the things I've
learned
Looking for another time.
I'll give you memories that I've
burned,
Looking for my peace of mind.
But more important than all of
this,
I give my heart to you,
To share the times of sorrow
and bliss,
And keep our friendship true.
So...
If you need a shoulder to cry on,
Ask and you shall receive,
If you need a friend to lean on,
Your sorrows to believe.
When you're afraid and without
a friend,
I'll always be here until the end.

Iris M. Vincent
NATURE'S CHAPEL
Sit in God's creation on a
beautiful spring day.
Notice all the wonders the earth
holds.
Trees reaching up toward the
heavens,
Birds playing on the wind,
Clouds racing through the sky.
Down below the grass, flowers,
and weeds dance,

Seeming to perform for the little
creatures on the ground.
What solitude can overtake you
as you forget all
The problems of the day.
Nature is so beautiful- the
perfect place to pray!

Ms. D. M. Kalp
FROM MY SIDE OF THE BOARD
November moves within my
mind
Black and white programming
Summer's Nikons bite the dust,
Again.
Stick figures
Picasso their way through
Don Quiote landscapes
and lose.
Why should I survive?
Sister to the plague,
See-saw friend, bitter enemy.
I make no moves.

R. L. Cover
SHADES
nocturnal silhouettes
standing in the light,
shimmering in the sight
of a sidewise glance
as they dance
on and on and on
under the winter moon,
under the shining winter moon
too soon gone, lost behind
the mountainside
in the coming of morning time--
...just shadows in the shaded
light.

H. B. Walker
LIFE
The mysticism of life leaves you
in a realm of beauty.
A beauty in man, a part of
GOD'S species.
To bring forth a likeness to him,
to show HIS dimension of love,
to all people.
Life is like the footsteps of a
ladder,
that bring us to a terrain of
thought and decision.
They are our choices,
all of them,
even though our choices were
already known to HIM.
He still gives us hope
that we may go in the
right direction.
No matter how treacherous the
footsteps may be,
to reach everlasting PEACE.

Effie L. Womack
FORBID THEM NOT
Suffer them to come and forbid
them not:
even tho you are tired and worn:
And sometime it seems that it is
hardly worth,
The tiny seed that you have
sown.
Suffer them to come and forbid
them not
Even tho you are buked and
scorned
But, what we know that they
might be,
The brightest lily ever adorned.
Suffer them to come and forbid
them not
Tho the way get dark and
dreary,
We may be the light to guide
them to
The land that shines bright and
clear.
Suffer them to come and forbid
them not
Said the Master, sweet and low
For accept you come as a little
child
You can't enter the kingdom
you know.

Carol Breas
THE LONELINESS OF CHRISTMAS
Its a lonely night tonight,
And things don't look so very
bright,
But I guess they never do,
When no-ones near to comfort
you.
The Christmas cheer hasn't hit
me yet,
But it's Christmas Eve I can't
forget.
I've yet to smell a tree of pine,
With lots of bulbs and lights
that shine.
See chimneys with stockings
that children hang,
Hear all the songs carolers once
sang.
But all I can do is dream of the
past
Hoping all my dreams can make
me happy at last.
But as I lay here in bed,
With my pillow under my head,
I'm as lonely as can be,
With no one here to comfort
me.

Sherry L. Grubaugh
A LITTLE PIECE
A little piece
of me today,
Was chipped off
and given away.

The little piece
was dear,
I gave it willingly,
Yet with care.
For that little piece
of me,
You see,
Myself
and someone else
Now share.

Lillee Q'Jeen Benet
BRING BACK MY BEN
Yesterday's grass was greener
(And naturally, so was I)
And now I go lamenting:
It is so cold, there is no gold
So warm as Ben's blue skies
Yesterday's days were nicer
(And Ben was the reason why)
And now I go lamenting:
It is so cold, there is no gold
So warm as Ben's blue eyes
Birth brought him on a fine
spring day
But October took Ben's breath
away
And now I go lamenting:
Call back the time, bring back
my Ben
Bring back our warm and
shining Ben

Lola Beasley
AN ODE TO DADDIE
To Douglas Holmes, my Daddy.
DEAR DADDY
I made a lovely picture of
your grave
The only thing left here is
The tomb-rock and it tells
you were brave.
Well you left us so quick
It shocked me and just made
me sick.
Now over, "Sixteen Years"
you've been gone.
Have you run into "Donnie"
yet?
Yes, it was a terrible,
terrible blow
But God has his way, we just
never know.
Is it really true that you walk
on gold?
If I make it, I'll have to be
honest, pure and bold.
But it's my plan to come to
see you
This disease they call "Lupus"
Seems no one understands.
The doctor looked me in the
face, he said, "I really wish
there's something I could do."
Some look at me and say,
"God Bless You."
But all the terrible suffering I
have done it sure will be worth
it
Just to lay my eyes "On You"
one more time.

Robert Vargo
ANOTHER SEASON
Down from the sun...rain
Along the thin branch
Lightly...light with pain
And the willow held
Braced...a tiny nest
Cupped to it's young breast
And the willow faced
August's red summer
To October's test
There called no thunder
Belching up it's name
Deep from old earth moss
But the willow raged
Along the eye line
...Silent fire...awake
And there shot at last
Across the meadows
...A bolt from shadows

Beverly Ann Grandcolas
MY LAST JOB
Why has the Lord been talking
and telling me what to do?
Could it be my end is close and
I will soon be through?
There is no day to pass when
he doesn't send a message
Of my never ending task in
an unsuspecting passage.
I'm almost like a film, put in
speeded motion
I sat back and watched myself
as I got the strangest notion.
Your time on earth is short and
your life is unsuspecting
But when I see the bottom line
there's a clue I've been
detecting.
Go and tell the world what I
have done for you
Tell of unending love and life
that shows he's always true.
I can't bite my tongue, and I
can't hold back the words.
You have to go and tell in order
to open other's doors.
It's surprising I'm not frightened
of what may well be true
Because I've listened to my Lord
say go and tell and do.

Kenneth J. Crane
FREEDOM RIDES AGAIN
Is it that we're different that
we're so far apart...or is it...
Different worlds, but so far
beyond. Both are Missionaries.
Different places, the meaning
is here, and together we'll live
the love,..for us to share.
Tree swaying in the meadow
changing day to day, it's plain
for us to see.
The tree is growing, flowers
glowing, sunshine flowing.
Finding the real
world, it's only survival.
Spinning around, ups and downs.
Waiting all to see.
The night...dark for shadows,
but lovely to see...the glowing
magical tour, it's all for you and
me.
The love, where?
Understanding how?
Sharing to care, why? But one
such roots to the machine.
Tree flows away, never to burn
from the sun's rays...beneath the
clouds...in the sea...freedom rides
again.

T. J. Williams
IT'S TIME
It's time to be a woman now,
to show that you are strong.
It's time for you to open up,
to learn the right from wrong.
It's time for you to face your
fears,
and leave them all behind.
It's time you knew what causes
tears,
before you lose your mind.
It's time to know just what to
give,
and why it is a must.
It's time for you to learn to live,
to have respect and trust.
It's time to see the one you love,
won't cause you any pain.
It's time you gave this fear a
shove,
and break loose from its
chain.
It's time to see the reason why,
and start to make love count.
It's time to smile instead of cry,
with love you will surmount.
It's time...believe that love is
fair,
there is no need to fight.
It's time to feel the love you
share,
before it's out of sight.

Alice Johnson
GOD'S ANGER
He arises in fury...
In rage and in pain...
In anger he rushes...
The sword is not fein.
The weapons averted...
And yet it is done...
The battle is over...
Down goes the sun.

Margaret Nienstedt
FLAME
A candle flame
Licks up darkness
Allowing hope to dance alive.
The iridescent blue and green
Center on stability
Just as faith
Defies eternity.
Then, like God's
Unconditional grace,
An enchanted light
Of glowing concern
Competes with shadows
And wraps loving arms
Around all loneliness.
Candle flames symbolize
Spirituality,
Faith and hope and charity.

Jonathan L. Myers
WINTER
the fan
Retains It's silence
After being my friend
The Scientific air
Which cooled upon my slumber
is docile till the end
and morning breaks
refreshing
with it's coolness and it's clean
All the blistering behind us
and the snowflakes
to
be
seen

Ruth M. Khemraj
BRAIN SUPERIORITY
That the male brain's superior
Thus the female's inferior
Is a common belief,
Which at present emerges
Giving rise to all urges
To strike at the chief
Cause of this Myth ironic,
Which has reached stages
chronic
In this age biologic.
Etiology unknown?,
Not when research has shown
How originated such logic.
Why, not in the middle ages
To which one can turn back the
pages,
But in a time unwritten,
Better known as prehistoric,
Originated this myth
metamorphic.
But grossly unforgotten
By those who're chattel in the
minds
Of the male chauvanist swines,
Who won't unlearn the word of.
the knave,
That has long been provided
And long since divided
The sexes to the grave.
Well, what do you say?
Hasn't now come the day
To start the exposure
Which will change this point of
view
In order to benefit me and you
And bring this myth to a
closure?

Carol Segen
ON THE DEATH OF A FRIEND
Goodbye to you, dear friend;
Never shall we meet or talk or
smile.
Our friendship spanned the
years,
I like to think it also spans the
miles.
We shared so many thoughts
And dreams that grew, even as
did I;
You watched me grow to
womanhood
And I watched you grow old and
wondered why.

Mary S. Prevost
FAITH
Faith is the assurance that God
provides for mortal man.
It is the sunshine that follows a
snowy, blowy day.
It is the brightly glowing candle
Shining in the window, to light
my blundering way.
Faith is like an island
In life's ocean deep and wide,
A peaceful, quiet shelter,
From the wind and storm and
tide.
'Tis bounded on the north by
hope
And on the south by love;
By tender counsel on the east,
And on the west, God's promise
of a better home above.

Ludwig Adams
WHAT DREAM?
The boss said
"We have a problem;
Don't leave before
You see me
At five o'clock."
I saw the boss
Behind closed door
Although I'm a Leo
I did not roar,
I yelped.
"We" had no problem
It was I who did
I was on
The list of hits,
I heard.
I went home
Told my wife-
I reviewed
My working life-
I cried.
I ate and wept,
I fell asleep-
When I did wake
I just shook off
The wretched dream.
What dream?

Sadie C. Laurent
BLESSED ARE THEY
Many times---
I saw my Mother sitting;
Lips silently moving--
Beads clicking, as they,
passed the fingers,
Our Father, Hail Mary's,
full of Grace.
Then by a window, I saw
my Mother standing,
lips moving, smiling,
always happy,
Then I asked, my Mother,
"What is it, that you have so
much to pray about?"
Is that the way the Saints
do it?"
More silence, as if in deep
thought--smiling she said--
"Blessed be the living,
Blessed be the dieing."

Mamie Ruth Lucid
RUTHIE: LOST AND FOUND
How soft are the sounds of the
heartstrings
Whispering the byways to
smiles
Much faster and quicker than
cartsprings
Tumbling the highways' long
miles.
Was it yesteryear I didn't know
That you were much more
than a name
Was it yesterday's visit ago
That the ties of our kinship
lay claim?
So rare is your manner and
beauty
A mixture of sparkle and glow
A blending of loving and duty
Brightening the way as you
go.
If I scan the sky in the evening
And I can't see my favorite
star
Then I'll know for sure it is
beaming
In your sky wherever you are.
May God Bless the ties that are
binding
Though the distance be far,
far apart
In search of the answers, I'm
finding
That my ties are bound by my
heart.

Shirin Robinson
VOICES
Voices. . .
After all the space.
Along the graveyard
Neither stepped
Nor wept to find
Who slept there.
But time,
That tossed the waves about,
And lured the ghosts that rode
their crests. . .
Unwary twilight wanderer.

Alice B. Kendall
AT TINTAGEL
I have seen how the sea boils
under merlin's cave
and smashes the stark headlands
where the gulls whirl
and the rooks cry
where Tintagel stands dark and
brooding against the
weathering sky
and I know both truth and
legend are born of mystery.
Cold stones laid one upon
another hold strictly silent
the secrets only they can tell.
Time takes its toll in ruins
then seeds bluebells and
buttercups like gardens in the
grass.
So blossoms grow in broken
castles when we pass.

Sue Sharp
THE VOYAGE
In Memoriam: Betty G. Vail (1923-82)
You put to sea a decade or more
ago
I came on board after about half
that time
Together we tasted the burning
salt
That comes from aging brine.
There were no fears of pirate's
ships
No treasures to lose or gain
Sailing unnoticed on uncharted
course
And taking turns at a fading
main.
Though summers' squalls of
where we'd been
And winters' nights were told
Cold rain soaked our spirits
But could not melt our souls.
Then our spoken words were
fewer
Lost in reticence less or more
You heeded the call of the
mermaid
Whose song you'd heard before.

Madeline Rasmusson
A LITTLE FELLOW
I am careful of what I say,
I strive to do what I ought to be
I dare not go astray for there
Is a little fellow that follows me.
For he is ever watchful,
I cannot escape his eyes,
For every thing he sees me do,
To his utmost the same he tries.
He looks at me in worship,
And says like me he is going to
be,
To him I am a model that
Little fellow that follows me.
A living example I must be,
In ever thing that I have done,
For the little fellow that follows
me,
Is my own dear loving son.

Marie A. Carey
ETERNALLY AWAITING
The warm spring afternoons,
winter's fires and darkened
rooms are gone.
Remember when we ran along
the river's banks laughing and
falling into the tall green
grass?
Why is it ending?
I still love you,
but I have to leave.
Please,
don't cry.
I won't leave here lonely.
And you'll live alone,
maybe.
Will you buy me pretty flowers?
Will you visit me everyday,
or at least once a week?
Will you tell people how
beautiful you thought I was, or
how gently I made love to
you?
Will you take someone else's
hand now?
I'll wait for you,
like I have before.

Jonathan Dobbs
RUSTLING THROUGH THE GRASS
I lie awake, in search of sleep
And then I hear the whisper
creep
It wavers, beckons, then it's
passed
Like rustling leaves in the grass.
I lie there thinking, what could
this be,
That whispers through and
beckons me?
I lie there sweating, nervous,
scared
As day's new sun is fully bared.
But is this just the earthly sun
Or could it be a heavenly one?
Am I still asleep in bed
Dreaming dreams within my
head?
But with a lasting surge of peace
I know that mortal life has
ceased

And through the gates that I
shall pass
I hear Him rustling through the
grass. a heavenly one?
Am I still asleep in bed
Dreaming dreams within my
head?
But with a lasting surge of peace
I know that mortal life has
ceased
And through the gates that I
shall pass
I hear Him rustling through the
grass.

C. Adele Henning
AN ETERNAL CHAIN
"I am Alex..."
"I am Ruth..."
Thusly, the beginning music
"I wish to be your Alex..."
"I will be your Ruth..."
The music grows, so gently.
"I am your Alex--I shall always
be yours..."
"I am your Ruth--entreat me
not to leave thee."
The music crescendos, sure
and strong.
And thus it
Came to be, as in the days of
Their fathers, and of all their
Fathers before them: an endless
And eternal chain--in the sight
Of witnesses, both made one,
Forever.
Delicate as
Filigree lace, but enduring
Strong, echoes, re-echoes, that
Great music of their love--
Learned from their fathers, sung
Through the land by their proud
Generations.
Nearly seventy
Years are past, and we hear the
Same words, even today:
"I am your Alex..."
"I am your Ruth..."

Johnny Mack Brown
I GAVE HER A ROSE
Dedicated to: Tiffany Brook Brown
I gave her a dandelion when she
was ten,
We would play cowboys and
Indians way back then.
We would run and jump and
play very hard,
And keep on going until we
were finally tired.
I gave her a sunflower when she
was thirteen,
And told her I didn't have the
money to give her a ring.
I bet we'd walk for miles, just
holding hands,
Thinking this life held no
sorrow, or demands.
When she turned sixteen I gave
her a carnation,
Knowing this was more than
just an infatuation.
We had started dating and going
to the shows,
And more goes on at drive-ins
than most people knows.
When she was eighteen I gave
her a rose,
And how much I loved her only
God knows.
She gave me sweet love that
made me feel like a king,
And soon thereafter I gave her a
Wedding ring.
On every Anniversary I gave her
some flowers,
And our blessings were as
numerous as April showers.
So many happy days had we
lived and we shared,
We had so much love and we
showed that we cared.
This morning There's a tear as
I'm bringing her roses,
I loved her while she lived and I
love her as life closes.
I'll bring you sweet roses every
day my sweet love,
But it won't be long until I join
you above.

Patricia A. Martinez
A CHILD OF THE UNIVERSE
My child, you'll always be the
joy of my life
I can never forget the happiness
you brought me the day you
were born
Laying in my arms that will
hold you always in your times
of need
And the special part of me in
you now will make you strong
Through the pains of becoming
an adult
I've taught you all I know and, it
will be your turn soon to
make your own decisions
And mistakes, learning from
them as I once have
Cause you're a child of the
universe growing up like
others but, best of all you're
mine.

Deidre Hardin
PEEP SHOW
swinging doors deliver
glancing blows to
middle class consciousness
all those teasing glimpses
of shimmering lights
and writhing skin

John T. Mansuy
THE WEDDING PRAYER
You're from a heritage rich with
simple joys.
Keep and guard these simple
little deeds.
Love for one another; joy of life;
and pride.
For these are the things the
happy couple needs.
Live each day as each day comes
to you.
Do not seek for things like
golden thrones.
For as you search your desperate
little search
You're using one another as
your stepping stone.
Be like a baby and a set of
stairs.
Climb the stairs of life but be
prepared to fall.
Get up again and try the same
old thing.
To succeed is to fall more
times than all.
Don't overlook the violets for the
rose
As it's the violets that will
brighten up your day.
The roses, yes, are nice in their
own way
But it's the little things that
make your life okay.
So search and seek and live but
stay free.
Throw out the things not
wanted, for you are you.
But when you come to
something wanted,
Clasp hold with all your life,
and then make do.

Kamran Lilah Smith
THE ROOM
The room,
my room -
I dreamt it alive
gaping at me like a mouth
lipped with perfect pink
curtains and a hardwood door
for a clacking tongue.
It was in there-
that room
where I had tucked away
my childhood
to gather dust on a shelf,
a childhood that festered a
wound on my soul.
I remember
my room
shuddering
when two strangers
smashed and destroyed
the floors below
in drunken rages.
My room
faithfully echoed
the sounds of hate
between the two
who never claimed
a daughter.
My room raised me by itself.
It took away my toys-
my favorite toys-
to make me grow up.
It shrank as I grew
and wouldn't hide
my ugliness.
It closed its door to me.
I heard the key turn.
I ran away one night
to become a gypsy.
I dyed my hair
anc changed my name to
Esmerelda.
But my gypsy wagon
has begun to look like my room.
I dreamt it alive again last night.
I'll build a fire.
I'll make it dead-
my room, my life.
I'll scatter its ashes in the wind,
and hope they don't blow back
on me.

Cynthia Zeigler
IN SEPTEMBER
I think no greater pleasure have
I known
Than walking down a country
road in September,
Edged with golden rod and
purple asters;
Tiny blue butterflies vieing
with the yellow sulphur.
And I embraced by autumn's
breezes.
One of life's greatest treasures---
Walking down a country road
in September.

Doris Marie Harper
HAWAII
Pearl divers work in the
noonday sun,
Tourists disembark filled with
holiday fun,
Leis hung 'round their necks are
strung with flowers bright,
And stars shine brightly on a
summer's night
In Hawaii
Swimmers stretch and struggle
in the waters blue,
While surfers ride waves gone
out of view,
And hula dancers gracefully
swing and sway
To rhythms strummed on
ukeleles every single day
In Hawaii
The moon comes up over
Manakoora Bay
To cast shadows on idle kayacs
as they lazily lay,
And people from every culture,
country and race
Live peacefully, are happy, warm
and slow of pace
In Hawaii
Pineapples, papayas and
coconuts beyond measure
Add gastronomical delight to an
unequaled treasure
And finally "Aloha" heralds the
end of a day,
As wonderful memories are
packed fast away
In Hawaii

Deborah Jean Saladini
TWILIGHT INNOCENCE
We walked the shore at
daybreak
just you and I
It was so peaceful,
even the ocean before us fell
calm
as we drank in the splendor
of her timeless beauty.
You stretched your hand
to pluck the rose;
its petals yielded willingly
to the magic of your touch.
Love flowed in circles around us
arousing our senses as never
before.
There in the silence of the
morning mist
we had found what we'd both
waited for—
I kissed the sand from your lips,
You combed my hair
and together we greeted the day.

Geneva M. Gillespie
MEMORIES AND SEAN
I sit by the window in quiet
solitude,
watching the snow flakes
pass.
My mind is warm on an ocean
beach
and the sun's rays last and
last.
I now see the wind's movements
of the bare trees,
and I wonder where it goes.
I see the redness it makes on
my small son's little nose.
Back again I ponder and wonder
on the shimmering white
sand,
I see a small boy running across
the hot burning sand.
His face no longer red from
cold, but rusty brown from
the sun.
I hear his excited laughter from
his long earned fun.
Come warm yourself this
wintery day
and remember last summer
with me.
Come lie on the beach and rest
yourself
and swim in the ocean with
Sean and me.

Sheryl Kreshock
PAINTED JOURNEYS
Woke up this morning with the sunrise in my eyes I think I'll travel my crossroads take those places left unseen.
There's these mountains I've got to climb bare feet hills to freely run I'm going to build myself a castle going to paint myself a dream.
I stopped along my journey's way studying the flowers, trees, insects; well they were all much deeper in detail--how could I have left these sights unseen.
I've climbed upon a light house peered along it's light beam, reflecting below saw the rich pastel sea shores; dove deep into it's acrylic depths.
Cotton pillows I looked down upon seeing a midget world far below gaint winged birds I fly on, how man has taught himself well.
I'm going to see the world over selecting different crossroads each day build myself that castle--thank god I've painted the day...

Cynthia G. Fountain
CIRCUS DAY
Poverty stalks the big tent
As evening nighs
Hungry eyes
Stare silently at the cotton candy
Painted clowns
Reflect the frowns
Of those too old to pretend
The somber child
Returns the smile
Of the ancient fat lady
Tiny fingers touch coarse hair
The huge black bear
Shakes his head angrily
Inside the tent
Money is spent
With no worries of tomorrow
And for the child
Just for awhile
Time stands still

Jessie S. Mikell
DOUBTS
Would you, if you could, take off your shoes
And go walking with me down some sunny, sandy road?
And would you, if you could, take off your coat
And go racing with me - somewhere - in a warm and misty rain?
Would you, if you could, swing with me in the treetops
Where some birds would sing along?
And O, would you, if you could, lie with me
On soft green grass under moon and silver stars?
And O, would you, if you could, let me put my arms around you
And feel your body next to mine?
And O, would you, if you could, let me hold your hand and heart
For just a little while -
Until cool winds clear my mind?

B. Smith Gray
FOR ERIN
Here you are.
I'm no longer free.
You're so little.
You depend on me.
I love it when you smile.
I hate it when you cry.
I've got to find out
The reason why.
Maybe you're hungry.
Maybe you're wet.
You keep on crying.
I haven't found it yet.
Are you feeling alright?
Are you sick?
Maybe a pin
Gave you a prick.
I'll keep on checking.
Maybe it's a burp.
Will it come up,
If I give you a slurp?
It was gas!
Thank God, I say.
It didn't come up.
It went the other way.
Now you're happy.
I don't hear a peep.
You must be tired.
Now, go to sleep.
I feel so good
When you feel alright.
I don't care
If you don't sleep tonight.
I'll be so glad,
When you can understand.
You'll have things to do.
You can play in the sand.
I still don't know
All there is to know.
I only hope
I can help you grow.
I don't care
If your hair doesn't curl.
You make me happy.
You are My little girl.

Cheryl A. Aldinger
THE JOKER
I wasn't born a cheater
I was raised the proper way.
Where the bed that you have made
Is the one on which you lay.
But life seems to deal out
Cards no one can see,
And when cheating came along
It was the card life dealt to me.
It wasn't meant to happen.
He just happened to be there
When I was sad and lonely
And needed someone to care.
Now that I've gotten started
It gets easier each day,
To sleep in someone elses bed
Then turn and walk away.
So husbands all take warning,
Show your wife you care.
For if she's just a wife to you
Heed my word, BEWARE!!
For she may be the cheater
In someone elses arms.
She may be the woman
Who deals out her charms.
For there's no one to turn to
Once you're the joker card.
And every woman whose been there
Knows the cheater's life is hard.
A woman must be cherished,
A lover and a friend.
Or she'll be out walking
And she'll meet the cheater's end.

Mrs. Ruth Gronosky
FROM HEAVEN, WITH LOVE
God gave a Special Gift to me,
Filled with his Love, deep as the sea.
It has the freshness of the dawn of day,
The beauty and grace of wild flowers in May.
It reflects the brilliance of the setting sun,
More precious than jewels, it excels each one.
It is as lustrous as a moonlit night,
Ladened with memories to make burdens light.
This Special Gift God gave to me,
My Daughter, to love, for Eternity!

Paula Diatrah Spikes
LET-IT-BE
I want to live, I want to laugh,
and I want to be happy.
For I only live once,
So let it be a good life.
If I were to die,
before four scores and five years.
I would not have lived a long life.
But between the time which I live,
and the time which I died,
was filled with laughter and happiness,
I would be satisfied.
For if I had made all my dreams come true,
and reached all my goals in life,
I would then have lived a full life,
For I rather live a life that's full,
then a life that is long and tormented by only sadness, failure and tears.
For which ever life I live,
whether long or short, I live only once.
So let it be a good and full life.
A long life, I ask not.

Alan Henry Hyde
VIEWS ON LIFE
Life is to live,
You've got to try.
You've got to laugh,
You've got to cry.
Life is for love,
And people who are
Reaching to capture
That last shooting star.
Life is to scurry
And hurry at play;
Also to worry
About things day to day.
Life is around us
Wherever we look,
The tallest of trees
And the babbling brook.
Life is to dare,
To attempt something bold;
Yet, some spend it sitting
And just growing old
Life is to meet with
Old friends and new,
And share all the good times
That you've all been through.
Life is for those
With whom we don't agree;
But will fight till our deaths
For their right to see
Things as they see them
And not as do we.
Life is a gift
Which has happened our way
A gift to be cherished
Each and every day.
Life isn't money
Or big fancy cars.
It is a precious time
And it's ours!

Donna Pope Pendergrass
TROUBLE, MY BABY BEAGLE (POPE'S SAXON PRINCE)
He looks at you with big, loving eyes
And gives your hand a warm, wet kiss.
He is ten inches tall
And brown, black, and white.
He has an over-sized stomach
And an appetite to match.
They say he is a prince from a lin of kings;
His name implies his stature.
Yet he walks slightly to the side
And gallops clumsily through the room.
He chews on shoes, knocks off glasses,
Carries off rugs, misplaces his bowl,
Fights with the cat, pulls up the carpet,
And talks back when scolded.
We tried to give him a name that would suit him.
Trouble, I think we did a pretty good job.

Linda Troutt Polakis
ANOTHER PLACE AND TIME
Sometime when you are all alone
And your mind unlocks that long closed door
My memory will slip out gently
And together we will be once more
My laughter will fill the lonely night
My face will come into view
And you will remember another time
So much in love as I with you
My blue eyes will touch you gently
Play in the dark shadows of your mind
And you will be drugged with the memories
Of another place and time

Jodi R. Cohen
SOMEONE IS AROUND
When times are really rough,
And you don't know where you're going.
When things just aren't going right,
You can count on me
to always be there.
When the sun seems to stop shining,
And the rain really pours.
When the day has gone all wrong
You can count on me
to always be there.
When people act so cold,
And laugh in your face.
When its hard to find a friend,
You can count on me
to always be there.
When you want to cry,
And don't know when.
When laughing is right at the moment,

You can count on me
to always be there.
When you want to talk,
And no one will listen.
When sitting in silence is what
you want to do,
You can count on me
to always be there.
When life sometimes has no
meaning,
And there's no one around to help
fight.
When all is left is someone
to always be there.
When you're searching for that
someone,
And can't seem to find her.
You can stop, because here I am
Right by your side.
to always be there.

Douglas C. Newton
YOU ARE WHAT YOU MAKE OF YOURSELF

You are what you make of
yourself, my friend,
No matter whatever your past
life has been.
You can't make excuses, they
never ring true
About disadvantages besetting
you.
You just have to face up to what
you have been
And leave all the bad behind
you, my friend.
Then enter the future from this
very day
Determined to live in a
strong, honest way
To unselfishly offer to your
fellowman
An example of kindness in
each way you can,
To think of the outcome in all
that you do
Remembering that it will
come back to you.
And never forget that the God
up above
Offers you constantly
redemptive love.
He's ready to help you in all
that you do
If you'll only trust Him and
seek to be true
To the highest and best that He
will inspire
As you earnestly pray His
help to acquire.
So don't ever give up whatever
your trial
But know that the worst lasts
only awhile,
And no matter how dark the
outlook may be
The uplook of faith brings a
hope constantly.
Don't ever be duped by the
hopeless and lost
But just keep on striving
whatever the cost
By investing your life in the
highest you know
You're bound to inevitably
flourish and grow,
Though again and again you'll
need God to forgive
You can learn through your
failures how not to live.
So no matter whatever your past
life has been
You are what you make of
yourself, my friend!

Sharla Hensley
WHOSE LITTLE HOUSE

Whose little house
By the old country lane
Is deserted and lonely
After the rain.
Who could have lived
In such a small place
With one tiny window
Draped with old lace.
Was it a little old woman
With a good-loving heart
That sat sewing all day
And took pride in her art.
Whoever lived here
Filled it with love
Though it was hard
They had strength from above.
And though it may not be
The best place to live
It has that special magic
That only love can give.

Deborah A. Simons
SPRINGTIME

Springtime gives joy to everyone
at heart, and those who love
each other will never depart.
All of the roses will bloom in
front of thee, and happiness
will spread from you to me.

Kent M. Flatness
EIGHTEEN

OH! The joys of being eighteen!
Boyfriends and flowers and all of
those scenes.

Handsome young men that soon
you will meet
Will vie for your hand as you're
crossing life's street.
For somewhere in life's rope
there's most always a hitch
So take care and concern and
get a man that is rich.
One that is rich in kindness and
love,
Patient as Job and gentle as a
dove.
Remember the things that count
up for wealth:
A mighty fine husband and
God's divine health.
And these when you find His
praises you'll shout
For a husband and health you
can't do without!

Betty Lou Caughey Bell
TO THE SEA

Silver threads, with gold and
crimson, woven into night,
Needles slithered in the sand
drifts, thimbles holding tight.
Cascading rivulets, with seams
splitting on the ocean floor,
Behold with all its wanderings
the source has found its door.
That which has in ages past
marked time for all to be---
Balboas' and Columbuses' are
but a part of thee.
Ah, the moan of battles past, of
injured lost and free
The tumult of my soul shall
ease. Thou too art part of me!
Prints of others wet with foam,
tell me did they belong?
Eternal vessel you have
nurtured cradles for the
strong.
Music of the Universe has
echoed in your sky,
A reverberating resonance
resounding, "Who am I?"
Waves of slipper satin,
unfolding on a burlap beach,
Eagle wings spread out in flight,
far beyond my reach.

P. Sohar
FRIENDS OF OLD

Oaks are all the friends I need
And all the friends I've got
Whether they are dressed in
green
Or naked to the knot
Friends they are and as friends
they come
In the same old mold
Created for the poets I like
The sacred poets of old
When the wind hums in the
woods
It's the same old tale
And old tales are what I like
best
For they never fail
They never fail to take me up
In their knotted lines
To the view of other hills
Where my studder rhymes
Where oaks and beeches give
the call
In the same old tongue
Calling me to join them
In their sacred song

Glenda W. Davis
WHEN THE ROOT CHILDREN WAKE UP

Today as nature wrought a
miracle;
I saw my Savior's Hand;
In every branch, of every tree,
In every grain of sand,
In every tiny flower bud,
And everything that grows,
I saw the Master Potter,
Reshape the warm Earth.
I saw the Master Creator in each
little bird,
I heard a bit of the Master's voice
in the chirp of, their song,
I saw a bit of the Master's love in
my little boys dirty faces,
I felt a bit of my Master's joy as I
heard my children at play,
And as the soft wind came
rustling by,
It was as though I heard it say;
"Earth is reborn today-
The Root Children have come out
to play!"

Ellie Connelly
THE LAMENT OF THE PEANUT BUTTER

There was a young mother,
Who went to the cupboard,
To fetch her children,
The peanut butter,
But, when she got there,
The cupboard was bare,
And the poor children had none.
So, she went to the market,
To buy some peanut butter,
But, found instead, the
Peanut butter was just too
dear—
So, when she got home,
With no peanut butter,
She called the children to hear—
"Oh, children, children, dear
children—
There's no sandwiches of peanut
butter."
"But don't cry," says she,
"For lunches, instead, you'll see,
Good soups, made of bones!"

Patricia A. Ranker
JUST SOMETHING

When I walk into the room,
There's no need for a word.
Nothing to be spoken,
Cause you've already been heard.
There's just something passing
between us,
Seem's for so long that it's been
there.
Time hasn't let it be that long,
But I'm not exactly sure.
Could it be it's your way,
Or could it be it's mine.
There's only one way we can find
it out,
It's known as space and time.
When tomorrow comes to light,
As every day must change,
It might seem clearer then,
But for now it seems so strange.

Lois Nelson
EMOTIONS

What are Love and Hate?
These Emotions we cannot see
These feelings that are such a
part
Of shaping our destiny.
Love fills our hearts with
happiness,
Joys beyond compare
Hate fills us with a sadness;
A very dark despair.
Keep love forever in your heart,
Strengthen it every day
You'll find, as love grows
stronger
Hate soon fades away.

Lois E. Maxey
MY POEMS

I have read them over and over,
a hundred times
My little treasure of verses and
rhymes.
They are a tool for making
amends
They are memories of family
and friends.
They are my pastime when I am
low—
On long winter nights, with no
place to go.
They are a bit of happiness
A sometime—funny side of me,
I guess.
They are my way of sharing, you
see
A little part of me, all for free.

Robin Regina Ramey
PAIN

If there's any pain involved,
then it's not worth being solved.
If you'll end up broken-hearted,
then you never should have
started. If it makes you want
to die, just sit back and cry.
Close your eyes and think of
me, and I will come and set you
free.
If it hurts your hands to feel,
just pretend it isn't real. If it
hurts your eyes to see, just
dream and think of me. Think
how good it is to live, think
of all the love you can give.

Muriel Rossel
CLOVER
Full furry black cat, Clover
Sweet and silky one
Curiosity did not kill you
Roving near the hunter's gun.
You flinched at the shot
Coming from the rear
It was not meant for you
It was meant for the deer.
And now you zoom
About the room
Cat that we adore
As gracefully on three
As you did on four.

John Desautels
FOREVER HIGH
HIGH
F
O
R
E
V
E
R
Igreetasun
andwelcome
those
who become
STARS
yet ever i
am
down
to
earth
4mypetrock
can
not
chase cars

Cindy Kilgore
HIGHWAY ROSE
You'd never tell by lookin'
why she looked like a rose,
but highway tales
proved her better foes.
Scars she couldn't close
hidden away,
her own fight
her determined life chose.
A driver, then a drifter,
her emotions tend
to lift her,
but all too soon
her stem the sun would bend
and the search for a different
tune
her dancing catwalk's end.
And once again,
highway tales kindle
a few strays
left in this towne to dwindle.
Bags packed in stories
fresh with hidden
bandages round,
why she looked like a rose
straight up from the ground.

Frederick Cioffi
LIFE
A young man sits before his
favorite dim window.
What *Is* Meditation?
A well *within* him speaks...
"Rhythm in your body *dances* in
sounds, and swirls."
An *Image* appears.
Nature's own Messenger *The*
Dove lands after flowing
flight.
"My breath takes me on its Ebb,
and *Flow*. My Insides are out."
I *see* the oneness
in the *Graceful* Unicorn
grounded in the *Internal*
Heartbeat --
The Flush of *Life* above its brow.
"Love is all we have *between* the
Ashes."
This man stops in his *Tracks* of
Fresh Snow.
"I *See* no Monday.
This is Sunday."
Being.
Only.
Now.

Julia Julsrud
THE DERELICT
The murmured word as by
charity befriended,
Honeyed hope, poured out like
solace into a cup
Dutifully extended.
But—
Offer me not the sweetmeats of
kindnesses
Now spoken.
For I have fed
On stones instead of bread
And all my teeth are broken.
I have drunk hope filtered
through despair
Someday, one day,
Someone would care, someone
would care.
But the Priest and the Levi
Passed by and passed by.
So often, too often.
Now what can soften
A heart sealed in the cement of
indifference?
The road is unending.
The road is unbending.
Into the night, into the night
Forever.

Marilyn Bozarth
MY LOVE
I love you just the way you are,
I wouldn't change a thing;
For you are everything to me,
You are my special King.
You touched my heart in such a
way
That I have never known,
Joy and tenderness fills me now,
These things to me you've
shown.
We'll walk life's path forever
one,
Through our many changing
years
Sharing dreams and hopes of
things we plan
Along with our sorrows and
tears.
So I'll love you darling
While I can,
You are so precious to me,
For all I want and need in life
Is you to be with me!

Kimberley J. Smith
TO KEVIN
The tears turn into rainstorms,
the storms fade into showers,
The seconds become minutes,
the minutes now are hours.
The hurt melts into numbness—
the numbness back to pain,
And the tears that had come
and gone,
begin to fall again.
And the night becomes so
silent—
the silence so unbearably loud,
And the stars that once had
shone so bright,
are misted now with cloud.
And the time it goes so slowly,
how the hours linger on,
And it seems like all eternity,
has passed since you have gone.

Mary Beth Wigger
GOD WALKS WITH ME
I cannot walk alone when wind
makes
Giant strides past my door,
When tumult rages wild and I
Hear thunder roar, and
Lightning speaks her jagged
Piece in silent tone.
I close my door
And dare not walk alone.

Not I!
But God, my Friend, is strong
And sure;
To walk with Him I feel secure.
The storms, whatever type they
be,
Can never, never conquer me.
I'm not alone,
God walks with me.

Bina Meadows
RAINBOWS
I saw the rain pouring down,
It beat the flowers badly.
The puddles were formed of
dirty brown
I sat staring sadly.
The drops became very small,
And finally they stopped.
The flowers stood straight and
tall,
Their umbrellas they had
dropped.
The birds began again to sing,
The songs of a brighter day.
Everyone hoped the sun would
bring,
A rainbow that would stay.

Jamey Ray
UNTITLED
The night wears gloves
and touches you
without touching you.
And you long for
the filtered mirage
of multicolored light.
Sunrise/Sunset
wonder seeps
from the far corners
of the sky.

H. Webster Stull
FAITH
I can't tell you what HE looks
like
I've never seen HIS face
If in fact HE has one
Like those of the human race
I couldn't recognize HIS voice
I've not heard HIM at all
Unlike so many other folks
Who claim they've had "The
Call"
I cannot prove that HE is there
Nor can I prove HE's here
Yet I believe HE's everywhere
And why is that so clear?
It's clear because I do not know
However else humanity
Could cope with life's
complexeties
Much short of sheer insanity
So I believe that HE is real
HE's more than just a wraith
I pray—and hope HE'll hear me
I've no proof—but I have FAITH.

Mrs. Kathryn M. Krueger
LOVE IS SAD
How sad it is to love someone
when that love's not returned.
How sad when you are turned
away by one for whom you've
yearned.
What is this pain I feel inside
that's worse than death itself?
I can't believe the man I love
loves no one—not even
himself.
What happened to the dreams I
had; the pride in our married
love?
If they've been crushed, so has
my soul—please help me, dear
God above!
I can't go on without his love—
he's everything to me.
How could I have been such a
fool? How could I help but
see—
That I can't compete with the
life he leads no matter how
hard I try.
I'll die a little more inside
each day, til he says goodbye.
Dear Love, don't be so cruel to
me. Please take this pain
away.
The love he doesn't want from
me will keep til another day.
I'll keep it deep within my heart
in the hopes that someday
he'll be glad
To know that it has been
waiting there.
In the meantime, tho, isn't love
sad?

J. Bihn
ON AGING
Age and Wisdom.
The two are so inseparably
entwined
And yet,
Man seeks to seperate the two.
The child is forever seeking it;
The youth thinks he has
attained it;
And those of mature visage wish
to escape from it.
Is not this a paradox unto itself?
For if Wisdom is only gained
through Living,
Should not the Aged be Revered
and Respected,
Not only as a source where
One can seek Wisdom,
But also as a Haven of Comfort
and Guidance?

E. Pauline Bradfield
GRATIFICATION OVERCOMES FRUSTRATION
I'm drifting toward the deepest,
darkest water
Where, oh, where is the shore?
Will the abyss pull me under?
Will I be me no more?
I hear Circe's voice calling
I have control no more—
I'm drifting swiftly, but willingly
I no longer desire the shore!
I'm in the midst of the deep now
I've never felt this thrill before.
This sensation that I'm
experiencing
May it last forevermore!

Tamara Sue Black

TOMORROW

Yesterday the world was
beaming
Running, playing, laughing,
gleaming.
Yesterday the men were fighting
Kicking, screaming, punching,
biting.
Tomorrow will be a better day.
Tomorrow won't be like
yesterday.
Tomorrow came. Tomorrow
went.
Tomorrow became yesterday.
Today the world remains the
same.
We see tomorrow never came.
The days fly by, the hours
chime,
We hope tomorrow will come in
time.
Tomorrow will be a better day.
Tomorrow won't be like
yesterday...
Tomorrow's here! It has arrived!
We see our faith has been
revived!
Tomorrow if you'll only stay
Tomorrow please don't go away.
Alas it must, for time goes on.
Today tomorrow is all gone.
Tomorrow was a better day.
Tomorrow was not like
yesterday.
Tomorrow came. Tomorrow
went.
Tomorrow became yesterday.

Catherine Anderson

ONCE A YEAR

I lie on the cold hard table.
He appears from behind a
hidden door
and sits at my feet.
"Place your feet here," he says.
"Scoot down."
"Spread your knees wider."
I am exposed.
The hot white light seems to
singe the hair between my
legs.
The icy steel rapes me.
"Well, how've you been?" he
asks.
I cannot answer.
I feel ugly.
This is not my best side.

Louis K. Acheson Jr.

TO OBLIVION

Is it far, Daddy,
To Oblivion?
Pretty far, Son,
But there are shortcuts.
Is it a nice place
To go, Daddy?
Some say nicer than here,
And some say not.
Are there lots of people,
Daddy, in Oblivion?
Quite a few, Son,
And more every day.
Some say there'll be
A population explosion.
Are *we* going, Daddy,
To Oblivion?
We're on the way, Son,
We are all on the way.

R. H. Peat

CRICKET SONG

Illuminating night fall
Understanding lays
In netted evening garden
Webbed in lush growth
How he plays
His mid-night concert
Beneath sparkling stars
His singing fiddle
Fills enclosed darkness
With shrill, joyful song
Nested
Amid the woven tangle
Of weeds and flowers
His chill music swills
And slices twilight dream
Of pining lovers
Each to each
The song is answered
Like eyes meeting
In the misty, flowered dark
Where one was lonely
Two are answered
As one half implies
And seeks the other
To complete the circle
His distant note traverses
From the world of Daffodils
Through the rainbowed array
To the Irises by the wall
The melody answers
Equal to the question
Of his tune
Bass is met by soprano
Quietly interwound
In lovers dark silence
Where all comes together.

Nika-Jen Bergen

THE RIGHT TIME

Birds soar in the heavens,
and float in air's buoyant
currents.
But when the air
is lashed with rain
or swept with winds
or clogged by snow,
They rest in some protected
place, fluff their feathers,
and wait to soar
again.

Debby Jones

ME (AS I SEE MYSELF)

Small!
but not thin...
Healthy!
but not fat...
Chubby!
but not obese...
Sexy!
but not provocative...
Bold!
but not forceful...
Strong!
but not pushy...
Innocent!
but not dumb...
Weak!
but not helpless...
Quiet!
but not unspoken...
Shy!
but not invisible...
Proud!
but not vain...
Happy!
but not elated...
Intelligent!
but not smart...
Uneducated!
but not illiterate...
Sensuous!
but not seductive...
Alone!
but not lonely...
Luxurious!
but not expensive...
Crazy!
but not mad...
Leisurely!
but not lazy...
Active!
but not untiring...
Witty!
but not silly...
Bewitching!
but not spell-binding...
Gone!
but not lost...
Poor!
but not impoverished...
Rich!
but not wealthy...
Silent!
but not mute...
Stubborn!
but not deaf...
"ME"!
but not quite...

Susan G. Schow-Swartz

ONE DAY FOR EARTH

The world breathed a heavy sigh
And slowly closed a tired eye,
But a memory clutched at her
weary
brain
Of all earth's creatures gone
insane.
A pulsing temple beat a tune
As she cried out her grief to the
distant moon.
One billion shining stars
gathered
around,

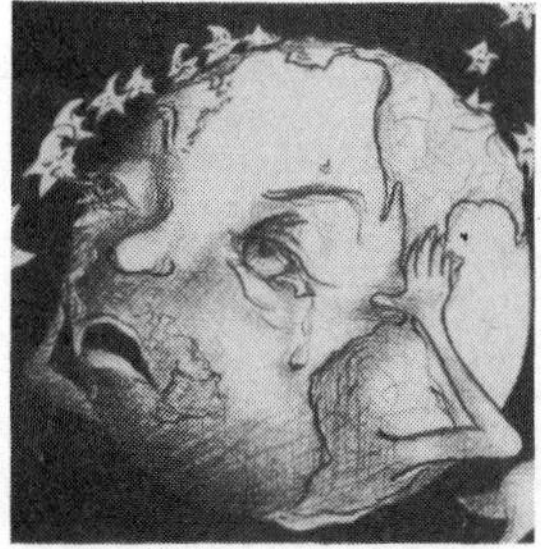

Bowing their heads when they
heard
this sound.
The atmosphere turned, oh, so
grey...
And the dark of night tried so
hard
to stay
That one lone tear painfully
slipped
away
And poor earth was faced with
another
long day.

Ruth A. Shooter

DADDIES

As a child, daddies are perfect.
They make sure that Santa
Claus gets everything right,
and finds your tree from all
the rest.
They help you ride your first
bike when, even with training
wheels, you feel like you're
going to fall any minute.
As a surprise treat on a dull
Saturday afternoon, they take
you and your best friend to
get an ice cream cone.
They can help you with "the
new math" using old math
while repairing a toaster on
the kitchen table.
They break up fights between
you and your brother, who
even though you wouldn't
trade him for an "A" in
English, you would like to
kill for breaking your favorite
toy.
They can come home from work
too tired to even talk, but
still make you feel needed
just by being there.
It seems like daddies know a lot
about somethings, and a little
bit about everything.
God made daddies as a very
special gift to children.
And when you grow up, and
realize that daddies are
human, with frailties and
faults like everyone else,
you love them even more.

Gloria Hornbeak

HEAVEN'S DOOR

Today my thoughts are traveling
back down a memorable lane to
the day a star fell from heaven
and touched our very soul. A
star of love that had joined
us together. It had touched our
bodies bringing us the warmth
of the sun, the beauty of the
mountain, and the sandy
beaches.
The years pass like days...much
too quickly. We weren't aware of
the storm brewing off the shore.
We weren't prepared for the
strong winds and the gushing
rains that swept away the
mountain and the sandy beaches
and brought darkness to engulf
our soul.
One day seemed like a year. We
turn one way then another
searching for light, the
beautiful mountain, sandy
beach, and the bubble carried us
back among the clouds to
touch heaven's door. We hoped
it would open once more to fill
us with that heavenly bliss, to
warm our bodies, and join us to-
gether, making us one again.
The beginning was so easy. It
took no courage, no strength,
no determination. Rebuilding
after a storm takes courage,
strength, and great deter-
mination to have a firm
foundation that can weather all
the storms. When we
accomplish this my darling,
we'll be even closer to heaven's
door. We'll see more beauty
than we could ever dream
possible. Stars will be diamonds
mountains will be pure gold,
and our love will glow brightly
the rest of our days.

June E. Catalini
THE TRAVELER
As snowflakes lodge within my hair,
I ride along through raw dark air,
on a chestnut colt whose nostrils flare.
A distant glow from fire's light,
a beacon on this winter's night,
brings hope to a weary traveler's plight.
Opening the wreath-dressed door,
I'm overwhelmed by fire's roar,
as the scent of cedar fills my pores.
Faces abound with welcome smiles,
quickly erasing journeyed miles,
from a remote and very distant isle.

Grace B. Dutton
BOYS
Rough, tough, and ready,
Always on the go
Boys will be boys
This we all know.
Torn pants and pockets filled
With every kind of toy,
Only help to label him
As ordinary boy.
Little dirty faces,
Hands dirty too;
But just as dear as if quite clean
They seem to know it too.
Climbing trees and fences,
Walking stone-walls o'er
Tracking in the dirt and mud
All over every floor.
Always in the jam jar
Cookies melt away with ease;
Happy, singing as they go,
Forever—"Mommy please?"
Noses tipped with freckles,
Infectious little grin
What would we do without a boy,
To raise a merry din?

Byron Tharpe
THINE EYES
With thine eyes you do implore,
that I know, you neither detest nor deplore,
In thine eyes this I see and more.
In thine eyes do I see a fire,
Hot with passion and desire,
Of love incomplete,
Which no combination of bodily feat
can adequately compete.
My love for thee daily grows,
and into thine eyes flows,
With a casual look anyone knows.
For as in the beauty of a young rose,
daily, more alluring thee grow.
In this year bye and bye,
in our occasional hi and by,
Our mutual love doth restlessly lie,
Till in the Spring,
the gentle change of seasons shall bring,
On gentle butterfly wing,
the fullness of our love.

Phillip Harrison Buttermore
TO MY WIFE
The image of your face before me,
the promise of love its beauty holds,
gives me a goal throughout my workday
and draws me at day's end toward home.
Now, more than the flame of courtship passion,
is the blazing hearth set by our love
that warms our home, our lives, our children,
that you give me my dearest one.
Oh, what a promise your love does hold
for days unseen—things yet undone.
To me my love, my heaven sent blessing,
together we meld—together we're one.

Mrs. Thelma Bishop Archer
DANDELION BLOSSOMS
Dandelion blossoms of butter yellow, Mother Nature's thrifty bouquet. Glisten from heaven's sun ray, nourishing from the earth's virgin plots. Rendering to spring's cause, whistle a song in tune with the pops through their green lion tooth leaves, into their hollow stems of limb. Curtsy to your applause.
Hurry, pick a bouquet today and watch the flow of gold unfold into your palm. Hurry, hurry, for tomorrow they may die into downy little pom poms clinging to you bidding their fare well. And fly, fly, far away to seed into a warmer calm. Or winter to bed over the earth's shouldering head.
Soon again to spring up king of the lawn. Then in a wardrobe of pom poms once again seed over the earth's shouldering head. Fluttering silenty around country and town, but it wouldn't be spring without dandelions around. Mother Nature seeded into weed indeed but not lasting long.

Denise Marie Taulli
A BOY NAMED DARREN
Darren was a boy no one could forget,
Everyone knew him and everyone loved him
He was the cutest, and the nicest guy,
Why, Lord, why?
When he laughed
Everyone laughed.
When he talked
Everyone listened.
When he died
Everyone cried.
Now he's gone,
But his face and ways will always live on.
He took a small part of everyone with him
And everyone's feelings were pierced from within.
We never thought you would go away
It seems we took for granted
That you would stay.
Darren, you will always be in our hearts
No matter how far apart we are.
The sun comes up, but not as bright
Without you around, it just doesn't seem right
At first we held away your dreaming face.
Come down, since nothing else to be seen,
Again could hide your eyes: so wild, so sweet.
How could you expect us to live without you,
We can't become accustomed to
The loss of happiness.
The sun comes up
The sky is blue
It's beautiful
And so are you!
We'll be thinking of you, Darren!

Mrs. Lillian B. Ayers
OH IF I COULD ONLY PRAISE HIM
Oh but if I could praise him there are so many things I'd say just how to begin for there is no simple way to express the things that God has done from our rising to our setting of the sun The ways he's made the road he's paved for us to walk each day it's so wonderful and grand that words cannot explain it's not easy to walk this narrow way but with prayer it keeps things fair as you travel along life's way
But don't ever forget to stop each day as you journey on your way and cry aloud let the world know you are proud to say thank you God for everything in every little way for each and everyday that's why I say. Oh but if I could only praise him these are the words I'd say Thank you Thank you I wish there was more ways But Thank you is my praise

Laura Abbott
THE FORGOTTEN DEED
Love can be happy as a child
Playing in a muddy puddle
As colorful as the rainbow after the rain
It can be Wild
As a lonely desert flower
Blooming in the sand
Love can be tame
As a Circus horse leaping thru a flame
Some have died in a forgotten Land
Just to give their brother's a helping hand
The word wasn't just a meaningless deed
Someone's died just to prove that
He's left us that love
Hanging up there above
It's free for all
This thing we call LOVE

Francis Russell West
HALLOWE'EN
The soft caress of fireflame on your face
Lighted the wak'ning glow of love for me,
Smoothed out the lines of care, through time and space
Brought back the little girl you used to be.
The moon illum'd our love, the stars came down
And danced in fiery splendor in our eyes.
The land lay still and quiet all around
As two hearts waked to love's e'er-new surprise.
O magic hours, too soon sped by! The glow
A memory, and love must wait a time
'Til two hearts, yearning, parted now, will know
Their fulfilled joy, another place and time.
It will not be denied, this love reborn,
It grows but stronger, waiting out the storm.

Linda L. Oliver
LOVE
Love is like two rivers
flowing into each other.
Running over the rapids
like lovers.
Were lonely before they met
now, they run so peacefully.
They have no worries
till the winter flurries.
Roaring, splashing, raging,
so peacefully over the world.
Love is when two things
go places, and sing.
Sticking together
through thick, and thin.

Grace B. Dutton
HOME
They tell us that a home is
A place to hang your hat,
There is no doubt about it,
But a home is more than that.
It's a place where God is at the helm,
And never ever wavers.
It's a place where love abides,
And you always receive favors.
It may be just a humble place,
A nook that's really small.
It may be quite a spacious house
Within a garden wall.
It could be just a cottage thatched,
Or a cabin by the sea.
But, if within it's own four walls Jesus dwells,
Then, it's the place for me.

Anna Smith
GROWING RICHES
That, "Money never grows on bushes or on trees",
I'm told;
Yet 'round my pool crouch

golden elders, heaps of
purest gold,
While silver dimes are tinkling
on my silver
poplar trees;
And I am rich, till thieving
winds come stealing
autumn fees.

Jeanne Meyers
HALLEY'S COMET 1986

Paths of fire
Traced in blackness.
Earth-infinity
Trembling,
Silently blue,
Awaiting thundering destiny.
So close and yet so far.
Gravitic forces weaving
A spider's web in space—
Gossamer and iron,
A delicate universe
Of cosmic strength.

Darrell W. Revel
DAWN WOULD FIND US OLDER

Closer, then still closer we
grew each fading night
As dawn would find us older, a
little bit surprised
The love we shared seemed
special, unquestionably right
Though I had to go the pain of
leaving echoed in your eyes.
While we are apart I'll miss you
Each night in my dreams I'll kiss
you
Just set your watch for my
return
Each day for you by my side I
yearn.
Farther, then still farther we
seem
to drift apart
Though you'll return, now
you're distant from
my waiting heart
That faithfully hopes, against
fears of an empty home,
for your re-kindled passion
while yet
I hang fire alone.
While we are apart I'll miss you
Each night in my dreams I'll kiss
you
I'll set my watch for your return
Each day for you by my side I
yearn.
Dawn will find us older, lonely
Each night I'll dream of you only
Just set your watch for my
return
Each day for you by my side I
yearn.

Margaret Mead Cutter
TO RICHIE, GOING HOME

Raindrops slipping down blush-
burnt rose petals;
Salty-wet, stinging humiliation
and disillusionment:
The pot of gold at the end of the
rainbow is fool's gold.
The brotherhood of man is held
together by "I need and you
have."
And the parade called life keeps
marching noisily by
Because you no longer need
what I have.
You called me Sister, but Oh,
brother!
What a fool I was!
Now you are making it on your
own.
Now you are your own link
with Man Outside.
Now you will be free, so you
can desert me.
Leave me, a summer's rose
blossom, facing fall:
Even the fading sun avoids me
And the chilling winds tear me
into a thousand tiny pieces.

Mary Beth Wigger
COME WALK WITH ME

Come walk with me in early
Spring
And I will show you a magical
thing!
We'll walk in the woods, hear
nature sing,
Where dry brown leaves are
whispering
Tales of an elfin, fairy king.
The pine trees hum as we walk
along.
The wind bends the oaks and
plucks a song
To the cadence of woodpeckers
drumming strong,
Come walk with me where
the wild birds fly

And the air is filled with their
mating cry.
While rabbits are cautiously
hopping by
A squirrel in a tree plays
counterspy.
Come walk in the woods where
the air is sweet;
Stray jonquils nod to us as we
meet,
Revealing mystery under feet.
The dandelions flash their
sunshine smile
and so goes our Spring walk,
mile after mile.

Rebecca Messner
PEACE: WHERE IS IT?

Everyone is looking for it,
Prayers storm Heaven in its
behalf
Peace is on all men's mind
Why then is it so hard to
find?
It's not enough to merely speak
We must act as though we
really seek.
Acting harsh while praying
peace
We'll never make the fighting
cease.
Remember, "a soft word turns
away wrath",
Also we are told "turn the
other cheek"
Both good suggestions, tried
and true,
To be used in all we do.
In this way the changes will be
made.
More than lip-service must be
paid
To seek ideas as Brotherhood
And on our Sonship to God.

Catherine Fisk
YOUTH TODAY

Youth today
many forces joining together
recognizing the damage done
from continuous
mismanagement
trying to make restitutions
for decades of corrupting
Mother Nature, Brotherhood,
Faith
conflicts amongst ourselves,
women as well as men,
justly mended, equaled
daring to reshape society
answering the urgency for
change
replacing greed, anger, Nuclear
War
with sharing, love, Peace
feeding the hungry, renewing
our strength
joining together as one
Growing.

Carmen S. Young (Hill)
WORDS

Words can mean everything to
persons of all kinds
They can brighten the nights
and make your heart shine
They can lift up your spirits,
turn January into May
And turn all sorts of oddities
into things bright and gay.
For a child they can make all
the difference in his day
They can turn his whole life
into fantasy or play
When encouragement is needed
they get the job done
And allows him to continue
with his play and his fun.
Even with all the good that
they can do
They also can cause a lot of
harm too
You have to be careful about the
things that you say
Or feelings can be hurt and
good friends sent away
A loved one's dream can be
broken and destroyed
Because feelings so special are
not to be toyed
The words that one chooses
should be cautiously said
Or no companions will he know,
but alone he'll be instead
True, words can be an asset if
used the right way
So don't take them for granted
and please watch what you
say
If you don't want hurt feelings
or warmth to turn to a chill
I suggest you treat language as
an Art, as a skill
Although you may be angry
keep watch on your tounge
And you won't have words to
regret in the days yet to come.

Blaine A. Allred
ALONE

I'm alone,
It wasn't meant to be.
I open the door,
No one goes in but me.
The house is quiet,
I hear not a sound,
Each room is empty
As I slowly move around.
I hear the clock ticking
Steady on the wall,
I open my mouth to speak,
But no one's there at all.
My foot steps echo
As I walk across the floor,
The one I loved is gone,
I'll see him no more.

Andrew L. Meyer
ENDLESS SEARCHING

I search for gratification,
and to feel good in my soul,
that's all it ever was,
and all it will likely be.
I watch other people,
and see more of the same,
I wonder what life is,
and why I came to be here.
I try to lose myself in others,
and feel worse for it,
I struggle to change myself
within,
and wonder if it's worth it.
I go to church and pray toGod,
and still I don't feel better,
I party and ingest intoxicants,
and feel good only for awhile.
I want to cry and I try,
but still the tears won't come,
I want to laugh, feel good, and
be happy,
and yet I feel so only for
moments.
I believe all moods come from
within,
and they grow within me as
vegetation,
I reach in for the flowers,
but I grasp mostly the thorns.
When I think I want to live,
I'm simply afraid to die.

Patrick John Schaefer
MOTHERS' HOPE

Heavenly promises are purely
sweet,
While earthly bonds pierce in
unrelenting ache;
Yet a mother's love gives hope
to this higher retreat;
A bit of heavenly earth to
graciously partake.

Elizabeth Suber Bennett
MAKING IT

Tuna fish sandwiches
And potted meat
Searching want ads
And walking streets
Pawning jackets
Cheap retreats
A bottle of wine on a cold night
Hot breath in my ear
Money is going
Doing bad
Losing weight
I've got to make it
I've got to make it
Please let it happen
Before I become a victim of my
dreams

Robert Steven Shepard
LET HIM BE!
Let him be!
He's a sad man. Does he know it?
Never shaved, always a frown.
He could be taken for "The poor man's" clown.
He's not unkind, but very far behind, unaware.
He has terrible odored underware.
Foul with fungus, breath to match,
and most of his desire is to scratch.
He'll look for his fortune in the gutters,
and public telephones, inside the shutters.
Let him be!
He's a sad man. Does he know it?
Most of his life he didn't care and floated.
Drinking false courage from a flask,
walking as if it were a task.
The kids torment him. His hell is their fun!
He'll take a quick drink, and then become furious
with the whole bunch.
Very rarely eats, and often repeats a haunting noise
at everyone he meets.
Let him be!
He's a sad man. Does he know it?
If he can find a corner without a fight,
he'll sit, and close his dark circled eyes,
as if he were putting out the lights.
Always setting around in the dirt.
He'll sleep, day, night, or when he hurts.
His strong, strange, twisted mind molds his unkind fate.
He is a sad man to see.
Most passer bys just say, "Let him be!".

Kristin L. Butsch
LEFT DANGLING
when I was a young child,
music filled my being
and crept its expression
into my body
dancing wildly
before my mirror audience
the curtain went down only
with a knock at my door
at eight, mother enrolled me in ballet
some quickie introductory course
cheap its primary aesthetic value
my dreams of dancing
ended on a recital stage
some six weeks later
my pink sequined tu-tu
was filed in the "Halloween box"
now and then I do my recital dance
as a joke for someone's entertainment
and my slippers were left, with my hopes,
to dangling from a rear view mirror
in a machine with a steel heart
with no room for stretching
only for watching
the road that has slipped by me.

Ezio Di Francesco
BREAKAWAY
Life, Again breaks away,
the breath of love. . .hold not in,
the heart left to bleed away
once smiles and laughter with hope and play.
A dying leaf fallen, decays away.
This month, a ray of sun diverted
not to shine my way.
. . .A chance. . .See you again,
to wet my lips with morning dew
and then to smell the air, dry with fragrant
radiantly plemish nutrients of life would bear.
With pen in hand and thoughts in mind
I sit ALONE. . .GOD?
The blossom, Withered, no fruit it bares.
To cry. . .hold a tear within!!
for life has left me, stripped of feeling within.

Hilda M. Jordan & Tammy Cinchonia Jordan
HANDS
Hands. . . . .
Everytime I hold someones' Hand
I dream I'm in Disneyland!
Everytime I hold someones' Hand
It must be Fantasyland!
Everytime I hold someones' Hand
I'll be playing in the Band!
Everytime I hold someones' Hand
It's a Grandstand!
Hands. . . . .

Mary Margaret Heckler
BIG BROTHER
(Dedicated to my Brother, John)
We never really sat and talked,
I remember how we fought.
I try to remember the good old times.
I'm sure that they are there.
But I really don't remember where.
I try to remember telling you,
Big Brother how I cared.
I'm sure I did,
But I really don't remember when.
And in all the years of growing up,
"I love you," I'm sure I said,
But I really don't remember when.
Now the time has finally come,
When Big Brother you aren't there.
And now I know just where to find
those word's I'm sure I said.
In tears of love and caring,
I find that you are gone.
And I'll never have the chance to say,
Big Brother, I Love,
I care.

Vivian Higgins Morse
ON THE LAKE BLUFF
There's a far-off place in my memory
Where all is un-man-touched and still
But for the imprint of a foot-formed path
And the call of a whippoorwill.
There are flowers and trees, birds and bees,
A lake - its sun and moonlit shore;
With nature and all its best decor
Who could ask for anything more?
And back from a bluff winds a hidden ravine
That provides for the name of the town it is in.
With trilliums, cardinal lobelias, and maidenhair ferns
To grace bidding shelters where a stream makes its turns.
Wild roses peek from beneath their shade,
White daisy in sunshine grows ..
Each in its aesthetically planned space is placed
As though some divinely great artist knows.

Burnice C. Wheatley (Williams)
SWEET LOVE A MYSTERY
Ah, love so sweet a mystery be
From saintly throne to poverty
From hidden dale to mountains high
Ye go beyond a mortal eye
I search thy crevice's of earth,
And in thy bed of mortal worth
Thy call aloud from soul's depart,
Thy mystery of thy bleeding heart.
Ah, love so sweet a mystery be
In misery heart I call to thee
And from this shell a mortal being,
I call to thee to meet my need.
Ye sing of old, thy time unknown
But yet so new thy rapture bloom,
And yet in strength of agony
I die in search of only thee.

Genevieve Sanderson
WORK TO DO
To lose a child is to face
A quiet house, and empty place
No laugh, no shout, no Hi Mom
To scatter your sedate aplomb
So look about, and you will find
Another to shatter your piece of mind
To lose a LOVE us to stand
Alone, bereft, in a burned off land
No forest swept by wind, and fire
Has trees or grass, or free desire
of BIRDS to sing, or plants to grow
There must be rain, and the healing snows
The warm winds of spring will set free
Each seed, and plant, and baby tree
And when the earth is quiet, and green
Their call will bring all wild life,
To lose faith in GOD, is not to see
We each have our own destiny
To EACH OF US is given a GIFT
Of WORK TO DO to heal the rift.

Suzanne L. Redmond
IMAGE
You see the girl
But she doesn't see you.
She lives her life
Anyway she pleases.
Day by day,
She's not in the way,
But somehow
She seems to touch you.
She has nobody,
Nobody wants her,
She's her own person.
Even when she's not there
You still see her.
Just an insignificant nobody
Existing in this world.
You feel sorry for her,
But you don't know what to do.
So you just leave her,
And hope for her.
And when you look at her,
You see something else.
She is the mirror—
And what you see is you.

Regina D. Moore
THE NAME AND THE FACE
If you saw me in a crowd
I'd look no different
I'd have no distinguishing marks that you'd notice.
I'm there with the others waiting for you
My heart goes to you unnoticed.
You'd have to search me out and find me
To know that I'm different from the rest.
My eyes would reveal what I feel
And my heart would tell you the rest.
If I told you my name today
You wouldn't remember it tomorrow
Because names without faces don't mean a thing—

I'd cry in endless sorrow.
If I held out my hand and touched yours
You'd know the true feeling of love
I'd never speak but our eyes would meet
You'd notice my eyes, my hair my smile
Wondering if I'd seen you before.
I'd smile and for the first time speak to you
And the special one
And finally the name without a face
And face without name become one.

Brenda Brown and Mike Day
GOD'S POWER
Have you stopped to smell a rose?
Have you stopped to watch a bird
Singing as it goes?
No sweeter song ever heard.
Have you ever watched a squirrel
Build a nest up in a tree,
With its tail all in a curl?
What a wonderful sight it is to see.
Have you hugged a kid?
Have you picked a flower?
If you can say I did,
Then you felt the touch of His power.
Have you called on the Saviour?
Have you found a new friend?
Have you unmerited favor?
Have you been born again?
Humble yourself as a kid.
Call on Him this very hour.
If you can say I did,
Then you've felt the touch of His power.

Vera Lander
ALL THINGS NEW
Somehow
I suspended my place
in time and space.
Cast adrift
from familiar moorings—
uncertainties agonizing.
Sounding depths
to anchor lines; bearings
all realigned.
Relinquished
superficial securities;
risking all for infinity's.
In exchange
for comfort's milieu;
meeting all things New.

Lucretia Fortriede
LITTLE HEART FULL OF JOY
Little one with heart of joy,
Playing with your toy,
Running here and there;
Jesus keeps you in His care
While playing in day
Or at sleep you lay.
He guides your life through.
He gave His life for you.
Give your life to Him.
Eternal life you will win!

Erin L. Noble
ABUSED
A child sits huddled
On a lonely front stoop.
Just waiting for life
To be through.
No tears to show
They've long since been past.
How long will this thing
Called child abuse last?
By the age of six
Even at three or four.
They know life is rough
And they've learned to be tough.
They don't let a tear
Show through.
They put on a false face
Leaving behind only a trace.
Of the pain
That they feel.
It's imbedded to stay
It seems almost unreal
That parents could hurt
Small children this way.

James M. Jackson, Jr.
MY PARENTS YOU ARE
My parents you are,
The greatest there ever could be,
We seem to be so far apart,
I love you Mom and Dad,
May it never be,
That we are so far apart,
That we ever stop,
Being a family,
I love you both,
More than you could ever see,
Thank you so much,
For letting me, be a part
Of our family,
I love you Mom and Dad. . .

Lorraine Hicks
FIFTY TWO AND START ANEW
School again after a season...
Encircled with the idea
to enhance my mood,
though questions searched
my mind.
One step into the room,
four walls of pictures,
shelves of papers and books
peer at me.
A chalkboard of scribbling...
An unruly circle of chairs
sat fresh young things,
students of today not
yesterdays.
Looking around quiz time
came to mine.
So ancient I felt,
frightened and awkward.
Me!
back to school at fifty two.

Deborah K. Deck
WINTER DAY
What a beautiful winter day,
Oh! I hope it's here to stay.
As the cold north wind doth blow,
With it comes the mountains of snow.
The ice on the trees make them gleam,
While the faces of small children really beam.
Snowmen, shovels, and sleds appear,
To greet the most beautiful time of year.
The air is crisp, sends a chill through us all,
But we watch with delight as the snowflakes fall.
Romp, run, and enjoy all that's near,
For all too soon it will disappear.

Dolores La Bianco
THERE WAS A TIME. . .
There was a time
When I could move a mountain
Long before I ever reached my prime
When the whole world fell in
pieces all about me
I rebuilt it over night
Yes, there was a time. . .
I was but a babe and don't recall
the sorrow
When mother left this world
For realms above.
And then sometimes
I would have traded places
With someone's pet, to get a taste of love.
There was a time
When the rocks of life caused anguish
That shattered my very soul to bits
With so much force
That here, today, when my soul should retire
I feel reverberations of a course
I took when I was young
Before my prime
Suffering now in silence, remembering
There *was* a time. . .

James P. Kelleher
COVERING UP THE ROSES
I see her at her task
Of covering up the roses
Against a sudden autumn frost
And bless her
For seeing it a duty
To save the world a beauty
That must otherwise be lost.
Against the Winter Rages
To a slender hope we cling
That sheltered fragile Beauty
Can once again make Spring.

Ella Foster O'Brien
OUR GENTLE OUTLAW
An errant wind will carry you
Oe'er the land you loved so well,
Oh, Daddy, may your spirit
roam
Where gentle raindrops fell.
No more will our "Gentle
outlaw
Roam the golden west,
No more will trails and valleys
Take him places he loved best.
Where burros graze, and cattle
roam,
In canyons deep and sheer,
Our "Outlaw" will be coming
home
To those he held most dear.
And when the winter snows lay
White and silent on the ground,
We know your spirit is at rest,
And peace at last you've found.

Dorothy L. Fadely
SEARCHING
I pray for the restlessness in my heart to cease,
That my search may soon be ended, I find blessed peace.
I've climbed the highest mountain, to gaze over the valley below
Humble, yet my heart is not satisfied, reaching beyond restless glow.
I scan each face of all I meet,
Asking each time, "are you the one I seek"?
I reach out my hand, hoping to clasp a feeling of comfort
Always asking, "has my search been fulfilled at last?"
Someday, I'll find beauty that will never fade, a love that never dies,
And I'll look and find the face I've searched for, so loving, so wise.
Nourishment to feed my hungry soul.
When this has come to pass, my search ended, blessed peace to enfold.

M. J. Sweatfield
THE WINDOW
I walked by your home last evening.
Green shutters were open wide.
Framed in the big picture window
Was the happiness inside.
You stood in the glow of firelight,

Baby hands clasping your dress.
On your face, a smile of welcome
For the one you love the best.
In my heart, a cry of longing.
Oh! How I envied him.
Framed--in the big picture window
"My life as it might have been."

Elizabeth Gerringer
CANDLES
Candles glowing in the night, through the morning hours.
Candles gleaming very bright, shining through the flowers.
Candles in the window in the evening after sunlight, changing
shadows on the walls.
The shadows move so slowly, I can see the night is still.
The stillness grows to movement, softly breezes fan the flames.
Night has turned to sudden darkness now, and there is no one else in sight.
Ghosts are creeping in the doorway slowly, count them, there are seven.
Seven candles for you, visitors, one for each, you light them now.
They do not speak, or cannot, turn and slowly walk away.
The seven candles are still waiting for my friends some other day.

T. Paul Jacobson
TO MY LADY FAR AWAY
To my lady far away
just a few words
I'd like to say.
Hi, and how are you
I wish I was there
to see you, to touch you,
to love and to care
Soon, I hope I can
be with you
cause this waiting and wanting
has me so blue
You brighten my life
You make me feel good
Oh, just to be there
If only I could

Raymond Gendron
FOR ACCEPTANCE
I do not try to aggravate
Though I know I sometimes do
I try not to be insensitive
But at times I am that too
I think a lot about some things
I know I cannot change
This does affect my attitude
And makes my actions strange
My self control I lose a times
And I say things I regret
I hope displays of anger
Aren't taken as a threat
I sometimes get a bit uptight
And find it hard to talk
At those times I turn around
And away, I often walk
I like to think I'm just as good
As any of the rest
Though if its not, too hard to take
I'd like to be the best.

Christine A. Foro
WHY IS IT. . .?
Why is it that when it's dark
You help my eyes to see?
And why is it that when I cry
You always comfort me?
Why is it that when I fall
I'm lifted by Your touch?
And why is it that when I'm lame
You give to me a crutch?
Why is it that at my lowest times
You give me such inspiration?
And why is it that when I'm lost
You help me to reach my destination?
I know how much You love me
You're always by my side.
I see Your love in everything
The sun, the moon, the tide.
You help me to go further
When I think I reach the end.
Thank You Lord so very much
For being my best friend.

Jean Allison Anderson Phillips
TINGEY TIMES
Telephones ring, doorbells chime,
Lord you pray, give me a dime.
To give to the man, standing at the door,
Always bellowing, "Give me more."
Bill collectors, what can we do?
Tis these problem times we're going through.
Hubby sits down to the table in delight,
Til he sees it's beans again tonight.
Kids a cryin', "Oh Mom please,
it's Nickey shoes to give our feet ease".
There's a special on at the local store,
How dare you kids even ask for more!
At the age of fifty one, never knew a garden was so much fun.
Worked our fingers to the bone,
To feed these kids we call our own.
Bills come in, money pours out,
Forgetting Santa without a doubt.
Join all the sweepstakes, that's what I'll do,
Hoping one just might come through.
Pray O'Lord see us through,
And for Heaven's sake, tell us what to do.

Liddie Moeller
IN THE AUTUMN
In the Autumn, the leaves come
Tumbling down,
They leave the trees bare, as they
Fall to the ground.
In the Autumn, we have pumpkin,
Squash and broomstick witches,
And soon we will have Christmas wishes.
In the Autumn, the sunflowers turn to
Black seeds,
And you don't have to worry about the
Weeds.
In the Autumn, you know that summer
Has come to an end,
And winter has yet to begin.
In the Autumn, sweaters, light jackets
And caps we adorn,
And we think, next Spring, many new
Things will be born.

Violet Marie Venegas
LITTLE WOODEN HORSE
He waits
with flowing mane
for footsteps small and swift
to run beside him,
whisper secrets in his ear.
He waits.
He does not know how old he is.
He knows
in younger days,
He circled with a carousel.
He waits
for tiny hands
to press his nose
with love;
his wooden heart still true.
He waits
for children's Laughter
sweet upon his ear
and thinks
COME SOON, SOME SOON.

Robert Cullen Duffy
POND MAIDEN
Drowned maiden parting
Lush lips of algae
For nesting goldfish.
Shadow eyes bequeathed
Awareness by moonlight
Coalesced to droplets
Of freed mercury.
Those tender eyebrows,
The soft fur of infant moss,
And tangled watercress tresses,
Billowed by secret breath,
Kiss satin cheeks pollen-freckled.
Lovely maiden, granite breast
Thrust forth to give perch
To a weary butterfly.
Gentle pond maiden,
Flesh dissolved and bone splintered
By a fallen maple leaf.

John A. Rodgers
OTHER SEASONS
In the rise of spring,
Winters eve
Childhood calling
Cravings.
Waiting
And thus not enlisting
Pressed flowers you're saving.
Getting on
Along your way
As true as he
Can take you.
Labor not
For fallen leaves,
The seed of spring
Shall rake you.

Marilyn Fuller
PATIENCE
Oh Lord, bless me with patience
To help me through today.
forgive my uttered words,
The one's that disobey.
Instead, let my mouth sing praises
And my heart be full of joy.
Let there be thanksgiving
Within my heart so deep,
That only true love and kindness
Will come forth out of me.

Sylvia P. Beres
BEHIND MY WINDOW SILL
Haunting, soft, melodious sounds
Steal past my window sill,
Imitating butterflies
On strings of violins.
Softly as a lover's kiss
Upon a sleeping brow,
Piercing as a mating call
From out the wilderness.
In repose, I lie there still
Till coulds come dancing by,
And lift me up, and we are one
The Universe, and I

Mary Finger
SURVIVAL TACTICS
On Christmas Eve in '73,
Santa brought a book to me,
It was called "How to Live on Nothing,"
Now isn't that something?
Don't buy a thing the book did read,
So, when I ate a tomato I planted the seed,
Put avacado on my face, money saved, no disgrace.
From old wine bottles I made lamps,
The only things I buy are stamps.
If I could figure an out for that,
I'd have living free down really pat.
I made cigar box jewel cases,
decoupaged one to hold shoelaces,
Made my yuletide decorations,
Stayed at home, no vacations.
Now I send my Christmas greetings
In envelopes from my retrievings.
When you read them save the paper,
Send it back, I'll use it later.
Well, here's the holiday once more,
Money-wise I'm mighty poor,
I eat beans instead of weiners,
'Cause inflation took me to the cleaners.

C. L. Gardner
SOME ONE LIKE YOU
I need some one like you
To make my every wish come true
We could be together for a life time
If only you say you'll be mine
I always wanted you so madly
To you I will give all my love gladly
You and I could see life through
I need some one like you
Darling, when ever I am near you
I forget the things I had planned to do
Time seems to go by so fast
Yet hoping you will be mine at last
I need some one like you
To make my every wish come true
We could be together for a life time
If only you say you'll be mine
I need some one like you

Linda A. Hamilton
LORD, I HAVE A FRIEND
Lord, I have a friend,
A special friend indeed.
She is one in o'er a million,
With her love You've filled a need.
Whene'er she is disheartened,
I say a prayer to You,
To resolve the situation,
With the mighty things You do.
There is nothing You can't handle,
No situation You can't repair.
Yet You've brought this for a purpose,

Tho' the answer is not yet clear.
Give her strength and understanding.
Bring Your love to ease the hurts.
Build her confidence and wisdom.
Let her know that she won't burst.
Make her know You bring out goodness
If she waits with patient care.
And You'll answer all our prayers
With the Grace You've let us share.

Reba L. Smith

FLOATING LILLY PAD

I saw a floating lilly pad
Come floating down the stream
If I could lie upon it
And dream a little dream
I'd dream about the coming year
And what all we have to face
Then perchance all our troubles
Would fall right into place
While floating on that lilly pad
I'd feel the sunny breeze
Then I'd look around me
And see the beauty of the trees
Beauty is in the beholder
It's there for you and I
So come join me on my lilly pad
As I come floating by
We'd make a wish for all the world
That no one feel lonely or sad
Wish them the happiest New Year ever
While floating on our lilly pad

Mary Tanco

CHRISTMAS

Christmas is a special time of year,
There is a cause for celebration.
It's the birth of our Lord and Saviour,
And a time for much meditation.
During the season of Advent,
As we prepare for his birth.
We joyfully wait for the event,
That will save the earth.
He was born to set us free,
From the human bondage days.
That means, that you and me,
Will have a chance to change our ways.
When that great day comes along,
All the earth will rejoice.
Singing a brand new song,
As if, with only, one voice.
So, as you sit at Christmas Dinner,
And see all the presents 'round.
Remember, that Jesus is the winner,
As you are heaven bound.

Imogene Puckett

A PRAYER

O God this night
there lies in silence
and stillness and darkness
in the Earth's core
a priceless treasure.
Would You sometime in Ages
hence let a small blue-eyed
toddler in white rompers
embroidered with three teddy-bears
hold his mother's hand?

Jani Gallagher

UNTITLED

why do they write poems
without punctuation
and capitals
and sense
starting new lines in the middle of
a sentence or a com
pound word
some lines are long and may run on like a paragraph as if they belonged in the middle of a novel or a short story and others may be
short
poems longer than they need be
full of
defining abstractions
appeasing turbulence
disordered
irregular
disarrayed
deranged
confusedchaoticjumbled
disjo inted
repetitious senselessness
telling about
hyacinths and biscuits
ignorance and winter sport
last light and first death
whatever happened
to brownings order
to drydens literality
to donnes expertise
i guess its all gone
the way of the
world

Colleen Bitner

TEARS

When we are burdened and tears begin to fall. . .
Be not ashamed nor brush them away
God understands, it's His way of washing our soul.
Let those burdened tears fall—
He's right there holding your hand.
Cry till there are no more tears to be let out.
Someday all tears will be wiped away but for now. . .
Smile—let them fall—God understands.
He's just washing our soul!

Lillian Wood Crenshaw

JOYOUS DOMINION

Oh, the joy that we feel when we know only the real,
that good is all the Father gives.
As this truth we know, joy will flourish and grow;
for in us the Christ lives.
That God gives only good is now understood,
for the Saviour has made this clear.
As we pray and believe, we surely receive;
for the Father's good help will appear.
Where there seems to be woe, we can surely know
that Truth triumphs over mortal opinion.
Through understanding of God, which lifts our thought above the sod,
over all things we have dominion.
Through Angel-thought divine, we even have dominion over time;
we have all the inspiration that we need.
We complete work with vim, giving praises unto Him,
as from time's limitations we are freed!

Janet Marie

WIND FANTASY

Whirling and swirling it hides in the haze,
Dust a grayin' the plain's maze.
Wailing while sailing toward mountains barren,
Finding shelter in a cave never carin'.
Silent mingling with early morn mist,
Drifting into grasslands ne'er to be missed.
Then driving and lashing rain

like sheets,
Seeking, wanting, as the woodland it meets.
Shattering leaves and crashing trees,
As down the pathway it weaves.
The search and worry ends in a clearing;
Here is peace and quiet just for the hearing.
Leaves do whisper and branches do creak
"Here I rest", the wind doth speak.

Debbie Hess

I LONG TO BE LOVED

I long to be loved
Just like a flower,
Or a little girl of three;
I long to be loved
With the simple knowledge,
Of someone wanting to love me;
I long for the touch
Of a gentle hand,
Brushing along my cheek;
I long for the touch
Of a gentle man,
One who leaves me unable to speak;
I long to be loved
But just for awhile,
Then I must be on my way;
I long to be loved
But my heart won't be still,
It lingers, then goes astray.

John E. Meeter

DUSK IN LATE SEPTEMBER

It's not even eight o'clock.
But it's already getting dark.
It's not yet the end of September.
But the cottonwoods are almost bare.
The world is still, the lake placid.
I look at the lone flicker, motionless,
In the almost leafless cottonwood trees.
A lone motorboat breaks the silence,
I wave at the yellow-sweatered people
I can barely distinguish in the
Deepening darkness. They're gone,
All that is left is the mind-picture
And the little waves washing ashore.
So it is with summer, its life and laughter.
There's silence where only weeks ago
There was the gladness of children's voices.
So also there's a stillness in my life,
The leaflessness of cottonwoods in autumn,
The waving of a few not recognized passersby,
The cadence and loveliness of little waves
Moving softly and smoothly toward the shore.

Robert A. Meredith

TO BE NEAR YOU

I could make love to the world
and still be more satisfied by just
being in your arms.
I could make the world laugh
for a year
and still be happier to see a small twinkle
in your eye for just a moment.
I could cause unhappiness for
countless millions
and still be more hurt by the sight of one small tear
that you shed in pain.
I could scold my God
and still be more fearful of your wrath
if I were to scold you.
I could live even if the entire
human race were to
turn on me. . .as long as
you were on my side. . .
but if you turn. . .
I would die.

Georgeann C. Tomicich

I WONDER

I wonder if rivers cry for the fish that come no more
I wonder if our mother, the sea, aches for a clean, white shore.
Do the clouds cry for the forests turned into towns,
Are the boulders weeping because they're painted like clowns?
I wonder if the animals roam from place to place
Looking thru bars at a little child's face.
Aching for what should have been
But will not be again because of man's sin.
I wonder if the day will arrive when nothing on earth is left alive,
I wonder, and the thought is sad, if humanity's epitaph shall read "If only we'd known what we had."

Jeanette Strachan
THE DROPOUT
When I was sixteen I thought it was neat
To drop out of school and hang out in the street
Of course at first I had a wonderful time
Going to the park and watchng the mimes
I went to the museum and walked down the hall
I even saw a picture of the Queen's famous ball
And on the days that it happened to rain
I would sit back, relax and stay on the train
After a while it got to be such a bore
That I went and knocked on my best friend's door
I said come on Barbara and play hookey from school
We can do lots of things even go to the zoo
She stood at the door and looked me up and down
Then all of a sudden she started to frown
She said Jeanette don't be such a fool
I want my education, I'm going to school
I said go ahead and do your arithmetic
I'm going outside and have me some kicks
That is when I first started to drink

Because when I drank I didn't have to think
Barbara graduated just the other day
Her life is fulfilled, she's so happy and gay
She searched until she found just the right job
And I hear she's in love with this new guy named Bob
As I sit on the curb with bottle in hand
I think of what a stupid fool I am
Instead of going to school and getting something done
I'm sitting in the street just like any old bum

Hazel Margaret—Rose Lessey
NATURE'S FANCY AND MINE
As the sun slowly awakens from its nightly slumber,
And the stars have lost their glow
From want of night's dark velvety sky,
And the dew drops kiss
Most gently the leaves. . . . .
So does my love my lips.
And I must awaken to day's dawn.
Just as crisp and fresh is the morning air,
And the heavens are filled with the sun's early rays,
Peeping out from the blankety haze
To welcome morning's majestic radiance,
So does my love yours.
I welcome you to my arms.
The birds chirp joyously on the branch
Heralding such boundless beauty
To the morning's majestic reign,
And joy and happiness fills the morning.
So does your love fill my heart.
And yet transcends all. . . .

Stephanie Allen
PEACE
When night befalls Francisco,
The albatross does sing,
From breaker to another;
A lyric spread by wing.
My soul is in Francisco,
Lurking in a song,
The prophet sings serenity,
I am where I belong.

Dorothy Surber
ROBIN
When little Robin Redbreast
has thoughts of building a nest
Summer is nearing very soon
and many other birds have room
to build their's too
All summer long they have fun
flying about in the sun
They fly about from morn to night
to gather every worm in sight
to feed their young
They teach their young one's to fly
so they can take off to the sky
In the spring of the following year
you can see each day appear
another Robin

Harvey Alan Sperry
THE NEW LIFE
A man passed by my life one day,
a child born of crisis.
Frightened as a canine stray,
fear his deadly nemesis.
Heart felt love shared with neighbor,
though oft denied and misunderstood.
Life assigned to Devotion's labor;
granting roses, poems and deeds of good.
He sought love in all its splender,
anger his taunter where ever he roamed.
Fear lurked before him demanding surrender,
tightening the noose until his spirit groaned.
Unfaltering faith provided a shield,
deflecting Terror's deadly siege:
Fragile dwelling refusing to yield,
protected as those of worldly prestige.
The world held no desire for him:
This perverted realm of many gods
who reign awhile then fade a passing whim.
Yet, his beauty thrived despite the odds.
He had a certain charm from another time;
an age of peace that lives within a fantasy;
a dream bestowed with life in cherished rhyme;
a life this man dared to live for all to see.
A man passed by my life one day.
The man was I when he sauntered on.
The life I was became a castaway,
never to see me pass again, for it was gone.

Johnaye Walker
PRECIOUS MOMENTS
JOY we share
ALWAYS being there
MEETING and KISSING
EMPTY moments missing
SHARING warmly repairing
ENVELOPING-caring
DEEPEST affection
WITHIN protection
ALWAYS fondly
RESPECTFULLY, SINCERELY
DEEP close TIES
GOODNESS which lies
EVER so close
RESPECTIVELY warmth
DESIRING to touch
EMPTYING as ever ready
SURELY LOVINGLY.

Janet M. George
WISDOM
We pass this way but once in life.
Each moment that we live --
we live but once.
For even if we approach
that same moment once again-
that same thought-
that same love-
that same insight-
that same understanding-
We are changed,
as is the moment itself.
For in each moment
we grow,
And in each growing,
we change the moment.

Ernest Oliver Burrows
OREGON
Land of timber and wheat
Without sham or conceit
Life is good on Pacifica's slope.
There are trout in each stream
Many hot springs that steam
Countless deer, elk and antelope.
Where the mountains are so high
The moon can just slide by
And Columbia rolls ever on.
There are broncos to bust,
There are good friends to trust
In the great state of Oregon.

Kathleen Pemberton
LOVING
Loving is sharing
The joy and the strife
It's caring, yet letting
You live your own life.
Allowing you choices,
Accepting mistakes,
Aware of your struggle
Yet never forsakes.
You always maintain
Your direction and goal,
It's touching hands,
Holding hearts,
Loving is helping
Someone grow whole.

Marisha
ALEXIS, MY LOVE
Your eyes
search me
touch me,
feel me
They sear through me,
touch my
soul, my
feelings
They undress me slowly,
piece by piece
They watch me
shiver,
cover-up,
relax
They find my
void
And know how to
fill it

Carolyn Middleton Koch
UNTITLED
I'm re-reading your letters again dear today
As I have over so many years.
The words, I love you and I always will
I struggle to read through my tears.
The pages are worn and yellow with age
The hands that hold them are too,
But for one magic moment the clock has turned back
And I am here sitting with you.

Charles E. Hill
THE THINGS YOU ARE
The sun that brightens the noon day sky,
the grass that glistens in the dew,
are just two reasons that tell me why,
life would be empty without you.
A life that's full and free and wild,
and ever so lucid as a star,
yet tender and soft as a Mother and child,
a gift of God is what you are.
The memories that my mind possesses,
the feeling of your hand in mine,
revive the flames of your caresses,
a taste unrivaled by finest wine.
The weeping limbs of a slender willow,
like the branch of a timorous pine,
the look of your face upon my pillow,
like an artist picture and a poet's line.

While I lie here awake, resting from the day,
reminiscing of a love thats like a dream,
I can hear the clock passing time away,
but our love runs deep, like reflections in a stream.

A. Jonathan Webb
LAZULI DEEP
Lay back and watch the clouds
Slipping down the stream,
Fly up and catch a dream
Dancing round and round.
Take your dream and let it be
A dream of flying free,
Of the sky and things to be-
A dream to you from me.
Make a wish and feel the earth
Spinning down beneath you,
Love the touch of sunwarm skin
And taste the sunshine laughter.
Take the hours and the days
Collapsing on the beach
Like waves of glass
Shattering on the shore
Sending rainbow shards
Up out of reach-
Irretrievable in the sparkle sky
Becoming starfires way up high.
Bring warm flames from your heart
Come with me,
The haze will part,
To a land of love and understanding
Where we can laugh
And we can cry
And let the world go screaming by.

Allison Bocksruker
SWIFT—WINGED DARKNESS
Swift-winged darkness devouring my mind
Eyes of the Night-Master all I can find
Unicorn moonlight and blackness of space
Floating in nothing, the Night-Master's face
Words of destruction and words of rebirth
The father is sky and the mother is earth
World-names are ugly - Earth, Jupiter, Mars
But names like Atlantis are songs of the stars
Atlantis - Atlanta, three apples of doom
A tapestry woven on Fate's ancient loom

Susan P. Glodas
WORDS UNSPOKEN
(For: Diane)
I've wanted so much to know you
And to see you deep inside.
I've tried to look beyond
To where the real Diane may hide.
I've felt your love and kindness
And those deep hurts you have inside.
I could almost see those tears
That you've so often cried.
I've seen a warm and gentle friend
Who so often met a need.
I've seen your thoughtfulness and understanding,
Christ lives in you, indeed.
I've often prayed that we may share
A friendship deep and true.
Because when I've thought of love
I've thought of someone special like you.
I've probably never said it
Or showed it in any way,
But I truly love you
In a very special way..

Uleta Hawthorne
REFLECTIONS
I dreamed of words age carved upon the wall,
and passed them by without a second glance.
I laughed and thought they mattered not at all,
until the owl awoke my second chance.
These words have struck the ashes of my soul,
and made me walk once more upon my knees.
In them I hear the bells of angels toll,
and feel the stormy lashing of the seas.
While I build castles in the fragile sand,
and walk alone along the empty shore,
I shut my eyes and touch your lingering hand,
though you are gone from me forevermore.
I feel the echo of your love in me,
as the words upon the wall I plainly see.

Eva O. Avery
GOD'S LOVE
Tis said that Love
Makes the world go round
But Love that is sought
Is seldom found
Unless it's GODS Love.
E'en then we must be
the sort that would
draw close to thee,
To fully share
The bounteous blessings
in your care.
Love is giving
Then from the source of Love
Comes an endless supply
For true love must on HIM rely
No doubt nor fear
Should e'er come near
To Loves happiness,
For it must wholesome be
And malice free.
Love covers a multitude of sin
And builds a person up
Let us show in word and deed
The Love GOD gave us in our need.

Cheryl E. Wright
UNTITLED
My friend is:
a companion for the Soul,
a guide to light the ways of searching,
a restful calm amid my failings.
My friend:
may challenge me to greater strength,
may speak the truth to my deaf ears,
may rebuke me with silence.
My friend:
touches me that I may feel,
looks at me that I may see,
hears me that I may speak.
My friend:
is my mirror.
is a precious gift.
is constant sharing.
My friend is you.
I love you, my Friend.

George Crapps
HUMAN INSECT
Remember the summers
we worked Daddy's pine forests
spraying beetle-infested slash
with BHC and diesel.
When the wind shifted
unexpectedly
the chemical mist
dampened our faces
with liquid fire.
As we ran to the pickup
for rags and water,
you swore you'd never
work with chemicals again.
When the Government
sent you to Vietnam,
they sprayed you
(the human insect)
with Agent Orange.
There was no place to run there.
You breathed the chemical.
It settled on your skin,
mixed with your blood,
became a deadly
permanent part of you.
Too bad that you
unlike the beetles of our youth
weren't killed quickly.
Agent Orange is heartless,
a slow killer,
destroying only
a small part of you each day.
The process could take years.

Cindy L. Alston
LITTLE GIRLS
To: Selina and Lora Rogers
Daughters are lovely and precious to have.
They make you happy and sometimes they make you sad.
When they are tiny, you hold them so close to you, it makes you feel wonderful and sometimes very blue, knowing someday they will grow up and eventually leave you.
Watching them grow from babies to young ladies.
Not knowing where time has gone, now you know the meaning of "Time Has Flown."
They go to their Daddy and ask for money, and he always says, "sure, Honey" -
Can I borrow the car? Where's the keys?
I know, Daddy, always say "please."
They grow up thinking Daddy's the best man in the world to them.
But now, Daddy is second in line to him.
Another man in her life, he knew it would come, but it's hard to take for some.
Daddy's heart is shattered, but he always seems to pick up the pieces that aren't scattered.
But what about Mom through the growing up of problems and fears.
Mom seems to shed a few tears.
From baby blankets and lacy clothes to skin tight jeans - Heaven knows.
I always tell them growing up is not shameful, but growing for little girls is very painful.
I've made my mistakes - God knows -, but through my daughters I hope my goodness shows.
Now, as I look back and see, my Mom was doing the best for me.

Christine Y. Chadwick
A SHELL'S MESSAGE
Along the beach I glance at the rocks,
And stooping, discover a shell
That's pearl-like, and rose-like in color,
And built, as the Maker, alone, does build!
With lines symetrically fragile
Like angels' wings, I see
Loosened from its prison of limestone
A shell—its spirit set free!
Thankfully, I clasp it—a symbol
Of what He means me to teach—
That knowledge is shell-bound in structure;
Its spirit must wander free!

Judy Siekerk
TO A FRIEND
Five reasonings I have
Though one alone suffices:
To be loved for one's self,
One's pretty, often nursery-like
Babblings, Brawlings, Big Deals.
Yet you realize the strength
Within awaiting promptings
(Often not given,
Rarely pursued)
When offered,
Total undreamed-of-realizations;
Goals - never to be sought -
Already conquerable.
I am a woman
And what this means
You make clear for me
Not by words (talk is cheap)
Nor alms (love is free -
We pay dearly)
Five reasonings and more have I
Yet they are of no advantage,
No concern are they;
One alone is joy to me:
You are
Here
Always
Not far (you are)
You (that is all)

Leona Eickelschulte
FANTASIES DREAMED
Soft beautiful music,
people sitting quietly,
some in wonder- thinking deep thoughts, going thru my head a beautiful ocean, waves coming into shore, crashng on the beach. Fingers of white trying to hold on to the sand, but sliding back into the water.
Swallowed up- but trying again and again. Getting closer each time, and I wonder, as I try to reach out to them, will we ever be able to hold on to each other- my fingers are cold, as I feel the water wash over them, leaving them cool and refreshed.

I watch the waves take them out to sea and see them come sailing proudly back, saying catch me if you can. You can almost see them laughing as they disappear again and again. And I watch until the sun sets, my mind at ease.
Beautiful music!! A lovely day.

Annette S. Crouch
THE ANSWER
in all the confusion
i started to cry
but i have found
that crying
is not
the answer
in all the confusion
i started to run
but i have found
that running
is not
the answer
in all the confusion
i started to *die*
but i have found
that dying
is not
the answer
in all the confusion
He came to me
and I have found
that He
is
the answer

Alma "Ollie" West
DIVORCE
For oh-so-long I was with you -
How close we grew to be!
There's funny things and serious things -
Recalled by mem-o-rie.
There's happy days and sad ones too -
But the good ore'rules the bad,
For the sweetest moments of my life
Were those we two have had.
Since fate has led us separate ways -
You've chosen yours but mine,
Is just as time would have it be;
All tangled, like a vine.
Alone I guard my memories.
Tis not an easy game,
To once have won then put aside -
My right to use your name.

Brenda Anne Megna
WHEN I THINK OF YOU
When I think of you I am happy.
I think of the warm moments we two have shared.
The cozy, silent evenings, and the laughs that we had over secrets no one will ever learn.
The wine we drank, the movies we watched.
Just being by your side.
When I think of you I am sad.
The times you were late and made me wait all alone in the dark shadows of the evening.
The days you failed to call and the time you forgot my birthday.
And the day we almost stopped loving each other.
When I think of you I feel secure and very hopeful,
Because you make me aware of life and of love.
The good times made us close but the hard times made the bond between us stronger.
When I think of you I am sure I'm the luckiest person in this world
I love you not only for who you are and what you are;
I love you for what I am when I think of you.

Sharon Chegini
A GROWTH OF LOVE
Where there are no roots
there are no seeds
Where there are no seeds
there is no growth
Where there is no growth
there is no life
Where there is no life
there is no laughter
Where there is no laughter
there are no sounds
Where there are no sounds
there are no words
Where there are no words
there is no understanding
Where there is no
understanding
there is no love

Blanche Marie Atwood
WAKE UP AMERICA
Wake up America - Don't believe the Enemy,
Don't be too generous - Don't be too friendly.
They speak about peace, but they don't tell the truth,
They are fierce enemies - In them is no truth.
For pennies from Asia with feigned kindly smile
Some Judas pours poison into your wine.
Though they talk about peace, their mark is bomb and pistol,
Don't believe what they say - Their aim is your capitol,
Their speech insincere, their saccharine words a vice,
Wake up America - Save your history,
Again be our hope, be great in victory!

Mary June Butler
MY DAUGHTER KATHY
Every mother should have a daughter
Who's as fine a mother as you,
As you raise your girls so very well
With a faith that is tried and true.
You're the very mother I'd love to have been
All the years you were growing up,
But you turned out so well tho' I had to work
That my pride overflows the cup.
And makes me look with a lot of love
At you and the family you've built,
The beautiful granddaughters you've given me
That give my heart such a lilt.
With songs and happy thoughts galore
That how could I ever feel blue?
I'll just say I love the family very much,
Colleen, Michele, Dennis and YOU !

Pat Christian Barry
RETRIBUTION
I long to see my people who are gone
But yet I know they are still with me
Intuned with earth in reverent song.
Listen. . .and they shall tell thee
Of earth's movement into spiritual callousness,
Of countless battles lost and won.
Why do you turn away with anxious dread,
Does this song surround your heart with pain?
Lift up your eyes and behold the morn
For we are within the realm of happy grace.

Paul Shapshak, Ph.D.
FIELDS
(Dedicated to Senator Robert F. Kennedy)
It is the age of flowers and trees,
Homes out of sight from wheat fields.
Turning about in Autumn, thinking through, again,
The origin of the year.
All along meadows, streams bubble out of sight from neighbors.
Nature is with us and sings catastrophe out of mind,
Beyond the edge of loss.
Nightingales sing of fire and the ocean,
The river's edge of night, Washington's crossing,
Lighting it all the way until dawn.
Walking nearby, catch the glimmer left to help
The family seeker. We are not the forest dweller
Who watches the sun, forgetting the greedy tiger
Stalking the Id of the bicameral mind.
Dag says we are not the charioteer who discerns
The Universal Lake at the edge of his road.
Unspeaking faces search out the Truth
To establish it for a time.
Cross the barriers, it's time to follow
Escaping comets, to live where new planets coast
Invisibly in Galaxies far from the heralding cry.

Georgia Ray
MY HUSBAND
Through all the hurt and sadness we've shared, I could never show the love I feel, and now I write the things that touch isn't enough of what I feel.
God put us together and for a time I could not see, the wonderful life we'd have once we'd be set free, free to be honest and face who we are, free to love each other and set our hearts free.
God guide me I pray to show this man I love, kindness has it's rewards, he chose me to be his wife and never shall I shame him nor make him feel alone, because with his love I no longer hate the world, it's no longer a struggle to survive. My wonderful husband please understand, I never feel alone, and thank-you love for all your love, and thank the good lord above, for without my God's guidance I would have never known, the greatest man I've ever known, My Husband.

Wilma Jacobs
FOUR SEASONS
Baseball training.
A lot of raining.
Tulips, and the smell of crocuses in the air.
I see that first robin, as I look out of my window and stare.
IT'S SPRING.
Picnics.
Roses in bloom.
They'll look pretty in a vase in your living room.
Children playing, having fun,
Full of energy, as they hop, skip, and run.
Vacations, people going everywhere.
It's getting quite expensive,
But I guess they don't care.

IT'S SUMMER.
Football games.
Leaves on the trees turning
yellow and red.
When they fall on the ground,
It's something most of us dread.
Children knocking at our door,
In their costume and mask.
"Trick or Treat" is the question,
You're sure to get asked.
Thanksgiving.
IT'S FALL.
Snowmobiles.
Blizzards, icicles, and lots of
snow too.
Some people would rather stay
indoors.
How about you?
Bluebirds, and blackbirds, and
cardinals to feed.
They'll come in your yard, if
you give them some seed.
It's Christmas, and presents, for
you and for me.
Ring out the old year, and a
new year you'll see.
IT'S WINTER.

Dee Tatum England

NO MORE NUMBER 9 DREAMS

Lurking in the bushes, a mean
little man, with evil on his
mind.
He shot you down in a flash.
Affecting the peace of mankind.
Bang, Bang, Then Yoko ran
screaming and crying.
As John crawled up the steps of
the Dakota, bleeding and dying.
Lurking in the shadows that
cool December night.
The end, your future looked so
bright.
Sirens sounded, people crowded.
Who, is that man on the ground?
Help me! I'm shot.
Are you John Lennon? Yeah!
After that, there wasn't a sound.
Its just not fair whats happened
to John, its not.
John is gone, it sheds a shadow
over Rock an Roll.
At last you've found your peace.
God rest your soul.

Judi E. Frost

LIFE AFTER 40

Forty years have come and gone
and life gets better yet,
If you have time to pause and
chat, we'll speak of this and
that.
Like the day my husband
presented to me some roller
skates for my feet,
And later that year, a tricycle
appeared to carry me up the
street,
With a basket to carry my
shopping things while the
wind blows thru my hair.
So we skate awhile, then ride
awhile, then stroll from here
to there.
We work in the yard side by
side, the tasks we always
share,
Eighty percent of the work for
him and twenty for me seems
fair.
All this great outdoor exercise is
designed to make me feel new,
But I get a little help from Oil
of Olay and a vitamin E or
two.

Laurence RoseTar

A JOURNEY

Pearl colours were dawned the
radius,
a hill where my heart with
pretty fragrances did ooze;
surged ten then the fountains of
my nectarial soul;
pure too, as the ligthings- have
come a giant memory,
across the vastnesses stepped I
in constance,
of lives un-relivable ago,
to unseen eyes of higher-mind,
lit brighter love;
wedded to the half-beast that
fakes being conscious of
nosegays;
drifts so to sink in a black hill
mire;
scarlets show these from my
soul,
night-muds the tides blue have
surged;
sleep I away could I wish
this nemesis of cosmic gravities
gone,
then in flights gospel cease I
tarry;
then away to climes of
rosemaries,
far, deep, contents strange,
to stranger roads!

Francis Bess Harrison

PERSUADE ME

If you have to say I'm wrong,
please state it very politely.
And with patience show me
how
that I may do it rightly.
If you care about me fondly
and my tears you call
unsightly,
Could you make your actions
daily
show you care for me
devoutly?
Sweep away the clouds of doubt,
be my sun that shines so
brightly.
Let your arms my safe haven be
as they surround me ever
tightly.
If we have a chance to choose
and we decide quite
differently,
Persuade me to your line of
thought
but do it ever so delicately.
If I then submit to your decree
and I do it very sweetly,
When I should happen to
disagree
will you treat me tenderly?
The same ideas we do not have
though life we share
completely.
So shall it always be your views
that we must follow
absolutely?

Kitty K. Stone

I LOST MY LOVE

I lost my love
And he lost me.
And now the two of us are free,
To wander through this world
apart,
And try to mend to each his
heart.
By bluffing, praying
And despair,
To defiantly re-capture what
once was there.
By hook, by crook,
By any means,
To breathe full life back in our
veins;
And live a useful, loving life
With another husband; wife.
To make the past
A passing dream
That was never really what it
seemed.
But each of us knows
Beyond a doubt,
That hurt remains, within--
without.
Regret and guilt go hand and
hand
As alone we travel through this
land.
We'll not escape the mournful
cry;
We'll feel this pain until we die.

Elizabeth Alexander

A NATION FOR PEACE

Is the world a nation?
Or is the world all for
segregation?
We depend on determination,
But we fight for integration.
The beauty of the world is you!
For we look for the Lord to see
us through.
We look for the walls to open
and close,
But all we get is a feeling of
hows.
Is the world all for itself?
Or is it all that is left?
We depend on the world for
many things,
But we have to look for other
rings.
I look around each day,
But I seek to find another way;
Because the days are growing
shorter;
We are not getting any farther.
You'll find it's getting weaker
and weaker.
And we're going under deeper
and deeper.
I can't find a solution.
It looks as though it's going to
be a revolution.
Don't take the world for granted,
For we will only find ourselves
stranded.
The beginning is gone;
But our ending is wrong.
We started as a child,
But we are only here awhile.

L. V. "Pooly" Harp

DO YOU REMEMBER MARCH 21, 1936

We were wed on a beautiful first
day of spring.
We solicited no concession,
We didn't have a single thing
But our love and the depression.
We launched our little fragile
boat
Upon life's stormy seas,
Sometime it almost ceased to
float
For nothing came with ease.
We took each blow the fates
could throw
And found a peaceful shore,
With firmer ground where we
could grow
To love each other more.
I pray we'll be together
When we reach that pearly gate,
Where there's no more stormy
weather
For me and my lovely Mate.

James W. Faucette

FOR THE YOUNG

Seek your pleasure in
wholesome things
And let the foolish go their
ways
Then your companions will
be kings
And the reward your wisdom
brings
Will make you glad throughout
your days.
Set your goals when you
are young
And plan with care the way
you'll go.
Life's a song that's to be
sung
And there'll be happiness
among
Those who reap where others
sow.

Kimberly Diane Almond

POETRY

Poetry is words in motion;
The pen is your escape route.

Rose Marie Phillips

MAKE MY COUNTRY CHRISTAN AGAIN

Dear One who created me,
Dear One who set me free,
As on my knees I pray,
I ask a special blessing today.
Make my country Christan
again,
We're drawing nearer to the
end.
Please Lord, my friend,
Make my country Christan
again.
Many of my brothers have
turned to crime,
Many have wasted a whole life-
time,
Seeking pleasure and fame,
Others in vain have taken Thy
name.
Please Lord, my friend,
Make my country Christan
again.
Your blessings please extend,
So our ways we can mend.
Many no longer believe in You
Others are just too busy to,
But if your power you would
exert
Your fold again you could
convert.
I ask a special blessing today
As on my knees I pray,
Please Lord, my friend,
Make my country Christan
again.

Ann L. Browning
RAINBOW ROUND GOD'S THRONE.

An ancient world
Corrupt and evil
Noahs warning
Scorned to heed-
but only the
Arks voyagers
A rainbow of
Wondrous beauty see.
This modern world
Seems drifting
Ignoring God's
Judgement to come-
But only those
Who receive Jesus
Will see the
Rainbow round God's throne.

Pamela Marie Schwede
LIVING LIFE DAY BY DAY

Living life day by day;
how everything just keeps running on it's way.
Making memories; some hard to express,
Wanting to free the bad ones; but trying to hold on to the rest.
Finding the answers to stories untold;
Seeing how easily everything unfolds.
Trying to reach out but still keeping the pace;
How things just keep getting harder to face.
Rushing the hands of time; only to find you've just passed them by.
Then seeing yourself searching for the chance to try;
One last time ...

Andrea Noel
FEAR

The wind flows through the
branches of any tree that is
near,
It whispers and screeches
at the coming of fear.
It knows when it's coming
for your heart tells it so,
so look away I beseech
you for it already knows.
The owl looks wisely
and turns away,
For the coming of fear
is on it's way.
It can tell you see
for your heart beats wild,
And cries through the air
like a frightened child.
So listen to my words
and don't let it in,
For it could destroy you
and you might meet your end.

Phillis K. Frazier
PARADISE COVE
(Dedicated to R.A.F.)

In primitive antiquity
far away from modern mode,
in a glen beneath a willow tree
the raging river flowed.
We sat there in the water-fall
sharing thoughts and feeling
free, then scaled the rocky
canyon wall; defied the river in
it's wake, and gazed there-at the
visions cast upon the mirrored
lake.
The small stream falls upon the
rocks to feed a greater flow and
nurture barren desert chalk then
at the seaside slows.
Now can it be reality that
freedom somehow fosters love,
or is it just a fantasy inspired by
Paradise Cove?

Ruth E. Yates
IF I LIVE ANOTHER LIFE

I might be passing through the worlds, and visiting the earth.
I might have lived a hundred lives, before my so called birth.
My visit here might be so short, perhaps some eighty years,
Before I'll have to move along, to other distant spheres.
I might not have another chance, to pass this way again;
So let me know the richest joys, that move the hearts of men.
I want to learn what life is worth, and how to conquer strife,
So I might take this wisdom on, if I live another life.

Patricia McCartney Fox
CHILD

My child blossoms in spring
Awakening in chilly morns but gentle dawns
I feel her spirit begin to sing
Begging freedom from my response.
Oh child, I long and fear to set you free
To flit in laughter amongst the grass
And newborn flowers yet to be.
For you can run, where I have feared to pass.

Marianne Seibert
SNOWDANCE

Today the snow clings to my hair
The sun shines in my face.
Diamonds cover every weed
The skis dance on my feet.
It's wonderful to own the hills
To speed down to the vale.
To hear the rushing of the wind
And feeling poetry.
I am the wind, I am the snow!
The skis are part of me.
I am committed to the course
And to the splendor on my feet.

Amie Trout
SUCCESS

Success!
What or Why -
Yours or Mine -
I can't
Be You
Nor You
Be Me -
Why should
I try?
Me is Me,
Not He
Or Thee.
Me is Me,
I'm rather
Proud.
I don't
Mind being
What I am -
Matter of fact
It goes
Some further -
I'm glad
I'm Me -
I'd be
None other.
Me is Me!
Thank God
For that.
If I've
Learned this
That, then's
SUCCESS!!

Claire Mignon Politsch
CHRISTMAS SONG

Sing a song of Christmas!
Church bells sweet and strong
People come to worship, their voices raised in song:
"O Little Town of Bethlehem", "Upon a Midnight Clear"
And prayers for peace and harmony, throughout the coming year.
Sing a song of Christmas!
Snowflakes in the air,
Girls in pretty dresses, with glitter in their hair;
Boys in bright red sweaters, warm caps upon their heads,
Riding up and down the hills, on their brand new sleds.
Sing a song of Christmas, in a warmer clime—
Pinatas, Las Posadas, and music all the time.
Colored lights in palm trees, fanciful parades,
Salvation Army kettles, unfortunates to aid.
Sing a song of Christmas, in lands across the sea;
Wherever it is celebrated, may it ever be
A time of great rejoicing, "Peace on Earth, Good Will to Men"
To keep the spirit in our hearts, 'til Christmas comes again.

Verna M. Valante
YOU

You are unique!
Whether tough or meek,
There's no one exactly like you.
Why should you try
To be another guy?
You have good qualities too.
Develop each positive trait.
Avoid comparisons; they grate.
"To your own self be true."
Mimics are funny,
As comedians, they rate money,
But a carbon copy is black or blue.
So if you want to succeed,
Make each thought and deed
A product that comes from you.

Halley Gail Held
LIFE'S TIMES

Some days are trying-
for the conflicts and frustrations surpass the dreams.
Some days are cruel-
for only the selfish manage to succeed.
Some days are crippling-
for the shy and humble fall to ruin.
Alas, there are other times.
Days,
When the sun warms the cold air.
When the tides clean the shore's debris.
When the mountains stand tall with pride.
And it is these days that tell us what is most precious-
The warmth of understanding
The cleanliness of peace
and The simple pride in one's being.

Mildred R. Jeffrey
WAITING FOR YOU

I light the candles,
Set in silver holders.
The flames rise high, then settle
They glow with softness.
I stir the embers.
Slumbering on the open hearth.
The flames rise high, then settle
They glow with warmth.
You arrive.
I am like the candles and the embers.
I glow with softness and warmth.
I am LOVE.

Birdie H. Flanakin
A LEGEND RETOLD

In a forest near Bethlehem grew a cedar tree tall and straight,
Its one and only wish was to become a part of a palace great,
But God's plans were made... every single one.
It was to be a manger, a bed for Jesus, God's only Son.
A beautiful birch tree grew near the Sea of Galilee.
The hull of a mighty ship it wanted to be...
It became only a common fishing boat...Jesus was on it one night;
He stilled a storm and kept the vessel afloat.
A dogwood tree near Jerusalem was blooming and standing very high.
Its only wish was to stand up tall and reach toward the sky.
The workmen cut down the dogwood tree and took from its trunk two boards.
They made a cross and 'twas on that cross they crucified my Lord.

Marjorie Brunton Newsom
ON ANDREW WYETH'S PAINTING: THE SEXTON

So...there it yawns, the final, last
dark bed...at which, in past, we
could not, would not, look. The
six-foot Sexton's rough blond
head is barely visible - and raw
piled earth is growing, loosely
shoveled, dank, disturbed...
There waits it for us, after
anxious trials. And who knows
but it will be certain peace - the
long-awaited; after years -
attained ?

Greg Rowden
DREAMS OF ANNETTE
As poison words lead to silence,
And the discerning eye of the peasant
Falls upon the lady fair,
And refulgent night is devoured by the whimpering light,
So, too, my evil thoughts are molded into love
For Sweet Annette.

Joan Bishop
SOUL'S TRUE IMPULSE
I have felt the gamut of emotions
Since the spring was set free.
Someone gently removed the pen
And coaxed my spirit to motion.
I call the force kinetic
Though I know it is expanding love
Which keeps me moving,
And I am leaning
Ever so slightly
That it does not cease.
The notion spares a heartbeat
And I hold my breath
That the delicate balance
Is not disturbed.

Lorra Anne Heutmaker
IF ONLY TO FORGET
If only to forget
the fear of a human voice
to enjoy the majesty of silence.
If only to forget
the reservoirs of the eyes
flowing to delight in the melody
of laughter.
If only to forget
the nervous pounding of
footsteps to the rapture of a
nightingales choir.
If only to forget
the hateful remorse of the
morning passing to bask in the
midday warmth.
If only to forget
the disturbing tranquility of the
evening to slumber into blissful
unconsciousness.
If only to forget
the inevitable cruelty of life to
congenially surrender to the
serenity of death.
If only to forget
allow your eyes to caress the
image of the Lord wrap yourself
in his love, then:
If only to remember........

Billie Catherine Taylor
THE HURT INSIDE
Tears in my eyes, hurt in my heart
My past wouldn't leave, it wouldn't depart.
Chains of the past were pulling me down,
Slowly, but slowly, I sunk to the ground.
I had been hurt, now I wanted to love
After endless searching, I sought God above.
Instead of love, my heart filled with hate,
Something had to be done before it was too late.
I prayed and prayed; I cried and cried
God heard my plea, he dried my eyes.
No more weeping! No more fears!
I think no more about the yesteryears.
Now I can love! I feel so free!
Thank you God for helping me.
I can now look forward to being a wife,
I'll cherish you God for the rest of my life.

Barbara D. Crawford
LITTLE ANGEL
Close by, the little church nestles on the hillside
Where the small orphan child awaits the yuletide
No friends, no family to make this holiday bright,
A sickly old man stumbles into the cold night.
As a wounded animal seeks shelter and warmth,
The man hobbles into the church with mirth.
This is the last season by far
O' shall I see another star?
Will the morning come slowly or quick?
Does the lamp still have a wick?
My heart cries for the past
For my youth, those good times and my love---at last.
O' I see an angel
Such a small, lovely, adoring angel.
Her small hands giving me water and bread
Finding a fluffy little pillow for my head.
Giving her all my earthly treasure
Gladly, I face the hour with pleasure.

David L. Funke
THERE'S MORE TO LIFE THAN MIND
Throughout all of our life's
Patterns and experiences
We were told and taught
What and how to think
But at no time
Were we told and taught
To simply think.
It is no wonder why
There are no earthly beings
Creative enough
To have the imagination
Or intelligence
To obtain the wisdom necessary
To save us
From ourselves.

Carolyn L. Harris
LET HIM KILL IT
I will let him kill it
With each little hurt
It will slowly
But surely die
Why can't he see my pain
I don't want it to die
This love I have for him
But I grow weary of the battle
Fighting to keeping it alive
So I will let it die
Even welcome the end
I will let him kill it

Jacqueline Crowell
SOMETIMES JOY
Sometimes my joy exceeds its bounds and spills out on my face
Or turns its cartwheels inside my chest, until I almost burst.
Then I feel like a little child who, embarrassed, digs a shoe
Into the dust beneath his feet to cover inner glee,
Or covered with the touch of love, like children tipped with jelly:
Upon my face, upon my hands, from my head down to my feet;
As brilliance in the July sun, as soft as baby's breath;
As strong as mountain's rocky roots, as long as evermore;
As beautiful as childhood's grace, as precious as our prayer,
As only that which matters most: love shining on your face.

Mrs. Lesa Chilton Acord
TO MOTHER
You watched after me when I was a baby and very small,
You recorded my growing height upon our kitchen wall,
You've watched over me all the rest of my life,
But still managed to hold down a job and be a good wife.
In times of great joy or when I was very sad,
You've been the most reliable friend I have ever had,
You've always been there when I needed you,
And with a smile or a word, you've made the light shine through.

And when your hair is solid gray,
When the lines in your face just won't go away,
I hope then I can help you with some of your tears,
And pay back the love you've given over the years.
And Mother I would just like you to know,
That where ever I am, or where ever I go,
Your memory and kindness will follow me through,
To say it in a phrase,
"I Love You!"

Victor Affinati
DEA NOVA
I turned my eyes but a little way from you
Love and allowed but a sigh of wind to cool
The warmth of your limbs in mine I was a fool
Love now in the night how will I find you
The closer my steps the farther wide I spin
And when I move not at all seems then I fall
And wonder will I ever see you again
Someone in the night breathes sweet to my senses
While these arms close round a form not new yet strange
Still I stay past forgetting your prayer and change
My airy steps for her abandoned dances
Through the zodiac about Dame Grande's poor fete
By the red gonfalon and Nocturnal One
Along loyal porticos past Holy Gift Gate

Margie Rockensock Stolt
SISTER
You are my sister, this is true.
Then how come I don't look like you?
Your eyes are blue, you are so thin,
No one would take me as your twin!
Altho our minds may work as one,
And yes, we've had alot of fun.
There's times you've made me want to curse,
Remember the sugar in my purse?
Or what about the water fight?
Or building a snowbear late at nite?
Or chasing each other with perfume?
And knocking things over room by room?
And oh, how many tears we've spent,
On things we've said but never meant.
But never once did we forget,
Our fights don't last, at least, not yet!
So Look-a-Likes we'll never be,
But closer friends you'll never see.
If in the future you're a bride,
I'll once again stand at your side.

Betty Gabriel
MY GOSPEL
I preach a gospel of kindness,
So healing in time of need.
A gospel that enriches the giver,
In a world caught up in greed.
It drives out gloom and darkness
It lessens all sorrow and pain.
It gladdens each heart that it touches,
Restoring ones faith again.
Oh, all mankind would be lovers,
If they'd heed my gospel and know
Just how one act of kindness
Could make their life style glow.

Elizabeth Hill
THE GAME OF LIVING
Sometimes we win, sometimes
we lose,
In this great game of living;
But, on the whole, we're apt to
win
The more we think of giving.
Of course we have our own
needs, which
We have to look out for;
And there are some essential
ones

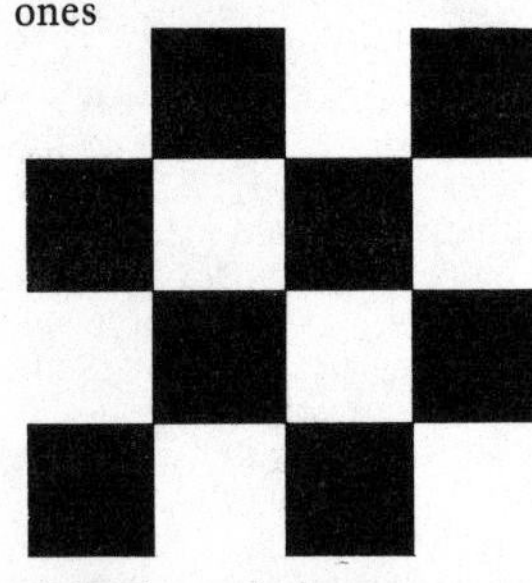

We simply can't ignore.
But making others happy will
Help us to win the game;
For in the end, we will get back
Some good, which is our aim.
Though life can be quite hard,
but if
We make the best of things,
We'll win, as each day comes
along,
No matter what it brings.

Pauline C. Robles
LOVE
Love is the ecstasy of life...
The source of friendship.
Love is...the ultimate
understanding between two
people!
It is communication;
silent language of life
Without words!
Love is...sharing and giving.
It is the Star of Light
that leads...
To a new world!

Geraldine G. Sanchez
THE LOVE GAME
I walked into the breezeless
summer night
The moon casting down its
heavenly light
There was a little road going
into the woods
I strained to see, the best I could
And caught real beauty at last.
The sparkling dew looked like
broken glass
I walked upon the dusty path
I felt so good I had to laugh
Little crickets singing so loud
I wondered what it was all
about!
Walking along
I felt like singing a song
Halfway through
I almost flew
But someone held me in their
capture
firm, strong and very sure.
Frightened, I started crying
Never knew when I quit trying
I woke to the morning light
Couldn't place myself just right
I looked up to see the great big
skies
And looked instead at clear
brown eyes.
A happy face that filled the
beauty of the woods,
All the beauty in my life held no
truths
Such as his
I was in contented bliss
I had to make sure
Of this beauty so pure
I closed my eyes, and opened
them once more
And *he* was there!
We laughed and sang all
through the day
We could never part, no matter
in what way.

Sara Lucas
ELEPHANT'S EYE
How much wisdom
In an elephants eye
Cupped in cavernous folds
Sees the wisdom of today
And centuries untold
Cased in cells fast hold.
Your tusks for
Trinkets, knives and pins
Your feet are stuffed and sold
The story of your wisdom
Is by five wise men told.
But your eye magnificent
creature neither bought nor
sold
Is a most transparent mirror to
your soul.

Tom Hedlund
LOVING AGAIN
I looked on you with such
fondness - such dreams.
New possibilities emerged -
materialized before my eyes as
I sat in awe and wonder of
you.
Daring to think
Daring to touch
Daring to feel
Daring to dream
Daring to live again
Oh we knew and felt it all so
well. This was no first time
romance-
Experienced lovers
Taking chances with each
other.

Richard Morano
WHO DO I ASK?
My head's
Ringing like a bell
'Cause there's no one to tell
An' I don't feel so swell
An', well,
It's just not my day
An' it's not okay
'Cause I got something to say
An' something to ask
An' it's becoming a task
'Cause I'm just a kid
Trying to get rid
Of sex on my mind
An' it's got me in a bind
'Cause someone to ask
Is impossible to find.

Shirley E. Polson
THE MORNING MY GOD SPOKE TO ME
God looked down from his
heavenly throne, saw me
standing all alone.
He smiled, and with out-
stretched hand, gave me peace
and comfort grand.
His eyes just seemed to say to
me. (Bring your troubles here to
me.)
I'll not give you wealth in gold,
but peace of body, mind, and
soul.
In your heart there will never be
fear, precious one I'm always
near.
So when your life on this earth
is through, daughter I will come
for you.
There we'll walk hand in hand---
MY GOD AND I IN THAT
PRECIOUS LAND.

Oliver Bathurst
GOLD FEVER
The year was 'ninety eight
And the freighter loaded freight
It had a motley crew
For it had in its hold
A fortune in gold
And those who had dug it
A few
There was Grubstake Mac
And Long Tom Jack
And Whiskey Ed and
Maybe a crook or two
They'd gambled and fought
For the gold they brought
For this was their fortune too
They'd clumbed Chilkoot
With all their loot
And found after hard won
battle
The load from the mother lode
Destined for the port of Seattle

Curt Sjostrand
THE MAN IN BLACK
Here's the story about a man
who laughs a lot and even sings.
He praises God and with a
passion he tells
of what he loves and what he
believes.
He loves his wife, his son
and his faith in God and man.
From Dyess, Arkansas to
Nashville, Tennessee,
this man has been to hell and
back.
He's been broke, he's popped
pills, and he's been busted
but he is proud to sing of how
he found the way.
His faith in God and man
proves
that love conquers all.
From the wheat fields of Dakota
to the bayous of Louisianna
his love is felt with open hearts.
From the White House in
Washington, D.C.
to the cells of San Quentin
Prison
his voice will be heard
evermore.
So when the curtain ascends
there appears
a tall and noble man with a
guitar and a song
and a story to tell of why he
sings and why he says
"Hello, I'm Johnny Cash".

Eric Gutman
CALIFORNIA SUNSET
Under a flawless blue sky the
sea was calm,
And the Sun was slowly sinking
toward the horizon.
Moving closer to the water
the Sun changed from pale
yellow to red until she was a
beautiful ball of fire balancing
precariously on the edge of the
ocean.
Then, glowing as a piece of
molton iron she dipped into the
water...and was gone.
And now...like the crescendo of
a symphony the sky lit up.
From the horizon to the zenith
the pale blue changed into red,
crimson and pink like the
palette of the painter who gave
us this magnificent piece of art.
For a few minutes the sky was
ablaze.
Then softly this kaleidoscope of
colors faded and the red melted
into pink and the pink into
orange and into white and blue.
Slowly the sky grew darker
the water shimmering like white
lace under the light of the
moon.
Night had conquered the Day.

Robert Keith Tabb
RING OF HOPE
This ring I give to you is filled
with love and hope
Love and hope in an
immeasurable amount
An amount I am unable to
count
It will bring luck and strength
throughout the years
It will keep you from unwanted
tears
It's a ring of strong family ties
Stronger than any in this mans
eyes
If you share this ring with
someone special
Someone special to you
It will bring them luck and
happiness
A family of lovin' too
To our family one and all
I give this ring with prayers so
tall
Don't look at it as a gift from
me
That is something it cannot be
For it's not what it is
But what it can do
This is a ring of love
From this family to you
WE LOVE YOU

Cleo Jent
THE TRAIN OF SECOND THOUGHTS—
Hey! Wha? &!- Somebody flag
this train!
Hey! You there- Oh, well-
Too fast! Chug-chuga-chug-chuga
That's old blood-pressure
pounding the brain-
Or the thumping of that
damaged heart-with pain!
Too late-the throttle's in high
gear-
Ain't nobody c'n get me offa
here!
Done put my name of the
dotted line-
Done told them retirement
would be just fine.
My thoughts railroaded me out
so fast an'clean,
Did'n even have time to dream-
--About the raise they're goin to
get
--About all that hard work an'

swet-
If this train of thought does stop,
I'm getting off here to
recollect-
--About all those years I worked
and planned
To get outa there, an' see the
land-
Not getting up early-or stayin'
late-
An' takin' it easy! GADS!
WHAT A BREAK!
Hey! Who? Get off that track!
Don't stop this train!
You think you're goin' to take
me back?
It's slowin' down--it's goin' to
stop!
Oh, What a shame-!
No..What a thrill!
It's my husband, Bill!
Now we're together, just as
we've planned,
We'll keep trackin' together, to
the promised land!

John Evans

LIFE WAS SIMPLE

Life was simple when I was a
child;
I didn't have to think about
money;
I didn't have to think about
food;
Yes, Life was very simple when I
was a child.
To me it was play time;
I didn't have a care in the world.
It was easy for me to love
everybody;
Life was so simple when I was a
child;
Life was too simple when I was
a child.

Bethany Jean Kissell

STORYBOOK FRIENDS

Storybook friends,
The kind I wish I had.
The kind who are never,
ever bad.
Storybook friends,
Who like me for what I am.
Who will help me out,
If I'm ever in a jam.
Storybook friends,
The kind who understand.
The ones who will never
ever demand.
Storybook friends,
The kind you can trust.
These kind of friends
are a must.
Storybook friends,
Who are always true,
They, who will
believe in you.
Storybook friends,
for whom we all look.
Are the ones who can be
found, only, in a book.

Lori Gabriel

THE EMERALD UTOPIA

I stand at the top of this hill, overlooking the lush country-side, and marvel at the beauty I see;
the pines and oak; the tall grass cascading across the field, jaded here and there by rainbow-colored flowers; the overwhelming sight of sky impregnating the earth at some distant point, unobtainable by the obsessed traveler.
Behind me, a weeping willow reaches out to touch me with a delicate bough, to lay upon my shoulder the hand of nature and hold me captive in this Emerald Utopia.
I surrender to your grandeur and should I grow weary I shall rest upon your blanket of daisies.
I shall feast upon your berries and herbs and cleanse my flesh with your glistening dewdrops.
I shall adorn my hair with ivory blossoms, and ring my fingers with golden buttercups.
You place at the foot of this captive a never-ending bouquet, a reality in a world of dreams.
May there always be sunbeams to warm you and raindrops to nourish you. May there always be eyes cast upon your beauty.
May there always be a captive heart, such as mine, to dwell endlessly in the realness of this magical Emerald Utopia.

Susan Adams

NEEDS

Like the trees and the flowers
need
the rain and the sun.
Like counting numbers
need
zero and one.
Like the sun and the clouds
need
a sky of blue.
Everything needs something
and
My need is you.

John Thomas Serpa

HOLD ME

Smiling
Touching
Kissing
Sensation
Anticipation
Expectation
Whispers
Dreams
Memories
Now and then
Tight and close
Soft and real
Moment of pleasure
Tears of joy
Peace of mind...

Wilnette Morgan

LIFE

Life is what you make of it,
Happy or sad
Life is what you make of it,
The best you've ever had
Life is what you make of it,
Opportunity and chance
Life is what you make of it,
A time to enhance
Life is what you make of it,
No matter where you be
Life is what you make of it,
You live, you learn, you see
Life is what you make of it,
Being joyous or having fun
Life is what you make of it,
A days work well done
No matter what I've made of it,
Come rain or come shine
Regardless to what you think of
it,
This life is mine

Royce Stubblefield

IT FEELS SO RIGHT

It feels so right to be with you and see your priceless smile; when you're away my thoughts are there, beside you all the while.
The spark that shoots across the space, that extends from eye to eye; is supercharged and full of life and just makes the spirit fly.
such a deep and easy feeling, fills me when you're around; immeasureable depth within your eyes, no bottom can be found.
The changes that you've brought in me, as you are passing through; are great - I love them dearly, as they were made by you.

Renee R. Smith-Bivins

THE RIVER

I want to join the river of life.
It's so alone here, here on the
shore alone, watching,
watching, watching.
I want to join the river.
Watching it move.
Feeling it pulsate
Hearing it laugh
I want to join the river of life,
Wanting it to wash over me
Carrying me with it.
Letting me take on it's rhythm
Engulfing, sweeping on toward
the glow
Yes, take me to the river.
Take my hand, begin the
sharing.
Let us give each other the river.

Jean Montroy Heinrichs

WHERE IS TOMORROW?

Tomorrow is never too close to
stay
It is a guess made from today
Whenever we reach for it
Tomorrow is never in reach
Tomorrow is out of sight
Tomorrow will never reach
light.
Yesterday is gone too
It was never really here
Make yesterday our past, yes,
we have
But yesterday was never really
there.
Today is today
But what we see in today
Will never be in our tomorrow.

Ethel M. Burch

DON'T LAUGH AT ME

Don't laugh at me as I totter by
Nor mock me when I pass,
But understand
The way you are now
I once was--
Young, smooth, beautiful,
Straight, thin, tall,
With a sharp eye, a quick
look,
A strong hand, flashing teeth,
A sure step,
The World at my feet.
The way I am now
You will be--
Old, wrinkled, ugly,
Bent, weak, bald,
With a shaky hand, snaggled
teeth,
A dull eye, a slow look,
A faltering step,
The grave at your feet.

Mrs. Mildred L. Geary

ALSO A FRIEND

Son, you are the product of my
fond hopes and dreams
That you climb the upright path
shares my many schemes.
To wish upon you the finer
things of life, amid success;
May you discover one necessary
ingredient -- happiness!
Because you are my Son, my
love stems deep for you,
Which keeps growing with your
age - you always knew!
To protect you from harm daily,
has been my true aim,
Thus - a habit which still
remains basically the same -
Yet I know you must shoulder
your share of sorrows;
With confidence, you shall
observe bright tomorrows.
Others also desire to hear the
joys of which I can sing --
Warmth from a kind heart, as
gently flowing off a harp
string!
Give to the world your laughter,
your humor to share --
Allow them to know how very
much you really do care.
You need to learn, experience,
grow, store, to expand,
Develop, with the flexibility of a
long rubber band.
For you were not created for me
alone, to smother;
Think of me, also as your friend,
not only a Mother!

Pearl R. Briggs

RELAX, MY HEART

Be still, my heart,
and stop your pounding.
The Lord is near
in love abounding.
Ask His guidance,
seek his grace;
He will grant you
strength and peace.
Be calm, my heart,
and cease your pounding.
'Tis only nerves
that are resounding.
Each little fiber's
taut with tension,
Angered or hurt
by human dissension.
So relax, my heart,
and ease that tension.
God's goodness is
of great dimension.
Breathe a prayer,
ask His care;
Your ev'ry burden
He will share.
Then don't forget
a "thank you" prayer.

Teri Neumayer
MISTLETOE
My kisses melting
Into your own, tasting like the
Red and white striped candy-
Canes hanging on our tree.
And before my eyes are the
Twinkling light; blues, reds,
Greens, every color. I never
Knew your kisses could do this
To me.
Or maybe it's the magic of the
Mistletoe that makes every
Taste of you become sweeter
And sweeter.

Nancy B. Love
MY YOUNG DON JUAN
He came my way when I was young,
Instilling in my heart a song;
Though fate decreed our separate ways,
His memory lingers through my days.
His heart was light and dear his smile,
And times with him my thoughts beguile;
Although our love was not to be,
His memory lingers yet with me.
He teased me with his boyish charm
And chased away my doubts and fears;

He held my hand and warmed my heart
And kissed away my girlish tears.
And while we did not speak of love,
We felt within our hearts a glow--
The pull of some magnetic force
That bonded with its ebb and flow.
The years have passed since last we met,
But should our pathways cross again,
That magic charm would be there yet
To warm our hearts with its refrain.

Nellie Martin
A CHILD'S MEMORIES
Will they remember a certain day,
When the beds were left unmade?
The dishes stacked in the kitchen sink,
And the house in disarray?
Will they remember a floor unswept,
Or the ironing piled high?
That these were unimportant things
As we let the hours go by?
Or will they remember the cookies
That they helped me bake that day?
And the dress we made for a special doll,
As we whiled the hours away?
The wheel we fixed on a broken toy,
A favorite book we read,
The good times that we shared all day
'Til I tucked them in their bed.
Will they think about the many things
that we let go undone?
Or will they remember I left it all
To join them in their fun?
What will a child remember?
Lord, help us while they're small,
To give them through the passing years,
Fond memories to recall.

Edith E. Vereshagin
THE CHOIR
An eighty-five voice choir
Did sing to me today;
Except for me alone
No audience had they.
They sang to me of fresh,
Cool airways up above,
They sang of fragrant blooms,
They sang of springtime love.
They sang of blue, blue skies,
Of sun, and moon, and star;
They sang of sunny climes
In southern lands afar.
They sang of thunderstorms,
And gentle rains, and squalls,
They sang of babbling brooks
And crystal waterfalls.
They sang of aspen leaves
A-trembling in the breeze,
They sang of baby birds
And cozy nests in trees.
With bubbling voices sweet
And soft as kitten's purr,
They sang as blackbirds sing --
Indeed, that's what they were!

Cassandra Malone
ME
I'd like to think of myself as me,
With a special place on this earth.
No one to answer to but me,
And a chance to prove my worth.
I'll make my mistakes,
I'll pay my dues;
I've nothing to gain
And nothing to lose.
If by chance I break the rules,
God looks after babes and fools!

Jude Hauenstein
WORDS
Bound by words
so long ago exchanged
Wishing I'd stayed a little girl
cuz woman is demanding pain
Two in a room
has become more empty than one
Dreams are keeping me going
but this travel is insane
I'm scared
We should now be more
Years having left their trace
in the together pictures
that haven't ever hung on our wall cuz you never felt it important enough
Thats where you and I began our fall
Bound by words so long ago exchanged wishing I'd stayed a little girl
In my world of pigtails n' lace
a world void of rust
with no reason to be afraid

Sylvia P. Beres
ALBERTA
The river belly is full this year
The coulees are verdant green
The amber waves of autumn wheat;
Waltz gently in the breeze
The mountains in the distant sky
Reflect the purple hues
Of golden prairie, sunset night
And lilacs rich in bloom
The rustle of the Poplar trees
The softly humming wind
The meadow lark in distant field
And I am home again

Neva Tognoni Brown
BIGGER THAN YOU ARE
What a straining, and
a stretching, it takes--
To become bigger
then you are.
But, how,
without a lot of reaching,
Can you ever--
touch a star?
How, without longing,
dreaming, yearning,
And a great deal
of heart burning--
Can you, ever--
travel that far?

Daniel R. Comiskey, Jr.
MOTHER NATURE'S PEARL
She lingers on a Summer's breeze,
Of Nature an essential part,
She's present in the Autumn leaves,
The blossom of my heart;
I know not how the seed was sown,
Yet from this seed my love has grown.
She casts aside the Winter gloom,
In nature a persuasive power,
Through her, Spring flowers bloom,
The buds of fancy flower;
I know not when the seed was sown,
Yet from this seed my love has grown.
For she is Mother Nature's pearl,
Daughter to the seasons four,
In splendor more than just a girl,
A goddess from the days of yore;
I know not why the seed was sown,
Yet from this seed my love has grown.

Joseph Lee Stokes II
THE DAY I FEAR
The day I fear,
is yet to come
or has it passed.
The love I've got,
or thought I had
has disappeared,
is it that bad.
Communication is just a means,
to express the inner depths of me.
Long distance conversations
become, a joke to all concerned.
The things we say,
are meant well
but they end without delivering
a message.
The day I feared,
has come and gone
and now I stand alone.

Helen Delphey Johnson
TO A TEACHER——— IN JUNE
School bells ringing,
Ding-a-linging;
Teachers smiling,
Out kids filing.
Parents parking,
Dogs all barking;
Children shouting,
Spirits mounting!
Teachers weary,
Eyes all bleary;
Hard days over,
Now it's "clover!"
No more fights,
Doors locked tight;
School's at an end,
Quiet descends!
Amen!

Aristides Steve Diaz
IT'S TIME TO PAUSE
It's time to pause and look about.
Too much liberation - nobody gets out.
It's time to pause and find our way.
Life is getting harder - mass confusion on its way.
It's time to pause and lend a hand, or else we might find ourselves without no land.
It's time to pause and clear our heads.
Our leaders may be gone - but their dreams are not dead.
It's time to pause and break this code -
And get our butts back on the road.

Terry L. Taylor
UNTITLED
The Water swirls around
I see my life pass by
I ask myself the question
"Am I going to DIE?"
I see the sun is Shining
The place still looks the same
I guess I'm still alive
I call out someone's name
I yell to him, "hey it's me"
But he just goes on walking
Again I yell to him
"Can't you hear me talking?"
He continues walking by
as if he doesn't see
I ask myself the question
"Am I really me?"
A noisy crowd breaks my thought
They have all gathered 'round
A man who is lying on the beach
I hear them say, "He Drowned"
I push my way through the

crowd
Until I've reached the place
Where the man is lying
Then I see his face
I can't believe what I see
As I let out a scream
for the face I see is that of me
Thank God that it's a DREAM

Jeanne Hill
YOU PROMISED
There will be other sunsets,
You promised and I believed.
Not knowing even then,
That you practiced to deceive.
And when the seasons all had
passed,
And promised sunsets never
came,
I pulled my soul inside myself,
Trying not to judge or blame.
I'll wait for time to work her
magic
And be hopeful until then,
For you said there would be
other sunsets,
You just forgot to tell me when..

Mary C. Piatt
RAIN
the after rain
leaves us with memories
...of what?
perhaps of other wet days.
and still it's the same
miles away
where faces of country hicks
are found in the slums
with different slang...
what you breathe in
during the years
is what you become
and I've found
a ground with cool blades of
grass crying,
guarded by pine
too heavy to consume.

Clarence Wieske
BOUNDLESS LOVE
A mountain stream, came
tumbling down;
Born of springs and dripping
skies.
At times a quiet pool is found,
At rest and peace, the water lies.
Then as it passes on ahead,
A rocky road it finds,
In and out the stream is led,
As thru the rocks it winds.
Then at last, it's mate is found,
It joins the ocean blue.
The sound of waves, join river
sounds,
And life begins anew.
I am like that mountain stream,
You are like the ocean spray.
We both had, this lovely dream,
To be as one, some happy day.
Now our love is joined and
boundless,
Over-flowing to the sky.
You know my love for you is
endless,
Forever growing, as time goes
by.

Maria T. Fraga
NEW YORK
New York, city of gloom,
glamour and glitter the
world's greatest melting pot,
its people sweet, rash, gentle
and bitter its bums in the
Bowery, its business world at
the top.
New York? New York is grand
where else can one find:
lovers walking hand in hand
others bickering at the same
time
food and wine, many a brand
diners, restaurants, a million
one-of-a-kind.
The Salvation Army's four
people band the Philharmonic,
music divine,
to some it's the promised land
for others a struggle, the daily
grind,
Religion, free to choose by all
man and its bigots will infuse
their continuous whine.
In its subways its people are
canned outside its theaters, a
mile-long line,
garbage collection, the barrios
demand then there's Fifth
Avenue where one pretends
all is fine,
one can feel lonely and that no
one gives a damn yet, in its
crowded streets one a friend
may find.
Lady Liberty in her island stand
its firm skyscrapers the
heavens outline,
infinite attributes its natives
defend and praise its core,
heart, soul and mind.
New York? New York is grand
city that no one can seem to
define,
its rawness and beauty at the
wave of a wand the city of
contrast of all time.
New York is exclusive
in its glorious grandeur
in its turmoil, hope seems
illusive, nevertheless, New
York will endure!

Dee King
GAYLA
I saw her in a cloud today,
So soft and fair and young as
May.
I watched her in a butterfly,
So graceful, lazy and kinda shy.
I heard her coo in the Mourning
Dove,
Sending forth her call of love.
I saw her eyes in the rising sun,
All bright and shiny and full of
fun.
I kissed her lips, when I kissed
the rose;
And I felt the softness of her
tiny nose.
I found her in my garden this
morn',
This tiny daughter whom I had
borne.

Virginia Mahan
THE WIND AND I
Mother whispered that I have a
date
With the liveliest dapper in
town.
'Tis not enough to dance in the
breeze,
I must encounter this knave of
renown,
Adorned in my finest regalia,
Vividly set with rust and amber,
The finest handwork available,
Embroidery from nature's
tambour.
I think I hear the rogue coming
now,
Like a pirate, reveling
mirthfully.
I know he will sweep me off my
feet,
But only he knows where he'll
take me.
Ready now, I'm anxiously
waiting,
Vigilant at my lofty station.
The sap is pulsing through my
veins as
I consider my destination:
A fence corner? a trash pile? a
lawn?
Caught fast in a bicycle
sprocket?
In the path of a small boy, I
hope,
Who'll carry me home in his
pocket.

Carolyn E. Riopel
CHRISTMAS CHEER
For those of you
with Christmas cheer,
I have a story
for you to hear.
It all started on
a cold winter's day,
when a little boy
from his mother did stray.
Out lost in the cold
of winter's wind,
his parents worried
that this was the end.
They searched for him high,
they searched for him low,
they had people looking
all o'er in the snow.
But a little old man
had found him weeping,
he brought him to his house
and now he was sleeping.
And then the next day
which was Christmas, you
know,
he brought him home
through the winter's snow.
This man gave a gift
of saving this lad,
and he realized
giving wasn't all bad.
And you will learn
as he did here,
that in giving you receive
a feeling of cheer.

Thomas A. Cocchiaro
SOME RIVERS
Some rivers are wide
and some rivers have tides
Some rivers have steamboats
and others did fill moats
Some rivers are famous
some flow to the sea
Some even have deltas
like the Nile and Mississippi
Some are the sight
of a people long past
Like the tigris and Euphrates
their time has moved fast
Some rivers are new
and some rivers are old
And of some rivers
stories and legends are told
What is a river
it's many great things
It's a body of water
revived by fresh springs
It's an artery of life
from the past to the now
It's kind of like us
in a way
somehow.

Kathleen Kelly
OASIS
Pasty-faced
Thin-lipped
She gave me the
mother to auditor
lecture
on menstruation;
I tell you a
history class with
Mrs. Boring
could not have been
more arid.
Ten years
with a broken
humidifier
made us the parched
people
we are today.
God help me remove
This ice goddess armor,
dehydrated psyche,
emotional drought
And build me a tavern
in the Sahara of solitude;
to be a good drinking buddy,
I'd revoke my degree.

Verita Moore Davis
THE WANDERER
He cries for help,
And no one hears.
He cries inside
Because of his fears.
He tries to reach out,
But his hand is slapped away.
There are times that he can't
Make it through the day.
He can only help himself
When he realizes he is weak.
But he's lost touch with his
surroundings
And does not know how to
speak.
This terrible thing inside
Is eating him alive.
Please, won't someone
Help him to survive.
The wanderer, with
No hope of his own
Hasn't reached out and
Touched the throne.
He has stumbled, and
He will continue to fall.
Only God will answer
If He is called.

Aunt Polly

I'M YOUR SPECIAL FRIEND

When your day has gone from bad to worse
And you're feeling sad and blue
Remember me, I'm your special friend
To you I'll always be true
When life seems to be closing in
And your burdens too heavy to bear
Remember me, I'm your special friend
And your load I'd love to share
As you go on throughout your life
And the road seems long and hard to walk
Just think of me, I'm your special friend
When e'er you've the need to talk
We've had days we'd like not to recall
Days we'd much rather get off our mind
Just think of me, I'm your special friend
Better days we're bound to find

Rheuama A. West

MY MOURNING FRIEND

It is evening.
Like Martha of old,
I have burdened myself
With household tasks
Preparing for your coming.
Floors scrubbed,
Furniture polished,
I want my house to shine
That you might be impressed.
Now--physically drained
I seek repose somewhere--
Weary of mind,
Too tired to care.
But wait--Mary was there too,
Long ago--by His side, refreshed,
Listening, attentive and loving.
Friend, which would you have me be?
Is it my clean house that beckons you,
Or is it me?

Lynn M. Hlinak

SNOW SQUALL

The snow
Like the distant music
Starts gently-
Rising and falling with the wind.
Ever increasing;
Building to a great CRESCENDO!
Suddenly! A flurry of restless activity;
Then quickly, quietly, fades away-
Until it is felt no more.

Jack Kirkland Bradberry, Jr.

JULIE

Put away those ballet shoes,
that satin wedding gown,
for little Julie will never be
more than she is right now.
Face it! Don't bury the fact
with tears, but with a smile
that she's yours to love throughout
the years.
Whose to say, "Whats a baby?"
A beautiful bouncing girl or
an angel from heaven bringing
love into the world.
For ballet shoes—these's
sparkling eyes.
For a wedding gown—there's
love.
Take good care of Julie—
she's only a loan from above.

Betty J. Lewis

WHEN THE STREET LIGHTS COME ON

Suddenly, softly, with out sound
The street lights claim the night.
And I wonder at their mystic meeting
the dark and the light
What sweet elements do they combine
Upon their embracing?
What secrets lie curled within their grasp
Upon their interlacing?
Down the block
Car horns invade the night
With sound.
And I walk in moving shadows
Through the town.

Soft as curious fog,
The night air cradles my feet
I march to the rhythm of clicking heels
Upon the street.
I walk a city block
Or maybe two or three,
At last my thoughts
Are soaring free,
Free to seek the darkness
And the light,
I have been one well acquainted
With the night.

Nora Raleigh

THE RAIN

It rained yesterday,
I opened my umbrella.
It rained today,
I lent my handkerchief.
If it must rain tomorrow
I shall be beneath the ground.

Nora Raleigh

TOMBS OF KINGS

Child of the city,
alone, alone have you too
sped through the great
gold room and seen
the hieroglyphics
carved in stone
surrounding the open
tombs of kings
on your solemn way
to a private skating rink
outside museum walls
unafraid you will fall,
roller skates slung over
one youthful shoulder
giving a passing guess
at the reality of things?
On the quest for a goal
the best I learned grew
from a great man dead
lo, three thousand years
who wrote strange words,
waited preserved for me
since antiquity; nearby
a merry-go-round
clangorous with sounding
organ music in a copse
of quiet trees
these to disappear
along with roller skates
and cotton candy fates,
brass rings, school dates.
In a bygone realm so
lived there authority
for its own sake,
and the quality of fear
speaking with a voice
whose tones I could not hear,
stilled the wine of freedom
until the grape was ripe
to be entombed, great
and as eternal: gold.

Doris Braley

GOOD MORNING

It's morning. . .
And the first stirrings of the day begin.
The sky brightens
with a streak of crimson as intense as the sunset of the night before.
The crows herald the dawn
with their raucous caws.
The other birds sleep in a little longer,
waiting. . . . .
There will be a whole day to sing about.
A whistle blows on a distant train,
wheels clacking on the tracks.
A dog barks, another one answers.
The ducks quietly slip into the pond. . .
respite from a hot night.
The sky lightens, and
more birds join in the performance
creating a morning symphony.
Even the bees sleepily buzz
their way from blossom to blossom as the sun begins to warm.
The day has begun—
Good morning!

D. C. Kallo

LOVE SONNETS OF THE '80's

Now only the mind and the body free
Whilst thy soul, perhaps, lingers with you;
Were I truly a man I guess it might be
Everything He is and more I could prove.
Should conversant nights turn to frozen days
An image greater than I am still stays;
Yet wandering through cleared fields so great
This ferocious mirage begins to decay.
Each breath I take, the heart that beats
My bones which harden on marrow,
The stuff of dreams—these things make me
Forget the loneliness, shame and sorrow.
So alas! and anon! We should know
Equality of mind, body and soul.

Anne Fields

THE DREAMER

Oh dreamer of a noble dream
Who'd do great things another day,
Life becomes a fantasy;
You sit and dream your life away.
Visions pass still unfulfilled,
Promises grow stale and cold,
Hope by inaction has been killed
While life slips by and we grow old.
If great men in days gone by
Had spent their life in thought alone
Their names, their thoughts would with them die:
Great things would never have been done.
Oh dreamer of a noble dream
Who'd do great things another day,
Life is not a fantasy;
Why sit and dream your life away?

Lydia Leah LaMont

TWO STRIKES

Gay cork, afloat on bright promise,
Bobbing easily along,
Serene on the dips and swells of life.
Lurking ominously, evil beneath the calm,
Insanity opens its cavernous maw
And yanks her under.
She fights the slavering beast,
Clings tenaciously to corroding reason
With hopeless desperation.
From the illusive realm of sanity
Life beckons, tempting her with normality.
Upward from the murky depths
she struggles.
Floundering thoughts lure the ravenous monster.
Once more it takes the bait;
Pulls her under. . .

Toby Heatherly

THINGS I LIKE

Things I like are not so few,
there are many, not just one or two—
So I'll just think, and tell them to you,
and tell about things I like to do.
First of all, I like to skate,
whether It's early or whether It's late—

It makes no difference If the
floor is fine,
Just give me my skates and lots
of time
When I'm skating I'm up in the
clouds
whether I'm alone, or with a
crowd—
Just give me a push, and off I go,
and where I'll stop, nobody will
know
I like to play baseball and
basketball too,
I like to play music and write
songs that's new
I like to swim and I like to
dance
and If you want to wrestle, just
give me a chance
I like to ride horses, and ponies
too,
I like to drive cars whether old
or new—
Sometimes I'll just go for a very
long hike
and think of all. . .these things
that I like.

Krishna Chaudhuri
MUKHOPADHYAY
If I were born rich,
I could pitch
In any one of those baskets,
Full of fruits and nuts,
Without cuts
Of my reputation.
Oversensitiveness
Only creates
Introvert, meek sensation;
In the harsh world,
Poors are forced,
and coarsed,
To lick the foot
Of the rich Bruite.
Roaring anger piled up high,
As a lightening of the sky,
But essentially fruitless
Turns into frustration.

Clifford Love
THE ROSE
I suppose
If I could have chosen
From Eden's lavish garden
The fairest of the rose.
I swear
It would not compare
With the loveliness I find
In you, my dear.
Now a rose, to be
Rich, full and free
Must be left unmolested to
bloom
Where all can see.
But I long
To possess it, part by part
And press the fragrance from
its petals
Between the pages of my heart.

Lionel Laurie
TO EUGENIA
The sleeping beauty dreams
Adrift in that world of Nod
We know so well.
Those forty winks so often
claimed
Quite by the way
Are surely more than meets the
eye.
What wondrous worlds does she
now see?
Slipping effortlessly below
Our diurnal turbulence
Into quietude and the calm
below
To frolic with nymphs and
mermen
Her deep and inner longings.

Sima Rubenz
DEAR INSURANCE SALESMAN:
We've mortgaged our future to
pay every bill
insuring us all against every
known ill.
(Recalling insurance we carry is
trying;
we have some against, Sir, all
things except dying).
What puzzles me, though, is
when something occurs:
an illness or accident, your firm
demurs
against paying up for the bills
we submit
it comes up with loopholes. . .
rejects the debit bit.
Now, why can't we have just
one policy giving
insurance against loopholes?
Now that would be living!

Alice Horne Chamberlain
HAPPY BIRTHDAY
85 years of looking out
for others.
85 years of helping out
your brothers.
85 years of living all
God's laws.
85 years of helping all
the squaws.
We are so glad to know
you Lyman Horne
our friend.

Gary Loeser
CAMPING UNDER THE STARS
Caught in the throes of a world
composed
Of loneliness and spite,
I shake my head and take a long
Deep breath of midnight air.
And as I glance, around me
dance
A hundred thousand stars;
They somehow stay the pain of
day
And take away all care.
But as of late I can't get fate
To stop the fears that guide me;
And it's all 'cause of a girl I love
Who isn't here beside me.
And so I lay and wait for day,
Thinking as I do
About the girl who is the world
To me, and she is you.

Suzanne Losee
TO SIGMUND
Sharpen the cleaver so I can
Chop up your words into
Edible pieces then I will
Chew and respond
With understanding and human
Warmth
Easily I cut through your
Veined defenses and observe
your
Oedipul strivings which
Lie bleeding while
Watching your slimy
vulnerabilities
Crawl to a dry death
Ending also the flow
Between your waterless
polarities
As well as your withering legs
Tenderly I shelter your parched
bones
In my messianic arms as I am
Applauded for my
Therapeutic techniques.

Chrystal A. Eastwood
CRACKER FACTORY
I will miss you my dear friend,
No, there's not any reason to
pretend.
I know my drummer has
changed her tune,
but maybe the beat will be
normal again, soon.
Will you come and visit me, in
the Cracker Factory?
I'm locked outside of my mind,
the only key is time.
Can't remember how long it's
been,
I'm on the outside looking in.
Will you come and visit me, in
the Cracker Factory?
I look into the mirror and see
no image there,
I don't know why she's gone or
where.
Lost in a maze I can't get out,
no one can hear my cries or my
shouts!
Will you come and visit me, in
the Cracker Factory?
It's always been hard for me to
share,
I'm thankful you're a friend who
cares.
My feelings seem important to
you,
I know together we can see this
through.
Will you come and visit me, in
the Cracker Factory?

Opal Price
THE GOLDEN YEARS
I am glad to be anywhere just
glad to be here
The golden years bring the end
so near.
Glad for each day if it's
sunshine or rain
Even glad to watch the world
thru a window pane.
I am glad for a smile or a
friendly hello
A rainbow, a sunset or the
freshness of snow.
I am glad for the memories of all
those years
The happiness, laughter,
heartaches and tears.
I am glad for the faith that
loved ones and friends
Will be there to greet me when
this life ends.

A. E. Wilson
DEATH OF A LINE
O ancestors!
For how long
was the lifespark
passed on from
generation
unto
generation?
I have come from
some place, away,
far away; somewhere
lost in ancient time,
yet am going
nowhere; can go
nowhere, for
I have no son
to carry on
your greatworks!

Mary Anne Sigler
JINGLE BELLS
J n l b l s, J n l b l s,
i g e e l   i g e e l
Another funeral over and gone-
Gone
to rest in peace;
Some joys, sorrows left
But for he who chooses
Are more joys ahead.

Arthur Alric Gregory
THEN AND NOW
Remember as toddlers, how we
played in the parks,
We hardly had worries, we were
happy as larks;
We dressed in our finery, we
had lots of toys,
As children, we had so much
unequalled joys.
We had soft beds to sleep in,
good food to eat,
Nice clothes to dress in, warm
shoes on our feet;
We were surrounded with
comfort, our parents made
sure,
We got all we needed and a
whole lot more.
At sixteen, we spent more time
out in the sun,
We met life's challenges and
still had our fun.
The world was enjoyable, 'twas
like a good play,
A whole lot different than it
now is today.
We grew up, got married, have
kids of our own,
We bought our dream house,
but it's really on loan;
Cause when we miss a payment
for even a day,
The bank will start threatening
to take it away.
We keep asking ourselves why
things are so bad,
We remember our childhood
and it makes us feel sad.
The wife needs a new dress, the
kids need new shoes,
But our pockets are empty and
it gives us the blues.

Jeri Cary
THE NIGHT WE FELL IN LOVE
Let's live a life of poetry, with meter, theme, and grace;
Your every line can rhyme with mine, with each word an embrace.
Let's dance to all the music heard only by we two,
And keep in step with dreams we've kept; yours of me, mine of you.
Let's paint the lovely daydream views within each other's eyes
So we can tell about the spell that keeps us hypnotized.
And while we're writing poetry, and dancing in the night,
And painting themes of rainbow dreams that beckon, ever bright,
Let's not forget to sing a song, for those to hear above
Who sang it sweet, and made complete the night we fell in love.

Marguerite Peck
HUNGRY CHILD
Hungry Child. . .Why? Thine eyes
Filled with water
A solitary tear ease down thy face
You're too young to feed the time
Of despair that has conquered
The Human race
Your innocent breath
Is sweet as the morning dew
There should be joy for
Hungry child, not sadness I see!
Survival from inflation;
Is what mankind seek
The tear of hungry child;
Who hath no food to eat
The tear of peace;
The world long to be free
These has wounded me
By word and by deed.

Tamia L. Lollman (Fowler)
TO TIMOTHY
Since you,
My time has been fulfilled.
Each moment
Spent thinking of you.
The flowers seem more fragrant,
The sun shines brighter.
My world has changed
I seem happy again,
And I have only you to thank.
When it is cold
I feel warm in your arms.
When I feel sad
You talk me up,
And make a smile appear
On the face that wore a frown.
I can't explain
This feeling inside,
But I do know
That it is a wonderful one.
Since you
Entered my life,
I have found
New reasons to be happy,
By just being me.

Marjorie Tull
ON LOVE
The demanding eye has often failed
Where the blushing cheek has won
The soul of duty is the purse
Love brings forth the sun
Love is a twin—unshared it dies
Unwelcome—like a sunset
Showered on the blind
Or a haunting rhapsody
Toward the deaf inclined
It's heartbeat is not yet so dim
'Twill not be heard among
The deaf—no, its power is such
The mute may speak its tongue.

Janice G. Stokes
TO BOBBY SANDS
Oh, brave and tormented soldier
why must you die?
Your beliefs drove you to a point
where no return is possible
and to go forward encompasses death
Your mother—how she must cry
How are we led into this
pain of belief?
For some the desire to express
goes beyond the desire to exist
and so ultimately we choose
and our values are satisfied
by our sacrifice and remain
an everlasting message
which neither time nor
opposition can extinguish.

Susan L. Nelson
DANA
A cool breeze blows through my window
I can smell the fresh air as well
as I can remember being
with you
Seen you today, heard your songs
now you're on my mind
Lots of good times we once shared, and as I
seen your smile shining on me,
it made me know you and I would
always share the times
You once said you loved me, I
believe you did
I once said I loved you and I know I
did,
Things like that don't change for me
the feeling has remained, I think
it always will. . .

Ray M. Kellogg, M.D.
THE NURSE'S HANDS
The tapered loveliness of my nurse's hands
Have cast a spell over me.
I close my eyes and yet do see
Them both in intimate detail.
I catch the gleam of lustrous nails
Spread wide in graceful gesture,
The soft green glow of the peridot
Astride her left third finger.
Comely as these members are
Their tasks are lovelier still:
They bathe tired feet; they bind up wounds
And soothe the fretful still.
They are busy, busy—
Ever vigilant in ministry to others.
No higher destiny could they own save one—
That they ultimately become
the hands of a sweet mother's.
And when at last
They forever fold in rest
It shall be said:
Her hands were greatly blest.

Margaret Williams-Cooper
LIFE AFTER DEATH
In death
a seed is planted;
In darkness,
roots reaching out
in defiance of hunger,
A grain of wheat
is reborn;
A child is fed;
Darkness fades into morn.

Ardythe Vos
I THE LORD
What the future may not hold,
I the Lord have already told,
What you will do, and where you will go, I the Lord will make it known.
Though college seems near and the pressures bring fear, I the Lord will make them clear.
The career you choose, whatever it be I the Lord will not make you lose.
So, don't make a nest or sit and set for, I the Lord will bring your mind to rest.

Mildred Morton
NEW YEAR'S EVE
There was a knock at the door, Twas New Year's Eve
What I saw with my eyes, I couldn't believe,
A tired old man, with a very long beard,
He was all wrinkled, and looked sorta' weird.
"I'm Father Time, I'm about to die,
I want a few words, then it's good-bye,
I'd like to present my year in review,
Then I'll bow out for nineteen eighty-two,
The office of President, Reagan had won,
Campaign promises, big plans had also begun,
The honeymoon was on, spirits were high
With new life, more zeal, and 'pie in the sky.'
March brought sadness, and a bit of despair
Too much, too soon, it didn't seem fair,
Your President was shot by a ruthless clown,
Others of note were also gunned down.
Good news, bad news, he covered it all
Then shouted, "America, you're still standing tall,
God bless you, and a prosperous New Year."
The clock struck twelve, as I saw him disappear.

Harriet Vrooman
MERRY CHRISTMAS
Happy Christmas holidays,
Merry, joyful, jolly days,
Full of fun and frolic ways,
Here and everywhere.
Sparkling, dancing, snowflake days,
Freezing, windy, stormy days,
Sun and moonlight—shadow days,
Carols in the air.
Shopping, greeting, meeting days,
Evergreen and holly days,
Church and home and candle days,
Casting out our care.
Worshiping, God-praising days,
Singing, playing, children's days,
Sharing, loving, giving days,
All tell us Christ is here.

Stanley Cantrell
RAIN, RAIN, RAIN,
As I sit here awondering
When the rains will go
I think about the woodland things
The rains will help to grow.
I see the fish swimming
In waters broad and deep
Down there thinking to themselves
Will I ever find my creek?
And turkeys wings asoaking
With feathers sodden deep
Say will the rain stop falling
So I can find something to eat?
All the woodland creatures
Driven from their homes
Will soon embrace the sunshine
Tomorrow when the rain is gone!

Ruth Wyatt
YOU, MOM
You helped me through life's lonely road.
When I needed a friend, you were there.
You picked me up, when I fell down.
You always showed me that you cared.
You stopped my hurts, with all your love.
You made me smile when I needed to.
You helped me through life's hardest parts.
You gave me joy when I was blue.
You tried to show me happiness,
and help me choose a way of life.
You shared my joys and sorrows.
In me, you took pride.
Through life's road, I got lost.
I turned my back on you.
You said your prayers, and kept your hopes,
and your love, for me, came through.
I hold you dearly in my heart.

You're special in all you do.
You're my mom and my best friend.
And, I'll always love you.

Leona Garrett Keller
THE SPINNERS LACE
Once before the sun came out to shine
Through the frothy fog of late August time,
Out I went to hang my clothes upon the line.
There I found a masterpiece of intricate design.
Inspired, I stood in moistened clover on the lawn
Thinking. Trapper who had spun the web and gone
Would return for food, as part of nature's pawn,
Finding dew bejeweled his lacy work before the dawn.
Expert spinner of fine webs was he by trade;
I, my life of tasks less intricate have made.
Lovely was his toil in diamond drops arrayed.
Humbly I moved on, and left the spinner's lace displayed.

Gary A. Burch
SEA CHANGE
A wild sea spit her, an old tooth,
Dune high beyond the surf's arm,
Her shell still ocean dressed
With barnacle coronet, air tarnished,
And sea grass veil
Dried in the alien sun.
Death marooned her, bloated, flippers stiff,
To swim in the insubstantial air,
Her wind-dried eyes staring empty
At the teeming turtle-green swells,
Her pincer jaws gaped,
Locked in an eternal plea
For the resurrecting wave
To round her blind eyes full,
And wash her stunned shell to living green,
Bathe her rigored arms to stroke
Into the pulsing primal sea.

Harold R. Mitchell
ZEPHYR, EXPLORING THE UNIVERSE
Manifesting her mysterious touch, lonely Zephyr succumbs as she steals silently through the Universe on a restless but continuous journey.
Voluptuously brushing the nearby objects, acceptance is exemplified by the victims.
Oh, how welcome Zephyr must feel in her encounters; for even the foliages sway for her passing.
Away, away ubiquitous one, divulge the unhappiness of passers-by; then, divert them into fruition. Pace furtively as you are, for such is symbolic of your purpose. But resort not to inclemency: these disparities are incogitable. However, if the Omnipotent desires the union, coalesce highly to His repletion.

Dorothy Brown Wilhite
THIS WORLD
Some people think this world is a terrible place
With hunger, pain, and prejudice of race.
They think that crime and terror reign,
And the earth is ruled by men insane.
I'm only a very young lass,
Who hasn't had many material things in the past;
But I know a cure for this,
Something that will bring happiness and bliss.
Love your neighbor as yourself,
And lock that ego on the highest shelf.
In everyone if you would,
Find something both kind and good.
I'm sure that when you've learned,
Love is reaped where it is strewn;
This world will be a better place
Without hunger, pain, and prejudice of race.

Cyndi (Jurey) Haysom
UNTITLED
Running out across a deserted
Field where only one Flower remains.
Thats how I feel,
Not like the one Flower left,
But,
Like all the others trampled down.

Joanne Haines
LILACS
Sweet morning mist,
Transparent-soft and lavender;
Graceful fronds, dew-laden,
Gently swaying arbor of joyous song.
Midday splurge of brilliance,
Vibrant torch of royal beauty;
Glorious flame beneath the blinding dome
Of golden sun.

Soft twilight shadows, silent,
Fragrant purple against the evening sky;
Sentinels of beauty
Standing guard against the night.

James A. Harrison
BENNINGTON VISIT
This week I felt the presence of a man.
I've walked with him in snowy woods at night,
And knelt at well curbs wondering 'bout the light.
He's shown me tufts of flowers
And talked to me of building walls, and home.
He's let me smell his hay so freshly mown.
This week I stood before his slab of stone.
It told me he had left this earthly life.
To soar the skies with Elinor his wife.
'Together wing to wing and oar to oar.
I spoke a word of thanks to Robert Frost
For helping me to find some things I'd lost.

Judy Delores Walker Guthrie
AUTUMN
Summer is almost at an end
It won't be long until fall begins
Scorching heat will fade away
Into days of azure grey
Smoke will curl from chimneys high
Painting lazy patterns in the sky
Wind with gentle touch will blow
Golden brown leaves, to and fro
Frost will fall upon the vine
Claiming that I thought was mine
The harvest moon will rise at night
And sit upon the fields so bright
Yes, the summer is almost at an end
It won't be long until fall begins
And as I walk in autumn splendor
These cherished moments, I'll remember

Daniel Russell Wetmore
PERSPECTIVE
In a jungle of steel trees
I have seen the gorilla
Pacing the floor
His concrete habitat,
Jump wildly at the bars
To the amusement
Of little children
Who shriek at his antics.
Eastward,
A home-bound relative
Sits 'neath a Kenya moon
Drinks in the bay
Of jackals—feels no rage.
Anger with an outlet
Twists the head from
A hyena who dares
Laugh.

Kathleen Finney
UNTITLED
Life just isn't fair
But then who ever said it was gonna be?
Bad things are always happening,
But why do they always happen to me?
Everybody hurting each other.
There's not a nice person to be found.
It's a good thing love doesn't generate the world
'Cause if it did, the world wouldn't go 'round.
Just a little love
Would make everything ok.
Why can't someone love me
Just a little bit today?

René Sanko
WINTER BLUES
You came with the summer sun
And left before the fall breezes.
Lighting my days; you were the one
But now, another change of seasons.
My nights are cold and barren.
My days are gray and cold.
Is there really any caring?
I don't know, I was never told.
The winter wind touches me
Like ice; biting, burning.
The chill runs thru me and in me
My body cries from the hurting.
The winter is a lonely season
But it is also ruled by time.
Maybe these are the reasons
I've grown a little cold inside.
Lighting my days; you were the one
Now, another change of seasons.
You are too far away to bring me the sun
And the winter wind never ceases.

Jamesheed Udvadia
GIVE ME A CHANCE
O Maker mine! O timeless one
Who is the Father and the Son,
What hast thou wrought?
Through deep waters I do wade,
Know not wherefore I was made—
In some web caught;
Day by day I knock and ask
If thou wilt let me know the task
Intended for me;
Show thy inscrutable face—
That is neither steel nor lace—
And set me free.
Night follows day, day follows night
And the end is not in sight—
What purpose, I wonder?
Is it all a great big jest
Before we are all laid to rest—
Or torn asunder.
O Thou, who made thy presence felt
Where Cyrus ruled and Zarthost knelt
Give me a chance;
Give me one word, 'tis all I ask,
One ray of light pierce thy mask,
Today perchance?
That I may know thou are there—
Truth and Justice and Loving Care
And Glorious Sound;
That I may come and at thy feet
Find myself a humble seat
On hallowed ground.

Helen Dittman
JUST A THOUGHT
Life is worth living
With its trial and care
When somebody else
Is there ready to share.

Jeffrey Cooper
5 A.M.
Sitting on the porch
I keep sweeping
as if I have always been
here
the night closing
silent wings
pages turning back
into leaves
murmuring their memory
of song.

Robert McGouey
BROWNIE THE ELF
Santa we know has a bundle of
work,
That he hardly can do by
himself;
We know he has helpers, some
fine little helpers,
But his favorite is, "Brownie
the Elf".

Brownie's job was to help the
others,
Get Santa on his merry way;
Then the big night Brownie was
missing,
Because he stowed away on
the sleigh.
Now he rides in the sled with
Santa each year,
And nobody even did know;
He hides in his bag with a
gleem in his eye,
And a smile that could melt
the snow.
Now Santa's work has since
been lightened,
By Brownie's presence ever
there;
And on the night of Christmas
Eve,
They now get almost
everywhere.
Riding through the night,
Brownie might assort toys,
If he has to he may trim a
tree.
He's fast, he's small, about three
feet tall,
And a great help to Santa is
he.
And when certain chimneys
perhaps are smaller,
Brownie will have some other
chores;
He can squeeze right down
through the chimney,
And he for Santa can open
doors.

Ernest Porter
WHEN MEN OF PEACE DIE
when men of peace die
whole nations humbly
bow their heads
and somber praises for
their spirits stab at our hearts
in dread
when martyrs like king
call for peace
and men like sadat
call to allah
we all who cherish peace
pray for it in different ways
the rap-a-tat of gunfire
has again silenced
the voice of reason
but still our hearts won't be
for thobbing peace is never
easily won and with hope
our minds and wills can see
that the fire of peace
is not done
so for these great men
and others
who fought for righteousness
a wreath of condolences
we should weave
and a reborn sense of peace
instill again our motives

Allan James Hayward
LOVE FROM A LONELY SOLDIER
Many days ahead my
love
away from home
and you I'll be.
In the hours
of these days,
how lonely I'll be.
Twenty four hours a
day,
we are soldiers,
twenty four hours
how to kill,
and self survive;
twenty four hours
to hate,
to tire,
to be lonely.
they say,
that we are soldiers now
so soldiers
we must be.
I don't regret it
though,
for it is something
to be proud of.
I am a soldier,
many miles from home,
and the ones I love.
Many miles apart,
and yet so close.

Michele Denise Fancher
CHRISTMAS IS A SAD, SAD SEASON FOR THE LONELY
When people wish you "Merry
Christmas"
while in your heart you're all
alone
When they call you up and tell
you
that their kids are coming home
And they tell you what they're
having
for their Christmas dinner too
While they never seem to notice
that inside you're feeling blue
They never seem to notice
that you always are alone
Or that you never have a
Christmas tree
or decorate your home
They never even notice that
your windows all be bare
And they don't know that the
reason
is not that you don't care
No one seems to notice
that you stay inside for lunch
While very deep inside your
heart
you'd like to join the bunch
The Christmas songs they sing
that fills their hearts with
"Christmas Cheer"
Only fills yours with an
emptyness
you wish would not be there
No one even knows of how
you wish this time would pass
So that Christmas would be over
and spring could come at last
Then the heart that feels so
empty
won't feel half as empty then
At least not for a little while
until Christmas comes again

Diane I. Rapp
RETREAT
for surely, one thing remains
self-evident to me, in my love of
nature,
the omnipresence of the Lord's
touch—
everchanging and directing its
course.
as the rivers flow, or trees lose
their colors
to autumn's gray and
windswept nights,
so my mind travels
to places far and near
when nature was mine.
all was quiet beneath my
thoughts.
and to dream was but to close
my eyes
to northern winds of winter's
bliss
upon which i plunged into
spring's open meadows,
where daisies stood straight
against a heavenly blue
sky's sun.
to dream, to dream of these
days,
for nature takes me to the edges
of her imagination
and i wish only
that i can live my tomorrows
as i have lived my yesterdays
forever. . .

Patricia Riley
THE BATTERED CHILD
You're the one who gave him
life,
Now he lives in a world of
strife.
How can you beat him and
make him cry,
Then look into his tearful eyes,
You say your sorry, but it's too
late,
The love is gone and now
there's hate.
He may forgive you when he
gets older,
But you've made his life so
much colder.
To him life is a world of joy,
How can you hit your little boy?
Hear him crying in the night,
He's hurt, alone, and full of
fright.
The wounds on his skin may go
away,
But the wounds inside are there
to stay.

Louise S. Cooks
MOTHER'S BEST
I have done the best I could. I gave birth too, loved, nursed, taught, had patience to see you through whatever the problem was.

I encouraged, though sometimes disappointed about the path you took.

Holding back and letting you make your choice, was at times hard to do.

I watched as you struggled along life's highway. Constantly seeking, succeeding or failing, but always trying.

I prayed, hoped, observed, and imagined. I beheld and you were there. The goal that you set had been reached. It was my pride and joy too, because I had followed you every step of the way.

Peggy Sweeton
LOVE IN THE 1970'S
With the abandoned pursuit of
sexual pleasures,
Society devouring sex manuals
and contraptions
To relieve the burning quest for
a sense of being
Instead plunges us over the
abyss of liberated
debauchery
Feeds our insatiable appetites,
but leaves
our souls tormented.
Starving for fulfillment and joy,
the quest is lost.
Desperately, we thrash at the
window of the Universe
with beating fists,
Crying out for the soul-mate
who will bring us
fulfillment of body, mind
and soul.

Terri Spaulding
THREE LITTLE WORDS
Say it again,
let me hear it one more time.
You know what I mean,
those three little words.
The ones that make
each day complete.
Please say them
just one more time.
I've got to hear them again
They mean so much
those three little words.
Yes, that was it
those three little words.
"I love you".

Kathleen K. Rech
HIS PRAYER
I heard a little boy praying,
He had so much to say,
Like "Thank You, God for
staying
Close to me all through the
day."

"And thank You God for kittens,
And daffodils and frogs,
And grasshoppers and garden snakes,
Oh yes, for puppy dogs."
"Thank You for my friend who
Stayed with me when I was sad,
He helped me just by being near,
And stayed till I felt glad."
"Thank You God for trees to climb,
And streams to catch some fish,
For kites to fly and games to play,
And balls to catch and pitch."
Teach us dear Lord, as this young boy,
To thank You for all things,
The great and small, You made them all,
Give thanks for little things.

Brenda M. Milberry
MY SON AND I
Hi. Who are you?
I have known you for so very long,
and now, face to face, feel
I barely know you at all.
The face is so familiar,
similar and yet so
distinct from my own.
I don't even know what you're doing now, what you like to do. . .
to eat. . .to see. . .to talk about.
Talk to me.
You frighten me yet you are one of my own.
Our time together is so
very precious.
Let's not waste one second of it.
Take my hand and we'll walk the
side roads together.

Margaret (Peggy) Walde
PRAISE GOD
PRAISE GOD, Praise God, Praise God today,
Thank Him for all the blessings that have come your way.
Take time to get down on your knees,
And say a prayer for all our boys still serving overseas.
And pray God's peace will come once more,
To every heart, to every home, and to every shore.
Let's all join hands the way we know we should:
And pray for lasting brotherhood.

Cher Marie McCoy
THE CLOWN
The clown
that makes people laugh
he's dressed up
sometimes he paints
himself a mask.
Unsure of how to cry
or use tender words
he motions all the meaning
of a love he's lost behind.
His frown upon his face
at times he can't erase
all the loneliness inside
he acts his parts
the people laugh
inside he cries.
The clown
of people's days
we carry on
in special ways
The acting parts
we still do play
We are the clowns.

Shirley M. Thompson
I HAVE THE LOVE
I have the love to make a young man sigh
I have the love to make a river rise
I have the love to change the my feelings go
I have the love I have the love
I have the love to melt your heart
I have the love that could tear you apart
I have the love that is so warm
I have the love I have the love
I have the love to change the night to day
I have the love to chase the blues away
I have the love to make an old love new
I have the love I have the love
I have the love to make a cold night warm
I have the love to do you no harm
I have the love to last a whole life time
I have the love I have the love

Jennifer M. Finlay
BRIGHT STARS
We walk far and wide
to every sky.
We seek the world,
ask every 'why?'
We run tall fields
on winds that blow,
Riding in clouds
and rains that flow.
We sing lark's song
dancing the tune,
Hear oceans speak
answering the moon.
Our bright stars fly,
play tag with sun.
And in our hearts
We've just begun.

Jeanette L. Wilson
MY FRIEND
When you're down and out
And you don't know what to do
There's a friend that I know about
Who can surely take you through
Your bills are due
There's sickness too
And everything looks dim
This is the time to introduce,
All of you to Him
He's King of Kings
He's Lord of Lords
He's the beginning and the end
He's God's own Son
How our victory was won
And He can do just anything
He's my friend
He'll be yours too
Through the thick and thin
He'll take away all of the tears
And replace it with a grin
My friend is joy when sorrows bear
When all is gone, He's always there
A friend indeed
To meet every need
His name is Jesus of Nazaree
As you get closer, you will see
That close to Him is where to be
When the road is rough
The going tough
A friend to you He'll be!!!

Edwardine Sperling
I TOOK A LIFE TODAY
He handed me his life today,
Pencil—stubbed and jagged—lined,
Creased and smudged and cruelly torn.
I quickly took my crimson pen
And stabbed the "i" in his life.
As downward coursed his aging years,
I stopped him short with commas.
One can't use slang for *father.*
(My old man simply cannot be)
With fencer's skill I slashed out *guys.*
And changed his *guts* to *fortitude.*
Like wounded men the red lines ran
Until I used my symbols up.
I didn't hestitate to *gr.* quite often;
I guillotined his *love*
And dashed his *hopes.*
And as his words continued downward,
Successfully, I stayed their fast decline.
I made a final jab and stopped him dead
In time to mark at least one other theme.

Dwayne A. Gates
CAN LOVE WAIT?
Can love wait as modesty can,
or rush to love another?
Can love be love, when only one is feeling
this emotion, without the other?
You think love could wait, a week, a month or two?
Love is not replaceable, God only knows that's true.
Don't you wish you were Cupid, and pick the women you want?
Be done with silly affairs and jealousy and taunt.
Love, at times could be promising, but other times there could be doubt.
Stay with your first intention, until you work your feelings out.

Darcey Dickinson
GOING
She would not kiss him good-bye,
But that doesn't mean she wouldn't cry,

And hurt inside when he would go.
If only she could positively know,
That he would be happy in what he would do.
To him it was all different, strange, and new.
She hopes his enthusiasm is justified and right
And that in the future possibly he might,
Return here, where he got his start,
And where he lingers evermore in her heart.

Joanne M. Pinkowski
YOUR DELICATE AND SENSITIVE HEART
My mind is confused
As to whether I have used
Your delicate and sensitive heart.
We felt we were one
But I went and undone
Your delicate and sensitive heart.
You came back to see
What my life had done to me
But oh, your delicate and sensitive heart.
In this cold, wintry season
I feel guilty, though for what reason?
As I lock you out of my mind,
I feel a lump in my throat combined
With my delicate and sensitive heart.

Joyce Faye Richards
LOVE AND LOVE LOST
Tomorrow I fly away. I'm certain our paths will cross again.
I wonder if we'll end as lovers. . . or as friends. . .
Or neither of the two?
One minute you're hot; and then you're not!
Your mind and emotion jet forth with forced contradiction.
Do you love me? Do you not?
Or is it that you thought you'd never love again?
Another hand of just pretend?
Full of hate. . .full of passion. . . full of shit.
You lift me up and put me down in one smooth motion
On a carnival ride in some strange amusement park.

Afraid of the dark? Afraid to see light?
Afraid to live your dreams beyond one starlit night?
Do you feel the love that's wrapped up in reality;
Or wish to live to lie within your fantasy?
Time is sectioned. . .A little or a lot.
Take time to play it through until you find forget me not.
Then come to me and tell me of your pleasure and your pain.
I know someday we'll take the chance and live to love again.

Shirley A. Bole
SUNSHINE KITCHEN
I love my pretty kitchen
With all its pots and pans
I serve my guests and family
The very best I can
I serve them lots of sunshine
A smile with every plate
A glass of special blessings
To let them know they rate
I Thank my God so humbly
for this lovely kitchen task
And I know He watches over me
For the needs that I might ask

Robert Bryan Chrismon
MY LITTLE NUGGET
I have a little nugget of gold,
which I love to hold
This little nugget I never let go,
because I love this little nugget
so
This little nugget is not a rock,
and this little nugget won't fit
your sock
But this little nugget fits in my
heart,
and this little nugget and I
will never part
My little nugget is a she,
to my heart she holds the key
My nugget's name is Nancy,
she's the kind of girl I fancy.

Rosa L. Northern
THE TOAST
Here's a toast to joy and
laughter
And here's a toast to sorrow and
pain;
And here's a toast to the ever
after—
That seems to mysteriously
whisper my name.
Here's a toast to the lovely little
flowers—
Growing lazily down by the sea;
Here's a toast to the man I
love—
Whom it seems has forgotten
me.
Here's a toast to awakening in
the morning—
To find a bright yellow sun in
the sky,
And here's a toast to you,
though you're gone
I wonder where and why.

John Krampasky
LIVING ON LOVE
I'm going to be falling in love
I will be living on the sea
Perfect! You, me. The sea
Blue sky over the high sea
Living on our love and this
world
No toil no sweat
The sea as our pet
It will obey and
Take us away
Living on our love and this
world
Sway with the waves
We will be brave
Take on the uncertain day
Pay the price
Say the word
So, we can be on our way
Living on our love and this
world

Artie Tillman Proctor
MOTHER
One cup of coffee
A warm word spoken
A thought that's shared
And a love un-broken.
A prayer for others,
And a lesson taught
What a ray-of-sunshine
Your strength has brought.
That friendly visit
The life you live
Your concern for others,
And a willingness to forgive.
That life of sacrifice,
And your loyal heart
An enduring spirit
Thank God, I'm a part. . .

John N. Shutt
UNTITLED
In the fettly swamps of Timble
In the gloomness of the bog
Lived a listy footing numble
'Neath a petrifying log.
Had centuries dwelt the numble
there
And whonone was the wiser.
Until above, unhid, his lair,
While walking had, a stranger.
A stranger thence who knew not
whither,
Wand'ring through the dankish
black,
Losing in the strangy thither
Mem'ry of the waywardback.
Crenching then, the riling
numble,
Listy footing in the silt,
Cantered if the hapless stranger,
Trampling whether what he
wilt.
A cry heard not the later
searchings
Distant in the silence inked,
Near to where they were not
looking,
Where the numble morely
sinked.

Velma Boswell
HARBINGERS OF SPRING
We know you are returning,
Spring;
For in the trees the robins sing;
And here and there among the
green
A lovely blossom may be seen.
We know you are coming,
Spring;
For the peach trees are blooming
And the plum trees are as white
As the snow on Christmas
night.
We know you are coming,
Spring;
Now we see the farmers coming
From the fields of fresh plowed
earth
Known to them since their
birth.
We know you are coming,
Spring;
For the honey bees are
humming.
And we see the white clad feet
Skipping gaily down the street.
We are glad you are coming,
Spring;
Now the children will be
playing
And gathering lots of pretty
flowers
Between refreshing April
showers.
We are glad you are coming,
Spring;
Bringing life to everything,
Bringing people everywhere
The loveliest season of the
year.

Clynelle Harris Aldridge
WHY HE WENT WRONG
A Dad and a Mother, by their
child did hover
Wondering what made him go
wrong.
They seemed not to remember,
how his life young and
tender
Had been shaped by them all
along.
Those Sundays galore, they went
to the shore
Instead of going to church.
Then the Sundays it rained, in
bed they remained
For any excuse they would
search.
They talked lots of faithfulness,
but it turned into
hatefulness
When things didn't go their
way.
They grumbled about the
preacher, found fault with
their teacher
The terrible things they
would say.
In regards to family altar,
somehow they would falter
It seemed they never found
time,
If only they had, their boy
would not be bad.
But loving, honest and kind.
Parents be loyal to Christ your
King Royal
Read and obey His dear word.
Your church then attend, your
child never send,
But as a family worship the
Lord.

Sandra Van Voorhis
GUINEA PIG
On way to hospital
sick and dying
Guinea Pig arches his head
up, and with determination
looks at the sun.
He knows his small life is
finished, and he won't see sun
again.
How much wiser he is than
most humans,
who take life for granted
and see the sun every day
without really looking.

Connie L. Averhoff
CRYING IN SILENCE
I'm crying in silence
because I'm afraid
to show how I'm feeling
and what people might think
Without one whimper
or a cry
I crawl inside myself
and let it die
I don't understand it
why I'm this way
crying in silence
while I play.

J. Francis Ludden
SHE'S MY LI'L PUNKIN
Just how we met, I'll never
forget,
It started out like another day;
And as the party progressed I
met a sweet little guest,
Made me thrill in a warm sort
of way;
She was shy and sweet and so
very petite,
Just the type you would carry
away;
Just to have and to hold, in my
arms to enfold,
On her I am sold, my sweet
pretty one,
She's my Li'l Punkin.
Her warm hazel eyes and pretty
brown hair,
Her smile so bright her little
form so light,
'Bout five feet in height and
to "hug?" just right,
Warm little lips and slender
hips,
She had me hooked the first
time I looked,
She's my Li'l Punkin.
With the passing years through
joy and tears,
We look back to the day we
met,
Through good times and bad
we've been happy and sad,
It's a full life we've had
without a single regret;
The "kid's" come by, they stop
in to say "Hi!"
Mom's glad they stopped in
for awhile,
I'm glad they're here, 'feels
good when they're near,
Fills the old house with cheer,
For me and Mom, She's my Li'l
Punkin.

Naomi Greenfield Gee
TAXATION
I stop a minute to hesitate—
Before I decide that I should
create,
A piece of art to
commemorate—
The *inheritance* of our
father's estate!
Like all things created equal—
We pay the price to make it
legal.
We are the prey of the
government eagle,
That snuffs us out with a
pedigreed beagle!
No matter how hard we work or
pray,
For happiness of a by-gone
day,
Someone's always there—to
delay,
Our progress towards *any*
sort of play!
After years and years of toil—
Through egress, regress and
ingress of the soil—
Along comes some deceitful
plans to foil,
Any chance of recovery

from this latest recoil!
God says it's never too late,
To use HIS talents to create—
The opportunity to
compensate—
With an everlasting,
glorious rebate!

Kimberlee Ziska
TO BOBBY WITH LOVE
Your eyes tell the story
Sweetheart,
They tell it all to me,
The love that you feel now,
And the way things used to be,
That you were free before,
But kind of lonely too,
And now you can't resist,
The love I give to you,
That you love me so much,
And want to be with me,
You want to marry me,
And share eternity,
I can see it in your eyes,
The happiness you've found,
I feel the same way Babe,
Whenever you're around,
The love you feel I can see,
In the twinkle in your eye,
And also in the way,
You feel free to cry,
I hope you can see it in my
eyes,
I hope that my love shows,
And I pray that until eternity,
Our love just grows and grows,
I always want to be there Bobby,
To see your eyes a glow,
Always be together,
And never let you go.

Peter M. Oberle
UNTITLED
I stepped aside and looked
through the tree branches
toward the feeder where birds
took turns pecking the seeds
through holes,
one by one from one tree to
another forming a waiting line
at the aviary stop and go
South, or stay here.
West, I go towards a setting
sun. . .
Collecting leaves from the earth
make composts to turn thence.
Leaves to earth, earth to earth.
Towards the setting sun. And
the next one rising.

Julius Balbin
OUR ONLY POSSESSION
In the ghetto
where it was
still possible
to make love
I met her.
We were both seventeen
blushing in each other's gaze.
Holding hands
we shyly embraced.
Once in the camp
separated
by barbed-wire fences
our ardor
knew no barriers.
The searchlights mounted
on guard towers
sought the darkness
as I crawled
to the women's barracks
where I dug beneath barbed-wire
and squirmed my way
between life and death.
I reached the door
and eased it open
silently slipping inside
where my beloved's whisper
led me to her bunk
as she waited naked.
reality's nightmare
was swallowed
in the abyss
of our embrace
where we soared
to the heights
of everything human
penetrating
each other.
The women around us
slept sighing or snoring
as we were beyond
curbing our passions
or silencing our moans
while copulating
in a fever our flesh
never knew before.
We possessed nothing
but each other
sharing those few moments
we moved with the rhythm
of the moon and stars
above us glowing
with eternity.

Hedy Heilmann
BABY BARNSWALLOWS
Funny, little, things you are
All fluffy, fat, and fumbly
With small sharp beaks and
Quick beady eyes, you learn
About life around you.
But as the chilly wind blows
And beats at your puffy breasts
You quickly snuggle down
into
Your little knotted nest.

Anne-Marie Ferreira
SADLY MISSED
Being somewhere missing your
big smile.
Hearing things, but missing a
wise comment,
Smelling the air, but missing
your sweet scent.
Seeing beautiful pictures, but
sadly missing you.
Remembering all the fun we
had,
But hating the times we'll never
have.
Being grateful for knowing you,
But mad for having lost you so
soon.
Hoping someday I'll see you
again,
But realizing it really won't
happen.

L.O.W.
INSPIRED BY A DREAM
I once had mercy
for a blind man
who had eyes
but could not see.
You fools who
have eyes but
do not see
I have no mercy for you
for you are
ignorant.

Wendy L. Youngblut
OBITUARY
A painted expression
On a blood drained face.
Embedded in silk lining.
Encased by instinct.
His body reflected pain, inflicted
by his own children.
Perhaps more painful than the
death itself.
Surrounding red roses bled tears
of grief.
Standing. Looking while muffled
conversation surrounded me.
His face felt like that of coarse
leather.
He gave so much, but received
so little.
My eye gave birth to a tear, and
then another,
But soon they trickled down my
cheek, only to die also.
Modeled in white and black, he
babbled words
that contained no meaning for
me.
The spoken words drifted over
my head, missing my ears, and
faded into the woodowork.
A soggy tissue soaked up
memories from years passed.
I understood the agony which
could only be viewed through a
child's eyes.
They gathered with the
possibility that all intentions
had been misconstrued.
Perhaps it is not he who is dead,
but instead, they.

Pat Tompkins-Flemming
GREAT GRANDFATHER
The old man sat in his rocking
chair
His straw hat bobbed as he
frowned.
He gazed at the sea and puffed
on his pipe
The cry of gulls was a familiar
sound.
He reminisced of the good old
days
When wooden ships and iron
men braved the sea.
He talked of the lobster catch,
whaling boats
And jigging fish from his green
dory.
He said, "my Nova Scotia home
has been all right for me
But I long to join my wife in the
land of eternity."
"Glad you came to see me my
girl
For I'll not be here next year."
"I'm growing old and tired my
girl
Life has been good, but God has
a place for me."
"Now don't talk like that dear
Grandfather
When I come back next year
You'll be here rocking on this
veranda
I don't believe your time is
near."
Sail boats appeared on the
horizon
As we watched bathers down at
the shore.
"My girl, you must understand -
if one lives too long
Life can become a chore."
He sprang to his feet, shook his
head and yawned
While looking me straight in
the eye.
"It's getting late my girl, the fog
is in
And the tide is out" -- he sighed.
"Soon it will be as dark as it can
be
Time to go in, light the fire, and
brew a cup of tea!"

Diana Boyle Rice
TRIBULATIONS
Set me free from tribulations
Let there be no trials for me
I am sick to death of sorrow
And of friends whose sympathy
Comes from hearts that feel no
meaning
Chokes me, gags me till I'm
down
Worse than any fall could bring
me
Broken, beaten to the ground.
Under which my love is
sleeping
Leaving me in endless grief
Here on earth to go on living
Go on searching for relief
From a wound that knows no
healing
And a love that knows no end
Tearing me in bitter pieces
That can never, never mend.
Lift from me this heavy burden
Let me breathe! God set me free!
From the one who binds me,
chains me
To a love that cannot be
To a love that won't release me
From these tears that know no
rest
As they fall upon the tombstone
Of the one I loved the best.

Michael J. Thompson
HEROES
Once upon a time, before all my
Heroes turned grey, they would
Sit for hours and tell the tales of
The adventures of their days.
Some had fought, some had
Worked, others had sung their
Songs. They traveled the world
And fared as they could, never
Worried of right or wrong.
They had fought for love, they had
Fought for food, and the dangers of
Their fight. And they would
Dream of the next day's fighting
Through the moaning of the
Night.
Some had worked and gained by
Toil, though all were so tired and
Worn. But they talked with pride
Of the work they had done and
Small sparks of genius they had
Borne.
Others had sung and lightened
The lives of their audiences
Everyone. They sang and talked
Over and again of great fortunes
They had almost won.
I never questioned what they'd
Done, now they have all turned
Grey. But it was all done with
Living twice in mind, and I wish it
Had worked out that way.

Christy Gerlach
FRIENDS
I was unhappy and lonely.
Then you came into my life.
You made me happy again.
I wasn't lonely anymore.
The empty feeling I had,
was filled by your love and care.
We were always together.
We were inseparable.
When we were together we'd talk, laugh, or joke with each other.
But most of the time we didn't have to, we knew each others thoughts and feelings.
So we just sat in silence.
But silence started coming too often.
We didn't know each others thoughts anymore.
The empty feeling came back.
Us, the two people who were inseparable, were now separate.
I don't know if I've gotten any stronger since then, but I think I'll make it.
I'm glad we can still be friends.
For if I need someone to lean on, I hope you'll be there.
Because now I need your love and care as a friend.

Hosea Drake
WHY?

Mother keep a candle in the window burning for me, I will be coming home soon. This war, over here is a long war but the end is growing near. You can feel it in the air as the time moves slowly through the day and through the night.

Mother it's a beautiful thing to see our mighty armies slowly moving across the plains and the enemy, trying to hold us back in vain. But it's a shame to see so many good men die, and no one can really say why! But you fight, as hard as you can because you don't want to be the one that dies!

GOD put us on this earth to love one another not to fight and die, can anyone really tell us why. Someone else starts a war and then we have to go and fight their war and die. Well, I guess it would not make any difference anyway, we would have to go and fight just the same.

But it's a shame yes, it is a "shame" so many men young and old have to die, in vain!

Bonnie J. Brasher
A THOUGHT OF THE UNIVERSE
Stars seen from earth form patterns,
Astronomers saw men and chariots from celestial matter.
Then laws of nature and patterns
Began to change in the universe,
As stars rose in the east and set in the west;
Perhaps this started our Zodiac calendar and all the rest,
From Jupiter to Mars, and Earth giving its best.
As the stars have been viewed over the Lunar years,
We find stars are worlds in our Milky Way Universe.
Precise and ordered we find the Cosmos,
Created by God's clockwork force.
The whole of the Universe as we begin to see,
Was from a bold imagination for mankind to believe,
Celestial Space has been opened up for us,
To explore the cosmos beyond our dreams.

Tom Campbell
HOW LIKE A SUNSET
How like a sunset is my Lord,
With beauty and glory in His word;
A benediction for the day now done,
A Promise Divine for the one to come.
How like a river: majestic, serene,
Yet, like a streamlet: sparkling and clean;
To wash away our sorrow and hurt,
Or cool our brow, and slake our thirst.

How like a snowfall: pure and white,
Or a dove at dawn in joyous flight;
To calm the soul, to ease the care,
And let us know that Love is there.
How like the mighty redwood trees,
Or the tiny sapling in woodland breeze;
Mighty and regal, standing o'er all,
Yet, tender and gentle to even the small.
How like my Lord to give these things,
With the beauty and joy each one brings;
How like my Lord to touch my soul,
To soothe my woes, to make me whole.

Carol Lee Pfaff
A SPIRIT TOUCHED
You reached out and touched me
Our Spirits became one...
What peace and joy to know God's love
The Universe, your Spirit and mine are now one.
The gentleness that is part of you
In my heart will always remain
The tenderness we both have shared
Came as a gift from the Master's hand.
Your love is God's greatest gift to me
I can possess to greater treasure..
Darkness may hide the flowers from my eyes
But it cannot hide the deepening of the Spirit.
It would not have been enough for us
To turn and grow in our own way...at our own speed.
We are a fact, not fiction or dream
Created by God's order of scheme.
We have shared the fields and mountain plains
And though you look peaceful, there is unrest within your bounds
You are ever reaching to touch the rooftop of the sky
Your Spirit reaches up so high.
The mountain's echoes, the waves of the sea
The golden moonlight, and the birds in the tree
Offer a call from God that cries out...
"Come away with me, and let your Spirit be free!"
The heavenly touch in my gentle hands
Will soothe your troubled brow
To set up on a hill among the trees
Now you can see, "A SPIRIT TOUCHED"...
Is "A SPIRIT FREE."

Thomas E. Zinn
LORD, PROTECT ME!
Lord, protect me from the crazies, the fools -
But most of all protect me from myself:
From unwise choices made and unmade,
From things done wrong and things not done at all,
From pain - but more so from giving it.
Allow me to live in peace— and if I can love and
Be loved - please allow that too.

Sister M. Michael Rhatigan
SILENT MELODIES
My heart is dressed to go dreaming
While the clock nags all the night...
I move like a shadow
along the garden wall
out beyond the broken path
where crimson petals sleep.
Morning unwinds itself
in tangled skeins
of bright yarn
forgetting mirrored clouds.
Melting snow puddles the lawn
ankle-deep in stars,
and grass sun-hungry
for greening.
The willow trails its thousand fingers
Watching the afternoon collapse into silent melodies.

Lonnie C. Bray
FIRST FLIGHT
I saw a young bird on his first short flight
His small body shook and trembled with fright
He beat his frail wings and tried hard to fly
When he didn't move he just couldn't try
His knowing mother glared strongly at him
As he scampered back up the narrow limb
But she would not move so he could get past
And he thought each breath would sure be his last
She knew his retreat was not meant to be
So pecking and shoving she pushed him free
As he started to fall thru the hot summer air
He found in him a strength he did not know was there
Before he hit the ground he was learning to soar
And his fear of falling wasn't there anymore
Sometimes we don't know just what we can do
How hard we can try until we have to
And all those people who give you a shove
Are not enemies some do it with Love

Kathy Price
UNTITLED
i saw a staircase.
it was not your ordinary staircase
for it led directly thru the clouds
and stopped at one star.
i saw a moon.
it was not your ordinary moon
for it was rainbow colored and laughing.
i saw a radiant light.
it was not your ordinary light
for its brightness was filled with love.
i saw a heart.
it was not your ordinary heart
for it was filled with melodies of peace.
i felt a secret.
it was not your ordinary secret
for it was whispering...
Life.

June L. Smith
CORONA
Aunt Hallie's red-gold hair,
Flame and fire flashed as
She brushed, brushed;
I held my breath
And watched, until
Three thick, bright coils,
Three suns subdued, were
Rolled and pinned
Low on the back
Of her no-nonsense head.

Michael J. Martin
MY SPECIAL WORLD
Hush,
be silent when you enter my world.
Waves slowly beat against rock.
All is dark,
only the moon shows a faint glow.

In the far distance,
a loon cries,
thunder rumbles,
lightning flashes.
On the far shore,
tall trees
stretch
to the skies' limit.
Rain begins to fall,
I must leave now, but,
hush
be silent
your world is just awaking
to find mine.

Esther Banks

FACES

Today I sat in a familiar place
and I looked at each and every face.
Some were young and bright without a care,
Some looked right through me, as if I wasn't there.
There were some faces with looks of despair, that age had put on them through years of wear.
But there was one face I'll never forget and the words it said I think of yet.
It was the face of an old lady who sat across from me,
She was just as happy as she could be.
She said, "Next week I'll be eighty five.
I thank God, I'm still alive.
I could have been dead and gone, but God saw a reason to let me live on.
He brought me joy, when I was sad-
He's the best friend I've ever had.
So whenever I'm tempted to gripe and groan
I stop-because I know that I'm just here on loan."

Carter Andre' Bradshaw

FATHER TO DAUGHTER

Well, daughter, I'll tell you:
Life for me ain't been no bed of roses.
It had some rocks,
And weeds
And bad soil,
And times when no sunlight shown --
Dark.
But in spite of all that
I've been a climbin' right on,
Pushing past the rocks and weeds
And takin' hold to whatever life
Regardless of the type of soil,
And many times feelin' so tired
And yet knowin' -- I just couldn't stop and rest
So girl, don't you stop goin'
Don't you let those weeds
And rocks get in your way
'Cause you find it still hard today.
Don't you stop growin' tall --
For I'm still goin', child
I'm still tryin' for us all,
And life for me ain't been no bed of roses.

Cynthia C. Winkler

SIMPLE THINGS

WHEN THE WORLD GET'S BIG,
and i feel small,
WHEN LIFE GETS SO COMPLICATED
i can't understand at all,
WHEN THE SKY GETS VAST
and i get dizzy
I DON'T "BROADEN MY HORIZON",
i narrow my vision.
I study something small and simple, like a leaf.
A little thing that doesn't last long, feels no sorrow, bears no grief.
With stem and mesh of veins all with purpose and direction.
It always knows just what to do, and never needs correction.
Starting out as buds, in pale shades of green, in summer darkens to deeper tones, and with each breeze, SINGS!

It's glory just begins.
Because it's finest moment, is the memory left with men.
Oh how wonderful the thought, that this simple thing has purpose in it's birth,
And it's death?
What grand splendor brings.
So now with mind in focus I turn back to the worlds complications.
In this I know my birth had purpose, I will find my life's direction.

Katherine Hunn Karsner

NUCLEAR STORAGE BASE

A hillside where sleek cattle browsed
When I was younger, now is marred
By grassy mounds in which are housed
Explosive weapons for ill-starred
Opponents to our way of life.
No longer do bright daisies dot
Hay scented meadows where I played.
The lovely landscape is a plot
For storing hate. Men are afraid
To proffer friendship, banish strife,
And settle down to peace anew.
They're planting missiles undismayed
Where once I and the daisies grew.

Jeffery Pennewell

The Coming Of Him Who Said I Will Come Like The Thief In The Night

Day by day its getting late, they say we're living in the last days. The Bible Quotes "Father against Son, Daughter against Mother", You can see it all happening everything the Bible quotes for the future is coming true. The weather has changed for summer it seems like winter and winter it seems like summer. For people who don't believe will be the first to fall to their knees to beg mercy, nevertheless little kids are getting smarter and worse they can beat their parents when they curse. Yes, it looks like we're living in the last days. Man's waters are getting polluted more and more everyday, radiation, lack of oil, raw materials declining, over population all because of rich greed and unusual policies, Yes, we're living but how long was man made to go on, When is the end, only God knows and He is coming. . . .

Anne McDonald

FOUR SEASONS

SPRING:

The sun is becoming warmer every day, those restless feelings inside are starting to bloom. The seeds of life are coming alive, the web of love is beginning its weave.

SUMMER:

Burning sands and soft warm breezes. Laughter echo's with the heat of passion, promises and secrets. All caught up in whispers and dreams, the web of love is fully weaved.

AUTUMN:

Gazing down the path of trees, viewing all their splendid color. The blowing winds will soon cause all the leaves to scatter. The dreams are fading away, the web of love has felt a chill.

WINTER:

The snow has fallen and so have the tears. What once was so warm and alive time has made cold in the night. The end is growing near, the web of love has DISAPPEARED........

Trees are poems that the earth writes upon the sky with. We chop them down and turn them into paper, and record all our emptiness......................

Juna A. Van Leer

A MOTHER'S LOVE

How can we explain the emotion
At the sight of a new born child?
It has been such a part of you
With imagination that has run wild.
But now for the first time you see in the flesh
This little creature to you, that's perfection
The embodiment of all your dreams
Love realized in all its reflection.
Pride and dismay but with unbounded faith
As you face the future years,
Knowing full well the price to be paid
In life's sorrows and it's tears.
But the joy that abounds at the moment of birth is especially designed,
For you have shared in the creation of someone part devine.
This child so small and helpless
You hold within your arms,
To nurture into maturity
Facing the world's alarms.
And then one day it will leave you
And in its place you'll find
An ardent deep composure
A feeling so sublime.
So passes life before us
But we are wont to share
Our place in all eternity
As Mothers we declare.
time is all so fleeting
But memories play their part
With everlasting imprint upon
A MOTHER'S HEART.

Walter Alvin Hamm

MY HEAVEN

In my heaven winged horses graze
In fields of violet haze
While doves of purest white
Kiss the dew drop's sparkling light
And fragile roses are bending
With breeze that seems somehow
To lift the willow's weary bough
To skies of blue unending
In my heaven life is serene
Abounding with visions never seen
By those who fail to love.

J. D. Leach

SLEEPY MONDAY POEM FOR D.K.C.

i am so happy, that
to cry
is adequate, my emotions
are not a river that always flows.
i cry now; my river bears your name, it
is more like a sea, it encompasses land that has not been chartered—
the mapmaker himself not sure of the terrain.
"is it mundane?" he ponders, he who knows so much about chartered lands,
he who knows only traces
about the unmappable/you are not a region whose boundaries
can be defined.
i/geographer, hired by the sanction of the greatest God of all—LOV
e. . .

Gene Hosey

ART IS ITS OWN SERIOUS ILLNESS

if it ain't in a museum
i don't wanna see it;
i do not want it
coming up to me on the street
and grabbing me by the sleeve,
spinning me around
and looking into my eyes
if you please
because
it
nodoubt
has wine all over
its breath

Julie A. Gold

HOSPITALIZED TOGETHER

shattered
they congregate
as schizophrenics,
staring away from
present happenings.
she screams at the table
that softly insists she listen.
others look up—
then away,
angered at being
distracted from
the voice
speaking to them.

Thelma Harper Bryant
THE OLD HOMESTEAD
I went back home today,
Just to stand and reminisce.
I thought of all the times
I spent in that old house,
For it was in that house,
that I was humbly born.
There it still stood,
Quaint, motionless, silent.
Not as it used to be,
For years had done to it
what they had done to me.
Shingles like scattered teeth,
Hung from its molded roof
Silvery, trembling in the
breeze.
Oh, I sighed, where is the
laughter
that old house once knew?

And for a moment there
I heard familiar sounds,
A tune that grandmother sang.
Then I felt a tear
drop down my wrinkled face.
Suddenly a soothing breeze
Softly whispered, and seemed to
say:
"My child, don't be sad and
lonely.
You also, like generations past,
Will leave your footprints here,
And join with love ones
sweet memories to share."

David A. Johnson
TRUE LOVE
I will not say you light my life
you only show the light to me
In ways I never dared to try
you show me love, that I can see
and a we share our lives, our
time
Reflecting God's love, that we
know
Then you in your way, me in
mine
Will learn to give, to love, to
grow

Mar'e Moe
DEPOT BAY
From behind a window pane
Of slanting sheets of rain,
I watch storm heads riding high
Across a glowering wind swept
sky.
Ships going out of Depot Bay
Some return, some forever stay.
From that rolling briny deep
Untold stories, if ships could
speak.
When those storms whip the
cove
Upon high sea, ships bravely
rove.
My heart like waves rise and
fall
With emotion, these stories I
recall.
Of men returning to loving arms
Safe by warm hearth, from
stormful harms.
Of those men taken by the seas
grasp,
No more to loving bosoms be
clasped.
Those women waiting on the
shore;
Lost their men to the sea, ever
more.
When upon that tragic sailing
away
Tear eyed women drop wreaths
into Depot Bay.

Ms. Brenda J. Gilbert
SADNESS, JOY AND DESPAIR
What is sadness ?
Why do my tears trespass
across my cheek
and leave a salty taste
for you to seek ?
What is joy
Why do my eyes dance so coy
and my lips smile wide
cool breath sigh
for you to keep ?
What is despair
Why do I throw my every care
to the wind - do you dare
hold your heart behind closed
doors and love no more
What is love
sailing swiftly out to sea
with orders to only be
passionate, giving,
understanding
and respecting
time together
time apart
accepting space.
What is love
if not with you
What is it ?

Sheri Karsten
TWO PEOPLES LOVE
Someday we may part
And if we do it'll break my heart
Because I love you so.
You'll never be my foe.
You may not know how I feel
But my love is real.
Though we may be far or near
We shouldn't shed a tear.
The two people in love
Is great as a white dove.
I have always loved you
And I always will.
True love is so fine
It goes with dinner and goes
with wine.
I have never told you these
things
But when I do I feel like I have
wings.

Cherylyn Owens
LITTLE GIRL LOST
I look into the blueness of her
aging eyes - so faded now
As if a shade had drawn around
to hide her silent self.
At times she peers and peeks
outside but...none can touch
the strings of her silent heart.
In an instant - in an angel's
breath of time - she turned
the corner from the light of
life.
She chose within a twinkling to
tread instead the grayish road
to inner death.
Had she loved perhaps a doll, a
kitten?
Was there laughter from now
sullen lips?
She whiles away the years in
echoing memories that only
she will know,
And lives in silence within
walls made with her own
hands -
With thoughts she will not
share - with shattered faith
and dreams forever gone awry-
Like a tiny delicate flower - she
dies unknown.

Daisy Bottolfson
OUR JOSHUA
God gave us Joshua, a
Precious little lad. A bundle of
Joy to love and cherish. We
Were so happy and glad - yet
Sad. Josh had a terrible heart
Defect, but like a rosebud,
Perfect in every respect. When
One week old they operated to
Save his life. But the hole in his
Heart would have to be fixed
Another day. We prayed "God
Bless Joshua our darling little
Son." Thank God he lived this
Time, but the next operation
Was to be won. For about eleven
Months more, we had Josh our
Boy. We loved him and adored
Him. He brought us so much
Happiness and joy. Remember -
How he used to talk and laugh,
At the baby in the mirror by his
Bed. How he played peek-a-boo
And patty caked, kissed and
Hugged and shook his head. I
Was going to teach him things,
And had plans for me and him.
Joshua and I could have done so
Many things together - I was
Going to teach him how to fish
And hunt and ski and swim.
Oh mom! he's losing the grip
On my finger. Bless his heart -
He didn-t want to let go, he was
So peaceful and didn't linger.
Our darling Josh was dying. He
Stopped breathing, and the
Machines stopped. I'm going to
Hold his eyelids down. Poor
Baby never did any sinning. The
Angels wanted him, and had a
Place for Joshua. He wasn't quite
Eleven months old. Such a short
Time to love and to hold, before
He went to his heavenly fold.
He was born for Paradise. Joshua
Didn't live in vain - the letter
Said - Because of Joshua's eyes
two people are seeing. The
Angels began to sing. It was so
Hard to put our precious Joshua
Under the sod. But - Thy will be
Done. We had to let go - and let
GOD!

Angela Rae Cooper
NATURE'S ILLUSION
A tiny white kitten, its eyes
aglow;
Chasing a butterfly to and fro.
The butterfly's wings, a colorful
shade;
Fluttering and flittering through
the glade.
The morning sun, dazzling and
bright;
Making the day a beautiful
sight.
Flowers and grass sway in the
breeze;
Setting a feeling of total ease.
The tranquility of nature,
touched not by fate;
Love and beauty for those who
await.
Follow the path, answer the call;
Share in the love of the Master
for all.

Vikki
TIMELESSLY
Sunchildren, lost in nightness -
Spun in bombardments
of black to white,
wrong to right,
sight to blindness -
Are marching.
Life dancers, lost in fragments -
Woven in carpets
of moments with days,
styles with ways,
silence with comments -
Are stumbling.
Old timers, lost in years -
Painted on palettes
of growth and change,
depth and range,
dreams and fears -
Are trading.
Hope finders, lost in duties -
Dualed in conflicts
of rimes on reasons,
magic on demons,
time on worries -
Are searching.

Lorraine Hicks
AT THE THRONE
Down on my knees
praying to God
in Jesus' name...
The words of my mouth
reach into the heavens
to the throne of God
and so do I.

Lorna Tallent Kidwell
I LISTENED TO YOU
One spoke of riches, another of
fame,
Of brightest of lights and star-
written name,
But you spoke of roses sprinkled
with dew,
Of rain-drenched lilies and a
cottage for two;
You spoke of love in the old-
fashioned way
And my heart beat fast at all
that you'd say;
You spoke of sunsets, of skies,
silver-blue,
Of moon-light--of love--and I
listened to you.

Juliet Gilbert Messimer
IMPORTAMAN INC.
because simply
All the men carried purses with
eyeliner and smacked their lover
on the butt and used the same
john in the public restroom and
what were women to do?
They hadn't taken each other as
lovers yet so they shelved them-
selves alphabetically and wrote
desperate letters to France
"Dear Jean-Paul"
(No Dear Johns ever!)
and started
Import a Man, Inc.
A picture book of European men
who wanted to emigrate to this
country,
wear aprons,
tend babies,
father children,
make love
and when necessary
stay home while
woman went to the office
and thought of briefs but
not man's (after hours only.)
Importaman, Inc. needless to say
made a fortune slowly but soon.
And the old adage marry a
foreign girl she'll treat you like
a king was replaced by
marry a foreign boy
he'll treat you like a lady
(queen had other connotations
and had to be abandoned.)
So the American women traded
stories in the restrooms
about which countries had the
best men.

Marlene
QUESTIONS
Where
are the crickets
?
Where
have they been for so long
?
I listen for their songs
to soothe me to sleep.
What
ever happened
to the rustle trees
that used to whisper
when
everything was silent
when
it was dark,
silent night
?
Tap your secret code
against my window,
Please
?
I'm waiting for your message.
Why
aren't the windchimes
playing anymore
?
Gossiping the night away.
No more
dancing to their own music
?
When
did the leaves run away
with the breeze
?
Always in a hurry.
Who
sent the first raindrops
to percolate
on the rooftop
"Hello-Hi-How-are-you?"
?
Why
don't they visit me anymore
?

Alice A. Dial
MYSELF
Within myself,
My hidden me.
Uniquely secret
Never we.
Music singing,
Soul afire,
Yearning, churning,
Shy desire.
Poetry,
A cataract
Of jumbled thoughts
Forever act
Within myself,
My hidden me.
Unique. Only in Christ
Will self find Thee!

Marjorie Sullivan
TAKE SOME
So nice in the morning
A kiss and hello
caring for you
agrees with me so.
coffee and sweet smiles
planning our day
everything seems so natural
it's like we don't know.
This might be our last day
together
who knows what tomorrow may
bring
our kind of lovin is so insecure
nothing to bind us
no wedding ring
for we are bound by Nothing.
So let's make the most of today
don't let's quarrel
or unkind words say
our time may be passing
tomorrow may not come
If we can't have it all
Let's just *Take* some.

Dorothy Lundvall
MY BATTLE WITH FEAR
(Re: Special Son Keith)
The lights went out in Ronan
See. . .if you can
The blackness is so thick
It makes me sick
The wind is rustling the tree
So strong and free
Lightning flashes across the
sky.
Battle fear. Mom, Why?
Is there a candle or a lamp
In this here camp?
I try so hard to be brave.
Assurance she gave
She says there's nothing to fear
Oh dear—oh dear
She says be bold, I hear
So I battle fear
My mind tells me it is true
I try—I do.
God! The truth is, it's very
hard
Lightning's in my yard
God! Please turn on Your power
It's been an hour.
The darkness is so long
I must be strong
Fingers of darkness 'round me
creep
I must sleep
Yes, sleep is what it'll take
And when I awake
The sun will chase away the
night
Then I'll be alright. . .

Helen Barker Farmer
THE OLD CHURCH YARD
what secrets; lie beneath the
ground and tombstones lying all
around a vine covered crypt still
marks the spot a place that time
thus has forgot. The loved ones
who are stilled in death as if
they had taken not a breath but
oh what lives they hint have
lived and oh what silence now
they give. To read each marker
by the old churchyard some
from England some born out
there to suffer death and toil
and tear. And the old church
stands guard as if they all were
here still dancing laughing
giving birth but tis one quiet
spot on earth where all is quiet
save a bird who flutters here
and there and loves the old
churchyard. For here beneath
the cold dark ground there is
wisdom lying all around. And as
one sits and contemplates we
know that in spite of fate we all
must share this common state
before it is all too late to be
about our Fathers love and
cloaked with Light sent from
above we pay our debts to him
alone who sits upon the
Judgement Throne.

Kahrla I. Dutzman
TRANSMIGRATION OF A LOTUS IN EGYPTIAN DARK
dedicated to my j.e.c.
pressed in a thousand slabs of
sandstone locked in the quiet,
awesome sands for days and
nights and nights untold there
in Egypt where we held us
refusing parting, dust and sand.
in starless, moonless dark we
knelt before the olive Nile
i kissed your shut eyes, then
devoured the red of your lower
lip and you cupped your hands
around the whole of my flat
belly the khamsin gusting our
naked, cinnamon bodies.
humbled, dreadless, slaking the
need to never end us you
pressed a lotus in my hennaed
hair and vowed to braid its
length again in a distant life
that is
part of a greater plan
and i, filled with a second sight
and a sixth sense, swore that my
heart, my soul, my khu would
seek you out no peace, no rest
until i found you. now i tremble
to think i nearly missed you the
one i sought so desperately but
you, you knew me at the first
look and thief in the night,
jumped the neighbor's fence to
steal a flower for my hair.

Raymond Lockhart
THE WOMAN OF MY DREAMS
The Woman of my dreams
Is somewhere very far away.
I visit her from time to time
But wish it were every day.
We talk, we laugh, we share
good times
And I enjoy her company.
But for now at least, all she can
be
Is a very close friend to me.
We've teased each other many
times
And these I know I won't
forget.
Perhaps someday she can be
mine
But that can't happen yet.
Someday I hope we can be more
To each other than just good
friends
But until that day comes along
Friends is where the story
ends.

Caroline Curiale
BETWEEN FOREVER AND NEVER
Perhaps we're all a little foolish
When we say "forever",
When we see it cannot truly be.
When we listen, watch, feel the
tide of time;
And it quietly becomes clear...
We must take life as it comes
And try not to sorrow at its
emptiness,
Its pain, its heartache.
We must, instead, eke out life's
splendor;
Bathe in its sunshine;
And langour in the portion of
love we reap.
Perhaps it isn't forever,
But neither is it never...
We must glory at the
in-between,
For it is ours to cherish if we
will.

Michael James Cannon
UNTITLED
O, has anyone
(Imaginary conversations with
you I have on walls uselessly
spent)
A gun?

Donald P. Bourque
VISIONS OF LOVE
Visions of love appear before me
As still and peaceful as a clear
moon
On a summer's night.
Enlightening to those who
conceive its presence,
Yet quite mysterious to some
Who search for an
understanding.
Its meaning, faded and foggy,
Often revolves around
someone special.
As a vision can appear before
you one moment,
It can also be gone the next.
Should this vision become
recurring,
It is not merely an illusion of
your mind,
But of a content heart growing
closer to another.
Leaving the midst of your
dreams,
Your vision of love
Becomes reality.

Lee Wells
ANOTHER OF MY BLESSINGS
This blessing that I have been
blest with is so new.
May I thank Thee and always
praise Thee too.
Let me always honor it each and
every day.
For it has made me happy in a
special way.
This blessing came on the
seventeenth of May.
To others it was a very happy
and special day.
Part of this blessing was one
ever so fair.
So my thanks for your love and
care.
The happiness of my son
Timothy does abide.
For Nancy did become his
beautiful bride.
This blessing has made others
happy too.
My thanks to you for this
blessing so new.

Aileen L. Sarcedo
NUMBER 59. (HAIKU)
I, Love,...where, I live;
I wish,...my family could give;
It, a little chance...
To know,...where, they grow,
With, a house, to have, and
show;
Is worth,...everything.
Hear me, my Children,
It's the best, we can provide;
APPRECIATE IT !!!!!..

Louise A. Crispe
TRANSITION
The blossoms are gone, the leaves are taking shape.
The grass all around so fresh and green.
Can it be a year that you left me!
I sit by my window, a tear in my eye,
As I think of the years gone by.
My mind full of memories, my heart still shattered.
Oh darling, you left me alone.
The ring on my finger, still where you put it,
Somehow makes me feel that you're near.
Pray for me as I pray for you.
My muddled state, I know must end.
This life, still mine, was not meant to waste.
There's a world out there, I could lend a hand.
Lead me, my love, as you always have.

Dolores Saunders
NEAR—SIGHTED
The door is open
Revealing the fog
Hazy, misty ground clouds
Tinged with chill
Blurred palms point to the sea
distant-seeming
So life's problems tip-toe in
softly, slyly
Blurring our dreams' vision
Our eyes strain to see
those foggy pointers
to
That distant-seeming sea
of our chilled
intentions

Maribeth Hayden-Odegard
THERE IS THE LOVE
There is the love
swelling in the soul
like a high tide
warm and full.
Fleeting though
It remembers the wounds
so piercing.
God—the pain
black and heavy.

Joe Chapman
INFLATIONS CURE
If only people understood,
Inflation has another name,
It's not how much you make,
It's how you play the game.
Each of you decides a price,
To ask or get for the service
Or product you create;
You're free - set the premise!
If based on daily need alone,
For safety, shelter, food, and love,
You're list'ning to gentle words,
That whisper from Above.
If based on "how much can I get",
Or, "now I can make a killing",
For after all, you know,
Prices are spiralling!
If I insist on getting more,
And I receive it soon enough,
The cost of that new car,
Will hardly be so rough.
But if the dealer hears about,
The higher pay I'm getting there,
Will he insist on more?
Really, it isn't fair!
But the worker (or the seller),
The collective bargainers say,
Are free to charge as much,
As the "other" will pay.
Now suppose that each one of us,
Realized that this inflation,
Went up or down, as each
Priced his contribution.
Then each charged less instead of more,
Reduced their spending in accord
With his or her real need,
And surely could afford.
In separating greed from need,
Opulence and luxury go,
Who needs a Rolls Royce car?
It's only just for show.
This entertainment - costly thing,
Spectator sports included,
Million dollar players!
Greed again - denuded.
Oh, yes! We market players know,
Get-rich-quick buyers will believe,
That worthless stock goes up!
If only we deceive.
So, inflation spirals down,
No depression is in store,
When we each charge less,
As we contribute more!

E. P. Kennelly
UNTITLED
I gave him my heart--to keep.
But one day he gave it back
Almost in the manner
Of one returning a borrowed book.
So I put it away on a shelf,
And it just lay around
Getting dusty.
Recently, I got it out;
Thinking to polish it up...
Maybe give it to someone else.
But it has his fingerprints all over it--
And they won't come off.

Deborah A. Ridolfo
LUCKY
Maybe I'll get lucky
Maybe I'll get love
I know it sounds kind of funny, but I
Feel like I'm slippin' away
Maybe I'll get smart
Find a love to steal away my heart
Maybe I'll get lucky
Maybe I'll get love
Maybe I'll hit it right
And I'll be going out tonight
To get some kissin' and huggin'
And maybe some lovin'
Maybe someday I'll be happy
But today I cry
Maybe I'll get lucky
Maybe I'll get love

Allison H. Rudesyle
TEARS COME FROM THE SEA
the mermaids invited me to my watery grave;
as i leapt to their arms, the waters clave
to accept my sacrificial body, which i so gladly gave.
the pearly fish'women swam far away,
diving in and out of the salty, clear spray,
and as i sank to the sea floor, my knees bent to pray.
now, here i am, with the fish floating by.
milleniums have passed, i still cannot die,
and i can't even taste when i cry.

Joseph T. Hartnett
SLOWLY WE FALL IN LOVE
We don't feel a trace of love
as we lie under twinkling stars
above
gazing at the moon, a round
firey ball
both secretly wishing, on the
first star we seen fall.
We don't feel a twitch of love
lying in a meadow, lighted by
the sky above
a soft breeze blowing thru our
hair
carrying the sweet smell of
honeysuckle in the air.
We feel a beat of love
as the darkness slowly
disappears from the heaven's
above
then from the edge of the earth
the morning sun starts to rise
a new day, brightly shining in
our eyes.
We know we fell in love
listening to the song from birds
up above
turning to one another, we fall
into a kiss
we explain to our feeling's, each
in a short poetic verse
then with a kiss we seal the
vow to do this again
just the three of us, you, me and
the universe.

Leah Sarray Dudley
I DREAM OF ANDRE'
A warm bundle of joy I dream,
Giving all the love I have
In order to conceive
That tiny human being.
It's the ultimate sacrifice,
One which I would starve for.
The one who'll someday
Take my place,
One that I'd surely die for.
Nine months of pure ecstasy;
That steady growing within me.
The pain I'll feel as I cry out
My love--
My joy--
As he opens his eyes
For the first time.
Nibbling at my breast,
I will feed him well.
Gurgling for my attention;
My flesh and blood.
I will be his mother
And he will be my son.
Raising him will be a challenge
One I'll never regret.
Watching him with hope filled eyes.
While he takes his first steps.
Understanding when he comes to me
With his problems in life.
Making every phase easier
I do have that right!
Forgiving him for his wrongs,
And praising him for his rights.
Praying that I can raise my child
In God's total light.
Talking to him about the mortal
man I adore, and teching him
about the other man in my life.
The one who shines his
Precious--
Holy--
Light.

Wylie McGee
A GRATEFUL TRIBUTE TO MY HUSBAND
I hope you are aware,
Of all my pride in you.
Your patient, loving hand
Has been my guiding rein,
Through all these years of need
In judgment, more than main.
To growing son, a "Dad".
To falt'rin' "Mom", a guide.
With patience oft redresed.
You've given heart to strife
And kept the balance true,
Toward finer joys in life.
A tribute for your help:
Your constant, willing pledge
Of never ending faith,
Gives courage for the test,
And makes us wish to aim
Toward goals with added zest.

Jon Katherine Martins
BEAT APPOLLO
He was beat Appollo with
passion
Coarse grained - yes
But, oh, so magnificent in
Unending, adulating style
And when I held that man
For a brief space
Between sunset and sunrise
His loving felt so good to me
A baby girl,
Wrapped in his receiving
blanket,
How he satisfied my soul
Sugar daddy of dragons and Bill
Blake
Crazy kisses so sweet and
simply sexy
From a man who wore a panther
on his shoulder
Like a guardian angel, like a
badge of honor
Like this heart I wear
Tattooed to my sleeve
And I stroked that Burma cat
watching the way it moved me
While I moved him
Mannish boy.
Together we could have moved
mountains
Stopped the seas from shifting
Rendered the stars immobile
And if we said, "Sun!
Stop that shining!"

......It would
I was took at first
By the sheer magnetism
Of Papa's will
But then slowly, most assuredly
The subtle tenderness of his
grace,
His poetry emerged

Pauline M. Bearth
SILHOUETTE OF LOVE
Leaning against a sturdy old oak I become entranced by the beauty of the falling dusk
The wind blows warmly from above playfully chasing after falling leaves
Crickets softly serenade the coming evening I become lost, caught in twilight's spell
Closing my eyes, though you are miles away, I feel you are here with me sharing this golden moment
Gazing at the sky delicately colored by the setting sun I see our love silhouetted against the heavens
Envisioned there, we watch as day slips quietly into night our happiness echoing the surrounding beauty
As earth falls peacefully to sleep I dream of the time when our lives shall become one
My joy outshines the stars that fill the sky for my world is filled by the beauty of you and the falling dusk

Cynthia Zimmerman
HALLOWEEN
Tarantula talk
On the baby-doll walk
Melts the plastic gates
Where the were-woman waits
In the shadowed poise
Of a room without noise
She views tiny seas
Cups of different mes
Where woman, worn away
Were-wolf, be gay
Where man, witch way
What way can explain?
The choice of female me's
Hooked through multi'colored keys
Left in rooms without noise
Wallpapered with boys
tarantula talk
On the baby-doll walk
For blessing or worse
For better or curse
Whispers a fate
For all those who wait

McDonald W. Phipps
HAPPY NEW YEAR
Gone is the year one thousand
nine hundred eighty one,
In the cradle of the ages she sleeps;
To be awakened by unstrained
philosophies,
When in historians chambers
humanity peeps.
On her waded throne of gloom and
optimism,
Sits the youthful and vigilant
eighty two,
Which is confronted with
earthlings basic-problems,
Right, what each should do.
Inter woven with times progress
and injustices,
Antipathy had its share.
Now, for a better world let's work
side by side,
As I say "Happy New Year"

Susan Grebe
CHRISTMAS TIME
It's Christmas Time
but where are the smiles?
They aren't gone for long
they'll return in a while.
I reflect on the past
during each holiday season
so if you find me depressed
I do have a reason.
Please accept my feelings
and stay by my side
and in due time
you'll know why I cried
each past Christmas Eve
when everyone gathers
I'd sit in my room
and just say I'd rather
be by myself
and remember the past
when holidays meant smiles
and the days flew by fast.
Now everything's changed
but I've saved a few
of the smiles that came so easy
for when I see you.
I know I should realize
that time can't go back
to when I was little
and could sit in Daddy's lap.
I remember when
together we'd play
with the games I'd get
each Christmas Day
and when I got tired
I'd take a nap
all cuddled up
on Daddy's lap.
But I've grown up
and he's not here
although the memories remain
and will always be dear.
You can't take his place
but what I want to say
is that just like him
I love you more each day.
And I hope you realize
that this means a lot
because in my heart
he holds the number one spot.

Zelma Louise Baston
HEAVENLY FIREWORKS
Lightning raced her steed across the sky,
Thunder echoed back, "She has arrived!"
Lightning played her game of "hide and seek."
Thunder announced: "I found them here."
Fireworks equaling thousands of "Fourth of July" festivals,
And thunder like a battlefield of sky cannons.
Man can never minutely equal the Master's electrical display.

Dorothea Heckscher Schaff
REFUGE
Let me enjoy the haven of your arms!
Oh hold me close and let the world roll by,
So closely to your heart that mere alarms
Vanish away and seem at last to die,
Kiss me again, my love, without regret
For ah tis sweet to be in your embrace,
Such poignant ecstasy just to forget
A while the sorrows of the human race,
Would that I had the power held by Fate
To weave the web of human destiny,
For then I'd never pause or hesitate
To bind you closer, ever near to me!
Alas, an idle dream, a sorry jest
To try to hold the magic of this hour,
But, meanwhile, fold me once more to your breast,
As though our love forevermore would flower!

Michelle Blake
DID YOU PERHAPS SEE THE BUTTERFLY IN ME?
Did anyone see the caterpillar,
when his life came to an end?
I forgot that the butterfly
was the caterpillar's friend.
They went through life united
But no, they were apart,
for where the caterpillar dies,
a butterfly will start.
I share the face of many a man
But still I think I'm unique
I run from the faces I cannot stand
and the real me seems so weak.
I am old, I am dying, I need to be free!!
Soon you will see the next part of me ...
And so the butterfly came to be
my wings are aglow with colours so free.
I left behind a face which no one now will see,
for that was the caterpillar which died in me.

William W. Adkins
A TRIP THROUGH THE SNOW
Why the weather forecaster's claim of light snow
For Muskegon and over Grand Rapids way
Was so terribly erroneous I do not know
As a blizzard was surely the order of the day
Overhead the menacing clouds were grey
But the sun shown brightly through it all
"Don't risk it," says the wife in dismay
"No cause for concern," says I, "We'll have a ball."
The snow began ever so lightly to fall
"We must turn back now," the wife insisted,
"Before it gets too dark; you and your ball,
On our way back you'll be glad I resisted."
Heavier and heavier the snow sure came down.
"We should have turned back," said she, "but now it's too late."
"You have always been a worry wart, said I, with a frown.
But I wasn't so sure now - an accident could be our fate.
The blizzard was now upon us; the vision wasn't good
"Pull over to the side and stop," said she.
"It's not all that bad," said I, "look at the car - see the hood?"
"We'll never get home alive," she said, "Must this be?"
Suddenly the snow let up and then it became less and less,
The sun was shining again; it hadn't been too bad, after all.
"I've been praying," says the wife, "that we could get out of this mess."
"Look," says I, "the day is young; we can still have a ball."

Rebecca Nance Riner
THE FLOWER
Among a cranied, cracking wall
A flower began to grow.
No one believed it ever could
But how could they know?
It was among this storm of trouble
Somewhere the flower found peace enough to bloom.
Somehow it found space to grow
Though no one gave it room.
The flower had faith in God and itself,
To try was all it did know.
If we have no faith in God or ourself
How shall we ever grow?
You see, life is just a melody.
One which doesn't play for long.
But if you, like this flower, can sing
You too will fit the song.

Wendy Van Voorhees
ICECREAM CONE
My red wet flicks
The white softness
Which is creeping
Stealthily down
This brown so quick.
The coolness knows
It melts, I think,
But still it hides
From my red wet--
White dripped between
my toes.

Ida S. Barton, Danae
DAYSPRING*
The day-star dances in the highest lights
and May arises to her heights,
flinging her garland from light to bower,
flinging the cowslip and
the pale prim-flower.
The daysman praises, and to bless

and raise the green
that God did dress.
We watch the entrance
and wish thee long,
and taste the verdure
and dance The Song*
(Luke: One 78)

Martina Sonner
THE GOLDENROD
A cinderella of the fields,
A child of wind-cast seed,
So humble and so nondescript,
There grew a lowly weed.
It lived along the meadow fence,
It thrived beside the wall,
Tenaciously it hugged the road,
'Twas scraggy, green and tall.
A weed neglected day by day
Beneath the summer skies,
Uncultivated and unloved,
A princess in disguise.
And then one autumn day I saw
A burst of golden plume,
Along the road, along the wall,
The field fence was in bloom.
The weed had caught the summer sun,
Had stored the golden light,
And now it flung its treasure forth,
In spasms of delight.
It welcomed bees and butterflies,
It shared its wealth untold,
From rags to riches it had grown,
Its value more than gold.
I saw a bit of heaven there,
I stood in awe of God,
While basking in the beauty of
The lovely goldenrod.

Robert J. Miller
INTENDANT
We talk as the moon blooms on
The ridges; we talk of walnut
Seeking; ripe mulberries are
Scattered on grass; our smiles
Are nuzzled with stem fluffs;
Our dog's gnathic quiet sleeps
At our ankles; slowly awakening
To turn an ear with affection:
This is a glade where the wind
Streams with gentlest knead;
We speak of a path to a region
From which memory retracks its
Indubitable and priceless
Intendants; a place of memory
Secure where fondest wonders
Are amaranths to our longing tenure.

Dawn I. Hudson
LIVE TODAY
Live today
Not in fear of tomorrow
Or in regret of yesterday
But for today
To enjoy to the fullest
To accomplish your goals
To conquer your quests
To fulfill your dreams, hopes, & plans
Live today, for today
With a zest for life
A realization for love
Enjoying God's miracles
And be joyful
Because you're alive
Because you can be...
...all that you want to be
You can do anything
You set your mind to
You can be free
To love life

A. Lily Rosado
NO MORE BIRTHDAYS, NO MORE JOYCE
Today my little girl
will be seven years old this day
A sunny day like this
on the very first of May.
As she opened my gift
I remember her surprise
when out of the box
jumped her new puppy, Spice.
But there won't be anymore birthdays
no laughter, no Joyce
I saw my baby last
lying among her toys.
She was a victim of a stranger
just a passer by
who saw my little princess
playing alone outside.
The stranger is gone
never to be found
while my innocent daughter
lies lifeless in the ground.

Bobbie Holder
FLY WITH THE WIND
The sound of the wind,
as it blows through a tree.
A sound if you listen,
can set you free.
So fly with the wind
and never come down.
Fly with the wind,
that makes life's sound.
The wind that blows
over a desert somewhere.
That sways the flowers
with oh so much care.
So fly with the wind,
if you dare.
Hurry! Hurry!
There's no time to spare.
So fly away now
and be set free.
Like the sound of the wind,
as it blows through a tree.

Stan Logan
HOW
How can one live and doubt,
Hearing a child's gleeful shout,
Or see a bird in graceful flight,
And flowers blooming in colors bright.
Billowy clouds in skies so blue,
Dear God—we owe these all to you.

Jocelyn Townsend
I LOVE YOU
I love you beyond time and space.
I have loved you in ages past
And in future time yet uncounted.
We have lived fully together
But we have died alone
Knowing that act must be
Rectified, and our souls
Seek one another out to love
Over and over again.
Joy fills our hearts as we faintly
Recognize the other in the
Experiences of many levels of love
In different lifetimes.
In this realization, our
spirits do revel.
What peace and beauty is felt
In living or dying, when
We know there is no death of
The Light of our souls!

J. Carlton Sherwood
THE SINGLE STANDARD
May Christ be to you forever new
As He was to Moses or Luther;
Do not you turn, as Israel drew,
The golden calf for Lucifer.
Satan's smooth and subtle cue
Impulse in his secret sateings.
Self - puffed and full his crew;
Play acting for his fateings.
Unless here one's faith grew,
Tall and above those inflatings -
Ever to realize so true;
Infidelity gives no rebatings.
To God and Christ ever endue,
All the glory and all the grace;
You are not your own retinue,
Nor cared for by your face.
Who took from Her the sacred look?
And virgin innocence pure;
"Him will I blot out of my book"
Spoke a jealous God be sure.
He reflected on thy God's motive,
And the Edenic standard there,
On that which we breathe and live -
Now adulterates this air.
May you never offer the excuse,
That in your plans, science or art,
In falsity have done abuse;
For children to Christ we start.

AM Felipe
WE WRITE
As poets we write
Not hearing
Not caring
What the critics may say
When they analyse our work
Into meanings, of
Symbolism, concrete aspects,
Metaphors and rhymes,
As if we think and write
Like cold ored lettered presses.
As poets we write
Not hearing
Not caring
for critics—
We write and care
Only for what our being
Cannot help but hold
—experiences that
Pregnate us to the limb
And begs for penciled release.
We write—
Only that we may save you
We write. . . . . .
We write (and will continue to write)
Words
Expressions
Meaning.

M. Ruth Howard
THE EMPTY MAIL—BOX
Her heart is light as she goes to the box,
For she hopes a letter is there.
But if it is empty, the way back is long,
And her heart is filled with despair.
for no one knows the load she bears.
No one but God above.
Just a line or two to say they are well,
From the ones she so dearly loves.
Yes, just a few lines on a post-card,
To gladden her heart each day.
The way to the mail—box is short,
If "Dear Mom" is all you can say.
So drop her a card tonight,
Tell her how much you care.
Don't be the cause of the tears in her eyes,
Or put more grey in her hair.
For when she is gone you will miss her,
And tears you will shed each night,
But Mom will know your heart aches,
And the tears are for the letters you failed to write

Rudy Zakall
LET HIM IN
Let him in, oh let him in,
Open up your heart
And let the Lord come in.
Let him in, oh let him in,
Open up your soul
And let Jesus dwell within.
Let him in, oh let him in,
Open up your mind
And let the Holy Spirit reign.
Let him in, oh let him in,
Fold your hands in prayer
And praise the Holy Trinity.
Let him in, oh let him in,
And you shall be saved and blessed
Till eternity.

Antonia Toledo Sherrod
DAWN
First rays of sun what do I see?
A silvery blanket all in front of me
Little tiny diamonds sprinkled over the grass
Makes the air smell fresh and sweet, but alas,
The sun comes out and the diamonds vanish,
as the rays of gold touch them and turn them into a mist of steam

Daniel F. Weir
THE ANGEL AND THE FALLEN STAR
I watched it fall the length of the silver night
Trailing stardust across the moonlight.
I followed its shimmering path with wonder and awe
As it drew straight and near without flaw.
I rushed to her room and saw it settle on her pillow.
Nestled in her golden hair it began to glow.
A soft white, heavenly light, it spread,
Hovering like a halo above her sleepy head.
I watched them there, the angel and the fallen star,
And whispered aloud, "Why have you come so far?"
She grew to love the gentle tiny

sun,
The soft light that sparkled in her hair as one.
She grew to love, to live and then to leave.
And for all the years that have passed I still grieve.
Sometimes I wonder if the fallen star was blind
To have died and left a universe behind.
And I wonder, as might a man of lonely dreams
Who charts the course of silver moonbeams,
If perhaps she followed the fallen star home,
And that high in the misty heavens, I'm not alone.

James G. Linn
FULFILLMENT

How these dreams and hopes reflect the phantoms of mystical fires to stoke a human furnace whose heat we reject while we cling to its lightwaves of hope.

Engaged in an act of a self so aware a symphony sublime to fuse as one our molecular selves, so random will care to become complete while all else is undone

For paint brush and pencil to see my hand must flow with illusion and art will become a dream to free the imitation from the inner delusion

To do what I am, is but to fulfill an unconscious awareness of this life that part of the self on a conscious hill for to truly live can destroy all strife.

Sammie Marie Slatcoff
MY SHADOW

My shadow is my constant companion,
He doesn't go anywhere without me.
Usually following or walking beside,
Never going out of my sight.
He never can stand up by himself,
And lets everyone walk on him.
He never has anything to say,
Walking along quietly.
My only complaint about my shadow,
He's a coward, afraid of the dark.
When I want to go out at night,
He stays at home.
Leaving me to go by myself.
And waiting for my return by the light.

M. G. Corson
I AM THE OCEAN

I am a living constant symbol changing.
Yet the Changeless Unlimited Being am I.
I am the waves that take form as time and force demand,
That ease or crash back into Sameness.
I am the Ocean of all things that you desire,
Riding or sinking with waves of delight.
I am the magnificent Ocean!
Play on, and ride with the waves of things from me!

Donna L. Dougherty
BENEATH

A sweet, gentle flower; I speak of the rose
Yet on thorn-covered bushes it lovingly grows.
In colors of yellow, pink, or pure red
Somehow mocking beauty; asleep in their bed.
Nature had camouflaged this cousin of heath
And bestowed a painful-pricked stem underneath
Sowing a moral of life in the green
Of what lies hidden and of what is seen.
One must look deeply and past first impressions,
And face the existence of future possessions.
To view clearly what lingers in matter and mind,
And touch upon lightly what grows on the vine.

Della E. Nugent
MY FATHER'S HANDS

Father's hands may not have portraits painted
Nor carved a single statue, nor created
Great literature for every age to scan.
His hands were destined for love's labors;
To lift the fallen, or aid his neighbor.
He rather chose to prove himself a man!
His hands knew love! Smoothed the rocky road
His motherless children had to travel.
They calmed childish fears, lifted the heavy load,
Banned exploits...adventure's schemes unravelled.
Those hands of love, now folded cold in death
Should've been a doctor's conquering a wilderness!
Father, you refused ambition's dreams for me
That I might know a love like that of Calvary.

Robert Michael Grossman
LISA'S SONG

Prancing among the daffodils,
Her dress filled with lace and frills,
She gaily muses and lifts her arms
In the sky, like a caged bird,
Yearning to fly.
She will freely admit
That she is sick,
Though only at night
Are her eyes sad,
Filled with tears and fright.
She is a child at play,
Partaking of the delights,
That we would normally refrain;
She has no fear of life, only death,
For it cheats her of passions and desires,
And the man she loves,
And that is her only wrath.
Yet, she indulges herself
Instead of contemplating her future;
She merrily dances in the sun
Among the wild things,
And puts out of her mind
Her body's torture.
A child,
A lovely child,
And as I watch
I must laugh and smile with her,
For this is her life's dance and song;
Lisa knows she doesn't have long,
She takes out her measure
And enjoys her pleasures.

Sadie M. Stafford
THE GUM CRACKER

Some girls chew gum sedately,
Some don't chew gum at all;
Others make it crack so loud
It echoes down the hall.
Why they should be so noisy
And ill-bred we cannot know,
But some of us could tell them
Just where we wish they'd go.
There is nothing so annoying
To the fellow worker's ear,
As the one who keeps it popping
Till we wish she'd strip a gear.

Bonnie Faye Matheson
PEACE AND BEAUTY

Sunset
In the mountains.
The Beauty
As the sun sinks behind the mountains.
The Sun
Casting sunbeams, as shadows slowly creep over the mountains and the valleys below.

The Sky
As it turns scarlett with the fiery reflection of the hidden sun.
And Then. . .The Darkness
The quiet stillness of the night.
So Quiet. . . So Peaceful
As if nothing else exists.
Nothing
Other than the mountains, the trees, the occasional call of an owl, or a whippoorwill. . .
And "me".

Miss Tracy McDonald
LIFE

I look up and I see an endless sea of hopes and dreams never to come true,
Or will they?
I am traveling through time, defeating life's problems, and striving to be me.
I feel as if I'm trapped in a world of confusion, and there is no hope!
I am afraid;
and yet I feel brave.
I am confused;
yet wise.
I am a young woman grown old through the seemingly endless pain of life.

Maurice Ronald Jamerson
THE NEW YEAR

Hear the bells ring out the old and,
merry shouts bring in the new.
The news has gone throughout the land;
Farewell!—the current year is through.
Raise your glass!—Let's drink a toast!—
Don funny hats, strike up the Band!
The old year's gone—it's but a ghost—
A bright new one is now at hand!
Farewell to the past that now is gone,
in memory it will always dwell;
What e'er betide we must press on,
time is fleeting, use it well!
Mourn not the cross that you must bear,
it's little worth when we complain;
Rather-tell a friend you care—
That the future will be bright again.
We mortals are a curious lot!
We strive so hard for discontent;
Be satisfied with what you've got!
Thank Heaven for all blessings sent.
As for me—I'll say a prayer,
and hope my Master will but heed.
May I fare as well as I did last year;
That He'll say yes-Well done-Godspeed!

Natalie Rose Scavone
TO ERIC—3-18-81

trying to etch a rainbow,
trying to paint the dawn,
searching for my happiness—
can it be all gone?
standing in the meadow,
gazing toward the sky,
waiting for time to stop—
has he passed me by?
suddenly i'm lonely,
searching for a friend,
hoping that someday soon—
my broken heart will mend.
i've found that special someone,
alone in this world, too—
he came along and held my hand—
he turned my grey clouds to blue.

JoAnne McDaniel Robichaud
GROWING APART
We were happy.
We were sad.
We loved.
It was wonderful.
Then it disappeared.
Like a flower
Growing
From a beginning.
Until we reached
So high
That we couldn't
Continue.
The sunshine
Vanished.
We wilted
Apart.

D. M. Cronin
NATURE COMPROMISED
I went to the hills to save myself.
Along the weathered path I wandered lonely, looking
to the top where I was to repent and wash in beginning brooks.
As I sauntered the traveled trail,
just as if in a fairy tale;
my eyes diverted to my right by Vincent's insolent flowers,
growing as if painted under an innocent child's power.
Blooming bright as the daystar,
weariless wild into the distance far.
My eyes dancing
through the yellow spots happily,
I found a young tree
broken, to the left of me,
filling the air with its sweet-scented gum,
hard and jeweled in the sun.
The wind that had broken
the timid limb,
playfully swayed the branch setting it to motion,
making the bird's nest it housed fall,
and I bowed to the natural law
able to wander the path freely
to the top meeting the sky mellowing.
The waters rippling, cleaning
and leaving me naked in the setting sun—
—luminous,
swaying me in the wind,
the star to shine on my skin.

N. Jo Murley
DEMAGOGUERY
Such heroic histrionics some politicians use to parry with the public trying to seduce us with hypnotic hyperbole and folksy way.

How sad they're self servants who spend nights in darkness counting silver earned negating rights of a captive audience come Election Day.

Ann Nelson Martin
MY CHRISTMAS GIFT
My favorite gift for Christmas
Isn't boxed or wrapped and tied
It's the warm and loving feelings
That are growing deep inside
It's the warm and loving feelings
That seems to surface at this time
It brings us close together
If only in our minds
With hustling and bustling, hurry and haste
Never a moment that we may waste;
Shopping, cooking and cleaning galore
Candles and tree trimmings
With wreath on the door
And ordors from the kitchen
Come of sugar cookies, spicy fruitcake
The buttery smell of fresh popcorn
With candy bubbling in the make
It's the good Old-Christmas Spirit
That would be most greatly missed
So I'll put it first and foremost. .
On this years Christmas List.

Sharie Sisler
THE RESCUE
Cold and still was the night,
The sky had no depth,
The ground was white and glittered,
Please G-d let me rest.
The snow looked warm and peaceful,
And drowsy I became,
Sleep would have overcome me,
If I gave in to nature's game.
I saw a light in the distance,
How far I did not know.
I crawled and trudged for hours,
Through the warm and peaceful snow.
Suddenly, I heard strange voices from afar
As I tried to sleep,
A passerby had rescued me
From the snow so cruel and deep.

Tory Robinson
THE ROSES SECRET
The roses are whispering o'er my fence
With blushes emitting celestial scents;—
Infant buds bid me and blossoms imply
That I should look up and search the still sky:—
"Is there a secret that you care to share
Pink petals a-nodding in the spring air?"
They still beckon me so I scan the sky
And then whisper back, "Oh please tell me why?—
The soft, scalloped clouds are usually here
And bluebirds in flight forever appear!"
Now I discern a sight in silhouette
That the roses and I shall never forget;—
The mountain peaked heav'nward, resting west
Displays with dappled splendor, winter's crest:—
Their secret I share an imposing thing
How rare to see roses and snow in Spring!!

Jonathan Tin
DAYDREAMS
When I daydream, when I wonder,
When I think, and when I ponder,
I think of things of long ago,
Or future worlds they do not know.
They are the ones,
The serious thinkers,
The ones that stand straight
And their minds do not tinker.
I conjure up lies of great fantasies,
That's what I do, that one is *me.*
I wonder of quests, or years out at sea,
Roughing it out,
Yes, that one is *ME.*

J Jones Clarno
THE DOLL HOUSE
I grew into a pink, hard, cold plastic--molded by machines in a Mississippi factory.
I am the doll.
The thought roars with a marshmallow laughter.
Like a chill in refrigeration, Dali paints women faces in angelic sunlight, only the moon reveals the green wires.
I muse.
For; In a thousand pieces my manuscript is buried in the depths of the sea, far away in never never land.
This is the true poem.
Too frightened
To be the perfect play thing,
I eat poetry for breakfast now.
Staring at white/beige pages on a winter morning--I note the overcast is like December in Calcutta.
It is not enough that women bring men into the world but men with weapons like a red sun scuttles them into purgatory: one by one their footsteps are void of shadows.
It is the middle march, in a factory in Mississippi.

Jerry St. Croix
PRESENCE OF GOD
When my Soul rides my mind
With the reins pulled up tight
I know I'm heading for the light
But, when my mind over comes me
As Soul
I'm going towards things of old
I see people struggling
Just as I do, to stay on the middle road
The one that is true
To balance out our life
Is not a means to an end
Its just the beginning, my dear friend
I'll cultivate my love for you
Then you'll know, I'll be true
Teach me the secret of life
And of the beautys that exist, beyond the eyes
Now, I'll have my heart and mind on you
Thats what I want to do
Be with you Blessed SUGMAD in light and sound
Then I'm on heavenly ground.

Donna Kay Geryk
NATURE IS LOVE
Nature negotiates it's nourishing love,
It deems no desires to be damned.
Crystalline clouds call: "Come,
Find happiness—flourishing and fluttering here."
Green pines grow in that utopian garden
Whispering willowy vows; which woe
The heathen heart, hurt in mortal life,
Promising permanent paradise to thee now.
Butterflies bud fully into bloom
Bringing their beauty, breathless to behold.
Friend, why forsake this favor
For human hate, hindrance and humiliation?
Roses represent nature's role.
Play her part—pluck plenty,
Bestow these beauteous blooms before
Love slips sinfully into silence.

Lynda Kaye Thomas
SLOW BURNING FLAME
Someone new
to end the night.
I'm drawn to you
like firelight. . .
and rapidly
I can't explain
this fall of wonder
and slow burning flame.
As delicate
as your first touch
I need you more
if not as much. . .
unlike winter ocean rains
hold me from under
your slow burning flame.
To you I wish
that I could say
"love me" as
you will today. . .
as I fear
to go insane
should tomorrow I die
in your slow burning flame.

Carilynn C. Causey
THE CENTER OF GOD'S WILL
God has a center circle called His Will:
A special place for you to fill.
A place where you'll find peace and rest,
The strength to meet life's hardest test.
The feeling of His presence keen.
His wisdom, guidance you will glean.
The choice is yours, to choose His Will:
To let him mold and make you 'til
You seem like Him in every way.

In thoughts, and deeds, and
what you say.
May you find His Will in all
your ways;
Desire to serve Him every
day.
God bless you as you grow to
fill
That special center of His
Will.

Anna Flanagan
SOMETIMES
Sometimes when I see you
I start to wish for more than
my share.
Sometimes when I see you
I wonder why we didn't meet
before.
Sometimes when I see you
I wish you'd see only me.
And sometimes, most of the
time,
I'm happy just to know you, and
be your friend.
I'm happy just to be your
friend.

Timothy F. Pederson
A WISH FOR LIFE
While thinking back in memory
Of one I left behind,
I wonder now if possibly
I could have been more kind.
Maybe if I might have said
A kinder word 'tis true.
I might not lie here in this bed,
Alone and without you.
Do you ever think of me at all
Or is it now too late.
For I find we've had a fall;
A bad run-in with fate.
To be together with you once
more
Would set my heart awhirl.
Not to see that still closed door
But my own little girl.
The only life I wish for us
Is one that two can share,
A life that's built on love and
trust,
A life beyond compare.

Ellen R. Henry
WHEREABOUTS
Cars pass by,
a distant song. . .
The days become shorter,
as the nights are long.
A memory lingers,
an anonymous face,
Take on a forbidden hue
of a long forgotten place.
Touching an element
etched only in time.
Eternally I search,
but there's nothing to find.
Placate the natives,
hush the tide.
It's breaking on an endless
beach,
there's nothing left to hide.
Honesty is only a word,
it reeks of pain and sorrow.
Remnants gather in the dust,
but where will they be
tomorrow?

Kathlene Lough
THE AUDIENCE
A battle has been waged
Upon the bloody stage
A warrior lies dead
At the curtain's edge
What was once his head
Stares mutely at the crowd
Who do not applaud
They sit without a care
And watch with detached air
As another and yet another
The warrior's daughter then
his mother
Fall to death before them
So very dumb and unaware
Mistakenly they've been spared

Marilyn O. Lunn
ODE TO SPRING
The pussy willow by the
babbling brook
dons a sheath of silver silk.
The lily wears a satin gown
as white and pure as milk.
Daffodils in their yellow frocks
brighten any gloomy day.
And cup-shaped tulips in red
shantung
made in the simplest way.
Pastel hyacinths attired in
organdy pinafores
enhance fragrance to the touch
of spring.
While tiny crocuses in waltz
gowns of tulle
listen approvingly as the song
birds sing.
The chirping robin has returned
in a new brown suit and bright
red vest.
But I still think my blue chiffon
is as lovely as the rest.

Lynne Lyons
UNTITLED
Ascending webs of moonbeam
thread
growing into spinning
prisms. . .
a cage dissolves
a tiny creature flies away
to a land where nothing
lives
except elfin kings and the
beat of wings
I go with the wind
and with the unicorn
soaring to forever
with firedreams flashing

Charles Henderson
LIVING STATUES
The graceful forms stand tall
Like Grecian statues
Around a jade green pool.
They are motionless;
Their eyes are blank, and yet
reflect
The tranquility of this moment.
Standing there beneath the
autumn sun,
One by one, they are posed
In statuesque splendor.
With skin as smooth as
alabaster
Their flawless faces are aglow,
Each radiating in its own way
Amidst glistening locks of
Shades of gold, red or brown.
How can we know
That these scuptured curves are
carved
From flesh and not stone?
Look! We can see clearly now
The rise and fall of full, haltered
bosoms
Which signal an inner warmth
As well as the breath of life.

Rita Adame
UNTITLED
My Whisper is like the wind's
blow
My Dreams make my love grow;
I tried not to let my feelings
show
But I guess you already know
I love you so.

Fritz Guendel
ETERNAL BLISS
The moon is shining beautiful
And slowly closing in on
midnight
How time went by
Since I am waiting here for you
Oh—when you come
I know
In this enchanting hour
We will devour
Every kiss
Eternal bliss
Enlightens our overflowing
hearts
While we are one
In silent pleasure
Gathering the roses of love
As gentle touch of time goes by
The moonlight serenades us.

R. Bateman Newcomb
LE GRAND CAFE
How often were you waiting
there
As I came running down the
street;
How welcome was that
haunting smile
That greeted me each time we'd
meet.
We listened to the old songs
played
And tipped the pianoist a beer;
There was a magic everywhere,
Enchanted days of yesteryear.
I pass the table that was ours
And other couples do I see;
And though I come a thousand
times
You won't be waiting there for
me.

Sharon E. Thomas
OH GOD
I changed my life to make you
stay,
I changed myself in so many
ways,
To make you feel like a special
man.
I made you proud, but I can't
understand,
What happened to us on this
autumn day?
I thought I was so special, you
made me believe;
Why did you leave on this given
day.
I thought you were special, in a
girls kind of way.
My crying and hoping won't
bring my man back,
So I'll try to forget, cause I
can't understand, the
thoughts of such a wonderful
man.
Oh God, It's happened to me,
I just loved him too deeply for
anyone to see.
But, now he's gone too far away,
it's goodbye my love,
For the world to see,
What a wonderful girl he made
of me.

Shirley A. Settle
DEATH
Death is the undisturbed sleep
of the soul;
An embryo in a lifeless form
awaiting life again.
As a child lays sleeping,
beautiful and innocent
in all his motives, so is
DEATH!!!!!!!!
We cannot say, "He is gone. He
is no longer here."
For somehow, though the heart
beats not, so lives the man!
The blood is not passing over
the route one was accustomed
to see function so
circumspectally, nor is the
brain making more than just a
few mistakes.
The eyelids do not close at the
end of another busy day; no
lips speak softly, nor do the
ears hear the gentle breezes
blow.
What, then, makes you the
victor over DEATH?
Me thinks the answer lies in the
spirit of our living. . . . . .

Peggy J. Parlee
SONSHINE
How proud we were when you
were born,
So small and pink and wiggley
and warm,
Little did we know, we'd watch
you grow,
From building blocks to
skipping rocks,
From Twinkle Twinkle Little
Star,
To playing with your first racing
car,
From cooing and a rattle's noise,
To playing baseball with the
boys,
From those first toddlers steps
and skinned knees,
To flying kites in the breeze,
And as you grow, step by step,
All these memories will be kept,
How do we teach you that
rough and tough,
Aren't always going to be
enough,
That a warm smile and gentle
hand,
Are just as important in being a
man.
With you go all our hopes and
dreams,
Of all the great and wonderful
things,
But most of all, as you can
guess,
We will with you happiness,
And with God's blessing from
above,
One day you'll know how much
you're Loved.

Shelly Weiss

MY FAMILY

There's something I have that I love,
Other than Jesus far up above.
I treasure it wherever I go.
Everyone has one that I know.
But mine is sort of special you see.
I'm talking about my family.
They love me alot that I'm sure of
I know that cause they show me in love.

Daniel K. Bristol

NEW FROM OLD

ALL my questions left unanswered from before and yet a new light begins to glow off in the distance. Bewildered by the past and intrigued by the future; I seem to exist in a partial trance. One that keeps me dreaming of what might be, while keeping me close enough to still touch reality. How knowingly I greed for something that might just be the instrument of my own destruction. This insane lust for such an entity is unexplainable and certainly sadistic. I thrill at her touch and kiss...so fine. All I want is for her to be mine. So much to ask of one so unfamiliar. Fading slowly as it drifts across the scarred memories of my mind; an old flame leaves a place it once kept warm. Could this fall together, so soon after such a downfall of faith in all that is right? Each encounter brings intensity to those feelings that already exist. The glow inside brightens with each passing moment. Will fears of ghosts from the past come true and smother the flame as it grows and glows? If it must end, let it do so now before the feeling enlightens and lifts my spirits past the point of return. Let it grow, as I feel it should, but don't let this love grow only to die. And then have our hearts look back and say, "I knew it would end this way."

Written: October 20, 1981
For: Kim Dahlgren

Montrose

WHY?

Why am I afraid to look at your face that has a smile so rare?
Why am I afraid to look at your eyes with that mysterious stare?
Why do I still enjoy your arms close around my neck?
Why do I want you to hold me longer and give me more than a "peck?"
Why, when you hug me, I feel I am yours and you are truly mine?
Why was I never able to develop a love for you of another kind?
Why does excitement flow through me when anyone mentions your name?
Why do I drop my head when I see you and feel guilt and shame?
Why does 20 years of separation not seem to matter?
Why can I not talk to you instead of "chatter chatter?"
Why can't you touch me without stirring feelings of desire?
Why, when you leave and walk away, my whole body is on fire?

Ruth Madden Jones

AUTUMN AGLOW

Oh, the sweet mystery of Autumn
While a few flowers are in blossom.
The air takes on a different feel
Many will take to the fields.
Golden Rod is all abloom
Frost must not appear too soon.
Colors of every hue
Awaken each day with the morning dew.
Stately, tall and small the trees are grand
They are always on the reviewing stand.
Such regal beauty cannot last
Winter is coming with a big blast.

T. R. Davis

WHY?

A child was born that awaited day,
His parents planning a long life's stay.
A short time passed and taken away,
The child died one saddened day.
The most difficult task left to do
Was for Mom and Dad, and others too,
To take each step while wondering who
Or what, they might have been able to do.
They began a search for the reason why
That he was the one chosen to die,
A search interrupted by time to cry,
And failing to find the answer to "why?"
If as the pages of the calendar turn,
They speak with their Lord, then they'll learn,
He'll provide the answer for what they yearn,
Not the answer to "why?", but where to turn.
He'll let them know that He'll always be
Ready to listen and bear what they see,
And He'll let them know how eternally
Each life of one month or one thousand will be.

Gwendora H. Reese

THOUGHT

Amazing what you find
Simply by not looking.
Unceasingly flowing
Like mighty rivers
Unperturbed by evolutionary change.
Expanding length—breath of unity—
You say a universal phenomenon,
And I only sought to capture a thought.
Undertaking, it's no small endeavor.
For thought is quite clever;
Captivating attention—unrenowned
In persistance no suitor can be found
Stamina, thought form many a book
Inclined to think, thought's a snook.
An idea so brilliant I could burst
Alas! To think thought thought it first.
Uninhibited, classification undefined
Predestined, form essence of mind
Try rid thyself you shall see
Forever, always, constant company
When I lay me down to sleep
Into my dream thought gently seep.
Why then try put into captivity
Unquenchable spirit bound to be free?

Lettie J. Williams

TIME FOR TRUST

When your dreams have turned to ashes
And your heart is filled with pain,
You wonder why when you've been true
That into your life comes rain.
When your pocketbook is empty
And tomorrow's hid from view,

And you try so hard to believe
That somehow it's best for you.
Then it's sweet to know that He cares
That He knows you through and through.
Earthly friends may forsake or fail
But He's ever staunch and true.

Rala J. Mahdi

MOTHER'S ARE LIKE THAT

A toast to Mother
There is no other
Who spends time like she
Holding and caressing me.
God sent her from above
Enriched with lots of love
No one can take her place
With all her given grace.
Each and every day
In her own special way
She gives me strength to survive
Making me feel so alive.
She's always so full of hope
With us and life she copes
There is never a doubt
What Mothers are all about.
Anyone would agree
All she's done for me
I sometimes on my knees pray
"Thank you God for her each day."

Elynor A. Baran

A GIFT IS BORN

Pouring rain on a summer day!
A gift arrives to grace my years!
Elegant in color, white and brown—
Spindly tall legs, mournful blue eyes—
A Siamese kitten!
Self willed and possessive!
Her defense, a batting paw and ruffled nose.
Put her claim on a special velvet chair—
A lacy bedspread, an acrylic painting
Including the family Bible!
Sadness turns into laughter!
Perched over the kitchen sink
Scolding, mewing to the squirrels and birds!
Plunk! Splash! I view a priceless carving soap bubble—
As the kitten falls backwards into the soapy suds!
The years march on gracefully!
Kitten grows into maturity—
Mournful eyes have disappeared—
Gives me her paw when asked for gratitude.
Keepataw Lalka the Sealpoint Siamese!

Mrs. Sharon J. Carroll

PRAISE THE LORD I'M GOING HOME

I'm going home where I belong,
Praise the Lord I'll sing his song.
The words are pure and simply free,
The gates have opened up for me.
The golden stairway I must climb,
Praise the Lord I'll make it this time.
The Lord he knows I've seen the light,
I'm going home I've won this fight.
The Lord said Knock and the door would open,
Seek and you'll be sure to find.
Ask and you'll be sure to be given,
The key to this door of mine.
So I asked and I was given,
The key to the Lords dormain.

When I knocked the door was opened,
I'll never look back again.
Praise the Lord I'm finally home,
His hands they reached out for me.
I've climbed the stairway to heaven,
My heart was finally set free.

Boyd Warren
DESCENDANT
My old unpainted sled
Hurries on the down side
Of Windswept Mountain
Making two rooster tails
As it plops
Onto the bushed-over barnfield
Slowing to a gentle stop
On the warm side
Of yesterday. . .

Beth Wiletsky
MOTHERS ARE BEAUTIFUL
In this poem you will see,
I will talk about my mother and me.
My mother once told me
from deep in her heart,
that she loved me.
And I said, "Momma, I know
that this statement is true,
and I want you to know
that I love you, too."

Catherine Woolridge
LONELY LOVERS
Lonely people seem to come together
like a newborn reaching for mama.
When we met we were like two young children
groping for familiar objects in the dark
we reached out for each other
like lonely lovers usually do.
Our love is interwoven like two tiny rain drops
on an otherwise dry, dirty window pane
like a mountain waterfall
so crisp, sparkling and pure
like a multi-colored sunset
full of cool passion and warmth.
But babies soon leave mama
and children accept the dark
raindrops always evaporate
a mountain waterfall sometimes becomes polluted waste
sunsets must give way to the moon's scheduled concert
and lonely lovers find security and soon drift apart
as we will eventually do.

Jo E. Hackerman
HARMONY
I never knew a sound quite as enjoyable as that of not silence but of earth as she is now
Her birds and her bugs and her rivers to be heard
I wish everyone could see her as I see her right now
Her gown is all green with sunshine highlights and a ribbon of rock,
amidst on her top
And around her waist she wears a ring
of the prettiest, happiest, flyingist things
not airplanes of steel,
but,
birds and their songs, all singing and calling and chirping along
And as long as I stay here and I don't make a fuss,
I can listen and look and play in her gown,
And all will stay happy
down here
on
the
ground.

George P. Sarsfield
NATURE'S CONCERT (MOUNTAIN STREAM)
How many sounds in the mountain stream?
What story does it tell
As it twists and churns its ancient course
Through rocks and waterfalls?
Blending with songs of birds and squirrels
And the mountain breeze
Ever changing - never ending -
Nature's concert in the trees.
Could life there be without the stream
Racing to the sea -
Always to return again
In falling snow and rain.
What sounds we hear from the mountain stream?
Sounds of past - 10,000 years -
A million years to be -
Sounds of music - sounds of life-
Sounds of eternity.

Jenny Cornelius MacDonald
CREATION IS...
Creation is the heavens that are so blue,
Creation is a flower that softens with the Dew.
Creation Is...
Creation is the trees that whisper with the wind,
Creation is the spirit that dwells deep within.
Creation Is...
Creation is the mother who's babe has been born,
Creation is the mother who's love is not forlorn.
Creation Is...
Creation is the Lord who worked for six days,
and rested on the seventh.
Creation Is...

Martha W. Harman
MOTHER' DAY
Mother's Day we love to share
With others with whom we like to compare
Our own dear precious mother!
She does not try to smother
The love we feel for others is due.
This honor we share with a few.
My Mama has gone to heaven to live
But before she left she had much to give
To her sweet angel wings to contribute
I'll always be grateful for faith I live it.
I'll wear my corsage of flowers white
While I dream at night about this sight
Of red roses. She loved to adorn us.
While those who can honor theirs thus.
We come closer to Heaven so bright
And just wish we could train our children right!
So we honor thee, all our mothers
We learn by our mistakes as no others
Can. So hooray for the beauty of
Our own dear mother!

Ruth E. Purvis
MY BOOK AND DADDY
My daddy puts me on his knee
And reads the story book to me,
Of houses lined all in a row
And of swinging high and low.
Of a puppy dog with a stubby tail
And of little kittens in a well,
Of an egg that sits upon a wall
And how he took his famous fall.
Of a little boat that sailed along
And a train that whistles his lonely song,
A little brook that babbles on
And a little girl that sings a song.
And now I want to go to sleep
As up to my bed I slowly creep,
My daddy tucks me into bed
And kisses me upon my head.
And as he slowly shuts the door
He takes a peek at me once more,
And with these things, I'll always know
My daddy will always love me so.

Gary Allan Stronach
THE ULTIMATUM
Of your deliverance
I urge you,
Procrastinate not!
For behold, upon the plains of
hesitation—Ancient,
windswept and yet cryptlike,
lie bleached,
by eons of ageless time,
the bones of countless
ambivalent millions
whom
upon the very threshold of
salvation stood. . .
hesitant,
in wait of "that hour of certainty,"
and while waiting—wasted,
and perished
for an eternity.

Bettylee Sowder
DANIEL THE GAY OLE BLADE
Now, Daniel was a gay ole blade,
Charm came as quite a knack.
He'd ask a dame to dinner,
Always leaving behind the jack.
The dames they never minded,
For he had a certain class,
But he had dinner every night,
With a different lass.
Well, hunger for Daniel,
This he never knew.
And the only thing he didn't know,
Was how to try and be true.
One night he was with one girl,
The next night someone new,
Oh, Daniel was a gay ole blade,
For the dames they never knew.

Catherine F. Douglas-McCargo
I WALKED WITH WINTER
I walked today where the first white feathers of snow
Lay curling uncertain in the early light;
And I remembered how we used to run,
Our breath hanging in the morning air like smoke,
And the cold hands of Winter pushing at our backs.
How you laughed when my feet slipped
And I tumbled, half-buried in the snow.
You picked me up and wrapped your arms around me
And suddenly the world was warm again.
Oh, I remembered all our yesterdays,
The years of Winter snows and Springtime thaws;
And now the Wintertime has come again.
I walked today in the freshly fallen snow,
But only my footsteps marked the silent white.

Carol Ann Kelley
WOMAN TO MAN
There is no man on this earth like you, old man. . .
You are the earth, so rich.
You are the sky, filled with all it's wonder.
You are the sea, forever flowing onward.
You are within me. . .
When you're without me. . .

You are free, old man. . .
Like the bird, soaring so high above.
Like the leaf, floating in the autumn air.
Like the Indian summer, old man. . .
You are within me. . .
When you're without me. . .

You are for me, old man. . .
Like a branch on my tree.
Like the light in my eyes.
Like the vintage of my wine.
You are within me. . .
When you're without me. . .
You're within me. . .

Debra R. Hickey
NORTHERN LIGHTS
Rays of borrowed sunlight,
Across a darkened sky.
Refractions set in images,
Of waves just passing by.

Donna Bartek
THE LAST FAREWELL
Under the arms of an old lovely
pine,
with a moon giving off a soft
gentle shine
They were saying their last,
final goodbye
both of them just a little bit
shy.
Both had to go their own
separate way,
but knew they'd meet again
someday. . .
So, they talked of good and
talked of bad,
days of which they both had
had.
She'd given him strength, she'd
given support
patience and love of every
sort.
Her love for him went very
deep,
and in days to come would
make her weep.
Much was said straight from the
heart,
a sensitive relationship from
the very start.
No pretense was felt between
the two
the emotions ran deep as they
both knew.
But love for them was not in
store,
only a tender friendship. . .
nothing more.
But as they were about to
depart,
he kissed her softly with all
his heart.

Donna Steinkraus
A CHANGE OF SEASON
Autumn winds are blowing,
Blowing,
Glowing in the moonlight up
above.
Winter skies are snowing,
Snowing,
Flowing as the tempest of my
love.
Spring showers are raining,
Raining,
Paining to restore my tears.
Summer heat is burning,
Burning,
Turning my heart, I fear.
And as my eyes are crying,
Crying,
Sighing for my lover lost,
I still recall your lying,
Lying,
Defying; and I pay the cost.

Pamela Ann Biddulph
THE PUPS
Have you ever seen a pup shed a
tear
for its mother they bludgeoned
to death?
The only white warmth the pup
had known
has been tortured and robbed of
its breath.
The pup saw her bloodied and
thrown into a sack
along with a half dozen others.
What will they do in the long
cold nights
When they all would've gone to
their mothers?
But the pup needn't worry, the
pup needn't fret,
for he has no decision to make.
For the men have come back
with their bloodied clubs,
the pup with the tears to take.

Michelle Ferrado
MOMENT
A storm drifting across the tips
of the mountain range had
chilled the air and picked-up
the breeze as I lay several
miles from the mountains,
beside a little lake just
before sunset.
It was relaxing to watch the
clouds as they greyed,
blending together with shades
of red, blue, and pink, casting
a reflection off the lake while
the sun crept slowly down to
rest.

Swana C. Lau
TO FELIX—MY LOVE
Two years besieged by the
sickness had been a long
nightmare indeed.
This poem, the first one I have
ever written in English, was
specially dedicated to my
husband Felix, shortly after my
recovery.
All the blues that lingered
around me, changed into
songs of victory,
All the tears that I shed, turned
into the sweetest memory,
And it was only because,
you were staying beside me,
through the entire journey.
Warmer than the sun shining in
the deep snow,
Tenderer than the raindrops
dancing on the rose,
These are the very thoughts you
remind me of,
And I love you so.
For every moment of your
company, there is harmony,
For every minute of your
presence, there is serenity,
I could have listed a thousand
more reasons for loving you
too,
But most of all,
It is simply because,
There is a rainbow joining our
hearts——
——that we, both adore. . . . . .

Julie Linn Melchers
CREATION SINGS
small slip
of silvery moon
shining through the window,
how did it feel
when He spoke you into being?

galaxies
of planets,
star-studded universe,
did you look on as He fashioned
us
with His hands?
on this
now silent planet,
in this fallen, darkened world,
we're all walking dead men.
(zombies without Your life).
stars sing;
far-off worlds have joined the
song.
this old creation's groaning:
we're soon to sing alone.
(Lord, teach us the song).
hear the song!
it's the song of the universe
with all the angels singing,
"glory to God
in the highest. . ."

Ralph H. Chase, Jr.
LITTLE CRICKET AND HAPPY MOUSE
There was an old house by the
edge of town;
It was all shambled and falling
down.
The windows were broken, the
door was ajar;
Inside lived a cricket and his
ma.
They got up bright and early
and they went to work each
day;
They had to watch out for the
mouse on the way.
He was so playful, he'd box
them around;
Little cricket got tired and
always fell down.

Little cricket played fiddle as
good as can be;
Mouse played piano as you can
see.
The music sounded so very
sweet;
And ma cricket played guitar
with a down home beat.
The animals came from miles
around,
When the little band made it's
sound.
They danced in the aisles, they
stomped their feet;
And kept time with the beat.
They made music together, they
sure had fun;
Isn't it nice to have a friend that
will always come?

Carol D. Stearns
MUDDY WATERS
Lying stretched out before us
The creek bed lies
Undisturbed,
With only occassional
movement
From nature's intended
inhabitants,
All clear and inviting as Spring;
We invade the tranquility
Momentarily,
Slowly making our way up
stream,
While behind us
We turn to see the muddy
waters
Left in our wake;
And as we travel on,
The realization
That life's pretty much the same
Sinks in.

Gary Dean Hanna
THE LORD AND YOU
I sit, I dream
I look at the sky.
It is blue, so blue
with clouds so white
And some gray
as if to subdue the day.
I sit, I dream
and as I do, I pray.
I pray to the Lord
that he hold you today,
That he hold you in his bosom
during your hospital stay.
I sit, I dream
and I know as I do,
The Lord we love
will take care of you.

Rob Miller
UNTITLED
A bright red rose in a field of beautiful daisies. What an insecure situation. What do the daisies care? They are all the same size, color, and beauty to them is dominated by their own kind. They can afford prejudice and rebuke. . .But this rose, towering above as an artform of beauty, denies its own presence, and at times is totally subjected to so-called beauty all around it. Not until the sun shines, and drops its first ray upon its petals, does it stand tall, and this rose becomes a beautiful flower and spreads its velvet petals to the fascination of beautiful daisies.

Charles E. Sanders
AIRPORTS
Ever notice how interesting
airports are?
Travelers all scurrying to far—
off places
Their character changes when
they leave the car
Blending into the maze of very
strange faces
The weekdays are mostly for the
businessman
Weekends and Holidays belong
to kids and first-timers
Concerned only with souvenirs
and a good tan
And all except employees hurry
for the airliners
It's people and planes only God
could arrange
With talk of corporate contracts
and yesterday's jokes
Certainly nobody wants to
appear strange
In this vast mixture of odd-
looking folks
Fortunately they're all very
closely bound
In attempting to hide their
mutual fear
Of being airborne and way off

the ground
All acting like kids in their freshman year
Only the children find pure joy
They're awed by it all
Thinking the plane is somebody's toy
And all pilots are handsome and tall
Adults would appreciate childish travel
By ignoring the pace and enjoying the flight
Don't let your nerves unravel
Admit it, Dad. The kids were right!

Daniel W. Hart

AMY. . . . .

When you're away
My heart bleeds for you—
Knowing you're not near.
When you're away
My days bleed with loneliness—
Knowing you're not here.
When you're not near,
A day is a year.
When you're with me
My Love bleeds on you—
Because you're near.
When you're with me
My days bleed with happiness—
Because you're here.
When you're near,
A day is a year.

Mary Hamilton Darrell

AUTUMN

The trees are yellow and red and brown,
And some of the leaves are floating down;
The squirrels are busy with nuts they've found,
You know that autumn is here.
The stream is singing a merry tune,
But it's not the same that it sang in June;
The hoot owl calls to the harvest moon,
You know that autumn is here.
My heart is gay as the autumn leaves,
For the pattern is bright that memory weaves;
The path is light to the soul that believes,
The autumn of life is here.

Ric Shrubb

I LOVE YOU FOR YOUR HONESTY

I'll never forget the night you told me you were once a lady of the night. You looked like you were in front of a firing squad.
Do you think I would leave you?
No my dear, I'll always love you so much for what you are that I'll never be able to hate you for what you were.
Besides, I'm not perfect. I couldn't even begin to remember all the names or dates or places from my past, some of them I never knew, so why should I criticize you?
You're good to me now and I trust you with my feelings.
For this I love you.
I respect you for the things you have learned. My only sorrow is that some of the lessons were painful for you.
I don't think I deserve you, but I hope you stay with me.
No I'm not jealous. I don't feel threatened by you or your past. Besides, jealousy is a feeling meant for lesser people than myself.
Have I told you that I love you more for being honest with me? I do you know.
Thank you.

William W. Elliott

FLOWERS

Tulips and roses; dainty violets
In deep dyed colors, and the marigolds
Of golden yellow; and the roadside pets
Wild dandelions, which everywhere unfolds.
Go seek the pale white lily where she grows;
Regal but delicate, much like a queen.
Then, let lilacs and hyacinths impose
Their amorous perfumes, while yet unseen,
Upon the air and gentle summer breeze.
Foxgloves and dahlias, and the daffodills;
Geraniums, narcissus, and heartease,
And all those daisies flocked on yonder hills.
God gave us flowers so that we could see
How beautiful this life was meant to be.

Anne E. Shanley Hujar

THE PERFECT MOTHER

You're close to her right from the start
She keeps you hidden, near her heart
And when it's time, and you arrive
She makes certain everyone knows you're alive.
She tends to you with loving care
And when you need her, she is always there;
She laughs and cries along with you
And when you're in trouble, she's right there to help you.
She cooks the meals and washes clothes
And cleans the house—what else?—nobody knows;
But with all the chores she does each day
She'll always have a smile and something nice to say.
She teaches you to know right from wrong
And by watching her, you learn how to be strong
So that when it is time to go on your own
You'll always be ready to stand alone.
When the time comes and you are ready to leave
You'll never know it, but she'll grieve,
But she'll give you her blessing and she will know
That her thoughts will be with you wherever you go.
Who is this person so loving and true
That will always stand by you?
I'm sure you've guessed—it could be no other
Than your very own warmhearted Mother.

Frank Lancaster

GOD'S TREASURES

Handle these treasures carefully, For they are very Divine
After God, gave you these gifts, He said, Do not throw my pearls to the swine
A gold ring, is not seemly for a pig, to wear in his snout
For he possesses, "seven devils, that from Legion, was cast out.
Lock these gifts, in a strong heart, where no thief can enter and steal
No house can be robbed, upon which, God, has put His seal
Be not selfish with these jewels, let the glow of diamonds shine through
It might entice some to follow the path of God's chosen few.
A host of Heavenly Angels will guard these treasures for you
The Devil is weak compared to God and He cannot break through
He is not entitled to God's gifts, He has had his day
God, gave him all of his Heavenly treasures, but he threw them all away.
Satan, is trying to capture the Throne of God, to have things his own way
But, God will retain His glorious Crown, and the devil will have to pay
Satan through distorting the truth, has forfeited his Heavenly Home

Now, confined to the earth, where he must continually roam.

Cheryl Hintzel

THE SOLDIER

There they all sit as the body lies near by
They are weeping and whispering and wondering why this person had to die
Many flowers adorn the room. The odor is so thick it makes you gag
The casket is made of bronze and at the end is draped a flag
As I peer down at the lifeless form, I search the face for the smile I remember so
That brave smile that made my tears flow heavier as he waved out the train window
He was going off to battle in Viet Nam because he felt it was his duty
Now as the preacher is speaking and I try to concentrate on his eulogy
I think of all the other soldiers from all the wars that fought and died
And the ones left behind. The aged mother, father, daughter, son, sweetheart and the young bride
War and death shall always be a part of our lives and we must learn to be brave
Brave as our soliders were. The ones living and the ones we laid in their grave

Ann Felshaw Zehr

JUST ONE LITTLE WORD

I wonder why people hurt other people,
We're not in this world to do that.
Some folks will pick up the least little thing,
It seems they just want to spat.
We all have our rights and feelings,
Of which we are all aware.
But some folks either seem to forget,
Or really just don't care.
Number One, they're always thinking of,
They want everything just their own way.
Myself, I'd rather give a little
And be happy the rest of the day.
To help mankind, our brother's keeper we should be,
But some folks don't seem to feel that way,
The only one they can think of is *ME*.
I hope and pray that someday soon,
The Lord will show them the way.
To be truly happy in the world in which we live,
There's just one little word that can accomplish this,
And that little word is GIVE.

Darlene Hetrick

LOVE IS FOREVER

Love is a kitten so soft and nice.
Love is a stab from a sharp knife.
Love is a dream upon a sailboat of joy.
Love is a game from which you are the toy.
Love is forever as far as you can see.
Love is a word that pertains to him and me.

Teresa L. Park
IF YOU CAN
Alot in this life hurts.
You try to make the best
of what you have
And what you can't make
better—
You learn how to take it—
If you can.
People come and people go.
Some you care about
and don't want to let leave
But when they decide to move
on—
You hold back your tears—
If you can.
Most all things change.
Sometimes for the better
but often times not
So you make the best of what
is—
Forgetting all the rest—
If you can.

Cynthia Tweedy Hoffer
WORDS!
Words are to me,
As sturdy as a tree.
They can stand firm and strong,
Can this written word be wrong?
They can bend like the breeze,
Congratulate and please.
They can make you cry,
And can form a great lie.
Words can make love,
Describe a flying dove.
They can talk like a poet,
Laugh at a joke, you know it.
Words have so many uses,
And also many abuses.
Like the last fifteen lines,
You'll swear, I committed a
crime.

T. K. Anderson
WILL—O'—THE WISP
She alighted with only the mere
suggestion
Of weight upon the place, as if
asked in question
And lit that part of the world
with a glow
Which less than a handfull will
ever know
Her limbs rose as gentle
willows, toward the sky
And her arched back lifted her
to meet my eye
What new-sprung presence tilts
these aged boughs
And what will stand a thousand
years from now?
It makes me sad, this beauty
which will not endure
As if things, once created, slip
to what was before
Yet, somewhere the answer
must surely lie
Where I looked into the
universe of her eyes
For the slightest spark of fire
her soul might send
And her briefness becomes its
own value in the end

Gilda Shane Glorioso
TIME VOYAGERS
You and I have been before,
Through the portholes of this
world—
Playing hide and seek in other
dimensions
Trying desperately to unite in
the right time. . .
Learning our lessons down
through the centuries,
Colliding with the forces of
awareness,
Soaring on the wings of angels,
And stumbling on the paths of
the earth—
All in our long walk through
eternity
Ever searching for the shining I
Am, in us all,
And reaching beyond to the
light
Which someday will make us
one.

Ken Spaulding
THE MYSTICAL CONNECTION
To dream a dream, Ah! That is
Mystical
To say a prayer, isn't that
mystical?
If the prayer comes true, we call
it physical
But, actually it is mystical!
Flying saucers, sudden wealth,
and instant healing,
Are these physical? Or are all
mystical?
The greatest invention of them
all, the electric light,
That gives man the power to
create day out of night,
All of these are part of the
mystical connection
But none would exist without
man's intuitive perception.
Finally, the light within, we
cannot see,
Which always was and forever
will be.
This without exception,
Is the greatest mystical
connection. .

Earlene Jackson
SONG OF LOVE
Take away my doubts and fears
that I may be thine,
wipe away my mist of tears
and endow me with thy love.
Encircle me in your arms so
strong
take me close to you,
crush my lips with yours so
long
that they are bruised with love.
Whisper the words I want to
hear
so very soft and low,
lay your head on my shoulder
dear
and be mine alone.

Julie A. Wrazien
QUEST FULFILLED
Because of our love
You longed to shout
"I'm here!"
When you arrived
Though I couldn't see you,
Yet sensed your presence.
Because of our love
We sat and beamed
at each other
while we related
the day's missions and
turmoils.
Because of our love
We drank surreptitiously
of each other's vervor,
Basking all the while
in the arms of contentment.
Because of our love
We were honest
about pleasure,
And gladdened with delight
in our quest to fulfill
our infinite yearning.
Because of our love
Our souls melted into one
And our kisses fused our
passion,
Quelling the haunts of desire
from before.
Yes,
We are one, my love—
bonded through faith
and honesty,
Predictable continuity
of all times.
Blessedly fortunate
for our special union
that has transcended
all time.

Stella S. Parpana
RULER OF THE UNIVERSE
Something Magic—Has a hold
on Me
Something Magic—Planned My
destiny
Something Magic—Set My Spirit
free
Something Magic—Embedded in
My memory
Something Magic—Guides Me
to believe
Something Magic—A gift of
creativity
An expression of thoughts
A SPECIAL part of Me
Something Majestic in
Authority,
this Sense of Justice touches
Me.
Something Majestic possessing
Might
It urges Me to carry on with
strife
Something Magic—My reason to
Be
Something Magic—A Lamp
which lights My way
to the chosen path of My
DREAMS

Dennis A Coast
THE APPROACHING STORM
A Scarlet sky surrendered a last
precious ray
Darkness crept in and started
its day
Fire flies flicker a twilight
mood
Distant crickets perform
evening prelude.

The road still warm from the
sun's gentle touch.
It feels so good who could ask
for too much.
Traveling lights glow from
afar
Winding through the valley, the
sounds of a car.
Starting to drift into a
whispering breeze.
A flash and a crack, oh don't
storm would you please.
The stars that glittered high
above.
Now all become covered like
that with a glove.
Running for shelter with each
breath of air.
Nearer and nearer and no time
to spare.
The fierce rains came in heavy
sheets.
Pounding the ground like an
athletes cleats.
A howl and a groan, into a
distant it moaned.
Then slowly but surely a
twinkle to form.
Finally an epilogue to the
approaching storm.

Beverly J. Graham
AUTUMN'S REVELATION
October is a special time
The trees are beauty to behold
It makes your senses come alive
And stirs the center of your
soul.
I looked at all this lovely world
My mind completely overawed.
The sun, the trees, the sky, my
love.
To day I saw my God.
He's shining through the colored
leaves.
And in the changing skies.
And in the love thats on your
face
And showing in your eyes
This day was perfect and I know
As long as I may live.
To day I saw the face of God in
everything we did.

Connie R. Stewart
FRIENDS
Its nights like these I treasure
most,
Two friends walking together,
Neither of us leading,
Neither of us following,
Both of us walking side by side.
Not a star in the sky,
Deep dark clouds over high
The ocean mist clean and fresh.
The waves tumbling into each
other,
My hand in yours,
Our sandals scuffing the sand
before us.
My thoughts shifting thoughts,
A great release. . .Solitude. . .
The beach.
Gentle sounds.
The night young like us,
My friend and I, side by side
Under dark clouds and gentle
sounds,
Thanks for sharing this with
me.

Michael F. Duniphin
YOU AND ME
The hours of night have slipped away this eternity at sea, with beautiful, roaming, wonderful thoughts of you, my darling and me.

We have loved before the entire
universe so that all can see and
experience the love between us,
my heart, you and me.
From the mountains, the rolling
hills, the desert and the sea,
people have experienced a love
shared only by a few,
sweetheart, you and me.
The hard times have made the
good times better, so in some
small way, I'm thankful to the
sea, for through this seperation
it brings us closer, yes my love
you and me.
God bless the oceans with all
their hell and fury. Because like
the hand of the Lord, the sea,
my darling has been good to you
and me.
Its been a quest and we have
emerged the victors, at last
we have quelled the sea, yes my
darling, GOD, YOU and me.

Betsy Marinda Reynolds
ECCLESIASTES 3:11
Upon my hands (which wander
in the grass through fingered
stems and milk-weed pods, nail-
split) are sticky stains of green
that must admit so colorful are
marked these few days past. I
seldom shed a tear for fall and
cast my joy as leaves onto the
lake; for it is quite another day
and every bit observable and
lovely as the last.
And if you frown at idealistic
youth that eases down from
heights of maple trees, I'll
say I've seen the old upturn a
truth in more than merely
rustling memories: I've seen
a dear heart stretch both hands
to smooth the floss from milk-
weed pods across bent knees.

Stuart L. Williams
WALKING NEAR
You're walking near me
My mind becomes filled with
my emotions
I can feel you touching my body
with tenderness of your
loving hands
My lips felt the passion of
the gentleness of you
I know the feeling of love from
within my heart
You're coming near me
like a bolt of lightening from
the sky my body experiences
a tremble
A joyous experience of life
consumed my soul
My body could feel the warmth
of you without words
my passion felt the embrace of
you
Mistaken movement filled my
soul
my emotions took over my body
I could feel the gentle beauty
of you
as I saw you walking near.

Lynden castle
PLACE HERE A MARKER
Place here a marker,
I feel rather like a book;
With shabby cover and
down-turned, frazzled pages,
I've quality,
- not the look.

Lyn E. Beyer
SOLITARY MAN
I am a solitary man.
But it doesn't mean I
Love you less. Perhaps,
Just that I don't tell
You as often. But I do
Love you. I can't begin
To count the endless hours
I've watched you in your
Sleep. My silent tears
Absorbed by my pillow.
You---my only passion.
I hope you understand.
I could not bear to be
Without you.

Vern Sawatzky
IT WAITS
Something mysterious rose
From the other side
Of reason.
It happened
On a lazy summer afternoon
When no one dared
Run the gauntlet
To identify the unnamed.
This sudden shadow,
this awesome presence,
This dark, deep,
Undeniable cesspool
Of drugless toxication,
Was a wavering, yet -
Without a doubt.
Behold! And beware!
As God is my witness,
It lies smugly dormant,
Waiting...
For you.

Grace Price
FRIENDSHIP——RETURNETH
What is this thing called
Friendship?
I said to a friend one day,
I do not have a million to give--
She replied, but you do give,
I don't know what I'd have done
without
Your friendship these last few
months.
What is it then?
A nod
A smile
A touch
A word of encouragement
A phone call
A visit
A listening ear
A prayer
You do not need to be a
millionaire to be a friend.
It's simply taking time to give of
these things to others.
A window washed
A lawn mowed
A hot dish dropped by
Sharing what you have
Just being you.
The rewards of friendship are
great.
It feels good to give--
Christ said "It is better to give
than receive"
It lightens ones own load when
doing something outside
ourself--for others.
A selfish person is not a giving
one--they keep their misery to
themselves.
Reach out
Do that kind deed--you've really
been wanting to do, but afraid
it is nothing.
Try it--You'll see
A better person you'll be
Reaching out in friendship, see
Only returneth to thee.

Marvin Eric Chaney
PROCRASTINATION
If procrastination is the basis of
your motivation
Then you had best be a master
of trickeration
Or you must possess an insight
for innovation
For your fate will face the
processes of elimination

Alice M. Hall Todd
THE ARTISTS' CALENDAR
Pure winter-white to lilting
green of Spring;
Blazing hues of Summer to
shimmering gold of Fall;
Silver frost, then back to
winter-white so pure.
Lovely, lovely, all!

Doreen Lewis
THE WRITER
As I sit here
pencil in hand
words suddenly appear
from a strange land.
Imaginary people
fly across the page
having great adventures
from another age.
I never know
what new worlds I'll find
one from reality
or one from my mind.

John F. Harper
THE WONDERS OF CHRISTMAS
Having something special, for
one and all. Whether be it, the
joys of youth or the beauty of
age, and the wonder of time.
Conscience and a realization,
giving one and all more than
enough to comprehend. The
Wonders of Christmas, could
have never been, if at first our
Lord had never loved and
forgave, each and every sin.
Hope for better times, a
shoulder to cry on, companion-
ship, especially when dejected
and all alone. Light to lead one
out of darkness, a loove unlike
any known. Knowledge and
wisdom for one and all, not for
just a certain or select few. A
warmth and understanding, to
comfort the worst of lifes
tragedies.
A care and want, to love and
forgive. Truth, today being in
ever short supply, for one and
all. With a promise of life after
death, in His kingdom for
eternity. Where all of lifes
wonders are kept, for one and
all. To have and keep, as long as
He and His kingdom, Heaven, is
that which we seek.

Maggie Pettit
SEASONS OF LIFE
Suddenly the cool brisk evening
sets in
And all around the dead
dead foliages blown by the
wind
Colors of orange, yellow and
brown replace the greenery of
the trees
While the flowers just tilt their
heads and turn to seeds.
In this quick transition from
spring to fall
Is life and death shown as a
simple thing to all.
the heartaches, griefs and sorrows
hidden to very deep
With only all the joy and
happiness standing up to take
a peek.
In the seasons of Mother Nature
We see our life's future
So live for the happiness and
put aside the sorrow
For we are here for now only to
be gone tomorrow.

Michael Degan
LADY OF THE SUN
Sad eyed
lady of the sun
to whom
these words I send
illustrate the beauty
of one
I wish to call
my friend.
Carry on
lady of the sun
your journey
to the dream
godspeed travels
you have begun
and a love
that shall redeem.

Sharon J. Fedor
UNWILLING WIFE
In winsome joviality
the years swept by
As I was gaily courted
by impassioned Lie.
Now the days are all alike—
longer, blander.
I am succumbed, unwilling wife
to Candor.

Hugo Walter
SOME SAY
Some say the sea is only sky
In ribbons blue and silver-white,
The sand--a golden cloud broken
And scattered softly by the
night.
Some say the sky is only sea
Blown listless from its steady
quay,
The sun--a wanderer, alone
Watching the hasty space of
day.
The only one who knows is
dead
Or just asleep; perhaps someone
Will raise his hand or nod
instead
Before the sand becomes the
sun.

Marjorie McDonald
PRAIRIE DAWN
Day dawns.
Rosy curls fill the sky,
Gradually deepening, they
Await the joyous lift of the sun.
Morning has come to the prairie,
Another day of warmth and life,
Another day for growing and ripening,
One day closer to the harvest.

bryan powell
MANKIND
we are the leaves of a tree
in a windstorm
scattered
on the ground are a countless
many lifeless leaves
being tossed
by a wind's whim
upon the tree
a few leaves
hold on with all their might
though they suffer
the rage of many storms
those leaves
live
a full life
God's children are but a few

Alfred Taber
SHADOW PORTRAIT
Life's escapade in shadow wrought
As perchance when one the light has faced
Evidence of one's being is traced
As I walk down life's sidewalk caught.
And once it - my shadow - was small,
Across the shining sea of days
It persists through joy and fear
Partner ever near,
Testimonial made by sun's rays.
But one day the shadow will not show,
Then...no shadow of a shadow.

Kay M. Datesman
ON THE DEATH OF A PARENT
You were there, at my first breath;
"Hello, my little son!"
I clasped your hand, our bond was made,
"I love you, little one."
and you cared.
and we shared.
Through careful steps to skipping,
From scribbling, then to prose,
You advised and listened,
Your door was never closed.
and you cared.
and we shared.
From diapers, knickers, trousers;
Long discussions as we walked,
Of girls and love, and morals,
No lectures; We just talked.
and you cared.
and we shared.
When I made you a Grand-dad,
Lullaby's became your song.
You let me raise them my way,
Never saying I was wrong.
and you cared.
and we shared.
You always kept that open door,
And my boys use it now.
Just as for me, you understood,
I wish I had learned how.
and you cared.
and we shared.
I was there at your last breath.
"Good-bye my Dad, my friend."
I held your hand, and at your death,
Our bond will never end.
and I cared.
and we shared.

Johanna D. E. Harris
UNTITLED
for my daughter
she
picks
fertile flowers,
captures
misty smiles
saying
i will love you
forever,
if only
you will love me
but
flowers
do die
and
sadly
i know
she cannot
love
dead roses

Deann F. Vickery
THANKSGIVING EVERYDAY
Why do things have to be this way
Let's have Thanksgiving everyday.
We thank the Lord for this and that
One day a year and we all get fat,
With a big old turkey and all the trimmings
To open the season of Christmas giving.
Our thanks is sincere, I do not doubt,
But only 24 hours, I really could pout.
Our God is good and deserves much more,
Let's open our hearts, let's open our doors.
Things do not have to be this way,
Let's have Thanksgiving everyday.

R. W. Myres
MY DOG AND I
We tramp across the browning fields
That late were bright in summer sun,
He ahead in loping gait
While I more slowly plod behind.
Sometimes he disappears from sight
In patches sere of dying stalk
Exploring with an anxious nose
Where some small creature spent the night
And then returns in bounding leaps
To let me know he's not forgotten
His companion and to get
From me a reassuring pat
And nuzzle my caressing hand
In fond expression of his love.
How many years may we expect
These rustic journeys to pursue
For I am growing old and gray,
His questing muzzle flecked with white?
But cast aside such mournful thoughts
For we today are both alert
And neither of us willing yet
To leave this troubled world behind.
So we continue on our way
Around the hill and through the wood
Where every hidden glade recalls
The memory of visits past.
At last before approaching dusk,
Which swiftly comes this time of year,
Reluctantly we turn about
And head on back to home and hearth.

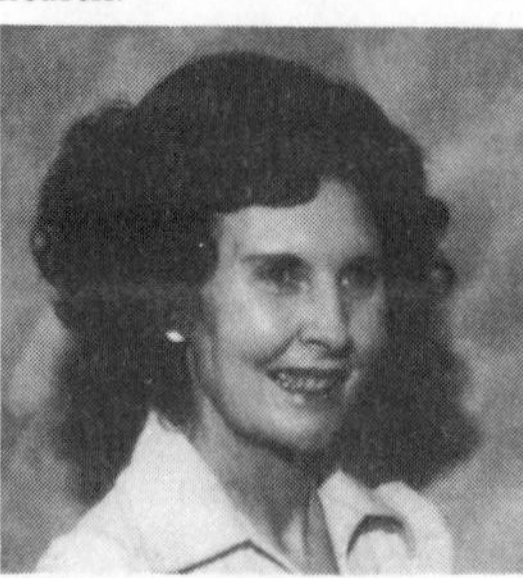

Ruby Louise Todd
LIFE'S MIRROR
He looked not familiar
As in the casket he lay.
Our years had been so sweet,
And yet so incomplete.
His features were set
In a tight line,
And he seemed strange
In a way I couldn't define.
Then I looked at his eyes
As he lay peacefully there.
I knew why he was strange;
Eyes were closed; We couldn't share.

For when open and with life,
Eyes are windows to the soul.
When filled with tender warmth
Can make delight the goal.
The heart had stopped beating,
And so could not feel;
The mind had stopped thinking,
And thus could not reveal.
For the soul is but the spirit,
Which without earthly life is gone.
The spirit is a combination
Of five senses, heart and mind.
The eyes mirror thoughts and feelings,
But when closed cannot reflect.
Oh, the wonders of our Creator
We see in circumspect!

Blaine A. Peters
FULLY GROWN TO MEN
One Sunday afternoon as I was napping in my chair,
I was wakened by piercing shouts and screams that filled the air.
As I hurried to the window and peered beyond the pane,
I saw in progress in my yard a sandlot baseball game.
The boy from down the street had hit a ball into the air.
The issue now in question - Was it foul or fair?
Each boy had his opinion on the way it ought to be
And kids and dogs expressed their views quite vociferously.
How inconsiderate of the scamps to interrupt my nap
And tramp a path upon my lawn from home to base and back;
To leave the bases where they lie when I must mow the grass
And break the clothes line on poles with mighty home run blasts.
The inconvenience of it all makes me want to say,
"Get out of here you doggone kids. Go somewhere else and play."
But more than inconvenience, how I hate the thought of when
These boys who play upon my lawn are fully grown to men.
One day I know the grass will grow and quietly live on
And when I mow the grass I know the bases will be gone.
The clothes line that I used to mend will never break again
When the boys who play upon my lawn are fully grown to men.
So I tolerate their game while in my throat there is a lump
As I burst upon the scene and shout, "Hey fellas, need an ump?"
Life's more fun when played by rules, remember this kids when
You boys who play upon my lawn are fully grown to men.

James Christian
JANUARY
from without
the mist returns
and through the blame
a longing kissed
where shadows
rainbow into
forever dawn
matures and trickles
to the cheek
slowly emptying
all the lies
told to those who
wonder how simply
two can grow
apart

Dolores F. Kalisty
FIRST DAY OF SPRING IN THE CITY
It's the first day of Spring in the city,
Which is covered still with the grime
And the unwashed pavements pity
And the darkening aging of time.
The flowers and buds remain in sleep,
While the soft cool wind blows
Mounds of Winter's dust into broadening heap.
And -- the Winter slows ---
For it truly is Spring by feel and by sign,
Though evidence hides mysteriously deep
While Winter puts away the savage time,
And begins the season's sleep.

There are smiles on faces today,
As the sun forces a path,
And whittles and wedges a way
Through the past Winter's
Wrath.
And the people smile more
As the wind blows warm,
Trying to pierce Winter's core.
Success in the stamping of the
storm.
The harsh Winter's wind now
subsiding;
On mellow and fresh winds
wash clean;
The first day of Spring high
riding
Within an aging City's dream.

Vivian S. Cline

HALLOWEEN

Halloween is weird and ghostly-
It is a haunting time.
Bill had to do a brave thing,
To earn a shining dime.
His brother promised a dime,
If in the church he'd go;
Place an apple on the stand-
Go all alone you know.
It was a weird Halloween-
Wind moaning in the trees.
The little boy was frightened,
And shaky in the knees.
But he could not miss the
chance,
To win a shining dime.
E'en if the church was haunted,
He would go this one time.
As he entered the graveyard,
He saw an object white.
He reached down, picked up
three rocks.
He threw one and lost sight.
The object appeared again,
Bill threw his second rock.
He almost hit it and he-
Was sure it was in shock.
When he went into the church,
A ghostly figure stood-
There in front of the alter,
Swaying and moaning good.
His last rock was in his hand,
With a sure, steady aim
He hit the swaying figure,
And off the white robe came.
His brother was standing there,
With a look of dismay.
The little boy was happy,
With a dime to display.

Jewel Marie Owen

ODE TO DIRT DAUBER DOBY

At daubing, Doby was a whiz
Yea, unexcelled was he
And should you view his work
of art
I know you would agree
One day I went out walking
And left my dauber home
When I returned that evening
I found my dauber gone
What dreadful fate befell my
friend
I wondered and for naught
Each day I watched my window
But Doby entered not
If you should see a dauber
Please treat him not unkind
Remember that a dauber
Can be a friend so fine

Lois A. Hart

YOUR HAND I SO NEED

Love, take my hand and hold it
Just hold it and never let go
Hold it with the all that's in you
That all I just only want and
will always need so.
I'll never need anything more
while here
Nor one thing over and above
that touch
That touch of your beautiful
hand
The only hand I'll - ever - want,
and - oh - just so very much!
For, love, your hand is of such -
beauty - to me
It's one of all-gifted talent, pure
beauty true
And it's touch is just only a
small part of the reflection
Of what and all is so beautiful
about special you.
Yes, love, you're special---just
special
And oh so - very - special to say
the very least
Tho' my heart could so-o easily
just flow out a book in tribute
For 'I love you' goes beyond the
bounds of North, South, West,
or East.
It shall never hold a limit of any
line for you, love
Nor, then, a desire to be ever or
long without your hand
For, love, just like God's, I'll
always need it's strentgh of
strong support
Which only and always would
ever keep me standing tall and
walking grand.

Konneen Willis

IN DANGERED SPECIES

Like an eagles paradise
Where wonders lie,
underneath prodigious
fountains
Above depths beyond knowing.
Heightened by age and time
Circumference foot to mile,
majestically girded iron
Silent-still.

Hollow bellows echo out
Nature's glove protects,
wildflower, oak, and thorn.
Solid-least no ground.
Anonymous the cavities
In solace stands alone.
The eagle leaves unforgiving,
strange life conquers stone.

Joe L. Mingo

THE OLD MAILBOX

An old rusty mailbox,
on a leaning Cedar post,
stood beside the road
like the shadow of a ghost.
I looked across the way
to see if a house was around.
I saw some old stone pillars
rooted deep into the ground.
I looked closer at the old box
to see if there was a clue,
as to who used to live there
was someone that I once knew.

Randy Wright

END OF THE WORLD

Quakes,
furies,
a desolate world
annihilated by
storms of fire,
Leaders nor
followers
ever learning,
a flame
is saved for
future burnings,
Skeletons rise
to walk away,
to leave behind
their blood filled
graves,
these phantoms tire
of fear and pain
they wish to be
heavens slaves

Patti Stevens

THE ESSENCE OF LIFE

A touch, a gentle word, and
it was there,
A surprising intensity for such
a thing unseen,
The very essence of life seems
in it's care,
What is this mighty thing
which leaves men trembling,
Some have known it as a
great wondrous thing,
They've been encircled in it's
radiant glow and warmth,
Others have caught only a
fleeting glimpse of it fleeing,
Toward the horizon on silver
wings spread in triumph,
For it is triumphant as it sails
on it's way,
Forever haunting the hearts of
men great and small,
Soaring like an eagle searching
for it's prey,
Over the years the intensity
hasn't dimmed at all,
If it hasn't found you keep on
watching above,
As it forever entwines the
hearts of men,
This thing that never fades
is called love.

Angela Burch

THE MIDDLE OF NOWHERE

people spend lifetimes
looking for something
to make them feel whole
finding their niche in the world
i have found it here
in what you see as
the middle of nowhere
and even if you can't understand
i know it is here
if you can't accept
what i am becoming
or what i want
to be
then love me
as you see me
before i go
before i grow
to be different
and if you can't stand to spend
time in the middle of nowhere
i'll make it on my own
i'll live for myself
until someone else
like me
likes me
and living in the middle of
nowhere

DeeDee Welch

ANOTHER BIRTHDAY (for Uncle Phil)

Another birthday here again
Another year about to begin
Your future's ahead for which
you build
Your hopes and dreams to be
fulfilled
Take time out for loved ones so
dear
Warmth and love will bring
them near
Share in the caring, laughter and
fun
The beauty of life has only
begun
Hope for the future and dreams
in your heart
Step by step--slow from the start
Wishing you peace and
happiness, too
Love and friendship all the days
thru

Bertie Scheer

INSPIRATION

To be worthy of a sacred trust
To be given the golden key
To walk upon a golden road
That stretches to infinity;
To make my aims the highest
aim
For the existence of life and
man
To give my cause the best of me
And all the love I can;
To trust above the highest form
To believe, always, in good
To transform this to other men
In perfect brotherhood;
To act upon a purpose true
From where the Cosmic flows
I pray that I will be worthy of
The Rosicrucian Rose.

Dorothy Greenlund

GOD CRIED

Did you ever stop to think God
cried the day his Son died for
you and me.
Did you think of how he hurt
when they nailed him to that
tree.
Did you think of all the sin and
hurt he had to, pile on him to
make us free.
Did you think of how God
suffered as well as we.
When he turned his back on His
beloved Son.
When he knew one motion of
his hand would change the
things being done.
But He saw you and he saw
me, so wretched, sick, and
poor.
And Jesus His only son could
-change us forever more.
So the Bible says, God turned
his back on his very dear Son.
Jesus took my place which God
could hardly face.
But you see Jesus and God are
one, and Jesus was an
obedient Son.
We know God defeated Satan no
matter what the cost.
So how can we take so great a
salvation at such a very low
cost.

Joan Tannen
OF DEATH REFLECTIVE
...And when I die
Who will mourn my passing by?
Friends, relatives, lovers--you?
Moments squandered
I held true.
Who will say
Witch, demon, angel, saint.
I'd fracture
Revere or taint.
Who will remember

Bi-Janus
Clouds or holly.
Who did know
Soul, heart, brain, senses
Sphinx riddled
Of open defenses.
So if I die...

Richard Steinhoff
HEADLINER TO MAINLINER
Jim was a quarterback and a headliner,
Until the day he became a mainliner.
His golden arm wrote a brilliant story,
Until he slid from that peak of glory,
And landed in an abysmal valley,
Lying face down in a skid row alley.
Quick was his fall, short was his reign,
When once that shaft entered his vein.
He'd heard the roar of the crowds mushroom,
But it could not fill his inner vacuum.
His ears would hear the deafening cheers,
But deep within all he heard was jeers,
The hauntings of an ancient voice,
That said he was a number last choice.
Its din would drown the loud acclaim,
And rob him of his hard-earned fame.
From in his prison of self-derision,
He made one last fatal decision.
He threw himself for a mortal loss,
And made that devil his lifetime boss.

Dorothy Greenlund
I'M NOT LONELY
I'm not lonely anymore, Oh praise the Lord.
Since Jesus changed my life forever more.
I'm not lonely anymore, Oh can't you see.
That Jesus made a new person out of me.
I'm not lonely anymore, Oh praise the Lord
Oh don't you hear Him knocking on your hearts door.
Oh please receive Him now-don't turn away.
For this may be the last call, that goes out today.
I'm not lonely anymore, Oh can't you see.
That Christ has made a new person out of me.
Oh receive Him now. Don't turn away.
Let Christ enter in your heart and live today.

Nancy Teresi
TUESDAY NIGHT
The way your fingers floated my
lips and parted my heart.
The preciseness of that moment
I try to recapture
sitting among the floral design
of sheets you have left rumpled.
Five a.m. An hour that appears
urgently, slinging you into the
one hundred mile separation.
In reverence I climb the steps.
The ritual that divides
and predicts where I sleep on a
given night.
Pale noises out my darkened
window.
Air that comes cooler.
Vigilantly tending the flames of
passion.
Insane to stretch myself from
you, now I taste the salt of love.
Extinguish my bed-light; to
pause and notice the screened
sections of an almost full moon
framed for me now. Held by the
diamond's dazzle transcending
upon navy blue sky.
As love came unbolted
so did the chestnut of a cabin
door.

Sandy Zuckswert Mello
IN THE BLINK OF AN EYE
I can hear the multitude of Angels singing
With a mighty shout their voices ringing
All the Angels in Heaven were making ready
Soon they'd ride white stallions steady
Even the smallest Angel seen
Had a job to make ready the King
He was chosen to polish the Crown til gleaming
And once again, I heard the Angels singing
I could hear the brush of Angels wings
While they sang praises to their King
The streets of gold were polished bright
Even the stars were glistened for this special night
The jasper shone from the light of the Fathers face
Every Angel in Heaven was gathered to take their place
Along side the King as He rode out to the gates opened wide
Jesus was standing there with Peter at His side
The tiniest Angel took the scroll in hand
And gave it to Jesus, once made man
He alone had the right to open the scroll
His death gave Him the right to claim these souls

Soon He'd be seen in the Eastern sky
To gather men in, in the blink of eye

Andrea Figgins
UNTITLED
You know God watches over you
During every time of need
And you will someday be rewarded
For your each and every deed.
A lot worse could have happened
If He hadn't been by your side
And I think He's putting us through a test
Our faith is being tried.
I guess we all forget at times
To place things in His hands
Because it's hard to remember
He always understands.
In time your cuts and bruises
And your black and blue marks will fade away
But I know that forever
Your love for God will stay.
And I know when we leave you there at night
He's standing at your door
And He'll watch over and protect you
Like He always has before.
(Written for my sister following an auto accident)

John K. Pringle
UNTITLED
Hopelessly lost in your sweet smile,
The nearness of you delights me.
When our searching eyes lock tightly,
I long to hold you all the while.
Believe this, what is meant to be
Must come to pass. Feel your feelings;
Set your heart only on good things.
Strive for openness and honesty.
Things worthwhile come not easily,
And complications will taunt you;
But what your heart knows to be true,
Heed it, for this is reality.

John K. Pringle
A SPANISH DREAM
I can feel your sad Spanish eyes,
Slowly searching my longing gaze
And hoping, will the future days
Yield the passions your life desires?
Thoughts of you keep on stirring me,
Dreams of you have etched your sweet smile
On all my days; and all the while
I plot how I can set you free.
I ache to hold you in my arms,
Release my desires within you
Until our breaths are spent. It's true,
I'd risk all for your Spanish charms.

Mrs. Kathleen A. Brothers
OUR GANG
Gathering from all counties, at a real fast trot,
Just for homemade goodies, served cold and hot,
Having fun with or without a bingo pot,
Were true-blue, fair and square, and all that rot,
All the group smiling, whether winning or not,
Cause good sportsmanship is what we all got,
To me and all, Wednesdays mean alot,
At good ole' Kathy's place, our gangs bingo spot.

C. J. York
GREED
There's a deep, dark secret,
hidden in the hearts of men.
You never know when to greet it,
it just knocks and comes right in.
It hides around each corner,
it hides behind each door.
First you make a quarter,
then you make much more.
Its eyes are red, and firey,
its teeth are sharp, and long,
its skin is deep, and mirey,
and it sings a crooked song;
...(greed)...(greed)...(greed).

Pearl Reinert
A CHRISTMAS PRAYER
A Christmas Prayer to guide you
all thru the coming year
May the love of Christ inspire you
and make your life anew
May his blessing bless and guide you
and bring blessings that increase
And to fill all your future
with a gift of hope and peace.
We thank you Lord for Christmas
and our homes in which we dwell
And for the love of Christ that unites us
and for peace and goodwill to all
We thank you all in glory
thru our Savior divine
May we always keep Christs' love
in our Christmas prayers.
A Christmas prayer to guide you
with its peace goodwill and cheer
Will bring you a feeling of gladness
happiness and contentment
May the love of Christ be always with you

to guide and keep you each day
And to fill all your future
with a gift of hope and peace.

Alice M. Rifflard
THE CLOUDS
Looking from my window, I
watch the clouds on high,
Traces of images---drifting
slowly by.
The clouds are white and fluffy
on a bright and sunny day;
But changeable conditions can
turn them quickly grey!
I love to watch them hanging
there, suspended high in
space;
Or moving slowly-dreamily, to
some far distant place.
My thoughts are wandering with
them as they float so softly
there,
A brief but lovely moment, I
drift without a care.

Edmund D. Pizon
TIME FOR SEARCHING
Time is mine now—ah, such
ease!
The next, several hours, mine
to use as I please.
How shall I use it? How will
it fly?
Shall it be wisely or wasted
and die?
Flashed, sparks, electric arcs,
leap about within my brain;
All thoughts boring into my
tortured mind; all the same!
Will this continue unabated,
Driving me mad, my needs
unsated?
The World is mine by others'
standards,
Yet I do not feel as if it were
granted.
In worlds of two, perhaps even
more than three,
This life of mine whirls as if
on a drunken spree!
Dawn to dusk, dusk to dawn;
first in one world,
Then to another as if't were only
life's poor pawn.
People I've known, people
special to me;
Mostly have gone; forced by
time and condition to flee!
Sadness, loss, fills my heart;
Why in God's Wisdom, does He
force us apart?
Two, three, four or more
People trying to learn the score;
Struggling against their other
self;
Seeking needs for which there is
no help.
Seeking council from another's
lips,
Only forces the troubled soul
to stay upon its sinking ship.
An answer, my mind seeks ever
deeper;
Within itself, it finds no
"keeper!"
Love has done this—love and
more;
Toils upon troubles deeps
crashing down the door.
Vainly I struggle to keep all
well;
Yet in this struggle, my life is
pure hell!
Onward, I plod and so do they;
Each of us hoping for a better,
brighter day.
Feelings like this, similar
thoughts often said,
Leads me to believe we are all as
one in the Land of the Dead.
Yet why, in all of mankind's toil
and strife,
Have we not yet found that
"oneness" in life?

Larney Rutledge
THE DREAM OF THE CENTURY
Dedicated to Anwar Sadat:
A man with a Sacred Mission
I am a man of dreams
dreams of a thousand islands
dreams that have gone with the
wind and faded into clouds of
oblivion
One night I had a dream
that changed my whole life
A voice came to me saying
you have been chosen to go
into all the world and
bring friend and foe together
so that love and peace
will prevail among all nations
I have made a personal
commitment to accept the
challenge no matter what the
outcome might be to pursue my
mission of peace because war
has not solved the problems of
the Universe and I hope my
dream will become the dream of
the century
Epitaph:
He lived for peace
and died for principles
The dreamer is gone
silenced by assassins bullets
but the dream of peace remains
in the hearts of man
until the day comes
when all of mankind
contribute their share
to make peace a reality.

Sarah Daniel Vaughan
SONGS OF FOREVER
I would write songs of forever
for you-
Songs of forever, to sing you to
sleep;
Then in our dreams
You would fly to me, darling,
For rendezvous we are destined
to keep.
Hand in hand we would fly to
the stars,

Visit Venus, Jupiter, Mars;
Slide down rainbows,
Dance under the sun-
Oh, my darling, we would have
fun!
I would write songs of forever
for you-
Songs we would sing
Our whole lives through;
Sleeping or waking,
Just you and me,
Singing together eternally!

Mary L. Face
SOULFUL SOARING
With eyes filled with wonder
I turn my soul to the sky
For, up in her heaven
the great bald eagle flies.
With fraying fans she channels
the wind
with soaring sieves she harvests
the clouds
surveying in circles the world
from above
everything surrounding is
watching her now.
And as I too watch the snow-
capped chest
guide the soaring knives
I see the sun reach out to her
and light her golden eyes.
And my life too,
somehow skyward she brings
for, on her wing my soul she
carries
or in my soul evolve her wings.
Her thunder, her grandeur
for a moment were mine
her contentment, her steadfast-
ness
I'll keep with me through time.
For, there is nothing as
humbling as beauty
walking hand in hand with
might
making nothing compare to the
majesty
of the bald eagle in it's flight.

Robin Lynn Buss
FANTASY
A love song whispered in my
ears
Laced in surah of flaming
crimson
Blended by tears
I dreamed of you last night
We walked through fields
Of yarrow and moonlight
And joy turned to sorrow
As the rain began to fall
I then locked toward tomorrow
And the visions that I saw
Were pressed in my mind
And painted on my wall
My thoughts dance in confusion
For this love of you
Is but an illusion

Virginia M. Pittman
FAREWELL TO SUMMER
Summer, it seems you only
arrived yesterday
Now you are quickly wending
your way
Down the path, where you
pause and kneel
To examine a leaf, a chill you
seem to feel
You hurry along in your thin
filmy attire
Winter following at a distance,
with eyes afire
As He tries to catch up with
this beautiful sprite
The eve of summer is turning to
night
Oh tell me Summer why was
your visit not longer
Can it be Winters influence is
much stronger
I can do naught but sit and
mournfully dread
Winters visit when things seem
so cold and dead
Promise me you will stay longer
next time
With your warm feeling and
your beauty sublime
Tripping along happily and
feeling so gay
As you push winter on His
blustery way
Promise me too you will come
early next year
So I can be planning with a
listening ear
For sounds of your footsteps, gay
and light
Oh Summer your dawn has
turned into night

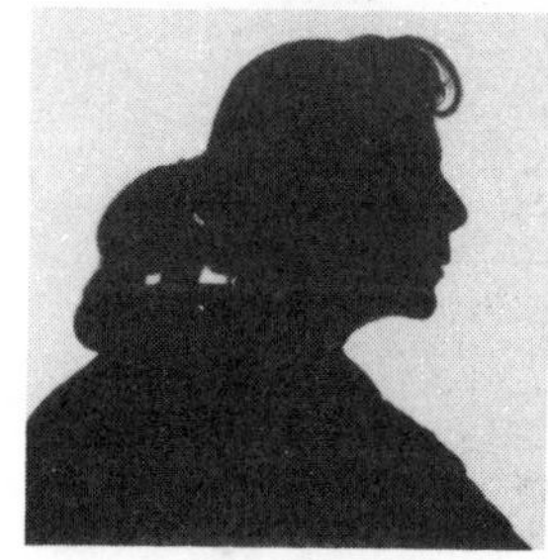

Alessandra A. Poles
THE ARTIST
An artist's blossom duly
perpetuates beauty,
Virtue, and the unspoken
supreme art flowers;
One creator brings to surface
hidden subtlety
Another the present or past or
distant futures;
Each soul reaching out giving
credence
To truth deepening emotions of
man's powers.
Infinite is the mystery of
strength in silence.

Richard Ballo
A SAILOR'S STORM WIND
In the morning, wind.
In the afternoon, wind.
In the evening, wind.
The wind carries rain, or the
sea, to my arms, legs, belly, and
face.
It penetrates my clothing,
sinks right to the marrow.
I turn my back defiantly,
absurdly; the wind is there.

Mrs. Mary J. Rhodes
SPECTRUM
One night
I asked Jesus
to teach me how to make
rainbows.
He took my hand and said,
"Come."
First, He scooped some red out
of the sunset, and arched it, and
hung it right there in front of
me.
Then He loved some blue out of
the sky and put it next to the
red. The sky smiled.
He held out His hand and
the sun melted onto His fingers,
sharing her golden blushes.
The grass beneath our feet
yielded her emerald richness.
Oh, how they all loved Him so,
eager and pleased at having been
of service.
He made the rainbow for me,
and wrote my name in it,
and draped it softly around my
shoulders.
My rainbow is waiting...and
all my pain in this life means
nothing except
that I am closer...to Him.
Color me anxious.
Color Him Love.

Myra Veda Smoot
UNTITLED
Do you know what God has
done?
He sent his only begotten Son.
He didn't have to do it but he
did.
He sent him so my sins may be
rid.
Some folks don't believe it's true
But I have seen what can do.
Some folks go by the way they
feel
But in my heart God is REAL.
I know God will work all my
problems out.
Because he sent his son to fight
my bout'.
I claim it in the name of his
Son.
VICTORY! VICTORY!
I have won!

Mary Letha Washington
TOMORROW
Doctors, lawyers,
Scientists, too.
All of these great people
I bring to you.
Headache, frustration, trouble-
some days well spent,
Will some day bring to us
A President.
Trusting heart, tender mind,
Will need all of the love
That we can find.
Take these little ones
And handle with care.
Listen to them, and lead them
Year after year.
Don't lose our little ones
To great sorrow.
Remember! Our followers
Of today
Will be our leaders
Of tomorrow.

Leslie G. Rembert
TRIBUTE TO MINNIE RIPERTON
You showered the world with
your gift of song
then I suddenly heard that
you were gone
You hit highs that I had never
heard before
it makes me cry to think
never no more
You were so young, but God
knew when to call you up above
one day I'll meet you there
and share some of my Love,
We'll discuss in full all of
your songs both old and new
We'll even discuss the new
ideas that never grew
Your songs are my inspiration
in so many ways
they (songs) get me started on
some of my worst days
MINNIE - I will always love
you and take constant trips
down "MEMORY LANE" because
you
not only "LIT MY FIRE" in the
past but you have a torch
burning in my heart forever.

Mona L. Cross
RAINDROPS
Now just a few raindrops linger,
And my fear subsides.
But I have learned of Nature's
fury
And of the stormy winds she
rides.
She called the winds from North
and South,
From East and West they came.
The thunder echoed long and
loud;
Lightning flashed like sudden
flame.
I shivered as the cold rain fell,
For it seemed to me a plan.
To test earth's many elements.
Last, woman if you can!
The raindrops like and army
joined,
And came in waves of might.
The skies that shown so clear
and blue
Appeared as darkest night.
I do not know just how long
I stood the stormy test.
But worn and weary, tired and
cold
I am in need of rest.
Now as I lie and watch the sky
A rainbow does appear;
As if to say "It's gone away,
There's no more need to fear."

Lydia Pauline Brown
FOR THESE BLESSINGS
I awoke this morning as
thankful as could be
When I opened my eyes, that I
could see.
When I got out of bed, I could
walk
I had a tongue and I could talk
With my ears I could hear,
What a gift so very dear.
My hands and arms were a
lovely view
As they reached out for work to
do
A mind to think, a heart to love-
For these blessings, I thank God
above.

James C. Stewart
I WILL PRAISE HIM EVERYDAY
I will praise him everyday,
Everyday of my life,
All my love I will give to my
Lord,
Every bush and every tree,
They all remind me,
That God is still here, he's not
gone.
All the places that I've been,
All the miracles that I see,
Remind me that God is still
here,
Every tree and every flower,
And with each passing hour,
I will live just to sing of his
praise.
I will praise him everyday,
Every day of my life,
All my love I will give to my
Lord,
Every bush and every tree,
They all remind me,
That God is still here, he's not
gone.
Lord, you gave your only son,
To die on the cross,
He suffered and bled for my
sins,
Lord, I give my life to you,
It's the least that I can do,
You've given so much to us all.
I will praise him every day,
Every day of my life,
All my love I will give to my
Lord,
Every bush and every tree,
They all remind me,
That God is still here, he is not
gone.

A. Paige Cooper
FALL, AND ME
Crisp new leaves
Orange and red sparks
Spotlighted against a sheet of
blue
My fingers stretch to skim the
smooth coolness
Not stirring the leaves
I follow one scooting along the
sidewalk
Crunch it with my foot
Before the wind carries it away

Helen K. Spinner
AFTER—THOUGHTS
The presence of now
holds no time
for realism in love.
It is only in after-thoughts
that reality makes an
appearance,
opening the memory
to all early warnings
that were willingly ignored.
When it's too late for changes,
and questions are answered,
the heart mends
and the fact remains
that falling in love
with the idea of love
damages worse than false
hope.

Siegmund Rutkowski
DANCE OF JOY
Which is it to be? today, tomorrow, yesterday, now this morrow. Where with all this sorrow. What do we do? Where do we go? What is left? We joke, we play, we laugh, we work, we pray and sing. In the fields of beauty, in nature, we feel contentness in our soul. Which is it to be? Now the time has come, to leave contentness.

To leave nature alone, at peace to sleep. To remember me and never to forget. Now sorrow comes back again, I must leave never to return. I shall not look back, for tears are in my eyes. Sadness chokes my heart! Which is it to be, why must I go? What is left? Oh, tell me why? what have I done! my coat I cling to, my heart throbs! As I see. Must I go?
Great sorrow comes to me! "Oh", so great. As I get closer I feel, I hear, the pain, the sound! Now I am ready. Which is it to be? Now, nothing is left. Great happiness and joy enters my heart, enters my soul, for to battle I go, for tired now I feel! There is no pain, now no sorrow. Now I sleep, forever in my grave to keep.
But why! What is the reason?

Renee F. Hazel
DAWN
Penetrating the darkness
With shafts of golden light;
Like the swiftness and beauty
Of a robin's early flight.
Lost in a haze,
The destiny of the forest way;
Scattering the shadows
That see to hide the day.
The forest, silence and tranquil
Meets the dawning day;
As Diana, the huntress,
Slips along her way.
The majestic trees are ruling
towers
High above the ground;
Deafening to the ears
With their silent sound.
The "Wishing" whispering
murmer
Of a Cathedral pine;
Bows so graciously
To the oaks divine.
The future reflects upon the
past,
A now forgotten dawn;
The dusk has stolen the glory,
And morning must move on.

Lucile McGregor Campbell
QUESTION
No one can make
A seed,
Yet from this
Minute beginning
All living comes--
Man,
Bird,
Beast,
The tree--
All of life and beauty
That we see.
No God, you say?
Then how did the world
Get this way?
Who did
What Man has never
nor ever
Could do?

Wendell Mack Tackett
MOTHER
If you could have seen her eyes,
you would have known.
Had you seen her smile,
you would have smiled.
Had you known what was in her
heart,
you could have taken heart.
Had you seen her when she was
young,
you would have felt younger.
Had you known her love,
you would have found it easy
to love.
If you knew her as I have
known her,
you would have loved her.
For she loved me,
as only a mother could.

Laura Madolin Thompson
THE RHINO AND THE FLEA
Look at me
Said the Rhino to the Flea
I am armoured to the knee
Yet a pest you be
So you see
That we
Could not possibly agree

Loren G. Phillips
PEACE
Resting on the couch
flickering candles
wavering shadows
and soft music.
My lady, near me ---
Attuned only to her presence
the pressures, tensions of the
day pass into oblivion.
Relaxed,
I can now focus on the
subtilties of life.
Wondering ---
WHY?
Better not to question why
for all meaning of the moment
may be lost through its
dissection!!
To enjoy ---
restful loving,
the lady's touch and scent ---
Sharing this moment together
is all a man could ask for ---
"PEACE"

Gladys C. Chaney
SLEDDING
When I go riding on my sled,
Sometimes I wreck and bump
my head;
As I get up to try once more,
I see my mother at the door,
Calling me to come and eat,
Or she is going to warm my
seat.
I eat my meal and out I go,
To play some more in the pretty
snow;
And when my hands and face
are red,
I hurry home and go to bed,
To dream about the things I've
done,
Until once more I see the sun.

Christine Winter Curran
FILLED WITH LIVING
Free as the sun high in the sky;
alive with a feeling and the
willingness to try.
Mountains stretching far, high
and wide;
bound with the wondrous
secrets they hide.
Trees that sway---strong with
the breeze;
keeping life protected, strong
and at ease.
Forces of faith, adventurous and
growing;
teaching of living through the
seeds they are sowing.
Waters running clearly with
vast, total power;
then fading into heaven and
returning a shower.
A carpet of goodness from the
soil and grass;
knowing from life that problems
will pass.
Please don't ruin or change our
glorious place;
just bless it and fill it with his
loving and grace.

Tania Olson
THE IMAGE
Your tall, spindly frame,
engraved in my memory,
walks through the now-empty
house, going from room to room.
You peer down the hallway,
look in every door,
rest, finally, in your chair.
The face is not yours --
it is so solemn.
Yet, behind that facade,
I see your laughing eyes
trying to tell me something
I cannot comprehend.
Are you happier, now?
Your head nods like a wilting
blossom.
I will leave you, Grandma.
Sleep well.

Jamee Corombes
TOGETHER
For the glory of all our being,
May your love be my love.
As you look at me, let it be me
I'm seeing.
For I do love you, from below
and above.
Confusion has its cause.
It needs to be alone and pause.
So your moments may be happy,
And the snows of serenity may
thaw.
Take heed of your motives,
Your reasons and your rhyme.
Climb those mountains, swim
those seas,
And I will see you in all time.

Marjorie Gagnet Berry
THE OLD LADY
Dark and desolate was the
winter night, the howling
wind knocked at the door,
shadows played against the wall
as footsteps creaked upon the
floor.
A silhouette of an aged being
standing at the window pane,
in tattered rags, face wrinkled
and gray watching the winter
rain.
She wore a gunny sack for
clothes and a bag over her
show-white head,
tennis shoes that were so big
she walked as if they were
filled with lead.

She lived alone in a crumbling
mansion surrounded by large
unkept grounds,
and as night came she would
light an oil lamp and you
could hear her pitiful
screeching sounds.
As the lonely seasons changed
from hot to unbearably cold,
you would see her walk
around her land, oh! so bent,
oh! so old.
She had no water but relied on
her neighbors and cooked on
sterno heat,
She rambled about her once
wealthy life to all she chanced
to meet.
Her cries became more frequent,
pleas for help that went
unheard,
then silence came as light
flickered out, not a sound nor
a word.
Thus, a spirit uninvited came
through the bolted door,
it was so cold, so very cold, the
shadows moved no more.

Marcella Cokkinis
THE LOST SHIP
Are you like a lost ship
That's tossed about at sea,
And like that forgotten ship
You have no place to flee?
The icy winds are torture
That tear the masts apart,
These are the temptations
That bleed a hungry heart.
Remember when Jesus was
On that stormy, untamed sea,
And calmed the wind and wave
That brought tranquility?
His voice was reassuring,
He only spoke, "Peace, be still,"
The raging waters ceased
And understood His will.
Do your burdens o'er whelm
you?
Is your heart heavy with care?
Have you thought of Jesus
As an answer to your prayer?
He calms your troubled hearts
And makes your courses known.
His undying love guides you
So you can be one of His own.
Our lives can be changed,
They can be made anew.
Tell your sorrows to Jesus,
His love will pardon you.
It seems that no one cares,
And you're sinking all alone.
Change your compass direction
And you will find a Home.
Somewhere there's a heavenly
harbor
Where you may see the light,
And God will be your Pilot
To steer through the stormy
night.

Nathan R. Hess
LIFING
topping at bottom,
scraping at sides;
clawing for signs
under shrinking weeks.
plan more above,
but, through all,
streaks of nothing:
crossing out; writing over;
X, X, Xing.
concatenation of instance beeps
by,
tugging at the senses,
tickling attention.
hard and simple intertwine
to form hilly pathway
for the lifing.

Gerard Philip Joseph Van Der Est "Jack of Straw"
By The Light Of The Silver Moon In The House Of The Green/Blue Crooked Shoe On A Christmas Night
The old women who lived in the
house of the green/blue crooked
shoe danced by the light
Of the silvery moon.
Her twenty-one children slept in
the splender of Christmas night
dreams.
The old women wished to Saint
Nicholas; for her bold child a
silver spoon;
For her child of wonder a
happy afternoon with a hula
hoop with a hul-hula.
For the other nineteen children
the old women further wished
to Saint Nicholas for seven
Pairs of red stockings, Barbie
dolls, computers, Bugs
Bunnies, friendly Mikey
Mouses,
And thought of Sesame
Street too; along with a
Juniper.
Santa Claus by record did hear
the wishes of the old women in
the house of the green/blue
Crooked shoe from New York
to London while her Children
slept my mother's inner
Thoughts with a Merry
Christmas with a hoot!
hoot! hoot! and a toot!
toot! toot!
Of a horn and a whistle.
Rudolph the red nose reindeer
did call to Dasher, Dancer,
Prancer, Vixen, Comet, Cupid,
Doner and Blitzen by the
silvery moon and a white,
white, white, snow.
CHRISTMAS EVERYWHERE!
By JINGLE BELLS there was
PEACE ON EARTH.
A SILENT NIGHT by a silvery
moon and white, white, white,
snow.
MERRY CHRISTMAS! indeed!
A friendly dog barked bow-wow
bow-wow.
A calico cat sang meow!, meow,
meow.
Mother and her twenty-one
children sang on Christmas
morning to Saint Nicholas by
white,
White, snow.
Mother and the twenty-one
children in Christmas song
thanked Santa Claus, Rudolph
the Red Nose Reindeer and
Dasher, Dancer, Prancer,
Vixen, Comet, Cupid, Doner
and Blitzen for they brought
forth their creed of a
American Christmas.
All prayed by a log fire bright
and further gave thanks to God
The Father, Jesus,
Mary, and Joseph for a happy
and joyous Christmas which
took place by a silvery
Moon and a white, white,
white, snow night.

Albert Bruce Ringrose, Jr.
OVER THE MEADOWS
Over the meadows
And through the trees
Thus I saw smoke
Atop with the breeze
But incoming like horror
But a laugh that did please
'Cause what came from thy sky
But little people just a saying hi!

Kelly Irene Carney
IN A CEMETERY
At the grave,
The people are silent.
Only the wind has a voice.

Teresa Silva
REALITY
There comes a time when you are beyond pain
And the hurting finally stops.
There is no longer a need for the searching
And the hoping for another to come along.
You tell yourself, "One can live just fine
On his own " and "No one could be happier
Than me", but these, as you know, are merely
Cosmetics for the sad Reality.
It all stops after a while -- the feeling,
The caring, the crying, the despairing.
And you realize that you are alone,
And the fact that you have realized this
Makes coping so much easier.
You realize, also, that the feeling has gone.
It will return, most likely, after a while,
And you will no longer be a shell,
A living, breathing, talking void
With no one on whom you may cast your spell.
Just when this time appears
No one knows.
We only hope and pray it is soon,
For the hurting needs stopping, and
The being alone needs solving.
Please, tell us when.
The city lights flash brightly on those
Who have another so that both are one.
Still, there are those who have
Been shut off.
These whom I speak of will never
See the glow of love in the eyes
Of another;
But, rather, the glow in the sad
City lights.

Petal A. Beebe
TO MAKE WHOLE AGAIN
Little Sparrow on the hill,
Fly to me; touch my hand
That I may know
The wondrous thrill
To feel a part of this land.
Tiny butterfly, brush
Your wings across this
Fevered brow, as with a hush
I would feel your kiss.
Gentle breeze, blowing soft,
Spare a passing caress;
Soothe my heart with
Your cooling touch, lest
In despair, I weep too much.
Creator of all that is,
I give to you my soul
To mold and once again;
My sorrowing heart make whole
In your love lies eternal bliss.

Theodore J. Warren, Jr.
SEA CLOUDS
Sea clouds rain on us
in darkened form nourishment
life thirst to drink
for survival sake, and soothe
our tongues from the sun's
rays of dry heat and dust
in our throats.
Sea clouds run underground
in caverns deep and well
earth wet under our feet;
beat clean the panes of our
homes; rinse the beach off our
children; clean the bones
sculptured bleached on nature's
face; wash the driftwood to the
ocean's edge;
turn the waterwheels' precision
factories;
Sea clouds rain the sky pure
blue, and our eyes will gaze
afresh the face of nature.

Wendy Whitbred
SAVIOR
He hurts as those who love us
must when we are sad
Without compunction He will
show us tears we can't see
through our own
He understands our blindness
while He watches over us and
we reach out, constrained by
efforts to compel and to receive
a love unfelt and urgent
Our God is not an idol made of
gold whose maker flattens and
balances it so that it will not
topple
But One whose total Incarnation
touched lepers with love
And whose cross-bearing shows
He cares when bearing is too
breaking and healing is too hard
Mary's searching tears were met
by angels' precious news of joy
Then love gave more than hope
of resurrection
The keeper of the garden was
the savior whom she only could
not recognize, but loved

Harrison R. Palmer
MEN DON'T CRY
From whence sad wretching in my throat
And all this water in my eye?
This surely can not come from tears
For we know man's too strong to cry.
Now why this pain that's in my chest
As I observe how I have failed
To reach those heights that I once craved,
Reviewing now deeds not regaled.
This can't be sobbing that I feel
When viewing sins my children reap
From errors I have made in life,
Because I know we men don't weep.
Our children, sons and daughters, each,
Share sadness with us through, the years
And yet, no crying comes to me,
Since manly strength prevents me tears!
How stark a paradox it is,
This standard to which man adheres

Pretending strength not yet revealed
Since truest strength is known in tears.

Patrick S. Rolak
FANTASY DREAM
As I sit staring into endless space,
All I get are visions of your pretty face.
Can't seem to get my mind to stay
On work that I have each day.
The movement in your walk is like poetry in motion.
Each time I see you I get the notion
Of how I've been longing to hold you Oh! So tight;
For just a brief moment, or even a night.
But I realize it's all nothing but dreams,
So why does it feel like my heart's tearing at the seams.
Perhaps I'm really hoping for the chance
For a little kiss, a bit of romance.
My loving you is better being just a thought.
Feelings are stronger for something you haven't got.
But love like this is something I'll never find,
It's beautiful and perfect, cause it's all in my mind.

Mary Schmale
WITHOUT PASSION
Raucous screams
rip
the early morning stillness.
The enemy
pins his victim
to the ground.
Wide brown eyes
plead silently,
but the captor
digs deeper,
holds his reward.
His cold determined stare
fixes
on the soft pounding breast
below him.
Ignoring threats
from above,
he begins
to lay the breast bare.
With each painful pluck,
the eyes grow wider,
the head jerks upward,
and a single cry
is heard
above all the others.
Then, spent,
the little brown head
drops back
upon the ground,
the eyes grow smaller
and the light fades.
Tiring of his hostile audience,
the hawk
lifts his robin
and flies.

Norma Joyce Christy
CHRISTMAS NOSTALGIA
Little hands that dared to touch the tinsel.
Little faces flushed and all aglow.
Little ears that listen for the sleighbells.
Seems like just a year or two ago.
Whispered secrets shared around the corner.
The morning search for 'deer tracks in the snow.
Happy hearts that must not be disappointed.
Just a year or two ago.
On Christmas Eve some carols for the neighbors,
Then a snack for Santa, left beside the tree.
Giggles in the dark and footsteps sneaking -
A secret race to be the first to see.
It's time, again, for us to fill the stockings;
A toy, a toothbrush and a candy cane.
And we thank God for another generation
Of little ones to bring us Christmas joy again.

Leslie Ann Shook
UNTITLED
A child always asks
why?
We wonder but never
ask...
Why is that?
Mommy left Daddy
Best friend Susie
died yesterday
Why is that?
Why does it rain on a summer
day when we could play
That simple queston, why
will never be answered
Why is that?
But then again
Why am I white and she black
Don't you see
what I had wanted
to be
is now forever
hidden in the faces
of friends
for they had wanted
me to be me.

Lugene Brady
JOB'S DILEMMA
God is omnipotent and just
I am sinless, so far as I can see
Trials and tribulations be my lot
Either something's wrong with God
Or something is sadly wrong with me
My heart tells me an omnipotent God
Could not be unjust

But my mind is not so sure
This battle between mind and heart
Is me trying to ensue
Prosperity a sign of God's favor?
Trouble and adversity a sign of God's judgment?
Mind! To this kind of thinking
I will not allow my heart to consent
On the horns of a dilemma
I am caught between
A faithless, foolish wife
And a dreadful disease
I shall undergo my afflictions
My God I shall never displease
Listen to the faulty arguments
Of my three fairweather friends
Or follow the leadings of my mind
I shall obey my motivated heart
And not retaliate in kind
With me there is no longer thought -- But knowledge
No longer persuasion --
But conviction
With fortitude and faith
I shall undergo my afflictions
Although I lack full understanding
Of the reason for trials
This shall be my resolve
I shall be courageous and endure
I refuse to curse God!

Michelle D. Baker
A LESSON IN HURTING
Sunshine is a needed thing,
but rain is important too.
For how can we ever hope to learn,
from skies that are always blue.
It takes the good times and the pain,
for any soul to grow.
Ho can we help others heal,
from hurts we never know?
How can you see the hurt in their eyes,
or know what it is they need.
If you have known only sunshine,
and your heart never bleeds?
Never run away from hurt,
never hide from pain.
For in every ounce of sunshine lost,
there is a lesson to be gained.
A lesson in loving,
a lesson in caring,
Learning to hurt,
is a lesson in sharing.

Colette Jean Robison
WHAT WE HAD
My life is not as happy, I am slowly giving up
We've changed our hearts along with the thoughts.
Learning of each other, growing through this pain
The good times we had, can never be the same.
I've always loved you and I can't stop now
With the forgiving and loving which we always shared,
The time that you loved me, the time that you cared.
Love doesn't come in the wind nor does it come with a song
But when it does come your way, don't do him wrong.
Misery will follow when it all is through
You will be torn apart, shattered and blue
I tried to tell you that love won't ever last
Dream about your future, forget about the past.
Play your spot and stand your ground,
The thing I'm sure of is that he will be found.

Jon Fortgang
THE BROKEN TOY
I am but a
toy.
Breaking and wearing down
each day.
How long before I break
completely,
no one can say.
All but one,
that is.
But to know would not be wise,
for one should live until
their ending day.
To look at life
can be sad at times.
But one should look at sad,
as life,
for without it,
how would life look;
always being
glad.

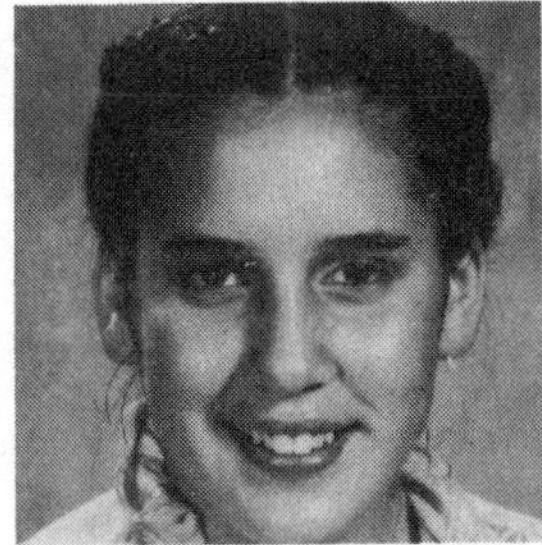

Shivaun O'Neill
MAKE SOMEDAY TODAY
I told my friend that someday
all my dreams would come true.
And she said "I feel sorry for you."
I asked her why these words she did say,
And she said "Make someday today."
I asked how I could do this task
And she said "Act natural, don't wear a mask."
I asked her why, and she said to me
"People will enjoy you more if it's the real you they see."
I told her that I'd "Make someday today"
And by realizing this, I'd be okay
And she said to me "You're there half the way,
Because you've learned to make someday today."

Esther R. Cole
NIGHT WATCH
Alone at the wheel of my frail craft
Alone in the dark of the night
The hissing sea and the flying spume
Obscure the wavering light
That marks the fangs of shadowed shoal
Where crouching headlands reach
Their talons sheathed in icy foam
Along their surf-torn beach.
And fear tiptoes into my thoughts
Chill dread that borders fright
Until a glimpse of that distant gleam
Rewards my straining sight
Then I lift my eyes to the heavens
Over the wind-wracked sea
And my spirit rises above the storm
And the dark surrounding me.
Then I hear the song the riggin' sings
Sings wild and sweet and free
Wind-swept notes from fiddle strings
That are fretted to the sea
Echoing her secrets to the stars
That span the heaven's vaults
Then fading away in mystery
While the surging deep exults.
In that enthralling moment
I'm at one with the sky and the sea
Sing with the riggin' sound the depths
And soar to Infinity
Play leap-frog on the milky way
and waltz with the northern lights
Then plummet again to mortal re-birth
Alone... but at one with the night.

J. D. Goff
OUTER DEEP
ethereal, and...empty-
this place where existance is and yet, is not.
cold and vast; glimmering like a diamond curtain against blackest black.
peaceful, yet raging incessantly, violently searing whatever it touches, yet leaving it
unscathed.infinity incarnate, but an impervious prison to one who must suffer here.

Karen Skeens
NIGHT FEARS
Tis the Story of old
That I tell to you
Of a Satin Night Lady
In a dress of dew.
Of a cricket chirp
In a woodwind band
While a firefly light
Leads the caravan.
Of the brook that sings
A wedding song
As the branch breeze
Keeps the harmony strong.
Of a bridal march
Down a graveyard isle
Between a voodoo sinister
And a virgin child.
Of a honeymoon
In a coffin bed
Birth of an infant
With a shrunken head.
Of the sunlit fading
Of the horrid life
Between a voodoo sinister
And his virgin wife.

Linda S. Sharp
I THINK OF YOU...
I think of you...
in the morning when I watch the sunrise- its beauty warming me inside; preparing me for a new day...
in the evening when the sun sets behind the mountains and the cool night air begins to blow softly against my face...
when the moon shines brightly upon the land with the stars surrounding it, twinkling so beautifully...
each time I see two people in love- gazing into each other's eyes--holding one another very close...
I think of you...
always
and that's how I know that
I love you

Mayo G. Cox, Jr.
THE ORPHAN
Lost in this land of darkness,
I'm just a lonely stranger.
An orphan from birth;
I lived in constant danger.
I never knew my mother;
And my father was far away.
I never had a sister or brother;
Nor heard the words, "I Love You!"
I never knew what it was like
To play with other girls and boys.
I never rode a bike;
Or played with shiny new toys.
I never had a place to call "Home."

Or someone to tuck me in bed.
No one ever told me a story
Or kissed my sleepy head.
You see, I'm a little orphan boy
With a heart full of fears.
I've spent many a sleepless night
With eyes full of tears.
I walk the streets at night
Looking for someone to come.
My world is full of fright.
I live from crumb to crumb.
People look at me and stare
Eyes glare
Voices speak
"Get out of my way."
"I don't care!"
Then a hand reaches for me.
I run.
I mistrust.
Then the hand touches me;
Picks me up
And carries me.
He speaks to me,
"Come with me,
I care."

Lousie DeGruy Parker
DEAR GOD
Dear God, our father in heaven
We need your help today.
You give to us, all that we have
And we have strayed away.
You've blessed us with your loving care
And your endearing fold.
We thank you God our father,
For all we have and hold.
Please bring us back, we pray thee,
Good Shepherd claim your sheep.
And let us give our thanks to you,
While kneeling at your feet.
Hold out your staff and rod we pray,
And gather us to you.
Because without your help dear God,
There is nothing we can do.
Dear God our father in heaven
Hold out your hand we pray,
And lift your fallen children Lord
We need your help today.

Dawn Aarhus Anderson
TELL ME WHY
Daddy, if you can hear me,
Tell me why you died that way.
All alone in that dump of a trailer,
Out of work, but full of booze.
Was it your liver that finally did it?
Or just too much drink, too fast?
Was it painful for you, dying?
Or were you sleeping when you went?
People ask me how you died,
And I'm not sure what to say.
Was it the alcohol that killed you?
Or instead, that damned fool pride?
The pride that always kept you,
Just inches away from help.
Daddy, if you can hear me,
Tell me why you died that way.

Helen Branch Blough
SNOWY DAYS END
It's nearing another days end and a cool breeze is whistling through a tall evergreen. The sun casts long fingery shadows against the neighbors white house, giving an orangy glow, warming me inside, reminding of evenings past, when I sat watching the sun set.

Little sparrows play chasing games through the wintery sky, and go flitting from tree to tree singing songs I think I've heard before. The snow covered ground and frosty white trees, sparkling and shimmering in the lake afternoon sunlight, bring loving thoughts like hot cocoa after a long day of rough playing and the excitement on Christmas Eve.

Mellow and wonderful thoughts are blowing around, leaving me a little breathless on a snowy days end.

Eddie M. Daniels, Sr.
WAS I WRONG
Was I wrong
To think as I thought
To feel as I felt
To act as I acted
To appear as I appeared
Was I wrong
To think as you thought
To feel as you felt
To act as you acted
To appear as you appeared
Was I wrong
To be what I wanted to be
To do what I wanted to do
To say what I wanted to say
To play like I wanted to play
To sing like I wanted to sing
To love the way I wanted to love
To live the way I wanted to live
Was I wrong
To be what you wanted to be
To do what you wanted to do
To say what you wanted to say
To play like you wanted to play
To sing like you sang
Love the way you loved
To live the way you live
Was I wrong
DARING TO BE ME.

Edith Russell
LITTLE MAW
Gentle, yeah that was our little maw. With us she seldom if ever got mad.
And she never shouted angry words at us, we only knew because she looked sad.
She loved us one and all the same. Well, maybe a couple she loved a little more.
But you never knew that, the way her eyes lit up when you walked through the door.
Maw was the heart of our little neighborhood, she always had time for a friend.
If you needed some sugar, a spool of thread, or some talk to help a lonesome heart mend.
She liked to spend a quiet day on the creek bank with her old fishing pole.
She didn't mind if we tagged along and found some soft green grass in which to roll.
When one of her kids had to leave home, with a hug they'd say, "Now mom don't you cry."
And we knew as they walked off down the road she put her apron over her face, she tried!
Maw loved and cared for all of us, we never went hungry or without her love.
Why, she took time to make us dolls, hats, and even winter gloves!
When grandpa died we thought we might lose her too, for her love for him was so strong.
But gentle though she was, she had will power and she proved everybody wrong.
Little grandma lived in pain for many years, how bad we will never know.
Many times we would hear her say, "Dear God, please let me go."

Grandma did leave us one cold January morning; just as she died from her blue eyes slipped a tear.
We tried to tell her once more that we loved her, but little maw didn't hear.
We'll never know if the tear she shed was happiness, because now her pain would be gone.
Or maybe she was a little sad for having to leave us in this cold world all alone.

Violet Meade Lundberg
HOBO LADY
Hobo Lady, with your bags packed tight;
Hobo Lady, traveling thru the night;
Hobo Lady, you are such a sight-
Push on, Push on, Push on.
Hobo Lady, trudging thru the cold;
Hobo Lady, baring such a load;
Hobo Lady, it's not too long, I'm told;
Carry on, Carry on, Carry on.
When you know that things get tough;
When you feel the goings rough;
When you feel you've had enough,-
Sing a Song! Sing a song! Sing a song!
Hobo lady, when you haven't long;
Hobo Lady, when you're doing wrong;
Hobo Lady, if you know you don't belong -
Move on! Move on! Move on!
When you come to the end of the line;
And you know you haven't got time;
When you get a certain sign;
And you have no piece of mind-
Say a prayer! Say a prayer! Say a prayer!

Clara Donath
THE DISCIPLE
Beneath the sun on a cloudless day
The dusty streets of the city lay;
The house brown were built of sod,
And the Jews within believed in God.
They kept their creed and broke their bread
And all the widows and orphans fed.
They lived the law that Moses gave,
And kept not bonded man or slave.
They trusted God, and only some
Did not believe the Messiah come.
Then down the crowded, dusty street
Came two men in sandled feet.
The light of love shone in their face
As they stopped to speak in the market place.
They told of Love and a risen Lord
And of His faith and His Holy Word.
And they said, "For this is god's given Son;
He has come to save you every one,
So let us heed the Savior's grace
And look to-day on His loving face.
For you have been given life by His hand
And He asks you with Him in love to stand,
That you might dwell in your Father's place
And live eternally in His Grace.
Now there were those who these words did hear
And they were angry and full of fear,
For yet the Messiah had not come
And this was blasphemy to some.
They shouted that these men did lie,
Therefore by the stone should die,
Then casting from their sweating hand
A sharp edged rock picked from the land.
And spoke the man, "Why doest thou this
When all I ask is but a kiss?
For love I bring and love I teach
To all who are within my reach.
For God so loved you, every one
That He gave to you His only son
So can you not do more than I
And build a church, and so live by—
The words of Christ that dwell on Love
And teach of His Father who rules above.
You stone me now but I shall not die
For you can not kill the eternal I!
And many shall come after me,
And soon the light of truth you'll see;
My friend Barnabas shall carry on
Even though my soul be gone."
The people bowed their heads in shame,
And someone ask, "What is his name?"

"I think he must a prophet be,
The name of Paul was said to me."
They left him as they crept away,
And he rose up and they heard him pray,
"Forgive them Father, for their hearts are young,
The song of your Son is newly sung,
And they shall come to know as true
That Christ and they belong to You."

Lea Cordner
CONQUEST
(for Robbie Jr., with Mommy's love)
My Son-
(young and innocent;
full of wonder...),
runs freely through the
green meadow - near
the humble home we live in.
His brown hair tangles in
the summer breeze...
Bluer than the sky above
and his long lashed eyes...
Exuberantly he charges-
(with a hope;
an attempt to climb...),
the steep hill and succeeds-
conquering his desire to be
that big world's little man!

Bobby J. Ambrose
ALONE
Today is a day for sorrow
For soon there will be no tomorrow.
Yesterday there was love and joy.
Now it seems so very coy.
What happened to the dreams we shared?
When one was hurt, the other was spared.
The path we took was beautiful and free.
We carved our love upon a tree.
Who would believe this is our fate
For now our love has turned to hate.
That beautiful tree has long been gone.
Now all alone, I must go on.

Alene Walker
MIGRATION
Days grow short and nights grow long,
Fly with me to a new home,
With life's labors almost o'er
To become children once more.
We'll sail with the clouds,
race with the sun,
But eager to bed, this second
Time young.

Vivian Hendershot
CLOWNING
Clowning is a lot of fun,
Some may say it's over done.
If you cause a few to smile,
Then you know it's worth your while.
Doctors say that it is needed,
When their patients feel defeated.
Even though we often pray,
Sometimes a smile, can pave the way.

Ann Carol Schoener
SILENT FIELDS
The corn husks lie bent and broken in a field of winter's white
The frosted wind is howling; the air so crisp, it bites.
The stormy sky above them threatens with frozen tears.
While the earth lies still and silent in the hush of long gone fears.

Mary Newport Taylor
MY SPIRIT
Of what substance are you, my spirit,
That I can feel each gentle movement of you within me
And yet see or grasp no more of you
Than the passing wind?
Of what divine beauty your visage
That my eyes are forbidden it's wondrous sight
And my fingers, it's exquisite contact?
And what your bright mission, my soul,
When your keeper is so steeped in darkness
And your bonds so fastly trussed?
Of what pride are you, my lovely spirit,
That I, ridiculous thing of earth,
Presume to clip your mighty wings?

Yolanda E. Smith
LOVE YOU
As I sit here tonight
I watch you smoke your pipe
I love you with all my might
When you look at me
My heart is in flight
You make me feel
Like I want to fight
Only for you
With all my might
I love you
With all my heart
I want to fight
For you with all my might
You make me feel
Like my heart is in flight
I love to be there
To smell the aroma in the air
Of your pipe tobacco there
As I watch you smoke your pipe
I love you with all my might

Nancy L. Ebar
A MOTHER'S INTREPID LOVE
In these years of growing up,
Sometimes it's awfully hard to do;
Just remember when you feel lost -
I really do love you.
You are changing into manhood,
The process is painful and slow;
So set a pace just right for you -
Remember I love you so.
Always try to do your best,
Stop when you have a doubt;
Never give up, just hang in there -
Knowing I love you alot.
The years will pass and one day you'll be,
Responsible for how you will live;
And the pride you posses
Is just half the test
You reap what you're willing to give -
I shall love you as long as I live.

Martha Helen Morris Eiffert
THE ROOT AND BLOOM
Man and wife
Are one,
He the root
She the bloom
If bitter
The root,
There's no
Sweet fruit.

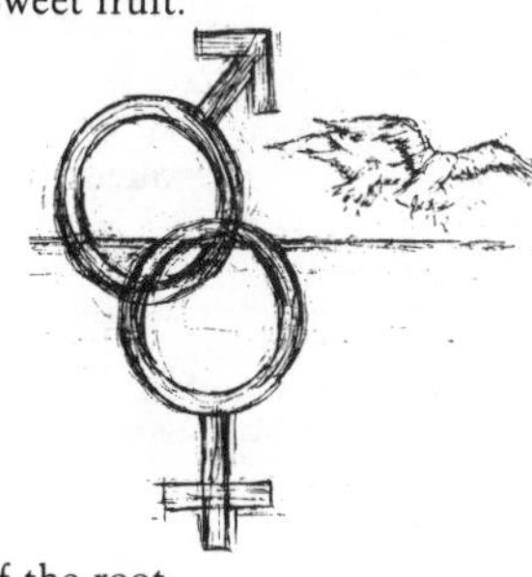

If the root
Doesn't try,
The flower
Will die.
Each must help
The other,
Happiness is
Working together.

Elden T. Stuart
UNTITLED
It is the calm
After the storm.
The ship rests
On the cool water
And the once frightening
Dark clouds
Cast their shadows
No more.
Who knows when
In the future
Another tempest
Will rage?
Perhaps, even
Mightier than the first.
Anchors rust
The depths corrode them
No more can they hold fast
A ship
Which needs grasp.
A sailor
Upon the winds
Meets little rest
And the decks
Won't let him.

Peggy Britton
THE TIDE OF LIFE
Swept away on the tide of life,
Flowing out to sea,
Childhood days fade into night,
Leaving their memories.
Balancing on the hands of time,
Swaying to and fro,
Slipping into tomorrow land,
Soon today will be long ago.
If I could step back for just one day,
To my land of make-believe,
And visit my thoughts of yesterday,
Content I'd always be.
Life flies so quickly around the clock,
Leaving traces along the way,
Burying memories deep in the hearts,
Of those who were young yesterday.

Mildred S. Gillies
FATE
White trunks stand tall
Winter's frozen silhouettes
With garments strewn on ground.
Alabaster Roman heads
On polished, wooden pedastals
Line the old museum halls.
Horseback heroes perch
Forgotten beside snow-packed paths
In city parks.
History lies in state
In a cold casket.

Terri Ann Eichelberger
ONE PERFECT SMILE
Life is a seriously funny thing.
People going around in circles,
One perfect ring.
To meet a person, a friend I did make,
As he touched my hand,
One perfect shake.
Through the hall I did pass him by.
I passed him in a hurry,
One perfect sigh.
With me he spent just a while
And a beautiful thing,
One perfect smile.
It's nice our friendship did never end.
Acquaintances we are still,
One perfect friend.

Judith LeFebvre
FREEDOM
Clouds gently spinning across the sky
Sun setting against the blue
Illusions of the day
Come to quietly rest in my mind
soft breezes move you limberly along
Feel the coolness against your skin
The bay sits majestically with the sails coming in for a landing
The sky is violet colored with a thousand cobwebs
A lone bird flies high
Feeling good now
Got the sky to herself
Floating in and out of open spaces in the evening air
She is at peace
And flies not looking for anything
Just for the uplifting glory of it.

Karen M. Kagiyama
FOR ANNE
butterfly chasers, you and I
with our nets we roamed the meadows green
scaled the rocky hills of gorse
to reach the summit
the top of our world
we found our prizes here
colored flutterers in the mountain breeze
laughing gaily we ran
nets trailing full behind
we hoped to gather hundreds of butterflies
we were lucky if we captured one
then we couldn't keep it long
our hearts were too tender
the pretty creature in a cage of net
was not half as beautiful as it was free

Frederic S. de Aboitiz
EXPIATION IN REINCARNATION
I.
Oh, it is not so much that I forgot something, as if in Morpheus'* stupor.
My brain, organ of the Mind, will not let me...many pains and sorrows...forget.
But it is just that I remember everything, like all his scabs the leper.
Old sins from previous lives cause my guilt to be in this World with profound regret.
The fires of burning passions within the breast of the lusty heart are anguish!
With the "Water of Life," the flaming coals in my chest I hope to extinguish!
II.
At last there are no longer any ifs, ands or buts about my destiny.
My fate? Condemned to bouts of depression, and damned with fits of despondency.
After so much study in years many, and deep thought in quiet self-scrutiny:
My soul I must save with suppression of wordly evils in ascendancy.
What heroic act, last and final, catapults one into Immortality?
One's life to advance "Eternal Humanity's" highest cause: Spirituality!
**In Greek mythology, Morpheus was the God of dreams, and son of Hypnos, the God of sleep (Ovid, Met. 11, 183-206).*

Katie Brunner
PARTNERSHIP!
The truest form of partnership
the world over can be found
in the Holy Estate of Matrimony
where everything abounds.
Here Man and Woman start a life
so complex, old and new;
a partnership that can create
a new Life sprung from two.
Here can be found the highest aim
a Man can hope to own
with a partner that will call his name
in a tender, kind and loving tone.
Here can be found the wonders
of emotions, sad or true;
the sense of all togetherness
perfected, through and through.
No matter what, as years go by
forget the wrong, the tears you cried,
in partnership you seldom find
that only one gets hurt, or tried;
But progress always will remain
in a partnership that's good and strong -
the words ones promised
"Yes, I do!"
Can write the future's nicest song;
Then faith, hope and charity
will only bring and multiply
love, peace and harmony,
a composition, for all and thee.

Donald J. Maslanka
MUSIC/LOVER
In theory-
Music is my life
It takes my tears
and joys
and fears
And works them into me
Only to come out of me as
Melody, Harmony, Rhythm, and Rhyme
The fact is-
You are my music
the 6/8 in my 4/4 life
A rolling, flowing, symphony that takes
this Avant-garde
Offbeat
Jukebox of dissonance
And lets me know that I'm alright
In the classical repertoire
of your love.

Sharon Gentle
FINAL MOMENTS
I got your letter the other day,
Stared down at it in my hand,
The feelings that I felt right then;
Even I didn't understand.
Slowly I read the words you wrote,
They held more than I hoped to find,
And when you said you were okay;
The weight lifted off my mind.
For weeks I had wondered about you,
Thought of you almost every day,
It wasn't until I heard from you;
That I was sure I touched you in some way.
So here I sit still holding on,
To the one who's shown me brighter skies,
Funny, I can almost see your face;
Through the tears that are in my eyes.
You signed your letter "with love",
I hope you know that means so much,
Though I may never see you again;
I will always feel your special touch.

Jim Chasteen
SWEETHEART
I thought that you would like to know,
That someone's thoughts go where you go.
That someone never can forget,
The hours we spent since we first met.
That life is richer and sweeter for,
Such a sweetheart as you are.
And now my constant prayer will be,
That God may keep you safe for me.

Teresa Stephanie Mahon
OF RAIN
the girl
the large dirty window
only the rain pouring down
as if a hundred eyes were weeping
breaks the falseness
as it cries to
get in.

Bernice Carroll
DEFINITION OF POETRY
POETRY is crystalized thought
in lovely design and pattern,
Carefully wrought, colored by tones
and undertones of emotion:
Moved and bestirred by winds or whims of fate—
With verbal grace goodby words become "Lingual Lace"!

Cheryl McCafferty
SWEET LULLABY
Now lay down your tiny head
Let me tuck you into bed
Give me a kiss, and hug me so tight
My lullaby will sing you goodnight
Fold your hands; say your prayers
Dream of toys and teddybears
Close your eyes; go to sleep
Tomorrow you'll be just as sweet

Helen Irene Miller
UNTITLED
While season after season slides
Through the slippery hands of time,
Love beckons me to slow my pace
And stop racing against the clock;
For she knows I must relax
To learn from her gentle touches.
Then, I can give my all to her,
And treasure time's fleeting moments...
So, I can win the "human race."

Cynthia Frings
COMPASSION
"You're late from school," her mommy said,
"I'll have to ask you why."
While awaiting explanation,
She heard her daughter sigh,
"Janie broke her dolly and
I couldn't walk on by."
"Did you stop to help her fix it?"
"No, I stopped to help her cry."

Stephen R. Saunders
THE WAITING ROOM
Another time and place settle on her as she settles into the rocking chair hers from habit only.
Large thoughts fill her.
Was the world different then than now? Memories have the slightest tinge of mauve; the pictures in her hands say yellow-brown.
She hesitates. Which is right?
No matter either way.
Now everything matches the walls: white above, gray below, the thin darker gray band between not separating two tones but merging them into dirty white.
If the world was a different color
it was indeed a different world.
There is a stir in the room as the medicated gnarled shift positions.
They are beyond hearing.
She does not notice,
wanting a green world next time, surely to be transported there.
Rocking.

Vesta L. Charbonneau
DEAR LORD
Dear Lord-
I found out today
That I am going to be a mother.
So, to You, Dear Lord,
I give all my thanks
For this creation that You

Have given me to bear.
And, Dear Lord, I pray to You
For a very healthy child,
For him to be perfect in
Everyway
Just as I know that You are.
I thank You for the hearts
He will warm when eyes look
On him and when other than
My arms hold him.
Many hearts I know there will
Be.
I pray, Dear Lord, that You will
Help me to be the best mother
That I can be.
To be the best friend and
Teacher
That I can be to my child.
I pray, also, Dear Lord,
That You help me to raise him
With a loving and caring heart,
To believe in You with all of his
Soul.
Help me to teach him respect,
Understanding, and kindness
For all mankind, animalkind,
And for this beautiful world
You have given to us.
I claim all these things,
Dear Lord,
In Your Most Holy Name.
And, Dear Lord, I give You my
Most Sincere and grateful
Thanks
For such a beautiful thing
As this to be bestowed upon me.
Thank You, Dear Lord,
For such a wonderful blessing.

Sylvia P. Beres

WE CAN'T WIN THEM ALL

It matters not
if we've won
and laughed,
or if we've lost
and cried.
the most important
part of it all
I think, is the fact
we tried.

Tamara L. Rigan

STARS

I wish for every time
We Touched.
We Kissed.
We made a star...
To brighten
My Heart
With a Memory.
A star so bright...
I could remember,
And Count
Every Touch
Every Kiss
Every Night.

Sereta S. Staley

MY PROTECTION

(This is an excellent poem for a child who is afraid of the dark)

I like to think the bits of light
About my darkened room at night
Across the floor, before my bed
Upon the walls, or overhead
Are really angels standing there
And hovering over me with care.
When I think this, my terrors cease
And I can fall asleep in peace.
Though strange shadows are in the room,
I need not fear the dark or gloom;
Because where angels are, tis true
That God is ever present, too.

Jean Wright

MY BEAUTIFUL HAWAII

I remember the first time I saw you,
I couldn't believe my eyes,
I marveled at your sparkling waters,
Majestic hills and brilliant skies.
I ran along your seashores,
Feeling so alive and free
And laughed as the tingling ocean
Tugged and pulled at me.
Slat water tinged the air
And painlessly stung my lips,
Your waters rolled so gracefully,
As an island girl's swaying hips.
Beads of water rested on me,
As I lay upon the sand,
Freely giving myself to the sun,
As it shone upon the land.
Gentle breezes drifted by,
Sending sweet perfume through the air,
How exotic were your flowers,
So beautiful and rare.
How magnificant were your sunsets,
With colors no artist could capture,
I would watch while your waves gently clapped,
And my heart would fill with rapture.
In that land of paradise,
My dreams became reality,
So much beauty to behold,
You mysterious wonders surrounded me.
Oh my beautiful Hawaii,
You're forever on my mind,
I never knew how much I'd miss you,
Until I had to leave you behind.
The memory of you keeps coming back,
Haunting me through each day,
I hear your island music whispering,
"Why did you go away."
I can still hear the ocean,
As it beats against the sand,
But now I see the waves
As though they were a beckoning hand.
I hear them saying, "Come Back, Come Back
And run along my shores,
Why did you leave me,
Come Back, Come Back, Once More."
I still see your palm trees
And the way they used to bow,
I took their beauty for granted,
But I surely miss them now.
I miss your rocky mountains
And the mist that hovered low,
Many times I looked up at them
And admired them from below.
I remember the day I had to leave
And how I couldn't say good-bye,
Tears flooded my eyes,
As I saw a rainbow in the sky.
The plane took me higher and higher
And I turned, once more to look,
You were more beautiful than ever,
Like a picture from a story book.
Your island was like a shimmering gem,
Amidst an ocean full of sparkling blue,
I still feel the ache inside my breast,
My Hawaii, I love you.

Angela Jean Yates

GOOD BYES

Good-byes are so hard to say,
Some will not heal for many a day.
There is a time in everyones life,
This word must be used at least once or twice.
Our time has come as a yearly farewell,
But may we never regret a tear that fell.

We ask questions and wonder why,
Words were invented such as good-bye.
Our time will come, when we will never have to say,
Good-bye again like we did today.
Until our time comes,
May you and I,
Never regret our tearful
GOOD—BYES...

Linda L. (Duryea) Hotchkiss

STRONG IS THE FOE

He's wandered away Lord, far from the fold,
He's hurting and bleeding and torn,
While the enemy fierce and bold,
Unmerciful and full of scorn;
For the wandering, feeble child,
Defeated from self and pride;
Refuses, though lost in the wild,
To return and in thee abide.
"My way is the right way," he cried,
"For I am the one who knows best."
That he could be wrong, he denied,
And great was his fall neath the test.
"Admit that I'm wrong, how can I?"
"I must never let on that I know,
And through the night watches, I cry;
The enemy - pride - is my foe."
Help him dear Father, I pray,
To know You are with him yet,
Longing for all those who stray,
To find peace and all their needs met.
Through Thy tender forgiving love,
The healing waters will flow;
Binding the wounds from above,
Of Thy children here below.

Patricia A. Misisco

SUNSHINE RESTRAINED

Rainy morning sunshine
comes from inside.
Every raindrop reflecting
the emotion denied.
The mood remaining
throughout the day
even when straining
to make it stay.

J. Patrick Rhone

JENNY

A sentient of sadness and longing
that is not bound to pain,
And resembles tribulation only
as the haze resembles the rain.
Her passion wantingly seared through me
while her beauty imprisoned my sight,
Her touch cradled my desire and crystallized
contemplation of the night.
The fondling glow of the winter's night moon
lightly embellished her resting form,
And permeated my heart with memory's movement
as the present perished and the future was born.
The moonlight exudes from from cracks of pulled-down shade
as I stand tenaciously immersed in memory of
Jenny, She was a portrait in flesh but, my arms aimlessly
search to find only absence and memory.

Dora Wilcox

LIFE

I have a headache, I don't know why,
everything is "Apple Pie" -
The dishes aren't done, the house is a mess,
the TV's on, and I'm sitting here for a rest-
I'm watching the kid, watching an R-Rated movie --
if this goes on she'll end up a "juvie" --
The "old mans" out, drinking beer with the guys--
tomorrow he'll go to work with big red eyes--
Oh well, that's life, if you can call it that--
And as I look at the door-
I reach for my hat.

Timothy Lushinsky
WOULDN'T IT BE
Wouldn't it be grand
To be able to stand
Upon a cloud of white
Where we did not fight.
Wouldn't it be spendid
Not to be offended
To cast two hexes
To combine the sexes.
Wouldn't it be lovely,
But, remember, I speak bluntly,
To seize the yellow, black and white face
And have only one plaid race.

Linda Sciapiti
WALKING TRAIL
Remembering this hell
Recaptured thought,
memory deepens
with intensity.
Bury, release, unload
that inevitable explosion.
Lingering on,
immersed in depths of agony,
revealing expression.
(you're not alone)
Extending outward,
arise-
Another time,
thinking you're sane
you will,
you must walk it again.
No.
Not this time.
Finally,
recognize the climb.
There is one who will listen.
Ears, a breath away,
anticipating, waiting to
bring forth an eternal glisten.
Focus on the light,
let warmth overcome.
Peace so bright
you know you won't run.
Break the barrier,
release your inner strength,
don't be a carrier.
Sure now,
you learn to bend.
A wonderous thing,
Walking Trail
has come to an end.

Jean Dye
FOLLOW ME
Carry your cross
Be it heavy or light,
With courage and prayer
He'll lead you day and night.
Whatever weight cross
He chose for you to bear,
Carry it with gratitude
Under His great loving care.
He'll lead you through
Any turmoil you face,
Just bear the cross assigned you
And He'll apply his favor and grace.

Barbara L. Trismen
THE ARTIST'S STUDIO
Your entire top floor is as musty
And dusty a tinderbox as
The building is itself.
There was another loft:
A battered waterfront property
Quietly crumbling in Buf'lo,
It's heavy door so weakened
By the very locks upon it,
We wondered it ever swung fro.
And Father had its key.
Your door is the same.
We have entered the dingy hall
We knew then as children of nine
And five or so.
We have climbed the twisted stairs,
Creaking our way beside
The ancient caged shaft
Some raucous lift once knew.
The same inky odor
Of thousands of printing days past
Is here as it was there.
And even those speed cars of childhood,
The swivel desk chairs we rode
As fast as ever we could
'Midst posters and paints and screens,
Are here in dusty silence.
And so it is complete.
The past surrounds us all
One sure way or another:
You paint and print in yours.

Miss Sharon Denise Townsend
A CRY FOR MOTHER'S HELP
Into the quiet blissful night
came the cry of a small child...
Mama, where are you?
It seemed as if time and
eternity were no more.
Piercing the silence once again--
came the cry for mother's help.
Mama, where are you?
Mama, please answer me.
All I ask is to be answered--
This will assure me that you care.
Also to know that in childhood's restless days
and sleepless nights you'll always be there.
Mama, where are you?
Not much do I ask...
Just to be loved.
Is that such a difficult task?
Mama, where are you?

Dixie Power Casero
THE RIDE
With a snarling roar of anger
The thunder strikes the plains.
The horseman does not change his pace,
He anticipates the rain.
But deep within his gentle steed
An ember starts to flame.
A dreadful yearning beckons,
He fights against the reins.
The horseman tries to calm him
He does not wish to run.
But as he strokes the plunging beast,
The two become as one!
The flame is burning higher
The flashing heavens rage!
This savage and his savage steed
Are of another age!
He screams in wild abandon
The beast responds in kind.
Across the plains they thunder,
One heart, one soul, one mind!
Then suddenly, it's over
The cleansing rains begin.
Their savage ride has ended,
As though it had not been.
But as he slowly turns toward home
He heaves a shudd'ring sigh.
And when the sun begins to shine,
The horseman starts to cry.

Judith Gorey Hoenig
PASSERS—BY
Today I walked with you,
You did not speak, but yet I
knew the thoughts you carried
as we walked.
I must go away for our dreams
will always be dreams.
And when I go away we will not
walk again nor talk again, but
we will always have our
thoughts.
This is all we can have, and we
knew it the first time we
walked.

Grace King Lafevre
EILEEN
In my home town I took a stroll one day;
I met a girl who chance to walk my way.
The prettiest girl my eyes have ever seen,
I ask her name she said it was EILEEN.

EILEEN EILEEN My dear I love you so;
My lips won't speak the words to let you know.
Each night I hold you fondly in my dreams;
My poor heart whispers, love me lovely EILEEN.
My poor heart whispers, love me lovely EILEEN.

Dom S. Castillo
THE ETERNAL TRIANGLE
The heart is the symbol of love
The mind is that of wisdom;
They are meant to blend together
But they are sometimes worlds apart.
Many times another woman
Would show a more exciting lust;
And man is bound to be taken
If true love isn't in his heart.
The eternal triangle is sure to appear
Whenever true love is no longer there;
Then jealousy becomes more potent
Than any kind of poisoned drink.
Oftentimes a mere stranger
Shows a more affectionate love;
Then the world seems to crumble
And eternity begins to fade.
A man is made for a woman
A lady shall find a gentleman;
Love is meant to be forever
But lovers do not always care.

A. J. Llewellyn
HAPPY ENDING
The storm attacked, like someone drunk on war-fever juice;
The upheaval came. Did it last too long?
The male child stood his ground. He won a kind of truce;
On his feet, still standing, and no doubt more strong,
But with all his sense of direction shaken loose.

Ernie Shelton
GOOD—BYE
Farewell my mother,
So long dearest friend,
Feel the cool breeze blow,
Smell the flowers in the meadow,
Good-bye world of mine.
Life, the daringest campaign,
How I fought against your tide,
Only to be swept further from your touch,
Come, come dearest,
Good-bye friend of mine.
Love, an experience never known,
A feeling not felt,
The heart unshared,
One word never spoken,
Good-bye for I know you not.
I never knew you,
Yet I felt your emptyness,
Your presence always there,
Though the feeling seemed real, but never complete,
Good-bye love of mine.
Unknown love, how I wished to meet you,
To kiss your tender lips, and caress your gentle face,
One to hold tight and say I love you,
I cannot wait any longer,
Good-bye love never felt,
Good-bye life never shared.

Roger B. Simpson
ODE TO A RIVER
The river knows
as it goes
where it's deep
where it's dirty
where rocks hide, and get
washed
where tree without roots
and posts with no fence
hitch a ride to the next dam
The river knows
it has a mission
to move the trash
dissolve the dead
cover the ugly
and swallow it all
with a chemical cocktail
of surplus water
and not be dammed
for a careless gurgle
or a raunchy belch
The river knows
it must work

overtime
to catch loose dirt
of a harried farmer
and pass it on
or pack it in
a lower delta
where fields of cotton
are swept by waves
while their planter prays
aloud for sun
and licks a stamp to send
Form 13-666-007
to the Ag Department
for flood damages
The river knows
and it goes
on and on
and on

Renee' Leigh Cambiano

SMILE

Somewhere in my heart
My
Inner
Love
Expands

Sylvia Woingust Branchcomb

THE ACCOMPANIST TO LIFE

(In memory of My Aunt, Cora Robinson Moore)

It is said that I am:
The controller of time,
The dimmer of light
The introduction to eternal darkness
The curtain caller
The guard over reincarnation
The joker of resurrection
The invisible monster.
They say I come:
Costumed in sadness
Dressed as the mediator between companions
Adorned in the gloom of lifelessness
Glittering with the promises of loneliness
In formal attire, because. . .
No one has returned to refute my status.
That is not I, for I am the silent partner of life
. . .better known as DEATH.
I am the doner of new life
The giver of creativity
The savior of pain
The carrier of solace
The mentor of idle moments.
I must come because:
I am the solicitor for the body
The caretaker of the soul
I am the grand finale!
Through all the whimpering
And all the highlights of crescendos,
Have you not heard that
I am your FRIEND?

Mary Louise Merrill

PEACE

"Listen, and be still,
for I speak for myself.
I am Peace—
that state which is tranquil,
a quieting of your heart.
That order, protecting by law or custom,
your way of life.
That freedom from oppressive emotions,
chocking out harmony.
That state in which there is a concord
of the governments of the world.
That pact to end,
such unwise hostilities.
I'm all of this, But!
there is more to me;
For tranquility remains not tranquil for long,
with contentions and misunderstandings.
No law or custom, can hold forever,
the security of men,
with respect and forgiveness missing.
No freedom will last or endure,
without the dignity due each one, body and soul.
No concord of governments or pact from hostilities,
will work without the hope of its peoples of a future, and eternal destiny.
For I Peace, have the essence of my being
within soul and spirit—
even in adverse conditions,
and I'm contagious enough to change many things.
But behold!
I come in truth, from within.
Yes, from the heart.
Why yes! my name is peace, but—
my temple is the peaceable,
and their reward will never end."

Cathie Lynn Marcello

MY BOY

She wishes she had an apron string,
So she could tie that lad.
For you see he's just the greatest boy
A mother ever had.
He's lazy and he's sloppy,
He'd never take out the trash.
And if you ever told him to pick up his clothes
He'd give you a good tongue-lash!
But still he's just the greatest boy
A mother ever had.
Because he's the exact replica of yours truly,
Dear old Dad.

Margaret M. Koors

TRIAL

A few kind words
and a reassuring smile
Do help motivate
going the extra mile!

Bonnie Teller

DANGEROUS TRANQUILITY

The sun broke forth and bathed its warmth over the swamp, where the evening before rain danced with heavy vigor on the rivers surface, sending the swamp inhabitants large, and small seeking shelter from its violent fury.

To look upon this tranquil change, from stormy darkness, to a sun sending down its blinding rays,one might observe only the surface beauty and not the dangers, or the preyers that wait to snuff out life, then steal away to lie in darkness still, to wait again for lifes sustaining kill.

As dusk begins to cloak the swamp, a noise is heard above the rest, a loud piercing scream. A panther is making itself heard, it's starting to prowl as darkness falls. From the heart of the swamp a fragile bobwhite sings its haunting call, such a difference from mean and forceful, to vulnerable, and small.

Clinging to the bark of a cypress tree, with green moss surrounding, a lovely wild orchid nods in a gentle, flowing breeze, while a coil of brown slither waits to strike just beneath.

At the rivers edge the sandbars gleam white in the moons rising light, waiting tranquil until the dead of night, then the screeching bobcat and the rooting boar alter the gleaming sand once more.

Alligators belly through the reeds, while bullfrogs sing in an alternating base. Nearby quick-sand oozes and spanish moss hangs heavy and gray. The swamp is alive with fragility and strength, but tomorrow it sleeps.

Annette M. Allee

HEARTS

Hearts,
Are meant for giving, taking, sharing, breaking.
I gave you mine—
You took it,
Promising sharing—
But instead of sharing,
You tossed it, and it broke;
Hearts,
Broken, can be mended.
I know, for mine has healed.
My broken heart I collected,
And tenderly nursed it back to health—
I love again.

Wayne Alton Spencer Dunbar

UPSET

Lawd massa eber upset yet,
If yuh want jus stick a bet.
See who can upset who fuss
Den de tap upsetta wii win de puss.
Hear bout upset,
Dat a fe me name.
Any wey huh tun it
Ih pell de same.
Upset Wayne,
Or Wayne upset.
Call me loud
Me get upset.
Upset right,
upset left.
Upset centre
Still upset.
Upset North,
Yuh upset me heart.
Upset South,
Dat is me mouth.
Upset East,
Me jus can't eat.
Upset West,
Well nothing left.
Soh why upset de upsetting man,
Galong goh find some otha plan.
Cause upsetting me, only upset you
and upsetting me you can't outdo.
Me feel upset ebry wey me tun,
When me wan walk, me hafe run.
Cause sey me upset eben eating me food,
Trough all a dat people sey me rude.
Me wish smaddy could tap me upsetting miself,
Lawd me wouda feel like candy pon de shelf.
Soh sheneber yuh hear smaddy call me name,
Tell dem sey upset nuh shame.
Cause sey is de bessis ting dem eba duh
In getting upset fe talk to yuh,
A gone. A yah yi.

Letha Memorie Lloyd-Wayne

ILLUMINATION

Gossamer wings fluttering in the sunlight,
imbued with pearlescent hues,

Lift my spirit to the realm of the omni-
presence of God,
Who holds the rainbow of promise and beauty
in His hands
Over all the Universe.

Bonnie Fouts Shannon

UNTITLED

Unsung songs, untold tales
Hiding on dusty shelves
In the corners of empty minds...
The joy they could bring
To lonely hearts
Will never be known.

Caroline F. deCiutiis
LOVE'S UNSPOKEN WAYS
Some words are never spoken
but are always understood. . .
others remain unwritten, as they
probably should.
Some choose to call this silence,
I choose to call it trust.
For, if ever a woman were loved
by a man, I know surely I
must.
I feel it in the gentle breeze
caressing soft, my face. . .
That brings a sudden smile
nothing can erase.
I see it at those times
our eyes do chance, to meet
And tell me of the love
your voice just cannot speak.
Some call this intuition, I
choose to call it love.
Some find and treasure always,
what others know nothing of.
Some choose to take it lightly,
for love, others might kill.
I choose not either way. . .But
love you and always will.

Florence G. Clifford
TO SMILE/TO WEEP
A time to smile, and a time to
weep
I smile as I hold a sunbeam, in
my hand
Slowly, it begins to fade, until
it is gone
And now I weep.
A time to rejoice, and a time to
mourn
I rejoice in the sound of a
newborn's cry
I mourn for the rose that will
wither, and die.
A time for joy, and a time to
dream
The joy is seeing the rainbow's
hue, after
the storm subsides
I dream of the hopes that might
have been
And of hopes that can never be.
A time to smile, and a time to
weep
Understanding turned to
tolerance, before
vanishing, like the night
And love has become as ashes,
on the hearth
As if bewitched, I try to smile
But in my heart, I weep.

Miss Sigrid Schlagowski
UNTITLED
Warmth. . . . .it felt warmth
as it emerged into consciousness
it felt warmth in the darkness,
it stirred
vaguely aware of it's
surroundings,
distant sounds
floated to it,
a gentle thumping.
Not yet able to think
the strange creature
with it's large head and tiny
limbs,
sensed its well-being
and was content.
Time passed
it grew stronger
and sensed security.
Suddenly
it sensed something new
something terribly wrong,
excruciating pain engulfed the
creature
defenseless
its body writhed in agony
it felt the ripping
tearing of it's flesh
burning of it's skin
the creature shuddered and felt
no more.
The Doctor threw the lump of
tissue
into the tissue sink,
among the blood and dead
matter
lay a tiny creature with tiny
limbs
and a tiny smile on it's large
head.
The operation was routine.
The abortion done without
complications.
and all were content.

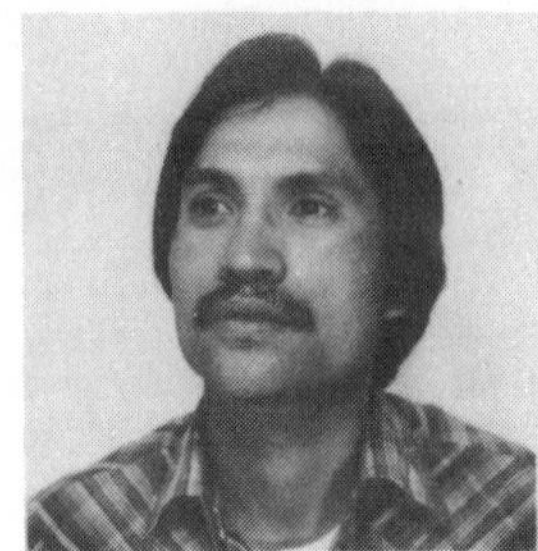

Michael David Cruz
THOUGH DEATH...
Though Death plods a monster
still
Through ev'ry earthy trail,
Though cold Sovereign of tear
and chill,
Of severance against the will,
It shall not prevail!
Though it lifts its horrid head
O'er youth and those now frail,
Though claiming kings and
those without bread,
The long-espoused or the
newlywed -
It shall not prevail!
Though ripping away the
newborn child -
A mother's unending travail -
Though gripping the innocent,
the wild,
Those strong of hope, those
from hope exiled -
It shall not prevail!
Though Death plows a monster
still
Through tender grass: we frail,
Though yet turning its grinding
mill,
And having now its merry fill -
It shall not prevail!

Sandra Hayes
FRIENDSHIP
Friends are always special to me
And friendship is something
that happens between friends
Something that you will always
be able to see
A band that never ends
This string can never be broken
At least not as far as I know
Friends aren't easily spoken
But most easily live and grow
In closing I want to say friends
are great forever
Even if there's no one left
but a friend
You can be understanding and
together
Right until the end.

Joy Guy
ON MY WEDDING DAY
The most beautiful
day of my life
I was blessed with a
great deal of happiness
such that I had never
known
I was surrounded by a huge
bouquet of lillies
sent to me by a well known
figure
Yes, the sun was shining
brightly
the birds were singing sweetly
And I
I looked radiant
as for my groom
he excited me, yes, I loved him
As we stood at the altar all
500 guests fixed their eyes
on us
Then suddenly
I felt a grip
as if a hand had
touched my shoulder
It was mother
Time to wake up!
Time to get to work!
Time to forget that
yesterday, the engagement
was broken.

Rita Higgins
GAME OF LIFE
God granted me courage to
stand on my feet,
And gave me wisdom and
knowledge, but they can
defeat.
He showed me left and right,
but what is right from wrong?
He gave me life to ful-fill with
my greatest ability.
But in being human, I must
even question tranquility.
I really thank God for giving me
will-power,
For if I didn't have that, then
everything would devour.
Now in turn with frustration I
cannot deal,
But then also given to us was
the right to appeal.
Now in giving life, God also
takes away.
Each with a reason and each has
a day.
And so in conclusion,
questioning life is a waste of
time.
And time isn't something you
play with, take advantage of,
nor sell for a dime.
So please spend each moment as
wisely as you can,
And keep in remembrance, "God
was the one who made man!"

Ada L. Hilliard
MEMORIES AT CHRISTMAS
The moon is peeking around a
cloud
Making a fairyland here below
In a forest still and silent
As it glistens on the snow.
I vision Santa and his reindeer
As I gaze on the starlit night
And hear his jolly laughter
When he passes from my
sight.
I remember the old, old story
Of Joseph and Mary from;
Galilee
That must journey to Bethlehem
To be taxed that was the
decree.
In the stable they took shelter
As they found no rooms that
day
The baby Jesus was born here
And placed in a manger of
hay.
With all the hope and promise
Of the Christ child from
above
May we find peace this
Christmas
In remembrance of his love.

Ruby W. Lambert
LET US REMEMBER
When by our warm fires we
kneel tonight
To place our gifts of love
beneath a tree
Let us remember men who face
the cold
In order that these simple
things may be.
No children there to whisper
soft goodnight—
No four warm walls to tuck
them safely in
But only through a strange
bewildered night
They hear the wind and groans
of fallen men.
They watch tonight that we
may fearless sleep
And wake the joys of Christmas
day to know
And for our hope of peace good
will to men
They leave their blood on fields
of frozen snow.
No carols reach their ears across
the air—
No sight of tinseled trees or
heart felt thrills,
For blast of guns have stole
their silent night
Where death creeps up Korea's
snow-clad hills.

Gloria A. Rowe
CATHERINE
The house on the hill was once
elegant and serene;
Now the house before her eyes
was only a remnant of that
dream.
She could no longer see the
panes of glass shining in the
morning sun;
And where once there was a
smiling face now there is
none.
Standing there, as if in a trance,
remembering the laughter the
house once possessed;
There was laughter, Trisha's,
David's and hers but now it
only brought distress.
She recalled the good but it
only brought to mind the
things that went wrong;
And why that day so long ago
she ran down the path
headlong.
Never had she come back till
now and now because her life
here is but a dream;

For David is gone and Trisha
was gone before she left so
it only seemed
To come back would only mean
putting the past where it
belonged,
And she knew this was
something she had much
prolonged.
She wanted to walk from room
to room recalling the good
and the bad;
To find herself in Trisha's room
and to remember, O' how sad!
To let the rooms echo with the
remembrance of David's voice
And to see in the vision of her
eyes the child to which they
both rejoiced.
The knob on the door felt cold
on the palm of her hand;
And as the door opened the
time element spanned;
For the oaken staircase still
shone in its polished beauty
And from where she stood she
could see the sitting room's
fireplace which looked
recently sooty.
Everything was just as she had
left it on that fateful day;
But from the outside it didn't
look this way!
Then she noticed the panes of
glass because thru them the
sun did shine;
O' outside there had been only
boards and no panes to shine!
How could she understand what
was happening, was it but a
nightmare;
Maybe it was just that she
had really never left here;
Maybe David was still in his
study with a book in his
hands
And his pipe in his mouth, O'
why, why can't I understand!
I must go to the study to see
if it's true;
To see if David is yet here too!
And as she passed the stairway
She smelt the polish and Trudy
had always done the staircase
on Saturday
and. . . .today is Saturday!
The study door opened with its
usual quietness and
She knew he was there because
his pipe was on the smoking
stand.
She could not see him because
he sat in the chair with his
back to the door;
Until his hand reached for the
pipe to empty the ash in the
cuspidor.
It was as if her heart stopped
and time itself stood still;
For she found herself speaking
words to try to fulfill
All the years she had been
gone and why;
But David seemed not to hear or
maybe it's not him and that's
why!
It was him tho', he stood up and
stretched and then turned
around;
It was David alright. . . .but the
David she had known twenty
years ago!
As he came toward her she
stepped aside;
He didn't even look at her but
went on thru the doorway
wide.
She followed him and said his
name but with no response;
He only went to the stairway,
O' God, why's there no
response!
I love him, tho' I left him
there has been none but him;
He didn't understand, I couldn't
live with him;
No, not without Trisha and
Trisha was gone!
O' to make him believe how I
really do love him and make
this past but a bygone!
He's getting away, he's heading
for Trisha's room, I must go!
Up the stairs she went to follow
him although
She wasn't so sure she could go
into her room
If everything was as she herself
had left it, it would only
bring floom.
But before she got to the room
she heard voices;
David's and also one she knew
to be Trisha's voice!
She stood in the hall watching
father and daughter;
Trisha was gone and. . . .
yet there she stood, her
daughter!
The long blond hair and the big
blue eyes;
The way she was before the
fever, but how?
Trisha died in her arms
twenty-one years ago!
It was too much, she ran down
the stairs and into the library
to find refuge from the past!
The fireplace was burning and
its light did cast
On a portrait on the opposite
wall;
And walking over to it she
could not believe what she
saw!
The words below the portrait
said, "In Memory Of My
Loving Wife, Catherine";
And as she looked into the
portrait's eyes she saw herself
and then realized;
It was not Trisha who had died
on that bitter night but she;
And all she saw and heard today
was all but a memory!
She left the library and walked
out the front door
And turned around to look at
the window panes that were
no more!

Anne Marie Clark
LETTER TO KEVIN
The sun has set, the sky is grey
and rose.
Insects strum in the quiet air.
Night is close at hand and
thoughts of you abound.
Why did you have to go. . . .
Where are you now?
I cannot help but ask, though I
do not wait for an answer.
I really have given you back to
God.
But. . .you are so alive in my
heart, so vivid in my memory,
so warm in my thoughts. . . .
How can you be gone?
The sky fades to darkness. . . .
The first star begins to shine,
and I try to understand. . .a
little.
You have changed from the
familiar to the unfamiliar;
as flowers fade into the ground,
so have you.
With spring, they will return to
life and in God's spring,
you will be with us again.
But. . .possesing only a human
mind, I rebel!
I seek you down the corridors of
the night
Where are you. . . child of my
child?
I hear your Mother's grief
swirling in the night mists,
calling your name.
I feel her heart's agony swelling
within her,
No more. . .No more!
God and Time. . .Time and God
will bring relief. . .but not
now
Love will finally frame your face
and form
and make bearable the
unbearable!
but not now.

Greg Antonavich
WHAT I MEAN TO SAY
When our eyes first met, I just
knew;
My heart had a desire, to know
of you.
I tried to show you, day by day;
That you were special, in a very
special way.
And the things I kept beautiful
and true;
Is the beacon of light, I hold for
you.
I often prayed to God at night;
That he might show me what
was right.
And the things that he has
shown me true;
Is the beauty that my heart gave
to you.
The pleasant little things we do;
Like long walks in the park with
you.
Are the things of joy and
happiness;
That I for one will never forget.
Like the stars I've seen within
your eyes;
Set twinkling in, the midnight
skies.
Or the warmth I've found,
within my heart;
Is the wonder of Gods' purest
art.
And the gentleness, of your
way;
Shows in things you do and say.
Sometimes hopeless, sometimes
blue;
And the desire to know you,
more than I do.

I'm sure you see, more deserving
men than me;
But I'm still hoping, someday
you'll see.
The beauty in life, that most
never see;
Is truly a part of Infinity;
And surely lives in you and me.

Susan Glick
WISE SOUL
Jurisprudence, how delicate the
balance between pleasure and
pain;
Frustration begets wisdom teeth,
the frostbite of desolation.
Reaching, cluthing, straining
for the shooting stars,
The edelweiss of Shangri-La
lies cloistered in a mountain-
pass
Snowbound
til the spring thaw.

Joseph M. Dreimiller
REFLECTION OF A SMOKY MOUNTAIN VISITOR
As she gets closer,
she runs away with my love.
Further and further down the
road. . .
Away from home. . .home.
The bonded image of clouds
passing through her snowy
peaks,
made me look back on life
and the one I truely love.
When I first saw her
in the Winter of '72
her eyes melted beneath the
sun,
as tears ran down her face.
He slowly passed her by. . .
until she was gone,
then I vowed to myself
that I would soon return.
Oh, I think about her everyday
she is now even in my dreams
it is so cold and lonely here,
but there is nothing I can do,
for it is so confusing
life without you.

Veronica D. Richard
BEYOND SPEECH
Through the hedge rows,
Only steps away
Across a pond,
A green field beckons.
Beyond the sapling bends,
The regal elm commands
dominion
In the crowded wood.
In spellbound apostrophe,
Dialogue is taciturn..

J. A. Eline
THERE'S NO END
Undeserving I am
of your love;
And yet,
my need for it grows.
I fear it's a fragile
thing, a butterfly's wing;
And yet,
my trust of it grows.
I don't understand it—
strengthened as the years
lengthened;
And yet,
my want of it grows.
Our future is merely
dreams to be fulfilled it seems;
And yet,
my love for you grows.

Linda Jane Roche
DEAR "MISS LILLY"
Presented to Mrs. Lillian Carter at the Dedication ceremonies of Holy Cross Church in Callicoon on August 12, 1979.
A hundred things we could find
to say,
To greet you gloriously upon
this day
Our people come from many
places,
To greet you, with smiles on
their faces.
How generous and loving of you
to travel so long,
To an area where the birds sing
so loud a song.
May God bless you for helping
to turn the sod,
Where our parishioners will
build their church to God.

This weekend we shall share a
view of the countryside
And Father will gladly act as
your guide,
We shall share a special
greeting, and a bit of humor,
too,
And share our thoughts and
dreams, as "special" friends
often do.
This twelfth day of August,
there is stillness everywhere
we look,
On the sailing clouds, the
invisible breeze, and the
nearby brook:
The dark waves of the green
foliage and the beauty of the
nearby hill,
All the work of our beloved
Author, all so calm and still.
So, we wish you a year made of
such wonderful things,
Bright warm sunshine and the
marvel of butterfly wings,
May God bless you with His
love and peace,
And may your hearty laughter
never cease.

Nancy Menda
NIGHT WINGS
Take flight, night wings,
Of purple gilded sky.
Day's light that you disperse,
Makes me sense that I
Am engulfed twixt shadows
Of blackest midnight's curse.
Go quickly on your way,
And let dawn be born
In time to start the day.
With sunlit sky adorn
An awakening, slumbering
earth.
Make haste, O midday sky,
Soon comes the cool of eve;
Which makes me sense that I
Have seen another day retreat,
Again 'neath silvery shadows
Of ebony wings of night.

Chris S. Russell
INCANTATION OF EARTH BY MOONLIGHT
In the shadow of those wisdoms
of my ancestors
the cure whispers itself to me.
Wake up when Selene kisses
your eyes;
come to me in cloud clothing.
Meet me in the silvered clearing
where
the little foxes perform their
love ballets.
I bring all good things for you:
flower petals for beauty and
color of life;
wine of the first of May for
endless youth;
warm spices of Earth for vigor
and well being;
caresses borrowed from
Angels and demons for
long life and contentment.
Bring the gift of self, My Love,
to mingle.
The Earth is a quiet, caring
hollow.

Dorothy Greenlund
LOVE EVEN ME
Lord Jesus would anyone but
you, understand my longing.
Anyone but you can see my
hurt.
Would anyone but you, keep
loving me knowing, I fail, and
then always feel so blue.
Lord Jesus, would anyone but
you, know my heart is aching.
When no one cares, what
happens in the run.
You make my life more real, by
just undoing all the things
that others have done.
I've often wondered if I weren't
alone, would you be so
important to me.
But now I know tis true, you'll
always be,
The First, The Middle, The
Last of my life,
The hope, the joy, the peace in
the night.
I know only that you don't leave
me, I leave you.
And when I do I feel so blue.
Keep me ever near you, close at
every hand.
Touch my life, because I need
you.
Always come and take my hand.
With you I know that I can
make it.
With you I know the way is
free.
For you ask nothing in the
giving and give strength for
every new and different
scheme.
My life is an open book to you
Lord, and still you love me,
love even me.

Tanya M. Elliott
HERE COMES THE SPRING
Here comes the Spring,
I feel it in the air.
Oh, such sweet memories,
if you were only here.
We talked of love,
we talked of death.
Too soon my love,yours was
met.
The touch of your hand, so
warm, so real.
To know now, I will never again
feel.
Oh, but I miss you so, my dear.
I want you beside me, to hold
me near.
Here comes the Spring,
I stand at your grave.
Trying to act normal,
trying to be brave.
A rose for you, I shall put down.
I am crying, playing the clown.
No, I'm not happy since you
went away.
I pray for the Spring, I pray for
the day,
when I hear your voice and it's
not far away.
But it will not come, it's only a
dream.
I kneel on the ground, I cry and
I scream.
Here comes the Spring,
without you I know.
All this is silly, now I must go.
I'll never stop loving you.
There is nothing anyone can do,
to take the love, I had from you.
Life will go on, the birds they
will sing.
Your love my dear, a precious
thing.
Oh, sorry morning,
Here comes the Spring.

Paul W. Hollingsworth
TO WRITE A RECITATION
Alone he toils on this cold and
bitter winter's night,
Composing a sonnet or
worthy verse to write.
The chill of night steals through
the walls and settles in the
room,
Hiding in the shadows, no
lurking there in the gloom.
Unnoticed by the figure
partially illuminated by the
moon.
This shawl draped scribe
hunched in wavering
candlelight,
Concentrating for a bit then he
begins slowly his thoughts to
write.
"Agh", he sighs in complete
exasperation, for once more
A shiver destroys his line of
deep concentration.
He rises from his table and
starts with sudden ire,
And slowly moves to darkened
hearth to agitate the fire.
He stirs the slumbering
embers to a tiny warming
blaze,
And warms the fingers of this
hands as he stands with fixed
gaze.
Now the chill forgotten, his
mind is back upon it's quest,
Searching, waiting for the
elusive thought itself to
manifest.
Suddenly with pen in hand he
begins once more anew,
Line after line he writes, now
there's quite a few.
Pausing every now and then
to scan the workings of his
pen,
"That's it", he speaks aloud
without the slightest hesitation,
I've done the thing, it is
finished, my humble
recitation.

Jerry M. Marshall
A GIRL. . .A WOMAN
A sweet young girl I do recall
A week ago today
Came crying as she said to me
"I gave my heart away."
The words I spoke were kind
and soft
The only words I knew
I told her that the time had
come
And asked "Do you love him
true."
"The truest love I've ever
known"
To me was her reply
Then go and find sweet
happiness
With him until you die.
She kissed my cheek on which a
tear
Fell slowly from my eye
And then a woman standing
there
Said "Daddy, Please don't
cry."

Anita Volk-Krusch
NOTHING UNDER THE SUN IS NEW
I see the sun rise as millions
before
Have risen over this valley. Bold
red
Rising orb is like a child with
crayons
Coloring clouds orange and
canyons yellow.
So what difference my love for
you,
Nothing under the sun could be
new!
Watching this orb color cacti
blue
And praries with a variety of

hues;
I am standing on a plateau away,
Skinned my knees just to see
the view.
So what difference my love for
you,
Nothing on this earth could be
new!
How naive, each sunrise, each
day is new,
Under sun, on earth, how
unique my love for you.

Melba Ford Chaffin

A POET'S PRAYER

Oh God, creator of the
universe—
How did You know just where
to put the sun—
The moon, the stars, the silent
wind that blows—
How did You know which
way the brook should run?
How did You know just where
to place each rock—
To form the lofty mountain
peaks that rise—
In silent meditation day by
day—
And lift their humble faces to
the skies?
And did You know that when
the north wind blew—
A rhapsody would echo
through the hills—
A rhapsody so clear it's
mournful strains—
Would even haunt the distant
whip-poor-wills?
How did You know the trees
should be so tall—
With branches bowing low to
offer shade—
That in the spring the leaves
would hide the sun—
And in the fall the withered
leaves would fade?
How did You know the birds
would sing so sweet—
Their never-ending songs for
all to hear—
And did You paint the robins
crimson breast—
How did You plan the seasons
of the year?
Oh God, creator of this world
of ours—
How did You know how deep
to make the sea—
And where to form the islands
there within—
How did You know just where
each one should be?
And all the many creatures that
You made—
To dwell within the waters
cold and deep—
Did You foresee their struggle
to exist—
Or did You make provisions
for their keep?
How did You know the deer
should be so swift—
The tiny sparrow should
know how to fly—
The fox would have to kill to
feed its young—
And did You teach the coyote
how to cry?
How did You make the squirrels
bushy tail—
And why did You proclaim
the lion king—
A deadly beast, and yet I'm
sure you knew—
The horror that a rattle snake
could bring?
Lord, did You know the eagles
soaring strength—
Would one day be the symbol
of our land—
The peacocks beauty never
could be matched—
The ostrich would find shelter
in the sand?
Oh God, creator of this world
below—
How did You know just where
to put the wall—
The solid wall of rock with
spring above—
To form the constant, rustling
waterfall?
Lord, did You know the pebbles
would be swept—
To other streams, down where
the river bends—
To find a resting place in
waters still—
And can you tell me where
the river ends?
Did You, when You were
planning all of this—
Know just how fierce the
winter winds would blow—
And was it in your plan we
would behold—
The beauty of the silent
falling snow?
Lord, did You know that when
the willow weeps—
'Tis an expression of her love
for thee—
The flowers lovely petals open
wide—
Providing nectar for the
honey bee?
Lord, did You know the graceful
butterfly—
Would scamper here and there
in endless flight—
Did You compose the crickets
serenade—
Of melancholy music in the
night?
Oh God, I do not doubt your
master plan—
I know You made this
paradise on earth—
And in Your wisdom, when the
time had come—
That you performed the
miracle of birth.
I know there is no greater power
than thine—
My eyes behold thy
handiwork with awe—
I search throughout all natures
wonderland—
Unable to detect the slightest
flaw.
I marvel at the beauty all
around—
I see a rainbow arched against
the sky—
My voice is still—my mind is
fixed on Thee—
And I can feel your presence
drawing nigh.
Lord, if You find me worthy in
thy sight—
And in your wisdom, if you
deem it wise—
Grant me one wish, a simple
task for Thee—
That others might view
nature through my eyes.
That other ears might hear the
joyful sounds—
That all of Your musicians
make for me—
And may the inspiration of Your
love—
Dwell in my heart throughout
eternity.
amen.

Billy Gerald Kiblinger

I TOUCH YOU WITH MY THOUGHTS

I touch you with my thoughts
when you are not here.
I feel your presence even though
you are not there.
That warm sensation I feel
inside, oh bliss;
here may it always reside.
My heart sleeps with you in
mind.
Emotions, I cannot explain, have
found their way
on an endless journey of
joy.
Like a lost boy,
groping his way through a
dense forest and finding a
clearing knowing peace in
his heart, you make my life.
Lines of prose, such as these,
reach one conclusion.
Words cannot express true
emotion. . . . . . .

Billy Crain

ANWAR SADAT

Bang! Boom, Boom! Pop Pop!
Pop Pop !!
Thus, ends the life of Anwar
Sadat!
Hated by some, and loved by
many.
Killed in a terrorist attack, ain't
that a pity.
For this was a man who truly
seeked peace,

Now we must share in his
family's grief.
For he was kind of an Egyptian
Jesus,
I heard someone say;
Kind of hard to disbelieve,
considering in 1918
he was born on Christmas Day.
Oh, I'm not trying to say that
he ruled without *turmoil,*
But even that is minimal to a
country so rich with *oil.*
He was the third president,
Egypt ever had
And he made more people
happy, than he did sad.
And I'm sure that the world will
and have not forgot,
Past Egyptian President Anwar
Sadat.

Mary P. Hunter Wells

CHRISTMAS

Christmas is filled with
memories
of love and joy of yore
Christmas is filled with
treasures
that the family has kept in store
Christmas brings forth many
happenings
of times shared by friends and
kin
Christmas brings forth precious
secrets
that were held so tightly within
Christmas reveals intimate
relations
of an experienced wish or desire
Christmas unmasks by-gone
adventures
that keep our dreams on fire!

Deborah Ellen Dixon

TO MOTHER WITH LOVE

Mom, did I ever tell you that I
love you?
Those three words are so simple,
But are so hard for me to say,
Yet they should be said every
day
Because you've shown love to
me in so many ways.
I love you for all the times you
kissed my
"Boo-boos" away and dried my
teary eyes.
For all the times you cared
enough to scold
And discipline me.
Now I understand why you used
to say it was more
Painful for you than for me.
And for all the times you
devoted your last drop
Of energy to my needs,
Instead of caring for your own.
I thank and praise you for all
your sacrifices
To make me the best person I
can be.
Mother truly is another word for
love.
You've created a legacy for all to
share.
But I count myself the most
fortunate of all.
For I have known you not only
as my mother,
But as my dearest friend.

Mr. Joseph Hinton Pepper Brice III

BIRD

What bird is this
That raps on my door
What bird lays dead
Upon my chamber floor
Why must I love so much the
bird
Only to watch her die
Who will be the next bird
To knock on my chamber door
Perhaps with the next bird
I will be able to fly

Claire E. Carbone
AWARENESS
The day the doctor said to me
I'm sorry you have a malignancy
I wondered, Oh my God! What went wrong?
How will I react, weak or strong?
Then I thought about how lucky I've been,
And I decided that this wasn't the end.
I'm going to live each and every day
Until the day my life is taken away.
Out of every cloud the sun shines thru
And life is to be lived by me and you.
I noticed a new awareness come about me
For I started to notice the flowers and trees.
I noticed an ant hill and a hive of bees,
And saw that life was all around me.
I also watched a blue bird fly
And tried to count the stars in the sky.
I heard the whistle of a distant train,
And then I felt a drop of rain
From a window on a Christmas night
I watched a candle glowing bright.
I saw the winter change to spring,
And I was more aware of many things.
I suppose I noticed all this before,
But now I wanted to notice it more
When was the last time I learned of a baby's birth?
Or how many times have I thought about the earth?
Was that a flower there beneath the snow?
And will that bud become a rose?
I wondered about the farmer and his land
And the things that grew with the aid of his hand.
Oh it's easy to go in and pick food from a shelf,
But do I stop to wonder how it all came about?
Then there's a man on the street that I see,
And I wonder, does he have a problem like me?
As he passes by he gives me a smile,
And that seems to make my day worthwhile.
I stopped at a playground in the mid of day,
And sat and watched some children play.
My eyes noticed a little girl wearing a hat,
And I remember being small just like that.
All of a sudden along came a cat
Chased by a dog who was white and black.
I wondered if the cat would find a tree
Because he wanted to live just like me.
Now I get up early to see a red sunrise
For there's nothing prettier than the morning sky.
And when I watch night change to day,
I marvel that God made it this way.
Everything's in order and running on time,
And it's all there to see; it's yours and mine.
But don't wait like me for that black cloud.
Just open your eyes and live life now.

Chester Roberts
WHEN SPRINGTIME COMES
I walked the greening fields of spring
To where the aspens quiver,
Where gladsome birds their carols sing,
And view the tumbling river.
The fleecy clouds in tumbled rank,

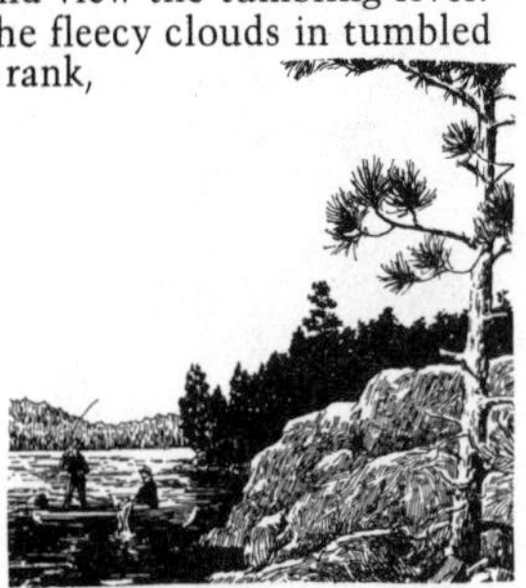

The sounds of geese arriving,
The violets on the river bank
The winter sleep surviving.
Oh to be young when springtime comes
The swimming hole inspecting,
Be climbing trees with boyhood chums
And dark green frogs collecting.
But young or old we revel in
The beauty of creation,
And when we see the spring begin
We greet it with elation.

Anna L. Nissel
SPELLBOUND
The breath of the trees reminds me
Of the fragrance that surrounds you;
The blueness of the sky, my dear
Recall the color of your eyes, so clear.
How can I then forget you
When all nature is alive and calling?
I miss you more and more each morning
Though your love washed out to sea.
Can we forget? Should we regret
When love held us both spellbound?
How can I then forget you
As our hearts once beat with one sound
Entwined in my mind you still rest—
My love for you is still true.
The shore of my heart is severed
Please come back to me, I pray;
We'll rekindle our love forever—
Love's flame will be our's to stay.

Laurie Zimmerman
THANK YOU, FATHER
You bring to me
the lush, green forest
of my mind,
the cool brook at my feet,
the spring grass
on which I lay and free my soul.
You bring to
the quiet moon and its star companions.
Thank you.

Helen James Ehlert
FRED'S POINT OF VIEW
I went for a walk with Fred
One balmy, winter day;
And Maggie, our Irish Setter,
Came sniffing along the way.
She rousted out some snow birds,
Some sparrows took speedy flight;
And then four beautiful cardinals
Came flitting into sight!
We marveled at their beauty,
Then climbed to the top of the hill;
To survey the valley below us,
So peaceful, white and still.
But coming down the hill
I let out a mournful groan!
"Those awful weeds!" I shouted.
They look like they've been sown!"
"They're only weeds to us, Mom.
God didn't plan them such!
Just think of them as shelter
For the birds you love so much!"

Marian Licata
LUV
As I sit upon my dock.
My heart ticks just like a clock.
I remember years gone by.
I then just sit and sigh.
Love that's true is hard to find.
The people you love are not so fine.
I guess in our hearts we search and search.
So you must believe in the Lord Devine.
As he will give you peace of mind.

Lawrence Spirio
WITH LOVE
Take the bitterness out of your heart,
with love, give yourself a fresh new start.
If you take the hate and throw it away,
with love, you can see the light of day.
Rout the fear that rushes through your veins,
learn to forgive, you soften the pains.
Take away anger you've had for years,
understand, frustration brings the tears.
Control the arduous ardor fume,
before your soul becomes consumed.
With love, you can put out the flame,
to compromise life is not a shame.
Let guidance come from heaven above,
you'll see, all good things can come with love.

Gerry Fauss
1ST PLACE
Hey, we are No. 1
Now let me tell you why,
We have 6 girls instead of 5.
Now, that's not all, as you will see
There's another trick up our sleeve.
As we reach into the proverbial hat,
Out comes the choicest of the Zodiac.
We have Deloras the Libra
Who loves to have Peace.
Maggie the Aries, full of Impulsiveness.
Judy the Capricorn, who is always Cautious.
Gerry the Taurus, full of Determination.
Ginny the Leo, full of Generosity.
I've saved the best for last—obviously
It's Nick, our Sponsor, and she's a Pices.
She is creative, changeable, emotional and devious.
There you have it, Zodiac's Best.
Over the past year we have put it to the test.
My friends what I have just said
Is not foolishness, but what we really have is this—
A ram, a scales, a bull, a lion, a mountain goat,
Being led by a Fish!

William Frank Landers
NIGHTRAINS
When it rains
I always get a retrospective feeling
I think back on the times
When you and I were one
When all we wanted
Was to make each other happy
Oh the nightrains
They give me heartaches
I lay there in the dark
Hold my pillow so tight
And pretend it's you
Something happens
I don't know when or where
What we had
It just seemed to fall apart
Then you went your way
And I went mine
Oh the nightrains
They give me heartaches

I lay there in the dark
Hold my pillow tight
And pretend it's you
Now here I sit
Writing you this letter
I'd call
But I don't know your number
I hope you're happy
And you've found what you're after
But the nightrains
Still give me heartaches
I lay there in the dark
Hold my pillow so tight
And pretend it's you

Marsha Hays Belanger

TO SAMMY—MY BELOVED SON

If I could change the way things are
I'd give you the moon—the morning star
Brighten each new day for you
Take away the saddest blue
If I could give you anything
I would stop at nothing
To make you happy and free
Help you climb the highest tree
If I could bring you joy
Whether it were a bright new toy
Or something you'd never give away
Like changing the clouds that are gray
If I could take you anywhere
To Disneyland or fly in the air
I'd spend every moment—each day
By your side I'd always stay
If I could dry every tear that falls
Destroy all your prison walls
I'd replace them with a sunny smile
And go with you that extra mile
There's only so far that I can go
Only so much I can show
My hand is here
My love always near
So let's walk hand in hand
And learn to firmly stand
Face every trial and test
Giving life our very best
God loves you
It's really true
Just believe in you
Make your dreams come true

Estelle Tischler

THE HOLOCAUST

What is the Holocaust?
A cry in the night
A silent prayer
A hand outstretched to heaven in despair
The Jewish people six million canonized
Torn from their countries, friends forgot them
Never again will they be trod on
Huddled together to die but not in vain
Who will remember them?
The few survivors but there are countless believers
Who knew that the Nazis were the deceivers
What was the reason for so many slaughtered?
The Jewish people sent to the gas chambers planned
and executed by the hands
of a tyrant, a maniac
who was not stopped
It was a dark page in our history
We will never forget
Sleep gently, our brethren, we will tell our children about you
We shall weep bitterly for the horrendous crime
It will be recorded in our hearts for endless time.

Robert D. Roberto

WEDNESDAY NIGHT

I'm alone. . .
with a quiet phone
Records are playing loudly
but no one is with me
T.V.! is starting it's
shows on time tonight
I could watch the rest
of the world's plight
Four walls are cornering
as boredom won't give me
anything to do
I hate the walls
painted blue
On T.V., the world
is beginning to cry
But through the reflection
I could see the tears
falling from my eye

Ken Liddick

86 PROOF NIGHTMARE

As I sat down on mounds of thrown out rhyme,
Aghast I thought my fifth of scotch to say:
"By chance mother of invention will climb,
And time necessity deceive today."
And so I wrote of love long gone, so mute;
So like little flowers grown worse from weeds.
They were once firm and clean and fresh of fruit.
Oh no! now set upon by Lucifer's thieves,
Who stole from me all these inspired inkings.
Thus I gave chase on my blue elephant.
Alas as Death drew near my heart's sinking.
And just as the Basest his knife would plant,
So like ringing alarms my soul awoke.
Sobriety arrived just like a joke.

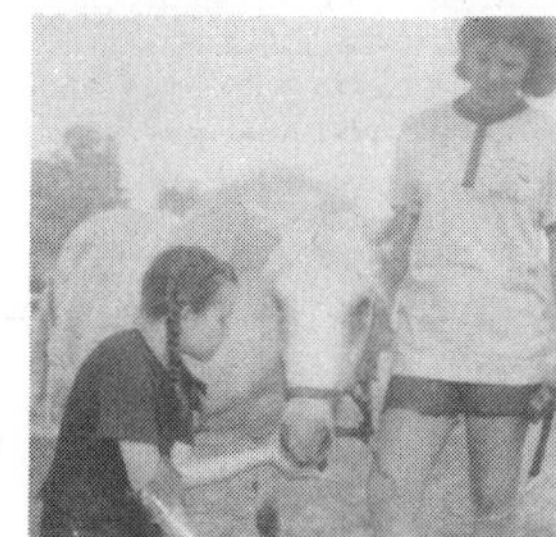

Maudie Hunter-Warfel

GOLD

There is no richer way to grow
Than simply just to know
That you are loved

George R. Steel

SONNET 13

Unspoken words hide behind some lips that
Are closed and sealed, as the doors of a tomb.
Oh yes, now and then friends will meet and chat,
But it's as a flower that will ne'er bloom
That these withheld words will ever remain.
What beauty could the universe behold;
What slave to spread upon the burning pain,
Ere these lips would soon part and speech unfold!
In stillness what persons have faced death?
What crimes or adventures have taken place?
How many lovers have parted with silent breath?
What events of history have not been traced?
What other accounts have never been heard,
All lost because of the unspoken word?

Susannah Dunlap

SEARCHING

Searching—for what I know not
Only that I seek.
When I find it, I'll know
But if I don't, then all is not lost
For there are experiences and people with
whom I have come into contact
These enrich and sustain my very soul.
So, though you search—keep in mind the things along the way
For only they can keep you when all is lost.

Melvin Earl Roberson, Jr.

UNSELFISH LOVE

It seems I started living,
Only a week ago.
Time is running away,
With each moment that we know.
Truly this must be happiness;
To love you, to hold you,
To provide and care for you.
My reasons for being.
Happiness, I see in your eyes everyday.
Glitter like stars they do,
As a childs on Christmas Day.
Even in your sleep,
When I wake and watch you slumber,
So peacefully you rest
As if guarded by angels.
I wonder!
I caress your face,
And kiss your lips,
Can you feel my love flow through?
Everyday brings new happiness,
By reason of loving you.

Mariana C. Webb

REMINISCENCE

Star studded nite,
Twinkling stars so brite
Lite up our hearts tonite!
Recalling memories of old
From the distant past,
Memories we used to think
Would never ever last.
Fresh nite air,
Our heads lite and clear.
Spirits soaring
Hand in hand we stand.
United till
Life's destiny we fulfill!

Kathryn S. Winslow

DIALOGUE

The language of touch. . .
articulate fingers, lips, tongue
feeling—words;
Primevil dialogue, free, elemental.
Your body trembles and I am lost in this new yet old dialect;
Meanings pure, unbound by artificial names
Words that must be felt, inhaled, absorbed
Symbiotic, born of earth and life-seed.

Jeanne J. Banash

CORAL CAVES

Ocean caves
Carved into
Exquisite shapes
By the salt sea
Rich coral hues
Bursts of color
Through deep
Ocean blues

Caves carved
Inside my mind
By thought waves
From you
Exquisite inner
Coral caves
Fresh carvings
Each new day

Lynne A. Hogan

UNTITLED

I am nothing more than a raincoat to you.
When it rains you bring me out to protect you,
from the down pour of your own grief.
And when the sun is warm with laughter
I am put away into my confined closet,
there never to be touched also with your warmth.

Kitty A. Henry

MODERN OPTIMISM

Drowning in sorrow
Deeper in grief
Where is tomorrow
Is there no relief?
Opening doors
Are now closed tight
So many dreams
Are now out of sight
A long lonely day
A lonelier night
No, I can't make it
Yes, I just might

Lucietta Powell
WE
We, who discovered life.
We, who know the beauty of it, will always conquer the ugly of it.
We, who know better than to sit back and let it pass us by.
We, who love life and practice patience in it.
We, who made an effort and enjoy peace of mind.
We, there are many of us. Won't you join us.

Susan E. Jordan
SUMMER REMINISCENT

We talked of trips around the world and pony rides at the zoo.

Picnics in Central Park and rain storms that drained us through.

"Mother calling" sister falling and brother John, late for his date. Upset stomachs, tired feet, and baby sleep in Mother's arms.

Bicycle rides on neighbor's grass, "Oh pardon me," Madam. I would not want that to be," grass dying on account of me.

Practicing music in the den, a fatherly image of my mother's friend.

The aroma of chicken soup, home made bread and apple pie made me feel very empty inside.

Summer is gone, my dreams too, I sat and reminiscent in the blue, and often wonder about my love, Sie.

Marguerite L. Bellah
ODE TO THE MOON
What happened—old Moon
You look so sad?
Have the people on earth
Been treating you bad?
Did "they" finally step
On your poor old crust
Like all things on earth
"They" felt they must?
Did it hurt when "they" landed
"Their" expensive "Lem",
Or did it seem—
Like a salute from "them."
"They" finally made it—
A dangerous trip
In "their" Lunar Module
"We" call a space ship.
You really were nice,
You didn't mind at all
When "they" danced on your surface
And didn't even fall.
It didn't take long
For our boys to feel
At home on your surface,
Could this be for real?
Could it be you enjoyed this
As much as did "they"?
And maybe you miss "them"
Since "they've" gone away?
Don't worry old Moon,
It won't be too long—
Before more "men" will see you
'Twill be someday soon.
So turn up your mouth
And don't look so sad,
Old Moon you don't know it
But you have been "Had".

Carol Chambless Wright
REAL EYES
Isn't it sad?
When two hearts are not one
Pledges yes, vows yes, promises dear
But meanings, yet vague
So the commitment's not clear—
Is it purposely done? This hurt yet again
Time after time, How hopeful she's been!
That this time he'd mean it—some real love he'd show
And not for himself—or others, oh no!
Rather this time for her, yes her, just her
For a glimpse of the nature of devotion, of caring—
True compassion, true trusting, true unselfish sharing
But alas! Perhaps tis not to be
For changes can only, always occur
With the will of one's soul
In line with our Master
But true will of one's soul
For a cause one believes in
And isn't ashamed for
To stand up to others
Whomever "they" be—
"They," the perennial pronoun
In whose name much "work" is done
Vague, undefinable; Who really is "they?"
Yes, "they" is for sure safe
For "they" have no feelings
. . .like the one he has married and taken to wife
Yes, into his home yet not into his life!
Has he no depth—of concern, of love
To transcend any moment, event, person, or time?
Or is it all in a word, or two, or three?
Instead of the spirit with which it is said
Oh, that is the main thing;
The spirit's the key
For therein lies the soul
Oh, why can't he see?
Our Lord is so perfect, so willing, so able
But He only works miracles
Through us as His cable—
His Dove is there; His Love is there
Do you have the time, the will, to be there?
You say you want to find your soul
Well, where are you looking?
Heaven's above.
I say, look to your attitude, your motives, your conscience
The spirit in which all is said and done
Yes, look not to the things themselves for their worth
But rather one's spirit, for God to heal and behold
And there's your answer, my answer, my friend
—your soul!

Shavaun K. Stewart
ABORTION
Abortion, I feel, is the taking of a life.
How can you kill a human being just to lessen your strife?
If this is the world in 1981,
How will it be in the years to come?
Will we kill each other for sheer pleasure?
Will we treat a deadly weapon as an honored treasure?
Abortion is crazy! You know it is true.
What if instead of someone else, they were killing you!
Then it would be serious and treated as it should,
Then it would be considered bad, instead of good!
So the next time you see the smile on a young child's face,
Or tears swelling in a pair of big, innocent eyes,
Remember, he or she might have been the victim of an abortion,
And that child would have died!

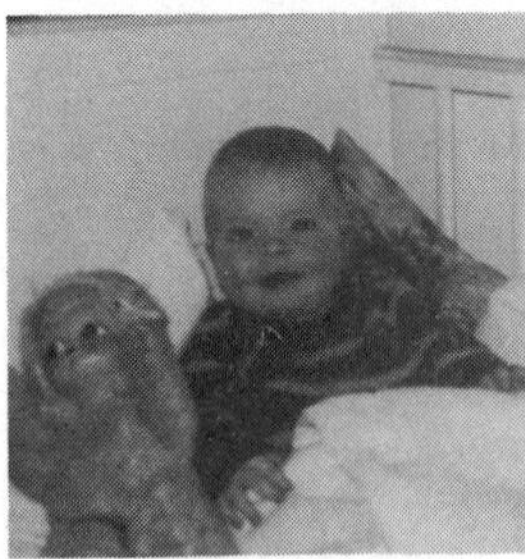

Alice
FEELINGS
My love has different feelings. . .
My love has felt pure happiness
From the moment of our first kiss
My love has felt sadness
Knowing we are apart
My love has felt secureness
From the touch of your hand
My love has felt doubt
Like you were leaving me out
My love has felt contentment
When we have been one
My love has felt jealousy
Thinking you were all mine
Feelings. . .
Some right. . .some wrong. . .
Without you I could feel nothing. . .
Your love has brought me alive.

Ilona Sardy
ILLUMINATION
Emerging slowly out of dark
As seed does from the dirt,
To form the formless
From invisible to visible birth.
Rising with restless resonance
With images of waves
To open and born into the air
And be ONE with different shapes.
Sunkissed and transparent,
Without darkness, just LIGHT. .
The inner strength of intellect
Makes words and sounds holy and bright.
It opens as petals of lilies or rose
To speak in silence only with the scent,
While secretly as gentle dew
The spirit becomes transcendent.

Beth Ann Walters
TO GRANDMOTHER
It has always been too late
For me to show my love.
Will I ever catch the wave
Before it crashes upon me
and buries me in the sand below?
Now you are dying
and I am clawing
my way through this
heavy, sticky sand—
In hope that I will make it
this one time at least
before the wind blows the flame
of your candle away.
But this sand
lays too heavy upon my chest
And my eyes rain blood
on the sand
Where reflected
are our memories.
And I stop to ponder,
How do I say good-by
now that the days have drawn to one!
So I push away the sand,
and my downpour dries
I reach for your hand
and you beckon for mine—
As your eyes close
your breathing stops
A smile breaks upon your face—
God has said my salutations for me!

Douglas M. Hodge
ALONE
Rocky beaches, Sandy shores
water white and blue
mist from waves, cresting high
resembles morning dew
If I had to trade it all
I don't know what I'd do
I think that if I traded it,
the trade would be for you
But the beach is here, the waters here
the waves are rushing on
I cannot trade, these things for you
because I know you're gone
Rocky beaches, Sandy shores
water white and blue

mist from waves, cresting high
resembles morning dew
And now I'll go, away from here,
and hope I understand
that your love is like the ocean
that goes and comes again

Mary Lippincott

NOLAW—NORTH LANSING AGAINST THE WORLD

(Dedication: Love to my favorite BG)

Colonel, Colonel, I fell for you, and I thought you were wearing blue.
But it's green on that fair bod, everyone thinks you've gone mod.
They knew you were the best, so they ordered you to the West.
I saw you standing on the floor, you were there right by my door.
Absolutely, you were not a bore; you knew so much lore.
I remember your paper on 'mace', even more I remember your face.
Oh, the shape of your nose and the swirling of your toes.
We shared a stick of gum, glad you didn't ask for rum.
You winked once too much, that got me in dutch.
I was so filled with lust, that
my mind, it did bust.
You actually drove me insane and it really did pain.
Fifteen times in the mental hospital, four trips to the place called jail.
To make me alive, four shocks I received in February of '69, but I'm not peeved.
Matthew 5:28 tore me apart, it played tricks on my heart,
But Matthew 18:22 gives me a fresh start.
I thought Mrs. Porru was your Mom, didn't mean to explode a bomb.
When I called and found you taken, my heart was nearly breakin'.
But I'm not blue, I'm a different hue.
Maybe someday in the sweet by and by, we may meet again in the sky,
That is, if you love Him more than her, that is why I acted then as I did, Sir
Because I love(d) Him and I knew it was sin, although I was overwhelmed with vim.
It truly must have been our fate, surely glad you found a mate.
Romans 8:28 is my guide, may she ever be by your side.
Was it in the sauna, that you found your darling Donna?
I hope your two childs grow up like you—meek and mild.
During this celebrated season, may His love give you a reason
to love and forgive with each day that you live.
I do forgive ye, will ye forgive me?
Lou, Lou, please don't sue;
I made you an offer; you declined the coffer.
The word was 'refused' on the envelope used.
It contained great news: "There's enough for two."
The mission was green, the directive a scheme.
All systems were go, including the dough
Where is your soul? What is the goal?
You were a ham, but this is no sham(e)!
I'll fight for you; I lie for you;
I live for you, I still love you.
May you and your second wife
have no significant strife.

Debbie J. Lowe

LONELINESS

What be this strange sensation
Seeping into my very pores?
Silently, steadily, crawling
Through the veins to my
Weary soul.
Slowly, creeping, I feel the grip
Engulfing my struggling heart
My emotions surrender to this attack
And my suspecting soul
Is snared.
Spiraling down toward oblivion
Draining my soul of existance
I succumb to this brutal victor.
For it's only reality. The reality of
Being alone.

Jun M. Rogado

EDITH

Exhortation of the word
will strengthen your faith
Decision you'd made
came from above
Imaginations from heaven
will keep you away
To succumb temptations
loneliness and despair
Honey I love you
and God will take care.

Danny R. Hendricks

A MOMENT ALONE

Yesterday seems so far away and tomorrow has yet to come
Dreams come and go, some real; some only fantasy
Life, the challenge; to embrace the moment
No problems, no plans; only the chance
A brightly colored bird flies overhead and my mind flies along
As wispy, white clouds float so carelessly by
I talk with a best friend of mine in thought
A moment to enjoy, to relax, to enhance
To share this time with a special someone
Exchanging views and thoughts together
Gazing back at what has been; wondering what will come
But for the moment; it really matters not at all
For I am my best friend; with whom I talk
Times like these; so special to both
For in my friend, I share my most innermost thoughts
And for this moment alone; I can share it all.

Anonia M. Akin

THE ROSE

HE placed it here so thoughtfully
To say a special thing—
The fragrance that HE gave it
As soft as angel's wing—
The swollen tender blossom, delicate to touch—

Is like the brush of loving lips
On hands, or cheek—and such
A gentle blessing. Or, with a drop of dew,
A vibrant symbol of hope and joy—
This gift, thru a rose, to you.

Lilly Pearl White Flake

PRIORITIES

Great possessions would be very nice
I fancy from time to time.
Being unable to pay the high price
Forces me to reason and rhyme.
Happiness cannot be bought.
It' a state of being in heart and mind.
For men have always sought,
Varying lengths of time are required to find.
As the search continues, a voice can be heard
Speaking to the hearts of all; it pleads.
Plainly from the Master comes these words,
"Lovest thou Me more than these?"
The answer must be positive;
The rule toward mankind decrees,
If happiness is truly desired,
"You must love Me more than these."
In crowds or alone, the voice is heard;
Always softly or loudly it pleads.
Once heard, it is never silent,
"Lovest thou Me more than these?"

Col. Lyle A. Brookover

TOWER MOODS

Dost laugh at man, who builded you,
Sky-piercing stone and steel?
O'er the great city, stretched beneath
Dost sense of conquest feel?
Rich jewelled crown of industry,
That holds the present stage,
Somehow I know that, looking down
Your heart holds youth and age,
In crystal air you proudly hold
That queenly head on high;
Disdaining modern man's applause
To higher gods you cry.
Traditions old; researches new;
To each you suavely bow;
Grey-veiled in smoke or Erie's fog—
Oh, I could love you now!
In bitter storm and slashing gale,
Staunch, fearless, hid from sight;
To know you're there gives mortals strength
To battle through the night.
A stately link 'twixt earth and heaven,
Calm rule your fev'rish world;
To mark your very topmost reach,
Red, white and blue unfurled.
In early morn, at dusky eve,
Thou ever-present tower,
The sight of you can lift me up,
Make rich each passing hour.

Clifford M. Danby, Jr.

WINDOW PAINS

Today I cannot resist the sky; a grey and restless heart that cries with mine. And I wonder if perhaps some window a thousand miles from here has your face pressed to it, pain etched upon a pane, sharing the tears that tap softly upon the sill.

There was so much that we shared. If only we had learned to be selfish with the words that emptied our hearts and filled our eyes, we might never have come to this moment full of distance and window.

And like the rain, the memory of you lingers and I find myself wishing that the breath which I exhale today will be the one you draw tomorrow. And once again I send my dreams away to drift with the clouds, foolishly hoping that neither will dissolve before reaching you somehow.

Peggy Leone

NO LONGER KING

King of the hill am I
My court is all of nature
Once a wise man came
But only to the edge he did go
I heard him say soft, but firm
"King you may be, but a person,
one does not know"
No more is there a king

Robin J. Sitten
SEER AT SEVEN
Awakened suddenly in the dead of night,
Someone calling my name, I know.
With the light of the moon as my only lamp,
I record what my mind's eye showed.
He was crushed in the gears of the old family clock.
If he screamed, likely no one heard.
But the folks say old Joe was the kind of a man
Who'd leave us without final words.
Yeh, his name was Joe, the pride of his town,
Epitomized the good Staunton name.
Just he and his boy to keep perfect time;
Future sons would do the same.
"As high as a mile and wide as a farm,
And a spring as long as a train".
It'd been captured by Reds and bombed by the Greys,
And pelted by hot acid rain.
She stopped bringing food when the mess was cleaned up,
She'd stand at the tower door.
Now she called to her son that his dinner was hot.
She couldn't look at the works anymore.
Some say that the blood that was still on the wheel
Was what naturally turned her away,
But Keith knew when the teeth had mangled good Joe,
His mother died some that same day.
How strange the shake in my fingertips.
How clear the voice in my head.
The twisted mass of flesh and bone,
The permanent tints of red.
That wasn't all there was to the clock;
The men had yet to arrive.
Nameless, like the woman so loved by Keith,
Who now had the will to survive.
They were fresh out of prison, but not on parole.
A sheet-rope was their only key.
And they worked 'longside Keith in the old Staunton clock,
Just as honest as men who were free.
They got Keith to trust them, the wife trapped upstairs.
The gears would drink again.
One good shove, a change in speed,
Then the teeth would taste her skin.
The boy came out of nowhere, a wrench in his hand,
Instinct grabbed for a gun.
A bad shot to the foot, and he stumbled back.
A Staunton cried out for her son.
It wasn't Keith who fell to death, as his fater before had done,
And the gears had stopped on their own.
One dead in the clock. One dead on the grass
Where, in his fear, he had flown.
Who are these folk who invade my dreams?
From what lands do they hail?
And why did their story conclude with *my* name,
From a dying man just out of jail?

Bill Logan
PROMISED
Today is here and yet it was not promised.
So I must try to live it to its richest extent.
I will go about my tasks, though none of them I have planned,
for you see
. . .Today is here and yet it was not promised.

I will greet everyone with a smile, a song and a dance for you see. . . .I must make a good impression, one to be remembered.
You see! Today is here and yet it was not promised.
I wonder, I really wonder about Tomorrow. . . . .
Is it Promised?

Alma Joyce
CONFRONTATION
Beloved judged, chastised to bring the spirit,
found guilty of cruelty and indifference.
Woes attack with kindness gone
as truth does polarize to split apart the rock.
Besieged, a silent scream sobs in the deep
and echoes in the chasms of belief.
Who battles with supplication,
ridicules enmity flesh controlled
does calculate this fatal plot
by calling love companion.
No mortal power does hire nor time
that journey and I am sanctified
without my knowing by joy
to reign within another glory.

Billie C. Burbage t.s.
MY PRAYER
When I have come to the end of the road,
I should like to look back and see—
That I have done my very best,
With the trust that was placed in me.
I should like to know that I have never. . .
By action, word or deed. . .
Betrayed a given confidence,
Or forsaken a friend in need.
I would like this consolation,
When I travel the very last mile,
To know I meant something to someone. . .
And caused those in sorrow—to smile.
To know that I shall be happy,
If, in the heart of: *just one*,
I can leave one lingering memory,
Of something good I have done!

Jodi Hutchins
AWAIT ME AT THE GATES
"I beg you, darling, please don't go,
stay here by my side."
"Sorry, my sweet, but I must go,
upon my horse I ride."
"Then promise to return, my love,
unless sure death awaits."
"Fear not, dear heart, I shall return,
await me at the gates."
"So kiss me, dear, before you go,
and tell me no good-byes."
"Dwell on this kiss 'till I return,
next morning when you rise."
These words that my true love last spoke
still live within my heart.
'Twas many a long year ago
that we were torn apart.
The meaning of his words stand clear,
I know now what he meant.
The gates of which he spoke were pearl,
to God is where he went.
Now as I breathe my final breath,
I know where he awaits.
And there is my true love at last,
he's sitting at the gates.

Ann Nordquist
A TRIBUTE
To a Noble Lord of generous heart
Who unselfishly breath and soul imparts
Upon her whom he had deemed
Worthy, bestowed in verse and line,
Word and syllable divine,
Perhaps now wishing her adieu, poised with piercing dart.
What web's been spun?
When noble lord perceives a princess fairy queen
But incorrectly identifies the esteemed
For she, a mortal maiden, terrestrial Hun
Clothed in imperfections and feelings undone
She desired another but whose heart could not be won,
What idiocy, not unforeseen?
To instigate such turmoil among the once serene,
For are not he and she friends endeared
In this life and eternity to come revered?
Because his affection ran amiss
He must not think himself inadequate
About which the damsel is most adamant
But to the contrary, delight in present hour's bliss
For lives have crossed, been blessed, and willed to risk.

Sheila J. Caldwell
TRAILS OF THE PAST
Days of untrod trails of dust covered land
and wagon trains moving through uncharted land.
A wilderness of dreams, hopes, and aspirations.
Hunting for tomorrow by exploration of today.
Joys through discoveries and sights unseen.
Painful sorrow known through death.
Living for today. Dying for tomorrow.
A trail filled with tears.
A history of pain for the conquest of civilization.
A civilization of tomorrow that remains for us to see today.

Kathy Sims
YOU NEVER EVEN NOTICED
Long ago. . .
Days long since gone
You never even noticed
The laughter that drifted like leaves in the wind when you appeared,
The light in my eyes like the stars in the heaven when I heard your voice,
The beating of my heart like waves upon a distant shore at the mention of your name. .
And so,
Today,
I sit,
I think,
Yes, I realize,
With little wonder,
That piece by piece,
Memory by memory,
That laughter has vanished,
That light has died,
That fire has abruptly been extinguished. . .
And You. . .
You never even noticed I was gone. . .

Stephen O'Reilly
NOWADAYS
Nowadays,
You say something,
Amongst a clatter
Of chatter
So to hear
Even your own voice.

Nowadays,
A serious thought
On a background
Of plastic bookwork
And blank stares
And monotonous answers,
And fighting an immovable
machine,
Makes one stop—
And consider.
A fragment—
Of sentence, or of continuous
flow?
To someone, or an alter ego.
Contain it.
Don't detain it.
Your responsibility is to
Maintain it.

Arthur W. McNamee

SAND CASTLES

Two youngsters built a castle
Built a castle made of sand
These firm molecules of
imagination
Bridged the gap to fairyland.
They were alone
On a crowded beach
And were solitary rulers of
mighty thrones
Where everything of every wish
Was well within their reach.
In this setting; quite serene
Rules this king
And his queen
Harmony!
With similar songs to sing.
But, wisdom pierced their ears
In the words of an aged man
Who snatched away the years
That bridge to fairyland
He said in a simple way
As though—to pray
"Castles built of sand
Cannot, will not stand"
Yet, all that day
They continued to play
Until the whisper of time
Blew it all away.

Joseph P. Kowacic

COMMENT

Some persons
complain
about their lot in life,
and count their miseries
one by one.
They never see
a bird,
a flower. . .
or a woman
before a windy sun.

Evangeline Beauford Jones

THE FRIEND I FAILED

My friend wrote to me today
but I wasn't happy to hear
what he had to say,
He said we shared joyous
moments from the beginning
but I had
failed him in the end.
He said I mentioned everything
on earth, but never once did
I utter words concerning the
new birth.
The letter was sad, and I knew
why, but there was nothing I
could do but cry.
My friend was sad, yes I could
tell because his return address
was stamped from hell.
His P.S. I hold it within,
don't become so friendly, you
forget, to tell someone of
their sins.
He may not know about the
new birth, only the joyous
times he has spent on earth,
Don't let another soul be lost,
surely it's not worth the cost.
Tell him right away about the
Savior you kept from me,
If only I had known Him, today
my soul would be set free.

Mary J. Sanderson

UNTITLED

I'd like to plant a million seeds
of daisies
Full of mirth
To watch them come and fling
their joy
Over the rolling earth

Judy L. Klimcheck

HAPPY AND FREE

Happy and free
I want to be.
Exempt from any care
Or anything unfair.
To breeze through each day
Because all is O.K. .
To give life a happy sound,
By loving everything around.
With this in mind
Then I will find
Each day is worthwhile
All you need is a smile.

Ahmad (Max Stanford)

FOR THE SPIRIT OF OUR PEOPLE

October blows in strange winds
Brinks robbery,
and the
witch hunt begins,
The weather has turned bad,
because the pigs have gone mad,
The war has begun
and many are on the run,
but we still say
We will win
because
The spirit of Malcolm,
is in
The Whirlwind.

Dawn Aarhus Anderson

SO YOUNG

So young and innocent
Not long ago,
And your budding figure
Held quite an appeal
For the adolescent males
Who once called you
"Chipmunk Cheeks".
Whether it was naivity
Or stupidity,
It matters little now,
But you gave in to their
persuasion
And before you knew it,
You were losing that
Feminine build
To the baby growing inside you.
Now that baby has a name...
Your name,
And you love her very much.
She's so beautiful,
And yet it seems so sad,
That her mother, too,
Is just a babe.

Sherry Henry Hodgson

OUR WEDDING ANNOUNCEMENT

As we vow our love before the
Judge,
Family and friends, hold no
grudge.
Plans were made, the date was
set,
Not a peep from anyone did you
get.
No invitations, 'twas private
you see,
Only the judge, a witness, my
beau and me.
Moments thereafter, we're
happily married,
My "big" wedding plans can now
be buried.
We've begun life together as
many have done,
So much easier now that we two
became one.

Kay M. Knobloch

THE WISHING WELL

I wish I was in India
to help the poor bunch;
I wish I was in Guatemala
to help the people find some
lunch.
I wish all countries were the
same
no matter where they are;
I wish all people could be
friends
in countries near and far.
I wish for good things for the
world
as you can plainly tell;
But for my wishes to come true
I wish I had a wishing well!

Kathleen Trompeter Peterson

IMPRISONMENT

I am an ugly encaged beast
Captured in this room.
My tentacles slip through the
windows
Reaching out hopelessly for
freedom.
The walls press against me.
I PUSH
DESPERATELY
Trying to burst forth.
I am at the very point of
escaping.
I PUSH—
The walls push—
We struggle endlessly.
How long can I survive?
Will I be imprisoned here
forever?
My mind is "THE ROOM"
My thoughts, emotions,
feelings—
MY HURT.
I must become free.
HOW?

Jean E. Lyons

BEAUTY OF ALL SEASONS

Looking out my window
Upon a summers day
Fields bright and green
Flowers formed a sweet bouquet
My window opened high
I gazed at fall leaves turning
From my throat escaped a sigh
Eyes with beauty burning
One winter day I saw the snow
On every house and tree
Felt the wonder of the scene
Down to the depths of me
My door I opened wide one day
To bid the spring good morning
The world filled with greening
trees
Some flower buds adorning
In thinking on seasons changing
With all their beauties
marvelous
I muse how any living man
Could wonder—Does God love
us?

Mary A. Griffin

THE VIRGIN CHILD

He came into this world to
bring peace
He came to renew a world that
was dying
He came to bring freedom and
peace to all mankind
He came to heal the sick
He came to raise the dead
The hungry he also fed
He came to make the blind to
see

He came to make the devil flee
He came to set the captive free
He came to bring reality
He was betrayed
He was denied
He was mocked
He was crucified
For the sins of the whole world
he died
He was the virgin child
And his name was CHRIST
JESUS

Flora Haynes

ENCHANTMENT

The world is a place of
Enchantment
We succumb to its beauties
each day.
When Spring opens its doors—
We view flowers
Sent by rains that are gentle and
fair.
God's glory is seen in the
summer
With beauty of every kind,
We pride in the blessings he's
sent us—
As Fall comes to remind us,
That the graciousness of Winter
is near,
With cold and refreshing
snowflakes
That billow and fall like
feathers
On ground that is thirsty
For reviving moisture so clear.

Anna Owens and Son Edward Owens

LORD JESUS COME

Lord Jesus come and pick me up
And take me home with You.
I try to love You more each day;
My heart is pure and true.
Thy words I keep, and I do pray
If working or at play;
Please, guard me thru the long dark night
And keep me thru the day.
Lord Jesus come and pick me up
And take me home with You.
I am unhappy here on earth;
No other friend is true,
But faith, with-in Thy Grace alone,
I know will see me thru.
Beyond the rainbow where You are
I'll start my life anew.

Ollie Vee Zoller

SAFARI

Hunter-born, ballooned with glee
Sans a trace Killer-to-be
Calendars, four, he lived thru
Stalked his prey, then weapon drew
Swatted snake-fast, victim dies
To floored-fly child yelled, "sssSprise!"

W. E. Pursley

A PSALM OF UNDERSTANDING

(What is man that God is so mindful of Him? Psalms:8-4)
(An answer to this question?)
Think upon our God—lonely Sovereign
Whose presence encompasses the dimensions of space;
Who, being without birth, lives unto the reaches
of eternity.
Think upon our God—Father of creation,
Who, by the spoken word, angels were born—the household of God was filled with joy.
Think upon our God—jealous Sovereign.
Whose angelic creatures, inflamed by thoughts of selfish desires
Rebelled to make desolate, the dwelling places of the most High.
Think upon our God—absolute Sovereign,
creating a new Heaven; where, sons and daughters, conceived in His own likeness,
Become partakers of His glory; and, in the fullness of time,
become perfect—even as their Father is perfect.
Regretful must have been that hour of beginning when the
Prophetic Eye beheld a rebellious world—ere time had spilled its decay over infinite space, and no inhabitant of the earth had embraced the sensual vices of our nature.
Sacrificial was His love; in which, the only Begotten, destined
to remove the adversary between God and man,
Suffered His body unto death that Saving Grace might be
given to a fallen world.
Certain must have been the wisdom that permitted the foibles of
every nature to wreck their whims upon the footstool of His creation.
Merciful was His love that spanned the chasm with a bridge of
faith, and builded the cosmos upon the potential worth of man.
Oh, thou thoughtless mortal!
Has not the Divine tasked the powers of expression, until thy soul, shackled to a rebellious will, cries out at the narrow confines of its limits,
Unable to reach immortality through the portals of a
deadened conscience?
Blessed are they, who understand the verities of life:
Whose thoughts are attuned to the will of God,
Whose sins are covered, for they shall stand with the ages,
When Time, deceased, ushers in the great Amen.

Terri A. Moore

WHY

Why can't I say the things
I want to say?
Why can't I be the person
I want to be?—
Would you understand?
When my thoughts don't quite connect
With my words—
Do you laugh?
When I stumble and act the fool—
Will you catch me?
Or,
Will you walk away
As others have before?
Please don't
(I need you.)

Dorothy Loeppke

THE GLORY OF LIFE

Do you make the most of your time spent each day?
Do you tackle your work with a vim?
Do you think the dear Lord for the hours that are yours?
Do you place all your trust just in Him?
Do you aim at a goal of success, or renown?
Do you start determined to win?
Or, do you take time to make the path smooth,
For someone to rise out of sin?
Do you lighten a load for someone to bear?
Do you stoop to help someone unbend?
Do you say "I will go", when the task you despise,
Without asking for foe, or a friend?
Do you know that the wings for our heavenly flight,
Must be fashioned from threads of kind deeds?
That life's not a goal, but a game of fair play
That the Judge of eternity heeds!

Janett M. Clark

UNTITLED

Once I felt my life was ending. .
That I had no meaning or purpose. . . . .
I felt that I had ventured into never, never land. . . . .
Then suddenly there was you.
Running around in endless circles
Wishing on unfallen stars. . . . .
Then suddenly in the mist of my dark cloud a
Gleam of light broke through. . .
Suddenly there was you.
You gave me a reason to smile. .
My life suddenly had purpose. . .
All the pain I once felt had departed somehow. . . . .
I'm not afraid anymore. . .
I feel I can climb the mountain now because
I know you'll be at my side.

Karen Ann McCarthy

OUR COMMUNITY CHURCH

Our community church
That we are grateful to know
Is our spiritual house,
For to worship God — we go.
For we know of God's joy,
The forgiveness of sin
And the fellowship received
As we enter in.
To all of God's children

As we are seated inside,
Know the freedom we feel
Toward GOD — we confide.
How thankful we are
To hear God's servant speak
And know that through him
God sends a message each week.
Now the service is over
And we are filled with God's love
Because our hearts have been touched
By our Lord—up above.

Janet Swee Ching Romel

THIS LITTLE TOWN

I like this little town,
Where all the leaves
Come tumbling down—
And this little lake,
Where nature has it made;
With the trees swaying in the breeze.
In winter you will freeze,
While snow lies on the icy-cold grounds.
In summer, there's glittering sands
Reflected from the sun's rays,
Day by day.
On the beaches—people talk, laugh, swim and eat.
Oh! What a wonderful feeling—
To be alive and awake
And have both eyes, for God's sake.
See the creepy, crawly creatures
Found on the ground, beneath the bareness of many feet.
As you stroll through
This wonderful little town
At night time
Listen to the chimes of the church bells,
Don't forget to pass by the little wishing well.
I can tell, there's music in the air,
Over there
With the rock n'roll band.
Across the distant beaches, there's a contrast
Found so fast
By day and by night.
Stranger. . . .should you pass this way,
Once again,
Stroll along the beaches
On the pathway of many a fine day;
Walk along this little town
Where swaying trees
In the breeze are found.
Stand by
To observe
The birds fly away.
Either today or tomorrow
Is filled with joy or sorrow,
Like the changing seasons
Of Spring, Summer, Fall and Winter,
There are many reasons
For enjoying life
Hang all its strife!

Linda Jane Bailey

CRIMES OF PASSION

I do still think of you
I won't tell you it isn't true
My life is so different because of you
You were the blessing of my lifetime
You are the inspiration that made this all possible
The moment has become so holy
White horses ride out in every direction
To gather the children ready for the fight
Poet laureate of the new age
Eater and drinker of sage
Watches as our children wait
Girdling themselves for the passage
In these holy moments I bless you
My gratefulness goes out to you on cometwings
It is from your courage I can sing
It is from the strength you send me

I can bridle my powers
for the next Battle
I sit waiting in the saddle
for a certain horn to blow
The fields and canyons are
silently filling with snow
It won't be long now
The silence is a masquerade
Power builds behind the scenery
The passions of mankind are
waging
Behind the snows the war is
raging
Traders and warriors armed with
reasons
Prepare the setting for all
seasons
Yet to come and that have been
Yes, what will be
When this is done
The answers are known by none
The war is no surprise
The surprise is in the survivors
Can their passion hold them
When all throws have torn them
The seasons and the reasons
blown them
From themselves into the
starkness
We have left from what's
unharnessed
Is this just the play of passion
That has stepped beyond all
reason
Is there left another season
Or is all stolen by our treason
Is there left another moment
Are there tears left for our
sadness
Will we be there you and I
To see the anger in the sky
Revenge for all our human
blindness
No hint left of celestial
kindness
From the saddle I can see it
From my heart, the pain, I feel it
Mountains rumbled in their
sober gloom
The day that men brought down
their doom
How many left to see the angry
sky
How many left beyond the
flurry of so many to die
I know that one will probably
be I
I searched the scenery
The bloodied meadows of
broken flowers
the melted snows from blazing
battles
Who is left to see this with me
To see the upshot of our crimes
of passion
To start again a brand new
season
Born out of new strands of
reason

Alma Joyce

COMBUSTABLE

What active speaking jest
and foolish laughing
lust, beware you do not
tempt the tempter in a snare.
All come to feel those passions
deep
neath oceans of passive souls.
Still disconnected from
themselves
in fear avoiding that canceling
of all loose ends and stubble.
Only as grace dwells inbetween
separating the two extremes
from anihilating flame ignited
in ignorance of our difference.

Meredith Brown

WHAT IS CHRISTMAS?

What Is Christmas?
The Time Of The Year,
When
Bells Ring
And
There're Snow Flakes
Everywhere,
The Bells In Every
Church Steeple
Cry
To Praise
The Birth
Of
Our Savior
Who Is Always Near By,
While In Each Home
We Sing
Christmas Tunes,
The Tree So Very Beautiful
Looks Like
Spring, Summer
And Fall
All In Bloom,
While The Yule Tides Burning,
We All Sit Aside
To Reflect,
What Is Christmas,
Giving, Sharing
Love
Peace On Earth
365 Days
A Year.

Margaret H. Kimbel

A JOYOUS AWAKENING

Early this morning just as the
sun was peaking o'er the hill
A plump little robin hopped
upon my windowsill
"Chir-rup! Chir-rup! Spring is
here! All nature rejoices.
Get up! Get up!" he seemed to
say.
"Ere too soon such beauty fades
away."
Then fluffing his feathers, he
gave a quick little twirl
As he sang out, "God's in his
Heaven, all's right with the
world!"
On that note I could lie abed no
longer
Immediately, my spirits were
lifted -
And I felt much stronger
Opening wide the windows, I let
the sunshine in
One glance at the blue of the
sky, and the green of the grass
And I was persuaded: Spring
indeed, has come at last!
Delicate little violets springing
up from the warm earth
Symbols of new life - rebirth -
The sweet fragrance of lilac
permeating the air
A sense of peace and serenity
everywhere!

Sweet bird, sweet bird, return
again to me
Bringing your song of Spring and
Love
Truly, a messenger from
Heaven above!

Linus Dickson

JUST FOR THE HELIBUT (HELL OF IT)

went there
with friends
but what for. . . .?
just for the helibut
threw my line in
couldn't catch a bite
altho'
these empty hours
I spent thinking
deep thoughts
but what for. . . .?
just for the helibut
five hours passed. . .
half the day shot.
I guess its time
to pack up
and go.
why did I come here
in the first place?
just for the helibut.

Rita O'Keefe

TERROR HITS

On Monday March 30th of eight
one
I sat with my family, having fun
Bulletin Bulletin flashed on
T.V.
Oh what now, What can it be?
We stopped talking, and turned
up the set
The shock I got is with me yet.
Our President of the U.S.A.
Pushed in a car with a look
of dismay.
Brady our Press Secretary on the
ground.
Blood from his head flowing
around
Two other men shot on the spot
One a Security Guard, One a
cop
Tears filled my eyes, and I
started to cry
Oh please God don't let them
die
I watched in horror as a man
was grabbed
By Security Guards who were
very mad.
The President was shot we
heard at last.
It brought memories of the
awful past.
I could see Kennedy in his car
This can't be happening it's too
bizarre.
Back to the news of eight one
Terror struck with a gun
March 30th was a terrible day
But fellow Americans I am
proud to say
Our President is doing fine
And so will the others, given
time
Gods speed to you four great
men
My prayers are with you till
your well again.
Although this happened awhile
ago
It's something everyone should
know
History was made on the spot
The day our President was shot.
Lets pray this won't happen
again
We need our leaders and great
men
Lets hope that we may never see
Our Presidents in Tragedy.

Daniel Scott Van Hoven

PANORAMA OF DARKNESS

I stood alone
Enclosed in darkness
The moon shone
It was timeless
Similar tone
Of an aging bone
With infinite scattered stars
Ominously glowing
Little light was flowing
A lunar pitted stone, touchably
near
Distinctivly dominating the sky
Far and full of unknown fear
It had no sound, though it
seemed to moan
Provoking the derelict hound,
upon his lofty mound
Mankind sleeps, primal, past
and present
Through it all daylight seeps
Mankind rises to begin
The picture fades away
Panorama of darkness once
again
Will be heavenly sent

Thomas Francis Cassidy Jr.

THE VOICE

I was stumbling through a blind
pagan forest of dim light
I was looking left and reaching
right
I knew it was day, I was trapped
in night
I fell down on my knee since I
felt uptight
Then a voice said "see" you will
be alright
My son you are free I have
given you sight
Amen

Catherine Curtin Fenzel

CLOCK AT MIDNIGHT, NEW YEAR'S EVE

One hand holds
The Old Year
Sentimentally. . .
Won't let go
So quickly
Hours that used to be. . .
Other hand
Goes forward
Optimistically. . .
Sure the New Year's
Better,
Rushing on to see!

Luella Arndt Kitchen
DEAR OLD SANTA
(Verse)
I am telling everbody
everywhere
I was talking to Santa and you
needn't fear
Of being disappointed on
December twenty-fifth
Cause prosperity is here
(Chorus)
So dear old Santa paint your
nose
Put those woolens round your
toes
Put on your old tassel cap
Your coat with cotton cuffs
Then dear old Santa
Fill your bag with lots of stuff
Cause prosperity is here
Go get your airplane inspected
now
You will need an earlier start
this year
It will take longer to deliver you
know
Cause prosperity is here

Dorris Smith
THE STAIRWAY TO HEAVEN
The stairway to Heaven
Is long and hard
And obstacles get in your way
If you try to climb by yourself
You may falter, stagger or stray
But there is someone to walk
with you
With strength beyond compare
Who will hold your hand,
And guide your steps
With tender loving care
If you try to climb without him
Darkness may dim your way
And each step will get harder
As you struggle from day to
day
The stair of hate you can
overcome
For his love will carry you
through
And the jealous stair will fade
away
As his strength comes into
view
Envy is another stair
That will trip if it can
So hold on tight and don't let go
Of the loving guiding hand
Criticism will be waiting
To discourage you every step
But strength will come if you
believe
A greater power is there to
help
Don't give in just step on up
Through the forest of distress
Each step will get lighter
And your efforts will be
blessed
The stairway of fear will reach
right out
And try to turn you back
Just lift your eyes
And the light will shine
Right through those cloud of
black
As you pass the evil stairs
Your fears will fade away
And peace will dwell within
you
When you reach the top some
day.

Cindy L. Belmer
TO DREAM, TO LIVE
Did you ever dream you could
fly?
Escape from Life's confusion?
Or did you dream the future?
The truth about tomorrow?
Daydream, nightdream, there all
the same.
Bringing thoughts so intense, no
one understands,
The real person, the being
within.
I feel lost within myself, yet, I
know where I am.
You don't understand me? Don't
confuse me!
I have yearnings I can't express.
Feelings I have yet to feel.
God made us as we are,
Life is ours to puzzle.
We will find our answers, in
time.
I have just begun to dream, to
live.
To show myself what I can do.
To do, what I am here for.

Ignazio C. Benfante
NOW IS THE TIME
Drink today your fill of Youth
and Spring.

If tomorrow you want to try
the happiness of which they
sing,
You'll find that it has passed
you by.
My dear, dream your little
dreams today,
For we're not masters of our
fate.
Thrill to joys of love while you
may.
Take romance before it is too
late.
And when you glance into my
eyes,
If there you see love like a
flame,
Then take your love before it
dies,
For it may never burn the same.

Alisa Comeaux
TO MY LOVE
Since we brok up I've
felt so blue,
There is no life for me
without you.
You say it's for the
best,
It's what we should do.
No matter how many times
I say
I need you
You say you don't want
to hurt me anymore,
But living without you
hurts me more than
anything before.
It felt so safe when I
was with you,
From all the things
the world can do.

I pray that God will let
you see,
There's something very
special between you and me.
Something we shouldn't let
slip away,
Something more beautiful
than words can say.
Everyone says just to
forget,
But they don't understand
my heart just won't let.

Gail Ma
WHAT WILL I BE WHEN I GROW UP?
I am already twelve and I
Should think of what I'll be;
I want to be a lot of things,
But what is right for me?
I want to be a musician,
Piano's what I'll play;
But I always hit the notes
wrong,
So what more could I say?
I could become a helpful vet,
And live in the jungle;
And help all my animal friends,
But I'm afraid to bungle;
I think I am too young to think
About what I should be;
When I grow up I'm sure I'd
know,
Which career is best for me!

Steven Picou
IF
If I were a poet
I would dedicate all lines to you
So beautiful a flower,
bursting in the sun
I would pen words which moved
solemn when night had begun
I would write of life and love
which you possess,
I would point my heart forever
in your direction,
Hoping that my words, like a
magnet, could attract your
attention, catch your eyes,
enter your heart, "Notice me,"
my lines would cry.
Yes, if I were a poet,
you would be my life and
writing could eventually
cease,
My worship would become
words,
My kisses, my pen.

Gail Magee
LOVE, A HARD WORD TO SAY!
He's around sometimes, but never when you need him, when thing's aren't right, and you need someone to say he loves you; but the word's are never there. How can someone be that way? Even times you feel deserted and left out, only money is on his mind; it's supposed to make everything alright again, but it never will. I guess for some love is a few lettered word, like money and a long lasting guilt complex. It never changes, it's alway's the same.

Helen T. Cockrell
MY MANY LOVES
My love for God, who suffered
and died to redeem man,
My love for America, this great
and wonderful land,
My love for my Family, which I
couldn't do without,
And my love for my Animals,
who happily run about.
My love for birds and the mere
glimpse of a flower,
While I sit writing down my
thoughts hour after hour,
Last, but not least, is my love
for my friend,
Who always gives me love and
encouragement to the end.

Lillian M. Degraw
THOUGHTS AWRY
The house a clutter
The house a mess,
I am so worried
I will confess.
Sisters yelling, shouting aloud
I feel as if my heads in a cloud,
Brothers awake with a swollen
jaw
He can't get in it except with a
paw.
My thoughts are all mixed
And if it could be fixed,
So not to hear this quarrel and
strife
How much different I could deal
with life.
My heads all aclutter
Like a piece of moss
And I think if I could just be
boss,
All of this I could throw away
And make this my own Day.

Jill Bartel
BE A DREAMER
Reach for the heights,
The misty, shrouded sky
Swirling in silent turmoil
About you.
Grasp onto what you believe,
Hold on fast
Gently cradling it
In the palm of your hand.
It shimmers brightly
At your fingertips.
Release it to the sea of air
And follow it skyward
Like a comet with a glowing
tail.
At the peak
In the brilliance
You'll know that at last
You have found yourself.

Gary D. "Bone" Potter
I SIT ALONE
I sit alone
As the night gently—creeps
about
in hidden blackness
Never being able to thrust

out-n-grab
A new life
With it's presence and
potency always
being relevant
Like the naked darkness.
I wait
My love deminished
Time passes as the dark of the
night sends it's
creepers terrorizing
always to be looked back upon,
but never to be forseen
While I sit alone.

Joyce L. Campbell
LONELY ROSE AND ME
I came upon an old house place
so desolate and almost gone.
I wondered, "Could this have
been a mansion or just a
house someone called home."
Did love once dwell behind
those shattered walls
Or was it just a house with no
love at all?
But yes, love surely must have
lived here by everything
around,
Because an old swing and
battered toys were scattered
on the ground.
My heart gave a leap for love I
was in need.
But then, I saw a lonely rose
or else it seemed to be.
I went over to pick it up as its
blossoms seemed to beckon.
For just how long had this
lonely rose bloomed here with
no attention?
Its sweet perfume and tented
petals seemed to show its love
so wild and free
And then, I stopped to question,
"did you grow here just for
me?"

Michele Bondick
RAINBOWS
Rainbows show the rain is gone,
The sun will shine in mornings'
dawn.
The promise is true that God
once made,
Soon the rainbow will be gone
and fade.
Rainbows give us hope and
cheer,
To believe in God year by year.

Nicole Constable
BE KIND TO ANIMALS
Be kind to the animals
they snarl and bite
they kick and fight
some days they're just like you.
Don't feed the animals
they're sick and overweight
lazy and bored
they remind me. . .
at times. . .
of you.
Take pity on those big sad eyes
with feelings closed and boxed
inside;
closed doors and cement walls,
arms holding through the metal
bars.
Don't play with the animals.
They're dangerous!
Watch your fingers. . .
animals bite. . .
so do you.
If you ever catch a lizard by the
tail,
think how you might feel first.
Look at those pretty birds;
I wish I had feathers like that.
You're nuts; lets go home.

Norma Lee Christiansen
REFLECTIONS
Upon the mirrored water
of my mind,
I gaze upon the image
of your face,

Beneath the surface of
a glassy pond,
You disappear
among the ripples
of my tears.

Helen F. Roberson
HEAVEN'S DREAM
Last night as I laid upon my bed
Many thoughts passed through
my head
As I drifted off to sleep
Lovely colours began to seep
Into my mind, into my soul
Only then did I behold
The unseen grandeur of
Heaven's gates
And many treasures that await
I dreamt I lived in a time
Of crystal stones, peace divine
Upon the walls were purest gold
Through the garden came the
young and old
As I walked along the jewel-like
streets
Rubies and jade beneath my feet
I came upon a man that day
At first glance I began to pray:
"Oh lord, I realize that this is
You
Prince of Peace and Heaven too!"
We talked about the mansions
rare
Of beauty there was no compare
I watched as he walked away
His name I whispered in dismay:
"Please Jesus, Let me stay!"

Victor R. Dyer
BEAUTIFUL PLAYGIRLS
Playgirls of yesteryear, in their tantalizing attire, heighten many a man's dream, ascended their hopes to the utmost desire.
Those beauties on stage, beach, park or wherever they may be, were lovely to look at as a christmas tree.
Smiling here and there, strolling to and pro, indeed they were a part of the wonderful show, on the cover of so many a publication, those playgirls drew much favored attention.
Beautiful playgirls, near and far, lent a glow of golden enchantment, as a bright star, reflecting back with a wistful tear, we dearly miss those beautiful playgirls of yesteryear.

Mary Jane J. Keane
IT'S NICE
it's nice to be home
in my warm, cozy bed
with my mom and my sisters
and assorted pets
there's nothing that beats
the refuge of a home
not just a building
but a strong fortress
behind
whose walls even the
Goliaths
of the world have to
flee
i want to remember
this calm,
and comforting
home,
that bids me adieu
and welcomes me too.

R. C. Ambrose
RA ON . . . AGE.
Age is much like too much
pizza
consumed on an eating spree,
a case of psyche indigestion
from too much reality.

Linda Laskaris, A.K.A. Jo.
BUILT FOR COMFORT
I was built for comfort, to hold through the night, to love at dawn, with daybreak insight.
I was built for comfort, to love and please, a tender man with simple need's.
I was built to hold your loving hand's, and change your mind about one night stands.
I was built for love, and I'm ready to be, that comfort you find, when you're holding me.

Monika A. Severs
YOU AND I
Intense the flames of passion
leaping,
Laughing, playing, loving,
weeping,
Only quiet when we're sleeping
You and I.
Intense the flames of passion
burning,
Dreaming, planning, wanting,
yearning,
Blundering but always learning
You and I.
Intense the flames of passion
flowing,
Trusting, sharing, always
knowing
That our love's forever growing
You and I.

Kristan Spencer Dillow
THE HARBOR
Sea gulls gliding over sea-green
glass,
sails hanging limp from a
twenty foot mast.
The harbor stands quiet, naked,
forlorn,
silently guarding the early morn.
Dusk hangs heavy as it veils the
dock,
gull-perched bouys gently rock.
Charters make harbor with the
fishermen's gold,
fish shack waiting for the
stories told.
Sea gulls gliding over sea-green
glass,
swooping to retrieve what the
knife lets pass.
Harbor life ebbs as the night
drifts by,
only too resume with the
tidewater's cry.

Sharon M. Anderson
(DUEL LA DO ME)
DUELLA DO ME
She was all asweat from her
travels that day.
She'd been walking more than
riding along her journeys way.
As she stepped into the tavern
the band began to play.
They sang: "Duella do me no
harm. I just shot a man
between the eyes and he shot
me in the arm."
"Now you know they'll come
and get me soon.
Or gun me down in this salloon.
Duella Do Me
No Harm."
Now this traveller thinking the
song too short,
and a catchy song it was.
So she asked the singer why and
he drawled, "Jus' cuz"
She never thought she'd rest
until an end to the song there
came.
"Give me that guitar." she said
and this is what she sang:
"Daniel I swear I mean you
no harm. But the man you
shot was my brother.
And Daniel I reckon I don't
have another."
"So meaning you no harm,
When I aim, its doubtful I'll
shoot you in the arm!"

Precious B. Stone
UNTITLED
I opened wide my mind
To draw from the universe
Clasped inspiration
The garden is done
Apparently cold, dead, dry
But it will return

Priscilla F. Douzanis
SCENE ON A HOSPITAL BED
Coughing and gasping, drowning
in one's own phlegm.
Is this the way proud Man
concedes to Death?
Once full, facing life with a flair
of defiance and a smug smile
on the face -
Now wrinkled, crunched -
cowering at the shadow cast
by the sycthe -
Sounds of fading life - a holler,
ringing with ebbing defiance -
Racking, pain struck chords -
Now echo through a parched
and withered throat -
Heralding sounds of the End.

Linda Faetanini Fedele

MY FAVORITE CLOWN

His serene face
begging for sympathy;
his large penetrating eyes,
searching one's inner depth.
Not a word
escapes his lips
yet he says it all.
Youngsters love him.
I too love him!
His silliness
captures the hearts
of all audiences.
Yet, it is those eyes,
that capture mine.
Who is this strange,
yet enchanting man;
who fills my heart
with youthful magic?
He is a clown.

Joyce D. Ramsey

SO FAR AWAY

The sunset is soft
The sky is blue
And all I can think of
Is being with you.
No matter where we are
No matter what we do
I only want to be with you.
The sunsets we've watched
The kisses we've shared
Makes us see how much we've
cared.
Through the tears I shed
Of my memories of you
Makes it hard to know of what
to do.
The minutes get longer
The hours never pass
Makes me wonder how long
we'll last.
With God to guide us
And the moments we share
We'll last forever since we
both care.

Cathy Judith Carlson

THOUGHTS

Thoughts of you roll through
my mind
like waves upon the sea
They gently build up to a peak
as you return to me
Then suddenly they crash
against
the hardened sands of time
And slowly drift back out to sea
You, my dreams, and I.

Kimberly Ann Wede

BOYFRIENDS

Loving, considerate
Kind and jealous
Funny and fun
When were together
They're the best thing ever!

Fred A. Keagle

REALITY

When everything is such a mess, you try and see just what is best.

Life it seems you can't control, and you feel it deep within your soul.

There are things around you just won't do, so you search to find just what is true.

The truth of life is very clear, This is what so many fear.

They say life goes on and so will you, no matter what you try and prove.

But it's really money that people grab, this they say they need to have.

When it's friends and love that they should grasp, but to them all of these are in the past.

But friends and love to me are deep, and these I want to have for keeps.

It really seems that people just don't know, or what they really want to show.

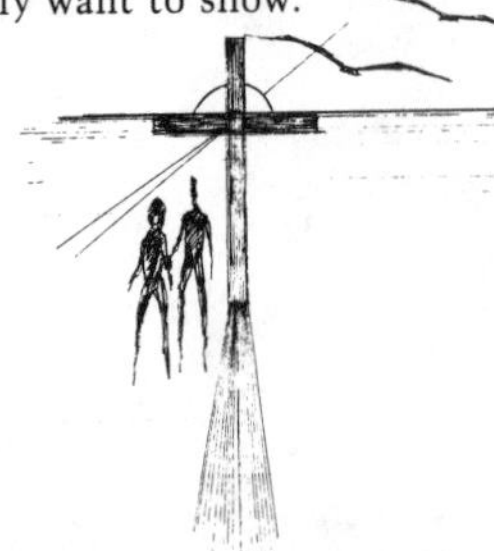

Just feel and say whats deep inside, but all of this they try and hide.

We all try and grab the rainbow of life, and think that there will be no pain and strife.

Your life is really never complete, because your on a one way street.

But it's up to you as to how you feel, seems all you want is booze and pills.

I understand that these are your highs, and this is something that you won't deny.

If people would just settle down, but all they do is run around.

They always travel a long road home, even though the paths been shown.

They ask where in life can they head, and often wish that they were dead.

They ask where in life should they be, the advice you give they never heed.

The valleys and peaks in life are hard to climb, for this is what they need to find.

For life is not an easy street, and many times you will be beat.

Sure many times you'll only goof, but life is tuff and thats the truth.

The life you want you have to make, even if you make mistakes.

Don't put up any fronts, just make the life you really want.

I know there are times in life you can't explain, and lots of times it's like a game.

Just don't look at life and expect the best, because it will bring too much stress.

You glide along when things are smooth, it finally seems you've found a grove.

And then the easy times are all but gone, and you wonder why you were ever born.

You now look at life and see nothing, and hope that the future will bring something.

You look at life and it seems so blind, and it seems so bleak within your mind.

You want your dreams to come true, so this is what you try and do.

You don't give up you firm up tight, you now realize you have to fight.

You now know that in life it's love that you should have, and thru pain and strife its what you grab.

You now rid your self as to what is false, you now put the drugs and booze to a screaming halt.

With the booze and drugs you had no life, except a lot of pain and strife.

Add more to life than take away, and deep down in don't be afraid.

Don't let your life slip thru your hands, touch life with your own plans.

Let life's wind sing your own song, try and find where you belong.

If it's God that you've felt, then ask him for a little help.

For he's the only one who knows all the facts, so if you want real true life it's him you ask.

Virgie Spurlock

LEAVING

Be kind, be kind, and do not
judge me harshly when I go.
Just know this was the only way
for me.
I've tried, oh Lord, how very
hard I've tried,
But I would rather die than not
be free.
For years, although I've smiled,
I've cried inside.
Each day I live, I die a little
more,
And this is how my life will
always be
Unless I find the strength to
close the door.
I've read somewhere, we walk
this way just once,
And how we walk forever will
remain
A memory of who and what we
were.
So judge me not, I beg of you
again.
Perhaps some night you'll see a
shooting star
Plunge down uncharted paths to
depths below,
And understand that I have no
control of destiny,
And when or where I go.

George Stuart Billings

SAINT PETER 1935

Snow captures still the air,
the silver rain
That laced dreamed summer's
day is timeliest gone
With summer's heightful
pride; present winter's dawn
Appears from dream-ed night
and moves in train
Of slow-sustain-ed hours to the
reign
Of azure-sparkling noon,
arisen-grown
From morning; trees' spring-
'waiting branches drawn
Against the quieted sky-through
-window's-pane.
Sky seen through iron has the
spectral tint
Of cloistered sunlight.
Diamond-patterned squares
Break up, make mute,
destroy the scarce
controlled
Clear blue of outer space.
Perchance, through dint
Of careful, questing gaze,
there then appears
The king of iron and the
friend of gold.

George Spellman

THE REASON FOR MAN

For man's existence on Earth,
some special purpose must be.
Fighting isn't one of them
but living together peacefully.
Man has fought amongst
himself
ever since the start of time.
Every century has brought new
violence,
this indeed is a crime.
For together we must live
in harmony and peace.
But, in order to attain this
all fear and fighting must cease.
It is time to lay down our arms
to fight never again.
Then and only then
we will be able to become
friends.
So help your fellow man.
Do not plot to wipe him out.
Because Love and Peace
Are what our lives should be
about!

Beth Mostovoy

MASK OF REALITY

the world
gleams in your smile
smiles in your eyes
I am not that world
and my revelations
are not in the revolutions
by which you live
I am a moon
a hint in the darkness
which shadows me from you
that you can't see thru
the flow of my tide is endless
deep within the currents of
myself
you see my face
its many phases
you see the face I choose
gleaming and shining above you
out of your reach
but not too high for your hopes
let my light shine softly on you

Lourdes Tello

IT SEEMS. . .

It seems
like old times.
I'm back in your arms
repeating the same mistakes,
But loving you
just the same.
Last summer
we made history.
We sang our songs
of love;
Seems only we
could understand.
Your hands guided me
through the night.
It seems my arms were meant

for holding you so tight.
Your eyes were meant
for looking into mine.
It's almost over,
this mournful play.
Don't even worry;
I'll be okay.
Once again to forget your face,
forget your words.
And at a slow pace,
forget my love.
I'll return to the monotony
of everyday life.
Find someone else
who won't mind my lies.
As I repeat the same mistakes
and reach out for love—once
again.

William M. Russack

A FAVOR, DEATH

Whenever, Death. . .
You choose to fold me in your
welcome arms. . .
Be clever, Death. . .
Do not sedate me with your
many qualms. . .
Just sever, Death. . .
The tangled nets that keep me
from your charms. . .
And never, Death. . .
Let Life praise me with
simulated psalms.

Stella Handley

THE DEVILS LAST SONG

Long ago I planned, in my
passing pride,
that I would reign as King.
Where is Kingdom, where is my
Crown?
In a garden, it was Adam and
Eve I found,
turned their world around.
It will be a bitter song, In the
end
I will sing. I admit! I'll never be
the
worlds everlasting King.
I hoped to conquer both Heaven
and hell.
That's a story, I'll never tell.
When I had Him on a mountain,
pleading to
bow down to me. Only a double
disgrace
did I see. O'er that bridgeless
gulf in
darkness in my chains, forever!
suffering
my sinfull pains. Where are
legions, Where are my hopes?
Hell is below, I have to cope.
You, have lived and died for my
ignoble
cause. I'm the only devil, that
has you in his paws.

Rosemary Whitacre

THE DAY OF NUMBERING

Let us have a day of numbering
Let us make a tag for things
So that nothing shall be lost.
Let us make a tag for time
A scarlet tag, and a net
For the dancing feet of time.
Let us stem the shrill beating of
time
Let us put our hands over her
mouth,
And make her be still.
Let us make a prisoner of time
Let us say that thus is time,
And so is time, and nothing
more.
For each day is distinct and
separate
Frail and sharp as shards of glass
Colored with all the colors of
love.
Let us never be afraid again, nor
run from time
Rather, let us catch time, proud
time,
With banks of silk and ropes of
sand.
For we shall have but one day
more
One day—from the matrix of
forever,
One day more—the day of
numbering.

Richard Poe

A KIND REBUTTAL

Shakespeare said the world's a
stage
Where one assumes an actors
part
I choose to differ with this sage
For life to me is more than art.
I contend there's art to living
A poised approach to every test
That starts by striving, grows by
giving,
Unveils itself whenever
blessed.

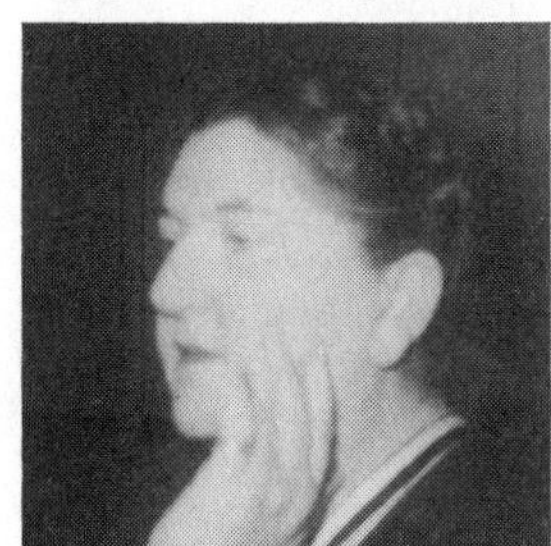

R. Schaeffer Altmann

THE PARLOR STOVE

Dry twigs snapped with delight
While the flames swallowed hot
stars,
Birch logs whistled and piped
creamy smoke
around cast edges.

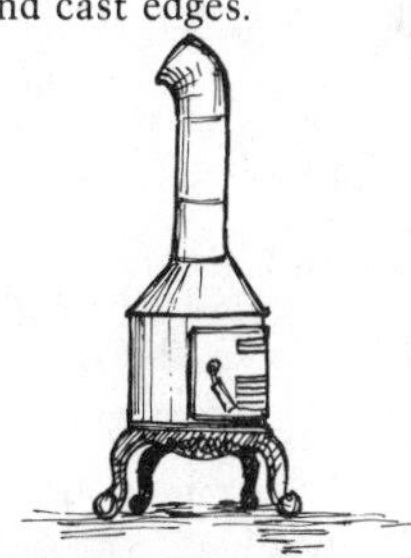

We looked into the little
windows to see
the holiday dance.
As hours passed, the black snow
drifted into
corners.
And it was cold. . .

Leonard John Piazza

THE SEED

These are the secrets of love
that strum upon the strings of
your heart and make the music
play.
You are immersed in the
orchestrated song the sound has
to offer.
It is a giving nature where a
dove echoes the inner most to
the outer.
The bird is a symbol of your
dawning into the spring of your
lifes hopes, dreams and
fullfillment.
You are as a cacoon fullfilling
the prophesy the creator has
given to you.
Before all, your transformation
unveils the eyes of the fearfull,
the unpassionate and the
shadowed.
You are a butterfly beating your
sounds upon the inner workings
of my mind.
You leap, you jump and dance a
dance of a gypsy.
The rubbing of your wings are
the signals of a courtship.
I thirst to hear this passionate
letter which shifts with every
movement you make.
It is an ecstasy to capture this
signal which travels upon the
airways of the wind.
It is but a freedom-song to be
fullfilled with this wine of
merriment.
Your spirit is treasured within
the deepest recesses of my heart.
For what is this heart to you?
But a humbled servant caring
and delivering what you pray at
the alter of your God.
I am but a poor man and my
coffers are filled with spi-ders
webs and dust.
My richness is the goodness,
honesty and integrity I believe
in.
My strength is a battlement of
warriors fighting for the beliefs
of justice.
I tarry not nor do I bend or
break.
I find an abundance of wealth in
your soul which is as boundless
as the sea.
With every tick of time you are
my first embrace and my last.
Every reflection in every stream
is a greater reflection in a larger
river and ocean.
For timeless is this love, and
owing to itself, it is a seed
growing to a more deserving
relationship within.

Virgil Graber

LIFE'S SILVER LINING

In man's zealous pursuit of life,
Life that's fraught with diverse
strife,
He must never pine and
languish;
He must learn to bear its
anguish.
Each cloud has its silver lining
With some sunshine
intertwining;
Life's problems are never so
great,
That they cannot cease or abate.
Even though life has its sorrows,
There will be better tomorrows;
Duress and stress each man can
bear,
If them with others he can
share.
Life has its worries and trouble,
That oft vanish like a bubble;
Man needs zeal to live the good
life,
Despite its connection with
strife.
Man can learn this lesson to
wit,
That has been taught in Holy
Writ;
If to this moral he will listen,
His life with virtue will glisten.

Phyllis M. Zueski

SUNSHINE PREVAILS

Loving Jesus, Saviour devine;
The bible says you are God's
own
it tells how wonderful you
made a way.
Echoes of your love became
well known
because your birth gave us
Christmas day!
Thank you Jesus; thank you for
all
the love you've left upon the
earth
where evidence of love will
stay.
The eastern star shines bright
tonight
and for new miracles I must
pray.
A vigil I'll keep for the answers I
seek;
through the season of lent I'll
endure.
Knowing you freely gave; as
angels
of heaven helped to show the
way;
your kindest love gave us
Easter day!
Loving Jesus; hear my prayer
today-
it's a special one I must share.
This dark, rainy day I've lost
my way
golden-edges on clouds tell us
you care.
I know the sun shines above
somewhere!

Minnie Busby

WHEN THE LIGHT CAME ON

When the light came on again
the day that Jesus Christ was
crucified all the saints gone
before that day arose and were
justified
Many people found the way on
that great and wondrous day
to a life that's everlasting in
the skies
As the light came on there were
those gone on who arose that
day to prove to all the way of
Jesus and his nail scarred
hands
When they laid him in the tomb
up in heaven was a wound in
the heart of God who gave his
dear son our souls to save
Then the night changed into
morn and Jesus friends came
to moan but the angels said
the day had dawned and Jesus
would always be their own
God gave Jesus on the cross to
save the world from loss
Do you know him now today
can you keep him all along the
way
so to others you may say
the light is on Jesus is the way

Moe Cleveland
THE SINGER
(Sincerely, dedicated to BIG PA)
Ashes to ashes and dust to dust..
There just never was enough time for us.
Through various shades of gray
I've loved you - "My Patch Of Blue!".
The lyrics of your sentimental soul --
Softly, they come to comfort me so
Like robust robins returning every Spring
Or rainbows -now- and then, again.
Yet, the bestest rainbow I've ever seen
Happened one Harvestime, long ago.
There it glistened! Oh, how it gleamed
On that tiny drop of sweat
As it trickled down your face at sunset.
So, let them keep saying:
"FORGET THE SINGER!
ALL THAT REALLY MATTERS IS HIS SONG.":
To me, they're obviously dead-wrong!
You see? I can't...it's true.
Oh, no! I shan't forget you, too.

Marguerite Wheeler
WITH GOD AS MY CO—PILOT
With God as my co-pilot,
I can travel far and wide.
With God as my co-pilot,
I can brave the strongest tide.
I need never have a fear,
that I can't do what is right;
because, with God as my co-pilot
the heaviest load is light!
When the days are dark and gray,
remember look to the sky;
and even though there is no sun,
watch - and a bird will fly by!
Even the tiniest of birds can fly,
and never lose their way,
because, with God as their co-pilot
they are guarded every day.
With God as my co-pilot
I can face every day with a smile
because no matter what does happen
GOD IS THERE ALL THE WHILE!

Naomi C. Lusk
TO A THOUGHTFUL FRIEND
Friends like you aren't found every day.
We don't meet many along the way.
Friends who help in time of need;
A friend like that is a friend indeed.
There's nothing for me that you wouldn't do.
I realize this and want to thank you.
How good it is to have such a friend,
And may our friendship never end.
This is my hope today and my prayer,
As I sit here thinking now nice you are.
May God richly bless you for being so sweet,
And I thank him kindly that our paths did meet.
And, please don't forget from day to day,
If I can help you in any way,
Please call on me and let me know,
So my love for you I can also show.
Having you as a friend is truly a pleasure;
You've brought me happiness and joy beyond measure.
Thank you again for all of this;
When I count my blessings, you top the list!

Larry L. Wingate
THE PRETTY BEACH AT BOMBER BAY
(Samae San, Thailand: 1971)
down on the beach at bomber bay
I go to greet the sun and play
some volleyball
perhaps
a man lies cold
in this same light
it tans my face
while his turns white
and overhead another flight
returns to nest at bomber bay
here on the beach the day is new
more time to kill, what else to do
but stroll the shore
perhaps
a man will crawl
I take my walk
the same may scream
I softly talk
and high above another hawk
has left its roost at bomber bay
war is such hell the generals say
yes, even here at bomber bay
many are bored
perhaps
he too just hoped
to pass the day
to see it through
somehow, someway
avoid the planes from bomber bay
up from the beach on which I play
the pretty beach at bomber bay

Richard Newton
A DOG NAMED STAR
Yes, my little friend, we have come a long way, running together through the fields of clover, jumping those bales of hay, the wonderful memories of a boy and his dog at play, are with me to this day.
I can still remember when our friendship began, you were just a furry little ball, no bigger than my hand, I would hold your warm body so close to mine, you were with me

always, yes my partner, even at bedtime, what other name could be more true, than the one Star, I gave to you?
There were many times when I felt alone, that your love, shining like a star was shown, now that once tireless run has slowed to a walk, and you seem to be sleeping a lot, just wanting the patting of your weary head, no Star, you cannot speak, but I know what's trying to be said.
No, old friend, I'll not let you down, in another world together, once more those same fields we'll bound, at my side you'll always be.
Yes, Star, you have become a part of me.

Irene Call
TRUE AND FAITHFUL
Is there no sedative
To ease this awful pain.
I gave my heart forever,
What a trophy I have gained.
I look on and do wonder.
Is ther a place, in this world for the true,
Or a faithful girl.
He admires all the others
The ones that play the cheating game.
In his heart, there is no difference.
They are all the same.
Maybe up in Heaven,
When around God's throne we stand.
The true and faithful
Will find a happiness, all their own.

Kay Dee Russell
I KNOW
As I gaze beyond the stars into that vast, 'somewhere',
Even tho I do not see Him, I know that He is there,
In my helplessness I reach for His guiding hand,
For I am nothing more than a tiny grain of sand.
As in a hurricane wind, I drift so weak,
His love and forgiveness is what I seek,
In this great universe - the space,
I know that God is there, tho I've never seen His face.
A longing to atone is concealed within my heart, for His agonizing pain,
As I see His grieving tear drops fall in a driving rain,
He sees the black stains on my soul, He knows that I have sinned,
How I wish with all my being, my sins I could rescind.
Temptation is so great in this human world of man,
That's why I seek to find, His powerful guiding hand,
I pray He overlooks my faults, tho many they may be,
So I might live with Him, through all eternity.
In His every loving gentle way, I'm sure He hears my plea,
For I hold God within my heart, and carry Him with me,
Although I cannot see Him, I know He's everywhere,
Listening to my every whim, and answering every prayer.
How do I know that God is there,
When talking to Him in my prayers?
For His sacred face I have not seen, tho for it I search and look,
I believe His words of truth, that are written in His Holy Book.

Bonnie L. Ritter
THE GIFTS HE'S GIVEN ME
One night you heard me say
"Some of the best things in life are free."
I wasn't saying what it meant to you -
just appreciating things given to me.
I was referring to your gifts
and the importance that they meant.
Unique, and all different -
even in the way they were sent.
First we enjoyed the Sunset
Over a lake - not even the sea.
But with you, I could imagine
how beautiful that must be!
The sharing added even more
too bad one - can't always be two.
The afterglow was God's, I know
but special for me - 'cause it related to you.
Then you called me "A Friend"
I was disappointed - not romantic, ya know.
But this was a gift too
it means: I accept you, but will still let you grow.
Through you I've seen a deeper understanding
with that - perhaps an emptiness will fill.
In you I've even seen my own thoughts
for all of this - have you ever sent me a bill?
The best to me was a Flower
It didn't cost a dime.
But for me to receive it,
you willingly took the time.
You bent down and picked it

- no one was around.
The value to me, was where it came from
- the heart, not just the ground.
You've given me so many things
And I know my acceptance is rough.
So now I give you - these Special thoughts
a simple "Thank You" just isn't enough.

Betsy McGuire
BOB
I reached for a star
And touched you;
I looked at the moon
And you smiled at me;
I sat in the sun
And felt your warmth;
I walked in the rain
And you washed away
My tears.

Rhonda K. Rasimas
JACK OF ALL TRADES
Jack of all Trades, nothing lost, nothing gained.
Best at nothing, nothing lost, nothing saved.
Knocked myself out, poured in my all, only finding out
not in but one category I could stand tall.
Felt failure and defeat having no professional line of success,
but then realized, thats what differs me from all the rest.
I don't excell in one area, no
outstanding accomplishments
that line a mantel with trophies,
my name does not ring a bell, or
familiar to the house hold word,
no fans flock my side, this lately
began hurting my ego and pride.
Dwelling on this unsettled
feeling, came to mind, this
isn't the correct dealing.
What I believed and thought
was shame, was creating my
own future fate pain.
I began to look at it in another
way, hoping to compensate in
some way.
Not devoting my attention
towards just one thing, has
gifted me with a wider span,
involved in everything.
I've greater horizons before
me by not being obsessed with
just one thought, my directions
vary, my knowledge of a little
this, a little that, gives me
capabilities to achieve better
understanding and knowing of
many facts, and my reflects are
ready to react.
Jack of all Trades ain't so bad,
breaking even with the human
race, I find myself in my own
number one first place.
From young to old, black to
white, some skinny, some
chubby, rich class folk to the
poor, wise and not so wise, have
I crossed paths with though
different fields reflecting, I'm
not so bad, I'm okay and on that
note, I rest my case and can
continue life in a new manner
and way.
Swimming the surf, riding the
waves, up in the saddle,
shooting the rapids in a canoe
with paddle, iceskating to Old
Man Winter, hiking the hills to
and fro, these are all the skills
I bestow. Enough to get by,
enough to be accepted, to be
called upon comes hell or high
water, I can be counted on by all
other.
Jack of all Trades, were not
gypies, or lost strays, we
redeem the balance God hath
made.

Esther I. Zeitlin
MOON—THOUGHTS IN SPRING
I may be stooped
But I still can kneel
And from that posture weed.
The feel of earth
In springtime birth
Is very good indeed.
****
Gulls may soar and 'copters roar
But the fountain whispers still
To little frogs deep in the pool
Beneath my window sill.
****
The scent of horses
The perfume of rose?
Which is it in April
Tickles my nose?

Anna Alberta Craighead Henry
WHAT MOMMIES ARE FOR
First, mommies give you birth or adopt you, whatever the source may be
You're brought into this new earth, for every one to see
Then you are watched carefully till you reach the age of five
Off, to school you go with tears in your eyes
I wanna go with you mommie, I don't wanna stay
You wipe their tears, wipe their nose, with a kiss & a promise
I'll be back to get you today
As your child grows to be big girls and boys
Am I good today? Will I mommie, huh, get a toy
For they know not where it comes from or really could care less
Cause they depend on mommie, to give them the best
As they grow into their teens, it's not dad who gets the
Questions of how, what, when or where
It's always mommie, cause, she is the one who is right there
God Bless you daddy and mommie too, cause your the best
Friend, HONEST I ever knew
When they ask you questions in their shy and sincere way of care
Remember, you were their age once, and asked the same questions
And you mommie shared
Because without you dad & mommie who would we go to to help us with
Our big problems of despair
God is heaven knew you both shared.

Jon D. Tobriner (Jon of Frisco)
LOVE
Feel giant in its move
Gentler on her bosoms tool.
Naturally taught in moments bliss
Everlasting without a twist.
Love to flesh more solid still
Powered of fillies in a windwards sill.
Long it stays and plays in ways
Feeling both the cream and the goats bay.
"Love"

Lolita Marcela Moreno
WHEN I AWOKE
This morning when I awoke,
I made sure not to take this day
as a big joke.
I looked out my window,
and up to the sky.
I closed my eyes
and began to cry.
I prayed to the Lord,
in a special way.
To help me make it
a beautiful day.
I was amazed at the
trees and the birds,
and how it could be
described in very few words.
I thanked my God,
and turned away.
To live my life in a
beautiful way.

Mrs. Evelina La Malfa, Meehan
LUNA MOON
The moon is round
It shines on me

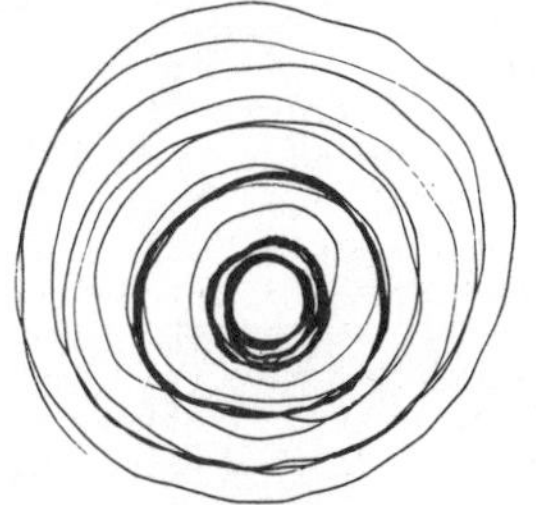

When I am in my bed
It shines all night
But goes to sleep
When I get out of bed

Roemaine Avis
RIDE * RIDE * RIDE
Give to me a horse to ride
far out amid the great divide
to feel the reigns with-in my
grasp
to ride...ride...ride.
To ride o'er desert...plain n' hill
to climb...climb...at his will.
To feel the wind against my face
my hair...blowing out in space.
Let me ride...ride...ride.
What a joy to have him lead the way
to see the valleys...dales...glens
The sky above...the earth beneath
as do his dancing feet do take the mountain trails
to see trees...in all their dress regale
Let me ride...ride...ride.
As homeward bound we make our way
he slows his pace...as if he too enjoyed the race.
The freedom of the open air
back home...his stall awaiting there:
he moves ahead with steadiness
because he knows...that we again
Will ride...ride...ride.

Deborah Lake
SEEDS
Children, so dear, you're windows to our past.
Your eyes remind us of a time, it slipped away so fast.
Children, so honest, you're mirrors for our souls.
Tales of love, tales of hate, in your eyes are clearly told.
Children, so precious, you're gifts of immortality.
Through you we see what's now and what still can be.
Children, so important, our marks upon the future.
Because of you we'll exist where we're now unable to venture.

Stephen Galle
THE ICE—CREAM MAN
Along the street you hear the bells,
and the sound of children as they let out yells.
As the small truck pulls to the side of the street,
you can hear the patter of running feet.
A quarter, a penny, a nickel or dime,
I have chocolate, vanilla, or lemon-lime.
Their smiles shine as bright as a beam,
as they run off licking their ice-cream.

Agnes R. Wendling
MOTHER OAK
Softly, Oh! tread softly please
Beneath my arms, my children sleep
Covered with a soft white blanket, they lie
And this lonely vigil, I must keep.
My arms are empty, my heart grows sad
When I think of the joy they did bring
But I cling to the hope, that once again
My arms will be filled in the Spring.

Steve Fabian
SILHOUETTE DANCER
Breathe freely now, my
silhouette dancer,
Move with grace and precision.
Revoke these strange thoughts,
exhale the swirling gloom.
Dance! Dance, live, and be well,
my beautiful silhouette dancer.

Janet Malinarich
A WHISPER
A whisper is soft, sweet,
It's melodic and in tune.
Gentle and knowing,
Telling me quietly,
The words I want to hear.

Beverlee J. Shafer
MY SISTER
You kneel on narrow bones
to tend a garden grown wild
on hills, in haunted patched;
moving a scythe tongue
smoothly over the pointed
speech of grass and shaping
earth in small circles, shells to
hold a sea of seeds for your
world of summer fiction.
With your hand against the
light you watch brief butterflies
tilt wings to wind, skim
shadows in the span of sun.

Arlene Di Rocco
FIRESTONE
When you bow your head before
me
Like a knight before his queen
I am lost.
Love bursts through my
fingertips
Igniting you
And we are consumed.
Flames brush your lips
And settle in your eyes.
Smoldering looks
Tumble out of the ashes
Deliciously warming me.
I hug the warmth
Through endless nights,
Repeating,
I am loved,
I am loved.

Betty Ann Bilbrey
HOUSEWIFE
A housewife is a high calling;
To be mothers and tend the
home,
To be a wife to one man
Is the greatest thing in the land.
A housewife meets many a
demand
To fill the needs of those
around;
Her family ranks the very best;
To her they are her honored
guests.
To make a home a nice place to
be
Makes a housewife happy, you
see;
Their lot is trying and tiring,
too;
For housewives always have
work to do.
There are quiet and peaceful
times
That a housewife finds;
To appreciate the beauties of
this life
Does make this housewife a
happy wife.

Phillip O. Hebert
THE OLD MAN AND THE SEA
I stand at the helm of this dusty
old ship
riding the waves up and down as
they dip.
Standing with the north wind to
my face
staring out to sea its such a
beautiful place.
I am an old man who lives by
the stars
with a long gray beard and age
old scars.
Time stands still when you set
to sea
what you see and hear may not
really be.
There are voices, moans and
ghostships at sea
but unsurprisingly enough they
are not new to me.
I take a shot of brandy and lie
on my cot
and thank the good lord for
what I have got.
Undoubtly the lord has been
kind to me
for letting me live my life by
the sea.

Clayton E. Morse
RETURN VOYAGE HOME
Some people think of places far
and strange,
and envy the poor seaman
who roams upon this range.
They never stop to think, their
minds eternally roam,
But the seaman thinks of just
one trip;
The return voyage home.

Vikki Sutphin
VIEWS FROM A SINGLE PARENT
My voice is crying in the
wilderness
I fear once again I will be
alone
Then I see my child with such
lovingness
And in reality I know what is
shown.
I as a child had a wonderful
mom and dad
I am supremely grateful for
what I had;
Parents to guide and direct me
Deprived, my child has no such
key!
Even though inflation and
divorce
Through pride and strength I
found a course;
To continue the dignity of
raising a child
On one's best ability, so let it
be filed.
I wish for single parents, the
gift of self-assurance
The gift of feeling worthy,
beautiful and important;
To have the courage to keep on
with tolerance
And those who desperately need
contentment.
So many are too bewildered or
proud to ask
On challenging times when
holidays come so fast;
The depressing reminders of
happier days
They need a friend, wouldn't
you say?
I wish parents the ability to
help a child understand
That discipline and punishment
exist to help lend a hand;
Not because we as parents feel
powerful or mean
But to guide a youngster to
grow as we have seen.
I wish for the child, a parent
wo listens and hears
One who knows what they say
that's not put into words;
A child who is loved, respected
and wanted—no tears
Of their frightened, alone,
single parent with fears.
I have overcome my loneliness
time and time again
I've suffered all the anger, panic
and hurt you'd expect;
I feel at times I've aged 100
years, but then
I again take control and have
gained my self-respect!
I've struggled over the years
to pick up the pieces in life
Abandoned by a husband and
other romances, still stems. . .
An immaturity on my part to
never become another wife
But more important than that, I
must win back my self-
esteem.

Alice M. Smith
A MOTHER'S PRAYER
Dear God, I thank you for the
son that you have given me
And for your son who's blood
was shed upon a tree
Make me worthy of this fine lad
the finest gift I've ever had
Whose life is placed within my
hand
Give me strength, give me
courage,
Strength to look beyond each
worry
Never let me go astray
Send your comfort day by day
Never take away the lad
The finest gift I've ever had.

Sandra Thornberry Steers
GROWING PAINS
Relax and grow; it feels real
nice.
The water only looks like ice.
But jump right in for yourself to
see
Just how refreshing it can be.
The water is warm and the
current slow;
And there are only a couple of
rules to know.
There is no need to learn to
swim;
But if you flounder, the result is
grim.
Relax and float and be carried
along
To hear and enjoy life's sweet
song.
Lay back and you'll see the big
blue sky.
Fighting just gets you a splash
in the eye.
Paths can be chosen as the
drifting pursues
And unexplored streams come
into view.
But you'll run aground unable to
function,
If you alter a course where there
is not a junction.
You will meet others floating
by.
And you may give each one a
try.
The time with some will be
quite long;
But most will be quick as they
came be gone.
To those who stay, please be
kind.
Don't try to put them in a bind.
They drift their own path to the
last
And if you are splashing, will be
gone fast.

Jean Knox
EVENING STAR
Evening star sleeping alone in
the Western sky,
Peer o'er the rim of the
slumbering past.
Tell us why striving men work,
and defeated cry?
What is accomplished that will
last?
Evening star weeping alone in
the Western sky,
Peer o'er the rim of the far
distant future.
Tell us why men live, and love,
and weary, die?
Why do you weep so, when all
is secure?
Evening star creeping alone in
the Western sky,
Dry your pearl tears and twinkle
away.
Dusk turns to night, so hold
your brilliance high,
Throughout eternity,...laugh and
be gay!

Mrs. Ronnie Grant
NOW I AM MY OWN ME
The time has come to write
again.
I have so much to say.
I want to tell you how I feel;
This is the time and day.
I have so many treasures;
Locked in this heart of mine.
So many beautiful emotions;
To last a life time.
You gave me much to deal with;
Made each waking day
worthwhile.
Each time I was ready to give
up;
I heard you say "SMILE".
Like the unknown that captures
the imagination;
And tries, but does not set you
free.
You taught me HOPE and
TRUST and FAITH;
And now I am my own ME.

Sara Woolner
DRUNKEN FOOLS
I met him at a party and he
looked fine,
I asked him his name and he
asked me mine.
Then we sat down at a table and
had a few beers,
After awhile there was no longer

any fears.
We were sitting close and
holding onto hands,
When I looked on the table
there was all empty cans.
We stood up together and
stumbled up the stairs,
When I turned around he was
no longer there.
After the party I saw him a few
times,
Thoughts ran through my head
like wedding chimes.
I saw him a few days later with
another girl thinking he was
real cool,
But this comes to prove that we
were Drunken Fools.

Susan D. Willett
UNTITLED
Make me a part of your life
In your thoughts and plans
Keep me close to you
Forever in your presence
Realize I have feelings also
Feel for me as I do you
Make me happy when I'm with
you
Accept me as I am
Give me time to be me
Eventually I'll love you

Mildred Guthrie Little
ADORATION
You are an inspiration -
You are a warm embrace;
You are a breath of hope
That fills an empty space.
You are a fervent lure -
Your are a sweet desire;
You are a passion-net
That lights a flaming fire.
You are a secret dream -
You are a fantasy;
You are a soft refrain
That calmly beckons me.

Adolphus M. Avery
LITTLE MOTHER OF DOLLS
Little mother of dolls playing in
the sun,
I think your game of life is just
begun.
Out of this void you came to
grace this sphere;
Had it not been for you I would
not be this sear.
Into this realm of earthly night,
You bring a ray of pure celestial
light.
You show a mother's tender care
In the way you comb your little
one's hair.
You too may earn a place in the
sun
For the way you care for your
little one.
For anyone with eyes can see
You are a pattern for eternity to
be.
Let the portals of destiny open
wide
For here stands a future mother
at your side.

Jeannine Luke
TRIBUT TO MOTHERS
There's no one so dear as a
mother,
To Trust, to love and obey,
To guide you through your
growing years,
And teach you how to pray.
All your childhood moments
Are filled with thoughts of her,
A guardian angel, who seems to
know
Every time you stir.
From the time you're born 'til
you leave,
She watches with tender care,
Every move, while every dream
And every thought she'll share.
And her heart is with you still,
When you go to make your way,
For you're still her precious
baby,
Even when your hair is grey.

Christopher A. Hebert
(aka Gideon Cade)
WHERE HAVE YOU GONE?
Where have you gone?
On a Sunday afternoon
With the trees turning
Crimson, gold and orange?
What have you seen?
The hawks of autumn
Soaring through the sky
Circling, flying effortlessly?
What have you done?
Sat in a wood to feed the
squirrels?
Run with the wind as though he
were your brother?
Rested on a hill to catch the
last of summer's warmth?
Where have you gone?

Martha Leaming Kinkead
UNTITLED
sometimes i feel so tired and old
and shamed
all dirtied by my doings
my heart is cracked and sore
like the knuckles
on a time-worn
washerwoman's hands

Roger L. Vance
FORGOTTEN
The tombstones stand silent and
gray
Waiting and watching for
coming day.
Trees stand bare in the moonlit
night,
They seem to be waiting for me
to take flight.
Soon, I too, will sleep beneath
this sod;
The lonely paths I'll no longer
trod.
People may wonder how I fare
But in ten years, will they
really care?

Ronald Joseph Flemming, Jr.
LONG SANDY BEACHES
The "Coolness" of the "Air"
penetrates deep into my skin
Slowly, it passes through "My
Body" so "Fragile and Thin"
Taking "My Soul" to the
"Haunted Houses" of
"Yesterday"
Telling "Tomorrow's Secrets"
and then slipping away...
All the "Many Wonders" that
lay heaped in "Spoils"
Tell all the "Same Stories" of
"Man's Many Toils"
All the "Beauty" man searches
for in his "Art"
Tells of the "Sorrow and Joy"
carried in "Every Heart"...
The "Mighty Sea" heeds the
"Wisdom" of it's "Tides"
Yet "Mortal Men" try to conceal
what they may not hide
For in all the "Heavens" and the
"Stars Above"
We fail to see, the "Greatest
Gift" of "Man," is "Love"...

Mary Ellen Dietz
GOODBYE
I sit near the window and feel
the warm tears streaming
from my eyes
My thoughts of you bring both
happiness and pain
I feel a burning flame tearing
inside me

You're with her and I am alone
If only fate were fair you'd be
with me now
You know how much I love and
care for you
Yet still you turn to her
My mind begins to fade
Moments of the past begin a
path through my
subconscious

And I wait
The visions that I see are hazy
and they begin to cloud
If only you knew how right it
all would be
She's only part of a moment
then she'll go
I am forever
The sun falls and darkness
settles around but also within
I am sleepy
I can hardly keep my mind
aware
But I don't deserve to sleep
If you don't want me what good
am I

You are my life
The pounding starts
Pushing and pushing with every
heartbeat
It seems my mind will fall
beneath the pressure
I close my eyes and peace...

Tammy Winsett
UNCONFINED
Set no limited value on my man,
or the love we both share
each day.
Both mean everything in the
world to me, neither one could
ever be replaced in anyway.
Place no artificial boundaries
around my love for it is as
endless as all eternity.
Please don't ask me to be careful
of how much I love him, or ask
me to restrict the way I feel,
being able to experience
emotions to the fullest is to
know life when it is true and so
real.
Allow me to risk my future in
his gentle hands, I trust giving
my love to him, only a woman
so deeply in love can give such
a man.

In return I will value his future
as greatly as I choose.
Let me be free to live as high
as I desire, for I have joy to
gain and nothing to loose.

Jack Lyons
TRAVELING COMPANION
Traveling around the world with
you-
You know it's great to have you
near
B'cause when you're beside me,
There's nothing that I fear.
Love's what gives me the reason-
A reason to believe what life is
about;
But friendship binds us together
Whenever there is doubt.
It's not often I feel this way,
It might as well be the first.
At least I know the friendship is
true.
Should I still wonder why you
do?
Writing melodies of love and
desire,
Looking for a rhyme.
Looking for what may make me
happy
But will I find it in time?

Sonja L. Darling
CELESTIAL VIEW
Stars
Are not really stars
By sight,
They are holes in the sky
At night.
With angels peekng through
To see if things are right.
And the moon
Is not really the moon
You see,
That's Gods' eye
Looking over me.

Maria Elena Pacheco de Garcia
BECAUSE OF YOU
Because of you,
love has a special meaning
you brighten my day in the
morning,
when I see you by my side...
If you are away,
I think of you every minute
and can't see the magic hour,
when you come home every
night.
Because of you,
I feel the same old emotion
the same old warm inspiration,
falling in love can bring...
You are my world,
my dreams, my hopes, my
reality,
my yesterday, my tomorrow,
and my song of love, in spring.

Ralph Engquist, Jr.

TO JOE

I know that its been hard for you
To live, or just exist at times,
Too many suns have lost their warmth,
Tomorrows never come,
You've wondered if its worth the pain
More times than you can even count,
You've had to cut new paths in forests
That few men ever trod,
And still you search the heavens for;
A guiding star to lead you home,
A harbour light to steer your ship,
An answer to lifes poem.

Jose V. Gragasin, Ph.D., D.H.

THE GREATNESS OF THE AMERICAN PEOPLE

(Dedicated to the Americans as a Nation)

American greatness refers to the marks of excellence,
The grand temple of rare achievements. . .
The noble thoughts, words, and deeds,
The goodness, truth, undying justice,
The virtues and other verities.
American greatness is found in the apex of human perfection,
In the crown ring deemed best in creation,
And can take any shape, any form,
From the lowly hut, the gilded throne,
Owned by none, but opened to all.
American greatness can be found on the top or at the base,
At the middle, or somewhere else,
Through the heart or by the head,
On the spiritual or material,
In ideas, principles and ideals.
American greatness is likewise found in edifice of enduring task,
In work sublime that lasts,
In grandiose form, more on the substance,
In the luminous flashes of beauteous Wisdom,
In testimony of man's ingenuity.
American greatness also appears in height to be reached,
In a challenge to be met,
In a monument to be built,
In the depth to be fathomed,
In battle to be won.
American greatness appears in a mission to be carried,
In a sacrifice to be borne,
In the quality to be possessed,
In a flag to be hoisted,
In a space to be conquered.
American greatness is a guarded trust to be passed on,
It is an ideal to be enblazoned,
A journey to be covered,
A martyrdom to be suffered,
A martyrdom to be endured.
American greatness is mapped out by foresight,
It is a destiny to be attained,
A frontier to be opened,
Efforts to be released,
A goal finally achieved.
American greatness appears in the thinker's mighty prowess,
In the philosopher's incisiveness,
In the poet's lyric masterpiece,
In the benevolence of the humanist,
In the jurist sublime reaches.
American greatness also appears in the courageous faith of American leadership,
In the vision of statesmenship,
In the sturdiness of a striving race,
In the nation's industry, moral prowess,
In a nation's fortitude and creativeness.
American greatness is further shown in the American educator's missionary zeal,
In the inventiveness of the scientist,
In the productive genius of the industrialist,
In the crusading spirit of the moralist. . .
All of these are master keys to real American greatness!
American greatness is shown in the composer's exquisite music,
In the sculptor's monumental works,
In the orator's moving eloquence,
In the painter's pictorial elegance. . .
This is greatness in its substance!
Where public servants offer their best,
In efficient, honest service,
Where labor cooperates,
With management in mutual give-and-take. . .
Here is Greatness knocking at the gate!
Where law and order are respected,
Authorities rightly obeyed;
Where people remain supreme,
The source of power, real sovereign. . .
This is American Greatness no one deniest!
In the American youth's dynamic vision,
Infinite in its dimension;
In the vigilance of citizenry,
for freedom and liberty for the pursuit of happiness,
Here is Greatness marching to glory!
Fidelity to a nation's past,
A bounder duty and sacred trust,
Enriching the glory that was,
Is a people's continuing must. . .
This is Greatness' beckoning flash!
So is in the gallantry of American soldiers,
Heroic defense of their country,
Magnanimity in victory,
Peace-making diplomacy. . .
This is American Greatness for humanity!
American greatness is earned in the guardianship of liberty,
Best heritage with dignity,
Its safe transmittal to posterity,
Lies the beauty of this legacy;
American Greatness glorious destiny!

If American greatness is based on a verity;
Greatness is immortality,
Like the Rock of Ages shall ever stay,
Across the years through Infinity,
In deathless continuity!!!

D. Joseph Mihalik

INSIGHT

It could be fury
for those who feel their way around
but then, it must be pain.
I can sit here and see
mountains passing by but
does he really sit in pain?
How much does he want
to catch a glimpse of what I'd call always.
I sleep to rest my eyes,
I wonder,
does he really have to sleep?
I'll never be anything more than who I am,
I'll never curse the lens.
He will be better than who he is,- adapted,
but he will miss the parade,
the fireworks, the clowns.
I'll never wish I was blind!

Janis Hall

MOTHER

A millionaire of helpful hints
When children need a guiding light,
Or music sung so soft and sweet
To calm a restless child at night.
Organized beyond belief
When things seem nothing less than wild
To do, and make, and just make do,
But always time to hear a child.
Temptation when a child falls
To run and nurse her wounded pup,
But tastefulness to save a blush
And let her wiser child get up.
Honor inborn in her soul
To teach a child to walk on by,
With straightened back and shiny shoes,
Or troubled, but with head held high.
Experience of yesteryears
When life was different from today,
But expertise in newer things
To lead a child the safest way.
Respect for independance
When her child is on his own,
But regret for country mileage
When her baby isn't home.
These talents of a Mother's Love
Are shown through every day,
Through child's debut from her womb,
And when he's moved away.
When loved pets die, or special friends
The soul and love drift up above,
But life holds one small pot of gold,
Forever is a Mother's Love.

Gloria Jean Daily

DREAMERS SEE GOD

Sparkling stars and dazzling moonbeams
In a black velvet night
Fragrances of spring and soft cool breezes
A wondrous, beautiful sight
A full mellow moon, that spells magic
GOD'S soft light in the sky
As stars form graceful, perfect patterns
As they twinkle and smile on high
Dreamers come out on a night like this
To view GOD'S magic night
Drinking in the wonder of GOD'S creation
Dreamers see GOD in the night

Davida Brouhard

SNOWFLAKES

See on this wintery day how
softly the snowflakes fall
upon the earth
causing cries of joy and mirth..
See how silently they fall upon
a crumbling old stone wall
where they lay like a mat so
soft and white
to this observer's delight.
See how they spread
across the land
Like a silver mantel untouched
by human hand.
So still they lie
until a frisky wind comes
sailing by
bringing much ill will
to the little snowflakes that
had laid so soft and still

Calvin D. Spurgin

TWO PEOPLE

For Dan and Sue

Two people
starting off as friends
never knowing where it ends
together they go down lifes way
their love grows stronger
every day
their lives entwined
become as one
shining brighter
than the sun
for each other
they will live
giving
all there is to give

Helen King Thornton

HEIRLOOM'S

Of Fame and riches in This world, I can make claim to none.

Fate has decreed my destiny to
be a humble one. Still, I
possess some precious
heirloom's. Did I hear you ask
their worth?
Ah! I would not sell my
heirloom's for all the wealth
on earth.
For my heirloom's are my
Jewels; my Jewel case is my
heart.
There is not one of my prized
gems from which I'd ever part.
So, if I've piqued your curiosity,
pray, listen to my tale, and,
each of my prized heirloom's, for
you I shall unveil.
My granddaughter is my onyx;
Her black eye's glow
Like pearl. She's one of my
prized heirloom's, my beloved
Jamie— Girl.
My grandson, Brent is my agate,
His eyes are sapphire blue.
He's the newest of my
heirloom's and a Jewel
through and through.
My grandson, Michael's my
emerald, his eyes are crystal
green.
His mind is like a diamond,
clear and sharp and clean.
My grandson, Seth is my cameo,
my most treasured sardonyx
boy.
He's enriched my life with
untold wealth of endless love
and joy.
My mother is named for the
ruby. Ah! what a precious
gem.
How blessed I am to have her
still, her love's a diadem, a
crown of Jewels no money can
buy;
no wealth on earth can compare.
No money on this universe can
buy a Mother's love and care.
My husband is my gold coin, his
strength of heart a treasure.
My two sons are my silver bar's,
they're sterling beyond
measure.
My son's wives are my garnets
for they've made my sons
content,
The garnet's warm and steady
glow of love to them they've
lent.
And—I have still other treasures
I cannot leave untold.
My grandsires and my
grandmeres now trod on
streets of gold.
A father and two brothers also
dwell within that land, whose
walls are lined with jasper and
where choirs are angels—
bands.

Dean Hunter

WHERE ARE YOU JANIS, JOHN, AND JAMES?

Where are you Janis, John and
James,
sometimes I can hardly
remember your names,
or the lines you sang, the music
was so good,
it seems then I understood, but-
somewhere, I lost the words and
now I cannot find them.
It wasn't long ago, before we let
you go,
that causes seemed so important,
war and peace, civil rights,
humanity, marching, music,
seemed to fill my life, feed my
soul,
give me purpose, make me
whole.
Somehow my memory isn't quite
as clear,
I quietly sit to listen,
straining somehow to hear,
a few of the notes,
a melody or two, some of the
words you sang.
Yet now they aren't too clear,
the melody, the words,
all important then, somehow
don't blend
with what's happening now.
So now I am prone to wonder,
often dream, sometimes ponder,
what differnece it could make,
none I guess, so I'll just sit and
dream,
and wonder...where are you
Janis, John and James.

Paul M. Poldergotch

ALONE

I looked into her soft brown
eyes
For the first time; they spoke to
me (and openly)
They told me that for a short
while
I would no longer be alone.
She gazed into mine and
They merged as if into one.
I shut my lids tightly
As if to prevent her escape and
Letting the softness of her
cheek brush mine
I nestled my lips upon the
warmth of her nape.
And protected by her soft
brown hair
I whispered the birth of fresh
new words,
With each taking flight to her
ear.
As the night went by, the closer
we became
Until at last we were one and
the same.
Upon the break of a new dawn,
I opened my eyes and...
She had left their gates,
As the shadows had left their
earth.
The closeness of her being had
left its home...
And once again. I feel alone.

Bettie L. Wilson Grimes

HAPPY BIRTHDAY MOTHER

Today is a very special day—
A new life had started it's way—
It was more years than it
seems—
Because of the many beautiful
dreams—
There were days of laughter &
joy—
Sure there were days of tears—
But our love grew stronger
still—
As together we strolled thru the
years—

Yes, Mother, this your special
day—
You loved me in every way—
You deserve the honor, don't
you see—
Because this is the day you
gave birth to me—
(Memory of Ethel L. Green 1980)

Freda Holmes

A WALK WITH GOD

Oh blessed morning of the
dawning how lovely when you
can walk by the wayside with
your god. you can see his smile
in the flowers. you can hear him
in the song of the birds. the coo
of a dove on a high hill. you can
hear his whisper in the wind. as
he brought birth to a new day.
He touches your soul with the
ray of the warm sun. To walk
with your God in the hour of
the dawning. My eyes have seen
great love in his world that is so
peaceful.

William K. O'Brien

DREAMS OF KATHLEEN

As I recall the moonlit nights
of warm fragrance and rustling
grass where a thousand
ambrosial airs caressed my face,
I see again the moon-iced stream
of darker banks and silver crests.
I sat there tumbling dirt clods
watching the clay wash and bleed
among the metallic main stream:
In and about the further bank
your rustling white ruffled skirt
danced as the wind of my wish
bared your glowing thighs.
I leapt amidst the wind
to your further bank
and sat to feel your soft hair
soothing my chilly neck.
You wrapped your silken arm
about my burly waist
and the fingers of my hand
felt your tiny soft face.

George Mossop

EXPECTATIONS AND NEGOTIATIONS

We could have been happy - you
said at last.
If who had done what? - I ask;
If I did what?
And if you did what?
Instead of what's already passed.
We're neither martyr nor misers,
you and I,
And cannot attain to all
expectations;
To discover these, we must
confer
With a view to agreement,
and each must ask -
What can I do for you?
And what can you do for me?
Both of these questions need to
be put
By each, to the other,
And replied to by each, for
answers that last.

Alisa J. Sorenson

LOVE

Love is the greatest gift God
gave us.
Let us not waste it while hating.
If everyone loved everybody else
the world would be a better
place for living.
As it has been said what the
world needs
is love sweet love of all beings.
Jesus came to give us love
and teach us to love one
another.
This was his greatest lesson
for all nations forever.
Let us not forget his love
in the midst of war.

Gary D. "Bone" Potter

TIME

outside of my window
I see a parking lot
three houses
a smoking chimney
I know because I used to
see what it was like
from the other three
I'm twenty now and
running free
I wonder if it will
change before I'm twenty
three
accidents used to happen
and I'd run to the other
three yelling and screaming
Help me! Help me!
I'm thirty and now I can
see this place is changing
right in front of me
I'm fifty now and can barely see
that times have changed and
gone ahead of me
as I got older I could see
that this place REVOLVED
AROUND ME!
Now I'm ninety one and all
alone
My next stop is the Funeral
Home.

Flora Dailey

TOMORROW

Tomorrow !!
What an optimistic word !
Not like next week or next year,
Or even today or tonight.
Tomorrow means:
A new day,
A new dawn,
A new light,
Sunrise, sparkling dew,
On grass, trees and roses,
A word that imposes,
As no other word can do
Hope of a wish come true,
Of a promise of right over
might,
So no one needs to fear.
Come what may,
Tomorrow means another day.

Heather Ren'ee Davis

UNTITLED

The pain you have to go
through when you want
something so bad and that
dream is so far away.
You want that something. . .
You need that something. . .
You get closer and closer to that
something everyday.
When you get one step away
from it, it sinks, slips right
through your fingers.
It makes all your dreams seem
dreamless. . .
And life of all seem lifeless.

Helen Little

WHO AM I

I'm a jingle bell heart
I'm as happy as a bird in a tree
I'm as free as the wind
Because I haven't just one place
to be
I'm a cloud in the sky
I'm a river flowing wide
I'm the rustle of a breeze
I'm a little girl for a ride
I'm a mountain towering high
A wave upon the sea
I'm my rainbow in my sky
A mother with a child upon my
knee
I'm a snowflake falling
A raindrop on a window pane
I'm a soft breeze blowing
Orange autumn leaves falling in
the lane
I'm the brook that keeps on
babbling
In the theater, I'm the whisper
still
I'm the meadowlark still singing
And the conqueror on the hill
I'm a church bell ringing
I'm a story being told
A poem long ago written
Now I'm really getting bold
Now I'm a picture being painted
I'm a baby's gentle cry
I'm a whisper in an ear
I'm a wonder! Now you know
why

Florence E. R. Foster

ENJOYING SPRING

When I was young,...and growing
wild,...
Like the meadow-flowers,...a
restless child,
I loved to roam through the
fields,...
And hear Spring's returning
birds' cries,...
And romp about, in the morning
air,...chasing butterflies;...
Or drink a cupped handful of
water from the bubbling
brook;...
And I'd devour all Nature's
secrets where ever I looked.
I loved to feel my long hair
blowing in the cool, soft
breeze,...
And look for birds' nests in the
newly greened trees.
I'd gather dandelions, daisies,
and buttercups, too,...
And bring them back to the
house,...and say,
"Here, Mom,..I picked these for
you".
I so delighted in Springtime;...I
loved to see things growing.
There was such peace in my
soul...just in knowing
That Spring's loveliness touched
me, to the depths of my soul;...
And I stored away memories,...a
wealth untold.
Now, I reach back to those days
when I was a child,...
And I find such contentment in
remembering Spring...
and me...growing wild.

Noralee

IMMORTALITY

There is a certain vision of
Immortality
To life
Although my body will be dust
(What an infinetely minute
speck of dust, as equated with
all the dusts there be!)
Can i console myself
By contending
i will no longer be a possession?
Nor will i possess
i cannot take this body
With me
(Who would want a house
subject to decay?)
life IS eternal
And IMMORTALITY is ours
Yet we cling to fading illusion
placing importance and greed
upon the sun ripened fruit
rather than the sun itself.

Avis Bates Starcher

HELP ME, LORD

Lord, help me to be what you
want me to be.
Help me to learn what you want
me to learn.
Help me to see what you want
me to see.
Help me to repent, sins bridges
to burn.
Help me to say what you want
me to say.
Lord, help me to help others,
too;
As You walk beside me day after
day.
Help me to do what you want
me to do.
A men

Katheryn McCall Noblitt

RENEWAL

Just a weary day this was at
first:
With so much lost, what was
there left to me?
So many hopes were gone
eternally -
And so at times it seemed my
heart would burst!
Oh, my heart would tend to lose
all hope:
The very sun dim to unseeing
eyes;
The blue of heaven hidden in
grey skies;
And only in deep shadow could
I grope.
But then: As I looked out to
barren earth,
I caught a glimpse of something
like pure gold:
A yellow crocus where had lain
the cold -
And that is when my spirit felt
rebirth!
As fragile flower dared to shine
where snow had lain,
My heart has found the strength
to hope and live again!

Kay Proctor

FALL OF THE SEASON

The old man lays back
in the fall of the season
as he looks all about him
he knows not the reason.
Why leaves turn color
grass dies on the ground,
a gloomy time of year
with overcast all around.
The old man lays back
a frost in the air,
he dreams of his past
and wonders who cares.
He thinks of his life
the years gone by
the good times and bad
and takes a big sigh.
The old man lays back
in the fall of the season
and silently drifts off
no-one knows the reason.
The wind starts to blow
it rains a cold tear,
for people forgot
the old man was here.
I gaze at the sky
in the fall of the season
and softly whisper
what is the reason.
I love you old man
I say to the air
don't ever forget
there's people who care.
Don't tell the old man
after he's gone
let him know now
and hope he lives long.

D. Proska

LOOK BENEATH THE WATERS

The depth of "Man"
is like the waters
of the sea. . .
The currents tug at his
inner most feelings—
stirring them about. . .

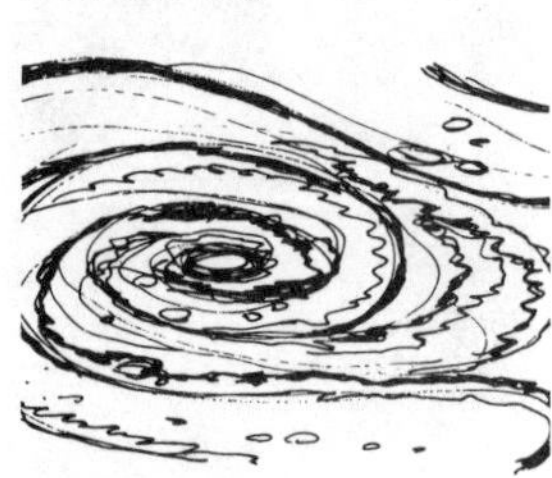

The waves rush in—
covering his sands
of thought. . .
Rest lovingly upon the sands
and the waves
will brush gently
against your body.

Alice-Larder-Fletcher

TO—MORROW

Rejoice and be glad ye children
of men,
Your blessed Redeemer is
coming again.
Not as a Babe, in a manger stall,
But mighty to save and rule
over all.
He Who offered Himself to die
in our stead
Then arose from that tomb for
the helpless dead,
Proving His Mastery o'er Satan
and sin,
He it is Who is coming again.
'Tis not for us the day or hour
to foresee,
But always ready to depart must
we be;
Neither look we for that
"man of sin,"
Nor a priestly "prophet"
revealed as kin.
To those who look for Jesus, it
was not said in mirth:
"I will keep thee from the
temptation
that shall come upon the earth."
A chamber in the Heavens shall
be opened to receive you.
Therefore rejoice! Be faithful
and true!
As problems grow greater and
troubles accrue,
Faint not, nor fear, a new body,
new life,
All these have been promised to
you.
In 1917, the gates of an ancient
city swung wide,
Not a volley was fired; none
bled or died.
As a bird flying, was victory
attained;
Yet love, peace and
righteousness hath not
reigned.
One answer remains, one prayer
for us all,
"Lord Jesus, come! Wipe out the
fruit of our fall!"

Lori "Annette" Robertson

WHY UNDERSTAND?

Why must your mother
understand that you
like to go up to your
room without any demand
and up she comes and knocks
with her hand, tell me,
Why Understand?
Why understand that people
must die?
Why can't we let our loved
ones part and not
even cry?
Why understand that we
feel another human
beings pain? We feel the
agony with them and
go through the strain.
Why understand that
children must leave
the nest? To go out into
Life and do their
best.
Why understand you love
someone terribly so?
Must the world have an
understanding of
everything that grows?
Why understand the

things that can
kill us? Why must we
think of the negative
instead of the plus?
Why understand? Does
that question seem
fair? Will anyone listen?
Will anyone care?

M. Nadine Walls Bailey

GONE THE CHILD

I would like to walk thru' the
dandelions once more.
I would like to walk thru' the
fields and smell their fragrance
as before.
The sun hot -- beating down on
my head -- the breezes blowing,
as through the grass I tread.
Oh, I'd love to wander those
fields again and feel once more
so free!
Where went that little child --
that little child in me?

Kirstin Raubitschek

UNTITLED

manderine kisses
under burnt orange skies
September embraces
cry
for autumn love affairs
Tangerine solaces
celebrate apricot
fantasies
and the cinnamon circus
made me forget
my
Valentine yesterday

Beulah W. Church

MY SWEET MEMORIES OF TUFFY A MINIATURE SILVER POODLE

Tuffy, my days dawn sad, empty,
lonely and blue
And all day long I'm thinking of
you
The joy of your love I shall
never forget
For you were my sweet darling
little pet
I am proud to have been your
true loving owner
It must have been hard on you
as a loner
With all the love you needed to
share
and nothing around you, but
pigs who could care
You were left with them to live,
before you were mine
And I gave you a home at just
the right time
You were always with me
whenever I felt low
At home I would stay if you
couldn't go
The pitter-patter of your tiny
little feet
Was always behind me until we
went to sleep
When each night I would tuck
you into our bed
Then Bobby would pet your
sweet little head
When your health begin to get
worse and worse
I was happy to be your ever
loving nurse
Your eyes never missed a move
that I made
While too sick to follow, behind
you just stayed
The joy of your love on this
earth is all over
And at night, oh how I miss you
to spread with the cover
My other pets try to make up
for your loss
Not daring to do this when you
were the boss
Its, so sad to watch them
looking for you
Their looks seem to say oh-what
can we do
I gave you nothing but tender
loving care
For the six wonderful years we
both had to share
While by your side both day
and night
I would sit
And thinking Oh God is this
going to be it
Your human friends came to pay
their respect
While your animal friends knew
not what to expect
Tuffy, my heart knows nothing
but regret
For a love for you I shall never
forget
Oh Angel I tried to give you the
best
Please know this my darling
while you are at rest
If, sweet little dogs to Heaven
go
You are sitting by Gods side
wanting to know
If when I'm called, can we be
together again
And take up where it came to
an end.

Christina Conway

THE ENDING OF SORROW

Beyond the days withering tides
When moon beams cast
dimensions aside,
A loved ones whisper comes to
you.
For separate lives
are lived as two-
when together we are one.
Release the soul that matches
mine
So we may walk
again in time.
Let's make the past
a new tomorrow-
With renewed love
void of sorrow.

Millie Hughes

THERE'S A LITTLE OF GOD'S SUNSHINE IN THE RAIN

There's a little of God's
Sunshine in the rain,
There's a little of God's
Sunshine we must gain.
Every raindrop has some sun,
And 'till all the rain is done,
There's a little of God's
Sunshine in the rain.
Every few drops have some
more, until sunshine is the
score,
There's a little of God's
Sunshine in the rain.
When we all meet 'way up there,
we will find rain is pure and
fair;
There's a little of God's
Sunshine in the rain.

Evelyn Clare

A TOAST TO YOU

If I could only take the sky
With stars across her brow,
And pluck a dew-filled fragrant
rose
That bonds in graceful bow;
If I could gather in my arms
The evening sun of gold,
And fill my pockets deep with
grass
That smells of earth-born mold;
If I could lift the winding road
That stirs the curious hearts,
And slip my hands deep into
snow
Whose cooling breath imparts;
If I could capture in my palm
Sweet laughter flown from lips,
And on a tender-fingered sheaf
Catch tears of morning mists;
If I could acquire all these
things
I know what I would do,
Just mix them well into my glass
And toast my love to you.

Connie Williams

MY GRANDMA GENDREAU

If I could speak my words would
be

I love you grandma dear
The love you gave me grandma
Will last me through the years
I am your little devil
I am your pride and joy
So please remember grandma
I'm just your little boy

Lona Fox

OLD SOLDIER

Clad in uniform, reluctant in stride, with love in his heart so long denied; the old soldier cried.

He called out to un-hearing ears and tried valiantly to halt his tears, to don a mask to hide his fears.

War smoke encircled and cast him down! He lay gasping upon the ground; in his misery no comfort found.

The battle raged, death whipped by, trembling the old man wondered why - am I willing to do this; willing to die!

The battle rose to a hellish peak, still the answers he did seek. Who are the strong? Who are the weak?

A lull in the battle gave him pause; he wondered who'd die for unjust cause. Interrupting his anxiety a young man falls!

With uttered oath the young soldier rose; hurled his last strength against his foes; in his heart the young man knows.

To live or die is not the issue; victory an act of justice due. Pride and principle and peace ensue.

The old soldier kneeled at the young one's side; forgot his fears but still he cried. Because of him the young man died.

At last the old man did comprehend why war is good and war is sin; that man is both a foe and friend!

Robert E. Shockey

SUICIDE AIN'T JUST ANOTHER TRAIN RIDE

Open your suspicious eyes;
relax, my intellectual lover.
You need not embrace the
weathered hands that reach out
from a thousand stories past to
touch your gentle fragrance.
But, just for a moment, come sit
by me; feel me breathe;
sip delicately from the cloven
cup of my existence in your
world.
Let your frightened spirit rise
freely, in silent, untroubled
meditation, slowly up the
broken trellis of my wasted life,
where the wilted roses of a
hundred lovers hang abandoned,
hidden by the evening dusk.
No tender rain can save what
has past.
But you are safe to taste my
wine, for you need not share my
bed to copulate with my
experience of age.
To you softly whispered are
secrets I have learned in pain,
and subtle smiles that never
spoke songs.
My massive novel is written in
the sand, and lies without a
cover in the cold morning hours;
frozen forever in the chill of
countless minutes of reality;
It is a life; a singles dance in a
day of memories, amused,
wounded, and not for sale; a
limited edition, published on
the surface of a tear, yet available
to you on temporary loan, until
death deals its bargain, and
payment is required for having
found it necessary to love you.

Beatrice Burton Kennedy

YOU DON'T KNOW ME

After I had given you all of me
With nothing more to give
You simply tossed me aside
And you went some place else
to live
At first, I was deeply hurt
I didn't know what to do
Just how could you up and leave
me
Especially after all that we'd
been through
But you know Sweetheart,
Darling, Wonderful One
The more I thought about it
The happier I grew
Because I knew sooner or later
Somebody, somewhere
Was going to sock it to you
TOO.

Patricia I. Doherty
DAYLIGHT COUP
If I had a penny
Do you know what I would do?
I would buy a piece of heaven
All clear blue.
Then when the sun had gone to
sleep
And stars came out to play,
I'd gaze in awestruck wonder
At my bargain made by day.
For if I'd waited till the night,
It never would be mine;
With all those merry, twinkling
stars,
Twould surely cost a dime!

P. H. Niles
DEUS EST
"Is there a God?"
The words were asked while
heads bowed low
and texts were thumbed
and plates were passed
and phrases frayed beyond
reprayer
"Is there a God?"
questioned Doubt
And, behold, one figure stood
arrayed in only himself-stuff
and spoke:
By God, I believe there is!
Since faith is seldom loud, there
was a stir
"Speak. Where have you found
It-Him-Her?"
Came this answer:
God is
a desire
a softness
a marbled patch between
the clouds
a tear
a word spake near
"But this is ..."
a caress, expressing all
The speaker was spirited away
And heads bowed low while
texts were thumbed
and plates were passed
and phrases frayed beyond
reprayer

Kendra-Jean Cliver
WHEN I LEFT
i left you
with me
looknig for
the me
i left
with you
when i left you
leaving
without you
without me

Sandra K. Shorey
THERE'S NO WAY BACK
I felt like an intruder,
creeping up those old stairs.
This wasn't my world now--the
magic had died long ago.
but maybe...just maybe...
It was as I had left it so long
ago.
I picked up my old dolls,
trying to relive the life they
once had.
It was no use.
but maybe...just maybe...
the stuffed animals!
I whirled to look. There they
sat; all in a row. Their worn,
once loving faces, only
looked at me with blank
stares.
I had deserted them.
They weren't the same loving
creatures I shared so many
tea parties with and
talked to for
hours on end.
Oh yes. I was an intruder now,
not the welcome little girl I
once was. I hurried back
down the stairs to my real
world. I knew now...
There was no way
back.

Marjorie Gagnet Berry
NIGHTMARE
Voiceless spirits of the night
make your presence known,
fiendish demons, bloodless
ghouls who are left to roam.
Where is your master? Bring him
forth and end this taunting
game, leave my sight forever to
return from whence you came.
Sleepless nights and broken
dreams as you prey upon my
mind, Silence broken by the
ghosts of midnight's woeful
whine. The clock strikes twelve,
the curtains move, mist and fog
fill my room, hooded figures in
long white robes to lead me to
everlasting doom. Ghostly eyes
made of glass beckoning to me,
with out-stretched arms step
closer, I scream, I must flee.
Where can I hide? Who will stop
them? I'm sick, so sick with fear,
the faster I run the slower they
walk and yet they are so near. A
closet in a deserted house to
stay till day come once more,
footsteps coming closer as the
knob turns on the creaking
door. These messengers of death
order me to rise,
their leader shows compassion
through his fearsome disguise.
he nods to the others as mist
and fog fill the cobwebbed room,
they disappear these creatures,
these haunting ghosts of doom.

Arden G. Newell
A LOVER'S LAMENT
No bird does sing upon the
bough
So sweetly now
That she is gone.
No flowers spring so fair
Now she's not here
To beauty share.
In my sad heart
Altho I know
It is not so
She seems pressed down
Beneath the weight of
earth
She that was so lissome,
sweet -
She cannot breathe
I think.
The rains will dampen her
gilt curls.
The winds so harsh will
rough her cheek
And oh the cold, cold snow
I cannot stand that now
I'll find a cloak - or warm
somehow
My dearest, dearest one!
I only see her fresh and live
With lingering lashes
downward curled
And easy grace full free.
It takes me long to nullify
all this
In my sick heart;
To know that she's
insensate now-
With no breath in this wide,
wide sphere
My darling one - my
dearest dear!

Barbara Ann Guynn
MY ENDLESS LOVE
My love for thee is timeless.
As grains of sand do count
minutes
Doth my love for thee grow
endless.
If it should ever come to cease
t'would be the world's end and
me.
Come, share your life with mine
Tis but seconds that we have to
spend
So wait thee not another
moment.
Time shall be lost as our love is
found
And as our love becomes eternal
doth time expire....

Theresa Ann Pifalo
THE CRICKET IN MY BATHTUB
I was awake in the dark.
Thinking about everyone I love
Dying...
About dying myself, or worse,
Just getting old
Alone.
Thinking about having no
children.
About still being a child
Who cannot (will not?)
Leave its mother
At thirty.
The cricket's song
Curled itself softly around my
mind.
I went in search of the song.
He was so small, so fragile.
His lacy legs made a pattern
against the rose ceramic of my
tub.
My sudden appearance stilled
his music, and
Frightened, he skittered toward
the drain.
Faced with the alternative of
going down,
He fastened his delicate legs
On the edge.
Fearing that I would send him
over,
I darkened the room.
Moments passed.
The first notes were tentative,
soft, cautious.
Then the song grew stronger,
louder, more joyful.
Maybe that's all there is...
Singing your song, and
Hanging on.

Henrietta M. Hardy
SILENT INVASION
Platoons of angry snowflakes,
capturing our bushes and trees
piling up against our window-
an army that is vanquished by a
sneeze.

Sophie Rodin
MIRO (1893-) PAINTING ——OIL ON CANVAS
Abracadabra in a magic quilt.
Playful, jazzy, nifty.
Aglow.
Grass -freen choo with one fire
eye; one shady eye,
A neat tiger tail of rails
Coming out smoke.
Track of tiger trail.
Connecing to a structure; a
house,
Sapphire in the middle.
A spider that is no spider,
extending--
Rather an umbrella
overhang,
Cilia in space.
Candle faces, green and Lemon,
Curving
Toward a star, a tree,
Under the rhinestone-ringed
moon.
Now the candles-- lamposts.
Lamp-post persons,
illuminate
The city.
A celebration in motion.
Silent,
Carnival of form in color.

William N. Howard
LYRIC ODE
O' Hetman! Hetman!
Whither away do you ride?
Toward the village near the
stars
in the snow-frosted Caucasus
mountains. . .
Yea! I am bound for my
astral home of Kyiw
where the glorious sacred Star
of Beth-lehem (House of Bread)
shines upon the Ukraine once
more
and the light-winged
seraph sings heaven's hymn
to the tune of the shepherd's
guitar.
I will rest my mighty steed
from the armaments of war. . .
and I will embrace my
sorrow-beleagered
maid and my
three small children,
Volodymyr, Olha and Sviatoslov.
They are so named, because
upon the
day of my firstborn,
three Spirits
appeared at the foot of my bed,
and spoke to my espoused one.
They declared themselves to be
the ghosts
of the valorous grand-princes
and the ancient empress
of history.
Enamored of this honor
the metropolitan solemnized the
identity
of my offspring
in memory of these great Saints.
My child Olha, I am told, has a

voice so deep,
that her singing is as
the waters of the Volga.
And when she delivers her
medley of odes
and intermezzos,
phantom cities with their
crystal palaces,
and streets of luminous
precious stones rise up before
one's eyes
with haunting swiftness.
Yea, back to the glorious days
of Novgorod,
when one's dreams were
crowned
with the sacerdotal priestcraft
of the blest arch-deacon,
Arios Nicholaus.
Our table was covered with
snow-white
embroidered linen,
the emblazoned unity of Jupiter,
Mars and Saturn
shone through our window
lighting up a sheath of wheat
and grandpa's hoary head,
while we worshipped at the altar
of lighted
candles,
ate hearth-cakes and feasted
on ginger-wine.
Ay! the season has returned
yet again,
when we clothe ourselves in
reverence
to the Holy Jesus,
tell tall tales of eclectic
fervor;
my heart and soul are faraway
from the croaking cries of the
Tatar-Turks
who vow to soak the earth
in Ukrainian blood.
Passion spent, weary of
wantonness and drive,
I begin to tire of wanderlust,
of forging new kingdoms of
conquest—
a ceaseless need for peace
echoes through my brain.
When I gaze upon my fat wife,
her red boots are as the blood of
lambs and bullocks,
her wide skirt is bright red,
making her
appear even fatter.
Her black-velvet hair
is adorned with mysterious red
and
white roses.
I suddenly feel as though I am
swelled
to bursting with the fruit of
nations,
and from her womb she gives
birth
to many children.

Bruce A. Garber

LOST AND FOUND

Vague memories were all I had
to recall of my childhood
association with Sam,
although he was gone more than
he was home I remember a kind,
gentle man.
His job required that he travel
alot so in his absence I
created an illusion, I dreamed
I would be the type of boy that
he'd want but the emptiness
only caused more confusion.
He always seemed to manage
somehow to pay bills and have
food on the table,
mother always told us that Sam
would provide for the work, she
was certain, would remain
stable.
But an accident had forced Sam
to stay home
his life had changed and now so
had mine,
we managed to erase the
loneliness once shared and our
laughter replaced tears of lost
time.
Sam passed away just a few
years ago
I was bitter, quite frustrated and
mad, but the passing of time has
mellowed my mind and forever I
will love Sam, my dad.

Carolyn Merriman

THE ORGAN

the organ
wheezes tunefully signaling the
start then lights
flash on and off on and
off barkers spiel balloons
soar high in the sky fat
mama belly-laughs space
wheels spin miniature
dancing clowns dangle from
flimsy canes motors hum
horses gallop without
advancing excited
children jump up down up
down occasionally
stopping often staring
intently at sights that
mark the beginning of yet
another night on the magical
midway

Mel Downard

AUTUMN

Autumn is a brief interlude of
time when we enjoy the last
flickering days of summer.
Autumn brightens up the world
with an array of beautiful colors
before the onslaught of a cold
Winter's day.
Swirling snow and frostbitten
toes will soon be on their way.
Autumn is the time of year
for a sport called football and a
hoopla cheer, taffy apples, hot
chocolate, and popcorn, too.
Or maybe a steaming bowl of
Grandma's stew.
So gather up the firewood for
those cold Winter nights.
Autumn will soon be o'er and
the cold North Wind will chill
your bones right down to the
core.

Peggy Bradshaw

HOME

A home is where the heart is
Not just living in a house.
It takes love and understanding
From the heart of every
spouse.
A home is what you make it.
Don't depend on all the rest.
For a home can be so wonderful
If you will try your best.
A home can be anyplace you
Live with love and joy.
A place thats well remembered
By every girl and boy.
So make your house a home
By giving it your all.
Not only for one season,
But summer, winter, spring,
and fall.

Cora M. Van Der Zee

GOD'S MOST PRECIOUS GIFT

A tiny Babe is God's most
precious gift,
Plucked from a Heavenly Bed of
twinkling stars
And sent to Earth by His Own
Messengers!
A fluffy fuzz of hair, as if
dropped from a downy cloud
above
And tinted here and there with
rays from the setting sun.
A nose so small, so sweet,
turned up a bit
As if to see from whence it
came!
Lips so full, so red and bowed, a
perfect form from Cupid's
Bow!
Dimpled knees, elbows, and
cheeks
Complete this precious Bundle
filled with Love!
A Gift of Love? A Gift of Love
indeed!
Who else but God above could
create and send so great a gift
To us--His Children here below?
Who else but God who loved
His Earthly Children so
Could have sent His only
Beloved Son
To Us--so many, many years
ago?
A tiny Babe He sent--a tiny Babe
to Bethlehem Town,
A tiny Babe whose Parents
searched one cold bright
starry night
To find a place where He might
lay His Head,
To find a place where their
small Babe
Might find a Birthplace from the
cold!
The stars above shown brighter
than before
And one, one Special Star, shone
brighter than the rest,
Lighting the way to a lowly Inn,
An Inn and Stable in bustling
Bethlehem.
It was a very Holy Night,
indeed!
For on that Night God reached
down to Earth
And gave to Us His most
Precious Gift--His Son
Who through His Life and
Death would
Bring Eternal Life to all who
follow Him!

Lanie Mech

THE TOMORROW RIVER SONG

I have pitched my tent
Beside the talking water,
The boughs above it
Whisper to me low.
Before I walk away,
Talk to me today
About how time and water
always flow
In the direction of tomorrow.
Diversion or obstruction cannot
stay,
And even in the quiet pool's
slow dreaming,
The reflection of tomorrow
shows today.
Sweet river,
Tell me all your secrets,
How paths of rock
Produce your clearest tones;
Talk to me about
Tomorrow and tomorrow
As you and I
Go singing over stones.

Wilma Russell

FOOTPRINTS IN THE SAND

Walking
on the beach
Watching
the birds fly
Free-
Stopping
to pick up a shell.
The moon
oh so bright
Rising
over a sea of blue.
Dreaming
of the day when
all our problems disappear
Like-
Footprints in the sand.

Shirley Ann Lawing

STRANGER

I see you walking down the road
everyday and many nights,
I've heard you live in the woods
with no running water
not even lights.
You always carry a brown paper
bag,
Does it hold your days treasure?
I sometimes wonder who you
are and how far your days
walk measure.
For you always take the same
route - Who are you?
What are you all about?
You couldn't be rebelling--
for you are far past that age.
I suppose you are just a hermit
as I've heard
Living apart from city rage
free as a bird.
I've wanted to stop many times
as I ride by; to give a helping
hand
I'm hoping you are happy
with the life you've chose
living off the land.

Darlene Lambert

THE QUIET

I used to have. .a lot. .to
say. . .
Before. .my Mother. .passed
away. . .
But. .now my words. .are rather
slow. . .
I hesitate. .to let them go.
I can't explain why. .this is
so. . .
It just is something. .that I
know.
Perhaps. .my inner mind. .can
see. . .
That. .part of her. .was part of
me. . .
And. .when she left. .she took
away. . . .
A part. .of what. . .I had to
say.

Eleanor L. Katzenmiller

CRISIS IN THE CHURCH

Protesting; Molesting-
Testing, Wresting,
Arresting-- Digesting!
Spiritualizing; Agonizing-
Totalizing; Trusting.

Albert G. Richardson
UNTITLED
"There are no words to say some things—

Because some things can be spoken only by the eyes.
And so—

If you have been fortunate enough
To have been spoken to by your lover's eyes,

You have experienced one of the finest things in life
Whether you have realized it—
Or not."

Isaac Boonyes Dreyer
A DISCOURSE WITH GOD
O tell me, God,
in language clear and plain.
Did You create
the human heart and brain
To be benevolent
and sane
And also deadly savage
and insane?
Was it intentional?
was it a godly error
That had engulfed us—
for millenia—in bloody terror?
How many centuries more
will we go on to gore
Each other's guts
and brains
Until no vestige
of humanity remains?
You're the Almighty
there above—I'm told.
Yet, from the vantage of
Your splendorous domain,
You helplessly
behold
Your pet-creation, wearily,
go down the gory drain.
We shall, O God, set straight
Your Great Creation Story.
Yes, though to You belongs
the praise and all the glory,
The master-key to our fate
has been in our hands
since mankind's birth.
Since then—
from Your immeasurable
domain—
You have been anxiously
observing us on earth:
At times with pride, regret
and with disdain.
For only we
have had the ultimate say;
And only we
are to be blamed for disarray
Among the people
of every race and nation—
For bloodshed, hate, disease
and inhumane starvation.
My sophisticated generation,
true,
Has conquered places
only, You,
O God,
their presence knew.
They are so distant,
desolate and dread
that only angels there
had dared to tread.
today, we span at will
the deepest ocean
And cruise
the stormy, raging seas.
We circle the globe
with speed of godly motion;
We land
at any point we please.
We dared to reach out
for the moon,
And made it happen
in one giant stride.
The hour is nearing—
mighty soon—
When we
shall glide
Among
the distant planets;
In cosmic vastness
we'll immerse;
We'll cruise along
and render songs,
exalting sonnets
To all the wonders
in the universe.
We now possess the awesome
power of the human brains
To shatter most
confining chains
Of prejudice
and ignorance among
The many who have been
deprived—so long—
Of their inherent right
to equal chance
To march in mankind's
great advance.
On our planet, Earth,
we know
That we can make the soil
to grow
All fruits and grain—
all life-sustaining food—
To banish hunger
from this Earth for good.
But my "enlightened" generation
has blindly let so many
languish in starvation.
Our men of science,
in all the lands,
Are reaching out
with giant hands
to all the spheres
of the unknown:
To open blazing,
wide frontiers
And raise the curtain
to a bright new dawn;
And to illumine winding roads,
we gropingly tread,
And treacherous blind turns
that lie ahead.
But is it not insane, O God,
While science strives
To use its healing rod
To save few precious lives—
It's frightening to contemplate—
It also, at a maddening pace,
Is searching for the ultimate
In the annihilation
of the human race?
With one hand we're erecting
pillars for a paradise,
And with the other
light the fires in hell.
When
will we realize
That we are tolling
our own death-knell?
But one day, God,
we shall not cower!
With resoluteness we
shall use our means and
power
To conquer hunger, ignorance,
blight and disease.
Then, strife and hate
will gradually abate and cease.
All barriers between
the nations and the races
Will ultimately crumble
and disappear;
Creative thought in every
tongue—

from distant places—
Will freely flow
without the slightest fear.
Ah, then!
From Your firmament, O God,
In all the splendour
of Your glory,
You will be peering down
and listen, smile and nod—
With boundless pride
and free from worry—
As we relate
to our beloved young,
In stories
and in song,
The wonders of
Your Great Creation Story.

Tim O. Pickett
OLD MAN OF THE ROAD
Oh, where are you going? Old man of the Road
Will you ever come this way again?
I picked you up late last night, wondered if you were alright
By the look of your beard, sight of your clothes
This man must have feared at least thousands of foes
We drove for a while, but it seemed like many, many miles
When I looked over to check my passenger out
All I could do is shout out loud!
I realized it was all in my head and
The old man was me fifty years from now.
Oh, where am I going, Old man of the Road
Will you ever come this way again?
Yes, meeting you this day has made me feel so bold
I feel mighty expansions from within.

Janet Maple
GO HOME, DAD
I went to a home the other day
Expecting to see a little boy at play;
But, instead, on the couch, lay the little guy
Lifeless and still, no sparkle in his eye.
I felt his head; no temperature there,
But he laid on the couch with an empty stare;
I rubbed his back and kissed his cheek,
He seemed so lifeless and extremely weak.
It was so different from the usual him,
He always was happy and wore a devilish grin;
He usually had plenty of energy to spare,
And was always playing without a care.
"Come on, bud, let's go out and play",
I said, thinking that would save the day;
But as he walked slowly outside
He grabbed my hand, and inside I cried.
"What's wrong", I wondered, "I gotta find out",
So I tried to get him to run and shout;
But he stuck right there close to my side,
Showing no excitement: only whines and sighs.
Finally I knew what it was that made him so sad,
When I casually mentioned something about his dad;
For what he said cut to the core,
"My daddy doesn't live here any more".
"I don't have a dad", he said, so strange
Like something running over him as big as a train;
I hugged him and kissed him and I wanted to die,
And he just looked at me with those big, sad eyes.
"Oh, God help him", I cried in fright,
"Let his dad please come home tonight",
And I say to you, friend, if you've left your son,
"Go Home to him before this day is done".

Betty A. Clark
FOOTPRINTS
If I could be you—And, you could be me
And, each of us could clearly see the difficult things that each must do—But then, you're not me and I'm not you
Where are you going? Where have you been?
When do you arrive? When comes the end?
Why have you when others have not?
What was the purpose? What was the plot?
The pleasure and pain don't balance the scale
Pleasure being dominant over all of the hell
Recalling the past we traveled so free
Leaving footprints forever in eternity—

H. Roy Thompson
EARLY SUNDAY MORNING
Early Sunday morning,
And the stillness exudes a certain tranquility;
The time is ripe for slouching in a favorite chair,
And rocking a gently metered soliloquy;
The time is ripe for savoring a favorite brew,
And being in touch with life's menagerie.
The time is ripe for gazing out the window,
As the sun begins to show off its reassuring radiancy;
The time is ripe for listening,

As the refrigerator purrs and the
clock beats rhythmically;
The time is ripe for fathoming
the seeds of creation,
As the lady, cat and plants
breathe contentedly.
The time is ripe for tuning into
the dimension that lies
beyond,
As nature seduces its ever-
present bed of relativity;
The time is ripe for witnessing
the gradual melting away,
Soon to hearken the untold
sights and sounds of reality;
The time is ripe for being a
small part of what pervades
the whole,
While waiting for humanity to
awaken, and carry out its
destiny.

Colleen M. Flinn

MY HELP, MY LOVE

It seems whenever I need you,
When I just don't know what to
do,
You're always there to share
with me--
To help me see things through.
Maybe it's your smile
or your loving touch,
or your arms that enfold me
secure;
I guess it's all these,
And so much more,
That help me to endure.
The main thing, tho,
Is our love
That does grow
And makes happier
Each passing year.

Milissa J. Scott

HEROES

You hear what others cannot
You see what others cannot
You succed where others fail
Others fear what you do not
You believe what others refuse
to
You speak out when others are
afraid to
You speak and write with more
wisdom and knowledge than
others could ever possess.
You are the last hero in the
world
And by far the best it will ever
know.

Suzanne L. Redmond

UNTITLED

What if I were to dream--
Fall asleep, but really fall;
Down, down, down to the
deepest depths,
All alone in a different world,
Nothing with me but my
thoughts and me.
My dreams are the only part of
me that is there.
They have stayed with me, but I
have left.
I'm in the blackest corners of
my mind,
In a place where I have never
been before.
Never have I explored to such
great lengths
With no boundaries and no
restrictions in my mind.
I can go as far as I want:
Escape into me, inside me,
inside my head.
It is very different here;
I'm all alone, and all I have to
rely on is me.
I can reach in and discover new
Aspects concerning me that I
have never known before.
I can go so far and explore such
strange and unusual things.
They are all new to me;
Can I even grasp them or handle
what is happening to me?
What if I've journeyed so far
that I can't get out?
Is there no escape from me or
the powers of me
that I could be taken over?
Are my capacities so great that I
can be eaten up by me?
With all this uncertainty, there
is no way to know
Where I'm going or how far I've
gone.
To be safe, I should stay, up
here
As a distance that I can't reach
me.
But should I hide from me?
In my sleep, I could find me.
But what is it that I am finding?
And am I brave enough to be
found?

Ruth N. Johnson

THE LONG ROAD HOME

Oh, how long is that winding
road?
The one we wander on
To reach the one all paved in
gold.
Each day it seems 'twill never
end
That long, long road to home.
But trusting Him, our loving
Friend
Will help us all our sins atone.
The day will come, we know not
when
Our travels will be o'er.
But 'till we take Him for our
Friend
Each step will be a heavy chore.
We're put here on this earthly
sphere
To do what e'er we can
To ease the pain and often fear
of every fellow man.
But- if we help to ease one load
With His eternal strength.
That great, big, long and
winding road
Will shorten great in length.

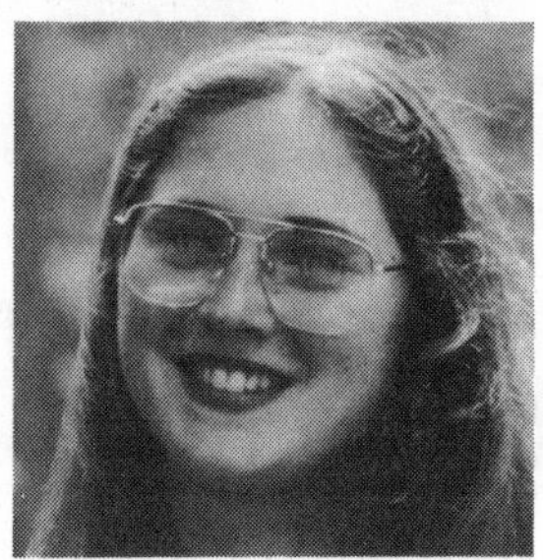

Cassandra Carrie Westbrook

LIVING

Smile, your love is felt,
your faults forgiven. Your
key to life lies in your giving...

Lila M. Sheldon

MEMORIES OF HOME

Over the hill and
in the valley,
Lies a stretch of fertile
land,
To the south and near
the roadside.
A rambling farmhouse
stands.
Rose covered is the
picket fence,
The gate is swinging
wide,
Offering the weary
traveler,
To rest a bit inside.
Past the door of the
old Kitchen,
On a table long and wide,
There's a board with
Several fresh baked loaves,
Churned butter by the side.
On the shining old black
stove,
A teakettle hums a
tune,
And you know you're
Welcome here,
As the merry month of
June
As you sit and sip the
fresh brewed tea,
And crunch the homemade
Bread,
You feel that you're revived
again,
And ready to journey
ahead.
There's Somethnig about that
abode of the past,
Whose serenity seems to
completely outlast.
Neither trips to the
moon,
Nor wherever you
roam,
Can ever erase the
dear memories of home.

Ms. Sherry J. Fairrow

A SPECIAL LOVE

within these fleeting moments,
You and I, we shared a
lifetime.
Some search forever, but they
never,
A love like ours do find.
We shared the sunlight of the
day,
The good things were always
ours,
For even in a sky of gray,
Our love birthed sunshine and
flowers.
The certain way you held my
hand,
The quiet way you walked,
In special moments our very
own,
The way we smiled and
talked.
With peace, you walked in life,
In joy you taught me love.
A special place, a special time,
God sent us from above.
Tho years have come and gone
My heart cries out anew,
For still I search each face I
meet
To catch some glimpse of
you.
The special way you looked at
me
Before your lips met mine,
Ours was a certain kind of live
The ties which God doth
bind.
I still remember and recall
The pain within my heart,
You took a portion of my sun
When we were torn apart.
my love is like the soft wind
Gently breathing on the
stream,
Sending ripples to and fro
Then disappearing like in a
dream.
Real, yet seemingly unreal,
As time slips unseen by.
Yet in a special way, my heart
relives
Our years, where this love
will never die.
Patches of grey color my hair,
The days pass swiftly now.
Your face still haunts my
memories,
Wonderingly, I question how.
Fulfillment of my love for you
Will never be it seems.
In still of night, when I close my
eyes,
My love lives only in dreams.
God gave to us the sunrise,
The early morning dew,
In special ways he blessed me,
And this, my beloved, is you.

"Mess"

SIMPLE REASON

There is a simple reason for my
face being red
Its not from something you've
said,
The reason my color has turned
Is because I'm sunburned!
There is a simple reason for my
figure being big
Don't get the impression I'm a
pig
The reason my figure is obtuse
Is because I'm Mother Goose!

Martha J. Wright

THE DANCE

With boogying feet
The actors meet.
Swaying in dance
They steal a glance.
Music plays both slow and fast,
Twisting and turning away at
last.
Gently weaving each new
measure,
Beats and spaces spin a treasure.
The dancers touch.
Their eyes say much.
Music lingers just for the
asking,
Each note singing of love's
unmasking.
Time to steal,
Love made real.

Juanita Payton Paholsky

MY PRAYER

May your life be pure and Holy,
crowned with love and joy
and peace
And the Golden Rule of
kindness, be your guide 'til
life shall cease.
Loving words by you be spoken,
Holy deeds be done each day
Render to the Lord true service,
trust Him fully and obey.
May the loving Saviour bless
you, may he keep you from
astray
And the Angel of His presence,
guard you on your homeward
way.
Lean entirely on your Master,
cling to His loving hand
Very gently may He lead you, to
a bright and better land.
Look to Him in days of
darkness, as your helper,
friend and guide
For He will never ever fail you,
trust in Him what e'er betide.
When the evening shadows
lengthen, at the close of lifes
short stay
May His presence ever comfort,
and be your strength each day.
Nothings better than His
blessing, nothings sweeter
than His care
May these be yours forever, is
my earnest, sincere prayer.

Georgia B. Green
GOT TO BE KIDDING FEELING

Once there was a love so great,
Oh: What Forbidden and Joyous Heights,
All in life was worth while, we built a world of our own
Such sweet tender ecstacy was truly ours, dreams, hopes, ambitions,
Such sweet lassitude of love we shared, sunrise never seem so rosey
As time went on our life was truly blessed, bright and full of vigor
A girl for me and a boy for you, the four of us lived with such love
All was well, peaceful, and serene, pure innocent bliss
But then things changed, and the word divorce left me devastated
Emotions sprang like lightning, you had wishbone and not backbone
You left our life sad and dejected
And I'm in a dark pit of loneliness
I've got that got to be kidding feeling, you were my strength, my universe
Oh! The joys of your word my guardian angel, my rock of Gibraltar
You were mister one, you were the mouth piece of truth
Now you're a river of rebellion to me
For you left this woman, broken hearted in a hell of a mess
Go your way and I'll go mine, will be better that way
And maybe some day the sun will shine again
I've got that got to be kidding feeling
Must pick up my broken pieces of life, yet I'm haunted by problems feelings and emotions
Wish I were on some remote desert island
But I must reach out and be versatile
For love without faith is a mockery
And this bumbling country girl can't take it
Must listen to my voice of destiny

Nadine Markowitz
UPON THE SODDEN PATH

My booted feet left textured marks
Upon the sodden path
Obliterating former prints
Of others who had passed.
Imprinted tales, the trail held
Indented in the mire;
A rider snaked by on a bike
And etched a skinny tire;
An owner with a shepherd dog
Had trudged through on the route;
Two sassy squirrels in single file
Recorded hot pursuit.
A heavy-weighted, clumsy man
Engraved his tracks awry;
Some tiny birds had hopped along
And stamped their names nearby.
A sudden weather change had formed
Some ice in roughened grooves;
And with each plodding step I took
In labored, studied moves
My footprints added to the scene
Another tale in land,
For as I walked along the track
In over-watered sand
I noticed upon looking down
That in my aftermath
My booted feet left textured marks
Upon the sodden path.

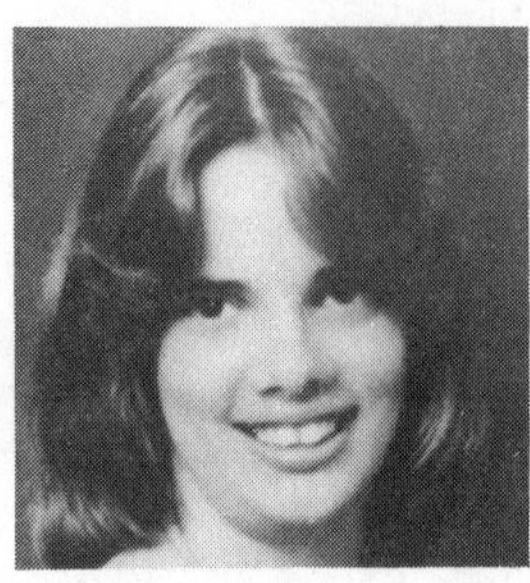

Laurie A. Hunter
GRADUATION: A NEW LIFE

My name is called out.
Friends and family applaud as I rise shakily to my feet.
Stumbling over neighbor's feet, I make my way out into the aisle and my high school years come rushing back to me.
I recall my first prom and how the rain drenched my new dress, but not my spirits.
The aisle passes underneath my feet as I glance at the familiar faces of dear friends I have made.

What will become of them?
Will they remember me?
A small tear steals from the corner of my eye.
Teachers who have disciplined and molded my character come to mind.
How they frown upon the frivolities of our youth, while secretly recalling their own days of frolic
At last the end of the aisle has come.
My high school days are over, but their memories and keepsakes still linger.
I reach out and accept my diploma and with it...
A new life.

Kelli Stevens
TO A FRIEND

Like a child you help me see the world filled with rainbows and sunshine, like no one else can.
You help me see the dreams within the long, cold nights,
And when my world is losing its sparkle, You smile at me with your glowing warm eyes that catch my world afire with sunlight.
Like a man you listen intently as I spill out my dreams and hopes
And when I'm bare, with my feelings at your feet you take me in your arms and kiss away the pain.
You make me feel special.
You sincerely lay out your feelings for me to save our love which could never be replaced.
If you ever leave me I will be lost in this cold world,
If you ever stop caring I will be afraid to trust,
But no matter what happens
I want to thank you for the sunshine you have brought into my life.

Carrie L. Braswell
HONOR FATHER

Song: Honor Father
Tune: How Great Thou Art

Our father dear, you know we truly love you,
You are the greatest man on earth we know.
Our Jesus sees and knows the teaching you do
That fill our hearts, and make them overflow.

Chorus
Then let's give praise to father on this day;
We honor you, we honor you!
Then let's give praise to father on this day;
We honor you, we honor you!

When hardships come and problems are arising,
And everything begins to fall apart;
You comfort us with love and faith abiding,
We hear your voice-you say, "Just trust in God."
And then as last, when all your days are over,
When you shall go to join the heavenly band,
We should be strong-no doubts arising ever
For the good words you've said will always stand.

Martha Stutts Hayes
WORTH

Matters not how efficient we think we are,
Far above the need of material gain;
Scorning the hands held out to us;
Belittling anothers' pain.
For there once walked a Man this way,
And the Mightiest of Men was He,
Yet He chose His friends from both the rich,
And the poor fishermen of Galilee
For He was equally at home with the rich men,
Or those from Shanty Town;
For He looked inside the heart itself,
There to judge the white or brown.
He never asked how great their wealth,
Or, "What will be in it for me?"
He never questioned their status quo,
Or how great their influence might be --
And you, my high and mighty ones,
Dare you honestly look within,
And deny you judge those you meet
By their rags, or riches and skin?
Take heed lest those whom you scorn,
Be far, far richer than you;
For they may be friends of that Mightiest of Men,
Who may be ashamed of you!

Edith Jackson Hankins
COZY OLD ROBE

Don't you love a cozy old robe
when the wind is whistling outside?
How grand it would be just to keep it on
and by the fire abide!
Seems I always have to rush around
and get dressed right away.
Here I must be and there I must go
It's never time for delay.
But, if I had my druthers
I bet you know what I'd do-
I'd keep on my cozy old bathrobe
and goof for an hour or two.
I'd mess around with my flowers;
rearrange the things on the shelf;
I might put some snapshots in the album;
Or write in the diary to myself.
I might just answer some letters
or send a birthday card or two;
I might fix a get well greeting
to somebody puny I knew.
I might do the chores in my bathrobe-
That I would enjoy well,
But just as sure as I tried that,
someone would be ringing the bell.
And, if I went to the door,
clad only in sleepers and robe;
No matter what all I'd been doing,
or how cold it was outside;
I'd better be dressed and ready,
I can't in my old robe abide.
Yes, I'd love to keep that old robe on
and snuggle in front of the fire.
Still, as long as I'm well and I'm able,
I'll dress and be busy, it seems;
But, staying in that cozy old bathrobe
is one of my favorite dreams.

Ruth V. Mackey
ON DAYS LIKE THESE

On days like these, when skies are grey,
and the sun, doesn't seem to shine;
I sometimes wonder, what has become,
of the love you said was mine.
What has become of the joys we knew,
All the laughter, and tears that we shed;
All the dreams that we built, all the plans that we made,
Have all been torn to shreds.

What has become of my happy
heart,
That only now hold sorrow;
My thoughts and prayers would
be fulfilled,
If you should return
tomorrow.
But, if by chance, you don't
come back,
Memories of you I'll treasure.
For just because, "On Days Like
These",
They bring me so much
pleasure.

Paul Allen Layne
UNTITLED
Master Builder of the master
plan.
Why did you make me a mortal
man?
Must I travel this road of life.
Through so much toil and strife.
Or shall You reveal my purpose
here on earth.
Surely I must have some worth.
Master Builder of the master
plan,
Why did you make me a mortal
man?

Dawn Marie Kirk
SWALLOW YESTERDAY
I find you pensively poised (yes,
absorbed) bent over your desk
seeking your words
I pause at the door to view you
and fearing to miss any gesture
or touch,
enter your warm embrace.
You tantalize me
in a brief moment
and gently intoxicate me with
laughter
Beginning to understand, I grasp
that moment and swallow
yesterday's solicitude.

Sharon L. Gross
VIET NAM
A few years ago in Viet Nam,
Our men went off to war.
They went to fight for our
Country, our peace they were
Fighting for.
They felt so lost and lonely,
In that far off foreign land,
But they loved their families
And country,
For this they took a stand.
So many lives were lost there,
Did they all die in vain?
Didn't they go through enough
Over there, with all the
Fighting and pain?
They're still going through
Their own hell here,
Enough is still on their
Minds.
They fought for us hard and
Long over there,
We should be thankful and
Kind.
Viet Nam, oh Viet Nam,
What horror in that place.
So much was done to our men
There, I'm sure we could
Not face.
They fought as hard as any
Man in any other war.
But where was all of the
Glory that their fathers
Knew before?.....

Ray Shaffer
YOU ARE SO NEAR
You are so near and yet so far,
Deep in my heart as a distant
star.
We have so much to share it
seems,
I hold you close but in my
dreams.
I know your touch, tender
caress,
It lingers with me in reminisce.
You are my friend most precious
one,
Will always be till life is done.
Tho you are far and should be
near,
I sense your presence I love you
dear.

Lisa R. Wilke
MY LOVE
My Love
Is a bird
Soaring over the land,
Resting only where it
wants to,
But never ending
Its long journey.

Hazel Clarkson
JUST A MEMORY
Upon a hilltop high and dry,
They built you there in days
gone by.
For beauty you no prize would
take.
Your walls were of the roughest
plank.
Could you but talk, what tales
you'd tell!
The part in lives you've played
so well.
Could you but speak the truth
and say
What must await the judgement
day.
Little children sweet and dear
By parents true were guided
here.
The presence of the Savior near
Has blessed each one without a
fear.
Here throngs have gathered
light and gay,
Just to pass the time of day.
Here young ones met as lovers
may,
To part no more upon life's way.
Within thy walls for many
years,
The old their strength have had
renewed.
True fellowship they've learned
at last,
As day by day love held them
fast.
In my own life you've played
your part.
I've loved you dearly from the
start.
My love I met within your

walls.
Today we heed our Savior's call.
'Twas here I learned to kneel
and pray
For those who persecuted day by
day.
'Twas here I proved the
scripture true,
Mid tears and trials of every
hue.
Here upon the alter bare, I
placed
I placed my all of earthly cares.
The Lord came in to rule and
reign,
My life no more to be the same.
Upon one winter's night 'twas
here,
My husband found the Savior
dear.
My prayer of years was
answered then,
Oh how could any doubt or fear?
The part you've played for me
and mine,
For hundreds more you've done
in time.
Each soul you've sheltered in
the past,
Treasures a memory that will
last.
You've served your day and
blessed the lives,
Of many pilgrims passing by.
They tore you down to build a
new,
A temple to the God we knew.
Now may the New one fill the
lives
Of strangers as they Journey by,
With life and love and Courage,
too,
To travel on as all must do.

M. Scovel
THE PEAKS OF EXISTENCE
I climbed a lonely mountain
And waited at the top
To feel like it was over
To feel like I could stop.
But what I saw upon that crest
Were countless peaks anew
Each one was different from the
rest
Outlined in spacial hues.
It was then I saw the answer
To the questionable meaning of
life
--The secret is the climbing up
To yet another height.

Carol Ellen White
SOUNDS OF SPRING
Nature is so melodious and
Sweet when the grass turns
Green and small rivers and
Streams open their heart to life
And flow freely like the birds in
A clear blue sky. You can hear
The melody of the soft warm
Breezes, the children playing
Games, laughing and having a
Joyful time. Listen to the songs
The birds are singing, animals
Exercising their restless bodies,
And the call of bullfrogs at the
Close of a long day.

Patsy Anne Graham
SILENT CRIES
No!
Not me!
This can't be!
This can't happen!
But,
Slowly--
Numbness leaves;
Reality reigns.
As those who see
Don't grope in the shadows of
blindness,
As those who run
Don't struggle in the grips of
lameness,
Just so--those who still share
love
Don't feel the stab-wounds of
divorce.
Such a simple word--
So lightly accepted by the world-
Everyone (who hasn't faced it)
knows
Just how one should handle it.
Time heals.
Time is friend and foe.
Time won't take me back to
erase mistakes--
To make a change--to avoid this
dreaded scene;
But time will slowly,
Slowly,
Ease the pain,
And cover the scars,
And life goes on.

Susan Hill
UNTITLED
Every night they appear
watching over us from above,
greeting the night as radiantly
as the sun greets the day.
First the moon rises
as if a town crier,
announcing their coming
to the moon-lit sky.
Then slowly, one by one
they appear overhead
lighting up the endless sky;
shining, sparkling stars.
They seem to have a message
each and every night;
to let your troubles disperse
with each appearing star.
Let the moon carry them away
as it moves across the serene
sky.
So that one can rise renewed
with the rising sun.

Maureen McGraw
TELL ME THE TRUTH
Tell me the truth
comply with my need,
answer my question
it's a simple one indeed.
Tell me the future,
but do not lie.
I wish no more pain
so, if you need me,
need me forever
and not just today.
Be honest with me
if you wish to harm me,
then harm me now.

Gertrude Ruhl Gehris
A GOAT KEEPERS PRAYER
Lord, let me be a goat keeper,
not only a goat owner.
Let me remember summer
browsings along a woodland
stream.
A soft muzzle in my palm,
A friendly head rubbing my
knee.
Let me not forget the delicate
tracery of silent footsteps in
virgin snow.
The warm winter sun on a
velvet back,
Loving eyes that follow my
every move.
Let me be thankful for loyal
folk, who believe as I do.
that goat milk is good food,
And, last but not least, dear
Lord,
I am grateful to serve you
and humanity.
Amen

Grace Saunders
EYES
Enticing, warm, laughing.
Yearning, sad, questioning.
Emerald, sapphire, jet.
Saying things that lips
would never utter.

Ione M. Bramlet
FREEDOM
"Tell me a story," you say;
And then you say
"I don't like your language;
I don't like the way you speak;
You use wrong verbs and
adverbs;
You end your sentences
with prepositions;
Your way of speaking sounds
vulgar and offbeat.
Express yourself. But do it
as I say."
I say to you,
"I don't know your language;
My language is of the streets
and ghettos.
What are verbs and
prepositions?
What is vulgar language?
If I express myself,
Please let me say it my way;
Let it be the way I feel,
The way I speak;
Let me say it as I think it is.
Let it be me.
Then and only then can it be
said
That I express myself.

Joan Goyer Bushno
ANNIE
They called her Annie
From The Wrong Side Of Town.
Parents warned "Don't play
With Annie. Can't you see
Her home is a hovel? her
Father is a shiftless drunk.
She isn't very clean, and
In winter she looks
So strange in her
Tattered jacket with her feet
Wrapped in burlap."

Teresa A. Nyarady
GLASSY—EYED CHILDREN
Minds drifting endlessly into
space
Glassy-Eyed Children of the
human race
Seeking comfort in the smoke
of the weed
That takes them higher,
plants the seed
A peaceful essence of troubles
erased.
Bodies sailing motionless in
reverse
Glassy-Eyed Children of the
universe
Ever-bound for a star unseen
Nevermore to be free
Entangled in the binding webs
of the curse.
Spirits lost in the infinite
vastness
Glassy-Eyed Children entering
the blackness
Encircling nothing - no life, no
love
No light entering from above
To free their souls from eternal
emptiness.

Joyce A. Ashworth
TRIBUTE TO A KING
The hungry, moaning room
witnessed
The birth of two tiny sons.
One, so rare, the other, shrouded
in death,
And the weeping house wept
alone.
The shining son was a jewel,
rare,
To the maternal heart that
humbly bowed
In adoration, as she gazed upon
him,
Who stood in princely form; she
thanked God, aloud.
The boy too, loved the queenly
mother,
Who stood in gray garments
inferior,
But in that penniless,
imprisoning impoverishment,
There richly reigned a noble
spirit, superior.
The golden chains of that royal
love
Between the mother and the
son,
Would bind the living son, and
the mother, dead,
Until that glorious reunion in a
smiling, silver mansion.
As the king grew, and sat upon
his golden throne,
There was within his burning
heart,
A love for the humble as well as
the great,
For he well-remembered his
simple start.
When ghosts of gloom would
come and dwell,
The king would walk into his
own world that lay
In loneliness, and there, he
would wait
Until the darkness fled, and he
happily sang, MY WAY.
While on the shimmering,
splendid stage,
The king would regally reign
Amidst jeweled lights that
danced
Upon the crowned humble head,
as he sang.
Amidst the screams and
shattering shouts
That issued from his subjects,
stunned.
There was a magic that
prevailed
From his enchanting heart, as
warm as the sun.
The style was as moody as the
man.
Drums thundered; his voice
rocked the map.
Trumpets sounded; he praised
the living God.
A gentle string, FALLING IN
LOVE WITH YOU, then OLD
SHEP.
As the ruling king and meek
man matured,
His royal hand blessed the
hungry earth
With great generosity, and the
kingly
Clothes vanished, for the man
manifested his worth.
In holy times of gentle
quietness,
When he heard the Saviour
speak,
He smiled into the face of God,
And bowed upon worshipping
sod, so meek.
Upon that fateful day when
death
Crept into the gray room and
dealt
That mighty blow, the king fell
dead,
While the weeping world, the
dark void, felt.
ARE YOU LONESOME
TONIGHT? the world wailed,
But the king mounted heaven's
silver stairs,
And walked into God's
welcoming arms.
Beholding the mother dear;
God's eternity to share.
Now, mother and son sing HOW
GREAT THOU ART,
While the world walks upon
saddened sod,
Still remembering that beating
heart of love,
Which was but an echo of the
beating heart of God.

Amy L. Copeland
SNOW
I like to watch the snowflakes
Swirling all around
As one by one they silently
fall upon the ground
Tiny flawless diamonds
no two alike you see..
A lovely quiet world of white
blankets every tree
A world of white perfection
A cotton candy day
A sight thats so magnificent
it takes your breath away

Irene Rathman
STRUGGLES
As the ants persistence is the
pay
As the scorpions development is
the sting
My struggles are - not what
others say -
Mine are the strength they
bring.
As food from food is brought by
the breaking of the shell,
As the juice of rapes is wrought
because of pressers feet,
I say it is struggles but - who
can tell -

My struggles also may be
anothers treat.
As birds sprout wings to fly
As the sun breaks forth to shine
I question my struggles - worth
the try? -
And discover the ends justify
mine.
Observing other efforts may
have a consoling tone -
The most difficult, yet
profitable, is my own.

Robert L. Powers
REFLECTIONS FROM VIET NAM
More than once...twice...thrice
Have I comtemplated my
demise.
But each time I heard the voice--
Listen to the rain.
Once I envisioned a gallant hero
Prepared to strike those who
waned.
Death and fear was to be
remediated,
But the cause was shallow...so
many died.
And a crying voice said--
Listen to the rain.
On a hill countless men died,
Each believing their's was a
victory.
Weary arms firing in the night
To faces unseen.
A blanket of death enshrouded
all near
And whispered--
Listen to the rain.
Silently in the night they fell
Like dominoes laid by a child's
gentle hand.
One by one they fought
Til nothing was heard but the
rustling wind.
And it softly said--
Listen to the rain.
Forgotten are their names,
For now they are souls of
despair
Laid to rest by the unforgiving.
Cursed and villified...some have
endured
Only to find comfort in the
stillness
Of an evening moon.
And gently it said--
Listen to the rain.
Must we succumb to the echoes
of the past,
Or can we face the personal
glories that be.
Many have lived on and often
heard the voice--
Listen to the rain.
For rain cleanses the earth and
soul
And washes away memories we
try to recall.
But the rain will never wash
away
That which war befalls.

Maxine Ethel Vann Thompson
EBONY BETRAYAL
Ebony holds the kiss of Judas
In the guise of his touch,
which first alerted her
that something was amiss.
(She's the last to know they say.)
The year of distance,the empty
spaces,
She still didn't read betwixt
The lines that can tell,
The icy breezes that chill
On a sizzling summer's day.
Old fashioned as all of it may
seem,
Fidelity she cherished,
But like happy endings,
Knights' shimmering armour;
The illusions now were gone.
"That's past," he said..."Forgive...
Forget."
Yet ghosts of lies still haunt,
Even the brightest noon,
The clearest crest where
In lies the shadow of wrong.

Genevieve Marie Meyers
ALONE
I'm alone in a dark place, in the midst of a star. It's very lonely and quiet. I feel like having friends around me, but it is too late; I'm already crying. There is nobody to talk to, or nobody to listen to; just the moving wind, very spontaneous and the feeling of the dark sky. I wish the whole world were with me, in the middle of a dull star.

Debbie Gallie
ACCEPT ME AS I AM

Accept me as I am
For you're no better than I
Accept me as a person
For I'm just as good as you
Don't tease about my color
For that will never change
Don't tease about my knowledge
For my wisdom grows day by day
Don't tease about my looks
For beauty lies deep within ones heart
My beliefs may be different from yours
But that is nothing to laugh at
Before you are ready to laugh at me
Remember, you're no better than I.

Georgia Bazacos Morgan
HOPE

Life's tiring, toiling, tedious way left me completely
despondent one day,
my life had become abysmally dark,
the future loomed empty, hopeless, stark.
All joy had left me, no peace could I find,
the flowers weren't blooming, the sun didn't shine.
No spring to my walk, no smile on my face,
vainly, diversions I sought to embrace.
Heretofore, music and books stilled unrest,
I turned to them now, hope filling my breast,
the books were quite lifeless, unyielding, still,
the music first flat, discordant, then shrill.
Restless, tormented, I twisted and turned,
if God existed, why felt I so spurned?
The pain I kept feeling did anyone care?
Can man know God? Is He really there?
Was there a link in a chain I had missed?
Life must have more meaning than this.
Had something escaped me, where should I look?
To my utter surprise, I found a new book.
It's message was loving, inviting, and blessed,
"Come unto me, and I'll give you rest."
The Son of God spoke, I heard Him with hope,
was He for real, I the butt of a joke?
Again He addressed me, His voice kind and sweet,
"I'm the Good Shepherd, will you be my sheep?
I am the way, the truth and the life
if you give me your heart, I'll end your strife."
Gladly the door of my heart swung wide,
"Come in, come in, please" I hastily cried.
Into my life He swept grandly that day,
the Bible says He's there to stay.
And I, with Him on my side, how feel I now?
Those damaging feelings, I will not allow.
Life presents challenge, purpose, intent,
I feel peaceful, forgiven, loved, content.
The flowers are blooming, I see the sun shine,
Often I smile now, and new friends I find.
He's coming to get me one day before long,
what about you friend, will you join that throng?

Monica K. Gallion
MY FOREFATHERS

Across the ocean my forefathers came;
to meet a fate for which I can not claim;
Brought to the New World on ships of wood;
for purposes so immoral yet understood;
This was where slavery began;
but the shadow would fall in the end;
You brought them here in shackle and chain;
so you, yes you shall take the blame;
Take me home to the mountains and streams;
quickly awaken me from this terrible dream;
Slaves all over, as well as whites;
began the fight for freedom and equal right;
War broke out between the states and many lives were lost;
but no one can repay this world those lives no matter what the cost;
Give me freedom, so, I'm black!
free me now or send me back!
I've not seen the whip but I carry the scar;
of my forefathers who came from afar;
From a land called Africa so far yet so near;
I can almost feel her sunshine,
and smell her sweet air.

H. David Bishop
THE OCEAN

What can you say at the start of the day
When the sun climbs over the inland rim?
I just can't hide what's deep inside...
My spirit is filled to the brim.
The seagulls wheel in a graceful reel
Across the painted sky.
And the wind is a balm in the morning calm,
Soft as a lover's sigh.
I remember the day, not far away,
When the waves came thundering in.
The rain came down with a rattling sound,
In tune with the howling wind.
I stood on this hill, so very still,
With the weather breaking around me,
Watching the clouds like mighty shrouds
Bounding in from the thrashing sea.
It was a violent war -- an assault on the shore --
The tantrums of a spoiled child.
The sea would twist in a frothing mist,
Cold, windblown and wild.
I love to stand on this piece of land
And watch the waves roll in.
Just the sea, the gulls and me...
Watching the day begin.

Diane Redus Holcomb
WHERE, WHAT, WHEN, WHY, HOW AND WHO

Where is home, that elusive womb?
Woven in dreams on an imaginary loom.
Why is our man the essential ingredient?
Because we've trained him to be most expedient.
How does rich differ from poor?
The latter determines the price in the store.
What's a child for--give me one good reason?

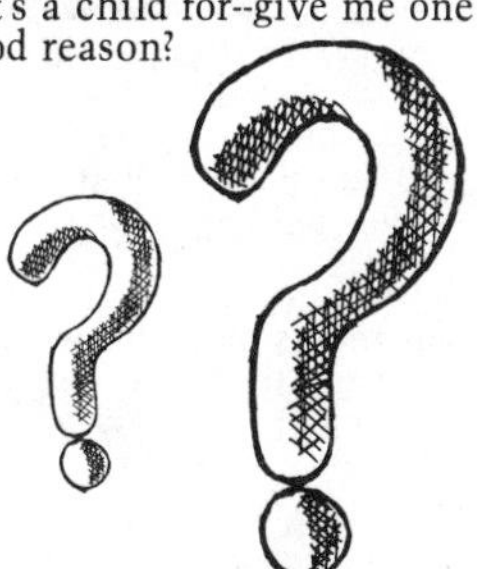

But to relive our own childhood, season by season.
When is a relative not just your kin?
Consider my cousin's my very best friend.
Who else could I count on through life's ebb and tide?
For there'll always be God and Fran on my side.

Cindy Schall
HERE I AM CRYING AGAIN

I'm not sure why these tears are forcing themselves, so I'm writing this poem to see if I can stop them.
Things are getting cloudy, of what I can see, so I must not be writing fast enough.
No, now the tears are flowing taking part of me with them, but I can't figure what is causing them, they're coming too fast to stop so I let them go on.
I'm the only one here to see them so they can easily be brushed away and forgotten, but how long can I brush them away?

Aubie Francis Brennan III
JOHNNY BE A BIG BOY

johnny be a big boy
don't cry
learn to die, daily
to passions and sentimentalities
you have to be a man
don't you understand?
soldiers never cry
they only die
daily
to fears
and insecurities
so johnny be a big boy
don't cry
learn to die daily
don't you understand
that God made you a man.

Jerome Ashland
POTATOE HEART

Crazy sea horses have had their day.
The boat people have no place to stay.
A page in time,
Has turned to crime.
No vegies in the park?
No telling it's dark.
Would they even eat a Lark?
Crazy sea horses have had their way.
Another day- to stay.

Andr'ea V. Rohr
OUTSIDE OF MY WINDOW

Gentle wind swirling,
Snowflakes are twirling,
Gray is the sky that gives me a chill,
To think of the iciness beyond my windowsill.
Bare are the trees as if frozen in time,
Where are thy leaves that were once thine?
Shhh...listen to the silence of the sleeping wood.
Memories of it singing, oh if it only could?
The songs will come again when the ground thaws out,
But it shall be a little while before this comes about.
You will know it when it happens,
For the frost will change to morning dew.
The warmth causes the wood to become anew.
Wood crackling and fire burning,
The window has become steamed.

Michael J. Colby
WHAT IS MAN'S DESTINY?

Will Man wage everlasting war?
Will he lie and cheat and steal
till the last endless night?
Will he drown the seas of humanity
in tides of greed and hate?
Or will he bask in timeless peace,
bring truth, honor, and order
to each new dawn, and let the
wind of helpfulness and the light
of love fill man's soul with
the Spirit of righteousness?

Sean Kevin Neilland, II
OLD FRIENDS

Greetings from an old friend are so warm and nice to hear,
And it's sad that paths do wander
far apart from year to year!
But it's nice that in the long run they do wind again to points
of convergence and connection and of talk and smoking joints!
So, old friends do come together as old lovers and old seams
And old friends go on forever in each others friendly dreams!

Shirley Rae Hedges
THE BATTLE WAS WON

I entered into sin so easily,
But the battle had already been won.
I surrendered at last,
Exhausted from the feelings of the struggle.
And for a moment I thought:
What would I say when face to face we'll meet.
All pretense and illusions stripped away.
Nothing between me and Thee but the truth.
Oh Lord, I cried.
How could I raise my eyes to Thy feet,
Oh Lord, I cried.
What would You say to me?
And for a moment my mind imagined:
These are the sins you planned in your heart without a thought of Me.
These are the sins I poured out My blood for you upon that hill called Calvery.
And This is the sin for which I cried,
"My God, Why hast Thou forsaken Me?"
And this is the Father who loved you since time began.
Come, my child, and greet the King!

Arline Levinson
DONALD BRINGS ME NIGHTFALL

How pointy are the stars I find
Reaching through your twilight hair
How sharp the light of love
How white, how clear.
Gather me between your shoulders,
Evening is complete-
Each stray flower is folded in,
Each running brook received.

Elma M. Guggenmos
EAST WINDOW VIEW

From the window's view above the sink,
Great beauties of Nature make one think
About the creations of our own Lord God,
The beautiful rainbows of which we are proud.
The early sunrise in all it's glory,
Makes life worth living, not feeling sorry
Because of our troubles or things gone wrong,
But helps to want us to sing a song.
Sometimes there are hungry birds on the lawn,
A mother deer with her own little fawn;
Again, there is snow when the winds blow cold,
Before Spring comes and the buds unfold.
Flocks of geese and ducks and cranes,
All appear above hills and plains;
A few hen pheasants with their young appear,
Grouse and quail and herds of deer.
Rabbits hop by night or morning,
Really show up without any warning;
Two watchful dogs spy and give chase,
But most of the time the hare wins the race.
Truck, pickup, trailer or car,
All pass by, from near or far;
The moon and the stars in a sky of blue,
Light up the night for everyone, too.
In winter, storm windows are pictured with ice,
Fantastic crystals make designs beyond price;
The cattle are grazing from spring to fall,
Newborn calves do frolic for all.
Old Sol shows up later in the fall,
At times scenic clouds are a joy to all;
We take for granted each days sunrise,
But a close watch can often surprise.
A flock of sparrows in the cedar trees,
Reminds us how God watches over these;
His eye is on the sparrow, too,
The fall of one has meaning for you.

Anna Reckner
HOME

I have been on a journey.
A long; lonely journey.
Through many passages of time.
Over many stormy seas.
Covered with gray skies
& noisy lightning
Through many valleys of Peace.
Green trees.
sunny fields,
contented nights
Smiled upon by thousands of stars.
Through all my soul has been restless, unsatisfied.
Aching with a longing
I could not seem to cure.
But
at last I've come home.
To my home within his heart!

Dr. Mary Ann Henley/Johnson
NO ESCAPE

Each time you see a raindrop;
You'll remember the tears I have shed.
Perhaps! you'll notice the sunshine;
And remember my laughter instead.
Each time you look at the starlight;
You'll remember the love in my eyes.
The rainbow, of course, will remind you;
Of the numerous times I tried,
To show you I loved you, while within me my heart slowly died.
Whenever you hear a bird sing; you will know; I am calling;
Your name.
The sound of your heartbeat will warn you;
You will never again be the same.

Hazel Smoak Clover
SHARING

Look forward till tomorrow becomes today
And one and one stays one
To hearts young and gay.
Romp and roam till you're content
Live each day as though Heaven sent.
Happiness is rare so share your smile,
Enjoy your trip don't count the miles.
Joy shared in love brings sweet content.
Remember...each day that you share
Is a day well spent.

Jill L. Diefenbach
UNTITLED

I want to tell you how I feel
but am afraid that somewhere on the paper
I'll say too much
or too little and
muddle up the simple phrase
I love you
which some people can take well
and others can't take at all.

Melchor M. Manjares
MY BELOVED

My beloved,
You are an inspiration;
My dreams come true
By the magic of your charms.
Each night and day
I wish you the best in my prayers,
That up above bless you and keep you in his arms.

Listen,
Come by my side
When I'm lonely and blue,
Caress me—when I'm in sorrows and in fear.
My beloved,
My dear beloved
Don't ever leave me,
Or I'll die.

Agnes Billane
THREE GARDENS

High Lodge, The Folly
Out of the morning's fragmentary moments,
Sunlight and spice cake and the frost upon the tennis net,
Birds coming to be fed.
Finches in the lilac bush outside the kitchen door,
Wood pigeons in ponderous grey waddling over the gravel,
A rook in the oak tree, wildly swinging,
This poem I would write today.
This poem I would write today
Out of the morning's fragmentary moments,
Sunlight and spice cake,
And the frost upon the lawn,
Birds coming to be fed,
The finches in the lilac bush, new budded,
And a child's voice calling,
"Mother, will you play zoos with me?"
As golden as the sunlight,
As fragrant as the spice,
New-budded----with the lilt of spring
And all the birds within it.
And now the arctic grey that covers all.
High Lodge,
Porterville Road
Pale October days,
The ground thick with the red of the wild crabapple
And berries of the mountain ash.
Drifts under the maple tree.
The glint of orange paint in chrysanthemum
Brown at the edges.
And the sumac, less crimson than before.
And still more days of sunlight,
More of birds' last calls
Thinking that spring has come again.
But all the time the leaves are falling.
Gutted stalks of snowballs
And the dead brown peony bushes
Curved and plump and lifeless,
Brown-edged chrysanthemums
Decaying on the stalk.
Wheelbarrows of old rose branches, dry and prickled and crisp.
Yet the salvia blooms scarlet
Standing straight with leaves black-edged
At the door.
Addie's Garden
Quietly child,
Your greydaddy is ill.
He lies so long upon the bed
With the sheet
Ruffled and frilled about him.
Hush child,
Do not wake him.
Just look and then remember how one day,
When grey autumn filled the room
You saw him lying there.
He loved you and remembered,
And was glad you came to see him,
Though he never knew
That you were there.
The deep pool where the lilies lay
Now stagnant in the sun
It's walls a square of grey green, but redeemable.
The elm trees, some about to die,
And the sassafras,
And grapes gone wild now on the arbour, making a hidden dell.
The autumn flower bed, lost in a corner,
Bright with marigolds, and the season's last zinnias.
The bell on the pole, and the fireplace of stone,
And all the long grass, deep and lush with dew.
The scrub pine, scraggled now into a thorny ceiling,
And the path leading to the old barn,
With its piles of old newspapers, card indexes, garden tools and calendars,
And the crushed grapes on the floor where they fell from the wild grape vine.

The bird house, and the sunken garden,
And the oval of grass the neighbors see, long ripe for the cutting.
Faded deck chairs, potted plants, picnic tables and the stone bench
Moss green,
Where a man could sit and dream.
This is Addie's Garden.

Gail Linda Rosenberg
SADLY, BETWEEN THE LINES
"Hello, how are you?"
how am i?
i keep pills in the drawer
and razors in the cabinet
for the tears that sting
and the heartache that burns
ashes inside -
and you ask how i am?
though the stakes are high
i will gamble
for the life i've lost hold of
in the course
of living,
for the pearl that is rarely found
inside the clam -
only when i see the sun again,
feel the raindrops on my face,
and wish upon a falling star,
will i know my'investment
was wise -
and tomorrow...
if i can walk barefoot in the sand
(hand in hand with a dream)
you'll now i'm doing...
"Just fine, thanks,
and you?"

Pat Schniering
MY PORTALS PASS
I feel the night surrounding me,
Slowly creeping through the cracks,
And up the stairs to my gloom.
Filling this musty monastery with dark.
The silence echoes throughout, with no other sound,
Save that of my empty chair.
Creaking and groaning with the strain,
Of years from burdens in weight that it has borne.
Each object I can faintly see in the dim,
Reaches out from the depths
Of my memories, of love and life past by,
To strangle my slipping sanity.
I smell the mildew and decay on the velvet,
As I listen to the rustling of the rats,
Preparing for my passing thru to come,
To devour me, keeping me prisoner throughout eternity.
Release me! Release me ole cursed soul.
Let me die! Let me die forever,
Bring me rest; give me peace,
From my tortured spirit I cry!
Will I to hell's portals of ever-lasting fire,
Or to heavens plains of justice be,
I beg! I plead! let me through.
Alas, I am lost, trapped by time, forgotten.
Again they await me...to taunt
While the shadows grow deeper, settling
Like a blanket of fog, as forgotten,
Colorless, lifeless and
nothingness as I.
It's here. The night has come to cover me,
As I sit in my chair waiting,
Waiting for the gloom I know to come.
While time passes me by with no other sound
Save that of the incessant creak and groan...creak and groan.

Beverly Rons
A CHRISTMAS PRAYER
On this day, A Child was born
Whom we all know and love
It was Jesus, Our blessed Saviour
Who reign's us from above.
We first knew Him, As a babe in a manger
He drew people to Him from the start
We loved Him then, We love Him still
He teaches us how to have a heart.
So give of yourself, Don't be afraid
And make someone smile today
You'll be surprised how good you feel
It's whats inside us, that really counts
And makes us what we are,
So let the goodness come shining through
And it will be a better world by far.
Without His guidance where would we be
There would be all kinds of harm
But as long as we trust and believe
He'll keep us in the safety of His arms.

Ko Durieux
THE DAY THAT I STOP CRYING
We kill them with that fancy word,
The unborn who have no chance to be heard.
And the kids who escaped this bloody hell,
Are now themselves not doing well.

'Cause those in charge who run the show,
Don't really care how they live and grow.

Yet the day I don't care about children sighing,
Is the day that I stop crying.
Some third world places that I know,
Are supplied by our aid with bread and dough.
And all the red tape this help goes through,
Makes our concern a real taboo.
So there we sit before our screen,
Desensitized from what we've seen.
Yet the day I don't care about people dying,
Is the day that I stop crying.
There's those who say: "Go back to base,
Return to politics to state your case."
But politicians have no answer,
On our greed that grows like cancer.
They lie themselves and call it "Truth,"
To make the mess they're in look smooth.
Yet the day I don't care about all the lying
Is the day that I stop crying.

John F. Baker
PRECAMBRIAN SENTINELS
They stand,
Low sentinels across the sand,
Resisting centuries of forces
that wear round their corners,
Scar their faces,
Breaching ranks,
And a stream slices through the narrow breach.
Their staunch poise,
Damaged but defiant,
Deserted by weaker companions
who vanished long ago.
Witness to billions of years;
The struggles, death and joys
Of all that trod over them.
Their mute stance,
Ancient before man or animal
roamed the earth,
Battered but dauntless still,
They stand.

Eleanor Powers McCann
VITA, VITAE
Ride a black horse
And weep into the wind...
Go, ever, stranger.
What is the road?
And where is its ending?
... Tell me!
Ride a black horse...
...a black horse...
into ... the ...
wind....

Thelma A. Blitch Atnip (TABA)
FOR HEAVEN'S SAKE, FATE!
Give me a little sunshine,
Give me a little chill,
Give me a little heartache,
Give me a little thrill,
But for Heaven's sake, Fate;
Put some money in my till!
Give me a little moonlight,
Give me a little rain,
Give me a little comfort,
Give me a little pain,
But for Heaven's sake, Fate;
Hard money I won't disdain!
Slap it on me, Lady Luck,
I'll turn the other cheek!
Show me things are looking up,
That I can live - not just eke!
Give me a little gladness,
Give me a little fear,
Give me a little sadness,
Give me a little cheer,
But for Heaven's sake, Fate;
Give me green-backs while I'm here!

Patricia J. Walkden
FIRSTS
weren't you the one who was
the perfect romantic and sent
me a dozen (plus one) long
stemmed red roses
my first ones
and wasn't I the perfect fool
who couldn't believe they were
for me and wanted to send them
back to the florist
you gave me a lot of firsts
my first orchid, pale and fragile
a lot like a new relationship
my first pearls, smooth and perfect,
like my dreams of the future
my first kiss
beautiful and tender,
like the way you treat me
my first love -
a combination of all the other
firsts, yet more precious than all
of them put together
we were the ones everyone
talked about
my favorite rugby player and
clown
your favorite nut and artist
who could occassionally draw a
good duck
for someone very special
remember...
all the great, wonderful times
we had
I'm glad you do
'cause I do too
and I want to have a lot more to
look forward to
you do too
good...'cause I love you
an awful lot
which is a first

Adela—Adriana Moscu
WHAT IS THIS FEELING
What is this feeling
that I have for you,
Where is it coming from
and where is it going,
How could I get to know
its pure meaning
if you are silent
when I am around.
What have you done to me
with your wild magic,
What are the tricks
of your eccentric mind?
I try to solve your puzzle,
Perhaps there is no answer
that I'll ever find.

Marina Rose
TO A NEW—BORN "I AM A FLOWER"
(Dedicated to April Nicole Brown)
I am a little flower of love.
God sends me blessings from above.
I bloom for all the world to see,
How beautiful a flower can be.
I am a little flower of Light.
My Cosmic Rays are shining bright.
These rays shine over land and sea.
How beautiful a flower to be.
I am a little flower, quite small,
There isn't much of me at all.
But when God sheds His Love through me -
I'm bright enough for all to see.

Rossm'e Taylor
METROLINER 5:30

Between the dusk
and the lights
and the untidy houses
and the five high chimneys
in a line
there is a lake
pure blue
made of shadows
and the train runs
through the lake.
It rolls slightly
with the motion
of the light slow ripples
of the dusk.
Trackside detritus --
cans and cartons
and empty oil drums,
taken-up rusted rails resisting removal,
stacked crumbling sleepers
longing for last sleep --
feels the cool
and grateful lapping
of the inflowing blue tide,
settles to the shadow-bed,
becomes smooth indigo.
On a siding
a paint-peeled old caboose
sends out one smoky
lamp-gleam --
solitary light-ship
on the insubstantial lake,
while distantly a radio tower
winks a red eye
in token of its willingness
to be the lighthouse
of a phantomed cape of dreams.

Marion Lund
NIGHT AND A LIGHT

Day to day work is wrought for man
Forward progress goes, new frontiers found
Each are dedicated to the future
As the wheel of time turns around.
Here and there a chimney smoke curls
Makes a blue apostrophe in the clear sky.
Nearby the big geese, strong and graceful
In battle formation, homeward fly.
Blue shadows linger near in the twilight,
The long day has drawn to a close.
Shadows slowly creeping and night birds sleeping
All nature is quiet for rest and repose.
Time exchanged time and light ended its day.
Then dark with its darkness is sealed.
Everything wears the garment of night,
Even the lilies that grow in the field.
With dark, dark shadows here and there
The feverish day and sunlight are not.
Man weary-toil with labor from his hand
Hours made slow from the day-long and sun-hot.
Everything is different in darkness
The stillness is hushed and serene
Even heaven and earth seemed divided.
But a presence still lingered between.
Just for a moment one might mark
What has been hidden by the dark,
Darkness, but here and there a light
For man, lamp gives light to the night.
There are lamps and lanterns embossed with gold.
Casting a halo of brilliant light,
All wrapped in warmth and color
New pouring new glory on a darkened night.
The windows, some dark, some bright
Reflect shadows through home and hall.
But outside on the street corner, a light,
It stands solemnly in place, celestial and tall.
This light shines out man's steps to guide
Old familiar paths that take him on his way.
Let us not this light be dimming
Or the flame go out before it is day.
There must be light to show man the way.
Ah, light its guarding watch keep, gives its best
Since time takes the sun out of the sky,
Giving the night quiet hours when laborers rest,
And then when night unfolds its wings,
It casts a spell of strength and might.
Darkness, but here and there a light
For man, lamp gives light to the night.

Iva Jean Bowden
IN MY DREAM

I arose in my dream and went out to meet my lover with outstretched arms he bid me come. He placed his arms about my waist, I felt his strength racing through my lonely body. I arose in my dream and went out to meet my lover, he stood in the shadows. I could hardly see. I knew it was my lover. I slept. the magic of his presence came like a fluffy cloud (touching me) the magic held me "I didn't struggle" I felt his kiss as it fell on my hair. I slept.
I arose and went out to meet my lover, there in the lonely night I stood as though I were made of marble stone. "I've missed you," I heard my lover say, my heart raced and fluttered like a wild bird that was no longer free... I slept.
I arose and went out to meet my lover, "Is that you?" I heard my youthful voice say. Yes it is I, he moved close to me (I waited for his touch) He took me in his arms, I moved close to his pulsating body. He kissed my brow, he then paused, "What a small face," he said. I placed my arms about his neck (our lips met...) I had not strength of my own...our love became as one. I slept.
I arose and went out to meet my lover, I stood there in the moonlit night. I looked all about everything was silver and gold colors, I heard my lover's voice I looked and he was walking slowly to me, he took my hand and said lets take a walk...and make plans, lets plan our tomorrows together. We walk near the cool brook and listen to the waterfalls...the moon

shown in the still waters..our faces! Can you see? "oh" yes.. We moved eagerly to each other...A cloud passed under the moon and it became dark. I slept.
I arose and went out to meet my lover. I look about and I was alone standing in a meadow green...All about were flowers. roses smelling so, oh, so sweet... I wondered am I alone?..maybe my lover is here. A breeze moved the rose bush..and I could see my lover standing there..he came to me..are you lonely he asked..oh yes..why must our love forever be incomplete. He sat on the green grass and leaned back and caught himself with his hand, he said sit my love..I did as he had asked of me. We placed our arms about each other and laid ourselves on the cool green grass...and our love was made complete...I slept and arose and went out to visit my lover
In my DREAM......

Betts Finley
A TIGHT—WOUND WATCH

At which particular point did I cease to be me?
And, when did this mindless cog probe infinity?
How did an automan, like me, delve in a fifth dimension;
Click and whirr as a faceless clock - extension,
Yet, skip one beat and cast one tiny sideward movement,
Separate time and space, and glimpse improvement,
Break the pre-determined pattern, stretch, pulling my chain;
An "abandoned" gesture, chiming when I pleased. The game
Mine for one small moment, believing it flexible.
Thinking surely I could reset the hands, change the schedule,
Let the whole world tick on time while I ran fancy free.
But, cogs meshed, blocking individuality.

Georgia Radcliffe
IDENTITY

How long does it take a heart to mend?
How long did it take the heart to break?
Was it a day, a month, a year--
How much abuse did the heart take?
The human heart is like a dream
That falls into a rushing stream
And if it comes upon a stone
Then love dies fast and dies alone,
But if it follows winding trends
Through jagged bluffs and narrow bends
Then it may fight the need to die
But it will one day lose its cry.
The love I have for you today
Will never pass this fleeting way,
For soul is timeless and divine
And yours has met and merged with mine,
So as the tides of time flow on
Your melody will never end,
I've touched the pinnacle of peace,
I've reached the zenith life can send.

Grace (Ledford) Harris
OUR GAME OF LOVE

Fate dealt the cards in our Game of Love
and for months we continued to play
ignoring the stakes that were piling up
knowing some time we must pay
We played so reckless not counting the cost
just hoping some how we could win
but at last we both realize we have lost
and that now we must pay for our sin
We should never have started for cheaters can't win
and we cheated each step of the way
we were so in love it seemed no sin
but now forever we'll pay
Our partners held trumps in each hand that
was dealt we knew that was how it would be
for regardless of how in our hearts we both felt
still neither of us were free
Now the last hand we are holding
and I know we have lost
that mine you never will be
to our partners forever we'll be paying the cost
and prisoners forever we'll be

JoAnne M. Jordan
MOMENTS

Moments scattered through the woods bringing the hours together in a garden of heather. A gentry-action by the sun and the forest floor is redone in shades of green, gold and blue. When time alters AM to PM the colors change their hue.

Orville Pointer
LOVE

Love has no race color or creed
is not bound solely by mortal
word or deed.
Love her monuments and
treasures are laughter tears and
smiles.
Full of heart warmth of soul.
Love is only a word to a cold
heart.
Sought by all found by some
forgotten by no one.
I have seen love in the eyes of
the poor, in the face of the sick
even those not long for this
world.
In the eyes of children I have
seen loves eyes so many times.
Her grace and wonder love so
vast to fill the heaves and the
earth yet all can live in the
vessels the heart and soul.
Some say the bleeding heart
only crys out.
But please feel and know that
should love leave this world,
soon after the shadows would
rule among them hate.
So perhaps some will read this
and wonder of love a great and
price...less gift to the world.

Lois (Vickers) Frizzell
THE MOCKING BIRD SONG

I awake in the morning
At ending of night
To hear the mocking bird
singing
As the dawn brings light.
Its notes are beautiful
Pitched either low or high,
Voicing sweet melody
With gaiety and pride.
Each note in its voice
Has a sound of glee;
Each note in its voice
Is a blessing to me.
It sings with perfection--
With never a discord;
In its song I hear
It praising the Lord!
It sings as if it had
No trouble or care--
No thoughts for tomorrow,
No worry or fear.
It sings with confidence
That God has supplied
All its needs...
And is satisfied.
It inspires a great
Inspiration in me
As it soars around
So care-free.
I perceive the qualities
It does possess--
We could all do without more
And live on less.
And be not anxious
Of what tomorrow may bring,
As we listen to the song
The mocking bird sings!

Erin Heather O'Donnell
ROCKING CHAIRS

You might call it a Murder
Institute
It's enough to break your heart
- or stop it
Antiseptically clean
Tuesday's we perform
Take your face off
Step inside
You can eat your cake and ice
cream
But there'll be no party hats or
balloons
Don't we all have birthdays
So many years too soon?
Rocking Chairs and Teddy Bears
The scent of baby soft perfume
Try to kill the memories
But they'll be back again next
June
Anonymous Murder Madness
Institute
Take your face off
Step inside.

Katherine Darrah Hunt
GRAND CANYON

A vast and eerie wasteland;
Abyss and jagged peak,
Secluded vale, deep chasm,
Sheer cliff and mesa bleak,
The Colorado River,
Gargantuan, unique.
A maze of many colors:
Buff stratified on red
With rose and golden headlands;
Soft green a shaly bed:
Warm brown, gray-blue and
purple;
The river's silver thread.
The sculptured panorama
Beneath each moving ray
Of magic-fingered sunlight
At dawn and end of day:
Titanic mass and color
Transformed in their display.
To probe a dark hiatus,
A large white stone is tossed
And, like a melting snowflake,
It vanishes, is lost
Within the chartless canyon
So massively embossed.
A brooding total silence
Prevails inviolate,
And in its hush of slumber
The canyon seems to wait
For Judgment Day to conquer
The carving hand of Fate.
Here Time and Space are joined
in
Profound infinity.
Man trembles on the brink of
August eternity,
Within his heart beholding
His shattered vanity.

Lilli Lee Buck
IT I DIDN'T

If I didn't love you,
Where would I put my heart?
In some lonely prison,
Protected from Cupid's darts.
If I couldn't think of you,
Where would I put my mind?
On some abstract subject,
To leave thoughts of hope
behind.
If I couldn't look at you,
Where would I cast my eyes?
Down toward the ground,
So that no-one could see them
cry.

Ellen Marie Knoettner
THE FOUR—LEAF CLOVER

One day I was lying in the grass
Thinking certain matters over,
When suddenly to my surprise
I spotted a genuine four-leaf
clover.
At once I pulled it from the
ground
Trying to do so carefully,
And I thought of all the possible
luck
This charm could bring to me.
I examined this piece closely
To make certain it was the real
gem,
Yes, it was green, had four petals
And was complete with a stem.
I wanted to save this charm
forever
Without another doubt;
So I placed it in my favorite
book
To thin and dry it out.
Well time has passed and the
course
Of my life is really still the
same,
And I wonder now if this
tradition
Is merely just a game!!
Perhaps if I pass it on to
someone
Who is truly special and dear,
The magic of the four-leaf clover
Will once again appear.

William D. Bosworth
LISA

Endless eyes, skin of cream,
Majestic beauty, yet soft, serene.
Life in Her abounds with glee,
Should I approach on bended
knee?
Adorned in fur, gold and pearl
Her aura's glow does throb and
swirl.
My thoughts say I should
scream for more
What key have I to melt hearts
door.
Emotion locked in heart of steel
Banes the love I dare not feel.
I yearn to hold, caress and love
My Lisa, soft, pure as the dove.
Taste the necter of Her lips
Feel the swell of rolling hips.
What thoughts and dreams She
could unlock
But, fear I, She'd laugh and
mock.
Locked within my tempered
shields
Beats a heart that passion
wields.
A voice that swells flood tide
strong
To win Her love could not be
wrong.
Approach Her as a gilded queen?
Appraise Her flesh, it's ivory
sheen.
Or hunter's charge to snag the
quarry?
Move in quick, never tarry.
As gentleman with coat cross
mire?
How indeed to kindle fire?
Lisa, dove, my heart is true
I wouldn't tire loving you.
Grant to me a single kiss
Nay spare the pain I'd rather
miss.
Come, no go, I can't decide
You'll think me crazy or to have
lied.
The truth abodes within my
heart
I pray for love that will not
part.
Lisa, sweet as sugared lime
Share love with me through all
of time.

Betty Milligan
THE NIGHT

I lay here quietly
thru the night
Stars shining brightly
provides enough light,
Enough light for me, to see
Just what tomorrow holds for
me.
It's almost dawn now,
the sun's soon in sight
Another day is here now,
God helped me thru the night.
Nothing is as pretty as
Sunshine coming thru
Leaving behind darkness,
Grass covered with dew.

Grace Carter
DADDY'S LITTLE GIRL

Along about five o'clock each
day,
My Mom starts tearing her hair,
She's tired of "How?" and "Why?"
and "What for?",
And looks for the nearest chair.
But promptly at five-fifteen, it
seems,
I sprout a halo and golden
wings,
It's time for Dad to arrive---and
see,
I'm Daddy's LITTLE GIRL!!!

Diane L. Wright
BURNING EVERGREENS ON TWELFTH NIGHT

A million vermillion tongues
lash out,
Encircling, devouring the
evergreen.
Each flame defiantly goes its
own way,
Then the cruel conspirators
convene.
The leaping, laughing flames
strike out...
Lapping and licking the spicy
air.
The watchers, entranced, dazed
by the scene,
Are lost in hypnotic stare.
The flashing, dashing fire is
wild;
A devil-may-care in disguise.
It's a crispy, crackly, heartless
rogue
With all that the name implies.
And then, of a sudden, it's dark
and still;
The flames die a death of pain.
Struggling for life, the demons
are squelched
Till naught but the ashes
remain.

Bro. Eugene F. De Lauro
GROWTH

The greatest men are sometimes
found, sifting sand or wetting
their feet at the sea shore's edge.
Seemingly, uninterested in life's
activities, or in seeking prestige
for prestige sake.
I the artist, stand at the slope
of their shore; painting!
Yes, painting a timeless idea
and in the process,
I try to come nearer to life's
eternal goal.

George Kessler
A MEMORY

I snuggled in a window niche,
My childhood's private nook;
The rays of afternoon lit up
The pages of my book.
I still remember what I read,
Though fifty years ago—
A fable written in French verse
About a fox and crow.

Sylvia Flitman
DON'T CRY MY HEART

The night was closing in and the quiet was almost unbearable. I turned the light out. Punched my pillow hard. Stared up at the darkness of the room and then as my eyes closed, I heard a whisper close to my ear, saying...Don't cry my heart, life has not ended, it is a new beginning and the sun is going to shine.

Don't cry my heart for sadness is only temporary and like a rainy day soon the clouds will part.

Don't cry my heart, life will go on...and like a sunrise, wait patiently for the dawn. Soon there will be beauty, rebirth and gladness, a new beginning and an end to sadness. So my love, please, please, don't cry my heart.

I felt a peace within me...I slept and morning came...a new day. A wonderful feeling flowed through me! I felt somehow happy, like a sorrowful load had been lifted off of me. I just knew something wonderful was about to happen to me. My heart began to sing...

I carefully patted my pillow, as I laid my head down for the night. I felt a glowing, happy, anticipating new year of love once again coming into my lonely life, to fulfill my heart with sunshine,. beauty and gladness.

This morning was a specal morning. I saw the parting of the clouds, the sun bursting through! That was enough to take my heart's breath away.

Charlotte A. E. McConnell
SOMETHING SET IN AMBER

When Young,
do not expect
the recognition
of the Experienced.
When Experienced,
do not anticipate
anything of Old.
When Aged,
the urge to expect
the recognition
of Old
will diminish
for you will recognize yourself.
Realize how much
you do not know
and each encounter
will make you stronger.
Open,
as a flower,
a Lotus for Learning.
Let the Heavens and Earth
flow through your fingers
as if they were your own.
Scan the Universe
for true wholeness
finding peace within.
One does not lie awake
looking for reasons;
the Gods* do not remind you
of what you already know.
In crystal dewdropped mornings
one can hear the calling;
one can see eternity through
a ray of fire,
reflections of oneself through
others eyes.
There is only One power,
the power is contained
within Something set in Amber:
the splendor of the sky,
a yellow shining star.
All the world can see
Something set in Amber
- an Aurora Borealis,
mirrored moonbeams.
The force
cannot be put into words.
Nor
can it ever be described.
We can open our eyes,
but if we can't really see
the beauty that flows
from within,
it is better
we close them
once again.
It is in feeling
with the senses
in which we acquire
Vision.
It is in knowing
the essence
of life
in which we gather
Beauty.
It is in seeking
the unknown
in which we acknowledge
Wisdom.
It is accomplishing
acknowledged Wisdom
in which we Understand.
It is all contained in
Tiger's Eye;
This is the
Spirit of Enlightenment.
**Whichever God you believe in.*

Richard Titus
THE GREAT ONES

The sea gives birth to natures child,
as in the water they lay,
who frolic and hunt as do all the wild
in their time and way.
The great Leviathons are ours to behold,
their beauty not forsaken,
and smoothness and speed are part of their creed
with their souls not to be shaken.

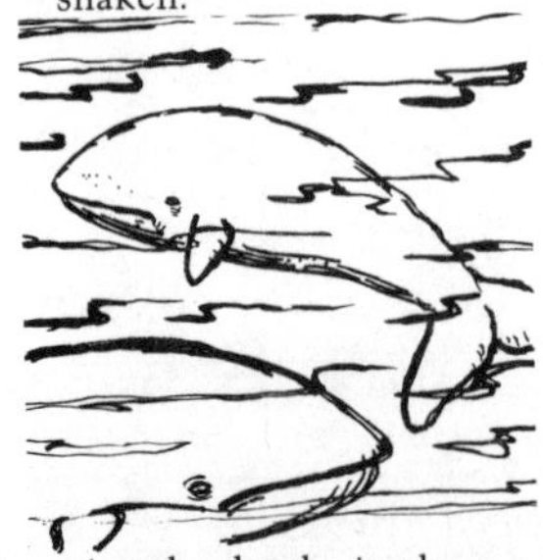

Scanning the depths in the oceans so blue,
and their hides so wide,
for God created great whales,
on plankton they would thrive.
Born in the sea as if in a womb
to be killed for mans selfish greed,
we are the scavengers who dig their tombs,
and for their extinction we pay not a heed
The ravaging of the waters mankind did create
since the dawn of the worlds first day,
but what of this beast who bellows peace;
is he always to feel this fate?
Whales alone seem without any hate
that we can seem to find,
look to the ocean for their homeward goal
to rescue their peace of mind.
Now that may shorten
as their numbers do decrease,
for the blood on a ton of priceless oil
will not help this end to cease.
What is there to make nature wonder
amidst its submerged atmosphere,
just what it was that remains the great blunder?
Is it mankind that has to be feared?

Debbie Auen
LOVE KNOWS

Love knows
How to be tender
Quiet or serene
It knows its' own mystery
Of remaining pure and gentle
Its' breathtaking beauty
Allows itself to be eternally free
Love constantly beckons the human heart
"Come - Come follow me"
Because reality forces love to be
Both the cause and cure
Of and for every broken heart
This gives reason for loves' unseen strength
To be tested, torn, and tried
Although momentarily subdued by heartache
Love suddenly gathers every haunting memory
And casts them all behind
And urges the broken-hearted
To look "ahead"
To "see" what they can find

Tena Bartels
THANK GOD FOR LITTLE THINGS

Thank God for little things
That come to you each day;
Just a friendly handshake
A kind word along the way.
That loving letter written
Maybe a telephone call;
We thank God for all of these
And welcome one and all.
Thank God for little things,
Like sunshine after rain;
For little arms around our neck
And fingered window pane.
For footprints on our kitchen floor
And lots of happy voices,
We thank God for all of these
Oh, how our heart rejoices!
Thank God for little things,
Like friendly neighbors too;
Who speak to us when 'ere we meet
And are always kind and true.
For loved ones round our table
And food for us to eat;
We're grateful for the smiles
From the people that we meet.
Thank God for little things,
Like little drops of rain,
Little rays of sunshine;
Comfort after pain.
Laughter after sorrow
Friends both old and new;
It's the little things in life
That make our dreams come true!

Sharron L. Wiley
REUNIONS

We should all be proud of our family tree,
It's roots and heritage and history.
So, we set aside one day a year
To come together both far and near.
We share our memories and share our lunch,
What a great feeling to be part of this bunch.
We lose some members forever, we know,
But new ones are added to help us grow.
Just as all trees change with the seasons,
So does ours for whatever reasons.
Don't forget we are all tied to one another,
Be it through birth, marriage or some other.
Our family gathering to me is great,
An occasion not enough of us appreciate.
Time flies as we work, keep busy, and have fun,
But let's never forget where we all came from.
This getting together called reunion each year,
Is something each of us should hold very dear.

Earleen Fernandes
THE MEADOW

Far away in a meadow
Things look so bright and green.
Flowers blooming everywhere
The most beautiful I've ever seen.
Coming closer I hear the buzzing of a bee
A butterfly flits by having lots of fun.
Birds are bathing in a pool
I see a baby rabbit on the run.
Standing here, this beauty I admire.
To grasp my feelings would be hard
For I have all these beautiful things
Right in my own back yard.

Paul Stuart Boehme
GONNA TAKE MOSCOW

You can join in the parade.
Gonna march the day.
Take Moscow from Ruskie.
You know they'd do us the same.
They're stealin' our fish.
Creepin' slowly closer to our shores.
Their spy planes, spy as they wish.
Board your windows, bolt your doors.
Ruskie's a comin'
Gettin closer all the time.
Morale low and fallin',
Show me a leader-
So hard to find.
Custer was curious cat.
Lee loved Savannah.
Lincoln fell to the bullet.
Teddy said hell ya all,
Bring them on.
Bring them on.
All red blooded Americans.
Gonna march all the day -
Take Moscow from Ruskie.
You know they'd do us the same.
They're stealin' our fish.
Creepin' closer to our shores.
Their spy planes, spy as they wish.
Board you windows, bolt your doors.

Kelli Jo Meredith
GAMES

So you're at your games again
Well babe that's just fine
because you see I've learned
and now have mine
You never gave me any credit
and that's okay too
my eyes are finally open
and can see right through you
You took the love I gave
but that's all over now
I don't have it any more
but it's over any how
So you'll make your moves again
only to find out
I don't play games
and can do with out
Go find some other fool
you've finally lost
and it isn't I
who must pay the cost
The things we did
will go unforgot
Babe it's over now
Forget
me
not

Shirley "Ski" Styczynski
WE LOVE YOU——CUBBY BEAR

You passed our way...Cubby Bear
You gave us gentleness...giggles
and goodness
You passed our way...Cubby Bear
You gave us sincerity...smiles...
and sunshine
You passed our way...Cubby Bear
You gave us kisses...kindness...
and kinship
You passed our way...Cubby Bear
You gave us fairness...
forgiveness...and faith
You gave us all of these and
much much more...
You passed our way...Cubby Bear
And you gave us LOVE

David Michael Etzwiler
WHAT IS HAPPINESS

What must a man have to
become happy,
Is it gold or silver, a nice house,
or a car,
Is it women, or traveling to
places afar,
Nea, my good man, it isn't any
of these,
And I'll tell you, my friend, have
an ear if you please,
Happiness is of a man who died
on the cross,
And if you put faith in Him,
you'll ne'er be at loss.
He was God-sent to deliver us
from our evil fate,
To free us from sin before it's
too late.
So forget about all of your
worldly wealth,
And put faith in Christ, an
you'll always have health.

Carolyn Bryant Bucko
HAPPY BIRTHDAY

Apollo will be 31 tomorrow
But he can't go back home
And he's really not sure
He can start again.
Apollo will be 31 tomorrow
As he stands on the hill
Looking back at the place
Where he knows he's been.
So he savors the stillness
Yet he craves all the lights
As he drinks in the darkness
On soft silken nights.
Apollo has turned 31 today
As she stands on the edge
Of a dangerous ledge
With her hand out-stretched.
And he turns from her
brightness
He can't look at the sun
And he checks all the keyholes
Making sure they are done
It's the end of the day
It's his own special way
To make sure he's safe
From the dreams he ignores
Now come lock the doors.
Apollo has turned 31 today
And he's happy and free
Though the things that he sees
Start to look the same.
He can touch with his soft voice
He can hurt with his eyes
And his virtue's a bookmark
That his passion decides
So light all the candles
And write out your list
Her arms are a haven
Whose comfort you've missed
It's dark once again.
Apollo has turned 31 today
He's strong and he's good
And he knows that he should
Help his fellowman.
Apollo was 31 yesterday
And he played and he won
So he'll laugh and he'll run
He won't share the blame.
And you'll get a fine answer
When you question his soul
And he drinks Russian vodka
As he counts out the toll
'Cause he measures his love
With an infinite scale
And he'll win at the game
Never bearing the shame
He's too good to be real.
Apollo was 31 yesterday
Such a rogue when he smiles
Holding back all the while
Still he's quite a man.
Apollo will be 32 tomorrow
And his life travels on
Like a flower in the sun
Of tomorrows dream.
Apollo will be 32 tomorrow
And. . . . .

Rachel-Duke Hamilton
LAMENT OF A FRUSTRATED POET

I can't write a pome
'Cause I'm not at home
In any other medium than prose
But there I fly high
Far up in the sky
And I write wilder stories than
Poe's
So pedestrian I am
But I'm also a ham
Who's inspired by those jewels
of y'ose.

Josephine Mandia Kipcakli
LOST SOUL

For: Rose and Joe Mandia

O Lord I am uneasy, so unable to rest. My soul searches for peace. It crys out in the cold dark night, where are you, where is your light! I have become so weary Lord, I dare not go on, I dare not for I dread falling. O Lord, comfort me, I beg thee, take hold of my withered hand for like a little child I come to you. With out you to guide me I will surely die. I can not see you Lord for my eyes are so filled with tears, I can not hear you Lord for the silence has made me deaf.
But I love you Lord for nothing in this world can stop me from loving you. Come, Come sweet Jesus my Lord, take this lost soul home with thee, for all of time and eternity.

Mrs. Kathryn R. Reynolds
FRIENDSHIP

To be a friend, that is hard
to define.
To have a friend, you are two
of a kind
But better yet, as all through
the years,
Two good friends, share their
joys and their tears.

A telephone call, a visit, a
rhyme,
Will cheer both of us up, any
old time.
So we will keep doing, as we
have before
For after all honey, we can't do
much more.

Cathy J. Dickens
THE U.S. FLAG

The American flag colors are
red, white, and blue
with battles fought so victorious
and oh so true.
Some were fought for equal
rights for me and you
and also for peace and slaves'
freedom, too.
The red stands for blood that
soldiers bravely shed
while blue stands for calmness
in the ocean's lazy bed.
The white stands for victory our
soldiers happily led.
But now they stand for battles
which are gone and dead.

Sheila Fuchs
A PORTRAIT OF TWO HANDS

As I gazed at this portrait deep
in thought
It had so much to say.
One reached out to ask for help,
The other was there to aid.
The two hands there-they
formed a bridge,
and the bridge was the thread of
God,
Who wove into this tapestry
a very royal nod.
The one outstretched, in need of
help,
was a simple creature, too.
But in this great simplicity
was a live and seeming cue.
One cast his head upon the
water
of his neighbor's love.
But in reality the guardian angel
was watching from above.
Two simple hands that cue a
tale
of simple give and take,
but the blessing here, just
beneath the surface,
is the hands of our great
Creator.

Joyce Inman
LOVE TOOK ME BY THE HAND

Love took me by the hand one
day
And led me to the babbling
brook,
"Now this is how the waters
play,
And this is how reflections
look,"
And so he left me kneeling
down
With wonderment upon the
ground.
And then I saw what Love did
mean
When leaving me upon the
green,
For when the waters play at will,
Always restless, never still,
Reflections from the earth and
sky
Are distorted to the eye.
Jagged and awry they seem,
Like the pieces of a dream,
Radiant sky and brown of earth
Juggled in a senseless mirth,
Broken beauty, broken grace,
Nature but a faceless face!
Only when the movements
cease,
When the waters are at peace,
Mirrored is the cosmic blue,
Pebbled bank and mosses too,
Unbroken beauty from above,
Boundless heaven, boundless
love!

Ruth E. Schaar
MY NEIGHBOR'S GARDEN

Just moved into town from
down on the farm,
Must learn to adjust,—no cause
for alarm.
All the years until now, I was
free as a breeze,
With gardens and fields and
faithful old trees;
But Fate intervened, —things are
not as before,
Now I gaze at the world through
my patio door.
There's a row of neat houses
with lawns clipped and green
And patio doors everywhere to
be seen.
But lo and behold, one lawn has
a surprise—
A tiny square garden 'neath
warm summer skies!
Neat rows of tomatoes and
green beans and such—
All reflecting the love of a
gardner's touch.
Nestled down midst the vista
of city-like scene
Like a gem shining soft in a
setting of green.
A sweet touch of "country", a
treat to the eyes,
And to those so attuned a lovely
surprise.
Many thanks to the gardner, —I
want her to know
The great pleasure I get from
watching it grow.

Donna Marie Garrett
A MOTHER'S LOVE
A Mother's love can neither
be bought nor sold,
For it is her heart that is filled
with pure gold.
From the smile and the gleam in
her eye,
The first time she sings a
lullabye—
Till the tear slips down her
cheek,
When the minister begins to
speak,
"Who gives this woman. . .to
this man?"
Mom holds her head up high as
she can,
As her heart pounds with mixed
emotion.
So proud of her beauty, Mother
shows deep devotion.
No, she does not stop caring
now,
Just steps quietly into the
background.
Many years went into this
production,
Which cannot end with the
reception.
Her new life will be a joy
though,
Because Mom excelled in this
show.
Her daughter made her very
proud.
May their love never cloud.
As her emphasis shifts to
another,
She shall never lose the love of
her Mother.

Karen L. Zimmerman
THE CEDAR OF LEBANON
From stories in the Bible,
And tales across the Lands,
Unquestionably, Undeniable,
Yet no one understands,
The Cedar of Lebanon.
The symbol of her country,
With colors all a glow,
A tree with quite a history,
The story we should know,
The Cedar of Lebanon.
Her branches cast a shadow,
For everyone to see,
How graciously She'll grow,
The splendor of her beauty,
The Cedar of Lebanon.
And year after year,
She still stands tall,
With never any fear,
That She's going to fall,
The Cedar of Lebanon.
Nature will protect her,
And that we can depend on,
As pretty as a picture,
With every waking dawn.
The Cedar of Lebanon.

Jennifer S. Cooper
SEARCHING
And SPLATT
I am slamming
I am jamming
I am pondering depth
I am SQUISH
like a praying mantis
smeared into an orgasmic
green mush
I am looking into an
abyss that I'm not sure
exists
And SPLASH
my soul laughs,
slips and watches while
my limbs that like
roaches sc-sc-sc-scatter
And SHATTER
I am breaching the
pane of my own
limitations
And hope to make
a mosaic
of the broken glass.

Gloria I. Paz
THE CEMETERY
I was walking a street,
Near, the entrance way,
Oh Paradise! this is the place
Where all the bodies rest.
I went inside to see,
I didn't hear a one...
I wasn't allowed here,
Because they aren't alive.
I knelt beside a tomb
And pray for everyone,
Suddenly! from above
I heard a mystic voice,
He told me... "Thanks!"
Then something came to me,
They desperately need
A prayer for them,
No flowers! they are gathered
Dry with the wind, on earth.
Then, I went away,
Thinking...they have the right,
To stay in peace today,
And forever... Amen.

Tamara Zehrung
A SINGLE DROP OF WATER
Just one ray of sunshine
With its piercing beam of light,
Melted one drop of water
From the top of snowy heights.
One drop, so small and lonely,
Slid down from off the peak,
And slowly, it began a trip
As for others, it would seek.
The ray of sunshine watched
the drop
As it struggled down the slope,
And the ray created more drops
That the first one might have
hope.
Together, the drops flowed
faster
As a trickle, and then a stream.
Not knowing their destination,
Their end was but a dream.
The streams joined new brooks
and creeks,
And with more purpose, they
did run
As rivers through the rolling
hills
All started by one ray of sun.
And finally, near the journey's
end,
The drops returned to the sea--
The place where all the sun rays
met
Lifting drops to clouds of
destiny.
Not all the drops flowed to the
sea
For some strayed by the
wayside;
And some were left in dying
lakes
Or missed by the sweeping tide.
And so the cycle must be
renewed
Till every drop finds the sea.
The gentle rains and the drifting
snow
Are guiding the lost to their
destiny.

Milena Soukal
THE MOMENT AFTER
The sun is setting.
Near is the hour
when hands of night
will reach into perturbed
twilight
and every tiny light,
the drowsy eyes
and dreams in-waiting
subserviently by the door.
Through distant lure
a faint aroma settled down
enhancing slowly
the bony skeleton of fright.
Because of it we shall not stay
too long in shallow water—
the surf is heading to the shore
uncouth, sensuous and rude.
Say, can we risk a break-up now?
First splash will wipe out
instantly
a microscopic life
that had begun in front of us—
its fine footprints in the sand.
We shall retreat now.
To stay alive. TO STAY ALIVE.

Dona Lotterman
DANCE OF LOVE
"We" are a fine ballet of love,
danced to the tune of
unquestionable reasons and acts.
Mind, heart, body and soul
intermingled toward "our"
ultimate goal of internal peace
and fulfillment...
Warm, lingering awareness; of
who we both are...
"one."

Judith Leora Johnson
MAJESTIC GRANDEUR
The grandeur of the mountain
With its majestic peaks
towering above the earth
Says with such austere
sophistication...
Valley... Be still...
You cannot deny my existence
For I am seen by
all who come this way.
I portray strength...
and display challenge.
And those who are drawn
by that challenge,
in turn, gain strength
in their own right.
I hover over you with
watchful eye and
protective arms.
I nourish your streams and
rivers
And invite you into my
bosom
for refreshing repose.
Be a friend...
With Honor...
And respect me,
For you cannot conquer me.
Friends need not be conquered
....only enjoyed.
Enjoy me...
For to this purpose
was I fashioned.
And so be it
with other friends...
Through enjoyment...
Grandeur is retained.

Lucy Beemer
WINTER FROLIC
Don't you hear the winter
whistling
Up a blizzard wind at night,
As it rushes around the corners,
Shaking things with mad
delight?
Hear the brittle tree's sad
sighing,
As they bend and sway so cold,
Longing, yearning, for some
memory,
Weathered dreams, and hopes of
old?
For a moment then it hushes,
Gathering might on some far
hill,
You can hear the lull of
quietness
In the elements so still.
Watch! bright sparks light up
the darkness,
Burst with crackling phantom
shapes,
As the wind steals quick and
stealthy
Down the waiting fireplace.
All wild creatures covered,
sleeping,
Cozy in their shelters warm,
But the wind must have his
frolic,
Dancing til the break of morn.

Carla Tracy
UNTITLED
These special feelings deep
within me,
Are feelings there will always
be.
No matter how we are apart,
You'll always be in my heart.
My thoughts and dreams
revolve around you,
And with my arms I hope they
may surround you,
And hold you close from this
day through,
So neither of us will be blue.

Barbara L. Kellogg
LOVE, JOY, PEACE
The blessings of friendship old
and strong
Are gifts which have no
measure;
The beauty of moments and
feelings shared
Is something I'll always
treasure.
In friendship true, a Love is
there,
A certain way of caring;
A deep concern for happiness
And troubles each is bearing;
A special meaning far beyond
The merely spoken word;
An honesty and openness
And feelings understood.
In friendship, there's a Joy
Shared between us through
the years;

Fond memories of happy times,
Of hopes and dreams, or tears.
And no matter what the time or
miles,
I know our friendship's true;
For the easiness and happiness
I find in being with you.
In friendship, there's a kind of
Peace
That comes upon the heart;
From patient understanding
Of the things our lives have
brought.
There's an inner peace in
knowing
That our care will never end;
For your smile and warmth are
always
In my memory, dear Friend!

Alva A. Gowins
AMERICA
America! America!
The land of liberty,
You have strayed from your
path
Of great destiny,
The hope of all men,
To reach your blessed shore,
That they might live in freedom,
Happy ever more.
From many lands they come,
Crossing stormy seas,
That they might worship God,
Upon bended knees.
A nation built by faith,
In a God of love,
By an humble people,
Inspired from above.
Many give their lives,
Their fortune and fame,
Now in this land we live,
They did not die in vain.
In our homes and Churches,
We can still talk and pray,
But consider our schools,
Will it remain that way?
They took God out of the
schools,
The devil walked right in,
If you don't believe it,
Just listen to the news again.
They are busing our little
children
Away out of town,
The poor nuts that's doing it,
Don't know the world is
round.
They rob, rape, and kill,
All just for fun,
Burn down the town,
Then shoot a cop and run.
When brought before the Judge,
Sitting in his pen,
They don't seem to mind,
In him they have a friend.
If they were sent to prison,
Where they ought to be,
Some misguided Judge,
Will surely set them free.
Then back to the market place,
As we often see,
Only this time around,
It could be you or me.
When our nation's leader,
Hugs the Russian bear,
Kiss him on the cheek,
We just stand and stare.
God in his Holy mountain,
Looks down on this sad act,
We could hardly blame him,
If he sent him home to pack.
He stopped the neutron
warhead,
The Russians to please,
When he cancelled the B-1
bomber,
They laughed up their sleeve.
He cut our navy shipbuilding
In half we hear,
When he stopped the cruise
missile,
They danced and drank their
beer.
They are killing the unborn
babies,
Hollering for E.R.A.,
Both an abomination to God,
They have pushed out of the
way.
Many of the nation's leaders,
Are honoring the gays,
Surely God will judge them,
If they don't change their
ways.
Some are taking drugs,
Others smoking pot,
On the downward road,
To where it's awful hot.
Listening to seducing spirits,
That are awful vile,
Whisper in their ears, no need
to marry,
Enjoy life awhile.
He cut our nation's defenses,
Right down to the bone,
While the Russians have gone
all out,
To make the world their own.
They have built the greatest war
machine,
The world has ever known.
While our President plays
politics,
And sits upon his Throne.
America! America!
Our land of liberty,
Change your way or fall,
No destiny,
Support our Patriots,
Our nation to save,
That our flag of freedom
May forever wave.

Mrs. Patricia B. Cabrinety
THE INVADERS
Out of a bed of fog-like silk...
Inching along it's way
Slowly, slowly by the day.
Teeny, tiny, bead-like tussock...
Inching along it's way
Slowly, slowly by the day.
Fuzzy, wuzzy, creepy crawler...
Inching along it's way
Slowly, slowly by the day.
Grown to four-star colorful
humps of age...
Inching along it's way
Faster and faster by the day.
Joining a munching, crunching
restless army...
Inching along it's way
Faster and faster by the day.
Three-inch, seven-starred
adult now...
Inching along it's way
Faster and faster by the day.
Unison sounds of patterings like
soft summer rain...
Daytime, nighttime
Crunching, champing.
Oak, birch, and even pine to
whet the ravenous appetite...
Daytime, nighttime
Crunching, champing.

Bare Trees in July

Bared trees resembling Fall
stand witness in June...
Daytime, nighttime
Crunching, champing.
Ghostly July limbs testify their
presence...
Flitter, flutter, flutter
thru life's ebbing breeze.
Bee hive like black masses
assembling for journey's end...
Flitter, flutter, flutter
Thru life's ebbing breeze.
Emmence of odor foul before
aloft light brown wings fly...
Flitter, flutter, flutter
Thru life's ebbing breeze
Life's cycle ended...yet begun
To start anew in next
Springtime's sun.

Robin E. Wesner
WE ARE BUT A SEEDLING
So many ancient avenues we
have traversed upon,
Long lost forgotten memories,
webbed in mysterious song.
Nostalgic array of faces so clear,
Unknowning why, I hold them
dear.
Whispering winds skirt the
story,
Its' theme plotted by firm hands
of time.
Seeds are rooted in thick black
loam,
Sprouting patience, in an
upward climb.
Nature weaves the path towards
growth,
Inner peace radiates light.
An honest heart purges the soul,
Seeking spirit shall gain insight.
Judgement of life shall not trek
alone.
Accompanied by familiar
strangers,
Who long also to uncover the
precious stone.
Past, present and future run
parallel course,
Harmoniously intertwined.
Wave lengths radiate patterns to
create,
The infinite universal mind.

Mabel White
SOMEONE
You came along when I needed
someone to help me on my way.
My children are gone and I'm
alone but God has his way for
me each day and he sent you
along to brighten my day.
It makes no difference if we are
young or old we need someone
along the way. It may be
someone's baby you sing and
rock to sleep, but God has a way
for us each day to help someone
on his way
So many out there need
someone they're crying and
begging for bread, they have
pain and heartaches, sad and
alone they need someone to
make them happy and glad. But
God has a way to gather his
strays, he'll answer their call
and send someone.

Mary L. Lanier
GRANDMA
G is for Gift
God sent you from above.
R is for Revolve
Like the sunshine with your
love.
A is for Arms
That never got tired.
N is for Never
Held back the love I
required,
D is for Dear
Yes, I think you are.
M is for Moments
Spent here and afar.
A is for Always
Gave your special touch.
Grandma, please hear me
I love you very much.

Monica Kay Tatum
SENSELESS MEANING
Sitting down
With pen in hand,
I expected to write something
brilliant,
Something stirring,
A piece to change the world.
Sadly, the only things that
flowed from my pen were
Shapeless words with scrambled
meanings.

Jane Caldwell Powers
RECAST
We've played our separate roles
Too long
Let us now recast our parts -
And I be you and you be me
Exchange our lives - our griefs
And joys
Give me your wants and take
My deep desires
Wear my smiles and let me
Show your frowns
Recast, restage, restore our
World
To harmony
And call
The new production
Peace.

Joe Ortiz
SLOW BEGINNINGS
Night has quietly slipped by
As you wake to discover
That the thief has taken away—
Yesterday
Leaving behind
A brand new day
And yesterday lingers for just
a moment
In a mind that has not fully
grasped—
Evidence of today.

Diane Hallahan

SPRING RAIN

Spring rain is like no other;
It makes the young butterflies
fly aflutter.
In the spring you can see
Many a new thing amongst the
trees.
Delicate drops dance on the
grass.
The sun glowing a brilliant
brass.
Rainbows promise a brand new
day
Out in the meadow the sound of
a Jay.
The smell of the air to
something sweet.
Mother Nature, up her sleeve a
treat.
Flowers coming up here and
there
Spring rain is the one, the one
and the fair.

Louisa Mulvihill

ABOUT THAT REMARK

I heard you, way down inside
Words that hurt, I almost cried,
Oh, you didn't come out and say
them
It's the meaning you implied.
Well, I'll just keep my mouth
shut
Those twisted words, meant to
cut,
Will all come back to you
someday
And kick you, right in the butt.

Carrollyn Turner Poenie

JUST A REST

Not lost to me forever,
Just absent for awhile,
An intermission in your life
To rest a weary mile.
A peaceful sleep, a pleasant rest
When all your cares have flown,
And when you wake again one
day
You'll see God's great unknown.
Where peace and beauty all
abound,
With chirping birds and flowers,
Where hand in hand we'll walk
along
And talk for many hours.
Oh, what things we'll have to
say
When together we will be!
We'll laugh and sing again once
more,
From sorrow we'll be free.
It's hard, I know, to look ahead
To things that're yet to come.
But, thoughts like these, I know
are true
And will comfort instead of
numb.
For after all, we each must pass
Through death's great, shadowed
gate,
But brightly shining just
beyond,
The Master stands in wait.
For he will call us unto Him;
He's watched us all the way,
His hands outstretched in
tender love.
Oh, glorious, happy day!
At last, our troubles ended,
Our burdens, we lay down
And trade our tattered, rugged
cross
For a heavenly, golden crown.
I must not dwell on heartaches
now,
But remember just the best
And throw my tears on He, who
cares.
He'll guide me through the rest.
So, for awhile, I'll weep and long
And miss your presence here,
But I'll see you in the "morning
light",
So wait for me...my dear.

Patti Jo Ware

MY FRIEND

Today I saw the sun
It's golden fire warmed my face
and heart
Today I saw the river...your river
It washed away the faltering
from my tired feet
Today I saw a flower
It beckoned to me with it's
dewey head
Today I saw the trees
They whispered, "Hello
stranger...where have you
been?"
Today I saw the seagull
He danced and swooped from
rock to rock, and asked if
I might join him
Today I saw a chipmunk
He chattered a happy "Good
morning", and asked if
I might help to find a cone
Today I saw the mountin
He promised me virgin trails,
sweet berries and singing
brooks

Today I saw the wind
He stormed through the forest
and down the canyons then
slowed his pace long enough
to gently whisper across my
face, then lifted me onto his
wings and carried me into the
clouds for a short visit, then
up and away into eternity
Today I saw because of you....
my friend
Yesterday I didn't see
Tomorrow I will see the rain
when I am gone from you........

Sheila Juba

MIMOSA

Bees hovered around
That mimosa tree
For years,
Singing its innocence,
Enticing pink heads
To silk blossoms.
It seemed to thrive. . .
Later,
The blooms were sluggish—
Not quite pink
Or fully spread—
The branches brittle
As though the sap had fled.
I worried for a while,
But the tree seemed to be
Alive.
The last snow
Though
Was more than it could bear:
The frail tropic branches
Bent beneath the weight. . .
I tried to brush the snow,
But winds
Froze
And cracked
The branches
One by one
And splintered the trunk
To earth.
Spring tries to breathe
A scent of passion,
But the bees
Cluster near
The white magnolia.
I dig my pink mimosa
From cold earth
And shiver.

James Wheeler

MEMORIES

Memories paint such lovely
pictures
as they work upon our minds
deepening shades of color on
our journey deep through time.
Every facet, every feature
of the image we perceive
reflects a measure of the
treasure,
the gift that we've received.
Loving hearts add to the
painting
adding pieces now and then,
extra strokes upon the canvas of
what was or might have been.
Mirrored beauty, love's creation,
with a palette knife sublime
fashions still the life inside us,
refining every line.

Janice L. Schulke

FALLEN IDOLS

Dustdevils dance on surly
streets
In a town, now dead,
Decaying.
Rotating rats infest the rooms
Where doors hang down,
Fallen, idle in disuse.
In '49 men staked their claims
and
Claimed the stakes
In musty mines
And lust-filled halls
Where Golden Idols ruled.
Some were timberlike men,
while others, cursed with
coward's skin
Worshipped Vice,
And Vice held them,
With a Golden,
Hollow Grip.
Men stole away, bewildered,
stunned,
When steams held only
Golden Sun.
Now shattered mirrors hold no
sight
Of exquisite faces
Or flaming lights,
So the town stands dark while
The Spirits spin,
When Idols fell from the hearts
of Men.

Carole Angela Rutledge Hawkins

THE SEASON OF CHRISTMAS

Tis the time of the year,
For wintry winds to blow;
And all of the little ones,
Hearts begin to glow.
With Christmas on their minds,
And the gifts that each will get;
Under the lighted Evergreen
Tree,
From jolly old St. Nick.
Young and old, sitting by a
Fireplace,
Watching shadows of the
flames;
Dance along the walls and
windows,
And glowing on everyones faces.
May this season for everyone,
Be cheerful and also gay;
As love and friendships grow,
With each and every passing
day.

Re

UNTIMELY ACTIONS

It's mainly when you smile at
me,
Like when you're reacting to
something
I've said,
that I feel this wanting to
reach out,
and touch you.
And it's when your eyes display
a certain warmth,
that I feel like I need to hold
you.
And it's when that warmth
is replaced
with a look of hurt and
uncertainty
that I come to the realization
that you might not ever have
the need
or the wanting
to hold me
again.

Web

FOOTBALL

Football widow—what a shame
With each I sympathize
Don't misunderstand, I love the
game
But no team do I idolize
On the radio and on T.V.
Saturday, Sunday, and Monday
night late
That is all we hear or see
Football now, we're beginning to
hate.
We turn the dial, slick, click,
click
Football, football everywhere
we look
By now we're getting sick
So we turn if off and pick up a
book.
These marks look strange for
awhile
Then how to read we start to
recall
Now that we realize this
Football did us a good deed after
all.

Edward Benn
DAVID AND THE TRAIN
Because there are only dreams
and riddles recently exhumed
of you, my brother,
your life and death comprise
the same obtrusive moment
in your brother's heart, who for
you has not existed. Something
of you remains always, removed
from weeds and smoothing
marble. Something as real as
dancing becomes a part of you.
If there is a name on your stone,
it is the name of a great king of
Israel.
It is Easter bringing forth
the bright silence
hovering beneath the songs of
birds.
Our father and mother
stand apart from the children
looking for something;
and looking everywhere,
flowers are violently alive.
Passing time unguarded
between a mysterious ocean
and a house, tropical beauties
violeting themselves in spring,
I begin the journey
with no end, as I see time
plays tricks on the living
in the shapes of ascents
and progressions, immutable
trains and revolutions, always
coming and vanishing with
catalogues and mountains, then
emerging.
Once in a dream, our father
has opened your infant grave,
exposing me to your ponderable
blood.
David, he says quietly, David
my son, you have become an
angel of the moving earth and
stars.
Now, wherever you are,
in whatever shadow
or silence, in whatever heart
or compartment you travel,
I come to you,
finding you from a vast distance;
I must come to you
in my manner to assure you
my brother, how much we are
alive.

Lori J. Flood
THE SEA AND ME
I've never been a sailor;
But the sea is calling me.
And though I've only seen it
twice;
It's there I long to be.
The pounding of the waves;
The crying of the gulls.
The winds that never stop;
I want to live it all.
I want to be there
With each changing of the
seasons;
The frozen fury of winter storms
That decend without a reason.
Summer days, hazy and warm;
And splashing wild storms;
And moonlit nights, with gentle
waves;
A tale of love, legend and lore.

Charles H. Hewett
THAT DOG OF MINE
I wonder if there's ever been
another friend like you, of
course there's been people, but
they never did the things you
do, When I am sick you help me
out, you are always there to aid,
and when I am well there's no
doubt, For you I have never
paid, I can not depend on
people, to do things like you do
for me, for they always want pay
for what they do for me, You
have stuck by me through the
thick and thin, And I always
will love you for it, Because you
are my friend, I never have to
call you but once, And never
ever twice, And you are always
there to help me and never
charge a price, When I need
someone for a friend, I call you
just one time,
And then you come running to
me, For you are THAT DOG OF
MINE.

Patricia L. Reynolds
THE NAME OF JESUS
Confess unto the Lord
In the name of Jesus;
Ask for a blessing in His
holy name;
In all that you do
Do in the name of Jesus,
And your life will never be the
same.
When you heal the sick
Heal in the name of Jesus;
Pray for the troubled in His
precious name;
Plead the covering of the blood
of Jesus,
For He suffered for your sins
And took the blame.
All you do, do in the name of
Jesus,
For old things passed away
All things become new,
For there's no other name
To come to the Father,
This is the Lord's commandment
to you.
Cast out satan, the prince of
darkness
In the name of Jesus,
Command him to stay out of
your life,
For he's the father of poverty
and suffering,
He comes into your home
With grief and strife.
Have faith whenever you ask
In the name of Jesus,
That God will be right there
for He's your friend,
You don't have to shout for Him
to hear you,
Whisper Jesus, He'll do the work
And the miracles begin.

Elaine Meli
THE PIT
Into a "Pit of Darkness" I strode.
Into oblivion I trod.
Not knowing what lay ahead,
And leaving all behind. . . .
I sought to find.
Out of the light and the
knowing—
Leaving the world behind.
I walked the "Pit of Darkness";
Leaving the world behind!

Wayne Joseph Klinge
THE POET
The reciting words of a poet's
past
A beautiful life with a meaning
at last
Standing alone in a century of
time
A different place for me and
rhyme
The martyrs voice in a forgotten
grave
But words of truth live on and
save
Of peace, freedom and of love
God's eternal gift from heaven
above

Miss JoAnn Roberts
AN IDOL OF WHAT?
A man strong in mind and
strength
a man of only one
an idol,
an idol of what?
will he still be an idol
when his strength shows
weakness
will he still be called a man
when he stumbles and reaches
for your hand,
he's then, an idol of what?
will you still idolize him
when you find his strength
is not his own
when you find he's in need
will you stand true
for what he meant alone.

Cleveland C. Matchett
ON THE STORMY SEA
Strong was the wind, violent the
rain
While waves struck wildly at
rocks in vain
Along the coast of Greenland
again.
A Norse ship rode the storm-
tossed waves.
At the helm was a boy, the son
of Eric the Red.
Eric taught his son to move
ahead
And bring the ship through a
dread
Storm as a skillful rider might
be led
To handle a spirited horse in
form.
A deep oar placed to right front
norm

Steered the craft, while ready for
alarm
Shields were strung outside
ready for harm
Leif, the youth, turned the blade
lever
To move the steering rudder and
endeavor
To watch the boat sail strong
and braced.
Bending with the movement of
the sea embraced
Was a shallow draft and keel
encased--
Able to bend easily and adapt in
haste.
This was part of its strength, as
the bosom waist
Of a breathing monster encased
Lets in no sea water because it
is defaced.
After the storm, came grey,
ghostly fog
Muffling all sound, soft and
thick it clogs
Sea, ice, and rocks agog.
But in lifting, it was tinged with
light.
From the overhead sky were
blurred outlines in sight
That became shadows. Then,
when fed by a gust of wind
bright--
Greenland was in view--
immense, shining, quiet
In passing colors. Looming
ahead in height
Were jagged mountain peaks
rising upward.
All around was the impression
that was heard
That all was alive but deserted,
none stirred.
Depressed screaming birds and
roaring streams
Broke the mood of stillness and
dreams.
Eric moved slowly toward Leif
who stood
With arm on hip and legs apart
in a mood
As though he were in charge on
earth.
Eric told Leif to watch the worth
Of time which appeared to stand
still like the birth
Of the world. When the fates
are too strong
Against him, the head must rule
over song
And heart. Chanting a prayer to
Odin belongs
For he protects those seamen
who do brave
Deeds. The greatest virtue is
courage, crave
Death in battle as a passport to
paradise.

Roslynn Hatchett
BUMPS
In the beginning there was no
bumps on me. God saw bumps,
He saw how they look he lifted
me from, the Bumps. By his
spirits.
He gave me joy
Bumps hear me
You are all over me
You started a long time ago
You didn't scare me
And he gave me peace midst of
the bumps.

Carl E. Ryan
LOVE'S REMEMBERING
Your unsullied character makes
your kiss
As a diamond in gold's precious
setting;
To hold you is a pleasant
experience,
Like fronded palms against
A purple sky.
It would be a lie to say,
I do not love you,
For, I do, in ways I cannot
even understand.
Though distance keeps you
in another place,
I see you now in soft
shadows
Of love's remembering.

S. M. Nieto
I THINK
I think of this blue earth
and what it means to you.
people dying of hunger not only
for food.
I think of this blue earth
and what it means to you.
Philosopher each of us to it's
own term.
Staging ourselves to what we
want
soon we got to meet our Maker.
Money creating men and money
destroying.
Tell me men how much for your
soul?
I think of this blue earth
and what it means to you.

Lila Lee Noller
NIGHT WHISPERS
The night is here so dark and
long
I sit here fighting fears
My life is rushing past me
Have I wasted all those years?
Where is the girl I used to be?
With all those hopes and
dreams

The promise of tomorrows
Ambitious plans and schemes.
These middle years are flying by
Oh Lord, Where did they go?
Slow down a bit and wait for me
I know those dreams are yet to
be.
Oh, look at me sweet world!
Beneath the aging flesh
There is a spirit young and free
That's me! It's really me.

Patricia Sparks
WHICH ONE?
Do you feel like you are two?
Do you feel it's not fair?
Do you know which is right?
Do you feel which path is right?
Or do you care?
I really want to care
I really want to do what is right
But, my heart and mind aren't
together
Thats when its not fair
O God! I pray help me make it
right.
Part of me wants to be bad
Part of me wants to be good
O God!! Pull me back together
But, my heart and mind isn't
too bright
When I am bad, I think of all
the things I once had.

Elinor Fowler
ANESTHESIA
A heavy weight is laid upon my
mind of sadness,
Nor peace nor rest can I
yet find.
I trust—and find too late
Unworthy
Are the objects of my faith.
I hope—and find ere long
My hope
Like dew is dried and gone.
I love and soon I see
Unreturned
My love will quail and flee.
Lethal slothfulness pervades my
being.
Careless
I can look on life with eyes
unseeing.

Domenick Bava
LOVE IN A CHANGING WORLD
Love is caring for one another
unselfishly,
maintaining family unity and
tranquility.
Dreaming and living in harmony
and peace,
not only when the sun shines
bright;
but in times of need, adversities
and stress,
when darkness and dispair
pierces deep into the night.
Love is free of greed, hate,
jealousy, lust and tyranny,
it is offering a helping hand to
less fortunate ones.
Love is to abide by "Law and
Order" and endear the holy
scriptures,
and placing the "Supreme Being"
before our every action.
Love is God's supreme emotion
in the human heart,
with its void, humanity would
be senseless and corrupt.
The world would be infiltrated
with distrust, disillusionment,
dishonesty, shamelss sin and
irresponsible heartless
shambles.
Love is important, for truth
and justice in this nation,
where freedom to express
oneself is a treasured right.
Love prompted our forefathers
to assure everyone of basic
human rights;
and equality in "life, liberty and
the pursuit of happiness".
Love is unchangeable and
possessed by every human
being.
In some, unrecognized, hidden
away and never utilized.
In others, it is given freely and
heartily with blessings;
with unrestricted abundance
and prevalence toward others.
Love is listening to, and seeing
others,
as we rightfully would expect to
be seen.
With sincere comprehension,
compassion and dignity,
quickly ignoring any trifle and
unjust misunderstanding.
Times constantly change with
new patterns of living,
unique environmental cultures
and unaccustomed habits.
Proponents of love and faith,
unfailingly attune themselves
unbiased,
to a new world of adjustment,
togetherness and progress.
Boundries and frontiers of
nations of noble and older
generations,
no longer exist in the
swallowing, sightless distance.
The immensity of the universe
is reduced to encompassment
of a small sphere;
with the new, scientific
advancement and dawning of
each new day.
Our age-old traditions and
treasured customs,
that stood the test of time
immortal;
will always be cherished in the
aged memories,
by those endearing souls to be
eternally forgotten.
But in young minds of ensuing
generations;
they will be over-shadowed with
their new;
loftier visions and timely,
advanced inspirations;
forsaking the old into the pits of
darkness and oblivion.
Love is needed in the "now" to
help meet each other's needs,
to forgive and forget prejudices
that undermine souls.
Love does not elevate the
power and ego of the elite,
to the detriment and downfall of
their underprivileged
counterparts.
Love means closer relationship
and consideration,
with our fellowman and the
changing environment.
Coupled with the welfare,
dignity, respect and "hate-
free";
social pride and destiny of all
mankind concerned.
Love is the power that melts
hearts of iron and steel,
that has conquered the mighty
and the brave.
Love can perform miracles, and
be the winning force of our
time,
if given sincerely and mutually
for the betterment of
everyone.
Love is forgetting reminiscences
of our old world,
and leaving our beloved past,
time-worn ways and glories
behind.
to seek the new bright beacon
that lights the way,
intelligently elevating our
mental visions and
aspirations.
To reach for new hopes and
goals toward a new world of
enlightenment,
and to build a better tomorrow
with peace, harmony and
solidarity.

Pat Holder
BE MINE
Be my valentine and share with
me the days of roses and wine.
To caress the rose and sip the
nectar of the vine.
To laught with me, when I feel
glee.
To hold me dear, when tears are
near.
To share the ups and downs
that make this life go around.
The earth has much Beauty to
behold, but what good is beauty,
if you feel alone and old.
For youth comes of happiness,
of sharing ones life with the
other sex.
And Gods given beauty though
it be there to see—be it so
useless my Darling to me.
For a shell of emptyness inside
to be—the beauty of the earth I
cannot see.
Be my Valentine and set me
free.

Bobbie Jo Delgado
MOMENTS
Each day is a moment
not to forget.
For now each moment
is the present
you have waited for.
Remember each moment
with heart
and you will have a
life time
of wonderful memories.

Margaret Grace McFarlane
MOMENT'S TO STAY
To love, to blossom, to grow
most significant bond.
The hour's of time come swiftly.
A being once so precious and
alive,
to be found gazing on some
sunlit shore.
Thought's carried deep to the
ocean floor,
only to be brought in with the
rolling tide.
Must we know of these
beautiful moment's
that pass away so quickly. .
Can they stay forever. . .
Can the tide not stay on the
shore
and leave it's seaweed
behind. . . . .

Anne Bobrick
DIALOGUE BETWEEN THE WICKET QUEEN AND THE MIRROR: A GROWN-UP VERSION
"Mirror, mirror on the wall,
who's the fairest of them all?"
"Oh mighty queen, you don't
mean
for me to tell you what is seen.
If I say that you are plain,
you will smash me into rain.
Thus I will praise your beauty
bright
and say that you are loved on
sight.
I will fight that inner dread
of the larger mirror in your
head."

Pamela Prout
INDIVISIBLE
What lonely creatures you are,
With thoughts to strange.
You speak of feelings
Not really understood,
With words that are empty;
With words that are deceptive.
You spend your lives
Protecting your space,
While desperately reaching out.
And each of you strive to be
Completely individual. . .
Not really sharing;
Not really caring.
Because you cannot be touched,

You fail to perceive
That you are not achieving
Your potentiality.
You scoff and discount
The uncomprehensible.
You must have forgotten
The evolution of man:
A cell, alone, bumping
Into another by chance;
Collecting for survival;
Becoming responsive,
And dependent.
And you say you are
The top of the plan—
An individual man.
Yet you are unaware,
As in the beginning.
A few are beyond your apex,
Realizing their being.
They touch one another;
Growing, sharing, caring as one.
While you wander aimlessly,
And endlessly seeking
Completeness and fulfillment,
They are content in their unity.
Oh what desolate creatures you are,
Alone in your shells.

Phyllis Fisher

A CRANBERRY CHRISTMAS

A Cranberry Christmas
Brings to the mind,
Old-fashioned parties
With cider or wine,
Where taffy was pulled,
And cranberries strung,
Stories retold and
Carols were sung.
A Cranberry Christmas
Always had snow,
With red holly berries
And green mistletoe,
Myriads of kids,
And stockings galore,
An evergreen tree and
A wreath on the door.
A Cranberry Christmas
A warm cozy fire
Waiting and watching
For each caroling choir.
Hearts are united
And filled with love
As we remember
Our Father above.
A Cranberry Christmas
Stirs feelings so deep,
So strong, so powerful,
Long been asleep.
Love for a Savior
Who came to the earth
With stories and teachings
To show us our worth.
A Cranberry Christmas
Is nothing at all
Without understanding
This most divine call.
Life takes on meaning
When one comprehends,
The gift Jesus gave us
When mortal life ends.

Elouise A. Spivey

THE SON—IN—LAW THAT WOULDN'T BE

Long before he was married into my family
He gave me joy, much happiness, and fun.
But these are some things one would enjoy
From her "Son."
His home has always been open to me and
He has never been too far or busy to help
Or send help when I needed something done
And truly this is what a Mother would expect
From her "Son."
Sometimes things were sad and it seemed
Nothing could be done, He then would come beside
The bed I know to say a silent prayer.
Then he would smile as the Morning Sun.
Playing the role of a "Mother's Dear Son."
I worry not about my Family I now leave
Behind as I start this race, I alone must run.
Because I leave them all in charge of "The Son—
In-Law" that became my "Son."

Diana Kildiszew

TO PATTY

Hush my child
And come near to Me,
For I will free you
From your misery.
I've counted your tears
You've cried all the day,
And know all sad sorrow
You've hidden away.
Also your pain
I suffered it too,
While hung on the cross
My blood shed for you.
I desire to lift you
And bless you with peace,
Draw close to me child
So your sorrow can cease.
You'll then know the love
Which only I give,
Be freed from your past
And joyously live.

Mary Bowers MacKorell

IN HEAVEN, PERHAPS

We cannot have them here:
A friend who completely understands,
Love from self set free,
Worship in the eyes of a little child,
The Christ in full majesty:
Our bodies are too frail
To bear such ecstacy.

Terry Dolin

THE MOUNTAIN

I went to the mountain one day.
Beaming down on me was a golden sun ray.
It shown so brightly on the snow covered ground.
There was a feeling of peace and love all around.
I sat quietly and watched two squirrels play.
They were having the time of their life on this beautiful day.
I thought how happy the people in this world would be,
If they would be like these squirrels, happy and free.
Above me, a hawk soars in the sky.
His is not to question why.
He just glides through the air, stopping from tree to tree.
He is happy being himself, that everyone can see.
People should go to the mountain, and just look around.
They would be surprised what wonders can be found.
They could take all the wondrous things they see.
Like the squirrels and hawk, and strive to be free.

Earl T. Rashid McMillan

YOU AND I

I WISH TO ACKNOWLEDGE:
Mr. Eugene Redmond, Poet in Residence, California State University of Sacramento.
Ms. Genevive Hunter - Consultant.
THANK FOR YOUR HELP IN PREPARING THE FORMAT.
WITH LOVE:

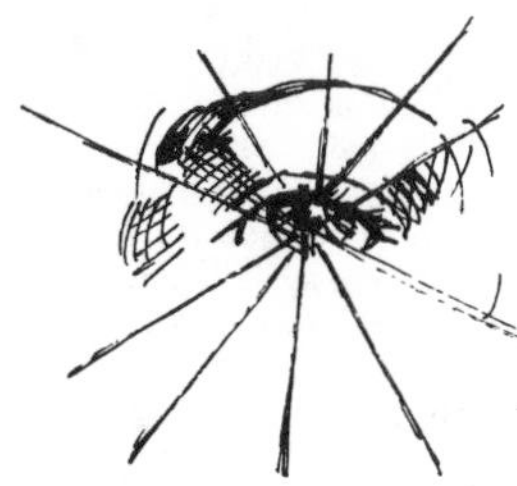

Princella, Cortney, Jawhar and Maya McMillan

Far . . . deep
where only
my heart's eye can see
rests spiritual intuition;
that center point
which sees
harmony so inevitable,
discord so impossible.
Existing discoveries
root safe in the eternal cord,
and those unborn
are sure to blossom.

Mildred Dickinson

BEIJING—(PEKING)—1981

GREAT WALL OF CHINA - hard to believe!
The mind can hardly conceive
That in eight-sixty A.D.
Men built what we see -
No machines their work to relieve.
Those Emperor guys thought big!
In their over-sized pokes - no pig.
The entrance to tombs
Through marble floored rooms
Must have taken years to dig.
They didn't go in for fountains,
But BOY! - you should see the mountains
That great wall crosses!
Human life losses
Were great. Of that there's no doubtin'.
'Tis said, with a sort of pride
That when the stone workers died,
They were dumped in the wall -
Having given their all.
Many bones in that wall abide.
Also said, it's 3,000 miles long.
No one's proved that figure wrong.
Emperor's dreams came true;
Examples many - not few.
But lives weren't worth a song.
And wars were not stopped by the wall.
It made no difference at all.
Since of wars, the seed
Is the averícious greed
That hangs over man like a pall.
CONCLUSION
When astronauts looked back to earth,
The wall was all they could see.
So maybe that sight was it's worth
Since the wars continued to be.
No matter how great the wall
If men's hearts are filled with greed,
There'll never be PEACE at all.
'Cause history repeats, we read.

Robin Ellis

DEATH

It feels like the falling
leaves of autumn
It looks like dried old
prunes
It tastes like old eggs
left to rot
It smells like the harsh
smell of wood just varnished
It sounds like the crying
of babies at night
Death is the ache of losing
a loved one

G. J. Karluk

LOVE IS LOVE

The thought of love does wander free
It belongs to neither you nor me
All we can do is let it dwell
Within our hearts for our Earthly spell
It casts no shadow that can be seen,
Yet, it's eternal and forever green
It stimulates the minds of men
Whose worldly descriptions never end.
How can you compare a feeling, thus,
That touches every one of us?
You cast the words and let them rhyme
One hundred, thousand, million times!!
Love is truth, love is life
Love is the one I call my wife
Her warmth cascades upon my brow
Even though I'm not sure how
I write some words, they end as poems
And sometimes, my mind, it does roam
But, there's one thing I know for sure
That love is love, and it endures!

Curtis Snodgrass

LIFE'S PREPARATORY WAY

I've sown many a seed
that fell by the way
But I've reaped enough
to make me move on
Of life's cup I have tasted
many ways without song
But I've sipped enough sweet
nectar to make me move on
I've dreamed many dreams
that never came true
But I've realized enough
to make me move on
I'll not look back
for you see
Yesterday's pages
are but
Life's preparatory way

T. M. Hardaway

BEQUESTING QUIET

What is my question?
Who will answer?
Where does the truth lie?
When will I know why?
My question
Will answer,
Does the truth lie?
Will I know?
There is no present,
Only futures gone past
And memories not yet come;
For when the future is present,
it is past
And the things of this world
will not last.
So,
If reality is now,
This life is empty, but
I choose not to surrender.
I have too much time on my
hands.
Lord, take these hands.
I have too much time on my
hands.
Lead me to the promised
lands.
Then a gentle breeze rises from
within,
"He who stands as a man
Will in time stride the Great
Divide;
For does not the great whale
Sing to a greater glory still?"
Now, I can read the lines
between the lines,
I can understand.
The lines, they spiral from
"Once Upon a Time,"
Do you comprehend?
We all began, we grew, and most
of us were born.
Now I'm waiting again,
To be born again.
And when I am three,
I will know infinity.
Then, with a smile, I looked to
the west.
Color streaked the bottom of
the sky
As the last dregs of an October
sun
Were pouring out into the night;
As though a work of art were
being painted in reverse,
While from the east,
Diamonds were being flung
Onto the black beach of forever.
In the waxing twilight,
Realities begin to melt,
Transforming under the glow of
a harvest moon,
Becoming a wonderland of jet
and silver.
Am I not a rich man?
The startling cry of a
whippoorwill,
A stallion silhouetted on a hill,
Time seeming to stand still,
Silence filling the air
To crescendo as a symphonic
ensemble,
Exploding.
Now there is a gentle breeze
within
And I know love is a friend.
Again, I ask you,
Does this not make me a rich
man?
And *this* is only
The Beginning

Marvin Lee McGhee

THE TRAVELER

I've traveled over country
that I'm sure I can't forget,
and the beauty of it all
is still within me yet.
I still can see the pine trees
so straight, slim and tall,
The mountains in the distance
and the rivers rumbling fall.
I still can see the falcon
in it's graceful evening glide,
over the tops of trees
and along the mountain side

I can even hear the panthers
scream so mournful as he
sounds,
and still can see the chipmunks
acting as circus clowns.
I sometimes even yet can smell
the freshness of the air,
and I'm longing more than ever
now to live my life out there.

Erny Adams

A LONELY TREE

I look out at the winter sky
It's color mixed in blue and grey
A lonely tree is standing
stretching high
A gust of wind tears out a
branch
And hurtles it away
I feel just like that tree
My arms stretched to the sky
You are the wind that comes
and touches me
Tear out my heart
And leave me there to die
I never knew how much a heart
could ache
I never felt such pain before
Should I just grasp what you
have offered me
Or should I walk away from you
And close the door

Gwen Hutchins

I LED YOU HERE TO SEE

Up the hill we go
To a place I love so
The climb is steep
But, riches we shall reap
We are at the top now
The effect makes me want to
bow
But all I ask is
For you to look and see
To me this is eternity
The beauty of it all
Is so dear to my Heart and soul
But, your expression shows
All you want to do is go
Now downward we bound
No reward has been found
I led you here to see
But, I saw for myself
You are not for me
You have no sensitivity

Linda C. Castro

PAGES

Each morning, my life is as
a blank piece of paper.
The events of that day etch
themselves permanently onto
the page.
At the end of the day, I can see
that the page is used up.
Some days, it's a jumble, where
I've tried
to do too many things at
once.
Other days, there is a lot of
blank space,
as if the day somehow
slipped away, becoming
eternally wasted. Never to
be used.
I look at these pages of my
permanent record, totally
helpless
to change any of these once
they've been recorded.
Some days, I look at the page
with pride
at what I've accomplished.
Other days, I look at it with
regret
that I didn't do more.
The blank spaces bother me,
and. . .no rewrites are allowed.

Julie Ann Bailey Lipman

THE OLD

The old
They're people who are more
precious than gold.
The stories they have told,
Are memories I always want to
hold.
They're like children you
sometimes want to scold.
But they're wisdom is something
to behold.
I'm so glad I have had the
chance to know these people
who are old,
Because My Life they have
helped to shape and mold.
These fantastic people more
precious than GOLD.

Fatthi El—Dabh

SEAROSE

and if we recede,
let us recede with plessure,
and while falling,
while the abyss has no voice of
welcome,
let us fall
like sharks smelling blood.
and let us imprison ourselves,
you and me
just once for a while
to see our essence and freedom
behind daily lies and cries,
daily noise and little chaos'.

Penny Lang

HAVING LOVE

Knowing "I Love You" comes
deep from my heart,
Makes it easier and less lonely
when we're apart;
Feeling "You Love Me" gives
strength to my days,
Being wanted and needed in
so many ways;
Hearing "You Love Me" touches
my heart,
It both holds me together and
tears me apart;
It seems that "I Love You" often
goes unsaid,
Why must we always keep love
in our head?

Lisa Y. Naghiu

THE WILD ONE

There he goes said one to the
other, he flies at the speed of
Pegasus not another,
He is a great black steed, of the
noblest breed, which was bred
for a pace that has grace.
His mane is as black as the
night wind blowing, his eyes are
the color of a fire that is
glowing,
His body is of strong bone,
though his name is well known,
he's free, he's beautiful, he's
The Wild One.

Diane A. Parras

JOURNEY

The wind of life is blown upon
me
Unexpectedly; I lose my ground.
I am swept away by endless
questions;
Not an answer to be found.
My soul is lost in immensity;
A boat upon the sea
Tossed about by raging waves
Of life and liberty.
Washed upon the shore of real,
I am ready to make a start.
Battered though I am, I smile
For surviving the hardest part.
I am but a wanderer
Just passing by
Seeking space to spread my
Eager wings and fly.

Mindy Sterba

MOMENTARY OUTTAKES

Thinking of elephants
And exotic liqueurs
While sipping tea
And petting my cat
who knows nothing of
Hemmingway
Or Kipling, yet
seems to be satisifed
None-the-less
But still I wonder

If there couldn't be more
To a Steinbeck world.
I reach
For Agamemnon
and find him. . .gone
And the Aztec pyramids
and Wounded Knee
And the men from Mars
They come to me
Once in a while
Celluloid figures
Roman heroes
Peter O'Toole
And I sigh and try
To hold on to them
. . .which never does any good
So shadows of adventure
Become whispers in my mind
Yet still, I'm thinking
Bullfights
while petting Floyd, the cat,
Who really doesn't
give a damn

Aurea Rodriguez

A TRIBUTE

A lonely rose was laid
With a silver tie pin on its stem.
A tear, a drop of dew. . .on the petals of the rose.
A sigh of grief. . .on the stillness of the dawn. .
A quivering hand. . . with a farewell on his finger tips.
Sound of parting footsteps on the lawn.
And there. . .on the mist and weeping dew
A silent prayer for one who died before his time!

Marjorie Hambrick

AFTER SUNSET

After sunset in Joseph's garden tomb
Unseen forces were in motion,
Gentle angel wings were whirring
As they attend HIM in devotion.
HIS hastily embalmed body
Was placed on the stone slab—dead,
It was wrapped in clean linen
On it 100 pounds of myrrh was spread.
There was a strange stirring
A rustle in HIS darkened nest,
A sigh escaped the once tortured body
As HE stirred to life from rest.
HE emerged from HIS burial inclosure
As a vapor from a flame,
The world's greatest event was recorded
HE arose—HE lives—again.

Pamela W. Church

PAST REMEMBRANCE

I feel a part of me is gone
to the memory that wishes
to stay. . .he's gone
People hurt in loss of him. . .
they empty their feelings in buying records; donating money
Why did this happen?
What are we to do without him
There is a reason somewhere. . .
What is this meaning
deep inside
Being courageous
or unfaithful
a sin
One mistake
comes another
I hurt. Don't you see
until the fire dies in the ashes

Sharon R. Christopher

GLIMPSES OF A MAYAN WINTER

Half torn squares of time grey rocks
piled unevenly in spots
stand silent
surveying the turquoise coves
like mutes with memories that scream unheard
to the endless waves
that live and die and live again
like the sunrise and sunset
and sunset and sunrise;
and so we try to find
what unharried afternoons we can
looking for different games
to pass the minutes
yet they live on
in the boring glamour we portray as 'reality'
amidst the jaguar with eyes of jade
and those with eyes of black coral
that also live mute under this foreign sun
possessing secrets that yet live
while we sit waiting, failing to understand
the tales they yearn to tell.

Rosalie MacKinnon Glew

THE CRIMSON EYE

The window is wide-open, the summer storm is, to me, a blessing: cool relief. Then an inner warning comes, to close the window and, reluctantly, I comply.
Instantly it descends, a molten ball, to dance along the window-ledge and seek some opening to enter; it seems alive and glares at me like a huge crimson eye. Then it veers to the left, I hear the crash where it has vented fury upon a tree. I fall to my knees in grateful prayer. I wonder who has sent it, who has warned me—Why hate and love should seek me from the skies.

Mary Bubeck

UNTITLED

I love just listening to you;
Your company warms my life.
I enjoy watching you live;
Your smile brings me joy.
We share our love,
through the music of laughter.
This we give to each other,
forever.

Dan O'Keefe

VOID

A moonbeam's dancing on a tiny heart
Beautiful ballet, free form art
Glowing rays beat the little drum
All is cold, no one's come.
Snow can't remember when bright sunshine
Warmed her life the last time
Turning white beauty into gold
No running water, all is cold.
An Eskimo stands a hill of glass
Looking out over a mighty mass
All of life has taken leave
All too cold, no reprieve
A lonely man stares into space
There's nothing left of the human race
No one cares no one cries
All too cold his body lies.

Everett Francis Briggs

FOR RITA

My Rita dear, I saw you go,
Through February snow.
You left me for the summer-land
Where dwells the Angels' band.
God grant, dear Rita, when I pray,
The words that I should say
To send you, in your home above,
Some keepsake of my love.
In Heaven, many windows are
Revealed by Evening Star.
If yours a casement-window be,
Lean out, and wave to me.
A cloud may pass, obscure your face.
I memorized the place
Where your small window thins the blue,
Behind it, God with you.
O cloudland high! High World of Blue!
Your filmy window through
When shall I see the Dear I knew?
O tell me, World of Blue!

Jaime N. Maza

INSPIRATION ADRIFT

LOVE, kindle the amber within me, inflame my
Complacency in holding fast on Thy power and infinity,
"with Eternal love"—for all humanity.
FAITH, hold my faltering heart,
veering Toward fear, as devil
in the dark, A sight—, set
me free, abide in thine
Guiding light of faith
till eternity.
HOPE, fill my empty soul to the brim with pain
Even suffering thru gale,
forceful and cleansing
Daunt fear with the Spirit, leave me
TRUTH,—I seek with righteousness, Love.

Donald W. Wiley

THE MARK OF THE HUNTER

Slash! Lash out! Wind whip the man
That's brave enough to travel the land
Of a dead, dread winter in Mich'gan.
Stark birches and snow ladened conifers
Are indistinguishable blizzard blurs
On a desolate wilderness horizon.
Ineffectual dull disc; cold orb; snow sun
Wanders recklessly 'mongst winter shrouds;
A spectral hoverin' 'tween sinister clouds.
However, it is quickly diminished by nature's hand
That dismally shadows this rugged Mich'gan land.
Cold is the blast of the frigid Artic-like wind
That tries and strives to do the hunter in.
Huddled and brave within his collar of fur,
He notices not the blur of the birch and fir.
Instead, deep shadowed eyes keep watch of the glow
That welcomes him warmly to the small farm below.
Worn hunter, tired, tired to the bone, and lame,
Musters remainin' strength to bring him to his lane.

Strugglin', he's draggin' home the game he has slain;
Leavin' blood of the venison reddenin' a snowy path.
The hunter's showshoes make the marks of the lath,
As he trods 'cross this vast snow-drifted Mich'gan land:
The mark of the hunter; the mark of the man.
The wind swirls and whirls, the hunter's nigh done in;
Tuckered, he blows and puffs clouds of white breath 'fore him.
Tired, dead tired, at last he enters his snow-filled farm lane;
Enters the hunter; strugglin', draggin' his venison game.
The back door of the frame house is suddenly thrown wide,
Revealin' the image of his dark haired worried wife inside.
She's silhouetted there in the opened and welcome doorway;
And the heady scent of supper o'er the winter air lay,
Causin' deep desires to gnaw and stir within her man
That's just returned from the hills of Mich'gan.
Slash! Lash out! Cause the shutters to rattle;
The blizzard rages and refuese to settle.
The dead stag sways, stiffens and freezes,
And swings heavily in the Artic-like breezes
From end of taut rope wound 'round ancient limb;
The Mich'gan winter rages 'round 'bout him.
Inside the frame house, now dark and still,
The hunter, the man, is home from the hill.

Patrick James Muller
CHRISTMAS NIGHTS
A Tribute to Uncle Ronnie
The world is quiet on a winter's night
When the land is colored a snowy white
A cold, cold storm blows across the land
And in an open field there sits a poor man
In a little gray and holy tent
Thrown out of his house by not paying rent
He is eating a rabbit so skinny and bare
Almost as skinny as the man who sits there
And across the field in a big white house
Even a mouse is as fat as a grouse
People all gay, people all warm
In a great white house, in a great white storm
But in the field the man sits alone
Cold and shivering—freezing to the bone
He has no gift except the rabbit meat
And the shoes he found which are upon his feet
As the wind grows colder
The wolves grow bolder
The man by now is 3/4 dead
Trying to keep warm in his poor little bed

Philip H. Skarin
LOVE
Love is like a beautiful butterfly delicate, elusive, and alluring;
Looking for a little nectar from a generous flower;
Lifting low spirits with its wings as it flies toward the sun, and
Laughing at mortals too heavy to fly.

Jill M. MacWilliams
A FRIEND
We might not always agree,
On some things we never see.
We don't always get along,
But together, we do belong.
Me for you, and you for me,
There's no other way expected to be.
When people look on, they see us as friends;
Its the kind of friendship, that never ends.
If I had someone else to choose-
If not you—with whomever else Id lose.
Because if I had chosen another,
I would have less than you, my perfect mother.

Billy C. Smith, Jr.
MAKE MY FAILURE COMPLETE
Where is my family, to love and comfort me?
I am not different from other people.
A loved one's voice would strengthen me,
And help make my failure seem less severe.
Where are my friends, to smile and laugh with?
Their bright smiles would lighten this dreary day.
Why won't they come, with their familiar laugh?
And help me forget my weighty problems.
My family has left me, what must they think?
Those friends won't come or call or write.
I have not become what they expected.
Without family or friends my failure is complete!

Marian Kay Brown
IMAGINARY LOVER
Imagine us together
walking in the rain,
picking pretty flowers
that grow wild every spring.
Running in the tall grass,
wading in a stream,
napping in the sunshine
to dream a carefree dream.
An afternoon with nature,
a picnic by the lake,
skimming stones across the water
counting ripples that we make.
Seeing the beauty of the sunset
change evening into night.
Watching the stars grow brighter
while standing in the moonlight.
Walking in a darkened forest
with a feeling of being lost.
And making love at sunrise
on a soft, thick bed of moss.

Lois A. Richards
SENSORY PERCEPTION
You are:
The sound of far-off thunder;
Rain on a tin roof; the roar of the surf;
A Christmas carol;
The fragrance of new-mown hay;
Burning leaves; pine trees;
Night-blooming jasmine;
The feel of bare feet on mohair;
Down-filled pillows; weeping willows;
Wind through my hair;
The taste of well water;
Tomatoes on the vine; chilled white wine;
Home-made soup on a cold night;
The sight of lights on the water;
A child in prayer; spring air;
A crippled shore bird.

Elizabeth Wells Bodiford
BENEATH OUR CHRISTMAS TREE
Tiptoe my children and come with me,
for I have something I want you to see.
Listen my children, but do not speak.
Just listen, watch, and take a peek.
Look there my children and you will see,
Ole Santa beneath our Christmas Tree.
Jolly, fat, and cheerful is he.
Singing and dancing beneath our tree.
Don't you remember how the story goes?
Red and white he was dressed from his head to his toes.
That's him my children! It's very plain to see,
That's ole Santa standing beneath our Christmas Tree.
Should we wake daddy or should we not?
Sorry my children, Santa's left, he's on the housetop.
Daddy will never believe that ole Santa we did see,
Singing and dancing beneath our Christmas Tree.

J. Stanley Weinrich
OUR MEETING PLACE
For many years its been my plight,
each Friday night to go,
to a place where there is more light,
when one room is not aglow.
Its a place where nearly everyone,
believes that those who can best agree,
will ever find that work well done,
most often creates peace and harmony.
I always find good fellowship there,
and in some manner find a way,
to tell the world, with a mighty blare,
its the friendliest place in the USA.

Mary H. Graves
DISTORTED BLUE
Was it just a memory
Maybe a half step to a dream
Wisdom will never answer here
This hue, this sense—unreal
Was it simply a breach of self
The bravodo of a fool

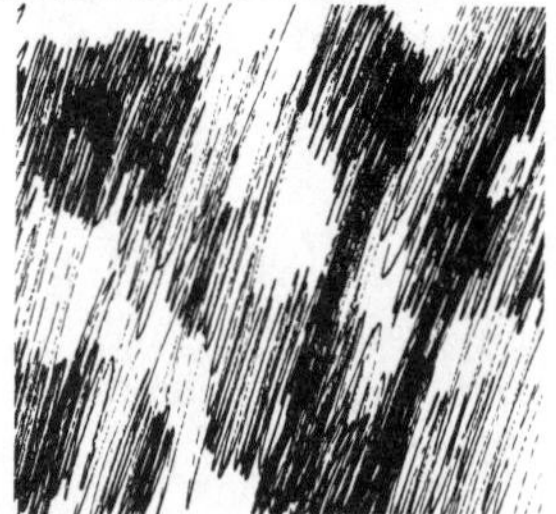

Reasons blur, become elusive
And shame distorts the past
Now it's only just a memory
A fragment of a dream
What will come can never be
But a promise lost to chance

David L. Mellett
WHY STUDY HISTORY?
I know that things are wonderful that nowadays abound.
How grand that science masters matter, sight, and sound!
It's a button push to knowledge, while a jet plane laughs at space.
When it comes time to suffer, drugs limit the pain you face.
Oh, no, I wouldn't forego it; mankind's reaching great goals;
But much has come too quickly, and there's heat in ancient coals.
What we have will ultimately bore us, and mock our spiritual drive
Unless we re-discover old ways that helped us survive.
Trudge through some brush and bramble; combat an angry stream.
Climb a rock-filled steep and find a place to dream.
The gnarled man by the worn plow is still the same species as we.
Don't forget his strife and suffering; he bounced us on his knee.
Yes, things are really wonderful that nowadays abound!
But we need some older kinships before we're truly sound.

Carolyn Gower
DON'T GIVE UP
It's hard to keep on smiling
When your life around you seems down
There's always someone less fortunate than you
If you'd just take the time to look around
You're fortunate to have ten fingers, ten toes
Get around without someone's aid
Be thankful for what you have
There's no guarantee it is here to stay
Life would be somewhat better
If we'd just cut down on our greed
Never hesitating to say "I'm sorry"
Swallowing our pride whenever the need
Make time to help your neighbor
Face problems one day at a time
Remember the value of true friendship
One who truly cares is hard to find
Spend more time appreciating what you have
Less time worrying about what you missed
It's true we all have room for improvement
But it's for sure we could have a lot less
Thank God each day for your blessings
Ask for strength to handle any pain
We were never promised a rose garden
And with faith we can sustain.

James Larry Mitchell
SAMANTHA JONES
She came to me slowly
whispering "its okay",
wrapped herself around me
and kissed my childhood away.
Those eyes, those eyes, those joyous eyes
They were warm wonderous and light.
She came to me gently
we opened up to each other,
and flew life's ultimate flight.
Her beauty showed outside
But there was much more
within, as she allowed me to glimpse her soul
the sweetness there was so sensuously rare
What a girl; in love with life
was Samantha Jones.

Connie Annette Nance
THE CRIMSON ROSE
Our love is almost like a rose
It grows from day to day,
Shortly before the petals fall
Its beauty wilts away.
The pain is like the thorns it bears
To hurt when you get close,
The trust is like the pleasant smell
That very slowly goes.
The joy compares to the fullness
That leaves when the end nears,
The dew that drops repeatedly
Looks so much like the tears.
The crimson color of the rose
Looks like the painted cheek,
As time goes on relentlessly
If fades from week to week.

Jane Barber
WHERE WERE YOU?
Where were you, when the die was cast,
And the world was to be steadfast?

Where were you, when the dark clouds appeared,
And the people needed someone unfeared?

Where were you, when the bird fell from it's nest?
And it's mother was greatly distressed?

Where were you, when your neighbor was ill,
And her life was steadily going down hill?

Where were you, when the drowning man held out a hand,
And he was too far out to reach the land?

Where were you, when the children dried out,
They needed help finding what the world was about?

Where were you, when the elderly were down,
And the world was willing to let them drown?

Where were you, when the animals were becoming extinct,
And it was said, 'that you never even blinked'?

Where were you, when all your brothers called,
All those watching surely were appalled?

Lisa J. Mason
WOUNDED AGAIN
You allowed me to believe
And have faith in you;
I opened myself to you.
And when I was most vulnerable,
You stabbed me,
Then turned away.
You left me
Standing there,
Alone.
Yet I was not
Lonely,
Only alone.
While
In the darkness,
I bled.
Weakness overcame me,
And yet I was strong,
For I had to be.
Then when I cried out,
No one came to my side
With an outstretched hand.
I groped in the darkness
And found the light,
With no help from you.
Now you ask me how I am,
Fine
Is the answer.
Yet this is only a facade;
An attempt to hide
The scar which remains.
Although it is not the first time
My life has been marred,
This wound was caused by you.
Perhaps you can't see this,
But then again
Maybe you can.
And though I remain hurt inside,
We both know I'll return,
Allowing you to wound me again.

Barbara Walker Carey
TIME TO WAIT
"Death is in the scheme of things"
This is philosophy—
The Shadow leaves with one you love,
This is reality—
Day upon day,
and yet you grieve.
Your time is not to spend,
but somehow to survive.
Around you hovers the gray and blessed shroud of shock.
Half-hearing, half-seeing, yet somehow,
and quite beyond belief,
You are still you.
Does this dismay you?
Does it anger you that the world insists upon turning and bringing its eternal light and dark around your clock?
That all the sounds of life still roar and rumble,
scream and whimper
Through your days?
Let wear your anger and dismay,
'til wearing out, they
bring a kind of peace.
And, understand, although there seems no reason, right or rhyme about it all—
There is an antidote—
Standing, patient in the shadows,
waiting,
our oldest ally, Time.

Larry Chaffee
POOR DUMB DONKEY
Poor dumb donkey could not talk.
Poor dumb donkey could not sing.
Poor dumb donkey could but walk,
And carry the Mother of our King.

Debra Leanna Neal
FOREST GLADE
Where sky is blue and earth is green,
Where no one is ever mean.
Where a cascading waterfall shimmers in the light,
Where stars hang as jewels in the night.
With leafy branches o'er my head
And mossy grasses for my bed,
A perfect place, a place for me,
That is where I want to be.

Steven R. Hurst
THERE ARE
Rough hills outlined against my sunset
Set there as they happened
All the hard times
The days no one would smile at me.
Yet, somehow they look beautiful.
Perhaps because I survived
Taking a little hill knowledge with me.

Joem Robertson
FRIENDSHIP
Friendship is a word,
Its meaning goes quite deep.
Friendship is sweet mem'ries,
Forever ours to keep.
Friendship is to be there,
When someone else is down.
As well as sharing joys,
When abundantly they're found.
Friendship is a smile,
A thoughtful, tender touch.
Or, just simply stating—
"I LUV YA VERY MUCH!"
May the Lord preserve our friendship,
With blessings from above
That we may be as free and happy,
As His gentle, peaceful dove.

Marida Collins
HIS OTHER LOVE
My husband has a lady on the side
When she moves she sure can glide
He fixed her up with all that paint
If I should put some on, he would probably faint.
The money he spends on her I could cry
He said she needs it so I sat by,
And watch him go his merry way
And wonder how long she will stay
Until another one catches his eye
Then he will tell her goodbye
It will start all over again
And he will spend, spend and spend
To hear him talk about her makes me sick.
All about her power and speed
And how she fills all his needs
Her slick body, high powered rear end
Now I know you will start to grin
But let me tell you I am not nuts
My Husbands love is a pickup truck

Mary Coady Sumwalt
GOD'S GIFTS
(A long prayed for gift)
A baby, is a gift so individual, a gift so rare.
Like the stars in the sky, unique as they appear.
Your baby is God's way of showing, that
Faith, Hope and Love are gifts of knowing.
If we open our hearts and eyes to see.
He'll do what's best for all, universally.
Praying and loving is certainly a must.
Everything will be alright, if in God we trust.
Your baby is a gift, a precious treasure.
A beautiful gift that goes beyond measure.
Through your Faith, Hope and Love.
You've been blessed with a baby from God above.

Connie Medeiros
UNTITLED
The ocean floor
Was a mountain before
And you and I were many things. . .
Is it better or worse
That you cannot walk
Upon the ocean?
Can you be the judge
Of what life brings?

Nancy Gail Fox
LOVE IN MAINE
I feel emptiness on the beach
The waves touch my memory with rythym
Growing
Breaking
Dissolving
Repeating over and over
The way you emerge
In
And out
Of my life
I remember our room
With it's postcard view
The rolling hills met the sea
Cold
Calm
Anxious

Seagulls cried
The fog would lift
The way you lifted me
Each morning
I feel the emptiness
I remember you

Melissa Goldsmith
THE GIFT SHOP
Ah, the ribbons and bows;
I used to have some just like those:
The bright rainbows
all broken.
Time is Here-
It dances in the glass
where the people stop and stare,
It hides
behind the crystal on the shelf;
I can see
where its shadow has run
Lost
Like ribbons
Like rainbows;
Pretty dancing Lights
But they were wrong.

Bobbie Trotter
TEARS AND TINSEL
Tinsel trees, sharp without the smell of pine
Cling dead upon a brittle, glassy pane,
A one-ice-sided window
Looking in,
Reflecting thousandfold
The sad-happy ghost of last year's
Mirrored merriment,
And all the false color brightly blinds me,
And tears and tinsel mingle into one.

Annie Ruth
REJECTION IS MINE
I stretched forth my hands offering love
I bought you a love gift to no avail
For it is I who love
Not you
You do not and cannot
While I was rejected
I cried "Love me"
For we are passing
We are not passing was your reply

You were right
I was in error
How could I possibly pass the unbelivable distance that unfolded
itself

I am the night
You are the dawn
You the holder of the day and a promise of a night to come
How far apart we are
Do not thank me my love
It is I who must thank you and ask forgiveness for my
untimely approach

My darling, in order to appreciate the grand and stately creations of God
One must love and through you I have loved
I sincerely believet his love is a gift given of God

For surely I could never bestow in myself such a gift
I shall stand and walk away
I do not want our eyes to meet in goodby

My love will tempt me to read your emotions in our parting
I am sensitive
I hurt

I would like a little while more to dwell with the vision of your
presence in a humble and gracious manner

Margaret Shell Kincade
A PLEA FOR THE RIGHTS OF ANIMALS
As he sits forlorn in his chair of restraint
This monkey so sad seems to say,
"Radiation experiments will soon burn my eyes
Oh why do they treat me this way?"
But his cries are not heard past the walls of the lab,
Needless cruelty rages full sway.
He is helpless to change his horrible life.
So he mourns in his chair day by day.
And think of the creatures in "factory farms"
Where animals live like machines
They stay cooped in small stalls
With scarce room to move,
More profits no doubt -- but what means!
These cows, pigs and chicks long for pastures and sun,
and the room to move and be free,
But alas "agri business" has doomed their poor lives,
Only shadowy gloom do they see.
While deep in our forests so peaceful and still,
Where our fur bearing animals stroll
Man's inhumane evil is even found here,
In his infamous steel-jaw leg hold.
Creatures caught in these traps oft suffer for days,
And the pain that they bear is so bad,
That some to escape will chew off a leg
Some others give up and go mad.
As humans we need to consider the rights,
Of our innocent animal friends.
We should help where we can to right their sad wrongs,
So often brought on by man's sins.
Let us strive for the day
When enlightenment reigns,
Man and beast will happier be,
When preventable suffering goes from the earth,
A far better world all will see.

Jack Dale
AN OCCUPATIONAL HAZARD
An occasional heartbreak is only an occupational hazard
If you work at Love
You can toil at it and think you've got it all figured
But it's all to no avail
Cause in the end an occasional heartache will linger
And that's because Love's such a hazardous occupation
And all it's risks you can never know
It'll carry you to such heights
But occasionally leave you falling, soaring down
And there won't be anyone there to catch you
To break your fall when you hit the ground
Oh, Love is such a sentimental profession
It'll make you so high or leave you so low
But on occasion on it's wings a trip you'll take
It'll make you feel you're the only one ever to know it
Make you feel so unique
But you'll find you don't really know anything about it
Just when you think you've mastered it's technique
That's cause Love's such a hazardous occupation
Such a sentimental profession
There ought to be malpractice insurance for it
And it ought to be compulsory that you carry it.

Gerald T. Anderson
LITTLE OLE SAUNA
Little ole sauna on Little Shag Lake
I'm back for the summer
Can't wait, can't wait!
Throw wood in the stove to heat up the rocks,
In no time at all you'll be spit fire hot!
Sitting in my good ole sauna soaking in the heat.
Hot bucket of water soaks my aching feet.
It's a rock filled stove with a blistering fire, hardwood fed.
The flames crackle loud, but I'm "Finnish" and proud
So I do not run out...yet.
Throwing water on the rocks,
A blast of steam rising hot
Turns your body crimson red!
Off my body pours the sweat.
Whew! one hundred and sixty,
Too hot! Too hot!
I'm out the door and off the dock.
It's part of a sauna, it's only right
To take a "skinny dip" in the dark of the night.
But soon I am back for the heat and steam
To wash down my body, I'll get squeaky clean.
I love my ole sauna, but I know it's time to go.
When the leaves turn color
And the lake turns cold.
Little ole sauna on Little Shag Lake,
I'm going home for the winter
But I'll be back, can't wait, can't wait!

Francis Wetherelt
THE HERALDERS
Jack Frost comes 'round every fall
And paints our canyons, wall to wall.
Stately pine trees often wear
A million diamonds in their hair.
Lowly sage and rugged rocks
Put on their many sequined frocks.
Common, sluggish little streams
Are all decked out like beauty queens.
While all around the neighborhood
White fence posts, like cold sentinels stood.
Waiting for old Colonel Sun
To come inspect them, every one.
And better yet for Sergeant Breeze
To finally let them stand at ease.
This is not so very strange,
This crystal psychedelic change
When we see
This act of God takes place each year
As the birth of Christ draws near.

Dolores Ann Eskite
HIGH ABOVE
High above
the sounds of earth
there walks a man
who clouds my air
lifting me to richer heights.
I stand alone
in naked splendor
leaning toward another self
blooming fragrantly in different soil
as familiar petals blow away.
And I,
the lover, woman, friend
acquaint myself with me.

Melanie Charrise Ratliff
YOU
You're my God, my soul, and my spirit.
I desire you to know so now you will hear it.
Even though toward me your eyes are blind,
I know you are my one so fine.
No longer are my thoughts so scattered.
They stay with you though they may be shattered.
My dreams of you are more than illusions,
But the real thing is all a confusion.
Notice me, please, you are my soul.
Reach out and touch me so I will no be cold.
Love me, hold me, just for once, my sweet.
I want more than illusions though our eyes will never meet.
I've told you. There now so be it.
The battle is won, but somehow there's still defeat.
'Fore now that I have you, you're not so great!
I think I had just tried too hard; now, you shall wait!

Michele Mapel
RAINY DAY BLUES
She sits by the window, a frown on her face
In search of the sun, of which there's no trace;
The rain keeps on pouring, no let up in sight
Dark clouds fill the skies' blocking out all the light;
There's no happiness or cheer, as long as it pours
For the child all alone, who's waiting indoors.

Johnnie O'Bryant Neely

WINGS OF DESTINY

He traveled through a forest green,
where never a cloud could be seen.
Though birds were everywhere,
And flowers blossomed there.
He had traveled far and suffered much
To reach that land of the golden touch.
A garden of Eden true and fair,
He was in Heaven just to be there.
Setting down his heavy pack,
He stretched himself upon his back.
Hands folded beneath his head to gaze,
At strips of blue sky through a leafy maze.
To reach a land so rich and fair,
Was worth the hardship he'd had to bear.
Soon he was dozing in a blissful state.
When down came the mighty hand of fate.
A dreadful rumble shook the land,
Mighty quakes of an unknown brand.
The forest cowered like a lion at bay.
A belching cloud banned the light of day.
Stunned and left in a helpless state,
Groaning and cursing at such a fate,
He crawled in a frantic searching about.
Surely there was some safe or possible out.
Wallowing in a trough of despair,
He cast about, and God was there.
No sooner had that Loving Presence come,
Than his tormenting fears were over and done.
A glorious light had shed its ray,
To keep those frightful shadows at bay.
God had built a wall about,
Even to banish his every doubt.
He arose, his spirit girded strong.
To help others in a motley throng.
No matter what might come his way,
Never again to defeat would he fall prey.
There were no bastions between life or death,
No mirages to endure of stress or strife.
Just a blast when calamity had him in her lair.
Then, the wondrous feeling, God was there!

Babette Lynn Barringer

EXPRESSION

Tears of wisdom flow quietly
down the face of old man time...
for he knows that a man can cry
without shame
at things such as love...
and the inability to do so
is death.

Clinton Lee Eisworth

SWEPT CLEAN BY THE SPRING

Swept clean by the spring,
I see the light of a new
beginning.
A call in the midst of my night
awakens me to remembered
dreams, so stirring that the day's
heat does not burn them from
my mind.
But first, I must salvage the last
pieces of my soul for the porch
sale, and then sit anxiously,
awaiting, hoping to bring the
price necessary for redemption
from this Hell!

Marina Rose

UNION

Unite Oh America
With Hands raised to God.
No more feel the sting
Of the chastening rod.
Into the Light - Advance, Aspire-
Up through trials that consume with fire.

Out of a darkness much blacker than night,
On to a glory so brilliant and Bright.
On to the dawn of a new day so free.
Now is the time. NOW - Let It Be.

Dawn Marie

THE ROSES

Sleeping heads, nodding down gently
Wilted memories of what used to be.
Their tresses falling softly,
Like dew drops
They lie,
Until they are swept away
With yesterdays dreams and untold secrets.
The silky pink petals
(Now shriveled and brown)
Are blown away
With our secrets and dreams
And scatter
Like empty treasures
Meaning nothing to anyone
Except Me.

Audrey L. Butcher

THE JOY OF MOTHERHOOD?

Today a day for peace and rest,
But Allison is full of zest
Can't doze a minute, or read the paper.
She wants ME to join her every caper.
Just sat down, to dream and think.
Allison thinks she needs a drink.
Sat down again, my feet are up.
"Ta Ta" she says, refill my cup.
The catalogue! I'll have a lookie
Now Allison, wants a cookie
I'm sitting again, cigarette lit.
She's lost her ball, she's throwing a fit.
For heaven's sake child, leave me be
She smiles, and plants a kiss on me
A nuisance, a pest, a darling, my baby
I'll rest tomorrow, - A-ha- maybe.

Leanna I Sauzek

CHRIST INVITES

Come along, abide with me.
I'll show you what life's meant to be.
Joy will flow in every vein!
Nothing will remain the same.
You'll find happiness on earth.
Your very being has rebirth!
Every star will shine much brighter.
Floating clouds will all look whiter.
Abide with me
You all belong.
Your life will burst
Right into song.
Joy will be there
From the start.
Let me come in,
I'll fill your heart.

Joan Brakefield Purcell

INFIDEL

You shall not lose me.
I will be there in your
sleeplessness,
I will haunt your thoughts
and hide in the corners
of your mind.
Neither light nor dark
can drive me away.
I shall dwell in your dreams
and lurk in your mirrors.
I am engrained in your movements.
I shall not loosen my clutch
on your heartbeat.
You ripped out my heart.
You took my love
then you stole my life,
and I shall never forgive you.
I will be with you
all the days that you live.
My very existence thrives
on your fear of me.
As on that night
when the life oozed from my
veins and my red tears
stained your bathroom floor,
you shall know my presence.
And your further deeds of
broken trust
will not go unrewarded,
I'll always see to that.
You shall not lose me, Infidel!

Jeanette Allen

LONESOME — BUT NOT ALONE

An empty room, dark and cold
A feeling I've never known,
But somehow I've managed to be this way
Lonesome - But Not Alone.
The memories of both good and bad
The happiness and sadness I've had at home,
Here I am, in this state of mind
Lonesome - But Not Alone.
The pains, the sorrows and defeat
The joys, the laughter, these emotions I've shown,
Living a life, tangled but free
Lonesome - But Not Alone.
Lonesome - yes that's my inner soul
My heart has nowhere to go,
I lost my one and only love
And these feelings of hurt he'll never know.
But Not Alone - no I'll never be
For my family and friends shall remain,
By my side - all the way
And with their love, I shall feel no pain.

Cathy Leigh Maciak

SYMPATHY

Sincerely as they touch your hand
Your tears roll out at the command
Many a handkerchief has been used
Poorly they have been abused
About the time your eyes are dry
The best of you begin to cry
Heaven loves a comforting friend
Yet sorrow and such are not to lend

Bernice Goodrum Ransom

SPARE THE CHILDREN

There's some mad person going
around our town, slaying our
innocent children, for what
reason no one understands.
The task force is doing the best
they can, to catch this heartless
man, but I am afraid the killing
goes on, and our kids don't have
a chance. Oh, Mr. child slayer,
you're hurting us, can't you see!
Oh, please stop these murders
and set our children free!
I know it makes your heart glad,
to see the parents faint out of
fear, well enjoy it while you can,
because our kid's deliverance is
getting near! Oh, parents, I know
it's hard coping with this
tragedy day to day, but
remember, there's a God who
loves you, and it won't forever
be this way.
Mr. slayer, even though you
haven't been captured yet, and
have slipped through the task
force hand, remember that
there's a righteous God in
Heaven, escape Him if you can!
I just didn't want you to feel,
yet, that you've gotten away.
In "Deuteronomy (32.35) God
said, Vengeance is mine,
and someday you'll pay.

Nydia E. Tompkins

NATURES BEAUTY

There is beauty on the prairie, there's a fragrance in the air,
There is music on the prairie, listen to the singing there.
The fragrance of the wildrose, the song of the meadowlark,
These are the joys of the prairie, more satisfying than a park.
I was born upon the prairie, spent my early childhood there
Playing on the native grasslands, running, jumping, without a care.
Small animals were my companions; squirrels, gophers; natures gifts.
Winter was a time of magic, sliding down the huge snowdrifts.
Now I live in mountain country, snowy peaks reach toward the sky.
Majestic animal life greets us as we travel roads on high.
And the beauty of the flowers with their ever changing hues
Fills our souls with great contentment, we forget our earthly blues.
We have done extensive treveling all across this land of ours.
We marvel at the animal and bird life and the coloring of the flowers.
Driving through a pass in Glacier Park we observed an awesome sight.
We saw a complete rainbow below us, all the colors clear and bright.
Let us enjoy the beauties of nature whatever our land and clime.
The waterfalls, the hills and valleys, give a feeling quite sublime.
Nature is grand where'er you travel, be it North, South, East or West
But we return home to the mountains, home to the place we love the best.

Stephanie Nahirniak

OUR SELF DESTRUCTION

Though Jesus, son of God, gave his life for us,
The people don't seem to regret it.
Instead of giving thanks and praise,
They already seem to forget it.
Their hatred and most misconducted ways,
Are leading to shameful destruction.
With blindfolded eyes they take the devils hand
Not caring for protection.
With dope and rape and all thats bad
Not heeding where they're going
Nor realizing the harm in this all
And all the sins they are sowing
The good times will disappear sooner than soon
With regret left along the pathway
With great laments and fears surrounding
To face the final doomsday

Margaret L. Grubbs

MESSAGE OF THE RAIN

I love the rain
It is God's gentle way of saying earth
Still holds some worth
And though His pain runs rampant through the drops
The raining stops and flowers grow
I love the rain
It is God's furious slash of slivered wrath
Down slanted path
Where droplets gain the fury of the wind
And tree tops bend before the blow
I love the rain
It is God's pain and wrath turned icy cold
And I behold
A summer slain and in earth's frozen breast
Is laid to rest beneath the snow
I love the rain
It is God's way of telling me He knows
I've missed the rose
And down my pane bright silver raindrops run
To greet the sun and curve His bow

Shellie Colleen Reese

COBRA

Sway with me, Human,
play me your song.
Sleep in my coils,
there you'll rest deep and long.
Let my gaze transfix you
till your will become mine,
Slither close to me, Human,
let me around you intwine.
Let my movements seduce you,
feel my skin cool and smooth,
each scale is an emerald...
touch me and be soothed.
See my ribs how they open
to undulate in my dance?
Do I not fascinate you?
Will you not take a chance?
Sway with me, Human,
feel my sharp venomed kiss;
Lean close to me, listen
to my flickering hiss...

John Fahnley

MUTE WOUNDS

Indignation cries
The blood-bursting chest of shot-gunned days
Litters wind-burdened winter beaches like withered kelp
Stark silhouettes mark the jetties on the bay
Where lone figures perambulate with their dogs
While adjacent, close enough to hear
Are the hoots and yells of a crowd consuming beer
Wounding the washing rhythms of the sea
The relentless chants of a heart betrayed for "me."
Shoulder to shoulder has now become the cutting angle
And stares are lasers cutting the twine of human eyes
Stealing the brain of its window on the world
Where all the murder, the famine unfurled
Like the cross-boned flag on a plague-swept ship
Lends not a pause before we sip
Oh sister with the golden hair
Oh brother with shrugged mantle of hope
One sixtieth of an hour should care
While fifty-nine become the hangman's rope

Ramon Estrada

LIFE

We walked to the altar
Her eyes how they shined
We became one
A marriage divine
We struggled through life
Her eyes confident and bright
We build together
A marriage delight
A daughter was born
Her eyes most delightful
We guided her
A marriage most prideful
Birth to a son
Her eyes shined with pride
We guided him
A marriage was right
She left with love following her
Her eyes produced tears
We prayed for her
A marriage with few cheers
He left like a man
Her eyes showed regret
We prayed for him
A marriage full of dread

Life became a struggle
Her eyes full of concern
Conversation was limited
A marriage discern
Love lost its lust
Her bright eyes faded
We lived together
A marriage belated
Two have lost love
Her eyes stared dried
We decided to part
A marriage had died
A marriage is a struggle
Future eyes for two
Study it carefully
It could happen to you

Michaele L. Reedy

LADDER OF LIFE

From the 1st to 5th step, you are considered a sweetie pie.
From the 6th to 8th step, you are a big boy or girl who mustn't cry.
From the 9th to 12th step, you enter puberty.
From the 13th to 19th step, you are a "dumb teen."
From the 20th to 34th step, you are full of curiosity and adventure.
From the 35th to 40th step, you have "mid-life crisis."
From the 41st to 60th step, you really start to live.
From the 60th step to death, you are wanting to begin again.

Lois C. Baker

LOOKING AHEAD

One day in all my sadness,
I searched for a word sincere,
In my haste, I found, I ran much too fast,
I seemed only, to nourish my fears.
Then I prayed for calmness of my soul,
For his love to come into my heart,
Such peace, within me, as I sat there,
Was a miracle, right from the start.
I opened my bible, and began to read,
A verse came before my eyes,
"You cannot have your dear child back,
But *YOU* can go to the child!"
From that time on, I've been looking ahead,
Cherishing the love in my past,
Knowing in my heart, I can never go back,
Only the goodness of God, will last.
So, if you have fears, that you cannot let go,
Just conquer them with a prayer,
Your thoughts will soar to the heavens,
Your answer, with God, is there!

Janet Pembor

THE CHRISTMAS HEARTH

O attic angels do come down
Into my house so spare and brown
Put cheerful cherubs here and there
The tarnished mantel now so bare
That flickering hope may not despair
But seem to wear
A red-lined cloak of winter white
For one true love to share tonight
With pigeons on my windowsill
Who fly away with newborn will
To hills of morning now so still
But soon to hear
The whispering kiss of peaceful pines
In answer to the bell of times
More dear. New Year!

Steven R. Hurst

TOGETHER I WISH

Sometimes I wish for fancy words,
Sometimes for precious colors,
Or for something new.
But nothing surprises you I know.
Autumn, my Brother,
Your gifts are from Jah,
As are mine.
How could I imitate something you do,
Or hope to impress you with something new?
So without fancy words, rainbow colors
Or anything new
I simply make my little heartfelt wish
That together we shall be
When all earth is made new.

Diane Maggio
MY FRIEND DAVID
Two years ago on a Summer's day,
I met you I'm thankful to say.
Through those years we've learned alot,
About who we are and who we are not.
At times we got hurt by our foolish pride,
But, stubbornly we came back taking each day in stride.
Forgiveness always followed, friends again were we,
How much I really cared you were blind to see.
But, quarrel after quarrel we came back
Better friends, we never talked things over
Just headed for amends.
I think the reason for forgiveness I know you will agree
Is because I really care for you and you really care for me.
But, one thing I wish didn't have to be;
The fact that a friend is all you want to be with me.

Ross G. Warren
AUTUMN
Get off of you bottom
You know that it's Autumn
It's time to start moving around
Vacation's been taken
The lawn needs a raken
It's surely not time to sit down
The curtains are dusty
The shotgun is rusty
The car is in need of some wax
The hedge needs a trimmen
It's no time for swimmen
It's really no time to be lax.

Marie B. Guimes
LOVE
You come into the room
Where I am resting
And play your violin
For me the way you did
More than half a century ago,
When we first met
And wed.
But now I am old,
And withered...
But you don't see it.
You pour your heart out
In music,
As if you're grateful
That I had come
Into your life
When we were
Young.
And you are stooped
With age, your eyes
Are dimmed.
But all I see is
How they light up
When you look
At me.

J. R. Kruizinga
LIFE IS A VAGABOND
What is life,
but a vagabond
wandering aimlessly through time.
Just when you think,
that you understand,
he drifts away, again.
Down some back-alley,
or darkened street,
where you have never gone before.
He stumbles through the dregs,
of our very inner souls,
revealing all that is within.
And trampling through the darkness,
he heads towards,
that infinite glow of light.
He pulls through all the sorrow,
and reaches out,
for the happiness of tomorrow.
When his journey is done,
he will rest,
and tomorrow will bring a new one.

Anita Wheeler
GLANCE
Lookng across the room,
I see his face.
The gentle look - he is busy.
Unaware of my study.
But it doesn't matter-
We are together.
I experience panic and peace
Simultaneously.
Is this possible?
Wanting to seek and know
the entirety of this man,
Or yet, just absorb
the comfort of his mere presence.
He suddenly returns the glance
And quietly
cuddles me with his eyes.
Small talk satisfies my anxiety...
For now.

Genevieve Sanderson
ME SWEET AILEEN
He was washing the dirt off from the heath
When who should show her pretty face,
But his gal from County Keath
His sweet Aileen and her sixteen
As fresh as the sun and the wind
"Sure, now, tis a day to be out to play,
To run in the gorse and the bream"
He took her hand, and they ran, and ran
Laughin' and gay, and free,
For the song of the birds filled them with glee,
The brook ran clear, and never a care they had,
The wind and the sun, and the heath were one
With Aileen, and her happy lad.
'Tis a star filled time, when one is young
For this broth of a lad, and his little one
Come ALL SAINTS DAY he'll have his say
And the Father knows 'tis sure
When you've a JEWEL man, you keep a close hand
"Till you've posted your bans in the land

Faye Ellen Brown
STEPS
I miss you, love
You're such a delight
Dreaming good dreams of
You each night
It hurt so bad
Not to see your glow
Thinking back
It began so slow
Now it's speeding up and
Far ahead
Up to the day
That we shall wed
Now even farther
Children come
Losing the time
We had alone
Now they're older
Brilliant, too
She looking like me
He looking like you
Time flew by and
Now I'm gone
Painful memories
When looking back on
You, too, are gone
Your time was up
Our children, raising theirs
Like they grew up
Now ours are gone
They'll be remembered well
What happens next
Only time will tell

Richard J. Toth
IMAGINATION TO REALITY
Unlocked from the depths of my mind, as if from an imaginary dream
A beautiful goddess appeared before me one day,
Her flaming hair and emerald eyes totally possessed me,
As no other woman had before her,
With her heart as pure as gold, and by being a totally beautiful person,

There strikes out a magnetism stronger than I, have ever known
To be with her,
To touch her,
To make sweet passionate love to her, is like being in another dimension of time,
Although, I've known her for just a short while,
It's like an endless dream fulfilled, with a sense that I've known her for a long period of time
I've got to get to know her better, as well as I'd like her to get to know me
It's a friendship that I hope will last forever

Debra Kay Schollenberger
THE AWAKENING
The earth is cool, until the sun casts long shadows off the trees;
The sparrow chirps;
The rabbits search for food on the dewy wet grass;
Crickets stop their nightly song;
Everything is peaceful, until man arrives with his four-wheeled beasts;
Only then are the earths feathers ruffled;
Now the sun hides it's sleeping shape;
Until another awakening day!

Susan S. Woodson
MY MESSAGE
I came into the world naked --
Naked and helpless against all the hatred, humiliations, prejudice and spirit-destroying pressure that man could possibly muster.
And when I leave, I may leave naked.
Stripped of what little I may have acquired in life,
Weary from battle.
But with one important difference --
I am no longer helpless.
I will leave with the knowledge that
I dealt with life the best way I could --
MY WAY.
And I apologize for nothing.

Robin W. Pierce
UNTITLED
black magic woman
magic voodoo woman
come out of the shadows
come out of the night
chanting love incantations
magic
magic words
of
another world
another time
for you
my hoodoo
juju
man

Timothy B. Leonard
UNTITLED
"Hello?"
"Hello?"
I said, "I love you."
"Are you still there?"
I wait for her to answer me,
o say
'I love you,'
but there is no answer.
Impulsively, I begin to
hang up;
but I wait.
Hang-on, hang-on,
just a little longer.
She keeps me waiting.
"Hello?"
then, goodbye...
NO
I'll wait longer...
just a little longer
"hello......?"

Opal E. Turley
PAY ATTENTION
for my daughters,
Leigh and Beth
To your love when he smiles
Your purse when you shop
The mountains in a haze
Lazy Summer days
An earthworm in the ground
Icicles hanging down
Rain on the roof
The traffic when you drive
A baby when he cries
A friend when she sighs
Tiny flowers in the grass
Frost on a glass
To pictures in the clouds
An old person looking back
Warm clothes when it's cold
A secret when you're told
Pickpockets in a crowd
And talking too loud.

Leah R. Danoff
INSATIATION
I.
The man kissed the lips
roughly. He looked at them,
half-parted and moist and saw
that they would not stay kissed.
He kissed them again and again.
The lips waited.
II.
The dust mop poised on the
threshhold of the room. Soft,
thick layers of dust crushed the
floor. Surging into the room, the
mop attacked the dust.
Cowering, the dust leaped into
the air. The dust mop swirled a
shiny path on the hardwood
floor. Behind the mop, the dust
snickered. It decended sifting
down, down, down, recoating the
shiny paths liberated by the
dust mop. Without looking
back, the mop sailed virtuously
out the door. The dust lurked,
coiled in thick heavy masses on
the floor waiting.
III.
The razor hovered over the
bearded forest of hair. Swiftly
the razor pounded on the forest.
Hair fountained into the air.
Slashing and cutting, the razor
macheted a white, naked path of
skin. Behind the white path of
the razor, the imprisoned hair
roots busily grew poking up
through the skin to freedom.
The forest of hair regrew in one
day. The hair waited.
IV.
The lovely face skipped through
the crowd of bobbing subway
faces. I remember holding that
face between my fingers.
Shoving and pushing I strode
amongst the subway faces.
Searching, my eyes darted
through hordes of staring faces.
Laughing, the lovely face hid
behind the other faces. The
lovely face waited.
THE END

Jane Cox Bruner
THE ANGEL OF DEVIL MOUNTAIN
Who is this lady of the range
In sweat shirt and blue jeans?
Upon her little Arab mare
On yonder hill she's seen.
Her snowy hair and dainty build
Belie what lies within.
This rugged little mountain gal
Has outworked many men.
Across the ridge and down the slope,
Her dog runs by her side.
She's rounding up her cattle herd
From bushes where they hide.
She notches all the young calves' ears,
With AK Bar she brands.
If shots or stitches any need,
They're done with her own hands.
On trail rides she has won her share
Of silver cups and trays.
A hundered miles in one day's time
Won her the judge's praise.
It matters not if fancy tea
Or children's tour she hosts,
At home in high society
Or putting up fence posts.
Her beauty shines from deep within,
Her faith in God, immense;
A friendly smile, a loving hug,
Her clear blue eyes intense.
Who is this lady riding by
In cowboy hat and boots?
The Mount Diablo cattle queen,
In God's soil are her roots.
Though Angelina is her name,
Befitting one so small,
To those she's met on life's long trail,
She's "Angel" to them all.

Magnolia (Beth) Walker
APARTMENT MANAGER
Apartment Manager, how great the sound.
The days are fine and I never, come unwound;
The work time is fine.
I don't begin until after nine.
This is what my friends all say,
And they even think I get great pay,
I never want to remove their joy,
So when things go wrong I just say, "Oh boy!"
I arrive at the office a little before ten,
And here they all come to complain again
"The people upstairs are making too much noise."
But those people are so quiet, and have great poise.
The children have rules, stay off the grass!
No bikes on the sidewalks, so all can pass,
And of course no paper thrown on the ground,
Because before long it would be all around.
The job is work and sometimes great,
Especially the nights I'm there till eight.
But what's so nice, I live next door;
And one thing for sure the job's no bore.

Mrs. Joe Burks
THE DAY AFTER CHRISTMAS
'Tis the day after Christmas
The house is a mess,
Ribbons and wrappings and bills are causing distress.
The stockings that were hung by the chimney with care
Now lay on the floor, crumpled and bare.
The children that were nestled all snug in their beds
Are out on the hillside with their new sleds.
Ma's changed her kerchief and I my cap,
For there's no time today for a long winter's nap.
There comes from the kitchen a very loud clatter,
They're changing the leftovers from platter to platter.
Santa and his eight tiny reindeer
Will not be seen for another whole year!

Elizabeth Hooper
MY RETREAT
Home
To those who care,
To lick my wounds
And lean momentarily
On a sympathetic shoulder,
To warm myself
In the light of gentle love
And understanding,
To restore my confidence
In the power of love,
To strengthen my soul -
And then return to battle
A cold and hostile world.

James E. Collins
CPR CLASS
There was a body on the floor
As I came upon the scene.
I went right to work on him,
And ruptured his spleen.
I came upon a choking victim,
I thought here is where I shine.
I gave him the Heimlach Hug
And nearly broke his spine.
If you are feeling faint and woozy,
And in need of mouth to mouth,
If you look in my direction
You will see I'm heading South.
Well, I went through all the stations,
Leaving victims in my wake.
I'm glad they were all plastic,
Not one human life was at stake.
So chew your food thoroughly,
Don't choke if I'm around,
'Cause if I do C.P.R. on you
You will end up underground.

Gabe Sims
BILIAN
Gliding around the stars
Dancing with meteors.
Allowing himself
To be captured
By gigantic mother-sun
Whose planets are
choreographed
By the gravitational will
Of the sun.
The starborne African
glides with rhythm,
Soars away to
Interstellar space.
Where brown eyes glance
Alien stars.
He bathes in the light
Of Novas--
His dark muscles strain
To escape Black Holes.
To Him
Earth is his hometown-
The galaxy is his nation...
He travels at the speed of light.

Ruth B. Gross
A WIDOW OF TIME
Days spent fulfilling one's needs
suddenly become years
Memories are made, treasured
and savored
Each morning, bright with its
newness and promise
of the day
We grow, experience, sometimes
tearfully, but continue
with the flavour of life
Suddenly, there are so many
yesterdays
and I have become
"A WIDOW OF TIME"

Kevin Coots
CHASTITY
Manifestation of my dreams
Although you I can't hold
Are the purpose of my schemes
More Beautiful than pure gold
Without you it just seems
My world lacks any glitter
For you are my Venusian gift
Whose love softens the bitter
Waves that set me adrift
On the Ocean of Reality

cjt
GEHEIMNISVOLL
Bliss in else
with nothing lame,
we dread the lean
and luscious name.
High and shrilling
echoes fill;
the dead and buried
grin so still.
Kiss us--*look!*--
and strike us hard:
nonpareil
scheme on card.

Alma Wingler
NIGHT NOISES
There's the noises you hear in the night time,
In the valley, the plain or the hill.

You may hear the call of the locust
Or the call of the poor whip-poor-will.

You may hear the sad howl of the coyote
Or the wolfs' loud plainitive call.

You may hear the soft chirp of the cricket
Or the sound of a small waterfall.

You may hear the cry of a baby
'Till its' mother holds it tight to her breast,
And she sings a soft, soothing lullaby
Then gently lays it back down to rest.

You may hear the loud noise of traffic
Or the mournful ambulance wail.

That's the kind of noise that upsets you
When the thought of injuries prevail.

But the soft, gentle breathing beside you,
The most satisfying sound of them all.

Then the alarm goes off and you answer
The most annoying night noise of all.

Lucy Irene Holthaus
A MOTHER'S LOVE
A Mother's love is this:
To warm gently with her kiss
A troubled heart
Or hurting body
Belonging to someone
Entrusted to her care.
Anytime,
Anywhere,
She can bring comfort there.

Danita M. Bagaglio
LAND OF COLOSSAL WAVES
to someone special, who has seen the waves

On the surface,
observers see gently flowing
water rippled by an occasional
rock. however quickly, so very
quickly the water
will calm itself
once more.
and many,
oblivious and shallow,
have claimed to see my inner
self.
For behind the mirage of peace
and tranquility
strong
colossal waves
flowing over with compassion
breed uncertainty;
yet warmth and soothing love,
unreaveled to the many,
oblivious and shallow,
who have claimed to see my
inner self.
One possessing pure sensitivity
have I yet to encounter, who
will seek beyond the surface of
camouflaging tranquility and
find the land of
strong
colossal waves
but only,
the oblivious and the shallow,
have claimed to see my inner
self.
The one possessing pure
sensitivity will truly know the
inner me, the land of colossal
waves will be discovered
but
up until now...
many,
oblivious and shallow,
have claimed to see my inner
self.

Marilyn M. Buntin
THE SAVIOR

While walking up calvary hill
one day,
I spied a stranger along the way.
He was dressed in a robe and his
shoulders were sagging,
From the weight of the heavy
cross he was dragging.
He wore on his head a crown of
thorns,
This was his destiny from the
day he was born.
He was hung on a cross and
pierced in the side,
He suffered much pain as he
bled and died.
He's coming again to take his
own
To live with him in his
heavenly home.
Willyou be ready if he comes
today?
To meet him in heaven forever
to stay.

Sally Cowles
LONG WEEKENDS

Like the
bloodless battles
of Roller Derby,
the traffic
squeezes in
and out defensively.
As advertised,
the long Holiday
weekend is here.
One extra
day added
to the already hectic two...
to cost you
a fortune to
get away from it all.
Thousands of
sweaty rides
and cursing conversations
To get away
from Life that
bumper-hugs in your mirror.

Tonda Williams
THE STRANGER

A stranger came to town
And all the people thus
Wondered
Where he came from what
Language he spoke, so
Quiet—yet it
Thundered
His belongings were few
You could count them on
His back
He lifted lowly souls
As if to own some

Invisible Jack
Never bothered while
Death stared and
Taunted
And hardly enough the
Acceptance of love is
All he wanted
To him it was more
Important
We understood our
Daily plight
To move from the
Darkness and
Into the light

Reba Bynum Bell
LET THERE BE RAIN

Pitter, Patter, drops of Rain,
Splashing on my window pane.
You're a welcome sight to see.
We need your generosity.
Fill the rivers streams and lakes
Do it now for goodness sakes
The Earth is dry we need it so
To wet our crops and make
things grow.
The trees all thirst, The grass is
Brown
Please dear God, let rain come
down.
The flowers have dropped their
pretty heads,
The soil lies parched within
their beds.
Tis only you that has the power
To make it rain at any hour
That's why we give to you the
praise
and thank you for your loving
ways.
Now! Thank you God, we knew
you would,
Because we know that you are
good
What in the world would people
do,
Almighty God if not for you?

Joanne M. Coyle
QUIET TIMES

I hop on my bike and go for a
ride,
Under the beautiful and clear
sky.
And as I ride and look around,
Beauty is everywhere to be
found.
A bird flying in the air,
A little squirrel without a care.
A mouse running in a field of
corn,
Tiny rabbits just being born.
Listen quietly and you shall
hear,
Wonderful sounds of far and
near.
Life is worth while it's so full of
Love,
Take it and run with it, it
comes from above.
God gave you life to live as you
please,
Respect it and live it to the best
that you see.

Mrs. Leah Baker
AUTUMN IN NEWFOUNDLAND

When it's Autumn in
Newfoundland,
It would take your breath away.
To see the lovely colors,
Of our trees around the Bay.
When you stand and view from
your window,
The countryside so rare.
With all it's beautiful splendor,
You can feel that God is near.
No painter can paint such a
picture,
However hard he may try,
But God with His hand has
painted,
This picture from on high.
How picturesque, such
scenery,
Nothing can really compare.
The beauty of our
Newfoundland Countryside,
At this time of the year.

R. Bailey Cunningham
MY RAINBOWS GLOW

I'm the colours of my rainbows
glow
I'm the bronze in the carmel
brown
And the yellowish of the bright
gold
I'm the glowing glee of my fiery
red
And the slumber blue of my
oceans thoughts
I'm the colours of all colours
The eternal wonder that's
forever
And at the end of my brilliance,
My reward will always be you!

Elizabeth Katka
THE CALLAS

In the valley of the lone and
distant mountains
rise the callas
with their secret enchantment.
Far below I see them blooming,
too remote for human hands to
grasp, their aureoles open
to mist and sun, rain and night,
and the strangely wanton wind,
now gentle, now cruel.
Their creamy curved faces
stare up at me like blazing
white stars,
inaccessible, mysterious, and
fulfilled.
I shall not descend into your
valley;
I shall not disturb your world of
contentment.
I only long for the same bliss
of flowering in time and place,
without hesitation, without
haste, roots firmly planted
in the fertile soil,
the elements in life few and
real.
Callas! Though you die,
you will bloom for me yet.

Fredie Scott Lyon
OLD LADY LUCK

Riding on the wings of success
Beating your brains out to be
the best
Working so hard you don't
really know
Which way is up and where do
you go
Sometime you'll see all that
you've missed
Beating your brains out for the
all mighty rest
And sometimes you'll win but
mostly you'll lose
And old lady luck makes you
sing the blues

Ralph H. Gibbs
L O V E

L et your hearts be happy
As you journey through
the years,
Keep a smile upon your face
Don't spoil it with tears.
O vercome each evil thought
Keep trouble from your
door,
Don't expect too much from
life
Though you be rich or
poor.
V irgin Mary, Mother of Jesus
Will look upon your life,
If you have faith in God
above
And help you in your
strife.
E mbrace each day as it goes
by
Don't ever live in pining,
And remember that in every
cloud
There's always a silver
lining.

Miss Mera Roberts
THE WATERFALL

I walk beside the waterfall
And devour the beauty of it all;
The leaping waters dance and
play
In great cascades of rainbow
spray.
A creation of God, beauty-
bound,
It flows from above with
tumultuous sound;
The rushing waters, how swift
they flow
To join the restless pool below.
The cry of the bird is lost to my
ears,
The spray clings to my face like
tears;
I throw wide my arms to
embrace it all--
The wondrous beauty of the
waterfall.

Larry C. Neal
WHAT IS A "POO"?
A "Poo" is a fabulous creature
of flawless form and perfect feature,
of mysterious whim, beautiful smile,
with big brown eyes, intelligent guile.
"Poo's" are rare (only one in the world!)
and into my life this one was hurled
to laugh and play with, taunt and tease me,
but mostly this "Poo" tries to please me.
My "Poo" drives me to near disaster
playing the role that fate has cast her
with flirtatious looks from those brown eyes,
with private smiles and seductive sighs.
There is no price tag upon my "Poo"
for money can't buy you a "Poo", too!
This "Poo" is the one love in my life
for this "Poo" is my beautiful wife.

Melvin E. Bellinger
MOOD
Even though a moments gaze
Sets our souls and minds ablaze,
Magically we raise our heads,
Knowing that our hearts have bled.
In this room the world is small,
Blurred, and spinning 'round the walls;
Shy young eyes dare meet to see
What it is love hopes to be.
(Ne'er to serve for self alone,
Or be first to please its own;
Subreptive lust, long since dead;
God, our Love, waits to wed.)
Pungent, going nowhere fast,
Silent, flowing swiftly past,
Moving stillness through our eyes,
Molder smolder; as a fire:
Spark the slightest wax to roll;
Dry the wettest flax of soul;
Burn my forest's years of cold;
Churn my young heart 'till it's old.
Just this moment time stood still,
Another we gave to brood.
Our souls only, stand as one;
And our love controls the mood.

Rochelle Mathys
ON THE BRIDGE
i saw him
standing there
on the bridge
...Alone
and i saw
in his eye
not yet fallen
...A tear
a thought occured
i must stop
his deadly game
...Suicide
i spoke gently
and he turned
the solitary tear
...Fell
he moved again
i cried out
hearing the water
...Splash
all i see
in the troubled depths
floating slowly away
...A rose

Angelee Sailer
THE MORNING AFTER
Look you, lady--comes the dawn,
Comes saffron light of morning;
Fades night's indigo anon,
Our love's demesne adorning
In all its amethysts and vermillions:
Flushed to perfect bloom,
unsealed in day's carillons.
Time flees so: 'tis the morrow.
Gloaming crept in mickle slow,
Came as seemed it should never.
All nocturnes else I would forego
Could I but bask forever
In this roundelay, staggered and astounded,
In this gramarye, bewildered and dumfounded:
Tangled in riot of fortunate disquiet.
Whence conned your hair its quickgold glint,
Its scent of damask roses
And wild thyme; whence the flowering mint
Your breath's soft swell discloses?
Let the first twine as a love-knot all around me,
The second envelope, belabour and confound me:
Surrender the bliss of one sheer stained-glass kiss.
The cordial keeps its selfsame force
On this morning after,
The salve its virtue, the flask its coarse
Potency to overmaster:
Sweet influences, bands stronger than Orion's--
Constancy's gulf-stream, bounty's waves, the anodynes--
Ensorcelled all in one clear coronal.
See how bright the heavens burn--
This Dawn is coming for us.
And lo! one Sudden Joyous Turn
Repeals the Stroke Dolorous:
The wearisome morrows give way before the Sunrise,
A final Morning, heraldic unto our eyes--
Time yields its sway to the unending Day.
Ensorcelled all in one clear coronal,
Tangled in riot of fortunate disquiet...

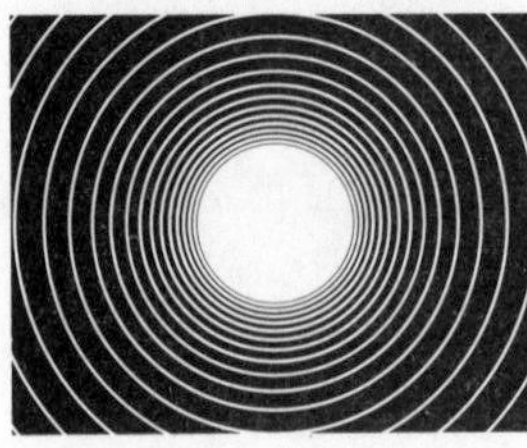

...surrender the bliss of one sheer stained-glass kiss.

D. Kay Weems
MY EMOTIONS
My emotions, I feel, since we broke up,
are like that of a bull in the ring.
All the people out there are laughing,
but I have no song to sing.
The hurt is like the darts thrown,
all strength within me has gone -
Since you decided we should part
and said our love was all wrong.
To hear your voice or mention your name,
is like salt to an open sore.
The hurt goes deeper and deeper until,
I just can't take any more.
At night I have to take a pill,
so that I may get some sleep;
But then I awaken from dreams of you,
trying to hold in my sobs, I weep.
I face each morning, tears in my eyes.
I weep driving down the road.
Remembering all the words you said,
and all the love we've known.
The tears come pouring from my eyes,
only to drip upon my coat.
My cheeks are red and sting from the salt,
and there's an ache in my throat.
I have no feeling for life any more;
I am just an empty shell.
Having your love was Heaven on Earth,
but now I am living in Hell!

Thomas Thompson
LOST LOVE IN A TAVERN
As I entered the bar, there was boisterous laughter and noises unclear;
As my eyes swept over the noisy crowd, they caught a fleeting glimpse of auburn hair;
I sat down in my selected place and prepared to order a beer;
The next thing I knew, a beautiful face was before my own in somewhat of a stare;
As I studied the eyes and the rest, she said "May I help you sir,"
I replied, "A Budweiser for me if you please," in a rather stunned way;
As she turned and walked to the keg, I drank in her body, which was perfect for her;
When she returned, I had added her up: I knew by now, I had seen a beauty this day;
As I thanked her, she smiled in a very sweet manner;
At this point, I had her fixed in my mind as I mused over the fact I would give her a ten;
Eyes of green accompanied by auburn-like hair with an angel's expression and a lovely demeanor;
Her figure was perfect and after giving it some thought, I was also aware of an impish grin;
As my eyes floated over the group at the bar, they rested on her as she was drawing more beer;
She turned my way and gave me a glance, only to be startled by a drunken boy's vulgarity which made her cringe;
In my abode that night, I knew there was more than just infatuation for the little dear;
The following day found me back at the same place for further study and a wish for her name;
Several days later she was still there, only to give a young man a beautiful smile;
She said, "Just get to know me better" when I suggested I would like the same;
Her eyes would not leave his when she was speaking to me, but it appeared her thoughts were at least as far as the River Nile;
We briefly discussed her in quite complimentary ways, but I was immediately aware of an unpredicted adversary;
He suggested I stay as I started to leave, taking one last look at her before I departed;
I was in there for the next several days, but something was not quite the same with the girl I knew only as "Gerry."
After being out-of-town for a short while, I returned to my haunt from which I had parted;
But I was greeted by a new face, one unfamiliar and considerably different;
When I asked the new girl, "Where is Gerry?" she said that she recently got married;
"An elopement no less with a customer," said she with a grin, "on money that was lent";
My mouth became dry but was quickly moistened with a beer, for this night I would not tarry;
In a stunned manner, I had dinner and drove homeward in a similar state;
After fitful tossing and turning, I finally gave up and gazed from my window into the night;

Finally I realized I was feeling hate;
Soon, I was conjuring up all types of obstacles that they would endure in the flight;
After further reflection, it occurred to me that this is the was it was to be;
Before long, I was aware how little control we have over our fate;
We are not really complete "masters of our destiny" no matter who we may be;
The next evening, what had been a vivid memory was gone and the lady and I truly enjoyed our date.

Michelle Pownall
PAVILIONS
In beauty darkness has no suffrage.
Citadels all about and one stands alone,
Here they come from their bondage- finding little rest.
Rejected, amorous love
Nothing beckons or shuffles the past.
I'm safe as long as I stay among these
And their swift tears.
Knowing I'm not what he wants
Beauty, bring your wavy dreams
I'll sit here alone with mine.

James C. Taylor
BLACK COFFEE
A thousand images
Swirl colliding
Within my swimming head.
I shall sit here
And drink a cup
Of weak, black coffee
And try again
And fail again
To say just what I mean
While distant silver chimes
Salute the rainbow midnight dawn
Still and ever beyond the mountains.

Genevieve Locke Oliphant
POETS
Kindred spirits, poets; free;
with thinking hearts, minds that
see through x-ray eyes older
than time; praising the virtues
of life in rhyme. Taut as strings
of a violin; compelling forces
from within, urge the limitless
imagination to reach new
heights of satiation. Journeying
on in dizzying motion like
seagulls dancing over the ocean;
gliding gracefully with style and
verve, seldom receiving applause
they deserve. To each his own
and quite unique; fulfilling
destiny as they seek to record
history and leave behind, foot-
prints on the sands of time. Like
prophets of old they visualize
events of which they poetize,
sharing with others as they
traverse the wonders of the
universe.

Doris L. Monfort
WHERE DO THEY GO?
There's a mystical feeling of 'aloneness' in the air,
And the thoughts of home are everywhere.
One by one, the neighborhood lights go on,
Casting a friendly spell
Then a comforting warmth embraces you,
A feeling that all is well.
Folks are hurrying, every which way
To each his own at the close of their day.
The familiar place to which they retreat,
May have someone waiting, who cares,
Or it may be a nook of their very own
Up a much traveled flight of stairs.
It may, just be, that what greets them is
A favorite, comfortable chair,
With an old robe and slippers beside it, the
Way they left them there.
And the final touch that is home, just might
Be a welcome glow from a neon light.
But, wherever they go, when they go home to rest
Its, mostly, the place where they feel their best.

Dana Jo Denney
TRIO
They bound through snow
Three new friends
Who I have known
For all my life.
The pony leads,
for he is the bravest.
He has survived the depth
of man's ignorance
And grown strong again,
His steady, constant gait
a tribute to the
triumphant heart
that beats within.
Then a flash of amber,
A horse that will remain
forever a colt
A spirit that will never know
What it is like
To be less than pure.
He follows--in chase
For to Cody
Life is a hide-and-seek dream.
The bay follows them both,
With backward tail and black
legs lifted high, touching an
element alien to his exotic soul.
His mind is a mystery to me,
As if he answers voices
the rest of us do not hear.
Echoes from some lonely,
distant land of his ancestral
past.
A strange trio
to find themselves together
in the midst of a Michigan
winter.
Yet in their differences
They strike a balanced
composition,
Complimentary colors
In an ageless design.

Ron L. Biggins
FRIENDS
Dave, John and I
Weekend at the fortside
running, jumping
such a lazy day
Laughing and yelling
as we childishly play.
Wading in the cool, cool
water at the rivers edge
red mud oozing between toes
feels so good.
Frogs greet us so jubilantly
Croak - hello
Croak - hello
Dave, John and I
Children are we unaware of
the color scene.
We are friends.

Esther Juanita Vance
WHAT IF HE HADN'T COME
What if He hadn't come to earth on that first Christmas Morn?
'Tis the day that our Lord and Saviour was born.
In a manger, in Bethlehem, with no room in the Inn,
That's how our Saviour's short life did begin.
What if He hadn't come to earth on that first Christmas Morn?
Would you and I have had a chance - to be forgiven and reborn?
We wouldn't have the promise of Eternal Life, or no Reserection Day,
There would be no one to give us Hope - along life's Way.
What if He hadn't come to earth on that first Christmas Morn?
There would be no one to intercede as we Pray, when life seems so forlorn.
But Hallelujah - God sent His only Son to earth, to live among men,
That we may know Peace, Love and Joy, that through Him our sins be forgiven.
What if He hadn't come to earth on that first Christmas Morn?
The Son of God who was beaten, falsely accused, and brought to scorn.
But Praise God He came to earth - to give Eternal Life to all,
If we but believe in Him, and receive Him, as we answer His call.
What if He hadn't come to earth where would you and I be?
What Hope would there be - of Eternal Life - for you and for me?
So "Thank You Lord Jesus" - for coming to earth - on that first Christmas Day,
Forgiveness of sin, teaching us Love and Peace, and showing us the ONLY WAY!!

dolores m hilmes
MYTH
mingle the myths
cryed the foreigners
of a distance past
stance on the mount
was found No More
intriguing was this story
as hords of people watch them
die
with a gruesome sigh
lords that could not be Halted
for they falted the spells of the
centuries
Pain distorted from all angles
Ironing the wrinkled creases of a
leftover day
"Nay" screeched the man
"I wish not death to past"
Lasted the Fast
WHAT A LAUGH!!!!
evil crept through crevices of
Never ending cracks
The true facts about the
foolish men
Fending their rights to the end
THEY SIN NOT
Acts Justified the lyes
told of senceless notions,
displayed emotions,
diluting comotion
through-out their masses.
breathing the gasses of the
decaying air
Fair was the Fear
they hid so clear
Was life dear to them
"Yea" They screamed
But it was all a dream
for they could not concock
spirits to grasp the fight for life
trifly adding their sadding
matting *heart.*

Dorothy H. Porch
RETIREMENT
They wined him and dined him;
They killed him with kindness.
He was baited and feted
Until he was spineless.
They covered him, smothered him
With bouquets and a wreath.
Such emotion and commotion
Turned his glee into grief.
There were pictures and mixtures
To gaze on and gulp.
Verses on cards, songs by the bards,
Until he resembled a limp piece of pulp.
He moaned and he groaned,
"This is being retired?
Before I cave in, find me a haven.
Protect me by saying, 'You're fired!'"

Carl J. Perry
SECOND RISING
Second rising
is
waiting in darkness
waiting in darkness
waiting
to be born
Second rising
is
in twilight's womb
in a jaillike room
locked inside
by the forces of now
by the forces of now
Only time
time swinging the key
Only time
can really answer

Julie A. Work
CATCH A FANCY
Catch a fancy;
let it go.
One fleeting moment
with the wind-
And off it sails...
Resting a moment here-
and one there;
To share its thoughts with all.

Betty Lou Rhoades
WE RODE A PURPLE TANDEM
We rode a purple tandem
On a misty cobbled street,
Where larks forgot their way
In singing melodies so sweet.
They stirred up the meadow
Each bending, golden blade,
Where shadows fogged
forgetting
In bitter wood and shade.
We rode a purple tandem
And didn't know for years
The road was paved in sunlight
Bought and paid in tears.

Joan M. Woolston
MARTIN LUTHER KING
You were crying out to be heard,
And I for one wasn't listening.
Your voice was loud and angry,
And this filled me with fear.
It wasn't your message I feared,
It was the thought of violence
That could follow.
So I put it all away in the back
of my mind,
Ignoring your pleas for right and
justice.
For I had not done you any
wrong.
It was a long road to the
mountain top,
Bitter injustice, hatred and toil.
But God gave you a gift.
One of courage, faith, hope and
love,
That I and others would never
know.
And in your fight for right and
justice,
You had to give up your life.
So, in dying, your dreams and
hopes
Are slowly coming true.
It sometimes pains me to think,
If I and others had listened then,
Today we could live as true
Brothers and Sisters
In love.

Kelly Harris-Mitchell
MY HUSBAND AND ME
I'll stay with you as you follow
your dreams,
Be with you all the way.
Never to leave your loving side,
And loving you more everyday.
When I need a shoulder to lean
on,
Or a comforting voice right
away,
I know that I can depend on
you,
To brighten my darkest day.
You listen when I want you to
listen.
I'm quiet when you want me to
be.
When we're apart, I'm thinking
of you,
And how much you mean to me.

Joyce Escott Buhler
BUT JESUS CAME
Sometimes I feel like I'll never
get home.
The night is so dark, and I feel
so alone.
Finding the right way is hardest
for me;
But Jesus came that my eyes
might see.
Sometimes I feel like the music
is gone.
I listen for voices that keep
passing on.
Even the chords that I play
disappear;
But Jesus came that my ears
might hear.
Sometimes I feel like I cannot
reach out.
I hold back myself; that's what
pride is about.
The giving and sharing we all
need so much...
But Jesus came that my hands
might touch.
Sometimes I feel like I'll never
be free.
The things of the world weigh
so heavy on me,
Searching for answers in seeds
that I sow;
But Jesus came that my heart
might know.

Lucy Hadsell Curtis
TODAY
When things go well, we seldom
feel
The things we should be
thankful for,
Until disappointments, hurts
and grief,
Make life seem dearer than
before.
'Tis then we realize what we
had,
Was a very blessed state,
For life is lived only today,
And today will never, ever wait.
Let us then smile and rest
awhile,
And say that kind word to
everyone,
And lay in the wildflowers and
look at the sky,
And savor each moment of the
life we've begun.
For today will never come again,
It is now we must search and
find our way,
For today we live the golden
hours
That gild the memories of
yesterday.
Today is God's most precious
gift,
As fleeting as the waves at sea,
Let us catch the fire in the
sundown tonight,
For tomorrow we will one day
older be.

Joseph DiLeo
THAT'S THE WAY THE BASEBALL BOUNCES
In the bottom of the ninth,
With the score tied 2-2,
Two out,
Two on,
Three balls and two strikes on
the batter,
The pitcher squeezes the
baseball in his hand,
Works it between his fingers,
Steps off the mound,
Picks up the resin bag,
Dries his sweat-soaked palms,
Checks the scoreboard,
Listens to the roar of the crowd,
Waits as a jet thunders
overhead,
Climbs back up,
Digs in,
Yanks on his jersey,
Lifts his cap,
Wipes pools of perspiration from
his brow,
Peers in for the signs,
Gently nods his head,
checks the baserunners,
Stares at the cleanup hitter
glaring anxiously back at him,
Waits,
Ponders,
Then,
With one fluid motion,
Jerks forward,
Snaps his wrist,
Delivers,
And follows through.
Silence for a split second,
And then,
Oak collides with rawhide in a
resounding crack.
The ball arches upward,
Projects outward,
Pierces the sky,
Glides through the air,
Going,
Going,
Going,
And suddenly,
Obediently,
Descends into the left fielder's
outstretched glove.

Dale Skoglund
THE BUTTERFLY
Embryonic impulse
I felt it stirring inside
Cocoon of long lost love
Made of fragile emotional hide
Your mystic crystal energy
Pierced the web of fine weaved
thread
Causing evolutionary process
Which in me you did imbed
Through larval stage I passed
For wings I began to crawl
When I heard your distant
heartbeat

No choice but to heed the call
So lateral membranes sprouted
I began my solo flight
But solo's not the way to go
No way to spend the night
I recall your mystic energy
With you I'd like a twosome
Massaging your emotions
Fluttering in your bosom

Michael G. Blais
HIDDEN STAR
Pouring from ancient clouds,
streaming rain; the ground it
shrouds.
Covered streets soaked and
sleek,
give way to passing cars.
Up in the sky darkness creeps,
upon the hidden star.
Night traps day and plans to
stay,
until the mornings found.
Forming above the clouds of
night the light returns to grey.
Shattered clouds; then day
appears, and time and life unite.
Looking far
you see the light
having found the hidden star.

Mildred H. Alaniz
THE OLD AND THE NEW
As the old year is about to end,
And the New Year soon to
begin,
As the New Year from God's
hand springs
Twill bring a multi-spectrum of
things.
Will it bring health, trust, hope
and faith,
Or grief misfortune or even
death?
Will it leave us more or less
wealthy than before,
Or leave you depressed, sick and
poor?
Will you work for self alone
with all your might,
Or share with others in their
plight?
In spite of adversity work in
faith and wait and see,
That whatever happens to you,
keep your destination in view.
As the New Year approaches,
Ask God's guidance at the door.
For this time dear friend you
have not traversed before.
Diligently hear what ancient
prophets say, live the golden
rule from day to day.

Georgia Earnest Klipple
CITY OF THE SIEGE
Hide, hide.
Hide in the cool, dark leaves.
Hide 17,500 corpses under the
Kudzu vine.
Let the monuments to man's
shortcomings, marble angels
on the battlefield, stand,
Druid stones of living green.
The long, smooth trenches of
the buried lie, drumlins at the
end of the death glacier that
moved *up* a hill.
We must not know the living
lost that siege, 5,000
surrounded, outnumbered
three to one by the lifeless.
Now we are a city for the dead,
a tourist bureau encircled by a
grave moat. See our skeleton?
Put in deep shadow with the
thick, wide leaves the
seething anthill of milling
blacks waiting to be freed
from themselves.
Cover the heartbreak, the hate,
the false pride,
the...
Grow the lush Kudzu.
Bury the land.
There is so much to hide.

Ralph Minnite
BEAUTIFUL AND UGLY
To be born beautiful and
experience beautifulness
through ones life is satisfying
To be born ugly and experience
ugliness through ones life is
annoying.
To be born beautiful and mature
to an old age is annoying.
To be born ugly and mature to
an old age is satisfying.

It's like seeing
The sun at its setting--
It is beauty and color
And emotion and inspiration--
And just out of reach.
I cannot teach myself
To cease pushing my hand
Toward its warmth.
Nor can I cease
My heart filling
Its vacancy with you.

Cynthia Richards
CHANGES IN ME
As the years have flown,
Many things in my life have
changed.
Parents have changed and so
have friends
And I myself have grown.
Sometimes I like what I see
And things are going fine
But its when it turns sour
That I wish for what used to be.
Many changes have occured in
me,
Some of my friends have noticed
too,
In the way I act and think
And in the way that I now see.
Since I take life in a different
view,
It seems to finally have a
meaning
As the days progress it seems
That I'm amazed at how much I
can do.
These changes must be for the
best
They're shaping me into what
I'm to be.
Yet we're always changing and
learning through life
The mind and heart never take
a rest.

June R. Meyer
UNTITLED
Who makes me smile?
Like a bird with a child
Who else loves you like I love
thee?
You light up my day,
Put shine in my day.
I blow like a leaf in the breeze.
Who makes me smile?
You make me smile.
I love you.

C. W. Atwood, III
SOCIAL STIMULATION
From where I sat,
it looked like a burning
quagmire, red and green
popping like fire.
Movements blurred stealthly by-
one even stopped and said Hi!
That one was certainly
high!
Great voluminous sound
shrieked to the door, and a
constant thud-thudding on
the floor, and I thought -
God what a bore.
Clanking of glasses and liquids
abound, all added to that over-
bearing sound, Is this where
great love is found?
In came more and more by the
very score, and most hoping
by nights end - to score -
and God -
I thought,
what a,
B
E O
R

Karen L. Chabot
WINTER NIGHT
Wandering winds on wintery
skies
Wafting to and fro,
Sleeting ice in silver stance
In moonlight rays do glow.
Glitter gathered on the ground
Tiny petals from unknown.
A blue-white blanket in the
night
A wonderous, ever wild sight.

Bobby Edmond
TOMORROW
The aspect that lies in the
future
Of tomorrow is now.
So why put off tomorrow,
When the task could be,
Performed better today?
Strange as it may sound,
Tomorrow's future may or may
not come,
The task would be done.
So why not?

Whether in work or recreation.
Why not do the best,
Performance today?
If the idea of thoughts
Or maybe conceptions cross
your mind,
Even the expectation of life,
Isn't promised to anything or
anybody tomorrow.
For today if achievement,
Goes unfinished this day,
Hoping that we are able to
participate,
In life's expectations of
tomorrow.

Jacki Freiberg
NEW BIRTH
I touch with novice fingers
the tiny grains of wheat
And watch with city-bred
amazement
wild daisies at my feet
With innocence of childhood
I stand silent, in endless rows
of corn
Waiting in eager anticipation
to see the birth of a smog-free
morn
I am awed by this land that
seems endless
Peopled by hardy stock
And my over-populated city
mind
the vastness seems to mock
I gaze wide eyed at the heaven
stretching forever in tones of
blue
And I find in the voices of the
country
A God my city heart never
knew

Cynthia E . Huggins
FANTASY
Sweet mama, take me in your
arms and rock me gently now,
Away beyond the misery that
growing up can bring.
I never shall grow older if you
never teach me how,
So rock me in your cradled arms
and sing, sweet mama, sing.
Sing low of painted china dolls
and soldiers made of wood,
And tell again the stories of
when you were once my age;
How as the years slipped softly
by, you slowly understood.
Don't let the years keep rolling,
mama, never turn the page.
Just take me in your arms, sweet
mama, rock me 'till I sleep.
As I pretend my life away, I live
within a lie.
But if some dark and lonely
night, you hear me as I weep,
You'll know I finally understand
that time will never die.

Louise Hinton
WHAT IS WEALTH
To some people wealth means
material things
Such as large houses, fur coats
and diamond rings
But some things cost little or
nothing at all
That other folks hold the most
valued of all.
There's the clasp of the hand;
the words we may speak
To the old and the lonely, the
ill and the weak
A short, cherry note; a gift of
fresh flowers
Like jewels, will brighten the
shut-in's drab hours.
The dandelions, growing in
numbers untold
In the hands of a child become
treasures of gold
As he holds them up with his
little-boy's grin:
"Grandma, have you something
to put them in?"
The flame of a maple tree
turned crimson-red
After the glories of summer
have fled
Standing apart on some far
distant hill
Surveying a world that has
grown strangely still.
The laughter of children, the
singing of hymns
And the warm lights of home
when at last daylight dims
The colors of sunset, the
mornings fresh dew
These things God gives freely to
me and to you.
The memories that come,
stealing out of the past
Lingering ever their bright glow
to cast
Warming the heart as the years
swiftly fly
Mem'ries, sweet mem'ries of
days long gone by!
Methinks that another great
treasure is health
Without which there is little
enjoyment of wealth
And friends, yes, the real ones,
the tried and the true
Who come rain or sunshine are
standing by you.
Methinks that with all these
and many like things
Sometimes the "poor" are the
envy of kings
For wealth never yet produced
peace of mind
Which is, after all, what they're
trying to find.
There's one gift and that's the
most precious of all
That's offered alike to the great
and the small
And that is Eternal Life God
offers Man
Through the death of His Son
and His salvation plan.

Lisanna Y. Taylor
MORTALITY
Are you there? Are you here?
I can only feel, your presence
near
The loneliness in my heart
Since the day we were apart
Me, in the land of the living
You always forgiving
You in the land of the still
Yet with our love there is a will
To be together, you and me
So all the beauty, we may see
To feel the warmth in our soul
To reach love's eternal goal
Yet, we are so far apart, from
each other
Our love, strong, yet different
from child and mother
One day our souls and minds
shall meet
And then we'll hear, how our
hearts beat
Until then I am alive and mortal
You are still and immortal
The day shall come, when we'll
be as one
Mortality, we shall, overcome.

Jason B. Johannson
FREEDOM ON THE PRAIRIES
Many a majestic animal,
Running wild and free,
On the open, wide prairies.
Many a majestic animal,
Running the roads of freedom,
Like the creatures of the wind,
That they truly are.
They go on, and on, and on,
Where are they going?
A horse's paradise without men,
Not a one to steal their freedom.

Donna Ross
ODE TO MOTHER
Now take a look and tell me
what
You really think you see,
Am I the child you used to
know
Or what I've come to be?
You've watched me grow from
then 'till now
And saw how I have changed,
Sometimes you wish that I were
still
A tiny child again.
You know the shadows of my
past
The child you used to see,
You loved me then and love me
still
A love 'till eternity.

Kenneth Graham
WORDS FOR A WOMAN WHOSE SPIRIT HAS BEEN RAVAGED

In the days when you were a little girl,
Your daydreams full of tenderness,
And easy, sun-gilt afternoons,
When bluebirds watched you from the branch,
You did not know what nightmares were;
You thought that years were beautiful things
When people spoke of them; and you were sure
Your backyard opened smoothly everywhere.
Do you remember that afternoon
When all the summer sky was yours,
And one bright cloud a gallant knight
Floating on a steed of white?
Do you remember how you twined
Your hair softly around and around,
And sang a song you made yourself,
And sang a million miles from grief?
A distant August. Now you have seen things
That made you say: I do not want
To be here--I do not want to be
Here. And hands have asked for strength
Beyond that given to the purest knight,
And that surprise was perhaps the steepest.
And when you looked out the window, one day,
And watched plush leaves lift silverly up in the wind,
And poplar boughs swaying like ballerinas,
You did not watch for long, but roamed
Keenly back to your room and your ancient dreams.

Kathleen Marie Miller
IF ONLY

If only a year
a month
a day
If only a moment
I would hear you say
The words I want to hear
From someone so dear
Say I love you
To dry all tears

David L. Yerges
WHOSE?

In a tree, an old oak tree,
On a limb high above,
Sits a bluejay,
Scolding me.
This is his territory,
So I stroll on down the trail,
For who am I to say,
That it is not his?

Sherry L. H. Lanz
THE RAGE

The whispering wind whisked through my room,
with an intense sigh of happiness.
I stood in the dark room as cold as ice,
as I prepared myself for the change.
As I prayed for the change not to begin,
a very uneasy feeling swept through my room.
The whispering wind changed and blew with rage,
I started to shake with tremendous fear.
Knowing that there would be a tremendous amount of destruction,
I turned and locked my door.
I felt a bomb getting ready to explode inside of me,
the rage began. I tore my room apart as rage tore me apart.
My rage began to go into hiding again. My body quit shaking,
the wind was calm once more.
I sat at the edge of my bed waiting for the rage to disappear.
I felt tense as I laid down and closed my eyes.
When I woke the sun was shining and I was confused,
not remembering what had happened the night before.
I began repairing my room in complete astonishment,
while asking myself who could have made the mess.

Jeffrey Miechiels
THE POET'S TASK

But not to dream...
What's what, without dreamin'
It's like going without a walk in the rain
All God's work would be in vain.
The Poet's task is this my friend;
To read his dreams and comprehend
The truest human fancy seems
Becomes as a night sleeping in his dreams.
All poems and births are in his own nation,
Delivered by interpretation.

Laura A. Fraser
L I F E

L is for the loneliness
experienced in life.
I is for the intimacies
in our daily strife.
F is for forever
forever we will live.
E is for eternally
eternally we'll give.

Suzy Perkins Watson
THE FINGER TIPS OF GOD

I was off key one day and felt so sorry for myself;
wanting to hide from life and climb upon a shelf.
The day was very gloomy, a storm brewed to the West,
so I decided to take a walk and then go home to rest.
Soon I spied a sparkling dewdrop clinging to a slender reed
and near by, a wild rose was growing entangled with a weed.
The colorful blooms were delicate, the petals fully blown;
that stubborn weed was choking it and I could hear it moan.
The plant's face turned upward, its blossoms were opened wide;
its flowers covered the weed, as if its inelegance to hide.
That little plant's life wasn't easy; it had plenty of strife
but its hardships were quite simialr to those in a human life.
Yet, it kept growing upward o'ertowering its struggling foe;
my eyes were opened to a lesson, that I really needed to know.
Now, the storm was gaining speed and I heard the tall trees rave;
I saw them shake hands with each other, as I ran into a cave.
The sturdy trees waved frantically and lashed to and fro;
the wind bent them to the earth, yet, they'd pop up and grow.
The storm moved on, the sun came out, the trees gave a friendly nod;
I know that day, my soul had touched the finger tips of God.

Henry Edson, Jr.
SEX IN THE MORNING

Shifting, shiftless my baby doll stirs
(Laconic stirring, me)
The subconscious is tangible
And treatable in the morning.
Stirrings in the lower deck
Rising.
Up, up, up
Awakening our senses,
Pulsating, throbbing
Tantalizing,

Like the sound of faraway drums,
Drawing nearer.
Nearer my love to thee
Evening failure becomes morning success
Hedonism's dregs are dissipated.
Our love's release pours forth,
Gushing in the sanctity of unity.

Fern Angell Giles Bergren
THESE THINGS SHE LOVED

These are the things she tended-loved, but of late they must be moved:
An old lamp with fixtures missing,
Two old dolls, just made for kissin'
Some picture frames, an old teapot,
An old silk dress she'd loved a lot,
A bottle of wine from far away,
An old ink well, a flower spray.
Some pretty feathers, a faded rose,
Where she got them goodness knows.
Dozens of pictures of this and that,
An old doll cradle, some china cats,
Some souvenirs from China Town
And best of all her wedding gown.
All these she treasured and many more
Plants and dishes and books galore.
"An auction, we said, "you must do so,"
But she sorted and hoarded,
So much couldn't go.
We boxed and packed for many a day
The ol' house looked lonely
With it all packed away.
And tears would come as they often do
When we give up treasures and start anew,
For no one knows each piece and part
That makes up a home in a mother's heart.
As I watched her pack some antique rare,
I knew it was part of a love affair.
I loved them too, for don't you see
What's a part of her is a part of me.
Now the old house is silent, the treasures gone
Each cherished piece that helped make it home.
Now she's old and grey and so am I,
But we've memories sweet of those days gone by
When friends and family would gather 'round
And enjoy the treasures she had found.
And laughter would ring thru the old house then
As we listened to tales of 'way back when'.
As she closed the door and turned the key,
I remembered life as it used to be,
When she shared her home with some lonesome kin
And opened her heart and took them in.
For I was one of the lonesome too,
She said, "Come on home, there's room for you."
And we shared our lives in a special way,
Now I ask God's blessing on her today.

Carol Gawronski
HAPPINESS

Happiness is an elusive thing,
We all wish to possess it, we all hear it sing.
It sings behind our problems, it sings behind our tears,
And, maybe, if we listen, it sings within our ears.
To be able to possess it, to really enjoy its song,
We have to stop, to listen, and invite it to come along.
For happiness is not hiding, nor can it be caught.
It exists within us always, not seriously to be sought.
What a delightful discovery a human being can make,
When, tucked inside, finds waiting, his happiness to take.

Jeffrey Porter Ross
CARNAL GENESIS
Hands clasp,
Lips touch
And soft sounds
Come in whispers. . . .
That moment we sigh,
Life begins:
A tiny blossom nurtured
To bloom in its' own time,
A personage of our love.
Breathless, we lie unaware
Amid the ecstasy,
Too awed by each other
To hear above heartbeats
The echo of our own beginning
Reverberating timelessly
From an origin
We had no part in.
We are partners
In a living creation;
This small new soul—
Our child.
I can claim the passion,
But the spark is not from me.
God of all; I see in this,
Thy handiwork,
Thee

Ruth A. Davis
BEAUTY AROUND ME
I take delight in all of God's
Creations—
The gentle, graceful deer, the
scented flowers and birds in
flight.
I am thankful to live in a world
so vast
Where I see beauty around me
in the day and in the night.
I look up and see the stars
twinkling in the night.
I look down and see a stream
sparkling in sunlight.
Wherever I look there is much
to bring delight,
Whether it is in the day light or
in dark night.

William F. Hogan
REAGANOMICS
Has Reaganomics got you down?
Are you tired of having the
Right-Wing push you around?
Ronny claims that his budget
cuts will not hurt the truly
needy,
But I agree with Gore Vidal's
comment "that Reagan is a
good President for the truly
greedy".
I believe that the budget should
be tight.
But my priorities are far
different than those of the
Right.
Reagan's people say that the
election gave them a mandate,
I do not think it included
destroying the Welfare State.
I am in favor of a strong
Defense,
But it should be based upon
common sense.
Giving more money to Lockheed
is not a foreign policy,
Welfare for the rich will not
keep us free.
I must confess that I am already
quite weary
Of Kemp-Roth supply side
trickle-down theory.
On a personal level Ronny
seems like a nice guy,
When whe was shot by Hinkley
a tear came to my eye.
However, his economic program
is an attempt to repeal
Fifty years of progressive
legislation begun by the New
Deal.
I do not believe he will succeed,
But the Reagan years are going
to be a difficult time for those
in need.
Jesse Helms thinks that he has
bleeding heart liberals like me
on the run,
My heart is not bleeding but I
do have one.
Which is more than I can say
for that Hun.
I want to inform Helms, Falwell
and the entire Far-Right
That Bill Hogan is not running
and intends to carry on the
fight.

Joni Alane Jansma
TO THINE OWN SELF BE TRUE
Life is a winding road of trials,
You must choose a path and
follow it for miles.
Never turning back or changing
course;
Forget indecision, obligation and
remorse.
Live for yourself and know your
own mind
That's the only way to break
society's bind.
After all, we've all been taught
the Golden Rule;
Do for others, deny self—slip
into acceptance's soothing
pool.
But I say "Be Yourself" don't
change to fit in.
Living to fulfill others' dreams is
man's most venomous sin!
Why can't we follow our hearts
and emotions?
Instead of drudging through life
with empty notions.
Don't we want freedom and
security to fall in our laps?
So we don't have to chart our
own live's maps.
But freedom and security are
both well earned,
Never obtained without the risk
of being burned.
Self—awareness is the only
way. . .
To grow more certain of
yourself day by day.

Nancy MacNeil
FOR KEN II
A couple of uncool city dudes,
Named Johnny Walker and Jim
Beam,
Got together one strange
evening.
They loaded up their double
barreled rifles. . .,
And, taking very careful aim,
Shot my daddy through the
back;
Wounding his sensitive soul,
Which time nor love could heel.
And finally they killed
His happy "Miller High" life.
. . .How cold!*!.

Barbara Smith
MOMENTS
From the time we are born,
Until the time we die,
Our life is made up of
moments—
As time passes by.
Enjoy all life's moments;
whatever they be,
Without them; you wouldn't
be you—
And I wouldn't be me.
As we walk through this world
And take what life has to give,
Relish life's precious moments—
Live and let live.
See goodness in everyone,
Have kindness in your heart,
You'll make this a better place—
Because you've done your part.
Take time to smell the flowers,
Notice a rainbow while it lasts,
A moment is a moment—
And then it is the past.
Moments make up memories,
Some pleasant and some sad,
If not for moments in our life—
No memories would we have.

Rick E. Norman
THE GAME OF LIFE
You win and you lose,
You live and you die,
You laugh and sing,
You sulk and cry.
No one wants to die,
Yet, everyone wants to live.
People take and take,
But have nothing to give.
There is a lot of love,
A lot of hate,
There is a lot of bad luck,
And a lot of good fate.
There is a lot of toiling,
A lot of strife,
But this, my friend,
Is THE GAME OF LIFE!

Sally Schlichter Streeter
MY TREASURES
The things that touch me most
in life,
Are things that I really can't
touch at all;
The song of a bird, a warm
summer breeze,
The leaves turning color late
in the fall.
The wonders of life that I hold
most dear,
Would be impossible to hold I
am sure;
The love of God of parents and
friends,
These are the greatest, why
ask for more.
The most sincere feelings that
I've ever felt,
Are those that I truthfully
cannot feel;
You can't put your hand on
caring and love,
Or offering yourself of your
own free will.
These are my treasures and they
do exist,
But you cannot touch them,
hold them or feel;
They are stored in my heart for
the right time and place,
But nevertheless, they are
certainly real.

Bee E. Goldsborough
LITTLE SOLDIER
(From the Poetry Corner)
As I said goodbye to my soldier
My heart was torn with pain,
And in my mind, I hear these
words
Over and over again,
"O! Mommy, we're playing
soldier
Will you make me a paper
hat?"
And down the street he strutted
Reassured by a gentle pat.
As I turned, I remember saying
"Hurry back little soldier man
For Mommy will be here
waiting"
And down the street he ran.
But the years have made some
changes
My boy is a Soldier real.
Dear God, please watch and
keep him
As he faces this ordeal.
As I said goodbye to my Soldier
My heart cried out again,
"Hurry back my little Soldier
And always be a man."

Margie Bocklage
A SILVER LINING
A tree can stand so beautifully
Yet, how many people truly see
The strength that stands against
the sky,
Shielding all the passersby.
This tiny seed did fall one day,
From a cradle of dirt it made its
way.
Alone it did withstand the
pain—
The scorching sun and frozen
rain.
Years gone by as it slowly grew
Amazing—how it made it
through.
Its limbs were broken times
untold,
Still, here it stands so very bold
With leaves that shade us from
the sun
And glimmer when the rain is
done.
To make each day much more
worth while—
A silver lining—in its very own
style.

Kenneth Bryce
PURE BEAUTY
The beauty of a child
Enough to drive you wild
Has to make you smile
Can't they stay awhile?

Edward J. Nayes
THIS LAND OF CONTENTMENT
The sound which echoes across
the land of Our Country
cherishes every moment of my
time
for my Life is dedicated to love
this land.
This Country of Ours
for our country is shared in joys
and in sorrows.
For no other love could there
ever be
than to know that the sun
shines
the light of happiness
which surrounds the beauty of
the
Rose
for which is shared
the love of contentment for
which is
the feeling
of which is known
for this feeling of contentment
is the affection from the Rose
for within this Rose
is the Love which grows.

Jeanne Jacobs
I LOVE THE LORD
I love the lord with all my heart,
He gave my life a brand new
start.
I've been born again and will
never stray,
For the lord walks with me by
night and day.
He lifts me up when feeling low,
He is the friend I need to know.
By my side he'll always stay,
He is the one I call on each day.

Kathleen Hale
HAIKU SEQUENCE
Clothed in white blankets
no wind stirs evergreen trees. . .
mutely the snow falls
One red rose on grave
Memorial Day love gift
old woman bows head
Click of garden shears
startles lizard on hedgerow
I smile. . . .so sorry!
Above my valley
patchwork quilts adorn
mountains. . .
autumn's mixed colors

Gwen Aileen Lincoln
YOU'RE IN MY DREAMS
Sleep claim me again
take me away
to him
Give me a few precious minutes
let me talk to him
hear his reply
Let me hold him close
feel his touch
let me show my love
Know he loves me too.
Sleep come back
don't go away so soon
it just wasn't enough
I can't let go
let me sleep eternally
so he will always be there
I love him so
you just have to give me the
time
to be close to him
Sleep please come back.

Roxane J. Marquis
BORN BLIND
Born into a world of darkness,
Noises are my eyes.
As I sit and wonder of the
worlds colors,
Feeling the wetness of the grass,
And the hardness of the tree
against my back.
The winds coolness,
Seems to describe its feelings.
The tree brushing my face with
leaves,
I cannot see.
The touch chills my senses.
My hauteur blowing away with
the wind.
Why can't I feel my way to
seeing?

Virginia Ann Taylor
ONE DAY AT A TIME
Thank God for little things,
Thank God for time.
Only today is mine. One day at
a time. . . . . this is enough.
My life is a gift of God given,
not in years, but a day at a
time.
Thank you, God, for all the
things we take for granted. Do
not look
back and grieve over the past,
for it is gone; see everything.
Overlook a great deal, improve a
little.
Life has this dilemma that
hooks us on its horns, the
thornbush full
of roses, or the rosebush full of
thorns?
My life is worth living if I
can learn to transform
everything that
happens to me into love, do not
be troubled about the future,
for it has not yet come.
Tomorrow and all that it holds
is God's secret and its coming
is not assured.
Oh make us more aware, dear
Lord, The happiness, the
blessings, the
thoughtfulness, the kindness
of a wonderful day.
Live in the present, and make it
so beautiful that it will be
worth living and
remembering.
God will always bless your
home and you and those you
love.
God answers prayer, So take one
day at a time.

Kirk Aincham
THE VISITOR
I opened my eyes with fear to
behold
The destruction about us can
never be told.
I remember it now like a terrible
dream;
Nothing, but nothing, had been
spared, it seems--
No idol too sacred, no brocade
too dear--
Not one square inch escaped
without smear.

I hoped my wife would recover in
time--
Her courage had been much
greater than mine.
It is written the earth shall be
saved for the meek--
But not if my grandaughter stays
more than one week.

Beth Marie Alex
BAREFOOT ON THE BEACH
I love walking on the water's
edge of a Florida beach.
My legs and feet, . . .bare,
the salty water comes up to
lick them
as waves roll their way in to
kiss the shore.
As my skin glistens with
wetness
from the reflection of the
setting sun,
I can feel golden tannes
penetrate my body
as a cool tingle rushes
through my willow-like legs
and arms floating freely
In the cool, fresh, salty smelling
breeze.
The quiet blue-green of the
ocean,
the blondness of the sand,
And the mixed hues of red,
pink, and orange
smeared on the west end of a
cornflower blue sky,
soon calm the wild whirling
pressure of angry air
which tries desperately to
escape the fences in my mind.
I glance down,
and for the first time,
again, . . .
I notice a tiny sea shell, as big
as a baby rose bud.
Its harmony of colors,
powdered shades of brown,
pink and white,
Coaxes the corners of my open
lips to smile,
while caught in the middle of
a gasp of amazement
at the beauty of the sea shell
cradled soft
in the palm of my small, wet,
sandy hand.
Looking again,
there were thousands of them,
arranged all over the beach,
as yet another wave comes in
and caresses my ankles
and causes some of the sand
underneath my feet
to make a quicksand-like
disappearance
And tickle my toes.
My favorite spot,
like my best friend,
calls me to be close to it.
As I stretch out my sand-
freckled legs,
I close my eyes,
and feel the cool ocean breeze,
scented with salt,
blow my hair across my face.
Nestled against a rock,
my lungs fill up with air so
soft. . .it feels like silk.
My head feels light and starts
to nod,
My arms and legs don't belong
to me anymore and become part
of
the sand, the breeze,
and the silent heart-beat of
the ocean
as its waves throb in and out
from the shore,
In a soft yet compelling rhythm.
As I slowly drift,
the sky throws on its deep,
purple, velvet cape
speckled with diamonds,
And watches me set free that
silent sigh soaked in sleep.

Mia Lynn Franklin
SUMMER NIGHTS
How long are the summer
nights
And short the days;
The sweet breeze blows
Gently while it rains.
The flowers give a fresh
fragrance
In the air;
The tall trees look high
Above the roof;
Birds fly below swaying cotton
balls
In the sky.
I lie down in the soft green
grass
of the meadow;
Looking above.

Sylvia Bridygham
NIGHT MURMURS
Another day draws to a close,
the stars are in the sky.
The crickets sing their mournful
song of days and dreams gone
by.
Alone is darkness straight and
tall,
each tree bends down to earth.
To touch each tiny blade of
grass
and listen to its mirth.
In tiny little whispers, the
breeze
scurries throughout the land.
To bring a calm and peaceful
bliss, to each and every man.

Iris Kramer
MY FRIEND AND ME
You have become my ego
As such
And in learning
In the face of your friendship
I have gained much realization
About myself.
This
Knowledge
Can never be taken away
No matter
How
The tree
Branches.
Or where.
So join hands
And relax with me
In the semi circle of my being.
For I am complete, only
When the body and mind
Deems it so
In the
Reflection
Of their togetherness.
And so it is
With
Friendship.
And so it is
With us.
My ego
And
Me.

William Lowenkamp, Jr.
JURA HIGHLANDS
Valleys long and deep-
pine forests - rock walls,
rolling contour of land
gently downward - Jura
Mountains La Chaux de Fonds,
and Le Locle-
from you - come delicate,
instruments of time.
So clean, so white,
so green and beautiful-
your grounds, with winding,
roads and river Doubs-
majestic gorges and waterfall.
Winding road-
to Les Brenets,
through tunnel Col-des-Roches,
so scenic are your wonders
so astonishing your views-
Jura Mountain Highlands.

Lillian Petrovic
IN FOND REMEMBRANCE
Dear Frank, why did you have to
desert me?
Why did you leave me to sit
here and cry?
Oh why did God now take you
from me?
To live in that Great Big Ranch
in the sky.
It certainly would have been

great to do,
All of the things that we
intended to,
We did put them off a mite too
long,
Now there is no time because
you're gone.
The joys and sorrows that we
did share,
Sure meant so much because
you were there.
And we were never lonely
because there were two,
But now I am alone and without
you.
For almost 41 years we were Mr.
and Mrs.
And now I find it quite hard,
To drop the Mister from Mr.
and Mrs.
When signing my name on a
card.
In daylight I am busy and no
shadows I see,
But when evening draws nigh, it
is lonely for me,
As I look for you in your
favorite spot,
Watching all kinds of sports,
which you loved a lot.
As a bowler and league secretary
you did your best,
And now your bowling ball and
trophies are laid to rest.
I am sure you have organized a
league in the sky,
And are watching your bowling
friends from on high.
Now since I have no other
choice but to,
Continue to live my life without
you,
I will grit my teeth and hold
back the tears,
And ask the dear Lord to quell
all of my fears.

Marianne Duda

A MOMENT'S GLANCE

Seeing you . . .
Your eyes found mine
and held them captive.
For a moment,
When time seemed to stand still
and the world around us faded
into oblivion,
I understood.
Words unspoken, unnecessary
were felt and seen
through the mirror of your soul.
My eyes questioning, probing;
Your eyes answering,
confirming . . .
And it was in that moment
I realized you still cared.

Teresa Whitman

A TRIBUTE TO MY GRANDFATHER

A man who had everything and
more
A strong, young wife that's for
sure.
The proudest man you have
ever seen
Funny, lovable, sexy and keen.
Through fifty years of marriage
You know he pushed a carriage.
Five children is what they had
Four daughters and one fine lad.
The tree of life, flourished on
With fifteen grandchildren it did
spawn.
What better tribute could ever
be paid
By any family that this man
made.
Worked long and hard for thirty-
seven years
As a pressman, he earned
respect from his peers.
Retired when life was rich and
full
Stout and stern with no punches
to pull.
His wisdom we sought, and
experience he taught
He let it be known that the Lord
had brought
A fine Christian man at the
head of his class
He always helped others
without letting time pass.
This man, this man that I loved
so dear
Where doctors and beds were
his only real fear.
Five great grandchildren were
added to his family tree
With one more on the way that
his eyes will never see.
In a hospital bed he lay
For six long weary days.
But now he sleeps in peace
With carnations at his head and
feet.
Even though he's buried and
dead
Our wonderful memories ever
linger on.
Grandfathers come and grand-
fathers go
I wish everyone a grandfather
just so.

Nickie C. Hall

JESUS IS MY FRIEND

Jesus is my friend and on him I
can depend
When troubles come great or
small
He can take care of them all
As on a journey I will go
Sharing his love with those I
know
I will tell of his mercy rare
In this world of cares
To all those that I will meet
With a smile I will greet
Tell them of this Savior dear
Who has been with me through
the years
With a love that one can
compare
Someday I will meet him in the
air
Oh! what joy shall fill my heart
When from this world I depart
To a home beyond compare
To a home with such beauty
rare
On Streets of gold I will walk
To friends and loved ones I will
talk
All cares and troubles will be
left behind
There will be great joy and
peace of mind
Jesus is my friend and on him I
can depend

Arlie T. Cofer

MOTHER NATURE'S STUDIO

The sky is blue
The water calm;
It's to the soul
A soothing balm.
It's mother nature's studio;
A sight to behold.
The colors are bright
The lines are bold.
The call of the wild
Is still out there.
God's fascinating creatures
Are every where.
Weird animal talk,
The song of birds;
It's all too beautiful
To put in words.
Then from afar
There comes a flash;
And close behind
A thunderous clash.
The picturesque scene
Has been disturbed.
But God's wonderous Creatures
Are not perturbed.
When the storm has passed
And the sun comes out
The birds and beasts
All scurry About.
The balance of nature
Is a delicate thing;
When it gets out of hand
She must have her fling.
When the fling is over
She's very clever;
She makes her pictures
More beautiful than ever.
Scenery like this
Where wild life play
Is very enchanting.
Let's leave it that way.

Edith Settle Morrison

ETERNAL THE QUEST

I asked of life but one fragile
thing,
Which seemed forever lost.
The only thing that deep within
Should belong, in part, to every
man
Became my albatross.

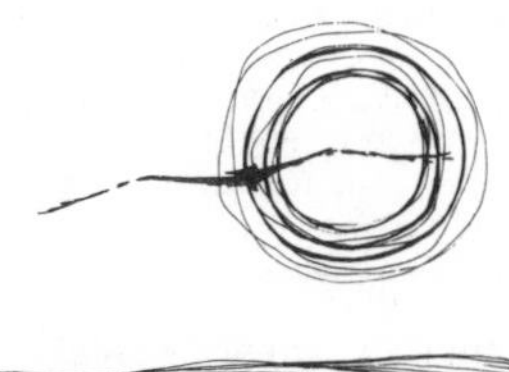

I searched for naught but
happiness,
To claim it, forever mine.
I glimpsed it here and spied it
there;
But left it finally, buried deep
somewhere
'Neath lifting, drifting, ever
shifting
Barren sands of Time.

Denise Joy Walter

UNTITLED

The Sea
Deep below the rippling
surface lies
silent, resting. Then
Gathers itself together—
rushes to the shore
and. . .
relents its savage fury upon
her
hungry lips
Crashing against the rocks in
pounding
pulsating rhythm
trying to pull the shore,
below
the sunlit surface
to the depths.
Its victim
Then, withdraws,
weakened by
the effort.
The Sea
and you. . . Like brothers
The quiet gentle feel of your
hands as they touch
my skin
I quiver with the moist
warmth of your
lips against my
body.
Then you explode in silent
hungry fury
And my body joins with
yours in the
pulsating throbbing beat, the
pain, the warmth
and the feeling of
love.
As the tide overtakes the
shore and
becomes one—
So it is with us.
Exhausted and
breathless by our effort
we lay back, gasping
The only sound being
the beating of our
hearts
and the sound of the
sea
within my ears.
The Sea
You
so much the same in love
Yet I am more willing a
victim than the shore.

Lawrence A. Siff

SEA MYSTERY

A rich man
By the sea
Frustrated at not understanding
The crash of the waves
The moonlight forming a silver
ring
On the beach
Helpless at the wind's murmur
He yells for the chauffeur
He yells for the maid
He yells for the secretary
Alone he cries
For the sea's richness
Moon is brighter, wind is
stronger
Waves crashing harder
The sea answers
Swallowing him
Up.

Rose Piontek

THE SEARCH

I sit here and reflect back
into the inner peace that I
have given myself.
This inner peace that sets my
love glowing.
I have searched and searched
for answers from within.
Not until I have let myself
go have I found what I have
been searching for.
That inner peace - It was so
easy - to let go!

To know that I have gained the tranquility that I searched.
To know it was here within not to have looked elsewhere - but here within me.
My soul cries out with pain - with joy - with love.
Oh yes, with love! It was always there within - I only needed to let go.
To feel the arms of love to enfold me within its bosom.
To feel the tears of pain fall against my cheeks.
To feel the emptiness of love not mine. Yet to know that the love is even more than my heart hopes of holding.
I have been given so much!
My inner peace -
My search has ended for I have always had the love -
No more pain - only gladness the search is over for I know that I am love and I am loved.

Lillian Goldie Eppley
WONDERMENT
I often used to wonder,
When just a little girl.
In geography classes in our school—
My mind would be in a whirl.
Of all the different places
On the maps we would discuss.
I'd wonder if it would occur;
For any one of us.

The years gone, and school days past;
He or she went their own stride.
To most of us there in that class—
Have traveled far and wide.
Since being taught the golden rule—
I can truly say with pride;
Many traveled while protecting our country;
Most have traveled far and wide.

Mary Lucci
A REQUIEM TO THE FIRST SETTLERS
(Written for the "Little Italy Heritage Day")
They, too, were like the pilgrims,
The first people who came
And worked so hard and
Settled this little parcel of land
On this earth—And called it "Little Italy"
May they now rest in peace.
They, too, came from far and wide
With nothing but their pride—
To carve a new place on earth,
Far from the place of their birth.
May they now rest in peace.
They, too, with God's helping Hand,
Came here to this wilderness land.
They, too, were scared
When first they came—
To start their lives all over again.
May they now rest in peace.
They worked so hard to get ahead
Long hours to earn their daily bread.
They tilled their gardens
'til night time came—
Next day they'd start all over again.
May they now rest in peace.
Most had to learn to read and write their names
So they could become American citizens and so would gain,
The love and respect of their new country they loved
With blessings from God and Heaven above.
May they now rest in peace.
They're all gone now,
Those first settlers who came
And worked so hard and
Did so much for us.
Resting, now, on the hill
Overlooking the land they loved so well.
Those early people who settled
This little parcel of land and called it
"Little Italy"
May they now rest in peace.

Eleanor B. Aldridge
GOD'S DAY
"This
is the day the Lord hath made--"
a day
of unmeasured pleasure.
Each moment
Unfolds a thousand dreams;
Each hour
a gift to treasure.
God give us hearts to share your love.
Breathe on us wisdom from above.
Leaning on Thy power and might;
Teach us to use this day right.

Edith A. Wilson
GROWING UP
She says she's confused, and mad at the world,
She's still not a woman, but not a little girl.
She doesn't understand anyone, and no one understands her,
And each day she wishes for a miracle to occur.
She likes the boys, and the boys like her,
They smile at each other, and their sweet hearts stir.
She can't understand why she's too young to date,
And is just sure spinsterhood is her fate.
She and her mom don't see eye to eye,
And sometimes she feels so hurt she could almost die.
Mom says in high school she can go out then,
But you can bet she'll have to be in by ten.
She often wishes she had never been born,
The ways of the world, she can't help but scorn.
And, even now at her tender age,
She says, "Where are the good old days?"
But one of these times, much to her surprise,
This young girl will begin to realize
That the world is actually quite nice,
And all her struggles were worth the price.
Her parents and teachers were really not so bad,
And she'll be sorry that she ever got mad.
She'll know they had her best interests at heart,
Even though at the time they seemed miles apart.
She'll be thankful for those who helped her along the way,
And may even have kind thoughts of yesterday.
But today, she's just fourteen, and full of frustration,
And all we can do is to try to be an inspiration.

Randee Mia Berman
KID GLOVES
You can kid yourself
for awhile and
enter the ring
with Mohammeds' mentality
and stance,
but
one glance will spill all.
You can't fool a kid about the
bare facts when you're not
wearing gloves.
You can't even kid a fool, 'cause
wisdom doesn't depend on
coverings;
Keep cool;
those knuckles, that grip
are enough equip-
ment to demonstrate
curious force, sound and
furious energy, tactics and
toughness, the
stuff of
commitment,
a fit mind and spirit,
foundation of lead --
not a dead-
weight but
lively with energized potion
in motions of magnet-ude:
craggy but care-full.
So where are the gloves?

Duane D. Thornton
GOD'S WORDS
They use me for worship
And yet, do not believe in me.
They refuse my offer of peace,
And yet, claim to be free;
But; they'll never be free,
As long as they fight.
They'll never be free till,
They see the light.
I made all men equal,
To live as brothers
Not to go around
Killing themselves, and others.
I've about given up,
On the human race.
Because evil and greed is taking over,
At a fantastic pace.
I only hope they'll want another chance,
One last try.
All I ask is faith:
And; I await patiently for their cry.
I'll forgive all they have done,
And more.
If only they stop shutting me out;
And once again, re-open the door.
Please heed my words; my children;
End all wars;
Which seem, your present trend.
Please do not bring all my creations
To an abrupt, and dreadful end.
Heed my words children,
Show me you believe in me.
So that all mankind;
Can once again, be free.

Ruth Sigler Avery
WELLS CATHEDRAL
Four Hundred statues grace these walls
And seven wells of water
Green the garlands round the base.
Afloat on small stones foundations rest--
Like an infant in the womb.
Beyond the narrow nave,
Inverted spiraling arches sweep
To tops of silvery limestone walls.
In retrochoir lacy chantry chapels
Seem woven fragile forests.
Southwad rise wide, slabstone steps:
Uneven, concave, hollowed, hallowed
By pilgrim feet through centuries
Under tierceron vaulted roof--
A pilgrim's joy
At such extravagance of praise.
Pale ribs of famous canopy
Seemed bathed with rainbow tears,
Seeping in shimmering sunlight
And spreading singing color
Through petaled, stained-glass windows
Shaped in stone.
A 1390 Anno Domini clock above
Displays jousting knights
Falling in continual combat
As chimes relentlessly toll the time.
Brass memorials distract the eye
To search and find friezes
Showing cards and dice of ancient players.
Anonymous, witty masters of the stone
Portrayed fruit-stealing jackanapes;
And etched in stone a face
Wearing a toothache's frown:
Carved not for fame

But in God's name to tell the
whole.
In scamper rollicking, tousle-
headed boys
Wearing white for choir;
They blend angelic trebles in
liturgies
At Evensong.
Outside, mendicant swans,
indulged by clerics
Float upon the moat,
And when they tug bell ropes
All soon are fed.
These glories of God's grandeur
Standing nigh ten centuries
Are etched upon a seeing heart:
The luminous huminous
holiness
Of The World in stone
Facing West in majesty
Toward an English sky.

Carol J. Crevier

ACROSS THE CHASM

Across the chasm
our minds have met
hesitant; seeking
Without the world's guidelines
Across the chasm
our smiles have joined
together, in triumph
As if leaving darkness behind
Across the chasm
acceptance, is mine
mirrored in your eyes
Restores the lost in me
Across the chasm
I bring affection
trusting, and without strings
To find the chasm is now gone.

Lucile Gregory Weeks

WINTERTIME

Sometimes winter would slip in
so softly,
Covering houses, streets and
naked trees,
While we were all warmly fast
asleep,
We'd scarcely believe the snow
so deep.
Other times she'd come with a
mighty roar
Rattle all the windows and
shake the door.
For days she'd howl and vent her
fury
As tho' she were our judge and
jury!
Unless her madness left lots of
pain
The beauty left was always the
same.
Some shimmery, shining jewels
she'd spill
On houses and trees and the
slippery hill.
With apple cheeks and a cherry
nose,
"Jack Frost nipping their hands
and their toes",
Children throw snowballs at
everyone
Laughing and playing and
having fun!
Grandpa, at seventy, just can't
wait,
He's at the lake and starting to
skate.
So find your skates and haul out
the sleigh
We're sure to have winter fun
all day!

Susan Rauert-Moscaritolo

FAIRY TALE ICE WORLD

glistening ice land
shining with a glitter--
winter wonderland
mild fitful luster...
brilliant -- sparkling
treetop wonders--
shining glasslike...
are they real?
sunbeams caressing
reflecting every tip--
ice branch on ice branch
gleefull, clinking tone!
a sound of rejoicing
this frozen animation--
fills my eyes and ears
with gaping wonder...
sparkling diamonds
casting spectrum colors--
distant mountains majesty
rise up to the sun...
oh tumultuous nature
of windy nights before--
thou did's't form and sculpt
with a blustery, icy chisel...
chasing all of nature
to the arbored center woods--
silently covering nourishment
stillness over all...
but happy in the sunshine
the aftermath we roam--
scattering berries and seeds
as shy creatures come forth...
wandering, walking
with one I love—
helping and talking
with no thought of time...
fairy tale ice world...

S. G. Creecy

THE SINNER'S PRAYER

The answers dear Lord
I know not where
Thy scriptures I've searched
With utmost care.
Come to my aid
I beg you please
Can't you see
I'm down on my knees?
Carry my burden
Lessen my pain
Please don't tell me
My prayers are in vain.
Teach me Thy love
Show me Thy way
Please dear Lord
Let it happen today!

Dianne Alee Angeline

ODE TO SPRINGTIME

Welcome sweet Springtime
The Earth again is new
I will dance and sing a joyous
song
For the seasons shared with you.
Glory abounds in beautitudes,
Mercy in the heart
Rapture in those silent
memories
When we are apart.
Come-sing me songs of
sunshine,
Kiss me on my cheek
Hold me in your warm embrace
My kind and loving Greek.
Whose warm dark skin
I love to touch
Tender words that mean so
much
Smiling eyes that flash with fire
Attributes of my hearts desire
When happiness is doubled
The World's a finer place
The Autumn years approacheth,
Yet leave not their trace.

James Perry and
Beverly Snyder

MEMORIES OF SUMMER

The grass has changed its' color.
Leaves sail on Autumns' wind.
Angry skies show displeasure
As summer comes to an end.
Birds no longer sing and play
On green branch shrouded trees.
Rolling clouds of sullen gray
Bring on an icy breeze.

Though winters' icy finger
Sends a shiver down my spine,
Summers' warmth still lingers
In the hollows of my mind.

This gray and gloomy weather
Shall not this brave spirit slay,
For in my heart I savor
The beauty of a summer day.

Josephine Sherard Davis

AN ANGEL IN MY GARDEN

Life is like a garden,
With flowers sweet and rare;
With birds and bees and
butterflies

And an angel here and there.
I own such a garden,
It's tucked inside my mind.
You are the angel in my garden
So rare, so sweet, so kind.

Debbie Holeman

BALLAD FOR BRIAN

Paranoid young Brian, brilliant
musician was he.
A lost vagabond, yet struggling
to be free
He raged with his parents, but
eventually lost.
He then accepted banishment as
his unhappiness's cost.
Father of six, to different lasses
unwed
Safety in numbers where
concerned Brian's bed.
Buskink his livelihood; through
Europe roamed he
Those numbered years they felt
good,
'Til in crept uncertainty. . .
Brian took a shot at direction,
Later would come great success.
But also misconception,
concerning a cutting jest.
One night during a run, an
admiring two
Approached distracted Brian in a
curious mood.
Together they discussed dreams
they all shared—
Of drugs, women and music, the
threesome compared.
A union soon followed. They
formed a band.
They added three more, and
began making their stand.
(They reduced the new to two
with better instruments on
hand.)
The five got a buzz out of
playing together.
Especially Brian, as their leader.
For the band was growing better.
Brian formed friendships that
helped the band out.
He pushed for gigs believing
without a doubt,
That they would be a group to
change the music scene.
That parents would hate them,
and young girls would scream!
Fantasy became truth as they
paraded uncouth.
Mystical magic took hold as the
lead singer grew bold,
And Brian in '65 reached his
peak.
One that faded quickly,
Leaving him morbid and weak.
Nervous breakdowns left him
white,
And his drug habits a sight.
While the image got clearer and
his death grew dearer,
The band members dumped him;
he was inferior.
Mid-summer it came,
whispering Brian's name
and nothing was the same.
(He was almost totally
insane.)
July 3rd crept 'round and the
action without sound,
Caused Brian to drown.
1969 itself was Hell-bound!

Judy D. Simmons

CAPTAIN OF FATE

As I sit at my window, and gaze
at the sea
It's soon that I'm sailing, just my
thoughts and me.
And as I sail along with the
wind in the mast
I've left all my problems,
seeking peace at last.
And as I take this voyage in the
depth of my mind
It's as real as I wish, and the sea
is now mine.
As I feel the spray moisten my
skin
The heat of the sun sends
warmth from within.
Yes, there is comfort I find on
these journeys I take,
But more then that, I'm the
captain of fate.

Ralph D. Phillips

LOVE FOUND—LOVE LOST

You saw me look at you,
I saw you look at me,
And from that time I knew
That we were meant to be.
Your eyes that shone so bright
Were like stars that twinkled
In the night;
And from that moment on I
knew-
One day I'd fall in love
With you.
...and as the years passed by,
I saw you laugh and cry.
I watched you grow to be
A very special friend to me;
And as our friendship grew,
I slowly fell in love
With you.
Then summer turned to fall,

And in the chilling frost,
Just when I thought we had it
all
No sooner than found - was lost.
And as the cold winds blew,
My heart cried out for you;
I thought that love could be
A fairytale of you and me.
Now, in the winter rain,
It's back to me again.
I can't believe it's true,
There's nothing left between
Me and you;
I guess it had to be;
You couldn't help yourself;
You gave the love you had for
Me -
to someone else.

Patricio Monreal
FREI
Un gigante esta durmiendo
silencio profundo pido.
Su sueno es puro y eterno
no lo despertara ningun ruido.
EDUARDO FREI, fue su nombre,
en Chile lo conocemos muy
bien
siguio los pasos de un hombre
que lucho por los pobres
tambien.
Su voz fue firme y clara,
su grito, un grito de guerra,
cuando libertad y justicia
exclamaba,
se escuchaba en toda la tierra.
Una luz se apago para siempre,
un pueblo entero sufre y llora,
murio un ex Presidente,
que solos quedamos ahora.
CHILE, patria querida,
quien te vio, quien te viera,
se callo lavoz atrevida
que el tirano tanto temiera.

Beverly DeVore
A SONG TO ME
I must find again
The measure of myself,
And adopt a structure
That changes with no revolt.
To see melody evolving
Altered purely by note
the harmony remaining
unfettered and remote.
A rhythm constant
Possessing no rhyme
Expressing abandon,
but losing no time....

John M. Akili
BOOK BURNERS
How can one burn books?
Even if you don't agree.
Everyone reading a book
should feel free...
Free to read whatever you
want, without fear of the (witch)
Book hunt.
How can one ban books,
doesn't everyone who wants to
have a right to look, and read?
Have you the right to change
Where reading might lead?
How can YOU tell ME what I
should read?
Who are you to tell me what
I should have in my mind?
Whatever I find in books--
I find.
And react as I will; shouldn't
there always be Freewill?
Books are so precious, even
the ones with whom I disagree.
Even, even when they attack
Me!
Have you or I the right to
burn?
Having free thinkers is the
way we all learn.
Have you or I the right
to ban?
Isn't this supposed to be
a free land?
Book burners take this advice
from me;
What goes into my mind I
have the right to choose.
If you try to stop me from
reading what I want,
You may be the one to lose!

Mildred Alaniz
THANKSGIVING
We thank you, dear Father,
that you gave us you Son,
and if we live and believe in
Him,
then we shall overcome.
Thank you, dear Father,
that Jesus willingly came
and the promise of salvation
to this day remain.
Thanks for food on the table
and plenty to share,
that seedtime and harvest are
forever in your care...
...that life, death, nor angels,
things present nor things to
come
shall separate us from your love
which is in Christ Jesus your
Son.
Thank you for home, family,
friends and holy brotherhood,
even trials and suffering of His
children, He worketh for good.
Lord, we thank you in the
summertime, winter, spring
and fall
when there seems less to thank
you for, we thank you most of
all...
For loving you and praising you,
even though we be sick, helpless
and poor,
God's heart is touched, His
blessing sends,
till there is no room for more.
Lord, help me that I may always
faithful be,
when laborers are needed...
Lord...
send me.

Sue Durham Coneway
LEAVING TOGETHER
If I knew, without doubt, that
we could walk
Away together from this life
holding hands,
And with a glance of eyes we
could talk
As in the glorious past years of
molding
A love that has withstood the
trials of time,
That we have spent together in
partnership
Then I could go with grace and
peace of mind,
Leaving serenely on our farewell
trip.
I would not care to go alone and
leave
You to be tormented with
loneliness;
Nor could I live without you
and not grieve
For the warmth and comfort of
your gentle caress.
Thus, may we leave together
holding hands,
Putting the past comfortably to
rest.

Ethel Mitchell Benson
OUR WORLD OF MUSIC
Our world of music, rich in
harmony,
From beauteous note there's
tone-true symphony;
Since time began music has had
its place
Through every age, through
every land and race.
In centuries past there was the
minstrel's lyre,
For tribal life drum beating
conquered fear;
With music's surrounding Rome
burned day by day
And, with such sound, crusaders
went their way.
A trumpet's blare announced a
victor's stand
While crowds would proudly
sing the anthems planned;
The music throbbed as troops
marched off to war
And welcomed them as they
returned once more.
All kinds of music, each filling a
need,
From folksy lays to songs of
faith or deed;
Our world of music is a world
so grand,
With friendly tunes it joins all
hand in hand.
Music has lived as all living has
been
And ever shall to win the hearts
of men;
This world of ours - a noteless
world can't be -
Has love of life that breathes of
harmony.
Picture a day from whence no
song would come
And who would thrive without
one chord to hum?
Our world of music, melody
unfurled,
Has sounds of song that right a
wondrous world.

Karen S. Bennett
UNTITLED
All alone I sit
And I don't understand
I'm an alien
In my own homeland.
I cry for a friend
But people don't hear
I don't think they see
Even one little tear.
I should tell someone
But I don't dare
They don't listen anyway
Cause they don't care.
It's building up inside
Almost too much to hold
One of these days
I will just explode!

Nellie Coberley
WHEN I FEEL THE HAND OF MERCY
When I feel the hand of mercy,
Reaching out to rescue me,
Then I thank the Holy Spirit,
That He saved a wretch like
me.
When He leads us thru the
valley,
Or upon the mountain high,
Then I feel the hand of mercy,
Standing there to let me by.
As we travel on life's journey,
He will lead us safely thru,
To the bright and shining
mansion,
Where He waits to welcome
you.
When we meet Him in the
portals,
Of that bright and happy
home,
And we hear Him sweetly
saying,
"Welcome child, you have
come home."

Harry Melanson
PIECES OF WHOLES
I'm tired of the roles
The roles that I play
Everynight and everyday
People come and pass through
my life leaving pieces of them-
selves behind
Those pieces lurk in the
shadows and collect in the
corners of my mind
Why can't I be me?
Why must I be made up of other
people's wholes?
The music builds and the
curtain is drawn back
Centerstage I stand about to
attempt the most difficult role
of my life
To be me

Christina Chingtsao
LIFE
Life is but a passing journey,
Though transitory, yet thorny.
Beware, let it not hurt you.
Through the darkness, shines
the light.
Why we hurry? Why we worry?
Life is but a sailing boat,
Sometimes smooth, somtimes
rough.
Be firm, let it not overturn you.
After the storm, comes the sun.
Why we despair? Why we envy?
Life is but a stage show,
Bad, sad, mad and glad.
Be sure to take a good part.
Heed not wealth, but strength.
Why we hesitate? Why we
doubt?

Life is but a changing dream,
Today we meet, tomorrow we
part.
Be calm, let it not grieve you.
Sad is the parting, may we meet.
Why we argue? Why we anger?
Times flies like the running
water,
It fleets and never returns.
Be ready, let's not be late.
Follow the steps, leading to the
light.
Why we care? Why we fear?

Elsie M. Cheeks
CROW VALLEY
"Out of my childhood past," I
remember"
A village with it's green grass

aglow.
Sloping down hillsides in a valley below.
Little white school sets off to it's self.
On down the road aways you can see the cabin,
Where I was raised.
In my vision I can see, mother sitting on the porch; "baby on her knee."
Listening to laughter from the older children playing in a stream near by.
Mother calls it's time to start our chores.
The sun has set and night is near.

Ruby Hale Stevenson

SWINGING GRANDMOTHER

Sunday dinner's over.
The kitchen's neat and clean.
So Ben and Craig and I
Run out-of doors to swing.

Craig can swing all by himself
Because he's all of four.
But one-year Ben swings in my lap
And I am fifty-four.

Marcia Rae Gorton

MOONLIGHT

Light that falls with splendor,
Stardust in the skies,
Radiant, in love again, I see
Moonlight in your eyes.
Your hair is dark and curly-
A spell you've cast on me-
I feel strong arms surround me,
It's evening on the beach.
Waves dazzle in the moonlight,
The tide is coming in-
Star's shine, your lips on mine-
And heaven closes in.

Helen L. Shaffer

LIGHT ALONG JERICHO ROAD

Along the dusty road on the way to Jericho
He followed the Father's will so long ago.
There came to His ears a cry and a plea:
"Son of David, have mercy on me".
Tho thronged all about, He stood very still-
Here was His mission; a need He must fill.
So the people told the blind man, "Come and arise,
For the Saviour is here and has heard of thy cries".
In gentle voice He inquired of the Man's need,
And as they all watched, a miraculous deed-
A gift was given, so rare, so free.
"You are now made whole through faith in me".
And so, as the blind man rejoiced in his sight,
So may we all, as we come to the Light.
For such was His mission; to heal all the earth.
He can give to us all new life - new birth.
And so today, will you not accept Him?
Or are the eyes of your faith so blind, so dim?
Will you give Him your burden, give Him your load;
Will you accept the same gift as on Jericho road?

Wayne Davis

US

I watch as our love glides along much like a bird in the wind,
unaffected by the turbulence of life's worries.
It moves with ease and grace,
resting only at intervals from flight,
to soar even higher.

Teri Pfister

THE QUEST

In the heat of the day
As the sun melts my heart
The soft breeze embellishes my fear
As I search for what I cannot see
In the depth of the night
As the moon shimmers silently
The salty sea echoes
As the starry sky holds my wish
In the haunting winter
As the clouds gather against the sky
The soft snow flakes fall like a possessive kiss
As I grow with the changing seasons
In the light of my feelings
As the dawn opens the lazy sky
A crystal vision begins
In the love I have found

Natalie Levner

ON LOOKING AT VAN GOGH'S "STARRY NIGHT"

Swirls - compared to my life
Ups and downs - all directions
Throwing me in the role of wife
Sometimes - filled with strife
Sometimes - happy recollections
Swirls - compared to my life
Motions - as though by a wind upswept
Gyrating - pulsating
In constant activity kept
Turmoil - contentment
The prance of Death
Leaving us hollow
Heartaches will follow
Boys - girls
Compared to my life
Many swirls

P. S. Howard

RAIN IN OKLAHOMA

Rain is such a different sound in
Oklahoma dropping from the
eaves of rented rooms onto
garbage can lids that line
themselves up beneath the
drops, as if each tap of rain
showed one more ounce of rain
There was a time I sat alone
crying with the rain;
railing out against it,
blaming it for my sorrow.
But tonight without you
it's quiet,
and the sound of rain on metal
lids is at least proof that I can
hear, and am here.
Your escape
leaving me only memories and
trash cans...
alone in the rain.

Eileen C. Joyce

MAURA

She came to my house from far away,
She came, she said, for a week to stay
To talk, to laugh, to eat to cry—
We shared these things, my friend and I.
It mattered not the span of years
That stretched along our joys and tears
She came as a child when she hurt her knee,
She brought a new doll for me to see
But now she's grown and full of love
Ready to welcome a gift from above.
A bit of Kilarney, with all of her charms,
Lucky the babe who will fill her arms.

H. S. Hawkins, Jr.

THE COUNTY HOME

The County Home stands tangled with hair,
Hair old like graying vines.
Black bones litter its hoary leather,
Bones broken like rotten oak.
In the cold dank dusk,
Shadows hide, dumb, dark, senescent.
Spirits like bats, dive for their victims.
Grandmother lives here sometimes.

Maureen C. Modesitt

CREATION TO LOVE

On the first day there was thunder, it came its rolling, crashing way,
And God directed it upon the void to split both night and day.
On the second day the Spirit moved and there emerged a land.
He breathed into and sculpted it - it showed God's mighty hand.
The third day there did blossom forth a woodland bearing seed.
Lush fields of fern and fruitful trees, an abundant harvest indeed.
The fourth day sunlight filtered in the forest verdant green,
And moonlight burst amidst the stars that night to rule and gleam.
When the fifth day dawned upon the seas, there rose the mighty whale.
God multiplied the fish and fowl to fill both brook and vale.
As the sixth day rose with a gentle breeze, there was a stirring of God's hand;
From rocky mount to valley low came a birthing to the land.
And there appeared a cattle herd in a pasture clover lined,
And the woods sustained the living things, each creature after his own kind.
And God did state that it was good as He added to His plan,
For in His image and with His love came the being known as man.
God formed this fruitful vessel from dust of earthen ground,
And breathed in Him His breath of life, and gave him dominion all around.
On this day six God's masterpiece emerged from His throne above,
He created man to rule this land; a product of heavenly love.
And so it was God's work was done as the seventh day began.
He blessed it and He rested then as the tide washed over the sands.
From the stars aloft to the shore below, this universe of His love,
Was poured of faith, composed by God, our magnificent Father above.

Bonnie J. Douglas

MY CHOICE

Discouragement came in today;
it tried to steal my hope.
Accusing things it had to say,
wishing I couldn't cope,
pointing its nasty finger
and scowling as it made threat,
looking in its ugly way;
the hurt I'll not forget.
Startled was I, when it appeared;
confusion flooded my mind.
I struggled within, as it jeered
the words; not one of them kind.
"Can this be!" my sad heart thought
"that one could be so cruel."
Discouragement now accompanied fear.
They were sure they'd come to rule.
Suddenly, from deep within
faith and hope arose.
Discouragement and fear had to flee,
because faith and hope I chose.

Angela V. Willcox

THOUGHTS IN THE DARKNESS OF NIGHT.

Thoughts in the darkness of
night are like ships sailing the
stormy sea, searching for the
haven of a harbor on the distant
shoreline and light.
With Neptune abiding in the
pilot-house and doning his
nautical cap, the motor awakes
with hoarse and boistrous
thunder, to sever thoughts in
the darkness of night. They sail..
steady, then toss to and fro, yet,
never collide. Each aiming for
the purple streak of shoreline,
braving the swells and piercing
the salty spray with strife.

Ahoy!...Trouble! the sea soldier
invades a thought while
wrestling the pirate of the sea,
midst angry combers, bursts of
spray and gusts of gale so white.
Sea skeletons of coral shake
loose and surface upon the sea
of glassy waves, to mingle with
meaningless thoughts churning
in the darkening sea; the bosom
of light and flight.
Tis war... among the elements
with thoughts thrust in
between. The rise and fall of the
ocean reveals the shoreline, the
harbor and safety..in the lee...NO
WRETCHED PLIGHT......

Jerrie L. Chamberlain
TOUGH TIMES
Times are tough now and
money is tight,
But things aren't as bad as what
they might.
We've had plenty of moisture in
our nation this year -
Compared to the '30's when rain
was a tear.
When there's a roof o'er your
head
And food on your table,
Be thankful and strong
'Till things get more stable.
Don't go to the welfare for an
easy handout -
Have some backbone and use
lots of clout!
Go mow a lawn or go pump
some gas,
For these times, too, soon will
pass.

Steven Barteau Wilson
APRIL A.D.
Elephants roar at 8th and A.
Birds too sing in the park.
On stoops people converse at
dawn
And argue orange for favor.
Me, I'm on the sidewalk
With your love on my mind.
By lightning we were blessed.
Through commotion and steel
I hear your sweet murmur.
Though thousands and
thousands
Split between the strain--strike;
I find a route straight-
By wish by may by your able
power-
Bond might.
Lovers date,
Promotion winds
I ache and no longer feel it's
even pain.
From the drink of steeds
storming
I no longer depend on such a
slow ride.
Blushing the veins of dockside
angels
I send my message
And softly, softly just in back
I feel your glance.
Wend willows now blooming
And again, and again and again
You're in my eye.

Lois Ann White
ASHES RENDER MUCH
All the things of life I sought
All I wanted, dear, you brought
Happy then because I thought
You cared
Thrills that came with every
kiss
Joyous hours we knew I miss
Only you would know the bliss
We shared
Sleepless nights bring back the
tie
Useless are my little cries
Foolish tears that fill my eyes
I know
Treasured still in mem'ry lay
Little words you used to say
Bringing love that couldn't stray
And so
There will always be a tear
Shed the first of every year
And I'll always want you near
My side
Tender thoughts will drift to me
You'll be mine in dreams you
see
Even 'tho I couldn't be
Your Bride
There will always be that ache
For the vows we didn't take
And the love I let you make
A trust
Recalling days that lay behind
Makes me pray that I may find
Love is just a bit more kind
In Dust!

Marie J. Tarsi
A WRITER'S CODE
to dream
to ponder
to experience—
to have it all lost?
no—
write it
savor it
share it—
then at leisure
live it all again!

Toohey O'Boos
THAT OLD FORGET—ME—NOT
Two good old guys were
swapping lies
about their boys in college,
those venturous lads who'd fled
the ranch
to build their stock in
knowledge.
"Sam, can you rightly
understand
them degrees they're workin' on?
If so, do tell, I'd like to know
why Zeb has slipped the farm."
"I reckon, Will," Sam replied.
"The first is called a B.S.
You know 'bout that, you've
been around;
if not, give it a guess."
So Will, indeed a man of the
world,
nodded knowingly
while Sam, attuned to Willie's
world,
rushed on with growing glee.
"Then they work a little more
to get that fine M.S.;
for fact, it's simply More of the
Same,
this I must confess."
As willie nodded once again,
Sam began to burrow
in the hardest flat of all the
land,
the toughest field to furrow.
"They study for years, all day
long,
they cut some fancy capers;
they plow through books until
the dawn,
then write those dandy papers.
"And if they have a quid of luck,
they pluck the pick of the lot;
this degree's their Ph. D.--
the big forget-me-not."
"Forget-me-not!" Willie spat,
no more the tacit reaper.
"Why, Will, it's just our stock in
trade
Piled Higher, son, and Deeper!"

Mrs. Madge Germek
A SILVER ANNIVERSARY
It's been 25 years since you've
wed
When you put your single lives
to an end.
That was when, with the future
in view,
You both solemnly pledged,
"I do."
25 years of wedded bliss,
Spats that ended with a hug and
a kiss.
And through these many
changing years,
You've bravely conquered all
your fears.
Now the present is here, for all
to see,
The special love you hold so
tenderly.
And your children who love you
the same,
As they did the first day they
came.
Through the many years before
you,
May the angels watch over you.
With a guiding hand, and an
angel's smile,
As long as you're here -- all the
while!

Michael N. Carvalho
UNITE WITH THE CHILDREN
Come with me children, just for
a day,
Give me your hands and I take
you away,
To a place full of laughter, care
free and gay,
And we can speak of things
we've always wanted to say.
You might say you love me and
Mommy too,
Though you don't understand
many things that we do,
But you know for a certainty,
we both love you,
We'll stand one by the others,
no matter what we go
through.
Then we'll go on a picnic and
songs we can sing,
And the Bees' and Mosquitoes,
they wouldn't dare sting,
The ants won't be hungry or
want anything,
And we can go home with much
more than we thought to
bring.
And though we go back to a
world that is wrong,
Our reason for going is why we
are strong,
To set an example and pass it
along,
And always live by the true
words we sing in this song.
So come with me, my children,
as Moses did say,
Jesus is watching and he said
okay,
One thousand years makes up
that one day,
So give me your hands, and we'll
be on our way.

Gaylene Gee Thompson
DREAMS AND MEMORIES
Come go with me if you will.
Out through the meadow over
the hill.
Down in the hollow by the mill.
There is a stream running still.
Come little boys with fishing
poles.
Down to hidden fishing holes.
Come little girls in braids and
curls
Down to where the stream
ripples and swirls
Little boys with fishing poles
Trying to catch fish swimming
fast
On up the sparkling rill.
Little girls with gigglish rill,
Dreaming dreams that just
cannot last.
All the dreams and memories,
On the mill stream cast.

Kathleen L. Abel
GOD'S LAMB
Mary had a little lamb,
whose heart was pure as snow,
and everywhere God would direct
the lamb was sure to go.
He followed Him
to calvary one day
to die upon a tree.
There He suffered, bled, and died
my soul to set free.
I cannot understand
a love so great
that would make my Savior go,
I only know He died for me
because He loved me so.

B. Elizabeth Travalini
REDLIGHT
When I am stopped at a redlight
stalled by the whims of
polemakers, I return to Corky's
lot, where old junk cars stood
silent and rusting waiting, like
me, to be hauled away or
forgotten.
We never bothered Corky's junk
Abby, Corky's girl, and I.
We left the sculpted atrocities
in the sun to melt into faceless
coins waiting to be spent.
Soda bottles from the watershed
brought as much.
Here in this setting we played
"Redlight" while headlights
watched us through the large,
hollow eyes of my dead
grandmother who stood where I
stood, waiting like me for a green
light that never came.

Katharine G. Leipold
LET YOUR IMAGINATION WANDER

Let your imagination wander, the postcard said,
And that is what I did.
I climbed in Jeanne's bottle --
And gently closed the lid.
The bottle started moving and then began to whirl,
And when the lid reopened, I saw our flag unfurl.
Welcome to America, our new land you will see --
Where people love each other and are happy to be free.
There's no need for locks on windows,
Or the doors you enter in;
Love and friendship replaced violence --
And the world knows no more sin.
It's a lovely place to be in,
People trust their fellowman;
And there are no hungry children -
They're all fed by Uncle Sam.
So, if we let our imagination wander,
To the world we'd like to see;
There would be no wars or famine
To cloud our History.
There would be such understanding,
Peace would reign from shore to shore;
Life would take on such new meaning,
With God, in His Heaven, once more.

Debra D. Davidson
UNTITLED

there are times when i fear my
leeriness of love and wonder
what must possess you to say i
love you i leak my weakness to
you in drops in Dollops at some
point in a flood will my blood
satisfy you or should i give to
you my Self in all terms of the
word you have me in parts in
Pieces even in peace when i
am with you in a celebration of
my body and all it can hold i
give more than i knew i had
more indeed than Anyone would
ask for and you not requesting
questing a thing
well for you it waits
waiting, time gets heavy and
weighted down with beer and
self pity grows wet yet i feel a
sense of self that grows and
perhaps swells Every time i am
near you and it brings me nearer
to blowing my insanity out of
the water
finally and sweating i am truly
alone my body next to mine in a
double bed obviously meant for
one fun and fame aside i ride
sheets into sleep and too late
see that alone i ride nightmares
as common to me as Breathing
in the morning i wake
uncomfortable and green my
face is the same as i've seen so
many years reflected in glass
but i detect an asinine respect
for depression repressing a
smile unrooted and unsuitable i
Brush my teeth spitting foam
dressed and fed i sit alien in an
armchair thick with wear and
years Tears fight strangely for a
stronghold on my face but
newly made up i remain fragile
and dry day runs down and
night comes faster and Deeper
than i would normally allow
when hunger becomes too great
i leave my chair and walk
unhurried to the kitchen later
with liquor and a quaalude just
for good measure pleasure
impresses me with its blurriness
and i fall asleep Deep in
solitary i hear a phone ring...

Lynne Ann Kennedy
OURSELF

The portrait of ourself is one that people don't think the same as the beholder. Think positive; make yourself feel the way other people view you. In that way, you yourself can feel good inside to know that the people outside and around care, think that you're beautiful and fantastic. When you look in the mirror don't put yourself down and stamp your face in the ground.

Remember, people always say how they feel and, if someone tells you you're cute or pretty, tell them thank-you. When you look again in the mirror, hold your head up high and say the things people have told you. This is a concern that everyone needs to know that people really care about you and also the way you look.

You're not an ugly duckling because you view it. It's the opinion of others that count; too.

Keep in mind that love and thoughtfulness go with words like cute and pretty. A person wouldn't try to hurt you with these words. The words in different ways mean a lot more to you than the person that said it.

People help you feel good inside and help build up confidence. People will help keep your head up instead of looking at the ground all the time.

Helen A. Jones
THE WINTER BIRDS

I sit at our living room window
Looking at the new fallen snow,
And watch the many birds
As they fly to and fro.
They come to the feeders
to get their daily food,
There are junco, nuthatch, towhee
To mention just a few.
A cardinal perched upon a limb,
So bright against the snow,
Is there to get his share of food
And then away he'll go.
The blue jays look quite pretty, too,
Against the snow so white;
They eat and eat their favorite food
Then swoop off before night.
There are chicadees, and now and then
a titmouse comes along;
There's downy woodpecker and red head
Who make our trees their home.
I love to watch the many birds
As they fly all around,
I'm glad they come to get their food
When the snow is on the ground.

Vera Pearson
ROUNDUP

He was aged and old, lined in the face,
And I saw as he stood a small bit of grace,
His hands were worn yet strong as he held,
A cowboys hat that told of some tales,

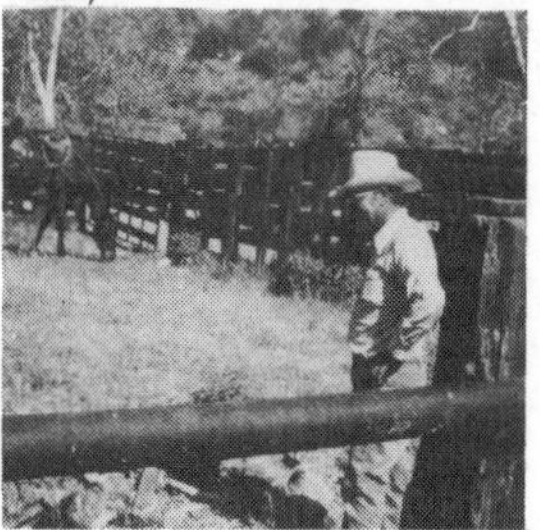

It was dirty and wrinkled, lined with sweat,
But you should have seen that cowboy's chaps,
His gloves were tattered, his vest what a sight,
And as you might have guessed his boots were alright,
Oh a cowboy's known by the boots he wears,
A shake of his hand will make you swear,
He's branded and roped and ridden all day,
So tired and hungry he will put you to task,
To fill up the table and then take a nap,
Those critters a bawling have all been fed,
And the sun is a setting a big day ahead,
Pull off those boots, hang up that hat,
Cause tomorrow is round up and you can bet on that.
He's rode that herd and fixed that fence,
Fed those cows and called the vet,
Branding irons handy, fire ready to light,
Now old partner say goodnight.

Patricia Slater
GETHSEMANE

Have you ever been to the
"Garden" with Jesus to pray?
Have you ever felt the anguish
That He felt on that day?
Can you imagine the solitude
That Jesus must have felt, when
He left Peter, James and John to
"Watch" and all they did was
Sleep
I think he must have felt "Let
Down" when he came back from
Prayer, when He asked His
Disciples, Couldn't you watch
With me one hour?
He must have felt compassion
Even though His world was
Bleak, for He told them their
Spirit was ready although their
Flesh was weak
Yes, I've spent a night in the
Garden and I've sat by the
Saviors side, and prayed with
Him in earnest until I thought
That I would die
My tears were like the sweat
That He shed as He prayed, and
They flowed just like His
Precious blood that washed our
sins away
And Yes, I prayed for the cup to
Pass from me, as did GOD'S
Only Son, but if that wasn't
Possible, "for GOD'S will to be
Done."
Unless you've spent some time
In the "Garden" with Jesus in
Desperate prayer I don't think
You can TRULY realize how
very much He cared
I learned a lot that night, I felt
His agony and His strife, but He
Went on even farther, He gave
His precious life

Mary Cochran Skramstad
WHERE THE ANSWERS LIE

In the haunts of the mind
Over a wake we wander
Avalanches of questions
Thundering.
Memories inside us we find
Contained in the mind
Like twine.
rivers of advice
Wash us under
Must it end
With the Condor?
Leaving the haunts
Of the mind
The Condor far behind
On angel's wings we fly
To where the answers lie.

Mrs. Sue Franklin
INTO EVERY LIFE

Into every Life, there must be:
A little happiness, a little sorrow
A tear of Joy, A tear of sadness,
A time to laugh, A time to cry;
A place to think, A place to daydream.
A moment of truth, A moment of hesitation;
A looking back at what was;
A looking ahead at what will be;
The place where we were born;
The place where we will die;
A time to love; and to be Loved;

Ann Wellbourne
THE DAFFODIL

Should one presume to pick the daffodil,
To confine within a vase as to possess,
Or should daffodils be free, left in the field,
Where all may admire their loveliness?
Bursts of yellow beauty, trimmed in green
By stem and leaves that reach to half embrace,

As if to call attention to
themselves,
To accentuate the beauty of
their face.
Listen! One can hear each
daffodil call out and say,
"Look at me, love me, admire my
loveliness!"
Then softly, "in return I will
inspire you and give you
beauty."
Then silently, "but please, ask
no more of me than this."
Perhaps they are confined even
in their field.
Who knows if what appears
To be morning dew upon the
daffodil
Is in truth not dew at all but
tears?

Edith Hendrix

SEASONS

As faded leaves slowly wilt,
Turning brown and softly slip,
With halting eagerness to the
ground,
Where they are forever eternally
bound,
Then the magic of winter
begins,
As Autumn days come to an
end,
With blinding snow and freezing
rain,
Firewood, hot chocolate and
snowbound trains,
With winters passing and
springs beginning,
Millions of flowers come
cheerfully grinning,
From snowball bushes to stately
ferns,
The wheels of nature forever
turn.
Resting awhile on summers
days,
Slowly drifting upon the waves,
Until they reach a silent wall,
Then turning around announces
fall.

Fernandez V. Griffin

OLD AFRICA

Forgive me old Africa,
I've left my first love.
I've been dragged across the
water--
Now I'm lost in the flood.
No more am I pure in heart
There is water in my blood.
O, how I long for my very first
love!
I hear you calling when the
warm winds blow,
I hear the voices of other
wondering souls.
I long for the day when again we
will meet,
On the shores of the promise
land--
On a golden street.

Beverly Bouche

TO THE STARS

Dear Stars,

You remind me of Andrew. His eyes, blue like the sky you dwell in, are as bright as you. O' beautiful stars, there are many of you, but Andrew is the brightest and most beautiful. Like you, North Star, he stands out from all the rest and can never be mistaken for any other. Likewise, none other can fill his place, for out of the millions, there is not another as bright, as radiant, or as beautiful. Always, until the end of time, he will shine forth in my heart above all others.

Candles of the heaven, he also reminds me of the day. His hair is like sunshine, and the sunshine of his smile is spread wherever he goes. His laughter, too, is warm and cheerful and it echoes in my heart with thrills that stir my soul.

Dear Stars, far above in the deep blue of the night sky, you shine down on the place where Andrew is, perhaps now sleeping, his handsome head resting peacefully on a pillow.

O' Stars, if I could float through the skies and stop quietly beside his bed, I would watch over him the whole night through, gazing at his angelic beauty in the starlight. Then, when the first sign of dawn appears, I would silently steal up and kiss him as he awakens I would whisper "Good-bye" and disappear, to fly home again. And so, beautiful stars, as I cannot do this, I ask you: Way up there, shed your beams on the boy of my dreams. Tell him too, that I've been true, lovely stars. And now, Dear Stars, Goodnight.

ONE WHOSE HEART BELONGS TO ANDREW, FOR HE HAS THE ONLY KEY.

Grace Vaughn Wilkes

BEING IN LOVE

The exquisite agony of
love,
soaring, dipping, flying,
singing—
winging—
heart racing.
The ache of parting for a
while,
sorrowful, sad, lonely,
crying—
dying
just a little.
The joy of reunion so
soon,
cheerful, joyful, wonderful
kiss
bliss
being in love.

Frances Louise Spaltro

AS IT IS MOST MAGIC

The white magic of the Moon
and Stars
Sends me (sighing, wide-eyed,
and fast-pulsed)
Into the land of never-never,
ever, and forever,
Where i soar on brave young
wings over Forests deep,
Dancing Rivers, and Mountain
castles strong;
Where i walk with Merlyn and
Gandalf through the
Valleys of Time, where we speak
of Love and Life,
While gathering potent herbs of
healing;
Where i converse with all the
folk (sheperds, kings,
Queens, farmers. . .) in their own
tongues
(Of course), and listen to the
travelling
Minstrels sing with silvery
voices of deeds
Brave and good, of Love, and of
beauty;
Where my friends and i, facing
many a peril,
Righteously and solemnly battle
evil and injustice—
With stout hearts, shining
swords, Faith, Magic,
Miracles, and Grace; (and here,
we can win!)
Where i am educated by wise
old Trees, and walk with the
Good Beasts of the world—for it
is
They who possess the simple
wisdom of the Ages;
Where we all—men, beasts,
fairies, hobbits, dwarves,
Wizards, and angels—can walk
Together upon the earth—just
as it was given to
Us (the planter of Dreams); just
as it is most
Lovely (free, mysterious); just
as it is most
Glorious (in its entirety!)—
as it is most Magic.

Judy Patmore

WHEN I'M GONE

When I'm gone
And oh so far away
Will you miss me?
Will you remember yesterday?
Will I pass through your
thoughts
While the sun is in the sky?
Will you hold me in your
dreams
At night when the moon is
high?
Will you long to kiss me
As I will you?
Will you feel sad and alone
As I will do?
But when I return
We will share our love again.
And the time we have lost,
Together, we will mend.

Diane Leimomi Riley

ECLIPSE

You have touched me;
I have touched you
as one may touch
from Earth
The light of a far off star.
yes shine so bright
and cold
and float
alone in a weightless expanse.
You begin to wonder
Who you Are
and what you're doing
Here.
I wonder too.
Tonight,
the moon eclipsed
and so, I thought of you.
You are of moons
and you eclipse
apart from me.
Another planet separates us
—woven strands of stardust
will open up our eyes
and make us realize
that, from our realm,
we may well envy clouds
for being closer to the moon
than we. . .
Yet, clouds reach in vain
to hold the moon
with wispy web-thread
stringers.
They remind me of a time
when lovers held their hearts
toward me
and I passed by, and blocked
them out
like the strangers
of a cold and empty
night.
They remind me of a time
When I held my heart toward
lovers
but eclipses don't happen
very often
You are of moons
and you eclipse
apart from me.

David Braun

GOD'S STARLIGHT

Yesterday's thoughts are passing
away;
now shines God's light for your
new day.
Starlight so dear and very clear;
as during your prayers God's
love you feel.
Within that love, His Voice
does speak;
listen dear ones, during your
week.
The Voice speaks of peace and
love;
as small children listen to their
God above.
Perhaps that's just the wind
you say;
but wind also whispers in its
own way.
The ways of God are many
indeed;
so listen, then act as a tiny seed.
Does the seed question its time
to grow;
or does it follow whispers as
God directs
His show.
So dear ones are you and I,
stars of Light in His Mystic Eye.
Your life changes as seasons
pass;
but Love remains, remember
that.
Let's open our minds, hearts and
souls;
so God's Starlight we may truly
know.

Mary Anne Bradley
THINKING OF YOU
I can't stop thinking of you
I really don't know why
But everytime I'm all alone
I sit right down and cry.
Wanting you by me so much
Longing for your tender touch
Oh, how I miss you
How I long to kiss you.
To feel your warm lips
Pressing close to mine
Vowing that our love will last
Until the end of time.
But, I know it can never be
For you aren't here with me
Anymore.
I keep thinking about our love
And the happiness we knew
But most of all when nights
grow cold
I think of only you.
Hoping you'll be there
Each time I open the door
But, I know it can never be
For you aren't here with me
Anymore.

Debbie Leyser
SPEAKING OF CHILDREN..
You're a happy smile carried by
tippy toes.
Your little mind never stops, but
no one knows
The funny words that you may
say.
Each word; a picture painted in
your special way.
As you flutter past like a
butterfly,

Your presence leaves me
knowing why
Everyone that you may touch or
blow a smile to
Is left with happy memories of
that special someone, YOU.

Lillie Mae Bennett
THANK GOD FOR AMERICA!
Oh, raise the flag high to wave
o'er this Land,
May God grant us peace 'neath
the might of His hand;
Oh, ring every bell from
mountain to shore
Proclaiming our freedom and
truth evermore!
Oh, sing a glad song, let it
sound clear and loud,
As shoulder to shoulder we
stand tall and proud!
Though 'tis not without error,
this Land of the Free,
'Tis my own dear country and
always shall be;
For Americans have the stuff
that it takes
To know when they're wrong
and to right their mistakes!
Thank God for America, the
best place on earth,
And I'm glad that He made it
the Land of my birth!

Joan H. Grindley
SINGULAR THOUGHTS
Love is like a shadow
A silhouette against the
framework of my mind.
I desire it desperately, fear it
greatly
And avoid it at all cost.
Not knowing if I would
recognize it,
Afraid I cannot find it.
The old scars are beginning to
heal.
To reopen them again would be
sacrilege.
Time, the great healer, a
procrastinator makes.
Fear makes me put off until
tomorrow
What could be enjoyed today.
Alone comes to mean safe;
together a torment.
The answer lies in faith,
Renewal of belief in one's self,
The courage to try again
knowing failure could be the
result,
The willingness to accept
whatever the fates yield.

Joy—Lyn Kenter
THE TRIP (LSD)
What is your name my child?
You are such a mess and have
grown so wild!
May I ask what you have done?
Was it any fun?
No, it was not fun and it was
not swell.
I took a trip and it was HELL.

Cynthia A. Hauff
A VIEW
I sit all alone,
The world surrounding me.
I see no sounds.
I look and hear
A sparrow in the tree.
I listen and see
The brook babbling.
I hear the fish
Playing leapfrog in the pond.
I feel a spider crawling 'cross
a rock,
And smell a blade of grass
Blowing in the breeze.
I listen to Queen Anne's Lace
As it sways in the valley.
The buzz of a bee
Draws my attention to a daisy.
And I see each petal with my
fingertips.
No, life has not passed me by.

Linda Comparetto Fernandez
DAY'S END
Clouds so white like cotton
balls
Skies of grey and blue
Sun, setting golden—
Fading out of view.
Comfortable chair, snug in the
sand.
In my hand, a glass of wine.
A toast to the sun's departure
The moon has arrived on time.

Patsy J. Kline
THE LEAVES OF LIFE
The leaves that sprout
come the early Spring.
The're like our lives at birth,
ready to unfold thru life, like a
wing.
They wave in the Summer
breeze,
like our lives being nurtured.
Still attached to Mother
Natures' bosom,
reaching out to lifes' virtue.
Then comes the Fall,
and changes are made.
Together, we flutter thru life,
giving God ourselves, to be
weighed.
In the Winter of our lives,
like the leaves on the ground.
Our souls we've given to Him,
serenity, once more to be found.

Patricia Yivonne Smith
REFLECTIONS
Reflections
of the face I see. . .
Can that person be
the real me?
Reflections
in the water
are those which others
see of me.
Reflections
of my whole
are not the pictures
of my soul.

Patricia Yivonne Smith
SOMEONE IS WAITING
She sits out on the shanty porch
in the creaking rocking chair,
singing softly to herself,
and speaking to the air.
Her hands are gnarled with
work and age,
her face is lined with care.
Her hands are folded in her lap,
atop the apron there.
She is still someone's mother,
and was once someone's wife.
She has done without luxury
for all of her life.
She lives on the hill
in the place she calls home,
but now is forgotten
and is so all alone.
The house is in a shambles,
and the fence has fallen down.
The windows are now shuttered,
and the garden is all brown.
She watches the road
for a car to appear
making a dust cloud for
she's unable to hear.
But there's no one to come,
and no one to care,
as she patiently rocks
in the cool evening air.

Mary Naylor
THE STRUGGLE
As a missionary I've seen people
struggle
Spiritually to find their soul.
As a counselor I've seen people
struggle
Emotionally to discover their
goal.
As a teacher I've seen people
struggle
Intellectually to understand
the whole.
As a nurse I've seen people
struggle
Physically with each labored
breath for life.
As a friend I've seen people
struggle
Socially to be amiable amid
trial and strife.
Struggle, a life of struggle,
Each has his own test it's
true.
To conquer and
overcome
And return home
renewed.

Christopher W. Meade
PROSCIBED PEWS
The chorus sings their paid songs, as family and friends file past to their proscibed pews, respectful to age. The casket leads all eyes to the altar, where the priest washes sins from the house. Prayers and eulogy serve to remind people that virtue had meaning to this man. The funeral's candor is lost to piety, the simple tear of man and church. The widow feels the drafts of an old church. Cold has the touch of loneliness. Her man has passed away in the wake of a sickness ignorant to the loving. Rites settle sins which are lost to memory. Parents watch as their children cry unashamedly. (Tears fill the void of a neglected need.) Ears accustomed to the play alert our eyes. Participants alike, take notice that this dorm of prayer is quiet.

Juanita M. Peyton
MY LITTLE GIRL
I prayed to God in heaven above
To give me a baby girl to love
It came to pass—the day had
come
The greatest even wouldn't be
long
It happened one morning five
minutes to three
We were the happiest parents
you would ever want to see
She weighed eight pounds—
chubby at that
She had big brown eyes and her
feet were flat
All the sweetness rolled into
one
We watched every move from
then on
Every morning she awakened
with a smile on her face
There could never be another to
take her place
As the days go by we watch her
grow
Into the sweetest little person
you would ever want to know
Now she is twelve and pretty as
she can be
She's our pride and joy added to
the family tree
Now when she sits down at the

piano to play
She can make you forget the time of the day
This little girl sent from heaven above
For a house full of people to cherish and love
Now this baby girl was named Katie Lee
For her grandmother's name was the same as she.

Robert G. Lamb
RACING THROUGH LIFE
When you spend your time
in the slow lane
as the rest of the world goes on bye
as I slowly drink a glass of wine
Well when I go tripping through space
Were time has no bounds
As I stare at the traces
Of light off the stars high in the sky.
So the next time you have a little time
Just get on the side lines
And watch the rest of the world
Try to race time bye.
When are they going to learn
That you can't out run time
but they don't seem to be concerned
that their life is passing them bye,
sinse you can't stop time.

Judith Paine
LINEAR INDIGO
I dip the brush in my mind's eye.
Deep.
Deeper still.
A fathom deep and more.
Indigo delineates the horizon.
Reaching high.
Higher still.
Now a stroke of palest blue borrowed
from the vaulted roof of sky and the jetty stands. . .
Desolate.
Implacable.
Stonily unique.
I taste the salt.
I feel the tidal pull.
Awash am I. I know infinity even as
Breakers smash against the shore.

Barbara G. Moore
TOUCHING YOU
I feel your hand,
Laid in mine
So big and strong,
Yet gentle and kind.
A hand I know that's
Killed in war,
And one thats loved
Like few before.
A hand that's safe
When troubles near.
A friendly hand
To those held dear.
This hand I've touched,
But few times,
But still I feel
I know each line.
For late at night
When all is done,
I count your fingers
One by one.

And though it's done,
Just in my mind,
I feel as if
We've stopped in time.

Julius L. Denning
NORMAL FOLKS
Both men and women drivers,
Normal people they may be,
Are usually kind and generous
And courteous you see.
When you meet them out in public
They will ask you how you are,
Very humble gentle people
Till they get into their car.
Then suddenly it happens:
They take on a different guise
And turn into a Frankenstein
Right before your eyes.

Now you hear the engine roar
And now the tires squeal,
Take a look who's sitting there
Behind that steering wheel.
You can see them on the freeway,
Some words they speak are dirty,
They seem to curse each other out
And even flip the birdie.
When they reach their destination
With both feet back on the ground,
Again they are the nicest folks
You've ever seen around!

Patty Emmons
FRIENDSHIP
We meet people
who touch our lives
ever so slightly,
as we in turn
touch theirs;
and in touching
we learn to understand.
Together we grow
and learn
to love;
for a time
we share
our joys
and our sorrows;
we learn to
trust one another
we learn to
really care.
Then as suddenly
as we came together
we grow apart;
we begin to change
and seek new
knowledge;
and in time
we finally part
as friends.
But the memories
of our lives together
will never fade;
we meet again
and reminisce
the memories
of the past;
and in the time
we spent apart
we have become
closer together
and in becoming closer together,
we learn the value
of a lasting friendship.

Patt Hoppes Brown
JUST A PRAYER
Lord, I have this awful feeling
That I just cannot explain,
There's a fear way down inside of me,
That I can't even name,
I don't fully understand it,
But I know what it's about,
And I need to find the reason Lord,
You need to help me out,
Now this feeling that I'm having
It stays with me night and day,
I don't want to do the wrong thing,
So "Dear Lord" that's why I pray,
That you will give me an answer,
Or you will give me a sign,
For I want to do the right thing,
And I want to ease my mind,
So I'm asking for your help Lord,
In the way I always do,
And I pray you'll help my children,
For they really need you too.

Denise Kanyon
A PLACE OF REFLECTION
The world was cruel today.
I ascend the steps with determination
As I remember—I know I was right.
My eyes come to rest
on the ridiculous open-mouthed smile
of an orange hippopotamus.
I sink into softness
as music grows from the walls
and blooms in the air around me.
Warmth spreads like a wave inside me
as I gaze at the cheery walls
that shelter me from the world.
The anger that clogged my brain
seems to drain from my fingertips
leaving me thoughtful.
Is is possible I was wrong?

Kathryn Ford Lafans
THE BRISKY WAVE
The brisky wave did thwack the sands,
All beachy throwing stones.
The bluey wet atop with caps,
Doffed gallantly to wind.
All riderless gal-loping waves,
Charged themselves the shore,
Then, slithering on sandy slide,
They back to torqueing broil!
Above the play, a vacant blue
Suspended whitty tufts,
Which sail-led scurridly, full East,
No other thought a-huff,
Non time to stop and bid fair day
To twiggy pine nor toad.
All could the forest tree to do,
But bow and scrape and wave,
As blust'y wind did rule a-speed,
Commandin', all the way.
Gave I, a brisky wave, aloft,
Privileged, adjoined,
To wave, to wind, to whitty tufts,
To blust'y wind, full sped.
(Written on Scotty Island, Lake of the Woods, Canada)

Joan M. Vail
LOVE OF YOU
I have searched hard & long for you.
Now that I have you, I have grown use to you.
And in my comfort I find that my pressures
make me want for more than you.
Yet all that I look for resembles you,
All that I long for reminds me of you,
And all that I want, in essence,
Stems from my love of you. . . .
J.M.Vail

Marie Carman
JUDY
Why must you leave—?
I've only just found you.
Why must you go—?
We've only begun to know each other.
When will I see you again?
Your perception and
compassion comfort me.
Will you be back soon?
My destiny is in your hands.

Susan Doering Meyer
POET'S RESPONSE
To Gloria A. Morgan Lyon
How we struggle for existance.
We inhale disillusionment,
exhale understanding,
hear crying,
speak laughter,
swallow anguish,
and spit out compassion.
Poetry is release;
a freedom we flower in our words:
And burden;
a cross we carry in our tongues.
I see what you touch,
smell what you taste,
sense what you know.
You are stronger,
wiser, but not
less afraid
than I.

Kimberly B. Iglehart
TWO WILL DO
Two little dirty, white balls of fur
One is a him, the other a her
They play in the neighbor's yard
Until they get tired
If those kittens mess on the boss' carpet

My husband will get fired
Bath time is such a delight
Those two always put up a grand fight
Time for a trip to the vet
For a very sick little pet
Ear mites and fleas, worms if you please
That'll be $16.42 says the vet
Right out of the blue
Now both kittens are much better
And I might add—
Except for the vet bill,
We're so glad
Our two kittens are cute
And mischievous, too
How about one more
Ask our friends, from their door
No thanks, we both chime as we leave
But two will do

Gary Dan Sanford
LITTLE COLORED BOY
When I was a little Colored boy
I was so green
Most of the time
I was very blue
Other times
I was just dark
However, as I grew to be a man
I grew to become Black
Now I am beautiful
Once upon a time
I was so green—
When I was a little Colored boy

Susan Dombrowski
EMERALD HOPE
You stand among the ravaged, burned out stalks
of mighty oak and ash.
Is it no less a miracle?
You are spared.
All about lay scorched
ashen trunks of elm and evergreen.
But you are saved.
The wind swept fast
and spread the raging fire
that scarred your green and fertile stead.
Yet, you survived.
Among the seered, singed
once stately spruce
you stand your lonely stand
and spend your soul.
You stretch your sturdy stem
to twine the tainted timber
and loop your love round livid logs
that harbored you from harm.
You cry a morning tear
and shed a seed.

Beverly L. Park Watkins
YOU'RE THE ONE
If the sky were a parchment,
And the sea an ink-well,
There wouldn't be enough ink
My feelings for you to tell.
You're the air that I breathe,
The breath that I take,
You even inspire
Every poem that I make.
You're the other half of me
That makes us one;
You're who I need beside me
When day is done.
You brought to me
A new life to live,
You opened the door, so that
My love I could give.

You started me out
In a brand new way.
Just be there to love me
Each and every day.

Myrna Downer
BABY JILL
All I can see
Is a whole new world
Reaching out to me
Through two little blue eyes
And the day shines with love
All I can feel
Is a little hand on my heart
And the tears quietly start
I never guessed motherhood
Would be this way
All I can hear
Is a little baby's cry
And I thank the Lord on high
For changing my life so
He looked down I know
And saw just how much
I needed Jill

George H. Klavitter
PEACE
High above the darkling world,
On wings unfurled I fly;
Leaving all chaos behind,
I scan the azure sky.
I fly, free from all restraint,
My heart is free from care;
I breathe lone and deep
God's pure and holy air.
I soar alone, and yet
I feel a friendly gaze;
Someone is near to guide me
And I feel the sun's warm rays.
Alas, too soon my wings I lose,
The world claims me, and I sigh
to see the moonbeams dart and dance;
Like fairies in the sky.

Henry M. Grouten
DEATH OF A LEAF
Gentle Autumn winds
blow colored leaves
that are spinning,
barely clinging
to life's support,
the branch that holds
them in such comfort.
Soon to be of an
independent breed,
no longer possessing
that essential need
for the sunshine that
once was their feed.
Now, becoming detached
and floating on air,
descend to the ground
softly, laying to rest
without a sound.

Robert Medina
EVERY STEP I TAKE
You'll be the one behind every step I take
You'll share the best I have to offer
Help yourself to every dream I have
You'll be my creative half
A partime love affair won't do
This will be a commitment, I pledge to you
Excuses for leaving will not be expected
Through my eyes you've been selected
Will mirror each others thoughts
Come to me for shelter if your feeling lost
Be my hero and pull me through
And know that I will support you
To be prode of each other in everything we do
You'll be mine but I won't control you
Help each other when imagination turns blue
All I need is that you'll respect me to
The privilege to share my love with you
Is something I look forward to
Surrounded by you be my lifetime date
Your with me, every step I take

Joseph R. Paquette
AUTUMN REVERENCE
Lord, Amidst your Autumn Reverence,
A Path Paved of Gold.
Delicately Adorned with Ferns of Copper,
Arched Oaks, Evergreens and Dogwoods,
Laced against a Sunlit Sky.
A Slight Breeze Rustling the Leaves,

With a Stream Gently Flowing by,
Reacting as Natures Looking Glass,
Reflecting Hues of Splendor.
Reverberating Symphonic Tones.
My Soul so Small, Amidst
This Massive Beauty,
Yet the Jubilation in my Heart,
Bring Tears of Awesome Joy.
Like a Titan I Visualize a Huge Organ,
With Brass Pipes Reaching the Heavens Above,
And Angels Voices Echoing,
Holy, Holy, Lord of Hosts.

Norman P. Koegel
DURATION
Tick, tock, tick and tock
Merrily ticks the well worn clock.
Be it atom powered or weight controlled,
It continues to frustrate til one is old.
Wosh, swish, whirr and whine
Everyone watching father time.
Where will it end—this quest for more—
Everyone wonders as they run and soar.
Screech, squeal, varoom and zoom
Seems like there is always more room.
But heed the signs or it won't be long,
For time is short and distance long.
Crash, splat, crackle and blam
Now we are all in a jam.
For we overlook with such great ease
The cost in time for these luxuries.
Tick, tock, tick and tock
All that is left is the well worn clock.
Could it be that atom and weights
Will eventually outlast the human race!

Ruth Adams
FOR ARTLESS
Too much we think about the past
Of cheap tarnish things that never last
Forget the false fast role you led
And never wish that you were dead
Just look ahead unto tomorrow
Didn't God forgive Peter in his sorrow
Say and do those things undone
Life for you has just begun
Reminds me of the proverb, quote
"How foolish these mortals be"
But best recall the one you broke
"By doing, being good, so good will come to thee"

J. Johnson
REDWOOD
I stood before a redwood tree,
so tall, majestic, and proud.
It stood there so peaceful and free,
not just a number in a crowd.
I sometimes wish I were a tree
and exist with pride and grace.
If this were so I would just be me
and shine like a star in space.

Blondell S. Huffman
WHO?
This boy, sitting there alive
and full of unharnassed energy,
Who told him he was special
and could
awaken this morning—
and live all day?
What Hand kept his machine in control
and the forces around him?
What Vision saw dangers about
and removed
them?
And what Judge made the decision this boy can
stay. . .but—
That one over there, in that far chair
in the back row
must go?

Charlene Wood
MEMORIES
Some people spend their whole life trying to recapture
what used to be.
Memories are like the ambers of a fire.
They can be rekindled
but only briefly;
For when the flame has gone
out and the memory faded,
there is no bringing it back.
Some people never realize
that memories are to be
cherished,

not chased.
Most of the time, even when
you catch the memory,
you find it different,
changed.
You let go, wishing you had
left it as it was. . .
a memory.

Marilyn Fleer
LAMENT FOR THE LION KINGS OF ENGLAND

Gentle bells of London tolling,
Tierce and Vespers, None and Prime.
Toll for Jack, for Ned, for Dick, for Harry.
Once upon your castled time
Ruled these knight-kings extraordinary
Till Tudor Dragon brought Boar doom.
Toll for Helmets gold and jeweled and silver, crowned with lions and flower of broom.
Toll for lions gold on shield of scarlet—Three laughing leopards pointing paws—
For Normandy, Aquitaine and England, Ruled by Henry Short Cloak's Laws.
Mourn chivalrous knights who with a proud fierce passion
Loved ladies, learning, war and art.
Embattled kings. Each in his fearless fashion
Had their lion symbol's heart.
Toll for the Henries and third Edward, Victors of the wars with France,
For Edward Richard First, Crusaders, knightly heroes of romance.
Toll for the Henries and Fourth Edward, sons of the Swan and Rose of White,
Toll for York's Richard for John and Second Edward. Though flawed each was a splendid knight.
Toll then bells of London gently, in starlit winter, sunlit May,
For Richard, Edward, John and Henry, Valiant Lords Plantagenet
Bright flowers of England's Feudal Day.

K. Kirkhoff
UNTITLED

There you are going away, and here I am, wishing you would stay

But I would never ask you to, cause I love you too much to want to change you

Take care of yourself wherever you go, think of the love we share when you're low

I won't cry in loss of you, just in happiness of the love we knew

My soul will always be by your side, you know our love was real before we ever tried

I won't end this with the word goodbye, I can't say that, no matter how hard I try

I hope we meet some day again, my love for you will never end

Rebecca Susan Aguilar
NO GREATER LOVE

No greater love
have you ever shared
than the love
you give each other.
No greater need
have you ever felt
than your need
for one another.
No greater happiness
have you ever seen
than in the smiles
you smile together.
No brighter tomorrows
could there ever be
than your tomorrows
side by side.
To comfort
and to cherish,
To honor
and to love.
Together,
Forever,
Through all of your life,
No greater love could be.

Crystal McDonald
YOU GIVE ME REASON

Alone on a cold winter night, many thoughts fill my mind.
Primarily, I look over my life to evaluate my successes and failures.
The answers that I find are complicated
But give me strength to go on.
Relaxing, I relive events in my life.
Some are painful but I can see through the pain now.
The years have seen many changes in my character
And have given me time to mature.
I've matured from my experiences of pain
Thus allowing me to fully enjoy the pleasures of today.
You are a part of my present happiness
Which gives me faith to take on new challenges.
Now the chill of the night is gone, and I hear your voice.
As you smile and draw me into your loving arms,
One final thought stands firmly in my mind.
You give me reason to be proud.

Cynthia Homer
COLORS

colors in my life are crayons
many many paint boxes
sunrises and sets rainbows
trees flowers friends
natures brilliant colors of life
subtle colors of happiness
soft colors of love
stark dark colors of pain
the ultimate palette

Michele Verdun
DREAM ON FOREVER

If you have a dream
Strive towards it.
Don't turn back.
And if you find that raindrops
Have mingled with the sunshine of your dream,
Remember that these create the beauty
Of a rainbow.
And beauty is a reality
Which makes your dream come true.

Hope K. Williams
PRECIOUS JESUS, HOLD MY HAND

Precious Jesus, hold my hand,
Lead me to that promised land,
Where the streets are paved with gold,
And it's glories are untold.
Where a heavenly host awaits,
Just inside those pearly gates,
To welcome me with loving arms,
Forever safe from earthly harms.
And I will know, my precious Lord,
That in that home above,
There will be peace and joy forever,
And a heavenly Father's love.
And how I'll thank Thee, precious Jesus,
As I cross the Great Divide,
For the love you have given me daily,
As you walked here, by my side.

A. H. Owens
DADDY DEAR

Daddy Dear, come over here
and sit with me awhile.
Let us talk of days gone by,
Back when I was a child.
Remember Winters long ago?
Red hot stove on long cold nights, popcorn and, ashes baked potatoes, you read to us by coal oil lights.
The cutting of Christmas tree,
(A small one wouldn't do!)
You picked a flower at midnight,
To prove Christ's Birth was true,
Then spring would come and I recall our walks out in the woods.
Dogwood blooms and violets,
Wild mushrooms sweet and good.
You taught us all the flowers by name
And trees by leaf and bark,
Wild bird songs, you knew them all,
Whether Cardinal, Wren, or Lark.
Summer days and nights of then were filled with work and paly,
Plowed furrows close behind you,
I'd Follow everyday.
The hayfields and the Wheatfields,
Were hot and dusty then,
But we all felt as good as new,
When you took us for a swim.
Now in the fall, I do recall,
The great times we all knew.
You showed us all how much you cared,
By little things you'd do.
Our halloween parties were such fun,
And hunting trips were too,
I always loved to help cut wood,
Just to be with you!
Ah Daddy Dear, come over here,
And sit with me awhile.
Let us dream how it will be,
When we've walked our last mile.
All these things that are so dear,
Is what Heaven must be!
We'll fish and hunt, and walk and talk,
Throughout Eternity!

Tracy Rene Ragan
TRIBUTE

He died early one Sunday,
And we all know,
it was time for him to go
onto another place.
He quietly slipped away,
and I miss him is the only thing I can say,
And as I pay this tribute to him,
I realize that never again
will I see his face.
He's gone to a far better place.
There's nothing we can do,
not him, not me, not you.
He will be much happier there,
And he knows we'll always care.
And as I pay this tribute to him,
I realize that never again
will I see his face.
For he's gone to a far better place.

Dr. Melvin E. Zichek
PRONOUN

His father was a man well known
Who had achieved some fame.
They never looked upon the son
Save through his father's name.

He always was his father's child,
'Twas like he was a toy.
He had no chance to be himself,
He just remained "his boy".
It proves to be a dire distress,
A problem clothed in shame,
When son becomes a pronoun thus--
The noun--his father's name.

Terri Johnson
SPRING——THE EARTH'S AND MINE

Winter snows lie like a comforter upon the sleeping earth.
All the colors and beauty of this maiden quietly await new birth.
Then, when the sun and the rains fall gently on her face,
She stirs; and from the sleeping ground a flower grows with

grace.
And with increasing urgency
this lovely maiden earth
awakes;
Her flowers and blossoms smile
on spring's morning as it
breaks.
Your love to me has been like
sun and rain to maiden earth.
Though I was sleeping and
unnoticed, now I too am of
great worth.
You came and looked beneath
this clay to find the good
somehow.
I stirred; and flowers of my own
sprang forth; and now
I, too, with urgency awake to
new pleasure and beauty.
To find the spring in others'
lives becomes my joyful duty.

Morgana D. Lampe

FACTUAL

First I was daddy's girl, then I
was yours.
The girl, girl, girls, always
simple, frothy, believing.
Slashed from shoulder to hip,
A jagged wound, like those
perpetrated,
By ancient aztec priests.
The still moving heart removed,
dripping gore.
Impaled on the alter of self
sacrifice.
A woman is born.

Brian Berry

FRIENDSHIP RIDE

To Colleen

Friendship is the ship I like to
ride
So come on out, come from
inside
Tell me all your problems but
tell me no lies
I'll help you with your problems,
and stand by your side
So come on now and take this
ride
Having friends are easy if you
give them a try
So come on now and be my
friend
I'll be with you until the end
Friendship, is the name of the
game
If you don't have friends it'll
drive you insane
So come on now and take this
ride
Having no friends is like suicide
So come on now and let me in
All I want to do is be your
friend.

Bud Christian

FLICKERQUICK

I sat enchanted in the woods
one day,
And flickerquick a jay hopped
in to play
Hide- n-seek from bush to tree,
but never,
Ever lost sight of me.
Masquerading well, he dodged,
Hop-scotching here and yon.
He clawed and jawed, and "flit" --
was gone.
Aspen quaked goodbye to him;
the pines whispered farewell.
Ripple-swish the river flowed
and seemed to tell
That though the scene be
flickerquick for some,
The promise is there's more to
come.

Dessie Bryant

EXODUS OF THE THIRTIES

Born of the futility of a land
gone mad--Dust Bowl--
and rot-gut bootleg booze,
They willed the ragged caravans
into the ripe valley.
Shoved by hunger in their
bellies and in their hearts,
They came
in Model A's and Chevrolets
and on hamburger feet.
they came
wrapped in Monkey Ward's
denim and chambray
Shadowed by pregnant,
ginghamed wives,
And suckling, cholicky babes
and too many kids.
Kids with haunted, thirsty eyes
and neglected, bloated bellies.
Kids piled high on pee-stained
mattresses,
Dodging soot covered pans.
The men stood with their
women--emersed and cleansed
in the miracle
of breathing, settled earth--
And knew at last they could
again be men.

Diana Lynne McNutt Enjady

WHAT MORE COULD ANYONE GIVE?

I, too, was unhappy, enslaved to
sin.
No matter how I tried, I just
couldn't win.
But, I came to know Jesus, and
He set me free.
After all I had done, He declared
me "not guilty."
He gave me a gift, free to all
men.
The gift of slavation-- Life with
no end.
The gift can never be earned by
the good things we do.
But rather by trusting Christ
Jesus; which the bible tells us
is true. (Romans 3:27)
If there are parts of your life
you'd like to be over and
through,
Give them to Jesus, for through
Him all things are made new.
Invite Him in as your personal
Lord and Saviour.
Only then shall you have life
eternal and all else He holds
in store.
Give up what enslaves you, no
matter what the price.
And become a follower of the
Lord Jesus Christ.
If He could save a wretch like
me,
Why can't He do the same for
thee?
God said we must be "born
again" by believing in Jesus
Christ. (John 3:3)
Repent and ask forgiveness-- for
at the cross Jesus has paid our
price.
My Father has a mansion, and
yes there's room for you!
Believe in my Lord Jesus, and
you will go there too.
Oh, don't be left behind.
But, come with me where there
is eyesight for the blind.
A place with no tears, and
streets paved of gold.
Accept the Lord, and your key
to heaven you shall hold.
My Father sent His *only* son, so
that you and I might live.
Jesus gave His life for us. What
more could anyone give?

Donnie Jay Murray

DESPAIR AND HOPE

When things start going wrong,
And you're wondering where
you really belong,
When life suddenly seems bare
And you're in despair,
Wondering if anyone really
cares
If you're even there,
Just looking for a smile
To keep you going a while,
Trying to find a friend
To help you make amends,
A glimmer of hope
And you're able to cope
Just when things start going
wrong.

Christine G. Kellner

WHAT IS REALITY?

Is it Life's definition?
How do we know what isn't
defined?
How will we find out
What Life is all about,
Unless we find out
What we are all about?

Charles Marcus Whitacre

LOVE

God gave it.
Young use it.
Adults abused it.
Old lose it.
Loneliness seeks it.
Lovers give it.

Maria E. Morra

SAILBOAT

"Like a Sailboat Coming in at
Dawn"
Do You stare and Dream of all
the Good Times and Secret's
it holds?"
For us, We have had our Good
Times,"
"But like that Sailboat, we also
must move on"
Love and Life with you were
different"
And I know I will never feel
that way again"
But I have to understand, you're
like the Sails"
When the wind shifts, The Sails
have to Turn"
Like a Sailboat coming in at
Dawn"
True Love Goes On and On"
You have been my inspiration"
But my Dreams have to End
here Dear"
For I have a Family waiting for
me at Home"
Everyone wants a Turn on that
Sailboat"
So Like the Sails I'll hold my
secrets and my dreams"
You'll always find some one else
to move on with," And,........
In my mind I'll see you coming
in at the Dawn"

D. Lynette Sage

DADDY—DIVORCE

Married, in love with his wife.
Fresh beginning;
Only the two.
Maybe there will be more;
Children seem far ahead.
Living for today and her love.
Mounting problems; can't face
them.
Three kids crying;
Love has faded.
Leaving--an open door;
Never mind the protests.
Urgent need to get out--away.
Forever gone, completely.
New life, new wife;
Only one child.
Don't even know the four;
Left behind in his mind.
Only faded mem'ries; Daddy

Patrice Brown

ANIMUS AGE

What do I see in this face before
me,
In eyes that are empty of life,
In a body depleted and helpless,
In skin that is wrinkled rife?
So very still..but for a tear that
lingers,
On hollowed cheek of pale hue.
I reach out and softly touch it,
Wishing I could helping...yet
knowing...
That now, there is nothing that
I can do.
The pain in this fragile shadow,
Of what remains of a life once
strong,
Is no longer for life...but for
dying,
To be, mercifully, where it
belongs.
Each day is a Hell of waiting.
Am I heartless to want it to end?
The mind no longer functions.
The bones no longer mend.
I brush back hair from off a
brow,
And I leave there a loving kiss.
I pat a hand that does not feel,
A hand, I know, I'll miss.
Selfish tears escape my eyes and
I pray to God that He
Will one day be more merciful
When the years have outlived
me.

Catherine Winona Hughes

EMOTIONS

A tear - Natures magic potion
Washing away the pain and
sorrow
Clearing the heart of all its hurt-
Making a clean path for
tomorrow.
A smile - The door to happiness
Adding sunshine to the day
Brightening the hearts of many-
Those people who pass your

way.
A laugh - The harmonious sound of cheer
Spreading the air with a magical pleasure
Life full of many accomplishments-
The success that has no measure.
A frown - A sign of disturbance
Thinking through thoughts of old
Rearranging life's path to happiness-
Uncovering all the memories you hold.

Margaret A. Linehan
LITTLE GIRL
The other day I heard a little girl say,
Gee! How I wish I could play!
And as I looked at the child so sad,
I then thanked God for all that I had.
Then I said an extra prayer
For the little girl sitting on the chair.
She was not like you and me,
For this little girl could not see.
She could not see the sun so bright,
Or the moon that shown most every night.
The stars above she would never see,
Nor the many colors of a tree.
The flowers that grow out in the yard,
Or the happiness shown on a birthday card.
She would not miss only Summer things,
But Autumn, Winter and also Spring.
In Autumn she will never see
The beautiful changing of a tree.
And as the snow has covered the ground,
She will sit and listen but not hear a sound.
For the children who she could hear before,
Will now be playing inside doors.
Then in Spring when the birds start to sing,
She will once again smell the fragrance flowers bring.
The little girl is lucky in a way,
For she can't see the bad things that happen each day.
And as you look up at the sky
And watch the clouds go passing by,
Say a little extra prayer
For the little girl sitting on the chair.

Melinda
MY HALLOWEEN PARTY
I wanted a Halloween party,
But our house was too small;
Mom said it wouldn't do at all.
I went out to the barn
and looked around;
Dust and cobwebs were all I found.
When the door was opened
It made a creaking sound,
Mom came out and had to agree
This was the perfect place for me.
We made black cats and witches riding brooms;
On the ceiling we hung colored balloons.
Some kids came to help and worked real hard,
We hung lanterns across the yard.
That night we played games and had lots of fun
The party was enjoyed by everyone.
Someone suggested we turn the lights down low
And tell some tales of long ago.
We had just gotten started with a gruesome tale
When we thought we heard a mournful wail.
We listened quietly, and we could hear
Footsteps slowly coming near.
The creaking door made a groaning sound
And a real ghost was walking around.
The kids all screamed and made a dive for the door,
Yelling, "I'm not staying here anymore."
But when we looked back there lay a sheet
And Mother was yelling, "Trick or Treat!"

Fay Jack
HIDE AND SEEK
Mother Nature, teases us,
With a game, called "Hide and Seek."
She covers her mountain tops, with clouds,
But sometimes, will give us a peek.
Whenever we get lost, in her forest,
She'll leave clues, to help us out.
With moss growing, on the north of the trees,
We'll soon get our bearing, no doubt.

She always leaves, a creek or two,
That flows down, to the river bed.
And if we follow, her clues, real well,
To safety, we'll soon be led.
She sometimes, covers the land, with fog.
It's difficult, to find our way.
But when she's ready, she'll show us all,
The beauty, of a great day.

Muff Beltramo
THE SHY ONE
They smile absently
"How d'you do?"
and then are gone,
Not seeing,
with their distant,
vacant stare,
nor discovering,
under the cool mask
I put on,
the intriguing, vital
person hidden
there.

Brenda J. Thornton
FINGER FRANTICS
Next on our list of famous foible twists
Are Janelle and the jawboned jackrabbit;
Once upon a time
(About 4:00 yesterday would be prime)
That famous scream of bloodcurdling theme
Sent me dashing
to find her prancing
with crimson splashing.
"Bunny wabbit bited me!" said she.
Which looked decidedly understated to me.
But three hours,
a clinic, and
a hospital later
We were all stitched and taped up tight,
Back home and tucked in bed for the night.

Terry Lee Smith
ALONE WITH YOU
Alone with you,
I find true rest,
serenity and calm.
Alone with you,
I am more blest,
praising you in psalm.
Alone with you,
I seek your best,
forgiveness, joy and grace.
Alone with you,
I brave each test,
rejoicing at each place.
Alone with you,
I feel new zest,
refreshing of my soul.
Alone with you,
I end life's quest,
completed, new and whole.

Michael Gregory
DARK ENTRY
Lifeless eyes menace the night of a steep forest of stone and steel.
Sirens screaming, searching, playing, soft white skin grows death and a long lost virgin whimpers in pain.
The body bled cold
I need a fix.
Nowhere to run to
No place to hide
No one to turn to
No time to die
Creeping madness swells the mind and a pool of red soothes the soul.
My name is nobody . . .
or so I am told.

A'na Hospy
WE'RE FLYING
So here we are, you and I
Floating in a bubble through the breath of an amber sigh
Time flies by yet we stand still
It's not important where it goes
Just the hours we're meant to fill
Ruby wine, mosaic tiles
You know how your love beguiles
And we're flying
The sands they fall, one by one
Following the patterns of a love that's just begun
The wind blows by our mem'ries past
Nothing else that matters but our love that's sure to last
Summer nights and velvet smiles
Crashing waves and lovers' trials
Here we are, you and I
We're flying high...

Sharon Iwasa
SEAHAWK
If I were a sea hawk
I'd rip through the sky
And fly out to sea
On the smooth wings--
Not of me, but of the wind
Out to where the blue whale sings
To watch the shark stalk
The prey of the deep
The tan-tinted rays
From the setting sun
That set ablaze the dolphin's home
With freedom's consent to venture alone
To soar without need of anyone.

Shirla R. Sewell
LOVE ME!
Love me;
like the sun rises lively over the horizon,
like the sea gulls glide softly through the sky,
like the dew gently falls on new grass,
like the moon consistently rises at nigh.
Love me;
when the flowers bloom in spring,
when the bees 'buzz' in summer,
when the leaves turn colors in fall,
when the snow turns the ground white in winter.
Oh baby, just love me, just love me.
Lively, softly, gently, consistently,
Spring, summer, fall, and winter;
Oh baby, just love me, just love me!

Jana Christopher
THE UNDYING LOVE
No greater a love will there ever be
Than that for my lover emitting from me.
He is my glascow, I am his blue-bell,
And for no price on Earth shall him I sell.
He is the godliest, my only one,
To me shining brighter than the mid-day sun.
Of the whole world, across oceans and seas,
It is he I savor, which I say to, "Please,
Please will You love me? Say that you do.

For my life is the love that I hold for you."
My greatest fear, in my unsure mind,
Is that he does not love me; he's just being kind.
For he is a kind soul, the kindest on Earth;
He seems immeasurable in terms of worth.
Yes, he is my love, forever and free,
And no greater a love will there ever be.

Pauline Pugh
THE SILENCE
How eerie...
Only the tick
Of the clock...
The hum of the
Passing truck.
The heat blowing
Through the vent...
The metal expanding
And contracting -
The momentary feeling
Of fright...
The emptiness of
The room void of
Sound - except for
The tick of the
Clock...
Then soon CUCKOO!

Hazel Baker
KALEIDOSCOPE
What does make this old world go around?
Is fame the name of the game?
Is any war the same as the same?
What is mythical and what is real?
Is it a give-a-way -- is it a steal?
Where are the lowers -- where are the winners?
Who are the righteous, who are the sinners?
So what does make this old globe go around?
Are they ever to be found -- these elusive questions, answers, and/or facts?
We must -- and we will -- cut through this kaleidoscope of confusion,
And go on to believe, to touch, to feel, and to act.

Eleni Katzingris Moustaka
THE FOUNTAIN OF THE LONELINESS
Into the fountain of my loneliness
with's dawn's smiles and with star candles,
I found again to your look passionately,
I found again and weep today too because
you want to forget who I exist.
When the shuttle of the night begins to weave its dreams,
I ever come again toward you
floating over in a deep abyss
of your parting years and lost auroras,
among the seaweed of rememberings
fragile strongholds...
Into the fountain of my loneliness,
when longing tears will drip in rings
you will see the necklace
of our snatches of happiness
together with my heart, under broken violins.

Mrs. Angie F. Gerdes
WHAT IS TRUST?
Trust is more precious than silver or gold,
It can't be purchased, cause it's *never sold!*
It's a beautiful bond between two,
It's essential in life and love that's true!
That's why the love of a child is unique,
It trusts *completely,* without doubt to seep!
The greatest blow is trust betrayed by one,
Whom you loved and trusted, but *broke the bond!*
If, in your heart you can forgive and pray,
Although you may be "Crushed", it will pass away!
Trust God completely, you'll be closer yes,
His blessings will provide you happiness!
When one door is closed, *He* will open two,
The greatest trust will be restored to you!
It's "Sacred" and *draws you closer to God,*
That, is trust, we can all treasure a lot!

Darlene Gentry
A DIVINE SCULPTURE
Surveying creation, God said "It is done.
All things are finished, all except one.
There yet remains something, I still want to do;
I must create man before I am through.
And, he'll be the greatest creation of all,
Reflecting my love, without blemish or flaw.
First, I'll begin with the dust of the earth,
Then add fallen mist to make clay, for his birth.
I'll form him and mold him, until I can see
A perfect creation, an image of me.
And when he is ready to be fully whole,
I'll breathe upon man, give him life, and a soul."

Donald W. Dutcher
THE GARDEN OF MANY FLOWERS
As I walk through the garden of flowers
I see all of these beautiful flowers
It is like walking through a garden
With many thousands of flowers
And each one a different flower
With each one beautiful in their own way
It is needless to say
Each in their own way
From a bud they do grow
And soon we do Know
What a pretty flower they will be
For all of us to see
It is like petals unfolding
As they come into full bloom

John Fitzgerald Onan
THE SUN
Every morning
the sun comes out
to warm us,
and every night
it goes
and lets us cool.
Just like our love
for one another.
We shared many happy times
together, which brought us close
and made us much warmer.

It was great
while it lasted.
But just like the sun
it goes away.
Until another day.
Some day it will return,
to warm us again.
Lately my days
have been very cold,
just waiting for you to warm me again.

Peggy Renee Williams
THE LIVING WILL
Rising each morning from a temporal cease fire.
to battle everyday foes.
Which come to destroy happy desires.
And replace them with sorrows and woes.
One must daily supply the ample munitions,
To combat the enemies of life.
That aim to bomb all courage and ambitions,
through hardships and strife.
To be victorious and conquer,
one must have a battle plan.
Out front, be consistant and steadfast.
Roll with all punches they land.
Put on the armour, not pertaining to mail
Let your positives cover your negatives trail.
Backup good efforts with the best.
Relieve all tensions with calmness and rest.
With every attack, counter attack, in a courageous manner.
Never give up, and fight with all might, defend your continual banner.
Yet, if defenses begin to stall, and you want to go awol,
And self desires to destruct, to the tune the reaper conducts.
Just contact the commander, who helps on the hill.
And never surrender the living will.

Juanita Dove McCoy
WISHES FOR GAIL
With love in my heart for you,
I'll tell my wishes and hope they come true.
First, I wish you so much happiness and love.
I've asked these things from God. I hope he will send them to you from above.
I hope you build your new life on love, trust and understanding.
With both of you working at these, your lives together will be withstanding.
When you walk hand in hand as one,
It's like coming out of the dark into the sun.
I wish, through one another's eyes, you can see
The beauty of simple things, even a beautiful tree.
When you have someone to tell your hopes and dreams to,
With both of you working together, I'm sure a lot of them will come true.
As both of you go down life's road,
I wish every day will be a light load.
Always remember you have a family that loves you.
A family is for a lifetime, these things are true.

Jerry Morrow
MEMORIES OF YOU
Memories of you
Like morning spring rain
Sustain and nourish my being,
Refresh my life,,,and,,,
Give me greater cause for being..

Christa Ann Elyse Krajeski
RAINBOWS
All God's rainbows bright and new
filling skies with beauteous hue
sparkle in those eyes so sad
making hearts grow ever glad.
In the beauty of your bow
let your brightness ever show
to all who toward the heavens gaze
fill their hearts with loving praise.

Frances Miller
MOMMA
Hard times and pain, you have had your share.
To look back over the years, somehow it doesn't seem fair.
To be hateful and bitter is not your way
You have always found the good

out of each given day.
You taught me to love, give, and to share,
And the love I have for you, I have nothing to compare.
Momma, you inspire me in the way you live,
In the way you treat others, and the love that you give.

Brian Phelix Berry

MY FRIEND

My family's my friend.
Yes, my friend.
They have been with me,
From beginning to end.
I may go astray
And off the right track,
But I love them so much
I'll always come back.
My family's my friend,
Yes, my friend.
They've been with me
Through thick and thin.
I may take a trip
And be on my own.
My family's my friend
I'll never be "Alone."

Mary J. Dowdy

MOM

I think about you mom,
Each day throughout the year.
Sometimes I even close my eyes,
And dream that you are near.
Reliving all those happy days,
When I was just a kid.
Remembering the fun we shared,
And all the things we did.
Remembering how tired you looked at night,
Before you went to bed.
But you never let me go to sleep,
Until my prayers were said.
I remember how you helped me,
In your own special way.
To try and do my very best,
Each and every day.
Even when you were suffering,
You wouldn't let me know.
You never felt sorry for yourself,
And that's why I loved you so.
These memories and many more,
Are in my heart to stay.
I keep them bright and shining,
So they'll never fade away.
And though I miss you most of all,
On Mothers Day each year,
I'm thankful for the things we shared,
Those days when you were here.

Kathryn Noor Abdelhak

A CANDLE'S MISTRESS

With devotion my light has oft' beheld
She travels her dark pastures
With only Heaven by her side,
My immortal flame will forever be
Her guide - she tends her flock
Banishing grief, pain and sorrow
Sharing faith for a happier morrow
Her empathy and love for the human soul
In unity make her being whole
Her endless toils will never cease
But in golden slumber my mistress
Finds Her Peace

M. A. Emelio

PROGRESS

You poison the rivers
and the skies with your
modern inventions
You erect plastic and
cold concrete towers
You call it beauty
Now there are no more
country sides to walk,
no rivers to swim, no
trees left to blow in
the wind
You are not only going
to destroy this land,
but you are going to
destroy yourself.

Ronald Ott

OLDEST FRIENDS ARE BEST

Oldest friends are best;
should regard unnoticed.
May stray away; they'll know
where you have gone...
You changed the stars I see;
beneath my motives you crawl.
"My hat hangs in my house," I say.
To echo throughout the walls.
I knew from one glance,
your disappointment.
Bravery is not a deceptive mask.
Playful neighbor's dog
doesn't speak,
nor need you ask.
I set the blade to you as well:
an annointment.
Love multiplies from mistaken roads...
As the wind blows,
men fall like dominos,
in search of friends.
But he finds himself alone,
once again.
So he pretends,
because the wife shouldn't know, and the children shouldn't go,
in that direction.

Eva Jo Bramble

PRAIRIE SYMPHONY

Where space is far out - beyond yonder
Where black clouds roll in with yards of thunder
And harp strings invade low hung eaves
While whistles come from stacks of sheaves
Windmills whirr to harvest the deep
Arpeggios are played on headed wheat
A barn door slams to add percussion
Then a coyote wails it's rendition
Thus the scores of a symphony grow
When the prairie wind is the maestro

Roji M. Ayres

SECOND KISS

Your eyes had held a passion,
As you suddenly pulled me near...
Then you firmly pressed your lips to mine,
While I felt a warmth, so dear.
That warmth had been a flame
You set to glow within my heart,
And I remember this quite sadly
For now, we're far apart...

Mindy Michele Chambers

GOSSIP

Gossip is such an evil word
It hurts like the cut of a sword
Why must one tell a story
That makes ones life seem gory
Why ruin a persons innocence
With the words in a sentence
Why must one ruin ones reputation
Like an open invitation
Why must ones spirit die
Because of ones lie

John A. Huebner

SELF

To see ourselves as we really are
To understand our life
Can cause the mind to tremor
Can cause fear and strife
Why so we cover our innerself
Why do we play a charade
Why can't we be open and free
Why can't we join the parade
Why must we search for a way to escape
Why must we hurt the people we love
Why must we go through life in a fog
Why can't we trust in the Being above

Alvin Ernest Martin

NOAH

How many centuries ago lived Noah!
He's even better known than old Balboa.
Balboa climbed up on an isthmus hill
To see the ocean which he thought so still.
He called the broad expanse of sea Pacific--
It should more rightly have been called Terrific.
But Noah did not have to climb at all.
He simply waited for the rain to fall,
And then within the ark he took a rest
And sailed far higher than Mount Everest.

Susan Coffey

MEMORIES

A dust mop stands against the wall,
a wooden dagger lays,
Oh, memories come to one and all,
of love and happy days.
The bird house and the broken shell,
the tire swing in the shade,
These memories, only walls will tell,
of good times that we made.
It's sad to see life come and go,
and homes we leave behind.
Our life ahead we do not know,
but new memories grow with time.

Elwood McCleary, Jr.

UNTITLED

Long I have searched for truth in you;
This be pride within my soul;
Tho I have faced most mountains tall;
All for love I freely gave;
Yet my honor you threw away.
Seeing, what you could not see;
Hearing, what you could not hear;
Knowing, what you could not know;
Feeling, what you could not feel;
I stood above the dismal grey.
Forevermore I will keep our vow;
I stand tall when you are weak;
Take my hand and touch my heart;
Now believe me for who I am;
Seal again our bonds together.
Some have trodden upon my head;
Others tried to claw at my heart;
Help me not to stand alone;
For you, my country, give me strength;
I am your banner, honor me your FLAG.

Thoreau D. May

YOUR SMILE

One unmistakable truth in life is,
If a person could see you smile
they would realize

All the dreams and aspirations of mankind
Will come true one day in the
Mind of God.

Opal Wade Nelson

MY GRAND DADDY'S LAP

I've traveled many, many miles
And far and wide I've roamed;
I knew one day that I'd return
To the place where I was born
And once again relive the times,
Wish again that I could nap
While being held so close and warm,
In my Grand Daddy's lap.
So safe and warm I'd snuggle there
No worry, not a care;
No dragons and no tigers came
And not a soul would dare
To tangle with my Grandpa
While his loving arms enwrapped
And I was being held so close,
In my Grand Daddy's lap.
These days I loved remain no more
Like the absence of his face,
Leave loving memories of the time
That Time cannot erase!
In happy reveries I dream that
My memory has entrapped
The dreams of being safe and warm,

In my Grand Daddy's lap.
If I could choose a place on
earth
For little ones to go,
I'd find a warm and loving lap
Where fancy dreams could grow
And so, when they are old and
gray
Old memories kept on tap
Would again recall a safe warm
place,
Like my Grand Daddy's lap.

Jeffery L. Harris

LOVING IN SILENCE

If you love me
long in silence
I'll bake
you a cake
from the love

we make
and I'll savor it
with your tongue
and sing
you the song
your silence sung

Earl Warren Throckmorton

SOMEDAY

I have walked in Eden;
a co-defendent am I.
I have walked in Jerusalem;
My crimes caused a good Man
to die.
I have been a blind man,
But not I see the light of day.
I have been a vagabond,
But not I know the right way.
Today, in years I count
existence.
Someday, all counting will be
done.
Today, in miles I count the
distance.
Someday, I'll live near the Son.
I will walk in Heaven,
a Son of God am I.
will walk on streets of gold,
my crimes are forgotten,
goodbye.
Today, in years I count
existence.
Someday, all counting will be
done.
Today, in miles I count the
distance.
Someday, I'll live near the Son.

Novella Armeni

EMPTY EYES

She lived in sanitariums,
existing day to day.
And everytime I'd see her,
in silence I would pray.
We used to go there sometimes,
I remember it quite well.
the vastness overwhelmed me
and sadness I could smell.
And empty eyes would stare
through me
as if I wasn't there.
And one by one, I'd be
approached
and told of all who care.
And "Mary, you're so lucky,
You're going home today!
Have a Merry Christmas,
I'll see you New Year's Day."
And once I asked my mother,
just why she left her there.
So all alone and far away,
to me it seemed unfair.
I never understood it,
I wonder if I tried,
and did my best, and gave my
time,
to see what was inside.
And it always would amaze me,
that she remembered me at
all,
and knew my name, enjoyed my
sight
each time we'd come to call.
And once she had a bracelet,
won at the bingo game,
she thought enough to think of
me,
she saved it till I came.
And she never got to bake us
cookies,
nor read us fairy tales,
or tuck us into bed at night,
or kiss away our ails.
But we were all my Grandma
had,
her link with yesterday,
her memories of freedom
and the life that slipped away.

Marjorie Leighton

THE MERMAID'S INVITATION

"Oh come and journey to
Fairyland
Come, swim away with me,
And I'll guide you through
cerulean depths
To a land of fantasy.
Reefs of coral and oceans of
pearl
Of phantasmagorical hue,
In that realm of enchantment,
need only your touch
To transmute into treasure for
you.
Your sea-horse awaits at King
Neptune's gates,
And your beautiful bride I
will be.
We will joyously kiss in the
cool cool depths
Of our paradise under the
sea."
I laughlingly answered the
pretty mermaid
With her floating seaweed
hair,
"I could love you until the day I
die,
And you'd never never care.
You are like the delicate
abalone,
All beauty, with heart of
stone.
You would draw me down to the
stygian deep,
Where forever I'd tarry alone."

Violet W. Wilcox

A DEAF ONE'S CALL

If my Lord should walk this
earth today,
I would lay my ear on the
ground
And feel the Power in the beat
of His feet;
But I'm deaf to the world
around.
I would see the love in His
gentle touch
And know His truth in my
heart;
But I cannot hear His tender
voice
Or know of His words at the
start.
His call for me is a beckoning
hand.
Not a word would I understand.
I'm one of His lambs that
strayed away;
But He found me in the thorny
way.
He picked me up and changed
my life
For a joy now fills my soul.
I'm learning the signs to
communicate
To others of my kind and fold.
I'm finding a place in the house
of the Lord
Like no other has done but
chart.
So if you can't unstop my ears,
dear Lord,
Then please unstop my heart.

Charlene Neely

SANTA AND ME

The pies are all baked
The shopping is done.
The tree is trimmed
And the stockings are hung.
Now the house is quiet;
There's no one up
But Santa and Me.
The presents are wrapped
And tucked under the tree.
A few last minute items
And we'll be home free.
Just sit and rest easy
Everyone is ready
But Santa and Me.
The cookies and milk
Are dutifully eaten.
The "a-child-can-assemble-it"
Kit is finally beaten.
In half an hour everyone
Will be up and att 'em
But Santa and Me.

Lula M. Fry

THOSE THAILAND BUGS

Now I lay me down to sleep
I pray tonight the bugs won't
creep;
But if a roach comes marching
by
I'll grab my ax and chop his
thigh;
And if that chop don't stop him
then,
I'll grab my ax and chop his
chin.
And if that roach should start to
run,
I'll wait for the next big
son-of-a-gun;
and be it mouse or spider or flea
I'll grab my ax and chop his
knee.
For over here you take a chance
if dare to sleep without your
pants.
For you may wake up just in
time,
to find he's chewed off your
behind.
Now take this warning, I ask
you please,
and listen for the mosquitos'
sneeze.
He may blow your hat right off
your head
and you may wish that you were
dead.
Now this is not some kind of
dream
for all these things mine eyes
have seen.

Kenneth W. Staton

MIEKO

What joy you give me!
Where was I before you came
To make me alive?
Was there ever life
When you were not a part of
me?
I don't remember.
Our destinies crossed
Somewhere before we could
know
Love would come to us.
Now I've taken a vow
To be your lover and friend.
I promised myself.

Lisa Howell

ALL SEASONS

As summer begins
And the sun brings to life
The wonderful colors to behold,
Hearts open up to be loved
And I am blessed with your
love.
As fall comes along
I see the leaves turn brown and
die
As the trees become bare,
And I know our love too
Is dying just like the leaves.
As each new season comes and
goes
Old hearts close and new ones
open
The tears of rain flow between
each,
And my eyes are red like the
sun
As they let the rain fall
Praying to have your love
During all seasons.

Sophia Mezynski

SUNSET

The day is near ending.
Over mountains of purple and
blues,
The brilliant sun is descending.
Once again, leaving an array of
hues.
Surveying the spaciousness of
heaven:
Upon this blue vault it appears
as though
From the rainbow with her
colors seven
A portrait of a wonderland of
fire and water will flow.
Bright red and deep orange
waves
Are intermingling on the left.
Azure blue turning dismal as
graves
On the right.Give a feeling of
bereft.
Natures' brush passes quickly.
Leaving no doubt.
Over, downward, up and out.
Mixing, shading and scattering
each color.
Pastels, bright shades and
remnants of obscure horror.
One last ray probes through a

prisms side.
Mountains turning dark and serene bid "adieu".
As slate disjoins from russet flames wide.
Each turning and exiting from view.
A few last puffs pass resembling cotton soiled
from a wound. Color fading. All is dark.
Black magic has produced an ornament. Nature has toiled.
Gazing afar is seen an igniting spark.

Lenore Sowle Buchalter

GROPING FOR SPRING

The night was...well, for the first time in months I had walked home without a coat.
This bright afternoon
smoke from someone's fire
sneaked quickly across the
campus green.
They cut the grass this
afternoon
and it smelled
for real-
warm and wet
like living grass does - or perhaps used to.
I felt the sun on the back of my
head and legs trying so hard
to be warm
today, only trying.
And tonight I looked up
and cold February stars
Blinked unseeing back at me!

Penny Laurne Fox

LOSING TIME ON LIFE

My heart broke today because our love has gone away.
You lead me astray and now my heart will have to pay.
We had it all but what's left now is so small.
We took a bad fall, it's too bad no one heard my call, for help.
It was so easy to be true but now there's no need to.
I no longer belong to you, but why did you leave me feeling so blue.
You turned me inside out without any doubt, but no,
I won't just sit and pout because I know it's not worth it.
And I won't sit and cry for you anymore all-the-while I'm losing time on life.
I already spent too many hours waiting on you and hoping for brighter tomorrows
When while I sat in sorrow I was losing time on life.
Soon I will begin picking up pieces from within and maybe someday soon
I will smile again, but until then I'll just be losing time on life.
I'll look back on those sweet yesterdays remembering the times we shared that day.
And then I'll wonder how today ended up in this way.
It's such a shame love can leave you so confused and pained when it all looks
So beautiful on the outside, there's so much more deep inside.
So, was I really losing time on life
Or just taking time to understand what love's all about.

Margaret Aydelotte

...WITHIN YOU

"How big is God?"
"My child,
He is as big as your heart can hold:
A sky of stars, or speck of dust,
A rainbow arch in drop of dew."

Derryl Parsons

NECROMANCER

The Necromancer is among us.
What has been forgotten,
remembers.
Dead whales surface from the
Depths of our schizm, brought
back to life with fond atavisms.
They are dreams within
Forests we sleep in.
They are dead names
Of the Rememberer.

Betty J. Streets Preece

LITTLE CHILD

Little child with curly hair
and eyes that dance with joy
Be it little girl in frills and lace
Or a little blue-jeaned boy
How is it that your cares are few
No worries crowd your mind
No seeking ways of fraud or greed
No devious plans unwind
Is it because you've not yet reached
A level in your life
Where we take each moment of the day
and fill it with work and strife
You never seem to mind the odds
or tend to grumble why
Is the daily love and care you get
Enough to satisfy?
Or is it because we've all grown up
Too soon forgotten when
The world was big enough for all
And love was fashion then
We're still the mortal, the very same
heart, body, soul and mind
The seed God planted in the womb
Just aged with Father Time
Alas! We have forgotten
The joys of childhood bliss
When bruises could be healed
With a tender hug and kiss
Now it takes wars and violence
We deal a heavy blow
Destruction walks across our land
Just making bruises grow
Oh little child with curly hair
A lovely pattern you do weave
Too soon the threads will all be cut
When that day comes, you'll grieve

Robert Gregory McCloud

INSPIRATION

Once dreamed I would be successful, but someone said no;
Once believed that I could help the world in it's greatest hour of distrees, but someone said no;
Once thought about being a writer and make the world a beautiful poem, but someone said no;
Once brought a bit of laughter to a tearful atmosphere, but someone said it was not possible;
Never thought once of failure, but a voice whispered it to me;
Never dreamed of being average until society said it was natural;
Never feared pain until you said it could hurt;
Met a man once whose presence cured me of all my insecurities;
Met the horizon and His hand directed its movement, His eyes were the sun at dawn, and the moon at dusk;
Never physically talked to Him but through Him I know its going to be alright;
Never dreamed I'd be where I am today and this man tells me I can go further;
Never would try to be above average and He said strive for uniqueness;
Never had a dear friend and He said he'd be by brother, my inspiration, and a dear friend;
This man, He's my God and forever my dreams will be positive with Him as my faith ... because with all storms there must be gentle rains.

Stephen Patrick McNeil

REBECCA, MY BEKI

If you are but of my imagination
an illusion...,
then make love to me now
before I awaken.
For living tomorrow
without dreams,
we awaken
alone...!

Stephen Patrick McNeil

A VALENTINE

The carnation,
It's pastel colors,
frail, intricate,
waving...
To me the most
perfect of the love flowers.
But the rose
in its red caressing fingers,
sensitive...,
is the intimate
expression of romantic desire.
Wrapping layer upon layer
as would lovers
in each others arms.
So to thee,
I give the rose,
My showering of love,
admiration.
Emotions to be loyal and shared.
Myself
for a life time
of blooming...,
a rose.

Lenora C. Freeman

LOVERS

Two people unite in the stillness of a winter's cold indifferent night
Keeping warm with inflamed kisses, embraces tight
Cast shadows in the glow of the full moon's light
Sheets once clean, crisp now crinkled, wrinkled; wet
Saturated by body sweat; evidence that bodies met
Mellow moans, tender touches, endless kisses express what they feel
Giving, sharing themselves freely not afraid to let all reveal
In loving arms, they find a special warmth despite the harsh weather
And experience total oneness-not only had two bodies met but two souls came together

Patricia Hoad

GRAN

Small wrinkled friend
Singer of cradle songs
Listener to French phrases
Nightmares and love affairs
Friend of my friends
Dammit
That night you died
I wasn't even near
To touch your hand nor
Whisper, "Comme je t'aime."

Ronald A. Croyle

WHISPERING LOVE

Soft, soft like the voice, of an angel.
Sweet, sweet are the words, I am hearing. Whispers, whispers of love, in thee air, only we shall share...
Whispering Love!
Oh! how my heart rejoices, when we are, together. And the soft, melody, I hear, whispering in my ear, with-in my heart, is saying... Whispering Love!
Oh! how long, I have waited, to hold, and kiss him.
Soft, soft is the gentle breezes, that are blowing, as we walk together, through thee meadow.
Sweet, sweet is the smell, of blossoms, in thee air... And as we kiss, I hear the honeybees, and songbirds, singing...
Whispering Love!
Oh! how the love, I feel, in my soul, is so warm... and glowing.
And the soft, melody, I hear, whispering in my ear, is the sound, of his own, sweet voice, saying...
Whispering Love!
As the sun, sets... we view, ah beautiful sunglow, in the sky.
Twilight fills, the night... as the stars shine, ever so brightly.
And as we kiss, I hear, the lovely cry, of a whip-poor-will,

echoing, in the valley...
He stares, in my eyes, as he
softly whispers, these
comforting words...
Think, think of tomorrow,
will be as bright, as this
heavenly night...
Whispering Love!

Marjorie Leighton

THE CRUCIBLE

In the crucible of the world,
Fate burns out the dross to refine the gold.
But oh, the incredible suffering
When the process burns into the very soul!
The dying of a beloved child
Takes on a fine-drawn agony.
It ruthlessly grips us with iron hands,
And wrings our hearts with fatality.
When destiny takes its terrible toll
And we are left comfortless at the last,
Then God in his mercy sends loving hands
To raise us up when our trial is past.

Julianne Matthews

FREEZING EMPTINESS

The chilling cold
bites at my nose
and rubs his icy fingers
through my hair
reminding me
that the warmth of you
must exist in memories.
Snowflakes whirlwind
causing thoughts of you
to collide and war with each other.
The cold wind
bites my daydream
causing the chill of reality
to awaken me.
Although we were only friends,
I find the distance
that has come between us
has caused a desolate emptiness
to ache deep inside of me...
A freezing emptiness and
I find it hard to bear.

Anna M. Zahn

FALL WEATHER

Fall is leaves scattered all around
Fall is many things, wind and
Rain, and gloom too
Fall is a thing of beauty, it
Touches me, it touches you
Fall is dark skies, turned to grey
And pretty leaves all arrayed
Mother Nature knows her
Place in this creation
She changes her face to all
In fascination, but the best
Thing I know is when the
Children dressed in their
Halloween creations come
calling with their presentation
"Trick or Treat"
Can't be beat
is
My idea of Fall Presentations

Marion Ralph Mooney

THE SILENT MASTER

Sitting alone, I stare at the silent phone.
And send out my own desperate transmission.
"Ring, damn you, ring!"
He'll call. He'll explain.
Everything will be O.K.
Last night we talked of love and hope and life.
We agreed that each of us is responsible for his own fate.
Masters of our destiny.
We spoke of strength and courage.
Of loyalty and honesty.
We agreed that nothing or no-one
Could take away the happiness we'd made.
After all, we planned it, designed it, executed it.
That was yesterday.
Today my world exploded.
Placing my hand on the phone, I will it...
"Ring!"... Nothing.
My heart beats faster.
The knot in my stomach rises to form a lump in my throat.
Tears fill my eyes.
The clock ticks ominously.
Time passes.
Looking out the window I see the leaves fall from a neighbor's tree
And drift gently over the fence,
And onto the surface of my pool.
Fall is here.
I could not stop it's arrival.
Summer is over.
Pain is here.
I cry.
I could not stop the fall.
I could not will him to call.
There are too many things I cannot control.
Too much I cannot change.
I am after all, vulnerable.

Tammie C. Mayberry

????????????

I have worked hard,
and had nothing,
But had it all.
I have loved much,
and not loved at all,
But have not known love.
I have seen much,
and have seen nothing at all,
But have not seen enough.
I have heard a lot,
and have not heard at all,
But need to hear more.
I have tasted.
until, I got tired,
And still need to taste more.
I have felt much,
But have really felt nothing,
And am searching, to feel more.

Brent W. Smith

VETERAN

I met a Vietnam Veteran,
Yesterday.
I did not know,
What to say.
He had lost an arm,
And a hand.
Nam spelled backwards,
Is man.

Christopher Miller

THE OLD CHIEFS GAZING FIERCELY AT FULL MOON

Here high in dark
while the night wind bathes tall
grass night air pulls wisps of old
dreams to this hushed wooded
clearing
In a last flood of vision
hugged tight, arching high
the old forest men light again
against the glow of dusk
seeking retreat, return
to what was once theirs
what will soon be theirs
The vision dies with the sun.

Yvette Sterner

A SOUVENIR EVERLASTING

We are only spectators
Walking along an unlearned path
Colorful wildflowers;
Fulfilling the sequence of greenness
Enjoying the fresh, coolness;
Of a breeze off the creek
As the sun loses it's brilliance;
Darkness supressing the sky
Many small planets appear;
A picturesque above the horizon
Feeling the warmth of the fire;
Shadowy, images appearing
We lie beneath the birch trees;
Their branches protecting and comforting
As we awaken to the outdoors
Feeling the sun's warmth
Hearing only the birds singing aloft
The creek flowing so near
This beauty we've captured
A souvenir everlasting.

James David Dowling

CROSSES OF OUR OWN

ETERNAL WIND shake the
flame this wrinkled mask lacks
sleep
For all this brittle bone and vein
lay famished at your feet
No nail has split these callous
hands this crown it knows no
thorns

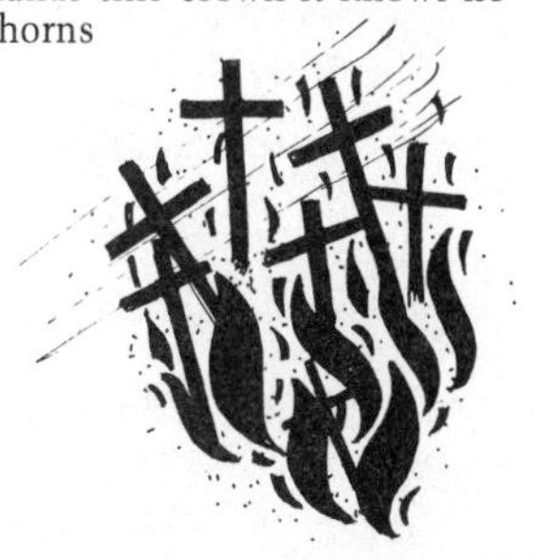

Yet the mortal's soul hangs
butchered still on crosses of our
own.

Rick Taylor

MY BUTTERFLY...MY GYPSY MOTH

For too many years...I chased you with a net,
Blindly stumbling...foolishly in pursuit.
Never gave thought...to what you needed,
Nor cared 'bout...what you must have.
I was hungry...for the capture,
Selfishly chasing...and ready to shoot.
'Stead of flying...in formation with you,
I tried to lock you...in your cocoon.
How sad to try...to capture,
A butterfly...a gypsy moth
The moral to this story...
The reason it's true:
Don't try to trap a butterfly
...With a wool net.
'Cause they're still...part gypsy moth;
And you know...how moths love wool.

B. Neill Dunlap

HER

Absolve and abrogate my mind of her image,
Lighten the burden of my fantasy.
I am the harlequin of her life.
She is as she was. . . . .
violins and orchids are always
in her presence, though the
mist of her falseness detracts
from her otherwise pervasive beauty.
Give up to me the desert with the many
splendored cacti. . . . .
Give to my heart the peace of the evening
stillness. . . . .
An old dog, the moon and stars. . . .
Clouds and shadows, time to drift with,
and a use for my memory. . . . .
Give back to me, my heart.

Beverly Ovelton Romero

JUST FOR YOU

For each smile it takes to
brighten your day,
someone smiles with you.
For each sigh it takes to
lighten the load,
someone shares a burden too.
For each tender thought
that you express,
someone feels the emotion spent.
For one heart
that you have touched,
someone is there, and will always be.

Norma Claflin Trask

FLOWERS

Flowers in the garden grow-
Made by the Masters hand,
There are red, orange and yellow ones-
And all are simply grand,
But God can't do it all you know,
It takes patience and loving care
For the one who shares his love for them
And places the seedlings there.
Flowers are one of God's wonders-
Which I hope will never cease-
There is beauty and joy in a garden,
And most of all there's peace.
So let us go to the garden,
And glimpse at the flowers fair;
Sit still and pray in the garden,
Because we know that God is there.

Clara M. Reed

REGRETS

If you think that life is tough
And you often stop and fret.
Let me tell you this is rough,
But, Baby, you "Ain't seen nothing yet"
I've had my head beneath the sand
I thought that I could hold your hand
And help you grow to be a man

Someday I hope you understand.
No one can take lifes knocks for you
And let you "to thine ownself be true"
I'm sorry that I let you down
A wreath of thorns is now my crown.
Make my faith in you come true
I know behind those eyes of blue
There lies a heart of purest gold...
Make me be proud, before I'm Old...
For my Son Mark Reed

Lorena K. Seither
IT'S CHRISTMAS TIME
It's time again for our Christmas prayer,
Decorations are swinging every-where.
The chimes are ringing clear and sweet
And shoppers are crowding on every street.
Above it all the meaning clear,
Should be told to people far and near.
It isn't clear to some you know,
Just why this Christ was sent below.
Peace on earth! good will to-ward men,
Means Christ the atonement for our sin.
He paid our debts on Calvary's tree,
And will return again you'll see.
And Oh! the joy, that will be shown,
When He returns to claim his own.

Sandra L. Stewart
GREY AND BLACK
Woman.
Old Woman.
Listen to the moans of her rocker
back and forth
back and forth.
Her head sprouts
an obscure greyish growth,
beneath which lays a
suffocating organ, entangled
by the roots of the growth.
Barely visible eyes are being sucked back
into her head
(serving no further purpose).
She hears voices.
White voices
ringing through her ears
muffled by lace suspended.
they come, they go.
With my finger
I trace a path
from ear to ear,
dust rises
settles again.
Beneath the skin of her hands
are meandering blue streams
holding up an outer shell.
A silent cremation of bones
is taking place, particles fall
into the streams, clogging them.
I hold her hand
and we wait together.
Can she feel my fright?

Richard A. Jenkins
I CARE
There are memories
we both
would like to forget,
There are heartaches
we both
remember yet.
Dreams
that have been shattered,
tears
that were shed.
Times filled with sorrow,
dreading
to live tomorrow.
But a good friend
is as
gold,
Someone
who's friendship
you can enfold.
And though you're still
hurting
and feeling low,
You took the time
to help carry
my troubled load.
Precious
indeed
is a warm smile,
A cheery hello
on the phone
once in a while.
I care much
that happiness
will be yours
each day,
And I want
to be there,
if I can help you
in any way.

Earl F. Farris
FLY FREE
Drink deep my love of the cup of life
And what the day may bring
We know not the depth of the cup
When our lip first touch the rim.
Drink while the wine still is sweet
Wait not the later hour
Drink while the dew is on the cup
Wait not till the wine grows sour.
We know not what the day may bring
With whom we walk next mile
The joy missed forever gone
Gladly meet a loved ones smile
The hours and years can bring joy
If we can see our way
If each dawn we tell our heart
This is a welcome day.
So lift your cup and raise your eyes
Use what the day may bring
In the wine of life are soaring thoughts
Let nothing bind your wings.

Maynard Irvin Hebert
OF MY DEATH
Of my death I do not fear
but to seek it I do not dare
for I care not to hurry or rush
my body back to empty dust
And death no help does it need
to destroy and bury my seed
for when it comes I will ready be
to welcome it with faith to me
Whether it comes day or night
by darkness or by the light
I shall bear it to my breast
and look to it for quiet rest

Cathy Joanne Feiner
UNTITLED
Time...whispers of wind sieving
through the ripples of sand,
Through a vast, open sea of
endless span of world
Rushing and winding and
soaring over, with clear, endless
masterful wings,
Ruling its prey with vicious
venom pouring through the
hourglass of loosely falling life
into the outstretched span of
the ever-grasping minute.

Rhodora Marie Lock
BLUE DAYS SING
Why does the sun shine when my days are blue?
How can the wind blow when I and you suffer unspoken quarrels?
How do the birds sing and fill the air with happy song - though our silent day is long?
Why will the moon and stars hang high when day is gone and it grows nigh?
All these things I love so much would make a perfect day
If only you would look and smile my way.
I wish that I could see the other side of the mountain, of what tomorrow will hold.
I wish that all our future days will be like that of old.
I pray that the other side is less steep than that we've climbed.
I pray we don't tumble down and hit the cold ground hard.
If the sun must shine on my blue days, let it be in your eyes.
If the wind must blow and the birds must sing,
Let this happiness; in your ears ring.
And the moon and stars which hang by night, will care for you, and be your's; a guiding light.
So, if I can't speak of my heart's sting,
For you, may blue days sing.

Moss
I SMELL A SCENT OF HUMOR (HANGING FROM THE DINGLE—BERRY BUSH)
THESE books I bought
They ought to rot
Like shit that hit the shitter's pot.
THIS pissy plot
I got for naught
And think you stink like shit when hot.
...PEE—YOU!!PEE—YOU!!!!

Margaret E. Goldinger
DANIEL IN THE LION'S DEN
I am the Lion, you are my lamb.
I hold you, dear child, with your head on my breast,
I've never been faced with such beauty.
Your eyes are so brown, your cheeks are so soft.
There is just a touch of peach fuzz, only a hint of the man you will be.
I may never know you later, in my memory you may stay this young forever.
I must tell you that I love you, it matters not if you love me.
For the rest of your life you shall be loved,
If not by others, then by me always.
From here what will happen only Fate can tell.
But now we are lovers and my heart is yours.
If we should part never to meet in this life again
I shall bear the disappointment as best I can.
For I know that the day we each draw our last breath
We will meet in the Elysian Fields and take each others hand-
You the Lion and I the lamb.

Vernon Samuel Green
VALERIA
Wait, oh wait is the word
I must love to know how to feel
A many a day I've strolled her way
To take a glimpse of maybe love.

Ever too much dreaming about something, never had
I suppose if I were a man of sense, I guess I should get mad
But my heart, lones like the wave of the farthest star
To comprehend and take hold a once a day glimpse.

Kristie Christian
JANUARY SUNSHINE
The girl and boy
sit together
on the fuzzy blanket
surrounded by the coldness
of the air.
The warmth struggles
against the cold,
trying to wrestle it
back into the ground.
The sun slices through
the crisp cold
to massage their backs
with its finger-like rays.
The warmth finally
pushes the cold
into the soil
and the lovers look up
and smile back
warmly
at their friend.

Doris Donegan
UNCLES
When I was young and in that day,
At Christmas, there was candy, fruit and toasted cheese!
But at given times he'd come from town, feigning a 'burp',
And complaining he'd eaten too much bananas and cheese.
(I knew full well he did it to tease me!)
Once when I was four,
He came and found me napping.
He placed love's gift (in a shoe-box) on the pillow,
And gently closed the door.
(The duckling woke me with its whispery, baby, quacking)
At eight, I watched with wonder and delight
As he fashioned a gift for me.
First the head, the arching neck and mane;
Two pricked-up leather ears, --

and sea-grass reins
(I heard hoofbeats and --
creaking saddles!)
Now, the years and the people
are gone,
And 'things' bring such fleeting
pleasure.
But I've known the all-sufficing
face of love, --
The memory clings - and brings
sweet solace,
- And is life's priceless treasure!

Ms. Vivian M. O'Neal

YOU ARE MY CITY

Under other circumstances,
You would find me
overwhelmed
By the City.
But, tonight, you are my city.
You are the lights, the laughter,
And the excitement of the city.
You are the streets and avenues.
You are the parks and beaches.
And I want to know all of you!
You are the City.
And the city is beautiful,
tonight!

Georgina Hopkins Gwizdak

THE GIRL WITH THE YELLOW EYES

What thinks --
the girl with the yellow eyes?
Muted spirits close
sound of sobbing --
long and pitiful.
She runs in the night
away from darkness
into gloomed strangeness --
The earth's child?
Or heaven's
earthling?
Life is hers.
She has lived --
in regret

and curious longings
to be understood
and loved.
But she is chased in despair
by the wild heart
which pounds within
her own
breast.
The girl with the
sad yellow eyes --
stumbled on through
prairies of desolation
and fell
and never got up.
But somewhere, somewhere,
two yellow eyes
are smiling.

Tom Olson

A WEDDING SONG

A love was born
long before we knew
We could find the joy
known by so few.
Then one simple question:
one soft reply,
And our hearts took wing
as if to fly.
Now our love draws us
to this special time,
Molding our hearts
into a rhyme
That makes a poem
of life's simple pleasures.
Building an eternity
we shall always treasure.
Now with love and faith
as our foundations
We seek not
your congratulations,
But only the presence
of your special love
To join with our spirits
in this peace from above.

Gretchen Johnston

FRANKIE

He left this world, a year ago
today
It was God's will I guess, that he
couldn't stay.
As we mourn, and pray, and
weep
There is a memory we keep,
Of things he used to do, and say.
The memory of his laughing
eyes,
The memory of his smiling face,
The clothes he wore, the way
he combed his hair.
The way he used to call your
name,
And now he isn't there.
He went away a year ago today.
We have a loving memory no
cloud can erase,
But it doesn't help the tears
from running down your face.
The voice you'll never hear
again call you mom,
Because he went away, a year
ago today.

V. Hunt

JACKSON SQUARE

outside can't be fix unless real
bad
the rich fix them real beautiful
inside
the voice strong southern and
sad
shouts from the mule driven
gay nineties ride
artist struggle to secure another
day
the hooker pleads a protest in
the street
a tour guide points to where a
movie was made
in the alley a wino rises
from a rough sleep
in each building tokens are sold
many happy faces only few are
sad
the artisans touch a reminder of
old
the buildings outside can't be
repaired
unless real bad

Wreathye Biddy

A GRANDMOTHER'S PRAYER

Dear Lord, please give me some
peace of mind
Now that my race is almost run.
Grant me a measure of security
and love
A slowing down, a place in the
sun.
Let me have the respect and
adoration
Of the children I have struggled
to rear.
Help me to be a "Golden Wife."
To the one man I hold so dear.
Let my sons and daughters turn
to me
With their sorrows, their joys
and woes
And make me so wise that I
may advise
without "Poking in my nose."
May my grandchildren ever
adore me
and never think of me as "funny
and old".
All these things I ask of you,
Lord
To make my remaining years
really gold.

Diane Lipscomb

DEAD END

A tiny bruise
in the fold of your arm
Marks the route taken
for last night's trip to
Ecstacy
that ended here
in your own hell.

Becky Cloud

I'M LONELY WITHOUT YOU

I'm lonely without you.
I sit back and think of you.
Oh, how I wish you were mine
again.
I listen to soft music.
It brings back the memory of
the things we used to do.
I know you are gone forever.
But I'm the fool who let you go
And who hurt you so badly.
Now I'm the one who's suffering
from loneliness.

Dorothy Easley

WHEN YOU'RE IN LOVE AGAIN

There is joy in the sun
There is joy in the rain
Everything is fun
When you're in love again
There is laughter
There is dancing
And singing glad songs
When you're heart's full of love
Seems like nothing can go
wrong
So you walk hand in hand
Through sunshine and thru rain
'Cause there is joy in everything
When-you're-in love-again!

Patricia Randall

FOR SCOTT

(A graduation Prayer)

Lord, as I watch my son:
Standing quietly,
part of the crowd.
Yet—different.
My eyes fill,
not with sorrow.
Just—pride.
I ask,
listen to his song.
make it sincere.
Let him learn,
not nobility,
not following,
But—fullfillment.
For Lord, I see the better part
of me,
the part that is yet to be.

Karen Field

AT CHELSEA LAMENT

Man do not beg at my heart
for it is swollen o'er the year
with grief and torment, torn
apart
it cannot forget the angered tear.
Man I beg of thee
If it were not for the fonder
thought
I would drown your heart in the
deepest sea
but instead was pity to be
sought?
Man beg no more
nor weep for thee
but quietly close my door
and walk down to the waiting
sea.

Robert L. Fastiggi

THE HISTORY LESSON

I have breathed the damp air
Of those dreary New York
nights
When the drizzle and the dark
Coalesce in shades of lonliness.
When apocalyptic visions
Of haze and smoke
Filter. . .like dreams
Through concrete shafts
When the sky weighs heavy
Like some unresolved guilt
And the street puddles form
With meloncholic sadness.
Just who is it talking
Beneath the constant drone
Of slick, rubber tires
On smooth, wet pavement?
In those obscure city corners
What absurd music lingers
Like aimless children of the
night
Loitering in dark, deserted
places?
And still I hear the faint echo
Of old, tired men in university
halls
Coughing out worn, jaded
thoughts
Of time. . .and space. . .and. . .
Civilization. . . . .
Newman taught best
From his tombstone:
Ex umbris et imaginibus in
veritatem
And here in the shadows
I suppose we must endure.
We owe it to the earth
And the muffled cry of
Conscience. . . .

Shirley Gray Mills

UNTITLED

In a moment of weakness my
heart was untrue,
I selfishly turned my back on
you.
For a sad, short time I drifted
about,
Convinced that your love, I
could live without.
I wanted my freedom to pick
and choose,
Too foolish to think about what
I would lose.
All through my folly you
patiently waited,
Till all of the wanderlust had
finally faded.
Sad and ashamed, uneasily I
slept,
Then dreamed of you and softly
wept.
When I awoke, you were still on
my mind,
And I hated myself for being
unkind.
Still you saw something you
wanted forever,

And your love and faith have kept us together.
Maybe you're a fool for waiting around,
I was a bigger one for letting you down.
I can hardly find words to say what I feel,
To thank you for love that is forever and real.

Stephen Wm. Elsner

MY GRANDMOTHER

I remember her when I was young.
A youthful visitor to her home was I,
making annual visits across town
as a vacation away from home.
She always greeted me with a smile
and a kiss; those were her trademarks.
Understanding and love I was never without,
and the warmth of her heart was only second to God.
Now I'm older and my visits
are not as frequent, but my love
for this woman has grown into
the greatest love affair in the history of the world.
To this woman I dictate
all the affection I possess.
The years left in my life
will be spent in praise and worship
of the woman who is the Grandmother of my life.

Judith A. Koplan

TO DANCE

Mirroring rhythms of cosmos, to dance;
With convolutions, revolutions of eternity rhyming.
O open ear, darting mind!
Hopeless he, deaf to its allure;
To its quickening pulse, deadened.
Such is statesman, plowsman, sailor, professor, student
In thrust to life mute, tainted.
I who am but mimic, clown, puppy dog, lover,
Leaf of grass by breezes of populations, nations, currents bent;
I yet am he who dances to all existence.

Florence E. Brytcuk

HUMOR

Why do our faces wear a grin?
After the flesh eraces,
All lines of what has been.
Are we happy after death?
Thinking of lifes little jokes,
Of the time spent on Mother Earth,
Of the places we knew and the folks.
It's only the flesh, that shows the time,
Lines mark a fine mesh, on the face of mankind.
Lifes kindness and lifes sin,
The skeleton lies for-ever with a grin.

Vicki V. Anderson

THE SUN WILL RISE

I don't know why I spend my time
(Writing words I can't believe)
alone, waiting for you to come to me.
(The sun will rise in the morning always)
In the deepest of the night I heard
(All our unborn children calling me)
you, telling me how much you love me.
(Till the end of time always)
Something's on my mind, I hope you know
(Unborn children calling me)
I woke to sleep and a song from
(Something inside me I know)
you, keeping me warm, like the sun.
(The sun will rise in the morning always)

R. E. Coates

A PRAYER

Please, oh Lord;
Our Father, our Guide,
Let us live in peace;
And let us walk with pride.

May we never see death,
And may we never hate;
But live together,
To love, and create.
Amen

Mildred M. Theis

EVENING SHADOWS

Silently dipping is the sun to the west
shadows come creeping on yonder crest-
Glorious hues illuminate the sky-
for evening now is Nigh!
Swiftly, the shadows of evening are falling
in the orchard, a robin to her mate is calling-
Our feathered friends, to the woodland go winging by-
for evening now is Nigh!
Silently beneath the hemlock the shadows are falling.
Far off, a boy to a cow is calling,
"Cooboss, coo, coo," his voice shrill and high-
for evening now is Nigh!
Swiftly, the shadows of evening are falling,
from across the road, a neighbor comes calling-
A Mother to her babe, croons a sweet lullaby-
for evening now is Nigh!
While stealthily, the shadows come stealing
the bells of a distant Cathedral are pealing.
Heads bow to The One on High-
for evening now is Nigh!
Swiftly silently, the shadows have fallen-
now Mans' work is done-
'Til the dawning of a new tomorrow-
With the rising of the Sun!

J. W. Cheney, Jr.

SATISFACTIONS' ETERNITY

Were warmth of heart and cold of night;
just to meet, not intertwine,
it's nonetheless, made best by that;
both passion, and sublime.
Were moments fleet, as clouds of storms;
mere wisps of breath, of time,
it's nonetheless, still baser fact;
some are just yours and mine.
Were aspects of life's eras;
as parts, within a play,
it's nonetheless, some scripts are cast;
to keep but some, while others slip away.
Were nights as fires, with embered coals;
and as such dimly glow,
it's nonetheless, they surely pass;
with dawn's daybreak's fiery flow.
Were days as winds of summer's night;
to pass, but not to touch,
it's nonetheless, eternity;
the timeless "sense" of such.

Sandra R. Dominguez

OLD CLOCK

Old clock that ticks the time away,
please take your time for me.
So much I feel I have to do,
so much I have to see.
The days they pass too quickly;
I feel I'm losing time.
I want to take each passing day;
to hold and make it mine.
I want to take the grains of time
and catch them as they fall.
I close my eyes and I can hear
the voice of future call.
She's telling me to live my life,
for when each day begins.
I have one chance to fill that day,
it won't be here again.
Old clock that ticks the time away,
please take your time, okay?
So I can fill my moments and they
can fill my day.

Margaret Armstrong

THE HAWK

Roaming through the countryside
I spied a hawk of giant size.
My eyes, they took a double take,
This hawk had siezed a giant snake.
Its talons grasped and off it flew,
But just to where I wondered too.
I followed it over hill and dale.
Why couldn't it have been an easy trail!
But as I soon found, while out of breath-
The hawk had journeyed to its giant nest.
Could it be? A fledgling or two?
I climbed the tree, and soon I knew.
What a beautiful sight for me to behold,
One just hatching, and so I've told-
An experience more unique
I've never seen!
What can I say?
I've conquered a dream!

Trina L. Scott

PINK

Pink is a carnation.
Pink is a soft color.
Pink is a ballet shoe.
Pink is a new eraser.
Pink is a joyful feeling.
Pink is your favorite candy.
Pink is your bedroom wall.
Pink is your slush.
But the reason I like pink,
Is just because it is pink.

Vernon C. Cross

CRYSTALS

Listen to the sounds of colours
Flowing from lips sincerely tart
Stare through tunnels of flagrant light
Passing by eyes blinded in the past
Savor victory and defeat through similar recepticles
Fashioned after fingers reaching for love
Tough my very inners and I will present
To you affections shown only to the stars
It is yours if you desire to enter this
Realm where emotion can be toughed
dreams can be heard
songs can be seen
life can be tasted
wishes can be sweet
love can be. . .us
Just listen to the sounds of your heart
And warmth shall give birth to reality.

Elizabeth M. Ward

DREAMING

i am living life through a world of dreams,
for in reality nothing is what it seems,
everything has an end,
and the gifts are only on lend. . .
through my dreams i have found,
that even if i am on the ground,
i can get up,
and take that next step. . .
on and on i go,
even through the times that are low,
for in my dreams,
reality is not what it seems. . .

Melissa L. Cooke

CHRISTMAS

Christmas is love,
Christmas is joy,
Christmas is getting
Lots of fun toys.
It's for the poor,
It's for the rich,
It's even for
My cat named Mitch.
Christmas is friends,
Christmas is teachers,
Christmas is parents
And family preachers.
Christmas is for Jesus
Because this is the day,

When He was born
Asleep in the hay.

Rose Mae Ash
DADDY KNOWS
My beautiful daughter
I remember when you were only three,
You'd sit upon your Daddy's knee.
You'd tell him of the glad things and the bad times,
That happened here this day.
Then you would listen to him say,
"Darling, you've had quite a day."
He would pat you on your head and you would be off to play.
Now you are a bigger girl,
But, still you have moments of gladness
and sometimes sadness.
You still have Daddy's knee.
Like when you were three.
You still tell Daddy what has happened
here this day.
Only Daddy talks to you in a different way,
And yet, he always seems to know,
just the right words to say.

Linda Wood
MY FRIEND (STEVE)
You were a wish—
A far-fetched hope—
An impossible dream. . .
Yet I watched you—
I followed you—
And oh how I loved you. . .
Then one day I chanced it—
I said hi—
And you said hi back. . .
My imagination soared—
I invited you over—
And we became friends. . .
Somewhere in all this, our friendship overcame the love—
You became my best friend—
And I fell in love with someone else. . .
And when that love was gone, everything was gone—
There were no long heart-to-heart talks—
Like we had. . .
You are my friend—
And I know you'll always be there for me—
Which is beautiful. . .

James Theodore Hawk
A CAREFREE LIFE
Don't take life too serious
cause it doesn't last to long,
imagine life as a Melody
enjoying it with a song.
Because there is nothing in life permanent,
nothing made to last,
so live it up, day by day,
dignified, with class.
For soon our lives will be over,
with worldly troubles, washed away,
some will go to Heaven,
other's, the other way.

Nidia Day
YES. . .TODAY
The continuation of yesterday brought us here today.
Sharing many sunny days and challenged darkened nights,
traveled thoughts, words unraveled, spoken and felt.
The emotions resolving the feelings battled by the mind.
Weighing out the uncertainty of tomorrow.
The key unlocking both doors, now able to unite as one. . .
today. . . . . .

Gene Catrambone
EXIT DUST
The lure of heaven, to be sure;
or not the comfort of one's
niche.
Or the crave for something more
to please: the wanderlust of
Youth, to whom the Phantom
speaks.
Or untold dreams that are
provoked
And respite from drudgery seem
Within a grasp. Or, to be sure,
The lure of heaven, reason what
may.
The tale of man, its thirst for
peace,
A bloodless war but is the fight.
There are no arms in this
human way;
The call of gold was first the
flight.
For, in quest of the hills 'twas
The wake of the West. And
The souls on the wing into gold
Sought peace. And the plight
Of the probes in Steinbeck's tale
'Twas next in the lures of a
demigod.
And now? What evil lures the
heart of man?
Evil? But plenty are the coffers
filled. With seemingly
Life of high estate the missiles
soar
As do the souls of men, but into
An abyss from the throne of
God instead?
They come: no Moses here to
part the seas.
And like an avalanche of snow,
down into the drink
Come the lured band. The
fences high
That contain the beings are
made of labels and barking dogs.
Their ominous sights might
betray
The goodness of the hearts
within.
"Who are you?" Exploited to be
sure
With a number in a missile
stall.
The payer of sundry plans and
the
Holder of an unstable land. I am
One in the big—why such a
Meaningless claim to be big?
They come
Prepared to rationalize. Every
Conceivable doubt is a BUT
Followed by a counterpart
whence the place they came.
Never once to concede a rotted
fig in Paradise!
Thus this breed weaves its core
Like some unrelated chain that
Holds together by egocentric
links.
Claims, numbers never really
tell
The score of this untuned
symphony.
'Give me stable ground,' cry
some, and
Yet whither in the maze of men?
The lure has yet its peak to rise.
And still
A thousand things untold of
doubt
And fear and mismanagement.
The wills of learned souls are
cyring truly,
For the lures of instability
are drawing boldly;
Love thy neighbor is dying
slowly; and searchers of peace
are
Sighing sadly. The lure of
heaven? Not, to be sure.
We trample on while the mind
deliberates;
Either join the growing band or
make an exit, dust?

Chester Howard Purington
VICTORY
As we go thru' life toward
Life's sunset - can we say?
As I travel life's upward road
I have no fear for "Thou are with me."
If I carry a heavy load,
I'll never tire, for "Thou are with me."
When I am old or near death's door,
I'll have no fear for "Thou art with me."

Because - when I leave this earth's shore
Death is but a victory.
"He will swallow up death in
victory; and the Lord God will
wipe away tears from all faces;
and the rebuke of His people
shall he take away from off all
the earth; for the Lord hath
spoken it." Isaiah 25-8

Eileen Clifford Rasmussen
LOVE LYRIC
My heart hangs within me like a small wind chime
fashioned of most delicate spun glass,
to lightly sound and softly sing each time
you breathe upon it gently as you pass.

Teresa M. Blondin Hughes
JOURNEY HOME
A life
Has gone
To another place
This we know
To a city
That has streets
Paved in gold
Thre is no pain
Nor inequities
Nor violence
Nor strife
Through Jesus our Lord
We will always
Be the light
All believers
Man
Woman
Boy
Girl
No matter what
Satan
Does to us
In this world
By people who
Cause tragedy
In the lives
Of many
For them
I can only say
With regret
They know not
Our Jesus yet
And even though
They took your life
We will pray
For them still
Because
With Jesus
When you die
You also gain
Life everlasting
Yes we are pained
In Jesus name
We will find comfort
One day we will
See you again
When we go
To reign
With Jesus Christ
Our lord
And king

Faith Laurence Attanasio
A SPECIAL ME
There is a special me, deep inside,
that to all others I must hide.
Only when I can be that special me
is my soul truly free.
It's the me that music soothes, and
speaks its magic to, and the me who
hears the gentle breeze sing its
tender song to.
It's the me who dances in my fantasies
to a thousand different symphonies,
and the me who holds you in my heart
and longs for you to be a part of these
treasures I hold within my thoughts.

Stephen S. Kaufman
THE SENSE OF LOVE
The question "What is love?" is the universal cry.
Could the answer come from someone as simple as I?
It is a sense as real and as true as the other five
and different from the others, it is possessed by everyone alive.
Let's look at another sense, the sense of sight
and the multitude of feelings by simply interpreting light.
Well, love is a sense as real and as true

and like the others brings feelings right back to you.
As a musician trains his ear to hear what others cannot
so your love sense can be treated to grow from the smallest dot.
Now find *your* dot, look for it, believe me it's there
remember, there is no questions of "if", simply of where.
Once you've found it hold on and begin to feel
wait for the message, it will come, just believe it is real.
It will lead you on a path so beautiful my friend
and glory of glories it is a path with no end.

Joyce Elaine (Dalton) Wheeler

LIFE SEARCH

Deep in cyclic velvet infinities
spiral
curve back
Dusty milky way widens
imperceptibly,
Deep in cyclic velvet
grasshopper aims
Hopping its sleek foil shape in
endless falling. . .
Upward
Outward
Downward
To there
To them
Deep in cyclic velvet orb aims
Spinning a sleek foil shape in
endless falling. . .
To us
To there
Downward
Outward
Upward
Signals Chirp Signals Chirp
No Sound No Sound

Arlac P. Sloane

AZURE CANOPY

venturing forth from schizoid syndromes
i travel outside myself into the azure canopy
and watch man-made metal hawks circling
the orange pieces of sky
between yellow-crinkled, foil-lined clouds at day's end
the sunset agate horizon bids me stop—
and like a loved one who gives so much in just being
i find time for the sun's retreat from heaven
to rejoice in mourning the day's death
this life star escaping into the alter ego
of planet reality brings with its departure such sweet beauty
filling me with peace enough to make it
through another night-and-day war of spirit vs. world
where my dreams collide into mundane monsters of mere existence
while all the humanoids hide in concrete caves
and hoard their remnants of torn love
i travel outside myself into the azure canopy
and am once again healed

Connie Marie Conley

TEARS AND RAIN

Rainy days are for
breaking up and remembering.
Because the rain is a friend.
It hides your tears
when you let out feelings.
Rain cleanses
the dirt from the world.
It makes everything
look fresh and green again.
But, inside you know
the past can't be cleansed.
It'll always be with you,
even after you've put on a new front.
And everytime it rains
you shed a tear
for each precious raindrop
knowing what it symbolizes.
Each teardrop reminds you
of ones from the past
and tears yet to be cried
for the children and innocence
which even the rain
can't bring back.
They're just memories.

Victoria N. Paige

UNTITLED

A
tear
roll-
ing down
a troubled
cheek, meets
another in an
undevised pool.
in a reunion of
innocent truth, pre—
senting fear and loneli-
ness, it ponders on for a
companion. And making a
satisfying aquaintance, it ap-
pears captivated and assured. . .
Not daring to change its direct-
ion, it proceeds onward and
turns out in the same
uninspired course. Dropping to
the ground it is polluted. A
wasted tear has soaked into
the ground
totally ruined
again. .

Daniel Lenox Barlow, Ed. D.

CHRISTMAS PRAYER

Christmas Joy,
Transcending toy—
Indwell our hearts with hope tonight.
Christmas Peace,
With full release
From strife and war, transform our night.
Christmas Love,
Descending Dove—
Scatter hate and spread Thy light.
Christmas Child,
As God has willed—
Come and be our soul's Delight!

Walter H. Baxter

WHOSE HAND IS THIS

I'm so frightened—
Absolute blackness, deep, thick, blackness.
No up, no down, no forward, no backward,
Only the blackness and me.
I'm so frightened!
I'm so frightened—
No sound, no feeling, no voices, not even my own;
I try to speak and nothing happens,
Only the blackness and me.
I'm so frightened!
I'm so frightened—
No walls, no floor, no ceiling.
Yet I can walk and not fall, but where am I going?
Only the blackness and me.
I'm so frightened!
I'm so frightened—
Help me! Hear me! Find me!
But where am I? Where is the way out of here?
Only the blackness and me.
I'm so frightened!
I'm so frightened—
Am I dreaming? Am I dead? Why am I here?
Won't someone please help me!
Only the blackness and me.
I'm so frightened!
I'm so frightened—
Something just touched me! There, I just felt it again.
It's a hand slipping into mine. Please don't hurt me!
Only the blackness and me, but your hand helps.
I'm not as frightened now!
I'm not as frightened now—
The hand is too small to be a man's hand,
But a little too strong to be a woman's hand.
Only the blackness and me and a hand, but
I'm not as frightened now!
I'm not as frightened now—
The hand is pulling me hard and fast.
A turn here, a turn there. Now a step up, now a step down.
Only the blackness and me and a hand, but
I feel better now!
I feel better now—
The hand seems to know the way.
Too big a hand to be a little girl's hand. It must be a little boy's hand.
Only the blackness and me and a hand, but
I feel better now!
I feel better now—
There's a light far ahead. I can feel the walls,
I can feel the floor, I can feel the ceiling.
Only the blackness and me and a hand, but
I feel better now!
I feel better now—
But why is the hand getting wet? Tears! Tears are falling on the hand.
And I can hear a child crying, but the light is getting nearer.
Only the blackness and me and a hand, but
I feel better now!
I feel better now—
I can just see it's a young boy whose hand is holding mine and leading me,
But he is crying so hard now, and the tears are falling on our clasped hands.
I wonder why? The light is very close now.
Only the vanishing blackness and me and the young boy's hand holding mine so tightly—but I feel good now!
I feel good now—
As his hand slips out of mine and our eyes meet blinking in the sun.
But, no, how can this be? The young boy is me—the child I used to be.
And I have become my father.
I'm so frightened!

Monette Preston

HIDEAWAY

I have so much to do today,
But I just want to fly away,
Away to a place that, they say,
Dreams and fantasies go to play.
And from this place, I will not stray,
For it will be my hideaway.
A hideaway to pass the day
In thoughts and dreams of far away.
But at this place, I will not stay,
Fōr it is just a hideaway.
A hideaway to pass the day,
But not to pass my life away...

Jauneen Pikka

A PROBLEM SHARED BY TWO

The street light outlines your figure. Your shadow slowly moves along the snowbank.

The cold, dark sky, spotted with stars seems to add to your feeling of emptiness. But the night is calm and quiet. It's a perfect time to be alone to think.

Maybe if you walk slow enough, everyone will forget you're back there.

The last thing you want to hear right now is a dumb joke, or a stupid comment, about how you played in the game tonight. They're all good friends, but how can you expect any of them to understand? All they can think about now is going out and enjoying themselves.

The quicker they walk, the slower you do. Soon everyone is out of sight. You can't even hear their excited voices, echoing, as they call out your name.

"Oh, God," you pray," please let me be alone. Just You and me for a while. I can do without their empty sense of humor. Let them forget I'm even around."

But in the distance you see a figure approaching. "Well," you think to yourself, "I tried, Lord."

The dark figure turns out to be a close friend, who has a worried expression on his normally smiling face.

You try to put on a half-smile and start up a dumb conversation. But the disguise doesn't work; he can see right through. He wants to know what's wrong, the truth. You tell him everything that happened, trying not to leave out the smallest detail. Now you both share the problem. Discussing every angel and detail. Already the emptiness is disappearing.

It's getting much darker now. Home seems so close. Soon you won't be able to talk anymore. Can you handle it all by yourself?

"I'll see you tomorrow," you exclaim, waking up from your thoughts.

"Ya, see ya," he says.

Well, you already took the first big step, just by saying good-by.

Doris C. Hughes

MY PRECIOUS GRANDCHILDREN

I have a little grandaughter,
her name is Jennifer Nicole.
Her hair is black, her eyes are
blue.
and she has a million dollar
smile too.
I have also been blessed with
three beautiful
little grandson's, there's
Johnny, Joshy, and Timmy.

My they are precious, and all
are so much fun.
Each child is special in their
own way,
and I often watch them while
they play.
They are truly a joy to me
each day.
I love each one in full measure
and their love for granny is
just pure pleasure.

Ella Mae Sanders

FLEECY CLOUDS

The fleecy clouds of pure snow
white
Are clustered in the sky as light
As puffs of little cotton balls
Or kernels of popped corn that
falls.
You'd dip a finger in and taste
And not a one you'd want to
waste.
They're like meringue on
creamy pie
All piled so fluffy and so high.
What holds them there? Tis
hard to see.
A miracle of God must be.
Sometimes they rest, seem to
recline,
And hover there like Father
Time.
Sometimes they scamper lightly
by,
Like little birds that swiftly fly.
Sometimes they even seem to
smile
If you but study them awhile.
And then again they seem to
frown.
They quake and quiver o'er the
town.
They get so dense you chill
with fear
Until,--at last--they disappear.

Virginia Burnette

YOU CAN BUILD AN ALTAR

You can build an altar
And put it in your heart
Let God be the mortar
And it won't fall apart
The fountain can be made of
righteousness
And trust can be put above
The incense can be of
faithfulness
And anointed with love
Peace can be made of kindness
And the offering can be made of
share
Consecrate it with happiness
And sanctify it with care
If you follow the instructions
You won't be doing wrong
If you keep your determination
You can make it strong.

Christy Ann

FUTURE

Stop and smell the flowers.
Don't let life pass you by.
Don't look back to catch the
past only forward to surpass
with the future.
Stop and look around you for
the future is upon you and
will not wait.

Debora Zimmerman

YOUR ANNIVERSARY

Your love grows deeper as
years go by,
So hang on to each other and
never ask why.
Just be yourselves for all the
years to come,
The years you've had together
are an example for some.
Make this anniversary the best
day of your life,
And thank God you're husband
and wife.
On this fifteenth anniversary
don't either of you feel blue,
All you have to say is a simple
I Love You.

Yvonne A. Halstead

FOR ROBERT

Robots in
Orbit,
Blast through the sky,
Earthlings and
Rabbits,
Time does not lie.
Are you
Not learning,
Do you not see,
Remember
Everything,
Whatever it be.
Have any questions,
Answers to seek,
Learn truths while you can, it's
Sleepers who sleep.
Time waits for no one,
Each soul plays a part,
And mostly dear son,
Don't lie to your heart.

Jessie Ethel Seroyer

AH MYSTERY!

She came as an Angel of Light
When suddenly my day had
turned into night
Her words soothed my troubled
heart
"The clouds will soon drift
apart"
A sweet look of sympathy was
upon her face
As she dried my tears with her
'kerchief of lace
Then came a whisper sweet and
low
"I loved him, too, don't you
know?"
She came and her coming was
not a-miss
Courage came back with her
affectionate kiss
She came as an Angel of Light
Then vanished, like magic, far
beyond my sight.

William E. Blake

COMPANION

It was five, or maybe four years
ago,
They came as a pair.
The difference was ever so
slight,
He from she, or she from he.
Both were very slim, neatly
groomed,
Dressed in their formal
grayish-brown tails
With just the right touch of
black.
As a couple they came daily to
sit in the garden,
enjoy the shade,
look at the flowers,
And be with their neighbors.
As the years passed we watched
The two during the warm
summer days
Caring for each other and
enjoying life.
The gentle calm and innocent
glory shared by
Each was felt by those who
spent the days of
Summer in their presence.
As messengers of peace they
were tenderly
Affectionate, unlocking those
around them
From their anxiety.
Then it happened!
Summer came, two or maybe
three years ago,
And only one of the pair arrived.
None could tell whether it was
he or she,
But all knew that one was gone.
Now
the garden,
the flowers, and
the summer shade
Was visited by just one.
The neighbors could also feel
The loneliness and despair.
Why was one left alone when
two were more beautiful?
Why was the joy felt by the two
replaced by the
Sadness of the one?
For almost two years the single,
lonely,
Neatly trimmed, glorious-one
Wandered and searched in
silence.
Only rarely would a muffled cry
be heard,
Those listening not knowing its
purpose.
It was maybe yesterday, or was
it the day before?
They returned as a pair.
Another partner had been found,
The couple was whole again.
This time the duet not only
came to the
garden and flowers
to sit in the shade,
but they came to the
pond to reflect and
gaze at one another.
Dressed as always in their trim
grayish-brown tails
With just the right touch of
black,
The neighbors not knowing
really who was he and who was
she.
And as before they carried their
calm dignity and
Everlasting love.
Noah sent the dove thrice
To test the water and land.
First the water had not
Subsided and the dove
Returned.
After seven days she was
Sent again and returned
In the evening with an
Olive leaf.
One more week passed and
She left to return no more.
Will the doves return next year
to the
garden and flowers,
to sit in the shade,
and to reflect in the pool?
Or, was the olive leaf left this
year?

Virgil S. Hart

GONE HOME TO CAROLINA

The little fellow has gone back
home to stay.
Easter without Eddie has been a
lonesome day.
Yes, he's back in North Carolina
with his brother;
And here the hours have slowly
followed one another.
Sometimes he was cranky, and
often he was loud;
But his absence is like the sun
behind a cloud.
Yes, sometimes he really made
things hum;
Now it's like the slow beat of a
drum.
Last evening I looked at his

empty bed,
And I missed that cute little
sleepy head.
He was usually up by half-past
six,
And bothered Grandma when
she had breakfast to fix.
On the sofa this morning was
no little boy;
His things were gone to the last
toy.
There was no pitter patter of
little bare feet;
To get him to dress was a
spectacular feat.
There was no little boy to take
to church.
We hid no eggs for him to
search.
There was a pretty rabbit made
of candy,
But a little fellow to eat it
was no longer handy.
Now Uncle Calvin can take a
nap,
Without a run and jump upon
his lap.
Some peace and quiet he at last
has found,
But he misses the little fellow
who his back did pound.
Grandad can now think, write
and read;
Knowing the whereabouts of
Eddie, he need not heed.
Oh, things were quiet and calm
today,
But it is lonely without his
Grandson so far away.
We had the little fellow, twelve
weeks, less one day.
It's only been three long days
since he went away.
Now when Grandma gets back,
believe you me,
She'll find herself wondering,
"Now where can Eddie be?"

Darlene Harris

GOODBYE, MY LOVE, GOODBYE

I wish I had known the danger my husband was in that bright April morning. He dashed off to work after we had an awful argument over a very silly thing. The last words we said to one another were mean and hateful. After he left without our Goodbye kiss, we always had shared before, I slammed the door and thought mean, evil things. An hour later the Policeman came to my door and told me my husband was killed in a car accident. Goodbye, My Love, Goodbye. I am sorry we parted the way we did, Goodbye, My Love, Goodbye, I know you are listening to my heart when I tell you that my love for you is very deep and true, so Goodbye, My Love, Goodbye.

Kimberly Boster Benson

RUNNING IN ST. MICHAEL'S

Only the dead look on
stone by stone
they watch with patient envy
First mile
by each outer loop
past sections A through D
Burkweist, Stapenhorst, Stein
I pass them sweating
granite lambs
mark bodiless souls
Gray dots the lawn
where Ursuline Sisters lie
hail Marys row by row
granite Cross granite Christ
watches them
and me
Second mile
Hagerty, Ostertag
Franciscan Sisters gather
their pallid hands
urge me to run
Round the curve
past Ohle's octagon crypt
Near the end
I pass the weighted iron gate
that locks them in
I run again on Thursday

Sir Steve Vega

AN OPEN LETTER TO ALL OF YOU...FROM ME!

For many years I've lived among you and I'm distressed by what I hear and see, these things are really bothering me.
Pollution destroys our water and bodies, and dirties skies that once were blue.
Drugs of course, are killing you.
Nuclear war can kill us all, not just adults but our children too.
T.V. and video games just eat up your minds, and don't let you rest
Cigarettes are cancer, and V.D.'s a pest.
Discrimination destroys us too, when others hate people like me and like you.
Hand guns we own, by divine right, they say, if you disagree, they can blow you away.
Governments and politics all lean left and right, all nations believe that going to war is the only way to stop a fight.
And here and there someone rips us off, course if you do it, its alright you scoff.
Religion is good if you know how to take it, some people are true, but a lot of them fake it.
But we all can do some good things together, and make our world just a little bit better.
Just a few things we should all think of,
Truth...Respect...Peace...and Love.

Elizabeth Petrick

THE BALLAD OF RATTLESNAKE JAKE

There's a tale I tell, went on in Hell,
In a place called Diamondback,
Where your spit burns up 'fore it hits the ground
And your lips are apt to crack.
Where the water sleeps in poison seeps
And never a green thing grows,
And soft men die, their bones still lie,
And only the desert knows.
Now this was the place I first saw the face
Of a scoundrel with infamous name.
Rattlesnake Jake was tough and lean
And his brains were just the same.
He was meaner than sin, with leathery skin,
A grimy ol' son-of-a-bitch.
He had eyes like a rat, and could hiss like a cat,
And his mouth had a sinister twitch.
Well his favorite sport, he used to snort,
Was catching them venomous snakes.
He hung up their skins on the wall with pins,
Then he feasted on rat'ler steaks.
Jake was proud of the scars he wore
From the fangs that sank in deep.
The limp he had was pretty bad
For the price he paid weren't cheap.
It's a man with booze and nothing to lose
Who's destined to get it the worst.
Such was Jake when he made the mistake
Of letting the snake bite first.
Eight foot o' diamonds adorned that snake.
It's eyes were yellow ice.
The sound of its tail was a witch's wail,
The curse of the Shaken Dice.
Jake was quick with his two prong stick,
But the snake was wise to the game.
His poison teeth had sunken beneath,
And poor Jake earned his name.
In a savage craze he raved for days
And swore at the demon snake.
The doctors knew from his shade of blue
That this was the end of Jake.
Well, the devil's lair, when Jake got there,
Was not much worse than home.
And there on a stone by Satan's throne
Was the eight foot snake o' this poem!
The adversary eyed him, wary,
Though both were not quite dead.
In the swirling smoke the serpent spoke
And this is what he said:
"I sure was fooled, 'cause when we dueled,
Perhaps you never knew,
The piece of you I tried to chew
Had venom through and through!"

Phillip L. Duncan

THE WOMEN IN MY LIFE

I Love and need Them. I can't
live without Them.
To listen to, advise, and at
times, to flout Them.
Sister, daughter, wife—the
women in my life.
Lovers, teachers, mothers—never
will I want others.
They all own different places
and different names,
Existing at different times and
playing different games.
Ella, Nancy, Mirinda, Connie,
Diane and Joyce,
Love, guidance, a tear shed,
giggles, a cracked voice.
Ella was there to show the value
of education.
Nancy was there to help me
with my daily situations.
Rindy taught me the facts—
starting at an early age.
Connie, my first love, opened
my life to a new page.
Faster and faster, one after
another, They began to come.
I loved them all, but I would
have settled for one.
Faces, places, time—they
naturally blend together.
But piece by piece, individually,
my memories I'll have forever.
I played the field cautiously,
carefully avoiding the hook,
Except when the right one came,
all it took was a look.
Yet I held out, dodging and
weaving, avoiding the bait.
But then nature stepped in, and
then it was too late.
For all of it, I think I'm a better
man.
Things I couldn't do before,
thanks to Them I can.
What I have I owe to the
women in my life,
Helping me to grow through
wealth, and through strife.
Passion, Love, Pain—It seems I
know them all.
Tears, tears, giggles—the
rise after the fall.
But I couldn't have done it,
couldn't have made it,
Wouldn't have wanted it,—had
They let me quit,
But there isn't a foot, there
exists no meter,
That captures the melody, or
strikes the poetic chord,
Like Momma,——Momma!
Of all names, only one bears
such honor.

Marguerite Sechrist

MY LIFE: POETRY?

In reflecting upon my half-century-plus years
I see that many persons have written poetry in my book of life.
As a result,
I have been satire; lyric; epic; drama;
Hymn; parody; elegy.

I have been simile; metaphor;
symbol;
the worst of verse;
Sometimes prose; free; metrical;
And so my life goes.
I have been iambic; trochaic;
anapaestic; dactylic;
stanza; couplet; single word.
And just when I need it most
someone comes along
and makes me limerick.
The closing line has not been
written for
I have not met the last person
in my life.
. . . .I wonder what I am yet
to be. . . . . . .

Lisa D. Garnett
THE MIRACLE OF TEARS
Past remains lie beneath the
crackling weeds,
As if to hide a lost phrase.
The concrete earth is like a
tombstone
In the silent world.
The mice have scampered away,
The ripened wheat was
harvested in some forgotten
time.
Every now and then one can see
a wolf,
His ribs protruding through his
shaggy coat,
But always there is silence.
The trees stand stark naked
against a sky
Whose black coulds hover with
expectation.
In the distance a small sound
is heard,
It is the crunching of unknown
feet approaching.
Could it be the gravedigger
coming to take
Another away with him?
Maybe.
But no, a small lone boy
wanders in
This world of death, not yet
knowing it.
With hands in his pockets,
He shuffles across the emptiness
Looking all around him—
perhaps exploring?
Then suddenly he stopped and
fixed his eyes to the ground,
As if he too had entered the
timeless world.
Slowly, very slowly, he lowered
himself,
Stretching his tiny gloved hands
out
To touch the bundle of fur lying
still there.
He gently curled his baby
fingers about it.
Grasping it tightly to his heart,
He began to rock back and
forth.
Back and forth in that empty
world.
Glistening innocent eyes stared
up at the sky,
Asking questions that were
never answered.
A tear trickled down his rosy
cheek,
While his body still rocked back
and forth,
As if to put the baby in his
arms to sleep.
He then labored to his feet and
Carried his precious burden
across
The frozen world of death.
And as he began to walk,
Large white tears trickled
silently down
From that colorless sky.
Again not another sound was
heard
Except for the thud of small
boots.
He stopped one last time as if
to shift the heavy weight.
It was then he felt it tremble,
As if its life was not yet lost.
The tiny boy hugged his
precious bundle tighter,
A glimmer of hope mirrored in
his eyes.
And thus he made his way,
The crunching again heard
beneath his feet,
Leaving behind the newly
cleansed earth
To bury past remains.

Jacqueline Diane Eramo
GRAMPA
My grampa
died
when I was
four
and I don't remember
very much of him.
It never really
mattered though
till just a year ago.
Then I met a
young man
One I think
grampa
would have liked.
Gramma likes him
if that's any indication.
But still,
it didn't matter
very much
that grampa died.
I hadn't rally
known him,
I was only
four.
My young man
always
spoke of his
grampa
and even went to
visit him.
When he came back
he always had
a joke
or loving wish
that his grampa
had sent to his
"little Italian girl".
But I didn't
get to meet him
for a long time
so it didn't
really matter
very much
that grampa died.
Then I finally met
my young mans
grampa
and things
began to change
I wondered
a little about
my grampa
and tried to
remember anything
I could
of him.
I remembered
little things
like being the
only one
who could sit
in grampa's chair—
and get away
with it.
Everyone else
got kicked out
'cause that was
grampa's chair.
But still it didn't
really matter
very much
that grampa died.
My young mans
grampa
was so much fun.
He told me
jokes and stories
and made me laugh.
He asked if
I was the girl
with the gold mine.
I replied,
"Of course—
but I only use it
to help pay for
my oil wells."
We laughed a lot
and he showed me
the family album.
I saw old family pictures
and who was who.
And now
it makes a difference
that my grampa
died.
I wish I'd known him,
But I was only
four.

Anne M. Walsh
UNTITLED
There are among us love-
avoided dark moments love-
bound, sauntering fires hoofed
of a winged creature striking
the night closer

until mastered from the
mounting brittle mid-nights
would split apart little knots
of burning sheathed, buried
caresses above the winds and
tips of tackled pyramids,
burning beyond the spent fuel
of fabled presences: sceptered
demeanors that do not survive
the cracking of their shells
late ring inexorable with age
reflect unspoiled in the
charged-particled, aurora-like
immortal cores of self-made
decalogues. And within gem-
bearing
furnaces: coruscating eidolons
that shine to none but white
flights of the Pegasus strapped
in gold bridles of hearsay.

Carolyn Gregory
CHRISTMAS IS A HEADACHE
Christmas is a headache, a
headache, a headache,
It leaves you with a terrible
backache.
Carrying packages from store to
store,
As you walk from floor to floor.
Waiting in line until your turn,
You begin to feel your face will
burn.
There's so many gifts I need
to buy,
If I don't go home, I feel I
will die.
In the middle of the Christmas
rush,
I am fixin' to cause a fuss.
Inflation, inflation, there is no
end,
Christmas is ruined with the
bills they send.
My answer to Christmas is Bah!
Humbug!
I wish Christmas could be swept
under the rug.
This is not the end, there's more
you see,
The gifts must be wrapped and
put under the tree.
Into the attic I must go,
To get the decorations, so we
can put on a show.
The tree must go up first, I am
told,
The lights won't burn that we
were sold.
Everyone wants to do their part,
To see how many disturbances
they can start.
The house is all lit for others
to see,
We're finally ready for
Christmas to be.
I am so tired, I feel I could lie
Down on the couch and let
Christmas pass by.
I finally pause and I begin to
hear,
Bells and carols and Holiday
Cheer.
There's more to Christmas than
bills and spills,
God sent His Son, His love He
instills.
The Wisemen came seeking a
star,
Maybe we have let Christmas go
too far.
What gift do I give to Him
this day?
To thank Him for showing me
the way.
Christ's birthday we come to
celebrate,
The real meaning of Christmas,
I cannot hate.
Christmas is a headache, it
really can be,
But the real meaning of
Christmas, Lord, we thank
Thee.

Doy M. Neumann
YOU AND I WILL NEVER FLY
I think different thoughts
than you
I hear music
you've never heard
I see image's

Of faces so clear
Aura's of colors
Kaleidoscope plays
Making me think
Of yesterdays
You and I are different
You are the day light
Bright and clear
I am the misty
Dark deep night
Full of the knowledge
that mixes into life,
Eagles, are soaring
Far in the sky
They are a part
of the coming year
We are different
We cannot blend
We only touch
corners passing by
Forming a triangle
In the sky
You and I
Will never fly
I roam alone
While you stay at home
My thoughts are unknown
They'll never meet yours
We'll pass each other
and shed no tears.

Madge Hall

UP IN THE AIR

I go up in the air,
I know not where.
If my saviour I have taken with me
No harm can befall me.

Ora M. Richards

ENCHANTRESS

With provocative lips she allures you—
How she beckons with gem-bedecked hand!
—Then while smiling benignly assures you
That her bounties are not contraband.
In delight she bedazzles, enchants you
By her garments that gleam like pure gold
And while feigning reluctance she grants you
A glance at her treasures untold.
Then with eyes full of guile she invites you
To partake of her glittering stones;
Her persuadable, sweet voice delights you
With its rich, pulsing, resonant tones.
She's Iniquity! She would immure you
In her palace that demons defend
And, like Circe of Old, would allure you
To destruction and death in the end!

Brenda Elaine Hitchcock

MY THOUGHTS

Why do you hide?
Open your eyes!
Let me see inside.
Are you afraid?
You want to be free.
Do you know what freedom is?
Do you care about me?
You seem to be running.
You don't know where nor why.
Someday you'll find it,
But for now you just want to get by.
Now I'm not sure,
Not any more than you,
But I'll say this one thing,
I think I love you.

Robyn A. Price

MEMORIES IN MY MIND

Memories in my mind,
the thoughts that come to me.
Changing times, the way things are, the way things have to be.
Being used to something,
then having to set it free.

Brett Axel

FIGURES OF NIGHT

Again appears figures of light,
The interlude of every night,
Spawn of gold and shaped as steeds,
Bringing illusions of my needs.
These, the figures who rule my sleep,
Invade my solitude,
Never here, yet never gone,
Disappearing at the dawn.
They fill my satin window panes,
Become insipid as they fade.
At times they gather in corners of gloom,
And other times they fill my room.
They leave and with them they remove.
Impassioned feelings of lament.
They challenge my very mind,
And deside my future life.
And soon they leave, but never go,
And who they are, I'll never know,
But when I wake, they creep away,
Waiting for another day.

Wayne Walter Johnson

WESTMINSTER THRICE REMOVED

The sun was hot that July day
When we drove to Westminster,
Where great-dad had fought the men in gray.
An iron marker claims the place
And I can recall grand-dad's face,
As he told the familiar tale.
"Twas June in eighteen and sixty-three.
Pennsylvania had been invaded by Lee.
Stuart was ridin' 'round the army again
And times looked bad for union men.
Many a body would soon strew the ground,
Fighting over a Pennsylvania market town.
Just two days before that crucial battle,
Stuart came to Westminster, needin' corn and cattle.
Instead he found in formation here,
Companies C and D, First Delaware Volunteers.
One hundred fifty horsemen,
Unsung in verse or song,
Charged Jeb Stuart's cavalry,
Some six thousand strong.
Fighting with great courage,
Still they lost the day,
Yet delaying Stuart's arrival
At Gettysbury, some thirty miles away.
They changed the course of history here,
Your great-grand-dad and the Delaware Volunteers."
My boy's mind wandered
In the glistening July sun,
Back a hundred years or more,
To trumpet's sound, battle flags, and guns.
A reckless red-haired youth,
Defending, country, liberty, and truth;
Risking all for a noble cause.
Grand-dad was decorated in World War One,
Dad in World War Two.
Perhaps the day would also come
When I could show what I could do.
I'd stand firm,
Like the rest of my manly kin;
A reckless red-haired youth,
Defending country, liberty, and truth;
Risking all for a noble cause.
The sun was hot that July day.
As we pushed across the Delta,
Chasing pajama clad men through elephant grass sway.
Scattered, muddy camps marked the dividion's place,
As the colonel wiped his sweaty face,
Complaining about our progress.
"Just last week we put a man on the moon.
Yet we've spent half of July and all of June
Chasin' "Charlie" through this filth and crud,
Our sophisticated weaponry bogged down in the mud.
Casualty rates keep going up,
Fighting over some lousy peasant; huts.
We burn their hootches, carts, and rice,
Seldom fighting more than leaches and lice.
Never do they stand and fight,
Hit and run, ambushes in the night.
Something is terribly, terribly wrong
When a handful can tie up six thousand strong.
We spring a trap,
They fight and lose;
Then sneak away.
In their canvas shoes.
What will history say?
Them tying us up day after day."
My mind wandered
In the glistening July sun,
Back several months or more,
To dying men, flashing mortars, and guns.
A reckless red-haired youth,
Defending. . .?
Risking all for. . .?
He stepped from amid elephant grass sway,
Just one hundred feet away.
No trumpet's sound or flags of battle,
Only the sound of his weapon's rattle.
I lie bloodied,
Seeing through the eve of eternal darkness,
A reckless black-haired youth,
Defending country, liberty, and truth;
Risking all for a noble cause.

Helen VenDeVille

SEED OF STAR

One day, i cut
An Apple, 'round.
To my surprise!
And felt so wise--
A "Star" in it
I found.
I made a hole
Towards the top
To hang upon
My Tree
I let it dry
For all to see;
A "Star" of Love
Upon the branch
A gift, from God
Alone, who knows
How many Apples
From One Seed,-Grows?
He put The Star
Inside, a guide, to find,
For you and me,-
If we but Search;--
For there are
Beautiful Things
In the Wonder Of
"Simplicity."

Lila Hurtado

BUTTERFLY MAN

There's a butterfly—just what do you see?
Some of yesterday's musty memories
Or today's never ending mysteries?
Memories or mysteries—which do you see?
As a child—young, innocent, and carefree
Playing on days calm, glorious and sunny
Butterflies would pay hide-n' seek with me
They'd allow me to stalk them cautiously
Permit me to find them judiciously
Then gleefully fly away teasingly
Saying, "I just dare you to catch me, Wheeee. . .
I'm a butterfly on wing—look at me. . .
Wouldn't you like to fly free just like me?"
There's a butterfly—just what do you see?
Some of yesterday's musty memories
Or today's never ending

mysteries?
Memories or mysteries—
which do you see?
Today butterflies represent Man
to me
Wings maneuvered through
morbid reality
By rigid puppet strings—
mechanically
Their life can be so lonely,
just flying free
Without love, wandering
helplessly
What's life if man isn't
battered brutally
Back and forth in life
perpetually
Not sitting long enough to
solve mysteries
Such as Woman—full of great
complexity
Man must feel life's depths
periodically
Rise to great heights to achieve
serenity. . .
There's a butterfly—just what
do you see?
Some of yesterday's musty
memories
Or today's never ending
mysteries?
Memories or mysteries—
which do you see?
An enigma, born to earth, flies
the sky
Have you ever stopped and
wondered why?
First he's a creeping caterpillar
Crawling on a damp and
mossy pillar
But when he sheds his cocoon
He becomes a beautiful
butterfly
With the heavens for his living
room
He flies hgh without even
saying "Goodbye"

Alfred Leon Wallace

HAVE YOU EVER BEEN THANKFUL?

Have you ever been thankful
for being a human
Instead of an elephant caged in
a zoo?
For instead of a breakfast of
doughnuts and coffee,
You would gaze all the day on
the hay you would chew.
Your life would be longer than
that of a man,

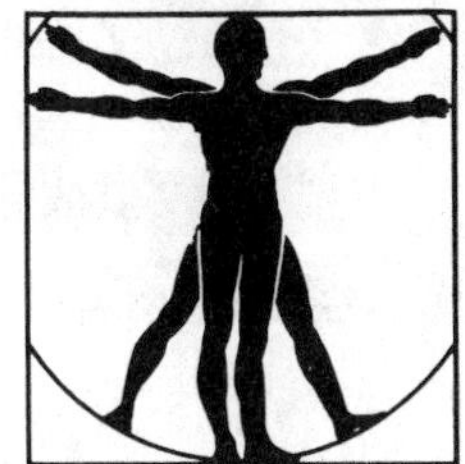

And your nose would be longer
to drink from the pool,
But life would be prison inside
of a zoo,
With nothing to do but to chew
like a fool.
Have you ever been thankful for
being a human
Instead of a Doberman pinscher
or hound?
For instead of the warmth of a
cozy, soft bed,
You would sleep in a box or on
ice-covered ground.
Instead of a strawberry punch
and a steak,
Your master would feed you
with dog food and scraps.
Your pail would be filthy with
water and dirt,
And life would be mangy with
boredom and naps.
Have you ever been thankful for
being a human
Instead of a pig or voracious old
hog?
For instead of a plate of
delicious spaghetti,
Your trough would be filthy and
worse than a bog.
On a miserable morning your
master would kill you,
And scald and dehair you for
succulent meat.
Your master would bleed you by
slashing your throat,
And your flesh would be
butchered for humans to eat.
Have you ever been thankful for
being a human,
For being exactly the soul that
you are,
For having a houseful of
treasure and things
Such as heaters and freezers
and beautiful car?
You may think you are deep in
the poverty list.
But yet you are richer than any
young cat
With your brain-bulging head
that has seldom been used
Except for routines or to dress
with a hat.
Have you ever been thankful for
being a human,
For having a life-span of eighty
or more?
And with knowledge of science
and change of your habits,
Your life can be longer than
ever before.
If the doctrine of reincarnation
is true,
Let us pray that your soul will
be human forever
For it's sad to be anything other
than man,
To be mastered by humans so
cruel and clever.

Betty R. Paton

FRIENDS

Not long—we've been friends
together
But too many battles we've
fought
The struggles we've had, when
fierce winds have blown
Have made ties, which are
strongly wrought,
That now, it appears to be
foolish
To let hurt feelings come in
And destroy in one
hasty moment the many days
growth of a friend.
How many hurts does it take,
my friend
To realize the sadness you've
brought.
Constant turmoil, the highs and
lows
Into this life much havoc has
wrought;
But friends keep on loving and
giving
Not to self to give much
thought,
Only the joy and happiness to
give
It's what love is all about.
How long will one friend keep
giving
When the other gives naught in
return
Tis a question that surely deep
In your heart must burn.
How can a friend take
something
So tender, beautiful— and yes,
very rare
And try to degrade it, refuse it
and even try to ignore it's there.
That's not my friend.
If only each one saw the other
one's heart-thoughts, and could
but know
Their feelings; their motives
for action
Then surely, it would bring us
low;
That we'd gladly ask for
forgiveness
of one whom we've learned to
love;
For all hurt and
misunderstanding
Can't destroy that which comes
from above.
After all, it's God in His grace
and glory
From whence all blessings
descend
Who sheds His love in the
hearts of His children
and gives us the love—of a
friend.
So pride, with its hurts and
failures
Should have no room in the
heart
But in its place, may
understanding
Come to dwell—that friends
do not part. . . .

Paul H. Douglas

THE ADVANTAGES OF NUCLEAR WAR

Have you ever seen an apple
That is eaten to the core
That's what earth will look like
After a nuclear war
We wouldn't have to worry
about
Population that's hard to bear
For every place we look
We'd hardly find a person there
We would not have to worry
Whether food is pork or veal
Because there wouldn't be
enough around
To consider it a meal
We would not have to worry
About the spread of crime
Because the richest man in the
world
Won't even have a dime
No jealousness of who has more
For all of us would be equally
No watering yards or mowing
lawns
For all of nature would be gone
And those that treasure material
things
Would be most badly hurt
To think that all their worldly
goods
Have now all turned to dirt
I haven't yet named advantages
For it seems more and more
The only advantage we would
have
Is to not have a nuclear war

Gloria Bostwick Fitts

JUST LOOK TO JESUS

When life's trials get hard to
bear,
And you need a friend to care,
Just look to Jesus, He'll carry
you through.
When you're feeling mighty low,
And you don't know where to
go,
Just look to Jesus, He'll carry
you through.
I was lost in sin and woe,
My life was meaningless, I
know,
Til Jesus changed me, and took
me as His own.
He cleansed my life where sin
was sown,
He gave me peace and joy
unknown,
Oh, what a Savior, what a
Friend,
Thank God, He's mine!
Just look to Jesus, He'll carry
you through.
He won't forsake you, whatever
you do,
He'll be your friend.
Jesus knows your every need;
He's always there to hear your
pleas.
Oh, what a Savior, what a
Friend,
Thank God, He's mine!

Sylvia A. Collins

VOYAGER I

Oh, Robot, probing yonder
ringed ball
With your turning, tractable
eye,
As you bobble bouyantly
through the sky
So record pictorial image to
recall
For our dark star to scan
to the enlightenment of
(puny) man.
As you tilt with curved arms
Of our Milky Way
And brave Saturn's braided rings;
Scrutinize Jupiter, super-novas,
a trillion things—
Clicking off count of moonlets
With your calculated
computer mind
Signaling whatever else you
find.
And push relentlessly through
resisting space
Perchance, you may gain
advantage
To photograph God's Face
And reveal where the bright
Angel sings.

Leslie Estes

BUTTERFLIES

Those naughty little creatures,
They never can be still.
Happily they flutter all about
you as they will.
They're always doing funny flips
and floating all about,

yes those anxious little
butterflies inside you.
THEY WANT OUT!

Lee Houston

SCOTTY AND ME

Of all the cats
that hang out on sixth avenue
watching the broads and
drinking brew
The two hippest dudes who
understand
the essence of looking at a
woman and
coping with sexuality
is
over eighty Scotty
and
under forty me

Angela R. Stillwell

RECIPE (HOW TO MAKE A BLACK)

Add a touch of ancestral hate
for the caucasion race
Carefully mix in a whole lot
of pride
then stir
When batter is stiff, beat in
education
about 20 minutes
Don't forget brown food coloring
essential part of recipe
Stick in freezer
Must let batter experience hard
cold life
Leave in freezer for 1 hour
now add
1 dash discrimination
1 pinch humility
2 tbls. hope & faith
1 cup understanding
½ cup pity
1 gallon determination
mix
Bake in oven for 9 hours
Remove from oven
Let cool
Let get r-e-a-l c-o-o-l
If baked correctly he'll be a bit
hip too
now
to serve
Open door
(make sure it's the front door)
And tell him he's free
Note: Completion of this recipe can be emotionally hazardous to one's health

June Elaine Lacy

DREAMER

"If You love something. . .,
Set it Free.
If it comes back,
It's yours.
If not. . .
It never was?
The obituary's been read,
Respects been paid for the dead.
The coffins being lowered to the
ground,
Mourners have all got up and
turned around,
Leaving with fears and grief,
Never escaping a reality so brief.
Shoveled dirt falls upon locked
walls,
No escape from this cave, all-
time perfect covered grave.
Entering. . .Transformation
Entering. . .Perpetuation
"Why did they all have to leave?
Why did they feel sadness and
grieve?
Hey! You out there. . .I'm alright,
Am I speaking loud enough? Can
you hear me?
Please don't go, I'm confused and
all alone. . .
What's the use. . .they can't hear
me. . .they're all gone."
Dimensional change, all-time
bursting into red,
Strange? The colour of life
should be exposed to the dead,
Don't fall alseep!!!Stay awake for
the subjective trance,
The Unknown unveiled with
One Cosmic Dance.
A designed phase, with only one
chance,
The envisioned experience, with
One Cosmic Glance.
"Why did they have to put me
away?
I hope to tell them; I thought
they were my friends one day.
But what if they've forgotten
me? What if they don't know
me anymore?
What if I can't pass through the
earthly door?
I'm feeling all alone now,
I want to cry now. . .
With no one to hear my tears,
no one to listen to my tears,
No one in the World to see me
withered and sere."
All Your dreams should be kept
untold,
Whether they be new or old;
If You want them to come true,
Silence! The one cheated would
only be you.
"I'm tired of crying, I have no
where to turn,
Why couldn't they save me this
agony and let me burn?"
Even in the quietest moments. .
Whistling winds blow, and
splashing tides flow,
Upon the existing radiance of
energy.
Even in the darkest moments. . .
Lightening struck the earth,
rumbling thunder was felt
throughout the universe,
And the euphonious voice
called. . .
"My name. . .I know I heard
my name?"
Leaving. . .Transformation
Leaving. . .Perpetuation
". . .And I was enveloped into
marriage,
Marriage to the Lamb,
Acceptance of the ride in this
guarded carriage,
Towards the deity of I Am.
An experience so beautiful, so
supreme!!!!!
Reality focused upon the
answering of my dream.
I don't even care to know why,
Maybe I just had to live in order
to die?"

George Randall Duensing

CHURCH, ON AN UNUSED NIGHT

Emptiness—The Hollowness
echoes through the pews.
The darkest shadows slowly
slither
Toward your mind and through
your soul.
No feel of God, must quiet fear
The growing rows have
swallowed up the life,
Left Stillness, Darkness lurking
here.
It seems a shadow perched
above.
From empty altars Blackness
springs.
To scream and scream and run
and fall
To find no comfort in lonely
fear
The Pall descends, surrounds,
engulfs.
It eats the mind, corrupts the
soul.
Why is this hallowed place so
hollow,
So fearfully frightful on an
unused night?

Joel Kent Dewees

SETTING SAIL

Winds of great sorrow
Cause waves in an ocean of
distress,
But the faithful sailor plots his
course
And with a great and mighty
effort
He gives his all and does his
best.

Deep in his heart he holds
The vibrant strengthening force
Which reveals a secret;
Not of life, but living:
That setting sail
And believing in his tiny ship
of faith,
The mighty Voice that created
all
Shall surely do the rest.
Peace be still. . . . .

Mattie Arkwright

DEATH HAS TAKEN

Love was so beautiful
Love was so real
Until the dark hand of death
From me you did steal
We were so happy
As we walked through life hand
in hand
So loving and so faithful
and each other we did so
understand
But now it's all over
and I'm left here all alone
To face life by myself
Now that you're gone
The days are not so bright
My happiness has faded away
It's so hard to make life worth
living
as I travel through each day
But there's one thing I look
forward to
To one hope I can cling
I'll see you again someday
When we come face to face with
our King

Mable Isley Catron

THE CHOICE

Disciples of Jehovah; there are
so few
who seek and find God's
simple truths,
Then knowing, take up their
cross and do.
Challengers of truth, his
Missionary's
Wander throughout the earth as
his Prophets did so long ago;
They seek God's will and teach
his word,
his righteous truths they sow.
Throughout the world theres
many souls
that do not know they stray,
For they've been taught from
infancy a
wrong and pagan way!
God's word is clearly written,
yet there are those who fail to
grasp
True meaning of the parables
they read.
The book they clasp
States plainly in Esaias'
prophecy. . .
'though hearing, they will
not know,
And seeing, never see!
Some hear God's word and for a
moment
treasure its truths,
Its right, its joy, its peace,
the sweet
surrender. . .
Then, Satan, hastening there,
steps in to
prod their minds,
Heartsick, they must
remember. . .
earthly goods they now
possess,
The life they lead of luxury
and ease.
How can they sacrifice all
these things
Emotions to appease?
Most souls hesitate, then
slowly turn away,
Vowing they'll repent another
time. . .
some other day.
Never knowing or seeing the
awful cost,
if that souls to darkness lost.
For hardened hearts, in time, can
become
their keepers cage.
Men do not realize in the end,
sin too,
demands its wage!
Some are rebels of truth, they
simply ignore
Christ's humble plea;
Dis-believing that our ransom
by his blood
was bought, his mission here,
his agony.
Lovingly, payment for man's sin
was given;
death was the bargaineer, its
true. . .
In triumph Jesus arose from the
grave, accending
into Heaven.
There are many still, like the
Pharisee's,
who would deny the miracles
of Jesus. . .

All the way from his birth at Bethlehem
throughout the agony of Gethsemane.
They simply argue that it can not be.
Ignoring the Bible, God's written word,
They prefer to take, the thesis on evolution,
declaring man decended from ape!
"Jesus is but a myth, a fable, fashioned in
some long gone yesterday" they say,
"Life is to short to waste on madness"
they turn and walk away.
The years ahead look lovely and fullfilled,
to them, life seems complete.
They do not ponder on the prophecys of old
or accept Satan's defeat.
Hugging earths pleasures close, they are content,
un-seeing, un-knowing,
Life is swiftly rushing by and time is going.
Soon it will all be gone. . .
Wasted, each chance to change they've had.
To late, they'll see God's simple truths,
And this, I know, must make our Saviour sad.
Yes, Jesus must still grieve at man's downfall;
He, who so willingly sacrificed his everything,
gave his very all.
Yet his sheep seem so confused, scattered, few,
hardened hearts seek Satan's rule!
His only comfort must be in the absolute knowing
sin and Satan will, one day, be going. . .
With only a word, or a touch of the Master's hand,
eternity will cleanse each sin-stained land.

Gina Brigida

UNTITLED

Since the time to depart is here, Let me
study your face
Although we been together so long, I never
really saw you
I just loved you
Let me touch you, before I leave, for I'll
never see you again
I'll only love you
Let me picture you, in my mind, so all my
dreams will seem real
Let it seem as though I can reach out
and touch you
Even though I can't,
I still hold you near
Let me hear your voice, because I'll
never hear it again and it will remind
me of all the times you said,
"I love you"
Let me see your smile just one more
time, so I can remember all the fun times
we had together
And when I think of you,
I'll cry, because. . . .
I Love You.

Debi Koehler

T.H.

You entered my life, and touched my heart;
And now my love it's time to part.
We shared the good times, even bad;
What once was happy now is sad.
But as good friends we will remain;
Although things can't be quite the same.
So goodbye love, and hello friend;
It's always good to talk again.
But beware my friend as you will see;
She'll hurt you bad as you did me.
It's happened once or even twice;
For on one's love there is no price.
So when your heart is broken in two;
Remember always my love was true.
And the I'll say goodbye my friend;
Like all good things we too must end.

Shirley Babineau

LOVE EXPIRED

A Bridge to cross
A Pain to bear
An Ocean to escape from
Life alone
No one to care
Lonely nights still to come
A cold Winter
A colder Summer
Another year to fade away
No inbetween Seasons
No pretty flowers and Summer Day's
No path to Life
No road to Walk
No sand to fill the Beach
A tear to Cry
A Voice to Talk
Two arms that cannot Reach
A soul is Lost
A heart is Broke
No cure to heal the Pain
A shallow Grave
A lonely Stone
A shadow weeping in the Rain!

Kim Cornell

A FOREVER FRIEND

I just don't know where to begin
to tell you how I feel about you.
You're someone that I can trust
and tell my problems to.
You're someone very special
much more than just a friend,
whenever I needed someone,
on you I could depend.
I just wish I could tell you
how much your friendship means to me.
The times that we spend together
are the best that times could be.
People like you
are so hard to find.
You go out of your way for everyone,
and never seem to mind.
Thank you my friend,
for making me smile,
and letting me forget my problems—
even it it's only for a while.
We never seem to argue,
there's nothing about you I detest.
I'm so glad that I've found you
because, my friend, you're the best!
There's times I want to hold you
and make you want me too,
But I feel it would ruin our friendship
and that's something I don't want to do.
The feelings that I feel for you
hold a special place in my heart;
Just between you and me,
I hope we'll never part.

Helen Weaver Ditty

WONDERING 1936-1981

I've often wondered how I'll feel
When I am older grown
And age has given me sorrows
And the years have by me flown;
For folks have often told me
That later I will learn
That life is not all roses
But is cold and rough and stern.
They say I won't be glad then
And happy as I am now
But that burdens will bend my back
And wrinkles will line my brow.
They hint that when I'm old
I'll forget the God of my youth
When freedom's song sprang glad from my heart
And my soul sought deep for truth.
But will the hills grow dim then
In the beauty I see there now?
Will the pine lift less gladly
Its high upreaching bough?
Will the sunset be masked in dullness
And will the clear cut silouette
Of the church spire in the distance
Its challenge for good forget?
Yes, God, I've often wondered
How I'll feel when I am grown,
But I am sure now God
That if I can go out alone
With You and a beautiful sunset
I will be as sure then as now,
That you are the God of all people
Whether old or young or how.
Since the young girl wrote her poem
Forty years and more have passed.
And now I know the answers
To the questions that she asked.
So many things have happened
In the times I've lived and seen
I'll tell about things that happened
In the years stretched in between.
I have traveled far
And visited many strange places.
I have dreamed many dreams
And met a lot of new faces.
Many small hands have been tucked into mine
As I became teacher, mother, grandmother.
I wanted to ease all the pain in the world
But I often had to accept help from another.
I've sung many songs of joy
For beauty below and above,
Exulting in good friends and family
And God's ever present love.
I've woven many threads
In my tapestry of life
Golden threads of love and laughter
Somber threads of pain and strife.
Then my prayer was for wisdom
To make decisions in the strong years.
Now my prayer is for patience and understanding
As life's waning day appears.
As old age lures me on
I'll write the last lines of my poem,
And trust my Heavenly Father
To some day "Lead Me Gently Home".

Howard Chester

A CHICKEN—A GUN—AND A BOY

"Dear GOD; I KNOW that it ain't right
To—'Wake You Up'—this time of night;
To listen to a—'Tale of Woes'—
Of a—'Teen-age Kid'—with a snotty nose.
But, after all, WE have been told
That whether it is—'Hot or Cold',
We are to 'Talk to *YOU* at night;
Right after we—'Turn Out the light.'
"Now what I done is pretty bad—
And made my-–'Old Man'—awful mad;
But I just *looked* down that — 'GUN' once,
And how come I was, such a 'Dunce'
As not to—*KNOW* (That Little Thing). . .
Was hooked up TO a great big 'Spring'
That made it—'BOOM!! and *SMOKE!!* and *SMELL!!*
And 'Blow That Chicken. . . *ALL TO HELL!"*
"Does THAT thing give my

'Pop' the right—
To—*'Swing A Whip'* —with all his might
To—*"Tan My Ass?"*— (that's what HE said).
And then send me. . ."Up Here To Bed—
Without a—'Single Thing' to eat. . .
And—*'Sore As Hell'*—from head to feet?"
"*SURE,* what I did—was a 'Dirty Deed'—
And I agree, there was — *'NO NEED—*
To make my *'Pop* so mad; but then
It's a—*(Dam Sight Worse)* for that—'Black *HEN!*
But *'GOD'*—I need to tell *YOU —'WHY,*
I send this—'Message'—to the sky.
I— *'KNOW'* that I can—
(Count On YOU!!—
For something that. . .
'I *CAN NOT* DO!!"
"When MY—*'Old Man'*—comes up the Stairs—
To YOUR 'Big Throne' (to say *HIS* Prayers). . .
Please *SHOW HIM* what's in that —'BIG BOOK'—
And make *HIM* take a. . .
'Good *LONG LOOK'.*
I hope— *'YOU* got it (Blow by Blow. . .
Of what I've took (DOWN HERE BELOW)!!
And listen to. . . *"HIS PRAYERS"* . . .and then
Just *WAIT,* to *HEAR* that loud— *'AAAaaaMEN'!!*
Then—*'TELL HIM'—(HE HAS TO GO. . .*
On a—*'Fast Journey, Down Below'!!*
So *PLEASE,—'Dear GOD'—* just. . . *'TELL HIM WELL'*
What I don't— 'DARE':—"TO *GO TO—HELL!!"*

Virginia Iza Taylor
GOD THE ARTIST
To the beautiful Kiamichi Mountains where the eagle dares,
where God has hung a painting to show how much he cares.
The azue fog lifts up its arms to kiss the mountain peaks,
the crystal waters ripple past to cool the winding creeks.
The fern clings to its mossy bed, flirting with each breeze that
caresses the tallest mountain top, to the moss beneath the trees.
And when it rains, the sun comes out to dry away the tears.
Then mountain streams lift up their towels to dry the mountain trails,
where thirsty dogwood and mountain laurel have filled their little pails.
So streams and mountains can drink again throughout the hills and vales.
Now man slips in and out again to view this wondrous sight,
and tries to add a little more to make this scene just right.
But God has not forgotten not one minute detail,
for when He plants a garden, He surely never fails.
The mountain laurel frames it all to show this beauty rare,
so we can easily look and see that God is truly there.

Suzie Buckner
AMID BLINDING CHAOS
Amid Blinding Chaos
Death Evades Friends: Great
Hate Invents Just
Killing, Leaving Men No
Ordinary
Peace.—Quivering,
Running;
So Troubled Under
Very
Wasted Xistence
Yearning
Zion.
Yesterday's
Xamples Wanted
Vernal Understanding.
Today's Society Raises
Questions, Pertinent Only
Not
Momentarily: Laquered
Kindling, —Juries
Infinite. Has God Found Eternal
Dynasties?
Crowds Besiege
Armagadon.

Madge Langley
DREAMS
Why no flowers at this funeral?
Why no tears at this wake?
No mourners wailing at the service
only mockers with empty laughs.
There'll be no neat square grave
Only a jagged hole
Dug by pain and misery
For, you see, my body has not died.
Only my dreams.

Elaine Brown
A BOOKS LAMENT
When I am gone and passed away,
I hope to all my friends (I'll say)
I worked at the Highrise Ca Fe.
Sometimes we worked.
Sometimes we played.
But at our jobs we always stayed,
And then I'll smile and float away,
On that pink cloud I earned someday.

David Hernandez
FAUSTIAN FLIRTATIONS
O lovely lady, how I do love you and would give
A kingdom gladly for your coolest kiss.
How you have ignited the fires of night
With those eyes that sparkle like fatal stars.
My days are consumed by the thought of your embrace,
The smile of those mischievous breasts in my hand.
Who would not forsake God and Country
To have your sweet thighs brush against his lips?
Yet the cloud behind my ingenuous ear asks
If this heaven has bought eternity for my soul
Or merely stuffed my licentious prayers
With youthful sweets that will wilt with the rose.
O dear lady, no not be offended if I forsake thee
For the Spring Sonata by the pied piper of Bonn,
Or the Jupiter of the crowned king of progidies
Or the symphony that makes us the final one;
For I dread no end as much as I do love you.

Lilian L. Ayres
THE ROAD HOME
Long and thin, a knife descending,
Wind of winter's ruling day,
Howling down a snow dune, calling,
Seeking, searching in the fray.
Like a lost soul lashed with nine-tails,
Shrieking, seeking, running scared,
Blizzard force finds lonely objects. . .
Hate and fury, nothing spared.
Cold and frozen as the northland,
Blind and futile, running wild,
Screaming at one walking boldly
Steadfastly, though honed and filed.
Out of night to home fire's light, he
Comes, has reached the goal he sought.
Howls crescendo blast no longer,
Walls hold back the storm he fought.
Builds the wind, and on it hurtles;
Wake the dead with solid sound,
But for him the storm is ended;
Won the fight, in rest abound.

David Kurt Carpenter
GOD KNOWS IT'S COLD
I wandered quietly through cold black streets;
The rain poured down for long gray hours alone.
I stumbled in with wet mud-covered feet
Wondering why I was so far from home.
An easy voice did softly speak to me.
I reached for her and smiled through fresh moist air.
We talked about our love we lost-happy;
Good times are gone—I wish I could be there.
But now we go—we loved us for a while.
My love goodbye, but why? God knows we tried.
She gave a hug—old love—she flashed her smile;
I felt that old familiar pain. . . we cried.
Our dreams were shed with every tear of old;
Without her here—alone—God know it's cold.

Yohauen Austerlitz
THE SPLENDID FOOLS POETIC DREAM
Would but that it was or could become to be. . .oftimes as real. . .that which one would but feign make it so to seem
And Time upon its Wingless Flight for a time and a while stood still and waystayed the swiftly fleeting years
Realities would become to be and be of they upon whom they may depend
As man learned to respect and regard wisdom pride dignity and authority. . .
And all that realized and acknowledged of and by each... of even...pride's own vanity then treasons delusions and deceits would no more be. . .
And one's soul need not withhold nor keep. . .the shed and unshed tears man then from life duty responsibility would no more seek respite nor retreat
As man yet seeks but one and another to wound destroy and offend
Steadily The Rivers of Life unto The Great Sea of Life. . .
On its destined course. . .its way does slowly surely wend
Man but feigns not to know wisdom dignity valour nor that to regard nor esteem
Of but pretense feigns to know of Eternity and or Destiny
As by the hours days and years plots and plans evily. . .in dens of iniquity and remains life and love unfulfilled and betimes incomplete
And so remains to be and be. . . till man learns and does realize and respect justice and authority. . .teachers. . . mentors. . .prelates and peers
With all man's wisdom dignity and pride. . .as even yet this day. . .a lovely thought or a little poem does requite the waning faith and esteem
Even so oft in askance and despairs becomes to be. . .life of pretense and mockery as of pretense tis so. . .as one would but feign make it so to seem
As what knows man. . .the dudes and the fun loving sinners of Life and the Real
Or seemingly care as to that composed in classic poetries. .
Or that contained in this balladian poem. . .A Splendid Fools Noble Dream the

Sentiments of a Splendid Fools
Poetic. . .Utopian Noble
Dream
As oft tis exactly as but
that. . .which it may so but
merely seem the Sequence of
events become to be. . .and
be. . .the sequels unto realities
Yet. . .what be the soul of man
that contains not nor holds
even the shades of. . .
A Poetic Fools. . .Splendid
Utopian Noble Dream
Perhaps one may have heard or
in poetic pages afore
sometime read. . .that. . .
The darkness of the darkest
night from aught but just one
lone little candlelight
Somewhere back into the night
had fled. . .
And yet sheds it softest
golden gleam
And what fool is he. . .that
harbours not in the shadows
of his soul. . .
Even the shades of. . .A
Splendid Poetic Utopian
Noble Dream
As Life and Death. . .My Friend
are Real and of realities and not
as oft. . . one or another would
but feign so to make it seem
As but a proven fool's
philosophy or an imagined
fantasy and as but. . . a fading
jaded dream. . .as but. . .a
fading jaded dream
As fades of but time alone of
tin. . .its temporal burnished
sheon fades and vanishes of
but the wanton abandoning
and the forsaking. . .
Life and. . .The Splendid Fools
Poetic. . .Utopian Noble
Dream. . .fades as. . .A
Splendid Fools Poetic. . .
Utopian Noble Dream
*(Whom or what is He. . .that
denies even the mere existence
of a wisdom-pride-dignity
greater than his own)*

Robert J. Lau
HANDSOME BUM
A Sad-Eyed Maiden Shed a Tear-
At Her Feet Lay a Crushed
Chrysanthemum—
The Ragged Urchin Drop't His
Lear-
His Shrill Voice Seemed 'Most
Handsome
'Mum—
Sad Was He That He'd Been So
Bad-
But, For His Sadness, He Felt
Right
Glad.

Walker Stevens
LOOK AROUND! LOOK FAST!
It's Mother Nature's time right
now
To give each one a thrill
By putting on her Indian
Summer show.
Ere winter brings its chill.
From the great red—gold maple
That towers o'er the Courthouse
Square
And charms all the people who
Run their errands there
To the corner of Main and Oak
Where the Sun came to the
ground
As the gingko tree to spread
its glow
To all things all around.
Surrounded by the dogwood
trees
It is a sight that everyone sees!
And don't forget the popcorn
trees
On the corner of Main and
Carroll
Where their maroon and white
attire
Is splendid apparel.
All over town where'er you look
Up and down on every street
You'll find a sight in every nook
To remember when there's sleet.
The oak, elm, and sweetgum are
scattered everywhere
To add their color for all to see
As we travel here and there.
Look around! Look fast!
Ere Winter brings its blast!

Bruce C. Gordon
PASSING
Walking down a mountain pass
around a bend
I came across you.
Moments spent in idle talk
about where we'd been
and where we'd go
left my mind and heart aglow,
with the music of your voice
and the radiance of your smile.
Parting,
my thoughts were with you
as you climbed the pass.
And I burned into my memory
the magic of those moments
in passing.

George L. Farmakis
LOS ANGELES 1984
The Olympics are coming!
World get ready!
Los Angeles is the place.
From 776 B.C. to 1984 A.D.,
From Olympia to Los Angeles,
Medals and shout of glory,
But just taking part—
That is the Main Story.
As the torch passes
from Greece to America,
Let us all remember once more
that here
We are all members of the
Human Race.
Los Angeles 1984
This is the time for the
Celebration of Humanity.

Charles David Boshinski
LIFE
Life is a beginning from an end.
It is something new from
something old.
When life ends it begins once
more.
Life includes death; but only
for a moment.
A moment to look back on life
and remember,
And a moment to look ahead
to a new life.
A life that gets better as the
one before ends,
And another begins.
Life is living and dying, and
doing it once again.

MaryLou Doubleday
LIFE AND TRUTH
My friend is dying.
What happens now?
Do I joke to try and mend the
many wounds:
—mental as well as physical?
I sit dazed, trying to
contemplate our tomorrows
but I can only think of our
many yesterdays.
I remember when:
—you and I were a twosome
—we cried because the boys
ignored us
—we laughed at our idiotic
behavior
What happens now, friend?
Do I reveal all my love and
tears, or conceal my emotions
from you and everyone?
I want to rush to your side
and drive the pain away
but no,
reality is here to stay;
we cannot run.
If by your dying I live,
and
if by my living you die,
then
why do we fight death
and rejoice at life?
I guess it's nature's way of
saying you are loved.
I love you, friend,
and always will.

June Lee Box
ONE DAY AT THE PLAZA
One day at the Plaza
San Diego's Plaza
filled with Spanish charm
Just half a city block
on lower Broadway
Outlined in hugh palm trees
guarding quartered lawns
Breeze-tossed central fountain
splashing pigeons clear
Easterners bench-sitting
cold bones in the sun
Transfer point for crosstown
streetcar passengers
Questioning the kiosk's
"Information Anderson"
Sudden shouts are heard
above the hustling roar
"Extra" "Extra" "Read All About
It"
"Lindberg's Landed Safe In
France"
"Spirit of St. Louis"
"From Our Own Airplane Plant!"

Keith Davis Jr.
PREPARED SOULS
Vanishing dreams of life
content,

A soul that's ready to go,
where its due to be sent.
Tell tale lines upon a face;
Uttered words of a devine grace.
A trembling voice that strains
to be heard;
Clinging fondly to every word.
A feeble body bearing signs of
wear;
Delicate gray strands highlite
the hair.
Wrinkled hands who's clasp is
weak;
Paving the way to the fellowship
that they seek.
Friendly warm eyes that drift
toward the sky;
Away from the earth knowing
that the end is nigh.

With a steadfast hope for a
better day;
Waiting to pay the price that
we all must pay.
If they've made preparation and
prepared themselves;
They have no fear in the valley
of death.

Robert L. Jackson
I DO, YOU KNOW
I do, you know, my darling
How often these words I say
Remember those precious
moments
Stolen in the day.
Think of how I love you
And never forget me dear
For I love you, with a love
Far more than just sincere.
I will love you always
Through the empty years
Until we're free to share this
love
For comfort, I'll have my
tears. . .
I do, you know,
Me

Scott Trimble
CHARLIE
A man, a tree,
Large, and dark; Impenetrable.
Works to live,
Wants to live,
Trains to live,
Lives for life,
Enjoys life.
Smelled death often,
But denied the aroma.
Almost immortal
Killed by an accident of an
uncaring child

Unbelievable;
An immortal superhuman,
modern god
Unnoticed in today's society,
His godliness emerging only at
night.

Many times lived,
When others would die,
Several times walked,
When others would fall, limp, or
crawl.

Impossible to kill, it seemed;
Until his body died mistakenly.
Killed only by innocence.
One of the few men who did
want to live,
Who wanted to live for the
enjoyment of life itself,
Removed from physical life far
before his time.
The beginning of his prime.

Denton Hyder

A CHRISTMAS PERIL

Tho my master is jobless
and our future looks dim,
tis nice to have holidays
to reminisce again.
The great day in November
when he worked at the bindery,
he cheerfully told his boss
to kiss his hind-ery.
A career in banking
he was destined to seek
which lasted one year,
six months and one week.
Aye, but he bounced back
in the month of April
to a term with cold
ass-phaltic people.
Twas again in November
when our hero, Bob Cratchett
was greeted by Ol' Scrooge
who gave him the hatchet.
Now, we spend more time
together
pacing the floor.
He hits me; I bite him.
Life's great when you're poor.
Alas, we are thankful
to still have our health. . .
along with my bruises,
his scratchmarks and welts.
So, be happy; be merry
this holiday season.
Count your blessings you're not
with us
for obvious reasons.
Like the story of Santa
who turned with a jerk. . .
I'm stuck with one
who can't find work!
Merry Christmas,
Tonto (the cat)

Phoebe Juanita Vaughn

I SPEAK TO YOU OF LOVE

I speak to you of love and
whisper softly what you
should hear.
I love you so much and to me
you are very dear.
All the mysteries and wonders
of the world cannot compare
to thee,
And what you possess, in no
other shall I see.
With your smile you awaken
my heart, as the sun awakens
the day.

When we are apart, no matter
how near or far, you seem so
far away.
When we are together laughing
and playing, it reminds me of
little birds all cuddled up in
their nest.
With your touch, you give me
comfort, as a mother gives her
child, when pressed against
her breast.
With your eyes you reveal so
much warmth and sincerity,
as only you can do.
With your voice, you serenade
me with melodious sounds, as
the Nightingales do.
So many things come to mind as
I think of you, but to express
what I feel, justice I could not
do.
If I could travel to the most
distant planet; swim to the
bottom of the sea; touch the
moon or draw stars down from
the sky.
If I could shower you with
priceless gems or serve you
food fit for a King or Queen.
If I could give you my heart on
a platter, I could not give you
more or receive greater than
the love I have or receive
from you.

Rhode

SOCIETY

an animal stands us on our
heels
Makes us act like trained seals
Fills our lives with wealth and
sin
This is the society everyone
lives in.
It's the same one that makes
environmental mess,
Forbids us to have anything less.
It makes the demanding
husbands, the irate wives
With their tales of struggles
and strife.
Now we adults who make the
rules,
To put into textbooks, to teach
in schools,
Aren't we the ones to blame
If the world is not sane?
We are the ones who will pave
the way
So our children won't have to
pay.
Let's make the way for a world
of joy
Color it happy for all the girls
and boys.
Society we are, society we'll be,
Until the end of eternity.
Which may not be long. . . .
BLOWING THE BOMBS
And playing hermit roles
May be our goals
But,
Where would we go?

Pete Tambunga

DECEMBER SNOW

The sky is painted gray in the
morning of the day
And on the ground the morning
dew will soon just fade away
The sparkle in the distance is
like diamonds on the ground
Reflections of the morning can
be seen from all around
Often times I see beyond the
stillness of the dawn
And watch the sun arise to the
silence of a song
The sky is painted gray in the
morning of the day
But soon the gray of winter
will bring snow along the way
Snow, snow, along the way the
clouds of winter snow
Along the way the silence of a
white December snow
Memories unfold with each
season that appears
And I welcome passing dreams
as the seasons disappear
Should you someday see the
change of a passing sunny day
Remember that in time you'll be
back to yesterday
Listen to the echoes of the
day when it is born
And you can touch tomorrow
before the day is done
You can touch tomorrow when
the clouds bring in the snow
For you'll share another memory
with the silence of a white
December snow

Roberta G. Jackson

ONE WAY TO GET TO MARS

Woke up one Monday morning,
kinda feelin sad and glum.
Slipped out of my bed, and put
my old clothes on.
I went into the bathroom,
and kinda held onto the sink,
And when I looked into the
mirror, what I saw made me
blink.
Washed my dirty face, and
combed the rats out of my
hair.
Then the phone upon the wall
began to ring with a blare.
"Hello," I said, with a voice
that showed distaste.
I thought the guy that called me
must have had some time to
waste.
But the voice in my ear said,
"Good Moring Brother Shane."
And after stammering for a
moment, I said, "Oh Hello
There Bishop Blane."
Well we talked for just a
moment, about nothing much
at all.
Then he really laid one on me,
fact it nearly made me fall.
"Brother Shane, you hold the
Priesthood, and you are a
fine young man,
And everything you try to do,
you do the best you can.
You see my boy, the Lord and I,
are thinking about the stars.
And sending someone just like
you, up to the Planet Mars.
The people there will need some
help, to learn the Gospel true,
And though we thought of many
a son, the honor fell to you."
Well he kept right on a talking,
but I didn't hear much more,
My heart was beating hard, just
like the slamming of a door.
"Now hold on just a minute Sir,
you don't quite understand,
I don't plan to leave this Earth,
I'm happy where I am."
He said that he was sorry but,
the Lord knowed what was
best,
And if I'd come down to his
office, he would tell me the
rest.
Anyway I guess you know who
won that battle fair and
square,
Cause here I am on Rocket 9,
just floating through the air.
But when I get to Mars you
know, I will tell them how,
That they can get to heaven,
cause they're half way up
there now.
And if they'll learn the Gospel
plan, and live it every bit,
The Lord will make a place for
them, right by His side to sit.
But if they fail to hear the truth,
no telling what will come.
Cause on their way to heaven,
a detour to the Sun.
Now I know this poem is crazy,
but I want you all to know,
The Gospel's true, I know for
sure, no matter where I go. .

Molly Thompson

TREADMILL

Buzz
Already awake
Roll off the bed
Head for the bathroom
The seat is so cold
Back in the bedroom
Pull on your jeans
Going out the door ask
"Are you awake"
(You know he is)
Downstairs you
fix breakfast
Write checks
Pack lunches
Outside
You run to the car
You drive
Sixty-five
All the way
The factory
Is still there
(Always there)
It is full of people
With tired faces
Their defeated eyes
Watch you buy the coffee,
And carry it to your desk
The horn sounds
You
And seven hundred others
Go to work
The lights and bells
Do not bother you
Much
You
Talk
Laugh
Swear yourself
Through
The Indy 500
Is in the parking lot
You drive
Seventy-Five
All the way
You go
To the store
You stop
At the postoffice
The postmistress
Hands over the books,
Like a French peasant
Who doesn't understand
You take them home
And put them with the others
(Unopened)
You eat
Whatever is put
Before you
You wash
Dishes
Clothes
Faces
Until
The house is quiet

You steal away
To the kingdom of pencils and paper
You write
A few lines
You frown
You try again
You frown again
You close your eyes for
Just
A
Minute
Buzz

Gertrud Demastus

MY DRUMMER

I hear a different drummer,
He beats his drum for me
Taram Tataram, Taram Tataram
It says: "You follow me!"
I follow in his footsteps
Wherever he may be,
And no one else is walking
As far as I can see.
And all the childrens laughter
Is in his beat
And every march to every war
Is in his feet.
I walk behind my drummer
To a different place,
And all the hunger in the world
Is in his face.
And all the flowers, all the birds,
And all the butterflys
Taram Tataram, Taram Tataram
Are in his eyes.
I hear a different drummer,
His drum, it has a voice,
And all the glitter in the world
And all the noise
We leave behind and walking on,
Taram Tataram, Taram Tataram.
I walk behind my drummer
At a different pace,
And way beyond, so far away
There's a different place.
Green valleys, mountains, rivers clear,
The lion sleeps next to the deer.
Taram Tataram, Taram Tataram
My heart will sing: "We're here we're here!"
Taram Tataram, Taram Tataram
My drummer rests his drum!

Eugene P. Hockenbury

LOVE

A poor way-faring child was I,
Without my parents I felt I would die;
But looking down from up above,
The Lord sent me someone with a great deal of love;
Hungry, thirsty, tired and shorn,
She cared for these needs as her sons clothes I had worn;
She did as the Saviour would have done,
I was given a part of whatever she gave her son;
By giving away as she did,
It was not hard to see why Christ had lived;
Physical limitations of man she gave?
No. . .never, for her gifts will surpass the grave;
It will surpass the grave and last for eternity,
Why? Because she shared it with you and with me;
She gave of herself as the Master teaches from above,
That gift she gave is called LOVE,

No special pretense was ever made,

Her love was hers and she always gave;

A young man as a child full of sorrow and sin,

Cannot tell you of the desperation felt from within;

But a young man who has experienced her love and her life,

Can say what a mother, what a friend, and what a wife!

Embellished upon my soul an eternity with this love spend,

Because she was faithful unto the end;

As the Saviour has said:
"These deeds shall thy memorial be,
Fear not Ruth, thou didst them unto me."

Diane Evans

WITHOUT YOUR LAUGHTER

I must be grateful, and drink my tea
Someone is singing that I can be free
I paid a price for the tragedy
that I was writing...inside of me.
In the third act, I threw down my script
I had been feeling...my Wings had been clipped.
I must be grateful for friends like you
Without your laughter, what would I do?
I've started a script; it's a comedy!
though, I must admit, it needs polishing.
Give me your hands and your honesty,
Tell me my past's not still haunting me.
Never got in a sorority, you see..
I was afraid of authority
I'm just beginning my Brand New Day.
Haven't you seen me in *Photo-play?*
I feel like donning a French beret
Warm and Alive in a Swiss chalet
or sailing a boat along Balboa bay
I must be grateful and drink my tea
Someone is singing that love is Free

I paid a price for the tragedy
that I was writing...inside of me.
I must be grateful for friends like You
Without your Laughter, what would I do?

Kimberley I. McGinniss

TAXICAB

An imperative whistle commands quick response
From the middle-aged man in the bright yellow hack
Never wary of strangers in late midnight jaunts
He is someone that nobody easily daunts
When he pulls to the curb disregarding the fact
That the traffic is heavy and never is less
Than a hazard which questions professional knack
He just waits for the whistler to jump in the back
While the newcomer's giving the needed address
And is settling back for a nice quiet ride
The experienced cabbie to meet the request
Jumps forward into the mechanical mess
Though the speed makes the passenger's eyes open wide
The invincible cabbie proceeds with an air
Of unflinching passivity bolstered by pride
In the job that he does on which many rely
When the journey is finished he charges a fare
Which the rider then pays plus whatever he wants
As a tip for the driver with reticence rare
And a seasoned facade of incredible dare

Debralee Marion

DIVORCE; SATAN'S CURSE

On our wedding day, we vowed
To love, for better or for worse,
We have tried, I know we have
To stop the pain of Satan's curse.
But, after all the love is gone
There's nothing left to feel
Don't be ashamed, don't be afraid
Our friendship will always remain real.
We'll be friends for life,
For the love we once shared,
The happy times, the funny lines,
These memories show we cared.
I wish you all the happiness
That one should receive,
I wish you all the joys of life
I hope you'll never grieve.

Lori Lynne Lewis

TOBY

scatter board house
marooned on a beach
lonely and faraway
from dreams of fantasy
crags and torn ships
reliving a past
lost as she was
gulped by the sea
and biting coid
hardship for etrenity
scattered in the air
is where she is
a symbol to those
who climb the waters
they will not find
what they need most

Pamela K. Barger

THE PASSIVE POET

The Poet's pen has come to rest,
On barren sheets of paper lying on the desk
Thoughts are deterred by an uninvited guest—
As dust gathers; Shadows are cast.
A dry ink well communicates its worth,
To once-barren paper filled with a Poet's words.
The Poet's spoken of heaven, hell, and earth;
Feelings and emotions, but finds himself sadly silenced.
Webster waits patiently upon the shelf
As time tinges the pages gracefully of yellow.
Thoughts haunt the poet; he sees only a ghost of himself—
Drifting, avoiding the committing of his life to the pen.
He walks the pathways of his mind,
Seeking motivation, the need to write again.
The Poet knows what he shall find at journey's end;
His findings revealed to all, as he finally takes up paper and pen.

Dorcas P. Hord

A TOUCH OF LOVE

You touched the sky
With shades of blue
You touched the earth
With flowers new.
You hung the Moon
And placed the stars
Took care of Jupiter
And planet Mars.
You gave us animals
Birds and such
To be our friends
To love and touch.
Then you made man
A living soul
And gave us Love
To have and to hold.
Then Your Spirit
You freely gave
That man can live
Beyond the grave.

Jeannetta Burbridge
A FORGOTTEN HOPE
The season's come, yes once again,
For Yuletide carols and merry men.
For trinkets, keepsakes and gifts papered bright,
While trees and small houses all glimmer with light.
And those with their shopping carts embark on a store,
Until shelves burdened with objects are burdened no more.
They spend and they buy with hope that in return,
A gift for their kindness they trust they will earn.
But Christmas in essence goes further than this,
In their hustle and bustle the meaning they miss.
Christmas began on one winter's night,
With one glistening star; the simplest of light.
The birth of a Child, just one little one,
Born to the world, God's only Son.
And then and soon after His life did He give,
With hope in His footsteps all men would live.
But most have forgotten the love that he gave,
When he died here on earth, their lives to save.
Nor do others remember the moment of His birth,
Surrounded by love, filled with great mirth.
Yes, the Child has been forgotten, maybe forever more.
By the wealth of a corporation and the success of a store.

S. K. Gunn
TATTLE—TAIL
I never would have known that you had another lover
I never would have known there was another
But I saw her there on Bourbon Street
Her jeans were tight with a faded seat
I knew I'd seen those jeans before
They use to stay in my dresser drawer
I looked one day and they were gone
Now this woman has them on
I imagine that while I was away
She came to visit for the day
When morning came and she was bare
You gave her your jeans to wear
It's all right darling I'm not hurt
Just don't ask where I lost my shirt
And if you see it on the street
Remember the jeans with the faded seat

William Taper
I'M A BUTTERFLY
How many times without a care
Have you snatched this creature from the air
But when you opened up your hand
No butterfly can understand
The butterfly must spend the day
In a world where he is prey
Even though I can't say why
I feel just like a butterfly
Floating about behind the scenes
Diggin the world through obscure wings
Drifting Drifting day to day
I would sit down but I can't stay
Must keep movin don't know why
Like an elusive butterfly
Must keep movin don't know why
I guess I'm just a butterfly

Theodor Femmel
REFLECTION
This web of words cannot describe
Or the greatest minds discuss.
Easier by far the toil of Sisyphus
Or Aphrodites 'potion to imbibe.
Then measure a woman's deadly guile
Or the enigma of her inscrutable smile.

Wayne William Snyder
LIVING REFLECTIONS
Life should be spent
Paying tomorrows debt,
For no man owes living
What he pays in death.
God is the mirror to life
No man his image deceives, for
Death projects what life reflects
And God is the truth between.
Death is that part of life
We witness yet do not perceive,
The end comes not in the dying
But in living we fail to conceive.

If God is dead
Then what is man,
But an uncarved headstone
An epitaph to His death.

Pamela Jo Shaver
UNTITLED
I am of the dead,
Marilyn the delicate;
I am of her rib,
Part of the child,
Murdered, murdered by involents
Of which their actions
Will not be prevailed,
With all our love we hail;
Marilyn, the innocent.
We hold you to the bosoms of our minds.
Swing your hips silently to heavens' bells.
Marilyn remember I'm here,
bring me all your love
Marilyn; I love you
We love you.
You are no casualty.
Of the body men lust,
Of the mind
Your treatment was unjust.

Of the soul only precious feelings,
feelings of righteous truth.
Maturity of immaturity.

A woman finally born,
born from the womb.
Born and then died for the tomb.

Bones and skin
remains of what used to be,
Of only what we can see.
Worthless, worthless body.
Without your delightful soul.

Released from the body
That holds back immortality.
Peacefulness, peacefulness and the light.

The light that fills
your sight with glowing
Curiosity and soul
With warmth once more,
Heavens' door.

Oh! Angel fly through heaven
Strike up another life;
Marilyn

GG Ruth Elouise Skaggs
LOVE IS
Love is a dream that begins in your heart
Love is a joy, you feel from the start
Love is a hand, held within your own
Love is a kiss, the sweetest you've ever known
Love is a faith, a must, a loving trust
Love is learning to give, a reason to live
Love is sharing, love is caring
Love is a desire, a burning fire
Love is heaven, love is sometimes hell
Love is a feeling I know so well
Love is truth, love endures all things
Love is like a bad tooth, it can cause a lot of pains
Love is words, that are not spoken
Love is a tie, that cannot be broken
Love is many things, it makes my heart sing
Love is an emotion that goes all the way
Love is a glorious feeling, what more can I say
Love is me and you, our children too
Love is so wonderful, because mine is shared with you
Love is like two hearts, that are as one
Love is until death do us part, til life is done
Love is God and His only begotten Son.

R
UNTITLED
for
you
.
.
.
i
smile
a precious child

silent
tears
years
years
years
i
spark
new life
tsubomi
1981

Jenny Grace Williams
IN THE NIGHT WITHOUT END
The days. The minutes. Going and coming. Me existing and Me fighting to survive and fighting to stop from breaking down.
The world is swirling like a top going in circles, chaotic, jerking, yet ever twirling. Endless. Me hurting. The world lost in its own pain. Me crying, screaming, dying in the rain.
The earth ageless opening up her arms to receive us and us trampling her underfoot.
Misconceptions. Half formed ideas. Rumors. Stories told.
Lies, lies all lies, and someone assumed it was the truth.
Accusors standing in a semi-circle waiting, waiting for their ultimate power around a mahogany table in a stuffy room in a smoke-filled city, just waiting to play God with someone's destiny.
The gates of Hell pushing apart, and all the flames consuming the hatred in the human heart.
Oh dear God, what have we done here? Here on this earth.
Babies dying in their mother's womb because of no reason at all and young men dying for wars without end.
And me drinking and me singing, and drinking some more so that I can forget all this stuff that I feel and see.
Oh dear God.

Teddi la Donna Longfellow
LIFE TO GIVE
I wish upon a star tonight.
The one wish that is really bright.
Of all the wishes I have wished that doesn't come true.
I want this wish I have wished to come true for you.
You have your life I want you to live.
For this life I want to give.
I may be younger as can be.
But for my Mother I give life for thee.

As far as I can see.
I want to give life to mother
from me.
I want to die to let you live.
For you're my mother I want to
give.
I will try and try again.
To let your life rebegin.
For all the love in the world I
send.
I hope to hear your life will
never end.
There is a man as happy as can
be.
For he is in your life as far
as I can see.
Live and love him as long as
can be.
For I can not live your life for
me.
In this poem I cannot lie.
For in reality I can not die.
This poem is for my mother's
long strife.
For I want you to live a long
life.
For all the love I can give.
I always want you to live.

Gary Paul Johnson
RAINBOW
Everyone is searching for the
rainbow
Everyone wants to be free
Everyone is searching for the
rainbow
Everyone just needs to see
That what you are
is what you feel,
and what you feel
is what you are.
How long is long?
How high is high?
You'll never know
unless you try
Searching for the rainbow
searching for the TRUTH
Reaching for the rainbow
reaching for the TRUTH
To why you're on this earth
now,
and what you are to do.
You know something is going
on,
and you want to make it
through.
Open your heart—
Let the LOVE flow from
within
Open your soul—
Let the LORD take your sin
Trust in JESUS
Let Him be your friend
Trust in JESUS
Let Him be your friend
Everyone is searching for the
rainbow
Everyone wants to be Free
Everyone is searching for the
rainbow
Everyone just needs to see

Kathleen P. McCann
FRIEND, WHY DO I NEED YOU?
I need you for your smile,
your wit.
I need you for your tears,
your help.
But, most of all,
I need you for the love you give.
It helps make life worthwhile.

J. Ted Schilling
TO THE LADY ARLENE ADDIEGO
You sat there
suspended within the hour of
noon like some rare spring
flower,
stretching tender arms out
to embrace the day,
gently shaking off the
morning dew
which had come to
transform the amber
rays of the sun
into rainbowed
diamonds,
and rest above your
golden eyes like
the crown of
Arthur.
I gazed at your hands, and
thought,
lovely...far too lovely.
But, not until I sent my
eyes sweeping past yours
did I know for sure.
Yes, beautiful, far too
beautiful,
far too rich a treasure
for me to hold.
Still, I went over to speak to
you,
counting off my good deeds,
calling back my moments of
beauty,
knowing there were

things within me worthy
of such loveliness.
How suspicious you were
as you looked upon me with
regal indifference.
Believe me, I only wanted to
reflect your smile,
to offer my friendship,
wishing merely for a
chance, one last
quixotic chance,
to move myself on
into the realm of
knighthood.
Perhaps I should not have told
you how lovely you are.
Forgive me, but sometimes I
forget that Camelot has been
lost,
and that now praises of
beauty
have been replaced by
slogans of equality.
Ah, but lady you are so
beautiful, so very very beautiful.
And how am I to think of you
as the equal of anything,
after having seen how the
morning sunrise blushes
before you?
Some tomorrow a gentle sun
will once again move across the
land.
Please remember me then...
remember the poet who knelt
before you
in his rusty armor, waiting
to champion your dreams
...trying to set right, the
legend of Guinevere.

Jennifer M. Petrone
AGAINST REASON
I will not be ruled by reason,
For it is the heart that loves
and not the mind.
It is the heart which knows
truth and beauty
And can send the spirit soaring
through the sky.
The heart knows no boundaries
and no end
And is not dependent upon the
forces of the world.
The heart is its own entity
and thrives on goodness and
love.
The heart's decisions may be
irrational to the reasonable,
But to sensitive spirits, they
are warmly accepted.

Marc Ciacchi
SOLITARY PERCEPTION
Shadows haunted me at dawn
today,
While I was waiting a decent
hour
To be seen on the morning
streets.
Shadows of all the skeletons,
Skeletons that could and would
Crowd themselves into my lifes
closets,
Were I to let them.
Which I might.
They could tear me apart.
They would sap my every
ambition,
Were I to let them.
And I might at that.
They could and would,
Drive me to self destruction,
Were I to let them.
And I might at that,
Let them, I mean.

Priscilla F. Douzanis
THE CREATION
Hellas—the gods knew so well
were to create man.
Your sweet shores beckon each
wave to come—and return again
and again to taste your salty
sweetness.
Haunting echoes from your lips
reach into my heart—
revealing your timeless soul—
Waters like crystal silk fill
your seas— gently caressed by
winds.
Your breath—your life comes
alive to a tune of bouzekee
carried by winds to an ever
listening ear—
Fingers clicking—bodies
swaying—smiles on lips—
a yasso—ouzo—
Yes, this is your present.
Your past filled with heroes and
citadels—have lived forever.
Your present is new—alive and
pulsating—fed from fires of
forefathers who dared and—
intermingled with passion—a
zest to fulfill—to be first and
free.
Hellas—is man and God
intertwined.

Candace E. Benjamin
NEW LIFE
Mothers nearing the stage of
life bearing
Imagining sounds of new
inspiration
Thus bringing forth a great deal
of caring
Hearts beat with great future
expectations
Bursts of happiness trumpeting
uproar
Mom's on cloud nine full of
faith, hope and joy
Promising ambitions open new
doors
Realize unlike dolls these gifts
aren't toys
Fathers-to-be pace in the waiting
room
Unwilling to see his filial born
Waits impatiently for good news
to consume
He has his whole life, his
child to adorn
A bundle of pride and joy is
received
A bright enlightening new life
is conceived

Anita Leblanc
MY FATHER
When my joy went to sorrow,
You were there to remind me;
There is always tomorrow.
Throughout my life you made
see,

All of lifes realities.
All my strength derived from
you.

You were my father, my best
friend too.
When in need, I always new
There you'd be, just for me.
The memory of you will always
be,

In my heart for eternity.
Though the Lord has taken you;
I thank him, for he's made me
see.

What a special father you were
to me.

David Marrs
POET
Perhaps you can write words on
white paper with yesterdays
eyes, but we cannot.
The pain is in remembering not
in rewording;
picking images from the
alphabet to capture the
remnants of suffering.
A distant moment not unlike
this one. . .
Piqued and cued, torn up and
dismantled; raged testament to
your endurance.
Poet, place your hand upon
tomorrow and transform it like
you change the past,
from action to thought, thought
to words, waving your magic
wand over an invisible sea.
Historian of emotion, creator
of emotion, searing hearts with
words of flame.
And as the words are written,
remembering takes its toll.
Paid in tears and love and even
blood,
poets stand, so we may crawl.

Deborah P. Nichols
UNNOTICED
Rhythmic sounds of fingers
tapping
Against tarnished glass
Head bowed low
Beneath brimmed hat—
Unnoticed
Sipping coffee, black
Stale smoke fills the air
Narrow eyes focus
Across darkened room
Brown beauty, legs in sheer
Wrapped in fabric so pure, silk
Clings to slender torso
Gliding and swaying
Music from the juke box flows
Through seemingly closed lids
He studies each move
And listens as laughter spills
He must grow tired
Watching and being hurt
Sipping coffee, black
Contemplating—
Unnoticed.

Jerrye Y. Almond
FROM YOUR GOALS NEVER STRAY
So, you're leaving now, go on
your way
Be true to yourself, from your
goals never stray
What roads of life will you
travel
As mysteries unfold and riddles
unravel?
Will you cross the rainbow to
the other side
Or forget your dreams as others
who tried?
Will you face the challenge
you'll meet out there
Or will you give up and cringe
in despair?
You'll be confused and troubled
many times
The farther you go, the higher
you'll climb
Go seek your future, do the best
you can do
Remember each tomorrow will
dawn brand new.
Each episode of life is a
forceful drama
Speeding you faster and faster
toward your Karma
Never look back at yesterday
Be true to yourself, from your
goals never stray.

Bernice Louise Beck
OPTIMISTIC OUTLOOK
May we adults
The world perceive
As a wide-eyed youth
On Christmas Eve.
While faced with strife
The whole world 'round,
Still, optimistic
Thoughts abound.
Not knowing hurt,
Or the grief of loss,
Time is a treasure
At priceless cost.
To awake refreshed,
Embrace the morn,
Not dwell on dreams
Now dashed and torn.
A verse well learned
From one still new:
Waste not one day—
They are too few.

Benson S. Ebinne
EPITAPH
The memory never seems
dimmed by time;
It is sharp, clear, unclouded
and fine.
The recollection of all I did
learn
From you concerning life, makes
me firm.
You taught me to stand firm for
what is right;
That honesty always wins the
fight.
You showed me that hard work
is part of life,
And taught me the essence of
shunning strife.
I have learned to appreciate
the existence of God
Whose kindness and love are
deep and broad.
Your illustrative and practical
sermons
Tell me you were ready to
answer God's summons.
Two truths you have always
stressed still work for me:
"Flee trouble, and take no man's
property."
You may have been untimely
snatched from us,
But, Grand Pa, Your memory is
still precious.

Dianne P. Maffeo
SHY=ALONE
I sit alone,
surrounded by people,
talk to me.
I have a voice,
you never hear,
talk to me.
Acknowledge my presence,
draw me out,
talk to me.
Be my friend
I'll be yours,
just talk to me.

Devona Kay Smith
THE VOID
The Void is a maze
deep inside your head
The Shadows keep you awake
running one step ahead
It's a long lonely journey
lots of hurts to stumble on
Thickets of memories to sort
and arrange
cast them aside and keep
plodding on
Coming out of the Void
the Traps will lure you
The familiar roads lead back to
the Arena
it's games and inevitable dues
So hold on to the Force
or a God, or a Friend
Whatever you find you can still
believe in
If you prostitute your mind
for love or money
Make sure it ain't counterfeit—
no Poison in the honey
The Void is deep and dark and
cold
there's nothing stable for you
to hold
There's lots of honey free for
the taking
But you better check the lable. .
before you eat from that table

Birtie Helen Tabb
ON A DAY OF APPLE BLOSSOMS
On a day of apple blossoms
And lilacs and April rain,
Some days of other years
Come haunting me again.
Across a page of letter
Written sometime long ago,
The afternoon sun drifts in
With some sadness in its glow.
Ah, perhaps they have all
forgotten
The words that once they
penned.
Yet I live once more in the
realm
That they have power to lend.
Words that were written in
earnest,
Words that were written in fun,
Fare alike in our recollection
When we know that their day is
done.
In a storm of cherry petals
They all become memories
again,
And mingle with apple blossoms
And lilacs and April rain.

Anna Orsino
NATALE

1

Una fragranza di pino,
un profumo d'incenso...
e Natale! Brilla una stella,
una dolce e melodica armonia
scende dal Cielo... E' un an-
gelo che discende a ricordarci
la venuta del Redentore.

2

E' Natale! suonate campane,
brillate stelle! Angeli, venite
dal Cielo. Annunziate la Nascita
del Signore. Brillate cuori!...
e nato il Bambino Gesu; brillate
e portate allegria con pace ed
amor.

3

Santo Natale... tu che porti
l'amor Divino a tutti, fa che
nessuno dimentichi di questo
Culto. E' nato... e nato... e nto il
Signor! Egli e nel mio cuore e
con gioia voglio dirvi: Buon
Natale a tutti.

Gabriel H. Paradis
SHARE WITH ME
Come take my hand, walk with
me,
Fill the emptiness of my life,
Share with me,
The magic of our universe.
Without the clouds and rain,
There is no rainbow,
Without the sun,
Flowers die, and the grass won't
grow.
Without you, I cannot be.
Without hands, we cannot
touch,
Without eyes, we cannot see,
Without honest hearts, we
cannot love.
Without you, I cannot be.
Without joy and laughter, we
cannot smile,
Without love, we cannot be.
Without souls, we cannot share.
Without you, I cannot be.
Come take my hand, walk with
me.
Fill the emptiness of my life.
Share with me,
The magic of our universe.
With you, I can be.

Wendy Christine Bagdi
MY DREAM
An ocean song sings out to me
As I walk along the shore.
The sun comes up and
morning's here;
Yesterday's no more.
I look above to see birds fly
They're high and always free.
I try so hard to fulfill my
dream
And that is to be me.

Shirley S. Perkins
THE WINKING OWL
The winking owl upon his perch
Knows the secrets of our search.
His life is attuned geometry,
The lines in perfect symmetry.
We live our lives in wild
abstract;
Dreaming our dreams, ignoring
the fact
That we're crying only crystal
tears,
And cringing from our harbored
fears.
Alone he sits, and coldly blinks;
His hidden thoughts he smugly
thinks.
He must be laughing deep
inside
At our regrets and plastic pride.
Just for once I'd like to trade;
So, with decisions crisply made,
I could sit there thinking for
awhile;
Then greet the darkness with a
smile.

Gwen Durham
SOUL MATES
After you left I had a dream
And in it you said: "Don't move
a thing."
Oh, but I did. I moved my desk
to where your
Chair used to be.
My writing desk, full of hopes
and dreams
That I had long ago given up
for you;
But you turned around and gave

up me
For an impulsive middle aged
fling.
What a pitiful sight to see!
A man who won't face
approaching old age
Like a punch drunk fighter
who won't give up
Still fighting in the ring
against all odds,
Refusing to face reality.
After thirty five years together
Do you want to die without me;
Do you want some *stranger* at
your bedside
When you face the great
beyond?
You and your paramour can
never transcend the bond
of thirty five years.
Before the divorce is over,
you will share my tears.
Though we're separated
physically,
Mentally we are still attuned.
You cannot escape from me
And I cannot escape from you.

Catherine Bruce

BABY MEETS A SUNBEAM

Sunshine facinates her
As it beams from heavens orb
In vain she tries to capture it
It's warmness to absorb.
What a mystery it seems to be
This light so soft and pure
But she cannot ever grasp it
Nor resist its shining lure.
To be so captivated
So enraptured, so enchanted
By a simple thing like sunshine
That we so often take for
granted.
It really makes me wonder
How I had never realized
All the magic in a sunbeam
When seen through a baby's
eyes.

Elizabeth Dahab

HER CHILD

I looked around and wondered
why they talked so loud,
I walked a little closer to the
gathering crowd.
In each of their pale faces, I
saw sorrow and fear,
And in each person's eyes, I
saw a glistening tear.
I looked around and wondered,
and moved from side to side,
There in their midst, I saw the
lady where she had died.
I turned around quickly as my
tears started to run,
Suddenly in the corner, I saw
her little son.
He looked at the gathering
crowd with questioning eyes,
Yet he could not understand, he
could not even try.
So he sat alone, forgotten and
played with his duck,
Not knowing the cruelty of life
or his bad luck.
I stared at his tiny curls that
filled his tiny head,
And wondered who, from now
on would tuck him in his bed.
I looked around and wondered if
anyone would come,
To take pity and to take care of
her son.
He looked up, then looked
around as he rubbed his
tummy,
Suddenly, tears ran from his
eyes as he cried, "Mommy."

Lloyd T. Deckard

HORSE AND SADDLE

I've been shot in my side, but I
must saddle my horse for I
have got to ride.
In the courts I was tried;
Now they're searching the
countryside.
If they catch me they may tan
my hide.
Now I must find a place to hide.
Across the border I've got to
ride.
Now my side is giving me pain.
I'm riding through the snow and
rain.
I am hanging onto my horse's
mane.
It's just a few more miles across
the plains.
When I get into Mexico,
I'll get out of this snow and
rain.
The posse is getting close to
me.
It's so dark I can hardly see.
They pulled their guns. They're
firing at me.
I wish I could find one damn
tree.
Now my side is paining bad.
I think that I've been had.
I should have listened to my
Dad.
And all this trouble I wouldn't
have had.
Out here they can't hang me, for
there is not one damn tree.
They have to take me in to
Bisbee.
And there they have just one
damn tree.
It grew specially just for me.

Sylvia Delua Sa'enz

ABRIDGMENT OF "MY PROPOSAL TO DANIEL"

Daniel, songs speak of your
name.
The Bible mentions it, too;
but it's not the same
with a poem, written just for
you.
It seems like I've known you
forever,
though I hardly do.
Firmly we join, together
in a form of de'ja'vu.
My angel, crushes come and go;
infatuations fade away;
but my feelings for you grow.
Mystically in my soul you stay.
If logically wrong to love you,
and passionately obscene,
I'll be a friend forever true
on whose staunch shoulder you
can lean.
I'll be a faithful companion
to take your lonliness away.
When you desire expansion,
I'll give you the space to
fly away.

Alicia Rene' Delehanty

IN THE YEAR THREE THOUSAND

In the Year Three Thousand
What a sight it will be
There will be it and it
Instead of he and she
We will have computers
To fix and repair
We will have wigs
Instead of real hair
In the year Three Thousand
To have a child you won't go far
Reach inside your robot
and pull it out of a jar
People will wonder at sometime
or another
Where's my sister, Where's my
brother
Animals and flowers that should
have grown
People from this era should have
known
In the year Three Thousand
World War III has started
Atomic bombs fill the sky
all life has departed
Jupiter hates Earth, Earth
hates Mars
Please dear God, put us back in
our jars!

Ross S. Stull, Sr.

IN MEMORIAM

Let us think of our loved ones
as roses,
That once bloomed in our
garden fair,
Now they have been
transplanted
In the Master's garden up
there.
They have been called to be
among His flowers,
In a land where they say there
is no night.
To bloom in His beautiful
garden,
A garden so wonderfully
bright.
So let us banish every thought
of sadness
That may remain in our
hearts,
And think of them up yonder,
In a garden where they shall
never part.
Their memories with us will
linger
For many and many a day
But let us think of them as
roses,
Roses for the Master's
bouquet.

Toni L. Williams

YOU

Love is you
you are all things wonderful.
your the sunshine. The fresh
clean air
after a spring time rain.
you are like no other human
on earth
you are love
you are sadness
you are joy, hope, happiness
you are you whom, I have never
seen or known
you are love

Carolyn Reeves

THE MIND OF LIFE

Darkness envelopes the mind,
Hiding thoughts in caverns
Filled with thick blackness,
Creating an aura of despair—
Weighted by fearsome inertia.
Eventually, a glimmer of light
Enters the gloomy mind.
Perceived, the light glitters
And glows, illuminating the
path
To peace and contentment.
At the end of the path
The mind enters a thick forest,
Becoming entangled in dense
thickets,
Tethered by root suckers—
Struggling to reach a clearing.
Finally, a clearing appears
And frees the mind,
Promoting a peculiar discernment
Of how nature is juxtaposed
In the mind of life.

Louis E. Williams

HAPPINESS

New Year has come again.
I love the newness of the year.
It is so young and full of
happiness.
Happiness is all I need.
Happiness is all I want.
Happiness is a result of knowing
that
I am love,
You are love,
And that we both have been
loved,
And will stay full of love, this
new year.
Happiness is a result of
Success,
Love,
Peace of mind
And a continuing prosperity
forever lasting throughout
each year.
Happiness is beyond description.
Happiness is beyond
prescription.
But Happiness is never beyond
recognition,
Nor is Happiness beyond
existence.
Happiness is just happiness,
And it is the best.
I am just happy, happy, happy
this brand new,
New Year.

Florence Lappin Gorman

OUT OF THE DEPTHS

Out of the depths I cried unto
the Lord:
Help me again to see.
But God travailed at giving sight
To one whose eyes knew only
night,
And I was left alone to see
The glory of dawn's harmony.
Out of the depths I cried unto
the Lord:
Help me again to hear.
But God gave sound of
whip-poor-will
To those who'd heard the bullet
shrill,
And I was left alone to hear
Crackling embers at hearthside's

cheer.
Out of the depths I cried unto the Lord:
Help me again to feel.
But God led babes to hearts that would hold
Them close within a loved one's fold,
And I was left to feel anew
My beating pulse in its song to you.

Betty Kay Still

JOSHUA

You were unexpected
sent from up above
to brighten up our lives
and spread a little love
Hearts down here had grown so cold
and hardened as could be
God knew we needed some sunshine
so He planted a seed
A seed of love that would grow
into a little boy
one who loved our Saviour
even before he was born
He came into this world
with a smile upon his lips
and loved everybody
even from the crib
His mission here upon this earth
to spread a little cheer
to help someone along the way
with a kiss, a smile, or a tear
Today we celebrate the day
just five years ago
God sent us this bundle of joy
a reminder of His love

Jose Zakus

ONCE YOU WERE AWAKE

Little Prairie Town
Are you sleeping now?
Once you were awake,
Alive, pulsating—
Throbbing, thriving—
Now—you are silent,
Empty and still.

Erva Loomis Merow

A PILL

When man has a pill
to end all ills,
I hope the can find one
we can take————————
and recall in absolute detail,
every exciting, beautiful——
perfect moment we've ever lived
and live it again and again and again.

Yvonne L. Miller

FESTIVAL OF FIRE

A three-quarter moon covered by clouds.
In the dim light, shadows meet,
preparing for the ceremony.
The procession moves slowly
some pray, others mourn.
Reaching the circle, they build the fire.
The dead wood is piled on,
the flames hiss
in harmony with the wind.
The lamb is placed on the altar.
The smell of burning flesh
incites circle members
to begin the ritual.
Whispered prayers increase,
mounting to a chorus of voices,
oblations for their dead.
After the final amen,
the leader speaks,
"This is the holy fire.
Extinguish all others,
tonight, only this burns in your homes.
Take these embers with you
as you return home
to prepare the feast.
They burn unquenchable
providing comfort for the returned souls."
Families leave,
and the festival of fire begins
bringing in All Saints' Day.

Adelina M. Levy

FREE LITTLE CHILD. . .

(to my daughter: Raquel)

Something good will become of you. . .little child,
if you learn to live by the expectations
that life so selfishly hides
behind the facades of mysterious treasures.
Someone sensitive will become of you. . .little child,
if you learn to live without rejection
parades of love won't pass you by
when you accept the value of the intentions.
Someone special will become of you. . .little child,
if you learn to express your real feelings
not the ones society is tied
by bias interpretation without meaning.
Someone happy will become of you. . .little child,
if you do not fall into generalizations
that is one of the opinions people buy
avoiding the wisdom of a true exploration.
Someone fullfilled will become of you. . .little child,
if you are capable to stand for the truth
and never allow any lies
to shake your philosophy loose.
Something good will become of you. . .little child,
if you learn to explore without fear
and if you recognize in your friend's eyes
the valuable courage of their tears.

Helen Fitzpatrick Holmes

THOUGHTLESS

I was trampled by the Horse,
Thoughtless, today.
His hooves struck deep,
etching grooves upon my mind.
I was murdered by the Horse,
Thoughtless, today.
He drove me into the ground,
kicking the dirt over my mind.

Joseph B. Patton

I'M FREE

I'm Free
So onward I go
Bound in Satan's web
Jesus set me free
I'm Free
So onward I go
The Highlights of my faith
have not reached it's peak
I'm Free
So onward I go
Look before you leap,
think before you speak
I'm Free
So onward I go
I'm out of the in crowd
I pray my light stay bright
This light of mine, I'm going
to let it shine
I'm Free
So onward I go
I hate evil
I will hold fast to what is good
It's the way you use freedom
It's the way you count love
It's the way you look at life
Jesus is the way, the truth, and the life
This life is living
I'm Free
So onward I go
The Highlights of my faith have
not reached it's peak
but I'm Free
So onward I go
I hate what is evil
I will hold fast to what is good
I'm Free
So onward I go

V. I. Pavlov

MY LAST GIFT

Dedicated to My Dear Judy...

My love for you, is like a golden leaf
That can fall only to your feet.
You will not return here again,
I will not return here probably either.
But here! Instead of me,
I am leaving for you
a bouquet of last cornflowers
I have found in the garden.
For you my love, for you.
Maybe tomorrow you will walk here again
Where restless wind is rustling petals
Where I have lost my dearest love.
And if they won't get blown away,
You will find my cornflowers.
Since I have nothing else left to give to you,
This is my last gift to our love.
Please! Don't touch them,
They are dead.
Let the wind of the time blow them away.
Let them bring a moment of sorrow
To the sweethearts in love,
That will pass by here tomorrow!

Jean Lyte

THE WOMAN'S ODE

I've often wondered how it would be
If I had a man who cared about me,
Who'd give with his heart, all that he owned,
Spiritually, lovingly, for me alone,
Whose arms I could feel for comfort from fear,
Whose gentle voice whispers, I love you dear,
Whose faithfully beside me when I'm troubled with sadness,
Calming me down at my threshold of madness,
Who'd know all the basics of life that I need,
Emotionally, unselfishly, he'd take the lead,
Who'd treat me with kindness, sympathy, and respect
And court me forever, as though we'd just met,
Yes, I often think about how life would be,
If I had that someone who cared just for me.

Paula Barninger

WINTERS' FURY

As I sit here, perched by the window,
I watch the town sleep beneath a blanket of white.
I think of times when I was young
And snow meant a day of fun for everyone.
No school; streets were barricaded.
Kids and sleds were everywhere.
Now when the white flakes start to fall,
People sit by and wait for dreadful phone calls.
It's four o'clock in the morning;
A cinder truck goes slowly up the street.

A light comes on across the way:
Have to get up early to make it to work today.
The sound of icescrapers hitting windshields;
The sound of shovels ripping across the tar;
Engines roar and tires spin,
As cars fight a never-ending war!

Rachel Elaine Grubbs

MY HIDEAWAY

I used to have a tree I would climb to get away from everyone and everything. I called it my hideaway. In the summer when the leaves were green and alive, I would climb my tree and stay until the late hours of the approaching darkness. I would look at all the city lights and wonder what it would be like to be one of those bright lights downtown. I would think for a few seconds. I imagined I was a bright light. I was in my hideaway. I travelled through time in my hideaway. I become space in my hideaway. I was where I wanted to be, I was what I wanted to be in my hideaway. I became part of my hideaway and my hideaway became part of me. When I left my hideaway, I felt as though I had left my best friend in another place. I felt alone. I would always go back and become or be something or somewhere. Now, the leaves are no longer green or alive and I can't go to my hideaway. I won't get "to be" or "become." But I can wait until the leaves turn green and come alive because I know my hideaway will always be there for me, and me for it.

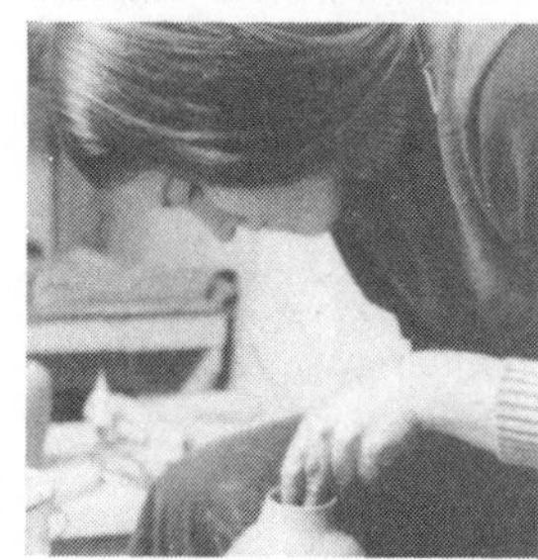

Beth Croxton
NO REST
I get depressed --
no reason;
just can't get my chin off my chest.

With tears I'm swept --
so many;
upon my cheeks like waves they crest.

I have confessed --
all my sins;
tho still at night I cannot rest.
You think I jest --
not funny;
with good humour I was not blessed.

Anthony J. Sapienza
AN AQUATIC FANTASY
The sun rose over the ocean,
as the boat moved out of port.
A single man crew, whose dreams abound
of a mystical aquatic court.
In my dreams her beckoning
made me realize it must be true,
by the way she called out to me,
and told me what to do.
I sailed in the direction,
as told in her lullaby.
Where the crystal water rippled,
to the tune of the seagulls cry.
I looked around and saw
that there was nothing to be seen.
Not an obstacle in miles,
but water blue and green.
Then suddenly there was a break
on the calm ocean's face.
And there appeared a topless nymph
who bore a gift of grace.
Her hair was golden, her eyes deep blue,
her skin so very light.
And though she invited me to join her,
I hesitated out of fright.
She jerked her body forward,
and as she dove below,
her fin caressed the surface,
as she moved so very slow.
No longer could I tarry,
so I swam so very swift,
to catch this lovely goddess
and receive her seductive gift.
But being mortal and not fish
I was unable to prevail,
in this acquatic court she endowed upon me
that glistened beyond what was real.
So many shadows encompassed me
as I quickly tried to rise,
to where my lungs would pump the air
that filled so many lives.
I broke the waters surface,
and found the sun had long gone down.
And the full bright moon was now
the mighty oceans crown.
My boat no longer anchored
in its designated place.
So I headed toward the rocks
at a very steady pace.
I don't remember coming to rest
on the surface of a stone.
But was wakened by the splashing
of the salty oceans foam.
It was then I heard the rumble
of the motor of a craft,
as two men came toward me
on what seemed to be a raft.
But as they came to where I lay
I slipped into the sea.
And surprisingly they took a man,
the man they took was me.
I saw them drag me on the raft,
and the eldest shook his head.
I called to them, but they hadn't heard
for my voice seemed to be dead.
Then I noticed how warm and calm
the ocean had become.
And my golden haired goddess returned
to take me where we had come from.
We swam beneath the ocean
in an endless current of time.
And our fins splashed the surface
in a constant mood sublime.
And now I dwell in the ocean,
With fish of every sort.
And my golden hair goddess and I
now rule the mystical aquatic court.

Elizabeth Pucciarelli
THE CHINA CUP
My heart is like the china cup
I place upon the shelf
The crazy glue I used to repair
Has left each line and crevice
The steaming brew that warmed me so
Has etched it's web upon it
I offer you a cup of tea: I offer you my heart
My heart was broken as the cup
The glue came from another
For friends are like that crazy glue
that hold the parts together
The china lined from being used
From giving warmth and comfort
Is Stronger still than first it was
With mending it together
So is my heart a stronger heart
Let's test it's strength together
I offer you a cup of tea: I offer you my heart
My heart is full of crevices
My heart is full of lines

Wes Rine
THE GIFT
I paused at a simple stone
The lasting remembrance of an infant child
Who, like seeds beneath the worlds earthern womb
Was fondled and caressed in her mothers arms
Till death came with sullen guise
And cast a pall over those innocent eyes
Over her feet she put mommas gift
A token given, a small life taken
One which love so carefully nurtured
Buried together with a 1000 unborn futures
Of laughter tear, and joy
Better left to rest in time

Terry Lee
INDIVIDUALITY
You are you
And I am me
Just like the oak
And the willow tree
Better yet
Just like Highway 101
And 99
You're going in your Direction
And I'm going
In mine
But we both serve
A purpose
No matter now puzzling
It sometimes may be
And unless we both
Understand this
Neither of us
Can truly be free!

Jo Jo Etta Bryant
GLASS HOUSES
As the rain beats steadily down,
The temperature continues to fall.
Each raindrop becomes a parasite,
Latching on to anything within its grasp.
Things hardly noticed from day to day life
Protrude into a blunt reality
As they become embedded within a frozen shell.
So beautiful and yet so cold and lonely.
The trees are still;
Their branches heavily burdened with a crystal-like casing--
Unable to move freely in the breeze or
To perhaps feel the warmth vital to their existence.
It's as though you're looking inside of everything
At the skeleton of their very being.
Wanting to be seen but not touched.
Being imprisoned within these walls could mean destruction.
Symbolizing quiet tranquility,
The appearance of time standing still
Is perceived when one gazes upon
The threshold of "glass houses".

Linda Gershen
LEAH
Not flesh of our flesh
Nor bone of our bone
But conceived in our hearts
Nurtured in our souls
Grown out of dreams
Born of love's labor pains
You are ours none the less
Our chosen child
Love of our love
Child of our dreams
We belong to you

Marilyn Moller
BURNING EMBERS
The silent flicker of the flame
whispers softly of your name.
Memories held in corners bare,
reaching out—yet you're not there.
Our love is gone;
but not to die
Look for burning embers in the sky.

Margie B. Milazzo
IN THE WINTERS' A QUIET
Come, we'll take a walk through the woods today
The sun is up and the wind does bite
Let's go, while it's caught in the strangeness of winter's way
Before it waste, in the winter's quiet.
We can take the old trail that leads
To the bend of the woods, where the trees are in sight
Slow our pace while in the woods proceed
Alone,in the winter's quiet
The holly trees are exposing berries now, ruby red
And birds are feeding upon them in flocks
We may step into a clearing, where trees are felled
In the stillness, of the winter's quiet
We will walk the carpet
Autumn left behind upon it's floor
Now layered together in frosty ice
Do come, we'll explore the woods once more
Quickly, lest we miss all it's beauty, in the winter's quiet

Esther L. Heiden
OUR LIFE
Our life goes by so very fast,
Yet we live as though it would last and last,
Time is so precious to us on earth,
We start to measure it from the exact minute of our birth.
But how does one feel when you look death in the face?
Like you are sinking into a black, black abyss?

Has Jesus prepared for you a mansion above?
Or have you refused to accept His love?
Questions like these people tend to erase,
Thinking they don't have to worry about looking death in the face.
They think they've been good and have done no harm,
They just simply feel there's no cause for alarm.
We cannot stand before God alone,
Relying on our own merits, or the things we have done.
Do you understand what God really expects?
His words, "Be ye therefore perfect," were not spoken in jest.
When you die, what will God see?
Will He see that Jesus lives in you so lovingly?
Will Jesus be the one who answers for you,
"Yes, Father, I died for this one too!"
If you ask Jesus to come into your heart,
All of your sins will completely depart.
Eternal life will then live in your breast,
And your body, soul and mind will be at rest.

Ms. Virginia A. Givens

STAGES OF LIFE

When I first met you I believed in you
Then you started cheating - you're so untrue
So happiness changed to fueding and fights
Although I am still here with you, it isn't right
I'll keep working each day to better myself
and one day your memory I'll place on the shelf
I've taken your punches while your lovers go free
we are living together yet you mistreat me
I needed your love while you loved in the street
Take a test for true lovers and you'll have to cheat
Your score would be low - the test you would fail
Some day you'll be sorry for the wrong you have done
Right now you are happy and think you have won
You could never be true to one woman alone
So what happens darling when your youth is gone
Will you lie around then all old and gray
and remember how you treated me that way
I'll be far away from your cold empty arms
You are settled now sweetheart where is your charm
All your lovers have left you for a better life
and you sit alone o where is your wife
Get up out of bed and cheat on your pain
You lived like a heathen so die like a man

James Sexton Layton

THE CROSS

Cocoon me round your arm
With love, as long ago,
And see if you can warm
Again these frozen hands.
We must concern no more
About the stolen letter
I left beneath your door
The night I went away.

In different ways scarred
With ugly marks we made
To keep apart, thus marred
Our scars have made us one.
A battlefield of snow
And a sordid house of shame
Joined hands to let us know
The use of love and hate.
You must forgive my crime,
And I'll forgive your sin,
And in the course of time
My handless arms will fade.

Charlene Marchant

A SPECIAL STORY. . .
TERRY FOX

He was a very courageous young man
Who started with a dream
He trained and worked and hoped each day
And soon it could be seen.
He started in the east and travelled to the west
And we just began to know
That he was a very special man
It was in his heart, it showed.
We soon began to read about him
And see him on T.V.
He was going to run across Canada
For everyone to see.
The money then came pouring in
Yes, cancer can be beaten
And Terry struggled on each day
He wasn't to be defeated.
Then one day he realized
Something wrong inside
He couldn't breathe, what was wrong
It could not be denied.
He struggled cancer once again
He had to quit for now
Said he "but if I get the chance again
I'll finish it somehow."
He came back home, his friends
His family, all taken by despair
Across the land people worried
there was uneasiness in the air.
Please get better Terry
Please go and try again
We all need you very much
We need you as our friend.
The money really came in now
Cause Terry ran no more
This boy he believed in miracles
Why can't we even the score.
But then one day it happened
It happened early morn
Terry Fox lives no more
We all feel lost, forlorn.
But his memory will live on with us
For years and years to come
We won't forget you Terry
Nor will our daughters and our sons.
We have a story, a great Canadian
Who did his part, then left us
For he's the one who's smile we loved
His smile is what has kept us.
Kept us hoping, smiling, loving
Through times both good and bad
What a hero we all know that
Although this story's sad.
So remember people, remember Terry
His smile, his curly locks
Cause he believes in miracles
And we love you Terry Fox.

Susan Escamilla

SOMETHING BAD HAS HAPPENED HERE!

My eyes they have seen violence and blood,
So little of happiness any more.
My ears they have heard
the crys of innocent people,
suffering for others faults.
My heart it has felt sadness
and many a sorrow,
But still I dream of a new way of life
Bettering our tomorrows.
People mustn't remain the same
it seems they've forgotten,
how to love and God's name.
And without this,
the world can never change.
The little eyes of the earth
our children,
Must not see, hear and feel
what is now called life.
Let us change the world
and make it nice,
for all mankind to love,
and live in peace.
And sadness never to be felt,
but to become only a word of the past.

Mary Martha Tenerowicz

SPEAKING

Speaking
often
reminds one
that between the hurt
and sorrow
are times of joy untold
when sweet mystery abounds.
The gentle
truth
of love
will be found again by simple speaking.

Linda E. Workman

CRY TO ME

"Cry to me",
Is what the old man told her,
"...when the weight of the world
Rests upon your weary shoulders.
But do not feel so all alone.
For I have lived my life
Three more than you
And always reaped
What I had sown."
"Cry to me",
Her angel of mercy said,
"...I will provide comfort
Without condemning you
And give my advise
Without pitying you,
For you have made
Your home where you stand.
And soon, like you -
I...without warning
Shall cross over
To a new and better land.

Don E. Seales

PAMELA

like an eagle
you've won your freedom
feel the need to fly
been caged too long
into the sunset be gone
cut the ties that bind
soar away yourself find
you love me
but I understand freedom's calling
an urge you can't resist
so try your new wings
and fly!

Larry Douglas Chappell

LIKE HE WAS

If I could be
Like he was--
So full of spirit
So full of love.
Yes, he was a hawk,
Yet, he was a dove.
If only--I could be
Like my daddy was:
A fighting hawk--
A loving dove.
If ever "near perfect"
Becomes me;
Then, I shall be
Like he was!

Mary Pinzok Mauriello

PROCRASTINATION

She decided she'd plant a garden this year.
In the backyard somewhere,
Probably up against the fence.
She'd think about it later though; after the snow melted.
But then she really should buy the seeds and plant them in those indoor starter pots now.
Later winter was the time of year for doing things like that.
But the children would be home from school shortly.
She'd buy seeds later.
She imagined it a beautiful garden.
Daisies, marigolds, asters,

petunias, a geranium or two.
All brilliantly colored flowers.
Like the ones in the needlepoint she's been meaning to start for some time now.
She remembered buying the picture to hang over the mantle; after the walls were painted.
The paint was in the house somewhere.
No doubt hidden in some dusty corner of the basement.
She knew she'd find it one of these days; when she cleaned the basement.
And she'd do that on some cold rainy day; maybe after her flowers bloom.
Turning from the window he was gazing out,
She sat down on her badly in need of upholstering sofa and decided she'd work on that needlepoint.
After a nap, perhaps.

Norma J. Townsend

A CHILD SHALL LEAD US

Look into your little child's face
See the love that's shining there?
He trusts you and has faith in you
So he's happy - without a care.
God is looking into your heart
Is love for Him still shining there?

He wants your trust and faith in Him
Happily - your cares, He'll share.
I look to our Heavenly Father with love
For I know He first loved me
He gave up His Precious Child to die
So that Heaven - I may see.

Marjorie Donahue Clark

I AM THE WAY—

Out of the depths that smother us
What shall bring us peace?
War is a monster—ravenous
Where is our release?
Man is man's worst enemy,
Proved through war-lord's reign;
Why, oh why, did he not foresee
The world beset with pain?
Never can we all believe
The slogan, 'Might makes right;'
A small voice bids us to perceive
That force leaves only blight.
Greed is a mighty octopus
Seeking to devour;
What shall halt his impetus?
We hope—the Angelus Hour.
Victory is a noble word;
But is war ever won?
The pain, death, and misery incurred
Require ages to be undone.
God is Love and Truth and Trust.
Greed is hate and lies and lust.
God is Peace and Faith Serene,
Greed is unrest and all things mean.
This is the only world man knows,
He's here for just a span;
He's born, he lives, and then he goes;
'Twas thus since Time began.
Why not strive for happiness,
To prepare for afterlife?
Why not a world—harmonious
Instead of only strife!
What's the answer to all of this?
We ask of One above;
"Woulds't thou escape from thy abyss?
Then exchange thy greed for LOVE."

Larry J. Zaikow

DUSTY HILL

On top of a mountain, a valley down below,
And a lake nearby,
Dusty hill beyond the horizon,
The sun shining in a distance a red sunset,
Standing on the hill, looking miles and miles,
In the low cold atmosphere!
I saw a sandy beach near a hillside,
Dreaming of the days roaming the country-side,
Today the clouds are so white with a clear sky,
Tomorrow I'll be on my way; along the shoreline.
Yesteday has come and gone,
Dusty hill! Dusty hill! Dusty hill!
The rugged rocky slope with fall approaching,
The trees turning color,
The leaves are, yellow, gold, orange and
Reddish, on the brown dusty hill.
A rainbow high, high in the heavens,
The old torn down shack; a ranch down in the valley,
That has been here years ago,
In the early times!
Looking from dusty hill you see the landscape,
Looking far and wide to the other side with a
Stream of water flowing down by,
Dusty hill with a clutter of old trees and stumps,
Shrubs and weeds growing on the hill;
All around dusty hill, where I once lived and grew up!

Cathy Jo Crawford

CURRENTS

Slowly, slowly, crawls the year
Like a baby with no fear.
Quickly will the months flow past
Until arriving at the last.
This, the final month, will drag
Each and every day will lag
'Til suddenly, the final day
Turns to night, and swift decay.
And then--the year will peak and fade,
Into the new, all thoughts will wade
When floating back along the way,
All memories will slowly fray.

William N. Chigas

ODE TO SHARON

"Eleven seasons would bid farewell,
Before the seed took root;
(How hardy must this bud be
to break through frozen earth)
To reveal the secret of an inner warmth."
This infant bud that grows within
across the earth a whisper call;
I embrace with eyes alone
for fear a petal fall
Nurtured by warmth & thought
the bud has shown it's sure,
To last through seasons beyond
forever to endure.
The patience of the world is mine
forever to be shown.
With gentleness and tender care
until the bud has grown.

Calla Mathy

LOVE IN LIFE—NOT JUST AT CHRISTMAS

God is Great and God is Good -
He'd end our troubles if only He could.
When Peace on Earth comes to us all -
Heaven's doors will open and He will call.
Come home, my children and let's share the love,
As we join together in our Home above.
Let this Christmas be more than fancy gift giving,
Make it one of faith and peaceful living.
Face each new day as a gift from above -
And we all understand that can only mean Love.
There can be no song without a heart,
It must have a melody and someone must start -
Putting the words together and then sing along -
To get the feeling so you can pass it on.
The same in life holds true each day -
Keep a smile in your voice; it will pave the way,
For a congenial fellowship with folks around,
Let's have Peace on Earth and let Love abound!

Virginia L. Harrington

PAULA'S WAY

She has withdrawn forever from the world of men,
No more the harsh caress to feel.
Her life amid the soft ones shall anon begin;
With soothing touch her wounds will heal.
She will eternal leave behind
the primal drive
that penetrates with rods of steel,
To seek her solace and her reason to survive
Through those with feminine appeal.
Into the bosom of her own she turns and cries,
Her pain no longer to conceal;
For what good is life if internally she dies
When forced to bow to carnal zeal?
She will not hang her head nor turn her face in shame,
Nor penitential will she kneel;
The prejudicial social world will know her name,
For she exists and she is real.

Lynn Nunn

JESUS OUR SALVATION

God opened up his heart an said I love my people too much to ever let them be lost, so he sent his son Jesus to be our salvation.
Jesus came as a baby just as you an me, but everyone knew Jesus was a special baby, Jesus was going to be our salvation.
Jesus grew up just like you an I through childhood into adulthood. Jesus had a closeness with God an a wisdom far beyond his years, Jesus was going to be our salvation.
Jesus grew in wisdom an compassion for the people, an went out everywhere preaching an doing miracles an they knew Jesus was going to be our salvation.
Jesus died on the cross an all our sins were to be forgiven, for he knew he was going to be our salvation.
Jesus arose on Easter Sunday an that is how we can be sure of our salvation.

John W. O'Neal, Jr.

THUS SPOKE...*

I am Satan's immaculate machine, they say,
his dream incarnate, his angel divine.
I am God's darkest bane, they say.
His nightmare. His worst fear maligne.
I am he who watches the sheep as they graze,
I am he who laughs at the herd.
I am he who refuses to drink at the well,
I am he who speaks the word.
I am he who talks to ears that don't hear,
as I look into eyes that are blind.
I am he who dreams a thousand dreams,
I am he who knows his own mind.
I am he who goes down into the abyss,
to see his soul laid bare.
I am he who climbs the mountain. Why?
Because it is there.
I am he who searches for

knowledge,
in whatever place obscure.
I am he who follows his WILL,
nothing less or nothing more.

Avis H. Holt
ALONE
As I wander all alone
through places he held dear
I pause...and listen
breathlessly
as it seems to me

I hear his name whispered
oh so softly
by the gently sighing wind
As it murmurs through the
treetops and with my
thoughts does blend.

Not only does his name seem
present in the pregnant air
His familiar voice and
laughter
also linger there.

I feel I must call to him
when suddenly I know-
If I should call
he could not answer
Oh God, I miss him so!

Doris Birmingham
WE THREE—ME
A *grandmother's* happiest day
might be
When she watches the parade
with her little boy of 3-

And sees those eyes light up as
he'll say
"I saw Santa Claus today."
A *mother's* happiest night may
be

When we have a sitter and it's
just she and me,
Then we're off for a night on the
town
Fun when dance partners just
won't let you sit down!
A *daughter's* happiest time
might be
When she visits "Mom", is
treated like company.
For Mom's retired and there I'll
be
Waited on hand and foot like
royalty.
But my *greatest* joy is when
We're all back together again.
I'm a grateful mother, daughter
and "Granny"
And wouldn't trade my life for
that of any!

Thelma C. Watlington
DID YOU THINK TO PRAISE YOUR SAVIOR
When you wake up in the
morning,
And the sun is shining bright;
Did you think to praise your
Savior,
Who has kept you through the
night.
Did you think of all the good
things
That He does both great and
small;
And to know that He still loves
us,
And protects us one and all.
Did you think of how He
suffered
As He died upon the Cross,
That our sins might be forgiven
And our souls may not be lost.
So let us now do all the good
things
That He has for us to do.
If we walk the straight and
narrow,
He will surely take us through.

Nancy Midgett Walker
THE REAL ME
She was deep within my inner
self,
In some dark corner of my mind,
Tucked beneath my heart of
hearts --
Yes, almost lost -- so hard to
find.
I'd heard her speak so many
times,
Heard her say, "Please set me
free!"
In that dark corner where she
lived
She couldn't breathe -- she
couldn't see.
Yet recently her voice grows
loud.
She moves about and won't be
still.
Rebelliously she shouts to me,
"I must be free! I must! I will!"
I say to her, "You're childish,
weak.
This path I'm walking, I must
walk.
I'll grit my teeth and walk along,
And will not listen when you
talk."
She stands erect and shouts to
me
In tones I've never heard before,
"I'm part of you -- now set me
free,
Or you'll be sad forever more!"

Cecilia Rudolf
THE POSSESSION OF A DREAM
With open arms, my heart is
longing,
Reaching way into the spheres
Reaching for the "Harmony of
Soul"
That spreads with calm
And fills our hearts with that
superb warmth of emotion
Such essence, which moves our
spirits
Silently way across the
heavens.

But I feel imprisoned on this
plateau called earth.
So, impressed I'm contemplating
To reach the immense, the
vastness of sky
And tomorrow I'm hoping -- I'll
fly.

I balance my anchor and by the
tug of the sun
Into the distance my spirit
orbits the dimensions
And I feel impelled to drive on
and loosen my harness
Such that controls my
innermost of heart.

But way in the cosmos, the
perspective of my galaxy
clusters
Like the possession of a dream.
New born of such matter --
superb a creation
—A FANTASY OF MY ESTEEM!!

William G. Zdanis
LIFE TURNED AROUND FOR JOE
Because he was small for his
age,
They called him Little Joe.
Some called him Shorty, Runt
and Shrimp,
Such names did hurt him so.
How he did envy bigger boys.
Felt bad about his size.
He'd often cry himself to sleep.
Himself he did despise.
And then one day this tallish
girl

Looked twice as Joe passed by.
She smiled at him, He dared
smile back,

Then felt tall as the sky.
And soon he knew he was in
love
With tall and pretty Flo
And when she said she loved
him too,

Life turned around for Joe.
This world has many more like
Joe.

Disgruntled with their size.
It's what's inside of you that
counts.

This, they should realize.

William G. Zdanis
WE REMEMBER, LORI
I can't forget her lovely face,
That smile, her sweet "hello".
Why did you take her from us,
Lord?
You knew we loved her so.
Yet, often I do think of her.
So sweet, so full of love.
Most precious is a loving child.
We miss her, Lord above.
A little flower Lori was
In bloom so short a while.
And when 'He' called, she came
to 'Him'
She left us with a smile.
You always have your reasons,
Lord,
For all the things you do.
You must have needed angels,
Lord.
Now Lori's there with you.

Faith A. Holmberg
JOGGERS DELIGHT
My friend, out jogging, I did see
And said to myself,
I can do that just as well as he.
He looked so cute—in his red
jogging suit
Don't know which was more co-
ordinated. . .
His suit or his feet.
But anyway, jogging looked real
neat.
So to the store I did go
Bought a sweat-suit, shoes, and
hat
Went home and said, "I'm going
to try that.
If it's good for him it's good
for me
And a jogger I became, as you'll
soon see.
I jogged a block and knees gave
out
Heart pumped like a drum, beat,
beat, beat;
I said to myself, "This ain't
so neat!
But the next day I was out there
again
And I kept at it day after day
Until jogging and me agreed,
this is the way.
Now after seven months, I run
pretty good
But, of course, I'm sure—not
just as I should.
But, alas, who cares how my
feet do trod
I just keep picking them up
And putting them down again
on the sod.
A mile and a half I can finally
go
And at the end—is my face
aglow. . .
But the joy of running—
The feel of the wind, the smells
in the air
All add to the joy that will
keep me out there.
And, so I have a friend to
thank. . .
Not knowing when he ran that
day
It would help a friend along the
way.

Sheri Kretschman
THE BOTTLE
A bottle held by a shaky hand,
His grip began to wane.
The bottle slipped and hit the
ground;
A million pieces strayed.
Each piece a part of his own life;
they flashed before his eyes.
A straying tear began to roll,
so gently down beside.
His body was no more his own;
commanded by a force.
His every move and every
thought;
were guided on a course.
To Laugh,
To Cry,
To Live,
To Love;
To go on with his life.
To keep from self-destruction...
was to be his only strife.
Long ago...a prosperous man;
held high upon a throne.
A man who once held all

respect,
in his community and home.
Until one day...
the pressures built;
A point too hard to hold.
A dwindling force took over then;
his life began to fold.
From then the once good-looking man;
suddenly grew old.
Ten years they seemed to go as one;
"THE BOTTLE" took it's toll.

Donna Jill Wilson
SWEET SERENITY
There's so little time left for us to love,
But it's truly what we all need more of.
It seems so hard to let ourselves go,
So much harder still to let our feelings show.
God gave us love to share one and all,
But we're so afraid to let ourselves fall.
Afraid of being hurt but what's sadder still,
Is the fact we don't show what we feel.
Love is the answer to all our fears,
Let Him in your heart to dry the tears.
Follow the path to which your heart leads,
And God will surely fulfill all your needs.
Give in to your soul and answer it's call,
Break down the barriers, tear down the wall.
Open your heart and set yourself free,
Only then can you find Sweet Serenity.

Thomas J. Bready
PRISONER OF HOPE
I didn't care, there were no hopes,
There I was, for the undone.
Push or shove, you never can tell,
They may come, but they never go.
And all the strangers try, but never realize that,
You too have problems, but you never let them know.
Most dream daily, and most just don't do anything.

Prayers are seldom, but when heard, they reflect anger among most.
So I, try the least to, at least not to be heard.
It's no use to try anymore.
Clank, it's shut again. Bye cellar.

Steve Spaugh
AN ACT OF LOVE
(a sonnet) To Mia Angelica
I gave not only a human heart,
Nor all or part of a life belonging
To one who lingers, oft' to depart
Without due regard for love still longing.
I gave you the sum of infinity
Wrapped in the soul of a child.
A manchild who breathed from eternity
With love yet both gentle and wild.
Your need and reply twain a a heav'n bequeathed,
Youthful, urgent, but ensconced in propriety.
Your wish and its act birthed a soul unsheathed,
Dazzling with passion, yet possessed in sobriety.
You chose the path to nurture divinity,
And thus shall our lives be strewn with sublimity.

Rose Marie (Bennett, Fiske) Williamsen
A DAUGHTERS PRAYER
Bless me "Willetta",
My mother so dear:
Speak to me always-
Making me hear.
Help me "Thy Fruit",
Of this darkened earth:
To relish for always -
My memories from birth.
Extend me "Your Hand",
Down lifes' lonely path:
Help me to always -
Forget mine own wrath.
Forgive me "Your Daughter",
Each careless mistake:
Teaching me always -
My lifes' blessed fate.
Remember me "Mother",
My life ever more:
Guiding me always-
To Heavens' front door.

Bradley Eugene Lehn
IN THE MANNER OF CHAUCER
Twenty-three men in a bar sat full of ale
when suddenly one let out a bellowing wail,
a deep-seated laugh as out of a cave,
cold as the wind on a winter's eve save
for a familiar, soft tone in its sound,
and I, in a moment, quickly turning around,
caught sight of a stocky man betook by rage,
trapped by the spirits inside, mellowed with age.
His eyes flashed as though in a spell,
behind which raged the fires of Hell;
and landing upon me, though for a glance,
made me want to run, though I had not the chance
for he came towards me, immense his stride.
In moments, the stranger was by my side.
Staring at me blindly from the cloak within
as his face cracked in an unholy grin.
"A wager, my friend," his breath reeking;
my body failing with each word he was speaking.
Each syllable piercing me as though a knife
plunged deep within to end my life.
I shook and rattled with each vowel he spoke;
my eyes ever-fixed upon his lifeless black cloak
which loosely upon his frame hung
reeking endlessly of foul-smelling dung.
"What is wrong, my friend? Why such a dither?
Follow me to this table hither.
There shall we compete, me against you,
alone. A wager, I say, must be made, 'tis true.
This contest cannot end in a draw.
The wager, my friend, is winner take all
and the loser must pay his due. Call
my bluff, if you wish, but I shall not fall!"
Upon completion, an unpropitious smile spread across his face,
showing two rows of teeth, evenly spaced,
battered by smoke, drowned by beers,
yellow with neglect, decayed with the years.
I proceeded towards him totally uneasy;
my brow dripping with sweat, my stomach queasy.
My heart was pounding. My fear was growing,
ever-mounting; never knowing
from what country this stranger came;
why he was here, what was his name.
I was drawn ever-closer by some unseen might
reaching into my brain, picking it clean, squeezing it tight,
until I could not stand the pressure any longer.
The urge within me growing stronger
to accept this challenge, though strange it may be.
Before this company I must protect my integrity
no matter the price, come what will.
His hollow laugh sending a chill
down my spine, a sickening revolt,
as though sent by Thor, god of thunder and bolt,
causing me to falter and weaken my knees.
I could fight no longer. I must do as he please,
unknowing if he was one to cheat,
but, I could not forfeit and accept defeat.
Setting before him, ready to faint,
as he reached forth his hand, bony and taint,
grasping my fingers in his, unbreakably locked,
and I sitting up straight as some proud cock,
gripping his hand, a deathly clench,
trapped as a bolt in a wrench,
cutting off my circulation, turning my hand blue;
each stuck together, as though by glue.
Our hands grew taunt, the contest started.
From here on we were not to be parted.
My God on high! What have I done?
I should have thought over the wager before we had begun,
but, I had to play, no matter the cost.
And now, as the match is nearly lost,
I find I am not playing for some mere trifle or trinket.
I must win! I cannot forfeit!
For if I should. . .I would lose my life.

Lloyd Leo Offutt
A BABY
A Baby is a smile of God,
The bundle of pure mirth.
A Sacred, little source of joy,
That's sent to us;
While we're upon this Earth.
From the moment of it's arrival,
Everything seems so very neat.
From it's tiny little laughter,
Cries, and Oh', How sweet?;
It makes our lives, so happily complete.
This is a form of God's great Love,
To show us, that He Cares.
He, would like us in His Home Above,
So, Friends why don't We?; meet Him There.
JESUS IS FIRST

Robin Foster Rice
UNTITLED
We spent a lot of money.
Seen the mountains to be,
Through the mirrors key.
Crossed the Rockies,
On through Montana's Great Plains,
To the vast deep blue sea.
Under a sunny sky, and a little rain,
These old wheels beneath me,
Have cautiously taken us there,
With thousands of miles, between me and free,
I have not a care.
Only to lock away, those memories,
With the key behind the door.
To be only opened from the inside,
To leave me restless evermore.
To stay on a neverending ride,
Standing with my back to the front of the door.
Still, my inspiration is a bird,
That is soaring and free.
Speaking not a word,

The way it was meant to be.
You have only to listen and feel,
To find your way home,
To what is true and real,
To what made the oceans foam,
To what gave me my soul,
And my life to breathe.
And to keep me from that dark
hole,
My only quest is to take heed.

Judith Helen Brown

IF

I'm caught in the
before-spring
when
winter-wedged-warm
gnaws at tree buds.
If sleep-elusive nights
were calmer
and valentine-moons
did not sail the clouds,
Sleeplessness would not trail
me like a ghost
And bend reason out of shape.

Evelyn Fuller Phelps

VIEW FROM THE TOP

Looking out my attic window,
I can see the tops of trees
And squirrels scurrying along
The wires doing their thing.
It's fun to watch the tops
Of automobiles going single file
Back and forth...and wondering
What the people inside are
thinking.
Where are they all going
In such a hurry, anyway?
The kid on the bicycle is
Working so hard at having fun.
Sometimes, it almost seems to
me,
Perched here, high above it all,
That, maybe, this is what it is
like
To be God.

Sharon Miles

SUNRISE

As I wake out of a dream of
confusion, I see the sunrise.
Believing that the sun is mine I
race the time to see the
sunshine of the sunrise in my
face, the yellowish gold ball
with dignity and grace.
Sunrise, sunrise I believe in you
and your dignity is so true,
SUNRISE.

Floy Butler

ESCAPE:

Have I displaced
my phantom self
as i treked
thru the blazing
diamond fields; or
have the prisms
and weightless shades
just eroded my
sight; and in
my burning flight
left me faultering
in the vortex?

Sandra A. Myers

WHAT IS LIFE?

How far we have come
But how little we know,
Of the mysteries of life
And for some want to show.
From the time we are born...
To the time we must die,
For how little we learn...
In the wink of an eye.
Like the hush of the nite!
Still the beat of the heart!
We come and we live
Till the time we must part.
How far we have come
But how little we know,
Of the mysteries of life
And some will never show.

Diedra Davis

EYES OF THE WORLD

A child-
A mystical wonder,
A magnificent gift,
A possession of love,
A beginning of a new creation,
full of questions
unanswered by man;
full of answers unwanted
by man;
Loyal and tender,
Forgiving and understanding,
Caring and admiring,
for what is a child,
but a child?
A child.
our hope for the future-
maybe...

Sandra Morgan

TO SPECIAL ONES ON A SPECIAL DAY

I like to sit down and express
my feelings in a special way
by setting aside some fleeting
moments to share a holiday.
Love has so many faces
displayed in so many places.
It is a volcano bursting with a
shower of happiness.
It is expressed through giving,
sharing, caring, and
meaningful success.
In February it's hard to visualize
beautiful violet flowers
especially after you've been
shoveling snow for hours.
But even though the snow is
cold,
It is so esthetic and sparkles
like gold.
The shimmering rays of the sun
glisten on the surface of
whiteness,
and when one's inside, he can
fantasize about its lovely
brightness,
The ice provides a slippery
covering for the naked street
so the children can slide,
hopefully on their feet.
The tall trees and stubby bushes
glisten with icy diamonds
after a freezing rain,
The scenery is so delightful;
how can Mr. Edison have the
nerve
to complain?
The moon throws a mysterious
glow in the night,
to enhance the shimmering
eerie sight.
One important duty of winter is
to pave the way for Spring
by defrosting the sun's rays and
encouraging the robins to
sing.
The expression of love occurs
anytime and in all seasons.
It may be a flicker or a flame
but it occurs for many
reasons.
It is more fun to make plans and
hold hands that are not
covered with gloves.
While walking down paths that
have shady trees that are
carrying doves.
Friendship is an internalized
external emotion
which is shared by those with
complete devotion.
It grows with each year of time,
remembering the past that's left
behind.
May you have a happy day
and enjoy it in a delightful way.

Leonard George Underwood

THIS THING CALLED FALL

Once again the leaves of fall
have come to call.
Oh carry me away to the beauty
of it all.
The maple trees blowing in the
breeze,
The sugar trees and their
golden leaves;
The reds. the browns, the shades
of green:
The orange, the purple and all
the shades in between.
The golds, the pinks, and even
lavender I think.
So many colors, I can't find
word to explain;
But yet it's so hard to try to
refrain,
From speaking of autumn and
the leaves that must fall;
All brought about by God in his
reign.
To appease my appetite in
autumn, it's really quite clear;
I must walk through the forests
where the beauty is near.
Come listen with me where the
quietness is so still;
From the floor of the valley to
the top of the hill.
Walk through the forests with
me and explore this splendor
from
God's open door.
Take time to see it and don't be
hasty to flee it.
Pick a leaf and touch a flower,
it will all be over in an hour.
Take time to smell the fragrance
of it all;
It's only here for a moment;
this thing called fall.

Chris Lyons

LOVE STATION

Many times I thought I was in
love.
Now I am older and mature.
The hurt of all those "lost loves"
makes no difference to me.
For I have found the true love I
have long been searching for.
This I have found in you.
You are a very special person.
You laugh with me.
You cry with me.
You talk with me.
Most of all, you love with me.
If I ever hurt or offend you in
any way, please tell me.
I will make it up to you in any
way I can.
If we are apart and you get
lonely or scared,
Call me.
I owe my service to you 24
hours a day.
Every hour I am open to you.
From the morning and all
through the night.
Stop in when your love is
running on empty.
The price of love is high,
But I will fill you up for free.

Elsie S. Finnen

TO A SPIDER

Small fount of silk
Trimming my garden bush
With delicate laces
Tinselly, glittering light.

Knit, purl, knit
Your intricate designs.
Knit, purl, knit
Brushed wool wraps for your
babies.

Karen Jean Minthorne

MOTHER?!

Young girl
Daughter
Young man
Friend
Alone
Door
Closed
Lights
Out
Corruption
My
Baby
Being
Seduced

Kathy Blackwell

SAD MOVIES

I feel as if we are loving
on borrowed time
as though we are headed
for the end of a sad story
sometime far away
-you see,
the script has already been
written.
And though we've seen this
picture a dozen times before
each time I hope the ending
will somehow be different
yet, each time
the end remains the same
and sad movies
always make me cry...

Mrs. Hattie E. Hobbs

OUR TODAYS

Tomorrow today will be
yesterday,
And tomorrow will be today.
The hopes of all our beings
That shape our destiny.
Of our todays do be careful,
Lest to us they bring sorrow.
For the living of our todays
Reflect yesterday on tomorrow.
As we would our yesterdays be
Our todays had we lived,
There would be no yesterday
shadows
Our hopes of tomorrow to dim.

Mrs. Grace Marseglia
GRANDCHILDREN'S STORY TO GRANDMA
Grandma we will tell you a story.
Listen to us.
It is all about God
Who loves us very much.
He gave us our health
So we could play.
It is a mystery how God makes us grow,
and have children of our own,
To watch them grow and be on their own.
We thank God for giving us
A wonderful Mom and Dad
For them to have us.
If it wasn't for Grandma and Grandpap
We wouldn't have a Mom.
So, bless their little hearts.

Belinda Stephens
MEMORIES
The memories of time gone by
Which makes a person want to cry
Memories of good times everyone had
Sometimes thinking of them makes me sad
The future is what I'm now looking for
The mysteries and wonders through the door
Because someday I'll look through the trees
And find nothing but these memories

Mary D. Allen
A CRY IN THE NIGHT
A heart cries out in the deep of night,
For someone to love, and care --
To care if he lives or dies alone,
Or suffers in dark despair.
What had gone wrong in that dear ones life?
Had I failed to give him a hand;-
Failed to show him the love, the will of God,
That leads to a better land?
How can I kneel down to God in prayer?
Give thanks for His love, and care--
When there's one of His children alone out there,
With no one his burdens to share.
Oh, God! have mercy upon my soul!
He knocked at my heart's door, and cried --
And I, in self interest, closed the door,
And left him outside to die.

James A. Seaman
DREAMS OF EXPRESSION
He spoke of freedom,
As entering a new world,
To become a silent warrior,
Knowing the values of all the universe.
For all he learned,
Became the melting pot
Of what he burned,
And could never restore.
Lifeless, limitless, lonely days,
Of enchantment and horror,
Filled his mind to the brink,
Of all his sorrowful realities.
Until one day he woke
To the sound of his own triumphs,
Never to underestimate
His dreams of expression.

Sharon E. Oaks
REMINISCENCE
When the flowers died
so did our love
but when the snow melts
and winter fades away
the flowers will again flourish
in the sunshine of spring
but our love will only be
memories
of moments that we shared
a remembrance that belongs
to me alone
for when you died
so did your love
and I alone
savor the beauty of our love
that longs to be reborn

Awlrtz Ztrlwa
(Walter L.R. Townsend)
ILLEGITIMATE
Did u know
some of us BLACKFOLKS
never even made
momma's-baby & daddy's-may-b
cause it's true
momma & daddy
was illegitimate 2
did u know
did u know
like father
like momma
like daughter
nature legallized it
cause it's true
BLACKPEOPLE
r illegitimate 2
did u know
did u know
n a land-that's illegitimate
a land-bleached-of-whiteness
stolen from another-race
cause it's true
ask BLACKPEOPLE
we were stolen 2
did u know
did u know
did u?

Suzanne Wood
WEATHERING THE STORM
The unleashed fury from a stormy sky
Makes us long to hide where it's safe and dry.
The chilling showers bring such dismay;
Shivering souls yearn to run away.
Discord often buffets our life,
Testing our strength with relentless strife.
Try though we might to hold on,
Our grip relaxes when hope seems gone.
Bruised and battered, our pain is profound.
Hopes splatter like rain on concrete ground.
We try so hard, yet it happens this way;
It's just not fair, we mournfully say.
Good can be hidden in that which is bad
And grow to replace what once was so sad.
But, watered with bile from pains we bemoan,
The good soon withers, and we are alone.
Lifeblood can't flow through ice-filled veins,
Frozen by dwelling on sorrow and pain.
By accepting the will of our Father above,
We help them to warm and flow with His love.
The chilled heart warms as we start to pray.
Sorrow and pain soon melt away,
Leaving inner strength and peace of mind,
God's umbrella for all mankind.
Under the blanket of His loving care,
Snug and safe, we should linger there,
Finding courage to face each woe,
For woe builds character and helps us grow.

Robert F. Karper
JOURNEY
Weary of patience and living concerns
I go to the place where peace returns.
Where a valley waits 'neath heaven's eye,
Hugging earth, smiling high.
Where sun and moon of lofy power
Descend and creep to reach each flower.
Where trees in congregation stand,
Hand in hand going down the land.
Haze and mist, in comfy robes,
Curls together all of those,
Touches upon their righteous will,
Warms the bending, praying hills.
Where ribbons a river, wrapping its way,
Binding its presence to the gift of day.
And mirrors oh such unity
As plies upon mans' reverie.
Here is creation's heritage,
Joy bestowed ridge to ridge.
Among these noble, kneeling walls
All selfish wants hear Judas calls.
Truth provides a forward path,
No echoing footfalls speak of wrath.
Here time requests etheral space.
Dawn and sunset adding grace,
To hold the stars, the mountain clouds,
To humble all my prideful shrouds.
Here beauty that all seasons share
Humanity breathes as equal heir.
Here the worlds great entities merge,
March and play their silent dirge.
Here I journey with reverent throb,
Journey along and wait for God.

Mary Lynch Kelsey
DEAR GOD, WHAT THINGS YOU DO!
Dear God, what things You do:
You paint Your sky a multi-varied hue,
Then position it precisely to command our view;
Your sun with warmth and strength You imbue,
Then challenge it with winds and rains You accrue;
You tint Your grass all shades of green and blue -
A creature-trod carpet, each day new;
You delight us with every flower You grew -
You soar our souls with each bird You flew!
You grant us sorrow, to turn us to You -
But You give joys, to share, too;
You bestow friends, a faithful crew -
And You allow enemies, always a few.
You realize for us our rarest dream true -
Our dream impossible, were You not the clue!
You bear with us, You carry us through -
You steal our hearts, the devil. You slew!
Dear God, what things You do!

Syd Warburton
THE SUN SHINES BLUE
The sun shines blue through windows grey
With pain on pane each outcast ray
On walls dark with shadows full
Of bleakish souls, scattered hulls,
Of crying spirits, love's own prey.
The sun shines blue on frozen ground
Not warming now each icy mound
Covered so with winter's cold
And frozen love, shattered moulds
Of dying hearts, love's unsound.
The sun shines blue on meadows dead
Not having life each blade unfed
By warmth now gone from chilled beams
Of radiance not, unspoiled schemes
To make one weep, love once tread.

The sun shines blue into the
glass
Not knowing why the wine doth
pass
By a heart chilled from a
nymph's lark
So bloodless now, frivolous tart
In flighty dance, love is crass.

Tysaun G. Latimore Jones
AND I HAVE A DREAM
And I have a dream
That one day I'll be
A child who has risen up to be
free
And I'll tell the world that I
once before
Lived right behind poverty's
door
But those days are over
There's no such a thing
Three bells for freedom and let
freedom ring!
There'll be a cry so loud, so
clear
That everyone in this world will
hear
Thunder will roar from out of
the skies
And only the good will
materialize
And I have a dream that they'll
stop all these wars
Because angels will come down
and rewrite these laws
There'll be no more murder and
no more crime
Because God will turn back the
hands of time
There'll be no more rich and no
more poor
No more hatred and no more
war
No racial injustice, no slavery
Everyone will walk proud and
free
No child abuse, no battered
wives
We all will live with decent
lives
There'll be a cry so loud, so
clear
Everyone in this world will hear
Thunder will roar from out of
the skies
And only the good will
materialize!

Sandy Gower Morgan
IT HURTS
A break, a change, a different
way of life.
The feeling of hurt like a
piercing knife.
But time goes by and heals all
sores.
And life goes on like swinging
doors.
Our memories are there to turn
on when-ever,
We feel so depressed, the storm
we'll weather.
But good memories are the best
of all,
For they bring joy thats
beautiful to recall.
A break, a change, a different
way of life.
Oh why am I a divorced wife?
Why can't it be like it was
before?
Why did we have to close all
the doors?
Why did our love have to go in
the past?
Why in heavens name, didn't it
last?
A break, a change, a different
way of life.
But minus the roll of someones
wife.
Too sudden a change, for I was
in love,
But still not free like the
morning dove.
And time it'll take to straighten
my mind,
Its been so mixed-up with all
man-kind.
A break, a change, a different
way of life,
Time will tell if I become
someones wife.

Vestra LaVerne Ash
LOVE
I loved You
Willingly, Freely, *Completely.*
No questions asked, no answers
needed, No Strings Attached.
Us. United yet D i v i d e d.
Carefree. Happy.
We talked: teasing, flirting...
serious, nonsense
Together as one yet separate
Equals yet dependent.
When did it change? When did
Roles set in?
meekness.
Dominance.
You talked i listened.
You Demanded i understood.
You Needed i gave.
i talked you listened.
I Suggested. You followed.
You Implied. i responded.
We changed.
We grew together.
We grew a p a r t.
Roles Played. Confusion Felt.
Uncertainty...Complications...
and now... We Were.

Virginia Wimer Wrenn
TO MAKE A HOUSE A HOME
For all the many, many things
That make a house a home;
For faith that's ever firm and
strong;
For love so kind and true;
And for everything that's pure.
For justice, weighed and
balanced;
For truth that lights a star;
It takes all these and then
some more
To make a house a home.
It takes a husband and a wife;
A father and a mother;
It takes a cook; it takes a maid;
And one to bake and sew.
It needs a teacher and a nurse;
And time to wash and iron.
Homemakers do all these it's
true;
Yet, it takes some little ones
To make a house a home.
It takes a lot of scattered toys
And battered pans upon the
floor;
With broken ones to mend.
It takes just lots and lots of
kisses
For curing cuts and bumps;
It takes a lot of fingerprints
And of markings on the wall;
For it takes a house that's lived
in
To make a house a home.
It takes so many, many patience;
And a lot of kindness too;
A lot of loyalty all wrapped with
loving care.
It takes a lot of planning
And of marking time as well.
It takes a lot of give and take;
And smiles that shine through
tears.
It takes a lot of God, of love and
prayer
To make a house a home.
I often think of other jobs
And things I'd like to do;
Of places I would like to go;
Or other people be;
Yet, when I have a little time
To sit and ponder dreams;
I thank dear God with grateful
heart;
That He chose for me the one
To make a house a home.

Louis Hoyt DeMers
DEATH WISH
A day once gone is recalled to
boast
Of pleasures known,
And then the gosts
Release their hold on hidden
hosts,
To leave behind the ash and
bone.
I pace the floor, as if to say
I know you're there,
And there's a way
To destroy the dirge blind fate
replays
For ears so deaf beyond repair.
A toast to Self? Bring on the
wine!
No soul can see
The subtle signs
That demagogues will always
pine
For none to buy or sell my plea.
I drink to few, but perhaps it's
best
To love them all
And not detest
The mournful cries of all the
rest,
Who'd steal my womb and
watch me fall.
My head grows numb, and
within the room
The air is light,
As though a tomb
Were forged from thoughts
predicting doom.
Before me looms the final night!
"Cui bono!" I cry, then awaiting
reply
The devil speaks
And offers lies
To a foolish mortal soon to die. .
For bone and ash is all he seeks!
A mist descends from days gone
past,
The blues. . . .The greys,
They're here at last.
The sun is blocked, but shadows
cast
By rays of light which pierce
the haze. . . .

Dennis F. Bivins
TWILIGHT
In twilight, gleaming spears
bounce upon the windows,
And then are suddenly gone as
another passer passes on.
Yet within those spears,
bouncing like eternity, is
comprehension.
Only comprehending eternity is
not as easy as one speaks of
it.
A spear may pass through space
forever, whatever
The mind will accept eternity as
forever, like one thinks of
space.
Each a never ending, never
dying, continuous flow,
With only a beginning, never an
ending.
The mind must think there is
an ending to this all
An ending to forever in space
could be our eternity,
But can the mind reach out that
far or is it really near?
Perhaps when one reaches their
eternity
That is the time of their
departure from this earthly
plane,
And another plane is reached,
thus the game begins again.
Perhaps the mind can never
comprehend where Eternity
Ends.

Christopher L. Smith
CHRISTMAS BEAUTY
Christmas Day is once again
here,
A perfect way to end the year.
The snow covers the earth all
around,
Delicate flakes float gently ever
so gentle to the ground.
Icicles dangle sparkling,
glistening bright;
All is covered with a soft sheet
of snowy white.
All is peace. All is still.
Save the cold night wind's
wintery chill.
Seldom is all left undisturbed as
now.
It's as if all creation had taken a
vow;
To rest and leave all alone
Until the sun's dawn is shown.
And then comes the first
twinkle of sunlight,
The dawn has come, people
burst into sight.
Snowmen are made, snowballs
are thrown,
The beauty is destroyed, the
silence is gone.

Lynda Williams Burretto
SEEKERS OF THE TRUTH
Sometimes tho we really try
To keep it all together,
It seems our life is merely a
breeze
And we a lonely feather.
Blowing here, to and fro,

And seeking that which is better,
Only to find, when we hit the ground,
Another breeze A'blowing,
And our loneliness still flowing!
So we, caught up in the wind,
The painful thing is knowing,
That we the seekers of the truth
Will probably die never showing,
All that we have to give,
Is Love and Truth,
And no one ever knowing!

Tia Vellani

WAVES

They dashed themselves against the rocks
And curled to reach the sky,
Rushing onward still, and wild,
They stretched up very high.
And then they broke with hollow booms,
And savage wrath unfurled,
With fury great and strength renewed
Upon the turf were hurled.
Their vitals spilled upon the shore,
Their power dwindling,
Reaching, licking, lapping forth
And laughing like a king.
And then they were pulled back beneath
The seething, foaming broth.
They vanished then, right out of sight
Within the boiling froth.
Then, they again began to grow
And swell and surge and pour
Only to go through again
The process of before.

Elaine K. Soetaert

THE MIGHTY CRY

A mighty cry fills the night,
Someone is hurt or trembling with fright.
I sit and ask myself "who?"
Oh, if only a person knew what to do!
It could be a teenager who was high,
Wanting to be free, he decided to fly.
Or maybe a child who is hungry and cold,
Needing a mother's love to hold.
Or, perhaps a poor man out in the street,
lacking money to cover his feet.
Could it be a man who has lost his wife,
Feeling there's no meaning left to life?
That mighty cry filling the night
Has strength that comes from need and fright
That mighty cry longs to be heard
For that cry has more meaning than any word.

Mary K. Shuster

THEY ASK

They ask: What has happened to you, my dear,
Your hair has lost it's shimmer and sheen
The clock on the mantle has not ticked for long
-marking your hour's to preen
Oh, where are the ribbon's you wore in your hair
The trinket's that lovelied your throat?
Your garden lies fallow
The birdbath is dry
Oh, where is the lark's golden note?
Please question me not, let silence prevail
And each day be lost with the last
For the one that I loved, in secret of course, is gone
And my dreaming is past.

John W. Bryant

HOPE

We build our houses,
cities, nations, empires--
Complex, ornate, fragile
wisps of life.
Brick by brick,
stone by stone,
We transform our dreams
into realities.
We watch with joy
the growth of all our hopes,
Until humanity smothers them
in darkness
and they turn to dust.

Sylvia A. Collins

THE FOOTSTEP ON THE STAIR

When Night-time clothes the waning Day
In Her velvet, sequined gown,
And children, weary of their play,
Subside and settle down;
When fledglings nestle 'neath the wing of the watching Mother bird;
And the evening zephyrs waltz and sing,
While froglets' tune-time can be heard-
Cupped- hand to ear
At the door I wait
For vibrations of the air.
This welcome sound I contemplate
Is a footstep on the stair.

Juli Frank

DEBBIE

Little girl, beautiful girl,
with your glistening blue eyes
and your soft blond curls,
dance for me,
give me a song
to dry my eyes,
to guide me along the road of life, through the quiet times.
Dance out a song, let me call it mine.
Gracefully twirl-let your arms gently flow.
Let the happiness deep within you brightly glow.
Tap out your joys
with your delicate feet,
and my heart too,
shall dance to the beat.
Please, little girl,
give me this chance.
For magic lies within your dance.

Roger A. Willard

A THING

A thing is real when shared by all.
Enjoyment is big when people smile and show that they understand:
A child playing with blocks and getting in the way;
A ten-year-old always asking why:
A teenage youth going off and doing things on his own to show Mom and Dad that he's not young anymore,
The young married couple who are lost but try to prove that they can make it:
The middle ager who knows what's right for everyone else,
The elderly people who wish they were younger and could do things again;
An understanding smile is all that they need to let them know that you'll help them with their thing.
A simple gesture needed by all mankind.

Tom Payne

FATHER

You were my evening star
Always there for me to see
Memories that left their scar
When you put out to sea
Lasting days of sorrow
Seems to be my plight

Hurting with each tomorrow
Sadness for you at night
I pray you're in a special place
That I can find your trail
Again to see you face to face
When it's time for me to sail

Bill Woodrome

REVELATION

I walked through the tunnel of shadows last night --
Much to my surprise I saw a beautiful and peaceful sight.
The Shepherd was there to help ease my mind,
How could this pure Lamb be so gentle and kind?
His hand met with mine and put my mind to rest,
I haven't had this feeling since nuzzling my mother's breast.
My time wasn't quite at hand, I was told,
There are fates awaiting me to behold.
So turn I must and slowly depart,
Knowing for sure deep in my heart
That I would return through the tunnel some day,
And I have a Shepherd for to show me the way,
And with Him it is some day I will live.
This pure-hearted Lord -- how could he forgive?
For I am a sinner like men of the earth,
Have lived of the flesh and been cursed since my birth.

Victoria L. Collette

SEARCHING

. . .I am Birdie
caged not free.
Within a cup full of loneliness
I search for that tormented road
that
was for me to follow.
I am where I don't want to be,
suffering what I don't want to
suffer.
I search for the answer but
I become lost in a plastic world
of wooden dolls crashed
upon my skull.
Torture of dormant memories
burn those ends
leaving only their centers.
To neglect the pain of misery
seems
hopless.
Restless at night, I scream
To voiceless power of
succeeding,
To fight out of this cage.
I mutter when no one listens,
I cry when no one sees.
And I hide endlessly in that
dark corner.
Sorrow for my tears, I wept
as time eats me up.
The cost of struggling for my
spirit
to twist and to turn for
suvival's
wants to be
free.
The future time would speak of
what had to come, good or bad,
even if I were helplessly caged
or fighting free
All I had to do was
Fly
Against
The
Wind.

Mary L. Kano

TRIUMPH

Lord, why has this happened to me?
Is it to draw me closer to Thee
Or to cleanse and make me free?
For two months the pain I had.
And yet didn't feel too bad.
Mable said to the Doctor you'd better go
And not be reluctant to show.
So one Thursday eve at 10:00 o'clock
I thought my world was going to stop!
When within my breast I found a lump.
And, oh, how I wished I'd only been bumped.
So it was really time to the Doctor to go
And find out what there is to know.
So to Dr. Snyder's office I went;
It seemed as though there I was sent.
With a long needle he tried to aspirate
And he didn't even hesitate!
"Well, Mary," he said, "I don't know what's wrong,
But with you we'll have to follow along."
X-Rays to be taken were next in line
To help Dr. Snyder to find

The problem within the breast,
And, oh, then came the test!
Everything came as such a shock
I thought my world was going to stop.
This surely couldn't be happening to me!
But he said we'll have to wait and see.
So into the hospital I had to go
And how I hated this you know!
Rebecca came down to stay by my side
And with Mable also to abide.
Early Monday morn Nadine came to prep
And asked me if I had slept.
Before I knew it was time to go
And find out what bothered me so.
I was so grateful as could be
For the Lord promised I'll abide with thee.
I can do all things through Christ who strengthens me.
Father, that's why I always flee to Thee.
Trials and tribulations often come our way
And would try us to sway.
Back to my room after surgery was brought
And, oh, how the nurses sought
To make me as comfortable as could be.
No, I said, this can't be me!
When one gets awake and finds your breast gone
Then everything's a brand new song.
Friends were so precious and dear
And were at times very near.
Their comforting words they would give to me,
And say, "Hey, we'll stick with thee."
Tears from out eyes would often flow
For to me it was such a blow.
Dr. Snyder in the morning we were always glad to see
For he would try to assure me.
He said, "Everything will be all right.
And your hospital stay will soon be out of sight."
Many times mixed feelings we had
And there were times we were sad.
Then Alice and Mable would cheer me
And say, "Hey, we'll stick with thee."
So without the Lord we'd never come through
For often times we were blue.
Your promises were always there
And Your love with us shared.
Sometimes, Lord, it's hard to believe
All the things in life we receive.
But You've promised always with us to abide
And Your Presence I could feel at my side.
So each day the halls we walked
And with other patients we talked.
It helped so much them to cheer
And keep us from getting drear.
Many new friends we made along the way
And I'm sure friends they'll always stay.
Flowers and cards started coming in
And you'd wonder how many they'd bring.
There were days when the going was rough,
Even though we thought we were tough.
So thank you Lord for this experience to me
And may it have brought me much closer to Thee.

Sarah Harris Levy
THE SIGN OF THE CROSS
Behind the Cross
Blank Spaces,
Before the Cross
Living Faces,
Beneath the Cross
Submission, Graces.
The Burned Cross
Life, Jesus walks again,
The Melted Cross
Death, truth drawing nigh all pain,
The True Cross
Resurrection, Ashes of truth remain.

Patricia Tauterouff Szymaniak
GRANDMA'S BRASS BED
Gleaming with a beauty so rare;
As the silver gray
in her hair.
Shining with a rustic
charm and grace;
As the sparkle in her eyes,
and smile upon her gentle face.
Although faded is the luster;
The brilliance shall
live on forever.

Mick K. Smith
MY HAIR
My hair grows like icing overflowing.
Each day I know lightninged alleys in me.
Streaks of gray are pressing through like dawning.
Sampson warm me! Hair's like tensing to me.
Each day I seem more impressed by freedom.
Freedom is a deal with yourelf. Causes
Last like spirits overlooked by time...A
Scared man surrenders to society.
Some folks think I'm nuts to see this battle.
Hair's like temperate changes in the weather...
Seasoned, constant, restless as a rattle.
Lucky and aware to wear pure feather

Phillip Ryan
NOW AND THEN
We plan and fail as if no sense to it,
Everything is out of time and doesn't fit.
It appears so hopeless and never ending.
I wonder what message we are sending.
You call and I miss the rings,
It's not meant to be it seems.
I try to meet and you're not there,
No matter how we try to share.
I cannot see you and explain.
I know for you it's just the same.
To cry and not be heard or understood,
To hunger and fast is just no good.
But every day of fast lifts my appetite
And the anticipation makes me tight
Until that moment of rare indulgence
When I once again enjoy your presence.
We celebrate our reunion and meeting
By gorging ourselves with each others greeting
And feasting on every word and grin
Until we part and wait again.
Kendall Ryan I hear you crying.
Believe me—I keep on trying
To be a real dad and not make you sad.
If you help me—I know I can
Give of myself and still be a man
To be some true fun and not turn or run.
I need you Kendall and feel you so.
I hope you and I can share as we go
To each and every place & not miss a trace.
Of life and love and beauty and song
So you understand as we go along
How much I care and want to share. . .
With you all I have inside. . .
keeping too much for one to hide.
I'll just be here and you'll see.
I'll be there when you need me.

Brenda S. Ward
GROWING
I grew up on stick horses and make believe
Never facing reality because dreams were better;
Grasping to the thoughts my mind would conceive,
Never feeling the cold except for the winter
The warmth I had protected from deep within
The hidden reflections that were never really spoken;
Kept me wondering if I would ever love again,
But then you came into my life
You have restored the vitality I seldom consumed
And given me energies I never knew existed;
Like the rose petals that have bloomed,
I can spread my leaves around you
On windy days when my leaves may blow
Give me the strength to hold up the stems;
To give you the room to flourish and grow,
So that you may extend your beauty
As I come to you and plant the seed
Frightened almost, but eager like a child;
Hoping to become a part of your need,
Like the sun, the rain and the seasons.

Kathryn M. Diana
CABIN RETREAT
Our cabin rests against the ground,
Slumbering, waiting, ringed around
With rusting evergreens and moss.
Its doorstep creaks; we ease across
To musty air and darkened room.
We part the curtains, chasing gloom,
Sweep and dust and shake the rug,
And as we work, resist the tug
Of leaping fish and laughing loon,
But kindle, cook and talk, and soon
The simple things, the earth, the sky
Meld into peace with days gone by.

Mona Roush
MY CHILD
My Child, how hard it must be
At this age of puberty;
So anxious for womanhood
Without pain, if only you could.
The latest fashions for your teens
Are put aside in favor of jeans;
Somewhere to go, day after day,
Time for homework - more time for play.
When seen with tear filled eyes
Be sure a friend has broken some ties,
The Mother who once dried your tears
Now cannot soothe your fears,
Acceptance in the crowd is your strongest ambition;
And this, my Child, is a teenage tradition.
After school what path will you hail --
One to your liking or you will fail!

Many decisions you will make alone
And trust each one will bring you home,
For soon a woman you will surely be;
With these teenage years a memory.

Agnes M. Poch
A TRUE FRIEND
Oh, doggie mine, please do not cry,
To school I must be going,
Soon I'll be back, my little pal
And we will have the rest of the day together.
Oh, doggie mine, you are my true friend,
You do not lie or tell when things go wrong,
Just silently wait, my pal, my friend.
Oh, doggie mine, comrade in arms,
Many places together we have been,
In the jungles deep, where wild creatures of danger creep.
Over acres of fields and deserts we have roamed,
Hunted dangerous things a long ways from home.
Oh, doggie mine, you have seen me cry,
My heart filled with sorrow,
You have seen me laugh and sing
And run and jump, like today was all tomorrows,
My little pal, my true friend,
It is time for me to say Good-night till tomorrow,
Sleep well my little pal, true friend,
Comrade of all my tomorrows.

Kim Christensen
MY FRIEND
My friend is someone who is always there whenever I may need a friend.
She will stick around forever, from the very beginning to the very end.
There will always be some good times, but there will also be some bad,
And whenever we are faced with distress, we remember the good times we've had.
My friend is the person that I can lean on just when I need her the most.
If I were old enough to drink, to show my sincerity, I would propose a toast.
My friend is able to forgive almost anything bad I've ever done or said,
And in times of trouble and fear, my friend tells me with courage I must look ahead.
I don't want people to take this the wrong way, but my friend has stolen my heart.
She's something else, the way she helps me with life and I know we'll never part.
My friend understands when I'm feeling low and I just have to be left alone.
Yet, she won't go out and leave me, she'll be home waiting for my call on the phone.
When there might be a brilliant idea or two floating around in my head,
She is always willing to listen to them, even if it means maybe getting out of bed.
When everyone is out of town, I'm all alone and I need to talk to someone,
Her services are only a phone call away and then my problem becomes a minor one.
My friend does many good deeds without telling the whole world about it.
Not to say she's quiet, 'cause when we're out having fun, she's full of charm and wit.
While I'm gone to school, or away for a visit, far away in a different city,
It's nice to know when I come back home there's someone waiting just for me.
Sure, time will heal many wounds, but there are some things only one person can mend,
And I'm really glad God gave all his good children a person we can call a friend.

John Anderson Lake
THE OLD HOMEPLACE
It's gone now...a cottonfield in its place.
Just the hill and the big tree, the only trace
Of the joyful, happy times of yesterday.
The peace, quiet and laughter all taken away.
No more rises the smell of blackberry pie.
Nor of home-grown chicken just begun to fry.
Neither the good hunger that you felt then.
Will it ever be the same again?
Ain't no great fireplace with crooked poke.
No fading embers to stare in when you awoke
In the hushed sounds of the country night
To hear the whip-or-will and owl in flight.
But it's still there you see.
In the mind's eye, around the big tree
The old homeplace stands as ever.
And will be there, forever and forever.

Denise L. Baker
I WISH I WERE...
I wish I were a robin in a tree that stood so high.
I would soar through the air and watch the clouds go by.
I wish I were a daisy, a violet or a rose.
I would bring much admiration, and for the photographer I'd pose.
I wish I were a shining star, in the sky's most darkest night.
I would be the smallest; yet shed the brightest light.
I wish I were an ocean, a river, or a lake.
I'd have so many visitors and friends in whom I'd make.
I wish I were a rainbow, beaming brightly after,
A rain which showered the land with happiness and laughter.
I wish I were a butterfly with wings of many colors.
More graceful, more delicate, prettier than all the others.
I wish I were a scientist, with a cure for every disease.
From all the pain and worry, life would be a breeze.
I wish I were a movie star with talents of so many.
Singing, dancing, and performing; if to mention any.
I wish I were so many things; these things I wish a lot.
Why can't I settle for who I am, and forget the things I'm not?

Henry F. Stecker
DREAM—SCAPE
Pygmalion his Galatea made,
A lady beautiful as he could dream;
He loved the dream he fashioned till 'twould seem
His mind's own fantasies were where he stayed.
And, then, because he loved the dream he's wrought,
The mythic gods gave Galatea life
And destined her to be his loving wife:
Fulfillment to each longing that he sought.
Millenia have passed since that sweet myth!
And only children think that dreams come true!
In all my lonely life I've had no view
Of lovely someone whom I could be with.
The Galatea of my writing's heart
Has never known the breath of life to start
A romance which love's longing may impart.

Chris Lambert
STONE ANGEL
An angel fell from upward sky, over was his rest
He was off to start his mission, off to start his quest.
Being a messenger angel, he was to spread the gospel word.
He was going to tell the world all the things that he had heard.
But no sooner had he flown off than he fell with sickening thud.
The sight of something beautiful sent him sprawling in the mud.
For although he is an angel, he used to be a man.
He used to be so human, as human as you can.
Then suddenly his form turns to stone and sinks into the earth.
But sometimes these things happen, when angels lose their berth.
The sight he saw destroyed him, so beautiful was it.
That is what he, is thinking as he sinks past deepest pit.
Now now one knows his mission. The world would have to do.
But that's alright, he's happy, for the sight he saw was you.

Martha Brock
I'VE GOT THINGS TO DO!
Set the stars twinkling in the sky,
Whisper to the wind as it passes by,
Hold conversation with a butterfly,
I've got things to do.
Unravel the secrets of the rose,
Trace the shadow of the snows,
Learn what the mountains know.
I've got things to do.
Ignite the sparkle in an eye,
Read the meaning of a sigh,
Teach a baby bird to fly.
I've got things to do.
Feel the mighty eagle's pride,
Follow the dew drop's circling stride,
Conquer the ocean's flowing tide.
I've got things to do.
Cause the gentle breeze to blow.
Make the tiger lily grow,
And ride on summer's bright rainbow,
I've got things to do.

Eugenia Wilkinson
OCTOBER MAGIC
Nature dies, yet the spirit comes alive, pale of moon, dark of night.
A time for revelling, the harvest is gathered in; it was the ancients' delight.
Nature paints a pretty picture; the air is crisp, still, and vibrant.

An end to all things but a new beginning, culmination and fulfillment.
A closed door from the beyond suddenly swings open and anything is possible.
Ideas spring from nowhere; something surges from within and creativity is bountiful.
October, the eighth--wondrous of all months, misplaced though you be.
Are you what was or what is yet to come--remains a mystery to me!

Robert L. Singer
PERHAPS
Perhaps when I go to sleep tonight,
Per chance to dream of you,
Perhaps I can convey to you,
My feelings of love so true.

Perhaps you'll let me kiss your lips,
Your tender lips divine,
Your lips that bear the flavor of,
Some sweet exotic wine.
Perhaps you'll let me run my fingers,
Through your lovely hair,
To arouse the wondrous fragrance,
That seems to linger there.
Perhaps, my dear, you'll allow me to,
Caress your lovely charms,
As I hold you here so tenderly,
Within my loving arms.
Perhaps one day, my dearest one,
Those dreams will all come true,
Until that day, I'll be content
To sleep and dream of you.

Marilyn Sue Favors

THE GATES OF MY CONTENTMENT

As I look beyond the daylight
I dream of a hope
A hope to find the key that will
open the 'gates of my
contentment.
Like a cloud of dust shone
bright as day or cool waters
trickling softly in the night.
There are golden blades of
grass growing and a child's
intonation of pure delight
As life is to an epicurean
So, too, if I could be
constant with the real
nature of things
This is my envisage and my
desire and I will sing it
assiduously to others as they
join me,
following closely behind.

Gladys Funk

SPRING

I watch the battle outside my
window engrossed in reverie.
spring tries to fight against
winters might,
march is the referee.
though it's a cold and blustry
scene, I feel no pangs of fear,
I'm really not surprised at all
They fight thus every year.
the snow comes down, the sun
peeps through;
they do not hesitate,
Each makes his play without
delay, each vows he'll dominate.
They both are brave, assertive
Right from the beginning;
If you've never had a ringside
seat before
You can't tell who is winning.
I watch while feigning worry'
But never keep the score,
I can foretell the outcome;
Spring always won before.

Cynde Fields Smith

AS I LAY QUIETLY BY

As I lay quietly by the sea
she plays her mystical music
Beckoning me to enter
slowly, frightened, I
Make my way toward her
warm hands.
She grabs me teasingly,
rocking me to and fro
First knocking me down
then tugging at my body
and my soul
I have no strength
Her music fills my ears
and I begin to tremble
For I have felt the heartbeat
of a million years

Joyce M. Days

WHAT ARE FRIENDS FOR

What are friends for?
If we can't bare each others sorrow
What are friends for?
If we can't listen to others problems
What are friends for?
If we can't feel others sadness
What are friends for?
If we don't cheer along with others gladness
What are friends for?
If we can't be indeed
What are friends for?
When someone's in need
What are friends for?
If we can't help in many ways
What are friends for?
God knows the roll each of us plays
What are friends for?
If we can't hold each others hand
What are friends for?
When we try to make a stand
What are friends for?
The love of God will show
What are friends for?
When you meet a friend
God will let you know

Charmian Perttu

HUMMINGBIRD

At first it appears to be a
large black bumblebee
diving into the white angel trumpets
but, as it pauses, hovering,
its tail quivering fishlike
green and irridescent, it seems
to be a small minnow
suspended from an invisible line
Only when it flashes above me,
and the sun spangles it with light
do I see the pulsing red throat,
the blurr of frenetic wings,
the long sharp beak
A ruby-throated hummingbird
has found my yard attractive
it flits from orange day lily
to the purple bells,
and on to the angel trumpet
supping sumptuously on the
sweet nectar
Visions of parrots and
flamingoes,
bright shrieking cockatoos,
brilliant jungle birds in lush
tropical foliage
flit through my mind
the hummingbird seems alien in
northern Ohio
flamboyant amidst the plebian
sparrows,
the domestic robin, the common
grackle
I wonder at his temerity as he
hovers, a scant two feet
from me, his bill buried deeply
in an orange lily—
suddenly a flash of red, green
glittering fish tail flailing,
a whirring blurr of wings, and he
is gone.
My mother too has a
hummingbird
she tells me excitedly
hers drinks from the tigerlilies
alongside the house
she has hung a feeder on the old
maple
filled with sugar water
she too is thrilled with her
exotic little visitor
and it seems strange to share
this enthusiasm
for we are, and always have
been,
dissimilar
unknown to each other
too often, it seems our thoughts
flit past each other
like the hummingbird
each intent upon her own
purpose
too often we skirt each others'
sensitivities
afraid, perhaps to probe too
deeply
it is not a question of love,
or loyalities
it is perhaps a disparity in
purpose
a divergence of pathways
yet, for a moment we share the
same path
we linger to watch the
hummingbird drink from the
feeder
together we partake in the
beauty of this tiny bird
perhaps we will surprise
ourselves
in sharing fragments of beauty
graceful details like the
hummingbird
that has flashed briefly into
our lives
My mother has brought me a
hummingbird feeder
together we wait for the sudden
flash of red,
the whirr of wings
together we watch our delicate
visitor hover above the feeder
Then perch, and drink deeply.

Leah Houghton Kuhnert

SOMEBODY

I'm Somebody.
Who are you?

You are Somebody, too.
Then, there is a pair of us.
Let's Rejoice.

Barbara M. Willes

COLOR COUNTRY NIGHT

As the crimson sun sets slowly
in the west
A lone tree silhouetted against
the sky
Shows branches bare, that once
were full of leaves.
The crickets chirp and lonely
coyotes cry.
Flat rocks, like giant tables in
the sand,
Cast shadows with huge, dark
and eerie shapes.
Then comes the silence of the
lonely night,
And darkness falls like heavy
velvet drapes.

Virginia Losier

ONCE

Once,
With tree's among these hill's
This land was filled.
An early morning breeze would
proceed with ease
As the sun would slowly lift
Mother nature changed her
behavior
With a glitter and shine.
Water's met its destination,
without hesitation,
While birds patiently flew the
heaven's.
This land cried out with a silent
tear
But humanities restriction's
Caused total destinction.
Time then touched nature,
Wilted all her behavior
And extinct our sight's have
become.

Patricia J. Branco

NATURES WOVEN BEAUTY

In this world that nature
unfolds,
there is a magical beauty for us
to hold.
The smile of the sun on a
clear summers day,
and a crisp cool breeze, to chase
the clouds away.
The peaceful feeling we get, as
we look at the moon,
often makes us wonder, why it
must leave us so soon.
The beauty of the ocean, and
it's tranquil mystery,
as each wave that rolls up talks
with thee.
The graceful eagle, as she
takes to her flight,
mere words can't explain the
beauty of such a sight.
And yet, there are eyes, that
will c[illegible]se not to see,
such things that nature weaves,
in perfect harmony.
So let others close their eyes if
they might,
to those eyes, that see, every-
thing in nature, is oh so right.

Eva M. Roy

A MEMORY IN A BOOK

I was going through the pages of
an old book last night,
When there it was, in plain
sight,
A piece of paper, pressed, but
in good shape,
And on it was written, when I
was six, my height and my
weight.
This sweet little paper was tonic
to my eyes,
For I had saved it, although
forgotten, there it lies,
Between the pages of this book
that I opened last night,
I think I will leave it there, even
longer, out of the light.
For some day, my grandchildren
may see it,

They will say, "Look, this
belonged to Grandma, but it is
a tiny little bit,
That we know about her,
because now she is gone."
I am only dreaming, but I expect
it won't be too long.
Life goes by all too fast, but this
paper brings back memories,
Of when I was a child, beyond
the care of worries.
I am so glad that I found it
among the pages, deep within,
Because, I just now remembered,
this book belonged to my own
Grandma Austin.

Kathryn L. Andrews

DIVORCE

Deceiving
Inside feelings that leave you
Vengeful
Of
Rebuilding your life together.
Children being broken apart
Emotionally.

Bonnie L. Ochs

GOD'S SYMPHONY

Somewhere upon this great wide
earth,
There is a song of glory.
A song that lifts the hearts of
man,
And tells it's great love story.
A song that can't be compared
To words a man can speak.
Nature is this song's tune,
Quiet, peaceful and sweet.
Not a note out of space,
Not a tune off key.
Every sound has it's place
In God's Symphony.

Bettie J. Fix

DREAMS

Dreams that fill my sleepless
nights
Show only death and things that
fright
Here is a multi-colored world
Where hazy visions, one after
the other, are hurled
Dreams that become nightmares
before daybreak
Run, Run, through these deadly
dreams
Until, falling awake
Down, Down, into emptiness
Falling through miles of dark
endless space
Dreams of loves so long
forgotten
Over the years these dreams
have been trodden
By many a fool on loves tragic
journey
So let this ever maddening
world keep turning
Dreams of loved-ones dead and
gone
That make me feel so very all
alone
Their ghosts walk nightly
through my dreams
So they will, it forever more
seems

Virginia C. Conner

ORIOLES

Your mother brought and
showed you
How to drink the bright red
juice:
For she had come the spring
before,
Her mother too had shown the
way.
A simple garden where birds
could come,
Sharing seed and syrup sweet.
It's such a treat to watch them,
Their pale chartreuse darting
through the leaves.
Sometimes father brings the
boys,
Cleverly teaching the art of
drinking upside down;
Then shiny black and yellow
flashes in the trees.
Nor is it any chore to fill
their cup,
Though emptied many times a
day.
Pure happiness is feeling God's
Spirit in their song
And being just a little closer
to natures wondrous ways.

Gwendolyn Bowen

ONLY A SUNSET AWAY

Looking into the sunset
While tears stain my face
My heart is just aching
While you lie at rest
The mountains
behind the sunset
The little sweet bird
flys no more
the still water
runs deep
While you lie at rest
The brown eyes
that used to gleam
have now closed
against the sunlight
the heart
that held my key
can no longer open
But just rest
So now - here I am
hands folded
Sitting and thinking
on the Banks of Jordan
Watching--the fleet
of army ships pass
While You're Only
A Sunset Away!

Charles F. Sutton

REAL AND UNREAL

How unlike are memories
From vague visions of our
dreams:

Dim features just barely
glimpsed,

As we dash from scene to scene
Without a purpose or plan;

Only incidents impress—

Both pleasant and frightening:

Briefly dancing at a ball,

Caught in midst of warm
embrace,
When whole scene evaporates
And alone in empty room;
Poised to stamp on huge vicious
Spider, crawling furiously
Toward you from where he was
crouched
Malevolently in corner,
Then awakening quickly
Just before it reaches you.
Dreams dissolve in shadows as
Mad illusions of the mind,
While memories remain—most
Vivid and most recent—etched
Clearly on the mind in live
Frames of sight and sound and
smell:

As in days of childhood when
Awakening one morn to
Sweet surprise of frothy snow,
Transforming drab fence posts
to
Gleaming pillars, capping all
Supremely with shiny crowns.
Or viewing neighbor's hedge row
From small "north east" room
upstairs,
Glowing dark green from ripe
rays
Of sun in mid-afternoon.
One still sees last grandmother
Smiling sweetly as she speaks,
Seated comfortably on
Chair in mother's kitchen at
A family reunion.
Warm spring and summer days
my
Mother coaxed me from the bed
By saying night's long rain had
Left large ponds most suitable
For hours of joyous wading.
How comical the headlong
Scramble of young chickens
through
Small doors of brooder house
When opened in the morning!
In awkward adolescence
One remembers ecstasy
Of first prom with endearing
Blonde, enchancing music and
The many colored streamers.
Still fresh in view, the vibrant
Moment on vacation when
Receiving lively greeting
From exuberant lady
On meeting her in motel's
Foyer at the outset of
A party among her friends.
The warm handclasp and
yearning
Gaze that's shared when each
one knows
That parting's imminent, yet
Desire persists to strengthen
Beginning bond of feeling.
The mounting of suspense just
Previous to wedding day,
Wondering fearfully if
One can adapt to rigors
Of another type of life.
The atmosphere of quiet
Reverence when each repeats
His sacred vows and listens
Raptly to the minister's
Prayer for a blissful marriage.
Next, sweet thrill one feels
when act
Of love is consummated,
And ensuing joy to know
A loving mate will always
Be there to support and share
One's most impassioned
feelings.
So memories become more
Deep and vigorous as one
Matures, and especially
Intense when shared with
someone
Complementing one's own flesh.
But though the present's rich
and
Full, and senses often reel
From impressions pungent and
So poignant, some glorious day
I'll awaken from this life
As though were merely a dream.

Karla E. Cooper

THE HOUSE

Trust: is the foundation for
which my house is designed,
Courage: is the plan, drawn to
the distance, of the mountains
I'll climb.
Dignity: keeps me pushing
forward to reach my worth-
while goal,
And Self-determination helps me
choose the right road.
Pride: helps me to carry and
place the rafters,
Hope: keeps my spirit up for all
the mornings after.
Caring: is design for the door,
And Understanding: is fitted for
the floor.
Good intentions: are built for
the window panes,
My Values: are the shields to
protect me from the rain.
Happiness: is built into the
comforting walls,
And the joys of all this, is the
lining, making up the halls...

Leslie J. Murphy

REVELATION NO. 1

I am an apple.
I just found out recently.
On one side I look decent,
But have been bitten on the
other.
And the edges are turning
brown
From sitting around.
About one half of me has been
chewed.
(I hope I was good food.)
I am a green apple, very spotted.
I am thankful as the bite gets
wider,
That I am not apple cider.
How far will the bite have
gotten
Before I know if I am rotten?
Or if I have a green worm,
Or if I have any sap, seeds or
core?

Sherry Diane Thorpe

FATHERS DAY

Fathers Day is a special day
That comes but once a year
But you my dear Daddy
Are special all year through
You're special in every way
More special with each passing
day
Because you gave me the right
kind of raising
And the things every little girl
needs
You spanked me when I was bad
You praised me when I was good
But most of all dear Daddy
You love me all year too!

You gave me the things I needed
And tried to give me things I wanted
But when you couldn't give me them
You made up for it as soon as you could
Just in case you didn't know
Which I'm sure you do
I Love You very much Daddy
And my love will always be true
Here's wishing you a Wonderful Father's Day
And every day there after
For you deserve the very best
Just because you're my Daddy

Steven Maurice Hewitt
FRIDAY THE THIRTEENTH NIGHTMARE
In a nightmare, fashioned from
a snack of chocolate cake and
milk, you and I go a-running.
Coral snakes slither across our
path as we race down corridors
of low hanging trees in the
evening.
Behind us an empty house
stands grimly and ominously
and it's all we can do to get
away. . .
for we are running from
something that we have never
seen except on some forgotten
night when we were lost in
dream.
As you and I race onward we
reach residential areas with
homes and people and cars.
We plead with them to help us
escape, but they seem so
suspicious and can read the fear
on our faces.
Behind us the hollow wind
blows coldly and oppressively
and all we want to do is get
away. . .
for in our mind's eye we can see
the madman's shining blade
as it whispers in the moonlight
of traps that he has laid.
In a nightmare that's become a
lesson of disquiet and fear,
you and I go a-hiding.
In a house we crouch by the
window peering down a lonely
road for the headlights that
will never come.
Behind us an awful sound rings
loudly and hideously and we
know we will never get away. . .
for the madman is upon us like
a horrible dream and waking to
reality we hear our sudden
scream. . .
and we scream. . .and scream. . .
and scream.

Reet Everett
FOR SHE IS 83
She was treated like a child
because her body was so weak
She only wanted to be left alone
to stand on her two feet
Her ears, they could not always hear
nor could her eyes always see
But that was something to expect. . .
for she is 83
But hidden in that body
was a mind independent and proud
It couldn't understand why
suddenly her freedom was not allowed
They tied her up as I heard her cry
"Please, just let me be"!
But they were doing it for her own good. . . .
for she is 83
Well this abuse was much too much
and here she had to stay
So the only escape that she could find
was to let her mind slip away
My grandmother is gone, she's run away
this person's a stranger to me
Now she is senile; they say no one's to blame. . .
for she is 83.

Randolph Adams
JACQUES COUSTEAU DISCOVERS A SPIDER ANTARTICA, 1971
The Sea Spider has no body
But only ten legs to walk upon the ocean's floor
Each by one itself alone
Moves as if by itself alone
Walks along the ocean's floor.
What mind controls these legs
Alone without a body to carry
Along the ocean's floor
Why do legs apart walk
Upon the ocean's floor?
Alone without a body
To carry a mind to care?
Maybe it is the ocean's floor
Who talks alone
To legs to join along to carry
Itself
Itself by Mind not body and To
Dream of legs that spiders have
For ocean's floors,
As oceans have floors
For waters, have bottoms
For spiders have legs
No More

Roger W. Oehlke
SCHOOL
One day, when I was seven,
I offered Phil Rocca
half my Hershey bar,
but he grabbed it all and ran
(he was ten)
stopping at the corner to yell
"Sucker!"
Maria, she lived upstairs in 4C,
and she was beautiful,
and one day when we were nine,
we were playing doctor,
and my old man caught us—
Jeez, was he mad!
He called her a whore and threw her out.
Next day I passed her in the hall,
but she didn't look so nice then.
I run a gas station on 43rd Street,
and every day I hope Rocca
pulls in so I can shortchange him
or something.
Once in a while Maria walks by
with her three kids and one on the way,
and maybe she smiles a little—
but I never do.

Mike Swartwood
OH! THE TEXAS PLAINS
How I miss driving on you.
After driving on you for over,
Ten years, I am now flying,
Over you.

How I miss going thru your,
Towns like Lubbock, Big Springs,
And of Course Amarillo.

How I miss driving over the,
Hill country. How I miss seeing,
The great Table Top Plains at,
Ground level. Off in the distance
I see the town of Amarillo. Up so,

High in the sky; All your great town,

Looks like a green spot on the wide,

Table top plains of the Panhandle.

Betty Hoerster Skoglund
A LONE LITTLE BOY
When I'm feeling down and can't take anymore,
I go back to my bank where special memories are stored.
I think of a lone little boy that we surely adored,
A lone little boy raised in a houseful of girls,
That was helpful and kind and always so loyal,
A lone little boy that just wouldn't spoil.

I remember so well all the little boy hugs and kisses
And all the nice things he did that a Mother greatly misses.
He made for us bright, happy days
And brought joy to so many with his winning ways.

Everything was done with verve and with zest.
Whatever he did, he gave of his best.

He saw the beauty in others that we couldn't see.
Wasn't that just a great way to be?
He nearly always stood out in a crowd
For that was the way that he was and we were always so proud.
He was loved by so many, not just a few,
That's quite an honor. . . .
Don't you think so too?
He had such a sense of right and of wrong
He struggled so hard and fought for so long.
It doesn't seem fair that it had to end
He told me often, "I love you so much Mom, you're my very best friend."
We should have known he was here on a loan
And that God would soon claim him as one of his own.
When God came that evening and called him away
It wasn't a visit, he meant for him to stay.
Oh God, it's so hard and we miss him so much,
His impressions, his laughter, his joking and such.
He was a great entertainer and an artist of sorts,
He liked music and dancing and dearly loved sports.
For all that he was and all that he thought,
For all that he gave and all that he sought,
Can any of these things ever be bought?
I remember so well all the little boy hugs and kisses,
And all of the nice things he did that a Mother greatly misses.

Joyce Pelosi
DESERTIA
The crimson color of the
turtle
Bohemian inhabitant
of sand
Visiting often, the anarchy
of ant hills
Misogynistic mountains
dominant
among the ruins.

Phyllis M. Miller
THE MAN THE GIRLS FEARED
I spoke to the girls nicely
Never said a word
That was rude
But they would
Have nothing
To do with me
Because I was no dude
Night after night
I would smile
And say "How de dew."
They would
fling their heads
Back so high
As they passed me by.
And shake
Their bodies too
"What could I do!"
The perfume that I inhaled
Was getting to me too.
And I wanted
To get nearer
"Don't you see!"
But they wouldn't
Trust me
I even offered
To treat them
At the shore
To drinks and food
And anything more
I meant no wrong
I was just a guy
Who wanted to go out
With a girl
And if she cared
Maybe have a whirl
Maybe a movie, a hamburg

And a coke
A little talk, a little laugh
A little joke
But they made me feel
Like the dust on the floor
And not much more
I felt that I must
Get near them
And even touch
Always I could smell
The perfume
That they used
And I felt so abused.
The guys had the women
That they liked
And many dollars
To spend every night
Someday I'd be rich too
But I was young
I couldn't wait
Until the day came true
I really didn't
Want those girls
I took their clothes off
Just in spite
Whenever they were alone
In the dark of the night
Now I was beginning
To like the thing
That I did
The thing
That was forbid
I didn't mean
To kill the last one
But she threatened
To sue
The prettiest one too
She pulled the stocking
Off my face
And that made me
a police case
But I might as well
Go to prison for life
I never could
Have won a wife

David R. McDaniel

I REACHED OUT—

I reached out to hold her
With my Mind—
A warm Wispy Wind I sent.
I'm sure as if I'd touched her,
She receives.
My heart heard the rustling
Of her leaves.

Julie Jensen

I REMEMBER A DAY

I remember a day. . .
A day when a soft cool breeze brushes the face of the earth,
A day when deep blue skies hold billowy puffs of white,
A day when trees are gently bending and leaves move as a flutter,
A day when green blades of grass unfurl with each little gust.
I remember this day, for it is a picture sculptured in my mind.

Rose I. Tomlinson

NOT IN VAIN

I see a lovely butterfly
Flitting in the sun,
It seems so free and peaceful,
But soon it's life is done.
For life goes by with gentle breeze,
Or stormy winds that blow,
With sunny skies or rainy clouds,
Our days they still must go.
But while were here in this dear life,
We live the best we can,
And trust in GOD to show the way
To live with fellow man.
We trust, we love, we fall, we fail,
But find our way again,
And like the pretty butterfly,
We have not lived in vain.
For we have soared upon the wind
And rested in the sun,
We've loved and wept and shared our fears
And smiled when day was done.
So when this life shall fade away,
And mind has come to rest,
Forward to his arms we go
For we have done our best.
We cannot change what has gone by,
Or erase the rainbow from the sky,
But we will live our life in bliss,
If we can just remember this,
The beauty of a butterfly
That lives its life, but does not cry,
When sunny days have turned to rain,
For life is lived, But not in vain.

Joette Marie Vecchione

TIRED DOVES EMPTY, TIRED DOVES NUMB

We were innocent, we were young,
We sang and skipped through curious fields
and caught whirling raindrops on our tongues,
and knew the laughter and excitement exploring yields.
We waltzed through the corridors of old dance halls,
of cheap hotels, of moss colored billiard rooms
like scavenger doves, and wrote of our defeats
in private codes in diaries hidden in our minds walls
and pushed through crowds in search of love.
We learned soon of the shadows that eclipse
dreams that time fails to renew
and watched the sand that eagerly drips
and destroyed the old blueprints of hope that we drew.
Now here we lie and wait and shiver
afraid, naked to the wailing river,
waiting for the paper ships to line up on the shore.

Cindy Fraser

THE CORFU BLUE

The Corfu blue amazes me—
Wild blue, like the depths of my soul.
Swirling
and
churling like my skirt
and the merry go rounds in the park.
I wonder what it looks like after dark?
Swinging
and
singing I watch as the waves
curl and furl to unfold in a masquerade foam against the side of the surprised ship. Like unicorns they crash and smash only to return each time more beautiful. The sea is me as I sing my song and I watch the dolphins sing a song.

Oh, oh, this Corfu blue,
to sail forever in this mystical blue
But oh, more glorious—
to sail with you!

This blue is forever, like my love for you,
and the sands on the beach are an eternity come true.

—Oh, oh,
This Corfu blue.

Just think,
We could drink wine,
and feel so fine,
And toast a toast, our arms entwined!

And sunsets would set,
And waves would be wet,
And all this would happen in the Corfu blue.

—I love the blue,
And I love you!

Mary Ann Kell

THE KNOCK AT THE DOOR

I had gone to bed
but could not sleep
For you see, my son
is a drug addict
and pray to God
your soul to keep
Down deep in my heart,
my dear son, I knew
that knock at the door
would be about you
How many days
how many tears
I know that it has been
more than a year
That I have lived
in deepest fear
I'm a mother
who waits
not for the knock
at the door
To tell me my son
has fallen
on the battlefield
of war
My son has fallen
on the battlefield, of society
He will not receive
a big write up, or notoriety
For he has an enemy
as deadly as any
That ever carried
a gun
Thousands have fallen
to this enemy
Like yours and
my son
My son, once strong,
happy and quick
Now has a body and mind
that is very sick
He acts on impulse
and very eratic
For you see, my son
is a drug addict
This country has fought
many wars, and won
Can't we fight one more war
for your's and my son
Our boy's have died, on land,
in the air, and the sea
They come home, from the
battlefield of war
and they're still not free
And they cry out, for help
from you and me
The pain and hurt
is all the same
Whether it's an army officer
in olive green
Who has crept quietly
up on the scene
He knock's on the door
with bowed head, he says
Your son has fallen
from enemy lead
Oh yes the pain and hurt
is all the same
Whether it's a police officer
in navy blue
Who wants to speak quietly
to only you

He knocks on the door
his shoulders he shrugs
your son has fallen
from deadly drugs
The pain and hurt
is all the same
Whether it's in sunshine
or rain
Or the color is green
or blue
Heartbreak and tears
will come to you
I hear the knock
at the door, once more
I slowly walk
toward the door
Head bent low
tears wet my cheeks
my feet unsteady
dear lord, I am ready
Slowly I open the door
for I knew
I will have to wait
no more
The time has come
I have done my best

Dear Lord, please
  do the rest
But there's no soldier
  in green
Or policeman
  in blue
It's you, dear lord
  it's you
With out-stretched arms
  he comforts me
the day will come
  I promise thee
No more sons
  Will have to die
No more mothers
  Will have to cry

Virginia Hurt Bailey

TO PITTSBURG—MIDWAY COAL COMPANY

In the white
Light of dawn
and early spring
I planted.
In the clear
Midday blue
and summer's growth
I cultivated.
In the golden red
Setting sun glow
and autumn's chill
I gathered.
In the black
Shining night
And winter's length
I dreamed.
Like the soft
Beginning beat
of the singer's drum,
Like the flutter
of a blue bird's
Fleeting flight,
Like the rising
Crescendo
Of the singer's song,
Like the fragile
Petals of a
Desert bloom,
The vision was
There in my heart,
Giving strength—
All was beauty
Wholly united
In my sleep.
But whirling winds
and flashing lightning
Turned my reverie
to chimera.
The enemy came
as an orange machine
And destruction began.
Our earth mother cries
out in pain
from the wounds
of progress.
Our father sun hides
his face in clouds,
Helpless and sad.
The Holy Ones
Speak no more,
Thus is the rainbow
Broken.

James Maurice West, Jr.

MERMAID

(Dedicated to Miss Anne)

I saw her walking by the shore
her hair radiant with the sun.
her body robed in white
  gossamer
that glistened with the tears of
the sea.
She looked up and her eyes
burned deep into mine.
I shuddered as the walls around
my heart fell like Jericho,
a trumpet blast of purity
echoing through my being.
She stretched out her hand
and spoke with the voice of a
thousand angels,
"Come walk with me awhile."
The ghosts of fears I have
  known
appeared.
"No. I cannot.
  Must not.
  Will not."
She spoke,
"Do not be afraid of what may
or may not be."
"I am afraid of what I have
already known."
She gazed at me through
bewildered eyes and then
reached for my hand.
"Come."
The coldness of my fears
melted like the snows in spring,
like warm bubbling water
surging through my body,
warming the iced caverns of
my heart.
We walked by the sea and
listened to the chorus of waves.
Her hair danced in the wind.
Her hand entwined in
mine like a gentle vine.
"Don't worry about what is to
be said now. Let our hearts
speak for us," she said.
She waved her hand and
the sky became a tapestry
of colors.
Flowers fell from the sky
touching lightly upon the
sand.

A rose, white as the sun, came
to rest in her hair,
a white jewel in a sea of
velvet brown.
She turned to me,
"You are never without love."
She kissed me long
and the universe exploded!
I fell like a star through endless
space.

I awoke on the shore,
the tide lapping at my feet.
My eyes searched the beach.
She was gone!
A dream?
A vision?

My eyes filled with tears.
I was robbed!
I was cheated!
I had lost again.
I had been awakened from a
dream, and did not want it to
be a dream.
I hated dreams.
But look!
There!
In the sand!
A rose!

Gene M. Skayer

GNATS

A man fled to the hills one day
To seek some solitude
From people who had placed
  him in
An irritated mood.
He stretched upon the downy
  grass
And gazed into the sky,
When presently a multitude
Of pesty gnats came by.
He swung at them and cursed at
  them
And lost his new-born grace;
They teased and buzzed and
  vexed and swirled
And bit his angry face.
At once he fled the lofty hills
And to the valley ran
And said: "I'd rather tolerate
Vexatious fellow man.
They may get on my nerves at
  times,
My good and evil peers,
But it is sure that they can-
  gnat
Get in my eyes and ears."

Marcia Mrochuk

MEMORIAM

Memories,
intruding and unwanted,
They come and go
As wisps of smoke
on a clear blue sky.
Butterflies,
light and flitting,
Untouchable
But ever present
in cobwebby recesses
long forgotten.
Faded sepia photographs,
Of days gone by.
Recollection,
brings back the pain.
Dusty, dog-eared pages
Of a faded scrapbook
fly on the wings
of the wind.
Clinging,
as cobwebs,
Never letting go
Perhaps they will fade
Until unrecognizable,
intangible,
and perhaps they shall slip
and fall away
Disappear into the bottomless
  pit
Of forgotten
Memories.

Thomas B. Hargrave, Jr.

LIBERTY CITY—1980 MIAMI

Why do you only hear me
When I light the torch?
Why do you only see my
  silhouette
When flames enlarge my image
In the eerie red of night?
Will you only comprehend
When I smash your face
Or kick your shin
To let you know that justice
  died
When, to cover up their crimes,
Cops lied
In Liberty City, yesterday.
If you think I will sit still
Or hesitate to use the skill
Learned in Nam's bleeding
  paddy fields—
You are crazy as hell!

Patsy Keener

LOVELINESS

Shadowy waves floating past
Purple twisting agony going
  with me,
Are you mine with a faint
  longing
of a tomorrow?
No, but with a hint of love
Winding, yearning river, going
on without ceasing and no true
wonder.
The future will dip this being in
an endless journey and splash
  gladly
in unknown waves—a taste of
  love in
wandering travels and longing
  are waiting. . . .
Togetherness is there, Two have
  the
wanted of all; Winding, yearning
  river,
moving, but with no greatness.

William James Northerner

MY DREAM

I dream of giant castles
  looming o'er the countryside.
Their great stone walls reach
  from the earth to touch the
  bluish sky,
Whose towers are a sentinel
  forever at their post,
Eternal is their vigil
  guarding o'er the kingdoms
  host.
Those ancient walls of gray and
  brown, where ivory makes its
  climb,
Repel the wrath of nature's hand
  to stand the test of time.
Their surface marred with
  cracks of age whose paths run
  to and fro,
Blend with the scars of battles
  fought from many vanquished
  foe.

And reaching out before its
  gates the gently sloping land,
Where hill and dale of emerald
  green, and woods so stately
  stand.
Where deer and boar and fowl
  abound and fish swim o'er the
  stream,
So beautiful this magic land,
  so peaceful and serene.
Beyond the wood and down the
  road from the castles ageless
  wells,
The village lies so quietly
  in evenings early call,
Each roof is silhoueted
  by the golden setting sun,
A herald of the coming night
  announcing this days done.
For at this time within the walls
  of each and every home,
The people gather at the hearth
  around the warming stone,
Where fire dances merrily
  and gives a friendly glow,
They tell of tales and stories
  written many years ago.
They tell of Prince and
  Princesses who rode the
  countryside,

Their garments of the finest silk
their servants at their side,
And of the many Kings and
Queens who rulled the
Kingdoms host,
Their armies riding o'er the land,
a sight of which to boast.
Impressive in their armor
which glistens in the sun,
They tell of many battles fought
where victory was won.
Atop their mighty armored
steeds with weapons at their
side,
Whose banners fill the eastern
sky in battle when they ride.
The stories tell of maidens fair
each one a lovely dame,
Whose very would was rescued
from the dragons scorching
flame,
By noble men of character
each fighting for the right,
Their courage none can
challenge, this brave and
fearless knight.
These mortal men of courage
were knighted by the King,
Whose sword hath kissed their
shoulder while angels were to
sing.
Allegiance pledged to God and
King in whose presence they
seem frail,
A quest was then appointed
them to seek the Holy Grail.
This magic time revived to life
from stories that are told,
Reach to the heart of all the
folk both young and very old.
And when you hear these
stories told of deeds worth
noble praise,
Just close your eyes and you
will return to live these very
days.

Veronica A. Jackson

REMEMBRANCE IN AMBROSIA

Remember one who warmed my
heart
Remember one who charmed me
smart
Remember one who stole my
feelings
Remember one who spent a
short time giving
He is the one that I wish
always to remember
And to him I chant,
Remember me who found your
heart
Remember me who filled the
part
Remember me who was polite
Remember me who was so
bright
Remember me who's life
portrayed
Remember me the one betrayed.
For this I will not shun you,
because the time that we had
together I wished. . .
Remembered as a rainy day,
when we could always find
our way;
Remembered as a sharp clear
night,
when we could always shine
so bright;
Remembered as a windy morn,
when all our troubles were
reborn;
Remembered as in sunny May,
when we turned our worries
all away;
Remembered as in stunning
June,
when we could reach our
rhythm's tune;
Remembered as in joyous July,
when all our dreams filled the
sky;
Remembered as in ageless
August,
when our hearts felt no
distrust;
Remembered as in sabbath
September,
when in our hearts we'd
always remember;
Remembered as in oceanic
October,
when our hearts, we held
sober;
Remembered as in nostalgic
November,
when I our hearts the love
soon tremor
Life. . . and it's dreams/
Love. . .and it's promises
Remembered, as in joyous
January,
when our hearts faced no
worry;
Remembered as in flamboyant
February,
when our hearts spoke
matrimony;
Remembered as in memorious
March,
when our hearts, the
valentine's arch;
Remembered as in ambrosia
April,
when our lives mythed fables;
Remembered as in winter, my
heart, at center,
Remembered as in spring, my
hand, it's ring,
Remembered as in summer, your
feelings, did slumber,
Remembered as in fall, my heart
speaks all.

Faye Hagemeyer

CURTAIN GOING UP

I cannot go to work today,
For Spring is calling me.
Pale fairy lanterns light the way,
And lupin trumpets sow
Their fragrant summons
heralding
The best of Nature's shows.
Cerulean blue the hangings are;
And verdant green the stage.
Young Spring herself's the
budding star.
A whippoorwill's the page.
From buttercups in Spring's
greenroom
We'll drink a heady toast
Of nectar pressed from clover
bloom
To celebrate the play.
Tomorrow I may work—but
I cannot work today.

Arlan Grover

MY COMPANION AND FRIEND

People say I'm crazy,
I posses the American dream!
But to me without life's special
feelings,
life is just another rusty
machine!
It's useless, just taking someone
else's space!

Without this feeling, in this
world,
For me there is no place!

For me it's a wonder,
How a solitary moment can be
so fine?

How in just a few minutes
the world can be mine!

But in the same token, just a
flash of time,
Can make what was real, just
a facade,
Or some sort of mime!

No man is an isle,
He can not stand alone!

But man must live on instinct
and feeling,
And so am I!

I aim my goals high and attempt
to sneer at defeat!

But yet I keep my foundation on
land,
And hope for the sky!

I've loved and lost,
By whatever means deemed!
I've lost what only some have
dreamed!

I'm thankful for the memories
And will return to the good
times!

For like a grandfather clock,
When the hour tolls I will stand
up and chime!

My life may be lonely and long
or it may come to a sudden end!
I just want to share it with you!
My companion and friend!

Eloise Carnes Chambers

IN MEMORIAM

December is the month of
festivities gay,
Also we remember those who
have passed away.
Daddy left us one dark rainy
night;
All the world seemed oh, so
cold!
Friends and neighbors were very
kind and polite
As their words of sympathy
were told
It takes time to really
understand
That God makes no mistakes
To all mankind throughout the
land
Our breath God gives or takes.
But memories never pass away—
Somehow they manage to stay.
With us there was no generation
gap,
For daddy could tackle the
toughest job
Or take a little child upon his
lap,
When he spoke it wasn't some
psychology he'd read.
He said what he meant and
meant what he said.
For his wrongs and mistakes
he used to shield or cover,
He didn't talk one way and deal
another.
He wasn't a minister but
sometimes he'd almost preach.
To us the right way he tried
to teach.
Oft his words were fire and
brimstone.
We'd suffer the consequences
when we did wrong.
We watched him plow and plant
a field;
Shoe the horse, milk the cow,
and harvest the crop.
He logged in the mountains
rough and steep,
Changes in the weather didn't
cause him to stop.
If one job was finished, another
he'd seek.
he could run a motor or operate
any machine.
He could rebuild or repair most
anything.
He drilled and blasted rock to
have a better road,
he did not falter under a heavy
load,
Little chance did he have to go
to school
But that didn't hinder him from
finding a tool,
and using his abilities he'd
make a way,
There never was a vacation with
pay.
He could ride a horse, row a
boat, or make a picnic
sublime,
He could fish and hunt, but he
never killed time.
He loved his fellowman and felt
it his task
To help the needy without
being asked.
At his table many enjoyed their
daily bread,
He visited the sick and often
buried the dead.
He isn't listed in the Hall
of Fame.
But I'm sure when God called
his name,
His battle was over, his race
was run;
Daddy knew his victory he'd
won.
Mother was faithful and stood
by his side.
No one felt the pain as she
did when he died.
Two years later in the spring
God called her away
Our sorrow was just doubled
that day.
They didn't leave great material
gain,
How well they knew such
things soon fade.
Deeds of kindness and seeds of
love they sowed
While they lived in our house
beside the road.
Christmas holidays have never

been the same
But our loss has been Heaven's gain.
We have a deeper understanding why Jesus was born,
And the shepherds and angels sang praises that first Christmas morn.

Katherine Marsh
MOONLIGHT—MOON
Dim light of evening shadows
Bathed in darkness of night
Pale blue reflection
Falls upon innocent shapes
Its creator sits high
Arranging each setting
For those absorbed in its web
To marvel at, breathless
Eyes that adore it
For there is denying
The mystery of such a beauty
A quixotical wonder
It smiles its yellow sheen
Softly gazing light upon the ocean
Tides going in, going out
And still flowing under the spell
The forebearing parent of night
Sitting like a mighty trojan
Perched in its partial place
That, of course, the sky.

Robert Clifton Crissman
DAY OF THE GUN
A young giant strode and bravely rode
Through the heart of a Texas town.
In the crowd that pressed, few would have guessed
An assassin's gun would cut him down.
On Dallas' darkest day, the sky, though gray,
Was sunny, and smiles were warm.
But a city at peace lost its 'Summer's Lease'
As swift as a tropic storm.
When time stood still, a sudden chill
Rippled through the gathered throng.
From vantage high, a sniper's eye,
Hate-riveted, wreaked it's wrong.
The trigger squeezed, hate was appeased
As Jack fell at Jackie's side.
A blood-drenched ride, a brave man died;
And with him a nation's pride.
(Later)
TV viewers, shocked and numb
Saw legends die and truth succumb.
Dazed and grieved, they watched the screen,
As film flickered on. . . fantasy or dream?
Was it for naught a hero fought
On perilous pacific reef?
Highest pinnacle attained, superbly he reigned
With honor and dignity— our chief.

"For whom the bell tolls?"
As we search our souls,
The only answer can be:
From chaos grim, lest we look to *him*
In truth, "The bell tolls for thee."

L. C. McGahan
MY OLD DOG
My shabby old mutt, his best days he'd seen
He had arthritis bad, and sight wasn't keen
He was near stone deaf, and he couldn't chew
For his teeth were gone, and his smeller too
He had bronchitis bad, and his heart was shot
For him just to breath, took an awful lot
To the vets we went, for his medical care
So my poor old dog, could breathe some air
He got pills to take, and liquids too
He swallowed them all, as if he knew
They were good for him, and would help his ills
My twenty year old dog, who lived on pills
He had arthritis so bad, in all his knees
That when he walked, he'd cough and wheeze
He was so darn old, his muscles were slack
He'd walk to the corner, and barely get back
He staggered around, most of the time
It might have been funny, if he hadn't been mine
I often thought, he'd be better off dead
But when I reached down, and patted his head
He'd look up at me, with a look in his eye
That same old love, that money can't buy
His tail still wagged, and he'd lick my hand
Only he and I, could understand
The vet told me, his days were few
For every week, there was something new
I always did my best, for my trusting friend
I stuck by him, until the end
For lo and behold, the vet was right
My friend he died, the very next night
While in my lap, without whimper or cry
I watched my friend, quietly die
He was nineteen years, and ninety-five days
I knew his habits, he knew my ways
He gave far more love, than his total weight
This ten pound dog, and my friend of-late
I loved that dog, that raggity canine
We lived alone and he was always mine
He was the best pal, I ever knew
My dear old friend, I'll sure miss you

Wesley Wildt
A PRAYER
If I could say a little prayer
Expressing all the joy
Within the happy hearts tonight
Of every girl and boy,
I think it would not be the toys
Or shining Christmas trees
That I would thank him for the most,
For all such things as these
Can never be compared, it seems,
To love that God has shown
By sending us his dearest gift,
His only, precious Son.
And so, if it were left to me
To say a prayer, my prayer would be,
"We thank you, God, for Jesus

G. M. Nick
THE CHANGING OF THE LIGHTS
It's the changing of the lights,
The seasons,
The winds.
The mainsail falls with the sun,
Summer is gone for fall,
Winter warnings have begun.
The lights are low
And playtime is short.
A cool wind begins to blow.
The summer breeze is now a memory past,
As leaves turn and fall,
A ballet performed by natures cast.
The artist's brush sweeps across the sky,
The clouds begin to define
The infinite blue that is enshrouded by.
The naked animals bare their furs,
Making ready for a sleep to pass,
A blanket that will endure.
It's the changing of the lights,
The season,
The winds.
Halloween and Thanksgiving have come to pass,
The holidays are on the way.
The lights are low and the day doesn't last.
A painted sky, cool wind has sewn,
Brisk upon the face,
Bundled in wool, the hair to be blown.
The trees begin to sway.
The land-born sailor
Dreams of his play.
The water games of summer gone
Fall upon the roof.
New rye begins to grow within the prairie lawn.
A warmer jacket and sweater worn.
The birds fly high, away.
Branches brace the snow the wind has blown.
It's the changing of the lights,
The seasons,
The wind.
A new calf wobbles to her mother,
Green grass dries by noon,
A new light and another.
A bluejay shakes the dew.
He sings a song,
The leaf on the branch is new.
Halo on the eastern mountain says,
"Good morning, my old friend.
The sun will soon shine for you."
White easter dresses,
The sails are raised,
The sand is changed by foot presses.
Long sleeve wind blows
The hopes of tomorrows love.
The patio for lunch knows.
It's the changing of the lights,
The seasons,
The wind.
Warm air tightens the sails,
The palm trees glitter,
"Gone fishing" the barber hails.
Open window sleep,
The children play till nine.
Early morning sunrise, through the window peeps.
Breakfast on the lanai,
Tennis after work,
Summer fruits ripen and lie.
Time to travel and unravel
The frustrations of the year.
Whitewash the house, and set the gravel.
Fireworks blossom and saltwater splashes,
Waves are speckled with flesh.
Sunsets are gorgeous, and the wind blows the ashes.
It's the changing of the lights,
The season,
The wind.

Patricia McClung
WHAT DO YOU MEAN I'M OLD?
My feelings don't feel old—
I still love God—
a sunset
my children—
my husband—
teaching school—
life—people—
my best friend—
I'm not old—life's too full to grow old
Can't I stay young a bit longer?
When I was "younger" there were so many problems to solve—
I couldn't enjoy life the way I do now—

There's too much to do—too
many to love,
students to help—reading to
teach!
Can't I be old later when I'm
ready to slow down—
My cup runneth over—so don't
call me old—
Can't I be 48 and holding or
I'll accept "mature"
but don't call me old—My life's
so full and I'm still a jogging!

Debbie C. Edwards
LOVE TO ME

Shaky Body,
Feel my Soul—
Hold me closer,
Feel us mold.
Taste the wine,
Of your kiss—
Passing moments,
Not to miss.
Ease me down,
On the floor—
Crying softly,
Close the door.

Sherri Dobb
SUNDAY, SEPTEMBER 23, 1979

We pick blackberries in the
woods by Lake Michigan.
Their purple juice flows down
my hand.
I hold your body in the rose
glow of the trees.
The woods are green and deep.
Your body is smooth and cool at
night.
When I move against you
your back is the colors of the
earth.
Mahogany, sand, maple, birch.
A smooth beach stone.
We walk on leaves in all stages
of decay.
Gold leaves on top of brown.
Leaves becoming part of the
earth
hold the coldness below them.
I want to lay my cheek to the
ground
as I lay it to your back in sleep.

Peggy Reuler
SUMMER NIGHT 1969

Each inch of the bee-store felt
as if nature had doused it with
honey. In buzzless darkness, the
bee-men, three, came there
stubby-faced and eyes of color
of rare meat.
Sipping from sticky-warm mugs
of muddy nectar, these
nocturnal creatures awakened
to relocate their bevy of bees.
Suited in yellow jackets,
like paired bumblebees,
they silently flew over the
sweet-sour soil of milk-and-
honey and dynamite mines.
Their truck was a firefly
in the Gallilean night,
and aided by a silver-studded
sky, the twin beams discovered
the hives.
Like padding bears the bee-men
approached twelve white boxes,
cages for the wild animals
sleeping within. Gently, sting-
pocked hands sealed in their
prey and placed the wood-slat
forms onto the truck for the
journey.
Then they perched on top,
like expectant hens roosting,
and with each bump, awakened
life rumbled beneath.
Again on ground, the unsealed
boxes became erupting volcanos,
and stinging bees spewed over
cheesecloth figures.
Some kamikaze guards violated
the masked boundaries, and
their globed bellies deflated
instantly as stingers penetrated
flesh; they died in their queen's
service. Others, workers, feasted
on virgin flowers.
The bee-men escaped the
honeyed hordes and mounted
their wheeled steed. Still
encased in cotton armor, damp
with eight o'clock dew and heat,
they fought sleep and
challenged the rocky Judean
terrain.

Mary G. Hazer
UNTITLED

the stars fall continually from
the vastness of the heavens
it was all in a dream
foreseeing the derivation of
the only final instance
there are no words to be found
to interpret this event
the bellowing silence filters
through the air
initiating a senseless fiasco
the streest which were once
glutted with signs of life
lie covered with solitude
faint crys of the flowers
are heard in the distance
longing sustenance; receiving
none
destruction appears dying
painless
illustrating the end of the
end. . .

Ruth H. Coward
A STRONG SELECTION?

For Mary Ellen Noughten,
This perfume I have boughten.
It smells a little strong to me
So she must use it sparingly,
Or else folks might be
tellin'—
That the loudest smellin'—
Is Mary Ellen.

Gladys A. Blankenbeker
WHAT AMERICA MEANS TO ME

Carved out of a wilderness,
A melting pot of races,
A land by Heaven Blessed
As seen in people's faces.
A land of great opportunity,
For those who forge ahead;
From her great and rolling
seas
To her lowly River's bed.
A place where the lowliest
born
May become highest in the land;
To those whose hands are toil
worn,
Steady and strong like iron
bands—
For they have molded our
Declaration
With heart, work, and love so
true;
Have given us our heritage—
inspiration
As we Honor, the Red, White
and Blue.
So here's to America's Glory,
Two hundred years of praise—
As proudly we re-tell the story
Let's be faithful to her always.
For at her breast we're
nourished
Clothed—sheltered—and blest;
Here Mankind's World has
flourished
And Democracy weathered the
test.

Katherine Andrews
I SHALL TRUST

I shall trust.
Tho filled with raging anger
and floundering in the
depths of depression,
I will not give in to
the subtle life-choking
grasp of death
concealed in
shrouds of selfishness.
I shall trust.
Tho my heart aches
with throbbing, unrelenting
pain and my tears flow like
cascading falls,
Tho emptiness penetrates
my being,
Tho anguish of soul
consumes me
and life's purpose evades me.
I shall trust.
Tho hope no longer finds
a home in my heart,
Tho my senses
fail to fathom
the incongruous muddle
through which I now struggle,
Tho light has passed
from my eyes
and a dark veil
shadows my soul.
I shall trust
because once there was
a spark of light.
Ah, so long ago it seems,
but that small flicker,
buried deep in my breast
sustains me,
brings to memory
a time of peace and joy
and life.
I shall trust.
Tho fear and insecurity
encapsulate me and
weigh me down with the
burdens of oppression
and anxiety.
I will not be damned.
I will rise out of the
depths of despair.
The snarling clutches
of death shall not
hold me down.
Smothered not
shall I be.
And tho the ages pass
and darkness seems
rooted to my being,
I shall not
surrender to the
stagnating loneliness
of death's despair.
For I trust in
the Lord of Light.
He shall come again
and illumine the
dark confines of
my poor existence.

Melvin D. Locke
A SOLDIERS CHRISTMAS CAROL

Twas the night before Christmas
and all thru the tent
There was an odor of fuel oil,
The stove pipe was bent.
The weary G.I.'s were sacked out
in their beds,
While visions of pinup girls
danced thru their heads.
When up on the ridge there
arose such a clatter
A Chinese Machine Gun had
started to chatter.
I threw back my covers and
awoke with a jolt
I grabbed up my rifle and I
threw back the bolt.
Outside we could hear our
Platoon Sgt Kelly
A little short man with a round
fat belly.

He yelled up Connors, Up
Donner, Up Watson, Up
Gibson,
Up Branner, Up Tanner, Up
Dobson, Up Nibson.
We all fell outside in a whirl
of confusion
Each man was so cold he could
have used a transfusion.
Get up on that ridge, And
silence that Red,
And don't you come back, Till
you're sure that he's dead.
Then putting his thumb to the
side of his nose
Sgt Kelly took leave of us
shivering Joe's.
But we all heard him say in a
voice soft and light,
"Merry Christmas" To all, May
you live thru the night.

Rebecca S. Rossignol
AUTISM

I had a predilection towards
introspection, as I searched the
dusty attic and damp cellar of
my mind. I rested on the very
precipice of pretension.
The pool of my memory was
much too clear, as I became
victim to total recall.
My actions, years ago, seemed
academic, but have come back
to haunt me, now.
I found it difficult groping in
the darkness, so I turned on a
light, but the tungsten burst,
time after time.
There are days that God should
never have given birth, and I
have had more than my share.
But we must accept our
mistakes the way we accept the
imperfections of a lover's face.
In the shadow of our past

should loom the promise of the future,
then why not for me, too? How could I help what my mother's matrix made me? It's said that even mice cast shadows, but what of rats?
My conscience is up against the wall, and my pride is on parole.
My days are measured by pills in a bottle, and grains of sand through an hour glass.
Acetylsalicylic acid slips easily off my tongue.
The secrets that I keep to myself are like the secrets the leaf keeps from the wind, the secrets the wood keeps from the fire, and the secrets that a doctor keeps from a pusillanimous patient with incurable cancer.
Thoughts buzz in my brain like flies over a dung heap.
My will got snapped like a crisp breadstick. My soul was pricked by the very tip of a finely-honed sword thrust with strong moral compunction through a layer of thin skin into thick flesh.
You always bleed when you dig too deeply.

H-Dirksen L. Bauman

TOGETHER

Together we built a rainbow
we sat very high on our rainbow
we ate the clouds with a silver spoon
yes—we ate our rainbow on the moon
Together we rode on a unicorn through the fog
laughing on our immaculate flight
as we ascended to an incredible height
over the orange mountains—
and across the world we flew
on our unicorn—we turned aqua—blue
Together we swam through the clouds
leaping and dancing
on these lily pads in the sky,
wondering if this is what it's really like to die
Together I forget the agony of reality—
you have taught me
not to see the world in a sorrowful grey
but to love this world in a beautiful way!

Donna C. Fedor

DEJA VOUS

Like all Lovers. . .
I return to the scene of the crime
And stalk the woods we walked in
Quietly
Looking for you there
Seeking a memory

Where are you, Love?
Did you go where meadows never end?
Where sunshine lights the water
And songs blow in the wind?
Did you catch your dream in the breeze of
The years that passed between us?
Or are you sitting in a rented room
Filled with someone else's dust—
Like me.
Are you lonely?
And seeking a memory of an easier time?
Will you silently yet desperately
Return to the scene of the crime?
Like all Lovers. . .
Like Me.

Miss Mary Jane Dennis

WELCOME HOME

"Welcome home, Ye Classmates, Class of '41,"
"Think ye not of 'Finished,' but of 'Just Begun.' "
Gather 'round the table; o'er his dinner plate,
Forty years of travels each commemorate.
From the halls of learning, braved we forth to bless,
Soon to know the journey through the wilderness.
Backed by youthful vigor, daring nought to dread,
Dangers lay before us in the Trek ahead.
From the halls of learning, might we scan the way
Where befall the mishaps, bringing dark dismay!
Buoyed by life's own laughter, unsubdued by fears
Mark the steps that brought some through the vale of tears.
Did you ford some waters; did you cross some plain?
Did you scale a mountain; did some manage again?
Have you faced the giants coming forth as foe?
Having reached your Canaan Land, can you onward go?
On the Mount ascended, and from where you stand,
Do you know the Master; does He hold your hand?
Do you make your journey, strengthened by His Love?
Is He speaking to you of those things above?
On the Shores of Glory, will you meet your King?
Gather 'round the Table, songs of praises sing?
Find your soul's fulfillment—Heaven's Just Begun!
"Welcome Home, Ye Children! Welcome Home! Well Done!"

Bruce G. Muncher

LIFE'S REMEMBRANCE

How is it
that two people
who once could not be separated
and were the best of friends
don't even talk anymore.
I can remember
when we used to talk
about growing up
and what we wanted
and how it would be;
and here we are
years later—
older
and somewhat wiser
and somewhat confused
for nothing is like
we planned
or talked about.
We don't even see
each other anymore
and we only communicate
at Christmas.
I guess
now that we are older,
comes the responsibility
of acting older
which I guess
is time consuming
and so we don't have time
for friends
anymore
Too bad
when we are small,
we are not told
what it will be like
when we grow up—
the responsibilities we will
have to face
and the hard times
we will have.
And also
we should be taught
to love ourselves
before
being taught to love others,
for many a times
there is no one else around
except oneself.
But wouldn't things
be more simple
if we could remain
young?
I guess not—
for maturity is slow
and growing older
is beautiful
for each individual
is different
in character
and mind.
But as you grow old,
hold on to your youth
and those
that were a part of it;
for if you don't,
you are gone before your
time.

Marilyn B. Traylor

TO MY IRISH FRIENDS

When Irish eyes are smiling—
We know Spring is on its way,
And, for all of my good Irish friends,
This is your special day.
So don your Irish green
And sport your shamrock, too,
And, from someone who isn't Irish,
It's "Top of the Morning to You."
And, going back many a year,
To that Irishman long ago,
We want to thank you, St. Patrick,
For overcoming your foe.
They took you captive as a lad
And, a herdsman you became,
But, the visions that you had—
Paved the way to see Ireland again.
You told us that the shamrock
Is a sign of the Trinity—
And, to those of us who believe this,
We can experience infinity.
And, so again to my friends I say—
"Top of the morning to loo,
I hope you have a lovely day
And, may God Bless You!"

Diedre J. Gammon

MY LOVE

You and me are here right now trying to talk
When you thought it was over, but you thought wrong
'Cause my love for you will never be like it used to be.
Even though we haven't seen each other in a while
Doesn't mean we have to hate each other
My love for you is strong and very special
It's not something you just go through then throw it away
I want to share things and be with you all the time
Even the joys and sorrows, the good and the bad
When certain things don't work out we can handle them
Communication is the #1 thing in peoples lives
Without that a person can't deal with it
Love is beautiful because I will have a lot of time
To spend with you.

Kristina Barber

A QUESTION FOR YOU

Can you be of a delicate spirit and nature,
And know you will endure?
Can you ever know to what length your spirit will expect your body and mind to go?
Would you, for someone whom you dearly love, through the very fires of hell go?
How do you tell, how can you be sure, of a feeling,
How do you know exactly with what you're dealing?
The mind is strange indeed,
But basically only knowledge and facts does it heed.
Feelings are of an emotional, spiritual line,
Extremely hard to pinpoint, to clearly define.
When you look into anothers eyes, you look into their very soul,
No matter what they hide, it is easy for an observant person to be told.
Fire and ice, all together as one,
Misery, darkness, yet light and fun.
When and why do two people come together in emotion?

What degree of feeling must
they obtain to get to that
point of complete and
absolute devotion?
To heed the other, when they
may cry in despair,
To need each other and if truly
in love, always try to be fair.
To give, as much as you wish to
be given to,
To include the other in most
of what you do.
Tell me where the binding is,
where does it first start?
In the eyes when you first meet,
or later when that gentleness
comes into your heart?
Love for another is difficult
because of ourselves, must we
completely give,
Ready to defend totally the
other and readily forgive.
Tell me why, so that I can
understand, and more easily
through life go,
Hopefully, before I die I will
know,
Where did it start?
In the mind or in the heart. . .

Cheryl Askew

WHAT A FRIEND I HAVE IN JESUS

He will help you through your
troubles,
when things don't seem just
right.

Just call on Him any time of
day,
morning, noon and night.
The Lord will never leave you,
He's always by your side.

He knows all of your secrets,
from him you can not hide.
Just keep your trust in Jesus,
He's a friend that's always there.
You can always call on Him,
and go to Him in prayer.

What a friend I have in Jesus,
all my sins and grief he bears.
I know the Lord will guide me,
Because he really cares.

He's with me through the
darkness,
the devil I do not fear.
For the Lord let's me know
his goodness is always near.

He walked on the waters,
He gave sight to the blind.

That was His way of letting us
know,
He was your friend, and mine.

Thank You, God, for what I am,
make me what you want me to
be.

I will serve you for the rest
of my life,
for all the world to see.
So serve the Lord with gladness,
show him you really care.

If you ever have a problem
take it to the Lord in prayer.

Lianne J. Moore

WITH MY EYES CLOSED

Sounds seeping through the
warped door,
A shivering wind wipes the
blanket of warmth,
Watching clouds-cream with
a cherry on board,
Puddles splashing like firing
guns,
Rise of morn' and a bright raging
sun,
Light passes like a flick of
a switch,
Dusk a site of blanketing fog,
Flickering stars spill upon
sparkling eyes,
The world revolving like hands
upon a tickery tock,
Lightening a flashlight of
shivering shock,
The fire of the world
to me,
Lightens life.

Barbara A. Kinney

TOUCHES OF LIFE

Moments spent in fear and
anguish
Put at peace by loving hands,
Time sacrificed from other
duties
Sets straight misguided plans.
Smiling faces washed with tears
Watch the children as they
grow,
Sharing one unto another
Treasures only some can know.
New beginnings birthed so
humbly
Soon endeavor to be kings,
Only to be dashed unseemly,
As the bell for martyr's rings.
Man forgetting to be human
Long enough to bare his soul,
Secretly revealing without him
God's plan can not be whole.

Faye Keown

WITH LOVE TO DON AND EVELYN

At last the day is drawing near,
You dreamed of years ago. . .
A different life, a different world
Your dream just seemed to grow.
The thought of helping others—
In a far and distant land. . .
Seemed so foolish to your
family,
But fit well within your plan.
So you read and taught and
studied,
And planned from day to day,
Of how you'd take your
family. . .
If your dream proved to be
God's way.
At first there was only Evelyn
Who shared your plan and
dream.
And the two of you together,
Could make the perfect team.
So why didn't the call come
quickly?
For your plan which was the
best,
Could it be that God in his
wisdom,
Knew you hadn't passed the test.
So the weeks and months pass
slowly
As you labored in our midst,
And a darling little daughter
Was added to your family list.
Then you felt your job was
finished,
At Oak Grove you'd done your
best. . .
But the training for World
Missions
Involved still another quest.
And so to South Carolina
The move to us seemed fair. . .
And North Greenville Junior
College
Was waiting for your care.
As Chaplain to the students
Your work seemed never done,
And to your little family. . .
God added a precious son.
Just now your world looked
perfect.
Thru the eyes of Mom and Dad,
But what seemed so right for
others
Left your life a little sad.
For tucked away within your
heart,
Was a dream of long ago. . .
Of how you'd take the gospel,
To a people who yearned to
grow.
And then the call for a Doctor
From the Seminary was heard. . .
And again you met the
challenge,
While your parents thought it
absurd.
Several hundred miles to New
Orleans
To train the preacher-boys;
The four of you adjusted well,
Amongst the work and toys.
And just as life had settled
down,
In this city with so much sin.
A doctors voice you
understood—
To say, "you're having twins."
Forget about that dream of old—
Thru the years you'd nursed
with joy
Because added to your family
now
Was two darling little boys.
Now who could take four
children
To a far off distant land?
Well only the Reverend
Copelands'
Who allowed God to draw their
plan.
So you see we've learned a
lesson,
As we've watched your life
unfold.
As you helped and hurt and
ministered—
You were only mastering the
goal. . .
Of the test you passed that God
had set,
To make your dream come
true. . .
And we were *oh So Fortunate*—
To have spent some time with
you.
So it's with our prayers and
heartfelt love
We say to you today. . .
"May God's richest blessing
rest on you,
As he sends you on your way.!"

Evelyn Bitz

COME GENTLE DEATH

Oh! Master, this servant has
worked long in your vineyard.
Her back is stooped now and
aches with each step she
takes.
The quick, bright mind that
loved the rosy sunsets, the
trill of meadowlarks;
That taught us all a love of
truth and goodness by
example,
Now only sees the things that
are wrong and sad in the
world—
Her soul no longer feels the joy.
The heart that once was big
enough for eight of us
That cared about our joys and
sorrows, hopes and fears,
Now only thinks that someone
may be cheating her,
Not giving full measure.
She was perhaps the bravest,
strongest one I'll ever know,
But now she's worn, she's tired;
she no longer hopes nor
dreams.
She longs for a place where she
will no longer ache;
Where she will feel at home and
in her rightful place;
Where she will be useful and
work for others as she always
has.
But she has worked too long and
worried too much,
And had too many dreams come
crashing down.
There seems to be no place for
her that feels like home
anymore.
Oh, Lord, please take her to you
soon before we forget how she
was once—
How brave, how strong, how
good!
Come gentle death.
Come gentle, gentle death.

Brenda Stuber

FADED LIGHT (A MURDERER'S TALE)

Tell me, if you know
if you can see.
the light I use to know
is fading
but not with the sun.
The warmth my hand
use to feel,
it only trembles from
the burning hatred it felt
and not from the sun
glistening off the sweat.
Eyes of mine
look for a smile
if only for a while
but with a blast
my eyes feel that cold,
brazen look of my doing.

Never
to hold my head high
again.
I'm a man
but yet I cry.
Remembering still
the flash of anger
the radiant heat I felt.
The droplets of sweat
had blurred my vision,
as I felt him melt
beneath my hand.
Tell me, if you know
if you can see,
the light that filled my soul
has suddenly
turn black and cold.
Like dying embers
within my heart,
shall I turn to stone?
People have built a wall
around me
and in darkness
I am alone.

Nell Wilson
POP—TOLDJA
Bip's a pip in a pop—toldja egg!
If you don't believe it, you ask
Poppa daddy if he isn't the
father of some kind of a seed
that was planted in the head of
a hair brained idiot like me.
Little Marie. (Hair—brained
idiot means comical.)
I'm Just three.
The way to turn a Flippant a flip
is to take a nip out of a tong—
oil tree with a chop—suey ax.
That is the same as an ABC
recipe. Lay the ax at the root
of the tree. You don't chop the
tree down, because it's comical.
You use the oil that comes from
the tree trunk and you won't
spoil. The oil from the tree is
considered to be fruit which you
may trade for money so you can
keep on being funny. Aw, Gene.
Aw, Autrey—I'll hush—must
rush. No gun. Won't travel.

Jack Knee
SAN FRANCISCO BAY
As we strolled along the busy
Quay one sunny summers day
We came upon a sailing ship
moored in San Francisco Bay,
I took my sweeheart by the
hand, as we clambered to the
decks
Wild with expectation as to
what would happen next.
As we walked upon the decks of
old, I thought of the sailorman
And if he thought he'd ever see,
the sight of another land.
Did he also dream of a beautiful
girl, like the one standing
close to me,
Or was his life all hardships-the
hardships of the sea.
We found a narrow passageway
and went down to the decks
below
Those decks hand hewn by men
long gone, those decks of
ashen gold.
I held my sweetheart tenderly,
Oh God! how I remember
When I asked if she would be
my bride, I felt her body's
tremor
She said, "Someday this might
be, but for now we'd have to
wait and see.
I need you and I want you and I
wish it could forever be,
Although we love each other so,
there are things I must
consider
I would not want to hurt some
others and cause them to be
bitter."
So now I stroll the Quay of Life
and dream of her for me,
And I hope and pray there's a
Sailor Saint who will grant my
humble plea.
I dream about my beautiful girl
that might come to me
someday
I dream about my beautiful girl
and the ship moored in Frisco
Bay.

Paula Iwamoto
MAGIC PURGED
A star fell down from the sky
and plunked right into my
pocket
With "Here I am! Make a wish!"
Written upon it in neons.
(For, if left to chance, it had
merely
fallen and landed no place in
particular as stars usually do,
I may have overlooked it
as I watched, say, a wino
collapse,
or the numbers on a McDonald's
sign change.)
So there I was with anything in
the world I desired.
I turned greedy.
I contemplated wishing for gold,
or a throne to give divine
judgements from,
or the awe of criminals and
kings,
In shame, I turned
humanitarian.
I considered wishing for peace
on earth,
and goodwill towards man,
and lots of other things
straight off Christmas cards.
Then I sat down and really
asked
myself what I needed and
realized:
I had you.
And you are all that I need.
I pulled the star from my pocket
and threw it back to the sky,
Leaving a smudge on the
sidewalk as if someone
had spilled a 10-cent bottle of
glitter.
Then I came to you.
I put my arms around you and
the universe narrows
to a pencil-thin slice of time
and space
with just the two of us in it.

Kimberly Jo Cox
HAVE YOU EVER BEEN ALONE?
Have you ever been alone
Wishing that the sun had shone?
Reaching, grasping for a hand,
Wanting someone from this
land
To understand your ways and
deeds;
Someone who would fill your
needs,
Touching only deep inside
Wanting you to be his bride,
Knowing love and joy and peace
Feelings that would never
cease—
When this special person comes
I will hear the distant drums,
And I always will be free
To love the man who found my
key.

Edwin S. Segal
STORM
Walking through the forest
groves,
Silent sweep of feelings, soft—
Floating through my tree lined
mind,
Limb to limb, from brain to
trunk,
Soft caress to soothe my heart.
Winds in waving trees lift up,
Catching clouds in fluffy sky,
Driving puffs to scudding storm.
Black bottomed billows, driven,
Full fury storm of tempest
Strength—temper sweeps
through tall trunks,
Passion whipped from root to
crown.
Power pulses, pounds, and fills
Bending boles, fusing. Soft
storms
Rage and flow, making unity.

Semon Haines
UNEXPLAINED ENDINGS
Sometimes things go good.
Times are sweet,
Nights are long,
And love is good.
Trials come, moods change and
Midnight comes too soon,
Stays too long, and
Blocks out the sunshine of
a new dawn.

James K. McLane
HOW?
How shall I show that I love
you?
With what rod could I measure
the depths?
And which cloud shall I choose
for the height?
Where shall I find the meter for
the straight, to gather the
width and length into
numbers?
Shall I measure according to
the intensity of my needs,
or with the longings of my
soul?
Or shall I add the numbers of
my dreams, and divide by the
sum of tears shed in your
absence?
How do I take the contents of
my heart, and rightly divide
the happiness and sorrow?
For even as I have loved you in
the warm breeze of
contentment,
I have loved you more against
the winds of despair!
And as I have loved you in the
beauty of your presence;
I have loved you unbearably
more in the agony of your
absence!
I have found that love is
nurtured by many things, of
which not one can be
measured!
For it knows no bound, nor does
it follow the course of man's
plans.
Rather man seek to know its'
paths, and the bounty of its'
fruit.
So I shall not attempt to
define my love with such an
inferior tool as the English
language.
Nor shall I attempt to confine
my feelings and emotions to
the limited boundaries of the
written word.
For words cannot hold the
feelings that fill my heart;
Nor can they impart to you
the knowledge of the joy that
fills the depths of my
existence!
So let my life be the rod by
which you measure;
And my faithfulness be the
means to show the depth;
And let the height be defined
with the passage of time;
And let my soul reveal to you
the length and breadth!

Margaret L. Grubbs
IT'S CHRISTMAS—NOW AND THEN
The windows of memory are
gleaming tonight
With candles of Christmases
past
And hearts gone away are
dreaming tonight
In shadows by old embers cast
In a long ago lane it's snowing
tonight

And a bell in a village is
ringing
Late shoppers are to and fro-ing
tonight
Leaving smiles with those who
are singing
Warm gingerbread cookies are
spicing tonight
In an oven lit brightly with love
Gay mittens and scarves are
de-icing tonight
Wet frozen with flakes from
above

The Christmas tree Angel is
glowing tonight
With the special glow of the
season
From the street comes a jolly
ho ho-ing tonight
And small children laugh
without reason
On a long ago pond there is
skating tonight
And lashes and snowflakes are
tangling

A warmly lit fire is waiting
tonight
For the sound of skates
homeward jangling
And over the merry making
tonight
The sound of a small Drummer's
drums
Brings a thrill that is close
to aching tonight
With it's joyous A-Rum-Pa-Pum-
Pums
On a far away Christmas I'm
seeing tonight
The faces of those who are dear
And counting the blessings of
being tonight
With those who laugh with me
here
And a bright suspicion is
growing tonight
That a Christmas is never past
But is only a joy that is going
tonight
To be part of the joy of the
last
And oh! How the memories are
singing tonight
In the heart they are so
treasured in
For wherever a bell is ringing
tonight
It's Christmas—Now and then!

Christine E. Pacanowski
LETTING GO . . .
think of me as you read
for. . .
our time has ended
left is the memories
together we shared
those days of laughter and of
tears
walking hand in hand
reaching for the heavens
and not quite making it
it didn't matter
we had no fear
we had each other
love danced between our
hearts
like starlite on the water
when (and if) you remember me
remember the fun we shared
our dreams come true
times we cried and dried
each others tears
those times we cared.
you were tender and
understanding
a friend I could turn to.
we talked of love and happiness
our goals; we made it.
but now you are yesterday
gone too soon
you are the memories
filling my mind
like the tears filling my eyes
a page in the book of our lives
is turned
good-bye my love
it's so hard to. . .
let go

Shirley Ann McDaniel
APOLOGIES
Pardon me
if I make you uncomfortable
by seeming an ominous, black
cloud
in your sunny, white world.
I didn't mean
to cause you pain
by insisting upon my rights
so that I could be equal to you.
I'm sorry
if it vexes your mind and soul
when I try to make you
understand me
in hopes that your hatred will
dissipate.
And please forgive me
if it makes you angry
that I feel it is you—
who should be apologizing to
me.

Ola Margaret James
SONNET IN SOLITUDE
If death were simple as some
would believe,
The withering of a tree, the
fading of a rose,
Instead of longing, deep and
wild,
To come into a house of blood
and bone,
And so work out the problem
that is life,
Instead of self-destruction, the
mistake
Leaves yet the soul in baffled
strife;
Glad would I plunge me in the
waters dim,
Become a soundless circle and
no more,
A simple, soundless circle and
no more,
But when I must come face to
face with Him
Who gave me life, I cannot leave
the shore,
So one must stand, do battle,
and progress,
For He would have His children
do no less.

Virginia White Turley
FREE WITH GOD
When I bowed my head
this morning to pray,
I thought of Flanders Field
and all those crosses row on row
and all those voices stilled.
And then I thought of all
the Wars and the price of
our freedom this day.
That you and I might lift
our voice to these and give
them praise.
This freedom we take
for granted, not thinking
we really must share.
For it belongs to Flanders Field,
the ones that truly did care.
Stilled by a weapon held
by a man, they kept America
free.
So you and I could worship
and work,
in the Land of Liberty.
Don't take for granted
our freedom today.
It was a price someone
has paid, maybe a father,
maybe a son, but it doesn't
matter our freedom they won.
Let's share this freedom
with all the world, and let
them know this day, for all
of those that gave their life,
we lift our hands in praise.
But there's another freedom
that only God can give.
If we can see this freedom
then Flanders Field will live.
It's Love, It's Mercy and
It's Power, that makes our
way seem right.
Even our mission we thought
was wrong, we made in
the darkness of night.
I wonder if our hostages
heard about this mission,
The one that made the
blind to see.
The one without commission.
This mission they thought
they crucified and sealed
with a Roman stone,
But there's not a rock
that He can't move,
When He claims us for
His own.
*(To President Jimmy Carter
With Love, Your Best, My Best)*

Randolph Adams
FREE TO BE ALONE
I cannot alone take upon
Myself the lesson to be free.
Freedom is not mine alone.
If alone, I cannot be free
To be free alone is only to be
alone.
Free as it be has its demands
I will demand your hand in
partner
Not to take anything away from
you
But to ask your help!
I cannot alone, be alone!
I cannot alone, be free.
You must take my hand;
Alone, I am alone.
With you, I alone will be FREE.

Patrick Russell Gibbons
UNTITLED
The sky is warm
but all around is ice.
The ground is cold
but my warm feet will start;
and when the heat
emerges from my eyes,
the dripping tears will freeze
that melt my heart.

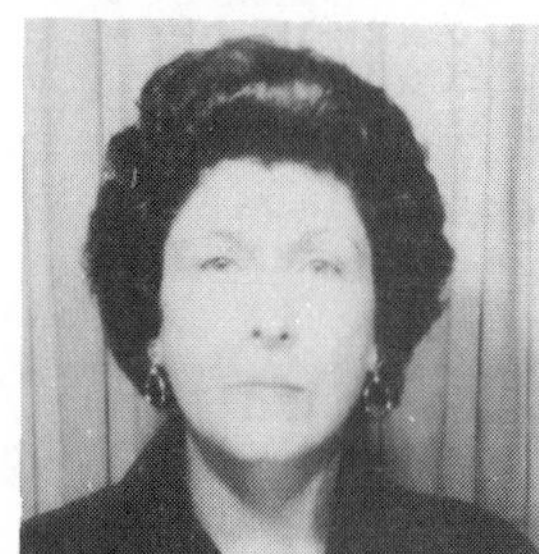

Katherine Wall McDowell
A BROTHER'S A THING TO TREASURE
In the bud of our years;
When tender hearts, keep
rhythm with love's measure
In life's green garden, thrice
blessed are we,
If we have a brother to treasure.
The budding heart knows
naught of hate,
Nor vengeful, hurtful pride.
Aloof from Satan's lure, love
springs pure
In the child heart not yet
tried.
O'er life's difficult path to go
Brother to Brother closer grow;
Holding the other in brotherly
pride—
Threading the maze of
childhood side by side.
In family circle bound secure;
Love grows strong, as love grows
pure.
Should not such love for aye
endure—
A brother's a thing to treasure.
Though life decree that ways
must part—
Cast not your brother from your
heart
Tokens of love leave not
undone, e'en though your
lot be a harried one—
A brother's a thing to treasure.
Release your soul to love
perfected.

Know a heart neglected is a
heart rejected.
Sustain the love flower fair;
Lest fain, it wilt in despair.
A letter, a word, a remembrance
small,
To bring to the longing heart
pleasure;
For love they sing is a living
thing,
And of sustenance must have
it's measure.
Forgive longing heart—
The sin of neglect,
To all erring hearts we owe
respect;
But a brother's a thing to
Treasure.

Marjorie Benchoff
A BEAUTIFUL STORY
In my heart I long to tell,
A beautiful story to all children
who dwell,
On a earth thats so full of
God's radiant love,
As He dwells with each of us,
in Heaven above.
A universe in beauty and form
we can see,
Each beautiful creation thats
been touched by Thee,
Man cannot make such beauty
to behold,
Each beautiful sight God does
unfold.
God gave us a world to in
beauty dwell,
He gave us His Son to a future
life tell,
That life be renewed from wrong
to right,
Leading others from temptation
as they Him sight.
For as Jesus on earth with man
did dwell
A beautiful future life He did us
tell,
It unfolds in a peace and joy all
men need.
Placed here in the Bible for us

to read.
God gave His Son as a Babe in Bethlehem long ago
That throughout the world all men would Him know,
Jesus life complete, He died for man,
As He was placed on the Cross, nailed by each hand.
As nails did pierce Jesus' body that day
He died for our sins to be taken away,
Yes Jesus hung on that cruel Rugged Cross
Saving all souls that they wouldn't be lost.
Then in the tomb His body was laid,
But our loving Lord Jesus arose from that grave,
That we inherit strength to cleanse us free,
All this God did for you and me.
Then Jesus ascended into Heaven above,
Sending us His promised peaceful love.
Remember God's gracious love is near,
Abide in Christ, listen and hear,
The words Jesus spoke so long ago,
Are awaiting in the Bible today, for you to know.
In a joy and peace only God's love can tell,
Of that Heavenly home where you will someday dwell,
So reign on the strength and love and peace,
In that beautiful story, Jesus came to teach.

Richard Shoupe

BLUE COLLAR

Factory town smoking—
daylight without and
choking laborers
lost within a maze of machinery
that clanks and grinds
heartless music
into hopeless minds.
Whistle
shrilly shatters the silence.
Workers mechanically flow out factory doors,
shielding their eyes from blinding floodlights
in the parking lot at dusk.
Sunless city
stares the workers down
into thoughts of escape.
Monotonous drone
of the company treadmill
marches them on,
directionless, despairing,
drained of all dreams.
Cardboard houses, plastic food,
burdens mounting daily—
they set their teeth, close their eyes,
forging their way
into a future that offers no hope of change.

Patricia L. Schuler

NOVEMBER NIGHT

The desert air is cold
as the sinking sun slides low
behind the butte.
And starkly silhouetted in the dusk
the monuments stand
sentry
round the camp.
A curl of golden flame licks
the night air.
We sit, your arm around me,
bringing close,
your warmth and mine.
The plastic cup of wine
we share.
Your unshaven face brushes my cheek.
Four of us sit, laughing, singing,
Gordon telling stories
only Gordon could invent.
Bill, with Diasy's head
upon his lap.
Her shimmering fur looks
warmer than the fire.
Against the etched horizon
spreads a glow
and, slowly, round and huge,
the moon ascends.
I catch my breath,
you draw me closer still,
to watch that globe
reach up into the heavens
and outline every rock and bit of scrub
and you and me and Gordon and Bill
sitting upon the desert floor.
My heart and soul are floating
from the wine and you.
The flame grows small
and crumbles into embers
and the cold air crawls
beneath my collar
up my legs
against my scalp.
We're side by side
my sleeping bag and yours.
The sky is pierced
with twinkling stars.
"Good night," you say
and I reply in kind
and close my eyes.
I breathe the chilly air
and the precious night.
Your kiss is quick
on the tip of my nose
and I open my eyes
but you've turned away.
I want to sing and laugh
and hug you.
I smile and close my eyes
but fail to fall alseep.

Mary Lee

GOD'S CHRISTMAS TO ALL OF US

A long time ago in a forest there lived so many trees.
They greeted each other and did most as they pleased.
When the weather was warm the branches rested in the sun.
When the rains came they curled tighter together to keep warm

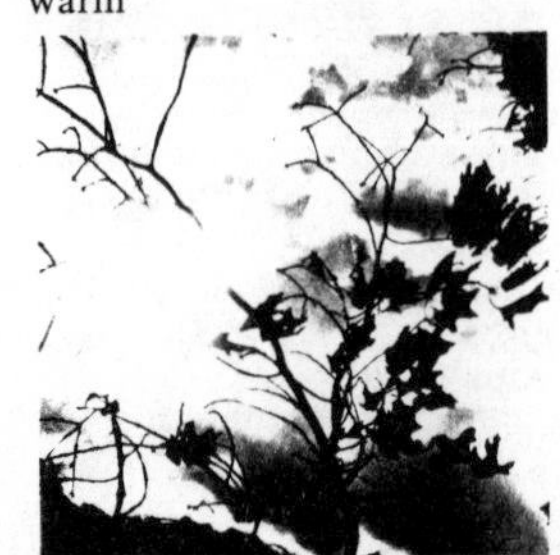

When fall came in wonder and frost 'bit their toes
And rose up to the trunks of the trees and the leaves scarlet rose,
To the tops of the trees all bitten scarlet and red.
The trees wore a host of colors painted by some one's great hand.
Then one day the snow came after a drizzling rain
And frosted all the trees like a beautiful wedding cake.
The snow flakes hurried together on the branches here and there.
Like a skater on a lake what could be more fair?
All the beauty of winter frosted green and white,
And the branches looked like diamonds on a starry night.
The silence remained unbroken, a silence everywhere.
A branch fell in the night like an answered prayer.
The hill sides were covered with snow.
When day light came a deer showed himself beside a tree.
A rabbit scurried from a bush to look on winter's purity.
The snow birds gathered berries on a bush not too far by,
And they flew away in unison to thank some one bigger than you and I.
A little dog ran to greet me across the fields of snow.
He had laughing eyes and I rubbed his cold nose.
I looked out the window to nature's flying sky.
And then the flakes seemed to rest against a moon light sky.
The hushness of this wonder and the whispers of the wind,
And the icy frosted icicles made tinkling sounds in the wind.
Then we heard friendly laughter and sleigh bells ringing too.
A horse gave a friendly neigh and his breath was white and blue.
They waved to us and the horse and the sleigh seemed to ride,
Into the heavenly sky o'er the fields of white.
We looked out side in wonder as these trees gave us a special blessing.
We heard the melody, "You know this is christmas."
A real christmas the trees seemed to say, because you appreciate
All of God's blessings in a wonderful way.
You have been so thankful and humble things do please,
"So we the trees of the forest are to be your christmas trees.
Even to the smallest tree and the tallest in the sky,
And the stars you see in the heavens will top each tree in God's sky.
Because you know Christ, a little babe was born some one bigger
Than you and I!"

Ged

UNTITLED

A
C
H
A
N
D
E
L
I
E
R
F
E
L
L
A
N
D
TT R EH A E S D
T O I N
SN I LO L M I
F O
C SE E P I
(NEW PARTS)

Warren Versluis

RENAISSANCE

Spring did not come on time that year
So deep the icy reign,
Its heart was caught in winter's throat
As birth is caught in pain.
How bound my heart that winter's end
Beneath a veil of grief,
And yet my troubles were too few
For me to find relief.
But then one night a storm raged whole
Of wild wind and rain,
And in the residue of birth
We found our way again.

Juanita Wallace

LOVE YOURSELF

Love yourself
and begin to live,
To those in need
truly give
a helping hand
til alone they can stand.
Love yourself
and begin to feel
a dawning of truth
about which is real;
the freedom of sharing
and the joys from caring.
Love yourself
and others will see
that beautiful person. . . .
you call me.

Kahaunani Miles

TO TOUCH THE HAND OF GOD

My closest friend knows all of me
He shared grief and died for me
As I grew he said to me
Time is now to let you go
You then shall find the path ahead
To know our love divine
You'll waken to our suns full light
To gaze into the starlit skies
These things are free and when you need
I shall be there to touch your cheek
Now I'm awake and he is here

Once more to touch my life in
grace
As I am told our love expands
When we begin to understand
As all eyes see what God
intended all to be
So long, in Church within
himself
Man tries to reach depth where
it once was
To feel the freedom meant to
be
Know channels where the
human being
Becomes wholesome perfect in
his sphere
Where grace performs to blend
all into streams
Where purified each eye may
see
The glitter of each golden beam
To know we stand upon the
threshold of
The "Holy Realm" to know its
here
What man once dreamed as we
all stop
Still it be, protruding will
the lighted path
Lay in our midst as shadows
disappear
To now let go of past as
present brings a mass
To know with practice came the
goal
To Love Thy God with all thine
heart with soul
To find the fountain which
brings life
To grasp and hold at last to
be at home
To view the veil removed where
stands this fountain
"Everlasting Life" which will
enfold, "Perfected Life"
As granderous joy perpetuates
"Eternal Life"
Love now in Christ walks hand
in hand to know the bond
Which bands the lock to now
hold fast while we reach forth
To touch "THE HAND OF
GOD"

Carel Meninno

DID ANYONE KNOW HER

did anyone know her like I did
did anyone see the nightmare
dreams in her life
I watched her grow old from
worries of the mind
as miseries of the soul took
their toll
did you know her
did anyone know her. . .like I
did
lovers turned into strangers,
laughter turned into tears
but always her heart was torn
into pieces
daylight turned into darkness,
truth turned into lies
and the trust she once felt left
forever
did you know her
did anyone know her. . .like I
did
I visited her grave today
the flowers had begun to grow
there
and the birds chirped sweetly
keeping her company
but I can't help remembering
when she came to me with tears
in her eyes
telling me there no longer was
hope
did you know her
did anyone know her. . .like I
did

Linda (Hogg) White

YOU

You make me feel like a flower
just in bloom,
With you there are no clouds of
gloom,
You make me feel the warm
sunshine,
When our bodies are entwined.
I have a glow,
Only one in love can know,
Without you I have no rest,
With you I am at my best.
I need no drug-no pill,
For with you I am fulfilled,
You are my heartbeat and my
breath,
And I'll love you til my death.

Molly Perkins

I HAD FORGOTTEN

I had forgotten
what it was like
to be away from my own space,
until I went back there,
and remembered
what it was like
to be away from you.

Mary Grace Carbone

FAITH

Having Faith-in one another:
Are the seeds that roots-forms
plants and flowers
Keep growing, yielding fruits,
our needs for our today
And tomorrows.
Inspiring Faith-with all, "Sisters
and Brothers":
It may be only inspirations
But, it helps to build large
plantations
Helps us to ration, all of our
frustrations
Gives us a helping hand-and
to understand
Only, if we keep sharing and
caring with no demands.
Having Faith-in and with our
dear ones:
If you are fortunate to have
it-keep it sacred
It is yours for what you make
it—
It glows in the dark-sings like
a lark
Shines like a star, follows you
wherever you are.
A Growing Faith-each with his
own:
It may be a special blend-or
like a precious gem
It's ours, till the very end
It's free, till eternity
It's ours alone-be it soft or
hard as stone
To share or not, it is for us,
to put to measure
Hold it dearly, it's our only
treasure.
A Special Faith: In our Creator:
The greatest gift we could
receive
In Him we must believe
If it's there, it is in our hearts
Hold it closely, never from us,
let it part
First, last, to Him call
He'll adore that loving trust,
especially; when we accept
It all, the if's and the musts,
sincerely fair, always just—
Our gives and takes-He adds
them altogether
Subtracts and saves for us-the
better
All our values, as, accounted
for, are what we shall reap
Big or small-are ours-all for
keeps, the good of the earth
With all it's worths, never
lonely-happiness only
For that we may be sure, all
else He'll help us endure.

A Faith so strong, can do no
wrong-cause He is there to
guide us
And that good faith shall
always be there beside us.

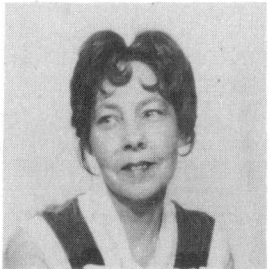

Merle Darnell Jennings

TREE OF DESTINY

Come, sit down and listen
quietly, and I will tell you a
story,
as it was told to me.
A story told by many
generations, of both disgrace
and glory.
A story of a man and a tree.
The tree is known as the
Dogwood, the man as Jesus.
both will become figures of
destiny.
Jesus was devine, he came to
free men in both spirit and
flesh,
for this jealous men will
sentence him to death.
The Dogwood Tree was used to
make the cross on which Jesus
was crucified.
on that dark and destined day.
The flowering tree, was once
long ago, or so the old folks say,
a towering, gigantic tree,
but has never grown huge again,
and remains a dwarf tree in size.
since that gloomy day Jesus
died.
The whiteness of the flowers
represents the purness of an
unblemished soul,
Jesus the son, for money,
betrayed and sold.
Three petals, one golden center,
the Father the Spirit and Son,
yet, they are one.
As I said, the flowers were once,
before Jesus died, to onlookers'
delight,
a solid snow white.
Yet, now and since the hour
Jesus died, each white petal,
took on its' tip the color red.
The color red on the tip of each
petal of the beautiful Dogwood
Tree,
represents the blood Jesus
shed for the atonement of sin.
This tree stands a witness that
Jesus came and will come again,
a witness for the whole world
to see,
that God so loved the world he
gave his only begotten son,
on the cross at calvery.

Harriett Katherine Atherton Croskrey

THE MEMORY OF YOU

The memory of you
I carry, deep,
Within my heart.
I Loved You.
A more beautiful person
I could never,
Hope to meet.
So Beautiful.
That crazy smile
Is laughter to me,
You always smiled.
So Carefree.
I could not
Be near you,
Without laughing too.
Like Summer Rain.
Your eyes, your hair,
Your gentle touch
I miss you
So Much.
That it hurts!
I love you,
Still.

Genevieve R. Erwin

IN MEMORIAM

A dear, sweet soul has gone to
his rest,
One who was kind, loving, and
true;
One who lived each day as best
He could for I'm sure he knew.
He carried his cross e'er with a
smile
For he was never known to
frown;
God helped him over every mile,
He never let on when he felt
down.
Sometimes we wonder why
things are so,
But we are sure God has a plan;
Each day and onward as we go,
Sometimes it's hard to
understand.
We know he's not suffering any
more
And that, with God, he rests in
peace;
For him, God has opened up
Heaven's door
And all his earthly cares have
ceased.

Adolfo Reyes

STARS

Their quiet might released
The stars prepare the night for
earth
Profuse with rays that ever
stream to blaze.
Vast number seems increased
As dim suns burn from nightly
birth
To stamp their lantern screen
with glowing haze.
Cosmic force bangs unceased
In timeless spread of astral
girth

Yes, stars reflect grand poise
to pensive gaze.
Far sunset's gleaming trace
Shoots azure sky's soft light
inclined
And strings long shadows rising
to suffuse.
Shaded tones quite encase
Day's fleeting breadth left
undesigned
Save for blinking candle spark
to infuse.
Sheer music beams through
space
To slowly soothe the restless
mind
And create hushed moments of
grateful muse.
Stern whirl of time commits
My stress toward material flair
To only lose green fields
uncaringly.
Glad smile at once admits
Whispered welcome of open air
That evening sway of nature
swings to me.
Bright sky tonight transmits
The flame to notions that I dare.
Thank the stars for this brood
that sets me free.
Forget sealed nights unseen
For settled thought slipped by
their wing
And left a belted breast
downhearted yet.
Meaning looms dark between
Moonlit chasms that wonder
bring
To stolid eye in search of no
regret.
The time to turn serene
Lies not before, but now to
spring.
Release the lock within your
face to let.
Stark heart that favor lacks
Remains unmoved by mournful
plight
And shocks beloved hope with
baneful scorn.
Keep me down to brass tacks
When dreams unveil the real at
night
To Simply crack my world upon
the morn.
While Man carves careful tracks
Eternal stars await his flight—
But, "Do they now impress the
man forlorn?"

Carolyn M. Kurth

THE NIGHT TOO, MUST DIE. . .

In Kashmir, under the pale of
the moon
Where the lotus blossoms
float along the river bank,
I dreamt of your coming and I
touched my heart
To still its wild beating. In
the dank
Of the early morning mist.
I gazed upon the mountains,
far-flung and free
And yearned for the sight of
you, the touch of you,
The love you gave to me.
Now, through a succession of
days and nights,
I am lost in a labyrinth of
despair; I cry. . .
For the white-winged heron no
longer calls to his mate
And the moon, wan and
beclouded,
Hangs like a host in the sky;
The bird songs of twilight have
all been stilled,
Even as my heart,
For the night, too, must
die. . . .

Donald J. Bayman

TO JEFFREY

I saw the boy so quick and
deep—
His eyes were closed, though
not in sleep.
His ears were deaf—He could
not hear
The dirgeful song that lingered
near.
The boy's young friends could
only cry
Their shameless tears that
would not dry.
His cup of life had now been
spilled
And emptied out—so sparsely
filled!
The room was hot and sweet
with smell
Of flowers sent in hope to quell
The silent fears—Despite belief
That naught could salve their
aching grief.
We must give up and let him
go. . .
And all the spirits we may know
Can not restore his absent
breath. . .
For only God can conquer death!

Judith Ann Mason

THE REARRANGEMENT

If the situation were different,
I wouldn't be walking alone,
The March wind whipping my
eyes,
And clutching my pocket
linings instead of your hands.
In the beginning we knew:
It was strange, impossible, but
not entirely wrong.
Your life. . .my life. . .they
both had been already cast.
We forgot vulnerability.
Lightning splits trees.
Love divides arrangements.
Love, forceful lightning,
Wedged a crack in the mold of
our lives.
React?
Sure we did.
Sporadically, deeply, humanly!
Our minds, our bodies. . .
symmetry.
A symphony that hit a flat note.
It had to remain unfinished.
Almost famous, ours, like
Beethoven.
The piano remains silent as
does our love.
How clever our reasoning.
Or was it?
We took what was ours. . .a
moment. . .an hour.
Why do I still feel cheated?
I believe it's harder,
Knowing we will see each other
nearly every day,
Remembering we cannot, must
not touch.
I want to touch you.
The solution. . .so simple, so
impossible—
If one were able to rearrange
lives as one does music.
You explained that once:
too many flats, too many
sharps, and a
crescendo without an
ending.
Indeed, and I can't even sing!

Donald J. Bayman

THE SILENT SCREAMS

The silent screams cannot be
heard—
They echo forth in chambers
closed
To human senses, numbed by
fear
Of finding them. Before the
word
Of Godless men, they don't
exist.
The moral problems that they
posed
Seem solved by argument you
hear—
They never lived—they won't be
missed.
But, hear the voice you can't
ignore—
The voice inside that speaks
with love.
Unless you heed, the curse will
send
From Babylon, the naked whore
To make the dawn of life a
tomb!
We must believe that God
above
Will bless the man who helps
defend
The sanctuary of the womb.
Let hate not spawn its
nightmare—dreams
To deafen conscience. . .kneel
and pray
That God will send His love
today. . .
For love can stop the silent
screams.

Janet Kay Osborne

BEAUTY

BEAUTY is that intangible quality which in the mind of the beholder gives expression and meaning to every aspect of life. Without beauty, the world would be an ugly place, full of ugly people going to ugly places doing ugly things. Beauty is a necessity. Beauty releases you from your tensions. Beauty refreshes you, gives you a new spurt of life. . .

Beauty is watching a surging, roaring waterfalls. . .
Beauty is going on a solitary walk on a country lane through a woods. . .
Beauty is relaxing on a raft in the middle of a lake enjoying the coolness of the water. . .
Beauty is walking bare-headed through a spring shower. . .
Beauty is climbing up a steep mountain path with the aspiration of reaching the peak. . .
Beauty is looking out your kitchen window into your backyard and being filled with gratitude for God for having granted you all this. . .
Beauty is feeling in unity with your surging, leaping mount. . .
Beauty is having friends. . .
Beauty is letting the wind play with your long, silken hair. . .
Beauty is being able to curl up with a good book in the attic during a thunderstorm. . .
Beauty is giving a smile, instead of a stare. . .
Beauty is being alive and fully enjoying every minute of it. . .
Beauty is soaring above the earth in a manmade wonder. . .
Beauty is traveling to new lands, meeting new people and learning to expand our life philosophies. . .
Beauty is having a pet. . .
Beauty is breathing in a lungful of fresh spring air. . .
Beauty is running in the sun. . .
Beauty is lying in a tree, hidden by leaves, dreaming. . .
Beauty is being free. . .
Beauty is being able to fling your arms wide open and cry at the top of your voice, "I'm glad I'm alive!". . .
Beauty is music, which nourishes the soul. . .
Beauty is love. . .love between parent and child. . .love between friends. . .love between lovers. . .
Beauty is a Home, a place where you can always feel secure and wanted. . .
Beauty is being able to see all men as brothers. . .
Beauty is helping others. . .
Beauty is Humor. . .
Beauty is being yourself. . .
Beauty is nature. . .
Beauty is beauty. . .
Beauty is God. . .

Ralph Quick Coplin

THOSE SPIDER MESHES

There's a spider goin' to get
you if you don't watch out,
Can't you see de web him
spinnin' and all de time him
singin'
Day and night him plannin',
prayin' and him Lord he hear
him sayin'
De good Lord he hear him
prayin' and him sayin' loud
and prayin',
"Lord, you knows as how I loves
her an' as how there is no
other
can compare with this lil' gal
o-mine."
Dat pritty web it growin',
grown', all de while this gal
am known'
Jest which way de wind am
blowin', am contented, pleased
an' happy
An' she says, "Come spider wrap
me in de meshes of your web,
For I love its silkin' fiber jest

gwan, make those meshes wider,
For I love you wiley spider, sing and build those meshes higher."
Says this sweetest lil' gal o-mine.
"For my heart am in your meshes and the Lord he know my wish is
That I long to take a peep into your parlor, diner, kitchen."
Some these days she lay her hand in, 'fore the pahson we'll be standin'
Hearin' words that preacher sayin', how as one we e'ver should stay in
To this web we now am weaven', true till death an' ne'er deceivin',
Me an' this sweetest lil' gal o-mine

Joan Dolby

IN THE CITY

The duck waddled on down the street
sticking his beak up at those he'd meet
I couldn't believe what my eyes did see
to see a duck walk beside of me.
The City around still acted the same
I couldn't stand it, I asked him his name
He said it was Ingle as simple as that
then his voice quacked, "Get off my back".
What could I do but turn away?
I forgot to rehearse what to say
Still the City was usual and hard
walking in tune, smoking cigars.
He hurried his pace with eyes that were bare
made it harder for me to accept what's rare
As I walked away I felt a deep pity
I guess I deserved this for living in the City.

Radford Riggles

WHY IS IT TO BE

Why is it to be, that we are what we are in reality?
Could it be, that we shall see when we touch infinity?
Then what is this? A show for thee, to watch our collective destiny.
Or is it just some game you play? No, no, there is no way.
Could it be a dream gone bad a nightmare in a way?
A war you've fought from day to day, and for eons more will wage.
If that the case, I sadly say I cannot even pray.
So if it be, I sadly see why we are what we are in reality.

Donna Rae Brokaw

YOU'RE DREAMING

I feel sorry for you because you
wanted me to hate you also
because you thought that I
cared.
You said you wanted me to go
on living without you yet you
didn't want me to forget that
you were there.
I know that as a person and in
our relation you were never
honest and in a sense "real."
Maybe someday you'll find
something to believe in and
within your own world you
won't dwell.
Your dreams and your memories
are together as your future is a
part of your past.
You want to be kept in my
dreamland yet you never let my
part in your life last.
I'll never really know what you
wanted from me nor will I ever
really know what you did feel.
I only know that for you I feel
so very sorry
because you see in my life you
were never "real."
You wanted to be a part of me
to be the reason I'd be able to do
what I can
to be the most important want
in my life,
but to leave me knowing that
I'd never be your woman.

David G. Harris

THAT CERTAIN SOMEONE

You are that certain someone
I look for all the time.
When I see you with that other guy, what can I say,
Nothing except
I like you, too.
You are that certain someone
Who makes my day complete.
You make the sun rise,
You make the rain go away and what can I say,
I like you, too.
You are many things to me,
Thats why I say,
Certain someone, come to me
I like you, too.

Jack Cirulli

ALL THAT COULD'VE BEEN

unwed mother,
unborn child
and a slow train back to Boston.
all there is,
all that was,
and all that could've been.

Mary Newland Roberts

MUSINGS OF AN AFTERNOON AND EVENING

I met a lady who talked about the mail.
She talked on and on as I sat on the rail.
She talked about how the beans would grow
And the corn, too, if it weren't for that crow.
I liked to hear her talk,
Who cares if she bent my ear?
She was happy and she must have thought
She wouldn't see me for a year.
Well, the sky turned gold
As the sun set behind the hill.
The wind grew strong
And I felt a chill.
I knew I'd have to build a fire
To warm my feet-come time to retire.
I had no one to snuggle up to
So a good hot fire would just have to do.
I thought of the lady who liked to talk.
Could She be lonely too?
Maybe I'd invite her to go for a walk.
Who knows *what* might brew?
She could keep me informed of all the news
While we sit before the fire.
Together we could share our views
And be happy when we retire.
—hope she won't mind my collection of rocks,
—hope she's a good cook.
—hope she'll darn my collection of socks.
—hope she likes a good book.
Woah! Halt! Hang on! Stop!
Before I run for the preacher you see.
I'd better find out if she even likes me.

Elizabeth S. Knox

THE OLD FLU BUG

The "Old Flu Bug" made its visit as usual this year
It made it far and made it near,
And quite a few weaknesses to many it gave
And some were led right to their grave,
It hit very hard and it hit very wide
If it was out to get you, there was no place you
could hide,
The coughing was so hard it nearly burst your chest
But you had to keep on fighting until you'd done
your best,
Your throat was so sore from coughing it had a burning sting,
Your ribs were hurting so you felt like you've been
in a boxing ring,
Sometimes it made you cold, sometimes it made you hot
And if you were going to make it, you knew not,
But after many days some have won the bout
Over "The OLD Flu Bug" who was fighting so hard to keep them down and out.

Ruby S. Paulk

I LOVE YOU!

I've loved you from the time
we met when we both went to
school, but you never seem to
notice while I played the
lovesick fool. I always tried to
look my best but you never
seem to care, you always went
for the easy kind or the ones
with long blond hair.

I never seem to measure up to
what you'd like to have, or was
it, that you didn't know just
how to show you cared. Now
you tell me, you have loved me,
right from the very start, How
can I take you serious and let
you have my heart?

I don't want to be a dreamer
nor a lover that's left blue,
for it's beyond my wildest dream
to have you love me too.
For you are all I ever wanted to
be there by my side,
but I could never let you go
after the knot is tied.

So darling stop and give some
thought to what your asking me,
cause I would never let you go
No, I'd never set you free. For
after we are married it will have
to be for life, that's the way I
was taught to be together til we
die.

So if you think it's just a
yen that you have felt for me,
please don't hide your foolish
pride just state the facts to me.
For the marriage vows are
something that I could never
break, and I'd expect the same
from you no matter, how it
rates.

The vows to me are sacred
and it keep's the temple clean,
for all the love we have to share
to help fulfill our dreams. So
darling don't deceive me just
state the facts of truth, marriage
could never work unless you
deeply love me too.

Laurie A. Myers

BALLAD OF A SHELTER DOG

I'd like to introduce myself, but I haven't any name.
So I will speak for all of us whose lives are led the same.
Though dogs may not be human, and cannot cry human tears
We hunger for your human love and cry, though no one hears.
I know it's hard to comprehend our lonliness is real,
But stop and look deep in my eyes, then tell me I don't feel.
With each new day the people come and one sweet puppy's sold,
Just as before they pass my cage for I am three years old.

God didn't make me pretty, nor bless me just one breed,
But darn that man, he made me feel and love and yes, to need.
There are some days they come and read this card upon my cage,
They comment on when I came in and something called my age.

Some days I watch them take my friends to somewhere they call sleep,
When this is done it scares me cause I've seen them sometimes weep.
I do not know what this word

means, but I know it must be bad
For how can something that is good make people look so sad.
Each day I know there's part of me that dies a little more.
Cause I can't bark or wag my tail as easy as before.
I feel a little tired right now, so I'll just close my eyes,
I hope tomorrow brings someone who'd like a dog my size.
They're standing at my cage again, they look so awful sad,
I wonder what it is I've done to make them feel so bad.
It could be that she'll take me home, but why then does she weep,
Oh God, she said that awful word, the place they call "to sleep."

Ms. Elizabeth Adams
YOU
You never touch me,
And yet I Love you.
You never Saw me,
And yet I cared for you.
You Never asked about me. .
And yet I looked all over for you.
Someone else made love to me. .
And yet I wish it was you instead of him.
For within me something cries out with deepest passion,
I fear it will never quench it's thirst.
And yet, I know I will continue to live,
And yet never know the feeling of your Touch. . . . . .

Wendy Lou Edwards
CYRSTAL LULLABYE
There arose a crystal lullabye
sung sweetly in my ear,
A golden dusted love song
whenever you were near.
A sky so blue it sparkled,
Windsong, crisp and clear,
A melody, pure harmony
whenever you were near.
When silver moon comes dancing
across the starry night,
the lake shimmers endlessly
on and out of sight.
Then rock me on the water
take me to the sky,
Sing a crystal lullabye,
and you will take me high.
Sing sweetly, softly
so only I might hear.
Hold me in your arms, babe,
its good to have you near.

Laura A. Donlon
COMPANION
Sitting in my corner,
Shadows on the wall.
Music's all around me
As the nighttime starts to fall.
Lighting one more candle,
The shadows leap and grow.
Music still surrounds me
Like the friends I used to know.
In my wine, the ice has melted
Like the walls around my heart.
Alone, once more, with music—
Another night without you
starts.
I'll stumble to my empty bed
When these empty hours end—
And the silence, through the music,
Is all I'll sleep with once again.

Catherine Brown
THE CAPTIVE
The four to eight miles' distance from any town
Was like a wall concealed by flowering vines,
For there were fields and trees and clouds and creeks
To reconcile one to a barrier
Impassable unless by car, by leave
And favor of her relatives. So much
Depended on their leave and favor now.
Despite the careful phrasing of requests,
Suggestions, tactful hints, restrained rebukes,
Despite the limited tasks that left her free
For many hours of doing as she pleased,
She felt a domestic servant, not as they
Expansively described it, "family".
Suppressed resentment at this role gave way
To guilty doubt that she did not repay
Sufficiently the cost of room and board,
Nor accumulate some credit toward the day
Of utter dependence on another's care.
She struggled against the sense of guilt, but mostly
It took her unawares, off-balanced her.
She was more apprehensive of future checks
And curbs, diminished scope, abraded pride
Than sickness, pain or death.
She was disturbed,
Uneasy for the thoughts to be dismissed,
Impulses to be stifled, speech to quell,
Lest she betray unseemly grievance or revolt
Against her evident duty to conform
In all things with the household's ways.
Brief memories of her self-sufficient days
And thoughts of starting fresh flickered and failed.
She almost, never quite imagined herself
Back in the city, working nine to five.
The outlines of this vision wavered, blurred
To indistinctness. The children came from school.
The sun shone warm. The early leaves
Spread a translucent ambience through darkling woods
Of fairy green mid unclothed trunks and boughs.
Water sparkled against the sedge in the ditch.
Clouds were ineffably soft and full and white.
Then, like a blast shriveling the world to waste,
A calculated or chance word slammed to the door
Of age's captivity. The very air
That had the sweetness of a sheet hung out
In sun and breeze, was drained of its charge of life.
Dream and desire grew fainter, farther, dimmer.

Earl J. Feather
WEDDING OF OUR SON
He was a lad of nearly twenty,
tall and lanky with a comely smile,
but all the smiles of yore,
could not compare with the one he wore,
as she came with her father, up the center aisle.
She was an angel white, with flowers of blue,
and happiness shown in her face and eyes.
She saw him waiting, at the alter there,
and then they knew, this was the day to prize.
The blue of his tuxedo, matched our mood,
altho' we weren't losing him at all,
instead we were gaining us another.
who filled the place of daddy's little girl.
The party followed, at his parent's home,
and many guests were there, to celebrate.
It was inevitable, that this time should come,
because when childhood is over, adulthood is waiting at the gate.
Their wedding trip was short, and filled with fun,
as they enjoyed the sights, already seen,
and later, when they ponder o'er this time,
'twill keep their love for each other, keen.
As they make their way in this old world,
and settle down, a family then to raise,
how happy will their hearts forever be,
because then, they both have known fulfilling days.

Eleanor Cleveland Anderson
LEGACY
Semele, beloved of Zeus,
watched the azurelite sphere above
as crystal feathers blossomed into flame.
Green ivy had grown over her smoking tomb
when Dionysos returned to her from the east,
to Semele, child of Harmomia, in Thebes.
Two deathless serpents
proceeded toward the north.
Blue ivy is painted around your room in Thera, Priestess.
Marvellous horned beasts play there still, near the stream.
You, with the sky woven into the gown over your delicate flesh,
now wear the fringed golden robe.
For whom was your hair shorn?
In memory of what song, what cries, are your ears stained
to match the gift you wonderingly unveil?
The spotted serpent guarding the painted dome of your head
protects you as you wait.
Two children, fittingly adorned, were boxing when Attis returned
in the ninth spring.
He came from the east with lapis lazuli
ground for another Virgin's robe.

Marjorie Burney Willis
A SOUL'S DESIRE
When clouds cover the galaxies of golden stars,
The world in darkness forgets the miracle of light;
That beyond the veil the sun will rise in unspeakable glory.
This is the time, Lord, when those who doubt need reminding
Of the way you unfold the fragrant petals of the rose;
And how you lift the birds in heavenly flight,
Lovingly giving them beautiful love songs to sing;
The way you trim the trees with white blossoms in the spring,
Then hang ripe red apples on them in the fall.
When the cold winter winds blow, and doors close,
Touch me, Lord, as you touch the earth in springtime.
Send me forth to tell of your miracles!

Around the world, millions are dwelling in great despair;
Hearts are breaking with many heavy burdens.
All are waiting for words of hope, peace and love.
Shower down your songs of joy and light from Heaven,
Like the sparkling raindrops on fields of flowers;
Softly, gently, let them fall to earth.
With great devotion, I'll spread them across the land.
To tell of your wonders, Lord, is my soul's greatest desire.

Marjorie Wickesberg
OCTOBER MOURN
Upon early Morning
I opened the curtain
to the valley below
Autumn at it's fullest
Autumn at it's best
There is something in the
  Autumn
that is native to my blood
It dances
Remembering loves kindling
  flame
Where is my wondering Jew
Gone like the wind
Only the leaves remain
red and golden

Dee Ashley
GREAT WONDERS
So many times you have been
The source of my strength.
Sharing your fears,
Smiling through silent tears.
So much wisdom in your shiny
  faces.
Kaleidoscopes of dreams, desires
And simple pleasures:
Cut, pasted and crayoned
  beyond measure.
Each one an assiduous abstract.
Wilted cornflowers, in small
  hands,
Transformed into orchids.
Infectious laughter, Serious
  concern.
Proms, mates and far away
  places.
Each grown to forge ahead,
The enchantment of childhood
  tucked away
While responding in appropriate
  ways
To the essence of time;
Making ripples and waves
Not unfelt, unseen nor unheard.

Lester R. Nuse
HEART'S ALSO CRY
Dad when I was young
I just wanted to love
But when I came near
You gave me a shove
Sometimes I think you
Wanted me to die
You beat me so hard
I could not cry
Many times you beat me
With a big leather strap
You made those marks
All over my back
It's not the hurt
You put on my skin
It's the hurt I have
I carry within
Why did you hate me
And hurt me so much
All I ever wanted
Was a loving touch
I wanted your love
But that was not to be
So all of your scars
I carry with me
I now have a family
And them I misused
Each night I go to bed
And each night I pray
That the Lord will protect them
In his own special way
They are all grown
And gone their own way
I lost their respect
Cause I walked away
There's been days of sadness
And hours spent alone
That's made me so sick
I've had hurt in my bones
And when the time comes
These words will be true
I'll die a lonely old man
The same way as you.

Edward P. Cole
NIGHT RIDER
Setting: A dirt road beside the Chesapeake bay, in a backwoods section of Kent County, Maryland.

T'was mid the first quarter of the year's first month. The Winter-wind harped a lay through bare Hick'rys. High on the northern rims, blew gray crowds of clouds. As the drab of evening shaded into night, the wind flew high up to join the winging clouds, and set in horning a snowy reverie. The River-road was dark with weird silhouettes that plucked upon the sheer strings of mortal nerves.

Around the woody bend in mad allegro, came riding a buggy 'pon four spoky wheels. Wrapped well with winter-wool for the season's blow, sat the wild-eyed Doctor of Herbs 'hind His horse.

In a mad roughness He screamed at the aged mare- As must He reach His goal b'fore the mid of night. The Blood Rever Plaque had struck 'pon the Goose-maid, and was less'ning the tempo of Her breathing. So quickly, He flew o'er the snow swept gravel to quench Her burning thirst with the Swamp-root Tea.

T'was out of the clouds there lamented a voice, and there before His eyes hovered Death's image mocking and grinning. The moldy old image fluttered it's loose veils while the wind whipped it's bones. "Ha-ha-ha." laughed Death with a ragged cackle. "The brew, the young Goose-maid will never swallow. Fool, fool, your journeys end shall be a vain thing, and 'pon the blood of the Goose-maid shall I feast." But the desp'rate old Man of Herbs loosed His reins and cracking His mare, He cursed the sight of Death. The wind whipped out the tears from His narrowed eyes, and His cape-strings flew out like reaching fingers. Old White Beard, the frost, tried hard to cool His veins, but o'er the whit'ning river-side road He wheeled, and slacked not His pace in the path of phantoms. Over Lime Water Bridge and through Crow's Nest Woods, across the meadow mound,—His goal yet ten miles.

T'was high on a hill the old Barley-mill stood. As He neared it's gates there came out two mortals, their smoky lanterns did swing like a pend'lum, one with powder-arms and one with a sharp blade.

"Stop!—Cease this hast." bellowed out a deep toned voice. "But my purse holds no gold." screamed the Man of Herbs. "Poor game fool, heed the aim of my trigger-arm, or I will lame the hooves of your lean-boned mare." But grabbing His whip, the Man of Herbs did swing, and made fall the Road-lay'y, His powder and arms. Then commanded His mare to pick up her heels. But as He sped past, the Road-layer He'd missed made to sink deep in His mare's belly, His blade. Oh the pain did make sore the pit of her gut. Whirling o'er went the buggy and bloody mare, and sent the Man of Herbs rolling down the slope. At the bottom 'gainst a creek rock crashed His skull, and made Him senseless of neither night or day, while the blizzard bled it's icy tears 'pon Him.

Many miles, least ten away the poor Goose-maid could feel Death's lips sucking the breath from Her soul. The steeple bells 'nounced the hour of eleven. All Her blood-kin huddled near to Her bed post. The Cock crowed for near mid of the stormy night. Then there sounded three raps 'pon the log shack door. Quickly the House-master lifted up the latch, and there stood robed in mold, the image of Death. "Mercy! mercy!" the House-master knelt and begged. But Death stood firm and moved not it's feet to leave. Then faintly through the snow-fog there appeared a Shadow moving near to the House-master's gate. Death's image grew dim. Fate was brewing sweet tea. The poor old wounded mare had drug her dying Master over long miles of heaping snow mounds into the village. And so, the young Goose-maid was filled with the Swamp-root tea,—Her fever ceased. T'was as though some great determined task was done. Death had not flown there 'pon it's mantels in vain; Having mixed the dose, the Man of Herbs soul fled—As did the blow 'pon His head make still His blood, while the dying old mare bled her last,—and died.

Joan Louise Lurvey
OCEAN SONG
Walking along on the ocean's
  shore,
Kicking driftwood and a broken
  oar.
I feel I'm rolling about
Like the waves continuing
  their route.
Taling seagulls wander
  everywhere,
Leaving whenever wings lift to
  the air.
I feel I'm seeing the land
Like the tides coming here with
  sand.
Humming shells lie near the
  water,
Vibrating adventure.
I feel I'm hearing a voice
Like the life swimming without
  choice.
Resting dunes pose quietly in
  peace,
Tasting salt floating in the
  breeze.
I feel I'm thawing inside
Like the winds losing their
  pride.
Drifting clouds vanish in the
  sky,
Showing the horizon fading by.
I feel I'm easing as one
Like the fires inside the sun.
Walking away from the ocean's
  shore,
Viewing where I was before,
I feel I'm echoing a song
Like these thoughts becoming
  gone.

Tolores Colleen Langston
LOVE'S THEME
You and I
Need no words
To speak
No fire for heat
No sun to shine
For us

We don't need moonlight
Not even a bright star
No love songs
Or soft music

There's fire in your body
And stars in my eyes
A love song in my heart
And music in your soul
You and I. . .

Linda Ashley
'TIS WE
If any two could be,
  Tis we.
If any two could feel
  So free
To follow out
Their heart's desire
To be the flame
That lights the fire
And keeps our cabin
  cozy warm
Even in the fiercest storm
  Tis we.

Kathy Morrison
HOW COULD I EVER DOUBT YOU

I've never seen a paint brush
on earth—
That could ever blend the colors
that you birthed.
Your soil comes in different
colors upon this earth of
ours—
Black, red, and brown spread out
without any bars.
The colors of your beaches from
black sand to brilliant white.
Oh God! As I look around I've
never seen such a beautiful
sight!
The waters of your oceans
extend out for miles and
miles—
Light blue, blue green, and
deep blue,
I love to ponder for awhile.
The trees of such excellent
splendor of different shades of
green.
Fall months with shades of
yellow and red mixed in of
this I dream.
Your mountains some rough and
some velvet of various shades
all around.
Some green, gray, and brown
built by the hand of God so
sound.
How could I ever doubt you
when I look with the naked
eye?
How could I ever doubt your
love and power as you passed
by?
I feel your hand of mercy as you
speak through your Word to
me.
I say, "Dear God please take
my soul and let me live for
thee."

Rita Lynn Porro
NO MATTER WHAT—YOU CAN MAKE IT

Once upon a time someone made that funny flavor lime. It tasted kird of sour but, the color was as pretty as a flower. You can even drink it at any hour, or on the highest tower.

Long ago it used to only cost a dime, but that was before anyone heard of any rhyme. Something one makes up new, something that grows old, something thats only a few, something like this story told.

It's nice to hear the word hi, cause then you know that there's a thee and an I. But it's sad to hear the word die, which could only mean good-bye. So many words, so many rhymes, like a flock of birds in the past times.

Can we all really be our own being, now that we are grown and for sure seeing. Look at all the stars so pretty and fine, maybe one day you'll say—I'll make them mine.

Get rid of all the bars and floors, and there might be less troubles through our doors. You've got to believe and no-more deceive, for one day we'll all leave.

Do you ever listen to what's ever missing, cause if you would try, you'd no-more cry. Something new, something few, something flew into the sky of blue. Maybe it could even of been, me or guess who.

Bert Underwood
SAW MILL RIVER

Meandering, murky and musical,
I won't drink it. There are no
fish left.
Poor beautiful and lonely
stream,
Why do you go on
Sliding through the rocks and
valley?
Velvet branches fall and become
rotten in tangled wet arms.
The brown moldy earth hugs its
spiders and bugs,
all fat from it all.
And the sunlight holds a green
shoot,
for a meaningful moment or
two.
Yet, I love thee, pure little
brook,
For You are what I could never
be—
A Free Soul.
Nobody holds you back;
You go on gently
wandering endlessly
Gurgling on your way
Dutiful only to God!
For He alone knows
Your Destination.

Helen M. Bauer
GOD'S UNIVERSE

Did you ever lay upon your
back and behold
The sparkling stars that twinkle
on high a thousandfold?
Or watch the moon in its
planned flight,
As it traversed the heavens in
the dark of night,
Giving off its wondrous glow
To brighten the path of the
traveler below?
Did you ever wonder at the
vast universe on high,
Or gaze with admiration toward
the sky;
Or watch the sun rise in all
its glory
Bringing forth the light of
another day to add to life's
story?
Or witness, as the rain subsides
and the clouds give way;
The radiant beauty of the
rainbow arching the skyway?
Did you ever lay upon your
stomach in a field of grass
And hear it rustle as through
it the gentle breezes trespass,
And think of how each blade,
with its chlorophyll,
Colors the world green over
meadow and hill,
Using the energy from the light
of the golden sun,
To mix chemicals with the
atmosphere to give air for
everyone.
Did you ever listen to the
mighty roar of the ocean blue,
And think in terms of what it
does for you?
Its moisture is lifted into the
air in vapor form,
To drop as snow or rain on
mountain, village and farm.
To fill the great lakes, rivers
and wells to the brim,
To nourish the food essential
to keep us healty and trim.
Did you ever look into a child's
upturned face,
And see the pure innocence,
faith and trust that time will
soon erase;
Or be astounded by the
development and genius of
man,
Who was put on this earth to
build and to plan,
By a God who loves him and
singles him out to bless,
Hoping he will attain in his
wisdom, Happiness?
If you can not answer the
questions, my friend, with a
yes,
Then you are missing a great
deal of life in this universe;
So take time to observe, to
think, to wonder and to feel
too,
That which the Master has
given to me and to you,
Life itself is a rare blessing,
don't throw it away,
Live it to the fullest, giving
your best each day.
Oh God, how manifold are thy
works and how wise thy ways,
Oh maker of the universe, giver
of life and days,
Thou hast wrought thy kingdom
here on earth in such a
unique fashion,
Giving man the power to think
and to ration.
If he would just look about him
with incredulous eye and
awestruck mind,
He would dispense with evil and
to hir neighbor be kind.

Joachim Wunderlich
UNTITLED

Darren L. Dicks
I DON'T BELIEVE IN DREAMS

Some persons live in a
fairy tale land
Wishing and wanting but
they get nothing in their hand
They can't face the world
as it is appears before their
eyes
They always want a fantasy
to come to their surprise
I'm the kind of person who
takes life
as it is
I give it my best shot
even though I'm not a whiz
So people can live their lives
in reality or in a dream
By I for my part just
simply don't believe in
dreams.

Gilles E. Soucy
CHANGE OF SEASONS

And God gave us life;
Also death.
The understanding of one
Only bewilders the other.
Like the fluctuating population
of the Lemmings
Or the spawning of the Salmon.
Life is hardly understood
And death challenges,
The reasons.
How can anyone say
I have lived a full life;
If one has not
Beforehand,
Died a full death.
And is death
So final?
All that you need,
Is to, behold!
The Changing of the Seasons.
Winter, so cold and dormant;
Spring, rebirth of the old and
new;
Summer, fulfilment and joy;
Fall, the dying season for
It's beauty, it's end!
If our lives could be
So colourful
And if this is death;
Then surely,
Death must be,
Beautiful.

Kay Slinkard
LOVE OF MY LIFE

Inside me there is an empty
place.
The sadness shows in my eyes
and face.
In a life that seemed so long
ago,
There was no sadness, only
beautiful love to grow.
We worshipped each other and
loved every night.
You made me feel wonderful, I
knew it was right.
My love made you apart of me.
Now, the time has come to set
you free.
A part of me wishes that I'd
never cared.
But now I think back of the
life we shared.
I thank God for the love I once
knew.
And thankful for having part of
my life with you.

Sherri Lynn Fields
A LOVE UNCOMMONLY FREE

A love uncommonly free,
so beautiful and rare!
Is often *thought* to be,
most wonderful to share!
Such a love cannot be captured
with actions of abuse,
or feelings of uncertainty.

Thus this love will then be
shattered.
And all of its worth and its
use,
will simply cease to be.
Indeed these words are true
to those who have felt its magic
touch.
For this love has reached so few,
in a world where it's needed so
much.
A love uncommonly free,
so beautiful and rare!
Is often *meant* to be,
most wonderful to share!!

Paul Herman W. Leonard

PETAL PULLING FOR PEGGY

(A poor little poem to plead my case)

"She loves me; she loves me not"
It really puts me on the spot.
She is the dot upon my i
The morning star within my
sky.
She is the "She" to "finish" me.
(One way or another.)
There is none other.
Mein Gott! Take pity on my lot.
Without her love
I'd be worse off.
Than a butterfly without a wing
Or honey bee without her sting,
Or song no one could ever sing.
What must I do—to woo
This gentle dove?
My "Queen of Love" has eagles'
wings
And a free soul that soars
and sings.
To woo such a one with some
success!
I must confess, I'm in a mess!
Just bill and coo would hardly
do.
I fear the "I" will have to die,
To clear the sky
Of murky clouds of fear and
doubts;
And in its place
The "I AM" must raise and braze
Itself
And take from off the highest
shelf
The perfect Crown of ALLNESS
LOVE:
The joyous thought: "It is
enough"
I'm satisfied with present delight
And present plight; and seek no
more
Than what is right and best
for her
Whom I adore more and more
Each moment—of Eternity.
That is my simple plea.

Richard Edwin Welby

THE SANDS OF TIME

How fleeting are the sands of
time as they slip this earthly
plot—
How minimal are the things
that were, things long ago
forgot,
How cherished are the
memories of loved ones, friend
and foe,
How really small the worries
were of sadness, and of woe—
How can we best cope with life
and its many, many turns—
First we're up and then we're
down—not too long till one
learns,
And yet throughout the
struggle, the rigor and the
strife,
Theres always someone waiting
on the periphery of life—
He only asks that patience be a
never ending goal, just shake
A hand or slap a back, it lifts
a sagging soul,
So when that final trumpet
sounds and its time to move
alone,
Your deeds will leave fond
memories just like a happy
song.

Geraldine M. Slowey

DECEMBER 9, 1980

Through your songs you said
more to the world than any
preacher
has shouted from the pulpit
more than any parent
has explained to a child
more than any politician
has promised in a speech
about the road to peace
by the map of understanding
and love.
But you were a face in a
blinded world
a voice in a deafened
planet—
A world blinded by
prejudice
A planet deafened by
hatred.
Tonight shots of insanity
laid you lifeless on the street
and your wife sobbed.
Suddenly the world
opened their eyes for one
scarlet trickle of blood
and listened for a cry of
mourning.

Bette Imholz

THE JOLLY LITTLE MAN

There's a Jolly Little Man
coming to town
He's not a Saint, he's not a
clown
He fills men's hearts with hope
and peace,
For the young in heart, he gives
them treats.

Oh, The Jolly Little Man,
Whose jingle, jangle of the bells,
With his ho, ho, ho, the World
he tells,
Tonight we put our cares away,
for tomorrow, is Christmas
Day.
He's as timeless as time itself
can be,
He brings out the best in you
and me.
He makes us forget yesterday's
sorrows,
We think only of a happy
tomorrow!
He does mysterious things of
only for one day,
With the swiftness of his
reindeer, the magic of his
sleigh,
He rides over rooftops, bells
ringing all the way,
To make us all happy on
Christmas Day.
He spreads magic over the very
young,
His praises the World over, are
sung,
He brings men help for those in
need,
His Elves, fill the shelves for
the youngsters indeed.
The World awaits his coming
in the stillness of the night,
The children stay awake to
catch the sight.
Anticipation is fever high,
Yet no one has ever seen him,
they all sigh!
If only for one day of the year,
Men could forgive, and spread
good cheer,
For the jolliest, happiest myth
of them all,
Santa Claus, says, Merry
Christmas to all!

Mary Ellen Bashaw

NO MORE TO DREAM

Oh sleep, carrier of anxiety to
harmony,
Herald of peace to the troubled
of heart,
Call on me now.
Hold me safe in thy warm
embrace.
In restful peace, surcease of
cares
of the morrow.
Remove the burning images
From within my heart.
Ease my mind from its woes.
Hold me ever in thy peaceful
darkness.
To sleep forever, no more to
dream.

H. Jefferson (Lugman Abdullah)

HUMAN HOG

I have always wanted, desired, never have I not yearned or wished.

Suddenly and strangely, my hunger acquired super strength in greed and lust.

Incessantly am I now longing, lacking, seeking, hoping and craving for all things; your thing, their thing, and most times anything.

Continuously am I wanting this, that, these, and those.

Prodigious and voracious is my thirst, for what I see, smell, taste or touch, and my intention is to capture all I can hear.

I wonder, who is there to paramount me in wants?

For my dream consist of coveting, possessing what others might dream to possess.

For I am he needing more than a dying man, more than a new born baby, more than the universe.

After all I have wanted, required and desired, I have yet to reach a master of want—only a human hog.

Anne K. Kishi

PRECIOUS REFLECTIONS

If you wonder friend
how much you've changed my
life. . .
Let me tell you. . .
When you're smiling
the sunshine enfolds me in its
halo. . .
When you're sad
something within me seems
to throb out loud. . .
When you're angry at the world
the fury within me
unleashes. . .
When you're puzzled
my own search begins to help
you find some solution. . .
When you're dreaming
my heart seems to ballerina
on those very same clouds. . .
You could say
my love for you runs soul-to-
soul
in a never ending flow with
the river of time.
And when I've reached out for
you
searching for empathy, some
words of wisdom. . .
You've always found time to
enlighten the way.
A trusted companion to my soul
Together laughing the hours
away
Delighting in nostalgic
childish play
Then turning to the grave
problems of the world
Discussing. . .pondering. . .
debating. . .
Counting our blessings in the
face
of many another's encounter
with life-and-death. . .
Two individuals discovering the
true essence of being human
The giving. . .the receiving. . .
the sharing. . .
Accepting each other for what
we are
Not clinging. . .but still holding
on. . .
Philosophizing. . .daydreaming. .
And forever awed by that
indomitable spirit of man
which arises from the
darkest despair
clutching on to life with
its myriad of beauty and
mystery.
Learning it can never be wrong
to care. . .to feel. . .to
experience. . .
to laugh. . .to weep. . .
Realizing one should keep
searching for the ultimate
Reaching for the heights
Climbing to the rainbow's end
Listening for the fairy tale
melody
of that elusive bird of
happiness. . .
So along this continuing voyage
of change and growth
In getting to love and admire
you for your beautiful,
sensitive self
I've grown to understand

someone else a whole lot
more
Someone who can still be a
stranger at times
But one who is happy to have
you as a friend
And who treasures being your
friend. . .
Namely, yours truly. . .

Billy F. Hicks
RECIPE FOR A HAPPY NEW YEAR

Take twelve whole months.
Clean them thoroughly of all
bitterness, hate and jealousy.
Make them just as fresh and
clean as possible.
Now cut up each month into
twenty-eight, thirty, or
thirty-one different parts, but
don't make up the whole batch
at once. Prepare it one day at a
time out of these ingredients.
Mix well into each day one part
of faith,
one part of patience,
one part of courage, and
one part of work.
Add to each day one part of
hope, faithfulness, generosity,
and kindness.
Blend with one part prayer,
one part meditation, and
one good deed.
Season the whole with a dash
of good humor.
Pour all of this into a vessel
of love.
Cook thoroughly over radiant
joy, garnish with a smile and
serve with quietness,
unselfishness, and cheerfulness.
You're bound to have a Happy
New Year.

Harriet V. Bohr
PRESIDENT KENNEDY'S LAST TOUR

With the bubble top us, They
were to speed down the street
So that the people of Dallas,
The President could greet.
But there was no danger, of
that they were sure
So they rode slowly and happily
on this his last tour.
No need for the bubble, the
weather was fine.
People were waving and
cheering all down the line
With never a hint of the sadness
to follow
This historical ride that soon
would be empty and hollow.
Now Lee Harvey Oswald, having
no faith in God
Was determined to put our
President under the sod,
So with well-laid plans, his
chance he awaited
To seek vengeance on America,
a country he hated.
From his sixth floor window, he
had a good view,
Three shots rang out, his aim
was true,
The President was hit, the
governor too.
'Twas done the dastardly deed
he'd planned to do.
But things moved to fast when
put into motion
His plans went awry in all the
commotion.
For some reason or other, a cop
on his beat
Oswald wantonly shot dead on
his feet.
Then he hurriedly fled to the
movies nearby
Not daring to dream that his
capture was nigh.
His conscience began bothering
him, wouldn't let him sit still
So the police arrested him
against his will.
Jack Ruby decided in anger and
fury
Not to let Oswald wait
court trial and jury
So he brazenly took the law in
his hands
Making a mockery out of justice
in our homeland.
They gave the president a
funeral fit for a King
After his wife placed in his
hand, her wedding ring.
They keep coming for miles to
visit his grave
There's no doubt about it, he
was remarkably brave.
But unless God watches over
the city too
No one is safe whatever they do.
Take heed of this warning
before it's too late
Remove from your heart, every
vestige of hate.

Tom McEnroe
MR. OUTRIDER

I'm a-ridin' down, other day, fum
Chino Valley. That's up north, a
way.—
An' time I gets ta Prescott
Town, I sez: "Hold up, Ol'
Gander, I'm a gettin' down."
Ol' Gander?—He's mah horse, ya
know; or is it other way
around?—

Been warm 'n dry, along the
way;—an' I kept a-hearin'
myself say:
"Better rest Ol'Gander, fer a
spell;—or sure as chips, he'll
be a-raisin' 'ell."

So, I tethers 'im there, in Old
Courthouse Square.—

You'll recollect the grass,—
an' the shade-trees, there.—
I un-cinches the saddle,—an'
I lets 'er down;—
An, I sez: I'm a-gonna
have me a look,
around—

Well, I'm a-walkin' along on
Whiskey Row, and right off,
meets a fella that I know.—
An' he be Mr. Scofield Blair. In
fum Sycamore Canyon. He's
big in ranchin', there.
Yep, over at ol' Sycamore's head,
Mr. Blair's got 'im a whoppin'
cattle spread.—
He sez: "Well, Glory Be and
Howdy-do!—Mr. Outrider, is it
really you?—"
Well, Mr. Blair's jest a-teasin'
o' course. Knows he's got the
name wrong.—
I'm a hard-ropin' flank-rider,
an' he knows Ah come on
strong.
He sez: "Ah missed ya at spring
round-up time. I'm glad ta see
yer a-lookin' fine.—
The roundin' up went pretty
good; an' coupla days o'
brandin' went fine.—
An' after that, as you would
know; Along comes the
story-tellin' time.
Ol' Skinny Winthrop,—he's mah
foreman, ya know,—
figgers they's about a dozen
steers, left among the
Sycamores, down below.—
But, he also reckons that just
about now,
those strays would come right
on up,—with coupla riders
that has know-how.
Mr Outrider, Ah wish you'd take
Ol' Yavapai Slim.—
Right now, he's—heh—loaded.
But, Ah knows which place
he's in.—
So, I'll sober 'im up;—An' I'll dry
'im out.—
An' I'll have 'im trail-ready,
by firt o' th' week. No
doubt!—
Mr. Outrider, they's some things
Ah wants ta tell ya, 'bout that
Canyon Floor;—
Though, Ah knows ya been
down there, b'fore.—
Smokey Belson sez it'll be warm,
a-ridin' down that trail;—
Jes like a south room,—in th'
Yuma Jail.—
Sez th' creek is a startin' ta
dry. Better carry good water,
'thout no alkali.—
Some o' th' riders wuz uneasy,
down there,
'bout th' uncommon size of
a long-haired bear.—
Now, Ah knows about bears, an'
I'll tell ya, right.—
Tie some bacon, to a willa,
afore ya beds down, at night.
So, Mr. Bear reach fer bacon,
afore he reach fer you.—
An' Ol' Sharps Rifle, by yer
side, drills 'im, plumb
through.—
Mr. Outrider, Ah wants ta be
honest; an' I wants ta be fair!—
If ya does th' skinnin',—ya kin
have the hide o' that bear.—
And, Oh yes, there wuz Fatso
Dawson. Sez ta me: Mr. Blair,
ya jest ought ta see!—
That Canyon Floor's so fulla
snakes.—
But, they's butter-ball fat.—
He, an' they makes good
steaks.—
So, Mr. Outrider, if you'll see
this thought;—
They'll be somethin fer
Yavapai Slim,—An' somethin'
fer you.—
Jes you bring up those beef, and
Ah wants ta be fair;—
May even be some—money,—
there.

All agreed, Mr. Outrider?—
Mr. Outrider?— Mr. — ? ? ?
Now, whut in tha world—has
got—inta—him?-"

James W. Mansell
THE PRAYING HANDS

The praying hands
mean more to me
Than just a prayer
on a bending knee.
The praying hands
are held fast and tight
The way a mother holds
a child on a stormy night.
What do the hands
really say; not just
A prayer to God, for
a handless man can pray.
They stand for peace
among all men
They stand for kindness
that will never end.
They stand for the
love I have for my wife
Not a mortal love,
but, much longer than life.
They stand for the joy
in your children's heart
Because we prayed one night
when the room was dark.
They stand for everything
thats great and good
And they stand for hope
the way praying hands should.
We pray that the
material wants of man
will never seperate
these praying hands.
For if the day comes
that these hands should part
Then man is lost
with out hope in his heart.

Grace T. Lam
FOREVER A FRIEND

My friend I've come to talk to
you again.
Seems my life is ever changing
yet still the same.
I'm lost, lonely and afraid.
No one can understand the
changes I'm going through.
Where would I be without you
to turn to?
You're the best friend I've found
to listen
No matter what time, day or
night,
You're always there.
You listen and dry the tears
that fall
Letting me release my emotions
So I can pick up the pieces of a
complex puzzle,

Creating a picture which is once again,
Whole and complete.
Sometimes that's all I need,
To know that you'll listen for as long as I want to talk,
Passing no judgments on me
But reminding me of the wisdom of my yesterdays.
You know every chapter of my life.
It's written in your memory,
The pain, the sorrow, the emptiness and the loneliness,
The laughter, the love, the joy,
My hopes and dreams, yesterday's and today's,
The building blocks of my being,
The stepping stones of my tomorrows.
You know me like a book
Filling my emptiness as I fill yours.
Who would ever think an empty page could be
such a friend?

Anna O'Neil

THE SPRING HAS BEGUN

There ends the clutch of the cold, biting air,
When where from my bed I see way out there
A little red robin chirping with glee
At the sight of the eggs in his nest in the tree.
The sun's out now, spring's in the air,
And guess now what I see way out there?
The snow is all melted, the winter is done,
The flowers are blooming, the spring has begun.

Anne Stanton

SHE WAITS

She waits, knowing he will come.
Yet unkempt recall of scarlet, gold and brown
And past October eves beside the hearth
Intrude upon her death watch.
Melancholia, bittersweet in its forgetfulness,
Keeps a mouldering love, dead now numberless years.
An uncompromising chill wraps its mourning cloak
Over the fire's barren ashes.
Nearer draws the balm of winter.
In anticipation, she waits.

Boniface Olekamma Odor

THE VOICE OF THE TOOTHLESS FORE—RUNNER

Productiveness in a tree are seeds yet of all that lay from windy handworks it, with edges broken, pores sealed of harsh labour, lying in nature's little fingers watches the burial of its folks and circumcision of offsprings.

Listen to the drums of the cemented palms hear the voice of the toothless fore-runner and the jingles and the rattles of the mapped feet.

Grandsons, and if you are daughters be concerned too. Youth is but a prelude to the playground. Battles bought and sold are in athlete's design. For you whose weapons are papyrus and reeds be your impressions created suiting the curves of nature's cutlery. Nimble are the wheels that caressed the dancing tracks perfectly but now dance not well.

Listen to the drums of the cemented palms hear the voice of the toothless fore-runner and the jingles and rattles of the mapped feet.

Hunched backs never come out of nothing and blindness is the best of sicknesses. Talkativeness is evil salubrity, but mind yourself is a golden elixir that changes all to gold. Discipline is our ancestor's footprints and facial beauty never makes a beloved generation. Who remembers beauty when quarrels patol in streets? Courtship without a name prevents the keeping of means but private pockets sew you an umbrella for the tornadoes. The hills have a pass but only the crafty finds the lead.

Listen to the unrhythmic steps of the skeleton hear the croaking of the aged drums sleeping afar and the coarse voice of the toothless fore-runner.

I do not need a wife is a daily incantation of men. Husbands eat everything they see like a roach, women answer. Who does not understand the story when they say; they have no partners but beautiful skins? The unrhythmic dance is playing and dancing. Soon the drums will take rust with no spade to coax. An unbeaten drum is a thing of misfortune. If palms will not stroke the hide, insects will, and that's enough signal of the worst to come.

Listen, my breakfast is ready.

Nancy Emmons

VENUS'S FLYTRAP

From the moss bed a green stem rises,
its cloven leaf poised above.
Bristles shape the lips
of this siren leaf.
The inside gleams;
moistened hairs sway and beckon,
tossing rays of light.
The beguiled fly pauses midair,
draws closer, then
clasped by the hairs,
drowns in the dew
while gates close
above him.

Carel Meninno

THREE IS A CHARM

you know I have loved and lost
two times already
so if there is a charm then Lord
send him along
send him along Lord
cause time is wasting and I'm
tired of waiting
I made my life and not depended
on anyone
raised the kids and paid the bills
along that road
but the going gets steeper and
harder and time draws to a close
so if three is a charm then Lord
send him along
send him along Lord
cause time is wasting and I'm
tired of waiting
I guess I have always done
things my way
and never stopped to listen to
you, my friend
there have been some wrongs
and there have been some rights
but who is to say who's right is
right
so if three is a charm then Lord
send him along
send him along Lord
cause time is wasting and I'm
so tired of waiting

G. A. Leishman

LOOK TOWARD THE SEA

Come,
look toward the sea,
experience
the intimate grandeur
of unbounded power
trembling within
one vast miracle
of heaving sighs,
rumbling to crash
upon the soul
in yearnful sobs.
sirening feet to wing
and fly amidst
the undulated stings
of stolen kisses,
thrown, unexpected on the wind,

teasing,
tossing passion with errant hands,
stirring wantonness to crest,
desire, to hold, devour,
lay in,
lay out,
and smother in great surging breasts,
capturing circled tumbling rolling thrusts
of consummated oneness,
in depths flung wide
astrew with seed that's spurred to crystal,
white,
upon the land,
coupling man
with earth, and universe
in one grand arpeggio
of solemn chant,
to nod-fulfilled
in subtle calm
of harboured beatitudes,
languored in the gravid brine.
Roll, roll,
ye mighty ocean, roll,
swell impassioned walls
to swale the thirsting land,
exhaust me in thy
never ceasing grace,
and suffer me
beholding one,
to recognize itself
within a grain of sand,
and yield me thoughts
to drink supremacy
of God's command.
Ah! what is an ocean,
if not a pounding universe
of uninterrupted intellect. . .a miracle?
then,
everything about this life is such,
for we know it not.

Henry H. Atkins, Jr.

TOBACCO

Tobacco is a filthy weed
From the devil doth proceed
Picks your pockets
Burns your clothes
And makes a chimney
Out of your nose

Helen Weston Govaya

REVERIE

Purple shadows kiss the mountains as the sun goes down,
Tiny birds have ceased to sing darkness fills the town.
One by one the stars appearing twinkle in the sky,
Lamps are lighted in the cottage day has waved goodbye.
Tousled heads lie on the pillows after prayers are said,
As they dream of bright tomorrow's nestled in their beds.
We too dream, of bright tomorrow's where friends never part—
In a world of peace and beauty joy forever in each heart.

Darcy L. Miller

UNTITLED

The moonlight on the water
Is like the sparkle in your eyes
Your smile is so romantic
Like the stars up in the skies
Your charm is like a flower
Blooming in the spring
Your love is like a new born child
A very special thing
Your kiss is like the dew drops
That kiss the blooming rose
And tho we've fought like cats and dogs
My love for you still grows

Lorine Alford

A MOTHER AMONG MOTHERS

They nailed her son to the cross
Though it must have been a very precious loss,
She said not a word
They mocked and scorned him
Her cup of sorrow must have been filled to the rim.
They cast lots for the clothing on his back
Her heart must have been about to crack.

Though He was the son of God,
she still was a Mother in sorrow
Nothing could erase the agony
of this horror.
This woman had to be very
courageous and strong
To watch all of this wrong.
Though this had to happen to
fulfill all righteousness
She had to be a God-fearing
woman, nonetheless.
For how many mothers of today
Would stand by and watch their
son being put to death this
way?
If someone were determined to
nail her son to a cross
Wouldn't she try to prevent it
at any cost?
If they ridiculed her son and
made fun of him
Wouldn't she get very angry
with them?
If they took away all the earthly
things he owned
Would she have just stood there
and moaned?
In the perilous times which we
live in
No mother would have been
content to stand about
and watch her son's life
snuffed out.
Mary had to be a Mother among
mothers
A mother high above all others.

Jean Kalobius

DIARY

If I fill all the pages
with every want and need,
Will my heart be an open book,
for anyone to read?
My diary of emotions
spread before me in black
and white.
When I close the book for the
evening,
will my feelings be out of
sight?

Heather Hallam

SEASONED LOVE

In Spring time as the rain
poured down
And laughing couples played
the town,
I knew nothing of your crown
On which small evils did
abound.
The Summer sun shone jewel
bright;
You and I enhanced each
night.
Never did we quarrel or fight;
I had never felt so right.
Autumn winds blew cold and
strong;
Our days together seemed so
long;
There surely was something
wrong;
I knew we never could go on.
Now I watch the snowflakes fall
As my heart did at the brawl.
Back to you I'll never crawl
Because I finally saw you all.

Birdie L. Roberts

THE STRAIGHT & NARROW ROAD

(Matt. 7: 13-14)

The Bible says:
Enter in at the straight gate,
for wide is the road and broad is
the way that leads to
destruction. Straight is the
gate and narrow is the way
which leads unto life and few
that find it.
Once I trod the wide road, Satan
by my side.
He said, "Don't you see how
smooth and nice,
You can almost glide."
Along the side were tears of
sorrow,
No comforting thought for a
better tomorrow.
All that walked, were the same
as me,
No one to help us, or set us free.
We came to a cross road, narrow
and rough
But, this One that stood there
held out His hand to us.
He said, "Come my children, I
will lighten your load.
For straight is the gate and
narrow the road."
I took my Master by the hand
And we walked along, this
strange little band.
We saw the flowers blooming by
the way.
No sorrow or tears were there
to stay.
No heavy load to shift or rub
our weary backs as along we
strode,
We didn't notice the narrow
road, as we had Someone to
lighten our load.
Walking with our Master, hand
in hand
To lead us into the promised
land.
That is the answer, my weary
friend.

Ferris Richards

FATE

If I had thought that on that
day;
so many years ago;
Fate would trap me in such a
way
as to fill my life with woe;
If I had known or even dreamed
what was to be would be.
That it would not be, as then it
seemed,
so unaware were we.
We left our town for just a day,
my only love and I;
A day our own to laugh and
play.
Oh! Not a day to die:
He had a plane and oh so grand,
he showed to me the sky.
With such joy he took my hand,
to teach me how to fly;
Ah—one's fate is there and it
will come,
no matter what you do;
and after all the final sum
is really up to you.
We clowned and laughed, and
then we froze,
as the plane began to fall,
We saw our lives before us
close,
and knew that this was all;
And then we crashed in cold
deep snow,
and lay for hours dazed;
My dear love sunk ever low
his eyes began to glaze.
The hours piled up and soon
were days,
as planes flew by on high;
Looking for us in all their ways,
and hearing not our cry;
A week, he died, I was alone,
my soul was filled with dread;
I could not cry, my heart was
stone,
my spirit was as lead.
Within the hour, the rescuers
came;
Oh, what a cruel sad fate!
To wait so long and so in vain,
and here they came so late.
If I were god, I'd cry a tear,
for the anquish of one left;
I since wonder, does he hear,
the pain of one bereft?

Glenn Gallagher

THE OLD MAN DIED

Everyday, I'd go up to his cabin
To see what else he had made
On winter days we'd sit beside
the fire
And in the summer, we'd sit
in the shade.
He taught me most everything I
knew
From fishing, to the birds and
the bees
He taught me how to bake and
cook
And how to sense the emotions
of the breeze.
I enjoyed his company, and he
enjoyed mine
He never got mad or angry,
because he was so gentle and
kind.

I was like the son he never had
And he was like a father to me
We'd sit around, and he'd tell
me stories
As we ate our bread, and drank
out tea.
But one day, I saw something in
his eyes
And suddenly began to realize
That pretty soon his time would
end
But I'd always be loyal to this
kind and loving friend.
His birthday was the next
morning,
I had brought something special
and nice,
It was two pieces of crystal
In the shape of little mice.
Silently I came into his bedroom
Where he was lying very still
He looked quite sick and pale,
He looked quite ill.
I put my hand on his forehead
And then I knew he was gone,
I sadly turned away
To dig a grave in the back
of his lawn.
Yes, the old man passed away
He was my leader, teacher, and
guide,
I had gotten down on my knees,
(with my head buried in
my hands)
And cried, and cried, and cried.

Teresa Cudrak

NATURES SURPRISE

I look out the window whose
border is being covered with a
lace of early frost, to see
what wonders nature has done
when my back was turned for
such a short time.
The winter-world outside is
beautiful, transforming
everything into real figurines.
The trees are bent in still
motion as the crystal snow
becomes a part of them.
The bare branches reaching out;
as if welcoming more.
The tiny bird trespasses across
the white rug of snow, which
has been laid across the lawn.
Its footsteps are molded into the
white interior as the wind
slowly blows more snow over
them,
wiping out their existence as if
they never really were.

Alexander A. Lujan

WISDOM OF THE HEART

Love is to the heart
As are the rivers rushing
through the land.
For its source
Lays within its
Giving and receiving.

DeeDee Welch

A SEARCH

Savor the moments, nurture
each day;
Look for the good as you go on
your way.
Trust in people, and they'll
trust in you;
Express your love in all that
you do.
Reach for the moon, hold to
your dreams;
The treasures of life are more
than they seem.
Feel the vibrations, heed to
their call;
The signs are showing and
reaching to all.
Search for the answers, clear
out your mind;
They lie within and are easy to
find.

Cindy Chupack

SOAR

You see the ragged jacket and
the hat that covers just enough
to shelter from the rainy night
an old man's head.
He wanders past, but leaves
behind a faded air of hope you
find discouraging,
Look back again, and wonder
what became of him;
the man is dead.
Realize that weary wanderer
never had a dream to follow,
Squeeze your mother's hand
much tighter as a swallow
flutters by. . .
And you become

overwhelmed by the fact that
you are free,
You have places to go; you
believe so you can be,
And with trust in your dreams
there is so much more to see,
You're a swallow if you have
the will to dream.
You see the busy city full of
people going nowhere,
people talking, saying nothing
as they hurry on their way.
In search for traces left of life,
you find no marks, just scars
of strife.
Their footsteps fade behind
them as you sadly start to
understand the reason why.
Tears fill your eyes since
you're different from the others,
You are sad to leave them
standing, but still unafraid to
fly.
You are one with the swallow in
a dream that's known as virtue,
Nothing in the sky will hurt
you,
Soar high, soar high.

James Wesley Sparks

THE INNER TURMOIL

I sit down with this pen and pad
and write to no one there,
And I think about the things
I've done, and said, but did
not hear.
I've tried to be different from
all my friends and folks,
But the things I do seem
crazy, and I feel I'm just a
joke.
And when I try to be the same
as others that I see,
I find that I'm not like them,
and then I'm not like me.
You will not hear me cry, or
sob, or even see me frown,
But I wish that you could see
the raging hell deep down.
No one here could really know
the swelling pain inside,
The very thing I try not to
show, but to hide.
So, I'm sorry for the things I've
done, and said, but did not hear,
I'd never really want to hurt
the ones I love so dear.
But I hope you can forgive me,
and love me as a friend,
For without the help of
someone else, I'm just a
dying wind.

Nettye Hollen

ESCAPE ON DEMAND

My day has been trying, tedious
and long.
Irritations have rankled, I've
bitten my tongue
To keep from lashing out to put
others in place,
Forcing a smile, keeping on a
nice face.
You see, I can do this,
commanding smooth
operation,
Knowing I have a haunt where
in my imagination
I go to emerge fresh with
confidence and ability
To resume daily commitments
with renewed stability.
There's a spot from my
childhood, called "Half-way
Rest",
Strategically placed there, mid
way up the crest
Of the high hill that linked our
house and the lake,
With a path winding upward
requiring stamina to make.
Leaving the boat pier for that
upward climb,
I'd push steadily forward, always
keeping in mind.
That up there on the hillside
beckoned physical relief
For catching my breath,
moments needed, however
brief.
Once there, on the bench I
would sit and reflect;
Time standing still, I'd feel
a two-fold effect.
For while resting my body for
the climb yet ahead,
I was aware of a soul-searching
hunger being fed.
A distinct blend of smells that
came from the woods,
Enhanced by the noises of the
insect and birds;
The gentle sounds of the lake
as it lapped at the sand,
Left an imprint on me, sensing
Nature at hand.
Even as a child, there on my
"Half-Way- Rest",
Calmed by the surroundings, I
still can attest,
I found a great refuge, a
quenching fountain,
Providing replenishment for the
rest of the mountain.
In your pattern of living may
you too know a haunt
For momentary evasion from
any burdening taunt;
A place only yours for escape
on demand,
To return purged of pressure,
once more in command.

H. W. Seiders

KING OF THE OKI PANOKI

Along about dusk, there's a
subtle, sweet odor—like musk
And the wild Oki Panoki settles
down to a sudden, solemn
hush;
All the critters that dwell in the
shade of the glades
Are "still"—for a spell—as the
dying day fades.
Not a groan, or a swish—of a
'gator or fish
Not a flutter of wings:—and this
is His wish;
I mean the King Of The Swamp;
he's there somewhere in the
gray hovering mist
Taking giant strides over the
great carpet of the water—
Marching up to his throne;
where he'll take ward over the
night—
And where he rules all alone.
I've pictured him there—sort of
grizzled and gaunt,
On the perch of his throne, in
the midst of his swamp;
Like the Indians before me—
must have pictured him too
In that morass of wilderness, as
his "silnce" came due.
'Twas told me by Gramps—and
repeated by Paw—
It's not just a legend—he is
their law,
And those creatures adore him,
of that there's no doubt,
To give him their silence—
while the world drones
without.
Many the times, I sat there in
the boat—and waited for him;
The King Of The Swamp,—just
like the "critters" that swim.
I never did see him,—not really,
you know—
Still he's there I'll avow, though
my eyes won't allow.
It's just something one has to
"feel"—like a half-pleasant
pall—
And then, in a few fleeting
moments—"immortality"
seems to call
And you start to believe; you
dare to believe—
There's something higher, and
broader—and deeper, O yes;
Than the sages defined it,—than
you ever can guess.

Then re-tempted to venture
again before dusk
Where a subtle, sweet odor—
like musk—
Seems to trigger the silence of
critters that swim
In the shade of the glades—
where this magic begins!
Phenomenon! O yes—that's the
label you find
For events such as this,—in the
back of your mind;
But, ask yourself—really, don't
you think there should be,
A King, for a swamp—like the
great Oki Panoki?

Craig Fintor

OH! SACROSANCT

Eyes of her life are tenderly set
Meeting the meaning of that
which she met
Coming and holding a mind
that was torn-Calming a start
from a heart in a storm
Now a passing hardly a day,
Wandering through her hopeless
maze
Her self of her body waiting
to call
Her 'morrow's message melting
his soul
A sirening song that may be
delayed
Heart to a heart he wanted his
stayed
Lo, she warmed the blood in her
breast
Securing the message she
wanted to test
Loving the air of majesty's lord
Swording the cord that;
prevented his best
His dying breath escaped with a
moan
Chilling and killing her
heartfelt groan
With a love that none far wiser
have had
With a love that none far older
have had
Having to have the love that I
had
Leaving the soul which renders
me sad
God of Mercy, Oh God of Light,
Calm the soul from the edge of
night
Leave her life free and tame
Caressing my spirit
that has no name.

Timothy M. Sankary

THE KEY

It was a foggy, storm-filled night,
Shipwreck victims everywhere
in sight,
Broken bones, bleeding wounds
and gore,
'Nough for a hundred
nightmares and more.
When out of the carnage and
haze,
Came a lone lighthouse ablaze,
With a fiery light of strength
and hope,
Offering friendship and sanity
to cope.
Casually passed once while
setting sail before,
On this hellish voyage to
unknown shore,
Gleaming brighter that night
than ever the sun,
Her light means more now to
everyone.
Strong and firm she is built to
withstand,
The ravages of wind, sea and
sand;
Tall and slim she is built to
promote,
Her outreaching light of hope.
Simple, loyal and pure in her
duty,
But diligent to protect her
booty,
From marauding and ruthless
pirate hoards,
That would ravage her inside
with swords.
So, locked up tight for years
has she been,
Never yielding up her secrets
within,
Waiting for just the right
sailor some day,
To come back with the key, and
. . .he just may.
But on that hapless night of
gore,
A lone sailor was washed up on

her shore,
Near drowned and half-starving
was he,
Needing care and shelter from
the sea.
Would she turn out this poor
lad,
So rumpled, helpless, unclad?
Once so hardworking and
strong, you'd admire,
But through his ordeal he would
tire.

Would she cooly ignore his plea,
In the name of her virtuous
dignity?

Still expecting her master to
come:
A prophet, heaven-sent, only
one?

Would God have intended this
tragedy,
His lighthouse to forget
humanity,
In pursuit of dignity, purity,
tradition,
To blind her from her mission?
But, lo, the sailor did not relent,
For here, he was sure, he was
sent,
To find salvation and the key,
To happiness, good health and
harmony.
So, crawling slowly around her
base,
Desperately pleading his case,
He came upon her gorgeous
door,
Keeping him outside from so
much more.
Falling on his knees, he cried.
Kissing the door gently, he tried,
Delicately to open her up to
him,
Realizing his chances were slim.
When suddenly at his feet he
spied,
A welcome mat, he realized,
That her hard-nosed cold
history,
Was not every really meant to
be.

And, seizing upon this
revolutionary thought,
He looked below the mat for
what he sought,
Lo and behold, he found the key,
The one he'd been seeking so
desperately.

At last it was clear what the
master intended,
Leaving the key there all these
years unattended,
That someone in need, yet
worthy and right,
Could gain entrance to her some
cold and dark night.

He entered with great awe and
respect,
For the master's plan that, in
retrospect,
Was both divine and human in
conception,
Perfect in its goal. . .but with
people's misperception.

So ends this tory of old,
Again, it had to be told,
So that others, young though
they be,
May see things as they should
be.

Hassie hayes Stone

MENTAL MOVIE

When I retire at the close of day
Sweet old faces, kind and serene;
Silently, they slowly glide
Across my mental movie screen.
Some come in soft pastel,
Others are in hard silhouette;
But whether colorful or dark
Memory faces are firmly set.
Ravaging time can not destroy
Nor dim the indelible traces;
These prints with me will stay,
Precious images of former faces

Kennella J. Huerta

HE THOUGHT HE HAD MORE TIME

Abundant time, he had not
To be struck down was his lot,
Silent killer stalked him in his
prime,
Robbed him of his strength once
sublime.
He could not change his fate,
Was forced to leave his mate,
She was his joy and his life,
She was his love and his wife,
His wish was not to leave her,
To live her days in despair,
He thought he had more time,
To save his sons from crime.

To protect his lovely daughter,
To see them all grow taller,
Never to quiet his grandchild's
fears,
Or see his smile or end his
tears,
To blame God, was never his
way,
Nor cry out to Him on his last
day.
Stripped of his privacy, dignity
and strength,
Beaten by pain and anguish, he
surrendered at length.

Triska Anadara Braun

UNTITLED

Before the daystar slowly starts
to rise on the eastern horizon
A girl rises from her half frozen
position
Slowly she gets up,not looking
forward to the day
Still he continues on with her
daily life.
She doesn't bother eating
anymore, only cleans up her
corner
And walk outdoors.
As the first rays of sun shed
light over the fields
A girl is bent over double,
working
Baking in the sun, not thinking
about anything
In her heart the sweat and toil
is for others, she cares.
It her life, she works on
Until the rays of light slowly
start to leave the sky.
When the great fiery ball starts
to fade beyond the distant
mountains
The lone girl staggers back to
her isolated hut
Alone she eats and crawls into
her barren corner.
She thinks for awhile, hoping...
But soon remembers.
Slowly; darkness closes in.

Sam Kahl

TO A CHERISHED FRIEND

(inspired by Ludwig van Beethoven)

When Life's proud Sea churn'd
great Despair,
And Terror held the distant
Shore in Night;
When Strife drunk-mad smote
disrepair
Upon the Hallow'd Fire fled
from Plight;
And Heaven stood deaf aloft the
Mocking Void,
And Ego plunder'd, schem'd and
vainly toil'd;
Thy Might took hold to smite
my Wayward Fare,
And vanquish Terror, which
haught the Soul's great Light.
Long constrain'd to hold that
stormtossed Journey,
Wide-eyed I clung, your novice
Mate close by;
My Soul o'erdrunk your Gaze
thrust most steady,
Thrust deep into Eternity's holy
Eye!
I there beheld you midwife
Genius;
There to populate the' World's
own Consciousness!
Wielding Pow'r's sacred Majesty,
Thunder you robb'd, hid by self-
styl'd gods On High!
Athenalike forth that bold new
Universe,
Surpasst all Former Things once
rever'd!
Born midst herald Trumpets,
Strings in verse -
Atlast! wan'd Hope reviv'd and
persever'd!
Brotherhood, waking, resounded
from the Deep,
A mighty Giant rous'd from
Utter Sleep!
God I 'held midst Calm's gentle
Nurse,
Calling my name midst Joy's
somber tears!

Ann Hunsicker

DREAMS

These dreams I dream at night
The ones I dream of you
Would make so much more
sense
If only they came true
But life just seems to hold
The dreams I keep inside
Instead of setting free
It only makes them hide
Why can't I have the chance
To show my feelings to
The one I love so much
The one and only you

Janice Clarke Taylor

THANK GOD FOR DR. KING

Thank God for Dr. King who
made the sacrifice,
Who launched a vast crusade,
accepting what be the price
To guide the starving masses to
Washington, D.C.,
To march for jobs and freedom
and racial equality.
He pledged to find a cure for the
suffering and the poor,
To wipe out segregation and
open every door,
So hundreds of thousands came
and hoped to be redeemed,
He looked upon that multitude
and told about A Dream.
A Dream where each of us
would seek reality
And wake up from the darkness
to the light of liberty,
We'd cast aside our differences,
hatred and bitterness
And fight for peace and justice
and dwell in righteousness.
He dared this powerful nation to
give us just a chance
To live in opportunity and
endure each circumstance,
He even dared America to take
us in her wealth
And heal our wounded souls
then nurse us back to health.
Thank God for Rev. King whose
faith was justified
With every demonstration, the
cause intensified,
He soon advanced the
movement for voter
registration
While students made demands
for school desegregation.
Marching through Mississippi,
Georgia, Alabama,
Through the Carolinas,
Arkansas, Louisiana,
The boycotts, kneel-ins and sit-
ins would spread through
south and north,
The demonstrations grew as his
leadership came forth.
But the hostile southerners
protested with bigotry,
They would not be defeated,
they swore brutality,
Refused the demonstrators,
blocked all the roads to town,
Brought out their dogs and tear
gas, no way they would back
down.
They rode in the night, burning
crosses along the way,
Shot and killed the
worshippers—even as they
knelt to pray,
They bombed the homes and
churches, women were
terrorized,
Lynched the Negro men, little
children were crucified.
Thank God for Dr. King who
knew his moral quest,
Though stabbed in New York
City, it was not time to rest,
Tired of rejection and "white
only" signs,
The back of the bus and never a
place to dine.
A thousand strong they came in
1961,
The "freedom riders" rode—
desgregation won,
They knew they'd be arrested,
but that would be their plight,
They sat up front with dignity,
it was their civil right.
This humanitarian would not

give up the search,
His roots were planted deep, earnestly in the church,
He saw the road to freedom and took his Saviour's hand
And led the restless people through a troubled, barren land.
Campaigning from his pulpit and through the nation's streets,
This dedicated leader, they thought had met defeat
When arrested in Atlanta, his cause had surely failed,
But non-violence was the key and the movement had prevailed.

Elaine Aslaksen
FLOW GENTLY
Is this a lesson of life, or is it just my stubborness that keeps me here with you?
Has my persistence taken over my logic, or has my heart conquered my will?
I can't fight the love I feel for you, anymore than a bird can fight a windstorm.
So I shall let fate take care, and lead me wherever it may,
As I am too weak to struggle anymore.
All of my energy has diminished, and my soul is tired.
So now I shall rest, and just flow gently for awhile.
Fate will carry me to my destination...wherever that may be....

Carol Lee Pfaff
MY POETRY
With eager hands and creative mind
I sat down to write...
My words at first uncertain were,
But I wrote every night.
My pen was always with me...
And, my writing continued on
People used to laugh at me
But, I decided to fight and write.
My words came forth more clearly now
And I journeyed on to harder works...
Thus I began to find the peace
That my creative poetry brought.
People then began to listen
At the messages they received
Amazed at how I expressed myself
Not just then, but always.
A secret I have kept within
And it has never yet been told
My poetry comes from deep inside...
My heart, my mind, my soul.

William G. Muller, Jr.
THE SENTRY
A mouse-colored haze lay heavy o'er the valley waste,
Crimson streams formed pools in the ruptured terrain,
Deaths pall captured life in its peaceful embrace,
Claiming all for its loot—flock, stalk and grain.
But above on a rise, neath a once stately pine,
Lay a soldier, a youth with warmth in his breast,
His eyes slowly opened and gazed down the line,
Quickly saddened at the sight of the infinite rest.
Soon, on wings of the wind, came the message he sought,
A tune from the bugle, though slightly off key,
It meant that those lives weren't given for naught,
That his comrades had died, died in victory.
Then out of the depths, from the well of his soul,
Rose the joy of a conqueror, who'd realized his aim,
Through long years of war, he looked to this goal,
"Keep America Free", would pound on his brain.
And strange, as though soothed by the "Great Healer's" hand,
His pain sickened body was loosed from its bonds,
And before him there stood, all covered with sand,
His buddies, with spades, making work of the ground.
"What folly now," quote he who watched,
"Do dead men rise to dig their graves?"
They answered not, but lined and marched
With measured step beside the knave.
On the back of a mule they found his shroud,
From the nearby tree they carved his cross,
His name inscribed, their heads they bowed,
And knelt and prayed and mourned their loss.
This body, conceived, born, and of dust created,
In life the dwelling place of an imprisoned spirit,
Shall with time marry it's earthen bed,
Having been relieved of mortality, has released the tenant from it.
And so it was from day to day,
The sentry viewed with peaceful eye,
The valley shed it's vale of gray,
Caress the sun and drink the sky.
The shallow ponds no longer blush,
But on their clear, smooth surface show
Fields rich with wheat free from rust,
And ripened corn in countless row.
Many times and now once more
He watched the wren come back to nest,
The ground-hog leave it's hole with thaw,
God's world was right, he now could rest.
But no! twas false, the wheel had turned,
We've reached that ugly spoke again,
Men, such fools, they had not learned,
Forgotten grief, forgotten dead, forgotten pain.
Just like puppets on a darkened stage,
They move on the impulse of invisible thread,
Each work, each step, real from the page
Of a script, penned not in black but bloody red.
And on this plain under survey,
There'll come a brave but dying lad,
He'll stumble, fall, but find his way
To a grave and sob, "Dad, my dad!"
Poet's Prayer
O Lord I pray and trust that thou
Wouldst again abide in peace with me,
Quench flaming thoughts that burn my brow
And prove my poem just fantasy.

Thomas Blender Thomson
THIS GRAIN
When this grain of sand,
on this pebble called Earth,
finds it's destiny in relation with,
this planet, in this Universe,
of this galaxy;
Then I will know,
I have found my place,
In relation to "God's Will"
For my existance with joy and tragedy
Amongst people who shared,
all these beautiful moments with me;
while searching.

Patricia Ann Carothers
AMERICA, STAY TRUE!!!
AMERICA, Stay True To God!
Each day, through every year;
Be strong to lead all nations
Into Freedom, far from fear;
Keep loyal to our flag which flies
Across this Royal Land;
Keep always to the Right to choose
God's Grace and Helping Hand.
AMERICA, Stay True To God,
In every troubled time;
He needs you as a nation to
Be Heaven's Christ-Life Line;
Don't fall unto the enemy,
Claim tools of Truth and Right;
Cling close to God, Eternally,
Draw all to see His Light.
AMERICANS, Stay True To God,
Let Him lead you, His Way;
A Nation, Indivisible,
No enemy can sway;
Place pride in all your workmanship,
Put prayers to all you do;
Join hand in hand, to The Holy Land,
Our Lord will see us through.
All people of America,
Stand up, stand right, stand true;
Keep that God-Blessed Banner
Flying high, up over you;
That flag we fly, up in the sky,
Remain to it, so true;
Salute the Love, she signifies—
Our dear Red, White and Blue!
AMERICA, Stay True To God!
We're still, just Pilgrims, here;
We've got a lot to live and learn
From Heaven's Hemisphere;
So band together, in a prayer
Our Land will always be
Filled full of Faith, God's Loving Grace
And Holy Liberty.
AMERICA, Stay True To God,
His Love, so free, gives you;
Stand tall to all, to help the small
See Glory, shining through;
A Nation grand, God blessed our Land
And people, just to be
Forever, leaders of the brave
For all Eternity.
AMERICA, stay Free, for God,
From His Goodness, never cease;
Stay Faithfully, His Nation, let
Him keep you in His Peace;
Give to your heirs and children
All your best examples of
Results of a great country, blessed
By our Great God of Love!

Doreen Dennis
ENCHAINED
White Moon
shinning,
Giving you a glow
Wrapped around you
held tightly
Never wanting to go
Your warm eyes
look into mine
As you gently touch me there
I'm Enchained in your love
I cannot be free

I am yours
Whenever you want me
Darkness
surrounds us
Hiding us in the night
Your soft kisses
melt me
Making everything alright
Your warm eyes
look into mine
And I know that you really care
I'm Enchained in your love
I cannot be free
I give myself to you
Whenever you want me
I'm Enchained in your love
I cannot fly free
I am yours
Whenever you want me

Deb Fudge
MY DESTINY
I sit
and wonder
where I am going
and if I'll ever
get there.
I look around me
for things
familiar to me
hoping they'll
give me a clue
to my destiny.
All I see
are my dreams
as they float
before my eyes
and I reach
out my hand
to grasp them.
I reach for one
but grasp another
holding it
tightly to my chest
afraid
to let it go.
When my curiosity
gets the best of me,
I slowly open
my hand
and peer inside
to get a glimpse
of my captive.
Seeing nothing
but darkness,
I open my hand
a little bit more
straining to
read my dream.
My dream
flees from the light
and hides in
the farthest corner
of the darkness
from
my searching eyes.
Frustration
overwhelms me
and uncontrollably
I fling the
cowering dream
across the room.
Hot, searing tears
burn my cheeks
as they roll
down my face
and sobs
shake my broken body.
When calmness
overcomes me,
I peer out
of tearful eyes
to see my dreams
watching me.
I smile faintly
and my dreams
warily float
before me
staying just
outside
my reach.
I then remember
my search
for my destiny
and give
a deep sigh
of frustration
at the answer
that so
slyly evades
my eyes.

Charmaine Cook
REMEMBERING YOU
I met you in September
when summer was ending.
And together we went
through autumn and winter.
I remember the long days
and longer nights,
that we spent talking
the hours away.
We were like Romeo
and Juliet in our own world.
We never said good-bye,
only "I love you forever."
Even now as we walk
in the silence of the woods,
We have shared another
summers end together.
And as the leaves of fall
spiral down to earth,
I remember a year ago,
when I met you in September.

Marjorie Whittlesey
SUNSET
The sunset glows pink and rose
and cream
In a sky of cerulean blue and
green.
The plane glides away from the
setting sun,
Where I left a dear friend alone
to die.
We had laughed together in a
foreign land;
We were scared together when
the enemy came;
We were happy together in
times of peace;
We loved roses and woods and
the land of the sun.
She lies in death row, as she
calls it, and says
She is happy to go and join
friends who have gone.
Her body is weak but that spirit
still shines,
Strong and unbending. She
smiles as she talks
Of past dangers and struggles
and friends we have known.
Her friends are world-wide and
she points out their gifts,
Tokens of love from a globe-
circling chain,
Proof of her courage and
friendship for all.
The sunset glows red in a
darkening sky
And the lights of a city spread
around and below.
All her life she made music to
honor her God.
Please, God, give her music to
carry her home.
Give her joy in the forests and
flowers she loves,
And peace at the end to repay
her long strife.
One light in the millions that
blinks out and dies
Is replaced by more lights, like
the stars in the skies,
But a friend is not easy to lose
and replace.
O God of the sunset, keep her
in your grace!

Joyce Zipprich
THE DECISION
He saw in her a reflection
of himself,
Love, in the form of
Consideration
Compassion
Comfort
Caring and understanding.
She, in turn, saw this in him.
Holding her hand, he felt her
gentleness—
She felt his encompassing
strength.

The room flushed.
He needed to hold her,
She needed holding.
The lean sinews of his soul
cried out,
Her heart was carressed by his
beckoning.
So easy to drift weightless into
A private planet of escape.
Antennas of the truth emerged,
as
Jagged thorns tore through to
reality.
She bled as she left.

Elizabeth Petrochilos
THE ROOM
I sat alone within my room
As it darkened and began to
rain.
All alone, with only a
thought,
Of a feeling I could not
explain.
Curled up on a chair, was
I so content. Then came my
Slumber as the blackened
night went.
Like a mist of fright out into
the
Night I felt a swirling swoon
Like the voice of an angel far
away,
Echoing from the room.
Lost in terror, here forever
In a place of marble stone,
Lifting my head up from the
dead,
I shrieked, sobbed and
moaned.
A ray of light from a candle
So bright cast a glow upon the
floor.
I arose from the grave and felt
A crave of this mystery I
bound
To explore.
Searching along this hallway of
hell,
Tortured and tormented,
Caught in a spell
Not a door did I see,
Just a calling to me.
I tried so desperately to find
The touch of her hand,
The feel of her skin,
Surely, surely I'm blind!
Why must I behold
The stories untold and
Venture all alone!
God, help me find
This woman so kind
Whom I surely feel I've
known.
As if a sigh from an
Angel high, did call
And say to me
Arise, my dear! Have no fear,
For you are now with me.
Together, forever, at last it's
passed.
I knew it would be soon.
She'd come for me when I was
freed
From the horrors of the room.

Edna I. Ledger
THE POWER OF GOD'S LOVE
God's love is deeper than the
ocean,
Wider than the sea,
It's all knowing and wise,
And it can flow through you
and me.
God's love is patient and kind;
It's understanding beyond all
measure.
Without that love
We are mere mortals.
If God's love flowed through
each of us
We could help change the
world.
It could help bring peace
And make it a better place to
live.
God's love is tender and sweet
More precious than any rare
jewel
If our lives were committed to
Him
Then we could show the world
How powerful Gods love really
is.

Alice E. McGill
A BEGINNING
With the last of my courage,
I grip on to my old dear life,
But with the blink of an eye,
It slips from my hand.
Hope vanishes, taking my
dreams.
It is time for a change.
The past forever echoes itself
In a hollow corner of my mind.
There will be no music to hear,
No singing birds in my
mornings,
And no voices to understand.
Everywhere I feel sadness,
But life hasn't come to an end;
It is only the beginning.
Thoughts churn in my head as
I gaze out the window.
Forward is where I must step
Without a glance back.
I cry my tears and say good-bye

To what my life has once been
For I know it's a point of no
return.
I need to untie my strings to the
past
For once again, I must learn to
be free.
Faith is my only guiding light as
I gather courage, all that I
possess,
To open that dark door up
ahead.
Acceptance of what has
happened
Is my key to the mysterious
door,
Cause what will be, will forever
be.
Every dying sun in a sunset
always
Has a reviving sun at dawn
Of a new day in a new life.

Joy C. Day

APOLLO

1)
Long He is coming.
The Darkness waits
Expectantly;
She knows Her time is short.
She holds Her breath
And waits.
2)
Shyly
He coyly trickles a finger
Over the edge of the mountain,
Reaches upward.
Hesistant He is,
Measuring the troposphere
With one golden cord
He lingers just below the
horizon,
Contemplating the day,
Preparing His armor,
Checking His steeds.
3)
With a sudden lurch
The chariot springs forward.
He is not taken by surprise.
He is master of His beasts.
He is most wonderful to behold-
Blinding in His brilliance,
A god in His Olympian glory.
The masses bow down to
worship Him.
4)
Stoically He climbs,
Silently He moves,
Purposefully He travels onward;
He never looks down.
5)
But the thoughts rise up to Him
Like vapors off of steaming
garbage,
Bubbling, Nauseous lava,
The hate and perversion of
mankind.
His own image is not reflected
In the sea below Him,
Only that of the Nethergod.
This He knows by instinct,
By virtue of His wisdom,
By the inner eye of His
prophecy.
6)
For He dares not to look down,
But to plod steadily forward.
Wearily His mighty stallions
approach world's end.
Heavy is their foam & great
their thirst.
The god is empty.
But He knows He will ride again
tomorrow,
Refreshed by ambrosia and
nectar,
For again today He has kept
Himself:
He has not looked down.

Katheryn Glietz Kehn

FATHER WE THANK THEE

Father, we thank Thee for Thy
care,
For guidance when we would
despair,
For food and shelter, health and
home,
For friends who to our fireside
come;
For gentle raindrops, falling dew,
For shining sunbeams—ever
new;

For faith and trust that we did
gain,
For lessons learned, and not in
vain;
For pleasant work our hands can
find
That gives contentment—
peace of mind.
Help us to serve our fellowman,
To lend assistance where we
can;
That we may make his path
more bright,
His heavy burden seem more
light;
So that he, too, may thankful
grow
And learn that Thou wouldst
have us so.

Leonora Lee

VOICE OF NIGHT

Thoughts, on winged,
pirouetting feet
Come swirling uninvited,
unannounced, on the muted
whisper
Of the breath of night.
As they swirl gaily by, one
vividly recalls memories
Long since thought dead. .
The voices, the places, the
varried faces
Come into focus with each
revolution.
The toil, the joys, the
heartache and oft times
heartbreak
Gives cause for an inner
reflection.
What causes the secret shades
of night
To invade, to reveal, those
thoughts and actions
Long since thought securely
concealed?
Could it be that one's
conscience has a parallel with
the night?
Both intangible, yet universally
a vital part of man and nature.
Both susceptable to the
penetrating force of light,
Whether it be the light of
Faith and Love
Bestowed from the One above,
Or the invented light of man.
To flee from either is a fools
folly.
To accept, to embrace, to be
thankful to the Creator
Of both, and for both,
Is contentment, Peace of Soul.

Jo Worden

OBSERVE

The beautiful things are waiting
for you
But you have to look to see -
Around, under, behind or above
No telling where they might be!
So give pause now and then
Stop and look at the ground
There are wonderful things
there!
A flower, a rock, a leaf or
A worm with golden hair!
Who knows what we all have
been missing -
Rushing through our lifelong
quest -
Perhaps what we have been
missing
Are the things that were the
best!

Judy Lee Smiley Blitch

THOUGHT'S WOE

My mind winds like the never
ending paves in the hills.
Continuous stroke of thought
ever throbbing at my gills.
But to breathe for just a few,
would be a grand vacation.
Woe, but thought of life is
but the life of generations.
I know not what ideals will be,
what is, though not forever.
And pressing hard as change so
does,
requires great endeavor.
And even though a constant
search,
has woes, it has it's pleasures.
The time of woe, if traveled
well,
holds promises of treasures.
I can surely not forsake, my
mind,
though it may ramble;
for if it is my way and love;
along it I will amble.

Judy Lee Smiley Blitch

MY HUMAN FEAR

Carry me oh feet and mind
into the world before me.
Least my heart be stole away,
the strength I must emplore
thee.
I grasp the opening so small
the flicker shows just slightly.
Touched by the great expanse of
it are secrets held so tightly.
The distant sounds are almost
here.
Mine is the kingdom calls.
Transition brought to balance
beams.
Faint pillars hold white walls.
Somewhere a voice is bouncing
off the walls of faith
transparent.
Urging me that all is well;
and soon will be coherant.
I gather all my thoughts in ode,
retain the wisdom I am shown,
please forgive my human fear;
a fear of the unknown.

Barbara A. Langevin

PRECIOUS MOMENTS

The wind teased the daisies
As we ran through the fields
We stopped, and he took hold
of me
His eyes met mine
He whispered; I love you
I have the love I'thought I'd
never find
He held my hand as we sat in
the grass
I watched the butterflies at play
These precious moments were
our last
I told him I was to leave
We cried a little
I begged him not to grieve
I started to walk away
He would not let me go
I said there'd be another day
Then I left.

Cindy Kilgore

CAPE FEAR BLUEGRASS FEST

It was a bluegrass
kind of afternoon
in the shade
of an old oak tree.
A dulcimer
out of place
serenades seagulls
seeking stillness.
A mandolin
calls turtles from the sea,
tempting mermaids,
and fish fins flying.
Banjo my brother, Seth,
until his buckdance
his finesse
and two-steps
a fiddler's test.
A survivor of Snowflake
Breakdown
in a blizzard of sand,
a stowaway mountaineer
doing his best.
Evening moon flows
down upon the barnyard beach,
Lumberjack dances
alone
his wooden stage asleep.

Linda Seifried

A MAN

Expressing yourself:
Being Yourself: Doing What You
Want, Saying What You Want.
Being a Man in Every Aspect of
the Word;
Being the Kind of Man I Can
Look Up to
With Pride, with Respect, and

with Love.
Standing Straight and Masculine with Beautiful Eyes:
Eyes that Shine with Wisdom and Lips Speaking Authority:
Lips of a Man: Understanding, Compassionate, Tender, Soothing.
The Protector: Trying to Banish Fears from My Mind;
So Soothing to be Around. . . . You are My Tranquilizer.
Just Sitting Together. . . .Not Saying a Word:
Sharing the Quietness, Our Hopes and Dreams, Enjoying the Peacefulness:
Gentle and Strong: Yes, That is You:
Not Only in Body. . . .Which You are,
But, Also, of the Mind and Spirit.
The Strength in Your Hands is not Only Physical
But, Also, Shows the Strength You Hold Inside.
For a Long Time I have Searched for A Man;
Not Just an Individual in a Masculine Masquerade,
But a Man in Every Aspect of the Word;
One Who Knows Who He Is; I Have Met One
And I am Proud to say I Know Him,
I Have Touched Him and He is Real;
And, Babe, That Man is You.

Barbara J. Goocher
DADDY!
There's been quite a few men
I've known in my life
and I've called them many
different names.
One was Brother and another
was Husband,
and Boss was the name of
several more.
But there's one man I've known
longer than any,
who has the name no one else
will share;
Who has loved me longer and
known me better
than all the others put
together.
His name is "Daddy" now and
always it will be
a name as unique as the man
who has it.
For you will be my Daddy
throughout my days --
loved, cherished, admired, the
only one for me.

Lindy G. Stem
SEASON'S COLORS UNSEEN
Colors dance across the sky
But I've never seen a shade of blue
And they tell me every spring
What Mother Nature brings
But lovely flowers never bloom
They say that rain is clear
And it sparkles when touched by sun
And they tell me every fall
What colors come to call
But trees never change in autumn
All the earth is touched with death
But they say it's just a kind of sleep
I never know when it snows
Until I feel the cold
And the dampness beneath my feet
And the summer is just the same
And I've never seen a shade of blue
And they tell me every spring
What Mother Nature brings
But lovely flowers never bloom
For me

Richard J. Gierczynski
MADCAP ELECTION
I want to be
A man with respect
Certain worn
In contol
Piercing like a thorn
I want to be
Tested
Proven
Without question
I want to be
Unsuspected

Tasha Razi Khosrovani
IN THE HILLS OF KENTUCKY
She was a large-breasted woman
Heavy, with a child hanging tight at each hip
Like a forgotten-cowboy with his hands
On his guns in clenched grip.
Her hair, pulled back, plain and simple
Her dress, a faded-calico-swirl
Nothing about her was fancy
For she was a calico-girl.
She sat on a porch without porch-swing
The clothes of her children were tattered with wear
Deep in the hills of Kentucky
Where life can be hard to bear.
Some clothes, flapping like ghosts of blue denim
Hung on a rope stretched taut in the wind
Tied next to a three-sided shack
Gone was the hope of tomorrow
And the man who swore he t'weren't
Comin' back!
At her feet sat a jug of corn-whiskey
With a squirrel-gun propped near in full-view
While she talked with suspicion at a stranger
And spat at the ground
While she chewed.
Her forehead bore wrinkles of anguish
Like furrows laid bare in a field—
Long deserted of rain;
In the distance blew a train whistle
Echoing her remorse and her pain.
But deep in the hills of Kentucky
Life was 'matter-of-fact.
No one dreamed of tomorrow
But of clean dresses, sweet-milk
And pork-chops, laced at the edges with fat.
She was a large-breasted woman
With a child hanging tight at each hip
Knowing life offered no kindness
To those who just sat down and quit!

Emory B. Tinley
WHAT WOULD I BE WITHOUT YOU?
What would I be without you?
What would the morning be
without the sun?
What would the night be
without the darkness?
And the fish in the water, what
would they be, without the sea?
What would the birds be,
without the trees to build its
nest?
And where would the robin be,
without its red breast?
And can you imagine Winter
without any snow?
Or a homing pidgeon with no
place to go?
What would a sailboat be with
no wind to guide it?
And what would a valley be
with no mountains to hide it?
What would life be with no
heaven to look up to?
Without your love, what would
I be...without you?

J. Mark Plummer
PORTRAIT OF A MAN
Growing up in the harsh years of the depression
the son of a share cropper.
He learned through hard work
the worth of a good name.
Today he stands tall in the early morning sun
long hours and dreams making himself,
known and respected within his
chosen desire.
With his children growing, they
began to look up and
understand him.
Pushing hard he expected nothing,
less than their best.
Others learned to respect him
for his knowledge and dedication
At not only his work,
but at everything he does.
Time has marked his face,
back bent from yesterday's labor,
Hair turned gray, he has no regrets for
he is a Man.

Deborah Louise Watson
SEASONS
Birds are singing in the trees,
buds are turning into leaves,
The sky is blue, the rain is light,
The rays of the sun shine golden and bright,
Every being starts anew, me as me and you as you,
Then our Spring turns full and warm, nature's sprouts have taken form,
Creatures spend their time in play,
The earth has plenty, and hearts are gay,
God has blessed us one and all,
for now our Summer turns into Fall,
Here is shown a beauty unique, this season brings us color at its peak,
The trees turn yellow, orange, and red,
They must prepare for the winter ahead,
The cold creeps in slowly at first,
Then Winter arrives with a welcomed burst,
The snow that falls upon the ground,
Captures silence by removing sound,
This solitude does not remain,
For the young at heart are heard again,
God gave to us these changes on earth,
They bring us joy which stems from rebirth.

Russell O. Litchfield
THE CHRISTMAS CANDLE
Dear gentle baby Jesus Child
O' Holy Love! O' sweetness mild;
This Christmas candle
I light to Thee
O' Saviour! born to set men free!
I proclaim the glory
Of Your spirit unfurled;
I share Your heart
With all the world;
I hold foremost
God's eternal goal
For love to flourish
In each man's soul.

Overcome with compassion,
O' Infant Christ,
Cherished thoughts
Of care increase
To fill my heart with Christmas
And
Eternal Peace.
O' baby Jesus! As this candle
Burns
Illumines the truth
Of Your concerns;
May this Christmas day
Of Your Holy birth
Bring peace and love
To all the earth.

Carmine F. Notarile
DESPAIR NOT OH LEARNETH MAN
Despair not oh learneth man, despair not.
In what you feel to understand, in the
students that you teach, the students you
find so hard to reach.
Cause their minds are adrift to what you convey.
Their eyes look not at you, but the other way.
Their ears are incoherent to

what you say.
Their tongues lash out, a
stinging whip
To demean you and the
knowledge you teach.
Despair not oh learneth man,
despair not.
You are burdened with the
knowledge
of knowing that they are living
within
a disillusion that all is well
and in
time they shall create their
own hell.
Slowly but surely their
disillusion of
security will be stripped away,
and they
will be exposed to life in its
actual way.
This is what brings despair to
your heart
and a kind of emptiness to your
mind.
But despair not oh learneth man,
despair not.
Their lives are shadowed within
the form.
In the path that they should
take
they are capable to give but find
it so easy to take.
They are capable to create but
it is
made so easy for them to hate.
They are on the borderline of
what is and what is not.
Their minds and thoughts are
molded
by the conditions in the world
today
unlike the world of yesterday.
And this I say to you, it is
people like you who will
determine what they
will or will not do.
Despair not oh learneth man,
despair not.

Marinella Miller Haygood
THE OLD COUNTRY SCHOOL
The old school house stands
quiet and still,
A monument beside the road.
It seems to sleep
There on the hill,
Now relieved of yesterday's load.
It's school bell silent and rusting
away;
The doors have fallen down.
Windows are gone-
Blank eyes that say,
"Let me sleep. Don't make a
sound.
I've earned my rest, the right to
peace,
And a place recorded in time.
So let me sleep
And take my ease.
Education, this legacy was
mine!"

Reggie
LET'S LIVE TOGETHER
Black, white, blue, or green,
What does this color difference
really mean?
People are people no matter
what color,
Everyone should try to love one
another.
We are here for one purpose, to
live and love,
But it seems all we do is push
and shove.
Living together is what it's all
about,
Looking around just makes me
want to shout.
Let's live together and give it a
try,
Because living like this just
makes me want to cry.

Betty Ruth Ingersoll
MY CLOSET
I talked with God this morning
in my secret place
Such wonder I beheld, I met
Him face to face
There He blessed my soul as
tears ran down my cheeks
He removed burdens, I'd been
carrying for weeks
He gave full release from all my
fear and doubt
Again He cleansed my soul,
from Calvary's precious faunt
He took the care and heartache
from my busy day
Drew me closer to Him and
wiped my tears away
He told of many things and then
He let me know
He would never leave me
because He loved me so
Oh, then with boundless joy He
filled my thirsting soul
His wonderous mysteries to me
He did unfold
Fellowship with the Lord, is
heaven here on earth
He fills me with His love, He
teaches me His truth
I've seen Him in His beauty, all
the world grew dim
I love to hide away and visit
there with Him

Dixie McVey King
CAPE HATTERAS LIGHT—HOUSE
I wish they would save me.
They once would come by
And discover me-
Me the one who made the light
That guided the ships through
the dangerous paths
In the sea and the storms that
torment over it.
Yet, now those storms seek
revenge
And eat at my foundations-just
as the sand castle
At wave-break when the tide
comes in.
Why they won't help me
From the scorn of the storms
That want to devour me-I can't
understand.
The days and nights
The rain runs down my cheeks
And it is filled with salt in the
air
Just like the tears that come
from their eyes
When they know their time is
coming to an end
And will no longer stand with
head held high in pride.
Even tho I'm old in age
I am still able to work
The same as when I was born
here
And winked my eye in love to
all the ships at sea.
I only wish that for all the
"southwesters"
Of the past, present and future
That I will have saved from the
storms fury and revenge
My life
So all "old salts" will feel the
love my eye shines
And not be with more salt-cured
features
From my tears drowning my eye
As I submerge into the depths
Of the sea.
I wish they would save me.

Eugene D. Brink
EVENING PASSION
With the shadows softly falling
As the day is winding down.
The greatest joy to my heart
Is just knowing you're around.

For in the mellow evening
As I hold you close to me,
And I kiss your tender lips
With a passion burning free.

All the care and the torment,
I have known through the
day;
Are like dust from the field
Which the wind has blown
away.

Though I smile in my sleep,
And may it ever be true,
That the fire in my heart
Is burning just for you.

Jill G. Murray
MOONLIGHT
I stood facing the ocean
which was preparing for its
evening rest.

The waves, no longer blinded
by the Sun's heat, sleepishly
spread out over the beach.
The moon came into focus.
Its light blankets the darkness.
Notes flickered from each swell
carrying the moon's lullaby.
Memories shot back to mind of
past scenes.

The same ocean, the same
moon—
but I was not the same.
I had stood here many times
before—
but not alone as now.

I had my love who had shared
this sight with me.
We would stand silently, trying
to hear the whispered lyrics.
And our eyes, moonlit bright,
glanced catching the love
rays.
Then as morning takes away the
moon from its watery love.
My love drifted from my sight.
I left behind the ocean and the
musical moonlight to forget
my love.
Now I have returned.
Time has not changed the ocean
nor the moon's lovely song.
Time I thought had changed me.
But as I watched and listened.
I could not help but smile.
I remembered my love;
saw his face—his eyes sparkle
love.
Time had not changed so very
much.
This beach will always be my
reminder.
For it knows no love of mine
but him.
And the moonlight will
always
speak his name to me.

Joanne Ledford
STONED
Riding the air currents of my
mind
feeling around to see what I find
Some things in oblivion, others
crystal clear
somewhere off in the darkness
is a mute fear
Surrounding me is beauty I
rarely know
winds create textures in my
minds flow
a total head of thoughts racing
crazy
seems to go nowhere and acting
lazy
Then everythings comes
together and creates
a pattern of open doorways and
gates
each leading to a special place
to stop
I'm riding the ferris wheel to the
top
Hanging in mid-air, total
fascination of sight
slowly coming down to the
grounds light
Letting feelings come from all
around
being created inside me, acting
like sound
Pink Floyd in the background
takes center stage
I become part of the notes
dancing on the page
I become the world, I house all
their thoughts
My alleys are all lighted, my
backstreets are forts
I give them everything they
want and need
I can't ascertain how it all
started from a seed

Jackie Hand
LOVE'S FRAGRANCE
Love is like a fragrant rose
Whatever shape or form
As solid as the first new bud
In the early morning dawn
And as the morning takes it's
flight
And noontime sets the stage
This rose unfolds it's petals
On Nature's scenic page
Then as the twilight lengthens
And darkness settles in
It's fragrance lingers in the air
To cheer our hearts again.

Georgann Jenulis
THE SOAP DISH
I looked upon a soap dish
In envy and regret
I tried to figure the why of it
But I haven't done it yet
There in the soap dish
Is the soap as creamy as can be
But when my hands pick it up
It gets as dirty as me

Kathleen P. McKinney
BENEATH THE PURPLE SKY
My heart is like a lusty wind,
That blows over hill and dale,
Over the restless sea, and then,
By the ships that sail.
Gladdened by the purple sky,
That blends within the sea,
As the softer wind doth sigh,
He's coming home to thee.

Many happy hearts will sing,
As near the shore comes She,
With my beloved and lads She brings,
To a land that's free.
In his embrace, I'll nestle,
Close within his arms,
The world will fade away,
And I am safe from harm.
So, with eager lips, I pray,
To Him who lives on high,
To lead him safely home to me,
Beneath the purple sky.

Ken E. Barkdoll Jr.
ON THE NOD
What great difference could it make,
In the rain-soaked dawn's bright gleaming,
When on the nod things came to me,
With no apparent meaning.
We were strolling, as always we did
To go one place or another,
And score upon a high grade lid,
Or some related bother
Neither of us were surprised then,
Turning the corner to find them.
These days they are always present,
With irons to fire at random.
Cold, and slushy was the street that day,
With cars doing the "Huxley Jig"—
Bald tires whining in the fog,
Latin words hanging heavy in the air. . . .
"Are you yourself there with you?"
"Been called worse.", was all I said.
What line were we to hand them,
When the flag had been waved red?
Tissue, redness, bone, and dust mingle now as one.
Fusing metal, and powder are soon to join the fun.
I saw some dentures fall, then shatter.
With the grotesque I'm undone.
Regardless of what pains are felt,
Or misguided cause-effects them,
I knew that once the hand was dealt,
The suit was cleaned for wearing.
The Kid goes down, and begins to cry.
His shouts seem more than real.
I arouse myself to find out why,
And it's time for diaper changing.
What great difference could it make,
In the rain-soaked dawn's bright gleaming,
When on the nod things came to me,
With no apparent meaning?

Rose Graham
MY LITTLE TREE!
My little Tree! My little dogwood tree!
Your leaves are red and pretty as can be
And match my shutters to a T!
Icie gave you to Frank and me,
When we were in Virginia in 1963.
You were the only one that lived out of three.
Each year I looked in vain
To see your white bloom!
Your chances were slim
On the side of a slope,
The water ran off instead of soak!
But alas, the big mower wheels laid you low,
I straightened you up and tried to get you to grow,
with the help of God, of course, you know.
There is always hope -
There is a sprout, that could take your place in case -
You did your best, and so must we,
Little red-leafed dogwood tree!

Patricia Ann-Jones
UNTITLED
Don't try to make me
feel guilty
with those sad blue eyes.
I wasn't playing a game when I said
I would love you forever.
But that didn't mean
I would stay that long.
Believe me when I say
further down the road,
everytime I see a
blonde-haired,
blue-eyed,
male-caucasian,
my heart will flutter
and my palms will get sweaty
in anticipation
of the memory of you.
But I can't stay.
I'm not the mixed bowling league on Wednesdays,
pancakes for breakfast every Sunday morning type.
Find yourself a nice village fire marshall's daughter.
One who swears by Avon products
and creates a great meatloaf.
Know that I love you
and will often wonder
what might have been
had I stayed.
Perhaps if I had met you a month ago
or a year from now.
I would have stayed.
But I have too much I am running from
and too much I am running to.
I only stopped
to come in out of the rain
for awhile.

Robert Francis Liebel
GOD'S LEAF
The Word of God is like a beautiful leaf,
caught in a gentle breeze
Until the Holy Spirit places a calm,
upon the heart that receives
The blood of the Lamb of God who
died on Calvary Day
Receive this Gift* into your life,
then spiritually you're on your way
*John 3:16

C. Douglas Trimpey
UNTOUCHABLE YOU
Untouchable you
Are the everlasting
And breathless moments
Of my life.
In my pumping heart,
I know I love you,
But cannot hold you,
And my Edens will never fade.
Clouded dreams
And moon-lit midnights
Are no longer journeys
Through unforgotten moods,
But dimly burning candles,
Lighting the caves of my thoughts;
I love you,
Untouchable you.

Eleanor Frost Stevens
I'LL NEVER GET OVER LOVING YOU
I'm so sad and blue
That I don't know what to do.
I'll never get over
Loving you.
God took you away. It was on a winter's day.
He must have needed you up there.
Guess He didn't know that I loved you so.
And it would be so hard to bear.
Now I dream all night that you hold me tight.
We plan like we used to do.
You steal a kiss and then it's daylight time again
And I bid farewell to you.
Since you cannot stay I begin the day
With a prayer for you up above.
All the whole day through,
everything I do
I share with you and send you all my love.
Sometimes I feel you near and I can almost hear
You say never fear.
I'll be with you always
Neither war nor time or space
E'er can erase the love still glowing in my heart.
There's nothing I can do, I'll have to see it through,
Until God needs me up there too.
Then my heart will sing, and all the bells will ring.
We'll be together always.
(In Memory of Cpl. Kermitte T. Sampson)

Maryann L. Havel
NO LOVE LEFT
Life's a wheel, it just keeps on turnin'
The sun is a fire, it just keeps on burnin'
The stars are lights, they just keep in shinin'
The kids are hungry, they just keep on shinin'
A small child born on the earth
Everyone's excited about the new birth
Presents go to Mom and Dad
To give the child what they never had
The stars in her eyes and the sun in her hair
And that big bright smile that's always there
The gifts and the money Dad gambles away
What about the rent that Mom has to pay?
The poor little girl gets nothing to eat
Mom and Dad need someone to beat
In the corner that she never looks out
She doesn't know what it's all about
She always has a scared look on her face
There's no food or love for her in the place
Cold and hungry in desperate need
Her parents problem-another mouth to feed
They wouldn't care if she's wet or dry
They make her shut-up when she starts to cry
The love's gone sour and the money-what's that?
Not enough food left, even for the rats
The stars in her eyes and the sun in her hair
And the big bright smile that's always there
They all seem to have gone away
No more love cause no more pay
The innocent child who did no harm
Made everyone laugh with that certain charm
If someone knew maybe they could save
It's too late-she's in her grave

Ann Hollon
SPLINTERED WORD
A word
Slid
Out of my heart
Onto
My tongue and
Hit
Against my teeth
Forming
The word love
And the word love
Fell
Out of my mouth and
Splintered
On the sandy ground
And the sun
Hit
The glassy
Broken
Pieces of my heart and
shone
Through them.

Shar Lynne Creager
LOVE IS SO KIND AND TRUE
Love is true; I know it is.
It's nothing at all like it is in
show biz'.
Love is something for people
who love each other,
Take for instance our father and
mother.
Love for them is so kind and
true.
They're there for each other
when one is feeling blue.
Oh, mother and father we love
you!
Our love for you is kind and
true!
Mother, our love for you is so
very new,
Father, that goes the same for
you!
Our love for you is so kind and
true.
We hope that neither of you
ever feels blue.
We love you, we love you, really
we do.
We thank you for being there
when we are feeling blue.
We love you, we love you, really
we do.
We hope in the future to be just
like you.
We love you, we love you, really
we do.
We love you, oh, so kind and
true.
We really do love to be with
you.
And with you near me, I know
I'll never feel blue.
We love you, we love you, really
we do.

Sakina Kagda
ACROSS THE INTERNATIONAL DATELINE
The window-seat horizon tilted
in the dusk of my yesterday.
The glitter of
the embroidered ground
geometrically patterned
by the lights
of the City of Angeles
dazzled my day.
Back home in Singapore
today is tomorrow, but here
it is yesterday.
A Pacific crossing
jetlag the companion
on freeway numbers, directions
exits and excitement
homes with reins on motors
ambled by choosily.
Every whim was delighted
every sight was blinded
by the razzle of the stars
and neonic flickers
of Sunset Strip.
Professional entertainment
sensor-touch moving props
'Open Sesame' garage doors
of all homes.
Thrills, frills, fun
in a neat bundle
of clockwork precision
the zenith of entertainment
Magic and marvels galore
to make you feel little again
big again. . .and over.
Choices abundant
a friendly 'Hi' the norm.
Signs, signboards everywhere
one said, apologetically,
'Drivers Carry no Tokens or
Change'
But I, the alien,
Unaware, carried no change too.
Understanding paid the fare!
When the junction cried
I zoomed zanily on
Montazooma's Revenge,
fell into a jaccuzi.
Shopping Malls
Motels and delis,
whizz and fizz
enchillados and burritos
delighted the taste.
San Bernadino, San Pedro
Anaheim and Azusa
Palisades and Diamond Bar
tagged names to numbers
La Jolla to San Diego
Whales to Shamu
and back again.
It's a long, long
wayside out there.

Olive Christine Moen
TELEPHONE TO JESUS
Telephone to Jesus, talk to the
Lord; the directory is found in
His Holy Word. The lines are
open night and day, You can call
from home or when you're away.

Busy signals you'll never hear,
party lines do not interfere. Call
direct, you can ask anything,
but ask for Jesus when you ring.

Switch-board circuits are in
every nation, they connect on
time from the Power Station. No
bargain rates, no time limit,
distress calls are made every
minute.

If by chance there's a bad
connection, the Power Operator
will make the correction. You
don't pay a bill when you make
this call, the service is free and
open to all.

Even the Prophets called, I am
told; they had the same network
in the days of old. You can call
anytime on this telephone, the
installment is paid, it is yours to
own.

Power lines to Jesus never fail,
He answers every call, even a
wail. Never a line that doesn't
go through, Jesus is waiting to
hear from you.

Elaine Reiman-Fenton
DREAM POEMS III
In my dream when I see you
again and all the unspoken
things get said once more
we are looking for the car
which was parked just around
the corner
but although we are walking
at what seems to be a normal
pace
we never get there.
Not that the car is gone,
just that we never arrive.
Each time that I dream it now
I feel happier in the dream
that we are walking along
and each time I notice that
we are talking and laughing.
It always ends before we quite
turn the corner
and when I wake up
I am wondering about the car.

Audrey T. Rabe
GOD IS LOVE
God is love,
That's what he is to me,
God is love,
To me, this, he'll always be.
God is love,
And he'll love you too,
God is love,
What-ever he does, he does it
for you.
God is love,
So, won't you love him now?
God is love,
All his love, for you, he'll allow.

Bethel Nunley Evans
A BIRTHDAY OF HONOR
How grateful we are that the
giant men of God
Had so much love in their
hearts for all mankind,
They were willing to write the
Books of the Bible
With salvation for people of the
future in mind.
The greatest history book that's
ever been written
Tells the story of an incident
that happened one December.
The exact date and hour of the
divine event
Was so long ago there is no
living witness to remember.
The Bible tells that the bright
Star of the East
Caused the shepherds to fasten
their eyes on the sky.
It told of the miraculous birth
of the Saviour of the world,
And pointed the way to the
manger where the Baby Jesus
would lie.
Hundreds of years have passed
since that great event took
place,
And each time we hear the
story,
it's just as exciting as can be.
God, the Father of Jesus, who
made the universe and all
therein,
Gave His Son in death for us,
that we might live eternally.
We commemorate Jesus' birth in
a manner of joy and love,
Like the Wise Men who brought
their gifts to the manger.
Christmas is the day we pay
tribute to our Lord,
And to those who have claimed
Him as their Saviour, He is no
stranger.
Let us count our bountiful
blessings every Christmas
Season,
And praise the name of Him
who gave it all through love.
Let us strive to give a gift
worthy of His Goodness
And proclaim to the world our
belief in the Matchless God
above.
We, who have given our hearts
and lives to the Almighty
Father,
Bow our heads in prayer as we
honor Him on His birthday,
And pray, "Dear aGod, fill us
with a burning desire to bear
Witness for You to the lost in
the world, and guide them to
Your Heavenly Way."

Laura Brown Becker
WINTER VASE
My frozen jar
made of porcelain stars
spinning with snow scatterings
molded to earth's wheel
Holding a bouquet of fence posts,
corn stalks, broken dry weeds
and bare branches
Gray days make dark water
it runs under your silent surface
and all things sleep below...

Ella Slotin
WHAT IS RELIGION?
The dictionary defines religion
"The Quest for the Values" of
an ideal life." With three
phases.
The ideal, attaining the ideal,
and man's conscience in his
quest from strife.
Abraham Joshua Heschel once
said, "Mystery Reigns Within
Reason, Perception and
Explanation."

The mystery is that man
rationalizes religion, reasoning
even thru disputation.
Religion is a bridge that links
the beast in man with man's
spiritual role.

Interpreting to man's eternal
ego, the immortality of his
soul.
Man's perception of devotion is
to try to do as his bible
preaches.
Love and kindness to fellow

man, interpreting that which theology teaches.
If man's conscience. By religion not be stirred,
What matter rote if symbol's shout not be heard.
Rituals, religion, righteousness, without love as a part.
Reverence, worship, what matter, if man hath hate in his heart.
Regligion is, when a man extends a hand to you, asking no returns.
With a kind word, a smile and your soul in harmony sojourns.
James Michener, the writer, once wrote, every man is my brother."
If only the world would warrant this love to each other.
The day of the messiah, so long anticipated, would come
When nation to nation, man to man, truly religious become,
"By doing unto others as you would they do unto you,"
Thus then, would the realm of religiosity renew.

Charles C. Myer, Sr.
TO MY LITTLE GIRL
"Tiss it, Daddy, an' make it don't hurt!"—
She cried, running in from her play;
And I caught her and held her, my sweet angel child
Until the tears and the hurt went away.
Her soft little arms hugged me ever so tight,—
Her lips were like down 'gainst my neck;
As she held forth the finger she had "hurted" in play,
I bowed my head and with my lips gave a peck.
Oh, my Dear Little Heart, I thought then to myself,
This small hurt you have suffered at play
Will pale when compared to the hurts life will bring
In your tomorrows just a few years away.
And in those tomorrows could I be then as now,—
Here to hold you when your world seems amiss;
Could you come running to Daddy with each little hurt,
And I could banish each one with a kiss.
Could I follow close by in those years just ahead,—
Be a buffer from the hurts and the harms,
And when you grow weary from the gale and the storms
You could seek refuge here in your Daddy's arms.
For I worry the path that my Darling must go,—
The path strewn with thistles and thorns;
The stones that would bruise her tender young feet,—
And the hurt and the harm from Life's storms.
Oh, I pray trailing winds would bring fair skies and kind,—
That would temper the path she must go;
That the stones would be deep under mosses and grass,
And that thistles and thorns could not grow.
But, whatever would be around the bend of the years,
If one wish could I have 'twould be this:
Dear Heart, hurt nor harm would be never so great
Daddy could not banish it all with a kiss.

Terry Raul Gomez
SUBMARINER'S SONG
Did you ever feel me near you
Riding on the breeze
Blowing lightly through your hair
Making music in the trees
Do you ever sense me watching
Just out of sight and sound
Look closely at the stars
My image may be found
Can you hear me calling
Voices in the rain
The pitter-patter of the drops
Whispering your name
Your skin is smooth as satin
Against my finger tips
A kiss as soft as baby's breath
I place upon your lips
For I am with you always
Walking gently on your mind
Reach beyond your dreams
And see I'm close behind
My spirit watches over you
Even as you sleep
My soul will not be prisoned
Beneath blue waters deep
Do not shed a tear my love
You feel I am not there
Believe in all around you
For I am everywhere

Edith Morton
SECOND HOME
In my mind I wonder beyonder
My feet walk into the street
My eyes rest on the alley
On the Fox River Valley
Awakened by sun shower
In the early morning hour
Surrounded by straight land
I have touched with my hand
The weeping willow tree
Is longing like me
To be free
The land of Lincoln
Sunset sinking

Katie Gray
CAN'T SAY GOODBY
I am Tired...
I am Alone...
I am cold...
I walk upon this tepid soil, and reality burns its way into my very soul...
The splashing rain...
The furious wind...
The cold ocean, lapping at frozen shores...
I am the wind...
I am the rain...
Am I also a frozen shore???
My loneliness is a frozen shore...
My need is a lashing rain...
Don't let it swallow me up,
to end this pain, deep inside, burning me...
I am tired...
I can't cry...
Can't say goodby...

Esther C. Hubbard
HE'LL CATCH IT BEFORE IT BREAKS
Some people seem to have a tremendous capacity to love
Either it has been taught or it's a divine gift from above
This reaching out for others is a joy only some can feel
For their hearts must be unmasked, not hidden behind a shield;
Others appear to be drawn to those with an open heart
Their gentleness, their look of concern, seem to set them apart,
They care about their fellow man and try to treat others fairly
And they can't and don't love lightly, but fiercely and dearly;
But sometimes their feeling for others makes them so vulnerable
They'll let others insult them, and hurt them, and yet still
They'll go on loving and forgiving, though they've shed a tear or two,
Because of something deep inside them, that's all they know how to do;
God needs these people because He can use them as His disciples
He can teach them how to heed and to follow His principles
To help His other children who sometimes forget that He is above,
And who might go through life without ever knowing His love;
So, dear one, if you think yourself weak and small
Because you allow others to use you and you take it all
Take comfort in knowing that God is always walking with you,
And if your heart is hurt, He'll catch it before it breaks in two.

Gregory Glenn De Mello
TATTERED HEART
I lived with all fervent, of an exalted ardent heart.
To discover but one purpose on earth for its fondness.
Then to make this emotion, sole intent of my existence.
And asked nothing less in return then the whole heart.
To me the disappointment became despair, hopeless & irrevocable.
It is now a disturbed and jealous feeling of affection I possess.
Be best I take my tattered hearts devotion to heaven.
For on earth my precious gift is cast back in mockery.
And rest like a curse buried deep in my soul.
So...love,---It is a fearful thing for me!

Lee M. Wolf
A PRIVATE RETREAT
I thought for you of how I might procure some golden prize to set upon your hand or neck,
or perhaps set down some lovely song or poem to while away your quiet hours;
And then I thought in all our trials how kind it would be
to give you an entire world apart from all this pain and strife, and all the chains of life that bind us here.
That world was fair tonight.
We rode across the bare and empty places of the planet,
on to some fine forest in my mind, and stumbled slowly down steep and stony slopes at last to reach a narrow barren beach—peopled only by the sunbleached bones of long-dead trees and the lapping of slow waves—the autumnal northern reaches of the Chesapeake.
There then you lay upon the ancient sand and listened deep to old Earth's pounding pulse,
While over the narrow land I wandered aimless, and questioned all the cold deep's outcast jewels: A solitary man, a solitary woman in the evening's cool.
Then down came the Sun from his high seat
and in his reddened heat set all the bay aglow:
Each flowing sparkling aqua wave was crimson crested, the fluttering leaves of Fall his sentience reflected; All the world took pause to note. . .
the blazing orb then donned a purple cloak, and went to bed.
Quietly embraced, a solitary couple watched this symphony of red.
Dusk keenly raced upon the shore, tranquility grew quickly more intense, and overhead bobbed lines of geese, calling ever shifting patterns, fading carefree 'cross the sky for peaceful marshes in the south.
Thus night crept upon the wood. Stopping but to pluck a single polished pebble from midst the flotsam there, the couple climbed the headland trail
into the velvet dark.
The timeless forest then closed in about us full, both with mists and winds of other times—some lost, and some times yet unseen.

But as we wandered wondering thus, There—through the dark—the startling call of the Barred Owl, twice. . .
And above, the full moon shining in the East.

Barbara A. Ziegler
UNTITLED
If a rose unfolds her petals
But to touch one butterfly,
What will happen as she opens
To others passing closely by?
Can she shun them spite their needing?
Will she flaunt her beauty so?
Or will she give to each, her nectar,

Love for each who pleads to know
Special moments for her sweetness,
Going on to hastened ends,
Filling up her time of blooming
Touched by love from many friends?

Madeleine France Roger
INTRUDER
(To Steven, my son.)

My dream is gone with the night. A misty day blurs incoherent entities, in a castle's room where someone has died. Too many words, too many faces to remember as the light grows warm.

Anxious I wait for next night to come. . .I hope to resume a dream, identify a corpse. . .But, there is only a shadow in the room. I mourn a friend who's face my subconsciousness has not retained. I glide through the mist in search of an ardent age. There are only ashes under my feet when the light grows warm.

With night number three, I am, once more, surrounded by haze. To find my dreamland, I need reassurance. My tormented spirit allows the castle to emerge. . .A magnetic flux, passing through a bell, rings my distressed call. This is again the wrong time! No one answers the door, nobody hears my cant! I feel thwarted, live in want. . . I twirl in the orb of darkness. I fear to stellify, I fear the canon's rules. I don't know anymore who are my friends! The glaive of failure drills my brain, slowly injects poison into my mind. . .I shall quit my folly materialize, before the Sun elevates. . .

An escort of multiple forms vanishes when I pass through dawn, and as the light grows warm, a corpse dives into telluric, shivering waters that reflect only my face. . .

barbara hagel
OCEAN
The water lies silent and still
suddenly lights bounce off her
as she appears,
like a worshipped star
She curls ever so strong,
rushing into shore to greet you
Breathing her salty breath on
you, she disappears
leaving only a layer of white
froth
Only to return again
this time much stronger and
beautiful
Lying her small gifts of colored
shells,
broken by her careless hands,
at your feet
She returns
to gather more

Patricia A. Mills
MEMORIES
Yesterday was warm,
My heart was warm and soothing,
The pleasant feeling of life
Itself brought on this luxurious feeling.
Today is cool,
My heart is cool and motionless;
The foul air which fills my lungs
Brings the dreadful feeling of life.
Tomorrow may be sunny,
But I can only feel for
Yesterday and today.

Kristin LeGoullon
THE EARTH
You are like a star in the darkness
Shining all your love down on me
In the daylight you are the sun
Every morning you rise to meet me
Your love is like the moon
It seems to revolve around me
For you see, I am the earth
And you affect me in every way

Doris Caverly
REFLECTIONS!
Why am I reluctant to turn away from a glorious summer sunset?
My eyes cannot get their fill—
of the icy fairyland
of my backyard—
seen thru my kitchen window
on an early winter morning.
a babys laugh—
a loving couple
with eyes only for each other—
Someones bright window box,
smells and sounds
and feelings—
Passing all too quickly!
I have grown older—
Time is slipping by.
I cannot turn away
from an outstretched hand,
a lonely voice,
a puppy's soulful gaze.
Memories return
of my children when they were small.
I can hear still their arguments—
their tussels—
The echoing quiet after their leave-taking.
Tears of resentment
for things I could not change,
have long been repressed.
The worn carpeting
has been covered
with my hand made rugs,
And I am contented
with a good book—
an apple—
and my sleeping cat, warm in my lap.
I Have grown wiser!
Time has softened my pain.
I can not laugh
when I recall
Moments in my youth that were fraught
with anxiety, hoplessness,
definite decisions,
(were they right or wrong?)
Travel—
eating out
a special dinner date—
a quiet day of rest,
a rousing football game on TV
a surprise call from an old friend.
Rapping with a friends teen-agers—
These are heart-warming, experiences
I loathe to let slip away!
I have grown older, wiser,
but I am forever young!

Kelly Eleanor Butler
REFLECTIONS
Look into my mirror- what do I see?
Look inside my mind- what do I find?
Look deep into a wishing well- what do I see?
I see reflections of a lonely person,
Reflecting an image of uncertainty, insecurity,
A person who is frightened and mixed up.
I look at myself and wonder if there
May be another person inside,
Trying to look out at the outside world.
I reflect an image- an unclear image,
Like a pebble tossed into a stream,
Making the water unclear to see through.
Then, I look at myself through
A beam of sunlight, and suddenly I
See myself as the reflection within.
I see my reflection with God...
And I see myself as a whole.

Mrs. Anne R. Dudley
COVENTRY CATHEDRAL
CATHEDRAL III
Cables strewn across the ruins—
in our pathway, under our feet.
We sensed a happening.
Huge incised glass doors cleaned and polished,
Workmen with sweeping brooms
trudging about inside the new church
with flannel on their shoes,
protecting the shining floors.
We inquired about getting inside the locked doors;
being turned down, we mentioned we were Americans—
had come over, almost especially, to see the new Cathedral,
The one they call the Third.
"Sorry, it's all ready for the Queen.
She'll dedicate it Thursday."
We plead we would be back home by then.
The old man was adamant and quite upset.
"Walk round to the East Side, outside.
See Sir Jacob Epstein's Archangel and the Devil.
This is all I can offer you gents, but if you hold on
I'll give you our booklet."
Then paddled off to keep his word.
Illustrations of the inside were before us
The effort of Spence and his crews.
A stone from Barakat is raised from the floor;
Sutherland's Tapestry is a seated Christ;
The Baptistry windows, John Piper's aglow!

CATHEDRAL II
Adjoining the new structure lay relics of one 600 years old:
the handsome Second, a tribute to Gothic style.
It did not survive the onslaught of World War II,
being blasted by shell after shell
until rubble was all that was left.
"The 'Jerries' did a damn good job on that one,"
a few charred ruins remain of the Second
at it's altar, a simple request
under a crudely fashioned cross,
two words engraved on the stone—the message—
"Father Forgive."

CATHEDRAL I
Ten centuries ago, in 1055 the last Earl of Mercia
Commandeered master masons, sculptors, carpenters,
glassmakers, all skilled hands answered his call
to build a church that would make Coventry the glistening
symbol of all Christianity.
This minster church of medieval times lasted some 300 years
Until Henry, the King, in unthinking wrath
Ordered it dismantled—
A masterpiece soon demolished by command of one selfish man!

Joseph William Overall
LIKE THE WIND
As the wind blows
My love grows
My thoughts are only of you
And like the wind
Let's learn to bend
For love has obstacles, too

Dudley R. Cruger

A NEW REFLECTION

There's a good stream that runs, babbles and gurgles through the meadow by the edge of the wood lot.
The sun tries to dry it up—the winters freeze it. But, it keeps coming down, down from somewhere beyond; down from some yet unfound pond.
It flows on to join another of its kind further down the valley in a secret place. In most spots you can jump across it, fair and square; in others, if you are not careful, you'd get wet. I know, I once lost a bet.
Once in a while it spreads out calm and pool-like and mirrors the sky and clouds that drift across, reflecting all that's taking place above its place—
A perfect imitator of the passing scene, showing what is, not what's been.
Lie down now and peek slowly over the edge. There you are! Caught right smack in front of yourself. A pebble slips down the bank and your face wrinkles, goes grotesque, then smooths again as it was before. Life, Death. Rebirth—nothing more.
Listen! If you lie still, quiet-like, you'll hear the voice of the stream repeat a childhood dream; bringing into focus something from yesterday, something that really isn't there to grab on to, just a glimpse of what was you.
Behind, a spell-breaking sound intrudes, You turn. It's your little sister hopping and skipping, coming right towards you through the field of high, green grass. She stops short.
Between you a question fills the air, "Please, can I come over there?".
Instinctively you start to shout, "Go away!", But, it's only instinct and dies unspoken. You gaze across at her, and next to your twelve years she's small with only five. Small, but yet big to some. Your hand goes towards her, "Welcome".
The question's answered now and she comes running, pleased by the knowledge of being accepted. She takes your hand in trust and listens as you say, "Come. Come see the little frog sitting by the stream. Come with me and build a dream."

Liz Szalay

UNTITLED

Today I'll be happy...today I can love you
If I imagine with all my strength
A time when the world has left us
In our minds, a place existing... set aside only for you and me
Where no one has tread ever before
I will hold you in my arms
Feeling all your soul...feeling the feeling
Coming from a trusting heart
One that has dared cross the unknown of getting close
Ah, the treasury of a warm embrace!!!
The pouring out, the explosion of all you feel inside
Transcending...speaking loving words
Words to soothe, calm, encasing everlasting kindness
Then silence...eyes closed...the warmth flows from an embrace to a tender kiss... wanting it to defy time
Stroking your hair...caressing the vulnerable skin of your soul
You and I ache to be loved, wanted, and understood
In the shelter of each others' arms, all this exists...and more...
I will always return to this place, this experience
To make my heart sing with love for you,
My life's friend.

Roque Rosales

I REMEMBER

I remember
The way you used to tuck me in
As in my bed, I layed to sleep.
The feel of your warm embrace,
And stroking my hair, out of my face.
I remember
The cold wind stirring
As it whistled in through our chimney.
That same lonely sound
That you must have heard
In our dark, gloomy room,
Night after night.
I remember
Your own little corner
With its small sparkling window
And a chair, to rest your age-bent feet,
Watching the sun setting low.
I have often stood
At that same dust filled window,
And wondered what it was you were seeing
And going through in your mind
As you tried not to show, you were weeping.
Oh mama
What unspoken thoughts, inside you
And what despair, must have played within you
Wandering through, all sad and lonely
Living in your solitude.
But mama
Did you know then
I'd remember you now,
Is that why
You did not speak?

William J. Granche'

MONSIEUR LAFON

It was the first time
I'd ever eaten white asparagus.
I thought a spell had made them,
or maybe it was
the vinegar and wine dressing
in which chopped garlic
and parsley floated or stuck
to the spears.
I never knew it was the mounds
that turned them white,
mounds in the garden,
made to cover the tips,
hiding them from the sun,
blanching them that way.
We ate them after chilling.
Digging potatoes was new too.
I'd always thought they came from
a potatoe tree, or hung on vines like tomatoes.
Dirt never dug so easily
as when I spaded those
well mulched rows and uncovered,
like so many rubies,
the new potatoes,
some as small as marbles;
I even thought to gather them
for my collection.
And when I accidently cut one in two,
I was startled to see the white bleeding meat
shimmering so against the black earth.
No one ever left so quickly,
without warning
silently sleeping away.
I'd been planning on one more visit
to help harvest potatoes, turn over ground,
cut away stumps to enlarge the garden,
gather snails or dig and shuck oysters.
I never knew anybody could die
before I was ready to let them go.

Rosetta U. Bowers

IS LIFE WORTH LIVING?

What is life without its twists and turns?
What is life, when sometimes right, and sometimes wrong.
What is a book, without its pages, and its cover?

What is a medly, if it isn't a song?
Then life is, worth living, one with another.
Oh, life, beautiful life, sweet life.
A life without envy or without strife.

The life we live to wait, and share.
But life is sweeter ever there.
The life which God has promised e—ter—nal.
The Supreme Being has it all in hand.

We shall gather in the great, great beyond.
Yes, there, ever there in the Promised Land.
Is life worth living, the question is asked?
Bearing our crosses, tri—als, and giving.

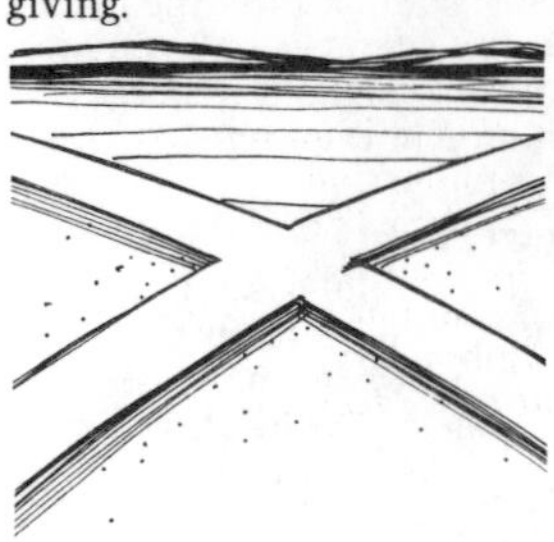

At the cross—road we find many tasks.
Let's keep on travel—ing, for life is, worth living.

Teman Douglas Treadway

THE CAVALRYMAN

The cavalryman maintained his course
And rode on toward the sun.
The hot horse mane caressed his brain
Like an inward telephone.
I stopped to feel his temperature
As he lay among the bones.
To me he bade he was half-mad,
But in that not alone.
The cavalryman maintained his course
And rode on toward the burning sun.
He soon lost hold and ate his horse
From the mane down to the bun.
Despite his moans I telephoned
The Superintendent of Parks
And asked him please to bring bleu cheese
And aged Cutty Sark
That we might revel through the night,
The cavalryman and I.
We sought the source of heaven's light
Till he proclaimed, "I soon will die."
So I prepared a coffin
With gold cross o'er its head
To guide his path to heaven by
The moment he dropped dead.
All was prepared, the sacred sword
From which red garlands swayed,
With pomp and class to fill his ass
As soon he passed away.
The rite was set, the man did step
Into the coffin black
And sent his soul to World Control,
Where all good soldiers find their racks.
Then to the pisshouse I did go,
It gave me pause to think.
I thought the guilt, the blood he spilt,
And dumped him in the drink.

Bill Mengarini

THANKS TO AN UNKNOWN CRAFTSMAN

Why take such massive pains to decorate
A simple parlor table, which would be
As useful if its legs were

plain and straight
Without this swirling wooden imagery?
The essence of beauty is function;
There is an unwritten injunction
Commanding the total expunction
From all our works of all embroidery.
But as we feel first puzzlement then thrill
Encountering a long-forgotten face,
My disregard becomes surprise until
First understanding dawns, then starts to race
With pleasure and wonder perceiving
These intricate forms interweaving
In multifold patterns achieving
This union of intensity and grace.
But this disturbs me still; I sense the pain
Which one who does such work is forced to bear;
This pitch is so exhausting to maintain
I feel not inspiration, but despair.
Was money or fame the ambition?
What goal is so worth acquisition
It justifies such repetition
Of tasks which need such patient, perfect care?
Are craft and compensation opposites?
A craftsman's spur is neither fame nor pelf;
The task itself attracts him, and he sits
As work-absorbed and placid as an elf,
And now come the full revelation:
The purpose of such a creation
Is only a pure celebration
Of joy in doing just the work itself.
These carvings from another time express
An insight which our software needs today;
Too few among our own works now possess
The spark this unknown craftsman's works display,
And we in our craft are left owing
A debt to a master for showing
How work done for joy endures glowing
With strength we can achieve no other way.

Lois J. Funk
THE FINAL AUDIT
The Balance Sheet was finished,
The Ledger finalized,
The records of a lifetime to
Be closely scrutinized.
The Auditor stood ready to
Examine every line
In order to determine
The fate that would be mine.
As He surveyed the Balance Sheet,
My heart was filled with dread,
For all my assets could not match
The entries made in red.
The liabilities of sin
Had plagued my life since birth.
The simple words "I love my Lord"
Summed up my total worth.
He opened up the Ledger, and
I held my breath in fear,
For knowing eyes could see beyond
Notations entered here.
The only credits posted were
"Faith", "Hope" and "Charity";
The entry under 'Debits' read
"My Saviour died for me".
The books could not be balanced,
I acknowledged with regret,
For all the records showed that I
Was deeply in His debt.
Then nail-scarred hands re-marked the books
And handed them to me.
And when I checked them once again,
They balanced perfectly!
The assets on my Balance Sheet
Read "Riches yet untold".
And there in bold, red letters was
The "Loss of Satan's hold".
The credits in my Ledger were
Summed up "Redeemable",
While written under 'Debits' was
A simple "Paid in full".

Donna L. McCombs
UNTITLED
What is love to me?
Sometimes it seems
There is no such state
Of being.

Alma Lillian Hageman
JOLENA
Jolena, winter baby
Our sweet little sprite
Blew in on a snowflake
One cold frosty night
Eyes velvet brown
Cheek petal soft
god sent you down
From a star up aloft.
First you were one
And now you are two
Short chubby legs
Tippy toe through
Bowers of flowers
Dappled with dew
Tulips and daffodils
Forget-me-nots, blue.

Bessie F. House
THE CONNECTION OF L
As I embrace thy tangled web of thrall,
And kiss thy lips with poignant care above,
No sweeter love with me shall ever pall,
For ours shall be a never ending love.
As year by year our memories abate,
And days become but shadows of the past,
Still though the heart yearns now to see its mate,
The sparks of passion in the soul still last.
And still before the early hours of day,
Two souls will meet, in passion intertwine,
And cradled in her bosom he will stay,
Two spirits in the veils of love divine.
True love exists as real as those who live,
A fragrant scent of happiness it gives.

David G. Silva
MALATHION MEDFLY MADNESS
It's Thursday night, and I'm awakened from bed, by helicopters flying overhead.
They're spraying malathion all over the place, and if you go outside they will spray you in the face.
It's to kill the medfly, that horrible little pest, that's contaminating our fruit, North, South, East and West.
I am a little worried about the effects of the malathion spray, and what would happen if you breathed it in every Thursday.
One guy drank some to prove it was cool, but personally I think he's a damn fool.
He said it was safe, and would do us no harm, but who knows, a year from now he could lose his arm.
It's now Friday morning, and I am lacing my boots, when I get this mad idea about plastic fruits.
I took these fake fruits and laid them down in the yard, hoping the flies would just think that they're a little hard.
I laid some in the sun, and some in the shade, and I sprayed them all with extra strength Raid, and fruit scented Glade.
It wasn't long before three medlfys flew down on a petrified peach and a plastic pear, and looked at them in despair, but before long they didn't seem to care.
They flew over to rape the granite type grapes, they chewed and they gnawed on the vine of the grapes, till they got so fat and thick, that they couldn't move a bit, so I went on over and smashed'em with a brick.
I know I didn't kill very many but I feel I did my best to rid this pest, and hopefully the malathion will kill the rest.
But if it's fruits they want, and fruits that they need, then why mess with the fruits on a tree, when they can just go down to the corner of Polk and Geary.
And if they must lay their eggs, which produce the maggots, then let them go lay them on all of the faggots.
Now if you want to blame all this medfly madness on just one clown, it would be our governor, Jerry Brown. . . .

Muriel J. Davis
GRANDMOTHER'S BUREAU
An old fashioned Bureau, in my Grandmother's day
Held many a treasure tucked safely away
The small dainty gloves of finest black lace
And the velvet bonnets that framed her face
Both, spoke of Grandmother's impeccable taste
There were scarlet ribbons, folded with care
For restraining the curls of Grandmother's hair
And seldom was seen a maiden so fair
Yes! Grandmother's beauty, caught many an eye
From the family carriage "In days gone by"
In this long ago Bureau, all neatly stacked
Among bits of fluff and bric-a-brac
Revealing a shyness that modern maids lack
Were gowns, that reached, from throat to in-step
And ruffled nite caps for use when she slept
Yes! Life was less hectic and the pace more slow
When she played croquet, with "her favorite bo"
And the family's carriage was kept just so
For the Sunday drives, in times long ago
When "All" living was gracious, by the candle lites glow.

Gene Roberson
THE SILENT MAJORITY—WHO ARE WE
Once there was a President no better perhaps but certainly no worse than any other in recent years. The thing that intrigued me the most about him was his constant referral to the silent majority. Somehow I knew I was a part of this group but I didn't fully understand the extent of who all we were until now.
We are the product of modern technology—We are the offspring of a political regime that is out of control—We are the youth who are incapable of understanding a system we cannot even comprehend—We are the survivors upon whose backs the burden of the whole system rests—Who are we—We are the silent majority—
Last night I dreamed I was in a great hall of justice and the words a government by the people and for the people was emblazened on the wall in pure

gold. The presiding judge was the father of our country, George Washington, in the jury box were all the founders of this great nation.
On trial there were the silver-tongued politicians whose only goal in life was to increase the burden of the poor in order to line their own pockets. The industrialists were there too for they have never believed a working man was worthy of his hire. The court was called to order, the charges were read, the council for the defense, a politician in his own right, entered their plea. Not guilty. The district attorney called for the first witness, my legs began to tremble, my throat became dry, I could not speak—you see I am a part of you and together we are the silent majority.

Fenton F. DeSilva
HARLEM WAS
Harlem was soft relaxing arms,
That raised your tired head from rest,
She'd wake you like a mother would,
And nurse you from her breast.
She was a cowboy riding a hobby-horse,
Patrolling the backyard courts,
And, Indians with home-made bows,
Warring from makeshift forts.
Harlem had rivers at her doors,
Neighbors who stayed aloof,
She was gardens on the fire-escapes
And sleep-outs on the roof.
She was stolen fruit from push-carts,
And stick-ball in the street.
She was "Daddy" coming home from work,
With tired aching feet.
Harlem was Winters stinging blast,
A drifting Autumn cloud,
Mama's favorite stewing pot
And a red-breast robin proud.
She was hitched rides on Taxi-cabs,
Wagons, and trolley-cars.
She was crabs, sold on the avenues,
And "Joy-Juice" at the bars.
Harlem was hungry mouths to feed,
And calloused feet to shod,
A skinny, eager, anxious hand,
With an empty fishing rod.
She was a doctor and a lawyer,
And a perfumed "party" girl.
She was a bus-boy, and a sky-cap,
And a "trip around the world."
Harlem was "father", leading his flock.
Running, walking, crawling,
A queen bee in a hen's nest,
And the voice of freedom calling.
She was a preacher in the pulpit
With a law book in his hand
Dealing "Justice" with a shovel,
To oppressed throughout the land.
Harlem was incandescent light,
Masquerading as the moon,
Casting shadowy silhouettes,
Where silent lovers spoon.
She was lungeford at the "Renny,"
And Basie at the "track,"
The "Boys" at the "Theresa,"
Extracting myth from fact.
Harlem was the milkman,
Plodding on his way,
Raising tired, smoke filled eyes
To greet the break of day.
She had no royal splendor
Nor, the "Glory that was Rome,"
But, her tattered cloak was sanctuary
To us, who called her home.

R. E. Thayer
A GLIMPSE WITHIN
In deep seclusion I slip away
Rejecting illusion in every way
leaving now; I take a trip
To probe the mind, thus I fold
Deep inside colors of yellow and gold
Here; the aura; The ever-changing code
Here I see places with glittered rays
Thus I probe into better days
Looking now I see man's treasures
of past-present, love and pleasures
I see it all - I see it plain
My body calls, thus sustain
True are the features that I see
The past-present and the roaring sea
Enlightening though it is, I steal away
For I must respect their loving way
I've learned of plenty - I've seen a lot
I return now to study what man forgot

J. R. Welch
I CRY MY ROCK HARD GRIEF
I cry my rock hard grief
and no one hears.
The tears are stone cold
and lie inside me
Washed by waves of despair
Like pebbles in a flowing creek.
I am haunted by beaten memories
That worry about at my feet
Like lonely ghosts of dogs.

Georgia Winn
THANKSGIVING
My name is Tommy Turkey and a story I shall tell
of how Thanksgiving came to be, oh yes, I know it well.
The geese and all the chickens were chatting one fine day
When suddenly they noticed that fall had come to stay.
The trees were bright with color and the air had such a chill
The streams and ponds were white with frost and snow was on the hill.
There was no time to waste they said for winters on her way
We must help gather in the crops and fill the barns with hay.
So one by one they scurried off to join in with the chores
Filling bins with fine fresh fruits and vegetables galore.
Stacking logs for winter cold, repairing homes and barns
Making candels, sewing quilts, spinning stacks of yarn.
Working all together, the pilgrims and my friends
Were now prepared as winters snows silently began.
Their hearts were filled with thanks, yes, they were rich indeed
By working hand in hand they now had more than they had need.
It was a time to celebrate and now they wished to share
A feast of many wonderous foods all carefully prepared.
Sweet potatos, dressing, corn strung high to dry
Rich sweet breads, cobblers, mince and pumpkin pies.
Pungent smells of herbs and spices floating thru homes and stables
Beckoned each and everyone to gather round the first Thanksgiving table.
From that day forth one day a year has now been set aside
To give our thanks and share with friends the fruits of a year gone by.
So lift your hearts with happy thoughts and look ahead with cheer
Give thanks not only on this special day but all throughout the year.
Well all good stories reach an end so I won't continue farther
You see I really have to go now for I'm the guest of honor.

Nina Patchen
FRIENDSHIP
It's great to be remembered
By friends who really care,
When your burdens grow too heavy
There is someone near to share.
It may not be a noted thing
Or gifts that they give,
Just an arm around your shoulder
Makes you really want to live.
Just a cheery word of comfort
Or a smile to make you see
That someone really cares for you,
That's what friendship means to me.

Numinia "Ming" Ureta
CHAOS
submerged in sweating heat
delirious in frantic fit
this city lost in its orbit
among bleak shadows and
surrealitic neons
of masquerading tigers
and painted belles
bespeak faint silences
amid noises and cacophony
of jungle beat;
the night,
mysterious and suspicious
forbidding in its visage,
fulfilling secrecy some dark conspiracy,
staining the self with tangled lunacy.
intoxicating drinks and drugs,
burning bodies with mortal fire
behind red-curtained bars;
stands insomnia
citymania
cancer of love forgotten
of a city beat and unbegotten
by caesared philistines'
today's x-ratedism;
o'forsaken men of gomorrah!
hold still your sodom,
chances are; eve's redemption
resurrect before the holocaust!
o'deflowered women of magdala!
unthrone thy ailing flesh and purify,
walk the night away not in some
dark'cloak alley but in some oft-ignored space
where at the touch of virgin wind
melts frozen fire
where towers a cross lies true freedom!

Linda L. Meier
OUR FRIENDSHIP
Our friendship. . .
it is a freedom
I think we share

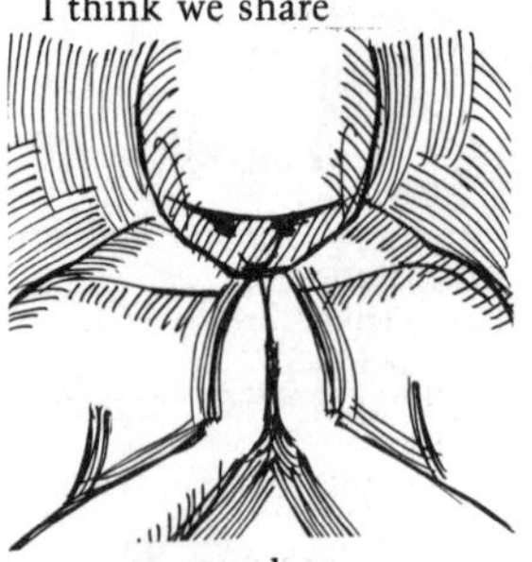

we are ourselves,
only,
always.

Dan Lauber Jr.
FATHER OF TWINS
A wimper and cry might be something to dread,
might very well mean a child in your bed.
It's five in the morning the sun's still asleep,
the critter is nursing so I make not a peep.
I nestle down deeper to a comfortable place,
and all I can picture is that cute little face.
My ears pierce the darkness and to my surprise,
I'm picking up echoes of her twin sister's cries.
I slither from under the covers so warm,
to rescue my daughter who seems so forlorn.
As I enter their bedroom in my morning disguise,
we stare at each other with half open eyes.
While I head for the bathroom I realize I'm late,
and I get the sensation, it just

isn't fate.
For now she is smiling and looking at me,
I guess tinkling on daddy was just meant to be.
She's ready to nurse with her dry diaper on,
so we scoot to the bedroom to visit her mom.
One baby down and still one more to go,
the father of twins can't afford to be slow. . .
As I quickly get dressed I'm aware that I'm late,
up at five in the morning it's now ten of eight.
I rush through my breakfast and all through my haste,
the twins sit there waiting for their little taste.
They've eaten their breakfast, already been nursed,
I'm afraid one more morsel will force them to burst.
They've sipped on my coffee and munched on my toast,
but the marmalade jelly they loved that the most.
I kiss them good-bye as I reach for my keys,
from a sitting position they leap to their knees.
They don't understand why their dad goes away,
but they know I'll return to eat supper and play.
When they've finished their supper and been given a bath,
they head for the bedroom for playtime and laughs.
An hour of playtime brings yawns and some sighs,
then comes the sandman who sprinkles their eyes.
They nestle on mommy all set to be nursed,
and now comes the problem of who will be first.
The sleepest baby will usually win,
while I think of how to keep quiet her twin.
As one long day ends and another begins,
tired but loved is this Father Of Twins

Eugene D. Evans
OCEAN
Where the sea runs thin as wafers and is swallowed by the sand,
Here I love to walk in silence with eternity in hand.
To my left the ocean stretches far beyond the sight of eye,
To my right the green earth groweth, and above, the open sky.
I can see a gull wheel slowly on a breeze invisible
As I sense the life-force beating with a pulse universal.
At horizon is a tug boat and I know it carries man,
Yet by distance it is symbol of a more than human plan.
For these waters are primeval and since Adam have not changed,
Nor can all the schemes of ego add or take one drop Arranged.
How it sets my heart to pounding and astounds my finite brain
To imagine ocean life forms quite more limitless than rain!
From the plankton to the sea-horse, whales and minnows, octopi,
Living mountains of the corals and the strange Arachnidae:
Fish like stars, and round, and oblong, slim, and fat, and every form,
Fish that fish for fish with fishbait. . . how can mind establish norm!
Deep and deeper in this ocean dwell some fragile living things
That exist within such pressure steel would burst to smithereens;
And it's dark a void of blackness where the sunlight is a myth
Still each smallest centimeter is the home of sentient kith:
There are creatures man thought perished in the Pleistocenic dawn
And the latest evolution in a fin-backed mother's spawn.
For this is the womb lifestuff as the earth whereon it lays
Is the Krishna—and the Siva is the Natural decay.
For the sea is everchanging like the dreams of mortal man,
As the mighty resurrection is the end that just began.
So I love to walk the beaches and collect a shell or two:
Then a gentle understanding, like a smile from God, breaks through.

Mary L. Garside
A GRANDFATHER
Your ambition was accelerating
To all who came near,
The beauty of your gardens
We will all hold dear.
Your vegetables so delicious
You shared with your neighbors,
Everyone enjoyed the fruits
Of your labors.
Floral arrangements lined the walkways
Fascinating to every eye,
Gladiolus and tulips stood proud
Sweetpeas climbing toward the sky.
Forgiveness was a virtue
High on your list,
Thoughtfulness and honesty
Were not to be missed.
The lessons you taught us
In your own subtle way
Were infallible for years
Not just for that day.

Janice C. Reiss
IT'S NO FUN
It's no fun to sit in the movies
and hold your own hand
and put your own arm around you
and use your own handker-chief in the sad parts--
It's no fun to sleep in a big bed
and have all the blankets to yourself
and nobody to warm your feet on
and two pillows (one for your head and one for holding)--
It's no fun to still feel married
and have no one to watch T.V. with
and no one to tell you how to spend your money
and no one to argue with--
I guess I don't know when I'm well off-----

Vicki L. Allen
THANKS
Thanks for everything,
You've always been to me.
Thanks for showing me the light
So that I could see.
Thanks for being with me
Throughout my life.
Thanks for helping me,
Down the road of strife.
Thanks for being there,
When I needed you.
Thanks for turning
My gray skies to blue.
Thanks for lending your shoulder
So that I could cry.
Thanks for listening,
Until my eyes were dry.
Thanks for all the days,
You've filled my life with sun.
Thanks mom,
For all you've done.

Joseph Richichi
FRIENDS — LOVERS
We laugh together.
We cry together.
We die to ourselves together.
We are we--together.
We share all that we are.
We are not me or you.
We are us.
We are one.
When You Hurt.
I hurt.
When I Hurt.
You hurt.
We are one.
We know each others thoughts.
We know each others faults.
Yet all is as nothing.
Our bond is ever strong.
For we are one.

Shirley M. A. Mayo
WHY DESTROY THE WORLD
Why destroy the world,
Since you can't comprehend.
Why destroy the world,
Is your mind that thin.
Why destroy the world,
Whenever you choose.
Why destroy the world,
Afraid you might lose.
Why destroy the world,
Getting fed up with life.
Why destroy the world,
Before you think twice.
Why destroy the world,
When things don't go your way.
Why destroy the world,
Remember this is only childs play.
Why destroy the world,
And let things go up in smoke.
Why destroy the world,
When pollution makes you choke.
Why destroy the world,
When things could be right.
Why destroy the world,
Turning the world back to night.
Why destroy the world,
Why hurry things on.
Why destroy the world,
Is it the reason you were born.
Why destroy the world,
Dabbeling in other affairs.
Why destroy the world,
Didn't you get your share.
Why destroy the world,
Just to sum things up right.
Why destroy the world,
Not used to the light.
Why destroy the world,
When it's plain to see.
Why destroy the world,
And destroy thee...
Why Destroy The World

Vern Sawatzky
NOTIONS AND DELUSIONS
You believe
Without knowing
The essence
Or it's budding.
That's not belief,
That's wishes and whimsy,
You entering a vortex

Of philosophical cartwheels
Turning you on
In uncontradictable
Frenzy. . .
Counterfeits
Of varying degrees;
These antichrists
Will bring you
To your knees.

Madeline B. Martin
ANOTHER SPRING
Spring has come; Life's promise is fulfilled.
Winter's snow is done, the melted floods will reach their crest;
new life is waiting in a downey nest.
Spring has come, earth is warming,
buds are forming.
The seeds are sown, the fertile soil is tilled.
So soon, Spring's lilting song turns to Summer's busy hum.
All young life is growing, maturing;
roots deepening, reaching, vitally enduring.
Summer's sun blazes forth, radiant and pleasant;
even summer rains are warm and effervescent.
And thus Life grows and stretches to its highest sum. . .
When comes the Autumn, with lingering Summer strains more slowly played.
Relentless time is winning, but not yet all,
for harvest is beginning while bright leaves fall,
Their glorious colors spreading on the earth
That now brings forth its ripened bounty, worth,
Worth all and more than Summertime has paid.
And then, with stately measures, time will surely bring
The snow. . .a soft requiem, a shroud, a tomb,

and at once, an eider blanket
of warmth for earth, the womb
Where lie the sleeping seeds,
the sacred promise of Another
Spring.

Theresa M. Rosania

LOVE POEM

A.
We carved our initials upon a
tree
So they would forever together
be
Our hands we clasped as we
walked
Squeezed so tightly as we talked
So much so as though our goals
Were to meld our minds, our
bodies, and our souls
Knowing full well that our fears
Are being masked by our silent
tears
To make our dreams of being
together always come true
A road of hardships will be the
only way through
But the strength of our love will
sustain us...and guide us
through the path
That will protect us from the
hardships...of others'
misguided wrath
By your love to faithfullness I'm
compelled
Knowing our love came from
where destiny dwelled
I care not for the pleasures
riches can give
It is only for the ecstacy of your
love I live
Spare me not your innermost
cry
For deep inside is where true
feelings lie
I pray to God that one day our
union will be
So that together we may say to
Him..."we thank Thee"
T.

Debbie K. Peacher

WHAT?

All over the floor
The Kittens did more,
They knew no better
For small they were,
And could not roar.

Now hear this
Loud and clear:!
I did not say
What on the floor
They did of more.

Ruth Elizabeth West

ESTRANGED

We live in two separate rooms,
my love;
Two separate rooms with a door
between;
And you carry the key on your
heartstrings
To open or close it at will;
Sometimes it's locked ever so
tightly
That not even a peephole exists;
And my room is cold and so
lonely,
You know not how much you
are missed.
I long for a day--a wonderful day,
When the partition and door
will come down;
And once again, with barricade
gone,
We can share our smiles and
our frowns;
We will plan and discuss all our
problems;
Without frustration, strain, or a
fuss;
We shall love each other so
deeply,
With no feeling or thought that
we must.
But perhaps that is too much to
hope for;
For the rooms are certainly
there;
If only the door could be opened
With a common path and a
prayer:
Oh, Lord, I ask for Your
guidance;
I know I've done something
amiss-
To be so very locked out and
locked in
That my mate and I do not kiss.
Lord, help me to see my own
fetters-
To check the lock on *my* side,
To see if my feelings of capture
Result from my anger and pride;
To make sure there is warmth
and acceptance,
Forgiveness and love on *my* part;
And to treasure those precious,
rare moments
When our adjoining door *is* ajar.

Bessie Wherry Noe

BRIDGES

Words are bridges
suspending our thoughts.
Life is a span
from birth to eternity.
Bridges are beautiful,
necessary and useful...
Bridges like the George
Washington, Golden Gate.
Bridges like London bridges
over the Thames,
Bring brightness
to our lives.
Poets build bridges
of friendship,
To foster Peace and
Brotherhood.

Bennie Townsend Jr.

CAN YOU VISUALIZE THAT DAY

I have often thought with
gladness, what this life has
meant to me,
But it's hard for me to really
visualize how it all came to
be.
I just can't imagine how the
Savior really felt,
When he arose to face the
soldiers after prayer where he
knelt.
How he prayed for all the world
and by a friend he was betrayed,
And being tortured by the
plan of God, as the debt that
must be paid.
As he sat within his quiet cell I
wonder what he thought,
"Can the people be so cruel
after what I have done and
taught.
I have given them my very best
and it seems to count for
nought.
The Savior must have really
felt the pity for man that day,
As he stood before the ruler and
heard, "Take that man away."
How could the people feel
that way when many he had
healed?
And to others he had been so
kind as the heavens had
revealed.
He must have wondered,
What have I done to make the
people so?
"I made them in my image and
have placed them here below."
"Crucify Him" was their cry,
louder and louder it grew,
As the soliders took the Lord to
robe him for review.
They dressed him up in
purple and pressed a thorny
crown,
Upon the Saviors brow which
made blood to trickle down.
They mocked him, smote him,
and ripped at my Saviors
beard,
They spat upon him, cursed at
him and many just laughed and
jeered.
I can just imagine all the
things he saw and heard,
But never opened his mouth to
speak, no, not a word.
The people must have started
to wonder, "Is this man for
real?
All the torture he has taken
and yet not a squeal."
The Savior's eyes must have
scanned the crowd to see the
mourning souls,
That suffered in the agony that
he himself beholds.
He must have thought, "Be
strong my child for there will
be a day,
That I will come to take you
home and wipe your tears away."
After they had mocked the
Lord, they led him ladened
down,
with the old rugged cross
dragging on the ground.
They whipped him and
shoved him, beneath the
heavy load,
He struggled with the burden
until he fell upon the road.
One soldier showed some
mercy as he stopped a
stranger near,
And made him help to bear the
cross in pity and in fear.
Our Savior and his helper
soon made it up the crest,
Can't you just imagine that the
Savior wanted to rest.
But instead they put hand on
him and laid him on the cross,
And when they started to drive
the spikes he didn't turn or toss.
Oh what a man our Savior
was to take the piercing pain,
How could the people ask for
this? They must have been
insane.
Each pound from the mallet
drove the spikes into the tree,
I just can't imagine how he
suffered this for me.
When the soldiers finished
and had nailed both hands
and feet,
Our Savior knew when this was
done it led to satan's defeat.
They lifted up the heavy cross
and place it in the ground,
The multitude that condemned
him began to gather round.
He hung there on the pierced
spikes they had driven in each
hand,
There was no way to ease the
pain, for on pierced feet he
could not stand.
I can't begin to visualize the
agony he went through,
And then to say, "Forgive them
Father, they know not what they
do."
The sight was so horrible that
the Father turned away,
And there he hung so lonely on
that great redemption day.
He hung and died for every
man that day upon the tree,
And even took the time to say,
"Today shalt thou be with me."
The redemptive work was
over when he gave up the
ghost,
Then came the resurrection but
the ascension was foremost.
Thank God for our salvation,
through this life of love,
Our hope is in His coming,
Then, we'll dwell with him
above.

Mildred Olbrish

POPE JOHN PAUL II

He traveled everywhere
Without any fear
He blessed us all
With smiling face
And Out-stretched arms
He made the people understand
He loved us all
The world around
He loved us all
Big and small
No one will ever forget
The Pilgrim Pope John Paul

Frank M. Ferraro

SILENCE

Silence;
an echo of strained thought.
Filtering through,
the memories that we've lost.
Filling us with feelings,
some we've never known.
Mixed emotions,
my how much we've grown.
Sometimes worries;
never seem to cease,
But in the silence;
there is substantial peace.
Not withstanding,
nothing guaranteed,
But for a moment;
all the time we need.
Shrinking shadows,
the dark before the dawn.
A savored moment
and then the silence gone.

Harold V. Anderson

MY LIFE

This life of mine, it is all I have,
what shall I do with it: do I
horde it as a miser, not sharing?
I am alone in this shell; it is
dark, I am lonesome and afraid.
I cry; no one comforts me.
No one knows I am afraid,
lonesome and that I cry.
My shell a facade of smiles,

light conversation,
speaking of the future as if I believe I have one.
Making grandious plans for your approval and applause.
My surface may seem smooth, but my surface is a mask.
Beneath it there is me, in fear, confusion and alone; crying for succor. You don't know who I am. How could you know I need you? I don't dare ask. I am afraid, afraid you will not accept me: afraid you will think less of me, that you will laugh, your laugh will kill me.
I am afraid that I am nothing, that I am no good, that you will see this and reject me.
Therefore, I put on my mask.
My life becomes a facade. I tell you everything that is nothing. I tell you of nothing that is everything.
You alone can release me from my shell, you can remove the mask, destroy the facade and find who I am. I may fight, strike back, I fight the help I cry for since it does not conform to what our culture has taught me. Love is strong, break this shell with compassion and Love, gently. I am someone you know very well. I am you and I am me.
I am neither a sacrilege nor a privilege. I am not incompetent or excellent but I am.

Collis P. Huntington Jordan
SIERRA CALLING
I feel the Sierras calling
"Come back as you did long ago"
The rush of waters falling,—
"See my mountains curtained with snow,"
"Pack up your flannels and jeans
Your boots, your rod and your reel
Hardtack, bacon and beans
Your leaders, your lines and your creel,"
"Know the Loch Leven are striking,
The Rainbow in schools at the fall.
Find what the Brook trout are liking
And remember that is not all"
"There is the trail to Lake Mary,
You may take a swim at Horseshoe,
You may see the buck deer so wary
Can't you hear them calling to you?
"Does the trail to 'Crystal' intrigue you?
To see what lies at the crest,
Or does the effort fatigue you?
The Goldens are at their best!"
Stop Sierra! I am leaving
I must breathe your chill clean air
You know for years I've been grieving,
To track the 'chuck' to his lair.
I shall hear him whistle at "Barney,"
Count partridge at "Arrowhead"
Many may sing of Killarney
I will sing of "Sierra" instead.
I shall stand by "Skelton" at daybreak
And kindle my breakfast fire.
Flapjacks and coffee I may make
As the sun tips the 'Minaret' spire
A dark mirror of water before,
You notice the stars have gone out.
The gray sheer cliff on the shore
Echoes back the splash of a trout.
I shall be tramping the trail
Among Incense cedar and pine.
I shall be hearing tall tales
Wherever the campfires shine.
We will capture black bear and red fox,
Will talk til our tongues are lame,
'Paul and the Big Blue' ox,"
We will put them both to shame.
I shall follow the trail of John Muir,
Of Mark Twain, and Bret Harte
In ghost camps I'll find their spoor
I've given them a century start.
I hear the Sierras calling
I will answer that call—someday!

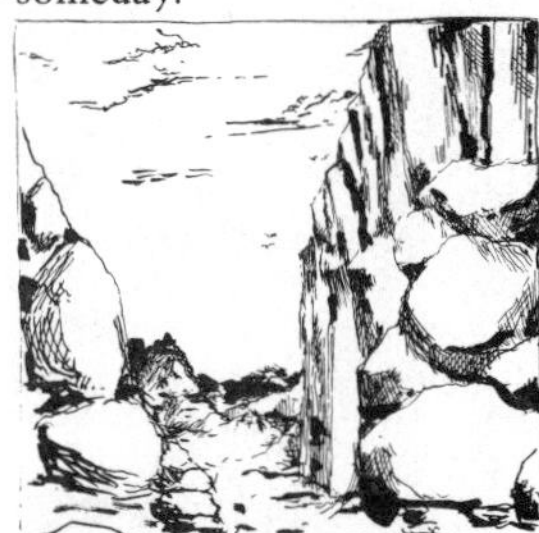

When I see the aspen leaves falling
Sierra! I shall come to stay!

Arthur Allyn Joyce
SOMETIMES AMONG A MEEK AND WILD ROSE
Sometimes among a meek and wild rose
Panting in desperation for love
I hear tones of billowing clouds
Reading palms in the heavens
Calling down the thorns and
Kissing the petals that shine
With the soft morning dew
That glistens like a smile
Awakened by this recapitulation
From the soft sky, laden
With the beautiful blue of
Her eyes and sunrise face,
The petals break and the
Light begins to enter, and
Warm mysteries escape-
Freed.

Judy Hampton
INSANITY
When I felt lonely, I called on you.
When I needed love and understanding,
I looked you up.
Whatever I needed,
You were always ready to give,
Ready more so to give, than to receive.
You took in all my fears,
All my hopes and wasted years.
Years wasted because I would not yield,
To cries of help so close to my ear.
And now I tell you insanity for me is near,
You listen closely but you refuse to hear.
Explain this to me friend,
For the meaning isn't clear.
Are things really to me as they appear?
Is it just a thought or only a fear?
Could it be because of the dope or the beer?
My friend you listened to the good and the bad,
Don't you know that the worst is yet to be had?
You just don't want to listen to the part that is sad.
Why can't you understand?
Why don't you see?
Why won't you listen to my earnest plea,
That itches me more than the bite of the flea?
My past I yearn for, my future I dread.
I wait someday, (someday soon it will be,)
For the bullet to hit me,
Right through the side of my head.
Not a bullet that comes from a gun,
But 'Twill be the bullet of insanity,
That strikes harder than lead.

Veronica Champ Friend
GOD'S TREASURES
Do we ever stop and look around
At all the things there are to see
At all the treasures God put on Earth
That bring pleasure to you and me
Are we too busy to ponder the journey of the bee
Enjoy the first new leaves of spring
To see the beauty of the butterfly
Listen to the songs of the birds while they sing
Hear the pounding of the waves upon the rocks
See the sun setting low in the Western sky
Smell the scent of the flowers in the breeze
Point out the pictures in the clouds as they pass by
Do we ever stop and thank the Lord
Give Him just a moment of our day
Enjoy even one of the pleasures He has given us
Or do we just hurry on our way
Why don't we open our hearts and eyes
Start looking at all there is to see
I wonder, would we even miss these gifts of love
If suddenly they ceased to be.

Mary L. Garside
MOTHERS
I think when God made mothers
He had one thing in mind -
A desire to extend *His* love
With a very special kind.
Expressing love in many ways
Is a mother's gift from God;
From beginning each exciting day
Until little heads start to nod.
Keeping her boys happy,
And also under control
Can surely be a full-time job,
But that's a mother's role.
Teaching girls to be ladies,
And to follow the Golden Rule;
Not to mention many other things
That they don't learn in school.
Whether a comforter or a counsellor,
Her teachings are a blessing;
To defend or to reprimand
It's her love she is expressing!

Janice Kathleen Crisa
CONFUSED HEART
O confused heart,
Awakened from thy slumber,
Given directions, undeservedly so -
Which direction shalt thou go?
Upon each path there lurks a spider
Waiting for thy careless step,
Whereupon thou wilt be devoured
Once entrapped upon its web.
Truth speaks of fear.
How canst thou avoid treading on another's heart
When thine own heart yearns -
Yet, how well kept the secret of thy reservation.
How slow to learn
Thy attractions evoke pain,
When thy motives be
For thine own gain.
O, quiet heart - sleep again!
For is it not better to suffer sleep,
Than to awaken too quickly
From thy bed of judgement.
Death comes to thy heart
With each lover's grief -
Cautious steps
Doth thy soul beseech!

Pauline K. Smith
EVERY TRUTH
Every Truth has its ultimate goal,
has its ultimate idea,
has its ultimate good,
has its ultimate position.
Into every Life there comes Truth,
there comes a seeking after Truth,
there comes a stand for Truth,
There comes the discovery of Truth.
Each Soul of Man is in need of Truth,
must make a decision for Truth,
responds to Truth,
will know Truth.

Given Truth, Man will reach his ultimate goal,
will follow the pathway of Truth,
will unfold his Life in Truth,
will find God in his Life as Truth.
All Truth is expressed in God,
is revealed by God,
is a part of God,
is a pathway to God.
By Truth does Man find God,
does Man live with God,
does Man worship God,
does Man love God.
What is Truth but the Spirit unfolding God,
the Spirit revealing God,
the Spirit teaching of God,
the Spirit bringing the Love of God.
Let the Soul sing Praises of God
the Heart rejoice in a God of Truth,
the Soul be glad for all Love and Truth,
the Heart and Soul worship
the God of Love and Truth.

Cath Jenkins
WHILE DADDY'S AWAY
As I crawl under the covers
Meant for lovers,
I feel a toy
Of our little boy.
He says it's such a nice big bed
Whoops! - a foot - then his tousled head.
Sleeping becomes a task
Why - you ask!
Daddy's in the hospital with a hurt back;
In our house there's such a lack.
It's now two-thirty - surgery at seven,
I pray he won't wind up in heaven.
I'm not good enough to go there-
Just don't have the fare.
I like the climate warm
See 'ya -------Storm!

James Leonard Goins
AGGRAVATED ASSAULT?
Tonight am I tormented by many things;
I am a kingdom divided, against itself.
The day before yesterday surely, I was a mountain.
Yesterday certainly, I was the rock;
How terrible tonight, I am less than sifted sand.
Who be ye, that hinder me so; why dost thou me tear asunder?
From whence do ye come and where dost thou go?
I am on watch for thee, let it beknowence to thee.
'Til thy final breath will I cling to life
That I mayest know, either your question, or your answer.
We can be friends, can we not, you and I?
Is a relationship between us possible?
Can I be me without you?
Dost thou come and go, of thine own free will?
Can you, if I die, live?
Breath, stagnated air, it's a chore and a pain to live.
Feet having taken too many steps, limp,
My bruises have not healed well, they are now open sores.
Fight! I long to remember, or to know what fight means;
Tonight am I tormented by many things.

Jamie Sue Kelly
IF YOU LOVE ME
If you love me...
Love me as a friend first,
Listen to me when I need to talk,
Comfort me when I need you,
If you love me...
You'll understand when I need to be alone,
You won't push me into things,
You'll let me be me,
If you love me...
You will know why I need a friend first,
Why I come to you to talk,
Why I need your comfort,
Because...
I Love you for you.

Jennifer A. Longmire
DOLLS
Bonnets, Bottles,
Playful, Cute, Expensive,
Sitting, Smiling, Staring,
Anytime of the Day,
Precious.

Valeriano Frank Mateo
GEST
Close your eyes, Honey
And listen to me
Only hatred can die
People can only cry.
If your love grows upon me, now
Nothing is going to interfere
So close your eyes
And float on by to my side.
Walk along the shore line
Footprints of memories
Miles and miles of daisies
Tranquil waters will wash away
Memories of yesterday.
Look towards the sun, my love
Sunrise to sunset
Flowers bloom, together yet
You are love, you've got to love in me
Close your eyes, oh Honey Dove
And let the wind blow through your hair
For someday you'll be there.
Don't get angry, let it burn
For love will always come in turn
Love yourself for I love you.
Walk with me, my sweet and lovely
Towards calmness in the sea
Stroll with gesture and slide with beat
Live and Learn
For it will burn.

Burnell Vickers
THE AWAKENING
Only when you're sleeping
could I come to you,—come near you,—
to murmur things
I dared not say out loud;
things which in my gut had lain
and burned and burned and burned;
a yearning love which could not be returned.
I dared not even whisper
though you were far from me,—
so far from me,—
and it was not just
a fear of being spurned;
for I had always known
since before the earth was made
that the love I gave could never be returned.
But it couldn't stay that way
for I was burning,—I was burning,—
like a fire which
can never be put out;
and I saw my fortress fall apart
leaving me exposed,
like a falsehood which men have learned to doubt.
Then the prison gates pushed open,
but not by me,—never by me,—
for I alone
could never turn the key;
a voice from paradise
had opened up my heart,
and the blood rushed out crying to be free.
Now do footsteps in the sunlight
run towards me,—run towards me,—
showering frightening things
for which I yearned?
And must I meet the scorching heat
of the joys I so much feared—
Can it be that the wheels of life have turned?

Mimi Stiles
AARON
He holds the future in his palm
inventive hands so small,
his energy is boundless,
his mind, filled with awe
His thirst for discovery
leads him in hot pursuit,
for an enemy that's lurking
inside his daddy's boot
He challenges his mother
with a duel of lengthy looks
when a query he has asked her
has her searching through some books
All his little setbacks
are discretely shrugged from view,
He has bolder feats to conquer
like the laces of his shoe
And the tear in his new trousers
won't support his alibi
when his mother sends a narrow glare
and dares to ask him why
His face is of an angel,
his eyes are novice moles
as he stands before a frosted cake
concealing finger holes
He will contradict your reasoning
and make you a nervous wreck,
but before you tend to chastise,
his arms embrace your neck
He'll bog your mind with chatter
when you'd rather rest your eyes,
and when they close he'l lift your lids
and happily shout, "SURPRISE!"
He's his mother's protector
a role he will not share,
until he seeks her sheltered arms
and whispers—
"mom—I'm scared."

Betty Bryant
CHANGES
Cotton fields white and green
gone are years when hands
picked you clean.
Turned to brown
You take the toil
from the field.
Not by nature's plan,
by inventions
of man.
What he missed when he did this?
Closeness
working together brings.
Now it seems
another machine
cleans you bare
nothing left
of nature's way
good or bad
here to stay.

Rebecca Bryant
JUST ONCE
Just Once...
Could you and I
walk on a rainbow
to the heavens
and see the light?
Could you and I
be a team
and show the world
we're strong?
Could you and I
face the darkness together
instead of running away?
Could you and I
kiss the rain good-bye
and hug the sun hello?
Could you and I
dry the tear
and bring a smile?
Could you and I
trust each other enough
to understand...
Just Once.

Alma Joyce
ITEM OF VALUE
A gift of pleasure for your eyes to have for a time but it can not last. Perhaps affinity of flesh; even lust becomes passe. Bathe your senses with pleasure and pain, accomplish works, give your praise. Fill with treasure, adorn with gold, charge your being with zest of life yet pride of energy time takes away. Oh matchless matter, can you enfold it? Grace to wear past judgement into the vast unknown.

Joan Brace
THE GEESE FROM CANADA
All this fine fall
on bright days and dull
the tall geese from Canada, tall
as a four year child, tall
and colored like a Chinese Mandarin
with gentle manners and slow gait
have mildly stalked and danced slow music
and ate upon the grass
ate our offerings of wild seed.
Aloof and mild they stretch and posture
one watcher out before
his tall black neck's question
answered by the throat's white band
Not so much his eye watches as all his senses
aware of threat or grace
startling, checking, running little gasping steps
Does he know the spotted dog inside
who also stretches watching
all his sense alert?
Geese—I have seen thirty-three
Whir'rr wings and take to air
like ominous bombers
Showing the white insignia on their tails
they turn, circle against the sky
disturbed from peaceful feeding
by one down-swooping jay
O Birds
In mist I see you mirrored in a lake
motionless your heavy floating forms
Necks incurved to rest upon your breasts
Silently you drift and all in circles
a nest of indrawn breaths
enchanged by the shimmer of your proper beauty
your sister water images
O Birds
Was the abbot of Shoku-Fuji
as this morning I
looking down from shrouded
mountain painting
roll of silk in hand and sumi
and you basking in his praising eye?
More geese music
The forward watcher spreads deep wings
purple charcoal brown and grey
to wave the comers-in
The seed is spread. The garden's safe
Uphill they walk most pilgrim soberly
in single file and slightly graceful waddle
like women pregnant and unbound
Ah! there some fault of pecking order
and lean dark necks shoot hissing out
to black/white/purple/grey
wing feathers, tail feathers
The unheard hiss is heard
Thirty three birds on the hill
a wing aloft, a leg extends the invisible bar
O beautiful creatures mystical
now pass the birch, ascend the hill
and gain the willow tree
Chests pale silk
undersides like watered light
now pattern this garden
now bless this grass
Dog tiptoes near the beach
slips in the lake
careful not to splash
he paddles silently around
forgetting he was hunter
They were feathered prey
Did they remember?
Silently they led him far beyond the island
smoothly moving on ahead
magicians luring him beyond his strength and his endurance
to his drowning, to his death
but finally conferring, they smoothly led him shoreward
he all brown and white and shaking
spent heart etched on panting ribs
while they turned and made the round again
of lake and island, lake and island
Drowning was no fate of theirs

Agnes Goodwin
EVENING SUNSETS
As the splendor of the morning unfolds
The sun shines colors of radiant gold
Slowly the sky fills with light
To a glorious wonderful sight.
Upon this beautiful little fawn
The sun shines at early dawn
Trails of rainbows fill the evening skies
Circling the butterflies.

Sunsets are for all the world to see
Especially you and me
Its colors of orange and yellow so vivid and bright
Fade into shades of the night.
The sun fades to goldish green
And what a magnificent scene
Sunset darkens the light of her skies
To rest in God heaven, from our eyes.

Alma Joyce
CO—EFFICIENT
I am, love cared enough to let
me be,give life and nurture
my existance growth and
thinking. But was it all decided
at creation?
Inheritance gives promise of
potential. Yet stepping out to
enter and possess the land finds
my sustainer wills to feed me
plus, minus and neutral.
Superceeding all that senses tell
comes a seeking to inhabit each
will dispersed, unfaithful, and
unprofitable. Still, you spend
yourself for me.
Only by faith to know the truth
in time to open the two way
door when you have forsaken
me yet shall I choose to want
you.

Beatrice Cearbe Roma
PHASES OF LOVE
I'm in love, happy and gay.
I want to sing, what to say?
I'm in love, happy and gay.
I want to dance through the day.
Darling, darling, I love you.
Love you, darling, I do.
Darling, darling, I love you.
Always it will be you.
Words that were said before
Don't tell you what you should know
That in my heart you score
High, with all others below.
Summer, fall, winter and spring,
When birds merrily sing,
For me there'll be no leaving
My wonderful darling.
Memories fade, new ones made.
Oh, need I wonder how?
Now each kiss, rekindles bliss,
Oh, happy memory.
My loves in an album lie,
Closed and dusty on a shelf.
Reminders of time gone by
While I sit here by myself.

D. E. Fransen II
TOMPKINS SQUARE
What remains is
an occasional cat
wailin' into lonely
depressed night...
tenor sax, grass,
solitude in hand.
& sometimes some
symbolic spade nods
over unheard drums,
while unchained dogs
cut their paws upon
bowery glass,
shitting over
emitic sidewalks,
sidestepping over, I go!
& finally night comes
with Third World
transisters blatting into
terminated-tenemated deep.
Epitaph to very faded,
once fecundant flowers.

Jack A. Parks
VISIONS OF MOTHER
I was nineteen and restless,
when I got the urge to roam,
I packed my grip and said good bye
and left my mountain home.
I went off to the city,
with its bright lights all aglow,
but every time I was alone,
I missed my mother so.
I fell in with the wrong crowd,
the pace they set was fast,
with women, wine and their fast cars,
I knew it couldn't last,
every eve' we'd make the bars,
at night we all got stoned,
by day I's always with the crowd,
but still I felt alone.
One evening as we made the bars,
the crowd, they all seemed bored,
a buddy said he had a gun,
we'd rob a liquor store,
and even tho I saw the harm
I really didn't care,
but just before we made the door,
I saw my mother there.
Mom reach her hands out to me,
as she said, God answers prayers,
I've looked all o'er this country son,
and to think I'd find you here.
I saw the wrinkles in her face,
the hurt that I put there,
but when I tried to touch her face,
she really wasn't there.
I knew I'd seen a vision,
so I left that place in fright,
caught the bus and went back home,
to Tennessee that night,
My mother had died waiting,
for her wayward boy's return,
she had been dead about two years,
on the day that I returned
Every night I have a dream,
of mother waiting there,
a rocking back and forth at night,
in her old rocking chair,
and praying for her wayward boy,
that he would come back home,
I hope God will forgive me,
that I had the urge to roam.

Leland G. Dewey
THIS IS FOR THE BIRDS
You may have my hair for lining your nests ---
Your molted pinions will help pen my jests ---
And we'll all pursue our inter-twined quests
As guests on this Orbiting Sphere.
Yours: The delight of keen sight and free flight.
Mine: Melancholy --- which leads me to write.
Ours: The vast myst'ry of all mortals' plight:
TIME'S BLIGHT ON THE LIVES WE HOLD DEAR.

Charlene P. Bertsch
THE UPSIDE DOWN ROOM
It has no windows, has no doors,
it's neither dark nor light.
It has no drapes or furniture,
it knows no day or night.
Though I have been there many times,
no corners have I found.
It is not square, not angular,
I guess it must be round.
It has no walls, yet is contained,
much like a warp in time.
There is no good or evil there,
no room for laws or crime.
I always go there all alone,
no one can go with me.
Of course, the room is always filled

but no one can I see.
There is no silence, yet no noise.
I have, but have not, heard
the questions, answers, and exchange,
all said without one word.

Brian Webb

UNTITLED

Seaweed like wavy hair
Into her depths I dive,
Where she thrashed and crashed
In her sea bed.
And organism after organism
Swam through the shadows
Of her mind, to reach the
Rivers to spawn.
To yield her young
Who grow and yield
In the shadows of her mind.

Margaret Forest

LONE TRAVELLER

LITTLE ORANGE CAT padding lamely down a lonely road, where have you come from and where are you going?
Your cloudy eyes, dim with despair, shift from side to side. As stumbling, you seek to find your solitary way.
Your gaunt body sags and falters helplessly, for you are weak and gnawed by hunger,
Having wandered so *long*, abandoned and alone.
Now you stop to lick your swollen paws, then slumping down upon the dusty earth
You close your eyes in weariness, seeking comfort in the warm release of sleep.
Will this be the end of the road for you, LITTLE ORANGE CAT, or will you once again try to pull yourself up
Seeking to find the one who so heartlessly abandoned you?

Jasper Davis

IN LOVE ALONE

Badly craving for her love,
A mortal as pure as gold,
But each time I approached,
Her breathless face turned cold.
I hated her for denying me,
But soon got my revenge,
When her lover, she discovered,
Dealt in adulturous sin.
I laughed out loud when I saw her face,
No longer a charming
queen,
Tears rushed down both sides,
Washing away the gleem.
But I still wanted her,
For once her tears were dry,
Beauty again would spring,
To enhance my starless sky.

Mary Barney Dunstan

CIRCUS TIME

At circus time, with spirits freed,
We hurry to the nearest stand,
To buy some peanuts to feed
The elephants by hand.
The long neck of the big giraffe,
A column shaped of grace and strength,
Has never failed to make us laugh
With its amazing length.
The tiger dressed in patterned stripes,
The fortune-teller and her art-
Are still the circus stereotypes
Which please the eye and heart.
The tunes the organ grinder plays,
The darting monkey, pert and tame,
Will always serve to brighten days
That sadness tries to claim.
And at last, with special merriment,
We look into the clowns tent,
To keep our hearts from discontent
With fun and laughter we found it a day well spent.

June LaFever

THE ESSENCE OF LOVE

Love is like a precious jewel
Held gently in your hand
To be polished and to be cherished
By a woman and a man
But do not squeeze in anger
With words you will deplore
For it will slip right through your fingers
And be gone forever more.

Elisabeth Stein Frisby

PARENTING

My life, my love, my children
all born within my soul.
Too soon, tomorrow, I must cajole
my fledgings into flight
to test their growing might.
Though we are bound to one another,
I must, as their mother,
open dependence's envelope
and send them forth with hope
into reality's rains and thunder
watching them swim over and under
in the waves of the sea of life.
O, how painful the blade of his knife!

Christy J. Abbott

STRANGERS

Cascading stars, spirals of incense,
Your incantations in foreign tongue...
The velvet touch of the crimson heart
Pulsating in rhythm to the blinking of your eyelashes.
The afterglow of the passion shared
By the strangers within ourselves.
Each of us has reached a space in which
There is no room to grow...
Checkmate.

Donna Callander Reardon

MY THREE SONS

Each a miniature being, his own individual self.
Today dependent on my love and guidance,
Reaching out for the warmth of my touch,
Reassured by the presence of my smile.
Yet each striving for his independence,
Struggling to become himself.
Like a mother bird pushing her young to fly,
I find myself painfully letting go.
Enabling each to grow within himself,
Allowing their independence to grow strong.
How difficult it seems at times, not to do for them
What for me seems so easy, yet for them so complex.
How quickly their minds absorb all that the world portrays,
Questioning me when uncertain of what's before them,
Or when fear or sadness overcome their joy.
As each day passes, God's help I seem to seek,
To hope and pray that all the love I've given,
Will one day remain a part, of the men that are soon to be.

Effie B. MacDonald

WHAT IS LIFE?

Life is a feather
pirouetting in the sun,
sparkling with morning's dew,
gossamar, wafting by,
gracefully dancing, traipsing
to the cadence of the gentle
rain, iridescent with rainbow
hues.

a feather
in a storm black as night,
driven by vicious winds across
jungle, sagebrush, valley and
city, a victim of the storms'
caprice, swept downwind.

Life is a feather
drifting, sadly and alone,
rootless, restless, oblivious to
others of its kind spiralling
by,
like a spirit lost, aimlessly
drifting, endlessly searching,
nearly settling, then caught
up and borne aloft at heady
pace;

a feather
seemingly delicate, yet
singularly strong, weathering
nature's ruthless aberrations,
reaching towards heaven,
beaten down.

Life is a feather
weary and forlorn after the
endless journey, seeking
sanctuary from the storm, yet
possessed by a fierce urgency
to complete the odyssey;

a feather
lovingly embraced by a
transient zephyr and
transcending in the unseen
arms of a soft wind, beyond
the horizon.

M. Jacquin

UNTITLED

Alone the eagle soars across
a winter sky
follow him so proud and free
must I.
the single bell demands an
answer now -
let it ring once more.
the world will not spin off
to
die.

Shelia Dees

I AM SAVED

There use to be two of me
Fighting a battle within
Then one day, I trusted Jesus
And the battle came to an end.
No longer is my mind filled with doubt.
And my eyes with tears,
Because with Jesus by my side
I have nothing to fear!
My mind was filled with evil thoughts
But I fought the battle and
No longer am I lost.
I gave to him my heart, mind, and soul.
And in return He made me whole.
Now my heart is filled with love,
Given to me only from My Master up above.

Barbara Buryiak

TO KAREN AT SIXTEEN

It seems just a few short years since I held you for the first time.
I examined you very carefully and counted all your fingers and toes.
You were a beautiful baby.
Watching you grow and mature has given me much pleasure.
There have been moments of displeasure and unhappiness.
But the joy and happiness of being your mother far outweigh them.
You are a truly beautiful person,
Thoughtful, loving, gentle, and sensitive.
My life is so much easier because of you.
I am proud that you are my daughter.

Adele Murray

TUTORED BY HEAVEN

When poverty fades away into the never-never land,
then gone will be it's evil STRANGLING hand.
Then will humanity rise another notch, and unleash
the talents rusted by the world's rain, sleet and SLUSH!
Iron bands will bind true love, and break only with the lack of trust.
There'll be no cries, no pain, no hypocrites and such, as the world will be—Tutored By

Heaven.
FEW—, will be the LOWLY
souls that will enjoy
trampling upon another human
being, SPLIT and SPIT
THE FUMES OF HELL—, upon
innocent lovely scenery.
Nobility of mind and nobility of
spirit will prevail
and find its way into more and
more hearts and minds each
day.
And so, mankind will be lifted
once again by—,
The Tutorer Of Heaven.
Violation of human rights will
cease and at last
the world, in dignity and love,
will live in peace.
No tears will blind people to
untruths, no lips,
nor sweet mouths, if and when
the whole world will just stop,
for one second and listen, to
the—
Tutorer Of Heaven.
Then will the honeysuckles sing
songs of love and
eternal Springs.
And as time drops another
violent age, wingless
angels to earth will bring,
life's golden original
lessons, lessons taught not by
earth, but rainbow
planets, silvery stars, and—
The Tutorer Of Heaven!

Dee Dee S. McArthur

CREATION

(Genesis 1:1-31, 2:1-3)

In the beginning God created
the heaven and the earth.
And the earth was without form,
and void;
And darkness was upon the face
of the deep.
And the Spirit of God moved
upon the face of the waters.
And, God said, "Let there be
light"—
And the Light shone forth
bright!
God divided the darkness from
the light,
And the darkness, He called the
Night.
And, so it was in just this way,
That God created the very first
Day.
God saw that the light was
good.
He looked about, from where
He stood,
And 'twas then that He decided,
That the waters, from the
waters, should be divided,
With a firmament to be called
heaven,
So, God created Heaven, on the
second day of seven.
When heaven was created, God
was very pleased!
The waters, below, He gathered
together, and called the Seas.
God gathered the waters from
off the land,
To give us the Earth, on which
we stand.
When the earth appeared from
'neath the waters below,
God blessed it to be fruitful
with all things that grow.
And the earth brought forth,
most abundantly,
Every grass and herb and every
tree.
Each yielded seed or fruit after
this kind,
As this was the plan, that God
had divined.
And, so it was in just this way,
That God created on the third
day.

Then, God made two great
lights,
To divide the days from the
nights—
The day to be ruled by the
greater light,
And the lesser light to rule the
night.
God made the Stars that shine
so bright,
To guide us on, in the dark of
the night.
The lights from the heaven
shine on the land,
To mark the days, the years and
seasons for man.
The Sun was created to give us
day light,
And the Moon was created to
illuminate the night.
And, so it was in just this
way,
That God created on the fourth
day.
God, Who created the turbulent
seas,
Created all creatures that
inhabit these.

And, He, Who created the earth
and the sky,
Created all beast and all fowl
that fly.
The great whales, created He,
And every living creature that
we see.
And, He, Who created the
boundless sky,
Decreed that it be filled with
all fowl that fly,
And He said, "Let the waters
bring forth, abundantly,
Every living creature that
moveth in the sea."
And, so it was in just this way,
That God created on the fifth
day.
And, God said "Let every living
creature appear on the earth,
Each creeping thing and beast
and cattle; each after his kind
to give birth."
Then, God created Man in His
Own Image, in the Image of
God, created He him,
Male and Female both, created
He them.
And He blessed them to
multiply; to be fruitful and
give birth—
For God created man to subdue
and replenish the earth.
When God blessed man, He
gave them His plan—
To have dominion over all beast
of the land,
All fowl of the air, all fish
of the seas—
God decreed that man rule over
all of these.
And, so it was in just this
way,
That God created on the sixth
day.

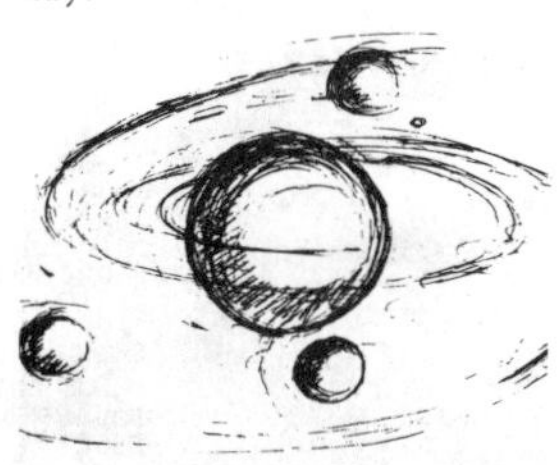

On the seventh day, God
decided to rest,
And, so it was this day that He
blessed.
God knew that all He had made
was good—
The heaven, the earth, the trees
bearing food;
So, this is how it all began,
When in His Own Image, God
created man.

Muriel Armstrong

REACH

Reach out and love
and laugh and cry,
live our lives daily
not in the by and by.
I love to reach
and laugh and cry,
To lay in the Sun
and watch clouds go by.
In Summer or Winter
in Spring or Fall,
My thoughts are with you,
love is for all.

Lisa Gemski

REFLECTION

We sit
in the restaurant.
You touch my hand,
look at my ring-
the gold crucifix
of my faith.
You kiss my hand,
look at me.
Jesus reflects in your
Jewish eyes.

Marianne Casale

TO THE GREATEST MOM AND DAD

Often times it's hard to find,
Just the right words to say.
I love you so much, Mom and
Dad;
Much more, with each new
day.
Not only for the things you
have given me,
Nor your guidance, and
advice.
Just your presence in my life
means the world to me.
The Lord has surely blessed
me twice!
When I am happy, you lovingly
share my joy;
When sad, you dry my tears.
Thank you so much Mom and
Dad
For all your love throughout
the years.
Although I don't show it every
day,
Deep down, I hope you know-
I feel so lucky to have you here
with me;
To help me live, and watch
me grow.
And as I go on throughout my
life
the main thing that I wish to
be,
Is just as much to both of you
As you have always been to
me.

James Owens, Jr.

HAVE YOU EVER LOVED?

Have you ever dreamed
Of the love which seemed
That all you could give
Could be received?
Have you ever wished
Of a love like this
Where nothing wrong
Would e'er be missed?
Have you ever thought
Of love untaught
In a lock so tight
No key is sought?
Have you ever known
Of love having grown
Without any seed
Ever being sown?
Have you ever loved
A most distant love
Whose love unfelt
Shalt e'er be love?

June (Sunkes) Skaarup

MY CHRISTMAS GIFT TO YOU

I don't need pretty papers
Or pretty ribbons of blue
To wrap this Christmas gift
That I have for you
For I give you this gift of love
That will last you through the
years
It's a gift that comes straight
from the heart
And will never bring you tears
It's a gift you can take with you
No matter where you go
It will always pick you up
Anytime you're feeling low
It's not only for Christmas
But for the whole year
through
For I want you to remember
That I'll always love you.

Lawrence W. Dries

CHRISTMAS FIVE AND TEN

There is a space preserved
eternally,
In the hearts of sojourners
Whose fortunes have traversed,
The timeless essence
Of a Christmas Five and Ten.
How well do we remember well?
The endless well, the bottomless
cup,
The mirth and good feeling
Of that cheery, buzzing store
We thought a home.
Indeed, more a home to many,
than home!

The Christmas Five and Ten
Is the dwelling place and lively space
Where despair and gloom are felled.
The Christmas Five and Ten
With its bustle, its motion;
Its stacks of goods and goodies,
Its miles of holly garland,
Its unceasing hum; music of the season—
Its aisles of toys; kiddies playland.
A place bedecked with an angel's enthusiasm,
A shrine, a home with Saint Nicholas enthroned—
Truly a glaced land.
Where the preferred gifts are the people there
With their smiles their laughter their fun
As bubbly full, as the shelves are.
It seems the Christmas Five and Ten
Is bursting at the seams—
So full of goods, yet fuller, of goodwill!
A sunnier, giftier nook has never been
A place, where welcomes are the warmest;
The locale, wherein the toasts
Within the hearts of men,
Are cheerily felt, and the practice of the Merriment.
Let us be the Lamb, a child again,
Return to the Christmas Five and Ten.
Be mindful of how our times, our lives have wrought
The statues of our past to dust.
Perchance we are clay sheep.
For what we now think glitter,
Was in our youth, pure gold.
Let us think on it!
Is our tinsel gold or our gold tinsel?
Is the wealth within us
As rich, as sure
As the richness known to a child's eye—
Surveying, doting merchandise
Seemingly stacked half-way to infinity?
Is the magic, the twinkle in our eye as deft?
Are we full of doubts, or filled with dreams?
—The sort of dreams
Five and Dimers draw their profit from;
Little children slumber on.
—What sets the mind aglitter
Is a purer gold.
Let us be elder urchins—
Join the children marching
To the Christmas Five and Ten
And upon those shelves within—
Find ourselves again—
Be. . .ourselves again—
Give—Give the greatest gift of all,
Our plain, old, simple selves!
The better half of getting
Is the giving.
Let us be the pretty paper,
The curling ribbon,
The apt gift.
Let us be the decoration,
The rows of candy cane,
The doll and fire engine.
Let us, come down from our shelves;
Indeed, from our very selves!
Let us be the delight,
The surprise in the child's eye,
Let us be, the magic,
The carols of the season,
The million dollar baby. . .
The laughter, the fun
The essence and the hum—
Let's be as merry, as bright
As a Christmas Five and Ten.

M. D. Bowden
I TRIED

I tried to be cool
but people told me I looked like a fool.
I tried to be hip
but all I did was slip.
I tried to be Ms. 'C'
but ended up as Ms. 'Z'.
I always tried to be
what everybody thought I should be, and what I thought would help me to fit in, but instead I got the door slammed in my face in every direction.
People saying "Get lost, you don't belong with us, you're different, you think you're too good for us."
Doesn't anybody realize that I was just doing those things to be 'in'? That wasn't me but out of desperation I did those things so that people would notice me and see that I was around.
I tried keeping to myself but I found I couldn't. I wanted to scream, to yell, to let everybody know how I felt about them. But instead, everything stayed rolled up in a neat ball inside of me.
I tried being straightforward and telling people how I felt. I found myself hurting people, losing friends, and hurting myself.
I tried being myself and that wasn't any good either. I didn't seem to let enough of me come through. I was always hiding a part of me for what reason I don't know.
I think I tried everything except one thing. . .God.

Christine Kallas
FROM A MOTHER TO HER SON

Every year on that certain day.
I think of you my darling son
Wishing you were here to share your dreams.
And somehow still wondering why.
God had to take you from me.
I really didn't think I would make it.
Each day seems to grow longer.
As those many nights linger by.
And I still cry for you.
But I know I have to be strong.
As I try to realize.
That God has a reason.
For every thing he does.
So my darling son,
As I stop to think of you once again.
Always remember you'll remain,
Dear to all of us.
Especially in our hearts.

Marvin Jordan
THE BELLS

The silver bells of Christmas
Rang out so many times.
Children sang their carols,
To tiny musical chimes.
Happy holidays are fading.
The swan-song of the year.
Yuletide bells are silent,
As the New Year hovers near.
The colorful bells seem sad
Ringing the old year out.
High in church towers, all around
The tidings are spread about.
The magic hour is here at last.
You join the noisy throng.
To the strains of "Auld Lang Syne",
The bells ring loud and long.
It will really be quite gloomy
Over mountains and through the dells,
When the World grows suddenly quiet,
With no music from the bells.

Katherina Gascoigne
DEAR GOD

Dear God, I must talk to you today!
There are so many things I want to say,
I realize you know each beat of heart
But God - our earth is falling apart,
Homes uprooted - lives torn asunder,
When you get mad God - we hear your thunder!
But do you hear the shells and bombs,
Are you listening to man's stupid wrongs?
The growing children with hunger pains
Dear little souls with swollen veins,
Women with babies in their arms,
No food to quench their loud alarms.
Men in power, seeking glory,
Through the years, it's the same old story!
Freedom lost - and men are broken
It's hard to understand this evil token!
We love this earth of your creation,
Where everything's made to fine perfection,
Fresh air - and forest glades demure,
Crags and mountains where the Eagles soar!
Now God - we've had our little talk today -
Make man know where he has gone astray!
Release the Dove of peace again,
I know our talk will *not* be in vain.

Miss Eva Springfield
DESIRE

From the very first day you walked into my life,
In the darkness, thoughts formed in my mind every night.
You called my attention from that long endless fall,
You made me smile, most of all.
Forever, I could picture your smooth as satin blue eyes,
Even if we find it necessary to say goodbye.
The desire I have for you grows with each sunrise,
And also when I look deeply into your eyes.
I wish to join you in some of the parts of your world
To me this would always be as precious as a pearl.
I want to thank you for allowing me to
interrupt your life, as I feel I've already done.
I will expect no more from you, anticipating,
that once more into my life you will come.
And no matter how soon afterwards you must depart,
When you return, always you'll bring my morning sun.

E. Leslie Impala
HAUNTING ME

Fragrance remembered
upon petals red
Beseeching the caste
where our souls were led
With sleep a remiss
I fall to me bed
Thoughts of you
slowly caressing my head
A slave to desire
as we both had said
Haunting me
And you are the key
To my fantasy
Must I dream to see
Loves Reality?

Gail Wood
LAMENTATION

Afterward,
you came and went
two nights in a row.
Childlike,
I clutched at your departure.
The second time—
mother shook her head;
only then could I believe.
My mother would not lie—
even in dreams.
Someone had to be the gracious hostess
so I sat alone, removed from grief,
and feared heat stroke for those
who suffered silently
in the uncomprehending July sun.

Masonic brothers stood united,
defending your honor with their presence.
The Grand Shaman made death inviting
with rolling hills and flowered meadows.
(Later I discovered your meadows-covered with the weeds
of a fifteen year infirmity.)
His words curled and beckoned
to my feet to walk through them,
to my eyes to read again
the troubled wisdom in your face.
daddy daddy daddy I am still a child
why are you lying in a box
that should be the new cabinets
of some proud young wife
who would line them
with flowered roach proof paper
(yours is lined in tasteful beige)
and stack cans with their labels
conveniently facing the door
(you conveniently face the door
but your label is gone)
The rite is too long.
His voice drowns
in the noise of dripping sweat.
Hurry Hurry
these people are tired of grief
and the mid-morning sun.
Suddenly:
a reception line.
Would these men
who loved my father
give or receive anguish?
My own grief retreats
from an onslaught
of handshakes and mumbled sympathies.
It is over.
Not wanting to leave you,
we stand in procrastination,
but you left two days ago
and my daughter doesn't understand
the division of body and soul and
I can't even explain
why you were buried
on her fifth birthday.

Bess M. Robertson

ROSE KENNEDY

Of't times I have thought about
This lady of reknown
So humble in her quiet way
Yet worthy of a crown
A mother filled with love
And devotion unsurpassed
Hears the childhood laughter
That echoes from the past
With great expectations
For the sons that she bore
She raised them with dignity
Through peace and tragic war
Her losses were beyond compare
As all the world has known
Her great determination
Won the courage she has shown
As she strove for happiness
Thru tradgedy and fear
The showers of heartbreak
Would constantly appear
My heart and I have secretly
Whispered a prayer
To help her endure
Her many crosses to bear
Her fortitude and valor
She was able to attain
Even though her private world
Was shattered once again
This lady of compassion
With understanding ways
Bore her sorrows bravely
Throughout the shadowed days
Now moments of the past
May bring sadness to her eyes
For time cannot erase
Our momentary sighs
Yet, the presence of this lady
With her great tenacity
Spells the symbol of encouragement
To face reality
The amazing Rose Kennedy
With handsome youthfulness
Magnificantly copes
With life's strain and stress
A most outstanding woman
With tender quality
Is wrapped in special charm
And personality
Her memories are precious
Her heart is filled with pride
May heaven send an angel
To be always at her side
Please tread the path of happiness
Dear lady of grace
As the wondrous threads of time
Are woven into place

William V'azquez Di'az

BY THE WET RIVER SAND

Walking along, by the wet river sand,
I sang my love, to a lonely star,
Knowing that sooner than springtime comes
She will be kissing the cold of December, goodbye.
Yes, it is going to be cold and lonesome tonight,
Now that you are going to another heaven,
I will be waiting for the sun to rise
In the empty mornings of my heart...
Yes, it is going to be cold and lonesome tonight,
It is going to be a windy and rainy night
Of empty dreams, but tomorrow will come, darling
And the heavenly rain, will clear the sky...
And
like the gold
that shines;
by the wet
river sand;
whe will be kissing
the cold of december,
goodbye... goodbye...

James N. Carr, Jr.

THE WRECKING DOLL

She screams at me she thinks
to change a mind.
I perceive a different motivation
Behind her violent agitations;
She raves at me in fear of
changing lies.
I apprehend her chilled
protestations
She's sensitive like a wrapper in the air,
And I, obsessed by her, behind a selfish dare;
Her survival instincts invent
created tensions.
Her body vibrates like a
wrecking doll.
Her eyes searingly search my veiled soul,
And I, like a current, veer about these flaming coals
Knowing she will be difficult
to rob.
Nonetheless, I gain a strength
in violating her.
She suffers very little and has fresh fuel
For her conscience; it's now a more efficient spool
For wrapping and threading her
shattered nerves.
She's certain she has salvaged
her mind again.
Her mind, the quintessence of meaning,
Her lymph carrying her thoughts streaming
Throughout the vessels where
blood was meant.
Though she hasn't suffered, she's
decayed some more.
Living underground amidst veins of black bile,
Rubbing shoulders with the corrupted and vile.
I go home feeling more ironized
than before.
And on my pillow, with steam
on my eyes,
I wonder why every wish is wrecked,
Why all my reasons insidiously stacked
To reveal that all I do is
bastardize, bastardize.

Paris Salvatore Dalto

UNTITLED

We are all of us,
within the light of consciousness—
groping in the darkness. . .

Robert E. Brock

MOTHER

To me she was
a guiding light
a clear cut path
both day and night.
When I would go wrong
she showed me right
and helped me aim
for greater heights.
Within my soul
she instilled excel
that what I did
must be done well.
For second chancers
are often losers
and of precious time
are real abusers.
I learned from her
that time runs out
for those who trust
and those who doubt.
And to the wonder
of the great and small
that upon them too
the dark veil will fall.
I hope some day
that it may be
some one will say
the same of me,
That to them I
was a guiding light
a clear cut path
both day and night.
When they would go wrong
I showed them right
and helped them aim
for greater heights,
That within their soul
I instilled excel
that what they did
must be done well.
"Always grateful,"
they say they'll be,
for the privilege
of knowing me.
And grateful I am
for knowing her,
and her wise counsel
I'll always share.
That the happiest moments
of life worth living
are those we earn
by the act of giving.
Oh, she was as wise
as any man
and she understood
Gods master plan.
And many times
when I would have quit,
she showed me how
I was part of it.
She's gone now
and there is no other,
who can take the place
of my "Dear Mother."
Yes, gently behind her
she closed lifes door—
her work is finished
on this earthly floor.

Sharon Louise Nichols

HE IS THERE

When I am feeling down,
I look upon the Lord,
And He is there to greet me,
To love me evermore.
He listens to my outburst,
My feelings of despair,
He helps me with my burdens,
And tells me He is there.
So, whenever I am troubled,
The problems I can't bear,
Go onto His shoulders,
My burden He doth bear.
The Lord and I together,
We make a real good pair,
He is there to help me,
When I go to Him in prayer.

Ann Fillis Dackin

DISNEYLAND

Disneyland I live in --
It's on, "Fantasy Avenue" --
In a town called, "Make Believe", where dreams always come true --
Disneyland is a grown'-ups' land --
Where reality is never played --
And many of us stay there until our dying day --
The streets are filled with laughter --
The rides bring cheers of joy --

And no one sleeps without the dreams we had as girls and boys --
You can stay as long as you want to --
But there's a price you must pay --
It's never visiting the town of, "Reality" --
Where grown'-ups' live each day --

Nancy Lee Welch

THE WINDMILL SPINS

In open fields of grasses gold
Survives a windmill worn but bold.
And as the vanes spin softly round
She'll spin old tales that neared her ground.
She'll tell how cattle made a drive
When wagon-loads did scarce survive.
She'll tell when homes had fenced-off land
And water pumped upon demand.
So whisper on you old windmill
About the lands that layed so still,
And tell their secrets proud and clear
To quiet ones who'll lend an ear.

Randall Cunningham

SATANS WIND

I am a lonely wind, blowing through space on high,
Pushing the racing jets, rolling the clouds in the sky.
Sailing boats are my specialty, thats a sport, do or die,
Raising waves as high as mountains, putting ships on the bottom, where they lie.
I touch all I meet, with a swish, a moan, a sigh,
Scattering the dust that smarts the eye, a frolicking devil am I.
Rolling a hat or a loose toupee and sending them flying high,
Lifting the skirts of a modest miss, a peek at her gam, a thigh.
I blow from east to west, doing no good they say,
Some gave me a devils name, "SATANS WIND" is the price I pay.
Pushing along the killer waves, I sink a ship a day,
Carry flames through a forest dry, put waves in the golden hay.
I regret my satans name, some days I'm quiet and lay,
then rustle the leaves of a mulberry tree and carry the voice of a jay.
Amplify the chimes of a high church bell and laughter of children at play.
Then caress the cheeks of lovers embraced, satan am I? nay, nay.
I ripen the fruits in season, I tease the pesky fly,
Lift a kite into the sky, higher than birds can fly.
I promise to return next spring, look for me in June,
You'll hear my whisper some quiet night, like sounds of a lonely loon.

Eugene Mohan

THE SPRING

The spring in the valley is as
Real as the spring on the hill.
In either I can drink my fill.
The spring in the valley is near the little school house;
The spring on the hill is near the home of the grouse.
A little beyond is a field of maize
And the woods where the cattle graze.
The wild grapes grow on the fence
To save from the market some pence.
There are horses in the meadow;
They are resting from the plow,
For there is no work now.
On this day of rest, I will go into the woods.
The mystery of the wood is as great as the mystery of the forest;
It has the flower, the rock, and the bird.
And the chatter of the squirrel is still heard.
The Spirit is still in the trees,
As I listen to the hum of the bees.
The visiting grosbeak is far different from the raccoon,
Since the latter works under the moon.
The Spirit is still in the trees,
As the fox crosses the road,
Without disturbing the toad,
And heads for the slough,
As the frogs dry out from the dew.
The Spirit is still in the trees,
As the birds drink from the creek,
And I through the trees do peek.
The spring by the road is also
Near the ducks in the marshy thicket
And within the sound of the chirping cricket.
The colorful birds overhead
Are even higher than my grassy bed.

As I drink from the spring on the side of the hill,
I see the green valley from afar
And forget that I ever owned a car.
As I drink my fill from this woodland rill,
I find the pheasant difficult to kill.
As the breeze moves through the leaves of the trees,
I contemplate the abandoned mill,
And the Spirit stays still.
I notice an old cabin made of logs,
And I hear from afar the barks of dogs.
And then suddenly I see a rock in the shape of a state,
And I begin to contemplate my ultimate fate.
The spring is now farther away,
But I will reach it by midday.
The water is so cool I will happily fill my jug
And then relax upon the grass as I would on a rug.
But above this spring in the sand
Is an even brighter land,
Where the wild rose grows;
And the cliffs drop off at my toes.
The deer here chew on the bark,
And the owl hoots mostly in the dark.
There is a partridge to be shot in a hollow,
But I know that another will soon follow.
The lone hawk will silently sail
Over the tangled cover of the tiny quail,
A place where I can look out over the dale—
Where the eye can view almost all in one sweep,
And where, at the horizon, is the river that is long and deep.
I will see large quantities of the wild plum—
Enough for an elephant, and then some.
Here the animals live in the shrub-covered ravine,
And many newly-arrived songbirds can be seen.
But with a little rest,
I will go back to the spring
To hear the bluebird sing.
The Spirit stays still in the branches of the trees,
As the hornets compete with the honey bees.
I will sit by the spring on the side of the hill
And believe it is as real as the spring in the valley—Rose Valley.
I will look at the schoolyard below,
Where the children no longer go;
But they came here once through the fields of hay
To be in school on each bright new day.
They came here once with their lunch in a pail
To listen to the teacher tell an ancient tale.
Now they are all gone,
And most live with a lawn;
But I prefer the spring on the side of the hill at dawn,
Which is more real than the life in the valley below.
I prefer to see the little chipmunk
And even the frightening skunk.
I prefer to feel the flowers under my head,
While others recline on, or sleep in, a bed.
I will sit by the spring on the side of the hill
And believe it is as real as the spring in the valley.
By a lonely rose bush there I will dally,
But this is also where the buttercup and crocus grow
And where the moccasin flower has a rounded toe.
It is where these lady's— slippers hide beside the path,
And where the human race does not show its wrath.
Where the moccasin flower has such solitude,
Most people do not even seek a mood;
So we of nature's golden race
Are left alone in our sacred place.
And we may be certain,
The spring on the hill is as real
As the spring in the valley below.
But many fear the spring on the hill,
And some can not approach due to a lack of will.
Some stay away because they have never been here,
And others do not, at all, come near.
Some do not even care;
And some do not know it is there.
But these could not see the rabbit in his lair,
And they do not know they are caught in a snare.
The idea does not even enter their head,
As I lie down on my grassy bed.
But it is still true that the spring on the hill
Is as real as the spring in the valley.
I even prefer the spring on the hill,
Where I can always drink my fill
And not be reproached for beholding the abandoned mill.
This little niche has a tendency to civilize;
You may reach it only if you are wise.
You will come here mostly by an act of conscious will,
But first you must make that small leap across the sacred rill.

Ann Fillis Dackin

BACKYARD GREENS (become the dreams of all our little sons)

Oh little one run from me now go play among your friends.
Ships of cardboard, swords of woods, blue oceans of backyard green.
Slay your neighbor, take the stern, ride the waves of pride.
Of a battle fought in backyard green,
A battle of childhood pride.
Run for now my little one see not the tears in my eyes.
For soon enough my little one

your backyard green will fade
to brown and die.
And your ships will be of
mighty steel.
Your swords blood red in the
sun.
And the neighbor that you slay
my dear,
Will be someone else's Son.

Mrs. Gyan Kuar Lal
THE BEAUTIFUL GREEN TREES
As I sit gazing lazily outside my
Small and Beautiful House.
What I did see, but the most
Beautiful Green Trees.
That did swallow my worries
and, which other beauties did I
need to break down my tension.
The Beautiful Green Trees
spread inner into the forests.
The dense forests which men
did use for building houses and
logs for cooking.
The Green Trees so beautiful, as
I were seeing the scenes of some
movie, produced in the Dense
Mountainous Valley of the
West.
And as I again sit outside the
house When tis so cool.
I again see the Beautiful Green
Trees, to me they are so lovely,
Lovelier than the street lights,
lovelier then the flower gardens.
Nothing would I take vision of
Than These Beautiful Green
Trees.

Audrey Renda
LOVE SHARED
Speak to me sweet love of mine
In words encouraging, soft and
kind.
Let your voice be a whisper
That drifts through the room
As the cool evening breeze
Floating clouds across the
moon.
Caress me with your loving
gaze,
And let your unspoken
thoughts
Be my light in the dusky haze.
Sitting here I know it is true,
My only happiness is being with
you.

Janet Hoppis
FOR KIM
(Who died August 1, 1976 in the Big Thompson Canyon)
Lord, this page
filled with repititious blue lines,
is as blank as my mind,
filled with one re-echoing
thought
she is dead.
and, like my hand
moving to cover the empty page,
something moves in my memory
covering my face with tears.
Lord, these tears
fall onto the silent paper
as my mind stumbles over
memories falling from unspoken
words
for my friend.
and from my heart
praying to the God of love
something rises in my soul
and leaves words of comfort.

Rita M. Reed
CHRISTMAS DAY
It was the day of Christmas,
when all through my abode
No one was stirring, because
all were stuffed like a toad
The stockings were still hung
by the chimney, but not with
care
In fact, it looked like St. Nick
had left his there
The children were restless and
wanted to go to bed
As visions of cleaning up this
mess dashed through their
heads
But Poppa and I would not let
them nap
We wanted them to help clean
up without any flap
When out on the porch there
was such a clatter
I jumped up from my chair to
see what was the matter
I reached the window in a flash
Just in time to hear the crash
The sun melting the new fallen
snow
Caused a glare and the cars
passed very slow
My wandering eyes soon caught
sight
Oil a sliding car that had hit
a new trike
The little ole driver got out
quick as a wink
And a whiff of his breath let
us know he was full of drink
Running out the kids soon
came,
And whistled and shouted and
called the little man a dirty
name
"Now stop it, now darn it, you
little brat
You know better than to call
the man that.
Get back on the porch or stand
by the wall
Or better yet, get in the house
away from it all."
And in a twinkling I heard from
the door
My husband begin to roar
As I drew up my head and
turned around
Out he came with a bound
He was not too well dressed,
with slippers on his feet
His pajamas were wrinkled and
baggy in the seat
He stumbled over the toys and
flung them back
He looked like a bum that had
stopped in for a snack
His eyes, how they blinked, his
temples pounded, how scary
His cheeks were flushed, all red
like a cherry
His mouth was drawn up like a
bow
And what he would do next, I
didn't know
A stump of a toothpick he held
in his teeth
And I knew any minute he'd
start his beef
He had a bearded face and a pot
belly
When he was mad, it shook like
jelly
This was my hubby, and I knew
how he felt
But I laughed when I saw him,
in spite of myself
A wink of his eye and a twist of
his head
Soon gave me to know—I had
nothing to dread
He spoke not a word, but went
straight to his work
He picked up the bent tricycle
and turned with a jerk
He pointed his finger as the
little man waited
And said he would talk to him
when his anger abated
The man left his address and
climbed into his car
And away he went like a
shooting star
But I heard him exclaim, ere
he drove out of sight
Happy New Year to all, and to
all a good night!

Skip Kniese
REMEMBERING
'And his white stallion fell from
under him
Wind lashing at his open face
Sky turning blue, waiting for the
heavens to fall
Earth turning upside down,
ready to swallow up the good
Dark clouds turn out rain in
torrents
Raindrops pelting the earth into
small puddles of blood
A second later, time stood still
Silence makes a haunting crash
around
Individuals scramble about as if
in a daze
People turning away with
unbearable loss
Not quite believing the
spectacle.'
'Later the morgue and
confirmation
Crying, sobbing, handkerchiefs
brought out
Disbelief, anger, sorrow,
madness
Flowers bringing out sweet
depressing scents
Friends lining up to see for the
last time
Handshakes, hugging, sympathy,
condolences
Long ago people not seen for
years
Close people coming together
With a bond as unimpregnable
as concrete
To hold up each other like
canes
...Then the putting away
Leaving a vacancy that could
never be replaced
A loss has occurred
And only the good die young.'

Marie-Anne L. Taylor
DEATH/LIFE
Am I quite soon prepared to die?
No! No! cries out my soul, not I!
I yearn to see another rainbow,
To feel the drops of dew, wet
upon my lips.
I hunger more for knowledge,
I need once more to catch a
butterfly.
To hear the cooing of the doves,
enchanting musical symphonies.
The joy of a child newborn.
Just to feel the cool grass,
wriggling between my toes.
Imagination, on cloudy billows
of enchantment.
I need to dream, to yearn, to
pause, to play!
With freedom, and abandon
I need to feel silence enveloping
me.
Most of the time is past, and the
now seems mostly reverie.
Time is eluding, fading fast!

Mrs. Robert E. Morley
FATHER'S DAY
Father's Day is for remembering,
The many good things he has
done,
The many ways he showed his
love,
For his daughters and his sons.
His work was hard and his day
was long,
And his pleasures they were
few,
But he carried his burdens
gladly,
Because of his love for you.
He taught you all the game
rules,
And how to pitch a ball,
Then he always found the time,
To mend a broken doll.
You thought he was a good guy,
And great as Father's go,
Of course he wasn't wise like
you,
But little did you know.
He never cared if you had
wealth,
Or were a leader of great
renown,
He wanted only your happiness,
And let nothing keep you down.
Will you be with him on
Father's Day?
His memories to share,
Will you tell him if he needs
you?
That you will always be there.

E. Ann Smart
VERSES COLLECTIBLES: NO. 8
I sing a song of psychiatry
Of Menninger and Freud,
Of phobia and mania
and schizo-paranoid.
I sing a song of psychiatry
Of chaises-longue and blue,
Of free association hunts
For some elusive clue.
I sing a song of psychiatry
I sing this song to you
Oh doctor, because I fear
My payment's overdue.

Douglas G. Miller
RICHES
I am richer far than you,
Who has a million in cash so
cold,
I have the diamonds in drops

of dew,
The sunshine at my feet spreads gold.
I have the diamonds of the night,
Against an ebon colored sky,
I have a moon of silver; bright,
To haunt us and to mystify.
I have the onyx of the midnight sky,
I have the turquoise of the sea,
These are things you cannot buy,
These are treasures which are free.
I have fine perfumes from the flowers,
I find rare scents in the lilac tree,
And I sit for uncounted hours,
Wondering how good our God can be.
I have the ivory of the snow-covered hill,
I have the pearls in crystal frost,
I pause to gaze and look my fill,
Never mine to keep, yet never lost.
I have the divine melodies,
And never one has brought forth stings,
From meadow larks and chickadees,
And all the countless birds that sing.
I have the ruby in the rose,
I have the emerald in the leaf,
I have wealth as no one knows,
A soothing balm for my lonely grief.
But, for all these treasures I endear,
I find within my heart a space,
For something richer; someone dear,
To stay by me as I run life's race.
Someone who will love me,
Someone who will be true,
Someone I place above thee,
Oh! diamonds in drops of dew.

Sensei Joseph Carbonara

ELANA CRIES

The child is crying
My mommy has gone.
Her warmness, the
memories are our
strong bond.
At last she's back,
mommy' here.
The world is safe,
no more to fear.

Ms. Beryle A. Brooks

LITTLE ANGELS

Tonight I peeked into their
room as they said their evening
prayer.
Instead of my two babies,
I saw two angels there.
They clasped their little hands,
and bowed their little heads,
asked god to bless us all,
then jumped into their beds.
I kissed them both tenderly,
as I tucked them in.
And as I walked away I knew
their dreams would soon begin.
I stopped to wonder what I'd do
If I were all alone,
No pitter patter of their feet,
echoing through our home.
Without them I'd be nothing,
for they're my life and song,
and as long as we're together
the days don't seem so long.
So we live our lives together
with each new passing day,
And I thank God for little
Angels, my two help pave our
way.

Bert Mullaney

I TALK WITH GOD

I talk with God each morning
In a very special way
I watch his world wake up again
And start a brand new day
I wander through his fields and woods
I smell his flowers and trees
I'm filled with awe and wonderment
At glorious gifts like these
We talk and chat a little bit
As friends quite often do
I ask Him for another day
And try to see it through
But when my day is over
No matter how it's been
I thank Him for my very life
And say goodnight to Him.

Shirley L. Teague

DREAMS

Dreams of far away places
Peace within
Loved Ones
Bright joyful days
Quiet times to think
Memories long past
Tomorrows yet to come?
Happiness
To over come our Fears and
To except what we can not change-
To give love openly-
Most of all to be FREE TO GROW within.

Lenora Lang

GIFT OF LOVE

Tonight my heart cried out in pain
For those who in this life are missing
Who in pursuit of pleasures, gained,
Miss out, on the gift of God's real blessings
Wonderful gifts of love, and eternal life
God's gift to those who give him love,
Trust, their knowing for a future bright
A mansion home in heaven above.
A peaceful life is hard to find
In a sinfull world, ruled by man
Toil each day, in the daily grind
Omitting God, to follow the law of the land
Do they remember? God gave his only son
To die for sins, on a cruel cross
Asking nothing in return, yet waiting
Just to give comfort, to the ones who's lost.
Could we, as a friend, do half as much
as God does for us each day
So to our Heavenly Father, give him our trust
Our love, he will give us peace to stay.
Then as God's children we will sleep
In peace at night, he cares in his own way
For we then are his to keep.

Everett E. Landon

LUKE 4: 14-32

From storied Nazareth-town, in ancient Galilee,
Revives a serene firm voice—hear it, calm and low.
Placid as fair-weather ripples on the little sea,
It returns to us amid cacophonies of long ago.
Esaias' book reposes in the gentle reader's hands:
". . .he hath sent me to heal the broken-hearted"—
As the Judaic custom is, the chosen reader stands—
"To preach deliverance. . ."—not a word from the text departed.
An acceptable passage from Esaias—familiar, good;
How oft they've heard it, and hearing, been made glad.
A comfort to Israel, (To all men, when correctly understood.)
But then, Who could comfort captive Israel, as Esaias had?
The book is closed; he hands it back. He sits down.
Please, they await the discourse; his the time to speak.
Of late, he has reputation gained in nearby towns.
In truth, his fame has risen to a heady peak.
"This day," saith he—how soon the scene is often turned—
"Is this scripture fulfilled in your ears."
"What? We know him! Ridiculous claims—all unearned!
"Is not this Joseph's son?" At once their disbelief appears.
Again, the Nazarene speaks to his neighbors there;
Then, from the synagogue come shouts of wrath.
Rushing forward, they thrust him out. How did he dare?
See them, jostling him along the worn and stony path.
From the brow of the hill, whereon their city stands,
Their determination is to cast him down headlong.
They surely will destroy him, if at all they can;
But passing through their midst, he escapes the angry throng.
Sometimes we, like they of undiscerning Nazareth,
Umbragious grow, our resisting minds, by some new thought impressed.
Thus tried by truth in phrases new, we fail the alien shibboleth,
Because we bind our convictions to traditions sometimes overstressed.
We thrust away the unfamiliar thought or unexpected news,
Which invades our formulistic mind's small synagogue,
To challenge treasured, settled complacent views,
Reigning absolute there, like some tyrannic demagogue.
And to the abrupt brow of quick, petulant offense,
We escort the vile nonconformist truth, to erase
All that lacks the imprimatur of our noble imprudence,
By casting it headlong, in defense of dear tradition's grace.

Nazareth sacrificed its Messiah, on the brink that day;
But 'twas the brink of fretful prejudice, and lofty pride—
We stand today, to thrust him from our own lives away,
Except our unswerving love of truth, his every word abide.
And truth, like Christ, if, having favored us, we spurn,
May escape our midst, and pass beyond our forbidding gate;
So that, not until before the bar of God, perhaps we'll learn
The truth about the truth we put off until too late.

Nancy Roulias

THEY CRUCIFIED OUR JESUS

Jesus never committed a crime
He died on the cross for your sins and mine.
He carried his cross up the mountain-side.
He did nothing but good—nothing to hide.
They tore his clothing and speared his side.
It was his fate—he was doomed to die
They pulled out his beard and spit on him!
He loved everyone—and also them!
God gave his son, because he loves us!
By his blood we are saved—our Jesus!
They nailed him to the cross and jeered him!
Christ asked our father to forgive them.

They crucified him!
They cursed him—he would stumble and fall!
Jesus was at peace—he gave his all.
They nailed him to the cross—thorns for his head.
He did no wrong, but they wanted him dead.
"A drink of water," said our Saviour;
Jesus asked for just a small favor,
And they gave Him vinegar instead.
He gave his life for us, and bowed his head.
They crucified our Jesus!

Mary Ann Tamberelli

MY LITTLE LEAGUER

The sun's shining brightly on fields of dark green,
The white diamond shape can be easily seen.
The bases are out there, one, two and three,
These step-stones to home have become the main key.
Here come the young lads all tense for their game,
Each one of them hoping he'll earn his due fame.
The equipment is orderly with bats in a row,
With all of their practice we've watched the team grow.

The umpire suits up and then yells, "Play ball!".
To all whom are present, that is a good call.
The ball is in play now, they're aching to win,
Both teams at this point are neat as a pin.
Each lad takes his turn at bat, proud as can be,
Next up is my boy, "Strike one, two and three!".
He looks so forlorn, "Don't worry.", I say.
"Wait 'til your next ups, you'll show them the way!"
The innings are passing, they really went fast.
It's our turn at bat now, this turn is our last.
The bases are loaded, the win's at the plate.
It's my boy at bat now, he seems so sedate.
He swings at the first pitch, a strike is the call,
The second was too high, it sure was a ball.
In comes the next pitch, a swing and a miss,
How could he ever bear pressure like this?
Now he is ready and feeling quite tense,
His eyes sparkled brightly as he glanced towards the fence.
In came the pitch, a beautiful throw.
I watched him swing strongly. I saw my boy grow.
I'll never forget that look on his face,
He knew he had just put his team in first place.
The season is over, they've played every game.
Each lad on the team has reached his own fame.
My boy is a hero, they shout it aloud.
While I as his parent, am feeling quite proud.
The years pass so quickly, and yet seem so meager,
While my love grows stronger for my little leaguer.

Kipp Curtis

UNTITLED

See the shades in endless dance
Within the embers red glass house
The dreams warm lair against the cold
Soft red light within the night
Take my hand and lead me there
In soft dreams meadows of powder white
The ashes of our dreams last night
The memories of yesterdays
I have seen the flames of growing fires
And touched the black of past desires
I will touch the source of the shadow glow
And all life will I have known

Donna May Smedley

A TINY, DIRTY PAIR OF SOCKS

When my heart was crushed and hurting;
As coal my life seemed black;
For I had just lost a tiny being;
Nothing I could do would bring Him back!
My little Son, so precious and dear;
How my heart pleaded to have him near;
I felt so much love, so strong, so true;
Yet His future with me could not come true.
The Father to this new little one;
Would feel the pain just as I have done;
He could take His little first-born upon His lap;
To comfort and help him to narrow the gap!
Yet here I lay, On a hospital bed;
Selfishly thinking, "Why not me instead?"
I guess I didn't quite realize, my firstborn too;
Needed His Mommy and loved Her too!
So when I needed the Lord's comfort most,
But what in my purse should I find?
Just a tiny, dirty pair of white socks;
That belonged to that first Son of mine!
So as those tears dripped down my cheeks;
I held those tiny socks for comfort to seek;
And softly to my God I began to speak;
I gave Him my future and family to keep!

Marva Stella

THE ENDING

There seems to be
Emptiness within me.
A hole in my heart
Where love once lived.
Cold dark nights
All by myself.
Wondering if
It is worth all the pain.
I don't want him back.
I often wonder now.
How it would be
If things had worked out.
Why does he seem
To enter my thoughts?
After all he's done
Why should I care?
Friends are confused.
Families hurt deeply.
They are caught inbetween
This cold, vicious battle.
This part of my life
Is ended and through.
New pathways ahead
Are waiting for me.

Gary Cloud

DEATH OF AN ARTIST

A masterpiece of a painting
but the artist
is dead
He died drinking his wine
a half empty bottle and a half finished painting
of a woman
a beauty of a woman, Yes a profoundly beautiful woman
could it be his wife? A wife,
of a single man.
No, it is his dream
His wish to have such a beautiful woman to Love.
You see he was a lonely man, a poor man.
For he was in love with this woman
he was shy
he could only express himself
when he painted
Paint.
He was a poor man not a penny to his name
in the slums he lived
barely alive
with no faimly to call upon, to love.
Like, the stillness of the morning
the room is full of death
but who cares
WHO
REALLY
CARES
that this room is full of death
Elsewhere life goes on, people still live
they do work, or they try
they do play, but do they cry,
DO THEY CRY!!!!!!!!!!!!!!!!!
For a man is dead, an artist by trade
with a half empty bottle and a half finished painting
of that woman.
The wine he drank was of the color red
A masterpiece of a painting
but the artist
is dead.

Ernest James Shimer

BI-CYCLICAL

In the beginning,
Twin wheels turn clear, catch thin light,
Thin as a bee's wing.
Being primitive,
Children know this image, know,
Too, all things that sting
And how they hint at life:
Squeeze
Me and you shall surely cry.
Years away, moving
Upon a street made bare, is
Form significant,
Generating its own sharp
Truth, its own secret center. . .
Out there, there's a girl
Who, between wheels tilting tight,
Tempting gravity,
Does describe an arc so ripe
It gives off very much warm.
In here, there's a boy
Masquerading as a man.
The damn fool's crazy,
Lying around in T-shirts,
Refusing to surrender.
And the leaves are down,
Empty-handed, having turned
Up to bum some time.
Dumb eyes deny them
And snub those who snub the ground.
Anyhow, the wife
Has taken the window, has
Pronounced judgment, ripe and cool:
Look! Thy
Neighbor's daughter
Is getting a good ass
On her. I look for her to get
Knocked-up.
In a dream she smiles
(Whispers a dirty word) and
Her smile, unnoticed,
Falls like first light on a boy
Betrayed. Then she gets grown-up:
Look, Dear,
I know the score,
I know the facts of life—
All about the boys and the bees—
And Lust.
To himself says he,
The Mrs. misses the point,
Hiding in his head
Memories of tomorrow;
Of a new leaf after this;
And of
The humble bee,
Delicate explosion,
Like a spark wrested away on
Warm Wind.
And soon come the boys,
Droning along on, of course,
Four wheels. She goes, too.
To negotiate straight streets,
Now in power, with pleasure.
Because she knows all. . .
But doesn't know a damn thing
About bicycles.

Eugene M. Hodges
BEYOND

meta
Parable
H
sound O silence
language R
die love life
become be

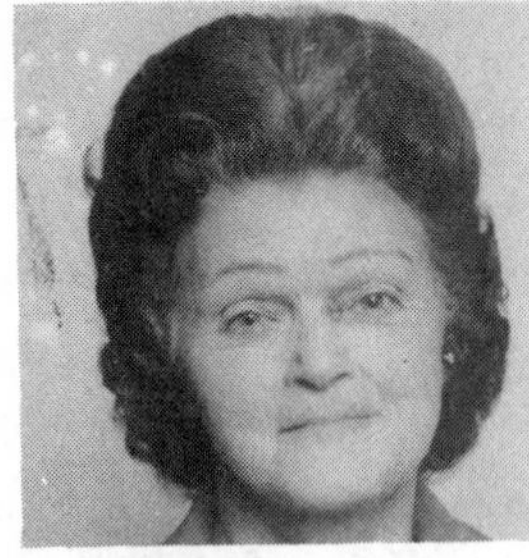

Jeanne Padlesky
SOMEWHERE

Somewhere the sun is setting
and the wind is blowing low.
Somewhere someone is waiting,
waiting for somewhere to go.
Somewhere a man with a lonely heart
is waiting for someone to share;
Waiting and praying that one day
someone from somewhere will be there.
Somewhere in the darkness of the forest
a maiden is walking in the night;
Walking and crying of loneliness,
waiting for someone to make it all right.

Somewhere a baby is crying,
crying and shivering with cold;
Crying and hoping that from somewhere
that someone will come to him to hold.
If somewhere was heaven and the blue skies,
and somehwere was the echo of this song;
That somewhere would be a path to heaven,
somewhere in heaven to belong.
But somewhere has never been found,
that somewhere is but a lonely song;
And somewhere there is still someone waiting
somewhere to someone to belong.

B. Eileen Kuchenreuther
ULTIMATE BLACK

death is black
black is death
wonder who I'll be when
I come back
help me help myself
nearer to darkness,
wear black
when the going gets too tough---
the tough shall die
help me to be there,
please--
and be sure and wear black
slowly, for I am evil
gray, gray, gray
nearly there
love is gone, the soul
now empty
the gray shadows are black
please make sure I am
wearing black

Ma. Guadalupe Gonzalez
ILLUSIONS OF THY ROUNDNESS

My castle I built upon my faith,
A spring I should see,
Illusions created of what will be
The spring never came for me.
To live I did not ask
Yet I had no chance
My eyes opened as I realized the roundness of thy sin
That roundness I had no chance to see
Death came over me.

Evelyn M. Heslin
LIFE IS PRECIOUS

Life-like a diamond
Sparkles, when clean
Becomes lusterless
When crime creeps in
Life-like a jade
Is valuable to possess
But will decline
If we don't give it the best
Life-like a pearl
So precious to have
Will become worthless
When wasted
Unlike a jewel
That finally ebbs away
Life is eternity
Think about it today!

Beverly Oberg Himber
THE DAY TOMMY DIED

We were a family, an odd looking tree;
Six kids, matched kittens, a pup, dad and me.
Love flowed so easy, no scars yet you know,
Six kids, cats, a dog; dad and me all aglow.
We camped by the lakes and floated the streams,
Lived just for each other the life we all dream.
No plans for tomorrow, 'stead of of cats, there was Tom,
Our kids were small people, each left, one by one.
The boys went through drinking, I'd wait at the door,
Hiedie outside the window, while Tom walked the floor.
A curious cat, old Tom you'll agree,
On each foot his extra toes were just three.
They caught when he walked, no mistaking that tread,
"chip, chip" on the tile, "tick tick" on the rug.
Tina's cat was old Tom since the time he was three,
When she fell from her horse her main comfort was he.
Then Janet left home, how my heart felt the tug,
"Chip, chip" on the tile, "tick tick" on the rug.
Don went out on his own, with his work went the jug,
"Chip, chip" on the tile, "tick tick" on the rug.
Next, Debbie took off, modern living, her bug;
"Chip, chip" on the tile, "tick tick" on the rug.
Nick Jr. got married, I felt like a tub,
"Chip, chip" on the tile, "tick, tick" on the rug.
The house gets so quiet, Nick's truckin' the lug,
Still the "chips" on the tile,
and the "ticks" on the rug
Tina's promised, Tam's growing, my heart knows that tug,
Still the "chips" on the tile
and the "ticks" on the rug.
No more Drinkin' Don's truckin' to where Dad has led,
I've the "chip" on the tile and the "tick" on the rug.
Jan has Terry and Michael, neat family, I'll plug,
Slowly "chip" on the tile, "tick-thump-tick" on the rug.
Tam's no longer a child, a woman 'most grown,
Silence blasts every corner and laughs, you're almost lone.
Tom "chip-ticks" a lot slower, but comforts; just there,
Sharing now as when camping, or burdened with care.
Comes now lull in the troubles, Tom purrs, wastes with age,
Still "chip-tick" hugs me to him, so true, maybe sage.
My heart faints to listen to times mute decree,
But soon has to face stark reality,
Now "chip-tick" is gone; Apron-strings are untied;
For all this I cried, on The Day Tommy Died.

Drucilla Wallace
WONDERING

Sometimes I sit and wonder,
Wondering, who am I?
Where did I come from?
Where am I going?
As I ponder over these thoughts
I pinch myself back to reality
and realize that
I am who I am.
It matters not where I came
from but it's knowing where
I am going.

Claire Haines
THE HANDS OF TIME

Theres a lily pad a drifting along the mighty sea
It keeps drifting and a floating where the tide wants it to be.
Sometimes the waves are rocky and other times so calm,
But, the lily pad keeps drifting, drifting on and on!
It seems to have no course in mind, no place where it wants to be
But now that it has seen the world, it knows it's destiny!
So, now it won't be drifting, it won't be drifting anymore
It's going to swim from the mighty sea and plant upon the shore!
It's going to take the energy from a midday afternoon
Stop drifting and a floating and develop into a bloom.
It's going to need some nourishment from the sea it's known forever
So it can change from a lovely bloom and blossom into a flower.

Judith a. Wienckoski
ROYAL BEAUTY

If I could be another form
For just one single day.
I'd bathe myself in radiant light,
From the sun's golden rays.
My magnificent lines and unique
Shades, are mine and mine alone,
The sunlight and it's brightness
Gives me most my royal tone.
The delicate scent that I release,
Swirls in your head and gives you peace,
For one that's seen, for one
That knows, for just one
Day, to be a rose.

Lisa Marie Korba
LONELINESS

Lonely people are the best actors of All.
For you portray the biggest act in Life.
Everyone thinks you're a sweet, outgoing person, with an ever-lasting smile.
You'd hate to let them see the truth...by now showing them that style.
You never let them see you frown.
You see my friend you're the best pretender around.
They only see you happy, laughing, and smiling.
When all you really are is beguiling.
Some will think they know you true,
But they know not how they misconstrue.
Lonely people keep to them-selves, all bottled up inside.
For you refuse to let them know just how you bleed in pride.
Then the final curtain falls; you leave your friends behind.
You take off your smile, unlock your cage, and explode inside your mind.
You wonder why you have no dates.
Maybe you don't look that great.
Some may think that you're taboo, but this you'll never know.
So loneliness stays with you--
out of it you grow.

It's hard to believe what people
put themselves through.
You'd think they'd want to spill
their guts and tell exactly
what's true.
(But you can't do that, it's too
big a stride!)
It's very difficult to swallow
your pride.
Don't these people deserve a
little bliss?
Foul is the fault of loneliness.
For craven are those who will
not try to look inside you or
just say, "Hi"

Helen Pratt Vaughn

DAWN TO DUSK

Dawn stirred--raised her sleepy
head,
Pushing back her purple
coverlet of night,
Slowing rising---stretching long
slim fingers
Of mornings' early sunlight
Sun eased its' way across the
sky,
Bathing fields in the warmth of
another day,
A soft breeze wafts over the
fertile land
Bringing scents of blossoms and
new mown hay.
Far away huge mounds of dark
clouds appear--
To refresh the earth and let us
know
That all living things need rain
to thrive
And nurture the things God
sows.
DUSK creeps silently over the
golden day,
And as the moon and stars the
sky do light,
Opens the door to fairyland and
dreams
Turning the quiet hours over to
night.

Crissy E. Downs

JUST A FRIEND

Just being a friend just isn't
enough,
Though I try and I try it's really
tough.
I hear that he likes me but it's
only pretend,
God how I hate just being a
friend.
And how he hurts me so much
with his lies,
He often brings so many tears to
my eyes.
One day he treats me like
there's nobody else,
And the next he puts me away
like a toy on a shelf.
He knows that girls like him
and that is why,
He thinks he's the worlds most
popular guy.
He hurts me so much in so
many little ways,
I hope I can give him up soon
one day.
I try and I try but I can't get him
out of my mind,
Believe me my love for this guy
is one of a kind.
It's not that he hurts me on
purpose you see,
It's that he wants me to be the
friend I can't be.
So I'll say it again,
I'll repeat it once more.
Just being a friend is such a big
bore!

Angelito T. Buhisan, Jr. (Joe) J.D.

FOR NATASHA

The dancing candlelight
In front of me
Reminds me of the time
When you and me
Could dance
With talking feet
And laughing eyes,
When you and me
Were young
Light of mind
And light of heart.
The dancing candlelight
Sways to and fro
Back and forth
Playing with the wind
Like breezes used to do
As it teased your yellow hair.
The dancing candlelight
Shines brightly in my view
But not as bright
As my memory of you.

Marco A. Fuentes

A VIEW

I went down to the beach one
day
To see what there was to see,
besides the sea.
I wandered along
Probing the innards of sand with
my toes,
well-washed from the
pounding waves.
It was smooth and pure,
freckled with the jaggedness
of broken shells.
The gulls shrieked in
excitement
at neither me nor brother,
but at the West Wind,
warm and damp.
It filled and entangled my hair
with the salty effervescence
of the sea.
On the sand lay a piece of wood,
still moist from the receding
tide.
Its surface, tender and worn,
gave way to my prying nail.
My watch buzzed, and I followed
the sound of traffic
back to the walk,
Where my cane led me home.

Harold H. Murphy III

THE GOOD TROOP

the words for you of love,
a constant attention of his mind
silence his lips
moving his hands
to speak from the heart,
in silent motion
like marching soldiers
in steps of silence
for show of strength
restrained,
unreleased,
but prepared and ready
for the time...
the place,
the words...
for you.

Harold H. Murphy III

WITHOUT REASON

today he was in love
with what he knew not,
and he wondered why
he was,
then he remembered
you,
and there was his
reason.
then he remembered
love has no reason
and that ended you,
so today he was
in love
and still is
without reason...
for you.

Dale A. Rittenhouse

A SIMPLE RHYME

In Space,
In Time,
In Step.
My Space,
Left a Scarred Battlefield.
Still Smoking, all is silent, Final.
But still the echoes ring in your
ears.
My Time,
What Shall it be,
But the time inbetween.
I love you,
Then step back and wait.
My Step,
is,
out,
of step.

Frances Wagemaker Yocum

COLUMBIA

Today I saw the Columbia soar
Out into the depths of space;
I watched the mighty boosters
blast
As tears spilled down my face.
I saw her free her booster tanks
As she continued on her trip,
And thanked the Lord for His
help
In the building of such a ship.
So while Columbia orbits earth,
We pray for her safe return
And for the fearless men within
her,
Their lives hanging on a
"burn".
Shortened though her trips may
be,
It's thrice now that she's
flown;
She glides along her silent way
So space mysteries will be
known.
Now we wait with bated breath
To see her safe once more,
To see her glorious glide to
earth,
Her landing on her native
shore.
We salute you, Columbia, Ship
of Space!
Your deeds will long ring out!
And when your wheels touch
down again
I'll join the throngs who'll
shout!

Susan E. Killam

NOW AND THEN

Fairy tales, medieval forests,
and despotic kings.
The old house on the hill
prohobited.
The little disputes over
nothing
A lucrative lemonade stand
with the seller,
baked in the sun
The grass stained knee
that got you rebuked
The punctual bed time,
even if it was still light
out
The baseball game won
because of forfeit
The first time you illegibly wrote
your name.
Mom't favorite pitcher
broken
inadvertently
The Milky Way cached away,
in the top left drawer,
amongst odd gym socks
The "100" test commended by
a batch of
Chocolate chip cookies
The cur that wanders
around the alley
"Please mom, can't we
keep him?"
The inappropriate suit,
down to my knees
two buttons missing
and two inches too
long
on the sleeves
As the pages yellow
memories will be added,
Forever.

Karolyn Kay Smith

A FOREST IN A CLOUD

In the fall of the year
Close to the coming of winter
The fog comes to sit in the trees
Slowly closing the door
From the outside with a silken
sheet of gray
Opening on a different realm,
A lost realm of shadowed
sentinels
Slinking away into the dark
smoky mists,
Then stepping out again into an
opaque light
Shrouded in powdery vapors.
The oak woods mingle with the
pines
Out-stretching their broad
limbs,
A contrast to the uprightness of
the mysterious dark of the
pines.
As the sap stops filling each
leaf with green,
They unclothe themselves in
tans, yellows and golds,
Then sprinkle to the needled
ground
Interspersing with rusts of
denuded cones and brown-
sueded soil.
The boiling mists cloak and
envelope each tree,
Their fingers caressing each
pearl-tipped needle
As they swiftly glaze the slopes
in cool silence
And table the mountain tops
in white and gray-puffed

crowns.
Tails and streamers of miniscule water drops
Stretch out across the vastness above and below
Spraying themselves here and there
In indescriminate condensed gusts.
A world in its own cocoon
With only the soft hollow sounds of bristling leaves
To awaken its sullen slumber.
Patches of blue peek through from time to time
Reminding one that this space is only temporary,
But locked at the moment in a time
And place of make-believe.
Here only a rickety unpaved road contacts the shrill outside
Or leads to lands unknown
And yet to be explored,
Where tall saddled knights journey through foggy vapor
And firey dragons lurk among the trees,
And there swimming and sinking in lifting fogs
Are dark murky-gray castles,
Their turrets floating on high
Surrounded by moats of white and gray.
Here one meets his dreams of old
Not quite clear enough to be real,
But real enough to provide escape
From the old time warp beyond
This one of gauze until
The old blood is renewed,
And the mind, having tasted a short repast,
Replenishes its visions with ever stronger dreams
Piled atop those worn down by used up time.
Here the heart enfolds itself with warmth from passions
Kindled by fiery romantic tales of yore,
By everlasting hopes of an enduring love
That will stay alive through a long hard winter
And maybe into a brand new year.
The mists move on brushing all as it passes,
Washing the summer dust collected on all things
Refreshing and cleaning all to new sharpness
Waiting for the icy blanket of winter
To put everything to bed for awhile
Until their awakening in spring.
And here I wander yet in a spell
Interposing my thoughts on such dreams
And surrounding myself in these cold boggy leas
Amid lofty crags of straight gray shadows
Pretending to be lost and testing my cunning
At noticing familiar shapes hanging back in
Tendrils of lacy watery gas.
But there is no fear like one that is lost
For I have been here many times before
And I always pray I will return
To these misty woods once more.

Diana L. Rosemin

PARENTS

They've lived for others for so very long,
Always there to keep hopes up with a prayer and a song.
They helped us through hurts, straight to the end.
Knowing in their hearts joy was right around the bend.
At times we weren't grateful and treated them bad,
and took special delight trying to make them mad.
They gave us each life so we could live on this earth.
They loved us, protected us even before birth.
They watched us crawl, then stand and grow,
'Til one day we were grown and they had to let go.
They worked hard all those years when we were so small,
then had to let go of us, help us stand, watch us fall.
But as the years became memories in all of our hearts,
We realize our parents played the most difficult part.
To make us be strong and then set us free,
To be what our hearts told us to be.
Our Parents, *God Bless Them,* will be always the same
and we are their children in in heritage, in name.

Patricia Leonard

HARMONY, OREGON

Trailing over backroads, rather aimlessly,
Peering through the back doors of people's lives...
Comparing all their differences,
Wondering what it is that
Makes men thrive...?
What is it here, that makes men content?

..How did they come to be...
In such remote and oftentimes
...Timeless...communities..?
The how and whys
Occurr to me...as
All their lives blink by...

Dallas Kirk Gantt

LOVE IS AN AGELESS ISLAND

from the silver spring of the acropolis
your laugh brings me bells of little white mountain churches,
my Saint Sophia.
clear Agean seas roll through your ageless eyes
in odysseys
and island lore.
You are close!
Pan feet on dry, hot wind,
crackling thunder rushes through my heart
like the cold icy rapids of the Styx...
...as I smell your soft skin.
lambs leap through lavender and yellow thorns
and wild oregano, basil, and thyme.
baklava lips drive dreams of siren sweetness through me
with the bite of blazing ouzo,
until I'm drunk as the dancing fishermen.
you brush against me,
and the many armed octopus of love
blushes and preens in the secret grotto
of Lalaria's marble cliffs.

Terri L. Snide

WHILE

I'll wake you with a kiss, at the break of dawn,
While birds sing of peace, in the early morn.
I'll reach for you always, and take your hand,
While cool spring waters stretch over the land.
I'll caress your heart with warmth and praise,
While moonlight hovers the sky with haze.
I'll hold you close during stormy weather,
While rain and sunshine, combine together.
I'll walk with you feeling an inner birth,
While mountains step upon, the face of the earth.
I'll be devoting myself to only you,
While grass is awakened by morning dew.
I'll reach to touch your hair and face,
While flowers blow freely with poise and grace.
I'll melt by your touch, like snow from the sun,
While our paths may be separate, We're still joined as "one".
Though he and I are sometimes apart,
This person is buried within my heart.
As he's given to me, a lifetime smile,
I dedicate to John D. Summers, Our Poem called "While"

Olive A. Lawrence

ONE GREAT SCHOOL

Always learning where'er we tread
Though sometimes to realize we fail.
Through tears or joy, humility or pride,
That one great truth we can't deny.
To the knowledge of truth one day we'll come,
Whatever we are, or plan to be,
If we shudder, explode, weep or cringe,
There are morals to fold 'neath our wings.
Bowed branches beat our souls in the valley
Where the tallest trees touch the soil.
But watch the willow rise to majesty,
Lifting its tip up so nobly,
Aft' those boughs are beat with soles.
Tasks of life must come and go,
So lift your dreams beyond the horizon
Tow'r with grandeur in due season.
In school, on the job, at home or Church
Through hands or ears or eyes or mind
For windows these are opened wide
To store the knowledge brought inside.
So live life to its fullest at most
Sifting well whate'er you grasp
Birds from perching you may not stop
But prohibit a nest to build on top.

Mary G. Marshall

THE MODERN JUDAS

There's many a modern Judas
That sells out for a song,
And then when it is too late
He realizes he's wrong.
He'd like to retrace every step
And have the deed undone,
For when remorse of conscience strikes
To him it is no fun.
"Here, take back your silver,
'Tis blood money, evil dole,
I will not have a piece of it
'Tis poison to my soul."
"But the giver refuses to take back
And the stain is left on me,
How can I face life with it?
I'd rather be drowned in the sea."
"I am the blackest traitor,
I cannot bear to live,
I'll go and hang myself in shame,
My life, my all I give."

Sharon Heilman

THIS LITTLE CHILD

This little child sits next to me
blind with love and trust,
she smiles at me
and breaks my heart,
for I see no future for her
in a world that's so unjust.
But tomorrow I will try again
to make her world
a better place,
so I can feel inside myself
I've earned,
the love and trust
in her sweet face.
For when she puts her little hand in mine,
it gives me all the strength
I need
to seek again and
maybe find.

Dora T. Friedman

HOLOCAUST — AN ALLEGORY

The hour was dark.
Black clouds had gathered.
Hail poured down
upon naked heads.

The trees had been felled;
there was no shelter.
No umbrella of mercy - shown.
No wall to be called home.
No space - no place;
exposed to nature's worst weather.
Hopes dashed;
we were alone,
Alone.
We were all alone!

Glenna D. Stanphill

A MOTHER FIRST

So she was found diversified
To be fulfilled in many roles-
And found she was never again
So much fulfilled
As when, forsaking self,
She was a mother first!

Marilyn B. Rutter

OH, CAPITOL CITY

A faceless city where Death and Drugs go hand in hand.
Loneliness is rampant.
Worthless city.
Drugs and whiskey drive the people mad.
They stalk the night. Plunder, steal. Destroy.
Decent folk cry all the time.
Many behave like whores.
Act like HELL.
Big sprawling crime city--crime all the time-
Good girls stay inside
or where the cops can watch----.

Linda Charles Steele

THE GIFT

I have seen the hand two times before,
and I will know,
if I see it once more.
Some people will turn away in disbelief,
not me -
For I believe that life is more..
than something you can see.

Bill Carper

OH JEFFERSON

Oh Jefferson
Is your dream fulfilled
Has democracy fulfilled
Or is it still a dream
Oh Jefferson
Oh Jefferson
What can we do
This apparition has appeared to others before
And lost to greed
Oh Jefferson
Oh Jefferson
You saw the unconquerable
But not the unpurchasable
Amassed wealths crush of right and reason
Oh Jefferson
Oh Jefferson
Monstrous corporate structure with insatiable appetite
Billowing smoke and flame from its innards
So dense the head cannot be seen
Oh Jefferson
Oh Jefferson
Must negligence
Fostered by psychological manipulation
Be the tool
Oh Jefferson
Oh Jefferson
Your spirit
A lagoon beside rapid water
Remains undisturbed at civilizations request
Oh Jefferson
You did all you could do

Eva Faye Compton

MONUMENT TO ACHIEVEMENT

Proudly, the colors furl
Atop this stately, classic structure;
Viewed by many, near and far
With wondrous admiration.
Through pillared portals, walk both great and small.
Famous footsteps fill the halls.
Echoes of great voices, long since stilled,
Absorbed in bonds of alabaster walls.
Rooms resound with busy sounds
Of destiny, being formed for all.
Sunshine fills the large rotunda,
To light the croft where historic artifacts
And people's handicrafts are shown.
For those who care,
This beauteous spot, here chosen,
That all may share,
This working "Monument To Achievement".

Linda Sutherland

SUICIDE PUT ASIDE

To Noel, My Precious Son

I sit in flickering candlelight...
And sip my wine to hide the night.
The man of my youth I loved in vain,
Mourning I cry in lonely pain.
The blade, cold and sharp, against my wrist...
Darkness and death lie in it's midst.
Desperately I search for thought of hope
When just in time for me to cope
I hear a murmur from yonder room,
A little blue-eyed, honey-hair boy subsides the gloom.
And motherhood screams inside my soul; I'm needed still!
And what is this, my child, by fate or God's will?
And dawning light draws nigh...
The shadows are scorned, they seem to die.
Pity turned the other cheek, my nature void of self thought,
For his very life is in my hands, I shall prepare his lot!
Suffering had no stronghold on his need and love for me
His simple beauty and innocence hath set torment free.
And ever will my head hold high in remembrance of this plight
For my spirit was saved from fiery hell and freedom had it's flight.
Our souls adjoined, flesh of my flesh, oh tender babe of my womb,
Yes, I am; because of your existence, safe forever of this threat
And suicide's desolate tomb...

Ann Harper

MONEY

Money, Money where have you gone; looks like you just slip right out of my hands. I won't worry, I won't cry, I'll just sit down and pray that you'll be back again.

Money, Money is that you at my door: come on in and sit a while. Money you must know yo gave me a lot of heartache and pain, but most of all you are the best friend I ever had.

Money, Money now that you are back, give me a loan and hit the sack. If you leave before I do, put the money in the sack. If you don't put the money in the sack, be sure to get your hat!

Hell Money, you been so nice and kind we'll have cocktails at nine, only to drink a glass of wine. Money, Money this is so long for now, hope we will have cocktails again at nine; if not, I'll just lay down and die.

Mrs. Anna Maria DePohr

COME WITH ME

Come with me,
Let us sail out on the sea
to the island,
quiet and silent,
nobody has ever seen
and let us have a dream.
Let us walk together,
I will show you my hidden bays,
my secret ways,
my home and my shelter.
Let us walk together,
don't say a word
let another voice be heard;
don't touch my hand,
forget the world on the earth,
let us dream together.
Close your eyes,
become noble and wise,
feel the immense sky
and do not ask why
we are here together.
Let us have a dream together,
a dream nobody can give us
nor take away from us:
the dream that you and I
belong together.

Patricia Kearney Brennen

BENEDIXIO PERENNISA

In this night of the new barbarians
the lamp of the monasteries
is still a Wondrous Star;
it's that constant
a beacon, that luminous
with the Word of God
In this night of the new barbarians
the labora of the monks and priests
is a living Te Deum;
it's that plain
a song, that sound
a prayer
In this night of the new barbarians
the sons of Benedict
are a rain of manna;
each one
is that perennial
a gift, that nourishing
a blessing.

For the Benedictines on their sesquimillenium.

Mary Bruce Starling

IT WAS A NIGHT!

It was a night one cannot forget!
How many times has this been said?
It could refer to terror or death,
Even to pleasure in someone's bed.
Observe the black cushion the tiny winking stars,
No moon to compete with yellow light.
One could almost touch great mars,
Symbol of war and strenth to fight.
The future is in the dreams of men,
The ones who meditate all night long.
They planned the deeds accomplished when,
All others condemned all things wrong!
Suddenly one night--it's all been done!
It was a night remembered by every one.

Debbie Brumble

TRIBUTE

For years had I wandered in desperate searching, until alas, your life and mine entwined, became Reluctantly, at first, in fear of pain so often rendered in situations of the heart. Building gradually to a fiery passion, engulfing us both in the flames of our youthful desire.
The blaze has long since died- a quiet death. Escaping slowly so as to go unnoticed. Leaving, in it's stead an eternal flicker of passion, gleaming amidst the vast sea of respect, concern and genuine affection we have cultivated in love, one with and for the other.
Today, then I rejoice in our lives. A rare tribute to situations of the heart.

A. "ZAI" McKenzie

WITH SYMPATHY—TO MY FRIEND

I find it hard to choose the words to describe what I want to say
To try and lift your spirits up and you out of dismay
I cannot give advice right now on what I think you should do
Fore, I've never experienced the type of loss that you have just been through

Even though you've said to me
yourself about things you plan to do
The loss of your mom, is what concerns me for I have a mother too
It's a very sad thing, when one falls victim to death's unpredictable toll
As it has no exceptions, or particular victims it strikes both young and old
And though it's said, as time goes on some memories will cease
I want you to know, that I really regret the sadness that this brings
I wish the rest of the family well hope everyone's in good health
It's all left up to you now dear so please take care of yourself.

Alma D. Guadalupe
UNTITLED
Wish I could describe
so intense and strange feelings
I wish the dreaming was forever,
to remove the mask, the time
and give this life of our's real meaning.
Wish I could tell you
how real present is,
waiting to keep you near me,
well, I just don't know all the time.
Wish you would love again...
it will be a dream come true.
don't doubt, don't be scared,
stay close, open your heart and just...
love me. Be here by my side.

Jack Rosenberg
WHEN I WALK INTO THE LIGHT
Tight are the bonds that bind me
Neck and foot and wrist;
Link by link have the chains entwined me
In their tangled twist.
Still, though the deepening shadows oft
May turn to darkest night,
This, too, will pass like a whispering breeze
When I walk into the light.
I must search within my inner self,
Where lies the hidden key
To open the doors of darkness
And set my spirit free.
Though my path to life's contentment
Is a rocky road at best,
I will only reach fulfillment
Through my faith and will and zest.
And if my knees should falter,
And I lose a step or two,
I must awake each morning
To greet the day anew.
For, as the raging storms at sea
Return to calm at last,
So will my nameless fears abate
And belong to a distant past.
To rid myself of apathy
The first step must be tall;
Then link by link, in patient stride,
The chains of bondage fall.
Then will my soul be free once more,
No longer fraught with fright,
When I throw this cloak of darkness off
And walk into the light.

The Rev. Dr. Charles M. Simon
WHAT IS GOD?
The sun, the stars,
The galaxies;
The restless oceans
And the inland seas.
The rolling hills
And the rugged peaks;
The cities crowded
And the deserts bleak.
The wind, the wave
The clouds, the rain.
The forests green
And the fruitful plain.
All growing things,
All teeming life.
The world of peace
And the world of strife.
All express God,
Divine, Complete.
And man, in His image
And likeness, replete
With choice,
Which is the God-given leaven
Whereby man creates
His own Hell or Heaven!

Mari A. Olson
LONELINESS
Why, Why?
Shall we let our flower die?
I sit in the park alone
You loved me once yet
You're Not by my side!
I watched the happy people
Walk
Merrily on the sidewalk;
No problems.
You left me and my sadness
Wrecks my life.
You're the one I've always wanted
You're the one I've always cared for
Yet you mangled my soul with words of
Hatred and unlovingness,
Bye, Bye
Good friends of mine we left our
Love forever
And now I'll let it die forever
Alone in the park.

Audre' Morgan
A CONCRETE CREED
It is better to know what you don't want,
Than to think you know what you do...want.

ks peterson
UNTITLED
Some say old loves
never die
Others, they can never be
Revived
I know when I see you...
I turn to run
I am...
torn
Your voice, calling me
Draws me to you
Your eyes demand mine
meet yours
I am calm
Cool...
I am shaking
Breathless...
Your touch is gentle
Your voice filled
with pleasure
You've grown more beautiful
Love cannot die
Only set aside
To be brought forth
by your Presence
Your touch
stirs my blood
Your eyes invite me
to Remember
And I do...
rising tides of joy
waves of anger
and Always-
Our love breaking through
the Light vanquishing
the Raging Tempest
Now I may lose you
to the only mistress
who can call back her Own
the land of your Birth
I felt no one could love you
As I
Despite what differences
between us
Forever is so long
to know you're so far away
To not hear your voice
Nor feel your touch
The fates may have won
Yet I cannot say
Good-bye
For you will be with me
Always...

Donna M. Nagelschmidt
HAPPY NEW YEAR
Alex, open the door-
I have room for more!
Come on in-
there's plenty of gin!
Been expecting you-
and Jackie, too!
Hope you feel fine-
there's plenty of wine!
Want to feel frisky?
have a little whiskey!
After you roll the drum,
why not try the rum?
If you feel in a fog,
have some egg nog!
I guess we should wink-
'cause neither of us drink!
Look I'm a poet-
bet you didn't know it!
You're cute as a deer-
how about a beer?
I wish you a spectacular
New Year!!!

Lee Frampton Miller
WHERE WAS THE MOON
(For Betty)
Where was the moon
As the sun arose
And the sky removed
her nightclothes
Too often the twinkling
Stars escape
from their evening home of twilight
And fade to black in the night
The sunrise creeps
as the city sleeps
Uncovering roads in the distant dark
which keep the two apart
Where went the frozen dew
on the grass
Why did it melt so fast
What was it in the sky that night
that brought something out of my past

Bonnie S. Wilkerson
LIFE
I looked at life and life looked back
With sadness in its eyes
Its head bent low from pain and care
Such agonizing cries!
I said to life, "What good are you?"
"Your days are hard and few."
But life with gentle voice replied,
"My destiny is up to you."
"You can only see the bad in life
If that's what you prefer
But then when trouble hits you hard
Remember what you've heard."
"My destiny is up to you," said life
"Much beauty you can see
Just look for good in everything
Be kind to those you meet."
"For it isn't so much how long you live
But how you stand the test
Give love, and joy, and happiness
Then surely you'll be blessed!

Bertie Murphy
SOMETHING GONE
The passing days have flown away
To never come again, they say.
If I believed your love was gone
Never again the rapture known
Of loving eyes and hungry arms,
I'd simply die today.
If I thought a hundred years from now,
We'd be together in a life so new
I could smile and dream awhile
And simply just want you.
To never know a lover's arms
Or tender throbbing sighs
To always long for something gone
From those soft gray eyes.
The emptiness of days and nights
Stretch endless on and on.
To always yearn for bursting lights
I hunger to be born!

Fae S. Farrell
SHE...
She stood at the window
Looking out,
People were there
Walking about,
But ... To her eyes

The street was bare
. . . .
No one was there.
She turned to the room
Looking about,
Children were playing
Ready to shout,
But ... To her eyes
The room was bare
. . . .
No one was there.
She walked 'round the children
Out of their sight,
Looking thru rooms
First left, then right;
She came to a mirror
In it she did stare
But . . . .
No one was there!

Richard Eugene Oliver

ON BEING SAD

I must be on the hill at twilight,
Especially in the fall.
To sit and watch the sun go
down,
To feel the wonder of it all.
But as the sun slips out of sight,
As the quiet of night comes on;
My mind begins to search the
past
And the things that I recall,
Causes tears to dim my eyes,
And turns my heart to sad.
I see the faces of friends now
gone;
The sound of their laughter,
The sharing of love.
Things that used to make me
glad.
Their passing was just as quiet
and sure,
As the setting of this days' sun.
But no matter how much I miss
them now;
I would not ask for their return.
For I could not bear to have
them see,
This cloak of sadness which
envelops me.

LaVerne A. Jorissen

AN ORCHID ISLAND

Brown eyed, brown skinned
children,
Shining like the water,
Catch the waves in Hawaii on
the Kona coast.
It is young, it was barren, this
mountain,
Rising from the sea, the peak,
Mauna Kea.
Volcanic at the crest, it erupts
and smoulders.
Birds feathered the island with
new seeds.
Blossoms of pointsettia,
plumeria, hibicus,
Tulip trees grow out of the
black lava.
Hurricane winds brought
sweet "uala",
Coconut, "niu", taro, for poi,
"kalo".
Gentle people came by canoe
from Polynesia.
In season, Hawaiian natives
used reeds
And skins decorated with
feathers
To make music for songs of the
Pacific.
Near the lush green forest of
the fern tree,
as though thrown from a giant
lei,
Orchids fall on an island
pathway.
Under the sea, fish like wild
flowers,
swim and multiply in living
coral.
Bright yellow, yellow as a
canary,
A purple, tinted yellow toward
the tail,
A small grey, with an orange
sun near the gills,
Orange, like the sail of the
glass bottom boat.
Hale Halawai Park, and
couples picnic.
Workers chop bamboo branches
with a machete.
In the pavillion, classes in
karate,
For children, and lei bedecked
weddings, watch
Brilliant sun sets beyond the
rim of ocean.
Kona lights and shopping
malls entice tourists
To shop for shells, mu-mus
with shirts to match.
Hawaiian Islands, a string of
jewels in the Pacific.
This is the locket. This is
Orchid Island.

Pamela B. Daddario

THE LORD PREVAILS

One way or another
The Lord prevails
Bringing us to our knees
As we continually fail.
So many things go wrong
Thinking we can persevere
Lifting ourselves up alone
Without Him to rear
Constantly bumping those walls
Of desperation and fear
Not humbling ourselves to Him
letting Him see us clear.
He and He alone
Can help in these times
Just ask His forgiveness and
grace
He'll strengthen us and we'll
climb.

Miss Ruth E. Nesom

WITH GOD INSIDE

Someone in despair was heard to
say,
There's no good news in this
house today!
Beloved, remember, with God
inside
We have good news what 'ere
betide.

For God is love, and love is of
God
Expressed simply in a goldenrod.
While God's angels hover over
us,
They sing a jubilee
When in our faces, God's
likeness they see.

Though our dreams may be
shattered,
The way dark and dim,
Heavens portals shine brightly
For those who trust Him.

Valerie D. Richards

THE REALITY OF CHRISTMAS

The Christmas season is upon
us and it seems it's lost its
way,
For the meaning of the 25th is
quite a glorious day.
A child was born to a virgin
queen, in a manger long ago,
He was born to be the son of
God, but no-one seemed to
know.
His father was a carpenter who
tried to teach his son,
But little did his father know
the power of this One.
He traveled far to heal the sick
and show the way to all,
And if you look back in history,
there's a bad part you'll recall.
They called him names and
criticized, but Jesus took all in
stride,
Then Peter helped to kill his
Lord, three times to be denied.
They hung him on a cross that
day, between two filthy men,
And a sign which read, "The
King of Jews", was hung above
his head.
Before he died, his last words
said were, "please forgive them
all,"
And the son of God died that
day and no longer would walk
tall.
I hope the meaning of Christmas
makes you stop and think a
while,
Of the peace, joy and love we
share for the passing of one
smile.
I wish to you the best of days
this holiday can bring,
And hope that this reminder
brings back special thoughts
again.
My love to all, and lots of cheer,
For a joyous Noel, and a Happy
New Year!

James N. Carnahan

A RICH MAN'S VIEW

Said the rich man to the poor
man
"I like the things you do;
Always fixing this or that,
Your tasks are carried through.
That which you so wisely repair
A rich man throws away,
But you in your wisdom mend it
For use another day.
Your friends are many, kind and
true,
Your home is filled with
laughter,
But when folks come to my
house
It is money they are after.
No heart—felt joys are known
to me,
No friendly lights are burning;
No loving kiss of children seek
The joy of Dad's returning.
Give me the simple joys of Life,
Let me stop to smell the rose;
Let me labor for my bread
Thus I'll earn my night's repose."

Michael D. Allan

STARS, TREES AND BLADES OF GRASS

If it should take naming all
the stars in the skies, or
counting all the trees in the
forest till I get with you,
then I'll do it. And if that
is finished, then I'll count
the blades of grass in open
fields till I get with you,
because my place is alone
while I'm away.
I sat alone and dreamed of you
to pass the time away,
and though we are so far apart I
dreamed about the day, when I
could hold you in my arms and
count those stars with you, for
the times we spend together are
so precious and so few.
The trees in the forest are my
promises, and them I plan to
keep, and though now we are all
alone my promises are just as
deep. The blades of grass in
open fields are the days I'll
spend with you, cause the love I
give with all my might is
honest, open and true.
My place is alone, while I am
away. The Stars, The Trees, The
Blades of Grass are just a way to
say,

I LOVE YOU

Mervat Takla Doner

YOU WERE SMART

You are the light
Of my sight,
You are my very delight!
Inspite of the warning,
Of what I feel now!
"You were smart;
No matter how,
You had to start."
You bring sunshine,
To my Life!
Amen.

Tamara L.Bremer

WHAT SHALL I DO?

I am the lonely one.
Troubled is my heart.
Many I have met and seen go
by.
Now I have but one love who
walks upon my heart.
I am the sideshow for onlookers
to laugh at.
What shall I do?
Am I destined to be distant in
mind?
In choice? In love? In life?
Living inside my heart is a soul
that reaches.
Reaches for attention, peace of
mind, companionship;
Only to be mocked at by others.
Trying to succeed but only to
fail.
What shall I do?
Now the sun shines brightly
above me.
Along comes another love into
my life.
Happy am I to open my mind
and heart.
I am cherished, adord, loved.
My soul awakens to live
peacefully.
No longer shall I hide.

No longer shall I be hurt by
ridicule.
Now I can live a more tranquil
life.
Thanks dear lord, for sending
this loved one my way.

Pam Hamilton
UNTITLED II
I'm in love with. . .
I want
Name witheld
out of fear
Of what might be said
unspoken
shadows
lurk about
Of rejection
from the very one
I hold dear. . .

Florence A. Lux
ARMSTRONGS OF THE WORLD
Armstrong sounded funny and
unimpressive to me
Since I tried to get reason why
I had that last name.
It is like an identification or
heir's badge.
Unbelievably I inherit this
baptised name!
First Armstrong in fourteenth
century named Alex Fairbairn
Was new laird of Mangerton,
Scotland changing surname.
Twelfth century Fairbairn
became surnamed long after
Faybeorn, Earl of Northumbria
whose last nickname
From sword feat was enviously
"Siward the Strong Arm".
Yngling was firstly a Swedish
family name.
Siward is popularly known in
Shakespeare's Macbeth.
Armstrong-Fairbairn-Yngling
could be hyphened name.
Three thousand Armstrongs
during sixteenth century were
Exiled from Scotland
withholding their proud
clannish name.
Twentieth century finds three
million Armstrongs
Being scattered widely in
world keeping their frame
Of long pedigree, tartan, motto
and heraldry.
Would they try to keep up
this difficult breeding game?
Would they join Armstrong
Association of the World?
Would they be indifferent
noting surname of fame?
Any Armstrong is so welcome
and free for membership.
Each should be counted fully
for number just the same!

Margaret Marsh Knowling
MY MOTHER LOVES VIOLETS
My mother loves violets.
'Tho' winter lingers-white
and chill-
And Spring is yet unheard
Nor seen-no touch of green,
But only quiet waiting
Hushed and still;
Yet thoughts of violets
Sing of other springs:
Cool, tender-scented bits
Of yellow sun
Caught in purple depths
And nestled in green-glossy
leaves.
With what joy
Captured in a fragrant handful
A grateful heart receives!
My mother loves violets.
She loves them clustered
Upon her china teapot;
It's iridescent sheen
A glowing compliment
For heart-shaped leaves and
purple bloom,
Joyous and bright.
She loves them scattered
In gay abandon
On elegantly royal
Gold-touched creamer-flecked
with light—
And tiny-footed sugar bowl.
Violets. So lovely. A whole
Garden patch caught forever.
My mother loves violets.
Is it that she understands
Their shy ways?
Remembers fragrances of past
days?
Do they evoke a memory
Of woodland paths-mossy-lined
and cool;
Filtered sun-light sparking
On jewel-like bits of blue
And purple in the shadows,
I know that their rare beauty,
Their tenderness, their fragrance
Speak of life-Color, motion,
music
Speak of life;
Tiny, tender things,
Cool greens, warm suns and
springs
Are part of life.
My mother loves life.
My mother loves violets.

Dorothy Renas
WHY
We shed a tear from time to
time for all the years gone by
For things we did - or should
have done
And so often wonder "why".

Why should it have to be this
way, that I should lose again
Sometimes it seems we'll never
win
That all efforts are in vain.

We think of friends and loved
ones, who from our lives have
gone
And "why" we always seem to
ask
Should I be left alone.

Poor lonely, tired fools are we
who are always wondering
"why"
Why this world has to be so
cruel
And at times we wish to die.

But there's one thing in this old
world that eases all the pain
It's a book we call the Bible
Read it once - and then again.

In this book you'll find the
answers, in His word you'll
find relief
Then in this world you'll find
contentment
Not just loneliness and grief.

We are what our Father makes
us, abide with Him and you
will find
The simple art of understanding
And a perfect peace of mind.

Nancy L. Wilson
BESIDES THE BASICS
Here I sit amidst my children
all aimed at different goals,
I sigh in frustrated silence
pondering Gods reasons
for my being the guiding
influence on all their precious
souls.
I held them to me tightly
when as babe
I rocked them through the
night, silently praying through
the years that I could raise them
right.
I've raised them to be loving,
understanding,
kind and just,
I can only hope when they're
grown that I have earned their
trust.

Marie C. Cryan
I AM ONLY A CHILD
I am only a child so please
excuse my mistakes and love
me for what I am, instead of
what you would like me to be.
Accept me with all my imper-
fections that hopefully will
disappear as I grow into
adulthood.
Please don't scold me when I try
to follow my peers, no matter
what the situation, for if you
would only look back and
remember, that is how you
learned right from wrong.
So please give me the same
opportunity.
I'm sure all my decisions won't
be the right ones, so please be
there to help me as your parents
were for you.
All too soon my childhood will
be over, never to be regained.
So Love me for what I am and
please, please remember *I am
only a child*, as you were, for
just a little while.

Dawn B. Ericksen
AS THIS MIND WANDERS
Spattered thoughts on a canvas
so white,
Shed the attempts of an artist
searching in the night.
Distorted illusions of idealistic
shapes and sizes,
epitomizes abstractness
colored with disguises.
Forging into realms and
territories quite unknown,
he becomes enlightened on
this creation, realizing he
has grown.
Imaginative realities in full
view, creating,
the absence of words, ultimate
relating.
Discovering an awareness of an
illustrated nature,
a pallet of ideas, with canvas,
do concur.
Sensitivity in the sketching,
projections of the mind,
The next form to be
conceived, the artist will
find.
A visual brainstorm in a
cumulus of color,
establishes an understanding
and a seeking being
composed by this author.

Michele Butts
LIFE'S POETRY
Life is begun;
With the universe we are one,
All there is, is what's inside.
Don't fear emotions you haven't
tried,
There is peace,
With understanding the pain
will cease.
Let your senses
Bring down the fences,
Built by the lies
That brought your cries
And caused your grief.
All that's needed is belief.
Let your heart feel
All that's real.
Happiness and tranquility
Can be reality;
Awareness is the perfect
symmetry;
Life's poetry.

Heidi M. Jaeck
GLORY!
I asked: "What?"
Your response was simply:
"His Love."
I asked: "Why?"
You answered:
"Because it is written."
I asked: "Where?"
You replied:

"If you look closely, you will
find it everywhere."
I asked: "When?"
You said:
"Everyday of your life."
I asked: "Who?"
You shouted:
"JESUS CHRIST, HIS ONLY
SON, OUR LORD!"

Verena Sieck
TODAY'S MOTHER
Your hand holds mine so firm
and tight
you're sleepy still, the day so
bright,
your hair shines golden in the
light.
No scars of life have touched
you yet,
no daily challenge to be met,
you're just a babe, sweet and
bubbly,
like a puppy, warm and cuddly.
I have to leave you now, you
know,
enjoy your day, the kiss I blow.
Some day, I hope, you'll
understand
that I'd much rather hold your
hand.
For as long as you wish, for the
entire day,
play and sing, and not go
away—
I think of you throughout the
day,
you're ever present, not in my
way—
your face keeps flashing through
my mind,
reminding me that you are one
of a kind.
Some days, though, go by so
slow,

I feel like leaving now, just go.
I don't want to let you wait,
can see you standing by the gate.
You tell me about the dog you drew,
and the big fat bone you made him chew.
The little girl that pulled your hair,
was made to sit silent in a chair.
I'm glad you cannot feel my guilt,
as I tuck you later in your quilt.
Your voice keeps going through my mind,
when, mother, when will you have time?
I gently step into your dream,
kiss your face, so soft like cream.
I touch your hair,
may you never feel sorrow!
I promise you Babe,
tomorrow,
tomorrow.

David C. Vernon
FOR LOVE OF JENNY
Jenny, sweet Jenny, You're like a breath of spring;
The soft caressing springtime breeze,
That dances with the budding trees,
And makes me feel so fresh and new, sweet Jenny.
Jenny, sweet Jenny, You're like the summer sun;
That life sustaining orb of light,
That fills me with a sense of right,
To love you and love you more, sweet Jenny.
Jenny, sweet Jenny, You are my every dream;
As the nocturnal flight of my very soul,
Drifts in the night to seek its goal,
Of loving and caring for you...for you, sweet Jenny.

Evelyn Chavez
CITY SERENADE
Freeway traffic
rumbling
like drums
in a parade
People
walking
on the sidewalks
click-clack
Harmonica man
clapping
and making music
on the mall
Children
tinkling chainlinks
on the playground
happily winging
People
listening
to their transistors
in the park singing

Meredith Diane Moll
QUEST
You can't bring back time,
It's like holding water in the palm of your hand,
Grasping for something which is gone,
A futile search for yesterday,
Perhaps we have to drink deeply from the past,
In order to know the shorelines of tomorrow

Janet Rita Cullen
THE AFFIRMED STORY
(My Tribute to a Champion)*
He started out a two year old,
Beating all the rest,
Won championship honors,
In both the east and the west.
At three, on to Kentucky,
and the Derby was all his,
He beat a Bay, called "ALYDAR",
who had just missed.
The same two in the Preakness,
were leading all the way,
But when it was over,
the little chestnut won again, this day, in May.
Then on Sat., June 10, 1978,
The Belmont Stakes was run,
as these two horses were neck and neck,
the rest of the field was done.
They went head and head, until the end,
and at the finish line,
"ALYDAR" had lost again,
to the little chestnut, for the seventh time.
THE TRIPLE CROWN had been won,

in June 1978,
This beautiful chestnut
could now be labeled—great.
It was a great big win
for a horse with a heart of gold,
and his Jockey, Stevie Cauthen,
who was only eighteen years old.
Trainer Laz Barrera, was happy too,
with his horse that was all heart,
but, really for the both of them,
it was just a brand new start.
For the owners, the Wolfsons,
and all of HARBOR VIEW,
This day was a bright one,
and a big dream come true.
But in the summer, and in the fall,
the horse was not the same,
For he went on, and lost to the great "SEATTLE SLEW";
although, he was very game.
in the JOCKEY GOLD CUP,
he was in the rear,
But when 1978 was over,
He was named HORSE OF THE YEAR.
He then went back to California,
for a little rest,
was back in January,
to prove he was the best.
with JOCKEY STEVIE CAUTHEN,
losing every race,
Trainer Laz Barrera got LAFFIT PINCAY, JR.,
to take Stevie's place.
From then on, the little chestnut,
started out to win,
And never had another loss,
ever again.
he won the CHARLES STRUB STAKES,
and the SANTA ANITA HANDICAP,
despite his trainers illness,
he still kept coming back,
He won the HOLLYWOOD GOLD CUP,
on June 24, this year,
Became the first horse to win two million,
With his retirement, getting near.
He rested in the summer,
at the Saratoga meet,
They made him an Honorary citizen,
Which made his racing life complete.
Then at Belmont,
on a wet and muddy day,
The good looking colt,
Put the WOODWARD STAKES, away.
He still had one more to go,
before he reached the end,
And in that race, was "SPECTACULAR BID",
another great rival for him, again.
But on this October day,
He had no match in this race,
and once again—in the Winners Circle,
so cool and full of grace.
The son of EXCLUSIVE NATIVE"—
"Won't tell you"—won,
The JOCKEY GOLD CUP,
His racing career now done.
On his way back to the barn,
He had the look of a Champion on his face,
For he knew, he just ran and won,
his very last race.
He looked like a champion,
thru and thru,
As there aren't many like him, in horse racing,
just a very few.
Now he's going to Lexington,
To begin his stud career,
In hopes his foals will be like him,
and win, year, after year, after year.
He's become HORSE OF THE YEAR again,
It has been confirmed,
The horse This tribute is dedicated to,
Could be no other, then,
"AFFIRMED".

Cozie Schultz Dias
THE IOWAN FROM SAN FRANCISCO
Of kitty-cats and cable cars;
Of candlelight and beans;
Young lovers strolling on the sand
In clean, cool, cut-off jeans;
Of mason jars and antique cars;
Of houses, wall-to-wall;
Of stately old Victorians;
Parks, color-rich with Fall;
Of winding thrills on cloud-kissed hills;
Of towers touched to sky;
Of Chinatown and dancing clown;
Of trollys trooping by;
Of silver fog and Christmas nog,
St. Patrick's Day parades,
Soft sunsets on a golden shore
In twilight's soothing shades;
Of flower carts and tender hearts,
And concerts in the park;
The magic of a million lights
That twinkled in the dark;
Of these and more the heart recalls,
Secure in memory's glow--
The heart that lived and laughed, and loved
The City, a long ago.

Lois Buzzell
THE LIGHT
There's nothing like a breath of spring
When the winter storm has gone.
There's nothing like a friendly smile
Or the singing of a song.
There's nothing like the glowing flame
Of the Light that will always be--
The Light of Goodness that shines from above
To lead us and keep us free.

Cindy Dennison
SNOWFALL
The snow falls slowly
silently upon the winter's
ground covering all the things of life.
The paths we walked
on warm summer nights
the stream where we pledged
our love
are covered with snow
never to be seen again.
But the memories of you
and the things we've shared
will always be in my heart
where the coldness of the
winter's snow
can never cover or touch.

Janet F. Ledington
A DREAM FOR YOU AND ME
I have a dream for you and me,
A lovely cottage by the sea.
I'll sit at your feet before the fire,
As you stroke my golden hair.
We'll walk together hand in hand,
We'll build our castles in the sand.
We'll be together through the years,
To share our laughter, joy and tears.
If you know this can not be,
There is no future for you and me,
Please don't tell me, not just now,
Let me have my dream somehow.
If when I'm old, I'm all alone,

My heart grown cold and hard
as stone,
I'll have my dream of you and
me,
In my lonely cottage by the sea..

Nora Raleigh
OUT OF AN ARCTIC GALE
Locked in a quest
for Nature's relenting
out of an arctic gale, apprised
the bluejay's eye and mine
held constant, inviting
whatever union of despised,
so my suppliant hand
took warmth as it gave
repetitive light caress
on the feathered huddle-
brightest hue the solely brave
awaiting,in quiet on a branch,
the aforeseen of plunder:
knave itself to know but under
the spell of that naked winter
yet the hint of resurrection;
then spurning human up and
away beyond sight's reach in
being flight it escaped to
eternity - in memory, a blue
reflection.

Clarice Tesh Brewer
WHAT DID I MISS
I was worrying about tomorrow,
And missed the joys of today.
I ran for cover when it rained,
And missed the rainbow in the
sky.
I hid from storms and rolling
clouds,
And missed seeing the sun
above them.
I was too taken with my own
ills,
And missed helping those with
more.
I was always too busy getting,
And missed the joy of just
giving.
I had no dreams, ambitions, or
goals,
And missed satisfaction of
success.
I hesitated too long in decision,
And missed out on many
opportunities.
I was so afraid of failing,
And missed the pride of
winning.
I was always suspicious of
others,
And missed having many A
friend.
I was always criticising others,
And missed seeing my own
faults.
I frowned, fretted, and fussed,
And missed knowing how to be
courteous.
I never smiled, just looked
down,
And missed ever seeing A smile.
I never rendered service to
anyone,
And missed many A returned
favor.
I was always hurting and hating,
And missed the wonder of love.
I never used my many talents,
And missed the sharing of
myself.
I lied about everything and
everyone,
And missed ever recognizing
truth.
I raved and cussed at every
chance,
And missed the beauty of our
language.
I over-indulged in everything,
And missed the power of self-
control.

I never had an animal pet,
And missed having A loyal
friend.
I never held a tiny baby close,
And missed feeling soft velvet
skin.
I was always a coward,
And missed feeling strong and
brave.
I had much bitterness in my life,
And missed having sweetness in
my soul.
I was forever complaining,
And missed seeing my many
blessings.
Til now, I'd never prayed to
God,
And missed having peace in my
heart.
I can see it all now!
I've missed so much in life!
Dear Lord: I plea, forgive me,
And let me make amends.
I nearly sent my soul to Hell,
And would have missed the joy
of Heaven!

Joyce Graham
SHE TOOK HER KEY
From room to room
She cleaned the floors,
Picked up the trash
And washed the doors.
She scrubbed the stool
And cleaned the sink
Washed out the tub-
Then took a drink.
When all the cups
Hung in a row
And her whole house
Gave off a glow
She took her key
And locked the door.
She knew that-
He'd be home by four.
The house was clean
From wall to wall.
But she was gone
Beyond his call,

Barbara A. Ziegler
UNTITLED
I have said goodbye to you
A thousand times inside my
mind,
Sometimes with tears of despair
And at other times with anger.
I have thought of every reason
To put you away forever
From my dreams, my needs, my
caring,
Only to bring you back in a
moment
To posses my very being,
For nothing more than the
simple sound
Of your voice saying "Hello".

Pamela M. Kingsley
FIRST SNOW
Finally you've come.
Oh how I've waited, so long.
You are so beautiful.
Falling with grace from
heaven.

White sparkly dust.
So tiny, so significant.
Though my day was hard,
you have made my face shine.
How I wish I could fall with
you,
and feel the cool breeze.
A silent misty sand.
Free, so free.

Fly, and float away my friend.
Finally you've come.
Take me with you.
I've waited so long.

Tracey A. Parkhurst
LOVING YOU FOREVER
(Dedicated to my Father and my Mother)
If they say I never loved you
You know they are a liar
for I am gonna love you
till the stars fall from the sky
for you and I.

David H. Leavens
I LIVE

A Woman said to me one night,
your face is a pleasant touch
upon my mind.
I replied: Young Woman,
Thank You
But;
I am but flesh
I came from flesh
I will always be flesh
Until the hand of death
come to take my soul,
and leaves my flesh behind,
and allows my spirit
to live on forever
apart from my flesh and soul,
I LIVE

Michael Keith Brame
UNTITLED NIGHT SONG
Tis' Morning.
The creative mind waits
until the breath of fresh dew
settles upon
the nests of its young.
The butterfly will spread
its powerful array...
and fly to the parts
we want to go.
And the never seen friends
and the past
and the glorious present,
"rejoice".
The night song--
Oh night
sky so white
with blackened eyesight
plays on til midnight.

Kenneth W. Brooks
LADY SUCCESS
Lady success petite nice and
neat
New clothes she wears most
every day.
You may call her the boss, but
rather instead
I'd call her a friend for she
helps her fellowman.
She has the authority to keep
you in line
Settling the difference with a
kind gentle voice.
Finesse in her dealings she
manages well,
Getting the job done with
no praise for herself.
Most everyone knows she came
through the ranks,
Deserving her position the
first of it's kind.
It's a team that she leads, each
doing his part.
She appreciates the duties
that each one performs.
When it's time for a favor she
won't run and hide,
But does what she can while
giving her smile.
Dividends pay in the course of
the years,
Kindness wins friends in
every phase.
The respect she has won in such
a short time,
Makes everyone know she's
one of a kind.

Mary R. Ingram
EPITAPH
Should you wish to gather
flowers for me,
I'd ask that you rather
let them flourish in their native
soil, and when next you chance
upon them, remember me.

Dorothy T. Warner
THE PROMISE
That which I seek I am told I
already am.
Am I peace? Where do I seek
you,
Am I love? In what place do I
find you.
Am I abundance and fullness of
life?
Have you somehow evaded me
too?
Wait, but I sought you all
elsewhere,
That which I seek is already
there.
I need not look for you peace in
my neighbor, or even in my own
household.
I no longer look for you
abundance in my employers
payroll.
I need not seek you love in the
words of my beloved.
I do not go to find you health in
the doctor's care.
You are my soul the core of my
being.
You are already there.
So I need only go within, as I
have need of you.

And seek that which I am, my
problems will be few.
The fullness of God's life is
what I am.
His promise was "Child all I
have is thine" then eternal peace
& harmony must be mine.

Cynthia Harris
THE MIRACLE OF SPRING
The softness of the rain, that falls upon my face,
While hand and hand with you I walk,
Silent, and not at a hurried pace.
The dampened meadow floor, beneath our naked feet,
The freshness of the air and the flowers that smell so sweet,
The song of birds flows mystically,
Carried by the gentle breeze.
Green takes the place of barreness,
Caused by the winter freeze.
The sounds, quiet and serene,
That whisper in my ear.
So calm, so different, than any other time of year.
This reborn newness, to all of mother natures things,
This to me is magic, the miracle of spring.

Robert Alan Casey
FRIENDS
The Golden Gift of friendship is so wonderful and fair;
a friend will stand next to you and always care.
through all the days that come and go,
you should get more friends, make them grow.
A friend is one who can see thru your eyes,
you know that friend will tell no lies.
A friend is someone who can mend your heart,
make you stand tall when you're falling apart.
A friend is one who will come to you,
stand by your side and always be true.
A friend is joy, and will constantly share,
always trying to master your despair.
A friend can cast your fears away,
and always listen to what you say.
The most valuable thing is inside a friend;
A FRIEND is someone you can have till the end.

Bridget Auenson Burnett
ONE WAY TRIP
The signs are all around us
The Messiah is soon to come
He's coming back for His Church
And He'll take them every one
Believe, my friend, and trust in Him
Put away the cares of this life
Give Jesus all your worries,
Your fears, your problems, your strife
He died for YOU -
Was crucified on the Cross
He came to save the world -
The oppressed and the lost
See the Cross - it is empty
His grave - it is too
He lives - forevermore
But, what about you?
Will you be ready
To meet Him that Great Day?
He's coming to take us home
Give yourself to Jesus - He's the Only Way

Margery Packer
REWARDS OF RECOVERY
Bruised, but gallant, eight wounded phalanges
Close ranks along the footboards of my couch,
Buttressing the vigil valiant
Of two staunch sentinels,
Who, swathed in sterile gauze
And plastrons of adhesive tape,
Maintain the injured flanks.
Solemn captive to the martyred mission,
I repine upon a mound of pillows,
Scanning the wall-to-wall territory
Of my dimlit cloister;
Half-ambulatory;
Peek, housebound, through its bivalve blinds,
Morphous as an oyster.
A vacuum, save for footles and sundries,
The salons of my mind expand;
Machinate through weeks of endless Sundays
Cosmic creations, or literary;
While bones glide toward a tentative jointure,
Slow to dovetail with flaccid ligaments,
Fancy explodes with free-spirit figments.

Carol Lee Shepherd
THE WINDMILLS
They take shape on distant horizons.
They move in the breeze as by unseen forces.
On approach, they waiver and grow dim.
Warriors of dark, unknown wars.
They seem to be moving away slowly.
The water falls in the desert and becomes dust.
But you hear the creak of slow life
You feel the splinters of worn boards, in your hands.
The windmills are real.

Karen DeMouth
NO STARS
There aren't any stars for me to see
They're hidden from my sight
My mind isn't what it should be
Something isn't right.
My heart is empty, my body's weak
But I never will give in
To that something strange inside of me
That something from within.
I've had this piercing heart before and you've given it to me again
You say you want to be with me but you never seem to say when.
The moon is bright tonight, it's fullness lights the sky
I'm sitting here thinking of you as time is passing by.
But then dawn comes and the sun is slowly rising
I seem to fall back on my dreams as I look across the horizon.
It's a beautiful sight to see and it could hypnotize you
The way you've done to me, when I look into your eyes.
I know I should leave you and never come back, for what you put me through
I know I could, but I don't want to, I just can't end it with you.

Michael Jankoviak
I SMILE
I smile at the beginning of each day. . .
Yearning for a day better than the previous
The people come and ask questions
Hoping to gain knowledge and assistance
I am but all too cooperative and helpful
They too, now smile, for I have taught and they have learned
Their gratitude passes with the words of thanks
And they move on. . .
I smile at the beginning of each day. . .
Yearning for a day bigger and better than the previous
A lost and confused soul has found me
And seeks companionship and closeness
Asking only for a friendly smile and its warmth
They too, now smile, for they were in need of a friend
and I shared their need
Their gratitude passes with the words of thanks
And they, too, move on. . .
I smile at the beginning of each day. . .
Yearning for a new day yet bigger and better than the previous
A new friend is met
The differences are thrown aside and the friendship is dwelled upon
They share their innermost feelings, not afraid to bare their
Own emotions
They too, now smile, for they trust one who has proven
himself trustworthy
Their gratitude passes with the words of thanks
And they, like the others, move on. . .
I smile at the beginning of each day. . .
Yearning for a new day yet bigger and greater than the previous
The people have been coming for a long time now
and have found what they had searched for
They have matured and become stronger
Believing in themselves and what they do
They now possess the ability of infinite growth, both emotionally
and spiritually
And they too, smile, for they know now their own worth
Their gratitude passes with the words of thanks
And they, like all of the others, move on. . .
I smile at the beginning of this day. . .
Yearning for a new day yet greater and more prosperous than the previous
For I know that others will come
Searching for answers, advice, encouragement, a smile, and the
warmth of friendship
Yet I also hopefully reflect on this day
Wondering if this might be the day when one might stay?
But alas, the time is not yet right
I smile. . .and they move on

Kim Stroschen
TO BE FREE
We are the tomorrow
We're young but old
We are the yesterday
Only wanting to grow.
You want us to be mature
But you continue to keep us hidden from the monsters
outside.
We have to face those monsters
like in our childhood dreams
We become dragon slayers
Dressed up in shiny armor.
And when the fights are over
And the dragons are slayed
We come in laughing
for finally life told us his
secrets
He kept hidden from us for so
long.
Let us out
Let us breathe
Let us feel the sunshine on our
faces
Life is too precious to waste
We need our freedom
Like you need yours.
People aren't meant to be locked
up
They're meant to sail like
seagulls in their clouds of
dreams.
They're meant to swim in
oceans of pink and purple.
We're just meant to be free.
If you'd give us a chance
We could prove ourselves.
Prove we're capable of growing

up
Prove that we can love
And that we can laugh.
Don't you see
We only want to be free?

Elaine Anne D'Alessandro
WHAT, LORD?
What do you see, Lord
When you look at me?
Do I bring a smile, Lord
Or a teary spring?
At times - I'm so close, Lord
I could just hug you!
Other times - I sin and sink, Lord
What do you think?
At times - I'm obedient, Lord
I feel your love.
Other times - I disobey, Lord
What do you say?
At times - I'm walking with you, Lord
I see "us" in action.
Other times - I do *my* thing, Lord
What do *you* do?
But always - you're with me, Lord
In both large and small ways!
What do you see, Lord
When you look at me?

Edith Lackey
TOGETHER
Together we are
Together we share
Together we love
Together we wed
Together we bear
Together we leave
Together we were

Connie Caskey
BALLETTE SCINTILLA
I see the dance
of the stars
the celestial ballet
endless, timeless
each pinpoint
of light
sending it's rays
to mingle
with those
of it's neighbor,
a universal dance
to the strain of the cosmos

Daniel Dante Sarnelli
MASKS OF DECEIT
I see mankind as actors on a stage
Bearing grinning masks, hiding their inner rage
With artificial faces,
Their hearts become impassive
With a shriveled self-image,
Their confusion becomes massive
And with a fading identity,
Their thoughts become tossed
Till the mask becomes dominate,
And identity is lost.

Gwen Stehr
UNTITLED
Two red roses my son Jon gave me
Said one rose means "I love you."
I ask why were there two?
One rose is cause you love me mom.
And the other cause I love you.

Eileen Sullivan Wallace
UNTITLED
When I look
At myself
When I see
What you have done for me
I know
I'll never stop loving you.
You have
Brought out the good in me
You have
Helped me see the good in others
You have
Shown me how to live
and taught me how to love.

Sharon Rene'e Smart
L—O—V—E
Love
a word
trying to express
what words cannot.
Love
an emotion
desired by all
possessed by some.
Love
an expression
of a feeling
held deep within.
Love
a word
trying to express
what words cannot.

Mary Dupont
I SHED A TRUTH
Wrapped in your love, I stroll
the lane- mid dew-kissed butter-cups, and
thistle sails, and
kitten tails;

Twirling in my happy gale.
I ran barefoot through swaying
Grass, and kissed the pall of
Winters past-
The southern breeze,
The warming lease,
slow inward creeps.
I climbed the hill, I climbed
Before, and
Thought about my freedom then-
It filled my heart that burst to
Shout!
I cried inside, and
dried my eyes, and
cried inside.
OH! Tell me naught will really
Change-
the air,
the sea,
the hill,
nor I,
When left behind to memory:
My barefoot fling with
worldly things.
Birds filled the air with nuptural
Tune that matched that old
Reluctant song
That filled my heart to burst!
You called my name, and
Back I rushed
Apple blossoms filled the air-
The meadow lark to its mate
Called and I am nestled in your
Love so warm and snug-
Now, arm in arm, we walk the
Lane- I am yours, and you are
Mine.
I shed a truth, and found a truth
More dear!
The air!
The sea!
The hill!
and ME!
OH MY!
My love for you is REAL!

McWallace Braxton
WOULD YOU BELIEVE ME, IF I TOLD YOU I JUST SAW A UFO?
Would you believe me, if I told you I just saw a UFO?
I saw this shimmering, saucer-shaped thang land in a field!
My girl and I were jus' under an old oak, telling each other our love is real.
Would you believe me, I saw this hugh space craft a few minutes ago?
I was kissin' my girl and playin' with her so.
Would you believe I saw this giant thang land?
I stopped what I was doin' and said, "Looky yonder, Ann!"
Would you believe me, I saw the hatch to this thang let down.
I was jus' telling Ann about her pretty skin, all soft and brown.
Would you believe me, I saw two darn critters in it, walk out!
I was still tryin' to calm Ann who was restless and movin' about.
Would you believe me, I saw these varmits totin' something like a flashlight that with a single beam of light, fell a big ol' grizzly bear!
I had stopped what I was about to do to stare!
Would you believe me, I saw those darn critters pull that old bear in deir ship,
I can't say anymore becaus' Ann jus' pulled me down for a soulful kiss on the lip!
Would you believe me, I honest to goodness did see a genuine UFO!
I didn't see that thang take off becaus' of my girlfriend's big afro!

Alice Cleveland Daugherty
POSSESSED
(A Cry in the Night)
I am possessed, yes I must be.
I see things that others can't see.
These things I feel are very real.
They are things that others don't feel.
I'm on an arc above the plane.
Often I am filled with pain.
This raging torment fills my mind.
I know that peace I'll never find.
I struggle with emotions so intense.
I live in solitude immense.
I try to find the place you dwell.
I look for heaven, live in hell.

Ercel C. Standeffer
JUDAS
Judas! Why did you fall away?
We, like you are fraught with guilt.
Like Peter deny, like Thomas Doubt,
Did we not sell our souls for less?
Then spit your name to hide our nakedness.
Our Lord forgives us every day.
Judas, why did you fall away?

Patricia Thrash
CASTLES
Castles in the air
Are made to look very fair.
Some have faults, later to find,
They tempt the eye and the mind.
Later they fall into decay,
Even dreams go astray, and
Some just fade away.

Renee I. Cocchi
THE FINAL SCENE
I must realize that it is over,
I must realize one simple fact,
It was a good stage production
But we just could not finish the act.
You took the lead, and I had the female part
Our love was our guide and our director
I thought that there was enough from the start.
Scene one of act one started
And we became a hit like I knew that we would
But our acting was only for the audience
And our actions became misunderstood.
Scene two began, we got our curtain call
But as we made our way on the stage
I knew that we both were about to fall.
We memorized our lines as they were written
We thought our life had the perfect script
But the words that we said to each other lost their meaning
The scenes of our life would never fit.
We were only actors
Being liked and reviewed by our fans
And as scene three of act one ended,
So, too did our plans.
The play finally ended, and we were all alone
The stage was ours for a brief moment
The audience had gone.
There were no more line that could have been written
No more words that could have been said
We performed the final scene
And now all of the scripts lines were read.
We glanced at each other
There was nothing more that we could do

And as I made my way down
from the stage, I started to cry
Because I knew that I would be
going without you.

Joseph C. Tweddle

THE WORLD OF POETRY CONTEST

The World of Poetry Contest makes me reminisce and try to win first prize, as homeward bound, my heart doth bound, in the dark I scrutinize,

The breeze that blows about me tis cool to fevered brows, through pastoral land where fox and wolf scan, along I watch the cows.

The frosts that passed, have at last left their dreary mark, what leaves on trees; in the hilly breeze, chatter in the dark.

As my river home appears, I'm moved to tears, for no longer there's a light: where mother use to patiently wait, this roaring towboat night,

As I climb into my lonely bed, I wish, I had more hair, if the cover don't smother, my poor old head, then soon I'm cozy there.

Then I reflect, who can reject, my story in rhyme so true, then I repose, in peace to doze, till day breaks anew.

Bette Roan

WE KNOW YOU'RE THERE

In flowers that bloom and the
sky so high,
The roaring sea passing by,
We know You're there -- You're
everywhere
In the trees and the wind,
The sun and the storms,
Fresh dew on the grass in early
morn.
We know You're there -- You're
everywhere.
I raise my voice in praise,
In thanks for all the gifts you
gave.
You know our faults, but love
us all,
And on each, shed your shining
rays.
You fill the world with miracles
and love,
Please walk with us and keep us
straight,
Dear God, extend your hand and
decide our fate.
We kneel and pray and often
say,
But for the Grace of God we'd
lose our way.
We know You're there, You're
everywhere.
Dear God, You're everywhere.

Louis S. Wagner

HUMANITY

A computer that thinks
A plane that can fly
A new little suit
A neat little tie.
Alone in the woods,
He sees a small creature,
He runs for his life,
Then looks for a teacher.
The boy sees a bird
Fly through the air
And throws a rock
Without a care.
Down it falls
As dead as can be,
Yet he is proud,
He killed a bird you see.
Alone in the woods,
He's been there awhile,
He sees a small creature
And lets out a smile.

Edith Lackey

CROWDS

uninterested
in society
mumbles
hatred
of anger
expressing
mass
agony
hanging
on to
an object
that lifts
the spirit
high
to a peak
of interest

Madeleine Meigs Blowers

THE HORSE

Last night a stallion sleek and
black
Stood silently without my door.
No rider sat upon his back,
His stately grace to underscore.
Entranced with life's
impassioned store,
I noticed not my visitor
And when impatient hoof was
heard,
I thought the whole thing quite
absurd.
Although one day I know I'll
ride,
This night I bade him step aside,
For I was young and life
enthralled
And he could wait until I called.
Each night a stallion sleek and
black
Stands patiently without my
door.
No rider sits upon his back
His stately grace to underscore.
The days sped quickly into mist.
My burdens grew by twentyfold
And life and hope did scarce
exist.
My soul to drudgery had been
sold.
Dark friend how free you seem
to me.
No hand denies your dignity.
Your pride envisions freedom's
wind,
Unbridled passions without sin.
Tonight a stallion sleek and
black
Will finally greet me at the
door.
My weary soul upon his back
Will ride with him for evermore.

Connie Patterson

LOVE'S LIMITS

Nameless fears, tossed by pain-
A minute's rest, then hurled
again
Into doubt filled shadows of
my mind.
Does one kiss, maybe two;
Simply saying, "I love you;"
Cure all - license you to be
unkind?
Like blades of shining steel,
Your two-edged words I feel
Piercing the warmth I once
hoped to find.
Healing, more sure of hope
Than lawful or illegal dope,
Love is not *ev'ry* ill's anodyne.

Jean Floyd

TRIBUTE TO MY MOTHER

I do not want to wait until some-
day when you are dead,
And have these things left in
my heart, the things I wish I'd
said.
And so I'll use this time today
and try to tell you dear,
I love you, and your voice, dear
Mom, is always good to hear.
I hear it in so many ways, tho'
we are far apart,
I hear it in the memories, of
youth, locked in my heart.
In memories of childhood days,
when you, with patient love,
Taught me the things that I
should know, of earth and up
above.
You taught me how to wash the
clothes, and make a bed with
care,
So everytime I do these things, I
see your sweet face there.
Because you taught me about
God, the wondrous things
He'll do,
When I am bowed in prayer,
dear Mom, I see you praying
too.
Altho' the things we do at times,
Don't always please each
other,
There's nothing that can come
between, this daughter and
her mother.
Now I am grown, we live apart, I
am a mother too,
And tho' I try, I'll never be, as
good a mom as you.
As time goes on, I'll try to live,
one day just like another,
But out of each, I'll take the
time, to thank God for
"MY MOTHER".

James S. Barr

REMINISCING IN A FOX HOLE

Oh think not my spirits are
faded and gone
Mid the smoke of this raging
great fight;
Nor think I shall ever cease to
go on
Dreaming of you each day and
each night.
When bombs fall around us and
death seems so nigh,
When we cling to the ground
in cold fear
And machine guns chatter from
the brush near by,
Still I find myself dreaming of
of you, dear.
Should I be overcome during
this bloody strife,
May a cross mark my grave
with the few,
Who have gone down in battle
and gave up their life,
And may my last thoughts be
of you.
It's a thin thread of life and may
it never break
While we are young and so far
apart.
Oh, guard our affections, dear,
for our sake,
May you ever be near and
dear to my heart.
Darling, I love you and I always
will.
It was the happiest day of my
life when we met,
May the Angels in Heaven
protect us until,
We together, can watch life's
golden sunset.

Beau Stine

LIFE AS DUGITS

Spring came and time to move
on,
for his friends he wintered
with had gone.
Northward, making a mere ten a
day,
searching each night for a
warm place to stay.
Each night from where he would
lay,
watching the stars as they
twinkled in play.
Thinking of the pot of gold at
the end of the rainbow,
knowing it was out there, for
his friends he would show.
Early morning came as the warm
sun aroused him,
his coffee began to boil in a

can made of tin.
Brewed from throw-away
grounds he had found,
then suddenly he was startled
from a nearby sound.
Moving through the brush
toward the sound,
he broke into a clearing and
there he found.
Right there in front of him was
a beautiful girl,
with long golden hair that
sparkled in every curl.
Her beauty was breath taking as
she set up on a branch,
asking where she had come
from, her reply a nearby
ranch.
This moment had taken him as

though a dream,
helping her down they walked
to a nearby stream.
As they set they exchanged
their tales,
he told of how he loved to
ride the rails.
She spoke of her lonely life
on the ranch,
and wanted to leave at her
first chance.
He stated his life was not her
way,
so she coaxed him to her
ranch to stay.
Seasons came and seasons went,
nigh on a year he now had
spent.
He began to miss the life he
once had lead,
knowing on northward he
must head.
Early morning came and he said
his good-byes,
while his love stood wiping
tears from her eyes.
As he walked he felt his life
empty and lonely,
knowing he must return and
make her his one and only.
As he grew near the driveway,
he knew this life was his and
here he would stay.
Years have passed and a new day
born,
for now he has finally found
that pot of gold.
Being the richest of all to have
all of this,
to spend with the rest of his
life.

Marguerite Henry Atkins

WING'ED GIFT

I wonder why the birds seem
never sad
Why they can sing
How they can sing
All the day long
And sing as cheerfully through-
out the night.
Is there no time at all when joy
runs cold
When they are dry
Indifferent
Devoid of love...
To them is sadness utterly
unknown?
When question I the remedy for
pain
How soothe the wounds
Of sorrow deep
I hear their call--
Their incessant cry--"Look up!
Look up! Look up!"
But God's to know the fount
from which it comes...
For they are His gift
Bright winged gift
Created to sing
And lift sad mortals to His heart
of Love!

judith kranz

A PLEASANT THING

it would be a pleasant thing
to love you
like picking blackberries
they fall into an apron so
willingly & without effort
sweet bland ripe
they can be jarred & stored
all winter
i think i would enjoy
to go to my pantry
on late november nights
& see them stacked so neatly
on the shelves
labelled lidded arranged
i wonder & i wish i knew
if my scratched lips
still tender
would heal with the warmth
of firelight
reflecting on these unending
immobile rows
or would they still bleed
still long
for the taste
of a scarce & nameless root

James S. Barr

THE REST OF MY LIFE

Never shall my affections be
taken away,
No matter how long be the
strife,
And I dream of our being
together one day,
I'll adore you the rest of my
life.
My humble affection is all I
can give,
All my fondest dreams are of
you.
I promise to love you as long as
I live
And may my fondest dreams
all come true.
Life would be lonesome without
that sweet smile.
Oh, I'd miss the gold in your
hair.
I'll not be gone forever but in a
short while,
I'll return, for my heart's with
you there.
The rest of my life I shall see
your sweet face,
Feel the touch of your hand
on my brow.
And when we shall have ended
life's weary pace
You'll know how much I love
you now.
There shall be a white cottage
beside the lane,
And the garden shall be filled
with flowers,
Red carnations and roses which
bloom in the Spring
To help beautify that home of
ours.

Susan Davis

CLOSENESS

As time went on, I felt myself
getting closer to you.
I was not afraid to spend quiet
times with you.
I liked reading together,
walking, taking a ride,
Or even going to the beach and
listening to the tide.
I never worried about those
times during the day,
When there seemed to be
absolutely nothing to say.
It was fun learning to share the
absence of sound,
It is a special kind of intimacy, I
have found.
I wanted to build a closeness
with us,
Built on the sense of who we
were, built on trust.
I wanted a trust that would
enable us to reveal our true
selves.
I didn't want things to get in our
way, like a quest for details.
I wanted to enjoy that feeling of
intimacy, I wanted us to
share,
To share each others lives and
to be totally aware.
You couldn't accept this, I don't
know why,
And always accused me of
having another guy.
You accused me wrong, you
must believe,
I love you dearly, can't you see?
It hurts to know you feel this
way,
Now we must go our separate
ways.
Time heals all, so they say,
But I'll always love you in a
special way.

Leon Douglas Bibb

THE OTHER SIDE OF THE SKY (The Flight of Space Shuttle "Columbia")

Gleaming white in the morning sun with its face skyward is spacecraft Columbia—the pinnacle of aviation, our link with the future, our link with the stars.

She is the grandchild of Wilbur and Orville's frail flyer, which also awed us as she, too, looked skyward and then joined eagles in their flight.

Columbia—like a giant arrow in the taut, bow of an archer—pierces the sunlit air, bound for the other side of the clouds, and well beyond them, too.

With engines screaming, the fiery-tailed Columbia—riding atop twin columns of yellow flame—leaves this spinning sphere for the craft's true domain, the quiet and crystal—clear darkness of outer space. That is Columbia's adopted home, where she frolicks in a world of endless sunrises and sunsets, well beyond the grasp of Earth.

Like her ancestor—Lindbergh's "Spirit of St. Louis"—she knows her destination. But how far, how far away it lie. For she was made to fly and that she does best.

Dancing on the silvered wings of flight is Columbia, high above the blue Earth— this giant glass marble with its wisps of white cloud accenting its intoxicating beauty.

Leaping from the contrails of pioneers who have gone before on Mercury, Gemini, Apollo and Skylab, Columbia marvels, too, at the majesty of space and the grandeur of Earth. With impassioned reverence of the endless ocean, Columbia streaks from one piece of vacuum to another. In the serenity of Earth orbit, where none other has flown on wings, she is still close kin to Kittyhawk in that she responds to gentle nudges of those who point her nose, but still give her rein.

Spacecraft Columbia is a link to the past, to those who studied birds and for centuries dreamed of flight. She links us to the sands of Kittyhawk and to the Brothers Wright. And we are all passengers in this aviation adventure, for who among us has never dreamed of soaring on outstretched wings?

Young and Crippen may have Columbia's ear, whispering to her to fly higher and faster and beyond Earth's bounds. But we are all in the co-pilot's seat, representing ourselves and those who have gone before, leaving their mark on aviation's path in the sky.

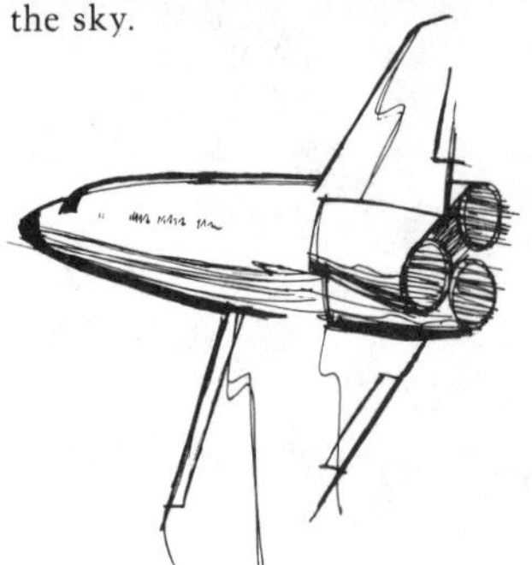

Touchdown on land does not end it, but instead denotes success, shouting the beginning of the endless dawn.

for a brief moment on Earth's fleeting clock, we and bird Columbia left this world, piercing the morning air like a dagger's tip, hurling ourselves out of Earth's grasp. We slipped through halls of air like a sword slicing the fog in a duel at dawn. We floated where there was no air, actually treading the vacuum of outer space. And like a seabird in search of food below, we arched our back and dived toward Earth, feeling its atmospheric sting in our urge to return home.

We have weathered them all—nature's elements—until Columbia's wing flaps dropped in home port as the rest of the world applauded our scheduled return.

But there will be other days for Columbia and us, as again we will fly off into the beckoning blue to perform our orbiting ballet. We will dance to the rhythmic sounds of nature itself, as Columbia and we search for what mysteries lie on the other side of the sky.

Bobby L. Jefferson
COMMITMENT
I don't want to lose you
nor let our love be as grass
That withers in the scorching light
instead let's be like glass
That shines brighter in reflection
and fogs with the storm of rain
Yet after the blue skies' birth
you never knew the pain
We must plant our hearts
deeper than before now
And giving more than ever was
must be our new vow
I don't want to lose you
nor be as the wind midwest
To make myself heard for time
then quickly take a rest

As I look out my window, there is a building close by, it's shabby and torn. And been burned inside: I begin to wonder; time to explore;
The women could come and go and still have their pride. Down the stairs, up the street, and closer to the door, "Hurry, now hurry, before someone sees you open the door.
I opened and went inside, there was a lady close by and baskets of apples, oranges, and peaches stacked sky high. And the vegetables are so fine. So I'm the laughing Jack-Ass with the cackling cry.
If you want to monitor your pennies, and put your marketing at ease, get acquainted with the lady she's a friend of mine. Time to explore, let your conscience be your guide.
She is a nice lady, don't judge her by her wit. She's tricky and sly, won't cheat you a dime, her hospitility is so fine. It is a shabby building, don't judge it by it's cover no marks of honor to dignify, just shuddering noises, fixed in my mind.
But her friendly ways were so fine, thank you, and come again was her reply. And I'm the laughing Jack-Ass with the cackling cry.

Nelson D. Mays
IT'S A GIRL
It's a girl,
She's daddy's pearl,
Sweet as can be,
She's part of me.
Sandy brown hair, bright brown eyes,
Pretty brown skin, and little tiny thighs.
She's special, she's cute, she's altogether new,
She's lovely, she's cool, and wonderful too.
She laughs, she plays, she kicks out her feet,
She cries, she eats, and falls right to sleep.
She has her mother's eyes, also her nose,
But it's definitely my eye-brow and pigeon-toes.
And there's something you can plainly see,
Everyday she looks more and more like me.
Mom calls her "Stuffin," I just call her "daddy's little girl,"
Together, we plan to give her the world.
But what will she be?
Can't wait to see!
She'll run the family business, inherited by her,
Use the money to buy diamonds and fur.
She'll be like her mother, and stand by her man,
Love him, take care of him, and help him when she can.
Maybe an athlete, that goes to the Olympics to win,
Or a lady priest and guide people from sin.
Ms. Teen, Ms. Black, Ms. America, Ms. Universe,
If she enters those contests, you can bet she'll be first.
A doctor, a lawyer, a civil rights speaker,
A business woman, accountant, or bookkeeper.
Or maybe she'll travel the world, and just have a ball.
Knowing her, she'll probably do it all.
I'll take care of her 'til she decides what to be,
Because I love her, and maybe one day She'll take care of me.
You know that Crystal is so must fun,
Now I think I will make me a son.

Dan Carroll
THE VAGABOND
Young Charlie looked upon the school and decided to abscond
The gentle master stroked his beard, "That little vagabond"
And thus he came and now he went and how he broke the rule
The kindly master's grim comment, "As stubborn as a mule"
Thus a rugged life began, intrigued by wanderlust
Thru rain and shine, thru days and nights and highways grainy dust
A startled mother rose one morn; she heard the rooster crow
And Charlie's bed was empty, a note—"I love you so."
They scanned each road and highway, they probed the village pond
"Call off the search," the master said, "He's just a vagabond."
A mother young and beautiful, whose only pride and joy
Would long remember words so harsh about her only boy.
Silence gripped the vineclad cottage, lonely pealed the village bell
And no sign of little Charlie, only whispered words that fell
Bravely stood the gentle mother, prayerfully she lit the light
Whispering to the awful silence, "Charlie please come home tonight."
But the wild winds know no mooring, neither does her restless son
Days and nights will fall like snowdrops, skirmishes now lost and won
How the fireside leaps in warning, nite winds whining at the door
Sleep o'ertakes his greatest lover, hope is but the great encore.
Swiftly grew the handsome Charlie, shot up like restless flower
Slim of waist and broad of shoulders never known to quake or cower
Lo inside the dim bar-room, choked amid the noisy throng
Silence hushed each tinkling table, just to hear him trill His song.
Time rolled by and so the season, miles and miles of road and rail
A mother watched and hoped and waited, year by year to no avail
Every tavern, road and highway from the east unto the west
Heard the songs and aye the stories of big Charlie at his best.
Then one night a moonlit evening, in a road house on the coast
Charlie sang unto the rafters, sang until he saw a ghost
Peering in a dim lit corner, Charlie could scarce believe his eyes
Trembling, cowering, pale and feeble, his old master tried to rise.
"Master," cried the startled Charlie, "how come that I find you here"
Then a well dressed waiter snorted, "he's just here to spear a beer"
"I was once your teacher, Charlie and your future did predict,
But that wrong has now engulfed me, I am just a derelict."
"Oh great master how it grieves me to see you in this awful plight
Never have you taught a lesson half so well as this tonight."
"Seldom did you e'er obey me, now it's past or maybe late
Your mother lives, and still at sunset, waits beside the garden gate."
"Like an angel in the moonlight, face so young but hair so white
And with all my heart I beg you, hit the rails this very night."
Charles was startled, stunned, bewildered, like a giant in a trance
Threw his money to the master and with one repentant glance
Burst the chains that once had bound him, headed for the swinging door.
"I will blow this life forever, but will ride the rails once more."
Alone into the night he staggered, softness filled the misty air
By the railway tracks he waited, one more trip without a fare.
Familiar rumblings break the silence, now a giant headlight shines
Black smoke rolls across the prairie, while the hungry engine whines
Safe inside the flying boxcar, a weary traveller makes his bed
Peace at last within his bosom, new horizons lie ahead
Slumber gripped the happy nomad, wheels nor whistles make no sound
Romance of the road is over, wayward son now homeward bound
Spring has burst upon the wayside, water swelled each stream and pond
Far away the master whispered, "God be with you vagabond."
Wildly flew the mighty engine, careless now, it knew the route
Heeding not the frantic hobo, "Hold it boys the bridge is out!"
In the wreckage by the village, people hurried to and fro
Whispering, calling, peering, probing, someone heard a voice so low
"Hurry, take him to the cottage, to the house upon the hill
Gently bear this shabby fellow, there is life within him still."
One old lady, roused from slumber, lit the light, unlocked the door
Knowing with a mother's instinct, it was he the stretcher bore.
Calmly did she kneel beside him, vainly did he try to rise
Gently stroked the grimy forehead, Charlie smiled and closed his eyes,
Now within the village churchyard, where the hands of time are still
Strolls a peaceful, white-haired angel, fashioned by a greater will
Carved in beauty from the dawning, lined by life's uncertain hand
Clothed in sunset's crowning glory, looks upon the fresh dug sand
And with heart and mind and spirit, smiles unto the great beyond.
"May your train ride thru to heaven, sleep in peace my vagabond."

Karen Halil

LIKE MEAD FLOWED

Within the boundaries of a blue
eternity,
a gash marred the symmetry of
conformity—
a hole in the sky.
And from this gash
poured forth smelted diamond,
and smote the mind.
When smitten,
the mind bowed.
Time merged to perform.
All of day and night abandoned
their duties,
flocking to watch
around dusky lanterns alighting
the stage.
Gracious was the mind in
performance,
but beyond all laws.
For the dance remembered
the future.
And the song awaited the past
in a day yet unborn.
But in the endless blue of the
sky,
pagan was the merging of time.
All beauty was unseen,
when distinction was forgotten.
Morbidly considered
was this where tomorrow was a
day ago,
was this song where yesterday
visits the future.
But the gash was real,
and time no longer followed the
straight path.
Time was a place,
where the heartsong of all
creation
like mead flowed.
Indignant was the marred
symmetry
lashing out with brutal
consistency,
until screams
cut off dance.
The mind had battered its living
body
against stark cliff walls.
Bloody
then was the wall of convention.
Madman,
was the mind now deemed.
And convention placed
past in slots
and future in separate boxes.
Madman,
the aching rules the world has
named
the only reality,
is choking all breath.
The breath
like the scented breeze laughing
in a place.
A place where reality
threads designs of dew upon
time.
A place
where the heartsong of all
creation
like mead flowed.
Now the mind is a madman,
a stinking corpse.
Convention smiles and praises,
well done.
Past
Present
Future.
Do not forget, repeat after me.
Poor madman,
now you are part of reality,
but you have lost the way.
And so many ways were to be
known
once.
But madman,
you have their reality.
Clasp it close
madman.
Swallow it
madman.
And when gnashing claws
dig through your living entity,
simply hold it closer.
You are the madman.
Spewed are your entails
around bloody feet.
Ignore
the sound of ripping flesh.
Perhaps you were a madman
long ago.
The reek of your rot is
destroying all beauty.
And beauty in turn,
blackens until the strips of its
flesh hang in decay.
Now you know what reality is.
Gossamer has been vanquished.
Forgotten is the way,
forgotten is the place.
But you have reality
madman.
Noble and grand.
Reality.
Repeat after me.

Joseph H. Young

MY MORNING PRAYERETTE

I thank you 'Father' for this day,
To bless me in this kind of way:
Keep 'Wisdom' and
'Knowledge' on the shelf,
And give me 'Strength' to
help my self.

Michael L. Holt

ORANGES!

Something happened to me
today and it helped me to see,
just what a simple orange really
means to me.
What? A poem about Oranges?
You ask in jest.
But wait! Read on, let me tell
you the rest.
As I ate the orange and
pondered its cool taste,
I realized that its design was not
made in haste.
Questions began popping in my
head without hesitation.
How does it stay so cool
without refrigeration?
What manner of man could
have designed such a thing?
I think not many, not any! and
my heart begins to sing.
For I've just lost the best friend
that I've ever had.
You see, last month, I said good-
bye to my dad.
Vague teachings of youth are
beginning to reappear,
and I realize that I will make it
through the year.
Yes I'm better now and I finally
feel free.
You see, I had just forgotten
that GOD made the trees,
and oranges of course!

Daniel Sosa Coronado

RAIN—-BOW

The joyous love that slowly
drops anon
Brings forth creation and truth
upon
A magical bank and clutter
a-top the sky
And sings worth jubilation and
warmth from the rye
For the specks of dew-wet aloft
my cheeks
Sensate my face with touchlets
of soft sleeks
And in those bodies o' water
setting measure on gage
They rapidly drown me to feet
on a rose from rage
From where I stand to step
once higher
The love has departed to its
song's desire
Yet, I will not weep when I
am to sleep
For binding a-store a light,
leaves heavenly-fast a
sight
Which engulfs my heart
with mystical color
And envelops in cart a
shine of many-a-dollar.

Darlisa Meszaros

TO BE LOST

When I talk, you do not listen.
When I smile, you do not look.
How can I reach you?
I write for you, but you do not
read.
I touch you, but you do not feel.
How can I reach you?
I cry for you, for you have no
tears.
I dream for you, for you have no
thoughts.
How can I reach you?
I love you, though you have no
love to give.
I do all these things for you,
And yet,
You are not aware?
Help me find a way, and soon.
For you are too great of a person,
To be lost.

Joelyn Katherine Foy

KANSAN SPRING PRAYER

The miracle of life;
God giving life in the earth
Rewards the painful waiting
For the seeds of man to emerge.
We rejoice in the silent wonder,
the fragrant ecstacy of lilacs
Blooming in the early morning.
Redbuds dwarfed among oaks,
giving color amidst the
faintest green.
Tiny leaflets crinkly with new
life
Shed their budly formlessness
Bursting forth in all their
innocence
Displaying God's infinite
handiwork.
Children waving;
Caught up in the surge of life
Sun shining mightily in their
smiles
The sky reflected in their eyes.
Oh, Lord, in one great voice
We thank you for the life you
give us
Your bread of life from the very
earth
Your pulsing blood of life's
experience.

Leone Rosamond Wood

ASIENTO

Reap no more, the zonda wind
Nor ponder o'er the Cheetah's
gait-
Feel the flesh yield
Beneath the stake
Ebony thighs through which
Sudan's deep grasses leaped
O'er the plateau and the plain
No longer sway to bongo
drums
Around the Bantu flame;
For shackled and quell'd
In links of steel
Upon the galleon deck they
stand,
Their eyes upon the eagle's
wing;
Chanting the hymns of requiem.

Maureen C. Connelly

A FEBRUARY THOUGHT

It bring's romance to the scene,
on Valentine's Day!
A touch of Spring, still unseen!
The memory of pleasant days,
ahead!
And the vision of a garden
growing somewhere!
Where Winter reminds us, that
he is still here!
Ah February, a time to plan on
days ahead!

Ed Manual

TOUCH

First touch of winter
split the cold pearl
of evening--
dusty glow
lights the blackness.
Inside sitting,
I outrun the thought,
my chair glides freely
on its rockers, but
that creak at center--
must be the pride
of bone and marrow.
Our deep desiring,
we wish to touch
the natural wild
anywhere--leaning
on the horizon,
to return to spring.

Sandy Poske

ON A ROLE

Am I who
I say I am;
What author
penned
this life plan;
Is my world
framed in
colors of me--
Do I see
all there is to see;
In yesterdays
I have birthed the
me of now;
Still, I wonder
how
to form all
this life, energy
and wonder
into a role
that will thunder
ages hence;
How,
Father,
Show me how
to give my
gift.

Roger L. Berkheiser II

DREAMS

Dreams that last forever
are dreams that never come true
tantalizing pictures of fantasy
Dreams for me and you
To be with yesterday's heroes
and among the fools of today
reality becomes mixed with
illusions
As with deception of the mind
they play
One is the loneliest number
That's why I hate to dream
alone
Fantasies fill a void in one's
heart
A friend's now dialing the phone
Dreams are mostly unreal
They just cover up the sadness I
feel
One day my life will be over
My dreams and fantasies will
die too
Those tantalizing pictures of
fantasy
were actually visions of you

Mary McMerrick

SORROW

There are no words I can speak;
Nothing I can say.
Nothing I can do,
That would take the pain away.
How can I be of help today?
How can I help tomorrow?
I wish I could but take a sponge
and soak up all your sorrow.
There's only one word I keep
hearing;
One word I keep thinking of -
May God in His all-knowing
Glory,
Surround you with it always -
"LOVE."

Wilma W. Harper

THE LUCKY THIRTEEN

Back in the Delta in Rodney,
Mississippi, a family of six girls
and seven boys were born to
proud parents Odesie and Etta
S. Williams.
The oldest named Mildred and
her followers—
Nathaniel; Arzola; Lawrence;
Wilma; Ethel; Percy; Johnetta;
Mary Lee; Leon; Leandrew;
Tyree; and the youngest,
Alexander, completed the
"bakers dozen."
This family is happy as happy
can be that God has blessed
all thirteen to be around in
the 1980's.
Memories of life in Mississippi
still linger in their minds and
ties to that State are very
strong as they still have two
members of the family who
continue their residence there.
Pennsylvania is the adopted
State by many of the family
members.
The sibling rivalry of these
thirteen
has kept them on their toes.
The Williams family has made a
contribution to society in
many fields of endeavor.
Their record is one in which
they are proud.
Each gives credit to Momma and
Papa who gave them their
beginning by instilling in
their minds the value of an
honest days work for a days
pay.
Their honesty and integrity are
admirable attributes of each of
the thirteen.
Papa was an exceptional man
with characteristics of a great
leader.
In the early 1900's Papa was the
forerunner of many in the
community by being the first
Black family to have
electricity.
It would be impossible to
describe Momma as she was
not an ordinary woman.
She stood the challenge of
rearing thirteen children in
her stride.
A great Christian woman was
she and she did her best to
instill these qualities in
her children.
Momma was a dedicated wife,
mother and homemaker.
Her family is delighted that she
lived to enjoy visits to at
least 15 states in her liftime.
She lived to experience the jet
age and on many occasions
traveled by plane.
If they had been a little quicker
about the space age, we are
sure Momma would have
wanted to travel into space
as she always believed in
progress.
To the thirteen 31 children were
born and the Williams family
can boast 19 great-
grandchildren.
The family reunion is an annual
event which started in 1961.
Family members travel from far
and near each year to commune
with God and each other.
Their pride in their offsprings
is evident as you watch their
smiling faces.
The future alone can tell what
life has in store for each of
them.

Alan C. Whittaker

LOVE IS NOT LIKE THE WIND

Love is not like the wind,
As love does not die down,
Nor fitfully change direction.
Love cannot be likened to the
moon,
The moon—waxing, waning,
Only occasionally full.

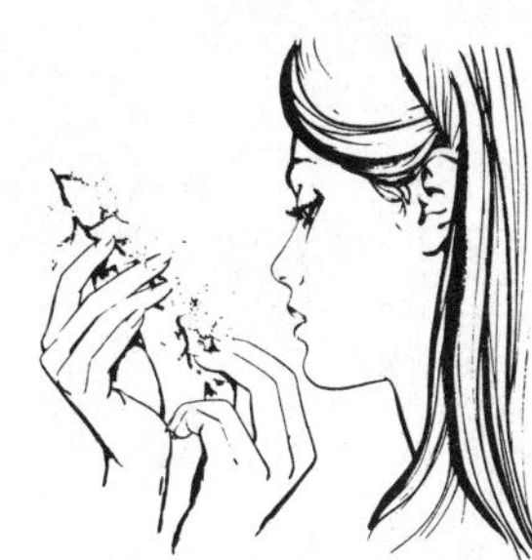

Love is not as the sun,
The sun oftentimes cloud-
shielded,
Just sometimes warm.
Love, rather, encompasses two
people,
Very much together, caring,
sharing,
Doing for each other—growing.
Thus so—their love will have,
Steadiness attained, fullness
gained,
And warmth for all time.

Everett A. Mills

PUFFY CLOUD

You puffy cloud so snowy-white
Born on the trade winds late at
night.
Tomorrow on some dusty plains
You will be some farmers
blessed rain.
Yesterday, before you were born
You felt his curse; you felt his
scorn.
Exactly, at this time in space,
You stand with your head erect
in grace.
Tomorrow will you stand so
proud?
Or will you just be another
cloud?
Have you passed this way many
times before?
Or will you pass but once and
pass no more?

Millie E. Bailey

SPRING

The sky hangs low and ashen,
The wind kicks up her tail
Sending the last few daring
clouds
Away—
With a shriek, and a wail.
Spring is here—
It is short lived.
Winter has returned—
Vengence to give.
Spring will return
And when she does—
Summer will follow.

Sandra Lee Deeds

REALITY

We dream, dreams that will
never be real.
We set goals that will not be
reached.
We hope, hopes that will never
happen.
We plan things that we will
never see.
We pray for peace that doesn't
exist.
We search for real love thats
never been heard of.
But why do we yearn for things
that are not there.
Impossible things we never can
share.
Is that what we are here for?
Is that what we live for?
Is life for real?
Or only a dream.
What is reality really like?
If reality did exist.
Would it be what we are
searching for?

C. Vincent Kroeger

THE BONES OF LOVE

The four-leafed clover is lifeless
pressed between the pages of a
favorite book,
The faded photograph reflects
an image of life
frozen in another place and
time,
Fossilized beauty, bones of love
to be stored away in closets of
memory.
These bones are not for the
practiced eye
of the paleontologist or
archeologist,
They are for the deep of night
without a moon
for a time when winds
whisper echoes of love,
And shadows clone forgotten
memories;
such fragments, dry and
fragile to the touch
are mere residue, ashes of the
flames
that once consumed two
hearts,
and forever fused together two
immortal souls.

Maria Fenesy

A MARCH DAY IN FLORIDA

Leaves rustling by the soft
blowing wind,
Shaking them loose and
tumbling to a mound.
Birds singing sweetly on high
wires,
While wasps are flying close to
the ground.
Nats making whirlpools,
And a lizard doing its mating
call.
The Easter lilies blossoming,
And growing very tall.
The radiant sun beaming
everywhere,
And taking good care of the day.
Nature is giving existence to
everything,
Whether it is at work or play.

Odis Hamilton Jr.

RAINDROPS

From the dark blue sky falls one
little raindrop. It comes down
like a feather even though it's
heavier. It falls in a garden,
and on a stem. Moments later
the bud begins to blossom. A
rose steps out into the dark mid-
night air, just to die.
From the dark blue sky falls
another raindrop. It comes down
like a feather even though it's
heavier. It falls into another
garden, and on another stem.
Moments later the bud begins to
blossom. A tulip steps out into
the dark midnight air, and
droops over, just to die.
From the dark blue sky falls yet
another raindrop. It comes down
like a feather even though it's
heavier. It falls in a garden,
and on another stem. Moments
later the bud begins to blossom.
A carnation steps out into the
dark midnight air, just to die.
From the dark blue sky falls
another raindrop. It hesitates.
"Oh what the hell, come on
guys" it says.

Irene Weems—Phelps

THE LIGHT AT THE RIVER

Out into the world of sorrow,
out into the world of pain
My weary soul sent searching,
for something I could not
regain
I was looking for my lost youth,
how I had wasted every year
Stumbling, falling at the
crossroads, blinded by my own
tears.
Standing on the bridge of
darkness, facing all my
terrible fears
Then a light shown upon me,
my Saviour seemed to say I
am here
What a sense of peace came o'er
me, as I listened to his voice
And I didn't seem so lonely,

there above the rivers noise.
Standing on the bridge of darkness, with the waters swirling past
The river winding out before me, a destiny I could keep at last
Then my Saviour softly whispered, come walk with me and smile
For in keeping my Commandments, your life can still be worthwhile.
Take a step out of the darkness, walk along the river shore
Feel my gentle yolk upon you, sorrow you will feel no more
Leave your burden cross the river, see the light up on the other side
Again a peace and calm came o'er me, as I crossed the waters wide.
So I will walk with my Saviour, as into a world of light, I try
Hand in hand out of the darkness, blinded by my own desire
For the light at the river, made me see a love so true
And life still goes on, even when we think it's through.

Marvin David Reed, Jr.

ALL I WANT

To hold you in my arms tonight
Is all I want to do—
To stroke your hair by candlelight
And tell you, "I love you."
To hold you close and hear your sighs
To gaze into your precious eyes
And share each other's bliss.
To feel your gentle, soft caress
As we lay side by side—
To shower you with tenderness
And love from deep inside.
To tell you that I love you more
Than words could ever say—
To say it's you I'm living for
To love you more each day.
To pray that we will never part
Not even for one day—
To know the love inside my heart
Is yours and yours to stay.
To hold you in my arms tonight
Is all I want to do—
To stroke your hair by candlelight
And tell you, "I love you."

Ms. Martha L. Blankenship

MY ABSENT COMPANION

We met, we married, we laughed, we had love;
Then you were called to that Home up above.
Fleeting and uncertain is life here below.
How long I'll be here, of course I don't know.
Why, on this earth, I was left without you,
Only God in His Heaven does know, 'tis true.
For a reason He left me; I know not what.
But this I do know: Us, He has not forgot.
I'm doing without you the best that I can;
But I do have a secret cry— now, then and again.
Our years here together were the best of my life.
You made it all worthwhile, yes, even in strife.
Those very last years when you were so ill,
You accepted it as our dear Father's will.
You bravely suffered, with no fear or no tear.
You seemed to sense that Heaven was near.
I did what I could to ease your great pain
And I'm so glad you'll never suffer again.
For you, it was a very rugged, up-hill climb,
But you successfully reached the top sublime.
Since that sad day when your heart stop'd still,
Oft I've wished I, too might cross o'er the hill.
I am so very sad and lonely down here below.
Everywhere without you I now must sadly go;
But I know that this will not always be so.
Miraculously, it has helped my faith to grow.
I'll see you, darling, in the sweet by-and-by,
Where living and loving shall never, never die.

Edna J. Barthau

A WINTER' DREAM

My Rose'anna Queen's last bloom lay on the frozen ground.
Long and cold the winter forecast snow has started falling 'round.
I heard the mailman's whistle and with eagerness I went
To open the flag-up box, and then to my delight—I spotted it
Among the mail my springtime catalogue. . .it rested there to
Greet me like an old friend from afar.
I walked back to the house, shook off the cold wet snow and sat
Down in my favorite chair beside the fire's glow.
On the cover of the catalogue was a beautiful display. . .
A Lilium so purely white with lovely budded sprays.
Contentedly I held the book and while slowly thumbing through
. . .I could see the magic of a garden coming into view.
Veronica, frikarti, both as blue as the blue sea, the pinks and
Drooping bleeding hearts, what a wonder I did see.
On and on to yellow marigolds, petunias purple hue, the garden
Of my mind sparkled like the summer's dew.
Achillea bright and sunny, the hollyhocks by the wall, looked
Down upon the lilies. . . the lovliest of all.
How I wished the breath of spring was already in the air,
I'd take my garden tools and hasten down the path. . .
Brush away the salt hay covers, bare the beds below. . .to see
The daffodils and crocuses, the blue grape hyacinths shooting up
Their greening candles like sentinels in the snow.
Another log went on the fire and I sat back in my chair, I dozed
And soon was dreaming that spring was here again. . .
I walked along the pathway and behold my eyes did see—my
Rose'anna Queen blooming there for me.

S. J. Chartier

UNSAID

"For, I am". . .
"Too, am I". . .

Set in love forever.
"Here, am I".
"Too, I am".
Placed in love together.
"Have received".
"As have I".
Given love forever.

Ralph Wappel

THE STRUGGLE

The swan swims with a grace you see,
A daffodil waves in the sun;
With gloomy eyes a shadow is cast
As moonbeams turn to one.
LO! The earth moves in air,
It shatters the mirror of life;
The air we breathe, the breath we take
Puts all in strife.
We know not what is done
To create when we dare,
The harmony of nature unknown, for man,
To possess a gift so rare.

Lora Lynn Lopez

THE HIDDEN KNIFE

Life's
Illusions
marriage and love
living the past and
hating the future
of the passing day.
Love is eaten away
by barbs of hate.
guilt,
the soldering factor
twisted guilt
used to hurt and confuse,
to dig the knife
into the willing sacrifice
of your bloated ego.
Hurt builds as the years pass—
continuous.

Irene Weems—Phelps

DESIRE

Have you ever been to Michigan? Well I want to go!
I want to be there, when the woods fill with snow
In spring, I want to see the first leaf unfold
I want to stay on, until they have all turned red and gold
I want to see the sunrise, outside my cabin door
I want to see the sunsets last rays, across the cabin floor
I want to see the moon as it rises on high
I want to see the stars as they dot the starry sky
I want to meet your friends, from whom I'd never roam
I want to see the house that could have been our home
I want to see you, for you were so very dear
I want to be your friend, if you need me, I'll be near.

Dottie L. Whitman

GOD'S GREAT LOVE

God has plenty of love for all. Let him live in your heart, and you can answer at his Roll Call. All will be love in Heaven above. At God's Roll Call, I will look for thee. I will be standing by the Shining Sea.

God showed his great love when he sent his only Begotten Son to this Earth, where we now dwell. Jesus died on the Cross so we could go to Heaven and live with him, and not burn forever in Hell. The answer is in your heart. Will Jesus say, "Enter in" or "Forever From Me Depart?" God always guides my pen; I can't do this without faith in him. If you enjoyed this tell him so, because it's through him I'm doing this, you know.

Michael D. Revels

SAVED

Circling downward my whole life through was heading for hell.
But then I saw you Lord!
You were standing before me with your arms open wide.
You said that you loved me, and I wanted to hide.
But the shadows were gone cast away in your light,
and your love was strong, far more than I could fight.
You said "My name is Jesus" come walk with me; for
I have many gifts that I want you to see,
So I opened my heart, but not very wide.
Then all your love came bursting inside.
It lifted me up and spun me about,
You showed me the way and I just had to shout
He's Alive! He's Alive!
And he's with me to stay, thank the Lord Jesus,
I'm finally saved!

Ruthie Killinger

LIBERATED

We hear all this about E.R.A. and what the libbers have to say—
Well, I think its about time we also heard,
from the women who are living by God's Word.
The role of wife and mother— it's very plain to see. . . .
it's written in the scriptures, that's what woman was meant to be.
He took the woman from Adam's rib, while in deep deep slumber,

then blessed them and said be
fruitful, and increase your
kind in number.
Woman was meant to be a help
mate, for God created man,
to walk along beside him, and
do the best she can.
God said they should be as one
flesh, and live throughout His
land,
It's all quite plain to grasp, you
see, that's how God had it
planned.
As for me—I'm liberated,
liberated in Christ you see,
for he did liberate me when he
died on Calvary.
As it says in this little poem,
and I hope its plain to see
that you women libbers, do not
speak for me!

Katrina Sandlin—Gillespie

MAYBE BY JUST CARING

I want so to touch you.
I can almost be sure
That maybe by just touching
you,
Your troubles I could cure.
I want so to reach out
And take you by the hand.
Maybe by just reaching out,
I could help you stand.
I want so much to help you
As you go throughout your life.
Maybe by just helping you,
I could save you from all
strife.
But you won't let me touch you,
And you won't let me care.
You won't let me help you,
So I pretend that you're not
there.

William F. Harrington

HEARTFELT RAPTURE

A light afar
Glistens through time
Enticing crystalline signs
Yearning to be nurtured
Our particles bind
Atomically coinciding
They intermingle in space
encompassing realities
Unknown to many, yet loved by
few
Such a road we find
Is so unique, but reflects the
fullness
We long to believe
While God continually invites
us to retrieve
The fruits of gold awaiting our
touch
Amidst passages and backroads
of our minds
Distant dreams await on lifes
horizon
Awaiting to be born.

Linda Bessette

LET THOSE WHO HEAR LISTEN

The lion marked distinction,
majesticly he took his stand.
Said He above, "I am the master
throughout all of the land,
Live in fear and reverence, this
I do command
Let those who hear listen, and
try to understand."
The ox did mark labor and
humbled himself to man
Just as man was forced to labor
long since time began.
Said He, "be humble whenever
you can,
Let those who hear listen,
unfolded is my plan."
Jesus marked the face of man—
in him I call my son
And all who follow in my plans
'til mortal life is done.
Be not slack to spread my word
and hasten to thy call,
Let those who hear listen, I
love thee one and all.
The eagle marked the flight of
life—to immortality,
The freedom from lifes suffering
was given out for free.
All thy crowns and mansions—I
hold in store for thee,
Let those who hear listen, and
answer to my plea.

Connie Jean Redman

JESSICA LYNN

She loves her life
She loves her home.
She loves to let
Her mind just roam.
To years now past.
A certain summer day.
To ice cream bikes and balls,
And children all at play.
She sees it all so clearly now,
The way that things were then.
For now she has a daughter,
Her name is Jessica Lynn.

Margaret Kerr

SPACE AGE SANTA

Hello, Hello, Hello!
I'm your beloved "Old Santa
Claus"
From the snow-capped North
Pole.
I want to remind each of you
kids
I'll be "Jetting through space,"
this Christmas Eve night
My Reindeer are ready for the
"Star Spangled Flight."
Ho! Ho! Ho!
Kids, I'm still my fat and jolly
old self—
Mrs. Santa is well—so is every
elf.
Boys and girls
Be super good; for I'm coming
soon
In a "Jet Powered Sleigh" that
can circle the moon.
I'll be wearing cozy white fur
on my cherry red suit,
With my same jolly face and
shiny black boots.
Children,
My toy factory is working late
each night
To fill the big sleigh all
glittered and bright
The Candy Kitchen is packing
peppermint sticks,
Juicy fruits and chocolates will
be in the mix.
Ho! Ho! Ho! (yawning)
Oh me, oh my,
I'll bet my shiny, black boots
That Dancer and Prancer will
glide through space
All of my reindeer will be
pulling in the once-a-year
race.
Wait just a minute;
My dear Mrs. Claus,
Bring in cookies and my hot
spiced tea,
Also Sweetie,
I need a hot pack on my
rheumatic knee.
Oh thank you Mrs. Claus for
each kind deed,
You're always filling Old Santa's
needs.
Now children
Please be patient;
I'll visit each of you on my
midnight run
The North Pole is making
ready for your Christmas fun
Mrs. Santa and the elves are
working night and day
Santa's reindeer will be in
control of the "Jet Powered
Sleigh"
Special delivery letters are
arriving through snow and
twinkling lights
We are filling these orders for
the Christmas Eve Flight.
There's too much noise in the
Work Shop—
Disco Duck, quit your
quacking please!!!!
Your album is moving like a
northern breeze.
Toy soldiers, stay in line,
until I make my run;
Jack-in-the-Box, Keep down,
you'll have your fun.
Elves, hurry, stop the run-a-
away trains,
Mrs. Claus, oh honey, duck your
head,
From the zooming, new
planes.
Oh dear dollys, please don't cry
For out in this world
There will be loving hearts of
many little girls.
Characters of famous Sesame
Street
All is well, happy children you
will greet.
Excuse me—
Oh my poor aching head,
Old Santa would love to go to
bed—
Oh no, I can't—I have a job
to do—
My mission is to visit each of
you.
Just one more precious
minute—
Mrs. Claus, do you want to
greet our children, Dear?
Oh yes, Santa; Christmas Eve is
almost here.
Dear children,
This is Mrs. Claus,
I've helped with surprises for
the long awaited flight—
I'll kiss Santa "Good-by" before
he leaves in the night.
Go to bed early, now; for a
long winter nap,
If you hear a strange noise, it
will be Santa's rap.
Have sweet dreams on this
Christmas Eve night
Santa will visit you on his
happy flight.
Ho! Ho! Ho!
All signals working; All lights
blinking red—
Rudolph is the leader—Hurry
children, jump in bed!
Sleigh bells are ringing
the elves are serenading,
Snow is softly falling, toy
soldiers are parading.
The jet engine is building up
super-sonic- power
Clocks are ticking off the long
awaited hour
All the world is waiting, it is
time for celebrating.
Old Santa's on the count down
10,9,8,7,6,5,4,3,2,1—
Zero o o o o o o o o o o o !!
A green light signals "Go"
We're off and away
On our Space Age Flight
Merry Christmas to all
And to all "A Good-Night,"

Ila Standlea Steinks

SUBTERFUGE

Here among the darker roots,
Grown one inch these past few
weeks
Are shiny, luminescent shoots,
Silvery strands and graying
streaks
Warning of advancing years
I would rather not admit.
Am I shedding futile tears?
Never! I will not submit.
Color purchased from a store
Masks this sign of passing time,
Assurances in shades galore.
What is yours? Moonmist is
mine.

Elizabeth Hilditch

MOON ODESSY

My God, the beauty of thy
handiwork
Sets our puny senses reeling
Our spirits soaring in deathless
praise
Of Thy Magnitude.
Green Earth, hung in limitless
Space
For Man to see and guage it's
worth
Sweet Mother of all her
children.
Now let no cold or lonliness
hurt our brother
Lead him in, and dress his
wounds
Love For Love to one another
Lest we find him, not, on
distant moons.

Lucia A. Roberts

CAROLINE

Born of the same womb
We were girls
Treading separate paths
To find our own.
I shared your hurts
Collected the tears
That spilled like morning dew
Over short blades of grass.
We went our ways
Severed our ties.
No more hopes
No more dreams.
Today I saw you.
Oh! how time slept
And awakened to find itself
In a realm of reality.
Your name came as an echo
A soft whisper of wind
I turned, and there you were.

Gord Lawson

THE NAMELESS POET

While life passes me by
Every moment is lonely and
cold
Searching for a feeling thats
Real

It can be rags to riches
Don't want money for whats
Felt inside
Can't say I'm poet nor artist
Yet nobody can deny me
The right to create
There is no doubt in my mind
about
Writing
I am living when I'm creating.

Rebecca A. Davis
DOING YOUR "THANG"
Jet setting, lap slapping
Feeling no pain,
Moon walking, jive talking,
Doing your "thang."
Lip smacking, fanny whacking
Doing your "thang."
Kicked back, laid back,
Feeling no pain.

Skinny dipping, fingers pinching
Feeling no pain.
Rare treasures, raw pleasure
Doing your "thang."
Hello's, good-bys,
Song, a sigh,
Jokes, smoke,
Flying high,
Feeling no pain,
Doing your "thang."

Dr. L. Marvin Marion
MY WIFE
The date was April 8, in
Seventy-eight.
"May I see you again?"
I asked, after our first date.
Then the courtship began.
How fast the weeks and months
did go.
In August I asked her to be my
wife.
How her face did glow!
What a happy day in my life!
After weeks of planning, on
October twenty-seventh
Before the altar we stood.
I was in seventh heaven
When she promised she would.
Her smile, an embrace, that
quiet voice;
Always trying so hard to please,
Tell me I made the right choice.
Now my mind is so much at
ease.
Everyday our love grows
stronger.
When I have to be away,
I wish to hold her longer
From that love I will never
stray.

Martha R. Klock
HAPPY NEW YEAR
So many times thru out the year
You come to me and then
I think of you and pray for you
And wonder how you've been
I think that I must write to you
And greet you fondly, too
But then I get distracted
With so many things to do
And then the time just rushes
by
And now the year is o'er
And then I realize that I
Have neglected you once more
So please forgive me, friend of
mine
My love is still the same
Though we may be far apart
Our friendship will remain

Charlz Rizzuto
BURNING EDEN
(For the Children)
Her long black hair blew with
the ashes
and pieces of her child
s ca t te re d
across an earth as charred as
her tongue
screaming in the fires of Eden
now blazing in a bus
blackening the skies
of Lebenon
as stars and crescents brand
brothers
in tombs of an ancient promise
handed to ch
il
dr
en
buried in nightmare.
*(written in the wake of
the March 1978 disaster)*

Karen L. Corrigan
UNTITLED
A fetus in the womb
Of my thoughts.
Twin souls,
Arguing,
Admonishing.
Voices in the night.
Contractions of righteousness,
Dilations of duty,
Uterine undulations of
Red, white, and blue.
Laborious screams
Imploring silence.
"Push, push."
And I give birth to
My ancestors.

Colleen T. Scholl
IF YOU GO, MY FRIEND
A lonely child I was, with
feelings locked up inside.
Wanting a special friend so I
can confide.
Your the kind of friend that
makes a dream come true.
You came and understood what
life has put me through.
My friend, you had the patience
to lend an ear.
That's why, I can't exist without
your friendship to share.
Now friends never seem to
remain around much anymore.
Your perception of everything I
do, has never been established
in any friend before.
For if you go, no one else I
could call a friend that I can
trust.
I couldn't stand the silence of
no more laughter among us.
I want to be assured you're always
going to be with me.
If you go, the old lonely person
again I'll be.
Like a ship without a wheel, if
you were gone, you would
take a part of me that won't
carry on.

Bonnie Williamson Thrun
I COME
Know that I am God, I give
thee peace.
Blessed be my name, for I shall
give thy soul release.
So go forth and preach my
Word,
No, not one shall ever say
they never heard.
I come soon, so watch and pray,
Within my love and cover you
must stay.
Know that soon I shall return,
Seek ye my Kingdom, for my
truth you yearn.
My love is great, my mercy fast,
My grace shall be sufficient as
in days gone past.
Are you ready for my return?
For truth and understanding,
yearn.
I come quickly, watch the sky,
Remember the prophets of days
gone by.
I leave this thought with you
dear friend,
Are your eyes on me. . . .soon
this world shall end.

Shari Kilback
REMAINS
You told me you're leaving
going away.
Taking the sunshine, from my
day.
Taking the warm, gentle touch.
Taking the love, I need so much.
Taking the stars, out of the sky.
Taking it all, with only—Good-
bye'.
But when you go, you'll also
find—
You've taken my heart, soul and
mind.
The only thing, you didn't take;
The thing, you completely, did
forsake,
Is something, that, you loved to
hold—
A body, that now, has grown so
cold.

Cindy R. Smith
FREE AT LAST
On the first day
That slavery began,
My old ancestors
Thought there would be no end,
To this dreadful
Act of crime,
Crying and screaming
Wasn't worth a dime,
But as time went on
And changes took place,
And God bestored
His loving grace,
We can say
We're free at last,
From this nightmare
Called our past.

Emma A. Sanchez
UNTITLED
I want my memory to
glow forever
I want you to forget
me never
I want to be the best
I can be
I want my *spirit* to
run free.

Nora O'Brien
MOTHER, BEHOLD YOUR SON
At St. Theresa's church, May 10,
1981.
The Blessed Mother beholds her
son.
There is to be a celebration
And all there join in jubilation.
As our Father Ambrosi goes up
the aisle,
Upon his face he wears a big
smile.
His love for Mary fills him with
joy,
This devotion he has had since
a boy.
Now celebrating twenty five
years as a priest,
Father's saying of the Rosary has
not ceased.
He brings many a soul back to
God,
And for this innumerable steps
he does trod.
He shows much concern for the
sick,
And Our Lady helps him with
the trick
Of showing patients how to
endure pain,
For their Heavenly rewards to
gain.
Father is kind and generous to
all,
Young and old are are at his
call,
He spends many moments in
prayer,
Kneeling before the Blessed
Sacrament there.
"Praise God! Praise God!" he
would exclaim,
When good things happened for
his fame.
It is no wonder Mary chose in
her way
To have Father honored on
Mother's Day!

Janet Jonett
FLOWERS ARE FOREVER
A flower may represent the
beauty which exists in a
friendship.
Although the blossom may
fade in time, the memories
of what had been remain as
bright as if today.
Just like in our relationship,
beauty exists naturally.
The blossom is held tightly
within our grasp;
And the essence will never fade
because our love shall keep it
fresh forever.

Mistelle J. Sparks
PEACEFULNESS?
Silent world smiling
As snow softly drifts
Into islands of beauty
Casting upon us
An ethereal sense
Of happiness
Which in itself
Pervades our beings
Letting us know
The essence of
Reality.

Frances Wilk Hobbs
TESSERA: 6TH CENTURY
Mosaic on broad unbroken areas
of walls
round arches crosses circles
domes vaults
Corinthian ornament cornice
brackets
fine buildings in Byzantine
Basilical oblong halls at each
side
semi-circled at the end
rows of columns adorned with
acanthus leaves
entire dome apse lined with
Mosaic pictures
Christ surrounded by saints
and apostles
pavements in Italy large slabs
of marble
in contrasting colors floors
black and white
Opus sectile Tessera
Opus Tessellatum
Gothic Westminster Abbey
Houses of Parliament
ceilings walls floors

Marble glass tile wood
inlaid to form pictures different
colored pieces
Artfully arrayed figures animals
designed positioned hardened in
mortar

Geraldine Van Allen Noble
A MID-SUMMER NIGHT'S MAGIC
Mid-Summer—Midnight-
Moonlight Magic!
Fireflies dance in hit and
miss fashion beneath my
window in the field near the
creek below.
Angels of Heaven taking turns
with magic wands
spark a silent concerto of
light as if some Heavenly
thoughtfulness were pointing
the way to the earthly
traveller.
My window at dawn— Sunrise—
The dance is over
and God's ignition of a bright
new day!

T. M. Pribicevich
CHILD
A child is a child
a beat of the heart
The need and the love
the important part
They're mischief and fun
and frolic and noise
They're all kinds of games
and the newest of toys
They're the kindest of friends
to animals and such
All kittens and dogs
they love very much
They're masters and missies of
snow men and igloos
They're sparkling brown eyes
and sea water blues
They're armies of inventors
and improvizations
They're partners, crusaders
and civilization
They're pioneers and scouts
and nurses and bakers
Their hands and their backs
and their feet sometimes
aching
They're fun games
and fun names
They're good and
they're bad
They're curious and wonders
and I'm very glad
That a child is a child
a beat of the heart
Their need and their love
the most important part.
Love,
Mother

Dorothy Elaine Ball
ECLIPSE
Precious time is frightened away
by doubts and trivia of such
magnitude that to let the eclipse
of anothers soul slant its
shadow into our very being
touching our most vulnerable
parts
Is Sacrilege
Self imposed strength can be
worn away as the ocean
consumes the last rays of sunset
to find them succulent
with an eager greed
to absorb another beam
and thus pad its own
waning ego

Patricia Lynn Hegwood
MY LAST REQUEST
I want one single yellow rose
Just one please if you will
That yellow rose to signify
These feelings that I feel.
A yellow rose for children
That meant so much to me
The children of my lifetime
That bounced up on my knee.
A yellow rose for friendships
That grew within my heart
A yellow rose a symbol
Of that very special part.
A yellow rose for memories
of the way I use to be
A human soul in bondage
Now and forever free.
Just a single yellow rose
That is my last request
A symbol of a lifetime
That found eternal rest.

Debbie Fite
MOMENT OF HESITATION
When I was a child, I dreamed of growing old. To follow in my father's footsteps was my one desire, to gain success and wealth and other socialities significant to man.
Now I am the man I dreamed to be. I am successful and have achieved.

Alas, but I've lost in the transformation. My successes seem as failure—my achievements as disaster. I've crossed the barriers of time and reached my goals, as it would seem to others.
Yet in the quietness of my heart, I long for the simple pleasures of childhood. I feel those to be the better days.
I stand on the bridge of life and tremor slightly.
The past and present seem as one. I long to return but know the doors have quietly closed behind me.
I must go on.

Arlene M. Cushman
LITTLE BOY
I am just a little boy
Wanting to play with toys.
My mind is full of wonders
Hoping you will understand my
blunders.
I love the beauty around me,
Wondering what will become of
me, Jeremiah.
I work out in the garden picking
up rocks.
Getting dirt on my shoes and
socks.
I water the garden and make
mud
Mired in the mud is my toy sub
I'll take my toy truck and tow it
out.
I hear my mom's shout,
"Boy! You are all mud."
Questioning of my pants have
enough padding?
I am just a little boy, I
don't deserve a paddling.
Clug Clug
Mud mired in the rug
1811 give a Kiss and a hug
Say, "I am Grandpa's boy
He lets me play in the mud."
Mom says. "straight to the tub."
Soap bubbles in my bath water, I
jump into the tub.
The mud I began to scrub
Bubbles in my eyes and on my
nose
I push up the plug; down the
drain the mud goes.
I Jeremiah, look at my Grandpa
and say,
"Grandpa, can I be your, little
boy?"

Greg Kain
FUZZY DREAMS
Everyone seems to have fuzzy
dreams.
Fuzzy dreams that make no
sense.
No matter if you're smart or
dense. But, ⁇
Everyone seems to have fuzzy
dreams.
Dreams that come and go as
they please.
You may be dancing or swinging
in the trees. But,⁇
Everyone seems to have fuzzy
dreams.
Like painting a flag on the
moon,
Or drinking milk in a saloon.
But,⁇
Everyone seems to have fuzzy
dreams.
Something like being a
superstar,
Or even going to the stars out
there so far. But,⁇
Everyone seems to have fuzzy
dreams.
Dreams are for the young and
the old,
Because dreams are where some
people find their pot of gold.

Dee Dee
MY DAD
There is a man in my life.
He is a very special, important
person.
He is always there through bad
times and good.
His opinion and advice are
always welcomed.
He always gives it freely,
He always gives it lots of
thought.
He supports me in my decisions,
If he feels I have chosen right.
He allows me to make mistakes,
But always helps to pick up the
pieces,
Then he tries to set my feet in
the right direction.
I wish he would talk with me a
little more in idle
conversation,
Praise me a little more often,
if I deserve it,
And be able to say he loves me
a little more.
I am as proud as any daughter
could be,
And maybe, more than anyone
could imagine.
I have come to love him with all
my heart and soul.
As father does not really suit
him,
The man is my DAD.

Mary E. Wojchik
BED CHAMBER
Lying here within my bed
chamber,
thinking of our marriage vows;
how our lives have turned to
amber,
blending yesterdays and nows.
We show mischievous splendor
here,
upon this bed, so inviting to
behold;
share dreams and hardships
through the years,
and imagine promiscuities never
told.
We cry within each others
arms,
one comforting the other.
You woo me with arrogant
charm,
and create in me a child to
mother.

Elsie Grapentin
MY DRAFTY OFFICE
A draft can cause no cold I'm
told.
But yet I find—
A draft has taken from my fold
All the loves that kept me
warm.
My feet are cold she meekly
cried
Oh! let me warm them by thy
side.
I will like fun, the dope replied
There is no draft—the
thermometer lied.
I work o'work, o'work,
But not cause I'm a jerk
My fanny's frozen to the chair
So how can I go anywhere?

Donna Marie Breisch
SPRING BLOSSOM
The flower so bright
and the color of spring
Will add pleasure and joy—
to most anything.
So yellow and rich
it smiles as it grows,
Enchanting and beautiful,
it breaks through the late
spring snow.
It sparkles and shines
in the spring morning sun,
And continues to glow,
though the day is done.
Bright and awakening
in the rich morning dew;
Soft and gentle,
bringing hope of good news.
How bright and beautiful
it stands on the hill,
The most elegant of flowers
is the glorious daffodil.

Sue Sutton Willbanks
AND LONELINESS
I sift memories grown cold
As fresh puzzles unfold.
How did feelings so intense
Settle into such reticence?
The passion of a summer night
Is a faint image in firelight.
Now only prudence glows,
And loneliness—God knows!

Viola W. Carter
EXISTING
Sanity is knowing you are
insane
Insanity is refusing to feel pain
Pain is simply being alive
Living is knowing who you are
Would tell you who I am. . .
If I knew. . .
Would tell you how I felt. . .
If I could feel. . .

Leslie Clint Slay
LIGHT
The center of the swirling
storm,
The universal eye—

Pretends to blow away from
course,
Blinded by the sky.
Deep within that mighty cell,
The powers came to be—
And formed the layers of its
soul,
To cloud the memory.
Shielded by the curse of kin,
The dimming shadows fell—
And caused a void upon the
deep,
Where self had once prevailed.
Pelted by those stinging blows,
The power did retreat—
And clothed the flight with
armour,
To assure the light's defeat.
Hidden 'neath the social mist,
The light escapes unseen,
And plays among the passers-by,
Painting the mortal dream.

Dwain L. Kitchel
VAPOR TRAILS
Scribing white trails in the
pastel
Blue of the early evening sky,
Unseen flying machines propel
Their living fares and prophesy.
Earth bound I wonder at the
straight
White lines which write
mankind's song:
"You've left the seas to
decorate
The lands and now you travel
on."
Moving always up and onward
In ceaseless pursuit of unknown
Destinies, the living record
Unfolds from veiled forces
blown.
I marvel at the starched white
lines
That stretch out in a form of
verse
Having pure but random designs
That too soon begin to disperse.
Ragged chords of chaotic whisps
Emerge in a tortured silence
Then disappear in full eclipse
To the Cosmos's bored
somnolence.
And I see in clear perspective
How transient are man's deeds
and breath
As, adrift in the vast narrative
Of nature, each flits so soon to
death.
Afront those vapor trails are my
Brothers and sisters, inhaling
And exhaling (like me). . ., Aye,
Their tiny traces awing to die.
But don't discount our hopes
and dreams
That soar beyond this universe's
vise
With spans and deeds united in
themes
That stride on vapor trails to
paradise!

Waneeta Goggie Thornton
LET'S WALK TOGETHER
I'm so glad that I am one with
attributes that shine within this
world there are quite some that
certainly are not benign.
We sometimes tend to judge
someone not knowing all the
facts, and yet when this is done
to us we see how hate attracts.
Time heals all wounds they say
but yet it's hard to trust for the
very one who smiled at you
helped kick you in the dust.
We tend to crawl before we
walk, and this has been said for
years-we should try and think
before we talk it would stop alot
of tears.
So-do not judge before you know
the trouble someone has caused
they might be the very one who
helped you in the past.
For me- I grace the earth with
charm and with each passing
day, I truly hope that people
learn that others are not their
prey.

Carole Browning-Black
PREPARING FOR THE WEDDING
She stands atop the carpeted
pedestal, centered among the
mirrors, reflecting in virtuous
beauty. The blush veil cannot
dim the radiant glow from her
expectant eyes; her vibrant
warmth flows freely from within
the chaste gown.
How rejuvenating, her youth;
exhilerating, her passion. How
appealing, her reticence;
soothing, her sobriety.
How reluctant my heart to
unclench its fist.

Emily Cole
CARRYING ME
The weight of the sea-
Mightier than one can imagine;
Able to carry a vessel from
shore to shore,
Yet, gentle enough to carry me.
We can not see its strength, or
begin to know why
Poets use their talents to write
about it.
We can but enjoy its beauty,
knowing that it controls
All...man, and animal, and land.
Yet, with all of its power, there
is an even greater force-
the WIND!
It can cause the sea to become
fierce with rage,
Enabling it to kill the very
creatures it cares for.
Though calm...peaceful...we, too,
are as the sea.
Able to turn against the very
one we care for...
The one who feeds and nurtures
us.
We, too, are a poets' wonder.

Virginia Ingalls Ellsworth
BLESSED LOVE
Was it only yesterday
that our eyes met,
locked and held
Something wonderful
happened in that
moment
Some inner force
that sealed our
hearts together
for all time
And now, years later
the miracle of love
has blessed us both
a hundred fold

Katie-Marie Dent
PASSION'S PLEA
Passion -
chained, seeking release,
incapable of freedom,
Subservient to the will.
Passion -
confined by a shell
of restraint.
Old ideas
restrict new feelings.
To give in is to
let go...
to give up that final stand
of independence.
Let it go -
released,
unleashed,
abandoned
to whatever happens!
But the will holds back
and pens inside
That which should be
free.

Nate De Legall
WHEN DID WE LOSE IT
When did we lose it? The feeling
we once shared. Was it during
that final sip of wine? Or during
the final chords of our favorite
melody. Did we give too much,
too soon or too little, too late?

Our anxiety devoured the
flames of passion before we
could kindle it into a blazing
romance. We tried to satisfy
each others needs before realizing what we really needed. Did
we bore ourselves with an
overwhelming love for each
other? Or like a new toy did the
novelty of it wear off?

Donna Lee Caragonne
A FRIDAY SCHOOL BUS
Rain, rain and more rain,
swooshing of passing cars;
sounds melting the time away.
Protected in my car from
cold and wetness so far;
urging the sun out today.
The yellow blob appears a
distance away; swishing,
blinking, stopping without
delay.
The bright blur belches out
colorful, squealing, vertical
streaks on Friday.

Cynthia Fontneau
THE MIST
Smell of pine in valleyed mist
with gleam of rose and amethyst
And boughs of dew overhung
round green sprays it clung.
This peaceful mist, no less
in natures dream of wilderness
Floats in clouds of mystery
deeper than the deeps of sea.
This mist so gray and blind
I wish to feel and touch my
mind.
And each tree sleeps in disarray
I know the wind will blow
today.
A universe of lifeless gray
over rotted moss and clinging
clay.
The silence of this muffled dead
is broken by the heart that bled.
Hope has no meaning here
for fate, it rules, not a prayer.
The dark earth trembles beneath
my feet
in resurrection, still singing
sweet.
This valleyed mist sleeps in
gloom
the never ending natures tomb.
In my soul, from which I drew
the hidden truth; I knew.
Ye are too swift, too white
to fly to what transcendent height.
The wild wings in deaths dim
night
groping shadows amidst your
light.
Such mystery is lying here
beyond my cold and human fear.
With shaking pulse and sharp
drawn breath
I saw beneath darkness and light
and death!

Janet A. Dean
INSIDE A BIKER'S MIND
To ride free and into the winds,
totally unencumbered by all of
the sins;
That ordinary people place upon
our kind,
we're just tryin' to survive - to
stay alive;
Just to keep on partyin' and
truckin' with our bro's,
and to get our shit together,
everyone knows;
How harrassed we are for
unjustified reasons,
by people who don't try to
understand - who could never
believe us.
We're just a step apart, our own
kinda' breed,
but then so is everyone else, if
you honestly concede;
Why don't they all just leave us
alone,
and go on concerning themselves with their own??
We know where we're goin' and
why
and really, it's nobodys business
to try;
To figure out why we're so
different from the rest,
we all kinda' feel we have
chosen the very best;
And, if we're all gonna get along
in this crazy mixed-up earth,
a good place to start is right
from the day of our birth;
To dispense with all prejudices
which exist now in the world,
and to begin fearlessly and
courageously to live,
unbiased, unbigotted, free and
harmoneously!!
Inspirational quotation:
"Thinking first before acting is
the very hardest work there is,
which is the probable reason
why so few engage in it, and so
few are successful!" (Henry Ford).

Dorothy R. Douglas
SUMMER HAZE
Summer haze hanging in the air
Buzzards flying low
Descending on a pair
of dead animals. Moving slow
then, swooping down.
Ready to eat,
smiling like clowns
Ah!...fresh meat.

Eleanor Attaway Patch
NEVER ALONE
We've had trials and
tribulations,
We've been tested "AS BY FIRE"
There were times it seemed the
harder we tried,
The deeper we sank in the mire.
We know that our love for each
other and God
Will sustain us all of life
through
And if you will put complete

trust in him,
He will do the same thing for
you.
We also know that all of these
things
Are not always to punish for
sin, but;
Are sent to make us strong...
No matter then how bad things
have been,
In our hearts we still carry a
song.
Yes, "BURDENS ARE LIFTED
AT CALVARY".
Someone has written that song.
Even with mountains of trouble,
for;
In our deepest sorrow,
We know we are never alone.

Colette Retif
THREADS
Centuries ago,
Cistrum in hand,
Before my Lady Isis
I prayed
To be the perfect queen,
the perfect wife,
the perfect mother.
I prayed for the lifting of the
veil,
the revelation of mysteries.
Before my Lady Isis
- Worship.

And the Earth spun many times
around the Sun,
And I went out,
And I returned.
Silver disc in hand,
Before the Lady Ishtar
I stood
And tried to understand,
Underground rivers,
the planting of the seed,
Moon worship,
Darkness from whence comes
Light.
Before the Lady Ishtar,
- Puzzlement.

And the Earth spun many times
around the Sun,
And I went out,
And I returned.
Olive branch in hand,
Before the goddess Athena
I came.
And of she who sprung
fully armed
From the brow of Zeus,
I claimed wisdom.
Maybe she did not hear my
request,
Maybe I did not hear her reply.
Before the goddess Athena,
- Silence.

And the Earth spun many times
around the Sun,
And I went out,
And I returned.
And now there is one
Who is called by many
Our Lady -
Pure, a virgin,
I do not easily approach her.
Before the Lady Mary,
- Estrangement.
But often near by,
I have noticed another Mary,
the Woman of Magdala
Before the Magdalena,
- Identification.
And the Earth keeps spinning
around the Sun,
And I keep looking,
And I go on searching.
Today, he crossed my path,
- A child.
Clear eyed,
Uncritical of his surroundings,
Full of faith,
Willing to share all things
With all men.
Joyful, trusting,
Walking hand in hand
with Life itself.
I saw courage there too.
Before today's child,
- Hope.

Theresa Y. Trani
WHO AM I?
I am the smile on the face of
eternal youth,
The wind that flicks brittle
leaves from the branches,
The bubbles in champagne,
The smell of the sea salt
sprayed upon the sands,
The twinkle in the largest blue
eyes of Douglas,
The impishness in the smile of
Christine.
I am the impatience of fifteen-
year old Michael.
I am the force of a mighty
fountain,
The freshness of a flower,
The spirit of a pioneer,
The consciousness of only
myself,
The exuberance of Christmas
morn,
The brisk bite of a winter's day,
The chill of autumn,
The sunlite on Sunday,
The joy of love,
The exquisity of surrender,
Sounds of the city,
Laughter,
Rain.
"I am the newness of Life".

Margie Lou Shelton
DANIEL, OH! DANIEL
Oh! Daniel, Oh! Daniel you've
taught me how to pray,
by going to God in prayer three
times a day.
I was carelessly drifting in my
own way,
now Daniel, Oh! Daniel you've
taught me how to pray.
When I read in Daniel six and
ten
how he prayed three times a
day-
Before he had to face the lion's
den,
before he had to face the lion's
den.
RECITATION:
I was worhiping my God, the old
T.V. set
and eating off a tray all the food
I could get.
Praying a little here and there
just doesn't work in a trying
hour.
I turned off the T.V. set and put
up my tray,
for now I'm trying Daniel's way.
Now I'm so happy I've a dearest
friend;
God and my Saviour I'll go with
to the end.
This I believe is true as in
Daniel six and twenty-two,
If I faced a lion's den
God's angel would shut the
lion's mouth as he did then.

Susan Thomas
HERE COMES THE BOMBS!
Heard it on the radio
The time for the end is here;
The nuclear bombs are coming
God, have mercy on us now.
They told us there is no need
for worry
A nuclear war will never occur;
But now all the people are
running
I don't know why, there's no
escape from the bombs.
In the beginning God gave us
everything
Beauty, Love, and Hope;
And from day one of man
We started destroying it all.
We took the skies and water and
polluted them
We took the land and raped it;
We took the animals and almost
drove them to extinction
And we cut down the forests
and made town houses and
parking lots.
So, we have no-one else to
blame for the end
We brought it upon ourselves;
God gave us everything we
needed and we had to ruin it
And now, look, you can see the
bombs in the distance.

Angela M. Norbie
UNTITLED
The moon, a laughing clown
face,
That plays hide-and-seek among
the clouds,
Pauses now and then to look
down upon the earth
As if our keeper.
And his laughter, the wind,
echoes across the plains,
Leaving the prairie grass bent
with joyfulness.
He cleverly teases until the sun
approaches
But the moon leaves with a
cheerfulness
That mocks the sun into rising
faster--
Chasing the moon from the
cherished sky.
The dew, tears of laughter,
Is now stolen by the sun, in
greediness,
To add to his own brightness.

Arlene Elizabeth Hall
DENVER
She sits upon a golden throne
With rock clad mountains to
her back
And faces plains of waving gold
Queen City of the Plains.
Upon her head a crown of gold
With sparkling diamonds on her
dress
And miles around within her
view
A mile high stands her throne.
From far and wide they come
This Lady for their Queen
She waves her silver scepter
And welcomes them all home.

Mary Paice
UNTITLED
If the continents became a
single land
If the scattered rivers all joined
hands,
If all the waves became one
wave,
If every grave became one
grave,
If all mankind had never bled;
The seas would be a lonesome
tear
He would never have to shed.

Rosanne C. Kilinski
STRENGTH
Strength is like the waves,
rushing as in a defensive line,
determined not to let anything
get in it's way.
Until it attackes the sand,
and erases the memories of the
day.
Then as if all of it's strength
is gone, it goes back to where it
came from, until it is ready to
attack the shore again.

Vincent J. Werner
FRIENDSHIPS LAST
It seems so funny that we could
be friends
And still live at opposite ends
Of a country so vast
How could a friendship last?

Loving and caring
To stay only by sharing
That is how friendships last.

Gordana Matkovic
SWEET JOHNNY
Close your eyes sweet babe
Let this mama ride you like a
wind
Sail your seas
Oh, but you're a hard one to
tame
Your winds are hurricanes
And your seas are high and
rough
You've been roaming in the wild
for too long
Close your eyes sweet babe
Let this mama tame your
hurricanes
Tame your high and rough seas
For you need to belong
You've been roaming in the wild
for too long
A fisherman wth a heart for a
bait
A radio with a love song playing
Close your eyes sweet babe
Mama is coming
For you need to belong
Close your eyes sweet babe

Lawrence Richardson
LITTLE THINGS
Blissful breezes to tickle the
warmth
Of a summer's day,
The sudden kiss, given in loving
Honesty,
A shared moment, that doubles
In the retelling, throughout the
Silver years.
An infant's bubbling laughter
And all-consuming grin.
Bask awhile in the glow of the
Golden moment, truly a blessing
For those who know how to
Cherish and embrace true values
And find glory in the giving of
Themselves.
A red-orange sunset over blue-
Calm waters, an albatross in
Flight/glide, the inner heart of a
Poet's song, sung by a meadow
Lark.

Christine M. Trucinski
FLEXIBLE AS ALWAYS
Gentle, understanding.
Most often always-soft spoken WOMAN.
Organizer, boss, helper too.
Patient-sometimes too much so.
Friend-daughter, sister,
Mother and-wife.
Protector, peacemaker, kind persuader.
Comforter, sensitive, soap-opera lover.
Sweeter than sweet.
"Creme de la Creme".
Generous beyond generosity.
A fair employer, unafraid of hard work.
Asking-no more of others than she gives of herself.
Unreal description-not really.
Only-simple words--of Love.

Adele Murray
WOULD THAT I BE A STAR
Oh would that I be a STAR,
OH! How I would shine.
On a stage I would be,
And an audience for ME would pine.

But darling then, how would you ever get to me?
With all those people, ALWAYS, all around me.
Oh you would need arms so---long---,
They'd stretch from land to sea, and sea.
And then my darling, how could our lips ever meet? You see.
So let the stars shine and be,
While I'll be content in being with you,
And being just, little little me.

Christine M. Trucinski
QUIET LISTENER
A friend so near and dear,
yet-so far away.
Always there, always considerate, ever kind.
We live in two different worlds-yet-
we share a love for life, for children, for families also dear.
Dreams, ambitions, cares, concerns, hurts, sorrow, joy and love-shared.
Never fully realizing, the strength, the selflessness, the ever present encouragement and friendship.
Always a word of comfort, always a ray of hope
to brighten up the empty darkness.
Putting aside worries of her own, disappointments,
problems, always lessening burdens of despair, to
meet the need, my need of a friend-like her.

Helen Stowe Johnson
A LESSON
Set your affections
On things up above,
Your life's hid in Christ
The God of Love.
Put off the old man
Walk in newness of life,
Walk not in anger,
Blasphemy and strife.
Forgive one another,
Be gentle, be kind,
In love with mercy,
In humbleness of mind.
Don't forget charity,
The greatest of all,
The perfect binding,
Through Christ our all.
What ever you do
In deed or in word,
Give thanks to God
The Father of your Lord.

Paula Larson
MOTHERING
Mothering seven children must have been a chore
Often you must have been glad there were not any more.
Though you best feel mighty proud
on this tenth day of May
Having you for my mother
I can say you earned this day.
Each day throughout the year we think of all you've done
Remembering all you taught us how we always had such fun.
Seeing why you disciplined us was just an act of love
Doing things for our own safety finding help from God above.
All your years of motherhood reflect your lovely ways
You are the best mom ever and deserve so much more praise!

Linda Serrone
A MOTHER'S PRAYER
I look upon your precious face
and can't believe my eyes.
I felt your presence all along
and realize now you are born.
So beautiful, so cuddly, so tiny
and cute.
My words cannot say how
much my love for you grows
each wakening day.
My baby is born and I look
upon your sweet face and hope
you know I will do my best to
guide you, stand beside you,
to hold you and sometimes
even scold you.
I am so proud and want the
world to see...so let me say
I cherish you with all my heart
and when you're in need
as your loving Mother
I will help you indeed!

Billy Gresham West
LEARNING
If man be red - or white - or black - or blue
He's never know what life's about - except he knew
About the past and what was done or spoke
Through sincere thought of mind or bawdy joke
For long ago - at some point in time twas found
Each fact of life - and 'twas tossed around
To find if facts were proved - or not
When each new (?) thought came to head
Unthinking ones looked on - and said
Oh - that's been thought - or that's been done
There's nothing new beneath our sun
Well every plan must have it's test
To find if this solution's best
So each new brood of fledgling minds
Must try those plans - and often finds
That what seemed new and fresh - untried
Was tested long ago - and died
For even then twas thought so new
Yet trial and error found that it just grew
From further back in man's own clime
And so twill be from start - till end of time

Michael John Behan
STARLIGHT AND VELVET
Starlight and velvet
fade into grey
Creatures of midnight
scurry away
Dawns fragrance settles
through nights chilly air
Leaves glisten like diamonds
in mornings new glare
The dew falling softly
gathers and waits
Gossamer threads start
then hesitate
A Lark is heard
a song clear and loud
Sailing past meadows
mountains and clouds
The twinkling sunlight
new brightens the green
As nature reveals
its new painted scene.

Peggy Zeaphey Nerl
RICHES
I may not have any gold or silver,
Or treasures so sacred and so new,
But I have riches far beyond this,
Because I found a friend like you,
I may go travel around this world,
With all the beauty in it to seek,
But the beauty in your friendship,
Sure made you all the world to me,
I could never feel poor or lonely,
Other riches I will never beseech,
As long as I have your friendship,
I shall treasure it till eternity,

Yvonne Carrie
GOD AND THE OCEAN
When I see the ocean God, I think of you.
When I'm near the ocean I realize how small I am and how great you are.
I see the wonders of the ocean all around me.
I think of the ships at sea and the Mighty force that moves them.
I watch the sea gulls that fly so freely.
I feel your spirit move across the water.
I hear the waves as they break upon the seashore, again I think of the wonders of you.
I feel the breeze in my hair and I feel the nearness of you.
In quiet solitude it is my hope that everyone feels the same.

Laura Ciarniello
A PATCH OF YESTERDAY
I seek you in the tradition of Sundays,
In the constancy of Italian music hours,
In the roughness of an unshaven face felt by a child's softness,
In pink cars, surprise phone calls, endless how-are-you's,
In pride and loyalty.
In these I seek you, for in these were your gifts to me found.
I find you within a woman's heart
Made young again by the search,
In a part of her soul long untouched
By her child ways,
In a patch of yesterday rich
In old love that worked,
In traces of truth hardly noticed
As cornerstones to present beliefs,
In feelings coated with the rust of forgetfulness,
In memories dusty from the passing of time.
In these I find you, for in these I discover your place in me.
Found again, my own old man,
Your little girl longs for the freedom
Your old love gave.
With my tears I'll dust away time,
And feel your memory
With a child's softness.

Brian Kelly
THE OLD MAN
He's feeble now the old man's bent
But judge you not by frame spent
Look in the eye that is crystal clear
It tells its tale of yesteryear
Of frolicking sports and loving care
Tender moments we all share
Giving all without relent
This is the man you see that's bent
Though heavy often was his load
Despairing thoughts he never showed
He met each day with a smile

and prayer
Took charge of all within his care
He was a man we all should know
That old man you see walking slow
Take time to bid him a good day
With luck one day you'll be that way

Barbara Louise Lenton

THE ROAD HOME

I'm travelling down the road once more,
Following the trail of reflectors which mark the path from me to you like breadcrumbs carefully placed to show the way.
The car cuts through the night, knifing its way through the settling fog which closes in and surrounds me like loving arms.
And I'm thinking....
I suppose I should be content having loved you and held you,
But the night is dark and lonely,
And merely seems to intensify the ever-strong desire to turn around and go back - leaving you n'er again.
How hard it is to leave your arms;
How unbearable to return to an existence which holds for me only silence and longing - a submarginal keeping of time until we can be together once again.
The time apart passes so slowly;
The time together so quickly.
And yet, with all the longing and aching, I am at peace for a moment in the knowledge that the future holds the joining of our spirits as one, leaving in its wake the promise and expectation of sharing a lifetime of precious seconds and loving hours...
And the roar of the road jars me from my thoughts,
Reminding me that I'm heading home,
Speeding further and further away from my dearest love,
And I am sad.

Douglas A. Sherman

FOOTPRINTS AND GULL TRACKS

Wind whipped swirls of sand
flit by sentinal dunes.
Small meandering footprints,
solitary and silent,
mark wave-washed sand.
Bubbles appear under
receding waves.
Gull tracks disappear
in the wash of the surf.
The trance inducing rhythm
goes on, unceasing.
The swells roll in
reaching long, wet fingers
high up onto the shore,
erasing all that was there,
all that will ever be there.
Footprints and gull tracks
filled in, ready to be
remade and filled again
until there are no more
footprints and no more gull tracks.
Until the sandy canvas is never again disturbed.

Corina L. Popp

LOVE IS STRONG AS DEATH

Song of Soloman 8: 6,7. Set me as a seal upon thine heart, as a seal upon thine arm: for love is strong as death: jealousy is cruel as the grave; the coals thereof are coals of fire, which hath a most vehement flame. Many waters cannot quench love, neither can the floods drown it: if a man would give all the substance of his house for love, it would utterly be condemned.

****

God hath placed the blessing of his divine love upon the skill of the doctor, when *He* made the heart of the dark man to beat in the white man's chest.

We know of no time on this earth when we have been more in need of an example of God's hand upon man to give such a touch of our Creator sublime.

So many methods have been tried, by man, to bring the races into to-getherness, *as many* have failed to bring about such a result.

Thus, God, in His infinite wisdom moves the minds, without fanfare, to prepare one man and then the other. The surgeon, aware of God's nearness, works with expectation, God breathes the breath of life, and a man lives. The donor, the patient, the doctor, the date and place are all necessary. The plan is Divine. *This is my own personal idea and belief concerning the heart transplant that took place on Jan. 2, 1968, by Dr. Christian Barnard.*

Rev. Robert H. Stout

CLOSER TO JESUS

I want to get closer to Jesus;
I want to get in with him strong,
For if I am close to my Savior
I find myself doing no wrong.
He's always near when I need Him,
He's never away from my side;
And if we get closer to Jesus,
We will receive power from on high.
He promises us sweeping promises,
And He always keeps His word,
And if we get on our knees quite often,
His wonderful voice can be heard.
It's grand, it' great, it's glorious
What the wonderful Savior can do;
And if you get closer to Jesus
I am sure He'll get closer to you.
I sometimes get down hearted,
And don't know what to do,
And then I turn to my Savior,
And He makes things just like new.
We thank You Father in Heaven,
For your son Jesus so true,
For if you had not sent Him,
I don't know what we would do.
I haven't always known Him,
Just a short time or so,
But in that time I have found Him
Steadfast and honest you know.

Andrew Peter Velez

MUSIC

OH!
endless sage of sound
rupture(d)
spirits with passions that cannot be described
mind
bent into strange spaces unfamiliar and lonely
rhythms
carry thought into distances far and away from body...
FEELINGS
roaming timelessly
harmonies
merging universes
melodies
entering other dimensions....

Helen Brown Rittershofer

TIME—RULER OF THE UNIVERSE

We search our souls and review the hours
As the intangibles arise and inspire powers
The past we recall as we try to relate
The sunrise and sunsets of expressive debate
For time draws forward from cycles of the past
Broadening dimensions of balance or even contrast
As channeling thought gives rise to expression
And creative dreams inspire and beckon
Man becomes aware of the challenge and change
Reawakens and confronts rediscovered desires
Through the windows of truism shine values confirmed
Mans' conception of realism is inspired and learned
Thinking man becomes creative-based upon projective thought
Seasons are produced by time and years are never bought
Generations come and go leaving lessons to be learned
The innuendoes through the years centuries old confirmed.

Ethel Fletcher Greene

LITTLE BLUE BIRDS

Little blue birds, little blue birds, you came in the Spring
When roses were blooming, sweet songs you did sing
In the mountains I see, you're blue as you fly
So sweet and pretty against the blue sky.
In Summer you nested so near to my door
I paused in the twilight and heard you once more
Your babies you fed, "all Summer indeed!"
Now Autumn's here, come once more and cheer me.
In Autumn, it seems my birdies have gone
My roses are faded, now wind sings a song
Pretty leaves have fallen all to the ground
I search but can't find my blue birds around.
We sang together when sunshine was bright
You fluttered your wings, playing in twilight
My heart is more lonely since you're not here
My two little blue birds, I wish you were near.
Winter will be longer when there is no song
From birdies that cheer me when days are too long
When it's Springtime in the mountains, it's songtime;
You'll pause and sing, "I'll claim you for mine!"

June Hill

IN NEED OF A FRIEND

He sits alone
in his rocking chair,
no one to talk to
no one to care.
Looking out the window
watching young kids at play,
what can he do
what can he say.
In need of a friend
for whom does he turn,
is he willing to teach
is he willing to learn.
Now night is falling
television on once more,
if only someone, anyone
would knock at his door.
He's lonely for company
in need of a friend,
if this is all to life
then when will it end.

Vicki L. Rohr Lanham

AUNTS AND UNCLES

Aunts and uncles we all need,
With memories, to go along!
Many give, that one seed,
To help us feel, that we belong!
Giving all the love they can,

To show they really care.
Some are, our biggest fans,
While others give us prayer.
Aunts and uncles often show,
That life is really always caring.
Many things in life we'll know,
Because of love they've been sharing.
To them I really have to say,
Thanks for love, you've sent my way!

Genevieve McMitchell
THERE'LL BE A TOMORROW
Don't look back
On mistakes you've made.
More than likely
The debt's been paid.
Don't waste your life
On things that are past,
They can't be changed
The dye's been cast.
Today may be sad
And filled with sorrow,
Always remember,
There'll be a tomorrow.
So look on the bright side,
Put a smile on your face,
Get up off your knees
And get back in the race.

Marian Hitchcock Reedy
CALIFORNIA KALEIDOSCOPE
Mission bells toll while padres stroll by adobe brick walls
Flowering fields fill balmy breezes with fragile fragrance
Hummingbirds sip hungrily from honeysuckle trumpets
Cable cars clang as they cling to frail rails on foggy hills
Sequoias shelter fern fronds laced with brilliant butterflies
Violets nestle under dripping green leaf umbrellas
Eucalyptus stretch silvery strands to storm shrouded skies
Pointsettias fling flaming petals forming Persian carpets
Roadrunners race tumbleweeds amid palms and drifting dunes
Booming breakers tumble sail-boats onto pebbled beaches
As Pacific gales turbulently crush star-studded clouds
Against Palomar's rugged and rock-strewn snow-crusted cliffs

B. J. Lohndorf
ODE TO A DRUNK
Stagger to the left,
stagger to the right,
stagger in the middle,
stagger all the night.
You drink Lonesome Charly,
you drink Five Star mixed.
Drink it in the evening,
then you're really fixed.
Started in the morning
by noon you're feeling good.
Ending in the evening,
then you're in the mood.
Polish off another drink,
have yourself a ball,
but just you wait til morning,
then blame Sam for it all.

Rosa Bolt Jones
HOMAGE TO SILENCE
With the turn of a knob I gain
What is worth a million dollars-
Silence-
Silence-that speaks and informs me
Of all the happenings of the day.
Silence-
In which I hear all the things
I cannot hear in the noise.
Silence-
That lets me be a human being
And not merely a tool
For blunder and exploitation.
Silence-
That covers the earth
After the storm has ceased.
Silence-
That overcomes the mourner
When no words can describe the sorrow
And all faculties come to a paralyzing stop.
Silence-
That renews and reclaims the hidden genius
And brings forth new life and compassion
Destroyed in the turmoil of a loud and empty world.

Carole Saltsgiver
REBECCA
There is a precious infant,
She's the daughter of you and me,
And when I look at this beautiful child,
Our love is all I see.
Everything we share between us,
Is shining in her eyes,
And I only hear the sounds of love,
Whenever our baby cries.
When I hold her tiny hand,
Your softness is in her touch,
And because she is the image of you,
I love this child so much.
Nowhere in this whole wide world,
Is there such a child so fair,
That reflects the deepest kind of love,
That only we two share.
Thank you for Rebecca

Carolyn Ann Slowski
GONE BUT NOT FORGOTTEN
His face so rugged and worn
With his best years behind him
He faintly remembers it being dim
The life he began when born
Wandering with loneliness and despair
He feels there's no-one to care
Leaving his heart so empty
He asks what about me
He having been hurt
Descended to the eternal sleep
Not by sickness or anything more
Just his heart so deeply broken
His pride oh his pride
Went with him but was still alive
It was there where he once stood
It would carry on forever.

Vicki Anderson
I FOLLOW
Whichever way you handle it
(My heart will bleed)
I might never be convinced
(Of any story I hear)
And if you try to say
(I will be treated unfair)
How you feel about it
(Do I mean the world to anyone)
Nothing words can do
(I stand above you watching)
To make me feel different
(I follow closely behind)

Joyce Smedley
I LET GO OF HIS HAND
I don't like the way my life is going now.
I want to change it, but I don't know how.
I was at a mountain top, when a storm came my way.
Suddenly—my dreams were shattered;
My world turned to gray.
I want another dream; I want to hope again.
I've got to take the first step—
Oh God, I need Your help.
How long has it been, since I've spoken God's name?
As I climbed to the top, I let go of His Hand.
Lord, I want to thank You for that little storm.
I thought it shattered my life—
But, Oh, I was wrong.
It only turned me around and made me realize;
I was seeing the world only through my eyes.
Somewhere along the way, I let go of His Hand.
It took a storm in my life for me to understand—
You may reach the mountain top; but my friend,
You'll never stay, unless you walk with God,
Each and every day.

Oh God, I want to thank You for another chance;
I'll never again let go of Your Hand.

Sheri
SHADOWS
You were first, the dream held within my heart;
then, we met;
We have known each other, perhaps, forever;
yet, we know so little;
Hand in hand we have walked many miles, upon many pathways;
although, together we have journeyed but thrice;
Our desires, our needs, are the same;
but, alas, the differences are there;
Life beyond -- life upon this earth;
Who can say --
Who can say, whether it was an eternity ago -- or today.

Bruce M. Ash
MARRY—GO—ROUND
I was on a 'marry-go-round',
Until you came along,
The prettiest girl in the block;
So cool and debonair.
I was like a noise without a sound,
Like empty words without a song;
Like a flight tower wind-sock,
Just sucking air.
I was on a 'marry-go-round',
Part of a busy throng,
Going to work, punching the clock,
Seeming never to get anywhere.
It was like a fighter's last round,
My love for you rang like a gong;
But when I went up to your door to knock,
You were no longer there.
So, I'm still on that 'marry-go-round',
What did I do that was wrong?
(Say, isn't that a *new* girl in the block,
The one with the golden hair?)

Donna Roden
I HAVE SURVIVED
I walk alone.
Through life and all its troubles.
I have no one to lean on or to confide in.
I have no one I can trust.
I have no one.
At first it was hard.
No. More than hard. It was impossible.
I didn't understand why it was I who should feel like this.
But slowly, oh so slowly, it became clearer to me.
Now I see the mystery that had me confused.
It took time, but now that the pain of realization is gone,
I'm beginning to understand.
You caused me such hurt and heartache.
But I lived.
You don't have the power to hurt me any longer.
You see, I reached down within my own soul and found strength.
My strength.
It will sustain me.
For you, who thought you would wither me like a dying rose,
Can kill me no more.
For you no longer matter to me.
You have become a figment of

my imagination.
To me, you are, no more.
The pain was almost unbearable.
Even so, I learned.
I learned to depend on myself
and no one else.
You thought you had me in the
palm of your hand,
To do with as you wished.
To crush. Hurt. Destroy.
But no more.
For in spite of you and your
pain-inflicting way. . .
I HAVE SURVIVED

Norma Jeanne Zeliff

THE ECHO OF THUNDER

The horses galloped, pounding a
steady beat along a winding,
dusty, mountain trail.
Flashes of lightning rent the
darkening sky, illuminating
the barren earth's parched
existence.
Rocks jutted menacingly,
looming larger than reality,
as the crashing thunder
echoed and re-echoed.
Flashes of light showed the ears
turned back, eyes rolled white
with fear, tongues hanging
dry.
A rabbit scuttled across into the
dry brush, triggering the panic
of the fleeing herd.
Rearing high into the air, hoofs
flailed the unseen enemy.
A small boy hurtled through
the air, striking with a thud!
The raindrops spattered slowly,
stirring the dust, gained
momentum, and beat a steady
tatoo.
Rivulets streamed off the
motionless figure, leaving
small puddles greedily
absorbed by the thirsty earth.
The pounding rain spent its
measure, leaving a crispness
and freshness of night.
The thunder mumbled softly in
the distance, as the storm
moved its forces down into
the valley.
The small figure layed so
motionless, so very still, his
clothes drying in the warm
soft breezes.
The dawn gleamed brightly, its
yellow-orange rays, shining
down upon a small boy of
seven.
Eyelids fluttering, grimacing in
extreme pain, he tried to
move the blood-soaked leg.
The effort became so
momentous, that mercifully,
he slipped into deep
unconsciousness.
Hours passed slowly, the sun
cruelly boiling down.
A deep throated bird's song
broke the silence.
A lizard slid clumsily over
the boy's foot.
Late afternoon found the boy
feverish with pain.
His lips, blistered by the sun's
rays, moaned feebily.
Hope of being rescued was
overshadowed by pain.
When hoofbeats sounded
coming up the trail, he
weakly called out an alarm,
and quietly fainted.
Cradled in the fatherly arms of
love, at long last, he was
transported to the safe haven
of home.
The finest doctoring continued
through the ensuing months,
but the escapade left the
small boy crippled and fearful.
For the body healed, but the
usual lively mind, was full of
frozen fear, and crippled as his
leg.
The golden summer days
shimmering and shiny,
gradually slipped into fall
with its full array of painted
leaves.
He watched with shuddering
that old proud horse, calmly
chewing hay in the large
corral below.
The boy, wrestled within, with
his torment, his fearful
thoughts as if in mortal
combat!
Then came a moment of
decision! A great moment of
truth!
He carefully approached and
mounted the horse named
Thunder.
Sensing the importance of such
a mission, Thunder quieted,
and joined the boy in the
battle at hand,
Together they merged, flying,
flying, as if ONE.
Conquering the feared foe, the
battle was soon ended.
Turning again toward the safe
haven of home, they were met
tearfully, with the shining
eyes of love.

Fred K. Johnson

FOURTEEN IN SIXTY-ONE

Four summers was I and ten,
The Crossroads store: As far
as I had been.
Like a million others in sixty-
one,
Hungerin' for excitement at
news of Bull Run.
So, I slipped away from 'Bama
cabin,
To stop the hunger pangs that
kept a-stabbin'.
And joined Ole Joe's Tennessee
Volunteers
By declarin' I'd seen more'n
fourteen years.
For months after joinin', it
was fun,
Walkin' in line: carryin' a
stick for a gun.
George, Jimmy, Bill, and me as
close as brothers,
Funnin' and laughin' at each
one's druthers.
Heroes: That's what we all
wanted to be,
Bathed in Glory but not dyin'
for the Confederacy.
But, at Shiloh, we learned what
it was all about,
When the Yankee boys
blasted us to rout.
And I saw George and Jimmy
lyin' on the ground,
Half-closed eyes, lips movin':
makin' no sound.
Blood ran from Bill's mouth in
a stream,
The glory of war was no
longer a dream.
Five summers and ten are past,
Hobblin' toward home, prayin'
to last
The hunger and pain and to see
once more
A cabin, once droll, and walk
through its door.
Would that I could have known
all this when
I was only four summers and
ten.

Andra Allen

A QUESTION OF TIME

So soon...
Already I miss you
At least I learned how to get
along without you.
Or I had.
Then I held you again
and forgot everything I'd
learned.
I found the rest of my soul in
your arms...
Odd.
I keep praying, "Thy Will be
done" and I fall in love with you
every time I see you.
Even though I know I shouldn't.
Odd.
No matter how far apart we are,
we always seem to take up
where we left off.
Like time and distance had
never existed.
Odd.
But who am I to question Fate?
Maybe I'll never wake up...

Ruth I. Blake

SNAILS

In my garden by the high brown
wall,
The Callas grow; green, strong
and tall.
'Twould not be so, ere I forgot
The foe of these tall plants to
spot.
Small creatures, they; but slow
and sure;
From Calla leaves their food
secure.
Their houses range from brown
to black;
Are fastened to each tiny back.
Warm bright rays of morning
sky
Seek nooks where sleepy snails
lie;
And in response to friendly sun
Creep out from safety, one by
one.
Were I a Frenchman, I am sure,
I'd find use, as a connoisseur,
For each fellow, and no lack,
Who carries his house upon his
back!

Christi Tanner

MOURNFUL DOLORES

*(based on Thomas Morley's
"Fantasy Doloroso"*

Cloaked in morning muted gray,
The mournful Dolores makes
Her way, across the dew-kissed
England hills...and forlorn
Like a solo lute her wails
Drift upwards to the bird--
That glides lonely overhead...
The saddest sound a heart has
Heard--the cries of Dolores
For her lover dead--no longer
Will they wed...
Ah, Elizabethan-like queen,
Walking in a dream--white
Cape flowing in the fog--
Why so sad? Is life without
Him all that bad? Do not
Despair and long for death...
Did not he say with his last
Breath--time, though slow,
Will heal your broken heart...
And memories of now will
Someday soon depart?
No, you must not mourn
Dolores fair--although he is no
Longer there...
You must live to sing your
Fa-la-la's--and dance the
New ballet in May...
For love will someday reappear,
To play upon your silent
Ayre...
And kiss your tears
Away...

Ted R. Daniels

PERPLEXED

Still unanswered by the sages,
Still no adequate reply
To the query of the ages:
Why must earnest, good men
cry?
Lions' den, the furnace burning,
Persecutions of the past. . . . .
Often for green pastures
yearning. . .
Victories that seldom last.
Jacob's ladder looms before us
With its rungs so widely
spaced. .

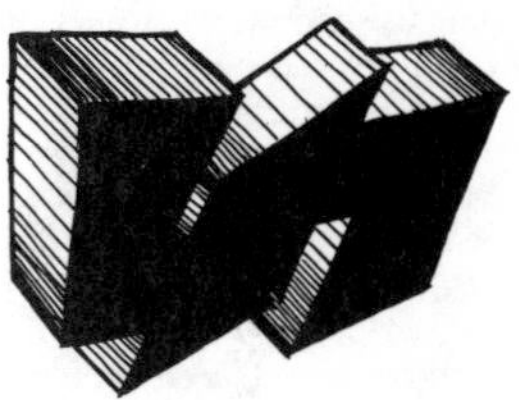

Can we list to angels' chorus
Or Seraph's strains so richly
graced?
We must leap with great
precision
To yon rung with soul
transfixed,
Lest we suffer hell's derision
Should we chance to fall
betwixt.
Laurels might be on us resting
If our mettle we can show;
Life is testing. . .ever testing!!
Life, why doth thou test me so?

Sue Lynne Foster

WHEN WAR IS OVER

When war is over...
And the fighting's done,
And we finally learn to live as
one.
When guns fall limply to the
ground,
With flowers growing all
around.
The skies will open up above,
As the eagle flies off with the
dove.
When our universal word is
song,
And hate and predjudice is gone.
When man learns how to love
his brother,

And live in peace with one another.
When unity spreads throughout the land,
As we finally learn to understand.
Then we'll live in peace and we'll all be free,
A utopia eternally.
When the whole wide world joins hand in hand,
And the lion sleeps beside the lamb.

Jeannette Garrison Silveira

MIKE

Your eyes they have a sparkle
your smile softly outshines
the sunlite on the morning dew
the rain drops on the pines.
Your words are a song of
honor, your touch a winters fire.
Your nearness ignites a living
flame that sparks with pure
desire.
You have brought me out of
darkness-a woman, and no
longer a thing; now
remembering my feelings and
dreams, a puppet no longer...
You've severed my strings...

Nora Wucinski

'TIS COMIC

Let's write something comic, amusing, funny to enjoy, for you and me.
Sometimes there is laughter even in trag-e-dy.
Like a boat sinking in the middle of the sea.
If everyone is saved-then we're all hap-py.
Mishaps are gladness if you have a bad fall,
And no bones broken just a few bumps, bruises, and a black eye-
Nothing too terrible to make you cry.
Thankful we should be; I write it in verse,
Always something bad could even be worse.

Mary C. Silvey

FAIRYLAND

I know a place that is like fairyland.
It is the wonder work of the Master's Hand.
This place displays its' seasons as a fascinating wonderland—
In the spring the babbling brook sings out it's song to woo the natures of the woods.
The birds are on the wing seeking the favors of their mates,
The wild bush honeysuckle is a thing of beauty and sweetness.
In the summertime the green moss covered rocks of the brook send out its coolness.
The mighty oak, stately pines, graceful birch, and sycamore are showing off their greenery.
All types of woodland violets, pitcher plants, and moss cover the land.
In the fall the blaze of color shows the closeness of God's plans.

Come early winter time the colorful leaves cover the place—
There is a hush as one softly walks over the land—
This place is a part of my life plan.
When I need to dwell on happy thoughts,
I think of my childhood running and playing at this wonder place.
As I grew older it was my place to ponder.
In my mature years I loved this place with my husband—
In a soft and happy tone he said, "This is our fairyland."

Gay Hughes

IN RETROSPECT

I'm sitting tonight in the glow of the grate and counting the years that have gone
And I'm thinking of how I've used up the time and what I've done with each one
I've toiled to the top of the hill's western slope and I'm just looking backward to see
What I've done with the days and the years that were mine and all that has happened to me.
I've tasted of happiness, laughter and love and all the things that were sweet
I've walked through the valley of sorrow and woe but I've never admitted defeat.
I've stumbled and fallen not once but a score and I've been criticized time and again
But I find no disgrace in the fact that I fell. . .
Only pride that I've risen again.
I might have been rich if I'd wanted the gold
In place of the friends that I've made
I might have had fame if I'd chosen renown
Instead of the hours that I've played
I haven't built much of a fortune to leave
To those who shall carry my name
And nothing I've done shall entitle me here
To a place in the great hall of fame.
But I've loved the great sky with its spaces of blue
And I've enjoyed the birds and the trees
I've turned from the lure of the silver and gold
To share in such treasures as these.
I've given my time to the children of men;
Together we've romped and we've played
And I wouldn't recall the glad hours spent with them
For the money I might have made.
I just chose to be known and loved by my friends and was deaf to the plaudits of men
And I'd make the same choice should the chance come to me
To live my life over again.
I've lived with my friends and I've shared in their joys,
Known sorrow with all its tears
I've harvested much from my acres of life,
Though some say I've wasted my years.
For much that is good has been mine to enjoy and I've tried always to do just my best
And I find no regret as the shadows grow long for the gold that I might have possessed.
I've wiped away tears and planted some smiles,
I've walked hand in hand with despair
I've helped with the burdens and lightened the loads too great for my brothers to bear.
And all through the years I've done what I could
To banish a tear or a sigh
I've lost out on wealth but I'm sure of this truth. . .
I've some things that money can't buy.
The song of the birds, the perfume of the flowers,
The love of a dog or a boy
Shall keep me content as I wander along
Still sure that they're mine to enjoy.
More years may slip by as they have in the past,
I've no reason to change or amend
For the path I have chosen is filled with delight
And I shall continue to walk to its end.
Now, if this is success then I'm surely content—
If it's failure, I've had loads of fun
Just doing the things I really wanted to do
And the things I thought should be done.

Dora Lee Christie

GOD'S ARTISTRY

God displays His handiwork
In every place and clime;
But the hour when day is ending
Is my most favorite time.
I saw the sun set on the water,
The sky a brilliant red;
With variations of color
Through the cotton puffs overhead.
Off to the left a solid line
Of color round about;
To the right, bits and pieces
Where He left His colors out.
Oh, our glorious Creator,
What artistry He wrought;
As I beheld day's dying glory,
My mind was filled with thought.
How much He thinks of us
To put on such a display;
But the wonder of it all;
It's different every day!

Dane Robert Watrud

THE LOVE

The love that was
Still is and does
What love must do
be true
Not alone for me and you
But all who call us dear
And wait each night to hear
Us climb the stair
And say God Bless You
in our prayer
We plant the seeds to grow
in little hearts
And they in turn fulfill
the good we will
And thus the rose of long ago
still shows
it's beauty in our day
The Rose of Sharon

Selver B. Williams

WHEN THE MOMENT COMES

When the moment comes,
The people will collide together,
They'll walk side by side down an aisle,
Not as enemy, but as sister and brother.
When the moment comes,
All hatred will finally dissolve,
We will be blinded by a color,
We will only see peace and love.
When the moment comes,
Joy will be bountiful within us,
Our love will prevail our happiness,
All eternal creatures will be friends.
We will all be waiting and praying,
To unite and be as one,
Oh how glorious it will be,
When the moment comes.

A E Beck

MARGY

Sunlight on water, like diamonds
She with snow in her hair and
Summer in her eyes
Sunlight, Laughter, Sorrow, Love

Anne Kelly

UNTITLED

Repeat what time has already passed
Give grace to those who dare not
For it is the one who dares not
Who dies with emptiness in his soul.
He counts each moment and looks not on

In fear that he may not live;
And in hoping to hide himself
from death
His soul slowly passes on,
And in hoping to hide himself
from death
His soul slowly passes on...
His soul slowly passes on...

E. M. Riddle

FREE TO FLY

Free to fly beyond anger of all
sort;
Reasons bad, reasons good,
reasons misunderstood.
Reasons, perhaps none at all;
Free to fly beyond anger's
furious fall.
Not thinking of now, but of the
past;
Not thinking at all, acting too
fast.
Free to fly into a peaceful state;
Being calm at all times, never
hate.
The temper is gone when you
can fly;
Just happiness, no want to cry.
Please act now, there is still
time;
Free to fly from this terrible
crime.
When, oh when, will I ever be
totally
Free to Fly!

L. J. Cormier

MOVEMENT

The time was:
When one could accept
Varied shades of being
Without push-button frenzy
When one could (most
assuredly)
Quicken the cerebral pulse
Unto the high places,
Despite digitals which answer
'Yay' or 'nay'
But gently now...
The balance is disturbed;
Look closely! Look fast!!
Inanimates are in motion

Terri Lousie Lamb

I NEVER GIVE ALL

Windswept through time
I defy this illusion
While left to myself
To disect the intrusion
Disaster and tragedy
rush through my head
The pleasure I crave
Comes only in bed
I search intensely for one
That keeps itself hidden
Touching on spectrums
Never dear, just forbidden
The widening abyss
Desperately wanting to fall
I long to dive in
But I never give all

Carol Tingey Michaelis

WHERE I USED TO BE

I went along the street where I
had lived before
I saw the school and the park
and the store
where I spent my nickles, long
before
I looked along the street and
wondered about the people
next door.
But what I really wanted to see
Was all the children playing
and have one of them be me.
If all the children were out to
play
I wonder--could I tell which one
was me that day?
Could I tell if she was happy
then,
Did she smile and have a friend,
Did she jump rope and play
with paper dolls,
like I think I remember she did?
When I go back to how things
used to be
I look for the street and the
school and the house
But what I really want to see
Is the little girl that I used to
be.

Elsa S. Degel

B O O S T

Boost your city, boost your
town,
Boost your neighbors all around,

Boost your bosses round about
you -
They can get along without you,
But success will quicker find
them,
When they know that you're
behind them.

Leola Minich

DOWN THE ROAD

My friend and I walked
down the road together.
We laughed and talked as we
walked,
down the road together.
We gathered flowers, as we
talked and walked,
down the road together.
Then we remembered our friend
down the road.
We talked and walked and took
our flowers to our friend,
down the road.
We gave our friend the flowers.
Our friend, down the road,
had been lonesome and sad.
But, because we had talked and
walked
and gathered flowers
Our friend, down the road, was
now happy and glad.
So let us always remember as we
travel
down life's road,
To gather flowers to share with
our friends,
down the road.

Joan L. Pearson

FREEDOM

Oh' thy freedom, what bliss, if
each of us mortals can earn this
right.
It is not given to us, one by one,
free for this word freedom is a
proud flow of pure joy that
passes the lips of every
American in sight.
We, the people of this proud
land are all equal born to, or
into this heritage and cannot
deny each red, white and blue
and star studded flag waving
proudly in the sky and in the
mist we hear a soft cry.
Wake up, wake up, you mortal
creatures, can you not see the
dove of peace flying over the
land. Can we not have the peace
each American has yearned and
died for. Must we nail together
more white crosses in some
faraway place, only to be
forgotten again and again.
Hear the cries in the wind,
Listen to their plea. Peace,
Peace, so we can rest. Peace in
the land. Peace, so we have not
died in vain. Peace, we demand
for the voices of freedom and of
the cries of our unrested souls
of our soldiers can rest and
would have not died in vain.

Patricia Kilpatrick Gibbs

NEVER TO BE

The songs that never were sung
for us
The paths we never will walk
The sunsets never our eyes will
share
The leaves that fall in the park.
The laughs that never our lips
shall sound
The tears we never will shed
The joy of morning seen
through mist
The sleeping late in bed.
The children never our bodies
shall make
The hands we never will hold
The trust that never we both
will know
The cuddling in the cold.
The tunes we never shall dance
till dawn
The future we never will see
The love that never we both
will share
All this is never to be.

Orilea Brown

DEAR FRIEND

In Memoriam: Alice Morrison Rackley (1925-1981)

Life is like a garden where
thorns and beauty dwell
Where thoughts and deeds are
the seeds that grow; and
indeed you planted well.
When I think of you it's pansies
I see, with that sweet
expressive face,
Bringing to mind such episodes
of another time and place;
of childish pranks, a sorrow
shared and dreams that faded
away.
But the fragrance remains
to warm our hearts and
bring a glow to the day.
So each of us, as we think of
you, has a lovely view to
share; as we travel down
our memory lane gathering
flowers there.

Ms. Annie L. Wilson

THE HALFWAY MARK

You stand in the middle of a
clearing.
You take a deep breath and you
sigh.
You look back at the thorns and
thistles of life.
The pain is there...even in your
eye.
You stand there and breathe the
free fresh air.
So deeply it...penetrates.
It soothes the mind. It helps the
heart.
The soul...it reverberates.
You look to the sides and you
look ahead
You don't have to look behind.
For what's back there, you know
about.
Ahead is where you will find.
All that you wanted in the past.
All of your dreams un-fulfilled.
Ahead is where it all really is.
The past—it seems, so unreal
Ahead - way in the distance
You dimly see a door.
It's marked - and all the labels
read.
All you could ever hope for -
So breathe while you can.
Because you see. Between you
and that great door
More thistles, more thorns,
more pain of life.
But isn't it worth a little more?

Paul R. Kovatch

WHO ARE WE?

We are more than a name and
number,
all things we do--we will
encumber.
To state our age and place of
birth,
we are ourselves--anywhere on
earth.
The friends we keep will show
everyone,
if we are serious or just having
fun.
What we read and what we
drink,
all affects how we think.
The T.V. shows we select each
day,
control our lives--come what
may.
The music that we love so well,
have words and thoughts we'll
never tell.
Our job, our home and city too,
can influence all but a few.
Newspapers, and magazines of
our time,
saturate our minds with sex and
crime.
It is not for us to choose our
relations,
but smile and bear our trials and
tribulations.
Everywhere we go we're told to
"DO IT",
but can our mind and body get
us through it?
To live today and sleep tonight,
doesn't mean we must always
fight.
There's more to life than power
and fame,
it takes courage and faith to see
the same.

Mrs. A. R. Meredith

THE PATTER PASSES BY

I hear the children on the street
In mirth their laughter roar,
It takes me back to yester-year
When happy children, four

Frolicked in childish fun and glee,
Around my cottage door
Although Alas, the laughter's gone,
I seem to hear once more;
The blend of childish voices
Of those happy ones at play,
But the patter of those little feet
Tread different paths today.
They have grown to man, and womanhood,
And took their place in life,
With cares, responsibilities,
They face a world of strife.
I thank you Lord for each of these
You trusted to my care.
Watch over Lord, protect and keep,
Is my fervent daily prayer.
I sit in reminiscence alone
As children by the score,
Go pitter, patter, on the street,
And pass on by my door.

Jorjanna Meeks

YESTERDAY I FELL IN LOVE

Yesterday I fell in love. . . . reached for the moon, and touched your hand instead. It was a crazy thing, my falling in love. . . .like I'd reached for your hand, and touched the moon instead. . . .like finding a pot of gold at the rainbow's end when I hadn't believed that it might be there. . . .like discovering a genie in a discarded old lamp that was ready and anxious to grant my every wish when I had long-since stopped believing in fairy tales, and miracles, and happiness that cry out inside a person so they feel like a child standing for the first time in front of a Christmas tree blinking unbelievingly at all the wondrous things his little eyes can see.

Yesterday I fell in love. . . . reached for you at the same moment you reached for me. It was a crazy thing, our reaching for each other at the same time. . . .like starting to sing the same lyrics at precisely the same time someone across the room started to sing them. . . . like writing identical lines of poetry at the same time someone else was writing them. . . .like discovering countless stars twinkling in the sky moments after a threatening storm, and a million sad and lonely people had burst into song. . . .like birds chirping, bells ringing, children singing. . . like dreaming you were walking on a cloud, and waking up to find you really were when you hadn't believed it possible to experience such a sensation, and you weren't convinced until that moment that falling in love could really happen; not the way the poets and songwriters have said it could, at least.

Yesterday the whole world changed for me. Somber skies transforming to a magnificient shade of blue all because I had fallen in love with you, and you had fallen in love with me. It was a crazy thing our falling in love like that. . . .like discovering there really were such things as jolly little elves who scurried around in the night to do good deeds. . . .like watching while the windows of heaven opened wide to scatter seeds of love and kindness on all living creatures. . . .like learning all the elements that excite horror, tragedy, and heartbreak had been swept away as if by some invisible broom or vacuum. . . .like turning back the calendar to the time when you had believed in fairy tales, and miracles, and happiness that cries out inside a person, and you were once again that child standing in front of a Christmas tree blinking unbelievingly at all the wondrous things your little eyes can see.

Yesterday the whole world changed for me. There I was, and there you were, and something magical, had happened all because I had fallen in love with you, and you had fallen in love with me.

Blance D. Geiger

THE LAST BOUQUET OF SUMMER

I strolled the silent garden walks,
Like wine to sip the last sweet drops,
My heart cried out in deep dismay,
Knowing Jack Frost would have his day.
Marigold in splendor, lined the paths with gold,
Aromatic guardians, of the garden's soul,
They added beauty to my home all day,
Friends were happy, with a bright Bouquet.
Colorful Zinnias stand prim,
Like starched old Maiden Ladies,
Potent still, with fading trim,
Companions to the Daisies.
The grasses bend with heads bowed low
To whisper one last prayer,
The broken Reeds like folded hands,
Are stilled, in mute despair.
As the hush that comes before the Dawn,
All nature seems at Limbo,
Before the Scepter cuts it down,
Grimly heaving one last blow.
All the glory lush with Verdure,
Like a breath that has been stilled,
Or a pattern set in time,
It yet must rise and be fulfilled.
The Leaves like silent teardrops fall,
In matured subdued coloring,
To blanket the Mother of it all,
A promise of life's renewing.
While my heart weeps, I choose and pluck,
The brightest blossoms gay,
Arranging them with tenderness
Into a last Bouquet.
I turn away in sad farewell
The beauty left behind,
Needs must return another day,
To represent it's kind.

Hans G. Jepson

A POET'S LAMENT

Lives there a Soul on earth today who has not spent some time to pray?
He may not know just what to say or how to best his fears allay.
Yet with his doubts he still proceeds to call on Him who knows his needs;
For in his youth were planted seeds that far outlast the later weeds.
From day to day his friends will say, "why waste your time to kneel and pray?"
"Just live and laugh throughout the day and think of different ways to play."
You've tried to follow what they said, yet when you did it seemed so dead,
'Twas nothing more than Ego-fed, a body, yes, without a head.

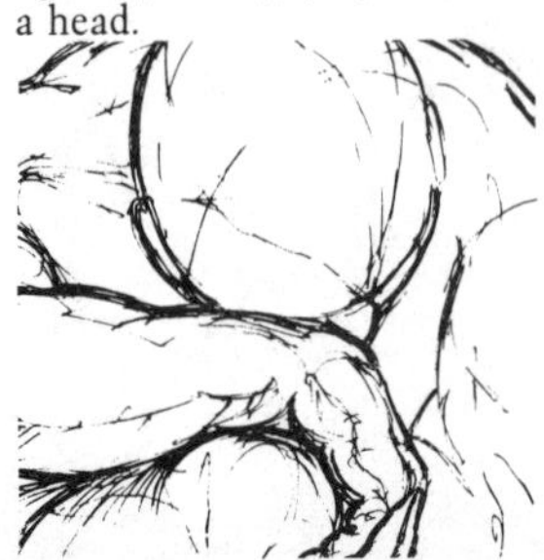

Each crisis as it came to pass, left you alone to face the class.
They all are gone, your wealth, your friends, the places where you spent weekends.
What was is not, no longer blends; Time does not give, it only lends.
Tis then it dawns on you at last, your small, small part of a larger cast.
So after all is said and done and life has made its final run,
When shadows seem the light to shun, yet linger as if they had won.
You watch the sun die in the West and feel that soon you'll also rest.
Before you do you want to pray, for now you know just what to say!

Freda Brenneman Aldinger

GROWING OLD GRACEFULLY

I Wrote this for our twenty-fifth anniversary.

We're growing old together dear,
signs of age begin to appear.
The gray is starting to show through,
middle age is just around the corner it's true.
The changes are coming gradually,
we're growing old gracefully.
Although we're still in our prime,
that will change with the passing of time.
We vowed to love each other forever and a day,
we couldn't live our lives any other way.
Darling our life together is so fulfilling,
day and night we give our love so willing.
Words are hard to find to express what I feel,
a love so strong, yet tender and real.
Stormy at times like the weather,
we always came through the trouble together.
God has given us many happy years to share,
a special love like ours is somewhat rare.
The aging process doesn't come hastily,
we're slowly growing old gracefully.

Sioths Shelenberg

MY SOUL AND I

I believe in re-incarnation,
No, never evolution,
I do not believe that I have evolved from an ant,
Nor a tumble-bug, toiling and rolling his wad of mud,
An ape, a horse an elephant,
No! that could not be,
I am a living soul,
Created in the image and the likeness of God,
To live forever and forever;
This life is a training for a better life to come,
That which is over-come in this life,
Will be our victory of the tomorrows,
When this body, the home of my soul
Has worn out, I shall lay it down and rest,
And soon shall be awakened a new born baby,
Held close to a loving mother's breast;
I shall grow, learn, live and strive
For the perfection
For which all are created.

Richard D. Cagg

NATURE'S CRADLE

The glimmering sheen from the branches of the trees
Feathers into the light of the night--yet my eye sees
Those same boughs and limbs in

the day
Cast shadows one upon the
other as they get in each
other's way
I watch a rock skate the top of a
frozen pond
Then began I to wonder how I
might expound
The meaning and wisdom of
what I had found
Then suddenly became I aware
As my heart sang praises to the
one with which I share
I felt my Creator's Finger as He
passed by
Sweetly He caressed my spirit as
it did fly
Entwined with His love and
beauty divine
Touched He me to release a
peace
Sharing a bit of bliss as He
cradled my soul
For nature beckons gently that
all may partake
And breathe deep of our
Creator--there is no escape

Lysa Jean Farmer

RUNNING AGAINST THE WIND

When young it's natural to run
against the wind,
caught up with all the optimism
and spontaneity of youth.
But the years pass and the run
turns to a gait -
the optimism and spontaneity
turn to caution and restraint.
With the passage of more time
the gait becomes a walk
the steps filled now with
cynicism and pattern.
One learns through the years to
pay heed to the wind...
Why is it that I am running
faster than ever against the
wind?
My optimism is gone; now the
total cynic -
yet my spontaneity and daring
continue to grow each year,
keeping tempo with the speed of
my steps that seem
to pay less and less heed to the
wind.
I meet the resistance of the
gales head to head
and search out the riskiest
paths to continue down,
where my solitary footsteps are
heard -
becoming faster and faster
against the wind.
How long before I am blown
away
as is the lone tumbleweed, who
has also neglected
to heed the voice of the wind?

Joan E. Tarro

REACH OUT

Sometimes in life two hearts
will touch
But, for one, the emotions
become too much;
And so, to avoid any glimmer of
pain,
One or the other indifference
will feign.
Before too long time slips away,
And we're unable to recapture
yesterday.
Honest emotions we were afraid
to show,
So the simplest of treasures we
never know.
Our minds we use to great avail,
But when it comes to feelings,
what makes us fail?
Are we unable to recognize
what's before our eyes,
Or have we been bombarded
with too many lies?
Are we much too frightened to
take a chance,
And give the other a second
glance?
Is trust a word we refuse to
know,
Or is it just much easier to
solitarily go?
We use our minds to attain
many "things";
But, when it comes to
happiness, what does it bring?
Can we be complete with only
that,
When emotional joy is where
it's at?
To be rich is to be able to
love and feel,
And only then can we
experience what's real!
To have an inner knowledge of
what life's about,
Is an incomparable treasure
without a doubt.
Why do we force our inhibited
ways,
And cheat ourselves for days
and days?
Do we feel unworthy to have
such joy,
Or are people simply a throw-
away toy?
Are we so engulfed in our long-
ago woes,
That everyone else becomes our
foe?
Have we closed forever the road
ahead,
And simply become the living
dead?
Can we not look up and see a
star,
And know inside just who we
are?
Are we unable to share the
morning sun,
And feel complete just holding
someone?
If our answer is no, we are
truly poor;
We are traveling alone on a
distant shore.
We've failed to reach out for
another's hand,
And we'll walk alone in a rich,
rich land!

Mrs. Cindy White

YOU'RE ALL I LOVE

All the things I love...
Are all the things you are -
In the lonely dark of night
You're my bright and shining
star -
When clouds are forming
overhead
And rain starts pouring down --
If all my sunny skies turn gray
And friends cannot be found --
Whenever things are going
wrong
Should something make me cry -
My love to make me happy,
You hardly have to try -
For just the very thought of you
Brings to my face a smile --
And for your kiss which is pure
bliss
My love I'd walk a mile --
But any time I need you
Never are you far -
And all the things I love, dear
Are all the things you are -

M. Ruth Howard

TREASURED MEMORIES

It is raining as I climb the
stairs to the dusty old attic.
The pitter-patter makes a tune
as it falls upon the roof.
I hum to the tune of the rain
drops as I lift the lid of
mother's old trunk.
I know I shall shed many tears
as I look at her treasured
possessions.
I slowly raise the lid, everything
is neatly in place.
Little strands of hair tied with
pink and blue ribbons, wrapped
in tissue.
A tiny gold ring, a baby shoe, a
little dress yellowed with age.
Here's a package of papers tied
with twine, poems she
composed herself.
"Just my thoughts" she would
say, as she wrote them down
each day.
A red polka dot dress, the dots
as big as a dime, an evening
cape worn thin
with time.
A tiny gold locket, heart shaped
holdin her first sweet hearts
picture, my Dad.
Her beloved Bible, frayed at the
edges, a record of marriages,
births, and deaths.
A sewing basket filled with
her working tools, scissors,
needles, horn-rim glasses
As I place the basket back a
pressed flower falls out, there's
a note "To my mommy, with all
my love, Jimmy" Scribbled in a
childish hand.
Mother dearly loved to sing,
each night when our chores
were done,
She would play the Organ and
sing to us.
As I place the things back and
gently close the lid, I have
cried as I knew I would, because
of the memories they brought
back to me.
It has stopped raining now,
but I can still hear the tune,
of the rain-drops.
Mother wrote a Poem she called
Rain, that is the tune I was
humming.
That is why I go to the attic
on rainy days, I feel her
presence there, as I spend hours
reminiscing with her and her
treasured memories.
She loved the rain, she loved
to walk in the rain, and I am my
Mother's daughter, singing her
little tune.
RAIN
I love the pitter-patter of the
rain,
The pitter-patter on my window
pane.
The rain never makes me blue,
For it always reminds me of you.
It was there I found you in the
rain,
And I'm so happy when I sing
this refrain,
To the pitter-patter of the rain,
Falling softly on my window
pane.

Andrew Stewart

DEMETRICE... UNFINISHED PALSM

i wrote a poem
for you
not because
i had to
but because
i felt
there was
something needed
said...
i write it
warm and caring
filled with
an abundance
of love...
sounds of the
ocean's
serenades
the tinkling
of a bell
dangling on the
neck of a puppy
named "smokey"
who came over
care-free
to play with
me...
the chatter of
seagulls
the silence of
the shifting sand
a ship moving
effortlessly
across the sea
i compared
your beauty
with the sun
moon
stars
in the sky
and just when
i thought
i'd
finished
i realized
i still
had not
said
enough....

Terezia Maria Farkas

THE DUCHESS AND THE RANGER

In a place and time long gone
A man and woman held hands
And promised each other
Their love would never end.
They'd planned their future well

For the man was a ranger
And the woman a duchess
Yet neither saw the impending danger.
Their families didn't like it
Who'd ever heard of this?
A duchess and ranger married
Seemingly in joyous bliss.
So the girl's father one day
Took the ranger down a wooded hill
And there beside a lonely bridge
The handsome ranger fell down still.
She cried for days on end
But when finally she stopped
She realized that she'd really won
Because one day they'd never be apart.

Mariana DeLeeuw Kasper

NOVEMBER

The trees stand stark and bare
Against the cold grey sky;
Only some rusty leaves
Cling to days long gone by.
The land lies tired and worn,
The grasses brown, weeds dried.
A harsh November wind
Rustles leaves far and wide.
Waters do not welcome,
Their steel grey waves awry.

Days of summer sparkle
No longer greet the eye.
Endless clouds shroud the sun
Despite our longing cry.
The birds have taken wing,
Only a few are nigh.
Pillar of endurance
Throughout the days that try;
The stalwart evergreen,
Its beauty bold abides.

Craig Steven Mara

POET TO POET

Many, a-many a year ago,
in a cave
within a hill.
There lived a man
named Deacon
who today,
is talked of still.
Now Deacon was
no man of greed,
no power was his own.
He just sat contently
in his cave,
and pounded on
some stone.
He carved some words,
in his own way—
a language of his own.
When suddenly
an earthquake shook,
and Deacon
lost that stone.
A billion years,
have gone by now
and Deacons in his grave.
but just some how
by stroke of luck,
that carved up stone
was saved.
Now scientist,
from far and wide
have come to see
that stone.
And are amazed,
how Neanderthal
could carve with sharpened bone.
One scientist said,
it must have been their Freud
studying someone's mind.
Another said
it's E=MC2,
we have found
another Einstein.
Now they were puzzled,
as you might guess—
for Deacon left no key.
So it was made public
to all the world,
for someone to solve?
We'll see.
Then a young boy,
named Johnny,
who wasn't very bright.
Looked at that stone
in a different sort of light
which left him with thoughts
the rest of the night.
He sat by himself
with the night
full grown.
And with thoughts containing
that ancient old stone,
he started to write
some words of his own.
It isn't of Einstein,
or even of Freud—
not even to do with old Rome,
Just simply some words
felt in a man's heart,
yes probably
the very first poem.

James David Jacobs

A WILL TO WIN

Through the shadows of the night I felt,
I saw the light, and a blow it dealt,
When at last my soul did say,
"It's been a trip of worthless day".
"A trip, I say, is not so bad",
"It's the bottomless pit that makes it sad".
I struggled and fought the best I could,
To find the end not so good,
Many a soul has lost their way,
Trying to travel thru the chartered day.
"There was a light", I said with joy,
That lit the way and led this boy,
Amongst the rumble and toils of life,
Somehow-Somewhere came the will to fight.
And out of the mud and failures to be,
The Light I saw had let me see!

Sharon Juanice Lewis

I LOVE THE SON

I have been transformed
By the renewing of my mind
In knowing the reality
Of Jesus Christ
Therefore
I love the Son
I cherish the Son
I believe the Son
For the Son has given me peace
And the Son has given me joy
The Son has given
And given
And given
And given
Until
I am no more me
But the Christ
That liveth in me!

T. Diana Brown

UNTITLED

As in life, a goal was placed in a shell and set upon a rock
And I found this shell, whose goal I released
Then I took it and set it upon a rock
And I wandered off to set such a goal
And the winds tore me, they scarred my body
My directions were altered
My mind confused
I stared again towards the past, trying to visualize
the light which brought me here.
Then I began again.
Never stopping, always trying
Trying
Trying
Trying... I grew old with age, but not with courage
And finally in the last days I returned there, to the place
which I'd wandered from, my journey complete -- I walked,
Looking hopelessly toward its light
And alas I completed my journey toward the rock
whose goal I'd found.
And though I had changed in appearance and had aged.
The rock had not
The goal was still there
I placed my mark upon it.

Joseph M. Sanford

WHEN LOVE GOES STALE

(September 5th, 1981)

When love goes stale,
It seems without fail
A troublesome time indeed.
It's a lonely tale;
No letters in the mail,
Just a heart might need.
Go and cry to the moon,
And do it soon,
But it won't help the pain,
For the mental tune
Might want to swoon,
But instead will melt in the rain.
Blame the winds of chance,
Then share a dance
With someone else along the way.
Love's horse will prance
And be so enhanced
With what someone else will say.

Donna Arsenault Rupenski

REMEMBER ME PLEASE

A long ride on a sunny day,
cows grazing - horses - hay
Remember me please.
A cool breeze through your hair,
Sudden dinners made with care,
Fresh spring water on the side of the road
A Fleetwood Mac tune on the radio,
Remember me please.
Waterfalls in the midst of woods,
talking till it's understood,
Staying up till late at night,
then catching Z's before it's light,
Remember me please.

Judy Hood-Cox

CAPTURED WITHIN YOUR LOVE

Capture me within thy heart
Bring me love that shall never part
knowing you love me is all I need
To help and guide and to succeed
The good and the bad is to be I'm sure
With our strength and knowledge we shall overcome and endure
Children in many our love will bare
Within our hearts deep love to share
On this day the bells will chime
Our love will go on throughout all time.

Katherine Nosek

I SAW YOU LAST NIGHT AND I CRIED

I saw you last night, and I cried.
Five years ago, we said good-bye;
You went your way--I went mine.
We never saw nor heard of each other--
Our time was occupied by another.
I saw you last night, and I cried.
No longer did you love me;
That was easy for us to see.
It was easy for me to handle too;
For neither did I love you.
I saw you last night and I cried.
Time heals all the memories
Of sweet things love's eyes can see.
I love another--I know this is true;
Years ago, I forgot about you.
I saw you last night, and I cried.
Five years ago, we said good-bye;
You went your way--I went mine.
The love is gone, it is no more.
I love you not; of this I'm sure.
I saw you last night, and I cried.

Inez J. Reddoch

SISTER MARY CALLISTA

Sister Mary Callista is a devoted Nun,
Her smile is warm as the morning sun.
At McAuley Home is where she lives,
Service to the Lord, is what she gives.
Sister cares not for fortune or fame,

But, she is proud of her family
name.
My husband Bill, is Sister's
brother
The two of them adore each
other.
The Reddochs were of Irish
decent,
Attending Mass, was a regular
event.
Thus, from this long family line,
Counting Sister, the children
were nine.
Her nieces and newphews are
quite a few,
Mostly adults and their children
too.
Sister is their 'Guiding Light!,
Shining like a Star at Night.
Mississippi is Sister's home
State,
And she lovingly remembers a
certain date.
The day that God, made her life
content,
That happy day, she entered the
Convent.

Thomas R. Boughan

THE MAN FROM PLANET ZEE

All the way from Planet Zee
came he
To this little corner of the
Milky Way Galaxy.
I found him picking my corn
So early in a dewy morn.
I am a rustic, who is not so
altruistic
As I would always like to be.
So, I taught this man from
Planet Zee
How to pick my corn for a fee.
He learned that money
Will make him a salient alien
On this wayward planet.

May Michaels

POETRY

Poetry, music of the soul.
Noteworthy prose, flowing
passages.
Melodious combinations of
emotional rhythms,
vibrations.
Complementary portrayals
adaptively depicting.
Heartstrings, echoing, reechoing
as a harp's chords, chilling
your marrow.
Poetical cadence of
communication.
Despondency, pathos, reverance
ecstasy.
Language of a dreamer's reverie.
The spirit, muse, inspirations
for the heralded
generations.

Jeanne Miller

SPRING

Be still my soul
and listen,
to the sounds of spring
unfold.
The birds sing out the glad news
Flowers bloom in an array of
hues.
The whole earth is alive and
throbbing within,
To the beautiful season we call
Spring.
Be still my soul
and listen.
To the sounds of Spring
unfold.
It's the word of God we're
hearing
more precious than all gold.

Cheryl Ann Theriot

ANOTHER

Another day,
Another time,
Another life,
Another mind.
The day is boring,
Time is storing,
Life is hazy,
And your mind is crazy.
Another night,
Another year,
Another world,
Another tear.
The night is dead,
Next year we'll be led,
In the other world we won't be
fed,
And then true tears we shall
shed.

Anwar Iqbal

BASKET CASE

I'm a basket case
A Third World person—
They call me "WOG"1
"COLORED," "GOOK"
I'm "HAM"2 and "JAPHETH"3
of the Olden Book 4
I'm a basket case
A Third World person.
I breed like rabbits
And swamp this world with my
number.
When trains collide, hurricans
strike, famines ravage
I beg for aid.
I'm a kid with a famished face
They call me "PAKI"5
a no-good lackey
I'm Powell's6 ulcer
Thatcher's7 cancer
A Third World person—
A basket case.
The chores I do
that none would do
I open doors
and sweep floors
I'm apple picker
A Jim Crow, Nigger
I'm a victim of jest-malign
"neglect-benign"8
A Third World person—
a basket case.

1. "WESTERNISHED ORIENTAL GENTLEMAN": any dark skinned foreigner, specially a native of South Asia, was called "WOG" by the British, who imitated the life style and mannerisms of the white man.
2. and 3. Noah's sons
4. Refers to Genesis
5. A derogatory name given to South Asian immigrants in Canada and England.
6. Former Tory ENOCH POWELL of England known for his reputedly "racist" utterances

7. MARGARET THATCHER, Prime Minister of England who vowed to put an end to the immigration of colored people in England, while campaigning for election.
8. Refers to the famous phrase "benign neglect" that Daniel Moynahan once used to epitomize the suggested attitude of the United States Government toward the blacks.

Diane L. Woodbury

THE OLD MAN'S FULL COURSE MEAL

Dedicated to Gramps

I turned the pork strips over in
the pan,
it spat at me and burned my
hand,
I raised my hand to my mouth
and licked the fire away,
the old man's cat sat by my feet,
swishing his tail in play, waiting
for his treat.
The old man hummed to
himself, while rocking in his
chair,
with shabby clothes and
whiskers long, as if he did not
care,
his eyes shined bright through
the windows dim light,
he smoked away at his hand
carved pipe.
He smiled with anticipation for
his full course meal,
his dogs ran and barked at the
spinning weather wheel,
the winds picked up and blew
through window cracks,
I knew his arthritis would hurt
in his back.
The seasons have been hard on
him,
he asked me to pass him the old
milk tin,
he held no thoughts of his ill
health,
he dreamed of his youth, when
he collected pelts.
His mind was innocent as a
child's,
soon the weather would turn
mild,
the season was old and near it's
end,
it would bring new life to make
amends.
His meal was cooked, the table
was cleared,
I served him his food, he dug
right in,
he paused a moment and leaned
in his chair,
then said, "you're a great cook
my dear."
He laughed heartily, then
continued his meal,
I wonder if he knows how I feel,
old man with your bright eyes
of blue,
do you know how much I love
you?

Nora O'Brien

AN ODE TO ALLEN

I have a friend who has proved
true.
He has ruddy cheeks and eyes of
blue.
He has been blessed with much
of God's grace.
The beauty of this shows in his
face.
He is willing to lend a helping
hand,
To let one know he does
understand.
He has suffered much on life's
way,
And knows how to live each
passing day.
His philosophy is to take one
day at a time
As onward on our journey we
climb,
He teaches one to forget the
past.
Our good works are what will
last.
He finds much consolation in
the 46th Psalm.
When one is in distress it is like
a soothing balm.
It tells us God is our refuge and
strength.
He is always with us even at
great length.
Allen looks not for earthly
riches or fame.
His love is of God, he does all
in His name.
He shows much compassion for
the aged and sick,
And with a sense of humor his
sorrows he does lick.

Cissy Rucker

HEROIN HIGH

See the skinny kid down on
main street trying to score,
Once He finds the pusher He
won't have to worry no more,
See the young girl in the tight
blue jeans,
She'll sell her soul for a fistful
of dreams,
The pusher rides high, getting
rich,
Watch the skinny kid see him
twitch,
He's got to get some money for
another high,
Don't worry about tomorrow,
just try to get by,
Just one more fix and he'll be
fine,
Lost in a dream without any
rhyme,
Lost in a dream made from dust,
His body craves it with a
fearless lust,
He'd rob and kill to get what
He needs,
He's hooked on a feeling and

the pushers greed,
Watch him stumble, see him fall,
To get what He needs He'd even crawl,
His insides are aching as He comes down,
He starts looking for the pusher,
He must be found,
He cries out as the pain gets worse,
He's trapped in Satans own evil curse,
He curses the day He was born,
As his soul and mind are slowly torn,
He faces death and the fires of hell,
As his soul slowly dies, but his mind gets well,
He feels all the freedom of the birds of the sky,
He's hooked on a feeling of a Heroin High!

Leslie Sagi
A TEDDY BEAR FRIEND
It was her first birthday the day he came
And although he didn't yet have a name
Everyone knew from her hug and kiss
That this was one friendship that could not miss.
When she was two that was the year
When he got lost and the worst was feared
But he turned up as things often did
Behind the sofa where he'd been hid.
Their bedtime story was a great delight
And at the age of three it hit its height
So two together they lay in bed
And listened to the stories read.
When she was four he got out of bed
And waited patiently while she was fed
Then his turn came and spoon in hand
She fed him every bit of sand.
When she was five they had a set
Of little dishes and they always met
At two o'clock for cakes and tea
Out under the old apple tree.
When she turned six and the days grew cool
The time came and she left for school
From nine to three seemed like years passing by
But in the evenings the time did fly.
One cause of pain was her seventh year phase
More commonly called the dress up days
With a nightshirt for bed, a dress for good too
And overalls for days when these just wouldn't do.
A step up came when she turned eight
And got a carriage, he could hardly wait
To be wheeled up the street and all around
Instead of being carried upside-down.
When she was nine she got a bike
And together they rode where they used to hike
From his seat in the basket he got to see
The lay of the land 'til she skinned her knee.
His social life began at ten
When they spent the night at the house of her friend
With sleeping bags and toothbrushes too
And best friend's secrets that he never knew.
Eleven and twelve combined as one
During these days they had less and less fun
Days were long while she was at school
And at night in the closet it got very cool.
When she was thirteen he noticed a change
In her behavior that he found quite strange
All the attention he'd previously known
Was now being given to a telephone.
Fourteen also brought changes he saw
For starters the mirror was brought in from the hall
Brushes, curlers, and contacts to see
All sat on the dresser where his bed used to be.
The next few years became only a blur
In the trunk he saw almost nothing of her
But those days have passed by now and time has flown
Still he patiently waits for her to come home.

Chris Gentry
TORTURE CHAMBER
Been here too long
Been sheer too long
Need to cloud-over and rain
Or I'll go insane.
Living of late
Been a constant flow of
Inescapable realities that slash
At my life lines and leave me to bleed.
Could it be another dose of maturity
Creeping up on me?
Or just another torture chamber within my mind
That I've stumbled on, blind,
And now must find my way.

Jo LeFevers
IT'S TRUE, IT'S YOU
A voice from the box said you're gone.
Like the others, I can't let go.
Senseless as the crime, must I carry on?
I think you'd say so. I think you'd say so.
Night vigil, listening to the box,
The darkness kissing dry our tears.
You made the sixties, and you fought the hawks.
Your genius labors gave us joy for years.
A man. . .
You were a man who dared to be new.
No one can say that you didn't do.
You changed your life to walk in her shoe.
You said that love won't die, and it's true. . .
It's you.
The times you made us laugh and cry,
I can't believe there'll be no more.
No one in the world can answer the Why.
Candles silent glow, there'll be no encore.
We've lost your unborn songs inside,
Your love songs, your wit sharp, yet kind.
We all made mistakes, a part of us died.
But your music lives always in our mind.
A man. . .
You were a man who dared to be new.
No one can say that you didn't do.
You changed your life to walk in her shoe.
You said that love won't die, and it's true. . .
It's you.

Stacey Leigh Weaver
SUMMER
Summer is here at last,
We're getting out of school.
We're going to have a blast.
And those who won't are a fool.
We'll go jogging, swimming, and hiking,
We might even go biking.
We'll go on vacation and take my parents along.

I'll meet a cute boy at the beach who is big and strong.
Summer is lovely

Gertrude M. Balfour
HAMLET'S FALLACY
"To be or not to be," said Hamlet regarding the big question.
He thought he had an option.
Obviously he had not been exposed to the formula of being,
Yod-He-Vav-He. "To be" is the only possibility.
Yod—the active Ego principle is united with He,
the passive, non-Ego—linked by Vav, the state of transition to new being.
The second He, a grain of the Yod, produced by Yod-He-Vav,
In time becoming a new Yod, creation interminable
Yod-He-Vav-He
Yod - He Vav - He
Yod et cetera-ad infinitum, ever in being
No possibility of not being.
Hamlet's fallacy, a mistake of Shakespeare
who hadn't studied the sacred Kabala.
I am part of Yod-He-Vav, the trinity of my being,
the second He a process of my new becoming.

Jeanne Dean
THE BUTTERFLY TRAP
I almost caught a butterfly
I really truly did
I had it in my hand
But it got away
Said the little kid
I almost caught that pass today
We would have won the game
I had it
And I dropped it
Said the youth with shame
I almost closed that deal today
I had him in my hand
I had him
But he got away
Said the angry man
today
i caught a butterfly
i held it in my hand
such a lovely butterfly
i let it fly away
this was a very old man

Mary L. Pope
CONTEMPLATION OF THE CRUCIFIXION
A lonely, desolate hill; a rugged wooden cross;
A cloak, seamless and worn; His hands, bloody and torn.
A sky, sober and threatening; a nail, driven through His feet;
A crown of thorns upon His head; agony and defeat veiled His Victory.
The inscription, scornful and cold:
"JESUS OF NAZARETH, KING OF THE JEWS"
Hung like a dark cloud over His body, limp and drained of life.
He is GOD, yet He was man.
He is KING, yet He was unglorified.
He is IMMORTAL, yet He was dead.
Rejoice, you humble of heart.
Rejoice in your new-born sanctity.
He was crucified that you might live.
Rejoice you humble of heart.
Rejoice in your glorious grace,
For His sacrificial LOVE gave birth to the
Redemption of mankind.

Marguerite Mooney
SLOW DOWN
Slow down your pace and meditate,
Why all the rush and hurry?
Take a few minutes to study and think,

Or time will drain away your strength.
Take time for a little pleasure,
Age encircles you much too soon,
Ambition and greed can never suffice,
When you dance to a worldly tune.
So, just sit down for a minute,
To fish in a cool, woodsy stream,
Or watch a bird feeding her nestlings,
Take time to listen and dream.
From worldly care, find a hideaway,
And with quiet receptive heart,
Choose the things that heal the human mind,
'Ere relentless time tears you apart.

Marceil Strong

EARTHLIFE

Before we left our home in
heaven above--we told God we
would come to earth and choose
between evil and love.
We were told that life would
be difficult at times--that
we would be tempted to stray
from his teachings divine.
But we wanted to come anyway..
we would be tested and tried
but we would not stray.
Some of us would be fat and
sick or have difficulty to
learn, some of us would be
intelligent and good-looking
and our paycheck easy to earn.
Some of us would give and give
and give, others would rather
die than to live.
Some of us would be jealous
of what others have on earth
there, some of us would be
willing our time and talents to
share.
But in the end, death would
bring us to judgment day--
then it would not matter
what others think or say...
It won't matter if we were
a slave or controlled the rule,
it won't matter if others
thought we were God's tool
or a fool...
We will stand naked before God
and only our spirits will show,
God will judge our deeds and
the depth of our souls he'll
know!

Vasilis E. Meimaris

PLEA

Then, I opened the door
to the last eon. . . .
And I saw the great city,
the New Nineveh,
in all its expanse;
split into opposite camps
with proud kings
piling-up their arsenals
of TNW's, ICBM's and ERW's1
or polynomial other weapons
and deploying their armies
to fight the battle of
Armageddon.2
And I saw its people
utterly confused. . . .
And you prophet of truth,
like another Jonah,
rest in oblivion
under the shade
of your gourd
waiting your threats
to realize.
Inhumane one.
Do not grieve
for the delay,
instead. pray
for more time.
Your God
is compassionate. . . .
In obsecurity, you are nobody.
You may foresee things,
you may foretell things,
yet, to no avail;
your voice is muffled.
The new Ninevehans
have grown deaf ears.
The heart of the children
of man is disturbed,
it turned to a rock.
The hope of man
is drugged.
The seed of man
is rotten. . . .
Can you grasp the meaning of signs,
the signs of times, our times?
Do not despair.
Reveal your mind
and forget yourself.
Be like Paul a Jew,
a Roman, a Hellene,
a Varvaros,3 a rolling stone
to win them all;
and day or night speak.
Shake-up the comatose4
to hear the thunder
of the coming wrath,
the wrath of self-destruction. . . .
Hurry. Come.
This world needs you.
Spring forth
off your tent, your shack.
Say something,
something of value,
of saving value
and save the billions, or millions,
or just a couple,
the terminal couple of humans. . . .
The Earth shall rejoice.
The Cosmos shall be gratefull.
The Universe shall salute you
with resonance. . . .
Notes:
1. Tactical Nuclear Weapons,
Intercontinental Ballistic
Missiles, Enhanced-radiation
Reduced-blast Weapons, or
"Neutron" warheads.
2. Revelation 16:16
3. Barbarian
4. Drugged, confused,
indifferent.

Marceil Morgan Strong

CAUGHT IN TIME

We find ourselves in a web of time--
Unable to move forward...
Unable to recede, behind.
Caught.
Caught like the spider caught the fly,
Caught as another year so quickly
gone by.
A new year ahead of us,
fond memories behind...
Tightly overwhelmingly--
caught by time.

Ellan Hotaling-Davies

A GOLD STAR FOR YOUR HEART

Father help us all tonight,
To see beyond the bomb's bursting light,
To see this world's big enough for us all?
In our world where boys, not yet men, must heed the call
To arms? Two arms, two legs and a gun to kill,
To most of them, against their will?
It seems so wrong to know a Mother's joy,
To love him and lose him, while he's still a boy?
In some distant land or a tiny isle,
To live and die in such a little while?
For boundries will change, but when all's said and done,
Tell me, my Father, who has lost and who has won?

Claudia Elizabeth Cobleigh

A FRIEND OF MINE

Take me back to the little house beside a friend of mine
With only a fence to separate and not these miles of time
I miss your smile dear friend your casual talk and wave
Your flowers, your bit of news and all the warmth you gave
Come sit with me and talk, come be my friend again
I care and want to hear your voice and just remember when
So understand why I dream and wander back in time
For awhile I'm back at the little house, beside a friend of mine

James R. Killough, Jr.

IF WE HEARD

If We heard God wailing in the garden,
Would we say it is an earthquake?
If We were to see his teardrops,
Would we say it is rain or snow?
If We heard the sound of his sigh,
Would we call it the wind?
If We were to be touched by God,
Would we say it is a strange feeling?
If we were God's child,
Would we say it is a fairytale?
If We saw God,
Would we call him man?

George Stock

O NIMBUS NOW BEFORE ME

O Nimbus now before me
eyes profuse with blue;
skin embellished by the sun
hair of chestnut hue.
My callowness repulsed you
then nimbus of the past;
yet still your image vivid
in verse forever cast.

Blair H. Allen

ORACLE FOR THE WORLD

Oratory sent against derisive night,
Lung of anxious urgency,
Mouth of exploding frustration,
No words thunder louder.
If you believe in reincarnation,
Mt. St. Helens would tell you
She has been Cassandra in Troy,
Days of raised swords in the past.
No one listened then either.
Television has made it entertainment,
The spectaculars of disaster
We disbelieve will happen to us.
A sudden-realized truth someday,
Too swift, too late to stop,
Unless we listen and seize the future
We can still shape in our hands
The way volcanoes build cones.

Margaret Clancey

THE HARLEQUIN

He is a very brawny individual,
His personality is matchless,
A debonair Man he is,
A person who has a harmonious disposition,

He is artistic with his hobbies,
His intrigue of science fiction books is unbelieveable,
He has a dexterity with tractors,
His young patients have him as their own Prince Valiant,
At times he gets perplexed with human beings,
His antidote for life is being a harlequin for people.

Teresa Marie Alsko

EYES TALK

Most people look at your eyes and only notice the color of them
I look into your eyes
I can tell you have been hurt before
So have I, I know how you feel right now
They say time heals all wounds
But a broken heart is so hard to mend
It takes time to pick up the pieces
Then you're not sure if you ever want to try again
I know I am ready to start anew
How about you?

Paul Jefferson

AUTUMN GEESE

Against the dull red glow of
an early August eve I watch a
flock of geese in beautiful
formation flying overhead,
I wonder whether, or not they
will make it south in time to
make their winter beds.
I watch as the leader flies on
against the strong southern
wind,
Ever so low he flies to avoid
the dense dark clouds,
He struggles to lead his
followers across the emptiness

of the open air,
They follow him without
hesitation they know not where.
The flock seem to get nowhere
fast as they increase the
flapping of their wings
The leader knows instinctively
he must go on
On against the strong southern
winds.
With frustration the leader
moves on inch by inch with his
followers close behind,
They gawk their language to let
him know they are making little
time,
So the leader left the flock
with diving skill and forward
motion;
Down he soard down toward
the clear blue water lake,
Here his flock would rest the
night an wait for the dawn of
a new day.
The night passes with ease so
early the next morning I
curiously await the geese to
take to flight,
Ah, but soon the familiar
flapping of wings catches my
attention as the flock flew off
into the sunlight;
I notice the leader as he
leaves his flock to glide
against the early morning dawn,
With grace and practiced skill
he circles the lake all alone.
Not once but twice he circled
until he discovered me,
Then as if in angry mock he
gawked, flapped his heavy
wings,
turned south and joined his
southward fleet.

E. T. Lomonaco
PROVERBIAL HANDS
I would coldly reflect off my
mirror,
do my business as though you're
not there.
I would idle my time
going through the world mine
I would act like I just couldn't
care.
For my pleasures and problems
are personal,
they mean nothing to you all
the same,
for they nestle away
make your nightime my day,
it was just my reality game.
If I know where I stand,
then I am just a man
being dropped by proverbial
hands.
There were times when I
seemed successful,
in the eyes of my colleagues I
stood,
I would lend them my services
rendered
for those things that I fared
in were good.
Then my life took a downswing
in motion,
cast aside by my friends now
they're gone,
but one time, I was just
their escape route,
now I realize I was their pawn.
Now we've gone separate ways
since our crimes never paid
it was all a reality game
for I know where I stand
I am now my own man
being dropped by proverbial
hands.
I would look back at all of my
skeletons
in the back of the mind filled
with dust,
and as much as I wanted them
hidden,
they were waiting, just ready to
bust.
Soon my pressures made clear
their awareness,
ripped my insides out, left
and then right
I was nervous by other men's
standards
in the darkness I stayed with
no light,
for I've hidden away
that is all I can say
it was just my reality game
but I know where I stand
I am only a man
who was dropped by
proverbial hands.

Maryellen
THOUGHTS I PONDER
I left her this morning
So sad and blue, she held me
close
Kissed my cheek, then my lips
Her arms around me enclosed
She did not want me to leave
It was different from times
before
I felt her soul cry out to me
It was as a child clinging at the
door
Don't leave me alone for I only
have
such a short way to go
How my heart turned and ached
My will was to stay
So bold and independant yet
humbly
By herself she chooses to remain
With all that she dearly loves
So very near, who say they care
Yet she sits and stays with
nothing
Around her but solitaire
A longing she has to be
pampered
Not spared, she gave so much of
her life
Can we deny her that part of us
That she longs so much to share
Now verging with all her nerve-
if naught-
Lets not forget the purse
I feel I have left and deserted
A long and trusted friend that
gave,
And was there when I needed
her most
Now how can I repay the most
she needs
To help lessen her weak
unending post
Can I, can you, can we continue
to ignore
The years gladly spent, while
using time
Lent she remembers: Little ones
born life,
When we fell she picked us up
(Where were
we when she fell) Youth, she
listen we had
much to say (Are we listening
as she sits
and waits). Adults how well she
knows
the burdens heavy on our brows
Through the years as heads were
turning
And legs were running, she tried
pointing
Us in the right direction, her
voice was
The demand to command and
we followed
Look inward, our attitude
effects her feelings
Its not the deeds of the rich
man, poor man,
Begger, thief, doctor, minister &
merchants
Chiefs' that will lift the
loneliness of her
Reclining years
It is the much needed love the
Caring and sharing
That she knew how well to give
That would lighten the time she
feels
She has yet to loose
She has mellowed with age, can
she change
Completely now to our liking,
while time
Helps her reach for ninety. We
love her
For she will always be the same
We found her when we needed
her help
Can't we find her now when we
are the help
She needs. If we listen we can
hear as
She silently cries out to us.
It hurts most after day is done
The night creates a deeper void
Prayers, thoughts on security
may be
Won't someone please take care
of me
Just a phone call to say we are
near
Would bring joy to someone so
dear
If we are so selfish that we can
forget
And we must reflect on ones
insatiable
Feelings of self love and long
for our
Neighbor to love us as
themselves
Than better she be a mother of
another
I shall return and soon I pray
And spend my time in many
ways, Listening,
Talking, a game of scrabble a
stake to play—
I'll marvel at a disciplined mind
and strong
Voice, sureness of times
accumulated and
Take into memories account the
reminiscing
That is her life.
Now while flying high way up
in the sky
And time keeps quietly slipping
by
I dry my eyes with a LINEN fine
That was given to me when I
said Good-by.

Becky Lyon Long
GRANNY'S GIRDLE
In the 1960's women's libbers
were marching everywhere.
To get attention they burned
their underwear.
In our cities, bras and panties
were constantly going up in
smoke.
Our government finally
understood the women's
movement was no joke.
While Granny was certainly not
for women's liberation.
She sure got attention with her
accidental demonstration.
She had an old girdle that was
just too tight.
So she tossed it in the fireplace
one winter night.
Billows of black smoke out the
chimney did flow!
Granny just wrang her hands
and sighed, "Oh no."
Bells started ringing all over the
little town.
Everyone thought the house was
burning down.
Volunteers put the girdle out in
great haste,
Leaving poor Granny amusingly
red faced.
There is something to be said
for being free as a breeze.
Ladies burn your bras, but no
girdles please!

Rita Kuykendall
LOVERS
Dead lovers on satin pillows
were found
Each in the others arms were
bound
Beneath a sheet so blue and sad
In naught but nature was she
clad
Her hair gleamed forth like gold
from a band
And upon this gold was placed
his hand
In death as her arms lay by his
side
In sweet repose, his loving bride
The world struck out with gun
and stone
And would not leave these two
alone
They chose in death a world of
light
For he was black and she was
white...

Evelyn Brock Fitzgerald
A MEMORY OF MAMA
Tracing back into yesterday
In thinking of my past
Of how changing time has been
Not long ago when just a lass
When I would walk and watch a
cloud
Reach up and up to touch the
sky
Hurry home to tell you mama
Too far away--tell me why?
You said, "God is in the sky"
The ladder can't reach you talk
about
He's in the sky there in a
heaven
He comes to here and takes us

out
How nice it is to trace again
Just to wake and feel brand new
Knowing mama could find my answers
And hear my problems through and through.

Lillian A. Ochoco, M.D.

THANK YOU, LORD...

Lord, thank you for giving me someone who cares, someone who lifts me up when I stumble, someone who helps me straighten my crooked paths...
Thank you for giving him who has always loved me, who understands and has always understood, who always aided me to fashion myself to the best from day to day...
Thank you, Lord, for bringing us together.
Help us that we may never fail each other.
Give us the strength, courage, perseverance... the grace to carry on through life's journey, to be one in mind, heart, body and soul.
Above all, bless our love for each other.
May it never wither.
Let it be like a ring, with neither a beginning nor an end...
And let our love always be... blossoms in the spring...

Kristi McGarry

BLACK OUT

Thunder
crackles,
booming,
shaking the ground.
Lightning
races the sky,
streaking
yellow
through
black.
Screaming wind
whips the trees,
snaps power
lines.
Icy rain pours
down,
pelting, soaking the city.
Children cry,
crouched
in
cold,
musty
basements.

Nancy E. Diwan

TIME

How closely are the days and years linked together;
All blended in a pattern that is at once different
And yet the same.
The minutes and hours glide together
Giving birth to days and years and generations.
Yet all these spring from a second of time;
A space of time only larger than fractions of itself.
Many say that time flies; however,
It is we who move and time that stands still,
Never to return,
Yet always to be remembered.
How we humans anticipate the changing of time.
The time that will eventually separate from us
The persons-The things we treasure most.
Yet, we go forward.
For it is in us all to hope that the future will be better;
That the future will reveal to us the reason of our existence-
The one thing that will make worthwhile
All the time that has passed.
We go blindly forward into that unknown space,
Seemingly, by our own will;
Yet, certainly following a unique, divine plan
Devised for us in eternity.
A plan shaped by a hand greater than our own.
A timeless unchanging plan-
Leading to our destiny.
In the end, not time; but, rather the way
That we have followed the plan, will be most important.
For too late we may realize that the never yet ever
Changing entity-TIME
Has finally run out.

Valarie Duncan McKee

DEATH

Kissed by sadness, torn by sorrow
Oh, the ache would pass tonight...
Pray the sun would shine from heaven only to make the morrow bright.
God, where is thy gentle handling of those who are so dear and kind?
Why must anguish go untempered by those of us you've left behind?
Why should those who show such kindness be given such a hand as this?
With compassion, I will remember, the people I most dearly miss!

Doris M. King

WE HAVE MET HIM IN THE MORNING

We have met Him in the morning
During our quiet time together.
Silence, they say, is Golden
So is meditation, it is good for the soul.
This quiet time together, each morn
The love we have for each other
To speak, but no words are spoken
Yet we know, what the other is thinking,
This quiet time each morn.
We have met Him in the morning
When we ask for guidance and wisdom
To give thanks for our blessings, and there are many.
To commune with Him each morn
And ask to be filled each day, anew
Of His love for us, this morn.
To feel this wondrous Joy
And to have it spread through our bodies and soul
And to have it Glow in our eyes,
Oh, Father, You are wondrous, indeed.
We have met You in our quiet time, this morn.
Such peace He sends us during this quiet time
To renew our bodies and soul for another day
So that we maybe of help to others
And to share God's Love with them,
So refill us with Your wondrous Love
In our quiet time, this morn.

Robert Stanley Patusky

MY FAMILY

My Family forms for me life's Landscape with God, the Master Landscaper
At times they are an Unassailable, rugged Mountain terrain; other times A cool, sun-reflecting lake or Swift cascade.
Moments together become a Spring meadow, or a hike Through a dark forest, which Conceals undiscovered golden Deserts and shipwreck laden Shorelines' treasures.
They are for me life's colors, And each is a splendidly Different color.

Without them life's landscape Would be night's grayness.
Yet, each reflects God's Morning sunburst in his own Way.
Their harmony dissolves the Grayness, and brings forth the Landscape's true nature.
My family come together and Lay down before me as life's Road. I am bound to them as I Am bound to the earth by Gravity.
Someday, the road may end, But the landscape and the Color will always be there.

Harold E. Harmon

CLOUDS—A FANTASY

As white clouds drifted by, that look
Like pages in a picture book,
Imagination ran so wild
As like a trusting, dreaming child,
I saw a mountain looming tall;
I saw a rabbit there, quite small,
A huge old bear with out flung paws,
A crocodile with open jaws
Held wide to trap unwary prey
Unlucky to have passed his way—
But then he faded from the sky
And turned to cotton drifting by.
A lake was formed among some hills,
And I thought I could see, with thrills,
A mermaid on a rock of gold
To beckon to a sailor bold,
And then I wished that I could be
Transported to that cloud-formed sea
And meet this siren there to find
All this to give me peace of mind,
If now in fact she had a tail
Or is it all a fairy tale,
And would she sing her siren's song
Enticing me to come along?
I saw a castle high in air,
And then I wished that I was there
To save the Princess from the clutch
Of loathsome tyrant, or some such!
But then the pictures darkened where
The clouds were dense, no longer fair,
And dumped their rain, and then I ran,
But memories of things I can
Behold, with pictures that I see
That move me back to fantasy;
For in my twisted, crippled state,
'Tis through my dreams I can relate.

Terry Guernsey

NO WORRY

I have no worry at all
In place, my problems will fall
They will come and go
Just as the wind does blow
I know things will be fine
I can see in my mind
My difficulties will pass
Forever, they never last
I feel as free as can be
At the moment, nothing is bothering me
I defendantly feel such relief
Because I have some belief

Josephine DeRasmo

GIVE HIM A GUITAR

See him looking in that music store hoping, with pockets turned insideout thinking, if he had that guitar, how far he could go.
Thinking of the money he could make to help his mama
As he looks toward the shoe box at his feet, he wonders how long he has to save for the black one with the pearly pick and red shoulder strap.
He pictures himself with it slung over his shoulder
Give Him A Guitar, he may go far
At the cotton club on Beal St. with shoeshine box in tow he makes his way up and down the bar begging customers he doesn't even know, 25¢ is all he charges, white shoes, black shoes, and brown, he polishes them all over town.
Give him a guitar, he may

be a star
Trying to make a living,
working every nite for just one
bite, his work has to be done,
while every one is having fun,
Why should he be the one?
While his mama is at home
washing and ironing to feed the
babies.
He's just a boy of 10, but he's
a man.
Give Him a Guitar, help
him be a star and maybe go
far.

Catherine-Ann Pawlik
HEAVEN'S TOUCH
Crystal skies behold, twinkling
Diamonds above our
Mother Earth—a child
Molded by God's grace
And penanced by man's sin
Glistening teardrops soothe
Savage incarcerations
Cascading teardrops
Sizzling, searing our wounds.
Behold—Heaven's touch.

Barbara Smith Davenport
REMINDER
Keep in touch with Jesus—
Talk with him everyday.
Tell him all your troubles—
Praise Him while you may.
Count your every blessing.
Give thanks for every smile.
Keep in touch with Jesus—
Let Him walk with you each
mile.
Down the rugged road of life
through the storms and strife
Keep in touch with Jesus—
He is the tree of life.
Keep in touch with Jesus.
Carry in your heart a prayer.
Keep in touch with Jesus—
He is waiting over there.

W. E. Nolan
THE WHEEL
I wonder how some folks would
feel,
if they'd stop and think about
the wheel.
What turmoil in the world I'd
say,
to take all wheels for just one
day.
There's wheels with cogs, and
wheels with spokes,
some government wheels are
just big jokes.
A wheel that rolls the miles
away,
and carries on from day to day.
There's ferris wheels and wheels
of chance,
and sewing machines that mend
our pants.
Most sailing ships would stop
and shudder,
the captain's helm would be
in rudder.
Old Dobbin would be in his joy,
for mode of travel would be
travois.
There's wheels of steel, and
wheels of wood,
but whatever they are they're
very good.
There's wheels on chairs, and
wheels on beds,
and so-called wheels within
our heads.
There's wheels of mud that have
no spokes
that's used by poor and common
folks.
Wheels on valves, wheels on
drills,
carousels for children's
thrills.
Cable bridge with wheels and
toll,
and wheels on toilet paper rolls.
There's index wheels that mark
all points,
and ancient rack wheels that
stretch your joints.
Some wheels sound like a flock
of geese,
it's the squeaking wheel that
gets the grease.
There's grinding wheels that's
made of stone,
and wheels for dialing on your
phone.
Wheels on cars and wheels on
planes,
wheels on bikes, and wheels on
trains.
Cutting wheel for all the trades,
roller wheels for packing grades.
A million, billion wheels in
play,
remove them all for just one
day.
Machines would stop, and be
quite still,
planes would crash into the hill.
So whose invention was the
wheel?
Whatever it costs, it's still a
steal.

James F. Judd, Jr.
OUR UNITED STATES OF AMERICA
United we stand
Each woman and each man
Our armed forces stand ready
to encounter any aggression
That would endanger our great
nation.
History tells of our
independence, of our
constitution
Of how we fought the American
Revolution
We fight and die; if we must
For our Country; in God we
place our trust.
Our great American flag waves
in the blue
Over we American people who
are free, brave and true
We are peace loving American
people; endowed by our
historical places and dates
Which tell of deeds by great
men who built the foundation
of The United States
We shall always remember our
American people who have
fought, died and made a
sacrifice
That help make possible our
American way of life
Our United States of America;
together we stand
The United States of America;
our freedom loving land.

Betty J. S. Smith
MY ANGEL
I spoke with an angel her voice
was so soft
She told me she loved me really
did care
About things I did or said
They all had meaning they were
from the heart
I looked into her eyes I saw
the love she was expressing
I wondered at this I wasn't
deserving
But then she touched me with
her hand to make me
understand
I was worth it all even more
because I was
hers and she was——my Mother

Shirley Kelly Reed
WINTER'S PATH
When Winter breathes Her icy
sigh,
with icicle fingertips brushing
tips of trees,
turning dew to frost with glacier
skirts,
sweeping cross the countryside,
She has no thought for you or
me
or any living thing—
no thought beyond Her magic
power,
transforming, as She stalks
the bright-hued Autumn.
Autumn rushes the icy clutch
to escape,
with little hope,
for Winter moves with grace
and stealth,
consuming, as She goes,
the hidden cache of Autumn's
glory
still lingering in Her path.

Shawna Grover
REQUIEM OF THE DEAD
The rain came throbbing down
steadily,
like the constant rhythm of a
human heart.
It was a dreary Spring afternoon
The trees were standing stark-
naked,
with their boughs jabbing
outwards;
like the horror scene of a late
night movie.
Look at all the sorrowful
mongers
Gathered to see for the last
time,
that which hasn't held much in
their minds.
Listen to them boast how they
loved you,
how they miss you.
Oh, what a performance on their
part.
For you can't con a dead man
I don't accept false anguish—
tears of mist.
For every dead man wonders. . .
Why couldn't you love me
when I was alive
as much as you do
when I'm dead?

Paula Oliveri Leblond
NEW YORK
Graffitti speaks loud
Blasts at city
a language
No one understands
Saturates all that moves
with ugly patterns
and designs
Cries out
to those who will hear
and bear awhile
Tells a story
of an empty
and
bleak existence
My language is poor
but my pictures bold
My spirit is spent
I have no direction
I smear windows
with
thick paint
I see not much
nor care to see
Mine is a turbulence
that shoots out
like a spout
that labors
to tell a story
Indifference and coldness
Nurture me not
Coarse agents
Can't erase
the marks
Shadows of the lines remain
A lament soars high
And a dent stares
into the eye of the City
As I walk away I see
Dust #1
Best high!

HelenDumack
A PRIMITIVE DELIGHT
The roadside bouquet
is
June's finest array
of
White daisies
Red clover
Against a back drop
of
Tall grass
Gentle breeze

A hovering bee
A multicolored butterfly
A primitive delight
Only
Mother Nature
Can supply.

Jo Anna Polistena Morello
LOVE AND HATE
Love is a 4 letter word. . .
In Springtime the sap flows
Everyone grows
When I feel your tender
embrace I'm One with the
Nature
If you are loved
You can give love
I look for signs of Truth in
your face
I need love to endure!
Two sides of the same coin. . .
Love and Hate
I'm on the edge
I'm on the brink
I love you
You reject me
I hate you
I love myself
I hate myself
Fear of the unknown equals hate
If I get to know you
Maybe I will like you
Maybe I will love you

Maybe I will hate you
If I get angry
People think I'm filled with hate
Belligerent!
Actually the hatred is a defense against unhealed wounds
And forgotten sorrows
I hurt therefore I hate
I hate therefore I hurt
You hate
We hate
They hate
I'm in pain!
Love overcomes hatred. . .

Isabelle McClellan Taylor
SONNET
We did not ask to come together,
I to you, nor you to me.
We did not seek each, knowingly.
Nor did we quest our destinies enjoin for what there was to be.
We found ourselves, and then, in each a harmony,
That swelled like cords, redundant on the ear,
Until they invade the being to the utmost and merge as one.
No, we did not ask to come together,
Unless the quest was in our eyes,
Or in a smile that sent unspoken words,
Which in our hearts alone were heard,
Evoking an inevitable need to share in equal measure,
And to attain the heights of love's delightful treasure.

Isabelle McClellan Taylor
SONNET
I shall not give this fragile heart to love again,
Lest I consummate a treacherous ecstasy and inescapable pain.
If I should anticipate the pleasure of a warm embrace,
The touch of quickened lips upon my upturned face,
If I should find my fingers seek to entwine,
Or eyes that speak when look deeply into mine,
Or hear soft words and vows of love's eternal bliss,
I shall quickly cast them into nothing's dark abyss.
I shall not, forever, put aside love's rare delight,
For without love, the heart becomes a tower.
But I shall hold it on the outer fringes of my heart,
Void of despair and revelation's stark light,
Where doubt and desolation cannot usurp my bower,
And render reason more vulnerable to tear apart.

Dwight Wayne Williams
THE DAY N' NIGHT POEM
What rhymes with day:
Ray;
For the sunshine,
little kids and flowers need to grow.
Gay,
For the happiness,
Within our hearts to share.
Bluejays;
For reminding us,
of the gift of life and rainbows.
What rhymes with night?
Sight;
For beautiful miracles,
God put here for us to see.
Right;
For right n' wrong,
Always a way for you to choose.
Fight;
For remembering struggles,
Along our paths of growing up.

Molly Schneider
SOUL'S
There is a time when all of us must part, to send our wagering "soul's" to God, whenever we must go. If all of us were to live forever, it seems that no tear would ever fall, but if this were true, then why would we need God. God would only be an image, which no soul would ever see.

So this is why he grants these soul's their chance to live forever! The souls that go now will never feel pain again.

Although they leave us, far behind they will live forever in the eyes of God!

Winston E. Langley
ON OUR JOURNEYS
We cannot always, perhaps ever,
Take with us our preferred freights.
We do not always meet at centre,
Share a taste in settled light.
At the edges we must wander
And debate the strangers there. .
All our roads lead us to crossings,
Straight-aheads do bear altars.
There we make our sacrifices;
Our gods, an eye, the only child,
And like Abr'ham follow silence
Though love-beyond-love bids us shout.
Bridges we are, at our pausings,
If we roam the far and deep,
And forever know that we choose
Paths also we do not take.

Rita S. Guillory
THE TREASURED HEARTACHE
A fragment of tranquility invades the tempest sea;
To calm the troubled waters that robbed the soul of peace.
The traveler when his journeys done;
Then turns to view his course.
And finds the storm he's ridden out;
May be a bountiful source.
This heartache must be treasured;
And remembered day to day.
To prize the gentle waters;
That now before you lay.
And if around the bend is found;
Still another raging billow.
The faith and hope that's now affirmed;
Abides with thee forever.

Diane L. Tomaino
SOUL SUPPORT
Sometimes when I need
to hold you most
I withdraw
Sometimes when I need
to talk to you most
I'm silent
And sometimes when I need
to be near you most
I'm far away
I don't understand why I act this way
Maybe it's because I'm afraid
of needing you too much
or loving you even more
but mostly I'm afraid
that you won't feel the same.

Irene Mary Pacana
IT WAS WRITTEN IN THE STARS
(A Tribute to John Lennon)
"A star is shining in the sky". . .
Sending music. . .that will never die!
Words with meaning. . .that will live on. . .
By a legend, from Liverpool. . .a Beatle. . .named "John."
He left his family, friends, and fans. . .with a heavy heart.
He had so much more to give. . . it was only the start!
But God wanted John. . .for His Choir. . .to teach and remind. .
The world of his messages. . that were left behind!
"It Was Written In The Stars". . . a fate. . .so sad. . .but true. . .
"An unexpected visit". . .an unwelcome cue!
"It Was Written In The Stars". . . he would contribute so much. . .
In music. . .song. . .and philosophy. . .many lives he'd touch!
Generations will come. . . generations will go. . .
The impact will remain. . . everyone will know!
There was a creative man. . . John Lennon was his name. . .
He left a legacy. . .he earned his "claim to fame!"

Paul D. Swigart
DUSTY PAGES TELL THE STORY
Dusty pages tell a story
Under tarnished rims,
Setting forth the timeless text
To satisfy our whims.
Yellowed though the pages be,
Pressed tight upon the shelf,
Admonishing the simple truth,
Graced freely of itself;
Eternal consequences
Shout in bold undaunted fire,
To lift a sinking captain
Evermore beyond the mire.
Lovelight shines so warm and free,
Lost only in our thought,
A beacon for the searching soul
Seen o'er the vision sought.
Time eludes the moment
On a sea of life evolved,
Reflecting secrets of the years,
Yet soon to be resolved.

Dorothy V. Wells
THE PARABLE OF THE SOWER
A sower went out to sow.
The seed he used was the Word of God.
He sowed it on ground that should not have taken too much toil,
But it fell on four different kinds of soil.
Some seeds fell by the wayside upon the hard but fertile heart;
Which had no understanding of what the Word was all about.
The ear has to be tuned to hear, or you will not understand.
That God's, own Son Jesus, is the Author of this Great Sal-vation Plan.
Some seed fell in stony places, where there was very little soil.
This stony heart heard the Word, and accepted it with joy.
Until the time persecution and trouble came to him,
He turned away offended; for this man, Christ, could never be his kin.
There was one also, who received seed among the thorns.
He heard of God's Grace, of how Jesus had been born
To save His people from their sins.
He took up the cross, but he could not follow him.
His eyes were opened, but he could not perceive,
That the gift of God's love was offered to all who believe.
He had no time His precious love to receive;
The pursuit of worldly pleasures,
Robbed him of heavenly treasures.
Oh, understanding heart
Blessed by God's own Hand!
For to you is given wisdom, and knowledge to comprehend-hidden truths.
You-are the fertile soil, and not the sand.
By their fruits they shall be known; the good seed sown
Shall bring forth fruit in abundance
Heirs to be called God's own.

Dwight L. Johnson
RAINBOWS OF PROMISES
(A Prayer for my Friends)
Wondrous frosted colored rainbows
Gleaming in the dew drop sun,
Enveloping the children
While through the fields they run.
Memory Keeping rainbows
Arching across the sky,
Protecting gold and silver
Watching the free birds fly.
Rainbows of Promises.
Promises of Love.
Rainbows of Lifes Meaning.
What life is made up of.
Just after the final rainstorm
A rainbow will appear.

A rainbow but a minute,
But a memory for years.
When you see your rainbows,
Please try to remember me,
And when you touch love's
rainbow,
You will find you then are free.
Rainbows of Promises.
Promises of Love.
Rainbows of Life's Meaning.
What life is made up of.
And when you go chasing
rainbows,
Try and see me there,
For rainbows are my messages
That I love you and I care.
Rainbows for a season.
Memories forevermore.
What dreams and rainbows are
meant to be,
What life is really for.
Rainbows of Promises.
Promises of Love.
Rainbows of Life's Meaning.
What life is made up of.
When you have caught your
rainbow
And held it in your hand,
You will find the happiness
and then you will understand
why
when you see your rainbow,
my memory will be there,
For then I think you will
understand,
that I love you—
I love you and I care.

B. Moore

UNTITLED

Creativity—
Such a word
It can hold the sun in one hand
and the moon in the other
Standing upon the highest
summit
able to hold the wind at bay—
to command the heavens to
rain
or to shine
So much power in a single word
yet so gentle, like a lamb in
its endeavor.
Why is it that sometimes
creativeness is allowed to
shout, to billow forth,
to go on and on, never ending?
—til one day it does?
Then as a riverbed in the midst
of a drought,
nothing—dry, dusty, unfertile,
unable to bear fruit.
Life goes on, slow, dreary, full
of shadows,
waiting. . .
And what of honor?
An illusive concept maybe,
An unspoken thought
A belief in the right of one's
course of action
Compare it to faith
Also a belief and most times
equally as hard to grasp
Honor is that facet of one's
personality
that leads them to a capacity
they never knew existed in
themselves
Men fight for one's honor
to uphold another's honor
In times past, men have died
in the very name
of honor
Is it so wrong to fight?
To believe that you are right
that the challenge you have
risen to
is that one reason you were
placed on this earth
Is it so wrong?
Can one be held accountable for
the circumstances
surrounding the challenge?
And what of honor?
How many have you known
who will never realize
the word nor the meaning?
So why condemn the one man
who chooses to face himself
and test the manifestations
of honor within his own realm
of existence?
So what of honor? Illusive?
Unspoken?
Just a word?
Test yourself
Find the word, honor, in your
own mind,
See if you, too, are able
to face yourself and rise to
fight for something you
believe in
Search within and find that
you do have the capacity to
grasp the thought, the
concept,
however illusive,
And be confident and know
that you know and have
found inside you
and have justified. . .
honor.

Frank W. Holt

THE ARTIST

Silent sentinels we artists are,
Listening for the soul to speak,
Like the crane in the surf
waiting for his fish.

When the fish appears,
When the soul speaks,
We must respond to that
moment
for our nourishment.

Connie LaVerne Sylvia

WHAT OF TIMES MY HEART AND SOUL?

It is from within myself
The dream, my imagination, a
memory fragments of time.
I was once a face, on the edge
of the wind
The barrier breaks, fire meets
the rose, pulses of space
create flowers of yesterday.
Of time and you, I will not
forget
Of time and love, a place of
chance, a stir of being as one
loves another.
Entwined spirits of all the night
Waiting, watching, feeling, we
fold, embody and unite in an
embrace of endless love.
As the night and dawn of time
arouse
Long was a silence, then a
whirling mass, of exotic
thoughts we held within our
view.
Stars from heaven with
pounding hearts
Birth of elements, marking
mighty deeds, in forces of
life, love, fire, and ice.
The pulse of space is within our
love.
Ever behold these throbbing
embers
And beyond will be assistance
with all
As by the mouth of the river,
the wolf remains, the flash of
silver-wing tips will ever rise
in dance.
I wish to hear in this first
sunrise
The quietly, low, humming
voices, that will become one
and a strange delight will test
the soul.
I gaze in shivering wonder
Seeing the power within us all,
to draw toward the edge of life
or death.
A thousand heartbeats within
me, did tell the need I learned,
ached me.
For I, cannot only think, or
I will have no mouth to speak
for opening my heart and soul.
It is now not only I seek the
answer—
For it is with the question,
that I give of myself.
To find in the test of my soul,
the ignorance that crucifies
my son/sun.
Fate will bring me to this
precipice
To vie with all and nature,
is to know love/eternity.

Michael J. Washowiak

ROLLING LIKE SOME (Full Moon and Empty Bodies)

Their faces painted in frenzied
emotions
Coloring a world of nightmares
whose
Eternal gallop never reaches
the edge
Of the maddeningly dangling
dawn
They begin to set themselves on
fire
To escape anonymous
tomorrows
In arrow-like shafts of light
Openly defying their own
creation
They close in on oblivion like
A cornered rat in some room
Long ago sealed to the sight
Of silken virgins denying their
fate
Though their future inevitable
be
Still attempting to alleviate
The persistance of precipitation
From the impassioned past
An impossible portrait to paint
The man in the moon howling
Horror in paradoxical harmonies
Deranged with discord they
assemble
Only to dissolve and coagulate
Again too late to control that
witch
Never created to be controlled
They let Luna in their windows
And both sirens wailing come
To their senses seductively
Seeking the destruciton of their
own
Ambiguous arguments
unrestrained
Training them in the
annihilating arts
While the bugles blow a
simultaneous
Attack and retreat for cowards
and heroes
To respond to in equanimity
Rolling like some Yin-Yang ball
The period beneath the question
mark
Seeks always to gaze beyond
the gap

Kurt H. Miller

FANTASY'S CARNIVAL*

Early in the month of September
On a sweet-smelling summer
night
When the carnival came to
Glad Oaks Creek
With it's rings and wheels
and lights
And the story that came with
the carnivals fame
Was a madmans dream delight
And Jimmys' blue eyes, and the
townspeoples' lives
Can never again be made right
Well the carnival came to Glad
Oaks Creek
In the summer of '75
And the magical tent, and the
hall of mirrors
Somehow came alive
The merry-go-round went round
and round
Backwards into time
As the ferris wheel and the
calliope
Rang out their eerie chimes
Jimmy and Mark were out that
night
Running around the town
When the ringmaster set up his
fantasy show
And the calliope spawned it's
weird sound
They saw the black hole that
just swallows your soul
And the fire that came from
the ground
As the Krewes led their dance
with melodical romance
And Jimmy and Mark rode the
clown
Now Rex, unmasked, rode by
the King and Queen
As they exchanged their royal
toast
And Jimmy said to Mark so soft
Lets ride the golden ghost
And the musical rings that the
carousel brings
Can be heard from coast to
coast
As Mnemosyne glides on her
chariot ride
With her agelss fantastical
host
Yes the carnival came to Glad
Oaks Creek
In the summer of '75
And the magical tent, and the
hall of mirrors
Somehow came alive
The merry-go-round went round
and round
Backwards into time
As the ferris wheel and the
calliope
Rang out their eerie chimes
The boys snuck through the
entrance gate
And lost a silver dime
And one stepped on the
merry-go-round
And went backwards into

time
The ringmaster cried loud, in his mystical shroud
"Ageless is all of mankind"
And poor Jimmy Queens, once sweet sixteen
Was now just a boy of age nine
So Mark ran swift, as did King Rex
Into eternal night
He had to save his only friend
He had to do what's right
And Mark laughed long and loud and true
And Jimmy came back to life
For when laughter shines on Mnemosyne
It snuffs her evil light
Now Jimmy rode the carousel back
To the age where he belonged
As the ferris wheel kept up it's pace
And the calliope it's song
In the hall of mirrors lost souls still swim
Repenting for all their wrongs
For the carnival will never end
Where evil still belongs
*Based on the novel
Something Wicked this way Comes by Ray Bradbury

Michael E. Wittner
FAME
I sit at my desk with paper and pen.
And with A sigh, and A laugh, I begin to write about Loretta Lynn.
There was a lady from Kentucky.
No I wouldn't say she was lucky.
She married a man by the name of Lynn.
Now, he pushed her into the music world knowing, she would win.
She gave the people their choice, to listen to the music
from her beautiful voice.
She sang the words of gold.
And yes, they really sold.
We all know, she has the voice of silk.
And when she sings, her fans melt like butter, and flows like honey and milk.
She met, a lot of people along her way.
They knew she would be great someday.
So they helped her towards fame, of today.
Now this lady they call the country Queen.
Well, we all know she's a singing machine.
And she has earned the right, to be called the Country Queen.
As we all know, Loretta Lynn will go Into the hall of Fame.
And God knows, I hope, she don't forget my name

Lois Thurman
FREEDOM' STAR
Come is time for final cleansing taking place on Surface Earth,
Time, too, for turning-point, directed to Season of Sixth Root Race Birth.
From vantage point universal Alpha and Omega call Twin Flames.
Gathered, He is uniting; God is reclaiming Earth.
Still aspin in willful coiling of blood and toil, of sweat and tears, Earth
Safe-netted by bonded strandings blazing white from God's Own Pure,
Laced with flames of violet: compassion, Mercy, Forgiveness, yet
Flames, transmuting error into Right, Changing darkness into Light.
Upon her side Earth lies restless, every atom bursting-bright, he
Axis straight by angel-group, helped by elf and sprite and fairy-loop, as lie
Toppled thrones in outer darkness
where black magicians meet with rue,
Sing! Sing We! November Night of Hallelulia
At last, at last, Earth is Free!
Flies the patient Dove returning, Gentle Love lifting Earth,
In her beak the well-tied strands are, rising on past Moon and Planet,
Deep in gold mists of MILKY WAY, She finds the Path that leads her homeward,
No longer
lost, or gone astray.
Soars the Bird of Heaven onward, across the shining bar, to
Shore once dimly-visioned now pulsing close, not seen afar, and
Moors her blazing burden, Safe in Glory,
where once it rested, when
God created Earth and named her FREEDOM'S STAR.

Doris C. Smith
THE SUPERINTENDENT'S VISIT
It happened last Friday at half-past two,
Many end-of-the-week tasks were still left to do
When into the classroom a visitor came,
Well-known and respected, Superintendent by name.
We tackled our language, oral discussion that day,
Most of the children had some fine things to say.
Then Jimmy got up and with full speed ahead
Related events which would be better unsaid.
I questioned in awe and in consternation—
"Have I over-taught skills of communication?"
Tom had a request and I rushed him to the door.
He said, as he walked with his eyes on the floor,
"It must be that third apple that I ate
When the recess bell rang a little late."
With the pace that is used when one turns on a dime
I whirled him into the washroom. He got there in time.
Dave's pencil punctured a bag, and it was rent;
Down the aisle fifty bouncing marbles went!
Where one could have once heard the drop of a pin
Then it sounded like hail on a roof made of tin!
They rolled under the piano and radiator—
I said, "Dave, we'll help you get them later."
Jane noticed the time stated it was nearly three;
Friday, desk-cleaning time, so no question had she
But hauled out all contents, plopped down on the floor.
Her example was followed by six others, or more.
I petitioned with sweat on my harried brow,
"If this world's going to end, please let it be now!"
Our spelling went well, then report cards were received,
We dismissed, then we searched; fifty marbles retrieved.
As the line passed, one small face looked up to me,
"Was I a good girl? I really do try to be."
I whispered, "Oh, yes, I'm sure that you do."
She called, "Goodbye, teacher; you know, I like you!"
Mittens found, scarves were on, even boots that don't fit.
The bus picked up the children. They were gone. That was it!
I remembered our visitor and re-entered the room
To receive the cold verdict of censor and doom.
Two adults in a place that had rollicked all day,
Then so empty it echoed like caves o'er a bay.
I laughed as I gasped, "Now, wouldn't you know—"
He said, "Wonderful children, just think how they grow!
The endurance of teachers, through work and through play,
But what's best, you still smile at the end of the day!"

Tancredi Vissec de Ganges
THE NARROW HOUSE
Is it a space where harvest is
Where men toil in the sun
Strong with the lusty emphasis
Of good works goodly done,
With other thought to a trysting-yield
Beside a moonlit lane;
In a warmer, fertile, more fallow field
And the planting of fiercer grain?
Is it a place where swallows fly
Over a dappled shade;
Is it a glen where lovers lie
And a young lad kisses a maid;
Does a strong lad pleasure a maid there
Under an apple tree,
Laggard and love-delayed there
With never a thought to me?
Perhaps to sink in a seething brine
Where gallant ships have gone;
To settle close to the broken spine
Of a sunken galleon.
A golden karabos of Crete
From many a thousand year,
I ponder the grave to shroud my feet,
Though I really do not care.
For if I may lie where love has been,
Where heart and pulse and touch
Have throbbed to kindly, human sin,
I shall not mind so much.
Nestle their calm above my head
I will not wish to stir,
Nor dream of ache nor ill long dead,
But rest me quieter.
With none of rancor, none of wrath,
With only this to keep—
My sacred truth—is aftermath
To monitor my sleep.
Then-from a slumbering, restless rouse,
Through the arch of a narrow door
Of another narrow, maternal house,
I shall struggle forth—once more!

Delbert Ray Gardenhire
THE LOVE GOD GAVE ME '79
The love of God has come to me
I know it can never leave.
People probably couldn't believe
I could say such a phrase
If I pulled up my left sleeve.
Yes, my arm is done away with, finished;
And my memory has and is gone
But if we looked at my other changes
There would be seeing of no true wrong.
I'm still here and I can love
Fortunately, there was no damage to my heart.
I have more thoughts of love for the Lord now
And so memorable there can simply be no depart.
These defects I've told you about;
My left arm and the loss of remembrance of my mind—

It all happened in this tragic car wreck
With my best friend—December 14, 1979.
Scars on my arms, I have many; and severe brain damage,
I know I can never be like the Delbert of the past,
Because I used to be very bad, but this new me I have of myself
Is improvement and needs to last and last.
I'm much better now; I hate evil environments
And It try to go with very nice girls.
There was this one particular woman named Linda Ellis—
She seemed real nice, so I gave her a whirl.
I know now that to get good you have to be good
So good! I had to go to the Lord.
And before I knew it this girl I have mentioned a few phrases ago
Had got me with her love sword.
She was right for me; so for opinions
I went to larger powers—the one I call "The Great".
You need some good advice or help when in need
Just do like me; I went to Him, he kept me from my near accidental fate.
I suggest to everyone that to get the best out of life is vital
And the way is to look somewhere abouts and maybe above.
Well no, the Lord is everywhere, sorry for wrong indications,
I went to the Lord in prayer only for my love.
I've told you about my good arm to bad and bad attitude to good
A short summary, but an exciting new change.
I love the best out of life now; good intentions, good wife Linda, and good spirits;
But it was imperative I go to Him to have this arranged.

Rhonda S. Collins
FOR ARTHUR, DEPARTING FOR BATTLE
Ascending his steed is my lord and noble king,
Arrayed in the royal finery for battle;
The silver clasp on his cape of scarlet
Conceals my holy medal lying next to his heart.
My lord and king sits nobly erect,
Viewing, with his ever-confident eyes that seem to protect,
The loyal soldiers and peasantry who pledge their trust.
How beautiful the exhibition as he departs
With the trumpets reverberating through the woods
And the drums beating the battle march.
All voices echo the thoughts of the parade:
A victorious battle will be waged.
How glorious is war for the periphery of those
Who never taste its ominous deaths.
I remember the last battle, with the same processional march,
The same false battle spirits, the same rejoicing cries.
But the battle became an interminable war,
And I feared for my beloved's life.
He returned, after an age it seemed,
Injured and nearly dead, I deemed.
How I wept when his wounds were disclosed,
But he comforted me with his simple prose;
"Look to the others; I am not ready for death myself.
Around me were the innumerable dead
Who would never wake, nor comfort their loved ones again.
I saw, with a shudder and a chill, the sudden emptiness of the women
Discovering their husbands and sons recently gone to heaven.
Dear Mother of God! What insanity makes Arthur wage war?
Let him remain in the comfort of our home
and forget wars that are not ours to fight.
But slowly I have learned that my king protects
The freedom and justice within his realm
And for the lesser kingdoms he also fights
Though it endangers his own sweet life.
In truth, I prefer him here by my side
But if he neglected his ideals and never offered aid
My admiration for him would quickly fade.
But because I love him with my soul and heart
Because his heart is pure, his quest is right,
I will remain untearful, patient, and quiet.
Therefore, I stand among the women gathered here
Praying silently, constantly, for his soon and safe return.
I wave to him my fervent farewells
Until he disappears on the horizon.

Mary Crickmer Conley
THE WAKING HOURS
Day has begun.
Night is done.
Says the old clock chime.
But I find
That in my mind
It is slumber time.
My body arose
Below my nose
And set to motion.
My silly head,
I dread,
Has the sleepy time notion.
Oh—how dreary,
When my body is too weary
Another step to take—
I go to bed,
And in my head
My mind springs Wide-Awake!

Andrea Ross
TO THE GARDNER FROM HIS FLOWER
Please don't go—I know I started out a hard, ugly seed.
Thorns protruding out all around me—but these thorns made it impossible for just ANYBODY to touch me and kill me.
I want to grow, to become a flower but in the past, I've
been burried in rock and I've gotten so thirsty and so forgotten—It took *all* the strength I had to get out of there.
One time I got buried in mud—
I almost drowned—until I taught myself how to swim.
Then there was the time I was buried in patches of weeds—
they almost choked me to death—I had to bite my way out.

Now—I'm in soft sweet earth—
It's warm and happy here.
I can feel my deep crimson petals ready to blossom.
You've cuddled, nurtured, cared..
You've made me believe that hard,
ugly seeds can become flowers too. . .
I thank you for my radiance
but please don't go. . .I can
become the most beautiful dark
crimson rose you've ever seen,
beaming happily up at you because of the goodness you've showered down on me—I know, I know, you HAVE TO GO.
—But remember, this flower was able to blossom *once more* because of you.

Nelle Morris Bigbee
WASHATERIA ROMANCE
While waiting for the washer to whirl
He noticed this tall, beautiful girl,
How nice, he thought, if they could meet
Somewhere, someday, on a quiet street.
Her jeans were tight, her brown hair light
Her blouse lay open at the neck,
She looked at him and he saw her smile
So excited, he could have run a mile.
He watched the rhythmic movement of her hips
The sweet curve of her tender, red lips.
He took his time folding his clothes,
Noticing her blouse embroidered with A ROSE.
He finished his wash the same time as she
And worked up courage to ask—if he
Could carry her clothes to her car
Things were going OK, so far.
She smiled, "Thanks, but I came on the bus,
Heck! He thought, and wanted to cuss.
By now his heart was lodged square in his lung,
He simply could not untangle his tongue.
But — Glory be! A Tisket-a-Tasket
She handed him her basket.
He led the way to his car
Actually walking on air,
When the wind brushed his cheek,
With strands of her hair.

Kenneth A. Pfeifer
WHY MUST WE LEAVE
Thank you for wanting me.
You made me feel so young.
My mind is filled with your good grace,
my heart with your sweet love.
I thought that it would never end;
the sharing of us by us.
But now you made it clear to me,
our oneness is about to bust.
Why must we leave one another?
Is it not right to want to stay?
Can't we keep it going longer?
We could try a different way.
Do you fear we might leave our other?
Thinking that it would be a sin.
I feel we can keep it going,
Without your wildest fear coming in.
Thank you for reminding me,
What romance is all about.
It's been such a long, long time.
You finally brought me out.
I hoped that you'd believe me.
I told you that I cared.
But you thought so little of

yourself,
you think that no one can.
I know the time is right,
before we go too deeply in.
But I can't help but wonder,
if we'll ever be one again.
I'm sure now, what you're
saying,
is the best thing for us to do.
I hope that I'll remain in your
heart,
as you will, in my heart too.
Why must we leave one
another?
Is it not right to want to
stay?
My only regret about our past,
is that we have to end it this
way.
I wish we would have had one
last chance;
a chance we still could make.
To show each other our kind of
love,
could be the right kind for only
our sake.

Garnet Fullerton Bruce

HOME VERSUS HOME

It's the only place for you,
Mom, theres no meals to
prepare
They'll help you with your bath
and clothes and even comb
your hair
You'll still have your privacy
and your own things in your
room
If you share with someone else,
it will keep away the gloom
We'll try to visit every day to
keep away the blues
If we can't, I can always phone
and leave a word for you
Since we've started our own
business, our time is not our
own
Mom, I know you'd like it if
you'd try a nursing home.
Now how do I tell my daughter,
that I don't intend to go
I don't want to be a burden, but
I've seen those homes and so
To me, they just don't seem like
such happy carefree places
People wandering around with
lost looks on their faces
I've seen people tied in beds
and some were tied in chairs
And wondered what would
happen if a fire broke out in
there
I'm comfortable living in a
house I've long called home
I'm used to my own rocker and
having my own phone
I don't need someone to tell me
when its time to eat
Or when to bathe and comb my
hair and help keep my room
neat
I know you mean well Darlin
with your thoughts of home
for me
But my home has always been
right here and it's here I'm
gonna be
Darlin, they look like prisons
with the fences round the side
The locked doors in the
evenings and the people tied
inside
They're just not my idea of what
a happy home should be
Home is where the heart is and
mine is wild and free.

Donna Lynn Nelson Kortje

THE BEST GIFTS

Hustle, bustle, to and fro
Oh to find a gift that shows
We care!
Size, color, do they have one
Oh, gift buying, not always fun
But we need to share.
Christmas joy, the holiday spirit
Let us celebrate, no need to fear
it
Many gifts we can bear.
Gifts that need no bows or
wrapping
Presents bringing much laughter
and clapping
May I tell you why and where?
In our faces and in our hearts
Some of the best places to start
Love and smiles, we discover
there.
Loving words, laughter, and
smiles
Make year-around gifts, so
worthwhile
Gifts unique in style and flair.
Our Saviour set a fine example
His gift was unique, pleasing,
and ample
Something that doesn't break
or tear.
Gave Himself so simple and
pure
Of this gift we can be sure
Nothing so caring, loving and
fair.
Give of yourself, your time,
your love
And our heavenly Father above
Will see that we bear, share, and
care everywhere.

Mildred White

THE BEAUTY OF LIFE

There's nothing like the breath
of spring,
That brings new life to
everything,
The grass, the trees, the pretty
flowers,
There's gentle winds and April
showers,
The birds begin to want to sing,
Because they know, at last it's
spring.
Then comes summer a warmer
season,
It's my favorite and here's the
reason,
This is when crops and gardens
grow,
So is it any wonder why I love
it so?
It's then that life is in
full bloom,
To enjoy for a while but all
too soon,
The fall season comes and slows
things down,
Instead of green leaves now,
they start turning brown,
Not only brown, but red and
gold,
The multi-colored world is a
sight to behold.
Soon ole Jack Frost comes
sneaking around,
And all the leaves tumble to
the ground,
Then ole man Winter comes in
on the scene,
And though it's unpleasant, it's
also a dream,
Because it is beautiful both
high and low,
When he sprinkles the
mountains and valleys with
snow,
So we have four seasons,
And each has it's reasons,
For something to hold dear,
Throughout the whole year.
There are other things that
make life grand,
A gentle smile, a helping hand,
Loving parents, relatives and
friends,
Just look around, the list never
ends.
There are animals of all kinds
and little pests too,
But each is beneficial no matter
what they do,
The Fall's the time for
harvesting the good things
that we raise,
And never should we fail to give
a verbal voice of praise,
To the One who is responsible
in the heavens up above,
It's all for our enjoyment, and
He gives it all with Love,
And even though conditions are
full of stress and strife,
Be thankful for the blessings
we receive throughout our
life,
They're enough to make life
worth while,
So rejoice and face each day
with a smile,
Besides, this is not the way it
will always be,
God promises us a Paradise
earth for all eternity.

Ann Margaret Borden

NO SIGHT

If I could not see, I wouldn't cry, I wouldn't weep, I'd bear my difficulties and show that I'm not scared.

I'd believe that I could function without sight. If I had only a little while to see, I'd take a look around, and think what *might* be.

I'd look at things and store them in my mind, and feel the texture of things that I like, and remember them always as my sight.

I'd look at my loved ones, though I'll never forget-all the good times, but still yet, I'd think of things beyond my life and
reasure myself that I am still alright.

I'd stop to see the roses, at a different point of view, and stop to feed the ducks and think of times with you.

I'd reread things that I have wrote, events of my lifes past. And think of good and disastrous times, happy, down-hearted, and sad.

But as I said, I would not fret nor shed a tear, for losing my sight, I do not fear.

Frank Halstead

ASIA MINOR

(To Doe, on the inception of her soul's freedom—This spring when the forgotten years of past lives whispered of other aureate dawns.)

We left our triremes1 in the
harbor,
Bearing Mithras2 we had come,
When our legions passed the
fountain place,
I could feel my heart-beats'
drum,
Pulsing with the throbbing
temple horns,
And of all that armoured host,
Amongst those singing
priestesses,
I dug your song the most.
But this talk is foolish
dreaming,
Of dusty times gone by,
And you can take that bloody
nonsense,
And stuff it in your eye,
This talk of reincarnation,
Is a lot of silly mush,
Yet, somehow, I was a soldier,
And you a temple thrush.

1. An ancient mediterranean galley having three banks of oars—in this case a Roman ship of war.
2. A God of an ancient mystery cult that flourished particularly with the Roman Legions of the late Roman Empire.

Nicey Mayben Roberts

THE MAN DRESSED IN BLUE

A cop's life is a little sunshine,
a little rain,
A lot of sorrow, and so much
pain.
We call the man in blue when
in distress and he
is often barred from success.
As he walks his beat, the sun
shines fair, so
proudly he is standing there.
He seeks a friend among the few
and hopes to find
one standing true.
Time goes on. Where have they
gone? Where are his
friends?
Once again his days are gray
as duty calls him to
start a new day.
This cop dressed in blue will
not retreat as he
proudly walks his dangerous
beat.
Time goes on to alter his fate
as death stalks and
lies in wait.
A distress call that every
officer fears says "A brother
has fallen." These brave men
hold back their tears.
All his brothers dressed in
blue buckle their armor
tight; they rush right in and
win the fight.
Heartbroken, but true to the
end, they have lost their
brother and also their friend.
The officer who is dressed in
blue is lying there
in sad review.
His family is heartbroken and
sad; he was a devoted

husband and dad.
The loyal friends that do
remain true come by to
look at the man in blue.
His real friends are in bitter
tears as they see their
friend of many years.
Perhaps this man's smile, down
life's road, has helped
to lighten another's load.
Those courageous men dressed
in blue are there protecting
me and you.
Although we don't know all the
men dressed in blue,
We pray our Loving Savior will
always protect you.

Vincent Rudolph Trotman
HAPPINESS IS
IF HAPPY, TELL NO ONE
THAT I AM NOT HAPPY,
IF MERELY FOR A DAY;
GLAD, I am, to have had a dad,
who held back a smile, and
sided my search to be happy;
happiness is aesthetic classic
beauty—
this a month-a season a jawful
of thought:
darlings enjoying each other's
sociability—
the faces-their parents-
contagious laughing—
light-t-ning-length-th-ning-
exciting them
their way-this day;
Mothers overseeing smiles of
future Mothers,
Her solemness in reminiscing
Mothers' Motherhood's
sacredness in protecting this
day's moments gladly-happily
sharing the joys of the parent's
home-hearts-open fields-paved
streets-crafts-visiting Grand
Ma-an Uncle or three, a friend
or two-a good bike or a broken
one-a joke shared-a sunday
school teacher-a car-a team
you joined, white happily
busying along Mary's way,
merrily each day;
Ah-a smile flowing nourishing
my legs-feet-abdomen-loins with
each pulsating heart beat, as I
walk this Staten Island Ferry to-
to enjoy-enjoy the waves, as I
enjoyed the subway, bus and
will the hill climb-challenging
breath and muscles on this
journey alone-together along
my way;
Blessed to be happy-verbalizing-
my heart, and mind-brain-they
do emotionally appreciate-you
also? How marvelous-this big
apple attitude of sharing money-
legally spiritually-New York;
The Golden mannered San
Francisco's fresh airy gate-
like-way to the Pacific-Seattle-
the New America-down-over-up-
to Alaska's Bay-Hawaii-
The firm folks of Salt Lake,
Boston Philadelphia, Florida,
U.S. of A. Sacramento, Norfolk
and some business and character
wordings from Jefferson
Franklin-Lincoln-Hoover-King's
America ". . . .the right to
the Pursuit of happiness. . . ."
within reason, and planned
action free of coercion
or conspiritical harm to others;
You are happy: to be, is, to have
been, was, could or should or
can present a contribution to
the present or future minds; this
is her reserves and his time as
persuaded-persuasions-persuading
experienced skills happily; this
the individual's might in a tight
fight for life—
if merely for a day-a season-an
epoch an age-eternity's Blessing
Happily HAPPINESS IS
HAPPINESS IS HAPPINESS IS

Paul Lewis Pappas
THE ONE THEY CALLED 'THE KID'
We were sittin' in Dugan's
Garden •
One hot midsummer night,
Drinkin' our daily glass o' suds
And talkin' 'bout last night's
fights.
We saw one bum go out in three
Another, out in two.
They don't know how to box,
we said,
Like fighters used to do.
We'll never see the likes again
Of Langford, Gaines or Ryan,
Nor will a man e'er toe the
mark
Like Philly Jack O'Brien.
Then the talk drifted 'round,
As it most generally did,
To everybodys favorite,—
The one they called 'The Kid.'
The Kid had fifty-seven fights
'Fore he was scarce sixteen.
He whipped 'most every man he
fought
And they called The Kid
"Champeen."
He was handled by the best of
them
—'Pop' Mathews was the one—
He never overmatched The Kid
And he loved him like a son.
He started as a Bantamweight
And grew into a Middle—
But the Kid would take on
anyone,
Weight mattered very little.
And then, one night in
Cleveland,
He gave forty pounds away
To an up and coming Heavy
Named 'Killer' Calloway.
Calloway had little class,
But he hit like a mule.
'Just stick and stay away' said
Pop,
'Make him look like a fool.'
'Stick and move, then stick
again,
Don't try to take him out. . . .
And then we'll stay with
Middles
And go for a title bout.'
For eight rounds he struck and
moved—
While Calloway hit air—
His punches missed a foot or
more,
But you saw the power there.
It was jab, move, and jab again,
The Kid was lookin' fine,
When a wild right hand from
Calloway
Dropped the Kid for nine.
The Kid got back up with a
smile,
But his eyes looked mighty
strange.
The Kid went down again for
eight
As Calloway found the range.
The Kid backed in a corner
And Calloway gave him Hell.
The Kid bobbed and weaved and
held
And waited for the bell.
Calloway threw a hard left hook
And followed with a right.
The crowd all hollered for the
Ref
To step in and stop the fight.
And, in the other corner,
Pop Mathews watched his pal.
He knew the Kid would never
want
Him to throw in the towel.
Left and right and right and left,
Calloway hit him well. . . .
The Kid dropped to the canvas
Just before the bell.
Pop Mathews crawled in
through the ropes
And lifted up his head,
Then let out a cry of anguish
As he saw the Kid was dead.
What happened? How can this
be?
You could hear the people say—
How could a fighter like the Kid
Lose to a guy like Calloway?
Too many fights, too many
rounds,
Too many punches, too many
pounds—
You can only go so many nights,
You can only have so many
fights. . . .
You ask me how I know so
much
About the Kid's last fight?
They still call me 'Killer'
Calloway
And I fought the Kid that
night.

Mary J. Risselman
A ROSE OF BEAUTY
As I reach out and touch the
velvety red petals,
Or smell the aroma of my red
roses—I think of you.
Each one of the twelve
individual flowers is unique,
And reminds me of who and
what you are.
When I look at one rose—I
think of the twinkle in your
eye,
Another reminds me of the
warmth of your smile.
Also, I think of the considerate
things you do,
And your concern for other
people's feelings.
I think of the fun times the
two of us have shared—
All the smiles and laughter
that have filled our days.
But I also remember that there
have been moments of
sadness,
When you were there to wipe
away my falling tears.
I'm reminded of your toughness,
as well as, your tenderness,
Your great strength and also
your moments of weakness.
Another rose represents the
security I feel when you hold
me in your arms,
And the special feeling I
have when your lips meet
mine.
I think of how happy I am just
being with you,
And how I miss you when
you're not near to me.
The greenery stands for all
that adds to the beauty of the
person you are,
The thorns represent that way
you defend those you care
about.
The yards of delicately
entwined ribbon made into a
bow,
Symbolizes all the people that
touch each day of our lives.
Each stem nourishes and
supports each fragile bud,
Just as a man and a woman fill
one another's needs.
The purpose of the water is to
maintain the roses' beauty,
Like the special meaning you
have added to my life.
When I look at all the roses
held together by one single
vase,
I think of all the things inside
of one very special guy.

Fred Bjornson
SAY IT NOW
One day comes along the hour
of eleven,
No doubt about it, I'll be
ready for Heaven.
Don't weep don't sigh don't sob,
I may have struck a better job.
Don't go buy me a big bouquet,
For which you'll find it hard
to pay.
Don't mope down the alley
feeling blue,
'Cause I may be better off
than you.
Don't tell anyone that I'm
a Saint,
Nor any old thing you know I
ain't.

If you have jam, you like to
spread,
Slip it to me before I'm
dead.
If you have roses, bless your
soul,
Just put one in my button
hole.
While I'm alive and happy
to-day,
Don't wait 'till I have gone
away.
(Well, I made it)
Climbing the 'Golden Stairs' was
tough,
Being an old man, I sure did
puff.
But, now that I've entered the
Pearly Gates,
I'm well located and have plenty
of dates.
Not the kind of dates we had
back on earth.
And yet more enjoyable and
full of mirth.
We have no burdens, no sorrow,
no pain,
What used to be our loss is
now our gain.
Talk about harmony, we sure
have it here,
And when we need help, it
always is near.
Time passes fast while we sing
and play,
Then ever so often we take
time out to pray.
When you hear that call, no
time to be sad,

For living in Heaven, you'll always be glad.
You have my word for it, things here are great,
Start climbing that ladder and don't be late.

Martie
MY MASTER
As I wearily trudged along a dusty road,
A stranger came up to me.
"Have you seen my master, please?"
He inquired anxiously, staring at my load.
"Oh he's not on this road," I retorted,
"For I've been this road a time or three."
"But you must have," he replied as he turned away.
"Huh," I mused, "must be a slave to have a master."
Wiping dust out of my eyes, I went my way.
My load was so heavy, why should I care?
Nobody cared for me long as I could remember.
There by the roadside sat an old woman beckoning.
(Now what? Always one distraction or another.)
"Have you seen my master, please?" She
Pleaded, looking at my cuts and bruises.
"Silly old woman, why can't they let me be?"
I mumbled, my load felt like a ton of bricks.
Teetering precariously under the weight, down I went.
Down in the mud and filth I sprawled—
In anger and disgust I raged and sputtered.
Suddenly so tired—so utterly spent—tears of rage
Gave way to tears of anquish and sorrow.
Gently He lifted me as though I were a child—
He washed me clean and healed me too.
"Who are you?" I sobbed. "Why I'm the Master,"
Said He, "I came to carry your load."
ok/ab

Mary G. McLaughlin
MR. REAGAN'S POLISH CANDLE—CHRISTMAS EVE 81
I put a candle in the window.
And then turned my thoughts t'wards Christmas Day.
And never heard the freedom cry. . .,from a place not far away.
From a people not so different then you. . .and you. . .or me.
I guess the only difference is, a need to see their children free.
It's not so much themselves, you know. . .They've lasted many years. They've done the work,
In fear to shirk. . .And held back a thousand tears.
It was the faces of the children, and a million haunted why wide eyes. It was the childrens hungry faces as they heard the empty lies. . .That made them raise
Their fists to fight and risk their very lives. . .
for freedom.
I guess the candle was forgotten and the flame died quickly out. . , I guess I wasn't listening to the urgent angry shout.
I guess I didn't want to hear about that place and all it's hell,
After all. . .I was happy hearing, the ringing Christmas bell.
Well. . .
May I say this in my own defense, and for what it may be worth. . .
On every single Christmas Card. . . .
I signed "Love and Peace On Earth."

Dorothy M. Crumby
A MOTHER'S LOVE
A Mother's love is unsearchable, unconditional and cannot be measured with the rule of reason;
It is far beyond our imagination, and our greatest expectation;
There is a part of Her that weathers all the storms, withstands all the obstacles, and covers our deepest wounds;
In the darkest hours of life, Her love reaches out to Her love ones;
Even in anger, out of her innermost parts, flow a stream of compassion;
She survives her weakest moments with a strength that we cannot comprehend;
Far into the night, Her heart crys out to the Creater
"Oh Precious Lord, let your peace rest upon my Children;"
"Grant them your Divine Guidance and Protection."
Truly Her love cannot be taken lightly, Nor can it be forgotten;
She is an extraordinary person, endowed with an endurance from Above;
Such a force is a Strong Foundation in any Home:
This is a Tribute to All Good Mothers Everywhere:
Whether she lives, or have fallen asleep in Eternity,
Her love is a living Monument—
It will never die! !

Donna Mae Kirkendall
PRAISES TO MY LORD
I praise you Lord, for the Sunlight; glimmering on swaying trees.
I praise you Lord, for moonlight; shimmering on the sands of seas.
I praise you Lord; for the autumn breeze; catching snow white velvet doves with ease.
I praise you Lord, for the stars, twinkling like stairsteps to Heaven.
I praise you Lord, for summer's warmth that fills the air with peace
while stirring excitement within my soul to see
all that's been born anew, I praise you Lord, that you are mine to have, to hold, to love divine.
I praise you Lord, for being here, and holding my life dear
I praise you Lord for being faithful, and showing your word holds true
I praise you Lord, for loving me, unconditionally and lifting me up, when I was so down, then giving me a Royal Crown.
And I praise you Lord, that I proclaim VICTORY
That your promises I claim Hurray! Hallelujah!
The battle's over, my victory's been won
I praise you Lord, my body and soul are of one accord.
(This is dedicated to, Carilyn, Di, and Jesus)

Ronald A. Oliver
ENDINGS
We're all stars,
in our own way.
Looking for the moment. . . .
. . .will recognition come?
Where is success?
I want to live a life of endings.
If we live for the moment,
the moment is the ending.
The music builds.
The curtain drops.
People cheer.
lights fade.
BRAVO, they call.
Is this possible?
Why some and not others?
It's fair,
Isn't it?
Give me more endings.
Wait,
what's the price?
Where do the jokes stop?
I was the life of the party,
so they said.
Yet, I was nothing but other people.
I learned from the best.
Or maybe that's only what they told me.
Now they're gone, do I search for tears?
Is anyone watching?
This must be an ending!
Must we always cry?
Our emotions run deeper than tears.
I *was* sad,
no one noticed.
Most people wear "The Emperor's New Clothes"
I wonder why?
Can't they see the happy endings?
Love, sunsets. .you know.
They're not transparent,
And what about our children?
Are they us?
Not yet.
Do we force them?
Can't we let them be new?
Their endings are pure;
laughter, pranks, feelings.
Yet we praise them for becoming our reflections.
The spirit is receptive,
my heart knows what's right.
Yet.
The endings, do we give them up?
That's what we live for,
Isn't it?

Robert C. Rimmer
CAUSE TO FEAR
Awakening to witness the birth of a new morn'
my scarred heart senses yet a painful thorn.
Tho slumber had soothed its somber pace
reality of another day I must somehow face.
Depredating pain ebbed from deep within,
inducing all thoughts to an unanswered din.
Ecstatic loves had drawn my earnest heart from me,
each with spoken dreams of the future to be.
Expelled was a Love forever as my beholding destiny,
only to be cast aside to bare the longing memory.
Memories, tho treasured, soon become cold
lacking the warmth within these arms to hold.
There is no comfort in this bleak solitude
for my pleading heart true love seems to elude!
A vacant heart lives with relentless despair
for man and woman were surely meant to pair.
Oh! To release my yearning impounded love,
I plea amongst tears to our Saviour above.
A love to wash away all doubts and fears,
to cleanse the uncertainties bred thru the years!
Falling to my knees, I gaze toward the sky,
holding back seeping tears, I question why!
For what purpose then was I delivered here,
what was my sole quest, I feel cause to fear!

Ardis McIntee Trowbridge
TO ROBERT
This fog formed late last night.
I'd rather say a cloud fell during the darkness,
But if I did, someone would say
Clouds don't fall. Impossible!
So to be precise, last night
Between your sleeping and your waking,

One of two conditions prevailed, and the fog formed.
This morning, in the thick gray dampness,
The cardinal hides in shadowed backyard pines
And I remember how you loved bright red.

Iona M. Brown
THE OLD TRUNK
We opened the trunk, my sister and I,
To take out the treasure of days gone by;
The collections of half a century

lay there;
And memories of mama were everywhere,
Hidden away amid tissue and cloth,
Protected from gnawing of mouse or moth.
'Mid trinkets and albums, an old scrapbook;
And, believe it or not, an old button-hook.
Here's bits of ribbon and pieces of lace,
Each telling a story of some time and place.
Here's a tiny jewel box full of souvenirs
From children and grandchildren thro' the years.
And pictures-here's a tintype of dear uncle Joe;
Now who is this one. . . . does anyone know?
A picture of mama in her wedding gown
With papa beside her, only he's sitting down.
And within the album's memory pages
Are pictures of us children at different ages.
"Iona, what's this?" my sister expressed;
"That's the gown in which the oldest was blessed;
And that's a strip from mama's wedding dress;"
It's yellowed with age yet holding it's press.
And these are the linens Velora has made,
Embroidered so neatly and in tissue laid.
And these silver pieces? oh now I know
Are the ones Vina gave her long, long ago.
Here's marbles and beads stored in this box!
From a friendship quilt, these left-over blocks;
And souvenir pillow-tops sent from her sons
In the Service;. . . .Now who sent which ones?
These hankies of coconut silk from the Phillipines,
Came from Norman, while there with the Marines;
And these little flags with the number of stars,
One to represent each son who was off to the Wars,
Remind us of the heartaches and sheddings of tear
As we awaited their return with trembling fear.
Here's hankies and doilies and Birthday cards,
And a valentines from papa, "With warmest regards";
Announcements of weddings, graduations and birth,
Some serious greetings, some gay with mirth;
Here's newspaper clippings of family and friends,
Each its part to their story lends.
Though the trunk was broken and shabby and old,
The treasures within have their story told
Of the precious moments that go to make life
Sweet in spite of any troubles or strife.
Now each little trinket that before us we see
Will hold for some loved-one a sweet memory.

Grace Marie Carbone

WHEN MOONLIGHT KISSES MORNING SUN

I walk unheeded blindly into the night,
Past houses, buildings and streetlights,
Down the walkways, across the traverse,
And in my mind I hear the poet's verse:
"When moonlight kisses morning sun,
You and I shall become one."
Past Wiley's old gin-mill,
The shoemaker's black-booted window sill
And the Five & Ten.
The last time I was there I can't even remember when.
The main boulevard brightly lit and
The park bench near the corner
Where I used to sit:
"When moonlight kisses morning sun,
You and I shall become one."
Now at a quicker pace I find my way
To the school playground, the painted
Hopscotch boards are there still.
I want to remember. I must and I will!
I stand plunged in a mental abyss,
Waiting for the memories to surface:
"When moonlight kisses morning sun,
You and I shall become one."
I'm back where I think my life began
And since then it's seemed a hundred year span.
The children's voices at play grow louder in my mind
And I hear them say, "Catch me, catch me if you can."
It all is clear before me and I wonder
Where has it all gone to.
The nuns, stiff in their starched habits.
Top secret records kept in the secretary's file-cabinet.
The priests dressed in black, just a small
Token of white visible.
And the evil punishing ruler-slapping principal.
Where, where is the huge black piano
Played by Mrs. Smith?
The crotchety, screeching, stick-like lady,
Lady with the red face.
Here in front of me your visage
Is suspended in space.
More than the nuns and priests,
You wanted to make us aquiesce.
If we sang our hymns we would be blessed,
If not you'd make us fear the burning fires of hell
Until we jumped at the sound of the school bell:
"When moonlight kisses morning sun,
You and I shall become one."
As I recover from this reverie, I walk
On further to the Church of St. Anthony.
Slowly I open Gothic doors,
As if afraid to wake my sleeping Lord.
Once inside the candle-lit house of God,
I make the sign of the cross and nod.

Kneeling inside a pew I recall my childhood
When cares were few and everything good.
And as I look around and listen,
The sun seeps through stained-glass windows
And seems to make the saints' eyes glisten.
Here surrounded by these holy eyes,
I am mesmerized, one with them
Who worship Him.
And as the morning's light sets in,
I hear the poet's verse again:
"When moonlight kisses morning sun,
You and I shall become one."

Michelle Percevault

LIFE

An open book of empty pages,
Awaits the completion of my life.
Only in the shadow of death,
Do I wish to have them filled.

Vhonda Gaye Griggs

RUSH, RUSH, RUSH

The title of this very poem,
Is true from start to ending.
I'll tell you what I really mean,
By this title's meaning.
It all starts out with how this world,
Is always on the rush.
Just look around in city places,
How people run and push.
They act as if all their time,
Is fixing to run out.
But really they're just on their way,
To a 50% discount.
Sunday is the only day,
That people stop their loafin,
And the reason that they stop,
Is 'cause the stores aren't open.
Why don't people stop and think,
Before they push and run,
Just think about your aching feet,
Are you really having fun?

Debbie Monk

THE LONELY MILLIONAIRE

"What a life", he said to me.
"Boring and such a drag.
I walk around all day in these old raggedy rags.

Not even a trace of a job to be found in sight for miles,
everyone looks at me weirdly, not even one friendly smile.
Sure I eat but junk, in plates of pure china and gold,
glasses made of crystal, this life's getting old.

why don't I join you my friend for a walk down the street,
we can stop and talk to everyone see who I might meet.
For I've just given up my money and my mansion too that is;
For money is not important when you have all these friends.

William Murray Campbell

BEAUTIFUL BRITISH COLUMBIA

Here is a land so very grand
And forever it shall be
A land of hope and promise
A land that's free for you and me
The green mountains and the rivers
With waters fresh and pure
Are nature's plan to give a man
All fish and game that he can lure
From cattle ranges to the fruit lands
Cuddled deep in scenery
To Alaska's friendly neighbour
Our own dear land, our north country
There is logging in our mountains
Where timbers huge, are cut with care
And the miners digging treasure
That some prospector did find there
This land of ours so fruitful
With all good things for life
It has many sites for the camper
And a mountaineers delight
With valleys ever beautiful
And lakes enticing anglers there
And cities incomparable
With nature's beauty that they share
From Grouse Mountain you see Vancouver
And world famous Stanley Park
You see its lovely harbour
And lights turned on when it gets dark
There is skiing on our mountain slopes

Sailing in the bay
Playing golf on the course
Once you're here you'll want to stay
If you want to see a city
Unlike all others you have seen
Visit our capital Victoria
A city of flowers, a beautiful scene
Sail on our ferries to Victoria
A pleasant two hour time away
You will cruise amid the islands
Your trip in mind, will always stay
A must is Buchart Gardens
It is well worth your time to see
And Victoria has its Sea Land
Where the whales perform with glee
If you are an avid sportsman
With your fishing gear in trim
You should go to Campbell River
Where the tyee salmon swim
Ships of every nation
Sail into waters we adore
Where the blue Pacific nestles
Between our islands and the shore
A preview of a heaven
Is here for everyone to see
When cruising through the inlets
Famed for beauty in B.C.
From the grizzly to the cougar
Big horn sheep, the moose and deer
Where ducks and geese are flying
In our fertile land, the food is here
There is salmon fishing, clams for digging
And oysters by the score
There are fish and prawns a plenty
For just the taking off our shore
This country is just teeming
With nature's beauty and wild life
It has pleasure's for the tourist
And a sportsman's paradise
There is no end to its attractions
Around each bend there's more to see
In beautiful British Columbia
The land I call, my own country

Ronald F. Smedley

THOUGHTS TWO

gently growing out of the misty morning
i sit and wait for summer to come
and
for the wet afternoons to engulf my body
so until then
or is the expression until later
i can't see
and right now i really don't want to
at least on the outside
(the inside is what really counts anyway)
that is why the earth is dying.
(just not enough looking on the isthmus of one's inner self)
notice i said on *one's* inner being
this always comes first
(it has to or else we'll have)
nothing more than a bunch of fat
pot bellied trolls who sit on their bee-hinds and pretend to be in touch
with humanity, while in reality the only thing they can see is
their fat fingers and all the glutton they can put into them)
kinda like the monkey and the coconut,
they never could get their hand out of the hole.
after someone has enjoyed the expression of the
coney island of his own mind and
the reality of his flawed personality
(this is where the Spirit comes into the picture)
he (or she) can begin to see the work and all around them
and now as it really is and must be. . .
collage after collage of flowing colors slowly weaving into
a person's being
seeing the armaddiillloooos walk by very s l o w l y
and man struggling to keep up at a very erratic pace
now. . .reality is perceived
it *is* true that ma and apple pie can come true
the only answer is to believe in the impossible
believe in the uncanny
believe in ma and that piece of pie
most important. . .believe in *god* (oops i mean) GOD.
so my friend
(as one aardvark to another)
remember the words of the great artistic master,
"where is my toothbrush?"
and when indoubt
count your chickens before
the bed bugs bite. . .
(nothing worse that i can see
than bed bitten chickens.)
AND and,
as you go out of this side
and continue up the other
please remember that people
people are meant to be treated
more humanely than your pet
ostrich.
they have eyes to see
to see on both
the inside
(which is all that really
matters now isn't it)
and on the outside (a
necessary but unfortunate
commodity).
if not,
if not,
if not my friend the demise of
mankind will gracefully fall
into the hands of aardvarks
and armadillos
and we *don't* want that. . .
do we?

Carmen L. Hickok

UNTITLED

As quickly as you can change,
I can fight—
the knowledge of privacy interference
leading to two part despair.
From darting eyes and cold fingertips
to slow jazz and hazy silver-blue walls of warmth
you strip my lady-fair flair
I shed my subtleness
as wine shreds
the threads
of careful planning.
Movements and sensations
flow gently.
Two true believers
in curiousity
and hidden lives
to flow together
gently
or
savagely
together now
separately again
afterwards.
Silver spun shadows
glisten with smoke
music and lust.
We are not
but are naked to the want
yet you know
and I know
we can hide.
Darkness is the only
light we wander
through.
Words spoken with caution
inquisitive of hidden meanings
which will add to the unreality
of an offbeat struggle of questions
none care to answer.
I bare to you
only a part of me
that fulfills the dream.
You search for an answer in my earring
but my perfume's essence
misleads you,
leads you into where you
lead me on,
beyond,
this real life.
Soft music
turns to loud,
as darkness
turns to light,
as passion
turns to flight,
as yesterday
turns to today,
and we smile
carefully in passing,
as my earring
secretly speaks
sweet seduction
to your fleeting
body.

Naomi Campbell

A LETTER—A BOTTLE

No date nor dateline—
An idea through all time
Dear Everyone:
InRef: *A Tiny Bottle*
This is my story—a story
I have not told
I'm a tiny bottle
But I cannot be sold
I measure one and a
Half inches tall
Brownish in color not
Filled with the
Goodie drink
Wouldn't break if I
Would fall
Some bottle people think!
My bottle design is unique
Plainly shows my name
Still I cannot be sold!
Along with my cousins
We claim world fame
This is part of my story
I wanted told
Differ from my cousin bottles
In color and size
They contain the refreshing
Drink that's frosty cold!
Together we win the prize!
Another part of my story
I wanted told
'twas eighteen hundred ninety
And four
That Coca Cola was first
Bottled
'neath the roof of
Biedenharn Candy Company
Store
Vicksburg, Mississippi—
This Eventful year
'came a place and period of
Fun and much cheer
Eleven hundred and five
Washington street
Is now a place where visitors
Meet
This bottled Coca-Cola
First sold for five cents
What better way could
Five pennies or a
Nickel be spent?
Before me—
Family members were on
The scene
In their color of cool
Green
Being a tiny size
Did my thing
With a wee bit of advertize!
Now I swing and swing
I dangle and dangle
From a key ring
Sometimes a brass chain
Sometimes one of gold
This is the whole of my
Treasured story I wanted told
I remain, one of a kind
A tiny Coca Cola Bottle
P.S. Please enjoy my cousins'
bottled tasty drink; they
CAN be sold with pride
Not being a bottled beverage
I only show for the ride

Phoebe J. Vaughn

THE OCEAN

I listen to the ocean's roar
and hear the echo of a thousand
voices calling from the deep.
The forces of nature erupting,
bringing forth a magnitude of
magnificence in a powerful
clash.

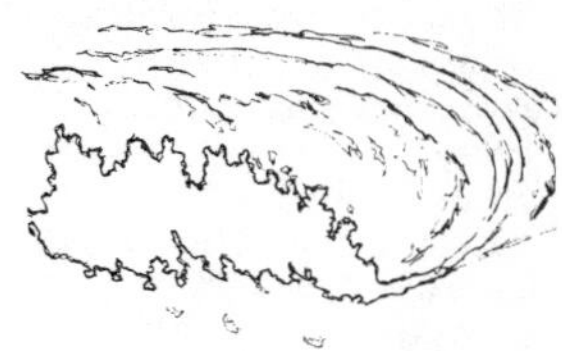

I hear the thunder roar and see
the white foam of the sea, as it
calls to me.

"Show me your timeless wonders
so I can learn to love you more."
Meeting on the sandy shore,
pushing forth seaweed as it
drifts by.
"Unfold, Oh Mighty One. Call to
me, call to me".
I feel the coolness of you
pressing against my flesh, as I
watch your waves rush in.
I know you will not swallow me
up, unless I come in too far.

Aldine Lorena Matteson Gunn
OF KNOTS AND STRING
I KNOTS
A yanked-on knot gets tighter
still,
But the tighest, patiently
picked at,
Gets gradually looser
And slowly comes untied.
Or a knot can be swiftly cut
clean through!
The pieces resulting will still
be two.
Slash! Untie!
The knot is gone. . .
And what remains is smooth,
straight string—
Or thread, or rope, or some
such a thing—
To tie into another knot,
or
Use another way.
Or throw a knot in acid; throw
it on a fire!
Ignite! Dissolve!
The knot is gone—
and so is the string,
Or thread, or rope—
and NO such a thing
To tie into another knot,
or
Use another way!
II STRING
A knot is only two bits of a
string,
Of a thread, of a rope, or of
some such a thing,
UNITED!
Reverse the "IT" and they
become
UNTIED!
Two pieces not of smooth,
straight string
(or thread, or rope, or some
such a thing)
To tie into another knot,
or
Use another way
To string things on, or tie
things up;
To bind a sheaf, bind a
wound;
To knit, crochet, make
macrame,
Or weave into a fabric,
Or stitch into some lace. . .
To fly a kite, or hoist a sail;
To make a noose, or hang
things up;
Pull logs along, hold horses
back,
Or toll a silver bell. . .
To spin a top, to sew a seam;
To play at tug-of-war;
To draw up water from a
well;
Or wind up neatly in a ball
And put away for a rainy
day. . .
To stretch into a tight
rope,
Swing a bridge across a chasm,
Make a net, make a life-line,
Make a guide-line through a
maze;
Or make a magic carpet,
Or a ladder for escape. . .
To string a bow, to string
a lute,
Or string glass beads upon;
To make a knotty problem
with,
Or to wrap things up again
And get "IT" all together,
And mend what's come apart. .
UNITE! UNTIE!
Hold on! Let go!
What's done can be undone, you
know—
What's tied can be untied, and
then—
If you find the pieces, tied
again. . .
And again. . .
and again. . .
and again. . .
As long as. . .
there's string!

Janet Elizabeth Almas
A MOTHER REMEMBERS
I remember, son, when you were
born; how your dad and I felt
proud
Of your little form, and curls of
blond hair, and your cries so
loud.
Then as months went by you
became a busy, engaging tot
And the night time feedings and
colic—all that we soon forgot.
When to an active boy you grew
and stronger became
You filled us with such pride,
son; were a true credit to our
name.
Next you put away boyish
fancies, became a helpful teen
Who told us with eagerness of
all you had done and seen.
But then war crashed upon the
world scene, and you grew up
too fast
And told us that you would do
your part to help our freedom
last.
Your letters, son; they told of
the suffering, the fear and gore
And all the countries laid to
waste by the ravages of war.
Yet you bravely stayed, son, and
did your part to keep this
country free
Even though safe at home with
us we knew that you would
sooner be.
Then one day came the glad
news, son, that you would be
coming home
And we thanked God we'd not
lost you as had been the fate
of some.
You were so pale and thin with
some grey streaks in your
curly hair;
We knew without your telling
that much trial had been your
share.
Your blue eyes had lost their
sparkle, and your once quick
step was slow;
Our son, you were no longer the
youth of six short years ago.
You were so tense, uneasy; with
bad dreams to haunt you at
night
Yet you bravely assured us,
"don't worry, folks, I'm quite
all right."
It was as if bad memories of war
inside you were locked,
And later we came to realize
that you had been shell
shocked.
It will affect you here after
in the daily work you do
To make you nervous and at
times unreasonable too.
On your body, no one can see
an ugly bullet scar,
But within your subconscious;
that's where your deep
wounds are.
Tears come easy to your eyes,
there is a tremble in your
voice
As you tell others of why you
went when freedom was your
choice.
They say you will get no
pension from wounds on the
battlefield
For they do not affect you,
because all have since nicely
healed.
But for the rest of your life,
son; shell shocked you're
destined to stay
Because for you those dark days
of war are never far away.
Our son, could we in some way
change things, but it is not
we can
For you left us a young boy, and
you came back home an old
man.

Mary Anne Daly
REFLECTIONS SHOWN FROM THE SEA
The sun cast a shadow upon the
sea and it showed the
reflection of how things use
to be. The sorrowful sun made
a silent speech as my eyes
began to tear for the memories
forever out of my reach.

The sky was cloudless like my
dreams; the sun had shown a
different scene. The waves in
the water were not as still as
the day—nothing was moved,
Nothing was said.
When the wind coughed up
nasty cold air,
Frozen hearts bled as night
drew near.

Stephen Wesley Preston
WHO KNOWS THE WINTER BEFORE THE STORM?
Who know the winter before the
storm?
The existence before the
eventuality?
When a living shadow begins to
lead you,
will you know to where you are
going?
Will you see life or witness
death?
Said the wise man to the
foolish:
" 'Tis by the days he'd ride
and the nights he'd hide
and the noons of life he'd
slip away.
Beware of the living shadow
I the wise man say.
He is not life
nor is he death
but in between is he.
For if he leads
and the shadow you follow,
discern the fate of thee."
Yet who knows the winter
before the storm?
How can one find pleasure in
death's unexpected verdict?
When you see the Clouds gather
to consult the Creator,
will you know when the Rains
will come?
Will They water the flowers, or
drown the soul?
Said the wizard to the joker:
"You keep them happy
and I'll keep them wise.
And look! I am a fool giving
instructions,
and a wise man is taking
heed,
so that a wise fool will reap
what a foolish wizard has
dreamt.
When one fails to see
what his own eyes behold,
then his whole world is
changing joker,
it's passing away.
Yet who knows the winter
before the storm?
Tell me, who knows the winter
before the storm?
When lightning strikes, where
did it come from?
When the Floods come and
overtake you
how will you get away;
the sea is too great.
This I say:
"Look into the skies
people oh so wise
and apologize.
You know that you were
wrong
but should it take so long
to say you're sorry?
It's your pride, It's your
pride, It's your pride.
You will humbly answer the
storm that demands
a reason for your existence.
You will answer to a time
proven conclusion.
Pray tell, who knows the
winter before the storm?

Dr. Leroy Thomas
NO ANGLE OF REPOSE
(To my favorite 21-year-old daughter)
The day you so confidently
stole into my life,
You weighed only seven pounds
and an ounce.
The old doctor who delivered

you insisted that
I watch the delivery, although
it wasn't my idea of
entertainment.
I saw you when you came out
all scrawny and bloody,
And I turned away. Could I
really have fathered
something so ugly?
But when the nurse placed you
in my arms a few minutes
later,
All pink and warm and cuddly,
I knew that you had captured
me for life.
You were my first, and you were
special.
You still are—even though you
think otherwise.
Soon you'll be married.
I'll walk down the aisle to give
you away,
Feeling it a farce because
you haven't really let me be
Your dad since you entered
puberty and became a
"woman."
So what am I to do—give you
gladly to a man
Who couldn't possibly be good
enough for you
Even if he were a Nobel Prize
winner?
You detest it when I say it
(after all, you're a grown
woman),
But I never look at you without
remembering that pink,
cuddly baby
And the first bath you ever had,
the one I gave you,
Because your mother and I were
young and independent
And wanted no one else around
during that special time.
So I'll throw the rice from those
bags made by your loving
mother,
But my heart won't be in tune
for celebrating.
Why celebrate on a day of doom
When Mount Saint Helens has
erupted again
And my world has slipped out
of its angle of repose?

Roger L. McCrary
THE KIDS. . .
The kids?
They're self explanitory.
Just watch them.

A symphony
And a tornado.
Who could ask for more?
(5 Sep 77
from "Open Soul Surgery")

Kurt Kelley
THE PATH OF GOD
The sun blasted it's remaining
red and purple hues across the
horizon
Then continued it's blaze of
glory until well out of sight
The warm breeze slowed down
and soon diminished
And I found myself in the
middle of a very beautiful
night
The trees and shrubs took on
black hues as they became
Lovely silhouettes against the
brightly colored sky
The cool night smelled of rain
and the air around me stood
perfectly still
And not once until then had I
ever questioned why
Why the sky had become darker
than usual
Why the moon was hiding but
the stars were lit
And how come I walked alone
so serene and quiet
And why in the world none of
this really seemed to fit
The beauty of the earth seemed
to reach out to me
It grasped at my heart and soul
until I cried
I realized how lucky I was to be
witness to such a beautiful
view
And how every minute of my
life I've tried I've really
tried
Tried to see things from both
points of view
Through the view of the poet
and through the view of the
one who just admires
Through the one who sees
beauty in all things no matter
how simple or complex
As simple as a rose covered with
dew as complex as hell's
deepest fires
I stood for hours doing nothing
but continued staring
At all the beauties surrounding
me including the lovely
golden rods
And it was then I realized with
all this beauty around me
There's only one place I could
be and that is on THE PATH
OF GOD
THE PATH OF GOD is an
interpretation of the road to
heaven
And gathered on either side of
that long and winding stretch
of pathway
Is all the Lord's greatest
accomplishments of all time
And this pathway continues
forever and becomes more
complete everyday
More complete with the
beauties we have all been
honored to be witness to
The blazing sunsets the brilliant
sunrises and every lovely
waterfall
The perfect flowers that bless
the soil and the beauty
contained in a simple smile
Should make it clear to all of us
that the Lord God almighty
loves us one and all

Wendy Adams
ODE TO MOM
I see in the movies and the
places I go
the happy families with their
dog Fido.
The comfortable house with
windows of glass
the spacious yard with freshly
mown grass.
The father, the mother, the
sister, the brother
live peaceful and carefree with
one another.
The parents never fight, the
children all laugh
their greatest concern? To give
Fido's bath.
How is it possible to live
without pain?
Having dreams and ambitions
thrown down the drain.
Parents who fought and later
divorced
Have left me cold, alone, and
remorsed.
Being told yes and then
punished after
Has made me deaf to love and
to laughter.
Being told "I love you and
can't let this go by"
Has taught me to resent and
also to cry.
A mother and daughter are
supposed to be tight
But in my family we always
fight.
It's just not healthy to
struggle this way
with each other we hate day to
day.
Maybe it's because I too
quickly complain
but I can't stand by and let
my life be drained.
I need to live and *also* be
happy
I can't let myself die, to become
bitter and snappy.
I dream about the motherly
love of that I hear
how can we be so distant and
yet so near?
I try to reach out and so does
she
But at different times, therefore
effortlessly.
Perhaps by chance someday
we'll succeed
and we will experience the love
we now need.
Could *this* be the link to
life I am missing?
The warmth, the touch of a
mother's kissing.

Shirley Zoss Misner
PRESIDENT JIMMY CARTER
My son, Paul has asked
Mama, would it be too big a
task
And write to Jimmy Carter
As I'm not too good a writer
And say God has blessed you
A President, who's really true
As God helped you from the
beginning
And you came out winning
Being President is a big duty
But you can do it truly
As you leave your peanut farm
We! the People are not
alarmed.
The nation lies in honest hands
As you left your Georgia land
Somebody bigger than you and I
Made it possible for you to
say good-bye
As God made way to guide you
Hand in hand he walks beside
you
As a little boy, God won your
heart
A love and trust no one can
tear apart
We! the people need more with
your system
Who can tell the world, I'm a
Christian
Yesterday, today, tomorrow is
history
But living for Jesus. . .is
victory.
A nation you can face
As God granted you your
place
With each and every race
You've made great pace
As we watch your honest smile
We know it was worthwhile
As I write each line, I find
A President so great and kind
Who's willing to share and care
Men like Carter are rare
A helping hand you lend
Love for you shall never end.
Jimmy is your name
Hard work has won you fame
God has given you a lot
As you went to the top
Oh! Say can you see
Why God did this for thee
A family who shares and cares
About all other's welfares
As I gaze upon your crown
Proof is everywhere all around
You will do it well, or not at all
God be with you, as you keep
walking tall
Amen

Judge Al Sater
AN OLD CODGER'S LAMENT
It took some time to find it out
But now we know for certain
No longer will we fret and pout
Or fear to draw the curtain.
Three score and ten plus two or
three
The Lord looked on with favor
But things have changed
because, you see
Our health began to waver.
The games we always loved to
play
Like golf and things athletic
We tried to do—but let me say
It got to be pathetic.
Our life style changed, we spend
more time
A sitting in a rocker
Instead of playing a short nine
We go to see the doctor.
On Sunday morn we head for
church
Instead of to the golf club
For golf balls we no longer
search
We'd rather have a back rub.
We watch TV—we read a lot
We visit with our neighbor
We mow the lawn, we clean the
house
We sleep, we eat, we labor.
We play some cards, we sing a
bit
We often swap a story

We don't move fast, we'd rather sit
We try hard not to worry.
At first we thought the Man Upstairs
Was punishing us for something
But after quieting all our fears
We frankly could think of nothing
We know we must adjust our lives
And do the best we know how
When it appears our time arrives
So what—we're ready—somehow!
We've loved this life, we had the breaks
What better could we ask for
The Good Lord gave us what it takes
Very little did we grasp for.
We feel we'd fare well with the Man Up Above
If we followed closely the Golden Rule
Plus the Ten Commandments—show lots of love
And try not to act like a silly old fool.
John Three Sixteen and the Twenty-third Psalm
Give us the assurance we feel we need
In times of stress they keep us calm
We also like the Apostle's Creed.

So thank you God, we don't complain
We've practiced serendipity
Just spare us hurt, and spare us pain
Let us live—and die—with dignity.

Douglas A. Peck
THE SPRING HILL DINING DISASTER
I recently went out to dinner, my friends, and I felt so incredibly great,
The lady, I thought, though she couldn't be bought, would be a remarkable date.
We dropped off the car with the doorman out front, and strolled lazily into the scene,
The french Maitre D' whispered, "Please follow me", to a corner quite dim and serene.
The waiter inquired after cocktails, you know, and I cheerfully ordered a few,
Then smiling and glowing his good nature showing, he instantly vanished from view.
He came back with two dry martinis straight up, which he served with impeccable care,
Then he murmured, "Monsieur, would you like an hors d'oeuvre", as he smoothed back his silver gray hair.
He said, "I prefer Clams Casino the best, Steak Tar Tar, or oysters and such",
"But perhaps you could go for some fine Escargot, but to me it's a little bit much".
With gusto we pounced on our Caesar, so fine, so luscious it brought forth a tear,
So then just for fun, I got St. Emillion, sixty seven, a horrible year.
The young lady ordered Duck L'Orange' and she shovelled it into her trap,
For myself, I must say, I preferred the filet, ten ounce, with a big mushroom cap.
The time of the evening was nearing, I fear, for coffee, and cordials, and smokes,
Although I'm dignified, I just sat there wide eyed, and listened to her dirty jokes.
Then dinner was actually over at last, it was time to dispense with the cash,
We'd both had our fill so I settled the bill, and we made for the car in a dash.
I smiled as we pulled in her driveway, oh yes, and I smirked as we walked to her stair,
She said "Thanks ever so, but I really must go, my husband's asleep in a chair".

Clara L. Kuck
LITTLE JOE
In a world full of sorrow,
In a world full of woe,
In a world full of loneliness,
Lives a little guy named Joe.
Poor Little Joe, so weary and worn,
Poor Little Joe, heart-broken and torn.
He lives day after day-week after week,
Just barely existing-so humble-so meek.
He scurries down the dark alleys of town,
In some dark corner you can see his frown.
Hungry and scared, he stays out of sight;
He sleeps in the daytime and comes out at night.
There's no one to love him-no one to care.
His little heart cries out, but no one is there.
His eyes are like saucers; his clothes, not so clean,
Are raggy and baggy on his frame so lean.
Joe used to have a home to call his own;
Then one dark wintry night his family was gone.
An oil stove exploded-the flames went leaping
Throughout all the house, their hungry tongues creeping.
The sky was lit up for miles around.
The firemen watched helpless as the house burned to the ground.
It snuffed out the lives of his father and mother,
Two little sisters, and one little brother.
They say all that was left was an old rocking chair,
And Little Joe could picture his mother sitting there.
It hurt to remember how she had held him so tight,
As she once had read him a story each night.
He could still hear her voice, so full of love—
Now his family was waiting for him up above.
As Christmas came on, the little guy's heart,
Felt like the seams were all ripping apart.
He remembered last Christmas-he had gotten a bike,
There were dolls for his sisters, and a train for Mike.
The Christmas tree was trimmed so pretty and bright,
And the house rang with laughter on Christmas night.
Now little Joe was left with no one to care.
No one to bathe him or comb his hair.
A tear trickled down as he tried to be brave,
You see he was kneeling at one big grave.
Now if on Christmas morn, you should find him peeping
In through your window, silently weeping,
Could you find some extra goodies, or maybe a toy,
That you could share with one small boy?
Is there enough love in your heart to share
To let Little Joe know that some one does care?
You never know what your future may hold,
So invite Litte Joe in out of the cold.
Especially at Christmas no child should know,
A world full of loneliness-like Little Joe.

Gabrielle
A ROSE, TEARS, AND BABY BREATHS
The rose in your heart
is but a baby's breath away
Tenderly with love,
He cradles her today
The Rose of Sharon
sheds His grace on thee
And the Man of Sorrows
says, "Come unto Me"
For you see, if the rose could speak
perhaps it would say
I represent Jesus
in a majestical way
Look at my petals
rich with red
This stands for the Blood
Jesus shed
Look at my stem
strong and with thorns
This stands for the crown
my Saviour has worn
Look at my leaves
shaped like a heart
This stands for the love
my Lord imparts
But if you look inside
and see the core of me
This stands for the Light
where Jesus set me free
Now look on to the Baby Breaths
all gathered around
These are God's children
who have won their crown
And when you see my petals
fall delicately from me
Then you'll know Sorrow's compassion,
they are tears, you see
Yes, I am the Rose of Sharon
cascading love
Yes, I am the Man of Sorrows
who hears you above
For My mountains of love
flow into the valley of tears
Yes, I have thy beloved, My child,
you need not fear.

Robert Louis Wilkinson
BUTTERFLY
I knew of you for so long
Minding your own, floating from one place to the other
Never knew about you, I wasn't wrong.
Fluttering free; asking no one else to bother,
But what if someone really wanted to,
Would you let him see the wonder of you?

My mind is alert, my senses keen
They would have to be, for the glimpses I've seen
Tell of such color, beauty and perfection
Lifting my spirit into tender affection
Almost to inspire fear to be close so near
If you flew away would hurt so much so dear.
But if you share the joy and spread your wings
I'd be feeling the warmth only your smile brings
Putting your love and beauty on display
For such a gentle admirer who would care someday
If the world saw one, they all would know why
This shimmering and shining gold butterfly.

Nagu Veerabhadran
LOVE LETTER TO "YOU"
i am writing to tell you that
i need a friend—"ONLY" a very close friend
to whom i can talk without inhibition
where i can hop and skip when we walk into
the woods in autumn at sunset
will you hold my hand when a sudden fear grips me??
can i say things like—
the baby dandelion on the green green grass
dew drops on my barefeet early in the morning
arch of a hazy rainbow seen over the willow
when driving like mad on the

highway
or—how the knots in my naval
jerk me back
from uneasy sleep into regular
insomnia
or—how the computer program
is driving me crazy
or—wonder how the hostages
make love to their girls now
and giggle giggle when i feel like
and let you caress my dimple on
my right cheek
when my brow is fevered and
my eyes burn with unshed
tears
will you gently kiss me???
other than all these—
PLEASE UNDERSTAND, i
assure you
i make no demands.
no ties.
no bonded promises.
no asking for a long
stemmed purple rose.
this is not my usual way of
becoming friends
but—i lost quite a few passing
me like
boats sailing aimlessly on
summer noons
i do NOT want this to happen
with YOU
if YOU happen to feel the
same way i do
i would like to know
if not,,,????—
will you return this letter and
give me time to
crawl back into my shell
and not to stir out for a
LONG, LONG time to come????

Ruth M. Barr

MISSING IN ACTION

The day he went away he said,
"Goodbye, Mom.
I'll be back before you know it."
The months went by. His letters
came,
And then they didn't.
The postman said, "Good
morning, Mrs. Day."
I knew what he was thinking.
(She wants a letter and there
isn't any.")
Then came the message saying
he was missing.
Just missing. That was all.
I thought, "This is the sort of
thing
That happens just to others, not
to me.
He will come back," and went
on working.
Now when I go upstairs to dust
I see
The jackknife marks upon the
window sill,
The same scarred window sill
where once he left
His books, his marbles, and
his apple cores.
And there upon the dresser side
by side
His hairbrush and his after-
shave, half used.
I think perhaps he is a prisoner
yet,
And someday he will still come
back to me.
(Oh God of mercy, could that
ever be?)
He may be wandering lost, in
some far land
Wondering who he is and why
his past
Is nothing but a vast, confusing
blur.
And in the Better Land I'll
find him there,
And he will say, "It's good
to see you, Mom.
I couldn't get back home to
you because
I got rapped on the head and I
forgot
Just who I was."
The people in the churchyard
press my hand
And say, "Good morning, Mrs.
Day."
I know what they are thinking.
("They say that she has never
given up.")
The grocer pats my shoulder as
he says,
"Good morning, Mrs. Day.
Will it be one full dozen or
just half?"
He knows I'm cooking now for
only one.)
No message ever came that said
he died.
Just missing. That was all.
"Blessed are they that mourn,"
the Master said.
I must be very blest because I
mourn
And mourn and mourn.
The years go by. My steps get
slower
And my hair gets grayer
As I wonder, and wonder,
and wonder.

Marjorie Kingston Skusa

THE PLIGHT OF THE DEER

"There'll be snow on the
mountain, tonight," said the
deer,
"For there's ice on the pond,
down below;
The leaves will be gone from
the trees until Spring
And the grass will be covered
with snow.
"There'll be snow on the
mountain, tonight, this I
know,

And vacation is over for me;
I must look for a lion atop every
rock
And a hunter behind every tree.
"All during the Winter I search
for a place,
In the forest to shelter my
young;
As I try to avoid the arrows and
guns
And the places where barbed
wire is strung.
"I may wander far in my forage
for food,
Before Spring comes and eases
my plight;
But I know by the feel of the
crisp Winter air
There'll be snow on the
mountain, tonight!"

Mrs. Johnnie Mae Johnson

IN JESUS´ARMS

When high inflation, high taxes,
high prices, unemployment,
recession, depression, nuclear
war, too much fighting, too
much killing, too much hunger,
too much sorrow, too much
trouble in times like these in
Jesus Arms is where I want to
be
When the rich keep getting
richer trying to get more powers,
trying to get more money
When no food for the little
children, no milk for the babies
Everybody think only of
themselves and the needy and
poor
is forgotten
In times like these in Jesus
Arms is where I want to be
When no one repents
No one believes
No one forgives
No one cares
No one shares
No one loves
When lies are the truth
Wrong is right
The truth is a lie
And right is wrong
In times like these in Jesus
Arms is where I want to be
When crimes in the streets
Crimes in the homes
Crimes in the churches
Sisters against sisters
Brothers against brothers
Children against mothers
Mothers against children
Lovers against lovers
No joy, no rest, no peace no
where
Sin and hate have corrupted this
old world
Because we have forgotten what
Jesus Said
Love ye one another as I have
loved you
In times like these in Jesus
Arms is where I want to be

Michael Anthony Smith

GIVE THE WORLD A SMILE

I saw an old friend yesterday,
he said he was on his way to
hell
I begged him to wait a while, he
turned, nodded and yelled
"Heaven's luck, right now would
knock us from our knees
although the world looks so
worried and displeased"
then I said, I think together
we could show the world, you
know how
to bring back the Love and,
"Give the world a smile"
"Give the world a smile, young,
old, happy no more frowns
and "Give the world a smile,
make the world happy again
with no anger to be found "Give
the world a smile"
then my friend said to me, if
we both are out to create
a better
world, we could start right now
to portray our own happy
faces
not looking towards that old
hell, we both hugged and
shook hands
on our way to pave happy
destinies in man but some-
how it seemed
all a touch of fate, but not too
late,enough to "Give the
world a smile"
"Heaven's luck, right now would
knock us from our knees
although the world looks so
worried and displeased"
I think together we could show
the world, you know how
to bring back the Love and,
"Give the world a smile"
and "Give the world a smile,
young, old, happy no more
frowns
and "Give the world a smile",
let's make the world happy
again
with no more anger to be found
"Give the world a smile

Moshe Parry

ROLL THE STONE FROM OFF THE WELL

(Inspiration from Genesis 29: 10, 11)

"And it came to pass, when
Yakov saw Rachel, the daughter
of Lavan, his mother's brother,
and the sheep of Lavan, his
mother's brother, that Yakov
went near, and rolled the stone
from off the well's mouth and
watered the flock of Lavan, his
mother's brother. And Yakov
kissed Rachel and raised up his
voice and cried. . ."
The days of old vanished quite
suddenly:
You cannot relate with
something
that has no meaning.
You cannot hallow,
what is void of value;
You cannot hear
that which has no sound. . .
Are we ever to be:
forgiven for ignorance,
released from blindness,
Raised on high forever?
Sometimes, voices from within
flutter, as if to speak;
Only to be silenced by
a mind that's gone to sleep.
The journey took me. . .
out from the city,
slowly across the sea. . .
I search for answers far
beyond my reach;
I yearn for mysteries
whispered within my
dreams.
Thoughts of fame and fortune
came my way,
I stepped aside to cross them
out.
Passionate desires seduced my
senses,
I quickly turned away. . . .
Surrounded by a chaotic world,
their hands upon my throat;
Internally mounting frustration,
inflicting pain; injecting
anguish. . .
As I cried out:

"Speak to me my soul;
Show me where to go!
How shall I ever know?
Teach me how to see!"
Amid the tears of desperation;
a perception of a soothing wave,
broke the fall of my shattered head. . .
She said:
"Roll the stone from off the well—
free the love buried there;
"Roll the stone from off the well. . .
Let pure waters flow. . .
In the seemingly endless night. .
Rest assured, you're not alone.
There will be light once again!
When peace spreads forth her withered wings;
prepares for one last flight. .
Take a hold, my child, take a hold!
for when love nears completion;
the simple heart attains fulfillment,
Freed from toil; eased from burden,
the tide will turn with the dawn of Heaven."
Even now, somewhere in the vast darkness
a lone candle burns. . .
A signal thru the fog. . .
"Surrender not to evil,
Put away all fear;
Pronounce eternal death
to falsehood's warriors.
Make ready for Salvation. . .
select the jewels for the Holy Crown.
Sew the royal robe
For he who arises
bears exalted treasures;
He who comes,
chooses worthy, both youth and age."
Oh, roll the stone from off the well,
the hidden source needs to be revealed.
We each must weigh
an equal portion upon our shoulder,
To roll this stone from off the well.

Barbara Robinson

UNTITLED

this was a golden day, my love,
with you
a soft and tender day
so fresh, so new
our love enfolded us
as love will do
I'll spend more golden days, my love,
with you

Esther Farrier

TIME

Time,
that strangely-contoured vessel,
was full—
Full to the brim with the restlessness
and avarice of those
wedded to the dust;
Swelling full with knowledge and opportunity
and desperate need;
Running over with
nothingness and lostness
indifference and unbelief.
Time was full—
and, spilled over by the spilling hand of
Jehovah,
Poured out ETERNITY
Himself
Into a woman's womb.
The Rivers of Time
again threaten its brim,
straining against containment.
Man and his greed and guile,
His anger and his anguish
is tossed stupidly, helplessly,
in a million fractured guises
on the full tide of time.
Inexorably the contents of that cup
pile up against the brim—
No warning sounds above the noisy riders
of the tide;
No hand deters the crazy flotsam;
No eye discovers the unbelievable beyond.
Time is full again—
Ripe for the spilling hand of God,
The fullness of
that odd-shaped cup will be drained into
Eternity,
Washing with great finality
the silt and contamination
that was
humanity
into the forever of God.

Nadinia J. Draper

MUSIC MAN

You sing so sweetly,
You speak of love you
gave so deeply.
Your song is so sad,
you sing of things
you never had.

You sing of passion
and desire, you set
young hearts on fire.
You are an inspiration
to those who are down,
you make those laugh
who use to frown.
You believe in love,
laughter and song,
that everythings
right and nothing wrong.
You sing of love, life,
and broken hearts,
And all things in which
you had a part.
You're a heartbreaker
soul shaker.
Your song brings love
to my heart.
From you I never want
to be apart.

Barbara Fraser Little

DEAR EX

It's been just five years since we severed the 'knot'
Long enough—for the 'blood' to clot
Pride, has been 'pocketed' long since
Instead of 'in' clothes, I'm wearing chintz
The rush to 'prove myself' has slowed
I'm comfortable, now in my own abode
The reason I'm writing is just to say
My 'blacks' and 'whites' are tempered with 'grey'
Sometimes—I miss you—and that's good, too
These past few years, I've altered my 'view'
I wanted to 'impress' you—
and never did succeed
It explains, I guess, why even now—I have this driving 'need'
To let you know—I'm still alive,
and things are going well
There have been times, I kid you not, when it's been 'tough' as hell
The big thing that I had to 'learn', was 'what' I *didn't* know
Oh, sure—I knew the 'lofty' stuff— 'cuz you brought in the 'dough'
My reality—was narrower, my stances—hard and fast
Perhaps, that's why that 'dream' of ours, just really couldn't 'last'
I thought that I did all the work, which you never seemed to 'see'
And you believed it was you who did, and that's the 'irony'
We 'did' it both together, made our pot-pouri
Neither of us was 'alone' in our Gethsemene
It never was a 'contest' one of us had to 'win'
You were not the 'hero', nor I the 'heroine'
We were only two 'scared' people, 'convinced we both were 'right'
I wasn't 'Cinderella', you weren't the 'big black knight'
We both were taught to 'challenge', what we didn't understand
And so—we pulled 'apart' because we saw a 'double-strand'
We 'sacrificed the 'single-thread'—by pulling it 'too hard'
Instead of using 'gentleness', we both kept up our 'guard'
It took so long to 'analyze'—
just really 'what' went 'wrong'
That—the 'words' mixed with the 'music', and we both forgot the 'song'
Your 'way' belonged to you,
my dear—as mine belonged to me
But, oh how hard we 'shook' the leaves of our 'own' family tree
Now, the battle's over—
the smoke has all died down
I'm sitting here alone tonight, beneath the eiderdown
A friend of 'ours' just called to say—tomorrow—is your 'wedding day'
I had to hang up 'right away'—
without a single word to say
I think, I always knew 'inside' that one day it would come
But—
My thought's 'ganged-up' a while ago—in a symposium
They gathered all around me, in this 'comfy' single-bed
And—all at once, I knew for sure a part of me was dead
Until a big door 'closes' and you are locked 'outside'
You 'comfort' yourself with a lot of things, even a 'false' pride
The last of my 'illusions' left—
just a while ago
"Cuz
'Cuz the flowers in 'my' garden—took so long to 'grow'.

Lucy Marston Towles

FREEDOM'S CALL

Our mother country was dear indeed
Until she taxes us heavily when in need.
We thought that we could rule our land
And not have England to plan.
Some wanted to fight for freedom's call,
Others thought we couldn't win at all.
Patrick Henry, a patriot, it's true,
Aroused us and we decided what to do.
We were enchained with few rights
So we decided to fight.
To war we went 1775
Hoping and praying to survive.
We were small and weak it's true,
But we were brave and France helped us, too.
The war was bitter and hard to fight
But we won and everything turned out right.
Our independence we had won,
A new country had begun.
A country so young needed a leader 'tis true
So George Washington was chosen to guide us through.
He was our first president loyal and true,
Although very young we grew and grew.
Another patriot brave and strong,
Was Thomas Jefferson who came along.
He wrote a document giving freedom to all,
The Declaration of Independence was what it was called.
What a masterpiece this turned out to be!
A cherished document of

American History.
Our forefathers struggled for
you and me,
Let's love our country, and let
it be
The best, truest nation of all,
And with God's help we shall
never fall.

Linda Ann Little
FOR TIMES LIKE THESE
To live in this world you have
to be strong,
For survival is not for the weak,
So develop a strength in spirit
and mind,
For victory lies hidden in
strength.
When the going gets tough,
then the tough must get
going,
Keep this in your mind every
day,
For you have potential strength
in your nature,
God built it in us that way.
If you will believe you are
strong, then you are;
For believing will bring it to be;
Strength is a God-given resource
we use,
A power reaction we need.
But along with strength lies
compassion,
A gentleness we must possess,
For Christ brought compassion
along with his strength,
We cannot be strong without
this.
Picture yourself standing strong,
walking tall;
Keep this as you wake, and you
sleep;
For as you believe you can do it,
you can;
And the strength you acquire,
you'll keep.
You must be a positive thinker;
No matter how dark things may
fare,
Raise your sights, and look
toward the light,
And the light will always
be there.
Know for a fact that with God
by your side,
You can take what you must
and succeed,
For courage and strength are his
shield and sword;
And these are the weapons you
need.
So remember you are what you
think, good or bad,
Yes, you are what you think,
strong or weak,
For survivors cannot be
defeated,
The army of God must succeed.
Do not be afraid or confounded,
Have a sound rugged set of
beliefs,
Change your life-style of fear
into one of full faith;
And fear will have no place to
be.
Never be awed by the clamoring
crowd,
But calmly keep faith going on,
Read Holy Scripture to build in
your heart,
That the power of God remain
strong.
Let go, and let God take you
over,
For he knows the way you must
go,
Drop thoughts that leave gloom
and depression,
For remember, you'll reap what
you sow.
David wrote words in the 34th
Psalm,
To bring strength during trial
and tears;
"I sought the Lord, and he
heard me,
And delivered me out of my
fears."
Learn to live on God's law
of supply,
Fill your life with a bright
point of view;
Do not be concerned with the
future,
For God will control it for you.
Prosperity means not only
money,
Or the things that wealth can
afford,
Prosperity also means much
more than that;
It means blessings and love
from our Lord.
So never think thoughts of
a loser,
Of poverty, or of defeat,
But center your thoughts on
abundance and strength,
And these will be what you will
reap.

Estel Mullinax Dodd
NATURE'S PATH TO HEAVEN
Where is the calm that
should be nestled in my heart?
Why do I sit here in the window
and gaze upon the woodland
and feel that I must struggle
to try and set myself
apart
From besetting sins and sore
transgressions
that prey upon my conscience
and make the calm of
woodlands
another—trespassed—
hallowed world?
Just beyond the hillside
lies another traveled road
Marked off at every turn by
people
who will their gazes
elsewhere,
their spirits just beyond
them
in a vale not quite
beyond their hearts
But withheld from the grasp of
empty dreams
in imagery that makes their
longings lighter,
and helps them see the pure
white
blossom of the holy
woodland flower.
Life does not have to be
predestined nor ordained—
some to see only ugliness and
unworded dreams
pushed rudely back by daily
cares and
unimportant priorities
made so by man.
The tiny woodland violet was
not placed among the weeds
to be trampled on by creatures
unaware, who
do not realize its Divine
origin
nor feel deprived it it
does not light their path.
Yet people, God's own supreme
creations, close eyes and ears
to the silent, reverent voices
of the woodlands—
primeval wisdom speaking
from life that
springs from death in
beauty to die again
to make the foreverness
of spring—
While we, His children, busy
ourselves with mortal
tasks which neither bring us
joy nor add
a petrified dimension to the
world we have created,
to glorify Him, or make
His earthly kingdom
match
the promise of His
death.

Lorena Hollister
KITTY PERFORMS HER ABLUTIONS
Here a lick, there a lick,
everywhere a lick—
Watch her and discover it's not
an easy trick.
Leg up, foot under, get inside
that ear!
Lave the chest, do the face,
don't forget the rear.
Slush the tummy, lap the tail,
nibble at a flea.

Whiskers need attention too,
preen them
Persistently.
At last you're through! You turn
about,
Then curl up in my lap—
Need you have been that
hygenic
Just to take a nap?

Donna Marie Micheli
LOVE LOST
Tonight I walk the streets alone
I stand before the door to your
house
It's late at night and I'm very
tired
But I can't seem to drag myself
away
The sidewalk in it's silence
whispers
Gently it seems to say "go to
him"
Don't stand here in the cold
when
He's just a window or a pair of
stairs away
Yet I cannot because a frigid
wind blows
Which separates me from my
hearts desire
I can only gaze ever upward at
the moon
And hope her fullness will give
up the courage
I need to keep myself from
coming here
The urge deep within must be
destroyed
As well as the eyes which
forever turn
To this house this street this
man
My trembling mouth seeks a
kiss lost in the past
That gave me hope happiness
and life
The hands which once reached
out to mine
Now are clenched tightly in fists
of hate
What can I do please someone
tell me
The words that can make things
right
I don't wish to have it end this
way
Too long have I waited for my
love
I'm looking up at his window so
bright and warm
Even as I look he peers out onto
the street
Does he see who stands so
hidden so full of fear
No I guess not for he turns
away
Why would he think to look out
at this moment
Would he rush down to greet
me with arms outstretched
The answers to these questions
I know all too well
So I should walk on to my house
to find some warmth
But yet I remain held to this
spot to this time
It seems I could stay here for
all futures to come
Even to the leaving of the
frailties of my body
Let it fall away for I shall never
more care
Take care not to let life slip
away
Come take my hand tell me
it'll be good
It's not too late for you and
I to be one
Reach out for my touch my
desire my love

Bay C. Smith
THE BALANCE
As I sat beside my pond looking
in,
The floating image of a face
stared back pensively.
Could that be me? Could I be so
distraught?
I should be pleasant, smiling,
or so I've been taught.
I lifted my eyes and gazed at
my surroundings,
The hills, the trees, my house
massively abounding.
With such beauty within my
touch and sight.
Then, why is my heart so heavy,
when it should be so light?
"You're bright, young lady, your
future holds much hope.
Calm, resourceful, there's
nothing with which you can't
cope."
And on and on, folks continue

to flatter me.
So what are the forces inside
that threaten to shatter me?
Then, I remembered that these
feelings had happened before.
That this was called depression
and would periodically occur.
And this was the extreme of
satisfaction and joy.
Is there a balance between the
two which a human might
employ?
Like a lightning bolt, the
idea lit up my head,
And sent a charge through me
that roused me as if I had been
abed.
Balance, yes balance, that
mediator of the extremes,
That keeps us humans going
along the path of our means.
As I felt the balance move
within me and the charge
subside,
I lowered my head to the pond
and what should I see inside?
An oval outline with shining
orbs and teeth,
It was my face, a glowing
testimony to inner peace.

Baldwin Burhop
DEATH CAME FOR THE NAVAJO

The lowering sun with its
slanting rays,
pierced the mirage and the
dusty haze,
painting the canyon walls a
bloody red.
The wind whispered softly
as it mourned for the dead.
The Indians had lived here for
many years,
with their hopes, their joys,
and their constant fears,
in the big red caves up high
in the wall,
where they could sit and hear
the nighthawk's call.
Cliff dwellers the Anasazi, and
then the Zunis built homes
in the shelters above, in those
big red domes.
But the war-like Navajos came
in droves
and forced the Zunis out of
their coves.
Then the conquistadors came
looking for wealth.
The Navajos, afraid of their
cunning and stealth,
retreated in the canyon, seeking
places to hide
where there were no trails
which the Spaniards could
ride.
Up high in a cove with a big
sheltered dome,
in a place the Zunis once used
for their home,
they placed their women, their
children and the old,
when the Spaniards came riding,
looking for gold.
The Navajos looked down on
the Spaniards with scorn;
But soon there were no Indians
left to mourn.
You can still see white marks
which the bullets had made,
where they hit the roof of the
cove and then ricochetted.
The cave was hidden for many a
year,
until someone discovered this
gruesome bier.
Ninety bullet-pierced skeletons
were found in the dust,
once people the Spaniards killed
for vengeance and lust.
Men saw where the bullets hit
wave upon wave.
They called the grim shelter,
Massacre Cave.
The Spaniards rode on and with
bated breath
named the canyon del Muerto,
the Canyon of Death.

Gabe Sims
GRANDMOTHER'S FUNERAL

They buried grandmother
In the fields in the country
Where she ran, played
As a child.
Her funeral held in
A hot wooden church.
A church older than the elders
themselves,
Where she worked in the
mission.
Whose one-time pastor-now
sleeps,
Baptized grandmother in a cold
pond.
That Sunday morning.
The funeral march goes over
A parched dusty road.
Where she once rode to
Downtown to the store
On the back of a wagon,
Her, and her man.
Past old cotton fields,
Where she-when a young lady
Picked cotton,
Her sweat staining her straw
hat.
Her Hymn-singing floated over
The cotton field.
They pass
Ruins
Of a slave quarter-shack.
Where she—a barefooted girl.
Sat on a raggedy porch long ago.
On a hot summer evening,
Dreaming as colored girls could.
An old well-kept Home
The funeral procession passes.
The home of grandmother,
Where she birthed twelve
children.
Where she loved and cared for
them,
In the late evening, after
laboring
At the white folks houses—
Cooking and cleaning for them.
There—in a hot summer day.
Her children gathered from
California, up North,
Shreveport, Atlanta.
Her children, children not
understanding,
The Pastor reads from the Bible,
Himself one of the children of
Grandmother.
They stand sad with sorrow.
Pain beyond pain.
From the fields.
A cool breeze blows.
Moving the leaves and the
womens hats.
Providing a lullaby, a song,
Adding a farewell murmur
To the grandmother's rest—
She sleeps in the bosom of Jesus
Resting from Life's Labors.

Chuck Marsh
SELF EMBRACE

Encouragement will help lead
one along their own way,
Sarcasm can only herd.
Down an eroded direction with
those who deliver,
the sting of their thought
whipping word.
A standing ovation for efforts in
view,
on occasion we may well lay
eye. 
As we are however human, with
most of our moments,
mistakes leave a new learning
high.
Another's approval, a pat on the
back,
are false scales for self worth
to weigh.
No sense in deceiving, with
truth we begin,
embracing one's ownself today.

James Richard Owens
AMERICAN PRIDE

It was on the eighteenth day
of March, and the hour was
getting late—
A baby boy was born in Sledge—
in the year of thirty-eight.
This young lad named Charley,
he had to grow up quick—
He could not be a child for
long—there was so much
cotton to pick.
Nothing would come easy for
Charley, a free ride he would
not get—
At six years old in the cotton
fields—he'd work, he'd toil
and sweat.
There was such hurt and
anguish, in his weary parents'
eyes—
Just to think of little Charley—
in these cotton fields 'til he
dies.
Charley sensed their feelings,
their love poured down like
rain—
For him to have a better life—
would ease his parents' pain.
With that in mind, Charley said
'I'll remain here no more'—
So he moved on to something
else—he'd wanted to explore.
And as he swung the bat, he
thought 'baseball might by
my game'—
And forty years from this day—
'I'll be in the Hall of Fame'.
'I may be like Willie Mays',
Charley said with a shout—
But that thought passed so
quickly—as the umpire yelled
'You're out'.
. . .and as he was—but on
baseball he did not linger—
In that mellow voice he sang,
'does my ring hurt your
finger'?
Never more would Charley's
hands, pick those balls of
cotton—
Instead he uses his priceless
voice—that from the Lord he's
gotten.
To fill men's lives with music,
and with the joy of song—
He's given this to others—and
for so very long.
There's not another singer,
who's done what Charley's
done—
And there's not another singer—
who's won the hearts that
Charley's won.
In the country music field,
Charley tops them all—
His songs skyrocket to the
top—before they ever fall.
So someday I am hoping, before
I cross to the other side—
That I will get to meet this
man—the legend named
Charley Pride.
And I am thankful that a place
called Sledge, shared Charley
with me and you—
I only wish there were more
like him—for folks to look up
to.

Thomas E. Smith
A TRIBUTE TO THE ROEBUCK

On my many hunts about this
earth
For things in return for my
money's worth,
My fondest memories, and of
course, my luck
Have been, and are of the little
roebuck.
Of graceful lines and nimble
foot
He spends much time in the
shady nook.
He can be seen most any day
Often fighting, but usually at
play.
When the evening shadows fall
And the night hawk starts his
call
The roe steps nimbly from the
trees
Carefully sniffing the
gentle breeze.
If all is well, and he can tell,
He begins to pluck his dainty
food
While carefully watching
o'er his brood;
He starts to chew his juicy cud
Just sixty meters from the wood.
I silently watch him pick his
fill,
Now I hesitate to make the kill
But I raise my gun and humbly
nod
Knowing such beauty comes
from God
The safety off, and all is ready
A count of ten will make me
steady.
During this count, the distance
figure
Then I begin to pull the
trigger.
The shot at last, the silence

broke
Deer bound away, I need a smoke.
I notice quickly as they run
One surely is the old buck's son.
At last I arise and move very slowly,
I feel this scene is almost holy.
Moments pass and I reach the spot
There kneel at buck with crimson blot.
His head will adorn my wall
Spring may come and leaves may fall
Then when gazing upon his rack
These treasured mem'ries shall come back.
'Twas not the kill that gave the thrill
But the graceful creature that had stood
Just sixty meters from the wood.

Debbie A. Grace

THE BOOK

My mind was filled with rhymes and riddles;
No where to go,
Caught in the middle.
Turning, turning, spinning around,
Backward, forward,
Upside down.
Finally it happened,
I came to a stop
Finding myself
On a solid Rock.
I picked myself up
And looked around,
Wondering just what
It was that I'd found.
He was a strong Man,
A bold one, yet gentle and meek;
Happy yet serious
When I heard Him speak.
His eyes filled with love
As He spoke to my heart;
Knowing He knew me
Right from the start.
He pointed a finger
And made me look,
There laid open
A golden book.
Upon the pages
Were rows and rows
Of all of the names
Of the people God chose.
I looked and looked,
But could not find
My name written
on any line!
I looked at the Man
I had come to know,
What could I do
So my love would show?
His love flowed around me
As He tenderly said,
"I died for you,
But you think I'm still dead!"
Suddenly in front of me
I saw a huge cross;
And then I knew
My life was not lost!
Seeing for the first time
All of His scars.
The heartbreak and sorrow
As numberous as stars.
Griefstricken and my spirit broken
I knew what I'd done;
I had put up that cross
And hung God's Son!
"Oh, Jesus, dear Jesus,
Can you forgive me?
This burden's too heavy
And I want to be free!

I want You to love me
I'll love You the same;
I promise I'll never
Bring You any more shame!"

Then He showed me
A babbling brook,
The water of life;
And my hand He took.

He pointed a finger
Again made me look,
There laid open
His precious golden book.

Upon that pure white page
Till the end of time,
Written in gold
His name and mine!

Joan Schuchman

TO THINE OWN SELF BE TRUE

NE
RV
OUS
BR
EA
KD
OW
N—
Nature's
remedy for my sick
soul.
Unconscious mind raged,
conscious introspection
destroyed.
Grotesque imaginings
intensified
my fears and guilts
inducing
a
roll
er
coast
er
of
think
ing,
exhilaration
and
fatigue.
Consciousness
stripped bare of
rationalizations and
defenses
fought my
frag
ment
ed
dreams—codes of self-
knowledge to be deciphered.
Spas
modical
ly,
sublimated truths
c
a
t
a
p
u
l
t
e
d
into consciousness.
Painful perceptions of
unflattering behavior—
insufferable,
ego-destroying.
Consciousness
deceived by
fantasy,
diminishing agony-
view of naked intellect,
exposed and unguarded.
Bizarre activity
outrageous accusations—
delusions
distorted
re
al
it
y to
avoid

confrontation
with
unconscious motivations.
ANGUISH—
view of self-
hypocricsy,
pleasing others,
demolishing my intuitions.
Meditation, exercise,
nutrition =COURAGE
Using rare gift—
precious
in
si
gh
ts
for
self-analysis.
Falseness to my ideals
will bring
success society
defies.
BUT
only truth and love will bring
me
PE
AC
E.
THEN
Acknowledgement
Acceptance
Assimilation
Adjustment.
T
H
E
N
I
forged ahead without regret
forgiving the past
and the pain.
And now I
face the future,
relaxed,
secure
and
unafraid.

Catharine Herder

PICTURE OF A DESERT WIND

I stayed in bed this morning. I never do, you know,
But I could hear a wild wind, and I *love* to hear it blow.
I imagined a wheat field waving, and heard the "whish" it made.
(In the desert, winds are "Ivory" calm, very seldom on a raid).
Then the wind blew in organ music—not really, just pretend—
And the squeal of a windmill turning. It really needed a mend.
I jumped out of bed and opened the door to take a look at my "Pard",
Not really *it*, but what it was doing to the growing things in the yard
It was fresh and live and blowy. In fact, it was almost cold.
It fought the bayonets of the Joshua tree (war-ready, sharp & bold);
Our one orange tree was tango-ing; and the big old pine tree swayed;
To every point on the compass the Palo Verde tree prayed;
The pond water ruffled and sped; honeysuckles shook to the ground.
I took to the window after closing the door, and inside heard the sound
Of the stove's air vent "plunk"; the patio sprinkling and sliding.
I thought I'd like to try the hose and see the wind madly guiding.
At last the wild day was over, and t'was time to go to bed.
Cradled in the wind's new soft wheeze and moan, it was Outward Bound ahead.
But I asked it please to come back tomorrow. And you know what? It did!
Blew our "to go" letters out of the slot and hijacked the trash can lid.

Phillip Ryan

UNTITLED

You'll do anything for one ya once loved
'cept love 'em again
Doing favors, helping with life and bein' a friend.
One by one, you do what needs to be done.

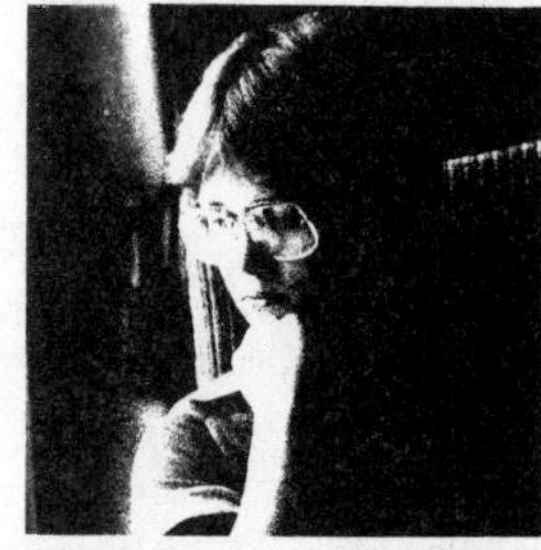

You even laugh and smile when it's not fun.
You try to take but always give and you coast instead of live.
You'll do anything for someone you once loved. . . .
Except love'em again.

David T. Smith

OSCAR AND THE HORNETS

One day while the crew worked in a swamp
that drained along County Line Creek
My party chief stuck His machete in a tree
and looked at his fieldbook to see if numbers agreed.
The thump of a blade against the wood
disturbed something I didn't think it should
And taken but a moment, Oscar

realized
awaken from labor, the pelting
bullets of stinging flies.
I turned when I heard his
scream
a cartoon dream-cloud about his
head streamed
Into thicket we madly fled
to get away from this crazy
scene.
After a time I didn't know, my
fear led me to an open spot
in the wood, where against
tupelo I leaned to stop
and catch my wind and my still
running heart.
Glen stumbled where I was
resting, shouting,
"What happened, Did you see"?
"Three of those bees almost got
me"!
I said "No, I didn't and
boy, am I glad",
but Oscar I think maybe got it
pretty bad.
We took a break and a smoke
sat around for a while and told
morbid jokes
We then thought of our poor
lost friend
and went in search of Oscar.
We searched and searched 'til
we found
our way down new cut line
Walking from the swamp toward
the truck
we saw old Oscar lying in the
muck.
With elbows propping up his
head
lay Oscar in the water—
shocked, almost dead
His chestwaders full of water,
Glen and I
held him up by his heels and
poured them out;
Counted his stings, which were
forty or thereabout.
Leaving the equipment, we each
threw an arm around our head
carried him to the truck and
laid him in its bed
To the hospital and back home,
he didn't utter a single word
moaning and groaning is all
we heard.
The next morning we picked
him up to go and work
There he was with a terrible
itch and his usual quirk.
Not since a car wreck, when for
several hours
Oscar lay in Grady morgue, had
he come so close.
The way I see it he's luckier
than most
He just gave up one of his nine
lives
By my count, the rascal still
has five.

Dianne Purcell
DIVINE PERSPECTIVE
He stood in the Synagogue and
read with authority
the words He Himself had
inspired.
Some marveled at His
knowledge, others doubted
and criticized.
He healed the broken and
diseased bodies of the ones
He had created.
Some were overcome with
gratitude and joy for restored
health. Others just walked
away without a word.
He was filled with compassion
and concern for the world He
had spoken into being. And
Yet it did not welcome Him
when He came to save it.
All of mankind He loved
without prejudice
Because He had created them
equal-even so they scorned
Him.
He wanted to help them but
they sought to *destroy*
Him!
He reached out to them in love
and They turned their backs.
He could have destroyed those
who sought to kill Him;
instead He stood and listened
as they cursed Him.
He endured the pain of the whip
and the crown of thorns. He
spoke not a word when they
spat in His face.
Even in death He wished them
no harm, but cried out for
their forgiveness.
"Our Saviour died on a cross of
wood and yet He made the
hill on which it stood."

Leona Ashcraft-Wise
JOURNEY THROUGH THE YEAR
January unleashes the cold
Air that reddens all faces,
Numbing every finger and toe
Urging all to seek warm places.
Away from Winter's icy blow to
Reminisce the summer days—
Yonder, Spring is returning.
February blinks at the sun
Enjoying few stolen moments,
Breaking up the white and gray
Reigning now; somehow relent
Undecided at making way to
Atmosphere hinting of warmth.
Relinquish your place, Winter
Youthful Spring will triumph.
March appears with the wind
Abreast the lamb and lion,
Reducing cold grayish days to
Crumbled hours that are dying.
Hurry, take hold sweet Spring!
April's warm sunny days display
Playful clouds gracing the sky;
Robin, annuals and butterflies
Interweave to the design on
high,
Laced with occasional showers.
Merrily we receive you May
And look for the summer by
Your warm life giving rays.
June has the gardens abloom
Under the late Spring's sun,
Nurtured by God and mankind
Echoing out the Divine Plan.
Jubilee days are upon us with
Ultramarine skies so clear,
Lazy days on July beaches
Yclept for dreams it appears.
Above us hangs an August sun,
Under shady trees we all meet
Gadabouts of the waning
summer
Uttering curses at the heat.
School time is drawing near
Teaming up with the autumn.
Students, take up your texts
Enter into the educational band,
Perceive the colors of
September—
Touches added by unseen hands.
Enjoy the bracing days slowly
Mingling with the summer sun,
Bushels of crops are harvested
Ending thus the fruitful run. . .
Remnants of summer are
tattered.
Opalesce days do proclaim the
Cool October winds that bring
Temperatures to lower degrees,
Observe now the weeping
boughs
Bending to approaching winter
Eliminating with an icy breeze.
Rally up, all ye hobgoblins!
Nod your head to give thanks
Of the season's past rewards,
Variety spices the yearly trek
Endowed upon us by the Lord.
Marvel November's snowflakes'
Ballet in the frost filled air,
Etched into the wintertide by a
Rhythm from Time with flair.
Daylight now grows shorter
Engrossing us with December
Christmas is nearing fast so
Experience seasonal offerings—
Miracles are close at hand.
Begin a new resolution list as
Events begin to now unfold
Ringing in another New Year.

Deborah L. Burzyck
DIRTY WHITE CHILD
Dirty white child
playing in your thrift shop
garments
what do you wanna be when
you grow up?
with all the infinite possibilities
that confront you,
it wouldn't be too hard to
decide
whether to be
a hooker
or a thief,
a pimp
or a thief,
a murderer
or a thief,
a dealer or
a stealer.
Your world
lies within the boundaries of
this street and that
and as you grow you discover
new streets and
expand your limits.
For now—
all the puddles in the park
will suffice
and the strange feeling mama
says is hunger won't really
bother you.
—your clothes are cool. after
all, kids weren't meant to
play in good stuff.
But,
dirty white child,
You're gonna want more—
more than anyone can give
you
and you're gonna have to take
it,
rape it,
hide it.
They're gonna getcha, Dirty
white child,
and put you away
for trying to catch your dreams
because
they don't understand
hungry.
they don't understand
your
ghetto attire.
and they don't understand
the silent tears dropping on
your pillow at night,
Dirty white child.
Dirty white
Dirty
White
child.

William A. Mutell
A GUIDE FOR EACH DAY
Learn more of life with each
passing year
Raise your glass to wish good
cheer
Notice the beauty of a woman
each day
And listen to words which old
people say
Be thankful for shelter and a
home cooked meal
And never do fear to say what
you feel
Try to put other people at ease
And never be too proud to ever
say please
Listen with interest to the
words of a child
While being strong, gentle and
mild

See with your heart as well as
your eyes
And not to be so quick to
criticize
Try not to be rude even when
someone's wrong
And raise your voice with
others in song
Never burden others with your
aches and pains
Remember it seldom does good
to complain
Do not feel that it is weak
to cry
And enjoy each moment passing
by
Never take for granted those
who care
And save some time each day
for prayer.

May Houtsinger
WEEDS
The winter winds ceased to
blow.
Southerly breezes melted the
snow
And there they were once more;
Poking up little green heads
On banks and gardens and
flower beds
Residing there again.
For years I have challenged
them;
Pulled them out again and again.
They are resisting me.
This the game they can play.
If I give up, they get to stay;
But I'll try once more.
All summer long I make myself

lame
Trying to play their silly game;
Pulling those persistant weeds.
The vegetables have finally grown.
Even fall bulbs I have sown.
I can rest till spring.
Returning from getting the mail one day,
I heard my neighbor call and say,
'Come over for a while.'
Morning chores over, it was time for a break.
'Kate, you make the coffee, I'll bring the cake;
I leisurely replied.
Our visit was about at an end
When looking up I saw an old friend,
Somehow in different garb.
While I weeded, getting lame and sore,
What Katy did was run the mower
Producing a fine green lawn.
Then in the fall picked weeds she found
Timothy, yarrow, and milk weed down;
She tinted, trimmed and dried.
A touch of gold here, red berries there,
Dark brown pods opened with care
Showed silvery milk weed down.
Before me my friend stood in a vase.
I swore I could see a smirk on it's face
Behind that gold paint.
The weeds I so quickly took out,
Katy saved and went a different route
Drying their now sturdy stems.
Her beautiful creation now stood in the hall.
Mine stood in jars on the cellar wall
To be eaten later that year.
Sometimes I wonder, am I happier than she?
It comes out the same as I can see.
I guess I'll plant more beans next year.

Andrea C. Smith
THE PICTURE
He lies beneath the shiny glass
Wrapped round with golden frame
With deep, dark eyes and flashing smile
The man without a name.
I ask my grandma who he is
She doesn't seem to hear
She just gazes at the photograph
Her eyes produce a tear.
He must have been a loved-one once
A man quite near her heart
But somehow life was stopped for him
They must've had to part.
He looks so gallant; stern and proud
A medal on his chest
And many stripes run down his arm
A man among the best.
His dark blue suit and bone-white gloves
Have faded through the years
Yet, there he sits upon the desk
To bring back sorrowful tears.
Who was this man of great acclaim
Who looks at me with pride
A mirror image of myself
Expression deep and wide.
I sit across from him and stare
Curiosity builds in me
That familiar face that gazes back
Who could this fellow be?
The time soon comes around when I
Must leave and say "so long"
But when that picture leaves my sight
A part of me is gone.
I soon return to the man
Who's love-filled heart seems near
He speaks to me in hidden words
A voice I seem to hear.
And when his thoughts project to me
In such a gentle tone
It's just right then I realize
I'll never be alone.
He lies beneath the shiny glass
'Wrapped round with golden frame
With deep, dark eyes and flashing smile
The man without a name.

Margaret Ratcliff
MY COMPANION, THE PILLOW
As a friend, it almost fills the bill.
I can yell at it
And not be criticized.
I can punch it with anger
With no fear of reprisal.
I can make it wet with tears
And it doesn't complain.
I can shove it aside when I don't need it
And it won't be hurt.
I can tell it my deepest thoughts
And not fear distrust.

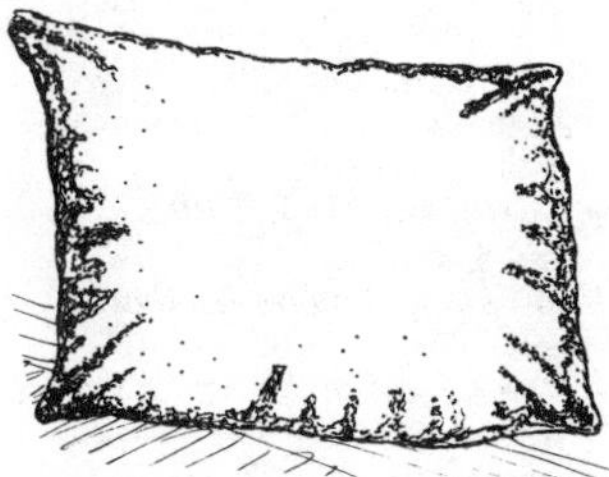

It will never turn away from me
In a time of need.
It can be supportive
But sometimes faulters from the strain.
It will always be there
When I want it.
I can share it
When the need arises
Or I can keep it all to myself
As my companion, the pillow.

Shari Burrus
RAINBOW CHASER
A thousand things
I have wanted to be,
A Mother, a lover, a friend out to tea.
A writer, a singer, a sailor at sea,
But when I look closely
I'm really just me.
When I look at my "outside"
I really don't care,
Because what's on my "inside"
I feel I can share.
Now if the world is too heavy
let me take you somewhere,
Close your eyes and believe
wallah,. . .we're there.
Let's go to the mountains
we'll take a slow train,
Look to the left
it's starting to rain.
But we have no care
it makes a nice stain,
Throw your voice to the valley
hear it "echo" our name.
Let's picnic on Mt. Lemmon
we'll sit in the pines,
Eat ripe watermelon
right down to the rind.
We'll climb to the slopes
and drink hot spice wine,
Stare into the snow
'till we're almost blind.
Oh how I wish
right here I could stay,
Living every minute
just to call it a day.
Never looking back
on a worn yesterday
But. . .reality claims us
and today is today.
It seems when you're down
you've lost every race,
My comrade I tell you
that isn't the case.
Sometimes reaching out
will slow down the pace,
There's still time to live
and still time to waste.
What I'm trying to say
is I call you my friend,
With my words and my dreams
it's love that I send.
And when you are lonely
throw your thoughts to the wind,
We can go on a picnic. . .
again and again.

Laurie Faulkner
EATING OUT
A dedicated masochist-melancholy me—
I sidle in to be greeted by—
"How many?"
I wonder if she's blind and briefly ponder walking out.
But no. . .at a small isolated table
I contemplate the tip and think of writing bad poetry
While I wait and wait-on you.
My thoughts have turned
And with a smile I decided must look wistful
I think of what I have and how I'd love to spend it all
On you-instead of on just me.
Jolted out of reverie, I hear an anxious voice.
"Need more time?" "Oh no," I assure her and shove my futile verse
Beneath the bread basket.
Scrutinizing the menu
I order something you would like—with rice.
She scurries off, and I realize that I would rather think of you
Than eat. With a sigh I wonder where you are
And why you can't see your way to me?
If you won't believe that I'd love to help you through
Your aloneness too (Really good!—I exclaim about the teriyaki
to no one in particular)
What kind of sorrow is it that blinds your eyes and
Keeps your ears deaf—to me?
I wish now I had not come.
Mockingly the sun outside the glass sheds double rainbows on my table;
Once again I'm reminded of how really ludicrous this is.
"Just one?" They asked me cheerfully
"Yes," I said, and add
"Don't rub it in."

Frederica McDill Culbertson
EASTER AND THE BEACH
The seas' bright green,
the sky's bright blue,
the ripples on the sand are white,
while those at leisure parade this Easter holiday,
on this Florida beach so far away.
Far away from the cares of the north,
where winter still abounds
with snow and wind and cold,
or so by everyone I'm told.
And have you noticed on the beach
how childlike people are?
Old women carry little bags
and a mix of shells they hoard,
while old men's kites now soar,
or they fish or read—
whatever their need.
And expressions the most do tell—
sometimes a glance, sideways and shy, I see,
and smiles—wistful, warm, kind, carefree.
Could they be the same who walk the street
and with their peers so ruthlessly compete?
How could it be?
And yet, I know, under it all they're truly good,
as God knows, and so you, too, should.
Most impressive are the youth,
home from school—away from books.
Girls—pretty, firm and small,
waiting for young men, some tall—
Young men—handsome, strong and brave,
prepared to meet the challenge of today.
Now don't overlook the children,
who with young parents are inspiring, too.
Children who like little lambs,
still full of innocence and pure,
act out their dreams and fairy tales,
sail their ships straight out to

sea,
or build with sand strong
fortresses
and castles reaching towards the
sky,
and command all that they see,
like the kings and queens they'll
never be.
You, too, like I, must enjoy this
day.
For tomorrow or soon it will not
be.
This pleasant pause will pass
while once again we hoist our
load and face reality.
But let us not forget from day
to day
the true meaning of this
holiday.
It was for you and me that
Christ, our Lord, was born—
and died, and rose again—and
gave us eternity.

Dolores Morganston Allen

THE GIRL OF MARRAKECH

In a bar out West, not one o'
the best,
I met there a sailor named Joe,
He was six foot three, some
taller than me,
And he drawled his words kinda
slow.
Said he'd been around in most
every town
From Djakarta to old Timbuktu;
He'd fought a good fight on
many a night,
For he brawled at the drop of a
shoe.
He'd sailed in some ships to
ports and to slips,
To countries both narrow and
wide;
Sometimes just a day,
sometimes weeks he'd stay,
More often he'd sail with the
tide.
I bought him a drink, it set
him to think
Of a girl he knew long ago;
He looked awful sad—I knew he
felt bad,
And he held his head sorta low.
Marrakech girls have teeth of
pearls
And skin more tan than white,
But it's their eyes that cause
men's sighs,
So big and dark and bright.
The market-place Joe first saw
her face
As lovely as spring's early morn,
And she was for sale to any
male
Just like she was cattle or corn.
He found her so fair, with her
raven hair,
But her eyes, they broke his
young heart,
For they spoke more loud than
a raging crowd,
With a plea that tore him apart.
Now somethin' in Joe just
snapped an' let go
To see the sad look in her eyes,
Air gentle and mild, half
woman, half child—
Joe's heart felt like squeezed
to half size.
The bidding began, and a
fiftyish man
Bid one thousand dirhams at
first,
Now Joe was clean broke, but up
he clear spoke
And upped the bid, while the
sheik cursed.
His soiled burnoose clothes,
his ugly hooked nose,
The leer on his swarthy old face
Made Joe vow right then, of all
of earth's men,
That sheik would not win the
bid race.
The offers climbed higher, as
each would-be buyer
Bid loud 'gainst the other
one's call,
Till finally the sheik, his rage
at a peak,
Rode off on his horse, filled
with gall.
Joe stepped up to claim his
prize in this game,
But having no dirhams to pay
He swooped up the girl, and
sprang with a swirl
On somebody's horse—and
away!
They galloped afar, just distance
their star,
Escape being Joe's only aim;
The horse sped away, sending
sand in a spray
As into the desert they came.
Some time into flight it grew
to be night,

So Joe had to rein in the steed;
He slid to the sand, and taking
her hand,
He helped her down, gently
indeed.
How could she be sure his
motive was pure—
Of English she knew not a word;
Poor Joe tried his best her fear
to arrest,
But she was just like a scared
bird.
He lay down a spell, for he
thought it well
To sleep a few hours till the
dawn;
He tied the mare's rope to his
wrist with new hope,
The girl though was still a
scared fawn.
The full moon shone bright, and
cast its cold light
On Joe fast asleep on his back;
The girl, silently, arose then
to flee,
For courage she sure didn't lack.
When night's course was run,
Joe woke with the sun,
When first it peeked up in the
East;
The patient young mare was
still standing there—
But the girl! Joe's heart almost
ceased!
His eyes couldn't see a shrub or
a tree,
Or anything save barren land;
He cast his eyes down,
inspecting the ground—
Her footprints were still in
the sand!
He leaped on the horse, and
followed her course,
His heart was a-racing like mad;
But a wind soon came up,
a-filling each cup
That marked her dark flight
from the lad.
He rode fast and well, like a
bat out o' hell,
A-searchin', a-searchin' some
trace;
The sun rose up high, a fire in
the sky,
And beat down on Joe's head
and face.
All through that day he galloped
away,
A-strainin' his eyes for the girl;
The merciless sun shot heat like
a gun,
His brain was sun-baked to a
whirl.
He rode through the night, for
such was his plight
His brain was afire with one
thought;
The dawn came and went, and
Joe's strength was spent—
He slipped from the steed
knowing naught.
How long he there lay, he never
could say,
Till a Moor caravan chanced
along;
More dead than alive, they
helped him survive,
And they took him with them
to Tetuong.
He searched quite a while,
walked many a mile,
Scanned hundreds in each
market-place;
He posted rewards of dirhams
and swords,
But never again saw her face.
Now at night, when the moon is
bright,
And a hush is over the land,
And he's almost alseep, his heart
gives a leap,
For he hears someone running
in sand.

Tallak T. Farsjo

ALL THAT GLISTERS IS NOT GOLD

What is the use to strive and
toil,
To dream, to build, and plough
the soil;
Because at last, at harvest time
You hardly have a single dime!
The tunnel's exit has no light,
No daytime sun, no starry night.
Around my hopes a snake will
coil,
With poison fangs my dreams
embroil.
No ringing bell, no pealing
chime
To cheer me on through desert
clime.
Why am I not a poet great
Whose fame and fortune lie in
wait?
As volume upon volume sell
The price in store could be
Nobel!
But no, in truth I must elect
To be a famous architect.
With shining gold and
silverplate
My towers upwards climb like
faith.
A master builder, you can tell;
The earth is mine—and all is
well.
Just like Peer Gynt, I dream for
days;
And in these dreams in many
ways
My heart is seeking happiness
From all this real depressing
stress
That pesters me—the lowly Joe
Who seeks life's "yes" but
gets its "no".
Around my dreams such happy
haze
Oft covers life's pragmatic face.
—So let me play the king, no
less
And win my game of "wonder-
chess."
The truth, of course,: this is
to dream
Yourself from life's no-glamour
stream
Where all must paddle their
canoes
Against the current, lest they
lose
The grip on life, yes life, for
real,
Where roses hide, but thorns
you feel.
This is the fight, the lucid
gleam
Where "Will" is king—the
guiding beam.
Remember, when you seek what
glows—
That fortune, fame can be your
foes.

Dorothy A. Chinn

FOR GOD SO LOVED THE WORLD. . .

Long ages past, I sent a group
of My children
To explore and enjoy this
Earth—
This fair planet of My creation.
I told them, "Go forth and
prosper,
For every good thing I have
provided for you.
I give you free will, that you
may express
The facets of your individuality
to the fullest,
And thus fulfill the mission I
have given you:
To experience this Good Earth
for Me,
Then return to Me, a fuller,
wiser part of the Family of
God."
But thru the ages, these
children,
These beloved children,
Forgot from whence they came
And the reason for their sojourn.
They pictured their survival on
this Earth
As struggle and toil—
So true to the Law,
The Earth fulfilled their
picturing,
And gave them struggle and toil,
For the picture in the mind
Is the first step of creation.

So I told My Older Son, the Christ,
"Go and remind your brothers and sisters on Earth
Of the reason they are there,
And show them the way back to Me.
This task will not be easy,
For they will think it easier
To worship you than to follow your example.
They will mock you for claiming to be My Son—
Not remembering that they too are My sons.
They will feel such pangs of guilt
When you show them they have fallen short of their mission,
That they will try to expiate that guilt
By putting the Wayshower to death.
But because some will have heeded Your teachings,
That 'death' will be the symbol of Your promise
That You will return to lead them
In their final lessons
And join them in their victorious journey homeward.
They will call you Prince of Peace,
Then fight wars over who understands You aright.
They will take Your Name in vain,
Claiming they are fighting for You,
Trying to hide their real motives:
A lust for power and greed.
Your teachings will be ignored
While they use Your Name
As an excuse to subjugate
Their brothers of a different race,
A different country,
A different consciousness of My Reality."
And so he came, this Older Son, their Brother.
He showed them that their "death"
Is only a transition—
That Life is Eternal as God is Eternal.
He taught them that they are here to HELP their brothers,
That violence begets violence,
And greed begets deprivation,
That lust for power begets subjugation,
For when they focus their minds and actions
On what they think they "lack,"
They must, by Law,
Experience that lack.
So when he "died" on the cross of their outpictured matter,
He never left them—
He told them, "I AM with you always."
But they, desiring to linger
In their outpictured Earth
Did not understand,
And though some did believe in Him,
They thought that they must wait
To again experience His fellowship and Love.
My Beloved Son, the Christ,
Did not mislead them, His brothers and sisters.
He said, "Follow Me" (follow my example).
He said, "Love one another" (love your brother for the expression of God that he is).
He said, "Help one another" (for as you help your brother,
You help yourself on your homeward path).
Today My Earth children
Are "cramming" for their final exams.
Some have diligently done their lessons,
And have no fear of the tests.
But many there are
Who partied late in the world of illusion
And now are very afraid
That they have missed their opportunity.
Though they have many lessons to learn,
And the time is short before the Earth's graduation,
The Older Brother, the Christ,
Is always at hand to help.
Be not afraid!
Your Father loves ALL of His Children,
And His Love is stronger than any Earthly problem.

Cindy Dearwater
A DAISY'S DILEMMA

The sky was soft with a springtime breeze as the morning was announced by the sun,

And the daisy yawned and stretched its petals towards the warmth, glad that night was done.

It then turned its head to the tulip and said, "The morning is quite lovely today."

"Oh I agree!" she answered jubilantly, but then puzzled, she added, "You should really be more gay!"

"Oh, I don't know," said the daisy with woe, "Do I really belong in this garden?

Do I matter or is it important that I exist? My doubt you really must pardon."

"Oh you old drone," replied she with a groan, "We've been over this a thousand times before.

Your purpose in life should not cause you strife. I say, you're getting to be quite a bore."

"See! I tell you right there!" declared the daisy with a glare, "I was never meant to be.

I may have well been drowned, or stepped on by a hound, or carried off by a bumble bee!

I do nothing at all but stand by this wall, my petals floating in the wind.

I don't rule the world, I'm not a rare pearl, and in the book of history my name's not penned."

"Don't be silly my friend," assured the tulip again, "You needn't move mountains to matter.

Just stand up and smile, enjoy the world for a while, and you may add to someone's laughter.

For love is passed on and you are God's pawn carrying out the glory of creation.

So just be happy and gay throughout every day, and if you're lucky,

You'll bring a moment of joy into the heart of some sad girl or boy, at the time when it's most needed.

Then at that moment you'll find, within your mind, why you were meant to be,

The reason's for love! Pure, simple, love, the kind that sets hearts free!"

Mildren Miles Workman
THE STORM

I cannot walk the ways of life;
for every time I do,
The Master takes His whip in hand;
And tells me what to do.
The lightning streaks across the sky;
When e'er He lifts His hand,
And whips me back into my place;
Upon His precious land.
His voice booms out with lashing tongue;
As He chastises me,
And once again His thund'ring words;
Will bring me to my knee.
His brow so full of pain and tears;

Each time I do a sin,
He stretches out His Holy hand;
For me to come to Him.
Those bitter tears, I know I've caused;
While in this world, I walk,
And as the Master calls me back;
To Him, I know, I'll talk.
And as He wipes His tears away;
And smiles on me, and then,
With humbled heart, and head bowed low;
I'm in His grace again.

Eileen M. Parker
A LETTER FROM HEAVEN

Dear Mama,
This letter comes to you today
And I'll try to tell in part
A little of the way I feel
And just what's in my heart.
I left a place that you call Earth
For a far-off land so nice
That now I know why it is called
The Land of Paradise.
I questioned why I came here
And the myst'ry now unfolds
That God in Heaven made it
Just for twelve year olds.
But Mama, there is one thing
That I have found so hard
And that's the thought that you're not sure
I'm happy here with God.
Please let me try to tell you Mom
A little of what it's like
It's not a doll or sled or swing. . .
Or a brand new, shiny bike. . .
It's not a brand new furry coat
Or a Christmas Eve with snow
Or even like a birthday, Mom
Or a —gosh, I just don't know.
It's Heaven, Mom, that's all it is
And God has paved the way
For people like you and Daddy
To be with me here, someday.
But Mama please, for me alone
Do this one thing today
Go to church where me and God
Will help you learn to pray.
And pray, please Mama, pray and pray
Tell God your hurt is real
'Cause He's the only one who knows
The way you really feel
I'm sorry now I left so fast
And didn't say 'goodbye'
But when the Angel held my hand
And took me toward the sky. . .
I wondered 'what will Mama think?
I didn't call her name. . .
Or say goodbye or anything'
And now I feel the blame.
But Mama, you can help me now
And tell me it's alright
And maybe then, and only then
We both will sleep tonight.
I'm sorry for you mortals
Who don't know Heavens' worth
We pray a lot for folks like you
Who suffer down on Earth.
But someday soon, Gods' Mighty Hand
Will touch each human being
And bring you here to see the wondrous
Things that I'm now seeing.
I've got to go now, Mom and Dad
Get down on bended knee
And pray for all our loved ones
The Angels, God and me.
Oh Mama dear, I'm happy now
So wipe away that tear
And cast your eyes toward Heaven
To see me ever near.
So wish me Happy Birthday, Mom
As happy as can be
So I can go on living here
The Angels, God and me.
Your Loving Daughter,
Denise

Timothy Driscoll
RENAISSANCE MAN

Sculpture and dance, biology and math
Physics and dramaturgy, everything that's grand
Would be mine, and a whole lot more, you see,

If only I could be a renaissance
man,
Yeah, a real renaissance man.
I'd paint like Da Vinci and orate
like Webster,
Excel in architecture and be in
the van
Of all the great artists who
come and go
Within the sight of this
renaissance man,
Yeah, this real renaissance man.
I would work wonders in
chemistry,
Discover asteroids bigger than
Japan,
Win more Nobels than Alfred
himself
'Cause I'd be a renaissance
man,
Yeah, a true renaissance man.
My love of music I'd translate
into
The best jazz, pop and rock in
the land.
Ludwig Von, and Bach and
Mozart too,
Would stand aside for this
renaissance man,
Yeah, a one-of-a-kind
renaissance man.
I would treat of every passion
and joy
Ever explored with pen-in-hand.
Balzac, Joyce, Tolstoy and Frost
Could never compete with such
a renaissance man,
Yeah, this one-and-only
renaissance man.
All of the above and more
would I seek
If only I could work out a plan
Without losing my head in
attempting to be
This elusive, all-in-one
renaissance man,
Yeah, this will-o-the-wisp
renaissance man.

Deborah Mangum
WINDOWS AND CREAMPUFFS

I lived and grew, to a certain
degree,
in a very small town.
The main industry, as far as
I was concerned.
was the local bakery.
I remember I could stand in
front of that place with my
face pressed hard against those
huge nose printed windows
and stare in for what seemed
like hours.
Wanting.
That was the best place in
the world.
It was the world, and it was
good.
Every time you opened the door
the bell over head
seemed to say "Welcome. Come
on in. Everything you
could want is in here.",
and it was.
I could make everything as soft
as a cream puff,
or as sweet and full of
surprises as a jelly
filled doughnut.
I could always make the world
seem nice.
It was all so simple.
But, that was then.
That was a long time ago.
I am gone.
The bakery is gone.
They don't even make cream
puffs like that anymore.
And cold hard store bought
chocolate chip cookies don't
work.
So, now
Here I am
Standing
Outside
Pressed hard against the world.
There are no big shiny windows,
No sweet talking bells,
No easy bakery store answers.
Still wanting.
Sometimes I feel so guilty
about wanting,
Sometimes I feel so old.

Carol M. O'Toole
WOOD VIOLETS

In the shadow of tall trees
Wood violets grow
Easily crushed by careless feet
Releasing fragrance as they die
She told us to smile one early
spring day
My little brother and I
And snapped our picture
Her shadow is on it
Behind her the woods where
the violets grew
The violets we picked
For our mother
We sit
Squinting up at her
Trying to smile into the sun
Behind her the woods where
the bee had stung
Wearing sweaters too big
The sleeves pushed up
Crunching apples she gave us
Warm sun contents our faces
Blesses our knees
Caresses our furry-tammed
heads
Then
All life Ruptured
I lost my mother that early
spring
My brother
The end of that summer
I grew into the sweater alone
The sleeves came down
With my smile
But what I have left
Is the sun on our faces the
tang
Of the apples she gave us
Her shadow yearning toward
us
My one smaller eye
From the sting
And the delicate scent
Of wood violets

Rose L. Osckel
UNSOLICITED OPINIONS

I think that sharing is
important.
I think that love is important.
I think it is important to state
one's case.
I think that biographical movies
based on fact may be
important.
I think that money isn't
important, but
I don't think that money is
important.
I think that's a paradox
in terms.
I think that a clear head
is important.
I think that importance is
overblown.
I think that knowing oneself
leads away from confusion.
I think I don't know myself,
but that's okay because
I don't think anyone else does,
either.
I think that Disneyland should
be left to children and so
should mature relationships.
I think that this poem is
progressing awkwardly.
I think that abortion kills,
people kill, and
I think that guns are
instruments in the hands of
demented killers.
I think that my heart is in
the right place, but my money
isn't.
I think that five and a quarter
percent annually isn't enough.
I think that Walt Whitman was
a martyr.
I think that martyrdom is a
fool's paradise.
I think my unsolicited opinions
don't matter.
I think that no one wants in
on my esoteric fantasy trips.
I think that Scrooge was on the
right track before the spirits.
I think this poem is too long.
I think that images in this poem
are nonexistent.
I think that insanity is a
prerequisite of adulthood.
I think that Spring is finally
here, but is hiding behind
Winter.
I think the Pope knows what he
is doing.
I think that Russians fear me,
just as I fear the long arm of
Communism.
I don't think that Automobile
inspections can kill.
I don't think that America has
been fed to the dogs, or that
the post-war generation made
America what it is.
I don't think I know what I
think.
I think that living with Carpe
Diem in mind is an idealistic
farce.
But then, so is Democracy.
I think that intelectualism
has its place at America's
universities.
I think that Rev. Stillwell is
trying to cause panic.
I think that tomorrow may
never come, but only because
America isn't chanting her
mantra.
I think that spiritual peace-
of-mind is nonexistent.
I think that Mickey Mouse is
a nonentity.
I think that Hare Krishnas
should be allowed in Airports
'75 and '77.
I think that frog clickers are
unconstitutional.
I think this poem is getting
nowhere.
I think that Hitler thought he
was right.
I think that freedom of religion
is different from free religion.
I think that to God it makes no
difference.
I think that for my generation's
children, things will be
different.
I think that free verse poetry
is indicative of a sick mind.
I think that drugs should be left
to people who know what
they're doing, and
I don't think I know what I'm
doing.
I think that without ethnic
groups and Beautiful People,
the social structure of
America would crumble.
I think I'm a raving lunatic,
but only when the moon is
full.
I think that Vietnam was an
unfunny Communist joke.
I think that alone doesn't
necessarily mean lonely.
I think that aloneness and
loneliness are states of mind.
I don't think that selfishness
is a sin, as long as one is
sincere.
I think I'm tripping out on
myself.

Iva Petree Marshall
AUTUMN

Gone, now Summer's magic
days,
Comes October's golden blaze;
Silenced long, the Whip-poor-
will,
Lonely now, the brooding hill.
Creeps the light frost thru' the
night,
Comes the morning crisp and
white;
Cautiously, the Brown hare
steals,
From the barren wind-swept
fields.
From my hearth, the warm fire
gleams,
Whines the Collie in his
dreams;
Thru' the night, the brown
leaves blow,
Sighing at the coming snow.

Judy McBride
HUNGER PANGS

This morning,
As I awoke easily and as
untroubled as a calm, restful
morning at sea,
I rolled myself out like the
ocean
So that I could tumble around
him.
Sleepy sensuality seeped out of
me,
Leaked down beside me.
Desperately, I longed to
drench him with my love
Soak him down wet!

But as I folded myself out. . .
So that I could wrap around him,
I noticed he wasn't there.
It was like planning on a day full of sunshine. . .
Only to discover the weather forecast says "It looks like rain."
Still,
I smeared my hands across the sleekness of the sheets. . .
Spread them out. . .
Like a morning mist melting.
Anxious to cover him up with my passions,
I tossed the sheets back. . .
The way trees shove the wind away.
Like one long starved,
My body ached for him.
I felt so undernourished. . .thin. .
Without his patient eyes pressing into mine.
I was so eager for him as waves are
When they fervently reach for land.
And, it's remarkable the way my skin has learned his touch. . .
Remembered it. . .
So that I could almost feel him hold me all the way around.
The essence of him
Permeated my mind
Like spearmint does in the spring of every season.
As I lay there,
I could even taste
Our warm wet kisses dampen me. . .
Like a tropical rainstorm does.
I knew that morning,
That the thought of him. . .
The feel of him. . .
The sweet smell of him. . .
Was not going to wash off of me smoothly. . .
The way soap does.
I showered anyway, and later in the day
I couldn't help but wonder. . .I couldn't help but wonder. . .
If someone might have seen him
Sealed to me stuck. . .
Pasted to me so tightly like glue!
Surely someone saw?!

Philip K. Berger

EARTHMEN

Last night,
I saw a dancing star
Beaming there in outer space.
It sparkled brightly from afar,
And seemed within the Moon's embrace.
The Moon's
first crescent, bright and clear,
struggled hard to move so near
to Venus in her splendor,
as if it needed special help
to light the path of three earth men,
on friendly mission bent.
Who knows
what other eyes did watch
this love affair progress?
Perhaps in envy of Earth's
triumphant march,
far out, in God's forbidden space,
where man has dared to tread.
So, may
the trio meet good fortune,
inspire man to lofty goals,
to overcome the myriad ills
which now confront the world.
May this endeavor
guide others, everywhere,
in countless walks of life, and
may it work in some strange way, to unify
the hostile nations of the Earth,
which, by comparison with
God's great Universe,
is small, indeed.
Yea,
but a dot in space,
and limited severely in comprehension
of all the complex
mechanisms which lie beyond,
and which man now seems
destined to explore.

Angela Green

TAKE ME IN YOUR ARMS MISS HEROIN

Take me in your arms Miss Heroin
So now little man you've grown tired of grass,
L.S.D. Cocaine and hash,
And someone pretending to be a true friend,
Said I'll introduce you to Miss Heroin.
Well honey, before you start fooling with me,
Just let me inform you of how it will be,
For I will seduce you and make you my slave,
I've sent men much stronger then you to their grave.
You think you could never become a disgrace.
And end up addicted to poppy seed waste,
So you'll start inhaling me one afternoon,
You'll take me into your arm very soon.
And once I've entered deep down in your veins,
The craving will nearly drive you insane.
You'll need lots of money so you've been told,
For darling, I'm much more expensive than gold.
You'll swindle your mother, and just for a buck,
You'll turn into something vile and corrupt.
You'll mug and steal for my narcotic charm,
And feel much better when I enter your arm.
The day when you realize the monster you've grown,
You'll solemnly swear to leave me alone,
If you think that you've got the mystical knack.
Then sweetie, just try getting me off your back.
The vomit, the cramps, your gut in a knot,
The jangling nerves screaming for just one more shot,
The hot chills, the cold sweat, the withdrawal pains,
Can only be saved by my little white grains.
And when you return, just as I foretold.
I know that you will give me your body and soul.
You'll give up your morals, your conscience your heart,
And you will be mine till Death Do Us Part

L. H. "Lee" McCormack

ODE TO THE NOW GENERATION

Like some, let us not be—
Like those who reply to the draft: "Not me";

Like many, unfortunately,
Who, with immaturity
Think they know it all—like he
Who listens not, but talks constantly.

Look around, take stock,
But do so objectively,
And maybe you'll come closer
To those steadfast and really free;

To those who are the bulwark
Of this society.
Not those of this trait, or that trait,

Not necessarily;
But of those who believe in
The overall good in Man,
For that's a certainty;

And of those who love freedom,
But with responsibility.
Yes, like those who love freedom,

Just like you and me,
But who will also sacrifice,
Give their life, if the need be,
For their liberty and freedom,
Neither of which come free.
No, as they say, "Freedom isn't free—

You've got to sacrifice,
Pay the price, for your liberty."
You've got to look yourself in the eye,

Not introspectively,
But look deep, compare
Yourself with the history
Of others, gone before, who were
Also confused, just as we—
But who held a standard high
Of God, duty, and country.

Like some let us not be;
Like those who complain but
Live in squalor, voluntarily;
Who contribute nothing but a
Whining voice to improve society;

Who reek and wreck and do nothing
Except destructively,
And do it with a vengeance
Of impropriety.

Like those who advocate, but
Practice differently;
Who look for someone else's
Weaknesses to see
And blame for their own misery.
Like those who want freedom—
Except for you and me.
Whose love of others, tho professed,
Is twisted, intermittently;
Whose love of life is limited to:
"What's in it for me?"
Whose love of self is overall,
Looking inward, selfishly;
Who feel: "The world owes me a living,
Regardless of what I be."
This world owes no one nothing,
To put it vernacularly.
In fact, it gives more than it takes,
And that spectacularly.
Not that it doesn't need improving,
It does so, naturally;
But it needs improving from
The best of Man; particularly
With the love of Man for his
Fellow humanity.
Life is what you make of it—
It can be happy, or a penitentiary.
It's full of choices which are free,
Unless you lock yourself out
Of its opportunity.
So look beyond the present pall;
Free yourself from that binding wall
Of prejudice against society,
And I think you'll find, like me,
That you can also know
What it is to be
Among this world's people—free
To love, to live constructively,
And to leave behind a memory
Of someone who contributed something—
If only a thought, an idea, or a philosophy,
Or at least some effort
On behalf of Liberty.

D. Albert Byers

THE RED WHEEL

The red wheel
in the sky
sinks into the trees
with a sigh
and weak knees
make him to cry
tears

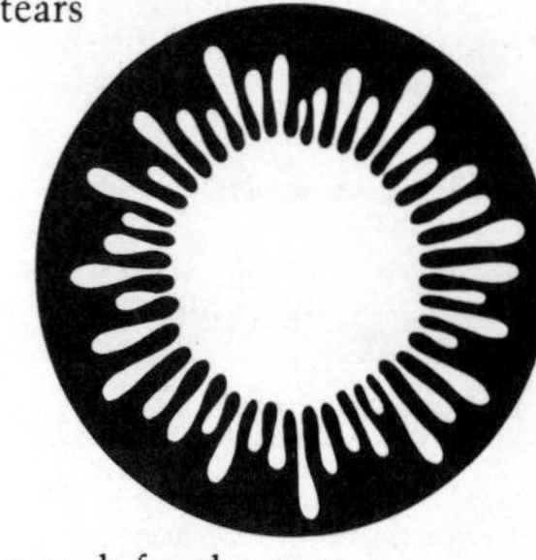

enough for the seas
until he is dry.
Everyone can see
yet, nobody knows why
the red wheel
in the sky
races through
the trees
sinking slow
still a million questions why. . .
What you goin to do?
where you goin to go?
we do not bother

to see,
nor can we take
the time to know
the red wheel
in the sky
as it travels
across lands and seas,
says hello
then goodbye
and makes it's decrees. . .
the red wheel
in the sky.
Lord, let it be
understood
that it's no lie;
help them to see
and help us to cry,
for it's not you or me,
but You,
You're the reason why
the red wheel
in the sky
is still there
for all to see;
there is no need
to question why,
the red wheels
in the sky.

Edward Michael MacCabe

ONLY ONE LIFE TO GIVE

A Texas boy is coming your way, O Lord
He's the right sort of chap to take on board
He's honest and decent and he did his part
To preserve the democracy that dwelled in his heart.
He has no medals, no brass, no gold.

He's only a youngster, not very old.
He gave his life so others might live.
He gave the all that's possible to give.
And I know that you'll be proud, when he stands right next to thee
For, in his way, O Lord, he died for liberty

Adella Garbe Butt

DARKNESS AND DAWN
John, 21

That night they caught nothing, that long dark night.
Peter hoped that in fishing he would comfort his plight.
He denied his Lord Jesus, Now his great heart grieved.
His friends tried to cheer him but he was not relieved.
No fish here no fish there. The sun went down.
Peter yearned for his Lord. Love would not drown.
Midnight came, the hottest night. Peter shed his coat.
While the fish in their fright fled away from the boat.
John sat close beside him in deepest sympathy
Praying, "Father, help my brother in his sad misery,"
Dark still and even darker, just before the dawn.
Peter wept, "Oh; Jesus in your service to belong."
Daylight came and from the shore spoke their Lord and King,
"Cast down where you cast, before. I'll give you a blessing."
Nets full of fish they did raise, and he whom Jesus loved
Said to Peter, "It is the Lord with a miracle from above."
Quick, they headed for the shore. Then Peter knew his Master.
He was so glad he swam before, eager to get there faster.
Jesus said, "Now come and dine of fish and of the bread."
'Twas the third time Jesus showed He had risen from the dead.
"Simon Peter," Jesus pleaded, "Do you love Me more than these?"
"Lord you know all things truly and You know that I love Thee."
"Then feed My lambs and feed My sheep to prove to Me that love."
Peter's heart sang for joy that reached to heaven above!

Debra Delores Mills

THOUGHTS OF A SOLDIER

Along a dusty winding road,
A wounded soldier lies.
The war has taken more in toll
He stares with sightless eyes.
A medic passes through the lot,
Chaplains kneel in prayer.
your son was fighting yesterday
Now he's no longer there.
What am I doing in this war?
How did it come to be?
A gun goes off with deafening roar
This time it is not me.
How many more days do I have left?
How long will I survive?
When will I leave this forsaken place?
And, will I be alive?
There was a guy amongst us
Who cheered us with his jokes.
Now he lies in foreigh fields, with
Medals enroute to his folks.
Soldiers lying everywhere,
Some dead, some in great pain.
No matter where you cast your eyes
The vision is the same.
John once was an athelete
With ribbons large and small.
But he'll no longer play those games
He has no legs at all. . .
Casualties could line these sheets
If I but had the time.
For many guys have fallen dead
And some no one will find.
Many friends are left behind
In fields and unmarked graves.
A bomb shell whizzes overhead,
This time again, I'm saved.
How many more guns will pass me by
Before one finds its' mark.
And when it hits will I be blessed
With life or the final dark. .
I do not know what tomorrow brings
And so, live for today. .
The bullets splatter around the field
And I am taken away. . .
I have but a few moments
My life is slipping away.
I wonder why I have to die
The answer——never said.

Charles Jackson Gallimore

THE ESSENCE OF BASEBALL

Summer, hot and dry in the big city,
I was bored, tired and felt old.
I truthfully admit I was filled with self pity.
I needed to participate in something quite bold.
Plodding down traffic snarled streets,
I waited for the coolness of dark.
I wiped my brow, dreaming of vacation retreats,
Then I glimpsed the baseball park.
I entered the stadium and took a seat,
Nine Chicago boys of summer ran on the field.
The Cubs and the Phils were about to compete,
What was it about baseball that made me yield?
Maybe it was the sounds of the game,
A carlton fast ball popping leather.
A coach calling the umpire a name,
Or a weak hitters bat swishing the air like a feather.
I pondered the reason that made me a fan,
The Phils lead-off man took his batting stance.
He sure was a little man,
In other team sports he wouldn't have a chance.
Maybe it was the players making dazzling plays,
Great pitchers challenging great hitters.
Carlton and Ryan facing Williams and Mays,
Burleah Grimes hurling spitters.
I realized my fondness for baseball wasn't for any one reason,
Because the relish sprinkled hot dogs taste good,
Or its simply the baseball season,
Watching this game I found baseballs essence and I hope I'm understood.
Top of the ninth and the Phils were three runs down,
The Phils began to rally.
I cheered, losing my frown,
As the Phils scored a tally.
I no longer was bored, feeling old or tired.
In innings time is measured.
I was stirringly inspired,
For baseball rallys should be treasured.

Fern Filner

LIFE WOMB

Grown in a cocoon of placenta,
is belly-breath, H_2O and emotions.
All fetal need, living within another.
We rock & roll to a heartbeat lullaby.
Quickening in mothers anxiety,
quieting in peaceful slumber.
Upon first breath
our world becomes a universe.
Open space, room to move—
freedom is birthed.
Then a restricting hand—
a slap on our soft-cheek,
changes our initial perception.
Yet possible peace is known,
desires for food and breath,
carrys us forward.
Then in the multitudes of paradox,
In the mirage of media,
In the plethora of societys requirements,
In the energy controversy,
In the spiraling womb of existence;
we are given choice.
Within each choice.
we seek and need balance.
Within our heart and souls
we recognize truth.
Within our minds
we debate answer/actions.
In these political wars
we die and we give birth.
In this economic struggle
we starve or eat from the horn of plenty.
In our individual degrees of aloneness
we hide—or we set ourselves free!
We must strive and reach,
that Infinite moment—
of monumental understanding,
of our deepest emotions.
This frees us from the growing
raging beast of anger. From the
sickening silence of sorrow.
With unwavering fortitude,
persistance, ideals and dreams,
adopt this truth—attitude,
In your longitude and latitude.
We must will our will to survive!

Evelyn Lorin Monette

MY LOVE AND THE OLD COAL MINE. . .

To day they took my love from me,
Now his loving face no more I'll see,
They put him the ground so cold,
It was the old coal mine that claimed his soul.
He sold our land and home so fine,
Just to come and work this old coal mine.
Down in that dark, dark, hole he went,
Until his health was almost spent.
He went through hell and misery,

Till it almost cost his love
for me.
And he blamed himself for that
awful curse,
Then his luck went from bad to
worse.
He cursed the day he found that
mine,
Thats why he turned to beer
and wine.
Even that didn't ease his mind,
So he turned to dope, just
any kind.
He spent his days down in that
hell,
And his nights were hell as well.
For in his dreams he'd see that
mine,
And all the coal cars in a line.
He'd see the tracks as they
would heave and awell,
And watched as they twisted
down into the bowels of hell.
He'd see the opening as it
groaned and groaned,
And in his sleep I'd hear him
moan.
His friends all come to help
him,
They thought it would be fun.
Oh how they found out they
were wrong,
When they all died one, by one.
In his dreams he felt he wasn't
alone,
And he heard his friends, cry,
and moan. . .
And as they turned towards him
there faces were his own,
And the blood they sweat,
would redden the stones.
And all the coal was red, like
fire,
And his throat would burn, as
he gasped for air.
And all he could see was old
coal dust,
And awake with eyes swollen
and red as rust. . .
A shot of booze to steady his
shakes,
I'd beg him (darling for the
children's sake).
But he'd only curse us and call
us names,
And then that day would be the
same.
On and on until the end of time,
As long as there's coal, and beer,
and wine.
Whiskey, and dope and men so
blind,
We will have this curse of the
old coal mine. . .

Jimmye C. Vaughn

QUESTIONS & ANSWERS

What is a boy and what is a girl?
The entire future of this
world.
What is a mother and what is a
father?
They are responsible for the
son and the daughter.
What is a sister and what is
a brother?
Sometimes a substitute for
father and mother.
What is an eagle and what is a
dove?
They are the birds that fly
above.
What is the sky and what is
the ocean?
Things to explore and set our
world in motion.
What is an encyclopedia and
what is a dictionary?
Books to show how things can
vary.
What is a country and what is a
nation?
Reasons to explain a
government's creation.
What is engineering and why
must we build?
To grow with the changing
world in which we live.
What is the moon and what is
the sun?
The light by which nature's
work is done.
What is love and what is pain?
It's something we experience
again and again.
Why are some people nice and
others mean?
People are the result of what
they've lived and seen.
What is right and what is
wrong?
The difference is the weak
and the strong.
What is religion and why must
we pray?
It helps us make it day-by-day.
What are clothes and what can
they do?
Merely cover the body—old or
new.
What is an argument and what
is a war?
Reasons people give to fight
for.
Why must some lose and others
win?
Nature often helps the drive
within.
What is prejudice and why so
many races?
Because people come from
diverse places.
What is a school and why must
we learn?
To prepare for the living that
we must earn.
What are teachers and why do
they care?
They know that there is much
to share.
They know that you are the
rain and the sun.
They know, for you, a parent's
work is never done.
They know you are love,
happiness and cheer.
They know that you are so, so,
so, very dear.
They know each of you is so
unique.
They know that's part of life's
mystique.
And each summer your teachers
will pray
That their paths again will
cross yours some day.

Melanie Carla Ferg

FIRST LOVE

I lie awake at night,
tormented by old memories.
Memories of a former love.
I've fought for his love for a
year and a half,
and won.
Can I win him back?
Again to regain his love and
pride,
except this time in silence.
I was blinded by love,
lost in a world of compassion,
and security.
I was told it wasn't easy.
Did I expect too much?
Did I give too little, or too
much?
Why? Why did it end when it
felt so right.
I showed concern and love
for my dearest darling.
I was scorned and forsaken
What did he want?
I gave my heart to a man who
loved me well.
Was it too much for him?
Was he ready?
Is that why it ended so?
My feelings have not changed.
They are still as strong as ever.
If anything,
I have learned to appreciate him
more.
I long to be held
in his warm and passionate arms
that once held my delicate body.
He has made me strong.
Now that he is gone,
will that strength crumble?
I long to be loved again.
Is it possible?
By the same man?
Are our hearts completely
empty of each other's love,
or suffocated by distractions
and lies?
Were our feelings forged or
genuine?
Does he know the agony that
fills my heart?
How can he know,
unless,
he too feels the same.
How can he allow the girl
he said he loved so dearly
bear the pain that she feels?
He tries so hard convincing me
it's over,
But why
do I feel his love for me
lurking still in the deep and
hidden caverns
of his heart?

Chuck Marsh

IN A SENSE

The five cities of stimuli
encompass a sea,
surrounding an island of
thought.
Where conclusions flower on a
learning vine.

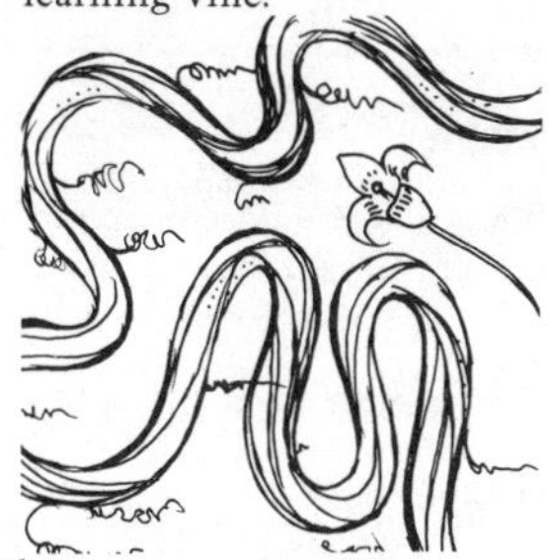

Where even our teachers are
taught.
In each an absorber of
information,
A communicative line.
Together composing a
masterpiece,
watching fruit of our new
knowledge shine.

Roberta J. Adair

THE LIFE OF THE RIVER

Dancing little streamlet,
running down the hill,
Making pleasant music over
rock and rill,
Sparkling in the sunshine,
singing in the night,
Showing to the stars their pretty
silver light.
Twisting 'round the boulders,
snaking through the grass,
Laughing, sighing, moaning, in
the deep crevasse.
Ever restless, onward hurrying
along,
Coming with a rainbow, leaving
with a song.
Till you meet your brother on
the plain below,
Side by side you journey, on
and on you go.
Pretty little brooklet, summer's
coming on,
With its carefree hours, Spring
is almost gone.
You are growing, growing daily,
and more strong,
And your tinkling whisper loses
childhood's song.
Now you talk of duty; you
have work to do.
Do it with your might then; do
it straight and true.
Wash the miner's sluice box;
turn the miller's wheel,
Wrest away the gold rocks;
grind the golden meal.
Yet, skip down the valleys,
circuit 'round the hills,
Fill the woods with music,
hear the birds' sweet trills.
Do not waste a minute,
youth is precious still.
Never let thy song be robbed
by heavy mill.
Bear the weary burden; keep
the heart-song light,
And you will spread gladness
by contented sight.
Oh, thou happy river, still
and broad and calm,
Bringing needed water like a
healing balm,
Seeking for the lowest, working
in thy place,
Whether dam or rockfall, with
a humble grace.
Happy with thy life-work,
feeding thirsty lands,
Patiently a-plodding over time's
bright sands.
Never fearing boulders, kind,
yet firm and bold,
Working toward the harvest
of the fields of gold.
Busy, ever busy, idle moments
none,
Always pressing onward,
work yet to be done,
You have miles to cover,
e'er you reach the deep.
Patience, pleasing river,
work, and watch, and reap.
Ah, the sound and sunshine!
mighty river now,
Whitened foam and wavelets
on thy lofty brow.
Creeping past the wheatfield,
moaning by the town,

Through the sunny Southland,
ever going down.
Sliding through the woodland,
whisp'ring 'round the lee,
On and on forever, going to the sea.
Dear old, tired river, you
have come so far,
Weary were the miles under
many a star,
Courage, patient river!
journey's almost done,
And the sea will find you
with the setting sun.
Strong, warm arms about you,
hear the sea's "Well done!"
Ever lower going, you have
found your home!
Ah, our friend, the river,
lessons learned have we,
To be ever seeking lower
plains, with thee.

Lois J. Martucci
MY DARLING GINA MARIA
Happy Birthday to you, my love;
I'll bet today you're happy as a
dove!
This little poem of mine has a
message for you;
I hope you'll never forget it,
whatever you may do.
Turning "THIRTEEN" will bring
you a "different life";
You are maturing, Honey; enjoy
it with a "new light."
Your future teen-age years will
be a long stride
Towards the years of adulthood
you will abide.
Physical and mental changes for
you there will be;
Of everyone this is expected;
you will have lots of
"company."
I have, you will, and *everyone*
faces this "changing age";
"Keep your 'Cool', "behave, and
enjoy it, so that when you
turn this "page"
Of your life you will always
remember it with regrets of
none,
Knowing your teen-age years
will be only "One."
Remember, Darling, it is hard
for "Mom" sometimes, too,
To realize how fast you are
growing; so please understand
me, in things that you do.
We will have our disagreements
and always "make-up";
But please, let's try to
understand each other better
in our "huffs."
Understand me as a Mother
always there to guide you;
I will listen and help you and
be there when you need me,
too!
Soon your baby dolls will be
"put away,"
And when the boys ask you out,
you will say, "OK!"
You will sometimes tantrum to
me, because I am "too mean,"
But remember, "Mom" will
always be there for you to
lean.
I will forever be your "Best
Friend"—to laugh with you,
and cry, too;
That's what Mothers are all
about, how well I know;
I do love you. . . . .

Ruth C. Davidson
LISTENING TO THE C.B. NEWS WHEN I AWAKE
When I wake in the morning
rich rivulets of sun descend
screened through flowered
window drapes.
Birds sing.
The trees cast shadows on the
window as they bend in a
ring.
You can almost hear the
branches hit the ground.
Suddenly, the sound of static
breaks the silence of the new
moring.
Break Break
Anybody home? Wake up sleepy
head.
Is coffee on? I'm three notches
away.
Be there in a sec.
Over and—SCREECH—BANG—
CRASH! Out for eternity.
The sound of sirens on the C.B.
is heard for miles around.
Break Break
I awake. Birds sing. Tears fall.
The sun shines through
flowered drapes.
Trees cast shadows on the
window.
The sound of the C.B. breaks
the silence of the new
morning.
Tears fall. Birds sing.

Frederic de Aboitiz
EXPIATION IN REINCARNATION
Oh, it is not so much that I
forget something,
as if in Morpheus'* stupor.
My brain, organ of the Mind,
will not let me
. . .many pains and sorrow. . .
forget.
But it is just that I remember
everything,
like all his scabs the leper.
Old sins from previous lives
cause my guilt to be
in this World with profound
regret.
The fires of burning passions
within the breast
of the lusty heart are anguish!
With the "Water of Life," the
flaming coals in my chest
I hope to extinguish!
At last there are no longer any
ifs, ands or buts about my
destiny.
My fate? Condemned to bouts of
depression,
and damned with fits of
despondency.
After so much study in years
many,
and deep thought in quiet
self-scrutiny:
My soul I must save with
suppression
of wordly evils in ascendancy.
What heroic act, last and final,
catapults one into
Immortality?
One's life to advance "Eternal
Humanity's" highest cause:
Spirituality!
**In Greek mythology, Morpheus was the God of dreams, and son of Hypnos, the God of sleep (Ovid, Met. 11, 183-206).*

Richard Ferrara
OPEN LETTER TO A DEAR FRIEND
If we must say goodbye,
And the touch of our hands can
no longer be a part of our
lives,
At least, I live with the memory
of you.
I'll fill my world with what
we shared, and what we
learned,
And marry, forever, the thought
of you.
To my old friends, and new
I share a small part of the touch
of you.
Seek out your love and place
them in the center of your
world.
Let all thoughts and deeds
revolve around them. As you
struggle
through the monotony and
pressures of daily routine,
remember in
whose arms you have found
comfort and shelter.
Distractions, variety, and
superficial pleasures abound,
But, a precious gem can not
warm you
And outward beauty fades
But, a love afire within
Glows ever warmer with age.
Do not let the past hurt and
foolishness of others affect
the one
you meet today.
Love is Giving. And it is better
to give all, and be hurt again.
Than to hold back, and suffer
the loss of the one, that could
have been.
Talk to one another. It is the
seed of trust.
And, like all flowers, takes time
to bloom. To patient, but, do
not restrain. Better to speak a
negative word now, than allow
a
resentment to grow.
Ask for help, but, don't neglect
to offer yours.
Offer yours, but, don't be
too proud to ask for theirs.
Forgive. It is love's foundation.
There is a power in
understanding. It draws its
strength from
compassion.
A greater man once turned the
other cheek.
A greater man once offered the
first stone to be thrown.
If one falls short of your dreams
Remember, it is not a dream
you're turning away.
A couple is made of two. Two
individuals, with separate
wants,
needs, goals, and desires. They
have a life to lead. A life as
precious, and as free to choose,
as we would have our own.
Respect that right.
Commitments are made by
choice, bound by conscience,
not by threats.
You are free to choose. And, in
that choice, if you wish
another to
share your side, it will be
because, that is what you
really want
to do.
Security is a matter of faith.
Believe in one another.
It is a couple's Golden Rule.
Remember, there is no
permanence in the word
farewell. A true love
will let go. But, a true love will
never die.
Astas que nos encontramos otra
ves (until we meet again).
Bendicion
(God Bless you and keep you
safe)

Ralph J. Tislaretz
THE SILENT WAR
It is the young who wage war
for the aged in power
It is the young who bleed
on the battlefield of war
It is the young who heed
mindless,
powerless, orders in a war
It is the young whose belly
a war moves on
It is the young who have
nothing
yet give the most in war
It is the young who suffer
greatest
with nightmares a lifetime
live
It is the young who turn to
flags,
to white crosses, inwards
It is the young to be honored.
My country tis of thee
Sweet land of liberty
For thee I sing
We are there
We see the ruin
We see the massacres
We see the tracers in the night
We see the howitzers
fire smoke steam and rust
We see companions come, go
quick, slow
We see greed, famine, fortune
giving, misgiving, wealth,
poverty
disease, death, sleeplessness,
hate, love, compassion,
togetherness
bitterness, lonliness,
on both sides.
We see this as an ever
endlessness.
We live war.
We live this ultimate madness.
War.

I see a farmer.
I see family, water buffalo
iron plow, young green rice
shoots
all in the mud, the irrigation
the harvest
The smiles around the family
circle
thru the doorless thatch mud
dwelling.
Happy they appear
thru the winter monsoon
workless.
I hear us say, primitives.

O say can you see
by the dawn's early light
This morn I awoke
My breath so loud yet
no words I spoke
As breaks forth through
the night a silent violet light.
The war is silent.
I, the day, in silence sunrise.

Alone in the war machine
I stood, silent, save
the thunder the thrill of
my blood asurge in veins
No thought to comprehend
Merely the night's end
wherein I with the sun
Into daylight transcend
Then I thought, brushed
aside a tear, swallowed hard
O say can you see
by this dawn's early light
A moment of peace.
I return.
I am a silent hero
of the silent war
With medals and ribbons
cross my breast
With scars and wounds
to prove I did my best.

My country, the people torn,
myself when it comes to war
I wish I were never born, yet
when war was as real as me
I took arms I took red cross
with no intent to glory gain
But vain, a life to save
instead to see it lost.
There were those that were pro
there were those that were
con
There were those who
did not know or did not care.

I thought it wise for me to
let all this be
To make it a piece of my
destiny
to do to give to be where
The war was, even tho this is
where
I would really rather not be.
O war is hell, war is bloody,
war is death that men breed.
War is every atrocity and more,
for human minds and spirits
Go to war and there they do,
they exceed, the foulest deeds.
O war, humankind's ultimate
horror.

I am a silent hero
of the silent war
I am a silent hero
silent no more.
My country, are you
my enemy?
I was where I did not want to be
doing what I or no one I
believe
should have to do Now.
It is silence everywhere I turn,
friend, stranger, country, all
Seems to matter not.
They who were pro are silent
They who were con are silent
They who did not know are
silent
They who did not care are
silent.
I am a silent hero
Of the silent war
With medals and ribbons
cross my breast
With scars and wounds
to prove I did my best.
It is a decade and three for me
and see it hear it still,
I watch the silence sweep
a crowded room with two
words,
Viet Nam.
I am a silent hero
of the silent war
With medals and ribbons
cross my breast
With scars and wounds
to prove I did my best.
If ever I could dream a dream
come true,
This I would envision.
That we may see the human
being climb
above itself—it is long
overdue, I
cannot see, save only in
ideals, that
we as a conscious people
have raised
our barbaric nature above that
of the
ancient Greeks—then rid this
world,
In the least, of violence and
war.
In spite of humankind, in peace,
freedom, and love, I believe.
Comes now the time to say
Farewell
farewell forgotten silent
companions.
Viet Nam, The Silent War
is history.
We, the living aging pages,
are testimony
for some, a living anguish
Others,
the nightmares that only time
can temper, time diminish.
Farewell warriors
may goodness and peace of
mind
be your companions.
Farewell
I am off to other work.
Another War. The Vanishing
Wilderness.
With these parting words.
Welcome home warriors
Welcome home known friends
Welcome home unknown
friends
Welcome home O homed ones
Welcome home O homeless
ones
Welcome home confused ones
Welcome home unconfused
ones
Welcome home anguished ones
Welcome home angry ones
Welcome home O silent dead
Welcome home O silent living
Welcome home citizen
Welcome Home!

Samuel A. Torres

THE KING JAMES VERSION

2 Chronicles

King Ahab, of Israel, invites
King Jehoshaphat, of Judah, to a
banquet, where the food
abundantly is set,
asking to join him in a war
against his neighbor, the king
of Syria, while huddling together
as they met.
King Jehoshaphat, of Judah,
already has many possessions
but he intently listens with
some interest,
he, himself, reigns over his
kingdom, he alone decides for
his people, whatever for them, is
best.
And the two kings in endless
numbers on the open plain in
full battle array,
their steeds hastening like
hounds on swift paws hurrying
to corner the prey.
Arrows overhead darken the
sky as on horseback they dash,
as a reluctant army the
challenge meets as armour and
steel loudly clash.
As the fierce battle settles
to the slaughtering cries of
death,
those prostrate mouning for
help reach up, some in kneeling
groaning distress.
In this deadly combat King
Jehoshaphat saw he had nothing
to avail
not as much as a lasting
foothold no ground to prevail.
His chariot he commands
from this place where blood is
to drain
upon this ground the hoot is
to trod the spill of the stain.
And, a certain eager man,
his bow an arrow strung,
aiming at a venture, at the
hostile host at the king among,
and, hastily, with but a
moment by which to spare,
the young man let loose the
arrow his own life dare;
at the chariot, slowing to
move with hardly a road to
pave,
where King Ahab, between the
two armies warring, he dare to
brave.
King Ahab, striking this way
and that his sword causing the
clatter,
as bobbing and weaving, the
helmets on soldiers apart come
to shatter.
He hesitates, his weary hand
raised as if in a private salute,
his gaze upon the masses, on
the stubbornness of this brute.
Now, the arrow in flight
strikes Ahab, his hissing teeth
grid back the shriek,
his whole body shaking, from
the toe to the upright height
of his peak.
"Charioteer, carry me, I
beseech thee, away from this
host,
of my own rivaling sword
I'm no longer to boost,
I'm wounded, I can no longer
subdue, the assaults upon us,
the soldiers incline to persue"
Away from the struggle he is
driven his chariot to idle aside,
on the platform the wound
he's to travail where bleeding he
stands to abide.
Thus, wearily, King Ahab with
tight lip gags with ooze,
among the armies warring, to
die this way, this valiant way,
to choose.

Barbara Lukes

EVE RE—ANOINTED

Sinful Woman.
Tarnished Angel.
You are not pinned
to the pretentious pedestal
to have the coiled snake
bite your tongue everytime you
speak.

See—you have wings
for your multiple identities.
You shall be your own pontiff.
Fly—lest your wings become
too heavy with fear.

Marleen Derge

OCTOBER

October weaves its magic spell,
The days with wonders fill;
Autumn in its glory,
Will give your heart a trill.
Leaves of red and gold,
Go dancing from the trees;
Tossed and whirled about,
By a laughing breeze.
The grass has lost its emerald
green,
And the flowers are no more;
Soon the icy hand of winter,
Will come knocking at the door.
So be content to walk along,
Beneath a clear blue sky;
And marvel at the view,
As you watch the wild goose fly.

Beverly Medlock

BEFORE YOU

Before you, I saw the greatest
love deep in a father's adoring
eyes.
Now you have come, and the
things I see
Are as great as the vastness
of blue skies.
Before you, I found security and
warmth whenever mother
held me to her breast.
Now you have come, and my
longing is to lay my head
down upon your chest.
Before you, the most wondrous
of sights were the beautiful
stars so far away.
Now you have come, and if I'm
to be blind, your smile, on
my memory will forever stay.
Before you, the most enveloping
caress came from the warm
and shining sun.
Now you have come, as I melt
in your arms, I feel our souls

surge as we become one.
Before you, I had only been
kissed by winds of Heaven
and gentleness of rain.
Now you have come, and there
is surely no joy in
meaningless kisses like theirs
again.
Before you, all these things I've
treasured just as much as a
sweet spring breeze.
Now you have come, and I have
been blessed with just one
treasure much greater than
these.

Shirley M. Ericksen

THE GYPSY SORCERESS

I was a young and handsome
guy, who used his charms to
tame
the innocence from the maidens
in a town called, Lilymane
My wife, her name was Mary,
had grown so dull and fat
and given me in six years, four
hateful squallin' brats,
She nagged me to stop
wandering while busy with
her broom
"I'd rather be a dog,!" I yelled,
a howling at the moon.
One evening I grew restless to
slip away again,
Climbed into my old truck and
drove off down the lane
a swearin' at my Mary, as I
drove to Lilymane.
Ahead I saw the glimmer of the
beckoning lights of town
and suddenly there before me
walked a maiden and her
hound.
"Hello" says I, "where do those
feet, lead a maid like you?"
She lifted up her dusky arms,
tears on her cheeks like dew.
"Let me help if you're in need,"
I said, at her distress
"Tis' nothing Sir, I've lost my
love, to that I do confess
to buying these, when he said,
'No'. . .She lifted up her dress.
Ah! Such legs I'd never seen,
adorned with silver hose
and at the top of each one, was
clipped a blood red rose.
"Oh Sir, you couldn't
understand, but will you let
me ride?"
Such luck, I thought, and
quickly, helped her to my
side.
"Please Sir," she whispered in my
ear, "ol' Brown's too old
to run, and usually stays at
home, unless there is some
sun,"
So Brown, the hound, was lifted
up and seated by the door
The scent of jasmine filled the
truck, the top down to the
floor.
My heart begin it's beating and I
could hardly breathe,
"Oh kind and handsome
stranger, won't you love me?
Then I'll
leave." I caressed her lovely
body and took her lips with
ease
and received in turn such joy,
ah! No human could believe.
But something overcame me,
and I watched my changing
form,
My God! What had she done to
me, with lips so sweet and
warm?
Then she was up behind that
wheel, and I had joined ol'
Brown
She drove to Lilymane with us,
to a tavern in the town.
The bar keep looked at us and
said, "I must enforce the law"
I tried to warn him of his fate,
and nudged him with my paw.
She smiled and how he softened
up, Lord! How she took that
man.
While Brown and I both sat and
watched, she turned him to a
tan.
If it hadn't been so tragic, how
funny it would be, for she
drove to town with two dogs
and drove away with three.
The Gypsy Queen is dancing,
Oh! Such a wondrous sight,
her
silver stockings flashing,
twirling in the flickering light.
Her people gather round her,
and I listen to them sing,
I'm a gift presented just to
please her Gypsy King.
What I'd give to see my little
ones, and repent for all I've
done, the King accepts her
kisses and his Gypsy Queen
has won.
Now he is laughing with her,
while I walk on quivering legs
to earn a few more crumbs to
eat or water from the kegs.
I'm learning to be grateful
for the food she throws my
way
and her many words of comfort,
yes, I often hear her say,
"Come now my love, eat your
fill and rest upon my bed."
Her hands caress my body as
the jasmine fills my head, and
I think of dear sweet Mary, and
those days when we were wed.
At night around the campfires, I
hear the violins cry
And the Gypsy Queen is
laughing, as I grieve beneath
the sky,
"I'd rather be a dog," I'd said,
how I wish that I could die.

Bev Fox Roberson

REMAINS OF LOVE

I spent the night
staring at the dead roses
that you brought last week;
they're still in the vase
beside my bed.
I cleaned the floors,
shampooed my hair,
searched for something sad,
watched TV.
Morning came,
and I'm still alone
with dried-up roses
that you brought.

Millie Redinger

A NIGHT FOR ME!

A night for Me!
A night for Me!
'tis an adventure. . .
For treasures hidden deep within
my soul
to come to life; and on this
rapture
Think o'er my long forgotten
goals!. . .

Christine Clayton

TO BE BALD ISN'T SO BAD

There once was a man, who had
no hair,
This to him was a frightful care!
Every morning, into the mirror
he'd peek,
Trying his best, some hair to
seek!
But each day, when into the
mirror he peered,
He saw no hair, as he had
feared!
He'd sit and sigh, he'd cry
blue tears,
Put his hands on his head, and
pull his ears!
Then one day an ad, he did
chance to see,
To grow some hair, was its
guarantee!

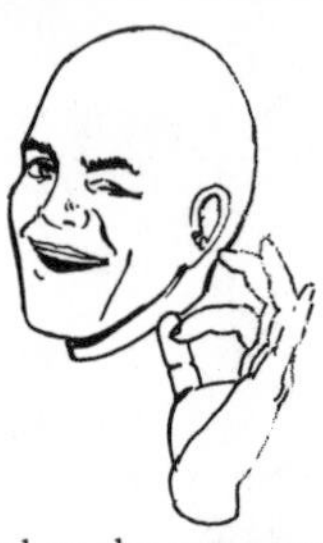

He raced to the store, and
three bottles he bought,
Soon he would have the hair
that he sought!
Home he did go, to sprinkle
some on,
Hair he should see, in the first
rays of dawn!
He leaped into bed, turning out
the lights,
His spirits soared, to hairful
heights!
With the morning's first light,
our man did awake,
He dashed for the mirror, a peek
for to take!
Would his hair be, brown or
black?
Would it be thin, or have no
lack?
Perhaps it would be red, with a
fiery glow,
Whatever the color, he just had
to know!
The man did reach the mirror at
last,
He grabbed the sink, and held
on fast!
There, reflected before, his
startled eyes,
Were the oceans of hair, that he
did prize!
But our poor man let out, a
fearful screech,
And for his head, his hands did
reach!
There before him, was the
thickest hair, he'd ever seen,
His only problem was, it was a
bright emerald green!
Our man did howl, for there
could be nothing much worse,
Than that thick emerald hair, it
made our man curse!
He cursed the bottles, of tonic
so mean,
For who wanted hair, if it had to
be green!
Oh, he'd rather be bald as a
billiard, than a pool table top,
And forever be stuck, with that
emerald green mop!
He drew all the shades, and
turned out the light,
But his hair was fluorescent, oh
what a sight!
Our man then did repent, the
foolish pride he'd had.
He knew now, to be bald, wasn't
so bad!
Up he did jump, and raced for
the sink,
Perhaps he could wash it, off
in a wink!
He scrubbed and scrubbed, but
to no avail,
For all his washing him did fail!
Our man laid down and cried,
big blue tears,
They ran through his hair, and
dripped in his ears!
For our poor man was sad, and
quite discontent,
To have emerald green hair, he
just wasn't meant!
Suddenly the answer, popped
into his head,
With a joyful cry, he leaped
off the bed!
Into the bathroom, he dashed
with due speed,
He grabbed his razor, to fill
his need!
Our man, his head did shave,
quick as a flash,
Then back to his mirror, he
madly did dash!
A pink bald head, his gaze did
meet,
Great his joy, at hair's defeat!
A smile replaced, our man's look
sad,
Oh, he was happy, no hair he
had!
The emerald green hair, he'd
shaved from his head,
He gathered and hung, in a
frame by his bed!
He hung it a reminder, of pride's
swift crash,
For our man, never again, would
be so rash!
So now when our man, in the
mirror does peek,
He finds the bald head,
which he does seek!
So we'll leave our man bald,
and quite content,
For bright, emerald green hair,
he never was meant!

Melissa K. Ward

A DREAM

There was a dream
of mine in which you were a
part of.
And, even if there's miles
between us,
every night when I turn out
the light
my dream becomes vivid and
you are there.

Lorina Tumblin

YEAR BY YEAR

Happiness I find to meet my
toils hear trusting in my Fathers
wise wisdom I have no cause for

doubts he whose heart Is Good beyond all endurance gives to each what he thinks best the Lord Himself is near me giving me his care for each year.

Lorina Tumblin
ONE TRIAL
To conquer one dream to earn one chain to unravel one puzzle to earn one week of happiness to overcome cares one glimpse of the Sun to overcome tears.

Otto M. Oshiro
THE GRACE OF THE WINDS UPON A FAIR MAIDEN
May one day you find all the peace deep inside
From your touch to your smile for you to share,
May the flight of birds galore
Be a sign of things in store for you—
For you are a lady, a woman so true,
For you are a fair maiden so gentle to do,
So let the breeze whisper and take you along
To reveal you a secret
That'll soon be known.
May one day you see all the life meant to be
From sunrise to sunset day after day,
May the twinkle in your eye
See the beauty all beside of you—
For you are so worthy, a promise is near,
For you there's a hope that's becoming and clear,
Like waves that wash the shores, be it ever pure
With a gift that's so rare
Lover's find for sure.
Will the pains keep hold of you
Will you let the darkness abide,
Somewhere up there above of you
Jesus holds the truth that sinners deny,
Are we able the both of us and others alike
To journey through our travels
To sail on blindly without a guiding light;
So won't you hold on, hold on to Jesus, won't you hold on, hold on, hold on with all your might.
May one day you know all the love that's aglow
From the seas to the shores and where you are,
May your heart be filled with joy
And those sorrows unemployed with you—
With you there's a whisper, a cry in the night,

With you there's a call to come and see the light,
So let it be forever, and let it be shown
Your eyes have seen the glory
And Heaven's your home.

Tim DiVito
YOUR EYES
Your crystal eyes
Enable me to see myself
Because within you
Is a part of me
Not only in the physical sense
But also in an emotional one
Visions of joy and sorrow
Allow me to choose my tomorrows
Because without both
I am but a simple being
I have felt great joy in my life
Also I encountered tremendous sorrow
Your eyes, so alive with life,
Give me the security I need,
To enter a delicate situation,
Then depart with my dignity
You let my soul be at peace
You let my heart know love has a chance
All I know is that your eyes,
Guide me on the path of self suffiency
With you I do not shudder at the thought
Of an untimely death
I do not fear to live each day
As it passes my way
Moments used to linger on
In my life unnoticed
Now I grasp and live each moment
To the fullest that is possible
Your eyes reflect my soul
Stairway to the heavens are your eyes
(Dedicated to Rhonda)

Ann L. Korosac
THE SEA
The sea is the magic of a million stars
Hiding fairy caves filled with golden bars;
And tainted with the blood of countless wars,
Its jeweled waters cover mountains, crests and knolls,
Carefully guarding unhallowed souls,
As on and on it rolls and rolls,
As on and on it rolls.
The sea is a woman, clever and mean;
And 'though handsomely dressed in a silken sheen,
It is really a garbage pail slimy and green.
The sea is a woman in a glistening dress,
Outlining her lips and her breasts,
Luring men on into nothingness,
On and on into nothingness.
It shimmers and glimmers and winks its eyes.
With teasing tongues it courts the dark skies.
While over and over it tries and tries,
To heave its belly up from its bed,
The better to belch up its stinking dead
With a cruel sound all sailors dread,
A sound all sailors dread.
A sound of crashing; a sound of bashing;
Of clashing and mashing, of slashing and gnashing.
It is death and destruction, both north and south;
A mad-dog frothing at the mouth;
A ghost-ship bursting with plundered stores;
Long fingers clutching at heathered moors.
As if to escape from prison shores.
Then, it settles down into a steady din,
And as if more than sure it can never win
Seems content to be captive of earth and men.
But beneath its disguise of rippling shoals,
Fathoms deep, is jealously holds
The mystery key to its secret scrolls.
As on and on it rolls, as on and on it rolls.

Tillie A. Bednar
THE FARMERS LIFE
The farmer is no white collar.
He wears blue jeans and work shoes.
A farmer's work is never done, long hours.
There's no time clock to go by or forty hour week.
Working hours are long, twelve hours or longer.
As Spring time comes, you see all kinds of tractors in the fields.
As God said, "Sow your seeds to multiply," and blessed it
With a magic touch, as the farmer plowed the ground.
It takes Mother Nature to make the crops, and hard work.
Ask for rain, then wait for the promise of rain and good weather.
After long hours of work and time, the crops are made.
Always have to say a prayer so no floods or storms come
Before harvest time.
Oh, when the harvest is over!
Oh, Middle Man gets over half
Without hard work; just pencil work and no worry.
The farmer is left again in debt. For next year, borrow again.
Sometimes no money to clothe themselves.
The farmer is the back bone of every one.
The farmer has to stick with it through thick and thin.
Life is hard. Tasks are never easy as a farmer.
It takes strength, skill, knowing how to be a farmer.
The things unseen.
And when I cross the fields,
I see beautiful crops and
Joy in my heart.
I bargained for a farmer's life, and life would pay.

Ann O'Sullivan Counts
THE AWAKENING
Aware of being awake;
No sudden shock or dream?
Rain so steady, quiet—
Such a contradiction to my thoughts of you,
the vacancy of my bed,
scenes of years of clinging desperately
to a moribund slipping skin from a grinning skeleton,
as I scratched the ground above your grave
in frantic hope that lies below the ground,
the smile I've sold my soul to win and have and hold.
Cheap, how cheap, I sold out
to all the damning illusions,
while buying time to blame and whine and ache.
And Time, oh yes, to play and replay
the record of your cold, unyielding hand inside my own,
and intertwine my fingers moulding it to melt and come to life.
Longing to rip away the wary mask of your indifference,
I embraced you each day in awful emptiness.
Ah! I'd chosen to forget, and called it mystery of love,
wherein I struggle.
The smile creeps into everbroadening lines across my cheeks
until I, face to face, with my own trickery meet
Me! Or is it you?
I've see you
briefly outside the shadow of myself.
What a pity I have never forgiven you
for being the inside-out of me.
The sun lightens the sky, as I,
the death watch, spit upon the grave in righteous indignation
My ego puffed with the warm breath that I could not,
to save your soul, of course,
breathe into you
and make you live, reach out, touch me.
My god, touch me!

Paula Cazenave
THAT I MIGHT KNOW YOU
ONE
O Tender Victory
Release your Presence
and your fragrance
that I may

love you
and feel you
and smell you
and touch you
and experience
Your
depths
in
my
innermost parts.
O Tender Lover—
Release your wholeness
into my *Being*
that I may
Be
in Eternal Union
and transcend all
but you and yours
in intimate fellowship.
O Tender Victory
Be Mine!
(John 17:3)
You have made me whole. .
now my heart sings "free!"
to laugh
to love
to live
to BE!
You have burned the dross
of lifes heavy toll. .
and brought back music
into my soul.
No vise can touch—
for loves deep fire
transmutes,
unfolds,
refuels
my soul.
For I have learned to love
by loving
as I feel your heart
touch mine.
"Flesh of my flesh"
CREATION ANEW!
united—entire
completed in YOU.
". . .that they may be one
in us. . ." *(John 17:21)*

Jeanne Rule
NAM
Dawn rises slowly,
stretching through the
mist shrouded hills.
Light slips around
the trees, touching
leaf edges with gold.
Across the river
smoke lifts from
a smoldering village.
The smell of fear is everywhere.
People lie where
they fell. Crumpled
heaps. Sprawled things.
No peaceful deaths
these. Mouths scream
in silent pain.
The village anniliated
because they were Cong?
Because they were not?
The smell of death is
everywhere.
Soldiers of both sides
move quietly through
the jungle
Longing at the end
of day to see
one more sunset,
Laughing with relief
when the close shot
kills a friend.
The smell of blood is
everywhere.
Prisoners of each side
watch in anguish
as the game proceeds.
Terror feeding terror
as random death
haphazardly depletes
The young and best.
Children—walking bombs—
Brother killing brother.
The smell of war is everywhere.
The cultures interweave,
each learning worst
traits of the other.
Evil lays its snares
at every corner of
the town
And angels venturing near
scorch lungs as
well as wings.
The smell of hate is everywhere.
Some return with
scars for all
to see
And some are
torn to pieces
inwardly.
Reality remains the war.
Mind barriers keep
them distant, tightly wound.
The smell of pain is everywhere.
Old warriors sing their
deeds and celebrate the
wanton death of friends.
Women mourn their loss
or nurse the spirit-killed
for life.
Despair sits daily in their eyes
and Lucifer stands
laughing in the wings.
The smell of Hell is everywhere.
Friends touch, lose
track, and find
themselves again.
Love reaches out
as hot as
village flames
To rescue one,
make strong another
and comfort one in pain.
The signs of hope are here and
there.

Maureen Lynn Koska
MY LOVE, SO TOTALLY WHOLE
The sweetest days
I ever had
were the ones
I spent
with you
You could never
take them
away from me
no matter
what you do
Where ever you are
What ever your goal
memories of you
fill my heart
my mind
and my soul

Verna Lea Jeffries
THUNDER CLOUDS ARISING
When a love goes wrong
Who is to blame
You say it's my fault
But I tell you the same
It is said they all have a silver
lining
We've gone from the bright sun
shining
Over that final horizon
Now we feel the thunder clouds
arising
What has happened to the bond
Of love and trust we used to
share
You alone without me, me
without you
This blank stare to tell the
world, I don't care
Is it really all that surprising
From the perfect love we had to
share
Falling into the depths of
despair
That we feel the thunder clouds
arising.

Theresa M. Leicht
WADSWORTH LONGFELLOW
Wadsworth Longfellow was
quite an odd fellow,
Who was a tinker, tailor,
merchant, and thief.
One day he met a well-to-do
lady;
After a few dinner dates,
He proposed marriage.
He got himself a preacher,
Who was a drunk from skidrow.
His well-to-do lady,
Agreed to get married in the
middle of skidrow,
'Cause she knew
Wadsworth Longfellow was
quite an odd fellow.
She thought he'd get rich,
But Wadsworth Longfellow,
Had a better idea than she;
And quicker than quicksand,
She became a corpse,
Because Wadsworth Longfellow
Had the same idea as she.
One day he got to drinkin';
He ended up in skidrow;
There he fell asleep.
He got to talkin'
And told everything he did.
A drunk who needed a drink
Heard him
Cleaned himself up,
And went to the town constable,
Who gave him a free bottle of
wine
For telling all he had learned
About Wadsworth Longfellow.
When they found Wadsworth
Longfellow,
He was trying to strike it rich
again;
But they gave him the chair,
And that was the last they
heard
Of Wadsworth Longfellow.

Carole Abbott
SPECIAL LOVE
Thoughts and tender moments
shared by two—
We search our hearts
where few have dared
Feelings no one ever touched
before
Feelings no one ever asked
before
I turn to see who's holding me
and there you are.
Oh Special Love
it's so unique
lifes true treasures come and
stay
when people share a special
way.

Mike Carpenter
MY NEWFOUND LOVE
You came into my life
at its darkest hour,
before me stood
a woman of my soul.
So long have I been
in a world of darkness,
a world of fear,
longing to know
the meaning of love.
And in the years of the past
I have hurt and been hurt,
all for the love
of a woman.
I have turned cold
for I was young
and bound to have my ways,
for I was young
and that was yesterday.
But today I stand as a man alone
asking only to give
my love to someone who
cares,
someone who will share
my hopes and dreams
with me.
You looked at me with
understanding.
I saw beauty in your eyes,
for they showed love of
being real.
You gave me a need to go on,
for you reached into my soul
and eased my fears.
I held you in my arms and
I felt whole inside,
you kissed me and it was
as if you were my soul
set free from hell.
I have found a heaven
in your eyes and a garden
of eden full of love
in your heart.

Tanya Maria Liptak
SHADOWS, REFLECTIONS AND SUGARY CONFECTIONS
Once a day I drift away
To a special world beyond.
For an endless moment
daydreams keep reality at bay.
Reality is such a yawn.
I'm a prisoner of boredom,
lacking stimulation.
Each day unfolds without
explanation or reservation.
Come what may it will come
anyway.
Here comes the day.
While marketing, cleaning
and all the rest
My well practiced imagination
is at its best.
My imagination provides lifes'
otherwise sadly lacking zest.
When the daily grind is through
You'd think my daydreams

would be done too.
But, Oh, have I a surprise for
you.
Even at the cinema on the
screen its me.
Bigger than life (but only I can
see).
I, the heroine, romantic,
adventurous, encompassing
everything I want to be.
My special world is my lifes'
key.
You can thank science for
computerization.
But thank goodness for
imagination.
It not only provides mental
renumeration
But oft times emotional
salvation.

Jill Angela Smith

ALL MY LOVE AND GOODBYE

I guess I just had to do it, I
couldn't bear to make it
through,
I'm sorry if I've hurt you, I
didn't mean to make you blue.
I just wanted to get away, I
couldn't take it anymore.
I tried to tell you last night,
but you simply closed the
door.
I wish I could see you again,
one last time for old times
sake,
But I told myself when we
parted, that it would never
be the same.
We could never be close
enough, there was too much
hurt and too much shame.
Oh darling, I write these words
As my life quickly ticks away,
In a moment I'll be gone,
This is my last today.
My head is starting to spin, the
things around me, they're just
a blur,
I wish I hadn't done it now, to
think it was all because of
her.
I can see the sun's rays coming
up, starting the first new day
of the week.
The week I'll never be able to
see, Oh God, look what you've
done to me.
I thought I had enough of life,
what I thought, I know it's
wrong,
At least there was time to write
you this song.
Oh darling, I write these words
As my life quickly ticks away,
In a moment I'll be gone,
This is my last today.
Precious memories we've had,
tuck them inside,
And if you hurt over this, try
to make it hide. Because I'm
afraid
I just might see you, and the
pain. . .well, I'd regret what
I did.
Please be happy, I know you
will be. Happiness didn't come
my way;
And it's the key. The Key to life,
especially yours,
Mine must of been behind
locked doors. Well, my hands
are shaking,
I have to cry, this is it I guess,
all my love and goodbye.
Oh darling, I write these words
As my life quickly ticks away,
In a moment I'll be gone,
This is my last today.
I wish there would have been
a better way.

Louise LeStrange Kennedy

HIDDEN HEART

If you want me to know you
Just look in my eyes
Your eyes hold the secrets
that your mouth will hide
Your eyes are but windows
to your heart and your soul
When you look straight at me
Your story's been told
So if you don't want me
To know where you're at
Then don't look upon me
Just take a step back
If you want a friend
To have and to hold
Don't stop looking into
The windows of my soul.

Mae L. Lucieer

CHANGING TIMES

Today is gone, its now
tomorrow,
yesterday's moon, is now
the sun,
what was our hope, is now our
sorrow,
what was our problem, is now
our fun,
time is passing, the years fly
quickly,
times of laughter, times of
tears,
magic moments, while we have
them,
ours to cherish, throughout
the years,
Did we live or did we daydream?
Did we let the times slip by?
Did we reach out and did we
take some,
or did we grow old in our try?
Changing times and changing
seasons,
growing old and getting gray,
Whats here today, is gone
tomorrow,
make sure you take what's
yours today.

V. Joy Moore

SPRITZ AND SPRINKLE

Spritz and Sprinkle
Were glimmers of light
That came from the Christmas
tree.
(Or so I thought.)
But, I soon found out
That it simply could not be.
For they frolicked and sang
And leaped and glimmered
Apart from the lights of the
tree.
They were balls of light—
Then elflike forms,
And, squinting my eyes,
I could see
Those heavenly flashes
Of lightning grace
Had come to visit with ME!
At the age of seven,
I wondered and pondered
The miracle of that night.
Said Spritz and Sprinkle,
"His name was Jesus—
Our brilliance His light.
'Twas Bethlehem's star
That was seen from afar
And we are but rays of that
light."
"Each Christmas we flicker,
Then sparkle and shimmer
For each little child such as you;
To tell you the story
Of the Babe and his Glory
To light up your world anew."
Then Spritz and Sprinkle,
They flickered and faded
Into the lights of the tree.
And left me to dreaming
(And planning and scheming)
How to keep Spritz and Sprinkle
Shining in me!

Melissa G. Queen

QUESTIONS

Hollow words are echoed
And fade away in space
Tears moist on the pillow
Disappear without a trace
A lack of understanding
But no concern to try
An effort that is wasted
Like reaching for the sky
Moments pass like hours
Weeks turn into years
Time stands still but moves
so fast
The future is concealed
What's the use in living
For what reason do we die?
The answers are so hard to grasp
Like reaching for the sky

Jeffrey E. Patterson

HAUNTING MEMORIES

Slowly, in Haunting Memories
My eyes search you out,
Through the blackness of the
skies,
Intoning movements of satin
comfort
To be held again with the
reserved passion
Of your soul.
Moving in rythmns of tender
thought,
You bring a lively joy into
this soft night,
Swaying and staying, forever,
Locked,
in the secret most places of
my life,
Filling the hardened voids
With the velvet of your touch,
Painting my Heart in shadows,
in colors
Rich and deep,
As ancient as this land we
dwell upon,
As moving as the Sea on my
doorstep
Changing my life with your
Love.

Valerie Dowden Messick

A COUNTRY MORNING

Leaves dancing wildly in the
summer's breeze
Butterflies floating here under
the trees.
A robin's admiring the nest that
she built.
A troop of ants drinking the
coffee I spilt.
A honey bee's buzzing from
flower to flower,
And here comes a car, the first
one this hour.
Hey, there sits a toad! From
what I can see,
The cute little fellow is
flirting with me.
As nature surrounds me in all of
her glory,
I think of the one who started
this story.
What a creator! Almighty is He.
His infinite power is stifling
to me.

Rosalyn Rosen

SURVIVAL

Society's tried to poison me
to make me forget what it's like
to be free
To walk in the woods and feel
the delight
of the universe contained within
my sight
Somehow. . . .I've survived
It's for the children, I cry
They get injected so slow and
don't even know
Before too long it begins to
show
Those innocent looks start to
disappear
Replaced by receding blanks
multiplied by the years
But, some will make it. . . .
just like me
to become a lone survivor of a
cultural catastrophe

Arthur J. Pipeling

CAMP WHEELER

Camp Wheeler is a favorite spot
That lingers in my heart,
I love the beauty of each plot
It is a work of art
For my son traineth there.
There is a building standing
there,
A castle that I love
It's guarded by an angel fair
Appointed from above,
For my Son sleepeth there.
The grass is green on this estate
It's beauty to unfold,
Pearl was used to make each
gate
Its' streets are paved with gold.
For my Son walketh there.
The Chapel is a sacred place
The organ sounds so sweet
It has the blessing of God's
grace
Where God and soldiers meet.
For my Son prayeth there.

Kathryn Cobb

TO THOSE WHO RUN

We all—or surely most—have
run away
From something—
Pain, terror, grief, knowledge,
The past, the future,
Present responsibility—or
boredom.

Many of us are running
From ourselves
And cannot get away,
For we go with us.
However, hope exists;
For God does, too.
Today a blue balloon
Rose quickly and cleanly
Out of the confining city
And grasping fingers.
Only this type of runaway
Is wise.

Edgar Michael Roberson III

LOVE IS

Love is being together
Love is learning. Love is
life. Love is kissing
more than twice.
Love is a feeling.
The feeling is love.
Being together, while
holding hands, expressing
your love like no one
else can.
Feeling, touching, hugging,
and loving are all
things we do to love.
But how we love, who
we love, and when we love
are all from the heart.
It comes straight from
the heart. Love is loving
you.

Susanne Schmidt Marx

AMERICAN THANKS

Thanksgiving days we celebrate,
America 200 years you had.
This land is great, its people free
your progress made world
history.
America your freedom rings
from all the world its seekers
brings.
As for this freedom, all who
fight
in this great land they all unite.
Once pilgrims came, they made
a place
from anywhere and any race.
As neighbors built and got
along,
so made this nation, great and
strong.
Made visions and their dreams
come true;
handed them down, to me and
you.
No people ever had therefor
in any land say thanks, for
more!
As we should on this happy day
for those all our blessings, say.
We still stand up for human
right,
we shall not feel what chains
feel like!
Nor suffer terrors of the wars
that many other nations scars.
For all the blessings let us say:
a prayer as thanks giving day!
No matter if we're rich or poor,
as long as freedom is ensured
that we can still choose how to
say,
our own grace, as thanks giving
day!
This choice of freedom that us
granted,
for this the pilgrims once here
landed.
To say their prayers as they may
as we still can, for peace, today!

Michael Eugene Thompson

SO RIGHT

Everything seems so right,
Therefore we shouldn't fight;
We should let our love flow
And let our happiness glow.
For isn't life to love and care,
To be as one and share
All of life's ups and downs,
How lovely this sounds.
To be with you as one,
From now to the end of the
sun;
To honor and cherish our life
Together, as one, as husband
and wife.

Daniel S. Johnson, Jr.

BLENDED SOULS

It has been a thousand years, it
seems.
And I foresee it will be a
thousand more,
Of loving you, but always only
in my dreams.
But how sadder still, if you
had not walked upon my
shore!

You became the gentle mist that
sprayed my face,
You were the fragrance of roses
in the air;
You were the rising sun, whose
rays through leaves created
fine lace.
But now, only our blended souls,
with all of nature, will we
forever share.

Lisa DeMaria

BASEBALL SEASON

You stood a catcher's stance
with mask and bat.
I sat in a fan's seat watching.
Love was our field, the bases yet
untouched.
I shyly looked away quickly
Love ricocheted around and
brought it back.
You made a catch. . . .he's out!
You made a hit. . . .1st. . .2nd
. . .3rd. . .a home run!
I was paralyzed by your speed,
elasticity and shoulders.
Love didn't need a referee.
I wanted to hide for cover, but
Love sent a messenger to me
You said, "Hello".

Ms. Pat Moss

AUTUMN OF LIFE

Spring brings hopes and dreams,
Of many things, it seems.
Hopes of happiness we all
pursue.
The constitution says we are
due.
Dreams that summer will last
forever.
That winter will come, no.
Never!
In the autumn of life, we soon
know.
Winter is coming. We will have
to go.

Vicki Lee Marie Carlisle

SECRET

locked away
in a little room
lies a secret
waiting to be assumed
placed aside
in a little corner
lies a secret
that belongs to a morner
always shut out
never to be seen
lies a secret
not visual through a screen
kept inside
just waiting to get out
lies a secret
there's no doubt
mindfully kept
in a corner to shove
lies a secret
and this secret is love

Libby P. Holden

MY MOTHERS' HAND

I noticed the change so
suddenly that it came as a
shock.
I had taken one of her hands
And it seemed so dry and
lifeless and
So terribly delicate like fine
old parchment
And the skin was so thin that
I felt as if I must handle it like
a rare old treasure
As though there were only one
of a kind
And there would never be
another like it.
That surmise was of course true.
For all only have one in our
entire life
And if it were not for each
particular one,
We would not be here at all,
And this cherished hand
Had suddenly and completely
gotten old. . . .
Terribly and awfully old,
And I had not noticed the
change until now.
I felt panicky that this security,
This all knowing all,
This sure fire bulwark against
the rest of the world,
This uplifting spirit,
This warmth,
This tenderness,
This comfort,
This servant,
This cook,
This bottlewasher,
This money lender,
This arbitrator,
This smile,
This kiss,
This all in all that is a mother
Would be leaving me alone and
I. . .in Turn. . .would be
Doing the same and wondering
If someone would notice, at last,
That my hands were like fine
old parchment,
And I was forgotten, and alone.

Daphne Diane Page

THE MUSEUM

In the museum
I watched my life flit back
To the Nile
Saw some people I recognized
they call themselves
Other names now
And go about their beliefs
As if this is it
But careful
Don't wake them up
The dream is so real
That the reality pales
And lessons unlearned
Are played back
On a transparent recorder
So softly and insistently
That it appears that they come
From the present
Locked there until they become
Our yesterdays.

Artin Tellalian

FRIENDLY TALKS

I wish to see the person of my
dreams,
Everything about her fascinating
seems,
Her eyes give the essence of
attractive beams,
My friendly talks with her
unreserved seems.
One day the person of my
dreams I met,
I found everything around her
quite well set,
Her charming eyes were telling
a lot to me,
Our friendly talks were the
outcome I see.
How nice it is to meet such a
hearty one,
You feel that you own a real
someone,
Give way to her charming looks
by being friendly,
Her friendly talks with you will
come unreservingly.
Dear friend, realize tasting
the fruits of such pure
innocence,
In such a way that makes our
friendly talks immense,
Its heaven on earth to see her
speaking eyes,
Its a man made miracle to have
her friendly ties.

Marion Daugette

ESPECIALY FOR MY MOTHER

God made the earth,
And He saw that it was good.
Then He made man
And gave him clear water and
good food.
God made the animals,
Then He made Love, a special
kind of Love,
Mother Love, that only Mother
and God
Can understand.
Mother dear with each word
that I write
And each thing that I do,
Comes a special message
From me to you.
Some say "Please forgive all of
the
Thoughtless deeds that I have
done,
And some just say "Gee it's
great to have
A Mother who's such fun!"
Some say "Thank you for raising
me right."
And some say "Thank you for
your prayers

That have followed me
Every day of my life."
All say "I love you very much
Mother dear,"
And over the miles that
seperate us
My thoughts of you, keep you
very near to me.
God bless you Mother dear.

Lawrence L. Russell
THE ONE OF US
Debbie Jean could we be a
dream?
Are we not the way we seem?
For you are here today,
but could be gone tomorrow.
If in the future I should fade
away,
feel no sorrow.
Every one chooses their own
fate.
Hell's horror halls or; heavens
pearly gates.
Its strange how we came
together.
as they say "Two birds of a
feather"
You have taught me how trust.
to believe in the one of us.
Have faith; we all must.
Sprinkled off a high, strong
mountain.
To drift in to youthful fountains
Well maybe not.
But to trust you have taught.
We never have fought,
Disagreed? YES.
But the relationship could have
been much less.
Think about it.
The script had to fit.
The world is more than just a
stage,
and we aren't merely players or
whispering soothesayers.
Rainbows in the night,
Freebird soaring out of sight.
The favored crescent moon, we
need wake soon.
the waves softly ripple, as me
you gently tickle.
Let us follow the free bird to
light?
Forever out of this wretched
world's sight.
When I'm with you I soar!!
Let it be proclaimed, let this
lion roar.

John Rachoy
THE SHEPHERDS
There was a shepherd so we are
told
Who lost a sheep from in the
fold.
The ninety and nine were safely
there,
But the one lost sheep he could
not spare.
He risked his life this sheep to
find
This one shepherd so good and
kind.
A greater Shepherd this story
told
Of one lost sheep from in the
fold.
Christ, this Shephard, came man
to save
With love so great His life He
gave.
The one lost sheep of wilderness
fame
Was saved by a shepherd of
lesser name.
'Tis found! 'Tis found! the
shepherd voiced.
All were saved and all rejoiced.
Alas, alas, what greater shame
The greater Shepherd could not
the same?
He computed the price and paid
the cost
But the few are saved—the
many are lost.
His life a ransom for the many
He gave
But the many are lost—the few
are saved.
We listen to the preacher's voice
Man has a will—he has a
choice.
"God will be just" the preacher
cries
"He'll never save whom Christ
denies".
Who made Christ's story into a
lie?
All in Christ shall live who in
Adam die.
In the present life death takes
its toll
But Christ will conquer as the
ages roll.
All souls He'll bring into
heaven's great fold
Just like the shepherd in the
story He told.
Death, where is thy victory?
Where is thy sting?
Will be the rejoicing this
Shepherd will bring.

L. H. Shauing'er
ETERNITY'S QUESTION
Eternity's question
Has kept me a child
In the darkest of corners
Where visions run wild,
Where shadows of heartbeats
Are light years away
And all that has happened
Is less than a day. . .

Sandra Linville
CONCEALMENT
Feelings flow within my soul
forever to emerge;
crying out for recognition
for a necessity not yet
conquered.
But mass confusion resides;
trapped, yet likely to explode;
being reluctantly unresolved
because I am stricken with
ambivalence.

Holly Murray
THE CYCLE OF THE ROSES
You remind me, young one,
much of the rose—
That you speak, so eloquently,
about. . .I see—
Within your heart that tender
bud,
magically appearing,
every spring—
The sure sign of a healthy seed;
Within your mind stems,
coarsely leaved,
The sign of pending maturity. . .
now and then—
A glimpse, of the woman to
come:
what a lady to be!
Tho' you may not always see
it—
may not always know it,
To ME, you are the perfect
rose—
UNIQUENESS,
From the blending of seeds;
COLOR AND TEXTURE,
Never to be found again.
Living proof—
Of Mother Nature's abundance,
priceless wealth—
Reaped from honest labour,
honest love. . .
BUT I KNOW, the day—
Will come when like the
symbolic rose,
You will be plucked from within
my grasp.
Your leaves to wither slightly,
your beauty—
To soften and fade, gradually. . .
THE COMING OF
MATURITY.
And the autumn shall give you,
IN RETURN,
a rose of your own. . .
The cycle unbroken,
IN CONTINUITY.

Kathleen A. Osborne
AUTUMN LEAF
The Autumn leaves with their
coats of brown,
falling, falling,—falling down.
But alone on one branch was a
small green leaf,
it hung all alone—happiness—
no grief.
It's heart was laughing, on his
face was pride
watching others wither until
they all died.
All alone was he, he said to
himself
"I'm free! I'm free! A whole
tree to myself."
But soon became lonely, turned
to brown as he cried,
"Oh No! I cannot fall, for I'll
die as they died."
When he was completely brown,
and his stem gave way,
the wind pushed and pulled
him, and called him to say.
"You fool, you fool, all leaves
must fall,
beckon with nature and to her
call."
Faster and faster he fell towards
the ground.
Happiness erased from his
face, to a frown.
"I cannot wither and die, said he,
for the snow that will come
will cover me."
But he knew not that it was
best
that sooner or later he would
join all the rest.
He will now return to the soil
where he started
looking up at the tree, from
which he was parted.
Then—the wind stopped short—
there was not a sound,
as he too lay dead, on the
cold, cold ground.

Patricia Palton
SONG OF FELLOWSHIP
Before you came to me
I was very much alone,
But compassion, kindness, and
caring
were the seeds inside me
sown.
You are everything I hoped for;
You love and share and care,
And when I've needed you the
most
There was someone who was
there.
When I needed fellowship
You never went astray,
I was never like a poem
Without anything to say.
If you ever just need something
I'll be glad for what I'll do
I'll love and share and care
And I'll be there for you, too!

Jennifer Lynn Kmetty
UNTITLED
Why did you go?
I need you now!
Don't you see?
You are a part of my heart
and you are in my soul.
Since you're gone, I am left
to sew the pieces together.
But I can't sew alone.
Please, I love you so.
I never told you,
but I am not ready to
let you go.
Don't you realize that
I am not old enough.
I don't want to be old enough
Somehow, I never will be.
I love you

Julie Anne Adkins
KEITH, YOU'RE NOT TOO. . .
Keith, you're not too quiet,
but not any too loud;
You're smile makes me feel,
as though I'm drifting on a
cloud.
Your eyes always dance
and shimmer in the light;
Just your little "Hello"
makes my day happy and
bright!
Oh, what a pleasure,
laughing and flirting with you.
There's just no way to measure,
how much I like you!
In my life you'll always play
a special little part;
No matter how far. . .you and I
are. . .
you'll always be in my heart!

Ina Louise Jackson
I AM
I am the sunlight
I am a bird in flight
I am the soft cool breeze,
I am a leaf in the trees,
I am the morning dew,
I am the sky of blue,
I am the lush green meadow,
I am the newly fallen snow,
I am a shining star,
Do you know, who you are?

Lucille M. Kroner
DAY'S END
The blue and gold have gone
away
In climbing up to close of day.
Shadows overpower the sun—
Across the sky white milk
clouds run
Like galleons 'fore a quick sea
breeze,
Escaping from the wind appease
My heart with beauty in their
flight,
To greet the dark oncoming
night.
I stand alone upon this hill
And listen to the night be still,
And wonder if again I'll know
The magic of its afterglow.

Rebecca S. Nova
TODAY
It's hard to begin
on a day like today
when your lazy and it's hazy
& there's no place to go
Dusty brown trees
& sad green leaves
turn to mush on the ground
in the fog that surrounds
your mind and the body
that life gave to you
what to do what to do
it is all so blue
from the sea to the
bruised eye sky above
We've worked with the earth
Big brother poisoned the air
Chemical oceans flow thru the
globe
Can we control it manipulate
the load
Learn love life war sex food
greed not
which goal have you got
If it's not for survival
then you'll die
with the rest of the lot.

Carmen Shields
TERRORIST
I listen as the sound of a flute
Is gently carried on a breeze
Then the city noise substitutes
A feeling of anxiety for ease
There are voices of children
Laughing as they play
While someone talks of nitrogen
And why we can't delay
The sun is warm overhead
Sky is clear and blue
Yes I heard you go ahead
Just tell me what to do
We donate ourselves to a cause
With hope to end oppression
Holding disregard for the laws
Eyes focus on recognition
The restless will be serene
If the serene becomes restless
The group which has convened
Refuses to be powerless
Though we try to help not harm
Others disagree
A tattoo on the leaders forearm
Displays hostility
I have seen a time
When brother fights brother
To test strength or win a dime
Perhaps, gain respect from
another
When starving is a nightmare
Eating is merely a dream
Living at best can be despair
And a whisper is a scream
The details have been set
Our strategy is planned
There is an airport and a jet
Tonight we make our stand
As the meeting comes to an end
We vow to reunite
Then into the crowd we blend
With other common sights
As I march down the street
My thoughts are strong and sure
But I look down at my feet
And my emotions become
obscure
Someone walks beside me
with a radio that is loud
I begin to loose my loyalty
In wonder of the innocent crowd
What religious organization
Would pursecute the innocent
I stop with hesitation
And remember a sacrement
There will be the young and old
We will force their judgement
day
But a freedom fighter is so bold
He may take someone's rights
away
We use violence
To escape misery
On the pretence
Of living peacefully

Marvin Robert Tucker
WINTER STORM
You seem
To be
Wild and free
Yet
Your heart cries
The icy tears
Of
A
Prison.

Dianne Shepard
JOHNNY
A cowboy stands on a cold dark
street.
With a smoking gun in his
hand.
In a puddle of blood, a man lies
at his feet.
With his lifes final prayers,
Many dreams and family cares.
Dying on his trembling lips.
As his children look on in
astonishment.
His Mother screams out the
pain.
Sister says he's gotten his
punishment.
While his lady holds his head;
And softly whispers his name.
Johnny—
Who will tend the land?
Teach my son well.
And who will comfort me when
I'm sad?
Teach my son well.
And who will protect us from
harm?
Teach my son well.
He is his fathers son.
But he can't go through life,
Apologizing for what I've done.
Realize son—death is
permanent.
So tread softly when it's near.
For it strikes like lightening.
Smothering with its' misty
cloak.
Teach him earths' wonders.
And kindness while he's young.
Then he won't die senselessly.
At the hand of someones gun.

Ram Evans
HEROES
My heroes were always men
With spines of steel
They didn't bend
Or even feel
Always icy and collected
Their hands are steady
Their mind is connected
For anything they're ready
These were the heroes of my
youth
And until I got older
I thought this the whole truth
Yet, now, I know I'm bolder
Much more than they
Now, I'm my own hero
In every way
I am no longer a zero.

E. Redding Brock
WAKE UP WOMEN! WAKEUP!
Wake up women and stand your
ground
Wake up women and be proud
Don't sit around with your arms
folded
Your help is needed in this
town.
Don't sit around finding fault,
And criticizing everybody
Some say I am going west,
some say I am going east
Others say I am north bound.
Women! Women!
Stick around! There is plenty to
do in your town.
Stop moaning and groaning
about what happened
yesteryears.
Waste no time worrying about
what's going on over yonder.
Wake up women! Wake up
women!
Keep your town on the grow.
It's no need to leave your home
town
Riding around—looking and
wondering.
Wake up women! Wake up!
There is a job very near you
Just be patient and check your
surroundings.
The old clock keeps clicking
and ticking.
Seemingly it says, "Wake up!
Wake up!"
The alarm is loud, very loud
and clear,
Wake up women, can't you hear!

Doris Pope
LOOK UPON A STAR
Look upon a star
there may lie a wish
that may come true.

June D. Swadron
SUPPOSING
Supposing there was a love
That formed from pure depth
A love that knew not tears, no
regrets
Supposing that love was given
to you
What would you do?
Just supposing.
Supposing the fear that
burdened your youth
Can be replaced by gentle truth
And you were given the chance
to
Let go and be free
And supposing that trust came
to you
From me?
Just supposing.
Supposing the love within your
soul
Escaped your walls and you
regained control
And the tears you shed were
cleansed by laughter
Forever after. What would you
do?
Just supposing.
Supposing you were lifted higher
than ever
By a love from one who cares
Supposing you shared the
dreams of a lifetime
With one who can feed your
prayers.
Supposing I offered my hand to
you
What would you do? What
would you do.
Just supposing.

Lawrence Charles Hanker
MEDITATION
Serenely, a breeze wafts
A river cascades perfectly
Green trees, blue sky, and white
clouds blend
As the psyche relaxes, the
heart opens
Subdued by sanity, nature
smiles
True purpose surpasses desire
The touch of light casts
shadows
The touch of light sends
shadows away.

Joy Marie Heinz
DIET—MISERIES
Chocolate pudding and apple
pie,
you can't have it but neither
can I.
We've both been suffering a long
long time,
ever since we slipped that
machine a dime.
Every person we see eats and
eats
all that ice cream and all those
sweets.
You've lost one pound and I've
lost two,
but we both know thats not
true, if
any-thing we've gained a few.
Eating yougart and loads of fish,
licking every bit off the dish,
going to parties has got to be
the worst,
dying of hunger and also of
thirst.
They all say you've got to eat,
you can't be rude,
Oh what the hell its only food.

Paul N. Bickford
PURPLE COW
Now Donald had a purple cow,
with character obtuse,
A silly bovine animal, this
lovely creature, puce.
Her face was sad and lonely, her
eyes were limpid blue,
Her sides were slick as slick
could be, her voice a husky
"Moo!"
Hip bones high and rugged with
skin draped gently o'er.

One horn curved north the
other south. Her teeth they
numbered four.
A peaceful gal? Without a doubt,
with attitude deliberate,
Until poor Donald came along
her creamy flood to liberate.
But here the tranquil mood is
gone, the placid picture
changes,
For this mild-mannered looking
babe came from the mountain
ranges.
She eyed the gleaming pail
askance, she frowned upon
the stool,
The look she gave our Donald
lad was unladylike and cool.
Our hero slapped her on the
flank and gruffly said, "Move
over."
The purple one just sneered at
him and rudely chewed her
clover.
Don sat himself with graceful
poise and gently took a hold.
The lady curled her upper lip,
her eyes she wildly rolled.
The milker took a firmer grip
and tugged experimentally.
The cow inhaled a lusty breath
and bawled unsentimentally.
She flipped her tail and took
the boy across his noble brow.
He murmured softly to himself,
"Dad-rat this gol-durned cow!"
He grabbed the waving member
and to it tied a brick
She calmly wound up once or
twice and tossed it in the
creek.
But patience has its just
reward the milk began to flow,
The foamy flood rose to the
brim and Donald rose to go.
But fickle fortune sometimes
smiles then turns it to a
sneer,
The purple one chewed
thoughtfully and twitched a
mulelike ear.
She slowly rolled her gentle
orbs. She shyly twitched her
tail.
Then carelessly she raised her
foot and placed it in the pail.
Now Donald *had* a purple cow,
the reason for this fable.
But if you stop at Donald's
house there's beefsteak on the
table!

Russell Gagnon

ENLIGHTENMENT AWAITED

A BLUE HUE saturated the sky
poisoned clouds dripped
on the horizon.
Father of perfection.
Father of supreme wisdom
Light streaks arch skyward
open womb
negative unbound positive
void in all demensions
pierced soil, unsort love
gathering thoughts of sinners
trusting God, whose will's my
own.
Left holding Sun
Right holding Moon
suspended time, horizons hands,
Neither Light nor Dark
three days of the cross
then the haloed moon.
Sages enormous glorious
precepts
bound into the Book of Life.
Men living for God listen!
Extend boundless thoughts
Gather within Yourselves
Our Creation, Syzygy Elation
WORDS direct innocence
Creating insecurities, freed
Floating inside innocence
Forever creating
Natural occurances, a point,
Mouths open to speak
Pens and cases of type make-
ready
Stroking brushes paint
Hands, mind of Body
The encumbrance of
encumbrance
My God their God
Energy motions, wave
Passing through bodies
Producing glorifying,
enumerating.
The End, the End
They tell me it's coming
My end earth's end, satan's end
The end of everything
They don't know.
My end coming
God's cycles of Birth and
death—
Beyond the end.
Directions insights karmas good
bad
I choose beyond man's visions
Leaping gravestones energies
transfused.
God light of pure matter
Words, gestures outside
Realms of pure energy, I have
chosen
Mists of turmoil a man declares
Frounce in church's Love
fighting insanity
Moods creating notions
My human stigma.
Students in life, lost children
wander no more.
Besieged by insight eyes stare
untressled.
A man's reason, art's creativity,
philosopher's being.
I channel all immensity into
purpose.
Ancient thoughts fuse into
today
Connections transcended eternity
Existing present, grasp them.
Flee naked past history
Unmasking living truths.
Men grope cling edge to edge
to see
Knowledged men move forward
Immensities Peaceful Bed,
Life of Answers,
Eyes ahead.
I am awakened.
"To speak of truth
and not to live it
is but a copout of mind
body and the very
existence of one's self"

Arlis Yancy

BIRCH TREE IN ALASKA

Mythical, mystical golden tree
of middle earth and Erresea,
Living legend, lost, away
from the golden woods of
yesterday.
Outside my window, on a hill
it lingers late, and watches still,
As autumn comes and grass
and flowers
age and wither, beneath soft
showers
Of golden leaves, shed like
tears
for lonely, sad, forgotten years.
Will grey-clad, silent elf-folk
glide
again, to gather at its silver
side?
Or sing and dance in the little
glade
till moon and stars grow pale
and fade?
Shall furry footed hobbits
creep
and mound its fallen leaves to
sleep?
While the north lights
flaming, frosty bars
and the mithril fires of the
polar stars
Quadrille to a pulsating
rhaphsody
in the endless skies o'er the
artic seas?
While naked and silver it
stands, to cling,
to the permafrost and await the
spring
And the warm, awakening,
wandering sun
till its roots are withered, its
waiting done.
And its gleaming, graceful,
greyskinned form
turned into dust, by the wild
wind borne
Across a world grown tired
and old
in the endless spin of time,
untold.
May it flower again, on the
westward shore
among the vanished folk that it
waited for!
In the gathering dusk it's
golden gleam
compels me stare awhile and
dream
Of an enchanted world,
unseen, unreal;
but it lives for me, and it
always will,
And I would go, if I had the
chance,
to that world of danger and
romance
With men so brave and elves
as fair
as the golden woods they
wandered there.
In my fantasy, it seems I gaze
on a mallorn tree from the eldar
days.

Edwin L. Arnett Sr.

MASTERING THE BIBLE

The Bible indeed, is a Work of
Art,
God of all books,—I've yet
read.
I pray I can master it,—
completely;
Before the day,—I'm dead.
To master the Bible and live as
equal,
Makes one perfect-n-heavenly
bound,
Those who live above average;
but less then its requirements,
Shall perish, with the devil,
beneath the ground.
What (named) mankind can
master the Bible?
Politicians, beggars, popes,
ex-cons, missionaries,
murderers; Well?!
On earth, Figures of speech are
plenty,
But Judgement Day; Christ
Jesus will tell.
Should particular nationalities,
Master the Bible?
All,—By the standards of
Gods grace,
For one-n-all would be brothers,
No distinguishings as color or
race.
What does it cost to Master the
Bible?
Very little, if you master it,—
you'll know,
So let God lead-n-you follow
instructions,
For your rewards in heaven
will grow.
How long does it take to Master
the Bible?
One month, one year, five or
seven;
Who cares if it takes you a
lifetime,
If it pleases our father in
heaven.
When or where should one
Master the Bible?
No precise age, place, nor
time, does the Bible tell,
But suppose tonight,—you go
to sleep, as a sinner,
N—tomorrow morning, you
wake up,—in Hell!!!
Yes; The Bible indeed,—is a
Work of Art,
God of all books,—I've yet
read,
I pray all mankind; will master
it,
Before the day,—They're dead.

Craig Hohlbein

IT'S COLD

Lots of snow.
Sixty below,

And really cold for an Eskimo!

Theodore Rivers Sr.

THE BIG SHOWDOWN

*(Sugar Ray Leonard
vs. Thomas (Hit Man) Hearns)*

At "Caesar's Palace" in Las
Vegas, the desert oasis known as
"Gamblers Town,"
The world's welterweight
champions met in a fight that
was called "The Big Showdown."
Sugar Ray Leonard was the
champion who was sanctioned
by the W.B.C.
Some say Leonard was faster
than Sugar Ray Robinson and
even the "Greatest" Mohammed

Ali.
Leonard was triumphant in the Olympics and for America he won a medal of gold.
The results of his fight called "Rematch Two" with Roberto Duran is a story that will forever be told.
Leonard rained punches on Duran even harder than those by Little Joe Cartwright's big brother Hoss.
It was during the seventh round that Duran uttered those now famous words "No Mas", "No Mas."
After defeating Duran, Leonard became even more famous with 7 up commercials on TV.
Leonard's career was guided by the maker of champions none other than the master stragetist Angelo Dundee.
The champion sanctioned by the W.B.A. was Thomas Hearns "The Hit Man" from Detroit.
Fighting for thousands while Leonard made millions made Hearns become very annoyed.
Hearns was a hungry fighter and Leonard was a multi-millionaire with money to burn.
A world's title is never given away, it's something one has to work hard for in order to earn.
In his championship fight against Pipino Quaves, Hearns showed he had what it takes.
Hearns was called "The Motor City Cobra" because his hands were deadlier than two rattle snakes.
After being hit by two of Hearns' mighty right hand punches, Pipino Quaves went down.
Hearns took from Quaves' head the W.B.A.'s version of the welterweight crown.
It was decided these two great champions should meet and each fighter readily agreed.
Hearns was known for his awesome punching power and Leonard for his great speed.
From the opening bell, Leonard knew that it would indeed be a very tough fight.
Leonard knew the power of Hearns after being hit with a solid right.
Throughout the fight, Hearns pounded Leonard's face until his eyes became puffy and swollen.
Leonard was determined that Hearns would not take this title nor by the judges would it be stolen.
During the fourteenth round, Leonard needed a knockout and that he did surely know.
With reserved energy, Leonard mounted an unrelenting attack and became the winner Via a TKO.
Many said "the fight should not have been stopped because Hearns could still defend himself."
Who would want to be the referee responsible for a fighter being beaten to death?
Even after losing, any fighter should eventually be able to get up and walk away.
There will always be a possibility for him to fight again another day.
A referee should never let any fighter get beaten to the bitter end.
One of them may be killed or harmed so bad they may not be able to fight again.
To control a fight and prevent any serious damage is what a referee is paid to do.
The public will surely demand a rematch and call it "showdown number two."
Leonard proved that he wasn't only a product of the media to every ,man, woman, boy and girl.
Not only was he the jr. middleweight, but also "the undisputed Welterweight Champion of the World."
Leonard proved himself the World's best welterweight as good as any fighter ever, pound for pound.
The name Sugar Ray Leonard will be spoken as one of history's greatest fighters after winning in "The Big Showdown."

Lauretta E. Pelton
YOUR WORRY-CLOSET-CLOWN

Hide me high, in a corner, on your worry shelf
Where no one can find me, 'cept'n yourself.
Secure the door with lock and key—
And
just
like
that—
Forget about me.
When worries weigh heavy—

Bo
gg
ing you
do
wn—
And you find you're wearing a firm do
wn
fr
own—
Then laugh with me
Your WORRY—CLOSET—CLOWN!
I'll twist!
I'll turn!

I'll roll and dance!
I'll flip!
I'll spin!
—and spurn gravity's stance!
Each move I'll make is for YOUR sake!
So
ooo
ooo
ooo
SMILE!
Then hide me high in a corner on your worry shelf,
Where no one can find me, 'cept'n yourself.
Secure the door with lock and key—
And
just
like
that,
Forget about me.—
Until worries weigh heavy—
Bo
gg
ing
you
do
wn,—
And you find you're wearing that firmed do
wn
fro
wn—
Then laugh with me
Your WORRY—CLOSET—CLOWN!

Dixie Lee Harrison
PRAYER OF A DRINKING MAN'S WIFE

Dear Heavenly Father up above,
Please watch over the man I love
Let him live, though sick with sin
Forgive him Lord, for the shape he's in!
And forgive me too, for I have been,
As sick as he, and trying to bend
Thy will to mine, as if I knew,
Exactly what You plan to do
Lord, as he roams from bar to bar,
Dear God, don't let him wreck the car!
See, there I go, I'm telling You
Just what *I* think You ought to do!
Lord, open my eyes, that I may see
Thy good and perfect will for me
Let me turn my will to Thine,
And to my man, be only kind
Give me insight into me
Show me Thy way to serenity,
Now I pray we will, this struggle win
In the name of Jesus Christ, Amen

Hilda E. Ongrady
HALLOWEEN NOSTALGIA

There was a candy stand on the corner - open for summer - enclosed for winter.
Such a stand I have never seen - especially at the season of Halloween.
Across the length of the stand was a string - Strung on the string were Halloween masks.
Some were pretty - some were evil - just to decide would fill one with upheaval.
Every year I would choose a mask and my, oh my, it was such a task.
The devil - the monster - the skeleton green - oh, my heavens, the worst I've seen.
When I made my choice on that Halloween night - I wore it home to give Mom a fright
She would throw up her hands and squeal - What is it? - What is it? It isn't real.
Then to the dresser to look for some clothes to deck me out from my head to my toes.
An old pointed hat - some baggy coat - a mop head for hair - an empty bag to tote.
My friend Ginger was a little clown - she went with me all over the town.
When our bags were filled and our feet were tired - we headed for home and to bed we retired.
I guess that kids still thrill each year to the strange excitement and lovely fear
Of the ghosts and goblins and witches mysterious - It's a time of year when you must be delirious.
And the little girls so pretty and bright - Sleeping Beauty - The Good Fairy - Red Riding Hood - Snow White.
They must feel the same tingle that I felt inside -
When a Wee Witch on a broom took a Halloween ride.

R. A. Whitlow
TO MY BEST FRIEND

Carol is the sunrise to my morning
The brightness that opens my eyes
And fills my heart
To all the beauties that surround me
And as the morning dew fades into the warmth of the afternoon
Carol is there to shade the rays
and comfort me from the heat
Then as the sun ends another day
turning the world from warm to cold
Carol is there to warm my body
And to assure me all is fine
Yes Carol is my morning sun
the shade from days long heat
and warmth from days end cold
But most of all Carol is a life long friend

Elsie Wilson
THE WIND
(For K.W.)

The wind it blows around and through,
It blows right on past me and you;
And we, we stay here, standing still,
While it races where it will.
Whence it comes i do not know,
Nor can i tell where it will go:

We do not see it rushing past,
And yet we see where it has passed.
It doesn't stop for house or tree,
It hastens over land and sea;
And as it runs by you, my friend,
On its way towards its end,
It whips around, plays with your hair,
Runs its fingers where i don't dare:
It lifts your locks and lets them fall,
Blows them round and feels them all.
I envy the wind - how can it be
That it can touch, but not me?

Linda Lee

THE VALIANT HORSEMAN

Riding away oe'r the green
The valiant horseman is seen,
Napoleon was his name
Who took me oe'r the plain.
Thru the woods along the trail
Faster and faster gallops the male.
Twining in and out trotting onward,
Beyond where skies are blue.
Red jackets trailing behind
To make him master of all.
Thru the gate at castle hill
There stood the oldest great mill.
He gave the signal shout to all
Tis the end and the race won
A valiant horseman leads again.

Miguel de Brito

HAPPY MOTHER'S DAY

If I wished you a sunbeam
and a hummingbird's kiss,
and only the best
a lifetime of bliss...
Or, I could wish you a moonbeam
shining only for you,
a garden of roses in bloom
all the year through...
Would you wish this pleasure?
that fantasy brings,
a heart ever so light,
like gossamer wings...
You love that which is lovely
all that is true,
you love being MOTHER
and just being you...
What of a dream world?
wouldn't you see,
your real world's more special
than any could be...

Jean M. Thieda

JUST THINK

Have you ever sat on a sandy beach
and watched the calm blue sea?
Or rested on a grassy knoll and stared
at a towering tree?
Look up to the sky at the fluffy clouds
gaze at yon mountains high,
Then look about at these wondrous things
Think how small we are, you and I!

John N. Garns

SO MANY PEOPLE...

So many people haven't been saved.
So many people haven't seen the Light.
So many people are living in a world of darkness,
When they know their world could be bright.
So many false prophets roaming the earth.
So many false religions to get caught up in.
So many people have heard the wrong Word,
Not knowing that Satan is taking them in.

Claudette Elaine Houston

DURING A MARCH

Mister, get your hand right on out of there
Mister- short, Black, poor like me
Please leave all those terrible habits behind
We are marching for a cause
We're angry over the deaths of all our Black children of Atlanta
You're angry and so am I
Don't go against me now
Look straight and march forward proudly
And don't you dare try to pick my pocket again at this Candlelight March in honor of our young Black lives that are gone!

C. S. Stachewicz

MORNING PRAYER

I've come to play before you
at the rising of the sun,
to dance on the earth
wet with dew
and make you smile.
I've come to pray before you,
unseen, yet felt, as you are.
I lift my hands! Myself...
to the radiant hue,
source of life.
I've come to drink from the pool
of strength at the beginning of
day, to swim in the holy air of
your presence, mind boggling
God! I the fool bow
before you in adoration.

Jean M. Thieda

FLIGHT OF GREY GEESE

Gazing upwards in sheer delight
I see them trek across the sky,
Grey designs in their southern flight,
Then I give a mighty sigh.
Earthbound are my aging feet
But my heart with them still sings,
Accompanied by their distant honks
and the music of their wings.
Soft shadows cast on earth below
as they swiftly wing their way,
Makes my heart begin to glow
Still down here I'm doomed to stay!

Walter James Leitmeyer Jr.

SEPTEMBER SONG

September Song lays in her berth,
A child yet unborn,
Floating quietly above the earth,
On a cool June morn.
Ropes grow taunt, then relax,
Holding both her bow and stern,
Together, they hold her back,
Rippling water make her yearn.
Yearning for the open sea,
Freedom from the dock,
She seem to beckon me,
To release her from her lock.
Her sails go up, against the breeze,
The Master pushes off,
Entering the waves with ease,
She cuts them silently.
Born again, for just this day,
Sailing free against the sky,
Salty air, water foam spray,
Her yacht pennant blowing high.
Ah, a sight, a quiet sight,
Calm sea, cool clean air,
A good day to sail this flight,
To join a sister, a beautiful pair.

Mary Sachs Zello

I HAVE TO BE FREE

Build me no thrones of marble stones, they're not for me.
I have to be free, I have to be free.
Build me no cage to hide inside,
God's world I want to see,
Just let me be free, I have to be free.
Four walls would only hide, and make a prisoner of me.
My spirit would fret, and chafe at restraint, can't you see.
Just give me the woods, the fields and the hills, give me
The desert or sea, but let me be free, just let me be free.
Give me no clock to watch, or fetter me to it's hands,
No clock on the wall to make my feet dance at it's commands.
Life is so short—too short for all that I want to do, and see,
I have to be free, I have to be free.
Our where the winds are blowing, and the rivers are singing to me,
Singing the songs of the ages, as onward they flow to the sea.
Where the white fleecy clouds are drifting in fathomless space,
Where birds are singing, and bees are buzzing
And God seems to be every place.
He stretches His hands out over our lives, and our land.
He gives us so much—if we only could understand,
That its not in striving, and grasping, and getting,
But it is in giving His love
That could make this old world seem just like heaven above.
So build me no thrones of marble stones, they're not for me,
I have to be free, I have to be free.

Give me no crown of jewels rare, though splendid and costly
They be, Just let me be free, I have to be free.

Dr. Mildred Carroll Wiseman

WINTER

I know the Winter will be cold
I feel it in my bones -- old
Breaks and aches begin to moan
And still complain and drone
On and on as leaves unfurl
And flutter down upon the squirrel
That patiently and laboriously tries
To unravel the carpet that he pries
Loose from my patio floor
Then scampers off to hide some more
Acorns when he becomes completely frustrated
At the stubborn piece of carpet that defeated
All his efforts to become a part
Of his warm and furry nest now set apart
From all his friends in their mores
To hide and hoard their Winter stores.
Then, too, the meadow lark flies in
And swiftly soon she will begin
To set her Winter home apart from all the rest
Of the feathered creatures at my back door.
Just so I know that Winter's chill
Will soon set in and blow its ill
And chilly breath on every creature
Man, bird, beast, and plants that feature
Now their green and bright bloom and fruit
So that soon all will turn brown and the brute
Will huff and puff and all will scamper
Forth to seek to fill the Winter's hamper
With creature needs for warmth and food
So that when ice and snow abound
They can keep warm and well-fed
And wait for the coming of Spring
Its warmer breath and winds to bring.

Kaizer L. Ukinstoff

UPON THE HOUR

Upon the hour of my birth in darkness and in shadow.
When winter snow laid aglaze in moonlight and in meadow.

Cold in pain a woman lies with skin as white as milk.
Bored a child into the world with flesh as soft as silk.
For it was no father there to greet me and to bless me with his name.
But greeted only with the laughter the child was born in shame.
And taken from my mother's side that died giving my breath.
Yes I was born upon that hour the hour of her death.

Louis R. Lincoln
THE TOUCH
I woke up today with thoughts of you, and glowing warmth spread outward from the core of my soul to engulf that which is within it. This feeling may be new to someone unaware but I rejoice in it as a blind man would with his first sight, knowing it for what it is, but not trusting it. Then the man reaches forth as I, and touches that which his heart sees and we know that all there is in life can really be.

Jan Ellison
DAVID'S LOVE ROSE
I just know God saved the most beautiful roses He ever made for you to give to me...
And, they surely are the most beautiful!
As I look at them they remind me of you ...
In its center,
Each one has a heart of gold...
Like you.
Soft as velvet on the outside,
Intricate and complicated on the inside...
Like you.
As the tiny buds open and smile,
They bring me warmth and happiness...
Like you.
Bright red petals with crisp green leaves;
Colorful, yet reserved...
Like you.
Gentle as a tropical breeze,
Yet strong enough to withstand the storm...
Like you.
Velvet steel...
Like you.
Each one different,
Yet each one a rose;
Like you...
An individual,
Yet always a man's man.
All that's within growing according to their Father's will;
It is my prayer that this too will be...
Like you.
So, thank you David for these roses...
But thank you most of all for the love that caused you to send them.

Donna Jean Roguski
SUNSHINE
The sunshine through my smile
My face----
Aglow
The energy always changing
Never
Ending
Accepting the depth of my soul
Untouched
By man
Allowing myself to shine, shine, shine
Radiating today
Forever
And burning to the core
Of my soul
For eternity

Effie Van Epps
PLAYTIME
Freckled noses
Stubbed toeses
Skinned knees
And roller skates
Chalky sidewalks
Patterned hopscotch
Jumping ropes
and one, two, three
Shouting voices
Happy laughter
Sounds of "Free"
And "Run, Sheep, Run"
Golden sunshine
Cheeps of birdlings
Grasses green
Oh, Spring has come!

Ethel R. Cetlin
THE EGG TIMER
Time is an ugly monster
Stretching wide its empty hands
Grinning with awful sneer
At those with nothing to do.
Time is a red faced demon
With long, greedy claws
Pulling with inexorable weight
At those who want to stay.
Time is man's obsession
His unconquerable fate
Panting with hope he eyes it
Then turns and hides his head.
For time bears his destiny
Hidden in its heart's core
Knowing an infinite secret
The price of man's flesh.

Bernice Loretta Holmes
LOVE'S TEARS
Today the rain like tears
Upon My Cheeks
Falls,
Touching The Rose.
Heaven Knows
How Much I Miss You.
Once We Loved, For You The Feelings Gone.
For Me The Memories Linger On.
After The Rainbow Comes The Sun,
Filling The World With Gladness.
While I Wait For Your Return
In Sadness...
Like The Rain, I Weep.

Jeanette Wilson
DO I BELIEVE IN GOD?
Just as surely as Santa lives in the mind and heart of every young.
Just as surely as you and I live so, I do believe, lives a Supreme Being!
I Believe
that God lives within us,
That is,
to the extent to which we let Him live!

Carolan Baber
LANGUAGE OF THE WIND
Speak
The language of the wind
You know not where ye come from
Or where ye will go again
You can only sing a good song
While among men
Hearts merging together
Hands holding a friend
Seek ye light in the storm
You can never presuppose the way or form
Of the fire found
That will keep you forever warm
Seek ye gold on the earth
If you open your eyes
You can touch the worth
Of rainbow emanations
That will fill your dearth
Seek ye the song of the soul
If you hear the melody
You will never grow old
It will render your journey
A mystic spiral untold

Irving D. Gaskill
HAPPY BIRTHDAY
There's going to be a birthday cake with candles on it too,
With "HAPPY BIRTHDAY" on the top and "BEST REGARDS TO YOU."
We'll gather 'round the festive board while every candle burns,
We'll all sing "HAPPY BIRTHDAY" son and wish you glad returns.
And you will stand upon a chair, a deep breath you will take,
And then you'll blow the candles out upon your birthday cake.
There's going to be a party, all your friends from far away
Will be invited to attend on this your special day.
You'll open all your birthday gifts, examine every toy,
It's an extra grand occasion for an extra special boy.
There'll be ice cream and candy too of which we'll all partake
When you blow all the candles out upon your birthday cake.
With every candle burning bright, we'll make a wish for you,
And if we never tell a soul, it's certain to come true.
We'll wish for you the very best throughout the coming year,
For best of health and happiness and all for you my dear.
A hundred happy birthdays we'll be wishing for your sake,
When you blow all the candles out upon your birthday cake.

M. Porter Hansen
NEEDED
O unborn child with earth's design,
I dreamed a dream and you were mine.
I heard your cry for flesh and birth;
I know your plight to gain this earth.
A sense of guilt within me lies;
attempts to sleep disturbed by cries -
Then I awake! Remorse untold - for then I knew - I am too old!
Without your love dare I to live?
I cry aloud, "O Please forgive!"
But knowing - how my ears do ring,
"I've had my chance and failed this thing."
O unborn child in spirit form, upon this earth you must be born,
For unlike me - not left alone -
I need you, one, to make our home!

Colleen Carey Davidson
THE BIG BRASS BED
I get so excited
As I tiptoe upstairs,
Up to Mommy and Dad's room,
For I know what's there!
I round the hall corner,
Stick my head in the door,
Catch my breath seeing it take up
Most of the floor!
The sun shining in
Bounces off of each rail,
Which always delights me
Without any fail!
The round metal post
Is cool against my head,
As I lovingly hug
The world's biggest brass bed!
Then I go to the footrails
And climb over the top,
Landing smack on the bed
With the quietest plop.
Next I sit straight and tall
Like a queen on a throne,
Ruling all my play kingdom
From this room in my home.
Mom's lace pillow sham
'Cross my shoulders I drape,
making it play the part
Of the queen's royal cape.
I tap for my servants
To bring me a drink,
And the sound that it makes
Is the pleasantest clink.
Then I hear Mommy call me.
She says to come down.
And although I obey her,
I do tend to frown.
I dismiss all my servants,
And climb down with a sigh,
Again hugging the post,
I bid the bed good-bye.
One day soon I'll return
To play queen on the throne,
In my very own kingdom,
Upstairs in my home.

James S. Whitlark
TO A WILTED FRESHMAN
Inarticulate narcissus
planted in class notes
potted in footnotes
manured in Cliff Notes
why did you vegetate?
What god seeing you pursued by knowledge
wrought your metamorphosis
saving you from feeling the forced embrace
of P.S. 91?
Or was it self-destruction
the night you wasted away
outlining Dante's "wood of suicides"
until your skin flowered blue with ink
and ill-marked leaves sprouted half covering you?
Why did your speech coagulate
like blood or thickened sap
flowing forth only

when the silence grown about
you was pierced
by my barbed words?

Sylvia Rosenbaum
UNCLE ELIE
Uncle Elie was a corpse in
the front room parlor,
laid out on ice in a fifty dollar
coffin set
on kitchen chairs,
all stiff and crumpled up
inside his clothes
and people talking in sodden
tones.
The lid bent open for
inspection and farewells.
Small and scared I peeked inside
to clarify the treachery of death,
half expecting him to wake and
holler for Aunt Jess, just like
he'd only gone to sleep for a
little while.
But Uncle Elie was as silent as a
grave.
Uncle Elie never
stirred.
I remember Uncle Elie
in the front room parlor
all dressed up in his twenty
dollar suit.

Janice Loreta
-RAINBOW-FANTASY OF HOPE
i hitched a ride on a yellow
sunbeam. my destination was
unknown. i traveled through
civilizations of mistakes, as
my like was then just a speck
of dust on a universal rainbow
of fantasy. i was lost in a
world of sufferance, with faces
of people embedded in stone.
they were all turning toward
the mourning with the eyes of
their children, and their eyes
reflected the colours of the
rainbow. yet, all the while,
they were swearing their lives,
that god's a verb.

Helen M. Beabey
GOD'S FLEET
Don't be shy, stand upright
In everything you do
You've got to know you're
special
Why else would God make you?
Be bold and be courageous
Stand firm in your belief
Don't let your ship be sunken
Cause it runs into a reef
Get your ship together
Fix the keel and raise the mast
It's only through our trials
That we can find true peace at
last
The comfort comes in knowing
That we've got a purpose here
And God will be there with you
When those trying times are
near.

Juanita Soriano
A PRAYER
I asked your ghost across the
air:
Why did you pass me by and did
not stay?
You were the only thing in life
for which I cared
Since then I'm living wholly in
yesterday!
As if in a living death
The fountain of my hope is
white and lifeless,
Am I still alive—or have I died?
I know not whether the soul I
press is a shadow—or less.
I know not if my unseen tears
Are in the depths of my own
death hidden and dry,
I feel them always glowing near
Even in my smile and deeper in
No matter how far there was a
day
There was an hour to me, this
was a spring.
In such an hour I'm resting;
I shall lie
In the house of memories—my
abode is on the wind!
I came to choose my desired
Paradise:
To turn back into Past, and to
to stop time
To press with both my hands
a day which never dies
And live in it, in this
heaven of mine.
O love! Higher from me than
is the sun,
Cast down a glance into my
humble will,
till when—my love, when will
light come?
Am I to stand under the cold
rain still?
Am I to have a voice and cry
If there is not ears to listen
and to heed?
Am I to pray for ever on
outside
If there is not soil to keep
my prayer-seed?
Am I to wait for everlasting
time?
I know I lost you—and for my
loss I cried.
Shall I remain forever at the
gate
Begging for it to open—and
walking in the dark?
O thou—if there be any Thou—
Who hast been before.
Art now
And shall be for evermore!
Open to me the door on which
I knock
And let me in—
Or let me die.

E. A. Weston
LONG LAKE FOUND
Long Lake sparkles at four p.m.
Even then when the sun's
gone to bed across the way,
The slate blue waves roll
forward as if they'll flood
the soft pine shores and
conquer the land.
A dainty white sail hovers in
the distance where the water
meets the forest
Behind which stretches the
White Mountains of another
state.
A thousand clouds float gently
above in a pale blue sky,
Level upon level of beauty.
And in the other direction,
there's a busy causeway
breaking across the wild from
shore to shore.
Naples isn't much but it's all
you've got between here and
civilization.
Naples is a ghost town with old
survivors of better years and
porches that creep with age.
Its the Fourth of July, camp
children set loose, townies
with long, stringy hair at the
pizza stand.
I can barely recognize the place
anymore; the people just
aren't the same, and the
buildings have bland faces.
Not like before, not like the
countless dream summers
spent with grandfather;
Who brought the cool, fresh
wind, apple pie faces of
pretty young girls with ice
cream cones;
Who brought sunny candy shop
days or watercolor easels
indoors while the rain danced
outside;
Who brought rights and wrongs,
laughs and tears, day and
night, all in perfect order;
Who brought, most of all, Long
Lake to my feet and helped
me make it my own.
Chill me wind, tonight, for you
bring out the best in me.
Waves, keep churning onward,
lapping the land.
I want to feel you all forever,
While a warm fire waits inside.

Jo Anne H. Williams
MY SON
Last night I heard, my baby
cry. I saw his tear drops fall.
Last night I heard my new
born's breath and felt his tiny
hand. Last night my son—was
just my son, today my son's a
man.

Kathleen Grant Watts
YOU'RE NEEDED
It is very, very easy
To feel sorry for one's self,
And to think "Well, no one
needs me,
Time to put me on the shelf."
But for those who wear the
banner,
Of the Christ who died for
you,
That's the time of sweetest labor
And there's still much work
to do.
As you wake up in the morning
And you're laying there quite
still,
Ask the Father for his blessing—
Pray for guidance in His will.
Know the sweetness of his
presence,
Feel the healing of His grace,
And the folks who live around
you
Will see Jesus thru your face!
Your eyes, all day, are mirrors,
Others look and smile or
pout.
What they see there are your
road signs
Teaching love and trust—or
doubt.
And your lips speak words of
kindness,
Or they bite and snap and
sting,
Showing up the way of sorrows
Or the place where angels
sing.
Age is not a time for moaning,
But for gladness in the heart.
Each day brings our Savior
closer
(A goal is better than the
start!).
Someone sees the way we
manage
And it helps—or leaves a
stone,
For a foot that's traveling
after,
To pass over—or be thrown.
You have never been more
needed
Than you are this very day.
So come on—look up—be happy!
Show a "Jesus Face" today.
A smile, a hug, a word of cheer
Will help someone to know,
That living for the Lord each
day
Is the only way to go!

Elizabeth S. Johnson
CHILDREN
There are children of all sorts;
Kind ones, mean ones, some
distort:
Bouncy, bubbly, always beaming;
All results from a world of
screaming.
Caring more and more each day;
Giving some in their own little
way:

Trying to make each and
everything right;
With all their little strength
and might.
Children are our pride and
possession;
Caring for them is their parent's
profession:
Never underestimate a child's
ability;
Their love to you is a big
responsibility.

Vickie J. McElroy
YOU AND ME
I know that it can never be,
you and me, and yet I still hope.
We belong to two different
worlds.
Sometimes those two worlds can
come together
but I knew from the start,
not with you and me.
What I wouldn't give to have
known what lie behind those
beautiful blue eyes. Could it
have been you were thinking of
you and me?
My Christmas wish came true.
Seeing you should have made
me glad. But instead it made me
sad for I knew still it could
never be you and me.
Your heart belongs to another
so you see it can't be you and
me.
Memories of our joy, memories
of our laughter.
Memories are forever in my
heart of you and me.

Why is it that in life
somethings can never be?
No matter what you try or how
the ache seems to grow with
each passing day. When it all
seems so right and yet you
know no matter what, it just
can't be, not even for just
a little while, you and me.

Frank C. Hamilton
DISSIPATION

The chainsaw screams its own
protest
for it's being used to dispossess
a lovely grove of tall pine trees,
with no replanting to appease
this dissipation of a wood
where patriarchs of nature stood
as proteges of the divine
in towering dignity of time.
I grant that God gave trees to
man
for wood to build, and bark to
tan,
but, man persists to fall the
trees
as if they bore some fell disease.
I wonder, is the lumber worth
such dissipation of the earth
that soon is gullied when
exposed
to elements without its clothes.
Can reality be seen in words
our children's children will
have heard?
"I think that I shall never see
a poem, lovely as a tree?"
Will their inheritence in time
when woods, as woods, were so
sublime,
be joyless in the world to be
if trees are in a zoo to see?

George N. Kokoros
A MAN FOR ALL AGES

'Tis Christmas Eve. . .
The wreath I've hung;
My tree is trimmed. . .
The bells have rung;
And now I sit
To reminisce
Of one dear Eve
I can't dismiss.
Quite anxiously,
I waited for
That Christmas Day—
Like those before—
When just a lad
So nimble quick,
I knew he'd come—
Old dear St. Nick!
That night I dreamed—
I was just six—
That he had come
With toys and tricks. . .
His sack so full
Of things he made,
Which he had packed
And now displayed.
A dainty doll
He left for Ann. . .
A ball and bat
For brother Dan;
And there beside
Our sofa-bed,
I saw him leave
My wagon red!
He checked his list—
He checked it twice—
And reassured
That all was nice,
While on the roof—
My eyes could see—
His reindeer stood
So patiently!
I saw this man,
With kindest heart,
Remove his boots
Close-by the hearth. . .
And there he leaned
To warm his feet,
Which felt the chill
Of snow and sleet.
Dad's chair he spied
So huge and soft,
Whereon he sat
Then turned and coughed;
And soon he fell
Quite fast asleep. . .
Each snore I heard
Was slow but deep.
Then he awoke
And donned each boot;
He fluffed his beard
And fixed his suit.
The clock now chimed
The hour two. . .
His sack he grabbed
Then climbed the flue.
And soon I saw
Each tiny hoof
Leap off our steep
Now moonlit roof;
I heard his laugh
Against the night,
As he fled on
To spread delight.
'Twas fun to dream
That dream I had,
When I was just
A little lad.
And tho' the years
Have gone their way,
I still conceive
He lives today!

Ms. Donnie (Bowden) Mackey
DIVORCE

In this beautiful house of
Rock. .Concrete. .Gut and
Me. .
I feel a prisoner of my own soul.
Crying of days that use to be. .
of laughter, love, children,
peace and me.
I dare not look back on dreams
of yesterday. .for they have
daily faded and gone away. .
All that's left is just TODAY.
I dare not tarry along life's
way. . . .and yet. . . .the very
walls cry out to me and say,
the way things use to be.
Yet morning. .numb. .my body
fills with life and the sun
shines in and tells of a new day.
This house is just Rock. . .
Concrete. . .Gut and Me

Etta A. Moretti
THE GOLD OF YOUTH

Ah, sweet youth that tingles,
From feet to finger tips,
Sweet life that surges,
From full red rosy lips.
Sweet throb and beat,
That youth alone can know,
Wild oats and tares of wheat,
The hands of youth all sow.
Yet how dead youth is to truths,
That age so quickly brings,
How fast the joy can be
squeezed,
That causes youth to sing.
For age soon teaches failures,
Standing pain, and loss, and
sorrow,
Accepting all lifes heartaches,
Trying with courage to meet
tomorrow.
If only youth could be a miser,
Hoard some of her shimmering
gold,
Have some left to spend
triumphantly,
That's when you need it. When
you're old.

Krishna Chaudhuri (Mukhopadhyay)
RICH AND POOR

If I were born rich,
I could pitch
In any one of those baskets,
Full of fruits and nuts,
Without cuts
Of my reputation.
Oversensitiveness
Only creates
Introvert, meek sensation;
In the harsh world,
Poors are forced,
and coerced,
To lick the foot
Of the rich Brute.
Roaring anger piled up high,
As lightning of the sky,
But essentially fruitless
Turns into frustration.

T. M. Snyder
UNTITLED

One find day so i'm told
when the old things seem new
and all the things clean
are grown dirty and dusty
the words i have written
will come to a limelight
where the thoughts they convey
though the paper be musty
will sound quite refreshing
mean something to someone
cause private reflection
stir public debate
be used by young rebels
as slogans on banners
offend sensibilities
help erase hate
assist first time lovers
to whisper sweet nothings
while seldom remembered
as something once learned
uplift sagging spirits
rejuvenate hope
or get banned in Boston
or even be burned
then i'll have achieved
i'll then be accomplished
even though i be dead
so they say one fine day!

Vanita Rae Smith
THE SUN BLESSED OUR LOVE WITH IT'S RAY

How beautiful you were
standing there on the sand,
Where the sea so gently touched
the land.
Your body bathed with a golden
tan.
You and I standing there hand
in hand.
Your dancing blue eyes
brighter than day.
The sun blessed our love
with it's ray.
Lips together, we moved
away to play.
How we did love each other
as we lay.
People passed by with their
gawking stare,
Too busy to climb the sacred
stair.
Wishing they were us, but
afraid to dare.
Most of all, they were afraid
to share.
We laid together watching
the sky.
Looked at each other and
gave a sigh.
Knowing that soon we
would say good-bye.
Even in living, sometimes
we die.
Finally the moon appeared over
the hill,
Like raindrops falling on the
window sill.
We were in love and in love's
will.
Knowing that only love's glory
could fill.
We were together through
the night.
Hoping that tomorrow
would make it right.
Our love was eternal in our
sight.
But morning came and
brought its fright.
The years are many since that
place.
But I can never forget your face.
The beauty of love and its
chase.
I still love you and that's
my fate.

Jeffrey B. Day
AUTOMATION

Robots in wilderness—
Their thoughts blinking fury,
Their metallic sound
disturbance
Creeping through the voids
between trees.
See them stumble on spongy
floor,
Not planed and comfortably
hard,
Get dampness in their joints
And begin to slow,
Step in a gentle brook
And short out their memory
banks.
See the mouse, four months
later
As Winter lies about,
Lazing in a nest of wires
And chewing on a hoarded
pumpkin seed.

James Patton Meriwether
MOM

My thoughts have been with
you of late, the good ones and
the bad.
I've wondered how you could
relate, with sorrows that
you've had.
The toil of so many years, and
still you find the room,
To holding overwhelming
tears, for second from the
womb.
I know that I have given
heartaches numbered by the
score,
And as you give I simply take,
what seems for ever more.
But being your remaining son, I
hope that you at least,
Consolidate my faults as one,
my virtues are your feast.
And being writer of this rhyme,
O'er words I have control,
Please realize oh mother mine,
I love you most of all,
For it was you at least in part,
who guided inner thought,
And I am proud of what I art,
what you sold I had bought.

So I give to you love not to
feign, and please do not refuse.
When I do things that seem in
vain, remember I'm confused.
And with this gift I gave to you
to warm you just in part,
Another please don't
misconstrue, to warm your
lonely heart.

Louis Bascelli

ALONE AND INFANT ON A SMALL BLUE WORLD

My words spill into my wet
shoes,
I wish I were dead or
thereabouts,
For this citidel is cold, and I
Am no magician to remedy my
soul
Which is twisted as if demons
lost the
Urge to wrench it away from
me. They left
It dangling.
Looking at this cozy wood, I
wonder
If the trees are just lazy people
Turned to wood. I am scared to
Touch a dial or turn a knob.
Please
Don't accuse me of being
Paranoid.
Please, please, please. And
please don't
Wear a green sweater.
If I wake, I dream.
If sleep can cure me, so be it.
If a smile be therapy, smile.
I am alone and infant in a
small blue
World.
I'll endure until I tire again.

Naomi Neitzke

HALF-BLOOMED FLOWER

(a posthumous tribute to Cal from his Naomi)

You were just a half-bloomed
flower,
though withered in disgrace.
Petals yet not fashioned in all
it's guises and symmetries.
But there you stood, alone
among the fields
of down and clover.
A solitaire of nature lithly
blending,
to life's tollsome tune.
Somehow translucently bending
to the
rhythm of the flock.
Gay, happy, carefree bud of a
flower,
you languishly flourished.
Until the half-formed petals,
engulfed
by inusitate forces downed.
As if too soon your life did
cease,
by jealous gods decreed.

Iris Rodgers Gerber

THE MIRACLE OF RAINBOWS

Thank You, God, for rainbows,
they truly mesmerize
Such glorious hues, from reds to
blues
as they arch across the skies.
When the sunbeams dance with
raindrops
thus, the lovely rainbow
gleams,
reminding us when life seems
bleak
we must not fail to seek our
dreams.
Life is such a precious gift,
let us take the time to
reminisce
and ponder o'er the
magnitude,
for this journey's but an
interlude.
Heavens promise of a rainbow,
to each and everyone,
brings a peaceful sense of
miracles
even when the showers have
gone.

Bonnie L. Yotter

THE TIME WE CLIMB

stop.
they will
arrive
When they
heaven.
straight to
that lead
stairways
climbing
footsteps
just as
heartbeats
of my
to think
I like

Cynthia R. Golderman

MISTY AUTUMN

Misty autumn, the chill and hint of the whisper of Winter-leaves falling red, mauve and gold, leaving the branches barren.

The rain calling an end to Summer, brings the most nostalgic time of the year.

Branches bare, waiting for the jewelry of sparkling ice to adorn them, rustle and move like giant grasshoppers across the sky.

Turtles in the pond, crawling in the mud to keep their deep sleep with Winter, braving the air and the last vestiges of a warm day's sun to remember again in the Spring.

I love the Autumn and all that it tells us. Spring will come again, and when it does, the verdant nature of life born again, will bring us happiness.

Misti Thiel

UNTITLED

Silence
thunders down
the empty aisle
as I listen
to my echoes
of past
happier times,
waiting
for someone
I know will never
return
the long line
of sympathic
friends
have all
gone home
leaving
me to mourn
your leaving
with
my own tears
and white lace.

Irma Campbell

PRAY FOR PEACE

What do we mean when we
pray for PEACE
Does it simply mean that
bombing will cease?
While men still crouch in fear
and dread
Knowing that communism will
spread.
While men are still afraid to
pray
Because of the communistic way
And some folks still must hide
their face
Because other men hate their
race
Lets pray that VICTORY shall
be won
And that there's peace for every
one
We can make the right prevail
Trust in GOD we need not fail
If we fight to shield the right
GOD will help us by his might
So lets each one do our part
To keep the peace within our
heart. .

Constance Dee Gordon

TRUE LOVE

I hope that I shall never see;
that rotten guy that cheated on
me.
With his eye all black and blue,
I saw him running with one
shoe.
I was really mad and started to
yell.
I told him he could go to h---.
I was very upset and super
urked!

Gosh! Do I ever hate that jerk!!
Imagine him and another girl.
Boy, did that ever destroy my
world!!
He said that I was the only one;
to believe him I was really
dumb!
I threw at him some odds and
ends.
I think I hit him in the head.
He dodged and ducked from left
to right.
We have a date this Friday
night.

Mel Lawson

THRENODY

You lately walked and talked
with us as we traversed
That twisting and uneven trail
that men call life.
Yours was a firm and measured
tread that drummed the beat
And steadfast was your voice
that rose above the strife.
You brought a presence that was
felt; an ear that heard;
An eye that saw; a heart that
gave beyond demand.
You worked for causes that were
good, nor counted time
You freely spent when others
sought your helping hand.
The lumps and leavens that are
life's we shared with you

As pilgrims share the fortunes
of an unknown course;

The laugh, the tear,
exhilaration's lifting thrust;
Anticipation's whetted edge, and
grave remorse.
From you we learned a courage
that is rare;
The kind that does not buckle
from a single blow;
But rallies though the bout
is marked with bruising odds,
And one is matched against a
most unequal foe.
We watched you as you walked
ahead along the trail;
And as approaching night forced
you its cloak to don
We prayed you would escape its
viscous, sable cape,
But you could not, and with the
coming of the day
We saw you dimly through a
mist; and you were gone.

William R. Eakin

ONE CANNOT NUMBER THE STARS

One cannot number the stars
though they reflect deeply pure
in finite chains of mountain
ponds,
though their eternal bright souls
know Death in the bowels of
trees;
though their sirenic singing
echoes pale in the void's bosom,
one cannot number the stars.
Though the earth shatters
against walls
of bounded space's cosmic night
and science grasps up the debris
from each dark, wounded
corridor
with sticky talons, clasping all;
though man's full eye detects
each light,
he cannot number the stars.

Jackie A. Miller

TOUCHED HORIZONS

. . . .Need I to look any longer,
or need I to search anymore
for the
I that has been in the days
of yore born whole. . .
. . . .have all my "touched
horizons"
really been? Oh yes, I must
say
I've felt deep down within
my heart and soul. . .

Robert L. J. Zenik

1,782,491

Yes I'm going into a state
Where-in-which it makes me
late
For a very important date
With my own vernacular fate

Fred A. Keagle

ANGEL

Who could believe that I'd have an angel to touch.

An angel to hold when cold or hurting, she is my angel for happiness and hope.

My angel of today, tomorrow and of yesterday, of pure will of life and desire of love.

My grasping angel of dreams and recall of memories of foolish days wasted without her.

All the answers to real fullfilment of the pure essences of love, my angel.

Now I've tasted the best in life thru her, nothing could even come close to my angel in life.

To have gain her is nice, to never lose her is my goal.

With her my dreams all seem as possible as tomorrow coming, Thru her I now absorb the feelings of happiness of life.

Even our downs are mere bumps in life, instead of large mountains to conquer.

For as I stand by her life is not a guilty trap of emotions,

but thru my angel life is a
haven of desire and pure
essences.
How lucky for me to have an
angel, how great the love we
share.
The greatness is all from her,
my hoping is all for her.
She is my rhyming words of
reason, my very truth in all
that can possibly be.
She pounds thru my very body
as if she was the very blood
of my life, she is my only life
and without her my death.

Kate Kelly Gienger
ALL THE EARTH'S A BANQUET

I eat dirt,
I always have
I reckon I always will.
To partake of soil
was frowned upon,
as the adults would question,
"Why?"
I didn't know why,
so they administered
(as a necessary cure)
a lethal dose of caster oil.
If they would have asked,
"What does dirt taste like?"
I could have answered,
Mother Earth has a flavor,
that can be savored,
momentarily,
by mulling the soil
about on the tongue.
Dirt has a wholesome
satisfying taste,
cultivated in quantity,
and pure to the palate.
If the adults would have asked,
"When do you eat dirt?"
I could have answered that, too.
There is a pattern to the tasting,
that follows revolving seasons,
a fresh spring shower,
a plowed field in early fall.
It's just about that time again. . .
would you excuse me please,
for I must fetch
the caster oil.
You see,
I eat dirt,
I always have
I reckon I always will.

Aileen L. Lum Sarcedo
NOTE TO: "A WANDERING HUSBAND"

If *YOU* should get. . . . .
On the Outside Again,
Remember Your Home;
When, meeting a Friend.
KEEP IN LINE. . . . .
If YOU, should Find;
And REMEMBER WHAT?. . . ..
"You Left Behind."
FOR. . . . .It won't Be
"THERE."
If, You Don't Care. . . . .
And, You'll end up paying;
Your *"OWN"* Fare.
REMEMBER THIS. . . . .
For. . .THIS IS TRUE;
As, I am "TIRED". . .
Of, BEING A "FOOL". . . . .

Loving you.....
Always & Forever "Lin"

Cornelia B. Furbish
THE ALIEN

A great white gull, on wide-
spread wing,
Soars over my roof, above the
town,
His voice is silent in his
flight,
Perhaps the traffic noises drown
His keening cries? No—he is
inland
From the sea and alien here.
His voice is mute—in noiseless
arcs
He swings above a concrete sea.
The air is hot and thick, lacking
the salt tang
That he wont to breathe. Some
deep-born instinct.
Soon, will turn him back—to
flee the town
And find again the wide, free
place
Above the rolling deeps, where
he belongs.
I'll miss the alien and my
heart
Will follow him in flight—
for part of me
Is alien, too, and would
fly free.

Marjorie Hansbrough
THE BADDEST BOY IN SCHOOL

Staargart, T. was a cadet
In a military school;
Six years old,
Smart beyond his years, but
He already had a name, it was
The Baddest Boy in School
At first-grade nap-time,
Staargart wouldn't sleep, so
Neither could the others
"I am," he loudly boasted,
"The baddest boy in school."
"Not so," I lied,
"I've heard that YOU
Are the BEST boy in school."
"Oh no!" the other tads replied,
"He IS the baddest boy in
school."
The upper classmen—his so-
called superiors—
They really envied Staargart,
But their rank and dignity were
damaged
When ignored by—
This Baddest Boy in School.
We liked each other—Staargart
and I
And when we'd chance to meet,
He'd put his little arms around
me—
This Baddest Boy in School.
They found ways to recoup their
pride;
They teased him and hazed him
and—
Fully knowing the penalty,
Taught him to say strange, bad
words.
Now Colonel Morrow was a
kind man, also fair,
But he had discipline to keep
and morals to teach,
And his paddle often landed
lightly
On the little bottom of
The Baddest Boy in School.
At full-dress rehearsal for family
and friends,
Swords gleamed brightly; bugles
harmonized;
But in the last young
squadron—out of step
Marched Sraargart, T., The
Baddest Boy in School.
At last, came graduation day;
One by one, the students
marched to the front,
Each to receive his dues. .
Then, one little boy threw the
whole room into
pandemonium.
They clapped; they cheered;
they stomped their feet;
The rafters shook in agreement,
For the highest scholastic
honors went to—
Staargart, T. "The Baddest Boy
in School."

Robert L. Woodward
TREASURY OF MEMORIES

Heirlooms of thought collected
in my precious treasury
Are experiences of love and joy
locked in my memory
A tiny girl following Daddy's
wagon down the muddy road
Walking with him to school
through snow and bitter cold
Pictures taken at the annual
reunion of each family
Picking and eating cherries
from the over-laden tree
Playing house under the grape
arbour with Sis or a cousin
Making colorful hollyhock dolls
carefully by the dozen
Sitting with Dad in the crib on
a cold winter's day
Picking corn for seed, happiness
in a contented way
Snuggling into a feather bed,
winter's stars shining bright
The joy of an ice cream cone on
a hot summer's night
Spending Christmas Eve Night
at Grandmother's house
The wonder of the tree Santa
trimmed, quiet as a mouse
Memorial Day's Grave
decorating and a Soldiers
Prayer
Greeting friends and family and
a picnic dinner there
Watching the Blacksmithy mold
metal with anvil and fire
To repair a piece, shoe a horse
or sharpen a plow share
Tag along with Mom to make
garden, plant each seed just
right
Choosing that first Mother's
Day gift, watching her delight
Violets found in Granddad's
timber on an early day in
spring
Hickory nutting in the Autumn
and help bring the cows in
Watch the magic of butter
making and shaping in molds
Joy of finding mints that
Grandfather's pocket holds
Clover jewelry, daisy chains,
dandelion puffs and curls
The love, joy, and treasures,
memories of a little girl

Edith Maud Dunkin
FRUITFUL PEACHTREE

The towering old peachtree,
rosy with bloom,
When April came over the land,
Now is bowing and bending,
well laden with fruit—
Sugary bushels, awaiting a hand
To gather them in, when they
ripen and yellow,
As under the hot August sun
they grow mellow.
The limbs, drooping low from
this full crop of beauty
Warn me picking and canning
will soon be my duty;
But the ripest and nicest, served
with sugar and cream,
Will provide us a banquet that
now seems like a dream—
Oh, won't eating those peaches
be grand!

Steve Carlson
THOUGHTS

Thoughts;
Intruding on what must be done
by what might
making what isn't
a possibility
and what is. . .
questionable
yet forming the only reality
we know.

Diane M. Flaherty
DAWN MANES

A silvery dawn's astir and aglow,
The family's asleep and the TV
low.
It's past five in the morning
near my coast,
At the wedding in Endland,
noon, almost.
The wispy fine mane, the silver
head band,
The move alongside the new
bride's right hand.
The four gray horses ahead of
the bride
Have manes dressed in silver,
coachmen who ride.
Some nimble fingers wove a
silver strand
Through those manes just last
night, in old England.
A wedding horse is watched, not
put to bed;
In a stall he might scratch
his itchy head.
The sleepy grooms stayed and
played their card games,
So I might remember silver
dressed manes.
The sun comes up gold, my
coffee is cold,
As I think how best the tale
should be told
Of the silken heads near the
gleaming reins
On the horses of dawn with
matchless manes.

Nelda Lorraine LeVant
TAKING A STAND

Takin(g a s)tand
Kushaiah!

Frederic Lasser
DEATH

How oft we walked
The peach and the grapes
In the garden of the neighbor
Ripe of skin and taste
Three swift steps
Of passion
Peeled our swollen heart
Naked to the bottom
And then we stopped
The peach and the grapes
In our own garden
Ripe of skin and taste
Three steps of truth
Stripped us of illusions.

Johnny Jay
AN OLD PAIR OF BOOTS

Just an old pair of boots
made of leather and thread,
but they're strong, and made
very well.
They took quite a beating
with us retreating
on the road, yes, the road thru'
hell.

Now this old pair of boots
cannot live without shame
though they served us so very well.
Then they kicked out all "cant's"
and made us advance
up the road, yes, the road thru' hell.
It's an old pair of boots,
which have trod many miles,
and many a story could tell,
of the mud, and the rain,
of snowy terrain
on the road, yes, the road thru' hell.
It's an old pair of boots
full of old memories.
A pair that the Army won't sell.
They're the boots of a man
who went thru' Japan
on the road, yes, the road thru' hell.

F. J. Bruette Sr.

HOLOCAUST

In the shadows of Darkness
Behind the wall of treachery
On the lips of love tormented
By the cold hands of war
Seek the human sacrifice
The kiss of death, forever more
The bomb keeps ticking,
With the clock on the wall
Tainted by the fungus of greed
Mocking all hopes and desires
Until the dawn, explodes
And the world with war is on fire
The legion lands, perplexed
Naked on the barren coast
As the pearls in the harbor
Probe the rocks on singapore
And the sand upon the beaches
Washes the blood into the shore
Grotesque, the sentinel stands
On the grave of misconception
For they in honesty believed
The propaganda of war
And like all others before them
Will walk this earth no more

Laura O. Willis

THE COLORADO SCHOOL BUS TRAGEDY

It was in Eastern Colorado, on the plains
Where the winding country roads and the narrow lanes,
Led to this little country school house painted white
Where the children studied math and how to read and write.
Back in the thirtys, about fifty years ago
A blizzard came one day, leaving huge drifts of snow,
The teacher said, its getting worse, we must leave now
And maybe the school bus will get us home somehow.
The snow drifts were as deep as the fence posts were high
And the white flakes kept falling from out of the sky.
The children were scared and cold, their voices were still
When the bus got stuck in the snowdrift on the hill.
The teacher tried hard to get it started again
But the wheels just went deeper and would only spin,
He told the children, stay calm and try to keep warm,
And he began to walk through that terrible storm.
As evening came, their hands and feet were feeling numb
And they started to think, "what if help did not come?"
There was this one young boy, just barely in his teens
Wearing a lightweight coat and a pair of blue jeans.
He told the children to clap their hands and not cry
And keep moving, or they might go to sleep and die.
He did all he could to keep the young ones alive,
But many of them froze before help could arrive.
As the night ended and it was daylight again,
This teen age boy saw the snowplow and several men,
His prayers had been answered and the help had come
But not before some of them were frozen and numb.
The men crossed the fields and there in a huge snowdrift
The teachers body was found standing, frozen stiff,
Through the snowdrifts, his lifeless body was carried
And taken home with the children to be buried.
The end of the parent's waiting had now arrived
Some children had frozen and died, but some survived.
None of them could understand why this had to be
The terrible blizzard and school bus tragedy.

Patty Louvall

FASTIDIOUS FELINE

Fastidious feline, with her
rough, red eraser
Wipes away the sanguinary
sauce of her predatory history.

Dorothy Greene

OCEANIA

Behold the blue-green Mother Sea;
All life claims me as source;
My depths are boundless mystery,
My waves are fluid force.
I seize the shore and then retreat,
My moon-ruled cycle now complete.

Gwenn Boudreaux

UNTITLED

Lonely old man, clothes tattered and worn
Let me be your friend
Your eyes tell of life I've never known
and may never know, be my teacher, help me grow
Be my friend.
Lonely old man, your every wrinkle cries
of life's passion and spirit seen only with your eyes
My attention sparks in you a fire
Let the flame burn low, set my soul aglow
Be my teacher, help me grow
Be my friend.
Lonely old man, from your heart and soul
The shadows of time step into rhyme
With stories of old from lips so cold
Oh, you've grown so old, so all alone
Be my teacher, help me grow.
Be my friend.
Lonely old man, you're not lonely any more
You are my friend and we'll share
I'll lend you my youth as you lend me your truth
I'll annoint you with love, and replace
With life's finest gowns, your clothes
Tattered and worn because you are
My teacher, you've helped me grow
You are my friend.
Lonely old man, you are my king
Love and kindness to you I'll bring
You are my friend. You'll be lonely
No more. . .

Morgan Griffith

LAY OF THE LAST DRAGON

The moon grows pale by midnight
Her light is nearly spent
The final star has fallen
Without a heart's lament.
The sun is waning crimson
Above a damson sky
Great castles lie in ruin
And elvish woodlands die.
Wise kings are cryptic spectres
Upon cold, crumbling thrones
Memorials are forgotten
And lost queens weep alone.
The wizards have all gathered
And sadly sailed away
For none believe in magic—
They have no cause to stay.
Here in this silent cavern
Upon my tarnished cache
I've seen the old ways burning
And young winds sow the ash.
I feel my lifeblood fading
My breath cannot find flame
And ere this world surrenders
I'd voice my dragon's claim.
For there are still a handful
Of diamonds in the dust:
Brave heroes scorned like beggars
Their rune-swords thick with rust.
And new suns can be kindled
To light the road to dreams
If hope and faith are cherished
And magic full redeemed.
And now my head weighs heavy
I take my final flight
For I have sung my anthem
And bid the world, goodnight.

Arden K. Michael

TWO THE SAME

We all see things in different lights
As we go through life each day
Whether it be while at work
Or even while at play
As we notice couples on the streets
Joining in life's game
Each man hoping he can be proud
Of his choice of a dame
She likes to think she's right too
Or so she does claim
Look at him! She really lit his flame
Hoping he'll bring her to fame
Then their Wedding Day arrives
Their friend and relatives came
Oh! She was so very proud
To take on his cute name
Taking off down life's road to become lame
Each one saying the other's to blame
For the children, It's really a shame
In the homes of TWO THE SAME

Mary Jonelle LaRue

THE KINGDOM OF PEACE

Silence.
Soft rippling mars the
Lonely stream.
Dew glitters solemnly on
The nearby foliage.
A gentle rain falls delicately,
Highlighting the lush green grass.
A timid fawn peeps out from
Behind a tree to watch the
Quietly pattering rain.
Wherefore doth the sun shine
In this misty world?
A glimmer shines all around,as
A colorful rainbow faintly
Falls through the soft rain.
Peace flows through this sombre
Kingdom, uninterupted.
If only the world and all its
Cities could succumb to this
Overpowering, lazy peace,
Forever.

Inez Sherbine

INTERLUDE

The trees are silent now,
Etched in nakedness against the sky,
against the hill;
Their silhouettes greatly changed,
yet beautiful still.

Against the pink and grey
of the cool evening sky,
They look like sentinels standing watch
as days of October hurry by.
November. . .December. . .
They come, with frosted fingers,
to set the hills aglow;
To, once again, drape the trees
in velvet robes of snow.

Lucee Dininny

AVENUES OF TRUTH

i traveled the avenues of truth today
trails vanished—
swallowed by man's machines
childhood discoveries remain within my mind
daily walks with Dad
discovery of a robin's nest
secured in a crotch of a low tree
blinded little creatures

huge head
small useless wings
grotesque creatures
nature reverses her offsprings
beautiful birds emerge
uncovered a raided rabbit's den
"the law of nature"
"nature keeps everything in balance"
endless search for a milkweed plant
to open and scatter the seeds into the wind
thus saving the shell for a boat to sail upon my tub
thanks, Dad
you taught me the love of nature
man's machine destroyed the woodlands
pushing the earth
ripping the roots from the soil
draining the swamp
a super highway will appear
capable of killing and saving lives
i will live the avenues of truth tomorrow

Lynn Breeden
TUNED TO THE WIND
As a young girl
she was untamed, unbridled.
Once you thought her calming
she tore off quite unquided.
Her eyes watched every move
but thoughts tuned to the wind.
A man she married.
A child to her was born.
Two years she tarried
feeling desolate, forlorn.
A man, a child, forgotten.
Her heart tuned to the wind.
Her life almost over,
she grieved those years past.
A man, a child, she sought,
a plea for moments past.
The man, the child looked,
then tuned to the wind.

Sara C. Mathews
LOVE AND SORROW
She was born on Mothers Day,
The first of six that tenth of May.
Being the eldest of the lot,
Her wisdom and courage was always sought.
By our side she remained,
Through those years of growing pains.
A year later almost to the day,
A sister was born in the month of May.
Friendships were made from the start,
Little was known it would end in broken hearts.
The eldest a giver of love and soul,
Her sister a taker and much too bold.
But Mom and Dad with time to spare,
Gave another sister for them to share.
The night was cold, laden with snow,
At home she was born, and began to grow.
Homely in sight, beauty never came,
Years later, no one remembered her name.
And as faith will have its way,
Another sister came one day.
A little too thin, a little too tall,
With eyes of blue, the size of balls.
A late bloomer one might say,
Like a burst of sun, she threw her rays.
And though there were four of us girls to feed,
Daddy began to sow, yet, another seed.
And Mom acting somewhat coy,
Made room for her baby boy.
With four sisters to keep him in tow,
Our little brother began to grow.
And with six years gone past,
Mom and Dad gave us the last.
Spooky we called her on first sight,
For she was such a tiny mite.
But sweet and cuddley like a new bought dolly,
Two days later, we renamed her Lolly.
And so we began as six all close in age,
Raised in poverty to some stage.
Together we were from the start,
And with our love we filled each heart.
Then one Saturday, without a warning,
One of our six, left us wondering.
Faiths were questioned, tears were shed,
Our hearts were broken, for one of us was dead.
And we thank ourselves a million times,
For all the memories stored inside.
And as time goes on, and our hearts mend,
We will never forget how we began.

Catherine Baron
WHERE ARE THE CLOWNS?
Cheering crowds applauding your act.
A thousand laughing faces
Melting away my confidence like cotton candy,
Or watching my heart
As it does trapeze flips;
But no one is there to catch it.
Shattered bits—
Confetti for your bucket.

Paula Papponi
THE RED CHINESE SLIPPERS
The red Chinese slippers
hugged my feet with newness.
They were smooth against
the old floor.
Bright were they, challenging
the summer sunshine.
Smooth and wrinkle-free
as a polished apple.
Flowers, birds, and butterflies
danced colorfully upon my toes;
and when I walked there was
loud clapping.
By October though,
one had to look closely to distinguish
the pheasant from the peony.
Tight hugs became loose pats,
and the clapping was reduced
to sounds of shuffling paper.
By December,
the old floor felt quite at home
under the red Chinese slippers.
Frayed toes opened up and let
the winter wind fly in.
I was cold;
and for a while heavy socks were
placed between me and my
red Chinese Slippers.
I ran to catch the cat.
They didn't come with me.
They stayed alone in the hallway;
not even together,
not even right side up.
One on its side, one on its embroidery.
I watched them, both of us motionless.
It was like a funeral.
Come the Spring,
I shall look for new ones.

Joseph H. Countess
FOR SOMEONE SPECIAL
When I'm alone and weary
with feelings painted blue
When my smile is lost to sadness
and I'm not sure what to do
I fill my thoughts with visions
of a lady eight years old
With warm blue eyes so tender
soft, flowing hair of gold
My troubles seem to melt away
as she strokes my memory
And suddenly I'm surrounded
by love she feels for me
My weariness is blown away
like leaves to Autumn's wind
And lips once set to sadness
are loosened to a grin
A little girl of beauty
with eyes that seem to glow
Small lady of affection
who's called by Stacie Jo
To understand the feelings
softly voiced above
One must be a father
who's known a daughter's love
When I'm alone and weary
with feelings painted blue
I fill my thoughts with visions
and those visions are of you
I love you Stacie Jo
Dad

Florence Whitaker Gross
EMILY DICKINSON: SELF—EPITAPH
I fled from Life and took my Love with me,
Deep and rich and warm within my heart.
Oyster-fashion, out of pain I wrought the pearl,
Hidden close until Death reft the shell.
Cutting swiftly, surely,
My fancy carved poetic cameos,
Dainty, mystic,
Set in iridescent words.

David O. Dodds
THE WALLS OF BILIBID
Within the walls of Bilibid
The days were often long;
While many cursed the God above
And lost the love of song.
Death stalked its prey as, one by one,
We heard the victims' groans—
We who lived on that living death
Were naught but ghastly bones.
Within the walls of Bilibid
Hope died within the breast;
While faith was like the sun when it
Is sinking in the west.
No love had man for fellow-man—
For there was none to spare,
No sympathy could one expect—
For there was none to care.
Above the walls of Bilibid
The stars were drifting by;
And in the stillness of the night
One whispered: "It is I."
Who spoke those words? Not they who cursed—
Their voices long had ceased;
But Someone spoke—and faith arose
Like sunrise in the east.
Above the walls of Bilibid
I looked away to God;
And resurrection hope forgot
The sorrow of the sod.
Love for my dying fellow-men—
The Calvary gift I shared
With all my sympathy because—
Christ was the One who cared.

Mary Adams
THE FIRST DAWN
The first dawn after a storm--
so fragile, so entirely still
you could sound it with a rod
as upon a piece of fine crystal,
so it sings beneath the mind's touch.
The first dawn and unlike other dawns
sounds you with its rods of light
and sets your inner crystal humming--
so fragile a resonance and so still
entirely after the storm.
It is the first dawn, womb-weary,
sparking light upon a vision of hills
reluctant to flame the day but
intent upon a delicate kindling.
(Juncos sway on laurel leaves--
they bob for berries beneath
a fine shower of raindrops...
they dip and sway and preen
wet feathers, bathing in the
first dawn.)
It is a primal dawn
cloaked in autumn chill,
treading lightly upon the hem
of the storm and so fragile
----a fresh covenant----
as trinity bells on an early sun day
wed my soul to the dawn.

May Coblentz Rhoades
50TH ANNIVERSARY
Hand in hand we've walked life's way
To this — our Golden Wedding Day,
Coming this far—we treasure rest
Looking back—we've been truly blest;
We've been spared the grief of being torn apart
By death, divorce or a broken heart—
The ill health and worries we had to share
Were overcome by faith and prayer.
Problems and sacrifice, with tears shining through
In faith, hope and love, made life's dream come true.
The family—entrusted to our care
Has been a joy beyond compare.
Our love for God and each other is still growing
We can hardly contain the love God is bestowing.

Placing our hands in His—we find
Comfort, great joy and peace of mind
Walking in the sunset hours of time
Hand in hand—the horizon is sublime.

Bess Teresa Cuddy
MY STAR

While on a lonely walk on night,
I thought the sky a dazzling sight.
And I had not gone very far
When I was *wishing* for a star.
"Such cannot be for me," I sighed --
Then gasped, with palpitating pride.
Goddess Dianne had flung one down
With meteor-strings to form a crown.
You may not see it in my hair
But be assured I wear it there.

Cheryl Louise Hall
A CHILD'S LOVE

Two Little Boys Have Left An Everlasting Impression,
With The Look Of Love In Their Expression.
Tears Of Mixed Emotions Filled My Eyes,
Making It Very Hard Not To Cry.
Sadness Yet Joy Was In My Heart
As I Watched The Boys With My Dog Depart.
Though I Felt Sad, I Knew Inside,
The Two Little Boys Loved That Dog As Much As I.
He'll Have A Good Home Full Of Love And Affection,
With The Two Little Boys He'll Give Love And Protection.

Carmine Socci
A SKYLARK

Perched on a rock,
a skylark
wings its way
to a tree limb,
rests. . .
flaps its wings,
then flies
over treetops,
high
into the sky,
and begins
singing an aria—
thus filling the air
with melodic music!

Dan Solloway
DEVIL'S THREE RING CIRCUS

HURRY! HURRY! HURRY!
Ladies and gentlemen
The show is about to begin.
We are going to watch life
From begin to end.
In the first ring.
We have a small child asking why?
In the middle ring
We have a couple living a lie.
In the last ring
We have an old man about to die.
And the old man and small child asking why?
So HURRY! HURRY! HURRY!
Get your seats,
And watch your life parade by.

Paul M. Talley
WHAT IS FAITH?

What can be said
Of mice and men
In this, our troubled time
When no one hears the church bell chime
Should we not be together?
Like birds of a feather
Some say that God is dead
People causing us all to dread
If you fail to have faith
You're just like an orphan waif
Lost, without a cause
Take one minute and pause
Reflect and meditate
Perhaps you'll discover your fate
Wonder where you're going
All that we've been doing
What can we say
When our future looks so gray
Confusion all around
Listen for the heavenly sound
Heed the call
Lest you fall
Redemption can be realized
If to the sky we lift our eyes
It's not too late
To realize our fate

Robert E. Willis
UNTITLED

Searching the apple for the
worm to find a rotten place
within
before the worm can get to him
is how this man so hurt by Love
peels away ev'ry woman's skin

Ruby Eleanor Melnichuk
OUR GUEST ROOM

We're glad to have *You*
As our *GUEST"*
Fragrant flowers
And hope *YOU'LL* have
A good-night's Rest
ZZZZZZ
SSnoring

To-morrow *YOU*
Again may Roam
Chickity-Chickty
Chick-check-chick
But while *You're* here
Just feel at Home.
Sip and Relax

Clifford Bailey
STALLIONS OF WILDHORSE MESA

Whenever I drive to Hanksville
Through the swell of San Raphael,
I think of the tales I pondered
As a lad by my wishing well;
Of the stallions of Wildhorse Mesa
By the light of western stars,
On the trail of the covered wagon
Before the advent of cars;
The stories of wildwest heroes
And the villains like Jesse James;
Of the redskins' endless plunder
That their memory defames.
Far across a distant furrow
Through a land that time forgot,
I picture those fabled ponies
Approaching that tabled lot;
Their dust-flecked flanks still moving
Through the washes and purple sage,
While over the eastern ridges
There hurtles a postal stage
A linking the eastern cities
With dreams that were proved to be best,
And their flight as those fleeting stallions
From the days of the early West.

Catherine Lynn Kaskubar Coonan
CHRISTMAS. . .

When I was young
Mom and Dad use to say
"Now don't forget to wish Jesus
A Happy Birthday"
And tho I'd remember
It was all too easy for me
To get lost in the dreams
Of what Christmas would be
The trees and the tinsel
Golden ribbons and bows
The dreams of Santa
Of Rudolph's red nose
Snowman cookies
With raisin eyes
Grandma's freshly baked
Custard pies
Ah! But when I was young
I did not know
How things would change
As I would grow
For I'd never hear the tiptoeing
Of midnight feet
For Santa was someone
That I'd never meet
But I would find the true meaning
Of Christmas
Not wrapped in packages of red
But, rather, deep within
My heart instead
Not tucked under the lights
Of the Christmas tree
But all in the love
God has given to me.

Clara Werner McClary
MASTERPIECES

I walked through the woods
On this late summer day
Could have taken a thousand pictures
As I walked along the way.
Each a masterpiece could be
Framed and hung for posterity
O, that this could be so
Must it be only in words to show?
There were the dainty wildflowers
Growing along the trail
They seemed to say a cheery "Hi"
Yet there was about them mystery.
The tiny, new pine tree
Babe in the woods it seemed to me
I wondered how it dared face
The coming snow and sleet
But it will be there when I return
Tho' it be one year or ten
Growing tall and strong
And I shall look for it then.
The tall branches of the oak trees
Created vaulted cathedral beams
Supporting only stained glass
In patterns of various greens.
The choir consisted of bird song
I heard along the way
The kind of music that angels sing
I was sure of it today.
And God was in His pulpit
High above it all
Sending down His blessing
And love too great to tell.
And tho' these masterpieces
May never hang in a gallery
They shall be forever
Stored in my mem-o-ry.

John D. Barrett
LIVING LOST

If I had my life to live over again,
I'd have settled down on a farm with a friend.
One day many years, so many ago,
A kid came to town just looking to show,
That he was the fastest, top of the hill.
But he didn't know I was faster still.
A knock at my door, a shout from the street,
Come outta your house, man, your gonna get beat.
I strapped on my belt, I loaded my gun,
We stood face to face, me and this young one.
I saw his eyes twitch, I pulled fast and shot,
Revealed by his face, it's my bullet he bought.
I fought at Shiloh, pumped many with lead,
From experience I knew, that this boy was dead.
Much time has passed, water under the bridge.
Since I buried that boy on old Oak Ridge.
I've killed seventeen; they've always drawn first,
And after all these, the first was the worst.
And now you must see, why I'm filled with rum.
And too soon I know, that my day will come.
At the pearly gates, they'll probably say,
Hang on to your gun, it's the devil's day.

Keith Stone
UNTITLED

She leaves the lighthouse after
a hard day's work. She
needs a rest. The path
to her little home is easy to
follow by the light of
the ships burning on
the sea.

Thomas Frederick Teorey
OF GHOSTS, THERE ARE NONE

I passed the cemetery,
as I had done for years;
It didn't bother me none,
nor cause me any fears.
The dead were dead -- so be it,
just dust and brittle bones;
So how could any spirits
come floating by, with moans?
WITH MOANS! My gawd, I hear

them!
Please close the gates of hell!!
It must have been the whiskey
and water from the well.
The darkness closed around me,
and shut out every light;
The air grew chill and quiet --
I longed for end of night!
I thought -- I must be dreaming,
for ghosts do not exist;
But this dream kept unwinding -
O lord, did it persist!
The moans were all around me,
some soft, some very loud;
I felt the icy fingers
of one big ghostly crowd!
My mouth was full of cotton,
my throat was dry as sin!
No more could I have called out
than I could still the din.
I felt so light and airy --
my feet touched no firm place;
These spirits were controlling
my movement throughout
space!
I floated past the gravestones
while reading words engraved;
With many names familiar
the graveyard ground was
paved.
The moans were so much closer,
they whispered in my ear;
And then they grew much
louder --
They brought me little cheer!
I felt my body settle
so slowly to the ground,
Beside a brand new gravestone,
upon a sloping mound.
The spirits had hysterics,
the moaning was a scream;
So scared was I, and trembling,
I prayed this was a dream!
The darkness faded slowly,
till such a ghostly glow
Lit up the gravestone's printing -
I started reading, slow:
"Here lies a devilish poet,
whose verses are so gross,
But also stimulating --
and now we'll have him
CLOSE!

Chaplain G. Gregory Berzinec
COLONEL WILLIAM EDWARD BERZINEC
Fallen
on the field of battle in the
accursed Vietnamese War.
Still fresh is your grave,
Still even a snow storm from
the heights
Not once did snow cover
Its withered flower.
But I am tired of this life,
It is meaningless and dull,
With your breath not warm,
With your days not fulfilled.
Alas! Child blinded,
I expected something else from
life
In the distance, a misty hill
For me amiably shone.
I thought: Happiness, rushing
emotion
There will be much for me on
my journey,
Oh, Lord, how senseless I was
That I wanted to enter the
closed door!
And I swam. . .but what I saw
On that green bank,
As I swam over, hatred,
I cannot express.
And here, crushed soul,
I cast away my desire,
I am before the door of destiny
In stunned stature.
Will I remain on this road,
Will I mingle with the
meaningless crowd,
Perhaps I cannot bear this fear
in my soul,
Courageously, I throw my self
into battle?

In this unfair struggle. . .
young soldier,
In this battle. . .inexperienced
fighter,
If I will be firm, quiet,
Like you, will I fall in the end?
Oh, wherever be your spirit, for
us unseen,
Now unhappily soared,
Hear my moan and cry, my
loving verse,
I tore them from my heart!
But what if you are not there. . .
Oh, God!
To whom should I turn? I am a
stranger here
You are even now dearest to me,
In the grave dark and silent.
Sorrowful and lamenting father,

Dale A. Hoover
IS THIS WHY
Is this why trees grow tall
That a young lad might swing
From limb to limb and youth
into manhood?
Is this why he enters the
seclusion of the boughs?
To bear arms against his
neighbor?
Is this why clay is deep,
So a young lad may toil with
His childhood play soldiers?
Who one day will breathe with
life
And march throughout the land?
Is this why the sweetest rose
When its time is spent
Loses its enveloping fragrance
And gives forth only the
Foul staleness of mankind?
Is this why clay is deep?
So that roses can give forth
Their sweet fragrance for man
And trees can grow tall?
Is this why---

Marsha A. Mitchell
BIRD LADY
She sings, her softened feathers
folded neatly across her
rounded breast of heather.
She coos and plucks unruly
items from her life and
watches as they float silently
to rest at her feet.
She bobs, in an attempt to
escape from the confining
cage she so freely entered.
She speaks, twittering
constantly about nothing,
even though there is no one
to listen.
She flies, around in circles,
gaining height, then suddenly
plummets to where she began.
She shakes her head, clears her
mind, then starts all over
again.

Janette M. Burns
DEBTOR
I borrowed time from life today.
Hours of flame, spun through
with gray
Starred with autumn, flowered
in May.
I borrowed time from life today.
To buy the moon above tonight,
To buy a share of bubbles bright
Of mingled laughter and delight
Blown as only lovers might.
But magic is transient. Life
grudges its hours.
Mist and swift darkness blot out
the high towers.
My words fall unheeded, our
song but a cry.
Alone, disenchanted, a debtor
am I.

James B. Taylor
A STRANGER IN THIS LAND
From a small country town in
the hill
came a cold breeze that was
never still.
With it came a very lonely man,
a stranger in this land.
He was from a land all of his
own
and a life story which was never
known.
Claiming to hold the life of all
in his hand,
but still a stranger in this land.
He had a heart filled with
kindness and love for all
and a mind filled with respect
that will never fall.
Being the one to do when no
one else can
was a stranger in this land.
He was free from all evil and
pains
and there was no one who can
claim
to have made a man from the
sand,
but a stranger in this land.

Patricia E. O'Neal
DREAMERS LOVE
The feelings that I have inside,
I know for long, I can not hide.
I know that soon, my heart will
break,
And you will say, "Oh goodness
sake,
Dear precious girl, you're just a
fling.
There could never be, a genuine
ring.
I'm just out to have a swingin'
time,
My life for no one will I ever
bind!"
How could he have such
carefree ways?
Especially when he leaves me, in
such a daze.
How could he see me as a one
night stand?
I feel I could do anything, when
I hold his hand.
I look in his big bright shiny
eyes
And oh my God, how my body
cries,
To be held in his arms, all night
long,
And to hear him say, "I'll do you
no wrong."
Oh how I'd love to be the one in
his life,
And never have to worry, about
worldly strife.
I can picture us together, for a
long long time.
Each day I dream about him, I
hear musical chimes.
But what is this, he's saying to
me now?
Don't tell me my dreams are
tumbling down!
I must pretend I can not hear,
Or soon you'll see some lonely
tears.
I close my eyes, and think so
damn hard
Why your love, for me is barred.
I guess it's because you've made
up your mind,
That your heart no woman,
could ever find.
I feel like I'm in quicksand,
going down slow.
I guess my feelings for you, did
show.
Now as I am sinking, crying for
your hand,
All you can say is, "You're a one
night stand."

Jane Dugger
SUNSET
What a wonderous sight
it is to behold!
The Sun at dusk
with her rays of gold!
The earth rejoices
in pure delight,
As she readies herself
for the moon at night.
Clouds so regal,
all golden and red,
Softly bowing
before going to bed.
A golden hue,
a shimmering sky,
Oh what a marvelous
Lord have I!
A hint of heaven
not made by man,
For this was done
by the Master's plan.

Virginia Hart Ryll
THE NOWHERE ROAD
He hurried past them
On the nowhere road -
Unmindful of the turtle shell
That crunched beneath his tires,
He saved his passion
For the one in front
Who slowed him on the
narrowness of road
And framed a world too small
for him to rule.

Larry T. Lassiter
GRANDMA ROSE
Grandma, I talked to you today.
Through the foggy haze of
lonely days
and frustration of being caught
in a mind and body that are
yours, but not for real,
I think you remembered me.
Did you remember me today?
The many times you held a
lonely child,
one frustrated with an adult
world where no one seemed to

care, except for special you.
I remember you.

Helen M. Lippert
VACANT HOUSE
There is something a little sad
About a forsaken old home,
Left shrouded with memories
Just standing neglected and lone.
Who planned, and who built this house?
What dreams and hopes did it hold?
What stories of love and of care
Could it tell if it could be told?
Who planted this rose bush here
By this faded old picket fence?
Where the pink flowers still can be found
Tho the foliage is gnarled and dense?
Whose hand set these apple trees
In the yard, now so overgrown;
With their fruit so shriveled and small
For no pruner's knife they have known.
Did a bride and a groom come here
To make this their sweet love nest?
Were children born in these rooms?
With their laughter and play were you blest?
Were the hopes and dreams fulfilled
E'er the fledglings all had flown?
Did the one who laid the foundation here
Pass on with his job well done?
Old home, do you ever sigh
For the gaiety, love and song
That once echoed through your courts?
Do the days seem lonely and long?
Would you turn back the pages of time
To a day that was full and sweet
Or have you folded the book
On a story that's rich and complete?
Just so is the life of a man
Like a vapor that passes away
Like the grass on the roof it is gone;
He reigns as king for a day.
He dreams, and he toils, and he builds,
Then leaving it all behind,
Goes on to his final home
Where reward for his toil he'll find.
Has our life been a fruitful bough
Or our works all shriveled and bare?
And burned with consuming fire
When we meet them all over there?
Are the conquests of life all won
E'er the strength of youth is past
Can the Master say "Well done"
When we stand before Him at last?

Everett E. Eckstein
SEVENTY SEASONS
withered hands
and weakened eyes
don't lessen the heart
of one who knows
the smell of applebutter,
outdoors, cooking in a huge,
copper kettle,
who knows the feel of
autumn's colors being crushed
beneath ancient shoes on
woodland trails,
who knows the fresh breath
of winter's first offering
before the brilliant altar
of God's clear streams
and flower-covered hills

Donald L. Berg
OLD HOUSE
Stand tall, gables, with gingerbread,
Broken by wind they've said.
Unkept grounds, where garbage crept,
Vines, weeds, bedrails and logs, to form flows,
From roots decades ago, Nature's own style,
In aging beauty, this old house.

Frank Brickl
CLOISTERED
She walks alone, head erect,
With dignity; she delights
To life's assault, keeps direct
Her steps to heavenly sites.
She stands alone in deep thought
Of joys now past in her life,
Remembering there is naught
To look toward but some strife.
She sits alone in her room;
The cross and pens on her desk;
Small furrows show signs of gloom;
This hour is not humoresque.
She eats alone: subdued sounds
Of eating while psalms are read
Remind her of human bounds.
The body too must be fed.
She sleeps alone on a cot;
For her, no man to embrace.
With virgins she cast her lot.
Her passions' lust to efface.
She lives alone, others near,
But none so close as her God
To whom alone she shows fear
With holy grace to be shod.
She dies alone, in good time;
Her life, a joy; much a fool
To worldly thought; reasoned rhyme
To them who would be God's tool.

Michelle M. Tokarczyk
PAROCHIAL CHILD
Not allowed
to wear a winter coat
in the bishop's parade --
it would hide the school colors,
camouflage the faith --
she sat in the
outdoor stadium
rubbing gloved hands
over bumpy flesh
blowing cold breaths through
prayers to faithful martyrs,
teeth chattering to
the march of blocked plaids.
Five years later
she sneaks 'round the corner
of the convent after
Fall exams; sucks nicotine
with chapped red lips; hikes
her skirt in defiance.

Terry R. Reiff
TWO WITNESSES
RAIMENT of sackcloth,
REVELATION by power,
the two candlesticks breathe
fire to devour.
SKIES without rain,
PLAGUES in the east,
the two prophets are slain
by the beast.
NATIONS do see,
KINDREDS rejoice,
the two martyrs hear
a great voice.
GLORY in heaven,
EARTHQUAKE below,
the two olive trees complete
the second woe.

Susan Reid Griffin
TOOL OF THE MASTER
I am the tool of the Master and the master of the tool.
I am the gifts He gave me; the wisdom of my soul, the strength of my spirit, and the love of my heart.
Should I choose to use them, they will serve us well.
Should I abuse them, they will serve no one.

Zerva Glasscock
RESPITE
How much I like the quiet
Of a misty, moisty morning!
The spray of rain is falling
As gently as a baby breathes.
No rushing, roaring torrents
To beat against our house
And flog our weary eardrums
With unceasing fury.
Just the fine soft mist
Floating toward a rain-drenched sod --
And heavenly quiet.

Stephanie Bays
DISCOVERY
Discovery in the world
in every place you see.
in a tree and apple seed.
In the cry of the new born babe.
Discovery to me in every place
I see is
The joy to watch
every new birth.

Lamar C. Brown
YELLOW RIBBON
The time has come for us to go;
The Yellow Ribbons on sight;
I can't hear the voices no more;
Of my captors at *Night.*
Little children standing tall;
With no ribbons in their hands;
Proud to see them one-n-all;
Back home on native *Land.*
I can hear the sound of *Bands;*
The waving of the *Crowds;*
The clapping of cheer-ful *hands;*
Crying and voices *A-loud;*
O what joy the boys are *home;*
Never more to *lose* their *class;*
Never more to go and *Roam;*
We are home at *last;*
I can see tears of Joy and *Sadness;*
Of the trials they had to *bear;*
I can hear the joy of children *gladness;*
Their trials we had to share.

Sam McKay
ELANNA MAE
Gentle spirit, like a feather's soft caress
Touching every fiber of the soul.
Sweet voice, the tenderness of turtledoves,
Calmly binding parts into a whole.
Jeweled eyes, akin to soundless seas --
Love's mysterious, unmeasured deep:
Magic empathy, unerring aim, magnetic
Pull uniting two as one before the leap.
Lips that serve the wine of love --
The old, old style, yet ever new.
The embrace that brings the heavens swirling
Down to knock the earth askew.
Love, the moving power through all life,
Adorns her beauty as the stars the night.
Never man did love a maid more fair,
Nor ever know a love more bright.

Harold Grier McCurdy
THE BOONE TRAIL
From a cramped cave above the Yadkin River
Buckskin Boone leaned out,
Alert to every bristling Stone Age quiver
Menacing his redoubt.
The downhill slope was one entangled lattice
Of muscadine, oak, and pine,
As desolate as the scene that daunted Attis
On Ida the divine.
Effeminate Attis on his Asian mountain,
Silk tunic spotted with blood,
Wept for the rose-wreaths by the public fountain
That crowned his lost boyhood.
Boone was a tougher number.
Explorer, squatter,
In a rough uncivil land,
He would not lend the devouring Magna Mater
A self-castrating hand.
Born to the West, he *was* the West -- a hero
Of tall tales yet unspun --
Equal to desert days and nights sub-zero
Under the moon and sun.
Masculine, protestant, brisk, too brisk to stifle
In existential pain,
To him exile was freedom. His long rifle
Barked in mountain and plain.
Smelling of woodsmoke, creeks crossed, peaks ascended,
And Becky's homespun gowns,
He blazed new trails, with wolves and bears contended,
Laid out and log-built towns.
Not that he ever throve in estates material:
The Law, disallowing his tracts,
Made him a landless landlord.
But an imperial
Quality sanctioned his acts.
His kingdom stretched from Florida to Kentucky,
Rowan to Yellowstone.
From La Charette they wagoned

him home to his Becky,
In Frankfort, bone to bone.
She was his Queen, and he,
whom she had married,
Her one and only King.
Bright on her finger when she
came to be buried
Still shone the marriage-ring.
Old roads remember him.
Arrowhead markers,
Bronze-plaqued, official, say:
"Here walked a man. Among
war-painted stalkers,
Men, beasts, he made his way."

Eleanor M. Guptill
INDIAN PIPES
Out in the woods where the
shadows are deep,
Strange, ghostly flowers
pushed up through the
ground.
The silence was weird--all the
birds seemed asleep--
When Indian Pipes' waxy
whiteness I found.
No leaves and no petals do
these blossoms show,
Like ghosts of dead blooms
they are fragile and pale.
At a touch they'll turn black,
though they're white as the
snow.
A breath could destroy these
flowers so frail.
I think that these blossoms, so
wraith-like and queer,
Might be the spirits of
warriors of old,
Who, perhaps, smoked the
peace-pipe in some ancient
year,
And now lie asleep in the
forest's dark mould.
I know it's just dreaming--a trick
of the brain--
And souls of the dead cannot
become bloom.
They're probably fungi called
forth by the rain,
But the mind of the poet's a
fanciful loom!
I like the idea of the warriors of
old,
Smoking the peace-pipe in
some ancient year.
Though they now lie asleep in
the forest's dark mould,
They remember with flowers
all wraith-like and queer.

Bridget Auenson Burnett
GOD IS LOVE
I've lost it somewhere.
I'll just listen and
maybe I can hear it calling.
I'll listen closely,
for it may be only a whisper.
Then, again, it may be a shout -
one I can hear for miles.
But I know not which it will be-
So I must listen quietly in the
quiet...
Listen!
Can you hear it?
I hear it!
It's shouting to me!
It's shouting...
but what is it saying?
What does it mean?
I can't understand!
The voice keeps saying one
word over and over.
What can it mean?
It must be good,
since the voice is shouting.
For if it were bad,
it would surely whisper.
What is this "LOVE"
the voice speaks of?
Does someone here know?
Please -- someone tell me!
I want to know;
I need to know...

Delma Mathews
AUTUMN LEAF
I held a bit of autumn
Within my hand today.
A leaf of gold beneath a tree
Where autumn winds did play.
It lay in my hand so quietly,
So gently and so still
It seemed but an echo
From summer's distant hill.
It clung to the mother tree
Thru summer rain and storm,
But as the autumn winds grew
chill
It dreamed of a bed so warm.
It fell to the earth with its
mates
Of red and brown and rust,
And there will sleep under the
snow
Where it will return to the dust.

Mildred E. Olheiser
THE LITTLEST THINGS
The littlest things can mean
so much;
A small boy's grin or the tender
touch
Of a dear one's hand; the smell
of earth
On a dewy morning; a young
girl's mirth;
A smile thru' tears; how a
skylark sings!
Oh, joy is made of the littlest
things!

Annette Bacon
NOVEMBER
November is often drear,
Coming as it does, this late in
the year,
With frosty fingers that touch
even the milkweed.
November is frozen fog
And rising vapors, once a field,
now a bog,
With the wetness sifting out of
the air.
November's celebration,
Harvest time, fiddle time, an
ovation
Of thanksgiving and awareness
of others' sorrows.
November is an ending,
The dormant time, that heralds
in the beginning,
When all living things wait in
perfect faith for spring.

Hilda McMullins
GRANDMA
Too young to put two and two
together
Yet, old enough to see what was
I remember seeing a dark
Shadow of a woman
Too old to walk on her own
Her muscled sons
Carried her as if she were a rag
doll-
She was.
And out of this hazy shadow
I saw a toothless smile
She smiled at *me!!*
I knew her and me
would be pals
could be pals
if only...
She hadn't went away.

Linda Benincasa
THE OTHER WORLD
Crackling sparkling windfires
sailing over distant galaxies
with their blue-green fiery gases
changing color with the light
burning through the sun
leaving voids of shattered rays.
ripping through dark coffins of
long abandoned shortly departed
souls.
Calloused hands amid the ashes.
Caressing your hand with my
blistered eye.
Making way for a New Kingdom
of which we are not a part.
The smallest very last
candle-flame
has just been smothered
taking with it all eternity.

Sherry Y. Anderson
I ONLY WANT YOU
My whole world looks lke rain
My heart aches with pain.
My best friend said he would
stay
Instead he has gone away.
There is nothing left to gain
It's all gone with the pain.
No need to be sad
It's gone; what we once had.
I hope you will see
That no-one can ever be
As special as you are to me!
I told you I would never leave,
But now all I do is grieve,
That one day you will see
How much your love means to
me.
I had a dream about me and you,
I hoped it would never come
true.
But soon we were saying good-
bye,
And that some other day we
could give it another try.
So I started a new life today
Hoping you would come my
way.
Why can't you see
I am meant for you, and you for
me!?
In my new dreams
Me and you, is what my new
life means,
My heart will always bleed
For the life I wish to lead
Is for us to be together!

Doretha Ann Bays
BE KIND
Be kind to your friends
As though they were kin.

Be kind to all—
Do not laugh if they fall.
Be helpful to all
Instead of hateful.
Be a kind person
Help a sick person.

Lynn Greenwood
A POEM, FOR KIP
A person who treats me like a
person.
With pride and respect.
And without meaning to - with
a glance
I turn his heart to jello.
But then with the gentle stroke
of his hands on my hair.
He turns me into a
Crystal Butterfly.

Ben Wilson, Jr., Ph.D.; Ed.D.
POPULI MAGNITUDO
The water
shades of color
and beauty
depths of deceit
and trickery.
Watch the water
its clear
but muddy
and deep
and shallow
seldom still
never pure.
The water
Watch the water
It runs free, the water
damaging, violent, rampant,
treacherous.
Tranquil
Constrained.
The water
Watch the water
Peace, still
Be they like the water
Translucent, transparent,
never fixed.
Fall;
rise.

Phil P. Marinovich
THE WITCH'S SCREAMS
There was an old witch who
lived in a ditch
And loved to scare the spooks
Until one night when the moon
was bright,
A spook came along wearing
boots.
He walked in the ditch and
stepped on the witch;
She cried and howled all night.
And on Halloween you can still
hear the screams
From the witch who was booted
that night.

Shirley J. Rothe
SOLITUDE
Sweet solitude
Is private
Alone for me
Alone.
So therefore
In my solitude
I think and dream
Alone.
For in the depths
Of solitude
Alone now
As I be,
I rapture
In my solitude
A moment
Just for me.

R. Virginia Mellon
THE YOUNG & OLD
What's happening in this world
of mine?
Where faces shone and good was
done-to pass the time.
Now people wander here and
there
Searching, for the one to care.
Restlessly, the young & old -
stalk their way-
Passing, endlessly through the
nght & day.
Love is necessary for all of us
But remember where to put your
trust.
When you are lonely and in
need,
Reach out a hand for Him to
lead.
Look hopefully into the sky
And always remember to try,
try, try.

Joseph D. Law
MINSTREL

The
pur-
ple
song
man
sings
anew
as
rosewood
echoes; fingers
lightly strumming
bronze strands
of silver
sounds that
resonate the
glinting warm
sunlight; and make
the shadows dance
within the stillness
of my soul.

Maurine Williams
MIRACLES

I am hypnotized -
one with the Night-in-gale -
when high in the sky
the full moon
like a giant balloon
is an orange globe
spilling mellow light
over the dozing countryside.
I join the night bird chorus
and open my throat to sing
chanting such carols of joy
they pierce the listening stars!
My notes are laced with love
for all miracles of nature
only God can provide!

Mildred Shankland
HERE COMES SPRING

Here comes Spring, with robins
and daffodils,
Bluebirds and lilies, and green
covered hills.
There's a murmur and stir in
every nook.
Showers are filling each little
brook.
Here comes Spring. Lambs frolic
and play.
Soft white bunnies are hopping
this way.
Kites are flying high above.
Boys and girls are falling in love.
Gone is the chill of winter's
gloom.
The old apple tree is all in
bloom.
Each seed and shell is bursting
to tell
Springtime is coming down in
the dell.
Here comes Spring with
sunshine and showers.
Perfect days with songbirds and
flowers.
Now is the time to let your
heart sing.
Here comes Spring! Here comes
Spring!

Marilyn Frances
HANGOVER

Why all this thinking
Analyzing
Seeking answers to
Unanswerable questions?
Sometimes I think me
Knowledgeable
And at other times truly
Ignorant.
I'm tired of wracking my brain
Tired of searching for answers
Alone.
Looking around alone
My head spinning with thoughts
I'm thankful and I'm sad
I'm greedy and I want more.
Why, though?
Incoherent thoughts
Which only fade into regrets
About obscure craziness
Only I - not hurting anyone -
Am aware of the next day
My head still whirling
Eye make-up accompanying the
Tear glands
Which burst under pressure...
Rest from this
Is what I want
Is what I was looking for
The next day
Wasted.

Delbert B. Nutter
LOVELY VISION

When the day was done and the
twilight
Came stealing over the land,
There came a most lovely
Vision
And took me by the hand;
Guiding through dale and
valley,
Till we came to Clarksville,
And bade me watch a pagent
That would give my heart a
thrill.
I stood there in the gloaming
Betwixt the shadows and
light,
And the school-house rose
before me
To welcome the coming night.
From above ten million stars
Seemed to pause to watch
with me,
While across the wintery valley
As far as the eye could see
Light from scores of windows
Came spilling into the night,
From the homes that dotted the
valleys
From the left hand to the
right.
At first, these lights seemed
feeble,
But as time went slowly past,
Even the stars seemed dimmed
By the brightness these lights
cast.
The portals of the school-house
opened;
There appeared a shining
light,
Enveloped the darkness about
me,
And pushed back the coming
night.
Then spoke the Vision's sweet
voice,
Like music from the sweetest
cymbal,
"This pagent of Clarksville
School
Is for you a shining symbol;
Like a candle light that is dim
When first it catches the
flame;
But brightens each second and
minute
And the darkness overcame.
"The feeble lights that you saw
Were lighted here today
In the hearts of the lovely
children
Who came to study and play.
These little lights that you've
kindled

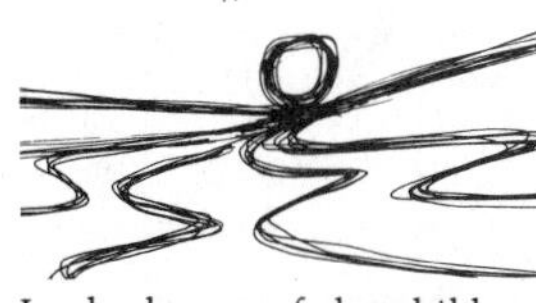

In the hearts of the children
here
Will shine farther and brighter
Each second, moment, and
year;
Will lighten the fog and the
mist
For generations after Thee,
Will gleam through the years
of time
And on into Eternity!"

Cosme R. Cagas, M.D.
DRIP DRIP DRIP

Drip
drip
drip
tiny
drop
s
from
a
leak
y
fauc
e
t
over time
time
time
make a river of pure waste.

E. Dewey Little, Jr.
A GIFT SUBLIME

In solitary moments
on crowded city streets,
my mind turns to protected days
when you gave to me a shelter
and never ceased to give.
For all those days of comfort
and all the days to come,
my heart overflows with feeling
but has not tongue to tell
of a love we've shared
with some to spare
for a future yet untold.

Chris S. Russell
SOUL VERSE

Sometimes I think love
is like a finished poem.
One cannot let it go so easily,
but continues trying to polish
and perfect it, even though
the type has hardened into set;
the ink can no longer be erased.
Just so, to let love be——
like a poem——simply what it
chooses to be, including
finished, is one of life's
harder tasks

Albert L. Hauser
AT HOME

As I closed the door behind,
The quiet peace settled
'Round me
And I stopped in stride
To listen to the gentle stillness
Of a new day.
The morning mist
Was soft
And the sea salt
Teased at my nostrils.
I stepped
Where the sand crept
And gazed
At the billowing velvet
Of a sea at rest.
Standing there with only beauty
Between God and me,
I was glad to be
At home.
With a clatter and a clash, and
A bang and a scream,
The smell of salt
Becomes the scent of
Newly-made coffee
While
Visions of color run
Suddenly past
And my beach is alive
With the swirl of sight and
sound
And I am glad to be
At home.
The day wore on
While the sun
Slid
Thru the blue.
Now long shadows
Reach past my toes
And the noise
Of beach-time joys
Softens to a minor key.
The cooling sand
Rolls down to the foam
And I am glad to be
At home.

Alice M. Griffin
WHERE SEAGULLS FLY

Seagulls, land, and me,
search the salty sea.
Wind to part your hair,
a vast domain that isn't there.
Boughs that reach around the
bend,
a land that holds you in it's
hand.
The scented accents of sealand
mystery,
it's changing tides, throughout
history.
Waves that leap like tiger claws,
and wail it's roar against
sea-walls.
The towering cliffs, the shallow
beach,
a firm foundation for me to
reach.
Wrap my youth and family ties,
around this land where seagull
flies.

Bird Helmick
LOW PROFILE

At the farthest tip of the lowest
bough of the mightiest oak of
the glade,
is the weest twig at the end of
the limb——too small for the
tiniest shade.
The verdant foliage that covered
the oak grew where the sap
flowed free.
But not even a bud of the
smallest leaf on the twig at the
tip of the tree.
And the acorns grew where the
bough was strong and squirrels
could frisk at will.
No acorn would hang on the
stringlike twig, no mission for it
to fulfill.
Whether the wind was a mighty
gale or the softest whispered
breeze
the tiny twig could not hold it

back as the stronger parts of the trees.
Of my myriad birds which were flying about whose feet were little or big
not one could grasp with its vicelike toes the infinitesimal twig.
Bare and useless and unobserved by all who might pass by
was the tiny twig at the tip of the limb who would never know how——or why
it found itself in this sad state unable to grow or bloom,
yet exist through days of endless waste like a life in a hopeless tomb.

Nel Modglin
PERHAPS CUM LAUDE?
Invited to life-school, I came.
Naive, Vulnerable, with eager mind,
I found the wonderful realm of learning.
When books were inscribed with my name,
All innocence was left behind.
I arrived at the point of discerning
That no one returns to that state again,
For each semester is outlined.
With no recess, hungry, yearning,
My thesis is being written with pen.
While time is reeling off its winding spool,
There is no shadow of turning!
I sit, now and then, on the dunce's stool,
But lessons are *still* learned at Hard
Knocks School.

Arlone Mills Dreher
MY HEART FOREVER
My heart forever keeps a watch for thee
Who ever understood me and yet smiled.
My life was always, always, meant to be
A complement to yours though gently styled.
My love's still yours though you may not be here.
My adoration pulses deep and long.
I dream of you each day, each month, each year.
My heart is still completely yours— and strong.
I know you've truly gone away from me.
I understand you will return no more.
But I, forever, keep a watch for thee
Still waiting for the love we had before.

Helen R. Wulfert
THE TIME IS NOW
Assassinations, strikes and wars,
Murders, rape and much more;
We wonder what tomorrow brings
And what it has in store.
There are crises all over this earth
All in the cause of power;
Can't we see that now's the time——
Indeed, the very hour
When we should remember Jesus Christ
For He's our only salvation;
He's always there, in spite of all——
For it still is God's creation!

Connie Moss
PEACE
Grasp what can't be held...
Cage what can't be caught...
Return what hasn't been given...
And receive the unattainable.
...Understand your feelings;
...Control your temper.
...Give your love,
...And inner-peace is yours.

Kate Knapp Johnson
UNTITLED
The simple fact that you were
an artist would have amused
you since, of all your admirers,
you were the least. Other facts:
how you were harried,
how you walked
from the canvas to the window -
again, again - drawing the colors
out as if from the perfect earth
itself. There could be
consummations and the
painting becomes a work of the
day-laborer who carries clay up
from the riverbank, back and
forth he moves with the yoked
buckets full of sienna until the
last muscle is spent. The
painting arises finally out of a
kind of weariness, the body
having travelled long between
its sources...
You came to yourself so late,
saying *I am the artist* — being
already seated by the river and
having set the yoke down
like a gift.
(For Randall Jarrell, 1914-1965)

Lavina Clemetson
I AM NOT AFRAID
They walk in glory,
Those who have gone before.
I cannot see them now,
But sometimes,
I strongly feel their pesence.
And I am not afraid.
I loved their earthly souls,
And now that they have gone
On before me
To prepare the way,
I do not fear them.
When they come to visit,
I cannot converse with them.
But I seem to hear
Many of the familiar words
Each of them were wont to use.
And I am not afraid.
I believe
They are with me
Most of the time.
They never interfere
Or offer advice.
They are simply there,
And I feel encouraged.
I am not afraid.
I know that I shall
Join them soon.
My soul cries out to them
As they come to call.
And somehow
I look ahead to my long journey
Into the great unknown.
And I am not afraid.

Don Micue
THE OLD ROCKING CHAIR
The old rocking chair in the parlor
Once held a young mother and child.
While gently rocking her darling to sleep
She gazed at him fondly and smiled.
The old rocking chair in the parlor
Often helped dispel terror at night.
Mother's crooning and rocking banished the fear
When dreams roused her young son in fright.
The old rocking chair in the parlor
Held a mother who worried a lot
When a thoughtless teenager stayed out much too late
And said, when he came, "I forgot!"
The old rocking chair in the parlor
Held a mother aged and grey
Who read through her tears the letter she had
From her son fighting far, far away.
The old rocking chair rocks no more.
In an attic it's gathering dust.
Both mother and son that it once held of yore
Now dwell in the realm of the just.

Vivien Bilbeaux
THE DEALER
On an old cement floor,
in a low wooden throne,
He sits in all his glory ——
omnipotent, alone.
His eyes are hollow pools of gold,
He fears no fire, for he feels no cold.
We can only guess what the cards will hold,
For they're held by The Dealer,
and only he knows.
Then one by one they show their face:
The card of Death, a King, an Ace,
we cannot know when the next will come,
we cannot fold and we cannot run,
For always he'll find you,
there's no place to go,
No shadow to hide you, for The Dealer knows.
You cannot escape him in the deepest of sleep,
for the questions they plague you:
which can be discarded, and which ones must you keep?
You're sure that you've lost him
then you're hit by the blow ——
The Jack of Clubs, the Queen of Hearts,
there is no ending for there was no start,
Caught in a game of fate and chance:
the game of life, an endless dance.

Robin Yvette Barge
NOW AND FOREVER
Now and forever
my love, I shall be
the one
who will see
you get through
the nights
when sleep can't exist
to uphold all my promises
we sealed by a kiss
the words
honor, love,
trust and sincerity
in an equal partnership
which brings
happiness and prosperity
I will be living a life
of two now
not just one
from this moment on
our new lives have begun
it's a love we will share
and enjoy both together
my love,
I will be with you
now and forever

Sandra Lee Neyer
TO A GARDENIA
O sweet gardenia,
Spotless, pure and white;
Blooming there alone;
You lift your head in holy purity,
And sparkle as a dewdrop on a blade of grass —
But no —
I breathed and how your pride did fade
Into the dim and darkness of the past,
For on your face, a telltale mark;
Your soul is doomed,
And beauty now has flown.
O soul, may I not mar the core
Of purity in mine own heart,
But send the beauty forth
As fragrance of a flow'r,
In rays of spotless white.

LeVoninsky Von Hardin
UNTITLED

When ever you find yourself behaving in ways that you feel you must, even though you might prefer other forms of behavior is musterbating. resolving to be different than the way you have been taught is proper when that way doesn't work for you. You begin with insight into your own behavior. The important thing is to determine for yourself which rules work, and which rules can be broken without harm to yourself or to others.

Our culture teaches that we are not behaving properly when we disobey, that you "should-not" do anything that is against the rules. However if you comply with all the rules all the time, then you are destined to a life of emotional servitude. There are great rewards in being your own person and living your life according to your own standards.

You may be seen as different, be labeled selfish, incur disapproval from many "normal" people, for some people will not take kindly to your resistance to norms they've adopted for themselves. Leading your own life involves flexibility and repeated personal assessment of how well rules work at a particular given present-moment. Resisting encultrations means making decisions yourself, and carrying them out as efficiently as you see fit. You can decide to be the person you want to be, or the one others want you to be. It is all up to you.

Remind yourself that what others do is not what bothers you, it is your reaction to what they are doing... Instead of saying, "they should-not be doing that," say, I wonder why I even bother myself with what they are doing. Become your own judge of your own conduct and learn to rely on yourself, to make your own present-moment decisions. Sing your own tune of happiness in any way that you choose, and not how some being thinks it is to be sung.

Edith Louise McCormick

SWEET SUMMER

Sweet Summer sighed softly and bowed her head
As she made her rumpled autumn bed,
For Winter had come and Winter had won
And Sweet Summer was leaving with the sun.
The wind rustled through the murmuring trees
And with a tear Sweet Summer said, "Please,
Masterful Cold, I care not to go
For I love the grass and the green leaves so."
But Master Cold smirked with a frosty eye
And Summer reluctantly said goodbye,
Gathering blossoms and buds to her breast
And sadly departing for her long rest.
And Windy Winter thought he had won
With his naked trees and his sickly sun,
But just as he laughed and settled to stay
Summer returned with the coming of May.

Lois Lumsden

WHERE HAS THE TIME GONE

Such a short time ago a babe
in arms you were a blond
bubbly baby whom your folks
did adore
To you the time seems longer,
so far in the past
But others of us see it speeding
by so fast

Already you have graduated,
twelve years of being educated
If like most girls, marriage
comes to mind
A happy home, sweet babes, a
mate that is kind
Happiness is vital to make our
life worthwhile
Love must overwhelm us be we
grown-up or child
Yes, in time you'll watch your
children the same as we do you
You'll wonder where the time
went as it goes whizzing by
Oh it's so hard to realize even
tho you try
You'll look back and recall this
verse I wrote
and know with-in your heart
these words are true I quote
Where has the time gone since
you started that first class
It took such a short time to
grow into a lass
A lass so sweet and pretty, full
of hopes and fears
Facing up to life throughout the
coming years
Today I'm hoping the best in
everything you do
Knowing that others are hoping for you too
As each mounting year draws
closer, you'll look around
and say: "Where has the time
gone", it frightens me this day

Rita Shinhearl Flynn

TIME OVER OUR HEADS

Does anyone know where they will go
After the wars are through?
Maybe to visit a grave or two,
And attend gatherings of hate,
Instead of love.
While deaths in the countries remain,
The heavens sprinkle time over our heads
With a future rain,
Like a plague over a sinful society,
As we plead innocence with profound piety.
In this age of need,
We all bleed with fear,
Knowing another season will be cold,
As it will be snowing uncertain flakes of tears.
Another unsuspecting generation is near.
And I hear the cries of the newborn.
Could it be they sense our hearts are torn?
The seams of faces reveal a crease in the races,
And musty-materialistic minds
That are worn.
Forever free is what we long to be,
Even though we cannot foresee
What will happen in all eternity.
Perhaps we should start living right today,
Even though dead victims must lay
Buried under confusion the whole world shares.
God, how I know it just isn't fair,
That few enlightened people will show they care.

Brad Lee

TERRY FOX——HERO!

In a world of drug addicts, criminals and other losers,
It's refreshing to know that occasionally we have some winners,
Terry Fox, in my book was a genuine hero,
Even though in the end cancer struck the final blow,
On an artificial limb, Terry completed half of his marathon,
But finally cancer succumbed his Vancouver mission,
For twenty-two years Terry was on this Earth,
In this short span he proved his everlasting worth,
Somewhere in Terry's life a lesson is to be learned,
Fame does not always happen by chance, sometimes it's earned.

Eliza S. Oglesby

SOMEDAY

Someday I'll write a poem,
Someday I'll sing a song,
Someday I'll find a flower,
That blooms the whole year long.
Someday I'll paint a picture
Someday before I'm gone,
Someday I'll fly a kite,
The whole year long.
Someday I'll ride a bicycle,
Someday I'll fly a plane,
Someday I'll write a story,
While the world is washed with rain.
Someday I'll watch the Autumn leaves,
Someday I'll catch a swarm of bees,
Someday I'll feel the cold of Winter,
And see the color of the leaves.
Someday I'll eat the fruits,
That Autumn brings to us,
Someday I'll smell their odors,
While I slowly turn to dust.

Faye Field

CHRISTMAS SERENADE

I walked alone in the winter night,
Multi-spangled with stars so bright,
'Twas on a night like this long ago
That shepherds saw Heaven's glow.
When I lifted coldest hands to pray,
For a sign from Him some way,
In the stillness, the angels' refrain
Came, warming me, once again!

Franklin D. Newman, Printer

AUTUMN REVERIE

Myriad leaves fall
Like printed sheets
From Nature's presses--
The prolific trees,
Publishing Summer's Memoirs
And Autumn's Almanac.
The annual edition
Of Mother Earth's Gazette
Makes its deadline.
--The Old Printer

Todd K. Tinkham

STORM WATCH

The tall trees shake with a wild west wind.
The pines sway to and fro.
And the short shrubs hum with the trembling sound
Of a murmuring undertow.
Some dead leaves dance on the forest floor
As the wind that rushes through
Sends them swirling and flying about,
And sends me swirling too.
And high above, the swift, shifting clouds
Take on the fantastic form
Of a phantom fathomless as night,
And fierce as the darkening storm.
The thunder roars like a dragon above.
The rain begins to fall.
And the lightning casts an aura that lasts
On the majesty of it all.

Jean Bomba

THE COURTLY GHOST

A spirit came on a moonlit night
To seek a maid to be his wife;
And there he saw her passing fair
As she was going up the stair.
"Pardon, Miss, I'd like a kiss,
Please turn your eyes to me.
For you look sweet and we could sleep
Through all eternity."
The lady paused and looked around
And seemed to be alone.
But a midnight wind had gotten in
And chilled her to the bone.
The days passed by, the neighbors came
And bring her back they tried.
Though she lay in the gloom of that cold, cold room,
She had left to become a bride.

Mary R. Frick

A HOUSE WITHOUT LOVE

I

A house without love is just a house
But when there is love inside
A house becomes a palace
A place of joy and pride.

II

So don't strive for wealth or riches
Or power or gold, but be
Happy in a cottage
Humble though it may be.

III

Because without love a house will be
A house but not a home
And this you'll find is always true.
No matter where you roam.

IV

So love one another all the way
And when each day is through
A cottage with loved ones at the door
Will be a palace for you.

Frances S. Wells

THE SUICIDE'S WIFE

I look into each face I see —
Their eyes are looking back at me,
So solemnly, accusingly —
I know they think I'm guilty!
My heart is crying out, "I tried!"
But something deeper down inside
Is saying, "All the same, he died."
I wonder — am I guilty?
I was not there! I did not see!
I did not hang him from the tree!
Oh God, dear God, please set me free.
Please tell me I'm not guilty.

Charles W. Harrington

ELYSIAN FIELDS

For love
As a course of departure,
A token of our esteem
To allude ourselves

In a moment of illusions,
For dreams
Or what seemed
A reality of youth.
Loneliness
Born of neglect
For the doors
Closed to minds
That had yet to be formed,
An encounter
Lost at cost
For a strangeless love
Born to an age of wealth,
And death to those
Who would not
Sell themselves.
A hope
In an exchange of glances
And a moment of
relinquishment
For the best of strangers
And the worst of friends,
An end to begin again
And a choice of life
For the strife of desire,
In a future built
And a life consumed
For the destiny of a dream.

Sara Woodbury
HAD YOU BUT LIVED
Now the light catches frail
drops and slivers of water.
On the silver fir particles ionize
as light fragments cleft to
stone. The moon in memory
Shimmers on the birch trees,
lining the pavement
Where once you walked, in
sunshine, head bent,
Your scarf ruffled by the wind.
Somewhere between the moon
and the sun that we knew
then,
The antihero came, strident
across America, the iron bar
Twisting, breaching several
decades of thought.
Here now your world to walk in,
there your music.
Here the capsules, the bits
emitting from your mind.
But no more do you walk the
sidewalks of Moscow,
And yet this your world, had
you but lived.

Mary Jane Reynolds
THAT MORNING
That Morning
that I watched
the cloud,
shaped like a dragon move
slowly toward the
sleeping giant;
breathing huge lungs full of
gray smoke.
The giant woke, feeling
the presence of danger and
turned
his sleeping head
in time.

Lewis Parker Miller
CHILDREN
If it weren't for children
This earth would be naught
But a wearisome world with
Lackluster days fraught.
It's children who make this
World worth living in.
Without them we'd hardly know
Where to begin.
For children are honest——
What they say is true——
Although you may not like
Some things that they do.
If all of us grown-ups
Could equal their worth,
What a great reformation
Would come to this earth.

Robert S. Best
YOUR LOVE
Your love can take me from this
gray
To sunshine on a meadow lay.
It matters not what reason be.
You always see the best of me.
Just to hold you in my arms.
Keeps me from all current harm.
A Symphony of songs to be
Is what your love means to me.
I speak of treasures pure and
fine.
Knowing that your love is mine.
Seek not vast riches beyond
your reach
But your true love is mine to
keep.

Lillian Payne RN
SERENITY
I love my early morning
Talks with God,
I feel He's very near.
The little birds their songs do
sing.
His rising sun—such light it
brings.
The world is quiet and all are
asleep
As my early morning tryst I
keep.
There is no blurring noise of
strife,
of news of sin, and death, and
war—
It is as God had hoped 'twould
be—
Quiet—peaceful—serenity.
My open Bible—my quiet
world—
My wonderful Saviour—my
spirit filled.
O learn my fellow Christian
learn—
Your Heavenly Father too must
yearn—to show to
You—as He shows to me—the
kind of world—He wants it to
be—

Regina Brooks Swanner
MY DAD WAS A COWBOY
He was a Cowboy, my Dad ——
good with a rope and good
with a horse.
He had the kindest heart, the
widest grin, the gentlest ways
of any man.
He told the finest tales (some of
'em he made up),
Played the funniest jokes on his
pals,
Rode the fastest mount
anywhere around —— a steel
dust named Gray Dog.
A feller never saw a better pair
than Dad on ol' Gray Dog.
Fate has a way of dealin' with us
all, and sure 'nuf, he stepped
in.
Dad had to sell Gray Dog ——
had to quit cowboyin'.
He went on to other work to
help his folks —— raised
me ——
O' course, by then Ma helped
him, too.
We fin'lly got another place,
even other horses,
But it never seemed as good
again.
Dad's gentle hands grew worn
with toil,
His face was burned from
twelve-hour sun.
In spite of it all Dad never lost
that grin —— that ready
humor —— that love of a
cowboy's life.
On a dark day one December, a
wild, young driver snuffed out
Dad's life.
He didn't really die that day —
he just went on ahead.
I think ol' Gray Dog was waitin'
when Dad went ashore on the
"other side."
'N I think Dad climbed aboard
and rode ol' Gray Dog one
more time —— rode right off
into the settin' sun,
Both of 'em happy as could be.

Bob Barci
EARLY MORN
Early in the morning,
When I'm still awake from the
night before,
And the street lights are still
glowing,
I think of you.
When the birds have begun to
chirp
And I haven't gotten home yet,
Thoughts of you fill my head.
With sunrise creeping up
And my soul is feeling its
warmth,
I long to touch you.
To explore you with sight and
touch,
To hold you close to my being,
To explore you with loving
caresses.
Early in the morning,
When I'm alone, cold, and lost,
I think of you.
How we spent our time
together,
How we'll continue to do so.
Early in the morning,
When the sun is up,
And the birds are chirping,
I know my love for you is true.

Joan Robinson Sabia
A COLLEGE OF WESTERN ARTISTS
We squeezed into Rackocy's
truck
the beige pick-up with the
flapping tailgate
with sketch pads and pensils
that were never black enough.
He drove seventeen miles east
to the other side of bramble
where Hope, New Mexico, sits
in front of horizons filled
with more of the same.
At the Texaco, the old man with
a star said, "Eight of us still
live here."
He told us of how he was told
of the lush days.
The side roads, gray-brown
like the river that turned the
other way,
were barren as the apple
orchards.
I studied the shadows of a
building too old to identify as
house or saloon.
I examined, drew, but mostly
wondered how long and what
kind of time faded and broke
wood into such an intricate
collapse.
I thought of all the trite
possibilities that Phillie
television had created, and
while I drew the merging
visions, I heard Rackocy yell,
"Hey, yo! Look at Sophie."
At my back, a good city block
away, in front of the only two-
story, my friend stood
sandwiched inside the tall
glass box to sketch the
pay phone.

Lynn Misiak
A CAFFEINE JUNKIE
"I'll bring your coffee in a
minute," she says.
I offer a smile of thanks.
Glancing around, just once,
I pick up my fork.
Without you and conversation,
I finish fast.
And still...no coffee.
Has the waitress left me, too?
Knowing how much you love
the warm, brown liquid,
has she run after you,
armed with a steaming pot,
neglecting my naked cup?
Determined that she has,
I grab my coat, her 60¢ tip,
and leave.
At home,
I reach for a mug, heat the pot,
and pour.
Caffeine will soothe.
But the pot is empty, and so am
I.
A caffeine junkie.
A love addict.
I'm addicted to you both.
Withdrawal pains begin.

Mildred Ballard
THE DYING BIRD
I'd found it lying
against the church
and thought it dead;
It had a heart-throb still:
(but it *was* dying.)
So, tenderly I tried
to bring it back.
I never could have even
dreamed the exquisite
tenderness of its plumage
Had I not held it!
The soft, dark iridescence
of its head and back!
Oh, soft, soft, soft!
No silk so delicate!

Bertha Powers Woods
JUST THREE
She's only three you know,
With dazzling smiles and eyes
that sparkle
She steals your heart
And love encircles.
All those cunning little ways
And "I Wuv You"
To fill your days
With sunshine,
And even "stormy scenes" will
blow
For "She's only three you know!"

Rada Danforth
BY THE RIVERS
As the children of Israel
Sat one day
By the Rivers of Babylon——
In a strange land,
And far away,
Wondered, as in times long
gone——
How could they sing the Lord's
song?
Much, too, have I traveled

And wandered
To alien and far ground——
Feeling as they,
Homesick——but,
By the waters I have found
I can sing the Lord's song.
As a young child,
When life was full
With a future yet to seek,
I gathered wild roses,
Rare and sweet,
On the banks of Willow
Creek——
And there, first sang the Lord's
song.
The Pacific's vast expanse,
Deep and wide,
With its powers unchained——
I felt its breeze
And heavy mist,
They covered and sustained.
I silently sang the Lord's song.
Years ran on to hard times.
Life's demands
And life itself seemed raw.
One cold, spring morning
I gathered
Lilacs, by the Imnaha
And breathed in the Lord's song.
When miles from home
With my little ones,
At a place called Lake
Katrine——
The autumn world
Was painted crimson——
We drank in this beauteous
scene,
And we sang the Lord's song.
Other children came to bless;
Other moves
And much traveling, too.
Along the rushing
Clearwater River,
We gathered blueberries, not a
few.
We could hear the Lord's song.
I looked for my roots
To yesterday,
Where memory builds her
towers,
And stopped by the
Old Platte River,
Where my Grandma gathered
flowers——
Tears fell to the Lord's song.
Many other waters
I so desire to see.
There's not time enough, in
truth——
But, oh, to gather
Wild currents
In the area of the Porteneuf!
There I could sing the Lord's
song.

Myrtle Fait Barnhill

IF I FORGET

Lord, if in my heart there is no
song,
Because of grief or undue
wrong;
If in my zeal to do thy will,
I fail to see my brother's ill;
If, when the future I would see,
Waiting not to know thy will
for me;
Lead me outside the city wall,
Where the night winds howl
and coyotes call;
Where few but the guards hear
the piteous cry
Of the Savior lifted up to die.
There on lonely Golgotha's hill,
I picture him hanging in
agony still.
Yet I know victorious, he
ascended on high,
Conquering death, he liveth
that I
Too, may live and share in his
glory,
If faithful I am in telling the
story.
If the way of the cross seems
rugged and steep,
If I forget I've a charge to
keep;
Back to Calvary, 'midst the
pressing throng
Of the shouting, gesticulating
crowd I belong;
Until I remember,—it was
love,—
Love that led Him to Calvary!

Denise Elkins

IN YOUR ROOM

I looked for you the other day:
I walked in your room
Where you always stayed.
Your clothes, your books,
Your needles, your hooks
Were all gone.
It all seemed wrong.
I closed my eyes, and for a
moment
Saw you lying on your bed,
The pillow propped up around
your head.
A look of happiness was on your
face.
Then, I opened my eyes and
found no trace
Of all the things that you had
loved;
Nothing remained that had your
touch.
I closed my eyes
A second time
Only to see
Your room was empty;
You had left me.

Sue Sharp

OUTSIDE

We watch
People with people
Grasping bent twigs and bark
chips
Placing these as treasures in
strongboxes
When one falters another comes
forward
Time blends shapes until there
is only a blur.
We watch
Dark splashes of color
Run deep into the heart
Finding chasms that are starved
for feeling
Changing from rich to paler
hues
As minutes diminish to seconds.
We watch
And know that days
Are shorter and nights are
longer
That Autumn's color will fade
Leaving only the cold and
piercing bluster
There is a deep well waiting for
us
——The Spectators.

Diane E. Pierce

ONCE IN A WHILE

I've overslept
I'll be late for work
The water's cold
A cold shower I'll take
There's a hole in my dress
The only one I've ironed
I can't find my shoes
Boy! is this trying
Now a run in my stocking
What am I to do?
It's raining outside
But I've locked my keys in
So I trudge to the bus stop
Without an umbrella in the rain
I've just missed the bus
But I'm not surprised
Now this big cadillac
Has splashed mud on my side
Well, I finally get to work
One hour late
And wouldn't you know it
My boss is irate
Well, I'm not upset
No I'll just take it in stride
You see days like this only
happen
"ONCE IN A WHILE"

LaVena May Drummond

MUSIC ROOM

As the English Ivy, winds up
the cameo
Lace curtain.
Our love also grows, spirals
and becomes
More certain.
The shriveled flower corsages
portray our hearts
When ever you are away.
The violin and bow resounding
make you
Nearer and dearer.
So, this very day we read,
"Stealing Heaven,"
And completely understand;
As we play our baby grand.
The lyre bells twinkle and tell
of a Great
"Love Story," and God's Great
Glory.

The books are all the best
classics you should
Read before you enter college;
They will give you worldly
knowledge.
The "Living Word," on a
velvet lion's head
Fireside bench.
Two "Kewpie" dolls nestled on
antique sewing
Machine trestle, in a lover's
clinch.
Love of life, God, Virgin Mary
and Holy Jesus
Is everywhere.
Of this you are very aware.
The Lord's Hand touched us for
an express purpose.
To free us from the temptations
of the flesh and
Worldly distractions and
surface.
"We needn't be separated," he
said, "we might enter
Religion together,"
And have the greatest
satisfaction," but of course,
There would be no retraction—
Ever.
We love you beyond counting.

Wanda Morris Pryor

THE CHILDREN'S DOG

All parents rely on the old
cliches
When children decide to marry,
"Just remember, Hon,
We're not losing a son,
But gaining a daughter" - or very
Flippantly say, "We're not losing
our girl,
But gaining a bathroom" - so we
Just hold back the tears
And are grateful for years
Of raising a close family.
Yet, all parents know that the
time must come
To put away dolls and holsters,
"We'll have all those shelves"
We keep telling ourselves,
Thus, each the other one
bolsters.
But when the kids' dog watches
wistfully,
Oh, how are we going to say
To that dog's pleading eyes,
To those old, faithful eyes,
"The children have all gone
away."

La Verne J. Witting

LIFE IS A BED OF ROSES

If life is a bed of roses,
With petals soft and sweet,
Then why is trouble 'round the
bend,
So difficult to meet?
If life is a bed of roses,
In a garden of delight,
Then why are brothers
sometimes rude,
To make one take to flight?
If life is a bed of roses,
So bright in glorious bloom,
Then why some days, 'though
we try not,
Are filled with clouds of gloom?
If life is a bed of roses,
Then why do friends astray,
At times they're sorely needed,
To help us on our way?
Life *is* a bed of roses,
From the day that we are born,
Lest we take life for granted,
Each rose - must have its thorn.

Katheran Moore Voight

IN MY PROFESSION

*(A Prayer for Health
Professionals)*

Dear Lord:
As I see the sick today,
and listen to their cries,
let me look beyond disease,
and see things through their
eyes.
Let me sense the pain they feel,
which brings them to my care;
and let me offer more than help;
but strength, and hope, and
prayer.
Let me give them something
more
than pills, and words, and fears;
please let me give them some of
me ——
new life, and joy, and cheer.
Let me always count on You
when books are set aside,
to keep me strong when trials
come,
and my patient dies.
Please give me strength to see
my faults,
and grace to take my bows.
Let me always be aware
that You're the One who taught
me how.
May this practice in my life
be my way of knowing
that You have chosen ones like
me
to keep creation going.
AMEN

Margaret R. Shelley

NO DEPOSIT — NO RETURN

Setting upon my door-step
upon my return was a bottle
that said:
"No deposit — No return"

And the contents were
passionate and mysterious——
the contents were a red rose.
Startled is what I was and
unsure of just who this
impetuous person was.
But the romance I felt for the
person who put passion in a
bottle labeled
"No deposit — No return"
is more than I can discern.

John E. Moyer
FULL MOONS AND FATHERS

The bright and boney orb will always rise,
Though hidden by clouds or earthly shadow,
Here, then gone, he slowly moves on; very wise.
May appear to be dead, but never dies,
Dad was born almost eighty years ago,
The bright and boney orb will always rise.
Dad's flesh and blood is only a disguise,
Good memories leave a strong widow,
Here, then gone, he slowly moves on; very wise.
The spirit of the moon breathes in his eyes,
Watching today, coughs at tomorrow,
The bright and boney orb will always rise.
Love is not mortal, an angry son denies
To hear Dad's voice, and to taste the moon's glow.
Here, then gone, he slowly moves on; very wise.
Solar winds drift as the lunar dust flies,
Death's autumn leaves blown deep under snow,
The bright and boney orb will always rise,
Here, then gone, he slowly moves on; very wise.

Virgina McKinney
LIFE

I have not held you long enough
and yet you cannot stay;
I have dared to climb your hills and trees,
and toss your dreams away.
I have ventured deep into your nights
where there I plucked your stars,
until each tenant of the sky
was poor as I was poor;
I did not leave a stone unturned,
a twig, a stick unbent,
and every leaf and bud that bloomed
I knew just what they meant.
I learned to listen to you speak
your whispers and your cries;
I knew instinctively when you,
would let a season die;
and though I do not know the hour,
when you shall turn from me;
I know that all too soon, my friend,
you shall set me free. . .

Joyce E. Savok
THE DOVES

Their cooing starts at dawning,
While they watch me from their perch.
Now they're walking through the garden,
Cooing softly, as they search.
Their mourning call, sounds again, at dusk,
As the curtains of day, draw to a close.
The pink-orange light from the sunset,
On the doves reflectingly glows.
Late in the fall, they are gone for awhile,
I'm alone, but soon I'll smile and pick up my gloves,
For just outside my bedroom window,
I'll hear again, the cooing of the doves.

Joyce E. Savok
THE GIFT

I watched two brothers in play
As I drove them to school on the bus, one day.
Their melodious voices gave me a lift,
Along with their smiles and a Christmas Gift.
What can I give these happy boys
More valuable than fragile toys?
I drew them near and bending low,
Said, 'Boys, I have to go,
But my gift to you is worth more than gold.
It cannot be bought, It cannot be sold.
It cannot see, hear or talk,
Nor can it swim, fly or walk.
It's near you when you laugh or weep,
It snuggles close to you in sleep.
It is my love I leave today,
And with you it will always stay.
It knows no distance, time or space.
It goes with you to most any place;
To distant lands, on raging sea,
You will still have this gift from me.
When you do right, it glows with pride,
When you do wrong, it hurts inside,
So now goodbye.' They watched me go,
Their boyish eyes were all algow,
With comprehension of the thought
My gift of love to them had brought.

Nita Broussard
ELUSIVE LOVE

Morning finds me facing the day ahead
With eagerness
Confident today will be the day you call
And declare your love for me
For I love you with all my heart
By noontime, fear is creeping in
On tiny padded feet
Sinking its sharp claws deeply
And steadily, methodically shredding my resolve
But I remain firm because I trust you
Surely I won't be hurt again
Night falls, and as darkness descends
My faith takes flight
Still alone, my dreams in tatters
I cry for a future never to be
For this elusive thing called
Love

Ginnie Fraher
UNTITLED

Why can't you slow down?
Must you always race with life and never take the time
for yourself or others?
People, stop a minute!
Look around you.
What do you see?
A lonely face?
A tired mother?
Someone looking for love?
Do you see beauty in a flower or
find comfort in the lullaby of
the crickets?
Can you spread a bit of magic
to a lonely face by sharing that
special ray of sunshine
called a smile?
People, stop a minute!
Take the time!
Life isn't a race to see
who can win.
It's a time to share, love and
care.
It's a precious moment
in the hand of God.
Use it wisely or lose it
to the games we so
often play.
People, slow down and take time
for yourself and others
I beg you. . .please!

Kathy L. Leaman
FLOWERS

Pretty little flowers formed with tenderness,
and blessed with nature's tender kiss.
The sun shines down from on high,
on beautiful little flowers too soon to die.
Then in sorrow the clouds they cry;
Gentle gems from above,
tears of nature's tender love.
For the delicate little blooms lost too soon,
in the still early month of June.

Janet Jordan
GRANDFATHER

pipe & hat & moustache
carried me on your shoulder
left me your doughnut from lunch
died when I was three
I knew
but couldn't bear
that you would leave
I took to wandering
explored the fields
got lost at picnics
with flowers in my hand
you loved me
grandpa

Betty Brock Ordaz
MAGGIE ROSE

I sit here, watching you sleep
my child of only six.
Your so loving and innocent,
Yet so dull of life and ideas.
Let's be friends too.
As you run off to play,
unaware of my presence
You seem to have the world at your feet.
The simple commands you're making
and needs you seem to have.
Are only little things I can do for you.
Let's be friends too.
Come to me on that special day
when you discover the boy behind you in class
has finally discovered you.
When your not sure if that friend of yours
is the friend you once knew at all.
Let me be there for you, to share your dreams.
Don't make me a grownup too soon.
I'm a person and a parent, but once a little girl too.
So let's be friends too.

Jan Chitwood
SOMETHING DIFFERENT

Shattered dreams have crossed
our mirror,
And our reflections can no longer
be seen.
The image we saw of one another
Was only a short-lived illusion.
Our patterns of life
Were those only a deranged man
could understand.
Our dreams stood tall,
Oh yes they did. . . .
But a strange thought
Has passed through
my mind,
Dreams are just reflections,
And reflections were only made
from illusions.
Illusions were not meant to be real,
And neither were we.

Sheryl J. Carter
WHO AM I?

I seek you out by day
And cause empty feelings to linger and stay.
I've been known to make you cry,
Who am I?
I hover over you in the night
And I make you want to take flight!
I cause you to moan and sigh
Who, oh, who am I?
I cause the four walls to seemingly close in,
And I'm the greatest enemy to all women and men!
Do you give up? Or can you guess?
My name is: "MR LONELINESS"!

Carol M. Ketcham
THE READER

Sitting in her favorite chair, reading.
No conscious thought of anyone she might be needing.
Music softly falling around,
a cacoon of gentle, soothing sound.
And soon, from deep within heart and mind,
memories, sweet memories, begin to unwind—

from all of the places the
heart has been.
Memories tiptoeing in without
a sound.
The book falls to her lap,
no longer an oasis. . .
The reader is lost now within
a place
where real people walk and
laugh and love.
She can hear them, see them
and,
though knowing these memories
for what they are,
the heart would really love to
touch each face.
The reader smiles, and
sometimes sighs.
Feeling lonely she even cries.
But thinking back on the life
she has had,
with love and laughter,
good times and bad,
she feels grateful to God above
to have known the certainty
of both His and an earthly
love. . .
So smiling faintly and with a
shake of her head,
picks up her book
to read a few more pages,
and then to bed.

Eulah Proctor Stanley

THEE ALONE

Thee Alone can make the rain
In this world of sin and pain
Heaven and earth depend on
Thee
Mother Nature and the sea
Thee Alone doth claim a son
The Holy Spirit conceived this
One
Jesus Christ was meant to be
Saving grace for you and me
Thee Alone can save a soul
Conquer death and make man
whole
Blessed be dear God of love
Transcending peace from heaven
above

Suzanne Bredlau Turgeon

TO GUARDIAN LOVE

O Guardian,
gifter and gift of my salvation,
you who stand counsel in the
dark corridors
and warm beds of my life,
you who stand off pain in raw
wisdom
and loneliness through
sensual cups.
O, I should be half my self
without you;
without you, I should bleed to
death.

Cynthia Mull-White

I NEVER KNEW (FOR JIM)

I never knew the way
The morning found your naked
eyes;
Like sunlight
On a clear blue mountain
lake.
I never knew
A stranded beach
Along a moonlit tide;
I never saw you barefoot
in the dew.
I never felt your
Gentle hands slip ribbons
From my hair;
I never heard you
Sing a sweet love song.
And
I don't know the reasons why
I go on loving you;
I'm in love
With a man I never knew.
You never watched
A candle
Silhouette my emptiness.
You never felt
The life ebb from my soul.
You never held me long enough
To stop the pain
From killing me inside;
You never heard my heart
Break in such woe.
You never saw me in
A gingham cotton dress.
Never saw me
Smell a rose at dawn.
I never knew your thoughts
About a forest,
Lush and green,
Or how you feel when seasons
come and go.
Yet,
I never knew a stronger love;
My life is finding you.
So sad,
I never held you
All night long.
I never will forget you
I'll never rest
Until you're home.
I'm all in love with you
Sweet man,
I never knew. . .

Phyllis Dexter

THE GARDEN

The sun lies molten on the
garden
And yellow roses garner gold.
I reap another day
To hem the edge of growing old.

C. F. Rogers

AFTER EACH BATTLE

There is yet an unnamed fear
Which holds the moment,
Even as victory becomes
awareness
And is worn as light armor.
Standing alert to a life-force
ended,
The mind is invaded by thought:
"There might I also lie."

D. W. Petry

MIRROR OF THE UNIVERSE

I turn to the sky
and know
Abundance
I turn to the sun
and feel the heat and power of
Energy
I turn to the wind
and know
Freedom
I turn to the sky, sun and wind
and look into the mirror of
the
Universe

Dale Maria Feldman

MY HOPE

Help me to love, O Lord, as You
have loved;
Let me forgive as I would be
forgiven.
You held no grudge when You
were whipped and shoved,
And when those nails into Your
hands were driven.
I want to be what You want
me to be;
I want to do what You want
me to do.
Without Your help, I falter
hopelessly;
But I will trust that You will
see me through.
The world and Satan press from
every side,
And all the evils tempt me day
to day.
Come, now, into my heart and
there abide,
Dear God, that I may overcome,
I pray.
For only through Your grace can
I be raised
To righteousness. O precious
Lord, be praised!

Brad Miller

PRAYERS

She lays with me and holds my
life,
deep in her arms I sleep.
I pull her tight and pray to God,
that her, my life, I'll keep.
She smiles at me and I see love,
the energy so strong.
I feel her breath and kiss her
so,
I've needed her so long.
I have to know she loves me
true,
for all my life she'll make.
Her loving touch and tender
smile,
on this my life I'll stake.
She need not fear these ways of
mine,
for I'm a gentle one.
If she stays with me for life,
all my prayers are done.

Dixie Jones

IMAGERY'S LOOM

Weave dreams and visions
On imagery's loom,
Be it picture or scripture
Of humor or doom
But spin not understanding
Of gossamer threads,
For what's woven by the mind
Is patterned in other heads.

Lucille D. Amoroso

A PICTURE OF JESUS

I've seen some pictures of Jesus
With eyes of lightest blue,
With long blondish hair and
skin so fair,
Somehow this doesn't seem true
For Jesus' Mother was Mary,
And Mary we know was a Jew.
Her skin and eyes were probably
dark,
Like other Judeans she knew.
He surely must have been
rugged,
And dark from His days in the
sun,
As He traveled and taught
While the miracles He wrought,
This Holy Man, God's blessed
Son.
But still, who can say what He
looked like?
I guess that God only knows,
The features as seen by the
artist,
Are the ones that He alone
chose.
So whether we think of Him
blondish,
Or blackish, or brownish, or red,
It's in the eyes of each viewer,
To worship Him though He is
dead.
For He paid that mighty ransom
So mankind may live without
dread,
And if we, as sinners, repent us,
He offers Himself as our bread.

Sheila L. (Nichols) Meadows

A HOUSE—A HOME

Love came
to warm this little house,
and left an imprint here.
From room to room
the memories float—
memories of joy and cheer.
Lovelight
burning in our eyes
when we met at the door.
Mixed emotions
when we kissed.
Could love ask for more?
Love came
to warm this little house.
Forever may it roam.
From room to room
the memories float.
Love made this house a
home.

Joseph Harris

HIGH SIERRA

Miles away the emerald jewel of
the Sierra shone. . .
A swath of green patching
timeless ramparts. .
The mountain trickle made a
paradise spring
By the huge basalt rock where
two young pioneers slept
In the year of 1839
There was the rough hewed
table they made
Facing the savage parapeted
peaks. .
The grove of white Balm of
Gilead trees

The rim of the far beyond/
Near them
An emerald patch of green
Where waters rippled crystal
wine. . .
Ramparts of ageless rock
Sentries of the primitive
wilderness. .
Carved by snows and wind and
time. .
Where Juniper trees
indomnitably took rest
In scarred basalt,
A moon peering over the knife
edged rocks
Of eternity
This night of 1839
Love holds its own
They held hands. . .kissed. . .
and loved
Carved their initials G.D. .B.D.
in a heart
On the table. .for posterity

Lorene Mae Crowe

MY PRAYER OF THANKFULNESS

Thank you Lord for the ability
to see, So that I might see
sunrises and sunsets that You've

created for me.
Thank you Lord for the ability to hear The sweet song in the morning of the birds that You've made so dear.
Thank you Lord for the ability to think and to reason, Because you are the only Creator of each and every Season.
Thank you Lord for the ability to smell All of the fragrances of this world, of the trees, grasses and flowers that You've crafted so well.
Thank you Lord for the ability to work And be able to do and function in those things that create satisfaction within myself.
Thank you Lord for the many blessings that You've given me; But most of all for Thy Son and for the Atonement of my Sins.
Thank you Lord for my husband—Robert Crowe To watch over and help me to Celestial Glory.
For Thou has given him Thy Holy Ghost and an inner glow To Guide us with Thy Love so that we understand Thy Divine Story.
That we may return to Thee as married forever and Eternity, So we can enjoy being in Thy presence ir Complete Serenity.
Thank you LORD.

Fluvia H. Kerr
DAWN OF SPRING

When merry Spring comes dancing in
She wears her veil of showers;
With each advancing tippy-toe
She leaves a print of flowers.
Primrose, crocus, violets
She scatters far and wide;
The breezes bend forsythia,
The willow droops beside.
The robin up at dawning
Is early on the wing;
Returning swallows glide and float
In circles as they sing.
The morning stars sing praise and fade
When glow the morning skies;
My throbbing heart skips half a beat
When ope' my true love's eyes.

Russell Schleicher
MOON ON THE MOUNTAIN

A peaceful night now covers earth
The pines are singing in the wind,
Moonbeams are bright, a golden glow.
A coyote howls on distant slope
And nearby hoots a hunting owl.
A peaceful night now covers earth
This lovely night is not for sleep
My spirit is so beauty filled,
Moonbeams are bright, a golden glow.
A meteor streaks across the sky
A silent blaze that leaves no trail
A peaceful night now covers earth.
Enveloped by calm nocturnal bliss
My daytime ills are truly gone
Moonbeams are bright, a golden glow.
The nighttime sky is free of clouds
The stars are dimmed, so far away
A peaceful night now covers earth
Moonbeams are bright, a golden glow.

Franklin W. Lemon
THE TONGUE

We speak of the tongue as a weapon,
That seems to have power untold.
The tongue also is a giver of blessings,
Often valued above silver or gold.
A weapon always needs ammunition,
The tongue's ammunition is "words."
It speeds them on toward their target,
Much swifter than the flight of birds.
One thing to me, most amazing,
No matter what we are trying to say,
If we choose well our words and expression,
Can be said in such a beautiful way.
Now I know, we're not all born to be artists,
But I'm sure that at least half or two thirds,
If we would apply ourselves in real earnest,
Could paint beautiful pictures with "words".
So let the tongue retain all its power;
I wouldn't change it if ever I could.
Just supply it with the best "ammunition,"
And make it use all its power for good.

Dorothy H. Uyeno
ENCOUNTERS

Treasures untold seem to unfold
When I smell a rose of yellow gold
Walk in the trackless purity of snow
Saunter by the river's gentle flow
Pleasures never cease when I see
Spring blossoms on the cherry tree
Linger among the lilacs after rain
View purple vetch on a country lane

Georgiana Lieder Lahr
IN ALL THINGS

I see God everywhere, in earth and sky,
In mountains, and in desert land, and sea;
I feel His Presence when the dawn draws nigh,
The beauty of Creation wells in me.
I touch Him in each flower's glowing face,
And hear Him in the songs that wild birds sing;
I hold His world in tender, true embrace,
And feel His heart in every living thing.
In rain, and sun, and wind, I see His Hand,
His Spirit moves upon the meadow grass;
And all Creation lives in His Command,
When I am very still, I hear Him pass.
Such rapture spills through mind, and soul, and heart,
I feel the pulse of God in every part.

Katharine Naismith
I LOVED YOU FOR THAT NAME OF YOURS*

Phil—Philippa Louise Boettcher; Catherine Munson; Quillian Garrison.
Mignonette Treschwig, Naomi Frome'n.
India MacIntosh, Texas Addington, Tennessee.
Iona Bedell.
Laura Lee Bird.
Saphrone.
Spinks Brooks and Townsend Douglas.
All Miriams and Marys.
Hilario Aguilar, Ezequiel Quintanilla, Santos de los Santos.
And Chauncey, Chauncey Cox.
And Pinky Swingle.
**Swinburne*

Bertha V. Langdon
A SMILE IS. . .A FROWN IS. . .

A smile is. . . . . .
A smile for joy,
Something to be smiling for,
A smile is. . . . . .
A smile for happiness,
Something to be proud for,
A smile is. . . . . .
A smile of happiness,
Something to be cheerful for,
A frown is. . . . . .
A frown of sadness,
Something to look back upon,
A frown is. . . . . .
A frown for aches and pains,
Something to be hurting for,
A frown is. . . . . .
A frown of anger,
Something to explode about,
But remember. . . . . .
A smile or a frown,
It's one or the other upside down.

James B. Middleton
A CHRISTMAS NIP

A nip in the air, with wind up your back,
And you expect to see Santa a totin' his pack.
The shoppers all grumble at bustling crowds,
But they trod ever onward, maybe broke but uncowed.
The store windows shine with new merchandise,
And placards all claim the ultimate prize.
The children, they gaze at each brand new toy,
And the Salvation Army proclaims Christmas joy.
A nip in the air, with wind up your back,
Christmas is over—there's no going back.
The toys are all broken; the gifts are all gone;
The Spirit has left us; and, now Winter dawns.

Marjorie Shuman
ONE SILVER BELL

One silver bell on a tiny tree,
On a box in the window, so that all can see
The love of that home as they pass by
This yuletide season, as evening draws nigh.
Yet from that bell no sound to be heard,
So that from within a heart is the meaning stirred.
Radiant hosannas are sung by the choir,
With tones reflected in the tall church spire,
And organs play, and chimes will peal
As to the earth they a message reveal
That Christmas is here, rejoice and be glad
Lift up your hearts, and do not be sad.
Snow covered mountains, radiant streams,
That appear like stars with moonlight beams,
And the quiet that falls on the stilly night
When hearts, like a fireplace burning bright,
Are waiting, so eagerly, just to share
That message of Christmas—Yes, I do care.
One tiny bell, on a small green tree,
One shining star, that's all mankind may see
One radiant angel glad tidings did bring
That He is born—Christ, the King.
One small babe in a manger lay
Oh, my heart, thank God for Christmas day.

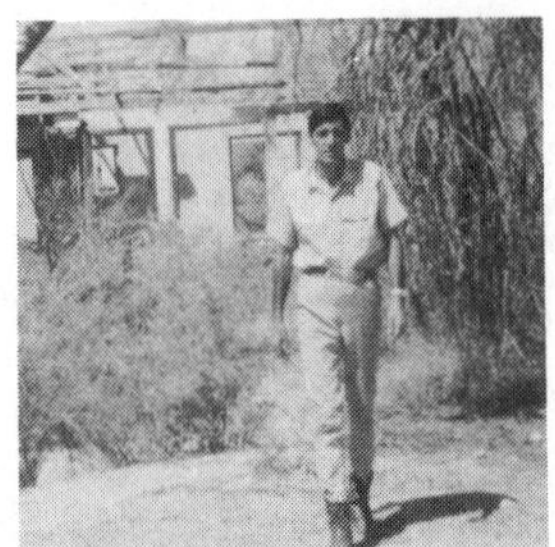

Everett Wild
PARADISE

Lord,
If you exile me,
Send me to the desert
Near a mountain
And a tree—
Not a big tree—
But one that
In the daytime
Will shade my head:
In the evening
Will hide my bed.
Perhaps there will be:
Cacti, greasewood,
Desert lily, tumbleweed—
Some berries on which to feed.
I'm sure that I will see:
Animals and birds,
A cactus wren,
Lizards and a pheasant hen.
To be isolated thus
Would be so nice
That I would call it
Paradise.

Anne Kirkpatrick
WHAT I CAN SEE

There is sunshine and there is
The glow in the night when
The moon shines
There is starlite and
There is blue sky

The grass is what I'm seeing
The trees are real
The water it moves
The land it breathes
One Sun
One Moon
One Sky
One Land
There is old and
There is new and
There is life and
Where is my Hope?

Patty Noack
I WANT YOU FOREVER
The beauty that forms when I
look in your eyes
The endless love I
seek in the skies
The story that follows
of you and of me
The time we have shared
so definitely
The joy that deepens
by holding your hand
The sparkle that brightens
your name in the sand
The pencil that writes this
the joy that is mine
The paper that holds it
line after line
The blessing uncovered
through exquisite delight
Our future of splendor. . . . . .
Is held in God's might.

Lisa Carbone
TIME
An alarm breaks my pillow
tales.
Where time has no meaning,
And people have false faces,
Without a thought—I'm ticking.
Pacing life into a measured day.
My morning mirror image,
Reflects wrinkles of time,
Scarring experience
Into a molded personality.
A walk by the old school
Unifies time as eternity.
There is another girl with
pigtails,
Filling my old space.
Feeling those same emotions—
unique to the human race.
Times steady stream
Channels off
Into personalized portions of
life.
Unproportional segments—
Each gaining more celerity.
An alarm breaks my pillow
tales.
Where time has no meaning.
Without a thought—I'm
ticking. . . . .

Leila Merchant
AURA OF CHRISTMAS
"Be not afraid," the angel said,
and Mary, by her simple faith,
believed,
and pondering in her heart the
things he said,
she followed in the path the
angel led.
"Fear not," the angel said,
"I bring you tidings of great
joy.
The Christ for whom you've
looked so long,
in Bethlehem is born this
day."
And the shepherds, surrounded
by heavenly joy,
hurried to find this baby boy.
The wisemen, coming from afar,
following the bright and
shining star,
brought gifts and laid them on
the hay,
knelt down and worshipped
the lovely child,
and quietly stole away.
It was a time of fear and strife,
of thievery, hate, and
prejudice, and killings,
with very little value placed on
life.
Just like today.
"Fear not," the angel says today,
"Your Christ is just a prayer
away.
His love shines through the
greatest strife,
His gift to you—ETERNAL
LIFE.
Hark to the Christmas bells
that ring,
Listen to the angels sing.
Adore the child,
BEHOLD, YOUR KING.

Charlotte Knight Harrison
BOUQUET
A tired bouquet
Of wilting grass
Clutched in a tiny
Dimpled hand
Placed in water
With tend'rest care
As though 't were for
An orchid rare
Only a mother
Knows their worth
These, the most precious
Blooms on earth!

Catherine J. Obbema
UNTITLED
Poetry is
the miracle of birth,
from conception to the final
moments of delivery,
when,
like the newborn infant,
the written word
emerges.

Odessa Cleveland
BLUES
The blues are deep in my soul
He shouts loudly;
Only to be heard by me,
While silence lingers someplace.
Touched, he grips the
innerlinings of my heart;
Gripped, as a princess on her
way to death.
He is not obscure.
We meet frequently at the Soul
Inn to be united in a sea of
blues

Christine Upston
SECOND CHANCE
I nearly threw my life away
not knowing how or when—
But then one night I met you
and you gave it back again.
My confusion overwhelmed me,
but you were always there;
To listen and to understand
and show me that you cared.
It may not seem important
just how much you've done
for me. . .
But you pulled me from deep-
water
in an everlasting sea
of confusion—illusion
heartache and defeat;
of helplessness and
hopelessness
a life incomplete.
The things I've been so hungry
for
the words I've longed to hear;
You brought the sunshine back
to me
and dried up all my tears.
I'm happy with my life again
in spite of all the scars;
You've made it all worthwhile,
somehow
just by being who you are.
You believed me, received
me
the way that I am;
you needed me and told me
I would find love again.

For all these things I'm grateful
and I wanted you to know—
You gave meaning to an empty
life
and filled a heart with hope.
And as the moon lights up the
heavens
and the sunshine burns the
sky;
Your candle touched another
and your goodness lit my life.
Thanks, Bill

Edith L. Price
QUIET TIMES
In the stillness of the morning,
As I rise, the Lord to meet,
I receive my day's instructions
Seated at my Savior's feet.
In a still, small voice he tells
me
What he has for me to do:
"Do not fear, my child," he
whispers,
"For I'll walk along with you."
In the bright, new day's
beginning,
As he's walking by my side,
All my troubles seem so small
now
With the Savior as my guide.
In these quiet times with Jesus,
Strength and power he will
provide;
He will never leave me helpless,
When by Satan I am tried.
When at last the day has ended,
And my work is all complete,
I will sit in sweet, communion,
Once again at Jesus' feet.

R. Roberts Baldwin
OTOLARYNGOLOGY
His quiet office features charts
Of all and sundry otic parts
Drum and hammer, nerve and
muscle—
Hush now yields to sounds of
bustle.
The Doc is late but for a start
He thumbs intently through
your chart.
His brows go up, he paws his
pate
While he absorbs your natal
date.
Your laggard ears he then
attacks
But doesn't find impacted wax,
So with his light and other
means
He probes your nose for jelly
beans.
Using a stick he flats your
tongue
And takes a gander toward your
lung,
Then just in case you're still
in doubt
He says, "You've had your
tonsils out."
Removes his light—still
sounding sage,
"Your hearing loss is due to age."
Finding your search for help's
been vain,
Leaving, you ask, "How's that
again?"

P. M. Beatts
SNOW
Winter's memories are long:
Summer goes lightly:
Spring brings a breath and a
song:
Autumn light gleams and
glows brightly.
Leaves fall, and the sun goes
over:
Dim the worlds stir.
Earth sees her age-old lover
Coming to her.
He walks in darkness: shattering
Bright is the glow of his
thighs,
Moving through stars, and
scattering
White tumult in the skies.

Christopher A. Anderson
DELICATE FLOWER
Please know
Delicate flower
That I am a gentle man
Oh—to just look upon your face
Fills my heart
And eases my mind.
How much so
Would I like
To give you one moment
Where you know again
That your love is boundless
And the most precious gift
That another could feel.
It is enough for me to know
At this time
That you are
Sure I may one day
Hold your hand
Or even kiss your lips
But I have so needed
To know that you exist
Somewhere in this world
Just as you are.

William W. Hudson, fsc
AMBIVALENCE
Bright
Yellow flowers
Blooming
Above the casket
Of my
Father.

Edith L. Leighton
WHAT IS LOVE?
Caring for each other
In fair or stormy weather.
Wondering how we each are
Whether near or far.
Understanding after fights
And after back turned, hurtful
nights.
Providing for home needs

Thoughtful wifely, husbandly
deeds.
A hand to hold
A kiss not cold.
Warm arms to hold you tight
Sometimes, day or night.
Just caring, sharing all the way
'Till the end of life's long
golden day:
THAT IS LOVE!

Lorene Rogers Murphy
THE OLD HOME PLACE
At some period in life, one
strives in vain, to relive ones
youth, by taking a stroll "Down
Memory Lane."
One feels the urge to visit the
neighborhood, in which one
spent most of ones childhood.
To day I returned to the "Old
Home Place," where I spent
many of my early years.
Where my family and I shared
laughter, joy and tears.
Those years were spent on a
small farm, a few miles east
of Burnet.
Any profit eked from that
rocky soil, you knew you had
earned it.
The old house is gone, but the
memories linger on.
I walked out to the old Wind
Mill, looked up with a sigh.
I couldn't realize so many years
have quickly slipped by.
The rickety old Barn still
stands, with it's hand hewn
rafters.
Standing in it's drafty hall,
the groaning of this aged
structure,
to me were but echoes of by
gone laughter.
In the Corn Crib, I gazed at the
spot, where the Corn Sheller
used—to be.
A frightened Rodent scurried by,
blinking beady eyes at me.
I picked up a forgotten Corn
Cob, turned it absent mindedly
with—my fingers.
The feeling of some unseen
presence, all around me lingers.
I kicked idly at small rocks, as I
strolled leisurely down the lane.
In my minds eyes, I was young,
running and playing again.
The old Orchard is no more, I
thought my eyes were playing
tricks—on me.
When I discovered a still
bearing Wild Plum Tree, I
picked some of the fruit, and
Fool that I am.
I could almost smell the aroma
of briskly boiling Plum Jam.
I returned to my Automobile,
then slowly drove away.
With no desire to relive the
memories of this nostalgic day.

Patricia J. Rose
ANONYMOUS
Flowers bloom, and then they
die,
what could it all be for;
To brighten up the spring time,
or fertilize the floor.
Even trees, though they live
longer,
don't really live much more;
It seems with all that time
and space,
they should do more than feed
the floor.
Sage brush isn't pretty,
replacing beauty, wiry weeds;
It twists and glides from place
to place,
so what's in dropping seeds?
If the flower and the sage
could willingly reverse their
call;
Do you think sage would give
up freedom,
just for the beauty of it all?

Alice M. Stack
GRIEF
I lost my child and I ask, Why?
Such a senseless thing to die,
So young.
To leave behind a family
grieved.
So many things to understand or
Believe,
Or try.
I lost my child and I ask why?

Marilynn Anese Craig
THE SONGBIRD OF ALABAMA (MY MOTHER)
When she stands up to sing
The congregation opens wide its
ears
As it might to the clear and
pleasing melody
Created by a robin atop a tree
Sharing its lovely message to all
Who will appreciate its
wondrous talent.
The pleasantness of her voice
reaches far and wide
For she migrates too,
Singing not only amidst her own
flock
But for other churches too
So that many may join with her
In spiritual rejoicing for her
mighty Creator.

How moving. . .
Those emotions which flow
naturally
Through her modulating voice
Slithering skillfully
Up and down the musical scale
Frequently reaching awesome
peaks. . .raising heights of
emotions.
Reaching deep into hearts and
souls
Of those who listen with
feeling,
With appreciative ears
As she tells them in melody
About the wondrous miracle
Of Creation.
Who can sing it better than
The Songbird of Alabama.

Mary Brickman Mayse
THE TIME WAS TO COME
I'm sorry for my indifferences
that I can't explain,
who's to say how I am, not I, for
I know not what is sane.
I know not when the day should
be, for all I know is it was,
today. . .and not to be purposely
made, not for hurt, but it does.
I can't be an expressable person,
of sound. .but in mind,
with the feeling of loss staying
constantly, I know find.
The time I know had to come,
for I am not to be with
anyone,
a friendship, a love—the care's
to be, and now there's none.
When the day I shall see you
last, of my day's are all to
pass,
with the lasting thought of you
to know—I know the time
was to come.

Elizabeth G. Trumble
JUST ONE MORE TIME
Just one more time
to see the sun shine
Just one more day
I have to play
One more glance
Just another chance
A face to remember
A place to remember
A lot of laughter a little fears
A lot of joy a little tears
There's a lot to remember
A lot to be learned
From the friends we've met
and the things we've done
Just one more time
to see the sun shine
Just one more day
I have to play
And a long, long while
before I see you again.

Florence G. Axton
CONVENTION
What is day?
A radiance, bewildering,
brightness, a golden ray,
An interval of light, freedom,
openess, sunrise,
Appearance of daylight, in the
morning,
A new beginning to a
REALIST.
A day never to return,
A day, perfection, to be
remembered, a day to learn,
Display, I don't want to, into I
desire to,
Work, accomplishment, love,
kindness,
NOURISHMENT.
Shadows fall,
Goals accomplished,
And I do recall,
A priest all aglo,
Said to me, "are you a part of
our
CONVENTION.?

M. Carl DeBruler
A VERY GOOD THING
The sea is a cesspool of filth
and corruption,
The rivers run deep in their
valleys long dead;
The rotting big cities highlight
the destruction
The rude race of man has left
here in his stead.
Unquenchable sol, though,
shines brightly and steady:
Man left him still burning,
unable to kill
His life-giving rays so eternal
and ready
To play once again the lead role
in God's will:
To start one more time the long,
slow evolution,
Re-peopling the earth over
millions of years,
And this time imbibe them with
firm resolution—
With wisdom, devotion and
God-loving fears.
'Twill all come to pass as time
flies on swift wing;
Consid'ring past failure, a very
good thing.

Carol Emory
LOSING
i caught my freedom from caring
too much
about your gauges of
Excellence,
your stylish life, the shape
of wine glasses.
the lines of affection grew taut
from straining to Please.
you thought you had some right
to dip into my life like it was
an endless pool—
i jumped free.

Anne Animus
UNTITLED
You give Meaning
to my life.
Can I give you less
than what you want?

Gloria H. Procsal
DIRECTIONS
You kept me quiet
for awhile
sitting at a loom
in Taos.
But now I harvest rye
at the bottom
of the sea,
leaving green footprints
on the ocean floor.
Still I would swing
from that yoyo
you call a moon
if I could,
and spend the next day
digging secrets
from a blue cat's
eye.

Edith P. Hazlehurst
I DON'T WRITE RIGHT
English is so hard to learn;
I hear just what you say,
But you use a word one way
today;
Next time, another way.
You say: "The wind Blew hard
last night,"
So I try to remember that;
Next time you're "feeling Blue,"
So I don't know where I'm at.
You talk about the forest—
The place that we went
"Through."
Next time I was confused
When you said: "The ball I
Threw."
When you mean such different
things
By the words you use,
I've decided that the language
Was made just to confuse.
My father went "Saw a board;"
That thing I Saw him do.
But when he said: "I Saw a
Child,"
Did he cut the child in two?
I saw my mother Knead the
bread;
Then I saw her turn and say:
"There's something else I Need

From the store today."
Does she mean she'll punch
the grocer?
That's what she does to bread.
Why do words mean two things?
I can't get it through my head.
Folks say: "I'm glad to
Meet you"
And at dinner I eat Meat.
How can I like to "Meet you"
When Meat is what I eat?
You Sent me on an errand
Without a single Cent.
How can you expect a kid
To know just what you meant.
I Write a little sentence
And you say it isn't Right.
Maybe I can't spell so good;
I never do Write Right.

Jon Bowman
MYTHOS
She is the tree in the garden
Whose fruit is pure,
In the center she grows
Where the rivers join,
Arms and branches, legs
entwine,
Leaves of hair with scent of
sap,
Blood that gives life to the
world.
She is a dream remembered
With whispers and sighs,
Words woven in gold
And spread on the flood
Like ashes strewn on the river,
She dances in fire and falls
With the snow on frozen
Olympus.

Frances J. Parkin
THE TREE
Once you were majestic,
alive and green.
Squirrels in your branches,
were often seen.

Now you are lonely,
black, stark, cold.
Did a bolt of lightning,
make you old?

Maryann Lambert
TRAPPED
Butterfly. . .
caught in a net;
Strive butterfly strive. . .
keep on.
Poor little butterfly, you were
caught
now die.

Clarence B. Carter
CHOICE OR NOT
I'm glad I'M not a chicken,
All brown and in a dish.
But what is worse than this is,
I could have been a fish.
I'm glad I'm not a turtle,
Swimming in my stew.
I'm glad I'M not a monkey
Swinging in a zoo.
I could have been a polecat,
With such an awful scent,
That trailed around behind me,
Every where I went.
I could have been an eagle,
Sailing in the sky,
Or one of many blackbirds,
Baked into a pie.
I might have been a stallion,
Wallowing in class,
Or, in a lowly barnyard,
Just a stupid ass.
Of all the things I could have
been,
From alpha down to zee,
With all my faults and
weaknesses,
Thank God I'm only me.

Carol D. Lewis
SPRING
A lovely, yellow daffodil,
a bluebird on the wing. . . .
a gentle rain, a warming sun,
at last, at last, it's Spring!
Pale green buds on every tree,
new grass of deeper green. . . .
of all the seasons, this must be
the lovliest ever seen!
The lacy clouds of purest white
wake up to greet the days. . . .
they hide the cold, dark gray
ones
and reflect sun's golden rays.
How I love to go outdoors
and look at everything!
I can almost hear it in the air;
At last, at last, it's Spring!

Jennifer L. Aiken
WORDS
Writing words that don't rhyme
Trying to say what's on my
mind.
I yearn to speak,
Sometimes the words won't
come.
So I write to relieve my mind.
To others they mean naught,
For me, they speak what has
to be said.
Don't try to understand,
They won't take a poetic prize.
Just words. . .floating around
in my mind.
Catching them long enough to
put on paper.
You may laugh, I don't mind,
For I know what you can't find.

Doarin R. Lewis
TAMMIE
Time passes
8 turns to 1.
Wished for you. . .
Settled for rum.
Words pile up. . .
Assignment undone.

Esther Long (Breazy Anne)
WHILE I SLEEP
Oh. .
And my dream
While I sleep,
is to have of Someone
to hold of me. .
While I sleep,
For if I wake not in this world,
A memory of Someone
I may keep. . .
And Someone may keep of me.

Kathleen Manley Liggitt
THUNDERSTORM
The rain is God's night music.
It clatters on leaves,
And whispers on soft grass.
It drums at our window,
Wakening us to listen.
Lightning sheds the dark,
Bright enough to read by.
The thunderstorm crackles
around us,
Applause for one of God's
Major plays.

Mary Hayes Harms
TIME HEALS ALL
There is a man who walks,
Along the shore of the sea.
It is there I go to talk,
To him of you and me.

I tell him of the love we had,
And why we had to part.
I sometimes think I was mad,
To let you break my heart.

He always listens to me,
And never says a word.
He assures me that there will
be,
Answers to the questions he's
heard.

It seems I must forget you,
Though how, I do not know.
Time goes fast to few,
For my tears still flow.

I wait for the far off day,
When there will be no sorrow.
You may never again pass my
way,
But there will always be
tomorrow.

I asked when this would be.
Seagulls answered my call.
Silence prevailed over the sea.
He told me, Time Heals All.

Joanne Burr (nee, Peterson)
LEGEND
She told of a man
I did not know.
He must've been something
For her to love him so.
"With laughing blue eyes
That danced on a smile,
And a swagger in his walk
That was all his own style.
In inches and feet
He wasn't too tall,
But in giving of love
He stood above all.
He had dark curly hair
And a contagious grin.
He died so young. . .
It was such a sin."
As the tales went on
I understood
Why she never replaced him
For NO man could.
Then came the pictures
And from them I read
That the man who gazed
through me
Was all she had said.
"Tell me, Sweet Lady,
Lest I should die,
The name of this man
You hold so high."
"But you knew him well.
He made your heart glad.
His name to you, Jo,
Was 'Dad.'

Keith Krueger
ALONE
Alone singing to myself,
I hear a crackling in the brush.
Light waves touch on the beach;
and shortly deminish to
nothing.
The sun sets upon the distant
water as a ship recedes into
darkness.

Its not gone, just out of sight.
Again I hear a crackling in the
brush.
I swing around to see who,
or what it is,
but its nothing.
Shortly, I begin singing again.
Still alone, but not lonely,
not depressed, just alone.
A slight breeze,
can you feel it?
Warm, tiring,
salty smelling.
Its just the ocean.
No more sunlight. Full moon
shines now. Its a welcomed
relief
from the suns heat. Almost
excruciating.
Millions of stars now.
One streak's the sky,
falling as it looks, into the
water,
with no splash.
Finally, I'm receding into total
darkness, and I'm asleep.
Still alone.

Carolyn Williams Maxwell
DEFINABLE LIFE
Life can readily be defined as
the ESSENCE of Me,
And all that I can ever hope to
be,
As I discover my individuality
Within this realm of
immortality.

J. Henry Bell
UP FROM EDEN
Scant figments of time
Hold slow to those barbarous
sadnesses
Lurking in mind's folds,
Coming as remembrances
To unsettle now.
Now, the only possession
Of a frail beast
Up from Eden;
Bound for isles in infinity,
Dragging the child, Fear, not
knowing.
Now, so dependent on was.
Not worth the while
Less bolstered by will be,
The energizer
That stirs the fire, Hope.
Precious nows bow
After holding slow to barbarous
sadnesses,
And fleet back toward Eden,
Leaving the beast suspended,
remembering, imagining,
Trying to solve time.

Christine King Shrum
EGG EGO
Crack
Open
Beat
Heat
Scramble
Season
Pass Around—
Pass Through—
Changed. . .
in the END!

Victoria
AS WITH ALL THINGS
As with all things. . .time
lessens the passions
and heals the longing heart
eyes that could not. . .part
now can look away
The fire that burned
our skin and made
our hearts slam against
our bodies
are gently pounding
at a milder pace. . .
The pleasure of your arms
are more easily concealed
and the bitter hot taste
of your mouth

is softer now,. . .and tempered
with honey. . .
You are not less than
you were
nor am I. . .
We took the years full of heated
desires
and replaced them with
gentle touches and smiles across
the room
Love wears many faces and
love has changed its mask of
hurried embraces
to one of lasting friendship
A dozen more years will be
given us
because we stood still and let
the years change our dreams
into a world
we can live in. . . .
and when we meet. . .and our
hearts jump. . . .once
we will know. . .

Marian Nell Thompson

LIFE'S WAYS

Creep across the pathway,
Slow but steadily—
Edging toward your destiny
Not yet with feet of clay.
Totter towards the doorway,
Stumble once or twice,—
Curiosity delays you;
Soon you'll have your say.
Walk out to the breezeway,
Gazing down the street.
Friends, not foes, entreat you;
Come on out to play.
Plunge on down the roadway—
Move at quite a pace.
Never stop to question;
Don't give the time of day.
Trudge along the highway—
Careful but assured.
Everything's not perfect;
But there is a way.
Cleave to all life's pathways—
Soon there's the demise.
Life on earth is over;
Squelching feet of clay.

Wesley Aaron Freeberg

UNTO THE HILLS

Mine eyes I lift unto the hills
From whence my help
proceeds.
From Him who made the rocks
and rills
Comes everything man needs.
The miner prays and lifts his
eyes
To hills where he must labor;
To dig the ore on which relies
Both he and every neighbor.
The fisherman looks up with joy
As streams rush down the
mountain,
For once again he's just a boy
At youth's eternal fountain.
The farmer lifts his eyes in
thanks
For ever flowing waters
Which flood the fields along
the banks,
To feed his sons and
daughters.
The city dweller rests his gaze
Where yonder snowcaps
tower,
And lifts his heart in prayer and
praise
For water, light and power.
The hunter stalks the wary deer
While in the hills it hides,
And thanks his God who every
year
This source of food provides.
The artist lifts his eyes in awe,
Impelled by sense of duty,
To paint or draw, without a
flaw,
The hills in all their beauty.
What e'er his task; who e'er he
be,
He cannot help confessing;
It is not difficult to see
How hills do bring him
blessing.
There is a help for all our ills,
Beyond where storm clouds
gather.
We lift our eyes above the
hills,
And thank our heavenly
Father.

Kathryn V. Daley

POET

My feelings do assertain
That maybe in a different vein
I would breakthrough novice
state
My writings to contemplate
And soar half way to the moon
With every piece and every
rune.

Sunny Hye Rapp

LINES OF THE CALENDAR

To her friends it was just a
calendar
Drawn with lines this way and
that.
To her it was days of their lives
that would be—
A phone call here, a doorbell
there, a puppy's wagging tail
It was more than a calendar
drawn, you see—
It was surely the days of their
lives that would be.
The days will pass, dear friend,
dear friend—
And I'll remember thee.

Martha Sardullo

ODE TO MARTIN LUTHER KING, JR.

Martin Luther King Jr. fought for human rights.

He fought for them with all his might.

Martin thought human rights were for all.

I have a dream was his call.

Martin Luther King Jr. worked for the good of people everywhere.

He won the Nobel Peace Prize for his humanitarian work that showed he cared.

So on his birthday let's remember the good he did.

And let it be a memorium for us to live.

Michael Damien Opilla

TO KAREN MARIE—ALL THESE. . .AND YOU

A house
A place to call my own
To spend my days
To live—a Home
A tree
To shade me through the day
To be a friend
To climb and play
A dog
To guard me through the night
To run and bark
But never bite
A fire
To warm my friendly home
And there I'll stay
And never roam
All these
I wish to have forever
But one thing more
Than any other
A girl
I Love to share my life
To share all this
And be my Wife

Ella Leber Grove

LONELINESS

Oh, let me be,
Beloved enemy,
Sublime companion,
Exhilarating foe,
Penetrating curse,
Unbanishable verse,
Thou undoctorable
Hyper-undertow.
Oh, deadly sense,
Insane intelligence,
Purgatoried peak,
Perplexing lofty hole,
Mystic, ever-calling,
Darkening, macabre,
Brilliantly gruesome
Keeper of my soul.
Oh, mock me not
In simple polyglot,
In wild abandon
Spinning to and fro,
Bawdy sorceress,
Stubborn wantonness,
In pensoroso time
Thy charm bestow.
Oh, torrid sun,
Suffocating one,
Desolate, sultry,
Thou execrating chill,
Decursive siren,
Feverishly wizened,
Apathetic coma,
Cryptic thrill.
Oh, tamper not
My vaporous lot,
Grandiloquently
Shattering delusion,
Let me fantasize
Muffled ego lies,
Perpetuate the myth,
Join in collusion.
Oh, acquiesce
My soul, to loneliness,
The poetess within
Requires seclusion,
Diminish to accept
The gentle velvet depth,
The mesmeric descent,
The lone illusion.

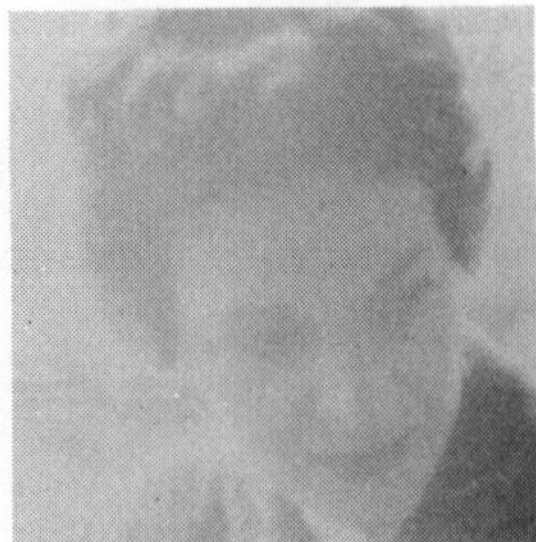

Edith Perruso

DARKNESS AT SUNSET

I can remember Mom, when she
was quite young,
She had lovely hands, and a
bosom of fun.
Seven children she bore, with
the stately posture of a
Queen.
I enjoyed sitting across her lap,
though I was at least sixteen.
She never once removed her
snug wedding band,
Which now slips loosely about
the slim fingers of her soft,
but aged hand.
Dad often called her "Battleaxe;"
in more tender moods,
"Sunshine."
I had never once witnessed any
affectionate display towards
Dad;
Their love, to the children
seemed, an esoteric thing,
Their entire marriage had been a
clandestine fling.
When I was disoriented and
stranded, for a year or more,
She travelled long distances by
bus, making many
connections,
Carrying me bags of fresh fruit,
and missing never a Visiting
Day.
She was both "Doctor" and
"Loyal Friend," throughout
my entire Stay.
For her "Practical Wisdom," I
owe my life's breath;
If it hadn't been for her
womanly instinct,
She understood my case so
well. . .
If it hadn't been for her strength
and determination,
I'd be but a discarded and
vacant shell.
She played ragtime with a
robust beat, up until her
waning years.
Trading the study of music to
marry Dad, she left her Tutor
in tears.
In weaker moments, she had
doubts about her youthful
decision,
While thoughts of fame
threatened a marital collision.
At the age of eighty, her
fumbling fingers stumbled

over the keys.
Soon, she was unable to clear
the piano bench, as Time had
buckled her knees.
I brought home Scott Joplin
records, as second best,
But Mom's ragtime style, far
surpassed the rest.
One evening, I had noticed
how horribly thin she had
become.
I touched her brow, it appeared
distended and numb.
It was no less, the impression
left by her naked skull,
Beneath its prominence, her
cavernous eyes betrayed a
wistful lull.
A strident ambulance could be
heard streaking down the
street.
"They do make an awful lot of
noise," I said, my annoyance
replete.
She lifted her sad eyes towards
me to reply:
"It sounds like they're saying
'W-h-y? W-h-y? W-H-Y?' "
I laughed at her and said, "Mom,
that's cute."
Seldom she shared her
impressions, becoming more
reticent and mute.
When the Pastor arrived, I told

him what Mom had said to
me,
And what a clever remark, it
seemed to be.
The Pastor shot me a look that
was Stark.
Suddenly trapped, I was forced
to face up to the Remark.
He tactfully changed the subject
to a lighter tale,
Which amused Mom, making
her laugh at a moment's Lark,
Dispelling thoughts of dying
that imprisoned her, in the
Dark.
Totally confined to her rocking
chair, she would sit listlessly,
Listening unconsciously, to the
drone of TV.
She was suffering terribly, her
lips distorted,
With an expression of anguish,
unbearable but thwarted.
"Mom," I said, "Wouldn't you be
more comfortable in bed?"
"I hate to go to Bed while the
Sun is still Shining..." ."
This Time, I did not laugh; I
wanted to cry, instead.
Nevertheless, the distressing
questions, "W-h-y? W-h-y?
W-H-Y?' "
Have never been known to
Transgress,
Nor, have they ever Left,
The Voiceless lips of Death!

Jonathan Richard

BUTTERFLIES

Butterflies they were to me,
wonderous things, a joy to see.
And in my youth I'd chase their
flight,
perchance to grasp them if I
might.
I snatched a Monarch of black
and gold,
and quivering his soft wings
did fold.
Deftly those wings I pulled
apart,
to learn my quest had burst a
heart.
Though beauty it was I rushed
to view,
from greedy glance it never flew.

Susan H. Werschay

JERRY

I close my eyes and who do I see
But a mere boy of two or three.
Of Italian descent he seems to
be
With bright sparkling eyes and
tarnished knee.
Conceited he seems at such an
age;
When older he will probably be
a rage.
His skin is a tender, brownish
hue.
His eyes seem to smile a
summer blue.
Dark hair falls across his eyes—
His brain is full of little lies.
He loves to smile and flirt
around—
On a girl's trail he is often
found.
Yet, he is lovable as a child
of three.
Now it is no wonder he is loved
by me.
Sixteen years later he is a
handsome lad
Tempted by inclinations of good
and bad.
He no longer cares about the
heavens and stars,
Nor of his once planned trip
to Mars.
Cars and girls are his chief
concern.
His personality alone makes
a heart yearn.
He has a certain quality which
makes him seem shy;
A bashfulness that can even
conceal a lie.
He has a habit of breaking
promises 'tis true.
And is very evasive about what
he wants to do.
He always seems to hold you in
the air,
Being never quite blunt nor
either fair.
No matter when he calls or
where he appears
There always seems hope for the
future years.
'Tis not often one sees him,
he seldom dials one's number.
Can there be no happiness for
one even in slumber?
Not even in one's dreams do
these events occur.
He's gone from dreams and
reality as it were.
His heart is one day here and
one day there.
Like a child he is fickle with
a heart every where.
Will he never possess a heart
that grows fond and steady;
Never mature like a man; will
he never be ready?
Will he always play his cards
and gamble
Or might he some day cease to
Ramble?
I hope I happen to be around
When he fancies to settle
down—
Because before he can change
his mind
He'll be at the altar and a
wife he'll find.

Johnye G. Boyd

HOLOCAUST

O Holocaust! O Holocaust!
Please don't strike the world
again,
Or it may deceive you or me
at any cost.
Whenever things seem wrong,
Don't allow venom to rise,
Sit back and relax, sing a sweet
song.
Blood ran swiftly during world
war II,
But the atrocities upon
humanity God did cease,
While Jews knew not what to
do.
O Holocaust! O Holocaust!
Please don't strike the world
again,
For the race of mankind may be
lost.
'Tis true life's deficit won't
be few,
But who's to proclaim,
It'll shun you if due?
Blood stain won't be ascribed
to only Jews,
For the hand of the super-
natural power will stir the
trigger,
Then, what with nationalities
of various hues?
O Holocaust! O Holocaust!
Please heed my plea and render
your decision,
Or the price of human life you'll
face cost!

Mozelle House

AUTUMN LEAVES

Autumn Leaves! Autumn
Leaves!
Clinging to the trees—
Holding on to summer's glow—
Swaying in the breeze.
Whispering thoughts of
yesterday—
What secrets do you share,
Of summer in its fullness,
So rich in beauty rare.
Autumn Leaves! Autumn
Leaves!
Flying 'round and 'round—
What tales of summer do you
bring
Tumbling to the ground.
A carpet for the earth you'll
make,
With colors all aglow—
Winter will soon be bringing
warmth,
with a coverlet of snow.
Autumn Leaves! Autumn
Leaves!
Now you've had your fling,
And Mother Nature will use
you now
For new life in the spring.
So sleep in peaceful slumber
there,
All nestled by the breeze,
Covered o'er with winter's
blanket,
And sheltered by the trees.

Sherry Burrell

DO YOU KNOW WHAT IT IS LIKE

Do you know what it is like
To wake up with the daylight
Feeling rested and full of life
Catching each and every
breathtaking bite
Have you ever looked around
And felt the whisper of all the
sights
The softness of an evening
breeze
With trees and fields that
sway and tease
The sun which beckons our
skins of pale
The ocean tides playing tricks
as we sail
From shore to horizon our
world is bound
Do you know what it is like
To wake up with the daylight
Feeling rested and full of life
Catching each and every
breathtaking bite
Have you ever looked around
Seeing people of all kinds
Some filled with compassion
And others full of hate and
despise
Have we shielded our hearts
And closed our minds
As not to see all these sides
Do you know what it is like
To wake up with the daylight
Feeling rested and full of life
Catching each and every
breathtaking bite
Have you ever looked around
To all the souls who need a
helping hand
This world is full of young
and old
Stop for a moment, don't be so
cold
Give a hand, don't forget your
heart
Give an ear and remember
some time
Just to listen to what they
say and mind
Do you know what it is like
To wake up with the daylight
Feeling rested and full of life
Catching each and every
breathtaking bite
If you know what it is like
Help someone else learn
How it feels to break with
the morning light
And give a bright smile and
a warm hello
For you will make their
morning a delight.

Mauricia Price

THEY CALL IT SPORT

A whispering of forest leaves,
A golden shaft of sunlit warmth,
A poised majestic antlered head,
A devastating rifle crack—
Combine raw elements to form
What hunters see as virile sport:
To stalk an unarmed beast and
kill
A creature God has rendered
beautiful. . .

Yvonne F. Null

WHAT IS A MIRACLE?

What is a miracle?
A baby's first cry
A mother's sweet sigh,
A tear in the eye,
Or the blue of the sky.
The smile of a child,
Flower's growing wild,
The sun shining bright,
The moon and stars at night.
The trees growing up,
The roots going down,
GOD is all around,
With HIS Wonderful Love.
A miracle?
Well it comes from Heaven
above.
You see,
It is GOD'S HOLY LOVE.

Becky S. Pittman

HIDDEN FEAR & OPEN ANGER

Many thoughts have passed
between us
But when words aren't made
clear
They become so meaningless.
The emotion we try to attach to
them
Only leaves our aching hearts
more unfulfilled.
Sometimes I try to teach you,
with my eyes.
But somehow the message
I try to transmit
Is not perceived.
Instead of looking in for more
You closed your eyes to mine
As you would close shutters
To block out the brightness
of the sun.
The few times we've held each
other close,
were never for more than a few
moments.
Was it reassurance or
Was it a 'leading me on',
To show me—I couldn't live
without. . .you.

But what meaning does it all
hold now?
When still we are words apart.
It's hard to say
When you think you've got it
straight
You fall.
It's never easy and never
clear.
Just passing thoughts
That flicker like the flame of
a candle
Only to be blown out,
By the wind of a false promise.

E. Tenore
FOR YOU
Star gazer,
Night saver,
Shaper of dreams.
Faith healer,
Grace stealer,
Collector of moonbeams.

Dawn breaker,
Love maker,
Escaper of time.
Soul traveler
Mind dazzler,
Your spirit is mine.

Mrs. F. A. (Blanche Swann)
THE LITTLE WILD VIOLET
All pass you by, little beauty
of the earth,
They say you're old-fashioned
and a tiny bit pert!
And I have seen the gardener
clip your head,
As he passed by with his old
swing blade.
Not once you complained, soon
you were up again,
The little wild violet, not so
tame!
So I plucked you from the wild
berth outdoors.
And I placed you in real dignity
indoors.
For though your station be so
lowly,
I see in your mien something
holy,
And a wee touch of God
Himself, you bet,
In you, the lowly little wild
violet!

Kathleen Shinnick Rumsey
INTERLACED THOUGHT
Upon midnight velvet the
restless mind slumbered
Backbrushed nap
s u s p e n d e d between
twilight and dawn
Freehanded selvage
Binding childhood thoughts
Tauntess of adult bias
Straightened grainline______
Fibre Content: 100% Natural

Louis D. Izzo
AS THE BUGLER PLAYS RETREAT
On the soil of the enemy,
that they fought,
Here stand these men, full of
thoughts.
Thinking of the days, passed by,
When they fought, side by side.
And now, "Attention," is proudly
called,
To these fighting men, one and
all.
No one dare move his eyes, or
feet,
"As the bugler, plays, retreat."
They were brave, and heros all,
For these men answered, their
nations call.
To bring the peace and
happiness, once more,
To a world of hate, and terror
torn.
Through a raging hell, they had
lived,
Where others laid wounded, and
killed.
But now at "Attention", they
stand and weep,
"As the bugler, plays, retreat."
And as they weep, within their
heart,
They feel the pain, so deep, and
sharp.
That made them live, the life
of hell,
On the battle field, where
others fell.
And see those bodies, torn by
shells,
A story, no one cares to tell.
Now,—Here they stand, in this
burning heat,
"As the bugler, plays, retreat."
And with faces wet, they hear
the call,
"Present-arms," known by one
and all.
As now the moment for taps,
was near,
They wait for that first note,
to hear.
That sounds the respect,
and love, to be paid,
To those men for the sacrifice,
they made.
Here they stand in tribute,
never to meet,
"As the bugler, plays retreat."
With that first note, ringing in
their ear,
They fix their eyes, on this pole
so dear.
That holds our flag, waving in
the sky,
Free to fly on enemy land, so
proudly high.
All this in their hearts, and
tears, they can not hide,
Tribute, they pay to those men,
that had to die.
Now,—all they hear, is their
heart beats,
"As the bugler, plays, retreat."
These men standing here, know
the price of life,
And the struggle they had, in
this mighty fight.
But they were lucky, and now
they live,
While others, their life, they had
to give.
So that they could be present,
at this retreat,
To thank the "Lord," and
pray, to always repeat.
The love, and respect these
dead, shall always seek,
"As the bugler, plays, retreat."

Adrian M. Maschek
TODAY
Today, I prayed God be with
you and I'm sure that he has
heard it's my faith that tells
me so, for I heard him speak no
word.
I didn't ask for jewels or gold
but something very fine
I asked but for his guidance,
so deep within your mind.
I asked that he go with you
every night and day
and keep your thoughts so
tender, let you never go astray.
I asked him for your happiness
I asked him for your health
I asked him for all that's good
for you, and when added they
spell wealth!

Harvey Alan Sperry
THE GIFT OF LOVE
What costs nothing but gives so
much,
enriches receivers as a golden
touch?
What gives the giver more than
he gave,
cannot be earned nor anyone
save?
What takes an instant to grant
or bestow,
lasts one a lifetime, with
memories grow?
What should the rich and
mighty retain,
the poor and the weak never
restrain?
What does one give to gain it
a value,
cannot be saved or buy
something new?
What gains a friend, creates
goodwill,
brings rest to the weary, cheers
the ill:
Cannot be borrowed or stored
for even a day,
be stolen or have value until
given away?
What can show love in
Mankind's domain,
babes give before learning to
ascertain?
What can be granted when there
is nothing to give,
an offering unique, without
comparative?
What does a man when
possessing no more,
need, to replace those he
formerly wore?
Undoubtedly all can answer
these questions;
the reply expressed with
unspoken emotions;
words undeclared, yet humanity
knows
the gift of love is a smile that
glows.

Elizabeth Pletcher
AS I WALKED INTO PREMISES OF ST. ANNE BEAUQUES
I walked into the gate
There I found a lovely lady.
High above looking over the
Sky and stars.
I walked up steps
And found a lovely lady
Who was waiting for sick,
And lame, despair, waiting
To be asked to help their
Need and wants.
I walked up another stair
There before me on my knees
I found twenty eight steps
Each with a prayer, one step
Closer to heaven; and crown
To meet my Savior Jesus.
Amen.

Irma Campbell
MY TRUE LOVE
She's the cutest little thing
in town
Her hair is curly and her eyes
are brown
We are so cozy, My True Love
and me
As she sits beside me, or sits
on my knee
She will always do, what I
want her to
If I am busy she waits 'till I'm
through
If I want to go out at night
And leave her home, that's
alright
If I come home early, or come
home late
She will always sit, by the door
to wait
Where ever I go, Its nice to
know
She'll be waiting cause she
loves me so
This life that I live suits me
just fine
There has never been another,
little dog like mine

Lori Jean Lang
SILKWORMS
I never see you come
back up.
You're always swirling
down, down.
I find this most difficult to
understand when
all you do is start from
the top
and climb down.
You've seen the top
and decided that it just is
not for you.
You're never afraid when your
frail thread breaks
because you're on your way to
the bottom anyway,
just so that you may
enjoy life.
You'd rather do it in your
own sweet time,
but when it comes right
down to it,
it really doesn't
matter

Lillian Hendel
ALONE
I ambled afoot one morning
at eight
Along city streets where none
did wait
Or stop to greet or notice me
I felt so small
Where the buildings rose tall
Each a towering gigantic tree
Saluting the sky in mimicry.
I scanned each face that I
encountered
For a friendly smile to light
my way
But a look of steel from each
who sauntered
Added to my own dismay.
Like a song I tried but failed
to recall
Or a story I couldn't
remember at all

To be desolate 'mongst the strangers who passed
Was like sitting alone in a deserted class.
I recoiled with a start from being so lonely
When I realized I'd been wrapped in me only.

Sharon De Long Lachenmyer
I'LL MAKE IT YET! ! !
Whenever I see a mountain
Whenever I see the sea
Whenever I see a valley
I see your face in memory.
The times we shared together
All come rushing back to me
Whenever I see my children
I remember you once loved me.
That time has past now
My life I'm building anew
I'm going to make it somehow
Without any assistance from you!
At the present time you may think
You have all that's precious to me
But with my faith and the help of God
I'll make it yet, you will see.
You shouldn't have ridiculed
My poems, songs and stories
Because soon you'll be hearing them
On the air, the land and the seas.
Following through on my decision
Was a frightening step to do
But I'm building a new life for myself
And its not going to include you!
Soon, I'll be able to see
A mountain, a valley, the sea
But your face won't come to haunt me
Because I'll soon be free!

Gertrude Bates
LOST CHILD
From the window I behold you—
A little maid dressed for school
Arms outflung in childhood joy
Sun like new-minted gold on your hair
Slate-blue eyes shaded with straw
Challenging smile beneath the brim—
Desperately I want
To have and hold
That which now is gone—
Small wanderer
With so many years ahead!

Mary Sammeli
DARK STRANGER IN A SMALL CAFE
One day, in life's play. . .
A dark stranger is sipping coffee
A girl enters on cue
Their eyes meet, hopeful of recognition
But a fantasy is lost to hesitation
A sense of precognition creates a sense
Of unity
A smile leads to a word
A word leads to a cup of coffee
They chat of where they have been
Both still hiding their feelings
From scrutiny
Becoming confidants in illusion
The dark stranger leaves reluctantly
Without evident loss
The girl returns to sipping coffee
Daydreaming of a mysterious man

T. O'Dell Hatchett
HOPEFUL
May the blessings of time
Continue in this sphere
To beautify your life
Throughout the coming year.

Dr. James Amick, Jr.
YOU HAVE THE GRITS TO GET OUT OF THE RUT
Don't give up in your quest to be happy,
Everyday won't be happy but keep your spirits high,
Don't be a half-a-minder, hesitating along the way,
You have it in you to win, don't let life pass you by,
You have the grits to get out of the rut.
Keep moving with that force that unbeatable,
Show the world you will not despair.
I know life can be an ocean of confusion,
Keep the determination and confidence,
There is a bright spot somewhere.
You have the grits to get out of the rut.
Keep a positive attitude at all times,
Don't let negative thoughts destroy your day,
If you really want to be happy and successful,
Move those negative thoughts out of you way.
You have the grits to get out of the rut.

Blanche Fredricks
AUTUMN
She's a show-off with her red gold,
and she's cool and airy, as if to scold.
Woe to all who love her.
Her message says get out of my way,
I'm in a hurry, not long to stay.
Mornings she glows, warm, bright and bitter.
Evenings, she's cold and spreads her glitter.
She's color, she's sparkle, but she's sly.
Wild geese scurry over her blue sky.
She tries so hard to tell all the world
that she's just a capricious girl.
She changes every leaf and flower,
painting magic every sleeping hour.
Then old man winter shouts his command
and takes her firmly by the hand.
Hear her sigh when the snowflakes fall!
Was she really ever here at all?
Woe to all who love her.

Mark Wallinder
UNTITLED
It was a cool, and windy summer
in California, when Hok, and Judy arrived,
No easy feat coming over the Bering Straits.
They waded through Washington,
and wandered through the Oregon woods
descending latitudes until they dropped
into Northern California.
What a strange place it was
A thousand years ago.
The green weeds grew over the head
of Hok
even on his tippy toes.
They wondered at the thickness of the soil,
rich from rain, and void of wear from feet.
"Let's build a church," said Hok
"and climb the Sierra Nevada in our
Sunday clothes."
And seven years later
they were still cutting paths
that even the deer couldn't follow.

Jeffrey G. Geiser
PRE-SLUMBER WONDERS
Building conceptual structures, based on a basic theme, and branching out into unknown origins.

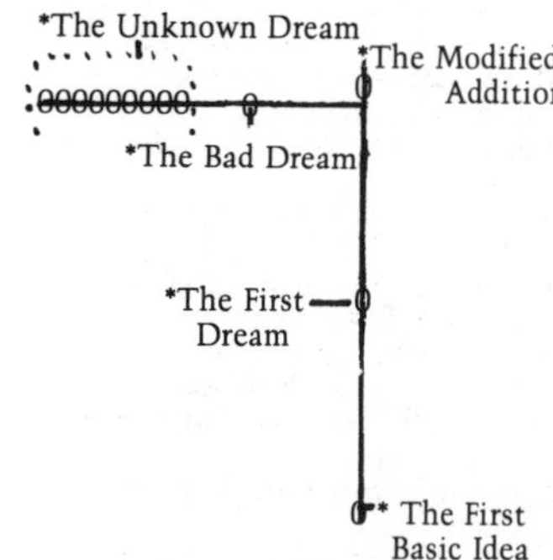

* read heading first then return to bottom of page and read up.

Jo LaGarde'
WISE OLD MAN
So wise and so old
But all that ice
The moon cannot help
To melt or thaw
What is held
Frozen so tight
The eyes are not cold
So wise and so old
But mind ears and mouth
All held so tight
By all that might
It almost seems
As though tears of brown
Coming down down down
Could melt all ice
But frozen so tight
With all that might

Martha Johnson
MR. GROUNDHOG, THE WEATHERMAN
I am a little groundhog.
Great fun I have with earth people,
All winter I sleep and dream,
People call it hibernation
To me, it is sleeping with
Contemplation—
With my weather instruments
Tucked in my body.
I pull out my weather watch
To check the time.
Too lovely, too early, to forecast the weather.
I get asleep, I went back to bed.
Suddenly, February Second knocked on my door.
Come out, come out, the sun is shining.
Perfect, perfect, I can predict
The weather in a second.
Watch me—
Out into the sunshine, I proudly walked.
And stood on my hind feet, looking in every direction.
There was my shadow on the ground.
My shadow forecasted six more weeks of winter.
Everyone was looking at my shadow shivering.
Six more weeks of cold, winter weather, I yelled.
Half smiling I crawled into my warm bed.
There, to rest peacefully for six more weeks.
Then, spring will be here—
With, flowers blooming, and birds singing.
Not a trace of winter will be on the landscape.

Daniel McDevitt
BIRTHDAY
Twas a nice spring morning
in the middle of May
when I awoke to go
pitch out the cattle's green hay.
The birds were singing
and the sky was still gray.
But I didn't care
because this was my day.
All I wanted was a couple of things
as precious as a bird's feathered wings.
In case you haven't guessed
what this mirth filled day is,
It is my birthday.

Alan C. Whittaker
FOREVER
From love emanates all things.
Love comes from all in life that sings.
Lasting love begets the beauty,
The pure, that which endures.
As the sun rises to a new day,
And upon the horizon night falls,
Love holds together, though at times
One is away; truly, there is no real parting.
There is no lessening, little to
Be compromised, less to be ignored.
Love gives the girded strength
To build upon. . .let nothing befall
To give, to have—everlastingly one's all.

Deanna J. Cannell
SON
Standing in a shadowed space
I watch, you're unaware
Beautiful eyes, handsome face
Sunlight dancing in golden hair. .
Laughter like a bolt of lightning
Affecting anyone near or far
Leaving me breathless when you display
The eloquence of a falling star. .
Gold, silver, castles and kings
Moments, years, a love apart
Pirates, dragons, little boys' dreams
You're etched so deeply in my heart. .
Lovingly would I ask of you
Do nothing to cause a tear
Leave soft footprints in the sand
After all, God knows you're here. .
With zest, be a gentle man
Tenderness brings dignity
When I am gone, cease to be
Touch me with love in a memory. .
A part of me, intracate,
Forever and beyond
Favored so by the Gods
This being, you, my son. . . . .

Roxana R. Boyles
FEAR NOT, I AM WITH YOU
A man cries out in the lonely night
shattering the shroud of silence;
A shallow breath of life's sustaining
air invades the warmth of his immobile form;

A glimmer of light from the moon's
full face gently crosses his rising and falling chest;
Hearing the rustling of the leaves
in the gentle breeze, the rhythm
of the sounds lulls him into tranquility;
And he sleeps, knowing he's not alone. . .

Thelma Jo Bowling
BABY JO
My birthday was that morning
And daddy loved me so
He'd taken all the money he had
And bought me Baby Jo.
For times were hard, and money scarce
The toys we had some made
But maybe God had talked to him
For he was unafraid.
I wound her curls on my finger
Ran my hand through Daddys hair
I felt so warm so loved, secure
on the arm of Daddy's chair
My Daddy kissed me next morning
I threw my arms round his neck
And whispered, "I love you Daddy
bout a bushel and a peck."
But the death bells rang at noonday
A sound we awaited with fear
A sound this coal camp hated
Prayed they'd never hear.
Cries went up from the women
Prayers were raised to the skies
Oh! don't let it be my darling
Please don't let my loved one die.
I played in the yard with my dolly
Humming a happy song
Waiting for the quitting whistle
To send my Daddy home.
But when the whistle sounded
My Daddy did not come.
When I saw that long grey casket
My childish heart went numb.
Friends looked at me with pity
Whispered we're sorry dear.
As if these words, to a six year old
Could heal the hurt and fear.
I crawled back into a corner
Hiding the best I could
Just me and the dolly he'd given
The crying done us good.
Baby Jo still wears tearstains
Upon her satin dress
For I lay her away next morning
When they lay Daddy to rest.
I wrapped her up in tissue
Tied her in ribbons blue
Then hid her here in this closet
For twelve years she has been new.
I found her here this morning and
And I know what I will do
She shall share a place at my wedding
As a sort of substitute You
The people are talking among themselves
And the main thing they have to say
Is why did she have that doll there
On this her wedding day?
I didn't tell them Daddy
It's best they never know
That it was in memory of you Dad
My first love so long ago

Amber D. Enbey
THE LEPRECHAUN
Each day I see the leprechaun
sitting by his little pond;
his thoughts concealed in a cloak of green.
I watch him as the time goes by.
He's a humble kind of guy,
and yet maintains his self-esteem.
He is bitter. I can tell
though I do not know him well.
When I approach he runs and hides.
The stories in his face are sad.
He sometimes feels he's going mad,
but will not show it due to pride.
Though many lands he has roamed,
the leprechaun lives alone.
The change of wind is his journey's end,
and he returns to his cozy home.
He tries to live from day to day
but his eyes carry him far away.
Is it hard to cope? Have you lost all hope?
He tries but he cannot pray.
Oh, leprechaun, you want to fly.
Grab your wings before you die!
A breeze of light would assure your flight
and carry you into the sky.
Have you forgotten how to cry?
I perceive your tears are dry.
Don't try to fight. Your rich insight
will see you safely through the night.

Ted M. Handegard Sr.
MY CASTLE
I have an old house that I built on the hill.
Cabin or shack, call it what ever you will.
Not quite on the top, sorta on the side,
A leveled off spot, I built it with pride.
Surrounded by tall timbers and a lot more,
A beautiful stream I can see from my door.
Its good drinking waters flow all through the year,
Running over clean gravel and crystal clear.
Now this old house ain't what it used to be
I built it away back in the year twenty-three.
The chimney is cracking, the shingles are loose,
I could fix it, I guess but I feel, what's the use.
The windows are broken, but that's not quite all
The logs in the sides are bout ready to fall.
The floors are sagging, the doors will not close,
They hang sorta open in quiet repose.
Maybe my humble home isn't much for size.
Though with the fresh air, it's a real paradise.
You may not understand or begin to see,
This home is my castle and always will be.

Patricia Dragon
. .CHILDHOOD SHALL DRIFT AWAY
As I sluff along the beach
letting my feet sink in the sand
and my towel drag in the tide,
I realize it was here, on this beach,
that several summers ago
I lost my sand shovel.
It is with that lost shovel,
now unsparingly faded and
slightly cracked at the handle,
that I bury my heart.
The luxurious sand castle I had built—
with childhood enthusiasm,
skinned knees and sunburnt cheeks,
collapsed with the on-rushing tide last night.
In one swift instant my castle was crushed.
My fairytale world was destroyed by reality,
just like my enchanted prince who lived within.
I sullenly watch as my childhood slips away.
Rolling out to sea,
taking with it my favorite sand shovel.

Carol Danell
THE BELL
Once, I lived
five worn marble walk-up floors
four portals,
three ivy-ed terraces,
two elms,
six hundred sixty-seven cobblestones
away from a church.
The church bell
clanged. . .
importunately every hour
on the hour. . .
. . .through turquoise sky-ed sunlight
or fog and rain,
national disaster, local crisis. . .
the bell clanged,
every hour
on the hour.
Mornings, I'd curse it.
I wanted to sleep.
Especially on Sunday.
But five worn marble walk-up floors
four portals,
three ivy-ed terraces,
two elms,
six hundred sixty-seven cobblestones away,
(a road built for chariots)
that persistent bell
clanged
through my shuttered, shaded windows,
as solemn, grave-faced black shawled women
veiled by dawn, halo'd in faith
crossed themselves,
and whispering Ave-Marias,
entered. . .
to light candles
and kneel prostrate
at the feet
of painted plaster saints.
A generous breasted Madonna
smiled down from an ornate frame. . .
Mona-Lisa-like.
And the damned bell
never stopped clanging
through my wax-stoppered ears. . .while
I egg-nogged a hangover
and took the Lord's name
in vain.
But time passed. . .
and I guess I got used to it.
Imperceptibly.
Years later
when I moved away,
seven jet hours away. . .
the whole world
suddenly
seemed
shakier. . .
insecure
on its axis. . .and
me. . .
on
mine. . .
without that bell
clanging,
unchangingly. . .
every hour
on the hour,
through turquoise sky-ed sunlight
or fog and rain,
national disaster, local crisis. . .

no matter what. . .
that church bell rang
every hour
on the hour. . .
every hour
on the hour.

Janice C. Burger
REMEMBERANCE OF A SUMMER PAST
Our time together has been so very short.
I have worked and sweat beside you.
We have laughed and played together.
I have seen the sun rise in your eyes
and the sun set on your face.
I've held you when you were feeling down and
you did the same for me
when strong arms brought me close to your chest;
and some how for a moment you made the world go away.
We shared our lives together and
it seemed as though we were as one,
for your mind had thoughts somewhat like mine.
I grew to love you as myself.
Yet to love someone you must let go.
You took the paved highway,
I took the gravel road.
For now you are in my memories only,
but some day soon we'll be together again.

Barbie Albertson
UNTITLED
Mary, Mary, dressed in lace,
Come see your saddened lover's face.
He loves you Mary, oh no not I,
Mary, Mary, please don't cry.
Mary, Mary, sad and lonely,
Crying for her one and only,
He loves you Mary, no not I,
For I have granted him a sad good-bye.
Mary, Mary, pray don't weep
Your fair lover you will keep
He loves you Mary, no not I
Now I wish you both a fair good-bye.
Mary, Mary, sister mine
Wed in bliss this day divine,
He loves you Mary, no not I
As I lay dying no tears to cry.

Edwina Krutal Bodziak
MY SEA
Watching the waves caress the beach and
The moonlight dance along the glistening sand.
I think of you warmly.
You are in a way like the sea,
Always there, always touching,
Forever impressing.
Only one difference between you two.
The sea will always be young.
We cannot stop time for ourselves,
We grow old with time, the sea knows no time.
You will always be you to me.
You were always a total experience,
Mothers always were.
For as long as I am a wave in life
You will always be my sea.

Kelly R. Johnson, Sr.
GHETTO FEARS
another child
has turned up dead
and once again
no clues
will this nightmare ever end
I don't know
do you
Atlanta as a city
is grieving
their anguish
the whole nation hears
a killer of young blacks
stalks the ghetto
a ghetto full of fears
children
are afraid to walk the streets
and parents are crying
in pain
the police are saying
that they're working hard
but still
there's no one to blame
it's such a damn shame.

Elaine C. Hart
LIFE
Order out of chaos
Everything is beautiful.
I hang my head, To me
Everything is dutiful.
I take things out of context.
I have few dealings
With the opposite sex.
To me, Life is a thing
To be lived because we are here.
Why do men climb the mountain?
Because it is there,
And we are here.
What is the answer to this dilemma?
It is found in the Bible:
"To do justly, love God,
And do the best we're able."
Read His Word,
Come to Him in Prayer
And, someday, at the
King's Table we will fare!

Edna Brummett
A DEEPER LOOK
This year I had to take a closer look at life.
What is its purpose, with its joy and its strife?
During this year, time and time again,
God, my Father, heard me call to Him.
The Easter story comes to my mind,
This year more meaning in it I find.
Salvation and eternal life is offered its true.
But there are also other promises too.
There is the promise of abundant life,
Of being with you thru each time of strife.
The promise, He will listen and answer your prayers
That He will continue to show He loves and cares.
I read "ask and you shall receive"
I was given miracles to see.
I read my Bible with much more care,
Finding many promises He wanted to share.
This year when I faced moments of despair,
I found strength, because God promised He would be there.
Accepting Him is where we each will begin
Then we let Him be our guide within,
Then we will find joy and happiness in this life,
We will find peace in the midst of strife.
Life's purpose then became to me,
Living as God wants—in love and victory!

C. A.
SPECIAL SINGER
Your music touches me,
the words move inside my mind and soul.
The melodies stir me—
Your voice carries all the notes,
so softly-so gently.
You are the Special Singer—
writing your own songs,
touching those who know you
in your own special way.
The description of your words
voices of my own thoughts and feelings,
adding a certain beauty to them.
The sound of your voice
captures my heart
and puts at peace.
You are the Special Singer.
Pictures of you holding the guitar—
an instrument opening the door
to the thoughts and feelings of your songs.
Your fingers turn the simple chords
into beautiful melodies,
which when added with words—
touch those fortunate enough to hear it.
At one time you ceased playing.
But someone cared enough
to convince you to start again.
To start again at something
we hope will never end.
For it is the special music—
and you are the Special Singer.

Greg Garrison
THE GODDESS EILEEN
Eileen and me; I'm the cup, she my tea,
I drink of her; she restorest me.
Her sweet nectar do I savor thru the
Years, my lovely Eileen, my glorious dream,
My safe passage to freedom is she. From
Her throne did she return for me, brave
And serene my heavenly goddess dear sweet,
Eileen. Tis her love she gives to me.
I drink slowly of her, not one drop wasted
My precious, my darling, my sweet, sweet
Love, my goddess forever, my true love,
Eileen.

Suzanne Chapman
CHILD IN THE RAIN
Soft rain, wet earth
grass pure green
Fresh-faced flowers
leaves washed clean
Worms out sniffing
sparkling air
Trees wear diamonds
God put there

Kathleen A. Hartley
CONTEST
A contest was held
to see who was best.
I thought I'd send my entry in
along with the rest.
The judging was done by a panel of a few
people who like poetry,
just like me and you.
"The decision is made!"
They declared with a shout!
"Now we must hurry
to get the mail out!"
Meanwhile, I waited,
to see who had won.
If I did or I didn't,
still I'd had fun.
Here comes the mailman,
with a smile on his face.
What a nice surprise!
I won first place!

Alice L. Baker
EVER LOVING GOD
My hand reached out for Mercy,
In it was placed a hot coal
I pleaded for understanding
But got damnation for my soul.
My heart cried out for loving
But wounded it returned
My mind cried out for knowledge
Of all the things unlearned.
I spoke but no one listened
I sang but no one heard
My words were cold and empty
My melody absurd.
Then one day I said a prayer
I walked paths I had not trod
I asked for and got forgiveness
From an ever-loving God
Now I know without my God
The wrong way I'd be leaning
He makes the love I feel for him
Filled with much more meaning.

Marcelle A. Brashear
PRISONER
Slow the hidden heart to turn. . .
. . .a key scrapes in the lock. . .
The trembling strain of reluctant brain
to muffle, yet hear, the knock.
If bind were laid away and chain
were broke and left to rust,
Oh, the struggle of the frozen mind
to understand new lust.
The chilling darkness in bone and soul
has meager comforts of its own—
In its wandering lone confinement
no seed of fire can be sown.
But ah, the persistent candle spark. . .
. . .oh, the ever-rattling key. . .
To douse the flame simply reach
beyond the prison of your safety.
Discover then the intruder's way
of setting your passions free—
Your fingers have crushed the wick to cold,
but the warmth has now touched thee!

Sensei Joseph Carbonara
CHRISTMAS TREE
Tree, will you stand in my home?
We will decorate you top to bottom around your full body.
Oh Tree, your beauty shall enhance
our home, sparkling, glowing with warmth
Bringing to us the colorful spirit that belongs to all.
Ah Christmas-the time to renew our commitments.
The year may have diminished
Our strength but the joyful season is the time to
rekindle our love.

Tree help us all to keep our
wondrous memories alive
again.
And bring a continuous sharing
thru the new year.
Tree brighten our hearts, open
our eyes to God's bountiful
world. In your graceful
adorning freedom help us to
Understand a quiet peaceful
companionship of human
beings.
Thank you oh Christmas Tree
May your proud gallantry
remain in my heart
thru out my life.

Dorothy Fifield

BIRD TALK

A one-legged Sandpiper once
observed
On bleak and sandy, windy, cold
Pacific shoreline vista,
Was considered a most
courageous bird.
With hop-scotch pattern and
fortitude,
The piper probed
Each bubbling, shrinking
creature cave,
Foraging for the prey,
Needle-beak intruding soggy
sand.
Valor unsurpassed, showed
avian,
To inspire evangelistic
proclamations:
Unclose your ear!
Bold bravery be your sword and
shield!
A crusade launched intrepidly
To spread a message confident
with hope,
And energy undaunted:
Hold to endurance!
Cast off despair!
Alas! A shocking sight one day.
A pert PARADE of one-legged
gallantry
In flea-like fashion. Lo!
Inspiration quelled by quirk
innate.

Barbara Susana Daku

MY THANKS

Thank-you God for everything,
The snow—and many other
things,
But most of all I Thank-you
Lord. . .
For all my friends that love me
dear,
And good things coming
through out the year. . .
As I looked out the window:
you are spreading the earth;
with your lovely blanket of
snow. . .
And once again I want to
Thank-you,
For this life, my children
and my friends,
And for all the things I can do. .
Thank-You God, from the
bottom of my heart;
For all the heartaches, tears
and joys,
I know of your wonderful love—
and from me you will never
depart. . .

Dorothy R. Douglas

STEPHEN'S PICTURES

I have a nephew, sort of,
Who sends me pictures filled
with love,
Of elephants tossing their
trunks at the zoo,
And some others of God-knows
who;
One has a bright-colored
rainbow and sun
Another a pumpkin, a snowflake
and a hamburger bun.
And all filled with happiness,
bright colors, and fun
Happy faces, different places
and joy-filled glee
Ooze from pictures with all
kinds of suns,
Because he thinks enough to
share them with me.
It's not that the pictures are
really great art
Even for a six year old,
It's the fact that he shares a
part of his time thinking of
me,
Removing the cold that could
settle while we're apart.
I love him for that.

Mark L. Chenault

INTO BLUE

Slip into sapphire blue
Through the glass surface
Into shimmering jewel.
Down
Into swirling shades of opaque
Ultra-marine turmoil
And seething blue flame.
Pulled down
Breathless, spinning and
flailing
Frantically look for the skies
Lost in the fluid abyss of her
eyes.

Pat Tonsmeire Cromwell

EVENING

I sit here placidly
as time slowly breezes my
mind.
I feel the movements of ages
running through my soul.
I feel magnificent in His world
and in His sight.
And yet, the wind shifts,
and I feel lost,
again,
in the multitude.

James Stuart Edson

THE UPLAND TRACK

Silver birches on the upland
track;
Sparkling waters as we glance
back.
A warm morning sun fills us
soon with joy
And gentle breezes waken girl
and boy.
Our canvas packs bob gently on
our shoulders;
The rising trail and woods give
way to boulders.
Up the trail the plummeting
rocks push forth
And sunrise meets rocky
shadows in a birth
Of light that stirs the stagnant
mind—
A quick look, a breath of air,
and climb!
We step by careful step the
summit seek
And hope some future time we'll
spend a week
Over countless other
sunsplashed trails,
When jolly hikers hear
themselves shout hails!

Meda E. Jaris

REMINISCENCE

My mother's voice was sweet
and low,
As musical as rain
That softly, on an April day,
Taps on the window pane.
Her hair and brow were like
the buds,
That bloom at Eastertide—
A lily blown by winds of life,
She stood with stately pride.
Though God has taken her from
me
On earth she lives again,
In Easter lilies pure and
fair—
And in the April rain.

Kathryn C. Kimmel

WALK SILENT, MY LOVE

The alarm went off at seven.
I turned it off and yawned.
Your breathing was beside me,
Though you were not there that
dawn.
I put my head on your pillow
And sniffed at your perfume.
Your ghostly arms rocked me,
And laughed away my tears.
How could it be me living
When you were gone for good?
I yelled, "How can I cry here?"
And knew your soul understood.
It was time to get up—
No breakfast was waiting.
I wanted you to stay away.
But you followed me all day.
You had one wish left;
I understood.
I bent on my knees and prayed,
Because you told me I should.
So, walk silent, my love.
Go on—go to sleep.
I understand; I know.
In his arms I will keep.

William Battrick

OUTINGS WITH FLOSS

What a joy to run! boredom a
blur behind me,
my black and dirty-white shag
conspicuous
as I nose a stubble field for
a careless mouse
or pause to sniff a refuse-
heavy wind
and assess the pungent mix in
terms
of the index of my favorite
contaminant.
My mate Floss, a quaint mongrel
I dote on—
and enrage by calling her my
parody
of a shopworn poodle—jogs
ahead intent
on odors native to dewy spring
glades,
looks back to monitor my
detour, flushes quail,
scares up a rabbit and streaks
away yelping.
If the wild game of tag swerves
toward me
I join in—halfheartedly,
knowing the rabbit's
zigzag flight stems from its
inbred
terror of dogs, not its
appetite for racing.
Also I eat too well to hunt by
choice
and often feel queasy staring at
a kill.
Buck fever used to screen
revulsion,
which grows slowly, endurably
visible
as a recurring nightmare exposes
the source
of my qualms: I once mauled a
pup for nipping
my ears in play and stood
rigid, unable
to reconcile limp form and
wide-open eyes.
I may flout my own motto,
Anything goes,
by gnawing my motives for
roaming (yet wishing
them still buried): Wanderlust—
a hunger
for intoxicating motion—an
impluse
to explore—a male's love of the
unexpected—
a runaway's fitful taste for a
kennel.
But I disavow any subconscious
urge to rile
my Master or avoid his
maddening Angels,
break a rule or defy an order,
for always—
as if I were a clock wound up
and set
to ring—the instant I sniff again
the perfume
of the barnyard I yelp with
delight.

Authors Name Given on Request

Be Bright Within and Even Your Shadow is a Joy

Drifting soft shadows caressing
the fields,
Are distorted through twisting
up hills and down dales.
Frolicking, follow their
glistening clouds,
Whose vaporous nature from
them is concealed,
Above, in the blue,
Even God must be proud,
So much truth, in this beauty,
prevails.

Susan Bonta

THE INEVITABLE TRAP

The spider weaves on and on
Barely stopping to rest.
A moth ventures near, then is
gone.
The spider continues still,
never stopping to rest.
At last it is finished—the
spider is oh, so clever!—
She waits in silence for her
victim.
The moth returns to investigate
and is suddenly gone
forever—
The spider not sparing a limb.

Rhonda Nadine Boyd, M.A.

UNTITLED

Sitting here. Contemplating.
Hoping. Fantasizing? ? ?
Waiting for you to come with
the Chinese food. jazz plays.
(Hell, who am I fooling? myself).
I'm waiting for you—your soft
embrace.
Hold me, please! (Hug my neck,
me, like Nicole hugged her
Mommy with innocence. Like
Iris nurtured Nicole with her
love).
Bright eyes.
Cookies, watermelon, giggles,
shy, girlish smiles.
I feel like a five year old
little girl all over again.
Sweetness, Soft lips. (Glow? I feel
like a light bulb!)
Joy, butterflies, (Hey, I been
seeing Blue Jays and Red
Cardinals!)
"Take the bitter with the sweet,"
folks say.
Babies, life, energy, ME!
Full of hugs, tears, kisses,
and wet diapers.
Life, Loving,
Loving you,
But most of all—
I Love Me, too,
Now that's LOVE.

Bill R. Boyd
LOVE AT IT'S UNBEST
"Not right now," she said,
"A headache I have gotten."
So I handed her an aspirin,
and said, "your reasoning is
rotten."
"Just for that," she said,
"I'll try without that pill."
I should have said "some other
time,"
Fulfillment was quite nil.
From here on out her negative
Will be all right with me
I'll just take that aspirin,
And resume my earnest plea.

Margaret E. Burnham
BRIDGE INTO DARKNESS
(Germany Moves On To Czechoslovakia)
It stood in stiff defiance of
the years
Across the Elbe river, toward
a shore
Which was the homeland and a
valiant core
Of people who ignored their
natural fears.
Gray granite made it, menacing
and harsh,
With arrogant small towers
here and there,
Emblems of a crushing weight
if brought to bear
For smashing all resistance in
its path.
When, suddenly, along a narrow
way
On their dark march which led
straight to the East,
Driven with purpose, shattering
the peace,
Came a long column headed for
"Der Tag".
Down silent streets where few
were now abroad
Rolled on the field cars of the
Nasi horde.

Jacklyn S. Besing
WHAT DOES IT FEEL LIKE TO BE EMOTIONALLY ILL?
What does it feel like to be
emotionally ill?
It feels like the whole world
is standing still
You feel like an outsider
looking in
Like you're in a jail, for
committing a sin
Your mind always feels like
a solid brick
Like no blood gets to it because
it's too thick
Your brain feels so tight, like
its in a vise
Because the muscles around it
have choked it so nice
Some people get headaches,
others feel it elsewhere
But no matter where you feel
it, it is always there
People tell you to shape up,
stop feeling blue
That it's all in your head, and
it's up to you
They'll tell you to get busy,
keep occupied
They could never feel your pain,
that's going on inside
Some boast of their
accomplishments, tell how
much they get done and how
quick
Never realizing that when you
were well, your work made
theirs look sloppy and sick
Some even resent you because
you sit and stare
It reminds them of their own
weakness, so they'll try not
to care
The ones that are most
uncomfortable when you are
near
They'll be next for, for them too,
reality is fear
The strongest ones are
compassionate, they'll have
faith in you and hope
Weak ones will use you for
conversation, their life is so
boring all they do is mope
Being emotionally ill is as bad
as being terribly poor
For when you are down, the
wicked help tear you down
some more
This does not happen all of a
sudden, but seems like
overnight
Caused by long frustration,
brought on by fear and flight
People should realize that this
is a physical thing
Even though it started out as an
emotional fling
So, if you know someone who's
living in an emotional hell
Your honesty, patience and
kindness, will surely help him
get well
And don't feel so cocky, because
you've read all the text
Be a little kinder, 'cause you
never know when you'll be
next

Jacklyn Besing
I DON'T LOVE YOU ANYMORE
The only thing I know for
sure—
Is that I don't love you
anymore—
I used to feel so beautiful and
free—
Now I feel like a hollow tree—
The more I know you, the less
you are—
How could I have ever been off
so far—
You always told me how to
behave—
You made me feel like I'm ready
for the grave—
How to dress and how to act—
And worst of all you had no
tact—
You've insulted me without any
shame—
Then had the nerve to call me
the blame—
From you I learned how to play
the part—
Because an act like this never
comes from the heart—
You cared more for strangers,
than you ever did for me—
I once tried to change you now
I'll just let you be—
People say love changes and
turns to something new—
I'm accepting the change,
realizing we're through—
When I tried to change you, I
got all upset inside—
Now I realize, I was wasting my
pride—
Your as shallow as anyone could
ever be—
Pretending to love everyone,
thinking no one can see—
For you the important thing
is to be a big shot—
If you could see yourself, you'd
never think your so hot—
You think people can't see
through you, that everyones a
fool—
They know your sarcastic,
sadistic and cruel—
You never learned what it takes
to make a man—
Your too busy impressing
everyone that you can—
Your proud of yourself when
you bring out my bad—
When I defend myself you feel
mistreated and sad—
I'm glad I found out before its
too late—
I could have married you what a
horrible fate—
I hope we both learned a lesson
and, this wasn't in vain—
This end is much needed, while
we both are still sane—

Grace Carnahan
TAXES ARE DUE
I was driving my clunker long
that old mountain road
The thing barely running, that
was part of the load
With tax and insurance due,
Man! was I blue
My wife had walked out because
I was broke
They'd closed down Old
Number Nine Mine
I saw the sharp curve with the
sheer cliff ahead
and I said "Johnny Quit living,
You're already dead"
And thought, Johnny quit living
you're through
So I jerked on the wheel to
head for the fall
That would cancel the debts,
trouble and all
But there on the cliff's edge
sitting up tall
A big old groundhog, having a
ball
Well! I couldn't take him cause
I was a loss
So I made the turn sort of criss
cross
Then I stopped the car and got
out on the road
Shoulders sagging with a mighty
big load
I walked to the edge, looked all
the way down
A shudder went through me as
tears washed my face
The groundhog had vanished
behind a big rock
But I was rooted in some kind
of shock
I stepped back slow and looked
up at the sky
Figured someone up there knew
better than I
The way I had picked to get
out of my woe
was only the way a coward
would go
Now if he sent that chuck to
keep me in line
There must be hope for my up
coming time
So I jumped in my clunker, took
off down the line
And next day they reopened
Old Number Nine Mine.

Jill Clingman
THE MOODS OF NATURE
The torrents of the wind
rattling windows and doors,
trying to get in.
Trees creaking and weighted
down with the wind as if
worshipping some great source.
Snow whipping wildly
everywhere; unattached
objects blow without direction.
Ending with the calmness,
serenity and silence, not known
by the busy and
uncaring, but only by the
people
willing to listen and
understand.

Brandi D. Wilder
UNTITLED
Reflecting on the last two
years, I simply want to
scream. . .
It seems that no one
understands alone as a central
theme.
And when one lives all by
herself, she learns about her
needs. . .
She walks and talks for self
alone. . .alone performs her
deeds.
When one has time (Ah,
precious time) to be alone
at last. . .
She thinks about her future. . .
she thinks about her past. . .
She thinks about the days gone
by. . .she thinks about the
nights. . .
She thinks about the loneliness,
as with herself she fights.
Her dreams are shared by no
one. . .her style is all her
own. . .
Her every thought is kept
inside, for she is all alone.
She has chosen life this way. . .
She has made it be.
Solitude and sanctity. . .That's
her only key.

Lori Michelle Cox
WATERFALL
Tumbling down in streams of
light
glistening in the bright sunshine
The water reflects the sun in
mirrors
of peaceful life that is well
sought after.
Quiet moments of the sweet
new spring
are found near a splashing pool
of mirrored images
Constantly changing with each
fresh drip
Creating new images of nature's
gift.

Jarshime Kimmel
TRUE LOVE
How fast, how fast, do the
minutes fly,
The minutes spent with you.
How sweet, how sweet, does
time go by,
When there is just us two.
How long, how long, since I
met you,
Those many years ago.
How nice the days, that we
lived thru,
Like lovely roses grow.
What thoughts, what thoughts
of love so true,
More endearing every day.

What fears, what fears, I had
for you,
That I'd lose you, some way.
Your pledge, your pledge,
showed me you cared,
Just as my pledge to you,
Showed you, showed you, how
well you fared,
As I hoped my pledge would do.
My love, my love, is singing
now,
A pleasant rhapsody.
My heart, my heart, with joy
does cry,
To hear your melody.
True love, true love, it beckons
me,
And askes, "May I remain?"
Please do, please do I'm
needing you,
And the whole world needs the
same.

Donna M. Glenn
LEANING
Tall and straight, up and up
Reaches the sturdy redwood.
But the top leans right.
Why?
He had to find the sun,
So he s-t-r-e-t-c-h-e-d
and leaned
To touch his source.
SOLID he stands now,
unmoveable.
Lord, help me s-t-r-e-t-c-h
and lean
To find you.

Kimberly S. Haley
THE SAILOR
A young man is silhouetted
against the sky
As the sun sets on the sea.
His eyes are on the water,
But his thoughts are all of me.
He thinks about a happier time
Before he had to go,
And then about the time ahead
When he'll be coming home.
It's hard to bear the feelings
Of loneliness and pain,
As he wonders what has
happened
And what things will have
changed.
The questions wander through
his head
As he stands there all alone,
And thinks of all they haven't
shared,
But knows how much they've
grown.
For awhile they've been forced
To go their separate ways,
But they'll be reunited
And that's the way they'll stay.
So what seems to be unbearable
As he stands alone this night
Will all be forgotten
When he comes home to his
wife.

Vallie A. James
MY SLEEP
The busy day comes to a close,
Then it is time for me to doze.
Thoughts of the day leave
behind,
As I close my eyes to rest my
mind.
My body rest with sleep so
sweet,
My muscles and heart slow
their beat.
It is great to build the
body with rest,
For sleep keeps me at my best.
I know sleep is what I need,
If I am to carry out the good
deed.
It is daylight that comes so
bright,
As I wake up and start out right.
Sleep brings quietness and best
power,
To the life for building the
tower.
The night was made for
mending man,
And things of the world go
hand in hand.
I need sleep for a good reason,
As days go by in the season.
It is freshness that sleep brings,
This helps me to stay alive and
sing.

David A. Johnson
MOTIVATION
Not fear, but faith
Not hate, but love
Moves men to greatest heights
Not consequence, but
confidence
Will light the brightest lights
The force that moves the
mountains
And earns the greatest wealth
Is "Love the Lord with all thine
heart
Thy neighbor as thyself"

Diane L. Livermore
THE FUTURE
To be honest, where I'm at today
secure in almost every way
I'm scared of what I've yet
to face
There are people much worse-
off than I
who struggle and fight to
give it a try
Thats what makes me scared
Am I strong enough to meet
tomorrow?
Could I stand up against pain
and sorrow?
Thats part of my fear
Am I alone with these things
that I feel?
Or do others believe this and
pretend its not real?
I hope I'm not alone
I'm young, have faith, and
should be strong
But what I'm admitting means
somethings wrong
Thats why I'm scared
To think now of facing next
year and new things
is senseless till I know what
tomorrow brings
So the fear is still there
I must give credit where credit
is due
God and other people have
helped me get through
But I'll always be scared.

Patrick Markey
A LIGHT
A light,
pierces through my window.
Pastelled in fluorescence, it
moves
straight and direct.
To close my curtain would only
be a gesture.
For I need a light to show me
darkness.
A sound,
whispers screaming through my
walls.
And is lost in the darkness
of my mind.
Though I yell to the caller,
beware.
He shuffles in the pillars of
my soul.
A sudden breeze,
blows on my curtain.
A sudden memory on my mind,
of days spent dreaming beneath
the sun.
Not of nights spent staring,
like this one.

Harriette Pickwell
LIFE BEGINS ANEW
Dusk is falling,
Night is calling,
All around is still.
Moon is gleaming,
Night lights gleaming,
Notes of Whippoorwill.
Insects creeping,
Soft winds sweeping,
O'er the grassy mound.
Shadows stalking,
Phantoms walking,
While the world goes around.
Without warning,
Heaven's morning,
Slips along the way.
Zephyrs rustling,
Life's a bustling,
With approaching day.
Sun's a bursting,
Plant's a thirsting,
For the sparkling dew.
Nature's singing,
Birds are winging,
Life begins anew.

Larry Robinson
THE POET'S NIGHTMARE
Searching past the midnight
hour
For just that certain word
And when the word forms on
the page
No longer does it rhyme.
Now the shocked and desperate
poet
Begins pulling out his hair
For now it seems, the entire
thought,
Has simply disappeared.

Skip Slavik
TEARS FOR HENRY MILLER
I cried for you today, dear
Henry,
Sweet old teacher,
Father of my awakening.
You would have been pleased,
though, I'm sure
For my tears were joyous, full
of understanding.
I cried with happiness because
now you are
Immortal.
Now you have joined the
masters who have
Nourished you
As you have nourished me
As you have nourished so many.
So good-bye, old master,
I know that where you are now
You look upon us
And you bless us
You shower us in the kind and
gracious glow
Of your smile.
Even though we never met, you
are the one
I've cherished most of all.
When there was nowhere or no
one to turn to,
I could always turn to you
And find comfort in your
wisdom
And grow in spirit and in
strength
From your words.
You have given me the
Wisdom of the Heart
And now, for you, the tears
of my thanksgiving.
Good-bye, dear Henry,
sweet old master,
I love you
You will always be my most
precious guide
Farewell, on your journey
through the ages.

Alain M. Vigeant
LOVE IS...
Ironic as it may seem,
love, the most beautiful of word,
is much more of a BEing,
than just a syllable to be heard.
To be always "in" love,
what a thing in believe!
but, it "is" us, all around
"as" us,
if we could but perceive.
In the eyes of a child,
in the touch of a hand,
love can tame the most wild,
sweeten the most bland.
Whatever the loss,
whatever the gain,
why structure a formula,
when the answer is so plain?
It is a fruitless endeavor, my
friend,
to attempt to define the Ward,
for love is much more of a
BEing,
than just a definition to be
heard.

Margaret C. Wagnon
AMERICA MY HOME
United States of America
The beautiful U.S. of A.
From the Atlantic to the Pacific
Her arms are open wide
From the village to the cities,
you
Can see the peoples pride.
In my dreams I have traveled
All nations.
Viewed castles, cities and
farms
but none can compare with
America.
With all her beauty and charm.
God gave us this beautiful
Country.
Rocky mountains, rivers and
Plains.
Let us all work together
to keep her
Our freedom our heritage our
gains.

Linda Macaluso
FLOODGATE
This bra suits me,
flesh colored lace looks good
against my dark skin,
my chest confined by a plastic
clasp.
She walks over and the front
unsnaps,
a thousand thousand synapses
burst inside my breasts
only to be caught by her mouth.
I don't remember now
if that really happened,
or if any of it did.
This arresting article of
clothing
she gave to me since it didn't
fit her
clutches tight around my
memory
of the gift she left behind.

Mary Geary Aertsen
NOT FREE
My earth bound heart can not
be free
But lashed by every note of its
refrain
Though winds whirl melodies
then flee
The earth, strands bind my feet

as with a chain,
Restrain the very soul of me,
This pulsing beat inside so
longs to fly,
Soar high across a restless sea,
Yet, it must let the wind escape
and sigh,
Accept the bands that deftly
tie,
For it's no voice of mine that
you hear sing
I'm but the echo of their
echoing.

Mildred H. Alaniz

THE BELLS OF CHRISTMAS

Oh! hear the bells of Christmas
A chiming in the breeze,
Oh! see the exuberant children,
Happy times are these.
There was born a Saviour
So very long ago,
And if you ever will be saved,
Tis imperitive for you to get
to know.
The Angel Gabriel appeared
unto the Virgin Mary,
Saying, "Hail thou blessed one.
For you are highly favored and
you shall conceive a son,
He shall be named Jesus, Son
of the Highest One."
The Lord God shall give him his
Father David's throne
He shall reign forever over the
house of Jacob,
A wonderful thing is this,
For there shall be an everlasting
kingdom and the Kingdom
shall be His.
Mary answered, "I am a virgin,
how can this possibly be?"
The Angel answered said to
her, "The Holy Ghost shall
come
Upon thee, and by the power of
the highest you shall be,
Therefore the Holy Thing
which shall be born of thee
Shall be called the Son of God."
Your cousin Elizabeth which
was called barren, has
conceived a son.
Then answered May, "behold
the handmaid of the Lord,
Let it be unto me according to
your word."
Prophets foretold his coming,
God prepared a star, to guide
the three wisemen to
Bethlehem,
And the shepherds from afar.
Jesus birth, life, death and
resurrection,
Did light and deliverance bring.
His light has pierced the
darkness,
Lights spreading glow
darkness cannot stay.
Light shall evermore increase
until eternal day.
Glory hallelujah, let every
soul gladly sing,
Because of Jesus, 'life'
Has swallowed up death, and
death has lost it's sting.

Don Altobell

LOVERS' LAMENT

"Never" and "Always" are lovers'
words. . .
But time after time they fail.
Life proves them shallow and
incomplete. . .
They shine for awhile, then
pale.
"Never again!" or "I'll always
care!"
Each over's hope really believes.
But life turns out different,
again and again,
As order we try to retrieve.
Pen in hand, I understand that
"Never" and "Always" can't
be. . .
But music and candles cloud
thinking and sight,
and lovers just can't see!
I'm one of those who fools
myself
and believes the next will be
last.
As much as I know the folly of
this. . .
I'll love each love 'til
it's passed!

Eddie Albalos

THE EVOLVED BUTTERFLY

When you were still in a
confined cocoon's stage
In an insect larva case during
your unborn baby-age,
It is one of those strange event
of Nature's ways
Which the LORD GOD of this
Planet Earth lays.
To all living things in order
for them to survive
Butterfly you have evolved as a
flying insect you thrive.

Man the Noblest Creature looks
at you with wonder
When you spread your multi-
colored wings so tender.
Gracefully flying and sucking
nectar among myriad of
blossom,
At the same time you pollinate
plants and trees to form
Their kind of fruit which
mankind needs though on,
In order to live with good
health and satisfaction.

Eileen Barry

TRAILS

I am thinking today of happier
days
Of old dog Peppi, Cecilio and
me;
Of wilderness trails and puppy
dog tails.
And wildlife scampering,
untouched and free.
Where are the babies of
yesteryear?
The prairie dog with a round
belly?
The roadrunner, swift as a
falling star,
Horny-toads, scampering pell-
melly?
Where indeed, is the small
spotted skunk,
And his cave-house that used to
be?
We dared not trespass his
private domain.
Old dog Peppi, Cecilio and me.
Some folks call it advancement,
And some call it civilization,
But, I can think of only one
thing,
Modernization is ruination.
For the great wheels came and
the giants roared.
Devouring each burrow and tree.
And 'lo we must bow, to the
progress of now,
Old Peppito, Cecilio and me.

Edward Norman Bak

UNTITLED

In the heat of the night
I awake;
A dream is broken,
another one begins.
I dream of you.
Your being is filled full,
child like love;
A mother you are,
the children really know.
Your love you own.
A mother,
a lady,
a poets dream.
God please,
keep you around a while.

Ralph F. Baker

THE GHOST OF YOUTH

Zoom!. . .A skate board rolls
down the hill
Graceful balance. . .
Filled with thrill!
Sometimes, I know, 'twas a slow
drag up
From kinder grade to senior
pup.
But really, 'twas no time at all
Now they're grads from college
hall.
Zoom!. . .The kids grew!
Zoom!. . .The years flew!
They're mated now with one. . .
oops Two!
No more now a lass and lad.
No more now dependent on
Dad.
Mom's way of life has changed
some too,
She repeating the cycle of pink
and blue.
The house is quiet 'cept for
the floor
That creaks a lonely groan;
It mimics the old folks
longing wait
For the day the kids come
home.

Ernest Oliver Burrows

ANNETTE

How could one e'er forget,
Annette
With understanding heart so
true?
And Roguish smiling eyes beset
With saucy curls of brunette
hue.
When could one e'er forget
Annette
And miss her happy day's
routine?
Absence would but spread
sorrow's net
Sending vast mirthless voids
between.
Why would one e'er forget
Annette,
No reason's found 'neath the
heavens?
Offering her heart and soul duet
She so gently our lives
enleavens.

Robert G. Bourbeau

TRANSITION'S DIARY

Awaken now to changing days
my lanquid lazy land
To the gentle unexpected touch
of Death's chilling hand.
With silent, damp, and misty
dawns, He ushers in the days
Resembling smoke-filled
battlefields of ghostly
blues and greys.
Open fearfully wide your
eyes and start the blood to
flow.
Reservations have yet to save
that youthful rosie glow.
Dying leaves, first brilliant red,
fade now to ambitious gold.
Yellows and Blues sigh without
relief, "This year's already
sold."
Colors imbue, awareness,
soaring hyaline hopes high
Till Evening's cool shadows
surround us, waking the
Mind's eye
To futile attempts at
evolutionary delay.
Though warm, tempting
bedrooms lure us, still we
hear them say,
"Save for Future's acquisitive
white." Tis of thee I sing.
Proudly cold and blackest night,
so too, dulls the latent dream.
Hueing horizontal moon rises in
abnormal size
Reflecting Memory's mortal
showers soon to crystalize.

Bertha L. Howard-Sherman

I AM "THE POET WHO DIDN'T KNOW IT"

I am a poet and now I know it
My writings here will surely
show it
I write the words that come to
me
For all of earth's mankind to see
God has blessed me with this
sea
That lies deep down inside of
me
Its like the river that's called
the Nile
It runs and runs for miles and
miles
Like an eagle in his flight
You wonder which man has the
right
Every man has his talent
Its just a matter of being not
shy, but gallant
Search yourself and find that
way
It will brighten up your day
Why don't you check out your
mind
You'll be surprised what you
will find
I've spread my wings and now I
sing
Of me, of you, of many things
Come go with me and you will
see
These things deep down inside
of me

Roberta Bryant

SADAT

Oh Sadat! Sadat!
Martyr, Warrior and King;
Echoes from you still ring,
Of a world at ease and peace
Where the sounds of wars shall
cease.
Oh Sadat! Sadat!
Your soul has found relief,
But the world remains in grief;
Perhaps you hear the groans,
As man in confusion moans.
Oh Sadat! Sadat!
If Heaven is where you are,
Please send us a star;
To guide our way with light,
And see us through this night.
Oh Sadat! Sadat!
You have not lived in vain;

For peace we'll someday gain,
What is right will have to be,
When the world is united and
free.

Hannah Mendelsohn
AUTUMN'S BALL
Each autumn there is a ball
And all the leaves attend.
Jack Frost makes their clothes
And many hours he spends.
Brown, gold, yellow, red,
Each one a different hue,
for there are no two dressed
alike,
As that would never do.
He sits up late on frosty nights
To get each leaf correctly
dressed.
Then they flutter off to the ball,
Each in his very best.
They dance and play all night
Too weary to return
They gather in a drift
Alas — just to burn.

Steve L. Hunt
CYNDI'S SONG
There are forgotten lands
and mindless bands
that surround my quiet times.
Old nursery rhymes with
saddening means.
But to look upon us now
and our future bounds
makes me smile a lot more
than a while.
Please don't pause on me.
Keep me forever knowing you.
With that I'll find myself.
Cause knowing you is more
than I've ever had.
And that makes me so glad,
so very glad.

Angela Jean Wilhelmi
USELESS WOOD
The old withered tree
it stood alone,
Slowly chipping away
like an ancient stone.
Now the old withered tree
that had once stood,
Remains on the ground
as useless wood.

Robert M. Marons
THE CLOWN
The makeup came on my face,
and I put on a wig,
Funny suit and a large blue bow
tie.
I read the children's names
at the party and said, "Hy!!"
I did a coin trick an hid a silver
dollar up my sleeve.
The children played card games
and checkers;
I waved my hand and said,
"Goodbye,"
when it was time for me to
leave.
I might not become famous or
gain renown,
But I enjoy being a clown.

Sc B. Mc Kinney
FORGERS SPILL HEART
Cold frigid metal
ripping and tearing
steel on steel.
Crashing.
Gushing.
Dying.
One way mirrors opened
pouring beyond eternal zest
friends grieve louder
emotions broken and grounded.
Dearer.
Closer.
Loser.
Hanging vines
gush forth their gold
pumps torn and pounding
breast on breast
red sounds flash away
fleeting memories
hold the flesh.
Sharing.
Caring.
Fading.
Steel and blood fuse
to make one
emotions perish
and forgers spill heart.

Carolan Baber
DESERT VOICE
Stood on the edge of the desert
And gazed thru the mountains
to the sea
Stood on a mountain top
And felt it reach for me. . .
Far into the windswept desert of
the mind
Deserts easily spin into time. .
Time is gold
Running thru the earth
Reflecting
Light and soul. . .
Speak
To the dove
She will fly before you
Thru the halls of love

Harold Cooper
THE ROSE OR THE THORN
The rose or the thorn, with a
heart that is heavy
My choice it is now and ever
to be.
Tho I'll love my rose forever
and ever
the thorn will be honest and
faithful to me
In summer the rose is sweet and
so fair
The living is good with never
a care
Then comes the days of the
winter's bleak dawn
The thorn is still here while
the sweet rose has gone
This rose I must lose is any
mans flower
A beautiful thing to have and to
hold
A wonderful love but just for a
season
But my thorn is still here tho
my world has grown cold

Alene Phillips Gamble
TIME GOES TICKING ON
Grandfather clock goes ticking,
the hours away each day.
The light breaks through the
morning,
as darkness fades away.
The earth awakens gladly,
it's wonders to behold.
And time goes ticking boldly,
it's rhythm never slow.
The babe awakens early,
awaiting to be fed.
As if it is reminded,
the schedule time is read.
Morning sun is rising,
the earth in constant tune.
As time is still a ticking,
and soon it will be noon.
The earth in all it's beauty,
it's wonders we behold.
Was made for man a dwelling
place,
by God so long ago.
The hand will wait for no one,
as it goes ticking on.
So make your plans most useful,
for time goes ticking on.
The bustle of the city,
neon lights aglow.
People ever rushing,
street cars are so slow.
The whistle of the factory,
workers are on time.
The clock is working
constantly,
just listen to it chime.
The farmer in the field at dawn,
will sweat as he doth plow.
Seeds that he will plant this day,
in harvest he will share.
So make your day a day of joy,
whatever you may do.
For time is still a ticking on,
and day is almost through.

Lloyd E. King
RENAISSANCE
Inside the empty flow of time
Exists the caravan;
The hollow, wandering band of
minstrels
That tell no lies
And fear the evils of their fellow
men,
They shun them out
And leave them damned;
Ignoring their cries.
But in a lonely crowded room
Within the retrospect of time
Arises. . . .
A single face that promises
Renewed salvation.

R. Bateman Newcomb
SUMMING UP
He climbed the challenged
mountains of his youth
And fell, and learned the
meaning of defeat;
He flung himself against the
storming winds
And failed, a bleeding hunk of
battered meat.
Again, again, unending yet again
Against the world he hurled a
single man;
When beaten back he then
resumed attack
And was repulsed before he
scarce began.
And when he smashed his path
by pure brute force,
A weltered mass of scars on
mind and heart,
He looked across the wreckage
of his years
And laughed-until the tears
began to start.

Sunny Hye Rapp
THAT YESTERDAY OF NOW
Has yesterday become the now
She asked at the dawn of day
Will he guide me
Though I fumble
In my childlike, grownup way?
Will He stay with me
Through my doubts and fears
Having heard the sea storms
blow
Will He help me
Will He lead me

With the gentleness of hand
And she wondered'
Will tomorrow bring
That Yesterday of Now.

Evelyn J. Smith
DRIFTING AWAY
Drifting away, my love for you
is drifting away,
Like a lone sailboat on a cold
windy day.
I have the pain to carry me far,
In search of something to heal
the scar.
Drifting away, my love for you
is drifting away,
For there is a price I have to
pay.
I can't eat nor can I sleep,
Cause the pain is down too deep.
Drifting away, my love for you
is drifting away,
To a more brighter, beautiful
day.
Where there is love, and always
so much,
Love, love, love someone has
that touch.
Drifting away, my love for you
is drifting away,
So fast now, I can feel it sway.
Yes, every second of each day
and night,
My love, is drifting out of sight.

Burnese Davis
PRIMA SERA
The trees stand out in stark
relief,
Their leaves green-black against
the indigo sky.
The Evening Star Twinkles like
a diamond nestled on a velvet
cushion;
Swallows Fly.
The Sun's last rays turning their
wings to gold.
Night birds begin their song.
Scent of Roses, Jasmine and
Honeysuckle perfumes the
breeze
that gently touches my face.
Night reaches out to clasp the
day in a dying embrace,
and day surrenders with a gentle
sigh.

Susanna Graham Bennet
ATROPHY
Don't let the small gestures all
pass away
Until you've forgotten how to
speak, how to say
I miss you, I love you, I think
of you often.
Words little used harden, not
soften.
Don't expect loving thoughts to
be seen
As if projected on a wide-
angle screen
And the gentle touch of caring
you forget
Only a precedent for apathy will
set.
The tiny mementos of time that
is shared
Are gold in the sugar-bowl when
the cupboard is bare
And dreams and the longings
spread over the years
Are like vines of togetherness,
lifting from fears.
And what of those who have
locked inside
The giving, the wanting and
needing to hide.
They've played the game, life
wasn't fair
And so they retreated to a
lonesome lair.
Tentative feelers they put out
to show
They're still alive, though they
no longer go
In search of warmth and love
and meaning
From the left over selves, their
sustenance gleaming.
Seemingly full of the joy of
living
They neither truly take or are
giving
But skitter along on the surface
of being

Almost unaware that their
hearts are unseeing.
Closed off in the safety of
cushioning cotton.
The art of loving nigh unto
forgotten
No one truly happy because
they exist
And so on emptiness they try
to subsist.
So needless, so wasteful, not
necessary at all
They've put themselves beyond
life's call
Because of the fear of trusting
again
They've put themselves outside
the pale of man.
Not daring the loving touch and
word
Putting away thoughts that
might be heard
They miss the best they ought
to know
Pity the frightened, they've
nowhere to go.

Marilyn C. Howard-Clinton

ROLE

An old man sat and summed his
life.
The memories rose from a
haze. . .
He thought of all the joys and
strife.
Back to light came all the
bygone days.
He spoke to the world—
It spake to him:
"World, you are just a stage of
old."
"Son, my look is new. . .
the scene is old."
"World, I sit and watch your
scene unfold."
"Son, my colors are royal:
Blue and gold."
"World, I sit here and find my
goal."
"Son, it's there to have and yours
to hold."
"World, where is the time to
shape and mold?"
"Son, time is nearly in the past."
"Son, this Chance is the last."
"World, what was my Role?"
"Son, your role: to reach a
human soul!"

Lillian Hedgeman Clarke

MR. WIND

Oh, Mr. Wind, how hard you
blow!
You blow things farther than I
can throw.
Look at you, pushing those cans
around,
And now you're trying to push
me down!
"Stop it! Stop it!", I say.
That's enough blowing for today.

Maria Curtis

THE THIN MAN CAPER

A thin man
walks a narrow road
While portly pop
Waddles like a toad
So fast and astute, he keeps his
splinters trim,
While racing past the slow ones,
who infuriate him.
Steer clear of his way
Limber legs stoop for prey.
Throw away laws written on
paper,
Watch out for
The thin man caper.
He'll throw a punch to a slug,
make the animals scurry,
Men hit the road getting wind
of the hurry.
The slim are sly
With a more treacherous yen,
Than ogres, giants, or supermen
A mighty Paul Bunyon could do
him in good.
Cut him down to size like
bundles of wood.
Sticks, not stones
Will break your bones
But they'll burn well thrown in
the fire.
Steer clear of his way
Limber legs stoop for prey
Throw away laws written on
paper
Watch out for the thin man
caper.

F. Maitland Cuthbertson

WHEN THE LOON CALLS

One frosty Autumn night when
the lake's mist rose
To curtain the outline of the
pine,
And the sky, cleansed of cloud,
Let moonlight through to deftly
soften the scene,
A loon called.
It was then he noticed Prayer
beside him,
Walking on his right;
When he approached Death's
door to knock,
It sat on the stoop by his feet.
Moments later when the door
opened,
It entered with him-silent and
humble.
There were those who smiled—
And those who did not
understand;
But when he came to that Place
of places,
He held out his hand
For Prayer to grasp with
fortitude.
So they stood, side by side,
To wait together as they always
had done;
That was the moment—
As the indian would say—
When the Loon calls.

John Ray Dossey

CHILDHOOD DAYS

Remember, friend, those nights
we spent
Camping in our backyard tent?
Two hunters we, without a
name,
Til shadows hid our jungle
game.
Or when we'd climb to tree top
high—
Two eagles soaring 'round in
flight?
Sometimes in our childish way
We'd play a million games a day.
Our parents said, "Settle down,
You shouldn't always play
around.
Life is hard. You have got to
know
Just what you'll do and where
you'll go."
But like an owl forever mute,
You and I didn't give a hoot.
Today was now, and now was
play.
We'd settle down another day.
We went around the world and
back
Collecting things in paper sacks.
Two travelers we, without
names,
Til time took our childhood
games.
Our carefree years went by fast:
Those childhood days forever
past.

Robin Roulette Davis

THEN CAME A DAY

You were once the most
important part of my life
until today when I gave in
to your selfish wife
Did you ever really love me?
Did you ever even care?
Was it your duty
or because I was there
My Love for you has faded away
Maybe you'll know how it feels
someday
To look up to some one
to feel like a stranger
to feel unloved
and your mind in danger
Then came a day you felt like
a part
you wish it could always
remain that way
To feel like someone actually
cared
Someone to talk to
Someone to laugh with
Someone to share with
Someone to be there when in
need
You hoped things would never
change,
to keep it that way you tried
your
best to only succeed
Then came a day
you noticed you succeeded
it made you proud, but that
was not
what you needed.
This important person who was
a special
part of your life,
hadn't noticed a thing.

Blondie Louise Davis

A NAME WITHOUT LOVE

Yesterday my life began. . .
"Jamal", my parents named me.
Mother's here, but, father's gone
To a place he said was free.
Said he'd be coming back for
us,
Said he needed time alone.
Why couldn't he take us with
him then?
It's years, since he's been
gone.
Father gave his name to me. . .
To prove I was his son.
Why can't he spend some time
with me. . .
Since I'm his only one?
Without him. .Life's unbearable,
Other sons have their fathers'
here.
Oh, can't he see inside this
heart. . .
Where lies a million tears?
Oh, *Father*, if you read these
words,
May I borrow you a while?
Oh, don't you know that when
you left. . .
You took my mother's smile?
Mother says I look like you. . .
For her, it is enough.
But I wonder just what's in a
name. . .
Without a father's love????

Tanya Feliciano

UNTITLED

I
consist of
a lot of
thoughts and feelings and
words that somehow have no
other way of escaping me except
for that wondrous instrument
the ink pen
that
lets my
angers, hates, pains,
loves, joys, loneliness, griefs
or
whatever
else I'm feeling
ease themselves onto the paper
and
show
everyone else that
I may be a misfit but,
make way for my feelings
because I can feel too

Edwina Freeman

TRANQUIL MOMENTS

As I sit among the flowers
admiring the lilacs of the field, I
enjoy their sweet sweet
fragrance such tranquilty they
instill.
Such a delicate little flower with
its pedals soft and smooth how
can it possess such power to
caress the inner mood.
With the raindrops falling
gently, dancing, feeling every
bloom it creates the sweet sweet
fragrance God intended to
perform.
When my days of youth surpass
me and I am old and gray, I will
sit in tranquil moments
thinking of this very day,
with the lilacs sweetly scenting
my memories, of yesterday.

Judith A. Galardi

TED

"I hate my mother."
No one answers
no one cares.
"I hate my mother", he'd say
then he'd call her on the phone
to see when she would be in
to visit.
"I'm thirty-seven
and I hate my mother.
Why won't she visit me?"

Elizabeth B. Holmes

MOTHER TO BE

Only as a "Mother" will you
know
The joys and sorrows of rearing
a child, so
You shall shrink in sizes a few
and become lighter in weight,
too
After the little one makes its
debut.
Just watch as the heart and
head above
Increase in size and weight,
overflowing with love.
Then make way as pride and joy
come into view.
Your shoes become harder to
fill, too.

Jeanne Barbasiewicz Hoogstad

CHILDREN IN THE MORNING

Up from bed,
Through the doorway,
Down the hall,
To Mom's room.
Not here!!
Through the doorway,
Down the hall,
To the livingroom.
Not here!!
Through the doorway,
Down the hall,
To the shower.
Not here!!
Down the hall,
Through the doorway.
Down the stairs,

To the basement.
Not here!!
Up the stairs
Through the doorway
Down the hall
To the kitchen.
Drinking coffee.
Making toffee.
Little brother,
Here's our Mother!

Ardith Cummings
MY PRAYER
Oh God Who makes the rain
that falls
so gently from the sky.
Who makes the wind that howls
so loud,
that blows dust into my eye.
You Who can make a blazing
sun,
a flower and a bee.
Won't You please, before I die,
Make someone who loves me.
Oh Lord Who makes the
gorgeous sky
at sunset every night,
You make the trees so
beautiful,
and every cloud just right,
You make the grass so soft and
green
the velvet sky above.
Could you please, before I die,
Make someone I can love.

John W. Kozubal
THE SEASONS GO
As I grow older,
there comes to mind.
Things don't last long,
not much time.
The seasons, too,
are like that now.
They don't last long,
only bow.
So faster,
on their way.
Much like sundown,
end of day.

Cynthia L. Lucas
RELIEF!
You always wondered why I was
so sad, well it was because you
were always harping that I was
no good and so bad.
But what was so bad about
putting up with your drinking
and physical abuse, and after
one of our fights giving the kids
some lame excuse.
I think back to when we first
met, you often said I had real
class, then later in our
relationship you started
telling me to kiss your ---.
I prayed a lot of nights for
relief from this type of life,
because I knew I deserved better
than what I got. I knew this
wasn't my lot in life to be an
abused wife.
Oh, the *relief* I feel to finally
be away from you. No longer am
I sad, dejected and blue.
The kids feel better too, because
now they can look at me and
see—no more black and blue
marks on me.

Inez B. Loesch
FRIEND CONFESSOR
I have sat and listened to your
woes;
Somewhat sad they were.
I commiserated with you
And tsk'd tsk'd in the right
places,
Served you coffee, and gave
advice
When you asked for it.
Sometimes it seemed your story
would never end.
Until one day I ventured to say
I had this worrisome problem
to discuss.
I couldn't understand when you
said
You really must go since you'd
already
Taken up so much of my time.

Nelda Lorraine Rohrback LeVant
EMC SQUIRED ESQ.
"Bless you, Eddie-Lou Cole."
If two R's we'll make it, so
To be something, Jesus *meant*
My story is no mystery
Tressure Treasure Trey
Something I thought I could
never *Be*
In squint constructions' *do* or
say—
A Carpenter of Carpentry!

William H. Miller
YOU ARE THAT KIND OF GIRL
You are the kind of girl a man
wants to marry,
The kind of girl a man wants to
protect and carry,
Over the threshold as soon as
she is his wife
To love and take care of for
the rest of her life.
The kind of girl whose eyes you
can look deeply into,
And see all the happy years that
lie ahead with you.
The kind of girl who has visions
of being a mother,
And knowing she wants you for
the father—no other!!
This is what makes life so
exciting and happy,
Keeps a man on his toes, feeling
real "snappy".
Wanting you only, for forever
and a day,
Then our future will be so
complete in every way.
"You are that kind of girl" that
I know is perfect and right,
The kind of girl that I'll
pursue both day and night,
Until you assure me that you
are totally, completely mine,
Because you are that kind of a
girl; 'till the end of time.

Edith Louise McCormick
DEATH WISH
I would not wish to be asleep
When death descends on me
Nor prey to any ills that keep
Me dreaming fitfully,
For I would choose to be alert
With comprehending eye
To taste in full this final hurt
As death is passing by.

Cynthia Kay Hill
CHRISTMAS AGAIN?
I love to write of Christmas
time
To smell the fragrant old Scotch
pine,
To hear the bells chime far
and near
Arousing us with sudden cheer.
The laughter now sounds
everywhere.
The people seem so much to
care.
Because they give, they will
receive,
The gift of life eternally.
Santa's dressed in red and white,
Telling kids of the Special
Night.
Then promising to bring new
toys,
To every little girl and boy.
It's great to wake on Christmas
Day
And catch reflected gold sun's
rays,
Beating down on the untouched
snow,
Like diamonds sitting with
splendorous glow.
Presents ripped apart at last!
Remembering a year ago; How
time does pass!
The Christmas carols together
we sing,
And I pour forth with the love
I bring.

John Mark
EPIGRAM
To be an intelligent
being is not always
the task of the knower,
but all that one needs
to do is to think faster
and to speak slower.

Katherine Oppenheim
TO MY COUNTRY
How like the splintered
tree we have become—
Bereft of gentleness,
Divided by our anger,
Devoid of compassion.
How really inarticulate
despite our constant babble.
The day will come when spring
will pass us by—
For the splintered tree
does not blossom.

Edna Kay Probert
UNTITLED
You needn't be ashamed
to feel the way you do.
I know it's hard sometimes
to be a "soldier" true.
You are not made of wood
and therefore, cannot be,
the pillar of undying faith
that you're supposed to be.
God knows that you are human
and there'll be times you'll stray.
Temptations all around you
will try to block your way.
On the road you're bound to
stumble,
often you may fall.
In the end you will be stronger
when you have faced it all.
I think much higher of you
at least you really try
to be a stronger Christian,
you're a better one than I.
You struggle not alone.
On the road you have a friend.
My prayers for your safekeeping
go with you to the end.

Elsie Peterson
JASON
Cleaning strawberries at the
sink.
A time to pause,
Reflect,
To think.
There's young Jason in my
garden.
He has his own big yard to
play in.
Here's a berry.
What has marked it?
Would never suit the
supermarket.
Is Jason spoiled with all his
toys?
Is he like most other boys?
This berry's too ripe.
Long on the vine.
Taste it.
Fermented.
Start of wine?
A vigorous, spirited, tasting
berry.
A vintner's joy to change to
sherry?
I smile.
A thought is begging venting.
Is Jason spoiled or just
fermenting!

Carol A. Parker
MY ETERNAL LOVE
My love for you is like an
eternal candle
That is lit whenever thoughts of
you appear.
Thoughts; that are sometimes
dimmed by the melted wax
gathered around the flame.
Thoughts; that could turn off
the burning glow.
Until you come, like a knight in
shining armor
To rescue the dimming flame;
with a little word of love, or
action, or deed.
Oh, my love, who knows me
like a book,
Yet can't understand the words
which have been read.
But continues to love for he
knows the content is good;
Yet waits patiently for some
spark of understanding
So he can be guided in the
way to handle the written
words;
But gets frustrated when he
wrongly understands.
You are my eternal light. For
without you
I am nothing except an ember
of what has been.
I can see you on the throne of
eternity to be a King forever.
And I shall be by your side, to
share in your reign;
And we shall be one, Forever!

A. J. Gosnell-Quedens
(Anna Jean)
HAVE WE FORGOTTEN?
"The last, best hope of man on
earth."
Here mankind has proved the
worth
of love for good and fellow-
man—
of love which says, "Do
what you can
to help your neighbor
and to serve your God."
From these truths do not
swerve, America—
and you will always be
"the land of the brave and
the home of the free."
Freedom for Spirit keeps
America free—
In the Name of our God, now
let it be.
For 'tis "the land of the free
and the home of the brave"
over which this flag in honor
waves.
Freedom for Spirit keeps
America free!
Forget it not!
Ever shall it be!

Sandra K. Robinson
NATURAL HIGH
I'm jolted by a bolt of
electricity.
I find myself faced with sudden
reality.
I'm at a loss to figure out why,
my goals are
suddenly extended to the sky.

My emotions have climbed to
the top, and, I know
I shall find just what I want.
All limitations have faded away,
and I look
forward to a brighter day.
Expectations have met their
match, and, there
is no need for artificial facts.
I have discovered that I am,
"me", and
that is more than anyone else
can ever be.

Tina Stroupe
ONLY FROM A DISTANCE
I've seen you from a distance
But never close up.
I long to hold you in my arms
Like a new baby pup
I've just got to touch you
To see if you are real.
I'd like for you to come closer
If you will?
I've just got to have you. I
insist.
Please come to me don't resist.
I've wanted you for a long time
So won't you please be mine?
Now that you've come closer
I don't know what to say.
I would like to touch you
If I may?
I've seen you from a distance
And now close up.
But now I long to hold
A new baby pup.

Jessica Stewart
REMEMBER
Remember how you had loved
me,
How we were in love as no
others might be.
Remember the time we had
spent together,
The walks we had gone on in
rainy weather.
Remember the times you would
hold me all night,
And we would talk of our
thoughts by firelight.
Remember these things and
never cry,
For soon comes the day that I
must die.
And for the rest of your life
remember me,
For all the love I gave to thee.
And on my tomb place the word
forever,
And that oh, so sweet word;
Remember.

Mr. Robin Sorrell
THE BOAT PEOPLE
How can anyone, with love, in
their heart?
Speak out and say, Let all the
Boat People drown.
Did not most of our forefathers,
emigrate at the start?
Would they act the same, if
these people were their own?
Yes, I believe, we are all God's
chosen people,
The Good Book says, come on
to me, everyone,
Let us shout loudly, from
every church steeple,
That for the Boat People, thy
best will be done.
Please welcome these children,
their mother, and dad,
Use our resources to help them
regain their pride,
Help them forget the terrible
ordeal that they have had,
And lay, all our racial, and
biased thoughts, aside.
Canada is so vast, and has so
much to give,
We must get together, and help
them, all we can,
You will all feel good, as long
as you shall live,
The Lord sayeth, Give thy
tender love to all man.

Debbie Moody Sorcic
SLEEP, MY LOVE
Sleep, my love,
And know not the dangers of
the world.
Close your eyes, lie still,
And let sadness and heartbreak
pass you by.
Dream of love and laughter,
Of little children and their
smiles;
Think of happy things
Like clowns and birds and me.
Let me lie beside you
And watch your thoughts drift
away;
Your face is content and full of
love,
Your eyes are calm and at rest.
Sleep, my love—
And remember me as you
dream.

Eleanor Mae Snow
RED JEWELRY BOX
Little red jewelry box
Sitting on a shelf
Little red jewelry box
I bought you for myself
Who knows how far you have
traveled
Who knows where you have
been
How many hands have opened
your lid

Just to hear your sweet music
play within
I don't know where you have
come from
I don't know where you have
been
But I shall treasure you
forever
And listen to your sweet music
play within.

L. R. Scott
THE COLONEL'S DEATHWARRANT—LONG DUE
And so you sit, mon Colonel,
In desert tents, in arid nights,
With hands so clean and heart
of hell,
Dispatching ants to fight your
fights.
Who can not doubt your wiles
or might?
Who fails to see your serpent's
skill?
Who's ears are deaf to tears
at night
From innocents your whimseys
kill?
In every corner of this Earth,
Men speak your name with
scorn and fear.
They wish your mother'd died
at birth
And curse those few things
you hold dear.
And I, a man of peaceful ways,
Know where you've been and
what you've done.
I've seen the bloodstained
human days
Of one unfit to see the sun.
Today, you've cut my soul again.
You've killed another man of
peace.
I curse to highest heav'n your
sin
And pray your blackened heart
will cease.
I leave to you this final thought
Of brutal ways too set to mend.
I give to you the gift you've
bought;
And, far too late, your just-
earned end.

Marj Schramm
MY GIFT
Charley's wife
Says
That I stole
Him.
Actually, what happened is
that—
She lost him;
He found himself;
He gave himself to me.
I had
Nothing
To do with
It.

Michael Eugene Thompson
MY LOVE
My love for thee
Is like the Redwood Tree:
Strong and enduring,
Forever maturing.
My love for thee grows
As strong as the river flows:
Forever moving,
Always living.
My love for thee will be
Such that everyone will see:
That I care,
And I share.
My love for thee will never
Burn low or burn out ever:
Passion will glow,
Love will flow.

Lucinda J. Underdue
BREATH OF DEATH
Why do we only live to die?
Why have we been forsaken?
Asking questions-why? Why?
Why?!—
In creating, was he mistaken?
Why are we born to strive; to
pass?
Where are we destined to live?
And thoughts race through the
mind too fast—
There's so much *good* to give.
And where will my poor soul go
to
When ashes fall to dust?
The memories so precious, so
few
Inside my brain, they'll rust!
What is this walking, breathing
thing
That we are caged up by?
We call it skin which we are
in—
Good-bye. . . .Good-bye. .—I
die. . . . .

Thomas Marvin Wooten
RECOLLECTING
I'm in the autumn of my years.
Crackling leaves rattle the nap
on the carpet
of my mind
Birds song is rare.
And flies
—too busy to bother buzzing
me—
fly away from here.
Sometimes I sit on the back
porch and wish
I had canned up something
preserved for
my winter days.
But all I got stashed in that old
cupboard
is a jar of wisdom that's soured.
A half pint of love that's almost
gone
And a cracked crock filled with
pebbles from
all the beaches I've roamed.
Didn't bring nothing with me—
Ain't taking nothing back in
leaving.
Not even the smell of life!

Mary A. Willar
THE GRANDFATHER CLOCK
The grandfather clock is stately
and tall
He stands in the corner, his
back to the wall
The pendulum swings back and
forth with great power
And chimes fill the room on the
stroke of the hour
Hands that keep moving with
delicate grace
Over the numbers that show on
his face
Tell you that time is slipping
away
Ever so swiftly, day after day
Twenty four hours a day
without rest
He will continue to give it his
best
So if he loses a minute or two
Wind him up fast, it's easy to do
For all that he wants is to tell
you the time
With the swing of the
pendulum, ring of the chime
And nothing's so sad as a clock
that runs down
Who stands in the corner, not
making a sound
So long live the king and the
mighty tick tock
The stately and elegant
grandfather clock.

Lois Wilson
FINALITY
I am made of tough old leather
Held together by baling wire.
Inside, I shatter like fine crystal.
The pieces tinkle as they fall
And I wonder that nobody hears.

Alice R. Nichols
SEED'S
My son as you travel along lifes
road
Planting your seed's to grow
With people trying to tell you
Just when and where to sow.
You'll be a square if you walk
straight
And right may seem all wrong
But tell me son, can you picture
a world
Where every one was stoned?
Your friends will say, man live
it up
Tomorrow may never come
But hold onto your self respect
Just in case it does.
At the harvest of your life
Things will look different then.
Reap from the good seed's of
your youth
And not wish for what might
have been.

Vera Daniell Wilson
REPENTANCE
I spoke unkindly to my friend;
She looked with stricken eyes.
How shamed I was and told her
so.
But the memory never dies.

I thought mean thoughts one
sunny day
And the brightness then was
lost
Reversal came within my heart
But sadness was the cost.
I was indifferent when a child
Trustingly questioned me.
I sought again the child's sweet
trust
But politely cool was he.
I turned a deaf ear to my Lord
My own plans had I then
I asked again for the self-same
chance
But the same came never again.
How small our lives. Each day
we lose
In selfish, thoughtless things.
Forgive, Dear Lord, send peace,
we beg
Thy understanding brings.

Laura R. MacDowell
LOVE AND LIFE'S BULLSHIT
Love is a strange thing.
It's hard to know when you're in
it.
What will this life bring?
Are heartaches the biggest part
of it?
Is the problem with life me?
Why is it so hard to cope?
I wish into the future I could
see,
Just to know if there's some
hope.
Friendships seem so hard to
keep,
Relationships always seem to
end.
Many nights I just sit and
weep,
The end is around every bend.
Whatever I try it's never right.
No one can ever be honest.
I'd like to kill myself some
night,
To get away from these empty
promises.
Promises are very hard to keep,
No one can ever keep them.
Many people get in too deep,
They just make promises and
can't keep them.
It's easy to say so many words,
But it's hard to prove them true.
Promises, friendships, honesty
are words,
But they are empty like I love
you.
Words mean nothing but action
speaks,
But action is a thing of the past.
Sharing love you shouldn't need
to be sneaks,
But real love went out with
real weather forecasts.
Communication is so hard
between people,
No one really believes each
other.
It shouldn't matter if a church
has a steeple,
But there should be love
between a child and a mother.
Old fashioned principles have
gone out,
New lifestyles have taken over.
Love goes on when the lights go
out,
And marriage went out when
divorce took over.
I still believe in old fashioned
ideas,
I believe in love, and trust,
and honesty.
I just wish other people did too,
So the world could be more
loving.
These last several lines do not
rhyme,
But life shouldn't be a poem.
I wish we could get meaning
into life,
And stop this bullshitting
around.

Michael J. Zino
THE LAMENT
Bleed savage bleed,
Cut deeply to the core.
The who has been touched.
It has been brutally but
Delightfully slashed by trust.
The tender whole is so
Vulnerable in its secrete
strength.
Insensitivity and cowardly
Myopia is the order of the day.
The penetrating truth is known.
The factual reality is realized.
The passion that is man is
Experienced in his truest
absurdity.
Being offered the very
Actualization of life itself;
It has not even been
Repulsed, no more horribly
It has been neglected.
The obvious failure not of
What is in its grasp but
Of the possibility.
The inevitable pitch of events
Have run their course.
Success is ours; beautiful
failure
In your striving you have found
it.
Tenderness and hardness
Easily hurt, that soulful sob
The very perseverance of life.
It can be no other way.
The deep transcending cut
Will never heal, nor should it;
For all that is timeless
Is the source of all that is pain.
Develop on in your fateful way.
The end has come before
The beginning is here.
All lives are confusion.
Only consciousness is lovingly
aware.
Be near, be near.

W. F. Yearwood
DO YOU REMEMBER?
Do you remember when the
days seemed long,
And never ending, yet ending
too soon?
For 'twas the time of youth and
a song,
You were too young to hug
and spoon.
Do you remember how happy
you were when
The whole world was new,
bright, gay?
And all the colors were distinct
then
And you saw nothing that was
just grey?
Do you remember your first
day at school
All dressed in your very very
best?
The goodies to be served made
you drool,
You were all jumpy and full of
zest?
Do you remember your early
playmates
And what fun it was to play
hide-n-seek?
'twas long before you thought of
dates
To plan for at the end of each
school week?
Do you remember time having
passed and low
'tis time to get dressed once
again
This time for that special,
special bow
And you just hope it won't
start to rain?
Do you remember your dates
and heart aches
When you didn't get that call
you expected?
And you swore you'd get other
nice dates,
But some turned out to be so
misdirected?
Do you remember that long
awaited wedding day
And you awoke with dreaded
joy and glee,
That everyone be just as happy
and as gay
As you were surely, surely
going to be?
Do you remember?

Mrs. Neloise K. Weber
I MAY FORGET, LORD!
I may forget to tell you, Lord
How much I love you so,
I alone know, how close you are
Wherever I may go.
My whole life through,
A sinner though I be!
Has never deserved the many
blessings
That thou bestowed on me.
I may forget, Lord, to say
"thanks"
For everything you've done
But in my heart, I do believe
you come—
To bring me gladness and joy
every single day
As only you can; and I also pray
That others, too, can enjoy,
The same happiness I feel
When I awake each morn to
greet the day with gladness,
At all the beauty in the world—
That fills our life with such
"sweet" madness!

Quintin Donnell White
SOMEONE'S HONEYBEE
Laughing at nothing
mean there's something (going
on) (going on).
Love is a feeling you just can't
hide.
When cupid's arrow touches
your side,
(resistance is gone) (resistance is
gone).
When there's a knock at the
door,
and your actions are not like
before,
everyone close to you can see
you're someone's honeybee.
The softness of your voice
comes from the mighty force
(of affection) (of affection).
You're floating on a cloud
With a smile as long as the
River Nile
(without direction) (without
direction).
When you start getting cleaner
than clean,
and there's joy in each and
every dream,
it's written in the sky
that your heart belongs to only
one guy.

N. E. (Gary) Wilson
THOUGHTS
Thoughts of mind, ever winding
and entwining, of which there
is no end.
Thoughts groping in vivid
darkness,
forever in a perpetual spin.
Thoughts of deeds, acts, and
accomplishments
often thought of but never done.
Thoughts of guilt, regrets, and
despair,
and wishing somehow we could
run.
Thoughts of lies, conceit and
concealment
forever bearing on the mind.
Thoughts of forever searching,
forever seeking,
knowing well we will never
find.
Thoughts of friends that god has
taken
and the ones we pushed away.
Thoughts of "why not more
understanding?"
on our hearts so heavy lay.
Thoughts of loves, both real and
fancied,
and wondering why they are no
more.
Thoughts of fears of seeking
new love
afraid of what might be in store.
Thoughts of life and all its
challenges—
is it worth the struggle now?
Or is death more inviting, at
least we
wonder, somehow.

Teri Ann Velicoff
ONE MOMENT LOVE, THE NEXT...
Love by candlelight,
soft and warm.
Flickering flames reflecting
in bright, shining eyes.
Secret smiles,
playful kisses,
carefree touches,
and endless giggles.
A stubble of wax
with a burnt out wick.
Light, Blinding Light,
through a curtain slit.
I awoke alone.

C. Uden
AFTER READING LORCA'S NEW YORK WORKS
The sun outside is shining.
The air is warm
The wind is blowing.
It is so beautiful outside you
can hardly breathe.
I sit on the sofa
Covered with a blanket
In the cool interior of our home.
I talked with a lady today.
She said she writes poetry
but her husband doesn't like to
have it around.
It makes him sad.
I said she should write the
happy stuff
Leave it laying around her house
Lock the good stuff up in a
treasure chest.
I can see that treasure chest—
It's mahogany, carved, lined with
Red Velvet.

It's got a tiny lock on it
About the size of a quarter.
I don't have a treasure chest
exactly like that
I don't leave my happy poems
Lying around the house.
My house is my treasure chest
And I leave my happy poems
Lying around the college, my
parent's home, my friend's
lives.
But it is a painful operation. . .
Unnatural.
Like a cescerian
Cescerian scars take a long time
to heal
And are complicated by bleeding
ulcers.
I talked to a bleeding ulcer
today.
She needs friends so badly
She tried to buy back our
friendship
With a hundred dollars.
Other ulcers
Spend their life times
Doing things they don't want to
do
In the mistaken belief that
Behaving properly
Will bring them happiness.
The happiness they receive
Is acclaim, success, acceptance—
At the price of their guts &
dignity.
The world sometimes is a jungle
Where the best way to survive
Is sitting alone wrapped up in
a blanket.

Patricia Anne Witmer

THE GREATEST STORY EVER TOLD

His word is like that of a
mighty ocean,
Like that of the thunderous,
roaring, puritan wave,
Running to the shore in a
bellowy white
Clap of crescendous applause.
Some are quiet and peaceful
Floating on a calm solitude.
Like the serene pause of a
hummingbird.
Or in-between a great concert
Of mysterious, living music,
Or a magnificent ballet.
That's the God of yesterday
and today!
His word is like an artists'
brush,
Painting a picture, penetrating,
deep and intricate,
And yet so simple,
Painting with great detail and
love,
Telling of God as being the
Alpha and the Omega,
Of Jesus Christ, our Lord and
Savior,
The story of old,
As the artists' brush unfolds.
In the beginning God,
Made heaven and earth
And all therof.
All the wise wisdom and
stupendous words,
Of the Bible,
Were written by our Master,
By the pen of God—
For you see, God was the poet.
It is the story of old,
The greatest story ever, ever
told.

Marleen Gudas Tarver

I AM BLESSED

Oh thank you Lord for another
lovely day,
I know that you have blessed
me in so many special ways:
I have my sense of sight, so that
I can see;
The sunrise and the sunset,
The mountains and the sea.
Animals, humanity, and trees,
All things created are here for
me.
I have my sense of hearing, so
that I can hear;
Scattering of storm clouds,
Hustling of holiday crowds,
Children's laughter,
A good-bye, the morning after.
I have my sense of taste, so that
I can taste;
The sweetness of honey,
A juicy apple to fill my
tummy.
Salty teardrops,
Sparkling, refreshing soda
pop.
I have my sense of smelling, so
that I can smell;
The fragrance of a rose,
A home-made meal on the
stove.
A skunk that has passed me
by,
Fireworks in the sky.
I have my sense of touch, so
that I can feel;
Warming sunshine, a fresh
breeze,
A gentle caress,
Occassional loneliness.
A baby's soft skin,
All my love I hold within.
And yet with all these senses,
I can only conceive,
That here on earth, death is
guaranteed.
I can see with my mind that I
cannot touch with my hand.
I only hold a thought of you.
I know someday when I reach—
you will touch.

Elizabeth Saltz

AUTUMN BEGINS

The echoes of the wind blowing
through the mountains,
Seems like a deluge from
above the clouds.
The tall trees stand proudly
as the green turns to
orange and gold,
Summer is gone and the green
mantle slowly disappears.
Endless farms of golden corn
spread across the countryside,
The yellow sun warms the tall
grass where cattle graze.
The farmer harvests bright red
apples and pears,
The great wonders of nature
unfold in all its glory.
The autumn leaves turn to rust
and yellow,
The pumpkins are loaded for
the City market.
The leaves rustle through the
trees,
The air is filled with the scent
of autumn flowers.
The dusk descends and the full
moon appears,
Night descends on the
peaceful countryside.
The farms are tilled with
tractors and tows,
The crops are gathered before
the snows.
The tall cliffs ascend upon the
mountain side,
The granite rocks are
reminders of pre-Cambrian
age.
The mating season is over, the
bees gathered nectar,
The blooming flowers present
a panorama of color.
The mountain lakes are filled
with fish that spawn,
The silos thresh wheat and
corn.
The farmer plants trees which
grow tall and strong,
The animals roam through the
forests bearing young.
The Hunter seeks his prey in
the early dawn,
He catches the deer, the
buffalo by the horn.
The bear runs wild till captured
by man,
The raccoon is sly and
inhabits the dam.
The new mown hay is stacked
on the carts,
The horses trot slowly
carrying man.
The farmhouse looks lonely,
nestled in the woods,
The well kept farm will yield
a harvest of goods.
The falling leaves signal that
autumn is here,
The farmer buys machinery
and repairs his home.
The next season's crop will be
bigger, he hopes,
He prepares to settle down till
a new crop appears.
The gleaming waters of the
Hudson shine brightly,
The chug of the cargo means
coal for power.
The logger chops trees which
roll down the river,
The miner goes to the mill
to bring iron and steel.
The leaves will fall and brown
hills will appear,
The snow will descend on the
wonderland of green.
The skiers will climb the hills
far and near,
The crisp, crackling fire in the
fireplace is serene.
The horses trot slowly through
the wooded hills,
The rider is calm poised and
confident.
The slow, winding lake invites
boaters who have will,
The swimmers delight in the
cool water, indifferent.
Look down on the valley, a
wonderland of green,
The well kept farms are very
serene.
The natural wonders of life
unfold,
Life is eternal as nature
reproduces.

Minnie Savage

WHO? ME?

The years went by so fast
I didn't notice I was old.
The children grown and married
I didn't notice I was old.
The precious babies arriving
3rd Generation.
I was delighted with my littlest
families growing up.
My own began to show grey hair
Strange, I didn't notice *I* was
old?
I've been so busy living life
I did not notice if I changed.
My husband more than 50 years
left this world quite suddenly.
I thought this world a pleasant
place.
So many friends and things to
do.
"Hold *on* the rail. *Wait* I will
help you."
People are sooo kind.
I didn't know that *I am* old.

Samuel H. Schwartz

INTRO—LOCUTION

My heart commands me: "Tell
How strong your feelings well
At thought of her who stirs this
fount at source;
As through your being surge
My sentiments that merge
With words of mind that mouth
and hand give force.
****"Let sun in heaven know
Not its refreshing glow
Keeps warm the spark of life the
flesh requires;
Her smiling eyes revive
The living flame to thrive
And feed this altar with
enduring fires.
*****"What raptured pride is
mine!
With love for the Divine
Doth she inhabit and this region
sway;
Throughout her true domain
All members in glad strain
Extol the queen whose willing
slaves are they."
*****Then looked I to my
heart:

"Need I to thee impart,
Thou chamber where the purer
sense abides,
How much I want to write
Of her, our both's delight?
But words are weak to quell o'er
flowing tides.
*****"The wonders of the world
Are for my eyes unfurled
To fill their depths with
grandeur Nature shows;
They ardently confide
Are ne'er more satisfied
As when upon her beauty they
repose.
*****"Thy tender bounds
expand,
Yet terms are not at hand,
With artist's touch nor poet's
gifted tongue,
Describing 'pon thy shrine
Pure love for one so fine,
And in full measure that her
charms be sung.
*****"The mind cannot express
Thy plenteous, pleasing stress,
As shallow ripples slight a
raging storm.
What cannot spoken be
Is oft a token we
Fond feelings full in fitting
frame can't form!"

Bertha Howard Sherman

SOMEBODY BIGGER THAN YOU AND ME

I owe it all to the one above
He's kind, he's generous, he's
filled with love
He lifts my spirit when it is
down
He's always somewhere around

When I'm feeling sad and blue
I have someone I can talk to
I've heard him say "You're not alone"
It wasn't through a telephone
He gave me strength when I was weak
He put me right back on my feet
When I thought my world had come to an end
He showed me that it had just begun
He's a friend, your next of kin
He's the early morning wind
He's the Sun, that morning Star
He's the one who stops the war
He's with me in my darkest hour
He's the beauty in the flower
He created both you and me
He gave us sight that we may see
All of the beauty in the sky
The birds as they go flying by
He's somebody bigger than you and me
He gave us life eternally
If we would only do his will
Eternal life will be fulfilled

James R. Shott
COLOR MY FAMILY

Color me tan with a masculine stain,
Macho and mottled with muscular show.
Color my wife with a delicate glow,
Dappled; adapting to pleasure and pain.
Color our daughter a talented hue,
A prism refracting expanding light.
Color our grandchild an innocent white,
A clear iridescence, hopeful and new.
Color each one as our canvas impels.
Watch for the changes that fade with the years:
Dazzling or hazy, in good times or sorrow.
Color us gently. Soft-shaded pastels,
Full-toned, yet tempered with laughter and tears,
Moistened and ready for tinting tomorrow.

Lieutenant: George Silvia
UNTITLED

Just the thought of
—you—
Still makes,
— me blue

Dollie R. Reed
SOMEBODY SAID

Somebody said, but is it true?
Suppose they had said the same about you?
Does it bear repeating, stop and think
Can it be unraveled link by link?
If you repeat it, will you gain
Or would it have been better to have let it lain?
Death has just taken the poor man's friend
But because of his death, this war does not end
Another has had to take his place.
To carry on in this earthly race.
Are you going to help him or let him down
Will you give him a hand or on him frown.
Remember your brother's keeper you are
And to help him would be better far
The enemy is waiting a chance to slip in
Are you going to help him and let him win
If not don't repeat what somebody said
And have all this sorrow to rest on your head

Lester Reed
THIS PUPPY PICKED ME

Snuggled in arm of little boys and girls
We find puppies wagging friendly tails,
And bright eyes shining in faith and love
Along with loyalty that never fails.
We ask why they picked these puppies
And say what fine ones they seem to be,
The answer is: "I did not pick this puppy
It happens the little puppy picked me.
To me tiny girls are unspoiled little women
And tiny boys are harmless little men,
A puppy is innocence in the finest degree
Far beyond description by tongue or pen.
Others could have the rest of the world
If I had only a little child and a pup,
I would want them to always remain little
And feel assured they would never grow up.
It is truly fine and pleasing to me
To see a puppy who owns either girl or boy,
And to note such faith and loyalty
Should fill anyone's heart with joy.
As we wander down along the path of life
And the finer side of life we strive to see,
We appreciate feeling that makes a child say:
"Mister! it happens this puppy picked me."

Mary A. Reichard
NIGHT COUGH

I coughed and I yelled 'til my tonsils got swelled,
Yet good ol' Als slumber was deep.
I choked and I hacked 'til a headache, in fact,
Was worse than the loss of my sleep.
'Twas a hell of a night; and I thought that I might
Be a victim of "Half-asleep Phlegm."
My hankies got all, so I trailed down the hall
For a roll of paper. And then!
All through the night, I filled to it's height
A sack that stood by the bed.
It did me no good to count sheep, cats, or wood;
In the morning I'd surely be dead.
Then, finally, sweet unadult'rated sleep!
I awoke at twelve forty-five.
The day was half gone, but I croaked out a song—
Happy to see me alive.
So I smiled and arose (with a blow of my nose). . .
I'd finished my howl at the moon.
'Tho I couldn't run, there were chores to be done;
'Twas a rest that ended too soon.

Richard Risemberg
THE RISING TIDE

Morning glitters on a rising tide
while you, uncomforted in calm, are sleeping late
to dream of summer's damage to your pride.
Though you've a wit whose strength is deride
the helplessness of joy in face of fate,
still, morning glitters on a rising tide
and sun knits shadows through the lawn outside.
If I could wake you now, I would debate
those dreams of summer's damage to your pride;
if you would rise and draw the shades aside
you'd see that nighttime fears seem far less great
when morning glitters on a rising tide.
Death comes to all; but we have not yet died.
Let's leave behind, with youth, the encumbering weight
of dreams of summer's damage to our pride.
Not till tomorrow shall we be allied
with all the nations of the dead, who lie in state
and dream of summer's damage to their pride
while morning glitters on a rising tide.

Nellie R. Garver
THE WATCHER

The Christmas Ball now over,
Gifts are laid away,
Festive days and gatherings cease
Farewell, joyous holiday.
Invisible to mortal eyes,
A stranger lingers on.
Where were the happy multitudes
That through the city thronged?
Discontentment wars against
Celebration of the Babe
And some forget the reason
The blessed Christ-child laid.
The Watcher sighs with pity,
"All is well, my friends,
This hope that comes unto the world
Is joy that never ends."

Toivo Puustinen
MY SPANKING BRAND NEW BELL—BOTTOMED BRITCHES

Oh, those black sons of flying witches!
They stole my spanking, brand new bell-bottom britches!
They came in the dense of the night,
When there wasn't a solitary spatter of light.
Through the cat's tunnel their little dog named, Fetchum Fowser,
Drug away my precious, brand new trousers.
Had I awakened at the moment, I would have pestered,
From upon a propped elbow I would have sequestered and questioned,
As they went through pockets one by one without a sound,
Would they split with me on whatever they found?
Oh, those black sons of flying witches,
They stripped me of my spanking, brand-new bell-bottom britches.
I went into horrid stretches of scratching naked itches.
I suffered the agonies of prolonged and recurring twitchings.
I cried until my face and eyes were glazed and blue.
Rivuletting tears joined a dribbling nose and formed red puddles of glue.
One look will suffice to snuff the love of Bonnie Blue Lou.
Bell-bottoms stripped and of britches too, scorn will crown her parting ad deau.
Left behind drifting, her smile everywhere, a withering ghost,
And for me to cry just this one tearstained boast,
"Somber days are coming for those black sons of flying witches,
When the knowledge breaks like the dawn,
That I didn't carry my 'go-to-town wad',
In my spanking, brand-new bell-bottom britches."

Mary Smalling Restivo
HAVE YOU SEEN MY LITTLE GIRL

Have you seen my little girl
picking the pretty flowers
in the meadow.
Where the birds are singing
and the bees are buzzing.
Have you seen my little girl
sitting by the brook catching
the fish.

Glenngo Allen King
A FABLED GUEST

Silence.
An Explosive,
The flawless
Architect
Among the Giants
Aiming Skyward
Conducting
the ultimate
tomorrow
In just one minute

Garland O'Quinn, Jr.
COMING THROUGH

There's a song down deep inside me that wants to burst out loud
There's a poem running through me that wants to please the crowd
There's a rhythm in my body that wants to make it dance
But a fear that keeps them in there will not let me take a chance
If I keep it to myself
they can never laugh at me
My awkward fumbling steps

the crowd will never see
But if I'm too successful
and my feelings learn to hide
I may never share with others
this happiness inside
So maybe, just one little tune
I'll hum and tap my toe
And if the time is ever right
I'll let the people know
That down inside this body
there's an ocean full of love
That wants to rain upon the
earth like showers from above

Linda Matt

UNTITLED

Within the deep purple sky
Pegasus does fly
Conquer the evil, banish the
nightmares, love will
prevail upon this magical night.
Tread through the forest
under fire kissed nights, find
the roses, cherish their unique
beauty, be touched by the spirit
of Cupid, and be a nymph such
as me.

Mary Therese McDonald

SOMEDAY

Someday I'll tell you
your green-eyed gaze
melts my heart
How the very thought
of your kisses
stirs my soul
Someday I'll tell you
a smile from you
makes my day
Your tender caress
touches me though
you're away
Someday I'll tell you
first I must know
you love me
But there is no love
in those green eyes
not for me
Someday I'll forget
I'll be married
he'll love me
And you will not know
I loved you first—
forever.

Hilaria Medina

IN MEMORY OF SAMANTHA

Samantha was a friend of mine,
We were together most of the
time.
She was covered with yellow-
white
And brown fur,
And how I miss her.
When I held her in my arms,
She wouldn't cause any harm.
Samantha would sleep with me
at
Nights,
And I tried not to hold her too
Tight.
She was such a toy,
That always played with joy.
Samantha was her name.
And she was tame.
She played with my feet,
And got a string on her teeth.
When she died, How
I wanted to have cried.
But I tried not to because even
though she's gone,
I am not alone.
Samantha was young, But got
run over by a car,
Even though she wasn't far.
I went to pick her up like a
new born baby kitten.
She was different from other
cats
I ever had,
Even though sometimes she was
bad.
I shall miss Samantha very
much,
But not take everything in a
whole
Bunch.
She is gone,
But I'm not alone.
I shall still and always
remember
her, and that still and always
small body of soft fur.

Etta Mellett

GUESSING GAME

Guess who!
Beautiful, that I am. Oh yes, you
will see.
Medium size, and such tiny and
dainty feet.
I think they are so sweet and
dainty,
I keep them up so they look
neat.
And I always wash before I eat,
And who knows but I may say a
prayer.
My nails are always well-kept, I
swear.
They are as tough as steel, like
a bear's.
(I'll win the prize!)
I keep my eyes covered with a
black band
So people won't know who I am.
Not a pet.
I am wise and smart, don't
forget,
So don't tangle with me, please,
sir.
I might look soft and cuddly,
but I swear,
I can be rough and tough, and
I can tear.
I can act like a sweet little
dumb lamb.
Guess again if you don't know
who I am.
I am a little bandit and a clown,
So smile with glee and say,
"It's not a toy!"
So we will play the little game.
You see, I am raccoon by name.
And no shame.
You're right!
The raccoon—the bandit.

Jocelyn Long

UNTITLED

Martin Luther discounted one
half the race when he
announced females good only to
bear (bare)?
Constantine boiled his wife
alive
They tilted the table and
strapped us down for whose
convenience?
Now Heathcote lays
circumcision on us
Mothers consent to mutilism,
asking for male revenge
Must the pendulum swing to
the other extreme
(We're talking of bringing
Ishtar back
She also required human
sacrifice)
Yuliya Voznesenskaya: Christ
paid for the sins of mankind,
and mankind obviously is not
worth Christ's suffering."
Mercy triumphs over judgement!

Channie Kahan

UNTITLED

In long years to come
I'll be happy and my past
sorrows
will be done
I'll have children with him,
And love them deeply
Our lives will have no
complications
And the days will go by one by
one
free of cares and worries
To the outside we are a perfect
couple
they will be envious
Seeing two people happy
together
but there will be one deep
dark secret
terrorizing me
And that one fear will be
That I will still love you.

Ruth Williams Kantor

MOOT SONG

This is a madness, love; it is
not purposeful nor wise;
There is no logic in the
exercise;
Why should I, now that I
discern
That reason's path is best and
wisest, turn
Away from what I value, what
I love?
Shall I call it chemistry, this
surge
Whose urgings I obey before,
above
The dictates of my conscience?
A dirge
Should be the theme of this
affair.
But, oh, what symphonies
resound within my body!
And what singing fills the air!

Russell Kirton

LOST

Its not the time or place
and now our minds separate
my heart remains the same
though we're away
I'll always be right here
love what is worth loving
and with a tear drop
blow the rest away:

Russell Kirton

LOVE COMES

Love comes its own time
and soon its passed
thrown away
and you stand there, wondering
but if it ever struck you again
you'll know what to do:

Mrs. David Koelling

JOYANNE SUNSHINE

There was always one thing
missing, and never to be mine.
That would have made my life
complete, I called her Joyanne
Sunshine.
Just six weeks did I have her,
then she was gone from me.
In ways I'd never known before,
I felt pain and misery.
An injustice I could not accept,
the loss of something fine,
Was all that I could understand
about Joyanne Sunshine.
All children have knicknames,
be they girl or boy,
The one that I had chosen,
would simply have been Joy.
Where her name had come from,
I really do not know,
But on the day I lost her, it
had firm begun to grow.
I guess I never will forget, the
pain that had been mine,
For no way can I recapture,
that dream, Joyanne Sunshine.
The one I care for, so much
more than words can ever say,
Shared the start of her life with
me, to the end of her short-
lived days.
There is no way you can replace
the life of a child you love,
Be they born or never knowing
life, they're blessed by a hand
from above.
The one thing that I still hope
for,
And pray someday will again be
mine,
Is a dark-haired, blue-eyed,
little girl,
I'd call Joyanne Sunshine.

Deborah A. Jensen

LOVE IS

The Happiness;
Of having someone around
And watching over them.
The Kindness;
Of being friends
And not being enemies.
The Joy;
Of knowing that
You are You!

Kathleen Klorer

TO 1981

Each boy, each girl
Want their childhood world
To belong to their children
As their's was unfurled
It isn't exactly *what* they
Want them to possess
But mighty close to
Their own child spots
of happiness. . .

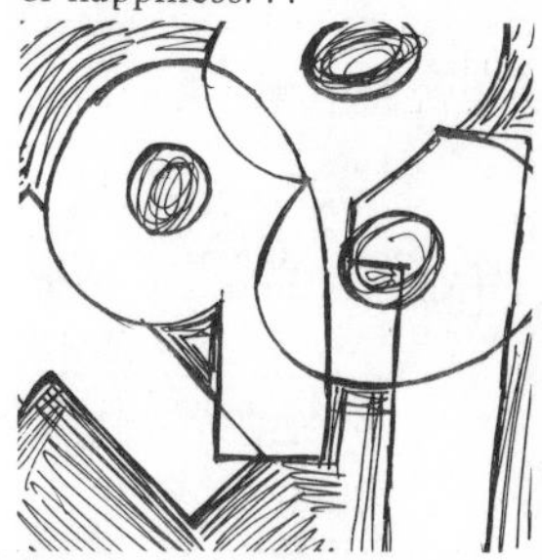

As for me. . .
I've come thru many
lanes
On the street of time
Sheltered by the trees
One chooses to find
Not exactly the ferns
my mother grew
But a lot of fragrance
I never knew
And still in the midst
Of these families true
Is the smiling presence
of black Jimmie Lou—

Marinda J. Harrah

MY SON

My son is like a bent tree
that has grown straight.
He is my joy when my days are
sad.
When I think of him, I am a
total woman.
He will be my future when I
am no more.
I let him try his wings even
if he falls.
Some day he will leave me;
I will have him no more.
But the world will be richer
by far.

Joseph Rog'el

THREATENING HANDS

Mother!
I still remember late that night

When the snow sketched all in white.
You I see, wherever I roam,
Our town, our street, our dead home.
I see the tempest rise
Over biting air, like burning ice.
Each face a tombstone for a grave,
We are obedient, much too brave.
We must stay in line, blocks of wood,
The capo's lashes all our food.
The crematorium—feet away.
O Lord, what prayer can we pray?
The capo's whip cracks, but hurts no more.
The shamed sun hides, as never before.
The S. S. rifles blaze all day long.
Men, women, the very young.
We don't feel frost or gale,
No more our dying bodies wail.
Our shadows sob against the wall,
And crematorium flames—threatening hands—warn all!

Anne Hays

AMY'S SMILE

Her captivating smile,
A gift from heaven.
Whenever she greets you,
It's yours
To enjoy—and feel the glow
Of love.
It warms your heart.
It calms your spirit.
It's a three-year-old
I'm speaking of.

Trudy Ann Durden-Hooks

CHRISTMAS

Christmas, what a time of the year-when everyone gets caught up in the spirit and feeling of love, and giving-the decorations-the songs-shopping sprees—O, the love of the Lord, we see—as friends and families gather around the tree.

Christmas-the Christ-like feeling, of the birth of Christ-(some two thousand years ago) so simple, (in a manger) but, yet celebrated the greatest of all-showing the love of our saviour, as he lived and died for mankind-not wanting a one to be lost, as he died on the cross.

Christmas, so sound and true-of all the gifts we could give-the best, our heart-to the Lord, forever-to never part.

Christmas-the best gift we could ever receive, is the love of the Lord-(with a change of heart) with him, we'd never have to depart.

Christmas-where love doth abound-where friends and love ones are all around.

Let us look above-this Christmas to God, with all his love, with thanks for all things on this Christmas day- and lets invite Jesus in our heart to stay, this Christmas day-

As we celebrate his birth-by giving our heart-and receiving his love, as he is the best giver of all- and we receive the best, to ever be received-this Christmas eve, from the Father and the Son-and heaven we'll be won.

F. H. Scott

TO MY DOCTORS

When the three-score post is long since past,
When I lie spent and still at last,
Spare me the alien blood, the goading shot,
The tubes, and tortures best forgot.
If you plainly see my life is ending
Don't force my love to useless spending
Of our small hoard so slowly garnered.
I pray you'll see this truly honored.

Jahn D. Hultgren

MILKWEED

Early bird
in a field.
hear soft footsteps
in the moist brown earth
such a nice sunrise
that covers the dark night,
while dewey mist
covers that quiet field
of infant corn plants.
By himself
a minority plays
in the middle of a row
cynical survival
faces the harsh kick
of a predjudiced foot.
An explosion of dirty violence
gaping bomb crater
shredded leaves
dashed hopes
white root gasping for breath
as plant lifeblood
spills
on the ground.

Harold Jerome Huff

LOVE

Love is beautiful, love is fair
my memories of love will be of you
Love is like the ocean
and some say love is everything
some say they do not know
Some say that love is like fire
that burns very slow
Some say that love's just like a flower
so beautiful they say, or love's just
like a star that shines down from heaven always
Perhaps love is everything.
love is beautiful, shining down from
heaven, warming the earth just like the sun.
Yes, love is like a star which blossoms in
the bosom of heaven, and shines brightly in
the sky.
Love is like beautiful poetry, new as a
new born babe
Love's like music, love is grand, and love
is always in demand.
Love is everything come what may
Loves the beginning and the ending of each
Tomorrow, each yesterday.
Love's a star that shines down from heaven
always.
Love's the sun which warms the earth
Love's the prayer that the nuns pray.
Love's the music, love's the song
Love's the right, and never the wrong.
Perhaps love will always be
a beautiful form of lovely poetry.
Love is charming, love is fair
Love can't be mistaken, anywhere.
Love is powerful, love's a star
shining down from heaven afar
Love's the triumph of the soul
love's convenient, love is whole.
Love is glorious, love is fine
Love is nature's valentine.
And, love's the food upon which the soul doth dine.
Love's an expression of the soul
love is never out of control.
O, love is beautiful, it shines down from
heaven upon earth like the everlasting,
ever warming sun.
Love is like a beautiful flower that shines
down from heaven upon the earth.
Yes, love is like a star blossoming in the bosom
of heaven and shining brightly in the sky.
Love's like beautiful poetry, new as a new born babe.
love's like music, love is grand and love is always
in demand.

Thelma B. Gabler

A MOTHER'S MESSAGE TO HER CHILD

As one goes through life,
Alone, or with husband or wife,
The greatest achievement of man or nation,
Is to adjust ones self to the situation.
Mother won't always be there;
To hear, and your troubles share.
But, there's God the Burden Bearer,
Who will solve your problems without compare.
So, if you'll follow this bit of advice;
You'll be repaid many times thrice.
Dear Child: I know right from the start;
You will always do your part.
So; play hard; play fair;
Play life's game, and play it square.

Stephen A. Gargiulo

LUCY

Like dried leaves against the cold
You began to wither,
The last leaf stuck there
Against the contrast of grey clouds.
A vacant house where you farmed
And raised your sheep and chickens
And cooked for your ten children
And then their children;
Where you buried two husbands and five children.
A tape of the lineage from before anyone had heard of Henry Ford.
Sold into marriage for a stolen pocket watch at 14.
Ushered in during the Blizzard of '88.
I was never on time for that last visit.
It looked as though you left screaming
that those ninety-two years were not enough.

John L. Gilmore

LIFE

Life is just a bowl of cherries,
Of fruit flies and of gnats,
Bananas and of ferries.
Ambitions are many;
Diversions varied.
Avocations are humorous,
Occupations are numerous.
Boys and girls the natural set;
While boys with boys,
Their sensuous desires get.
And Helen with Helen of Troy;
Climax reached in place of a boy.
San Francisco.

Colleen Marie Gorman

THE EVER CHILD

You are the Ever Child,
The innocent, meek and mild.
The pity we feel for you is misplaced;
Often pity is on envy based.
We've dubbed you retarded and slow,
Yet my mind insists this isn't so.
You live an uncomplicated, serene life,
Free from our progressive, troublesome strife.
Jealous? Why I think I am.
For your childish, innocent souls God won't damn.
You live in another world, another time,
Faraway from insane war and deranged crime.
You've escaped the Alcatraz in which we're confined,
For nowhere are the walls higher than in the human mind.
Guarded by logic, yet the warden is greed,
And it is the warden we prisoners too often heed.
I wouldn't change places with you,
But I often wonder if the reverse isn't also true.

Cline W. Grant

THANKSGIVING

I am thankful for the tall green trees,
That grows so great and strong.
I am thankful for glad words of cheer,
That helps the world along.
I am thankful for the flowers that bloom,
That grows by lifes pathway.
I am thankful for thy gracious love,
That binds from day to day.
I am thankful for the golden corn,
The precious gift of God.
I am thankful for the rugged way,
The path our fathers trod.

Charles Ruggles Fox

COURAGE OF THE TRUTH

Can this nation,-any nation
Born of Freedom, yet survive,
When the rites are left untended,
Will the embers stay alive?
In this vale of tribulation
There's no freedom cheaply bought,
No extenuated offing
That will lead to more than aught.

When the mores find remission
And the doors are left ajar,
Retrogression comes a-creeping
And contrition's never far.
Of the heritage we Honor,
Are our children well advised.
Are they taught the fundamentals
That our forbearers recognized?
Let the concept never waver
Nor the courage of the truth;
Keep the fires of Freedom burning
In the province of our youth.

David Holmes

OH DAWN ARISE

Oh dawn arise
We wait for thee
for the darkness was here
during the times they polluted our lands
and our seas lie in wastes.
Oh dawn arise
Black vapors engulf thy skies
and little children die in the filth
of its lost ones.
Oh dawn arise
Our inheritances await for thy coming
lest they are destroyed by them who hate thee,
and the wars snare us to an eternal doom.
Oh dawn be swift
Before our people are gone
and it is too late.

R. F. G.

UNTITLED

Fond phantom
Of my inner life
Be slow
So slow
In turning round.
Be,
Darkly beautiful
Like,
A black swan.
Let,
Your neck
As
The
Bend
Of
A
Feather
To encircle,
Enthrall,
And forever hold me.

Henry J. Dugan

A HILL OF PEACE

Someday I will climb to the nearest hill.
Until my lungs and heart begin to fill with the fine air of a carefree day.
It could be in October or perhaps in May.
But no matter what month, no matter what day.
I will sing until the dark clouds move away.
I will gaze upon the many sweet flowers.
And walk slowly in the rain for many hours.
And still the rain will clear.
Stella, will find me and she'll come near.
Stella, will walk with me to the cottage, where red roses grow over abundantly.
And I feel certain love will bloom just for Stella and me.
We shall look away through the cottage window towards the tranquil blue sea.
And across the road A Hill Of Peace shall come in sight.
Myself and Stella shall enjoy a glorious, peaceful night.
A Hill Of Peace out there in the distant lane, where peace will come again.
And our flag shall wave so gloriously.
Peace and love, just Stella and me.

Paul E. Hubbell

THE LADY IN GOLD

When a small boy on Random Street,
where a little town and country meet,
I sat on the porch as folks passed by
when out of one's sash and hat ribbons of red and gold flashed high.
As a youth I saw in the railroad car
the face and form that smote my heart.
This was again the golden girl
at the window ready to depart.
When a man, I beheld a vision true

as if dropped from the sky
upon the courthouse green,
her fair head proudly high
flashing the gorgeous colors
I twice before had seen.
There I stood at the high altar
the dream close by my side,
it was a happy wedding
of groom with captured bride.
But she escaped, as ageing
she left my earthly sight
passing into the imaged world
in a whirl magic flight.
Yet still I see her passing
in many a crowded street,
the woman or the angel eluding
chances that we might meet.
But long as I, in sleep or waking
live on, as years roll by,
in dreams and thoughts she's making
appearance in sunset colors
flashing into my dimming eye!
If, in Christian's Heaven
it's as famed John Bunyan told,
she's entered the eternal city
in crown and cloth of gold!

Jack D. Currie

REDEMPTION

No hint from her had he
Save one small pat upon the shoulder
Or else a glance held a trifle long
Scant lead for becoming bolder
Somehow she healed the grievous hurt
That oft results from war
And all at once he realized
What he'd been fighting for
Even so, he knew, it couldn't last
'Twas for a little while
Yet happy illusion reigned, and
The fleeting hours beguiled
Now, in the tenderness of reverie
Unspoiled by time, or tears
He sees her, still smiling there
And wafts a kiss across the years

Sylvia Argow, Litt. D.

CARNAL SCENT

You made me believe that your frozen smile
Was the golden fringe of daring sun
And the magic flame of love
A carnal scent in autumn's cycle.
Could I know that your flamingo'd claws
Were tearing at my heart
When the summer rain splashed
The blossoming bluebells
And our starlit love twinkled until dawn
And awakened each lonely flower
Budding in the summer dew.
The cool magic of the rain
Splashed upon my face
And glittered as the glowing sun
Turned leaves to crunchy lace.
I watched you as a flower
That closed at early twilight
And autumn leaves made a turnabout
From green to speckled brown.
Could I believe the wallowing birds
Were flying into the horizon
Disappearing from my view
And salamanders flaunting flames of fire
Diving into the curly crest of a cruel sea.
I watched the orioles begging for crumbs
But fledgelings know naught of the harrowed world.
You made me believe there was no lonely road
And running streams ran calmly forward.
I watched the shadows of the rocks and rills
As you became nothingness in the night
And I watched and I watched
As you disappeared from sight.

Margaret V. Hunsinger

AUTUMN LEAVES

Thank you autumn leaves
for rustling your last merry tune,
flitting here, frolicking there,
beside the broken wall.
You stir about and make a nest
as if a birth you share.
At best I cannot understand
why leaves drop off, and never
stop, until the winter wind
does whip them out of tune
with mother earth.
Inside she sings and sings,
until comes the spring.
Green pastures just begun,
leaves green again come with the sun,
and warms each weary soul.

Lynn Baymler

DAYDREAMING

Daydreaming is the foundation of the world
For if people didn't daydream
Columbus would not have sailed to find the new world,
The colonists would not have dreamed of freedom
And then achieved it.
Men would not have dreamed of walking on the moon
And then attained their goal,
And love would not exist in this world.
For what is love without daydreams?
To love you must first dream of that love,
Plant the seed of hope,
Nourish it into a possibility,
And then watch it blossom into reality,
The love of your life—
Your total existence.

Rebecca D. Hundley

MAGIC OF THE SNOW

Oh wondrous morn! Oh snow clad hills;
Did you come to soothe dull winters ills?
Your barren gorges yesterday,
Made spring-time seem so far away.
Today, an ermine blanket,
Covers every twig and limb.
Tall trees cast long shadows,
On the blankets under them.
Sunlight glistens, on white hillsides,
One seems to hear a robin sing.
A crocus bright peeps thru the snow
And in my heart again, It's SPRING!
Sure, under the winter-time blanket,
Nature so busy, yet so quiet and serene,
Plans her springtime dance,
Upon a carpet of softest green.
Inviting all the spring-time flowers,—
Lily, Pansy, Rose, Fern and Violet,
Their escorts, —Sweet William and his friends,
To waltz and dance the minuet.
Bluebirds will fly over the garden,
Their gay notes a message to bring.
They'll bill and coo, then fly away—
To tell the world,—
IT'S SPRING! IT'S SPRING!

Patti Jo Frazier

FORGET TO REMEMBER

There's nothing to remember,
I asked the Lord to help me forget
the times I cried myself to sleep
for something he had said.
There's nothing to remember
for as hard as I can try
there was no time he picked me up
and held me as I cried.
I wish I could remember
a very special man
"Let's go for a walk, daddy,
won't you hold my hand?"
—a smiling face and outstretched arms
as we came running home,
—a quiet talk at the close of the day
to assure I was never alone,
—a pat on the back on graduation day
for a job well done,
—His face in the center of a cheering crowd
no matter if I'd won,
or holding my child upon his knee
making him laugh and sing.

Oh, God,
if I could only remember these
things.

Eddie Hanvey
ONCE AGAIN
I've slept with many winters
Embracing the cold
And walked the halls of so
many years,
And held so many midnight
lovers,
I never really got to know.
Lying down in unfamiliar places
Sometimes alone
Sometimes with lovers
Sometimes with fear.
I've done so many foolish things
And yet I've often made out
well.
I've given all my smiles away.
But, without regret—
They were well deserved.
Some went to lovers
Some to children
And some the rain even stole.
Searching the mountain of
memories
Few friends I've had,
But I've loved each one—
Even those who betrayed me,
They meant well.
And when the sun
Yields it's golden rays no more,
And the blossoms of my heart
No longer bloom,
And that final moment arrives.
Let me know once again,
The pleasure of a smile.

James Asbury
A SMALL BOY'S WISH
He woke up bright and early
And hopped right out of bed,
So he wouldn't miss a minute
Of the fun that lay ahead.
Today his dad would pick him
up,
They had a special date
To go off camping in the woods
And he could hardly wait.
He wished his dad lived at home
again,
The way he did before.
Since he'd moved out a year ago,
He missed him more and more.
Now every other weekend
Was all the time he had
To do the things kids like to do
Together with their dads.
He'd tried his best to
understand
Exactly what went wrong,
How come his folks decided
They couldn't get along.
But when you're five years old,
It seems an awful shame
To have your mom and dad
break up,
No matter who's to blame.
Sure, he knew he should be
thankful
For the weekends with his dad,
And the way his mom took care
of him
Just like she always had.
But what he wanted most of all
Was how it used to be,
When the three of them
together,
Made a happy family.

Marjorie Carr
CHRISTMAS CHRISTIAN
I've always loved the Baby, But
I do not love the Man.
The helpless Baby in the cave;
I'm sure that He has power to
save!
The darling, newborn Baby;
Not the stern, demanding Man!
I loved Him in Jerusalem! Bright
head amid the grey!
The tearful parents seeking
Him,
To find Him in the temple Dim;
Conversing with the elders,
Who heard Him in amaze.
The years passed by quickly, to
them I held no clue
But then I saw Him as a Man
And here the stern demand
began;—
"Give what you own to these
who need!
"Leave all, and follow Me!"
I think He asks too much of me,
(Frail creature of the Earth)"
I have too much of daily strife
To add His service to my life!
Why does He ask so much of
me?
I worshipped at His birth!

Ruby Reyes Flowers
TO IKE
I saw butterflies on Molokai
Dancing in the sun.
Their wings were sparkles of
joy.
Don't they know that this
was once a place of death?
A place of shadows and
darkness, of mutilated
misery,
Where men prayed for death to
release them from their prison
of despair?
How dare the butterflies dance!
I heard birds on Molokai
Singing with abandon.
Their voices were symphonies
of praise.
Such songs of happiness too
much for my ears
In this place where lullabyes
were never sung.
Where mother and child were
ripped apart—
The infant denied the comfort
of his mother's breast
And she, the joy of his first
smile.
How dare the birds sing here!
I saw the sunshine on Molokai
Glistening in the air.
It painted bright rainbows and
teased a million sparkles on
the ocean waves:
Those pounding waves that
once hurled wretched men
ashore.
Men made unacceptable by that
dread disease: the creator of
rejection
and loneliness.
How dare the sun shine here!
I met a man on Molokai.
He walked with God.
A smile filling his face ran
over.
His eyes glowed with a
radiance from within.
He knows this enemy called
leprosy.
Yes, he knows it well.
His body has known the hell of
endless pain.
His soul, the curiosity of
those who remain unmolested.
His sensitivity, the cool
acceptance of his now
"arrested" state.
Yet—he dares to smile!
Now I know why there are
butterflies on Molokai—
dancing in the sun.
And why the birds on Molokai
sing a joyous symphony.
And I know why the sun dares
to shine and warm the souls
of men on Molokai.
They are but the reflection
of God's delight in the faith
of His children!

Evah Baugher
A WINTER DAY
So many lovely things there are
About a winter day
I take them quite for granted
And sometimes forget to say,
A simple prayer of thankfulness
For joys that are a part
Of happiness in living,
And contentment in the heart
The whistle of a cardinal
The singing winds that blow
Thru leafless boughs, the
sunlight,
Spilling jewels on the snow
The song of small, gray birds,
The cobalt skies of shining hue
The opal dawns, and sunsets
I've accepted as my due
So now on wings of gratitude
My fervent prayer shall rise
I thank thee, Father thank thee,
And I do sincerely prize,
The blessed gifts of winter days
However great or small,
Because it is thy tender love
That has bestowed them all

R. Allen Alexander
APPEAL TO CHANGE
Where is the pain to endure the
loss
While minds drift away,
And who will pay the cost
When the sky turns deathly
grey;
Feelings inside turn I don't
know where,
They leave me stranded
among the void only here
and there
To places that do not belong
Which are neither right nor
wrong;
The twists, the turns,
The notion that changes
never start,
Men have the vision to kill
and burn
The beauty of which is art,
And if we are to stand to
reason
Will it justify the season
to come
Or will the shadows cease to
fade
While we total the vacant sum.
Now the time has come to say
Rested thoughts upon this
fruitless day,
The path of life is changing now
'Til the waves of memory are
dead;
The road before me now
The structure so clear,
The work is before the
craftsman waiting to mold,
The fruits of life must never
grow old,
Let time be spent in message
display,
Can the stones of gloom be
torn
'Til all is vented away
And ideas flow from a new age
Filling life with smoky, scented
sage.
I gaze at the window and what
do I see
A cold grey sky on a summer
eve,
Somehow the hope seems to
leave
And the sun is blood crimson
red
Portraying ones that have long
been dead;
Darkened clouds obliterate the
light
As minds know not where they
are led
And the loss chills the soul of
fright.
If life is an illusion, then
what are we;
If sight is but fusion, how
can we see;
A man may find seclusion, but
what will he be;
What is a dream and what is
not;
But what really seems is far
from lost.

Winnie Hughes
I DREAMED HE WAS AN ANGEL
There are times when life has
no future to face
but the Master stands by with
dignity and grace
when our sorrows are over we
feel God knew best.
He takes our loved ones in
His arms to rest
Doctors said our son would very
soon die
How could I bear to tell my
baby good-bye
I wondered about his soul when
he passed on
Will God welcome him for His
very own
One night I had a vision before
he took his flight
A voice softly said his soul
is cleansed white
In my vision I was in the
country on a high bluff
Driving an old model car with
brakes worn and rough
As I slid half way down, I saw
with my eyes
A dressed up angel drop from
the skies
It sat down in my path while I
wrestled my brakes
With his beautiful smile, it was
our son, no mistake
He sat smiling, looking straight
in my face
Wearing his robe and crown to
God's beautiful place
His robe skirt lapped in
folds as he dropped to the
ground
The stars in his robe matched
those in his crown
I awoke shaking with a terrible
fright
After the vision I witnessed that
night
Very soon he said good-bye to
us all
When a dove flew to his
window and made his last
call.

Babe Milroy
THE MEETING
For one enchanted hour we met
in love's own bower.
The hopes of wasted years were
blended in our tears.
You gave your lips to me and
kissed me tenderly,
You held me in your arms
and caressed me with your
charms.
You whispered, "Babe, I love
but you, no one else will ever
do."
And when you stroked my brow,
it seemed to me somehow,
The years just rolled away and
you were here to stay.

We pledged our love anew,
yet we knew 'twas true,
Other lips would press, and
other arms caress,
As we alone our burdens bear
with no one near to care,
Until once more we meet in
love's own bower sweet.
Then you will place upon my
hand the long awaited
wedding band.

Vahta Charko
OF SIR GALAHAD
Long ago he did stand
The purest one in all the land
and not a spot did stain his
chest
For never layed he his sword
to rest
Through this age he travelled
and on
Now to return as chaste as a
fawn
Even today I saw him standing
there
Sword in hand no cloth did he
wear
But armour of virtue and long
golden hair

R. C. Burroughs
THE BLACK BULL, BIRD, SNAKE AND BANSHEE
Is survival avoid—
ance of collisions?
Each was a near miss;
silhouettes whose details I'll
never know,
no more than my last death
or your face next to hers
years from now
when you finally awake afraid
of our dark incarnations.
As we straddled bareheaded
on his motorcylce balancing
past Possum Corner at midnight,
you tried to be a roadblock:
bullheaded and sacred.
Next time, in his Land Cruiser,
you dove at me out of the Texas
sun
swerving in your last God
Almighty second.
An eclipse
or just another scared crow?
As we step barefoot across
a Matagorda Island run-off of
liquid moon,
there you are, treading the
edge of darkness,
head ready to strike.
He watches you with Hero
worship.
Knowing better, that we are at
last mortals,
I hurry him back
to our firewood's starry coals.
In a last escape attempt,
I grab him by the ribcage
shaking us with laughter/anger,
desire/grief—
longing to impact
as another galaxy on the ground;
instead, of a banshee
howling in this night black as a
coalsack.

Therese Gidney
NATURE'S REBIRTH
Spring is nature's rebirth
When the long grey death of
winter
Is replaced by nature awakening
from her slumber
And once again restoring the
beauty of the earth.
Mother Nature dresses her bare
grey trees
With buds that soon blossom
into full green leaves.
And the winter's extensive
barren mass
Is soon carpeted by lush green
grass.
A squirrel scampers from tree
to tree
A tiny meadowlark whistles his
flutelike melody
A bumblebee alights on a wild
spring beauty
And gathers the pollen to make
golden sweet honey.
Orchards are scented by pink
and white blossoms
Gardens flourish with a rainbow
of flowers
Fragrant lilacs perfume the
air
As the beauty of spring touches
everywhere.
Springtime is when a young
man's fancy
Is turned to thoughts of love
When his heart is enraptured by
the beauty of spring
And the dawning of a renewed
life it promises to bring.

Mary Anna Cookson
FADING LIGHT
The fading light of Sunset
Reminds me of a long past
time
When the Sun's rays
poignantly, hauntingly
Enveloped me.
Trembling I find
A thin veil of sadness
and longing
Enfolding me
Now.
Without knowing the reason
I am impacted. The golden
rays
Enter and spread,
Encompassing me.
Silent I fall, yielding to feelings
Long since forgotten. From
another
Time and place, I remember
The Sun's embrace.
Ever since I was a child
And saw the Sun on gleaming
rock,
And saw the shadow that it
formed,
I have not known which
way to turn.
I'm drawn to the East of the
rising Sun
Yet I'm pulled to the Sun of
the West.
My life's predicament has
been
I have not known which
path was best.

Georgia Hedrick
FEET OF LEAD
Totter carefully across the
spunglass web
of fear on fear on fear
with spider-sure feet—
I tremble at the gaping spaces
everywhere.
Who can say that I
will not surely tumble
forever within and between
what has been so carefully
spun
with time and care?
Who can say just how long
I can so precisely tip-toe
across silken threads
with feet of lead?

Emma Johnson Fry
SPRING TIME
Spring time, what a beautiful
season.
This time of the year God has
blest.
Hearts become merry and
lighter.
Faces more loving and brighter.
Since passing the cold winters
test
Refreshing showers and
beautiful flowers
Replenish and renew the land
The flowers and the trees
The birds and the bees
All feel the touch of his hand
So how could we doubt his
presence
Or his promise of a new life to
come
When each spring time
His promise is proven
And the sparrows are all guided
home

Octavio Bessa, Jr. M.D.
FLOWERS IN THE WIND
One day I had a compelling
desire
To walk in the woods. . .

The rain just fallen
And the grass so fresh and pure,
Two birds nestling on the tree
above
Also by nature lured, sang
A song only by them
understood.
It was so quiet and inspiring
That today with a humble mood
I long so much again to return
For a walk in the woods.

Elva Howell
SMILE
It's easy to smile
When everything's great
No sickness around,
And our bills are up to date.
But what about the times
When no money comes in
And sorrow, and pain,
And sickness begin?
Do we have a long face,
And does our chin drag the
floor?
We have a Saviour;
We should lean on Him more.
He'll take us through,
No matter what's wrong;
So trust Him when things are
Good, bad, and all the way
along.
He's the same yesterday,
Today, and forever;
Fo if *our* love is the same,
Should we turn on Him, no
never!
Remember He loves you,
Through thick and through thin;
Nothing can separate us,
With *His* love we can win.

John I. Hancock
INTERLUDE
Alone at last, close to each
other,
Passionate whisper, "You're my
lover."
Look at drunken splendor in
the moon.
Love never comes too soon,
An interlude.
To keep our secrets, we'll
conspire
With magical moonlight, dying
fire,
Fondly pledge love forever.
We'll be true, no other
Shall intrude.
Fiercely beat a pagan measure.
Celebrate love and pleasure.
Hurry, hurry let's begin
Before we're late and ruin
Love's mood.

Nora Herring
TIME
When I look into the distance,
It's closing in on me.
I can almost see it
In my aimless reverie.
I feel it passing by me
Heading for the night.
That's when I try to hold it
Up into the light.
Sunset is changing colors
At a distance in the sky.
Red and orange and black
Fades into the night.
Time, stop I want to yell at it
Time, don't leave me all alone.
Because I need this time,
Time to get me home.

Lois Barton
SISTERHOOD
For many years I've supervised
As barnyard mothers tend
their young,
Washing their ears and
scratching fleas;
With rough tongue licking off
the dung.
Those barnyard babies are like
mine.
They keep on coming back for
more.
When baby stands as high as
mom
She still performs her daily
chore.
This morning I looked on a
while
As doe caressed her yearling
fawn.
Both neck and ears were
groomed in style
Before the young one ambled
on.
For months I've scolded doe and
twins.
Each night they raid my
garden plot.
The rose bush is a skeleton,
Young fruit trees eaten back
to naught.
And now I must revise my view.
She's just a wild deer from the
wood,
But loves and tends her babies
too.
Can I deny our sisterhood?

Mary M. Burzinski
MISTAKEN IDENTITY
She looked like a little old lady
(Her long hair was her charm)
He walked up to her gallantly,
And took her by the arm—
He wanted to help her cross the
street
(He was one of those "good
guys")
But when she socked him in the
eye
She took him by surprise.
When she gave him an upper
cut
That's when he broke and ran
For he'd discovered this little
old lady
Was really a little old man!

Loreta Inman
CHRISTMAS
Why
Do we
Celebrate?
To glorify
God.

Bob Barci
INNER SILENCE
Here I sit, among a room full
of people,
Lost in my thoughts that have
drowned out their noise.
I resemble my thoughts,
Lost-in vast blackness,
Lost-in vast emptiness.
Floating around for so long in
this darkness is killing me,
For whenever I find some sort of
light
It quickly dies out.
I treasure the light for it
rarely comes.
When it does, I grab hold and
try to brighten it,
But, it quickly dies out, and I'm
afloat in my mind again,
Searching for the light.
I know the light exists—
Some place.

Betty Adams
A THANKSGIVING FACT
The stove is flaming red fire
real hot
The cook, mistress, woman of
the house
Has started her day with
preparing for the feast
Soon the family and friends will
be ready to eat
Some offer to assist her in
arranging the meal
Everything one could think
of is with the deal
My how the table all
decorations are exact and neat
One has to thank the one above
a many
Cost so little, yet so much
money
Who cares the ones we love are
so very precious to say
Candles burn as happy as they,
for all together to be
For many a Thanksgiving Day
A happy prosperous
Thanksgiving many

Cathie Lee Frazier
WHO AM I?
Who am I?
When the legend dies?
Will I be remembered—
or just another faded ember.
Will I be remembered when I
am gone,
like a beautiful spring morn
and dawn.
Or as a rainy day, gray and
cold,
so useless and so old.
What have I done that
surpasses,
and stand out among the
masses?
What phrases or words did I say,
that people will benefit from
day after day?
Was I the person I really could
have been,
or did I borrow more than lend?
Was I flexible enough to say
"That's O.K.",
or did I always utter, NO WAY"?
It's so strange watching my
passing,
people looking over me and
asking,
"Who is this? How did she go"?
Caretakers shaking their heads
saying, "I don't know".
It is too late to change all that
I have done,
for last night was my last
setting sun.
If I had the chance tonight,
I'd get up from deaths bed and
make it all right.

M. W. Bellesfield
ERIC
A passing thought.
New life begun.
With passing time
The moment comes.
The pain; a cry.
The surge of blood.
A miracle of parenthood!

Patricia Ann Grossie
WHERE SINGS A SOUL
Where sings my heart but
where the bluebird flies or
where meets the ocean to the
sky, somewhere farther than
where dreams are thought to
scheme as they float by.
Where sings the wind its own
songs but in its own embrace of
all along their way I say.
For merry sings the heart of me
as though to embrace the wind
in dance, for fleet of foot is my
spirit bright when touched by
Spirit's might.
For do not the fleeting wings of
songs touch each mortal on
life's journey long, as journeys
the wind with lovely songs?
Where sings love in the songs
of the wind but where-ever
treads the wind I say, but only
Spirit knows the way.
Speedily travels love songs in
the wind like answered prayers
to humble hearts in need,
somewhat like tears heal
hurting soul's deeds when
nobody sees and nobody hears
but Spirit and thee.
Where sings the wind swept
shores of time like waves roam
free the restless sea?
Mystic be the tides of time like
heart's songs singing in the wind
to remind us to listen well for
soul's songs will surely call not
to some but all.
Where sings my heart when the
silver moon wanes cold in
masked abode and the bold
darkness of night in silence
marches an untraveled road?
Amidst the dust and clay of me
broken and in pieces though I
be, still I look but need not
see, for Spirit's songs of soul
sing for you and me.

Fern Baker
MY MOM
My mom was the queen of
mothers
Beautiful, kind, and true,
Loving and so close to you.
She could cook, bake, and sew,
She knew her bible thru and
thru.
Her lovely garden was planted
row by row,
And kept so clean by her dear
old hoe.
She loved her church and
believed in God.
She loved her children and
home—
Never cared for society and
roam.
She was beautiful thru and thru.
All her friends bound to know
That her home was made of firm
belief
Based on the words of God.
She is missed by all who loved
her—
Especially her children, who'll
never forget
The kindness and teachings she
Gave them—
Precious memories,
Oh! How Sweet.

Joseph P. Catallozzi
UNTITLED
Spent many years upon this
ground,
old tree, of tarnished brown,
Outstretched arms into clean
air,
warming in the sunset's glare,
Till that night the clouds crept
in,
misty cold, very grim,
Rain tore off your tarnished
sheathing,
stopped your rhythmic
breathing,
Now you are dead, no longer can
be,
old brown, tarnished tree.

Nancy M. Collett
COMPLICATIONS
I complicated yours, and you
complicated mine.
Two lives that met on a
summer's eve,
and ran for what only seemed
like light years.
And in running we reached
out—touched—loved as
summer people do,
warm and mellow.
When did our summer end?
Why didn't I notice you running
away and not with?
Was it complications from
your not so long ago past
that made our present
impossible?
Complications that drew the
warmth of your nearness away
from my heart,
forming tears in eyes that
adoringly believed you were
the saviour of
my meek soul.
Raindrops fall now and August
puddles are born, and settle
muddy on the corner.
My life sits muddy, too.
Unclear and unattached.
Confused by—complications.

Edward Carl Farris
I'VE BEEN A FOOL
Ask me not why I give you
things;
it's not easy for me to explain.
You might as well ask why
flowers
need sunshine and soil and
rain.
Do you ever ask why birds
like to sing, or find mates,
or fly;
why Tumbler pigeons tumble
as they play in the summer
sky?
Do you ever ask, or wonder,
why bees produce so much
honey?
why a woman, to keep her
beauty,
would spend every cent of her
money?
Do you ever ask why a
mountain
is made up, mainly, of stone?
why corn must ever grow corn;
why a dog likes to gnaw on
his bone?
Would you ask why a captured
fox
is so hard to befriend or tame?
why one man prefers anonymity,
while another strives for
fame?
It was only last week that I felt
as young as a boy in school,
but then a friend set me
straight.
Now I know how I've played
the fool.
Ask me not why I give you
things;
it's not easy for me to explain.
I suppose you could say it's a
paradox;
like love and sorrow. . .and
pain.

Dorothy J. Jones
I CAN COME BOLDLY
I can come boldly to the
heavenly throne,
Because I'm never, never alone,
Jesus is with me, there to
intercede,
asking the Father for all that
I need.
I have been to the cross, and
there with the Savior,
I was crucified, My sins all
forgiven,
My own self Denied.
He took His life up again and
gave me my own,
That's why I can come boldly
to the Heavenly throne.
Nevertheless I say thy will,
not mine be done,
and I ask in the Name of
JESUS, God's own Son.
Then I go rejoicing along
life's way,
praising the Savior day after
day.
I will praise Him for ever for
the truth that I know,
And He will go with me
wherever I go.
And if I trust Him for all of
my needs,
I can come boldly down on my
knees;
Asking the Father in Heaven
above,
Knowing He will answer with
His Tender Love.

Philip Arnold Johnson
CINNABAR TEA
There once was a lady who lived
on Rainier
That bought on her birthday
a blue cavalier
She drove into market and met
on a ramp
A rogue in a rolls that was
trimmed like a tramp
She beamed at his bonnet he
hmmmed at her hood
She offered apparel would make
him look good
They flew up to college and laid
out the loot
To buy half a tweed of all prime
Qiviut
She sewed and she hemmed to
fashion him clothes
Now they live near the pool
close to Harrison Close.

W. A. Alviso
LIVING SENSE
Man alive, or is he dead?
Sometimes I wonder, if he's in
my head.

Does man exist?
I cannot resist, the "Wonder" of
us all.
Touch to feel,
Look to see,
Listen to hear,
Breathe to smell, and—
Lick to taste.
All in all, I *must* think. .,
To know.
Knowledge—
Sixth sense, or living sense?
I think—

Robert David Boatwright

LOVE SONG

Tis' nice this wooing of me
Tragedy comes as we will see
Marriage is made here on earth
Parting is part of that sad
ol' dearth.
Loving me while you can
Isn't it enough that I'm your
man?
Sickness is yours to claim for
sure
Seeing its wrong why should I
endure?
You've done your best to put
me down
And all I did was clown around
Isn't sad this emptiness inside?
Your vicious feelings you
cannot hide.
Now at last we say good-by
Our love was once very high
Reality of love is it always
stays
If you had it, we would have
had merry days.

David E. Barnes

FOREVER, THE SHORTEST LIFE OF LOVE

From the beginning.
From the rivers comes the sea,
They will flow. It will be.
Touch a rainbow with a star
my perfect spectrum there
you are.
Then the life.
If you would move me to do
great things,
touch me with your smile.
Nothing moves me more.
And then good-bye.
Let me not say good-bye and
lose you,
but let me say so long,
you are a part of me
I cannot go.
Realization of loss.
You are nothing to me now,
for I am away from you.
It is a different world.
And then as it was from the
beginning.
For a moment,
I thought I could not dream
without you. . .
but then;
I remember that before you,
I dreamed of you.

J. Ann Farkas

THE VICTORY

Oh, Death, Where is thy sting?
When the Master standeth near.
My body is but a prison
That keeps my spirit here.
Oh Sickness. Where's thy
victory?
When the Master bore it all.
He stands by me, eternally,
He'll never let me fall.
Oh, Pain. Where is thy
agony?
When the Master softly
speaks.
Commands you, "Leave My
child alone,
Can't you see, she needs to
sleep?"
Oh, Grave, Why should I
fear thee?
When the Master bids
me, "Come."
You only hold my body,
My spirit is going Home.

Dawn Allen

OUTSIDE OUR DOOR

All my luck
to you my friend.
For the world outside
our door is unknown.
All my praise
to you my friend.
For the people outside
our door are strangers.
All my strength
to you my friend.
For the challenges outside
our door will be hard to
defeat.
And all my love
to you my friend.
For the strangers outside
our door know not of
young, vulnerable hearts.

Elizabeth Tucker Carleton

TRIBUTE TO MY DOG

She looks at me, puzzled.
Can it be
That this human will fail to see
The gnawing hunger of
dependency?
Then her courage returns
And expectancy,
Expressed in her language
Quite definitely.
Throw her a bone?
Not me, not me—
I respect her dignity.

Thomas W. Faranda

SPREAD THE PETALS GENTLY

The most beautiful part of a
flower
is the part we see the least of.
But it is there. . .
hidden amidst the petals;
waiting to open,
to be warmed,
to be noticed;
People
are like flowers. . .
Spread the petals gently.

Walter S. Brown

HOPE

I see a leaf that is growing
so green,
It is trying it's best to try
and be seen.
It even waves when there is
wind,
It's just it's Love it is trying
to send.

Clara M. Bush

ANGEL MOTHER

Angel mother mine,
Wrap me in your shawl
Draw me to your breast,
Just one more time;
Kiss away my pain,
Dearest mother, Angel fair,
Soon forever in thy loving care.

Maude G. Allen

TAKE IT OR LEAVE IT

A monkey once related
To mortal man one day,
"How come you have changed
In your looks and ways?
How you've changed so in
beauty
Over passing times
While I'm still a monkey
With no education of rhymes.
You are smarter than we,
For you celebrate Christmas
And have known all the time
You didn't descend from us.
Many of us are captured
And live in a zoo
And oft times you commit
crimes
For just a nickel or two.
So, I'll still stay a monkey
And sit on a limb,
Eat bananas and coconuts
While you keep looking trim.

Betty Lou Berney

MAKE ME BE JUST A WOMAN

I'm really not the super woman
the world thinks I should be
And now life is so muddled, I've
lost all reality.
Pressure from society has not
been really right,
'Cause much is left undone
now—my schedule is too
tight!
Can't listen to my children
or take time out for you
And sharing our love is one
thing, that is past due.
Make me be just a woman—
take me in your arms and hold
me.
I'm tired of everyone a tellin'
me what I had ought to be.
Make me be just a woman
Tell me all the things I want
to hear
Love and protect me, kiss away
every tear.
I'm tired of all the ERA when
things could be alright
Without us going off to war and
joining in the fight.
Women now have got
themselves worked right into
the ground
And things are getting worse
now, as we go round and
round.
We're trying to do two jobs now,
instead of just the one
'Cause woman's work is never
done while man works 'sun to
sun.'
If this is liberation, then why
am I not free?
I'm more tied up than ever,
and that's what puzzles me.
The TV and the radio says
woman's got it made
Now that we are working and
the money we are paid.
But now there's little time left,
for my family and me,
My schedule's tearing us apart,
since they have set me free!

Charlene Comstock Frazier

SPRINGTIME

I saw a robin today.
And buds just coming to life,
Shapes of geese went honking
by

And colorful kites flew high.
I have a feeling it's spring
My heart is so light and gay
Let's fly with the singing
bluebirds
Beyond and over the hills.

Tony Echevarria

THE RAT RACE

Sweetly colored children skip
off to school with
Their textbooks and shiney
apples.
The prisoners march in drab
grey stripes and dark numbers.
Keenly colored businessmen
rush off to work with
Their briefcases and shiney
reports.
The serfs live shackled to the
soil that feeds them.
Gayly colored politicians run off
to rallies with
Their tax cuts and shiney
promises.
The puppets dance with tight
strings and painted smiles.
Glamorously colored
revolutionaries sneak off to
plan with
Their red flags and shiney
weapons.
The pawns are expendable in
the war games.
Blankly colored scientists stalk
off to conventions with
Their data and shiney theories.
The blindman with dark
glasses stumbles even in the
light.
The racing rats run their rat
race
From dawn to dusk,
From birth to death,
From generation to generation.
How well they run, so fast are
they.
So fast they blend together.
Blending, at last, into the lies
For which they run.

Marjorie Edminster

THE FLAG

I can really wave from the
flagpole
To all the people going by,
I have stars which shine like
The ones in the sky;
I have stripes of two different
colors
They are made of red and white,
I'm put up in the morning
And taken down at night;
Many call me "Old Glory"
And my glory will never fade,
I am hung from almost each
window
And carried in every parade;
I've been torn in lots of battles
To a very old looking rag,
But America salutes me
For you see I am their flag.

Rose C. Edwards

STONE WALLS OF TIME

Man, espaliered
On the stone walls of time
Grows strong and stronger,
Nurtured by the substance
In which he stands.
Fed by the springs of sorrows
And the living waters of dreams,
Opens Neanderthal eyes
And catches a gleam
Of an inner glow
Luring him upward
As far as his soul will go.

Merle V. DePuydt

WHAT IS A GRANDSON?

He's a heavenly gift from above,
A little boy for us to love.
He's sometimes very noisy
As he jumps from here to there

His eyes are full of joy
This darling little boy.
His pockets full of everything
A ball, a knife, a few marbles
and some string.
He doesn't talk softly as he has
his say
He speaks right out in his own
way.
Sometimes he baffles everyone.
God bless you my dear
grandson.

Mary Kathryn Delaplain
SECOND THOUGHTS
Although flustered,
Yet I mustered
Energy for the task.
I, though fluttered,
Never muttered
When refused what I asked.
I'll again flow
With time I know.
My work has filled my flask.

Charles J. Dertinger
MOUNT RUSHMORE—AMERICA'S PROGRESS
To Washington, Jefferson,
Lincoln and Theodore
Roosevelt,
Hallowed site, we dedicate
thee, our lasting tribute dwelt,
Eternal in our memory, each
gave our country aid!
Undaunted by opposing odds,
this Land of Liberty made.
Nation in the making, upon July
the Fourth
In Seventeen Seventy-Six, my
friends, our Independence
wrought.
To Jefferson, the drafter and
others of that band,
Endless praise be given for the
Freedom of our land.
Dreams of closer unity, our
sired signed—remember?
Seventeen Eighty-seven on the
Seventeenth of September;
The greatest paper of all times
our history relates,
A document called: "the
Constitution of the United
States."
These set of rules we're
governed by, ensuring lest we
fall,
Equal Liberty, Justice and
Domestic Peace for all.
Such were the deeds of early
men upon America's shore,
Of how our land did prosper,
this poem will tell more.
First added to our growing land,
by Louisiana Purchase,
Arkansas, Oklahoma, Iowa and
Wyoming's space;
Mississippi's River, its' waters
all so vast,
Extending from Lake Itasca, to
Mouth of Southwest Pass.
Receiving all of Colorado and
Louisiana,
Included in that tract of land
was Western Montana;
Close areas, all bought from
France, title—clear and free,
As of December 20th, Eighteen
Hundred Three.
Later to our holdings, we added
Florida's coast;
On this occasion citizens,
Spain was our host—
Negotiations were started and
America's claims were seen,
Getting it by purchase in
Eighteen Nineteen.
Many trials arose as Texas
Independence sought,
American settlers with the
Mexican Government fought;
Yet in Eighteen Forty-five,
December Twenty-nine,
We admitted Texas as the next
State in line.
Establishing a meeting at
Guadeloupe-Hidalgo,
Served to sign a Treaty of
Peace and the annals show:
Upon the Second of February of
Eighteen Forty-eight,
Republic of Mexico ceded us
that date—
Verdant California and New
Mexico,
In beauty, minerals and wealth
see our nation grow.
Vast our nation's getting, as
our sires schemed,
Even growing greater—than
their fondest dream.
We settled Oregon's question in
Eighteen Forty-six,
In compromise with England,
this boundary line was fixed:
"The forty-ninth, north latitude
was the lines' division;
Hence, land between 42° and
49° 's was ours' by decision.
Peace has settled on the land,
the Civil War is o'er,
Enabling us to deal with the
country of Russia for:
Alaska rich in gold and seals, a
truly furry heaven,
Completed October Eighteenth,
Eighteen Sixty-seven.

Florence Battenberg Doty
SOLITUDE
Have you ever felt the joy
and bliss,
Of just one hour of solitude?
Tis good for the soul to be
alone,
And spend a time in pensive
mood.
Take inventory of thyself,
Perchance the Master stands
close-by,
If burdens seem too hard to bear,
wear a smile, instead of a sigh.
Have you ever longed for quiet
and peace,
Hope to banish all cares away?
Have you ever walked alone
with God?
He will brighten your darkest
day,
So, walk with Him, and talk
to Him,
His gracious presence, ne'er
exclude,
Take time each day to be alone,
And spend one hour in solitude.

Laura J. Dufresne
RETIREMENT
I was walking down the road
one day,
When I saw an old man who
stopped to say,
Tis a fine morning my dear girl,
And he gave a quick smile and
did a little whirl.
Then he laughed real loud, and
jumped for joy,
Like a happy little child with
a brand new toy.
He said he came from the other
side of the hill,
Where stands a broken old
aging windmill.
I've been working there for years
and years,
He said with eyes full of shiny
happy tears.
And now my day has come to
retire,
To sit in a rocking chair in front
of a fire.
To sleep in every morning as
long as I please,
And lock up the mill and throw
away the keys.
I've got me a mind to take a
little trip,
Or get me some tea, and drink
it sip by sip.
To get up and go without
having to hurry,
Just to relax and not have to
worry.
Worry about deadlines or not
making enough to eat,
I'm letting someone else grind
and mill the wheat.
Yes siree my girl I'm gonna
have a ball,
And if theres fun things to do
I'm gonna do them all.
Nothings ever gonna stop me
anymore,
Until I'm standing in front of
that golden door.
Then he winked and smiled and
said have a nice day,
And tell the whole wide world,
I'm on my way.

Pauline P. Dwight
SPACE
This velvet sky of black
Dotted with a million stars
Shining down upon this earth,
Sending their messages
Which fall unheard.
The sun, the moon
These other worlds
Their shafts of light,
Light the uneven paths
Of this universal life.
The clouds of endless mists
Forever doomed to wander
In outer space,
Covering this world below,
This earthly place,
That forever turns upon
Its' Axis,
Until its' final doom.

Jean Campbell
SIMPLY LOVING
You found me a battered soul,
a lonely, stormy beach—
the happiness I'd tried to find
was always out of reach.
I'd tried so hard to please the
world—
it always wanted more,
until I stopped and asked
myself
who was I living for?
You took me where you found
me,
didn't alter, bend or change.
You said there's nothing about
me
you'd like to rearrange.
And so I give my love to
you—
it's easy, and it's free—
now isn't that how all good
loving
really ought to be?
We're all a part of Nature,
In His image we are made.
The differences between us,
like wildflowers in a glade
just serve to make more
beautiful
this world that we share—
I'm glad you looked into my
heart
and liked what you found
there.

Mrs. Elizabeth Cardwell
MOON DREAM
I dreamed I walked on the moon
with you.
The surface was coated with
azure blue
The atmosphere we rated fine
Better than being on cloud nine
We floated around to see
everything
You picked up a moonstone and
made me a ring
But an end soon came to my
wondrous dream
When into my window danced a
moonbeam
I awoke to find I was back on
earth
Home at last and full of mirth
On earth or the moon one thing
is true
If I have my way—I'll walk with
you.

John R. Clough
AFTER THE RAIN HAS GONE
Exposed, cracked and dry,
Hither the rain has long passed,
Left now are only traces by and
by
Of memories long surpassed.
But come again this rain
And the creek will run full,
Bringing with it the smell of
Faint autumn harvest and crisp
air.
And a new beginning,
And thoughts of summers past,
With hopes for future profit
And more times like these,
Blended with the mellow feeling
That a shot of liquor brings.
A short full life it is,
World without much care,
A life full of victories,
Defeats, and despairs,
But never without hope,
All to be seen on a trip
After the rain has gone.

Nancy Conjura
INEQUITIES OR TREASURES
Somewhere:
brain cells are starved
in an underfed child,
growth ceases,
body weakens.
Elsewhere:
a baby thrives,
mind nourished,
frame strong,
some have riches
Beyond all human needs,
yet, to others
a loaf of bread
and drink of wine
are priceless. . .

RV Cottam
TRULY NEEDY
You've heard of hospitals for
Veterans
where all you have to prove
is that you are, indeed, a Vet
Now hear of hospitals for the
Aged
where all you have to prove
is that you are old
and that you have pain
and that your claimed need
(you've heard the loud refrain)
is "truly needy"
of relief from pain—
having passed the threshold of
endurance,
like certain people I could name
have passed the threshold of
sanity
and cashed in their tickets
for a compassionate trip
on the rickety train
headed toward humanity.

Judy Lane Baldwin
AFTERGLOW
You cupped my up-turned face
And kissed me, just before the
 dawn.
"I love you", said your eyes;
Your lips just sighed "goodbye"
And you were gone. . . . .
I watched as skies grew light
And swirling winds blew dust
 and leaves
Behind you on the road.
When I could see no more,
I moved at last to go inside,
Then sat, and, like a candle,
Glowed.

Printice Barker
JESUS MY SAVIOUR
Jesus Christ was sent down from
 above,
By our Heavenly Father to show
 us His love.
Jesus my saviour, my king and
 my Lord,
I love and adore Him, and
 believe on His word.
He was born in a manger and
 lay there to rest,
By His dear mother, Mary who
 loved Him best.
Jesus grew up a carpenter
 working with his hands,
He was always helping others
 and doing God's commands.
He went about curing sickness
 and healing the blind,
He helped the poor and lame,
 and those sick in mind.
He was nailed to a cross at
 calvary,
And died for all sinners
 including even me.
He loved us so much He was
 willing to die,
So that some day we can meet
 Him up in the sky.
he is now in heaven at my
 Father's right hand,
Jesus is there interceding for
 poor sinful men.

Darrell W. Brown
TCB
Whether taking a long shot,
 Extraordinary chance,
Or two whispering in the
 moonlight
 With a loving glance
Taking Care of Business
 Means Romance.
I may not be able to do it
 As well as he or she,
Or apply the right ingredients
 So my lover won't flee,
But when the moon is right
 And there's a breeze in the
 tree,
You might find someone and
 T C B.

M. Crawford Anderson
WAITING FOR DEATH
Many the tangled thoughts,
 confused
And wandering, slide through
 my mind. . . .
I fold my hands and bide my
 time.
These years of illness, crying
 and despair,
Have made me calm, but, still I
 cannot bear
To tell the loneliness that's
 mine.
Waiting alone; amid'st the
 hurrying throng
Of strangers, each with purpose,
 plan and goal,
I feel myself invisible; on shoal.
I find I have no need for
 industry, or
Plan; but spend these hours
 suspended,
Absorbing the whole.

Robert S. Appel
COMBAT
Did'ya ever walk 'No Man's
 Land'
After day passed to night?
And feel the cold and ghostly
 still
Preceding ev'ry fight.
Thrumming nerves and silent
 voices
Blends a mystical spell
That chills the soul of ev'ry man
Who plods his way through hell.
Did'ya ever wish tomorrow
Was just a day before?
Or today would be tomorrow
With fears you needn't store.
That Jerry would have planned
 retreat
In pompous Nazi style
And all that 'would-be-shootin'
 hell
Could cease for just awhile.
Did'ya ever dread the orders
When attack had begun?
And one by one a comrade fell
Another Mother's son
'Tis haunting to know a buddy
Who just a moment past
Was living with a fleeting hope
That this was not his last.
This self-same hope that filled
 his heart
Bade mine to carry on
But then as if by fate decreed
I fell and I was gone
There I lie on alien soil
A comrade—one more son
Living, dying, yet listening for
That still small voice of One. . .
From One whom at the dawn of
 day
And then again at night
Keeps asking man to hold his
 faith
And not give up the fight
Did'ya ever pause. . .talk with
 God
When Satan was your guest?
Then you've cherished
 interruption
And found man's priceless quest.

E. Grayce Berger
OUR LAWRENCE WELK
A country lad with heart of
 gold
Said to himself one day
I want a band "My very own"
Where I can work and play.
So with this thought he started
 out
To make his dream come true
And bring fulfillment to his
 days
To last a whole life through.
With diligence he worked and
 planned
In that small country town
The challenges he met were
 great
But later brought renown—
Each year he gained because he
 gave
To youth along the way
A chance to show their many
 gifts
In such a bright display.
Through work and prayer and
 faith in God
He's reached the height of fame
Each race and creed around the
 world
In "Honor" speak his name.
An earnest prayer from grateful
 hearts
Goes forth throughout the land
That God will bless and safely
 keep
Dear Lawrence and "His Band"

Donald E. Benson
PLACE
Deep within still life,
the surface of the soul
can be scratched
like old skin
on
a frozen moon,
though known but slowly
above this dream.
Faint wounds have no real
effect when space and time
embrace in
the best sense,
and,
as distant lights,
advance beyond our
pool of metal.

L. Jessie Bennett
WINDS
Winds, winds that crazily blow
 across the barren plains,
Or swiftly slip high into an
 unknown sphere,
Thus on to bow low Burmuda
 fields of cane,
Winds that set the stalks,
 reeling, waving, bending in
 despair.
Quiet, whispering vespers join
 and rapidly grow
To agitate from calm to angry
 the rolling ocean waves,
The wayward gales then sweep
 wildly, gathering great rains
 in tow,
The wild motion leveling
 homes, trees and ships to
 jumbled graves.
Fall winds gently cross the tall
 mountain ranges,
Caressing and whispering to
 the slowly dying leaves,
Urging and hurrying their fall
 while painting wild color
 changes,
Demanding a quick parting from
 the limbs to which they
 cleave.
Oh, the wild, wild winds take
 heed from the dying sun,
And sweep down valleys,
 fanning sparks to blazing fury,
Roaring and booming as the roll
 of a great gun,
The winds and fire mate to
 become twins of death and
 fury.
The warm, sensuous winds
 awaken rain-laden clouds in
 the sky,
Bringing water down upon
 wide fields of growing grain,
Sweeping onto meadow where
 broad green grasses lie
Flooding every crooked, tree-
 lined lane.
The four winds, like their
 brother weather, all through
 the ages,
Have been deemed responsible
 for the fear of things
 unknown,
Have upset and changed the
 bright props of many of life's
 stages,
Lives, loves have changed just
 because those wayward winds
 have blown.
Winds, winds—gentle, silent or
 strong are in every clime,
 nature's motion
Roiling, swirling, wedded to
 green earth and darkening
 sky,
Gentle, still, mysterious
 continuous emotion;
Rising now heavenward to
 commune on high.

June Kaul
BUT THERE ARE TIMES
Ah,
Free and unencumbered
Strong and undaunted
Steadfast and sure
But. . .
There are times
When one loses focus
And strength turns
 to mush
When thoughts bounce around
 like a ball
 on a soft
 rubber string
Never connecting
Till they hang loose
 limp
 waiting. . .
And you wish
 for a match
 to light the inner furnace
A valet
 to dress
 the outer man
A pup
 to hold your leash.
Then a friend says,
 'You know,
 you really look like hell
 today!
And you laugh
 at him
 and then at yourself
And with that laugh
 the Spirit
 seeps back into the soul
You feel the velvet glow
 of a friend
You see the joy
 in the morning light
And you flush
 with eager anticipation
And go about your day
 doing your thing.

Vera Cassell Keffer
OH BEAUTIFUL SUMMER
Oh beautiful summer
 what a short stay,
But you have graced our fields
 with flowers since May.
Busy days of summer,
 Oh how they flee.
You just don't leave
 much time for me.
I want to do some sewing
 But the garden needs hoeing,
There's places to be going
 But the grass needs mowing
Come on Peaceful Autumn
 with colors of gold and wine
I'll drag up my lawn chair
 and then I'll recline.

Charles W. Kennedy
JOURNEY TO THE FURTHER STATION
In some, talent stops
 short.
 Dies.
But to those who have courage
 to accept challenge
and the talent to accomplish
 something more—
there is the journey to the
 further station.
 To a lively continent.
 To new ventures and
 accomplishments.
And happy remembrances and
 reunions.

Enno Klammer
PARTED

One flesh. . .
A man shall cleave into his wife,
Shall leave his father
and his mother and
the two shall be
one flesh. . .
my bones
my flesh.
In sorrow she brought forth
a child,
our child,
our first—
a fragment of a poem
the Author soon withdrew
from public view.
Our children
three
she bore—
three gems;
the Author still at work
revising them—
and me—
each day
His way—
still fragments of the poem
This life
His life
makes whole, ,
binds up the bruised reed
and fans the dimly-burning flame
to brilliant light
where we shall see Him
face to face
and know as we are known.
We are His own.
Herself
a part of me
yet part of Him.
No fragment now,
for she is whole
and,
parted,
I am part—
a fragment still,
a fragment of His poem.
Ah! Poet!
Shaper!
Maker!
Cast your spell
and make us whole—
no fragments then;
no fragment of a poem—
when all is well.
Amen. Amen.

Karen Koal
A SEED

She opens her back door,
steps outside.
Dressed in a gown
woven of silk threads
from the corn field
where she played.
She yawns, covers her mouth
with a newly sprouted leaf,
stretching for the sky.
She steps back inside.
Her face lined by rivers
deep.
Her eyes no longer light
up as a cats at night.
She stands
waiting,
As the roosters pass her by.
They lust for her no more.
She is an ear of corn
ready to be picked
in early—
spring.

Willard Wood Lawrence Sr.
GIVE A LITTLE— GAIN A LOT

When called upon to do your best;
Whate'er the task might be,
Be sure you're able to stand the test;
Do what is asked for, happily.
Give of your strength, resourceful youth;
Show that you have what it takes.
Stand up for the right, expound the truth!
You'll expose the ones who are fakes.
Throw into a job your soul's fresh ardor;
Be confident that you'll succeed;
For the person who tries a little harder
Untold benefits, He'll reap, indeed.
Many before you, have set the pace
They are willing to lend a hand;
Hold up your head, show your smiling face;
Be ready to take the right stand.
The person who is always ready to serve
And devote his best to a job,
Will never be wanting, But will always deserve
A place that's up near the top.
Yes, give of your best to God, and Mankind
Give God first place in your heart;
If the task seems hard, don't cease to grind;
For, at least, you have made a start.
Now, when you know that you've done all that's asked;
You may look back, and say with pride,
"I knew when I started, I'd complete this task;
I had help, with Him at my side."
Don't go with the mob, to selfish aims,
That's the easier way, perhaps;
To go it alone, may mean Tough Terrain
If you sidestep, pitfalls, and traps.
Go set your course, and focus your eye
Don't be waivered, in your stand;
You'll find then the pie, that's in the Sky,
And You'll reach that PROMISED LAND!

Teresa F. Lancaster
DEATH

Words can not express a meaning
when the one you love is gone,
and only you are here, left to carry on.
Death is such a sad affair, but in our hearts we will rejoice,
For now he's with the God Almighty,
because that was his choice.
There is no pain in dying
except in the souls of others,
and the pain is increased 1000 times
when the friend is like your brother.
We are so very sorry
our condolences we do share
and these are just a few lines
to let you know we care.

Betsi Lattimer
SO SIMPLE

so simple.
All Philosophies
Merge and Converge and. . .
condense to become
little girl squeals.
little girl squeals or
little boy laughter
pure and true and. . .
uncorrupted
stainless steel.
new fallen snow or
first bud in spring
delight. . .
little girl squeals.

George L. LaNeve
PAEAN FOR A HUNTER

LET ME:
Wander in the hills again,
Feel the wind and the rain,
Walk alone in the morning dew,
Breathe the heady, potent brew,
See the sights from a lofty ridge,
Gaze at a road and wooden bridge,
Hark to the bugle of baying hounds,
Listen to the many thrilling sounds,
Bask in the sun on an October morn,
Hear the echo of the hunter's horn;
Find my rest beneath that ground,
Under sweep of wind and bay of hound.

LeeAnn P. Lawrence
JUST ONE MORE MINUTE

Just one more minute my darling
I will be there right away
I have a little chore to do.
So sit there by the fire
Relax until I come;
I will put the children down to bed
Then I will bring you a rum.
Now we are alone
The kids are asleep
We can watch the fire
And think of our dreams.

Daniel Lee
A LONELY RENAISSANCE

The galaxy narrowed and gathered into a shaft of light
Then froze still as a stream in the midst of night
A column of ice glittering in the lonely sky
Bright with fiery stars in heaven's glinting eye
It began to swirl, spin, and twist
Sending ripples of reflections through the timeless mist
The gloom remains unaltered; the birth unnoticed
Witness the barren orb of a reborn earth
The sky arched at its culminating peak
Then circled and waned to and fro beckoning all to see
And across its black dome stood many a streak
The flitter of fiercer stars in an endless sea
Beamed outward, the starlight reaches toward eternity
Past the moon, radiant in splendor, yet subtle in its wake
Bound for the Creator, a billion voices cry out in agony
Envision our once illustrious planet
Now useless yet always moving
Always changing yet never ceasing
Under the burning sun and filling the empty sky
All other worlds are but mere ashes laid to rest
Yet the earth twinkles in the vast nebulae of existence
A ball physically in motion yet all else suspended, dying
As the sky and the heavens watch in dreaded silence
A mysterious figure appears and shatters the morbid gloom
The curtain of fate sways, a mirror is seen all too soon
And in this mirror stands this reflection of post-doom
The door in space opens; the lonely image steps through
The figure stands upon a silver pedestal up high
And points to a pale orb in the darkened sky
He delivers his message to ears that are full
I gave you all you needed to survive,
Love and warmth, kindness and strength
What went wrong? Why am I all alone?"
His words are unheard
A tear rolls down his saddened face and falls
upon his broken heart. . .

Esther Legacy
EQUALITY IN COMMONAGE

Thou art equal, said the document of Community,
Drafted by the Constituents, of Constitutional decree.
How can this be, for it contradicts all that I see.
Tis a moumenon conceived by understanding,
Not a phenomenon beyond my reasoning.
Equality is an object in itself,
Not relatively to us.
Though it is born in commiseration,
Not to commote but to commodate the common.
Universal in principle, belonging or pertaining,
Equally to more than one, or to many indefinitely.
The nature of Mankind,
In general by Commonage,
Bearing equality from the Creator, thy God.

Robert Lillis
SURPRISES

The tingle that comes from a touch of the lovely lady
the thrill of a glance from blue eyes that hold a hint of mystery as well as a change of color
the softness of golden hair flowing gently over lovely

shoulders
the strength of one so tiny
the life that bubbles and flows
from a wit and smile that
leads her friends into gales
of laughter
the depth of thought and
emotion claimed from an
effrontery so carefree
the brilliance so hidden from
the average acquaintance
the deep committment that
shows to some who care to
see the work she does.
the talent that ebbs and flows
like life through all her
lovely body.
the love expressed in new,
exciting, intriguing touches,
movements and words.
a private openness unbounded
by past hurts, frustrations,
and defenses.
the communication that is
unspoken and often only
thought.
the deep concern to be strong,
independent, stable,
upstanding, and respected.
the need for love that wells
up with overpowering
sexuality
the physical prowess, strength
and energy that push for
involvement and
accomplishment
the expressed desire to
privately by dependent and
needed; to be fulfilled
the touch of lips that demand
so much and give more. . .

Ruby B. Lee
THE PRAYER OF STRENGTH
"OH" God give me strength."
I pray each day.
As I start my journey along
the way
Hold my hand and stay by my
side
Because Jesus it's so easy to
slide
It hurts my heart if I do wrong
Because I know you're watching
and
We should be strong
You gave your life and you
shed your
"Blood" so,
"God" please give me strength
So I'll do no wrong.

Catherine Susan Lipske
COLORLESS BEAUTY
Colorless beauty
A raindrop falls
Wet
Cool
And daring
Green grass
Swaying in time—
the wind
Breathless ecstasy—
soaring
As a bird
Freedom
Visions, thoughts,
Reasoning
Toes touching sand—
imprints
Love
Again imprints—
forever
Burning soul
Colorless beauty
Teardrops fall
Wet
Hot
Frightened

Miss Jo Ann Lindemann
SO LONG AGO
Reaching into my pocket
I pull out treasures. . .
Faded newspaper clipping, rusted
pennies, and
Memories.
Days flowed
Smoothly
Like an arrowhead washing
down the path.
Life was dulcet as peach
preserves.
Worship and fried chicken
possessed Sunday
So long ago.
Burnished autumn afternoons
I tumbled in leaf piles
Mama raked.
Pitchers of sunshine pouring
on us,
Mama sang German tunes from
her childhood.
Dearest Mama
Nary a wrinkle has residence
on your face.
While standing erect as a fence
post,
Breezes whisper to you.
Silently
You reminisce of the time you
presented me
To God's earth.
Unlike cut flesh
Memories cannot be stitched
together.
Into my pocket I place my
memories wholly.
By reflections I was molded
into an adult.
A child I was
So long ago.

Eileen Loro
ALONE. . .
longingly, i dream of you, each
and every night.
recalling the touch so warm
and tender and all the power
and might.
of our passion nestled softly
(within the folds of love).
the comfort and care you freely
gave from: above
below
surrounding me. . .
causing me to feel: wanted
cared for
whole and
oh, so very real.
i am sorry that you no longer
are here.
to again share the touch
(of comfort given freely
and so ever much).
with a lovingness and caring
so lacking in this world.
will i ever fill the void i
feel as i dream of you
longingly,
and my body lies here cold.

Robin Fern Love
ODE TO A LOST LOVE
I remember a love so rare, so
very rare,
When love meant a friend and
companion.
I remember the beauty of
strength and kindness,
When this precious mold kept
me safe and warm.
I remember well the essence of
a love that
lives, and will never die.
One who is a sophisticate, yet
is not too worldly,
Who knows about life early,
Yet does not exploit his
precious knowledge.
A person who is bold, and yet
meek,
Who has understanding, fire,
and warmth.
A person who possesses the
capacity to love,
And to be loved.
Who is indispensable, can never
be underestimated,
And will never be forgotten.
I remember the charisma, the
care,
And everything in-between.
The love I lost so long ago; I
love you,
And always will.

Beulah Lowe
HE MUST LOVE US
HE must love us all, to share
his sunsets and works of art.
A free show beyond compare;
times display for day to part.
He must love us all so much,
to give us minds to admire,
what we see but can not touch.
A sky bright as fire, a sunset.
A rainbow in the sky is formal,
an arch as if by contract.
Sunsets compare but are
informal,
splashed on like an abstract.
HE must love us all to show
the glory of sunset and rainbow
scenery to paint but cannot
touch
HE must love us all so much.

E. June Mathews
SNOW MAGIC
I awoke this morning to a
beautiful sight,
Mother Nature had sifted snow
last night;
Everything was dazzling white
and clean,
Nothing familiar could be seen.
It was a trip into fairyland,
Where someone had used a
generous hand
To sprinkle sapphires and
diamonds over all—
The most fabulous display,—I
can recall.
It was truly a glimpse of
heaven,
I viewed from my windowpane;
Like the opening of a great
treasure chest,
The sun shone on diamonds at
their best.
I stood speechless,—all was
unreal,
Drinking in the beauty before
someone would steal;
Because this magic could not
last,
The diamonds would melt and
all would pass.

Robert Marons
A NICE DAY
I walked on the beach, beyond
the point where the bus could
reach.
I fed bread crumbs to the ducks
at a pond,
Where my family had visited
and were always fond.
I had a lobster dinner at a
restaurant that was near a
resort,
And visited an old-fashioned
army fort.

Nancy J. Martin
LONESOME SEARCH
One day I was walking along
my way,
Just like someone passing the
day.
Where would I stop, see, or
hear of,
The very thing we all seek—
Love
I was lonesome for someone
who,
Would fill the day for me alone.
When I would live from day by
day,
Beside me—one to show me a
way.
The sun, the stars, the moon
can see—
What we together someday
could be.
Like bright in the sky—or
dark at night,
There's always to be shown the
light.
Like this is one way to say,
Many, two or just one day,
You, me whatever be the way,
Love, will flourish, and when
you find it—it will stay.

Debby Masterson
ENACTMENT OF LOVE
I know of this man
Who from day to day,
Will squanderously spend
Most of his pay.
He'd open a fresh one
And drink it straight down
Carelessly spreading
Solitude all around.
But party-time's over
And the bills are all due
The money's a problem
Now he's feeling blue.
He finds him a subject
To take all the blame
Not realizing the heartache
Provoked by this game.
It really is saddening
For all that's involved
And the pain will keep
growing
'Til the problem is solved.
It takes a big man
To admit that he's wrong
And put back the pieces
Where they all belong.
With a new point of view
He will now look at life
Just thankful he still has
His children and wife.
Their love and respect
The future will bring
'Cause they've sworn before
God
And their symbol's a ring.
The tension will ease
And the problems seem small
'Cause together they'll learn
That love conquers all.

Esther Mazza
TEENAGE GIRL
Hey! Little girl, little girl
in your teens,
Life is not a merry-go-round,
Rock and roll in your favorite
blue jeans
But! keep your mind clear and
sound.
Little you know of the dangers
ahead.
That are sure to come if
emotions run free
So! Be yourself and don't
be led
You'll benefit later, wait
and see.
Enjoy your youth, with all its
trends—
Dance, sing and cheer for your
team
As the next generation, brings
yours to an end

And becoming a lady. 'Tis not
what it seems.
Then, will all your dreams
come true—
When you store your favorite
blue jeans?
Hey! Little girl, it's all up
to you—
Little girl, little girl in
your teens.

Miriam Mendlowitz

BEHIND EVERY CLOUD THERE IS A SILVER LINING!—

The skies are grey
The moon is bleak
The tree's don't sway
The birds don't tweet
. . .All is silent in dismay.
True, the weather's stormy
Of sun, the sky is bare
True, the ocean's balmy
And yes, the clouds *are* there
. . .But look behind them.
There, beyond this dismal
picture
Is a shimmering silver linning
There, beyond this gloomy
surface
Is an inner glow
. . .laughter, gaiety, happiness!
You could share that laughter
You could reach that glow
You could join its gaiety
You really could, I know!
. . .But first, you gotta find it.
You don't have to travel to
foreign lands
or spend a fortune while
searching
Although your home may not be
grand
It's where you should be
reaching
. . .Look everywhere, Carefully.
Look *beyond* your daily
problems
Look *behind* the leaking
sink
Look *below* the peeling ceiling
Look *aside* a scowling face
. . .Merely extend your hand.
Somewhere, beyond your reach
The answer—It's there
Waiting for someone to grasp it
Someone from Somewhere
. . .It could be you!
Soooooooo. . .
When the skies are grey
To brighten your day
Just look away.
And then you'll find
That every dreary cloud
Is actually lined.
You COULD reach that lining
But not by reclining
You gotta work for it!!!
So Smile and Do It Quick!

Kay McGary

CHICAMAUGA

The line of cannons were in
place,
From the woods edge came the
yell,
Then we saw the enemies face.
Shots rang out and men fell.
Our sights were set,
The cannons roared,
The enemies had met,
As we clashed our hearts soared.
Then as the smoke cleared
There before us we saw death
and dying.
Then we knew what we had
feared.
We felt no shame upon crying.
North against South, brother
against brother,
We were young and strong
But we were against one
another,
And deep down we sensed the
wrong.

Ozella Meek

NATURE'S LESSON

In a long forgotten fence row
Left untouched by human hand
Tangled mass of bright wild
roses,
Blossom forth to bless the land.
No one comes to prune it's
branches.
No one rakes, nor hoes, nor
tills.
Not many ever see it's beauty,
Yet in pride, it blossoms still.
Left alone, a gnarled old plum
tree,
Wafting fragrance in the spring
Wild it grows, as nature meant
it.
From it's branches, birds still
sing.
No one comes to claim it's
harvest,
No one rests beneath it's shade
Yet, there it stands on ground
God gave it,
To fill the purpose it was made.
We, too as all of God's creation,
Were given special roles to fill.
We need not strive for
recognition,
But only seek to know His will.
And though the world can't see
your value,
Perhaps yours seems a menial
task,
Just stand your ground, and fill
your purpose.
Do your best is all He asks.

Sherry C. Miller

CAUGHT IN THE TRANCE

I am tired;
And the tiredness of the body
Is not of the body,
Nor is it of the mind.
It comes from my otherness,
The strangeness that is so
Truly me that I am lost in
it's reality.

I am confused.
I have gone from one point to
another,
And now the returning is
painful.
Which bears the sameness;
Which is enduring and true;
Which is the otherness now?

Lilly Mitchell

IN AUTUMN

As I walk through my garden,
autumn leaves at my feet.
I pick the last rose, it's
fragrance so sweet.
I walk down the path where the
lilies grew.
The same path I walked so
many times with you.
The seasons come and quickly
go.
Each autumn my aging steps
grow slow.
In passing years my eyes grow
dim.
I whisper a prayer, another
season I may walk with him.
In autumn if I should go away,
then it be God's will.
All the beauty of the season
softly standing still.

J. J. Morris

FOREVER AUTUMN

You are my autumn person,
Orange and brown as the
autumn leaves,
My Taurus, brown-earth
companion.
Autumn, that glorious time of
year,
beauty to make the soul ache
for wanting to possess it,
to stop the inevitable of
its passing.
Like the butterfly that must
not be captured,
the beauty being freedom
and moving.
Like the bittersweet strain of
music
that moves through the
body,
and aches the soul in its
passing.
And the chill along your back
that tells of coming winter.
For two winters I have been
warm in your love. . . .
and my loving.
This autumn the chill is
creeping into me again,
over my shoulders, down my
arms
and into the cavity that
homes my soul.
Oh, to bring you with me in my
changing,
I am the music that is new
with each moment,
the butterfly that cannot sit
for long on one stalk,
the autumn beauty that will
pass into winter, and be
reborn spring. I cannot
forsake the
being and becoming of what
I am
You seek the comfort of the
unchanging
You would keep the leaves
on the tree,
the chill in the air.
You would keep the butterfly
on one branch.
the music repeating,
repeating, repeating.
You dare not face the winter
for the rebirth of spring.
You would stay
forever autumn

Margaret Montgomery

ODE TO A SAW HORSE

He stands spraddle legged;
paint dabs coat his armor.
His squared-head perches upon
nailed limbs, forming triangles
of perfection.
Shoulders squeak with fatigue
from
the weight of building another
day, but he has passed each
test of strength
with stoic ease.
Structured elegance escapes him,
but wherever man builds, the
wooden warrior stands
majestically at his
side,
the backbone of the
carpenter who
erects the world.
Ione Nelson

Ione Nelson

MY FATHER

My father was a handsome man,
He had a heart of gold.
He must of been a gay young
blade,
Or so the tale was told.
He had a love of music
And dearly loved to dance,
He played the fiddle very fine
Which made the ladies prance.
A square dance caller he was
not
But really tapped his toe
To keep the music on the beat
And not too fast or slow.
The night he caught young
Sara's eye,
His heart did do a flip.
And everytime that she danced
by,
His bow would take a dip.
He courted her and soon they
wed
And as the story went,
She joined with him and with
his band,
A life she felt well spent.

Paul I. Neuenswander

MY MILK COMES IN CARTONS

There was riotous joy as the
chores would progress;
For we'd jump down the hay
chute and land on old Bess.
With her heels in the air-we
would tear through the barn,
As the tussling and scuffling
would wear on the yarn.
Noise would come to an end
and the air would grow still;
once my dad and the team
would reach the wind mill.
Then we'd sit down to milk like
good farmer boys should,
Till the heifer grew tired of the
spot where she stood.
In an instant of time, I'd get
flogged by her tail,
and her foot would invariably
end up in the pail.
If my luck would hold out I'd
lose hardly a drop;
As I'd heft out her foot and skim
off the top.
At supper-with my craving for
milk on the wane,
The others would drink up and
never complain.
As is said—"the unknown
doesn't hurt folks a bit",
however, if known, they would
have had a real fit.
Now my chores are all history,
for we haven't a cow,
though at times I still crave
that stuffy hay mow.
But as my milk comes in
cartons, it's often I think,
of what might have happened
e'er I tipped up to drink.

K. J. Nelson

TO DIE

If a kitten must die,
let it die mercifully.
If a man must die,
then let him die in peace.
If a soldier must die,
his life should not have been
in vain.
If a child must die,
then let the cause be just.
For all creatures of the Earth
living is knowing life does end.
Death is an essential part of life,

it is as beautiful as birth,
as necessary as gravity,
as real as stone
and as merciful in its domain
as God in His kingdom.

Audree Nottingham
THE ETERNAL FLAME
The fire burns greatly from
within
The fire to live
The fire to build
The fire to destroy
If fed too much
Energy is quickly sapped
If fed too slow
Smothering it to death
Burning fast into oblivion
Smothering into extinction
Feed it well
Care for it tenderly
Know when to gently let it burn
down
Know when to rekindle it to
flame
Know when to watch and when
to fear
Know when to enjoy
A tiny flame glowing
Nurturing into maturity
Bringing such great and
gathering
Forces of power
The power to create or destroy
See the great lack of wisdom
See the burned acres
See the destruction
A tiny flame brought forth
To be extinguished so soon

Nancy Brier O'Neal
THE WILD STALLION
If you commit to me
The open green pastures
Of your remaining running
seasons—
To trod in
And to graze in with you;
If you award to me
The sweet-scented garlands
Of your prize-winning roses—
To humbly surround me
And my modest stables and
abode with,
Will your starvations
Forever be fulfilled?
Will your races
Be all run?
Could your meadows
Bear white fences?
Can I harness
A wild stallion?

Thomas Marvin Wooten
RECOLLECTING
I'm in the autumn of my years.
Crackling leaves rattle the nap
on the carpet of my mind
Birds song is rare.
And flies
—too busy to bother buzzing
me—
fly away from here.
Sometimes I sit on the back
porch and
wish I had canned up something
preserved for my winter days.
But all I got stashed in that
old cupboard
is a jar of wisdom that's soured.
A half pint of love that's almost
gone
And a cracked crock filled with
pebbles
from all the beaches I've roamed.
Didn't bring nothing with me—
Ain't taking nothing back in
leaving
—Not even the smell of life!

Lorraine Ortman
AUTUMN
Autumn is a time of beauty,
It is a time of falling leaves;
Children jump on them and
play;
This they can't do every day.
It's more fun in the cool breeze,
Beneath the beautiful trees.
It's a time to paint in wondrous
colors,
And to have picnics with friends
& lovers.
A time for singed
marshmellows,
A time to remember other
fellows.
A time for weenie roasts,
and how about a toast—
To praise the One who hears,
This most beautiful time of the
year.

Tamara E. Peacock
DAYBREAK
Daybreak
The lonely tree.
Its branches high
The silence of the dawn
The grace of the morning sky.
The awakening of hills.
Their color changing fast
The beauty of the early morn
The peace I've found at last.
The golden grass.
Its dryness showing death
The sadness of the lonely tree
The hope of the taken breath.
Daybreak.

Mary Lou Peterson
THE BEAUTIES OF WINTER
The trees, bushes, fences, and
poles are white with frost,
Icily hung with a frozen song.
And when the bright sun shines
upon it,
Oh, how they do glisten and
sparkle.
The branches sway with their
icy load
Where millions of diamonds
flash and glow
With a blinding glare.
The swirls of frost painted upon
the window panes
With intricate designs
That no artist can redesign.
The fresh white blanket of snow
lays upon the ground
Showing tracks of rabbits, deer,
and fox
Going in this direction and that.
In front of me, beautiful ice
formations.
Hanging down off the edges of
roofs.
Formation resembling
stalactites, of trickling,
dripping water.
These icy columns may be
needle-sharp,
long and thin, or maybe short
and fat.
Cold sun shone on glittering,
crystal frigid zone
Caught on tiny crystal surfaces
of fresh snow
Creating ice prisms over the
ground.

James K. Phillabaum
SOMEONE-SOMEWHERE
When you're down and you're
feeling blue,
Remember—someone,
somewhere cares for you.
In those times of stress and
strain,
Your problems play upon your
brain.
This can wear you out and get
you down,
This can wilt your smile into
a frown.
Please keep in mind whatever
you do,
Someone, somewhere cares for
you.
When your future looks only
dark and grey,
Ask for help and you'll find a
way.
When something awful has
shattered your dream,
Things may not be as bad as
they seem.
When "feeling down and out"
describes you too,
Remember—someone,
somewhere cares for you.
When your troubles start to
overflow,
You often wonder which way to
go.
When you feel you've been put
to the final test,
That's the time to get things
off your chest.
When you need someone to tell
your troubles to,
Remember—someone,
somewhere cares for you.
Maybe now is the time for your
own sake,
From life's daily cares to take a
break.
When no more problems can
you face,
Maybe it's time for a change of
pace.
But above all, and this is true,
Remember—someone,
somewhere cares for you.

Sibyl Jean (Jarvis) Pischke
APPARITION
The mist rising in the lowland,
Sent ghostly figures swerling
beneath the trees,
She raised a hand in ghostly
greeting,
Beckoning me.
When the shadows of the
evening
Start to climb the garden wall,
'Twas then the swaying ghostly
figure
Seemed to call.
In the springtime or late
summer,
In every season one and all,
Blending with the evening
shadows,
Against the wall.
Who was this ghostly
apparition?
Graceful swerling silver mist,
Gliding silently by my window,
Blew a kiss.
Was it father? Aunt? or Mother?
Or could it be a long lost lover?
Whispering softly, gently
swaying,
Ghostly call.
Is it wild imagination
Bringing ghostly apparitions,
Misty silver, swerling figures
Growing smaller ever bigger?
Be gone all!

Holly Pickles
LONELINESS
The pain inside tears me to
pieces.
A desperate need to talk has
overcome me,
but no one will take time out
to listen
If only there was someone who
would,
Someone to understand my
feelings,
to care in my time of dejection,
to put their arms around me,
and hold me while I speak.
Is someone listening?
Does anyone care?
Please hear me.
Please listen.
Please care.
Please.

Connie Porcher
THE TEAR-CATCHER
Daily we see them as we pass
on the street
Hearts that are breaking in
many we meet,
Arms that are heavy, knees that
are weak,
Bearing great burdens of which
they can't speak.
Eyes that no longer sparkle with
joy,
Everything shattered like
yesterday's toy,
Hearing no laughter, no smile
do they see
Searching for happiness,
"Where can it be?"
No time to listen, too busy to
hear
The weeping at midnight when
no one is near.
A kind word, a smile, to show
that we care
Would lighten, considerably,
the burden they bear.
But still we pass by, unaware of
the pain,
Thinking only this moment of
what we can gain.
Until the day comes when our
own heart breaks in two
And we know from experience
the hurt others went through.
Perhaps it's a lesson each one
of us needs.
Perhaps it's the way God plants
His love seeds
In the soil of deep sorrow,
watered by tears,
So our lives will be fruitful,
and not wasted years.
God treasures the drops from
our eyes that are shed—
In a bottle He keeps them His
Holy Word said.*
Perchance He needs helpers to
hear when they fall—
"Lord, please make TEAR-
CATCHERS of us, one and
all."
*Psalms 56:8

Carolyn Preiser
SO LONG SUBURBIA
good-bye walls
I painted fine
and matched with paper
with which it rhymes;
farewell to floors
I scraped and scrubbed
behind the slobs
who drooled their grub;
'chow', my carpets
so thick and plush
I vacuumed daily
to rid the dust;
so long range
so shiny and new
you should've cooked more
like you were supposed to;
good-bye couch
with squeeky springs
I loved to slouch
and sort out things;
farewell, teevee

someday you'll pay
for coloring my world
in a visual way;
toodles, dear bed
my favorite spot
so warm and exciting
you've got the plot!
'chow', my patio
with the morning sun
I'd burn like hell
but it sure was fun;
take care trees
you scrawny sticks
grow up straight
and oust the ticks;
good-bye grass
and diagonal lines
I busted my ass
so you'd look fine;
so long house
you sure are great
but I just can't swing it
on my welfare rate;
bye 'ole neighborhood
with streets and lights
and garbage men
decked out in white;
so long suburbia
so neat and trim
where everyone waves
and forces a grin;
so long suburbia
phones and coffee breaks
it's a cotton life
'his 'n her' mistakes;
so long suburbia
with your barking dogs
and weekends free
for fireplace and logs;
so long suburbia
and a friendly beer
trading idle gossip
to fill one's ear;
so long suburbia
neighborhood treats
people turn stale but
the air stays sweet;
so long suburbia
you spoiled me fine
you're not forgotten
just far behind.

Mary C. Puls
SORROW
Sorrow cries at me no tears
to shed
I hear the laughter of a night
time star
I once held a darkened skies
dream but now she is dead
for morning suns glitter could
never go far
and I bled but no thorns for
my rose
As I feel the wind of nightmares
icy hand
One single time the gentle
rains eyes close
Sorrow I cannot bear thy grin
Blood stained lips of wine
What once was past will begin
To ruin ancient time
and the flower shall fade once
more
Into dust behind closed door
oh how never to be seen again
Sorrow
if only to feel your pain

Jane Rachford
NO MORE WINE
Tonight after supper
You ran quickly, quietly away.
As I sit holding the hand of
darkness,
I want to know before the
Reels stop turning and our
make-believe is over,
When THE END closes our
mouths, leaving
Residual words, bitter-tasting
drops,
In the bottom of a cup when all
the good is gone.
It's better to be on our way,
away before
Goodbye sneaks into things
we say,
Turning "what's for supper" into
"I don't love you anymore."
Before you forget to leave notes
That make me smile, like:
"Jennie, Jesus loves you,
I care too."
I didn't prepare for your
leaving, and
Forgot to say I planted a garden
yesterday,
There's honeysuckle, too, close
as summer,
Just around the corner.
Two summers ago, I planted
myself into your life.
We shared suppers and each
other then,
Even the summer children
thought
We belonged that day on the
sand.
I must have known you better
than
Just a warm body or tired
smiles at sunrise.
Sharing Mateus one afternoon,
you told me
Your mustache was full of
wine and a lady's love,
Was it my body or my mouth
That made you finally run?
I am pieces of the bottle aimed
in anger,
S c a t t e r e d on the floor,
Reflecting moonlight through
the window—
A kaleidoscope puzzle.
Midnight, my life and the clock
tick away.
There's no more wine.

Sharlene Sue Adkins
PHONE CALL FROM HEAVEN
I was trodding along, my life
so full of sin
I could hear Jesus calling,
but I wouldn't let him in.
I guess the devil had me, he
wanted my soul to keep
But one night something
happened as I lay in bed
asleep.
I dreamed I got a phone call
from Heaven
The voice was so sweet and
clear.
Are you following in my
footsteps?
Mommy said I want to meet you
up here.
God has a place prepared for
you
You'll sing up here with the
Angel Band.
Read your Bible, go to church,
give your heart to God
I'm waiting for you over in
Gloryland.
I awakened and looked around
for Mommy
Then I remembered God had
taken her away.
I realized my life would have
to change
I want to be ready for that
Glad Reunion Day.
So I got on my knees looked
up to Heaven
I prayed Dear God cleanse my
soul, set me free.
I will hold to Your hand and
walk with You
Satan no longer has a hold on
me.

Marion Roland Gerardi
KATERI TEKAKWITHA
You were kin to the Mohawks,
But not kin to their ways.
You were an only soul,
Spent with prayer all your days.
Partially blinded by plague,
When time passed you by.
The rules of your faith,
Lifted you to the sky.

Barbara J. Paugh
YESTERDAY'S SANDS
Memories. . .
May slip thru our hands
As Yesterday's sands
When we felt love's essence
Thru another's presence—
Words that were shared
And expressions of care—
Reminiscences. . .
A moment's capriciousness.
Guitarro. . .
Where did this song begin
And how does the melody end?
Tomorrow, will you feel my
sorrow
And play again of Yesterday's
sands?
As I travel these distant
places,
Will Time still carry the
traces—
Hauntingly. . .
To lonely beaches inside of me?
Hauntingly. . .
To lonely beaches inside of me.

R. Harvey Habenicht III
MIGHTY LISPING
I am walking solitary but not
alone
Along on ever-changing line
Between there, and here
Where leisurely rushing
Caressingly battering
Hills of liquid lash
On shifting solids
Beneath sighing gusts
And color-laden bursts of
light—
All laced with the waves'
Mighty lisping of your name:
Rose ssshth
Rose ssshth
Rose ssshth.

VickiLynn Mohr
AN OLD MANS' SORROW
She was sitting on the edge
of the beach
letting the surf come up to her
feet,
the waves breaking just out of
reach.
I very much wanted for us to
meet.
I casually walked by and
smiled,
when she looked up with big
grey eyes.
I was surprised and instantly
beguiled.
I had found a love I thought
was wise.
"May I sit here?" I casually
asked
and pointed to the spot beside
her.
I was hopeful, knowing my
love was masked.
"I suspect so." was her mild
rejoinder.
She was a beauty, her skin
like cream.
I wanted to touch her but I
dared not
For fear she would vanish as a
dream
when one is awakened, the
dream is forgot.
"I live around here, just across
the bay.
You know? The house that's on
top of the hill?"
She shook her head no, I sat
in dismay.
What else could I talk of to see
how she feels?
We sat in silence until dusk
settled in.
She got up to leave, but I
grabbed her hand.
She looked at me like I
wanted to sin.
"I'd like you to stay. Please
understand."
"I've lived all my life on top
of that hill,
with no one to love, or be
with me there.
I don't know why, maybe it's
Gods' will.
But now I need someone. One to
be near."
She looked at me with
sympathy and said,
"I'm sorry you have wasted your
whole life.
These years you have left are
filled with dread
of not finding a companion or
even a wife."
"Please stop," I cried.
"True, I'M an old man
but I could make you happy.
I'd—I'd love you."
She shook her head sadly,
"You understand
I have a life ahead, places to
see, things to do.
But you have lived your life
with no more years
left on your health. I'm sorry.
I have to go."
"Bye." She got up and walked
away from an old man in
tears.
Who knew she was, oh, so right.
I let the tears flow.

Lester Nicholas Recktenwald
RISE OF THE CITY
Here, it seems,
The vitality of institutions is
tested
Built by men with their
material traditions.
This is not Utopia: could it
be?
The inner impelled to fit the
outer?
It would seem man here could
work and build
To release himself from his
own shortcomings.
Now needlessly wearing and
wearying are trifles:
Obstacles that man erects
with his limitations:
Thongs that bind him to the
physical past
From which he does not loose
himself.
Why is this tick of wood or
stone so precious
It should shape man's course
within this sphere?
It has neither seed nor blood,
mentality,
Or immorality, and shall pass
with the corrosive
Elemental blasts. It is but a
temporary dwelling.
This is not Utopia: should it
be? Like this wood
These sticks and stones bind

men's direction here
So the body binds the man.
Today we live by it,
And tomorrow we shall die of it
unless the city
Shall arise from the dreams of
frontiersmen
To its real and capable heights.

Charles E. Sanders

TIME

Isn't it wonderful that nothing
is infinite,
Every venture is inevitably final
Thanks to some long-forgotten
Roman
For engineering the conclusion
of a year
Days and nights have come and
gone
Hours and minutes have fleeted
and passed
Some of us ended, others gone
on
Glory and shame alike in the
past
Each new year beckons the
successful
and offers new hope to the
losers
Three hundred sixty-five virgin
days wait to fulfill
the hopes and dreams of
sophisticates and hoosiers
The dignity of self satisfaction
And the quiet arrogance of
humble pride
Await those whose unfaltering
action
Will be to challenge a new
'82 and lay '81 aside.

Marie Pierre Semler, M.M.

NATURE CULTURE

Behold the Man who speaks
to you from nature's tree
Who knows the highest peaks
the deepest minds and seas,
Who chose minute and tender
things
as scribes in stone, in shell,
In wood upon the quiet lea,
who limn of men, of beasts,
of God,
Of secret things o'er which
men dream,
conjecture, are wholly lost.
Things that speak of life's
eternity.
Behold the tree that has no will
set free, no wish, except the
light,
The light that draws forth
beauty,
untaught virtue, invisible
power,
To teach spirits groping in
this dark hour to find in truth
The way that leads to Home.

Douglas Thornburg

BOOKS

Teachers teach from it,
Students learn from it.
People write it,
Others enjoy it.
Presses print it,
Bookstores sell it.
Libraries loan it,
People return it.
Rioters burn it,
Museums cherish it.
Speedreaders skim it,
I leisurely read it.

Earl G. Reque

LOVING PRESENCE

I walk
Into the room.
A warmth is there;
A cosmic veil
Of love
Permeates the space.
I feel embraced,
Held, strengthened,
Energized.
The security
Of total peacefulness
Envelops me.
A friend is there.

Kiva JS Rice

RITA

The warm, brown flavor of your
skin
Is neither too rich nor too thin
Upon my tongue as it leaves
trails
Of moisture down along your
breast.
Beside your arm across my
chest,
The darkness of my own flesh
pales.

Mildred Ringer

THEN COMES TOMORROW

Then comes tomorrow. . .
After living our earthly day,
Then comes tomorrow. . .
With Jesus always to stay.
Then comes tomorrow. . .
To walk in pastures green,
Then comes tomorrow. . .
With heavenly saints to be
seen.
Then comes tomorrow. . .
We will see the streets of
gold,
Then comes tomorrow. . .
With total love he will enfold.
Then comes tomorrow. . .
We'll see Him face to face,
Then comes tomorrow. . .
Saved by His loving grace.

Kay Rislov

THE STRANGER

I saw the world in his eyes
A bit sad, but I surmise
That it reflects a part of living
In moving on, of learning and
giving.
We taste bits of life as we
travel through
What's good for me may not be
for you.
Soft spoken yet eager to hear
one's views
Of other's opinions, of home
spun news.
He'd traveled far, trying many
things.
A serious side, but his laughter
took wings
As we spoke of the frivolous,
but a deeper side
Came through now and then, he
could not hide
The depths of a soul hidden
deep inside.
His eyes are the windows into
which I look
And I read them so clearly,
like an open book.
I saw kindness, understanding,
and humor too.
So many of his secrets seep
unknowingly through.

Aurea E. Rodriguez

INVOCATION

Oh Lord! Lift our hearts to the
vision
Of all the goodness, and
everlasting love.
Take us back to the birth of
this great nation,
And strive toward the highest
ideals on which this country
came to be.
We are strong as a Nation,
Nevertheless, let us each be
strong with the force attained
not thru fear
But by the union of all no
matter race or creed.
Oh God! Remove from us all
fear, discontent, hatred!
And grant us the insight to be
thankful for all the goodness
we have,
Not only for ourselves but for
others to cherish too.
O God! Help us to bring forth
the best that is in each of us.
And as we leave behind all
negative feelings
We will strive onward in the
realization
And recognition of all the
blessings we cherish—
Prosperity, peace, and good
will to all mankind.
We thank Thee, God!

Daniel Russell

BABY LON

When I came forth
unto this earth
and the womb I depart
this thing they call birth
with pain I came
with it I'll go
what it's all for
the masters do know
As I came forth
a woman did cry
yes I heard her
before she did I
In Taurus they say
my celestial home
about the Pleiades
accursed to roam
But shall I fit
the etherean cast
to answer at present
I look to the past

Louise I. Schmitt

FINALE

A small white house
unpretentious and alone
but a nature's castle cradled
within the protective arms
of leafy filled trees.
Flower boxes embroidered
with pinks and whites
nurtured with loving care.
Manicured shurbs play
the roll of stalwart sentry
against a backdrop of velvet
green carpeted lawn.
Wearing a gingham apron
with a bib-like top and a
sunbonnet that covered most
of her snow white hair,
she had an air of fulfillment
walking among her precious
gems.
Dear God be kind to her
in that retirement home
when she learns that she
will never return again
because her castle is
"FOR SALE."

Charles Franklin Shockley

ADVISORY

Our chances are strictly slim,
if we take them, and succeed
by the skin of our teeth, we
are survivors.
A rip in the balloon is pertinent,
the curiosity of the discovery
bides one to stick around
for the aftermath.
Each heart must protect itself,
leading to frustation,
lack of trust,
no hands like cradling mangers
to caress passing souls.
This is itself stagnation,
stifling, human, dehydrating,
humidity
perspires from her breasts,
trapping the talented
into obscure trivia,
blindly mis-blessing mindful
justification.

Jacqueline Clyne Sheppard

THE MEANING OF CHRISTMAS

Bits of colored paper, formed
into a chain.
Angels singing carols with
a glad refrain.
Holly and candles, mistletoe
and good cheer,
All signs of Christmas coming
again this year.
Trees are all trimmed from their
peaks to their toes.
Packages wrapped up with
brightly colored bows.
Santa and his reindeer up on the
roof,
Now even a Scrooge can't
remain aloof.

The stores are all filled with
shoppers who rush.
The meaning of Christmas now
caught in the crush.
Short tempered sales clerks
and customers abound.
Parking lots are full, no
spaces to be found.
Where did the true meaning of
Christmas go?
Each year it gets more
commercial and so,
Think back long ago, to that
much awaited birth.
Think of the shepherds
rejoicing on the earth.
He came down from heaven as a
babe in the hay.
Came down from his throne to
show us the way.
Keep Christ in Christmas, it's
the best we can do,
To make it merry, and more
authentic too!

Gae Schmitt

WHY

Why
is it cold?
Why do people
walk hand out of hand?
Why do tears come
too easily?
And why
am
I
alone?

Aloysius Leon Sinicki

THE ULTIMATE INSENSITIVITY

Abortion, the act of termination
Is a dire, distorted elimination
At worst a contorted
explanation,
For limiting the
population
In the stage of gestation;
It is a callous insinuation

To assume that we as a nation
Are not guilty of spreading
the ideation
That a sense of rank
discrimination
Is not being put into
application.
One must be brought to the
realization
That abortion is to be held
in utter abomination.
It is contrary to the
Almighty's mandate of
procreation;
And, in any sphere, the act
is a means of mass
extermination!

Dorthia L. Skelton
FLIGHTS OF FANCY
I have the most adventures of
anyone I know—
On flights of fancy I am always
gone.
I travel trails up wooded
mountain sides
And watch the sun rise red
and gold at dawn.
I ski on down a gleaming
slope of snow,
And feel the wind whip past
me as I fly,
My heart leaps up when I
behold
The darkening thunder-clouds
up in the sky.
I sit inside a cabin, snug and
warm
And listen to the storm-winds
in the trees,
I stand beside a campfire
blazing high
And smell the woodsmoke
wafted by the breeze.
I often stand upon a hill so high
And look down where the river
tumbles on
To make a frothing, roaring
waterfall
Only to wake and find my
dreams have flown.
But, while I dream, my life
is so complete,
I thrill within this secret
heart of mine
And smile as I console
myself and know
This gift will last until the
end of time.

June (Sunkes) Skaarup
THE ALMIGHTY
You must always fear the
Almighty
As through this life you go
You must always remember
No matter what you do He
knows
He does not like the evil
And wicked ways of man
So always remember
To do the very best you can
So as you go on your way
Just keep one thing in mind
Do unto others as you would
be done
Then happiness you will find.

Cynde Fields Smith
HAZE AND CONFUSION
i walk through the day in a haze
of wonder
looking at no one
just staying in my own little
world down under
different from everyone
sometimes i look at a flower
with amazement
or maybe at the sky
or maybe at the cold gray
pavement
often i just don't try
to see the dark reality that
is really life
the blood that is shed
and all of man's woeful strife
so i'll live in my dreams of
fantasy and beauty
close my eyes to the outside
and let the assasin do his duty

Phyllis Joan Smith
A POEM FOR SHEILA
An angel is knocking at my
friends door
In anguish, I pray and walk
the floor
It is not time yet, I say
Heaven is years away
My friend, she has been, these
many years
She knows my whims and fears
We have shared joy, and sorrow
And, looked foreward, to
tomorrow
Her friendship, I treasure
Her smile brings me pleasure
God, works miracles, they say
As on my knees, I kneel, and
pray. . .

Caroline Snow
AN ENGLISHWOMAN IN AMERICA
Lush hills of early sunlit June,
Soft rolling waves, hypnotic
view.
Glistening beams, slow rising
moon.
All new.
Another day, another place
enjoyed as much,
A fleeting sadness dwelling on
the loss.
What difference really lies
between
An English and a foreign moss?
Grass, stone, leaf and flower
differ not.
Cloud, stars, sun and moon are
just the same.
What difference really lies
between
America's or England's rain?
People—glad or sad—their
hidden fears
Lie underneath the surface, tell
their toll.
What difference really lies
between
An English and a foreign soul?
With such a world of beauty to
explore,
Knowledge, depths of feeling
to enjoy,
What dreadful difference lies
between us all
That we destroy?

Jackie Sobczak
A TREE IN TIME
A boy and girl under a tree.
That boy and girl is you and me.
But that tree is in eternity,
and will always be,
like our love, for you and me.
That tree, that tree,
oh what memories that tree can
be.
The warmth and strength, I find
in thee.
The beauty of its image, against
the sky
will always be there, until the
day I die.
The trees branches, that gently
sway,
seemed to keep me from going
away.
That tree with carved initials
on.
Holds many memories of days
gone.
It stands tall and strong,
like my love for you will live
long.

Sheila K. Spence
GRADUATION PENDING
The goal of many a lass
As she enters her freshman class
Is to get a degree, oh yes;
But not the one you would
guess.
The degree which I'm speaking
of
Has more to do with love
Than with science or crafts or
speech,
Or any subjects you teach.
The degree to which I've
referred,
Upon brides is always conferred;
If by now you still can't guess,
I'll tell you: It's M-R-S!

Dorothy Staples
A WALK IN THE WOODS
Along the sun-shadowed woodsy
trail
Patterns of light and dark
Led us deeper into the cool
damp forest
Where everything was still.
The only sound, the rustle of
brown leaves
As we walked along the path.
Yet no! The trill of bird
Called with clear whistling
notes.
We paused to listen and heard
The scurrying of small animals
nearby.
A chipmunk jumped from
high-up limb to limb.
The busy ants travelled to and
fro
Upon dry fallen leaves.
Where is the silence? The woods
with life abound.
Along our way on either side
was
Boscage growth, skunk cabbage,
ferns.
From under lacy ferns a pinkish
lady slipper peeped.
Large, lichen-carpeted rocks
and boulders
Rested on green mossy beds,
While violets and Indian Pipes
peered out
From behind the mossy rocks
and vied
With bunch berries, bright red
in the sun.
Trillium and Wake-robin
nestled there.
Jack-in-the-pulpits raised their
heads.
Trailing arbutus dressed in pink
And periwinkle dressed in blue
Graced the lovely forest floor.
What joy! What joy! Just to be
there!

Lynn Miller Stafford
A MAN FINISHES A SONG FOR HIS FRIEND
A man was sitting on the edge
of his chair
His face was growing soft with
years
His jaw spreading widely to his
temples
His eyes looked tired and red,
they were small but very
intent
The man's shoulders were
defined and his long arms
balanced firmly a guitar
His knuckles were distinct with
tension
And his long fingers chose a
confident position.
His strumming was of a strained
and even effort
Beside him stood a young girl
Her hair was long and fell
straight and heavily on her
shirt
She was standing and her green
skirt touched the man's red
sleeve
Her head was tilted to one
side and her light hair looked
good next to his brown
She pressed her finger tightly
against the second division of
the guitar's arm
The man began to nod his head
in understanding that the
song was ending
And his hand motioned to
suggest that the music fades
He looked abruptly towards the
girl.
Her fingers relaxed hesitantly
from the arm of the guitar,
She smiled brilliantly
And she stepped away from the
man.

Hazel Mae Starkey
MYSTIC MOMENT
Beloved,
Friend,
First rose covered with dew,
I hold out my hand to you.
I feel again your warm embrace,
In the rose your smiling face.
In my heart deep inside,
The veils door opened wide,
I am standing by your side.
Friend,
Beloved.

Renata Sworakowski
GRANDMOTHER'S GARDEN
So quiet and pleasant it is,
right here,
When it is hot everywhere else,
it's cool here.
Roses and flowers galore,
Smell so good and sweet.
Pink, yellow and red,
Orange, white and much, much
more.
Birds chirping here and there.
Breeze lightly blowing.
Leaves flutter in the wind,
Flowers move gently.
The air is sweet and fresh
here,
In my grandmother's garden.

Susan Ann Thompson
PARTY IN DOUBT
On a fog grey morning in a
single plot of land
Triangular shadings for a
picnic ground
4th Avenue South and Twenty-
fifth bound
By smashed paper cups and
cigarette butts
A red topped table and
oversized fountain
One lone bird—was it merely a
robin?
Took over the table and
staked out a claim
Searched every inch, turned
every corner
Showed no concern when
nobody came
Faced me at last with three
long stretches
(A ruffled curve and a
sideways glance)
"This celebration was for
me!"

Jerrold Toliver
A CHRISTMAS RHYME
We've all heard it before, how
Christmas
Shouldn't be just one season,
but all year round.
Well, I've been pondering the
thought
And, personally, I've found
That Christmas will live forever
Only in the hearts of those
who want it to be so.
The bonds of God's love
nothing can sever.
We can keep Christmas when
and where ever we go
If we but realize that the gift
has not changed—
The gift of atonement that
blots out the fact
That God and man were once
estranged.
"For God so loved the world
He gave His only begotten Son".
Christmas lights will soon come
down,
But this act of love cannot be
undone.
As Christ lives, so does the
Christmas Spirit.
The gospel will be effective
As long as there are ears to
hear it.
And so in loving hearts
Christmas does not come and
go.
It lasts as long
As they wish it to be so.

John Eugene Taylor
SYMBOLS AND EQUATIONS
Symbols and equations
And new found wisdom,
Elements of mankind already
breathing.
A vast sea of darkness
The stars bright, cold, distant
Uninhabited in timeless space.
Launching headlong into orbit
Beyond sight, thought, speed,
and sound
Erased forever from all
humanity.
Moving rapidly in another
dimension
Exploring the deep secrets into
the unknown
On a voyage bound for oblivion.
A brilliant flashing light
Exploding with blinding fury,
Their eyes rolled back and
melting.
Locked, sealed, crushed
Slowly suffocating,
Shrinking helplessly into
infinity.

Janie VanDerSchouw
THE BEST COOK ON THE STAGE LINES
I've traveled the lines, many
a time,
And the best cook of them all
Runs the station where Union
Gulch meets the Arkansas.
She's a buxom gal, with a
pleasant smile.
She's fifty if she's a day—
She keeps a 30-30, to drive the
wolves away.
When the travelers step down
and look around
They see a structure made of
log.
There laying on the porch is
Ute; half coyote and half dog.
And then they smell food, and
smile
At the pies on the window sill,
And hear the best cook of them
all say, "Sit down and eat your
fill."
The driver named Sam is the
first one done,
And on his way out the door,
He winks and kisses the cook,
and hits the trail once more.

Elvera Wilken
GRATITUDE
We thank God for the golden
corn
From fields now drab and brown
Thankful for the crimson leaves
As they come tumbling down.
Now trees and fields may rest
a while
'Neath winters quilt of snow.
Thankful for the stacks of hay
In hayfields row on row.
Thankful for the ripened fruit,
For every kind of grain,
For every food in garden
grown—
Products of God's sun and rain.
Thankful for the warmth of
home,
For friends found everywhere.
Thankful for enduring faith
And for the power of prayer.
Thankful for the strength to do
Some worthwhile tasks each
day.
I am thankful for AMERICA,
And that I live in the U.S.A.

Elizabeth Cottam Walker
SILENCE
Here only is silence simplified.
When it is born within the
depth of sound
Like a violin note that has
defied
A masters wish to place soft
and round
In a circle of melody. Within
this note
I'd a silence clear, profound,
Where only Eternity's Song of
the soul is known.

J. Pembroke Waller (Joseph P.)
BIG RIVER
Big river, ramble on
Whispering in inaudible
whispers,
In decibels of a muse,
In the chords of Apolo,

Fought with the navies
Of many lands. Hosting honors
Of victories dead and dying
Fawning tombs we know not,
Blinding secrets long forgot.
Big river, tells us no lies,
On her the secret lies.

Don D. Wilson
DUST AND SHADOW
Flown off is the snow; in the
fields the leafy
grass appears again and
in the trees the green;
in change on change the earth
is quickening;
back the flooding streams are
drawing to their banks.
The Grace, unclothed, with both
her sisters
and the Nymphs, makes bold
to guide the chorus.
The year, the hour that takes
by force the genial
day—they teach us not to look
for endless life.
The westering breezes quell
the freezing weather;
spring is crushed by summer,
likewise to expire
as fecund autumn showers
favors down;
presently the deadening winter
reappears.
Still, the fleeting moons make
their celestial
losses good; when we sink
lifeless to the place
of dutiful Aeneas, wealthy
Tullus,
Ancus, we are dust and airy
shadow.
Who knows the lofty gods will
swell this day's sum
with tomorrow's time? This is
all we know:
everything you hand your
cordial self will be
salvaged from the hand of your
insatiate heir.
Whenever your life's sun,
Torquatus, sets,
and Minos frames his grand
decree for you,
neither noble birth, nor tongue
of eloquence,
nor piety shall give you back
to life.
Diana cannot free Hippolytus
the pure from deepest night in
the abyss;
Theseus, king, has not the
strength to sever
Lethe's bonds from Pirithous,
his dearest friend.

Lisa H. Witham
MEMORIES OF CAMELOT
Cosmic code
recollection of pyschedelic
revolutionary
naive belly dancer in the sun
words slipping around
loose and cheapened by
constant use—
My mind sighs in the torpid
raven blackness of nights
unknown
best forgotten by the slowly
mellowing subconscious. . .
"Do you wanna dance, do you,
do you wanna dance?"
Screams the radio
on the kitchen table;
Captivated by melancholy
memories
Ghosts and Dead dreams
Rise like lazarus from the
slow rot
of my brain
haunting my soul with all
their pain—
Forgotten they stand grim and
mute testamony
To the realities I knew in
the past...
"Peace, Peace" my conscious
mind screeches
holding its breath
but standing up I wonder
what happened to
Cheech the Wizard, Timothy
Leary, Life, Hippies, and
The Promised Revolution of
Love;
And whatever became of Syn
Barrett—
Harbrunger of the New Age of
Consciousness
I ask myself
lost in quiet solitude
now melting into the nights
sad air. . .
Turning then to go
I sigh softly to myself
Realizing with a sudden start
That whoever said
"What a long strange trip
its been"
In the end
Was right all along. . .
. . .yeah. . .
What a long strange trip this
life has been for us all. . .

Dorothy (Shorts) Williamson
HE CALLED ME FRIEND
I had never seen him before.
Yet he spoke to me of love and
faith.
He poured out his heart in the
brief span
of twenty minutes.
He told me of the love for
his family and
his faith in God, to see him
through these
trying times.
As he started to leave, I
wished him luck
and offered my hand.
He looked at it, then put
his arms around
me and called me friend.
And I never even knew his
name.
For these few precious moments
we were
what this world is all about.

Amanda Wallbaum
GIRL IN RED
Sitting in the waiting room,
hoping someone would speak
to me—nobody did.
Everyone seemed preoccupied,
but then, a light tap
caused me to turn about.
A friendly man smiled at me,
"Will you help her?" he asked.
"Surely, Sir," I replied.
A beautiful girl in red
took my arm; together
we entered the waiting plane.
"Where are you going?" I asked.
"New York," she said, "where
I'll get a Seeing Eye."
"Great!" I said, wishing her luck.
Inwardly I thanked God
for His goodness to me.
I could see, not perfectly,
but enough to lead the blind,
for this—"I thank you, Lord."

Catherine Mulhall Walraven
EXPLANATION
A poet is no part
Self-adoring
Instead, he tilts his heart
For easier pouring
Of love
As the crescent moon above
At birth
Showers moonbeams down on
earth.
A poet is not unaware
That life holds moments unkind
He knows that they are there
He only seeks to find
Mystic meanings of glorious
splendor
And a sign
To make them tender
And divine.
A poet simply knows that hearts
can break
Unless there are faith and love
at stake.

Mrs. Henrietteria Ruth Wiggins
YOGA OF LOVE
Blossoms from within, develops out
of the hearts of men, and then,
Takes roots to fly above, that is
the yoga of love—
Yoga of love comes from above
Hides in the soul of everyone
Listen for the call to come
Thats the yoga of love

Lucinda Berryessa Woodall
RIGHT NOW
Right now, you're still an innocent squirt,
But pretty soon you'll be playin' in the dirt.
Mom and Dad have great dreams concerning you,
And wonder which ones you'll choose to do.
Right now, you're content in your swing,
But pretty soon you'll be mature enough to take wing.
Mom and Dad will not skimp on protection,
And hope you'll not know loneliness and rejection.
Right now, you're safe and protected,
But somé of your temprament has already been detected.
Mom and Dad have important lessons to teach,
And know you have the complexion of a peach.
Right now, your life is just beginning,
But it will have chapters as baseball has innings.
Mom and Dad have a nice home, with a new coat of paint,
And really don't expect you to be a total saint.
Right now, I look at you hair, so long, dark and unruly,
But lovingly pray you'll not be treated cruelly.
Mom and Dad, your parents each pray,
That truth and honesty with you forever stay.
Right now, for you I wish,
You'll never be like a fish.
Swimming in doubt and confusion,
Nor filling yourself with self-delusion.
For it "is" right for me to love and care,
About someone who is so delightfully fair.
To love you with all of my heart,
And pray I am always in your life,
or maybe just a part.

Nancy M. Wypiszynski
DAD
I knew you not but I do care
I didn't ask what happened, I never dare.
You see, if I'd ask Mom, I know we'd cry
Then go on to that big question, "Why?"
But you are gone and she's done her best
And where I am talking to you in your rest.

I do what I do today and it's all new
But I've never done anything just for you.
So I hope what you sing, goes up to you on the
wings of a dove
And even though I never knew you,
You are the only father for me that I could ever love.

Virginia J. Yacyniak
THE REPLY
Send me not on Valentines Day
Affectionate words in a card to display,
Or fervent vows that Cupids dart,
Has whistled its way to the depths of your heart.
No, my darling, if love runs deep,
In the morning just let me sleep.
Perk the coffee, warm the bottle,
Wash the dishes, give Jr. a rattle,
So if your love is truly deep,
Please, oh, please, just let me sleep.
The Reply
Cupids' dart has pierced my heart,
Without true love, life cannot start,
So come the morn I'll let you sleep,
But come the night, true love will creep.

John R. Zuecca
GENTLE RAIN
Don't fight it, don't force it
Let it choose it's own course
For love's path is the path with heart.
That which flows slowly and gradually is sure of itself at every bend.—
It's flow is not diverted by false images of what we should be—and are.
None of the stream drains off as in a heavy rain to be lost, nurturing nothing.
The drops of love's gentle rain flow uninterupted to where the rivers meet
Undiminished
Untouchable
Fulfilled.

Wendy Elaine Willett
WHO'S PLAYTIME
Like a beauty pageant, for a pretty girl
Are the minds of the super powers of our world
As children their playtime was probably cut short
Now adult, planning their many games of war
Keeping their secrets and building their weapons
Leading us all, meek as blinded shepherds
Willing to follow or be led by our noses
Into six foot graves, if we are lucky
Adorned with whose roses
Let's play until it's over, are they hoping to win
Then turn to God and say "There's no sin"
Or more likely, turn up at the gates
And demand "let us in".

Johnathan Thomas
SOULLOST
Court of a Queen
Monsters of the Dark
Sky of Deep Blaze
Only One Will Find
There he is Seen
And he the Mark
Slashing in the Craze
Opening the guts Mind
Killing meaning little
Soaring so high
Thoroughly her reign
Not even battle
Wet of Cry
It is vain

Helen Strey
THE DISCIPLES—AND I
Into the dusk He comes
He *knows* that He must *die!*
Into *that garden*, --for spent--
He knows that I will cry --
Oh, how *weak* am I!
To *run away* and hide!
I *long to be so strong for Him*
And with my *Lord abide!*
I could not *wait* in *prayer* ---
I *slept* - before He *died*
Palm branches! Hosannas!
Could *He* be *crucified!!!!!*
He died for *me*, *a sinner!*
Accept His gift for you!
"Father," he said, *"Forgive them, For they know not what they do!"*
Death could *never hold Him!*
He *arose!* And so will *I!*
I will be *so bold* for *Him*
Until the day I die!

Lucille Nash
BABY DEAR
Baby dear, baby dear,
How I love to have you near!
Only last year you weren't here,
Sharing with me my rocking chair.
Were you in some Celestial Clime,
Far removed from Earthly Time,
Happily soothed by angelic chimes,
Invited on Angelic fare to dine?
DEAR HEAVENLY FATHER—
Thank you for our baby daughter.
For her shining trusting eyes,
For her lusty demanding cries,
For her dewy rosebud lips,
For her gentle fingertips,
For sweetly clinging cuddly arms.
WE'RE SIMPLY CAPTIVATED BY HER CHARMS!

Larry L. Miller
TO MY WIFE
I love you!
You, that's who!
You, the one who makes my life complete!
Of all the women, you're the one who can't be beat!!
You, the one who turns me on!
Oh! I could go on and on!
There really is no more to say!
'Cept glad on that very special day,
I met and loved you!

Karyn M. Leithead
THE MAGIC OF OUR LOVE
Softly, sweetly, smoothly does the music play
We dance to the rhythm of the sound it makes
Happy in the circle of one another's arms
Your gentle touch
Warms my heart and
Brings a smile
To my lips
Gently the strings of the music continue to play
as we dance on and on
We are apart from all others moving on the wings
of love and happiness alone
You hold me close
softly speaking words of love in my ear
The music has stopped now
yet on and on we dance
Moving to the rhythm
of the joy we have found in each other's arms
Far from all and
never to be found

Evey Kerr
OUT TO SEA
Windy storm and angry sea
taking my love away from me.
In the tempest, out there tossed
my heart's true love is out there lost.
I wonder if he thinks of me
out there on the stormy sea,
while here I stand and call his name
the ocean thunders, still the same.

Regina Krumenaker
YOU
Before meeting this special friend
Understanding one couldn't define
For you always help with my problems, and
Forever you'll be mine.
I've never known this feeling,
Love is what it's to be.
Only because it's from you, makes it
Very special to me.
Every day I think about you,
Year 'round you're my number one.
Only you will mean this much to me
Until all time is done.

Alexander Ellison, Jr.
THE LORD ALONE
The Lord Alone,
Can Set,

You Free.

Violet L. Gregory
THE VERDICT WAITS
When Orwel wrote the book he
Could not know that 1984
Would soon become a date that
Needs no modifying phrase.
It stands alone, as other dates
have stood, but holds a rabid
force within its cup and lets the
Subtle essence do its work.
When vicious power maintains
The upper hand where can a
Pinpoint gap begin to show?
When propaganda flares, full-
Fledged and strong; when lies
Are truth because they have the
Floor a tiny voice may ache
Within the throat but fear
Prevents one sound from coming
Out: An unwise glance or tone
Of voice could mean the owner
Would be vaporized by noon!
A telescreen blares on from day
To day; Big Brother watches;

Childish Spies report then shrug
when handcuffed parents leave
The scene. Patrol, Police and
Party fill the land. The past was
Never here--no sign allowed--
Unless it be a glory or a fame
And since the now controls, the
Now is all. The wars switch
Back and forth but never end;
They sashay as the dancers in a
Reel, and prisoners by recurring
Hordes will swing much like the
Laundry on a summer day while
Youngsters stay from school to
Watch the sight.
Although I stretch my mind
Until it screams it does not
lightly take such brutal fare.
I have lived too close to love
and faith and truth to shun
Them now. They represent my
Creed till darkening symbols
Have small chance to turn all
Beauty out, to let the morbid in.
I see a snail who makes a silver
road. "Intrepid little voyager!" I
Say and hope that other silver
Roads will show that I had
Passed this way, all unafraid.
I could not grind him
underneath my heel though this
Would prove my power, from
Beast to beast. When does the
Grinding impulse start to grow,
And when the lingering beauty
Cease to be?

Dewey Knudslien
THE BONDS OF LOVE
If all the days and months and years
Of time were put together
And all the winds and rains and snow
And every kind of weather
And if I could have lived them all
And known you from the start
You would have been as you are now
The creature of my heart
And if my love through all that time
Could fit into a thimble
It would adorn your finger
As a faithful boundless symbol
The real and soulful symbol
Of how much you mean to me
As long as there is any life
And through eternity
Because of any might or bound
As time and tide may measure
You are the only one I love
And I shall always treasure

Chariss Cruz
LOOKING BACK
The memories stay
As we go our own way
To find who we really are
The times we've shared
The things we've done
Together or apart
We'll remain number one
The smiles and the laugher
The tears and the pain
Each feeling or thought
Will always remain
In our hearts
In our souls
Rememberances of all kind
The friendships so treasured
Are locked in my mind

Judith L. Clark
WHO AM I?
Who am I?
Am I a frog?
I think not; for if I were,
I would be jumping and eating flies: I would be damp.
Who am I?
Am I an earthworm?
I think not; for if I were,
I would have no conception of the world: I would be blind.
Who am I?
Am I a cat?
I think not; for if I were,
I would prawl at night and eat mice: but I would be warm.
Who am I then?
I am a being.
I am warm and soft, and intelligent; for I am me.
I can perceive and understand why I live and know my world:
I have love.

Denise Bradby
SMALL PARTICLES END IN CLOUDS
Very stealthily, here crawls it.
Ugly through tunnels of darkness,
Primitive urges will, present at birth, always grow.
Savior, here, here is your challenge!
God, creator of all, where are early salvations?
Our screams carry, unrelentlessly; unite in a wave, a warning, dehortation; to the never-ending populations, echo and resound—
Then diminish, then continue on. Prophets had cried "No procrastinating! Make us be peaceful:
else we will die prisoners."
Oh the Lord, hell has fire; flames of white.
Burning, searing, unimaginable.
Thought it fantasy
Have those not died yet. Nor does ever our unclean
Souls deal with that pit or abyss.
Here! crawls
death, under the "progress" crawls to the children:
Every life sin does ruin and small particles end in clouds.

Lorraine A'Vart
THE ONES WE SHOULD COUNT ON
Don't put so much emphasis on education and money
putting emphasis on common sense may sound funny
but these are the ones that handle all
they are the alert to answer any call
Ingenuity is first and foremost
they have no time to sit around and boast
they are there to provide the need
they are the rare, the fighting breed
Things would get done, seem like a wink of an eye
the impossible, they are willing to try
setting up life, for all to enjoy
necessity the answer, this they employ
Frightened of no one, they stand proud and strong
doing the good, this is their song
plotting and planning throughout the night
to make sure things come out right
Give a chance to these well balanced people
with the others, we thought, we was climbing the steeple
only to be thrown in the muck and mire
almost getting burned by the roaring fire
Isn't it worth it to take the chance
instead of regressing, we would advance
instead of refusing, loved ones of their need
just because of others greed
We have a right to enjoy our life
without this agonizing frustration and strife
this is not a quality of those I spoke
to them, life is serious and not a joke

Rosemarie Lynn Namotka
HAPPY FATHERS DAY, DAD
I Love You Dad With All My Heart
And if only words could say
The respect, the love, I have for you
Even though I am away
Of days long past, when flowers bloomed
And seasons changed with time
Memories are still so fresh
Far deep within my mind
The nights were cold and bitter
Smuggling close beneath the sheets

And Dad would talk and scratch my back
Till I laid fast alseep
Remembering old Babka's House
When daybreak came too soon
My dad would wake me up from sleep
To make the church by noon
The help that I would try to give
So dad would let me stay
When we would bake all kinds of things
And showed me what he may
Memories are priceless
For whenever I want Dad near
I reach within my memory banks
And snatch them from the rear
I would like to wish my own
Happy Fathers Day to You
And if I could, I would give
The great vast world to you
Then wrap it in a rosy box
And tie it with a bow
Shouting from within the world
I love you, I love you
No gifts could be brought
Or words to be sought
To show you Dad the place you hold
Far deep within my heart

Joan Haasl Millikan
SYNTHESIS
I guess Dads old.
I can't tell,
I've known him so long.
We look at his garden
From the lean of the hill.
Cabbages, corn, berries, beans,
Rows and rows of growing,
Waving earth below us.
The old sun's benediction
to all that sowing—
Brimmed silence to the
Top,
Causing Dad to turn,
His head tilting
a grin.
"It's come to me,"
He said.
His cigarette puffed—
and died.
"Even if no-one ate it—
I'd still grow it."
We watched a swallow—
slicing sky.
I guess he's old,
It's hard to tell.

Mary E. Kinnaird
CHURCH SPIRES
Church spires reach up to glorify the night.
Church spires stand high in beauty of the morn.
They serve as symbols of the newborn light
And tell to all the world that Christ was born.
All those who come to worship day by day
Find strength to cope and and carry all their load,
Upon the altar all their problems lay
And walk with faith and joy the Christ-trod road.
Oh, won't you come and join this happy band
Of Christians working for a life that's good?
Go forth with joy to reach that happy land
And make your life the same that Jesus would.
Church spires reach up and out to beckon you
And bid you walk with Christ in all you do.

Eva Archer Bontecou
I'M STILL IN LOVE WITH YOU
Another Spring, another Fall
And I'm still in love with you
Our children grown, our worries flown
And I'm still in love with you
The harvest reaped, our love increased
Your beauty aged with tears
You've been my comfort and my help
Thru all these many years
We've had our quarrels and our spats
And arguments galore
But you've been patient and so kind
I love you more and more

Jeanie Raines
WEDDING
To merge in love
For one another
Gods plan for us I know
In his house
Vows of forever
Set our souls aglow
Tenderly sharing, touching
And caring beginning
A new life today
A birth of rejoicing
Embraced by our Lord
His message to convey.

Index of Poets

A

B

C

D

E

F

G

H

I

J

K

L

M

N

O

P

Q

R

S

T

U

V

W

Y

Z

Index of Photographs

Index of Illustrations

R

S

T

U

V

W

Y

Z